# Encyclopedia of

# Monasticism

## Volume 1

## A–L

# Encyclopedia of

# Monasticism

## Volume 1

## A–L

*Editor*

WILLIAM M. JOHNSTON

*Photo Editor*

CLAIRE RENKIN

Fitzroy Dearborn Publishers
Chicago and London

**British Library and Library of Congress Cataloging in Publication Data are available.**

ISBN 1-57958-090-4

First published in the USA and UK 2000

Index prepared by AEIOU Inc., Pleasantville, New York
Typeset by Sheridan Books Inc., Ann Arbor, Michigan
Printed by Sheridan Books Inc., Ann Arbor, Michigan
Cover design by Peter Aristedes, Chicago Advertising and Design, Chicago, Illinois

Cover illustrations: Tibetan thangka, image courtesy of John C. Huntington, the Huntington Archive (Volume 1);
Jean Fouquet, *St. Bernard, Abbot of Clairvaux*, image courtesy of Giraudon/Art Resource, New York (Volume 2)

# CONTENTS

# FOREWORD

Innumerable people have collaborated to bring the *Encyclopedia of Monasticism* to fruition. At an early stage members of the Board of Advisers counseled on selection of content and recommended possible contributors. Certain members of the board have gone beyond the call of duty in resolving dilemmas, proposing innovations, and bolstering confidence. Among the stalwarts, I owe special debts to Mathew Ciolek, Janice Glowski, Penelope Johnson, Martin Repp, Bruce Venarde, George Weckman, and Father Paschal Baumstein, O.S.B. Without their support and ingenuity, I could not have executed this project.

A most pleasant surprise has been the initiative taken by many contributors in suggesting collaborators, proposing new entries, and commenting on editorial issues. I feel particularly indebted for insights offered by Bhikkhu Bodhi, Mathieu Boisvert, Mahinda Deegalle, Marek Derwich, Charles Frazee, Alexander Golitzin, Luis O. Gómez, Rita Gross, Frank Hoffman, Andrew Huxley, Gereon Kopf, Whalen Lai, Steve McCarty, Michael Prokurat, Chris Schabel, Mary Schaefer, and Simon Wickham-Smith. Many others volunteered suggestions or answered queries. Everyone involved personified the collegiality of monastic studies. It is the least factionalized field of research that I know.

No less exhilarating has been the willingness of contributors to supply photographs for their own articles and those of others. In particular, Chris Schabel (of the University of Cyprus) – photographer extraordinaire of Christian monasteries – has supplied more than 130 images for the project. Mary Schaefer (of Atlantic School of Theology, Halifax, Nova Scotia) generously offered images of choice sites and liturgical details in Italy, France, and Ireland. John Powers (of the Australian National University, Canberra) made available his unrivaled collection of Buddhist monastics in action, particularly in Korea, Ladakh, and Sri Lanka. He also kindly arranged for David Moore to supply some extraordinary images from Japan. Steve McCarty (of Kagawa Junior College on Shikoku Island, Japan) provided photographs of rare sites and activities in Japan. John C. Huntington graciously provided images through the Huntington Archive of Ohio State University, which is administered by the ever helpful Janice Glowski. In addition, colleagues in western Massachusetts loyally supplied an array of indispensable images. I am profoundly grateful to Professor Marylin Rhie of the Smith College Department of Art for her extraordinary photographs of Chinese, Korean, Javanese, and South Asian monuments. Robert E. Jones of the University of Massachusetts History Department graciously furnished photographs of Russian monasteries.

To those who have never edited a reference work, I say the following: today a publisher's computers and their able operators perform tasks that might otherwise seem insuperable. My admiration for reference book editors who flourished prior to 1980 has increased immeasurably. One reason for the proliferation of reference books since the late

1980s lies in the economies of brain and time effected by computers. No less beneficial is e-mail. For a period of almost two years I have exchanged e-mail with collaborators as widely separated as Japan, Taiwan, Australia, Sri Lanka, Cyprus, Finland, and Canada, not to mention the United States and countries of Western Europe. I have experienced on an almost daily basis an interlocking of scholarly endeavor and monastic commitment that spans the globe. Like so much else, research on monasticism has become globalized. In both conception and execution this book embodies that fact.

It has been an unfailing pleasure to work with the staff at Fitzroy Dearborn in Chicago. Their editorial director, Paul Schellinger, conceived the project and granted it room to grow. The commissioning editor, Chris Hudson, tracked every stage of the project, persevered in resolving issues great and small, and never flagged in his enthusiasm. He gives new meaning to the words "reliable," "efficient," and "courteous." This book is very much his product.

William M. Johnston
Editor

# INTRODUCTION

The *Encyclopedia of Monasticism* emerged as a result of its publisher's intuition that the time is ripe to undertake a conspectus of monastic life past and present – its practices, doctrines, lifestyles, spiritualities, and art as pursued in Buddhism and Christianity. It is the privilege and duty of a reference book to scan methodological horizons, to assemble data, and to offer panoramas of past accomplishments. A further set of tasks involves redefining the needs of a field and reorienting it toward future agendas. The *Encyclopedia of Monasticism* performs both types of functions, recapitulating the past as well as anticipating the future.

Any reference book in religious studies is likely to bring together data in fresh combinations and to focus methods in novel ways. This reference book does so to an unusual degree, and this for several reasons.

The *Encyclopedia of Monasticism* is the first work in any language to examine monasticism past and present, devoting nearly equal attention to three great strands. Stated in chronological order of their emergence, these are: Buddhist monasticism, Eastern Christian monasticism, and Western Christian monasticism. In the present work, comparisons within each of these strands abound, and to a lesser extent among the three traditions, particularly between Eastern and Western Christian monasticism and between Buddhist and Eastern Christian monasticism. The latter juxtaposition is treated in the entry "Origins: Comparative Perspectives" by Mathieu Boisvert; "Monasticism, Definitions of: Buddhist Perspectives" by Mahinda Deegalle; and in a cluster of articles by Whalen Lai such as "Images: Buddhist Perspectives." This *Encyclopedia of Monasticism* is inherently comparative, above all in the topic articles designated "Buddhist Perspectives" and "Christian Perspectives." In addition, cross-references indicate a multitude of potential comparisons, as does the unusually detailed index.

A second challenge has been to select from and then to balance the many methodologies available in what may be called Buddhist and Christian monastic studies. During the past 30 years, scholars in older disciplines such as history, art history, philology, and liturgical studies have expanded their repertoire of methods and assumptions. In addition, entire new fields have emerged in the humanities, including women's studies, cultural studies, and postcolonial studies. Paralleling ferment in the humanities has been expansion of the social sciences of religion. Although the examples that follow come entirely from the English-speaking world, French, German, and Italian scholars have been at least as imaginative. As exemplified by Bryan Wilson, sociology of religion plots comparisons of context on an ever wider geographical and methodological canvas. As epitomized by Paul Pruyser, psychology of religion has devised entire new vocabularies in the wake of Freud, Jung, and Erikson. Equal ferment animates anthropology of religion through the innovations of Victor Turner, Mary Douglas, and Clifford Geertz. Phenomenology of religion has likewise undergone a revolution, not last through the reconceptualizations of Mircea Eliade, Ninian Smart, and their students. More broadly, study of spirituality and spiritualities keeps on expanding. Within monastic studies proper, archaeology, gender studies, and regional social histories have burgeoned. Such a cornucopia of methods at once challenges and frustrates a reference book editor. Not all innovations or approaches can be applied or even mentioned, yet as many as possible need to be represented. That has been attempted here not least by commissioning articles on "Historiography, Recent" of Eastern and Western Christian monasticism and on recent breakthroughs (e.g., "Archaeology," "Dialogue, Intermonastic," and "Plainchant"), by featuring unusual entries such as "Fishing and Fish Culture" or "Humor," and above all by encouraging authors of more than 60 "Buddhist Perspectives" and "Christian Perspectives" articles to propose fresh, often arresting, juxtapositions.

A third challenge has been to incorporate a worldwide upsurge of interest in the study of monasticism. Contributors to this volume reside in some 25 countries and describe monastic life in almost 50 countries. At the start of this project no one could have guessed the intensity of commitment or the range of talents that the project would elicit. This is a reference book that was, as it were, waiting to be written. A mere handful of the articles adapt material published elsewhere, and many entries represent the first of their kind. Some propose novel comparisons (e.g., "Initiation: Buddhist Perspectives" or "Master and Pupil: Buddhist Perspectives"). Others achieve unprecedented comprehensiveness (e.g., "Mount Athos, Greece," "Orthodox Monasticism: Slavic," or "Tibetan Lineages: Gelukpa"). Still others pioneer a new conceptualization of a vast topic (e.g., "Historiography, Recent: Eastern Christian," "Historiography, Recent: Western Christian," or "Spirituality: Eastern Christian"). A few tackle an entirely new field (e.g., "Internet, Buddhist and Christian," "Mount Meru," or "Bön Monasticism").

Articles divide into five types: Persons, Places (the monastic histories of countries, cities, and individual monasteries), Topics (both Buddhist and Christian), Roman Catholic Monastic Orders, and Perspectives (both Buddhist and Christian). Persons eliciting coverage include founders, reformers, scholars, mystics, and other foundational figures. Countries (or in some cases regions) number 45, with additional articles describing sites within 15 of them. Countries whose monasticism is less well known receive ample coverage (e.g., Australia, Bulgaria, Cyprus, Ethiopia, Romania, Vietnam). Regrettably it proved impossible to secure an article canvassing one all-important country: Italy. Fortunately, major Italian sites such as Florence, Rome, Assisi, Bobbio, Subiaco, and Monte Cassino (as well as Italo-Greek Monasticism) receive essays (not to mention abundant photographs). Themes range across history, sociology, theology, liturgical studies, gender studies, and the study of art and music. Entries on Roman Catholic Orders embrace monastic and contemplative ones of all centuries but not the active order of clerks regular that emerged in the 16th century or after. Thus 17th-century contemplative orders like the Visitandines and Trappists are delineated, but the Jesuits and Daughters of Charity are not (except for occasional references as in "Canada"). Buddhist Perspectives and Christian Perspectives comprise essays on concepts (Anticlericalism, Solitude), practices (Meditation, Prayer), customs (Clothing, Food), current concerns (Persecution, Contemporary Issues), scholarly controversies (Gender Studies, Laicization of Spirituality), and monastic pursuits (Gardens, Music). Taken as a whole, these are among the most distinctive articles in the *Encyclopedia of Monasticism*. All entries, even those with a general title (e.g., "Bible Interpretation," "Critiques of Western Christian Monasticism," or "Pilgrimages, Buddhist") examine monasticism specifically rather than the religion as a whole.

Except in one or two comparative entries, the *Encyclopedia of Monasticism* does not encompass Hindu, Jain, Daoist, or Islamic monastics or confraternities. Instead it was decided to focus on the two religious traditions that most conspicuously foster monasticism: Buddhism and Christianity. In this work, monasticism is defined as a single-minded commitment to religious life conducted apart from the surrounding society (almost always in celibacy and relative poverty) and following a rule that usually involves emulating or obeying a founder. So defined, monasticism, whether Buddhist or Christian, generates tension between two options: life in community (cenobitism) and life as a solitary or hermit (eremitism). Venerable ways of combining these two options abound, particularly in Eastern Christianity (e.g., *lavra* or *idiorrhythmia*). The *Encyclopedia of Monasticism* examines at some length permutations of these options and of the problems of definition that result (e.g., "Monasticism, Definitions of," "Origins: Comparative Perspectives," and "Spirituality: Eastern Christian").

A few words about usage. Although the title "St." appears in entry headings (e.g., "Francis of Assisi, St."), generally it is omitted from the text of articles, except where the context is liturgical (e.g., "Hymnographers") or generic ("Christianity: Overview"). Dates of birth and death of major monastics are provided in every article. Dates for Christian personages are taken from F.L. Cross and E.A. Livingstone, editors, *The Oxford Dictionary of the Christian Church* (3rd edition, Oxford and New York: Oxford University Press, 1997) and *Lexikon des Mittelalters* (10 vols., Munich and Zürich: Artemis, 1977–1998). Dates for Buddhist persons are taken from John Bowker, editor, *The Oxford Dictionary of World Religions* (Oxford and New York: Oxford University Press, 1997). For rulers and popes, the dates in parentheses designate the reign, not the lifetime. Many Greek names have been latinized (e.g., Evagrius Ponticus, Gregory of Nazianzus) as have certain Russian ones such as Nilus of Sora. Bibliographies have been supplied by the author of each article. The works cited range widely and are published in some 20 languages.

One of the most place-bound of human activities, monasticism fascinates a growing number of persons, including some who have yet to set foot in a monastery or encounter a monastic. To satisfy such readers, an *Encyclopedia of Monasticism* must encompass an unprecedented array of approaches, methods, regions, lifestyles, and liturgical practices, both Buddhist and Christian. Nowadays hunger for information and for encounter is nourished and exemplified by the explosion of monastic websites. As Mathew Ciolek's article on "Internet, Buddhist and Christian" shows, during the two-and-a-half year gestation period of this *Encyclopedia*, the number of websites concerned with monasticism has doubled several times over. A number of these are listed at the end of articles. At first glance, the placelessness of the Internet appears to clash with the groundedness of monasteries. Yet the two opposites appear to attract, for most Christian monasteries (and orders) and many Buddhist ones now maintain one or more websites, where laypeople pay "virtual" visits to locales that they may never behold in person. Strange as it may seem, monastics comprise some of the chief protagonists and beneficiaries of religious use of the Internet. That is why websites are listed at the end of many articles of this book.

One way to assess a reference book is to identify clusters of articles that might invite publication separately. The *Encyclopedia of Monasticism* contains articles that could constitute books on the following topics, among others:

Medieval Western Monasticism: Orders and Leaders
Medieval Western Monasticism: Comparative Essays
Christian Monastic Spirituality: Liturgy and Mysticism
Eastern Christian Monasticism (particularly Egyptian, Greek, and Russian)
Christian Monasticism: Recent Changes Worldwide
South Asian and Tibetan Buddhist Monasticism
East Asian Buddhist Monasticism (China, Korea, Japan)

Monastic Rules in Buddhism (Vinaya): Historical and Comparative Essays
Buddhist Visual Art and Its Role in Monasteries
Christian and Buddhist Monasticism: Comparative Essays
Christian and Buddhist Monastic Arts and Ritual

On the Buddhist side, unexpected richness has accrued from persuading up to a dozen authors to write on aspects of Buddhism in areas such as Japan, Tibet, or South Asia. Thus the *Encyclopedia of Monasticism* enables readers to scan a spectrum of contemporary views about Indian, Chinese, Japanese, Korean, and Tibetan Buddhist monasticism. The diversity of information, methodology, and ethos astonishes. It would have been impossible to impose terminology, much less an ideology, on such a heterogeneous team of scholars, but probably none of the contributors anticipated the fecundity of approaches that emerge, notably as regards Indian, Chinese, Korean, Japanese, and Tibetan Buddhist monasticism. In the cases of Japan and Tibet, individual schools and traditions, sites, masters and – in some cases – eccentrics, critiques, and works of art are appraised from as many as a half-dozen perspectives. A polyphony of scholarship resounds. Anyone who may think that monasticism generates monotony will discover that the opposite is true.

To illustrate the interweaving of themes, one can cite the topic of Tendai monasticism in Japan. It is discussed in articles on "Buddhist Schools/Traditions: Japan," "Tiantai/ Tendai: Japan," "Japan: History," "Japan: Sites," "Mount Hiei, Japan" "Mountain Monasteries, Buddhist," "Ennin," "Saichō," and "Marathon Monks." Yet because of differences in methodology and focus, hardly any overlap ensues. Similar multiplicity attaches to other Buddhist topics such as Gelukpa schools in Tibet, Theravāda Buddhism in Sri Lanka and Thailand, not to mention Chan/Zen in China, Japan, and Korea. Articles on the latter countries survey schools, teachers, controversies, customs, arts, methods of meditation, and monastery routine (for the latter, see particularly "Chan/Zen: Japan"). Present-day Korean monasticism is delineated in "Korea: Recent Changes" and "Korea: Sites." Such variety will help to disperse whatever narrow-mindedness may linger from the rather skewed vision of Zen that D.T. Suzuki disseminated in the West two generations ago.

On the Christian side, profusion blossoms concerning major European countries, particularly England, Ireland, France, Germany, Spain, Poland, Greece, and Russia. As cross-references show, the first three centuries of Christian monasticism (A.D. 250 to 550) are treated in unusual depth, as is monastic spirituality (particularly in liturgy and meditation), both Buddhist and Christian, of all periods and regions. Major syntheses such as the articles on "Liturgy: Western Christian," "Martyrs: Eastern Christian," "Monastics and the World, Medieval," "Spirituality: Eastern Christian," and "Theology, Eastern Christian" reconfigure their topics.

Polyphony concerning Western Christian monasticism is if anything the richest of all. Benedictine monasticism gets examined in at least 40 articles on persons, places, themes, and Christian perspectives. Notable among these entries are "Benedictines: General or Male," "Benedict of Nursia, St.," "Benedict of Aniane, St.," "Scholars, Benedictine," "France: History," "Schools and Universities, Benedictine," "Theology, Western Christian: Benedictine," "Liturgy: Western Christian," "Office, Daily: Western Christian," "Lectio Divina," "Abbot Primate, Benedictine," "Congregations, Benedictine," "Cluniacs," "Monte Cassino, Italy," and "Subiaco, Italy." A cluster of articles examines monastic rules: "Augustinian Rule," "Benedict of Nursia, St.," and "Regulations: Christian Perspectives." An unusual series inventories acts of asceticism in "Celibacy: Christian," "Devotions, Western Christian," "Hermits: Eastern Christian," "Holy Men/Holy Women: Christian Perspectives," "Self-Mutilation, Christian," and "Transvestite Saints." The diversity of data, interpretations, comparisons, bibliography, and websites generates innumerable routes of reading, both within and beyond these two volumes.

As regards Eastern Christian monasticism, a similar array of interpretations concerning the Near East (i.e., exclusive of Greece) can be assembled from articles such as "Origins: Eastern Christian," "Origins: Comparative Perspectives," "Pilgrimages, Christian: Near East," "Hermits: Eastern Christian," "Hagiography: Eastern Christian," "Theology, Eastern Christian," "Archaeology: Near East," "Liturgy: Eastern Christian," "Spirituality: Eastern Christian," "Stylites," "Armenia," "Egypt," "Syria," "Israel/Palestine," and "Jerusalem, Israel." An equal or greater amount of material pertains to monasticism in Greece and in Russia. In a unique synthesis, the article on "Libraries: Eastern Christian" canvasses monastic libraries in 10 countries across 17 centuries.

As always in religious and historical studies, cross-cultural comparison taxes the resources of terminology. To ease the burden, the *Encyclopedia of Monasticism* provides a Glossary of basic terms in both Buddhist and Christian monastic vocabulary. Many of the terms are from Pāli or Sanskrit on the Buddhist side and Latin or Greek on the Christian side. Comparative scholarly terms come from many sources, including art history, study of liturgy, and the sociology of religion (particularly that of Max Weber and Ernst Troeltsch in the articles by Whalen Lai on Buddhist parallels to Christianity). No attempt has been made to impose a uniform language of comparisons. Such rigor would have been both premature and intrusive. In the year 2000 scholars shun Procrustean uniformity, not least concerning a phenomenon as flexible as monasticism. Monasticism surely owes some of its present-day appeal to its diversity, adaptability, and even unpredictability. This book celebrates that plasticity and the rules that nurture it.

These volumes offer diverse opinions about the significance of monasticism in civilization. Monastics are presented here as (to name a few) contemplatives, builders, rulers, missionaries, inventors, theologians, scholars, rebels, spiritual seekers, moral exemplars, and pioneers of gender roles. What all these assessments have in common is their focus on monastics as intensifiers of endeavor. Because monastics tend to live in tighter communities than do their neighbors, monasticism focuses energies as in a microcosm. Monasticism concentrates the mind. This notion raises the question of what, if any, macrocosm do monastic microcosms mirror? Does monasticism mirror social realities such as class, gender difference, or colonial interfaces? Or does it mirror social aspirations such as love of neighbor, preservation of tradition, and networks of collaboration? Or spiritual aspirations that involve meditating, invoking the ultimate, or anticipating the life to come? Part of the fascination of studying monastics and their ways of life and worship lies in exploring larger realities that the communities purport to encapsulate. Monasticism invites us to project onto it our priorities either for betterment of life or critique of its flaws. For practitioners, monastic life intensifies social realities and spiritual aspirations, and for outsiders it can clarify allegiances and sharpen choices. By stimulating the imagination, monasticism mirrors, if not all things, at least the essential things.

This then is a book for scholars and other inquirers, whether secular or religious, who are interested in monasticism in any of its manifestations, past or present, male or female, Asian or Western. Lineages (whether within orders, cities, or countries) are traced, terminology is defined, controversies are addressed, methodology is dissected, spirituality is evoked, new perspectives are broached, and bibliography is deployed. A cornucopia of monastic experience, refocused and reappraised, awaits. As might be expected, not a few articles in this book marvel at monastic achievements. Notwithstanding many shortcomings, monasticism is one field of human endeavor that can inspire awe. This book helps to show why.

William M. Johnston
Editor

# ADVISERS

Baumstein, Paschal, O.S.B.
Bray, Dorothy Ann
Ciolek, T. Matthew
Collett, Barry
Flood, Gavin
Freedman, Paul H.
Gilley, Sheridan
Glowski, Janice M.
Johnson, Penelope D.
Repp, Martin
Rippinger, Joel A., O.S.B.

Silber, Ilana Friedrich
Strong, John S.
Talbot, Alice-Mary
Thurman, Robert A.F.
Venarde, Bruce L.
Ware, Kalistos T.
Weckman, George
Wiesner-Hanks, Merry
Wittberg, Patricia
Zaleski, Carol

# CONTRIBUTORS

Alexakis, Alexander
Alfeyev, Hilarion
Alldritt, Leslie D.
Allison, Robert W.
Amstutz, Galen
Anderson, Wendy Love
Appleby, David
Arnould, Alain, O.P.
Ashley, Benedict M., O.P.
Auslander, Diane Peters
Bangdel, Dina
Baumstein, Paschal, O.S.B.
Beliaev, Leonid
Bell, David N.
Bellenger, Aidan
Belsole, Kurt, O.S.B.
Berman, Constance Hoffman
Bisson, Thomas N.
Black, Jill
Blackstone, Kate
Bodhi, Bhikkhu
Boisvert, Mathieu

Boland, Vivian, O.P.
Bradley, Ritamary, S.F.C.C.
Brassard, Francis
Bray, Dorothy Ann
Breeze, Andrew
Brodman, James W.
Callahan, Daniel F.
Carbine, Jason A.
Cardman, Francine
Carney, Margaret, O.S.F., S.T.D.
Casey, Michael, O.C.S.O.
Caswell, James O.
Chandrasekhar, Chaya
Chaney, William A.
Chaoul-Reich, M. Alejandro
Chase, Mary Jane
Chewning, Susannah Mary
Chirapravati, M.L. Pattaratorn
Chryssavgis, John
Ciolek, T. Matthew
Coff, M. Pascaline, O.S.B.
Cohen, Richard S.

Coleman, Simon
Collins, Roger
Constantelos, Demetrios J.
Constas, Nicholas P.
Copsey, Richard, O.Carm.
Cornelius, Michael G.
Coureas, Nicholas
Cowdrey, H.E.J.
Cunningham, Lawrence S.
Curran, Mary Bernard, O.P.
Dandelet, Thomas
Davis, Cyprian, O.S.B.
Deal, William E.
Deeg, Max
Deegalle, Mahinda
Derwich, Marek
Dessein, Bart
Dilworth, Mark, O.S.B.
Dinzelbacher, Peter
Eden, Bradford Lee
Egan, Keith J.
Elkins, Sharon K.
Feiss, Hugh, O.S.B.
Flanagan, Sabina
Foard, James H.
France, John
Frankforter, A. Daniel
Frazee, Charles A.
Friedman, Russell L.
Funk, Virgil C.
Glidden, Aelred, O.S.B.
Glowski, Janice M.
Goa, David J.
Golitzin, Hieromonk Alexander
Gómez, Luis O.
Gonneau, Pierre
Goorjian, Taline
Gosling, David L.
Gow, Andrew
Green, Bernard, O.S.B.
Grendler, Paul F.
Gross, Rita M.
Haile, Getatchew
Hale, Robert, O.S.B. Cam.
Harris, Elizabeth J.
Harris, Ian
Hart, Patrick, O.C.S.O.
Hatlie, Peter
Hayes, Dawn Marie
Heirman, Ann
Hen, Yitzhak
Herbel, Richard G., O.S.B.
Hester, David Paul
Hillis, Gregory A.
Hirschfeld, Yitzhar
Hoffman, Frank J.
Hoffmann, Richard C.
Hollerman, Ephrem (Rita), O.S.B.
Holt, John
Hongladarom, Soraj

Howe, Elizabeth Teresa
Howe, John
Hughes, Kevin L.
Huntington, John C.
Hüsken, Ute
Hutchison, Carole A.
Huxley, Andrew
Hyers, Conrad
Irwin, Kevin W.
Izbicki, Thomas M.
Jaffe, Devra
Janes, Dominic
Jestice, Phyllis G.
Johnson, Penelope D.
Johnston, Elva
Jones, Charles B.
Jones, E.A.
Jones, Norman L.
Jorgensen, John
Jorgensen, Wayne James
Jotischky, Andrew
Joyce, Timothy J., O.S.B.
Kabilsingh, Chatsumarn
Kalas, Veronica
Kavenagh, Terence
Kawamura, Leslie S.
Keefer, Sarah Larratt
Kelly, Joseph F.
Kidder, J. Edward, Jr.
Kieffer-Pülz, Petra
Kimura, Takeshi
King, Sallie B.
Kinnard, Jacob N.
Kirchner, Thomas L.
Kleine, Christoph
Kollar, Rene
Kopf, Gereon
Kosuta, Matthew
Krawchuk, Andrii S.
LaFleur, William R.
Lai, Whalen
Law, John Easton
Lebecq, Stéphane
Lehmberg, Stanford
Lewis, Todd T.
Lindberg, David C.
Lipschutz, Julianna
Lishka, Dennis
Logan, F. Donald
Madigan, Kevin
Marra, Claudia
Mathews, Edward G., Jr.
McCallum, Donald F.
McCarty, Steve
McGuckin, John
McLaughlin, Mary Martin
McMahan, David L.
McMahon, Patrick Thomas, O.Carm.
McWilliams, Philip E.
Merkley, Paul A.

Mews, Constant J.
Mills, Frank A.
Mills, Martin A.
Minnich, Nelson H.
Mitchell, Margaret M.
Moorhead, John
Morris, Adam
Nguyen, Trian
Nicholson, Helen J.
Nietupski, Paul
Nolan, Mary Lee
Nuth, Joan M.
Nyberg, Tore
O'Loughlin, Thomas
Opsahl, Erhard P.
Oravez, Catherine
Pagani, Catherine
Papadakis, Aristeides
Parsons, David
Payton, James R., Jr.
Percival, John
Peterson, Michael D.
Pietsch, Sigrid
Podskalsky, Gerhard, S.J.
Popović, Svetlana
Porceddu, Laura
Postles, Dave
Potts, Cassandra
Powell, James M.
Powers, C. John
Price, Richard M.
Proksch, Nikola, O.S.B.
Prokurat, Michael
Ramsey, Boniface, O.P.
Ranft, Patricia
Rausch, Thomas P., S.J.
Reader, Ian
Rees, Daniel, O.S.B.
Reinders, Eric
Renna, Thomas
Repp, Martin
Reynolds, Frank
Rippinger, Joel A., O.S.B.
Roumbalou, Maria
Rubenson, Samuel
Ruffing, Janet K., R.S.M.
Sagovsky, Nicholas
Salgado, Nirmala S.
Samuel, Geoffrey
Schabel, Chris
Schaefer, Mary M.
Shaffern, Robert W.
Sharf, Robert H.
Shaver-Crandell, Annie
Shevzov, Vera
Shinohara, Koichi
Shore, Jeff

Shuck, W. Glenn
Silke, John J.
Simons, Walter
Sinclair, Tom
Skinner, Mary S.
Smith, Katherine Allen
Sommerfeldt, John R.
Sørensen, Henrik H.
Stewart, Columba, O.S.B.
Stewart, David
Stoudt, Debra L.
Sullivan, Donald D.
Sutera, Judith, O.S.B.
Swearer, Donald K.
Tannous, Tarek
Tatz, Mark J.
Teasdale, Wayne
Tedesco, Frank M.
Tegeder, Vincent, O.S.B.
Teteriatnikov, Natalia
Tierney, Mark, O.S.B.
Timbie, Janet
Timko, Philip, O.S.B.
Tiyavanich, Kamala
Touwaide, Alain
Tucker, John Allen
Tunstall, Lee
Turner, David, O.S.B.
Vanden Broucke, Pol
Venarde, Bruce L.
Verbist, Peter
Vess, Deborah
Vidmar, John C., O.P.
Vorenkamp, Dirck
Vu Van Thai
Walsh, Michael J.
Walsh, Michael J.
Warneke, Sara
Wathen, Ambrose G.
Weckman, George
Wells, Scott
Wickham-Smith, Simon
Wickstrom, John B.
Wiles, Royce
Willis, Janice D.
Williard, Brian
Wilson, Liz
Wiseman, James A., O.S.B.
Wittberg, Patricia
Woods, Richard, O.P.
Wortley, John
Wright, Wendy M.
Yorke, Barbara
Zagano, Phyllis
Zaleski, Philip
Zieman, Katherine

# ALPHABETICAL
# LIST OF ENTRIES

# THEMATIC OUTLINE OF ENTRIES

## TRADITIONS

Buddhist Lineages and Traditions
Chinese Buddhism
Japanese Buddhism
Korean Buddhism
South Asian Buddhism
Southeast Asian Buddhism

Tibetan Buddhism
Western Buddhism
Eastern Christian Monasticism
Western Christian Orders
20th-Century Issues
Comparative Topics

## PERSONS

Founders of Monastic Institutions and Orders
Scholars

Women Monastics
20th-Century Leaders

## PLACES

Countries and Regions
Cities and Locales

Individual Monasteries

## INSTITUTIONS

Rules

Governance of Monasteries

## PRACTICES AND PURSUITS

Liturgy
Music
Spirituality
Asceticism

Theology
Scholarship
Art and Architecture
Economic Activities

# TRADITIONS

## Buddhist Lineages and Traditions

Asia, Central
Buddhism: Overview
Buddhism: Inculturation
Buddhism: Western
Buddhist Schools/Traditions: China
Buddhist Schools/Traditions: Japan
Buddhist Schools/Traditions: Korea
Buddhist Schools/Traditions: South Asia
Buddhist Schools/Traditions: Southeast Asia
Buddhist Schools/Traditions: Tibet
Burma (Myanmar)
Chan/Zen: China
Chan/Zen: Japan
Chan/Zen: Korea
Chan/Zen: Vietnam
China: History
China: Sites
Disciples, Early Buddhist
Esoteric Buddhism in China and Japan
Forest Masters
Holy Men in Power (Hierocrats), Buddhist

India: Sites
Japan: History
Japan: Sites
Kathmandu Valley, Nepal
Korea: History
Korea: Recent Changes
Korea: Sites
Kyoto, Japan
Ladakh, India
Mahāyāna
Marathon Monks
Mount Hiei, Japan
Mount Kōya, Japan
Mount Wutai, China
Nara, Japan
Nation-Building and Japanese Buddhism
Nembutsu
Nepal: History
Nepal: Sites
Patrons, Buddhist: China
Patrons, Buddhist: India

Patrons, Buddhist: Japan
Patrons, Buddhist: Korea
Saṅgha
Sri Lanka: History
Sri Lanka: Recent Changes
Sri Lanka: Sites
Syncretism in Japan, Buddhist
Taiwan
Thailand
Tiantai/Tendai: China
Tiantai/Tendai: Japan
Tibet: History
Tibet: Sites
Tibetan Lineages: Gelukpa
Tibetan Lineages: Kagyü
Tibetan Lineages: Nyingma
Tibetan Lineages: Sakya
Vietnam
Women's Monasteries: Buddhist
Zen, Arts of
Zen and the West

## Chinese Buddhism

Bodhidharma
Buddhist Schools/Traditions: China
Chan/Zen: China
China
Critiques of Buddhist Monasticism: Confucian
Daoism: Influence on Buddhism
Daoxuan (Tao-hsüan)
Esoteric Buddhism in China and Japan
Festivals, Buddhist
Holy Men in Power (Hierocrats), Buddhist

Huaihai (Huai-hai)
Huineng
Huiyuan (Hui-yüan)
Mahāyāna
Missionaries: Buddhist
Mount Wutai, China
Mountain Monasteries, Buddhist
Patrons, Buddhist: China
Pilgrims to India, Chinese
Pure Land Buddhism

Scholastics, Buddhist
Shaolin, China
Shenxiu (Shen-hsiu)
Taiwan
Taixu (T'ai-hsü)
Tiantai/Tendai: China
Topography, Sacred (Buddhist)
Visual Arts, Buddhist: China
Zhiyi (Chih-i)
Zhuhong (Chu-hung)

## Japanese Buddhism

Aum Shinrikyō
Buddhist Schools/Traditions: Japan
Chan/Zen: Japan
Critiques of Buddhist Monasticism: Japanese
Dōgen
Eisai (Yosai)
Ennin
Esoteric Buddhism in China and Japan
Fujii, Nichidatsu (Nittatsu)
Hakuin
Holy Men in Power (Hierocrats), Buddhist
Hōnen
Ippen
Japan: History

Japan: Sites
Kōan
Kūkai
Kyoto, Japan
Marathon Monks
Mount Hiei, Japan
Mount Kōya, Japan
Mountain Monasteries, Buddhist
Nagano, Japan
Nara, Japan
Nation-Building and Japanese Buddhism
Nembutsu
Patrons, Buddhist: Japan
Peace Movements, Buddhist

Prophethood, Japanese Buddhist
Pure Land Buddhism
Rennyo
Saichō
Shikoku, the Pilgrimage Island of Japan
Shinran
Suzuki, Daisetz Teitaro
Syncretism in Japan, Buddhist
Tiantai/Tendai: Japan
Visual Arts, Buddhist: Japan
Warrior Monks: Buddhist
Zen, Arts of
Zen and the West

## Korean Buddhism

Buddhism: Inculturation
Buddhist Schools/Traditions: Korea
Chan/Zen: Korea
Chinul

Korea: History
Korea: Recent Changes
Korea: Sites
Mahāyāna

Patrons, Buddhist: Korea
Visual Arts, Buddhist: Korea
Wŏnhyo

## South Asian Buddhism

Abbot: Buddhist
Anurādhapura, Sri Lanka
Architecture: Buddhist Monasteries in
    Southern Asia
Asaṅga
Ashram, Influence of
Aśoka
Bodh Gayā, India
Bodhidharma
Bodhisattva
Buddha (Śākyamuni)
Buddhaghosa
Buddhism: Overview
Buddhism: Inculturation
Buddhist Schools/Traditions: South Asia
Buddhology
Cave Temples and Monasteries in India and
    China
Councils, Buddhist
Critiques of Buddhist Monasticism:
    Indo-Tibetan

Dharamsala, India
Dharma
Dharmapāla, Anagārika
Disciples, Early Buddhist
Discourses (Sūtras): Mahāyāna
Discourses (Suttas): Theravāda
Economics: Buddhist
Fasting: Buddhist
Festivals, Buddhist
Hermits: Buddhist
India: Sites
Jain Monasticism and Buddhist
    Monasticism
Kandy, Sri Lanka
Ladakh, India
Libraries: Buddhist
Mahāpajāpatī Gotamī
Mantras
Missionaries: Buddhist
Nālandā, India
Officials: Buddhist

Patrons, Buddhist: India
Pilgrimages, Buddhist
Pilgrims to India, Chinese
Rules, Buddhist (Vinaya): Historical
Rules, Buddhist (Vinaya): Monks
Rules, Buddhist (Vinaya): Nuns
Saṅgha
Scholastics, Buddhist
Social Services: Buddhist
Spirituality: Buddhist
Sri Lanka: History
Sri Lanka: Recent Changes
Sri Lanka: Sites
Stūpa
Ten-Precept Mothers as Theravādin Nuns
Theravādin Monks, Modern Western
Travelers: Buddhist
Visual Arts, Buddhist: India
Women's Monasteries: Buddhist

## Southeast Asian Buddhism

Angkor Wat, Cambodia
Bangkok, Thailand
Borobudur, Java, Indonesia
Buddhadāsa
Buddhism: Overview
Buddhism: Inculturation
Buddhist Schools/Traditions: Southeast Asia
Burma (Myanmar)

Chan/Zen: Vietnam
Examinations, Theravādin
Festivals, Buddhist
Forest Masters
Hermits: Buddhist
Missionaries: Buddhist
Mongkut
Mun, Ajahn

Nhát Hanh, Thích
Novices, Theravādin Rituals for
Peace Movements, Buddhist
Taungpila Sayadaw
Thailand
Vietnam
Visual Arts, Buddhist: Southeast Asia
Women's Monasteries: Buddhist

## Tibetan Buddhism

Asia, Central
Bön, Influence of
Bön Monasticism
Buddhist Schools/Traditions: Tibet
Critiques of Buddhist Monasticism: Indo-
    Tibetan
Dalai Lama (Tenzin Gyatso)
Deities, Buddhist
Dharamsala, India (Tibetan)
Gampopa

Kathmandu Valley, Nepal
Labdron, Machig
Ladakh, India
Lhasa, Tibet
Meditation: Buddhist Perspectives
Milarepa
Mount Meru
Nepal: History
Nepal: Sites
Padmasambhava

Sakya Pandita (Sapen)
Tibet: History
Tibet: Sites
Tibetan Lineages: Gelukpa
Tibetan Lineages: Kagyü
Tibetan Lineages: Nyingma
Tibetan Lineages: Sakya
Vajrayāna Buddhism in Nepal
Visual Arts, Buddhist: Tibet
Yeshe Tsogyel

## Western Buddhism

Buddhadāsa
Buddhism: Western
Buddhology
Contemporary Issues: Buddhist
Dalai Lama (Tenzin Gyatso)

Dharmapāla, Anagārika
Internet, Buddhist and Christian
Nhát Hanh, Thích
Peace Movements, Buddhist
Spirituality: Buddhist

Suzuki, Daisetz Teitaro
Theravādin Monks, Modern Western
United States: Buddhist
Zen and the West

## Eastern Christian Monasticism

Archaeology: Russia
Architecture: Armenian Monasteries
Architecture: Eastern Christian Monasteries
Armenia

Bulgaria
Egypt
Elders, Russian Monastic (Startsi)
Ethiopia

Greece
Hagiography: Eastern Christian
Hermits: Eastern Christian
Hesychasm

Historiography, Recent: Eastern Christian
Iconoclasm (Controversy)
Italo-Greek Monasticism
Lavra
Libraries: Eastern Christian
Liturgy: Eastern Christian
Maronites
Melkite Monasticism
Nestorian Monasticism
Office, Daily: Eastern Christian

Origins: Eastern Christian
Orthodox Monasticism: Byzantine
Orthodox Monasticism: Slavic
Philokalia
Pilgrimages, Christian: Eastern Europe
Pilgrimages, Christian: Near East
Romania
Russia: History
Russia: Recent Changes
Russia: Sites

Seasons, Liturgical: Eastern Christian
Serbia
Spirituality: Eastern Christian
Stylites
Syria
Theology, Eastern Christian
Ukraine
Vision, Mystical: Eastern Christian
Visual Arts, Eastern Christian: Painting
Women's Monasteries: Eastern Christian

## Western Christian Orders

Anglican Monasticism
Antonians
Augustinian Canons
Augustinian Friars/Hermits
Beghards
Beguines
Benedictines: Female
Benedictines: General or Male
Bridgettines
Camaldolese
Capuchins
Carmelites: Female
Carmelites: General or Male

Carthusians
Cistercians: Female
Cistercians: General or Male
Cluniacs
Dominicans: Female
Dominicans: General or Male
Franciscans: Female
Franciscans: General or Male
Gilbertines
Grandmontines
Hospitallers (Knights of Malta since 1530)
Maurists
Mercedarians

Premonstratensian Canons
Protestant Monasticism: Lutheran
Protestant Monasticism: Waldensian
Servites
Templars
Teutonic Order
Trappists
Trinitarians (Mathurins)
Vallombrosans
Victorines
Visitandines

## 20th-Century Issues

Buddhadāsa
Buddhism: Western
Butler, Cuthbert
Casel, Odo
Chapman, John
Contemporary Issues: Buddhist
Contemporary Issues: Western Christian
Dalai Lama (Tenzin Gyatso)
Dharmapāla, Anagārika
Dialogue, Intermonastic: Buddhist Perspectives
Dialogue, Intermonastic: Christian
   Perspectives
Fujii, Nichidatsu (Nittatsu)

Griffiths, Bede
Haid, Leo Michael
Hume, Basil
Internet, Buddhist and Christian
Keating, Thomas
Knowles, M. David
Korea: Recent Changes
Le Saux, Henri
Leclercq, Jean
Main, John
Marmion, Columba
McInerney, Michael Joseph Vincent
Mun, Ajahn

Nhát Hanh, Thích
Peace Movements, Buddhist
Russia: Recent Changes
Schutz, Roger
Sri Lanka: Recent Changes
Suzuki, Daisetz Teitaro
Taixu (T'ai-hsü)
Theravādin Monks, Modern Western
United States: Buddhist
Wolter, Maurus
Wolter, Placidus
Zen and the West

## Comparative Topics
(each of the following topics elicits separate entries discussing
Buddhist and Christian issues)

Animals, Attitude toward
Anticlericalism
Asceticism
Body
Clothing
Contemporary Issues
Death
Dialogue, Intermonastic
Fasting
Food
Gardens
Gender Studies
Governance

Hagiography
Hermits
Holy Men/Holy Women
Hygiene
Images
Initiation
Laicization of Spirituality
Libraries
Liturgy
Master and Pupil
Meditation
Monasticism, Definitions of
Music

Officials
Origins
Persecution
Prayer
Regulations
Sexuality
Social Services
Solitude
Spirituality
Timekeeping
Travelers
Worship Space

# Persons

## Founders of Monastic Institutions and Orders

Aidan, St.
Antony, St.
Asaṅga
Aśoka
Basil the Great, St.
Benedict of Aniane, St.
Benedict of Nursia, St.
Bernard of Clairvaux, St.
Bodhidharma
Boniface, St.
Brigit, St.
Bruno, St.
Buddha (Śākyamuni)
Caesarius of Arles, St.
Cassiodorus
Chinul
Clare of Assisi, St.
Columba, St.
Columban, St.
Cuthbert, St.
Daoxuan (Tao-hsüan)
David, St.
Dōgen
Dominic, St.

Eisai (Yosai)
Ennin
Francis of Assisi, St.
Francis of Paola, St.
Fujii, Nichidatsu (Nittatsu)
Gampopa
Gregory I (the Great), St.
Gualbert, John, St.
Guéranger, Prosper
Hilda, St.
Hōnen
Huineng
Huiyuan (Hui-yüan)
Ippen
Joseph of Volokolamsk, St.
Kūkai
Le Saux, Henri
Macrina, St.
Mahāpajāpatī Gotamī
Martin of Tours, St.
Milarepa
Mongkut
Mun, Ajahn
Nilus of Sora, St.

Pachomius, St.
Padmasambhava
Pirminius, St.
Rancé, Armand-Jean de
Riepp, Benedicta (Sybilla)
Sabas, St.
Saichō
Sakya Pandita (Sapen)
Schutz, Roger
Sergius of Radonezh, St.
Shenoute of Atripe
Shinran
Stephen of Perm, St.
Taixu (T'ai-hsü)
Taungpila Sayadaw
Teresa of Avila, St.
Theodosius of Kiev, St.
Wilfrid, St.
William of Hirsau
Willibrord, St.
Wimmer, Boniface
Wǒnhyo
Zhiyi (Chih-i)

## Scholars

Albertus Magnus, St.
Alcuin
Ambrose, St.
Anselm, St.
Bacon, Roger
Baker, Augustine
Basil the Great, St.
Beauduin, Lambert
Bede, St.
Bernard of Clairvaux, St.
Bonaventure, St.
Buddhadāsa
Buddhaghosa
Butler, Cuthbert
Casel, Odo
Cassian, John
Cassiodorus
Chapman, John
Chinul
Chrysostom, John, St.
Climacus, John, St.
Damian, Peter, St.
Daoxuan (Tao-hsüan)
Dharmapāla, Anagārika

Dionysius the Pseudo-Areopagite
Dōgen
Dominic, St.
Eckhart, Meister
Eisai (Yosai)
Evagrius Ponticus
Gregory I (the Great), St.
Gregory of Nazianzus, St.
Gregory of Nyssa, St.
Griffiths, Bede
Guéranger, Prosper
Hildegard of Bingen, St.
Hōnen
Hrosthwitha
Hume, Basil
Isaac the Syrian (Isaac of Nineveh), St.
Isidore of Seville, St.
Jerome, St.
Joachim of Fiore
John of Damascus, St.
Keating, Thomas
Knowles, M. David
Kūkai
Lanfranc

Leclercq, Jean
Luther, Martin
Marmion, Columba
Maximus the Greek, St.
Merton, Thomas
Palamas, Gregory, St.
Rabanus Maurus
Sabas, St.
Saichō
Sakya Pandita (Sapen)
Sergius of Radonezh, St.
Shinran
Suzuki, Daisetz Teitaro
Symeon the New Theologian, St.
Taixu (T'ai-hsü)
Theodore of Stoudios, St.
Thomas Aquinas, St.
Walafrid Strabo
William of Hirsau
Wolter, Maurus
Wolter, Placidus
Wǒnhyo
Zhiyi (Chih-i)
Zhuhong (Chu-hung)

## Women Monastics

Abbess, Christian
Beguines
Benedictines: Female
Brigit, St.
Carmelites: Female
Catherine of Bologna, St.

Cistercians: Female
Clare of Assisi, St.
Claustration (Cloister), Rules of
Contemporary Issues: Western Christian
Desert Mothers
Dominicans: Female

Double Houses, Western Christian
Elizabeth of Schönau
Franciscans: Female
Gender Studies: Buddhist Perspectives
Gender Studies: Christian Perspectives
Heloise

Hilda, St.
Hildegard of Bingen, St.
Holy Men/Holy Women: Buddhist
    Perspectives
Holy Men/Holy Women: Christian
    Perspectives
Hrosthwitha
Julian of Norwich
Labdron, Machig

Lay Brothers and Lay Sisters, Christian
Macrina, St.
Mahāpajāpatī Gotamī
More, Gertrude
Mystics, German Monastic: Female
Radegunde, St.
Recluses, Western Christian
Riepp, Benedicta (Sybilla)
Romania

Rules, Buddhist (Vinaya): Nuns
Ten-Precept Mothers as Theravādin Nuns
Teresa of Avila. St.
Thérèse of Lisieux, St.
Transvestite Saints
Women's Monasteries: Buddhist
Women's Monasteries: Eastern Christian
Women's Monasteries: Western Christian
Yeshe Tsogyel

## 20th-Century Leaders

Buddhadāsa
Butler, Cuthbert
Casel, Odo
Chapman, John
Dalai Lama (Tenzin Gyatso)
Dharmapāla, Anagārika
Fujii, Nichidatsu (Nittatsu)
Griffiths, Bede

Haid, Leo Michael
Hume, Basil
Keating, Thomas
Knowles, M. David
Le Saux, Henri
Leclercq, Jean
Main, John
Marmion, Columba

McInerney, Michael Joseph Vincent
Mun, Ajahn
Nhát Hanh, Thích
Schutz, Roger
Suzuki, Daisetz Teitaro
Taixu (T'ai-hsü)
Wolter, Maurus
Wolter, Placidus

# PLACES

## Countries and Regions

Armenia
Asia, Central
Australia
Austria
Belgium: History
Belgium: Sites
Bulgaria
Burma (Myanmar)
Canada
China
Croatia (Hrvatska)
Cyprus
Czech Republic
Dissolution of Monasteries: Continental
    Europe
Dissolution of Monasteries: England, Ireland,
    and Wales
Dissolution of Monasteries: Scotland
Egypt
England: History
England: Sites
Ethiopia
France: History

France: Sites
Germany: History
Germany: Sites
Greece
Hungary
India: Christian
India: Sites
Ireland: History
Ireland: Sites
Israel/Palestine
Japan: History
Japan: Sites
Korea: History
Korea: Recent Changes
Korea: Sites
Latin America
Nepal: History
Nepal: Sites
Netherlands
Poland
Portugal
Romania
Russia: History

Russia: Recent Changes
Russia: Sites
Scandinavia
Scotland
Serbia
Spain: History
Spain: Sites
Sri Lanka: History
Sri Lanka: Recent Changes
Sri Lanka: Sites
Switzerland
Syria
Taiwan
Thailand
Tibet: History
Tibet: Sites
Ukraine
United States: Buddhist
United States: Western Christian
Vietnam
Wales

## Cities and Locales

Ajaṇṭā, India
Angkor Wat, Cambodia
Anurādhapura, Sri Lanka
Assisi, Italy
Bangkok, Thailand
Bobbio, Italy
Bodh Gayā, India
Cappadocia, Turkey
Cîteaux, France
Cluny, France
Collegeville, Minnesota
Częstochowa (Jasna Góra), Poland

Dharamsala, India (Tibetan)
Echternach, Luxembourg
Einsiedeln, Switzerland
Florence, Italy
Fontevraud, France
Fulda, Germany
Gethsemani, Kentucky
Istanbul, Turkey
Jerusalem, Israel
Kandy, Sri Lanka
Kathmandu Valley, Nepal
Kiev (Kyiv), Ukraine

Kyoto, Japan
Ladakh, India
Lhasa, Tibet
Maria Laach, Germany
Melk, Austria
Meteora, Thessaly, Greece
Monte Cassino, Italy
Moscow, Russia
Mount Athos, Greece
Mount Hiei, Japan
Mount Kōya, Japan
Mount Wutai, China

Nagano, Japan
Nālandā, India
Nara, Japan
Rome and the Papacy
St. Gallen, Switzerland

St. Riquier, France
Santiago de Compostela, Spain
Shikoku, the Pilgrimage Island of Japan
Solesmes, France
Subiaco, Italy

Taizé, France
Vadstena, Sweden
Vienna, Austria
Whitby, England

## Individual Monasteries

Beuron, Germany
Bobbio, Italy
Bodh Gayā, India
Cîteaux, France
Cluny, Abbots of
Cluny, France
Collegeville, Minnesota
Częstochowa (Jasna Góra), Poland
Echternach, Luxembourg
Einsiedeln, Switzerland
Fontevraud, France

Fulda, Germany
Gethsemani, Kentucky
Iona, Scotland
La Trappe, France
Lérins, France
Lindisfarne/Holy Isle, England
Maria Laach, Germany
Melk, Austria
Mont-St.-Michel, France
Monte Cassino, Italy
Mount Sinai, Egypt

New Skete, New York
Reichenau
Santiago de Compostela, Spain
Shaolin, China
Solesmes, France
Subiaco, Italy
Taizé, France
Vadstena, Sweden
Whitby, England

# Institutions

## Rules

Asceticism: Buddhist Perspectives
Asceticism: Christian Perspectives
Augustinian Rule
Benedict of Nursia, St.
Benedictines: General or Male
Canons Regular, Origins of
Celibacy: Buddhist
Celibacy: Christian
Christianity: Overview
Claustration (Cloister), Rules of
Columban, St.
Contemporary Issues: Buddhist
Contemporary Issues: Western Christian

Crusades
Education of Christian Monastics
Fasting: Buddhist
Fasting: Eastern Christian
Fasting: Western Christian
Fugitive Religious
Governance: Buddhist Perspectives
Governance: Christian Perspectives
Initiation: Buddhist Perspectives
Initiation: Christian Perspectives
Monasticism, Definitions of: Buddhist
    Perspectives

Monasticism, Definitions of: Christian
    Perspectives
Novices, Theravādin Rituals for
Oblates
Recluses, Western Christian
Regulations: Buddhist Perspectives
Regulations: Christian Perspectives
Rules, Buddhist (Vinaya): Historical
Rules, Buddhist (Vinaya): Lineage
Rules, Buddhist (Vinaya): Monks
Rules, Buddhist (Vinaya): Nuns
Vocation, Christian

## Governance of Monasteries

Abbess, Christian
Abbeys, Territorial
Abbot: Buddhist
Abbot: Christian
Abbot Primate, Benedictine
Anticlericalism: Buddhist Perspectives
Anticlericalism: Christian Perspectives
Arhat
Ashram, Influence of
Augustinian Rule
Bishops: Jurisdiction and Role
Canons Regular, Origins of
Cathedral Priories (England)
Christianity: Overview
Church Councils, Recent Catholic
Claustration (Cloister), Rules of
Cluniacs
Congregations, Benedictine
Councils, Buddhist
Critiques of Buddhist Monasticism: Confucian
Critiques of Buddhist Monasticism: Japanese
Double Houses, Western Christian

Economic Justice, Buddhist
Economics: Christian
Examinations, Theravādin
Exile, Western Christian
Fugitive Religious
German Benedictine Reform, Medieval
Governance: Buddhist Perspectives
Governance: Christian Perspectives
Gregory I (the Great), St.
Gregory VII
Heretics, Christian
Initiation: Buddhist Perspectives
Initiation: Christian Perspectives
Jansenist Controversy
Lavra
Lay Brothers and Lay Sisters, Christian
Monastery, Christian
Monastics and the World, Medieval
Monk-Bishops
Nation-Building and Japanese Buddhism
Oblates
Officials: Buddhist

Officials: Western Christian
Orders (Religious), Origin of
Papacy: Monastic Popes
Papacy: Papal Pronouncements
Patrons, Buddhist: China
Patrons, Buddhist: India
Patrons, Buddhist: Japan
Patrons, Buddhist: Korea
Patrons, Christian: Lay
Patrons, Christian: Royal
Peace Movements, Buddhist
Reformation
Rome and the Papacy
Social Services: Buddhist
Social Services: Eastern Christian
Social Services: Western Christian
Ten-Precept Mothers as Theravādin Nuns
Warrior Monks: Buddhist
Warrior Monks: Christian
Women's Monasteries: Buddhist
Women's Monasteries: Eastern Christian
Women's Monasteries: Western Christian

# PRACTICES AND PURSUITS

## Liturgy

Ambrose, St.
Benedict of Nursia, St.
Beuron, Germany
Chrysostom, John, St.
Cluniacs
Death: Buddhist Perspectives
Death: Christian Perspectives
Death Rituals, Buddhist
Devotions, Western Christian
Gestures, Buddhist
Guéranger, Prosper
Hymnographers
Iconoclasm (Controversy)
John of Damascus, St.

Lectio Divina
Liturgical Movement 1830–1980
Liturgists, German Monastic
Liturgy: Buddhist
Liturgy: Celtic
Liturgy: Eastern Christian
Liturgy: Western Christian
Mandala
Marmion, Columba
Novices, Theravādin Rituals for
Office, Daily: Eastern Christian
Office, Daily: Western Christian
Plainchant
Seasons, Liturgical: Eastern Christian

Seasons, Liturgical: Western Christian
Solesmes, France
Spirituality: Eastern Christian
Spirituality: Western Christian
Taizé, France
Visual Arts, Eastern Christian: Painting
Visual Arts, Western Christian: Liturgical
    Furnishings
Wolter, Maurus
Wolter, Placidus
Worship Space: Buddhist Perspectives
Worship Space: Christian Perspectives

## Music

Beuron, Germany
Festivals, Buddhist
Guéranger, Prosper
Hymnographers
John of Damascus, St.

Liturgy: Eastern Christian
Liturgy: Western Christian
Music: Buddhist Perspectives
Music: Christian Perspectives
Office, Daily: Eastern Christian

Office, Daily: Western Christian
Plainchant
Solesmes, France

## Spirituality

Aelred of Rievaulx, St.
Arhat
Ashram, Influence of
Beghards
Beguines
Bernard of Clairvaux, St.
Bodhisattva
Celibacy: Buddhist
Celibacy: Christian
Celtic Monasticism
Charism
Death Rituals, Buddhist
Deities, Buddhist
Devotions, Western Christian
Dharma
Esoteric Buddhism in China and Japan
Festivals, Buddhist
Gnostic Cosmogony in Buddhism
Hagiography: Eastern Christian
Hagiography: Western Christian
Hermits: Buddhist
Hermits: Eastern Christian
Hermits: Western Christian

Humor: Buddhist
Humor: Christian
Iconoclasm (Controversy)
Intercession for the Dead, Buddhist
Jansenist Controversy
John of the Cross, St.
Julian of Norwich
Kōan
Lavra
Lectio Divina
Life Cycle, Christian
Mandala
Mantras
Marathon Monks
Martyrs: Eastern Christian
Martyrs: Western Christian
Mount Meru
Nembutsu
Penitential Books
Pilgrimages, Buddhist
Pilgrimages, Christian: Eastern Europe
Pilgrimages, Christian: Near East
Pilgrimages, Christian: Western Europe

Pure Land Buddhism
Recluses, Western Christian
Relics, Christian Monastic
Repentance Rituals, Buddhist
Self-Immolation, Buddhist
Self-Mutilation, Christian
Spiritual Direction, Christian
Spirituality: Buddhist
Spirituality: Eastern Christian
Spirituality: Western Christian
Stūpa
Stylites
Suger
Theology, Eastern Christian
Trappists
Virtues, Buddhist
Vision, Mystical: Eastern Christian
Vision, Mystical: Western Christian
Visual Arts, Eastern Christian: Painting
Vocation, Christian
Zen, Arts of
Zen and the West

## Asceticism

Antony, St.
Bodhidharma
Body: Buddhist Perspectives
Body: Christian Perspectives
Bruno, St.
Buddha (Śākyamuni)
Buddhaghosa

Carthusians
Cassian, John
Cathars
Chinul
Damian, Peter, St.
Desert Fathers
Desert Mothers

Dōgen
Eisai (Yosai)
Elders, Russian Monastic (Startsi)
Ennin
Evagrius Ponticus
Fasting: Buddhist
Fasting: Eastern Christian

Fasting: Western Christian
Forest Masters
Gampopa
Guigo I
Hakuin
Hermits: Buddhist
Hermits: Eastern Christian
Hermits: Western Christian
Hesychasm
Holy Men/Holy Women: Buddhist
     Perspectives
Holy Men/Holy Women: Christian
     Perspectives
Hōnen
Huaihai (Huai-hai)
Huineng
Isaac the Syrian (Isaac of Nineveh), St.
Jerome, St.
Joseph of Volokolamsk, St.

Kūkai
Labdron, Machig
Macarian Homilies
Macarius of Alexandria, St.
Marathon Monks
Maximus the Greek, St.
Milarepa
Mount Athos, Greece
Mount Hiei, Japan
Nilus of Sora, St.
Padmasambhava
Paisy Velichkovsky
Palamas, Gregory, St.
Peter of Alcántara, St.
Philokalia
Rancé, Armand-Jean de
Recluses, Western Christian
Sabas, St.
Saichō

Sakya Pandita (Sapen)
Savonarola, Girolamo
Self-Immolation, Buddhist
Seraphim of Sarov, St.
Shenoute of Atripe
Shinran
Solitude: Buddhist Perspectives
Solitude: Christian Perspectives
Spirituality: Buddhist
Spirituality: Eastern Christian
Spirituality: Western Christian
Stylites
Symeon the New Theologian, St.
Teresa of Avila, St.
Theodore of Stoudios, St.
Trappists
Wŏnhyo
Yeshe Tsogyel
Zhiyi (Chih-i)

## Theology

Abelard, Peter
Albertus Magnus, St.
Ambrose, St.
Anselm, St.
Augustinian Friars/Hermits
Augustinian Rule
Basil the Great, St.
Benedictines: General or Male
Bernard of Clairvaux, St.
Bonaventure, St.
Carmelites: General or Male
Casel, Odo
Christianity: Overview
Chrysostom, John, St.
Cistercians: General or Male
Dionysius the Pseudo-Areopagite
Dominicans: General or Male
Evagrius Ponticus

Franciscans: General or Male
Gregory I (the Great), St.
Gregory of Nazianzus, St.
Gregory of Nyssa, St.
Humanism, Christian
Isaac the Syrian (Isaac of Nineveh), St.
Jansenist Controversy
Jerome, St.
Joachim of Fiore
John of Damascus, St.
Liturgical Movement 1830–1980
Luther, Martin
Macarian Homilies
Marmion, Columba
Mystics, German Monastic: Female
Mystics, German Monastic: Male
Palamas, Gregory, St.
Philokalia

Sabas, St.
Spirituality: Eastern Christian
Spirituality: Western Christian
Suger
Symeon the New Theologian, St.
Theology, Eastern Christian
Theology, Western Christian: Augustinian
     Friars/Hermits
Theology, Western Christian: Benedictine
Theology, Western Christian: Carmelite
Theology, Western Christian: Dominican
Theology, Western Christian: Franciscan
Thomas Aquinas, St.
Victorines
Vision Mystical: Eastern Christian
Vision Mystical: Western Christian

## Scholarship

Albertus Magnus, St.
Alcuin
Ambrose, St.
Anselm, St.
Archives, Western Christian
Bacon, Roger
Baker, Augustine
Basil the Great, St.
Beauduin, Lambert
Bede, St.
Bernard of Clairvaux, St.
Bible Interpretation
Biblical Figures and Practices
Bonaventure, St.
Botany
Buddhadāsa
Buddhaghosa
Buddhology
Butler, Cuthbert
Casel, Odo
Cassian, John

Cassiodorus
Chapman, John
Chinul
Chrysostom, John, St.
Climacus, John, St.
Collegeville, Minnesota
Critiques of Buddhist Monasticism: Confucian
Critiques of Buddhist Monasticism:
     Indo-Tibetan
Critiques of Buddhist Monasticism: Japanese
Critiques of Western Christian Monasticism
Damian, Peter, St.
Dharmapāla, Anagārika
Dionysius the Pseudo-Areopagite
Discourses (Sūtras): Mahāyāna
Discourses (Suttas): Theravāda
Dominic, St.
Echternach, Luxembourg
Eckhart, Meister
Education of Christian Monastics
Evagrius Ponticus

Gender Studies: Buddhist Perspectives
Gender Studies: Christian Perspectives
Gregory I (the Great), St.
Gregory of Nazianzus, St.
Gregory of Nyssa, St.
Griffiths, Bede
Guéranger, Prosper
Hagiography: Eastern Christian
Hagiography: Western Christian
Hildegard of Bingen, St.
Historiography, Recent: Eastern Christian
Historiography, Recent: Western Christian
Hrosthwitha
Humanism, Christian
Hume, Basil
Internet, Buddhist and Christian
Isaac the Syrian (Isaac of Nineveh), St.
Isidore of Seville, St.
Istanbul, Turkey
Jerome, St.
Jerusalem, Israel

## Art and Architecture

## Economic Activities

# A

## Abbess, Christian

When, in the second century, groups of women who had made the difficult and dangerous decision to devote themselves to chastity and to the Christian ideal gathered together for protection and support, the oldest among them would instruct her sisters in the principles and practice of their new life. From this beginning the role of abbess of a monastic community expanded to include not only spiritual and educational obligations but also financial, administrative, political, social, and legal duties. For at least the first thousand years of female monasticism, financial reality, as well as the cultural associations of authority with wealth and social status, ensured that women of means who were adept at handling money, administering estates, and utilizing connections with powerful males would be those best remembered for founding and maintaining successful communities. However, these foundations often contained women from all conditions of life, for example, former prostitutes and slaves mingled with nobles, widows, wives, and virgins. Maintaining harmony undoubtedly required extraordinary skills. Tough and able, these founders were businesswomen, social workers, stern disciplinarians, and often exemplary ascetics, devising relentless daily schedules of work, study, and prayer.

Wherever it was introduced, the Christian movement during its early stages welcomed women in active roles. Gradually, however, Roman cultural beliefs, such as those expressed through the teachings of Paul and many of the early Christian fathers, circumscribed the parameters of women's participation as the new religion became an established institution. Early female monastic leaders in the East, prevented from acting in a priestly capacity, were slowly pressured into seclusion and silence. However, their lives both inspired the successes and foreshadowed the difficulties of the great abbesses of the early Middle Ages.

On the frontiers of the Roman Empire, the period of conversion to Christianity created a "golden age" for Christian abbesses. In Ireland monastic communities were the first "towns," providing a context in which all sorts of people could live and work together outside the small family unit. From the very beginning Irish women were founding and administering hundreds of such institutions, most of which had disappeared by the 10th or 11th century. We know the names of only a few of these women, and then only because they were considered saints

(i.e., extraordinary women who could work miracles). However, in the stories of their lives their human side can often be perceived. Brigit, the late fifth- and early sixth-century foundress of Kildare, and her successors were in charge of both male and female monastics in a foundation that was a major ecclesiastical power in Ireland for centuries and that launched a widespread network of daughter houses. Yet we see Brigit churning butter or gently encouraging one of her charges who was struggling with temptation. Moninna founded and cared for a community of 150 women and ended up battling demons for possession of their souls by dressing in animal skins and ploughing the earth with a wooden hoe. Such was the respect due to the spiritual power of these abbesses that they negotiated with kings and lords for the release of hostages and the cessation of hostilities, yet they taught their charges reading, writing, and Christian philosophy with humility and patience. The hagiographies, or saints' lives, of the Irish abbesses emphasized how compassion and charity often created misgivings among their nuns, who feared their leaders would give everything away and leave them with nothing. Brigit's active preaching and Moninna's brave example greatly helped to define and popularize Irish Christianity.

In Anglo-Saxon England abbesses were usually queens or related to royalty and came to the Church as widows or wives. Their physical motherhood underscored the ancient attribution of abbesses as mothers to their communities. All abbesses of this time were expected to be learned, but the Anglo-Saxons put special emphasis on wisdom. Abbesses such as St. Hilda were famed for training future bishops and advising kings. Saint Leoba was proficient in the works of the Church fathers, ecclesiastical law, and the decrees of Church councils. Their hagiographers emphasized the importance of discipline and obedience in their lives, and by the eighth and ninth centuries this emphasis facilitated obedience to the Roman Church (which demanded the strict seclusion of women). Hilda herself hosted and participated on the losing side at the Synod of Whitby (664), which decided that northern Europe would follow the Roman rather than the Celtic Church.

Although regional differences existed between the way early abbesses were depicted, their responsibilities were similar regardless of time or place. Abbesses were expected to maintain and protect their communities in a still pagan environment under constant threat of violence, plague, and famine. Even after the

Western world became thoroughly Christianized, life was precarious, and rich monastic lands, especially those in the hands of supposedly vulnerable women, were always a target for rapacious lords, worldly bishops, and marauding barbarians. As the Middle Ages progressed, abbesses struggled to balance demands from the Church for their strict claustration against the needs of their communities, including basic financial needs that required interaction with the outside world as well as a need to perform their works of charity and tend to the sick. These women also battled accusations of vanity and sexual improprieties from a secular and ecclesiastical world that was unable to believe that a community of women could live without male supervision. Some of these accusations were justified. Some abbesses were inept and others morally deficient, but those who fulfilled the requirements of their position must have been heroic. The value of these women in bringing people to the Church and vice versa is inestimable. In modern times Christian abbesses face many of the same challenges and difficulties in their ambiguous and often dangerous task of maintaining Christian ideals in the face of social reality. As in medieval times, many choose to obey the Church and remain in seclusion, but others choose to follow Christ by acting out their beliefs among the people.

DIANE PETERS AUSLANDER

*See also* Benedictines: Female; Brigit, St.; Contemporary Issues: Western Christian; England: History; Governance: Christian Perspectives; Hagiography: Western Christian; Hilda, St.; Ireland: History; Liturgy: Western Christian; Women's Monasteries: Western Christian

## Further Reading

Alexandre, Monique, "Early Christian Women," in *A History of Women in the West*, edited by Georges Duby and Michelle Perrot, Cambridge, Massachusetts: Belknap Press of Harvard University Press, 1992
Bitel, Lisa M., "Women's Monastic Enclosures in Early Ireland: A Study of Female Spirituality and Male Monastic Mentalities," *Journal of Medieval History* 12 (1986)
Cloke, Gillian, "This Female Man of God," in *Women and Spiritual Power in the Patristic Age*, A.D. 340–450, London and New York: Routledge, 1995
Gilchrist, Roberta, *Gender and Material Culture: The Archaeology of Religious Women*, London and New York: Routledge, 1994
Hollis, Stephanie, *Anglo-Saxon Women and the Church: Sharing a Common Fate*, Woodbridge, Suffolk, and Rochester, New York: Boydell Press, 1992
Johnson, Penelope D., *Equal in Monastic Profession: Religious Women in Medieval France*, Chicago: University of Chicago Press, 1991
McNamara, Jo Ann Kay, *Sisters in Arms: Catholic Nuns through Two Millennia*, Cambridge, Massachusetts: Harvard University Press, 1996
Millinger, Susan, "Humility and Power: Anglo-Saxon Nuns in Anglo-Norman Hagiography," in *Distant Echoes*, volume 1, edited by John A. Nichols and Lillian Thomas Shanks, Kalamazoo, Michigan: Cistercian Publications, 1984
Ridyard, Susan J., *The Royal Saints of Anglo-Saxon England: A Study of West Saxon and East Anglian Cults*, Cambridge and New York: Cambridge University Press, 1988
Schulenberg, Jane Tibbetts, "Women's Monastic Communities, 500–1100: Patterns of Expansion and Decline," in *Sisters and Workers in the Middle Ages*, edited by Judith M. Bennett, Chicago: University of Chicago Press, 1976
Schulenberg, Jane Tibbetts, "Strict Active Enclosure and Its Effects on the Female Monastic Experience (c. 500–1100)," in *Distant Echoes*, volume 1, edited by John A. Nichols and Lillian Thomas Shanks, Kalamazoo, Michigan: Cistercian Publications, 1984
Schulenberg, Jane Tibbetts, "Female Sanctity: Public and Private Roles, c. 500–1100," in *Women and Power in the Middle Ages*, edited by Mary Erler and Maryanne Kowaleski, Athens: University of Georgia Press, 1988

# Abbeys, Territorial

Territorial abbeys, formerly known as abbeys-*nullius*, are monasteries that possess an extraordinary, geographically defined exemption and jurisdiction. In the Catholic Church, all monks of exempt orders (e.g., Benedictines and Cistercians) enjoy personal exemption, meaning that in matters of internal governance the religious is accountable directly to the Holy See. *Nullius* status enlarges on that personal prerogative by affording a territorial exemption. This removes the monastery itself and whatever pastoral area assigned to it by the Holy See from the boundaries and influence of a diocese or bishop. Thus, in effect, an abbey-*nullius* is its own diocese, and its abbot is "ordinary," holding ordinary jurisdiction within his allotted territory. The term "abbey-*nullius*" is meant to indicate *abbatia nullius dioecesis* (an abbey of no diocese).

The origin of this status is shrouded, but a few threads of its history have been uncovered by modern scholars. Both Monte Cassino (Italy) and Einsiedeln (Switzerland) have claimed to be the first abbey-*nullius*. Einsiedeln's claim is stronger, although it has not always enjoyed privileges as great as those granted to the Italian monastery. Nevertheless, it is clear that *nullius* exemptions came into existence no later than the ninth century, and thereafter their concept, status, and privileges remained reasonably consistent.

Because territorial abbots act as ordinaries, they are sometimes allowed to receive episcopal consecration. However, that privilege is granted only as a matter of local tradition or personal favor, never because of any jurisdictional entitlement. Nonetheless, by right of office abbots-*nullius* are permitted to exercise the rights, functions, privileges, and duties of bishops, except for those that require powers indebted to episcopal consecration (e.g., the power to ordain men to major orders). Thus, the abbot-*nullius* is truly a functioning head of a diocese; indeed, his quasi-episcopal status was explicitly affirmed in the 1917 Code of Canon Law. As external marks of this dignity, an abbot-*nullius* is entitled to use episcopal colors (e.g., in clothing and

The United States' only territorial abbey had a history typical of such monasteries. Belmont Abbey (in North Carolina) held "diocesan" rank from 1910 to 1977. Originally it governed eight counties, but in 1960 its "diocesan" territory was partitioned to consist exclusively of the monastery's own grounds (seen here), about 600 acres.
Photo courtesy of Belmont Abbey Archives

heraldry) and has precedence (e.g., in processions) over conventional abbots, even over archabbots.

Significantly for abbeys-*nullius*, the monastic chapter has always retained the right of electing the abbot and thus of electing the ordinary of its diocese. After election, the chapter's choice is submitted to Rome for approval. However, a *terna* (listing three candidates for the ordinary's throne) is not needed, as it is in conventional dioceses. Instead, as the practice developed after the Council of Trent, the monastic chapter's nominee required the approbation of both the curial congregation for religious (as with conventional abbeys) and the congregation that dealt with bishops (as with candidates listed on a conventional diocese's *terna*).

For monasteries this diocesan status was a mixed blessing. Unlike purely honorific distinctions (e.g., archiabbatial status), it imparted real powers and bestowed rank rather than mere precedence. It also imposed serious obligations. Among these were oversight of the local Church and reports to Rome. Repeated absences of the abbot were also necessitated. For example, he was expected to attend bishops' meetings and even to participate in ecumenical councils; the abbot ordinary was

obliged to undertake the periodic *ad limina* journeys to the Holy See; and, within his separated territory, the abbot, like a bishop, was required to make the various visitations of parishes and to preside at confirmations.

The distraction imposed by pastoral duties was proportional to the territory attached to the abbatial diocese. This varied considerably. In some cases an extended missionary area was administered by the monks (who might employ secular priests to assist them). However, it was not uncommon for the *nullius* to be restricted to the grounds of the abbey itself.

Canon law has dealt variously with territorial abbeys. Initially, the law addressed abbeys-*nullius* as independent, subdiocesan jurisdictions (rather like a vicariate-apostolic). However, with the issuance of the 1917 code that perspective was revised. In this newer code the focus was placed on the person of the ordinary rather than discussing the *nullius* in terms of its separated territory. Accordingly, because within his own territory the abbot-*nullius* exercised jurisdiction comparable to a bishop's within his diocese, the *nullius* was transformed from being subdiocesan to being quasi-diocesan. Thus, in effect, the 1917 code enhanced the status of abbeys-*nullius*.

Church interior, territorial abbey (Benedictine) at Pannonhalma, Hungary, 13th century.
Photo courtesy of Chris Schabel

The number of territorial abbeys has varied through the years, seldom exceeding 60. Those whose status was mainly honorific tended to endure, whereas those that initially addressed a real pastoral or missionary need usually found their diocesan character terminated once a local diocesan clergy was established.

After the Second Vatican Council (1962–1965), abbeys-*nullius* were generally accounted to be historical anomalies. Virtually all those that still existed were merely honorific, having (at most) a token diocesan territory. Two conciliar shifts in pastoral theology had discredited *nullius* jurisdictions. First, the Church at this time reaffirmed its traditional position that an ordained bishop was the proper head of a pastoral territory. Second, the Church no longer recognized the propriety of maintaining dioceses as historical testimonials. Pastoral care was to be the criterion for a diocese's existence.

Finally, under the reign of Pope Paul VI (1963–1978) the creation of new abbeys-*nullius* ceased. Then, on 23 October 1976, the Vatican issued a *motu proprio* titled *De Abbatiarum Nullius Dioeceseos Innovatione*. It called for the gradual termination of abbeys-*nullius* throughout the universal Church. Suppressions began immediately, the first taking place in the United States at Belmont Abbey-*Nullius* in North Carolina on 1 January 1977. When the canon law was revised in 1983, even the title "abbey-

*nullius*" was abolished, replaced by "territorial abbey," a term that reflected the current (and pre-1917) understanding of such jurisdictions. The suppressions continued under this newest code of canon law until, within a mere 20 years of the issuance of the *motu proprio*, four out of five of the precounciliar abbeys-*nullius* had lost diocesan character.

Unlike the cathedral-abbeys of England, abbeys-*nullius* were real, independent dioceses that contributed significantly to the establishment of a strong local Church. Whereas the English cathedral-abbeys derived their status from being attached to a diocesan see, abbeys-*nullius* governed the Church in their own specified territories, exercising full, ordinary authority and legitimate, canonical, diocesan jurisdiction. Although cathedral-abbeys and abbeys-*nullius* are not uncommonly confused, in both character and practice the disparity between them was substantial.

PASCHAL BAUMSTEIN, O.S.B.

*See also* Abbot: Christian; Bishops: Jurisdiction and Role; Monk-Bishops

## Further Reading

*Acta Sanctae Sedis* (1865– )
Bachofen, Charles Augustine, *Rights and Duties of Ordinaries*, St. Louis, Missouri: Herder, 1924

Baumstein, Paschal, "An Abbatial Diocese in the United States," *The Catholic Historical Review* 79 (1993)

Benko, Matthew A., *The Abbot "Nullius,"* Catholic University of America Canon Law Studies number 173, Washington, D.C.: Catholic University of America Press, 1943

Chokier, Erasmus, *De Jurisdectione Ordinarii in Exemptos*, 1629; as *Codicis Iuris Canonici*, Vatican City: Typis Polyclottis Vaticanis, 1871–1881, 1917, 1993

# Abbot: Buddhist

When the Buddha established a monastic community (*saṃgha*), it was envisioned as an order of wandering mendicants (*bhikṣu*) who left the home life and subsisted solely on alms given to them by the lay community. The vinaya rules stipulate that monastics were expected to live under trees or in temporary shelters and were allowed to remain in dwellings for extended periods of time only during the rainy season (*varṣa*) retreat, when travel was difficult or impossible. The rainy season habitations were generally of two kinds: *āvāsa*s and *ārāma*s. The former were demarcated and maintained by the monastic community, and the latter were generally donated by wealthy patrons. Each habitation contained individual huts in which monks could shelter. As these establishments grew, the entire area was often designated a *vihāra*.

During the Buddha's lifetime the eremitic ideal was maintained, but it appears that within 200 years of his death more permanent monastic establishments began to develop. Initially these were intended for use during the rainy season retreat, but increasing numbers of monks began to reside in them for longer periods, the result being that they expanded. As this trend continued, *vihāra*s began to acquire more buildings, administrators, staff, and libraries. A number of offices are mentioned in Indian vinaya literature, including a superintendent of novices, a superintendent of buildings, and a superintendent of food, but the office of a single person in charge of an entire monastic complex appears to have developed rather late in Indian Buddhist history. The structure of the early monastic community was based on a republican model, and the Buddha is said to have steadfastly refused attempts to institute a hierarchy. For example, when his cousin Devadatta asked him to name a successor, the Buddha reportedly said that there was no need for any person to become head of the order. What hierarchy existed tended to be based on seniority and the general acclaim of the community.

However, in other parts of the Buddhist world the establishment of Buddhism in a particular region was generally thought to coincide with the founding of monasteries, and these

The abbot of Pulguk-sa Monastery, South Korea, beginning the evening meal.
Photo courtesy of John Powers

commonly had a single monk who oversaw the affairs of the community. Outside India cenobitic monastic establishments have always been the norm (although there are small communities of eremitic ascetics who adhere to the paradigms of the early Buddhist community). In these organizations there is normally a hierarchy of offices, with an abbot at the top. For example, in Thailand the abbot of a monastery (*chao awat*) is perceived generally as representing the organization as a whole, and so he should be a person whose comportment is above reproach and whose learning enables him to adjudicate disputes with impartiality and in accordance with the vinaya. There are a number of formal requirements for abbots in Thailand: a candidate must have spent five years in the monastery and must be at least 25 years of age, and there must be no serious objections to his appointment from the other residents.

In eastern Asian traditions the abbot often plays a crucial role in determining the direction of a particular monastery. Numerous examples exist in Chinese Buddhist history of a new abbot (Chinese, *shang-tso*) taking charge of a monastery and changing its doctrinal orientation. Thus, for example, a monastery that had traditionally been devoted to Chan training might become a Pure Land (Ching-tu) establishment, and although individual monks might continue their earlier practices, the tenor of the monastery will generally shift, and those monks who are uncomfortable with the change in orientation might move to another monastery that is more congenial.

Chinese monasteries have three main administrative positions: *shang-tso*, *ssu-chu* (rector), and *tu-wei-na* (superintendent). The *shang-tso* is usually a senior monk who is respected for his probity and learning and often for his meditative attainments. Many abbots spend little time in actual administration and function mainly as figureheads who are thought to embody the ideals of the community. The actual administrative duties generally fall to the *ssu-chu*, who is in charge of such things as construction and maintenance of buildings, and the *tu-wei-na*, who is responsible for details relating to the daily lives of monks and the monastery, setting the times for the chanting of sūtras, meditation sessions, meals, and general upkeep of the grounds.

The situation is similar in Tibetan monasteries. The abbot (*mkhan po*) is generally a senior monk of long standing who has distinguished himself in learning and comportment. In the dGe lugs pa (Gelukpa) order, the abbot will generally have been awarded the *dge bshes* (geshe) degree and in the larger establishments would invariably have earned the highest level of distinction (*lha ram pa*). Because of the complexity of the scholastic curriculum that is the basis of training in the major Gelukpa monasteries, the abbot is expected to be someone who has thoroughly mastered it and who has also distinguished himself in dialectical debate and who is thus able to function as a repository of the tradition to which the monastery belongs. In other Tibetan orders, such as the bKa' brgyud pa (Kagyü), there is a formal program of training for abbots, and only those who demonstrate exceptional ability are given the title. In all Tibetan orders there is a vast curriculum of study that must be mastered by the abbot as well as a complex liturgical tradition that he is expected to maintain. In all Buddhist traditions the abbot plays a key role in the continuation and propagation of a given tradition. Although the day-to-day administration of a monastery is generally handled by others, the abbot is expected to provide spiritual direction and to embody the ideals of the group in his actions and teachings.

C. JOHN POWERS

*See also* Buddha (Śākyamuni); Buddhadāsa; China; Governance: Buddhist Perspectives; Hermits: Buddhist; Holy Men/Holy Women: Buddhist Perspectives; Master and Pupil: Buddhist Perspectives; Officials: Buddhist; Patrons, Buddhist: India; Rules, Buddhist (Vinaya): Historical; Saṅgha; Thailand; Tibet: History

**Further Reading**

Dutt, Sukumar, *Early Buddhist Monachism: 600 B.C.–100 B.C.* (Trubner's Oriental Series), London and New York: Kegan Paul, Trench, Trubner, Dutton, 1924; revised edition, London and New York: Asia Publishing House, 1960

Foulk, Theodore Griffith, "The 'Ch'an School' and Its Place in the Buddhist Monastic Tradition (Zen, Japan, China)," Ph.D. diss., University of Michigan, 1987

Lamotte, Étienne, "The Buddha, His Teachings and His Sangha," in *The World of Buddhism: Buddhist Monks and Nuns in Society and Culture*, edited by Heinz Bechert et al., London: Thames and Hudson, and New York: Facts on File, 1984

# Abbot: Christian

An abbot is the superior of an independent (*sui juris*) monastery, called an abbey, in which he exercises full spiritual and temporal power within the limits drawn by law and monastic regulations. This title is used among the Benedictines, Cistercians, and Trappists; in some other monastic orders and congregations (Camaldolese, Cluniacs, Olivetans, and Vallombrosans); and among the majority of the Basilians, the Regular Canons of St. Augustine, and some of their congregations and orders (Laterans, Arrouaise, and Norbertans). In the early Middle Ages, this title was used also with reference to superiors of secular clergy who were devoted to *vita canonica*. The abbot's counterpart in Eastern Christianity is the *hegumen* or archimandrite.

The word *abbot* (Latin, *abbas*) is derived from the Syrian Arameic *apa*, *abba*, employed in the New Testament in reference to God and translated as "father" (Mark 14:36; Rom. 8:15; Gal. 4:6). In the early stages of monasticism, the title of abbot was applied to charismatic anchorites who gathered around themselves disciples who wanted to learn the secrets of monastic life. Their position was based on the authority of "Father" and "Master" of a voluntary community of anchorites. With the creation of organized forms of monastic life (cenobites), the word *abbot* became the title of the superior of a community of monks, successfully superseding the term *provost* (*praepositus*), which was used for a time (e.g., in the Rule of St. Augustine). Gradually

Abbot's tomb, Abbey of Villers-la-Ville (Cistercian), Brabant, Belgium, 13th century.
Photo courtesy of Chris Schabel

the term *abbot* became reserved for superiors of independent monasteries, which were in turn called abbeys.

It was the Rule of St. Benedict that established the name for the superior of an independent monastic community as well as his position and role. In the Rule, St. Benedict refers to the abbot as the "successor of Christ" in the monastery (*Christi agere uices*, 2.2; 63.13) and as "Lord and Father" (*dominus et abbas*, 63.13) of the whole community. The nature of his power is not only administrative but above all charismatic; it is rooted in a paternal authority that unites the monastic "family" and in particular in the spiritual authority derived from God. In this sense respect paid to the abbot, even in a simple invocation of his name, is an act of faith.

Accountable to God, the abbot guards the purity of the Rule (2.6; 3.11; 64.21), and his principal task is to lead souls of fellow brethren to salvation. In his actions the abbot "is to help rather than to lead" (64.8); he is to be guided by the apostolic principle to "convince, plead, reprimand" (2.23); he is to be governed by compassion (64.11), prudence, providence, and circumspection (64.12, 17); and he must avoid all exaggeration (64.12). While making decisions he should ask the entire community for advice (3) or, in less important matters, seek the opinion of the council of elders (3.12). Nevertheless, the final decision "must depend mostly on his judgement" (*magis in abbatis pendat arbitrio*, 3.5).

The role of the abbot, his personality and energy, proved vital for the community and abbey. An abbot belonged to the local political elite. Abbots of affluent Benedictine abbeys held a position equal to that of bishops; quite often, especially in the early Middle Ages, they were appointed bishops. Rich and influential abbots traveled with large retinues and were frequent guests at royal courts. More and more often they became involved in politics and economic life. Some of them (e.g., at Farfa, Fulda, and Monte Cassino) ruled sovereign principalities. In these circumstances spiritual guidance of the monastic community was often transferred to the abbot's deputy, called prior, who represented the monastic community's interests, especially during the ruling periods of secular or commendatory abbots.

The fact that abbots exercised both administrative and spiritual leadership reinforced a deeply rooted tradition that shunned the changing of spiritual leader; out of this tradition developed the notion that an abbot should hold office for life. Enshrined in Justinian's constitution of 530, from the 13th century this principle was assailed. In newly established orders the principle of a limited term of office for monastic superiors gradually evolved. It was accepted by some Benedictine congregations founded in

Abbot's stall, France, probably Artois or Picardy, early 16th century. Oak, 329.6 × 336.3 × 83.8 cm. The Cleveland Museum of Art, 1999, purchase from the J.H. Wade Fund, 1928.657.
Photo courtesy of The Cleveland Museum of Art

of this kind were common during the period of the so-called secular abbots in the 9th to 10th century, again in the late Middle Ages, and later when the institution of commendatory abbots (i.e., persons receiving the usufruct of monastic benefice and its revenue yet without spiritual jurisdiction) was widespread. This institution, although formally forbidden by the Council of Trent (1545–1563), survived until the 19th century.

With the appearance of secular and commendatory abbots, a need arose to safeguard the temporal needs of the monks by establishing the so-called common (conventual) table on a certain part of the estate. The income produced by the common table was used to care for the monks' needs. The remaining estates and income of the monastery constituted the so-called abbot's table and were designated for the exclusive use of the abbot. This income usually was used to cover the buildings' maintenance and repair costs and some other prescribed expenditures of the monastery. The earlier ideal of abbot, expressed in the Rule of St. Benedict, was revived by the monastic restoration of the 19th century.

Today an abbot is elected by the conventual chapter in a secret vote for the term prescribed by the order's or congregation's constitution, that is, for life, or for an indefinite term, or until reaching a certain retiring age, or for a set number of years. He must have been professed at least 10 years, of legitimate birth, at least 30 (originally 25) years old, a member of the same abbey or at least of the same order or congregation, and an ordained priest (or on his way to becoming one soon), and he must receive a consecration and abbatial blessing from the diocesan bishop within three months (originally within one year). On that occasion he receives the attributes of his power: a copy of the Holy Rule of St. Benedict, crozier, ring, miter, and pectoral cross. He is also granted the right to use a throne with a canopy as well as to confer tonsure and minor orders on his religious. Since the Middle Ages abbots have been allowed, by papal privilege, the use of pontificals (i.e., of insignia and ceremonial proper to bishops).

Canon law distinguishes at least three types of abbots. A regular abbot (*abbas-regularis*) governs his abbey. If he enjoys episcopal exemption, the abbot is accountable only to the pope and authorities of his order. He has ordinary jurisdiction in the external and internal forum over all persons belonging to the abbey. An abbot-*nullius* (*abbas-nullius*) has episcopal jurisdiction over all persons (clergy and laity alike) in the territory subject directly to the abbey. Abbots who are superiors in various religious congregations may use special titles (e.g., archabbot, *abbas-generalis*, *abbas-praeses*, or abbot-primate).

In formal address an abbot is titled "right reverend abbot," but his religious would address him as "father abbot."

MAREK DERWICH

*See also* Abbeys, Territorial; Benedict of Nursia, St.; Bishops: Jurisdiction and Role; Cluny, Abbots of; Economics: Christian; France: History; Governance: Christian Perspectives; Monk-Bishops; Officials: Western Christian; Origins: Western Christian; Patrons, Christian: Royal; Regulations: Christian Perspectives; Visual Arts, Western Christian: Liturgical Furnishings

Glastonbury Tor with the tower of the chapel of St. Michael, Glastonbury (Somerset), England. Richard Whiting, the last abbot of the Benedictine Abbey of Glastonbury, was executed here in 1539 for refusing to accept dissolution.
Photo courtesy of Chris Schabel

the late Middle Ages and in the modern era and, with time, even by some black monks' abbeys. Usually the abbot served for three years.

Initially an abbot in office appointed his successor (e.g., Pachomius and the Rule of the Master), but the Rule of St. Benedict (64) established the principle of having the abbot elected by all monks in the monastery. In practice, however, numerous exceptions occurred because of the abbot's position and social role and because of the gradual feudalization of the office. Frequently, temporal powers (king or prince), Church authorities (pope or bishop), and (especially in the early Middle Ages) the founders of the monastery or their descendants and local feudal lords intervened in the selection process. Abbots imposed by these persons could be selected from among the monastery's own monks or come from another abbey; the latter solution was common during the period of monastic reforms. However, most dangerous was the appointment of a monk belonging to a different order or even a layperson to the position of abbot. Incidents

## Further Reading

Constable, Giles, "The Authority of Superiors in Religious Communities," in *La notion d'autorité au Moyen Age: Islam, Byzance, Occident: Colloques internationaux de la Napoule, session des 23–26 octobre 1978*, Paris: Presses universitaires de France, 1982; also in his *Monks, Hermits and Crusaders in Medieval Europe* (Variorum Collected Studies Series), London: Variorum Reprints, 1988

Felten, Franz, *Äbte und Laienäbte im Frankenreich: Studie zum Verhältnis von Staat und Kirche im früheren Mittelalter* (Monographien zur Geschichte des Mittelalters, 20), Stuttgart: Hiersemann, 1980

Felten, Franz, "Herrschaft des Abtes," in *Herrschaft und Kirche: Beiträge zur Entstehung und Wirkungsweise episkopaler und monastischer Organisationsformen* (Monographien zur Geschichte des Mittelalters, 33), edited by Friedrich Prinz, Stuttgart: Hiersemann, 1988

Fracheboud, André, "Le Portrait de l'Abbé aux origines cisterciennes," *Collectanea Cisterciensia* 48 (1986)

Giordanengo, Geneviève, "La fonction d'abbé d'après l'œuvre de Geoffroy de Vendôme," *Revue d'histoire de l'Église de France* 76 (1990)

Hegglin, Benno, *Der benediktinische Abt in rechtsgeschichtlicher Entwicklung und geltendem Kirchenrecht* (Kirchengeschichtliche Quellen und Studien, 5), St. Ottilien: EOS Verlag der Erzabtei St. Ottilien, 1961

Hilpisch, Stephanus, "Entwicklung des Ritus der Abtsweihe in der lateinischen Kirche," *Studien und Mitteilungen zur Geschichte des Benediktinerordens und seiner Zweige* 61 (1947)

Lemaître, Jean-Loup, "Les compagnons de route de l'abbé de Cluny au XIIe siècle," in *Istituzioni monastiche e istituzioni canonicali in Occidente (1123–1215): Atti della settima Settimana internazionale di studio Mendola, 28 agosto–3 settembre 1977* (Miscellanea del Centro di Studi Medioevali, 9), Milan: Vita e Pensiero, 1977

Lienhard, S.J., "*Sanius Concilium*. Recent Work on the Election of the Abbot in the 'Rule' of St. Benedict," *American Benedictine Review* 26 (1975)

Penco, Gregorio, "La figura dell'abate nella tradizione spirituale del monachesimo," *Benedictina* 17 (1970); also in his *Medioevo monastico* (Studia Anselmiana, 96), Rome: Edizioni Abbazia S. Paolo, 1988

Salmon, Pierre, *The Abbot in Monastic Tradition: A Contribution to the History of the Perpetual Character of the Office of Religious Superiors in the West* (Cistercian Studies Series, 14), Washington: Consortium Press, 1972

Vogüé, Adalbert de, *Community and Abbot in the Rule of St. Benedict* (Cistercian Studies Series, 5), 2 vols., translated by Charles Philippi and Ethel Rae Perkins, Kalamazoo, Michigan: Cistercian Publications, 1979, 1988

Vogüé, Adalbert de, "The Abbot, Vicar of Christ, in RB and RM," *Word and Spirit* 6 (1984)

# Abbot Primate, Benedictine

Pope Leo XIII (1878–1903) had an orderly mind, and his clarity of thought was offended by the various factions that had arisen in many of the religious orders. During his pontificate various Franciscan groups were affiliated into the Order of Friars Minor, and three different orders of reformed Cistercians joined to form the Order of Cîteaux, Strict Observance (commonly referred to as Trappists). When Leo turned his attention to the "Order of St. Benedict," he saw what seemed to him to be the greatest confusion and the greatest resistance to "reform." According to oral tradition, he took a look at the Benedictines and called it "ordo sine ordine" (an order without order).

There was much to justify such a remark. Until 1893 the congregations existed side by side without any bond between them, having in common nothing more than a professed allegiance to a particular Rule that none followed literally. Apparently as early as 1886, the pope had determined that the same sort of approach to amalgamation being undertaken among Franciscans and Trappists should apply to the Benedictines, for on 4 January 1887 he sent a letter to Archbishop Dusmet of Catania, a Benedictine of the Cassinese Congregation, expressing his desire to reopen the old Cassinese Collegium Anselmianum with the intention that it should serve as a theological college for all the independent congregations that described themselves as Benedictine. In one part of the letter, he said, "As the forces of those who are united together are stronger, the hope of better things in the future will be much firmer if the various members of the Benedictine order, scattered far and wide, were to coalesce as if into one body, with one and the same laws, and one and the same government." The letter went on to propose the restoration of the college at St. Anselmo as a first step in this process.

In certain Benedictine circles these words seemed ominous because it was feared that they presaged some such piece of unification as Leo XIII effected in the case of the Franciscans and Trappists. It is difficult to believe that such was not his intention. Nothing further was heard of the matter until 1893, when in April a meeting of all Benedictine abbots was convoked at Rome for the laying of the foundation stone of the new College of St. Anselmo. Acting in the pope's name, Archbishop Dusmet, by this time a cardinal, laid before the abbots a series of proposals from the Holy See. Included in the topics proposed for discussion were the creation of an abbot primate to oversee the Benedictines and the organization of the new college. The assembled abbots were invited to submit a response.

The pope proposed that although all the congregations would retain their existing structures and officials, an abbot primate would be created to oversee the business of the whole order. The abbots rewrote this to assert that the abbot primate would not have the right to change officials within a congregation. They also changed the title of the proposed new primate to "representative" (this more accurately describing his relationship to the Benedictine congregations) and stated that he should have no jurisdiction within existing congregations. The pope further proposed that the primate be elected for a 12-year term by the presidents of the congregations; the abbots responded that the electors should rather be all active abbots. Finally the pope proposed that although the primate would reside at St. Anselmo, the superior of the college would be a rector; but in their response the abbots suppressed the office of rector, suggesting that the superior should, as customary for Benedictines, be the abbot of St. Anselmo. In effect the abbots' reply had eliminated not only the office but also the title of primate.

The pope's brief, "Summum Semper," involved a compromise, accepting the suggestions of the abbots but retaining the title of abbot primate. The abbots had failed to prevent the establishment of a primate but had succeeded in preserving and protecting the independence of the congregations and individual abbeys from outside interference. Although there would now be an official called the abbot primate of the Benedictines, the abbots had seen to it that he would be kept busy with the affairs of St. Anselmo rather than having a primary responsibility to look after the affairs of the Benedictines.

The definition of the primate's positions, rights, and functions came in the decree "Inestimabilis," issued in September 1893:

1. Every five years the presidents of congregations must send the primate a report of the state of the congregation.
2. If problems arise within a congregation that cannot be handled internally, recourse is to be made to the primate, who shall do his utmost to compose the dispute.
3. If there is urgent necessity for an immediate visitation of one of the congregations, the primate has the right of making the visitation.
4. The primate is to see to it that regular discipline is maintained in the congregations.

Noteworthy here is that it is all very vague and, one might say, Benedictine. The only article that gives the abbot primate any sort of jurisdiction is the third, yet even here the language is explicit in regarding the situation as exceptional. Even should the primate act in such an emergency, he is to report to the Holy See for further instruction. One must conclude that the vagueness in the legislation is intentional and that Leo XIII acquiesced in the abbots' thwarting his original intentions to organize a more central authority for the "Black Monks."

Looking back at a period of more than a century since the institution of the office of abbot primate, what have been the results? No doubt they have been more modest than Leo XIII originally intended in his "reform" of the Benedictines. The significance of St. Anselmo in establishing personal relationships that cross congregational and national lines cannot be minimized, yet no closer juridical connections exist between the congregations than did in 1893 (other than the office of the abbot primate itself). Monasteries do exist that are not part of a congregation but are under the direct authority of the abbot primate. Abbot primates have generally encouraged these communities to affiliate with a congregation, and some have done so. Since the Second Vatican Council (1962–1965) and the adoption of the vernacular for the liturgy, there has been no common Benedictine version of the Divine Office. The abbot primate has been pivotal in providing guidelines and resources for the revision of the Divine Office in Benedictine monasteries, especially through issuing the "Thesaurus Liturgiae Horarum Monasticae" in 1977.

AELRED GLIDDEN, O.S.B.

*See also* Congregations, Benedictine; Franciscans: General or Male; Orders (Religious), Origin of; Trappists

## Further Reading

Butler, Edward Cuthbert, *Benedictine Monachism: Studies in Benedictine Life and Rule*, London and New York: Longmans, Green, 1919; 2nd edition, London and New York: Longmans, Green, 1924; reprint, London: Speculum Historiae, 1961

## Related Web Site
*http://www.italkey.it/MONASTERI/primate.html*

# Abelard, Peter 1079–1142

French Benedictine philosopher and theologian

Abelard was born in 1079 in Le Palais near Nantes in Brittany. His monastic career began on the heels of controversy and was itself controversial in its departure from the Benedictine value of stability. After his defeat of the realism of William of Champeaux (c. 1070–1121), he taught in opposition to William at Melun and Corbeil and later set up his own school either in or near the monastery of St. Geneviève. Following a disastrous encounter with Anselm of Laon (d. 1117), Abelard became master of the schools and was likely a canon of Paris. More controversy ensued when Abelard began an affair with Heloise (c. 1100–1163/64), the niece of Fulbert, canon of Notre Dame. When she conceived their son, Abelard secretly married her and placed her in the convent of Argenteuil. After the enraged Fulbert had Abelard castrated, Abelard took monastic vows at the Benedictine abbey of St. Denis in 1118 and began writing theological works.

Partly at the behest of Anselm of Laon's students, in 1121 the Council of Soissons condemned his Trinitarian theology and sent him to St. Médard. He later returned to St. Denis. He gained more enemies when he denied that their patron saint, Denis, was the Dionysius who had been bishop of Athens. Forced to leave the abbey, he founded the Paraclete near Nogent-sur-Seine in 1125.

Once again Abelard attracted a large following, and in 1126 he accepted the invitation to become abbot of St. Gildas. The monks reacted to his attempts to discipline them by attempting to poison him. His constant wanderings from monastery to monastery led Bernard of Clairvaux (1190–1153) to condemn him as a "monk without a home."

In 1128 news reached him that Abbot Suger (c. 1081–1151) of St. Denis had laid claim to Heloise's community at Argenteuil, where she had become prioress. Abelard met them at the Paraclete and installed them there in 1129; Heloise later became the first abbess. After his return to St. Gildas, in 1132 he wrote his autobiography, the *Historia Calamitatum*. It came to Heloise's attention by chance, and so began their famous correspondence. Although some scholars have questioned the authenticity of these letters, most modern scholars accept them as authentic. In the fifth letter of the correspondence, according to Betty Radice's numbering, Heloise requested a history of the order of nuns and also a rule more suitable for women than the Rule of St. Benedict.

Her request is puzzling in light of the fact that the Rule had historically been modified through customaries to suit the needs not only of women but also of varying locales and other circumstances. Abelard himself reminded her that many of her difficulties had already been resolved by dispensation and argued that the same institutions were suitable for both monks and nuns. Thus, it is unclear whether Abelard intended his rule to supplant the Rule of St. Benedict. In keeping with the spirit of moderation in the Rule of St. Benedict, he forbade excessive asceticism and self-mortification. He allowed the nuns to eat meat three times a week. However, he departed from the Rule by insisting that bread be made of at least one-third coarse grain and by not emphasizing manual labor. He required strict enclosure.

Abelard distinguished between nuns who were consecrated as virgins by the bishop and those who were not, yet on all women religious he conferred great dignity. In the sixth letter of the correspondence, Abelard argued that the consecration of virgins was prior in the order of grace to that of monks and that women had performed clerical roles in the past. He called the abbess in his rule a deaconess, a title that had not been in existence for abbesses since the eighth century and was then uncommon in the West. Like the early deaconesses Abelard's abbess was to be an older woman. In contrast to the customs of his time, the abbess was not to come from the nobility. Abelard's abbess ruled without a prioress, and he likened her power to that of a commander of a regimented army prepared to meet the assault of demons, an image drawn from the Benedictine Rule and other monastic documents. His use of imagery associated with male roles suggested an equal role for women in the monastic life.

Nevertheless, Abelard's rule placed women as "the weaker sex" under the guidance of men, who performed manual labor and presided over mass. Although a male community would be nearby whose abbot was technically the superior of the abbess, the abbot was not to question her will in any way or make decisions without her approval. The men were to vow never to consent to any oppression of the women.

Abelard's rule developed Benedict's notion of mutual obedience and attempted to re-create the community of the Book of Acts. He preserved the equality of women not through superiority as defined by Fontevrauld nor through subordination as defined by the Cluniacs but through the mutual obedience of equals. Although the Cistercian scholar Chrysogonus Waddell sees Abelard's rule as one of the most remarkable documents of the 12th century, the nuns of the Paraclete do not appear to have ever followed Abelard's rule, and he remains most well known for his controversial theological works.

Although Abelard continued to guide the nuns and wrote many sermons for them, he returned to Paris by 1136 to teach again at St. Geneviève, where John of Salisbury (c. 1115–1180) was one of his students. His controversial use of logic in theology eventually attracted the attention of Bernard of Clairvaux, who brought the matter before Pope Innocent II (1130–1143), and in 1140 the Council of Sens condemned Abelard for heresy

and excommunicated him from the Church. The pope later lifted the sentence, and Abelard retired to Cluny. He died in the Cluniac daughter house of St. Marcel in 1142. Although Abelard spent the greater part of his adult life as a monk of various monasteries, his constant wanderings led men and women religious of his day and ours to view him with suspicion. It was not until his last two years of life that Abelard earned the respect of his fellow monks. No less an authority than Peter the Venerable (1092/94–1156) praised Abelard as a man of prayer and humility who had graced Cluny with his presence.

DEBORAH VESS

See also Animals, Attitude toward: Christian Perspectives; Cluny, France; Fontevraud, France; France: History; Gender Studies: Christian Perspectives; Heloise; Hymnographers; Suger; Theology, Western Christian: Benedictine

## Biography

Born near Nantes the son of a Breton knight, Abelard studied with several teachers before becoming a lecturer in theology at Paris. Following his love affair with Heloise c.1116, he retired to the Abbey of St. Denis. Having antagonized the monks by challenging the legend of their foundation by St. Dionysius, he established a small community at the Paraclete near Troyes. Later Heloise became abbess there. In 1127 he became Abbot of St. Gildas before returning to teach in Paris. Peter the Venerable, Abbot of Cluny, rescued Abelard following the condemnation of his doctrines in 1140. After being reconciled to St. Bernard, Abelard died in a Cluniac priory near Chalon-sur-Saône.

## Major Works

*Dialectica*, 1117–1121
*Glossae Super Porphyrium, super Predicamenta, super Periermeneias, super Topica* (published together as the *Logica Ingredientibus*), 1117–1121
*Theologia Summi Boni*, c. 1119–1120
*Sic et non* (first recension, 1121)
*Theologia Christiana*, 1121–1126
*Dialogus I*, 1125–1126
*Historia Calamitatum*, 1132–1133
*Sermons for the Paraclete*, 1132–1137
*Commentaria in Epistolam Pauli ad Romanos*, 1133–1137
*Theologia Scholarium*, 1133–1137
*Ethica* or *Scito te Ipsum*, 1138–1139
*Apologia contra Bernardum*, 1140
*Confessio fidei*, 1140
Hymns (e.g. "O Quanta qualia")

## Further Reading

Benton, John F., "Fraud, Fiction and Borrowing in the Correspondence of Abelard and Heloise," in *Pierre Abélard, Pierre le Vénérable* (Colloques internationaux du centre national de la recherche scientifique, 546), Paris: Editions du Centre National de la Recherche Scientifique, 1975

Gilson, Etienne, *Héloïse et Abélard* (Essais d'art et de philosophie), Paris: Vrin, 1938; as *Heloise and Abelard*, London: Hollis and Carter, 1953; Ann Arbor: University of Michigan Press, 1960

Grane, Leif, *Peter Abelard: Philosophy and Christianity in the Middle Ages*, New York: Harcourt, 1964; London: Allen and Unwin, 1970

Grill, Von Leopold, "Die Neunzehn 'Capitula' Bernhards von Clairvaux gegen Abelard," *Historisches Jahrbucher* 80 (1961)

Luscombe, G.E., "Pierre Abelard et le monachisme," in *Pierre Abélard, Pierre le Vénérable* (Colloques internationaux du centre national de la recherche scientifique, 546), Paris: Editions du Centre National de la Recherche Scientifique, 1975

McLaughlin, Mary Martin, "Abelard as Autobiographer: The Motives and Meaning of His *Story of Calamities*," *Speculum* 42 (1967)

McLaughlin, Mary Martin, "Abelard and the Dignity of Women: Twelfth Century 'Feminism' in Theory and Practice," in *Pierre Abélard, Pierre le Vénérable* (Colloques internationaux du centre national de la recherche scientifique, 546), Paris: Editions du Centre National de la Recherche Scientifique, 1975

Murray, A. Victor, *Abélard and St. Bernard: A Study in Twelfth Century "Modernism,"* Manchester, Greater Manchester: Manchester University Press, and New York: Barnes and Noble, 1967

Newman, Barbara, "Authority, Authenticity, and the Repression of Heloise," *Journal of Medieval and Renaissance Studies* 22 (1992)

Sikes, Jeffrey Garrett, *Peter Abailard*, Cambridge: Cambridge University Press, 1932; New York: Russell and Russell, 1965

Southern, R.W., "The Letters of Abelard and Heloise," in his *Medieval Humanism and Other Studies*, Oxford: Blackwell, and New York: Harper and Row, 1970

Thomas, Rudolf, et al., editors, *Petrus Abaelardus, 1079–1142: Person, Werk und Wirkung* (Trierer Theologische Studien, 38), Trier: Paulinus-Verlag, 1980

Waddell, Chrysogonus, editor, *The Paraclete Statutes Institutiones Nostrae* (Cistercian Liturgy Series, 20), Trappist, Kentucky: Gethsemani Abbey, 1987

Weingart, Richard, *The Logic of Divine Love: A Critical Analysis of the Soteriology of Peter Abailard*, London: Clarendon Press, 1970

# Aelred of Rievaulx, St. c. 1109–1167

## Cistercian monk

Abbot of the Cistercian House at Rievaulx (Rye Vale), Yorkshire, from 1147 until 1167, Aelred owes his renown to his treatises on spiritual life. Son of a Saxon priest in Hexham, Northumbria, Aelred lived for a time at the court of King David of Scotland before entering Rievaulx around 1133. He wrote his most famous book, *Speculum caritatis* (*The Mirror of Charity*), in 1142–1143 at the request of Bernard of Clairvaux.

Aelred's spiritual teachings are based on two fundamental affirmations. The first is that the entire universe is informed by the creative energy and redeeming force of love – the love of a God who is love. Aelred is also convinced that human beings, al-though flawed by sin, are basically good and capable of the happiness for which they long. Human beings are entities whose essential components are a body and a soul. The soul functions in knowing (the intellect), in choosing (the will), and in perceiving, imagining, and remembering (the memory). To this traditional Augustinian triad Aelred adds the *affectus*, the power of attachment, which he describes as "a kind of spontaneous and delightful inclination of the spirit toward someone" (*The Mirror of Charity* 3.11.31). The body is good and so essential to human nature and its perfection that Aelred asserts that humans cannot fully enjoy the beatitude of paradise until their bodies are resurrected.

Human dignity derives from the Creator, in whose image and likeness humans are made. Through prideful self-centeredness, humans have lost their likeness to God (although not his image) and have exiled themselves in the misery of the land of unlikeness. Their re-formation in God's likeness is made possible through God's gift of himself in Jesus Christ, but this salvific process requires the ongoing response of human free choice. Thus, human perfection is a process of recovery, not a state of being.

The pilgrimage to perfection leads from humility (the perfection of the intellect in self-knowledge) to love (the perfection of the will). Aelred makes true love for self and neighbor the essential expression of the love for God that is necessary to human happiness. The *affectus* is perfected in friendship, the most natural and holiest of human relationships and a ladder by which to ascend to friendship with Christ and union with him.

For Aelred, meditation is the primary means by which one attains the humility of self-knowledge. Meditation requires intense activity of the intellect as well as the efforts of the imagination, will, and *affectus*. Aelred counsels meditation on and through nature, on the human condition, and especially on Scripture (*lectio divina*). Growth in true love (*caritas*) requires arduous effort to overcome false, self-centered love (*cupiditas*), an effort immeasurably assisted by the self-restraining practices of silence, simplicity, obedience, chastity, prayer, and unremitting service to others. Prudence and moderation in these practices are necessary to ensure that they do not lead to spiritual pride.

Those who follow this path to perfection might be granted, even in this life, the rapturous ecstasy of an experience of God. Aelred describes this contemplative experience through the images of spiritual intoxication and most often the embrace of the bridegroom, who both initiates and consummates union with his now beautiful bride, the soul.

Aelred's influence on monastic spirituality is demonstrated by the fact that Bernard of Clairvaux chose him to write what might be the defining treatise on Cistercian spirituality, *The Mirror of Charity*. Aelred's spiritual status was also enhanced by the *Life of Aelred*, written by his pupil and Rievaulx monk Walter Daniel. This work was widely circulated in medieval manuscripts and more recently in translation. Middle English translations of Aelred's *On Reclusion*, a treatise on the solitary life, were widely read in medieval England. Aelred's spirituality has become influential in the 20th century in both monastic and lay

Refectory exterior, Cistercian Abbey of Rievaulx, North Yorkshire, England, c. 1225.
Photo courtesy of Chris Schabel

circles, largely through the rediscovery and translation of his treatise *De spiritali amicitia* (*Spiritual Friendship*). The latter adapts Cicero's treatise *On Friendship*.

JOHN R. SOMMERFELDT

*See also* Cistercians; Humanism, Christian; Lectio Divina; Recluses, Western Christian; Spirituality: Western Christian

## Biography

Son of a Saxon priest, Aelred attended the court of King David of Scotland and then joined the Cistercian Order at its first Yorkshire house of Rievaulx c. 1133. Ten years later he became Abbot of Revesby and four years after that Abbot of Rievaulx, serving until his death in 1167. It was at the urging of Bernard of Clairvaux that Aelred wrote the treatise on "attachments" for which he is best known: *The Mirror of Charity*.

## Major Works

*Speculum caritatis*, 1142–1143; as *The Mirror of Charity*, translated and arranged by Geoffrey Webb and Adrian Walker, 1962; also translated by Elizabeth Connor, 1990
*De spiritali amicitia*, as *Spiritual Friendship*, translated by Mary Eugenia Laker, 1974
*Oratio pastoralis* (Pastoral Oration)
Life of Edward the Confessor
Sermons

## Further Reading

Dumont, Charles, "Aelred of Rievaulx's *Spiritual Friendship*," in *Cistercian Ideals and Reality*, edited by John R. Sommerfeldt, Kalamazoo, Michigan: Cistercian Publications, 1978
Dumont, Charles, "Aelred of Rievaulx: His Life and Works," in *The Mirror of Charity* by Aelred of Rievaulx, Kalamazoo, Michigan: Cistercian Publications, 1990
Dutton, Marsha L., "Christ Our Mother: Aelred's Iconography for Contemplative Union," in *Goad and Nail*, edited by E. Rozanne Elder, Kalamazoo, Michigan: Cistercian Publications, 1985
Dutton, Marsha L., "Aelred of Rievaulx on Friendship, Chastity, and Sex: The Sources," *Cistercian Studies Quarterly* 29 (1994)
Hallier, Amédée, *The Monastic Theology of Aelred of Rievaulx*, Spencer, Massachusetts: Cistercian Publications, 1969
Powicke, F.M., "Introduction," in *The Life of Aelred of Rievaulx* by Walter Daniel, Kalamazoo, Michigan: Cistercian Publications, 1994
Raciti, Gaetano, "The Preferential Option for the Weak in the Aelredian Community Model," *Cistercian Studies Quarterly* 32 (1997)
Roby, Douglass, "Chimaera of the North: The Active Life of Aelred of Rievaulx," in *Cistercian Ideals and Reality*, edited by John R. Sommerfeldt, Kalamazoo, Michigan: Cistercian Publications, 1978

Sommerfeldt, John R., "The Vocabulary of Contemplation in Aelred of Rievaulx's *On Jesus at the Age of Twelve, A Rule of Life for a Recluse,* and *On Spiritual Friendship,*" in *Heaven on Earth,* edited by E. Rozanne Elder, Kalamazoo, Michigan: Cistercian Publications, 1983

Sommerfeldt, John R., "The Rape of the Soul: The Vocabulary of Contemplation in Aelred of Rievaulx's *Mirror of Love,* Book III," in *Erudition at God's Service,* edited by Sommerfeldt, Kalamazoo, Michigan: Cistercian Publications, 1987

Squire, Aelred, *Aelred of Rievaulx: A Study,* London: SPCK, 1969; Kalamazoo, Michigan: Cistercian Publications, 1981

Stuckey, Marsha D[utton], "A Prodigal Writes Home: Aelred of Rievaulx's *De institutione inclusarum,*" in *Heaven on Earth,* edited by E. Rozanne Elder, Kalamazoo, Michigan: Cistercian Publications, 1983

# Agriculture, Western Christian

There is very little in the monastic rules about how monks and nuns should support themselves – except for the invocation of manual labor. The earliest monks and hermits in the desert of Egypt, the islands of Greece, or off the coast of Ireland must have lived primarily by gardening, gathering, and fishing. As successors of the Roman paterfamilias, most early abbots and abbesses must have assumed that they too would live from the revenues of landed estates like any other landlords. Certainly land given to monastic communities throughout the early Middle Ages was land with men and women on it, and conveyances of land often included explicit rights proper to lords over it – such as the right to hold local courts. For example, occasionally in the Carolingian polyptychs, we get a glimpse of the management of such estates, and efforts were made to reform monastic agriculture by bringing land directly under monastic management, as when later medieval English Benedictine abbeys attempted to reintroduce labor services.

The reform movement of the 11th century brought a new concern about the mixing of secular and religious in many areas of life. Criticism arose not only about lay ownership of tithes, lay investiture, and clerical marriage but also about monastic ownership, that is, the role of abbeys as lords of villages of men and women and their endowment of churches and their revenues. A new eremitic movement saw fit to return monasticism to an idealized primitive purity and poverty such as was thought to have been the case among the followers of Christ. Preachers of such apostolic poverty had a specific economic message – to make religious men and women less like secular lords – but this meant that monks and nuns must refuse to be supported by

**Monastic tithe barn, Abbotsbury Abbey (Benedictine), Dorset, England, c. 1400. One of the largest monastic barns in existence.**
**Photo courtesy of Chris Schabel**

Monastic barn, Glastonbury Abbey (Benedictine), Somerset, England, c. 1500. The barn now houses the Somerset Rural Life Museum.
Photo courtesy of Chris Schabel

"manorial" revenues. By the 12th century the emerging result was a new "monastic agriculture" practiced by members of religious communities themselves – not as overseers but as laborers.

This program of reformed monastic agriculture was adopted by nearly every reforming movement of the 12th century – in differing ways and to varying degrees, – but is primarily associated with reformers from Cîteaux and Clairvaux who were developing themselves into a religious order. Moreover whatever the date of the early documentation, the clearest outline of the tenets of this monastic agriculture may be gleaned from the earliest collected statutes and exordiums of the Cistercians and certain charters and papal confirmations. The basic principles entailed the use of monastic labor on newly consolidated monastic estates, called granges, from which earlier tenants had been removed. Ideally this depopulation occurred at once or was unnecessary because granges had been created out of what had earlier been uninhabited wasteland; this ideal has given the Cistercians an undeserved reputation as pioneers. In fact there were very few uninhabited areas to be had, and much of Cistercian acquisition was from previously established tenants. Some of those earlier secular inhabitants might have been the anonymous pioneers who were finding that they could not support themselves on such recently cultivated wastelands because marginal lands were subject to pe-

riodic flooding or because the returns on marginal areas dropped after several years of cultivation. Monastic groups such as the Cistercians were able to buy cheaply the rights of such peasants, to convert the most marginal lands back to pasture, to build expensive dikes to protect their agriculture, and to absorb the risk of periodic flooding. Whereas most Cistercian abbeys seem to have strung together into an individual abbey's estate a diverse group of such consolidated granges located at some distance from one another, other reformers, such as the Carthusians, apparently attempted to create a single zone surrounding the monastic compound from which all others were excluded.

The need for labor for such "new" monastic agriculture was answered by several additional innovations: a truncated reform liturgy; labor saving instituted by the construction of mills and the use of more efficient tools; the consolidation of fields; the removal of claims over monastic lands from other owners, especially tithe collectors (by episcopal and papal exemptions from tithes on monastic labor); by the widespread adoption of less labor-intensive animal husbandry (including transhumance) to replace exclusive cereal cultivation; the hiring of seasonal laborers; and the introduction of lay brothers and lay sisters who were often former tenants of land being acquired. Such lay brothers and lay sisters (*conversi* and *conversae*) were attracted by a status of economic security as well as by religious motivations, and the early equality of status for such converted adults meant that knights and other lords and their wives and sisters, as well as peasants, retired to a more holy life of laboring in the monastery. Only late in the 12th century is the existence of such lay brothers and lay sisters justified by an ideology that proclaimed that their work on the distant granges allowed monks and nuns to stay within their cloisters, and only somewhat later than that did a gulf in status begin to make the *conversi* and *conversae* begin to be treated just like other manorial tenants.

By the time that religious orders such as the Cistercians appeared, monastic reform agriculture had become well established. It coincided with a rapid acquisition of property and the economic choices that happened to be what economists would call extremely rational, albeit made out of 12th-century religious concerns. Monastic reformers consolidated individual granges but diversified the types of granges within an individual abbey's total estates, they introduced labor-saving equipment, laborers worked well because they were religiously motivated, and their being celibate meant that they had low dependency costs. Abbeys that had been granted tithe and other exemptions because they were poor, or had adopted a less expensive simplicity of architecture, and or had increased animal husbandry to preserve time for their liturgical duties could continue to expand their landholdings and recruit new laborers to be lay brothers and lay sisters. The new monastic agriculture worked well as long as expansion brought in new workers, but in the acquisition of estates such reformers also strayed from earlier ideals of apostolic poverty. As recruiting of monks and lay brothers declined, labor shortages forced abbeys to begin to rent out their most distant estates to farmers who paid fixed rents as well as to recruit tenants for planned towns (in Gascony, the *bastides*) created out of monastic grange lands. The success of the new monastic agriculture of granges and lay brothers lasted less than two centuries before most reform communities again were supported by villages of tenants.

This new monastic agriculture was practiced most successfully between around 1150 and 1215. It has often been associated with Cistercian monks and is often tied to tithe exemptions that have been seen as typically Cistercian. Yet it was not exclusively Cistercian and was certainly not limited to men's houses within the Cistercian Order. For example, the monastic historian Herman of Tournai, in his history in praise of the bishop of Laon (*Patrologia Latina* 156.1001–1002), remarks on the extraordinary ability of the nuns of Montreuil to work as hard as the brothers of Clairvaux – not at weaving or sewing but in the fields. Indeed by the 13th century it was primarily women's houses of the reform orders that remained popular and successful at this monastic agriculture – often because the nuns used it to support leprosaria or other hospital-type charities.

CONSTANCE HOFFMAN BERMAN

*See also* Archaeology: Western Europe; Carthusians; Cistercians: General or Male; Economics: Christian; Fishing and Fish Culture, Western Christian; Lay Brothers and Lay Sisters, Christian; Orders (Religious), Origin of

## Further Reading

Berman, Constance H., "Cistercian Development and the Order's Acquisition of Churches and Tithes in Southern France," *Revue bénédictine* 91 (1981)

Berman, Constance H., *Medieval Agriculture, the Southern French Countryside, and the Early Cistercians: A Study of Forty-Three Monasteries* (Transactions of the American Philosophical Society, volume 76, part 5), Philadelphia: American Philosophical Society, 1986

Berman, Constance H., "Cistercian Women and Tithes," *Cîteaux* 49 (1998)

Burton, Janet, *The Monastic Order in Yorkshire, 1069–1215* (Cambridge Studies in Medieval Life and Thought, 4th series), Cambridge and New York: Cambridge University Press, 1999

# Aidan, St. d. 651

## Monk of Iona, missionary to Northumbria

Aidan, a monk of Iona, founded the monastery on Lindisfarne from which Christianity spread through much of northern England. After the Synod of Whitby (664), the church in Northumbria conformed to the traditions of Rome. For a century the Anglo-Saxon Christianity of Cuthbert and Bede was famed throughout Europe until its monastic centers were extinguished by the violence of the Viking raids that began in the late eighth century.

Aidan was summoned to Northumbria by Oswald, who came to the throne after his victory at Heavenfield (634). The Christian faith was already known in Northumbria through Paulinus, chaplain to Ethelburga of Kent, who married King Edwin in 625. Paulinus, a companion of Augustine of Canterbury, represented the Roman mission and monastic tradition, whereas Aidan was formed in Celtic monasticism. Oswald had been impressed by the Christianity of Columba and the monks of Iona when he was in exile during Edwin's reign. He provided Aidan with an island base at Lindisfarne, close to the royal seat at Bamburgh. There Aidan founded a typical Celtic monastery from which he went on lengthy evangelistic journeys through the kingdom of Northumbria, habitually traveling on foot, preaching, teaching, and baptizing. The king closely supported his work and on occasion acted as Aidan's interpreter until his death in battle in 642. In the years that followed, Aidan's missionary work was concentrated on Deira (southern Northumbria), which was ruled by Oswin, a younger kinsman of Edwin, until Oswin was murdered on the orders of Oswy, king of Bernicia (northern Northumbria). Twelve days later, on 31 August 651, Aidan died at Bamburgh. He was buried on Lindisfarne, in the 17th year of his episcopate.

Bede records that Aidan was chosen for the Northumbrian mission because he was endowed with "the grace of discretion, mother of all virtues." He describes how Aidan gave to the poor the money or expensive gifts that he frequently received, on one occasion handing over his horse to a beggar. Such gifts were also used to ransom slaves whom Aidan then instructed in the faith.

Some of these men later became priests. Bede bears witness to his reputation for piety by recording miracles attributed to him, including the stilling of a storm. Aidan's timely intercession was said to have saved Bamburgh when it was threatened with destruction by fire at the hands of the marauding troops of Penda, king of Mercia.

Aidan was a dedicated teacher who encouraged his companions to follow his example, meditating on Scripture or learning the Psalms as they walked. From time to time he withdrew to the Inner Farne island for concentrated prayer. He selected 12 English boys for monastic education and training in the faith. Among these were Eata, a formative influence on the young Cuthbert (c. 636–687), and Chad, the first bishop of Lichfield. Aidan was responsible for the appointment of Hilda as head of a religious house at Hartlepool before she went on to found the famous double monastery at Whitby. Bede records how one night the young shepherd Cuthbert saw light in the heaven as the heavenly host took to themselves a human soul, which he later learned to be that of Aidan. So moved was Cuthbert that he gave up shepherding to enter the monastery at Melrose, eventually following in Aidan's footsteps as bishop of Lindisfarne and being numbered with him among the Northumbrian monastic saints. Although Aidan was remembered with admiration for his attractive character and his holiness, his cult was speedily eclipsed by that of the more dramatically austere Cuthbert.

NICHOLAS SAGOVSKY

*See also* Celtic Monasticism; Columba, St.; Cuthbert, St.; Hilda, St.; Iona, Scotland; Island Monasteries, Christian; Lindisfarne/Holy Island, England; Scotland

## Biography

While living as a Celtic monk at Iona, Aidan was asked by St. Oswald, King of Northumbria, to missionize that region. Consecrated bishop in 635, Aidan chose the island of Lindisfarne as his base. He strengthened Celtic Christianity in Northumbria just before the Synod of Whitby (664) would romanize its practices.

## Further Reading

Mayr-Harting, H., *The Coming of Christianity to Anglo-Saxon England*, London: Batsford, 1972; as *The Coming of Christianity to England*, New York: Schocken Books, 1972

Stancliffe, Clare, and Eric Cambridge, editors, *Oswald, Northumbrian King to European Saint*, Stamford: Paul Watkins, 1995

Wallace-Hadrill, J.M., *Bede's Ecclesiastical History of the English People, A Historical Commentary*, Oxford and New York: Oxford University Press, 1988

## Ajaṇṭā, India

The Buddhist caves at Ajaṇṭā are located in western India, about 220 miles east northeast of Bombay. One can presently count as many as 36 independent foundations, including monastic residences, stūpa halls suitable for communal worship, and detached shrinelets carved into the sheer 250-foot-high wall of rock that overhangs the Waghora River. Among the remains of Buddhist monasteries in India, those found at Ajaṇṭā hold special riches for both tourists and scholars.

For the tourist Ajaṇṭā offers some of the finest painting and sculpture anywhere. Many of the caves' walls are filled with colorful events from Śākyamuni Buddha's current and previous lives, with hieratic tableaus of buddhas and bodhisattvas, even with mannered depictions of the contemporary Indian scene. These monasteries' painted surfaces were organically integrated with sculptures of nymphs and buddhas, seamonsters, and wish-granting genies to create veritable palaces that one ancient patron described as rivaling those belonging to the king of the gods.

Naturally, Ajaṇṭā has proven a favorite subject for historians of Indian art. The site has received substantially less attention from historians of Buddhism, although not because of a lack of suitable data. Ajaṇṭā's paintings and sculptures are matched by an abundance of epigraphical records; moreover, the site can be

Cave 24 (*caitya* hall), Ajaṇṭā, Buddhist cave temple site, Maharashtra, India, interior with stūpa, Gupta period, c. A.D. 475.
Photo courtesy of Marylin M. Rhie

Overview, Ajaṇṭā Caves, India, 200 B.C. to A.D. 500.
Photo courtesy of John C. Huntington, the Huntington Archive

linked to specific texts, including Āryaśūra's *Jātakamālā* and the vinaya of the Mūlasarvāstivāda sect. Thus, Ajaṇṭā's artifacts represent a complex and vibrant form of local Buddhism and provide a witness to Buddhism as a constituent of Indian society. They provide a unique window onto how monasteries were patronized and envisioned in early medieval India and make it possible for scholars to reconstruct the human relationships that went into successive layers of religious construction.

The caves at Ajaṇṭā were executed in two distinct phases. The first phase, dated around 100 B.C. through A.D. 100, was responsible for two stūpas and three simple monastic dwellings. At this time the Ajaṇṭā pass was situated along a popular route from southern to northern India. Indeed, an early patron identifies himself as Kṛṣṇa from the town of Bāhaḍa, another stage on the same route. Although most of Ajaṇṭā's art comes from the second phase, some early painting that is unique in India demon-

strates a style simultaneously simple and sophisticated, and thoroughly charming in its use of line and color.

The second phase, responsible for most of the site's artifacts, can be dated around 460 through 480. All the major fifth-century patrons seem to have owed allegiance to the court of a single king, the Vākāṭaka overlord Hariṣeṇa. These courtiers include Varāhadeva, a government minister; Buddhabhadra, a noble become monk; and an unnamed feudatory raja subordinate to Hariṣeṇa. Indeed, this grand project was closely associated with Hariṣeṇa's reign. It was begun soon after Hariṣeṇa's ascension, having been a public display of the Vākāṭakas' power, wealth, and piety (the monasteries also likely served as military garrisons and waystations for merchants and pilgrims). However, Hariṣeṇa's family fell from power before the site was finished. Ajaṇṭā's caves were swiftly abandoned by both artisans and monks, resulting in their singular state of preservation.

Seated Buddha, Cave 1, Ajaṇṭā, India, fifth century A.D.
Photo courtesy of John C. Huntington, the Huntington Archive

In the long run Ajaṇṭā has proven far more important for Western scholars than it was for Indian Buddhists. The seventh-century Chinese pilgrim Xuanzang recounts that Dignāga, a fifth-century Buddhist logician and seminal figure in the history of Indian philosophy, once frequented these caves, but Xuanzang went only as a tourist. The exuberance with which he describes the physical setting and artistic marvels is balanced by his complete silence regarding the presence of an active Buddhist community.

RICHARD S. COHEN

*See also* Architecture: Buddhist Monasteries in Southern Asia; Cave Temples and Monasteries in India and China; India: Sites; Mahāyāna

### Further Reading

Behl, Benoy K., *The Ajanta Caves: Artistic Wonder of Ancient Buddhist India*, New York: Abrams, 1998; as *The Ajanta Caves: Ancient Paintings of Buddhist India*, London: Thames and Hudson, 1998
Cohen, Richard S., "Nāga, Yaṣiṇī, Buddha: Local Deities and Local Buddhism at Ajanta," *History of Religions* 37:4 (1998)

Interior, Cave 9, Ajaṇṭā, India, fifth century A.D.
Photo courtesy of John C. Huntington, the Huntington Archive

Ajaṇṭā, Cave 19, full view of facade.
Photo courtesy of John C. Huntington, the Huntington Archive

Fergusson, James, and James Burgess, *The Cave Temples of India*, London: Allen, 1880; 2nd edition, New Delhi: Munshiram Manoharlal, 1988

Mirashi, Vasudev Vishnu, *Inscriptions of the Vākāṭakas* (Corpus Inscriptionum Indicarum, 5), Ootacamund: Government Epigraphist for India, 1963

Mitra, Debala, *Ajanta*, New Delhi: Archaeological Survey of India, 1956; 9th edition, 1983

Parimoo, Ratan, editor, *The Art of Ajanta: New Perspectives*, 2 vols., New Delhi: Books and Books, 1991

Schlingloff, Dieter, *Studies in the Ajanta Paintings: Identifications and Interpretations*, Delhi: Ajanta, 1987

Shastri, Ajay Mitra, editor, *The Age of the Vakatakas*, New Delhi: Harman, 1992

Spink, Walter M., "Ajanta's Chronology: The Crucial Cave," *Ars Orientalis* 10 (1975)

Spink, Walter M., "The Archaeology of Ajanta," *Ars Orientalis* 21 (1992)

Yazdani, Ghulman, *Ajanta: The Colour and Monochrome Reproductions of the Ajanta Frescoes Based on Photography*, 4 vols., London: Oxford University Press, 1930–1955

# Albertus Magnus, St. c. 1200–1280

German Dominican friar, theologian, and philosopher

Albert the Great belongs to that band of university students and teachers who joined the Dominicans and Franciscans in the early decades of the 13th century. Born at Lauingen near Ulm, he studied at Padua, where he joined the Dominicans. He taught at Dominican houses throughout Germany and became professor at Paris in 1245. Thomas Aquinas (c. 1225–1274) was his student there and later his assistant in founding the Order's house of studies at Cologne.

Occupying himself with the full range of philosophical and theological questions, Albert took special delight in empirical observation of the natural world. "Experiment is the only safe guide in such investigations," he wrote (*On Vegetables and Plants*, 6.2.1). At the same time he says that "the whole world is theology for us" (*Commentary on Matthew*, 13.35). He stands alongside so many monks, nuns, and friars who not only contemplated the natural world as an expression of God's glory and wisdom but became vintners, beekeepers, gardeners, farmers, collectors, apothecaries, and so on. His interest in natural science means that Albert was more like Aristotle than Thomas ever was. In fact it was Albert who led Thomas and others in the task of "making Aristotle intelligible to the Latins" (*On Physics*, 1.1.1).

Albert undertook administrative responsibilities as provincial of Germany and as bishop of Regensburg (1260–1262). The Dominicans were generally reluctant to become bishops – both Dominic and Thomas had refused. Humbert of Romans (d. 1277) tried to dissuade Albert from accepting a bishopric, fearing that it would make it impossible for him to preach from that base of poverty that Dominic had deemed essential. A change of pope made possible Albert's early return to preaching, teaching, and writing, although he agreed to preach a crusade in Germany at the request of the new Pope Gregory X (1271–1276) and attended the Council of Lyons in 1274.

Albert was drawn into many controversies, especially those concerned with the interpretation of Aristotelian philosophy. He was also drawn into the increasingly bitter dispute with secular clergy deeply threatened by the emergence of the friars. In 1277 he defended Thomas' teaching, which had been declared suspect by the bishop of Paris.

Albert stands at the head of a German Dominican school, which differs in important ways from the Thomist school. Ulrich of Strasbourg, Dietrich of Freiberg, and Berthold of Moosburg developed Albert's work, using newly available Neoplatonist sources. Interest in speculative mysticism led Meister Eckhart (c. 1260–c. 1328), John Tauler, and Henry Suso to develop themes dear to Albert, such as the incomprehensibility of God and the importance of self-knowledge. Albert wrote commentaries on some biblical books as well as on the works of Pseudo-Dionysius. The popular *De adhaerendo Deo* and other works of spirituality and piety attributed to Albert are now regarded as works of later authors.

Known as "the Great" even before he died, Albert was canonized in 1931 and declared a Doctor of the Church. Patron of natural scientists, he continues to inspire those fascinated by the natural world, whether for its own sake or as a way of contemplating the Creator. One of the greatest of medieval scientists, Albert continues to be honored as an exceptional genius. In 1998 the German Federal Railways named one of its most powerful locomotives "Albertus Magnus."

VIVIAN BOLAND, O.P.

*See also* Agriculture, Western Christian; Dionysius the Pseudo-Areopagite; Dominicans: General or Male; Eckhart, Meister; Education of Christian Monastics; Germany: History; Mystics, German Monastic: Male; Pharmacology; Theology, Western Christian: Dominican; Thomas Aquinas, St.

## Biography

Born near Ulm, Albertus entered the Dominican Order at Padua c. 1229. He studied theology in Cologne before becoming a lecturer in various German Dominican houses. Between 1240 and 1248 he taught in Paris, where after 1246 Thomas Aquinas was one of his pupils. From 1248 he took charge of a new Dominican house of studies in Cologne, becoming Dominican Provincial of Germany 1254–1257. At the request of Pope Alexander IV (1254–1261) he defended the new religious orders before the papal court at Anagni. The same pope made use of Albert's abilities in other ways before appointing him bishop of Regensburg in 1260. The succeeding pope, Urban IV, accepted his resignation as bishop. Albertus returned to Germany and from c. 1270 again taught in Cologne. He exerted enormous influence on Thomas Aquinas and later German Dominicans such as Meister Eckhart. He was declared a Doctor of the Church in 1931.

## Major Works

*Summa de Creaturis*, 1236–1244
*De Naturi Boni*, c. 1238
*Commentary on the Sentences*, 1243–1249
*Super Dionysium De divinis nominibus, Mysticam Theologiam et Epistolas*, c. 1250
*De Intellectu et Intelligibili*, 1258
*De Animalibus*, c. 1260
*Super Ethica* (on Aristotle's *Ethics*), c. 1260–1270
*In Libros Metaphysicorum* (on Aristotle's *Metaphysics*), c. 1260–1270
*In Librum de Causis*, c. 1260–1270
*De Unitate Intellectus*, c. 1270
*Summa Theologiae*, 1270–1280
*Beati Alberti Magni Opera Omnia*, 21 vols., edited by P. Jammy, 1651
*Beati Alberti Magni Opera Omnia*, 38 vols., edited by A. Borgnet, 1890–1899
*Sancti Alberti Magni Opera*, edited by B. Geyer and others, 1951–

A work probably by John of Kastl (d. after 1418), *De adhaerendo Deo*, was falsely attributed to Albertus.

## Further Reading

Cross, F.L., and E.A. Livingstone, "Albertus Magnus, St.," in *The Oxford Dictionary of the Christian Church*, 3rd edition, Oxford and New York: Oxford University Press, 1997

Kovach, Francis J., and Robert W. Shahan, editors, *Albert the Great: Commemorative Essays*, Norman: University of Oklahoma Press, 1980

Libera, Alain de, *Introduction à la Mystique Rhénane: d'Albert le Grand à Maître Eckhart* (Sagesse Chrétienne, 3), Paris: OEIL, 1984

Libera, Alain de, *Albert le Grand et la Philosophie* (A la recherche de la vérité), Paris: Vrin, 1990

Tugwell, Simon, *Albert and Thomas: Selected Writings* (Classics of Western Spirituality), New York: Paulist Press, 1988

Weisheipl, James A., "Albert the Great (Albertus Magnus), St.," in *New Catholic Encyclopedia*, volume 1, New York: McGraw-Hill, 1967

Weisheipl, James A., *Thomas d'Aquino and Albert His Teacher* (Etienne Gilson Series, 2), Toronto: Pontifical Institute of Mediaeval Studies, 1980

Weisheipl, James A., editor, *Albertus Magnus and the Sciences: Commemorative Essays 1980* (Studies and Texts: Pontifical Institute of Mediaeval Studies, 49), Toronto: Pontifical Institute of Mediaeval Studies, 1980

# Alcuin c. 740–804

## Anglo-Saxon Christian theologian and scholar

Alcuin was born in Northumbria sometime around 740 and was educated in the cathedral school at York, then under the direction of Ælberht (d. 780). Nothing is known of Alcuin's family or ancestry, but that he did not progress in the ecclesiastical hierarchy beyond the rank of deacon might suggest that his ancestors were not very influential. However, his intellectual skills and the patronage of Ælberht, whose protégé he seems to have been, led to his succeeding his master as head of the episcopal school when the latter was raised to the vacant bishopric of York in 767. The young man accompanied the new bishop (whose see was elevated to the rank of archdiocese in 773) on journeys to the Continent. Contacts made in this way might have led to his being invited to teach at the court of the Frankish king Charles the Great or Charlemagne (768–814). According to the anonymous *Vita Alcuini*, probably written at Ferrières in the mid-820s, this resulted from a chance encounter between the king and Alcuin at Pavia while the latter was returning from an embassy to Rome to seek the grant of the *pallium* for Archbishop Ælberht's successor Eanbald (780–796). If so, it occurred in mid-March 781. Although it has often been assumed that Alcuin, who then had to return to York, went back to the Continent to join Charlemagne's entourage at the earliest possible opportunity, no evidence exists that would place him at the Carolingian court prior to the year 789.

In this year stylistic analysis has detected his role in the drawing up of the capitulary known as the *Admonitio Generalis*. He was back in Northumbria in 790, as can be seen in his letters, and he does not appear to have returned to Francia until 793, when he played a minor although not insignificant role in the drafting of the *Libri Carolini*, the formal response of Charlemagne's court theologians, written in the king's name, to the restoration of icon veneration in the Byzantine Empire at the Second Council of Nicaea in 787. Although in rank still no more than a deacon, at Charlemagne's request Alcuin played a vital part in the direction and the formulation of the *acta* of the Council of Frankfurt in 794. Also in the mid-790s, he was much engaged in writing various polemical treatises against the doctrines of Adoptionism, which first developed in Spain in the early 780s but were subsequently promoted in Francia by Bishop Felix of Urgell (d. 816), who was condemned at the Council of Frankfurt.

Alcuin had already been given the abbacies of St. Lupus at Troyes and of Ferrières by Charlemagne, and to these was added that of St.-Martin at Tours in 796. Here he retired from the court, now almost permanently based at Aachen, in the course of the same year. As testified to in his numerous letters, of which around 280 survive, he continued to be consulted by the Frankish ruler and by a wide circle of lay and clerical friends on a range of topics. His influence might have suffered some eclipse in 802, when the canons of St.-Martin resisted the authority of their diocesan bishop, Theodulf of Orléans (d. 821), in a dispute over sanctuary rights. Although Alcuin tried to justify their actions, his own health was failing, and he died on 19 May 804.

Although until recently this was a matter of considerable disagreement among scholars of the period, it is now generally accepted that Alcuin himself was never a monk in the sense of having taken formal monastic vows. Saint-Martin at Tours was also a house of canons rather than a fully monastic community. However, Alcuin's writings give him a special role in the history of monasticism. While at the court of Charlemagne, probably in the period 794–796, Alcuin helped draft the circular letter known as the *De Litteris Colendis*, or "On the Cultivation of Letters." Only one copy of this mandate survives, probably sent to the abbots and monks of all the major Carolingian monasteries. It requires them to devote themselves to the study of grammar, especially so that in reading and in copying the Scriptures errors should be detected and eliminated, as these could otherwise lead to confusion or the teaching of false doctrine. Alcuin himself was responsible for the composition of a series of short manuals of instruction, including an expanded version of Bede's *De Orthographia* and a grammar that served as teaching texts in many of the schools that were developed in the major Carolingian monasteries in the late eighth and ninth centuries. Something of the philosophical culture, especially in the study of logic, that he developed in the palace school has been recovered from teaching texts that he prepared with his Anglo-Saxon pupil Candidus.

These educational ideals were also put into practice by Alcuin himself at Tours, where he developed a major scriptorium that in the generation or two after his death became a noted source of Bible manuscripts. Many of these, of which several have survived, were of the stylistically corrected version of the Vulgate that Alcuin himself had worked on in the abbey in the late 790s. He presented a copy of this to Charlemagne early in 800 and another the following year. In the years following his death, deluxe Tours Bibles were produced both for several of the Carolingian royal and for other monasteries.

As master of the palace school, Alcuin directly influenced several of the leading scholars of the next generation, with many of whom he thereafter maintained a continuous correspondence. Other pupils studied under him at Tours. These included his own successor as abbot, Fridugis (d. 834). Some were sent from other monasteries specially to study at Tours. Of such external pupils the most famous is the Fulda monk Rabanus Maurus (c. 780–856), who would become the most prolific exegete and encyclopedist of the early Carolingian period and would also serve as abbot of Fulda (822–842) and archbishop of Mainz (847–856). In turn he would pass on the legacy of Alcuin's instruction to a further generation of pupils who came to study under him at Fulda. Among these were Walafrid Strabo (c. 808–849), later abbot of Reichenau (842–848), and Lupus of Ferrières.

ROGER COLLINS

*See also* Bede, St.; Education of Christian Monastics; France: History; Fulda, Germany; Hymnographers; Libraries: Western Christian; Manuscript Production: Christian; Rabanus Maurus; Walafrid Strabo

## Biography

A native of Northumbria and pupil at the cathedral school at York, Alcuin made his mark as a member of the court of Charlemagne during most of the 790s up to his death in 804. As abbot of St.-Martin at Tours, he revised the text of the Vulgate, wrote manuals of grammar, rhetoric, and dialectic, and penned hundreds of letters. Through his own efforts and those of pupils he helped to launch Carolingian scholarship.

## Major Works

*De Litteris Colendis* (On the Cultivation of Letters)
Letters
Grammar
Lives of the Saints (Willibrord, Vedast, Richarius, and Martin)

## Further Reading

Bullough, Donald, "Alcuin and the Kingdom of Heaven," in *Carolingian Essays: Andrew W. Mellon Lectures in Early Christian Studies*, edited by Uta-Renate Blumenthal, Washington, D.C.: Catholic University of America Press, 1983
Bullough, Donald, "Alcuin before Frankfort," in *Das Frankfurter Konzil von 794: Kristallisationspunkt karolingischer Kultur* (Quellen und Abhandlungen zur Mittelrheinischen Kirchengeschichte, 80), edited by Rainer Berndt, Frankfurt-am-Main: Selbstverlag der Gesellschaft für Mittelrheinische Kirchengeschichte, 1997
Bullough, Donald, "Alcuin's Cultural Influence: The Evidence of the Manuscripts," in *Alcuin of York: Scholar at the Carolingian Court: Proceedings of the Third Germania Latina Conference Held at the University of Groningen, May 1995* (Germania Latina, 3), edited by L.A.J.R. Houwen and A.A. MacDonald, Groningen: Forsten, 1998
Duckett, Eleanor Shipley, *Alcuin, Friend of Charlemagne, His World and His Work*, New York: Macmillan, 1951
Ellard, Gerald, *Master Alcuin, Liturgist: A Partner of Our Piety* (Jesuit Studies), Chicago: Loyola University Press, 1956
Ganz, David, "Mass-production of Early Medieval Manuscripts: The Carolingian Bibles from Tours," in *The Early Medieval Bible: Its Production, Decoration, and Use* (Cambridge Studies in Palaeography and Codicology, 2), edited by Richard Gameson, Cambridge and New York: Cambridge University Press, 1994
Gaskoin, C.J.B., *Alcuin: His Life and His Work*, London: Clay, 1904; New York: Russell and Russell, 1966
Godman, Peter, editor, *The Bishops, Kings, and Saints of York* (Oxford Medieval Texts), New York: Oxford University Press, and Oxford: Clarendon Press, 1982
I, Deug-Su, *L'opera agiografica di Alcuino* (Biblioteca degli "Studi Medievali," 13), Spoleto: Centro italiano di studi sull'alto Medioevo, 1983
Marenbon, John, *From the Circle of Alcuin to the School of Auxerre: Logic, Theology, and Philosophy in the Early Middle Ages* (Cambridge Studies in Medieval Life and Thought, 3rd series, volume 15), Cambridge and New York: Cambridge University Press, 1981
Wallach, Luitpold, *Alcuin and Charlemagne: Studies in Carolingian History and Literature* (Cornell Studies in Classical Philology, volume 32), Ithaca, New York: Cornell University Press, 1959; revised edition, New York: Johnson Reprint, 1968

# Ambrose, St. c. 339–397

## Bishop of Milan

Bishop of Milan, the capital of the Roman Empire in the West, from 374 until his death, Ambrose is perhaps best remembered today for the crucial role he played, through his preaching, in the conversion of Augustine of Hippo to Christianity. Given Augustine's pivotal importance in the history of Christianity, and of Western Christian monasticism, this would be reason enough to commemorate Ambrose. But his other accomplishments, particularly in the realm of spirituality, are also notable.

Perhaps the greatest of these was his promotion of the charism of virginity. On this topic Ambrose produced four treatises, one of which, entitled simply *De Virginibus* (On Virgins), deserves to be ranked among the finest Christian writings of its kind. Like his contemporaries, Ambrose saw virginity as superior to married life. Like them as well, he spoke of the virgin as enjoying a nuptial intimacy with Christ, and he drew upon the biblical Song of Songs, with its erotic imagery, to describe this intimate relationship. So highly did he esteem virginity from the perspective of sheer physical intactness that he asserted a virgin may commit suicide in order to avoid rape – an assertion to which Augustine would later take exception. Ambrose also reported the existence of what appears to have been a monastery of 20 virgins in Bologna, which would have been a rarity at this early date in the West.

Ambrose's second major, and related, contribution to spirituality was his emphasis on the cult of the Virgin Mary. Focusing precisely on her virginity – before and after the birth of Christ – he presents Mary as a model of how virgins are to live, particularly in *De Virginibus* 2.2.6–2.3.19.

Finally, Ambrose's biblical commentaries, including lengthy works on Psalm 119 and the Gospel of Luke, soon became part of the Western Christian monastic heritage. His tendency to

Atrium, Basilica of Sant'Ambrogio, Milan, Italy. Founded by St. Ambrose as Basilica of the Martyrs (380s), the church became Benedictine in 789. The Monks' Tower on the right (9th century) and the Canons' Tower on the left (12th century) predate the atrium of c. 1150.
Photo courtesy of Chris Schabel

Relics of St. Ambrose, St. Gervase, and St. Protase in the crypt beneath the High Altar, Basilica of Sant'Ambrogio (formerly Benedictine 784–c. 1470 and then Cistercian until 1797), Milan, Italy. Relics date from the late fourth century and the silver reliquary from 1897.
Photo courtesy of the Editor

focus on the moral aspects of a given passage provided spiritual nourishment for the monks and nuns of the Middle Ages whose struggle, after all, was primarily in the realm of the moral and ascetical.

Ambrose is generally characterized as a derivative thinker. His theology came largely from the Greek East; the writings of Philo, Origen, Athanasius, Basil, and others were accessible to him because, although a native of the Latin West, he possessed the ability to read Greek. This allowed him to be a significant conduit of Greek thought and spirituality to the West. What he lacked in originality he made up for with a strong personality and an often extraordinary gift for expressing himself. These traits, in combination with the prominence he enjoyed as bishop of Milan and his reputation for orthodoxy, ensured the ongoing popularity of his writings.

BONIFACE RAMSEY, O.P.

*See also* Augustinian Rule; Hymnographers; Origins: Western Christian; Plainchant; Scholars, Benedictine

### Biography

Born of a Christian family in Trier, Ambrose pursued the career of a Roman provincial administrator, practicing law and becoming Governor of Aemilia-Liguria. While based in Milan, he was acclaimed Bishop there in 374, although not yet baptized. As bishop he encouraged the conversion of Augustine in 386, and resisted demands made upon Christians by successive Roman emperors. He introduced Greek theology into a Latin-speaking community and pioneered the use of hymns in Western liturgy. He promoted monasticism, the cult of martyrs, and the Roman canon of the mass. He is one of the four Doctors of the Latin Church.

### Major Works
*De Mysteriis*
*De Officiis Ministrorum*

01-394

Camillo Pacetti, funerary statue of Saint Marcellina (Sister of St. Ambrose), Basilica of Sant'Ambrogio (formerly Benedictine 784–c. 1470 and then Cistercian until 1797), Milan, Italy, 1812. Photo courtesy of the Editor

*De Spiritu Sancto*
*De Virginibus*
*Expositio Evangelii secundum Lucam*
*Expositio in Psalmum CXVIII*

**Further Reading**

Dudden, F. Homes, *The Life and Times of St. Ambrose*, 2 vols., Oxford: Clarendon Press, 1935
McLynn, Neil B., *Ambrose of Milan: Church and Court in a Christian Capital*, Berkeley: University of California Press, 1994
Ramsey, Boniface, *Ambrose*, London and New York: Routledge, 1997
Williams, Daniel H., *Ambrose of Milan and the End of the Nicene-Arian Conflicts*, Oxford: Clarendon Press, and New York: Oxford University Press, 1995

# Anchorites. *See* Hermits: Eastern Christian; Hermits: Western Christian

# Angkor Wat, Cambodia

Today's Angkor Wat is a pilgrimage site as well as a tourist attraction. Until recently monastic culture has remained in the area, and Buddhist visitors have kept the pilgrimage tradition alive through the centuries. The temple consists of three parts: a central temple surrounded by three galleries and a moat around the complex. The Angkor plain abounds in temple complexes from before and after the Angkorian period, and these constitute the main resource for understanding the history and development of Khmer culture, in which Hinduism and Buddhism interact in unique ways.

Religious concepts from both Hindu and Buddhist traditions were introduced to Cambodia during Funan and the following pre-Angkorian period of Tchen-la. The Hindu religion was practiced mainly by the court, whereas Buddhism functioned more as the religion of the lower classes. Later both became part of a syncretist Khmer religion, as local cults became integrated in a novel spiritual system. Classical Angkorian culture developed from the 9th until the 11th century, reaching its culmination during the 12th.

The Angkor monarchy was established in 802 by Jayavarman II (c. 802–c. 850). He functioned as a "Devarāja king" in a cult in which the king embodied the highest level of priesthood. Under the influence of Javanese tradition, Jayavarman II followed a principle of social organization whereby material and spiritual levels of society follow the same symbolical scheme. Characteristic of this scheme was continuous evolution toward religious ideals, expressed in a vision of the Universe that was reflected in artistic and architectural languages of the temples. Accurate geometric design was repeated on different scales in temple, landscape, and town planning. In later times the cult of divine king (Devarāja) was transformed into a cult of a Buddhist king (Buddharāja) by Jayavarman VII (1181–1219), who built the temple Angkor Thom.

Originally Angkor Wat was erected outside the ancient city of Yasodharapura, which was the ancient capital of the Khmer kingdom under Sūryavarman II (1113–1145). Unlike other temples in the area, it was built facing west – toward the city – to express interaction between the two spheres of profane and divine. This also made the temple more accessible to inhabitants of the city. Other buildings probably existed inside the courtyards of the main temple, forming a monastery-town within the city. The ring galleries around the central temple have a symbolic meaning of which one detail can be seen in the composition of the gallery walls: the degree of openness of the galleries expresses the level of experience needed to enter various stages of the temple.

The first gallery, consisting of columns, has the external wall open, representing the openness of the level for the general public, whereas the internal wall toward the second gallery is closed. The second-level gallery shows the opposite pattern, with open walls toward internal space and closed walls toward outside, whereas the last gallery of the third level of the temple has only a portico, and the inner-most temple is completely closed. The symbolism evokes Mount Meru surrounded by a fence.

The temple's three levels have been connected both to specific priesthoods and to the rulers of the country. Different levels of the temple evoke different levels of teaching or spiritual achievements, where proceeding in the proper order was necessary for each visitor. This tradition parallels initiations known from Vajrayāna Buddhism, whose teachings are likewise divided into different levels.

The building's history falls into two phases, one starting from the period of construction and the other starting when the temple was transformed into a Buddhist monastery around 1200. Some traces of the first period's original cult can be deduced from the wall carvings, which are very accurate in detailing dresses, ritual objects, and scenery. Most of the stories came from Hindu mythology, which was combined with local stories representing, for example, Sūryavarman II, the king, whereas the inner galleries were decorated with heavenly dancers (Apsarās). Dancers were an important part of the personnel serving the priests and monks in the original Hindu-temple culture of Angkor. The personnel of one temple consisted of 18 priests, 2,740 officiating priests, 2,202 assistants, and 615 temple dancers. Khmers abandoned Angkor in 1432, after which it was lost for centuries.

Most of the furniture and movable objects of the temple have disappeared, but some are conserved in the museums in Cambodia (Phnom Penh National Museum) and in France (the Musée Guimet in Paris). Unfortunately, the temples of the zone are still being looted and artworks sold abroad.

This ancient civilization shared with Java a cult of royalty that promoted a peaceful ethical order in which spiritual progress and artistic representation of spiritual values were esteemed. The site was abandoned after the decline of the Khmer kingdom and became known as the "capital that has become a Buddhist monastery." European discovery occurred in 1580, and temple restoration began in 1860. Henri Mouhot wrote the first detailed description of Angkor Wat temple.

Religious cults practiced in the zone of Angkor can be deduced from representations of divinities from the zone. Based on collections in the Phnom Penh museum, one of the chief protector figures was Garuḍa, a Hindu mythological being with a bird's head, which is found throughout the temple as well. Other divinities include Hevajra, a Buddhist divinity of Vajrayāna tradition, whose cult was practiced at Angkor during the 12th and 13th centuries. Another divinity in the zone was Lakṣmī, a Hindu divinity who holds two lotus blossoms in her hands, very similar to the figure of Bodhisattva Padmapani (holding one lotus) found in the Chandi Mendut temple of the Borobudur complex in Java. Also present was the Buddha Maitreya, depicted with four hands and bearing a stūpa as a head ornament.

Prajñāpāramitā, the embodiment of the perfection of wisdom, further exemplifies the cults practiced in ancient Cambodia. Lokeśvara was connected closely to the King Jayavarman VII, who built the temple Angkor Thom, successor to Angkor Wat. The executive power was seen as embodying this bodhisattva, who directed efforts toward the welfare of others. For example, in an inscription on the walls of the hospital, Jayavarman VII declared, "All beings who are plunged in the ocean of existence, I seek to draw out by this good work. And may the kings of Cambodia who come after me attain with their wives, dignitaries and friends the place of deliverance where there is no more illness." During this period a number of hospitals, streets, and other public buildings were built for the general welfare. After the death of King Jayavarman II, a general return to Theravāda Buddhism took place, and more stūpas than temples were built.

Angkor Wat presents some common features with the Javanese temple Borobudur, for both incorporate the shape of a terraced pyramid with the central building representing Mount Meru. Borobudur has special water gargoyles in the form of dragons, or Makāras, which derive from the local mythology. Likewise, Angkor Wat has the Nāga-parapets and decorations, which reflect local mythology as well. At Angkor Wat the repetition of elements is built around two axes that extend in four directions horizontally and two directions vertically. The reflection in the water of the temples extends this symbolism. This differs from Borobudur temple, where the repetition and symmetry seem to be multiplied in ten directions. The Javanese terminology of Kāma-, Rūpa-, and Arūpadhātu are not commonly used concerning Angkor Wat, even though the division into three realms shows influence from Javanese cosmology. One example is the representation of heaven and hell in the low reliefs of the galleries of Angkor Wat, which at Borobudur become stories of the law of cause and effect in the lowest level of the temple.

LAURA PORCEDDU

*See also* Architecture: Structural Monasteries in East Asia; Borobudur, Java, Indonesia; Maṇḍala

## Further Reading

Bénisti, Mireille, *Rapports entre le premier art Khmer et l'art Indien* (Publications de l'École française d'Extrême-Orient, Mémoire archéologique, 5), 2 vols., Paris: École française d'Extrême-Orient, dépositaire Adrien-Maisonneuve, 1970

Boisselier, Jean, *La statuaire Khmère et son évolution* (Publications de l'École française d'Extrême-Orient, 37), 2 vols., Saigon: École française d'Extrême-Orient, 1955

Cœdès, George, *Pour mieux comprendre Angkor*, Hanoi: Impr. d'Extrême-Orient, 1943; translated as *Angkor: An Introduction*, London and New York: Oxford University Press, 1963

Dagens, B., "Angkor la forêt de pierre," *Découvertes Gallimard Archéologie* 64 (1966)

Giteau, Madeline, *Khmer Sculpture and the Angkor Civilization*, London: Thames and Hudson, and New York: Abrams, 1965

Grison, Pierre, *Angkor au centre du monde* (Architecture et symboles sacrés), Paris: Dervy-Livres, 1980

Groslier, Bernard Philippe, *Angkor, Hommes et Pierres* (Les Imaginaires: Art et archéologie, 7), Grenoble: Arthaud, 1956; translated as *The Arts and Civilization of Angkor*, New York: Praeger, 1957; revised as *Angkor: Art and Civilization*, London: Thames and Hudson, 1966

MacDonald, Malcolm, *Angkor and the Khmers* (Oxford Paperbacks), Singapore: Oxford University Press, 1987

Mazzeo, Donatella, and Chiara Silvi Antonini, *Civiltà Khmer* (Grandi Monumenti, 9), Milan: Mondadori, 1972; translated as *Ancient Cambodia* (Monuments of Civilization, 9), New York: Grosset and Dunlap, and London: Cassell, 1978

Stierlin, Henri, *The Cultural History of Angkor* (Great Civilizations), Geneva: Edito-Service S.A., 1983; London: Aurum Press, 1984

Swaan, W., *Città scomparse dell'Asia*, Istituto Bergamo: Italiano d'arti grafiche, 1967

# Anglican Monasticism

The first implantation of religious life in the Anglican Communion that was fully and explicitly "monastic" (insofar as it would correspond to the usage of that term in canon law) was the Benedictine community founded by Father Ignatius (Joseph Leycester Lyne, 1837–1908) at Claydon, Suffolk, in 1863. The community moved to Llanthony, Monmouthshire, in 1869. However, both previously and contemporaneously, there were many cases of communities within the Church of England in which a prominent place was given to components of the monastic tradition, and there were others that in the course of their history evolved from an immersion in apostolic activity to a more monastic pattern of life. The monastic spirit was far more widely diffused than simply in those cases that conform exactly to the canon law definition.

Some affinities with monasticism survived the Reformation. The Book of Common Prayer was an adaptation to universal use of the Breviary, and the daily recitation of morning and evening prayer was required of all the clergy. The cathedrals and colleges of Oxford and Cambridge retained a recognizably monastic imprint both in their worship and in their life as communities. However, the reformers and their immediate heirs were highly suspicious of monasticism itself, which seemed to them to aim at the creation of a spiritual elite and at salvation through good works rather than faith. The Reformers enjoined instead sanctification for everyone through family life and in the workplace. Nevertheless among the next generation of Anglican theologians, Lancelot Andrewes, John Bramhall, John Cosin, Herbert Thorndyke, and William Law were powerful voices who argued for the legitimacy of religious life and pleaded for the installation of monastic communities within the Church of England. The earliest attempt to implement this vision of the Caroline Divines occurred at Little Gidding, Huntingdonshire, where, from 1626 to 1646, about 30 members of the extended family of Nicholas Ferrar (1592–1637) practiced a life of retirement from the world. Their regimen involved prayer four times a day, regular fasting, night watches, and simplicity of dress. Although short-lived and concealed from the public eye, this single instance was enough to show to many long afterward that the Anglican Church could generate its own forms of monastic life, and that itself was a strong indication of its fundamentally Catholic character.

In the early phase of the Oxford Movement, two celebrated experiments in community life took place: Newman's at Littlemore (1840–1845) and Frederick William Faber's in his rectory at Elton (1843–1845). Newman indignantly repudiated the title "monastery" when it was applied to Littlemore, but the austerity, regularity, and withdrawal from the world did betray aspirations toward monasticity. And indeed the Tractarians' resort to the Church fathers brought home to them how central monastic life had been in the early Church. Newman had also discovered the Breviary through the Oxford lectures of Doctor Lloyd and had requested the former Spanish priest Blanco White to explain to him its intricacies. Newman retained a lifelong interest in Benedictines and wrote a treatise on their mission in the history of the Church (1858). It has been conjectured that he joined the Oratorians because he felt that they were the equivalent in modern times of the monks in the Benedictine centuries. By contrast Faber's community, even in its Anglican days, was heavily imbued with the exuberant Catholic devotion favored by its founder and after its corporate conversion would eventually develop into the Brompton Oratory.

After Newman's conversion to Rome, Edward Bouverie Pusey (1800–1882) was the leader to whom those Tractarians rallied who remained attached to the Church of England. Pusey was a man of heroic self-discipline and a rather somber spirituality who had considerable gifts for organization. One of his most signal achievements was to plant and foster several Anglican sisterhoods, beginning with that of Holy Cross in Park Village West, London, in 1845. This bold innovation would set into motion a mushroom growth of women's communities many years before a parallel development occurred among men. The sisterhoods answered the need of many intelligent and dedicated women to find an outlet for their energies at a time when most careers were not yet open to them. The sisterhoods also came to be seen as an assault on the acute social problems of industrial England at a time when the welfare state had not yet arrived, and this helped ensure their acceptability to a public that was not at all sympathetic to them on religious grounds. Nursing sisters were heroines of the Crimean War (1853–1856) and of the cholera epidemic of 1866. East London became the classic field of their operations, and these Anglicans modeled themselves on the Ursulines and the Sisters of Charity. However, intermingled with the staggering load of their social work were not a few items of the monastic tradition – community life, religious dress, recitation of the Day Hours of the Divine Office, and a general tendency to graduate from activism toward contemplation. The first hurdle to be cleared in this direction was the opposition of most of the bishops to religious vows. The nuns and their spokesmen declared that they had come to see the necessity and desirability of vows out of their own lived experience. In light of their usefulness to the Church (for they entered quarters where no one else could evangelize), the bishops conceded this point. Soon a few of these active communities began to feel a call to become integrally monastic, that is, to curtail their active involvements in order to take on enclosure, local stability, and the full Divine Office and to proclaim themselves Benedictines. Such is the history that nearly all the present Anglican Benedictine nunneries have in common, including those now at Edgeware (founded 1866), Rempstone (1857), West Malling (1891), and Burford (1952). The latter was hived off from the highly professional Sisters of Wantage. Isolated as they were at that time from the mainstream of Benedictine life in the Roman Catholic Church and its living tradition, the sisters had no alternative but to learn their monasticism from books and from their own trial and error. Their instinct was to take monasticism very seriously and to take it as a whole; for example, they used the *Breviarium Monasticum* and the *Missale Romanum* in Latin.

Let us now look at Benedictine communities for men. Father Ignatius' heroic attempt to revive monasticism in the romantic setting of Llanthony proved a magnificent fiasco and a cautionary tale. It was bedeviled by the impulsive and autocratic personality of its lovable founder, who, unchecked by any other authority and lacking contact with any experienced Benedictine, imposed excessive penances on his long-suffering subjects, while he himself was absent for prolonged periods, playing his other role as one of London's foremost evangelists. His final act of folly was to accept ordination as a priest from an *episcopus vagans*, René Vilatte, in 1898, putting him beyond the pale of the Anglican Church. His death was followed by the rapid dispersal of his community. The shipwreck of his hopes was in tragic contrast with the success of more active orders, such as the Cowley Fathers and the Community of the Resurrection, Mirfield, both in expanding and in acquiring "*ius civitatis*" within the Church of England.

However, the next monastic attempt in the Anglican Church bore not a few resemblances to that of Father Ignatius. The personal charisma of Aelred Carlyle (1874–1955), a former medical student, dominated his community, the Anglican Congregation of the Primitive Observance of the Holy Rule of St. Benedict. It was first located in the Isle of Dogs in London's dockland (1896–1898) and then, from 1906 on, on Caldey Island, off the southern coast of Wales, another picturesque but isolated setting. Carlyle too had grand building designs and a heady sense of abbatial prerogatives, but he was isolated both from any experienced Benedictines and from the mainstream of his own Communion. Even its High Church wing, notwithstanding the support he enjoyed from Lord Halifax, regarded Carlyle as belonging to the extremist fringe. The breaking point came in 1911, when he asked Randall Davidson, archbishop of Canterbury, for official recognition. The archbishop made this condi-

tional on a favorable report from a visitation to be conducted by Doctor Charles Gore (1853–1932), the Catholic-minded but firmly Anglican bishop of Oxford. Gore required that the Caldey monks abandon a number of Marian and extraliturgical Eucharistic devotions and that they comply with the Book of Common Prayer. Their refusal to make any concessions led them in 1913 to make their sensational submission to Rome corporately with the exception of a tiny minority.

However, it was this loyal remnant that, through their patience, their obedience, and the steady leadership of a series of wise abbots, ensured the survival of Benedictinism in the Church of England and its acceptance by the Anglican authorities. They moved to Pershore (1913–1926) and then to Nashdom (1926–1987) and are now at Elmore Abbey, Berkshire, having made a foundation in the United States in 1939, now St. Gregory's Abbey, Three Rivers, Michigan. Some of its members have achieved renown – Dom Gregory Dix (1901–1952) of Nashdom Abbey as a liturgical historian, Dom Anselm Hughes as a medieval musicologist, and Dom Bernard Clements as broadcaster and Vicar of All Saints, Margaret Street, the flagship of Anglo-Catholicism.

Another community that has found its way to full Benedictinism by a circuitous path and that was very much centered on the personality of its founder is Alton Abbey, Hampshire. This had originally been the mother house of the Order of St. Paul, founded in 1889 by Charles Plomer Hopkins to promote the spiritual and material welfare of seamen. Hopkins not only founded a number of hospitals and hotels for mariners but also took a prominent and trusted part in agitations to improve their working conditions. From the start his Order was vaguely Benedictine in character. It gradually concentrated all its far-flung activities in Alton and adopted the Rule in 1981.

A heroic monastic enterprise was that of the Monastery of St. Mary of the Cross, which lasted from 1918 to 1936. Father William Sirr had long been superior of the Society of Divine Compassion, a tiny community of very socially conscious Anglican Franciscans at Plaistow, again in East London. Feeling a call to a life of prayer, silence, and hiddenness, he moved to some abandoned stables at Glasshampton, Worcestershire, and, hoping that others would join him, devised a very severe Rule that combined Cistercian and Carthusian elements – so severe that he never attracted a permanent community and remained a hermit, albeit with a reputation for sanctity. However, in 1938 one of his friends founded the Community of the Servants of the Will of God at Crawley Down in Sussex, a community that still flourishes.

The condition of Anglican Benedictines today is certainly more modest both in numbers and in style than in their more colorful past but probably is more authentic to tradition, both Benedictine and Anglican. They enjoy excellent relations with their Roman Catholic counterparts and actively participate in all joint activities, such as abbots' congresses and regional active celebrations in former Benedictine cathedrals. The Anglican Church appreciates them as a native growth. Ecumenically they have a vital role to play, especially in disclosing to Orthodox

Eastern Christians the contemplative presence within the Church of England. Their patient and often painful pilgrimage toward a full and genuine monasticism has imbued them with a wisdom from which everyone can benefit.

DANIEL REES

*See also* Cathedral Priories; Chapman, John; Dissolution of Monasteries: England, Ireland, and Wales; England: History; Island Monasteries, Christian; Knowles, M. David; Missionaries: Christian; Office, Daily: Western Christian

**Further Reading**

Allchin, A.M., *The Silent Rebellion: Anglican Religious Communities, 1845–1900*, London: SCM Press, 1958

*Anglican Religious Communities Year Book 1999*, Norwich: Canterbury Press, 1999

Anson, Peter Frederick, *The Call of the Cloister: Religious Communities and Kindred Bodies in the Anglican Communion*, New York: Macmillan, 1953; London: SPCK, 1955; revised edition, London: SPCK, 1964

Anson, Peter Frederick, *Building up the Waste Places: The Revival of Monastic Life on Medieval Lines in the Post-Reformation Church of England*, Leighton Buzzard: Faith Press, 1973

Attwater, Donald, *Father Ignatius of Llanthony: A Victorian*, London: Cassell, 1931

Calder-Marshall, Arthur, *The Enthusiast; An Enquiry into the Life, Beliefs and Character of the Rev. Joseph Leycester Lyne alias Fr. Ignatius O.S.B., Abbot of Elm Hill, Norwich, and Llanthony, Wales*, London: Faber and Faber, 1962

Cameron, Allan T., *The Religious Communities of the Church of England* (Adelaide Nutting Historical Nursing Collection, AN 0440), London: Faith Press, 1918

Perchenet, Annie, *The Revival of the Religious Life and Christian Unity*, London: Mowbray, 1969

# Anglo-Saxon Monastic Reform. *See* Reform, Tenth-Century Anglo-Saxon Monastic

# Animal Husbandry, Christian. *See* Agriculture, Western Christian

# Animals, Attitude toward: Buddhist Perspectives

In Buddhist doctrinal terms "animals" refers to a category of sentient beings and to a rebirth form possible for all sentient beings in samsara. "Animals" (Sanskrit, *tiryagyoni*; Chinese, *chusheng*) is one of the Six Paths of samsara and one of the Three Unfortunate Rebirths, usually placed above hells and *preta* (hungry ghosts) and below humans, *asura*s, and gods. Their life span is not fixed in length, ranging from less than one day to a middle-length eon (in the case of a dragon king). Although less painful than rebirth in the hells or as a *preta*, rebirth as an animal is considered inauspicious. The *Lam Rim* text of Yeshe Tsöndrü explains, "Some make a home in heaps of dust; / Others breed in swamps of sewage. / Some bigger ones gulp down small ones; / or armies of small beasts devour a large one. / Variously killed for their meat, skin and so on; / Slaughtered in all sorts of different ways; . . . But all are very deluded and stupid, / not knowing what should be done or abandoned" (Rabten, 1984). Animals are also used for hard work or killed for sport. Rebirth as an animal is not an unfair punishment but rather the natural consequence of one's own karma. Animal rebirth is often associated with physical passions, especially lust: "great passions create beasts with hair and fur and mild passions produce winged and feathered creatures" (*Surangama Sūtra*, 1978). In some cases there are also patterns in the manner of rebirth from the animal state to the human state: the *Surangama Sūtra* says, for example, that foxes are reborn as "vulgar men," tapeworms as "vile men," and domestic animals as "men versed in the ways of the world." The karmic justice of rebirth as a domestic animal can provide some qualified sanction for the use of animals as beasts of burden.

Occasional references are made to the buddhas' and bodhisattvas' specific ministry to and care of animals (along with all other forms of sentient beings). In front of many Buddhist temples are ponds for "releasing life" (fish or turtles), and in some cases one may pay a small fee to release a bird. Temples are also refuges for stray cats and dogs. The famous Buddhist monk and expert on monastic discipline Daoxuan (596–667) is renowned not just for carefully removing the lice from his body but for placing them in a corner so that they would not be stepped on.

According to some sources ministry to animals goes beyond merely not killing them to the point of actually converting them. The Chinese monk Xu Yun once administered the Three Refuges and precepts to a cock who had been donated to a temple but was violent toward the other fowl. "Soon, the cock ceased to fight and stood alone on the branch of a tree; it no longer killed insects and ate only when given cereals. After a while, whenever it heard the bell and *qing* rung, it followed the monks to the main hall and after each prayer meeting it would return to the same branch in the tree. It was again taught to recite the Buddha's name and eventually crowed, 'Fo, Fo, Fo' [Buddha, Buddha, Buddha]" (Xu Yun, 1988). After the bird died in the Buddha hall, Xu Yun wrote, "Where did this being differ from the Buddha?" His autobiography contains similar episodes with a cow, a raven, and two geese.

Buddhist scriptures make use of animals extensively for rhetorical purposes, for example, to praise the Buddha as the "bull of men," as in *Vimalakirti* (Thurman, 1976), or "the Lion Son of the Sakyas," as in the *Lotus Sūtra* (Hurvitz, 1976). "Sharp of tooth and with claws to be dreaded," animals are also representative of danger from which a bodhisattva may save the pious (*Lotus Sūtra*).

Furthermore animal imagery is used to describe the unawakened mind, providing metaphors for spiritual states. The "burning house" metaphor of the *Lotus Sūtra* contains many animals representative of the horror of samsara: "bands of dogs. . . . In their struggle snatching and pulling one another, / Snarling, gnashing their teeth, and howling." Logically, then, the Pure Land of Amitābha lacks animals, as it also lacks the paths of hells and *pretas* (Gómez, 1996).

Animals feature in Buddha's biography in a number of ways. In the *jataka* literature we read stories of the past lives of Śākyamuni, as a monkey, rabbit, and so on. The leitmotif is always to demonstrate the vast accumulation of merit gained by the Buddha's innumerable acts of self-sacrifice. As a rabbit, for example, he comes across some hunters who are about to kill and eat some other animals and then throws himself onto their fire so that they need not kill. In this story the hunters not only spare the lives of their trapped animals, but they forswear their hunting vocation. This reaction is typical of the hunters and butchers in Buddhist literature. In Śākyamuni's biography horses and elephants appear as modes of transport and as witnesses to his marvelous power. A monkey and an elephant make offerings to him, and there is a tradition of a great gathering of all animals to witness his *parinirvāṇa*.

The issue of vegetarianism hinges on Buddhist attitudes toward animals. Was Buddha a vegetarian? The textual evidence suggests that he was not, and indeed most Buddhist monks in Asia do not avoid meat if they are given it. Today Japanese Buddhist clergy eat meat, although through much of the history of Japanese Buddhism a vegetarian diet was regarded as the proper norm for monks and nuns. Nonetheless the Pure Land monk Shinran used meat eating to make a point about the futility of self-effort in the age of the decline of the Dharma, and he got married for similar reasons. In Thailand monks of the minority Thammayut sect do not accept meat into their diet, whereas the majority Mahanikai sect follows the tradition of eating whatever is offered, even if it includes meat. In Tibet, tradition and Tantric doctrine allow for the eating of meat. Still, a strong vegetarian emphasis is distinctive mainly of Chinese Buddhism, where apocryphal sūtras were produced in which Buddha affirms vegetarianism for the monks and nuns. Also in China the Confucian ideal of filial piety was explicitly linked to the possibility that the animal you are eating might have been your own parent in a past life. Because of this association of Buddhist beliefs and vegetarian diet, Christian missionaries such as Matteo Ricci (1552–1610) specifically criticized vegetarianism as heathen. Similarly later missionaries used meat eating as a litmus test of the sincerity of converts who had previously maintained a meatless diet.

ERIC REINDERS

*See also* Aśoka; Bodhisattva; Buddha ( Śākyamuni); Daoxuan (Tao-hsüan); Discourses (Sūtras): Mahāyāna; Food: Buddhist Perspectives; Mahāyāna; Sexuality: Buddhist Perspectives; Shinran; Thailand

## Further Reading

Gómez, Luis O., translator, *Land of Bliss: The Paradise of the Buddha of Measureless Light: Sanskrit and Chinese Versions of the Sukhavativyuha Sutras* (Studies in the Buddhist Traditions), Honolulu: University of Hawaii Press, 1996
Hurvitz, Leon, translator, *Scripture of the Lotus Blossom of the Fine Dharma (The Lotus Sutra)* (Records of Civilization, Sources and Studies, number 94), New York: Columbia University Press, 1976
Khoroche, Peter, *Once the Buddha Was a Monkey: Arya Sura's Jatakamala*, Chicago: University of Chicago Press, 1989
Lu K'uan Yü, translator, *The Surangama Sutra (Leng Yen Ching)*, London and New York: Rider, 1966
Page, Tony, *Buddhism and Animals: A Buddhist Vision of Humanity's Rightful Relationship with the Animal Kingdom*, London: UKAVIS, 1999
Rabten, Geshe, *The Essential Nectar: Meditations on the Buddhist Path* (A Wisdom Basic Book), London: Wisdom, 1984; Boston: Wisdom, 1992
Thurman, Robert A.F., translator, *The Holy Teaching of Vimalakirti: A Mahayana Scripture*, University Park: Pennsylvania State University Press, 1976
Xu Yun, *Empty Cloud: The Autobiography of the Chinese Zen Master, Xu-Yun*, translated by Charles Luk, edited by Richard Hunn, Shaftesbury, Dorset: Element Books, 1988 (first published in 1974)

# Animals, Attitude toward: Christian Perspectives

Evidence for the attitudes of Christian monks toward animals is diffuse. This article deals with three kinds of clues: texts on abstinence from meat, agricultural evidence, and the place that animals held in three sorts of literature, namely, bestiaries, beast fables, and saint's lives.

The Rule of Benedict forbids eating meat of four-footed animals by any but the very sick (36.9, 39.10). Similar legislation was fairly typical among his monastic predecessors (Pachomius, Rule of the Master). The principal motivations for this vegetarianism seem to have been that meat was an expensive luxury and that meat nourished sexual appetite. Later Western monks tended to hedge on their observance of abstinence from meat. For example, Abelard (1079–1142/43) urged such abstinence on Heloise (c. 1100–1163/64) and her community. Heloise rejoined that women are less likely to be sexually affected by eating meat than men, although in the end the statutes of the Paraclete adopted abstinence.

In medieval Europe most monasteries maintained some ties with agriculture. The plan of St. Gall shows, if not reverence for animals, at least a reverence for order. In the southwestern corner of the plan are similarly designed buildings for horses and oxen, sheep, goats, cows, pigs, brood mares and foals, and their respective keepers. In the southeastern corner are a goosehouse and a henhouse with a separate house for the fowl keepers. Evidently, the animals were valued mainly for the by-products they produced: leather, milk, and eggs. They were given fine accommodations and resident caretakers.

Cloister of the "Canticle of the Creatures," Church of San Damiano, Assisi, Italy, early 13th century. Here in 1224–1225 St. Francis composed the "Canticle of the Creatures."
Photo courtesy of Mary Schaefer

Another clue to monastic attitudes toward animals is provided by studies of Cistercian agricultural practice. Established as a reform of Benedictine monasticism in 1098, the Cistercians valued manual labor, but after some decades it was mainly the lay brothers who operated their extensive farms. After 1325 most of their lands in England and Wales were leased to outsiders. Until then English and Welsh Cistercians had raised cattle, run dairies, and tanned hides, although cattle were never the cash crop that sheep became in the 13th century. Some evidence exists that Cistercians were superior sheep men, but no evidence exists that their attitudes toward sheep differed from the attitudes of their neighbors.

Literary evocations seem to tell us more about monastic attitudes toward animals than do historical data. The second-century *Physiologus* was written by an Alexandrian Christian. This book offered lore about animals and uplifting guidance for human behavior drawn from the characteristic activities of each animal. It featured North African animals and by the fourth century had been translated into Latin. The *Physiologus*, amplified with material from Isidore of Seville, Gerald of Wales, Hugh of Fouilloy, Bartholomaeus Anglicus, and other sources, became very popular in the 12th and 13th centuries. These amplified versions of the *Physiologus* were called "bestiaries," and many or most of them were monastic in origin. A typical entry consists of a quotation from Scripture, a fact (real or imagined) of natural history about the behavior of the animal, and a moral drawn from this for human life. Brunsdon Yapp and Wilma George (1991), professors of zoology and manuscript scholars, advance the theory that bestiaries were textbooks

written for students in monasteries. Many, but not all, of their pictures . . . are not only correct but highly original. . . . Bestiaries are not, as they are generally held to be, merely compendia of old wives tales and religious symbolism, amusing or boring according to your taste, but documents that are important for any serious history of medieval science.

Thus, bestiaries show both a desire to know the natural behavior of animals and a readiness to draw moral lessons from that behavior.

Beast fables differ from bestiaries in that the beasts in the stories speak. The "Swan Sequence" is found in a sequence collection from the abbey of St.-Martial in Limoges and seems to have been intended to illustrate Christ's redemption by depicting the renewed vigor that dawn brings to an exhausted swan flying above the ocean. The more complex, 11th-century *Ecbasis captivi* is by, for, and about monks. The New Law of mercy replaces the Old Law of strict justice, and so the weak calf-monk who has attempted to flee is given another chance. Both these fables show a willingness to make theological points through stories about animals. The characters of the animals are familiar to the intended monastic readers either from direct experience in the case of the calf, the fox, and the wolf or from literature through the *Physiologus* in the case of the lion and unicorn. The characterizations work because the monk-author and his monk-audience feel empathy for both animals and monks. Nothing is especially scientific or sentimental in these fables. Animals are neighbors, known well enough to appear as stereotypes but mysterious enough to fascinate and hold attention. At the very least their appearance in moral fables suggests that their treatment in day-to-day life involved a degree of moral constraint.

The lives of the Desert Fathers manifest a certain ambivalence about animals. Demons appeared to Antony (c. 251–356) in the forms of fierce or dangerous animals, but when wild animals damaged the vegetable beds in his garden, he caught one of the animals, held it gently, and said, "Why do you do harm to me when I harm none of you? Go away, and in the Lord's name do not come near these things again!" Thereafter, as though awed by his orders, the wild animals stayed out of Antony's garden.

According to St. Bede's prose life of St. Cuthbert (c. 636–687), one day Cuthbert left the monastery at Melrose with a servant to go preaching. They had traveled for a long time but still had a long way to go. Cuthbert asked the lad where he planned to eat. The boy said that he had been thinking about that question a good deal but had no idea what they could do. Cuthbert told him that those who serve God faithfully do not die from hunger. He looked up, saw an eagle, and said, "God can feed us today through her ministry." Later the eagle snatched a fish from the river, and the boy ran to the eagle, grabbed the fish, and returned to the man of God. Cuthbert told him to give the eagle ("our handmaid") the share that she deserved for ministering to them. The lad did so. Cuthbert and the servant turned aside to a village at mealtime and split the remainder of the fish with the householder who cooked it for them. The story needs little commentary. Nature's bounty must be shared with other animals; it is not humanity's alone. In the presence of the saint, nature's harmony is restored, Edenlike.

Bartholomew of Farne, a 12th-century monk of Durham, lived for 42 years as a hermit on Inner Farne. Eider ducks nested everywhere on the island. One day a mother duck was leading her brood to water when one fell down a crevice. She went and tugged at the hem of Bartholomew's habit. At her urging he then followed her to the crevice, and she pointed down it. He saw the duckling clinging to the cliff and climbed down and rescued it. The mother received the duckling back with joy. Thus, animals' hurts are analogous to ours; their instincts are analogous to our thinking, and their well-being is interconnected with ours.

In none of the cases cited here are animals sentimentalized much less divinized. The followers of St. Benedict generally lived in rural areas and at least in the early Middle Ages did some agricultural work themselves. They knew animals as companions, rivals, and sources of food, hides, and other necessities. Their willingness to use animals as moral exemplars shows a recognition that animal instincts mimic human virtue. The affinities between people and animals make it easy to cast animals as characters who portray monks in a fable. At their best human beings live peacefully with animals and look out for their well-being. Humans share the goods of the earth with them.

Saint Francis (1181/82–1226) left the comforts of middle-class life to share the wild animals' experience of foraging for food and finding shelter opportunistically. This might have given Francis and his friars a view of animals that was slightly different from that of the monks. Having accused the wolf of Gubbio of abominable crimes not only against animals but also against rational creatures made in the image of God, Francis convinced the wolf to enter into a peace treaty with the people of the town. On another occasion Francis rescued some doves and built them nests, so that they lived with the friars for a time. Saint Anthony of Padua (1193–1231) won over the people of Rimini by preaching to the fish. In "Canticle of the Sun," Francis praises God for and through all creatures, his brothers and sisters, without mentioning animals explicitly. Praise of the creator for animals and for all creation is probably what Christian monks would regard as their deepest response to the animals with whom they share the earth.

HUGH FEISS, O.S.B.

*See also* Abelard, Peter; Antony, St.; Bede, St.; Cistercians; Cuthbert, St.; Heloise; Isidore of Seville, St.

## Further Reading

Bell, David N., *Wholly Animals: A Book of Beastly Tales*, Kalamazoo, Michigan: Cistercian Publications, 1992

Clark, Willene B., *The Medieval Book of Birds: Hugh of Fouilloy's Aviarum*, Binghamton, New York: Medieval and Renaissance Texts and Studies, 1992

Donkin, R.A., *The Cistercians: Studies in the Geography of Medieval England and Wales*, Toronto: Pontifical Institute of Mediaeval Studies, 1978

George, Wilma, and Brunsdon Yapp, *The Naming of the Beasts: Natural History in the Medieval Bestiary*, London: Duckworth, 1991

Habib, M.A., editor, *St. Francis of Assisi: Writings and Early Biographies: English Omnibus of the Sources for the Life of St. Francis*, London: SPCK, 1979; Chicago: Franciscan Herald Press, 1991

Kardong, Terrence G., *Benedict's Rule: A Translation and Commentary*, Collegeville, Minnesota: Liturgical Press, 1996

Price, Lorna, *The Plan of St. Gall in Brief*, Berkeley: University of California Press, 1982

Sorrell, Robert D., *St. Francis of Assisi and Nature*, New York: Oxford University Press, 1988

White, T.H., *The Bestiary: A Book of Beasts*, Gloucester: Sutton, 1954; New York: Putnam/Capricorn, 1960

Ziolkowski, Jan, *Talking Animals: Medieval Latin Beast Poetry, 750–1150*, Philadelphia: University of Pennsylvania Press, 1993

# Anselm, St. c. 1033–1109

Italian-born Benedictine, archbishop of Canterbury, and theologian

Anselm of Bec/Canterbury (c. 1033–1109) was a monk (1060–1109), abbot (1078–1093), and for his last 16 years the archbishop of Canterbury (1093–1109). Although ordinarily assessed as a philosophical-theologian, Anselm considered most of his writings to be spiritual commentaries or, more precisely, spiritual responses rooted in the divine reality.

Saint Anselm was a native of Aosta in the Italian piedmont. Deriving his religious orientation from his mother, Ermenburga (a Burgundian), Anselm was moved as an adolescent to seek admission to a nearby Benedictine monastery (c. 1048). However, unable in this ambition to win the endorsement of his father, Gundulf, Anselm had to delay his vocation. Eventually, after Ermenburga's death, conflicts with his father led Anselm to abandon home and patrimony at age 23 (c. 1056). In a journey of about three years, he crossed the Alps and traversed Burgundy, then moved northward into the Loire valley and beyond. Although Anselm's original purpose likely was simply separation from Gundulf, his ambitions evolved into a quest for intellectual growth. Accordingly, in 1059 he turned toward the Norman monastery of Notre Dame at Bec. This abbey based its observance on *Regula Benedicti* (the monastic rule of St. Benedict) and had a school overseen by one of the great scholars of his time, Lanfranc of Pavia (c. 1005–1089).

After a year of study at Bec, Anselm entered the monastery as a novice (1060), professing monastic vows one year later. His profession was followed by a time of relative silence (1061–1063) in which his activities are largely undocumented. However, evidence points to a period of intense thought and meditation, for when Anselm emerged from this silence, the premises of his imposing intellectual work, although not yet articulated, seemingly were defined in principle. At this time the abbot of Bec, Herluin (d. 1078), appointed Anselm claustral prior and master of the school.

The pivotal point in Anselm's thought came in his 44th year in a revelatory presentment that occurred to him one day in the midst of the Divine Office. It resulted in the concise definition of God ("that than which none greater can be thought") for which he had long searched. From this time forward all his intellectual work – and the conduct of his life as well – would unfold in that definition's context.

Anselm's literary output as a monk at Bec is varied. Over his 15 years as prior (1063–1078), followed by 15 as abbot

St. Anselm of Bec/Canterbury – Benedictine monk, bishop, doctor of the church – is portrayed here in a window at the Abbey Basilica of Belmont Abbey (North Carolina). The window was executed by the Royal Bavarian Establishment of Francis Mayer and Company (Munich) in 1892.
Photo courtesy of Belmont Abbey Archives

(1078–1093), Anselm wrote and circulated prayers, meditations, and treatises while engaging in an extensive correspondence. A number of the prayers and meditations eventually were collected (especially from 1070 to 1075) for wider distribution among monastic and lay correspondents. Anselm's first treatise was a relatively standard logical discussion titled *De Gramatico*, written during his period of silence (1060–1063). It never exercised much influence and is often overlooked. Anselm then turned to the production of a treatise (eventually two treatises) on the being of God. In *Monologion* (c. 1075 or 1076) Anselm wrote of divinity and its several attributes. Indeed, chapter 16 of this work gives Anselm's only effort toward listing the attributes he believed to be innate in the Supreme Being.

*Monologion* is studied today as Anselm's earliest articulation of his concept of divinity but also because it typifies the method of his logic. Anselm's argumentation is discursive. Without being ruminative, his discussions advance according to a progressive discernment and revelation of what *must* be because of its truth. Any truth is true because of its participation in, and to the degree that it participates in, the Supreme Truth (divinity); and, according to Anselm's *De Veritate* (c. 1080), divine truth is to be understood as absolute, meaning that God is always as He ought to be. That is important to Anselm's logic and rational method because it establishes for him a principle of rectitude (*rectitudo*): because God is always as He ought to be, a line of truth can be traced – by deductively inquiring into what must be true in consequence of the Supreme Truth of the Supreme Being – that exposes all truth. This process of reasoning is effective because of God's absolute consistency and fidelity to Himself, His truth.

Anselm then goes a step further, creating a moral theology that flowers from the divine being. The Lord, in creating human persons, invests these creatures with a call – with purpose. For Anselm that purpose is as absolute as its divine author: as is taught by both Scripture and Benedict (Deut. 6:5, Matt. 22:37, Mark 12:30, Luke 10:27, and Benedict RB 4:1), a person owes God his whole being – all that he is and has. That precept is the foundation of Anselm's moral theology. He weighs morality in terms of a person's consistency with the Absolute Being, a conformity of (human) being to (divine) Being. This emphasis on divine/human alignment requires Anselm to revise theology's ordinary vocabulary as well. For example, what later generations would label "Godlikeness" is evocatively termed "similitude" (*similitudo*) by Anselm. Even more significant, Anselm renders his concept of "union" with God under the rubric of *concordia*, a preeminent accord of being and Being that he proposes in terms of going to God – entering Him – rather than under the traditional notion of a divine "indwelling" in humanity.

For Anselm this is more than a shift of vocabulary because it reflects the spirituality that he finds in *Regula Benedicti*. Anselm admits that Augustine is the source with whom he hopes never to be in conflict. However, the more pervasive influence on him – because he not only uses it, but also inculcates it as his own – is *Regula Benedicti*, to which Anselm was bound by both vow and affinity. He has a striking way of taking Benedict at his word.

For example, undoubtedly Anselm accepts Benedict's principle "*ut in omnibus glorificatur Deus*" literally and without reservation: God can be glorified in *all* things; and Anselm's understanding of God's vigilant presence – even though the Lord may often seem to be remote (Pros 1) – is precisely Benedictine (RB Pro).

In 1093 Anselm was forced to accept the Archbishopric of Canterbury. Reluctant to exchange his abbatial crozier for an episcopal one, Anselm tarried for more than five months before accepting England's primatial throne. In the end his decision was swayed favorably by a series of external affirmations of this revision of his vocation. These testimonies came from his Church overlord (William, archbishop of Rouen), his secular overlord (Robert Curthose, duke of Normandy), and most important from the monks of Bec. Having pledged to serve his monastery as abbot until death, Anselm's integrity would not allow him to accept the separation imposed by episcopacy unless it bore the monks' consent. They finally acquiesced, although begrudgingly. Thus, Anselm, because he believed himself morally obliged to ensure Bec's good abbatial governance, virtually dictated the selection of his successor, William of Beaumont. Some modern scholars dispute Anselm's reluctance to accept the promotion to Canterbury, but their theories are incompatible with what is known of Anselm's mind, his reasoning, and his integrity.

Anselm's reign at Canterbury (1093–1109) was a troubled period. England's kings – William II (c. 1056–1100, r. 1087–1100) and then Henry I (1068–1135, r. 1100–1135) – repeatedly quarreled with Anselm, most significantly over Church reform and councils (especially from 1102 to 1108), relations with Rome, knights' service, homage and investitures, and the prerogatives of the primate in regard to the bishops and bishops-elect of England and Ireland. These conflicts led Anselm twice into exile on the Continent (1097–1100 and 1103–1106).

One of the treasures of the Anselmian legacy is his collected correspondence. More than 400 letters are known today, many of which were first assembled during his own lifetime (c. 1086 and later) and perhaps edited. These are invaluable as a source for understanding Anselm's moral application of his spiritual principles and the pivotal role of Benedict's rule in those principles. The Benedictine perspective participated in most of the Anselmian precepts, which ranged from the general recognition that a person addresses God mainly by the goodness of his life to the specific reference (to RB Pro:4), often repeated, that it is the Lord who brings the person's good intentions to fruition.

Anselm's most notable theological works were produced during his episcopacy. On the whole these were written in response to current crises and disputes (e.g., regarding the procession of the Holy Spirit) and sometimes at papal summons. Foremost among these is *Cur Deus Homo* (1095–1098; Why God Became Man). In this work, taking his hermenutic from the feudal system (with which his contemporary readers would have been conversant), Anselm proposed what he called the "honor-of-God." God's honor consists in all that is due to Him, including the homage and obedience of all His creatures. By this principle, whenever God has not received His due (i.e., when a human person sins and thus fails to render God His proper obedience and respect), a deficit is created, requiring satisfaction. However, in the case of original sin, man's debt exceeded his ability to compensate. The willful removal of humanity from its native harmony with divinity had imposed an indebtedness so great that, even though it was the responsibility of the human person, only God could effect reconciliation. Thus, Anselm reasons, it was necessary that God should become man and give His life (the fullness of what is God's to claim of man), thereby satisfying the debt for all those persons who align with Him. In this way, Anselm concludes (with that astonishing simplicity that consistently marks his reasoning), redemption was won (by God and yet by man) properly and rightly. The desire of both God and man for reconciliation was efficiently satisfied while simultaneously providing for the integrity of God's honor. Subsequently, Anselm wrote a less formal and more eloquent edition of his *Cur Deus Homo*, titled *Meditatio Redemptionis Humanae* (1099; Meditation on Human Redemption).

Despite the originality and import of his theology, the most frequently studied Anselmian text is claimed by philosophers. Titled *Proslogion* (1077 or 1108), this brief spiritual treatise expounds on the necessity and character of divine being. Following promptly on *Monologion*, it provided a different but complementary treatment of his subject. Anselm's reputation today as an original intellect rests mainly on this work.

*Proslogion*, Anselm specified, gives a single argument (*unum argumentum*) for God's necessary being. Nevertheless, the common scholarly practice has been to isolate from the whole a core argument (using only chapter 2, or chapters 2 and 3, or more). Since the 18th century, this detached portion has been called (perhaps inaccurately) the "ontological argument," or "proof," of God's existence. Actually, rather than seeking to prove divine being, Anselm employs the Lord's reality as a premise of the argument. He even writes most of *Proslogion* in the second person, addressed to God in the form of a meditation.

After an initial chapter that begs God's intimacy and expresses the author's longing for surety of the Supreme Being, Anselm shifts into a brief, reasoned affirmation of what he realizes he has always known. This affirmation is the passage commonly called the "ontological argument." Preserving his personal tone and addressing his narrative to God, Anselm begins by defining God as "that than which none greater can be thought." He then notes immediately – before giving any further "argument" – that the Lord's existence must be true. Anselm's rationale is that a person can conceive of this Being *only* as One who exists; otherwise, it would still be possible to conceive of a greater being (one who does exist). Thus, it follows that the Supreme Being cannot be otherwise: God must exist, or else He would not be as we know Him to be (i.e., the One than whom none greater can be thought). When one accepts this definition, Anselm contends, the only reasonable conclusion is that God exists.

Afterward (apparently in the year following), Anselm's reasoning was challenged by Gaunilo, a monk of Marmoutiers.

Among his various objections (*Ad Gaunilo Pro Insipiente*), Gaunilo charged that the mere thought of a perfection does not necessarily indicate a corresponding reality. Anselm's response to Gaunilo (*Ad Gaunilonem Responsio Anselmi*) was that, in this one singular and exceptional case (i.e., divinity), existence really is necessary. Indeed, not only does God exist, but He cannot not exist. Even the mere concept of God affirms the necessity of His reality: His perfection demands existence. Moreover, it is right and best that He exist (i.e., it is a matter of rectitude). Finally, Anselm states explicitly in chapter 5 of the *Responsio* – clearly articulating the point that was the undercurrent of his argument throughout – that God is and is as we believe Him to be, a fact that demands not only that He exists but that He exists *necessarily*. His truth necessitates existence. Only a fool, Anselm says with the psalmist (Ps. 13, 14:1), would deny God.

This argument has become one of the most debated concepts in philosophical theology. Although generally challenged and discounted, its originality and the profundity of its implications have ensured an enduring eminence in religious and philosophical discourse. However, in weighing the content of the "argument," it is important to remember both that the whole *Proslogion* gives Anselm's *unum argumentum* and that Anselm thought the exchange with Gaunilo so important that he specified that from that time forward it should be appended to *Proslogion*. It is now reckoned to be part of the argument.

Anselm's life is peculiarly well documented. Both of his secretaries, Eadmer and Alexander, were conscientious in preserving the Anselmian legacy. In Eadmer's (c. 1060–1122) case that even involved disobedience to Anselm's instructions to destroy such documents. Thus, contemporary, firsthand stories of the archbishop's life survived, most notably in Eadmer's *Vita Anselmi* (1109–1125; *Life of Anselm*) and his *Historia Novorum in Anglia* (1109–1114; History of Recent Events in England). These are recognized today as models of balanced and insightful historical documentation. The contribution of Alexander to this legacy revolves around a collection of sayings that were purported to be the maxims of Anselm.

Anselm's struggles against the crown served in union with his reputed sanctity when, in subsequent days, his veneration was at issue. Thomas Becket (c. 1118–1170), an archbishop in similar circumstances, was the first to petition Rome (1163) to raise Anselm to the dignity of the altar. Although no documentation exists to indicate any canonical recognition of his holiness, Anselm's liturgical feast was celebrated from that time forward in England and eventually on the calendar of the universal Church. Also, in accord with this new dignity, Anselm's remains were translated to a place of honor in the cathedral at Canterbury. Since 1734 he has been recognized as one of the Doctors of the Church, being titled *Doctor Spei* (the Doctor of Hope).

When Anselm died in 1109, he left behind a dissatisfied English episcopate and crown. However, among those closest to him, especially the monks and his numerous correspondents, he was immediately revered, being seen as a miracle worker and a heavenly intercessor. For later incumbents of Canterbury, Anselm would epitomize the status and recognition that were proper to that see; and, according to the medievalist David Knowles, Anselm is recognized today as the exemplar for both Benedictine monks and Benedictine abbots.

PASCHAL BAUMSTEIN, O.S.B.

See also Devotions, Western Christian; England: History; France: Sites; Lanfranc; Scholars, Benedictine

## Biography

North Italian by birth, Anselm entered the Benedictine monastery school at Bec, Normandy, in 1059 whose leader was another North Italian, Lanfranc. In 1063 Anselm succeeded the latter as prior and 15 years later became abbot. He visited England several times to review his monastery's land there and to see former monks of Bec. In 1093, after the archbishopric of Canterbury had been vacant for several years, King William Rufus (1087–1100) nominated Anselm. Having accepted reluctantly, the latter upheld the autonomy of his office against royal claims to appoint bishops, and twice he spent several years in exile in Rome. Anselm's Latin treatises rank among the most influential in Western theology, and his statement of the ontological argument for the existence of God (in the *Proslogion*) remains fundamental. In the early 18th century he was proclaimed a Doctor of the Church.

## Major Works

*Monologion*, c. 1075–1076
*Proslogion*, 1077 or 1108
*De Veritate* (On Truth), c. 1080
*De Incarnatione Verbi* (On the Incarnation of the Word), 1095
*Cur Deus Homo* (Why God Became Man), 1095–1098
*De Processione Sancti Spiritus* (On the Procession of the Holy Spirit), 1102
*De Libero Arbitrio* (On Free Will), c. 1108
*The Prayers and Meditations of Saint Anselm with the Proslogion*, translated by Benedicta Ward, 1973
*Anselm of Canterbury* (collected treatises in four volumes), edited and translated by Jasper Hopkins and Herbert Richardson, 1974–1976
*The Letters of Saint Anselm of Canterbury*, 3 vols., translated by Walter Frohlich, 1990–1994

## Further Reading

Baumstein, Paschal, "Anselm's Intellect and the Embrace of Bec," *Faith and Reason* 14 (1988)
Baumstein, Paschal, "Revisiting Anselm: Current Historical Studies and Controversies," *Cistercian Studies Quarterly* 28 (1993)
Eadmer of Canterbury, *The Life of Saint Anselm, Archbishop of Canterbury*, edited and translated by Richard W. Southern, London and New York: Nelson, 1962
Eadmer of Canterbury, *Eadmer's History of Recent Events in England*, translated by Geoffrey Bosanquet, London: Cresset Press, 1964
Southern, Richard W., *Saint Anselm: A Portrait in a Landscape*, Cambridge and New York: Cambridge University Press, 1990
Vaughn, Sally N., *Anselm of Bec and Robert of Meulan: The Innocence of the Dove and the Wisdom of the Serpent*, Berkeley: University of California Press, 1987

# Anthony, St. *See* Antony, St.

# Anticlericalism: Buddhist Perspectives

Buddhism was from the start monastic. Through a series of councils and textual elaboration, the form and complexity of Buddhist monastic institutions changed over time. Certainly the *saṅgha* developed far beyond the relatively simple set of initiation procedures and monastic rules that appear to have been instituted by Buddha. Laypeople were never excluded from the grand enterprise of Buddhism, but throughout most of Buddhist history the laity have taken a subordinate position. To uphold the status of monk or nun requires control over ordination, and this leads to criteria of inclusion and exclusion as well as regimens of discipline and mechanisms for expulsion. The most common form of anticlericalism in Asia has been an attack on the dividing lines between cleric and laity, on the very category of the monastic, which has been contested on numerous occasions: by rulers, by anti-Buddhist polemicists, and by Buddhist reformers.

Many rulers in Asia, even pro-Buddhist ones, have sought to control aspects of the *saṅgha*. Taking on the role of the *cakravartin* (wheel turner), rulers have at times "purged" the *saṅgha* of its "impurities" by enforcing stricter controls on entry (through quotas on ordinations or added stipulations), by extending secular law into the jurisdiction of the Vinaya (monastic code), and by expelling certain monks and nuns. In some cases, then, attacks on clerical institutions have been phrased in pro-Buddhist terms. In other cases no such rationalization existed, and the goal was simply the extermination of the *saṅgha*. Such violent anticlerical persecutions occurred sporadically throughout history, but perhaps the best known include the persecution during the Hui-chang period in China (c. 843–845), the Communist-inspired iconoclasm of the Chinese Cultural Revolution (1966–1976), and the violence in Tibet since the 1950s. In Japan the slaughter of monks during the civil warfare of the 16th and 17th centuries and the anti-Buddhist movements of the early Meiji period (1868–1870s) come to mind.

A rich tradition of anti-Buddhist discourse has fueled state control and persecution of Buddhism. Erik Zürcher (1959, 1972) has categorized the anticlericalism in the fourth and early fifth centuries in China into roughly four types of arguments: (1) political and economic arguments, which emphasize the threat of Buddhism to the state; (2) utilitarian arguments, which assert the uselessness of maintaining monks and nuns who produce nothing; (3) arguments based on feelings of cultural superiority, or xenophobia; and (4) moral arguments, which consider such monastic behavior as celibacy and leaving the home as unnatural and thus immoral. To this list one might add any number of further permutations. Of course pro-Buddhist polemicists have responded to each area of concern: (1) by praying for the welfare of the ruler and the state, (2) by producing "merit" and helping the laity produce merit by teaching them law-abiding conduct, (3) by asserting a more global perspective and/or negating the value of territoriality, and (4) by developing discourses of Buddhist filial piety. The celibacy of monks was a problem in eastern Asia, where a son's obligation to continue his family lineage was so strongly asserted. In Thailand a tradition of temporary ordination allows men to ordain for a short period and return to lay life without stigma.

From the 13th century on, Western Christian discourses of anticlericalism come face to face with Buddhism in cultural encounters between East and West. Initially there was hostility toward Buddhist monks as idolators and heathens. From the 16th century on, Catholic missionaries in China asserted the supposed ignorance and venality of Buddhist clerics as a means of distancing themselves from Buddhist monks in the eyes of both the Confucian literati in China and the anticlerical Protestants in Europe. In the 19th century a flood of Protestant missionaries imported their own traditions of anticlericalism. Their reports on Chinese religion repeatedly assert the similarity of Buddhist and Catholic monasticism, almost always with a negative value judgment. In some cases missionaries drew from native anti-Buddhist rhetoric, so that we find two opposing religions (Christianity and Confucianism) sharing hostility to Buddhist monasticism.

Traditions of anticlericalism can be found within Buddhism as well. The emphasis on minute rules of monastic discipline did not always sit well with some Mahāyāna monks, whose doctrinal rhetoric emphasized a bodhisattva's intentions and vows, that is, the spirit of the law rather than the letter. Although the Mahāyāna continued the institution of monkhood, its critique of earlier forms of Buddhism (which it labeled Hīnayāna, "the lesser vehicle") involved a qualified negation of the distinction between cleric and laity. One seminal Mahāyāna text, the *Vimalakirti-nirdesa Sūtra*, features a layman, Vimalakirti, whose enlightened wisdom is considered on a par with that of Śākyamuni Buddha. Vimalakirti demonstrates the limited understanding of one monk after another. The ideal figure of the bodhisattva is almost always depicted as a layperson. The strong motif of nondualism in Mahāyāna thought could also be applied to the dualism of cleric/laity. As Mahāyāna developed in Asia, a number of groups pushed the logic of this nondualism and rejected the institution in varying degrees. Some Buddhist groups, such as the Japanese Pure Land sects, broke down many (but not all) of the barriers between lay and monastic status. The best-known of these reformers was the Japanese monk Shinran (1173–1263). Shinran married, calling himself "neither monk nor layman" (*hiso hizoku*). The soteriological basis of his actions (and the Jōdo Shinshu tradition he began) lies in the radical faith in Amida Buddha during a time when it is no longer possible to achieve enlightenment by one's own power, even by ordination. To place one's faith in the saving power of Amida was also to reject the salvific power of any of one's own actions, including ordination. Such self-powered efforts can actually prevent one's salvation because of the danger of deluded pride. As a more recent example, the Chinese monk T'ai-hsü (Taixu, 1889–1947) also claimed to have transcended the clerical status

in accordance with the intellectual tide of Westernization of his time.

Buddhism in the United States now includes a number of monastic centers, although most of the impetus has come from Asian immigrant communities. With some exceptions American Buddhists have been little interested in the clerical institution. Meditation, practiced in Asia almost entirely by clerics, is now mainly a lay activity in the United States and has also become popular among middle-class laity in Asia. The pervasive Protestant critique of monasticism and ritual and the American culture of individualism have meshed well with certain anticlerical aspects of the Buddhist tradition.

ERIC REINDERS

*See also* Buddhadāsa; Buddhist Schools/Traditions: Japan; China; Critiques of Buddhist Monasticism; Prophethood, Japanese Buddhist; Pure Land Buddhism; Rennyo; Saṅgha

**Further Reading**

Ketelaar, James Edward, *Of Heretics and Martyrs in Meiji Japan: Buddhism and Its Persecution*, Princeton, New Jersey: Princeton University Press, 1990
Wright, Arthur F., "Fu I and the Rejection of Buddhism," *Journal of the History of Ideas* 12 (1951)
Zürcher, Erik, *The Buddhist Conquest of China: The Spread and Adaptation of Buddhism in Early Medieval China*, 2 volumes, Leiden: Brill, and New York: Humanities Press, 1959; reprint, with additions and corrections, Leiden: Brill, 1972

# Anticlericalism: Christian Perspectives

Skeptical attitudes toward the clergy are a complex phenomenon in European history that only incidentally touches monasticism. Whether Jesus himself ever taught about organization among his disciples is uncertain, but some sectors of the early Church held a power structure to be inimical to his message (cf. Mark 9:33–37 and Luke 9:46–48 but contrast Matt. 18:1–4 and cf. Mark 10:42–45 and parallels). However, a system of offices (e.g., preaching and teaching) can be seen emerging in the very earliest Christian documents (Paul's letters, the *Didache*). Rooted in synagogue structures and paralleled among other first-century Jewish sects, this apparatus grew, and by the following century a system had emerged with three tiers: a single bishop (sole community leader vested with sacral authority as a divinely chosen "apostle" standing in relation to the community as Jesus had stood to the original disciples), a group of presbyters assisting him, and a further group of assistants and deacons (as described in Ignatius of Antioch's letters). Within this structure a process began that focused sacral power (e.g., only a bishop or, failing him, a presbyter could preside at the Eucharist), administration, and doctrinal authority in one of the three groups, and here originated the notion of a "clergy" distinct from the rest of the people (the *laos*, "laity").

By the time of the Council of Elvira in Spain (306), the clergy had emerged as an elite with a corporate identity of three components: (1) it was the conduit of the divine favor, will, and presence; (2) it was bound by its own discipline code; and (3) it was a socially distinct, all-male group whose right to control was vouched for by sexual abstinence. A few years later this tight empire-wide system of control was a central attraction of Christianity in the eyes of Emperor Constantine (306–337), and his demand for uniformity in practice at the Council of Nicaea (325) reinforced the clergy's distinct identity as a force within the imperial constitution. In both the East and the West, subsequent centuries saw an elaboration of that position whereby clergy became an elite socially, sexually, legally, educationally, and in terms of administrative power. Within the religious sphere that power was almost complete. In other areas, such as education, they held a virtual monopoly. Within the "temporal order" clergy were a distinct estate, often providing administrators, usually also large landholders, and sometimes exercising temporal power directly, for example, as elector-bishops in the Holy Roman Empire or administrators of the Papal States (still vestigially at the Vatican).

Although few links exist between monastic ideals and Christianity's clerical structure, monks were fully integrated within it and thus were also the targets or victims of opposition to it. Insofar as monasticism involved a "retreat from the world," it was structurally similar to the notion of the clergy as a separate sacral group. Although often unordained, monastics were legally clerics (defined as "having the tonsure") whose life and behavior was governed by canon law, and they were treated as being on the clerical side of the cleric/lay divide. Moreover monks in holy orders (priests, deacons, and lesser ministers) were legally no different from any other clerics, and abbots exercised jurisdiction similar to that of bishops. Monastics also participated in the larger government of Christendom through being elected pope (e.g., Gregory the Great, 590–604) and in the administration of temporal rulers (e.g., Alcuin [c. 740–804] at Charlemagne's court). Some monasteries were civil powers; for example, the abbot of St. Gallen was also a secular ruler during the Middle Ages, and the abbey owned many estates outside its direct government. Even those who shunned such involvements – a position espoused ever anew by monastic reformers – still needed to administer their own estates, and so they too participated in the clerical and landholding systems.

Anticlericalism during the medieval period was often little more than rage against rich landowners, and such rage became anticlerical in the case of monastic estates. In the later Middle Ages, it was often the guise under which kings, such as Philip IV (1285–1314) of France, sought to bring all power securely into their own hands. Attacks on the clergy were akin to those on the nobility and motivated by a desire to vanquish alternative power structures and collectors of revenue. Although the notion of a priesthood and of a distinctive role for monastics was challenged at the Reformation, these attacks are only incidentally classed as anticlerical. Anticlericalism, in its classic form, was a product of the Enlightenment in France, where its theory was outlined by Voltaire and Diderot: clergy perpetuated false myths that enslaved mankind, their role as the First Estate abetted their own power, and they obstructed reform by justifying the nobility's right to rule. Thus, during the French Revolution (1789–1799) monasteries became a primary target: not only did their confiscated lands provide revenue and their buildings accommodations for prisons, military academies, and the like, but their removal from influence, especially over education, was seen to advance the revolutionary cause. The destruction of St.-Germain-des-Prés (the Paris monastery and home of Maurist scholarship) is a good example of ferocious anticlerical zeal. The same period saw the disappearance of Cluny, Clairvaux, Cîteaux, and many other French abbeys. This form of anticlericalism – attacking everything connected with the Church as hostile to the ruling government – has been a feature of totalitarian regimes of whatever ideology ever since.

Today a newer anticlericalism has emerged within Christianity, as many theologians and groups deem the concept of a "clergy" to be a false path. These anticlericals see clergy as incompatible with the notion of mutual service, in which each community member has a distinctive contribution and witness to make to the whole. This attitude is expressed both in writing and in the rejection of distinguishing social badges, such as religious dress. Whether these movements can alter long-established patterns of thought and behavior, whether good or bad, within Christianity remains to be seen.

THOMAS O'LOUGHLIN

*See also* Asceticism: Christian Perspectives; Bishops: Jurisdiction and Role; Cluny, France; Critiques of Western Christian Monasticism; Dissolution of Monasteries; Luther, Martin; Maurists; Persecution: Christian Perspectives; St. Gallen, Switzerland; Schools and Universities, Benedictine

### Further Reading

Berthelot du Chesnay, C., "Anticlericalism," *New Catholic Encyclopedia*, volume 1, New York: McGraw-Hill, 1967
Laeuchli, Samuel, *Power and Sexuality: The Emergence of Canon Law at the Synod of Elvira*, Philadelphia: Temple University Press, 1972

# Antonians

The community of St. Antony of Vienne was an order of regular canons (this meant that the members were under the jurisdiction of local bishops, unlike, e.g., the Cistercian Order) founded in 1095 around the relics of St. Antony the Abbot, sometimes called St. Antony of Egypt, who was born on the west bank of the Nile in the mid–third century. Athanasius (c. 296–373) called him the founder of asceticism. Orphaned at age 18 he took up the life of a hermit in the desert, remaining closed in an abandoned temple for 20 years, during which time demons attempted to frighten him by assuming terrible shapes. In 311 he left seclusion to help the Christians in Alexandria who were being persecuted by Emperor Maximinus (308–313), and again in 335 he went to Alexandria at the request of Athanasius to speak against the Arians, whereupon he retired again to live in solitude in the desert. His remains are said to have been taken to Alexandria in 561, then to Constantinople, and then in the tenth century to a Benedictine priory in the village of St.-Didier-de-la-Motte (today called Bourg-St.-Antoine) near Vienne on the Rhône in southern France. There the Order was founded out of veneration for their miraculous healing power, sometimes called St. Antony's fire. In 1095 a young noble from the dauphinate named Guérin, after gazing at the saint's arm, was healed of ergotism, called the "*mal des ardents*," a disease contracted from rotten grain, especially rye, not uncommon in the late Middle Ages. The young man's father founded a hospital for this disease and a community of ten men around it. In 1298 a bull of Pope Boniface VIII (1294–1303) made them an order of regular canons living under the Rule of St. Augustine. Their constitution was modeled after that of military orders (thus they were called the "Soldiers of St. Antony"), and their habits were black with a blue linen cross (in the shape of the Greek letter T [tau]). In the early years of the Order, all the members were noblemen, and they were assisted, in their service to the afflicted, by people called *donati* or *conversi*, some of whom were women.

The Order expanded rapidly and, in addition to ergotism, also treated skin afflictions. At its height it had 369 hospitals across Europe, stretching from Portugal to Hungary and from Italy to England and Scandinavia. The Order underwent an internal reform in 1477, mainly concerning the administrative standing of the many abbacies, whether of greater and lesser preceptorship. In the late 15th century, difficulties arose in some cities over the administration of the hospitals; many secular rulers wanted to consolidate these into a single, large hospital in each city (such is the origin of the *Ospedale maggiore* in many Italian cities), and the process of unification of hospitals and the control of them was in many cases contentious. Documents of 1477 list 192 preceptors in the Order; at least 200 houses in France, 100 in Italy, and 40 in German-speaking lands; and houses and hospitals in many other countries. In this period many secular rulers were patrons of the Order, supporting houses and hospitals within their territory and sending gifts to the central house in Vienne. The kings of France and dukes of Milan, among others, sent treasures and money to the monastery in the dauphinate, often competing with one another in largesse. Some cities that did not have Antonine houses agreed to pay an annual tribute to the Order instead.

Pilgrimages to the central house were common in the late 15th century, and these were undertaken by many people. In 1479 Bona of Savoy, the duchess of Milan (widow of Galeazzo Sforza and regent for Giangaleazzo), sent two ducal singers to Vienne, and one of them asked on her behalf for the sacred wine of the Order to be given to her minor son Giangaleazzo, the duke. Petrus Guérin, notary of the Diocese of Tours and a prominent officer of the Order, recorded that the singers had made the pilgrimage and seen the arm of Antony but that the officials would not release the wine to the duchess because, according to the constitution, it could be given only to men of the

Order. Nevertheless they agreed that the young duke could receive the wine at the next general chapter meeting in Italy (implying that he would be received into the Order then). Surviving sources for the liturgy include an oration and responsorial verses for the blessing of the water and the wine of St. Antony. An elaborate ritual was performed for the induction of noblemen into the confraternity.

In the 16th century the Order declined sharply. In Germany territorial disputes arose among the houses, and in France Calvinists burned some of the houses. In Portugal the Order was extinguished, and its holdings and property were transferred to the Jesuits. In 1616 another major reform of the Order caused a division between the houses and patrons despite the intervention of the papacy. In addition ergotism was no longer an epidemic, and this improvement, together with the growth of Protestantism, caused many more houses to be closed. In 1775 the Antonines were merged into the Order of St. John of Jerusalem (the Order of Malta). The remaining 211 Antonines were made chaplains of the Order of Malta, and with them the Antonine property was also transferred. Although measures were taken to enable the Antonines to retain their identity within their new Order, these proved insufficient, and they were absorbed by it.

In iconography the saint is always depicted as an old man with a beard and staff and usually with animals, especially a pig. The feast of St. Antony is observed on 17 January, and farmers bring oxen, sheep, and goats to the church to be blessed on that day. Many towns raised "the pigs of St. Antony" and sold them to pay for the feast. Although the original parish near Vienne is now closed, that city still holds a commercial fair featuring animal husbandry on the saint's day.

PAUL A. MERKLEY

*See also* Antony, St.; Augustinian Rule; Canons Regular, Origins of; Hospitallers (Knights of Malta since 1530); Origins: Eastern Christian; Social Services: Western Christian

## Further Reading

Advielle, Victor, *Histoire de l'ordre hospitalier de Saint Antoine de Viennois, et de ses commanderies et prieurés*, Paris: Chez l'auteur, 1883

Hertling, Ludwig Freiherr von, *Antonius der Einsiedler*, Innsbruck: Felizian, 1925

Hovorka, N., *Leben und Versuchungen des heiligen Antonius*, Vienna, 1925

Nooderlos, P., "La Translation de S. Antoine en Dauphiné," *Analecta Bollandiana* 60 (1942)

Ruffino, I., "Canonici Regolari di Sant' Agostino di Sant' Antonio," in *Dizionario degli Istituti di Perfezione*, volume 2, Rome: Pauline Editions, 1975

# Antony, St. c. 251–356

Egyptian hermit and a founder of Christian monasticism

Saint Antony's career is known to us mainly through the famous biography written soon after his death by Bishop Athanasius of

Alexandria (c. 296–373). According to the biography, the *Vita Antonii*, his parents were rich Christian landowners. The place of his upbringing is not given but in later sources is identified as Coma, close to present-day Boush on the Nile about 60 miles south of Cairo. The biography tells us that at the age of 18 or 20 he was left alone with a young sister after his parents died. Having listened to the words of the Lord to the rich young man (Matt. 19:21), he soon afterward sold all their possessions and became an ascetic. After having picked up the necessary knowledge from other ascetics and spiritual teachers in the neighborhood, he is said to have locked himself up first in an empty tomb and later in a deserted well. His struggle with all varieties of demons attacking him during his years of isolation is vividly depicted in the biography. The description of his appearance after 20 years of isolation (chap. 14) is famous for its allusion to the *Life of Pythagoras* (c. 550–c. 500 B.C.). Antony is said to have "maintained utter equilibrium, like one guided by reason and steadfast in that which accords with nature." To escape pressure from the people seeking his help, he left the Nile valley after an unspecified time of teaching and healing and settled in the interior desert about 85 miles east of the Nile.

Antony's subsequent career brought him to Alexandria twice, first to support the martyrs in the time of Maximinus (A.D. 311–313) and later to support Athanasius against the Arians. The later visit is confirmed by the index to the festal letters of Athanasius. In his later years Antony alternated between this "inner mountain" and the "outer mountain," the place near the Nile where his disciples stayed. A visit to him by the disciples of Pachomius shortly after the latter's death (A.D. 346) is recorded in the lives of Pachomius. In Antony's biography a very long and a shorter sermon, both centered around how to gain peace and defeat the demons, give witness to his teaching. Stories about his encounters with philosophers and Roman officials give evidence to his reputation as both a wise man and a patron of the afflicted. According to the biography he died at the age of 105 and was buried in a place not revealed to anyone. The date of his death, A.D. 356, is confirmed by Jerome in his work *De viris illustribus*.

In addition to the *Vita Antonii*, Antony is known from a wide variety of sources, more or less independent of the biography. Most important are the seven genuine letters, which give a good insight into his spiritual and theological ideas. From the letters it becomes clear that Antony was not totally unlettered but was familiar with popular philosophy and the theological traditions of Alexandria, especially the legacy of Origen (c. 185–c. 254). On the basis of these, Antony teaches the return of all intellectual beings to their primordial unity through the attainment of spiritual knowledge. Other writings ascribed to Antony, including the Arabic version of the letters attributed to his disciple Ammonas (d. before A.D. 396) and an Arabic rule, cannot be considered genuine. In the sayings of the Desert Fathers, the *Apophthegmata*, Antony appears as the undisputed pioneer of the monastic tradition and the most famous teacher of later generations. The Pachomian sources reveal both his importance for the emergence of monasticism and the tensions between the es-

tablished cenobitic, strictly orthodox movement and the more fluid anachoretic tradition. Antony undoubtedly was a historical figure who in the earliest decades of the fourth century became one of the leaders of the development from village asceticism to desert monasticism.

The fact that all later sources on early monasticism refer to Antony as the father of monasticism confirms his pivotal role not only for Egypt but also for Palestine, Asia Minor, and the West. Many of the first generation of monks in Egypt and Palestine are said to have been his disciples or the followers of his disciples, and many stories are known about monks going to Egypt to visit him or the place where he had lived. Little reason exists to doubt that the monastery of St. Antony, still inhabited, goes back to his first disciples and occupies the place of his inner retreat. His position as the father of monasticism is further strengthened by the general acceptance of the authenticity of the seven letters, which not only connect him firmly with the traditions of philosophical and theological teaching of the spiritual masters of Alexandria but also provide a link between this tradition and the spiritual writings of the great monastic authors of the late fourth and the fifth century. Through his letters Antony helped formulate some of the basic ideas of early monastic theology, and his influence can be felt in the writings of Ammonas, Evagrius Ponticus, and others. However, his main impact comes through the *Vita Antonii*, which has been one of the most widely read texts in the history of monasticism. As the first biography of a monk, it influenced later hagiography and helped shape the image of the desert monk. The Latin translation is known to have influenced both Jerome, who wrote a companion to it (the life of Paul the hermit), and Augustine, who refers to the impact of it as decisive for his conversion. In the Middle Ages many adaptations appeared, especially in connection with the foundation of the Order of St. Antony in France in 1095. Antony is also one of the most favored saints in iconography in both the East and the West. Representations of his temptations by painters such as Matthias Grünewald and Hieronymus Bosch are only the most well known. In modern times his life has inspired novelists such as Flaubert in *The Temptation of St. Antony* (Paris, 1874) and painters such as Salvador Dalí.

SAMUEL RUBENSON

*See also* Animals, Attitude toward: Christian Perspectives; Antonians; Asceticism: Christian Perspectives; Desert Fathers; Egypt; Ethiopia; Evagrius Ponticus; Fasting: Western Christian; Hagiography: Christian Perspectives; Hagiography: Eastern Christian; Hermits: Eastern Christian; Humanism, Christian; Jerome, St.; Origins: Comparative Perspectives; Origins: Eastern Christian; Pachomius, St.; Pilgrimages, Christian: Near East; Regulations: Christian Perspectives; Retreat, Christian; Vocation, Christian

## Biography

Known through the *Vita* written by his friend Athanasius, the hermit Antony looms as one of the very earliest Christian monastics. About 269 he undertook a life of abnegation and c. 285 withdrew to the Egyptian desert. Around 305 he came out of solitude to organize his followers into a community of hermits living under a rule. Around 310 he withdrew once again, settling at what is known as Der Mar Antonios near the Red Sea. He is universally acclaimed as one of the founders of Christian monasticism.

**Major Works**
Seven Letters

The so-called Rule of St. Anthony is not by St. Antony.

**Further Reading**
Athanasius, *The Life of Antony*, translated by R.C. Gregg, New York: Paulist Press, 1980
Bagnall, Roger S., *Egypt in Late Antiquity*, Princeton, New Jersey: Princeton University Press, 1993
Brakke, David, *Athanasius and the Politics of Asceticism* (Oxford Early Christian Studies), New York: Oxford University Press, and Oxford: Clarendon Press, 1995
Dörries, Hermann, *Die Vita Antonii als Geschichtsquelle* (Akademie der Wissenschaften zu Göttingen), Göttingen: Vandenhoeck and Ruprecht, 1949
Gould, Graham, *The Desert Fathers on Monastic Community* (Oxford Early Christian Studies), New York: Oxford University Press, and Oxford: Clarendon Press, 1993
Rubenson, Samuel, *The Letters of St. Antony: Monasticism and the Making of a Saint* (Studies in Antiquity and Christianity), Minneapolis, Minnesota: Fortress Press, 1995

# Anurādhapura, Sri Lanka

Situated in the dry, northwestern region of Sri Lanka, Anurādhapura became one of the most influential monastic centers in Asia during the period from the third century B.C. to the end of the ninth century A.D. Its monastic history began when a mission from India, led by the Venerable Mahinda, allegedly the son of Aśoka (ruler of the Mauryan Empire c. 269–230 B.C.), converted the local ruler, Devānaṃpiya Tissa, contemporary of Aśoka, to Buddhism. Ensuing royal patronage enabled Mahinda to found a monastery in Anurādhapura, the Mahāvihāra, thus "establishing" Buddhism in Sri Lanka. He was joined by the Venerable Sanghamittā, his sister, who founded an order of nuns, bringing with her a sapling from the tree under which the Buddha gained enlightenment.

A complementarity formative for Theravāda Buddhism grew between state and monastery. Monarchy protected the monastic community and endowed it with land to provide for increasing numbers. The monastic community supported the monarch. From the city monasticism spread to other parts of the island, notably Rohaṇa in the south and Kalyāṇi (Kelaniya) in the southwest. For over 200 years the Mahāvihāra dominated with an orthodoxy rooted in the Theravāda Vinaya tradition brought by Mahinda, a tradition based on oral transmission of the Pāli texts. In the first century B.C. a process of division began when

Remains of small temple at the Abhayagiri Monastery, Anurādhapura, Sri Lanka, c. fifth century A.D.
Photo courtesy of Marylin M. Rhie

the Abhayagiri Vihāra was separately endowed. In the third century A.D., a secession from the Abhayagiri led to the formation of a third group, the Jetavana Vihāra. Each undertook massive building works, forming a veritable city of monasticism.

The Abhayagiri became known for its openness to new doctrinal developments, including those that were to develop into Mahāyāna. At times this led to acrimony between the orthodox Mahāvihāra and the Abhayagiri, culminating in the fourth century A.D. when 60 Abhayagiri monks were expelled for heresy. However, all three monastic groups flourished in the city and eventually worked together. The early fifth-century Chinese pilgrim Fa Hsien gave an estimate of 5,000 monastics for the Abhayagiri and 3,000 for the Mahāvihāra.

Notable among scholars of the city was Buddhaghosa, who came to the Mahāvihāra from India in the fifth century A.D. His works – the *Visuddhimagga* (*The Path of Purification*) and commentaries in Pāli on most canonical works – are still the touch-

King's Pleasure Garden, Anurādhapura, Sri Lanka, 14th century.
Photo courtesy of John C. Huntington, the Huntington Archive

stone of orthodoxy for Theravāda Buddhists. Notable among the city's literary skills was the chronicling of history, seen in the *Dīpavaṃsa* (The Chronicle of the Island), compiled before the fifth century A.D., possibly by nuns, and the first part of the *Mahāvaṃsa* (The Great Chronicle).

Strong international links developed with Burma, China, and India. In the fifth century A.D., a delegation of nuns traveled to China to give ordination to women in Nanking, establishing a lineage that still exists.

Çola invasions from South India in the ninth century A.D. eventually necessitated abandoning Anurādhapura in favor of Polonnaruwa. Re-reclamation began only in the 19th century. Today the ancient city is a major place of pilgrimage. The tree grown from Sanghamittā's sapling still lives. International funding has enabled impressive restoration, especially of the massive stūpas linked to the three monastic groups. Monastic communities of monks and nuns (now contemporary nuns rather than fully ordained nuns) have returned, but Anurādhapura is no longer a national monastic or political capital.

ELIZABETH J. HARRIS

*See also* Architecture: Buddhist Monasteries in Southern Asia; Asceticism: Buddhist Perspectives; Manuscript Production: Buddhist; Patrons, Buddhist: India; Sri Lanka: Sites

## Further Reading

de Silva, K.M., *A History of Sri Lanka*, Delhi: Oxford University Press, Berkeley: University of California Press, and London: Hurst, 1981

Dhirasekara, Jotiya, *Buddhist Monastic Discipline: A Study of Its Origin and Development in Relation to the Sutta and Vinaya Pitakas* (Ministry of Higher Education Research Publication Series), Colombo: Ministry of Higher Education, 1982

Gombrich, Richard, *Theravāda Buddhism: A Social History from Ancient Benares to Modern Colombo* (Library of Religious Beliefs and Practices), London and New York: Routledge and Kegan Paul, 1988

Gunawardana, R.A.L.H., *Robe and Plough: Monasticism and Economic Interest in Early Medieval Sri Lanka* (Monographs of the Association for Asian Studies, 35), Tucson: University of Arizona Press, 1979

Panabokke, Gunaratne, *History of the Buddhist Sangha in*

Bas relief of elephants, west side of tank, Royal Pleasure Gardens, near the Isurumuniya rock temple, Anurādhapura, Sri Lanka, third century B.C.
Photo courtesy of John C. Huntington, the Huntington Archive

*India and Sri Lanka*, Colombo: Postgraduate Institute of Pali and Buddhist Studies, University of Kelaniya, 1993
Rahula, Walpola, *History of Buddhism in Ceylon*, Colombo: Gunasena, 1956; 3rd edition, Dehiwala, Sri Lanka: Buddhist Cultural Centre, 1993

# Aquinas, Thomas. *See* Thomas Aquinas, St.

# Arahant. *See* Arhat

# Archaeology: Near East

*Coptic Monasteries*
The foundation of Christian monasticism was based on the ideal of a life withdrawn from the world and wholly turned toward God. This eremitic tradition emerged in the Thebaid, or Tabennesis, in nothern Egypt between the late third and the fourth century. Although the early hermits occasionally convened for common worship, they paid no attention to architectural arrangement. They used to live in caves or in tombs, to construct simple hovels, or to adapt existing structures for their needs. Eremitic tradition is studied archaeologically hardly at all.

The founder of the first monastic settlements (c. 320) seems to have been Amon, referred to by St. Athanasius in his *Vita Antonii* and by Palladius, Socrates, and Sozomen. Under St. Antony (c. 251–356), who spent 20 years in the desert in order to devote his life to God and to achieve spiritual perfection through solitary prayers, contemplation, fasting, and sexual abstinence, common life began to take the place of the purely eremitic life. Monasticism in its cenobitic form became a permanent institution with St. Pachomius (c. 290–346), who organized large communities of monks. There the essential features of cenobitism were established: life together according to a rule under the supervision of a recognized superior. However, the architectural arrangement of the early monastic settlements had been formed only by the end of the fourth or the beginning of the fifth century. Archaeology revealed a complex of buildings that was surrounded by a wall and included a gatehouse, houses for the monks, a church, a refectory, a bakery, a hospital, and a hospice for strangers.

Ruins of west "transept," Church of St. Symeon Stylites, near Aleppo, Syria, late fifth century.
Photo courtesy of Chris Schabel

From the Thebaid monasticism spread to Lower Egypt – to the Wadi Natrun, known also as the Nitrean valley and the Desert of Scete – about 50 miles south of Alexandria. Ammon of Alexandria (d. c. 356) and St. Macarius the Great (c. 300–390) are known to have trained many disciples there. Archaeological remains of the fourth-century *lavra* of St. Macarius have been found on the site of Deir Abu Makar, a ninth-century monastery still standing in the valley. Three other ninth-century monasteries remain – the monastery of the Syrians (Deir es-Suryani), the monastery of St. Pschoi (Deir al-Anba Bishoi), and Deir el-Baramus – which were built on the sites of fourth- to early sixth-century *lavra*s. Important archaeological studies were made of Wadi Natrun in the 1840s by Tattam, Curson, and Tischendorf and in the first quarter of the 20th century by Palmer-Jones and Hugh G. Evelyn White.

In the course of the fifth century, the Pachomian type of monasticism was developed further by St. Basil (c. 330–379). By the mid–fifth century, monasteries already had well-established regional plan types. However, the division of the Egyptians into Orthodox and Monophysites found no reflection in monastic architecture. In the course of excavations, it is impossible to say whether a monastery was Orthodox or Monophysite. The architectural setting of monasteries was influenced by both secular church architecture and military fortifications. It is supposed that their architectural arrangement was inspired by that of the Essene community at Qumran. At the same time the monasteries were as much agricultural structures as houses for prayer, for the monks had to be economically self-sufficient and to live from the proceeds of their work. Most monasteries were situated on the edge of a village and had access to the fields.

In contrast, in North Africa early Augustinian monasteries usually had no architectural setting that would allow us to identify them archaeologically. Thus, St. Augustine (354–430), in his *Vita 5*, mentions many monasteries in Hippo Regius, the ecclesiastical province of Numidia, including a small monastery that he had built for his lay monks in the garden of the community. On his election as bishop of Hippo in 396, he turned the bishop's house into a residence for his clergy, so that they lived a common life. There he described other monasteries in the vicinity of Hippo founded by Leporius and Barnabas, and Augustine's sister presided over a convent for nuns.

Excavations in Hippo Regius in the 1960s under the direction of E. Marec have unearthed a three-aisled, pillared basilica with the bishop's cathedra at the back of the apse and benches for the priests. Beneath the basilica were ruins probably of a pre-Constantinian house church surrounded by a group of buildings, mosaics, and graves. Marec believed that he had discovered the remains of the monastery in the garden described by Augustine, but that view has not won acceptance, and it is impossible to say whether this was a monastery at all.

In the fifth and sixth centuries, Egypt was already densely covered with a net of monastic complexes. Extensive archaeological excavations revealed complexes of the Red (Deir el-Ahmar) and White (Deir el-Abyad) Monasteries, both near Sohag, and the monastery of St. Simeon at Aswan.

A large monastery of Apa Apollo at Bawit, on the west bank of the Nile River, with rich sculptural and painted decoration, was excavated between 1901 and 1913 by the French Archaeological Institute in Cairo; most of the structural finds were removed to the Coptic Museum in Cairo and the Louvre in Paris. The monastery flourished between the sixth and the eighth centuries and was abandoned in the second half of the 12th century. Excavations revealed the remains of two churches, the North and the South, and a number of two-story structures, of which the ground floors were probably memorial chapels and the upper floors served as living quarters.

Some of the best-preserved wall paintings, dated from the sixth to the eighth century, come from the monasteries of Bawit and Saqqara. The scenes depicting Christ enthroned, Christ and the Virgin, Apostles, and portraits of St. Sisinnios and St. George are of particular interest (now at the Coptic Museum in Cairo). Much sculptural decoration remains in situ in the monastery churches.

### Development of Cenobitic Monasteries

The layout of fifth- and sixth-century cenobitic monasteries reflects the process of transition from solitary forms of life to more customary forms of monasteries of common life and is characterized by enclosing walls. However, the construction of high defensive walls developed no earlier than the ninth century. Usually an area first became known for a famous hermit who settled there, and then the concentration of hermits in it followed. The dwelling of the founder (or his tomb) was claimed after his death to be a sanctuary, and a monastery would gradually develop on the site. Thus were established monasteries of St. Antony and St. Paul, both near the Red Sea; the monasteries in the Nitrean mountains; and the monastery of St. Macarius in the Desert of Scete.

From the 1960s to the 1980s, a system of independent complexes was revealed by international expeditions of archaeologists at the fourth-century Kellia (Cellia) about 30 miles north of Wadi Natrun. It comprised separate groups of dwellings of celebrated hermits and their disciples. Hundreds of cenobitic cells were hollowed out of the ground and covered with vaults of mud brick. One of the complexes belonged to a large community; it consisted of courtyards with living quarters built along the perimeters and was surrounded by the wall. Another complex, which was also surrounded by the wall, might have housed no more than one hermit and several of his disciples. The third group of buildings comprised two churches, two towers, a large refectory, and several cells and definitely served as the center of the whole settlement, which was surrounded by numerous primitive dwellings. Most complexes comprise a vestibule; a single-naved oratory; offices; living quarters; rooms for servants, novices, and guests; and a courtyard. The walls were extensively painted, especially around the main area of prayer, i.e. the oratory niche. By the fifth century the whole system was enclosed by a low fence, although separate complexes were still independent. Kellia was most densely occupied in the seventh century; cells for monks often stood no more than 30 feet apart. However, the cells remained independent, although the new wall was erected around the old complexes, and the central complex was broadened out and fortified.

Almost from the very beginning, a necessary feature of these groups of cells was a central church; later a common refectory was added. From the mid–fifth century fortified towers (qasr) began to be built.

### Lavra

The forms of cenobitic monasticism varied greatly in Egypt. One of the forms, known as lavra, dates back to the first centuries of Christianity. The lavra was a synthesis that combined elements of solitary and communal forms of life. A type that survived until the 14th century had an organized, fortified center that was surrounded by numerous isolated unprotected cells is represented by Mustafa Kasif dated to the fifth century and by Der al-Dik dated to the sixth century; the latter site comprises 15 rock-cut cells, two churches, and a fortified tower.

Excavations at Esna in Upper Egypt revealed a very specially organized rock-cut lavra that was founded around the second half of the sixth century. It comprised two cenobitic complexes five miles apart. In one of the complexes, the steps led down to a subterranean square from which emanated a net of passages and cells, each sizable for a small community. The structures were similar to lavras found at the Wadi Natrun: Deir Abu Makar, Deir es-Suryani, and Deir al-Anba Bishoi.

### Syrian Monasteries

Both the eremitic and the cenobitic form soon spread to Syria and then to Palestine and Asia Minor. Among the most significant examples of early monastic architecture of the fifth and sixth centuries are those provided by the well-preserved complexes in Syria, the so-called land of stylite saints, where many monasteries were abandoned after the Arab invasion in the seventh century and thus underwent no modifications. It was there that G. Butler (1872–1922) studied, in only two years, 87 churches and 12 monasteries. His work was continued later by J. Lassus and G. Tchalenko. Innovative methodology, such as aerial photography, permitted important conclusions concerning the liturgical planning of churches, construction technique, types of crops, and so on. In Syria and Antioch a monastery appeared to be an important agricultural structure, and the village population depended on its wealth and prosperity; workmen from the local village served the needs of a monastery. Sometimes complexes dated to the fifth century were already surrounded by walls. At that time Syria was so densely populated that any possibility of eremitic life there is doubtful.

The layout of Syrian monasteries was arranged as an almost quadrangular enclosure. Excavations at Qasr al-Benat (c. 425) revealed remains in which the elements of refectory, dormitory, hostels, and auxiliary buildings can be defined. All these elements were set up to the north of the church and were linked by porticos. At the celebrated pilgrimage monastery of Qal'at Sim'an (c. 480), all buildings for monks and pilgrims were grouped around three sides of a courtyard to the south of the main church and were linked by corridors that connected the complex as the whole system. A usual feature of monastery planning in southern Syria was a rectangular atrium surrounded by a colonnade. Such an atrium has been revealed at the monastery of Umm is-Surab (489), where a two-story quadrangular living quarters was set up just opposite the north side of the church. Another type is represented by the complex of It Der, where the buildings were set up along the axial road to the church so that they comprised a forecourt, which might have been inspired by atriums of some of the emperor's larger basilicas. Similar monasteries are found in North Africa, where separate buildings were erected along the sides of the church and sometimes resembled contemporary Roman military fortifications, with massive rectangular walls and towers.

*Byzantine Monasteries*
At the fifth-century monastery at Dafni, Greece, the whole complex was enclosed by a massive wall, with a church in the center that was surrounded by buildings facing the church and arranged along the perimeter. These features were developed in monastic architecture throughout the Byzantine world under Emperor Justinian (527–565). From this time on the imperial conception, which comprises defensive structures and buildings for ascetic monastic life, began to exercise a decisive influence on the development of monastic architecture. Such an easily defensible monastery complex was built on Mount Sinai (c. 540). The tenth-century Great Lavra on Mount Athos, Greece, was built essentially in the same tradition. Auxiliary buildings and workshops were set up along the walls; lodgings for monks in large communities sometimes achieved four stories in height. The most important buildings, such as a refectory, usually faced the entrance to the church.

By the end of the early Byzantine period, plenty of monasteries had been located within city walls, especially in large cities. Their architecture and funeral complexes have been studied archaeologically most thoroughly in Istanbul. In 1906–1909 the remains were revealed of the fifth-century basilica of the Theodore of Stoudios monastery (Imrakhor Cami) with mosaic floors, graves of fathers superior, and the 13th-century late Byzantine crypt. The excavations were conducted by the Russian Archaeological Institute at Istanbul. Monasteries of Lips (Fenari Isa Camii), Pantokrator, and Chora (Kariye Camii) were excavated by the Dumbarton Oaks Institute in the 1950s and 1960s. The excavations were conducted by T. Macridy. P. Underwood, who studied the Chora monastery 1947–1968, had ascribed the

complex more precisely to the late 11th or the early 12th century, enlarged in the 1320s. He discovered and studied both the mosaics and the frescoes. Materials on the architecture were generalized by R. Ousterhout (Underwood, 1966–1975; Ousterhout, 1987; the excavations were generalized by Oates, 1960). Excavations conducted by A. Megaw in the monastery of Pantokrator revealed a complex that comprised two four-pillared churches dating from the 1120s with a *capella-memoria* between them. There he unearthed a floor paved by elaborate marble mosaic and, in the arcade that linked the South Church with the memorial chapel, remains of the burial of Emperor Manuel I (1143–1180), with the most significant Constantinople relic, "The Anointing Stone" (Megaw, 1964).

Slavic/Byzantine monasteries in the Balkans were studied by Russian archaeologists already in the 19th century. The results of the work allow us to conclude that the tradition of these monasteries was closely related to that of Byzantium, Western Europe, and Russia, although it was quite independent. In the 1920s A. Grabar paid attention to the Bulgarian two-story sepulchral churches and their close connection to the Caucasus (the Bachkovskii monastery, 11th century). (This topic has been pursued down to the present by Bulgarian and Serbian scholars Bobchev, Dikolov, Bakalova, Kirilko, and Penkova.) The results of architectural archaeology on the 12th- to 15th-century Serbian monasteries have been generalized; they reveal that, unlike the Western European one, no stable regional plan type had been developed there, although some basic principles can be traced: the perimeter of the walls formed a semicircle, and the main gate was placed just opposite the main entrance of the cathedral. (In contrast, plan types of both Byzantine and Russian monasteries follow the features of the surrounding landscape.) Numerous auxiliary buildings, refectories and kitchens, scriptoria and libraries, hospitals and hostels, and cells and warehouses were set arbitrarily, although a cross-in-square church was always placed at the very center of the semicircle because, according to S. Popović, of its symbolic meaning. Recently the materials on burial monuments of Serbian rulers were also analyzed by S. Ćurčić, D. Popović, and S. Popović.

*Rock-Cut Monasteries*
A special field of monastic archaeology pertains to rock-cut monasteries. These generally consist of irregular cavities excavated at several levels, linked by irregular vertical shafts and subterranean passages forming "underground cities" and bear some features of church architecture. Cave churches resemble built architecture: carved vaulting, columns or piers, blind arcading, cornices, and other elements imitate masonry work. Sometimes rich painted decoration is found. In the 18th and 19th centuries, the regions in Asia Minor, where the monasteries were widespread, were thought to be inhabited mainly by monks and hermits. Bin Bir Kilisse, a plateau surrounded by mountains, was populated from the fifth century to the turn of the 11th century. There about 60 churches have been revealed: basilicas, cross-in-square, and with domes. At the monasteries there survived refectories, *domus ecclesia*,

long-shaped dormitories, and huge rectangular courts sur-rounded by Justinian-era buildings.

In Cappadocia many rock-cut structures came to light (Tokali Kilisse, Göreme; Acik Saray), sometimes with brightly painted decoration, built between the 4th and the 13th centuries, that were multiplied from the late ninth century. Actually, their dating to the tenth century was proposed by Y.I. Smirnov and later confirmed by N. Thierri and L. Rodley. They were thought to house monks and hermits.

However, these monasteries were not built in isolated or remote places. They were linked with surrounding villages and cities by a network of roads, participating in a comprehensive social system and depending on local patrons. Burials, as well as donor images and invocations in the painted decoration, suggest that the patrons of cave monuments were usually of middle rank. Recently R. Ousterhout has challenged the attribution of all Cappadocian cave churches as monastic.

The monastic origin of such a celebrated complex as the remains of the so-called Alahan monastery at Isavria, between Selevkia and Ikonia, is also doubted at the present. The remains, 2,952 feet above sea level, were uncovered by U. Ramsey and Turkish archaeologists at the end of the 19th and the beginning of the 20th century and were studied by the British Institute at Ankara under the supervision of M. Gough from the 1950s to the 1970s. The complex, three basilicas, a baptistery, and a cemetery, set along a mountain terrace and linked by a colonnade, was dated to the period 457–491 because of two tomb inscriptions, one of which belongs to the architect Tarasius (d. 462).

Rock-cut monasteries are known in other parts of the Byzantine world: in Phrygia, in Midye in Thrace, in Sille near Konya, and near Chersonesos, Crimea, on the northern coast of the Black Sea. The Byzantine derivation of the Crimean rock-cut cities was confirmed only in the 1880s, and a similar debate on their monastic attribution is now under way. Excavations, taking place during the last 25 years, have proved some of them to be not monasteries but fortresses, unprotected settlements, or separate churches.

The Crimea was converted to Orthodox Christianity at the turn of the fifth century. However, monasteries multiplied mainly in the eighth century, probably because of the presence of Christian refugees whose property had been confiscated during the Iconoclastic controversy (726/27–843), when many Christian communities moved to the edges of the Byzantine Empire. Numerous rock-cut churches and chapels of Crimea (Eski-Kermen, Tepe-Kermen) have elements of architectural decoration (columns, cornices, arches), wall paintings, piscines, and cut-in-floor burials that are similar to those of Cappadocia, although the liturgical planning is simpler and the decoration more modest. Monasteries continued to be built until the Islamization of Crimea from the 13th to the 15th century. Some of the monasteries were founded by refugees from Armenia (Surb-Khach at Solkhat). Small islands of Orthodoxy survived until the 17th century under the protection of the Moscow principality (e.g., the Assumption rock-cut monastery near Bakhchisaray and Kachi-Kalionskii monastery).

Archaeological discoveries show that monasteries were built at the remote edges, both eastern and southern, of the Christian world and even beyond its borders. Excavations in Nubia revealed a number of three-aisled monastic churches, with a cathedra set in the middle of the northern one; an altar surrounded by a wooden barrier, with steps to a *bema* in the shape of an apse; and beyond the walls, from the north, a baptistery. In the Old Merv, Turkmenistan, Central Asia, monasteries were built in the form of an oval house (Giaur-Kala), with an isolated inner court surrounded by cells. In Kyrgyzstan, in the mountains of the central Tien-Shan, 12 miles from the Chinese border, was revealed a monastery in the form of a quadrangular stone building with a quadrangular hall, surrounded by living quarters consisting of 25 cells and auxiliary buildings, with cellars and wells (Tash-Rabat, 10th to 13th century). Notwithstanding all this, it was Old Rus' that became a direct successor to the tradition of Byzantine monasticism.

LEONID BELIAEV

*See also* Architecture: Eastern Christian Monasteries; Cappadocia, Turkey; Desert Fathers; Egypt; Istanbul, Turkey; Lavra; Libraries: Eastern Christian; Mount Athos, Greece; Mount Sinai, Egypt; Origins: Eastern Christian; Syria; Theodore of Stoudios, St.

## Further Reading

Badawy, Alexander, *Coptic Art and Archaeology: The Art of the Christian Egyptians from the Late Antique to the Middle Ages*, Cambridge, Massachusetts: MIT Press, 1978

Butler, Alfred Joshua, *The Ancient Coptic Churches of Egypt*, 2 vols., Oxford: Clarendon Press, 1884; reprint, London and New York: Oxford University Press, 1970

Butler, Howard Crosby, *Early Churches in Syria, Fourth to Seventh Centuries* (Princeton Monographs in Art and Archaeology), Princeton, New Jersey: Princeton University Press, 1929

Crawford, Osbert Guy Stanhope, *Castles and Churches in the Middle Nile Region* (Sudan Antiquities Service, Occasional Papers, number 2), Khartoum: Sudan Antiquities Service, 1953

Ćurčić , S., "Medieval Royal Tombs in the Balkans: An Aspect of the 'East or West' Question," *Greek Orthodox Theological Review* 29 (1984)

Evelyn White, Hugh G., *The Monasteries of the Wadi 'n-Natrûn* (Publications of the Metropolitan Museum of Art), 3 vols., edited by Walter Hauser, New York, 1926–1933

Frend, W.H.C., *Archaeology and History in the Study of Early Christianity* (Variorum Collected Studies Series, 282), London: Variorum Reprints, 1988

Gough, Michael, *Alahan: An Early Christian Monastery in Southern Turkey* (Studies and Texts, 73), Toronto: Pontifical Institute of Mediaeval Studies, 1985

Grabar, A., "Christian Architecture, East and West," *Archaeology* 2 (1949)

Hasluck, Frederick William, *Athos and Its Monasteries*, London and New York: Kegan Paul, Trench, Trubner, Dutton, 1924

Hoddinott, R.F., *Bulgaria in Antiquity: An Archaeological Introduction*, New York: St. Martin's Press, and London: Benn, 1975

Kirwan, Laurence Patrick, *The Oxford University Excavations at Fir.ka*, London: Oxford University Press, 1939

Lassus, Jean, *Sanctuaires chrétiens de Syrie: Essai sur la genèse, la forme et l'usage liturgique des édifices du culte chrétien, en Syrie, du IIIe siècle à la conquête musulmane*, Paris: Geuthner, 1944

Megaw, Arthur H.S., Theodor Macridy, Cyril Mango, and Ernest J.W. Hawkins, *The Monastery of Lips (Fenari Isa Camii) at Istanbul* (Dumbarton Oaks Papers, volume 18), Cambridge, Massachusetts: Harvard University Press, 1964

Meinardus, Otto Friedrich August, *Monks and Monasteries of the Egyptian Deserts*, Cairo: American University at Cairo Press, 1961; revised edition, 1992

Mileham, Geoffrey S., *Churches in Lower Nubia*, Philadelphia: University Museum, 1910

Mylonas, Paulos M., *L'Architecture du Mont Athos*, Benetia: Ellenikon Institoyton, 1963

Nicol, Donald MacGillivray, *Meteora: The Rock Monasteries of Thessaly*, London: Chapman and Hall, 1963; revised edition, London: Variorum, 1975

Oates, David, *A Summary Report on the Excavations of the Byzantine Institute in the Kariye Camii: 1957 and 1958* (Dumbarton Oaks Papers, volume 14), Washington, 1960

Ousterhout, Robert, *The Architecture of the Kariye Camii in Istanbul* (Dumbarton Oaks Studies, volume 25), Washington, D.C.: Dumbarton Oaks Research Library and Collection, 1987

Panofsky, Erwin, *Tomb Sculpture*, New York: Abrams, and London: Thames and Hudson, 1964

Popović, Svetlana, "The Trapeza in Cenobitic Monasteries: Architectural and Spiritual Contexts," *Dumbarton Oaks Papers* 52 (1998)

Rodley, Lyn, *Cave Monasteries of Byzantine Cappadocia*, Cambridge and New York: Cambridge University Press, 1985

Runciman, Steven, Sir, *The Eastern Schism: A Study of the Papacy and the Eastern Churches during the XIth and XIIth Centuries*, Oxford: Clarendon Press, 1955; New York: AMS Press, 1983

Shinnie, P.L., *Excavations at Soba* (Sudan Antiquities Service, Occasional Papers, number 3), Khartoum: Sudan Antiquities Service, 1955

Shinnie, P.L., and H.N. Chittick, *Ghazali, a Monastery in the Northern Sudan* (Sudan Antiquities Service, Occasional Papers, number 5), Khartoum: Sudan Antiquities Service, 1961

Tchalenko, Georges, *Villages antiques de la Syrie du Nord: le massif du Bélus à l'époque romaine* (Bibliothèque archéologique et historique, 50), 3 vols., Paris: Geuthner, 1953–1958

Teteriatnikov, N.B., "Burial Places in Cappadocian Churches," *Greek Orthodox Theological Review* 29 (1984)

Thierry, Nicole, and Jean Michel Thierry, *Nouvelles églises rupestres de Cappadoce: Région du Hasan Dagi-New Rock-cut Churches of Cappadocia*, Paris: Klincksieck, 1963

Underwood, Paul Atkins, *The Kariye Djami* (Bollingen Series, 70), 4 vols., New York: Bollingen Foundation, 1966–1975

# Archaeology: Russia

*The Field of Monastic Archaeology in Russia and Its Development*

In 18th- and 19th-century Russia, the field of monastic archaeology was developed very little. Scholars did not perceive existing monasteries and monastic centers as objects of archaeological interest; attention was directed mainly to well-preserved monuments of architecture. However, some exceptions should be noted: in the 18th century the Bel'chitsky monastery at Polotsk in Belorussia was excavated; in the 19th century Earl Sergei Uvarov, celebrated archaeologist, started exploration of the Pokrovsky monastery at Suzdal' aiming to find the tomb of Prince Dmitrii Pozharskii, defender of Moscow. From the end of the 19th century, several famous architects, such as V. Suslov and P. Pokryshkin, were actively involved in architectural restoration and to some extent in archaeological investigation of monasteries.

During the Soviet period, which interrupted development of all fields connected with Christianity, the achievements of monastic archaeology were quite modest. Only after World War II were a number of the most prominent monastic centers studied archaeologically, for example, the Pecherskaya Lavra in Kiev, Troitse-Sergiev monastery (43 miles north of Moscow), and Yuriev monastery in Novgorod. There was the only one period, from 1983 to 1993, when active archaeological work was carried on, during which the old Soviet bureaucracy had loosened its strict control over religious life in Russia and police-run monastic centers had become open to scholars. Vast excavations started in Moscow (Danilov monastery, the monastery of Epiphany, the monastery of Peter-the-Metropolitan, and St. George monastery) and in the Moscow region (Pafnutiev-Borovsky monastery). Vast excavations were undertaken in northern and northwestern Russia that have revealed a number of monuments of architecture and monastic necropolises (Krasnoholmsky-Uspensky monastery in Tver'; Hutynsky monastery in Novgorod; Spaso-Mirozhsky in Pskov and Snetogorsky monastery, near Pskov; and the Kirillov and the Ferapontov monasteries at Beloe Lake).

Now, after all church buildings and monasteries have been returned to the Church, archaeological work is allowed only when it directly serves Church interests, such as the excavation of relics or religious buildings intended for consecration by the Holy Fathers. Some of the recent investigations (e.g., Spaso-Andronikov monastery in Moscow) have been followed by numerous restrictions and resulted in damage and scandals. However, work on the necropolis of the Romanov dynasty (16th and 17th centuries) at the Novospassky monastery in Moscow proved successful. Of the 15 or 20 monasteries existing in Moscow at the beginning of the 15th century, only three have been seriously studied.

Although the field of monastic archaeology in Russia is very young, a great need exists for its further development. A vast number of early monasteries were abandoned and demolished and are known only from written sources. Massive destruction took place during three periods: (1) From the 1230s to the 1240s during the Mongol invasion in northeastern and southern Russia, many monasteries were burned and flattened. (2) In the 18th century in the reigns of Peter the Great (1689–1725) and later of Catherine II (1762–1796), a vast number of monasteries were suppressed and their lands vested in the crown. The reforms of these rulers resemble the Dissolution in 16th-century England. (3) The Soviet era was a dismal period for Russian monasteries. Violent Communist persecutions after the revolution in 1917 entailed the destruction of almost all ecclesiastical centers, including monasteries and parish churches, including impressive works of art and architecture.

*Monastic Architecture and Planning*
From the late tenth century, the liturgical practices of the Eastern Church had been carried beyond the Byzantine Empire into the principalities of Russia. In 988 Kievan Rus' was converted to Orthodox Christianity, adopting Byzantine culture as well. The earliest monasteries appeared in the 11th century on the contemporary territories of Ukraine, Belorussia, and Russia. Written sources from the 11th to 13th centuries mention about 70 monasteries and monastic centers; however, buildings from that period are very rare. Preserved complexes belong mainly to the 17th–19th centuries, and only a few to the 16th.

Neither early monastic planning nor architecture has been much studied. No archaeological evidence has been found that would permit complete reconstruction of a monastery from its beginnings until the present time. Nevertheless it is likely that architectural tradition in Kievan Rus' was influenced by that of Byzantium and later by that of the Princely States of Moscow.

Monastery planning varied widely in form; in an open field it might follow the relief of hills and valleys; in a city it had to be designed to fit the plot of land. From the late 15th century, we observe a tendency to develop an inward-looking quadrangular plan enclosed by a wall; throughout the 16th and 17th centuries and later, the plan became rectangular or square.

The general arrangement of buildings developed around the main "winter" and "summer" churches of the monastery, where three distinct functional zones can be defined: (1) a so-called sacred zone, approximately at the center of the enclosure, comprised of churches, a refectory, and a bell tower; (2) living quarters, consisting of monastic cells, hostels, hospitals, lodgings for the father superior (*igumen*), and so on; and (3) monastic workshops, warehouses, and other ancillary buildings, placed along the walls and in the towers and frequently outside the walls. Outside the walls also stood dwellings of the serfs, owned by the monastery, and a special church for certain ceremonies (e.g., weddings) that were forbidden inside the monastery.

Unlike in the West the early Russian monasteries had no uniform plan, for no attempt was made to group the main buildings around a forecourt or an atrium, and usually no dormitories for monks existed, only cells. All the early Russian monasteries were constructed initially of wood, albeit in time this was replaced by more permanent materials, such as limestone and brick.

Among the great variety of monastic complexes, rock-cut structures hold special importance. The larger monasteries, such as the Pecherskaya Lavra and Pskovo-Pechersky monastery, belong to the 11th century and can be seen as the final episode in the development of Byzantine ecclesiastical rock-cut architecture. However, rock-cut complexes were built in the 17th century (such as the Sviatogorsky monastery on the Oskol River and monasteries on the Don River and at the southern borders of the Moscow state) and even in the 19th century.

The history of Russian monasteries is poorly documented in written sources; the information provided by archaeology is usually more reliable and detailed. Contemporary archaeological excavations in Russia concentrate mainly on three points: layers of early settlements, foundations of monastic churches, and necropolises. The remains of monastic churches help determine the general stratigraphy and dating. During three excavation seasons (1985–1987), the remains of the monastery of the Epiphany (Moscow) were uncovered. Its stone cathedral, which was believed to have been built in the late 1330s, in fact was dated to the late 14th century and had a predecessor, a wooden church built at the end of the 13th century that had been destroyed, possibly by fire.

A popular notion exists that Russian monastreries were established deliberately in remote locations where no one else cared to settle. However, archaeological evidence indicates that from the early 14th century economic dependence forced the monastic communities to locate themselves in densely populated areas. The development of monasteries did not depend solely on internal organization but rather was to a large degree determined by external factors. The 14th-century monasteries were built near the estates and on the lands of princes or nobles who could offer protection and financial support. A considerable number of monasteries were founded inside the Kremlin walls, in the very core of medieval Moscow. The most ancient of them, the monastery of the Savior, was established by Great Prince Ivan the Kalita in 1330. Monasteries built beyond the city walls arose in the vicinity of a boyar's estate, on a main trade route, or at busy crossroads, easily accessible to tradespeople and pilgrims. A clearer picture began to emerge in 1983–1985 during archaeological excavations at the Danilov monastery (Moscow), about four miles south of the Kremlin. The establishment of the monastery in the early 14th century was confirmed archaeologically. Contrary to reports that the first limestone cathedral was erected in the 13th century, dating of the foundation places its construction in the 1550s, but the site of the first 14th-century wooden church was found. Archaeological finds such as rough handmade pottery, iron and bone tools, and spindle whorls indicated the presence of a late tenth-century settlement that was established near the ford across the Moscow River. The ford was used until the end of the 19th century.

Another popular misconception is that the Russian monasteries were built for both defensive and religious purposes. Study of their military significance was encouraged by official state atheism and often served as an excuse to protect a monument. However, archaeology proves that from the 11th to the 15th century the monasteries were not strongly fortified. No indications of ramparts, moats, or other defensive structures were found. Until the mid–16th century, the only protection was a simple wooden fence. The fortress-like appearance of the monastery had grown up during the 16th and 17th centuries, when wooden fences were gradually replaced by brick walls with towers. At this period several monasteries, such as the Solovetsky on the White Sea and the Kirillov at Beloe Lake, were put on a war footing. They were rebuilt as the czar's fortresses to quarter troops, to place cannons, and to store weapons reserves. Occasionally such a monastery was able to stand a many-months siege, as the Troitse-Sergiev monastery (43 miles north of Moscow) did in 1611. However, generally the walls of most monasteries were symbolic rather than defensive and might have been inspired by the idea of a monastery as the symbol of the Heavenly Jerusalem, as described in the Apocalypse.

A unique feature of Russian Orthodox architecture, the main gate (called in Russia "The Holy Gate"), was always constructed as a two-story structure where the upper floor served as a church and cannot be effectively defended. In rare cases when a monastery was to be used for military purposes, an additional fortified gate was erected in front of the Holy Gate, and additional platforms for cannons were constructed on the walls and on the towers.

Two- or three-story refectories built of limestone at least from the 15th century are of a special archaeological interest. Monks tried to save heat during the long, cold Russian winters, and a monastic complex for communal meals offered a perfect solution to this problem. It comprised an underground icehouse, a storehouse, a kitchen and a bakery (with powerful stoves that served also as heaters), and the main refectory hall, usually with a church. A system of inner channels, providing hot air and smoke from the stoves, run through the walls of the building. However, unlike in the West, until the end of the 18th century water supply was organized in the most primitive way, using only wells and springs, with "the Holy Well" as a compulsory element of the ecclesiastical center of a monastery.

The most significant archaeological evidence is provided by necropolises. Although artifacts in the early monastic graves are few, sometimes personal crosses – whether metal, wooden, bone, or leather woven – are found. More than 600 graves from the 17th-century Moiseevsky convent cemetery were revealed during Manezh Square excavations in Moscow in 1993–1995. Many skeletons were wrapped in well-preserved silk vestments embroidered with silver and gold thread. Finds from the site included carved wooden body crosses, ceramics, glass, and metal funerary vessels.

Excavations of monastic necropolises provide important information about the Russian Orthodox burial rite: vessels for Extreme Unction with the remains of the Holy Oil mixed with wine were left in the grave after the ceremony was completed. This tradition likely derived from that of the ablution of the bones in wine that was widespread in the Byzantine monasteries. From the end of the 14th century, small majolica bowls or pottery cups were used for this purpose. Rich 16th-century burials,

such as the tombs of Ivan the Terrible (1533–1584) and his sons, have provided a significant collection of European glass of a type that became widespread in the 17th century. From the mid–18th century, porcelain vessels of both local and European origin are found.

A number of early limestone funeral monuments were uncovered at the monastic cemeteries of the 13th to 17th centuries. Of particular interest are anthropoid sarcophagi – those with ridged gabled lid and tomb slabs with a schematic depiction of a human body. All of them provide evidence of the shared Romanesque tradition in the development of funeral monuments in medieval Europe and Russia.

During archaeological excavations, it is sometimes difficult to distinguish between secular and monastic burials unless inscriptions are found. However, in Russia inscribed monuments appeared only by the late 15th century; the commemorative texts follow brief Byzantine prototypes, mentioning only the date of death and the saint's festival of this day, the name of a monk, and sometimes his family and his baptismal name. The inscriptions never included either religious texts or condolences or blessings or hopes.

LEONID BELIAEV

*See also* Kiev (Kyiv), Ukraine; Moscow, Russia; Orthodox Monasticism: Slavic; Russia: History; Russia: Sites; Ukraine

## Further Reading

Beliaev, Leonid, *Drevnie monastyri Moskvy (kon. XIII–nach. XV vv.) po dannym arkheologii* (Ancient Moscow Monasteries), Moscow: In-t arkheologii, 1994
Beliaev, Leonid, "Arkhitekturnaia arkheologia Moskvy XVII veka" (Archaeology of Moscow Architecture: 17th century), in his *Kul'tura Srednevekovoi Moskvy: XIV–XVII vv.*, Moscow: Nauka, 1995
Beliaev, Leonid, "Drevnosti Danilova monastyria" (Antiquities of St. Daniil Monastery), in his *Kul'tura Srednevekovoi Moskvy: XIV–XVII vv.*, Moscow: Nauka, 1995
Beliaev, Leonid, *Russkoe Srednevekovoe Nadgrobie. Belokamennye plity Moskvy I Severo-Vostochnoi Rusi XIII–XVII vv.* (Medieval Russian Tombs), Moscow: Modus-Graffiti, 1996
Beliaev, Leonid, "Moscow: A Modern City or Archaeological Monument?," *Athena Review* 3 (1997)
Beliaev, Leonid, "Mystery Monasteries," *Archaeology* 4 (1997)
Buseva-Davydova, Irina, "Nekotorye osobennosti prostranstvennoi organizatsii drevnerusskih monastyrei" (Some Features of the Planning of the Ancient Russian Monasteries), *Arkhitekturnoe nasledstvo* (Architectural Heritage) 34 (1986)
Buseva-Davydova, Irina, "Monastyrskie kompleksy" (Monastic Complexes), in *Drevnerusskoe gradostroitel'stvo X–XV vekov* (Old Russian Town Planning X–XV), edited by N.F. Gulianitskii, Moscow: Stroiizdat, 1993
Denisov, L.I., *Pravoslavnye monastyri Rossiiskoi imperii* (The Orthodox Monasteries of the Russian Empire), Moscow: Izdanie A.D. Stupina, 1908
Zverinsky, V.V., *Materialy dlia istoriko-topograficheskogo issledovaniia o pravoslavnyh monastyriah v Rossijskoi*

*imperii* (Materials for Study on History and Topography of the Orthodox Monasteries of the Russian Empire), 3 vols., St. Petersburg: 1890, 1892, 1897

# Archaeology: Western Europe

With the exception of medieval parish churches, probably more monastic sites survive in Great Britain with visible masonry than any other class of medieval buildings. Monastic remains, like those of the Cistercians, are usually found in isolated places, whereas Benedictine remains are often found near or in towns. It is because monastic buildings are a source of potential deposits of material evidence that, in Great Britain at least, they are designated ancient monuments and are generally preserved for posterity.

However, as an empirical study archaeology cannot shirk its major task, which is to reconcile the visible monastic evidence above ground with evidence that is still hidden underground. In attempting to reconstruct a clear picture of monastic life, the archaeologist must use all resources available, including, where extant, monastic cartularies. In addition, in determining changes in the physical remains, it is advantageous for the archaeologist to carry out detailed study of architectural moldings, as recorded in the 19th century, as well as a study of the visible evidence of monastic cathedrals. In so doing the monastic archaeologist should be able to ascertain reasonable dates, at least where changes in the fabric of monastic buildings are obvious.

However, before any serious archaeological investigation is carried out, the landscape, in both towns and countryside, ought to be explored to determine why that site was chosen and how it was adapted to suit the requirements of a monastery. This should be accompanied by a close reading of the Rule of St. Benedict, together with a study of any extant statutes or constitutions belonging either to the order or to the monastery itself. This is even more important where no survey has ever been carried out.

Although monastic archaeology, in the broad sense, has long been connected with medieval studies, serious archaeological investigation began only in the 19th century. The Ecclesiological Society and the Oxford Movement are said to have provided the major impulse behind the early investigations. The main aim of such excavations was not only to ascertain the essentials of the monastic plan but also to unearth it, showing as much of the monastic buildings as possible. To achieve this, selective excavations were first made to expose the ground plan, and missing parts were then added using intelligent guesswork.

By the early 20th century, the methodology of monastic excavation had changed little, apart from examining and drawing important moldings found on the site. Most other finds were ignored, apart from tiles and tombs, which were seen as providing datable artifacts. The monastic cartulary or *Dugdale's Monasticon* was usually consulted to provide what was seen as datable evidence to support their findings. Up to the outbreak of World War II, the methodology used to excavate monastic sites went

unchanged. Moreover many sites in Great Britain had been cleared and guidebooks or leaflets produced, together with the publication of excavation reports.

Although this could be regarded as progress in monastic archaeology, any real advance was hampered by the same superficial methodology. Thus, any alterations beneath these latest floors remained undisturbed, and only those artifacts that were considered significant were recorded and published, and usually this meant that finds from earlier periods were largely ignored. In other words archaeologists still looked for the most obvious ritual changes and alterations to the buildings, especially where such changes involved part of the monastic plan. Cognizance was taken of earlier building campaigns, and notes were made to record where evidence was visible on the surviving walls or had disrupted the latest floors.

After World War II important changes took place in monastic archaeology. To better understand the monastery as a building complex that had developed to meet the needs of the religious community, architectural and documentary evidence was introduced to supplement the physical evidence of the excavated remains. Nevertheless, it must be emphasized that documentary evidence should not be allowed to contaminate the dating of artifacts, which need to be studied on their own. This means that dated or datable artifacts should be considered with extreme caution and not seen as something that gives a precise date to a monastic site. Moreover the evidence of cartularies must be placed within the context of archaeological investigation because recorded matter is not always so reliable.

Today the excavation, investigation, and recording of monastic sites is much more sophisticated, with every piece of evidence, from the earliest to the latest building campaigns, being deemed of equal importance. As a result, monastic archaeology has become more broad based, yet monastic investigation still focuses on the church and cloister. Of course the cloister embodies monastic life, thus its importance to the archaeologist.

Research in the 19th century made the Benedictine and Cluniac cloistral plan well known, but subsequent excavation of the outer precincts now needs to be redefined. Although aerial photography and field surveys have often captured the extent of the outer monastic precinct, these have rarely been followed up by a thorough archeological investigation of the site to reveal the full range of material evidence. Moreover, before beginning any archaeological investigation of the outer precincts, it is best to avoid any fixed ideas on either the layout of the buildings or their use.

Intensive archaeological excavation of the outer precinct of a monastic site can lead to the rediscovery of millponds, fish weirs, moated enclosures, mounds, and vineyard terraces only after a thorough search of the many surviving cartularies and court rolls. Conversely, only by carrying out field surveys of monastic estates and analyzing the physical remains can archaeologists compare their findings with the written record.

Archaeology has demonstrated important differences in the outer precincts of the monastic plan used among Cistercian and Carthusian sites versus those of the Benedictines. Thus, it is more than likely that agricultural and industrial buildings, such as blacksmiths' shops and stonemasons' sheds, will be found in the outer precincts of the Cistercian and Carthusian houses, where lay brothers did most of the manual labor, in contrast to the Benedictines and other orders, which usually took advantage of outside labor. Thus, it was not unusual for a town or village to spring up around the precinct walls of the houses of the Benedictines. Research into early maps can also explain how the village or town developed.

Unlike previous generations modern archeologists now have techniques on hand by which they can accurately investigate monastic sites from ground level simply by doing a magnetometer survey, which will enable them to find hearths and kilns of industrial complexes. Researchers can detect pits and ditches by using proton magnetometer and gradiometer or other resistivity surveys. Phosphate sampling can also be used to identify cattle byres and stables. The excavation of most monastic sites would perhaps provide evidence of other important features, such as buildings for storage and for the poorer traveler, especially where the monastery did not have suitable accommodation at the gatehouse. In addition, where such buildings have disappeared, a geophysical survey could perhaps plot the drainage patterns across the site, and this would allow the reimposition of these lost buildings on the ground plan. Finally, pollen analysis taken from buried soils could show what the land looked liked prior to the monks' arrival and before any boundary bank was thrown up and the fish ponds dug out.

Another potentially important source of evidence would be the excavation of monastic cemeteries. Only when monastic archaeologists seek the assistance of anatomists and paleopathologists – in order to examine the skeletons while still in the earth – will information be maximized.

Parallel with recent progress in monastic archaeology have come advances in theory that have led to the refinement of various approaches. These approaches promote sophisticated analysis of problems traditionally associated with monastic archaeology. Functionalism is a commonsense approach to explain how a monastery adapted to the many changes it faced during its lifetime. Processualism and the systems approach examine the long-term process of change within a monastery but are concerned more with the general than the particular. Thus, a single monastery can be studied as a religious institution or prayer house whose different components consist of the monastic church, chapter house, cloister, books, and liturgical equipment.

Another approach is structuralism, which considers how humans categorize things. This could be adapted to monastic archaeology by considering the monastery in terms of sacred and profane, good and evil. Thus, it could be inferred that the inner court represents the religious (good) aspect of the site, whereas the outer court represents secular (evil) aspect of the site. Contextualism marks a return to the traditional emphasis of medieval architecture, or the cultural history of a particular place (e.g., the Abbey of Cluny) in the 12th and 13th centuries, by examining the building schemes of the relevant abbots, the master masons (if known), and the relevant patrons. Within the contextual approach architectural history and art history also play an important part in any interpretation of the site. Finally, spatial analysis, which examines the use of space and its importance to the monastic environment, could be used.

In conjunction with modern methods of archaeological investigation, the monastic archaeologist now has on hand the computer with software that can create virtual three-dimensional reality such that almost any monastic site can be reenvisioned much more accurately than in artists' impressions.

One of the most important outcomes of a campaign of monastic archaeology is that a monastic ruin, like any artifact, becomes a direct link with the past and as such provides tactile evidence of the medieval world. In other words a monastic ruin (as distinct from a site museum) is a museum in which the historic past becomes a three-dimensional experience for visitors. This aim is furthered by correct interpretation of the site and can be achieved only by using the highest quality research and expertise so as to present the information in a way that will make it accessible to different groups. Explanatory text and graphics should also be provided in locations where they are most helpful and especially where visitors can interpret the site firsthand. Large-scale models can present a tactile impression of the monastery in the 16th century while illustrating and identifying its development and any post-Reformation changes.

Thus, an urgent task for monastic archaeology is to ensure that all open-ground sites have been properly recorded, using aerial photography, a ground survey, or a combination of both. Moreover architectural analysis, together with expertise in geophysical survey, should also be used to record both the visible and the invisible features of the monastic site. Furthermore, all unrecorded monastic sites remain at risk, especially those in towns. When an unrecorded monastic site is discovered during urban redevelopment, it is at once in danger. If national government is unable to sponsor or initiate emergency excavation work to save or record the site, then sponsorship, as has happened in the past, would have to be sought from local government or other sources. Much has been lost in the recent past, but all developers, whether government or private, must be informed of the importance of any monastic remains discovered on a building site. One way of ensuring this is for monastic archaeologists to publish the results of their work. Many excavations have been undertaken at monastic sites throughout Great Britain, but very little work was published prior to 1985.

Thus, the concerns of monastic archaeology today are not only with buildings – the church, claustral area, and outer precinct – but also with every aspect of monastic life. In other words the discipline is concerned with internal changes that took place during the years the community existed and how the community adapted to those changes.

PHILIP E. McWILLIAMS

*See also* Architecture: Western Christian Monasteries; Cluniacs; Dissolution of Monasteries: England, Ireland, and Wales; England: History; Spain: Sites

**Further Reading**

Aston, Mike, *Monasteries*, London: Batsford, 1993

Butler, Lionel, and Chris Given-Wilson, *Medieval Monasteries of Great Britain*, London: Joseph, 1979

Emery, Mike, editor, *The Archaeology of an Ecclesiastical Landscape: Chapel House Farm, Poulton (Cheshire) 1995* (Excavation and Survey Report/Chester Archaeology, number 9), Chester, Cheshire: Chester City Council, Department of Development and Leisure Services, 1996

Fletcher, R., *Space and Community Behaviour: Spatial Order in Settlements*, London: Academic Press, 1977

Gilchrist, Roberta, and Harold C. Mytum, *Advances in Monastic Archaeology* (BAR British Series, 227), Oxford: Tempus Reparatum, 1993

Gilchrist, Roberta, editor, *The Archaeology of Rural Monasteries* (BAR British Series, 203), Oxford: BAR, 1989

Greene, J. Patrick, *Medieval Monasteries* (Archaeology of Medieval Britain), Leicester, Leicestershire: Leicester University Press, and New York: St. Martin's Press, 1992

Morris, Richard, *Cathedrals and Abbeys of England and Wales: The Building Church, 600–1540*, London: Dent, and New York: Norton, 1979

Morris, Richard, *The Church in British Archaeology* (Council for British Archaeology Research Report, 47), London: Council for British Archaeology, 1983

Sackett, J.R., "The Making of Style in Archaeology, a General Model," *American Antiquity* 42 (1977)

# Architecture: Armenian Monasteries

From the first period, which runs from the early days of Christianity in Armenia in the early fourth century to the first years of Arab occupation in the seventh, little has survived to inform us as to the character of specifically monastic building. The great majority of surviving buildings are churches that are either certainly nonmonastic or else have no provable monastic connection. Those monastic churches that we have from this period are mainly small, single-naved churches with a rounded apse to the east, as, for example, the first church (fifth century?) at Tsitsernavank in Azerbaijan. Masonry and ground plans, as also the history of Armenian monasticism, suggest Syrian inspiration.

The early period shows a handful of examples of churches with centralized plans in which the dome rises at the crossing of two and sometimes four axes. Apses directed east, west, north, and south act as supports that stabilize the drum and dome while greatly expanding the floor area available to the congregation and expanding even more the space and spaciousness of the total interior. Further support and further expansion of the interior space are afforded by the corners between the apses, where a cylindrical niche, surrounded by thick masonry, rises from floor level to the base of the drum. One example is Artsuaber, to the northeast of Lake Van (seventh century). Besides the monastic churches many more examples of churches built in this form that were not part of a monastery can be found.

These churches, although having much in common with centralized plans in fifth- and sixth-century Syria, belong to a stage in the development of Armenian architecture, in the sixth and seventh centuries, at which the architecture can be said to have moved away from its Syrian origins. The churches are decidedly not from the same stable as sixth-century Byzantine architecture, yet some sixth-century Byzantine churches share certain features with the Armenian churches built to a centralized form. The shared features include the plan on two axes and exedrae placed symmetrically with regard to the axes. However, the presence of these features in the Byzantine churches seems to be owed to a Syrian origin rather than to any exchange between Armenia on the one hand and Anatolia and the Balkans on the other. Armenian architecture of the period (sixth and seventh centuries) does overlap closely with Georgian, and some plans are almost identically reproduced. This would appear to point to frequent interchange between Georgia and Armenia rather than to parallel but independent movements in each.

The second period of Armenian building runs from the late 9th to the 11th century, during which most of Armenia freed itself from the power of the Sunni caliphs. This period resumes in the 12th century, after the Turkish invasions, and runs to the early 14th century. In the latter leg of the period, building took place mainly in northeastern Armenia, where a series of princely dynasties lived in relative freedom from the nearby Turkish kingdoms and principalities, mostly as vassals of the Georgian kingdom or later of the larger Mongol or the smaller Il-Khanid Empire: the latter two were tolerant of Christianity until the end of the 13th century.

In monasteries the most common church design is one that is sometimes called the Armenian cross. In reality the latter is not a cross but rather a way of supporting a dome on a tall drum set above a single-naved church the body of which is itself tall and soaring on the interior. The church as a whole is rectangular; the apse to the east is narrowed so as to allow for a chamber on either side, and these chambers are entered either from the apse or from the west. The eastern supports to the dome are the corners at the entrance to the apse; the western ones are short walls built inward from the church's north and south walls. The four supports are connected by arches on which is supported a pendentive system. To the west the space might be limited by chambers built between the short interior walls and the west wall of the church as a whole. From the 13th century the nave walls and the drum become taller. As in other structural types, the dome is covered by a steep conical cap that greatly adds to the tall, tapering quality of the church's architectural character.

Other designs are found, especially from the 9th to the 11th century. For example, some four-apsed centralized churches exist at Hayravank on a promontory in Lake Sevan (11th century) and a many-lobed design at Khtskonk near Ani, again in northern Armenia. Domed triconches exist at Narek and Iluvank, both south of Lake Van. These resemble a four-apsed design, but the western apse is replaced by a vaulted rectangular arm that, together with the space beneath the dome, forms the nave. Hall-churches exist as well, generally with one but sometimes with three apses, in the regions south and east of Lake Van. These are found in both legs of the period, from the 9th to the 11th and from the 12th to the 14th century. These church designs can again be paralleled in Georgian architecture. Some differences exist; in the "Armenian cross" type, for example, the western support of the dome is generally a pair of piers.

Another characteristic of the period is the zhamatun, a large chamber normally built against a church's west wall. It served as a chamber for assemblies or else as a forechurch where some services were held. The earliest example is at Horomos near Ani (1038), but otherwise zhamatuns seem to have been built only in the second leg of the period, from the 12th to the 14th century. The most common structural type is that of a rectangular hall whose vaulting is supported on four piers. The central compartment of the nine is covered by a dome. The remainder of the nine are covered by vaults of various kinds, including domical vaults. The vaults and especially the dome receive a wealth of carved decoration. Otherwise the vaulting is contrived by means of two pairs of ribs supported on thick pilaster-piers, a pair of which is set in each wall. The intersecting pairs of ribs provide a skeleton that stabilizes the domical vault.

Another characteristic of the period is the survival of monastic complexes, especially in northeastern Armenia. Often there are several churches, more than one of which might have a zhamatun, and the complex that survives might include a refectory and a kitchen. The complex is protected by a wall, above which rises a group of churches, generally arresting to the eye by virtue of their height.

Building continued in the 15th and 16th centuries, but Armenia lost some of the wealth it had derived from international trade, and conditions were chaotic and violent, especially in the 16th century, when Armenia was the theater for repeated wars between the Ottoman Empire and the Safavid Empire in Iran. The real revival, which can be thought of as the third period, came in the mid–17th century. Building took place mainly in the districts of Nakhchevan and Julfa and in parts of Azerbaijan farther to the northeast, that is, generally in parts of Armenia benefiting from trade with Russia and the Ottoman Empire and more accessible to the Safavid capital at Isfahan, which itself was also a locus of Armenian monastic construction.

The churches are either basilicas or else based on the basilican plan. The latter category includes domed basilicas, in which the dome is supported generally on the ends of the apse wall to the east and on the first pair of piers in the nave to the west. Some cross-in-square designs are known; these are churches with a rectangular nave in which four pillars hold up a dome and provide support also for four vaults, each traveling outward from the dome to the external wall. Vaults cover the corner spaces.

TOM SINCLAIR

See also Architecture: Eastern Christian Monasteries; Armenia; Orthodox Monasticism: Byzantine; Syria

## Further Reading

Cuneo, Paolo, *Architettura Armena dal quarto al diciannovesimo secolo*, 2 vols., Rome: De Luca, 1988

Mango, Cyril A., *Byzantine Architecture*, New York: H.N. Abrams, 1974; London: Academy Editions, 1979

Mepisashvili, Rusudan, *The Arts of Ancient Georgia*, London: Thames and Hudson, 1972; New York: Thames and Hudson, 1979

Politechnico di Milan, Facoltà di architettura, *Documenti di Architettura Armena. Documents of Armenian Architechture [per] facoltà di Architettura del Politecnico di Milano [ed] Accademia delle Scienze di Yerevan*, Milan: Ares, 1968; 2nd edition, 5 vols., 1970–1972

Thierry, Jean Michel, *Armenian Art*, New York: H.N. Abrams, 1989

# Architecture: Buddhist Monasteries in Southern Asia

Buddhism, one of the world's true monastic religions, began using retreats and parks as "monasteries" from as early as the time of the Buddha Śākyamuni. During his lifetime Śākyamuni founded the Buddhist community that consisted of four orders of the faithful. They were the *bhikṣus*, or male mendicant professionals; *bhikṣunīs*, or female mendicant professionals; *upāsaka*s, or male lay followers of the Buddha; and *upāsikā*s, or female laity. The *bhikṣus* and *bhikṣunīs* were essentially wandering mendicants who sought shelter in forests and caves and begged for food. The *upāsaka*s and *upāsikā*s, on the other hand, were householders, members of the nobility, and those who lived a secular life. They did not necessarily seek nirvanic release but derived soteriological enhancement by obtaining merit through making altruistic offerings and supporting the mendicant community.

During the monsoons in parts of southern Asia, heavy rains and floods made it impossible for the *bhikṣu*s and *bhikṣunīs* to wander and beg. During these periods, places of shelter for the wandering mendicants became necessary. Thus, from the very time of the Buddha Śākyamuni, tracts of land, parks, and buildings were donated by the laity to accommodate the monastic community. These retreats were called *ārāma* or *saṅghārāma*, and, in literature on the Buddha's life, the Jetavanārāma at Śrāvasti is the most significant.

One of the Buddha's lay followers, Anāthapiṇḍada, invited the Buddha to visit the city of Śrāvasti. The advanced party of monks, seeking a suitable place for the Buddha to sojourn, agreed on a *vana*, or park, owned by Prince Jeta. However, when approached by Anāthapiṇḍada, who wished to donate the land to the monastic community, Prince Jeta was unwilling to part with the land. In the hope of dissuading Anāthapiṇḍada, the prince asked for an exorbitant price – that he be given as many gold coins as it would take to cover the entire land area. Eager to provide the *saṅgha* with the best *ārāma*, Anāthapiṇḍada, much to Jeta's surprise, agreed to the latter's offer. Unfortunately, with only a small section remaining to be covered, Anāthapiṇḍada ran out of gold and was unable to meet the required price. Regardless, greatly impressed with Anāthapiṇḍada's spirit of

Fig. 1: Anāthapiṇḍada's gift of the Jetavanārāma. Rondel on the *vedika* from Bhārhut, c. 80 B.C.E., Indian Museum Calcutta.
Photo courtesy of John C. Huntington

generosity, Prince Jeta donated the remaining land, thereby creating the Jetavanārāma.

The date of the Jetavanārāma story is undoubtedly later than the actual gift of the land. No gold coins from the fifth or sixth century B.C. have been discovered. However, by the time of the Bhārhut Stūpa (about 80 B.C.) the story was important enough in Buddhist literature to warrant its depiction in sculpture (Fig. 1). According to archaeological excavations there is little doubt that

Fig. 2: The "preceptor's hut" at Gum Bahal, c. third or second century, near Śankhu, Nepal.
Photo courtesy of John C. Huntington

the Jetavanārāma existed, and, presumably, many events related to the early layers of the Buddhist sūtras occurred at the site. The Jetavanārāma site has been excavated by the Archaeological Survey of India to the late Gupta levels (c. fifth century). Unfortunately, at this time no effort has been made to reach the earlier levels.

### Early Buddhist Monasteries

Major gifts of the Jetavanārāma type aside, the early Buddhist mendicants ordinarily took shelter in existing natural caves. Such natural caves are known at the sites of Gṛdakuṭa (Vulture Peak) at Rājgir in Bihar state, Pitalkhorā in Maharastra, Guṇṭupalle in Andhra Pradesh, Gum Bahal at Śankhu in Nepal, and Anurādhapura and Mihintale in Sri Lanka.

Subsequently caves sculpted out of rock cliffs and boulders were excavated in the environs of the natural cave sites. From at least as early as the first century B.C., the excavated monastic sites, as well as those that were to follow in the succeeding centuries, came to consist primarily of two types of buildings. The first type of building was the *vihāra*, or "station." The second was a building known in English as a *caitya* hall, or a hall housing a *caitya*, or sacred place. *Vihāras* provided the residential quarters for the monks and consisted of small sleeping chambers with a ledge for a bed in each and frequently a small niche for the inhabitant's belongings. In later *vihāra*s a series of such sleeping chambers were arranged around a square courtyard. In contrast the *caitya* hall differed from a *vihāra* in both function and structure. The *caitya* hall was the worship area and was used for Buddhist teachings. Whereas the *vihāra* was square or rectangular in plan, the *caitya* hall was generally apsidal with a stūpa at one end serving as the devotional focus.

### Brief Survey of the Development of Rock-Cut Monasteries in Early India

#### The *Vihāra*

Early examples of "excavated" monastic shelters in the form of rock-cut huts exist at Gum Bahal near Śankhu, Nepal (Fig. 2), and in badly damaged remains at Pitalkhorā in Maharastra, India. The name "Gum Bahal" is a Newari derivation of the eastern Indian term *Gumphā Vihāra*, literally "Vihāra of Caves." Vocative changes with syllables omitted is characteristic of Tibeto-Burman languages such as Newari. Thus, with almost no sound value for the final consonant, *gumphā* becomes *gum*, and *vihāra* (sometimes pronounced *bihāra*) becomes *bahal*. In the manner of typical early *vihāra*s, the caves at these sites are small boxlike structures carved directly out of the rock. The *vihāra* at Gum Bahal best exemplifies the earliest type of excavated rock shelters. The structure is two-chambered, with a small sleeping room behind an entrance area. The entire matrix of the rock mass is removed except for the walls and the ceiling. The presumably high cost of such excavations suggests that the shelters were probably used by high-ranking teachers. Oral history at Gum Bahal maintains that Buddha Śākyamuni himself visited the site and that he resided in the cave retreats for one rainy sea-

Fig. 3: Three views of the vihāra at Bhājā, c. 100 B.C.E., Maharastra, India.
Photo courtesy of John C. Huntington

son. Whether or not this visitation actually occurred, hagiographic and architectural histories support an early date for Gum Bahal, placing it in the narrow historical niche between natural caves and the more elaborate excavated complexes.

The excavated *vihāra* at Guṇṭupalle, Kondivte, as well as others at Pitalkhorā are more complex than the early boxlike structures and exemplify the developmental nature of monasteries in southern Asia. Although carved in stone the caves are close copies of contemporaneous wooden architecture. It is assumed that a fully developed wooden architectural tradition preceded and coexisted with the rock excavations of southern Asia. Unfortunately, because of the ephemeral nature of wood, no examples of wooden buildings survive. It is also believed that initially, wood craftsmen, rather than stone masons, worked on the design of several rock-cut caves. For example, at Pitalkhorā the exceedingly thin walls of the early *vihāra*, made of a particular type of volcanic rock, have collapsed because of the lack of tensile strength. These walls could have been designed only by craftsmen unfamiliar with the properties of rock. Moreover in several early caves in western India (e.g., Pitalkhorā and Bhājā), the methods of wooden joinery are carved into the rock matrix. The "joints" merely emulate wooden architecture and serve no functional purpose. The best preserved of these *vihāra*s is at Bhājā in Maharastra, India (Fig. 3). The structure is entered through a veranda that leads into a square room around which the sleeping chambers are clustered. The plain exterior of the cave belies the rich sculptural decoration, emulating wooden prototypes, on the interior.

As rock-cut monasteries developed in southern Asia, the design of the excavations moved away from wooden prototypes and began to use the rock matrix in a more organic and integrated manner. Further, many types of structures were added to the architectural vocabulary of a monastery.

Vihāra 3, also known as "Gautamīputra Cave," in Nāsik, Maharastra, exemplifies the next stage in the development of the

Nāsik Cave 3 (top left)
Bāgh Cave 2 (top right)
Ajaṇṭā Cave 2 (lower left)
Ajaṇṭā Cave 17 (lower right)

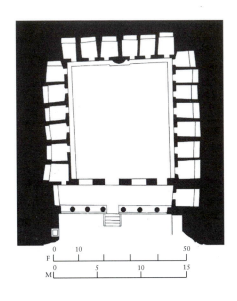

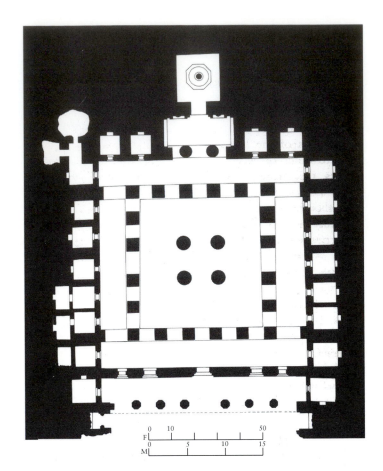

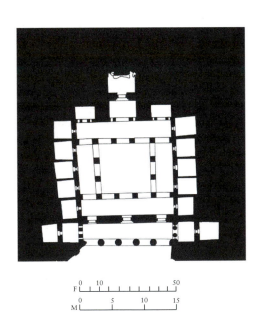

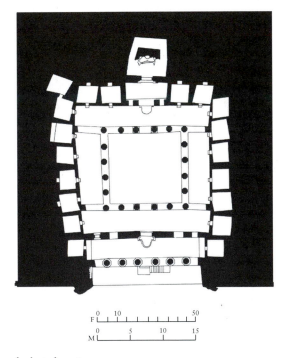

Fig. 4: Comparative plans of selected western caves.
Drawing courtesy of John C. Huntington, based on original drawings in *Art of Ancient India*, 1985

rock-cut residence hall (Fig. 4). The plan is more organized than in earlier caves such as at Bhājā, with cells radiating in a seemingly symmetrical manner from a central courtyard. The richly decorated veranda foretells the direction in which rock-cut architecture develops, coming to fruition in the succeeding years at the cave sites of Ajaṇṭā and Ellora.

Variants on the simple square-plan *vihāra* occurred from around the mid–fifth century and are evident at sites such as Bāgh and Ajaṇṭā. Although the sleeping cells were still arranged around a square courtyard, in Cave 2 at Bāgh, Madhya Pradesh, a shrine housing a *stūpa* was added to the back wall of the *vihāra* (Fig. 4). At Caves 1 and 2 at Ajaṇṭā, an image shrine was added to the back wall (Fig. 4).

With time, the modest rock-cut *vihāra*s were richly embellished with sculptural and painted panels and were meant to emulate the palaces of the gods and paradises of the Buddhas (see Susan L. Huntington with contributions by John C. Huntington, *Art of Ancient India*, 1985). For example, according to an inscription in Cave 16 at Ajaṇṭā, the *vihāra* is said to resemble the palace of the god Indra (Vasudeva Vishnu Mirashi, editor, *Inscriptions of the Vākāṭakas, Corpus Inscriptionum Indicarum*, volume 5, 1963, p. 111, verse 27). Thus, when a devotee entered

the cave he or she was essentially entering the paradisiacal environment of Indra's heaven, Trāyastriṁśa.

Specialized types of *vihāra*s also evolved and are evident at later Buddhist *vihāra*s at Ajaṇṭā and Ellora. In Cave 5 at Ellora the roughly square plan of most early *vihāra*s gave way to a longitudinal, rectangular form with long central benches and several subsidiary image shrines (Fig. 5). An ambulatory passage was added around one of the inner shrines, allowing the devotee to circumambulate the Buddha image within by walking around the entire shrine. In other caves, such as Cave 17 at Ajaṇṭā, a passageway was added within the interior of the shrine, allowing just the image to be circumambulated (Fig. 4).

The mature phase of the development of rock-cut architecture in India was marked by variants such as the caves discussed previously as well as by *vihāra*s developing into enormous multi-story temple complexes. Cave 12 at Ellora in Maharastra is an expansive structure consisting of three floors (Fig. 6), each different in plan (Huntington, 1985). The first and second floors were occupied by the monk's chambers, small cells, and image shrines. The third floor is a large pillared hall, richly adorned with sculpture. This might have served as an assembly hall or an area where advanced initiations took place.

Fig. 5: Ellora Cave 5, near Maharastra, India.
Photo courtesy of John C. Huntington

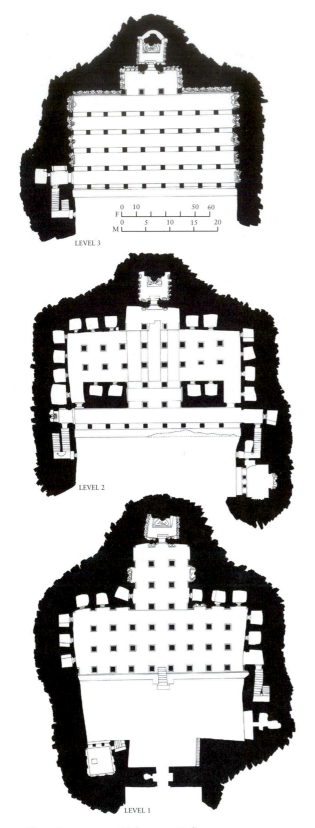

**Fig. 6: Ellora Cave 12, near Maharastra, India.**
Drawing courtesy of John C. Huntington, based on original drawings in
*Art of Ancient India*, 1985

*The* Caitya *Hall*
There is no demonstrable proof of just when the *caitya* hall became a standard feature of a Buddhist monastic site. However, there are rock-cut *caitya* halls at Guṇṭupalle, Kondivte, and a spectacularly large one at Pitalkhorā, all dating from the second or first century B.C. Both Guṇṭupalle (Fig. 7) and Pitalkhorā (Fig. 8) are obvious copies of wooden prototypes. Indeed, given the elaborate architectural conception of these excavated *caitya* halls, there is no doubt that similar wooden structures were far more common.

At both Guṇṭupalle and Kondivte (Fig. 9), the stūpa is enshrined in a circular cell with barely enough space for circumambulation. These caves were obviously designed for individual worship rather than congregational assemblies. By contrast the *caitya* hall at Pitalkhorā is a large apsidal structure in the manner that remains characteristic for several centuries to follow. Here the mendicants would have gathered to listen to the teachings of the Buddha as interpreted by the local preceptor or master of the Dharma. In inscriptions, *caitya* halls are called *gandhakuṭi*, or "fragrance hall" (Huntington, 1985), referring to the breath of the Buddha as he taught. This clearly indicates that *caitya* halls were not merely structures to house the object of worship but were active teaching venues as well.

A detailed analysis of the development of *vihāra*s and *caitya* in southern Asian architecture is well beyond the scope of this article. It should suffice to say that after several hundred years, for reasons unclear, rock-cut monasteries ceased to be excavated and that freestanding structural buildings made of wood, brick, and other material became the preferred mode of architecture. Whereas the development of monastic rock-cut architecture in southern Asia can be traced in a roughly linear manner, studying the development of freestanding monasteries is a more challenging task.

*Brief Survey of Remains at Freestanding Monasteries*
Most important monastic sites invariably grew and flourished along major trade routes that ensured continued lay support. For example, the renowned monastic complex at Sāñcī in Madhya Pradesh was located near ancient Vidiśā, an important trading center from as early as the time of Śākyamuni Buddha himself. Situated along the trade route between the western coastal regions and the central Gangetic plain of India, Vidiśā remained a primary mercantile and religious center for centuries to follow (Huntington, 1985).

Whereas trade routes and economy were some of the external factors that yielded monastic complexes, the sites were focused within around a place or object of devotion, such as a stūpa, a temple, or an image. Such focal points are the defining statements of the Buddhological essence and thus vivify and serve as generators of a monastic setting. For example, significant monasteries developed around the sites of the eight transformative events of the Buddha's life – *paribhogaka* relics – each marked by a stūpa. The first four events – the birth at Lumbinī, the enlightenment at Bodh Gayā, the first sermon at Sārnāth near Vārāṇasī, and the *parinirvāṇa* at Kuśinagara – are men-

Fig. 7: Guṇṭupalle *caitya* hall, Andhra Pradesh, India, second or first century B.C.E.
Photo courtesy of John C. Huntington

tioned in the *Mahāparinirvāṇa sūtra*. They are considered places appropriate for pilgrimage by lay followers. The secondary four sites – the Buddha's descent from Trāyastriṁśa heaven at Sāṁkāśya, the great miracle at Śrāvasti, the taming of the rogue elephant Nālāgiri at Rājagṛha, and the monkey's gift at Vaiśālī – had come into prominence by the second and first centuries B.C. The latter do not become part of a single text until a later date. However, they existed in narrative sculptural representations on the architectural railings of Bhārhut and the gateways of Stūpa I at Sāñcī from as early as the first century B.C. Located at or near significant political centers and serving as powerful places of pilgrimage, the stūpa drew in laity who, in turn, sustained the Buddhist *saṅgha*.

Although certain aspects (e.g., political, economic, and religious) of freestanding monastic settlements might appear obvious, specific information regarding the organization, design, and function is less evident. For example, the types of monuments that existed at a site or the precise nature of the activities conducted by the monks and laity are questions that are more difficult to answer. Whereas in rock-cut monastic sites it is clear that a *vihāra* and *caitya* hall served as the basic unit, in structural buildings no established formula is obvious. Largely built of ephemeral materials such as wood and brick, buildings within monastic complexes have left few remains. What remain are skeletons of architectural structures that provide limited information about building types. Moreover increased religious support and the burgeoning of complex religious practices called for different types of architectural structures to be constructed within each complex. These buildings appear to have included temples for specific deities and rituals, commissaries, storehouses, and so on in addition to the regular residence cells and teaching halls of earlier periods. The following discussion features disparate examples of remains at important freestanding monastic complexes that provide a glimpse into the rich variety

Fig. 8: Pitalkhorā *caitya* hall, Maharastra, India, second or first century B.C.E.
Photo courtesy of John C. Huntington

of architectural visions that arose during the last half of the first millennium.

The monastic complex at Nāgārjunakoṇḍa in the Kṛṣṇa River region of Andhra Pradesh, India, comprises three structures as opposed to just the regular two: a *vihāra* and a *caitya*

Kondivte        Sketch Plan Not To Scale        Guṇṭupalle

Fig. 9: Comparison of the ground-plans of Kondivte *caitya* hall, Maharastra, and the Guṇṭupalle *caitya*, Andhra Pradesh, both second or first century B.C.E.
Drawing courtesy of John C. Huntington

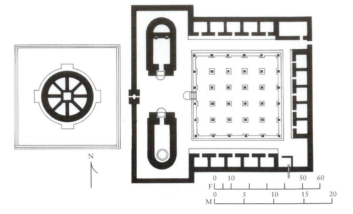

Fig. 10: Plan of a typical monastic complex at Nāgārjunakoṇḍa, Kṛṣṇa River region, Andhra Pradesh, India.
Drawing courtesy of John C. Huntington, based on original drawings in *Art of Ancient India*, 1985

hall. Here a stūpa-*vihāra* alignment from east to west is the central focus flanked by an apsidal image hall and an apsidal *caitya* hall (Fig. 10). The three-part configuration was used repeatedly at the Nāgārjunakoṇḍa site. Interestingly the bilateral symmetry of the two halls is also found in eastern Asia. For example, in the Horyu-ji in Nara, Japan, the *kondō*, or "golden hall," and the *to*, or pagoda, are located on either side of the central axis that leads to the *kō-dō*, or lecture hall. The significance of the three-part configuration implies that a distinction was made between the stūpa as reliquary of the Buddha and the image of a Buddha. Without inscriptions, specifically which Buddha is represented is impossible to identify. It is possible that Śākyamuni, Maitreya, or possibly even a Buddha of either the past or the future is depicted. The underlying meaning of the three buildings might represent the Mahāyāna concept of compassion and wisdom combining to form enlightenment. The stūpa in the first hall represents the compassion of the Buddha, exemplified through his life and activities as a teacher. The image of a Buddha in the second hall exemplifies the wisdom of the Dharma. Together they constitute the enlightenment of future Buddhas – expressed through the monastic community residing in the central *vihāra*.

One of the most interesting sites with a number of unique structural remains is Parihāsapura in Kashmir, India. Located along the way to Gandhāra, the Indic terminus of the Grand Silk Route, Parihāsapura's monuments are reputed to have served as models for Buddhist architecture all over Asia. At the site the remains of a basement of a large square structure with additional cells indicates that the building was probably a *vihāra*, a place for resident monks associated with the flourishing Buddhist center. However, the foci of the complex were two unique structures: (1) an 80-foot copper image housed within an enormous *caitya* and (2) an enormous stūpa. *Bṛhad*, or "gigantic," images of the Buddha became increasingly prevalent in Mahāyāna Buddhism from the second century on and conveyed the concept of the universality of Buddhist teaching. Buddhist Dharma was personified as enormous Buddhas. They were es-

Fig. 11: Painting of Lalitāditya's Caitya. West niche of the Sum-tsek at Alchi, Ladākh, India, c. 1075–1100.
Photo courtesy of John C. Huntington, the Huntington Archive

Fig. 12: Painting of Caṅkuṇa's stūpa. West niche of the Sum-tsek at Alchi, Ladākh, India, c. 1075–1100.
Photo courtesy of John C. Huntington, the Huntington Archive

sentially the visual manifestation of the Dharmakāya, or "body of the Dharma."

According to literary accounts, the *caitya* was built in the second quarter of the eighth century by Lalitāditya, the powerful emperor of Kashmir and a devout Buddhist practitioner (Mark Aurel Stein, translator, *Kalhaṇa's Rājataraṅgiṇī, A Chronicle of the Kings of Kaśmir*, 2 vols., 1900, 1:142). Only the plinth and a massive block of stone that would have supported the metal image survive today. However, a painted representation of the *caitya* at the Sum-tsek at Alchi monastery in Kashmir provides information regarding the monument's original appearance (Fig. 11).

The stūpa, the second major monument at the site, was also built in the eighth century by Emperor Lalitāditya's Tokhārian minister, Caṅkuṇa. Unfortunately all that survives of the structure is a complex cruciform base. However, a painted representation at the monastery at Alchi (Fig. 12) indicates that the stūpa

had a high base and a relatively small hemispheric dome. Above the dome rose a tall spire of 13 disks, reflecting the Tantric tradition. Caṅkuṇa's stūpa served as the archetype for structures in the neighboring regions of Ladākh, Nepal, and Tibet.

Another unique type of structure that has been tentatively identified as a maṇḍala hall occurs at Nālandā, the most influential monastic complex of eastern India. The presence of the "maṇḍala hall" at a major site such as Nālandā suggests that other monastic complexes in the region might have had similar monuments, thereby making such buildings a common feature of monasteries. In a literary account the Tibetan monk Dharmasvāmin, who visited Nālandā in 1235, mentions the presence of a Cakrasaṃvara temple that had survived the Islamic onslaught of 1199–1203 (George Roerich, *Biography of Dharmasvāmin: A Tibetan Monk Pilgrim*, 1959). Although no Cakrasaṃvara temple structure has ever been archaeologically

Fig. 13: Mahābodhi temple, Bodh Gayā, Bihar, India. Various dates of construction and restoration from c. 250 B.C.E. through 1984.
Photo courtesy of John C. Huntington

identified, it is possible that Dharmasvāmin referred to what is now known as Temple 2 at the site. All that remains of Temple 2 is a plinth with sculptural representations of a series of Hindu deities. These indeed might be a reference to the so-called exterior *vajra*s located in the outer rings of some Buddhist maṇḍala, including most forms of the Cakrasaṁvara Maṇḍala. Thus, it is possible that the temple was intended to be a three-dimensional maṇḍala, thereby justifying its designation as a "maṇḍala hall."

The Mahābodhi, or "Great enlightenment," temple, whose present structure dates to around the fifth century, is the focus of a thriving monastic settlement at Bodh Gayā in Bihar, India (Fig. 13). It is unique for two reasons. First, it commemorates the *vajrāsana*, or seat beneath the *pīpal* tree under which Śākyamuni sat in meditation. Second, it is a deliberate three-dimensional architectural "sculpture" of Mount Meru, the Buddhist world system as a sanctified mountain. The Mahābodhi temple indicates that pyramidal temples were probably a characteristic feature of monastic sites, along with residence cells, prayer halls, teaching venues, and so on. It is possible that the Mahābodhi temple type inspired several other similar monuments, including the "stūpas" at Rawak in Khotan, Vikramśīla and Nālandā in Bihar, and Pāhārpur in Bangladesh. These monuments are said to have had significant pyramidal towers, presumably also communicating the Mount Meru notion.

A detailed analysis of the various types of buildings at each monastic site is well outside the parameters of this article. In general it is sufficient to note that specialized structures at monastic complexes are dependent on local teachers, the supporting laity, and specific traditions practiced in the region. Overall a monastic complex can be divided into two types of structures. First, buildings such as residence halls, teaching or assembly halls, and accompanying devotional structures form the basis necessary for the routine functioning of the monastery. Second, the specialized forms of architecture, such as temples for specific rituals, maṇḍala halls, and so on, are offerings themselves, donated by the patrons to accrue *punya*, or merit. Together the two types serve to define the sacred environment within which the ultimate religious goal can be sought.

*The Monastic Universities of Early India*
By the eighth century and especially during the rule of the Pala dynasty (8th through 12th century) in eastern India, large monastic establishments known as *mahāvihāra*, or "great monasteries," served as universities. The monasteries housed thousands of monks who were trained by preeminent teachers of Buddhist philosophy and practice. Along with religious theory the curriculum also included grammar, linguistics, composition, debate, rhetoric, astrology, mathematics, Āyurvedic medicine, and the arts of music and painting. Such institutions provided students with superior educational facilities and produced some of the highest intellectual thinkers and creative minds of the time.

As recorded in both Chinese and Tibetan literature, Uddaṇḍapura, Vikramśīla, and Nālandā in Bihar were the important universities of eastern India. Today most of the buildings at these educational institutions are destroyed. However, what remains at the sites suggests that the premises of each university consisted of grand temples, large dormitories, refectories, libraries, and a variety of other structures.

According to Tibetan sources Uddaṇḍapura was a fully established institution by at least the beginning of the ninth century. The university was most noted for its extensive resources and large library. Indeed when the library at Uddaṇḍapura was burned in the Islamic invasion of 1200, it is estimated that perhaps tens of thousands of manuscripts were lost.

Vikramśīla was one of the major centers of esoteric Buddhism that flourished in eastern India. The proselytizer Atīśa, an important figure in the second propagation of Buddhism in Tibet, studied at Uddaṇḍapura and then acquired a high position at Vikramśīla. When specially invited by the king of Gu ge in Tibet, he is said to have transported 60 loads of manuscripts and goods carried on horseback. Through these means Atīśa transmitted much of the religious and intellectual knowledge of the university to Tibet (Susan L. Huntington and John C. Huntington, *Leaves from the Bodhi Tree*, 1990).

By all estimates Nālandā was the most influential institution. It was founded no later than the fourth century A.D., presumably at the birthplace of Buddha Śākyamuni's favorite disciple, Śāriputra. Its prominence grew during the Pāla period, and it was noted for high standards of education, selective admission, and challenging examinations (Huntington, 1990). Scholars from Tibet, China, and other neighboring countries traveled to India, especially to visit or study at Nālandā. The Indian Monk Śubhākarasiṃha, who transmitted and introduced the esoteric traditions to China, studied at Nālandā and was just one among the many progressive thinkers at the university.

*Conclusion*
It is clear that monastic settlements formed the core of Buddhist religious activities from the earliest of times. The Buddhist monasteries of India ran the gamut, ranging from modest communal areas to large, impressive imperial establishments. Monasteries were created and sustained for the protection of the political state. They also served as important institutions of higher learning that generated intellectual thinking. Thus, whether carved of stone or built of ephemera, a monastery was intended to exist "as long as the sun dispels darkness by its rays" (Mirashi, 1963, p. 129, verse 29). In essence the Buddhist monastery was an expression of faith and the profound belief in the benefaction of Buddhist teachings.

JOHN C. HUNTINGTON AND CHAYA CHANDRASEKHAR

*See also* Ajaṇṭā, India; Anurādhapura, Sri Lanka; Bodh Gayā, India; Buddha (Śākyamuni); Cave Temples and Monasteries in India and China; Disciples, Early Buddhist; Mount Meru; Nālandā, India; Stūpa

## Further Reading
Note: Unfortunately, no definitive publication of Gum Bahal has been published in Western languages.

*Archaeological Survey of India, Annual Reports*, various editors and locations, 1902–1929

Brown, Percy, *Indian Architecture (Buddhist and Hindu Periods)*, 3rd edition, revised and enlarged, Bombay: D.B. Taraporevala Sons, 1956

Cunningham, Alexander, *Mahabodhi, or the Great Buddhist Temple under the Bodhi Tree at Buddha-Gaya*, London: W.H. Allen, 1992

Dehejia, Vidya, *Early Buddhist Rock Temples: A Chronological Study*, London: Thames and Hudson, 1972

Huntington, Susan L., with contributions by John C. Huntington, *Art of Ancient India: Buddhist, Hindu and Jain*, New York and Tokyo: Weatherhill, 1985

Spink, Walter M., *Ajanta to Ellora*, Bombay: Marg Publications for the Center for South and Southeast Asian Studies, University of Michigan, n.d. [1967]

# Architecture: Eastern Christian Monasteries

A monastery is an architectural compound designated for the religious life of monks or nuns. Monasticism started as a lay movement in the third century. Originally anchorites were those who escaped from religious persecutions. During the Constantinian era Christianity was carried on by an official church and a mixture of diverse religious groups and sects. Dissatisfied with the unstable conditions of life during this period, numerous individuals, including rich and poor, men and women, and fools and criminals, began to retire to the desert for a solitary life of prayer and to search for personal salvation. As the number of such settlements continued to grow, they formed communities of monks and nuns that flourished from the middle of the fourth century throughout the Christian East and the Balkans. Anchorites gathered often around "loca sancta," such as an important pagan cult center, a famous hermit's column, or a martyr's burial site. Oratories and churches built near such sites became centers where hermits gathered for the liturgy. Although different in their local traditions, these communities developed two basic types of monastic life – cenobitic and eremitic (from the Greek for "desert") – that affected the architectural planning and function of their settlements. Pachomius (c. 290–346) in Egypt and Basil (c. 330–379) in Asia Minor wrote the first rules on communal monastic life and were leaders of the cenobitic movement. The latter spread in the Christian East, especially Egypt, Palestine, the Judaean desert, and Asia Minor.

In cenobia monks lived within a walled compound, attended daily church services, ate communal meals, worked together, and slept in dormitories. Pachomius' monasteries were large and housed several hundred monks. His cenobia had several churches, a refectory, dormitories, a meeting hall, a kitchen, a bakery, storage rooms, and stables. On a symbolic level the monastery was perceived by the monks as a heavenly city, or "Heavenly Jerusalem."

The eremitic style of life required living in isolation; hermits prayed alone or with one or two disciples. The earliest hermitages and cells have been excavated in Kellia in Lower Egypt. These are walled rectangular compounds consisting generally of a courtyard, a vestibule, a prayer room, and cells for a senior monk and a disciple.

The two styles of monastic life gave birth to the *lavra*, which incorporated both cenobitic and hermitic monasticism and spread from the fourth through the sixth century in Egypt, Palestine, and the Judaean desert. *Lavras* were usually located in rocky mountains, valleys, or ravines. The core of the *lavra* was a monastery similar to a cenobitic one. It was connected by pathways with a network of cells and small hermitages located in close proximity. Hermitages were different in size, technique, and number of buildings; they included cells (*kellia*), a chapel, a kitchen, a bakery, and storage rooms. Monks lived in cells or hermitages and gathered together in the monastery for the liturgy and communal meals on Sundays and feast days. The *lavras*' monasteries did not have refectories. Monks had their meals in the courtyard or in the church. The Great Lavra (present-day monastery of Mar Saba near Jerusalem), founded by St. Sabas (483) in the Kidron Valley, is one of the most elaborate examples. The monastery housed about 150 monks who

**Monastery Church, Secul, Romania, 1602.**
**Photo courtesy of Mary Schaefer**

South facade, Church of St. Symeon Stylites, near Aleppo, Syria, late fifth century.
Photo courtesy of Chris Schabel

lived in cells and small hermitages that were dispersed along the cliffs on both sides of the valley. The chief monastery provided food, secure protection, and spiritual guidance for the monks.

In the fifth and sixth centuries, monasteries played an important role in the spiritual, social, economic, and cultural life of Byzantine society. Emperor Justinian I (527–565) issued legislation that prohibited the confiscation of monastic property. Monasteries such as Qal'at Sim'an in Syria (473 and 491), Qartmin in Tur 'Abdin, the province of Mesopotamia, and St. Catherine's Monastery in Sinai (547) flourished under the support and protection of the emperors and government officials. Qal'at Sim'an was built on the site of St. Symeon's column. Its main *katholikon* has a cross plan with an octagonal center that contains St. Symeon's column and four basilicas adjacent to its east, west, north, and south sides. The topographic orientation of the monastery to the pilgrimage road and the nearest village, Deir Sem'an, was an essential feature. Pilgrimage centers in the Byzantine provinces were supervised by local church officials. The large pilgrimage complex of St. Menas in Egypt was carried on for several decades and completed 491–518. The building campaigns were conducted by the patriarchs and local bishops. A large three-aisle basilica with transepts was designed to ac-

commodate large numbers of pilgrims. Built on top of catacombs, St. Menas' shrine was transformed into a crypt that was adjacent to the west end of the church.

The network of pilgrimage centers in Egypt, Palestine, Syria, and Asia Minor promoted traveling and trade, stimulated the economy, and contributed to the spiritual well-being of citizens in these areas.

Depending on local traditions, regulations, and technique of execution, monasteries differed in size, shape, and number of monks. In general fifth- and sixth-century monasteries showed basic components that fulfilled the requirements for monastic life. The spatial organization of these components (consisting of ecclesiastical buildings, dwellings, and buildings for economic activities) was shaped by axial directions that coordinated with the functions of buildings. Similar to Roman military camps, monasteries had a rectangular or square plan and were surrounded by strong, fortified walls. The latter had a double function: it provided a "holy enclosure" that separated monks from the pleasures of the outside world but also served as a defense wall during wars or siege. The walls of large monasteries were built from local stone blocks, as at Deir el Abiad and the Sohag monasteries in Egypt. At St. Catherine's Monastery in Sinai, the walls were built from granite blocks and fortified with projecting towers and machicolations above the entrance gate. They were also decorated with relief crosses to ensure protection.

The monastery gate was oriented toward the road. It also provided a direct access to the monastery's main church, the *katholikon*, and chapels. Other buildings comprised a refectory, a kitchen, single- or two-story monastic cells, storage rooms, workshops, and stables. These buildings were lined up along the monastery walls. Large monasteries also had hostels and hospitals. Because water was scarce in these desert areas, monasteries and even small hermitages were provided with cisterns and irrigation systems. Cemeteries or cemetery chapels were located outside the monastery walls, as in St. Catherine's at Mount Sinai, or the Monastery of St. Gabriel at Qartmin in the Tur 'Abdin area. Monks were also buried in rock-cut *arcosolia* outside the monastery walls. Alahan monastery in Cilicia in Asia Minor is an example. Gardens, often with their own enclosure, were also set outside the monastery walls.

Single-nave or three-aisle basilicas were the most common plans for the *katholika* of large monasteries in Egypt, Palestine, Syria, and Asia Minor. Major churches were built of local stone; mud brick or regular baked brick was used for the construction of smaller chapels. Three-aisle basilicas can be seen in the pilgrimage centers, such as St. Catherine's at Mount Sinai, St. Menas in Egypt, and Qal'at Sim'an in Syria. Their longitudinal shape favored the processional character of the early liturgy and allowed space for monks and pilgrims. A spacious three-aisle basilica in St. Catherine's Monastery (built by Emperor Justinian in A.D. 547) had an entrance on the west facade. The *naos* was usually preceded by a narthex where monks gathered before and after the church rituals. There monks waited for the sound of the *semantron*, a wooden device, used to call for the community meal. Egyptian basilicas had a semicircular apse in their interior and a rectangular projection on the exterior. Some examples have a straight eastern wall on the interior. The central apse was provided with one or multiple bench-*synthronon* (a single bench or a series of benches arranged in a semicircle in the apse) with a cathedra, a bishop's seat, at the center. In front of the apse is a bema with the altar table at the center. A templon screen or a low parapet screen originally separated the sanctuaries from the *naos*. Some *katholika* included large numbers of chapels that could be attached to the east, north, and south walls, as in the case of St. Catherine's basilica.

Syrian monastic churches showed different liturgical planning. The main entrance to the church was from the south. A bema with clergy seats was at the center of the *naos* and not in front of the main apse, as in other churches of the Christian East. Churches in the Euphrates region, the Tur 'Abdin area, utilized a transverse nave plan for their *katholikon* and even chapels. The central sanctuary had two, three, or four lateral chapels dedicated to different saints and lined up at the eastern end of the church.

Refectories (*trapeza*) in Palestine and Syria were situated to the southwest or northwest of the *katholikon* entrance. In Egypt they faced the entrance of the *katholikon*. After worship and prayers, monks would proceed directly to the refectory for meals and continuous prayers. Monastic dining halls were longitudinal buildings with an apse. Pachomian communities had two-story refectories to accommodate a large number of brothers. Series of semicircular tables, stone or marble, were displayed on both sides of the hall with stone benches on the sides.

The presence of baptisteries in early monasteries attests to their missionary role in converting local populations to Christianity. Baptisteries were of different types and had different locations within the monastery space. In some cases small rectangular rooms were adjacent to the east or west end of the church. In a large pilgrimage church such as St. Menas, the octagonal domed baptistery was attached to the west end of the church and behind the saint's crypt as at Qal'at Sim'an. Octagonal freestanding baptisteries are also found in Syria, Asia Minor, and the Balkans. The sunken baptismal font was either circular or cross-shaped with two staircases on either side.

Massive stone towers were either freestanding or incorporated within the monastery walls. Two or three stories high, they contained chapels, library, living rooms, cells, storage rooms, water supplies, and latrines. The upper level of these towers was reserved for a chapel, and the lower story was used for living quarters. The most valuable books were hidden in places between the upper floor and the roof. Towers were self-contained and were used by the monks during emergencies. They were also used as places of seclusion for prominent monks.

The ecclesiastical rules necessitated the separation of the sexes in monastic male and female institutions (nunneries). The rule of *abaton* ("inaccessible") restricted male access to the monasteries by women, and vice versa. Novel 133 of Justinian (c. 539) prohibited entrance to monasteries by the opposite sex. Although double monasteries existed in Byzantium, there were attempts to discourage these institutions by the Novel of Justinian 123 (c. 536) and by later church regulations.

Monasteries played key roles in church politics, religious movements, and the spiritual life of Byzantine society. During the eighth and ninth centuries, the period of Iconoclasm, monastic life was suppressed, and monasteries often lost their buildings and assets. Monks, however, played leading roles in defending Orthodoxy. Theodore of the Stoudios' monastery in Constantinople took an active part in the polemics against the Iconoclasts. The victory over Iconoclasm was crucial for a new development of monasticism. After Iconoclasm a gradual revival of monasticism took place. A number of monastic settlements were established on Mount Athos, in Asia Minor, and in the Balkans. Initially these were small hermitages and *lavras* that emerged during the ninth and tenth centuries on Mount Athos, Mount Olympos, Mount Latros, and Cappadocia. The well-preserved, early tenth-century rock-cut hermitage of St. Symeon in Zelve, Cappadocia, is a typical example. It has a small chapel on the ground level with Symeon's tomb in the narthex. A narrow shaft in the rock behind the chapel provided access to the monk's cell. Symeon was able to climb up to his cell using cavities on the side walls of the shaft. His cell included two rock-cut beds, a table, and an oven. The unique phenomenon that emerged during this period is the creation of communities of monasteries within a single region, such as on Mount Athos or in the Göreme valley in Cappadocia.

The first anchorites settled on the Mount Athos peninsula in the eighth century. Starting from the ninth century, Byzantine emperors provided protection and benefactions for Athonite monks. The emperor established a *protos*, a governor of Mount Athos, in the capital, Karyes. In 941–942 Romanos I Lekapenos granted an annual subsidy of one gold piece for each Athonite monk as well as for monks in Mount Olympos (Bithynia), Mount Kyminas, and Mount Latros. Saint Athanasius came to Mount Athos in 957 and later founded the Great Lavra with the help of his friend, Emperor Nikephoros Phokas (963–969). His *lavra* was a large monastic foundation that became a model for other monasteries on the Holy Mountain. Different from the Palestinian type, it was a true cenobium. Monks lived together in the monastery under strong supervision of the *hegumenas* (abbot) and obeyed the rules of the *typikon* (the rules for monastic life). However, St. Athanasius allowed a small number of hermits to live outside the monastery walls in their own cells. The *typikon* of St. Athanasius was similar to that of the Stoudios monastery in Constantinople, which was a leading center of monasticism in the capital. The latter had an impact on the development of rural and urban monasticism in the middle Byzantine period.

Economic growth and government legislation during the 11th and 12th centuries stimulated the growth of monasteries. Wealthy individuals were encouraged to establish their own monasteries as a place for their burial and commemorations. Because of tax immunity monasteries gained more property and became wealthy landowners. Strong church leadership led to the regulation of monastic life and formulation of monastic rules (*typika*). The latter regulated monastic life and influenced the architectural and liturgical planning of churches and chapels. Monasteries were classified as imperial, patriarchal (*stauropegion*), episcopal, private, or independent. *Metochia* were a new type of small, subordinate monastery that emerged during this period. These were established close to monastery lands in order to manage the properties. Large monastic foundations also established small *metochia* in cities as residences for monks' visits, housing a small number of monks. The average monastery during this period could accommodate between 20 and 40 monks. The largest ones, such as the Evergetis and Pantocrator monasteries in Constantinople, had about 80 monks.

Monasteries flourished in both the cities and the countryside, attracting large numbers of pilgrims and promoting the economy. Rural monasteries were close to the roads and nearest towns and kept close ties with the cities. The Mount Athos monasteries communicated with the outside world by boats.

Because of their isolation from the outside world, holy mountains like Mount Athos were favorite sites for monastic settlements in the middle and late Byzantine periods. The design of a monastery involved collaboration between the patron, the abbot, and the architect. The architectural layout of Athonite monasteries shows an irregular trapezoid or polygonal plan, probably depending on the shape of a site. Monasteries continued to have strong defensive walls. The entrance to the monastery was marked by a niche for an icon or occasionally a gate chapel. Monasteries had freestanding towers, such as the one in the Hilandar monastery. The upper floors had a chapel, cells were on the middle floors, and storage rooms were on the ground level. Initially these towers were occupied by the leading ascetic of the monastery but were also used as watchtowers and as a place of refuge for monks during wars.

The axial orientation between the monastery gate and the *katholikon* continued to be important. The *katholikon* occupied a central position in the monastery courtyard, an innovative feature in Athonite monasteries. During feast days the space around the *katholikon* was needed for liturgical processions that circled around the church. In the 11th century the Lavra *katholikon* was reconstructed and received a new triconch plan that set a model for others, such as the Vatopedi, Iviron, and Hilandar monasteries. This plan was also utilized in the church architecture in the Balkans. The north and south apses of the *naos* provided new space and location for the monastic choirs. Two lateral chapels were also added on both sides of the narthex; the north one housed the tomb of the founder. The interior of the monastic *katholika* and chapels were lavishly decorated with holy images executed in mosaics and frescoes. Painted and mosaic icons decorated templon screens and were also used as *prosknetaria* icons.

A *phiale*, a fountain for ablutions, was placed in the courtyard and in front of the *katholikon*. It was used for the blessing of the water during the feast of the Epiphany. A cruciform refectory stood to the west of the *katholikon* entrance. After the church service monks went directly to the refectory for prayers and meals. This location of the refectory was typical for Athonite monasteries. Because of the large size of certain ecclesiastical complexes, other monasteries, such as Nea Moni on Chios and Hosios Loukas in Stiris, had refectories on the south side of the *katholikon*.

Imperial monasteries in Constantinople had a prominent location and were important stations during the processions at the time of church feasts, festivals, and special occasions. The Pantocrator monastery, the largest monastery of this period in Constantinople, is located on a hilltop facing the Golden Horn. It was built by Emperor John II Comnenos (1118–1143) as a burial place for the Comnenian dynasty. A *typikon* describes the layout of the monastery churches and buildings and sheds light on monastery life. It has three churches: the Virgin Eleousa (north), Christos Pantocrator (south), and the church of Archangel Michael (middle). The latter housed the tombs of the imperial founders. The exonarthex became a notable feature of large monastic complexes. The development of the narthexes has been interpreted as a reflection of liturgical functions, such as the rituals of the *diaklysmos* (when monks gathered together to await the summons to the *trapeza*), processions that commemorated the founders, and burials. In the Pantocrator monastery two churches, the Archangel Michael and the Pantocrator, were united by the exonarthex on their west side. The church of the Virgin Eleousa was open to the public, whereas the Pantocrator church was reserved exclusively for monks. Every Friday the icon of the Virgin was brought in a procession consisting of clergy and laypeople to the church of Eleousa and the imperial tombs for veneration.

A large number of monasteries during this period in both the cities and the country were established by holy men, after whose deaths these monasteries became pilgrimage centers. Hosios Loukas in Stiris, Greece, was enlarged in the early 11th century. A larger *katholikon* was added to the tenth-century church of the Virgin. The relics of St. Loukas the Younger, a local hermit (d. 953), were incorporated into a tomb that was built in the north transept of the new *katholikon*. Because this transept is connected both with the exonarthex of the church of the Theotokos (an earlier church on the site) and with the *naos* of the *katholikon*, the tomb was easily approached by two streams of pilgrims without clashing with each other.

Side by side with larger monasteries, small hermitages continued to exist. Another rock-cut and partially built hermitage of St. Neophytos (the Enkleistra) in Cyprus was founded by St. Neophytos in the 12th century. A relic of the cross was installed in the wall of his chapel. The presence of the relic attracted pilgrimage to the site during the saint's life, and this continued into the post-Byzantine period. The church has fine fresco decoration that depicts St. Neophytos above the altar carried by two angels to heaven. The architectural decoration and the relic of the cross were incorporated into the program of the church *naos* to illustrate the private and public goals of the Neophytos hermitage.

Monasteries during this period show a variety of plans for the *katholika* and refectories. A new, complex type of *katholikon* appears during the 11th century: a domed Greek cross octagon. It originated in Constantinople and developed in other areas, especially in Greece in the monasteries of Hosios Loukas in Stiris or Daphni near Athens. During this period some monasteries were literary centers; they had libraries and scriptoria (such as the one mentioned in the *typikon* of the Evergetis monastery) where monks compiled and illuminated books.

After the recovery of Constantinople from the Latins in 1261, Byzantium's poor economic condition led to the disturbance of civil life. Emperors Michael VIII (1259–1282) and Andronikos II (1282–1328) and church leaders, such as St. Athanasius, the patriarch of Constantinople, encouraged the rebuilding of old monasteries and shrines. Some shrines were restored and became spiritual and healing centers for the sick. The famous ancient monastery of Zoodochos Pege in Constantinople was restored during the reign of Emperor Andronikos II Palaeologos. The monastery had *hagiasma*, a miraculous fountain, and a mud bath. A baldachin above the fountain bore a mosaic icon of the Virgin Zoodochos Pege (a life-giving source).

The Hesychast movement in the 14th century led monks to place greater emphasis on the search for individual salvation. Hesychasm, a mystical system, inspired direct communication with God through practice and exercise. This movement promoted the increasing number of monks during the Palaeologan period and especially on Mount Athos. A group of monasteries, called *Meteora*, were established on rock spires in northwest Thessaly near Stagoi, where some monks from Mount Athos went. Monks were able to reach the outside world in a basket for provisions suspended from the monastery down to the ground.

Monasteries of this period became smaller in size. Their architecture is distinguished by an increasing number of chapels that were used as burial places for abbots and patrons of the monastery. Monastery *katholika* and chapels became a place for aristocratic burials. Excavations have revealed graves in the aisles of the St. Theodore *katholikon* of the Brontochyon monastery (1290–1296) in Mystra. *Katholika* in Brontochyon and the neighboring Hodegetria-Aphendiko monasteries had numerous chapels aligned with the side walls of the *naos* and a two-story chapel at the ends of their narthexes. *Parekklesia* were built to accommodate the tombs of the founders, such as the one in the monastery of Chora in Constantinople. It was placed alongside the south wall of the church. *Arcosolia* tombs, built within the thickness of the wall in the narthex, exonarthex, or *parekklesion*, became a striking feature of the Palaeologan burial places in the monasteries. In addition exonarthexes and ambulatories were built in new churches and added to old churches to unite the old and new buildings into larger complexes, such as the south church and exonarthex of the monastery of Constantine Lips in Constantinople, which was commissioned by Empress Theodora Palaeologina, the widow of Michael VIII, in the 13th century as an addition to the tenth-century church. Monasteries also had libraries where the collections of ancient books were gathered. The one in the monastery of Chora in Constantinople, as has been suggested, was built by a founder, Theodore Metochites.

Christian states in Bulgaria, Serbia, and Kievan Rus' fell under the influence of the Byzantine monastic architecture of the Balkans and especially of Mount Athos. The most distinguishing feature of Serbian monasteries is a circular plan of enclosure, seen in the 12th-century monastery Djurdjevi Stupovi in Serbia, the 13th-century Studenica monastery, and many others. As scholars have suggested, the shape came from pagan cult architecture and spread to medieval Serbian monastic foundations. As in Athonite monasteries the *katholikon* in medieval Serbian monasteries occupies the center of the circular enclosure. Their plans include narthexes and large, almost square exonarthexes. The exonarthexes occasionally displayed baptismal fonts, as in the cases of Studenica and Gračanica. Following Athonite monastic refectories the Serbian monastic dining rooms also face the western entrance of the *katholikon*. The one in Studenica, built in the 12th century by the Nemanjic dynasty, is a rectangular hall with semicircular tables. The 14th-century monastery of the Archangels in Prizren copied directly the triconch shape of the Great Lavra refectory. Monastery towers had chapels that were decorated with didactic subjects. A Canon for the Departed Soul decorates the tower chapel in the Hilandar monastery. In Serbian monasteries most of the dwellings, monastic shops, storage, latrines, and so on were aligned along the circular enclosure. This planning gave a more prominent position to their main *katholikon*.

Bulgarian monasteries followed the general plan of Byzantine monasteries. The earliest have survived in Pliska and Preslav.

The late ninth- or early tenth-century monastery of Patleina (St. Panteleimon) has a small square-domed *katholikon*. The refectory here is located on the south side of the *katholikon* like many found in Byzantium, such as Hosios Loukas, and Nea Moni in Chios. The *katholikon* was originally decorated with a large ceramic icon of the Pantocrator, which was uncovered, together with other ceramic tiles during excavations.

In 11th-century Rus', cities enjoyed prosperity because of the alliance with Byzantium. About 70 monasteries were established in Rus' before the Mongol invasion (1237–1240). The monasteries flourished in Kiev, Chernigov, Vladimir and Suzdal, Novgorod, and Pskov. Several monastery *katholika* are still preserved in Kiev, such as in the Vydubetsky monastery or the 12th-century Kirylovsky monastery. These are large buildings, built in fine brick and decorated with frescoes. The Kievo-Pecherskij monastery (The Monastery of the Caves) is the earliest, founded in the middle of the 11th century by St. Antony. It had great influence on monastic life and architecture. Only the *katholikon* of the Dormition of the Virgin (1073–1089) is partially preserved. The *Paterik* (The Book of the Fathers), written by the monk Nestor, contains a wealth of information about monastery life. According to the *Paterik*, the monk Alimpij went to Mount Athos and visited Constantinople, where he copied the *typikon* of the Stoudios monastery. Thus, the style of life of the Byzantine monastery was accepted by the Rus' brethren. The *Paterik* also reveals that this monastery was a literary center. It had an icon painter, also named Alimpij, who painted for the rich and poor to spread Christian piety and devotion among the local population. The *Paterik* also mentions the veneration of the image of St. Demetrios, whose cult came to Rus' from Thessalonika and the Balkans.

Monasteries continued to exert impact on Byzantium by providing spiritual ideals to its society. As pilgrimage centers they sheltered travelers and promoted devotion to holy images and veneration of saints and relics. As cultural and artistic centers, they greatly stimulated the development of Byzantine art and architecture. The conservatism and continuous imitation of ancient monastery building types contributed to continuity in the planning of monastic architecture. Regional techniques, architectural preferences, and different liturgical traditions affected the individual character of monasteries in different geographic areas. Patronage affected the choice of planning of the *katholika*. However, from the very early days monasteries continued to embody the image of a holy city where piety and prayer prevailed.

NATALIA TETERIATNIKOV

*See also* Archaeology: Near East; Architecture: Armenian Monasteries; Cappadocia, Turkey; Greece; Israel/Palestine; Istanbul, Turkey; Lavra; Meteora, Thessaly, Greece; Mount Athos, Greece; Mount Sinai, Egypt; Origins: Eastern Christian; Serbia; Syria

## Further Reading

Bridel, Philippe, editor, *Le site monastique copte des Kellia: Sources historiques et explorations archéologiques: Actes du Colloque de Genève 13 au 15 août 1984*, Geneva: Mission suisse d'archéologie copte de l'Université de Genève, 1986

Brumfield, William C., *Gold in Azure: One Thousand Years of Russian Architecture*, Boston: Godine, 1983

Bryer, A., "The Late Byzantine Monastery in Town and Countryside," *Studies in Church History* 16 (1979)

Burridge, P., "The Architectural Development of the Athonite Monastery," in *Mount Athos and Byzantine Monasticism: Papers from the Twenty-Eighth Spring Symposium of Byzantine Studies, Birmingham, March 1994* (Publications/Society for the Promotion of Byzantine Studies, 4), edited by Anthony Bryer and Mary Cunningham, Aldershot, Hampshire, and Brookfield, Vermont: Variorum, 1996

Charanis, Peter, "The Monastic Properties and the State in the Byzantine Empire," in *Dumbarton Oaks Papers*, number 4, Cambridge, Massachusetts: Harvard University Press, 1948

Evelyn-White, Hugh G., *The Monasteries of the Wâdi'n Natrûn*, part 2: *The History of the Monasteries of Nitria and Scetis*, and part 3: *The Architecture and Archaeology* (Publications of the Metropolitan Museum of Art, Egyptian Expedition), New York: Metropolitan Museum of Art, 1926–1933

Hirschfeld, Yizhar, *The Judean Desert Monasteries in the Byzantine Period*, New Haven, Connecticut: Yale University Press, 1992

Kasser, Rodolphe, *Le Site monastique des Kellia (Basse-Egypte): Recherches des années 1981–1983*, Louvain: Peeters, 1984

Lassus, Jean, *Sanctuaires chrétiens de Syrie: essai sur la genèse, la forme et l'usage liturgique des édifices du culte chrétien, en Syrie, du IIIe siècle à la conquête musulmane*, Paris: Geuthner, 1944

Mylonas, P.M., "Research on Athos," in *XVe Congrès international des Études Byzantines*, volume 2, Athens, 1981

Palmer, Andrew, *Monk and Mason on the Tigris Frontier: The Early History of Tur 'Abdin* (University of Cambridge Oriental Publications, number 39), Cambridge and New York: Cambridge University Press, 1990

Papachryssanthou, D., "La vie monastique dans la campagne Byzantine du VIIIe au XIe siècle: ermitages, groupes, communautés," *Byzantion* 43 (1973)

Patric, Josef, "Monasteries," in *The Oxford Encyclopedia of Archaeology in the Near East*, volume 4, edited by Eric M. Meyers, New York: Oxford University Press, 1997

Popović, Svetlana, *Krst u krugu: arhitektura manastira u Srednjovekovnoj Srbiji* (Biblioteka Umetnicki spomenici), Belgrade: Prosveta, 1994

Popović, Svetlana, "The *Trapeza* in Cenobitic Monasteries: Architectural and Spiritual Contexts," in *Dumbarton Oaks Papers: Number Fifty-Two*, Washington, D.C.: Dumbarton Oaks Research Library and Collection, 1998

Rodley, Lyn, *Cave Monasteries of Byzantine Cappadocia*, Cambridge and New York: Cambridge University Press, 1985

Sodini, Jean-Pierre, "Les églises de Syrie du Nord," in *Archéologie et histoire de la Syrie* (Schriften zur vorderasiatischen Archäologie, 1), volume 2, edited by Jean-Marie Dentzer and Winfried Orthmann, Saarbrücken: Saarbrücker Druckerei und Verlag, 1989

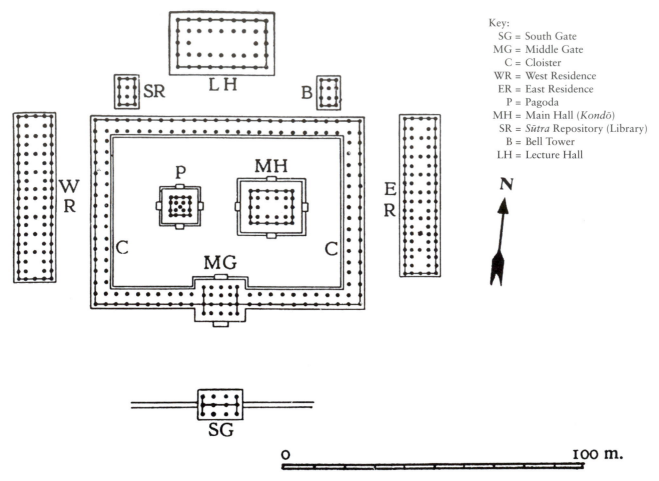

Key:
SG = South Gate
MG = Middle Gate
C = Cloister
WR = West Residence
ER = East Residence
P = Pagoda
MH = Main Hall (*Kondō*)
SR = *Sūtra* Repository (Library)
B = Bell Tower
LH = Lecture Hall

Fig. 1: Hōryū-ji, Nara Prefecture. Plan of original version without later alterations.
After J. Edward Kidder, *Early Buddhist Japan*, 1972, Fig. 36

Talbot, Alice-Mary, "Women's Space in Monasteries," in *Dumbarton Oaks Papers: Number Fifty-Two*, Washington, D.C.: Dumbarton Oaks Research Library and Collection, 1998

Tchalenko, Georges, *Villages antiques de la Syrie du Nord: Le massif du Bélus a l'époque romaine* (Bibliothèque archéologique et historique, 50), 3 vols., Paris: Geuthner, 1953–1958

Teteriatnikov, Natalia, *The Liturgical Planning of Byzantine Churches in Cappadocia* (Orientalia Christiana Analecta, 252), Rome: Pontificio Istituto Orientale, 1996

Teteriatnikov, Natalia, "Monasticism in Cappadocia: The Case of Göreme," in *Work and Worship at the Theotokos Evergetis, 1050–1200* (Belfast Byzantine Texts and Translations, 6.2), edited by Margaret Mullett and Anthony Kirby, Belfast: Belfast Byzantine Enterprises, School of Greek, Roman and Semitic Studies, The Queen's University of Belfast, 1997

Walters, Colin, *Monastic Archaeology in Egypt* (Modern Egyptology Series), Warminster: Aris and Phillips, 1974

# Architecture: Structural Monasteries in East Asia

In the South Asian homeland of Buddhism, stone was the preferred medium of constructing temples and monasteries, whether in the form of cave temples or stand-alone structures. However, in East Asia such buildings were most frequently made with a wooden framework, whose plaster walls and tiled roofs were supported by an elaborate system of bracketing. These materials were of age-old practice in East Asia and were adapted to the new context of Buddhism. The visual result was naturally very different, but in both concept and function some similarities to their South Asian ancestors could be seen.

Although many remnants of structural monasteries exist in China, the Chinese have not been much interested in the conservation of ancient structures of any kind. Exceptions do exist, but what remains of early structures often are only portions of once grander complexes. However, the Japanese have been much

Fig. 2: Hōryū-ji, Nara Prefecture. View of pagoda and Kondō.
Photo courtesy of John C. Huntington, the Huntington Archive

more attentive in maintaining ancient structures; and, since Buddhism first arrived in Japan in the sixth century, their first monasteries and temples were modeled on Chinese sources, from which Buddhism came. This was especially appropriate, as the character of Chinese architecture differed from indigenous Japanese architecture, which came to have Buddhist significance. Whereas Japanese architecture, as seen in Shintō shrines, rests directly on the ground, traditional Chinese architecture of important buildings, such as palaces and temples, is raised on a stone platform. Furthermore those same structures often consist of a building resting on top of a series of platforms, one on top of the other. This coincides with the concept of raising the visitor or resident above the ground and thus establishing a separation from the earth. In other words Buddhist detachment can be read into the very nature of Chinese architecture.

This can be seen at the Buddhist monastery of Hōryū-ji near Nara, which was first founded by Prince Regent Shōtoku Taishi (572–621). The present buildings date to the late seventh century, as the first monastery was burned to the ground in 670 but almost immediately rebuilt. The new original plan (Fig. 1), mod-

ified later, consisted of one gate followed by a double front gate piercing an enclosing wall raised on a stone foundation that was level with the interior. The two principle structures inside, which again were raised on stone platforms, are the pagoda and the Kondō, or "Golden Hall," placed side by side immediately in front of the gate (Fig. 2). The pagoda appears to be a five-story building but in fact has no provision to climb within it, nor originally were any images inside (although some were added later). Instead it represents the East Asian version of the Indian stūpa, or burial mound, that commemorated the one-time presence of the historical Buddha. In this sense it is an abstract diagram, whereas the Kondō is a rectangular, one-story building (with another roof added to give it some sense of visual equality with the pagoda) containing yet another raised platform, this for images. Simultaneously, these two buildings recall the complete extinction of the Buddha in the pagoda but recognize the later necessity to provide his image together with other images in the Kondō, including guardian kings at the four corners of the central platform. Outside the walled enclosure, although later incorporated within it, were separate buildings consisting of a

Fig 3: Tōshōdai-ji, Nara Prefecture. View from the front.
Photo courtesy of John C. Huntington, the Huntington Archive

Fig. 4: Dayan si (Big Goose Pagoda), Xi'an, Shaanxi. Rubbing from the stone lintel of the entry showing a scene of a temple front with images.
Photo courtesy of John C. Huntington, the Huntington Archive

Fig. 5: Murō-ji, Nara Prefecture. View of the Kondō.
Photo courtesy of Sakamoto Photo Research Lab

dormitory and dining hall on either side and at the back a library for sacred texts, a lecture hall, and a bell tower. Thus, the entire complex is self-sufficient in terms of both the daily lives of the resident monks and their religious needs.

Both the pagoda and the Kondō at Hōryū-ji offer provisions for circumambulation, but in temples that follow shortly thereafter this is much reduced or eliminated. This was likely because the pagoda was a building with no function other than that of an abstract symbol. Tōshōdai-ji, which is located in the western suburbs of Nara, was founded in 745 by a distinguished Chinese monk, Jianzhen (Japanese, Ganjin; d. 763). The large, single-roofed Kondō is directly in line with the now lost gate (Fig. 3). Twin pagodas were at the corners of surrounding wall (these too are no longer extant). Thus, what was of primary importance was an immediate confrontation with the images of the Kondō, and indeed they all face to the front, the back of the hall being unimportant. Much the same can be seen in a depiction on a stone lintel of a pagoda from China dating to about the same time (Fig. 4). Given the influence of the powerful Tang dynasty

(618–907) on the Asian continent, it is possible to take Japanese structures of this time as essentially direct replicas of Chinese ones.

The "Great Eastern Temple," Tōdai-ji, on the eastern edge of Nara, was also originally built in the mid–eighth century; but its twin pagodas were pushed outside the walled enclosure altogether. The original Kondō was of staggering size, and its cavernous interior was filled by a colossal bronze Buddha, both of which befitted a state temple and its capital (then known as Heijō). It is reported that over 400,000 carpenters and metalworkers were involved in its construction. Unfortunately it was burned and destroyed by earthquakes several times over the years; however, it was always rebuilt (only a small portion of the original lotus seat of the Buddha remains), and the present structure still remains awesome. It is surrounded by several ancillary buildings, including a massive log structure – the Shōsō-in of 756, which contains the treasures of Emperor Shōmu (r. 724–749) and gives a rich picture of the material culture not only of Japan but also of Tang China and exotic lands to the west.

Fig. 6: Hōō-dō ("Phoenix Hall") of the Byōdō-in at Uji near Kyoto. Overall view.
Photo courtesy of Sakamoto Photo Research Lab

As continental influence waned with the collapse of the Tang dynasty in 907 and as Buddhism had become firmly established in Japan, art and architectural forms increasingly took on a Japanese cast. Two buildings at two different sites can give some indication of the diversity of architectural practices in later Japanese Buddhist temples and monasteries. The early ninth-century Kondō of Murō-ji is located in the heavily wooded hills of Nara prefecture (Fig. 5), and its two pagodas are almost hidden well away from it. All the buildings are small in scale and very much a part of the surrounding landscape. One of several features of special importance is the thatched roof of the Kondō, a feature that harks back to indigenous practice as seen in Shinto shrines and even farmhouses. By contrast the "Phoenix Hall" (Hōō-dō) of the Byōdō-in at Uji outside Kyoto is a paradise of form and color both inside and out (Fig. 6). The building itself, completed in 1053, is in the form of a phoenix with outstretched wings (which are completely nonfunctional and even inaccessi-

ble), a central body, and a structure extending from the back as a tail. Twin bronze phoenixes at the ends of the crest of the roof emphasize this. It sits before a reflecting pond that gives the sense of a phoenix hovering just above the ground. Inside is a gilded and lacquered wooden Buddha (carved by the famous sculptor Jōchō). It is of remote Tang ancestry but made more sumptuous yet, being enhanced by a gilded openwork canopy with inlaid mother-of-pearl. The Buddha is surrounded by a lavishly painted ceiling, by carved celestial and other figures on the walls, and by paintings on the walls and doors of other figures and landscape scenes recalling actual Japanese scenery.

The Phoenix Hall is surrounded by a manicured park. This, together with the splendor of the building, tells of a Buddhist paradise made entirely by human hands. But paradise can be made by nature as well, as at Murō-ji. For whatever influence China might have had on Japanese architecture in earlier years, the sensitivity to the perfection of beauty – of whatever kind, from whatever source, and for its own sake – emerges as a special characteristic of the Japanese.

JAMES O. CASWELL

*See also* China; Japan; Kyoto, Japan; Nara, Japan; Taiwan; Worship Space: Buddhist Perspectives

**Further Reading**

Fukuyama, Toshio, *Heian Temples: Byōdō-in and Chūson-ji* (Heibonsha Survey of Japanese Art, volume 9), New York: Weatherhill, 1976

Kidder, J. Edward, *Early Buddhist Japan* (Ancient Peoples and Places, volume 78), London: Thames and Hudson, and New York: Praeger, 1972

Kobayashi, Takeshi, *Nara Buddhist Art: Tōdai-ji* (Heibonsha Survey of Japanese Art, volume 5), New York: Weatherhill, 1975

Mino, Yutaka, *The Great Eastern Temple: Treasures of Japanese Buddhist Art from Tōdai-ji*, Chicago: Art Institute of Chicago, 1986

Mizuno, Seiichi, *Asuka Buddhist Art: Horyu-ji* (Heibonsha Survey of Japanese Art, volume 4), New York: Weatherhill, 1974

Ōoka, Minoru, *Temples of Nara and Their Art* (Heibonsha Survey of Japanese Art, volume 7), New York: Weatherhill, 1973

Pirazzoli-T'Serstevens, Michèle, *Living Architecture: Chinese* (Living Architecture Series), translated by Robert Allen, New York: Grosset and Dunlap, and London: Macdonald, 1971

Soper, Alexander, *The Evolution of Buddhist Architecture in Japan* (Princeton Monographs in Art and Archaeology, 22), Princeton, New Jersey: Princeton University Press, and London: Milford, Oxford University Press, 1942

Soper, Alexander, "Architecture," in *The Art and Architecture of China* (Pelican History of Art, Z10), by Soper and Laurence Sickman, Baltimore, Maryland: Penguin Books, 1956; 3rd edition, Baltimore, Maryland, and Harmondsworth, Middlesex: Penguin Books, 1968

# Architecture: Western Christian Monasteries

The architecture of Western monasticism was shaped by several factors, the main ones being the site, the monastic plan, and monastic theology.

The choice of site, often one of great natural beauty, was crucial. Moreover chapter 66 of St. Benedict's Rule stated that monasteries should be self-sufficient, and essential buildings were usually joined to the south aisle of the church, although exceptions existed.

The monastic plan followed by most monastic orders emanated from St. Gall. It reached fruition at Cluny II and later at Clairvaux. Cluny added the chapter house to the east range, extending the monks' dormitory beyond St. Gall's square plan. This Cluniac arrangement was adhered to by every monastic house, apart from the hermits.

At Clairvaux Cistercian segregation kept lay brothers and choir monks apart. The former were accommodated in the west range, the choir monks' refectory being built at right angles to the south cloister walk. The later introduction of the day room into the south range resulted in further complications.

Monastic ground plans are similar, but each is unique, and very often the plan was adapted to suit the most unlikely places. Saint Martin-de-Canigou, Mont-St.-Michel, and La Sagra di San Michele are typical of such places, and Rievaulx is probably the perfect Cistercian site.

The cloister was formed by four open arcaded walkways with lean-to roofs, although some were perhaps glazed in the later Middle Ages. The preferred area was 100 square feet, but this was not always the case. The cloistral area not only depended on the site but also dictated the size of the buildings. Cloister architecture, like that of the churches, did evolve, producing substantial buildings of architectural merit, as the remains of Fountains Abbey illustrate.

In England, Norwich Cathedral has a wonderful late cloister (1297–1430), and Gloucester, with its fan vaulting, is even more exceptional. The arcading of these English cloisters is large, divided into four lights, filled with elegant tracery. Yet Romanesque cloisters are also exceptional, fine sculpture being used to great effect at St. Trophime, Moissac, and Santo Domingo de Silos, Spain. Saint Paul's-outside-the-Walls, Rome, is famous for its twisted columns of *cosmati* work.

The cloister became the nucleus of the standard monastic plan, providing the monks with access to the cloistral ranges and out-service buildings. Where practicable the important buildings were built around the cloister to form three ranges.

The chapter house, dormitory, and calefactory formed the east range. The stark basement chapter house at Dryburgh contrasts with the 13th-century polygonal chapter house at Westminster Abbey, one of the wonders of English monasticism. The impressive dormitory at Eberbach (German Cistercian) has a fine vaulted roof on short central columns. The day stairs at Maulbronn (German Cistercian) have a banister of fine cusped and molded encircled quatrefoils. Probably the finest night stair is at Hexham Abbey (13th century). The finest calefactory could perhaps be at Mont-St.-Michel. A sumptuous grand hall with two huge fireplaces, it has a fine ribbed vault supported by twin rows of columns.

The refectory and lavatorium formed the south range, and the kitchen stood nearby. The refectory at Alcobaça, Portugal (Cistercian), has twin central columns that give the impression of great height and space as well as lightness, whereas at Chester the refectory is a fine example of Benedictine simplicity and elegance, with tall, broad windows lighting the great hall. Gloucester probably has the finest lavatorium in England, with rather excellent fan vaulting. The great 14th-century kitchen at Durham Cathedral, by John Lewyn, still stands and is an excellent example of domestic architecture.

The prior's lodging, with guest accommodation and cellarage below, usually formed the west range. The prior's lodging at Castle Acre is a fine apartment, although its architecture is

**Exterior of Lavabo in cloister of Cistercian Abbey of Lilienfeld, Austria, 13th century.**
**Photo courtesy of Chris Schabel**

homely compared to that of Mont-St.-Michel, where the guest hall is a tall vaulted room with central columns and is well lit by twin narrow lancets. At Fountains the lay brothers were accommodated in the west range. The architecture of the undercroft – one long room – has majesty, while its simplicity is overwhelming. The north walk, attached to the church, was used for reading and recreation. Indeed evidence exists of game boards cut into the stone seats at Gloucester.

An infirmary always stood within the monastic enclosure. The infirmary at Much Wenlock, a handsome building in the Romanesque style, is still extant. Very often monastic out-service buildings are awe inspiring, such as the grange barn at Bradford-on-Avon, England, with its excellent wagon roof. Gateways to monastic enclosures were often buildings of great architectural merit. That at Lorsch Abbey, Germany (c. 770), is unique, being based on the propylaeum of Old St Peter's. It is a splendid example of classical revivalism. The upper floor was a royal reception hall, and the triple-arched undercroft became the entrance.

Monastic theology had a distinct influence on the architecture of medieval monasteries. The eucharistic liturgy at Cluny resulted in great emphasis being put on the east end, very often having a triple apse, such as that at Cluny II (955–981). At Cluny III, begun in 1008, the ultimate development produced one great central area at the east end for the liturgical drama, with a corona of chapels behind. When dedicated in 1130 Cluny III was the largest monastic church in the West. Paray-le-Monial, Sâone-et-Loire (completed by 1109), is a miniature Cluny III. The arcaded apse has an ambulatory, with the clerestory typically Romanesque. Great vaulting shafts emphasize the vertical, rising up to support the ribbed barrel vault. Paray gives a good impression of Cluny III's soaring heights, seen in Cluny's extant south transept. The proportions of these great churches tell us that they were nothing less than cathedrals.

However, the architecture of the early Cistercians is the complete opposite. Saint Bernard (1090–1153) considered Cluniac ornamentation, such as the light in the new east end at St. Denis, a distraction. This accounts for the exceptional austerity of early Cistercian architecture, especially at Fontenay Abbey (1139–1147), with a shallow square east end, flanking chapels, and low pointed vault. Most Irish houses followed this plan, indicating that an unusual measure of uniformity was applied at this time. The architecture of Cistercian churches changed after Bernard's death in 1153.

Romanesque developed regionally and nationally. The monumental quality of early German Romanesque at Hersfeld (1037–1144) is reminiscent of Roman basilicas. In Italy the church of

Bernardo Rossellino, Cloister of the Orange Trees, Benedictine Abbey, Badia, Florence, Italy, c. 1435–1440.
Photo courtesy of the Editor

St. Abbondio, Como (1063–1095), has tall piers, small clerestory, but no triforium. A great feeling of height is evident. Saint-Savin-sur-Gartempe, France (c. 1060–1115), one of the most impressive monuments of medieval architecture, is equally high, but here the piers reach roof level without a break. The groin-vaulted flanking aisles, of similar height, add to the amazing sense of space. The nave of St.-Madaleine, Vézelay (1120–1140), a magnificent example of high Burgundian Romanesque architecture at its best, is divided into bays by great vaulting shafts rising from ground to roof level. The lack of a triforium, as at San Abbondio and St. Savin, increases the impression of height, and the use of colored stonework lightens the structure. The early Gothic choir was begun in the 1180s.

San Zeno, Verona (1125–1135), a fine example of Italian Romanesque, has such an expanse of wall in the nave that it tends to minimize the arcading. Similar elements are found in the austere brick-built Norbertine priory at Jerichow, Brandenburg, begun in 1149. Ratzeburg Cathedral, Germany (late 12th to early 13th century), like Jerichow, is Romanesque brick, with the square nave piers supporting a clerestory and early Gothic vault.

The east end is apsed. The apse at San Frediano, Lucca (1112–1147), is an important feature, with its bands of red and white stone, the upper story forming a semi-rotunda. It has a fine, tall campanile. The interior is basilican in plan. In complete contrast is Santo Stefano, Bologna (c. 1150), an octagonal red-brick Lombard Romanesque imitation of the Holy Sepulchre at Jerusalem. The rough interior held the 12-sided shrine of St. Petronio, surmounted by an altar and a pulpit.

In Germany at Maulbronn (1146–1178), the nave has square piers and plain clerestory. A medieval screen (restored) divides the nave from the monks' choir, but the vaulted roof and Gothic woodwork are later. Eberbach, Germany (c. 1170–1186), also Cistercian, has a rather bare nave with huge square piers and minimal clerestory. The barrel vault is groined. Maria Laach (1130–1156) is a typical double-apsed German Romanesque church, having towers at both ends. The verticality of the interior, similar to the earlier Hersfeld, is strengthened by the square piers. The soaring towers and the three-story square east end at Murbach, Alsace (c. 1150), similar to St. Andrews, Scotland, are all joined by a roof, creating a wonderful sense of unity.

The most complete Cistercian monastery of the period is Poblet, Spain (founded 1151), and still in use. The church (1180–1196), based on Old St. Peter's, Rome, is a great work of early Romanesque. The rough stone and somber character of the interior lacks decorative frescoes. The tall eastern apse is filled with a Mannerist reredos. The enclosure wall must be the grandest anywhere, fortresslike with polygonal towers. One of the best Cistercian churches built on a grand scale is Alcobaça (1158–1233). The magnificent spacious interior, beautifully proportioned, is reminiscent of Vézelay, especially the wonderful apse of seven bays.

Early Norman Romanesque, first noted at Mont-St.-Michel (1024–1084), reached maturity at Caen in St.-Trinité (begun c. 1068) and St.-Étienne (1064–1077) with its magnificent long nave. At St.-Trinité the nave arcades are taller and narrower, but at St.-Étienne the proportions of the nave arcades match the triforium, giving it almost perfect proportions. Both churches have a clerestory passage, which became an important feature in Norman churches.

Cluny III is very important to the development of Romanesque, but it is in England where the most spectacular advances were made. After 1066 all English cathedrals and almost every major abbey were rebuilt in the new Norman style, influenced by Jumièges and Caen. Little of St. Albans' (c. 1080–1115) early Norman church still exists. The stout, square piers in the nave, triforium, and clerestory emphasize power rather than grace. Even the transepts and crossing tower, with triforium, evoke this sense of authority. The nave is mostly 13th-century early English and counterbalances the austerity of the Norman work. Gloucester's wonderful Perpendicular exterior belies the powerful Norman nave. The triforium, almost invisible, squats between tall, thick piers and arcades and tall clerestory windows. The arcading of the nave is not overwhelmed by the later ribbed vault. The choir, with the great east window, was rebuilt in a marvelous Perpendicular style.

Norman influence, from St.-Trinité, is seen at Durham (c. 1093–1133) in its twin western towers. Indeed at Durham a major technological advance was achieved with the pointed vault. Being much more secure than the barrel vault, it opened the way for soaring Gothic vaults. Durham, despite early Gothic elements and forms in the clerestory, is mostly Norman. The incomparable interior and the proportions of the Norman nave – with decorated piers and cross-ribbed vault (1120s) – is the finest example of Norman architecture. Similarly decorated piers are in the nave at Dunfermline and the ruined Cluniac priory of Castle Acre. Selby Abbey is one of a few complete English medieval churches, with evidence of Norman to early Gothic in the nave and transepts. One nave pier is decorated like those in Durham. The west front is early English with a late Norman doorway. The long choir is 14th century. The western towers were completed in 1935.

Tewksbury Abbey's Norman west front is exceptional, with great retaining arch, but Peterborough probably has the most remarkable west front anywhere in England and is one of most dramatic and audacious conceptions in medieval monastic architecture. It is 156 feet wide, being dominated by three huge 81-foot-high Norman arches. The gables are filled with wonderful arcading and rosettes of early English work. The two flanking towers with spires and pinnacles are 14th century. The proportions of this west front are almost perfect, making it indeed a tremendous achievement. The Norman interior complements the exterior. Saint Bartholomew's, Smithfield (1123), has the finest Norman east end and crossing in London, and the Norman architecture at Christchurch Priory, Hants, is of excellent quality. The pulpitum is late 14th century, and the choir is Perpendicular, with fan vaulting like the Henry VII Chapel at Westminster Abbey. This is one of the few churches that still has its medieval divisions.

Norwich Cathedral, begun in 1096, is also beautifully proportioned, its nave arcades and triforium being similar in height. Here, together with its long nave, is seen the influence of St.-Étienne, Caen. Norwich has the finest Norman apse and ambulatory in England, one that compares with any in Europe. The later ribbed vaulted roof and pulpitum date from 1446 to 1472. The Norman tower is the tallest in England. A complete contrast with Anglo-Norman Romanesque is Fontevraud in France. The church (c. 1120) has a tall apse and nave, but it is the vault with cupolas that are of main interest. The cupolas give the interior of the church a great sense of freedom and movement that most Romanesque churches lack. However, at Pontigny Abbey, France (1150), in the nave and crossing, the transition to Gothic in the Cistercian Order is discernible. The nave might have Romanesque walls, but the roof is an early Gothic ribbed vault.

The great leap forward from Romanesque to Gothic occurred in Paris at the great Abbey of St. Denis (1137), the seminal church for Gothic architecture. Only the ambulatory, corona, and parts of the west front belong to Suger's church. The choir and ambulatory, filled with larger windows and slender columns, contrast with the heaviness of the Romanesque, creating an area of light, spaciousness, and elegance. The affinity of the three divisions, together with other elements of the west front, prepared the way for the High Gothic in France.

Jedburgh Abbey, Scotland, might have remnants of a Norman choir, like Romsey Abbey, but the nave is transitional, the arcading supporting an early Gothic triforium and clerestory. Despite the excellent Norman door, the west front is early Gothic, with a delicate rose window filling the gable.

Although Canterbury is one of the first English monasteries in the new Gothic style, the choir, begun in 1175, is in the early French Gothic of William of Sens (completed by William the Englishman). Round piers with large water-leaf capitals support early Gothic arcading, reminiscent of the cathedrals of Paris and Laon. Despite this beginning English Gothic architecture developed independently from that of Europe, evolving, around 1335, into the Perpendicular style. At Canterbury the emphasis is on height, which Henry Yvele continued in his Perpendicular nave of 1378–1405, making it one of the finest English medieval churches. Westminster Abbey, although French in inspiration (influenced by St. Denis and Amiens), is nevertheless a very English church and still has its medieval divisions. Two campaigns – 1245 to 1269 and 1375 to 1520 – conformed with the original. The window tracery anticipated the geometrical. The Henry VII Chapel with fan vaulting is quite exceptional.

The Norman crossing, transepts, and choir of Carlisle Cathedral were replaced between the 12th and 15th centuries. Only two bays of its original Norman nave exist. The great east window (51 by 26 feet) (c. 1340) is the largest flowing traceried window in England. Despite later restorations Carlisle is a still a medieval building. At Hexham Abbey the choir is transitional, whereas the transepts are early English. The clerestory is a more sophisticated version of that at the nearby priories of Lanercost and Brinkburn. The church has great detail, especially the blind arcading in the transepts.

The Cistercian presbytery of Abbey Dore, Hertfordshire, is still in use. Apart from the early English east end (1200) and an ambulatory with five vaulted chapels, the church is transitional. The finest Augustinian nave in England is at Bridlington Priory, Yorkshire. Architecturally it is very important. Building began in the 13th century and continued into the 15th. The eastern arches of the arcades, the glazed triforium, and some clerestory windows are decorated. The western bays on the south side are Perpendicular.

Bristol Cathedral is one of the most original medieval church designs and perhaps the finest hall church in Europe. The sense of space is tremendous, and the architecture of the aisles is unique. The subtle use of vaulting bars transforms the walls into flying buttresses. The vertical effect of the aisle vaulting is awesome, assisted by tall traceried windows reaching up to the height of the presbytery, which is lit by four large lancet windows. Saint German's Priory, Cornwall, has a west front of great interest. The lower parts of the towers are Norman, whereas the upper part of the north tower is octagonal and early English; the southern tower is square and 15th-century Perpendicular. The late Norman doorway is one of the finest in England.

Much Wenlock Priory, Shropshire, has remnants of a fine 13th-century church with a ribbed vault, the nave perhaps being similar to Rievaulx. The choir at Rievaulx was completed by 1230, and the springers are still in place for the vaulting. The nave and transepts are Norman (1135–1140), but the clerestory is early English. The ruins of Rievaulx's nave indicate that the architecture would have been of a high quality, in keeping with Cistercian values. However, it contrasts with the austere nave at Fountains with its round piers, slightly pointed arcades, no triforium, and Norman clerestory. The nave architecture might be more sturdy than delicate, but it is still impressive. Yet the lofty and elegant remains of early English architecture in the chapel of the nine altars match Rielvaux. Two tall hexagonal shafts, like that in the chapter house at Westminster Abbey, supported the vault. Although Sherborne Abbey, Dorset, shows evidence of Saxon, Norman, and early English work, it is best known for the glorious Perpendicular in the presbytery and nave. The fan vaulting, the earliest in any major English church, is splendid.

In Italy evidence of the Gothic is found at Fossanova (1179–1208) in its Italian west front, the tympanum of which is decorated with *cosmati* work. Yet the interior of the church is austere, the arcades being supported by stout piers. Casamiri was built by masons from Fossanova (1203–1217), although the interior is early Gothic. Both churches have the cool beauty expected of Italian Cistercian churches.

By the 13th century in Germany, important Gothic churches were being built. One of them is Altenburg (begun c. 1255). Its rich and delicate architecture is not especially Cistercian. The apsed choir has a corona and fine traceried windows. The arcading is tall and slender, supporting slim clerestory windows, with a delicately traceried triforium. Chorin, Brandenburg, has a most spectacular west front (1334). The central bay, gabled with crockets, is flanked by smaller identical bays that are decorated with blind arcading. Three tall lancets fill the west front, which is rich in harmony.

In Austria Heiligenkreuz (1295), of Burgundian Gothic, is like a hall church. The choir (c. 1280) has three identical bays, with slender piers supporting a rib vault. The feeling of space is almost late Gothic. Zwettl, Austria (1342–1348), is also Burgundian Gothic and similar to Heiligenkreuz. Indeed the polygonal form of the hall choir made its first appearance here.

In Spain the emphasis in Santa Maria de Pedralbes, Barcelona (1326), falls on the walls. The three-story apse has no chapels. The architecture is delicate, for the thinness of the walls – and their absence of structural functionality – echoes the principles of Rayonnant architecture.

Hall churches for preaching were the friars' contribution to medieval architecture. The austerity of the Carcere, above Assisi, contrasts with the great Basilica below, proud and fortresslike and perched on the side of the mountain. The Basilica (1228–1253) has an upper and a lower church. It is an exceptional example of Italian Gothic. The aisleless upper church is more French in style, although the great wall spaces, with rather small windows, are decidedly Italian. The walls presented a challenge to fresco painters. The rather sturdy architecture of the exterior is softened by a fine rose window. San Francesco, Bologna (c. 1236), is the first mendicant Gothic church, with pointed arches, sexpartite vaults, and no tracery. The east end is supported by flying buttresses.

Saint Croce, Florence (Arnolfo di Cambio, 1295–1442), has an exceptionally broad nave (62.5 feet), but the emphasis is on the vertical. The apsed east end with a tall narrow arch is flanked by smaller ones. Slim polygonal shafts, with sculpted capitals, support tall pointed arcades. However, San Antonio, Padua (1232–1307), is more like a cathedral than a Franciscan church. Its east end with apse and corona of nine chapels is French in character. The west front, with five deep arches, is reminiscent of Peterborough, but the double gallery above is Lombardic Romanesque. The interior and exterior, with domes and turrets, were influenced by St. Mark's, Venice, giving it an unmistakable Byzantine appearance.

In Great Britain few friars' churches survived the Reformation. The Franciscan church at Chichester (1250s) has a five-bay choir. The five lancets in the east end and the twin lancets in the flanks have early plate tracery. This is a simple church, like the restored Greyfriars at Elgin, Scotland. However, the apsed choir of the Franciscan church at Salzburg, begun around 1408 by Hans Stetheimer, is opulent, with seven exceptionally tall and delicate shafts supporting a wonderful German-style lierne vault and the ribbing springing from the shafts. A remarkable sense of unity can be seen between the choir and its seven baroque chapels, which enhance the church's opulence.

The Dominicans also built spectacular churches. In St. Maria Novella, Florence (begun in 1283), the nave arcades rise up to roof level, with a circular window in each apex; ribs of the quadripartite vault spring from vaulting shafts. The interior is spacious and is an example of pure Italian Gothic. The Dominican church, or Jacobins, at Toulouse (1230–1292) offers a total contrast. Here central columns rise 90 feet with the apse like an English vault. The columns create a double nave, five bays long, that was used for preaching and teaching. It was a design common among French Dominicans.

Two medieval Dominican churches are still in use in Great Britain: Norwich and Brecon, Wales. Norwich has the finest remains of any medieval friary in England. Its aisleless choir, east wall, and some side windows date from the 14th century, whereas the remainder is Perpendicular. The broad-aisled nave has seven wide bays with a clerestory above. At Brecon only the early English choir of the 13th-century friary is still in use. The lancets are shafted, but the east window is of five lights.

The architecture of hermitages is quite different. Although there might be a cloister at Camaldoli and Grande Chartreuse, facing on to it are the cells of each monk. The 14th-century refectory at Chartreuse has a groined vault, paneled walls, and a wooden reader's pulpit of a later period. Mount Grace, Yorkshire, is the only Carthusian house in Great Britain with any decent remains, although a modern one exists at Parkhouse.

The Middle Ages witnessed a new phenomenon, the warrior monks, notably the Knights of the Temple. Their circular churches were built in imitation of the Temple at Jerusalem. The Holy Sepulchre, Cambridge (c. 1130), with a fine Norman door, is circular, being surmounted by a lantern. The Temple Church, London (1185), has a round nave with a western porch. It is an important example of early Gothic, and the extensive use of Purbeck marble in the arcading and upper stories is reminiscent of Westminster Abbey and Canterbury choir. The 12th-century church at Laon, France, is also circular with a porch at the west, whereas the rotunda of the 12th-century church at Tomar, Portugal, is supported on a central section with Moorish influences. Temple Balsall, Warwickshire (rebuilt 1290), is quite different. It is rectangular, with four bays, like a college chapel. The east window has five lights, and the side windows have geometrical tracery.

Because of the devastation of the Reformation, most medieval monasteries in Great Britain are ruined. Some have substantial remains, and others disappeared. Thus, it is in England that much of the archaeological evidence concerning European monasticism is to be found. It is in Continental Europe, where the ravages of the Reformation were less, that most evidence of monastic buildings endures.

PHILIP E. McWILLIAMS

*See also* Archaeology: Western Europe; Assisi, Italy; Austria; Carthusians; Cathedral Priories; Cistercians: General or Male; Cluniacs; Cluny, France; England: Sites; Florence, Italy; Fontevraud, France; France: Sites; Germany: Sites; Liturgy: Western Christian; Maria Laach, Germany; Mont-St.-Michel, France; Spain: Sites; Templars

**Further Reading**

Aubert, Marcel, *High Gothic Art* (Art of the World, 14), London: Methuen, 1964; as *The Art of the High Gothic Era*, New York: Crown, 1965; revised edition, New York: Greystone, 1966

Bony, Jean, *The English Decorated Style: Gothic Architecture Transformed, 1250–1350* (Wrightsman Lectures, 10), Ithaca, New York: Cornell University Press, and Oxford: Phaidon Press, 1979

Butler, Lionel, and Chris Given-Wilson, *Medieval Monasteries of Great Britain*, London: Joseph, 1979

Calkins, Robert G., *Monuments of Medieval Art*, New York: Dutton, and London: Phaidon Press, 1979

Conant, Kenneth John, *Carolingian and Romanesque Architecture, 800 to 1200* (Pelican History of Art, Z13), Baltimore, Maryland, and Harmondsworth, Middlesex: Penguin Books, 1959; 4th edition, New Haven, Connecticut, and London: Yale University Press, 1978

Fletcher, Banister, *A History of Architecture on the Comparative Method*, London: Athlone Press, 1896; 4th edition, New York: Scribner, 1901; 17th edition, London: Athlone Press, and New York: Scribner, 1961

Focillon, Henri, *The Art of the West in the Middle Ages*, 2 vols., New York and London: Phaidon, 1963; 3rd edition, Ithaca, New York: Cornell University Press, and Oxford: Phaidon, 1980

Frankl, Paul, *Gothic Architecture* (Pelican History of Art, Z19), Baltimore, Maryland: Penguin Books, 1962

Grodecki, Louis, *Gothic Architecture* (History of World Architecture), New York: Abrams, 1977; London: Faber, 1986

Huyghe, René, editor, *Larousse Encyclopaedia of Byzantine and Medieval Art*, London: Hamlyn, 1958; New York: Prometheus Press, 1963; revised edition, New York: Excalibur Books, and London: Hamlyn, 1981

Little, Bryan, *Abbeys and Priories in England and Wales*, New York: Holmes and Meier, and London: Batsford, 1979

Stalley, Roger, *The Cistercian Monasteries of Ireland: An Account of the History, Art, and Architecture of the White Monks in Ireland from 1142–1540*, New Haven, Connecticut, and London: Yale University Press, 1987

Stoddard, Whitney S., *Monastery and Cathedral in France: Medieval Architecture, Sculpture, Stained Glass, Manuscripts, the Art of the Church Treasuries*, Middletown, Connecticut: Wesleyan University Press, 1966; as *Art and Architecture in Medieval France: Medieval Architecture, Sculpture, Stained Glass, Manuscripts, the Art of the Church Treasuries* (Icon Editions, IN-22), New York: Harper and Row, 1972

Toman, Rolf, editor, *The Art of Gothic: Architecture, Sculpture, Painting*, Cologne: Könemann, 1999

# Archives, Western Christian

The main distinction between an *archive* and a *library* is one of function. The former has typically existed almost solely for the support of the institution where it resides, as a repository of documents unique to that institution. The function of a library is more universal: the items it contains might or might not be unique, but the collection's appeal is typically to a broader community of scholars. This overview will argue that that distinction is becoming less meaningful now than in previous centuries.

Archives certainly pre-dated the Christian era, notably in Assyria, Egypt, and Greece. So important was the work of recording and securing written tradition considered that even in pre-Christian settings this task was frequently deemed "sacred" enough to be commonly linked with the work of the temple (Hayes, 1907).

At the heart of monastic life lies a desire to find an ideal mode of life, one called out from among the crowds. The task of formulating that ideal is too rare and costly to risk it to oral transmission only: to some degree it can be said that something such as the Rule of St. Benedict or the *Life of St. Antony* will endure in writing or not at all. It makes perfect sense that monasticism and the discipline of archival service go hand in hand, although no one monastic could have anticipated how much the perseverance of the Church or, for that matter, the survival of Western civilization would come to depend on the disciplines of writing and preserving.

Religious communities of all sizes and traditions have always produced records. Whatever has come down to us, for example, of the *Life of St. Antony* (founder of monasticism) can be credited to those who not only listened and followed but also wrote and preserved his life and sayings. The writings of the early Christian fathers were no doubt preserved in primitive archives (Hayes, 1907). These require, where possible, preservation and storage with a view to later retrieval. It is quite likely that in large cities that served as diocesan headquarters early Christian archives were assembled on the pattern of the imperial government. Certainly it is true that we know what we know from the early centuries of the Church because of the labors of secretaries and archivists. This points to another distinction of the archive from the library: with the Church as the trustee of extensive landholdings, its archives would normally have incorporated deeds, contracts, and other documents of a purely legal rather than a scholarly nature. The modern distinction between judicial and ecclesiastical spheres of influence (and the types of documentation associated with such activity) was unknown in such a setting. (Note how frequently even today people have recourse to parish records in the process of seeking, for example, genealogical information.) As an indication of how important this gradually became, it is noteworthy that regulations on the standards for archives appear in the Council of Trent (1545–1563) as well as in the edicts of Clement VIII (1592–1605), Paul V (1605–1621), and Benedict XIII (1724–1730). These directives dealt with what sort of institutions (e.g., churches, seminaries, monasteries, and hospitals) would be expected to document their activities and what sort of papers ought to be preserved. Directions are given on what sort of locks will provide adequate security (Fink, 1967). Although these regulations did not take shape until the 18th century, this delay indicates the recognition that much had been lost, or at least loosely attended to, in the absence of such requirements.

What was finally stipulated was both universal and comprehensive: the local parish bore responsibility to keep close records of those baptized, confirmed, married, and deceased and the local diocese all correspondence from the bishop to the diocesan, provincial, metropolitan, and national levels of administration.

In the case of monastic archives, we can assume that a similar pattern was followed, with an addition that was to have far-reaching effects: the scriptorium, or writing place:

> The *scriptorium* was under the care of the precentor or else of one of his assistants called the *armarius*, whose duty it was to provide all the requisites needed by the scribes, such as desks, ink, parchment, pens, pen-knives, pumice-stone for smoothing down the surface of the parchment, awls to make the guiding marks for ruling lines, reading-frames for the books to be copied, etc. Most of these were manufactured on the premises: thus at Westminster the ink was made by the precentor himself, and he had to do it in the tailor's shop. The rules of the scriptorium varied in different monasteries, but artificial light was forbidden for fear of injury to the manuscripts, and silence was always enforced. As a general rule those of the

> monks who possessed skill as writers made this their chief, if not their sole active work. (Huddleston, "Scriptorium," 1907)

By adding scriptoria, abbeys such as Monte Cassino saw to it that not only its own records but earlier, often fragmentary portions of classical literature as well were saved from obscurity. "A medieval monastery was often rich in archives, containing rare manuscripts, beautiful chirographs, paintings, precious metalware, and documents pertaining to the rights of a people, the privileges of kings, and treaties between nations" (Hayes, 1907). Centuries after Benedict's death (c. 550), when the site was restored,

> the abbey's reputation reached its zenith, however, during the reign of Abbot Desiderius, who ruled from 1058 until 1087, when he was elected pope under the title of Victor III. Under this abbot, the most famous of all the series after St. Benedict himself, the number of monks rose to over two hundred, and the school of copyists and miniature painters became famous throughout the West. (Hayes, 1907)

Writing, copying, and careful preservation had a similar if somewhat more urgent place in later communities much farther West:

> A Celtic monastery consisted of a group of beehive cells around a central church or oratory, the other principal buildings being the common refectory or kitchen, the library or *scriptorium*, the abbot's house, and the guesthouse. Adamnan, after Columba himself the brightest ornament of the School of Iona, in his 'Life' of the founder, makes explicit references to the *tabulae*, waxen tablets for writing; to the pens and styles, *graphia* and *calami*, and to the ink-horn, *cornicula atramenti*, to be found in the *scriptorium*. (Healy, 1907)

The 20th century has witnessed both the worst and the best of times for monastic archival collections. Fink (1967) has noted that although the Holy See had created in the 1920s a commission on putting Italy's ecclesiastical archives in order, the effects of World War II were nothing short of catastrophic (perhaps especially the destruction of Monte Cassino). In the first decade of this century, an observer there could say that "the archives (*archivium*), besides a vast number of documents relating to the history of the abbey, contains some 1,400 manuscript codices chiefly patristic and historical, many of which are of the greatest value. The library contains a fine collection of modern texts and *apparatus criticus*, which is always most courteously put at the disposal of scholars who come to work on the manuscripts." Some of the latter were saved.

It is fair to say that such disasters have at least served to heighten awareness of the fragility and the irreplaceability of these resources, and diligent effort in the decades since the war has been evident. The great irony is that in technologies that had been predicted to bring the demise of the written document, archives found an unexpected ally. Not only have microforming initiatives had the effect of providing a more durable "backup" to deteriorating texts (see especially the *Hill Monastic Manuscript Collection* at St. John's Abbey, Collegeville, Minnesota), but the World Wide Web has served to provide digital images of these originals accessible in a manner that would have been unimaginable only a decade ago. Thus, the end of the second millennium heralds what might be the most exciting and dynamic era yet witnessed for the rich legacy of monastic archives.

DAVID STEWART

*See also* Bobbio, Italy; Celtic Monasticism; Collegeville, Minnesota; Echternach, Luxembourg; Humanism, Christian; Internet: Buddhist and Christian; Ireland; Libraries: Western Christian; Manuscript Production: Christian; Maurists; Monte Cassino, Italy; Scholars, Benedictine

**Further Reading**

"Archives," in *The New Schaff-Herzog Encyclopedia of Religious Knowledge*, volume 1, edited by Samuel Macauley Jackson et al., New York and London: Funk and Wagnalls, 1908

Bréhier, Luois, "Manuscripts," in *The Catholic Encyclopedia*, volume 9, edited by Charles George Herbermann et al., New York: Appleton, and London: Caxton, 1907

Collinson, Patrick, et al., editors, *A History of Canterbury Cathedral*, Oxford and New York: Oxford University Press, 1995

Fink, K.A., "Archives," in *New Catholic Encyclopedia*, volume 1, New York: McGraw-Hill, 1967

Hayes, P.J., "Archives, Ecclesiastical," in *The Catholic Encyclopedia*, volume 1, edited by Charles George Herbermann et al., New York: Appleton, and London: Caxton, 1907

Healy, John, "Iona," in *The Catholic Encyclopedia*, volume 8, edited by Charles George Herbermann et al., New York: Appleton, and London: Caxton, 1907

Huddleston, G. Roger, "Benedict of Nursia," in *The Catholic Encyclopedia*, volume 2, edited by Charles George Herbermann et al., New York: Appleton, and London: Caxton, 1907

Huddleston, G. Roger, "Scriptorium," in *The Catholic Encyclopedia*, volume 13, edited by Charles George Herbermann et al., New York: Appleton, and London: Caxton, 1907

Kekumano, C.A., "Archives, Ecclesiastical," in *New Catholic Encyclopedia*, volume 1, New York: McGraw-Hill, 1967

Krause, Martin, "Archives," in *The Coptic Encyclopedia*, volume 1, edited by Aziz Suryal Atiya, New York: Macmillan, 1991

Minnich, Nelson H., et al., editors, *Studies in Catholic History: In Honor of John Tracy Ellis*, Wilmington, Delaware: Glazier, 1985

Plante, Julian G., editor, *Checklist of Manuscripts Microfilmed for the Hill Monastic Manuscript Library*, Collegeville, Minnesota: Hill Monastic Manuscript Library, 1900

Rosenthal, Joel T., editor, *Medieval Women and the Sources of Medieval History*, Athens: University of Georgia Press, 1990

Sommerfeldt, John R., and Francis R. Swietek, editors, *Studiosorum speculum: Studies in Honor of Louis J. Lekai, O. Cist.* (Cistercian Studies Series, number 141), Kalamazoo, Michigan: Cistercian Publications, 1993

Stuard, Susan Mosher, editor, *Women in Medieval History and Historiography* (The Middle Ages), Philadelphia: University of Pennsylvania Press, 1987

**Related Web Sites**

*http://www.csbsju.edu/hmml/resources/resource.html* ("Hill Monastic Manuscript Library Resources")

*http://www.byu.edu/~hurlbut/dsciptorum/* ("DSciptorum")

*http://www.georgetown.edu/labyrinth/subjects/mss.htm* ("Manuscripts, Paleography, Codicology")

*http://rsl.ox.ac.uk/imacat.html* ("Bodleian Library: Towards an Image Catalog")

*http://metalab.unc.edu/expo/vatican.exhibit/exhibit/History.html* ("Vatican Library")

# Arhat

The word *arhat* is a Sanskrit term (Pāli, *arahant*) that means "being worthy" or "deserving." Someone is an arhat if, according to Theravāda Buddhism, he or she has attained *nibbāna*. It should be noted that the term *arhat* has been translated as "foe destroyer" (*dgra-bcom-pa*) by Tibetan Buddhists, who viewed it as a formation of the two Sanskrit words *ari* (enemy) and *han* (to strike, destroy). Although philologically speaking this translation is wrong, the idea that it conveys is quite exact, as attainment of *nibbāna* involves destruction of one's real enemies, that is, ignorance and the craving for existence. As such this spiritual ideal is valid for all Buddhists.

Because the Buddha abstained from designating a successor to lead the community of monks after his death, it appears that very early in their history Buddhists felt a need to declare who was entitled to impart and explain the teachings of their spiritual founder. For example, the story of the first council tells us that at some point only the arhat had this right: indeed, Ānanda, who had followed the Buddha for most of his teaching career, still had to become an arhat to be part of this council. Thus, in early Buddhism the problem of spiritual authority became closely linked to that of the nature of the arhat.

According to the Mahāsaṅghika, the first important schism of the Buddhist community occurred around 386 B.C. in relation to what constitute the signs of arhathood. It appears that a certain monk, recognized as arhat because of his wisdom, showed signs of weakness that called into question his status and consequently his authority. The controversy that arose from this event is better known as "The Five Points of Mahādeva." A monk of Pātaliputra, named Mahādeva, came to question the ideal of the arhat as it had been presented up to that time. Likely with the intention of rendering this ideal more accessible, he pretended that the arhat had five weak points. The first point advocated the idea that an arhat could be seduced by another; that is, he could have nocturnal emissions caused by erotic dreams. What the Mahāsaṅghika asserted here is the fact that the body of the arhat is still subject to natural emissions of fluid, such as sweat and semen. The Theravādin (Sthavira) objected to this view by saying that semen is not comparable to other bodily emissions in that it is exclusively the result of passion and thus is contradictory to the nature of the arhat's spiritual accomplishment.

The second, third, and fourth points raised by Mahādeva dealt with the omniscience of the arhat. The Mahāsaṅghika defended the view that an arhat can be subject to ignorance, have doubts, and be instructed by others. Their basic argument was that one should distinguish between ignorance (ajñāna) concerning matters of daily life, such as the names of people, and ignorance (avidyā) that keeps one in the cycle of births and deaths. The Sthavira did not accept this distinction and argued that any limitation to the arhat's omniscience diminishes his spiritual perfection. The fifth point, which seems somewhat enigmatic, proposed that entry into the Buddhist way may be accompanied by a sound, such as "Oh, sorrow!" According to Lamotte (1958) this last point might be related to what became an important controversy within Buddhism, that is, whether entry into the spiritual path is gradual or whether it is sudden. Indirectly the notion that the fully renunciate life of the arhat is the only means of enlightenment is here being challenged. To a certain extent the five points taken together can be viewed as some sort of manifesto promoting laypeople's aspirations to spiritual rights.

The five points raised by Mahādeva also attest to the development of two tendencies that do not necessarily exclude one group of Buddhists or another as regards the nature of the arhat. The first tendency is to view the arhat as a human being who, despite his spiritual accomplishment, remains subject to certain weaknesses. For example, one weakness that divided the different schools of Buddhism was the possibility for the arhat to regress from the state of arhathood. The second tendency is to regard the arhat as a superhuman being endowed with special powers, such as walking through walls and flying in the air. Some sects even argued that everything about the arhat, including his body and what came out of it, was pure. This second tendency most likely is responsible for the development of a cult devoted to the arhat in modern Buddhist countries. For example, in Burma and northern Thailand festivals begin with offerings to Upagupta, an arhat believed to bring prosperity and good fortune for those who petition him. Arhats such as Upagupta, because of their spiritual achievement and fields of merit, are considered sources of magical and protective powers. It is to be noted that such powers per se were never contested by the Buddhists throughout their history; rather the contested question was whether the powers were attributable to the arhat. It appears that those who viewed the arhat as a human being were responsible for the development of devotion to the buddhas and the bodhisattvas on whom devotees conferred a supernatural nature. It is perhaps in relation to this question that one should look for the causes of the shift of attention from the arhat to the bodhisattva ideal that occurred within Buddhism. There is no need to attribute it to an essential difference in terms of spiritual achievement. In other words, if for the Mahāyāna Buddhists the

bodhisattva ideal became superior to that of the arhat, this is due not, as is wrongly assumed, to what an aspirant does as a human being but rather to what he becomes as a supernatural being. In this respect the Theravādin, with their great arhats, can certainly match the compassionate bodhisattvas of Mahāyāna Buddhism.

FRANCIS BRASSARD

*See also* Body: Buddhist Perspectives; Buddhism: Overview; Buddhist Schools/Traditions: South Asia; Burma (Myanmar); Councils, Buddhist; Disciples, Early Buddhist; Hermits: Buddhist; Holy Men/Holy Women: Buddhist Perspectives; Mahāpajāpatī Gotamī; Mahāyāna; Origins: Comparative Perspectives; Thailand

## Further Reading

Bareau, André, "Les controverses relatives à la nature de l'Arhant dans le Bouddhisme ancien," *Indo-Iranian Journal* (1957)

Gombrich, Richard, *Theravāda Buddhism: A Social History from Ancient Benares to Modern Colombo* (Library of Religious Beliefs and Practices), London and New York: Routledge and Kegan Paul, 1988

Horner, Isaline B., *The Early Buddhist Theory of Man Perfected*, London: Williams and Norgate, 1936

Katz, Nathan, *Buddhist Images of Human Perfection*, Delhi: Motilal Banarsidass, 1982; 2nd edition, 1989

Lamotte, Etienne, *Histoire du Bouddhisme indien* (Bibliothèque du Muséon, 43), Louvain: Publications Universitaires, Institut Orientaliste, 1958

Walshe, Maurice, translator, *Thus Have I Heard: The Long Discourses of the Buddha Dīgha Nikāya* (Wisdom Intermediate Book), London: Wisdom, 1987

# Armenia

Although the history of monasticism in Armenia has yet to be written, the importance of monasticism for Armenian culture and letters cannot be overstated. It was the monks who, although they were not the only educated class, served as scholars, teachers, and leaders of the intellectual life in Armenia. It was they who preserved the cultural heritage during long years of war and persecution, and it was they whose great intellectual and artistic activity stimulated Armenia's rise to intellectual, political, and artistic prominence during the period of the Crusades. Finally, their work still shapes the cultural life of the Armenian Church today.

The origins of monasticism in fourth-century Armenia, like the growth of Christianity within its borders, show traces of two separate influences: Greek and Syrian. The early historians Koriwn – Łazar P'arpec'i, the *Buzandaran Patmut'iwnk'*, John Mandakuni, and a collection of homilies attributed to Gregory Lusavorich (the Illuminator), known as the *Yačaxapatum* – all bear witness that in the southern regions of Armenia were found numerous solitaries who lived that singular, rigorous eremitic life that was associated especially with early monasticism as it developed in Syria, remarkable for its resoluteness as much as its stark and severe extremes. Ełišē, one of Armenia's most illustrious historians, has left a brief description of these hermits who lived in individual cells with minimal clothing and who otherwise were completely subject to the elements and to the terrain they inhabited and ceaselessly engaged in night-long vigils. Although their numbers gradually diminished, hermits living such lives can be found in Armenian sources as late as the 10th and 11th centuries. However, in the northern and central parts of Armenia sources suggest that monasticism developed according to a more regulated, organized cenobitic pattern generally associated with Eustathius of Sebaste (c. 300–after 377), the friend of Basil of Caesarea (c. 330–379). As far as can be discerned, the development of Armenian monasticism from this initial stage normally followed the pattern set out by Basil, whose rules survive in numerous manuscripts and were plainly used in Armenian monasteries. This monastic development probably began to appear in the late fourth or early fifth century and not in the early fourth century, as claimed in the anachronistic account of Zenob of Glak, *History of Tarōn*, who attributed the impetus to Leontius of Caesarea.

Records concerning monasticism in Armenia during the fifth to eighth centuries are relatively sparse (often little more than a mention of this or that monk) as Armenia was embroiled in fierce religious battles with neighboring Persia, which sought to bring Armenia back to its Zoroastrian practices, with only a brief respite before the beginning of the Arab invasions in the seventh century. Nevertheless the foundation of a monastery by Tatul in the area of Aršarunik was succeeded by a monastery school that seems to have lasted into the 13th century. During this period the monastery of Makenis near Lake Sevan was founded, as were several others. It is rather startling that during this period Armenian monks seem to have made an impact on various forms of monastic life outside of Armenia. Although the number has been disputed, a seventh-century text of Anastas Vardapet lists over 70 Armenian monasteries in the environs of Jerusalem alone, and Armenians are often mentioned in early monks' lives and histories in both Greek and Syrian traditions, for example, in John Moschus' (c. 550–619/34) *Spiritual Meadow*, Cyril of Scythopolis' (b. c. 525) *Lives of the Monks of Palestine* (including Euthymius himself), and John of Ephesus' (c. 507–580) *Lives of the Eastern Saints*.

It is not until the period of the Bagratids, beginning in the late ninth century subsequent to the initial wave of Arab invasions, that a notable surge of interest took place in monasticism and monastic life. During this period it was monastic life that determined the direction of the Armenian Church. From this time until the 14th century, the building of monasteries and the number of persons entering the monastic life increased greatly. In the period between 874 and 953 alone, more than 20 monasteries were established throughout greater Armenia. Many of these monasteries were built near cities, villages, or castles of the nobles. The *Universal History* of Stephen of Tarōn, known also as Asołik, is an important source for the names and locations of a great number of monasteries founded during this period. These include the monastery of Narek, located south of Lake Van,

which became famous for being home to Armenia's most famous medieval religious poet, Gregory of Narek (c. 950–c. 1010), and the monastery of Gladzor, renowned for its intellectual life and its manuscript illuminations. In the 13th and 14th centuries, Gladzor was the crown of Armenian monasteries, producing such renowned churchmen as Esayi of Nich, John of Orotn, and especially Gregory of Tat'ew, perhaps the most famous of all Armenian teachers. All the teachers from Gladzor who went to teach in other parts of Armenia until the 17th century traced their intellectual lineage back to Gregory. Gladzor was also famous at this time for its manuscript illuminators, such as T'oros of Tarōn and Awag. In the northern regions of Armenia were also founded such famous monasteries as Hałbat and Sanahin. In the province of Siwnik' alone, the 13th-century historian Step'annos Ōrbēlean provides such a long list of monasteries, arranged by the cantons in which they are located, that the list makes up one of the longest chapters in his *History of Siwnik'*.

Although some of these monasteries survived for several centuries, many monks were forcibly evacuated during the Seljuk invasions of the 11th to 14th centuries. A few monks, such as those of Gladzor, simply relocated, whereas most others fled into Asia Minor, especially around Taurus and Cilicia, and began new monasteries there. This move unleashed a certain renewal of Armenian monasticism as many of these Cilician monasteries rose to great heights and won renown for their learning (boasting such figures as Nerses of Lambron, Nerses Shnorhali [the Graceful], and George of Skewra) as well as for their skill in manuscript production and illumination, most notably by such figures as T'oros Roslin and Sargis Picak.

Although monasticism in Armenia was mainly of a cenobitic type, the life of a monk involved both physical sacrifice and intellectual activity. Armenian monasteries tended to be walled enclosures with the monks' cells within the walls. Lashed by the harsh weather of the Armenian plains and mountains of the Caucasus, the monks were forced to live lives of great austerity. The ruins of many of these monasteries are still visible today and bear eloquent witness to how harsh such a life must have been. The intellectual regimen of the monks consisted of rigorous study of the great theological tradition. Above all, this consisted of study of the Bible, which also included patristic commentaries on the biblical books. In some monasteries (e.g., in Gladzor) one finds also a number of works of Aristotle and of Philo (c. 20 B.C.–A.D. 50), the famous Jewish philosopher of Alexandria, along with the only known surviving commentaries on his work.

A final but no less important phase of Armenian monasticism arose with the figure of Mekhitar of Sebaste (1676–1749), an Armenian Catholic who fled west to escape persecution by his Apostolic compatriots and who, with the permission of Rome, formed the Mekhitarist Order and founded a monastery on the island of St. Lazarus (San Lazzaro) off the shore of the Lido, Venice. A group of these monks later left and founded another Mekhitarist monastery in Vienna. Both of these monasteries are still functioning (although not as they once did) and are widely admired for the great learning of their monks and for their production of texts and studies in Armenian history and literature.

In the 18th and 19th centuries, the monastery in Venice produced hundreds of editions of Armenian texts, a number of important studies, and a dictionary of classical Armenian that is still unsurpassed. Both these monasteries have their own printing presses and still publish journals important for the study of Armenian history and literature. Throughout the history of the Armenian Church, monks were eager to pass on their learning to all who would be taught, and this learning remains the boast of Armenia today.

EDWARD G. MATHEWS, JR.

See also Architecture: Armenian Monasteries; Basil the Great, St.; Egypt; Israel/Palestine; Jerusalem, Israel; Origins: Eastern Christian; Syria; Women's Monasteries: Eastern Christian

**Further Reading**

Amadouni, Garabed, "Le rôle historique des hiéromoines arméniens," in Il monachesimo orientali, Atti del Convegno di Studi Orientali (Orientalia Christiana Analecta, 153), Rome: Pontifical Oriental Institute, 1985

Catholic Church, Disciplina Armena, volume 2: Monachismo: Studio Storico-Canonico e Fonti Canoniche (Codificazione Canonica Orientale. Fonti Serie 2-Fascicolo 12), Venice: St. Lazarus, 1940

Leloir, Dom Louis, "Le moine selon la tradition arménienne," in Armeniaca: Mélanges d'études arméniennes, Venice: St. Lazarus, 1969

Maksoudian, Fr. Krikor H., "The Religion of Armenia," in Treasures in Heaven, edited by Thomas F. Mathews and Roger S. Wieck, New York: Pierpont Morgan Library, 1994

Mécérian, Jean, Histoire et Institutions de l'église arménienne: Évolution nationale et doctrinale, Spiritualité-Monachisme (Recherches de l'Institut de Lettres Orientales de Beyrouth, 30), Beirut: Imprimerie Catholique, 1965

Sanjian, Avedis K., "Anastas Vardapet's List of Armenian Monasteries in Seventh-Century Jeruslaem: A Critical Examination," Le Muséon 82 (1969)

Sanjian, Avedis K., "The Monastery and School of Glajor," in Armenian Gospel Iconography: The Tradition of the Glajor Gospel (Dumbarton Oaks Studies, 29), edited by Sanjian and Thomas F. Mathews, Washington, D.C.: Dumbarton Oaks Research Library and Collection, 1991

Thierry, Jean Michel, Patrick Donabédian, and Nicole Thierry, Armenian Art, translated by Célestine Dars, New York: Abrams, 1989

Thierry, Jean Michel, Églises et couvents du Karabagh (Materiaux pour l'archéologie arménienne, 3. Publication du prix littéraire Kevork Melitinetsi, no. 26), Antelias, Lebanon: Catholicossat Arménien de Cilicie, 1991

Thierry, Michel, Répertoire des monastères Arméniens (Corpus Christianorum), Turnhout: Brepols, 1993

# Arts, Buddhist. *See* Visual Arts, Buddhist

# Arts, Christian. *See* Visual Arts, Eastern Christian: Painting; Visual Arts, Western Christian

# Arts, Zen. *See* Zen, Arts of

# Asaṅga fourth century A.D.

Mahāyāna Buddhist monk, scholar, and founder of Yogācāra school

Although various specific dates are offered for the life of Asaṅga, it is generally agreed that he flourished during the latter half of the fourth century A.D. He was born in the city of Puruṣapura (modern-day Peshawar) in northwestern India (now Pakistan).

What we know of Asaṅga's life comes mostly from the legendlike histories by Bu-ston and Tāranātha. The most authoritative historical source is that by Paramārtha, although the latter account addresses itself mainly to a biography of Vasubandhu, Asaṅga's younger half brother.

Within Mahāyāna Buddhism, Asaṅga is revered for having successfully demonstrated that the Mahāyāna represents genuine Buddha Dharma (against certain Hīnayāna arguments that the Mahāyāna was the creation of heretics); for founding the Mahāyāna school variously known as the Yogācāra, or Cittamātra, system of thought; and for establishing several Mahāyāna vihāras, or monasteries (perhaps as many as 25), all of which achievements are said to have caused a complete rejuvenation of the Mahāyāna in India.

At an early age Asaṅga went for ordination as a Buddhist monk. Although he initially joined the Sarvāstivādin (Hīnayānist) sect, before fully embracing the Mahāyāna he belonged for many years to the sect known as the Mahīśāsakas, famed for its great emphasis on meditation. Such early training was to leave a profound impression on Asaṅga. Under a teacher named Piṇḍola, Asaṅga studied both Hīnayāna and early Mahāyāna scriptures, notably the "Perfection of Wisdom" discourses, or prajñāpāramitā-sūtras. When he had difficulty comprehending the latter texts, Piṇḍola gave him a certain initiation, and Asaṅga set out to obtain clear instruction directly from his tutelary deity, the so-called Buddha of the future, Lord Maitreya. Here begins the most famous chapter in the life of Asaṅga. It is a story that is well known to every devout Mahāyānist. The great saint is said to have retreated to a mountain cave where for many years he strove in his meditations to have a vision of Lord Maitreya. Despairing of his unsuccessful attempts to glimpse Maitreya, Asaṅga several times abandoned his meditations, only to return to them after witnessing some other examples of fortitude and assiduity. After 12 years had elapsed with no signs of success, Asaṅga decided to abandon his practice

completely and, utterly disappointed, left his cave. On the outskirts of a town, he found a dog who had the lower part of its
body eaten by worms. Asaṅga became filled with compassion,
and just as he stooped to offer his own flesh to relieve the dog's
suffering, the image of the dog suddenly disappeared. In its place
Asaṅga beheld the Lord Maitreya, full of light.

Thereafter, it is said, Maitreya took Asaṅga with him up to
the Tuṣita heaven and there taught him five revolutionary new
"books":

1. the *Abhisamayālaṃkāra*, a treatise on the Perfection of
   Wisdom sūtras and practices
2. the *Madhyāntavibhāga*, or "The Discrimination of the
   Middle from the Extremes"
3. the *Dharmadharmatavibhāga*, or "Discrimination of
   dharmas and their true nature"
4. the *Mahāyānasūtrālaṃkāra*, or "The Ornament of the
   Mahāyāna Sūtras" and
5. the *Uttaratantra*, a treatise on the *tathāgatagarbha*, or
   the doctrine of "Buddha nature."

When Asaṅga's studies with the future Buddha Maitreya (or
with an actual historical person named Maitreya) were completed, he returned to the human realm and straight away set to
work for the benefit of beings. From this time forward
Maitreyanātha (i.e., one devoted to Maitreya) becomes the main
epithet associated with Asaṅga and his written works.

Asaṅga's first acts were to establish a number of monastic
abodes, the number of which is estimated to have been at least
25. While residing and teaching in one of these *vihāra*s, later
known as the Dharmāṅkara *vihāra* (namely, the "monastery
from which the Dharma again sprouted"), Asaṅga set down in
writing his profound understanding of the Buddha's teachings.
First, with the help of students, he put into written form the
"Five Books" dictated by Maitreya. Then he settled into composing his own treatises. A work attributed directly to him was
the *Abhidharmasamuccaya*, a brief compendium of the Abhidharma. This work was probably followed by Asaṅga's summary of Mahāyāna practice, the *Mahāyānasaṃgraha*. Finally,
and most important, Asaṅga began work on the *Yogācārabhūmi*, a mammoth encyclopedic work on "The Stages of Practice of (Buddhist) Yoga." The first division of the latter work is
further divided into 17 separate volumes, each called a *bhūmi*,
or "stage" (of the Buddhist Path), and the 15th among these, the
*Bodhisattvabhūmi*, almost immediately became a renowned Mahāyāna Buddhist treatise in its own right. Indeed when he had
completed the *Bodhisattvabhūmi*, Asaṅga's fame as a master expounder of the Mahāyāna spread far and wide.

Even as he completed these major treatises, Asaṅga continued
to instruct a great many *śrāvaka*s, or "Hearers" (monks of the
Hīnayāna tradition) in the doctrine of the Mahāyāna. One of his
most famous converts to the Mahāyāna was his half brother Vasubandhu, who for many years had been a main proponent of
the Hīnayāna. Asaṅga not only converted Vasubandhu but also
adopted him as his student. By doing so Asaṅga gained a cham-

pion of philosophical debate who would later compose influential texts for the new school that his brother was founding, the
Yogācāra. Because of Asaṅga's great erudition, he also came to
the attention of a king named Gambhirapaksa. That king became a royal patron to Asaṅga, and with his help Asaṅga
founded more monasteries. Thereafter the Mahāyāna once again
took root and flourished in India.

It is said that although the Mahāyāna had long before spread
in India, prior to Asaṅga's preaching it had declined. Some of the
monks could recite Mahāyāna sūtras but without understanding
their meaning. Tāranātha's account says that "even during the
time of the most extensive spread of the Mahāyāna, the number
of Mahāyāna monks did not reach ten thousand" and that "even
in the days of Nāgārjuna, most of the monks were śrāvakas."
However, because of Asaṅga's teachings and writings, during his
own lifetime the number of Mahāyāna monks reached "tens of
thousands." Thus Asaṅga is revered as the foremost expounder
of the Mahāyāna doctrine and as the compassionate instigator
of its rejuvenation.

Working together, Asaṅga and Vasubandhu fashioned the
characteristic ideas of the Yogācāra school. However, whereas
Vasubandhu was mainly a theoretician, Asaṅga's writings were
rooted in the practice of meditative trance. Accordingly "Yogācāra" means the "practice of yoga" and refers to the bodhisattva's path of meditative development. Although many
scholars normally view the two main schools of Mahāyāna
thought – namely, the Mādhyamika founded by Nāgārjuna and
the Yogācāra founded by Asaṅga – as being nearly antithetical,
ultimately the ideas constituting the two schools are not so different. Both had Buddhahood as their goal, both took the Perfection of Wisdom sūtras as their philosophical base, and both
saw themselves as preserving the Buddhist ideal of the "Middle
Way." The difference lies in the emphases and methods of practice advocated by each. Yogācārins emphasized *samādhi*, or
meditative concentration (the withdrawal of the mind from
sensory phenomena), as the means to accomplish liberation. In contrast, Mādhyamikas emphasized, through rigorous
philosophical dialectics, the doctrine of *śūnyatā*, or the "emptiness" (of independent existence) of all phenomena. The Mādhyamikas criticized the Yogācārins for tending toward
substantialism (of mind, or consciousness), and the Yogācārins
criticized the Mādhyamikas for tending toward nihilism.
Asaṅga's Yogācāra is generally (although erroneously) viewed as
propounding a form of philosophical idealism. Although some
Yogācārin texts might sound "idealist," Asaṅga was clearly
aware that consciousness too is ultimately "empty" of independent existence, and a detailed examination of his works shows
this.

In addition to its emphasis on meditative cultivation, the Yogācāra school introduced to Mahāyāna Buddhist philosophical
literature several important new tenets and theories. For example, it was the Yogācārins who introduced the theory of the
"three bodies of a Buddha," namely, that a Buddha possesses
three kinds of bodies, or *kāya*s: a *Nirmāṇakāya*, or magically emanated body in which to instruct ordinary beings; a

*Saṃbhogakāya*, or mystical enjoyment body in which to instruct advanced bodhisattvas during meditative trance; and a *Dharmakāya*, or ineffable truth-body. The Yogācāra also developed the so-called three-natures doctrine as a fuller description of the Buddhist two-truths theory. In addition, as a means of explaining how it is that ordinary beings become attached to worldly phenomena and thus prolong their suffering, the Yogācārins propounded the notion of the *ālayavijñāna*, or "store consciousness," as part of a sophisticated epistemological-psychological model for detailing the evolution of consciousness that creates the seeming reality of the subject-object duality.

JANICE D. WILLIS

*See also* Discourses (Sūtras): Mahāyāna; Japan: History; Mahāyāna; Nālandā, India; Tibetan Lineages: Gelukpa

## Biography

A pivotal figure in the emergence of the Mahāyāna, Asaṅga is known from legends about him and his half-brother Vasubandhu. As a scholar-monk active in the late fourth century A.D., Asaṅga (whose name means "without attachment") was born in what is now Peshawar. He and his half-brother formulated the basic ideas of what became the Yogācāra school. Five books ascribed to him were supposedly dictated by the bodhisattva Maitreya. Other works won acclaim for masterful exposition.

## Major Works

*Abhidharmasamuccaya* (Compendium of Abhidharma)
*Mahāyānasaṃgraha* (Compendium of the Greater Vehicle)
*Yogācārabhūmi* (Stages of Practice of Yoga)

## Further Reading

Bu-ston, Rin-chen-grub, *History of Buddhism Chos hbyung*, 2 vols., translated by Eugène Obermiller, Heidelberg: Harrassowitz, 1931
Paramārtha, *The Life of Vasubandhu*, translated by J. Takakusu, T'oung-pao, 1904
Rahula, Walpola, " Asaṅga," in *Encyclopaedia of Buddhism*, volume 2, Colombo: Government of Ceylon, 1966
Tāranātha, *History of Buddhism in India*, edited by Debiprasad Chattopadhyaya, translated by Lama Chimpa, Simla: Indian Institute of Advanced Study, 1970
Willis, Janice D., *On Knowing Reality: The Tattvārtha Chapter of Asaṅga's Bodhisattvabhūmi*, New York: Columbia University Press, 1979

# Asceticism: Buddhist Perspectives

Buddhist attitudes toward asceticism have changed and taken interesting twists in both doctrine and practice. Although within Indian Buddhism asceticism never became prominent, various later Buddhist traditions, especially in Japan, emphasized ascetic practices. This article examines various manifestations of Buddhist asceticism and weighs the changing perspectives within Buddhist communities toward asceticism as a form of religious training.

Nachi Falls on the Kii Peninsula, Japan, is famous for acts of asceticism. It was a major site of Buddhist-Shinto syncretism during the Kamakura period (1185–1333).
Photo courtesy of David Moore

*Indian Buddhist Asceticism*

The Sanskrit term *tāpasa* designated an ascetic. Its root *tap* meant "heating," "burning," and "consuming by fire." The term also meant "tormenting" oneself by subjecting oneself to suffering. In the Indian religious context, extreme austerities undertaken for achieving religious or magical goals were referred to as *tapas*. Ascetic practices were undertaken as a means of salvation, and their moral dimensions became evident when *tapas* involved the disciplining of the senses.

In India the ascetic practices pertained mainly to non-Buddhist schools. Buddhist texts often referred to non-Buddhist ascetic practices and gave accounts of their austerities. Non-Buddhist ascetics believed that purity and emancipation could be obtained by self-mortification alone. Although Śākyamuni Buddha disapproved extreme asceticism, he lifted the common usage of *tapas* out of its magical and mechanical background by transforming its meaning so as to bear a moral and spiritual sense. In this process, although *tapas* was redefined to indicate moral self-discipline in Buddhism, it was difficult to extirpate its original meaning of self-mortification.

Both positive and negative attitudes toward asceticism prevailed in Indian Buddhism. Although Śākyamuni disapproved asceticism, in later times asceticism crept back into Buddhism to a limited extent. According to traditional accounts Śākyamuni practiced severe austerities during his seven-year search for religious truth. In the *Mahāsīhanāda Sutta* (M.I.77–82), the Buddha recounts to Sāriputta the way he had practiced austerities in vainly striving to attain Buddhahood. Once he realized the futility of both severe ascetic practices and extreme indulgence of sensuality, he renounced both forms of extreme practices and recommended the middle path to religious liberation. This realization by Śākyamuni ranks as a great feat in India's search for religious awakening. In the strict sense Indian Buddhism opposed extreme asceticism and discouraged such practices. In the *Saṃyutta Nikāya* (IV.338), the Buddha condemned asceticism by asserting that an ascetic tortures him- or herself to excess, attains no profitable state, and realizes no knowledge and insight.

However, even within the Buddha's lifetime certain prominent disciples recommended severe forms of asceticism. For example, the controversial Devadatta, Buddha's cousin, after proposing a rigid and austere way of life for the Buddhist monastic, requested the Buddha to approve the Five Points as compulsory rules for all Buddhist monks (Vinaya 2.196–197). The Five Points are as follows: monks should (1) live in the forest, (2) subsist solely on doles collected from door to door, (3) dress themselves in rags picked up from dust heaps, (4) dwell always under a tree and never under a roof, and (5) eat neither fish nor flesh. Whereas Devadatta attempted to give an orthodox dimension to the Buddhist monastic practice, the Buddha rejected Devadatta's five-point proposal because of its severe ascetic nature. The Buddha believed in exercising one's own initiative in religious practice and did not want to subject religious practitioners to unnecessary obligatory rules.

Although the Buddha realized the futility of extreme asceticism, he left some space for those individual followers who were more inclined toward ascetic practices. Although the majority of the Buddhist *saṅgha* led relatively comfortable lives, certain prominent disciples, such as Mahā Kassapa and Subhūti, were keen to practice asceticism and preferred to live in the forest. For such serious practitioners the Buddha allowed the practice of the 13 *dhutaṅga*s (ascetic practices). Whereas the *Majjhima Nikāya* enumerates only nine, the *Vaka Jātaka* (no. 300) refers to 13 *dhutaṅga*s, and Buddhaghosa's *Visuddhimagga* (chap. 2) gives a comprehensive account of them, explaining that the 13 ascetic practices are not a part of the path leading to the eradication of desire but only a preparation for the path. The *dhutaṅga*s that bear ascetic dimensions aim at eliminating all forms of attachment. They are as follows: (1) wearing robes made of rags taken from dust heaps, (2) wearing only the three robes, (3) living on alms alone, (4) begging alms in regular order from house to house without discriminating between rich and poor, (5) eating one session only, (6) eating only from the alms bowl, (7) refusing any extra food after one has gotten one's due share, (8) living in the forest, (9) living at the foot of a tree, (10) living in the open air, (11) living in a cemetery, (12) becoming satisfied with whatever dwelling one gets, and (13) sleeping in a sitting posture.

### Theravāda Buddhist Asceticism

From the very inception of Sri Lankan Theravāda monasticism in the third century B.C., ascetic trends have prevailed within Theravāda practice. Anurādhapura, Sri Lanka's early medieval capital, contained forest groves (*tapōvana*) and monasteries for ascetics (*tāpasārāma*). Whereas the majority lived in temporary huts and stone caves, following the ascetic lifestyle of Mahā Kassapa and Subhūti, some preferred to live in forests and follow the 13 *dhutaṅga*s. Even today Theravāda monastics practice some of the *dhutaṅga*s even though such vows are not compulsory items in Theravāda monasticism. In contemporary Theravāda ascetic dimensions are found in the daily routine of the forest-dwelling (Sinhalese, *vanavāsi*) monastics in Sri Lanka, Thailand, and Burma. Historical documents support the prevalence of forest-dwelling monastic fraternities in ancient Sri Lanka, but in certain periods political unrest within the country weakened the very survival of such forest-dwelling fraternities. Nevertheless at critical times, for example, during the Polonnaruva period (1055–1235), the forest-dwelling fraternity at Diṁbulāgala led the reforms of the *saṅgha* initiated by Parākramabāhu I (1153–1186). Although the modern forest hermitages in Sri Lanka are rather recent, their late origins do not undermine Buddhist religiosity. Buddhist ascetics in the modern forest hermitages are highly respected because they attempt to display virtues and soteriologically efficient religious practices closely associated with asceticism.

### Mahāyāna Buddhist Asceticism

Within several Mahāyāna Buddhist traditions, ascetic practices acquired mystical and esoteric meanings. Nevertheless, asceticism has penetrated into almost all Japanese religious traditions without being limited to the two prominent Japanese esoteric Buddhist schools: Tendai and Shingon.

The Japanese language is rich in terms that convey the meanings of the English term *asceticism*. For example, *shugyō* means "ascetic practices" that are undertaken as spiritual exercises for the attainment of a particular religious goal. *Kugyō* (penance), which was mainly the training method of Indian non-Buddhists, is another category of *shugyō*. Its Sanskrit equivalent was *duṣkara-caryā* (austerity). Ascetic practices have become important aspects of religious training as a method of making one's "suffering" an effective means of attaining a religious goal.

In Japanese Buddhist practice "waterfall austerities" (*taki no gyō*) became popular rituals for purifying one's mind and body. Ablutions under waterfalls became increasingly conceived of as effective ways to get rid of one's evil dust from the secular world. The severe austerities of the 12th-century ascetic priest Mongaku at the Nachi waterfall became a famous model of severe asceticism. Within the Tendai *sennichi kaihōgyō* (The Austerity of

Encircling the Mountain for Thousand Days) practice as well, water asceticism came to play an important purification function. Until he turned 90, Hakozaki Bunno (1892–1992), the 37th *gyōja* (ascetic), arose at 2:00 a.m. to perform the water purification ritual *suigyō* at the two waterfalls at Chōjūin. Sakai Yūsai, the 46th *gyōja*, following his master, Hakozaki, got up at midnight and purified himself at the two waterfalls before departing for his daily *kaihōgyō*.

The Nichiren monks perform a unique "religious austerity" called *aragyō*. Although the Chinese character *ara* means "rough," "fierce," and "wild," as a compound *aragyō* means "asceticism." The *Buddhica* defines *aragyō* as "severe ascetic practices (*hageshī shugyō*) involving the act of secluding oneself in steep mountains and having ablutions in waterfalls for the purpose of accomplishing one's heart's desires." Nichiren monks perform the annual ritual retreat of the *aragyō* for 100 days from 1 November through 10 February at Hokekyōji, Nakayama, Ichikawa City, Chiba Prefecture. Onjuin, the mecca of the *aragyō*, contains the tomb of Nichikiyū (1663–1728), who drafted the rites and rituals of the *aragyō*. Whereas the fierce Fudō-myō-ō is the patron deity of the *sennichi kaihōgyō*, the female deity Kishimojin is the patron of the *aragyō*. Her Indian name is Hārītī; she was the daughter of a *yakṣa* in Rājagṛha. She killed the babies of others to feed her own children, but after encountering the Buddha she converted to Buddhism and vowed to protect it. For easy delivery and good health, Hārītī is invoked; in Japan her images bear a fierce face, and her hands form an *añjali* (salutation).

During the winter retreat of the *aragyō*, the ascetics live within the enclosed ritual space (which is functionally similar to the ecclesiastical *sīma*, or boundary, of the Theravāda tradition) and renounce all contacts with the outside world. By sustaining their lives with coarse clothes, plain food, and no shaving, from dawn until midnight the ascetics purify their bodies by pouring cold water over themselves seven times daily: the ascetics begin the day with the first bath at 3:00 a.m. and then continue the water asceticism at three-hour intervals at 6 a.m., 9 a.m., 12 a.m., 3 p.m., and 6 p.m. The last prayer service of the day is held at 11 p.m. They spend their entire time within the enclosed ritual space reciting the *Lotus Sūtra*, copying Buddhist scriptures, and devoting themselves to pious veneration of sacred scriptures with esoteric significance. More than 170 ascetics participated in the ritual at Hokekyōji in 1998–1999, and they often undertake the *aragyō* several times in their lifetime. The Nichiren school considers this *aragyō* ritual an esoteric practice and avoids any public exposure of it.

Fasting (*danjiki*) is a popular ascetic practice in Japanese Buddhist traditions. The most critical phase of the Tendai *sennichi kaihōgyō* practice centers around an asceticism called *dōiri*, which is constituted with a nine-day fasting (*kokonoka danjiki*). When the ascetic completes the 700th day of the *kaihōgyō*, he enters the period of the *dōiri*. During the nine-day fasting, which actually lasts for 182 hours, the ascetic lives without any food, water, sleep, or rest. This ascetic fasting is designed to bring the *gyōja* face to face with death. Although originally the

*dōiri* lasted for ten days, it was shortened a bit, as almost all ascetics died during the retreat. After the symbolic "last meal" (*saijiki-gi*), the *gyōja* arrives at Myō-ō-dō. While the *gyōja* performs 330 full prostrations, the guests depart, and the doors are sealed. The *gyōja* recites the *Lotus Sūtra* before the altar of Fudo-myo-o at 3:00 a.m., 10:00 a.m., and 5:00 a.m. During this retreat he finishes chanting the entire text of the *Lotus Sūtra*. Every morning at 2:00 a.m., the ascetic performs the *shusui* (water-taking) ritual. Chanting the *Heart Sūtra* he walks to the Aka Well located about 650 feet above Myō-ō-dō. He scoops up two buckets of water, carries them in his shoulders to the main hall, and offers them to the image of Fudō-myō-ō. Apart from this short departure from Myō-ō-dō, he spends the remaining hours sitting in the lotus position and silently recites the Fudō-myō-ō mantra 100,000 times. The *gyōja* Hakozaki Bunno had performed the nine-day fast of no food, water, or rest 36 times to purify himself as a preparation for the New Year.

Although early Buddhist traditions deemphasized the soteriological efficacy of ascetic practices, this attitude did not prevent later Buddhists from developing ascetic rites and rituals. Japanese Buddhist ascetic practice can be viewed as soteriological strategies that were required in the civilizational process of adapting and naturalizing Buddhist doctrines and practices in alien cultures.

MAHINDA DEEGALLE

*See also* Anurādhapura, Sri Lanka; Body: Buddhist Perspectives; Buddha ( Śākyamuni); Buddhism: Overview; Buddhism: Inculturation; Buddhist Schools/Traditions: Japan; Celibacy: Buddhist; Chan/Zen: Japan; Deities, Buddhist; Disciples, Early Buddhist; Dōgen; Fasting: Buddhist; Forest Masters; Fujii, Nichidatsu (Nittatsu); Governance: Buddhist Perspectives; Hermits: Buddhist; Holy Men/Holy Women: Buddhist Perspectives; Japan: History; Mahāyāna; Marathon Monks; Mount Hiei, Japan; Mountain Monasteries, Buddhist; Nation-Building and Japanese Buddhism; Origins: Comparative Perspectives; Spirituality: Buddhist; Tiantai/Tendai: Japan

**Further Reading**

Bhagat, M.G., *Ancient Indian Asceticism*, New Delhi: Munshiram Manoharlal, 1976

Bronkhorst, Johannes, *The Two Sources of Indian Asceticism*, Bern and New York: Peter Lang, 1993

Buddhaghosa, *The Path of Purification (Visuddhimagga)*, translated by Bhikkhu Ñāṇamoli, Colombo: R. Semage, 1956; 2nd edition, Berkeley, California, and London: Shambhala, 1976; 5th Edition, Kandy, Sri Lanka: Buddhist Publication Society, 1991

Carrithers, Michael, "The Modern Ascetics of Lanka and the Pattern of Change in Buddhism," *Man* 14 (1979)

Carrithers, Michael, *The Forest Monks of Sri Lanka: An Anthropological and Historical Study*, Delhi: Oxford, 1983

Doniger, Wendy, *Asceticism and Eroticism in the Mythology of Siva*, London and New York: Oxford University Press, 1973; as *Siva, The Erotic Ascetic*, New York: Oxford University Press, 1981

Eliade, Mircea, *Yoga: Immortality and Freedom*, translated by Willard R. Trask, New York: Pantheon, 1958 (original

French version published in 1954); London: Routledge and Kegan Paul, 1958; 2nd edition, Princeton, New Jersey: Princeton University Press, 1969

Fujita, Shōichi, *Gyō to wa nanika*, Tokyo: Shinchōsha, 1997

Hara, Minoru, "Tapo-dhana," *Acta Asiatica* 19 (1970)

Kaelber, Walter O., "Asceticism," in *The Encyclopedia of Religion*, edited by Mircea Eliade et al., volume 1, New York: Macmillan, 1986; London: Collier Macmillan, 1993

Kloppenborg, Ria, *The Paccekabuddha: A Buddhist Ascetic*, Leiden: E.J. Brill, 1974

*Onjuin*, Nakayama: Onjuin, 1998

Perera, H.R., Yoshirō Tamura, and A.G.S. Kariyawasam, "Ascetic," "Asceticism," and "Ascetic Practices," in *Encyclopaedia of Buddhism: Volume II*, edited by G.P. Malalasekera, Colombo: The Government of Ceylon, 1966

Rhodes, Robert F., "The Kaihōgyō Practice of Mt. Hiei," *Japanese Journal of Religious Studies* 14:2–3 (1987)

Stevens, John, *The Marathon Monks of Mount Hiei*, Boston and New York: Shambhala, 1988; London: Rider, 1989

Yalman, Nur, "The Ascetic Buddhist Monks of Ceylon," *Ethnology* 1 (1962)

# Asceticism: Christian Perspectives

Asceticism, understood as a partial renunciation of bodily needs to obtain spiritual benefits, has been a vital aspect of Christianity throughout its history. Ascetic practices, ranging from simple traditions of fasting and means of prayer to living a life of complete renunciation and self-mortification, spring from an emphasis on the transitory character of this life and the material world as well as from an urge to move from the exterior toward the interior. Christian emphasis falls as well on the fallen status of mankind and on suffering as an inevitable part of the history of salvation. The body, with its natural needs, is on the one hand highly esteemed as God's creation and a participant in the resurrection and eternal life and on the other strongly linked to sin and the domination of evil. To live according to the passions of the body is generally condemned on both ethical and theological grounds. Thus, strategies to control the body are, in most traditions of Christianity, considered an essential part of Christian life.

Historically Christian asceticism has its roots in the New Testament. In the Gospels, Jesus is described with ascetic traits, and his instructions to his disciples are often categorical in calling for renunciation of material goods and personal interests (see, e.g., Matt. 4:1–4, 6:1–34, 8:18–22, 10, 19:16–30 with parallels). The letters of St. Paul and others also strongly emphasize the direction from material to spiritual, from "outer" man to "inner" man, as well as a demand for total dedication to Christ, the Holy Spirit, and the new religious community (see, e.g., 1 Cor. 7:1–11, 25–40, 9:24–27; 2 Cor. 4:16–5:10; Eph. 4:25–5:20; 1 Tim. 2). Recent sociological research on the New Testament verifies the radical renunciatory character of the first Christian communities.

In the first Christian centuries asceticism was connected mainly with the calling to discipleship. Ascetic practices were an essential part of various duties in the congregations and in the spreading of the gospel as witnessed to in early texts, such as the Didache and the Apostolic Tradition. In some early Christian movements, especially in Syria and Asia Minor, renunciation of property (as well as celibacy) was even considered a duty of all believers. Ascetic practices rooted in pagan cults, especially those connected with preparation for initiation into mysteries and revelations through oracles and dreams, also influenced early Christian practice, as did philosophical reflections on how to be liberated from the urges of the body.

With the rise of the monastic tradition in the fourth century, asceticism achieved an institutional setting. Moreover it is in early monastic theology that we find the first outlines of ascetic education, the first instances of a psychological reflection on ascetic experience, and the beginnings of a theological interpretation of asceticism. The earliest monastic texts, such as *The Letters of St. Antony* and other monastic epistles, reflect philosophical notions related to Platonist tradition and the theological legacy of Alexandria known to us through the writings of Clement (c. 150–c. 215) and Origen (c. 185–c. 254). In early monastic narratives, such as the *Life of Antony* and the *Life of Pachomius*, asceticism is taken for granted both as natural to anyone who devotes his life to the quest for God and as witnessed to by the biblical narrative and its saints.

In the *Sayings of the Fathers* (*Apophthegmata Patrum*), thousands of stories and sayings of fourth-century monks are recorded, giving a wide variety of ascetic practice and instruction. Two main features stand out. First, asceticism is closley linked to repentance. Ascetic practice is seen as a sign of remorse, the road that makes it possible to stand in front of God, asking for and receiving forgiveness for one's sin. Second, ascetic practice is a struggle to overcome the passions that separate humans from God, a struggle to achieve spiritual independence and a true life. Here the notions of original nature, created in the image and likeness of God, as well as bodily resurrection, are linked to a transformation of body and soul in this life. The monk spends all his life under the liminal conditions characteristic of repentance and cultic purity, including self-afflicted pain and renunciation of what is otherwise normal.

Reflection on asceticism starts with Evagrius Ponticus (346–399) and the author of the Macarian Homilies. On the basis of his own experience and the teachings of his ascetic masters, Evagrius develops a systematic teaching that includes practical instruction as well as theological analysis. His teaching on ascetic practice involves an investigation into and classification of the various impulses and passions that influence man. The aim is to arm the monk with weapons in his fight to overcome the demons trying to subdue him. In his theological reflection Evagrius, developing the views of Origen, emphasizes the need for development, beginning with the material and practical and passing through a deeper analysis of the nature of things to a vision liberated from all images and notions. The Macarian Homilies, with their use of Syriac traditions, are less philosophical, basing ascetic education mainly on biblical models and an emphasis on personal spiritual experience. Asceticism opens the individual to experience the presence of God.

Although the establishment of monastic institutions under the control of the hierachy gradually put an end to many extreme forms of ascetic practice, some were retained, at least in the East. The most famous of these are stylitism and foolishness in Christ. The first was made famous through Simeon the Stylite in the fifth century and remained a feature of the Eastern Christian tradition until modern times. Here asceticism meant the renunciation not only of property and bodily needs (e.g., food, sleep, and social life) but also of movement, of freedom to act. Standing on a pillar for the rest of his life, the stylite made himself independent of space, placing his body outside society, visible but untouchable. The fools in Christ acted insane, mocking all rules for social behavior, thus making it evident that everything considered valuable in this world was actually an obstacle to spiritual life.

In the Eastern Christian tradition, asceticism has remained an important feature not only within monasticism but also in the life of ordinary Christians. On the one hand fasting is linked to the ritual life both as preparation for important feasts and as preparation for participation in the sacraments. On the other hand ascetic practice is considered important in times of crisis, as part of repentance and prayer and as spiritual exercise in preparation for special events and difficult tasks. To the Eastern monastic tradition, asceticism is fundamental. Novices are regularly asked to fulfill various ascetic exercises to subjugate their desires and attain a degree of freedom. Ascetic rules are important in order to remain on the path but are generally seen as provisional and often vary from monastery to monastery. More extreme forms of asceticism, both in matters of fasting and vigils but also in renunciation of social interaction and movement, are common and highly respected. Spiritual authority within as well as outside the hierarchy is widely regarded as dependent on ascetic life.

In the Western Christian tradition, asceticism became more closely linked to monasticism. Monastic rules, beginning with the Rule of St. Benedict, came to regulate the ascetic practice of the monks. In the 12th as well as the 16th century, monastic revival movements (Cistercians, Carmelites, and others), reacting against the lenient policy of the monasteries, introduced stricter rules. A strong link between ascetic practice and spiritual exercises was introduced by Ignatius of Loyola (c. 1491–1556). In the life of ordinary Christians, fasting remained a duty connected to certain days and periods of the year. In addition ascetic practices were connected mainly with penance. The Reformation, with its emphasis on "sola fide" (faith alone), criticized the entire monastic tradition as well as all kinds of ascetic practice. Thus, rules of fasting, pilgrimages, vigils, and various pious exercises were soon abandoned in Protestant areas. On the other hand strict codes of moral and strict ecclesiastical rules, especially in reformed traditions and in Pietism, emphasized an ascetic way of life.

From the point of view of systematic theology, asceticism is closely linked to Christian anthropology. Although early theologians, such as Origen, hesitated, Christian theology has generally embraced the body, because it was created in the image and likeness of God. With the acceptance of the teaching about the resurrection of the flesh, this means that Christian anthropology is based on a positive view of the body and gives a place to the body in salvation and consummation. Although Eastern Christian thought generally prefers to ascribe passions to inherent weakness rather than to inherited sin, the practice of at least some abstention from and renunciation of bodily pleasures, not to mention a life of passion, is seen as a possible and necessary exercise to maintain a spiritual life. The close relation of body and soul in the Bible and the dogma of the incarnation of the divine in Jesus Christ contributes to an understanding of the body as sanctified, a temple for the Holy Spirit. On the other hand it excludes any kind of asceticism that is based on contempt for and negation of the body. Even the most rigorous ascetic practice characteristic of early Eastern monasticism has as its goal the sanctification and transformation of the body.

Christian ascetic practice incorporates most varieties of asceticism found in other world religions. The most important forms are the reduction of food (fasting), of sleep (vigils), and of sexuality (celibacy). In addition to these are a wide variety of practices that can be termed ascetic. Some, such as abstention from private property or obedience to a spiritual master, are strongly but not exclusively linked to monasticism. Others, such as abstention from various forms of pleasure and entertainment, are connected with various forms of pietism. Extreme forms of asceticism, including standing on a pillar, being immured in a cell, or living like a wild beast, are known from early and medieval Christian tradition, mainly in the East, whereas the Western tradition has examples of extreme forms of voluntary suffering and self-inflicted pain.

Ascetic practices might be temporary, governed by either the liturgical year, such as fasting in Lent, or by sexual abstention prior to receiving communion or vigils at the time of the feasts. However, ascetic practice is also often connected to the personal situation, such as experiences of suffering, commitment of grave sin, or promises given. In addition to monks and nuns who follow stricter rules, some Christian traditions also demand a stricter ascetic life of all clergy, most notably the rule of celibacy for priests of the Roman Catholic Church.

Criticism of ascetic practice started during the Renaissance and flourished during the Reformation. Arguments against ascetic practice on the one hand indicted a Church hierarchy considered to be oppressive, demanding pious acts in exchange for various services of the Church, and on the other insisted on justification by faith alone and denied any system of merit and satisfaction. Howewer, the almost complete repudiation of asceticism that can be found in most Protestant churches of today has its roots in the liberal and social movements of the 19th century with their emphasis on the ethical/political side of Christian religion and their denial of every kind of metaphysical reality. However, recent ideological and cultural developments in Christianity show a renewed interest in the question of the body and thus in asceticism.

SAMUEL RUBENSON

## Further Reading

Brown, Peter L., *The Body and Society: Men, Women, and Sexual Renunciation in Early Christianity*, New York: Columbia University Press, 1988

Chadwick, Owen, translator, *Western Asceticism*, Philadelphia: Westminster, and London: SCM Press, 1958

Elm, Susanna, *Virgins of God: The Making of Asceticism in Late Antiquity*, Oxford and New York: Oxford University Press, 1994

Miles, Margaret R., *Practicing Christianity: Critical Perspectives for an Embodied Spirituality*, New York: Crossroad, 1988

Morris, Marcia A., *Saints and Revolutionaries: The Ascetic Hero in Russian Literature*, Albany: State University of New York Press, 1993

Vaage, Leif E., and Vincent L. Wimbush, editors, *Asceticism and the New Testament*, New York: Routledge, 1999

Weinstein, Donald, and Rudolph M. Bell, *Saints and Society: The Two Worlds of Western Christendom, 1000–1700*, Chicago: University of Chicago Press, 1982

Wimbush, Vincent L., editor, *Ascetic Behavior in Greco-Roman Antiquity*, Minneapolis, Minnesota: Fortress Press, 1990

Wimbush, Vincent L., and Richard Valantasis, editors, *Asceticism*, New York: Oxford University Press, 1995

# Ashoka. *See* Aśoka

# Ashram, Influence of

The word *ashram* has two dimensions in Indian parlance. The first usage designates a forest hermitage. It consists of an old, holy sage surrounded by a small "family" of disciples. The second usage incorporates the forest ashram into a pattern for the ideal life cycle with this as one of its stages.

The Sanskrit root *shram*, from which *ashram* is derived, means "to exert oneself." Thus, the ashram is a place of exertion, or disciplined striving after a goal. Within the diversity of Indian religions, this exertion can be ascetic and oriented toward the acquisition of spiritual power; it can be yogic, which is a method of self-development; or it can apply to philosophical reflection on the deeper significance of life and the world. The sage and his fellows in the ashram follow one or more of these paths in their woodland retreat. *Śrāmaṇa* has come to be used of ascetics or people pursuing a special religious program, especially Buddhist and Jain monks (at least by the time of Aśoka, c. 250 B.C.).

It is clear in Indian literature that an older, charismatic man provides the focal point of the ashram. It is not enough to say that he is the leader or even teacher of the group. He is somehow the living manifestation of the holy in the ashram. Others imitate him, learn from him, and derive from him their spiritual nourishment. However, it is significant to note that his leadership is not authoritarian, nor is it prescribed by any external rule or pattern. He might be like a father in the family but by no means an abbot.

The second dimension is the pattern of the four ashramas, or stages of life. Perhaps the name ashrama was given to this ideal pattern for the life cycle to convey the idea that each of the stages is an arena of exertion or perhaps as an extension of the term used for the third stage: the forest hermitage. It has been argued that the pattern of the four ashramas was created by the brahmanic tradition to syncretize many different styles of religion, integrating many options for religious activity into one harmonious course of life.

The lower castes, very young children, and women do not participate in this pattern directly. It is the young boy of a "twice-born" caste who leaves his family at the puberty rite (*upanayana*), enters the household of a teacher, and thus begins the first stage. It is called *brahmacarya* (cultivation of Brahma) and lasts until the boy is of age for marriage. This ashrama is characterized by study, obedience to the teacher (guru), and celibacy. The last element is so prominent in the practice of *brahmacarya* that it has become the dominant meaning of the word.

The second stage of life, *gṛhastha*, consists in the care of a home and family, the pursuit of economic and social well-being (*artha*), and sensual enjoyment (*kāma*). The authors of the *dharmaśāstra*s (code books) agree that this stage is the foundation of society, and they exalt it. We cannot understand the nature of the next two stages unless we note that they are not opposed to the natural family and its way of life but proceed from it.

When the head of a family sees his grandchildren born and has gray hair, the *dharmaśāstra*s permit him to go on to the third stage. This is where the forest dwelling finds a place in the system. This ashrama is called *vānaprastha* (derived from *vāna*, meaning "forest"). A wife may accompany her husband into the simplicity of the woodland hut, but continence is now the rule. This stage marks the beginning of preparation for death, a relaxation of the concerns that formerly enmeshed one but without the extreme cleavage from all ties that marks the fourth stage.

When seen in the context of the four ashramas, the forest stage would seem to offer no dynamic of its own. However, to describe the ashram (i.e., the third stage of life) as a place of transition would not indicate a lack of integrity and stability as much as it would underline the peculiar nature of this social structure; by nature the ashram is temporary and evanescent.

The fourth and last stage of life is called *sannyāsin*. According to the ideal pattern, when the forest dweller has achieved the necessary freedom from all attachment, including that to his hermitage and associates, he becomes completely homeless and wanders freely. He has then achieved, to the greatest extent possible in this world, the final goal of *mokṣa* (release).

The emphasis on independence of any place or person in the piety of the *sannyāsin* would seem to eliminate participation in a communal religious life. However, historically this has not been the case. Both Buddhist and Hindu monasticism find their roots in associations of *sannyāsins*. In the earliest Indian writings, we are told of *sannyāsins* gathering in bands and following one or another dharma (school of thought and life). The Buddha revolutionized this institution by permitting the monks to rest in one place together during the rainy season. From this temporary settlement the more or less permanent *vihāra* (Buddhist monastery) developed. The Hindus, much later at about the time of Śankara (around A.D. 800), proclaimed the possibility of remaining a *brahmacaryin* for life. This had the same result: the foundation of communities of celibate men oriented toward religious learning and activity.

In summary, the ashram, both as a place and as a discipline of life, appears in Indian culture as a social religious structure of a somewhat monastic type. It shares with a monastery the feature of a group of people living apart from the family or village, pursuing programs of life for self-improvement and religious goals. However, it differs from clearly monastic institutions by being impermanent, without written rules, and casual in authority.

GEORGE WECKMAN

*See also* Asceticism: Buddhist Perspectives; Buddhism: Overview; Critiques of Buddhist Monasticism: Indo-Tibetan; Deities, Buddhist; Griffiths, Bede; Hygiene: Buddhist Perspectives; Jain Monasticism and Buddhist Monasticism; Origins: Comparative Perspectives; Regulations: Buddhist Perspectives

## Further Reading

Kaelber, Walter O., *Tapta Marga: Asceticism and Initiation in Vedic India*, Albany: State University of New York Press, 1989

Kane, Pandurang Vaman, *History of Dharmasastra* (Government Oriental Series, class B, number 6), 5 vols., Poona: Bhandarkar Oriental Research Institute, 1930–1962; 2nd edition, 1968

Miller, David M., and Dorothy C. Wertz, *Hindu Monastic Life: The Monks and Monasteries of Bhubaneswar*, Montreal: McGill-Queen's University Press, 1976; revised edition, New Delhi: Manohar, 1996

Olivelle, Patrick, *The Asrama System: The History and Hermeneutics of a Religious Institution*, Oxford and New York: Oxford University Press, 1993

# Asia, Central

Two waves of Buddhist activity can be mapped in central Asia. During the first period, the province of Gandhara (in modern Afghanistan) exported its Graeco-Buddhism into Chinese Turkestan. Buddhism was popular among the Türks, and T'o-po, the last "great" khan, was a Buddhist who used his patronage to create a cultural and spiritual center for visiting Indian and Chinese monks. The Indian monk Jñanagupta spent ten years (575–585) at T'o-po's court and set up a committee to translate and catalog Buddhist texts.

After the Uighur immigration during the second half of the ninth century, Turkic Buddhism reached its peak of popularity, only to fade with the arrival of Islam in 1250. Many Buddhist texts in Chinese Turkestan dialects attest to the multicultural society that grew up during this period.

In Mongolia, a tolerant attitude secured a space for Buddhism to flourish, and it expanded rapidly under the patronage of Kublai Khan (r. 1260–1294) and the resident Tibetan monk 'Phags-pa, so that at one point the number of Buddhist religious had reached 200,000. It was only at the turn of the 12th century, when Gazan Khan (r. 1295–1304) converted to Islam, that interest in Buddhism began to wane.

For three centuries, Buddhism was all but lost from central Asia. After the conversion of the Ordos Tümet Altan Khan in 1577, a spiritual domino effect led to the conversion of almost the entire Mongolian population, a conversion that had profound political and social results. Itinerant monks settled down in inhabited areas and co-opted the local spirits to Buddhism, thus converting the people from shamanism to the Vajrayāna. At the same time, these monks established monasteries and began to reach out into the extensive networks of local nomadic tribes.

With the arrival of Sönam Gyamtso in 1578, and the conferring upon him of the title of Dalai ("ocean") Lama by Altan Khan, Tibetan influence in Mongolia was assured. Sönam Gyamtso's successor sent among the Mongols a permanent representative in the form of the Jetsün Damba Khutughtu, although over the centuries the importance of this figure has faded, so that now he is of significance only to the Khalkha Mongols.

As in Tibet, the scholastic achievements of the monasteries often outweighed the purely spiritual ones: it was often felt more important for Mongolian monks to study in a Tibetan monastery than to do retreat; and, on their return, they were accorded a level of respect more in keeping with a high lama. However, the intellectual influence of Tibet meant that, during the reign of Ligdan Khan, monastic scholars translated the Kanjur into Mongolian and, during the mid–18th century, made available the entire Kanjur and Tanjur in printed form.

Following the Communist revolution in 1921, Buddhism came under sustained attack from the central government. The attacks were sporadic at first, with some level of cooperation between the religious and secular hierarchies: indeed, the first ruler of the new Mongolia was none other than the Eighth Living Buddha, the Khutughtu Bogdo Gegen. On his death in 1924, the Mongolian People's Revolutionary Party (MPRP) was already moving toward an anticlerical onslaught, and in 1928 the first wave began properly to take shape.

Between 1928 and 1932, the government viciously attacked the religious foundations throughout the country, closing monasteries and sending monks away to work on the land. However, the force of this attack was at best chaotic (and all the more frightening for that), culminating in the great uprising of 1932, in which monks and laypeople together forced the government to relent.

These revolts challenged the very foundations of the new Mongolia. It left no doubt in either Moscow or Ulaanbaatar that the people were serious in their opposition: the party understood that the people needed to be placated and brought grudgingly to heel.

In July 1932, the Little Khural had the leaders of the rebellion executed, returned freedom of religion to the people, and reaffirmed the separation of church and state. On 8 July, the document "On Dividing the Property and Cattle Collected from the Conspirators" was published, ensuring the release of monastic property to those who could prove no involvement in the rebellion. Clearly, the aim was to divide the Buddhist establishment through a temporal and legal framework, as no explicit antireligious feeling was present. This law, and further tax-raising laws, was passed by the Great Khural in 1933.

In 1934, the council of ministers passed another law, requiring that each monastery take in a representative to sit in on meetings concerned with administrative business and thereby to be the eyes and ears of the party within the monastic context. Further laws were soon passed, forbidding, among other things, the giving and collecting of alms, the teaching of religion in schools, the building of new temples, and the ordination of all people under the age of 18.

This gradual and legalistic movement finally gave way, in 1937, to three years of systematic destruction of monasteries and the near-total elimination of monks, either to the Siberian gulag or to a quicker death at the hands of MPRP First Secretary Horloyn Choibalsan's secret police. In 1937, 75 monasteries closed and nearly 2,000 monks were executed; by the end of the following year, 760 of the remaining 771 monasteries had been closed.

Temples were kept alive to impress upon visitors the inequalities and extravagances of the monastic system: a few old monks were permitted to worship as a kind of living museum. In the years before the collapse of Communism, the buildings were retained as tourist attractions. Recently, a process of restoration and renovation has begun that will surely take many years and a great deal of money to carry through.

As might be imagined, monasteries in Mongolia tended to mirror the Tibetan model, with the largest complexes consisting of nearly a dozen buildings. In addition to the one major and several minor assembly halls (*tsogchun* and *dugang*, respectively), a monastery might consist of a number of small temples (*süme*), a general-purpose temple (*khürije*), hermitages (*keid*), and stūpas (*suburgan*) as well as residences for lamas and private quarters for the abbot, kitchens, storerooms, and outhouses. In addition to this, the larger monasteries had colleges devoted to philosophy, doctrine and protocol, demonology and demon suppression, mathematics, astrology, and divinity. Most monasteries were too small to have all four colleges: Urga, in Outer Mongolia, was one of only a few to do so.

Within the monastery, the *khutughtu* (reincarnate lamas) exercised complete spiritual and temporal power. Despite the dissolute life led by many of the lamas (and frequently recounted in folk songs), their learning and spiritual attainments went unchallenged, and the lamas retained the respect of monks and laypeople alike.

Beneath the *khutughtu* in the hierarchy were the main religious and secular officials (*khamba* and *shansotba*, respectively). Once the Manchu had taken temporal control over the monasteries, they appointed their own official, the *Da Lama*, to oversee administration; the importance of this official fluctuated with the Manchu's political strength. Of the other monastic officials, the *khamba*'s assistant (*tsorzh*) was the most powerful, although the discipline master (*yeke tsogchin gebdüi*), the chant master (*umzad*), and the treasurer (*demchi*) also exercised considerable power. In 1937, at the beginning of the purge carried out by Choibalsan's secret police, some 10,000 of these high officials remained, attesting to the amount of political strength that they wielded.

All the cattle, land, and possessions of the monastery were controlled by the *shansotba*'s deputy, the *nirba*, and in the years after the revolution, this arrangement proved to be a source of conflict between the collective farms and the workers who had spent their lives laboring for the monastery. The personal property of the *khutughtu* was exempt from external control, passing from reincarnation to reincarnation, increasing and decreasing with the *khutughtu*'s popularity.

Three principal monasteries and a number of smaller temple complexes exist in the country. The three main monasteries are the following:

*Gandan Khiid* (Ulaanbaatar). Gandan Khiid's full name is Gandantegchinlen, but it is generally called by the shorter form. Built in 1840, it is the country's largest remaining temple. After the revolution, it was spared to impress visiting foreigners, with its few resident monks overseen by the KGB.

Presently four temples exist at Gandan Khiid, all under renovation and payed for by the growing number of practicing Buddhists in Ulaanbaatar. The monastery houses about 150 monks.

*Erdenezuu Khiid* (Kharkhorin, Övörkhangai). This is probably the most important monastery in Mongolia. It stands within an impressive 400-square-meter walled compound, around the outside of which are 108 stūpas. Recently, the three temples inside have been renovated, and the monastery itself is an active place of worship.

*Amarbayasgalant Khiid* (Sant Süm, Selenge). This, the second most important monastery, is still under renovation.

In addition to these, several other monasteries are of cultural or religious interest. Among these are the following:

*Monastery-Museum of Choijin Lama* (Ulaanbaatar). Also known as the Museum of Religion, this monastery was built between 1904 and 1908 to honor Luvsanhaidavt, the brother of one of the Mongol kings. In 1938, after the purge, it was re-opened as a museum. Of the five temples in the complex, the most interesting are probably Yadamyn Süm and Amgalangiin Süm, which contain rare works by the famous national artist and sculptor G Zanabazar.

*Shant Khiid* (situated between Kharkhorin and Khujirt, Övörkhangai). Once called the West Monastery, this is the only surviving monastery in a region once famous for its religious activity. The significance of the temples in this area came from the fact that G Zanabazar visited them in 1647. During the Stalinist era, a group of five monks kept up the clandestine chanting of sūtras, often at great personal risk. About 50 monks reside here, and the monastery buildings are under reconstruction.

*Zayayn Gegeenii Khuree* (Tsetserleg, Arkhangai). For some reason, this large, ancient monastery was spared form the revolutionary purges of the late 1930s. When it was built in 1586, it was very small but was expanded in 1679 to include to five temples: at its height, it was home to about 1,000 monks but today to no more than 70. Behind the monastery is a large, almost vertical hill, Bulgan Uul, where some Buddhist inscriptions are still intact.

*Dechinravjaalin Khiid* (Ulaangom, Üvs). This small temple was founded in 1757 by Lamaav. At its height, about 2,000 monks resided here, housed in gers scattered among seven small temples. The buildings were all but destroyed in 1937, and in 1990 a few gers were erected to serve as a temporary temple while reconstruction work was done. About ten monks are on-site, along with some 30 students.

SIMON WICKHAM-SMITH

*See also* Holy Men in Power (Hierocrats), Buddhist; Liturgy: Buddhist; Missionaries: Buddhist; Tibet: History; Tibetan Lineages; Visual Arts, Buddhist: Tibet; Worship Space: Buddhist Perspectives

## Further Reading

Damdinsuren, TSeden, *Günzhiin Süm*, Ulaanbaatar: publisher untraced, 1961

Isibaldan, *Erdeni-yin Erike: Mongolische Chronik der lamaistischen Klosterbauten der Mongolei*, translated and annotated by Walther Heissig, Copenhagen: Munksgaard, 1961

Miller, Robert James, *Monasteries and Culture Change in Inner Mongolia*, Wiesbaden: Harrassowitz, 1959

Moses, Larry W., *The Political Role of Mongol Buddhism*, Bloomington, Indiana: Asian Studies Research Institute, 1977

Pozdneyev, A.M., *Sketches of the Life of Buddhist Monasteries and Clergy in Mongolia*, translated by Alo Raun, Seattle: University of Washington Press, 1972

Sinor, Denis, *Inner Asia: History, Civilization, Languages*, Bloomington: Indiana University Press, 1969

Storey, Robert, *Mongolia: A Travel Survival Kit*, Hawthorn, Victoria, and Berkeley, California: Lonely Planet, 1993

Sung-Yün, *Emu tanggû orin sadka-i gisun sarkiyan: Erzählungen der 120 Alten: Beiträge zur mandschurischen Kulturgeschichte*, translated and annotated by Giovanni Stary, Wiesbaden: Harrassowitz, 1983

# Aśoka d. 232 B.C.

## Mauryan emperor in India and patron of Buddhist monasteries

The importance of King Aśoka for the development of monastic traditions within world civilization is great. It consists mainly in the fact that he systematically sent Buddhist missionaries to foreign countries. In the long run this activity resulted in the patronage of Buddhist monasteries and eventually the worldwide spread of Buddhist doctrine. Thus, next to Gautama Buddha himself Aśoka is the single most important historical person to have set in motion the wheel of dharma. For Aśoka dharma meant concern for the welfare of others, religious tolerance, moral living, and nonviolence to both humans and animals (entailing pacifism and vegetarianism, respectively). As a wheel-turning king (*cakravartin*), Aśoka ensures a peaceful and prosperous – even idyllic – situation for his followers while he rules well enough to merit the dharma wheel. This is understood as a magical emblem of kingship that returns to the earth on the decline of an era. *Cakravartin*s have 32 marks of a Great Person, rule with dharma, and engender a Golden Age.

Although converted to Buddhism, Aśoka was tolerant of religions generally, as is evident from his edict on toleration. Religious interpretations of Aśoka emphasize his conversion and patronage of Buddhist monasteries, whereas sociopolitical ones emphasize that the art of rulership involves building consensus and unity through tolerance of all creeds. This difference in interpretation correlates with whether archaeological evidence from the rock edicts (as in the latter interpretation) is considered alone or whether textual evidence from the *Aśokavādāna* is admitted as well (as in the former, religious one). An *avadāna* is a popular narrative about the deeds of a significant person that typically emphasizes the importance of karma, faith, and devotion. Usually it is religious interpretations that are supported with reference to such legends, or *avadāna*s. Versions of these legends exist in several languages, such as Pāli, Sanskrit, Chinese, Tibetan, Japanese, Burmese, Thai, and Sinhalese.

It is noteworthy that Aśoka even supported the *Ājīvika*s, who were opponents of Buddhism. Indeed love to enemies is a hallmark of Buddhist doctrine and practice, so that for Aśoka (as for Gandhi much later) the religious and the political are one. There is no reason to believe that Aśoka 's conversion to Buddhism was insincere or contrived to a political end devoid of spirituality.

As the grandson of Chandragupta Maurya (c. 324–c. 300 B.C.), Aśoka was crowned in 269 B.C. and inherited an empire large enough to make him the world's most powerful monarch

The Great Stūpa, Sāñcī, central India, original stūpa from the time of King Aśoka (c. 250 B.C.), enlarged to the present size c. 150 B.C. with gates added c. 50 B.C.
Photo courtesy of Marylin M. Rhie

of the time. Aśoka ruled Pataliputra (present-day Patna or Bihar), including eastern Afghanistan and all of India except Tamil Nadu, Kerala, southern Karnataka, Assam, and Bangladesh. According to a legendary account, Aśoka massacred 99 brothers and was an exceedingly cruel ruler. What is more likely, as John Strong (1983) has argued, is that he murdered his stepbrother, the legitimate heir to the throne. In 261 B.C. Aśoka annexed Kalinga on the Bay of Bengal in a bloody battle. Contemplating thereafter the suffering inflicted on the people, Aśoka converted to Buddhism and became sympathetic to the civilizing force of religions. To bear injury patiently is preferable to retaliation, thought the mature Aśoka. In the Aśokan Rock Edicts, carved in stone a few years after the Kalinga conquest, Aśoka asserts that cultivating the virtue of patience is preferable to retaliating against wrongdoers.

After Kalinga, Aśoka propagated Buddhist dharma far and wide, beginning with his own household. He became a monk yet remained a king, and he propagated Buddhism in a reign that lasted about 40 years. One of the main ethical emphases of Aśoka was to cherish all life. Animals especially were given special protection. Coming from the Śaiva tradition, in which animals were routinely sacrificed for food, religious rituals, and sport, Aśoka gradually changed all that within his domain. He did so first by abolishing the royal hunt in 259 B.C., next by decreasing the amount of meat eaten at court, and finally, in 243 B.C., by regulating the whole country in its dealings with animals and prohibiting the slaughter of many kinds of animals. *Cakravartin* Aśoka's propagation of Buddhism extended to Sri Lanka through the work of his younger brother or possibly son, Mahendra (Pāli, Mahinda).

Aśoka ruled above all by attempting to stimulate an ethical change of heart rather than by manipulating the behavior of his subjects. According to the sage-king Aśoka, three primary duties are reverence for parents, elders, and teachers; noninjury to animals; and truthfulness. In all but the reverence for animals, the similarity between Aśoka's ethics and that of the Chinese sage Confucius (551–479 B.C.) is striking in the emphasis on benevolent rather than merely legalistic rule; respect accorded to parents, elders, and teachers; and sincerity or truthfulness. Indeed ideas such as truth, sincerity, and respect for others are hardly foreign to Buddhism. These ideas might have been part of a common stock of morality that linked China to India and India to the Greek world through trade facilitated by the interaction between highlanders and lowlanders along the way. In the Vinaya rules Buddhist monks and nuns are not to destroy vegetation, so it is interesting that Aśoka extends nonviolence to animals without speaking of noninjury to plants.

Aśoka was a *cakravartin*, a "turner of the wheel of law," whose teachings were set forth in the Fourteen Rock Edicts, the Seven Pillar Inscriptions, and the Legends of King Aśoka (*Asokavadana*, part of the *Divyavadana*). Aśoka required government officials to give instruction in morals and built stūpas (Buddhist reliquary mounds) throughout the kingdom. He also provided a great deal to his people in the way of social services. These benefits included development and provision of herbal medicines for both people and animals. Aśoka developed banyan-tree rest areas, cultivated mango orchards, and established wells along the main roads. He stimulated the establishment of inns, watering places, and animal shelters throughout the land. The official doctrine behind all this is that these acts enable people to become pious. The life and thought of Aśoka is somewhat paradoxical. On the one hand Aśoka opposed the slaughter of lower animals for food, supported vegetarianism, and insisted on the care of animals. On the other hand, regarding human life, he never abolished capital punishment or military control of empire, even after becoming a monk.

FRANK J. HOFFMAN

*See also* Animals, Attitude toward: Buddhist Perspectives; Buddha ( Śākyamuni); Councils, Buddhist; Governance: Buddhist Perspectives; Holy Men/Holy Women: Buddhist Perspectives; Holy Men in Power (Hierocrats), Buddhist; Manuscript Production: Buddhist; Master and Pupil: Buddhist Perspectives; Missionaries: Buddhist; Patrons, Buddhist: India; Scholastics, Buddhist; Social Services: Buddhist; Stūpa

## Biography

The third Mauryan Emperor in India, Aśoka ruled from 269 B.C. to his death in 232. In the eighth year of his reign he converted to Buddhism following a campaign in Kalinga on the Bay of Bengal. His Edicts proclaimed precepts of lay Buddhism on pillars throughout India. The sage-king built stūpas, patronized monasteries, and thought of himself as a king who turns the wheel of dharma (*cakravartin*). Aśoka probably did more to perpetuate Buddhism in India than any other individual after the Buddha himself.

## Major Works

Fourteen Rock Edicts
Seven Pillar Inscriptions

## Further Reading

Cunningham, Alexander, Sir, editor, *Inscriptions of Asoka* (Corpus Inscriptionum Indicarum, volume 1), Calcutta: Office of the Superintendent of Government Printing, 1877; new edition by Eugen Hultzsch, Oxford: Clarendon Press, 1925; reprint, Delhi: Indological Book House, 1969

Gokhale, Balkrishna Govind, *Asoka Maurya* (Twayne's Rulers and Statesmen of the World Series, 3), New York: Twayne, 1966

Smith, Vincent A., *Asoka, the Buddhist Emperor of India*, Oxford: Clarendon Press, 1901; 3rd edition, Delhi: Chand, 1919; Oxford: Clarendon Press, 1920

Strong, John S., *The Legend of King Asoka: A Study and Translation of the Aśokavādāna* (Princeton Library of Asian Translations), Princeton, New Jersey: Princeton University Press, 1983; Guildford, Surrey: Princeton University Press, 1989

# Assisi, Italy

Assisi is a township located on Mount Asi, near the center of the province of Umbria, Italy, 41 miles north of Rome. The ruins of the Roman temple of Minerva stand near the center of the town. Saint Rufinus, bishop of Assisi, was martyred there in 236; in the 11th century the cathedral of San Rufino was built to house his remains. Near the medieval well here stand the ruins of a tenth-century Carolingian monastery. Charlemagne

Courtyard, Church of San Damiano, Assisi, Italy, early 13th century. This was the first church that St. Francis repaired (c. 1206). St. Clare lived here from c. 1214 until her death in 1253.
Photo courtesy of Mary Schaefer

(768–814) destroyed the town in 773 during his war with the Lombards; he later rebuilt it, and with the construction of the castle known as the Rocca d'Assisi, Assisi became a major political force in central Italy. Assisi is renowned mainly as the birthplace of St. Francis (1181/82–1226). The sites associated with him have been preserved or, in other cases, transformed into major sanctuaries.

The Cathedral of San Rufino contains the font where Francis and Clare (1193/94–1253) and also Emperor Frederick II (1215–1250) were baptized. Francis would later preach his first sermon there, and the oratory where he often prayed is still preserved. The Chiesa Nuova was built in 1615 over the remains of the house that belonged to the father of Francis. It is built on the model of the Greek cross and contains the small chamber in which Francis' father imprisoned him at the beginning of his conversion. The convent contains many rooms in which Francis lived as a child, the cloth shop in which Francis worked as a youth, and a museum. Behind the church is the San Francesco Piccolino, the place where Francis was born. Francis renounced his inheritance and worldly goods at the Bishop's Palace, located near the Church of St. Mary Maggiore.

In 1206 one of the important events in the spiritual transformation of Francis occurred at the Church of San Damiano. Francis was praying in the ruins of the church when the image of Christ on the crucifix spoke and told him, "Francis, go and repair my church, which as you can see, is in ruins." Francis returned home, sold his father's cloth, and returned to St. Damian's. The priest, who knew Francis' father, refused the gift; Francis threw the coins he wished to donate through a window near the entrance to the church. When he became ill in 1225, Francis stayed here and wrote the *Canticle of Brother Sun*. After his death in 1226, his body was brought here briefly on its way to the Church of St. George. Saint Damian's is also associated with Clare, who lived here from 1211 to 1253. Clare performed several miracles here, including the multiplication of bread and oil, the appearance of the sign of the cross on a loaf of bread given to the pope, and the driving away of the Saracen and Tartar troops in the service of Frederick II; while on her deathbed Clare was said to have seen in a vision here a ceremony held at the Basilica of St. Francis. The Order of Poor Clares has its origins in San Damiano.

The Church of St. Mary of Rivotorto, named after a stream that runs along the left side of the building, was constructed in 1854 over the place where Francis and his followers stayed from 1209 to 1211 and where he dictated his first Rule. The Order of the Friars Minor was born here. While Francis was preaching in Assisi, his followers also had a vision here of Francis seated on a chariot that circled the location three times.

Francis often visited the Eremo della Carceri or Hermitage of the Prisons, whose name means "retreat" and "isolation." He stayed here between 1210 and 1211, and the grotto where he slept and the oratory where he prayed are still preserved. The hermitage also houses the tree associated with the story of St. Francis and the birds, the remains of one of Clare's habits, and other relics.

The basilica of Santa Maria degli Angeli, located at the foot of the mountain and begun in 1569 on the authorization of Pius V (1566–1572), was built on the model of St. Peter's in Rome and encloses the tiny little chapel, the Porziuncula, where the Franciscan Order had its origins. The chapel belonged to the Benedictines of Monte Subasio, who allowed Francis and his companions to use it. Clare renounced her worldly goods to follow Francis here in 1212. It was also here that Francis received the Porziuncola Indulgence, or the Assisi Pardon. Saint Francis threw himself into a thorn bush still located in the Rose Garden of the basilica after experiencing temptations of the flesh. His blood transformed the thorns into roses. Two angels appeared and brought him back to the Porziuncola, where St. Francis asked the Lord to pardon the sins of those who came here. The Indulgence, confirmed by Pope Honorius III (1216–1227) in 1216 and celebrated on 2 August, was the occasion for mass pilgrimages to Assisi in the following centuries. The walls and the apse are in their original state, and the frescoes on the facade date from 1830. On 3 October 1226 Francis died in a cell near the Porziuncola that was once used as an infirmary for the Franciscans and that is still preserved in the basilica. A statue by Luca della Robbia in the basilica is modeled on the saint's death mask. One can also see the cells of some of the first friars of the Franciscan Order and the fireplace room where they prayed in the old convent; the convent also houses one of the largest libraries in Umbria. The grandeur of the basilica disregards the values of the saint, known as "The Poor Man of Assisi," and stands in direct contrast to the simplicity of the sites enclosed within its walls.

The Basilica of San Francesco, located in the town itself, is one of the finest examples of Gothic architecture in Italy. It is composed of three sanctuaries, one on top of the other. The hill where the basilica was built was once known as "Hell's Hill," as it was the place where criminals were executed; after the construction of the basilica, it was known as "Paradise Hill." Gregory IX (1227–1241) laid the first stone on 25 July 1228, and Innocent IV (1243–1254) consecrated the basilica. The Upper Basilica is renowned for its frescoes by Cimabue, Simone Martini, Pietro Lorenzetti, and Giotto, whose St. Francis cycle is the basis for our modern image of Francis. The plan of the church is in a double T representing the Tau of St. Francis. The tomb of Francis is located under the altar of the Lower Basilica. The remains of Francis were brought here in 1230 from their original burial site in the Church of St. George. Sixtus IV (1471–1484) ordered the remains to be sealed; in 1818 Pius VII (1800–1823) allowed excavations to begin, and the sarcophagus of Francis was discovered. In 1824 a new crypt was opened; in 1932 it was redesigned and now also houses the remains of four of the companions of St. Francis. The habit of Francis, several other relics, and the bull confirming the Rule of St. Francis are housed in a room in the convent once used as the chapter house. The vaults of the Upper Basilica, several frescoes in the Lower Basilica, and much of the convent were heavily damaged in the earthquakes of 1997. Restoration of the Lower Basilica is nearly complete; work on the Upper Basilica continues.

Also damaged in the quakes was the Basilica of St. Clare, which was built on the site of the Church of St. George, where Francis was educated as a youth. The basilica houses the remains of Clare, several of her relics, and the crucifix of San Damiano that spoke to St. Francis.

Today the Diocese of Assisi is subject to the Holy See. It is home to eight monasteries and 18 women's convents, including the Abbey of San Benedetto, located two miles away from the Hermitage of the Prisons and built in the 11th century.

DEBORAH VESS

*See also* Architecture: Western Christian Monasteries; Clare of Assisi, St.; Francis of Assisi, St.; Franciscans; Visual Arts, Western Christian: Book Arts before the Renaissance

## Further Reading

Brooke, Rosalind, and Christopher Brooke, "St. Clare," in *Medieval Women*, edited by Derek Baker, Oxford: Blackwell, 1978

Cruickshank, J.W., and A.M. Cruickshank, *The Umbrian Cities of Italy*, Boston: L.C. Page, 1907

Gordon, Lina, *The Story of Assisi*, London: Dent, 1900; New York: Dutton, 1913; revised edition, London and New York: Dent, 1929

Habig, Marion, editor, *St. Francis of Assisi: Writings and Early Biographies*. Chicago: Franciscan Herald Press, 1973; London: SPCK, 1979; 4th edition, Chicago: Franciscan Herald Press 1983

Hutton, Edward, *The Cities of Umbria*, New York: Dutton, 1904; London: Methuen, 1905; 7th edition, London: Methuen, 1925

Ladis, Andrew, editor, *Franciscanism, the Papacy, and Art in the Age of Giotto*, New York: Garland, 1998

Lunghi, Elvio, *The Basilica of St. Francis in Assisi*. New York: Riverside, 1996; as *The Basilica of St. Francis at Assisi*, London: Thames and Hudson, 1996

Moorman, John, *Medieval Franciscan Houses*, St. Bonaventure, New York: Franciscan Institute, St. Bonaventure University, 1983

Moorman, John, *A History of the Franciscan Order from Its Origins to the Year 1517*, Oxford: Clarendon Press, 1968; Chicago: Franciscan Herald Press, 1988

# Augustinian Canons

The origins of the Austin Canons can be found in some dissatisfaction with the performance of the clergy by the 11th century and in a renewed attempt to revive the apostolic, communal life in the cause of reform. The reformers at the Papal Curia were concerned about simony, nepotism, private property, and clerical marriage with its attendant inheritance of benefices. One solution was to reintroduce a more effective rule of common life. Thus, the order of Austin Canons was constituted as the first of the new orders of regular canons, who had a pastoral role, being required to administer to the laity, but who were regular in the sense of living under the newly adopted rule of St. Augustine (*ordo novus*). They led a full common life, in contrast to those clergy who came later to be designated "secular" canons. The latter might still live under a rule, but it was an older rule (*ordo antiquus*) based on that produced by St. Chrodegang for his cathedral at Metz and authorized by the Council of Aachen in 816 (the *Institutio Canonicorum*), which was revised in the middle of the 11th century. The old-rule prescribed a collegiate organization with common use of cloister, refectory, and dormitory but allowed the continuation of private property. Thus, secular canons might lead a common life in collegiate churches but not the full apostolic life. The "regular" canons lay somewhere between canons and monks.

The Lateran Council of 1059, prompted by Hildebrand, the future Pope Gregory VII (1073–1085), encouraged the clergy to adhere more strictly to the common life by living under a rule, although at first that status and the rule were inchoate; the precept was reissued at the next Lateran Council in 1063. Within the next 50 years, communities of clerics were established to follow a stricter common life, especially in northern Italy and southern France under the influence of reforming bishops but without having adopted the formal Augustinian rule. The main centers of this reformed trend were in Lombardy, Tuscany, Burgundy, Aquitaine, and northeastern France (especially the diocese of Reims). Important houses in this new movement included those of Lucca, St. Lorenzo (near Turin), and St.-Ruf (near Avignon). Only in the early 12th century did the common life that was adopted become regularized as that of the Augustinian rule.

The basis of the rule was the exhortation for the religious and apostolic life contained in a letter (Letter 211) from St. Augustine, bishop of Hippo in North Africa (c. 396–430), to his sister, a nun, that, when adopted by a male community, became established as the *Regula Tertia*. Additionally, the *Regula Secunda* prescribed the daily observances for the rule. These two *Regulae* were probably accepted by some communities of clerics as early as the sixth century. The attraction of the *Regula Tertia* in the 11th century consisted both of its stipulation of a life in common for those performing a pastoral function and of its flexibility. Although it had similarities with the Benedictine discipline, it was less austere on the points of silence, fasting, and Matins. Nevertheless, in 1339 it was tightened up by Pope Benedict XII in the bull *Ad decorem*.

The new regular life was followed by several distinct orders of canons based on the Augustinian rule. The Premonstratensians acknowledged a mother house at La Prémontré and were distinguished by their white habit (thus the White Canons) from the Austin Canons (Black Canons). The Arrouaisians also acknowledged a mother house, Arrouaise (founded c. 1090), where Abbot Gervase (1121–1147) had adopted a stricter version of the rule of St. Augustine. The Victorines, established at the mother house of St.-Victor at Paris around 1108 by William of Champeaux, also devised a more austere version. In England, the male complement of Gilbertine houses also had a discipline

**Warming room next to the cloister, Lacock Abbey (Augustinian Canonesses), Wiltshire, England, c. 1232–1238.**
**Photo courtesy of Chris Schabel**

based on the Augustinian rule. However, the discussion here focuses on the Austin Canons *stricto sensu*: the Black Canons.

Whereas other orders that followed the rule of St. Augustine paid obedience to a mother house, the organization of the Austin Canons was decentralized. Chapters general were not introduced until after the exhortation of the Fourth Lateran Council of 1215, which required heads of houses in different countries to meet every three years.

The Austin Canons expanded prolifically and rapidly throughout Europe in the early 12th century. In England, a flurry of foundations occurred during the reign of Henry I (1100–1135) and his first wife, Matilda, who was an initial founder of an important house, Holy Trinity at Aldgate, from which several daughter houses were colonized. Henry founded five houses of the order and assisted the foundation of seven others. Many *curiales* or others associated with his court were founders as well. In southern France, bishops promoted these regular canons and, because they were unable to reform their chapters of secular canons, founded houses of regulars within their episcopal cities. In the early 12th century, this was a feature as well in England,

where some important Austin Canon houses were founded or refounded in or close to boroughs that were rapidly developing or expanding, reflecting the pastoral role that was anticipated of the Black Canons (even if it ultimately proved to be an unreliable expectation). Moreover, bishops in England promoted Austin Canon houses in the early 12th century. Nevertheless, few houses of Austin Canons were instituted as regular cathedral chapters, being resisted on the Continent by cathedral chapters of secular canons, whereas in England some cathedral chapters had already been colonized by Benedictine monks or were held by seculars. Exceptionally, the cathedral chapter of Carlisle was established for Black Canons by or in 1133.

Although Austin Canon houses received many parish churches from lay benefactors, (perhaps in expectation of a more effective pastoral ministry to be gained by a low level of material commitment), little evidence exists that the Black Canons performed that ministry. In a few cases in England, some parish churches might have been administered as priories with cure. However, it is evident that, especially in the towns, where population was expanding in the 12th century, the Black Canons failed to provide an adequate ministry, a fact that helps explain the popularity of the mendicant orders in urban centers from the 13th century.

In Germany, the Austin Canons were promoted in the early 12th century by Archbishop Conrad of Salzburg (d. 1147), whose initiative marked the inception of the order there. The popularity of the order was greatest in Italy, France, and England. In France proportionately more houses attained the status of abbey than did the large number of priories in England.

In numbers of religious and estates, the largest houses rivaled some of the older Benedictine houses, but most of the foundations were of small houses with slender endowments. Several strategies were available to donors, at minimal cost, in the establishment of these new religious houses, some of which related to the relationship between the regular and secular canons and other religious leading a communal life. For example, some Austin Canon houses were founded with the endowment of a parish church that in turn became the basis for the convent. Some hermitages were converted into small Austin Canon houses. The benefactions to Austin Canon houses consisted largely of advowsons of parish churches by which the appropriated glebe was returned by the laity to the Church in the form of the Austin Canons. Moreover, some colleges of secular canons were either refounded as Black Canon houses or appropriated to their use. Thus, part of the attractiveness of Austin Canon houses might have been the low economic outlay required of a patron to found a religious house, so that patronage of a religious house might be opened to a wider spectrum of patrons.

Consequently, the estates of many Austin Canon houses proved insufficient and the houses' survival tenuous. The result in England was the suppression of some of the smaller houses in the 15th century or their appropriation by another house; for example, the tiny house at Charley in northwestern Leicestershire (England) was annexed to its neighbor Ulverscroft. In 1519 Cardinal Wolsey issued *statuta* to be observed by Austin Canons because of their perceived laxness, but Austin Canon houses did not escape his suppression of some small houses to finance his academic college at Oxford (later Christ Church). Many of the houses that were sequestered in the dissolution of the small religious houses in England in 1536 were those of Austin Canons, and these were succeeded in the dissolution of 1539 by the larger houses, such as the abbeys of Cirencester, Leicester, and Osney. Some of the estates of the last became the endowment for the new diocese of Oxford.

The French houses continued their existence but suffered in the secularized atmosphere of the late 18th century, although Austrian and Swiss houses have a more unbroken continuity. The remaining French houses have formed the French Congregation, an association replicated in the Austrian Congregation of Canons Regular in 1907, which had as its president the abbot of St. Florian. The similar Swiss Congregation is led by the houses of St. Nicholas and St. Bernard (Great St. Bernard Hospice) and St. Maurice. The Lateran Congregation (Congregatio SS Salvatoris Laterensis) has the longest history comprising houses in Italy, Poland, France, Belgium, England, Spain, and the United States and having its origin in service at the Vatican basilica. In the 18th century, in Italy alone, it consisted of 45 abbeys and 79 lesser houses. It has been divided into six provinces, each presided over by a visitor or provincial; the abbot general and procurator reside in Rome at St. Pietro in Vincoli. In Italy, the order now fulfills the original objective of the parochial ministry, for the canons serve parish churches in Rome, Bologna, Genoa, Fano, and Gubbio.

DAVE POSTLES

*See also* Augustinian Rule; Austria; Canons Regular, Origins of; England; France: History; Germany: History; Liturgy: Western Christian; Poland; Scandinavia

## Further Reading

Bynum, Caroline Walker, "The Spirituality of Regular Canons in the Twelfth Century," in *Jesus as Mother: Studies in the Spirituality of the High Middle Ages*, edited by Bynum, Berkeley: University of California Press, 1982

Dickinson, John C., *The Origins of the Austin Canons and Their Introduction into England*, London: SPCK, 1950

Dickinson, John C., "Canons Regular of St. Augustine," in *New Catholic Encyclopedia*, volume 3, Washington D.C.: Catholic University of America Press, 1967

Lawless, George, editor, *Augustine of Hippo and His Monastic Rule*, Oxford and New York: Oxford University Press, 1987

Milis, Ludo, "Ermites et chanoines réguliers au XIIe siècle," *Cahiers de Civilisation Médiévale* 22 (1979)

# Augustinian Friars/Hermits

In 13th-century Italy three orders of hermits followed the Rule of St. Augustine: the Hermits of Tuscany (instituted as an order by Innocent IV [1243–1254] in 1244 as the only religious order ever founded by a pope), the Hermits of Blessed John the Good, and the Hermits of Brettino. Because of the similarity of the three orders, Pope Alexander VI (1254–1261), on 9 April 1256, formed them in a "Great Union" into one Order, the Austin Friars, or Hermits of St. Augustine.

The Order is famed for its charity, spirituality, and theological study of St. Augustine's teaching on the primacy of grace. To fulfill the Order's vocation to preach and teach, like the Franciscans and Dominicans, intellectual pursuits were very much to the fore. The English province had a house at Oxford University as early as 1266 and one at Cambridge University by 1289. Gregor Mendel (1822–1884), the founder of genetics, was an Augustinian Friar.

The Order is ruled by a prior-general and was formed into provinces as need allowed. Like the original Italian hermits who claimed descent from St. Augustine of Hippo (354–430), a claim difficult to prove, the Augustinians chose to follow the same Rule. Constitutions were drawn up to regulate the daily life of the Order and to encourage the friars to study Scripture, the

Nave of the Augustinerkirche, Vienna, Austria, 14th century. This church became the Habsburgs' court church.
Photo courtesy of Chris Schabel

teachings of the Church, and the writings of St. Augustine. According to the Rule the friars lived in common in poverty and in the spirit of charity toward one another, and because the call was to the eremitic life, the medieval *horarium* was severe, and as mendicants they often had to beg for their subsistence. The English friar William of Flete, known for his saintliness, sought the eremitic way of life at the hermitage of Leccetto (still extant). In 1367 he met St. Catherine of Siena (c. 1347–1380), a Dominican nun, and through his influence and direction she expounded her mystical doctrine, but in a decidedly Augustinian way.

Cardinal Annibaldi, protector of the Tuscan Hermits, had plans to expand the Order into Europe and England. From Italy the Order spread eastward into Poland and west across Europe through Germany, the Low Countries, and France and, by the late Middle Ages, into the Iberian Peninsula and as far as the Holy Land. The English province, founded in 1260, went on to become one of the most important in the Order. In 1280 the English friars opened their first house in Ireland, and at the dissolution of the monasteries 22 were in existence. Ireland became virtually independent with its own vicar-provincial.

The Order was decimated by the Black Death; 5,000 of the friars died out of a total of more than 8,000. This might partly explain the later fall in numbers, whereby England in 1538 had only 317.

The Augustinian friaries, like the mendicant houses, were beacons of prayer and the spiritual life while maintaining an active apostolate. The Augustinians were always strong supporters of the papacy and orthodoxy, defending both on many occasions from attack from both within and without. The renowned English theologian Thomas Winterton defended the doctrine of transubstantiation against his friend John Wyclif (c. 1330–1384). Indeed for centuries Augustinians held the important Vatican posts of papal sacristan and "devil's disciple."

Germany was always a center of activity. Johann Staupitz (c. 1468–1524) led the Augustinian Observantine reform, which became a separate order in 1506. Martin Luther (1483–1546) joined the Observantines at Erfurt in 1505. After his break with Rome in 1517, thus beginning the Reformation, the Augustinians became Luther's staunchest critics. Many of his contemporaries followed Luther, but not Staupitz. Indeed the Reformation caused much damage to the Order in Germany. Elsewhere property was confiscated and recruitment forbidden wherever Protestantism was victorious.

In England Henry VIII's Reformation completely destroyed the Austin Friars. Myles Coverdale (1487/88–1569), an English apostate friar, is more famous for his translation of the Bible into English. Printed in Antwerp in 1535, it influenced the King James Authorized Version. Thomas Cranmer (1489–1556) used

Cloister, Augustinian Friars' House, Erfurt, Germany, 14th century. Martin Luther lived here 1505–1508.
Photo courtesy of Chris Schabel

Coverdale's translation of the Psalms in his Book of Common Prayer, which is still used today. The loss of such intellects weakened the Austin Friars. John Stone, a Canterbury Friar, was the only one to remain steadfast in the Catholic faith. He was executed on 27 December 1539, the only martyr from the once great English province. He was canonized in 1970 by Pope Paul VI (1963–1978) as one of the 40 martyrs of England and Wales.

Although the Reformation caused irreparable damage to the Order, it did not destroy it. Further harm was done by the French Revolution, which not only destroyed the French province but unleashed wars as well, putting many European friaries at risk. Nevertheless the Order survived.

By the 16th and 17th centuries, the friars had arrived in the New World, sent there initially by the Spaniard Thomas of Villanova (c. 1487–1555). From there they converted the Philippines, traveling as far as Goa, later going to the Near East and Far East. In 1794 the Irish province sent missionaries to the United States. The new province was approved by Rome in 1796, and others were soon established in other parts of the United States and Canada. In 1842 a college was founded in Pennsylvania that eventually became Thomas of Villanova University. The Irish friars founded a province in Australia in the 19th century and landed in Nigeria in 1939.

Despite the dissolution in England, several Britons did join the Augustinians in Europe and, together with Irish friars, returned to England as missionaries. Although severely weakened, the Irish province survived the Reformation. Thus, an Augustinian presence appears to have existed in England even in the late 17th century. However, it was not until 1865 that the first real post-Reformation church of Austin Friars was founded in England: St. Monica's, Hoxton Square, London. The community consisted of Irish friars, and from that day forward they began to rebuild the former English province. Finally, on 8 September 1977, the English province was restored as the Anglo-Scottish province. The present provincial is an Englishman, the first since the dissolution in 1538. The Augustinian Order now has provinces worldwide.

PHILIP E. MCWILLIAMS

*See also* Augustinian Rule; Dissolution of Monasteries: England, Ireland, and Wales; England: History; France: History; Germany: Sites; Ireland: History; Luther, Martin; Poland; Reformation; Theology, Western Christian: Augustinian Friars/Hermits

### Further Reading

Burton, Janet E., *Monastic and Religious Orders in Britain, 1000–1300* (Cambridge Medieval Textbooks), Cambridge and New York: Cambridge University Press, 1994

Burton, Janet E., *Medieval Monasticism: Monasticism in the Medieval West: From Its Origins to the Coming of the Friars* (Headstart History Papers), Witney: Headstart History, 1996

Gregorio, Michael di, *The Augustinians towards 2000*, Rome: Augustinian, 1993

Gwynn, Aubrey, *The English Austin Friars in the Time of Wyclif*, London: Oxford University Press, 1940

Hackett, Michael Benedict, *The Austin Friars*, Clare: Augustinian Press, 1998

Knowles, David, *The Monastic Order in England: A History of Its Development from the Times of St. Dunstan to the Fourth Lateran Council, 943–1216*, Cambridge: Cambridge University Press, 1940; 2nd edition, 1963; New York: Cambridge University Press, 1976

Lawless, George, *Augustine of Hippo and His Monastic Rule*, New York: Oxford University Press, and Oxford: Clarendon Press, 1987

Lawrence, C.H., *The Friars: The Impact of the Early Mendicant Movement on Western Society* (The Medieval World), London and New York: Longman, 1994

Roth, Francis, *The English Austin Friars, 1249–1538* (Cassiciacum Studies in St. Augustine and the Augustinian Order, American series, volumes 6 and 7), 2 vols., New York: Augustinian Historical Institute, 1966

# Augustinian Rule

The Augustinian Rule, or Rule of Augustine, is a synthesis of several distinct but related documents, each of which in its attribution to Augustine of Hippo (A.D. 354–430) is still contested. Taken as a whole the Rule has provided the model for numerous religious communities in the Latin West, including the Premonstratensians, the Augustinian Canons at the Abbey of St. Victor, and the Augustinian Friars/Hermits to which Martin Luther belonged. It is still the rule of the Order of St. Augustine, descended from the Hermits.

The distinctive character of the Rule lies in its emphasis on the ties of community life and fraternal charity. Based on the notion of the "apostolic life" presented in Acts 4:32–35, the Rule exhorts its followers to "live together in harmony and be of one mind and heart in God: for this is the purpose of your coming together" (*Praeceptum* 1.2). This commitment to unanimity of heart and mind, through which the monks are called to "honour God mutually in each other" (*Praeceptum* 1.8), takes careful notice of the social conditions under which one enters the community. In the Rule it is important that social relations of rich and poor be neither replicated nor reversed among the monks. While the rich should not retain an attitude of superiority toward their poor brethren, the Rule also cautions that "monasteries should not provide advantages for the rich to the disadvantage of the poor. Such would be the case if the rich become humble and the poor become proud" (*Praeceptum* 1.7).

The particular observances recommended in the Rule are typically monastic: communal praying of the psalms, manual labor, common property, silence, obedience, regular reading, fasting, chastity, and fraternal correction. The text itself is brief and gives the impression of a summary more than of a code of conduct, so that some scholars have suggested that it represents a "reminder" based on oral teaching.

Essentially two elements comprise the Rule as it now circulates. The first is the *Ordo monasterii* (Regulations for a Monastery), which is for the most part a list of particular observances, including a rather detailed description of the psalmody. The authenticity of this document is widely disputed, as some have suggested that it is a much later document (perhaps of the seventh century), and others have wondered whether it comes not from Augustine but rather from his circle of influence, perhaps even from his good friend Alypius. Scholarly consensus, although not yet unanimous, has come to consider the second element, the *Praeceptum* (Rule), as authentically a work of Augustine's, dating from around 397. This text outlines more generally the purpose and nature of the Augustinian monastery and then proceeds to discuss in general the monastic observances as enumerated previously. Some have argued that a Rule for Nuns, i.e., the same rule applied to communities of women, precedes the Rule for Monks. The Rule for Nuns is found within Augustine's Letter 211, which is now believed by many to be authentic. However, recent scholarship tends to conclude that the masculine form preceded the feminine and that Augustine himself adapted the Rule for Monks to meet the needs of the community of women whom he addressed.

However, it should be added that the ease with which the Rule is shifted from masculine to feminine while preserving the same basic shape is one of its distinctive characteristics. Its brevity allows the general framework of a way of life to emerge without too much specificity. Perhaps this flexibility is why the Rule has appealed to so many different communities in the Latin West: it is intrinsically adaptable. The traditional final form of the Rule as it circulates today consists of the first sentence of the *Ordo monasterii* followed by the complete text of the *Praeceptum*.

Because it is so brief, the Rule can offer only the beginnings of an understanding of Augustine's teaching on monasticism. In Augustine one can see the blending of the monastic ideals represented by Athanasius' *Life of Antony* and the classical notion of the ascetic philosophical retreat into *otium* (leisure or retirement), which Augustine received in large part from Cicero. According to his account in the *Confessions*, it was on reading Cicero's *Hortensius* that Augustine converted to "philosophy," and it was on hearing the story of St. Antony that he fled into the garden at Milan and came to the point of final conversion to Christianity. George Lawless (1987), O.S.A., has demonstrated how these two ascetic ideals continued to influence Augustine from the moment of his conversion to the end of his life. Late in 386, Augustine gathered a community of friends in a villa in Cassiciacum. The community of the villa took shape more along the classical model of philosophical retirement, but every day began and ended with prayer. Augustine's written dialogues from this period might be better described as Christian philosophy than as spiritual instruction or any other similar monastic activity.

When Augustine returned to his hometown of Thagaste in North Africa in 388, his life acquired a more monastic shape. The household was characterized by the surrender of possessions, fraternal conversation, fasting, prayer, spiritual reading of the Scriptures, and intellectual work. However, only when he came to Hippo and was ordained a priest in 391 did Augustine first quote Acts 4:32–35, the "seed-text" of his monastic vision. The house he established in Hippo was the first to be referred to as a "monastery." However, it should be noted that this transition from the classical to the monastic was gradual and almost un-self-conscious, and the Rule still carries this double heritage.

In sum Augustine's monastic orientation, like the rest of his thought, developed and deepened throughout his career. Beginning from the classical Roman model of retirement from the world, Augustine developed a vision of community and even of shared contemplation within and at the service of the Church.

KEVIN L. HUGHES

*See also* Antony, St.; Archaeology: Near East; Augustinian Canons; Augustinian Friars/Hermits; Canons Regular, Origins of; Christianity: Overview; Liturgy: Western Christian; Origins: Western Christian; Servites; Spain: History; Vadstena, Sweden

**Further Reading**

Bavel, Tarsicius J. van, *Christians in the World: An Introduction to the Spirituality of St. Augustine*, New York: Catholic Book Publishing, 1980

Brown, Peter, *Augustine of Hippo*, Berkeley: University of California Press, and London: Faber, 1967

Lawless, George, *Augustine of Hippo and His Monastic Rule*, Oxford: Clarendon Press, and New York: Oxford University Press, 1987

Verheijen, Luc, "La 'Regula Sancti Augustini'," *Vigiliae Christianae* 7 (1953)

Verheijen, Luc, *Saint Augustine's Monasticism in the Light of Acts 4:32–35*, Villanova, Pennsylvania: Villanova University Press, 1979

Verheijen, Luc, "La Règle de saint Augustin: L'état actuel des questions (début 1975)," *Augustiniana* 35 (1985)

Zumkeller, A., *Das Mönchtum des heiligen Augustinus*, 2nd edition, Würzburg: Augustinus-Verlag, 1968; as *Augustine's Ideal of the Religious Life*, New York: Fordham University Press, 1986

# Aum Shinrikyō

The new religions of Japan that have emerged in the 19th and 20th centuries have generally been lay-centered movements. One exception to this has been the controversial movement Aum Shinrikyō, widely known for having committed a number of attacks on Japanese society, including the 1995 Tokyo subway attack. Aum is distinctive in modern Japanese religious history as a new religion centered on world renunciation and because, in an age in which monasticism had become an increasingly marginal

in Japan, it affirmed the importance of withdrawal from the world as central to the search for enlightenment.

The name Aum Shinrikyō combines the Sanskrit term *Aum*, signifying the forces of creation, preservation, and destruction, with the Japanese *shinrikyō* (teaching of truth). This fusion illustrates Aum's eclectic nature, drawing on Buddhist, Hindu, and Tibetan as well as Japanese religious influences. It was established by Asahara Shōkō (b. 1955) in the mid-1980s with a focus on achieving individual spiritual transcendence through yoga, meditation, and asceticism. Emphasizing the spiritual pollution of the body and phenomenal world, the movement stated that the only way to reach higher spiritual realms was by withdrawing and cutting oneself off from the corrupting karmic influences of the mundane world. Asahara was believed to be the only truly liberated being in the world, and followers needed to show absolute obedience to and receive initiations from him to improve their spiritual standing.

Although Aum also had lay members (of its total membership of around 10,000 in 1995, some 1,200 had renounced the world), its primary emphasis was on renunciation. The term used in Aum for renouncing the world was *shukke* (leaving the family), the same word as used in Japanese Buddhism for "becoming a monk." Like Buddhist priests Aum members, who were mostly young and well educated, assumed a new name when they did this. In Aum these "holy names" were based on the names of the disciples of the historical Buddha, and Aum's *shukkesha* (renouncers) regarded themselves as seeking to implement the simple, austere disciplines of early Buddhism in their lives.

In renouncing the world, members gave all their worldly goods to Aum and lived lives of extreme simplicity in its communes, sleeping in dormitories, rising early, eating a spartan vegetarian diet, engaging in meditation and severe ascetic practices, and working long hours for the movement. Commune members were expected to be celibate and to follow individual systems of practice ordained by Asahara. The movement developed a strict hierarchy based on spiritual attainment: besides the division between lay members and those who had renounced the world, the *shukkesha* themselves were divided into seven ranks, the highest below Asahara bearing the title *Seitaishi* (sacred great teacher). Ordinations to each level were carried out by Asahara, and each rank was distinguished by the color of the robes worn, from orange for the lowest ranks of *shukkesha* to blue for the *seitaishi*.

Asahara's teaching included powerful millennialist themes, announcing that the world was heading for destruction before the end of the 20th century. Originally Aum preached a mission to save the world; however, as it met with resistance to its teachings and because few people renounced the world to join its mission, it became increasingly convinced that apocalypse was at hand. It now preached that the world merited destruction – a prospect that was welcomed as a means of enabling the true seekers of Aum to attain spiritual fulfilment in a new realm. Combining martial images with a communal, world-renouncing focus, its members saw themselves as sacred warriors led by Asahara. They saw him as a messiah destined to bring salvation and to destroy evil in a holy war against the evils of the mundane world. Gripped by this martial mentality, Asahara became convinced that his movement was the target of a huge conspiracy that aimed to destroy it and decided that Aum should arm itself with chemical weapons to defend itself. It also began to engage in violence, after which many of its senior figures, including Asahara, were arrested and imprisoned in 1995. Many members left the movement, but around 900 remain, many continuing to regard themselves as monks or nuns with Asahara as their supreme spiritual master. They still engage in rigorous ascetic practices.

IAN READER

*See also* Asceticism: Buddhist Perspectives; Death: Buddhist Perspectives; Japan: History

**Further Reading**

Kisala, Robert, "The Aum Spiritual Truth Church in Japan," in *Wolves within the Fold: Religious Leadership and Abuses of Power*, edited by Anson Shupe, New Brunswick, New Jersey: Rutgers University Press, 1998

Reader, Ian, *A Poisonous Cocktail?: Aum Shinrikyō's Path to Violence*, Copenhagen: NIAS Books, 1996

Reader, Ian, *Religious Violence in Contemporary Japan: The Case of Aum Shinrikyō*, London: Curzon Press, and Honolulu: University of Hawaii Press, 2000

Shimazono, Susumu, "In the Wake of Aum: The Formation and Transformation of a Universe of Belief," *Japanese Journal of Religious Studies* 22:3–4 (1995)

Shimazono, Susumu, *Gendai shūkyō no kanōsei: Oumu Shinrkyō to bōryoku* (The Potential of Religion in the Modern Day: Aum Shinrikyō and Violence), Sosho gendai no shukyo, 2, Tokyo: Iwanami Shoten, 1997

Takahashi, Hidetoshi, *Oumu kara no kikan* (Escape from Aum), Tokyo: Sōshisha, 1996

# Austin Canons. *See* Augustinian Canons

# Australia

Christianity is barely two centuries old in Australia, and the presence of monasticism is even more recent, yet the 19th century saw four separate attempts to establish a community of monks on its shores, each in its own way intended to help evangelize that vast continent, much as St. Boniface (a model explicitly cited) had done for central Europe in the eighth century.

The earliest such attempt was also the most ambitious and unusual. In August 1843 the first Catholic bishop in Australia, John Bede Polding (1794–1877), an English Benedictine, officially inaugurated a monastery next to his cathedral church of St. Mary in Sydney. Its monks were intended to supply clergy not only for splendid cathedral liturgies but also for a network of small missionary priories throughout his enormous diocese. Polding, as much a romantic as a missioner, set up St. Mary's as

a cathedral priory, partly on the English medieval model and firmly under episcopal control (with his vicar general, Henry Gregory, as prior). His taste for the neo-Gothic in architecture and decoration extended to monastic practice as well, namely, the admission of numerous child oblates into his monastery.

Although never part of the English Benedictine congregation, 25 choir monks and 11 lay brothers were eventually professed for the community. However, the vision of an immense, monastic diocese soon foundered on its own inherent contradictions and impracticalities. The monastery was dragged down by this failure, by inadequacies of formation and Polding's unwillingness to allow the monks any independent leadership (despite the extended absences of both himself and Gregory). Transferred to Lyndhurst, the community was finally suppressed in 1877 by the second archbishop of Sydney (another English Benedictine).

Thousands of miles away, on the western side of the continent, Rosendo Salvado (1814–1900) and Joseph Serra (1810–1886), two Spanish Benedictines of the extinct Congregation of Valladolid, arrived in 1846 at the Victoria plains, about 80 miles north of Perth. Their focus was not the fledgling European settlements but the despised and endangered aboriginal population. A monastery and agricultural settlement, New Norcia, was founded and in 1867 became the center of a vast abbey-*nullius*. (The latter was eventually abolished 115 years later.)

In 1880, of the 59 professed monks in the community, only eight were priests, and for over seven decades (1908–1981), the real missionary effort was concentrated on Kalumburu, an isolated spot in far northern Western Australia. In contrast, New Norcia itself became largely an educational center, with schools and orphanages (in which only a handful of the monks were directly involved). The last of these institutions closed in 1991.

For at least a century after its foundation, New Norcia was essentially a Spanish outpost in the Australian bush, as reflected in its architecture and the composition of its monastic community. It is arguable that New Subiaco, a short-lived monastery (1851–1867) founded in the suburbs of Perth and especially favored by Joseph Serra, would have been more successful at promoting Benedictine values in the local Church than its rival ever was. Today, New Norcia, with its old buildings and museums, has become a popular tourist attraction. However, the number of monks is very much reduced (less than 20).

The fourth of these 19th-century foundations was made in the remotest location of all, when, in September 1890, a colony of Cistercians of the Strict Observance from the French abbey of Sept Fons transferred their unsuccessful foundation in New Caledonia to Beagle Bay on the northwest coast of Australia. This was not far from the later mission of Kalumburu, and the choice of site was driven equally by a missionary impulse. However, although these Frenchmen sought to evangelize the local aborigines, they also wanted to maintain a strictly contemplative lifestyle and a highly austere monastic observance (in terms of clothing, sparse vegetarian diet, heavy liturgical schedule, and so on) – all this despite backbreaking work to establish an agricultural and cattle-raising concern. The tensions inherent in such a project, plus the trying climactic conditions (heat, dust, annual wet season, and the ubiquitous mosquitoes), doomed the foundation to failure, and it was abandoned after only nine years.

Thus, of the four monasteries referred to previously, only one survived into the following century. Much more resilient were the two 19th-century foundations for Benedictine women, both made by Archbishop Polding of Sydney.

In February 1849 the archbishop inaugurated an enclosed Benedictine convent with two English nuns (one of them Henry Gregory's sister) on an estate (Subiaco) at Rydalmere near Sydney. The community gradually attracted recruits and in March 1851 began a small boarding school for the daughters of well-to-do Catholic families. The archbishop sometimes spoke of Subiaco as a sister community to St. Mary's, and he kept a tight control over its life. It was not until 1864 that the nuns were permitted to elect their own superior, and even after that date, Polding's successors in the archdiocese (especially Cardinal Moran) were quick to check any signs of independence.

In the lean years of the late 19th century, the monastery remained an island of English tradition in the sea of Irish Australian Catholicism. Its school was eventually given up in 1922, and in 1957 the community transferred to Pennant Hills. Less than 30 years later, the nuns moved from Sydney altogether and settled at Jamberoo on the south coast of New South Wales, where the abbey has both a flourishing guest house and a full novitiate. In 1978 a dependent house was opened on the central Queensland coast, and this small community (at Lammermoor near Yeppoon) is now autonomous. It has its own modest dependent house at Croydon in the suburbs of Melbourne.

In February 1857, with the assistance of a Sister of Charity, Scholastica Gibbons (1816–1901), Polding founded the first Australian congregation of active women religious, later known as the Sisters of the Good Samaritan of the Order of St. Benedict. The early constitutions and spirituality of this institute drew on Benedictine sources, but its original work was with destitute and oppressed women in colonial society. In the early decades of the 20th century, the congregation began to expand rapidly and in 1937 already numbered some 566 sisters. However, by this time its focus had long switched to school education, and the Benedictine element in its official legislation and ethos had also noticeably diminished (especially after the intervention of Cardinal Moran in 1889). Yet after the Second Vatican Council, interest was renewed in this early heritage, and in 1975 the Good Samaritans became part of the international Benedictine Confederation. The congregation is present in Japan (since 1948), the Philippines (1990), and Kiribati (1991), although its overall numbers are now declining (about 380 sisters in January 1998).

Apart from the steady expansion of the Good Samaritan Sisters, the first half of the 20th century saw only one additional Benedictine foundation in Australia: the Benedictine Missionary Sisters of New Norcia, established in 1935 by the third abbot, Anselm Catalan. These religious, always few in number, worked at both New Norcia and Kalumburu until the mid-1970s, when most of them returned to Spain. In October 1984 they were accepted into a much larger congregation, that of the Missionary

Benedictine Sisters of Tutzing, which still maintains a small presence at Kalumburu. However, in the decade or so after World War II, interest was renewed in Australia as a monastic site.

The Cistercians returned in 1954, but this time from the Irish abbey of Roscrea. The monks successfully established themselves on a thousand-acre property at Tarrawarra in the Yarra valley (near Melbourne), where they now support themselves with their cattle herds, craft work, and guest house. Perhaps especially through its liturgical life and the writing and spiritual guidance provided by some of its monks, this community (today numbering just over 20) has become a spiritual center of considerable significance in the Australian Church. (In the same year as Tarrawarra's foundation, Irish Cistercians from Mount Melleray established a monastery at Kopua, on the north island of New Zealand.) In addition, two modest Benedictine foundations in the Sydney area were made during this period, both of which have remained small in scale.

Monks of the Sylvestrine Benedictine congregation date their presence in the city from 1949. Since 1961 they have been settled on its northwestern outskirts, at Arcadia, where a monastery was gradually constructed. The community of 14 monks (1998) has a small beef-cattle herd and a guest house, cares for two parishes, and is involved in teaching and chaplaincy work.

Tyburn Priory, belonging to the worldwide Congregation of the Adorers of the Sacred Heart of Jesus of Montmartre O.S.B., was founded in Sydney in 1956 and since 1986 has been situated at Riverstone to the west of the city. This community leads an enclosed, contemplative life centered on the liturgy and perpetual adoration of the Blessed Sacrament. The sisters make profession to the congregation and may be transferred from house to house. (In 1996, a foundation was made in New Zealand, in the Diocese of Auckland.)

Two small Anglican Benedictine communities now exist in the southeastern state of Victoria. Saint Mark's Priory (founded in Melbourne in 1975 and transferred to rural Camperdown in 1980) has two monks and two nuns and the Community of Christ the King, formed in 1997 (in Wangaratta), consists of four transfers from another Anglican sisterhood.

However, despite its importance in the early history of the Church in Australia and the publicity sometimes given to particular houses, the Benedictine tradition now has only a minimal impact overall. Given the size and age structure of most of the existing communities, the future of Christian monasticism on the continent looks increasingly uncertain.

TERENCE KAVENAGH

*See also* Benedictines: General or Male; England: History

## Further Reading

Birt, Henry Norbert, *Benedictine Pioneers in Australia*, 2 vols., St. Louis, Missouri: Herder, and London: Herbert and Daniel, 1911

Claffey, Camillus, "Brief Account of the First Few Months at Notre Dame [Tarrawarra Abbey]," *Tjurunga: An Australasian Benedictine Review* 53 (1997)

Forster, Marie Gregory, "Benedictine Women in Australia," in

*A Man with an Idea: St. Benedict of Nursia*, edited by John Stanley Martin, Melbourne: University of Melbourne, 1981

Forster, Marie Gregory, "Subiaco: The Arrival of Benedictine Nuns in Sydney," *Tjurunga: An Australasian Benedictine Review* 54 (1998)

Hutchinson, David, et al., editors, *A Town Like No Other: The Living Tradition of New Norcia*, South Freemantle: Freemantle Arts Centre Press, 1995

Kavenagh, Terence, "Benedictine Monks in Australia," in *St. Benedict: A Man with an Idea*, edited by John Stanley Martin, Melbourne: University of Melbourne, 1981

Kavenagh, Terence, "The Sylvestrine Benedictines in Australia," *Inter Fratres* 40:1–2 (1990); 41:1–2 (1991); 42:1 (1992); 44:1–2 (1994); and 45:1 (1995)

Kelleher, Marilyn, "Sister Scholastica Gibbons: Co-Foundress of the Sisters of the Good Samaritan," *Tjurunga: An Australasian Benedictine Review* 50 (1996)

Malone, Marie-Thérèse, "Cardinal Moran and the Subiaco Constitutions," *Tjurunga: An Australasian Benedictine Review* 32 (1987)

McGlynn, Marie Gerard, "The Growth of a Religious Institute: Some Lists and Statistics Relating to the History of the Good Samaritan Sisters O.S.B., 1857–1937," *Tjurunga: An Australasian Benedictine Review* 39 (1990)

Shanahan, Mary, *Out of Time, Out of Place: Henry Gregory and the Benedictine Order in Colonial Australia*, Canberra: Australian National University Press, 1970

Stormon, Edward J., editor and translator, *The Salvado Memoirs*, Nedlands: University of Western Australia Press, 1977

# Austria

Christianity came to what is today Austria when that region was still part of the Roman Empire. Eugipp's *Vita of St. Severin* (d. 482) contains the first hints of monastic sites, or "cellulae," whose local identification is much discussed (probably Mautern in Lower Austria, Lorch in Upper Austria, and Salzburg). It is also an open question whether the so-called catacombs near St. Peter in the heart of Salzburg served as cells for an Irish community of hermits during the early Middle Ages. At the end of the seventh century, Bishop Rupert (c. 650–714) of Worms, invited by the duke of Bavaria to lead a new campaign of Christianization in his southern provinces, came to Salzburg, where he founded not only a new bishopric but also the first lasting monastery of Austria, dedicated to St. Peter. Following a custom of the Celtic Church, he made himself abbot, although already a bishop. However, it is not impossible that Rupert gave a new organization to an already existing small monastic community or that he revived a still earlier community. In any case St. Peter would emerge as the oldest Benedictine monastery in the world to exist without interruption from the date of its foundation to the present day. In 711 or 712 Rupert founded another monastery south of Salzburg, Bischofshofen, and somewhat later, again in Salzburg, the first nunnery, Nonnberg, where he installed his niece Erintrudis as abbess.

Further monastic sites soon followed that were designed to Christianize the mostly heathen population and to strengthen the rule of the Bavarian dukes and later that of the Franconian kings. These convents obeyed the Rule of St. Benedict. In 748 Mondsee (on the lake of that name) was erected by Duke Odilo II of Bavaria; monks from Monte Cassino accepted an invitation to form the first community. In 777 Duke Tassilo III (ruled 748–788) had a monastery built at Kremsmünster, an outpost against the Avars in the East. Around 800 St. Florian was dedicated to the martyr of 304. The invading heathen Magyars (Hungarians) during the first half of the tenth century burned many monasteries (e.g., St. Florian, Kremsmünster, and Mondsee) until they were defeated in 955. As in other countries of Europe, the early Austrian monasteries were centers of written Christian Latin culture in a sea of illiterate indigenous oral traditions, mostly of Germanic and Slavonic stock. Only a very few manuscripts have survived to testify to the work of the scriptoria

**Cemetery, St. Peter's Abbey (Benedictine), Salzburg, Austria. Founded in A.D. 696, St. Peter's Abbey is the oldest monastery in German-speaking Europe.**
**Photo courtesy of the Austrian National Tourist Office**

Stams Abbey (Cistercian), Tyrol, rebuilt 1729–1732. It was founded in 1273 in memory of the last Hohenstaufen Emperor Konradin by his mother Elisabeth.
Photo courtesy of the Austrian National Tourist Office

before the High Middle Ages. Codices were markedly influenced by Insular (i.e., Anglo-Saxon) patterns, as is the case with the famous chalice that Duke Tassilo presented to Kremsmünster.

In the 11th century the reform movement of Gorze and Cluny spread to these convents (St. Peter in Salzburg, Mondsee, and Kremsmünster), and there were several new important foundations of Benedictine monasteries by local nobles (e.g., Lambach, c. 1040). Nonetheless it was the Church reform of the 12th century that was responsible for a new flowering of monasticism in Austria. The main impact came from the Cistercians, who erected their first monasteries while St. Bernard (1090–1153) was still alive: Rein (1130), Heiligenkreuz (c. 1133), Zwettl (1138), and Wilhering (1146). Of less importance were the foundations of the Premonstatensians, such as Wilten-Innsbruck (1128) and Schlägl (1218). Like the Cistercians the Augustinian Canons were promoted by the Babenberg dynasty, which ruled Austria from 976 to 1246. Melk (a tenth-century Benedictine from 1089 to the present) and Klosterneuburg (11th century) developed into important monastic centers in Lower Austria. Because of Austria's geographical position near Italy, the mendicants arrived here very early from the south: in 1217 the

Dominicans in Friesach, in 1224/30 the Franciscans in Vienna, and other houses were to follow. Later the Habsburg dynasty, ruling from 1276 to 1918, invited Carthusians into the country: Mauerbach, founded in 1316, was their first establishment. Lay religious groups remained marginal in this country (e.g., the beguines in Vienna).

During the Counter-Reformation the Habsburgs installed the Jesuits and the Capuchins in their dominion. The former came to Vienna in 1551, where they joined the university, to Innsbruck in 1561, to Graz in 1572, and to Linz in 1600. The latter established their first convent in Innsbruck in 1593.

The late 17th and 18th centuries can be called the great age of Austrian monasticism, the Thirty Years' War (1618–1648) being over and the Turks having been defeated. Most abbeys were reconstructed in an extremely sumptuous baroque style, representing the victorious Roman Catholic religion (the numerous Protestants having been expelled from the Habsburg territories or driven into clandestiny) but embodying the pact between Church and state: large monasteries, such as St. Florian, Melk, and Göttweig, all possess splendid special suites for the emperor and his court.

When in 1780 Maria Theresia's son Joseph II (1780–1790) was enthroned, Austrian monasticism received a blow from which it was never to recover. In 1782 Joseph, wanting to put into practice the ideals of the Enlightenment, abolished all contemplative orders, accepting only those that worked actively in the fields of pastoral care, education, or charity. One-third of the more than 700 convents in the Habsburg territories had to close including around 140 in Austria itself. Because most of them had grown immensely rich, the emperor was also interested in transferring their estates to the state, that is, to secular clerics. Often these reforms were undertaken without any understanding of the cultural wealth of monastic traditions, so thousands of medieval manuscripts simply had to be destroyed. During the restoration of the 19th century, many convents were revived and recovered their possessions. Later many new congregations were established, especially those of caritative and educatorial female branches. Whereas the monasteries had always been centers of religious art in former times, in the 19th and 20th centuries their contributions in this field became unimportant. A new disaster hit the monasteries when Austria joined the Third Reich in 1938: more than 200 convents had to close until the end of the war.

Today the old monasteries, although inhabited by rather small communities, still exercise an important role in local economies, where they employ the local population on the extensive estates they own. At the same time they also have their place in tourism; several monasteries even have founded a union called "Klösterreich" to enhance their advertisements. During the last few years, many of these sites have been chosen by the counties' governments as places for historical exhibitions that attract large crowds. During the preparations thereto, the buildings have been restored so that today all the more important monastic sites are in a satisfactory state of conservation. Nonetheless the disproportion between the large historical buildings designed for hundreds of inhabitants and the small number of monks living there remains a problem, as it is difficult for the communities to meet the cost for conservation of their architecture and art treasures. Today about 2,000 monks and 7,000 nuns live in Austria.

*Monasteries to Visit*

Nearly all Austrian monasteries welcome visitors to the church and parts of the other buildings, some, to be sure, only in the form of guided tours. Proceeding from the West to the East, the most interesting sites are the following. In Tyrol the Cistercian monastery of Stams presents mostly 17th-century architecture and art. In the city of Salzburg are two outstanding monastic sites: St. Peter, in the very town center, with a Romanesque basilica adapted magnificently to the baroque style and surrounded by the atmospheric churchyard, and Nonnberg, the abbey of the Benedictine nuns, situated very beautifully on the castle's slope, with a late Gothic church, reredos, and stained-glass windows. Among the many well-preserved monasteries in Upper Austria, at least Lambach, St. Florian, and Wilhering must be mentioned. The first preserves the most important wall paintings from the end of the 11th century to be found in any German-speaking country, the biblical iconography of which conceals allusions to the Investiture Controversy. Saint Florian exhibits its gorgeous baroque rooms for the emperor and an important museum (with paintings by A. Altdorfer, among others). Wilhering possesses the most beautiful of all Austrian churches in the rococo style. Very rich is Lower Austria, too: the Cistercian monastery of Zwettl has conserved the original early 12th-century dormitory, chapter room, and an important Gothic church; Romanesque and Gothic Cistercian ecclesiastical architecture can be found in Heiligenkreuz, here embellished by excellent sculptures of Bernini's pupil G. Giuliani. Very extensive baroque sites, triumphantly built above the Danube, are the monasteries of Göttweig and Melk, the library of which contains many medieval manuscripts and rare books. In Klosterneuburg one finds the "Verdun Altar" by Nicolas of Verdun, an outstanding enamel altarpiece dated 1181. In Carinthia one should visit at least Gurk, with its Romanesque crypt built on 100 columns and its rich early Gothic mural paintings, and Millstadt, a Romanesque site with enigmatic architectural sculpture (12th century).

PETER DINZELBACHER

*See also* Benedictines: General or Male; Capuchins; Celtic Monasticism; Cistercians: General or Male; Czech Republic; Dissolution of Monasteries: Continental Europe; Premonstratensian Canons; Vienna, Austria

## Further Reading

Angerer, Joachim, and Gerhard Trumler, *Klösterreich*, Vienna: Molden, 1978

Bamberger, Richard, editor, *Österreich Lexikon*, 2 vols., Vienna: Österreichischer Bundesverlag für Unterricht, Wissenschaft und Kunst, 1966

Englisch, Ernst, *Ein Beitrag zur Geschichte der Bettelorden in Österreich von den Anfängen bis in die Mitte des 14. Jhs.*, Ph.D. Diss., Vienna, 1969

Friess, G.E., "Geschichte der Österreichischen Minoritenprovinz," *Archiv fur Österr. Geschichte* 64 (1882)

Hogg, James, *Die Kartäuser in Österreich*, Salzburg: Institut fur Anglistik und Amerikanistik, Universität Salzburg, 1980

Schaffran, Emerich, *Stifte in Österreich*, Linz: R. Trauner, 1962

Schmeller-Kitt, Adelheid, *Klöster in Österreich*, Frankfurt am Main: Weidlich, 1965

Tausch, Hildebert, *Benediktinisches Mönchtum in Österreich*, Vienna: Herder, 1949

Tomek, Ernst, *Kirchengeschichte Österreichs*, Innsbruck: Tyrolia, 1935

# B

## Bacon, Roger c. 1214–1292

English Franciscan scholar

Roger Bacon was born into a prosperous English family early in the 13th century. He was educated at the universities of Oxford and Paris and taught in the arts faculty at the latter in the early to mid-1240s. In the mid-1250s Bacon joined the Franciscan Order for reasons not revealed in any surviving source, but quite likely because of its reputation for sanctity and learning. He died in 1292 or soon thereafter.

The focus of Bacon's early teaching was Aristotelian philosophy, newly available in Latin translation. Indeed Bacon claimed to be one of the first to lecture on Aristotle's *Libri naturales* at the University of Paris. However, in the late 1240s or early 1250s Bacon's attention shifted from Aristotelian natural philosophy to other portions of the new learning – specifically, the mathematical and "experimental" sciences.

By the 1260s Bacon had become an outspoken advocate of mathematical and "experimental" science, campaigning to save this new learning from two opposite but equally worrisome dangers. On the one hand was the risk that champions of the mathematical and experimental sciences might pursue them for secular purposes as ends in themselves. On the other hand loomed the very real possibility that the leaders of the Church, fearing claims to autonomy by the new mathematical and experimental disciplines, would suppress them, depriving Christendom of what Bacon regarded as a treasure of inestimable value. Bacon's strategy was to adopt the middle position, which acknowledged the vital importance of the new scientific materials but made their value contingent on their subordination to the needs of Christian religion. This was St. Augustine's handmaiden (*ancilla*) formula, rearticulated and applied to the very different world in which Bacon lived, where the quantity of pagan learning awaiting handmaiden status was a great deal larger than it had been in Augustine's day.

Bacon adopted the bold position that nearly all the new learning was useful in these terms – that, firmly disciplined, it would serve as a vital resource for theology and the Church. However, if this claim was to have bite, it required illustration with concrete examples that would make clear just how mathematical and experimental science could serve the Church. This Bacon undertook most notably in his *Opus Maius*, an appeal to Pope Clement IV (1265–1268). Here Bacon presented the fundamentals of the mathematical sciences – *perspectiva* (the science of light and vision), mathematical geography, astronomy and astrology, and (a favorite Baconian idea) the universal radiation of images or force (*multiplicatio specierum*) – always with an eye to religious utility. He also mounted an appeal for "experimental" science, by which he meant both a methodology for the acquisition of knowledge and a body of lore (e.g., alchemy and the art of prolonging life) allegedly acquired by experiential means. The mythology that has portrayed Bacon's "experimental" science as a precursor of modern experimental science should be discounted.

Bacon's immediate influence on papal attitudes toward the new learning is unknown. His longer-term influence on developments in *perspectiva* was substantial, as was the application of his doctrine of *multiplicatio specierum* to 14th-century epistemology.

DAVID C. LINDBERG

See also France: History; Franciscans: General or Male; Humanism, Christian

### Biography
This Franciscan scholar studied at the universities of Oxford and Paris. It was probably at Oxford that he entered the Franciscan Order c. 1257. During the mid-1260s he wrote his encyclopedic *Opus Maius* for Pope Clement IV (1265–1268). For the almost 25 years thereafter he continued writing. It is reported that in 1277 the General of the Franciscan Order condemned his "novelties." He died, perhaps in Oxford, sometime in or after 1292.

### Major Works
*Quaestiones* on Aristotle, 1240s
*Opus Maius*, 1267–1268; as *The "Opus Majus" of Roger Bacon*, 3 vols., edited by John H. Bridges, 1900
*Opus Minus*, c. 1268
*Opus Tertium*, c. 1268
*Communia Naturalium*
*Communia Mathematica*
*Compendium Studii Philosophiae*, c. 1272
*Compendium Studii Theologiae*

*Roger Bacon's Philosophy of Nature: A Critical Edition, with English Translation, Introduction, and Notes, of De multiplicatione specierum and De speculis comburentibus*, edited and translated by David C. Lindberg, 1983

*Roger Bacon and the Origins of Perspectiva in the Middle Ages: A Critical Edition and English Translation of Bacon's Perspectiva, with Introduction and Notes*, edited and translated by David C. Lindberg, 1996

## Further Reading

Easton, Stewart C., *Roger Bacon and His Search for a Universal Science: A Reconsideration of the Life and Work of Roger Bacon in the Light of His Own Stated Purposes*, New York: Columbia University Press, and Oxford: Basil Blackwell, 1952

Hackett, Jeremiah, editor, *Roger Bacon and the Sciences: Commemorative Essays* (Studien und Texte zur Geistesgeschichte des Mittelalters, 57), New York: Brill, 1997

Lindberg, David C., "The Applicability of Mathematics to Nature: Roger Bacon and His Predecessors," *British Journal for the History of Science* 15 (1982)

Lindberg, David C., "Roger Bacon and the Origins of *Perspectiva* in the West," in *Mathematics and Its Applications to Science and Natural Philosophy in the Middle Ages: Essays in Honor of Marshall Clagett*, edited by Edward Grant and John E. Murdoch, Cambridge and New York: Cambridge University Press, 1987

Lindberg, David C., "Science as Handmaiden: Roger Bacon and the Patristic Tradition," *Isis* 78 (1987)

# Baker, Augustine 1575–1641

English Benedictine scholar

David Baker was born 9 December 1575 at Abergavenny, Wales, the 13th child in a well-to-do family of the established Church. He returned home an atheist after studying at Oxford from 1590 to 1592. In 1596 he went to London to read law. Three years later he was appointed recorder of Abergavenny. Traveling through the district, he had a brush with death on a rickety footbridge. He regarded his survival as a miracle and recovered his faith in God. He began reading theology and in 1603 was reconciled to the Roman communion.

Baker sought a religious community of moderate rigor and contemplative orientation and so joined the monastery of St. Giustina of Padua and took the name Augustine. He tried to learn how to do methodical meditation, but he could not, and he entered into a period of deteriorating prayer and health. In 1607 his superiors sent him back to England still a novice. In 1607 Baker professed his vows before Dom Sigebert Buckley, the last survivor of the Benedictines of Westminster Abbey. During the next 15 years, he was in England, sometimes actively serving as priest and minister and sometimes devoting himself mainly to prayer. He abandoned methodical meditations for acts of the will and aspirations. This led to passive contemplation, which he thought was exclusively the work of divine grace. He was then commissioned to do historical research on behalf of the English Benedictine Congregation. He performed this task well, and some of the results of his research were published in *Apostolatus Benedictinorum in Angliam* (1626; The Benedictine Apostolate in England).

In 1624 he became auxiliary confessor for the monastery of Our Lady of Comfort at Cambrai, the predecessor of Stanbrook Abbey. Two of the novices there, Gertrude More (1606–1633) and Catherine Gascoigne (1600–1676), were to be his distinguished disciples. He shared with them his knowledge of interior prayer and his favorite spiritual writings. Dom Frances Hull, the chaplain of the nuns at Cambrai, questioned the orthodoxy of Baker's teaching on prayer, especially its strong emphasis on the inner guidance of the Spirit. In 1633 the general chapter exonerated Baker. He was moved to St. Gregory's in Douai, where he lived a secluded life exempt from most of the daily conventual observances. Ironically, many sought his company and his spiritual advice. The community at Douai was divided between those who emphasized missionary work in England and those who preferred a more regular, conventual life. Baker's preference was for a very interior, prayerful and secluded life free of the activities of both missionary work and monastic routine. Baker was dismayed when the president of the congregation, Dom Rudesind Barlow, claimed Baker as a partisan of the party that preferred the conventual life. Baker wrote a position paper that included a satirical portrait of Barlow, who resented the paper and arranged an order sending the 63-year-old Baker to England as a missionary. Baker died there three years later in 1641.

Dom Serenus Cressey reworked over three dozen treatises written by Fr. Baker and produced the book *Holy Wisdom*, first published in 1657 and remaining in print almost continuously since then. The book is divided into three main sections: the internal life, mortification, and prayer (meditation, forced acts of the will, and contemplation). Dom Justin McCann compiled Baker's *Confessions* from autobiographical passages in Baker's commentary on the *Cloud of Unknowing*. Baker also wrote *The Inner Life of Dame Gertrude More*, which studies the stages of her inner development.

Augustine Baker has exercised a constant influence on English spirituality, especially among Benedictines. His emphasis on affective prayer has been a salutary counterweight to efforts to impose methodical meditation on those unsuited for it. His love of solitude anticipated the revival of interest in eremitical life during the last half of the 20th century.

HUGH FEISS, O.S.B

*See also* Butler, Cuthbert; Chapman, John; England: History; Exile, Western Christian; More, Gertrude; Spirituality: Western Christian; Wales

## Biography

This Englishman became a Roman Catholic and entered the Benedictines in Padua, Italy, in 1605. After being ordained to the priesthood in 1613, he worked as chaplain for English monastic houses at Cambrai and Douai. At Cambrai he was spiritual director of Gertrude More, whose Life he wrote. His posthumous *Holy Wisdom* influenced many including the disseminator of Christian meditation, John Main.

## Selected Works

*Apostolatus Benedictinorum in Anglia*, 1626
*Sancta Sophia: or, Directions for the Prayer of Contemplation*, 2 vols., 1657; as *Holy Wisdom: or Directions for the Prayer of Contemplation*, 1876
*The Inner Life and the Writings of Dame Gertrude More*, edited by Benedict Weld-Blundell, 1910
*The Confessions of Venerable Father Augustine Baker*, edited by Justin McCann, 1922
"Secretum Sive Mysticum, Being an Exposition of Certain Notes upon the Book Called *The Cloud*," in *The Cloud of Unknowing, and Other Treatises*, edited by Justin McCann, 1924 (6th edition, 1952)

## Further Reading

Gaffney, James, *Augustine Baker's Inner Light: A Study in English Recusant Spirituality*, Scranton, Pennsylvania: University of Scranton Press, 1989
Knowles, David, "Father Augustine Baker," in *English Spiritual Writers*, edited by Charles Davis, New York: Sheed and Ward, and London: Burns and Oates, 1961
Low, Anthony, *Augustine Baker* (Twayne's English Authors Series, 104), New York: Twayne, 1970
McCann, Justin, and R. Hugh Connolly, editors, *Memorials of Father Augustine Baker and Other Documents Relating to the English Benedictines* (Publications of the Catholic Record Society, volume 33), London: Whitehead, 1933
Rhodes, J.T., "Dom Augustine Baker's Reading Lists," *Downside Review* 111 (1993)
Spearitt, Placid, "The Survival of Mediaeval Spirituality among the Exiled English Black Monks," *American Benedictine Review* 25 (1974)

# Bangkok, Thailand

Thailand is a country of about 60 million people, 95 percent of whom are Buddhists, with 0.5 percent Christians (both Catholics and Protestants) and 3.5 percent Muslims, mostly in the four provinces in the extreme south of the country. Land was given to build both Christian churches and Muslim mosques. Thai people of any faith enjoy freedom of religious practice.

Bangkok is the capital of Thailand and is known locally as Krungthep (City of Angels). Its population of 10 million consists of all the three major faiths. Some of its churches and mosques have historical and architectural aesthetic value. The city was founded in 1782 with the establishment of Chakri dynasty, starting with King Rāma I. The present King Bhumipol, or Rāma IX, continues the same dynasty. The city's early period saw a great attempt to follow the model of the previous capital, in Ayudhya, which was sacked by the Burmese in 1767.

In the early part of King Rāma I's reign (1782–1809), the Grand Palace was built along with Wat Prasiratnasasadaram (Wat Prakaew; wat means "temple") to enshrine the emerald-colored Buddha image. This temple is unique in that it is attached to the Grand Palace, serving as a chapel for all royal rituals and ceremonies without monks in residence.

Another temple built during King Rāma I's reign was Wat Sudat, which housed Pra Si Śākyamuni, a large, beautiful Buddha image brought down from Sukhothai. Another temple, Wat Po, was renovated in this period and is situated immediately to the south of the Grand Palace. The remains of Pra Sisanpet, a renown gold standing Buddha image that was burnt down in Ayudhya, was brought here, and a chetiya was built over it. Wat Po is surrounded by about 300 stone inscriptions representing eight different fields of knowledge, including Buddhism, history, and literature. Thus, it is sometimes claimed to be the first university in Bangkok where knowledge is available for the public. With its proximity to the Grand Palace, the Wat is well maintained and is worth visiting; more than 800 Buddha images of various styles have been assembled from the Ayudhya period. In the same compound is the largest reclining Buddha, which has been in existence since the 18th century.

During the first three reigns, energy was invested in building temples; at the end of Rāma III's reign (1824–1851), more than 100 Wats had been both newly built and renovated.

When Rāma IV (r. 1851–1868) came to the throne, he immediately recognized the great burden of maintaining the existing Wats in Bangkok. A monk himself, he discouraged the practice that each king should build his personal Wat, and he allowed resources to be divided to maintain existing ones.

An important change regarding Buddhist clergy took place during King Rāma III's reign when Prince Mongkut, the crown prince who at that time was a monk, introduced Thammayut as a reformed sect of Budhism. This sect was supposed to be more scholarly in its interest and practice. Since then, the Saṅgha in Thailand consists of Mahānikāya, the older sect, and Thammayut, the reformed sect.

Two Buddhist universities were established under King Rāma V (1868–1910). One is based in Wat Bavornnives to serve monks from the Thammayut sect and the other in Wat Mahāthāt to provide education for monks from the Mahānikāya sect.

Today, the population of Buddhist monks is about 300,000 with a maximum of 10,000 white-robe local nuns (*maeji*). The number of the temple in the whole country is 25,000.

Two more temples need to be mentioned for their historical importance. The Marble temple, renovated in King Rāma V's period, has a uniquely beautiful architecture that combines Thai art with a Western influence. The main chapel hou See also ses a replica of Pra Buddha Chinarāt, a famous Buddha image in Pitsanulok. Another temple worth visiting is Wat Traimit, where one finds the only intact large-size gold Buddha image of the Sukhothai style.

CHATSUMARN KABILSINGH

*See also* Buddhadāsa; Forest Masters; Libraries: Buddhist; Mongkut; Mun, Ajahn; Thailand

## Further Reading

Audric, John, *Siam: Kingdom of the Saffron Robe*, London: Hale, 1969; as *Siam*, South Brunswick, New Jersey: Barnes, 1970

Bowring, Sir John, *The Kingdom and People of Siam*, 2 vols., Parker: London, 1857; reprint, Kuala Lumpur and New York: Oxford University Press, 1969

Keyes, Charles F., *Thailand: Buddhist Kingdom as Modern Nation-State* (Westview Profiles: Nations of Contemporary Asia), Boulder, Colorado: Westview Press, 1987

Waugh, Alec, *Bangkok, the Story of a City*, London and New York: Allen, 1970

Young, Ernest, *The Kingdom of the Yellow Robe: Being Sketches of the Domestic and Religious Rites and Ceremonies of the Siamese*, Westminster: Constable, 1898; New York: New Amsterdam, 1900; reprint, Singapore: Oxford University Press, 1986

# Basil the Great, St. c. 329/30–379

Cappadocian organizer of Eastern Christian monasticism

Basil the Great (*Basileios* in the original Greek), known also as Basil of Caesarea, is considered the father of Eastern Christian monasticism, father of institutionalized philanthropy, and a leading advocate of the use of classical Greek learning in the service of the Christian faith.

Born in Neocaesarea in the province of Pontus in Asia Minor to a wealthy family of three brothers and one sister, Basil received his elementary education from his father, a teacher. On the death of his father in 345, Basil moved to Caesarea of Cappadocia, where he continued his education and became acquainted with Gregory of Nazianzus (c. 330–390), with whom he achieved a lifelong friendship. Gregory provides much information about Basil's character and ministry.

From Caesarea, Basil moved to Constantinople, the capital of the Byzantine Empire, where he is thought to have studied under the famous rhetorician Libanios. Athens was the last stop; he moved there in 352 and studied not only philosophy, literature, and rhetoric but also medicine. Following the completion of his studies in Athens, in 356 Basil returned to Caesarea, where he rejoined his family and became a professor of rhetoric and continued his study of the Greek classics. During this period he was greatly influenced by the Christian teachings and by the example of the Christian lives of his mother, sister Macrina (c. 327–380), and brother Naukratios and decided to receive baptism. His desire to become better acquainted with Christian monasticism led him to undertake long trips and visit hermits and renowned monks in Syria, Palestine, Mesopotamia, and Egypt. His experiences in those places contributed to the formulation of his monastic ideal, especially in Egypt, where he met Athanasios (c. 296–373), the biographer of Antony and the founder of eremitic monasticism, and Eustathios of Sebasteia (c. 300–after 377), founder of a monastic community in Pontus. Both of them shaped Basil's conception of monasticism.

On his return to Caesarea in 360, Basil was ordained deacon, but because of the theological disputes there over Arianism, he distributed all his possessions to the poor and philanthropic causes and fled to Pontus, where he met his old friend Gregory of Nazianzus. The two lived like brother monks, studying Christian theology, including the writing of the great Origen (c. 185–c. 254). The serious illness of Caesarea's bishop Dianios made it necessary for Basil to visit him there. His stay in Caesarea became a turning point in his ecclesiastical career. On Dianios' death, Eusebios, his successor, retained Basil as his assistant. He was ordained presbyter and in 370 succeeded Eusebios as archbishop of Cappadocia. As archbishop he paid special attention to the needs of the poor, the sick, orphans, widows, and the needy in general, for whom he established a system of institutions, such as a leprosarion, orphanage, hospital, and old-age home, collectively known as *Basileias*.

In addition to many writings on education, theology, apologetics, hermeneutics, and liturgics, Basil became renowned in both the East and the West for his contributions to the moderate cenobitic form of monasticism. He introduced a monasticism that emphasized not only prayer, a liturgical life, and study but also work and social service. His *Asketika* include 13 books that prescribe ways of ascetic life, ethical admonitions, and administrative rules. Some of his ascetic writings were addressed not only to monks but also to all Christians. Most of his writings were translated into Latin, Armenian, Georgian, Arabic, and Slavonic early in the Middle Ages.

The most important of his *Asketika* were written in the form of questions and answers, known as longer and shorter rules. The central idea that stands as the basis of his ascetic philosophy is *agape*, or love for God and man. It is total love for God that leads to the monastic ideal. He relies on the Christian scriptures and monastic teachings of Eustathios of Sebasteia to formulate his own reformed cenobitic monasticism. He advocates moderation and believes in the formation of small cenobitic communities, in contrast to Pachomian coenobitic communities, where monks lived in the hundreds or even thousands (as Palladius the historian of monasticism writes).

The strength of Basil's philosophy and rules of monasticism lie in the fact that he harmoniously blended the eremitic spirit of St. Antony and the organizational principles of Pachomius. Basil's monastic theology combines both the letter and the spirit of the Holy Scriptures with the ethos and experience of the early Church. Basil's rules emphasize a Church-oriented monastic life conducted in the spirit of the Apostolic Church with its enthusiasm and commitment to a faith manifested even in martyrdom. This martyrdom, although of a new kind, is attained through the sacrifices of the body for the welfare of the soul. These sacrifices include poverty and purity of life, including virginity. Complete surrender to God's commandments constitutes the ideal monastic life.

Basil's rules on monasticism influenced early Latin Christian monasticism, including St. Benedict's (480–543) rules, which determined monasticism's evolution in the Christian West. In the Christian East Basil's rules were revised by Theodore of Studios (759–826) and have become standard in Orthodox Christian monasticism to the present day. Basil remains one of the most influential Christian theologians in both Greek and Latin Christendom.

DEMETRIOS J. CONSTANTELOS

*See also* Antony, St.; Benedict of Nursia, St.; Cappadocia, Turkey; Desert Fathers; Gregory of Nazianzus, St.; Gregory of Nyssa, St.; Hermits: Eastern Christian; Humanism, Christian; Images: Christian Perspectives; Liturgy: Eastern Christian; Macrina, St.; Origins: Eastern Christian; Orthodox Monasticism: Byzantine; Pachomius, St.; Regulations: Christian Perspectives; Spirituality: Eastern Christian; Theodore of Stoudios, St.; Visual Arts, Eastern Christian: Painting

## Biography

The brother of Gregory of Nyssa and Macrina, Basil received an excellent education before entering the monastic life. With his friend Gregory of Nazianzus he preached missions in the early 360s before being summoned to preach orthodoxy against the Arian Emperor Valens. From 370 to 379 he served as Bishop of Caesarea in Cappadocia. He played a major role in consolidating Orthodoxy. The Liturgy attributed to him, itself a longer version of early ones, may be in part his work.

## Selected Works

*Patrologia Graeca*, volumes 29–32, edited by J.P. Migne, Paris, 1857–1866

*Asketika*; as *Ascetical Works*, translated by Monica Wagner, volume 9, *Fathers of the Church*, 1950

*Hellenes Pateres tes Ekklesias*, volumes 1–10 (P.K. Chrestou and S.N. Sakkos, general editors), 1972–1974

*Bibliotheke Hellenon Pateron kai Ekklesiastikon Syngrafeon*, volumes 51–57 (Konstantinos G. Bonis, general editor), 1975–1978

Basil also compiled a *Philokalia* (from the works of Origen)

## Further Reading

Fedwick, Paul Jonathan, editor, *Basil of Caesarea: Christian, Humanist, Ascetic: A Sixteen-Hundredth Anniversary Symposium*, Toronto: Pontifical Institute of Mediaeval Studies, 1981

Morison, E.F., *St. Basil and His Rule: A Study in Early Monasticism* (S. Deiniol's Series, 3), London and New York: Frowde, 1912

Murphy, Margaret Gertrude, *Saint Basil and Monasticism* (Catholic University of America, Patristic Studies, volume 25), Washington, D.C.: Catholic University of America, 1930

# Beauduin, Lambert 1873–1960

Belgian Benedictine, Liturgical Movement leader, and Advocate of Church Union

This Benedictine liturgist, ecumenist, and monastic founder was born near Liège, Belgium, on 5 August 1873 and died at Chevetogne on 11 January 1960. Beauduin was educated at the minor seminary at St.-Trond and spent a very brief period with the Trappists before continuing his studies at the major seminary of Liège. Leo XIII's (1878–1903) social encyclical *Rerum Novarum* (*On Capital and Labor*) had been published in 1891, about the year that Beauduin entered major seminary. Beauduin was pro-

foundly influenced by the Church's social doctrine. Ordained in 1897 he joined the Aumôniers du Travail, a fraternity of priests who served as labor chaplains, in 1899. After they no longer had direct contact with the workers, Beauduin left the fraternity in 1906.

That same year Beauduin entered the Benedictine monastery of Mont César in Louvain. During Beauduin's time Mont César was a monastery of the Beuronese Congregation, which placed special emphasis on the solemn celebration of the liturgy. At Mont César Beauduin came under the influence of Columba Marmion (1858–1923), prior of the monastery and a theologian and spiritual writer whose inspiration flowed from both interior and external participation in the Church's liturgy. Much more than the external solemnity, it was Marmion's theological and spiritual vision of the liturgy that proved to be foundational for Beauduin's liturgical spirit. Formation at Mont César also drew Beauduin to other sources of Christian spirituality: Scripture, the writings of the Church fathers, and conciliar and other magisterial documents. In 1903, only three years before Beauduin entered Mont César, Pius X (1903–1914) had published *Tra le sollecitudini* (On Liturgical Music), which referred to the liturgy as the primary and indispensable source of the Christian spirit. This appreciation of liturgy as the source of Christian spirit was to remain at the heart of Beauduin's spirituality.

Immediately after his profession in 1907, Beauduin was assigned to teach a course on the Church. He developed it around the idea of the Church as the Mystical Body of Christ, thus anticipating by more than three decades the encyclical of Pius XII (1939–1958), *Mystici corporis Christi* (1943; *The Mystical Body of Christ*). At this time Beauduin also came to a personal realization that the liturgy lies at the center of the piety of the Church. He was instrumental in founding the Belgian liturgical movement in September 1909. In 1909 he collaborated with other monks of Mont César in beginning the periodical *Questions Liturgiques* and published his theological vision of the liturgy in 1914 as *La piété de l'Eglise* (*Liturgy the Life of the Church*).

Beauduin's interest in ecumenism and the Christian East began about 1920 and would consume much of his energy for the remainder of his life. In 1924 Pius XI (1922–1939) had encouraged the Benedictines to work for Christian unity, and in 1925 Beauduin founded the monastery of the "Monks for Unity" at Amay-sur-Meuse. In 1926 Amay began the publication of *Irénikon*, a journal devoted to Christian unity. Through Cardinal Mercier (1851–1926), Beauduin contributed to the Malines Conversations (1921, 1923, and 1925) and in 1925 proposed that the Anglican Church be united to Rome, not absorbed by it. Criticized for this remark Beauduin had to leave Amay in 1928, and his exile from it lasted until 1950. The Second Vatican Council vindicated Beauduin. Moreover, the monastery continued its ecumenical activities, moving to Chevetogne in 1939.

The monks at Chevetogne today cultivate contacts with Christians who are not in communion with Rome, receive guests, celebrate the liturgy in Eastern and Western rites, and organize theological colloquia. They also endeavor to introduce Western Christians to the riches of the Christian East. At the time of Beauduin's death (1960), the community numbered 35 monks (30 in 1995). The Byzantine church at Chevetogne was consecrated in 1957 and the Latin church in 1996. The monastery was raised to an abbey on 11 December 1990.

KURT BELSOLE, O.S.B.

*See also* Belgium: History; Beuron, Germany; Liturgical Movement 1830–1980; Liturgy: Western Christian; Marmion, Columba

## Biography

This leader of the Liturgical Movement and Advocate of Church Union was born in Belgium. In 1897 Beauduin became a priest ministering to working men. In 1906 he joined the Benedictine Abbey of Mont César at Louvain. There he founded the periodical *La Vie liturgique* c. 1910 to promote the Liturgical Movement. While at Sant'Anselmo in Rome after 1921, Beauduin became interested in Eastern Christian liturgy, and, in 1925, founded a monastery of shared Eastern and Western Liturgy at Amay-sur-Meuse, which in 1926 began to publish *Irénikon*. The community moved to Chevetogne, Belgium, in 1939, and Beauduin rejoined it there in 1950 after having been exiled in 1928 for incautious advocacy of Anglican reunion with Rome.

## Major Works

*Le piété de l'Eglise*, 1914; as *Liturgy the Life of the Church*, translated by Virgil Michel, 1926

"Dom Marmion and the Liturgy," in *More about Dom Marmion: A Study of His Writings together with a Chapter from an Unpublished Work and a Biographical Sketch*, translated by The Earl of Wicklow, 1950

*Melanges Liturgiques*, 1954

## Further Reading

Bouyer, Louis, *Dom Lambert Beauduin: Un homme d'Église* (Église Vivante), Paris: Casterman, 1964

Haquin, André, "La préparation du mouvement liturgique de 1909: Dom Lambert Beauduin et l'abbaye du Mont César," *Questions Liturgiques* 47 (1966)

Haquin, André, *Dom Lambert Beauduin et le renouveau liturgique* (Recherches et synthèses: Section d'histoire, 1), Gembloux: Duculot, 1970

Haquin, André, "Le prêtre selon Dom Lambert Beauduin, d'après diverses correspondances et notes de retraite," *Questions Liturgiques* 58 (1977)

Haquin, André, "La fondation d'Amay et l'exil de Dom L. Beauduin à En-Calcat," *Questions Liturgique* 68 (1987)

Lyons, Patrick, "Monks and Ecumenism: The Case of Lambert Beauduin," *American Benedictine Review* 48 (1997)

Martimort, Aimé-Georges, "Dom Lambert Beauduin et le Centre de Pastoral liturgique," *Les Questions Liturgiques et Paroissiales* 40 (1959)

Quitslund, Sonya, *Beauduin: A Prophet Vindicated*, New York: Newman Press, 1973

Rousseau, Olivier, "L'Expérience oecuménique du monastère de Chevetogne," in *Découverte de l'oecuménisme* (Le mystère d'unité, 1), Paris: Desclée de Brouwer, 1961

Rousseau, Olivier, "L'évolution ecclésiologique de dom Lambert Beauduin entre les deux conciles du Vatican," *Questions Liturgiques* 54 (1973)

*Veilleur avant l'aurore: Colloque Lambert Beauduin*, Chevetogne: Éditions de Chevetogne, 1978

# Bede, St. c. 673–735

## English Benedictine scholar

Bede was the most important scriptural commentator and historian of his age and the greatest scholar and writer of Anglo-Saxon England. He was born on lands given to the monastery founded by Benedict Biscop in 674 at Wearmouth in northeastern England, of English and recently pagan ancestry. He entered the monastery as a child at the age of seven and later transferred to the house founded at Jarrow in 682 under the leadership of Ceolfrith, for whom Bede always had the most affectionate veneration. It was one community sharing two sites. Bede almost never left Jarrow until his death; the farthest he traveled in connection with his researches was Lindisfarne to the north and York to the south. He never held office in his community but worked as a teacher and writer. He was ordained deacon at the age of 19 and priest at 30.

Benedict Biscop (c. 628–689) was a frequent traveler in Europe, making six journeys to Rome and bringing back books, glass, paintings, relics, and the archcantor of St. Peter's in Rome to teach his monks the Roman liturgy and uncial script. He made Wearmouth-Jarrow the greatest cultural and intellectual center in northern Europe. He devised a rule based on the Rule of St. Benedict and the rules of the 17 monasteries he had visited. At his death in 689, fearful that the abbacy should become a family inheritance, he exhorted the community to elect a successor according to the Rule of St. Benedict. Ceolfrith was elected and continued his work, doubling the size of the library. The number of monks in the joint community grew to 600. One of the great intellectual achievements of his abbacy was the copying out of three complete Latin Bibles (Pandects), one for each monastery and one as a gift for the pope. Each was made from the skins of 1,550 calves – a sign of the wealth of the community as well as the scale of the endeavor. Ceolfrith resigned from the abbacy in 716 and set off to die in Rome, taking the Bible with him. He died on the way in Burgundy, but the Bible survives at the Laurentian Library, Florence, as the Codex Amiatinus, the oldest surviving Latin Bible in one volume.

Thus, although Bede spent all his life at the very edge of the Christian world, he was at the center of its civilization through the books at his disposal and as a member of the community dedicated to scholarship. He wrote exceptionally fine Latin; he had considerable knowledge of Greek and some knowledge of Hebrew. He undertook the task of transmitting learning and skills, composing a Latin dictionary, a treatise on verse meter, a book of epigrams, an encyclopedia on natural phenomena, and a manual very widely studied throughout the Middle Ages on how

Tomb (16th century) of St. Bede in the Galilee (westernmost chapel, 14th century) of Durham Cathedral, Durham, England.
Photo courtesy of the Editor

else at Jarrow had fallen victim to plague in 686. Cuthbert was depicted as having power to tame nature and to bring it to a new harmony, expressing as it were his own internal integrity of spirit. Consciously writing in a tradition of Christian hagiography, Bede wanted to show that Anglo-Saxon England had its own saints.

His *Ecclesiastical History of the English People*, completed in 731, not only is the main source for early Anglo-Saxon history but also is still regarded as a distinguished work of history. Bede sifted evidence that he had gone to considerable lengths to gather and verify. Nevertheless the history remained in a genre similar to earlier Christian and biblical models, conveying a theological message, albeit handled with consummate skill. He was a vivid narrator. Some of his passages, such as that of Gregory the Great (590–604) calling the English slaves sold in the Roman market not Angles but angels or Edwin's councilor likening a human life to a sparrow's flight through a banqueting hall, have become part of England's common cultural inheritance. Bede's message is the triumph of the Christian gospel: through the preaching and example of the saints such as Aidan (d. 651), who is portrayed exceptionally warmly, and the steadfastness of Christian kings such as Edwin and Oswald, whose humility and generosity are especially emphasized, God's work prospered and paganism failed. Defeat in battle was not so much a setback for Christianity as it was another form of triumph: martyrdom.

One of Bede's long-lasting achievements was to have fused the Roman and other European monastic traditions with those of the Celts. A major preoccupation of his *Ecclesiastical History* was the confrontation between monastic missionaries from Ireland and Scotland, with their own customs and especially their own way of dating Easter, and the missionaries from Continental Europe. Although Bede presented the disputes and rivalries forcibly, he also showed the virtues of the Celtic monks such as Aidan and the successful merging of the traditions in figures such as Cuthbert.

Bede died in harness, having worked hard in his last days to complete the vernacular translation of the Gospel of John. He asked to be taken to the church and died singing the Gloria Patri on the feast of the Ascension on 26 May 735. He was acknowledged as "the candle of the Church lit by the Holy Spirit" by his younger contemporary Boniface (c. 675–754), whose English monastic mission brought Christianity to the Germans. In the eleventh century Bede's bones were translated to Durham Cathedral. In 1899 Leo XIII (1878–1903) proclaimed him a Doctor of the Church.

BERNARD GREEN, O.S.B.

*See also* Aidan, St.; Boniface, St.; Celtic Monasticism; Cuthbert, St.; England; Gregory I (the Great), St.; Hagiography: Western Christian; Humanism, Christian; Libraries: Western Christian; Lindisfarne/Holy Isle, England; Scholars, Benedictine

**Biography**

The incomparable scholar known as the "Venerable Bede" recounts his life in the final chapter of his *Ecclesiastical History*

to compute the date of Easter. These were ancillary to his main work, for he saw himself above all as a scripture scholar and wrote 25 works of commentary on both the Old and the New Testament, summarizing the interpretations and learning of past centuries. His scriptural work was highly regarded and much used throughout medieval Europe. The special status he accorded to Ambrose, Jerome, Augustine, and Gregory led to their recognition in the West as the Four Latin Doctors. Bede also made some translations of scriptural texts into the vernacular, hastening to complete the Gospel of John as he was dying.

However, his fame now rests mainly on his hagiographic and historical work. The lives that he wrote of Benedict Biscop, Ceolfrith, and the great hermit and bishop Cuthbert (c. 636–687) secured their reputations. Here he laid out a picture of monastic holiness that was both tender and affectionate. Heroic perseverance was represented by Benedict Biscop's tireless labors to create a great center of Christian civilization at Wearmouth-Jarrow or by the account of Ceolfrith and a little boy, presumably Bede himself, struggling to keep singing the full Office when everyone

*of the English People.* At age seven he joined the monastery of Wearmouth south of the River Tyne and in 682 moved to the monastery of Jarrow. There he spent the rest of his life except for brief trips to neighboring Lindisfarne and York. He was ordained priest at age 30, and died at Jarrow past age 60, having written major Latin works on versification, calendric calculation (of Easter), Biblical commentary, hagiography (St. Cuthbert), and above all his *Ecclesiastical History of the English People.* Since 1370 he has been buried in the Galilee Porch of Durham Cathedral.

## Major Works
*De Orthographia*
*De Metrica*
*De Natura rerum*
*De temporibus*
Life of St. Cuthbert, c. 721
*De Temporum ratione,* 725
*Historia Ecclesiastica Gentis Anglorum* (*Ecclesiastical History of the English People*), 731

## Further Reading
Bonner, Gerald, editor, *Famulus Christi: Essays in Commemoration of the Thirteenth Centenary of the Birth of the Venerable Bede,* London: SPCK, 1976
Brown, George Hardin, *Bede the Venerable,* Boston: Twayne, 1987
Hunter Blair, Peter, *The World of Bede,* London: Secker and Warburg, 1970; New York: St. Martin's Press, 1971; reissued, Cambridge and New York: Cambridge University Press, 1990
Mayr-Harting, Henry, *The Coming of Christianity to Anglo-Saxon England,* London: Batsford, 1972; as *The Coming of Christianity to England,* New York: Schocken Books, 1972; 3rd edition, London: Batsford, and University Park: Pennsylvania State University Press, 1991
Stacpoole, Alberic, "St. Bede the Venerable, Monk of Jarrow," in *Benedict's Disciples,* edited by D.H. Farmer, Leominster: Wright Books, 1980; 2nd edition, Leominster: Wright Books, and Harrisburg, Pennsylvania: Gracewing, 1995
Ward, Benedicta, *The Venerable Bede,* London: Geoffrey Chapman, and Harrisburg, Pennsylvania: Morehouse, 1990; revised edition, London: Geoffrey Chapman, and Kalamazoo, Michigan: Cistercian Publications, 1998

# Beer and Brewing, Christian. *See* Brewing, Western Christian

# Beghards

Beghards (Latin, *beguini* or *begardi*; German, *Begarden*; French, *bégards*; Dutch, *bogarden* or *begarden*) is a general term used in medieval Europe to denote laymen who led a life of quasi-monastic penance and devotion but did not take solemn vows and were unaffiliated with an approved religious order.

The beghards had their origins in the same movement that gave rise to the better-known female beguines, whose lifestyle theirs closely resembled. Cited as participants in a few early communities led by beguines around 1200, laymen, called "male beguines" (*beguini*), were first mentioned living on their own in small, all-male groups during the 1220s. Like the beguines, these men devoted themselves to chastity and good works (care of the sick and the poor); unlike most beguines they often led an itinerant existence that added to the suspicion that ecclesiastical and civic authorities cast on the whole movement. A chronicle written at Cologne around 1220 described such men as heretics, and in his *Life of St. Léocade* of 1222–1224, the French Benedictine Gautier de Coincy vigorously attacked them as religious "hypocrites" (*pappelarts, beguins,* or *begarz*), setting the tone for most medieval testimony on the beghards.

Despite their poverty and the high incidence of vagrancy among them, some beghards did form stable communities. Among the oldest of these must be a convent of *beguini* attested at Douai in 1246 and the larger and important community of beghards (*beghini, begardi*) mentioned in Bruges from 1252 on; other early convents of beghards in the southern Low Countries were those of Diest (1257), Sint-Truiden (1270), and Nivelles (1272). Outside this area beghards might have lived in convents as early as 1243 in Vienna and in Cologne in 1258, but the evidence for these dates is less certain. By about 1300 beghard convents existed in many cities and towns of the Low Countries, Germany, Austria, and northern France.

Most beghards worked as wool or linen weavers or aided in the preparation and finishing of the woven cloth. Those who lived in convents pooled their resources in a common workshop, where young novices learned the craft as apprentices. In most areas of the Low Countries, where textile guilds tightly controlled the manufacture of cloth, these convents were, from the late 13th century on, supervised by guild representatives who limited the number of looms in the workshop and put caps on their production. Consequently most beghard convents were rather small.

The beghards suffered greatly from the decrees of the Council of Vienne issued under Pope John XXII (1316–1334) in 1317, accusing beguines and beghards of heretical teachings. Most beghard convents ensured their survival only by adopting an approved rule, such as that of the Third Order of St. Francis, and by forming congregations under the auspices of local bishops. Although their orthodoxy was repeatedly questioned in parts of northwestern Europe in the later 14th and 15th centuries, beghards often fulfilled important social functions, supporting needy or elderly textile workers and providing vocational instruction. The last beghard houses were closed at the end of the 18th century.

WALTER SIMONS

*See also* Beguines; Belgium: History; Franciscans: General or Male; Heretics, Christian; Social Services: Western Christian

## Further Reading

Lerner, Robert, *The Heresy of the Free Spirit in the Later Middle Ages*, Berkeley: University of California Press, 1972

McDonnell, Ernest W., *The Beguines and Beghards in Medieval Culture, with Special Emphasis on the Belgian Scene*, New Brunswick, New Jersey: Rutgers University Press, 1954

Schmitt, Jean Claude, *Mort d'une hérésie: L'Église et les clercs face aux béguines et aux béghards du Rhin supérieur du XIVe au XVe siècle* (Civilisations et sociétés, 56), New York: Mouton, 1978

# Beguines

Beguines (Latin, *beguinae*; Dutch, *begijnen*; German, *Beginen*; French, *béguines*) are Catholic laywomen who lead lives of devotion and quasi-monastic discipline without taking permanent vows. They originated around A.D. 1200 in the southern Low Countries (present-day Belgium) and soon afterward were known in Germany, Switzerland, the northern Low Countries (present-day Netherlands), and northern France. They never formed a religious order or adhered to a single rule but lived in communities that drew up regulations for their particular use. At the height of the movement, in the late 13th century, joining a beguine community may have constituted the most popular form of religious vocation for women in the Low Countries and adjacent areas. Suspected of heresy beguines were persecuted in the early decades of the 14th century, after which many communities were suppressed. Nonetheless some survived into the early modern period and even enjoyed a new efflorescence during the Counter-Reformation of the 17th century; in Belgium and parts of the Netherlands, beguine communities continued to thrive until the 20th century.

The beguines are exponents of the vast movement for religious reform that inspired clerics as well as laymen and -women in the late 11th and 12th centuries, when Western Europe witnessed great social transformation. In the newly urbanized southern Low Countries, interest in a more meaningful religious experience based on the Gospels inspired growing numbers of laypeople to join new religious orders, such as the Cistercians and Premonstratensians, as lay brothers and lay sisters; others practiced evangelical values within the family home; and still

**Beguinage of St. Elizabeth, church (1605), Bruges, Belgium.**
**Photo courtesy of the Editor**

others adhered to dualist beliefs held by Cathars. Although their precise opinions and goals differed greatly, these reformers tended to reject the material wealth generated by the new money economy and were critical of traditional Church structures; the more radical among them also favored a form of lay apostolate, which the Church strenuously opposed. Around 1170 the activities of such lay folk in the bishop's town of Liège (Belgium) drew the attention of ecclesiastical authorities who condemned a reform-minded priest called Lambert (d. 1177) as a heretic for having translated Scripture into the vernacular. A legend dating from the mid–13th century and accepted as fact in many later, scholarly publications on the beguines claimed that this Lambert founded the first beguine communities. Although this attribution is certainly false, it has now been well established that Lambert was among the first clergymen to pay special attention to the spiritual needs of female lay parishioners and to encourage their religious ambitions. Lambert translated for them into French the Latin life of St. Agnes, the early Christian virgin, and this might suggest that the laywomen of his circle venerated the ideal of chastity or even virginity in much the same way as did the later beguines. Lambert is also known to have translated for his lay parishioners (male and female) the Acts of the Apostles, one of the key texts of the religious reform movement.

Shortly afterward women inspired by these ideals began living together informally close to a hospital, monastery, or church in several places of the Diocese of Liège. In Huy a small group of such laywomen assisted Juetta, a 23-year-old widow, who devoted her life to the care of lepers around 1181 and died as a recluse or anchoress in 1228. Another famous figure of the early beguine movement was Mary, a young woman of Nivelles, who around 1191 persuaded her newlywed husband to live chastely and to practice good works in the leper house of Willambroux, where a small community of like-minded women subsequently took up residence; Mary left them around 1207 to live as a solitary near the monastery of regular canons of Oignies, where she died in 1213. Her teachings drew the attention of the skilled preacher (soon bishop of Acre in the Orient and later cardinal) Jacques de Vitry (1160/70–1240), who in 1215 wrote an influential life of Mary of Oignies that celebrated her vocation in the world and defended it against its detractors. In a letter of October 1216 to his friends in the Low Countries, Jacques also claimed that he had obtained oral approval of the women's way of life from Pope Honorius III (1216–1227) in the summer of 1216, but that decision – if it indeed was made – was never officially registered and appears to have had little effect.

Around 1230 communities of such women, henceforth called beguines, took on institutional form by acquiring property, selecting a superior, and adopting internal regulations. These institutions (Latin, *beguinagia*; French, *béguinages*; Dutch, *begijnhoven*) are first attested in Aachen (1230) and Cologne (c. 1230), Leuven (1232), Cambrai (1233), Ghent (1234), and Namur (1235). (The formation of these beguinages may have been made easier by Pope Gregory IX's bull of 1233, *Gloriam Virginalem*, protecting "continent virgins in Germany," but was not initiated by it.) By 1250 almost all major cities of the Low Countries had at least one beguinage; the movement also spread from Cologne to the more southern cities along the Rhine (e.g., in Mainz by 1233) down to the Lake Constance region. In the following decades beguine communities sprang up in a wide area of northern Europe, from the northern Low Countries to Paris (where King Louis IX [1226–1270] established a beguinage modeled on Flemish examples in or before 1264) and from Saxony to Bohemia.

Two types of beguinages can be distinguished. The first, usually called "house" or "convent," was made up of a relatively small group of 5 to 15 beguines living together in one or two buildings, governed by a single "mistress" (or "Martha" in German lands). These beguines did not have their own church or chapel but attended services in the parish church with other parishioners. Founded by wealthy individuals (either noble or from the urban upper classes), such beguinages were often placed under the initial supervision of a member of the founding family; the spiritual care tended to be entrusted to the parish priest and to friars of the Dominican or Franciscan orders. This type of beguinage was most common in parts of the southern Low Countries (Artois, Hainaut, and the Liégeois) and along the Rhine, where certain cities had several dozen to 100 such houses during the 13th century. A second type of beguine institution, found only in the southern Low Countries, was the "court" (Latin, *curtis*; French, *court*; Dutch, *hof*), a complex of houses, convents for communal living, and service buildings at the edge of the city, with a church or chapel at its center and surrounded by a wall and sometimes even a moat. These courts offered prospective members a variety of living options: the wealthier beguines could build or buy a house within the compound and live alone or with a few companions, beguines of more modest means could rent a room in such a house or join a "convent" within the court under the direction of a convent mistress, and poor and elderly beguines found lodging in the beguine hospital or in specially designated houses of the court. The whole complex was governed by a "grand mistress" who ruled for a prescribed period assisted by other beguine officials. Such "towns within the town" could be quite large: the beguinage of St. Elizabeth at Ghent had about 610 to 730 beguines in the late 13th century, and St. Catherine's in Mechelen might have numbered about 1,500 to 1,900 between 1486 and 1550.

Unlike members of monastic orders, beguines did not take solemn vows. On entry into the community, they promised to obey its rule and superior for the duration of their stay. They had to live chastely and simply, but a vow of poverty was not required, and they could leave the community if they so desired. Beguines who could not maintain themselves through rents or other property income were expected to earn an income as nurses, teachers, or laborers in the urban textile industry; however, many communities set aside part of their resources to help poor, disabled, and elderly women; in some cases a beguine house was entirely devoted to the support of such women. The popular success of beguinages undoubtedly resulted from the supportive environment they provided for single women – often of rural origin – in medieval and early modern cities. Some indications exist that beguinages served as refuges for women wishing to avoid or escape an undesirable marriage.

Teaching was an integral part of the beguine vocation. Beguines taught young girls and boys reading and writing, foreign languages, weaving, and needlework. During the 13th and 14th centuries, many beguines also expressed the desire to explore spiritual matters and to bear witness of their mystical or ecstatic experiences. Because their potential reading audience was a lay one, they wrote in the vernacular. Beatrix of Nazareth (d. 1268), who was trained by beguines before becoming a Cistercian nun at Nazareth in Brabant, wrote one of the earliest mystical treatises in Dutch, *Seven Manieren van Minne* (Seven Manners of Love). Between 1250 and 1280 the German beguine Mechtild of Magdeburg (c. 1207–c. 1282) composed *Das fliessende Licht der Gottheit* (The Flowing Light of Divinity), and several anonymous devotional texts in French, probably written by beguines, have survived that might date from the same era. Perhaps the greatest beguine writers of the age were Hadewijch of Brabant and Marguerite Porète. Hadewijch wrote poems, letters, and visions in Dutch that are now regarded as masterpieces of medieval mysticism. We know practically nothing about her life, and even the date of her activity has been disputed: some have placed her around 1240–1250, but others suggest the early 1300s. The latter date would make her a contemporary of Marguerite Porète (d. 1310), whose French *Le Mirouer des Simples Ames* (The Mirror of Simple Souls) was condemned as heretical by the bishop of Cambrai between 1296 and 1306 and again by an inquisitorial panel that ordered her execution in Paris on June 1, 1310. Although her book was to be destroyed with her, versions of it in medieval French, Latin, Italian, and English have survived.

Marguerite's condemnation was not an isolated incident. From the very start the beguines' devotion, chastity, and mystical aspirations met with suspicion. Jacques de Vitry and others testified that "beguine" was originally a pejorative term, intended to mock and discredit the women. The word's etymology has been much debated. Sources from around 1250 maintained that it was derived from the nickname "le Bègue" (the Stammerer) given to the movement's mythical founder, Lambert, but that name does not appear in the original 12th-century sources. It has also been thought that *beguina* was an abbreviation of or allusion to *Albigensis*, the Latin name of the southern French city of Albi, a center of Cathar and other heretical activity. Although some sources indeed used *beguina* as a synonym of "heretic" and radical Franciscan tertiaries of southern France, known as "beguins," were condemned as heretics around 1300, the original meaning of the term was probably different. According to the most recent hypothesis, *beguina* was based on the old Germanic stem *begg-* and denoted a person who muttered prayers but whose piety raised doubts, not unlike the middle-French *papelard* (hypocrite) or the English *lollard*. Beguines were deemed suspect for a number of reasons: they were women who aimed to live chastely and religiously without observing monastic claustration or any of the traditional monastic vows; they sometimes claimed to have experienced mystical transports, which were always contested; and they were determined to study the Scriptures in the vernacular and teach on religious subjects at a time when this was forbidden to laypeople and to women in particular. Moreover, as urban economies around 1300 were hit by severe crises, authorities became increasingly disturbed by the great number of beguines who lived on the edge of poverty.

At first Church officials (e.g., in Liège in 1246) acted against beguines who wandered about without supervision. Preparations for the General Council of Lyons in 1274 focused attention on the irregular status and intellectual interests of beguines, and in 1277 and around 1284 German synods questioned beguines' orthodoxy. Marguerite Porète's case seemed to confirm the fear that beguine mysticism espoused antinomianism and fostered disrespect for the sacramental power of the Church. Her trial led to two decrees against beguines that were redacted at the Council of Vienne in 1312: *Ad Nostrum*, directed against "the sect" of beguines and beghards of Germany suspected of teaching certain antinomian beliefs, and *Cum de Quibusdam Mulieribus*, which ordered local Church authorities to disband all beguine communities except for those of "faithful women."

No reason exists to believe that German beguines ever formed what has been erroneously called a "sect of the Free Spirit." Nevertheless they certainly were attracted to mysticism and often lived in small, rather loosely organized communities that escaped close scrutiny by local priests; a relatively large number of them might also have been vagrants. This might explain why bishops in German lands took drastic measures after Pope John XXII's (1316–1334) publication of the two decrees against beguines. In some German cities beguinages were entirely suppressed; in others beguines were forced to join approved organizations, such as the Third Orders of St. Francis or St. Dominic. By the 16th century the few surviving beguines of Germany and France devoted themselves to the care of elderly widows and displayed little interest in spirituality.

In the Low Countries bishops and their agents repeatedly investigated the beguines' orthodoxy until the late 1320s. During this period beguines were often harassed, and their property was spoliated; many small communities, poorly financed, closed their doors. Most court beguinages survived, albeit more tightly controlled than in the previous age. Yet beguines retained many of their original characteristics, and individual beguines, such as Maria van Hout (d. 1547) at Oisterwijk and Claessinne van Nieulant (d. 1611) at Ghent, continued to be famed for their spiritual insight. The courts even enjoyed a remarkable renaissance in the 17th century: spurred by the Counter-Reformation's celebration of female chastity and economic conditions that once again drove many rural women to the city, court beguinages in Flanders, Brabant, and Liège regained the population losses that they had suffered during the religious troubles of the 16th century.

French republican authorities closed down most beguinages during their occupation of the Low Countries (1795–1815), but the institutions were revived in the course of the next decades. For example, in Ghent there were again more than 1,000 beguines in 1860. Overall, however, the number of beguines declined from 1900 on and especially after the mid–20th century. The total beguine population in Belgium dropped from about

600 in 1960 to 59 in 1977. The last surviving beguines now live in two beguinages of Ghent.

WALTER SIMONS

*See also* Beghards; Belgium; Benedictines: Female; Cathars; Dissolution of Monasteries: Continental Europe; Dominicans: Female; France: History; Franciscans: Female; Heretics, Christian; Holy Men/Holy Women: Christian Perspectives; Netherlands; Premonstratensian Canons; Women's Monasteries: Western Christian

## Further Reading

Hollywood, Amy, *The Soul as Virgin Wife: Mechthild of Magdeburg, Marguerite Porete, and Meister Eckhart* (Studies in Spirituality and Theology, 1), Notre Dame, Indiana: University of Notre Dame Press, 1995

Koorn, Florence, *Begijnhoven in Holland en Zeeland gedurende de middeleeuwen* (Van Gorcum's Historische Bibliotheek, 97), Assen: Van Gorcum, 1981

Lerner, Robert, *The Heresy of the Free Spirit in the Later Middle Ages*, Berkeley: University of California Press, 1972

McDonnell, Ernest W., *The Beguines and Beghards in Medieval Culture, with Special Emphasis on the Belgian Scene*, New Brunswick, New Jersey: Rutgers University Press, 1954

Schmitt, Jean Claude, *Mort d'une hérésie: L'Église et les clercs face aux béguines et aux béghards du Rhin supérieur du XIVe au XVe siècle* (Civilisations et sociétés, 56), New York: Mouton, 1978

Simons, Walter, "Jacques de Vitry," in *Literature of the French and Occitan Middle Ages: Eleventh to Fifteenth Centuries* (Dictionary of Literary Biography, volume 208), edited by Deborah Sinnreich-Levi and Ian S. Laurie, Detroit, Michigan: Gale, 1999

Wehrli-Johns, Martina, and Claudia Opitz, editors, *Fromme Frauen oder Ketzerinnen? Leben und Verfolgung der Beginen im Mittelalter*, Freiburg im Breisgau, Basel, and Vienna: Herder, 1998

# Belgium: History

The monastic history of Belgium has been affected above all by the country's geography. The plains of the north, along the North Sea, are traversed by several navigable rivers that became important arteries of communication and trade in the early Middle Ages and supported intense urbanization in Flanders and Brabant beginning around A.D. 1000; in the southeast of the country, the woods of the Ardennes hills impeded dense human population but comprised several valleys suitable for monastic settlement. Straddling the northern border between the medieval kingdoms of France and Germany, the country was always exposed to French (and Roman) as well as Germanic cultural influences, yet it also made original contributions to monasticism.

During the late Roman period (third to fourth centuries), Christian presence in the area was probably limited to a few urban centers. This presence barely survived the Germanic migrations of the fifth century but received a strong boost in the seventh and early eighth centuries owing to the work of Aquitanian and Irish monks, who established about 45 monasteries as missionary centers, mainly along the Scheldt, Scarpe, and Samber Rivers. The most famous of these missionaries was undoubtedly St. Amand (c. 584–679), who founded the abbeys of St. Bavo at Ghent, Nivelles, and Elnone (later to be called St.-Amand-les-Eaux), among others. The monasteries of Lobbes, St. Peter of Ghent, Sint-Truiden, and Stavelot-Malmédy also date from this era. All were established in collaboration with the Merovingian kings and regional nobility, who endowed them with very large estates; most monks and certainly all abbots belonged to the highest aristocracy. We know little about the organization of monastic life in these early institutions other than that they were governed by a combination of Irish customs and the Rule of St. Benedict and that many were intended for women or were double monasteries, in which male and female communities lived in close association with each other. Still, whatever the precise form and spirituality of monastic life in these institutions, their wealth, political and juridical power, and intellectual activity made them leading monastic centers for many centuries.

During the Carolingian and post-Carolingian eras (late eighth and ninth centuries), the existing monasteries underwent several changes that did not always contribute to monastic discipline. While the Rule of St. Benedict replaced the older heterogeneous customs, the widespread practice of appointing lay abbots often dismantled regular life; some of the monasteries were effectively transformed into chapters of canons. These circumstances eventually prompted reform led by Lotharingian monks, such as Gerard of Brogne (d. 959), Richard of St. Vanne (d. 1046), and members of the monastery of Gorze (tenth century), who reestablished discipline in houses entrusted to them and founded new ones, such as Gembloux (c. 940) and Ename (1063); the effectiveness of local reform explains why the Order of Cluny had relatively little influence in the Belgian area.

In the course of the late 11th to 13th centuries, population growth and greater social and geographical mobility, especially in the northern plains, contributed to the spread of new religious orders. Many originated in France and southern Europe: the Cistercians and Premonstratensians established almost 90 monasteries for men, women, or both (in double monasteries) between 1120 and 1250; the mendicant orders (Franciscans, Dominicans, Carmelites, Augustinian Friars, Saccites, and Pied Friars), who catered to the spiritual needs of the urban middle classes, founded about 50 convents for men during the 13th and early 14th centuries, mostly in Flemish and Brabantine cities. The unusual expansion of the Carthusian Order in the 14th and 15th centuries was due mainly to the support of the dukes of Burgundy and the local nobility associated with their court. Other new orders were local, such as the regular canons of Arrouaise, founded at the end of the 11th century in the vicinity of Arras, and those of the Crosiers, established by Theodore of Celles around 1211. The northern Netherlandish movements of the Modern Devotion (*Devotio Moderna*) and the congregation of Windesheim exerted a direct and indirect influence on several

Exterior of refectory, St. Bavo's Abbey (Benedictine), Ghent, Belgium, 12th century.
Photo courtesy of Chris Schabel

houses of regular canons as well as Brethren and Sisters "of the Common Life."

Perhaps the most striking aspect of monastic life in the late medieval and early modern era was the remarkable success of active religious orders for women. The Cistercians and Premonstratensians were the first to found numerous houses for female religious in the early 13th century. These houses gained fame for the superior forms of contemplative life they offered to women of the nobility and elite urban classes, such as Lutgard of Tongeren (d. 1246) and Beatrice of Nazareth (d. 1268), whose life stories circulated as guides to mysticism. However, many of their early female converts were lay sisters of more modest background who fulfilled menial tasks. The beguines, women without solemn vows who were involved in charitable care and gathered in hundreds of small and large communities, provided a popular alternative to the more cloistered monastic vocation. The numerous small convents of female Cellites and Franciscan Tertiaries that were formed in the late 14th and 15th centuries continued this tradition, although most of them adopted solemn vows around 1500. On the eve of the Reformation, there might have been about 100 beguinages and 150 convents for women of various orders devoted to the active religious life; their numbers

bear witness to the social services they rendered in this highly urbanized region.

Like elsewhere in Europe, the Reformation was a time of crisis as well as renewal for religious orders in the Belgian lands. The Benedictines, Carmelites, and Franciscans regrouped to form regional congregations or developed new, stricter branches that were quite successful within an ecclesiastical framework highly marked by the Counter-Reformation. The Jesuits appeared in 1542 and established several residences before the religious troubles starting in 1566; their loyalty to the Spanish cause earned them government support in the late 16th century, when the order blossomed to form more than 40 houses and gained a stronghold on higher education in the region until their suppression in 1773–1774.

Emperor Joseph II (1780–1790) of Austria ordered the suppression of all contemplative orders in 1782. After the conquest of Belgium by the French Republican army in 1795, all remaining monasteries and religious houses were forced to close their doors. Some of them reopened after Belgium's independence in 1830 owing to its liberal constitution of 1831 recognizing religious associations; in the following decades new congregations for men and women arose that were devoted to education and missionary activity in Africa (Congo, Rwanda, and Burundi), Latin America, and Asia. Since the 1960s vocations have dwindled in most orders. Nevertheless the orders of Augustinian Friars, Benedictines, Cistercians (Trappists), Dominicans, Franciscans, and Premonstratensians retain a strong presence.

WALTER SIMONS

*See also* Beauduin, Lambert; Beghards; Beguines; Benedictines; Carthusians; Chapman, John; Cistercians; Double Houses, Western Christian; France: History; Marmion, Columba; Netherlands; Premonstratensian Canons; Reformation; Willibrord, St.

## Further Reading

*Benedictus en zijn monniken in de Nederlanden*, 3 vols., Ghent: Stad Gent, 1980

Harline, Craig, "Actives and Contemplatives: The Female Religious of the Low Countries before and after Trent," *Catholic Historical Review* 81 (1995)

Milis, Ludovicus, *L'Ordre des chanoines réguliers d'Arrouaise*, Bruges: De Tempel, 1969

*Monasticon Belge*, Maredsous: Abbaye de Maredsous, 1890–1897; Liège: Centre national de recherches d'Histoire religieuse, 1960–1993

Montulet-Henneau, Marie-Elisabeth, *Les Cisterciennes du pays mosan: Moniales et vie contemplative à l'époque moderne* (Bibliothèque de l'Institut historique belge de Rome, 28), Brussels: Institut historique belge de Rome, 1990

Moreau, Édouard de, *Histoire de l'Église en Belgique* (Museum Lessianum, Section Historique), 5 vols., Brussels: L'Édition Universelle, 1940–1952

Sabbe, M., M. Lamberigts, and F. Gistelinck, editors, *Bernardus en de Cisterciënzerfamilie in België 1090–1990* (Documenta libraria, 11), Louvain: Bibliotheek van de Faculteit der Godgeleerdheid, 1990

Simons, Walter, *Bedelordekloosters in het graafschap Vlaanderen: Chronologie en topografie van de bedelordenverspreiding vóór 1350*, Bruges: Stichting Jan Cobbaut, 1987

Simons, Walter, *Stad en apostolaat: De vestiging van de bedelorden in het graafschap Vlaanderen, ca. 1225–ca. 1350* (Verhandelingen van de Koninklijke Academie voor Wetenschappen, Letteren en Schone Kunsten van België, Klasse der Letteren, 121), Brussels: AWLSK, 1987

Tihon, André, "Les religieuses en Belgique du XVIIIe au XXe siècle: approche statistique," *Revue belge d'histoire contemporaine* 7 (1976)

# Belgium: Sites

Although monastic institutions in Belgium have suffered greatly from the ravages of war, especially during the 16th, 17th, and 20th centuries, many sites recall the history of monasticism in the region and demonstrate its presence today.

One of the oldest and most intriguing sites is found in Ghent, where parts of the medieval abbey of St. Bavo are well preserved.

The abbey, founded around A.D. 639, was one of the wealthiest and most influential monasteries of the old county of Flanders during the Middle Ages but was largely demolished at the command of Emperor Charles V (1519–1558) for the construction of fortifications in 1540. In turn these were dismantled in the 19th century to reveal the remains of central units of the abbey, still visible today: the chapter room (10th to 12th century), the refectory, and the cloister (12th century), with its unique lavatory (*lavatorium*), an octagonal construction with a water fountain and basin used by monks to wash their hands before meals.

The prodigious success of the Cistercians and Premonstratensians can be gauged at several places. In Lissewege a monumental grange from the second half of the 13th century bears witness to the cultivation of lands in northern Flanders by the abbey of Ter Doest. At Villers remnants of the abbey church, refectory, and brewery from the 13th and early 14th centuries mark the site of the once famous abbey that was not only a center for 13th-century mysticism but also the burial place of several dukes of Brabant. Old and new are united in Orval, where the ruins of the 12th-century abbey, destroyed in 1795, are flanked by the present monastery, built under the direction of Henri Vaes (d. 1945), drawing on medieval Burgundian models (the abbey church is inspired by that of Pontigny). Like many other Cistercian and especially Trappist monasteries in Belgium, Orval is also famous for its beer. Most of the Premonstratensian monasteries founded in the 12th century were rebuilt in the early modern age. Fine examples of such complexes are those of Averbode (17th to 18th century), Leffe (16th to 17th century), Park at Heverlee (16th to 18th century), and Tongerlo at Westerlo (16th to 18th century).

Beguinages in several cities have maintained their medieval layout and monumental architecture, although most of the individual houses and convents that now remain within those compounds date from the 17th and 18th centuries. This is true especially for the court beguinages of Diest, Leuven (Louvain), Tongeren, and Sint-Truiden, where the original 14th-century churches remain largely intact; at the church of Sint-Truiden, wall paintings from the 13th to 16th centuries also provide insight into the devotions of medieval beguines. Other splendidly preserved beguinages are those of Antwerp, Bruges (currently inhabited by Benedictine nuns), Courtrai, Diksmuide, Ghent (Great Beguinage of St. Elisabeth, Small Beguinage of Ter Hooie), Hasselt, Lier, Oudenaarde, and Turnhout. Of the Great Beguinages of Mechelen (Malines) and Brussels, which from the 14th through the 17th century ranked among the largest in the country, only the baroque churches remain.

The monastic revival in 19th-century Belgium was accompanied by a renewed interest in medieval architecture. The Benedictine monastery of Maredsous at Denée and the beguinage of Sint-Amandsberg near Ghent offer harmonious examples of the neo-Gothic style much in vogue during the late 19th century. At Chevetogne the Benedictine monastery of the Exaltation of the Cross (originally erected in 1925 at Amay-sur-Meuse), devoted to Christian unity, has an ecumenical center and two churches: one in Novgorod style for the Orthodox rite and another in Western style for Catholic worship.

The most important monastic centers today are those of the Benedictines of Sint-Andries near Bruges (missions), Sint-Pietersabdij of Steenbrugge (renown for its *Corpus Christianorum* and other publications), Maredsous (publisher of the *Revue Bénédictine*), and Keizersberg near Louvain (*Recherches de théologie ancienne et médiévale*); the Cistercians and Trappists of Achel, Orval, and Westmalle; the Premonstratensians of Averbode, Heverlee ("Park"), Leffe, Postel, and Tongerlo; and the Franciscans of Sint-Truiden.

*Monasteries to Visit*
Averbode, Bruges (Wijngaard, in the old beguinage; Sint-Andries), Chevetogne, Ghent (St. Bavo; beguinages of St. Elisabeth, Ter Hooie, and Sint-Amandsberg), Heverlee (Park), Sint-Truiden (beguinage), Orval, and Villers.

WALTER SIMONS

*See also* Beauduin, Lambert; Beghards; Beguines; Benedictines; Carthusians; Chapman, John; Cistercians; Double Houses, Western Christian; France: History; Marmion, Columba; Netherlands; Premonstratensian Canons; Reformation; Willibrord, St.

**Further Reading**

*Benedictus en zijn monniken in de Nederlanden*, 3 vols., Ghent: Stad Gent, 1980
Colinon, Maurice, *Guide des monastères: France, Belgique, Luxembourg* (Guides Horay), Paris: Horay, 1977; revised as *Guide des monastères: France, Belgique, Luxembourg, Suisse* (Guides Horay), 14th edition, Paris: Horay, 1998
Declercq, Georges, editor, *Ganda en Blandinium: De Gentse abdijen van Sint-Pieters en Sint-Baafs*, Ghent: Snoeck-Ducaju en Zoon, 1997
Delmelle, Joseph, *Abbayes et béguinages de Belgique* (Collection Nouveaux Guides de Belgique, 2), Brussels: Rossel, 1973
Majérus, Pascal, *Ces femmes qu'on dit béguines. . . . Guide des béguinages de Belgique. Bibliographie et sources d'archives*, 2 vols., Brussels: Archives générales du Royaume, 1997
Sabbe, M., M. Lamberigts, and F. Gistelinck, editors, *Bernardus en de Cisterciënzerfamilie in België 1090–1990* (Documenta libraria, 11), Louvain: Bibliotheek van de Faculteit der Godgeleerdheid, 1990

# Benedict of Aniane, St. c. 750–821

Frankish Benedictine reformer and promoter of the Benedictine Rule

The Gothic boy Witiza, later called Benedict, was sent by his father, the count of Maguélonne near Montpellier, to train in arms and secular affairs at the royal court of Pepin the Short (747–768) and Charlemagne (768–814). During the Frankish expedition in Italy of 773–774, he witnessed his brother's accidental drowning, and this event seems to have acted as a catalyst in Witiza's conversion. The primary source for this episode and indeed for most of what is known about Benedict is the *Life of Abbot Benedict*, written soon after 821 by Ardo, a monk of Aniane and a disciple of the late abbot. According to Ardo, in the three years before the accident Witiza had experienced a growing disjunction between the secular lifestyle of the court and his inclination to devote himself to God. His entry into the cloister of St. Seine, near Dijon, in 774 thus aligned the outer and inner aspects of Benedict's life in the pursuit of monastic perfection. For nearly six years he undertook ascesis and embraced humility with enough zeal to attract attention, not all of it favorable, but Ardo reports that in the end his reputation at St. Seine's was so strong that Benedict was nearly elected abbot. To avoid this, and seeking a path more difficult than that of the cloister, he and a few followers went to live as anchorites where the Aniane River flowed through the family estate near Montpellier. When the rigor of this existence proved too much for his colleagues, Benedict established on the same spot a cenobium, consecrated in honor of the Blessed Virgin Mary, that offered a secure institutional setting for communal life. Ardo underscores the rugged construction of this first church and the simplicity of its liturgical appointments as reflections of Benedict's rigor. However, this outward austerity disappeared in 782, when with Charlemagne's encouragement Benedict constructed a cloister large enough for hundreds of monks and a fine new church furnished with precious utensils. What impresses the modern reader of the *Life* as a curiously abrupt shift in approach to the architectural and aesthetic aspects of monastic life puzzled neither Benedict nor Ardo, who could accept both the privation of beauty and its presence as the two aspects, one might say descending and ascending, of a single divine revelation.

Benedict made a conscious decision to adopt the Rule of his great namesake as the exclusive norm for the new monastery. Before the late eighth century, the Rule of St. Benedict was one among many used in the West, and often a single monastery followed more than one rule. Benedict of Aniane did not repudiate these other rules but instead, in a massive compilation known as the *Concordia regularum*, emphasized their harmony with the precepts of St. Benedict. As for the numerous matters of observance, discipline, and daily life not covered in the Rule, Benedict established a set of customs (*consuetudines*) at Aniane after making a careful study of those of other houses. Charlemagne favored Aniane with a charter of immunity and rich gifts that helped support Benedict's effort to reform monasteries in Aquitaine and beyond according to the Rule of St. Benedict and the customs of Aniane. This reform impulse intensified under Louis the Pious (814–840), who befriended Benedict sometime after 781, when he became king of Aquitaine, and continued to rely on the abbot's advice after he succeeded Charlemagne in 814. So that his chief monastic adviser could be close at hand, Louis the Pious made him abbot of the new monastery of Inden (Kornelimünster) near Aachen. Benedict was a major influence at the councils of 816, 817, and 818–819, which marked the culmination of two generations of Frankish ecclesiastical reform by differentiating the *ordo canonicorum* (order of chapter clergy) from the *ordo monachorum* (order of the religious) and stipulating in detail the rule and customs that each group should follow.

Endeavors to implement this legislation in practice, efforts that would occupy the remaining years of Benedict's life, had mixed results. The prospect of obtaining privileges and grants of immunity was incentive enough to ensure that the Rule of St. Benedict eventually became the single norm of monastic life in the Frankish realm. Yet regional and local customs never yielded to the *consuetudo* that Benedict of Aniane favored, and despite the efforts of imperial *missi* and envoys from Inden and other centers of reform, diverse customs persisted into the ninth and subsequent centuries.

Although Ardo attended as much to Benedict's holiness and exemplary personal conduct as he did to the abbot's extramural activities, within a few years of his death he was being referred to as the second Benedict, and later authors emphasized his role in the institutional reform of Western monasticism. In a few local traditions, chroniclers honored Benedict for his part in restoring older monastic establishments, such as that of St. Maximinus in Micy, where Benedict had sent envoys at the request of Bishop Theodulf of Orléans. More important, the customs of tenth-century Cluny were based on those of Baume, which had been reformed according to the observance of Benedict of Aniane. The first printed edition of the *Life*, published in 1638 in Paris by H. Menardus, provided the foundation for that of the Bollandist Gottfried Henschen a generation later. In the early 18th century Jean Mabillon (1632–1707) presented Benedict as the monastic collaborator of Charlemagne and Louis the Pious in returning Benedictinism to first principles. According to Mabillon the second father of the order not only reversed the process of decline that had weakened monasticism but also aimed at creating a Benedictine confederation with some sort of overall institutional structure. Although modern scholarship has shown that even the most sanguine ninth-century advocates of unity as a reform ideal did not think in terms of an "order" in this constitutional and administrative sense, Benedict of Aniane still deserves credit for making *vita monastica* synonymous with Benedictine monasticism until well into the 12th century.

DAVID APPLEBY

*See also* Benedict of Nursia, St.; Benedictines; Cluniacs; France: History; German Benedictine Reform, Medieval; Liturgy: Western Christian; Monastics and the World, Medieval; Orders (Religious), Origin of; Regulations: Christian Perspectives

## Biography

Following a military career under Pepin and his son Charlemagne, in 774 Witiza, the future "Second Benedict," joined the monastery of St. Seine near Dijon. After six years, by which time he was nearly elected abbot, he withdrew as a hermit to the banks of the river Aniane on his family property near Montpellier. In 782 he founded there a cenobitic community, which soon attracted hundreds of monks. He edited previous monastic rules so as to give priority to that of St. Benedict. Charlemagne's approval of Benedict of Aniane's practices made the latter's version of Benedictine monasticism authoritative in the West.

## Major Works

*Codex Regularum monasticarum et canonicarum* (Collection of Monastic Rules), edited by J.-P. Migne, in *Patrologia Latina*, volume 103, 1844–1864

*Munimenta fidei*, edited by Jean Leclercq, in *Studia Anselmiana* 20 (1948)

*Hucusque* (Supplement to the Gregorian Sacramentary), edited by Jean Deshusses, in *Le Sacramentaire grégorien*, volume 1, *Spicilegium Friburgense*, volume 16, 1971

## Further Reading

Kottje, Raymund, "Einheit und Vielfalt des kirchlichen Lebens in der Karolingerzeit," *Zeitschrift für Kirchengeschichte* 76 (1965)

McKitterick, Rosamond, *The Frankish Church and the Carolingian Reforms, 789–895*, London: Royal Historical Society, 1977

Semmler, Josef, "Benedictus II: una regula- una consuetudo," in *Benedictine Culture, 750–1050*, edited by W. Lourdaux and D. Verhelst, Leuven, Belgium: Leuven University Press, 1983

Semmler, Josef, "Benediktinische Reform und Kaiserliches Privileg. Zur Frage des institutionellen Zusammenschlusses der Klöster um Benedikt von Aniane," in *Institutionen und Geschichte: Theoretische Aspekte und mittelalterliche Befunde*, edited by Gert Melville, Cologne: Böhlau, 1992

Severus, Emmanuel von, "Benedikt von Aniane- Benedikt von Nursia. Gleicher Name- gleicher Geist?," in *Regulae Benedictini Studia: Annuarium Internationale*, Third International Congress on the Rule of Saint Benedict, edited by Bernd Jaspert, Hildesheim: Gerstenberg, 1982

*Vita Benedicti Abbatis Anianensis et Indensis auctore Ardone*, edited by Georg Waitz, in *Monumenta Germaniae historica*, *Scriptores*, volume 15, Hannover: Hahn, 1887; reprint, Stuttgart: Hiersemann, 1992 (excerpts of the *Vita* are translated into English in *Carolingian Civilization: A Reader*, edited by Paul Edward Dutton, Peterborough, Ontario: Broadview Press, 1993)

# Benedict of Nursia, St. c. 480–c. 547

Italian monk and author of the Benedictine Rule

Benedict was the founder of Subiaco and Monte Cassino in Italy and author of the principal monastic rule in the West. He was the subject of a biography by Pope Gregory the Great around 593, the second book of the *Dialogues*. Although its authorship has been disputed, the scholarly consensus affirms its authenticity. As the chief aim of this work is to demonstrate that sixth-century Italy could produce miracle-working saints, it needs to be treated with caution as a source of information about Benedict. Many of the details are colored by parallels that it draws between Benedict and Christ, Moses, David, Elijah, Elisha, and saints, such as Martin of Tours (d. 397). However, Gregory is careful to cite his sources (all figures close to Benedict), and the outline of the story is usually accepted as reliable.

Antonio Begarelli, St. Benedict, Church of San Pietro (Benedictine), Modena, Italy, 16th century.
**Photo courtesy of the Editor**

Benedict is depicted as coming from Nursia and going to Rome when young for his studies. Appalled by its sinfulness he withdrew from the city and became a hermit at Subiaco. After three years of solitude, he was asked to become abbot of a monastery, but his reforming ways were unpopular and led to an attempt to poison him. The poisoned cup shattered when he blessed it, and the broken cup is one of his symbols in art. He returned to Subiaco and gathered disciples whom he organized into 12 communities of 12 monks, each led by a dean. The Roman aristocracy brought their sons to him for education, and two of them, Maurus and Placid, became his best-known followers. Another celebrated miracle involved Maurus, who, under the protection of Benedict, walked on the lake at Subiaco to rescue Placid; here Maurus resembles Peter walking on the Sea of Galilee, and Benedict is like Christ. A local priest envied Benedict and attempted to poison him with a loaf that a crow took away in its beak – another symbol of Benedict in art. He withdrew to Cassino in southern Italy and there founded a monastery that was established on more thoroughly cenobitic lines. He was drawn into conflict with local paganism, and Gregory describes a number of occasions that showed his miraculous

prophetic insight. He met a leader of the Goths who was engaged in a bitter war with the Byzantines and prophesied both the decline of Rome to disease and famine and the destruction of his own monastery at Subiaco. Toward the end of his life, he was visited by his sister, Scholastica (c. 480–c. 543). She detained him in conversation throughout the night outside the enclosure by bringing down torrential rain with her weeping at his attempt to go back into the monastery. He died praying in church after predicting his own death.

Thus, Benedict was a contemporary of Boethius (c. 480–c. 524) and Cassiodorus (485/90–c. 580). The Rome that he knew when he was young was still the city of classical civilization, with its consuls and senate, fine buildings, and large population. The transition from empire to a Gothic kingdom in Italy had been notable for its continuity. However, he lived through a time of dreadful upheaval, of famine and plague, and of war when Italy was invaded by barbarian Lombards and by Byzantine

Stained-glass portrait of St. Benedict (c. 1910), crypt, Basilica of San Colombano, Bobbio, Italy.
**Photo courtesy of the Editor**

armies trying to reclaim the West for Constantinople. His life spanned the end of the classical world and the beginning of a new age in which monasticism was to play a vital role and his influence was to be enormous.

Gregory says that Benedict wrote a rule "notable for its discernment and its clarity of language." This short Latin text (about 15,000 words) is divided into a prologue and 73 chapters, in the last of which Benedict offers advice for further reading to advance deeper in the monastic way and calls his own "a little rule for beginners." Benedict's debt to earlier monastic tradition is evident, although scholars disagree about how far he is a disciple of John Cassian (c. 360–after 430) or of the more thoroughly cenobitic Basil (c. 330–379) and Augustine (354–430). Twentieth-century scholarship has also established his dependence on another sixth-century rule, probably also Italian, known as the Rule of the Master. Much of Benedict's text is a condensation and adaptation of the Master. An analysis of Benedict's use of his sources has clarified his distinctive monastic vision.

At times the ordering of the material is confusing. No overall structure is recognizable. The prologue and the first seven chapters, outlining the underlying monastic theology of the Rule, are drawn largely from the Master. Some groupings of chapters are fairly obvious, such as 8 to 20, on the Divine Office; 23 to 30 and 42 to 46, on penalties; 31 to 41, on the cellarer, property, mutual service in the community, and the sick; and 57 to 65, on skilled workmen in the community, admission of novices, priests and visiting monks, community order, the abbot, and the prior. However, links between these sections are less obvious, and the placing of a number of chapters seems entirely arbitrary. This has given rise in modern times to a number of inconclusive attempts to describe the process of writing and revising the Rule.

The essence of Benedict's monastic vision can be said to be an attempt to create a life in which monks can develop and sustain an awareness of God. His longest chapter, on humility (7), has as the first step of humility for the monk to recall "that he is always seen by God," a phrase repeated six times in the Rule. Awareness of God inevitably leads the monk to humility, a true appreciation of the relationship of creature and Creator. Obedience, likewise the first step in humility (5), is a response of love and generosity to God. Although he often uses military images, depicting the monk as battling for Christ, and constantly talks of monastic life as service of God and the community, Benedict sees the monk mainly as a listener in the school of the Lord's service (prologue). The root meaning of *obedience* is "to listen," from *ob-audire*. A monk hears God in the commands of the abbot and of the Rule, in the needs of the brethren, and in Scripture, to which he devotes about three hours of prayerful reading each day (48). Thus, silence is of central importance in the monastic life (6). Obedience should also make the monk transparent to his superiors and elders (4, 7). The awareness of God is anchored in the Incarnation and the Paschal Mystery: three times Benedict tells the monk to "prefer nothing to the love of Christ," and five times he says that the mainspring of the life is acting in the love of Christ. The prologue and the first seven chapters, where this

teaching is largely laid down, are a superb summation of the teaching of the tradition drawn very heavily from the Master.

Benedict's view of the abbot and authority in the monastery represents a significant shift from the Master. His first account of the abbot in chapter 2 derives closely from the Master and behind him from Cassian: the abbot is the master surrounded by disciples. However, this is at once balanced by a chapter (3) of Benedict's own creation on calling the community together for consultation. The abbot is not the sole source of wisdom and must listen to the opinion of others, even the youngest. More than the Master, Benedict emphasizes the pastoral qualities and role of the abbot in chapters on concern for the excommunicated (27) and an abbot's installation (64), which many regard as one of the wisest and most humane in the rule. Benedict says that the function of the abbot is to be a servant, "to benefit the monks rather than lord it over them" ("prodesse magis quam praeesse" in the neat Latin phrase) and that he should "strive to be loved rather than feared." He must be prudent, discerning, and moderate and needs to be chaste, temperate, and merciful. He needs to be aware of his own limitations and, above all, to show "discretion, the mother of the virtues."

Benedict also gives much greater prominence than the Master to officials whom the abbot appoints to share his pastoral responsibilities, especially the cellarer, who is depicted (31) as a man who must have similar qualities to the abbot, as his aim is also to serve and promote the welfare of the community. The novice master (58) is also a very important and trusted figure. On the other hand Benedict plays down the role of deans (21), who feature more prominently in the Master and expresses great concern about the prior (65) who could rival the abbot as an alternative source of authority if not appointed by him. Here it seems that Benedict is commenting on contemporary developments and problems in sixth-century monasticism. An important feature of Benedict's abbot is that normally he is chosen by the community (whereas for the Master he is chosen by his predecessor); since then this has tended to be the usual monastic way of selecting superiors. This established the centrality of the community as the source of wisdom and even, in a sense, of authority. Benedict also sees that at times the abbot might need to rely on the intervention of other members of the community to deal with monks with whom he cannot cope himself (27). Overall an emphasis on rank based on seniority in joining the community (63) allows for a class of seniors who should be treated with the greatest respect by juniors (71). Benedict has a very strong sense of the dynamics and organic nature of community and has an important chapter on obedience being owed not only to the abbot or the Rule but also mutually among the brethren (71), preceded by chapters in which he warns against protective patronage by any monk of another (69) or against anyone presuming to punish or strike another without authorization (70).

Benedict gives a full and original account of the Divine Office (8–20). It can be estimated that in his scheme nearly four hours a day were devoted to liturgical prayer. Eight daily offices spread throughout the day: vigils, lauds, prime, terce, sext, none, vespers, and compline. Unlike the Master, who has a daily service in which the monks receive Communion, Benedict makes no specific provision for the Eucharist, but unlike the Master he does allow priests to join the monastery or for the abbot to have a monk ordained priest for the service of the community, so Mass is probably assumed to be celebrated regularly. Benedict's account of the Office marks a shift from the Master that, given the later normative status of his Rule, was to exercise a decisive liturgical impact in the West. He abolished all-night vigils and the practice of simply following the psalms through the order of the Psalter. Instead vigils is a lengthy service of psalms and readings celebrated in the early hours of the morning, and the psalms appointed for different offices are chosen for their relevance to the Office and relationship with one another. He is insistent that all 150 should be sung each week but is aware that this is less demanding than was previous monastic tradition. It seems that the psalms were sung by an individual cantor with a communal refrain followed by a silent pause. His notion of the monastic life as living in the awareness and fear of God underpins his view of the Office as the regular intensification of this in the day (19). At the same time the Office is part of the monk's service of God (50), the work of God (*opus Dei*) to which nothing is to be preferred (43).

Benedict gives considerable attention to penalties and sanctions in monastic life. Twelve chapters are entirely devoted to penalties, and 27 others end with threats of punishment. Although a monk might be expelled from the monastery for incorrigible intransigence after repeated warnings, the most extreme sanction within the community is excommunication from Office and meals. This highlights the communal vision of the Rule. His view of sanctions, unlike that of the Master, is pedagogic, not retributive, and no penal code of offenses and corresponding punishments exists, although the application of sanctions is better structured and graded than in the Master. The abbot alone is the judge of penalties, and his discretion is complete, although he is repeatedly urged to play the role of healer. Perhaps the division of the chapters about penalties into two groups (23–30 and 42–46) is intended to give greater emphasis to reconciliation, as laid down in the second group.

A strongly communal dimension comes to the fore in the chapters on the cellarer (31) and the following chapters on property (32–34 and, again later, 54–55), the kitchen servers (35), the sick (36), the elderly and children (37), the weekly reader (38), and meals (39–41). Although due account is taken of individual needs, the main criterion in judging what is right about property or food is finding a reasonable communal standard rather than enhancing the ascetic renunciation of the individual. Service of the brethren is repeatedly emphasized as the main task of the cellarer and weekly servers and readers. Benedict takes a generous view of the sick and invents the idea of an infirmary for them, whereas the Master is full of suspicion that they might be malingerers. In the same way Benedict is far more positive than the Master about guests (53). Guests and the sick, as well as the poor and the abbot, are all people in whom the monk can meet and serve Christ.

Benedict seems to take a largely practical view of work, simply as a way of earning a living. Although he says that "idleness is the enemy of the soul" (48), he does not develop a theory of work as an antidote to sin as the Master does. He clearly sees work as part of a balanced life, but in the sole chapter dedicated to the subject (48) he pays far more attention to adjusting the times of meals and offices according to the seasons and to the importance of daily reading than to any consideration of what work the monks should be doing. The monastery should aim to be a self-sufficient economic unit to save the monks from external engagement (66), and produce is to be sold more cheaply than it is by outsiders (57). He sees heavy work, such as harvesting, as a burden that monks might have to shoulder out of poverty, perhaps meaning an inability to hire workers or rely on tenants (48).

Benedict's arrangements for admission of new members of the community (58) are a very significant development beyond previous monastic practice, including that of Cassian and the Master. He invents the words *novice* and *novitiate*. He depicts a yearlong novitiate when the applicant is under the guidance of a novice-master, a notable figure in Benedict's view, and lives in separate accommodation, a novel feature of his monastery. The novice hears the Rule read to him three times during the year, and if it is decided that he should stay and become a monk, in the presence of the community he takes vows of stability, fidelity to monastic life ("conversatio morum"), and obedience. This well-considered structure was to have immense influence on later monastic practice.

Benedict allows children to be offered as monks by their parents, whether nobles or poor (59), a practice expressly ruled out by the Master, who insists that monastic commitment must be made by people old enough to make a rational and informed choice. Child oblation was unusual in the sixth century, although it became more common over the following few hundred years. Later monastic practice firmly repudiated this feature of the Rule. Benedict differs from the Master too in allowing priests to be admitted to the community or monks to be ordained. This does not represent a shift toward the clericalization of monastic life, although these chapters (60, 62) were later to contribute to that. Rather it is likely that this was Benedict's attempt to preserve the independence of the monastery from external clerical control – clearly a lively issue in the sixth century as it was later, as can be seen from the correspondence of Gregory the Great.

Thus, Benedict's Rule was a persuasive summary and application of monastic tradition and a considerable improvement on the Rule of the Master. It was a successful synthesis of ascetic teaching drawn from Cassian and cenobitic practice drawn from Augustine and Basil. Shorter and more flexible than the Master, it allowed the abbot much scope to adapt its regulations, for example, concerning the order of psalmody (18), and in many places it remained deliberately vague. Thus, it was more workable. Its moderation and humanity had perennial appeal. It laid down a viable system of monastic government: a strong abbot, sharing his authority and pastoral responsibilities with others, and a community of which the abbot was the servant with a stable and continuous identity. Its organization of the Office, the training of novices, and the role of various officials were all new and proved enduring in Western monastic history.

Benedict's Rule became normative in the West from the time of Benedict of Aniane (c. 750–821) in the early ninth century. Before then it was often used in combination with other rules or monastic traditions, although the Anglo-Saxons and their eighth-century missionaries to the Continent did much to establish its preeminence. Almost the whole history of Western monasticism for the last thousand years has been a series of revivals and reinterpretations of the Rule. The discovery in the 20th century of its dependence on the Master and detailed analysis of its other antecedents have led to a more scholarly understanding of the text while also perhaps undermining any simple attempt to follow it literally today. De Vogüé's immense French edition has led to several outstanding modern scholarly commentaries, and the RB1980 edition is a superb resource for study of the text. At the same time, an explosion took place in the last quarter of the 20th century of popular translations and commentaries for lay readers. What impact these fresh readings of the Rule and its newfound popularity with a far wider readership will have on the practice and development of monasticism in the future remains to be seen.

BERNARD GREEN, O.S.B.

*See also* Benedict of Aniane, St.; Cassian, John; Cassiodorus; Christianity: Overview; Economics: Christian; Governance: Christian Perspectives; Gregory I (the Great), St.; Liturgy: Western Christian; Monasticism, Definitions of: Christian Perspectives; Monastics and the World, Medieval; Monte Cassino, Italy; Music: Christian Perspectives; Office, Daily: Western Christian; Officials: Western Christian; Regulations: Christian Perspectives; Retreat, Christian; Saints, Italian Benedictine; Scholars, Benedictine; Spirituality: Western Christian; Subiaco, Italy

### Biography

As told in Book II of Gregory I's *Dialogues*, the "father of Western monasticism" was born at Nursia and educated in Rome. Benedict withdrew to a cave east of Rome about 500. Having lived there for a time as a hermit, he began to attract a community of hermits and cenobites. Following local conflicts he moved further south to Monte Cassino c. 527, where he established a cenobitic house. His Rule, adapted from several earlier ones, has been seminal for nearly all subsequent monasticism in Western Europe and throughout the westernized world. His sister St. Scholastica is reported by Gregory to have established a convent at Plombariola a few miles from Monte Cassino.

### Major Work

Rule (*Regula*)

### Further Reading

De Waal, Esther, *Seeking God: The Way of St. Benedict*, London: Collins, and Collegeville, Minnesota: Liturgical Press, 1984

Eberle, Luke, editor, *The Rule of the Master*, Kalamazoo, Michigan: Cistercian Publications, 1977

Fry, Timothy, editor, *RB 1980: The Rule of St. Benedict in English*, Collegeville, Minnesota: Liturgical Press 1981

Holzherr, George, *The Rule of Saint Benedict: A Guide to Christian Living*, Dublin: Four Courts Press, 1994

Kardong, Terrence G., *Benedict's Rule: A Translation and Commentary*, Collegeville, Minnesota: Liturgical Press, 1996

Vogüé, Adalbert de, editor, *La règle de Saint Benoît*, 7 vols., Paris: Éditions du Cerf, 1972

Vogüé, Adalbert de, editor, *The Life of St. Benedict – Gregory the Great*, Petersham, Massachusetts: St. Bede's Publications, 1993

# Benedictine Congregations. *See* Congregations, Benedictine

# Benedictine Rule. *See* Benedict of Nursia, St.; Regulations: Christian Perspectives

# Benedictines: Female

For almost 1,500 years Benedictine women have been an independent force within the Christian Church. Benedict's identity remains shrouded in mystery, but his Rule and his life were effectively promoted by Pope Gregory I (590–604) in his *Dialogues*. Benedict first sojourned as a hermit at Subiaco east of Rome, still a spectacular monastic site with cells carved into the mountain. Following John Cassian (c. 360–after 430), whose Conferences he admired, Benedict was attracted to the eremitic life of the desert as well as to a more communal ascetic life. He designed, as he says, a beginner's rule, "a school in the Lord's service," to train recruits and make the celibate dedicated life (emerging as monasticism) more accessible to laypeople.

He warned his monks not to be gyrovagues (monks who wander from place to place) although wandering evangelical preachers remained influential and popular from St. Paul to Francis of Assisi and beyond. He thought the eremitic life advisable only for those who had first undergone long training in community, a wisdom perhaps garnered from his own experience. Benedictine monastics were to take vows of conversion of life, stability to the same community until death, and obedience to the abbess or abbot as if to Christ. They were to live lives of study, communal and private prayer, and manual work (rare for Roman aristocrats). There were to be only priests enough to serve the sacramental needs of the community, and all the brothers or sisters, regardless of social origins, were to be equal in Christ and even the least and youngest consulted on important decisions. Yet, not surprisingly in that day, the Benedictine monastery was no democracy, and considerable power was vested in the superior, who, after consultation, might make final decisions. In addition there was a functional hierarchy of seniors and juniors, professed and novices, officers and ordinary religious, with privileges and duties according to their rank.

Benedictine life is usually structured around prayer in the chapel seven times a day. Although this life can become routinized and relationships formalized, the potential of silence and intense community living affords the opportunity for deepening loving relationships with God and others. The seniors provide spiritual guidance for the juniors, as the abbas and ammas of the desert did for their disciples. The monastery is never without guests, who are to be received as Christ, and the religious interact constantly with the surrounding community. From their beginnings Benedictine monasteries were witnesses in the world, having been modeled on the first Christian communities described in the Acts of the Apostles.

That there were Benedictine women from the beginning is implied by the legend of St. Scholastica, who used to meet with her brother Benedict to discuss their way of life in a house between their communities. Once she urged him to stay overnight to talk longer, and he protested that he had to return home. When he would not listen to her, she prayed to God, who sent such a storm that it was impossible for Benedict and his brothers to depart. That was their final meeting, as Scholastica died soon thereafter. Benedictine monks and nuns have been partners since the beginnings, and the women have always had a voice in common decisions.

Thus, women religious began following the Rule of St. Benedict (RB) in the sixth century, but older foundations often had mixed rules and their own particular customs. The Rules of Augustine (354–430) and Caesarius of Arles (c. 470–542) were also popular with nuns; the convent of St.-Croix of Poitiers, founded by Radegunde (c. 518–587), might have preferred the insistence on enclosure in St. Caesarius' Rule that gave royal and aristocratic nuns who left husbands in the world a measure of seclusion and protection.

In theory each Benedictine house was independent. Nevertheless, bishops often wielded greater jurisdiction over women's houses than men's monasteries, which looked to visiting abbots rather than local bishops for supervision, especially in later centralized orders, such as the Cluniac and Cistercian. Efforts were made by the Carolingian reformer Benedict of Aniane (c. 750–821) to impose the Benedictine Rule, and later reforms, such as those of Cluny and Gorze, spread its influence. It is important to remember that even early monasteries with mixed rules and later active orders have been deeply imprinted with Benedictine values and practices.

Both the Carolingian and the Cluniac reforms insisted on the free election of the abbess without outside interference of either bishop or lay lord. However, bishops were required for the

Facade (18th century) and church tower (12th century), Santa Cecilia in Trastevere, Rome, Italy. Benedictine nuns occupy the attached convent.
Photo courtesy of the Editor

consecration of a new church or abbess, and they had jurisdiction over the clergy who provided sacraments to the nuns. Thus, a Benedictine women's house needed to work well with the bishop.

Most women's houses had at least a small male community of chaplains and often lay brothers who helped with the manual work. Especially famous were the Anglo-Saxon houses of women and men ruled by an abbess, but such so-called double houses existed as well in France, Germany, Spain, and Italy. The Venerable Bede (c. 673–735) writes of Abbess Hilda of Whitby (614–680), who nurtured five bishops among her students and hosted in 664 the famous synod that settled the differences between Celtic and Roman calendars and practices. At first she did not favor the Roman ways, doubtless including the RB, but after 664 accepted them graciously. In the 12th century such famous French monasteries of men and women as Fontevraud and the Paraclete were also led by abbesses. The correspondence of Abelard (1079–1142/43) and Heloise (c. 1100–1163/64) after she became abbess of the Paraclete discusses the application of the RB to nuns of the 12th century.

Benedictine monasteries fostered many women mystics and prophets, such as Hildegard of Bingen (1098–1179), who is becoming ever more popular today. The Convent of Helfta, under the aegis of two strong abbesses named Gertrude (1256–c. 1302) with mystic inclinations, accepted as a nun the beguine mystic Mechtild of Magdeburg (c. 1207–1282) when her writings were investigated by the Church. Not only did the Benedictine monastery provide a life in which mysticism, often revolving around devotion to the Eucharist, could flourish, but medieval Benedictine institutions were independent enough to offer a measure of protection to nuns whose new ideas might be critical of the clergy.

Benedictine monasteries were the center of lay communities (sometimes towns grew up around them) to which they offered all kinds of liturgical, educational, and health services. They supplied the processions and relics for saints' day celebrations that attracted pilgrims from afar. Carolingian and later monasteries provided schools for novices and local noble boys and girls. With relics came healings, and local hospices (part hospitals, part guest houses) were attached to many monasteries. The portery and church provided meeting points of nuns and townspeople, and the poor were often fed in special dining rooms or at the door.

Sisters remained very close to their families (often several entered the same house), and gifts and exchanges of land bound local aristocratic families to the monasteries that they founded, staffed, and endowed. Lay advocates were often engaged from leading families to defend the monastery and forward its legal and business interests.

Debate has arisen among scholars on two related questions. First, how freely did nuns enter medieval monasteries? Were they placed there rather than married off by their parents, or did they choose their vocations?

Second, how strictly enclosed were Benedictine nuns? Some documents do assert that a certain father made his daughter a nun, yet there are many examples of freely chosen vocations during the early and High Middle Ages. Alan of Brittany founded St. Georges, Rennes, to provide his sister and her friends a monastery where they could devote themselves to the prayerful life that they yearned for. Herveus, treasurer of St. Martin of Tours around 1000, founded Beaumont because a women's monastery no longer existed in Tours, and he wished to help a group of women attempting to live a monastic life among the canons of St. Martin.

Children, not old enough to make any kind of choice, were frequently dedicated to monasteries as oblates, but they were to make a decision whether to remain when they reached adolescence. Some very famous religious, such as Leoba and Hildegard of Bingen, were child oblates. Most ordinary entrants, bringing with them a gift or dowry, were admitted as young teens, the age at which they would also be expected to consent to an arranged marriage. Some people also joined monasteries much later in life. Widows were welcomed and brought some of their property as dowry. Wives who felt called to a deeper religious life or who perhaps wanted only to separate from an abusive spouse might seek entrance to a monastery with their spouse's consent.

Despite sporadic ecclesiastical legislation calling for strict enclosure of religious women, there is much evidence that sisters did go out to visit their families and on necessary business. For example, the nun Agnes was visiting her family when Leoba's Carolingian monastery was shaken by the crisis of discovering a dead baby in the reservoir just outside the cloister. The townspeople accused a nun of having given birth and then baptizing and drowning the infant – something that all denied except Agnes, who was away. Later she was exonerated when a poor, young woman boarding with the nuns confessed to the crime. Leoba's monastery might have followed a mixed rule at this time. Abbesses often visited royal courts, ecclesiastical synods, and other monasteries where they served as witnesses for charters, and for such business the abbess of Notre-Dame Saintes kept a horse. We have noted that the famous Abbess Hildegard of Bingen undertook preaching tours with the permission of the papacy. Likewise many documents show laypeople being received into a monastery, sometimes in the refectory, to transact various kinds of business. Families visited their monastic relatives with some frequency as well. None of this was seen as abuse in ordinary medieval Benedictine houses. After all, guests were always to be received as Christ.

Benedictine women's communities began to experience difficulties, often amounting to persecution, in the later Middle Ages and again in modern times. In difficult times aristocratic families favored men's over women's houses, and many women's communities that were poorer than men's were forced to close. The Cluniac Order sponsored only one official women's community, Marcigny, founded more than a century after Cluny's origins, although many Benedictine women's houses adopted Cluniac goals and programs. The same happened with the Cistercian reforms; abbots and reformers unofficially assisted women's communities in adopting Cistercian customs, but few official Cistercian convents with their privileges of immunity were in existence; thus, bishops supervised the Cistercian look-alikes as they did the traditional Benedictine communities, which often mitigated the intended reforms.

Competition for the best recruits was increasing among new orders (e.g., Franciscan and Dominican) and even among new styles of religious life not bound by the cloister and perpetual vows, such as that of the beguines. From the 12th century there was a desire to work with the poor in the world while living a contemplative life. Such a mixed active/contemplative life was permitted to mendicant tertiaries (who might even be married) and beguines but forbidden to women Franciscans or Dominicans, who, like Clare of Assisi (1193/94–1253), were enclosed as Benedictine nuns. Thus, there was a problem of reluctant enclosed Benedictine women in the later Middle Ages who secretly yearned for more active religious lives.

The issues of difference between Benedictines and the newer orders centered on cloistering (or even on living in established monasteries at all) and the interpretation of poverty: Benedictines held all things in common, but Francis called for absolute poverty of the community itself. There was also the evangelical preaching ministry of the new mendicant orders, who earned that name by begging if necessary for their daily subsistence rather than accepting property and rents to support themselves, as Benedictines did. However, Benedictine, Dominican, and Franciscan nuns – with some notable exceptions, such as Hildegard of Bingen – did not undertake begging or preaching missions and were required to accept sufficient property for the upkeep of their sisters, or else the number of their novices might be reduced by bishop or pope.

Later medieval papal bulls, such as Boniface VIII's *Periculoso* (c. 1300), began to insist on stricter enclosure, making it ever more difficult for the sisters to earn a living because they had to employ more outside agents who did not always act in their interests. Some houses resorted to dividing their income among the religious so that those with the highest dowries and best prebends lived in greater luxury than others. These nuns were not really living the Benedictine life but rather a kind of canonical life that permitted private property.

Late medieval and early modern communities also allowed things such as *corridies*, which permitted older laypeople who had paid a kind of insurance policy to end their days supported in the monastery. Other boarders ranged from young students in the monastic schools to wealthy noblewomen who had been discarded as mistresses. They did not always understand the monastic life or promote the best spiritual atmosphere. Through the revival of a practice known as the *commenda* (custody), kings (and sometimes lesser nobles) were able to appoint their relatives as abbesses of such royal foundations as Fontevraud. Such superiors might not live as Benedictines at all and frequently kept separate apartments to entertain their relatives and friends. The practice of "dumping" prisoners, the handicapped, and even the mentally ill in monasteries increased in modern times.

Monasteries were not dissolved as quickly in Protestant countries as had once been thought; many communities fought for their survival and beliefs, and others retained monastic lifestyles, with Protestants and Catholics coexisting for generations. Even Catholic countries became more reluctant to support purely contemplative communities and often urged the nuns to undertake work useful to society. Benedictine houses, all of which were required to be cloistered, developed schools and hospitals within, whereas new Catholic-Reformation orders, such as the Sisters of Mercy, the Ursulines, the Visitation Sisters, and Mary Ward's Institute, eschewed perpetual vows and the cloister as much as possible in order to work among the poor and the sick in hospitals and schools.

The Observant movement prior to the French Revolution sometimes quite violently reformed traditional Benedictine convents whether they needed it or not. This resulted in leaner, more militant communities that were sometimes able to resist dissolution in the French Revolution. The new Trappists, men and women, wandered from one part of Europe to another as refugees until they were allowed to return to France and their strict monastic lives in the early 19th century. The sisters of St.-Croix and other Benedictine women who were ousted from their convents rented houses, moved in with friends, and otherwise retained an underground monasticism until the crisis was over.

However, the pressure to work for a living was inexorable, and most Benedictine missionaries who came to North America to serve particular ethnic groups lived very active lives, working in much needed schools, hospitals, and parishes. Purely contemplative Benedictine women's communities in the United States are rare today, except for Regina Laudes in Connecticut and the Trappistines. Since the reforms of the Second Vatican Council (1962–1965), women religious have faced a vocational crisis. Many orders have given up the habit, divested themselves of schools and hospitals, and stopped staffing parishes. They have moved out to live in small groups in apartments and among the poor, finding particular ministries to suit their talents. Some have commanded professional salaries as college presidents, lawyers, and doctors in an effort to pay for the upkeep of their many older nuns. Others have become outspoken advocates of social justice and the poor and oppressed. Two excellent examples are Sister Helen Prejean (of the Sisters of St. Joseph), who has become an advocate of death-row inmates, and Sister Joan Chittister, author, activist, and former head of the American Benedictine sisters.

What is the essence of Benedictine life that cannot be compromised? And where are women Benedictines heading? Understanding the times and listening to the call of God are keys in the prologue of Benedict's very flexible Rule, which is now often advocated for the spiritual life of the laity as well. Prophecy, vision, and deeply contemplative prayer have marked Benedictine monasteries throughout the centuries, and the laity today find such monasteries, especially the more contemplative ones, a constant source of refreshment and retreat. Good liturgy and intentional Christian community have marked Benedictine houses, which in turn offer these as models to surrounding parishes and congregations. Benedictine monasteries continue to be ecumenical outposts and offer spiritual guidance and hospitality to people of all religious traditions. The ascetic life offers inspiration to the rich who are sated with material advantages and guiltily aware of the worldwide gap between rich and poor. Benedictines are engaged in the environmental movement and have spread worldwide with many new recruits from the Third World who teach about their cultures in increasingly multicultural communities. Governance by consensus and by religious superiors who no longer rule marks the Benedictines of today. Feminism flourishes in women's communities to the dismay of an increasingly conservative clerical hierarchy. As it has for many generations, Benedictine life offers single women (including many divorced) a vehicle for close relationships with other women, partnerships with men, and a challenging and fulfilling way of single life. Benedictine women are struggling toward new roles in church and society, often advocating behind the scenes for equality and priesthood for women and also combatting the feminization of poverty in the world.

MARY S. SKINNER

*See also* Abbess, Christian; Beguines; Benedict of Nursia, St.; Benedictines: General or Male; Cassian, John; Cistercians: Female; Claustration (Cloister), Rules of; Contemporary Issues: Western Christian; Double Houses, Western Christian; Fontevraud, France; France: History; Heloise; Hilda, St.; Liturgy: Western Christian; Mystics, German Monastic: Female; Oblates; Office, Daily: Western Christian; Patrons, Christian: Lay; Radegunde, St.; Relics, Christian Monastic; Social Services: Western Christian; Trappists; Vocation, Christian; Women's Monasteries: Western Christian

**Further Reading**

Centre Européen de Recherches sur les Congrégations et les Ordres Religieux, editors, *Les religieuses dans le cloître et dans le monde des origines à nos jours: actes du deuxième colloque international du C.E.R.C.O.R, Poitiers, 29 septembre–2 octobre 1988* (Travaux et recherches/C.E.R.C.O.R., 4), Saint-Étienne: Publications de l'Université de Saint-Etienne, 1994
Chittister, Joan, *Wisdom Distilled from the Daily: Living the Rule of St. Benedict Today*, San Francisco: Harper and Row, 1990
De Waal, Esther, *Seeking God: The Way of St. Benedict*, London: Collins, and Collegeville, Minnesota: Liturgical Press, 1984
Elkins, Sharon, *Holy Women of Twelfth-Century England* (Studies in Religion), Chapel Hill: University of North Carolina Press, 1988
Johnson, Penelope, *Equal in Monastic Profession: Religious Women in Medieval France* (Women in Culture and Society), Chicago: University of Chicago Press, 1991
McNamara, Jo Ann, *Sisters in Arms: Catholic Nuns through Two Millennia*, Cambridge, Massachusetts: Harvard University Press, 1996
Nichols, John, and Lillian Thomas Shank, editors, *Distant Echoes* (Medieval Religious Women, 1), Kalamazoo, Michigan: Cistercian Publications, 1984
Nichols, John, and Lillian Thomas Shank, editors, *Peace Weavers* (Medieval Religious Women, 2), Kalamazoo, Michigan: Cistercian Publications, 1987
Nichols, John, and Lillian Thomas Shank, editors, *Hidden Springs: Cistercian Monastic Women* (Medieval Religious Women), 2 vols., Kalamazoo, Michigan: Cistercian Publications, 1995
Norris, Kathleen, *The Cloister Walk*, New York: Riverhead Books, 1996; Oxford: Lion, 1999
Oliva, Marilyn, *The Convent and the Community in Late Medieval England: Female Monasteries in the Diocese of Norwich, 1350–1540* (Studies in the History of Medieval Religion, volume 12), Woodbridge, Suffolk, and Rochester, New York: Boydell Press, 1998
Privat, Edouard, editor, *La femme dans la vie religieuse du Languedoc: XIIIe–XIVe s.* (Cahiers de Fanjeaux, 23), Toulouse: Privat, 1988
Reynes, Geneviève, *Couvents de femmes: la vie des religieuses contemplatives dans la France des XVIIe et XVIIIe siècles*, Paris: Fayard, 1987
Schmitt, Miriam, and Linda Kulzer, editors, *Medieval Women Monastics: Wisdom's Wellsprings*, Collegeville, Minnesota: Liturgical Press, 1996
Schneiders, Sandra Marie, *New Wine Skins: Re-imagining Religious Life Today*, New York: Paulist Press, 1986

# Benedictines: General or Male

These were monks of the Rule of St. Benedict, Ordo Sancti Benedicti (O.S.B.), who made up a congregation of religious priests and monks without priestly ordination. The Benedictine Order is one of the oldest Christian orders.

The name "Benedictines" appeared in the 13th century in some national languages (Old French) and since the end of the 14th century in Latin sources; it has been in common use since the 17th century.

Originally the Benedictines were called "monks" (*monachi*), then referred to as the monks living in accordance with the Rule of St. Benedict (*sub regula S. Benedicti*). From the 12th century on, they were also called, from the color of their habits, "black monks," as opposed to the Cistercians, that is, "white" or "gray" monks. From the 13th century on, the name "Order of St. Benedict" (Ordo sancti Benedicti) has been in use.

The habit of the Benedictines consists of a black tunic girded with a leather belt and, on the top of that, a black scapular with a cowl. For the choir a black hood (*cucullus*) is worn by fully professed monks, whereas a cope is worn by temporarily professed monks and by novices.

The charism of the Benedictines is the search for God with the Gospel for their guide; their slogan is "So that God might be worshipped in everything" and *Pax* (peace); their motto is "Pray and Work" (*ora et labora*).

The Rule of the Benedictines was created by St. Benedict of Nursia (c. 480–c. 550), who wrote and augmented it from around 530 in Monte Cassino abbey. It is a modified version of the slightly earlier (c. 500–c. 530) anonymous so-called *Regula*

**Master of the Cloister of the Orange Trees, fresco of Benedictines at table, Badia, Florence, Italy, 15th century.**
**Photo courtesy of the Editor**

*Magistri.* Benedict also made use of the Bible and Scriptures of the fathers of the Church and founders of monasticism: John Cassian, Augustine of Hippo, Pachomius (in Rufinus' translation), Basil the Great, Jerome, Macarius of Alexandria, Caesarius of Arles, and others.

Characteristic features of the Rule are moderation, prudence, and a humane conception of monasticism. Thus, the monastic ideals of the East could be adopted to the mentality of the people of the West. Saint Benedict saw the monastic ideal in contemplative communal life and inner formation. Because of its general nature, his Rule allowed for adapting specific regulations on the internal life of the community and organization of abbey to particular circumstances while remaining faithful to principles.

The Rule consists of a prologue and 73 chapters not arranged in any discernible logical order. The first part expounds the principles of monastic life: abbot and fraternal community (2–3), spirituality (4–7), liturgical code (8–20), penitential code (23–30, 68–72), and organization of the monks' life (21–22, 31–57, 67). The second part is concerned with admission and training of members (58–63). The third part deals with election and responsibilities of the abbot and prior (64–65) and the fourth with claustration and gate (66). The last part, later added

to the original Rule, contains additional remarks and advice (68–72) and an epilogue (73).

The Rule expounds principles of stability of place (*stabilitas loci*) and of claustration as well as of maintaining balance between common prayer, *lectio divina*, manual labor, and recreation. It emphasizes inner discipline (humility, obedience, silence, and fidelity in everyday duties for the love of God), ideals of the Gospel, and imitating Christ.

On the destruction of Monte Cassino abbey, the autograph copy of the Rule was brought to Rome. Pope Zacharias (741–752) returned it to the restored Monte Cassino abbey. For fear of the Saracens, around 883 the manuscript was transferred to Teano abbey, where it burned in a fire in 896.

It was frequently copied. All the manuscripts are one of three types: (1) pure text (true copies), the most important of which is *Codex Sangallensis* (914), kept in the Stiftsbibliothek of St. Gallen; it was probably copied in 817 in Aachen from a copy made of the original manuscript for Charlemagne after 787; (2) interpolated text, a group to which belongs the oldest extant manuscript of the Rule *Codex Oxoniensis* Hatton 48 (Oxford, Bodleian Library) of around 700; and (3) mixed text, or *textus receptus*, which first appeared in the eighth century (first in the commentary of Paul the Deacon) and which has been the most widespread; it is based on the two earlier types, and its popularity is due to its corrected Latin and added explanation of a few unclear loci.

The Fourth Lateran Council (1215) confirmed it as one of four standing monastic rules alongside the Augustinian Rule and those of Basil the Great and Francis of Assisi.

## Commentaries and Customaries

Commentaries expound current interpretations of the Rule. The earliest was written by Paul the Deacon around 786 (*Pauli Warnefridi diaconi . . . commentarium*, Monte Cassino, 1880). Other early commentaries are *Concordia regularum*, written by Benedict of Aniane (*Patrologia Latina* 103.703–1380), and two written after 820: Smaragde (*Expositio in regulam Benedicti*, edited by Alfredus Spannagel and Pius Engelbert, in *Corpus Consuetudinum Monasticarum*, volume 8, 1974) and Hildmar's (*Tractatus Hildemari monachi in regulam s. Benedicti*, edited by Mittelmüller, 1880). Numerous commentaries were written in modern times. An important modern commentary is that of Paul Delatte (*Commentaire de la Règle de saint Benoît*, 1913).

Monastic customaries (Latin, *consuetudines*) define more accurately and adapt to needs of everyday life (and to local customs and tradition) the general regulations of the Rule. They define, in writing or in oral tradition only, detailed practices of everyday life of a particular monastic community. They aim at describing a peculiar way of life – customaries pertaining to meals, work, sleeping, or performing liturgy – during a day and a year. The importance of this sort of detail was first emphasized by the councils of Aachen in 802 and 816/17.

A basic collection of Benedictine customaries (including Cluniac) was published in the *Corpus Consuetudinum Monasticarum*, established at the suggestion of Kassius Hallinger.

## Monastic Organization

The Rule provides for an autonomous, self-contained community (66) headed by the abbot elected by this community (64). His power is unlimited (2, 63), yet he must take counsel with the seniors (3). He appoints officials, among whom the Rule names prior as his deputy (65), as well as deans (21), cellarer (31), novice-master (58), and guest-master (53). Later modifications led to the increasing the role of the conventual chapter (assembly of all monks). It elects, for a limited term, officers (the precantor or cantor and the sacrist being of importance), among them the prior, who thus becomes the representative of the chapter. The monastic property is divided into the *abbatia* and the *mensa conventualis*. An informal position of prominence is occupied by monks who have been living in the monastery for the longest time.

A Benedictine abbey is to be a self-sufficient microcosm that houses in fraternal community for the most part unordained monks (60, 62) who come from various social strata (2) and who are of various ages (37). In a monastery there are also the sick (36), excommunicate persons (44), oblates (59), and novices (58) as well as monks from other houses (61) and guests (53).

Later evolution lead to the proliferation of clerical status in the community and to its division (from the 11th to the 12th century) into two parts: choir fathers (priests) and illiterate lay brothers (*conversi*).

The monastic Benedictine community included also other social groups who were not monks but participated in its spiritual life: a few poor and old persons maintained by the monastery, residents (benefactors who, in their old age, were living in the monastery), founders and their families, patrons, sons of nobles admitted to the monastic school, and guests. Also affiliated were *confratres*, that is, persons, monasteries, chapters, or orders that through confraternity (philadelphia) with a Benedictine community acquired participation in the spiritual benefits of the Mass and other penitential practices. Their names were inscribed in the book of confraternity (*Liber confraternitatis*), and on their death their names were entered in obituaries (*Liber mortuorum*). There were also members of fraternities linked with monastic churches, servants of the monastery, and the abbot's *familia*.

Benedictine abbeys do not constitute a centralized order. They are independent units. Sometimes they form confederations of various organizational principles. Abbeys are subject to a local bishop or to the pope if they enjoy a privilege of exemption from bishop's control.

## Spirituality

A fundamental characteristic of Benedictine spirituality is "being with God," a goal to which monks aim through *metanoia* (i.e., everyday conversion). In their profession the Benedictines vow maintaining stability of place (these ties between a monk and his abbey are important characteristics of the Benedictine profession), obedience, and assuming a monastic way of life. Thus, they vow to serve God through imitating the obedient, pure, and poor Christ. The essential elements uniting the Benedictine community are liturgy, which for the monks is the basic source of inner life, and daily Eucharist. Individual Benedictine prayer is open and based on daily liturgy and on *lectio divina* (i.e., meditative) reading of the Bible and biblical commentaries, mainly patristic. Monks are "men of prayer." Their vocation is to benefit fellow men through their example of life centered on God. For a Benedictine the monastic community is the "school of the Lord's service," in which solitude and mutual bonds are equally important. This community is united by the abbot, Christ's deputy in the monastery.

Basic elements of the Benedictine tradition, accentuated in the Rule of St. Benedict, are labor and hospitality. Labor is the regular source of providing for the monastery and caring for the poor. Its importance is underlined by the motto "Pray and Work" (*ora et labora*). Labor meant first of all daily service work for the monastery, such as gardening, working in monastic workshops, and copying books. Burdensome work in field was performed by the monks, unless the labor was exceptionally burdensome; then it was not the monks' task. The Benedictines were expected to entertain guests in whom they were meeting Christ.

## Early History

Benedict of Nursia did not intend to establish the "Benedictine order." His Rule was written only for the abbeys that he established successively at Subiaco, Monte Cassino, and Terracino.

On the destruction of Monte Cassino by the Lombards (c. 577), the monks probably moved to the Lateran abbey, Rome, where they met the future pope Gregory I (590–604), who, in the second book of his *Dialogues*, popularized the person of Benedict. The first information about abiding by the Rule comes from the seventh century from the territory of modern France and England.

Saint Columban's (d. 615) activity led to the renewal of monasticism on the Continent. In the newly founded monasteries (e.g., Luxeuil), the more rigorous so-called Rule of Columban was in use. Soon, in unclear circumstances, it was supplemented by other rules, better adapted to realities of communal life, among them more and more often the Rule of St. Benedict. This observance is referred to as "mixed rule" (*regula mixta*), or, in plural, "mixed rules" (*regulae mixtae*), thus the name of the period when they were applied (seventh to eighth century).

It is certain that from the 620s the Rule of St. Benedict was, alongside the Rule of Columban, a part of the mixed rule. This observance is attested, among others, in the abbeys of Solignac (632), Rebais (635), Nivelles (640), and St. Wandrille (649). The increasing role of the Rule of St. Benedict is confirmed by transfer of Benedict's relics to an abbey in Fleury in 663. In 660 the Rule of St. Benedict was known in the south of France.

An important role in shaping the Benedictine monasticism was played by the tradition of "learned" and ascetic monasticism of Lérins and by the so-called "basilica monasticism" connected with monasteries established as basilicas founded at graves of martyrs (e.g., St. Martin in Tours, St. Hilary of Poitiers, and St. Denis in Paris) that were performing important liturgical, pilgrimage, and cemetery functions and in which prevalence of priests among monks was typical.

In England the Rule of St. Benedict was applied by the adherents to the Roman liturgy (Wilfrid and Benedict Biscop). It gained a broader following after the Synod of Whitby (664), often in a common observance with Irish rules, which were well adapted to local monastic traditions. The Rule of St. Benedict was transferred from England to the Germanic countries by monk-missionaries, such as Willibrord and Boniface/Winfrid. Boniface introduced it in the abbey of Fulda, established in 744.

From the Germanic countries the Benedictine Rule was transferred by missionaries to Slavonic lands, where it encountered the expansion of Eastern Orthodox monasticism led by Constantine/Cyril (d. 869) and Methodius (d. 885), the two brothers sent as missionaries from Constantinople to what is now Moravia and Pannonia. They adopted Slavonic into the liturgy that was accepted in abbeys on the areas populated by southern Slavs (Bulgarians and Macedonians in Dalmatia and Croatia). In central Europe the Latin liturgy gained the upper hand. In the 11th century there was a Benedictine abbey using the Slavic liturgy in Bohemia (Sázava). In the second half of the 14th century, Benedictines adhering to the Slavic liturgy from Dalmatia appeared first in Bohemia and then in Poland. However, their abbeys declined in the 15th century. Eastern Orthodox monasticism was strong in Hungary.

With the restoration of the Monte Cassino abbey by Petronax in 717, the Rule of St. Benedict returned to Italy, backed by popes. Its final triumph came by the 11th century. In Italy Eastern Orthodox monasticism survived for a long time. The "mixed rule" dominated on the Iberian Peninsula until the 11th century.

*Carolingian Age (Eighth/Ninth to Tenth Century)*
The growing popularity of the Rule of St. Benedict caused the Carolingians, beginning with Pepin the Short (747–768), to uphold it as a standard of monastic life (e.g., the "Germanic" Synod of 742/43). Imposing a single rule (Benedictine) and uniform habits (Synod of Aachen in 802) for all monks suited the centralizing policy of Charlemagne (768–814). He encouraged the development of abbeys, recruiting them for state service as so-called royal abbeys. Abbeys were, among others, to operate schools accessible also to laymen (813).

At the synods of Aachen in 816, 817, and 818/19, his successor, Louis the Pious (814–843), together with Benedict of Aniane (c. 750–821), the reformer of the abbeys of Aquitaine, brought about the separation of monks and canons. All monks were to abide by the Rule of St. Benedict and to follow the customs codified by Benedict of Aniane. Performing the liturgy and separating monks from the outside world were emphasized. In practice many monasteries were still following the "mixed rule."

Thereafter, the downfall of central authority, civil wars, and foreign invasions led to the destruction of numerous abbeys, and

**Monastery of St. Scholastica, Subiaco, Italy, 11th to 17th century.**
**Photo courtesy of the Editor**

the crisis of monastic observance was aggravated by interference of secular authorities in the life of abbeys. They were considered the private possession of a founder and his heirs (a so-called private monastery, or *Eigenkloster*). Institutions harmful to monastic life became common, such as "lay abbots" and advocates (*advocatio*) who, originally having been appointed to protect monasteries, eventually took control of them.

### Reforms of the Early Middle Ages (10th to 11th Century)

Benedictine monasticism retained its vitality, and by the early tenth century its revival began, aided by bishops and nobles interested in the restoration of proper monastic observance. The reformers wanted (1) to introduce strict Benedictine observance conforming to the tradition of Benedict of Aniane, (2) to liberate abbeys from secular influence (through free election of abbots), and (3) to ensure their economic improvement (through restitution of real estate).

The reform movement engulfed Burgundy, where the abbey at Cluny was founded in 910; central France (region of Orleans, Fleury, and St. Denis in Paris); and Lorraine (abbeys in Brogne, Gorze, and Ghent). Reforms were begun in Lorraine by Gerard of Brogne (d. 959) and advanced by Richard of St. Vanne (d. 1049) and by Poppo of Stavelot-Malmédy (d. 1048). They influenced the renewal of monasticism in the Ottonian Empire, where local centers of the reform were in the abbeys of St. Emmeram at Regensburg and in Niederalteich, Lorsch, Corvey, Fulda, and Einsiedeln.

The renewal of monastic life in Burgundy, France, Italy, and Spain was due largely to the Cluniacs. Their model of organization and monastic customaries influenced Wilhelm of Dijon (d. 1031), who carried out the reform of the abbeys of St. Bénigne, Dijon, Fruttuaria, and Fécamp, among others. Fruttuaria originated the reform connected with abbeys in Siegburg (1070) and St. Blasien. Very successful (more than 100 abbeys and influence in Bohemia and Poland) was the reform initiated in the abbey of Hirsau, whose abbot William (d. 1091) maintained ties with Cluny. In the tenth century Dunstan, Ethelwold, and Oswald of York implemented the reform of English monasticism, drawing on the experience of abbeys in Fleury and Ghent. The *Regularis Concordia*, adopted at the Synod of Winchester (after 970), introduced a uniform system according to Benedictine principles. Its characteristic traits were cathedral abbeys and priories. In the 11th century this task was carried through by Lanfranc and Anselm.

Growing piety as well as the social and economic transformation of the 11th to 12th century inspired some opposition to the Benedictine tradition of Aniane stock. This led to a search for alternative ways of monastic life based on the principle of return to sources (the Gospel, the Acts, and the original interpretation of the Rule of St. Benedict). Based on the Benedictine monasticism, new hermit orders came into being. They accepted the Benedictine Rule as their constitution, interpreting it through different customs and monastic statutes. Apart from the Camaldolese (1012), Vallombrosans (1039), Carthusians (1084), and Fontevraud (1100/01), among these new orders were the Order of Grandmont, founded by St. Stephen of Muret (1074), and the Wilhelmitenorden, founded by William of Vorcelli (d. 1142). Of great importance was the emergence of the new order of Cistercians (1098).

### High Middle Ages (13th to 14th Century)

The development of cities and associated growth of new orders (e.g., Dominicans and Franciscans) made the older monasticism, including the Benedictine, recede into the background. There were few new Benedictine abbeys, and the number of monks did not grow. The dearth of new foundations and of large land grants caused economic problems by the end of the 12th century, but these were soon overcome. The 13th century was a period of prosperity and influence for the Benedictines. Fresh ideas, mainly Franciscan, provided a new impulse for interpretation of the Benedictine Rule. On its base new congregations were founded in Italy: the Sylvestrines, founded by St. Sylvester Gozzolini (d. 1267); the Celestine Order, founded by Peter of Morrone, later Pope Celestine V (d. 1296); and the Olivetans, founded by Bernard Tolomei of Siena (d. 1348).

Natural disasters, epidemic diseases, wars (especially the Hundred Years' War between England and France), growing fiscal burdens of contributions required by the state and the Vatican, the Great Western Schism (1378–1417), and the dissemination of the institution of commendatory abbots were the principal causes of the crisis of monasticism in Western Europe in the 14th and in the first half of the 15th century. It was connected with the general crisis of Western European civilization. Only in central and northern Europe, which were less directly engulfed in this crisis, did Benedictine abbeys continue to prosper.

### Congregations of the Late Middle Ages (14th/15th to 15th/16th Century)

Already in the 13th century, the popes, from the time of Innocent III (1198–1216), attempted to impose on the Benedictines a centralized organization modeled on the Cistercian use of regular provincial chapters. Centralization was intended to ensure better protection against outside involvement and to create mechanisms of internal control of abbeys. These attempts were resisted by the abbeys, which were accustomed to independence. As a result neither prescriptions issued by the Fourth Lateran Council (1215), nor the statutes of Pope Gregory IX (1227–1241), nor the bull *Summi Magistri dignatio* (the so-called *benedictina*) of Pope Benedict XII (1334–1342) succeeded. Among other things the latter introduced 36 Benedictine provinces, triennial chapters, and visitators.

Only a grassroots movement of renewal changed the situation in the late 14th and early 15th centuries. New reformer congregations were established that were to play an important role in the Order's renewal. The most important was the reform of St. Giustina abbey at Padua, conducted in 1409 by Ludovico Barbo (d. 1443). The St. Giustina (De Unitate) congregation in Padua, established in 1419, was later called the Cassinese Congregation, following accession of Monte Cassino abbey in 1505.

It was a centralized organization, with abbots elected for a limited number of years, and its example influenced later congregations. Those shaped on its pattern included the Spanish Congregation of Valladolid (1489), which in the 16th century was extending to Mexico and Peru as well; the German Congregation of Bursfeld (1446); and the Hungarian Congregation of Pannonhalma (1514). The local reform center in Bavaria was the abbey of Kastl (1381), itself reformed under the influence of Prague. Almost at the same time, reform of Subiaco abbey influenced the reform of Benedictine abbeys in Poland, and Melk abbey (1418) became the reform center for Austria and southern Germany. In Germany an important role was played by the chapter of abbots of the province of Munich and Bamberg as well as by Abbot John Rode (d. 1439) and by Nicholas of Cusa, who served as papal legate from 1450 to 1451.

## From the Reformation to the Secularization (16th to 18th/19th Century)

The Reformation inflicted serious damage on many Benedictine abbeys and suppressed them in the countries where it triumphed (Scandinavia, England, and Scotland).

The Counter-Reformation and the Council of Trent (1545–1563) brought a recovery. The decree of the Council of Trent on religious orders (1563) prescribed the formation of Benedictine congregations that would soon come to the foreground. Congregations were established in Portugal (Lusitanian in 1566, modeled on the Valladolid Congregation, and the Congregation at Brazil in 1582), the Netherlands (the Exempt in 1569 and the Congregation of the Presentation in 1628), Switzerland (1602), Austria (the restored Congregation of Melk in 1617–1625), France and Germany (English Congregation in 1619), Bohemia (17th century), and Poland (1709). No congregation encompassing the whole of Germany was formed, but congregations active in Germany (e.g., Swabian Congregation in 1603, Congregation of Strasbourg in 1624, Bavarian Congregation in 1684, and Congregation of Augsburg 1685), together with independent abbeys, constituted a union centered around the Benedictine University of Salzburg (1617–1810). In France, apart from a few ephemeral congregations (Exempt in 1580, Congregations of Brittany in 1604–1628, St.-Denis in 1607–1633, and Allobroges in 1621, united with the Cassinese Congregation in 1674), an important role was played by the congregations noted for their scholarly interests: Saint Vanne (1604, modeled on the Cassinese Congregation) became itself a model for Maurists (1621), who contributed as well to improving monastic observance.

The Enlightenment, rationalism, and absolute monarchies of the 18th century proved inimical to monastic life. They eventually brought about widespread suppression of abbeys. In France the first dissolution took place in 1766, and during the period of the French Revolution all abbeys were suppressed. Benedictine abbeys were subject to suppression in the southern Netherlands (1796); Switzerland (1796); western regions of Germany (1802); Italy (1810); Baden, Bavaria, Württemberg, and Prussia (1803–1807); Silesia (1810); the Russian-occupied kingdom of Poland (1819–1864); Portugal (1834); and Spain (1835). Emperor Joseph II (1780–1790), in implementing the policy of so-called Josephinism, suppressed about 20 Benedictine abbeys in Austria, Bohemia, Hungary, and Galicia (i.e., southern Poland).

## Renewal (19th to 20th Century)

Already in 1802 the Benedictines restored suppressed abbeys in Hungary and formed a congregation headed by Pannonhalma, active in education. English monks who fled to England before the French Revolution founded abbeys at Ampleforth (1802) and Downside (1814). In 1830 King Ludwig I (1825–1848) of Bavaria restored an abbey at Metten. This gave rise to other abbeys that in 1858 revived the Bavarian Congregation. They were busy in running high schools. In 1833 Prosper Guéranger (1805–1875) founded an abbey at Solesmes that became a liturgical and contemplative center where renewal of Gregorian chant took place. In 1847 this abbey headed the Congregatio Gallica. Jean-Baptiste Muard (1809–1854) founded La Pierre-qui-Vire abbey (1850) with Trappist observance. This important center of preaching and missions was later absorbed by the Congregation of Subiaco, established in 1872. This congregation was formed as a result of reforms of Pier Casareto (1810–1878), who in 1843 introduced strict Benedictine observance in monasteries of the Cassinese Congregation, which had been restored after the Napoleonic period. He transformed Subiaco (1850) into a reform center.

In 1863 Maurus Wolter (1825–1890) and Placidus Wolter (1828–1908) established an abbey at Beuron, Baden-Württemberg, that gave rise to the Beuronese Congregation (1868), modeled on that of Solesmes and preeminent in the liturgical movement. In 1884 a Beuronese monk, Andreas Amrhein, established the missionary Congregation of St. Ottilien.

Restored abbeys in Spain belonged to Congregations of Subiaco or Solesmes. Abbeys in Belgium belonged to Congregations of Solesmes and Beuron. Of great importance was the founding of an abbey at Maredsous (1872) by monks of Beuron. In 1920 four abbeys split from the Beuronese Congregation to constitute the Belgian Congregation, now called the Annunciation Congregation. It unites abbeys in many countries of America, Asia, Africa, and Europe, including in Poland. In 1899 abbeys of Austria formed two congregations that in 1930 united into the Congregation of Immaculate Conception. In 1945 the Congregation of St. Adalbert was constituted in Bohemia, to which during the Communist era abbeys in other countries belonged.

In 1846 a monk of Metten, Boniface Wimmer (1809–1887), founded St. Vincent abbey (Latrobe, Pennsylvania), which gave birth to the American Cassinese Congregation, modeled on the Bavarian one. Swiss monks of Einsiedeln and Engelberg founded abbeys at St. Meinhard, Pennsylvania (1854), and Conception (1873), creating the Swiss American Congregation. Both are major centers of preaching and education. In 1827 Brazilian abbeys, once a part of the Portuguese Congregation, formed the Brazilian Congregation, which, having been abolished in 1855, was later restored by monks of Beuron. There are two congregations of Armenian Benedictines as well.

In 1893, on the initiative of Pope Leo XIII (1878–1903), the Benedictine Confederation headed by abbot primate was created. Its seat has been at the St. Anselmo College in Rome.

Now, at the end of the difficult period of Fascist and Communist dictatorships, a noticeable development of the Benedictine Order has been taking place. Since the liturgy was simplified by the Second Vatican Council (1962–1965), the Benedictines could be more involved in social activity. Now 21 congregations and 9,000 monks belong to the Benedictine Confederation; in addition, there are also the Olivetans, the Camaldolese, and the Vallombrosan Order, all associated with the Benedictines.

*Activity*

The Rule has permitted Benedictines to perform various duties, depending on the needs of the monastery. This has allowed abbeys to accommodate to the needs of the day as well as to local demands and customs.

An especially important role was played by the Benedictines during the early Middle Ages. After the 12th century their role declined. Nevertheless thousands of abbeys distributed over all Catholic Europe were deeply rooted in local communities and performed various functions. Their strength lay in comprehensive and complex ties with local communities. The real estate of Benedictine abbeys was usually scattered across a wide territory and intertwined with estates of local nobility. Local character and strong economic base were typical of Benedictine abbeys. For local communities they played the role of religious, cultural, and economic centers. Their contribution was important in economics, land use, food production, and the development of gardens and technology as well as in respect to timekeeping, gesture, and hygiene.

The Benedictines' contribution to culture and science was very significant. Thanks to their manuscript production, libraries, and schools, the heritage of antiquity could be preserved and cultivated. This contributed to the Carolingian Renaissance and to the blooming of European culture from the 11th century. In every century the Benedictines have produced scores of scholars. In the early Middle Ages they were creating European scholarship (Bede, Alcuin, Rabanus Maurus, Walafrid Strabo, Anselm, Suger, Abelard, Rupert of Deutz, Ordericus Vitalis, and William of St. Thierry). The Benedictines participated in every major turning point in European history (scholasticism, humanism). The Benedictine scholarly movement of the 17th and 18th centuries promoted Bible interpretation, theology, patristics, liturgics, lexicography, hagiography, and ancillary disciplines of history (paleography and diplomatics). In this respect, especially significant was the contribution of the Maurists and of the Benedictine University of Salzburg. This tradition has been revived during the Benedictine renewal of the 19th and 20th centuries by monks of Beuron, Collegeville, Maredsous, Ligugé, Maria Laach, St. Ottilien, and St. Anselm in Rome as well as by, for example, Prosper Guéranger, Ursmar Berlière, David Knowles, Thomas Merton, Jacques Dubois, Jean Leclercq, and Bernard Hume.

Always, but especially in the 9th to 12th century, many Church officials were Benedictines. In the period of their greatest blooming in the 10th to 12th century, the Benedictines aided secular clergy and played an important role in developing new forms of monasticism. Reformers of the early Middle Ages and new religious orders received Benedictine assistance and protection.

Abbeys were focal points for fraternities of laypeople, founders, and benefactors who wanted to earn salvation through participation in prayer and good deeds. The extent of this phenomenon is illustrated by thousands of names entered into *Libri fraternitatis* and the books of the dead (obituaries) at Benedictine abbeys during the 9th to 12th century. Its significance extended beyond the development of monasticism and evangelization into shaping of the medieval society.

The role of Benedictines in the Christianization and evangelization of Europe was critical. They provided the first missionaries in most newly converted countries. Benedictine missionaries, such as Willibrord, Boniface/Winfrid, Ansgar (apostle of Scandinavia, d. 865), Wojciech/Adalbert (apostle of the Prussians, d. 997), and Bruno of Querfurt (apostle of the peoples of the East, d. 1009), hold a secure place in history of Europe. Following this tradition Benedictines participated in the Christianization of Lithuania (14th and 15th centuries) and, from the 16th century, of the New World, including the territory that was to become the United States.

In the second half of 11th and in the 12th century, in the aftermath of the Gregorian reform, Benedictine abbeys received thousands of parish churches and chapels. At some of these abbeys, priories (to the east of the Rhine known as *praepositurae*) were created, consisting of a few monks dependent on the mother abbey. They performed economic functions and administered parishes, blending easily into local communities as priories most often occupied small buildings adjacent to the church. The influence of Benedictine abbeys on spirituality of local communities was profound and durable, as manifested in local prayers added to the *opus Dei*, in the influence of abbeys on the development of church songs, and in memoirs and stories related by people who lived near abbeys.

Benedictine abbeys have always been important centers of liturgical life, church singing, and music. Benedictine abbeys remain the leading centers of studies concerned with these issues.

Benedictines were instrumental in the development of the cult of relics and of pilgrimages. Numerous abbeys became important centers of pilgrimage-related cults. Some were established at the most important pilgrimage routes, catering to pilgrims and travelers, thus implementing the principle of hospitality. Many Benedictine monks were proclaimed saints.

Benedictine abbeys have been very active in caring for the poor, the old, and the sick; they furthered the development of hygiene and pharmacology.

A dense network of abbeys facilitated circulation of information. Despite the obligation to maintain stability of place, Benedictines have been known for their mobility, sometimes even for transgressing the norms of law.

In the modern world an important activity of a Benedictine monk remains, as it has been throughout the entire history of the

Benedictines, working in the monastic household, workshops, and garden. Much time is spent on ministry and teaching.

Abbeys operate guest houses, where they organize days of retreat for individual persons and groups. Many abbeys today have groups of oblates, that is, lay Christians practicing Benedictine spirituality.

MAREK DERWICH

*See also* Abbot: Christian: Abbot Primate, Benedictine; Christian; Benedict of Aniane, St.; Benedict of Nursia, St.; Beuron, Germany; Christianity: Overview; Claustration (Cloister), Rules of; Clothing: Christian Perspectives; Cluniacs; Columban, St.; Congregations, Benedictine; France: History; Fulda, Germany; German Benedictine Reform, Medieval; Guéranger, Prosper; Lectio Divina; Lérins, France; Liturgy: Western Christian; Maurists; Monasticism, Definitions of: Christian Perspectives; Monte Cassino, Italy; Oblates; Office, Daily: Western Christian; Orders (Religious), Origin of; Reform, Tenth-Century Anglo-Saxon Monastic; Reformation; Scholars, Benedictine; Schools and Universities, Benedictine; Solesmes, France; William of Hirsau

## Further Reading

*The American Benedictine Review* (semi-annual journal), 1950–

Batselier, Pieter, editor, *Saint Benedict, Father of Western Civilization*, New York: Alpine Fine Arts Collection, 1981

Benedict, Saint, Abbot of Monte Cassino, *La Règle de Saint Benoît*, edited by Adalbert de Vogüé and Jean Neufville (Sources Chrétiennes, 181–186), Paris: Éditions du Cerf, 1971–1977; volume 1: *Introduction*, translation and notes by de Vogüé, text established and presented (Prologue–ch. 7) by Neufville, 1972; volume 2 (ch. 8–73): translation and notes by de Vogüé, text and concordances by Neufville, 1972; volume 3: Neufville, *Instruments pour l'étude de la tradition manuscrite*, 1972; volumes 4–6: de Vogüé, *Commentaire historique et critique*, 1971; volume 7: de Vogüé, *Commentaire doctrinale et spirituel*, 1977; as *The Rule of Saint Benedict: A Doctrinal and Spiritual Commentary*, Kalamazoo, Michigan: Cistercian Publications, 1983

*Bulletin d'Histoire Bénédictine*, volume 1 (1907–1912) by Ursmar Berlière; volume 2 (1913–1922) by Berlière; volume 3 (1923–1932) by Philibert Schmitz; volume 4 (1932–1941) by Schmitz; volume 5 (1942–1956) by Schmitz; volume 6 (1957–1963) by Schmitz; volume 7 (1964–1969) by Daniel Misonne, Emmanuel Latteur, and Henri Ledoyen; volume 8 (1970–1974) by Misonne, Latteur, and Ledoyen; volume 9 (1975–1978) by Ledoyen; volume 10 (1979–1984) by Ledoyen; volume 11 (1985–1990), Maredsous, by Henri Ledoyen and Élisabeth Aymes; volume 12 (1991–1996), numbers 1–7 by Ledoyen and Aymes, numbers 8–12 by Aymes; volume 13 (1996– ), Maredsous, by Aymes (Appendix to *Revue Bénédictine*)

Butler, Cuthbert, *Benedictine Monachism: Studies in Benedictine Life and Rule*, London and New York: Longmans, Green, 1919; 2nd edition, 1924

de Vogüé, Adalbert, *La Communauté et l'Abbé dans la Règle de Saint Benoît*, Paris: Desclee, De Brouwer, 1961; as *Community and Abbot in the Rule of St. Benedict*, translated by Charles Philippi and Ethel Rae Perkins, Kalamazoo, Michigan: Cistercian Publications, 1979

de Vogüé, Adalbert, *Ce que dit Saint Benoît: une lecture de la Règle*, Maine-&-Loire: Abbaye de Bellafontaine, 1991; as *Reading Saint Benedict: Reflections on the Rule*, Kalamazoo, Michigan: Cistercian Publications, 1994

Derwich, Marek, *Monastycyzm benedyktynski w sredniowiecznej Europie i Polsce: Wybrane problemy* (Benedictine Monasticism in Medieval Europe and Poland), Wroclaw: Wydawn. Uniwersytetu Wroclawskiego, 1998

*I Fiori e' Frutti santi. S. Benedetto, la Regola, la santità nelle testimonianze dei manoscritti cassinesi*, Milan: Ministero per i beni culturali e ambientali, 1998

Kapsner, Oliver L., *A Benedictine Bibliography: An Author-Subject Union List, Compiled for the Library Science Section of the American Benedictine Academy*, volume 1: *Author Part*, volume 2: *Subject Part*; Kapsner, *A Benedictine Bibliography: An Author-Subject List: First Supplement: Author and Subject Part*, Collegeville, Minnesota: St. John's Abbey Press, 1949–1950; 2nd edition, 1962

Kardong, Terrence, *The Benedictines*, Wilmington, Delaware: Glazier, 1988

Linage Conde, Antonio, *San Benito y los benedictinos*, volumes 1–7, Braga: Irmandade de S. Bento da Porta Aberta, 1991–1993; volumes 1–2: *La Edad Media*, 1991–1992; volumes 3–4: *La Edad Moderna*, 1993; volumes 5–6: *La Edad Contemporánea*, 1993; volume 7: *Indices, Cartografia*, 1993

Schmitz, Philibert, *Histoire de l'Ordre saint-Benoît*, Paris: Maredsous, 1941–1956; volume 1: *Origines, diffusion et constitution jusqu'au XIIe siècle*, 1941; 2nd edition, 1948; volume 2: *Œuvre civilisatrice jusqu'au XIIe siècle*, 1941; 2nd edition 1949; volume 3: *Histoire externe: I. Du concordat de Worms au Concile de Trente*, 1948; volume 4: *Histoire externe: II. Du Concile de Trente au XXe siècle: Histoire constitutionelle*, 1948; volumes 5–6: *Œuvre civilisatrice du XIIe au XXe siècle*, 1949; volume 7: *Les moniales: Tables générales*, 1956; as *Geschichte des Benediktinerordens*, Ins Deutsche übertragen und hrsg. v. Ludwig Räber u. Raymond Tschudy Bd. 1–4, Einsiedeln, Zürich: Verlagsanstalt Benziger and CO, AG, 1947–1960

# Bernard of Clairvaux, St. 1090–1153

French Cistercian reformer and theologian

## Life

The life of Bernard of Clairvaux is known to us from various hagiographical accounts, beginning with the *Vita Prima* ("First Life"), begun during his lifetime by his friend William of St.-Thierry (1075/80–1148). In addition to these sometimes-exaggerated narratives, information can be gleaned from occasional references in civil and ecclesiastical records, especially those generated within the Cistercian order and from Bernard's own voluminous writings, especially the 547 extant letters of his epistolary corpus.

A critical biography is yet to appear. Late 20th-century studies of Bernard's life are marked by a methodological reserve, perhaps reacting against the exuberance of earlier claims of the saint's historical importance. Different models of sanctity have often influenced the presentation of the events of Bernard's life with the result that the complexity of his character and actions is commonly underestimated. A conviction is growing that Bernard needs to be viewed within the context of the intellectual and cultural ferment that marked 12th-century Christianity in the various regions of Europe. A widely accepted proposition is that it is imperative to understand the first half of the 12th century in its own right without viewing it merely as an expression of generic medievalism. This means paying attention to earlier and less known stages in the development of such realities as the Crusades, the Inquisition, the dualist heresy (later named Catharism), architecture, ecclesiastical centrism, universities, and scholasticism.

The usually accepted details of Bernard's life are quickly told. Bernard was the third son of the knight Tescelin, born at Fontaine-lès-Dijon, less than four miles from the ducal capital of Burgundy. After the death of his mother, Aleth of the powerful Montbard family, Bernard's education was entrusted to the canons of St. Vorles at Châtillon-sur-Seine. In 1113, at the age of 23, he and some 30 companions, many of them family, together entered the New Monastery (Cîteaux), at that time already beginning its expansion with the foundation of La Ferté.

In 1115 Bernard became abbot of Cîteaux's fourth foundation, Clairvaux, located in a narrow valley about 75 miles north of Cîteaux in Champagne. The first years of Bernard's abbacy were marked by the hardship typical of new foundations, by disabling health problems, and by rapid growth. However, within a decade Clairvaux itself had made three foundations, the total number in its line of filiation in Bernard's lifetime being 169.

Granted the uncertainties of dating, likely more than 50 letters exist from Bernard's first ten years as abbot of Clairvaux. From these it is clear that he was already beginning to have an impact outside his own monastery. He had begun networking, becoming involved in the business of the fledgling Cistercian order and in ecclesiastical affairs. At this time he also wrote his first treatises, *In Praise of the Virgin Mother*, *On the Steps of Humility and Pride*, and the *Apologia*, the latter being his major contribution to the Cistercian-Cluniac controversy. By the end of the 1120s, he had written a rule of life for the Knights Templars, finalized his treatise *On the Necessity of Loving God*, and composed a substantial theological work, *On Grace and Free Will*. A long letter to Archbishop Henry of Sens later circulated under the title *The Manner of Life and Duties of Bishops*.

In the small world of reformed monasticism in France, Bernard was becoming well known by 1130. In that year, following a double papal election, he became embroiled in the resulting schism on the winning side of Innocent II (1130–1143). During the eight years until the situation was resolved, Bernard was much involved in advocacy of Innocent's cause: moving around, attending councils, speaking to clergy and influential people, and writing letters. His high profile at this time led to his aid being sought in many unrelated situations concerning the reform of the Church and of religious communities. In addition, after the 1134 death of Stephen (Harding) of Cîteaux, the order's cofounder, and the subsequent confusion caused by the failure of his successor, Bernard's informal leadership within the rapidly expanding Cistercian order increased. In 1134 he was commissioned by the general chapter to head a team charged with the reform of the books of liturgical chant adopted under Stephen. Aware of the incongruity of his busy life, Bernard wrote about this time to Guigo the Carthusian (1083–1136): "I am like a little bird that has not yet grown feathers, nearly all the time outside its dear nest, at the mercy of wind and storm" (Ep. 12).

During the 1130s, despite many absences and the foundation or affiliation of 22 new daughter houses, Bernard continued to preach and write. The rudimentary versions of his sermons for the liturgical cycle came into being at this time, and the first 24 *Sermons on the Song of Songs* were redacted between Advent 1135 and 1138. In response to questions submitted by Hugh of St.-Victor (d. 1142), Bernard wrote a long letter (Ep. 77) that was later regarded as a theological tractate and christened *On Baptism*.

In 1140 Bernard was elected archbishop of Rheims but declined the office. Invited to preach to the schoolmen of Paris, he delivered a message that was later redacted under the title *On Conversion* and attracted many recruits to Clairvaux. In doing battle for the minds and hearts of the young, he was drawn into theological controversy with Peter Abelard (1079–1142/43), stage-managing the ecclesiastical trial at Sens (25 May 1141) and engineering the papal condemnation of the older man (16 July). The whole affair did little credit to those involved, although Peter the Venerable (1092/94–1156), the abbot of Cluny, later in the year mediated a reconciliation between the two principal adversaries. Bernard would continue to campaign against those perceived as heretics: Arnold of Brescia, Gilbert de la Porrée, and the dualists of Languedoc.

During the 1140s Bernard's activities were many and varied: intervening (not always appropriately) in ecclesiastical elections to ensure that offices were held by reform-minded candidates; arbitrating disputes; giving his support to bright young men such as Peter Lombard (c. 1100–1160), Robert Pullen (associated with the beginnings of Oxford University), and John of Salisbury (1115–1180); and responding to the appeals of many (including Hildegarde of Bingen) who sought his aid. Bernard admitted that he had overreached himself: "I know very well that I have presumed more than I should have done without paying sufficient heed to myself" (Ep. 218.3). His work with the group responsible for the reform of the Cistercian liturgical books was completed in 1147, the same year that the congregations of Obazine and Savigny were aggregated into the Cistercian order, the 27 monasteries of the latter group being attached to the filiation of Clairvaux. During this decade 32 foundations were made from Clairvaux. At this time also his new secretary, Geoffrey of Auxerre, began the redaction of his epistolary corpus and the collection of anecdotal material with a view to an eventual vita. Work on the *Sermons on the Song of Songs* and other sermons

Jean Fouquet (c. 1420–1481), *St. Bernard, Abbot of Clairvaux*. Musée Condé, Chantilly, France.
Photo courtesy of Giraudon/Art Resource, New York

continued, and between 1141 and 1144 he wrote the treatise *On Precept and Dispensation*.

In 1145 a former monk of Clairvaux became Pope Eugene III (1145–1153); Bernard's influence with the papal court increased considerably: "they are saying that it is not you but I who am pope, and from all sides they flock to me with their cases" (Ep. 239). Despite Bernard's request to be spared further involvement (Ep. 245; see Ep. 228), Eugene launched him against the dualist heretics, and then, following the call to arms in defense of the Holy Places, Bernard was recruited to preach what came to be called the Second Crusade. Beginning at Vézelay and crisscrossing Europe, Bernard called on able-bodied Christians to be signed with the cross. He thought of the crusade as a moral enterprise, a means of purging the Church of its accumulated corruption; he demanded unrealistic levels of conduct from the soldiers, reminding them of the holiness of their mission. He condemned unequivocally any persecution of Jews, such as had occurred in the Rhineland (Ep. 365). Despite Bernard's eloquence and the loftiness of the proposed ideals, the venture failed both militarily and morally. Bernard was left to bear the brunt of blame.

Bernard was now an old man: "I am weary and fainthearted . . . no better than an ant harnessed to a cart" (Ep. 280). Burdened by ill health, he allowed his sphere of activity to contract sharply. He authored a hagiographical life of his friend Malachy, archbishop of Armagh, and then composed for Pope Eugene a mature spiritual treatise about Church governance titled *On Consideration*. It was at this time also that the luminous last sermons on *The Song of Songs* (SC 80–86) were written. Bernard died on 20 August 1153.

*Writings*
Whatever prominence Bernard achieved was due to the quality of his mind and the warmth of his personality. Both features are evident in his writings, as they must have been in his eloquent discourse. Jean Leclercq estimates that of the nearly 1,500 surviving manuscripts of his work, about half are contemporaneous. The critical edition was published between 1957 and 1977 in nine quarto volumes comprising 3,693 pages. For most of Bernard's writings, modern translations of varying quality are available in many languages. A complete verbal concordance was published by CETEDOC in 1987, and a comprehensive index of scriptural citations exists.

Bernard wrote beautiful Latin. He had the knack of conjuring up reminiscences of traditional authors (especially the Vulgate Bible and the texts used in the liturgy) in a way that seemed fresh and original. This was probably because the sound and syntax of his writing was invigorated by assimilation to the vernacular. In some of his more homely works, such as the sermons *De diversis* and the *Sentences*, we find many colorful and humorous expressions and a wide variety of illustrative images drawn from both everyday life and literary sources.

Bernard's most common literary genres were epistle, treatise, and sermon. However, it was through the medium of the sermon that he demonstrated his literary brilliance. Rarely did Bernard proceed along anticipated lines in commenting on a text or teaching about a particular festival. He took for granted that readers had negotiated such trajectories for themselves, offering a counterpoint and usually going off in an unexpected direction in what seems like a stream of consciousness. However, closer analysis of the sermons reveals a high degree of coherence in his arguments, just as examination of the manuscripts shows how carefully he reworked his texts to ensure the effect he wanted.

Bernard was a right-brain theologian whose theological content and style belonged more with the patristic period than with the Aristotelians of the 13th century. His primary purpose in preaching and writing was practical: he had the intention of building up and strengthening the lives of others. In particular he sought to bring traditional monastic wisdom to bear on the issues faced by those seeking to live an evangelical life and to make some progress toward God through contemplation.

The content of Bernard's theology was mostly traditional. His writings on Christology and Mariology are powerful because of his eloquence and imagination – they make a strong impact on the reader – but he rarely expands the speculative frontiers. His most characteristic writing is that dealing with the dynamics of the spiritual life. Here Bernard shows himself clear-minded in his sense of priorities, attentive to experience, and very skilled in drawing together widely disparate biblical themes to provide stimulation and encouragement for those in his care. At the heart of his spirituality based on profound reflection on the essential compatibility of human and divine was a theological anthropology that is grounded in human creation as seen "in the image and likeness of God" and brought to a culmination in the incarnation of the Word. His vision of the human journey to God spanned all the phases of salvation history, just as it was relived in the life of every individual. We are *formed* as the image of God, *deformed* by sin, and *reformed* by the grace of being *conformed* to Christ; we look forward to being *transformed* in glory at the end of time. His innovative doctrine of the "intermediate advent," situated in the middle time between the Incarnation and the Second Coming, testifies to his capacity for rereading present experience in the light of salvation history. His explanation of the alternation between positive and negative moments in spiritual progress demonstrates both his intuitive mastery of human psychology and his gift of reframing experience in biblical categories. In all that he wrote, his priority was spiritual and pastoral. More often than not a specific theological stance is not stated explicitly; it is to be sought below the surface of his practical recommendations.

Bernard was acutely interested in the dynamics of human behavior, but he was never a moralist, in that he did not write ethical theory. He was concerned with the subjective component underlying external actions. In a literary career of nearly 40 years, his central theme is love. Love is our way of participating in the life of God: it frees us from the tyranny of selfishness and aligns our priorities with the divine plan. Love alone is able to satisfy the capacious yearning that is at the heart of every human endeavor. Such a doctrine corresponded closely with the aspira-

Abbey Church (Cistercian), Fontenay (Côte d'Or), France, 1139–1147. The oldest extant Cistercian abbey shows the barn-like plan preferred by St. Bernard.
Photo courtesy of Mary Schaefer

tions of Bernard's contemporaries and was a key component in his spiritual leadership.

This "moral," or behavioral, aspect of his writing not only was at the service of a general amendment of life but also promoted the reform of the Church and of monasticism. Bernard was a second-generation Cistercian. The austere, focused monasticism in which he had been formed dominated his evaluation of most situations, sometimes, as in the case of his recommendations to the crusaders, to the point of unreality. He projected the microspiritual world of individual conversion and spiritual growth onto the Church as a whole as well as onto many secular institutions that, in the 12th century, complemented ecclesiastical activities within a nominal Christendom. Bernard viewed his many external missions as contributing to the reestablishment of the divine "order" in human affairs and, as such, as not foreign to his essentially monastic vocation.

*Influence*

Bernard exercised the greatest immediate influence on his contemporaries as an advocate of monastic reform. His contribution was twofold. First, by reexpressing the ideals pursued by the Cistercian founders in ways that were attractive to his contemporaries, he increased the credibility of the Cistercian enterprise and drew to it many high-quality recruits. By the end of the 12th century, more than 500 Cistercian monasteries existed throughout Europe, from Ireland to Scandinavia and Eastern Europe, some with hundreds of monks and lay brothers. The mere existence of such a density of organized and somewhat uniform monasticism was not without considerable impact on the Church at large and on other forms of religious life. Second, as can be seen in his controversy with Black Monks, Bernard was a lifelong defender of the integrity of the ideals of the Cistercian reform: poverty, austerity, simplicity, and authenticity. He insisted that these values be expressed practically in lifestyle, external relations, architecture, liturgy, chant, and manuscript illumination. He successfully marketed these renunciatory values not only by personal example and charisma but also by presenting them in a context of affective Christocentrism and mystical ardour.

Around Bernard developed a Cistercian "school" of spirituality, whose members included William of St.-Thierry, Aelred of Rievaulx, Guerric of Igny, Gilbert of Swineshead, Isaac of Stella, Amedeus of Lausanne, Baldwin and John of Forde, and, in the next century, the Flemish mystic Beatrice of Nazareth and scores of other writers. Although personal and situational differences exist among the various authors, the "unanimity" of their lifestyle, literary sources, and aspirations gave them a common vocabulary, a shared value system, and a unity of vision that is clearly discernible throughout the extensive Cistercian corpus. All lived the rule of St. Benedict; all devoted several hours daily to liturgy, work, and *lectio divina*; all were committed to giving literary expression to the life that they shared; and all did this with fervor and verve. It was through Bernard that the austere reform of Cîteaux first found its own voice.

Bernard exercised great influence on the Cistercian order through his own line of filiation, his interventions at general chapters, and a large network of friendship and patronage. His presence was so pervasive that Jean Leclercq has proposed that Bernard should be regarded as founder. In 1159 a liturgical commemoration was authorized for Clairvaux. In 1162 a request for canonization was made, and three years later his official vita was published. Bernard was canonized by Alexander III (1159–1181) in 1174 and declared a Doctor of the Church in 1830 by Pius VIII (1829–1830). More recently, Pius XII (1939–1958) wrote the encyclical *Doctor mellifluus* in his honor in 1953, and John Paul II issued *Schola caritatis* in 1990.

Bernard's works were widely read and copied during his lifetime. In 1165 the Black Monks of Anchin completed a large three-volume set comprising both Bernard's collected writings and various texts written about him. His *Sermons on the Song of Songs* were translated into French toward the end of the 12th century. Many writings and axioms, frequently of an inferior quality, were falsely attributed to him, thus increasing his fame.

John of Salisbury attested to the power of Bernard's preaching. Bernard's eloquence and literary brilliance were often acclaimed, for example, by Thomas Aquinas and by Robert of Basevorn, who used him as a model in his 1322 treatise on rhetoric *The Form of Preaching*. Dante Alighieri was another admirer.

Erroneously, praise of Bernard as a stylist led to the implication that he was merely a pious author and not a serious theologian in the scholastic mold – not one who addressed the questions that they asked or who employed the methods of dialectic to find answers. The pseudonymous works did nothing to improve his reputation. Despite having become marginal in Catholic theology, Bernard was much appreciated by Luther and, in spiritual matters, by Calvin. After the Enlightenment, Bernard's conflict with Abelard was interpreted as a typical struggle of faith against reason; as a result Bernard was demonized in many intellectual circles. Controversies with heretics made him look intolerant. Enthusiasts for Gothic architecture dismissed his attitude to art as regressive. Decontextualized quotations on political theory made him appear as a supporter of the Church's temporal power. His involvement with the Second Crusade was widely condemned as an example of bellicosity, imperialism, and racism. Even within religious circles Bernard was often viewed as an example of the old-style churchman, combining a hard-nosed and ruthless exercise of power with a sentimental and untheological piety.

A bad opinion of Bernard survives, especially among those with no direct access to his writings. However, the scholarly situation changed in the latter half of the 20th century. Bernard's claim to be numbered among reputable theologians was brilliantly advanced by Étienne Gilson's 1934 monograph *The Mystical Theology of Saint Bernard*. The various congresses held in 1953 and the prodigious work of Dom Jean Leclercq began a process of reevaluation in almost every area of Bernardine research, a field that continues to ask new questions and demand new conclusions. A bibliography of secondary literature now exceeds 3,000 items. For example, over 70 papers were read at the 25th Medieval Congress at Western Michigan University in 1990.

Bernardine influence is felt especially in Cistercian monasticism and in the area of spirituality. He is read, taught, and written about very widely, and his works continue to be appreciated for their human depth and contemplative wisdom as well as for the poetry of his profound theological vision.

Michael Casey, O.C.S.O.

*See also* Abbot: Christian; Abelard, Peter; Aelred of Rievaulx, St.; Cistercians; Cîteaux, France; Crusades; Devotions, Western Christian; France: History; Guigo I; Hagiography: Western Christian; Holy Men/Holy Women: Christian Perspectives; Humanism, Christian; Hymnographers; Leclercq, Jean; Liturgy: Western Christian; Spirituality: Western Christian; Templars; Warrior Monks: Christian

## Biography

Born into the nobility near Dijon, Bernard and his brothers entered the recently founded monastery at Cîteaux in 1112. Three years later the abbot Stephen asked Bernard to found a new Cistercian monastery in a place of Bernard's choosing. He selected Clairvaux, where he served as Abbot until his death. He supported and in turn was supported by popes Innocent II (1130–1143) and the Cistercian Eugenius III (1145–1153). He preached the Second Crusade in 1147. Bernard remains the preeminent thinker of the Cistercian tradition.

## Major Works

*Sermones super Cantica Canticorum*, as *The Song of Songs: Selections from the Sermons of St. Bernard of Clairvaux*, edited by Halcyon Backhouse, 1990
*Sermones per Annum*
*De diligendo Deo*
*De consideratione*
*The Letters of St. Bernard of Clairvaux*, translated by Bruno Scott James, 1998

## Further Reading

Note: over 200 relevant titles may be found in the "Cistercian Fathers Series" and the "Cistercian Studies Series" from Cistercian Publications, University of Western Michigan, Kalamazoo. Articles on Bernard appear regularly in the journal *Cistercian Studies Quarterly*. Much of the new work on Bernard has been done in monographs written for the various centenaries: 1953 (death), 1974 (canonization), and 1990 (birth). The following is a select list of useful titles.

*Bernard de Clairvaux: Histoire, mentalités, spiritualité: Colloque de Lyon-Cîteaux-Dijon*, Paris: Éditions du Cerf, 1992

Casey, Michael, *Athirst for God: Spiritual Desire in Bernard of Clairvaux's Sermons on the Song of Songs*, Kalamazoo, Michigan: Cistercian Publications, 1987

Casey, Michael, "Bernard of Clairvaux: Forty Years of Scholarship," in *St. Bernard of Clairvaux: The Man*, edited by John S. Martin, Melbourne: University of Melbourne, 1991

Casey, Michael, "Cistercian Spirituality," in *The New Dictionary of Catholic Spirituality*, edited by Michael Downey, Collegeville, Minnesota: Liturgical Press, 1992

Commission d'histoire de l'Ordre de Cîteaux, *Bernard de Clairvaux*, Paris: Éditions Alsatia, 1953

Gervers, Michael, editor, *The Second Crusade and the Cistercians*, New York: St. Martin's Press, 1992

Leclercq, Jean, *Recueil d'études sur S. Bernard et ses écrits*, 5 vols., Rome: Edizioni di Storia e Letteratura, 1962–1992

Leclercq, Jean, *Bernard of Clairvaux and the Cistercian Spirit*, Kalamazoo, Michigan: Cistercian Publications, 1976

Newman, Martha G., *The Boundaries of Charity: Cistercian Culture and Ecclesiastical Reform, 1098–1180*, Stanford, California: Stanford University Press, 1996

Pranger, M.B., *Bernard of Clairvaux and the Shape of Monastic Thought: Broken Dreams*, Leiden and New York: Brill, 1994

Rudolph, Conrad, *The "Things of Greater Importance": Bernard of Clairvaux's Apologia and the Medieval Attitude Toward Art*, Philadelphia: University of Pennsylvania Press, 1990

Sommerfeldt, John R., *The Spiritual Teachings of Bernard of Clairvaux: An Intellectual History of the Early Cistercian Order*, Kalamazoo, Michigan: Cistercian Publications, 1991

# Beuron, Germany

The monastery of St. Martin at Beuron was first founded as a community of Augustinian canons around the year 1077. The Augustinian monastery was suppressed in 1802 and became the property of the house of Hohenzollern-Sigmaringen. The present Benedictine monastery, which is partially situated in the buildings of the Augustinians, was founded on 24 May 1863 by the brothers Maurus (1825–1890) and Placidus (1828–1908) Wolter.

Born in Bonn, Maurus and Placidus Wolter were ordained priests for the Archdiocese of Cologne (1850 and 1851, respectively) and later entered the Benedictine monastery of St. Paul-outside-the-Walls in Rome (professed 1857 and 1856, respectively). While in Rome the Wolter brothers met the widowed Princess Catherine von Hohenzollern, who had inherited the monastery property at Beuron, and with her support refounded Beuron as a Benedictine monastery. From its very beginnings monastic life at Beuron, and especially its liturgical life, was profoundly influenced by the abbey of Solesmes in France and its founder, Dom Prosper Guéranger (1805–1875). Abbot Maurus Wolter's particular contribution to Beuronese spirituality can be found mainly in his *Praecipua Ordinis monastici Elementa* (1880; *The Principles of Monasticism*).

Beuron contributed significantly to the new springtime of Benedictine monasticism in the 19th century. The community made its first foundation in 1872 at Maredsous in Belgium, and in 1873 Pope Pius IX (1846–1878) erected the Beuronese Benedictine Congregation. When the monks were driven from Beuron into exile during the Prussian Kulturkampf (1875–1887), that became the opportunity for the founding of Erdington, England (1876; since 1922 at Weingarten, Germany), Emaus in Prague (1880), and Seckau in Austria (1883). After the return of the monks to Beuron, other foundations followed: Maria Laach (1892); Mont César (from Maredsous) and Gerleve (1899); Jerusalem (1906); Grüssau, Silesia (from Emaus, 1919); Neresheim (from Emaus, 1920); Trier (from Seckau, 1922); Neuburg (from Beuron, 1926); Tholey (from Trier, 1949); and Nütschau (from Gerleve, 1951). The Beuronese Congregation, similar to that of Solesmes, also includes monasteries of nuns: St. Gabriel, Prague (1889; since 1920 at Bertholdstein, Austria); Maredret, Belgium (1893); Eibingen (1904); Herstelle (incorporated into the Congregation 1924); Kellenried (1924); Engelthal (from Herstelle, 1962); Säben (incorporated into the Congregation 1974); Varensell (incorporated into the Congregation 1982); Fulda (incorporated into the Congregation 1982); Marienrode (from Eibingen, 1988); and Aasebakken, Denmark (incorporated into the Congregation 1988). Political consequences following the defeat of Germany in World War I resulted in the separation of the Belgian monasteries from the Congregation and the displacement of the communities founded in England and Bohemia.

Besides its foundations Beuron's contribution to the Benedictine Confederation includes its generosity in providing personnel and funds for the Pontifical Athenaeum and International College of St. Anselm in Rome (founded in 1888) and the renewal of the Brazilian Congregation at the request of the Holy See (1895). In 1884 Father Andreas Amrhein, a monk of Beuron, founded the Benedictine Society for the Foreign Missions. From the foundation of Amrhein grew the Benedictine Congregation of St. Ottilien and the Benedictine Missionary Sisters of Tutzing. Around 1870, under the inspiration of Desiderius Lenz (1832–1928), Beuron began to develop its own stylized form of religious art that shunned naturalism and found its artistic inspiration in Egyptian and classical forms. The burgeoning liturgical movement was especially well served by Beuron's successive publications of the *Schott-Messbuch* (since 1884; Schott People's Missal). Regular publications from Beuron include those from the Vetus-Latina-Institut, which researches the texts of the Old Latin Bible (since 1949), and the monastic journal *Benediktinische Monatschrift* (1919; Benedictine Monthly), since 1959 published as *Erbe und Auftrag* (Inheritance and Commission). In 1999 the community at Beuron numbered 69 monks, of whom 24 are priests.

The monastery at Beuron, situated in the picturesque Danube valley in southwestern Germany, serves pilgrims and tourists through sacramental ministry, retreats, and a guest house. It also provides a slide presentation that introduces visitors to the monastic life.

KURT BELSOLE, O.S.B.

School of Desiderius Lenz, frescoes (1900–1913) and statues of St. Benedict and St. Scholastica (restored 1959), crypt chapel (1545), Abbey of Monte Cassino, Italy.
Photo courtesy of the Editor

*See also* Augustinian Canons; Chapman, John; Congregations, Benedictine; Germany: History; Guéranger, Prosper; Liturgical Movement 1830–1980; Liturgists, German Monastic; Liturgy: Western Christian; Maria Laach, Germany; Marmion, Columba; Missionaries: Christian; Monte Cassino, Italy; Plainchant; Scholars, Benedictine; Solesmes, France; Wolter, Maurus; Wolter, Placidus

## Further Reading

Benediktinerkloster Beuron, *Beuron, 1863–1963*, Beuron: Beuroner Kunstverlag, 1963

Buschmann, Johanna, *Beuroner Mönchtum: Studien zu Spiritualität, Verfassung und Lebensformen der Beuroner Benediktinerkongregation von 1863 bis 1914* (Beiträge zur Geschichte des Alten Mönchtums und des Benediktinertums, 43), Münster, Westphalia: Aschendorff, 1994

Engelmann, Ursmar, *Beuron: Die Benediktinerabtei im Donautal* (Grosse Kunstführer, 22), Munich: Schnell and Steiner, 1957

Hilpisch, Stephanus, *Benedictinism through Changing Centuries*, translated by Leonard Doyle, Collegeville, Minnesota: St. John's Abbey Press, 1958

Mayer, Suso, *Beuroner Bibliographie: Schriftsteller und Künstler während der ersten hundert Jahre des Benediktinerklosters Beuron, 1863–1963*, Beuron: Beuroner Kunstverlag, 1963

Merkle, Coelestin, editor, *Das hundertste Jahr: Zur Hundertjahrfeier der Benediktiner in Beuron 1963*, Beuron: Beuroner Kunstverlag, 1963

Petzolt, Stephan, "Die Gründungs und Entwicklungsgeschichte der Abtei Beuron im Speigel ihrer Liturgie (1863–1908)," Ph.D. diss., Bayerische Julius-Maximilians-Universität Würzburg, Würzburg, Germany, 1990

Pfaff, Maurus, "Dom Prosper Guéranger und Maurus Wolter," in *Commentaria in S. Regulam* (Studia Anselmiana, 84), edited by Jean Gribomont, Rome: Edizioni Abbazia S. Paolo, 1982

Rees, Daniel, "The Benedictine Revival in the Nineteenth Century," in *Benedict's Disciples*, edited by David Hugh Farmer, Leominster, Hereford and Worcester: Fowler Wright Books, 1980; 2nd edition, Leominster, Hereford and Worcester, and Harrisburg, Pennsylvania: Gracewing, 1995

Schöntag, Wilfried, editor, *250 Jahre Abteikirche Beuron: Geschichte, geistliches Leben, Kunst*, Beuron: Beuroner Kunstverlag, 1988

Senger, Basilius, *Die Beuroner Benediktiner Kongregation und ihrer Klöster*, Beuron: Beuroner Kunstverlag, 1989

Wolter, Maurus, *The Principles of Monasticism* (Studies in Ascetical Theology, 1), translated, edited, and annotated by Bernard Sause, St. Louis, Missouri: Herder, 1962

# Bhikṣu/Bhikkhu. *See* Rules, Buddhist (Vinaya): Monks

# Bhikṣuṇī/Bhikkhunī. *See* Rules, Buddhist (Vinaya): Nuns

# Bible Interpretation

No clear instances of monasticism exist in the Jewish or Christian Bibles. Some practices and social structures mentioned in both Scriptures anticipate later Christian monasticism. In this article the Western monastic use of biblical themes and ideas is reviewed. Although not specifically monastic, these items were interpreted and appropriated by monastic authors and sometimes given a special monastic application.

The Bible figured prominently in the daily life of monasteries. The Benedictine Rule prescribes activities that are pervasive throughout Christian monasticism. All the Psalms are chanted each week, and ten chapters of the Rule (9–18) are spent in assigning the Psalms to various offices. The Psalms and many other parts of the Bible are memorized and thus pervade monks' thoughts and speech. Daily reading and meditation (*lectio divina*) is prescribed in the chapter on manual labor (48), indicating its role as part of the business of the monk. Although it might have included other books over the centuries, this prayerful reading was at first mainly if not entirely taken from the Bible.

The Psalms and the other parts of the Bible are read or interpreted in ways that seem strange to modern readers and scholars. Historical setting and literary context are usually ignored in favor of allegorical and personal applications. First we note that the Psalms and other Old Testament readings are understood allegorically to refer both to Christ and to New Testament ideas and practices, using a style of interpretation found in the New Testament itself. More generally many items are allegorized so that they refer to more immediate concerns than the ancient situations from which they arose.

The Song of Solomon illustrates the difference between traditional, i.e. monastic, interpretation and historical exegesis. The latter focuses on the human love expressed in the poetry, speculating that the book is a collection of wedding songs. However, much Jewish and Christian interpretation understands the book in terms of the love between God and either Israel or the Church. Mystical and monastic interpretation applies all the imagery to the psychological dynamics of an individual's relationship to a beloved God. Bernard of Clairvaux's *Sermones super Cantica*

*Canticorum* (Sermons on the Canticles) are the most famous monastic commentary in this vein. Because the songs celebrate desire, they provide a map of the soul in its quest for God, encompassing both the agony of separation and the ecstasy of intimacy.

Monks meditate on biblical texts by turning individual words over in their minds, ruminating on every phrase. Spiritual reading is sacramental, assumed to be transhistorical, creative, and capable of transforming the reader. Exegesis of this type focuses on connotation, reminiscence, and imagery. Key words and images get associated with others in a creative, imaginative way, in an older form of what today might be called "reader response criticism." For example, the theme of wandering in the life of Abraham reminds monastics that they are strangers and pilgrims in the world. The desert periods in the lives of Moses and Jesus and the Sinai experience of Israel speak about the renunciation of comfortable life to be nearer God. This reminiscence style of exegesis relies on synonyms and even similarity in the sounds of words.

In addition to special interpretations of Old Testament themes and the creative association of words, a kind of literalism animates monastic exegesis. Some passages of the Bible are taken as injunctions or recommendations that were not necessarily so intended or interpreted. Two prominent examples of such injunctions are the seven hours or offices of prayer derived from Psalm 119's use of that number in verse 164 and the midnight office from verse 62. Specific numbers and images in the Psalms can be understood as rhetorical or poetic language but were interpreted by the Benedictine Rule (chap. 16) as divine justification for the offices of the monastic day and night.

The "evangelical counsels" constitute the most controversial examples of this biblical literalism. The Synoptic Gospels (Matthew, Mark, and Luke) present many radical and comprehensive pictures of holiness or life in the kingdom of God or of heaven. The intensified Old Testament laws in the Sermon on the Mount in Matthew are so rigorous that their fulfillment requires something like monastic existence. However, they might be interpreted to apply to ordinary life situations that do not require so complete a reformation of life. In this latter spirit they were seen as ideals toward which to strive, as eschatological sayings, as principles to be observed in spirit, or as impossible demands by comparison to which all lives are recognized to be insufficient and sinful.

Three options emerge: all Christians must become monks, or all Christians must strive to live like monks and fail, or Christians divide into two levels of expectation. Ascetic, or monastic, theology has adopted the third option. It argues against the first that these high expectations cannot be commands for everyone because in that case the nonmonastic's failure to obey would be sin. Nonmonastic Christians cannot be so easily condemned. The second option applies to all Christians and has generally been adopted by Protestants, but it does not satisfy the most serious seekers after holiness or biblical guidance. The task of monasticism in light of this dilemma is to preserve the rigor of Jesus' words within a larger community of forgiveness.

Under the third option the rigorous life indicated in the Gospel sayings obeys the evangelical counsels. They are understood to constitute a program of perfection beyond the normal demands of moral theology and salvation. They provide a set of techniques for achieving and manifesting a degree of holiness that exceeds the minimum. They are not for everyone but rather only for those certain persons with appropriate situations, time, and strength.

At least in the last few centuries, the evangelical counsels are often summarized as comprising poverty, chastity, and obedience. Poverty is a good example to illustrate various options in biblical interpretation. Renunciation of personal wealth and property so as to achieve simplicity in the wherewithal of life is a basic theme in all monasticism. In Hindu and Buddhist monastic life, poverty is reinforced by begging, a practice incorporated into the mendicant orders of Christianity, especially the Franciscans. Oddly the Bible nowhere endorses mendicancy and does not clearly endorse poverty in and of itself. Paul worked to pay for his food (2 Thess. 3:7–12), offers to pay Onesimus' debts (Philem. 18–19), and commends paying taxes (Rom. 13:6–7). Nevertheless, the words of Jesus to the rich young man that he sell all and give to the poor (Matt. 19:16–30 and parallels) famously inspired Antony to relinquish his wealth and adopt the anchoritic life.

Many New Testament passages criticize and warn the rich, notably in 1 Timothy 6:9–10 about love of money and in the diatribe that begins James 5. Luke emphasizes the dignity of poverty at many points and records Jesus blessing the poor without adding Matthew's qualifier "in spirit." These words could be thought to be rhetorical exaggerations, mere exhortations to simplicity in life and charity toward the poor. However, taken to heart in detail they mandate an economic structure and policy in which at least some faithful followers of Christ will possess little or nothing.

The story of the rich young man involves discussion of exactly this problem in interpretation. Jesus declares in words that have long bewildered exegetes that "it is easier for a camel to go through the eye of a needle than it is for a rich person to enter the kingdom of God." Peter questions the feasibility of the implied life program, to which objection Jesus seems to agree by acknowledging its impossibility for humans, albeit not for God. Peter then suggests that he and the other followers have left all, which seems to make them qualified as truly nonrich. They and others who make similar renunciations are then assured that they will receive compensatory rewards eventually.

If the end of that pericope is taken to recommend extraordinary renunciation, it provides a charter for monastic economy within a larger community whose dissociation from wealth is not as clear. Monastic renunciation not only repudiates the bad but goes beyond to repudiate what is legitimate. Wealth is lawful even though it might be dangerous or compromising. Matthew, unlike the other Synoptics, moves in this direction by making the rich young man's dispossession a matter of being "perfect" (*teleios*). Mark and Luke imply that he lacks this one thing in his program of obeying the law. They force the interpretive issue by

literally demanding poverty of all, forcing the reader to adopt the first or the second option.

One more theme can illustrate the character of monastic biblical interpretation and how it differs from other types. Obedience as a monastic discipline is associated with Jesus' calling of Matthew, "Follow me" (Matt. 9:9 and parallels). Each monastic soul hears that as a summons addressed to itself and as a reason to imitate Matthew, who abandoned his job and apparently everything else in which he was involved. Even more demanding is the saying that the disciple must "deny himself and take up his cross" to follow Jesus (Matt. 16:24 and parallels). More inclusive yet is the renunciation of family (Matt. 10:37, Luke 14:26), ending in the Lucan passage with the disciple hating "even his own life." This can become a mandate for mortification in physical as well as social and psychological forms.

It is significant that this language of radical discipleship is found solely in the Gospels. In the writings of Paul, the primary monastic inspiration comes from his positing a polarity between flesh and spirit. Neither Paul nor monastic readers necessarily think in Gnostic dualistic terms, although that possibility persists. The "flesh" is not an inherently evil material opposed to the spiritual but rather the old, sinful person at war with God. The struggle within the Christian person is an ascesis, described in athletic terms in 1 Corinthians 9:24–27 and in military terms in Ephesians 6:11–17. The warfare imagery emphasizes the role of the devil, who, by taking advantage of the flesh, intensifies the struggle. The theme of the self being crucified appears here also (Gal. 6:14).

Once more a choice in interpretation looms. Although the struggle between flesh and spirit might occupy one's entire time and energy, the communities whom Paul addresses as well as he himself are engaged in mundane life. The Christians of Corinth and Galatia are hardly submissive, obedient monastics, and the goal of community love and orderliness is not fully realized.

Finally we note the theme of the angelic life. As the resurrected are said to be like angels, that is, no longer married (Matt. 22:30 and parallels), so monks anticipate that state in their celibacy. Like the creatures, elders, and angels around the throne of heaven (Rev. 4, 5, 19), monks worship night and day. They anticipate the eschaton and the millennium here on earth.

GEORGE WECKMAN

*See also* Benedict of Nursia, St.; Biblical Figures and Practices; Lectio Divina; Regulations: Christian Perspectives; Spirituality: Eastern Christian; Theology, Eastern Christian

## Further Reading

Bouyer, Louis, *The Meaning of the Monastic Life*, New York: Kennedy, and London: Burns and Oates, 1955

Burton-Christie, Douglas, *The Word in the Desert: Scripture and the Quest for Holiness in Early Christian Monasticism*, New York: Oxford University Press, 1993

Campenhausen, Hans, Freiherr von, *Tradition and Life in the Church: Essays and Lectures in Church History*, Philadelphia, Pennsylvania: Fortress Press, and London: Collins, 1968

Leclercq, Jean, *The Love of Learning and the Desire for God: A Study of Monastic Culture*, New York: Fordham University Press, 1961; 2nd edition, London: SPCK, 1978; 3rd edition, New York: Fordham University Press, 1982

Pennington, M. Basil, *Lectio Divina: Renewing the Ancient Practice of Praying the Scriptures*, New York: Crossroad, 1998

Thils, Gustave, *Christian Holiness: A Precis of Ascetical Theology*, translated by John Farrand, Tielt, Belgium: Lannoo, 1961

# Biblical Figures and Practices

Monasticism as such does not occur in either the Jewish or the Christian Bibles. However, one can identify anticipatory elements, and these are said to prepare for and/or legitimate a phenomenon that emerged after these canons had been established. The article "Bible Interpretation" discusses biblical elements that are important to monks even though they might not be specifically monastic in the Bible. In this article specific features of monasticism are located in the biblical texts: celibacy, communal life for religious activities, and programs of religious discipline (vows). These features are often attached to certain personae or figures in the biblical narratives.

## Celibacy

Celibacy does not exist in the Hebrew Bible. It is assumed that everyone will marry and produce children if at all possible. The levirate law (Deut. 25:5–10) emphasizes the obligation to produce offspring. It can be assumed that deliberate abstention from marriage and sexuality would be regarded as disobedience of Torah and God. In the Hellenistic period the Wisdom of Solomon (3:13–4:1) defends the virtuous eunuch and barren woman, but without recommending their unfortunate condition as such.

The New Testament speaks more positively about childlessness. The saying on eunuchs (Matt. 19:12) offers the option of deliberate abstention from reproductive sexuality "for the sake of the kingdom of heaven" while noting that "not everyone can accept this teaching." A similarly optional celibacy is recommended by Paul to the Corinthians (1 Cor. 7:25–40), and 1 Timothy 5:3–16 recognizes a status of "widow" (differentiated from mere survival of a spouse) and recommends it with its sexual abstinence only for those over 60 years of age.

The most positive word on celibacy in the Christian canon elevates it beyond a simple option to holier status. Revelation 14:3–5 identifies 144,000 blameless men who have not "defiled themselves with women" as "virgins" (*parthenoi*) purchased or redeemed from humankind to be "firstfruits to God and the Lamb."

## Community

The Hebrew Bible mentions certain groups that anticipate monastic community insofar as they pursue religious activities that are not incumbent on other groups. The "sons of the prophets" (e.g., in 2 Kings 4:38–41) seem to have traveled and lived as a group, perhaps as apprentices to a "father" prophet. They exhibit behavior described as rapture, frenzy, or possession, and they perform instrumental music (1 Sam. 10:5–6, 10–13). Elijah and Elisha are the figures most closely associated with this phenomenon; although Elijah operates alone, Elisha clearly leads a prophetic guild. The Rechabites (Jer. 35:2–19) are not prophets but a family or clan. They apparently observe special restrictions: not drinking wine and living in tents rather than houses.

We know of the Essene communities from Josephus (c. 37–c. 100) and the Dead Sea Scrolls. The community at Qumran seems to have been at least semi-monastic, but it and the Essene movement do not appear explicitly in the Bible accounts. However, through the figure of John the Baptist and his disciples, elements of this ancient Jewish sect may be discernible in the New Testament texts. John may have been an Essene; he looks like an ascetic of some sort, and he has a following. Insofar as the Essene movement was monastic, it may supply the hidden background for the monastic character of the earliest Christian community.

The Gospels picture the band of disciples following Jesus as an incipient monastic community. They are homeless (Matt. 8:20, Luke 9:58) and have, at least during their preaching and healing mission, specific restrictions on possessions (Mark 6:8–9 and parallels). Jesus himself becomes a model for monks in his apparent celibacy, poverty, and homelessness. Many of Jesus' radical statements about life reform might have been directed solely at this small group. If so, the wider group of followers can be understood to be a supporting group for this inner, monastic circle.

In Acts (4:32–35) the communal economy of the Jerusalem church shares with monasticism the feature of common possession of goods. This is not a universal pattern in the New Testament churches, as other churches had money enough to make "collections" and share the proceeds with the Jerusalem church when it was in need (1 Cor. 16:1–3).

## Vows and Disciplines

The clearest example of a vow in ancient Jewish life is that of the Nazirite (Num. 6, apparently referred to in Acts 18:18 and 21:23–24). Whether temporary or lifelong, this vow imposed special prohibitions or regulations of life (not drinking wine, not cutting one's hair, and not touching a corpse). According to Exodus 27:2–8, people are vowed to God in some way, but this seems to be a relic of human sacrifice, and it is presumed that the person will be redeemed from the vow by an appropriate payment.

In Luke 2:37 the widow Anna is said to live in the temple night and day, fasting and praying. The real widows of 1 Timothy 5 also pray night and day. Mary Magdalene and John the Evangelist seem to be special friends of Jesus, and their devotion to him makes them models of monastic piety. The home of Mary, Martha, and Lazarus (John 11, 12) can be seen as a kind of monastery.

GEORGE WECKMAN

*See also* Bible Interpretation; Dialogue, Intermonastic: Christian Perspectives; Hagiography: Christian Perspectives; Master and Pupil: Christian Perspectives; Retreat, Christian; Seasons, Liturgical: Western Christian

**Further Reading**

Leaney, A.R.C., editor and translator, *The Rule of Qumran and Its Meaning: Introduction, Translation, and Commentary* (New Testament Library), Philadelphia, Pennsylvania: Westminster Press, and London: SCM Press, 1966

Vaux, Roland de, *Ancient Israel: Its Life and Institutions*, 2 vols., New York: McGraw-Hill, and London: Darton, Longman, and Todd, 1961; 2nd edition, London: Darton, Longman, and Todd, 1965

# Bishops: Jurisdiction and Role

Already in 451 the Council of Chalcedon stipulated the jurisdiction of a bishop over all monasteries within his diocese. In particular his was the right to allow the founding of a new monastery as well as to maintain and supervise all monasteries and monks in his diocese. His authority extended over the real estate and income of all lay inhabitants and monks and their obedience to monastic discipline, including matters of monks' contacts with the outside world and their activity in the society.

Later legal regulations kept these provisions in force. A decree of Gratian (12th century) reserved for bishops the right to establish new monasteries and visitation rights. However, it took away from the bishops the right to supervise monastic life and observance, leaving that to monastic authorities. A bishop could ordain a monk a priest only on consent of the monastic superior. Nevertheless a monk stood under the bishop's authority in all matters related to parish ministry.

A bishop's particular authority resulted from these general norms. He oversaw the election of abbot with respect to its conformity with regulations and conferred consecration and benediction on the newly elected abbot. Under certain conditions he could also depose abbots. The bishop enjoyed hospitality rights in monasteries and could impose certain taxes on them. In particular the bishop had the right to conduct, in person or through his representatives, visitations of the monasteries under his authority; to produce visitation records; and to redress any irregularities. Abbots and priors were required to participate in diocesan synods, either personally or through their representatives. Monks living in monasteries located near cathedral churches participated in its liturgy. Sometimes abbots and priors were members of cathedral chapters as *gratialis* canons and enjoyed the right to sit in the stalls.

Anchorites leading solitary life did not need exemptions in their relations with the ecclesiastical hierarchy. The emergence and diffusion of cenobitic monasticism made these relations more complex. From antiquity cenobitic monasteries in both the East and the West enjoyed strong ties with bishops. One line in

the development of early monasticism is even referred to as "episcopal" monasticism. This name emphasizes the close ties between bishops and the monastic movement: in the West this condition lasted until the 12th century and has remained in force in the Eastern Orthodox Church. Bishops were often recruited from among monks who in turn were bishops' closest associates, especially in diocesan work. Special relations between bishops and monasteries existed in cathedral abbeys and so-called bishop's abbeys, common in the Middle Ages before the Gregorian reforms. Their patrons were bishops (by virtue of foundation or for other reasons). Bishops played an important and positive role by supporting early medieval monastic reforms.

Nevertheless even the oldest abbeys were not free from a desire for exemption from a bishop's authority. A monastery with its real estate and inhabitants functioned as an entity in terms of organization, economy, and law. The diffusion of real estate, ties with branch monasteries, and various relations between abbeys resulted in a monastery's activity frequently overflowing diocesan borders. The emergence of centralized congregations and orders indeed required the implementation of exemptions. A monastery located in several dioceses, although subordinate to their centralized authority, was pursuing goals and tasks impossible to assess from the point of view of the interests of a single diocese. Leaving it within the framework of the regular diocesan organization could hamper further development and render the goals unattainable.

Exemptions became necessary in situations in which goals of religious orders coincided with goals of the entire Church and exceeded those of individual dioceses. This was the case, for example, with the Church reforms and the involvement of monks in ministry and external missions. Exemptions were supported by popes who perceived them as means of solidifying their power and by secular authorities (e.g., the emperor) who were striving to preserve their original rights of royal protection (*tuitio*) at the expense of bishops.

The name "exemption" refers to the practice of releasing a monastery or an order from the regular authority of the bishop of a diocese and placing it under the direct control of a superior Church authority (most often the pope). Its counterpart in the Eastern Church was *stauropigia*. Originally popes exempted only selected monasteries. Exemption became a distinct legal institution only in the 12th century and the first half of the 13th.

At first monasteries sought to protect their autonomy by obtaining the bishops' guarantee of noninterference in their internal affairs and then resorting to provincial synods in matters of dispute. The first known papal exemption was issued for the abbey at Bobbio (628). The number of exemptions grew as a result of the feudalization of bishops in the early Middle Ages and papal struggle to reform the Church. Monks were seen as valuable allies in this struggle. The exemption received by Cluny in the tenth century became a model for others. From the 11th century exemption was granted to numerous Benedictine abbeys and from the 12th century to newly established congregations and orders (e.g., Cistercians, Carthusian Order, Premonstratensian Canons, and military orders). This trend intensified in the 13th century and later, eventually encompassing all centralized orders.

Initially exemption was of passive nature; that is, it released the monastery's territory from some of the bishop's powers. It pertained to imposing interdiction on the monastery, excommunicated monks (sometimes also the whole *familia* and benefactors), supervision of the monastery's economy and discipline, visitation rights, and sometimes release from the tithes (especially newly imposed ones). Exemptions also allowed monasteries to exercise a free choice of bishop to ordain monks, consecrate an altar or a monastic church, or confer benediction on the abbot. From the late 12th century, some exemption privileges transferred to the monastery's superior some of the bishop's powers within the monastery or even its real estate. Such exemptions released from the bishop's jurisdiction not only individual persons (monks and *familia* of the monastery) but also the whole territory belonging to the exempt monastery, together with its inhabitants, as well as churches and chapels in its possession.

Exemption privileges were of various extent and practical importance. Whether bishops, who frequently were hostile to them, abided by these privileges depended on the current political situation. Often the issue of exemption caused conflicts.

The extent of exemptions was limited by regulations issued at the Fifth Lateran Council (1515) and at the Council of Trent (1563), and some popes (Boniface VIII, 1294–1303; Clement V, 1305–1314; and later Leo XIII, 1878–1903) precisely defined mutual rights and obligations of bishops and monks. It became a common practice to entrust bishops as representatives of the Holy See with a range of rights themselves to exempt monasteries and orders (e.g., visitation rights).

Thus, bishops retained their authority over a substantial portion of monastic life within their dioceses. In general they retained jurisdiction over parish ministry performed by monks, matters concerning the purity of doctrine, the tertiary movement, and lay brotherhoods active around monasteries. Subject to their authority were also nunneries not incorporated with the exempt male orders as well as numerous monasteries, congregations, institutes of consecrated life, and associations of apostolic life established by the bishop within the framework of diocesan law.

According to the *Codex Iuris Canonici* (CIC) of 1917, passive exemption was enjoyed by all male orders and those female ones that abided by papal enclosure and that were subordinate to the higher superiors of male orders. By a special indult, male monastic orders also acquired exemption. Their higher superiors held jurisdiction. After the Second Vatican Council (1962–1965), the whole idea of exemption has changed: it exists to ensure internal control of orders and monastics' readiness in service to the Church. On the authority of the new *CIC*, the bishop, in accordance with the principles of cooperation and coordination, cannot hinder or thwart monks in their work or disturb their inner harmony. Because of his responsibility for the whole ministry within his diocese, a bishop enjoys some authority over

monks and has the dispensing power (except for matters reserved for the pope or ensuing from general laws).

MAREK DERWICH

*See also* Abbeys, Territorial; Abbot: Christian; Benedictines: General or Male; Bobbio, Italy; Cathedral Priories; Cluny, France; Monastics and the World, Medieval; Monk-Bishops; Orders (Religious), Origins of; Patrons, Christian: Royal; Regulations: Christian Perspectives

## Further Reading

Becquet, Jean, "Les relations des monastères avec les évêques," in *Monachisme d'Orient et d'Occident: la vie monastique en Occident de st Benoît à st Bernard*, 19–20–21 septembre 1983, Abbaye de Lérins: Association des Amis de Sénanque, 1983

Boshof, Egon, "Kloster und Bischof in Lotharingien," in *Monastische Reformen im 9. und 10. Jahrhundert* (Vorträge und Forschungen, 38), edited by Raymund Kottje and Helmut Maurer, Sigmaringen: Thorbecke, 1989

Carpentier, R., "L'évêque et la vie religieuse consacrée," in *L'épiscopat et l'Église universelle* (Unam Sanctam, 39), edited by Yves Congar and Bernard Dominique Dupuy, Paris: Éditions du Cert, 1962

de Bonhomme, A., "Juridiction des évêques et exemption des réguliers," *Revue du droit canonique* 15 (1965)

Felten, Franz J., "Protezione episcopale," in *Dizionario degli istituti di perfezione*, edited by Guerrino Pelliccia and Giancarlo Rocca, volume 7, Rome: Edizioni Paoline, 1974

Fogliasso, Emilio, *Introductio in vigentem disciplinam de iuridicis relationibus inter religiones et ordinarium loci*, Augustae Taurinorum: Schola Typographica Salesiana, 1948

Gallen, Joseph F., *Canon Law for Religious: An Explanation*, New York: Alba House, 1983

Hourlier, Jacques, *L'âge classique, 1140–1378: les religieux* (Histoire du Droit des Institutions de l'Église en Occident, 10), Paris: Cujas, 1973

Knowles, David, "Essays in Monastic History: The Growth of Exemption," *Downside Review* 50 (1932)

Oberste, Jörg, "Klostervisitationen. Erträge und Perspektiven mediävistischer Forschungen," in *Les visites monastiques: Moyen Âge et Temps modernes* (Opera ad historiam monasticam spectantia, Series 2, Collectanea 2), edited by Marek Derwich, Wroclaw, 2000

Rencontre d'histoire religieuse, *L'évêque dans l'histoire de l'église: Actes de la Septième rencontre d'histoire religieuse tenue à Fontevraud les 14 et 15 Octobre 1983*, Angers: Presses de l'Université d'Angers, 1984

Walsh, M., "The Bishop and the Religious," *Clergy Review* 52 (1967)

Wathen, Ambrose, "Monastic Visitations: Historical Soundings," *American Benedictine Review* 39 (1988)

# Black Canons. *See* Augustinian Canons

# Bobbio, Italy

The Irish St. Columban (d. 615), driven from Burgundy, came eventually to Lombardy, where in 614 at the abandoned Roman fort of Ebovium he founded the last of his monasteries. As in Gaul, so here too his powerful personality attracted disciples from among Lombards, Franks, Romans, and Germans, and Bobbio was already flourishing at his death a year later. Under his immediate abbot-successors, Athalia (who had accompanied Columban from Luxeuil), Bertulf, and Bobolen, Bobbio continued to thrive as school of piety and learning and as bulwark against the Arianism of the Lombards. The monk St. Bladulf was put to death by the Arians. Meanwhile, under Bertulf, Bobbio became the first abbey to secure papal exemption. Bobolen introduced the Benedictine Rule as an alternative to the sterner Columban Rule. The latter was abandoned completely in the tenth century, and Bobbio joined the Congregation of Monte Cassino, becoming known as the "Monte Cassino of the North." Charlemagne (768–814) and later emperors endowed Bobbio richly, and its abbots – for example, St. Wala (d. 836) and the geometer Gerbert of Aurillac (the future Pope Sylvester II), made abbot in 983 – were notable figures in their times. In 1014 at the instance of Emperor Henry II (1002–1024), the pope made Bobbio an episcopal see. The bishops, chosen from the monks, continued to reside in the abbey, somewhat in the Irish fashion. Jurisdictional conflict between abbots and bishops inevitably ensued, and Bobbio as spiritual and intellectual center went into slow decline. The abbey became a member of the Congregation of Santa Giustina from 1649 until its secularization by the French in 1803. The bishopric, also suppressed in 1803, was restored in 1819 and became a suffragan of Genoa. One of its bishops, Anthony Gianelli (1838–1846), has been canonized. Today what remains of the monastery building (9th to 16th century) is a school, and the abbey church, with the tomb of Columban in its crypt, now serves the parish. The crypt was completely renovated in 1910, when the body of Columban was reinterred in a 15th-century sarcophagus.

Columban, with manuscripts from Ireland, founded at Bobbio one of the great libraries of the Middle Ages. Irish monks came in some numbers to Bobbio as well as to St. Gall (founded by Columban's disciple, Gall) and to Reichenau, enriching all three monasteries with manuscripts. However, Bobbio received

**Benedictine cloister (16th century), attached to Basilica of San Colombano, Bobbio, Italy.**
**Photo courtesy of the Editor**

books from Pope Gregory the Great (590–604) and from Italy, North Africa, and Spain. Copies of the classics, of heretical works, and of Greek texts were preserved in the abbey or quite often were palimpsested or sent on to Luxeuil (with which Bobbio remained in close relationship) to be palimpsested by the Luxeuil scribes. Thus, Bobbio preserved much classical learning while its scribes, Italian, Irish, and Merovingian (from Luxeuil?) continued, between the seventh and tenth centuries, to turn out codices, acts of the Councils of Ephesus and Chalcedon (useful against Arianism), dogmatic works, the *Liber pontificalis*, and (a special interest of the Irish) grammatical works. At Bobbio Irish art came under Oriental influence, whereas Irish liturgy was influenced by the Ambrosian. This Ambrosian influence is to be detected in the hymns and collects of the Antiphonary of Bangor, although it was composed in Ireland and brought by some Irish pilgrim (perhaps one Dungal in the 11th century) to Bobbio. Whether the transmission in the seventh century of the works of Isidore of Seville (c. 560–636) went directly to Ireland or came through Bobbio is in dispute, but the evidence rather favors direct transmission. Two of the Bobbio manuscripts now in the Ambrosian library (one, MS.S.45, apparently belonged to Athala and was written before 622) are written and decorated in the Irish style, but with use of dots that might be Coptic. It is a moot point whether the Bobbio Missal, now in the Bibliothèque Nationale in Paris, was composed at or near Bobbio or at Luxeuil or even in Ireland. Beginning in the 16th century, the bulk of the Bobbio manuscripts were carried away to the Ambrosian Library in Milan, the Vatican Library, the Biblioteca Nazionale of the University of Turin (a disastrous fire in 1904 destroyed or damaged most of the volumes here), and to other libraries.

JOHN J. SILKE

*See also* Bishops: Jurisdiction and Role; Celtic Monasticism; Columban, St.; Congregations, Benedictine; Ireland; Isidore of Seville, St.; Libraries: Western Christian; Monte Cassino, Italy; Reichenau; St. Gallen, Switzerland; Visual Arts, Western Christian: Sculpture

**Further Reading**

Bischoff, Bernhard, *Latin Palaeography: Antiquity and the Middle Ages*, translated by Dáibhí Ó Cróinín and David Ganz, Cambridge and New York: Cambridge University Press, 1990

Cipolla, Carlo, and Giulio Buzzi, editors, *Codice diplomatico del monastero di S. Colombano di Bobbio fino all' anno MCCVIII*, 3 vols., Rome: Tip. del Senato, 1918; volumes 1 and 2 corrected by Buzzi as *Studi Bobbiesi*, Rome, 1918

Comaskey, Bernard J., "Bobbio, Abbey of," in *New Catholic Encyclopedia*, volume 2, New York: McGraw-Hill, 1967

Concannon, Helena Walsh, *The Life of St. Columban (St. Columbanus of Bobbio): A Study of Ancient Irish Monastic Life*, St. Louis, Missouri: Herder, and Dublin: Catholic Truth Society of Ireland, 1915

Ferrari, Mirella, "Spigolature Bobbiesi," *Italia Medioevale e Umanistica* 19 (1973)

Kenney, James F., *The Sources for the Early History of Ireland: An Introduction and Guide*, volume 1: *Ecclesiastical* (Records of Civilization, Sources and Studies), New York: Columbia University Press, 1929; revised edition, Dublin: Pádraic Ó Táilliúir, 1979

Lapidge, Michael, editor, *Columbanus: Studies on the Latin Writings* (Studies in Celtic History, 17), Woodbridge, Suffolk, and Rochester, New York: Boydell Press, 1997

Mercati, Giovanni, *Prolegomena de fatis bibliothecae monasterii S. Colombani Bobiensis et de codice ipso Vat. lat. 5757*, Rome: Vatican City, 1934

Wilmart, André, "Bobbio (Missel de)," in *Dictionnaire d'archéologie chrétienne et de liturgie*, volume 2, edited by Fernand Cabrol, Paris: Letouzey et Ané, 1903

# Bodh Gayā, India

Bodh Gayā, located in the modern state of Bihar in northeastern India, is the site at which Śākyamuni is said to have attained enlightenment and become the Buddha; as such it has, since at least the fifth century A.D., been the most important Buddhist pilgrimage site in all of India. However, as a monastic center it has been of secondary significance and has never come close to rivaling the great medieval monastic universities that were located at Nalandā and Vikramaśīla.

The historical record of Bodh Gayā's monasteries is spotty and must be traced through occasional references in the accounts of the Chinese pilgrims as well as from the fragmentary archaeological record. Throughout its history Bodh Gayā has been of special importance to Sri Lanka and Burma. According to the Chinese pilgrim Faxian (fifth century), who did not himself visit Bodh Gayā, a monastery by the name of the Mahābodhi Saṅghārāma was built at the site to house Sri Lankan pilgrims. Xuanzang, who visited Bodh Gayā in the seventh century, records that a Buddhist monastery was established at Bodh Gayā as early as the fourth century by a king of Sri Lanka (either Upatissa I or Śrī Meghavara; the record is unclear). Xuanzang states that the Mahābodhi Saṅghārāma structure consisted of six different buildings and was occupied by some 1,000 Mahāyāna monks of the Sthaviravāda school. In the late 19th century, Alexander Cunningham and J.D.M. Beglar uncovered what they believed to be the remains of this monastery. Groups of Burmese monks, supported by a variety of Burmese kings, made regular trips to Bodh Gayā until at least the 19th century, mainly to make repairs to the temple. However, as Buddhism entered a long period of decline in India, the monastic presence at Bodh Gayā likewise began to fade, and by the 13th century, according to the Tibetan monk Darmasvāmin, only about 300 Sinhala monks remained at the site.

After several centuries of disuse, at the end of the 16th century Bodh Gayā entered a new phase of its monastic life; it was at this time that the deserted site was visited by a Śaiva Hindu, Gossain Ghamandi Gir, a member of a Śaiva lineage that traces its roots to Śankara in the ninth century. Gossain Ghamandi Gir's followers built a small monastery at Bodh Gayā in the

Mahābodhi temple, site of the Buddha's enlightenment, Bodh Gayā, India. Remains at the site date from the period of Aśoka and the first century B.C. The latest major restoration to the tower was completed in the 19th century.
Photo courtesy of Marylin M. Rhie

early part of the 17th century that has since been continuously occupied by a lineage of Śaiva priests. This monastery's status is relatively minor within the Śaiva monastic system – according to oral tradition it is ranked 36th among the 52 major Śaivite *mahs* – but it has served as an important anchor for Hindu pilgrims who visit Bodh Gayā in conjunction with visits to nearby Gayā (a major Hindu *tīrthā*). Since the end of the 19th century, the Śaiva priests have been at the center of a conflict over control of Bodh Gayā as monks and laypersons from Sri Lanka attempted to regain control of the site. This conflict was not resolved until the 1950s with the formation of a multireligious committee to manage the temple and its environs. An active Śaiva monastic presence still exists at Bodh Gayā, although in recent years, with the Dalai Lama frequently taking residence at Bodh Gayā, more Buddhists are flocking to the site. Amid a spate of Buddhist monastic building, in addition to the Sri Lankan and Burmese monasteries, temples and small monasteries operated by Bud-

dhists from Tibet, China, Japan, Thailand, Vietnam, and elsewhere are functioning.

JACOB N. KINNARD

*See also* Architecture: Buddhist Monasteries in Southern Asia; India: Sites; Nālandā, India; Pilgrims to India, Chinese; Sri Lanka; Ten-Precept Mothers as Theravādin Nuns

**Further Reading**

Barua, Benimadhab, *Gaya and Buddha-Gaya*, 2 vols., Calcutta: Chuckervertty Chatterjee, 1931–1934
Barua, Dipak Kumar, *Buddha Gaya Temple: Its History*, Buddha Gaya: Buddha Gaya Temple Management Committee, 1975; 2nd edition, 1981
Cunningham, Alexander, *Mahābodhi, or the Great Buddhist Temple under the Bodhi Tree at Buddha-Gaya*, London: Allen, 1892
Dutt, Sukumar, *Buddhist Monks and Monasteries of India: Their History and Their Contribution to Indian Culture*, London: Allen and Unwin, 1962
Leoshko, Janice, editor, *Bodhgayā, the Site of Enlightenment*, Bombay: Marg, 1988

# Bodhidharma trad. c. 470–543

## First Chinese patriarch of Chan/Zen

Bodhidharma (Chinese, Putidamo; Japanese, Bodaidaruma) in classical Chan/Zen was the genealogical link with India as the 28th patriarch from the Buddha and the first of the six patriarchs of China. Thus, he was accorded the worship due to a founding ancestor in Chinese culture, and his statue or tablet was installed on the altar in the Hall of the Patriarchs (*zutang*) in Chan monasteries. His icon was flanked by those of the founder of the monastery and of Baizhang Huaihai (749–814), the reputed creator of a distinctly Chan monastery and author of the Chan monastic rule, or of another ancestor. This iconolatry was instituted by around 1070. Bodhidharma's anniversary was celebrated on the fifth day of the tenth month in the lunar calendar with a ritual of ancestor worship led by the abbot. Furthermore, as the meditation hall was the most important site in a Chan monastery, the icon of Bodhidharma, or of Mahākāśyapa, the first Indian patriarch, was also enshrined on a dais in its center. Originally there was no such statue, it is claimed, because theory held that the mind is Buddha, and so the meditator had to look inward and not seek an external image. With time, however, ritualization generated a demand for an icon. Moreover, from the Song dynasty on, a Chan meditator was constantly confronted with Bodhidharma, for every time he consulted the abbot on his understanding, the monk had to prostrate himself before a portrait of Bodhidharma hung in the ante-room to the abbot's chambers, thereby reminding him of the determination of Huike in seeking the mind transmission from Bodhidharma. After all, Bodhidharma was crucial to the genealogical claims to a legitimate succession by way of the personal transmission of mind from Śākyamuni. Thus, when a pupil was made the heir of an ac-credited Chan master or became an abbot of a Chan monastery, he was given a scroll of certification (*fajuan*) on which his ge-nealogy was recorded, with Bodhidharma placed at the head of the lineage. It is unclear when this practice began, for portraits (*dingxiang*) of the abbots were used for this purpose from Song times as well.

### The Creation of the Bodhidharma Image

The image of Bodhidharma, in literature and art, has been trans-formed over time to suit fresh doctrinal developments and monastic concerns. The first mention of a Bodhidharma is in the *Luoyang qielanji* (547; Record of the Monasteries of Luoyang, cf. Jenner, 1981), which recorded the past glories of the Buddhist buildings of Luoyang. There he is portrayed as a 150-year-old Persian monk who praised the Yongning Monastery's nine-story pagoda as the greatest in the world by chanting *nama*s and pros-trating himself before it for several days. Bodhidharma had to have been in Luoyang between 516 and 526, for this pagoda ex-isted only for that decade. The picture of Bodhidharma is of a strange, foreign monk and the concern is the verification of the superiority of the pagoda, not with Bodhidharma himself. Thus, the mention of him as Persian (*Bosi = Fars*) is mistaken, for his name is Sanskrit, and Sassanian Iran was little known for its Buddhism, which, moreover, was Sarvāstivādin and not Ma-hāyāna. The author of this account, Yang Xuanzhi, probably mistook the name of the brahmin dynasty of southeastern India, the Pallavas, for the Sassanian dynasts, the Pahlava. This expla-nation would accord with the second-oldest document, the pref-ace to Bodhidharma's *Erru sixinglun* (On the Two Entrances and Four Practices), attributed to Tanlin, which states that Bodhid-harma "was a South Indian of the Western Region. He was the third son of a great brahmin king." The Pallavas, with their cap-ital at Kāñcī, were the only major brahmin rulers in South India; all the others belonged to the usual *kṣatriya* warrior caste. The third account of Bodhidharma, that by the Vinaya master Daox-uan, written by 645, drew on Tanlin's preface. A tentative recon-struction from these sources would be that Bodhidharma came by sea to South China in the 470s and then moved into Northern Wei, where he taught a meditation technique based on Ma-hāyāna. His teachings seem to have brought him into conflict with the mainstream meditation teachers, who taught elemen-tary or non- Mahāyāna methods. He gained two or three pupils (not including Tanlin, who was rather an amanuensis or assis-tant translator), one of whom was Huike. Hints exist that he was executed just outside Luoyang in the troubles of the late Northern Wei between 528 and 534.

Subsequently, mythmaking took over, creating the Bodhi-dharma legend. From around the early seventh century, a group of scholar-meditators who adhered to the *Laṅkāvatāra Sūtra* at-tached themselves to the charisma of Bodhidharma, and this is reflected in Daoxuan's post-645 additions to his *Xugaoseng zhuan* (Continued Biographies of Eminent Monks), in which he states that Bodhidharma transmitted only that sūtra. This idea was further developed in the late seventh and early eighth cen-

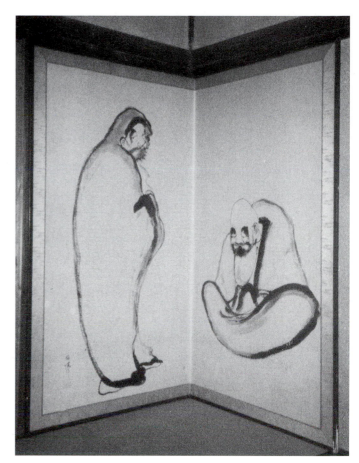

Ink painting on a folding screen in a Takamatsu City Zen temple of Bodhidharma (Japanese, Bodaidaruma), who transmitted Zen from India to China.
Photo courtesy of Steve McCarty

turies, as disputes arose over who was the legitimate heir in a lin-eage from Bodhidharma. The first to emerge was the faction around Faru (638–689), a pupil of Hongren. They affirmed the transmission of the *Laṅkāvatāra Sūtra* and proclaimed a lineage (but not a theory of a unilinear, one-patriarch-per-generation lin-eage). They situated Bodhidharma in Shaolin Monastery and claimed that he was poisoned by his rivals, possibly the scholas-tics of that monastery. Furthermore, this faction supposed a do-cetic death, in which he left his grave empty in the fashion of a Daoist immortal. He was allegedly sighted traveling west in the Pamirs by an official emissary. Huike is said to have severed off his own arm to gain the master's teachings. This group had a persecution complex, insisting that the transmission of the True Dharma was always threatened and so requires miraculous protection.

Shenhui (684–758), detecting flaws in these conflicting ac-counts, took the opportunity from 730 to paint a new picture of Bodhidharma as the transmitter of the Tathāgata (Rulai) Chan, who boldly told Emperor Wu of Liang (r. 502–550) that no merit was to be found in the external Buddhism of building monasteries, ordaining monks, or copying sūtras. The emperor, mired in this materialistic Buddhism, failed to comprehend, and so Bodhidharma departed north to Shaolin Monastery, where he conferred on Huike the ineffable Dharma, the *Diamond Sūtra* and a robe of transmission. The cues from Faru's version of the tale of the empty coffin were elaborated in a more Daoistic mode, with the statement that the sandal left behind in the tomb was now kept at Shaolin. Shenhui also asserted that an inscription commissioned by Emperor Wu of Liang was engraved on a stele at Shaolin. Shenhui's purpose was twofold: to attack the materialistic Buddhism of the court and the Chan groups patronized by it (namely, those of Faru and Puji) and to fabricate a theory of a genealogy of Chan patriarchs back to India in a single line of transmission, with only one patriarch per generation, this lineage confirmed by the handing over of a robe. Thus, this "true" Chan is that of the Tathāgata, Śākyamuni himself, which was brought to China by Bodhidharma. Shenhui made this first linkage of Bodhidharma with a lineage back to the Buddha of Indian patriarchs.

Between 774 and 781 the *Lidai fabaoji* (Annals of the Dharma Jewel through the Generations), a parochial but influential text issued by an opportunistic group in Szechwan, appropriated Shenhui's ideas. It called Bodhidharma by the name Dharmatrāta, claiming that he sent his pupils Buddha and Yaśas to China to preach. They failed in their mission, prompting Dharmatrāta to come to China, where he met Emperor Wu of Liang. The poisoners of Dharmatrāta are identified as Bodhiruci (d. 535) and Vinaya Master Huiguang, both of whom lived at Shaolin Monastery and who championed a translation of the *Laṅkāvatāra Sūtra* different from that used by Dharmatrāta/Bodhidharma. Soon after, the *Baolinzhuan* (Baolin Monastery Biographies), a lineage text of the Mazu branch of Chan, downplayed the transmission of the robe and replaced it with verses of transmission and predictions confirming succession. All the later, "standard hagiographies" of Bodhidharma were based on this text, without acknowledgment. In this text Bodhidharma supposedly was shown great veneration by the emperors of the Liang and Northern Wei dynasties, given gifts, and mentioned in dispatches sent between the two courts. The account is given greater verisimilitude through spurious, detailed chronologies of events and minor details of officials and predictions in profusion. The author forged the inscription by Emperor Wu of Liang and recorded that Bodhidharma was granted a posthumous title by Emperor Taizong in the Dali reign (766–779). Bodhidharma is even reported to have been an avatar of Guanyin, an equation that would later be significant. The motivation of the author was to seek recognition from the court and others that its lineage was imperially sanctioned and that the Correct Law is superior to secular law. The *Laṅkāvatāra* as the scripture of transmission was restored. Even Bodhidharma's burial place and date of death (6 January 537) are stated. Moreover, it provides a history of Bodhidharma in India, defeating in debate the leaders of six "schools" of Buddhism, likely meant to be read as lineage rivals of Mazu Chan.

The process of textual mythopoesis largely ended in China in the 11th century, for the disputes over rival lineage claims had ceased, as multiple "family" lineages from Huineng were now accepted, the list of patriarchs was settled, and the Song court gave its imprimatur to several sanctioned, standard histories of the lamplight transmission. Thus, these texts were rationalized and edited out the more deniable and outrageous statements in the *Baolinzhuan*, leaving the cleansed image of Bodhidharma that normally has been approved by the Chan establishment ever since. The only new incidents added to the Chan hagiographies after this time were of Bodhidharma facing a wall at Shaolin for nine years and Huike's request to have his mind calmed.

*Other Uses for Bodhidharma*
From this fixed literary image, new visions or uses for Bodhidharma emerged: as a cipher in the *gong'an* (*koan*, public cases), that is, the conundrums for meditation formed of instances of enlightenment meant to halt discursive thought; as an avatar in Japan; as a subject of art; and as a figure in folk culture.

Students of Chan in their meditation practice were continually confronted with *gong'an*, such as "What was the meaning of the Patriarchal Teacher coming from the west?" and the interview with Emperor Wu of Liang. The latter forms the first case of the *Biyanlu* (The Blue Cliff Record), probably the most popular collection of such public cases since it was published in 1300. Thus, Bodhidharma remained a constant emblem of Chan. Some see in the dialogue of Bodhidharma and Huike over calming the mind, which can be found in the *Long Scroll's* continuation of the *Erru sixinglun*, the genesis of the *yulu* (recorded sayings) and the *gong'an*, which were extracted from them.

In Japan Bodhidharma was made part of a trio with Huisi (515–577) and Shōtoku Taishi (574–622), the customary first true native Japanese Buddhist. In the legend Shōtoku Taishi, supposedly an incarnation of Huisi, a founder of Tiantai Buddhism, encountered a starving beggar, an avatar of Bodhidharma, on Kataoka Hill. This identification was made by Kōjō (779–858) to prove the transmission of the "one-mind precepts." Kōjō's master, Saichō (767–822), the founder of Tendai in Japan, not only promoted these bodhisattva precepts but also recorded the genealogy of Chan by means of Bodhidharma, and he claimed to have personally learned from the Japanese extension of a Chan lineage that was later transmitted within Tendai. This Tendai lineage and doctrine became the basis for the new Darumashū (Bodhidharma "sect"; historically an unattested name) founded by Dainichi Nōnin (late 12th century). Nōnin claimed natural enlightenment, without a master, through his study of these Chan texts, the most important of which were attributed to Bodhidharma. Taking hints from these radical texts, Nōnin established a "protestant sect" that soon attracted the condemnation of other Zen promoters. However, Nōnin's teachings seem to have been very popular. After Nōnin was allegedly murdered in a misunderstanding, the attack on the Darumashū as a heresy, especially for not being party to a lineage, led many of its followers to join a new group around Dōgen (1200–1253), thereby contributing to the formation of the Sōtō denomination.

Japanese Buddhist historians perpetuated the myth of the Bodhidharma encounter with Shōtoku Taishi. Kokan Shiren commenced the history of Buddhism in Japan, the *Genkō Shakusho* (1322; The Buddhist Writings of the Genko Era), with this tale, which was repeated in the *Honchō Kōsōden* (Biographies of the Eminent Monks of Japan) by Shiban (1626–1710). Indeed a Daruma Monastery was founded in Kamakura times at Kataoka in the Nara prefecture, and from the Muromachi period it was subordinate to Kyoto's Nanzenji. Hakuin Ekaku (1686–1768), the reviver of Rinzai Zen, had a pupil, Eryō Sakyō, who restored the Kataoka Darumaji (or Darumadera). Around the same time the Ming dynasty monk Xinyue (1639–1696) fled from the encroaching Manchus to Japan. His pupil Tenshū Hōrei (1659–1735) founded a Daruma Monastery on Shōrin-san (Mount Shaolin) near Takasaki City, Gumma prefecture. This began as a temple to worship Kannon (Chinese, Guanyin), but a dream omen, possibly from Bodhidharma, had it converted into a monastery dedicated to Bodhidharma, himself an avatar of Guanyin. This temple still belongs to the Ōbaku Zen denomination and has become a market for Daruma memorabilia.

Visual representations of Bodhidharma also mutated in China and Japan. They began as pictures of a slight monk, rather more Chinese in appearance than Indian and always in the act of transmitting the patriarchship to Huike. These illustrations, dating from the 11th to the 12th century, were likely related to the images of the transmission of the lamplight found in the halls of the patriarchs (*zutang*), the first of which, the Hall of the Seven Patriarchs, was erected in Shaolin Monastery by Puji (651–739), Shenxiu's pupil, and the second, the Hall of the Six Patriarchs, at Shenhui's behest in 752. These halls became common from about the tenth century on, as they symbolized the lineage of the monastic community and its abbot. Thus, the Indian features of Bodhidharma mattered less than his identification as the primal ancestor.

The earlier Chinese artists had only models of Indians in the 16 *lohan* (arhat) and Vimalakīrti. *Lohan* had earrings, high noses, deep-set eyes, and long eyebrows. As the *lohan* became more popular, in the 13th and 14th centuries Bodhidharma was given a more intense and Indian visage and was depicted as riding on a rush leaf over the Yangtze River on his way from Liang to Northern Wei. This last image probably derived from the *lohan* who "cross to the other shore" and a verse from the *Shijing* (Book of Songs), "Who says the river is wide? / On a single reed you can cross it!" *Lohan* were also partly assimilated with the Daoist immortals in paintings by the monk Guanxiu (832–912) on the basis of his dream visions of spiritual travail crystallized into a moment of time. Thus, Guanxiu painted Bodhidharma, whose empty coffin was a sign of a Daoist immortal, facing a wall in meditation with long eyebrows and a cape over his head. The Song literati, both monks and laity, Sinicized Bodhidharma, and black ink brush paintings of Bodhidharma were often given as presents to donors and patrons. This induced a simplification and greater emphasis on the brush strokes.

However, under the Mongol Yuan dynasty, which had far more contact with central Asia and India, more Indian features were introduced to the portrayals. A most immediate model was Dhyānabhadra (or Śūnyadiśya; Chinese, Zhikong; c. 1300–1361), whom Chinese said resembled Bodhidharma, as he had an emaciated dark-skinned face, blue eyes, and an unblinking gaze. Dhyānabhadra claimed that he was the 108th Indian patriarch of Chan and that his mother was from Kañcī. He frequently referred to Bodhidharma and Emperor Wu of Liang. Thus, in the Ming dynasty and later we find very Indian or "Persian" images of Bodhidharma alongside Chinese-looking, youthful depictions of him. Such contrasting images can even be seen in one location, Shaolin Monastery, but it mattered little, as the true (*zhen*) appearance of a saint was invisible.

In Japan the paintings included pictures of Bodhidharma meeting Shōtoku Taishi. The images of Tokugawa Japan were often humorous and irreverent, such as those by Hanabusa Icchō (1652–1724) and Suzuki Harunobu (c. 1725–1770) of Bodhidharma as a female or prostitute. Perhaps they were influenced by Hakuin, who gave his pupils many simplified, quick brush sketches of Bodhidharma as a fierce or introspective Indian monk. In his popularization of Bodhidharma, Hakuin was influenced by the Ōbaku monks, refugees from Ming China. Hakuin popularized Zen meditation by stating that good fortune (*fuku*) was the result of meditation and enlightenment. These were equated also with Bodhidharma, who consequently was made an item of folk culture.

The refugee monks from China also imported novellas about Bodhidharma, such as the *Damo chushengzhuan* (The Birth and Life of Bodhidharma). In China these 15th- and early 16th-century novellas, such as the *Damo chushen chuandengzhuan* (Bodhidharma's Incarnation and Transmission of the Lamp) by the layman Zhu Kaitai, were commercial products trading on Chan motifs. When they reached Japan they were further vulgarized in the booming popular culture of the Japanese cities. In this Bodhidharma was often made a figure of fun, being featured in books of humor and satire, in mad poems, and in haiku verses. Folk artists at Ōtsu drew pictures of Bodhidharma akin to those by Hakuin but in commercial quantities. Thus, Bodhidharma entered Japanese culture as Daruma, often a red-robed, self-righting doll or luck charm. Daruma trinkets are sold at the Daruma temples and special fairs. This was an outgrowth of the original attempt to popularize Zen meditation, but the commercial imperative came to dominate.

Likewise in Chinese folk religions or new religions, Bodhidharma was adopted as a patriarch, especially by the Qing dynasty Lojiao religion, which made him its first patriarch and produced literature about him called *Damo baojuan* (Precious Scroll of Bodhidharma). These scriptures were credited with a magical potency. These secret societies of boatmen took some of their motifs from Chan literature, and they equated Bodhidharma with Amitābha (Mituo Fo). Thus, Bodhidharma became a god who could save one from sorrow and provide happiness, just as in Japan but by a different route. Bodhidharma had almost returned to the image he had acquired in the *Luoyang qielanji* but with an elevated status. However, throughout he was always a founding ancestor and symbolized the transmission of a spiritual truth that prompted the establishment of the Chan Order.

JOHN JORGENSEN

*See also* Buddhist Schools/Traditions: China; Chan/Zen: Japan; Humor: Buddhist; Kōan; Zen, Arts of

## Biography

A semi-legendary first patriarch of Chan/Zen in China, Bodhidharma is said to have ventured from India to China, where he worked his way northward to Shaolin monastery. He practiced *zazen* (sitting motionless) for some years. He has attracted a vast iconography, including the Daruma dolls of Japan.

## Major Works

All works ascribed to him are of dubious authorship. The most likely to be of his authorship is *Erru sixinglun* (On the Two Entrances and Four Practices).

## Further Reading

Faure, Bernard, translator, *Le Traité de Bodhidharma*, Paris: Éditions Le Mail, 1986

Faure, Bernard, *The Rhetoric of Immediacy: A Cultural Critique of Chan/Zen Buddhism*, Princeton, New Jersey: Princeton University Press, 1991

Faure, Bernard, *The Will to Orthodoxy: A Cultural Genealogy of Northern Chan Buddhism*, translated by Phyllis Brooks, Stanford, California: Stanford University Press, 1997

Foulk, T. Griffith, and Robert H. Sharf, "On the Ritual Use of Ch'an Portraiture in Medieval China," *Cahiers d'Extrême-Asie* 7 (1993–1994)

Jenner, W.J.F., *Memories of Loyang: Yang Hsüan-chih and the Lost Capital (493–534)*, New York: Oxford University Press, and Oxford: Clarendon Press, 1981

Jorgensen, John, "The Earliest Text of Ch'an Buddhism: The Long Scroll," unpublished Master's dissertation, Canberra: Australian National University, 1979

Kido, Chūtaro, *Daruma to sono shosō*, Tokyo: Heigo shuppansha, 1932

Lachman, Charles, "Why Did the Patriarch Cross the River?: The Rushleaf Bodhidharma Reconsidered," *Asia Major* 3rd Series, 6:3 (1993)

McFarland, H. Neill, *Daruma: The Founder of Zen in Japanese Art and Popular Culture*, New York: Kodansha, 1987

McRae, John, *The Northern School and the Formation of Early Ch'an Buddhism* (Studies in East Asian Buddhism, 3), Honolulu: University of Hawaii Press, 1986

Sawada, Mizuho, *Bukkyō to Chūgoku bungaku*, Tokyo: Kokusho kankōkai, 1975

Sekiguchi, Shindai, *Daruma no kenkyū*, Tokyo: Iwanami shoten, 1967

Yanagida, Seizan, *Daruma* (Jinrui no chiteki, 16), Tokyo: Kodansha, 1981

Yoshioka, Yoshitoyo, *Dōkyō to Bukkyō 3*, Tokyo: Kokushokankōkai, 1976

# Bodhisattva

The term *bodhisattva* (Sanskrit, *bodhisattva*; Pāli, *bodhisatta*; Tibetan, *byang-chub sems dpa'*) consists of two words: *bodhi* (awakened, enlightened) and *sattva* (being). The word can be understood from the perspective of an effect and of a cause. From the perspective of an effect, the bodhisattva refers to one

Avalokiteśvara Bodhisattva, Candi Mendut, Jogjakarta, Java, Indonesia, c. A.D. 800, granite, over life-size.
Photo courtesy of Marylin M. Rhie

(*sattva*) who already is awakened (*bodhi*), and thus the Awakened (*bodhi*) Śākyamuni (*sattva*) can be understood as a bodhisattva. From the perspective of the cause, the term refers to a being (*sattva*) who is intent on attaining the awakened state (*bodhi*). Thus, although the bodhisattva in the causal state had not yet attained and experienced the awakened state, this bodhisattva is determined to attain Buddhahood (*bodhicittotpāda*) for his or her own benefit (*svārtha*) and for the benefit of others (*parārtha*) and thus diligently continues praxis (*yāna*) for those purposes (Yoshio Nishi, 1977).

The bodhisattva as an ideal came about in order to differentiate the *bodhisattva-yāna* that was expounded by the Mahāyāna tradition from that of the arhat ideal of the *śrāvaka-yāna* and the *pratyekabuddha-yāna*. The Mahāyāna tradition is rooted in the results of the second Buddhist council (approximately 100 years after Śākyamuni's death) held at Vaiśālī in which the Mahāsaṃghika school questioned and challenged the arhat ideal. It also criticized the monastic form of Buddhism and placed its emphasis on both the monastic and the ordinary believers of the

Statue of Maitreya in Alchi Monastery, Ladakh.
Photo courtesy of John Powers

Buddha-dharma. Thus, in contrast to *śrāvaka-yāna* (those who practice by listening to the Buddha-dharma) and *pratyekabuddha-yāna* (those who attempt to become awakened by themselves), the *bodhisattva-yāna* refers to the spiritual path of one who is intent on becoming awakened in order to benefit oneself and others. In other words, the bodhisattva in the state of an effect comes down from a lofty height to intermingle with the populace in order to benefit them, whereas bodhisattva in the state of a cause works diligently for the benefit of oneself and others.

A bodhisattva may be of the world (a worldly bodhisattva) or transworldly (nondual), neither attached to the world nor detached from it. The bodhisattvas that appear in the Buddhist scriptures are, above all, heroic. Very active and strong, they are usually handsome, educated, and virtuous and prove capable of expressing themselves well. In terms of praxis the bodhisattva practices the perfections (*pāramitā*), which according to some texts are counted as six and in others as ten. To the six perfections of (1) charity (*dāna*), (2) moral conduct (*śīla*), (3) patience (*kṣānti*), (4) endeavor (*vīrya*), (5) concentration (*dhyāna*), and (6) wisdom (*prajñā*) are added the perfections of (7) appropriate

action (*upāya*), (8) earnest wish or vow (*praṇidhāna*), (9) power (*bala*), and (10) highest knowledge (*jñāna*) to make up the ten perfections. These ten perfections, according to texts such as the *Daśabhūmi-sūtra*, are practiced in orderly sequence on each of the ten stages of spiritual development consisting of (1) the Joyful (*pramuditā*), (2) the Pure (*vimalā*), (3) the Luminous (*prabhākarī*), (4) the Radiant (*arciṣmatī*), (5) the Very Difficult to Conquer (*sudurjayā*), (6) the Coming Face to Face (*abhimukhī*), (7) the Far-going (*dūraṅgamā*), (8) the Immovable (*acalā*), (9) the Good Thought (*sādhumatī*), and (10) Dharma-cloud (*dharma-meghā*) (Har Dayal, 1932).

The first five of the six perfections refer to the bodhisattva's compassion (*karuṇā*) and the sixth one to wisdom (*prajñā*), these being the two qualities possessed by every bodhisattva. The first six can be seen as the cause, for without these six perfections a bodhisattva would not have the wing of compassion and the wing of wisdom to soar through the ordinary world in order to help others. Yet the mere act of soaring will not benefit sentient beings, for without the other four perfections as the effect, a bodhisattva would not be able to transfer to others (*parārtha*) what has been gained for one's self (*svārtha*). Thus, it is only when one possesses the three qualities of compassion (*karuṇā*), wisdom (*prajñā*), and the capacity to act appropriately (*upāya*) that such a being can become a bodhisattva who can benefit the world.

A bodhisattva who transfers merits to others for the sake of benefiting the spiritual growth of another can be called the "savior bodhisattva." It is this savior bodhisattva who vows not to gain the awakened state until all other sentient beings have gained such a state (*praṇidhāna*). It is this vow that kindles the bodhisattva's wish to attain the awakened mind (*bodhi-cittotpāda*).

There are generally four varieties of bodhisattvas: (1) Śākyamuni as a bodhisattva who has not yet attained the awakened state, (2) the general classification bodhisattvas in a previous life that appears in the *Former Life Stories* (*jātaka*), (3) a bodhisattva possessing a special path of practice, and (4) the Mahāyāna bodhisattva who has accomplished the various spiritual stages.

LESLIE S. KAWAMURA

*See also* Anticlericalism: Buddhist Perspectives; Body: Buddhist Perspectives; Buddha (Śākyamuni); Buddhism: Overview; Buddhist Schools/Traditions: China; Deities, Buddhist; Discourses (Sūtras): Mahāyāna; Holy Men/Holy Women: Buddhist Perspectives; Meditation: Buddhist Perspectives; Mountain Monasteries, Buddhist; Prayer: Buddhist Perspectives; Prophethood, Japanese Buddhist; Pure Land Buddhism; Scholastics, Buddhist; Self-Immolation, Buddhist; Sexuality: Buddhist Perspectives; Tibetan Lineages

**Further Reading**

The most thorough discussion on the bodhisattva doctrine in Sanskrit literature may be found in Har Dayal's *The Bodhisattva Doctrine in Buddhist Sanskrit Literature*, London: Kegan Paul, Trench, Trubner, 1932. A supplementary study into other forms of Buddhist works in China, Tibet, and Japan may be found in *The Bodhisattva*

*Doctrine in Buddhism*, edited by L.S. Kawamura, Waterloo, Ontario: Wilfrid Laurier University Press, 1981.

For a discussion on the cause-and-effect perspectives concerning the term *bodhisattva*, see Yoshio Nishi, *Daijō Bosatsu-dō no Kenkyu*, Kyoto: Heirakuji Shoten, 1977 (first published in 1968).

See Yuichi Kajiyama, *Bosatsu to yū-koto* (The Expression, Bodhisattva), Kyoto: Junbun Shoin, 1984, for a thorough discussion of these two aspects of a bodhisattva.

For a thorough discussion on the variety of stages, names of stages, and the perfections, see Har Dayal, *The Bodhisattva Doctrine in Buddhist Sanskrit Literature*, pp. 165–269 for the *pāramitā*s and pp. 270–291 for the *bhūmi*s.

# Body: Buddhist Perspectives

Like many other forms of Indian spiritual practice, Buddhist monastic training utilizes the body as an object of contemplation and as a locus of psychic transformation. Although known to distinguish bodily processes from psychic processes for the purpose of analysis, Buddhists do not ascribe to the notion (articulated by other religious traditions originating in India) that within every person exists an eternal psychic or pneumatic self that might be said to "have" or "occupy" a body. Thus, the path to nirvāṇa, or awakening, involves the entire human being as a psychophysical complex. The body is not separate from the mind; physical processes are dependent on mental processes and vice versa. Thus, for a Buddhist monk or nun to engage in meditation on the nature of the body and to cultivate bodily comportment through monastic discipline is to tread a path of physical, moral, and cognitive transformation.

Buddhist scriptures and meditation manuals composed for largely monastic audiences present a wide variety of meditations that focus on the body. Many involve mindful awareness of everyday activity – mindfulness of breathing, of the modes of deportment, such as standing and sitting, and of routine activities such as talking, eating, resting, and sleeping. Others are analytic in nature. The body can be broken down into its four material elements: earth/solidity, water/fluidity, fire/heat, and air/movement. Such analytic exercises are especially beneficial for overcoming the illusion of an enduring Self (Pāli, *attan*; Sanskrit, *ātman*). In the *Majjhima Nikāya*, the analysis of the body into its four material elements is likened to the quartering of an ox; once the ox is so divided, the generic concept of "flesh" militates against a recognition of the individuality of the ox. While members of other monastic communities in ancient India also practiced meditations on the physical elements of earth, water, fire, and air in the body, Indian Buddhists developed a uniquely Buddhist form of meditation on the body – a meditation praised in Buddhist scripture as the *sine qua non* of salvation. Known as the cultivation of mindfulness of the body (*kāyagatāsatibhā-*

*vanā*), this contemplative technique entails breaking the body down into its 32 constituent parts, including internal organs such as the heart, the liver, the spleen, and the kidneys. So detailed is the anatomic analysis in this cultivation of mindfulness of the body that scholars credit members of the early Buddhist monastic order (*sangha*) with a decisive role in the development of ancient Indian anatomic theory. Kenneth Zysk (1991) has argued that concern with ritual impurity limited the extent to which other (namely, brahminic or proto-Hindu) religious specialists could serve as healers or carry out empirical studies based on dissection. Strictures concerning the handling of bodily wastes from persons of different social classes and the disposal of dead bodies limited what brahminic caregivers could provide in the way of medical care and empirical research. With their relative (but, as we will see shortly, certainly not absolute) indifference to brahminic purity strictures, members of the Buddhist *sangha* garnered a great deal of empirical knowledge of bodily processes and led the way in medical advances.

*The Ambiguity of the Body*
If Zysk is correct in asserting that Buddhist monastic communities in India were less hampered by strictures concerning the handling of bodily wastes and dead bodies, this is not to say that members of the Buddhist *sangha* regarded the body as intrinsically valuable or that their conceptions of the body were untouched by concerns about bodily purity and pollution (Collins, 1997; Williams, 1997; Wilson, 1996). Cultivating revulsion from the body by noting with disgust the emissions from various apertures of the body, especially those below the navel, constitutes a preliminary stage of psychophysical training practiced by monastics of virtually all Buddhist denominations. With its orifices emitting mucous, ear wax, sweat, excrement, and the like, the body is conventionally envisaged as a festering pustule, a boil with many openings leaking pus. For monks and nuns who are afflicted by sensual desire, who view bodily pleasures such as eating, bathing, self-adornment, and sexual activity as inherently satisfying, to develop a sense of aversion toward the body by visualizing it as a miasmic pustule or by contemplating corpses in various stages of putrefaction is recommended as an antidote to sensuality. If the generic human body is likened to a leaky bag of filth, the female body is regarded as even more miasmic; this perception is perhaps due to the fact that it has an additional aperture lacking in males, an aperture prone to emitting periodic quantities of blood (Faure, 1998). In any case literary representations of meditations on the loathsomeness of the body tend to be overwhelmingly androcentric (Wilson, 1996). Such narratives, embedded in hagiographies of various denominations, brim with scenes of dying and diseased women observed by male spectators. Conversely male bodies rarely serve as objects of contemplation for women in these narratives. Instead women contemplating the foulness of the body observe their own aging bodies or those of other women. While Buddhist discourse declares all bodies to be impermanent and subject to disease, such hagiographies suggest nothing exists that is so effective as a female body to instantiate this cardinal truth.

As revolting as many of these accounts might be, one should not assume that Buddhists are phobic about the body. The aversion that such accounts induce is not an end in itself but a remedy for hedonism. Ultimately the outlook that meditators seek is neither attraction nor revulsion but indifference. Meditation on the repulsiveness of the body is sometimes described as a "bitter medicine" that may be discontinued once greed for bodily pleasures has abated. After having served its purpose as a corrective practice, disgust for the body ideally should give way to a more neutral attitude. Moreover, in comparison with the bodies of nonhumans, the human body has much to recommend it. Buddhists across Asia recognize that human birth is rare, and many Buddhists regard human embodiment as an essential prerequisite for achieving awakening (the exception here being eastern Asian Buddhists who recognize the possibility of inherent Buddhahood within the plant and animal kingdoms). Although our bodies might be of a gross material nature compared to those of divine beings dwelling in heavenly realms, we humans enjoy opportunities for awakening that gods and goddesses lack by virtue of the sublime material conditions in which they live. Rebirth as a god or goddess is a worthy goal for laity who might not be in immediate pursuit of awakening, but it holds little appeal for those monks and nuns who do not wish to postpone their awakening by hundreds of years. For them embodiment as a human being is a precious opportunity not to be wasted.

In a word much depends on perspective when evaluating the status of the human body for Buddhists. If treated as an intrinsically valuable thing, the body can obstruct the experience of awakening, preventing one from seeing things as they really are. However, when used instrumentally as a locus of meditation and insight, the body has immense value, more precious than a wish-fulfilling jewel. The Buddha is reported to have declared that the body, with its attendant psychic processes, is the locus of salvation, the path to a transcendent, deathless condition (Collins, 1997).

### Subtle Bodies, Salvific Bodies

Thus, the body might present the face of friend or foe, depending on what goals one wishes to achieve and how effectively one invests the body's resources in achieving those goals. Monastic training, like any regimen of physical training, develops capacities unknown to those without self-discipline. If one dedicates oneself to the disciplined cultivation of Buddhist virtues (i.e., salutary physical, moral, and cognitive states), those virtues will be instantiated in the form and appearance of one's body. As Susanne Mrozik (1998) argues, Buddhist texts promote the goal of bodily transformation, promising those who cultivate virtue sweet-smelling, beautiful, and healthy bodies, even while teaching that in their natural condition all bodies are smelly, impermanent havens of disease and death. Given this emphasis on bodily transformation through the cultivation of virtue, it should come as no surprise that Buddhists advocate contact with and contemplation of the bodies of Buddhas and saints known as arhats and bodhisattvas. Contact with such beings is salutary not only because such beings are virtuous and helpful but also because their discipline has transformed them to the point where their bodies exude medicinal effects. Like walking apothecaries Buddhists saints are said to heal disease on contact with the afflicted just as their words heal the disease (Pāli, dukkha; Sanskrit, duḥkka) that according to Buddhists afflicts all unawakened beings. Accounts of the salutary effects of beholding Buddhas, arhats (worthy ones), and bodhisattvas (future Buddhas) – or even formulating the aspiration to have such experiences – are commonplace in many genres of Buddhist literature. Seeing their radiant skin, bright eyes, and decorous deportment engenders serenity and joy; the sight is said to be at once tranquilizing and stimulating. This Buddhist emphasis on the benefits of seeing the body of the religious virtuoso can in part be explained by the southern Asian milieu in which Buddhism arose: many southern Asian religious traditions advocate the practice of participatory seeing (Hindi, darśan), whereby the observer participates in the sacrality of the observed by visual contact. If one cannot gaze on the bodies of Buddhist saints, one can nevertheless recollect the features of the body of the Buddha. The contemplative practice of recollecting the extraordinary features of the body of the Buddha, with its 32 major and 80 minor distinguishing marks, is common to all Buddhist traditions. The Buddha is also embodied in his teachings (Pali, dhamma; Sanskrit, dharma). Although some Buddhists insist that this body of teaching is the only proper object of reverence and that adoration of the physical form is misguided, Kevin Trainor (1997) notes that textual passages warning against attachment to the Buddha's physical form are outnumbered by passages advocating such devotion.

### The Gift of the Body

In accordance with the principle that the body has no intrinsic value but gains value through the manner in which it is used, Buddhists extol the practice of offering one's body to others out of compassion. Tales of the former lives of the Buddha narrate many occasions in which the Buddha-to-be offered his flesh to starving animals at the expense of his life. Where Theravāda Buddhists regard such altruistic practices as praiseworthy but not necessarily to be imitated, Mahāyāna Buddhists, committed to the ideal of postponing one's own final awakening out of compassion for all sentient beings, regard self-sacrifice as an essential component of the Buddhist path. In addition to offering their bodies as food for starving beings, followers of the bodhisattva path also gain merit by burning the body as an act of religious devotion. The locus classicus for the practice of self-immolation is an incident narrated in the Saddharmapuṇḍarika, or Lotus Sūtra. In a previous life the bodhisattva Bhaiṣajyarāja ingested copious amounts of flammable substances and then set fire to his body as an offering to the Buddhas. During the Vietnam war Vietnamese monks and nuns attracted considerable attention to their cause by performing public self-immolations in protest against the Diem regime, which had imposed restrictive measures on the practice of Buddhism and the activities of Buddhist monks and nuns. The burning of the entire body or parts of the body, such as an arm or a finger, is also highly extolled by Chinese Buddhists. In Chinese Buddhist monastic ordinations, the ordinand's willingness to make such an offering is signaled by the burning of several places on the head with moxa. Clearly the body becomes an essential element of religious practice where the sacrifice of life and limb for the sake of others is advocated. However, even without committing oneself to such heroic measures, one cannot embark on the bodhisattva path without regarding the body as an essential means of fulfilling one's bodhisattva vows. Central to the vows of the bodhisattva is the stated willingness to undergo billions of repeated embodiments in the cycle of rebirth (samsara) in order to help others achieve awakening. Paul Williams concludes that for Mahāyāna Buddhists, "compassion requires some sort of active embodiment" (Williams, 1997).

In contrast to the Mahāyānist emphasis on postponing final awakening for aeons and aeons, Buddhist Tantrism (Vajrayāna) emphasizes speed of attainment, promising the achievement of Buddhahood in one lifetime. The body is said to contain the seeds of Buddhahood, the prerequisites for achieving full awakening in this lifetime. Thus, the human body as a focus of practice is central to Vajrayāna Buddhism. Practitioners regard the body as a microcosm of the universe, with all its gods, goddesses, and other powerful beings. Such beings are invoked and their powers harnessed for the goal of full awakening by touching various parts of the body using special hand gestures and by chanting mantras or sacred utterances.

LIZ WILSON

*See also* Bodhisattva; Buddhism: Overview; Gestures, Buddhist; Hygiene: Buddhist Perspectives; Images: Buddhist Perspectives; Mantras; Meditation: Buddhist Perspectives; Self-Immolation, Buddhist; Sexuality: Buddhist Perspectives; Virtues, Buddhist; Women's Monasteries: Buddhist

**Further Reading**

Collins, Steven, "The Body in Theravāda Buddhist Monasticism," in *Religion and the Body* (Cambridge Studies in Religious Traditions, 8), edited by Sarah Coakley, Cambridge and New York: Cambridge University Press, 1997

Das, Veena, "Paradigms of Body Symbolism: An Analysis of Selected Themes in Hindu Culture," in *Indian Religion* (Collected Papers on South Asia, 7), edited by Richard Burghart and Audrey Canlie, London: Curzon, and New York: St. Martin's Press, 1985

Dissanayake, Wimal, "Self and Body in Theravāda Buddhism," in *Self as Body in Asian Theory and Practice* (SUNY Series: The Body in Culture, History, and Religion), edited by Dissanayake, Thomas P. Kasulis, and Roger T. Aimes, Albany: State University of New York Press, 1993

Faure, Bernard, *The Red Thread: Buddhist Approaches to Sexuality*, Princeton, New Jersey: Princeton University Press, 1998

Mrozik, Susanne, "The Relationship between Morality and the Body in Monastic Training According to the Śikṣāsamuccaya," Ph.D. diss., Harvard University, 1998

Pye, Michael, "Perceptions of the Body in Japanese Religion," in *Religion and the Body* (Cambridge Studies in Religious Traditions, 8), edited by Sarah Coakley, Cambridge and New York: Cambridge University Press, 1997

Trainor, Kevin, *Relics, Ritual, and Representation in Buddhism: Rematerializing the Sri Lankan Theravāda Tradition* (Cambridge Studies in Religious Traditions, 10), Cambridge and New York: Cambridge University Press, 1997

Trenckner, V., and Robert Chalmers, editors, *The Majjhima-Nikāya* (Pali Text Society), 4 vols., London: Frowde, 1888–1925; Boston: Routledge and Kegan Paul, 1974

Wijayaratna, Môhan, *Buddhist Monastic Life: According to the Texts of the Theravāda Tradition*, translated by Claude Grangier and Steven Collins, Cambridge and New York: Cambridge University Press, 1990

Williams, Paul, "Some Mahayana Buddhist Perspectives on the Body," in *Religion and the Body* (Cambridge Studies in Religious Traditions, 8), edited by Sarah Coakley, Cambridge and New York: Cambridge University Press, 1997

Wilson, Liz, *Charming Cadavers: Horrific Configurations of the Feminine in Indian Buddhist Hagiographic Literature*, Chicago: University of Chicago Press, 1996

Zysk, Kenneth, *Asceticism and Healing in Ancient India: Medicine in the Buddhist Monastery*, New York: Oxford University Press, 1991; corrected edition, Delhi: Motilal Banarsidass, 1998

# Body: Christian Perspectives

The "body" is the corporeal, material element in a human being. It is contrasted traditionally to the soul, as immaterial and immortal, and (especially since Descartes) to the mind, as the seat of consciousness. The drives, or passions, of the body tend to bridge this divide, but it was customary in the tradition to assign to the body those drives most directly connected to its maintenance and propagation, certainly the "physical" appetites of eating and sexuality, and often drives that, although not obviously physical, were thought to arise from them, such as anger and aggression.

The richest biblical material for a theology of the body is to be found in St. Paul. His emphasis on the resurrection of the body (2 Cor. 15), on the dignity of the body as the temple of the Holy Spirit (1 Cor. 6), and on the link between the physical body and the body of Christ (1 Cor. 12) laid the foundation for a high valuation of the body in Christianity. Modern interpretations of Paul's primary word for body – *sôma* – generally try to avoid soul-body dualism by taking the term as often as possible to refer to the human person as a whole; this obscures Paul's conviction that the material body possesses significance and dignity in its own right. In contrast Paul's use of another word for the physical organism – *sarx* (flesh) – might appear to denigrate the body, as he often uses the word to refer not only to what is transient in human life but also to what is positively sinful. The dominant Christian interpretation has always been to see this as a case of synecdoche, by which *sarx* refers to the whole person rather than one part of it; as such the term brings out the more negative aspects of human existence without linking them specifically to embodiment. Recent commentary (as in Martin's *The Corinthian Body*, 1995) has detected in Paul a picture of sin as a form of infection that invades the person from outside through the limbs of the body; the implication of this picture is that the body is not sinful in itself but is more easily invaded and taken over than what Paul calls the "mind" or "inner man." The physical vulnerability and mortality of the body make it a symbol for moral weakness in human beings. The consequence is an anxiety over the body as the permeable part of ourselves, singularly open to pollution, to an invasion by demonic forces most obviously displayed in disease and improper sexual relations. This picture was strongly reinforced by the sectarian spirit of early Christianity: the concern to preserve the holiness of the Church as the body of Christ from contamination by pagan society spilled over into anxiety over the purity of the physical body. Sexual renunciation and frequent fasting were recognized by the end of the second century as essential elements for a personal holiness that, going beyond the more modest requirements of the moral law, could embody the holiness of the Church itself.

In the monastic movement of the fourth and subsequent centuries, this picture became more subtle and psychologically perceptive. Such key texts as the *Letters* of St. Antony (c. 251–356), the *Conferences* of John Cassian (c. 360–c. 435), and *The Spiritual Ladder* of John Climacus (c. 570–c. 649) insist that sin originates in the will rather than the body but still attach great value to the mortification of the body on the grounds that the soul can

Lavabo, inside the cloister of the Cistercian Abbey of Lilienfeld, Austria, 13th century.
Photo courtesy of Chris Schabel

be acted on only through the body and that the body provides the best gauge of the spiritual progress of the inner man, which resists direct inspection. Fasting is established as the first of the virtues in the sense that it must be the initial step in a gradual process through which the self is discovered and purified. This makes the body both the locus of sin and the means for overcoming it.

What was the ideal state of the body? The greatest of the later Byzantine theologians, Gregory Palamas (1296–1359), defended an asceticism that aimed to reduce the body's dependence on physical stimuli from outside and to enable it to share in the soul's union with God. Contemporary Western speculation on the state of the body after the resurrection pictured a perfected body that has become changeless, stable, and impermeable with no need for nourishment, let alone sex. All these ideas attempted to transform the body into the perfect image of the sanctified soul; the messiness and changeability of flesh and blood, the dependence of the body on eating and digestion, its self-perpetuation through sex and procreation – all these characteristics were excluded as alien to the body in its "true" nature, that is, the nature that it possessed (at least in part) before the Fall and that it is destined to recover after the resurrection. In this context medieval hagiography delighted in saints who anticipated the age to come by sexual renunciation and such improbable feats as surviving on no food beyond the Eucharist. Saint Catherine of Siena (c. 1347–1380) died prematurely as a result of fasting from food and drink for a whole month. Modern writers have asked whether she and similar female saints of the later medieval period were the victims of what is now diagnosed as anorexia nervosa. However, what needs historical explanation is not just the psychological peculiarities of individuals but the attitude of a whole culture that stimulated pious women to express their spirituality through feats of fasting.

Emphasis on the instability and permeability of the body and its need to be dominated and ultimately remade by the soul had serious consequences for the status of women, as the relation of body to soul was thought to be reflected in the relation between women and men. Most cultures think of women as more firmly embedded in the physical world than men (most obviously in their role in childbearing) and of men as more capable of purely rational thought. This means that any spirituality that emphasizes the need for containing the passions of the body and attaining rational self-mastery plays into the hands of social conservatives who want to maintain the traditional hierarchy of the sexes. The developing cult of Our Lady, which unfolded in stages between the 12th and 19th centuries, might have restored a sense of the special dignity of the body and of woman as specially linked to the body, but this was frustrated by the development of a Mariology that, in contrast to the teaching of the Church fathers, played down the physical aspect of Mary's motherhood in favor of an emphasis on her faith and obedience.

The Second Vatican Council (1962–1965) opened the Catholic Church to a modern world that is concerned with social equality and personal freedom and thus is critical of the hierarchical structure of traditional society and of the associated emphasis on the subordination of body to mind. The body has been "liberated" through a widespread rejection of traditional ascetic practices, such as fasting and uncomfortable postures during prayer. However, behind the rhetoric is a retrograde tendency to think that the bodily, material element in our makeup deserves attention only insofar as it has an effect on the mind and feelings, as if it has no importance in itself. The body is further sidelined through optimistic spiritualities that emphasize the constant opportunities for growth and development: the aging body of the middle-aged and elderly was valued in traditional Christianity as a constant lesson in patience and humility, but in the context of the modern emphasis on growth and freedom it becomes an unwelcome appendage that is not to be allowed to diminish our self-image.

The abandonment of many ascetic practices traditional in Christianity, with their concern to act on the will through the body, has been balanced to a certain extent by the introduction into Christian spirituality of such Eastern practices as yoga and tai chi. It is as if, in order to become respectable again, asceticism has to break its link with the Christian tradition and appeal to outside sources. Sadly, traditional asceticism has been discredited by its association with a social politics concerned to promote self-discipline as part of submission to social control.

The body is not only the immediate object of self-mortification in traditions that emphasize self-discipline but also the immediate object of external coercion and control. The history of the body is in part the history of how society has sought to discipline and control its members. The regimented diets in traditional monastic communities were intended not only to tame the passions in the interests of self-discipline but also to express the subjection of the individual to the will of the community. The emphasis on moderation in eating and plainness of diet in pious households from the 17th to the 19th century was linked to the need of capitalist society for a disciplined and submissive workforce. Such influences are inevitable. The reaction in late 20th-century society against restraint in food and sex represents a reassertion of individual freedom only in part: it reflects also the economic interests of producers, who need a buoyant market of consumers insatiable in their quest for pleasure. Contemporary Christians in Western society have almost no interest in traditional asceticism, but the obsession with bodily health that they share with their non-Christian contemporaries becomes a new form of loss of freedom: it reflects the economic interests of the providers of "healthy" foods (usually the more expensive) and the interests of the medical profession, which practices a system of medicine that reduces the patient to a passive body in its power.

The third millennium needs a new spirituality of the body that will simultaneously pay more respect to the irreducible physicality of the body and restore its freedom. A positive valuation of the body as we actually experience it would need to start with the changeableness and permeability of the body as an index of the spiritual life, and this, it could be argued, must include openness to change, a surrender of rational self-control,

and a self-exposure to the world in loving trust in the providence of God. The traditional stereotype of women as more changeable and more emotional than men, as less self-assertive and more endowed with sympathy and the spirit of accommodation, could actually play a useful role here (on the condition that it is not imposed on all women): for instead of concluding that women need to be directed by men, the way could be opened for a reshaping of social relations and a civilizing of society through according greater weight to women's experience and the cultivation of "feminine" qualities or virtues.

Meanwhile the freeing of the body from the moral pressures of a restrictive ethic intensely suspicious of pleasure and emotion needs to be completed by a liberation of the body from the pressures of consumer society and the tyranny of the medical profession. Some real degree of bodily self-control needs to be practiced to give us the freedom to choose between pleasures. Meanwhile the perceived link between bodily health and the well-being of the person needs to be loosened up: we need to learn to react to disease or decay not by a panicky surrender of our bodies to the latest fads in medical treatment but by a balanced response in which the type and length of treatment remain the free choice of the patient. The traditional spirituality of accepting illness and disability in union with the Passion of Christ and in solidarity with the poor and afflicted remains an essential part of a healthy spirituality that upholds human dignity and freedom.

RICHARD M. PRICE

*See also* Antony, St.; Asceticism: Christian Perspectives; Cassian, John; Climacus, John, St.; Palamas, Gregory, St.; Relics, Christian Monastic; Spirituality: Eastern Christian; Transvestite Saints

## Further Reading

Ashley, Benedict M., *Theologies of the Body: Humanist and Christian*, St. Louis, Missouri: Pope John Center, 1985

Brown, Peter, *The Body and Society: Men, Women, and Sexual Renunciation in Early Christianity* (Lectures on the History of Religions, new series, number 13), New York: Columbia University Press, 1988

Bynum, Caroline Walker, *Holy Feast and Holy Fast: The Religious Significance of Food to Medieval Women* (The New Historicism: Studies in Cultural Poetics), Berkeley: University of California Press, 1987

Bynum, Caroline Walker, *The Resurrection of the Body in Western Christianity, 200–1336* (Lectures on the History of Religions, new series, number 15), New York: Columbia University Press, 1995

Clément, Olivier, *Corps de mort et de gloire: petite introduction à une théopoétique du corps*, Paris: Desclée de Brouwer, 1995

Coakley, Sarah, editor, *Religion and the Body* (Cambridge Studies in Religious Traditions, 8), Cambridge and New York: Cambridge University Press, 1997

Martin, Dale B., *The Corinthian Body*, New Haven, Connecticut: Yale University Press, 1995

# Bön, Influence of

The Bön religion is proclaimed to have been well established in Tibet by the time Buddhism arrived there in the seventh century A.D. The question of Bön origins has generated lengthy discussions among both Tibetan and Euro-American scholars, but because Buddhism was victorious over Bön, what we get are schemes of polemical work that remain hostile to the Bön religion. Dan Martin, who has studied this topic extensively, writes, "[s]tatements about the 'primitive animism of Bon' and its later 'transformation' or 'accommodation' (or 'plagiarism') have been repeated so often that they have achieved a status of cultural Truth" (Martin, 1991). Martin proposes that the way Bön existed during the last millennium "represents an unusual, yet quite legitimate transmission of Buddhist teachings ultimately based on little-known Central Asian Buddhist traditions" (Martin, 1994).

The relationship between *bön* and *chös* – both being equivalents for the Sanskrit word *dharma* (in the sense of Truth or Teachings about Truth) for Bönpos and Buddhists, respectively – remains a point of controversy even today. Some scholars, such as Per Kvaerne, consider Bön a non-Buddhist religion, justifying their claim by emphasizing such aspects as "concepts of religious authority, legitimation and history rather than rituals, metaphysical doctrine and monastic discipline" (Kvaerne, 1996). However, others, such as Martin, Snellgrove, and Kvaerne, in earlier publications, describe Bön as a Buddhist sect (albeit an unorthodox one) based on practice and doctrinal similarities. This article does not entirely endorse any of these stands but rather acknowledges these different perspectives toward teachings that share similar traits. Clearly, further historical research is needed. It seems that in the past both Tibetan and Euro-American scholars have neglected to examine Bön texts, silencing the tradition by deeming these texts to be unworthy of their interest. Some doorways, such as the eastern Tibetan "nonsectarian" (*ris med*) movement of the 19th century and the present Dalai Lama's recognition of Bön as the fifth Tibetan tradition might be helpful in bringing a broader acceptance and thus understanding of the Bön tradition as a whole.

The term *bön* has the same range of connotations for its adherents (Bönpos) as *chös* has for the Buddhists. Furthermore,

[f]or the Bonpos especially, the Dharma, whether it is called "chos" or "bon" in Tibetan, is not something sectarian, but it truly represents a Primordial Revelation which is again and again revealed throughout time and history. It is not only primordial, but perennial. The Dharma is not simply the unique product of a particular historical period, namely, [B.C.] sixth century North India. (Reynolds, 1991)

Significantly no word for "Buddhism" exists in Tibetan. Both the Bönpos and the Buddhists utilize the term "Buddha" (*sangs rgyas*) to define he or she who is enlightened or awakened. Etymologically "Buddha" refers to the experience of "clearing away" (*sangs*) the ignorance that obscures one's primordial awareness and "expands" (*rgyas*) its enlightened qualities. In other words Bön and Chös can be seen as different ways of expressing the teachings of an enlightened being, a Buddha, while affirming too, as most Tibetans believe, that there are as many buddhas as there are stars in the sky.

The traditional Bön account is that 18,000 years ago the Buddha Tonpa Shenrab Miwoche (sTon pa gshen rab mi bo che) came to this world to a region of central Asia known as Olmo Lungring ('Ol mo lung ring). Some believe this to be a mythic land described as an eight-petaled lotus under a sky that appears like an eight-spoked wheel. *Ol* symbolizes the unborn, *mo* the undiminishing, *lung* the prophetic words of Tonpa Shenrab, and *ring* his everlasting compassion. Bönpos themselves seem to believe that Olmo Lungring is both this imaginary mandala-like land and a part of this world, located to the west of Tibet. In the center of Olmo Lungring rises Mount Yungdrung Gutseg (g.Yung drung dgu brtsegs), the pyramid of nine swastikas. The swastika, or *yungdrung*, is a symbol of the indestructibility and everlasting wisdom of Bön, and the nine represents the nine kinds of teachings or vehicles that were taught by Tonpa Shenrab. These teachings spread throughout all of central Asia, first to the regions of Tazig (sTag gzig) and Zhang Zhung (Zhang zhung) and then to Tibet, Kashmir, India, and China. The major part of Bön literature is claimed to have been translated from the sacred language of Zhang Zhung, and today many Bön texts still have Zhang Zhung words interspersed with Tibetan. Some of their texts are claimed to have undergone a triple translation from Tazig to Zhang Zhung to Tibetan and others a quadruple one, originating in the divine language (*lha'i skad*) to Sanskrit and then to Tazig, to Zhang Zhung, and to Tibetan.

In these accounts Tonpa Shenrab was manifested as Chimed Tsugphud ('Chi med gtsug phud, "Immortal [Master] with a Top-knot") in his previous life, and Śākyamuni Buddha was a disciple of his called Sangwa Dupa (gSang ba 'dus pa, "Essential Secret"). After that life, during Tonpa Shenrab's time, Śākyamuni Buddha was again one of his main disciples, named Lhabu Dampa Tobkarpo (Lha'i bu dam pa tob dkar po, "The White Pure Son of the Gods"). The latter asked his teacher what could he do to help sentient beings, and Tonpa Shenrab told him that he should help the people in India, who were following religion with the wrong view. For that purpose Tonpa Shenrab gave Lhabu Dampa Tobkarpo an initiation so that in his future lives he would not forget the teachings. Thus, he was born in India as prince of the Sakya clan and taught following the instructions given previously to him by his teacher, Tonpa Shenrab, benefiting many sentient beings.

Bön teachings have been preserved mostly in Zhang Zhung (which was later conquered by Tibet) and Tibet itself. Some scholars, such as Martin and Reynolds, mention a probable connection between the term *bön* and central Asia. They instance Tazig (today's Iran) and the Sogdian/Iranian word *bwn*, meaning "dharma." Thus, "the Tibetan word *bon* might be a borrowing

Menri Monastery in Dolanji, India, of Buddha Tonpa Shenrab Miwoche, founder of the Bön religion.
Photo courtesy of Ligmincha Institute

from Iranian Buddhists" (Martin, 1994), a notion that would solidify the traditional claim that Bön originated in the Tazig area.

It is difficult to determine to what extent Bön and Chös incorporate each other or to locate where the overlapping between them is. Bön traditional accounts claim that Tonpa Shenrab taught the cycles of the Nine Vehicles or *yana*s (*theg pa dgu*) and the Five Doors (*sgo lnga*). The former and more popular cycle consists of four causal vehicles (*rgyu'i bon*, sometimes called "Shamanic" by Euro-American scholars) that included divination, astrology, medicine, ritual, and so on and that led to the four result vehicles (*'bras bu'i bon*) of the sūtras and tantras, and culminated in dzogchen (*rdzogs chen*, "Great Completeness"). Because all nine vehicles were taught by Tonpa Shenrab, they are all considered as genuine ways toward enlightenment.

Bönpos themselves distinguish three kinds of Bön, namely, primitive Bön; Yungdrung (g.yung drung), or eternal, Bön; and new Bön (bon gsar). Primitive Bön they see as an ensemble of the popular religions; Yungdrung Bön is the religion that claims its origin in the Buddha Tonpa Shenrab and sees itself as a separate religion from Buddhism, even when acknowledging similarities; and new Bön is the movement that began around the 16th century from the interaction and amalgamation between Yung-

drung Bön and Buddhism, especially with what later became the Nyingma (rNying ma) tradition.

Euro-American scholars usually doubt the accuracy of the dating that Yungdrung Bön claims for its structure of the nine vehicles, usually pushing the date not earlier than the eighth or even the tenth century A.D. Moreover Buddhists do not claim the causal vehicles as part of their teachings. In fact, even though they have incorporated some of those practices (and that is most likely what makes Tibetan Buddhism so unique in comparison to other forms of Buddhism), they appear to have a jealous feeling of exclusivity toward what in Yungdrung Bön are called the result vehicles. Euro-American scholars, especially those who consider Bön an unorthodox form of Buddhism, see the Bön teachings coming from the same source as Buddhism (namely, from Śākyamuni) but having arrived in Tibet at different times and through different routes, as Martin and others propose. Snellgrove, likely the creator of this theory, believes that the teachings that were later called Bön were a form of Buddhism (mainly tantric) that penetrated first to Zhang Zhung. When propagated to central Tibet, the teachings clashed with the Buddhism that had come directly from India. Clearly a Bön religion existed in Tibet before the arrival of Buddhism around the seventh to eighth century, but it is hard to determine what teachings functioned under the name of Bön. In particular there is debate about whether to include the dzogchen teachings, an issue that also occurs with dzogchen in the Buddhist traditions. The Bön tradition presents three dzogchen systems: the earliest and most important is the Oral Transmission of Zhang Zhung (*Zhang zhung snyan rgyud*), which is traced to the eighth century; the other two, Instructions on the *A* (*A khrid*) and Great Completion (*rDzog chen*), go back to the 11th century. Today Yungdrung Bön consists of all nine vehicles, and thus a common misunderstanding limits the Bön religion to the four solely causal or "shamanic" vehicles. This view will not be supported here, nor will the equally problematic identification of all Bön practitioners with the four "result vehicles."

Bön practitioners include both monks and lay practitioners. The latter are usually known as *nagpa*s (*sngags pa*) or tantric practitioners, who might live in organized communities or in solitude. They have very few vows in comparison with the monks; they can marry, have children, and work in the world; but they also spend a great deal of time in retreat and performing rituals for the villagers. There are also *chöpa*s, or practitioners of *chö* (*gcod*), whose practice centers in reducing one's own ego. *Chöpa*s are mostly *nagpa*s, but occasionally monks also practice *chö*.

This presentation of the Bön religion agrees with Kvaerne when he asserts that

Bon was not a sinister perversion of Buddhism, but rather an eclectic tradition which, unlike Buddhism in Tibet, insisted on accentuating rather than denying its pre-Buddhist elements. (Kvaerne, 1994)

M. ALEJANDRO CHAOUL-REICH

*See also* Asia, Central; Bön Monasticism; Buddhist Schools/Traditions: Tibet; Deities, Buddhist; Nepal: History; Tibet: History; Tibetan Lineages

**Further Reading**

Blondeau, Anne-Marie, "Les Religions du Tibet," in *Histoire des religions*, volume 3, edited by Henri-Charles Puech, Paris: Gallimard, 1976

Karmay, Samten, "A General Introduction to the Bon Doctrine," *The Memoirs of Toyo Bunko* 33 (1975)

Kvaerne, Per, "The Bon Religion of Tibet: A Survey of Research," in *The Buddhist Forum*, volume 3, edited by T. Skorupski and U. Pagel, London: School of Oriental and African Studies, University of London, 1994

Kvaerne, Per, *The Bon Religion of Tibet: The Iconography of a Living Tradition*, Boston and London: Shambhala, 1996

Martin, Daniel, "The Emergence of Bon and the Tibetan Polemical Tradition," Ph.D. Diss., Indiana University, 1991

Martin, Daniel, *Mandala Cosmogony, Human Body, Good Thought and the Revelation of the Secret Mother Tantras of Bon*, Wiesbaden: Harrassowitz, 1994

Norbu, Namkhai, *The Necklace of gZi: A Cultural History of Tibet*, Dharamsala, India: Information Office of His Holiness the Dalai Lama, 1981

Reynolds, John Myrdhin, *Yungdrung Bon, The Eternal Tradition: The Ancient Pre-Buddhist Religion of Central Asia and Tibet: Its History, Teachings, and Literature*, Freehold, New Jersey: Bompo Translation Project, 1991

Snellgrove, David, *The Nine Ways of Bon*, London and New York: Oxford University Press, 1967

Snellgrove, David, and Hugh Richardson, *A Cultural History of Tibet*, Boston and London: Shambhala, 1968

Stein, Rolf, *Tibetan Civilization*, translated by J.E. Stapleton Driver, Stanford, California: Stanford University Press, 1972

Tucci, Giuseppe, *The Religions of Tibet*, translated by Geoffrey Samuel, Berkeley: University of California Press, and London: Routledge and Kegan Paul, 1980

# Bön Monasticism

This indigenous tradition of Tibet traces its first monastic incursions to the late tenth century A.D., establishing its first large Bön monastic institution, Yeru Wensakha (g.Yas ru dben sa kha), in 1072. Yeru Wensakha flourished in central Tibet until it was destroyed by floods in 1386. In 1405 Menri (sMan ri) became the most important Bön monastery in central Tibet, reviving Yeru Wensakha's tradition, and located near its predecessor. In 1834 Yungdrung Ling (g.Yung drung ling) was instituted as another important Bön monastic seat in central Tibet continuing with Menri's tradition. Other monasteries were also established throughout Tibet, especially in the regions of Khyungpo, Kham, Amdo, Gyarong, and Hor, so that by the beginning of the 20th century 330 Bön monasteries existed in Tibet.

Notwithstanding what some scholars claim, it seems that dialectical debate training, or "definitions" (*mtshan nyid*), was present in the Bön monastic training from its inception, although probably not with the sophistication that the Gelukpa (dGe lugs pa) school of Tibetan Buddhism, brought in the 14th and 15th centuries. The latter influenced also Bön monastic training as a whole. Nevertheless the Bönpos (Bön followers) maintained their uniqueness because their system of logic and debate was based ultimately on the higher teachings of Dzogchen (rDzogs chen), or the Great Completeness school.

Bön higher teachings can be divided into three – the sutric path of renunciation, the tantric path of transformation, and the dzogchen path of self-liberation – and their curriculum included the intellectual understanding and the meditative experience of all three paths. These are structured under a system of nine vehicles (*theg pa'i dgu*) with three different presentations: the Northern Treasure (*byang gter*), the Central Treasure (*dbus gter*), and the Southern Treasure (*lho gter*), so called according to their place of rediscovery. The Northern Treasure is compiled from texts rediscovered in Zhang Zhung and northern Tibet, the Southern Treasure from texts rediscovered in Bhutan and the southern area of Tibet, and the Central Treasure from texts rediscovered in central Tibetan areas close to the Buddhist Monastery of Samye (bSam yas). These three nine-way divisions have their path delineated in steps of sūtra, tantra, and dzogchen, the latter always being the highest, the "unsurpass-able" way. The Southern Treasure is found in the "Glorious" (*gZi brjid*), the long biography of the founding Buddha Tonpa Shenrab (sTon pa gshen rab mi bo che), and is the most distinctive, inclusive, and widely used. It is also the most well known among Euro-American scholars, as it was partially translated into English as *The Nine Ways of Bon* (1967) by the English Tibetologist David Snellgrove in collaboration with Lopon Tenzin Namdak. The Central and the Northern Treasures divide the nine vehicles into three sets (of three vehicles each), calling them external, internal, and secret. The Central Treasure shows more similarities with the Nyingma (rNying ma) nine-way, in which the external includes the sūtra teachings of Mahāyāna and Hīnayāna, the internal includes the lower tantras, and the secret includes the higher tantras (where the last vehicle is dzogchen). The Northern Treasure has pretty much disappeared or declined, and in it the external refers to the codes of ethics, or vinaya, the internal represents the sūtra teachings, and the secret the treasure (*mdzod*), which here represents the dzogchen teachings. The Central Treasure is still taught in some monasteries, but the Southern one is more prevalent and possibly the one that best epitomizes the Bön spirit.

The Southern Treasure is divided into four causal vehicles (*rgyu'i bon*), the subsequent four result vehicles (*'bras bu'i bon*), and culminates in dzogchen. The four causal vehicles include divination, astrology, ritual of various kinds (such as ransom and ways of disposing adverse powers), medical diagnosis, and methods of guidance toward a better rebirth. The four result vehicles include guidance for lay practitioners who want to follow the virtuous path of the ten perfections, rules of monastic discipline, and exposition of the various tantric meditative practices together with their rituals. Dzogchen is explained as the final attainment.

Another way in which the Bön teachings are divided comes from the "Piercing Eye" (*gZer mig*), or medium-length biography of Tonpa Shenrab. It is called the Four Portals and One Treasury (five in all; *sGo bzhi mdzod lnga*), in which the portals include all kinds of teachings and philosophical explanations of sūtra, tantra, and dzogchen compiled as the iron, copper, silver, and gold volumes and the treasury as the all-embracing pure summit of the turquoise volume.

The Bön Canon contains the words of Tonpa Shenrab (*bKa' 'gyur*), including teachings of sūtra, tantra, and dzogchen as well as cosmogony, hagiographies, and prayers and the Commentaries of it (*bKa' brten*) dealing with different kinds of commentaries, narratives, and works connected with arts, logic, medicine, and poetry.

In the 1950s, with the invasion of Tibet by Communist China and their Cultural Revolution, Bön suffered together with all religious faiths. Lopon Tenzin Namdak was key in keeping this tradition alive in exile. At that time he was the head teacher (*slob dpon*) of Menri monastery in Tibet. After a first frustrated attempt, in which he was shot and wounded by Chinese soldiers (leading to ten months of incarceration), Lopon Tenzin Namdak managed to escape to Nepal by way of the small principality of Mustang. There he met Professor Snellgrove, who invited Lopon to the University of London through a Rockefeller Fellowship. After three years there, during which together they wrote *The Nine Ways of Bon*, Lopon Tenzin Namdak heard that his teacher, Lopon Sangye Tenzin, had also escaped successfully to India.

Thereupon Lopon Tenzin Namdak decided then to go back to India and take care of his teacher. In 1967, with the help of the Catholic Relief Service, he purchased land and started a Bön settlement with 70 families in the Himachal Pradesh village of Dolanji. A few years later, through the help of the Dalai Lama and the good offices of the Indian government, it developed into the first Bön educational center in exile (the Tibetan Bonpo Foundation), with the new Menri monastery as its center. In Menri a nine-year program leading to a *geshe* (equivalent to a Th.D. and Ph.D.) was established. In 1969 the successor to the deceased abbot of Menri was chosen by lot from among all the *geshe*s, and Jongdong Sangye Tenzin became the 33rd abbot of Menri. Assuming the spiritual leadership of the Bönpos in exile, he was named His Holiness Lungtok Tenpa'i Nyima. He presided over the Bön community and, together with Lopon Tenzin Namdak, the new abbot, ran Menri monastery.

Through the *geshe* curriculum Menri reestablished the school of dialectic, mirroring its previous one in Tibet. The purpose of learning through dialectical debate is to lead a student to better understand the philosophical basis of the teachings and deeper application in meditation practice. During this nine-year training, the monks follow a very strict schedule, starting with prayers before breakfast, around 6:15 a.m. (7:15 in winter), with a variety of teachings and practices during the whole day, concluding with dinner around 7:30 p.m. Some monks continue their studies at night, memorizing texts, praying, and so on.

The sūtra teachings are done over a period of six years and include various studies, such as logic and definitions, different kinds of mind, right and wrong perception, the successive stages of the path (as explained in the nine ways), different tenet systems of other schools, and monastic discipline.

During two years of tantra teachings, monks learn teachings similar to those of the lay practitioners, such as the preliminary practices (*sngon 'gro*), the introduction to the view of dzogchen, and the various kinds of outer and inner tantras (see the following discussion).

The last year is devoted to dzogchen, in which the monks develop further the point of view/understanding of this unsurpassed state. In addition subjects such as grammar, poetry, astrology, philology, religious arts, crafts, and medicine are distributed throughout the nine years of training.

Different exams are given during the course, and at the end of their training the monks must pass two comprehensive examinations: one on the main dialectics course and the other on the subsidiary subjects. These exams are performed in front of both the teachers and the students, who are allowed to ask questions on any of the topics studied during the nine-year training.

Beginning in 1977 Lopon Tenzin Namdak looked for property in Kathmandu, Nepal, to build a new monastery. He found a site near the Swayambhu stūpa, a place that had long been sacred for Bönpos as well as for Buddhists. In 1987 he established Triten Norbutse (Khri brtan nor bu rtse) there, taking its name from the original 14th-century monastery of central Tibet, which was destroyed completely during the Chinese Cultural Revolution. The new Triten Norbutse would also serve as an educational center for the Bönpos coming from different areas of Nepal. Although monasteries existed in Dolpo and Mustang, they did not provide a thorough monastic curriculum.

With the help of local Bönpos and financial support from different organizations in Europe and the United States, the monastery was gradually built. In 1994 the Dialectic School was established and a Meditation Group inaugurated. The latter was a four-year program for those who wanted to focus completely on meditation instead of dialectics. Each year is devoted to one of the four dzogchen traditions: the first three years for each of the main Bön traditions of Instructions on the A (A khrid), Dzogchen, and Oral Transmission of Zhang Zhung (Zhang zhung snyan rgyud) and the fourth for a special Bön dzogchen that has passed through an Indian lineage, the Yetri tasel (Ye khri mtha' sel). Every year is divided into two parts: the preliminary practices of that year's teachings and the main practices (dngos gzhi).

The preliminary practices include the study of texts and different practices of body, speech, and mind to prepare the practitioner to receive higher teachings. Among these are practices such as reflecting on impermanence, which tames the practitioner by turning one's mind toward practice; practices that purify the practitioner through offering exercises with the strong intent of wishing enlightenment to all sentient beings (bodhicitta); and practices that perfect the practitioner through exercises that include a brief version of chö (see the following discussion) and receiving blessings through devotion to one's teacher.

The main practices include meditation sessions for stabilizing one's mind and integrating with the appearances through the practices known as breakthrough (mkhregs chod) and leap-over (rthod rgal). During the last 100 days of each year, the students practice special breathing exercises (rtsa rlung) and physical yogas ('phrul 'khor).

The schedule of the meditation group begins at 4:00 a.m. (4:30 in the winter) and ends at 9:00 p.m. Each of four main meditation sessions lasts an hour and a half with teaching and study periods in between. Each day also includes the four offerings of smoke (sang), water (chab), burnt food (sur), and chö (gcod). Around 5:30 a.m. the smoke offering is performed (mostly individually) by burning incense and juniper branches. This is believed to exert a powerful purification effect on the place and is directed specifically to the local protectors and generally to all beings. Around 9:00 a.m. the water offering is done; this consists of fresh water being poured on flower petals and grains that are arranged in nine bowls in a circular fashion with one remaining in the center; it is considered a very pure and simple offering directed to all beings. It is common when performing this offering to request the deities to help sentient beings satisfy their needs or to reorient one who is lost. In the evening,

around 5:30 p.m., the burnt food offering is performed as a ritual directed mainly to the spirits of those who have passed away. It consists of burning all types of food, which give off a good smell, mainly roasted barley flour (rtsam pa), butter, oil, medicine, and grains – the smell being the support that satisfies all their desires. Finally at night, around 9:00 p.m., chö, or the visualization of offering one's own body, is performed. It is thought to be a very powerful means to help all sentient beings through generosity and to develop the altruistic mind of enlightenment. The ultimate benefit is to develop the nondual state of meditation. In order to increase the terrifying aspect chö is performed at night; doing it at night within the monastery complex prevents outsiders from being there and provokes a response of fear similar to that of a charnel ground or any of the other classical terrifying localities in which one is supposed to do chö. Monks of both the dialectic school and the meditation school participate together in many important ceremonies throughout the year.

In 1992 Tenzin Wangyal Rinpoche, one of the six geshes who graduated from the first graduating class (1986) from Menri monastery in Dolanji, founded the Ligmincha Institute in Charlottesville, Virginia. This institute, which has branches in Texas, California, Mexico, and Poland as well as centers all over the United States, Canada, Europe, and Latin America, aims to preserve the cultural and religious traditions of Tibet, especially Bön.

M. ALEJANDRO CHAOUL-REICH

See also Buddhist Schools/Traditions: Tibet; Critiques of Buddhist Monasticism: Indo-Tibetan; Deities, Buddhist; Discourses (Sūtras): Mahāyāna; Rules, Buddhist (Vinaya); Tibet; Tibetan Lineages

## Further Reading

Karmay, Samten, The Treasury of Good Sayings: A Tibetan History of Bon, London: Oxford University Press, 1972
Karmay, Samten, "A General Introduction to the Bon Doctrine," The Memoirs of Toyo Bunko 33 (1975)
Kvaerne, Per, "A Chronological Table of the Bon Po: The bstan rcis of Ñi ma bstan cjin," Acta Orientalia 33 (1971)
Kvaerne, Per, "The Canon of the Bonpos," Indo-Iranian Journal 16 (1975)
Kvaerne, Per, The Bon Religion of Tibet: The Iconography of a Living Tradition, Boston and London: Shambhala, 1995
Lukianowicz, Andrew, editor, Triten Norbutse Bön Monastery, Kathmandu, Nepal: Triten Norbutse Monastery, 1997
Mimaki, Katsumi, "A Fourteenth Century Bon Po Doxography: The Bon sgo byed by Tre ston rgyal mtshan dpal – A Preliminary Report Toward a Critical Edition," in Tibetan Studies: Proceedings of the 6th Seminar of the International Association of Tibetan Studies, Fagernes, 1992, volume 2, Oslo: Institute for Comparative Research in Human Culture, 1994
Norbu, Namkhai, Drung, Deu and Bön: Narrations, Symbolic Languages and the Bön Traditions in Ancient Tibet, translated by A. Clemente and A. Lukianowicz, Dharamsala, India: Library of Tibetan Works and Archives, 1995

Samuel, Geoffrey, *Civilized Shamans: Buddhism in Tibetan Societies*, Washington, D.C.: Smithsonian Institution Press, 1993

Snellgrove, David, *The Nine Ways of Bon*, London and New York: Oxford University Press, 1967

# Bonaventure, St. c. 1217–1274

## Italian Franciscan friar and theologian

Bonaventure was born in Bagnoregio near Orvieto, Italy, and at baptism was named after his father, John di Fidanza. The origin of his name as a Franciscan, Bonaventure, is not known. His mother attributed to Francis of Assisi the cure of her son from a serious childhood illness. In 1235 Bonaventure went to Paris to study the arts. He became a master of arts at the University of Paris in 1243. Probably in that same year he entered the Franciscan Order. At the University of Paris, he came under the influence of the Franciscan Alexander of Hales (c. 1186–1245). He incepted as a master in 1254 and then served as a regent master in theology at Paris until 1257.

In February 1257 Bonaventure was elected minister general of the Franciscan Order and for the rest of his life worked untiringly to bring about a unified Franciscan Order. The general chapter at Narbonne in 1260 instructed Bonaventure to compose a new life of Francis, which became known as the *Legenda Major*. This work became the official biography of Francis and was distributed throughout the Order. In recognition of these efforts on behalf of the unity of Franciscan life, Bonaventure has been called the Order's second founder. Although his administrative duties made it impossible for him to teach at the university, Bonaventure preached often to students and their masters at Paris and composed numerous works during his generalate that made a significant impact on the spiritual and mystical tradition of Western Christianity. Bonaventure composed his mystical masterpiece, *The Journey of the Mind into God*, in 1259. He structured this concise work on Francis' experience on Mount La Verna, where Francis had received the stigmata. For Bonaventure Franciscan life was a journey to contemplation; in fact, for him the whole Church is called to be contemplative. Bonaventure integrated the intellectual with the affective in his spiritual writings. His influence on late medieval spirituality was far-reaching. However, falsely attributed to him was the widely read *Meditations on the Life of Christ*.

Bonaventure stood in the Augustinian theological tradition but not slavishly so. Moreover, scholarship no longer permits him to be seen as anti-Aristotelian; rather, he was a Platonist who knew Aristotle well and made astute use of certain Aristotelian doctrines. Bonaventure's theology and spirituality, like the life of his model Francis, was thoroughly Christocentric. He, along with Thomas Aquinas, was much involved in the defense of the mendicants whose ministry in the universities was opposed by bishops and secular masters.

Bonaventure declined the archbishopric of York but in May 1273 was named a cardinal and consecrated bishop of Albano. He was active in preparations for and deliberations of the Second Ecumenical Council of Lyons. Bonaventure died on 15 July 1274, shortly before the close of this council. Pope Sixtus IV (1471–1484), a Franciscan, canonized Bonaventure in 1482, and another Franciscan, Pope Sixtus V (1585–1590), declared him a Doctor of the Church in 1587. Bonaventure is often referred to as the Seraphic Doctor. His feast day is 15 July.

KEITH J. EGAN

*See also* France: History; Francis of Assisi, St.; Franciscans; Theology, Western Christian: Franciscan; Vision, Mystical: Western Christian

## Biography

Giovanni di Fidanza, the "Seraphic Doctor," studied at Paris, where he entered the Franciscan Order c. 1243. From 1247 to 1257 he taught in arts until elected Minister General of the Franciscans. He codified the Order's statutes in the "Constitutions of Narbonne" (1260) and wrote the official biography of St. Francis (1263). He died during the Council of Lyons (1274). He inaugurated the mainstream of Franciscan theology.

## Major Works

*S. Bonaventurae opera omnia*, 10 vols., 1882–1902 (critical edition)

*The Works of Bonaventure*, 5 vols., translated by José De Vinck, 1960–1970

*Bonaventure: The Soul's Journey into God, The Tree of Life, Life of St. Francis* (Classics of Western Spirituality), translated and with an introduction by Ewert Cousins, 1978

## Further Reading

Bougerol, Jacques Guy, *Introduction to the Works of Bonaventure*, translated by José de Vinck, Patterson, New Jersey: St. Anthony Guild Press, 1964

Congresso Internazionale per il VII Centenario di San Bonaventura da Bagnoregio, *San Bonaventura Maestro di Vita Francescana e di Sapienza Cristiana*, 3 vols., Rome: Pontificia Facolta' Teologica San Bonaventura, 1976

Hayes, Zachary, "Bonaventure: Mystery of the Triune God," in *The History of Franciscan Theology*, edited by Kenan B. Osborne, St. Bonaventure, New York: Franciscan Institute, St. Bonaventure University, 1994

Quinn, John F., "Chronology of St. Bonaventure (1217–1257)," *Franciscan Studies* 32 (1972)

Quinn, John F., *The Historical Constitution of St. Bonaventure's Philosophy* (Studies and Texts: Pontifical Institute of Mediaeval Studies, 23), Toronto: Pontifical Institute of Mediaeval Studies, 1973

Ratzinger, Joseph, *The Theology of History in St. Bonaventure*, translated by Zachary Hayes, Chicago: Franciscan Herald Press, 1971

*S. Bonaventura, 1274–1974: Volumina Commemorativa Anni Septies Centenarii a Morte S. Bonaventurae Doctoris Seraphici, Cura et Studio Commissionis Internationalis Bonaventurianae*, 5 vols., Rome: Collegio S. Bonaventura, 1974

# Boniface, St. c. 673–754

## Anglo-Saxon monk and missionary to Germany

Boniface, Anglo-Saxon monk, missionary, bishop, and martyr, is venerated as the "Apostle of Germany." Born of a noble family in the kingdom of Wessex, he was named Wynfrith. At an early age he expressed a desire to become a monk, and his parents reluctantly presented him as an oblate to the recently established monastery at Exeter. Although the saint's vitae occasionally invoke the *Regula Benedicti* and later generations of Benedictines have been eager to claim him as one of their own, the monastic life that Wynfrith experienced clearly grew from a mixed tradition. Irish influence is evidenced in ascetic practices (vigils, fasts, and temperance) and a strong emphasis on the love of learning. Christian Gaul had contributed the *Regula mixta* with its selective use of the *Regula Benedicti* to monastic observance in southern England. Anglo-Saxon monasticism was fostered by, and in turn helped to strengthen, the "lord-retinue" pattern of a society that depended on a supporting network of kinship and patronage, something that the *Regula Benedicti* sought to avoid. A further discrepancy shows in a reference to Boniface's monks retaining some control over private resources, albeit for the purpose of almsgiving. The legacy of the Gregorian-Augustinian mission to England (597) resulted in Anglo-Saxon interest in Roman liturgical practices, erudition, canon law, and Church organization, although the monastic life it transmitted cannot be said to have been specifically Benedictine.

In his formative years Wynfrith is said to have been remarkable for humility and obedience, showing great promise in his studies, whether scriptural, grammatical, or rhetorical. Having outstripped the resources available at Exeter, he moved to Nursling near Southampton, whose abbot was renowned for his learning. The focal point of Wynfrith's efforts remained the practice of *lectio divina* (sacred reading) and exegesis. After ordination to the priesthood, he was in great demand as teacher and spiritual counselor in and beyond his community. The earliest items of his "correspondence," a unique collection of firsthand information about his career and vision, date from this period. Among his correspondents were abbesses and nuns who were unable to hear him in person. The letters bear witness to a high standard of education in communities of women and to Wynfrith's great regard for them. Many of the friendships formed at this time were to last throughout his life. Wynfrith was repeatedly chosen as royal envoy to the archbishop of Canterbury and through involvement in local synods gained insights into pastoral and disciplinary Church matters.

Then in 716 he felt called to join the missionary outreach of the Anglo-Saxon Church among the Germanic pagans. This movement, sustained almost exclusively by monastics, drew in part on the ascetic ideal of *peregrinatio* (pilgrimage) of the Celtic monks: it involved leaving everything, even one's homeland, for the sake of Christ. Another powerful inspiration was the example of the Gregorian mission to England in 597; this likewise had been carried out by monks. The consciousness of being linked to the Germanic peoples on the Continent by bonds of kinship added a further incentive to proclaiming the Gospel among them. Wynfrith's attempt to evangelize in Frisia in 716 proved a failure, but in 718 he set out again, traveling first to Rome, where he received the blessing and commission of Pope Gregory II (715–731). As a sign of loyalty to the successor of Peter, Wynfrith's name was changed to that of Boniface, an early Roman martyr. For three years Boniface worked closely with the Northumbrian monk Willibrord (658–739) in Frisia, then he left with a group of disciples for Hesse. Reports of initial successes in this region caused Pope Gregory II to call Boniface to Rome in 722 and to consecrate him as bishop for Germany without a fixed see. He also provided him with letters of recommendation to Charles Martel (714–741). In effect Boniface accepted secular patronage to gain a measure of security for his work and followers.

Throughout his career Boniface maintained close links with his homeland and his friends. As the scope of his activities grew, he was able to muster the missionary potential of Anglo-Saxon monasteries. He appealed to bonds of kinship and spiritual friendship, giving vivid accounts of the hardships of the German mission and offering monks and nuns the opportunity to be associated with him in this venture and its rewards. He asked for support through prayer, material aid (especially books), and personnel. His challenge helped refocus the monastic ideal in Anglo-Saxon England itself and called forth a generous response from monasteries and individuals, enabling him to staff "cells" in Amöneburg (722), Fritzlar (723/24), Ohrdruf (725), and Fulda (744). These developed from missionary outposts to pastoral bases and educational establishments for monks and clerics and soon began to recruit new members from the mission territories. Nuns followed his invitation as well, his relatives Thecla, Leoba, and Walburga among them. Monasteries for women were reestablished at Kitzingen, Ochsenfurt, and Tauberbischofsheim. They played a vital role in rooting the new faith among the German peoples by witnessing to the practice of Christian belief and worship in everyday life and developing into centers of culture and learning. Boniface also drew on his monastic following in his capacity as missionary archbishop (since 732) and papal legate (738/39) when consecrating new bishops. It might have been one of these, Willibald (700–786), another relative and former monk of Monte Cassino, whom he had recruited on a visit to Rome and appointed to the See of Eichstätt, who influenced his new appreciation of the *Regula Benedicti*. The reform councils of 742 and 743 held under Boniface's leadership stipulated uniform observance of this rule as a means to consolidate his achievement and to weld together the new foundations and the established monasteries of the Frankish Empire. For his "model-foundation" at Fulda in 744, Boniface sent his disciple Sturm to study monastic observance at Monte Cassino and to implement it as Fulda's first abbot. However, Boniface himself remained ultimately in charge of all his foundations during his lifetime. The witness of his contemporaries and disciples shows that they regarded him as their "Lord" and felt privileged to belong to his spiritual retinue. Monastics on both sides of the English Channel considered that his martyrdom at Dokkum, Frisia, by brigands in 754 (shared by over 50 companions) reflected glory on them as his followers. His personal and monastic charisma, embodied in his communities, continued to bear fruit for centuries in new foundations and through spiritual and secular learning. The historian Christopher Dawson remarked that of all Englishmen the one who exerted the most lasting impact in Germany was Boniface.

NIKOLA PROKSCH, O.S.B.

*See also* Celtic Monasticism; Exile, Western Christian; Fulda, Germany; Germany: History; Holy Men/Holy Women: Christian Perspectives; Lectio Divina; Missionaries: Christian; Monastics and the World, Medieval; Netherlands; Willibrord, St.

## Biography

Wynfrith, the "Apostle of Germany," was born in Wessex and educated in Exeter. He later joined a monastery near Southampton. In 716 the learned monk journeyed to Frisia (today's Netherlands) to assist Willibrord. In 719 in Rome Pope Gregory II instructed him to preach to the heathen, particularly in Germany, and in 722 ordained him bishop, albeit without a see. Active in Hesse and Thuringia for more than 30 years, he founded monasteries, organized worship, and became archbishop of Mainz c. 746. He was murdered in 754 by brigands in Frisia and his body was taken to Fulda for burial.

## Major Works

*Ars Grammatica*
*Ars Metrica*
*Epistolae*

## Further Reading

Dickerhof, Harald, "Zum monastischen Gepräge des Bonifatiuskreises," *Sammelblätter des Historischen Vereins Eichstätt* 71/72 Jg. (1979–1980)

Fletcher, Richard, *The Conversion of Europe: From Paganism to Christianity 371–1386 AD*, London: HarperCollins, 1997; as *The Barbarian Conversion: From Paganism to Christianity*, New York: Holt, 1998

Hyland, William Patrick, "Missionary Nuns and the Monastic Vocation in Anglo-Saxon England," *The American Benedictine Review* 47:2 (June 1996)

Levison, Wilhelm, *England and the Continent in the Eighth Century*, Oxford: Clarendon Press, 1946

Mayr-Harting, Henry, *The Coming of Christianity to England*, New York: Schocken Books, 1972; as *The Coming of Christianity to Anglo-Saxon England* (Fabric of British History), London: Batsford, 1972; 3rd edition, University Park: Pennsylvania State University Press, and London: Batsford, 1991

Proksch, Nikola, "The Anglo-Saxon Missionaries to the Continent," in *Monks of England: The Benedictines in England from Augustine to the Present Day*, edited by Daniel Rees, London: SPCK, 1997

Reuter, Timothy, editor, *The Greatest Englishman: Essays on St. Boniface and the Church at Crediton*, Exeter, Devon: Paternoster Press, and Greenwood, South Carolina: Attic Press, 1980

*Sankt Bonifatius: Gedenkgabe zum zwölfhundertsten Todestag*, Fulda: Parzeller, 1954

Schieffer, Theodor, *Winfrid-Bonifatius und die christliche Grundlegung Europas*, Freiburg: Herder, 1954; second printing with extended bibliography, Darmstadt: Wissenschaftliche Buchgesellschaft, 1972

Sladden, John Cyril, *Boniface of Devon: Apostle of Germany*, Exeter, Devon: Paternoster Press, and Greenwood, South Carolina: Attic Press, 1980

# Book Arts, Christian. *See* Visual Arts, Western Christian: Book Arts before the Renaissance

# Book Production. *See* Manuscript Production

# Borobudur, Java, Indonesia

The temple of Borobudur is one of the largest Buddhist monuments in the world, located in the Kedu plain of central Java. Founded around 800, the temple is known today mainly as a tourist attraction. Borobudur is the main temple of the complex, together with Chandi Mendut and Chandi Pawon. The complex is exemplary owing to a richness of philosophical language and

Chandi Mendut, Jogjakarta, Java, Indonesia, c. A.D. 800, stone.
Photo courtesy of Marylin M. Rhie

View of the great maṇḍala temple at Borobudur, Jogjakarta, Java, Indonesia, late eighth–ninth century A.D.
Photo courtesy of Marylin M. Rhie

has stimulated interpretations of its symbolism according to different Buddhist traditions. Although many studies have been made since Sir Stamford Raffles (1781–1826) discovered the site in 1814, no consensus has emerged.

The shape of the main building is that of a three-dimensional maṇḍala with a square base, rounded terraces, and a central stūpa. Formerly the complex of the three temples was connected by a paved pilgrimage road, leading east to west from Mendut to Borobudur. The stages of the Bodhisattva's path to enlightenment can be read in the main temple's balustrades, and some have argued that the entire pilgrimage route might have featured similar carved sandstone balustrades.

The circumambulation path starts from the base of the Borobudur temple and leads with a spiral-like movement through arches with protector figures (Kalamakara) toward the upper terraces. Walls and balustrades are carved in 1,460 panels bearing reliefs from different texts – *Karmavibhaṅga*, *Lalitavistara*, *Jātaka* and *Avadāna*, and *Gaṇḍavyūha*. The panels likely were originally painted, as shown by small amounts of white and ochre on their surface. Today the reliefs show a rough and porous sandstone surface whose preservation improves on the upper levels.

The main temple has Buddha statues inside niches and stūpas, where a special lattice in the stone walls of the stūpas makes them visible from outside. The statues of Akṣobhya, Ratnasaṃb-

hava, Amitābha, and Amogasiddhi stand inside niches in their respective positions, and Vairocana adorns the circular terraces. Some studies suggest that the basic maṇḍala combines two others: Garbadhātu- and Vajradhātu maṇḍalas. Many studies have attempted to establish which Buddha was the main figure of the temple, embodying as it were the essence of the general design. In 1842 an original statue was found inside the main stūpa but has disappeared. Different theses suggest figures such as Maitreya (the Buddha of the future) or Mahāvairocana (because of the importance of this cult in previous times in this area). Alternatively the whole complex might represent the nonduality of the Dharmadhātu. In both cases the temple's configuration would embody different aspects of enlightenment as described in *Gaṇḍavyūha*.

Another analysis can be done comparing the interior of the temples with the interiors of Chandi Mendut and Pawon, similar to the two interior spaces contained inside the main stūpa of Chandi Borobudur. This connection gives another clue for reading the symbolism, forming a link between apparent beginning and end points of the complex. The dimensions of the internal space decrease, proceeding from Mendut via Pawon to Borobudur, suggesting that one temple could be configured as contained inside the other.

The central statue, which was placed later, depicts a Buddha with bhumisparsa mudra, connected with Buddha Akṣobhya,

Stūpas at the top level of the great maṇḍala temple at Borobudur, Jogjakarta, Java, Indonesia, late eighth–ninth century A.D.
Photo courtesy of Marylin M. Rhie

already present on the eastern side of the monument, and Śākya-muni, the historical Buddha of our age, or the Healing Buddha – "the embodiment of the completion of all the tasks" – which can be read as a greeting to future visitors of the temple.

Chandi Mendut contains a statue of Mañjuśrī (who in some traditions was seen also as the Buddha of the future) seated in a chair (which is an unusual presentation) surrounded by Vajrapani and Padmapani. Characteristic of Chandi Mendut is the acoustic effect created within the terraced dome of the temple. By contrast Chandi Pawon is characterized by empty interiors with empty niches on the wall that did not necessarily contain statues.

The landscape around the temples has been changed by restoration as well as by natural forces. The environs of the main temple have been developed into a garden-park for tourists with a museum. In former times two rivers flowed from two sides, ending in a lake at the front of the main temple, which today is only dry land. Originally a monastery was situated at the south-eastern corner of the main temple. Today monastic culture is represented only by a Theravāda Buddhist monastery near Chandi Mendut. The temple, monastery, and internal garden show statues representing Buddha Śākyamuni's life.

The temples were built during the Śailendra dynasty, a golden age in central Java from 750 to 850. This kingdom exalted the ruler of the country as "the wheel-turning king" – an emanation of enlightened being. This philosophical system, known from both Hindu and Buddhist cosmology, finds expression in the architectural language of temples known as mountain temples. A similar tradition is found at a later period in the temple of Angkor Wat (12th century), Cambodia, a fact that allows us to compare this cosmology's expression within different preexisting cultures. The Buddhist and Hindu religions were practiced in different monastic centers of Java until the introduction of Islam in the country.

No scriptures prior to Borobudur temple survive. Some scholars explain this loss as being due to the use of perishable materials, such as palm leaves, whereas others believe that orally transmitted teachings excluded written documents. Documents found relating to the building include gold plates from 650 to 800 that explain 12 *nidāna*s in Sanskrit, and two documents mention a temple similar to Borobudur, one by King Sama-ratungga (824) and another by Queen Sri Kahulunan (842). One description of religious practice refers to the cult of Mahāvairo-cana, and one later text comprises a "guide for the construction of the temple," written 75 years after Borobudur was completed.

Architecturally the temple complex is articulated into differ-ent parts. A certain time axis is represented in the reliefs, where the Buddha Śākyamuni's past lives are presented on the lower level and the future road to enlightenment is shown in Sudhana's life story on upper levels. The main building is divided into three parts as a configuration of the three *dhātu*s: Kāma-, Rūpa-, and Arūpadhatu (i.e., sense, form, and nonform spheres of existence). The same division occurs in the two smaller temples of the complex as well.

This threefold division expresses three different ways of practicing Buddhism: ethics, meditation, and wisdom. Mendut is a place for worship, Pawon provides empty space suitable for meditation, and Borobudur conveys doctrinal scriptures. Another way of reading the division involves presentation of the three *yāna*s – Theravāda, Mahāyāna, and Vajrayāna – synthesized into one, perhaps a characteristic of Javanese tradition. In this view Pawon presents a crossing point between two different paths, Arhathood with Pratyakabuddha's way standing on the one side and the Bodhisattva way on the other. This thesis is confirmed by the existence of a Buddhist movement of the same kind in Indonesia, where all three Buddhist doctrines are compounded into one. The same principle recurs in various Vajrayāna traditions.

Two restoration projects have been made since the discovery in 1814, the first one completed 1911 by van Erp and the second started by Unesco around 1950 and completed only recently. The original appeareance of the monument has been maintained, except for the corner cut on the lowest terrace (known as "the hidden foot") in the southeastern corner.

LAURA PORCEDDU

*See also* Angkor Wat, Cambodia; Architecture: Structural Monasteries in East Asia; Maṇḍala

**Further Reading**

Bernet Kempers, August Johan, *Ageless Borobudur: Buddhist Mystery in Stone, Decay and Restoration, Mendut and Pawon, Folklife in Ancient Java*, Wassenaar: Servire, 1976

Boeles, Jan J., *The Secret of Borobudur*, Bangkok: Boeles, 1985; 2nd edition, 1989

Brown, Morton W., "Indonesia Rescues Ancient Borobudur," *National Geographic* 163:1 (January 1983)

Gómez, Luis O., and Hiram W. Woodward, Jr., *Barabudur: History and Significance of a Buddhist Monument* (Berkeley Buddhist Studies Series, 2), Berkeley, California: Asian Humanities Press, 1981

International Symposium on Chandi Borobudur, *Proceedings of the International Symposium on Chandi Borobudur, September 25–27, 1980*, Tokyo: Executive Committee for the International Symposium on Chandi Borobudur, 1981

Kandahjaya, Hudaya, *The Master Key for Reading Borobudur Symbolism*, Pustaka Karaniya, Indonesia, 1995

Miksic, John, *Borobudur: Golden Tales of the Buddhas*, Boston: Shambhala, and London: Bamboo/Periplus, 1990

Saccà, Lucilla, *Borobudur, mandala de pierre* (Cahiers de l'unicorne, 10), Milan: Archè, 1983

Soekmono, R., *Chandi Borobudur: A Monument of Mankind*, Assen: Van Gorcum, 1976

Unesco, *Borobudur: Beauty in Peril*, Paris: Unesco, 1973

Unesco, *Borobudur: The Conquest of Time*, Paris: Unesco, 1983

# Botany

Botany, the scientific study of plants and plant life, came into its own as an empirical science around 1830. Thus, botany as a systematic study was unknown throughout most of the evolution of monasticism. However, this is not to say that the study of plants or of plant life was neglected in the monastic community or that no literature was produced. Quite the opposite is true: large amounts of information (and misinformation) were available to and created by monks. The literature, much of it from non-Christian sources, had been assembled over a period of time and then redacted by the monks of the medieval age, unfortunately with few new ideas.

As with most of the medieval sciences, ideas about the nature and properties of plants came from two primary sources: the literary tradition, mainly Greco-Roman, and the folklore tradition. The literary tradition, although with skips and jumps, goes back to classical Greece. Monastic botany finds its roots in Theophrastus' (372 B.C.–287 B.C.) *Historia plantarum*, which reached the monastic community mainly through Pliny the Elder's *Historia naturalis* (A.D. 77). It can be said without a doubt that Pliny's work was the single most influential text on later medieval botany. The main source of information on the medicinal properties of plants was *De materia medica* by Dioscorides, popularized in the West by Galen (d. 199).

Whereas the literary sources were mainly scientific in nature, the oral folklore tradition might best be described as "homey." Here, handed down by word of mouth, generation to generation, was practical information about the values of specific plants for domestic and practical uses. Whereas the classical texts tended to mix scientific with philosophical discourse, folklore traditions were pragmatic, albeit often superstitious.

The two traditions rarely came together in any meaningful way until the end of the Middle Ages, when each began to look to the other. Up to that point the botanical learning that had survived the dissolution of the Roman Empire was mainly that of glossaries by monks and others who sought simply to identify plants and botanical recipes known to the ancients. Medieval Scholasticism, rather than promoting new plant studies as one might expect, merely facilitated access to the classical and Arabic texts. Thus, more people were informed, but little of new importance was accomplished. As the end of the Middle Ages approached, academics, many of them monks, with their medical and "craft handbooks," and the herbalists, again, many of them monks, with their Books of Secrets, began to recognize the contribution of the other to the overall knowledge of plant lore.

Perhaps the best work in this regard is that of the Dominican Albertus Magnus (d. 1280), who, between about 1254 and 1257, expanded the pseudo-Aristotelian work *De plantis* with his own contribution of three new books and several chapters to the original five books. This was followed by his botanical masterpiece, *De vegetabilibus*, which demonstrated independent research as well as a high respect for his sources, both classical and folklore. Of particular note is Albertus' clarity and precision in his descriptions of individual plants. Geoffrey Chaucer, in his prologue to the *Canterbury Tales*, draws attention to three other botanical writers: the Englishmen Gilbert Anglicus (early 13th century) and John of Gaddesden (c. 1280–1349) and Bernard de Gordon (13th century). Chaucer connects the three because each used a name of a plant in at least one of their works. Bernard is unquestionably the leading representative of Anglo-Norman botanical medicine. Of particular interest, considering that Bernard was probably not a monk (although he highly recommended such living and seemed to live as one), is the amount of writing he devoted to providing botanical remedies specifically for monks, such as an ointment to improve the sight of lectors. Early monastic contributors of note to botanical knowledge include Walafrid Strabo (c. 808–849) of Reichenau and Hildegard of Bingen (1099–1179).

Our primary source of knowledge about the contributions of medieval monks to the study of plants and plant life comes from monastic herbals. Although most of them are lost to us, every monastic community undoubtedly had its own version, compiled mostly as a result of trial and error. In general the herbal was a compilation of medical, pharmacological, and botanical information about plants thought to have therapeutic value. In addition to the herbal, the monastic *infirmarer* most likely had a leechbook and recipe collection, both of which disclose much about the monastic study of plants. The leechbook, a sort of a general medical handbook, contained all that was considered of value to a practicing physician, whereas the recipe book served mainly as a more detailed source of information regarding the preparation and compounding of medicinal herbs. Frequently the leechbook contained a series of interconnected sections dealing with the properties and uses of a specific plant in medicine. The recipe book, on the other hand, while containing material similar to that in both the herbal and the leechbook, was organized according to particular maladies. Of importance to the medieval physician (and to us in our understanding of monastic botany) is that the recipe collection contained not only "scientifically proven" remedies but those of folklore as well, with specific reference to the common, or folk, name of many species of plants.

Most data contained in early monastic herbals are descriptive morphologically (i.e., of size, shape, color, habit, and so on) and anthologically (i.e., of flower, fruit, and seed), with some space given to describing domestic uses and habitat. The last point is essential if one is to be able to find and gather the specified plants. Herbals often conflated closely related species, with common species simply having the notation that the properties were "known to all." All in all we can deduce that monks of the Middle Ages knew about 1,500 species of plants, although each monastery had its favorites, and their reputed value was debated from monastery to monastery.

Throughout history certain plants, because of their supposed poisonous, aphrodisiacal, or mystical properties, were regarded as sacred or holy. Two such examples are the fir tree of the Norse and the mistletoe of the Celts. Although such plants were either Christianized or their use prohibited, much botanical folklore has nevertheless survived to this day regarding mystically curative properties of certain plants. The lives of the saints, as well as works such as those of Hildegard and others, often seem to con-

done such use. Particular flowering plants, with their ascribed mystical properties, have come to be associated with a particular saint or a holy spring. Such a spring usually has a monastic connection.

Closely connected to botanical folklore is the practice of "liturgical botany," in which particular plants, because of their symbolic significance, become necessary to ritual. Two well-known uses of botanical liturgy are the use of olive oil in anointing and of palm fronds on Palm Sunday. In addition a few of the monastic rules and lives of their founders call for the blessing of plants. One such example it that of St. Columba (c. 521–597) of Iona, who required that his monks, after asking permission, bless a tree before chopping it down. Some folklore requires the use of plants in specific blessing rituals, such as use of lavendar to sprinkle holy water on the threshold of a new home. Closely related is "moral botany," a literary device popular among medieval monks. Moral botany is found in medieval plant fables, biblical stories, and sermons that openly allegorized (e.g., *Roman de la Rose*) or hinted at a particular symbolic moral meaning in a plant. To capitalize further on the "moral nature" of certain plants (e.g., "Crown of Thorns"), many monastic gardens had these plants growing in sort of a "moral garden."

FRANK A. MILLS

*See also* Albertus Magnus, St.; Bacon, Roger; Columba, St.; Gardens: Christian Perspectives; Pharmacology; Social Services: Western Christian

## Further Reading

Albertus Magnus, Saint, *Alberti Magni . . . De vegtabilibus libri VII historiae naturalis pars XVIII*, Berlin: Reimeri, 1867

Bashford, H.H., "Gilbert and John," in his *The Harley Street Calendar*, London: Constable, and Boston: Houghton Mifflin, 1929

Demaitre, Luke E., *Doctor Bernard de Gordon, Professor and Practitioner* (Studies and Texts/Pontifical Institute of Mediaeval Studies, 51), Toronto: Pontifical Institute of Mediaeval Studies, 1980

Reeds, Karen, "Albert on the Natural Philosophy of Plant Life," in *Albertus Magnus and the Sciences, Commemorative Essays 1980* (Studies and Texts/Pontifical Institute of Mediaeval Studies, 49), edited by James A. Weisheipl, Toronto: Pontifical Institute of Mediaeval Studies, 1980

Siraisi, Nancy G., *Medieval and Early Renaissance Medicine: An Introduction to Knowledge and Practice*, Chicago: University of Chicago Press, 1990

Stannard, Jerry, "Medieval Herbals and Their Development," *Clio medica* 9 (1974)

Stannard, Jerry, "Botany," in *Dictionary of the Middle Ages*, volume 2, edited by Joseph Reese Strayer, New York: Scribner, 1983

Weisheipl, James A., editor, *Albertus Magnus and the Sciences, Commemorative Essays 1980* (Studies and Texts/Pontifical Institute of Mediaeval Studies, 49), Toronto: Pontifical Institute of Mediaeval Studies, 1980

Wilms, Hieronymous, *Albert the Great: Saint and Doctor of the Church*, translated by Adrian English and Philip Hereford, London: Burns, Oates and Washbourne, 1933

# Brewing, Western Christian

Beer has quite a long history, dating back to the ancient Near East, where it provided a means of economic exchange and was consumed even by the elites, notwithstanding its often questionable quality. In early medieval Europe peasant women carried on the art of brewing, combining oats, spelt, rye, or any available grain to form a cloudy, highly viscous mixture. However, brewing, as we now recognize it, began with the monks and nuns of Western Europe as they advanced the science while also providing sustenance for both their bodies and their economic well-being. Although available research assumes men came to dominate beer production, nuns continued to brew, including Martin Luther's eventual wife, Katherine.

The Bavarian monastery Weihenstephan, founded in A.D. 724, is often cited as the oldest continuous brewing operation, but records prove misleading. The brewery at Weihenstephan was officially acknowledged only in 1040 after it received the *Gruit*, or brewing privilege – a right that included production as well as the sale of excess quantities. Doubtless Weihenstephan had begun much earlier, as had Weltenburg, also in Bavaria. Tax records indicate that beer provided a staple of annual collections as early as the eighth century, enabling us to trace brewing to early Bavarian monasteries, although the operations may not have been continuous or on a large scale.

The Swiss abbey of St. Gallen ushered in the era of megabreweries. Founded around 600 by St. Gallus (d. 627), the abbey struggled for years before reaching its peak in the 11th century. Like many medieval monasteries St. Gallen controlled a unique economy that featured large numbers of pilgrims as well as pious, or penitent, nobility. Relics, such as a thorn from Jesus' crown, provided the standard attraction; although occasionally, as at St. Gallen, legends accreted to the founder's remains, drawing large numbers seeking miracles. This placed the monks at the center of the medieval hospitality industry, as the crowds, who also brought gifts of grain and silver, required lodging and sustenance.

The monks sold their beer in three distinct categories. Honored guests enjoyed *celia*, made from barley and hops, whereas lesser pilgrims consumed *cervisa*, a beer made with wheat, oats, hops, and whatever remained from the *celia*. The monks also produced a beer for everyday consumption, called *conventus*, which they swilled in quantities approaching five liters daily. Each type of beer also required its own brewery and staff, with almost 100 monks required for the entire operation. Later, as St. Gallen increased in prosperity before embarking on a rapid decline, the monks left the labor-intensive efforts to serfs.

The profitability of beer declined markedly during the 11th century, as vintners discovered that grapes could be domesticated to the colder climates of central Europe. Specifically the *Riesling* strain of grapes came to dominate the most fruitful fields, pushing out the hop gardens that had become so prevalent. Also, as one might expect, shifting cultural patterns and the lower quality of beer made wine into a high-status beverage, further reducing the desirability of beer. These changes affected beer production for a brief period, but it soon reemerged from the cultural ferment.

Much of what follows can be charted through the study of an abbey founded in the 15th century, Andechs of Bavaria. Located on a mountaintop near present-day Munich, Andechs initially served as an estate for the ruling Wittelsbach family. However, it soon became a treasure trove for relics, ranging from the Virgin Mary's clothing to a tablecloth purportedly used at the Last Supper. Of course pilgrims flocked to the relics, encouraging authorities to build a chapel and monastery for the spiritual and material care of visitors. On the advice of Cardinal Nicholas of Cusa (1401–1464), Duke Albrecht III (1438–1460) founded a Benedictine monastery at Andechs in 1451. Albrecht granted the monks immediate brewing privileges and encouraged them to distribute their product widely.

Andechs developed much as St. Gallen had earlier, enhanced by its excellent location and generous benefices. Pilgrims were obliged to bring large quantities of grain and other goods and in return received lodging, beer, and access to priests. Visitors, as with St. Gallen, partook of refreshments on the basis of their social status, with only the highest nobility enjoying the signature brew.

Andechs, however, fell prey to the violent upheavals of the 17th century and was ransacked by the Swedes during the Thirty Years' War (1618–1648), with its fields left barren and its water supply contaminated. Rebuilding was hampered by labor shortages, lightning strikes, and frequent fires. The pilgrims returned, as did beer production, although Andechs came to be used increasingly as a supply depot for other regional monasteries, drawing the crowds to other locations.

However, the monastery faced its most dangerous threat in the 18th century. The Bavarian government increased taxation rates and made entry into monastic orders increasingly difficult. Distribution privileges were also withdrawn, meaning that monks could produce only for their own consumption, eliminating a lucrative trade. This pattern repeated itself across Europe, allowing state-operated breweries and private concerns the opportunity to drive most of the monasteries out of the beer business. The Napoleonic conquest of central Europe drove the final nail, and Andechs was secularized in 1804, sold to a certain Johann Lucass.

For the vast majority of monastic breweries, the secularizations of the early 19th century ended their operations. Often private groups simply bought the monastic property, which had been made available for sale by civil authorities, and produced their own beer, which they called "monastic" or "abbey" beer. But Andechs, along with a tiny handful of other monastic breweries, fared better. King Ludwig I (1825–1848) of Bavaria soon returned Andechs to the monks on the condition that it service the newly founded abbey of St. Boniface in Munich. However, to recover the monks needed time and money and were forced to sublet the brewery to various operators. Finally, by the late 19th century, enough money was raised to purchase new equipment and renovate the chapel and living facilities, bringing back the pilgrims in large quantities.

Today few authentic monastic breweries exist, but some Trappist breweries in Belgium have survived, and several of the Benedictine Order, including Andechs, still produce their brews in the alpine regions of central Europe.

GLENN W. SHUCK

*See also* Agriculture, Western Christian; Germany: History; Hospitality, Christian; Relics, Christian Monastic; St. Gallen, Switzerland; Social Services: Western Christian

**Further Reading**

Bikel, Hermann, *Die Wirtschaftsverhältnisse des Klosters St. Gallen*, Freiburg, Germany: Herder, 1914
Dornbusch, Horst, *Prost! The Story of German Beer*, Boulder, Colorado: Siris Books, 1997
Gebhardt, Bruno, *Handbuch der Deutschen Geschichte I–II*, 9th edition, Stuttgart, Germany: Union, 1970
Mathäser, Willibald, *Flüssiges Brot*, Munich: Süddeutschen, 1974; 2nd edition, 1996

# Bridgettines

Saint Birgitta (1303–1373), the founder of the Bridgettines, was born to a noble Swedish family. Her mother died when she was 12, and she was sent to live with an aunt. In 1318 she was married to the nobleman Ulf Gudmarsson. The couple had eight children. Ulf and Birgitta went on pilgrimage to Santiago de Compostela in 1341. Not long after their return, Ulf died at the Cistercian monastery of Alvastra. There in 1346 Birgitta had her first revelations and conceived the idea of founding a monastery in honor of the Blessed Virgin that would follow a rule given through her. In 1349 she traveled to meet Pope Clement VI (1342–1352) and obtain approval for her Rule. She lived the rest of her life in Rome, where she was joined by her daughter Catherine. She received further revelations, made various pilgrimages, urged the pope to return from Avignon, and called for the reform of the Church. In 1370 Urban V (1362–1370) approved her Order but placed it under the Rule of St. Augustine. She died in 1373 and was canonized in 1391.

Although the Rule of the Order of the Holy Savior, as Birgitta called her congregation, was joined to the Rule of Augustine by the pope and Birgitta's Rule itself underwent various modifications (e.g., a papal reviser changed it from a first-person revelation from Christ into a third-person document), it exercised lasting influence over the Order. It provides guidance for personal and communal discipline, a ritual for consecration, and guidance for constructing a monastery of 60 nuns under the guidance of an abbess, who would be joined by 25 monks led by a confessor general. Of the monks 13 were priests, four deacons, and eight lay brothers. The Rule outlines norms for the work of these groups. The abbess represents Mary; she governs the internal life of the monastery for both nuns and monks. The confessor general is the spiritual guide of the whole community. Both

these superiors are elected by all the members of the community. The Rule provides for a library as well.

The first monastery of the Order was established at Vadstena, Sweden, in 1369. Birgitta's remains were brought there in 1373–1374, when claustral life began. Her daughter Catherine remained in Rome to settle the affairs of the new Order before going to Vadstena, where she became the first superior and died in 1381. The bishop witnessed the consecration of the first members in 1384, and at the same time a strict form of cloister was established. The first abbess was blessed in 1388, three years before Birgitta's canonization. Although the early years of the Order were troubled by controversies over the presence of male and female religious in the same community, the Order quickly spread. Paradiso was founded in 1394 at Florence and in turn founded additional monasteries. From Vadstena came monasteries in England (Syon, 1407), Denmark (Maribo, 1416), and Poland (Lublin, 1412). In 1422 Martin V (1417–1431) forbade monks and nuns to live in adjoining monasteries. Under the leadership of Giovanni Ser Mini, prior of Scala Caeli in Genoa, some monasteries for men only were established in Italy, and a woman's monastery was erected in Genoa. The papal prohibition was soon lifted by Eugene IV (1431–1447) in 1435. This began a new surge in foundations, especially in Bavaria, the Rhineland, and the Low Countries. Some general chapters were held in the 15th century to help bind the 19 monasteries of the Order together.

The Reformation led to the closure or transfer of many Bridgettine houses. Among the surviving monasteries were seven in Poland founded from the initial house at Lublin. Altomünster in Bavaria and several houses in the Rhineland, as well as Syon, exiled from England to Portugal, and some houses in the Lowlands continued to exist after the storms of the Reformation subsided. Josephinism, the French Revolution, and the secularization that followed greatly reduced the Order.

Meanwhile a separate Order arose in Spain called the Recollect Bridgettines. Although they were influenced to some extent by the older Bridgettines in the Low Countries, they constituted an entirely different order. The Order had no male members in its monasteries, the first of which was begun at Valladolid (1651). This new Order made several foundations in Mexico.

Four houses of the original Order were restarted after the upheavals of the end of the 18th century: Uden in Holland, with its foundation at Weert, Altomünster, and Syon, which returned to England. These houses have only female religious.

Elisabeth Hesselblad (1870–1957), a Swede who converted to Roman Catholicism in the United States, entered the Order in Rome in 1904. She tried to bring the surviving communities into closer contact. In 1919 she opened a community in Rome. Her community extended hospitality to pilgrims, much as Birgitta had done. Some novices from India entered the community in Rome in 1937 and then returned to India and founded a number of communities. The Order she founded numbers 34 convents located in India, Europe, and Mexico. A group of men began a Bridgettine monastery in the United States, which eventually settled at Amity, Oregon. It is subject to the archbishop of Portland, Oregon.

Saint Birgitta's Order came into the world when large, rural religious houses such as she envisaged were having a very difficult time. Her Order developed in areas that were especially hard hit by the Protestant Reformation. Perhaps her most important contribution has been to lodge within Swedish tradition and patriotism her Catholic presence. Birgitta's intent was that educated priests in each community would provide instruction and spiritual guidance. In Sweden hundreds of sermons given in Bridgettine monasteries are extant. After these have been studied more thoroughly, they will provide a valuable window into the spirituality of the Bridgettines. Birgitta herself was much influenced by Cistercian monks, and the spirit of her Order has more to do with the older monastic spirituality than with Scholastic theology. Her own mystical experiences derived from close reading of the Bible. Her mystical experience and aims mirrored those of the prophets. Her visions are directed toward the Church and the world, calling both to conversion. Her *Revelations* proved immensely popular and was translated quickly into many languages. An excellent representative of the Bridgettine tradition is Richard Reynolds (c. 1487–1535), a humanist, preacher, and martyr under Henry VIII.

HUGH FEISS, O.S.B.

*See also* Augustinian Rule; Cistercians; Double Houses, Western Christian; Reformation; Scandinavia; Vadstena, Sweden; Women's Monasteries: Western Christian

**Further Reading**

Bridget, of Sweden, Saint, *Revelaciones extravagantes*, edited by Lennart Hollman, Uppsala: Almqvist and Wiksell, 1956

Bridget, of Sweden, Saint, *Revelaciones*, edited by Birger Bergh et al., Uppsala: Almqvist and Wiksell, 1967

Bridget, of Sweden, Saint, *Opera minora I: Regula saluatoris* and *Opera minora II: Sermo angelicus*, edited by Sten Eklund, Stockholm: Almqvist and Wiksell, 1972–1975

Bridget, of Sweden, Saint, *Life and Selected Revelations* (Classics of Western Spirituality), edited and translated by Marguerite Tjader Harris, Albert Ryle Kezel, and Tore Nyberg, New York: Paulist Press, 1990

Cnattingius, Hans, *Studies in the Order of St. Bridget of Sweden*, volume 1: *The Crisis in the 1420's* (Stockholm Studies in History, 7), Stockholm: Almqvist and Wiksell, 1963

Damiano, Piero, *La spiritualità di santa Brigida di Svezia*, Florence: Fiorentina, 1964

Ellis, Roger, *Syon Abbey: The Spirituality of the English Bridgettines* (Analecta Cartusiana, 68), Salzburg: Institut für Anglistik und Amerikanistik, 1984

Fogelqvist, Ingvar, *Apostasy and Reform in the Revelations of St. Birgitta* (Bibliotheca Theologiae Practicae, 51), Stockholm: Almqvist and Wiksell International, 1993

Gregersson, Birger, and Thomas Gascoigne, *The Life of Saint Birgitta* (Peregrina Translations Series, 17), translated by Julia Bolton Holloway, Toronto: Peregrina, 1991

Jørgensen, Johannes, *Saint Bridget of Sweden*, 2 vols., translated by Ingeborg Lund, London and New York: Longmans, Green, 1954

Morris, Bridget, *St. Birgitta of Sweden*, Woodbridge: Boydell Brewer, 1999

Nyberg, Tore, *Birgittinische Klostergründungen des Mittelalters* (Bibliotheca Historica Lundensis, 15), Lund: Gleerup, 1965

Nyberg, Tore, compiler, *Dokumente und Untersuchungen zur inneren Geschichte der Drei Birgittenklöster Bayerns, 1420–1570* (Quellen und Erörterungen zur Bayerischen Geschichte, N.F. 26, volume 1), Munich: Beck, 1972

Nyberg, Tore, editor, *Birgitta, hendes vaerk og hendes klostre i Norden [Birgitta, Her Works, and Her Five Abbeys in the Nordic Countries]* (Odense University Studies in History and Social Sciences, 150), Odense: Odense University Press, 1991

# Brigit, St. c. 453–c. 524

Reputed Irish founder of the Abbey of Kildare

St. Brigit of Ireland is the reputed founder of the monastery of Kildare, County Kildare, in the fifth century. The actual date of her foundation is unknown; no records and few archaeological remains exist that can be dated to this period. However, by the mid–seventh century the monastery was a well-established community and episcopal see, large enough and important enough to offer considerable rivalry to the churches and communities of St. Patrick, centered at Armagh, for the supremacy of the churches in Ireland. St. Brigit's monastic foundation was the first for women in Ireland and one of the few that have been recorded. Kildare also became a double monastery for both men and women under the rule of the abbess, the only one of its kind in Ireland for which any mention is made. Although eventually Armagh gained supremacy and the monastery diminished, Kildare continued as a monastic community, mostly of nuns, into the 12th century.

The origins of the saint herself are obscure and entirely legendary; some of the traditions attached to her can be traced to a pre-Christian Celtic goddess named Brigid, and her feast day, 1 February, corresponds to one of the major festivals in the pagan Celtic calendar. Her first known hagiographer, Cogitosus, wrote more than 100 years after her presumed date of death (524, 526, or 528, according to the Annals of Ulster), and his *Vita Sanctae Brigidae* (c. 680) is considered one of the earliest works of hagiography in Ireland. Cogitosus claims in his preface that he is writing at the behest of his brethren of Kildare and declares Kildare the head of "almost all the Irish Churches with supremacy over all the monasteries of the Irish" (Connolly and Picard, 1987). Cogitosus says little about Brigit's birth and early life, except that she was born of Christian parents and performed a miracle in her youth, after which she took the veil. The *Vita* then becomes a series of anecdotes relating conventional miracles of healing, providing and multiplying food, controlling the weather and animals, and protecting her household. He also records the unconventional miracles of Brigit hanging her wet cloak on a sunbeam and restoring an errant nun to virginity by causing the nun's pregnancy to disappear.

Brigit as abbess wielded considerable authority in her community; according to Cogitosus, she chose her own bishop, Conlaed, to perform the episcopal and sacerdotal functions that she was unable to exercise, but the real power and authority within the monastery lay with the abbess. The office of abbess of Kildare continued to be an eminent one; the abbess of Kildare commanded an honor price for death or injury equivalent to that of a bishop. This has led some to believe that Brigit was a bishop. *The Old Irish Life of St. Brigit*, composed in the ninth century, records that at her consecration as a nun, the attending bishop, filled with the grace of God, accidentally read the orders of a bishop over her (Ó hAodha, 1978); however, the same *Life* relates a meeting between St. Patrick and St. Brigit, when Brigit, lacking the authority to baptize a new convert, had to call on the services of Patrick. The names of the abbesses of Kildare are recorded in the Irish annals, along with the abbots and bishops, from the 8th to the 12th centuries, an honor given to no other female foundation in Ireland.

The final part of Cogitosus' *Vita* is devoted to a depiction of Kildare itself. He describes the church as a spacious structure with three chapels separated by wooden walls. The first wall ran the width of the church in the east part, and a door was at either end. Through the door on the right the archbishop and the chapter entered the sanctuary; through the door on the left the abbess and the nuns entered to partake in the Mass. Another wooden partition stretching from the west wall separated the men and women faithful, the men entering from the right and the women from the left. Cogitosus says little of the church decorations but does tell of painted pictures and wall hangings. On either side of the altar rested the bodies of Brigit and her bishop, Conlaed, in richly decorated tombs adorned with gold, silver, and precious gems, attesting to their status as religious leaders and to the wealth of Kildare. Cogitosus defines the monastery as a "metropolitan city" without encircling walls where kings kept their treasure and fugitives found sanctuary and says that "it is looked upon as the most outstanding on account of its illustrious supremacy" (Connolly and Picard, 1987). No other description of St. Brigit's church and monastery survives; however, it is apparent that a substantial and influential monastic community existed at Kildare.

The "supremacy of the churches" in Ireland passed to Armagh in the eighth and ninth centuries, but Kildare remained a monastic community until the Norman invasion, although not as a double house. Gwynn and Hadcock (1970) speculate that the men's community diminished in the 12th century to a few who served the cathedral. Between the 8th and 11th centuries, the community suffered variable fortunes, being plundered and burned on several occasions. The monastery of Kildare was important politically to the ruling family of Leinster, from whom were drawn many of its bishops and abbesses. In 1132, in an attempt to gain control over the monastery and install his own

choice of abbess, the king of Leinster raided the convent; the ruling abbess was raped, several monastics were slain, and the church was destroyed. The obit of the last abbess of Kildare is recorded in 1171. In 1185 Giraldus Cambrensis included in his *Topography of Ireland* a description of a perpetual fire at Brigit's monastery that was kept by the nuns within a sacred enclosure (the fire had supposedly been first lit by Brigit and was kept in her memory). Given Giraldus' other fanciful descriptions, this one is also dubious, but it does attest to the continuity of Brigit's community as a convent for nuns.

In the late 12th century, Kildare came into the possession of the regular canons of St. Augustine, and a Franciscan house was established on the site in 1254. The nunnery at Kildare continued in existence until the general suppression of 1540–1541. Although the cult of St. Brigit spread from Ireland to England and the Continent, St. Brigit did not leave behind a monastic rule, nor did her successors establish a major order. The importance of Brigit's foundation lies in its role as a prominent record in the history of women's houses in early Christian Ireland and the place of women in the early Irish Church.

DOROTHY ANN BRAY

*See also* Abbess: Christian; Celtic Monasticism; Double Houses, Western Christian; Hagiography: Western Christian; Ireland: History; Pilgrimages, Christian: Western Europe; Transvestite Saints

## Biography

St. Brigit (or St. Bride) may or may not have lived, for her name could be a version of that of the pagan goddess Brigid. Legend links her with Leinster and with the women's monastery at Cell Dara (Kildare). She is revered as the foundress of women's monasticism in Ireland.

## Further Reading

Bitel, Lisa M., *Isle of the Saints: Monastic Settlement and Christian Community in Early Ireland*, Ithaca, New York: Cornell University Press, 1990

Bray, Dorothy Ann, "The Image of St. Brigit in the Early Irish Church," *Etudes Celtiques* 24 (1987)

Connolly, S., editor and translator, "Vita Prima Sanctae Brigitae," *Journal of the Royal Society of Antiquaries of Ireland* 119 (1989)

Connolly, S., and J-M. Picard, editors and translators, "Cogitosus: Life of Saint Brigit," *Journal of the Royal Society of Antiquaries of Ireland* 117 (1987)

Gwynn, A., and R.N. Hadcock, *Medieval Religious Houses: Ireland*, Harlow: Longmans, 1970; reprint, Dublin: Irish Academic Press, 1988

Mytum, Harold, *The Origins of Early Christian Ireland*, London and New York: Routledge, 1991

Ó hAodha, Donncha, *Bethu Brigte*, Dublin: Dublin Institute for Advanced Studies, 1978

Ó Riain, Pádraig, "Sainte Brigitte: Paradigme de l'abbesse celtique?," in *La femme au Moyen-Âge*, edited by Michel Rouche and Jean Heuclin, Maubeuge, France: Ville de Mauberge, 1990

# Bruno, St. c. 1030–1101

German Christian monk and founder of the
Carthusian Order

The founder of the Carthusian Order was born in Cologne and
studied in the acclaimed cathedral school at Reims under Herimann. After Herimann had resigned his post, Bruno, at that time
master and canon at St. Cunibert's, Cologne, became schoolman
and schoolmaster of the cathedral school at Reims, where he
stayed for the next quarter of a century. Many of his former students rose to high rank in the Church and played an important
role in the struggle for ecclesiastical reform. Pope Urban II
(1088–1099) was one of them.

Bruno sided with proponents of the Gregorian reform in their
struggle to have Manasses of Gournay (1067–1080), a simoniac
archbishop of Reims, removed from office, and he did so despite
the fact that Manasses had appointed him his chancellor around
1075. Deposed from all offices Bruno found refuge in the castle
of Ebal of Roncy. After Manasses was removed by Pope Gregory
VII (1073–1085), Bruno returned to Reims (1080). Bruno's contacts with the papal legate Hugh of Die had played a role in his
deposition. In 1081 the cathedral chapter presented him for the
see of Reims.

Like many other high-ranking clergy of this epoch, Bruno decided to renounce offices, titles, and riches. With two companions he found refuge (c. 1082) in a hermitage in the forest of
Sèche-Fontaine (Commune Avirey, Aube; Diocese of Langres)
near Troyes, where he tried in vain to live as a hermit under the
spiritual direction of St. Robert (c. 1027–1111), abbot of the
neighboring Molesme.

Under these circumstances Bruno and six new companions
requested a place to build another hermitage from St. Hugh I,
the new bishop of the mountainous diocese of Grenoble, known
for his pro-reform views. The hermitage, La Grande-Chartreuse,
was established in June 1084 in a place called *desertum Cartusiae*, in a small valley 3,870 feet above sea level and about 15
miles from Grenoble. The new community received support
from Seguinus, abbot of La Chaise-Dieu (1078–1092). The first
charterhouse consisted of wooden cells for eremites, a cloister,
and a stone church in which eremites gathered for common
matins and vespers. Other offices, prayers, reading, and manual
labor were performed in privacy in cells where meals were also
taken. Only on Sundays and feasts did the whole community
gather for prayer and in the refectory. Two of Bruno's companions (who were not ordained) together with *conversi* handled the
material needs of the community.

In 1090 Pope Urban II summoned Bruno to Rome to become
his adviser. Bruno never returned to La Grande-Chartreuse,
where he made Landuin (1090–1100) his successor. In June
1090, fleeing with the pope from Emperor Henry IV
(1056–1106), he traveled to southern Italy, visiting Capua and
Salerno. In the autumn of the same year, Bruno declined the
archbishopric of Reggio and with papal consent continued to
live in seclusion. Later he traveled to Calabria, where, with the
help of Prince Roger of Sicily, he established his second colony of
hermits, St. Maria dell' Eremo (now St. Maria della Torre) in La
Torre at the Serra (now Serra San Bruno) in the mountainous
and forest-covered region of the Diocese of Squillace. Bruno died
there on 6 October 1101 and was buried in a charterhouse that
he had founded in St. Stefano del. Bosco.

Bruno never wrote a separate charter and did not intend to
established a new order. Nevertheless, he became a model for
those who wanted to seek God in seclusion.

In the Middle Ages the cult of Bruno was limited to the region
of Calabria. In 1514 Pope Leo X (1513–1521) canonized Bruno
*viva voce*, approving his cult within the Carthusian Order. His
feast (6 October) was introduced into the Roman liturgy in 1623
by Pope Gregory XIV (1621–1623). In 1674 Pope Clement X
(1670–1676) raised it to the rank of *festum duplex*.

MAREK DERWICH

*See also* Carthusians; France: History; Hermits: Western
Christian

## Biography

The founder of the Carthusians was a German, educated at
Cologne and Reims. For nearly a quarter of a century he taught
at the cathedral school at Reims. In the early 1080s Bruno took
instruction from Robert of Molesme, the future founder of
Cîteaux. In 1084 Bruno and six companions withdrew to the
mountains near Grenoble, where he founded La Grande-
Chartreuse. In 1090 Pope Urban II (whom he had taught at
Reims) summoned Bruno to Rome. Bruno refused the bishopric
of Reggio and founded the monastery of La Torre in the
wilderness of Calabria. He died there in 1101.

## Major Works

The most important sources for the study of Bruno's spirituality
are his two letters written at La Torre to Raoul le Verd and
to La Grande-Chartreuse community in which he presented
the advantages of the contemplative life (*Lettres des
Prèmiers Chartreux*, volume 1: *Bruno - Guigues - S.
Anthelme*, edited by M. Laporte [Sources Chrétiennes, 88],
1962; 2nd edition, 1988). Most probably he also wrote a
profession of faith (*Professio fidei*, ibidem). Doubtful,
however, is Bruno's authorship of commentaries on the
Psalms (*Expositio in Psalmos*, in *Patrologia Latina*, volume
152) or on the letters of St. Paul (*Expositio in epistolas S.
Pauli*, in *Patrologia Latina*, volume 153), works
traditionally attributed to him.

## Further Reading

Bligny, Bernard, *Saint Bruno, le premier chartreux* (De mémoire
d'homme), Rennes: Ouest-France, 1984
Gioia, Giuseppe, *L'Esperienza contemplativa: Bruno il
certosino* (Spiritualità, 3), Torino: Paoline, 1989
Gruys, Albert, *Cartusiana: Un instrument heuristique,
bibliographie générale: auteurs cartusiens* (Bibliographies,
colloques, travaux préparatoires), Paris: Centre National de
la Recherche Scientifique, 1976

Hogg, James, "Bruno und die Kartäusen," in *Mönchsväter und Ordensgründer: Männer und Frauen in der Nachfolge Jesu*, edited by Josef Weismayer, Würzburg: Echter, 1991

Hogg, James, "Le vite di San Bruno," in *San Bruno e la Certosa di Calabria: Atti del convegno internazionale di studi per il IX centenario della Certosa di Serra S. Bruno: Squillace, Serra S. Bruno, 15–18 settembre 1991* (Bibliotheca vivariensis, 4), edited by Pietro De Leo, Soveria Mannelli, Catanzaro: Rubbettino, 1995

Langraf, A., "Probleme des Schrifttums Brunos des Kartäusers," *Collectanea Franciscana* 8 (1938)

Mursell, Gordon, *The Theology of the Carthusian Life in the Writings of St. Bruno and Guigo I* (Analecta Cartusiana, 127), Salzburg: Institut für Anglistik und Amerikanistik, Universität Salzburg, 1988

Papàsogli, Giorgio, *God Answers in the Desert: Bruno, the Saint of the Charterhouse*, Parkminster: Carthusian Order, 1984

Posada, G., *Maestro Bruno, padre de monjes* (Biblioteca de Autores Cristianos, 413), Madrid: Biblioteca de Autores Cristianos, 1980; 2nd edition, 1995

Un Cartujo, "Familia e infancia de san Bruno," *Studia Monastica* 37 (1995)

# Buddha (Śākyamuni) c. 586–c. 483

Indian founder of Buddhism

*Life of Buddha in History, Legend, and Monastic Practice*

According to traditional belief, Buddha was born a prince but renounced the world. Traditional dates for Buddha are 586 to 483 B.C. Significantly these dates have been disputed in recent scholarship by Richard Gombrich, who prefers dates 120 years later. It must be admitted at the outset that the idea of "the Buddha" is to some extent a construction, for there is a much longer period between the death of Buddha and the emergence of the first written records than there is between the death of Jesus and the production of the first synoptic gospels. However, group recitation of Pāli scriptures by monks and nuns called *bhānikas* (reciters) provided continuity and to some extent ensured orthodoxy during the period before written documents. Thus, although *suttas* (discourses) in the Pāli language cannot be confidently said to be the exact words of the Buddha, they are the earliest texts for the study of Buddha's life and thought. The Pāli Canon remains the most authoritative set of texts about the life and teachings of Buddha. By contrast texts in Mahāyāna Buddhism are culturally and chronologically much further removed from Buddha's frame of reference. At issue here is the sort of truth to be found in Buddhism and the manner of finding it. In general Theravādins assume that the earliest texts must be closest to the true ideas of the Buddha, whereas Mahāyānists assume that Buddha speaks through a historical process in which later developments might be closer to the fullness of Buddha's message.

Accounts of Buddha's life and thought contain a mix of folk elements and intellectual doctrine. The *Jātaka*, stories of previous lives of Buddha, depict his birth as involving a sort of immaculate conception in which Queen Maya gives birth to him after dreaming of being touched by the trunk of a white elephant. Whether this myth explains what makes elephants sacred in India or instead exemplifies their general utility (which doubtless antedated the birth story) is a matter for reflection. In any case legend has it that Buddha was born in the Lumbini Grove, under a Sal tree, to which Queen Maya (or Mahamaya) had clung while giving birth. Thirty-two auspicious marks were seen on the body of the newborn indicating his potential for greatness. In the *Jātaka* Siddhartha's birth is depicted as surrounded by a great deal of pageantry, after which he performed heroic deeds. It was prophesied that the young Siddhartha would become either a world conqueror or a world renouncer.

Buddha's father, hoping that the young prince would become the former, provided him with every earthly comfort within the palace walls. Paternal prohibitions against travel outside those walls having been secretly violated, Buddha viewed with the help of his charioteer, Channa, four sights that changed his life. These four sights – old person, sick person, dead person, and renunciant – led to the Great Renunciation, in which Siddhartha embarked on his religious quest. Leaving the palace on his horse, Kanthaka, while all others were asleep, Buddha began a new life at the age of 29.

After leaving his wife, Yaśodara, and son, Rahula, in the opulent palace, Siddhartha became a wandering mendicant. As a practitioner of yoga in the pre-Buddhist meditative tradition, Siddhartha became a pupil of illustrious meditation masters, Alara Kalama and Uddaka Ramaputta. Having learned all they taught but judging it insufficient for complete enlightenment, Buddha went on to develop his own distinctive achievement. Even when abandoned by his friends, the five ascetics, who found his Middle Path between asceticism and sensualism not to their liking, Buddha persevered. The temptations of the god Mārā could not deter him. Buddha proved rock steady against both threats of violence and the seductions of Mārā's lusty daughters. Neither self-love nor love of another could be used to destroy him. Under the Bodhi Tree (*Ficus religiosus*), Buddha vowed on the banks of the river Neranjara not to stop meditating until reaching *nibbāna* (Sanskrit, nirvāna, "enlightenment"). The enlightenment experience emerged in the depth of the night from cultivation of *jhanas* (trance states). According to some accounts Buddha meditated for seven weeks and was sustained by a milk-rice offering. One way to understand the significance of Buddha's enlightenment against the background of pre-Buddhistic tradition is to say that knowledge of the destruction of the defilements (*āsavas*), the sixth *abhiññā*, is his distinctive achievement. From a Theravāda perspective he had now gone beyond one whose essence is enlightenment, the bodhisattva, and become the enlightened one, or Buddha. It should be noted that the Buddha's enlightenment was manifested in socially engaged action, for he did not withdraw afterward but embarked on a public teaching career. According to a traditional account, he taught for some 45 years after enlightenment and died at the ripe old age of at least 80. His death is on some accounts depicted as one for which he prepared and on other accounts as

View of the monastic site with Dhamekh Stūpa, site of the Buddha's first teaching, Sārnāth, India, c. fifth century (Gupta period) and later.
Photo courtesy of Marylin M. Rhie

one that happened unexpectedly because of poisoned food. Traditional belief holds that at death, as at birth, miracles occurred.

In one respect Buddha shows the virtuous path of the bodhisattva as Mahāyānists see it, as he did not go to final enlightenment (parinibbāna) but remained to help others achieve enlightenment. Ultimately the achievement of enlightenment led to the founding of the monastic order of monks and nuns, the sangha.

According to the Udanavagga, a Pāli text, his distinctive achievement is the understanding of causality. After his enlightenment Buddha preached dhamma, thus winning over initially skeptical associates. He adapted his teaching to the context and level of the audience, using "skillful means." There is some scholarly controversy about just what "omniscience" means and whether Buddha achieved omniscience. Unlike Jain leaders, such as his near contemporary Mahavira (599–527 B.C.), Buddha was not thought to be literally omniscient. However, Buddha is depicted as knowing all that is necessary for salvation. After an extensive teaching career, Buddha's parinibbāna (final enlightenment) came after eating some spoiled food (probably mushroom or pork).

The earliest form of Buddhist monastic life was that of South Asian and Southeast Asian Theravāda (Doctrine of the Elders), but Buddha's original ideas developed into East Asian Ma-

hāyāna (Large Vehicle) and Tibetan Vajrayāna (Diamond Vehicle) versions. Strictly speaking Theravāda is only one of the Hīnayāna schools, others being, for example, Sarvastivāda and Sautrantika. However, in popular use the term Theravāda is often used interchangeably with Hīnayāna. Because the latter term can mean not only "small" in the sense of elite but "small" in the sense of "lesser," it is not a respectful term to employ, and Theravādins do not usually use it of themselves. Mahāyāna means "great" in the sense of large or populous, as the large raft can carry many people of various psychological types and not only celibate monks and nuns. In general, three types of attitudes toward sexuality exist: repression, accommodation, and using it to transcend passion (Theravāda, Mahāyāna, and Vajrayāna, respectively). In any case Buddha's dhamma (doctrine) is to be used for crossing over and not for clinging on to, and neither Theravādins nor Mahāyānists make a fetish of doctrine. It is usually the Theravādins who are the more monastically inclined; sometimes they are criticized by well-meaning Buddhists of other traditions who would like to see the Theravāda tradition become more socially engaged. In fact Buddha himself was socially engaged, for after the enlightenment experience he did not withdraw from human contact but continued to teach.

At issue here is what being a socially engaged follower of Buddha means. Sometimes Theravāda tradition is criticized internally by the Theravādins themselves. In this way Buddha's thought can be continually renewed by being open to self-examination. It is clear, however, that the *dhamma* wheel set in motion by Buddha, the *Tathāgata* (enlightened saint), is wide ranging enough to accommodate celibate monasticism and various other lifestyles as well as it moves around the world.

Generally speaking, although there can be some overlap, Theravāda dominates in Sri Lanka, Thailand, Burma, and much of Southeast Asia, whereas Mahāyāna dominates in China, Japan, Korea, and Vietnam. Vajrayāna is dominant in Tibet and the surrounding region. Crucial to the development of Theravāda was the patronage of the successful King Aśoka who caused much bloodshed but later patronized religious, especially Buddhism.

### Representations of Buddha in Art: Aniconic and Anthropomorphic Traditions

During the first few centuries in the development of Buddhism, there were no anthropomorphic images of the Buddha. The early view on this was expressed by the Buddha himself, who, when asked by Ananda what the *sangha* would do after the Buddha died, observed that his person was of little consequence, as the Buddhist doctrine is eternal. In this "aniconic" period the Buddha exemplifies "presence as absence" in the sense that his presence is represented by such iconographic elements as footprints or the Bodhi Tree.

Whereas in early Buddhism Buddha was regarded as a human being who found an ancient path to enlightenment, a path that had been trod by numerous Buddhas before, the Mahāyāna encouraged apotheosis as foreshadowed in the numerous epithets showered on Siddhartha Gautama in the early Pāli texts. Here he is "Buddha," the Enlightened One (a term comparable to the term *Christ*). Buddha is styled "Tathāgata" (literally, "thus gone"), one who has lived the holy life and done what has to be done and will never be reborn. Numerous other epithets are also applied, such as *cakravartin* (turner of the wheel of Doctrine) and *bhagavan* (lord). Buddha is even *satthar devamanussānaṃ* (teacher of gods and men), for the gods – *deva*s, or "shining ones" – themselves are still in need of enlightenment. Whether Buddhism is "atheistic" depends on what exactly this term is taken to mean and which tradition of Buddhism one focuses on. What is clear is that in early Indian Pāli Buddhism, Buddha is depicted as neither a "god" nor an ordinary man but as a pathfinder in this eon. In this respect Buddha is comparable to his near contemporary, Mahavira, the Jaina leader. However, Buddha does not claim "omniscience," a characteristic attributed to their "ford maker" (*Tithankara*) Mahavira. As the parable of the Simsapa leaves illustrates, what Buddha knew and taught was small in comparison to what he knew and did not teach, which, like all the leaves of the forest, is nevertheless finite. Still Buddha is depicted as knowing all that is necessary for salvation. This is not so very different from the Roman Catholic understanding of papal infallibility, wherein the pope is said to know all pertaining to faith and morals with an unerring understanding. This is not taken to mean that he knows all facts about

the world or future events, such as what the weather will be like. Yet there is a difference. Despite the belief of Buddhists that Buddha's comprehension of *dhamma* (doctrinal truth) is perfect, they do not rely on him in the way that Christians often rely on their religious leaders. There is a rejection of anything except the authority of experience and experientialism (not to be confused with empiricism). Buddha urged his disciples to come and see (*ehi passika*) for themselves in a way that makes personal realization (not to be confused with empirical verification) paramount. Rather than accepting doctrine on blind faith in the way Buddhists saw the Hindi brahmins doing, everyone is to be a lamp or island (Pāli *dīpa* can mean either one) for oneself. The Buddha encourages rational faith (*akaravati saddhā*), not the baseless faith (*amulika saddhā*) of the brahmins, like blind men touching various parts of an elephant and taking reality to be limited to partial perception. There is a complex intertwining of faith and art in Buddhist appreciation such that anyone desiring to understand Buddhism is advised to supplement sūtra study with the study of the development of the Buddha image.

With the development of Buddhist figure sculpture, Buddha is typically depicted in seated meditation but also lying recumbent in *parinibbāna* and (more rarely still) in walking meditation. Although the development of iconography in the presentation of the Buddha image defies simple description, certain features dominate: the right shoulder bare, expressive of an ancient pattern of dress (reminiscent of a bust found in Mohenjo-daro); rings on the neck (representing the conch shell and authority of Buddha's speech); the elongated earlobes (emblematic of the Great Renunciation, princely jewelry having been removed); the hair curled like snail shells with possible solar symbolism; the third eye on the forehead (representing wisdom); the limbs often treated in a plantlike, organic fashion; and the gestures (*mudra*) expressive of tranquility, insight, and compassion. Typical gestures in seated Buddha figure sculpture include the *Dhamma-cakra-pravatana mudra* (turning the wheel of the law) and the *bhumi-sparsa mudra* (touching the earth to bear witness to Buddha's enlightenment).

### Language and Text

Pāli, the earliest language of Buddhism, was used to write the first Buddhist texts after a period in which the oral tradition of the reciters (*bhāṇaka*s) prevailed. Buddhist texts were written down several centuries after Buddha's death, probably between the second century B.C. and the second century A.D. After the codification of Buddhist texts by successive Buddhist councils, written texts developed about the life of the Buddha. These Pāli *sutta* (Sanskrit, *sūtra*) texts comprise the *Sutta Piṭaka*, one of the three baskets or *Piṭaka*s – Sutta, Vinaya, and Abhidhamma. The *Sutta Piṭaka* told of the life and teachings of Buddha, the *Vinaya Piṭaka* provided the rules of conduct for monks and nuns, and the *Abhidhamma Piṭaka* systematized the doctrine. The *sutta*s (thread of argument, straight as a carpenter's line) relate stories of the life of the Buddha recorded in discourses that were organized in books according to type. Thus, the teachings of the Buddha in the *Sutta Piṭaka* consist of the five *Nikāya*s: *Majjhima*

Buddha under the Bodhi Tree, Swedagon Pagoda, Rangoon, Burma, 18th century.
Photo courtesy of John C. Huntington, the Huntington Archive

*Nikāya* (Middle Length Sayings), *Dīgha Nikāya* (Long Discourses or Dialogues of the Buddha), *Saṃyutta Nikāya* (Gradual Sayings), *Anguttara Nikāya* (Kindred Sayings), and *Khuddaka Nikāya* (Minor Discourses). The Pāli Text Society's editions of Buddha's teachings are landmarks in the history of scholarship, recent work by Maurice Walsh is noteworthy, and some academic and religious groups have even put Pāli texts into CD-ROM format.

### Biographies of the Buddha

Major Buddhist schools have fashioned biographies of the Buddha throughout its history. In Theravāda there is the *Nidāna-kathā* (classical) type and the *vamsa* (chronicle) type. In contemporary Buddhism "demythologized" biographies of Buddha have been written. These emphasize aspects of Buddha's life that are compatible with scientific views of reality. One example is the biography of the Buddha constructed from Pāli sources by David J. and Indrani Kalupahana, *The Way of Siddhartha* (1982).

### Buddha and Monasticism

Buddha, together with *dhamma* (doctrine) and *sangha* (order of monks and nuns), forms the Triple Jewel (Sanskrit, *Triratna*). Revered by Buddhists, the Triple Jewel provides structure for the Three Refuges (*Tisarana*). This formula, namely, "I take refuge in the Buddha, I take refuge in the *Dhamma*, I take refuge in the *Sangha*" (recited three times), is used in initiation ceremonies for those who become Buddhists and as reminders for *sangha* members continuing on the path. It is thus clear that the relationship among Buddha, *dhamma*, and *sangha* is an integral one and that respect for the Triple Jewel plays an important role in the lives of Buddhist believers. It is clear that Buddha is regarded with a high degree of respect and reverence by believers. In the Pāli Canon Buddha is depicted as a man and not a god (*deva*). However, if one were to say that he is *merely* a man, that would be misleading in certain ways, first because Buddha instantiates an archetypal form of consciousness that has appeared before in the infinite past and will reappear at least once (Maitreya, Buddha of the future) and second because of the great reverence paid to Buddha, far more than would be appropriate for any human being. For example, Buddha-images in ritual context might become symbols and are then thought to participate in the power of Buddha. In this sense the figure can be regarded as "animate," but the "worship" of this figure is neither idolatry nor narcissism. It is not the stone or metal that is revered, nor is it one's "substantial self" (regarded as nonexistent by Buddhists), but rather the archetypal form of enlightened consciousness that was achieved, for example, by Siddhartha Gautama Buddha. Beings, including Buddha, are streams of consciousness characterized by continuity without identity of self-same substance. Consciousness is not an *ātman* (a permanent, blissful center of consciousness, as in Hinduism) and cannot rightly be reified or thought of as static.

Monastic practitioners of Buddhism have interpreted the life of Buddha as a model to emulate. This is so regardless of whether the ideal is the arhat that dominates in Theravāda or the bodhisattva that dominates in Mahāyāna. Buddhists who follow the arhat ideal emphasize celibacy as a precondition for the monastic life as well as the importance of working out one's salvation through meditation as an island (*dīpa*) unto oneself. Buddhists who follow the bodhisattva ideal sometimes permit monastics to marry and have families, seeing that one should be a lamp (*dīpa*) for oneself but that one's own salvation is intimately connected with the salvation of all sentient beings. Through the vow of the bodhisattva not to attain enlightenment until all sentient beings do so, great emphasis falls on compassion. In the development of Buddhist views about sexuality, one sees a change from repressing sexuality (Theravāda) to accommodating sexuality in the institution of marriage (Mahāyāna) to using sexuality either actually or symbolically to overcome passion (Vajrayāna).

Nagarjuna (c. 150–250 A.D.), the supreme dialectician of Buddhist tradition, on one interpretation shook scholastic Abhidhamma Buddhism from its ossified category-laden way of thinking back to a realization of the primacy of meditation practice. In this respect Nagarjuna returns to the original message of Buddha, for, despite the extensive use of logic to show the limitations of logic, Nagarjuna approximates the spirit of the Buddha as understood in Zen tradition, which often uses nonlogical means to show the limitations of logic. In Nagarjuna's message he paid homage to "The Exalted One," the Buddha, by beginning and ending his *Mulamadhyamakakarikas* (*Verses on the Foundation of the Middle Way*) with a salutation to Buddha. Thus, structurally the *Mulamadhyamakakarikas* resembles Anselm's version of the ontological argument in that Anselm begins with a prayer. Neither the *Mulamadhyamakakarikas* nor the ontological argument is addressed to those outside their respective circles of faith. In each case the text has a religious focal point (God in one case and Buddha in another) that is external to the text itself and without which the text would lack meaning. In sum, although on one interpretation Nagarjuna appears iconoclastic, the force of his logic goes to show the limitation of reason as applied to matters of ultimate reality and meaning. His overall presentation in the *Mulamadhyamakakarikas* only exalts the importance of Buddha, notwithstanding the appearance of iconoclasm.

Monastic practitioners in some Buddhist traditions (such as Zen) have put much emphasis on lineage. In this way one sees clearly the importance attached Buddha. Yet occasionally in Zen one finds what seems to be a shocking disregard of the Buddha – Q: "What is the Buddha?" A: "Three pounds of flax!" – or a seemingly sacrilegious saying, such as "Meet a Buddha, kill a Buddha." Zen masters varied and are not all from a mold; then, too, nonliteral interpretations of such statements are also possible. For skillful discussions of Buddhist ethics, see articles by George Bond and Mahinda Deegalle in *Pāli Buddhism*, the works of Damien Keown, and the *Journal of Buddhist Ethics*.

### *The Buddha, Buddhas, and Buddhahood*

Siddhartha Gautama Śākyamuni Buddha is the name of the Buddha, when by "Buddha" is meant the historic person who lived in Magadha of North India around the fifth century B.C. As "Siddhartha" he is the well-accomplished one; as Gautama he resonates with the power of the ancient *ṛṣi*, or seer, of the same name to whom are attributed some Rigvedic hymns; as Śākyamuni he is the sage of the Śākyan clan; and, most important, as Buddha he is the enlightened one. According to Pāli *sutta*s Buddha is depicted as a man who connected with an ancient path, himself neither a god (*deva*) nor Creator God (*Issara*). Yet even in this sense Buddha also has important epithets applied to him, such as "Tathāgata" (literally, "thus gone," a "liberated saint"). In a second sense, however, "Buddha" is an archetypal form of consciousness that manifests itself throughout Buddhist history. It is in this sense that there were previous Buddhas and will be a Buddha of the future, Maitreya. Pāli texts teach that there can be only one Buddha in each *kalpa* (eon). The idea seems to be that another Buddha cannot arise until the teachings of a particular Buddha have entirely disappeared. Buddhas arise only in a later part of an eon when beings can appreciate the message better because more suffering exists then. Although Buddha opposed

caste-based thinking and regarded as "true brahmins" only pure persons who followed the Buddhist path, Buddhas are traditionally viewed as arising in India (specifically, in the continent of Jambudvīpa) among the brahmins and *kshatriya*s. In yet a third sense, there is "Buddhahood" (viewed in philosophical terms as an abstract universal), in which case "religious emptiness" (*śunyata*) is what is meant.

In the development of Buddhism there are also "celestial Buddhas," such as Amitābha (infinite light) and Bhaiṣajyaguru (Medicine Buddha); "cosmic Buddhas," such as Vajradhara, Adi Buddha, and Vairocana; and "living Buddhas," such as Padmasambhava and Kūkai.

FRANK J. HOFFMAN

*See also* Anselm, St.; Asceticism: Buddhist Perspectives; Ashram, Influence of; Aśoka; Buddhist Schools/Traditions: South Asia; Buddhology; Chan/Zen; Dharma; Disciples, Early Buddhist; Gestures, Buddhist; Jain Monasticism and Buddhist Monasticism; Mahāpajāpatī Gotamī; Mahāyāna; Master and Pupil: Buddhist Perspectives; Origins: Comparative Perspectives; Patrons, Buddhist: India; Regulations: Buddhist Perspectives; Saṅgha; Spirituality: Buddhist; Visual Arts, Buddhist

### Biography

The historical Buddha, i.e. Siddhartha Gautama who became the Enlightened One, is known from legend, mythic retellings, and oral tradition. His life falls into three parts as prince, yogi, and finally the Buddha. Having lived as a prince until age 29, he fled to become a wandering yogin and practiced asceticism for six years until his body almost wasted away. Dissatisfied, he resorted to the Bodhi Tree (*Ficus religiosus*) at Bodh Gayā, where he achieved a breakthrough to enlightenment (*bodhi*). In the remaining 45 years of his life, he wandered in Northeast India accompanied by the faithful Ananda. As Śākyamuni ("Prince of the Sakyas") Buddha, he attracted followers who comprised the *saṅgha* (at first only men, and later women in their own *saṅgha*), delivered innumerable teachings of the dharma in the sūtras, and modeled the life of the Middle Way. At his death at age 80 in the town of Kusinagara, Uttar Pradesh, he attained final nirvana (or *parinirvāṇa*). Countless legends embellish the story of this most emulated of religious teachers. He left no writings, but oral transmission of his teachings was recorded in sūtras (Pāli, *sutta*s) during the reign of King Aśoka (272–232 B.C.).

### Major Works

Discourses (*sutta*s) in the Pāli Canon (Tripiṭaka) are attributed to the Buddha. What purport to be his words were transmitted orally for centuries before being recorded during the reign of Aśoka.

### Further Reading

Carrithers, Michael, *The Buddha* (Past Masters), Oxford and New York: Oxford University Press, 1983

Coomaraswamy, Ananda Kentish, *Elements of Buddhist Iconography* (SAMP Early 20th-Century Indian Books Project, item 10117), Cambridge, Massachusetts: Harvard University Press, 1935; 3rd edition, New Delhi: Munshiram Manoharlal, 1979

Dehejia, Vidya, *Unseen Presence: The Buddha and Sanchi*, photographs by K.B. Agrawala, Bombay: Marg, 1996

Griffiths, Paul J., *On Being Buddha: The Classical Doctrine of Buddhahood*, Albany: State University of New York Press, 1994

Kalupahana, David J., and Indrani Kalupahana, *The Way of Siddhartha: A Life of the Buddha*, Boulder, Colorado: Shambhala, 1982; London: University Press of America, 1987

Oldenberg, Hermann, *Buddha: His Life, His Doctrine, His Order*, translated by William Hoey, London: Williams and Norgate, 1882; Ann Arbor, Michigan: University Microfilms International, 1979

Rahula, Walpola, *What the Buddha Taught*, Bedford, Bedfordshire: Fraser, 1959; New York: Grove Press, 1962; revised edition, Bedford, Bedfordshire: Fraser, 1967; New York: Grove Press, 1974

Saddhatissa, H., *The Buddha's Way*, London: Allen and Unwin, and New York: Braziller, 1971

Suzuki, Daisetz Teitaro, *Buddha of Infinite Light*, Boston: Shambhala in association with the American Buddhist Academy, 1997

Thomas, E.J., *The Life of Buddha as Legend and History* (History of Civilization [Pre-history and Antiquity]), London: Routledge and Kegan, and New York: Knopf, 1927; 3rd edition, London: Routledge and Kegan, and New York: Barnes and Noble, 1949

# Buddhadāsa 1906–1993

Thai Buddhist monk, scholar, and reformer

Phra Dhammakosājān, better known by his self-appointed monastic name, Buddhadāsa Bhikkhu (Servant of the Buddha), was one of the most influential Thai monks of the 20th century. Born on 21 May 1906 as Nguam Panich, Buddhadāsa spent three years as a temple boy at Wat Pum Riang, a monastery in his hometown, where he learned to read and write and was introduced to Buddhist teachings and rituals. After he had completed his primary schooling and lower-secondary education in Chaiya, southern Thailand, his father's untimely death forced him to work in his family's business at age 15. Ordained a Buddhist monk in 1926, by 1928 he had passed the third and final level of the monastic curriculum and was invited to teach at the royally sponsored Wat Boromathāt monastery in Chaiya.

Subsequently two years of residency in Bangkok (1930–1932) to study Pāli left him disenchanted with rote learning, the noise and distractions of the city, and the lax behavior of Bangkok monks. He returned home in the spring of 1932, the year in which Thailand was transformed from an absolute to a constitutional monarchy, and soon thereafter established a forest monastery, Suan Mokkhabalārāma (The Garden of Empowering Liberation), known simply as Suan Mokkh. He rapidly gained a reputation for intellectual prowess, ability as a teacher, and innovative interpretations of Theravāda doctrine. By 1937 his history of the Buddha's life was being used as a textbook at the Thammayut monastic university, Mahāmakut. In 1940 Buddhadāsa attracted wide attention for a series of lectures at the Buddha-Dhamma Association in Bangkok. His plain language, unencumbered with technical monastic jargon, and his rational, demythologized interpretation of Buddhist teachings appealed to the new urban elites. Suan Mokkh continued to grow and expand, moving to its present site in 1944. Today Suan Mokkh also includes an international meditation center and training program.

Buddhadāsa's teachings have become the basic platform of reformist Buddhism in Thailand for both monks and laity. Several noted Thai social activists, such as Sulak Sivaraksa, acknowledge their indebtedness to his example and guidance. His books are taught in monastic and secular universities, and he remains one of the most widely published and read Buddhist authors in the country. He criticized mainstream Thai Buddhism's preoccupation with the externals of ritual and ceremonial, calling the intent to better one's self in the world as nothing but religious materialism. He interpreted nirvāna not as a far-removed ideal but as liberation from egoistic preoccupation. Rather than a goal achievable only after many lifetimes or requiring monkish renunciation, nirvāna is attainable here and now by all whose attachment to self is transformed into selfless, compassionate regard for others. His social and political teachings envisioned what he referred to as a righteous or dhammic socialism characterized by three fundamental principles: the good of the whole, self-restraint and generosity toward others, and respect and loving kindness. These teachings are grounded in the fundamental Theravāda perception of the mutually interdependent nature of all the universe. As Buddhadāsa put it, "The entire cosmos is a cooperative. The sun, the moon, and the stars live together as a cooperative. The same is true for humans and animals, trees, and the earth. When we realize that the world is a mutual, interdependent, cooperative enterprise . . . then we can build a noble environment. If our lives are not based on this truth, then we shall perish."

DONALD K. SWEARER

*See also* Bangkok, Thailand; Forest Masters; Mun, Ajahn; Peace Movements, Buddhist; Thailand

## Biography
Ordained in Thailand at age 20, Buddhadāsa ("Servant of the Buddha") dwelt at his own forest monastery outside Chaiya from 1932 until his death in 1993. A prolific and revered author (who wrote in Thai), Buddhadāsa grounded reformist (i.e. engaged) Theravāda Buddhism on the notion of the mutual interdependence of all things.

## Major Works
*Toward the Truth*, edited by Donald K. Swearer, 1971
*Me and Mine: Selected Essays of Bhikku Buddhadāsa*, edited by Donald K. Swearer, 1989

## Further Reading
Gabaude, Louis, *Une herméneutique bouddhique contemporaine de Thaïlande: Buddhadasa Bhikkhu*

(Publications de l'École française d'Extrême-Orient, volume 150), Paris: École française d'Extrême-Orient, 1988

Jackson, Peter A., *Buddhadasa: A Buddhist Thinker for the Modern World*, Bangkok: Siam Society, 1988

Jackson, Peter A., *Buddhism, Legitimation, and Conflict: The Political Functions of Urban Thai Buddhism* (Social Issues in Southeast Asia), Singapore: Institute of Southeast Asian Studies, 1989

*Radical Conservatism: Buddhism in the Contemporary World: Articles in Honour of Bhikkhu Buddhadasa's 84th Birthday Anniversary*, Bangkok: Thai Inter-Religious Commission for Development, International Network of Engaged Buddhists, 1990

Santikaro Bhikkhu, "Buddhadasa Bhikkhu: Life and Society through the Natural Eyes of Voidness," in *Engaged Buddhism: Buddhist Liberation Movements in Asia*, edited by Christopher S. Queen and Sallie B. King, Albany: State University of New York Press, 1996

Sivaraksa, Sulak, editor, *The Quest for a Just Society: The Legacy and Challenge of Buddhadasa Bhikkhu*, Bangkok: Thai Inter-Religious Commission for Development, Santi Pracha Dhamma Institute, 1994

Swearer, Donald K., "Bhikkhu Buddhadāsa's Interpretation of the Buddha," *Journal of the American Academy of Religion* 64:2 (1996)

Swearer, Donald K., "The Hermeneutics of Buddhist Ecology in Contemporary Thailand: Buddhadāsa and Dhammapiṭaka," in *Buddhism and Ecology: The Interconnection of Dharma and Deeds* (Religions of the World and Ecology), edited by Mary Evelyn Tucker and Duncan Ryuken Williams, Cambridge, Massachusetts: Harvard University Center for the Study of World Religions, 1997

# Buddhaghosa fifth century A.D.

## Indian commentator on Theravāda Buddhism

Ācariya (Teacher) Buddhaghosa is the most important commentator of the Theravāda Buddhist tradition and the individual most responsible for casting the Buddha's teachings in the definitive shape that they have assumed for the Theravāda Buddhist world. Coming to Sri Lanka from India in the fifth century and working at the Mahāvihāra (Great Monastery) in Anurādhapura, the island's ancient capital, he welded into a single comprehensive system the vast mass of commentarial material that had accumulated over the centuries. For most Theravādins today his works are second in authority only to the Word of the Buddha itself.

The *Mahāvaṃsa*, the Sri Lankan chronicle (in its second part known as the *Cūlavaṃsa*, 37:215–247), gives us a brief account of his life that, although dating from the 13th century and interwoven with legend, probably contains a kernel of historical truth. According to the chronicle, the future commentator was born into a brahmin family near the Bodhi Tree in northeastern India. After learning various systems of philosophy, he wandered over India engaging in debates until he met up with a Buddhist elder named Revata, who converted him to Buddhism. Revata ordained him as a monk with the name Buddhaghosa (Buddha voice, "because his speech was profound like that of the Buddha") and later sent him to Sri Lanka to translate the Theravāda commentaries from Sinhala into Pāli, the language of the Pāli Canon. Buddhaghosa arrived in the island during the reign of King Mahānāma (409–431) and studied the Sinhala commentaries at the Mahāvihāra under the chief elder Sanghapāla. When he asked for permission to translate them into Pāli, the elders first tested his abilities by giving him two stanzas to expound, and he complied by writing the *Visuddhimagga*. Recognizing his genius, the elders gave him free access to the old commentaries, which he translated to their approval. His task finished, he returned to India to venerate the Bodhi Tree.

The prologues and epilogues to Buddhaghosa's works provide disjointed scraps of information that can be used to evaluate this account. Although several features appear dubious, little is explicitly contradicted. Some bits of evidence point to South India as his homeland, but this is not conclusive. The statement that he wrote the *Visuddhimagga* before gaining access to the old commentaries is untenable, as the work is based squarely on those texts. None of the trustworthy sources tells us how long Buddhaghosa stayed in Sri Lanka or about his life after he left the island.

Buddhaghosa's undisputed masterwork is the *Visuddhimagga*, "The Path of Purification." In itself this book is not a commentary but an encyclopedic treatise on Buddhist doctrine and meditation, written to guide seekers of purity along the "straight way" to the ultimate purification, *nibbāna*. The author arranges the teachings of the Buddha into the three traditional stages of virtue, concentration, and wisdom but fills in these headings with a wealth of detail that testifies to the fecundity of Theravāda thought in the centuries after the Buddha's demise. Drawing on the old commentaries, he gives a pithy outline of monastic discipline, full coverage of all the 40 classical subjects of concentration, descriptions of the stages of insight culminating in enlightenment, and an elaborate account of Buddhist philosophical doctrine.

The *Visuddhimagga* does not stand alone but functions as the cornerstone of the entire exegetical method embodied in Buddhaghosa's commentaries on the Pāli Canon. In the prologue to each of his commentaries on the four main *Nikāya*s (*sutta* collections), he says that "the *Visuddhimagga* stands between and in the midst of the four *Nikāya*s and will clarify the meanings of (the various topics) stated therein." Thus, each of the *sutta* commentaries is to be filled in by consulting the *Visuddhimagga* for detailed treatment of topics that they mention only briefly.

Theravāda tradition assigns at least 12 commentaries to Buddhaghosa; each of these has an elaborate postscript, perhaps attached by the Mahāvihāra, that ascribes the work to "the elder who bears the name Buddhaghosa conferred by the venerable ones." Present-day scholars question several of these ascriptions but generally agree that he should be credited with the commentaries to the four *Nikāya*s and probably the Vinaya commentary. The Abhidhamma commentaries are also assigned to him, but this ascription is more problematic, as twice within these works the author says that he wrote them at the request of Bhikkhu Buddhaghosa, and it is unlikely that both author and petitioner had the same name. Possibly the other commentaries ascribed to Buddhaghosa were actually composed by a committee of which he was the chairman, a hypothesis that would explain the improbable number of texts assigned to him as author.

To appreciate the nature of Buddhaghosa's work, it is necessary to emphasize that the project he undertook was not to compose original expositions of the *dhamma* or to create an innovative system of philosophical thought. Rather his task was that of an editor and translator, and in his prologues he repeatedly asserts that he is relying strictly on the methods of exposition passed down by the elders of the Mahāvihāra. A body of commentaries had gradually evolved in India over the centuries, probably from the Buddha's own time, defining the orthodox Theravāda interpretation of the canonical texts and Buddhist religious practice. When Buddhism was introduced to Sri Lanka in the third century B.C., these commentaries were brought along, but whereas the canon was preserved in Pāli and was closed to all additions, the commentaries were rendered into Sinhala and gained in bulk as Sinhalese teachers added to them up to the first century A.D., at which point they too were closed.

Because these texts were preserved in Sinhala, the Theravādins on the mainland felt deprived of the keys needed to interpret their scriptures correctly, and it was to bring back these keys – translated into Pāli, the international Theravādin language – that Buddhaghosa came to Sri Lanka, probably at the behest of the Theravāda *sangha* in South India. However, Buddhaghosa did not simply translate the old commentaries. The quantity of material that had collected over the centuries was far too imposing, and thus in the very process of translating he condensed and streamlined the ancient commentaries (no longer extant), leaving behind a body of polished expository works marked by relentless precision, thoroughness, and an uncanny degree of internal consistency. These works, although far from infallible, provide indispensable aid in understanding the terminology and doctrinal meaning of the canonical texts as viewed from the perspective of the mature Theravāda tradition. In the course of exegesis, they also afford us many revealing spotlights on ancient Buddhist history and on monastic practice during the early centuries of Buddhism.

For example, the *Samantapāsādikā*, the Vinaya commentary, is a massive exposition of monastic discipline over 1,000 pages in roman script. The work begins with a history of the Buddhist order from the Buddha's death to the establishment of Buddhism in Sri Lanka. It then gives detailed explanations of the training rules of the monks and nuns and elaborations on the monastic observances prescribed in the canon. The work is of special value because it shows how the old masters of Theravāda monastic discipline sought to interpret the original rules in relation to the changed circumstances of post-Aśokan Indian society

and in the new milieu encountered in Sri Lanka. The author often quotes conflicting opinions of the Vinaya teachers and tries to adjudicate between them.

Although the man Buddhaghosa remains veiled from us in clouds of obscurity (which might well accord with his own wish for self-effacement), the measure of his success can be gauged from the esteem with which his work has been held by the Theravāda Buddhist world. For Theravādins from the fifth century to the present, his *Visuddhimagga* and commentaries are regarded as authoritative guides to the *dhamma* and a worthy fulfillment of the promise implicit in his name.

BHIKKHU BODHI

*See also* Anurādhapura; Sri Lanka; Rules, Buddhist (Vinaya); Scholastics, Buddhist; Sri Lanka: Sites; Virtues, Buddhist

## Biography

Born into a northern Indian brahmin family in the late fourth century, Buddhaghosa (whose name means "Buddha-Voice") converted to Buddhism and went to the Mahāvihāra in Sri Lanka for instruction. There he assimilated Theravādin teaching, which he summarized in the *Visuddhimagga* (*The Path of Purification*).

## Major Works

*Visuddhimagga*, as *The Path of Purification*, translated by Ñāṇamoli, Bhikkhu, 1956; 5th edition, 1991
*Samantapāsādikā* (Vinaya commentary)
*Sumaṅgalavilāsinī* (Dīgha Nikāya commentary)
*Papañcasūdanī* (Majjhima Nikāya commentary)
*Sāratthappakāsinī* (Saṃyutta Nikāya commentary)
*Manorathapūraṇī* (Aṅguttara Nikāya commentary)

## Further Reading

Adikaram, E.W., *Early History of Buddhism in Ceylon*, Migoda, Ceylon: Puswella, 1946
Gray, James, translator and editor, *Buddhaghosuppatti, or, The Historical Romance of the Rise and Career of Buddhaghosa*, London: Luzac, 1892
Hinüber, Oskar von, *A Handbook of Pāli Literature* (Indian Philology and South Asian Studies, volume 2), New York: de Gruyter, 1996
Jayawickrama, N.A., translator and editor, *The Inception of Discipline, and the Vinaya Nidāna* (Sacred Books of the Buddhists, volume 21), London: Luzac, 1962; Boston: Pali Text Society, 1986
Law, Bimala Churn, *The Life and Work of Buddhaghosa* (Calcutta Oriental Series, number 9), Calcutta: Thacker, Spink, 1923
Law, Bimala Churn, "Buddhaghosa," in *Encyclopaedia of Buddhism*, volume 3, fascicle 3, edited by G.P. Malalasekera, Ceylon: Lanka Bauddha Mandalaya and the Department for Cultural Affairs, Government of Ceylon, 1957
Malalasekera, G.P., *The Pāli Literature of Ceylon* (Prize Publication Fund, volume 10), London: Royal Asiatic Society of Great Britain and Ireland, 1928; reprint, Kandy, Sri Lanka: Buddhist Publication Society, 1994
Norman, K.R., *Pāli Literature* (History of Indian Literature Series, volume 7, fascicle 2), Wiesbaden: Harrassowitz, 1983

# Buddhism: Overview

## Buddha and Being Buddhist

At the most fundamental level, the Triple Jewel of Buddha, Doctrine, and Order is used to distinguish who is Buddhist and who is not. Buddhists take refuge in the Buddha, *dhamma* (doctrine), and *saṅgha* (order of monks and nuns). The first of these is Buddha, viewed as a historical figure. The earliest language of Buddhism is Pāli.

Siddhartha Gautama Śākyamuni Buddha was born a prince but renounced the world. Traditionally the Buddha is thought to have lived between 586 and 483 B.C.E., or "Before the Common Era" in Buddhist terms. Westerners may understand the basics of the complex Buddhist view of time by recognizing, first, that it is not Christocentric, and, second, that many previous worlds existed before this one. There were also previous Buddhas, and there will be a future Buddha. One Buddha is born in a particular eon (Sanskrit, *kalpa*), and another Buddha does not appear until the previous one has disappeared and his teaching declined.

The particular Buddha in the present eon, Siddhartha Gautama Śākyamuni (for our purposes "the Buddha"), was born in the pleasurable environs of a palace in North India (specifically Magadha). Siddhartha, whose life is popularized in Herman

A statue of Śākyamuni Buddha on Dobong-san mountain near Seoul, South Korea.
**Photo courtesy of John Powers**

Hesse's novel *Siddhartha* (1922), had a son named Rahula ("Obstacle"). After seeing the sights of old age, sickness, death, and renouncer, the young prince left the palace and embarked on the Great Renunciation. Before becoming Buddha he meditated under the tutelage of famous yogic masters. His enlightenment under the Bodhi Tree (*Ficus religiosus*) at Bodh Gayā is explained in the *Udana* as one of understanding causality. After this, being Buddha, or "one who is enlightened," he began teaching. Although a man and not a god (*deva*), Buddha is depicted as knowing all that is necessary for salvation. After his final enlightenment (*parinibbāna*), he was no more to be reborn.

One main emphasis of Buddha's teaching is the Middle Way (*majjhima paṭipadā*). In ethical and soteriological terms, this is a middle path between the asceticism of the Jains and the sensualism of Siddhartha's former princely palace. Neither the sensualism of the princely palace nor the asceticism of the Jains proved to be an adequate path (*magga*) in the personal experience of the Buddha. In terms of afterlife views, Buddha's teaching is a Middle Way between the annihilationist view (*ucchedavāda*) of Cārvāka materialism and the eternalism of the Vedic brahamic soul-substance view (*ātmavāda*).

Everyone must be self-reliant on the path, a *dīpa* (lamp or island) for oneself. This self-reliance is especially emphasized in the early tradition of Theravāda Buddhism and contrasts with the reliance on "other power" in some parts of the Mahāyāna tradition. This is notably not the case in the Mahāyāna school of Zen, in which self-reliance and the steep, sharp way to enlightenment is emphasized.

For several centuries after the final enlightenment (*parinibbāna*), group recitation of Pāli scriptures by monks and nuns, called *bhāṇika*s (reciters), provided continuity of *dhamma*. To some extent group recitation ensured orthodoxy in the period before Pāli *sutta*s were canonized by successive Buddhist councils. Although from a scholarly perspective these Pāli scriptures cannot confidently be said to transmit the exact words of the Buddha, they are widely regarded throughout both Asia and the West as the earliest texts for the study of Buddha's life and thought.

Being Buddha is something that, theoretically, any human being can accomplish in this very life. Viewed in this way Buddha is not only a historical figure but also and importantly embodies the possibility of self-transformation and enlightenment within each individual. In Mahāyāna Buddhism this is sometimes called the "Buddha nature." However, it is clear that early Buddhist emphasis on impermanence (*anicca*) – along with nonsubstantiality (*anattā*) and suffering (*dukkha*) as one of the Three Marks of Existence – would be logically incompatible with construing Buddha nature as permanent substance (*svabhava*). In the development of Buddhist tradition, the *dharmakāya* (truth body), *sambogyakāya* (bliss body), and *nirmanakāya* (appearance body) are the various bodies of Buddha. Parallel ideas for comparison and contrast in Christianity are the *Logos*, or Word; Christ as resurrected; and the Word made flesh, respectively. However, one should not think of these similarities as identities or overlook relevant contrasts.

Parinirvāṇa (Image of the Death of the Buddha, surrounded by his disciples), Swedagon Pagoda, Rangoon, Burma, 19th century.
Photo courtesy of John C. Huntington, the Huntington Archive

### Dhamma, *Oral Tradition, and the Pāli Canon*

*Dhamma* (doctrine or truth) is the second item in the Triple Jewel revered by Buddhists. Doctrine was initially mediated by oral tradition. *Dhamma* (Sanskrit, dharma) includes the Four Noble Truths and the Eightfold Noble Path. The Four Noble Truths (*cattaro ariya sacca*) are noble in the sense of being "worthy" (*ariya*) of pursuit. The first is that suffering or unsatisfactoriness (*dukkha*) exists. It is for convenience that "suffering" is the English term most often used to cover the enormous range of the term *dukkha*, from torment to a vague feeling that things are not alright in the universe. The second truth is that suffering arises because of craving (*taṇhā*) and ignorance, or not seeing (*avijjā*). The third truth is that suffering passes away (*nirodha*), nothing being permanent in the Buddhist way of thinking. The fourth of the Four Noble Truths is that a path to the cessation of suffering (*magga*) exists. This path is the Eightfold Noble Path (*ariya aṭṭhangika magga*): (1) right view, (2) right aspiration, (3) right speech, (4) right conduct, (5) right livelihood, (6) right effort, (7) right mindfulness, and (8) right concentration.

These eight may be summarized under the headings of *sīla* (morality), *samadhi* (concentration), and *paññā* (wisdom): (1) and (2) concern wisdom; (3), (4), and (5) concern morality; and (6), (7), and (8) concern meditation. Buddhists in the *saṅgha*, as well as lay practitioners, are expected to develop control of body (*kāya*), breath (*prana*), and mind (*mano*) in their daily lives. The hope is that control of the posture of the body, the inflowing and outflowing of the breath, and the awareness of mind altogether will lead to a lessening of the tendency to react instinctively under the grip of ideas of "I and mine." One should cultivate a thoughtful distancing from "likes and dislikes" in order to live authentically from a center that is not obsessed with craving.

The goal of practice is not simply a better rebirth, although that would be welcome. What the dedicated aspirant on the Buddhist path seeks is enlightenment (Pāli, *nibbāna*; Sanskrit, nirvāṇa). Enlightenment admits of a distinction between enlightenment in this life, in this very body, as shown in figure sculpture of the seated Buddha, and enlightenment in the case of any liberated saint (*Tathāgata*), such as Buddha, who will never again be reborn, as shown in figure sculpture of the reclining Buddha. In Pāli Buddhist texts when *parinibbāna* (final enlightenment) is used, one can be sure that the latter is meant, whereas when *nibbāna* (enlightenment) is used, the context must be examined to ascertain whether the former or the latter is meant.

Three characteristics of things are impermanence (*anicca*), nonsubstantiality (*anattā*), and suffering (*dukkha*). Impermanence means not only the poetic sentiment that "nothing that is can pause or stay," in Wordsworth's sense, but also the philosophical doctrine that "you cannot step into the same river twice," as Heraclitus (c. 500 B.C.), for one, maintained. "Nonsubstantiality" here means that there is no substance but only process. Thus, no *ātman* exists, if this means permanent substance. Consequently also no permanent God substance exists (e.g., Issara, or Creator God), for that would have to exist outside the nexus of dependent origination. All things, even the *deva* (shining ones), exist in causal nexus; gods too are in need of liberation. Suffering means that because all things are composed of parts and will eventually disconnect, no place exists, not even the princely palace of Siddhartha, where one can escape suffering for long.

In accordance with the belief in impermanence and nonsubstantiality, even individual persons are viewed as dynamic processes rather than as essentially static substances. Persons consist of the five aggregates (*pañcakkhandha*): form, feeling, sensation, disposition, and consciousness. Enlightenment is viewed as an individual accomplishment involves eliminating passion (*rāga*), hatred (*dosa*), and confusion (*moha*) in one's everyday life; purifying the heart and mind (*citta*); and achieving perfect irreversible enlightenment (*samyaksambodhi*) before going off in *parinibbāna*. This is a complex process that, barring exceptional cases, requires a cultivated calming of the mind (*samattha*) and *vipassana* meditation in a gradual movement toward enlightenment that takes many years, if not many lifetimes of rebirth (*punabbhava*, literally, "re-becoming"), in the cycle of birth and death that is samsara.

Lovingkindness (*mettā*) is part of Buddhist practice and is to be extended universally to all sentient beings. For monks (*bhikkhu*s) and nuns (*bhikkhuni*s), it is a violation of Vinaya rules (once one is confessed in the *sangha*) to destroy vegetation intentionally and without good reason. No specific "rebirth station" (*gati*) exists for plant life or vegetation in the southern Asian perspective, whereas some eastern Asian Buddhist poets after the time of the *Lotus Sūtra* did speak as if it had a particular *gati*. Cultivating a mind-set that is free from aggression, one that is "harmless" (*ahimsā*), is part of the Buddhist way. Although clearly Buddhists did not carry to such great lengths the *ahimsa* doctrine as did their predecessors, the Jains, nonharming is so pervasive that it is to be extended even to enemies. A lot of ground exists for interreligious dialogue between Jains and Buddhists both because of large-scale structural similarities of thought and because traditionally the two systems of Indian philosophy are classified (together with Cārvāka) as Heterodox. Heterodox schools are so classified because they do not accept the Vedas as divine revelation.

In concluding this section on the importance of *dhamma*, the shortcomings of seeing Buddhism only in terms of doctrine must be emphasized. Some well-established Buddhist sects, such as Zen, say that there is to be "no reliance on words and letters" and instead place more emphasis on the practice of "just sitting." This is also a tendency of many present-day Buddhist cen-

ters in Europe and the United States, and it recalls an early emphasis wherein Buddha claims to teach only suffering and the cessation of suffering. Overall basic *dhamma* as in the Four Noble Truths is seen on a medical model that diagnoses the ailment, the causes of the arising and passing away of the ailment, and the way to cure the human predicament of suffering. Thus, *dhamma* is understandable by anyone who takes the time to investigate whether there is anything in it for that person.

The *Sutta Piṭaka*, the *Vinaya Piṭaka*, and the *Abhidhamma Piṭaka* together are the Tipiṭaka (three baskets) of texts that make up the Pāli Canon, and these, especially the *Sutta Piṭaka*, are fundamental for understanding the subsequent development of Buddhism.

### The Saṅgha (Community of Monks and Nuns), Eastern and Western

The achievement of enlightenment (*parinibbāna*) led to the founding of the monastic order of monks and nuns, the *sangha* (monastic communities). In ancient India the most important of these monastic communities were those at Nalanda and Taksasila, where archaeological remains can be seen to this day. The Pāli term for monastery is *vihāra*. Far from being a grim abode, as the etymology shows, a *vihāra* is a place where one enjoys one's stay.

Generally speaking no distinct "sects" exist in southern Asian Buddhism, although in Sri Lanka, for example, one might distinguish Siamese, Burmese, and Rāmañña *bhikkhu*s. In China there were two schools of thought – the mystics and the Amidists (believers in Amitābha) – but this too is less a matter of sectarian division than of emphasis. It is in Japan that sects of Buddhism have flourished. In *The Essentials of Buddhist Philosophy* (1947), Junjiro Takakusu provides the outlines of this development.

Lay followers of the Buddhist path are expected to adopt the five precepts (*pañca sīla*): no taking of life, no stealing, no wrong (harmful) sexual relations, no wrong use of speech (including the true but hurtful), and not getting drunk or high on drugs. In applying these five precepts, particular Buddhist communities vary in the way in which the precepts are construed, being more or less conservative, depending on the context.

Requirements for *bhikkhu*s and *bhikkuni*s (monks and nuns) are more strict, and they must take vows of poverty and chastity. Normally these vows result in having only a robe, bowl, and staff (when aged) and not being married or having sexual relations. Details of the many Vinaya rules that monks and nuns must follow are set forth in *The Buddhist Monastic Code* (*Pātimōkkha* training rules).

### Outlines of the Historical Development

#### 1. Theravāda

Strictly speaking Theravāda is only one of the Hīnayāna schools, along with Sarvastivāda and Sautrantika; thus, Theravāda is not identical to Hīnayāna. Scholars such as Edward Conze, Richard Gombrich, David J. Kalupahana, and Ernest Frauwallner have written important works on the development of Buddhism. Theravāda has been the most resilient and successful of the Hīnayāna schools and has influenced our notion of what counts as "early Buddhism." The Pāli Canon, as we know it, is the canon of this particular successfully transmitted school. Because "early Buddhism" cannot easily (if at all) be given a precise chronological fix, it is best understood as a convenient term for texts of the Pāli Canon. The Pāli Canon consists of the Five *Nikāya*s, or Collections, arranged by length and type as follows: *Dīgha* (Long), *Majjhima* (Middle Length), *Aṅguttara* (Gradual), *Saṃyutta* (Connected), and *Khuddaka* (Minor). These have been codified by scholars in the Pali Text Society (1882–present) in England from the late 19th century. As a result a set of romanized Pāli texts and corresponding English translations have been produced on the basis of different recensions of manuscripts in several Asian languages. It was mentioned previously how an emphasis on self-reliance and being an island or lamp for oneself is a characteristic emphasis of Theravāda Buddhism. Linked with this is the idea that claims of knowledge should be based on direct personal experience. Knowing and seeing for oneself is consistently emphasized in the Theravāda tradition. This contrasts with both Jainism and Brahmanism. In Jainism the parallel to the Buddha ideal is the *Tirthankara* (literally, "ford maker"), one who assists safe passage to the other shore, in this case *kaivalya*, or *mokṣa*. In contrast to Jain claims of the "omniscience" of the *Tirthankara* (Mahavira in this eon), Buddhists saw Siddhartha Gautama as a man who found a path but was not literally omniscient. The Buddhist parable of the Simsapa leaves – in which Buddha is depicted as saying that what he knows and has taught is like the leaves in his hand, whereas what he knows and has not taught is like all the leaves in the forest – is best interpreted as a contrast between specific knowledge necessary for salvation and superfluous, abundant, but nevertheless finite knowledge that he has that is irrelevant to soteriology. Buddha often says that he teaches only suffering and the elimination of suffering. The implication is that he does not teach speculation. (Speculation is not the same thing as metaphysics. Buddhas may still have doctrines, such as rebirth, that are metaphysical.) Because the Buddha is not a speculative thinker, he teaches only *dhamma* that is true in the beginning, middle, and end. This doctrine is based on "rational faith" and not "baseless faith."

Consistent with his experientialist (not empiricist) emphasis, the Theravāda position cannot embrace speculation or blind faith. However, confidence and faith play a role, yet a different one than in brahmanic belief that the *Veda*s are revealed truths. In Buddhism it is one's own meditative experience and reflection that provides the key to truth, not memorizing or internalizing holy books. Thus, in contrast to monastics of the Jewish-Christian-Islamic "people of the book" tradition, the faith of Buddhist monastics takes a different form. Here there must be initial faith to come and hear the doctrine, to sit down by the side of the teacher, to check it out and see whether there is anything in it. There is also path faith, consistent with doubt and struggle, wherein the Buddhist monastic is learning and developing in confidence while practicing morality and concentrated meditation of mind that together, it is hoped, will yield wisdom.

Finally there is also non-backsliding faith as a hallmark of the liberated saint's achievement, which is hard-won and has no connection to confidence in what has yet to be experienced.

### 2. Mahāyāna

In one respect Buddha shows the virtuous path of the bodhisattva as Mahāyānists see it, as he did not go straightaway to final enlightenment (*parinibbāna*) but remained to teach so that other beings could attain enlightenment as well. This bodhisattva ideal is supposed (in general books on Buddhism) to contrast with the arhat ideal of Theravāda, the ideal of a reclusive practitioner of meditation. In point of fact significant overlap exists. A stark contrast might emerge, for example, by comparing one sector (e.g., forest monks) in Theravāda with one sector (e.g., the bodhisattvas after enlightenment) in Mahāyāna as represented in the last of the famous ten ox-herding pictures. Once again, however, because it is in the nature of Buddhism to avoid egoism and one-sided thinking, many practitioners see rather the unity of Buddhism than stereotypical dualistic ideas such as arhat/bodhisattva or sudden/gradual.

### 3. Vajrayāna

Vajrayāna (the thunderbolt vehicle of Tibet) practices visualization of deities in the context of meditation. True believers of the Vajrayāna way might see all Buddhism as leading up to their viewpoint. In this tradition Theravādins (called Hīnayānists, although Theravāda is but one of the Hīnayāna schools) are described as those of low capacity with poor motivation to save oneself, Mahāyānists as those of moderate capacity, and Vajrayānists as those of high capacity. Vajrayāna practitioners sometimes see themselves as on a fast track to enlightenment in Buddhist terms. Some practice guru worship, the *kalamitra* (spiritual friend) ideal, or psychoanalytic activity. In the process there might be an abandonment of critical perspective, yet there is a long tradition of debate in Tibetan Buddhism that makes its internal perspective esoteric and highly developed.

From the obscurity of the misty hilltops of the Himalayas, Tibetan Buddhism has emerged as something in the everyday consciousness of westerners. Monastics of Tibet, whether in exile in India or traveling to the United States and other countries as cultural ambassadors, have generated an enormous amount of goodwill and sympathy. Chief among them is the Dalai Lama. Tenzin Gyatso (1935– ), the 14th Dalai Lama, who has risen to the occasion. Films such as *Little Buddha* (1993) and *Kundun* (1997) have done much to popularize the Tibetan cause.

### Scripture, Pilgrimage, and Ritual

Scripture is important in Buddhism but is not used by monastics or even lay practitioners in the way it is in the Jewish-Christian-Islamic "people of the book" tradition, wherein Holy Scripture is regarded as divinely revealed. Buddhist scripture is a guide to a path that people had found even before there was scripture in this eon.

Pilgrimage is an important part of Buddhist life. In India there is pilgrimage to Bodh Gayā. In Japan there is the Shikoku pilgrimage and in China pilgrimage to four Buddhist mountains.

In general American Buddhists pay less attention to ritual than do their Asian counterparts. Harmony is an important idea in eastern Asian thought, which holds that lack of detailed attention to ritual matters in sufficient detail can result in a lack of harmony that has the consequence of generating unskillful karma. In southern Asia, although Buddhists rejected the brahmanic idea of sacrifice as in itself efficacious or meritorious, in time the Buddhist community developed rituals of its own. Although rituals are not the main focus, some rituals, such as the *Paribbājaka*, are important in Buddhism.

*Buddhism in Contemporary Life*

In addition to the ethnic types of Buddhism that have migrated to the United States and that supply support to various kinds for immigrant communities, there is also the phenomenon of American or Western Buddhism. Some American Buddhists favor social engagement, and others do not, but in general American Buddhists as a whole are more prone to social activism than are Buddhists in Asia. Certainly Buddhism, as a phenomenon spanning Asia, Europe, and North America, exhibits a great deal of variety and freedom of thought in its worldwide development.

The impact of interreligious dialogue on Buddhism is also apparent, as some in the West claim to "practice Buddhism" without "being Buddhist." (This distinction raises interesting philosophical issues about inclusion, identity, and definition that go beyond the scope of this article.) Often westerners see only the impact that Buddhism has had on Christianity. This is often understood in terms of the "inroads" made by Asian religions into what is seen as "our territory." The other side is either not seen or not presented, namely, how contact with the West has altered Buddhism. From traditional Buddhist perspectives it could be argued that Buddhist ideas shorn of cultural moorings in ritual and social life and lacking textually transmitted beliefs about the nature of reality make for an understanding of Buddhism that is really "out to sea."

FRANK J. HOFFMAN

*See also* Asceticism: Buddhist Perspectives; Bodhisattva; Body: Buddhist Perspectives; Buddha (Śākyamuni); Buddhism: Western; Buddhology; Councils, Buddhist; Dalai Lama (Tenzin Gyatso); Disciples, Early Buddhist; Discourses (Suttas): Theravāda; Hermits: Buddhist; Jain Monasticism and Buddhist Monasticism; Mahāyāna; Meditation: Buddhist Perspectives; Missionaries: Buddhist; Monasticism, Definitions of: Buddhist Perspectives; Origins: Comparative Perspectives; Patrons, Buddhist: India; Pilgrimages, Buddhist; Regulations: Buddhist Perspectives; Rules, Buddhist (Vinaya); Saṅgha; Spirituality: Buddhist; Vajrayāna Buddhism in Nepal; Virtues, Buddhist

**Further Reading**

Chang, Chun-yuan, *Original Teachings of Ch'an Buddhism*, New York: Pantheon Books, 1969

Ch'ên, Kenneth Kuan Shêng, *Buddhism in China, a Historical Survey* (Virginia and Richard Stewart Memorial Lectures, 1961), Princeton, New Jersey: Princeton University Press, 1964

Gombrich, Richard, *Theravada Buddhism: A Social History from Ancient Benares to Modern Colombo* (Library of Religious Beliefs and Practices), London and New York: Routledge and Kegan Paul, 1988

Gombrich, Richard, *How Buddhism Began: The Conditioned Genesis of the Early Teachings* (Jordan Lectures in Comparative Religion, 17), Atlantic Highlands, New Jersey, and London: Athlone Press, 1996

Hoffman, Frank J., *Rationality and Mind in Early Buddhism*, Delhi: Motilal Banarsidass, 1987

Hoffman, Frank J., and Mahinda Deegalle, editors, *Pali Buddhism* (Curzon Studies in Asian Philosophy), Richmond, Surrey: Curzon Press, 1996

Jayatilleke, Kulatissa Nanda, *Early Buddhist Theory of Knowledge*, London: Allen and Unwin, 1963

Kalupahana, David J., *A History of Buddhist Philosophy: Continuities and Discontinuities*, Honolulu: University of Hawaii Press, 1992

LaFleur, William R., *Buddhism: A Cultural Perspective* (Prentice-Hall Series in World Religions), Englewood Cliffs, New Jersey: Prentice-Hall, 1988

Lamotte, Etienne, *History of Indian Buddhism: From the Origins to the Saka Era* (Publications de l'Institut orientaliste de Louvain, 36), Louvain-la-Neuve: Université catholique de Louvain, Institut orientaliste, 1988

Puligandla, R., and David Lee Miller, editors, *Buddhism and the Emerging World Civilization: Essays in Honor of Nolan Pliny Jacobson*, Carbondale: Southern Illinois University Press, 1996

Rahula, Walpola, *What the Buddha Taught*, Bedford, Bedfordshire: Fraser, 1959; New York: Grove Press, 1962; revised edition, Bedford, Bedfordshire: Fraser, 1967; New York: Grove Press, 1974

Robinson, Richard, *The Buddhist Religion: A Historical Introduction* (Religious Life of Man), Belmont, California: Dickenson, 1970; 4th edition, Belmont, California: Wadsworth, 1996

Takakusu, Junjiro, *The Essentials of Buddhist Philosophy*, Honolulu: University of Hawaii, 1947; 3rd edition, 1956

Upadhyaya, K.N., *Early Buddhism and the Bhagavadgita*, Delhi: Motilal Banarsidass, 1971

Williams, Paul, *Mahayana Buddhism: The Doctrinal Foundations* (Library of Religious Beliefs and Practices), London and New York: Routledge, 1989

# Buddhism: Inculturation

*Southeast Asia*

In the course of its spread in the Southeast Asian countries (Burma, Thailand, Cambodia, Vietnam, and Indonesia), Buddhism quickly gained a foothold and eventually was able to establish itself as the dominant religious tradition. Buddhism brought both civilization and trade to the region and early on became closely connected with the ruling classes in the respective countries. From the eighth century on, Buddhism in most of the Southeast Asian kingdoms fell under strong influence from the esoteric tradition. Only very late, after the 11th century, did the anti-Mahāyāna Theravāda tradition gain a sufficiently strong foothold in Burma, Thailand, Laos, and Cambodia. Eventually Mahāyāna Buddhism was suppressed and driven out of

Three-storied pagoda, Yakushiji temple, Nara, Japan, early seventh century, wood.
Photo courtesy of Marylin M. Rhie

Southeast Asia with the exception of Vietnam. Here Mahāyāna remained dominant, and only several centuries later was Theravāda Buddhism introduced.

In the Theravāda-dominated countries, most members of the male populations join the monastics as novices for a limited period of time. All the major expressions of art and architecture in Southeast Asia are the products of Buddhist culture. Although numerous local spirit cults exist in the Theravāda countries, Buddhism remains the absolute and virtually the only spiritual tradition.

### Tibet and Mongolia

The introduction of Buddhism to Tibet proceeded mainly by conversion. Buddhism brought learning and civilization to the Tibetan plateau, and its religious institutions have dominated the country from the eighth century on. Monks in the Tibetan tradition are called lamas, and they enjoy a high position in society. Thus, Tibetan Buddhism is also called Lamaism. Buddhism has developed several distinct characteristics in Tibet and Mongolia. One of these is the system of the consciously reincarnated *tulku*, popularly known as "Living Buddhas." According to this

belief an important lama reincarnates himself life after life in order to liberate sentient beings. In effect this system constitutes a feudalization of Buddhism that is designed to retain leadership and control of important monasteries under a particular clan. Many elements of the original shamanistic tradition, Bön, have been absorbed into Lamaism, including blood offerings, possession of mediums, and a general preoccupation with spirits, including exorcism. In Mongolia, Buddhism and Shamanism function side by side.

### China

From the beginning of its introduction into China, Buddhism influenced the local traditions Confucianism and Daoism and in turn was influenced by them. In contrast to many countries to which Buddhism was introduced, foreign monks arriving in China were seen not as bringers of a superior spiritual and cultural tradition but as barbarians introducing barbarian culture.

In the course of history, the Chinese Buddhists composed a distinct literature of their own. This literature, which in addition to the canonical scriptures includes thousands of texts, is by far the greatest collection of Buddhist scriptures in any language. It exercised a profound impact on the further development of Chinese culture.

Buddhism was given a special outer form in the course of its meeting with and integration into Chinese culture. This resulted in the creation of distinctive iconography, sculptural styles, and temple buildings (including pagodas). Certain secular practices, such as burial of the dead, were practiced by the Buddhists alongside traditional cremation.

The Chinese inaugurated a number of new Buddhist schools that had never existed as such in India, including the Jingtu, Chan, Huayan, and Tiantai. In many ways these schools reflect distinct Chinese interests and purposes. Jingtu offered a method of deliverance that could be grasped easily by ordinary people; Chan shared the Daoist ideal of the ascetic and carefree sage; Tiantai supplied a highly developed system of graded practice; and the Huayan tradition provided a learned, metaphysical system that explained universal harmonization and integration. However, the development of different schools never created real and sharp sectarian distinctions as happened in Japan. Chinese Buddhism has always been characterized by accommodation and harmonious coexistence among the various schools. Thus, it can be argued that the Chinese "custom designed" Mahāyāna Buddhism to suit the temperament of their own culture.

### Korea

One of the main characteristics of Korean Buddhism is its ecumenical tendency. Although syncretism and harmonization among different schools, doctrines, and even foreign faiths is a common feature of Mahāyāna Buddhism, the degree to which conscious harmonization was effected is peculiar to Korea. In the course of history, many attempts have been made to create a kind of pan-Korean Buddhism that would share doctrines and practices.

Under the Koryŏ, Buddhism acquired a status comparable to that of national ideology and was always closely linked to the

**Siong Lim Temple, Singapore.**
**Photo courtesy of John Powers**

secular powers. Thus, Korean Buddhism is sometimes characterized as "Buddhism that protects the nation" (*hoguk pulgyo*).

From the Chosŏn period (1392–1910) on, Buddhism came under increasing influence from Confucianism, an influence that was most clearly felt in ways relating to monastics' conduct and ranking. A ranking system based on seniority rather than religious virtue came into vogue. This malpractice has remained in place to the present and to a large extent is to blame for the internal problems within the country's largest Buddhist denomination, the Chogye Order. As in Japan, Korean temples at certain points in history maintained armies of monk-soldiers. During the Chosŏn, Korean Buddhism became synonymous with Sŏn Buddhism, a trend that can still be seen. This does not mean that no other forms of Buddhism exist but rather that the others are commonly subsumed under the aegis of the Sŏn tradition.

### Japan

From early on, Buddhism in Japan enjoyed a close relationship with indigenous Shintoism. During the Nara period (710–794), groups of mountain ascetics practiced a combination of esoteric Buddhism and Shintoism in the mountains around the imperial capital. Although Buddhism has always been the dominant spiritual tradition in Japan, Shintoism has maintained a presence in the makeup of many of the Buddhist schools. In particular the Shingon, Tendai, and Hōssō schools feature many elements of Shintō. This is also reflected in the Buddhist pantheon, where many of the most popular deities embody both religions. The presence of Shintō shrines within the boundaries of many Buddhist temples testifies to the continued symbiosis between the two religions.

Japanese Buddhism has several distinctive characteristics. A pronounced involvement with military affairs down through Japanese history finds its expression in the many intersectarian conflicts that often involved armies of monks (*sohei*) fighting each other. In contrast to other East Asian countries, Japanese Buddhism has been greatly influenced by esoteric practices, and these are found as an integrated element in the otherwise rather sectarian Zen and Nichiren schools. Japanese Buddhism has also had a much closer connection to the imperial court than was the case in either China or Korea. Whereas only during certain periods did Buddhism enjoy deep links to rulers in these two countries, such ties were more or less continuous in Japan. Another characteristic is the relatively weak practice of the vinaya (rule) within most of the schools. This deficiency often resulted in decadent religious milieus governed by material wealth and political connections as well as in a strong homosexual tradition

The "wheel of becoming" (*bhava-cakra*), entrance wall, Rumtek monastery, Sikkim. Six destinies (*gati*) each occupy one sector: gods, demi-gods, humans, animals, hungry ghosts, and hell-beings.
Photo courtesy of John Powers

within the temples. Likewise the lack of a strong vinaya paved the way for the secularization of Japanese Buddhism that had begun with the Pure Land tradition in the late Heian period and reached its climax with the abolition of the celibate clergy under the Meiji (1868–1912) and the resulting institution of hereditary family-temples.

HENRIK H. SØRENSEN

*See also* Asceticism: Buddhist Perspectives; Bön Monasticism; Buddhism: Overview; Buddhist Schools/Traditions: Japan; Burma (Myanmar); China; Clothing: Buddhist Perspectives; Deities, Buddhist; Japan: History; Korea: History; Syncretism in Japan, Buddhist; Thailand; Tibet: History; Travelers: Buddhist

**Further Reading**

Bechert, Heinz, and Richard Gombrich, editors, *The World of Buddhism*, London: Thames and Hudson, and New York: Facts on File, 1984

Ch'ên, Kenneth, *The Chinese Transformation of Buddhism*, Princeton, New Jersey: Princeton University Press, 1973

Gernet, Jacques, *Buddhism in Chinese Society*, translated by Franciscus Verellen, New York: Columbia University Press, 1995

Jan, Yün-hua, "The Bodhisattva Idea in Chinese Literature: Typology and Significance," in *The Bodhisattva Doctrine in Buddhism*, edited by Leslie Kawamura, Waterloo, Ontario: Wilfried Laurier University Press, 1981

Jan, Yün-hua, "The Chinese Understanding and Assimilation of

Karma Doctrine," in *Karma and Rebirth: Post Classical Developments*, edited by Ronald W. Neufeldt, Albany: State University of New York Press, 1986

Jan, Yün-hua, "Patterns of Chinese Assimilation of Buddhist Thought: A Comparative Study of No-Thought (*wu-nien*) in Indian and Chinese Texts," *Journal of Oriental Studies* 24 (1986)

Lester, Robert C., *Theravada Buddhism in Southeast Asia*, Ann Arbor: University of Michigan Press, 1973

Matsunaga, Daigan, and Alicia Matsunaga, *Foundation of Japanese Buddhism*, 2 vols., Los Angeles: Buddhist Books International, 1974

Takeuchi Yoshinori et al., editors, *Buddhist Spirituality: Indian, Southeast Asian, Tibetan, Early Chinese*, New York: Crossroad, 1993

Zürcher, Erik, *The Buddhist Conquest of China*, 2 vols., Leiden: Brill, and New York: Humanities Press, 1959

Zürcher, Erik, "The Impact of Buddhism on Chinese Culture in an Historical Perspective," *Buddhica Britannica*, volume 1, edited by Tadeusz Skorupski, Tring: Institute of Buddhist Studies, 1989

Zwalf, W., editor, *Buddhism: Art and Faith*, London: British Museum, and New York: Macmillan, 1985

# Buddhism: Western

*Introduction to Basic Terminology*

The term *Western Buddhism* does not mean just "Buddhism in the West" but, rather, is used here to denote the range of Buddhist ideas and practices in English-speaking countries today. Thus, although doubtless in some way influenced by the existence of Buddhist Church of America (founded in 1899 by Japanese Buddhists) and other Asian groups, Western Buddhism is Buddhism adapted to the Western scene.

It is more typical of Western Buddhists than of ethnic Buddhists in the West to emphasize the necessity of the practice of meditation as an essential part of living a Buddhist life. Within Western Buddhism a distinction can be made between those who follow "socially engaged Buddhism" and those who emphasize the practice of meditation apart from any sociopolitical ideas. A similar distinction exists in a few ethnic Buddhist contexts, such as in the neo-Buddhist revival movement of B.R. Ambedkar (1891–1956) wherein many *dalit*s (untouchables) were converted to Buddhism in Maharashtra, India, beginning in 1956. Overall, however, the socially engaged Western Buddhists have much more in common with ecologists, feminists, and animal rights activists than would either Asian Buddhists living in Asia or ethnic Buddhists living in the West. Asian Buddhists and the ethnic Buddhists in the United States tend for the most part to be culturally conservative. In this way the influential popular Buddhist writer Thích Nhát Hanh (1926– ) may be viewed not as a radical in opposing the war but as a Vietnamese patriot and citizen of the world.

It is difficult to generalize accurately or to distinguish between Western Buddhism and ethnic Buddhism in the West, as the phenomena under discussion are ever changing and abound in borderline cases that are difficult to classify. Not all the phenomena can be easily labeled as either Western Buddhist or ethnic Buddhist because some Western-born teachers were trained in Asia and some westerners who are Buddhists have Asian ancestry. Thus, in what follows no "essentialist definition" will be proposed; rather, two distinct but occasionally overlapping sets of "family resemblances" will be sketched.

*Ethnic Buddhism in the West*

Ethnic Buddhism in the West provides a social support network for recent immigrants in communities where English is not the language first acquired. Different sorts of ethnic Buddhism tend to differentiate themselves in terms of which beliefs and devotional practices are followed, which scriptures are studied, and which particular teacher is followed in a lineage. Ethnic Buddhism is concerned mainly with the Buddhist way of life as mediated through a particular cultural framework (e.g., Sri Lankan, Chinese, Thai, Cambodian, Vietnamese, and Japanese) and not with spreading doctrine in the West. However, the Tibetan Buddhist monks, exiled from their homeland in Tibet to India, have proven to be enormously resilient and proactive in advancing the cause of Tibetan culture in the West. With support from charismatic academics, such as Robert Thurman of Columbia University in New York City, and media stars such as Richard Gere, Tibetan culture and its Buddhist religion and philosophy are being not just preserved but also disseminated in the West, especially in the United States.

The Tibetan situation aside, in the majority of cases ethnic Buddhism is not well positioned to cross boundaries to Buddhists of other cultural traditions or to the American population at large. Only a few centers, such as Ratanasara's Sri Lankan–based Buddhist interfaith center in Los Angeles and Bo-kim Kim's Won Buddhist Temple of Philadelphia and the affiliated seminary, are capable of reaching out somewhat to both Western Buddhists and Buddhists of other cultural traditions.

Despite its often insular character, ethnic Buddhism in the West functions both as a link to the homeland and as a bridge to the adopted land. To be sure its beliefs and practices may result in a "cultural lag" wherein the forms transmitted to the new country become ossified and do not keep pace with developments in the motherland. In such cases Western outposts can be of great interest for the study of the preceding culture.

*Characteristics of Western Buddhism*

Western Buddhism tends to deemphasize devotion (worship) and scripture, and many Western Buddhists have either no particular teacher or several teachers in succession. Often there is a "root teacher" from whom one goes on the path of experiential exploration through meditation. Western Buddhism also tends to be individualistic, with little emphasis on attire (e.g., meditation garments for laity and vestments for clergy), having mostly democratic *saṅgha* organization, a minimalist conception of ritual, and little emphasis on scripture study. Donations are encouraged but often not mandatory. Some differences of view regarding devotion, the sword of Mañjuśrī, and clerical vestments divide practitioners both among sitting groups and in some cases within particular groups.

*Historical Development to 1900*

Interest in Buddhism as a way of life can be traced to an 18th-century English scholar named William Jones. Born in London in 1736, Jones began his career as a lawyer and linguist. After being hired to translate several Asian historical and religious texts, he became fascinated with Asian culture. In 1783 he traveled to India to study Asian thought. Eventually Jones founded in Calcutta the *Asiatick Society*, an organization devoted to the analysis of Asian religion and philosophy. After Jones' death in 1794, the work of the society, published in its journal, *Asiatick Research*, continued. In 1805 the influence of Jones' work extended even to the United States, where many of his essays were reprinted in *The Monthly Anthology and Boston Review*. This journal was edited by William Emerson, father of noted American philosopher Ralph Waldo Emerson (1803–1862). The work made a lasting impact on the younger Emerson; in 1840, when he and fellow transcendentalist Henry David Thoreau (1817–1862) established their own journal, *Dial*, it developed a very Asian orientation and contained many essays on the teachings of Buddhism. In 1878 Edwin Arnold (1832–1904), an English journalist, published a book titled *The Light of Asia, or The Great Renunciation, Being the Life and Teachings of Gautama, Prince of India and Founder of Buddhism.*

On its arrival in the United States, the book was critically acclaimed and became immensely popular, going through 80 editions and selling almost a million copies. It is generally acknowledged that *The Light of Asia*, inspired by the work of William Jones almost 100 years earlier, introduced Buddhism to mainstream America. By the mid– to late 19th century, Buddhism became an extremely popular topic among American intellectuals. Thinkers such as Edward Morse, Percival Lowell, Henry Adams, and Thomas Edison belonged to Buddhist-related societies or published works on Buddhism. Journals with a Buddhist concentration, such as *The Monist*, *The Open Court*, and *The Buddhist Ray*, were heavily circulated. Westerners in international groups such as the Theosophical Society and the Maha Bodhi Society (both based in Madras, present-day Chennai) corresponded with Buddhist monks in Asia, especially those from Sri Lanka. The international headquarters of the Theosophical Society is located in Chennai on the estate of Annie Besant (1847–1933) and also operates the Adyar Library for its members and bona fide visiting researchers. Madame Helena Blavatsky (1831–1891) had, with Colonel Henry Steele Olcott (1832–1907) and William Q. Judge (1851–1896), founded the society in New York in 1875, and its teachings, although far from doctrinaire, tend to emphasize karma, reincarnation, and the unity of all life.

Two distinct developments in the 19th century facilitated the entry of Buddhism into the United States. On the Pacific coast increased immigration resulted in the arrival of Asian Buddhists who, as it were, brought Buddhism along with their baggage. This is "Buddhism in America." On the Atlantic coast Buddhism became an imported object of intellectual inquiry and interest.

This is "American Buddhism." Although subsequent development is complex and the distinction is not always useful for distinguishing East Coast Buddhism from West Coast Buddhism, it offers a useful starting point for reflection about the plurality of Buddhisms that exist today. In the United States one main difference is that between the "fresh off the boat" ethnic varieties of Buddhism and the "manicured" middle-class (i.e., "American") types of Buddhism. However, these categories cannot be regarded as mutually exclusive, for many borderline cases exist of phenomena that defy categorization as either "American Buddhism" or "Buddhism in America." For example, when an American lives in Asia long enough to become Asian in the realm of ideas and then returns to the United States to teach a traditional Asian way, what is being taught – Buddhism in America, or American Buddhism? Another problem is that a rigid application of this distinction would seem to imply the dubious proposition that ethnic Buddhists are somehow un-American. Thus, whereas the distinction has some use in certain contexts, it should not be treated as a precise designation to be applied in a categorical manner.

After gold was discovered in California in 1848, the subsequent gold rush brought many Asian immigrants to the United States. By 1870, 63,000 Chinese were living in California, most of whom retained their culture's traditions and Confucian-Daoist-Buddhist religious orientation. In 1853 in San Francisco's Chinatown, the first Chinese temple was established, and by the end of the century, 400 Chinese temples existed on the West Coast. In these nondenominational temples Confucianism, Daoism, and Buddhism could all be practiced at the same time and place. The Chinese made their way into the labor force all across the country, especially as primary workers in the transcontinental railway construction of the 19th century. The Buddhist population of the United States increased dramatically in 1898, when the United States annexed Hawaii, where over 25,000 Japanese Buddhists were living and working.

A milestone toward the legitimation of Buddhism in the United States came in 1893 at the World Parliament of Religions in Chicago. For 16 days in September, the Parliament provided a locus for discussion and interreligious dialogue with representation by major religions from around the world. A Sri Lankan Buddhist named Anagarika Dharmapala (1864–1933), himself deeply involved in the Theosophical Society, was such a popular speaker at the conference that he gained national media attention and celebrity-like status. He returned to the United States several times in subsequent years to lecture on Buddhism. On 23 September 1893, after Dharmapala finished a lecture in the Atheneum Building in Chicago, the audience witnessed Charles T. Strauss, New York City businessman and son of Jewish parents, take the stage alongside Buddhist monks. After a brief ceremony Strauss became the first person to convert to Buddhism on American soil.

*Buddhism in the 20th Century and Beyond*

In the 20th century Buddhism continued to gain momentum as more Chinese and Japanese immigrants poured into the United States. Compared to the Chinese variants, Japanese Buddhism remained more regimented and formal. Buddhism proved to be so fascinating to many intellectuals that Buddhism thrived in large cities, especially on the West Coast and in Hawaii. Until later in the century when Theravāda and Vajrayāna began to flourish here, Mahāyāna Buddhism (from China, Japan, and Korea) was initially the most influential. The two forms of Zen or Chan Buddhism (Japanese and Chinese, respectively), Soto (Japanese for "just sitting"), and Rinzai, also known as the "shouting and beating sect," were the forms that made significant headway. This stands in marked contrast to Europe, where interest centered largely on the Theravāda form of Buddhism prevalent in southern and Southeast Asia.

The proliferation of Zen was due mainly to the efforts of the Japanese monk Shaku Soen and his student D.T. Suzuki (1870–1966) at the turn of the century. Two other students of Soen, Shaku Sokatsu and Senzaki Nyogen, were also very influential in this regard. The latter established a number of *zendo*s (meditation halls). One of Shaku Sokatsu's students, Sasaki Shigetsu (or Sokei-an), was an important figure who established the Buddhist Society of America. In 1931 in New York the society became known as the First Zen Institute. The ensuing popularity created demand for qualified *roshi*s (Japanese masters) to instruct Americans who were eager to supplement their growing theoretical knowledge with supervised practice. However, Zen practice did suffer a setback during World War II, when, fearful of conspiratorial subversion, the U.S. government confined many Japanese in internment camps.

As the 20th century continued, Buddhism remained influential in the Asian immigrant community. It returned to the spotlight in the 1960s, when it became a subject of intellectual, philosophical, and theological interest at large. This was due in part to the popularity of writers of the "Beat" movement of the 1950s, such as Allen Ginsberg and Jack Kerouac. Buddhism has been discussed by thinkers as diverse as Alan Watts and Derek Parfit.

In the 1960s American enthusiasm for Buddhism gained ground owing to the hippie counterculture, in which images and ideas from Asian religions figured prominently. In the Haight-Ashbury district of San Francisco, this meeting of East and West took popular form. The result, for many 1960s seekers, was a hybrid between Buddhism, the peace movement, and the psychedelic drug culture. However, the vast majority of Buddhist teachers and serious American students eventually came to regard intoxicating drugs as counterproductive to the goal of having a clear mind that is free of illusions. Combining the psychology and philosophy of Buddhist and other Asian traditions, a 1970s Haight-Ashbury institution, the California Institute of Integral Studies, has survived in an accredited academic form as the California Institute of Asian Studies.

So many Buddhist meditation groups have been established that it is difficult to trace this development. With the establishment of the Tassajara Zen Mountain Center in California in 1966, a milestone in the monastic history of Buddhism in the United States was reached. In 1972 in California the Gold Mountain Monastery was founded by the Sino-American Buddhist Association. At Gold Mountain all five schools of Chinese Buddhism were active. San Francisco's Buddha's Universal Church (1963) was another important institution in spreading the dharma (truth or doctrine).

The 1960s and 1970s saw the influx of Theravādin and Tibetan (Vajrayāna) representatives. The latter began arriving in the 1960s, the major catalyst being the Chinese invasion of their Tibetan homeland in 1959. Three important refugee lamas – Tarthang Tulku, Chogyam Trungpa, and Kalu Rinpoche – established a number of centers. Of these, two that stand out are the Nyingmapa Center in California in 1969 (Tarthang Tulku's creation) and the Naropa Institute (Chogyam Trungpa's center of Buddhist study), founded in Colorado in 1974.

Interestingly it was early Buddhist Theravāda that arrived in the United States last. Two American students of this school, Jack Kornfield and Joseph Goldstein, established the Insight Meditation Center in Barre, Massachusetts (1976). Also at Barre the Buddhist Studies Center, directed by Andrew Olendzski and Mu Soeng, offers annual Nalanda Summer Institutes, which combine study and practice. They are similar in format to the Summer Seminars on the Sūtras, which combine sitting meditation with scholarly study of texts and have been offered by Juarez Bodhi Mandala in Santa Fe, New Mexico, since the 1980s. The Philadelphia Buddhist Association, operated mainly by Richard McKinney, is a center emphasizing Theravāda, Zen, and Tibetan traditions and was founded by the late businessman Ed Leitz and Professor Albert Stunkard, M.D., in 1986. It was established as a meditation center but has evolved to include a Sūtra Study Group, which deals mainly with Theravāda and eastern Asian Mahāyāna. Also in Philadelphia is the Tibetan Buddhist Center, which both teaches meditation and promotes understanding of Tibetan culture.

In "American Buddhism" American teachers of Buddhism typically operate their own religious organizations. Zen has representatives called dharma heirs, from both the Rinzai and Soto Japanese traditions, functioning in the United States. Japanese-trained Soto Zen teacher Dai-en Bennage operates Mount Equity Zendo near Harrisburg, Pennsylvania, where the teaching includes that of Thích Nhát Hanh. Bernard Glassman is abbot of the Zen Community of New York, which has a notably American influence and differs from the Soto tradition in which Glassman was trained in that the center operates a business in addition to meditation practice. Maurine Stuart is president of the Cambridge Buddhist Association, which also differs from the Rinzai sect of Zen tradition in that a woman is allowed to be abbot. Additionally her practice employs massage for correcting meditation posture instead of the famed stick of compassion, which is indicative of a change of customary rituals. Richard Baker was abbot of the San Francisco Zen Center in 1983, a position he had held since 1971, following disputes as to the role and authority of his position as abbot. This might be a particular indication of an emerging American Buddhism, for in Japan the authority of the abbot goes unquestioned, whereas American culture encourages the questioning of authority. As a new millennium begins, will there be a "New Age" of peace and tranquility with Buddhism as one of its driving forces? That remains to be seen.

FRANK J. HOFFMAN, BRIAN WILLIARD, TAREK TANNOUS, CATHERINE ORAVEZ, AND ADAM MORRIS

*See also* Abbot: Buddhist; Anticlericalism: Buddhist Perspectives; Buddhism: Overview; Buddhology; Chan/Zen: Japan; Dharmapāla, Anagārika; Dialogue, Intermonastic: Buddhist Perspectives; Forest Masters; Kōan; Meditation: Buddhist Perspectives; Nhát Hanh, Thích; Sexuality: Buddhist Perspectives; Shinran; Spirituality: Buddhist; Suzuki, Daisetz Teitaro; Theravādin Monks, Modern Western; Tibet; Zen and the West

## Further Reading

Bennage, Patricia Daien, *Zen Seeds: Reflections of a Female Priest*, translated by Shundo Aoyama, Tokyo: Kosei, 1990

Eppsteiner, Fred, editor, *The Path of Compassion: Writings on Socially Engaged Buddhism*, Berkeley, California: Parallax Press, 1988

Fields, Rick, *How the Swans Came to the Lake: A Narrative History of Buddhism in America*, Boulder, Colorado: Shambhala, 1981; 3rd edition, Boston: Shambhala, 1992

Hoffman, Frank J., "Contemporary Buddhist Philosophy," in *Companion Encyclopedia of Asian Philosophy*, edited by Brian Carr and Indira Mahalingam, London and New York: Routledge, 1997

Kapleau, Philip, *To Cherish All Life: A Buddhist View of Animal Slaughter and Meat Eating*, Rochester, New York: Zen Center, 1981

LaFleur, William R., *Buddhism: A Cultural Perspective* (Prentice-Hall Series in World Religions), Englewood Cliffs, New Jersey: Prentice-Hall, 1988

Phillips, D.Z., editor, *Religion and Morality* (Claremont Studies in the Philosophy of Religion), New York: St. Martin's Press, and London: Macmillan Press, 1996

Prebish, Charles, and Kenneth Tanaka, *The Faces of Buddhism in America*, Berkeley: University of California Press, 1998

Reps, Paul, compiler, *Zen Flesh, Zen Bones: A Collection of Zen and Pre-Zen Writings*, Rutland, Vermont: Tuttle, 1957; London: Arkana, 1991

Tworkov, Helen, and Natalie Goldberg, *Zen in America: Five Teachers and the Search for American Buddhism*, Tokyo: Kodansha International, 1994

# Buddhist Schools/Traditions: China

## Introduction

When dealing with Chinese Buddhist schools, one should bear in mind that the historical reality behind the concept "school" (*zong*) can at times be rather loose. Although it can signify an actual institution organized around a specific set of doctrines, or nominative scriptures, with a historical line of patriarchs and with its own temples and monasteries, it can equally well mean a loose organization consisting of monks sharing the same practices but not necessarily the same lineage. Alternatively it can refer to a nonorganized movement of Buddhists who share the same beliefs and doctrines. In addition a number of terms signify branches and subsects within a given school or denomination, such as "house" (*jia*) or "branch" (*pai*).

Institutionalized schools normally are characterized by their lineage of transmission. This means that they have a fixed history and that they generally remain faithful to the original teachings expounded by the founder and his immediate successors. Such a line of transmission is often upheld by sect histories, containing accounts of the founding patriarchs and their successors. Both the Tiantai school and the numerous Chan schools and subsects maintain a strict adherence to what they see as orthodox lines of transmission.

In the course of history a number of the Chinese Buddhist schools became associated with particular temples and locations. The Chan Buddhists monopolized a number of temples and mountains, such as Baolin, the site of the sixth patriarch Huineng's temple, and Mount Song, the site of Shaolin Temple, where their founder Bodhidharma is said to have practiced. In the same way the Tiantai school continued to remain powerful on Mount Tiantai, its place of origin. A holy mountain, such as Mount Wutai in northern Shanxi province, had numerous temples, most of which were controlled by different schools of Buddhism. Nevertheless at certain times the Huayan school was dominant there, and at other times it was the Zhenyan, the Chan, or the Tiantai. By the Song dynasty (960–1279), the government had set up a number of state monasteries that were not controlled by any one lineage or school. This helped abolish sectarian ownership over any one temple.

## Pure Land School (Jingtu zong)

The origin of Pure Land Buddhism in China goes back to the first translations of the Pure Land sūtras, that is, the larger and minor *Sukhāvatīvyūha*. Later it received further stimulation through the appearance of the popular *Guan wuliangshou fo jing* (Amitāyus Dhyāna Sūtra), a work of central Asian origin. The Pure Land tradition traces itself back to the White Lotus Assembly organized by Kumārajīva's (344–413) disciple Huiyuan (344–416) on Mount Lu during the early part of the fifth century. The tradition itself recognizes Tanluan (476–542) as its first patriarch.

The Pure Land school spread under the leadership of Daozho (562–645) and his disciple Shantao (613–681). Both wrote a number of tracts and commentaries on the Pure Land, and Shantao's became influential for the East Asian Pure Land tradition in general. As in Chan and Tiantai Buddhism, the Pure Land patriarchal lineage is partly fictitious.

The doctrines of the Pure Land focus on rebirth in Sukhāvatī, Amitābha's Pure Land. This heavenly realm, located in the far western reaches of the universe, may be considered equivalent to paradise or heaven in the Christian tradition. However, it is not a permanent state of grace but rather a station on the way to final nirvana. It is thought to have been metaphysically created by the vows of Amitābha to save all sentient beings who want to be reborn in his realm. The main practice in the Pure Land tradition consists of calling or reciting (*nianfo*) Amitābha's name (Nanwu Omituo fo) and to visualize his Pure Land. In

Longmen, Henan, Fengxian *si* (Cave 19), overall view.
Photo courtesy of John C. Huntington, the Huntington Archive

accordance with the Pure Land scriptures, one may be reborn into this paradise in nine grades, depending on the purity of one's karma. Even the worst sinner can be reborn in the Pure Land, provided that he or she utters Amitābha's name in earnest.

During the late Tang dynasty (618–907) and the Five Dynasties period (907–978), Pure Land doctrines and practices merged with both Chan and Tiantai Buddhism, and in time this syncretic feature became a distinct characteristic of the Buddhist tradition in China. In the premodern and modern periods, Pure Land Buddhism has been the dominant form of Chinese Buddhism. Pure Land worship is an integral part of the daily liturgy in all Buddhist temples in China.

The cult associated with the bodhisattva Avalokiteśvara (Guanyin) can be considered an offshoot of the Jingtu tradition. Over the centuries it became so infused with local tales and other religious traditions that already during the Tang dynasty it had become a pan-Chinese religious phenomenon. The main focus of the Avalokiteśvara cult is the island Putuo (Potalaka) off the shore of Zhenjiang, which is considered the holy abode of the bodhisattva by the devotees.

### Three Stages School (Sanjie zong)

This tradition was founded by the monk Xinxing (540–594), a charismatic and visionary leader who expounded the three ages

of Buddhism. In accordance with this belief, Buddhism enters three stages of progressive decay after the death of Śākyamuni until the advent of Maitreya, the Future Buddha. The Maitreya cult was highly popular in Chinese Buddhism of the sixth century, and as such Xinxing's teachings belong to this major trend. Using a special way of counting, Xinxing maintained that the end of the world was near. This belief in an apocalypse followed by a millenarian vision brought the school into direct conflict with the worldly powers. Furthermore the leaders of the Three Ages school are known to have fabricated a number of scriptures to bolster their claims and to have passed them off as genuine translations of Indian Buddhist sūtras. Many of the other works connected with this school were likewise considered controversial by the rulers, and the school was persecuted several times during the early Tang dynasty. Nevertheless, it was not stamped out entirely, and its scriptures continued to be circulated until the end of the Tang.

### Tiantai School (Tiantai zong)

Under the Sui dynasty (581–618) the first great school of Chinese Buddhism arose, namely, the Tiantai school with its center in Guoxiang Temple at the foot of Mount Tiantai in Zhejiang. Although it traces its lines back to the historical Buddha and to certain other Indian masters, the actual founder was the monk

Zhiyi (538–595), a master who combined meditation (*zhiguan*) with the study of the canonical scriptures. The *Saddharma-puṇḍarīka sūtra* was of special importance for Zhiyi, who wrote several commentaries on its meaning. The Tiantai school developed a special system for classifying Buddhist doctrines (*panjiao*). In accordance with this vertically ranked system, the teachings are placed into five categories, depending on the depth of their doctrines as understood by Zhiyi. The *Saddharmapuṇḍarīka sūtra* was classed together with the *Mahāparinirvāṇa sūtra* in the top grade as containing the ultimate teaching of Buddhism.

The Tiantai enjoyed unsurpassed imperial support throughout the Sui dynasty and was the largest of all the Buddhist schools at the time of the founding of the Tang dynasty in 618. Because of its close relationship with the ruling house of the Sui, the Tiantai school was suppressed during the first half of the Tang, but it again rose to prominence in the period following the An Lushan Rebellion (756–762). Toward the end of the dynasty, it was widespread throughout the realm, and in addition to Mount Tiantai in the south it also controlled most of the monasteries on Mount Wutai in the north. Under the Huichang Suppression (844–845) of Buddhism, it shared a fate similar to the one that befell the other large doctrinal schools of Buddhism, and many of its temples were destroyed. At that time many of the classical Tiantai writings were lost and had to be reimported from Korea later. The Tiantai school experienced a brief revival during the Northern Song dynasty and at that time split into two contending denominations: the Shannei ("Inside the Mountain") and the Shanwai ("Outside the Mountain").

## Sanlun School (Sanlun zong)

Another important school that arose during the Sui dynasty was the Sanlun, which had been founded by a Korean monk. This school is based on the study of *madhyamaka* philosophy and meditation. The three treatises, from which this school derives its name, are the *Zhong lun* (Treatise on the Middle Way), the *Bai lun* (Treatise in One Hundred Verses), and the *Shiermen lun* (Treatise in Twelve Sections). The main propagator of the school was Jizang (549–623), whose *madhyamaka* thought influenced Zhiyi, the founder of the Tiantai school. Sanlun teachings also played a role in the doctrinal makeup of certain lineages in early Southern Chan. The Sanlun school disappeared during the late seventh century, and its teachings were absorbed into the doctrines of the Tiantai and Chan traditions.

## Lu School (Lu zong)

The Lu school was formally founded by Daoxuan (596–667), a scholar-monk and student of Chinese Buddhist history. As indicated by its name, the Lu school centered on the study of Buddhist disciplinary codexes (vinaya). Although it maintained a line of transmission, it did not develop a strict sectarian structure. Nevertheless the study of the vinaya was considered especially important in certain temples. During the Tang the center for vinaya studies was on Mount Zhongnan to the south of the capital, Chang'an. As any person wanting to join the *saṅgha* had to undergo some training in the vinaya to be ordained, all Buddhist temples, regardless of their sectarian affiliation, ultimately had to follow the rules as laid down in the vinaya.

## Faxiang School (Faxiang zong)

Because of its close connection to the ruling house of the previous dynasty, the Tiantai school was denied imperial support during the early Tang, and patronage was extended instead to the Faxiang school, founded by the pilgrim-monk Xuanzang (c. 600–664). He returned to China in 645, bringing with him the Sanskrit scriptures, on which he based his teachings. In terms of doctrine the Faxiang school was based on a special branch of Indian *Yogācāra* philosophy, which taught that whereas phenomena are fundamentally illusory, the mind or consciousness (*shi*), which perceives them, is real. A central aspect of this doctrine deals with the classification of the characteristics of individual phenomena (*dharmalakṣana*), from which the school's Chinese name derives. Xuanzang's major work, the *Cheng weishi lun* (Treatise on Consciousness Only), contains the essence of the Faxiang doctrine.

The prominence of the Faxiang school was short-lived, and after the demise of Xuanzang's leading disciple, Guiji (632–682), it died out as an institutional tradition. However, the study of *Yogācāra* doctrines and of Buddhist logic continued within some of the other schools, and from time to time proponents of these aspects of Faxiang Buddhism were able to arouse attention in Buddhist circles. Such developments took place as late as the late Qing dynasty and the early Republican era (20th century).

## Huayan School (Huayan zong)

The Huayan school, which is based on the voluminous *Buddha-vataṃsaka sūtra*, traces its origin back to Dushun (557–640), although the real founder of the school was the third patriarch Fazang (643–712). Fazang gained access to the Tang court late in his career and presented a simplified version of Huayan to Empress Wu Zetian (684–704). His teaching is found in the work, the *Jin shizi zhang* (Tract on the Golden Lion), in which he set forth in a popular manner his understanding of universal interpenetration of all phenomena. The main teaching of the Huayan school focuses on the interpenetration of all phenomena and the total integration of the absolute and the relative realms and as such is one of the most speculative of all Chinese Buddhist schools. Like the Tiantai, the Huayan school developed its own system of classifying the Buddhist teachings.

Chengguan (738–838), who is traditionally considered the fourth patriarch but who never met Fazang, was highly influential in his own time and received many honors from the Tang court. He resided for several years on Mount Wutai, where he wrote his major works. Chengguan is rightly held to be one of the greatest philosophers in Chinese Buddhism. Following him as the fifth patriarch of the school was Guifeng Zongmi (780–841), who also had a transmission from the Southern Chan tradition. He authored a number of works in which Chan and Huayan doctrines were harmonized. The Huayan school died out in the course of the Song dynasty.

*Chan Schools* (Chan zong)

According to tradition Chan Buddhism was brought to China by the Indian monk Bodhidharma (d. c. 530) at the beginning of the sixth century. However, Chan as a distinct school of Buddhism was invented in China. It has its roots in the Buddhist *dhyāna* (*chan*) tradition that developed in the latter half of the Nanbeichao period (386–581). The practices of the early *dhyāna*, or meditation, tradition include a wide a range of methods, such as *śamatha*, *vipaśyanā*, visualization, and *buddhanusmṛti* (*nianfo*), all of which are practices leading to *samādhī* (deep self-absorption). A mastery of *samādhī* is considered necessary to attain enlightenment. The doctrinal foundation of the *dhyāna* tradition is based on several canonical Hīnayāna and Mahāyāna scriptures, both Indian and Chinese.

The later Chan Buddhist tradition, which takes Bodhidharma as its first patriarch in China, is a phenomenon that originated in the first half of the seventh century. Its early history is intimately linked with the Sanlun and Tiantai schools. It became a distinct school of Buddhism, with collateral lineages of transmission, during the second half of the seventh century. Most of these lineages considered Bodhidharma the first patriarch in China and the 28 in a patriarchal line going back to the historical Buddha himself. Bodhidharma was followed by five or six Chinese patriarchs, depending on the individual history of the sect.

By the middle of the eighth century, the Chan tradition consisted of two contending factions, the Southern and Northern schools, in addition to several lesser lineages. Each of these laid claim to the orthodox patriarchal tradition, and for several decades a virtual intersectarian strife with strong political undertones divided Chan Buddhism. However, all shared a doctrinal foundation, and on the surface little difference existed between Northern and Southern Chan. The real differences lay in the way in which the teachings and meditation techniques were practiced. Whereas the Northern lineages normally insisted that the process toward enlightenment took place gradually, the adherents of Southern Chan held that its attainment occurred instantaneously. The issue was settled by Shenhui (684–758), a leading master of Southern Chan who through clever rhetoric and political machinations established his supposed teacher, Huineng (638–713), as the sixth patriarch and thereby himself as the seventh. Although Northern Chan historically continued to exist until the end of the eighth century, it was eventually absorbed into the Southern Chan.

In the course of the ninth century, Southern Chan branched out into several lineages and gradually spread to all corners of the Tang Empire (618–906). In this period many Chan temples were established in the mountains and in the countryside, where the monks cultivated the temple lands and to a large degree became self-sufficient. The great masters from this period descended from the line of Mazu Daoyi (709–788) and included monks such as Baizhang (720–814) and his disciple Huangbo (d. 850). Most of the Chan lineages claimed to "transmit Mind-realization beyond the established teaching." A comprehensive and distinct Chan literature had developed by the middle of the

ninth century. It consisted of several genres of literature, such as sect histories (*zongshi*), tales, recorded sayings (*yulu*), recorded interviews between masters and their disciples (*wenda*), doctrinal works (*lun*), and collections of poetry. Important Chan works from this period include the well-known *Liuzu fabao jing* (The Platform Scripture of the Sixth Patriarch) and the *Linji lu* (The Record of Linji). Guifeng Zongmi (780–841) was an important Chan scholar who combined Chan doctrines with the teachings of Huayan Buddhism.

By the Five Dynasties period, the Chan tradition had divided into five major schools: the Linji, the Caodong, the Guiyang, the Yunmen, and the Fayan. In terms of methods of practice and doctrines, they did not differ significantly. What set them apart were mainly lineage and geography. During that period Chan Buddhism incorporated certain elements from the other Buddhist traditions, especially from esoteric and the Pure Land schools.

By the beginning of the Song dynasty, Chan Buddhism had become the largest Buddhist denomination in China. It controlled large monasteries that owned vast tracts of land cultivated by tenant farmers. These state-supported institutions housed up to several thousand monks (or nuns). During this period Chan Buddhism was dominated by the Linji and Caodong schools, which gradually absorbed the lesser traditions. It was also under the Song that the compilation of the great Chan histories, compendia, and *yulu* took place. They include the *Jingde chuandeng lu* (The Jingde Transmission of the Lamp), the *Wudeng huiyuan* (The Five Lamps Meeting at the Source), the *Zongjing lu* (Record of the [Chan Schools'] Mirror), and *Baizhang jinggui* (Baizhang's Regulations).

Many important Chan masters emerged during the Song dynasty, among whom Dahui Zonggao (1089–1163) from the Linji school was most influential. He developed the *kongan* method of meditation (also known as *kanhua*, "contemplating the word"). A *kongan* is a "spiritual case story" normally taken from the literature of the earlier Chan tradition. The gist of the *kongan*, i.e. the *huatou*, is the topic or theme used in meditation. Consequently an extensive *kongan* literature had developed by the Southern Song, including the *Biyan lu* (The Blue Cliff Records) and *Wumen guan* (Gateless Gate).

After a long period of decline, several important Chan masters emerged at the end of the Ming dynasty (1368–1644). Among these were Hanshan Deqing (1546–1623), a meditator and scholar-monk outside the traditional Chan lines of transmission, and Hongzhi (1535–1615). The latter popularized a combination of Chan and Pure Land teachings that became the established norm for Chinese Chan. During the late Qing dynasty (1644–1911) and the early Republican period (1911–1949), Chan Buddhism experienced a revival.

*Zhenyan School* (Mijiao/Zenyan zong)

Perhaps the most widespread form of Buddhism tradition during the Tang dynasty was the largely pansectarian esoteric Buddhist tradition (*mijiao*), represented by the Zhenyan school. Although the history of esoteric Buddhism in China went back to the third century, it the reached its zenith during the eighth and exerted a tremendous influence on Buddhism at the Tang court. The most prominent representatives of this tradition were Śubhākarasimha (637–735), Vajrabodhi (669–741), and Amoghavajra (705–774). The former cotranslated the *Mahāvairocana sūtra*, the central scripture of the tradition, with his disciple the Chan monk Yixing (682–727), who was also known for his knowledge of astrology. Amoghavajra, the third patriarch, was a highly industrious translator and author who produced more than 75 different works, including translations, commentaries, and ritual manuals. The Zhenyan school propounded a fairly systematic and structured form of esoteric Buddhism complete with highly elaborate rituals that included the use of mudras, maṇḍalas, complex visualizations, and *dhāraṇī*s. Several of the largest and most prestigious temples in Chang'an and Luoyang were controlled by adherents of esoteric Buddhism, including the Cien Temple, the Anguo Temple, Da Shanxing Temple, and Qinglong Temple.

By the middle of the eighth century, Zhenyan Buddhism held almost total sway over the Tang court and at the same time exerted a considerable influence on other Buddhist schools in the empire. Tiantai monks in the twin capitals came under increasing influence from the rituals and esoteric practices taught in Zhenyan Buddhism. At the beginning of the ninth century, the Zhenyan transmission was gradually diffused, and eventually esoteric practices were adapted by the other schools of Chinese Buddhism, especially by the followers of the Tiantai school.

When the Huichang Suppression of Buddhism took place between 844 and 845, most of the large Zhenyan temples in Chang'an and Luoyang were destroyed. This heralded the end of the formal Zhenyan school, although more syncretic and unstructured forms of esoteric Buddhist practice continued in the provinces. By the end of the Tang dynasty, esoteric Buddhism had become extremely popular in Sichuan (Shu), where it fostered a local variant that flourished until the middle of the 13th century.

*The Huichang Suppression of Buddhism*

During the Huichang reign (840–845), Buddhism suffered the strongest and most far-reaching and radical suppression to take place so far in Chinese history. From 845 to 846 the suppression reached its zenith in the regions surrounding the two capitals. Many monks and nuns were killed, and several thousand were forced to disrobe and resume the status of laypeople. Temples throughout the country were turned over to the government to be used as schools and for storage, and their treasures and art objects were destroyed. Statues and other objects of metal were melted down, and wood and stone images were vandalized. In this way enormous quantities of religious art were lost. The Huichang Suppression signified a radical change in the direction of Chinese Buddhism, as it toppled the large doctrinal schools Huayan, Tiantai, Faxiang, and to some extent Zhenyan. None of them was able to regain vitality after the suppression ended officially in 858. However, both the Chan schools and the Pure Land school survived the suppression relatively intact and arose

in the Five Dynasties period and the following Song dynasty to become the two most influential Buddhist denominations in China.

HENRIK H. SØRENSEN

*See also* Asia, Central; Bodhidharma; Chan/Zen: China; China; Critiques of Buddhist Monasticism: Confucian; Daoism: Influence on Buddhism; Daoxuan (Tao-hsüan); Deities, Buddhist; Economics: Buddhist; Esoteric Buddhism in China and Japan; Hermits: Buddhist; Holy Men/Holy Women: Buddhist Perspectives; Holy Men in Power (Hierocrats), Buddhist; Master and Pupil: Buddhist Perspectives; Mount Wutai, China; Pilgrims to India, Chinese; Pure Land Buddhism; Self-Immolation, Buddhist; Shaolin, China; Taiwan; Tiantai/Tendai: China; Tibetan Lineages; Travelers: Buddhist; Zhiyi (Chih-i)

**Further Reading**

Chang, Chung-yüan, *Original Teachings of Ch'an Buddhism*, New York: Pantheon, 1969

Chappell, David W., "Tao-ch'o (562–645): A Pioneer of Chinese Pure Land Buddhism," Doctoral thesis, Yale University, 1976

Ch'en, Kenneth, *Buddhism in China: A Historical Survey*, Princeton, New Jersey: Princeton University Press, 1964

Chih-p'an, Shih, *A Chronicle of Buddhism in China, 581–960 A.D.: Translations from Monk Chih-p'an's Fo-tsu t'ung-chi*, Santiniketan: Visva-Bharati, 1966

Chou, I-liang, "Tantrism in China," *Harvard Journal of Asian Studies* 8 (1945)

Donner, Neil, *The Great Calming and Contemplation: A Study and Annotated Translation of the First Chapter of Chih-yi's Mo-Ho Chih-Kuan*, Honolulu: University of Hawaii Press, 1993

Dumoulin, Heinrich, *Zen Buddhism: A History*, volume 1: *India and China*, translated by James Heisig and Paul Knitter, New York: Macmillan, and London: Collier Macmillan, 1988

Ennin, *Ennin's Diary: The Record of a Pilgrimage to China in Search of the Law*, translated by Edwin O. Reischauer, New York: The Ronald Press Company, 1955

Gimello, Robert M., "Chih-yen (602–668) and the Foundation of Hua-yen Buddhism," Doctoral thesis, Columbia University, 1976

Gimello, Robert M., and Peter N. Gregory, editors, *Studies in Ch'an and Hua-yen*, Honolulu: University of Hawaii Press, 1983

Gregory, Peter N., editor, *Traditions of Meditation in Chinese Buddhism*, Honolulu: University of Hawaii Press, 1986

Hsü, Sung-peng, *A Buddhist Leader in Ming China: The Life and Thought of Han-shan Te-ch'ing, 1546–1623*, University Park: Pennsylvania State University Press, 1979

Hurvitz, Leon, *Chih-i (538–597): An Introduction to the Life and Ideas of a Chinese Buddhist Monk*, Brussels: Melanges Chinois et Bouddhiques, 1962

Ishii, Shūdō, *Sodai zenshū shi no kenkyū* (Studies in the History of the Chan Schools during the Song Dynasty), Tokyo: Daitō shuppansha, 1987

Jan, Yün-hua, "Tsung-mi and His Analysis of Ch'an," *T'oung Pao* 58 (1972)

*Land of Bliss, the Paradise of the Buddha of Measureless Light: Sanskrit and Chinese Versions of the Sukhāvatīvyūha Sūtra*, translated by Luis O. Gómez, Honolulu: University of Hawaii Press, 1996

Lu, K'uan Yu, *Secrets of Chinese Meditation*, London: Rider, 1964; York Beach, Maine: Weiser, 1969

Lü Jianfu, *Zhongguo mijiao shi* (The History of Esoteric Buddhism in China), Beijing: Zhongguo shehui kexue chubanshe, 1995

McRae, John R., *The Northern School and the Formation of Early Ch'an Buddhism*, Honolulu: University of Hawaii Press, 1986

Osabe, Kazuo, *Tō Sō Mikkyō Shi Ronkō* (Essays on the History of Esoteric Buddhism during the Tang and Song), Kobe: Kobe Joshi Daigaku Tozai Bunka Kenkyujo, 1982

Pas, Julian F., *Visions of Sukhāvati: Shan-Tao's Commentary on the Kuan Wu-Liang Shou-Fo Ching*, Albany: State University of New York Press, 1995

Reischauer, Edwin O., *Ennin's Travels in T'ang China*, New York: The Ronald Press Company, 1955

Robinson, Richard H., *Early Mādhyamika in India and China*, Madison: University of Wisconsin Press, 1967

Sørensen, H.H., editor, *The Esoteric Buddhist Tradition: Selected Papers from the 1989 SBS Conference*, Copenhagen and Aarhus: Seminar for Buddhist Studies, 1994

Strickmann, Michel, *Mantras et mandarins: Le bouddhisme tantrique en Chine*, Paris: Gallimard, 1996

Swanson, Paul, *Foundations of T'ien-t'ai Philosophy: The Flowering of the Two Truths Theory in Chinese Buddhism*, Berkeley, California: Asian Humanities Press, 1989

Tanaka, Kenneth K., *The Dawn of Chinese Pure Land Buddhist Doctrine*, Albany: State University of New York Press, 1990

Tsukamoto, Zenryū, *A History of Early Chinese Buddhism*, 2 vols., translated by L. Hurvitz, Tokyo and New York: Kodansha International, 1985

Weinstein, Stanley, *Buddhism under the T'ang*, Cambridge and New York: Cambridge University Press, 1987

Welch, Holmes, *The Practice of Chinese Buddhism 1900–1950*, Cambridge, Massachusetts: Harvard University Press, 1967

Wu, Ju-Chun, *T'ien-t'ai Buddhism and Early Mādhyamika*, Honolulu: University of Hawaii Press, 1993

Yoritomi, Motohiro, *Chūgoku mikkyō no kenkyū* (Studies in Chinese Esoteric Buddhism), Tokyo: Daitōshuppansha, 1979

Yü, Chun-fang, *The Renewal of Buddhism in China: Chu-hung and the Late Ming Synthesis*, New York: Columbia University Press, 1981

Zürcher, Erik, *The Buddhist Conquest of China*, 2 vols., Leiden: Brill, and New York: Humanities Press, 1959; reprint, Leiden: Brill, 1972

# Buddhist Schools/Traditions: Japan

Japan owes almost all of its schools of Buddhist thought to sources in China, in some cases through the medium of Korean monks. Formally introduced at the court in the middle of the sixth century into a polytheistic culture with entrenched practitioners of Shintō ceremonies, the proponents of Buddhism were forced to "prove" its superior effectiveness through some form of magic. This they did with an indestructible "relic," and a Shintō diviner approved the continued use of the Buddhist paraphernalia. Accepted first by the aristocracy and much later by the populace as a whole, the magical element in Buddhism played a large role in its social expansion.

Not until the latter half of the sixth century were temples built and individual Buddhas or lesser deities identified. These were Shaka (Śākyamuni), the historical Buddha, solicited to secure the repose of an individual's soul in paradise; Yakushi, the Buddha of healing, petitioned to gain relief from an ailment; Miroku (Maitreya) as a bodhisattva, to encourage a patient but future quest for Buddhahood; and the Four Heavenly Kings (Shitennō), to provide security for the ruling family or the country. After the Taika Reform of 645–646, which concentrated power in the person of the emperor and organized a bureaucratic government along Chinese lines, Buddhism prospered as wealthy families competed with one another in temple construction, encouraged by the court.

From 710 until 784 the capital was at Nara, about which later writers speak as though here sectarian Buddhism had reached an early maturity, referring to the Nantō Rokushū, the Six Sects of the Southern Capital. However, the formal organization into sects with a hierarchical structure and branch temple relationships probably did not develop until later, perhaps to counter the rise of newly introduced sects. Now called the Nara sects, these are (1) Jōjitsu (introduced in 625), based on a treatise by the Indian priest Harivarman (fourth century A.D.), *Sattyasiddhi-śāstra* (Japanese, *Jōjitsu-ron*; Treatise on the Completion of the Truth), which in a negativistic way sees neither mind nor matter as existing, only the sūtras; the Void is ultimate Truth; (2) Sanron (Three Treatises, brought in 625 by a Korean monk), based on the treatise of Nāgārjuna (second century), *Madhyamika-śāstra* (Japanese, *Chū-ron*; Treatise on the Middle Path), which emphasizes dwelling in the "emptiness" with neither a positive nor negative attitude; (3) Hossō (654), based on a treatise by Asaṅga (fifth century), *Yogācārabhūmi-śāstra* (Japanese, *Yuga-ron*; Treatise on Yoga), which claims that nothing exists outside the mind (only ideas create the phenomenal world; known as Yuishiki "consciousness-only," it is also the Middle Path); (4) Kusha (658), based on a treatise by the Indian priest Vasubandhu (fifth century), *Abhidharmakośa* (Japanese, *Kusha-ron*; Treasury of Analysis of the Law), which expounds on the elements of the phenomenal world; (5) Kegon (c. 736), a Chinese sect of the late sixth century, based on the *Avatamsaka-sūtra* (Japanese, *Kegon-kyō*; Garland Sūtra), "universal causation by Ultimate Truth"; and (6) Ritsu (753), brought by the Chinese priest known as Ganjin when he came to perform ordinations, in the Rules sect, a Chinese sect emphasizing discipline and morality in the religious life.

Jōjitsu, Sanron, and Kusha have disappeared, being too similar to others or too abstruse or extreme to have survived. Hossō blossomed, in part because of a constant stream of Hossō propagators from China and Korea. The first great temples were Hossō – the headquarters is shared by the Kōfuku-ji and

The main cemetery on Mount Kōya, Japan, near the Okuno-in.
Photo courtesy of David Moore

Yakushi-ji in Nara, both with many related temples – its position strengthened by the association of all the temples built by Prince Shōtoku with Hossō, though only after his lifetime. The Hōryū-ji separated itself from Hossō in 1950 to form the Shōtoku-shū, a sect dedicated to the prince. Kegon is headquartered at the once-powerful Tōdai-ji and claims some 55 associated temples today. Ganjin was given land and built the Tōshōdai-ji in Nara for his company of Chinese priests. Ritsu (popularly called Ris-shū) flourished in a collegiate way and now lists over 20 related temples.

After Jōdo (the Pure Land concept) spread in Japan from the late tenth century, the veneration of Amida replaced that of Shaka, and Yakushi slowly disappeared from popular interest, it too largely absorbed by Amida. Emperor Kammu moved the capital from Nara, believing that his political plans had been thwarted by the Nara clergy, and settled in Heian (Kyoto) in 794. This cleared the deck for the introduction of sects that either were or became esoteric (*mikkyō*, "revealed"), namely Shingon (Sanskrit, *Mantra*, "True Word") and Tendai (a Chinese mountain and sect name meaning Heavenly Platform). A whole new pantheon of esoteric deities came in with Shingon.

Kūkai (posthumously, Kōbō Daishi; c. 774–835) was sent to China on one of the official missions, studied at the Chinglong temple in Changan, and returned in 806. Ten years later his request to establish a *shuzen dōjō* (place for practicing meditation) was granted, and he started a monastery in a remote mountain named Kōya in Wakayama prefecture. This became the center of monastic esotericism in Japan, the head temple named Kongōbu-ji, the original buildings arranged to form a maṇḍala, a magical diagram. Temples have proliferated on Mount Kōya until the plateau now boasts about 120 and is visited by multitudes of people whose purpose is to "commune with the Daishi." Through the centuries thousands have been buried in a large cemetery there, Okuno-in, to be near the saint. He himself is said to have simply gone into the Diamond Meditation (Sanskrit, *va-jradhyāna*), waiting to return with Maitreya, the Buddha of the Future.

In China Kūkai had qualified himself as "master transmitter of the law" (the process of learning the secret teachings at the master's feet) and had collected the ritual objects needed for the ceremonies in Japan. His extensive writings began with *Sangyō shiki* (Indications to the Teachings of the Three Religions), a comparative analysis of Confucian, Daoist, and Buddhist thought, which embodies the syncretism characteristic of much of later Japanese philosophy. The crowning work is *Jūjū shin-ron* (Treatise on the Ten Stages of Spiritual Development)

Exterior, Kannondo, Byōdō-in, Uji (near Kyoto), Japan, 11th century.
Photo courtesy of John C. Huntington, the Huntington Archive

grading religious experience on ten levels, culminating in Shingon's Tantric practices.

Developing a reputation as a miracle worker, by 810 Kukai had proved the effectiveness of his techniques at a time of national calamity by reading the *Ninnō-gokoku-kyō* (The State-Protecting Benevolent Kings Sūtra) and performing the accompanying ceremony (*Ninnō-e*) for the emperor, in the best eighth-century tradition. In 823 Emperor Saga appointed him chief priest of the Tō-ji (Kyō-ō-gokoku-ji, State-Protecting Temple), then under construction in Kyoto, with instructions to complete it. Among many accomplishments, including inventing the syllabary *kana* writing, he is credited with being the sculptor of 15 of the 21 wooden images of deities that compose a maṇḍala on the platform of the temple's Lecture Hall.

Shingon is best known for its dramatic art, resulting from illustrating the dual concepts of the Diamond (Sanskrit, *Vajradhātu*; Japanese, *Kongō-kai*, "permanent cycle") and Womb (Sanskrit, *Garbhadhātu*; Japanese, *Taizō-kai*, "material cycle") Worlds, as two painted maṇḍalas hung opposite each other to face the Buddha platform with all its precisely arranged ritual articles. Dainichi (*Mahāvairocana*), Buddha of Infinite Light, is the central deity, the source of all existence, through whom Buddhahood is attained in this life. Associated are five esoteric Buddhas of the Kongō-kai (Japanese, Ashuku, Hōshō, Amida, Fukūjōjū, and Dainichi) and of the Taizō-kai (Dainichi, Hodo, Kaifuke, Muryōjū, and Tenkuraion). On the bodhisattva level are the Five Great Kings of Light (Sanskrit, *Vidyārājas*; Japanese, *Godai-myō-ō*), the chief of which is Fudō (Sanskrit, *Acala*). When warriors of the later Zen persuasion found their symbol in this formidable, fierce-looking, sword-brandishing deity, Fudō became one of the most popular deities in Japanese history.

Saichō (posthumously, Dengyō Daishi; 767–822) also returned from China in 805, bringing with him the tenets of Tendai, the philosophical base of which is the *Lotus Sūtra* (*Hokke-kyō*), the gospel Gautama himself is said to have preached, also central to the Kegon sect. He had had a small temple on Mount Hiei, northeast of Kyoto, and to that he repaired, expanding it and requesting that it be named Enryaku-ji (Enryaku era: 782–806) and that it be permitted to perform ordinations. Both were granted after his death. In Tendai the ordinary man is believed to have the Buddha nature, so that enlightenment is achievable through meditation on the Buddha, coupled with moralistic behavior. The monks study the Triple Truth of Tendai: the Void, the Temporary, and the Middle Path. In 851 the temple formally adopted the practice of *nembutsu*, concentrating on the Buddha by repeating his name, the expression being a contraction of *Namu Amida-butsu* (Homage to Amida Buddha). The exercise devolved into incessant repetition, reciters fingering rosaries, groups moving large beads along ropes, and other activities accompanying street dancing.

The priest Ennin (794–864) visited China and on his return (847) introduced esoteric practices learned there, while differing from Shingon in that Tendai viewed esoteric and exoteric philosophies as reaching the same goal by different paths. Shingon saw them as running on two quite divergent courses. Typical of Tendai's efforts to harmonize, the view was inclusive, allowing different emphases to emerge. The later monks who propagated Amida and the Pure Land doctrines and Zen, as well as Nichiren himself, were all products of the Tendai school, each attesting to a better way of achieving enlightenment.

By today's count Tendai and its many subsects record a total of over 4,100 temples, but the count is very loose as the degree of relationship varies greatly. In practice some could be called Jōdo Shin-shū temples. Shingon lists over 12,000 temples, its definition somewhat more precise.

The encounter of one polytheistic religious system with another on different intellectual planes required some simplification of the upper plane if common ground were to be found.

Space could be made for additional deities, or for an overlay of existing ones, but displacements were out of the question. Buddhism had been presented to the Chinese through Daoist language. Gyōgi (670–749), a priest of Korean origin and a skilled engineer, exemplified the life of public service by building bridges, digging canals, constructing harbors, and setting up dispensaries and rest homes. For his saintliness and social contributions, Emperor Shōmu conferred on him the rarely used title of Bosatsu (bodhisattva). To Gyōgi is attributed the initial steps toward the mutual identification of Buddhist and Shintō deities, usually referred to today as *honji-suijaku* (also known as Dual-aspect Shintō), meaning manifestation from the original state. Most notable in the developing cooperation between the religions was the rise of the *jingu-ji* (shrine-temples), Buddhist temples built on the property of or near Shintō shrines for reasons of joint protection. Buddhist and Shintō priests were trained to conduct each others' ceremonies. Most of these shrine-temples were destroyed in the anti-Buddhist movement in the early Meiji period (1868–1912).

The magical element in Buddhism, which had been its initial attraction, continued to appeal and was enhanced by the uses of the Shingon mantra, the mandalas, and ceremonial paraphernalia. The emergence of Pure Land practices from the milieu of Tendai was a reaction against this excessive reliance on ritual and its magic, the effort having been started by Kūya (903–972), whose original meditations on the Buddha led him to take to the

Interior, Kannondo, Byōdō-in, Uji (near Kyoto), Japan, 11th century. This Pure Land temple of Kannon (Kwanyin) centers on laypeople.
Photo courtesy of John C. Huntington, the Huntington Archive

streets, reciting the name of Amida Buddha (*nembutsu*). Supported by the Fujiwara family rulers, Amida worship became the religion of the Heian court, and numerous temples were built by courtiers and emperors alike for their eventual retirement as monks.

The concept of being reborn in the Western Paradise was put into focus in a treatise by Genshin (942–1017), another Mount Hiei monk, written in 985 with the title *Ōjōyōshū* (Rebirth in the Pure Land [of Amida]). It detailed the process as dependent on faith and on invoking the name of the Buddha. Reception in paradise was just one more step in existence, a glorious occasion, the Buddha and his entourage of music-playing bodhisattvas coming down to receive the soul of the deceased into its new life (*raigō*). Unlike the view of the Nara clergy that called for considerable personal effort (*jiriki*), Tendai emphasized the grace of Amida (*tariki*, "another's power") as the main instrument of salvation. The ways of the Fujiwara became known as the Easy Path and, in popular consumption, degenerated into street chanting and dancing, thereby meeting the spiritual and social needs for a vast number of people. The era was colored by the pessimistic concept of *Mappō* (End of the Law), the last of three stages of Buddhism, this one marking the degeneration of Buddhist power and the disintegration if not total disappearance of its physical legacy, including the sūtras. Japanese Buddhists had dated the beginning of the period to 1052.

The evolution of the Pure Land movement into formal sects ran parallel with the development of Zen (Sanskrit, *dhyāna*; Chinese, Chan, "meditation") practices in Japan. Zen had been known to Saichō and had been in the Tendai repertory but made no headway at that time. Another Tendai priest, Myōan Eisai (1141–1215), returned from China in 1191 after studying Linzhi (Japanese, Rinzai) Zen and built the Shōfuku-ji in Hakata, Fukuoka prefecture. A treatise he wrote, *Kōzen-gokoku-ron* (Treatise on the Propagation of Meditation and the Protection of the State), a defense of Zen in three fascicles, antagonized the entrenched Tendai clergy and, despite his relative willingness to compromise, made Kyoto unfriendly. He went to Kamakura, where the wife of Minamoto Yoritomo (1147–1199), founder of the Kamakura military government (*bakufu*), espoused his cause, and the next shōgun, Minamoto Yoriie (1182–1204), promoted it. He soon built the Kennin-ji in Kyoto, which taught a diluted Tendai-Zen, before erecting the Jūfuku-ji for the succeeding Hōjō family in Kamakura, a pure Zen temple. Eisai brought tea from China, and as a result of his discourse on its medicinal properties, the aristocracy adopted tea drinking and the ceremonies that followed.

Rinzai is southern Chinese, emphasizing the use of kōan (essentially, paradoxical questions) toward the goal of sudden enlightenment. Another form, more northern Chinese, was propagated by one of Eisai's former students, Dōgen (1200–1253), also Tendai trained. In his travels in China, he had studied Caotong (Ts'ao-tung) Zen, in which daily work and a disciplined life play a strong part, but the primary method of discovering the Buddha nature within involves sitting cross-legged in meditation (*zazen*). Enlightenment can be a long, slow

process. On his return (1227) Dogen preached Sōtō Zen and lived and worked in Kyoto, where he built the Kōshōhōrin-ji, an exclusively Zen temple, but his intolerant attitude aroused the enmity of the traditional clergy and forced him to leave. He founded the Daibutsu-ji in Fukui prefecture in 1244, later named Eihei-ji, today one of the best-known temples for Zen training. The antipathy toward texts and images – which are only a distraction from the "realization of self" – is quite apparent in the scarcity of icons in Zen temples.

Zen had become a way of life for the military caste by the time the Ashikaga shōguns governed Kyoto (1338–1573), the aristocracy preferring the Rinzai approach. They and other members of the court built huge temples in the city's suburbs. These all suffered in the civil wars but are to some extent rebuilt and thriving religious institutions today. The Ashikaga shoguns employed Zen priests extensively as their educated elite in affairs of state and in business dealings with China.

As it moved down the social scale, Zen reached a diametrically opposite position to the philosophical questions in the sūtras posed by the Nara and esoteric schools. The samurai and the lower classes found in Sōtō the guidelines they needed for discipline and self-control. They built many albeit smaller temples. Sōtō, more than Rinzai, has incorporated Pure Land features in funerary rites, a fact that accounts to some extent for its greater popularity. The list of the branches of Rinzai today includes about 5,400 temples, whereas for Sōtō it is over 14,700.

One other school of Zen is Ōbaku, its headquarters the Mampuku-ji, a large temple near Uji. A Chinese priest called Ingen in Japan built it in the 17th century to retain the Chinese-style architecture and ritual, which is still the case today, with modifications, such as adoption of the *nembutsu*. Ōbaku claims an association of over 470 temples.

The Kamakura period (1185–1333) receives its name from the place on the east coast where the ruling Hōjō family set up its military headquarters. It was still necessary to monitor activities in Kyoto through representation there, since control of Kyoto brought control of the country. Power and position were maintained through military means rather than administrative maneuvering, the rulers coming from quite a different class than the effete and literate Fujiwara.

Reaction against degenerate Amida practices came again from the Tendai school, the first of the spokesmen being Hōnen (posthumously, Genku; 1133–1212), to whom is given the credit for the start of Jōdo-shū, Pure Land Sect, but actually formalized much later despite his animosity to sectarian organizations. However, the sect dates its beginnings to 1175, when Hōnen began to teach his convictions. These constituted a return to the content of the early sūtras, faith and recitation being inseparable. His persuasive treatise *Senjaku hongan nembutsu-shū* (Collection of Passages Concerning the *nembutsu* of the Selected Original Vow) of 1198 was written to champion the primacy of the *nembutsu* route. By claiming salvation through faith in Amida alone, Hōnen was imposing a virtual monotheism, limiting the range of choices normally open to a Japanese seeker.

When Hōnen reached too large a popular audience to suit them, the jealous Tendai clergy engineered Hōnen's banishment, but he was pardoned in 1207. The flagship temple of the Jōdo sect is the Chion-in in east Kyoto, said by Hōnen's followers to have been founded by him in 1211, a temple immense even by Kyoto's standards. Its monumental entrance gate, dating to 1633, is the largest in the country. However, it is not his teachings but that of a disciple named Shōkō (Benchō, 1162–1238) that the faithful now follow. Shōkō quoted Amida's 20th vow to the effect that the *nembutsu* is not the exclusive way to arrive at rebirth in the Pure Land.

Those not reborn in the Pure Land are consigned to one of the *Roku-dō* (Six Paths), the six lower states of existence, a kind of all-inclusive hades. These six realms are vividly described by Genshin in his *Ōjōyōshū*: heavenly beings yet unenlightened (*tenjō*), humans (*ningen*), fighting spirits (Sanskrit, *asura*), animals (*chikushō*), hungry ghosts (*gaki*), and hell (*jigoku*) – these translations vary. Elsewhere there are ten realms (*jikkai*). Like the heavens, sins and their corresponding hells are graded and are shown in the arts as naked figures in fires stoked by horrible demons, pots of boiling water, cocks tearing up human bodies with their beaks, ghosts eating corpses in a temple yard, ghosts snatching fresh excrement from beneath men and women, ghosts bent on infanticide at new births, and so on. Filth, depravity, and revolting behavior characterize the lower levels. Punishment is relative to the sin. Sins constitute such activities as failing to obey the Buddhist injunctions, murder, robbery, cruelty to animals, killing temple fish, selling watered wine (*sake*), and plying another with wine to take advantage of him or her, usually the latter. Fortunately, Jizō, the well-known deity of children, Japan's most beloved *bosatsu* who is always represented as a monk with shaved head, often in a row of six and wearing a red bib, will rescue souls from hell once repentance is assured.

New styles of monks appeared, known for their transient ways rather than monastic bases. Itinerant monks (*angya-sō*) were on constant pilgrimages; mendicant monks went from house to house begging for alms. Members of the Fuke sect can still be seen walking the streets with baskets over their heads, blowing flutes. Mountain ascetics (*yamabushi*), in the practice known formally as Shūgendō, climb sacred mountains to gain power in dangerous conditions requiring extreme physical exertion. Their home bases are usually Shingon temples. Religious associations (*kō*) of both men and women – which at best might be called quasi-Buddhist – are still involved in ascetic practices to gain spiritual power, such as fasting, eating only trees, standing under freezing waterfalls, walking on fire, climbing ladders on sword edges, and so on. Examples of monks fasting to the point of self-mummification in order to reach Buddhahood, the preserved remains garbed in priests' robes and given Buddha status, exist in several temples in northern Japan.

Women appear from the first to have been the majority of believers, especially in the Pure Land sects, and they staffed convents from the initial building of temples in Japan, but for long they suffered serious prejudice in Buddhist thought and practice. Among their disabilities was exclusion from the main precincts of Mount Hiei and Mount Kōya. Priest Dōgen emancipated them by proclaiming all humans to be totally equal, and Zen convents thrived from Kamakura times on, to the extent that some prominent nuns are known by name, notably Mugai Nyodai (1223–1298), with Hōjō parentage. In concert with the development of the Gozan temples in Kyoto and Kamakura (a term borrowed from China) were the Niji (or Amadera) Gozan (the Five Mountain Convents). Entering the cloister was almost expected of widows – of which there were many during the civil wars – together with taking the vows, the tonsure, and accepting the vegetarian diet and habit. Serious commitment, escape from crime and prostitution, avoidance of abuse, and desire to be culturally involved were among other reasons for joining a nunnery. Some, like their male counterparts, went into business or cultural activities. Failure in such enterprises often led to a mendicant's life or back to an earlier profession.

Jōdo's rich history and literature has lent itself to endless interpretations and numerous branches today. Most important, because it is the largest Buddhist sect, is Jōdo Shin-shū (True Pure Land Sect), which follows the thought of Shinran (1173–1262), a disciple of Hōnen, also once in the Enryaku-ji. He faced the same local hostility and was banished and later pardoned. Kyoto proved uncomfortable, and he preached in eastern Japan, where his simple living and teaching of faith in the saving grace of the compassionate Amida were accepted by multitudes of peasants. Notable is the fact that he broke his monastic vows of celibacy and married a member of the aristocracy, wore no distinctive clothing, and ignored the injunctions against eating meat. The people saw him as the bridge between the remote, scholarly, seemingly disinterested clergy and themselves. He established a pattern of family life for priests that was followed by a large number later, known as *zaike bukkyō* (staying at home Buddhism, i.e., a lay preacher).

One more reformer had the same Tendai experience but believed the sect had lost its original beliefs. Nichiren (1222–1282), an intense personality, sought out the seat of power in Kamakura and preached the worship of Shaka, the historic Buddha, through the *Lotus Sūtra*, the teachings of the transcendent Buddha, who had appeared as a man to save helpless humans, had "feigned" enlightenment and entry into nirvāṇa – all of which were elements of pre-esoteric thought and almost forgotten. He recommended using the mantra *Namu myōhō-renge-kyō* (Homage to the Lotus of the Wonderful Law). Nichiren wrote extensively, criticized other sects, accused the authorities of the breakdown of moral order, predicted national disasters, and thereby crossed swords with Hōjō Tokiyori (1226–1263), a former regent who was a committed Zen practitioner. These clashes resulted in successive exiles and a sentence of death, which was commuted. After returning in 1274 from exile on Sado Island, he claimed to be not merely a believer but a true disciple of Shaka, seeing himself as Buddha's main *bosatsu*.

The Jōdo sect lists more than six million adherents and more than 8,000 temples. The Jōdo Shin sect claims more than 13 million adherents associated with more than 20,000 temples today, this number fairly evenly but irreparably split between the Honganji and Ōtani branches. The Nichiren sect, the most intensely Japanese of all sects, is divided between the groups that call themselves Nichiren sect and Lotus sect. Rigid and divisive, by the 16th century it had split into nine distinct branches. There are about 6,000 Nichiren-related temples today.

Ashikaga rule was generally unenlightened, oppressive, and rarely devoid of local conflicts. The tendency in Buddhism to deny reality and withdraw from worldly affairs was exacerbated through reliance on Zen meditation. Although the simple life and self-discipline reinforced a fighter's confidence, it proved less than useful for administrative leadership. Patrons though they were of Zen temples, they were fighters first and could be very destructive of others' temples. Zen did not lend itself to the same kind of abuses that accompanied Pure Land practices, but there were many complaints of lax discipline in the temples. It was the warrior's religion, Pure Land the peasants' religion. Nevertheless the two were not exclusive. Aristocrats followed the time-worn custom of building a retirement temple, becoming a monk, and waiting to be reborn in the Western Paradise. After the military *bakufu* was established, the popularization of the Amida practices made this same goal available to untitled warriors.

Following the civil wars, much time and energy went into reconstruction. The Tokugawa regime (1603–1868) obligated every household to be attached to a temple as supporting parishioners (*danka seido*), a law not rescinded until 1871 at the peak of the Meiji government's anti-Buddhist movement. Nevertheless the ties had become so close that support did not dry up, and many people today remain attached in much the same way despite a 1947 American-inspired law intended to distance church from state. Conditions are changing rapidly due to extensive urbanization and the mobility of the population.

Buddhist temples are the link with the past, the custodian of the ancestral tablets. Income for the average temple – over and above voluntary donations by participants and spectators at special celebrations – comes from funerals, awarding posthumous names, one-week and 49-day memorial services, plot maintenance, and requests for special prayers and home visits. All these practices elicit cash donations. Temples with long histories and well-known arts have profited extensively from the domestic and foreign tourist business.

Most of the so-called new religions are, by and large, closer to Shintō than to Buddhism in that their main objective is to enhance this life. They usually have no philosophy for a future life; paramount are community life and philanthropy. However, those that emphasize peace and compassion or those that, like Nichiren Shō-shū (Nichiren Right Sect), dating from 1913, believe that Japan should be a Buddhist state have obvious roots in the Buddhist past. Nichiren to them is this age's Buddha. The sect has undergone a contentious history, its major doctrinal schisms arising over the relative value of different sections of the *Lotus Sūtra*.

Lay Buddhist associations are structured fairly simply, but most have experienced difficulty over rights of succession. The best known are Sōka Gakkai (Value Creation Society; 1937), Reiyūkai (Society of Friends of the Spirits; 1930), and Risshō Kōseikai (said to mean in full Society for the Perfection of the Nation and of the Community of Believers in Accordance with Buddhist Principles; 1948). All three trace their creeds to Nichiren, and all include shamanlike or oracular women at their inception. The founders have taken on *kami* status. To a great extent their appeal has been through an antiestablishment stance. Sōka Gakkai sprang from Nichiren Shō-shū, reaching prominence with the aid of a now dissociated political party, Komeito (Clean Government). Rather Shintō-like in being worldly oriented, members find happiness in the search for profit, goodness, and beauty. Reiyukai requires of its members daily offerings to the ancestral tablets and constant reading of the *Lotus Sūtra*. Split from it is Risshō Kōseikai, which also insists on the ancestral rituals but is deeply involved with social work both in Japan and abroad. All members participate in small-group meetings (*hōza*, "law," "seated") to discuss beliefs and problems.

However, Japan, unlike China, where little besides Pure Land and Zen remain today, almost everything once introduced – the Nara schools, the Tendai and Shingon esoteric sects, and the Pure Land, Nichiren, and Zen schools – still exists, the history having been a cumulative and then fragmentative process. Government records have listed 162 sects, almost all of which have subsects, branches, and offshoot groups. Outside the esoteric sects, most are Mahāyāna. The strength of each sect or religious group is better measured in number of temples rather than in claimed adherents. The total number of the latter exceeds the population of the country because people often list themselves as members of more than one sect, school, or religious group, in a reflection of the pluralistic attitude within Japanese religion as a whole. In this vein an instinctive Western effort to sort out the Shintō from the Buddhist elements is scarcely relevant. It might not be clear whether a deity is Shintō or Buddhist, a fact that actually makes the deity more useful. A Shintō altar beside a Buddhist altar in a family home today receives equal veneration at morning worship.

J. Edward Kidder, Jr.

*See also* Asaṅga; Asceticism: Buddhist Perspectives; Chan/Zen: Japan; Deities, Buddhist; Dōgen; Economics: Buddhist; Eisai (Yosai); Ennin; Esoteric Buddhism in China and Japan; Hermits: Buddhist; Hōnen; Japan; Kōan; Kūkai; Kyoto, Japan; Maṇḍala; Mantras; Mount Hiei, Japan; Mount Kōya, Japan; Nara, Japan; Nation-Building and Japanese Buddhism; Nembutsu; Patrons, Buddhist: Japan; Prophethood, Japanese Buddhist; Pure Land Buddhism; Rennyo; Saichō; Shinran; Spirituality: Buddhist; Suzuki, Daisetz Teitaro; Syncretism in Japan, Buddhist; Tiantai/Tendai: Japan; Zen, Arts of; Zen and the West

## Further Reading

Eliot, Charles, *Japanese Buddhism*, London: Arnold, 1935; reprint, London: Routledge, and New York: Barnes and Noble, 1959

Hori, Ichiro, editor, *Japanese Religion: A Survey by the Agency for Cultural Affairs*, Tokyo: Kodansha International, 1974

Humphreys, Christmas, *Zen Buddhism*, London: Allen and Unwin, 1957

Inagaki, Hisao, *A Dictionary of Japanese Buddhist Terms*, Kyoto: Nagata Bunshodo, 1984; 2nd edition, 1985

Kitagawa, Joseph, *Religion in Japanese History*, New York: Columbia University Press, 1966

Matsunaga, Alicia, *The Buddhist Philosophy of Assimilation: The Historical Development of the Honji-Suijaku Theory*, Rutland: Tuttle, and Tokyo: Sophia University Press, 1969

Nakamura, Hajime, I. Hori, and S. Noma, *Japan and Buddhism*, Tokyo: The Association of the Buddha Jayanti, 1959

Picken, Stewart, *Buddhism: Japan's Cultural Identity*, Tokyo and New York: Kodansha International, 1982

Saunders, E. Dale, *Buddhism in Japan, with an Outline of Its Origins in India*, Philadelphia: University of Pennsylvania Press, 1964; reprint, London and Westport, Connecticut: Greenwood Press, 1977

Suzuki, Daisetz, *Zen and Japanese Culture*, New York: Pantheon, 1959

# Buddhist Schools/Traditions: Korea

## Early Schools and Traditions

Most prominent among the Buddhist schools during the Three Kingdoms period were the Samnon school (Three Treatises school) and the Yŏlban school (Nirvāṇa school) founded by Podŏk (fl. mid–sixth century). The former was responsible for the rise of the Sanlun school in China and the Sanron school in Japan. The latter was based on the doctrines of the *Mahāparinirvāṇa Sūtra*. Both of these schools were fairly short-lived and had ceased to function before the Silla kingdom unified the Korean peninsula in 668. During this period the messianic cult of Maitreya was highly popular, and numerous images dedicated to the Future Buddha were made. This cult also had a great impact on folk religion and from time to time was influential in the Korean spiritual landscape.

## Kyeyul School

This school is said to have been introduced by the monk Chajang (608–686), who studied under Daoxuan (596–667), the founder of the Lu school in China. As the study and maintenance of the vinaya was obligatory for all monks in Korea, at one point in their careers monks from most of the other Buddhist denominations studied the doctrines of the Kyeyul school. Thus, its organization was basically nonsectarian. It was called the Namsan school under the Koryŏ. Traditionally the large T'ongdo Temple in the southeastern part of the peninsula has been the main seat for vinaya studies in Korea.

## Pŏpsŏng School

This school was founded by Wŏnhyo (617–686), one of the most charismatic and original thinkers of Korean Buddhism. Through his numerous writings, mainly in the form of commentaries, he set up a doctrinal system for harmonizing the various Buddhist doctrines. In contrast to the vertical system of classification (*p'angyŏl*), he created one that was horizontal in which the various teachings were ranked as equal. As an actual school of Buddhism, the Pŏpsŏng school was evidently very short-lived and does not seem to have outlasted its founder. However, as a tradition of Buddhism it played a major role in the formation of Buddhism not only in Korea but in the rest of East Asia as well.

## Pŏpsang School

This Korean version of the Chinese Faxiang school was founded by Xuanzang (c. 600–664). Although this tradition was formally founded by Chinp'yo (fl. mid–eighth century) during the Unified Silla period, several Korean monks had studied Yogācāra Buddhism prior to that time. The most important of these was Wŏnch'uk (612–696), who was one of Xuanzang's main disciples. His commentaries on the *Cheng weishi lun* and other works became so popular among Asian Buddhists that their influence even reached Tibet. During the Koryŏ dynasty the Yogācāra tradition that followed the Pŏpsang school was known as the Chaŭn or Yuga school. It was especially influential during the first two centuries of the dynasty and controlled a number of large monasteries and temples in the vicinity of the Koryŏ capital. During the second half of the 14th century, the Chaŭn school declined and by the early Chosŏn dynasty had virtually ceased to exist as an independent Buddhist tradition.

## Hwaŏm School

The Hwaŏm (Flower Garland) school was established in Korea by Uisang (625–702). Under the Koryŏ dynasty the Hwaŏm was the most influential of all the doctrinal traditions, and its teachings were so persuasive that they had a profound effect on both the Ch'ŏnt'ae and the Chogye schools. In the early part of the dynasty, it was due mainly to the efforts of Kyunyŏ (923–973) that the Hwaŏm school rose to power. One of the greatest Korean monasteries, Haein Temple, where the woodblocks of the Tripiṭaka are kept, once belonged to the Hwaŏm school. Although it ceased to exist as an independent denomination of Buddhism during the early part of the Chosŏn dynasty, it has left an unmistakable imprint on Korean Buddhism.

## Sŏn Buddhism

During the Unified Silla period, Sŏn Buddhism (Chan) was introduced from China by several Korean pilgrim-monks. This early Sŏn tradition was divided into nine mountain schools (*Kusan sŏnmun*), each with its own line of transmission. By the end of the dynasty, a number of these lineages had achieved considerable prominence, and often their leading monks were invited to lecture at the Silla court in Kyŏngju.

Sŏn Buddhism saw a great revival under Chinul (1158–1210) and his successor, Hyesim (1178–1234). With Songgwang Temple, located on Mount Chogye in South Chŏlla province, as their base, they propagated a new version of Sŏn Buddhism that integrated Hwaŏm philosophy and Pure Land practices with *kong'an* meditation. The tradition that Chinul had founded produced 16 national masters, and it continued unbroken until the early part of the Chosŏn dynasty (1392–1910). During this time it became very influential in many parts of the country and had several hundred temples under its control.

In the early 13th century, the teachings of the Linji (Imje) school was introduced from Yuan China. In contrast to the Sŏn developed by Chinul and his successors, which represented a local tradition, this "new" brand of Sŏn traced its lineage back to the Southern school of Chinese Chan. Whereas Chinul's Sŏn was based on the sudden enlightenment/gradual practice (*tŏnŏ chŏmso*) approach to enlightenment, the Imje school taught the method of sudden/sudden (*tŏnŏ tŏnso*). Eventually the Chogye and the Imje lineages were merged and became officially sanctioned as the Chogye tradition.

By the early Chosŏn dynasty, the Sŏn tradition had become the dominant brand of Korean Buddhism, a position it has retained to this day. During the 16th century a great Sŏn master arose, Hyujŏng (1520–1604), whose brand of Buddhism consisted of a combination of *sŏn* and *kyo* (doctrinal Buddhism). Although he was influenced by Chinul, he was not an original thinker but rather someone who preserved the tradition and invigorated it. Because his disciples are considered the founding fathers of nearly all the existing lineages of transmission today, Hyujŏng's role in the history of Korean Buddhism is extremely important.

### The Ch'ŏnt'ae School

This school was officially founded by the Hwaŏm monk Uich'ŏn (1055–1101) at the end of the 11th century, but the teachings and practices associated with this Chinese school of Buddhism had already been introduced in Korea during the seventh. The exponents of Ch'ŏnt'ae Buddhism did not add anything of importance to the Chinese works of this school, and only a handful of minor tracts written by Korean monks have survived. Although the Ch'ŏnt'ae school had ceased to function as an independent denomination by the early Chosŏn dynasty, it has been revived after 1945.

### The Pure Land Tradition

Contrary to the developments that took place in China and Japan, Pure Land Buddhism in Korea never developed into a school as such. Pure Land belief became established on the Korean peninsula as early as the late Three Kingdoms period and rose to prominence in the course of the Unified Silla period as a pan-Buddhist development. During the Koryŏ it became one of the most significant and influential forms of Buddhist practice, the popularity of which penetrated all levels of society, from the nobility to the peasants. As was the case with esoteric Buddhism, Pure Land worship was practiced by virtually all Korean Buddhists regardless of sectarian affiliation. Even in the Sŏn tradition, in which emphasis normally was placed on personal liberation, Pure Land practices were also prevalent.

### The Esoteric Tradition (Milgyo)

Both written sources and extant examples of material culture provide us with evidence that the use of *dhāraṇī*s and mantras was practiced by the Buddhists of the Unified Silla period. It is also known that a handful of monks studied Zhenyan Buddhism under Amoghavajra (705–774) in Tang China. Under the Koryŏ two schools of esoteric Buddhism existed: the Ch'ŏngji school, which arose around the middle of the dynasty, and the Sinin school, which supposedly was established during the reign of the first king, T'aejo (r. 918–943). It appears that the monks from these schools were very active in the many and grandiose esoteric rituals performed at the Koryŏ court.

HENRIK H. SØRENSEN

*See also* Buddhism: Inculturation; Chan/Zen: China; Chan/Zen: Korea; Chinul; Critiques of Buddhist Monasticism: Confucian; Economics: Buddhist; Korea: History; Korea: Sites; Rules, Buddhist (Vinaya); Wŏnhyo

### Further Reading

Buswell, Robert E., *The Zen Monastic Experience: Buddhist Practice in Contemporary Korea*, Princeton, New Jersey: Princeton University Press, 1992

Buswell, Robert E., editor, *The Korean Approach to Zen: The Collected Works of Chinul*, Honolulu: University of Hawaii Press, 1983

Ch'oe, Pyŏnghŏn, "The Founding of the Ch'ŏnt'ae School and the Reformation of Buddhism in 12th Century Korea," in *Religions in Traditional Korea*, Copenhagen: Seminar for Buddhist Studies, 1995

Han, Kidu, *Han'guk sŏn sasang yŏngu* (Study of the Thought of Korean Sŏn Buddhism), Iri: Wongwang taehakkyo, 1974

Hŏ, Hŭngsik, *Koryŏ pulgyo sa yŏngu* (A Study of the History of Koryŏ Buddhism), Seoul: Ilcho kak, 1986

Korean Buddhist Research Institute, editors, *Buddhist Thought in Korea*, Seoul: Dongguk University Press, 1994

Lancaster, Lewis R., and C.S. Yu, editors, *Assimilation of Buddhism in Korea: Religious Maturity and Innovation in the Silla Dynasty*, Berkeley: Asian Humanities Press, 1991

Pulgyo Hakhoe, compiler, *Han'guk Chogye chong ŭi sŏngni sa chŏk yŏngu* (Studies in the History of the Formation of the Chogye School in Korea), Seoul: Minjŏksa, 1986

Pulgyo Munhwa Yŏngu Wŏn, editor, *Han guk sŏn sasang yŏngu* (Studies in the Thought of Korean Sŏn Buddhism), Seoul: Tongguk taehakkyo ch'ulp'anbu, 1984

Pulgyo Munhwa Yŏngu Wŏn, compiler, *Han guk milgyo sasang yŏn gu* (Studies in the Thought of Korean Esoteric Buddhism), Seoul: Tongguk taehakkyo ch'ulp'anbu, 1986

Sørensen, Henrik H., "Ennin's Account of a Korean Buddhist Monastery 839–840 A.D.," *Acta Orientalia* 47 (1986)

Sørensen, Henrik H., "The Conflict between Sŏn and Doctrinal Buddhism in Unified Silla," *East Asian Institute Occasional Papers* 2 (September 1988)

Sørensen, Henrik H., "Lamaism in Korea during the Late Koryŏ Dynasty," *Korea Journal* 33:3 (1993)

Sørensen, Henrik H., "Esoteric Buddhism (*Milgyo*) in Korea," in *The Esoteric Buddhist Tradition*, edited by Sørensen, Copenhagen: Seminar for Buddhist Studies, 1994

Sørensen, Henrik H., "Korean Buddhism: The Pre-Modern and Modern Period," in *Buddhist Spirituality II: Later China, Korea, Japan, and the Modern World*, London: SCM, 1999

# Buddhist Schools/Traditions: South Asia

*Origins and Development of the* Nikāyas *(Schools)*

The development of different schools of Buddhism began quite soon after the death of Śākyamuni Buddha, perhaps as early as the fourth century B.C. The Buddha left a great number of discourses, which certain of his disciples memorized and passed along orally. However, he did not work out a thoroughgoing, systematic philosophy that answered all questions that might arise and thereby ensure internal consistency. Thus, his death left open to interpretation many matters regarding both doctrine and discipline. Moreover, the Buddha created no central authority for the *sangha* after his death, exhorting its members, according to traditional accounts, simply to follow his dharma, or teachings, and to be "lights unto themselves." Additionally the geographic, cultural, and linguistic diversity of southern Asia made disparate interpretations of the dharma likely. As Buddhists spread to different parts of South Asia, they developed their own local traditions and understandings of the dharma, resulting in a rather wide diversity of teaching and practice across the Indian subcontinent.

Although most if not all early Buddhist schools agreed on certain foundational ethical and doctrinal points, efforts to collect, interpret, and synthesize the teachings into a consistent system inevitably entailed disagreements on many issues. These disagreements, along with the multiplying interpretations of the dharma, led to a series of councils that attempted to solidify issues of doctrine and practice and to establish the words of the Buddha. The second of these, a council held by a group of learned elder monks (Sthaviras) at Vaiśālī 100 years after the Buddha's *parinirvāṇa*, was most important to the development of schools. The council was called to address points of discipline, such as whether to allow monks to use gold and silver, as well as one point of doctrine, namely, whether a monk's personal teacher's practices can be considered authoritative. The Sthaviras insisted that the texts, not one's personal teacher, should be the guide of every monastic, a position from which a group of monks from eastern India dissented. This group held a separate council shortly afterward and formed its own school, the Mahāsaṃghikas (those in the great assembly). Thus, the formation of the first Buddhist schools, or *nikāyas* (groups), if the traditional records are accurate, resulted from a division between the Sthaviras, or Sthaviravādins (teachings of the elders), and the Mahāsaṃghikas. From these two a number of other schools branched off, and further subdivisions followed at the third council.

Traditional sources report 18 schools that developed in the period from the second council of Vaiśālī until the fourth century A.D. Modern scholars have found evidence for as many as 30. Different sources list divergent numbers and lineages of schools, and the characteristics and doctrines of some are lost to history. Even the existence of some in traditional lists is in question, but the presence of many is confirmed by inscriptional evidence and the documentation of Chinese travelers in southern and central Asia in the seventh century. One traditional listing of the 18 schools of non-Mahāyāna Buddhism, each constituting a subdivision of the initial split between the Mahāsaṃghikas and the Sthaviravādins, is as follows:

Sthaviravāda
  Pugdalavāda (Vātsīputrīyas)
  Vibhajyavāda
    Mahīśaka
    Dharmaguptaka
    Kāśyapāya
    Theravāda
  Sarvāstivāda
    Sautrāntika

Mahāsaṃghika
  Ekavyāvahārika
  Lokottaravāda
  Gokulika
  Bahuśrutīya
  Prajñaptivāda
  Caitika
  Pūrvaśaila
  Aparaśaila
  Rājagirika
  Siddhārthika

Only one of these early schools still survives, the Theravāda, which thrives in Sri Lanka and Southeast Asia. The Theravāda Canon is the only complete canon still extant. Some canonical and postcanonical literature survives from a few other schools, and, although relatively scant, it does provide some valuable information on them.

*Doctrines of the Early Schools*

The *nikāya*s distinguished themselves from one another mainly on doctrinal matters and occasionally on issues of conduct. The Sthaviravādins claimed authority on the basis of remaining faithful to the teachings of the first disciples of the Buddha. They maintained against the Mahāsaṃghika that the arhat, a perfected Buddhist saint, is beyond the possibility of regression on the Buddhist path. They also asserted that neutral actions exist that have no moral consequence and that neither the transcendental Buddha claimed by the Mahāsaṃghikas nor the "person" of the Pudgalavādins exists. They also rejected the Sarvāstivādin notion that dharmas, the constitutive elements of existence, persist eternally.

The Mahāsaṃghikas held a number of doctrines contrary to the Sthaviras. Perhaps most important, they claimed that the arhat can relapse and that his perfection is not absolute. They also maintained that the sūtras were not the final word on the dharma and further that transmission of teachings outside the scripture was possible. Some groups of the Mahāsaṃghika, especially the Lokottaravādins, claimed that the Buddha exists eternally as a supernatural being and that his appearance on earth had been only a magical projection of his true eternal nature.

This idea, along with the notion of transmission of teachings outside the accepted canon, would provide important elements in Mahāyāna Buddhism. The Prajñaptivādins were also likely to have influenced the Mahāyāna, distinguishing themselves by the doctrine that all things lack substantial existence and are products of linguistic conventions (*prajñapti*).

According to Theravādin sources, the Sthaviravāda split further at the third council, dividing between Sarvāstivādins (those who teach that everything exists) and the Vibhajyavādins (those who make distinctions). The former became widespread and influential in northern India and central Asia, establishing monasteries throughout these regions and producing a number of important Abhidharma works. The school's name reflects its assertion that all dharmas have eternal existence. This doctrine arose to solve an enduring philosophical problem in the Abhidharma literature; that is, if the dharmas persist only momentarily, how can karma have long-term effects? To solve this problem the Sarvāstivādins claimed that dharmas actually exist eternally but become manifest only for a brief moment. Before and after manifestation they exist in a latent, unmanifest state. After a dharma is actualized and then returned to latency, it serves as an influence on future karma. The Sarvāstivādins also promoted the doctrine of the perfections (*pāramitā*s), which became important in Mahāyāna thought. This doctrine set out another vision of the path to enlightenment, that of the bodhisattva who fulfills the six perfections: generosity, morality, patience, vigor, meditation, and discernment.

Another influential school, the Sautrāntika (those who follow the *sūtra*s), claimed that the *sūtra*s alone contained the words of the Buddha, denying authoritative status to the Abhidharma. It responded to Sarvāstivāda's concepts of the eternality of dharmas by offering an alternative view of how karma works. According to the Sautrāntika every action plants karmic "seeds" that come to life later in life or in a future lifetime. This would become an important concept in the Yogācāra school.

The Pugdalavāda school taught a doctrine of the "person" (*pugdala*) that forms the basis for the five *skandha*s, or constituents of personal existence. Whereas according to other schools of Buddhism this doctrine was antithetical to the doctrine of no-self (*anātman*), the Pugdalavādins believed that the notion of a continuing person supplied the only way to explain the continuity of consciousness and memory from moment to moment and from lifetime to lifetime. The enduring person also serves as the basis for the capacity of karmic deeds to produce results and is seen as necessary for morality and kindness in interpersonal relationships.

Fragments of the doctrines, history, and geographic locations of other schools survive in references to them in the works of some of the previously mentioned schools. Judging from the records of Chinese pilgrims in India, most of the schools had disappeared by the seventh century. The only surviving school, the Theravāda, represents the lineage of the Sthaviravāda (retaining its name in Pāli) and is still strong in Sri Lanka and parts of Southeast Asia. None maintained a substantial presence in East Asia or Tibet, where Mahāyāna schools held sway.

## Mahāyāna Schools and Traditions

During the first or second century B.C., a new movement not explicitly allied with these schools began to take shape: the Mahāyāna. In calling itself the Mahāyāna (Great Vehicle), it drew a sharp distinction between itself and the *nikāya*s, which it referred to collectively as the Hīnayāna (Lesser Vehicle). Many scholars believe that the Mahāyāna developed in southern India out of the Mahāsaṃghikas, from whom the Mahāyāna seems to have derived certain important ideas. Some recent scholarship suggests that the movement originated with the laity and their stūpa worship, whereas others argue that monks devoted to the Mahāyāna's new scriptures were its primary founders.

Perhaps the most important innovation introduced by the Mahāyāna was the composing of new sūtras that claim to have originated with Śākyamuni himself but that modern scholarship places much later, beginning in the first or second century B.C. and continuing well into the common era. These sūtras contained many doctrines, attitudes, and values found in the canonical texts but also introduced novel elements, some reflecting the influence of specific *nikāya*s and some reflecting non-Buddhist influence. A number of the philosophical positions of the earlier schools were expanded and embellished, and much more room was made for devotion, not only to Śākyamuni Buddha but also to a growing pantheon of Buddhas and bodhisattvas, understood by the Mahāyāna as beings who have renounced the "selfish" nirvāṇa of the Hīnayāna in favor of remaining in the phenomenal world to help others attain liberation. In some Mahāyāna texts the Buddha is presented as a supernatural being unlimited in time and space or as one who is identified with the cosmos itself. Although the vast corpus of Mahāyāna literature likely was written by monks, many texts make a distinct appeal to the laity, sometimes elevating them to a status higher than that of monks.

The Madhyamaka (Middle Way) school, the most influential of the Mahāyāna, traces its origins to the second-century philosopher Nāgārjuna, who gave a systematic account of the pivotal Mahāyāna doctrine of emptiness (*śūnyatā*). He argues that all things, even the most basic elements of existence (*dharma*s) as well as all conceptual-linguistic categories and constructs, lack (or are empty of) permanence, separateness, and inherent self-existence (*svabhāva*). The hypostatization of categories and things prevents realization of the interdependence and temporality of all phenomena, a realization that constitutes enlightenment. Even Buddhist ideas are taken to be only conventional truths, although these must be understood in order to achieve the highest truth.

Another major Mahāyāna school, the Yogācāra (practitioners of yoga), also known as the Cittamātra (mind-only), Vijñānamātra (consciousness-only), or Vijñānavāda (those who hold the doctrine of consciousness), interpreted this notion of emptiness through detailed analyses of mind states. Yogācāra is often interpreted as a philosophical idealism that denies the reality of external objects and affirms the reality of the mind. More precisely, however, its notion that the world is "consciousness only" means that duality, or the sense of an ultimate distinction between subject and object is a construction of consciousness itself. In reality the subject and object are interdependent, their apparent distinction and independence being "merely perception" (*vijñāptimātra*). The two brothers, Asaṅga and Vasubandhu (fourth century A.D.), were the primary expositors of this tradition.

Later scholastic movements attempted to combine the Madhyamaka and Yogācāra schools, and other thinkers, such as Dignāga (c. 480–540) and Dharmakīrti (c. 600–650), developed important traditions of Buddhist logic, debate, and epistemology. The Tathāgatagarbha (Buddha essence) tradition drew on Yogācāra doctrines to present a more positive interpretation of ultimate reality than that of the Madhyamaka. Although this movement might never have been a school in the sense that the Madhyamaka and Yogācāra were, it initiated an important textual tradition with influential doctrines, especially the doctrine that all beings are potential or latent Buddhas; that is, everything contains Buddha nature.

Many Mahāyāna devotional groups flourished as well, worshiping celestial Buddhas and bodhisattvas, such as Amitābha, Maitreya, Mañjuśrī, and Tārā. Devotional elements were quite popular among followers of the Mahāyāna monastics, both laity and monastics. These elements played a crucial role in the emergence of another movement or series of movements that arose out the Mahāyāna – Tantra, or the Vajrayāna – which was well known by the sixth century. This movement constituted a departure from much in the previous schools and initially grew out of marginal groups outside mainstream monastic circles. Although the origins of Tantra are obscure, it is clear that in addition to integrating many elements of Mahāyāna philosophy it drew on earlier Vedic modes of thought, positing elaborate sets of homologies based on resemblance and emphasizing the chanting of mantras, or formulaic verses. Tantric texts (Tantras) deal with magic, astrology, and ritual as well as highly refined visualization practices designed to identify practitioners with their chosen deities. Some followers of Tantra were innovators who flouted monastic discipline by adopting practices specifically contrary to normative Buddhist teaching, such as meat eating, ritualized sexual practice, and drinking alcohol. Others worked to incorporate Tantra into the mainstream of Buddhist monastic practice, engaging in antinomian activity only symbolically.

DAVID L. MCMAHAN

*See also* Ajaṇṭā, India; Asaṅga; Aśoka; Bodh Gayā, India; Bodhisattva; Buddha (Śākyamuni); Councils, Buddhist; Deities, Buddhist; Disciples, Early Buddhist; Discourses (Sūtras): Mahāyāna; Jain Monasticism and Buddhist Monasticism; Mahāyāna; Nālandā, India; Pilgrims to India, Chinese; Repentance Rituals, Buddhist; Sri Lanka: History; Stūpa; Travelers: Buddhist

### Further Reading
Bereau, André, "Hīnayāna Buddhism," in *Buddhism and Asian History*, edited by Joseph M. Kitagawa and Mark D. Cummings, New York and London: Macmillan, 1989

Conze, Edward, *Buddhist Thought in India*, London: Allen and Unwin, 1962; Ann Arbor: University of Michigan Press, 1967; reprint, London and Boston: Allen and Unwin, 1983

Dutt, Nalinaksha, *Buddhist Sects in India*, Calcutta: Firma KL Mukhopadhyay, 1970; 2nd edition, Delhi: Motilal Banarsidass, 1978

Gómez, Luis O., "Buddhism in India," in *Buddhism and Asian History*, edited by Joseph M. Kitagawa and Mark D. Cummings, New York and London: Macmillan, 1989

Lamotte, Étienne, *History of Indian Buddhism from the Origins to the Śaka Era*, translated by Sara Webb-Boin, Louvain-la-Neuve: Universite Catholique de Louvain, Institut Orientaliste, 1988

Nagao, Gajin, *Mādhyamika and Yogācāra: A Study of Mahāyāna Philosophies*, Albany: State University of New York Press, 1991

Warder, Anthony K., *Indian Buddhism*, Delhi: Motilal Banarsidass, 1970; 2nd edition, 1980

Williams, Paul, *Mahāyāna Buddhism: The Doctrinal Foundations*, London and New York: Routledge, 1989

# Buddhist Schools/Traditions: Southeast Asia

One of the most remarkable characteristics of Buddhism is its migration from one geographic location to another. Buddhism lasted in its country of origin, India, about 1,500 years – leaving today only very few traces, mainly among the nonindigenous population in the northern parts of the country. The gender differentiation in vinaya rules permitted some effect on the longevity in this specific geographic location and historical phase.

Supposed life spans of Buddhism in different areas are conditioned by internal and external conditions. The migration has also been called "the pilgrimage of Buddhism," which permitted the development of Buddhism in surrounding countries, creating new forms of approach both in lay and monastic life.

The development is characterized above all by the tradition of Southeast Asian Buddhist kingdoms that evolved from Emperor Aśoka's example. They adopted the union of political and religious authorities, even though the introduction of Buddhism came through different paths, including the encouragement of King Aśoka himself, the activities of pilgrim-monks, and spontaneous interaction between societies due to trade relations. During the 11th to 15th centuries, known as the period of active expansion of Buddhism in Southeast Asia, most of the principalities and kingdoms in Burma, Thailand, Laos, and Cambodia were converted to the Buddhist religion. The knowledge came from Pāli texts originating in Sri Lanka of the fourth century and from interpretations or commentaries on these texts written by Theravāda missionary monks who carried the Dharma teachings to the capitals and also to the villages. At the end of the 15th century, temple-monasteries (*wat*s) were established in most villages throughout Cambodia and Thailand, Laos, and Burma. *Wat* originally meant a moral, social, and educational center.

The geographic and political history of the surrounding countries has fluctuated as geographic boundaries and names from ancient kingdoms have changed. Many regions came under the influence of European colonialism and can be grouped into today's Myanmar, Bangladesh, Vietnam, Laos, Thailand, Cambodia, Malaysia, Brunei, Singapore, Indonesia, and the Philippines.

Southeast Asian countries are often divided according to the main cultural influence active in them. Indian influence brought mainly the Theravāda tradition, whereas the Mahāyāna tradition arrived through Chinese immigrants. In these countries both cultural influences are usually present in different proportions and do not exclude one another.

Southeast Asian Buddhism is characterized mainly by four great historical high cultures – Pagan (in Myanmar), Sukhothai (in Thailand), Srivijaya (in Cambodia), and Sailendra (in Indonesia) – that were based on the Buddharaja cult of cosmology and religious principles according to the Mahāyāna Buddhist tradition. The Theravāda tradition of Southeast Asia is characterized generally by its multidisciplinary approach, knowledge of which is partly biased by Western descriptions of the religious impact on everyday life in these countries. Basic generalizations made regarding economic and gender issues are often misleading.

Because of the original local beliefs and spiritual orientations, Buddhism developed in both scholastic and nonscholastic forms, of which the latter was sustained and developed mainly by monastic communities. Such inclusive syncretism is characterized by Buddhist tales that assimilated the previously known local folktales and legends, often with mythological animals and protectors who survive in different artistic masterpieces as door guardians to the sacred space. Western philosophical and anthropological studies tend to overlook some of the syncretist moral values that pervade a wide range of religious activities.

An example of Buddhist legends and tales, deeply imprinted in the Southeast Asian folkloristic cultures, is the Legend of Upagupta as well as various animal stories, often narrated from Jātakas (i.e., Buddha Śākyamuni's previous incarnations narrated as stories). Upagupta is a saint well known in Southeast Asian Buddhism as the protector of Buddhist festivals. The story line never ends, and its loose ends can become connected to the listener's everyday life as an interactive part of the story.

Ancient Buddhist kingdoms are the most spectacular of the past presences whose social organization and cosmological views contributed to the historical moments inside the Southeast Asian cultures, examples of which are known today mostly for their incomparable artistic and architectural achievements. The glorious Buddhist kingdoms of King Aśoka's inspiration developed according to three patterns: (1) from a spiritually oriented society of Mahāyāna inspiration toward a materialistic society with an emphasis on interests of the individual in both spiritual and material organization, (2) from a spiritually oriented society of Mahāyāna inspiration toward transformation into another spiritual approach (as in the cases of Burma and Thailand) toward a Theravāda monastic emphasis or (as in the cases of Cambodia and Indonesia) toward other religions, and (3) from a spiritually oriented society of Mahāyāna inspiration into a so-called socially involved but still materialistic society. An example of the latter developments includes the transformation of Sukhothai with its high-culture society into today's Thailand with its sharp dichotomy between lay and monastic practices. Another example is

Burma, where ancient pagan culture, with an emphasis on the meritorious stūpa constructions, evolved toward involvement of an individual for a religious cause (as seen in Aung San Suu Kyi). Another trajectory moved from the Sri Vijaya and Sailendra dynasties into today's Cambodia and Indonesia, where eclectic religious practices strengthen or undermine national identity. In the case of Burma, a specific form of religion without further commentaries, based on the Pāli Tripiṭaka, has become the best-known form of "Orthodox Buddhism." In the "Pagan period" a Buddhist kingdom similar to the Angkorian period in Cambodia and Sukothai period in Thailand flourished, and some archeological evidence suggests rather a presence of the Mahāyāna.

Different studies have been made of the arrival and establishment of Buddhism in Indonesia, of which monuments such as Chandi Borobudur testify, even though today Buddhism is a minor religion there. According to some sources Buddhism became established in Java upon the arrival of Prince Gunavarman, a prince from Kashmir. This might suggest some common features in the religious activities of the two countries, a thesis that is supported by local legends of a certain Gunadharma having been the constructor of the temple of Borobudur. Further study is needed as to whether the temple was part of the introductory process or was constructed into the already established center of Buddhism.

Some forms of so-called popular Buddhism exist in today's Indonesia as well as in certain Theravāda institutions, which are secluded from the rest of the society rather than in active interaction with it because of political opposition (with some vandalism against temples). In both Theravādin and Mahāyāna traditions in Indonesia, emphasis is given to the principal moments of the Buddha Śākyamuni's life and previous lives, as evidenced from the architectural decorations. Tales of the Jātakas and Avadanas functioned as an introduction to the religion, after which the Bodhisattva's path was the main practice, pointing at the highest level to the dedication of the accumulation of merits for the sake of all sentient beings, as in the Sudhana's story carved in the upper gallery of the well-known monument Chandi Borobudur. The Buddharaja cult seems to have lasted no more than 100 years, but this very active period still influences today's life in central Java. Besides the ancient Buddharaja cult, other forms of Buddhism divide into popular and Theravāda cults, just as in many other Southeast Asian countries. Mythical biography of Buddha's previous lives has played a fundamental role in the structure and dynamics of Indonesian traditions and provides a unifying factor among the different schools from the past until present day.

Arrival of the Buddharaja cult in Cambodia probably came from Javanese influence, of which the evidence is mainly archaeological. Political changes in the country have replaced the original form of Mahāyāna cults with different more or less orthodox Theravāda cults, and in some cases political parties have used Buddhist precepts to promote identity. For example, a new Buddhist order, Dhammayut, was introduced from Thailand, where the role of mythology became secondary and the rationalization of the Buddhist theology the primary focus, with emphasis on studying texts instead of oral transmission of the religion.

Thailand offers a rich example of the social transformation of ancient traditions derived from the Devaraja/Buddharaja cults through the presence of monastic institutions sponsored by the royalty, days of national celebration, and the survival of some words and names of clearly Buddhist origin.

In Southeast Asia, Mahāyāna and Theravāda traditions developed both cyclical and linear views of a person's spiritual development. The cyclical notion, begun in great Buddhist kingdoms/political leadership, has been one way to practice the religion, where the leader was a symbolic emanation of an enlightened being. The king or other religious authority adopts the Bodhisattva's way of life as a lifework. The dichotomy between monasticism and lay life in former societies was overcome by the presence of a king who interacted with both sides, being the expression of Buddhist ideals in protecting the welfare of other sentient beings. Iconographic as well as didactic communication of Jātaka stories helped focus on the everyday life of laypersons, creating the possibility of religious practice without boundaries, where lifestyles emulate religious ideals. The crucial role of the Jātaka stories is evidenced from their architectural presences at Angkor Wat and Chandi Borobudur, where the stories simulated the presence of the Buddha for an individual or visitor.

This principle that Theravāda kings were protectors of Buddha fields of merit started from King Aśoka and at a mythological level from King Vessantara and led to development to the cult of royalty and the wheel-turning king in Southeast Asia, where rituals and the social orders were conceived as part of a cosmological system. This cosmological Buddhism has left traces throughout the region.

LAURA PORCEDDU

*See also* Angkor Wat, Cambodia; Bangkok, Thailand; Burma (Myanmar); Forest Masters; Mun, Ajahn; Thailand; Vietnam

## Further Reading

Blofeld, John, *Mahayana Buddhism in Southeast Asia*, Singapore: Asia Pacific Press, 1971

Brown, Robert L., "The Jataka Stories in Ancient Indian & Southeast Asian Architecture," in *Sacred Biography in the Buddhist Traditions of South and Southeast Asia*, edited by Juliane Schober, Honolulu: University of Hawaii Press, 1997

Lester, Robert C., *Theravada Buddhism in Southeast Asia*, Ann Arbor: University of Michigan Press, 1973

Matthews, Bruce, and Judith Nagata, editors, *Religion, Values and Development in Southeast Asia*, Singapore: Institute of Southeast Asian Studies, 1986

Schecter, Jerrold L., *The New Face of Buddha: Buddhism and Political Power in Southeast Asia*, New York: Coward-McCann, and London: Victor Gallancz, 1967

Sengupta, Sukumar, *Buddhism in South-east Asia: Mainly Based on Epigraphic Sources*, Calcutta: Atisha Memorial Publication Society, 1994

Somboon Suksamran, *Political Buddhism in Southeast Asia: The Role of the Sangha in the Modernization of Thailand*, edited and with an introduction by Trevor O. Ling, London: Hurst, and New York: St. Martin's Press, 1977

Strong, John S., *The Legend and Cult of Upagupta: Buddhism in North India and Southeast Asia*, Princeton, New Jersey: Princeton University Press, 1992

Swearer, Donald K., *Buddhism and Society in Southeast Asia*, Chambersburg, Pennsylvania: Anima Books, 1981

Swearer, Donald K., *The Buddhist World of Southeast Asia*, Albany: State University of New York Press, 1995

# Buddhist Schools/Traditions: Tibet

Tibetans today talk of four main schools or traditions (Tibetan, *chölug*, chos-lugs) of Buddhism in Tibet: the Nyingmapa (rNying-ma-pa), Sakyapa (Sa-skya-pa), Kagyüpa (bKa'-brgyud-pa), and Gelukpa (dGe-lugs-pa). To these can be added the P'önpo (Bon-po) tradition, which is closely affiliated with the Buddhist schools in its mythology and philosophy. Although this serves as an initial set of labels, it can be misleading in that these terms refer mainly to monastic "orders" rather than to bodies of doctrine or specific approaches to Buddhism. These orders are themselves made up of a number of smaller named "suborders" with a high degree of autonomy (e.g., Drukpa or Karmapa within the Kagyüpa and Mindrölling or Pelyul within the Nyingmapa). Each of these has one or more large monasteries that act as training centers and where senior lamas of the suborder reside. Smaller monasteries and religious centers tend to be attached by links of teaching and training to these larger monasteries, following their ritual practices and recognizing the authority of the senior lamas of the suborder. Even these relationships can be fairly tenuous, especially in the case of more remote monasteries.

The Sakyapa and Kagyüpa traditions were the first to emerge as identifiable schools. They originated in the 12th and 13th centuries, respectively, in the monastery of Sakya (Sa-skya), founded by the hereditary lama family of K'ön ('Khon) in west-central Tibet, and in a series of monasteries in central Tibet founded by the second- and third-generation disciples of the great poet-lama Milarepa (Mi-la-ras-pa, 1043–1123). The main Sakya monastery has remained under the control of the K'ön family into modern times, but two offshoots, the Ngorpa (Ngor-pa) and the Ts'elpa (Tshal-pa), developed in later centuries. Differences of philosophy and practice between these schools remain minor, with the Hevajra Tantra and the Lamdré (lam-'bras, "Path and Result") tradition of teaching remaining central to them all. From very early on the Kagyüpa developed as a number of distinct and autonomous subtraditions, of which the best known are the Karmapa (Karma-pa), Drukpa ('Brug-pa), and Drigungpa ('Bri-gung-pa).

The Gelukpa originated in the 15th century with the students of the great philosopher and reformer Tsongk'apa (Tsong-kha-pa bLo-bzang-grags-pa). The various major teaching colleges in the Gelukpa tradition all teach from school texts that present the position of Tsongk'apa and his immediate disciples with minor differences. Thus, the Gelukpa tradition exists in somewhat variant versions associated with the various component colleges of the great Gelukpa monasteries of central Tibet. The Gelukpa were numerically the largest and politically the most powerful tradition in premodern Tibet, and the Dalai Lama, effective head of state in central and parts of western and eastern Tibet, was the most senior lama of this tradition. Although individual Dalai Lamas might exercise great personal authority backed up by their political position, they were not, however, the formal heads of the Gelukpa tradition. This position was occupied by Tsongk'apa's appointed successor as Abbot of Ganden [dGa'-ldan] Monastery. In fact, for most practical purposes, individual monasteries enjoyed a high degree of autonomy.

The Nyingmapa (rNying-ma-pa) continue the earliest traditions of Tibetan Buddhism but for many centuries were based on small hereditary lama lineages. Having begun to develop a distinct institutional identity in the 12th and 13th centuries in reaction to the emergence of the New Tantra schools, they boasted many eminent lama-scholars and visionaries but did not possess large teaching monasteries until the 17th century. Much the same is true of the P'önpo, who again existed for many centuries, mainly as a tradition carried on by hereditary lamas, and only gradually developed large-scale monastic institutions.

As the Gelukpa became more politically dominant, links between the three other Buddhist orders and, to some extent, the P'önpo became increasingly strong, culminating in the 19th and 20th centuries when a group of lamas from all these traditions were active in the so-called Rimé movement (Ris-med), gathering and systematizing the various teaching lineages into collections that were passed on within all these orders.

The differences among the five principal schools concern not so much doctrine as the meditational procedures and ritual practice of Vajrayāna Buddhism. One major distinction derives from the contrast between the so-called Old and New Tantra traditions. The Old (Nyingma, rNying-ma) Tantric traditions are held to have come to Tibet in the time of the charismatic Indian guru and siddha Padmasambhava (Gu-ru Padma 'byung-gnas, Gu-ru Rin-po-che, active in Tibet in the late eighth century). They were supplemented by rediscovered texts and visionary revelations (terma, gter-ma) found from the 11th century on. The New (Sarma, gSar-ma) Tantras were brought to Tibet from the 11th to the 13th century by Tibetan disciples of a number of Indian siddhas and by Indian teachers traveling to Tibet, of whom the best known is Dīpaṃkara Atiśa (11th century). The Nyingmapa are closely linked to the Old Tantras, thus their name; the other three traditions are mainly New Tantra, although all today have some involvement with Old Tantra traditions, especially the Kagyüpa and Sakyapa. The important meditation and practice tradition of Dzogch'en is closely linked with the Old Tantric lineages and is again most significant for the Nyingmapa and least significant for the Gelukpa.

The P'önpo have a separate Tantric tradition of their own that is based, like that of the Old Tantras, largely on visionary material and that can be traced back to Tönpa Shenrap (sTon-pa gShen-rabs), the P'önpo equivalent to the historical Buddha Śākyamuni. They also have a separate transmission of the Dzogch'en teachings.

A second difference relates to the relative emphasis placed on yogic practice (mainly the meditation and ritual practices of Vajrayāna Buddhism) and on philosophical study. The Gelukpa tradition, which is by far the largest numerically, is noted for the great emphasis it places on philosophical study as a prerequisite to Vajrayāna practice. Teachers in the Nyingmapa and other non-Gelukpa traditions place greater emphasis on practice in relation to philosophy than do the Gelukpa and might encourage serious students to take up yogic practice at an earlier stage than do the Gelukpa. However, such differences are not absolute and all schools contain lamas and monks whose interests are mainly scholarly and others who are more committed to practice. For all schools philosophical understanding is preliminary and auxiliary to practice rather than being important in its own right.

The Gelukpa are also known for insistence on monastic celibacy as a precondition to serious Buddhist practice, including that of the Vajrayāna. Thus, although there are both lay yogic practitioners in the other traditions and lay yogic communities, this is not the case for the Gelukpa.

The crucial role of the lama-disciple link in Tibetan tradition means that all orders place vital significance on the lineages of transmission of the teaching, especially, although not only, in relation to the Vajrayāna teachings. Many of these lineages are traced down through named teacher-disciple links from Indian gurus of the 11th and 12th centuries or earlier who are believed to have received them from encounters with Vajradhara, Vajrayoginī, and other Tantric deities. Other lineages, mainly in the Old Tantra traditions, derive from more recent visionary contacts with Tantric gods by Tibetan lamas. Particular monasteries and orders are associated with specific lineages and the related Tantric deities, so that the Sakyas, for example, are famous for the Hevajra Tantra practices transmitted from the Indian guru Virūpa and the associated lamdré (lam-'bras, "Path and Result") teachings, whereas the Kagyüpas are known for the nāro chö-druk (naro chos drug, "Six Doctrines of Nāropa") and the Sūtra Mahāmudrā teachings. Both are associated with the Indian guru Nāropa, and are shared also by the Gelukpas, who derived from Kagyüpa lineages. Most major Tantric cycles have several different lineages of transmission.

Within the colleges (chödra, chos-grwa) of the major teaching monasteries, philosophical study and Vajrayāna practice were combined into an organized curriculum. Although certain teaching monasteries were renowned for special practices in which they specialized, students would usually attend those with which their local monastery or family had traditional links. At the level of liturgy and ritual practice, substantial differences exist between schools, suborders, and individual monasteries, relating in part to the different deities that they recognize as significant both as yogic patron deities and as monastic protectors.

To some degree philosophical differences between the schools pertain to their contrasting emphases on philosophical study or yogic practice. Thus, the more yogically inclined schools (e.g., Kagyüpa) tend to place more importance on tathāgatagarbha theory (Buddha nature) and Cittamātra-style philosophical approaches than on Mādhyamika, whereas the Gelukpa emphasize the primacy of the Prāsaṅgika Mādhyamika school, which originated with the great Indian scholar Nāgārjuna (c. 150–250). Differences in the interpretation of Mādhyamika exist as well, with the shentong (gzhan-stong) opinion, which emphasizes a positive conception of ultimate reality, again linked to yogic practice, being supported by a strong minority, especially within the Kagyüpa and Nyingmapa schools.

Although the Gelukpa have been the largest order since the 17th century and were politically dominant in most of central Tibet in particular, few areas were dominated exclusively by a single tradition. The Drukpa were especially strong in Bhutan (Druk-yul, or Druk Country in Tibetan), where the head of state until 1907 was a Drukpa reincarnate lama. The state of Derge (sDe-dge) in eastern Tibet was ruled by a Sakyapa princely family and contained many important Nyingmapa and Karmapa monasteries, and most of the major 19th-century Rimé lamas were based there. However, monasteries of all traditions could be found in all parts of ethnic Tibet until the destruction of monastic life after 1950. Lamas of most major lineages escaped to continue their traditions in exile and eventually to aid in the reconstruction of Buddhism within contemporary Tibet.

GEOFFREY SAMUEL

*See also* Body: Buddhist Perspectives; Bön, Influence of; Dalai Lama (Tenzin Gyatso); Deities, Buddhist; Gampopa; Labdron, Machig; Milarepa; Nepal: History; Padmasambhava; Sakya Pandita (Sapen); Spirituality: Buddhist; Tibet; Tibetan Lineages; Yeshe Tsogyel

**Further Reading**

Lhundup Sopa, Geshe, and Jeffrey Hopkins, *Practice and Theory of Tibetan Buddhism*, London: Rider, and New York: Grove Press, 1976; 2nd edition as *Cutting through Appearances: The Practice and Theory of Tibetan Buddhism*, 1989

Samuel, Geoffrey, *Civilized Shamans: Buddhism in Tibetan Societies*, Washington, D.C.: Smithsonian Institution Press, 1993

Tucci, Giuseppe, *The Religions of Tibet*, Berkeley: University of California Press, and London: Routledge and Kegan Paul, 1980

# Buddhology

There are several senses of the term *Buddhology*, and despite its wide currency in religious studies circles, at the time of this writing there is no other encyclopedia article in English on the term. The first thing to notice is that "Buddhology" is not identical with interdisciplinary "Buddhist studies," in which Buddhism is studied from a variety of disciplinary perspectives (such as history, religion, philosophy, anthropology, or art history). Yet in some specific sense or another, Buddhology may unfold *within* Buddhist studies. This article differentiates four senses of the term *Buddhology*: as hermeneutics, as exegesis, as the study of attributes of Buddha (Buddhalogy), and as ontology.

## Buddhology as Hermeneutics

In this sense "Buddhology" is simply the study of Buddhism conducted with or without detailed references to specific texts. In the broadest sense one does Buddhology whenever one interprets Buddhism. This process is one form that hermeneutics can take.

The salient fact on which Buddhology takes its point of departure in any eon (*kalpa*) is the enlightenment experience of a Buddha. Without the coming to be of a completely enlightened Buddha, an event that is believed to happen only once in an eon, there would be no context for Buddhology.

## Buddhology as Exegesis

In this sense Buddhology has been practiced since there were written Buddhist texts. In the broadest sense Buddhology in our eon goes back to Buddhaghosa (fourth century A.D.), who, in his *Visuddhimagga* (*The Path of Purification*), interpreted and categorized the ideas of the early Buddhist texts. As currently practiced in the writing of dissertations within academe, Buddhology makes use of present-day exegetical techniques and modern scholarly methods. Exegetical Buddhology in academic contexts is normally presented in a "nonconfessional" tone, meaning that the exegete does not exhibit religious commitment in the process of exegesis. This type of exegetical Buddhology is a distinctively modern approach to the study of Buddhism. It involves the application of critical scholarship to Buddhist texts by translating and/or making interpretive commentaries on them. Thus, Buddhology in this sense is a descendant of philology. This type of Buddhology can be understood as philology applied to Buddhist texts.

## Buddhology as Buddhalogy

In this sense "Buddhology" can be compared and contrasted with Christology; here is meant the study of the nature of Buddha, the attributes of Buddha, and the idea of Buddhahood. The modern term *Buddhalogy* was coined by Paul J. Griffiths. The teaching ministry of Buddha focused consistently on suffering and the elimination of suffering. Thus, Buddha is regarded as the great psychological doctor. In this sense there is a parallel issue to that of the attributes of Jesus and to questions about his humanity and divinity. In the Pāli Canon of Theravāda Buddhism, Buddha is depicted as declaring that he is a spiritually perfected human being who has connected with an ancient path and also that he is not a *deva* ("god" or "shining one") in a rebirth station of gods. On this view he was a man who became fully enlightened after having found the ancient footprints of previous Buddhas in other eons.

However, in the historical development of Buddhism there have been those who wished to deify Buddha. Early Buddhist texts in the Pāli language clearly depict Buddha as a human being (*manussa*), not a god (*deva*). The folk Buddhism of the *Jātaka*s (part of the fifth *Nikāya* or *Khuddaka Nikāya*) evolved in contrast to doctrinal material of intellectual Buddhism preserved in the first four of the five *Nikāya*s and provided the seeds for the development of miracle stories about the Buddha. Thus, in later Mahāyāna Buddhism, Buddhology (viewed as the study of the idea of Buddha and his attributes) takes a turn toward apotheosis. After his "final enlightenment" (Sanskrit, *parinirvāṇa*; Pāli, *parinibbāna*), the epithet "Buddha" (Enlightened One) – one of several attributes – became the main identifying term. In Pāli Buddhist texts the epithet *Tathāgata* (thus gone) is often used interchangeably with "Buddha" to designate

Siddhartha Gautama Śākyamuni. There are many other epithets of Buddha. However, at death Buddha is supposed to have said to those such as Ananda who mourned his passing that the *dhamma* is eternal and his person irrelevant. From this one might surmise that the attributes of a particular Buddha need to be considered in the light of an overall ontology.

*Buddhology as Ontology*
In Mahāyāna the theory of the three bodies of Buddha – *dharmakāya* (truth body), *nirmanakāya* (appearance body), and *sambhogakāya* (bliss body) – all contribute to the development of the idea of Buddha. The first, *dharmakāya*, is the doctrine body, the law body, or the embodiment (in Buddha) of truth. The second, *nirmanakāya*, is the phenomenal body, the manifestation body, or the transformation body, by which Buddha helps sentient beings on the road to enlightenment. The third, *sambhogakāya*, is the noumenal body, the bliss body, or the Buddha as communicating dharma to the bodhisattvas in contrast to his communicating with ordinary sentient beings as *nirmanakāya*.

In sum there is hermeneutical Buddhology, exegetical Buddhology, attribute Buddhology, and ontological Buddhology. Whereas interpretation can proceed at a general hermeneutical level in hermeneutical Buddhology, with or without detailed references to texts, Buddhist texts (scriptures) are crucial to exegetical Buddhology. The attributes of the Buddha are the focus of attribute Buddhology, whereas one can understand the larger picture with reference to ontology in ontological Buddhology. Ontological Buddhology shows a view of how all of reality can be of one body yet with three aspects.

Viewed existentially Buddha is what one may become: an archetypal form of consciousness awaiting particular manifestation. Attributes of Buddha thus serve as reminders of how meditation may produce real inner change, resulting in authentic behavioral change for the better.

FRANK J. HOFFMAN

*See also* Buddha (Śākyamuni); Buddhism: Overview; Buddhism: Western; Dharma; Esoteric Buddhism in China and Japan; Mahāyāna; Meditation: Buddhist Perspectives

**Further Reading**

Gombrich, Richard F., *How Buddhism Began: The Conditioned Genesis of the Early Teachings*, London and Atlantic Highlands, New Jersey: Athlone Press, 1996
Griffiths, Paul J., *On Being Buddha: The Classical Doctrine of Buddhahood*, Albany: State University of New York Press, 1994
Hoffman, Frank J., and Mahinda Deegalle, editors, *Pali Buddhism*, Richmond: Curzon, 1996
Kalupahana, David J., and Indrani Kalupahana, *The Way of Siddhartha: A Life of the Buddha*, Boulder, Colorado: Shambhala Publications, 1982
Nattier, Jan, *One upon a Future Time: Studies in a Buddhist Prophecy of Decline*, Berkeley, California: Asian Humanities Press, 1991

# Bulgaria

The earliest traces of monasticism in the Balkans, today nearly effaced, have been found in the Southern Dobroudža on the Black Sea coast. Abandoned rock monasteries were resettled by Bulgarian monks from the ninth and tenth centuries onward. Spiritual links between the monasticism of late antiquity and that of the early Middle Ages are the "classics" of the monastic fathers (lives and "Paterika") of Egypt/Sinai, Palestine, Syria, and Rome. The fact that the coast of the Black Sea became once again a monastic center after the official Christianization of Bulgaria (865) can be demonstrated by the monastery of St. Mary in Ravna (district of Varna), which has been a topic of research since 1978. An inscription of the consecration in the year 889 and more than 300 (or even 3,000) further inscriptions on walls (in runes, in Greek, and in the old Bulgarian language, the latter using either the Glagolic or the Cyrillic alphabet), as well as drawings of crosses, representations of men or of beasts, and symbols, allow us to regard this monastery (including also a scriptorium among his ruins) as a spiritual center. Other spiritual centers can be found in the two capitals Pliska and Preslav (and their surroundings); the latter excelled in the production of colored ceramics (remnants found in Tuzlaláka and Patlejna).

Bulgarian monasticism owed much to the disciples of St. Cyril and Methodius, who were expelled from Great Moravia and received a friendly welcome from the first Christian khan Boris-Michail, who himself became a monk in 889 after abdication. Especially prominent was the first "bishop of the Slavs," Clement, the founder of a literary school in Ochrid (at the monastery of St. Panteleimon) for preachers, poets, translators, and copyists. Later Nahum took over the same function in the capital, together with Constantine of Preslav. Another important man of letters (and translator of the Hexaëmeron/Šestodnev, Expositio fidei of John of Damascus) was John the Exarch.

However, the most important figure for Bulgarian monasticism in the first Bulgarian Empire (681–1018) was the founder of the national monastery of Rila, John (d. 946). Like Abbot Feodosij of the Kiev Caves monastery (d. 1074), John represents not the more numerous so-called *ktitor* monasteries (monasteries by feudal foundation), endowed by czars and boyars with large real estates (often as burial places for the dynasty), but rather the alternative type of cloister: half hermitages within natural rock caves that in the Nestor chronicle are said to have been founded "by tears, fasting, prayers, and vigilance." John came as a hermit to the southern Rila Mountains, where he gathered around him over the years 66 brothers. He did not leave any writings except a spiritual testament, disputed in its authenticity, in which he admonishes his monks to the common life, to orthodoxy according to the tradition, to keep away from kings and princes, to handwork and regular reading of patristic texts, and, finally, not to be greedy for money. Among the spiritual pupils of John we find Prochor of Pšinja, Gavriil of Lesnovo, and Ioakim of Osogovo (Sarandapor), who founded noteworthy monasteries in northeastern Macedonia.

At Rila, soon after John's death, a certain decadence is noticeable. It was amplified by the concentration of monasteries in the new capital of Tărnovo. A renewal came only in the 14th century, when Rila became an important book center for several centuries. The present paintings in the church were done during the 19th century (except the old 14th-century frescoes in the Chreljo tower). Meanwhile in Communist times the monastery was suppressed from 1961 to 1969, and then a few monks returned, living marginalized in the court of the monastery, which served as a tourist center. In 1990 they became autonomous again from ideological (state) interference.

A second, more important pillar of Bulgarian monasticism was the Athos monastery of Zographou, founded according to popular legend around 919. As with the Serbian monastery of Hilandar or the Russian St. Panteleimon, an intense activity of translators and copyists (in exchange with Greek monasteries) can be seen. The Bulgarian monk Paisij of Hilandar published his "Slavic-Bulgarian History" in 1762, a work that contributed to the national awakening. Today both Bulgarian and Russian monasteries are suffering from a lack of new monks.

During the second Bulgarian Empire (1185–1395), new monastic centers arose – once again divided into the two types mentioned previously: in the new capital, Tărnovo, and surroundings on the one hand, and in rock valleys, hardly accessible, in the northeastern part of the country (cave monasteries near Ruse and Červen) on the other. In Tărnovo emerged the Great Lavra (almost completely destroyed) among many smaller monasteries on the hill Trapezica. As can be seen from the large number of ceramic monograms of czars and patriarchs found there, the building was a very well equipped *ktitor* monastery. As regards this type, the criticisms of the Bogomils concerning the wealth, the empty ritual, and the moral decadence of the monks, as expressed in the anti-Bogomil tract of the priest Kozma (tenth century), are quite understandable.

A privileged place in hagiography and hymnography belongs to two monastic foundations in the neighborhood of Tărnovo made by two pre-Palamitic Hesychasts (pupils of Gregory the Sinaite), Teodosij and Evtimij: "Holy Mother of God" near Kilifarevo and "Holy Trinity." A fellow monk of Evtimij was Cyprian, later metropolite of Kiev and Moscow (d. 1406). Meanwhile Teodosij became the leading figure at the council of 1359 against the Bogomils. The most famous monk from the rock monasteries was the later patriarch Ioakim I (after 1235).

A special case among the monasteries, resembling the pan-Orthodox type of Mount Athos, is the Georgian foundation (1083) of the Petritzos Monastery (Bulgarian, Bačkovo) within the mountain chain of the Rhodopes, south of Plovdiv. At that time Bulgaria was a province of the Byzantine Empire, in which the Great Domestikos Gregory Pakourianos (d. 1086), at the emperor's service, could not only found a monastery but also imbue it with a specific aim: to protect against heretical doctrines spread by the Armenians resettled around Plovdiv (including Monophysite Paulician/Bogomil ideas). Frescoes in the "Kostnica" (house where the bones are kept; 12th century) belong to the high points of art in Bulgaria. The Georgian charac-

ter of the monastery was preserved until the end of the second Bulgarian Empire. It was not until 1894 that the monastery was definitely given over to the Bulgarian exarchate.

During the Turkish occupation, a new monastic center emerged in the Vitoša Mountains near Sofia; one of these new foundations (Dragalevski manastir) is now the residence of the patriarch. The remaining, relatively numerous monasteries for men and women need restoration and new vocations.

On the Roman Catholic side, on account of the conversion of former Paulicians (17th century), monasteries of the Franciscans, Capuchins, Jesuits, and later also of Passionists, Assumptionists, Sisters of the Eucharist, and Carmelites, were established.

*Sites to Visit*
Monasteries of Rila, Bačkovo, and Bojana (outskirts of Sofia).

GERHARD PODSKALSKY, S.J.

*See also* Archaeology: Near East; Architecture: Eastern Christian Monasteries; Greece; Libraries: Eastern Christian; Mount Athos, Greece; Orthodox Monasticism: Slavic; Palamas, Gregory, St.; Russia: History; Visual Arts, Eastern Christian: Painting

**Further Reading**
Atanasov, G., "Skalni manastiri v kraj dunavska Dobrudža" (Rock Monasteries in the Danube Dobrudža), *Vekove* 15:6 (1986)
Čavrakov, C., *Središta na bălgarska knižovnost IX–XVIII vek* (Centers of Bulgarian Literature 9th–18th centuries), Sofia, 1987
Čavrakov, G., *Velikotărnovskite manastiri* (Monasteries de Veliko-Tărnovo), Sofia, 1970
Dujčev, I., "Le Mont Athos et les Slaves au Moyen Âge," in *Le Millénaire du Mont Athos, 963–1963: Études et Mélanges*, Belgium: Editions de Chevetogne, 1963
Khristov, Khristo Dechkov, Georgi Stojkov, and Krăstiu Miiatev, *The Rila Monastery: History, Architecture, Frescoes, Woodcarvings* (Studies in Bulgaria's Architectural Heritage, volume 6), Sofia: Bulgarian Academy of Sciences, 1959
Kisov, Slavcho, *Bachkovski manastir*, Sofia, 1990
Kuseff, M., "St. Clement of Ochrida," *Slavic and East European Review* 27 (1948)
Kuseff, M., "St. Nahum," *Slavic and East European Review* 29 (1950)
Mavrodina, L., "The Ivanovo Rock Churches," in *The Bulgarian Contribution to the World Culture Heritage*, edited by Magdalina Stancheva and Dafina Vasileva, Sofia: Technika State Publishing House, 1989
Obolensky, Dimitri, *Six Byzantine Portraits*, New York: Oxford University Press, and Oxford: Clarendon Press, 1988
Podskalsky, G., *Theologische Literatur des Mittelalters in Bulgarien und Serbien (865–1459)*, Munich: C.H. Beck, 2000
Popkonstantinov, K., "Traditionen von Kyrill und Methodius im altbulgarischen Literatur- und Ausbildungszentrum des 9. und 10. Jahrunderts beim Dorf Ravna, Bezirk Varna," in *Symposium Methodianum: Beiträge der internationalen*

*Tagung in Regensburg (17. bis 24. April 1985) zum Gedenken an den 1100. Todestag des hl. Method* (Selecta slavica, 13), Neuried: Hieronymus, 1988

Prashkov, Liuben, *Monasteries in Bulgaria*, Sofia: Spectrum, 1990

Tachiaos, A.-E., "Mount Athos and the Slavic Literatures," *Cyrillomethodianum* 4 (1977)

Thomson, F.J., "The Origins of the Principal Slav Monasteries on Athos: Zographou, Panteleimon and Chilandarion," *Byzantinoslavica* 57 (1996)

Totev, T., "Les monastères de Pliska et de Preslav aux IXe–Xe s.," *Byzantinoslavica* 48 (1987)

# Burma (Myanmar)

When the Buddha visited Arakan in northwestern Burma to pose for the *Image of the Great Sage*, he predicted that his monks would have a glorious future in the country. His prediction proved correct: Buddhist monasticism continues to flourish in Burma. His reasoning – that monks would enjoy eating the locally grown paddy rice – is highly plausible: for at least 1,500 years Burma's monastic traditions have existed in symbiosis with Burma's distinctive technology of rice irrigation.

## History

Burmese monastic histories (the surviving ones date from the 19th century) trace a continuous history of monastic lineages back to Pagan's King Anoratha (1044–1077). These claims are corroborated by the surviving architecture, frescoes, and inscriptions from Pagan's classical period (1044–1210). The earliest Burmese name to appear in these lineages is that of Shin Arahan, whom Anoratha appointed as his chief monk. These histories say nothing about monasticism during the first millennium, but archaeology fills the gap. The Pyu city of Beikthano has a group of Buddhist buildings (stūpa, monastery, and shrine) dating to the fourth or fifth century. The discovery of the fifth-century *Golden Pali Text* in the Pyu city of Sri Ksetra shows that Pyu monks read the same Pāli texts as their Pagan successors and related to the king and queen in similar ways. Other first-millennium monks read the canon in a Sanskrit recension and followed the Hīnayāna traditions of North India. Burmese monasticism is certainly 1,000, probably 1,500, and possibly over 2,000 years old.

Two institutions peculiar to Burmese monasticism until the 20th century were the monastic role in education and the political role of the chief monk. Until the 1880s monks were responsible for all levels of education, from six-year-olds learning the alphabet to 26-year-old postgraduates studying the complexities of vinaya and abidhamma. Boys around the age of ten were expected to shave their heads and spend at least one rainy season living in the monastery. Students in tertiary education underwent a longer ordination: past the age of 16, all students at the monastic universities had to be ordained, although most postgraduates were expected to disrobe some time in their 20s to take up government positions. Instruction in less scholarly subjects was provided by the *pwe kyaung* monks. The phrase (literally, "a monastery that holds a festival") denotes self-funded establishments whose abbot offered instruction in topics such as astrology, surgery, elephant riding, boxing, and self-defense. The 19th-century monastic histories belittle the *pwe kyaung* monks: they reflect the views of the elite lineages in general and the First Maungdaung *sayadaw* (1753–1833) in particular.

The title of chief monk embodied a loose idea of monastic hierarchy. Most Burmese kings since Anoratha have chosen an inner cabinet of monks to live among the courtiers, ministers, and generals of the capital city. The most prominent of these received the title chief monk, but his functions would vary from reign to reign. He might be a great scholar, attracting monks from all over Burma to study in the capital, or a great meditator, who functioned as a magnet around whom powerful but unpredictable natural forces coalesced. Sometimes he was simply the only monk with whom an irreligious king could get on – perhaps the tutor who had taught him to read and write. Occasionally a chief monk would be a great disciplinarian and purify the monkhood by enforcing his personal interpretation of vinaya. This seems to have happened on the rare occasions when the king was domestically strong, externally peaceful, and interested in religion. The last chief monk (the Taunggwin *sayadaw*) died in 1938.

## Sites

Compared with the glorious architectural heritage of Burma's pagodas, Burma's monastery buildings are a disappointment. With few exceptions the monasteries and meditation halls are built of wood, whereas the shrines, stūpas, and pagodas are built of brick and laterite. Wood rots fast in Burma's climate. Few wooden monasteries built before the 19th century are left, although some modern monasteries incorporate carved teak panels from earlier buildings. The monastic university towns are of interest: Pegu, east of Rangoon; Pakokku, near the confluence of the Chindwin and Irrawaddy Rivers; and above all the Sagaing Hills, across the Irrawaddy from Ava and Mandalay. At Sagaing a network of paths leads for 15 miles from monastery to pagoda to cave to meditation hall. Along these paths pious donors have inscribed Pāli verses or erected wooden sunshading or put out fresh drinking water for passersby. Burmese architecture responds to its natural surroundings: the monasteries of Sagaing display this talent to the full. The average village monastery is unlikely to be an attractive building, but its position relative to the village involves the same dialogue with nature: the monastery will be positioned to take the shade from a clump of trees or perched on a ridge to enjoy a prospect of the pagoda across the valley. Town monasteries tend to the functional. The donor community will have built, to the highest standards of construction available, a modern-looking place in which monks can live, teach, and receive visitors. To find beauty in a breeze-block monastery in an industrial suburb of Rangoon, the connoisseur must continue to focus on how the monastery and the outside world, the sacred and the secular, interact. Passing from the street to the ordination hall, one traverses a liminal landscape of walls, gates, spaces, and boundary stones, each detail of which is dictated by the architecturo-legal sections of the vinaya.

Kubyankgyi, Myinkaba, Burma, 12th century.
Photo courtesy of John C. Huntington, the Huntington Archive

*Recent Changes*

The British conquest of upper Burma in 1884 forced Burmese Buddhism to adapt to new political structures. From 1885 to 1918 the British slowly learned to build a simulacrum of the chief monk's monastic hierarchy. Then, between 1924 and 1935, they stripped it of power. Since the departure of the British in 1942, Burma has been ruled by two foreign armies of occupation, two Burmese military juntas, a socialist one-party state, and a Westminster-style democracy. The two last-named governments attempted to replace the chief monk with a hierarchical structure of committees and courts as well as a system of government registration for all monks. The 1949 attempt failed. The 1980 attempt seemed to have succeeded, until the demonstrations of 1988 (in which monks played an extremely prominent role) revealed otherwise. Beneath the state-imposed hierarchy, monks had consolidated a civil society of their own. In the post-1988 repression, an unknown number of monks, especially from Sagaing and Mandalay, have lost their lives. Times at present are difficult, but history offers some hope: in previous centuries Burmese monasticism has managed to flourish under similarly adverse conditions. Until the 20th century monks were the guardians and exponents of Burma's classical culture. However, recently, first under English rule and now under military rule, monks have become the exponents of Burma's political aspirations and guardians of what is left of its precolonial identity.

Tourists are banned from areas such as the Chindwin valley, the Western Range, and the northern Shan states, where the most picturesque monasteries are to be found. Among the accessible sites, the Sagaing Hills and the nearby Mandalay-Ava-Amarapura region have the most to offer. However, at the time of this writing Aung San Suu Kyi, the victor in Burma's last elections, continues to urge tourists not to visit Burma.

ANDREW HUXLEY

*See also* Libraries: Buddhist; Manuscript Production: Buddhist; Novices, Theravādin Rituals for; Rules, Buddhist (Vinaya): Lineage; Taungpila Sayadaw; Theravādin Monks, Modern Western

## Further Reading

Aye, Kyaw, "The Sangha Organisation in Nineteenth Century Burma and Thailand," *Journal of the Siam Society* 72:166 (1984)

Ferguson, J., and E. Mendelson, "Masters of the Buddhist Occult: The Burmese Weikzas," *Contributions to Asian Studies* 16:62 (1981)

Forchhammer, Emanuel, *Report on the Antiquities of Arakan*, Burma: Government Press, 1892

Swedagon Pagoda, Rangoon, Burma, 18th–19th century.
Photo courtesy of John C. Huntington, the Huntington Archive

Ling, Trevor, "Burmese Philosophy Today," in *Asian Philosophy Today*, edited by Dale Riepe, New York: Gordon and Breach, 1981

Mendelson, E. Michael, *Sangha and State in Burma: A Study of Monastic Sectarianism and Leadership*, edited by J.P. Ferguson, Ithaca, New York: Cornell University Press, 1975

Pe, Hla, *Burma: Literature, Historiography, Scholarship, Language, Life, and Buddhism*, Pasir Panjang, Singapore: Institute of Southeast Asian Studies, 1985

Stargardt, Janice, "The Oldest Known Pali Texts, 5th–6th Century: Results of the Cambridge Symposium on the Pyu Golden Pali Text from Sri Ksetra, 18–19 April 1995," *Journal of the Pali Text Society* 21:199 (1995)

Strachan, Paul, *Mandalay: Travels from the Golden City*, Gartmore, Stirling: Kiscadale Press, 1994

Strong, John, *The Legend and Cult of Upagupta: Sanskrit Buddhism in North India and Southeast Asia*, Princeton, New Jersey: Princeton University Press, 1992

Than Tun, *Essays on the History and Buddhism of Burma*, edited by Paul Strachan, Whiting Bay, Isle of Arran: Kiscadale Press, 1988

# Butler, Cuthbert 1858–1933

English Benedictine scholar and monastic reformer

Edward Cuthbert Butler, born in Dublin, Ireland, on 6 May 1858, was educated in England at the Benedictine School at Downside, Somerset, from 1869 to 1875. On entering the monastery there in 1876, he completed his novitiate and formation at Belmont, Hereford, then the English Benedictine common novitiate. At Belmont he valued the full liturgical observance, absent from Downside (whose monks worked mainly on the mission), that was made possible by a large resident community. Furthermore, he discovered the writings of Augustine Baker (1575–1641); these were to make a lifelong impact because monasticism, for Butler, whatever its practical arrangements, was essentially a contemplative state. On returning to Downside he taught in the school (acting for a time as its prefect or head master) and continued his studies, acquiring an external B.A. and M.A. from London University. He played an active role in the movement for reform within the English Benedictine Congregation, which led to the Apostolic Constitution, "Diu Quidem" (1899). This restored normal Benedictine government to the English monasteries, with the monasteries raised to the rank of abbeys, abbots elected by their communities, and the powers of president and general chapter, dominant in the previous constitutions, proportionately diminished. Butler's researches on monastic origins gained impetus from this reform, and he was an obvious choice to become first superior (1896–1904) of the Downside house at Cambridge, Benet House, enabling the first generation of monks to study at the university. In 1898, with a fellow monk, he became the first Catholic priest to graduate at either Oxford or Cambridge since the reign of Mary Tudor (1553–1558). In 1908, when awarded an honorary D.Litt. by Trinity College, Dublin, he became the first Catholic cleric to be so recognized. In 1906 he was elected second abbot of Downside and remained in office following his reelection in 1914 until his resignation in 1922, when he went to St. Benedict's Priory, Ealing, London, where he died in 1933.

His long period, by English standards, as abbot of Downside allowed him, especially in his early years, to put into practice much of the monastic theory that he had been studying for so long. He worked to develop "Diu Quidem" and to reduce the number of outside missions, concentrating on the internal development of his conventus. His years of office witnessed a development of the community's liturgical life, an enhancement of the abbey's church's fittings, a separate Downside novitiate, and the encouragement of learned activities both in the developing school and in the academic pursuits of individual monks. The idea of Downside as a "model monastery" for the Congregation appealed to him, and when he succeeded Cardinal Gasquet (1846–1929) as abbot-president in 1914, he had enough support from his fellow abbots to be reelected in 1917. In 1921 he failed to win their confidence, and his subsequent resignation as abbot revealed that his reforming tendencies, which included the jettisoning of the remaining missions, proved too challenging for many in his community.

Butler's early writings included a number of articles for *The Dublin Review* and *The Downside Review*, which were intended to reply to the anti-Catholic historicism of Adolf Harnack (1851–1930) and other German historians on monastic and Christian origins. These were followed by his edition of Palladius' *Lausiac History* (1904) and by his critical edition of the *Rule of St. Benedict* (1912), to which he attached, as a kind of catechism for the first Downside novices, a *medulla*, or a summary of the Rule.

A wider audience, both academic and monastic, was achieved through Butler's *Benedictine Monachism* (1919), perhaps his most influential work; this is a distillation of his abbatial conferences, which not only surveyed monastic history and constitutional problems but also provided him with an opportunity to discuss his spiritual doctrine. More of this appeared in *Western Mysticism* (1922), a work that reflected both his abiding debt to Baker and his long friendship with Baron Friedrich von Hügel (1852–1925).

In his later years he turned to history, producing a two-volume *Life and Times of Bishop Ullathorne* (1926), which placed the Victorian bishop at the center of the events of his time, and another two-volume work, *History of the Vatican Council* (1930), which remains the most succinct account of the 1869–1870 proceedings. All Butler's writings were written in clear, almost stark style and were readily translated. Curiously his reputation both benefited and suffered from the work of his monastic disciple, Dom David Knowles (1896–1974). It benefited from the attention that Knowles gave it in his prolonged reflections on Butler originally published in *The Downside Review* and republished in *The Historian and Character* (1963). It suffered from the astringent quality of those reflections and from Knowles' implied criticism that Butler was not radical enough in his drive toward monastic reform.

AIDAN BELLENGER

*See also* Baker, Augustine; Chapman, John; England: History; Historiography, Recent: Western Christian; Knowles, M. David; Liturgical Movement 1830–1980

## Biography

Born in Dublin and educated at Downside, Somerset, the future writer and monastic reformer entered the monastery there in 1876. He participated in the reform movement that in 1899 restored autonomy to English Benedictine abbeys. While serving as superior of Downside's house at Cambridge (Benet House), Butler graduated from the University. From 1906 to 1922 he served as Abbot of Downside. There he encouraged pursuit of scholarship and reduced missionary activities. This discomfited some in the community, with the result that he retired to Ealing Abbey in London from 1922 to 1931.

## Major Works

*Benedictine Monachism*, 1919
*Western Mysticism*, 1922
*Life and Times of Bishop Ullathorne*, 2 vols., 1926
*History of the Vatican Council*, 2 vols., 1930

## Further Reading

Bellenger, D.A., "The English Benedictines: The Search for a Monastic Identity 1880–1920," in *Monastic Studies: The Continuity of Tradition*, edited by Judith Loades, Bangor, Wales: Headstart History, 1990

Clark, A., "The Return to the Monasteries," in *Monks of England*, edited by Daniel Rees, London: SPCK, 1997

Knowles, D., "A Memoir" and "The Works and Thought of Abbot Butler," in *The Historian and Character and Other Essays*, Cambridge: Cambridge University Press, 1963

Yeo, R., and L. Maidlow Davis, "Abbot Cuthbert Butler, 1858–1934," *Studia Anselmiana* 84, Rome: Pontificio Ateneo S. Anselmo, 1982

# Byzantine Monasticism. *See* Orthodox Monasticism: Byzantine

# C

## Caesarius of Arles, St. c. 469–542

Gallo-Roman monk and archbishop of Arles

Caesarius, a Gallo-Roman from Chalon-sur-Saône in Burgundy, was one of the great monk-bishops in Gaul who attempted to impose monastic ideals on the clergy as well as on the urban and rural populace. He represents the shift away from pagan Roman culture and toward the steady Christianization of Gaul. Trained at the monastery of Lérins, which was noted for its learning, he came to envision society in terms of biblical, patristic, and monastic principles, especially those of fraternity and communal charity. When he became archbishop of Arles in 502, then subject to the Visigoth Alaric II, Caesarius frequently called episcopal councils to promote such practices as canonical reforms, a uniform liturgy and Divine Office, stricter rules for the clergy, correct doctrine, missions to the countryside, and clerical preaching. At these councils he defended Augustinian views of grace and the Trinity and opposed the semi-Pelagian theories of free will. Caesarius expected the clergy, especially the bishops, to set an example of ascetic living and a Christ-like poverty and simplicity. A popular preacher who spoke plainly and directly to his congregations, Caesarius gave sermons on the themes of prayer, penance, fasting, social peace, pride, chastity, sobriety, Bible reading at home, compassion for the poor, forgiveness, virtues of the saints, and the Eucharist. He wrote a rule for a monastery of men that he enforced throughout the diocese. He composed a rule for nuns under the abbacy of his sister, Caesaria. This monastery for women remained his lifelong concern; its strictly regulated and enclosed cloister was an innovation at the time. His zeal for ransoming enemy captives got him into trouble in Arles, but he was exonerated by King Theodoric the Ostrogoth (489–526) in Ravenna and by Pope Symmachus (498–514), who gave him the pallium and made him papal vicar in Gaul and Spain. As metropolitan he worked tirelessly to Christianize parishes and dioceses in southern Gaul in accordance with quasi-monastic behavior. Although many of the canons of his councils were ignored by the Merovingian Church, the later Carolingians, especially Charlemagne (768–814), adopted a number of these reforms for the Frankish Church, partially through the advocacy of St. Boniface (c. 675–754). Caesarius' sermons became widely diffused in the West.

Caesarius' intention in advancing tighter episcopal control over suffragan dioceses was not to replace Roman officials with clerical ones but to exhort Christians to practice mutual love and responsibility. The bishop was supposed to be a pastor and a reformer. For him the monastery and the diocese were twin models for higher standards of conduct in the Church universal, itself an image of the heavenly Jerusalem. Caesarius' values were eschatological and penitential, not traditionally Roman and imperial. He died on 27 August 542.

A life of Caesarius was written shortly after his death. More than 250 sermons have survived, as have seven letters, two monastic rules, and treatises on grace: the Arian heresy, the Trinity, and the Book of the Apocalypse.

THOMAS RENNA

*See also* Benedictines: Female; Boniface, St.; France: History; Lérins, France; Office, Daily: Western Christian; Origins: Western Christian; Patrons, Christian: Lay

### Biography
Caesarius entered the monastery of Lérins about 490 and served as archbishop of Arles from 502 to 542. He negotiated with the Ostrogoth King Theodoric to make Arles the primate's seat in Gaul. Caesarius composed two monastic rules, one for monks and a lengthier one for nuns. They draw on the example of Lérins and show the influence of both Cassian and Augustine.

### Major Works
*Regulae Monasticae*
*Sermons*, 3 vols. (31, 47, 66), translated by Mary M. Mueller, 1956–1973; critical edition of the *Sermones* by G. Morin in *Corpus Christianorum: Series Latina* 103–104 (1953)

### Further Reading

Beck, Henry G.J., *The Pastoral Care of Souls in South-East France During the Sixth Century*, Rome: Apud Aedes Universitatis Gregorianne, 1950
Daly, William M., "Caesarius of Arles: A Precursor of Medieval Christendom," *Traditio* 26 (1970)
Klingshirn, William E., "Caesarius' Monastery for Women in Arles and the Composition and Function of the 'Vita Caesarii'," *Revue Bénédictine* 100 (1990)

Klingshirn, William E., *Caesarius of Arles: The Making of a Christian Community in Late Antique Gaul*, Cambridge and New York: Cambridge University Press, 1994

Klingshirn, William E., translator, *Caesarius of Arles: Life, Testament, Letters*, Liverpool: Liverpool University Press, 1994

# Camaldolese

The Camaldolese are Benedictines, and so their first founder is St. Benedict. However, they also represent a unique 11th-century renewal of Benedictine life, and so their second founder is St. Romuald (c. 950–1027).

The Sacred Hermitage of Camaldoli and the monastery below it, located in the Tuscan Mountains near Arezzo, Italy, were founded by Romuald sometime between 1012 and 1024. The etymology of *Camaldoli* is debated, but the word is possibly a conflation of *campus Romualdi*, "field of Romuald." In 1113 Pope Paschal II (1099–1118) gave the joint foundation some additional hermitages and monasteries that had been founded or reformed by Romuald, thereby allowing an eremitical-cenobitical congregation to form, headed by Camaldoli and thus called "Camaldolese."

Romuald, like Peter Damian (1007–1072) after him, was born and raised in Ravenna, and so was shaped spiritually by the Eastern Christian spirituality of that great coastal city. The son of a nobleman, Romuald entered the Cluniac abbey of St. Apollinaris in Classe (with its magnificent, immense paradisiacal and paschal Byzantine mosaics, which influenced his spirituality) to do penance for his father's murder of another in a duel. After three years in the abbey, Romuald received permission to retire into solitude. From that time on he alternated between solitude and community life and journeyed through central and northern Italy and even as far as Catalonia and the abbey of Cuxa. Romuald's prophetic, charismatic spirit enabled him to found and renew monasteries and abbeys, defend the poor, and even seek martyrdom as a monastic missionary, although this was not granted him. He reintroduced into Western monasticism the hermit's cell and the idea of the lavra, or community of hermits gathered around a common chapel, refectory, and other community buildings; and this is the model he introduced at Camaldoli.

His spirituality, rooted in the desert experience, is summed up in his "Brief Rule":

> Sit in your cell as in paradise. Put the whole world behind you . . . realize above all that you are in God's presence . . . empty yourself completely, and sit waiting, content with the grace of God, like the chick who tastes nothing and eats nothing but what his mother brings him.

Saint Bruno-Boniface of Querfurt, a contemporary of Romuald and his disciple, chronicles in *The Life of the Five Brothers* the warm communal spirit of friendship of the first monks of the Romuald circle and their zeal for solitude and for mission and martyrdom. Bruno-Boniface thus proposes this "threefold good" of fraternal community, solitude, and mission/martyr-dom, and this unity-in-diversity characterizes the Camaldolese charism down through the centuries, as it also typifies much of monasticism and, in a more basic way, three key dimensions of the Christian life itself. Indeed, it can be seen as ultimately rooted in the unity-in-diversity of the Holy Trinity.

From the end of the 11th century through the first half of the 14th, the Camaldolese congregation grew rapidly, especially in Tuscany and northern Italy, encompassing both monasteries and hermitages, and in both urban and rural settings. The early *Constitutions* (probably early 12th century) are "of remarkable discretion and breadth of view . . . the effect of the whole is one of balance and sanity and supernatural good sense. [They] reflect the true spirit of the Gospel of Christ and the wisdom of the greatest Desert Fathers" (Merton, 1957).

Camaldolese monks and hermits made a significant contribution to the emerging Christian humanism of the Renaissance. For example, Guido of Arezzo (c. 992–1050), "the father of modern music," developed the foundations of modern musical notation. Gratian (d. c. 1160) is considered "the father of canon law." His *Decretum*, rather than delineating a closed, rigid juridical system, sets forth some 4,000 patristic, conciliar, and papal decrees regarding all areas of Church life.

Lorenzo Monaco (c. 1370–1425), considered the most important Florentine artist of the first half of the 15th century, exercised a significant influence on Fra Angelico and other early Renaissance artists. Ambrose Traversari (c. 1386–1439), general of the Camaldolese order, pioneered ecumenical dialogue with the Eastern Church; he translated many of the Greek Fathers into Latin and participated in the Council of Florence. Fra Mauro (d. 1459), gifted mapmaker, gathered the data of returning explorers in detailed maps of a round world that indirectly influenced Columbus.

All this creative work occurred within Camaldolese cloisters (urban and rural), where serious monastic observance was maintained.

Later popes utilized the Camaldolese in reforming various monastic communities in Italy. In the 19th century the Camaldolese contributed a pope to the church, Gregory XVI (1831–1846). Very conservative in many ways, he also condemned slavery and the slave trade and greatly advanced the missions, encouraging the formation of native clergy. He founded the Egyptian and Etruscan museums at the Vatican and the Christian Museum at the Lateran.

Romuald left his disciples no other rule than that of St. Benedict, and the modern Camaldolese Congregation of the Order of St. Benedict has belonged to the Benedictine Confederation since 1966. Another congregation that includes hermitages only – the Congregation of Camaldolese Hermits of Monte Corona, which traces its history back to the 16th Century Blessed Paul Giustiniani (d. 1528) – is not a member of the Benedictine Confederation. In 1569 the ancient Hermitage of Fonte Avellana (Umbria), along with the congregation it headed, united with Camaldoli. An exclusively cenobitic Camaldolese congregation developed in 1616 and was reunited with Camaldoli in 1935 by Pope Pius XI (1922–1939). Now only two men's Camaldolese congregations exist; these share a common liturgical ordo and the same habit:

an all-white tunic with hood and scapular. The two congregations have houses mainly in Italy but also in Poland, Spain, the United States (Big Sur, California; Berkeley, California; and Bloomingdale, Ohio) as well as in India and Brazil. Several houses of Camaldolese nuns exist as well, in Italy, the United States (Windsor, New York), India, Brazil, and Tanzania. Notable recent Camaldolese include Cypriano Vagaggini, liturgist, peritus of the Second Vatican Council, and member of the International Pontifical Theological Commission, as well as Bede Griffiths (1907–1993), a pioneer in Hindu-Christian dialogue.

ROBERT HALE, O.S.B. CAM.

*See also* Benedictines: General or Male; Canons Regular, Origins of; Cluny, France; Damian, Peter, St.; Florence, Italy; Hermits: Western Christian; Humanism, Christian; Monastery, Christian

## Further Reading

Bossi, Paolo, *Eremi camaldolesi in Italia: Luoghi, architettura, spiritualità*, Milan: Vita e pensiero, 1993

Cataluccio, Elena Magheri, and Ugo Fossa, *Biblioteca e cultura a Camaldoli: Dal Medioevo all'umanesimo*, Rome: Editrice Anselmiana, 1979

Donati, Giovanni Gualberto, *L'Ordine Camaldolese*, Arezzo: Edizioni Camaldoli, 1964

Giabbani, Anselmo, *L'Eremo: Vita e spiritualità eremitica nel monachesimo camaldolese primitivo*, Breschia: Marcelliana, 1945

Hale, Robert, "Camaldolese Spirituality," in *The New Dictionary of Catholic Spirituality*, edited by Michael Downey, Collegeville, Minnesota: Liturgical Press, 1993

Hale, Robert, "Eremitical Life," in *The New Dictionary of Catholic Spirituality*, edited by Michael Downey, Collegeville, Minnesota: Liturgical Press, 1993

Leclercq, Jean, *Alone with God*, New York: Farrar, Straus and Cudahy, and London: Catholic Book Club, 1961

Matus, Thomas, *The Mystery of Romuald and the Five Brothers: Stories from the Benedictines and Camaldolese*, Trabuco Canyon, California: Source Books, 1994

Merton, Thomas, *The Silent Life*, New York: Farrar, Straus and Giroux, 1957 (see especially pages 144–171)

Pagnani, Alberico, *Storia dei benedettini camaldolesi: Cenobiti, eremiti, monache ed oblati*, Sassaferrato: Prem. tip. Garofoli, 1949

Vigilucci, Lino, *Camaldoli: A Journey into Its History and Spirituality*, translated by Peter-Damian Belisle, Trabuco Canyon, California: Source Books/Hermitage Books, 1995

## Related Web Sites

*http://www.camaldoli.com*
*http://www.contemplation.com*

# Canada

Three powerful thoughts console a good heart, which is in the infinite forests of New France or among the Hurons. The first is, I am in the place where God has sent me, where He has led me as by the hand, where He is with me, and where I seek Him alone. The second is that, what David says: according to the measure of the pains which I endure for God, His divine consolations rejoice my soul. The third, that one never finds either cross, nails, or thorns, without finding [Jesus Christ] in the midst, if one looks closely. (Kenton, 1925)

The temptation to assume that "monasticism" arrived in Canada with the first European missionaries must be resisted. Recognition that a well-developed spiritual culture was already in place has been slow in coming but is now increasingly established among historians. A more recent work, such as Hans Mol's *Faith and Fragility* (1985), devotes its first two chapters to outlining what can still be known about early spiritual traditions among the Inuit and "North American Indian" cultures. In its orientation to the role of the shaman, initiation rites, taboos, totems, and so on, indigenous spiritual culture had its own conception that some individuals from within a tribe, family, or village possessed unique spiritual callings, at least roughly analogous to our notion of "monasticism." Even before the well-documented saga of the Jesuits in Canada commenced, this sense of "the few for the many" – Mol refers to the shamans as "the experts on the spirit world, [who] exemplify the spiritual priorities . . . the brokers with the spirits" – nothing could be more clear than that survival, against the land and the elements, was the dominant motif.

Thus, monastic culture in Canada has always and everywhere been characterized by contrasts and tensions that have continued to play a formative role in its development. The narratives of French missionaries, in particular those from the Jesuit Order, are paradigmatic, as they broke the trail for all that has followed. Nothing in their European experience could have prepared explorers, immigrants, or clerics for the vast wildness of the Canadian landscape. The French explorer Jacques Cartiér is said to have preached to the native inhabitants of present-day Québec and Montréal himself on his first visit there in 1535 (Carrière, 1967).

One can scarcely imagine the shifts of soul and body demanded of members of religious orders, immediately on landfall in Québec, Nova Scotia (Port Royal), or Cape Breton (the fortress of Louisbourg). The Jesuit Order had existed for only less than a century when its first missionaries set foot in Canada, and inevitably their sense of calling was to be radically reshaped by the challenges presented in this new setting – from a civilization that had evolved within the nurturing framework of Christendom to a thoroughly animist setting; from a social culture characterized by settled villages and towns to nomadic life; from a geography of familiar and proximate horizons to one of unmapped, trackless expanses; from a reasonably temperate climate to a land of forbidding winters; and finally, and by no means least, from a culture where both French and Latin were well known to a place where one had to start completely over. Still, as it was with the habitants generally, so it was with the clerics: many fell victim to heartbreak, disease, and weather, and a few found within themselves untapped resources of strength and heroism.

The journals of the best known of these monastic pioneers provide a remarkable narrative. The Jesuit "Eight Martyrs" (canonized by Pius XI in 1930), who served with dogged determination among the Huron tribes on what is now known as the Bruce Peninsula in Ontario, are the best-known examples. On several occasions missions to the Great Lakes region in which Jean de Brébeuf was involved were turned back or failed. Of his departure on this last inland journey, he later wrote, "Several times I was completely baffled and desperate, until I had special recourse to our LORD JESUS, for whose glory alone we were undertaking this painful journey, and until I had made a vow" (Kenton, 1925).

Kennedy pays homage to the Jesuits' capacity to take what they had brought with them and apply it to what they found on arrival, as follows:

> While they strove to spread the faith by the accepted means of knowledge, adaptation, and eloquence, individuals often found themselves forced into independent action of startling boldness and originality. (Kennedy, 1950)

The Canadian psyche continues to be influenced to some degree by unique tensions and ironies: huge landmass/small population, the ongoing struggle to reconcile cultural tensions (no longer only English and French but increasingly from Western and aboriginal Canadians), and always the awareness of living next door to the strongest nation on earth.

In short this is a much different spiritual landscape than what the first Europeans found. To some degree that early frontier spirit was tempered over time by population growth and urbanization. Yet even at the time when missions (by now Anglican as well as Catholic) extended to the Canadian West, a similar pioneering spirit was characteristic of the activity of the religious orders. The late 20th century has seen a sharp decline in the base of adherents to traditional Christian groups, yet this scarcely means a disappearance of monastic life. Especially worth noting as countertrends is the massive and energetic influx of non-Western religious groups, notably Sikhs, Buddhists, Hindus, and (on a smaller scale than in the United States) Muslims. Broadly speaking these groups have arrived in this new territory with a fervor and dynamism reminiscent of that of the Jesuits of the 17th century. Mission activity, retreat centers, and so on are not unusual within these groups. Also worth noting is the monastic activity among nontraditional religious groups. Countercultural, vaguely "spiritual" alternatives to urban life began to appear in the 1960s, and their appeal was immediate. What is more surprising is that, in their more recent New Age manifestations, these groups have far outlived their original impetus. Thus, it would hardly be an exaggeration to say that some of the highest-profile and most dynamic centers of activity on Canada's West Coast, for example, come from within this sector rather than traditional religious groups (Bibby, 1993).

Few countries have experienced such a rapid cultural diversification in the late 20th century as has Canada. This rapid change has called on Canadians who consider themselves "settled citizens of long-standing" to accept and adjust to diversification. As in the past, monastic pioneers of Canada in this time bring their fervor to a vast, strange land where almost no one understands them or why they have come.

DAVID STEWART

*See also* France: History; United States: Western Christian

**Further Reading**

Bibby, Reginald, *Unknown Gods: The Ongoing Story of Religion in Canada*, Toronto: Stoddart, 1993

Campbell, T.J., "de Brébeuf, Jean," in *The Catholic Encyclopedia*, edited by Charles George Herbermann et al., volume 2, New York: Appleton, and London: Caxton, 1907

"Canada, The Catholic Church in," in *The Modern Catholic Encyclopedia*, edited by Michael Glazier and Monika K. Hellwig, Collegeville, Minnesota: Liturgical Press, 1994

Carrière, G., "Canada," in *New Catholic Encyclopedia*, New York: McGraw-Hill, 1967

Curran, Francis X., *The Return of the Jesuits: Chapters in the History of the Society of Jesus in Nineteenth Century America*, Chicago: Loyola University Press, 1966

Fournet, A., "Catholicity in Canada," in *The Catholic Encyclopedia*, edited by Charles George Herbermann et al., volume 3, New York: Appleton, and London: Caxton, 1907

Kennedy, John Hopkins, *Jesuit and Savage in New France* (Yale Historical Publications, Miscellany, 50), New Haven, Connecticut: Yale University Press, 1950

Kenton, Edna, and Reuben Gold Thwaites, editors, *The Jesuit Relations and Allied Documents; Travels and Explorations of the Jesuit Missionaries in North America (1610–1791)* (American Library, volume 23), New York: Vanguard, 1925

Mol, Hans, *Faith and Fragility: Religion and Identity in Canada*, Burlington, Ontario: Trinity Press, 1985

O'Brien, John A., *The First Martyrs of North America: The Story of the Eight Jesuit Martyrs*, Notre Dame, Indiana: University of Notre Dame Press, 1953

Pollen, J.H., "Society of Jesus," in *The Catholic Encyclopedia*, edited by Charles George Herbermann et al., volume 14, New York: Appleton, and London: Caxton, 1907

# Canons Regular, Origins of

The growing secularization in the life and property of the Church encouraged Hildebrand, the future Gregory VII (1073–1085), and Peter Damian (1007–1072), of Fonte Avallano, to urge that the *Ordo Canonicus* live the full apostolic life, as in the primitive Church. Official recognition by the Lateran Councils of 1059 and 1063 ensured the survival of the new Order of Canons Regular. Despite opposition the Order was perceived as a justifiable development in the Church, and indeed it became one of the lasting products of Gregorian reform. A revival in the study of canon law accompanied the rise of the canons. In addition the founding of eremitic communities, such as the Camaldolese, heralded a period of austerity and might have directly influenced canons to seek the primitive purity of the canonical life.

Although that was their earliest allegiance, early houses also sought to restore liturgical worship. However, they required a rule that gave authority to the ideal of the apostolic life, and St. Augustine of Hippo (354–430) provided that authority. Despite its great practicality, Augustine's Rule was not adopted until the time of Urban II (1088–1099), becoming the guide and symbol of the apostolic vocation. Saint Ivo of Chartres (c. 1040–1115) is perhaps responsible for the adoption of Augustine's Rule by the canons, who saw themselves being subject to Christ under the Rule of St. Augustine. The canons' rediscovery and rehabilitation of St. Augustine's Rule is probably their most important contribution to the history of the Western Church.

Yet it was only toward the end of the 11th century that Augustine was seen as their "founder," imparting his immense prestige as saint, theologian, doctor, bishop, and religious to advantage. Moreover the excellent practical nature of his Rule ensured that it would be adopted by many generations of religious. The earliest references to the Rule are found at Senlis around 1059 and certainly at Rheims in 1067 and at Soissons in 1089. By the late 11th century it was adopted outside France, and became universal by the 12th century.

Indeed the 12th century was well advanced before the term Canons Regular became common, yet Gregory VII (1073–1085) had used the title four times in his constitutions for the Order. The title Canons Regular distinguished them from secular canons, who did not live the common life. In 1066 it appeared in the foundation charter of St. Autbert, Cambrai, and that of St. Vincent, Senlis, around 1085. Only after several decades did they became known as Augustinian Canons.

Technically canons were not monks but rather clerics with a monastic character. They took the three vows, and their receipt of the surplice was as significant as a monk receiving the habit. Moreover not all canons were priests, ordination not being necessary for communal life, and as Christ's poor they sought a more perfect life. Superiors became known as priors, to whom the canons owed strict obedience as in monastic houses.

Following the Lateran Council of 1059, the canons existed mainly in and around Rome and central and northern Italy. Saint Frediano was the most influential and was independent, as Cluny was. In Rome St. Croce in Gerusalemme and St. John Lateran were centers of Canons Regular. By about 1085 the canons had reached Berghera in south Calabria, Switzerland at Great St. Bernard pass from about 1081 to 1086, and from there into southern France. By the early 12th century, the Order had formed in Austria, the Holy Roman Empire, and Spain.

In France the canons had houses in all three regions. An early influential house was St. Ruf, Avignon (1038–1039), and St. Quentin, Beauvais, became a model house of the Order. In northern France some canons' houses were abbeys, as were almost all independent houses. Although abbeys were rarely found outside France, Jedburgh in Scotland ranked as one, whereas in England most houses were priories.

The earliest English foundation was St. Botolph's, Colchester (c. 1095), the first of 274 priories. The canons' success in Germany almost matched theirs in England. The first Scottish house was at Scone (c. 1120). The spectacular success of the canons is perhaps explained by the fact that communities often remained small, thus requiring a smaller endowment – a fact that appealed to lay patrons.

No official bond existed among independent houses. Indeed the majority of canons' houses never belonged to an independent congregation but were as much a part of the diocese as were the seculars. In the early years the term *house of canons* applied as much to seculars as it did to regulars. Nothing much happened before the time of Innocent III (1198–1216) to form the Order into an administrative unit. Canon 12 of the Lateran Council of 1215 stated that every kingdom or province should hold triennial general chapters of abbots and priors of all religious orders. This included the vast number of houses of canons.

The Order experienced difficulties maintaining communication among houses spread across large areas. Unlike the great Benedictine houses, the canons were more localized and thus often lacked the resources to maintain themselves and to withstand major problems. Smaller branches, such as the Arrouise and Victorines, experienced even greater problems of this sort. Moreover, because many were bound by ties to a diocese, their survival depended on favorable circumstances. In any case canons' houses were more popular with episcopal patrons, for as an integral part of the diocese they proved useful, being subject to a bishop's jurisdiction, supervision, and visitation. Thus, the likelihood that disagreements would arise was small.

Although the Order had achieved uniformity by the 13th century under a common patron and government, the canons' vocation developed in different ways. Canons formed cathedral chapters, administered private and collegiate chapels, operated priories in towns, and managed hospitals, while some become scholars, such as Hugh (d. 1142) and Richard (d. 1173) of St. Victor. The canons' involvement in parishes, authorized unequivocally at the Council of Poitiers in 1100, was encouraged because of the apostolic life they taught by work and example. However, the Victorines and Arrouaisians, both strict orders of Canons, sought the eremitic life, and Arrouaisians were as austere as Cistercians.

PHILIP E. MCWILLIAMS

*See also* Augustinian Canons; Augustinian Rule; Camaldolese; Christianity: Overview; France: History; Gregory VII; Monastics and the World, Medieval; Monk-Bishops; Officials: Western Christian; Orders (Religious), Origin of; Victorines

## Further Reading

Burton, Janet, *Monastic and Religious Orders in Britain, 1000–1300* (Cambridge Medieval Textbooks), Cambridge and New York: Cambridge University Press, 1994

Burton, Janet, *Medieval Monasticism: Monasticism in the Medieval West: From Its Origins to the Coming of the Friars* (Headstart History Papers), Witney: Headstart History, 1996

Dickinson, J.C., *The Origins of the Austin Canons and Their Introduction into England*, London: SPCK, 1950

Easson, David E., *Medieval Religious Houses, Scotland: With an Appendix on the Houses in the Isle of Man*, London and New York: Longmans, Green, 1957; 2nd edition by Easson and Ian B. Cowan, London and New York: Longman, 1976

Knowles, David, *The Monastic Order in England: A History of Its Development from the Times of St. Dunstan to the Fourth Lateran Council, 943–1216*, Cambridge: Cambridge University Press, 1940; 2nd edition, 1963; New York: Cambridge University Press, 1976

Lawrence, C.H., *Medieval Monasticism: Forms of Religious Life in Western Europe in the Middle Ages*, London and New York: Longman, 1984; 2nd edition, 1989

# Cappadocia, Turkey

A rural, mountainous region in central Asia Minor (modern Turkey), Cappadocia encompasses about a 62-square-mile area bordered to the north by the Halys River, to the east by a famous salt lake, and to the southwest by the Taurus mountain range. The eruption thousands of years ago of several volcanic mountains in Cappadocia and the subsequent erosion over the centuries of the solidified volcanic ash created the region's distinctive geology and unusual landscape. At one time or another, many ancient civilizations of the eastern Mediterranean incorporated this area within their empires. From the fourth to the sixth century A.D., Christianity spread throughout the Roman Empire, whose eastern half developed into the Byzantine Empire. Situated firmly within the empire's eastern frontier, Cappadocia prospered. In addition to Caesarea, the capital of the province, urban centers and smaller towns grew, supporting many seats of bishops. From the seventh to the early ninth century, first Persian and then Arab raids through Cappadocia's territory devastated the area. By the ninth century the Byzantine Empire had regained its strength and pushed its Arab enemies behind and beyond the Taurus Mountains. A period of prosperity ensued as both local and foreign military and land magnates settled in Cappadocia. Security lasted until the late 11th century, when the Seljuk Turks, one of a series of invading nomadic tribes, conquered Byzantium's eastern frontier.

Cappadocia's fame as a center of monasticism is due largely to the Cappadocian origins of Basil the Great (c. 330–379), who wrote the basic rule of Orthodox monasticism. During Cappadocia's second period of prosperity, from the 9th to the 11th century, a large population settled in the region, carving hundreds of houses, monasteries, underground refuges, and storage areas into the soft volcanic rock characteristic of the area. They also carved numerous sites for worship, including parish churches, monastic chapels, private chapels in residential dwellings, and independent burial chapels. Many chapels were painted with saints and elaborate narrative scenes from the Bible. Images inside the churches of patrons as donors testify to a population of aristocrats, generals, laypeople and family priests, and monks.

The monastic population of Cappadocia did not live in orders such as those found in the Western medieval world but most likely practiced all forms of Byzantine monasticism, living in *koinobia*, in *lavra*, and as hermits. In all three lifestyles a monk leads a life devoted to God. In *koinobia*, or cenobitic monasticism, monks live and worship together while working toward the benefit of the monastery, engaging in administrative affairs as well as production for the monastery's self-sufficiency. In eremitic, or anchoritic, monasticism, a monk retreats from the world, usually to the desert, pursuing complete seclusion as a hermit. In *lavra*, monks live individually and isolated in the countryside but come together once a week for communal worship, thus achieving a compromise between the cenobitic and eremitic monastic forms.

In Cappadocia several rock-cut complexes preserve rooms with refectories that epitomize the cenobitic lifestyle. These rooms resemble known refectories built out of masonry that are found in the monasteries of Mount Athos. They consist of rectangular, rock-cut tables surrounded by benches. In cenobitic monasticism monks assemble once a day for a communal meal, while the abbot of the monastery sits at one end of the table. In the Cappadocian refectories a carved niche at the table's end identifies the abbot's seat. Most Cappadocian complexes and their refectories are small and intimate and probably served anywhere from 5 to 20 monks.

Several chapels seem to indicate that some monks practiced an eremitic lifestyle. These chapels are found rather high up in isolated cones and have a small number of loosely associated and poorly articulated rooms. Two such chapels in Cappadocia preserve painted inscriptions that refer to the donor as a stylite, who performed a peculiar form of asceticism that involved ascending a column or a pillar. While remaining on its peak, the stylite led a life of contemplation. Famous monks of the early Christian period in Syria developed this type of asceticism, an ideal toward which at least two Cappadocian monks seem to have striven.

However, most of the monks in Cappadocia probably lived in communities known as *lavra*. At Göreme, a site in eastern Cappadocia, one large, elaborately designed and painted church (the Tokali Kilise) dominates a group of complexes that are seen to have been monastic because of their refectories. Groups of monks might have dwelled in the surrounding structures while coming together on a weekly basis for communal worship in the largest church of the region. The variety and complexity of the rooms associated with the large number of churches and chapels in Cappadocia reflect the flexibility of Eastern Orthodox monastic practices, especially in the rural countryside of the Byzantine Empire. The confluence of all these types of structures, which remain mostly undocumented, makes Cappadocia both fascinating and unique, providing an untapped resource for the understanding of Eastern Orthodox Byzantine monasticism.

VERONICA KALAS

*See also* Archaeology: Near East; Architecture: Eastern Christian Monasteries; Basil the Great, St.; Desert Mothers; Gregory of Nazianzus, St.; Gregory of Nyssa, St.; Hermits: Eastern Christian; Images: Christian Perspectives; Lavra; Macrina, St.; Origins: Eastern Christian; Orthodox Monasticism: Byzantine; Stylites; Theology, Eastern Christian

## Further Reading

Giovannini, Luciano, editor, *Arts of Cappadocia*, Geneva: Nagel, and London: Barrie and Jenkins, 1971

Jerphanion, Guillaume de, *Une nouvelle province de l'art byzantin: Les églises rupestres de Cappadoce*, 4 vols., Paris: Geuthner, 1925

Jolivet-Lévy, Catherine, *Les églises byzantines de Cappadoce: Le programme iconographique de l'abside et de ses abords*, Paris: CNRS, 1991

Kalas, Veronica, "The Rock-Cut Architecture of the Peristrema Valley: Form, Function and Context of Byzantine Settlements in Cappadocia," Ph.D. Diss., New York University, 1999

Kostov, Spiro, *Caves of God: Cappadocia and Its Churches*, Cambridge, Massachusetts, and London: Oxford University Press, 1989

Mathews, Thomas, and Annie-Christine Daskalakis-Mathews, "Islamic-Style Mansions in Byzantine Cappadocia and the Development of the Inverted T-Plan," *Journal of the Society of Architectural Historians* 56 (1997)

Restle, Marcell, *Byzantine Wall Painting in Asia Minor*, 3 vols., translated by I. Gibbons, Greenwich, Connecticut: New York Graphic Society, 1968; Shannon: Irish University Press, 1969

Rodley, Lyn, *Cave Monasteries of Byzantine Cappadocia*, Cambridge and New York: Cambridge University Press, 1985

Thierry, Nicole, *Haut Moyen-Age en Cappadoce: Les églises de la région de Çavusin*, Paris: Librairie Orientaliste Paul Geuthner, 1983

Thierry, Nicole, "Cappadocia," in *Dictionary of the History of Art*, London: Macmillan, and New York: Grove's Dictionaries, 1996

Thierry, Nicole, and Michel Thierry, *Nouvelles églises rupestres de Cappadoce: Région du Hasan Dagi*, Paris: Klincksieck, 1963

Wharton, Annabel Jane, *Art of Empire: Painting and Architecture of the Byzantine Periphery: A Comparative Study of Four Provinces*, University Park: Pennsylvania State University Press, 1988

# Capuchins

By the beginning of the 16th century, the Franciscan Order was divided between two distinct ideologies. The Conventuals accepted revenues from papal dispensation, and the Observants preferred living solely by alms. This division concerning the Franciscan ideal of poverty caused a separation within the Order.

However, the Observants, through various acts of legal legerdemain, began to subvert their own ideology and find ways to accept monetary gifts, often allowing a layperson to accept on their behalf or by undertaking chaplaincies that had fixed stipends. Of course these customs did not go unnoticed by many of the more zealous members of the Observants, who considered these actions a legalized betrayal of St. Francis's ideals and unworldly simplicity. Thus, just as the Observants had separated from the Conventuals, the Capuchins broke away from the Observants.

The leader of the Capuchin reform was Father Matteo di Bassi (1495–1552), a member of the Observant community in the Diocese of Fermo. According to legend the friar had been attending a funeral and was returning to his convent when he met a beggar on the road. Father Matteo gave the beggar some of his own clothing. Shortly afterward the friar was in prayer when he heard a voice tell him three times to "observe the Rule to the letter." On hearing this Father Matteo arose; found an old habit with a long, pointed hood, or *cappa* (thus the name Capuchin); and set out at once for Rome. In 1525 Father Matteo received permission from Clement VII (1523–1534) to wear the Capuchin habit and live in the strictest poverty. Thus, the Capuchin reform began.

Although it was not Father Matteo's intention to initiate a new order of monasticism, his zeal and devotion quickly won him a set of followers. Two other friars, Louis of Fossombrone and his brother Raphael, sought to join Father Matteo and were quickly denied permission by their superiors. The two friars called on Clement VII, and on 3 July 1528, through the declaration of the bull *Religionis zelus*, the Capuchin Order was granted independence from the Observants.

The new Order quickly grew in size, owing partly to the fervor of its preaching and also to the large exodus of monastics from the Observants. Forming, like the Jesuits, during the Counter-Reformation, the Capuchins quickly became important as defenders of the Church. However, the Capuchins suffered a great blow to their influence when in 1541 their vicar-general, Bernardino of Siena, also known as Ochino (1487–1564), apostatized and joined the Lutheran Reformers. The scandal caused by his defection gave ammunition to those within the Church who opposed the Capuchins. It was only through the efforts of Bernardino of Asti, who pleaded their case at the Council of Trent (1545–1563), that the Order was saved from extinction by the Roman Court. Yet the Capuchin Order survived, and soon its numbers continued to expand rapidly, and with those numbers came a broadening influence, so much so that on 15 October 1608, Pope Paul V (1605–1621) decreed the Capuchins to be the spiritual descendants of St. Francis and no longer merely an offshoot of the Franciscan Order.

Throughout the 16th and 17th centuries, the Capuchins, along with the Jesuits, remained the most effective and important of the Church's preachers and missionaries. Their preaching was simple and straightforward, and the Capuchins were also renowned for working in the service of the sick, often following a pestilence to aid its victims. By the mid–17th century, the Capuchins had chapters all over the world: Morocco, Egypt, Cyprus, Canada, Ethiopia, and Brazil were just a few of the places where their influence had reached.

As the Capuchin influence continued to expand, the friars themselves gained in prominence with both secular and religious authorities. Often Capuchin friars were used as envoys and ambassadors for important missions. One such friar was St. Lawrence of Brindisi (1559–1619), who was sent as ambassador by the Holy Roman Emperor Rudolf II (1576–1612) to solicit an alliance with Spain and the Catholic League of Germany. The ensuing military victories in the Thirty Years' War were credited to St. Lawrence's work. Another Capuchin statesman was François Leclerc de Tremblay (1577–1638), better known as Père Joseph, who, as an adviser and political agent of Cardinal Richelieu in the 1620s, was dubbed "éminence grise."

As the 18th century dawned, the Capuchins became prime targets for the mounting criticism that was being leveled against the Church. Widely lampooned in both book and song, the Order nonetheless devotedly continued its missionary work. By this time Capuchin influence had spread worldwide, and having served for almost two centuries in the United States, the Capuchins were formally established there in 1857.

Today the Capuchin Order remains one of the largest and most influential. Almost 20 of their number have been canonized or beatified. At present about 12,000 Capuchins live and work in 76 countries, with a little over one-third of that number in Third World nations. The Order is characterized by monastics such as Padre Pio (1887–1968), the mystic and stigmatist who for 50 years bore the marks of Christ's wounds in his friary of San Giovanni Rotondo near Foggia, Italy. Many miracles are attributed to the wildly popular Padre Pio, and recently Pope John Paul II beatified the Capuchin friar.

Today the Capuchin Order may well be most widely known for having inspired the name for *cappuccino*, the popular form of coffee (so named because the color of the drink matched the color of their robes), but the Capuchins are certainly regarded as an Order rich in colorful historical figures and one integral to missionary endeavor. In a formal address of 5 July 1982, Pope John Paul II praised the Capuchins for pursuing a "truly brotherly life based on simplicity and evangelical charity, open to the meaning of the universal brotherhood of all people and indeed of all creatures . . . a most eloquent witness . . . to a society such as ours which is so strongly marked by inequality and by a spirit of wanting to prevail over others."

MICHAEL G. CORNELIUS

*See also* Francis of Assisi, St.; Franciscans: General or Male; Missionaries: Christian; Poland; Reformation

**Further Reading**

Bonilla, Víctor Daniel, *Servants of God or Masters of Men? The Story of a Capuchin Mission in Amazonia* (Pelican Latin American Library), translated by Rosemary Sheed, Harmondsworth, Middlesex: Penguin, 1972

*The Capuchin Reform: Essays in Commemoration of Its 450th Anniversary, 1528–1978* (Analecta ordinis Fratrum Minorum Capuccinorum, volume 94, number 5), Pittsburgh, Pennsylvania: North American Capuchin Conference, 1983

Cuthbert, Father, *The Capuchins: A Contribution to the History of the Counter-Reformation*, 2 vols., London: Sheed and Ward, 1928; New York: Longmans, Green, 1929

D'Alatri, Mariano, and Ignatius McCormick, editors, *The Capuchin Way: Lives of Capuchins*, Pittsburgh, Pennsylvania: North American Capuchin Conference, 1985

Messmer, Sebastian Gebhard, *The Establishment of the Capuchin Order in the United States*, New York: U.S. Catholic Historical Society, 1906

Ruffin, Bernard C., *Padre Pio: The True Story*, Huntington, Indiana: Our Sunday Visitor, 1982; revised edition, 1991

Third Order Secular of St. Francis, Capuchin Province of St. Mary, New York, New York, *The Third Order of St. Francis: Official Guide*, Yonkers, New York: Capuchin Tertiary Province of St. Mary, 1964

# Carmelites: Female

The original Carmelites were a lay community of male hermits who gathered in the opening years of the 13th century on the slopes of Mount Carmel at the southern perimeter of the crusader state. Through the first half of that century, as they migrated to Europe, their status evolved to be mendicant friars alongside the Dominican and Franciscan friars. However, unlike the Dominicans and Franciscans, they had no female monasteries associated with them.

Although initially no nuns followed the Carmelite rule, the Carmelites, at least in certain places, associated women members to the order as *pinzochere* (also called *conversae*, *oblatae*, or *mantellate*) lay sisters, who were under obedience to the prior of the local friars' community, took solemn vows, and wore the Carmelite habit while living in their own homes. In 1298 Boniface VIII (1294–1303) imposed the enclosure on all women in solemn vows, but this canon was not accepted by many nuns, much less by the *pinzochere* associated to the various mendicant orders.

When Nicholas of Cusa (1401–1464), on an apostolic visitation to the Netherlands in 1451, ordered women living in beguinages to adopt an approved rule, the beguines of "ten Elsen," who were under the pastoral care of Carmelite friars, applied to Prior General John Soreth for admission to the Carmelite rule. Their petition was accepted on 10 May 1452, and they became the first community of nuns affiliated to the Carmelite order. In the autumn of that year, a second community in Florence was admitted to the order. The bull of Nicholas V (1447–1455), *Cum Nulla*, gave the prior general and provincials of the order the same rights as their Dominican and Augustinian peers to admit nuns to the order. In the subsequent decades many houses of nuns were established in Italy, France, Germany, the Netherlands, and Spain. Frances d'Amboise (1427–1485), wife of Duke Peter of Brittany, established the monastery of Bondon, herself becoming a Carmelite after the death of her husband. She played a very influential role in the spread of Carmelite nuns in France.

The observance in the medieval Carmels was very uneven. Although not known for scandal, the life was often lax. Many monasteries did not observe enclosure, and nuns often lived off private incomes. Many obtained exemptions from the choir and refectory and even license to live outside the convent in the homes of family or wealthy benefactors.

The Monastery of the Incarnation at Avila was typical of this lax observance. Although the Spanish Church had been re-characterized by the small size of the community, its poverty, and its strict enclosure.

Teresa's reform initially met with the support of the Carmelite order, but as the reform spread, and especially as friars joined the reform (drawing both vocations and revenue away from the unreformed Carmelites), tensions began to build. In an effort to stem the reform, Teresa was ordered to confine herself to one monastery and found no new ones. However, her reform was too vibrant to be contained, and the Discalced Carmelites grew rapidly. After the death of St. John of the Cross (1542–1591), the Holy See juridically divided the Carmelites into two separate orders. The Incarnation of Avila remained with the Ancient Observance until the 20th century, as did most of the monasteries founded before St. Teresa. The communities that Teresa founded remained in the Discalced Carmelites.

In 1604 two of the leading disciples of St. Teresa, Anne of St. Bartholomew and Anne of Jesus, were invited by Cardinal Bérulle (1575–1629) to make a foundation in Paris. The cardinal, one of the leaders of the vibrant renewal of spirituality in France in the late 16th and early 17th centuries, used the Spanish nuns to establish the reformed Carmel, and when he was able to provide leadership from among his own disciples, notably Madame Acarie, now Marie of the Incarnation, the Spanish nuns moved on. Anne of Jesus went on to Flanders in the Spanish Netherlands, where she established the Carmel of Brussels. Anne of St. Bartholomew went to Antwerp as first prioress in 1612. Anne of the Ascension Worsley, an English recusant who had helped establish Antwerp, founded the first Carmel for English Catholics at Hopland-Antwerp. Another English-speaking Carmel was founded at Hoogstraeten in 1678. These Carmels eventually drew candidates from Catholic Maryland, and Hoogstraeten sent a foundation to Port Tobacco, Maryland, in 1790. In 1831 the community relocated to Baltimore, to which most Carmels in the United States can trace their foundations. About 13,000 Discalced Carmelite nuns reside in more than 900 monasteries worldwide. The Ancient Observance has about 900 nuns in 65 monasteries.

In the 19th and 20th centuries, several dozen apostolic communities of women have chosen to follow the Carmelite rule as active religious. Carmelite sisters engage in educational work, social work, nursing, pastoral ministry, and other services while following the Carmelite way of life.

Carmelite women have attained a particular prominence in mystical theology. Teresa of Avila, the 19th-century Thérèse of Lisieux (1873–1897), and 20th-century Edith Stein (1891–1942) are widely read, as are several other Carmelite women.

Since the Second Vatican Council, Carmelite women have dramatically diversified in the details of their lifestyle. Issues regarding the traditional habit, the particulars of enclosure, education, the nature of their service to the Church, solitude, relationship to external authority, the nature of the fast and abstinence, and other questions have revealed a wide spectrum of opinion on how the Carmelite heritage is to be lived out by women in the contemporary Church. From 1990 to 1991 monasteries of Discalced Carmelite nuns were given the choice

Discalced Carmelite nun at work in Little Rock, Arkansas.
Photo courtesy of Jim Young

formed by Ferdinand (1479–1516) and Isabella, and although the Carmelite friars of Castile were fairly observant, this monastery had successfully avoided dealing with its poor morale and tepid spirit. Founded as a *beateria*, the women of the Incarnation had become nuns only earlier, in 1513, and had never accepted the enclosure. Many nuns had been exempted from choir, refectory, and other common exercises. The community was huge, numbering over 100 nuns, and the economic conditions were uneven, as some nuns had servants and lived in spacious apartments while poorer nuns shared a common dormitory and ate from the inadequately provided common table. The nuns depended on frequent visits to and from benefactors. Teresa de Cepeda e Ahumada (1515–1582), a nun of this monastery, had undergone a personal conversion in 1554. She desired a more contemplative life and began to discuss the prospects of a new and more observant community with several friends. In 1562 Teresa was able to surreptitiously begin the new community, San José, in Avila. Following the example of Observant movements in other orders, Teresa called her reform "discalced," or barefoot, and she adopted the name Teresa of Jesus. Her reform was

of two distinct sets of constitutions, but even within each of these sets, the details of observance varies considerably. Far from being problematic, this flexibility is seen as an asset. The simplicity of the primitive Carmelite legislation has always left Carmel open to adapting the charism of the order to the particulars of time and place.

PATRICK THOMAS MCMAHON, O.CARM.

*See also* Beguines; John of the Cross, St.; Spain: History; Teresa of Avila, St.; Thérèse of Lisieux, St.

## Further Reading

Currier, Charles Warren, *Carmel in America: A Centennial History of the Discalced Carmelites in the United States*, Baltimore, Maryland: Murphy, 1890; reprint, Darien, Illinois: Carmelite Press, 1989

Discalced Carmelites Nuns of the Association of Mary, Queen of Carmel, *Carmel in the United States of America, 1790–1990*, Eugene, Oregon: Queen's Press, 1990

Saggi, Ludovico, "Originale bulla 'Cum Nulla' qua Nicolaus Papa V canonice instituit II et III Ordines Carmelitarum," *Analecta Ordinis Carmelitarum* 17 (1952)

Smet, Joachim, *Cloistered Carmel: A Brief History of the Carmelite Nuns*, Rome: Institutum Carmelitanum, 1986

Steggink, Otger, *La Reforma del Carmelo español: La vísita canónica del general Rubeo y su encuentro con Santa Teresa, 1566–1567*, Rome: Institutum Carmelitanum, 1965

# Carmelites: General or Male

The Carmelite Order had its origins in a group of penitent hermits around 1200 at the wadi 'ain es-Shiah on Mount Carmel, about three miles south of Haifa, Israel. The Order's first extant document is the formula of life given to the Carmelites between 1206 and 1214 by Albert, patriarch of Jerusalem. The primary focus of this formula was on a simple life of solitude and prayer in cells around a chapel dedicated to Mary. This formula of life said nothing of pastoral ministry. Anonymity marked the origins of the Carmelite Order, as its founder is not known, nor are the names of its original members, except a "B." as prior in a copy of the formula of life. This initial letter was later expanded to "Brocard."

Around 1238 Carmelites began to migrate to Cyprus, Sicily, England, and southern France. By 1291 the Carmelites had been completely expelled from the Holy Land. In mid-13th-century Europe the Carmelites found the mendicant orders of the Franciscans and the Dominicans flourishing. Consequently the Carmelites were unable to sustain their eremitic identity. By 1247 their formula of life, with some slight changes, became a Rule with increased cenobitic elements and with the option to make settlements not only in the wilderness but also in the growing cities of Europe. The Carmelites set out to make good on

their new mendicant identity by following the other friars into the cities. By 1300 the Carmelites in England were third in population among the four friar orders – the Franciscans and Dominicans ahead of them and the Austin Friars behind them. The Carmelites also followed the other mendicants into the universities and became a medieval student order. Known as White Friars because of the white cloak they adopted in 1287, the Carmelites became popular preachers and spiritual counselors. The Carmelite charism can probably best be characterized first by the notion of creative tension between solitude and community that has existed from the days of its formula of life and subsequently by the tension between solitude and ministerial community that began with the entry of the Carmelites into the mendicant ranks.

However, during the last half of the 13th century opposition arose to the new Carmelite identity as friars both within and outside the Order. In 1270 Nicholas, the Frenchman, prior general, composed an impassioned letter, "The Fiery Arrow," that lamented the presence of his brothers in the cities and urged on them greater fidelity to their eremitic origins. The Second Council of Lyons in 1274, after affirming the status of the Dominicans and the Franciscans, left the fate of the Carmelites and the Austin Friars for a later decision. That decision, in the affirmative, came in 1298 from Pope Boniface VIII (1294–1303). In 1326 the Carmelites received full mendicant privileges. Since then Carmelite men have never questioned their mendicant identity but have wrestled time and again with how their contemplative calling is best integrated into this identity.

The Carmelite literary tradition got under way in earnest in the second quarter of the 14th century. The lack of a known founder heavily influenced this literature, as gradually claims were made for Elijah as founder of the Order and for a special relationship of the Order with Mary. Later the brown scapular of Mary became the sign of affiliation with the Carmelite Order. The title of the Order became the Brothers of the Blessed Virgin Mary of Mount Carmel. A very significant collection of documents appeared as *The Ten Books on the Institution and Special Deeds of the Carmelite Religious*. Some of the texts of this collection claimed to date as far back as John XLIV, bishop of Jerusalem from 387 to 417. However, modern scholarship has shown these documents to be the work of the Catalonian provincial, Felip Ribot (d. 1391). The Ribot Collection did much to promote the role of Elijah as founder of the Order and, influenced by John Cassian's writings, also laid the groundwork for the later mystical orientation of the Order in the 16th century under Teresa of Avila (1515–1582) and John of the Cross (1542–1591).

Like other orders, the Carmelites undertook various reforms from the 14th century into the 16th century. The best known of the medieval Carmelite reformers was Blessed John Soreth, prior general from 1451 to 1471, under whose leadership the second order of nuns came into existence. In the 16th century Priors General Nicholas Audet and John Rubeo fostered reform, but it took Teresa of Avila and her collaborator, John of the Cross, to

Antonio Raggi after Bernini, Statue of Virgin and Child, Transept of the Discalced Carmelite Church of Saint-Joseph-des-Carmes, Paris, 17th century.
Photo courtesy of the Editor

restore effectively the Order's early emphasis on solitude along with a renewed mystical vision. In 1593, after the deaths of Teresa and John, the Discalced Carmelites became a separate order with particular strength in Spain and Italy. The Touraine reform, begun in 17th-century France, espoused a return to contemplative solitude on behalf of the original branch of the Order, now known as the Ancient Observance, whose initials are "O.Carm."; the Discalced Carmelites have the initials "O.C.D."

John of the Cross, saint and Doctor of the Church, is the most widely known male Carmelite saint. At one time, St. Simon Stock, purported scapular visionary during the 13th century, was widely known, but he is now considered mainly a legendary personage. Saint Raphael Kalinowski (d. 1907) did much to restore the Discalced Carmelite Order in Poland, and Blessed Titus Brandsma, O.Carm., who opposed Nazism in the Netherlands, died at Dachau in 1942.

The Ancient Observance and the Discalced Carmelite branches of the Order underwent the vicissitudes of the anticlericalism of the 19th century with consequent declining numbers and influence. Both branches have recovered remarkably and spread throughout the world during the 20th century. Since the Second Vatican Council, the two branches, both with headquarters in Rome, collaborate on various enterprises and have vigorously pursued the study of their historical and spiritual traditions with the aim of renewing Carmelite life and of making a Carmelite contribution to the contemporary renewal in Christian spirituality. Various groups of second and third orders are affiliated to the two male branches of the Carmelite Order.

KEITH J. EGAN

*See also* Augustinian Friars/Hermits; Crusades; Dominicans; Franciscans; Israel/Palestine; Jerusalem, Israel; John of the Cross, St.; Liturgy: Western Christian; Spain: History; Teresa of Avila, St.

## Further Reading

Cicconetti, Carlo, *La Regola del Carmelo: Origine, natura, significato*, Rome: Institutum Carmelitanum, 1973
Fitzgerald-Lombard, Patrick, editor, *Carmel in Britain: Essays on the Medieval English Carmelite Province*, 2 vols., Rome and Aylesford (Westmont), Illinois: Institutum Carmelitanum, 1992
Mulhall, Michael, editor, *Albert's Way: The First North American Congress on the Carmelite Rule*, Rome: Institutum

Carmelitanum, and Barrington, Illinois: Province of the Most Pure Heart of Mary, 1989

Rohrbach, Peter-Thomas, *Journey to Carith: The Story of the Carmelite Order*, Garden City, New York: Doubleday, 1966

Saggi, Ludovico, compiler, *Santi del Carmelo*, Rome: Institutum Carmelitanum, 1972 (see especially Saggi's "Agiografia Carmelitana"; this essay is missing in the following translation of this book: *Saints of Carmel*, translated by Gabriel Pausbauck, Rome and Aylesford (Westmont), Illinois: Institutum Carmelitanum, 1972)

Smet, Joachim, *The Carmelites: A History of the Brothers of Our Lady of Mount Carmel*, 4 vols., Darien, Illinois: Carmelite Spiritual Center, 1976–1985; revised edition of volume 1, 1988

Staring, Adrianus, editor, *Medieval Carmelite Heritage: Early Reflections on the Nature of the Order*, Rome: Institutum Carmelitanum, 1989

# Carthusians

Radical monastic groups sprang up throughout Europe during the turbulent 11th century. Named after their first foundations, Carthusians, Vallombrosans, Camaldolese, and Cistercians all shared a desire to live in solitude and poverty. They retreated into the forests and mountains of southern France and northern Italy, referred to as "deserts," and defended their withdrawal as a restoration of early Egyptian monasticism. Ultimately, this "new monasticism" described itself as an "imitation" of Christ, whom the monks envisioned as a poor and humble figure most closely united with his Father during desert retreats and in solitary prayer. The Carthusians became the most austere of these "new monks."

These groups appealed broadly to both clerics and laymen. Usually well born, such men often abandoned comfortable lives in a newly prosperous European economy to join these remote rural experiments. One of these was Bruno of Cologne (c. 1032–1101), a cleric who had risen in academic life to serve for 20 years as head of the cathedral schools at Reims. However, at age 52 he resigned this post and later explained his decision in language that evoked the conversion of St. Augustine from Book VIII of the *Confessions*: "[W]e vowed to leave the fleeting things of the world and lay hold of eternal things, and to receive the monastic habit." Bruno was joined by four clerics and two laymen with whom he retreated to the Benedictine abbey of Molesme, where he learned the monastic life from Robert of Molesme (c. 1027–1111), who would later found the reformed Benedictine Order of Cistercians. After three years, expressing a desire for greater solitude and austerity, Bruno and his companions traveled 300 miles farther south to Grenoble. The bishop made over to them a high and remote valley in the Chartreuse massif about 30 miles from the town. Here they built log cabins around a chapel, later naming the settlement "La Grande Chartreuse."

The first Carthusians tempered their solitary existence by retaining many components of communal cloistered life. They wore the traditional monastic tunic under a cowl and a scapular joined at each side by a distinctively wide band of cloth. However, the Carthusian habit like those of most reformed groups, was white rather than the traditional monastic black, an innovation that gave rise to rancor between the "old" and the "new" monks. The early Carthusians also adopted the conventional form of the monastic liturgy but radically altered its content. Basing their rite on the usages of nearby towns, especially Grenoble, they composed a new office, allowing only scriptural or patristic material. Hymns were not permitted, and they rejected the lengthy additional prayers and rituals that had accumulated in traditional monastic liturgies.

More innovative was their decision to create a "community of solitaries." Although the Carthusians retained conventional monastic structures, such as a chapel, chapter house, and refectory, they did not live in traditional dormitories; instead, each monk had his own private dwelling, or "cell." These cells defined the architecture of a Carthusian monastery (known in England as a charterhouse). They surrounded a common cloister and church and were constructed on two stories. On the first floor a woodshed led into a small workroom, and above that a small oratory contained a choir stall and kneeler. Beyond this was a library and a bedroom, all overlooking a small garden. Owing perhaps to the expense of this architectural elaboration and to a conviction that small numbers were essential to maintaining fervor, the membership in each monastery was limited to 12 monks plus a superior (modestly called a prior rather than an abbot), thus monasticizing the model of 12 apostles headed by Christ.

Long periods of solitude in the cell, always celebrated as the distinctive core of Carthusian monastic life, were balanced by a few hours of daily communal activity. The monks emerged at midnight to participate in the liturgical offices of matins; they attended a community mass in the morning (a later addition) and chanted vespers late in the afternoon. On Sundays and major feasts, the monks celebrated together the entire office as well as a conventual mass and ate together in the refectory. On these days an hour's walk was prescribed during which the monks were free to speak to one another of "useful matters." A longer outing of about three hours, called a *spatiamentum*, occurred every week, and once a year an expedition lasting an entire day was conducted through the monastery properties.

Meat was forbidden even to the sick, and on three days of the week only bread and water were taken, a fast later mitigated to Fridays only. During much of the year, the monks took a single meal alone in their cells after noon. The professed monks had some flexibility in arranging their hours in the cells within the traditional threefold framework of monastic life set down in St. Benedict's Rule for Monks: liturgical prayer, spiritual reading, and manual labor. Alone in the cell each monk chanted with full choir ritual those parts of the Divine Office that were not celebrated in common. Spiritual reading and intellectual activity had more prominence in Carthusian life than in the often anti-

Reconstructed cell, Mount Grace Priory (Carthusian), North Yorkshire, England, 15th century.
Photo courtesy of Chris Schabel

intellectual atmosphere of other reformed orders. Bruno, the order's founder, had a strong academic background, and later Carthusian tradition insisted on constant mental activity in the cells, often referred to as *otium negotiosum* (busy leisure or rest in activity). From the beginning Carthusian houses had extensive libraries and in later centuries often possessed the richest collections in their region. Indeed, the third element in traditional monastic life, manual labor, usually involved the Carthusians in some aspect of book production. Guigo I, the fifth prior of La Grande Chartreuse, wrote in the 1120s that books should be "made with the utmost care, that we might preach the Word of God by the work of our hand since we cannot do so with our mouths." Carthusian manuscripts became a standard of excellence, and this "labor" complemented the meditation over sacred texts that formed a core element of Carthusian spirituality.

The Carthusian focus on book production was made possible through easy access to parchment. Sheep raising was the only practical form of agriculture in the high and desolate places favored by the Carthusians. The tending of flocks and all other heavy work was the responsibility of lay brothers, or *conversi*, a new institution that formed an essential part of Carthusian houses. Like their fellow reformers, the Cistercians, the Carthu-

sians believed that the use of serfs and hired servants for agricultural work had contributed to monastic worldliness. Instead, the Carthusians, like the Cistercians and Camaldolese, invited illiterate laymen to join the monastery. Performing the usual tasks of medieval peasants while living in separate dormitories and negotiating all contacts with "the world," they wore a simple brown habit and recited a simple office of *paternosters* (Our Fathers) wherever they were working. On Sundays and major feast days, they joined the monks for Mass and a common meal. The number of *conversi* was limited to 16 to discourage the expansion of the monastery's possessions. A senior monk directed their work and oversaw their spiritual lives, so although the *conversi* remained peasants, they were full members of a prestigious social and spiritual institution. The careful attention given to their integration into the community spared the Carthusians from unrest among the *conversi*, a problem that plagued the Cistercians and other orders.

The fundamental shape of Carthusian life likely was determined during its first decades, although no formal constitution was drawn up until a half century later. In 1127 the *Constitutiones Cartusiae* (Customs of Chartreuse) were drawn up by Guigo I (prior from 1109 to 1136). Elegantly written, the

Large cloister, charterhouse, Pavia, Italy, 15th century.
Photo courtesy of the Editor

*Constitutiones* provided both a spiritual guide to Carthusian life and a summary of its customs. The Carthusians formed themselves into a religious order in 1142: nine houses of hermits agreed to observe the religious life as it was practiced at La Grande Chartreuse following the *Constitutiones* of Guigo under the authority of the prior of La Grande Chartreuse, who served as general superior.

Many more persons admired the Carthusians for their austerity than could endure the life, so the order grew slowly. From 1060 to 1200 only 37 new houses were founded, but between 1300 and 1500 the order underwent an explosive expansion, opening 160 new charterhouses. The order reached its greatest extent in 1514 with 196 houses, including 12 monasteries for women. Women's houses, also called monasteries, followed the Carthusian rule exactly, except that more time for conversation was allowed and the nuns shared a daily common meal.

A new intellectual vitality entered the order during this late medieval expansion. The traditional copying of manuscripts expanded to include composing many original works of theology and spirituality. These writings received wide distribution as the Carthusians shifted their expertise in copying manuscripts to printing books in the late 15th century. This productivity resulted in part from the influx of more members, especially academics, but the popularity of these new spiritual writings might also have sparked the growth in membership.

The Carthusians developed two distinct but complementary spiritual literatures that treated their main spiritual concern: the union of the soul with God. The first approach, the "affective way," emphasized similarities between God and humanity. The soul reflected on the humanity of Christ (his redemptive suffer-

ing and death) and on the life of his mother Mary. These meditations were designed to produce a strong movement of the emotions or "affections": tears of repentance and expressions of love and commitment to Jesus and his mother Mary. The rosary, a development that was emblematic of this affective way, employed a circlet of beads divided into sections, each devoted to one of the "mysteries," or major events of the life of Christ and his mother. These formed the subjects of meditation while the *Ave Maria* was repeated over each of the beads. Rosary meditations were developed by the German Carthusian Dominic of Prussia (1382–1461) and were spread throughout Germany by traveling Carthusians. Adopted from them and popularized by Dominican preachers, the rosary was transformed into one of the most characteristic and enduring of all Catholic devotional practices. A rosary hung from the belt commonly forms part of the Carthusian habit even today.

The second approach, the "negative way" (*via negativa*), emphasized the transcendence or "otherness" of God. Union with God was attainable only through the suppression of all positive thought and images, subsequent to which his otherness might be encountered. Carthusian writers developed their distinctive approach to this popular technique of mystical union through the writings of the late antique Neoplatonist mystic, Dionysius the pseudo-Areopagite. One of the most prolific authors of the later Middle Ages, Denis the Carthusian (1402–1471), expounded this "way" in many of his 174 volumes. A classic English work in this genre, *The Cloud of Unknowing*, is thought by some to be of Carthusian authorship. The author of the *Cloud* teaches that the soul can encounter God only by means of a supernatural love that alone can pierce the "cloud of unknowing," in which all sense perceptions and ideas are left behind.

A famous and often repeated phrase praising the Carthusians was first uttered in 1257 by Pope Alexander IV (1254–1261): *nunquam reformata quia nunquam deformata* (the Carthusians have never been reformed since they were never corrupted). This might be true, but they did not escape the worldly rewards of their high reputation for holiness, especially in the later Middle Ages. Bishops and other wealthy patrons encouraged Carthusian monks to build elegant monasteries in the great cities of London, Paris, Cologne, and Pavia. Powerful benefactors, men and women alike, dined with the monks, furnished their houses sumptuously, and were buried in the monastic crypts. Many monasteries owned extensive properties far beyond their walls, contrary to the prescriptions of the *Constitutiones* of Guigo, and other abuses multiplied: the Coventry charterhouse operated a school in which a defrocked monk was allowed to teach, and the list of one Carthusian monk's possessions included over 100 items of clothing, books, and furnishings, several of finely crafted materials.

The Carthusians were jolted out of this comfortable existence by the 16th century Reformation. Some went over to Lutheranism, whereas many others wrote tracts against the Protestants. These emphasized internal reform over institutional innovations and condemned violence, as Carthusian writings had done ever since Guigo I denounced the Crusades in the 12th century.

Nonetheless, the Carthusians did not escape the upheavals of the Reformation. Forty-four houses were suppressed in Protestant areas, and at least 50 monks were executed. The prior and some members of the London charterhouse were publicly hanged, disemboweled, and burned at the order of King Henry VIII (1509–1547). In 1562 La Grande Chartreuse was destroyed by Protestant Huguenots and lay in ruins for decades.

After the Reformation the order never regained the splendor and influence that it had shown during the later Middle Ages, although it revived considerably in the early modern period, especially under Prior Innocent Le Masson (1675–1703). Subsequently, the order fell victim to the forces of radical change in the late 18th and 19th centuries. After a systematic dismantling by the forces of the French Revolution and Napoleon, only 6 of the 200 original Carthusian houses remained open, none of these in the order's French homeland.

A rethinking of Carthusian identity and mission followed the Second Vatican Council in the 1960s, leading to a reemphasis of its early institutions and spirituality. Claustration has become stricter, and even traditional monastic hospitality has been discouraged as inconsistent with the eremitical vocation. Limitations on reading and publishing have been reinforced, and a traditional Latin liturgy has been retained in several houses. Some concessions have been made to modern conditions: individual monks now have more freedom to arrange their recreational time outside the cell, and, more significant, the status of *conversi* has been altered. A monastic life combining manual labor with contemplation but without complex choir duties or priestly ordination has proved appealing to modern aspirants to monastic life. Such individuals are usually of more varied background and talents than their medieval predecessors. The order has responded by conferring on the *conversi* the status and title of monk, previously limited to the choir priests. Moreover, every year each lay brother is freed from his usual tasks for a week of sustained prayer and meditation. These occur in the lay brother's cell in the main monastery, which has replaced the dormitory of medieval *conversi*. The brothers join the ordained choir monks more often, especially for colloquies and *spatiamenta*.

The Carthusians remain a small order, but they are reviving in numbers after two difficult centuries. Currently, 25 houses of men exist in 11 countries, as do five monasteries for women. In addition, three new foundations exist for men in the Western Hemisphere, one each in Argentina, Brazil, and the United States (Vermont).

JOHN B. WICKSTROM

*See also* Agriculture, Western Christian; Asceticism: Christian Perspectives; Benedict of Nursia, St.; Cistercians; Devotions, Western Christian; Dionysius the Pseudo-Areopagite; France: History; Guigo I; Libraries: Western Christian; Liturgy: Western Christian; Monastics and the World, Medieval; Office, Daily; Orders (Religious), Origin of; Spirituality: Western Christian

**Further Reading**

Note: there is no scholarly overview of the Carthusians in any language.

*Carthusian Spirituality*: *The Writings of Hugh of Balma and Guigo de Ponte*, translated by Dennis Martin, New York: Paulist Press, 1997

DuBois, J., and uno certosino, "Certosini," in *Dizionario degli Istituti di Perfezione*, volume 2, edited by G. Pelliccia, Rome: Edizione Paoline, 1975

Guigo I, *Coutumes de Chartreuse*, edited with a French translation "par un Chartreux" of *Constitutiones Cartusiae*, Paris: Éditions du Cerf, 1984

Hogg, James, general editor, *Analecta Cartusiana* (many volumes)

Lockhart, Robin, *Halfway to Heaven: The Hidden Life of the Sublime Carthusian*, London: Thames Methuen, and New York: Vanguard Press, 1985

Martin, Dennis, *Fifteenth-Century Carthusian Reform: The World of Nicholas Kempf*, Leiden and New York: Brill, 1992

Ravier, André, *Saint Bruno, the Carthusian*, San Francisco: Ignatius Press, 1995

Thompson, E.M., *The Carthusian Order in England*, London and New York: Macmillan, 1930

William of Saint Thierry, *The Golden Epistle: A Letter to the Brothers at Mont Dieu*, Spenser, Massachusetts: Cistercian Publications, 1971

# Casel, Odo 1886–1948

German Benedictine priest and theologian

Born at Koblenz-Lützel in the Rhineland, Casel entered the Abbey of Maria Laach in 1905 and was ordained in 1911. The community's distinguished tradition of scholarship and theological study was strongly developed by Ildefons Herwegen, who was abbot from 1913 to 1946. Herwegen, himself the author of 30 books and major articles, made Maria Laach a major center of liturgical research. From 1921, when Mass was said universally in Latin, largely silently by the priest facing away from the people, it was celebrated daily in the crypt of the Abbey Church with lay participation and the priest facing the congregation, anticipating reforms in Catholic liturgy by 40 years. Casel devoted himself to the theology rather than to the history of liturgy. He obtained doctorates in theology from Rome in 1914 and in philosophy from Bonn in 1919. The essentials of his liturgical theology were laid down in his early work, reaching mature expression in his *Die Liturgie als Mysterienfeier* (1922; The Liturgy as Celebration of the Mystery). From 1922 he was chaplain to the Benedictine nuns at Herstelle. He died there on Easter Sunday 1948, having had a stroke while about to sing the Exultet in the Easter Vigil the previous day. The last words he uttered were "Lumen Christi," the Easter proclamation of the Light of Christ.

This farewell was most appropriate. Casel's major theological contribution was to establish the centrality of the Paschal Mystery to Christian worship. He recognized this from his profound patristic learning. He was also part of the movement in Catholic theology that had begun with Johann Adam Möhler (1796–

1838) in Germany and John Henry Newman (1801–1890) in England. They had recovered the idea that the Church is a spiritual and organic union in Christ rather than an authoritarian or legalistic institution. The liturgical movement developed the same idea, especially in monasteries of Solesmes and Beuron. Above all Casel was himself a monastic scholar who was steeped in the tradition and practices of monasticism. He became probably the most eminent and influential liturgical theologian of his day, writing over 110 books, articles, and reviews and inspiring a circle of brilliant disciples.

Casel saw Christ as the revelation of the mystery of God and each act of Christ as a mystery, manifesting the glory of God in incarnation, suffering, and resurrection. These saving acts of Christ are made present and effective in the Church and its liturgy. The liturgy is not the commemoration or repetition of the bare historical events of Christ's life or simply a means of gaining the graces these brought. Rather, it is the means of participating in the mystery that those events themselves made present. Here Casel was offering a fresh account of the relationship of the Church and its worship with the life of Christ, a problem that lay at the heart of the Reformation. Some critics complained of a lack of philosophical rigor in his expression of his ideas, and very few scholars accepted his comparisons of pagan mystery cults with Christian worship. Nevertheless his ideas proved immensely influential in the development of Catholic theology and official teaching. Through him the Eucharist and the whole liturgy of the Church came to be recognized as the efficacious memorial of the mystery of Christ's death and resurrection, offered by the whole corporate body of worshipers through the power of the Holy Spirit. Thus, a Benedictine theology of liturgy – one close to Eastern Christian concepts – has come to permeate the entire Catholic Church.

BERNARD GREEN, O.S.B.

*See also* Beuron, Germany; Germany: History; Liturgical Movement 1830–1980; Liturgy: Western Christian; Maria Laach, Germany; Solesmes, France; Theology, Western Christian: Benedictine

## Biography
Born in Koblenz, Casel entered the Benedictine Abbey of Maria Laach in 1905, became a priest there in 1911, and went on to earn doctorates in theology (Rome, 1914) and philosophy (Bonn, 1919). From 1921 to 1941 he edited the *Jahrbuch für Liturgiewissenschaft*. From 1922 he served as chaplain to the Benedictine nuns at Herstelle, and it was in their chapel that he suffered a stroke at the Easter Vigil in 1948. Casel's theology of the mass as re-enactment of a mystery cult has exercised seminal influence on liturgical reform.

## Major Works
*Die Liturgie als Mysterienfeier* (The Liturgy as Celebration of the Mystery), 1922
*Das christliche Kultmysterium*, 1932; 3rd edition, 1948; translated as *The Mystery of Christian Worship*, edited by B. Neunheuser, 1962; as *The Mystery of Christian Worship, and Other Writings*, 1962

## Further Reading
Gozier, Andre, *Dom Casel*, Paris: Fleurus, 1968
Schilson, Arno, *Theologie als Sakramententheologie: Die Mysterientheologie Odo Casels*, Mainz: Matthias Grünewald, 1982

# Cassian, John c. 360–after 435
Transmitter of Egyptian monastic lore to the West

John Cassian, born probably in Dacia (roughly corresponding to present-day Romania), was attracted to Christian monasticism early in his life. Sometime – perhaps well more than a decade – before 400 he left his native land and traveled with his friend Germanus to Palestine, where they joined a monastery in Bethlehem. Cassian would very likely not have left the profound mark on Christian monasticism that he did had he and Germanus not felt moved to journey twice from Palestine to Egypt to see the monks who populated the desert there.

The results of Cassian's exposure to Egyptian monasticism, which must have occurred no later than 400, are evident in his two great monastic works: *The Institutes of the Cenobia and the Remedies for the Eight Principal Vices* (often referred to simply as *The Institutes*) and *The Conferences*, both composed in Latin. *The Institutes* were written sometime between 419 and 426 and *The Conferences* between 426 and 429, many years after their author had left Egypt and while he was living in Marseilles, in southern France, where he had founded two monasteries and where he eventually died.

Both *The Institutes* and *The Conferences* purport to summarize the monastic customs and teachings with which Cassian had become acquainted during his stay in Egypt. They represent an attempt to translate those customs and teachings into terms assimilable by the monks of southern France at that time who might have been familiar with the form of monasticism that had been promoted by Martin of Tours. Cassian appears to have disagreed with several aspects of this form.

*The Institutes*, by far the shorter of the two works, consists of 12 books. The first four deal with monastic vesture, the hours of prayer in a monastery, and the virtues (mainly humility and obedience), which are especially characteristic of the Christian monastic life. Each of the remaining eight books is devoted to one of the eight principal vices, or capital sins: gluttony, fornication, avarice, anger, sadness, acedia, vainglory, and pride.

*The Conferences* present a less systematic appearance at first than *The Institutes*. It is divided into what are claimed to be 24 interviews, or conferences, with 15 different Egyptian monks, touching on such varied themes as the vices, constant prayer, chastity, the role of divine grace and human free will, and promise making and lying. However, what appears to be a lack of system in the treatment of these matters is deceptive. In fact, the entire work is founded on a careful theological plan that is laid out in the first two conferences and that can be summed up as follows. The ultimate end (*telos, finis*) of the monk is the kingdom of God, but his more immediate, this-worldly end (*scopos*, *destinatio*) is purity of heart. To attain purity of heart, a monk must pursue the good at the expense of not only the bad but also the less good, or the indifferent, and to be able to determine what is truly good at any given moment, he must possess discretion, or prudence. Such discretion cannot be had without the assistance of a spiritual guide, an "elder" in the monastic life, who is one's superior at least in wisdom, if not in age. To this elder, one must disclose oneself completely and not conceal from him even one's most intimate thoughts; that requires humility. All this can be abbreviated by saying that humility makes discretion possible, the practice of discretion leads to purity of heart, and purity of heart is an anticipation of the possession of the kingdom of God.

In fact, of these four moments in the monastic or spiritual life, *The Conferences* focus mainly on discretion and purity of heart. They set their sights on the acquisition of purity of heart and offer an ongoing model of discretion in the 24 interviews that Cassian and Germanus have with the 15 monks whom they have approached, for, in effect, these monks perform the role of elders for the two young interlocutors. More than that, most of the 24 conferences promote the exercise of discretion by offering time-tried solutions to typical monastic problems.

The most famous of the 24 conferences is the 13th, titled "On God's Protection," in which Cassian takes issue with his contemporary Augustine of Hippo's theology of divine grace. Whereas Augustine (whose name is never mentioned in the 13th conference) held that a human being could not initiate or carry out any good work whatsoever without divine assistance, or grace, Cassian contended that, at the very least, some good works could be begun on a person's own initiative, without the intervention of God's help, although they could not be brought to completion without it. Both authors cite the Scriptures abundantly in support of their respective positions. The matter of divine grace vis-à-vis human initiative, or free will, was an especially important one in monastic circles, inasmuch as an overemphasis on grace to the detriment of human initiative – which seemed to many to characterize Augustine's theology – cast doubt on the whole monastic project. For if everything depended on God's initiative, or grace, why opt at all for the asceticism and general harshness of the monastic regimen, as God's grace could save anyone regardless of ascetical practices?

Cassian's dispute with Augustine, which unfortunately caused him to be looked on with suspicion by many Western Christians, who revered the bishop of Hippo, alerts us to the fact that Cassian did not write in a vacuum but was subject to the influence of others. Among those who influenced him more positively were, first, Evagrius Ponticus (346–399) but also Basil of Caesarea (c. 330–379), Jerome (c. 345–420), and the Fathers of the Desert, to say nothing of the Old and New Testaments and Stoicism and Neoplatonism.

The influence that Cassian himself exerted on the monasticism of subsequent generations, including that of the present day, is incalculable. Because he wrote in Latin, his works were more immediately accessible to Western, or Latin, monasticism, and they successfully transmitted Eastern and specifically Egyptian ideas, sifted through and modified by Cassian, to the West. Thanks especially to Cassian, who effectively rewrote much of the controversial Evagruis Ponticus, Evagrius' thought was made palatable and was popularized under Cassian's name. Benedict of Nursia (c. 480–c. 550) prescribed the reading of both *The Institutes* and *The Conferences* for his monks in his famous Rule in the sixth century, and Cassian was cited approvingly by many of the greatest figures of the Middle Ages, including Thomas Aquinas (c. 1225–1274). From about the middle of the 20th century, Cassian has been the object of renewed interest on the part of scholars who consistently view him with sympathy, even in his dispute with Augustine on grace. In addition, he continues to be read sedulously by monks and nuns not only in the Christian West but also in the Christian East, where his theology has always been held in esteem and his view of grace was never seen askance.

BONIFACE RAMSEY, O.P.

*See also* Augustinian Rule; Benedict of Nursia, St.; Chrysostom, John, St.; Egypt; Fasting: Western Christian; Hagiography: Christian Perspectives; Hermits: Western Christian; Humanism, Christian; Island Monasteries, Christian; Meditation: Christian Perspectives; Office, Daily; Origins; Regulations: Christian Perspectives; Spirituality: Eastern Christian; Spirituality: Western Christian

### Biography

Born in Dacia, John joined a monastery in Bethlehem and moved c. 385 to experience monasticism in Egypt. Having been influenced by Evagrius Ponticus, he was sent from Constantinople to Rome c. 404 by John Chrysostom. About 415 he established two monasteries near Marseille.

### Major Works

John Cassian: The Conferences, translated by Boniface Ramsey, 1997

John Cassian: The Institutes, translated by Boniface Ramsey, 2000

### Further Reading

Chadwick, Owen, *John Cassian: A Study in Primitive Monasticism*, Cambridge: Cambridge University Press, 1950; 2nd edition, as *John Cassian*, 1968

De Vogüé, Adalbert, "Understanding Cassian: A Survey of the Conferences," *Cistercian Studies Quarterly* 19 (1984)

Stewart, Columba, *Cassian the Monk*, New York: Oxford University Press, 1998

# Cassiodorus c. 490–580

Roman Christian monk and scholar

Flavius Magnus Aurelius Cassiodorus Senator was born on his family's estate at Scyllaceum (Squillace) in Bruttium. He grew up under the reign of Theodoric (493–526), who restored prosperity to Italy and governed a mixed society of Arian Goths and Catholic Romans with the Roman system of public administration. Cassiodorus was introduced to life at court by his father, who served Theodoric as praetorian prefect. The young man's talents were recognized by appointment to responsible positions: quaestor (507–512) and master of offices (523), succeeding his unfortunate relative Boethius (c. 480–c. 524). Cassiodorus' administrative ability and his success at promoting harmony between Gothic rulers and Roman subjects were also valued by Theodoric's successors, who made him prefect of Italy (533–536); Witigis honored him with the title of patrician. In 536 he attempted with Pope Agapetus I (535–536) to establish a theological school in Rome to rival the secular schools in the city, but the plan came to naught because of the pope's death and the astonishingly swift advance of Emperor Justinian's (527–565) army of reconquest, led by Belisarius, which entered Rome in December. The ensuing war against the Goths occasioned Cassiodorus' retirement from public life. Witigis surrendered Ravenna to Belisarius in 540 and was brought under arrest to Constantinople, but the war continued for two more decades, ravaging the cities and cultural institutions of Italy.

Toward the end of his career, Cassiodorus edited a collection of official documents, *Variae (epistolae)*, that spanned his 30 years in government. To it he appended *De anima*, a reflection on the soul, which marked the turning point in his life, not to philosophy as with Cicero and others, but to religion. For the next ten years, he worked on *Expositio psalmorum*, his commentary on the Psalms. This was his "conversion" piece, as the opening lines of the preface reveal: the burdens of office and the anxieties of secular affairs have been set aside to seek refreshment in Scripture.

After retiring, Cassiodorus spent some years in Constantinople and then, around 554, returned to the family estate, where he established two monasteries: one for hermits on Mount Castellum and one for cenobites, Vivarium, on Mount Moscius, where, around 562, he composed *Institutiones divinarum et saecularium literatum*, a detailed program of intellectual work for the monks. The preface tells of the plan he had once had to found a theological school in Rome, but now that teachers were no longer available, he was doing the next best thing by providing them with a library and a guide to its contents. Book I outlines a systematic, self-paced curriculum of theological formation for those who already had a secular education. The recommended readings indicate works for beginners and those for more advanced students (e.g., I 21.2). Book II offers a condensed treatment of the seven liberal arts for those who lacked schooling. To increase availability and dissemination of texts, Cassiodorus encouraged the translation of Greek works and the copying and correcting of manuscripts, especially for orthodoxy. At age 92, he composed *De orthographia* as a guide for the work of the scriptorium.

Cassiodorus promoted a view of the liberal arts that was becoming widely shared, namely, that the liberal arts had their origin in Scripture and, when studied in the context of Scripture, are reclaimed for the service of truth (I 27). Already in *Expositio* he had extolled the psalter as an inspired textbook of rhetoric and the liberal arts (e.g., Pref. 15; Ps. 150:6). In other words, what earlier generations of educated Christians had regarded as useful tools for understanding Scripture, Christians in the diminished circumstances of the early Middle Ages regarded as tools to be learned from Scripture. However, the aim of *Institutiones* was not only intellectual and academic. The entire program was designed for monks as a disciplined way of seeking Christian perfection, the attainment of which depends not on human effort but on God: learning alone does not make one holy, and the lack of it is no obstacle to grace (I 28).

Judging from *Institutiones*, Cassiodorus was probably no more than the monastery's lay patron. Two abbots are named. Monks were told to observe the rules of the fathers and the commands of their own superior (I 32.1). Cassian was recommended as a monastic guide (I 29.2). Beyond that, monks were to practice the corporal works of mercy, to instruct the monastery's peasants in Christian living, and not to tax them excessively (I 32.1–2). Those tested in community who aspired to something higher could withdraw to Mount Castellum (I 29.3). Monastic observance at Vivarium and at Benedict's Monte Cassino (c. 529) was probably similar, except for the monks' work. Benedict's rule (RB) enjoins manual work. His "school of the Lord's service" is figuratively a workshop where the art of Christian living is perfected (RB Prol. 45–50; 4.75–78). The difference between these two "schools" is caught in Benedict's and Cassiodorus' use of Jacob's ladder (Gen. 28:12) as an image of monastic progress. For Benedict the rungs of the ladder are the steps of humility, leading to perfect charity (RB 7). For Cassiodorus they are the commentaries of the fathers, which impart the meaning of Scripture and lead to contemplation of God (I Pref. 2).

Cassiodorus' *Institutiones* provides the most complete description of the type of Scripture-based education that was developing in the absence of secular schools. Even earlier a similar approach was being used at Lerins. Caesarius of Arles (c. 470–542), who was trained there, instructed candidates for orders in that way, and the Council of Toledo (527) ordered Spanish bishops to do the same. Isidore (c. 560–636), Bede (c. 673–735), and Alcuin (c. 740–804) would help develop the method further. Vivarium did not survive beyond the seventh century, but Cassiodorus' influence did in the form of textbooks, especially his *Expositio psalmorum* and *Institutiones* and particularly Book II, which served libraries as an acquisition guide. Vivarium's translation of Josephus' *Antiquities* and the translation and digest of three Greek histories of the early Church also lived on.

PHILIP TIMKO, O.S.B.

*See also* Benedict of Nursia, St.; Caesarius of Arles, St.; Cassian, John; Education of Christian Monastics; Humanism, Christian; Libraries: Western Christian; Manuscript Production: Christian; Monte Cassino, Italy; Origins: Western Christian; Patrons, Christian: Lay; Scholars, Benedictine

## Biography

A member of a senatorial family, Cassiodorus served the Ostrogothic kingdom in Ravenna until its collapse. During the 540s he joined Western exiles in Constantinople, only to return to Italy in 554. He established at his estate at Squillace, south of Naples, a monastic community known as Vivarium. Its library included a scriptorium for translating Greek texts into Latin. Although the library had been dispersed by the seventh century, its works were widely copied for centuries.

## Major Works

*De anima*

*Expositio psalmorum*; as *Cassiodorus, Explanation of the Psalms*, translated and annotated by P.G. Walsh, 1990–1991

*Historia ecclesiastica tripartita*

*Historia gothorum*

*Institutiones divinarum et saecularium literatum*; as *An Introduction to Divine and Human Readings*, edited and translated by Leslie Webber Jones, 1946

*Variae*

## Further Reading

Markus, Robert A., *The End of Ancient Christianity*, Cambridge and New York: Cambridge University Press, 1990

O'Donnell, James J., *Cassiodorus*, Berkeley: University of California Press, 1979

# Cathars

Cathars were groups of heretical Christians found in many parts of Europe during the 12th and 13th centuries. Despite doctrines that often seemed repellent and exotic to orthodox Christians, the Cathar way closely paralleled aspects of mainstream monasticism and responded to some of the same spiritual needs. Catharism flourished especially in the Languedoc area of what is now southern France. *Cathar* was probably derived from the Greek word for "pure," reflecting the desire of the Cathar elites to purge themselves of contamination by a sinful world.

The Catharism that arose in Western Europe was anticipated in the pre-Christian dualist cult of Zoroastrianism in ancient Persia as well as in certain Gnostic Christian heresies, such as Manichaeism. Common to these dualisms was a strict separation of spirit and matter into perpetually warring factions. The good God responsible for creating the realm of spirit confronts across time an arch-antagonist called Satan. The denigration of the physical world as Satan's evil creation was rejected by the mainline Christian churches of antiquity, and as a result the Gnostic heresies were eventually suppressed. However, the old Gnostic impulse revived in 10th-century Bulgaria in the heresy of Bogomil ("beloved of God"), an alienated Byzantine Christian priest. Bogomilism coupled a standard dualist cosmology with an uncompromising ascetic regimen that proved a potent mixture when it reached Western Europe in the 12th century. Bogomil-like heretics appeared in Rhineland Germany in the 1140s, and shortly afterward *Cathar* became the common term for them.

Meanwhile, clusters of Cathars had emerged in northern France and Italy and, above all, in the Languedoc regions of what would be southern France. Local Catholic authorities managed to contain the movement everywhere except in Languedoc, where massive outside intervention was required after 1200.

Meanwhile, the Bogomil-Cathar ideal of heroic self-denial fell on fertile ground in a Western society in which asceticism had become a central value among Christian reformers inspired in part by the papal revolution of Gregory VII (1073–1085). Developments such as the Crusades, the Gothic cathedral, and the founding of austere new monastic orders, like the Cistercians and Carthusians, reflected an intense desire to do great things for God.

However, Languedoc had remained largely unaffected by the vital religious currents flowing around it. The Catholic faith of the people of Languedoc tended to be less than zealous, a situation compounded by a local clergy perceived as indifferent in its ministrations and sometimes scandalous in its conduct. The Catholic bishops of the region seemed more intent on repairing

Bernardino Butinone, Fresco of Peter Martyr (c. 1202–1252), Church of Santa Maria delle Grazie (Dominican), Milan, Italy, c. 1482. Peter Martyr was born into a Cathar family and as a Dominican preached against the Cathars. The earliest Dominican martyr, Peter was murdered by a Cathar who reportedly abjured heresy and became a Dominican lay brother.
Photo courtesy of the Editor

their financial problems than on serious reform. Finally, secular political power was dispersed among quarrelsome petty princes who managed to thwart any effective central government.

It was, then, in a Languedoc split among weak local lords, secular-minded bishops, and a populace more or less perfunctory in its Catholicism that Cathar missionaries flourished after 1160. Traveling usually in pairs, they expounded their teachings wherever they could find a hearing. They preached the pressing need to free the soul trapped in the prison of the human body so that it could ascend to the spiritual God in heaven. Thousands were converted. Many thousands more, while remaining Catholic, proved sympathetic to the burgeoning Cathar communities, by now also called "Albigensian" after the town of Albi, where the movement was especially strong.

By 1200 four Cathar/Albigensian bishoprics existed in the Languedoc heartland, including one in the regional capital of Toulouse. The number of Cathars now numbered well over 100,000, supplemented by up to a million sympathizers who did not become formal members.

It was not simply the paralysis and indifference of local Catholic authorities that so enhanced Cathar fortunes in Languedoc. A combination of Cathar discipline and doctrine and the sterling example of the Cathar elite, called *perfecti*, provided positive incentives to conversion.

In the first place, Cathars, like Bogomils, imposed on their elite leaders severe dietary strictures that strongly appealed to those striving for salvation through self-mortification. To detach the Cathar elite of perfects permanently from the corrupting lure of the carnal, no food produced by coition could be eaten. Meat, eggs, cheese, and milk were specifically forbidden. Because animals were potential carriers of reincarnated souls, they ought not be killed. Fish were allowed because they were thought to reproduce by spontaneous generation. In addition strict celibacy was enjoined on the perfects. Sex and marriage as physical phenomena were regarded as obscene. Having children only trapped more human souls in the prison of the body.

Again this mortification of the flesh was required only of the committed elite of the perfects, who were relatively few. The role of the great majority of Cathar adherents, called "believers" (*Credentes*), was to support and venerate the perfects. Believers were not held to the same austere standards. They were allowed to marry, have children, and enjoy a meat diet. They could live a relatively relaxed lifestyle until death approached, at which time they could choose to become perfects. Meanwhile, they were expected to follow closely the simple moral code of the Ten Commandments and of Christ's Sermon on the Mount. Rejected in toto was the Church of Rome with its elaborate priestly hierarchies, sacraments, doctrines, and liturgy, all of which were seen as mired in sinful matter.

The single Cathar sacrament, the Consolation (*Consolamentum*), was a purely spiritual act administered in a brief ceremony by a perfect. It was designed to remove all sin and induct a believer into the ranks of the perfect. The *Consolamentum* imposed on the initiate the rigorous requirements noted regarding diet and conduct. Both men and women could become perfects, but the *Consolamentum* could be taken only once. If a perfect fell from grace, the only recourse was rebirth in human or animal form. Thus, most Cathars postponed the *Consolamentum* until the end, when the likelihood of relapse was minimal.

The doctrines of Catharism were especially abhorrent to the Catholic Church. For example, the Cathar Christ was not fully divine but only a messenger of the good spiritual God sent to awaken people to the true spiritual meaning of the Cathar religion and thereby escape the grim cycle of reincarnation. In addition, Christ only seemed to have taken human form and could thus never have redeemed humankind by dying on the cross.

Again Catharism would not be destroyed from within but only as the result of large-scale military action. In 1208, following the assassination of his legate in Languedoc, Pope Innocent III (1198–1216) proclaimed a holy war. Despairing of a peaceful solution to the Cathar challenge in Languedoc, the pope appealed to French King Philip Augustus (1180–1223) for help. The ensuing Albigensian Crusade (1208–1213) conducted against Languedoc by northern French barons proved to have been as much for personal gain as for repressing a dangerous heresy. Many thousands of Cathars were killed or imprisoned, and a papal inquisition mopped up the remnants of the movement. By the early 14th century, Catharism was no more.

With its dualistic thrust and doctrine of reincarnation, among other teachings, Catharism stood in striking contrast with the orthodox tradition of the Catholic Church. And if certain parallels can be found between the Cathar perfect and the medieval Catholic monk, the more obvious comparison for Catharism in general, and for the perfect in particular, is with the ascetic traditions of the East in India, Japan, and ancient Persia.

DONALD D. SULLIVAN

*See also* Asceticism: Christian Perspectives; Beguines; Bulgaria; Crusades; Fasting: Western Christian; France: History; Heretics, Christian; Spirituality: Western Christian

## Further Reading

Borst, Arno, *Die Katharer*, Stuttgart: Hiersemann, 1953

Costen, Michael, *Cathars and the Albigensian Crusade*, Manchester: Manchester University Press, and New York: St. Martin's Press, 1997

Duvernoy, Jean, *L'histoire des Cathares*, Toulouse: Privat, 1979; reprint, 1989

Lambert, Malcolm, *Medieval Heresy: Popular Movements from the Gregorian Reform to the Protestant Reformation*, Oxford and Cambridge, Massachusetts: Blackwell, 1992

Lambert, Malcolm, *The Cathars*, Oxford and Malden, Massachusetts: Blackwell, 1998

Le Roy Ladurie, Emmanuel, *Montaillou: Promised Land of Error*, translated by Barbara Bray, New York: Braziller, 1978

Loos, Milan, *Dualist Heresy in the Middle Ages*, 2 vols., The Hague: Academia, 1974

Runciman, Steven, *The Medieval Manichee*, Cambridge: Cambridge University Press, 1947; New York: Viking, 1961

Strayer, Joseph, *The Albigensian Crusade*, New York: Dial, 1971; reprint, Ann Arbor: University of Michigan Press, 1992

Wakefield, Walter L., *Heresy, Crusade, and Inquisition in Southern France, 1100–1250*, Berkeley: University of California Press, and London: Allen and Unwin, 1974

Wakefield, Walter L., and A.P. Evans, compilers, *Heresies of the High Middle Ages*, New York: Columbia University Press, 1969; reprint, 1991

# Cathedral Priories (England)

Ten of the 19 cathedrals in later medieval England were monastic in organization. Nine of them – Canterbury, Durham, Winchester, Worcester, Ely, Norwich, Rochester, Bath, and Coventry – were Benedictine priories, whereas the cathedral at Carlisle was staffed by Augustinian canons.

Although monasticism was an important aspect of the Celtic Church in Britain, cathedrals were not, and no institutions date back to that period. The idea of cathedral monasteries first came to England with St. Augustine (d. between 604 and 609) and his followers in 597, but it did not last long, if indeed a monastic cathedral was fully established at Canterbury. The Viking invasions devastated a number of religious houses, so that monastic life according to the rule of St. Benedict had virtually ceased to exist by the time of King Alfred (871–901). We know that Canterbury was staffed for several centuries by secular canons under the leadership of a dean, not a prior, and that a similar situation existed elsewhere.

Following the revival of monasticism by St. Dunstan (c. 909–988), a number of monastic cathedrals were established. During the closing years of the Anglo-Saxon period, Winchester, Worcester, and Ely, as well as Canterbury, had adopted this form of organization. However, it was the Norman Conquest that marked the beginning of a new epoch in English monastic history. The monastic cathedrals at Rochester, Durham, Norwich, and Bath were founded between 1080 and 1100, with Coventry following in 1102 and Carlisle in 1133. These establishments were to remain virtually unchanged until the time of the Reformation. Attempts were made to convert several more secular cathedrals, including Lincoln, into monastic houses, but these were unsuccessful. It is interesting to note that monastic cathedrals were a uniquely English phenomenon; secular organization prevailed elsewhere. The only other examples appear to have been Monreale in Sicily, where the abbey was made a bishop's see in 1176, perhaps with the English precedent in mind, and Downpatrick in Ireland, which was colonized by monks from Chester in 1188.

The monastic cathedrals were quite different from their secular counterparts. All of them housed much larger numbers of people. Seventy was often regarded as the ideal number of monks for a large Benedictine house, and the greater cathedral priories approximated that size. Like other Benedictine houses, they reached their peak shortly before the disaster of the Black Death in the 14th century. They then declined but had recovered substantially by 1500. At Durham, one of the largest and best documented cathedrals, the number of monks varied from 80 to 100 during the years between 1274 and 1348. There were 52 deaths from the plague in 1349, leaving only 39 monks in 1350, but the population soon returned to about 70 and remained there until 1539. Not all these monks actually lived in their mother houses. Several of the priories had dependent cells, and some monks were sent to study at Oxford and Cambridge, where they lived in monastic colleges, such as Durham College, Oxford.

The chief officer of a monastic cathedral was the prior. There were no abbots; the bishop theoretically possessed that office but in fact rarely interfered. The priors of the great cathedral monasteries were rich, prominent men. They enjoyed their own establishments within the walls of the monastery and had separate dining halls and kitchens, private living quarters, and servants. They often held country estates and in the early Tudor period might live there as country gentlemen. The duties of the prior were enormous. He was ultimately responsible for the buildings, the worship, and the finance of the cathedral and for the education, discipline, and salvation of the monks under him. He was

Benedictine cloister (c. 1388–1418) of Durham Cathedral, Durham, England.
**Photo courtesy of the Editor**

often drawn into politics because he was accepted as being the equal of the feudal lords of neighboring lands. The prior of Coventry even had the right of being summoned to the House of Lords in Parliament, a curious tradition, as the heads of larger and richer cathedral monasteries did not enjoy that privilege. The prior was assisted by a large number of subordinate officers, including one or more subpriors, a sacristan, a precentor, a receiver, a clerk of the works, an infirmarian, an almoner, and a guest master. Numerous laypersons lived within the precincts as well. Boys were being educated in the cathedral schools, and the so-called corrodians – generally, older men who were maintained for life on nomination by the king, the prior, or occasionally the pope – lived there as well. The monastic cathedrals held substantial lands and received most of their revenue from them. Their income in the early 16th century varied from about £2,500 at Canterbury to little more than £400 at Carlisle, the poorest house.

The cathedrals that were organized as Benedictine priories maintained the full round of monastic offices that had been sung in houses of Black Monks since the time of Lanfranc (c. 1010–1089). Generally, three great masses took place daily: the morning mass, the chapter mass, and the mass honoring the Blessed Virgin Mary, often sung in the Lady Chapel with more elaborate polyphonic music than was thought appropriate for other monastic services. The services sung by the Augustinian canons at Carlisle appear to have been similar but perhaps simpler. Chantry masses and obits for the dead were celebrated frequently as well. Shrines and services held at their altars were more important in the monastic cathedrals than in their secular counterparts, such as St. Paul's in London or York Minster. The greatest shrine was that of St. Thomas Becket at Canterbury, but St. Cuthbert's shrine at Durham was also famous, as were the shrines of St. Swithun at Winchester, St. Wulfstan at Worcester, St. Etheldreda at Ely, and St. William at Rochester. Miracles were attributed to such shrines, and pilgrims left large offerings at them.

The monastic cathedrals were exempt from the initial stage of Henry VIII's dissolution of the monasteries because they enjoyed revenues greater than the £200 fixed by the statute of 1536 as the upper limit of the houses to be closed. However, they were subject to suppression under terms of a second statute passed in 1539. Instead of being dismantled, most of them were converted into secular cathedrals, similar to the other secular cathedrals of the "old foundation." Monks might become secular priests or be pensioned off. In some places the former prior became the new dean, and it was common for former monks to be named members of the new cathedral chapter. For example, at Durham, 28 of the 66 monks present in 1541 stayed on in different capacities. These reestablished cathedrals came to be known as "cathedrals of the new foundation," and they received sets of statutes prescribing their organization and operation. Their income remained about the same. Indeed, the poorest cathedrals (Rochester and Carlisle) were granted additional revenues following the dissolution. Two of the cathedral priories, Coventry

and Bath, were dissolved. In both cases they had served dioceses that had two cathedrals; the Bishop of Lichfield and Coventry retained his seat at Lichfield, and the Bishop of Bath and Wells continued to reside at Wells. Bath Abbey became a great parish church, but the old cathedral at Coventry was dismantled (it was not the building destroyed by bombing in World War II).

Physical changes as well as constitutional ones followed the Reformation. A wave of iconoclasm led to the smashing of statues or at least (as in the Lady Chapel at Ely) their decapitation. Shrines were also removed (as at Canterbury) or defaced (as at Durham), and their wealth was confiscated by the government. The monastic liturgies disappeared, and all Latin services became illegal following the publication of the first Book of Common Prayer in 1549. Queen Mary (r. 1553–1558) did restore the Latin Mass, and she brought monks back to Westminster Abbey (her sister Elizabeth [1558–1603] turned them out again in 1559), but none of the cathedrals reverted to the earlier monastic form.

STANFORD LEHMBERG

See also Architecture: Western Christian Monasteries; Benedictines: General or Male; Bishops: Jurisdiction and Role; Dissolution of Monasteries: England, Ireland, and Wales; England; Lanfranc; Monk-Bishops

**Further Reading**

Duffy, Eamon, *The Stripping of the Altars: Traditional Religion in England c. 1400–c. 1580*, New Haven, Connecticut: Yale University Press, 1992
Finucane, Ronald C., *Miracles and Pilgrims*, London: Dent, 1977
Knowles, David, *The Religious Orders in England, III: The Tudor Age*, Cambridge: Cambridge University Press, 1959
Lehmberg, Stanford, *The Reformation Parliament 1529–1536*, Cambridge: Cambridge University Press, 1970
Lehmberg, Stanford, *The Reformation of Cathedrals: Cathedrals in English Society, 1485–1603*, Princeton, New Jersey: Princeton University Press, 1988

# Catherine of Bologna, St. 1413–1463

Italian Franciscan teacher and reformer

Born in Bologna, her mother's native city, Caterina Vegri spent most of her life in Ferrara, the city of her father's family, whose most prominent members were notaries, lawyers, and judges favored by the ruling Este family. As a young girl, according to her first biographer, Caterina spent several years at court as a companion to the young Margherita d'Este, cultivating there, apparently, the literary skills, as well as the artistic and musical talents, for which she was noted.

From the age of 13, Catherine spent her remaining years in the religious life. Entering a community of pious laywomen (*pinzochere*) named Corpus Domini, in Ferrara, she became a nun there in 1435 when the community was reborn as a monastery of reformed Clarisse, following the strictest version of the Rule of St. Clare. Ardent in support of this severe rule and in dedication to reformist Franciscan ideals, she gained a reputation for holiness as a devoted novice-mistress at Corpus Domini in Ferrara. In her early years there, she composed the visionary, semi-autobiographical treatise *Le sette armi spirituali* (Seven Spiritual Weapons), which she kept hidden until she entrusted it to the priest who attended her on her deathbed.

Writing for her sisters, especially her novices, she presented her own experience as a dramatic example of the tests, temptations, and weapons of spiritual battle. These were mainly temptations of the mind and spirit rather than those of the world and the flesh. The spiritual battle for which she would arm her nuns was a lifelong inner struggle to subdue the will and the self, to attain conformity with Christ not in his physical suffering but in his obedience and humility. This small book and her years of teaching and reformist activity mark Catherine's place in late medieval spirituality and monastic history, especially that of Italian religious women.

For more than 20 years, she molded the religious life of her community; her teaching helped make the community in Ferrara a vital center of Clarist reform in northern Italy. As her own spiritual reputation grew, the community saw a remarkable increase in numbers, from perhaps 20 to more than 100 in the span of two decades. Her fame as "a second St. Clare" also led a new Clarist Corpus Domini in her birthplace, Bologna, to choose her as its first abbess in 1456.

There, on her death in 1463, her sisters observed the physical signs of sanctity, especially the incorruption of her body, which is still claimed today for her remains in Corpus Domini, Bologna. The church is located a short distance west of San Domenico. A few years after her death, by 1470, this community acquired a printing press and published the first of several editions of Catherine's *Le sette armi spirituali*, which made it a 15th-century "best-seller." With her incorrupt body as the icon of her community and a focus of civic pride, she also became a "community saint" in a double sense, inspiring her sisters and her fellow citizens to the long and dedicated campaign that finally achieved her canonization in 1712.

Her first *Vita* was the work of Illuminata Bembo, a close friend of Catherine in Corpus Domini, Ferrara, and also in Bologna, who succeeded Catherine as abbess at Bologna. Bembo wrote two versions of this *Vita*, an earlier personal recollection and her longer *Specchio de illuminazione*, completed in 1469 but not printed until 1787, when it was published together with Catherine's *Le sette armi spirituali*.

MARY MARTIN McLAUGHLIN

*See also* Asceticism: Christian Perspectives; Clare of Assisi, St.; Franciscans: Female; Spirituality: Western Christian

## Biography

Born in Bologna, Caterina Vegri grew up in Ferrara, where she spent several years at the court of the Este. In 1426 she entered a community of pious laywomen (similar to beguines) in Ferrara and in 1435 became a nun when her community, named Corpus Domini, joined the Franciscan Second Order (Poor Clares or Clarisse). Catherine's dedication to strict interpretation of its Rule and her gifts as a teacher won her such a reputation for holiness that in 1456 she was chosen as abbess by a new Corpus Domini in Bologna, where she died in 1463. She was canonized in 1712.

## Major Work

*Le sette armi spirituali* (Seven Spiritual Weapons), edited by Cecilia Foletti, 1985

## Further Reading

Martinelli, Serena Spanò, "Per uno studio su Caterina da Bologna," *Studi medievali* 12 (1970)
Martinelli, Serena Spanò, "La canonizzazione de Caterina Vegri: Un problema cittadino nella Bologna Seicento," in *Culto dei santi: istituzioni e classi sociali in età preindustriale* (Collana di Studi Storici, 1), edited by Sofia Boesch Gajano and Lucia Sebastiani, L'Aquila: Japadre, 1984
Martinelli, Serena Spanò, "La biblioteca de 'Corpus Domini' bolognese: l'inconsueto spaccato di una cultura monastica femminile," *La Bibliofilia* 88 (1986)
McLaughlin, Mary Martin, "Creating and Recreating Communities of Women: The Case of Corpus Domini, Ferrara, 1406–1452," *Signs: Journal of Women in Culture and Society* 14:2 (1989); reprinted in *Sisters and Workers in the Middle Ages*, edited by Judith M. Bennett et al., Chicago: University of Chicago Press, 1989

# Cave Temples and Monasteries in India and China

There are two basic reasons for the existence of cave temples and monasteries, one practical and the other of religious significance. First, by excavating into a rock cliff the builders are saved the labor of quarrying the stone, shaping it, and transporting it to build a structure elsewhere. Second, suitable sites frequently are located away from urban centers – a fact that coincides with the Buddhist injunction to detach oneself from earthly concerns in the pursuit of final extinction (nirvāṇa). Buddhist caves are found in the homeland of Buddhism, India, and other Asian countries, especially China. Yet over time they came to appear very different and functioned in very different ways according to prevailing standards that range from the religious to the political.

Among the earliest cave temples in India is that of Bhājā, a short distance south-southeast of Bombay, which dates to about the first century B.C. (Fig. 1). Today all that remains is a *caitya* hall, or place of ritual practice, one of the major structures that constitute a monastic complex. The structure of the Bhājā *caitya* hall is modeled on a stand-alone building, complete with pillars and roof ribs, although these are not structurally

Fig. 1: Cave temple at Bhājā.
Photo courtesy of John C. Huntington, the Huntington Archive

necessary, as the whole is cut from the living rock. At the back of the long U-shaped cavern is a domical, unadorned mound. This represents the stūpa that originally was a burial mound to honor distinguished individuals but was adopted by Buddhists as an indication and ultimately symbol of the burial place of the relics of the Buddha – confirming his historical existence but not revealing its contents, for he had ceased to be a part of the cycle of birth and rebirth. Believers would practice the rite of *pradakṣinā*, which involves circumambulating the stūpa. In so doing they would replicate the cycle of birth and rebirth while seeking complete extinction, which the unseen core of the stūpa symbolizes.

At this date no image of the Buddha exists at Bhājā or anywhere else. This was honoring an ancient injunction:

The Lord has passed completely away in Nirvāṇa, so that nothing is left which could lead to the formation of another being. And so he cannot be pointed out as being here or there. . . . He can only be pointed out in the body of his doctrine, for it was he who taught it. (*The Buddhist Tradition in India, China, and Japan*, edited by William Theodore De Bary, 1969)

Doubtless for a variety of reasons, but especially so that believers would have some sort of mnemonic image of his one-time ex-

istence, these images came into existence in the first two centuries of the current era almost simultaneously at various sites in southern Asia. Being neither entirely human nor entirely abstract, these images adhered to the injunction. Thereafter images of the Buddha and ancillary figures flourished.

This evolution is especially evident in the Buddhist caves at Ajaṇṭā, the most elaborate of many Buddhist cave sites in India. One (Cave 10) is much like that at Bhājā and dates to about the same time. However, two others (Caves 26 and 19, Fig. 2), which date to the late fifth or early sixth century, although architecturally similar, have stūpas at the back with prominent buddha figures facing the entrance. In addition other details of the caves are rich with ornament and imagery, and all interior surfaces are richly painted with similar motifs. This applies also to a *vihāra* (Cave 1), the other main structure of early Indian monasteries that serves as a residence for monks and pilgrims in cells off the main room. They were surrounded by the richness of color and images on the ceilings and walls. There could not be a greater contrast between the austerity of the earlier caves and the richness of the later ones. Clearly the nature of the Buddhist adept has changed from one of the pursuit of abstract knowledge to one of being overwhelmed with ecstatic sensuality.

Fig. 2: Ajaṇṭā, Cave 19, interior view with stūpa at the back and a standing Buddha on the front.
Photo courtesy of John C. Huntington, the Huntington Archive

Buddhist missionaries from India reached China as early as the first century A.D., but it was not until about A.D. 400 that, owing to the remarkable talents of Kumārajīva, intelligible translations of India Buddhist texts became available to the Chinese. The early missionaries and later Chinese pilgrims who went to India seeking authentic texts and images largely followed the Silk Road through central Asia; this road had been established in the second century B.C. for purposes of trade between China and the West. Monasteries along the way, now mostly in ruins, provided way stations for them. Of these one complex survives: the Mogao caves at Dunhuang at the far western tip of Gansu province. They were originally begun in the mid–fourth century A.D., but what remains today is almost 500 caves dating from the 5th to the 13th century. They are in varying states of preservation, and considerable restorations have been done over the ages, but the painted plaster walls and stucco images remain as vivid testimonials not only to the strength of the alien belief and their devotees as they passed through the Dunhuang entrepôt but also to the developing eagerness of the Chinese to pursue its tenets.

Just as Chinese Buddhist adepts often had to radically change their cultural habits (such as giving up one's surname as a part of the separation from earthly attachment that is fundamental to Buddhism), they also had to adapt their ways of architectural and visual art to suit the new doctrine. This can be seen in Cave 257 at Dunhuang, dating to about A.D. 500, where the stūpa at the center of the cave resembles a structural tower with its four square sides (Fig. 3). (Similar caves at other sites go even farther by including descriptions of wooden structural members and tile roofs; see Fig. 7.) However, conceptually it is related to Cave 19 at Ajaṇṭā (which dates to about the same time), for a large niche encloses a central Buddha figure as well as ancillary figures on the front. In Cave 428 a story that illustrates one of the previous incarnations of the Buddha (known as *jātaka* tales) in the form of a tigress who sacrifices herself to feed her starving cubs is in the format of a Chinese handscroll (Fig. 4).

Once Buddhism became firmly established, especially in North China, where it had special appeal to alien invaders who had invaded the area and held it during the period of disunion of China (A.D. 265–618), Buddhism became increasingly powerful, even to the extent of being a part of the state. Under the alien Northern Wei dynasty (386–535), Buddhist institutions were used to put a distinctly non-Chinese stamp on alien rule and thereby justify it but also to serve as an arm of government, especially in the realm of planting, harvesting, storing, and distributing crops. This was a natural development from the fact that a Buddhist monastery should be essentially self-supporting for the same reason of detachment from the world mentioned previously.

Fig. 3: Dunhuang, Gansu, Cave 257, interior view with stūpa-pillar.
Photo courtesy of Langdon Warner, Asian Art Archives

Fig. 4: Dunhuang, Gansu, Cave 428, section of wall painting showing the sacrifice of a starving tigress from a *jātaka* tale.
Photo courtesy of Hon. Desmond Parsons, Asian Art Archives

This meant that the monastery acquired considerable wealth of its own from such activities, and this conflicted with the power that the court claimed as its own. Thus, using a patently transparent excuse the Northern Wei court instituted a wholesale persecution of Buddhism that lasted from 446 to 452, with the defrocking and even murder of monks and nuns, the destruction of images and monasteries, and other atrocities.

Yet on the death of the persecuting emperor, Wencheng, Buddhism was immediately restored. Perhaps as a means of atoning for the persecution or perhaps recalling an earlier comment by the head of the Buddhists that he was not bowing before the emperor (which the unattached monk would not properly do) but rather was bowing before a buddha and thus endowing the emperor with power even beyond this world, a petition was presented to the court by the then head of the Buddhists, Tanyao, to excavate five cave temples, each in honor of the first five emperors of the Northern Wei dynasty in a sandstone cliff at the modern village of Yungang, about ten miles west of Datong in northern Shanxi province. Each of these caves contains a monumental figure (about 50 feet for each) of a Buddha or a Bodhisattva at the center flanked by a few complementary figures.

Each stares out through his own window to the gathered masses of court officers, nobles, and likely common citizens. The central figure of Cave 20 wears a bizarre costume that is thought to copy one that Indian King Udayana had made of sandalwood (Fig. 5; the front wall of this cave that contained the window and a doorway has fallen away). This story was a part of the justification for the making of Buddha images, and this particular type can be found in innumerable versions in China at this time, especially at Yungang. It is hard to imagine a stronger statement of both political and religious power for its association with the historical Buddha, for the equation with a Northern Wei emperor, and for ostensibly being an authentic portrait first made for a king.

Whereas the first five caves at Yungang are impressive in themselves, 15 other caves at Yungang are of equal but ultimately different splendor (as is an extended series of smaller ones at the western end of the site). The differences include a greater variety of iconic images, complex decorative motifs (both of which were altered versions drawn from Indian and eastern Mediterranean sources), carved representations of the life of the historical Buddha (Fig. 6), and a robelike costume for the

Fig. 5: Yungang, Shanxi, Cave 20, overall view (the original front wall has collapsed).
Photo courtesy of James O. Caswell

Fig. 6: Yungang, Shanxi, Cave 6, scene of the birth of the Buddha from the central stūpa-pillar.
Photo courtesy of H. Iwata, Peking #349, Asian Art Archives

Fig. 7: Yungang, Shanxi, Cave 6, niche containing a seated Buddha illustrating the first preaching in the Deer Park and flanked by structural pagoda images.
Photo courtesy of H. Iwata, Peking #91, Asian Art Archives

Fig. 8: Maiji Shan, Gansu, view of the whole mountain.
Photo courtesy of De Silva Darbois

Buddha that is based on that of the contemporary Chinese scholar-bureaucrat's garment (Fig. 7), all lavishly painted. With the exception of being painted, none of these things is to be found in the five caves honoring the Northern Wei emperors. Unfortunately no reliable remains of other monastic structures exist at Yungang, although they probably were located at the site or very nearby. Being made of wood with tiled roofs, they have long since vanished.

It is likely that these caves were sponsored not by the court but rather by nobles, monks and nuns, and ordinary believers. Instead the court apparently turned its attention to the development of its capital city at Pingcheng (present-day Datong), including the erection of various temples as well as a 300-foot pagoda that itself undoubtedly was part of a monastic complex. The court built similar structures, including a 900-foot pagoda,

when it moved its capital south to Luoyang in Henan province in 494, as is richly described in a nearly contemporary account, the *Luoyang jialan ji* (*A Record of Buddhist Monasteries in Luoyang*), by Yang Xuanzhi. Thus, as far as the court is concerned Buddhism and its structures had become features of the urban rather than the country landscape.

Many other caves were still built in the countryside during the Northern Wei and throughout the sixth century or even later. One of the more spectacular, especially when viewed from afar, is Maiji Shan ("Haystack Mountain") in Gansu province (Fig. 8). It is peppered with about 190 caves dating from the Northern Wei and for some centuries thereafter. They can be reached through a complex modern scaffold, but unfortunately they are in a somewhat ruinous state. Nonetheless the effort to remove a monastery from urban centers remained for some, especially for those devoted to the faith and who expressed their detachment from the world through these precipitous excavations marked by difficulty of access.

By contrast, with the reunification of China first under the Sui dynasty (581–618) and especially under the long-lived Tang dynasty (618–907), Buddhism came to enjoy a second period of prosperity. The best evidence of this is the monumental Fengxian *si* among the many caves, including some of Northern Wei times, about nine miles south of Luoyang in Henan province (Fig. 9). Luoyang had been the last Northern Wei capital as well as the capital of several dynasties in earlier Chinese history, and it became one of two capitals of the Tang dynasty. The ground plan of the complex, which is now open to the sky, is about 98 feet wide and 114 feet deep. The principal figures of the Fengxian *si*, despite its monumental scale, constitute a microcosm of a temple complex. Along the side (or north) wall, which originally would have been matched on the opposite wall, one is confronted first by a well-muscled standing guardian warrior followed immediately by a well-armored guardian king, each about 33 feet high. Following them is a standing worshiper facing the altar along the back wall. There a panoply of images serves as a kind of altar to the temple. At the center is a colossal seated buddha figure of Vairocana, a cosmic Buddha, which measures just over 55 feet

high; he is flanked by Bodhisattvas at each end with large Luohan figures in between. In other words the sequence from front to back is the "gate" to a temple with dynamic figures keeping evil forces at bay, worshipers inside, and an altar of eternal images.

Although not of a monumental scale, perhaps the best representative of the splendors of Tang Buddhist cave temples is Cave 328 at Dunhuang, especially the west wall (Fig. 10). There a panoply of lavishly painted stucco images is found in a wide niche, including a central seated Buddha figure with standing Luohan figures to his side and seated Bodhisattva figures to their sides. Others extend into the space of the room (one is today found in the Fogg Art Museum of Harvard University). Bodhisattva and Luohan figures are also found painted on the walls behind. There are ten Luohan figures in all, referring to the first disciples of the Buddha, with the two sculpted ones representing the oldest and the youngest. It is remarkable how easily the transition is made between the sculptural images and the painted ones through the supple articulation and fullness of forms of both. This aesthetic is distantly related to Indian images as seen at Ajaṇṭā (see Fig. 2), but the latter are more abstract, whereas the Chinese images are almost tangibly physical.

This definition of images becomes a part of what is known as the "Tang international style" and is to be found in images from

Fig. 9: Longmen, Henan, view of the Fengxian *si*.
Photo courtesy of James O. Caswell

Fig. 10: Dunhuang, Gansu, Cave 328, overall view of the panoply of figures in a niche of the west wall including the surrounding wall as well.
Photo courtesy of *Dunhuang caisu*, 1978, pl. 47

Korea and Japan at the same time. It lingers to one degree or another throughout all later Buddhist images and testifies to the final adoption and adaptation of Buddhism to its new home in eastern Asia. Likewise Tang standards of monastery plans and their structures exerted the same influence abroad, especially in Japan.

JAMES O. CASWELL

*See also* Ajaṇṭā, India; Architecture: Buddhist Monasteries in Southern Asia; Buddhist Schools/Traditions: China; China; Missionaries: Buddhist; Mount Meru; Patrons, Buddhist: China; Pilgrims to India, Chinese; Stūpa; Visual Arts, Buddhist: India; Worship Space: Buddhist Perspectives

## Further Reading

Abe, Stanley K., "Art and Practice in a Fifth-Century Chinese Buddhist Cave Temple," *Ars Orientalis*, 20 (1990)
Akiyama, Terukazu, and Matsubara Saburō, *Buddhist Cave Temples: New Researches*, translated by A.C. Soper, Tokyo: Kodansha International, 1969
Caswell, James O., *Written and Unwritten: A New History of the Buddhist Caves at Yungang*, Vancouver: University of British Columbia Press, 1988
Caswell, James O., "The Significance of Local Styles in Northern Wei Cave-Temples," *Oriental Art* 44:4 (1998–1999)
Dehejia, Vidya, *Early Buddhist Rock Temples: A Chronological Study*, London: Thames and Hudson, 1972; as *Early Buddhist Rock Temples: A Chronology*, Ithaca, New York: Cornell University Press, 1972
*Maiji shan shiku* (in Chinese with full English translation, "The Rock Grottoes of Maichi Mountain"), Beijing: Wenwu chubanshe, 1954
Mizuno, Seiichi, and Nagahiro Toshio, *Ūnko sekkutsu*, 16 vols. (plates and text with full English translation), Kyoto: Kyoto Daigaku Jinbun Kagaku Kenkyujo, 1951–1956
Pelliot, Paul, *Grottes de Touen-Houang*, 6 vols., Paris: Librarie Paul Geuthner, 1914–1924
Spink, Walter M., *Ajanta to Ellora*, Bombay: Marg, 1967
Spink, Walter M., "Ajanta's Chronology: Politics and Patronage," in *Kāladarśana: American Studies in the Art of India*, edited by Joanna G. Williams, New Delhi: Oxford and IBH, 1981
Spink, Walter M., "The Archaeology of Ajanta," *Ars Orientalis* 21 (1991)
Weiner, Sheila L., *Ajanta: Its Place in Buddhist Art*, Berkeley: University of California Press, 1977

Whitfield, Roderick, *Dunhuang: Caves of the Singing Sands: Buddhist Art from the Silk Road*, 2 vols., London: Textile and Art, 1995

Yang Xuanzhi, *A Record of Buddhist Monasteries in Luoyang*, translated by Yi-t'ung Wang, Princeton, New Jersey: Princeton University Press, 1984

# Celibacy: Buddhist

The central place of celibacy in the Buddhist spiritual path can be seen from the fact that in Pali both are designated by the same word, *brahmacariya*, meaning "holy conduct." Before his renunciation, while still a prince, the future Buddha led a full married life, but when he went forth on his "noble quest" he entered on the way of holy conduct by embracing the practice of strict sexual abstinence. After his enlightenment he declared that he led a "life of celibacy complete and purified," and for his monks and nuns he made celibacy an essential plank of the monastic vocation.

The Buddha not only commended celibacy as an ideal but also knit it into the fabric of monastic life through the disciplinary code of the Vinaya. The third precept undertaken by the novice is abstaining from incelibacy. On taking full ordination the new *bhikkhu* is obliged to observe the *pāṭimokkha*, the monastic code of 227 rules. The first four rules form a group called the *pārājikā*s (offenses entailing defeat), so named because a monk who commits any of them automatically forfeits his status as a monk and can never be readmitted into the *saṅgha* during his lifetime. The first is sexual intercourse, defined as genital, oral, or anal intercourse, heterosexual or homosexual, active or passive, even with an animal; exoneration is granted only to unconsenting victims of rape. Even more stringent rules are laid down for nuns, who undergo "defeat" not only for intercourse but also for lustfully embracing, touching, or pressing the body of a man and even for meeting a man on a sexual rendezvous.

Lighter rules in the *pāṭimokkha* are intended to protect the monks from sexual transgressions short of intercourse. Thus, offenses of the *saṅghādisesā* class, which require a formal meeting of the order, include masturbation, lustfully touching a woman, and speaking lewdly to a woman; *pācittiyā*s (offenses of expiation, cleared by confession) include lying down in the same dwelling as a woman, teaching a woman the Dhamma at length without an intelligent man present, and sitting alone with a woman in a private place. Corresponding rules for nuns are found in their disciplinary code.

The Buddha did not restrict celibacy to abstinence from actual sexual union but spoke of seven subtle breaches of the celibate life. An ascetic may be sexually abstinent, but he is not perfectly celibate if he allows himself to be massaged by women, jokes and plays with them, stares into their eyes, secretly relishes their voices, reminisces over past encounters with them, looks with envy at sexually active laymen, or leads the holy life in the hope of being reborn in a sensual paradise (*AN* 7:47, IV 54–56). To protect his monks from the lure of sensuality, the Buddha often cautioned them about the dangers in closely consorting with women. More broadly he speaks of the dangers in sensual pleasures and compares them to a skeleton, a piece of meat, a flaming torch, and a charcoal pit (*MN* 22, I 130; *MN* 54, I 364–365). He also likens the gratification of sensual desire to the pleasure that a leper experiences by heating his sores over a brazier (*MN* 75, I 507).

The repeated emphasis the Buddha laid on celibacy for his ordained disciples has two explanations. One is the simple, practical reason that sexual activity issues in children, tying the ascetic down to a life of domestic obligations detrimental to his spiritual training. The second, deeper explanation lies in Buddhist doctrine. The final aim of the Buddha's path is liberation from the suffering intrinsic to the round of rebirth, and the Four Noble Truths show that suffering originates from craving. Craving has three prongs – sensual craving, craving for existence, and craving for annihilation – and sexual desire is the most powerful manifestation of the first: "I see no other form, O monks, that so obsesses the mind of a man as the form of a woman; no form that so obsesses the mind of a woman as the form of a man" (*AN* 1:1.1, 6, I 1–2). The Buddha includes sensual desire in virtually all the classes of defilements that must be eliminated to attain *nibbāna* – as a hindrance, a fetter, a bond, a flood, and a taint. Because sexual activity in deed, word, and thought only perpetuates craving, the quest for liberation requires the restraint of all expressions of sexual desire.

To overcome sexuality in its entirety, far more is needed than physical abstinence. What must be done is to eradicate craving as an underlying tendency of the mind, and that calls for systematic training. The training begins already with the precepts for the lay follower, including the precept to abstain from sexual misconduct. Devout lay followers are also enjoined to observe celibacy on the Uposatha days (the observance days of the lunar calendar) once or twice every two weeks.

For one entering the homeless life, celibacy becomes a full-time occupation laid down by the disciplinary rules, but physical abstinence is only a first step. To combat the subtle lures of sensuality, the Buddha instructs the monks to exercise strict restraint of the senses, reining in the mind from attractive sense objects. Monks are also taught to view women as mothers, sisters, or daughters, depending on age (*SN* 35:127, IV 110–111). The definitive conquest of sensuality is achieved by the practice of meditation. Because sexual desire is nourished by the perception of the body as attractive, to overcome the sexual urge the Buddha especially recommends "the perception of foulness" (*asubha-saññā*), that is, the meditative exercise of viewing the body as a compound of 32 parts – organs, tissues, and fluids – all individually unattractive (*AN* 10:60, V 109).

The monk can eliminate sensual desire tentatively with the attainment of the first *jhāna* (meditative absorption), in which the mind is "secluded from sensual pleasures and unwholesome states of mind." However, even with this achievement he remains vulnerable to the deep tendency of sensuality, which might surge up unexpectedly whenever mindfulness grows slack. To eradicate sensuality completely it is necessary to develop insight into the impermanent, unsatisfactory, and nonself nature of all conditioned phenomena. As insight matures, the sharp blade of wisdom cuts away at the fetter of sensual desire until, with the attainment of "nonreturning" (*anāgāmitā*, the third stage of awakening), the fetter falls away entirely. However, even the nonreturner retains a residue of nonsensual craving that will lead to a higher rebirth and thus has not reached the goal of the celibate life. This comes with the attainment of arahantship, the fourth and final stage of awakening, when craving is extricated at the deepest levels and the mind is fully liberated from all bonds. Thus, it is the arhat alone who can declare, "I have fulfilled the life of celibacy."

In all the early Indian schools of monastic Buddhism, basically the same Vinaya or monastic code was observed, and thus celibacy was a fundamental principle of all Indian Buddhist monasticism, whether of the Hīnayāna or the Mahāyāna system. Because the successors of these schools outside India – in China, Korea, Vietnam, and Tibet – inherited the original Vinaya, even today the monks in these countries are committed to celibacy as much as their counterparts are in Theravāda lands. However, in Japan, where the Vinaya heritage lapsed, marriage for monks came to be allowed during the Meiji Restoration of the 19th century, and thus today most Japanese monks do not observe celibacy, nor do the monks in those Korean sects that have been influenced by the Japanese practice. Vajrayāna Buddhism holds that the highest Tantric practices include sexual union, which is off limits to a monk bound by the Vinaya. This incompatibility has led to peculiar tensions in Tibetan Buddhism that its different schools try to resolve in different ways.

BHIKKHU BODHI

Abbreviations: *MN* = *Majjhima Nikāya* (by number of *sutta*); *SN* = *Saṃyutta Nikāya* (by chapter and *sutta* number); *AN* = *Aṅguttara Nikāya* (by chapter and *sutta* number). *Sutta* references to the *Nikāya*s are followed where relevant by the volume and page number in the roman-script edition published by the Pali Text Society.

*See also* Asceticism: Buddhist Perspectives; Buddha (Śākyamuni); Buddhist Schools/Traditions: South Asia; Gender Studies: Buddhist Perspectives; Novices, Theravādin Rituals for; Origins: Comparative Perspectives; Rules, Buddhist (Vinaya): Historical; Sexuality: Buddhist Perspectives; Tibetan Lineages: Nyingma; Vajrayāna Buddhism in Nepal; Visual Arts, Buddhist: Nepal

**Further Reading**

*The Buddhist Monastic Code*, translated and explained by Thanissaro Bhikkhu, Valley Center, California: Metta Forest Monastery, 1994; 2nd edition, 1996

Holt, John C., *Discipline: The Canonical Buddhism of the Vinayapiṭaka*, Delhi: Motilal Banarsidass, 1981; Columbia, Missouri: South Asia Books, 1983; 2nd edition, Delhi: Motilal Banarsidass, 1995

Horner, I.B., translator, *The Book of the Discipline (Vinaya-Piṭaka)*, 6 vols., London: Oxford University Press, 1938–1966

Tachibana, S., *The Ethics of Buddhism*, London: Oxford University Press, 1926; New York: Barnes and Noble, 1975

Wijayaratna, Mohan, *Buddhist Monastic Life: According to the Texts of the Theravāda Tradition*, Cambridge and New York: Cambridge University Press, 1990

# Celibacy: Christian

In general, celibacy is the state of living unmarried; canonically, this state is a freely chosen means of dedicating one's life to the service of God as a cleric or monk and especially as a priest. Although the adjective *caelebs* occurs (usually of men) in classical Latin, both it and the noun *caelibatus* were not often used in patristic and medieval Latin; they and their vernacular derivatives became common from early modern times. Earlier, the terms most characteristic of Christian asceticism were *virginity*, as the state of life of men or women who abstained from or avoided all sexual relations; *continence*, as a personal habit in thought and deed that arose from this state of life; and *chastity*, as a moral virtue of purity both outwardly and inwardly according to the demands of one's station but expressed most fully and fruitfully in virginity or continence. Against this background, celibacy stands in close relationship to the second of the "evangelical counsels" of poverty, chastity, and obedience, by which Christians are challenged to set aside earthly values and to respond freely and generously to the promptings of grace and the call of God.

In the New Testament, Christ spoke of the children of the age to come as neither marrying nor being given in marriage but as being equal to angels (Luke 20:34–36; Matt. 22:30); by a special grace, some chose virginity for the sake of the kingdom of heaven (Matt. 19:11–12). In the eschatological situation of the early church, St. Paul regarded the unmarried state as preferable to the married for those who could receive it; to married people he recommended periods of continence as bringing spiritual benefit (1 Cor. 7:1–8, 26–38). Such New Testament teaching was addressed to all Christians rather than to the clergy. The Pastoral Epistles envisaged bishops, priests, and deacons who were "the husband of one wife" (1 Tim. 3:2, 12; Titus 1:5–6; cf. widows in 1 Tim. 5:9); the emphasis was on good general character rather than a particular state of life.

As the early church developed, many clergy, including bishops, were married, although a premium was set on the single life. The Council of Elvira (c. 324) began a tradition of legislation by which bishops, priests, and deacons were required to abstain from their wives (in 419, a council of Carthage expressly added subdeacons). After the peace of the church and with its expansion, chastity and virginity were highly commended as marking off Christians from the pagan world and, within the church, committed from nominal Christians; they were especially appropriate for clergy and monks. From the late fourth century, legislators and writers campaigned ever more strongly for clerical continence, that is, abstinence from sexual intercourse within marriage. Married men continued to be ordained with the agreement of their wives, but the marriage of the already ordained was not permitted. Only with councils such as Gerona (517) and Toledo (589) did it begin to be suggested that a clerk in major orders should not live with his wife.

The issue of clerical chastity came strongly to the fore under the reform papacy of the later 11th century, especially with the zeal and determination of Pope Gregory VII (r. 1073–1085). The legislation of this time culminated at the Second Lateran Council (1139), which not only deposed clerks in the subdiaconate and above with wives or concubines from their offices and benefices but also declared null the marriages of such clerks as well as regular canons and monks. Nevertheless, the problem of clerical fornication remained endemic throughout the Middle Ages, involving even the Renaissance popes. In 1563, the Council of Trent condemned all sexual activity by the clergy, insisting on the superior excellence and blessedness of virginity and celibacy by comparison with marriage (sess. 24). By introducing the seminary system of clerical formation, Trent ensured for its legislation a hitherto unattained effectiveness. Following on from the medieval consolidation of the clergy as a canonically separate body, the council forged a close association between priesthood and celibacy in the Roman Catholic Church.

In the Eastern churches, a different development is apparent in the canons of the Council at Constantinople "in Trullo" (682), which forbade priests and deacons to marry after ordination; those married before it might keep their wives, with whom sexual intercourse was permitted except during a suitable period before liturgical ministration. Complete continence was required of bishops and monks. In due course, all parish priests were required to marry before ordination.

Early Christian legislation and admonition about clerical chastity emphasized the need for cultic purity in ministers at the Eucharist; it drew mainly on the law of the Levites in the Old Testament and on a sense that all sexuality was ritually polluting (Lev. 15). During their course of duty, Levites were separated from their wives. Christian priests were free of the Levites' necessity physically to perpetuate their tribe; especially when the Eucharist was celebrated daily, the higher demands of the new covenant required them to be continually chaste in mind and body so that their daily sacrifice might be pleasing to God.

Over the centuries, considerations arising from chastity as an evangelical counsel were also advanced. It represented conformity to Christ, as the source of priesthood who took flesh of a pure Virgin and lived as a virgin. It was called for by obedience to God, who appointed for men the distinct vocations of the virgins, the chaste, and the married. It was an anticipation here on earth of the angelic life that is humanity's true and eternal destiny in heaven. Pastorally, it set the clergy free from particular affections so that they might be available to others at all times and places. More mundanely, it prevented the misdirection and alienation of church property.

Thus understood, chastity finds especially fruitful expression in the lives of monks and nuns. The rule of St. Benedict made little mention of it, although *castitatem amare* appears as an "instrument of good works" (cap. 4). Chastity is taken for granted as a condition of the monastic life, as one of integrity and incorruption in body and mind, lived in the closest conformity to the example of Christ.

H.E.J. COWDREY

*See also* Asceticism: Christian Perspectives; Holy Men/Holy Women: Christian Perspectives; Monk-Bishops; Origins: Comparative Perspectives; Origins: Eastern Christian; Orthodox Monasticism: Byzantine; Sexuality: Christian Perspectives

**Further Reading**

Brown, Peter, *The Body and Society: Men, Women, and Sexual Renunciation in Early Christianity*, New York: Columbia University Press, and London: Faber, 1988

Brundage, James, *Law, Sex, and Christian Society in Medieval Europe*, Chicago and London: University of Chicago Press, 1987

Cholij, Roman, *Clerical Celibacy in East and West*, Leominster: Fowler-Wright Books, 1988

Constable, Giles, *Three Studies in Medieval Religious and Social Thought*, Cambridge and New York: Cambridge University Press, 1995

Denzler, Georg, *Das Papsttum und der Amtszölibat, Päpste und Papsttum*, 2 vols., Stuttgart: Hiersemann, 1973–1976

Frassetto, Michael, editor, *Medieval Purity and Piety: Essays on Medieval Clerical Celibacy and Religious Reform*, New York: Garland, 1998

Lea, Henry Charles, *An Historical Sketch of Sacerdotal Celibacy in the Christian Church*, Boston: Houghton, Mifflin, 1844; London: Williams and Norgate, 1907; as *History of Sacerdotal Celibacy in the Christian Church*, 4th edition, London: Watts, 1932

Sheppard, Lancelot C., translator, *Chastity: Being the English Version of "La chasteté" in "Problèmes de la religieuse d'aujourd'hui,"* London: Blackfriars Publications, and Westminster, Maryland: Newman Press, 1955

# Celtic Monasticism

This is a collective label rather than a term designating a particular mode of monasticism. It denotes the various Western European monastic endeavors in areas where Celtic languages were spoken, prior to the significant influence of Benedictinism. Thus, the term covers monasteries in Brittany until the ninth century, monasteries in England before the arrival of the Anglo-Saxons (late fifth century) and still later in what is now Wales until the arrival of the Normans (late 11th century), and in Ireland from the time of St. Patrick (mid–fifth century) until the arrival of the Cistercians (12th century). The term also covers those monasteries in present-day Scotland and England that were founded at the time of the Irish expansion into Scotland during the sixth to eighth century and those foundations on the Continent that were founded by Irishmen (e.g., Bobbio by Columban) in the period before adopting Benedictinism; however, the term must be used carefully (e.g., the name of St. Gallen in Switzerland recalls an Irish hermit, but it was not a "Celtic" foundation).

## Scholarship

Two problems confront any study of Insular monasticism. First, our sources are far less complete and accessible than for monasticism at a similar period on the Continent. Unlike elsewhere in Europe much material that might show us this monasticism close up (e.g., commentaries on Scripture from this milieu) remains unedited or without modern religious assessment. Second, interest in "Celtic monasticism" emerged in the mid–19th century among three distinct groups who envisioned a monastic landscape that served their own religious and political agenda. Although historians have conducted several revised assessments, the older views still capture popular imagination and are so entrenched that they resurface tacitly in critical studies.

The first group wanted to portray the Celts as a people forgotten on the edge of Europe who had preserved an ancient past that mocked the sophistication of the highly organized center but that was doomed to be swept aside. The Breton Ernest Renan (1823–1892) built up this picture of a rugged race of extreme people who as monks were unbridled ascetics, unlearned,

High cross with sundial, Monasterboice (County Louth), Ireland, tenth century. The sundial was used to calculate the canonical hours of worship.
Photo courtesy of Mary Schaefer

and despisers of subtle rules, laws, and theology. This model asserted distinctiveness from the tradition of Western Christianity, to which the word "medieval" was applied: what was "early medieval monasticism" in Italy became known as "Celtic monasticism" in Brittany. This view ignored the fact that these monks were among the first to produce systematic canon law and wrote theological works that, although anonymous, can only by externals be identified as distinct (e.g., through Celtic language glosses).

The second group were Anglicans who wanted to show that the "ancient church" of the British Isles was a distinct "branch" of the Catholic Church devoid of Roman allegiance. Again this demanded emphasizing any perceived difference. Thus, "Romanism" arrived only with the monk Augustine (seen as a "Benedictine" dispatched by Gregory the Great) in Kent in 597 and had its victory in a "great clash of cultures" at the Synod of Whitby in 664. Preceding this in England and continuing longer in Scotland and Ireland had been another church that was autocephalous, distinctive in discipline in its monasteries (including everything from relations with bishops to the style of tonsure) and radically different in theology. In sum this church was said to have been "very Eastern," as its monasteries "originated in Egypt, not Italy." The latter was a crucial point that showed that this church was similar to the Copts in its lack of relations with Rome. This view ignored the facts that no distinct rite existed in these Celtic areas (just typical local variations on the Latin rite), that the "differences" resolved at Whitby were minor and local, that "Benedictinism" was not a uniform system before the ninth century, and that Celtic monks traveled to Europe from the start and were not seen as theologically alien. Although to modern eyes "Celtic" monasticism might look "Eastern," the same can be said of all Western monasteries at the time if one observes them through the optic of Cassian and Palladius. For it is exclusively from these two works that Eastern features are derived, including the so-called Celtic ascetic practice of cross vigil (standing at night in water with arms outstretched), which is modeled on Evagrius Ponticus (346–399) as described in the *Historia Lausiaca* 38.11. Contrariwise the one distinctive phenomenon, the penitentials (which through Cassian had Eastern links and were so recognized by Theodore of Tarsus [c. 602–690] when archbishop of Canterbury in the 680s), were downplayed as being "too Romish" in their advocacy of confession and their links with indulgences.

The third group pursued a nationalist agenda, especially in Ireland, and made common cause with all who wanted to challenge the first two groups. Whereas the first and second groups wanted to emphasize distinctiveness by difference from the European mainland and sought discontinuities, this group faced a more complex task. On the one hand they demanded national recognition, and this required pride in one's people's past as a civilization with a distinct language and culture and a long history of independence. However, the Irish could not flourish as a doomed, forgotten, peripheral race nor as "an island people" separated from the Continent. The latter image was already part of English mythology and thus would not buttress an indepen-

vived only on the fringes, and with it all that is good, as a unique nonurban culture based on monasteries arose, and these monks made Ireland "an island of saints and scholars" who eventually reconverted Europe, and thus these monks "saved civilization." Enough historical details exist to make this myth look plausible, and versions of it can be adapted to serve several political causes: in France from 1920 to 1950 to play down German connections or equally in Germany to downgrade French and English connections. The case ignores the mass of evidence for the continuity of Christianity despite invasions. At no time was the Celtic fringe cut off. There was constant traffic in people, and all the fifth- to sixth-century Latin writers were known in Ireland (e.g., Eucherius, Cassiodorus, and Caesarius of Arles). This historical scheme looked at Insular art objects without contemporary comparative materials and rarely examined the theological writings. Furthermore it assumed that the absence of urban centers led to a "monastic church" without recognizing that although the law (in Latin or the vernacular) used certain monastic terms to cover every legal situation, there was no "monastic church." Rather in this society monasteries wielded political power and because of their schools and libraries stood out more prominently in the historical record than did other institutions of that culture.

*Origins*

Our evidence for the earliest monks in the fifth century is sketchy. Patrick (fifth century) assumed monks and virgins to be a normal aspect of Christianity and mentioned their presence among his converts (e.g., *Confessio* 41). Gildas (sixth century) mentions monks in Britain, and other evidence (from scraps of law to toponymy) supports this claim. However, our first secure evidence comes from the sixth century, when we see a number of monastic founders whose houses not only survived but grew over the following centuries into significant political entities, at the head of monastic federations. The foundations of Ciarán at

Graveslabs, Temple Ciarán, Clonmacnois (County Offaly), Ireland, c. 900.
Photo courtesy of Mary Schaefer

Temple Ciarán, Clonmacnois (County Offaly), Ireland, c. 856.
Photo courtesy of Mary Schaefer

dence movement in Ireland. Catholic scholars desired to rebut Renan and to show that the Catholicism of Brittany was a genuine expression of this people, whereas in Ireland the first Christians were held to be not a distinct "branch" but fully Roman. Without removing any of the boundaries they cherished, this group was able to achieve these multiple separations through the following scheme: Christianity spread throughout the Roman Empire and by the early fifth century had passed beyond its borders into a distinct political culture (Ireland). There a noble group received this heady new wine free from the corruptions of the Roman Empire. Just then that empire (now again perceived as "civilization") was destroyed by the barbarians. Faith sur-

Clonmacnois, Finnian at Clonard, Columba on Iona, the double monastery of Brigit at Kildare, and the work of Columban in the Vosges and finally in Italy, to name just some of the most famous, can be located in this period. To be sure, except for the deaths of Columba in 597 and Columban in 615, we have to be cautious about precise dates.

Each monastery should be seen, as with most monasteries in the period, as an individual response to the monastic impulse by someone who had experienced monasticism and then went off to establish either a hermitage to which others later came or a cenobitic community. The monastic sources that inspired these new foundations are remarkably similar to those that were inspiring new foundations on the Continent at the time, most of which later would become (progressively after 817) "Benedictine." These sources include Cassian (c. 360–after 430) along with the early monastic hagiography (by far the key inspirations); then Eucherius of Lyons (d. c. 450) and the other textbooks that came from Lérins – these provided a guide to exegesis and an attitude to the creation; and, by the seventh century, Cassiodorus (485/90–c. 580) as a guide to study. In the seventh century our picture becomes more precise, as Insular sources become sufficient both to write conventional history and to assess spirituality and theology. Thus, by the mid–seventh century we know that island monastics were producing a range of teaching tools and were deploying the entire range of Latin theologians in their own scholarship. Likewise we know that they could compare their monasticism with that of other monastic founders. For example, Gregory the Great's *Dialogi* were being read on Iona.

## Sources

Although dating the earliest documents is difficult, we possess several monastic writings that reflect conditions of the sixth century in the form of disciplinary documents, that is, penitentials and sets of maxims (sometimes described as "rules"). However, it is in the early seventh century that we find more developed monastic structures in texts, such as the rules of Columban and his other writings, which were copied and invoked widely for several centuries. From the same period we have the first theological writings – mainly didactic texts and commentaries on Scripture – and from slightly later we have the first hagiography. It promoted the particular monastic practices of one founder as a paradigm for other, smaller foundations to adopt by federation. The eighth century saw an expansion of those trends as well as the diffusion of Irish monastic materials throughout Europe (e.g., Adomnán's *De locis sanctis*). The relationships between Celtic and larger monasticism can be observed in Bede's writings.

At the end of the eighth century, two unrelated events took place that shaped Insular monasticism until it was absorbed into the Cistercians. The first was a monastic reform movement known as the Celi De (the companions of God), which invoked the standard reform themes of a more rigorous asceticism, a return to "original" purity of lifestyle, and a rejection of "corruptions." Its effects included a range of ascetic works and a new emphasis on a rigorous understanding of Christian life (e.g., the

preaching of Sunday in almost sabbatarian terms). The other development was the first Viking raids. They raided monasteries all over the Insular world, even those well inland in Ireland. The raids eventually led to a withdrawal of monks from more exposed locations and especially from the island monasteries around the coasts of the British Isles (e.g., Iona).

### Monasticism and Society

One theme common in much writing about Insular monasticism (especially in Ireland) is that it comprised a "monastic church" in which the monastery replaced the city and the abbot replaced the bishop as religious governor (the bishop being a liturgical figure exercising "the power of Order"). This misleading picture resulted from assuming that tenants on monastic land were representative of the larger society and from failing to recognize that in the absence of urban structures monastic terminology was used to describe the church at large. When fuller studies, especially of the legal materials (e.g., the *Collectio canonum hibernensis* compiled in the late seventh and early eighth century) have been carried out, a more accurate picture of these relations will emerge.

THOMAS O'LOUGHLIN

*See also* Archives, Western Christian; Benedictines; Bobbio, Italy; Brigit, St.; Columba, St.; Columban, St.; Evagrius Ponticus; Hagiography: Christian Perspectives; Hymnographers; Ireland; Island Monasteries, Christian; Lérins, France; Liturgy: Celtic; Martyrs: Western Christian; Missionaries: Christian; Monastics and the World, Medieval; Monk-Bishops; Origins: Western Christian; Penitential Books; Recluses, Western Christian; Spirituality: Western Christian; Wales

## Further Reading

Charles-Edwards, Thomas, "The Social Background to Irish *Peregrinatio*," *Celtica* 11 (1976)

Clancy, Thomas Owen, and Gilbert Markús, *Iona: The Earliest Poetry of a Celtic Monastery*, Edinburgh: Edinburgh University Press, 1995

Herbert, Máire, *Iona, Kells and Derry: The History and Hagiography of the Monastic Familia of Columba*, Oxford: Clarendon Press, and New York: Oxford University Press, 1988

Hughes, Kathleen, *The Church in Early Irish Society*, London: Methuen, and Ithaca, New York: Cornell University Press, 1966

Hughes, Kathleen, *Early Christian Ireland: Introduction to the Sources*, London: Hodder and Stoughton, and Ithaca, New York: Cornell University Press, 1972

Hughes, Kathleen, and Ann Hamlin, *The Modern Traveller to the Early Irish Church*, London: SPCK, 1977; as *Celtic Monasticism: The Modern Traveller to the Early Irish Church*, New York: Seabury Press, 1981

Kenney, James F., *The Sources for the Early History of Ireland: Ecclesiastical*, New York: Columbia University Press, 1929; New York: Octagon Books, 1966; Dublin: Pádraic Ó Táilliúir, 1979

Lapidge, Michael, and Richard Sharpe, editors, *A Bibliography of Celtic-Latin Literature 400–1200*, Dublin: Royal Irish Academy, 1985

Lapidge, Michael, editor, *Columbanus: Studies on the Latin Writings*, Woodbridge, Suffolk, and Rochester, New York: Boydell Press, 1997

Mayr-Harting, Henry, *The Coming of Christianity to Anglo-Saxon England*, London: Batsford, 1972; as *The Coming of Christianity to England*, New York: Schocken Books, 1972

O'Loughlin, Thomas, "The View from Iona: Adomnán's Mental Maps," *Peritia* 10 (1996)

O'Loughlin, Thomas, "Individual Anonymity and Collective Identity: The Enigma of Early Medieval Latin Theologians," *Recherches de théologie et philosophie médiévale* 64 (1997)

O'Loughlin, Thomas, *St. Patrick: The Man and His Works*, London: Triangle, 1999

O'Loughlin, Thomas, *Teachers and Code-Breakers: The Genesis Tradition in Latin 430–800*, Turnhout: Brepols, 1999

O'Loughlin, Thomas, editor, *The Scriptures and Early Medieval Ireland*, Turnhout: Brepols, 1999

Olson, Lynette, *Early Monasteries in Cornwall*, Woodbridge, Suffolk, and Wolfeboro, New Hampshire: Boydell Press, 1989

Ó Maídín, Uínseann, *The Celtic Monk: Rules and Writings of Early Irish Monks*, Kalamazoo, Michigan: Cistercian Publications, 1996

Sharpe, Richard, "Churches and Communities in Early Medieval Ireland: Towards a Pastoral Model," in *Pastoral Care Before the Parish*, edited by R. Sharpe and John Blair, Leicester and New York: Leicester University Press, 1992

# Central Asia. *See* Asia, Central

# Ceylon. *See* Sri Lanka

# Chan/Zen: China

Chan is the mature or late form of Chinese Buddhist monasticism. In recent centuries most Chinese monasteries were classified as Chan, and their residents were governed by a Chan monastic rule that was a guide to ritual procedures, offices, and general practice. This rule supplemented the detailed prescriptions of the Vinaya code, or *Prātimokṣa*, with its 250 prohibitions for monks (more for nuns) that governed all elements of personal conduct and that all monks had to obey. For the details of administration, individual monasteries also had a set of administrative procedures, the *guiyue* (an elaboration of the Chan rule), for each of the four sections of the monastery: the meditation hall, the guest department, the business office, and the sacristy (office of the abbot). From 1823 the Chan code was the *Baizhang Conglin qinggui zhengyi ji* (Baizhang's Pure Rules for Large Chan Monasteries with Orthodox Commentary), the name of which is derived from Baizhang Huaihai (749–814), the alleged originator of a distinctive Chan code.

However, this does not substantiate a sectarian identity for Chan. Rather, it is evidence of the diffuseness and fluidity of Chinese religion. Sociologically, in China, Chan was not and is not a sect or denomination despite having a legendary founder in Bodhidharma; a rule giver in Huaihai; its own canon, or *qinggui* (pure rule); a number of special teachings, such as sudden enlightenment; exclusive scriptures, such as the *Liuzu Tanjing* (Platform Sūtra); characteristic documents, such as the *yulu* (recorded sayings) of enlightening dialogues and sermons by Chan masters; and exclusive genealogies. Most Chan monks did not reject a wide range of practices, such as the chanting of the name of a Buddha that was typical of Pure Land. They obeyed the precepts of Vinaya, in addition to practicing meditation, which some even denied was Chan. Monks from non-Chan lineages also meditated, and from Song times most lived under this Chan rule in Chan monasteries. Thus, considerable overlap existed, and only in rare circumstances could the word *Chan* designate a sect or exclusive group. Because of this the Chan rule (the word *gui* meant a compass as used in building, analogous to the *kanon*/rule in Christianity) was the shared rule for mature Chinese Buddhism, a status that it gained during the Song and Yuan dynasties, when it was the most popular form of Buddhism among the elite and received the approval of the state.

*History*

Chan traces its origins to several generations of ascetics who did not reside permanently in monasteries during a turbulent period from the end of the Northern Wei period (534) until the early Tang. This brought them into conflict with the authorities, who had legislated that monks could not leave the monasteries without permission, whether to proselytize in the villages or to meditate in the mountains. They were condemned as vagabonds. By the early Tang, in the seventh century, a number of disparate groups appeared, most claiming a connection with Hongren (601–674). They either built monasteries on lands donated by patrons and relatives or lived in cloisters within monasteries under the prescriptions of the Vinaya discipline of the Dharmaguptaka, as interpreted by Daoxuan (596–667) and his successors, the Nanshan Vinaya school. All these groups claimed to practice Mahāyāna meditation, which was the path to, or was in itself, the realization or seeing of the Buddha nature. This realization was said to be sudden (*dunwu*), or all at once. Eventually, most linked themselves to the charisma of Bodhidharma through lineages of transmission, the dominant trope of Chan (and much of Chinese culture), which created unseemly disputes over the legitimacy of rival lineages. Yet as participants in a widespread movement in medieval Chinese Buddhism to privilege intention over form and deportment, they were concerned generally with the precepts (*śīla*), especially the bodhisattva precepts. However, the *Nirvāṇa Sūtra* that was translated by Dharmaksema in 421 was more compelling, for it stated that a recipient of the *śrāvaka* (listener/"Hīnayāna") precepts would not see the Buddha nature or the Tathāgata. Only those who accepted the bodhisattva precepts could see the Buddha nature and be enlightened. As the object of "proto-Chan" was to see the

Sculpture of Bodhidharma, patriarch of Chan Buddhism, Shaolinsi, Songshan, Honan province, China, gilt bronze, Jin dynasty, c. 12th century.
Photo courtesy of Marylin M. Rhie

Buddha nature and be enlightened, the bodhisattva precepts were a prerequisite. Thus, they debated the bodhisattva precepts and wrote liturgies for the bodhisattva-precepts ordination. Moreover, the "Hīnayāna" precepts, although necessary, in their view could not lead to sudden enlightenment, for they entailed a gradual accumulation of merit and implied lengthy preparation.

After a number of the "Chan" groups merged and more adopted the banner of "Southern Chan" (*nanzong*, the southern lineage), as propagated in the campaign of Shenhui (684–758), a stronger compulsion was felt to synthesize these ideas and formulate a set of guidelines for their monasteries. These guidelines were needed to supplement the Dharmaguptaka Vinaya and the state-imposed regulations (*daosengge*). An example of this was the *Platform Sūtra*, which essentially was a precepts sūtra that

supposedly was preached by Huineng before conferring formless precepts on clergy and laity at a precepts platform. The formless precepts directed vision to one's own nature, the Buddha potential in the mind. This was an extension of the notion that the bodhisattva precepts are mental and intentional and that the Buddha nature itself is the nature of the precepts, meaning that meditation/enlightenment/Chan could succeed only in conjunction with the bodhisattva precepts. The bodhisattva precepts were mental and thus formless, like the pristine mind.

After the rebellions of the mid–eighth century, the sale of certificates of ordination by the Tang court and its main agent, Shenhui, focused concern on the devaluation of ordination and the precepts. Similarly, the fact that the Vinaya was primarily "Hīnayāna" despite some Mahāyāna coloration added by the Nanshan school produced some misgivings. Many of the regulations or prohibitions were unsuited to Chinese conditions and were an inadequate bulwark against the secular laws directed at the clergy.

These questions apparently became acute in the "Chan" lineages south of the Yangtze River, where fewer state-supported monasteries existed. Baizhang Huaihai was made the symbol of the resolution of these concerns, likely because he had been ordained by a Vinaya teacher, Fachao, and yet had become one of the last pupils of Mazu Daoyi (709–788), an energetic and influential Chan master. Huaihai had also studied the Buddhist Canon at Foucha Monastery, where he might have realized the problems of implementing the Vinaya codes transported from India. Finally, he was given land for a monastery on Mount Baizhang by a donor. There he also associated with a Vinaya teacher, Ling'ai. It seems that he adopted a Chinese monastic custom of having the monks cultivate the fields and construct buildings. A series of abbots, not all direct heirs, succeeded to the post at Baizhang, venerating Huaihai as the founder of the monastery. Gradually, they began to institute some general procedures for the monastery that they or others attributed to Huaihai. This became known as the *Chanmen guishi* (Rule of the Chan Gate/Monastery), and it was possibly completed by the 11th abbot in the late ninth or early tenth century. The veneration of the abbot is suggested by the fact that no Buddha Hall was required, for the abbot himself was the representative of Buddha or enlightenment and was possibly identified with the Buddha Hall or the Dharma Hall.

The *Chanmen guishi* might also have been formulated in response to the state-approved Dharmaguptaka Vinaya interpreted by Daoxuan and Shenqing (d. 814), being based heavily on it but sometimes reacting against it. These codes were seen as inapplicable in some respects to the Chinese Sangha. Thus, the *Chanmen guishi* adopted customs developed in Chinese monasteries over the preceding centuries, such as agricultural production, cooking in the monastery, not begging for food, and corporal punishment for rule violations, all of which were forbidden in the Indian Vinaya codes and which some Chan monks regarded as "bodily bonds." Moreover, the *Chanmen guishi* tried to avert state intervention and punishment of the monastery's residents by taking on the responsibility for the punishment or expulsion of offenders, keeping all such events internal affairs of the monastic assembly. Finally, it enhanced the importance of meditation and the regulation of its practice by making the meditation or monk hall the key building and the abbot a meditation consultant. The simplicity of this primitive rule was due to a streak of asceticism that abhorred complexity.

However, these guidelines were too simple: the 250 precepts of Vinaya were still observed for the most part, as were the bodhisattva precepts. However, the increasingly Sinicized Sangha demanded more detail, for it was influenced also by the state and Confucianism, with its penchant for ritual and decorum. To avert such pressures laymen were forbidden to live in the monastery, and restrictions were placed on personal and monastic wealth. Further developments were created by the rhetoric of the Chan ideal of enlightenment within everyday physical activities and the agrarian slogans warning that one cannot eat if one does not work, something backed by Confucian utilitarianism.

By the Song dynasty Chan was the dominant form of monasticism and was perceived to be distinguished from the Vinaya school. It had imperial sanction and support, which forced the Chan rule to become more explicit and adopt a complex network of monastic offices and rituals as desired by the state. The bureaucracy even decided whether large public monasteries would be designated Chan cloisters or Vinaya or Teaching monasteries. Most were called Chan. One attempt to clearly codify the Chan rule and demystify the basic technique of meditation was made by Changlu Zongze. In his code of 1103, the *Chanyuan qinggui* (The Pure Rules of Chan Cloisters), he reiterated that Chan practice commences with the precepts while he introduced lists of formal assemblies and details of monastic bureaucracy and downplayed physical labor. Thus, the bureaucracy included a bursar, a fund-raiser, and an estate overseer. Around the late 12th century, this tendency to monastic wealth and state support became more pronounced when the Southern Song court established a hierarchy of monasteries in southeastern China, the so-called five mountains and ten monasteries. These were official monasteries headed by abbots appointed by the emperor. The monastic communities were to pray for the emperor and the state, which were threatened by enemies from northern China. This is reflected in the later codes, especially in the *Baizhang qinggui* compiled by Dehui on the orders of the Yuan emperor, Shunzong, in 1336. The Mongol conquerors promoted Chan, and so this code emphasizes prayers for the emperor's longevity and the monastic ancestors. The emperor is even described as a *Nirmāṇakaya*, a Buddha incarnate. This code, with only slight alterations, has remained in force ever since, and it is replete with directions on funerary rites, prayers for rain, and the set times for meditation but contains less on meditation itself. During the Ming dynasty this code was mandated for observance by all monks, not only Chan.

The complex bureaucracy of monastic offices in this code reflects the imperial administration with its eastern and western ranks as well as the great wealth of many of the monasteries. The prayers for the emperor, rain, and so on reveal the subordination of Chan and the Sangha to the authoritarian state. Yet the supremacy of meditation was somehow maintained, for in major "Chan monasteries," even into the 20th century, all the other monks and acolytes worked to support the monks of the meditation hall. The contemplatives did not work, but they lived, meditated, and slept in this hall, which was lined with meditation benches. The center, except for an image of Bodhidharma or Mahākāśyapa, was empty of impediments so that the monks could circumambulate after sessions of sitting in meditation to exercise their muscles and counter drowsiness. During the meditation terms, which usually lasted six months, the monks sat in meditation for about nine hours per day, the sessions broken by rituals, meals, circumambulation, and lectures. They slept little over five hours. The day started at 3:00 a.m. and finished at 10:00 p.m. To maintain such a demanding schedule, all the other monastic permanent residents – cooks, vergers, cleaners, administrators, and provisioners – worked to the routine sounded by the meditation hall. However, monks often went on pilgrimage in the summer, and very few took up the challenge of the 49 days of intense meditation, 15 hours per day, of the autumn session. The meditation monks were the elite; the other monks were their supporters, even if they held higher offices or status. Prayers, masses for the dead, and similar rituals were, at least in the ideal, elite monasteries, held to be of less consequence than meditation/Chan.

JOHN JORGENSEN

*See also* Buddhist Schools/Traditions: China; Critiques of Buddhist Monasticism: Confucian; Economics: Buddhist; Initiation: Buddhist Perspectives; Kōan; Master and Pupil: Buddhist Perspectives; Sexuality: Buddhist Perspectives; Taiwan

**Further Reading**

Bielefeldt, Carl, "Ch'ang-lu Tsung-tse's *Tso-ch'an I* and the 'Secret' of Zen Meditation," in *Traditions of Meditation in Chinese Buddhism*, edited by Peter N. Gregory, Honolulu: University of Hawaii Press, 1986

Chŏng, Sŏngbon, *Chungguk Sŏnjong ŭi sŏngnipsa yŏn'gu*, Seoul: Minjoksa, 1991

Colcutt, Martin, "The Early Ch'an Monastic Rule: *Ch'ing-kuei* and the Shaping of Ch'an Community Life," in *Early Ch'an in China and Tibet*, edited by Whalen Lai and Lewis R. Lancaster, Berkeley, California: Asian Humanities Press, 1983

Dumoulin, Heinrich, *Zen Buddhism: A History*, volume 1: *India and China*, translated by James W. Heisig and Paul Knitter, New York: Macmillan, and London: Collier Macmillan, 1988

Faure, Bernard, *The Will to Orthodoxy: A Critical Genealogy of Northern Chan Buddhism*, translated by Phyllis Brooks, Stanford, California: Stanford University Press, 1997

Foulk, Theodore Griffith, "The 'Ch'an School' and Its Place in the Buddhist Monastic Tradition," Ph.D. Diss., University of Michigan, 1987

Ishii, Shūdō, "Hyakujō kyōdan to Isan kyōdan: zoku," *Indogaku Bukkyōgaku kenkyū* 42:1 (1993)

McRae, John R., *The Northern School and the Formation of Early Ch'an Buddhism*, Honolulu: University of Hawaii Press, 1986

Nan, Huaiqin, *Chanzong conglin zhidu yu Zhongguo shehui*, translated as *Dhyana Monastic System and Chinese Society* by Huang Fu, in same volume, Taipei: I wên shu kuan, 1964

Satō, Tatsugen, "Chūgoku ni okeru Daijokai no tenkai-sanju jōkai ni tsuite," *Indogaku Bukkyōgaku kenkyū* 18:2 (1970)

Tanaka, Ryōshō, "Shoki Zenshū to kairitsu: Jubosatsu kairitsu o chūshin toshite," *Komazawa Daigaku shūgaku kenkyū* 2 (1969)

Tso, Sze-bong, "The Transformation of Buddhist Vinaya in China," Ph.D. Diss., Australian National University, 1982

Welch, Holmes, *The Practice of Chinese Buddhism 1900–1950*, Cambridge, Massachusetts: Harvard University Press, 1967

# Chan/Zen: Japan

The term *Zen* originates from the Sanskrit *dhyāna* (meditation), which was transcribed as *chan* when it was translated into Chinese. Then *chan* was transcribed as *zen* in Japanese. Zen is a school of Mahāyāna Buddhism in Japan. The two major branches of Japanese Zen are Rinzai and Sōtō, both transmitted from China and incorporated into Japanese culture. There is another branch of Zen called *Ōbaku*, which retains more Chinese style. Rinzai is known for its use of *kōan*, the series of riddle-like questions used to cultivate the mind and attain enlightenment. One of the best-known kōans, invented by Rinzai master Hakuin Ekaku (1686–1768), is "What is the sound of the one hand clapping?" Sōtō was transmitted from China by the Zen master Dōgen Kigan (1200–1253), who emphasized sitting (*shikantaza*) and wrote a very important philosophical work on Buddhism called *Sōbōgenzō*. Although Zen as thought and practice had already been transmitted to Japan in the eighth century, what we know as the independent religious order of Japanese Zen was established in the 13th century, when Myōan Eisai (1141–1215) and Dōgen went to China, learned Zen, were given credentials of the Zen Enlightenment by their Chinese masters, and returned to Japan to start Zen monasteries.

Although Zen belongs to Mahāyāna Buddhism, it differs from other orders of Japanese Buddhism in several aspects. First, it does not regard Buddhist scriptures as the source of the final authority on salvation. Rather one's own direct Zen experience is the source of salvation. Second, it emphasizes the authentic lineage of the Zen experience from master to disciple and claims that the Buddha's Enlightenment has been conveyed through many generations from Buddha himself to his direct disciples and on to theirs. Third, it is often popularly said that in contrast to the True Pure Land school of Buddhism, which teaches the Amida-butsu's (Buddha Amitābha) salvation (*tariki*), Zen is a Buddhism in which one must rely on one's own efforts to attain salvation. Although this remark is not completely accurate, it underlies Zen's rigorous self-discipline.

When Zen Buddhism was accepted in Japan, the warrior (samurai) class of the Hōjō family in the Kamakura shogunate controlled Japan. For various reasons Zen Buddhism was welcomed by the warrior classes. Later Zen was to exert some influence on what are often popularly represented as traditional features of Japanese culture, such as flower arranging and the tea ceremony. These originated in the 16th and 17th centuries. The so-called Japanese gardens also fell under Zen influence. Musō Soseki (1275–1351) designed and constructed the famous moss garden of Saihōji in Kyoto. Thus, some scholars, such as D.T. Suzuki (1870–1966), have said that Zen Buddhism provided the base for the traditional Japanese cultures.

Yet cultural expressions, such as Zen teachings (kōan), Zen drawings, Zen gardens, and Zen temples, are in fact the products and expressions of the Zen masters who have undergone many years of rigorous training, religious practices, and Zen experience. Zen experience is not attained merely by appreciating a Zen garden or feeling calm within the mind while sitting overlooking the hallway of the famous Ryōanji in Kyoto. Without appreciating the rigorous monastic life of Zen Buddhism, it is hard to understand what Zen is. Considering that even a Zen master starts as a novice in the beginning, this article will describe a path of discipline, life, and experience. Only by going through Zen monastic life can a novice become a master. Not knowing the daily ritualized life of Zen and treating a Zen master as just a scholar leads to a misunderstanding of him and his "artistic" products and expressions. This article explains the Rinzai monastic pattern, which in some respects is similar to Sōtō.

*The Beginning of Zen Life*

Zen monastic life is tightly disciplined and mannered. Zen monks in discipline, who gather around a Zen master, are called *unsui*, which is translated literally into "cloud, water." Their lives at a monastery begin with a harsh ordeal. One who wants to be accepted by a monastery is free to choose which monastery. Entrance into the monastery territory is called *kashaku*. On arriving at the gate, a novice lies down and bows by lowering himself on the ground with his palms up (*gotai tōchi*) three times. At the entrance hall (*Zantō tōchakujo*), he asks permission to enter in order to be initiated. Yet what awaits him is a harsh refusal. An elder monk (*ka'an*) meets him, scolds him, pushes him back out of the entrance hall, or sometimes throws him out to see whether he will show his determination to stay. A novice must force himself back and to keep a bowing posture while sitting on the front step for two days (*niwazume*). He is permitted to come in to stay in a small room only overnight. After two days' ordeal he is allowed to come in and stay as a guest in a small guest room (*Tanga-ryo*) without any lamp after dark. In the evening he must sit until 9:00 before he goes to bed. To sleep he is given only a narrow, thin mattress. The novice is allowed to sit still facing a wall in a room all day long for three days. This is called *tangazume*. One who successfully passes this stage is allowed to be initiated into the monastic life.

*Social Structure*

At this point it might be useful to examine the hierarchy of a Zen institution, which aims at letting each monk attain the goal of his monastic life. This explanation will help a reader imagine various roles of Zen monastic life. At the Zen monastery are two groups: *shike* (master) and *unsui* (monks). Among monks are two groups: *jouju* (those who are assigned special tasks and given titles) and *dounai* (those who are not assigned any special task). The former are usually senior monks and function as officials, such as *shika* (manager in charge of the temple hall), *huusu* (financial manager), *jikijitsu* (leader in charge of managing *zazen* in the Zen hall), *shouji* (agent in charge of looking after the statue of Monju Taishi and the monks in training), *tenzo* (in charge of cooking and preparing food), *densu* (in charge of managing everything at the main hall, e.g., reading *sūtra*, cleaning the hall, and reading and announcing the time), *inji* (in charge of serving *shike* [master], also called *san'nou*), and *fuzui* (an assistant to *huusu*, placed in charge of monitoring rice and wheat supplies and of managing *takuhatsu* [begging for alms]). *Shike*, *huusu*, *jikijitsu*, and *shouji* are called *hyouseki*.

A division also exists among *dounai* (those who are assigned no special tasks): *yakui*, who have a room in the *jisharyou*, and

The Kenchōji (Zen) temple, Kamakura, Japan, founded 1253, Kamakura period, *karayo* style.
Photo courtesy of Marylin M. Rhie

*daishu*, who manage a life in the *zendō*. In the *jisharyou* are *shouji*, a room of *ryoutou* for *jikijitsu*, a room for *jisharyou*, and a room for *jokei*. The eldest among *shouji* is chosen as *ryouko*, who will be in charge of managing *dounai* monks and of communicating between *jouju* (with their special tasks) and *dounai*. *Shouji* is also in charge of watching the back gate of the *zendō*, which the monks are allowed to use to enter and exit. Without *shouji*'s permission, *dounai* monks cannot go out of the *zendō*. *Jikijitsu* is in charge of the activities inside the *zendō* and of setting up *senkou* (the incense stick), which is used to measure time for *zazen* (sitting).

The rank of a monastic member depends on when he entered the monastery, the basic temporal unit being a half year, called *ichige*. The half year from February to July is called *u'ango* and the one from August to January *setsu'ango*. The former is counted as *kasei* (summer session) and the latter as *tousei* (winter session). In *ichige* are *seichuu* (a training period) and *seikan* (an interim between sessions). A novice is allowed to be accepted only during the latter. When a new session season starts, the monks are assigned new tasks.

This temporal unit is also used as a way to hierarchize the monks. The first session is called *ichige*, the second session *nigeme*, the third session *sange*, and the fourth session *sige*. During the first *ichige* a novice is called *shintou*. According to one's length of stay at the monastery, no matter what his previous secular status, monks who stay longest are called *koutan* and those who stay second longest *nakatan*, third longest *battan*, and so on.

### Daily Life

Daily life at a Zen monastery abounds in ritualized manners and prescriptions and instructions on behavior. Seen as a systematic manner to let each monk attain his purpose, all these ritualized formats are necessary. For example, no talk and conversation is allowed in the *zendō*, the *jikidou* (the dining room), or the bathroom. There are detailed ritualized manners in which to eat simple food together with all monks in the *jikidou*.

A day at a Zen monastery begins with ringing a bell at 3:30 in the morning in summer (4:00 in winter). The *densu* in charge first awakens *jouju* by ringing a bell while another *densu* prepares water (only a few scoops of water are allowed) for all monks to wash their faces and then opens the back gate of the *zendō*. Every monk wakes up quickly, puts his thin futon away on the shelf, and dresses himself. Only a thin layer of clothing is allowed, even in winter. When everyone is ready, the group proceeds in line quietly to the *hondo* (the main hall) accompanied by the sound of the ringing bell. There they offer the morning prayer and read the *sūtra*, followed by *baitou-zarei*, during which the monks sit together and drink a cup of plum tea. Then they take breakfast of *kayu* (rice porridge) and pickled daikon (giant radish). Each monk has a set of five wooden bowls from which to eat. There are detailed prescribed manners of how to hold bowls and how to eat. Before breakfast, they read *Hannya-haramitta-shin-gyō* (*Prajñāpāramitā hṛdaya sūtra*), they recite the names of the ten buddhas and other required scriptures, and after the meal they make other prescribed recitations. Daily food is very simple, but the monks are allowed to eat food prepared and served by their lay family on *takuhatsu* (on leaves when they beg for alms). In addition an individual monk may save some rice that he has received at *takuhatsu*, and when he has stored up a lot of rice, he may eat that lot of rice. During daytime the monks clean the buildings and corridors, sweep the garden, and work in the field. On the first, third, sixth, and eighth day of every month, they group together to go out to the town to do *takuhatsu*, for which there are also detailed prescriptions of behavior. On *takuhatsu* they are sometimes served lunch at a layperson's household. On the fourth and ninth day of every month, the monks shave their heads and clean the *zendō*, the *hondo*, and the toilet.

All these daily activities are not regarded as merely supplementing *zazen* practice. Nevertheless *zazen* practice is the central practice and experience of Zen monks.

Daily the monks must sit for a few hours. There is a prescribed manner to sit, to do *zazen*. Although it might seem easy to sit, it is better to do so under the guidance of an experienced Zen monk. When a sitting monk loses concentration and falls asleep, a watching monk walking forth and back in the *zendō* hits him on both shoulders with a wooden stick called *keisaku*. When a monk wants to receive *keisaku*, he can ask for it as well. During *oozesshin* the monks sit all day long from 3:30 in the morning until 10:00 in the evening for a week without breaks, except for going to the toilet and going out at meals. This requires enormous endurance of both mind and body. In addition each monk is given kōan by a *shike*, whom he must visit in order to present his answer to it. The *shike*, on seeing the monk, quickly knows whether he has anything to say. Even if the monk presents his answer, if it is not good enough, the *shike* simply refutes him silently.

While a monk is thinking about the given kōan, suddenly he might attain satori, or enlightenment. If he thinks that he has, he would go to see a *shike*, who would intuitively understand him and, if his satori is genuine, would give him a credential (*kenshou*). Satori may be a one-time occurrence but the monk continues to sit, deepening his understanding of his own satori. Afterward he might become a Zen master of some temple, but not all of those who attain satori will manage a temple. Conversely not all Zen monks who run a temple have attained satori. Among these Zen masters one who shows artistic talent might design a Zen garden, another might draw calligraphy and calligraphy drawings, and a third, if intellectually rigorous, might write a piece about kōan or an explanatory book on Zen. As this brief sketch of Zen monastic life shows, a rigorous disciplined life is fundamental for Zen masters and monks. This routine should not be forgotten when one is enjoying Zen gardens, Zen drawings, and Zen arts.

TAKESHI KIMURA

*See also* Buddhist Schools/Traditions: China; Buddhist Schools/Traditions: Japan; Critiques of Buddhist Monasticism: Japanese; Dialogue, Intermonastic: Buddhist Perspectives; Dōgen; Governance: Buddhist Perspectives; Hakuin; Humor: Buddhist; Initiation: Buddhist Perspectives; Japan: History; Kōan; Kyoto, Japan; Master and Pupil: Buddhist Perspectives; Nation-Building and Japanese Buddhism; Nembutsu; Prophethood, Japanese Buddhist; Suzuki, Daisetz Teitaro; Warrior Monks: Buddhist; Zen, Arts of; Zen and the West

## Further Reading

Note: many books on Zen Buddhism are available in English; the following list does not cover all the important works.

Abe, Masao, editor, *A Zen Life: D.T. Suzuki Remembered*, New York: Weatherhill, 1986

Abe, Rie, *Zen no Tera: Rinzaishū/Ōbakushū*, Kyoto: Zen Bunka Kenkyūjo, 1996

Aoyama, Shunto, *Zen Seeds: Reflections of a Female Priest*, translated by Patricia Daien Bennage, Tokyo: Kosei, 1996

Arai, Paula Kane Robinson, *Women Living Zen: Japanese Soto Buddhist Nuns*, Oxford: Oxford University Press, 1999

Atken, Robert, *The Gateless Barrier: The Wu-Men Kuan (Mumonkan)*, San Francisco: North Point Press, 1991

Bankei, *Bankei Zen: Translations from the Record of Bankei*, translated by Peter Haskel, New York: Grove Press, 1984

Bielefeldt, Carl, *Dogen's Manuals of Zen Meditation*, Berkeley: University of California Press, 1988

Chiba, Reiko, editor, *Sesshu's Long Scroll: A Zen Landscape Journey*, Rutland, Vermont: Tuttle, 1959

Dōgen, *A Primer of Sōtō Zen: A Translation of Dogen's Shobogenzo Zuimonki*, translated by Masunaga Reihō, Honolulu: University of Hawaii Press, 1971

Dumoulin, Heinrich, *Zen Buddhism: A History*, volume 2: *Japan*, translated by Gregory Alles and Paul Knitter, New York: Macmillan, and London: Collier Macmillan, 1988–1990

Hakuin, *The Zen Master Hakuin: Selected Writings*, translated by Philip B. Yampolsky, New York: Columbia University Press, 1971

LaFleur, William R., editor, *Dogen Studies*, Honolulu: University of Hawaii Press, 1985

Omori, Sogen, *An Introduction to Zen Training*, translated by Dogen Hosokawa and Roy Yoshimoto, London and New York: Kegan Paul International, 1996

Ryōkan, *Ryōkan: Zen Monk-Poet of Japan*, translated by Burton Watson, New York: Columbia University Press, 1977

Satō, Giei, Eshin Nishimura, and Bardwell L. Smith, *Unsui: A Diary of Zen Monastic Life*, Honolulu: University of Hawaii Press, 1973

Suzuki, Daisetsu Teitaro, *An Introduction to Zen Buddhism*, New York: Grove Press, 1954; London: Arrow Books, 1959

Suzuki, Daisetsu Teitaro, *Manual of Zen Buddhism*, London: Rider, 1956; New York: Grove Press, 1960

Suzuki, Daisetsu Teitaro, *Zen and Japanese Culture*, New York: MJF Books, 1959; London: Routledge and Kegan Paul, 1973

Tanahashi, Kazuaki, editor, *Moon in a Dewdrop*, San Francisco: North Point Press, 1985

*Two Zen Classics: Mumonkan and Hekiganroku*, translated by Katsuki Sakida, New York: Weatherhill, 1977

Yamada, Mumon, *Zazen no Susume*, Kyoto: Zen Bunka Kenkyūjo, 1998 (contains a list of Zen temples in each prefecture, including ones that are open to lay people)

# Chan/Zen: Korea

The introduction of Chan (Sino-Korean, Sŏn; Sino-Japanese, Zen) into Korea is attributed to the Korean monks Pŏmnang (n.d.) and Sinhaeng (704–779). Pŏmnang went to Tang China during the reign of Queen Sŏndŏk (r. 632–646) to study Chan under Daoxin (580–651), the fourth patriarch of the Chinese Chan school. Pŏmnang's disciple, Sinhaeng, also traveled to China and trained with the Chinese master Zhikong (703–779) of the Northern school of Chinese Chan, which advocated gradual enlightenment. Toŭi (783–821) is believed to be the first Korean monk to transmit the teachings of the Southern school of Chan, which emphasized the idea of sudden awakening.

By the end of the Unified Silla period (668–935), nine schools of Sŏn Buddhism had been established in Korea by Korean monks who had studied in China. These orders were called the Kusan, or "Nine Mountains," a phrase that refers to the remote mountain regions where the nine schools were located. Seven of these schools were connected with the Southern school of Chan.

Sŏn Buddhism emphasized meditation, introspection, and the path of sudden enlightenment, rejecting excessive dependence on the scriptures. Sŏn challenged the so-called Ogyo schools, or "Five Teachings," which had developed in the beginning of the Unified Silla period. These established institutions housed the more speculative and scholastic schools of Korean Buddhism and advocated the study of a particular scripture. Their influence declined toward the close of the Silla period. From then on Sŏn Buddhism became the prevalent form of Buddhism in Korea. It still constitutes the heart of Korean Buddhism.

In the Koryŏ period (935–1392) – generally considered the golden age of Buddhism in Korea – Buddhism enjoyed the patronage of the royal authority and was considered an important force in unifying the country, as it was seen as the base for an efficient government. Sŏn Buddhism showed remarkable development during this period. Buddhist masters functioned as preceptors. Even members of the royal family and the nobility entered monkhood. The greatest example is the monk Ŭich'ŏn (1055–1101), the fourth son of king Munjong (r. 1047–1083).

Ŭich'ŏn, originally a follower of the Hwaŏm (Chinese, Huayan) school, hoped to overcome the rivalry between the scholastic Kyo and meditative Sŏn schools. He attempted to unify the Kyo and Sŏn through the creation of the Ch'ŏnt'ae (Chinese, Tiantai) school. The monk Chinul (1158–1210), one of Korea's greatest Buddhist thinkers, continued Ŭich'ŏn's efforts to harmonize the Kyo and Sŏn schools. He advocated a combination of these two great branches of Koryŏ Buddhism into a school known as Chogye. Chinul's unique synthesis of Hwaŏm doctrine and Sŏn practice became the philosophical foundation of Buddhism in Korea. He is also considered the founder of the Susŏnsa, a famous temple known today as the Songgwangsa (Chŏllanam-do province).

The monk P'ou (1301–1382) was one of the most distinguished Sŏn masters of the late Koryŏ period. He studied during the Yuan dynasty in China (1279–1368) and introduced into the Korean Sŏn the practices of the Chinese Linji school (Sino-Korean, Imje; Japanese, Rinzai).

In the Yi, or Chosŏn, period (1392–1910), Confucianism became the national ideology. Buddhism lost its state patronage and was suppressed by the government. The Confucianists pressed the government for confiscation of temple lands, abolition of the tax-exempt status of temples, a drastic reduction in the number of monks and temples, and rigorous control of Buddhism. During the reign of King Sejong (r. 1418–1450), all schools of Buddhism were combined into two large schools: the Kyo (Doctrinal) school and the Sŏn (Meditative) school. Each school was allowed to operate only 18 temples, and no temples were permitted in the capital. Under Yŏnsan (r. 1495–1506) Buddhist monks were considered to belong to the lowest of social classes, and Sŏn monks survived by retreating to distant mountain temples. Hyujŏng (1520–1604), also known as Sŏsan Taesa, is regarded as the most prominent monk of this period and is the author of the *Sŏn'ga kwigam* (Mirror for Sŏn Monks), a guide to Sŏn practice. He is also known for his efforts to harmonize Sŏn with other schools. In other works he asserted the similarity of the aims of Buddhism, Confucianism, and Daoism. He is also considered a national hero because he organized an army of monks to fight the Japanese when Toyotomi Hideyoshi (1536–1598) invaded Korea in 1592.

After the ratification of the Korea-Japan treaty of Kanghwa in 1876, Japanese immigrants started settling in Korea. Through the activities of Japanese Buddhist monks on the Korean peninsula, Japanese Buddhist schools exercised an important influence on the revival of Buddhism in Korea. Under Japanese pressure, the ban on Buddhist monks entering Seoul was rescinded in 1895. The Korean monk Kyŏnghŏ (Sŏngu, 1849–1912), the first Sŏn monk of national distinction after Hyujŏng, restored the tradition of Sŏn Buddhism. He visited temples all over the country and founded various meditation centers. After the absorption of Korea into the Japanese Empire in 1910, the Japanese attempted to place Korean Buddhism under the control of Japanese Buddhism. A number of pro-Japanese monks favored merging the Korean Buddhist order with Japanese Buddhism. Yi Hoegwang (1840–1911) sought to merge his newly founded Won school with the Japanese Sōtō school of Zen, but a large group of Korean monks resisted. In 1926 the Japanese introduced the system of married clergy in Korea. This measure was a tremendous shock for the Sŏn school, which practiced celibacy, and for Korean Buddhist tradition in general. A dispute started among the Korean Buddhists and continued until recently.

Among the prominent Sŏn monks of modern Korean Buddhism are Kyŏnghŏ and Kusan (1909–1983). Kyŏnghŏ is known for raising the moral and disciplinary standards of Sŏn Buddhism. Kusan, Kyŏnghŏ's disciple, is best known for his international activities. He made many trips abroad to lecture on Buddhism and established a meditation center at Songgwangsa where foreigners receive training in Sŏn meditation. Today the Chogyejong (Chogye school) regards itself as the successor of the traditional Sŏn and is the largest among the 18 Korean Buddhist schools. The headquarters is the Chogyesa temple in the heart of Seoul.

POL VANDEN BROUCKE

*See also* Buddhist Schools/Traditions: Korea; Chinul; Kōan; Korea: History; Korea: Sites

**Further Reading**

Buswell, Robert E., "Buddhism in Korea," in *The Encyclopedia of Religion*, volume 2, edited by Mircea Eliade, New York: Macmillan, 1987; London: Collier Macmillan, 1993
Buswell, Robert E., *The Formation of Ch'an Ideology in China and Korea: The Vajrasamādhi-Sūtra, a Buddhist Apocryphon* (Princeton Library of Asian Translations), Princeton, New Jersey: Princeton University Press, 1989
Buswell, Robert E., *The Zen Monastic Experience: Buddhist Practice in Contemporary Korea*, Princeton, New Jersey: Princeton University Press, 1992
Buswell, Robert E., editor, *The Korean Approach to Zen: The Collected Works of Chinul*, Honolulu: University of Hawaii Press, 1983; abridged as *Tracing Back the Radiance: Chinul's Korean Way of Zen* (Classics in East Asian Buddhism), Honolulu: University of Hawaii Press, 1991
Grayson, James H., *Korea: A Religious History*, New York: Oxford University Press, and Oxford: Clarendon Press, 1989
Kamata, Shigeo, *Chōsen Bukkyō shi* (Toyo sosho, 1), Tokyo: Tokyo Daigaku Shuppankai, 1987
Vos, Frits, *Die Religionen Koreas* (Die Religionen der Menschheit), Stuttgart: Kohlhammer, 1977

# Chan/Zen: Vietnam

Thiền (Zen), a Buddhism of the low land-dwelling Vietnamese elites and not of the peasants or animist montagnards or Hindu Cham or Theravādin Khmers of central and southern Vietnam, was introduced into the Red River delta, which had experienced a Buddhism imported from China during the Chinese occupation and colonization (which lasted from 111 B.C. to A.D. 938). This Sinitic monasticism accommodated native animism and Cham influences, and Zen gained only a momentary foothold at best. However, literate monks were vital to the success of the early, independent Vietnamese dynasties, and hints exist that the popular cult of Huineng was introduced from Guangdong and was linked to the fate of the Lỳ dynasty (1009–1225). The Lỳ dynasts built many monasteries, but the Buddhism of the period was a mixture of esoteric incantations, ritual, and Pure Land piety. However, in response to a challenge by an increasingly influential Confucianism, some of the Vietnamese elite attached to the court, such as the monk Thông Biện (d. 1134), fabricated genealogies of eminent Vietnamese monks and famous monasteries

and linked them to Chinese Zen lineages. During the Trần dynasty (1225–1400), Emperor Nhân-Tông (r. 1279–1293), in the immediate aftermath of repulsing the Mongol invasions, became a monk and founded the independent, short-lived Vietnamese Trúc Lâm Zen lineage, which was heavily Confucianized. Despite such political connections the bureaucracy grew increasingly anti-Buddhist. The Chinese Ming conquest (1413–1428) imposed a blitzkrieg campaign of Confucianization, which was extended by the Lê dynasty (1414–1788). This policy severely restricted Vietnamese Buddhism, which by the late 16th century, especially in the north, came under the influence of Liên Tông (Lotus sect), a probable offshoot of the Chinese White Lotus sect.

Under the southern warlords, the Nguyễn, Buddhist centers were established around Hue in the former Cham territories. This attracted Chinese monks who were fleeing the Manchus in the 1660s. They introduced a Linji (Vietnamese, Lâm-Tê; Japanese, Rinzai) Zen that held Zen and Pure Land practice to be identical. As the Vietnamese pushed the Khmer out of the Mekong delta in the 17th and 18th centuries, they brought syncretic forms of folk Buddhism south while conservative Zen remained in the cities of central Vietnam, and the Lien Tong dominated the north. By the 18th and 19th centuries, the Buddhist order was Linji in name, but 80 percent of believers followed Lien Tong. Buddhism was also oppressed by pro-Confucian mandarins and French colonial policies, and anti-French rebellions were launched by Buddhists and Buddhistic new religions from the Mekong delta.

In the 1930s, inspired by the Buddhist reform movement in China, intellectual clergy led an "engaged Buddhism" of welfare activities, education, and modernization. However, Buddhism in the village pagodas (chùa), where only few monks lived, provided a mixture of Pure Land faith, spirit and ancestor worship, Daoistic rituals, and the veneration of Confucian saints. Thus, it is often collectively named *tam-giáo* (the three religions). Zen meditation was practiced only in the large city monasteries, where the Chinese rule was observed. In 1963 Mahāyāna and Theravāda Buddhists (mainly Khmers) formed the Unified Buddhist Church. It resisted the Ngo Dinh Diem regime and later the communist government, which in recent decades has restricted Buddhism, converting pagodas to secular uses, and made Buddhism an arm of the state. Zen is now subsumed in a much weakened syncretic Buddhism and in fact never dominated Vietnamese Buddhism except in rhetoric. Where it exists it largely follows the Chinese model.

JOHN JORGENSEN

*See also* Chan/Zen: China; China; Huineng; Nhát Hanh, Thích; Pure Land Buddhism; Vietnam

**Further Reading**

Duncanson, Dennis J., *Government and Revolution in Vietnam*, London and New York: Oxford University Press, 1968
Kawamoto Kunie, "Vetonamu no Bukkyō," in *Higashi Ajia shochiiki no Bukkyō: Kanji bunkaken no kuniguni* (Ajia Bukkyōshi, 4), Tokyo: Kōseishuppansha, 1976

Nguyen, Cuong Tu, "Rethinking Vietnamese Buddhist History: Is the *Thiền Uyển Tập Anh* a 'Transmission of the Lamp' Text?" in *Essays into Vietnamese Pasts* (Studies on Southeast Asia, number 19), edited by Keith Weller Taylor and John K. Whitmore, Ithaca, New York: Southeast Asia Program, Cornell University, 1995

Nguyen, Cuong Tu, *Zen in Medieval Vietnam: A Study and Translation of the Thiên Uyên Tập Anh*, Honolulu: University of Hawaii Press, 1997

Nhất Hanh, Thích, *Vietnam: Lotus in a Sea of Fire*, New York: Hill and Wang, and London: SCM Press, 1967

Porter, Gareth, *Vietnam: The Politics of Bureaucratic Socialism* (Politics and International Relations of Southeast Asia), Ithaca, New York: Cornell University Press, 1993

Thiên Ân, Thích, *Buddhism and Zen in Vietnam, in Relation to the Development of Buddhism in Asia*, Los Angeles: College of Oriental Studies, Graduate School, 1975

Trần Văn Giáp, "Le Bouddhisme en Annam des origines au XIIIe siècle," *Bulletin de l'École Française d'Extrême-Orient* 32 (1932)

Tso Sze-bong, "Li, Chen, Li sanchao di Yuenan Fojiao yu zhengzhi," *Hsin-Ya hsüeh-pao* 10:1 (1973)

# Chant, Buddhist. *See* Music: Buddhist Perspectives

# Chapman, John 1865–1933

English Benedictine scholar

Henry Palmer Chapman, as he was known before monastic profession, was born at Ashfield, Suffolk. His father was a senior dignitary of the Anglican Church, being archdeacon of Sudbury, and because the grandfather had been a London banker, the family had considerable wealth, so that the young Henry was destined to go to Eton. However, because of his delicate health, he had to be taught at home by tutors. This private formation may be the reason for his lifelong originality that often veered toward the eccentric but also for his very wide reading, and his mastery of music, art, and many languages, ancient and modern.

From 1883 to 1888 Chapman was an undergraduate at Christ Church, Oxford, where he obtained a First in Greats, an exacting course of Latin and Greek followed by philosophy. He went on to read theology first in the university and then at Cuddesdon Theological College. This was a High Church establishment, and it was natural that after his ordination as a deacon he should follow the Anglo-Catholic pattern and serve his first curacy at a church in the London slums, St. Pancras, which he found a searing experience.

However, in 1890 he joined the Roman Catholic Church and almost immediately the Jesuit novitiate. This again proved not to be the way forward for him, and in 1892 he entered the Benedictine monastery of Maredsous, Belgium, where his Cuddesdon

friend, Bede Camm, had preceded him. Maredsous belonged to the German Congregation of Beuron, whose hallmark was its strict discipline, the priority it gave to the Liturgy, and exacting scholarship. Chapman flourished here. He was ordained priest in 1895 and sent to join an English foundation that the Beuronese had made at Erdington, a suburb of Birmingham, where in 1905 he became prior. It was during these Erdington years that Chapman accumulated his vast knowledge of the Church fathers, which gave rise to the legend that he had read the whole of Migne's Patrology. Suddenly in 1913 the Anglican Benedictines on Caldey Island corporately converted to Rome. Their abbot, Aelred Carlyle (1874–1955), was sent to Maredsous to undergo a personal novitiate, and Chapman was asked by the bishop of Menevia to go to Caldey as temporary superior for a year, a delicate task that he discharged with tact and discretion.

During World War I Chapman served as a military chaplain and then was asked to join the Vulgate Commission in Rome. After he disagreed with his principal collaborator, Dom Quentin, on the methods to be followed in deciding between variant manuscripts, Chapman returned to England in 1922. In the meantime, because of wartime hostilities, his community at Erdington had returned to Germany, and in 1919 he transferred his monastic stability to Downside, where he became prior in 1922 and abbot in 1929, a surprisingly rapid promotion for a newcomer. Sadly he survived only half his term of office, dying in 1933.

Although his regime was brief and dogged by ill health, it was a very productive one on the material level: a daughter house was established at Worth, many new buildings were added to the school, and the church was embellished with choir stalls and an organ. However, clouds of crisis were gathering on the very level where Chapman might have been expected to be more than equal to coping with it. A group of younger monks led by Dom David Knowles (1896–1974) were alarmed at the encroachments of the school on to the pattern of monastic life at Downside. The trial of strength that ensued became an implacable one. The abbot was already very ill and resorted to peremptory measures, posting David Knowles to Ealing, where he soon severed his connection with Downside and went on to a brilliant career as a historian at Cambridge.

However, this sad final chapter should not force into the shade Chapman's outstanding achievements in scholarship and spirituality. In his *John the Presbyter and the Fourth Gospel* (1908), he entered the lists against Adolf Harnack's view that John the Evangelist was not John the Apostle but rather another John whom Papias called "the Presbyter." In *Matthew, Mark and Luke* (1967), Chapman contended for Greek Matthew as the earliest of the Synoptics, arguing against the prevailing consensus. He doughtily defended the Catholic interpretation of the early evidence for the papal claims against Bishop Charles Gore and other critics. However, in monastic history he took up positions that were ingenious, not to say bizarre: that St. Benedict wrote his Rule at the order of the pope and that his monastery consisted not of unlettered peasants, as believed by Cuthbert Butler, but of cultivated well-born Romans (*Saint Benedict and the Sixth Century*, 1929). The works that modern readers will find most illuminating are his contributions to the *Catholic Encyclopedia* on the early Fathers and councils and especially his article "Mysticism" in the Hastings *Dictionary of Religion and Ethics*.

However, it is above all as a guide to prayer and contemplation that Chapman has exerted a lasting influence. His aphorisms are often quoted. His *Spiritual Letters* (edited by Roger Hudleston, 1935) convey his doctrine all the more effectively because the book is not arrayed as a treatise but is addressed personally to his correspondents, clearly, briefly, to the point, and in down-to-earth language without any attempt at being impressive. Such discerning and qualified observers as Evelyn Underhill and Friedrich von Hügel have born testimony to Chapman's authoritative guidance in this field, the fruit both of firsthand experience and of that garnered from the many contemplatives whom he had encountered in his work of retreat giving. The thrust of his teaching was to reassure people who, worried by their inability to meditate, were actually ready to go on to the prayer of quiet, when the soul wants merely to be with God, not to think about him. Chapman was very conscious that different individuals need to be treated differently and not by any run-of-the-mill method and that spiritual directors should know when to withdraw from the scene. Whereas Cuthbert Butler was very much shaped by the teaching of Augustine Baker (1575–1641), Chapman's guiding light was the 18th-century French Jesuit Jean Pierre de Caussade (1675–1751) and his doctrine of abandon and the sacrament of the Present Moment. This led to Chapman being accused of Quietist tendencies by another Jesuit, Archbishop Goodier (*The Month*, 852, 1935, 493ss.). However, these charges did not attain much credence.

DANIEL REES

See also Anglican Monasticism; Baker, Augustine; Beuron, Germany; Butler, Cuthbert; England: History; Island Monasteries, Christian; Knowles, M. David; Liturgical Movement 1830–1980; Main, John; Meditation: Christian Perspectives; Spirituality: Western Christian

## Biography
After undergraduate studies at Christ Church, Oxford, he was ordained a deacon in 1889. A year later he joined the Roman Catholic Church and in 1892 entered the Benedictine house at Maredsous, Belgium. In 1913 he served as superior of the community at Caldey Island immediately after it had converted to Roman Catholicism. After serving as a military chaplain during World War I, he transferred to Downside abbey in 1919, where three years later he became prior and from 1929 to 1933 abbot.

## Major Works
*John the Presbyter and the Fourth Gospel*, 1908
*Saint Benedict and the Sixth Century*, 1929
*The Spiritual Letters of Dom John Chapman, O.S.B., Fourth Abbot of Downside*, edited by Roger Hudleston, 1935
*Mathew, Mark, and Luke*, 1967

## Further Reading
Brooke, Christopher, editor, *David Knowles Remembered*, Cambridge and New York: Cambridge University Press, 1991
Butler, Cuthbert, "Abbot Chapman," in *Downside Review* 52 (1934)
Hudleston, Roger, "A Memoir of Abbot Chapman," in his *The Spiritual Letters of Dom John Chapman, O.S.B., Fourth Abbot of Downside*, London and New York: Sheed and Ward, 1935

# Charism

The Greek word *charisma* (from the Greek verb *charizesthai*, "to do a favor") does not appear in classical Greek, rarely in the Septuagint version of the Hebrew Bible, but 16 times in the letters of St. Paul and once in 1 Pet. 4:10. The New Testament always uses the word to describe something God does or gives. At times, *charisma* simply signifies a generous gift from God, but in other texts it refers not to gifts that God bestows in a general sense but to specific gifts given by God according to need and from God's generosity. Thus, "Each has a particular gift [*charismata*] from God, one having one kind and another a different kind" (1 Cor. 7:7). What these gifts are in particular varies according to the specific context, as the list of *charismata* in Paul's letters differs. In 1 Cor. 12, Paul describes an impressive array of meanings for *charismata*, ranging from modest skills, such as a "word of knowledge," to more extraordinary gifts of healing and doing powerful works to the "gift of prophecy" and "every sort of tongue." In Rom. 12:6–8, the list is modified to encapsulate, first, prophecy and then service, teaching, exhortation, generous giving, helping, and acting in mercy. By contrast, 1 Pet. 4:10–11 lists as gifts the ministry of word and service.

In patristic literature, *charismata* reflects a similar fluidity of meaning. The word *charisma* has been applied to the Holy Spirit, the Baptism, the Eucharist, the priesthood, forgiveness of sins and chastity as well as the New Testament understandings of prophecy, miracles, and so on. Because the Latin Vulgate did not use the word *charisma* but, rather, words such as *gratia* (grace) and *donatio* (gift), medieval theologians did not use the Greek term. However, as the theology of grace evolved, they did make some distinctions that took into account the Pauline passages discussed previously. For example, St. Thomas Aquinas distinguished that grace given by God, by which we are sanctified, and those graces given for a particular need but that do not transform us and make us favorable to God. In the Summa (I IIae 171–178), Thomas discusses these latter graces (*gratiae gratis datae*, "graces freely given") and categorizes them as follows: gifts that relate to knowledge (prophecy, faith, wisdom, discernment of spirits, and knowledge); those that relate to speech (tongues and the gift of preaching); and, finally, those that involve action (performing miracles). In his reflections on the nature of "graces freely given," Thomas makes an observation that would become standard in subsequent theology, namely, that these gifts are given not for one's own sanctification but to help others come closer to God.

In the modern period, we need to distinguish two understandings of charismatic gifts. Since the turn of the 20th century, with the genesis and subsequent rise of modern pentecostalism, one strand of the Christian tradition has understood these gifts almost exclusively in terms of those religious experiences that emphasize ecstatic experience, the gifts of tongues, the baptism of the Holy Spirit, and those other outpourings that characterize the so-called charismatic renewal in either of its various Protestant or Catholic forms. The charismatic revival triggered a new interest in the gifts, and that interest, in turn, gave impetus to many theological investigations.

The Second Vatican Council (1962–1965), after some hesitations from those who saw charismatic gifts referring only to those extraordinary outpourings of the Holy Spirit (in prophecy, glossolalia, and so on), adopted a wider understanding of charism, that is, those special graces given by the Holy Spirit to "Christians of every rank" so that they might be made ready to "assume various works and offices, for the renewal and upbuilding of the church" (Dogmatic Constitution on the Church, *Lumen Gentium* no. 12). It is interesting that the same chapter of the constitution denies that these gifts need be extraordinary (*clarissima*); indeed, they might be simple and diffused in the church (*simpliciora*).

What are these gifts that "upbuild" the church? Commentators, inspired by the Pauline lists, have spoken of the charism of teaching but have also added catechesis, service to the poor, forms of social action, and other activities of the active apostolate. Once the church became accustomed to using the language of charisms for activities that aid in the edification of the church, it became easier to look backward into Christian history to detect in the tradition those gifts of the Spirit that were not tied directly to the sacrament of Orders (e.g., priesthood and episcopacy) but to those regular impulses by which all baptized persons, in the pursuit of the Christian life, also do so while aiding in the building up of the church. One theologian listed the following from the Christian tradition with no pretense to completeness: monasticism, asceticism, virginity, martyrdom, poverty, and mysticism as well as social services and the doing of theology.

In what sense can monasticism be called a charism? If one accepts that the monastic life is one way of being a Christian, one might further argue that this particular way of life gives to the church certain things that intensify its presence in time and space as well as its desire to instantiate insights into holiness. The decree on the renewal of religious life (*Perfectae Caritatis*) of the Second Vatican Council refers to monastic institutions as "seedbeds of growth" (*seminaria edificiationis*). The decree links that phrase to its earlier analysis of the role of monasticism in the life of the church. How precisely does monasticism add to the life of the church, or, to put it within our traditional vocabulary, how is monasticism a gift given for the good of others?

First, monasticism is available to baptized persons of both genders as a realizable way of living the Christian life. Despite the clericalization of masculine monastic life (an accident of history), monasticism is a lay movement that is offered as yet another way of being a Christian. Second, monasticism instantiates certain elements of Gospel living in an exemplary fashion: separation from the world; the value of work and the sharing of goods; the priority of prayer and work and the gifts of hospitality, silence, solitude, and retreat offered to others.

To enter the monastic life, then, is to do so in obedience to the grace of vocation but with the added dimension that living out the monastic life is both for personal Christian growth and a sign for others. In this way, we can understand monasticism as bringing to reality certain emphases of the gospels that otherwise might be absent or attenuated in Christian witness. It is for that reason that the abbot general of the Cistercians could write, on the ninth centenary of the founding of the order, that monks recognize the "gift we have received: our vocational charism." He then adds that this vocational grace is "for the sake of serving many others."

LAWRENCE S. CUNNINGHAM

*See also* Orders (Religious), Origin of; Vocation, Christian

**Further Reading**

Betencourt, Esteveo, "Charism," in *Sacramentum Mundi: An Encyclopedia of Theology*, volume 1, edited by Karl Rahner et al., New York: Herder and Herder, 1968

Kline, Francis, *Lovers of the Place: Monasticism Loose in the Church*, Collegeville, Minnesota: Liturgical Press, 1997

Malatesta, Edward, "Charism," in *The New Dictionary of Catholic Spirituality*, edited by Michael Downey, Collegeville, Minnesota: Liturgical Press, 1993

Olivera, Bernardo, "The Ninth Centenary and the Millenium: Church, World, Cistercians," *Cistercian Studies Quarterly* 33:4 (1998)

# Chih-i. *See* Zhiyi

# China

*Background*

Monasticism was alien to China. Introduced by central Asians in the first century A.D., Buddhism remained confined largely to the foreign communities for the first few centuries. The Chinese word for monastery, *si*, probably derived from the name of the office that handled foreign relations (*Honglu si*). A further barrier to Chinese entering the Sangha was the fact that the monastic rules were transmitted orally. The first authenticated translations of Buddhist scriptures were made by the Parthian An Shigao between 148 and the 180s, but they concerned doctrine and meditation, not discipline (vinaya). After the collapse of the Han dynasty in 220, ordinations might have ceased in

North China because of a lack of qualified monks to perform the ceremony in the prescribed manner, which required three masters and seven witnesses or, *in extremis*, five, all senior monks. This practice was not properly revived until after 250, when the first Vinaya texts were translated by Dharmakala.

The problem of ordination and lack of textual authority plagued the *bhiksuni* (nuns). The orthodox ordination of women, who constituted a separate order or assembly (*sangha*, *zhong*) because they had to observe more rules, required ten monks and ten nuns of ten years' seniority. They were difficult to find in this early period. The first nun, Jingjian, to receive the vows of a novice (*sramanerika*) did so in 317 and did not receive full ordination as a nun until 357. Yet this ordination was challenged by some monks. Around 429 a group of Sri Lankan nuns also disputed the legitimacy of all earlier ordinations of Chinese nuns. In 433/34 most of the Chinese nuns were reordained with the help of other Sri Lankan nuns.

### Northern and Southern Dynasties

Around 300 Chinese Buddhism was separated geographically into North and South by political events. The northern tendency favored a "state church," subordinating the Sangha to the state.

The Sangha prospered but at the cost of state interference. The Sangha's administration imitated the secular bureaucracy, and Buddhism developed mass followings of devotees and monasteries with vast estates.

Southern Buddhism was that of the gentry or aristocracy, which asserted autonomy of the Sangha. This Buddhism practiced a gentleman's Buddhism of tranquillity, filial piety, and metaphysical speculation, eminently suited to the noble monk who fitted the pattern of the traditional Chinese recluse hidden in mountain seclusion. This was a career option for the marginalized gentry. The North was ruled by non-Chinese, who used Buddhism as an arm of government, whereas the South was under Chinese rule and had few foreign monks. Buddhism developed along these two trajectories until the Sui reunited China in 589.

### The South

Under a series of weak regimes in the South, from 340 the Sangha asserted autonomy (i.e., a right not to literally bow to secular rulers). Some of the southern gentry and rulers were staunch Confucians, for they considered themselves exiles who had to emphasize their Chineseness to differentiate themselves

Qianfodong (Thousand Buddha Caves) at Matisi (Horse-hoof Temple), Zhangye, Gansu province, China, Buddhist caves and niches from the fifth century and later.
Photo courtesy of Marylin M. Rhie

Longmen, Henan, Binyang dong (Cave 3), interior view encompassing central seated Buddha and standing Buddha with Bodhisattva and Luohan in between.
Photo courtesy of John C. Huntington, the Huntington Archive

from both the "barbarian" North and the indigenous southerners. This conservatism manifested itself in attacks on the alien aspects of Buddhist monasticism. These Confucians asserted universal rule, (i.e., no state within a state). Thus, they objected to the Sangha as a rival institution possessing regulations that introduced a parallel law and rival authority. The monks replied that the Sangha rules were more akin to Confucian ritual and decorum than to secular laws and that the blessings (*fu*) brought by the Sangha assisted the state. When a military leader, Huan Xuan (369–404), took power in a coup d'état in 402, he challenged the independence of the order on the grounds that monks and nuns had participated in politics. The defense was led by Huiyuan (334–417), a pupil of Daoan (312–385), who had introduced a fuller Vinaya to the North and distinguished Buddhism from native Chinese thought.

The magnitude of the task that Huiyuan faced in bridging the cultural and ideological divide was enormous. Unlike in India, where religious communities were independent and rulers paid homage to monks and ascetics, in China the emperor was in theory supreme, being the Son of Heaven, who could tolerate no rivals for authority or independent associations within the state.

Huiyuan pleaded that the Sangha is not of the secular world. The monk dwelt as a traveling guest "beyond the limits" (*fang-*

*wai*) of the profane world. The monk is searching for the ultimate, eternal spirit (*shen*), which is the base for the superstructure of temporal appearances (*xiang*), the secular institutions and ideologies. Thus, monks can save the world only by being apart from the world yet within it. These guests must be provided for by the state so that the soteriological mission can be accomplished. Thus, the Sangha had to be autonomous and have its own rule. Huiyuan did concede that the state could purge the Sangha to maintain the purity of its membership. Furthermore, he claimed the Sangha had a civilizing role equal to that of good government, which assisted the state. The xenophobia of the exiles who saw Buddhism as barbarian could be countered only by declaring the similarity of Buddhism to native ideologies. Thus, for Huiyuan, Buddhism was the inner fundamental in civilization and morality, whereas Confucianism was its outer derivative.

The greatest cultural barrier to acceptance of celibate monasticism was Chinese familism. Filial piety meant that the individual had to serve the family and produce heirs to continue the worship of the ancestors. To display filial piety the body had to be preserved in its natural condition. The celibate, who shaved his head, left the family (*chujia*), and maybe mutilated his body, was accused of exterminating the family and even humanity and of doing to his body what the state did in punishing criminals. Daoan had attempted to give the Sangha its own family status by having the clergy take the surname of the Buddha, Shakya, or *Shi*. For the renouncers leaving the impurity of the family was to enter purity. Huiyuan contended that according to the Vinaya persons could not join the Sangha if their parents denied permission or if they were state employees. Huiyuan's senior, Sun Cho (c. 300–380), had gone so far as to argue that Buddhist filial piety was more comprehensive and efficacious than other forms could be. Achievement of sainthood by the monk-son increased the veneration directed to the father and brought parents greater bliss through rebirth in Heaven, a Pure Land, so that they no longer required the sacrifices of secular ancestor worship. Later it was claimed that as any being might have been one's ancestor, the Sangha's filial piety was more universal because it was directed to all beings, not only the clan ancestors.

### The North

The North was ruled by violent, non-Chinese despots. There was no question of the Sangha's autonomy; Buddhism was a tool

The main cliff (west side), Maiji Shan (Corn-rick Mountain), Tianshui, Gansu province, China, Buddhist caves founded in the early fifth century.
Photo courtesy of Marylin M. Rhie

of the ruler. However, the credulous, often illiterate military rulers were impressed by the magic of the Buddhist missionaries. Leading thaumaturges, such as the Kuchan Fotudeng (d. 349), who supposedly gained their powers through meditation and asceticism, became state-employed shamans who brought rain, cured illness, and predicted the future. The rulers also preferred the universal Buddhism over the particularist native Confucianism of their subjects. Thus, they encouraged central Asian or Indian translators to come, and so most of the Buddhist scriptures were translated in the North. State sponsorship rapidly expanded the Sangha in the North, an area that had over 80 percent of the Chinese population and that boasted a higher percentage of the population in the order, about 5 percent. The larger Sangha resulted in pressure to compile comprehensive monastic rules, something that Fotudeng tried to introduce. His pupil, Daoan, attempted to locate a complete translation of the Vinaya but, having failed, eventually wrote his own code of procedures that spread through the North and the South. This search continued. After Kumārajīva (344–413) arrived in China in 401, he translated the Sarvastivada Vinaya and introduced a complete school of Buddhist thought: the Madhyamaka. These ideas and his excellent translations of scriptures were sent through correspondence and a mass exodus of monks southward in 416 after a pro-Buddhist northern dynasty was overthrown.

The Tabgatch Turk Northern Wei dynasty (386–534), despite a persecution of Buddhism in 446–452, took northern Buddhism to its zenith. Buddhism became a mass religion. The Sangha had over 2 million members by about 525. The state and Sangha were identified with an implication that the emperor was a Buddha (or his earthly representative) and the patriarch of the clergy. After 405 the state created a bureaucracy of monks to administer the Sangha in parallel to secular officialdom. Monasteries acquired vast estates, and people flocked to become tenants, serfs, and servants of the Sangha to avoid state imposts. Thus, the state introduced laws to control the Sangha and a system of registration for clerics. Although it expelled those whom it considered undesirable, the wealth and corruption of the order led to increasing criticism.

Popular Buddhism in the villages and lay societies introduced the previously non-Chinese fear of hellfire as a consequence of evil actions and karma to create the beginnings of a Buddhist ancestral cult. In its later, classical form, this filial piety was directed more to the mother than to the father, the contrary of what was demanded by Confucianism. Mothers had sinned (*zui*) by having given birth to the son. To avert the hellish results of this sin, a son had to be a devout Buddhist and contribute to the order, which was self-defined as a field of merit or fortune (*futian*). Just as good crops are the result of past good deeds, so the harvest of merit for the ancestors and the donor could be gathered by planting the monastic field with the seeds of donations. Thus, elites and peasants, lay and clergy, all made offerings to monasteries so that their ancestors and relatives would be alleviated of their hellish tortures and be reborn in the Western Pure

Land through this transfer of merit through the Sangha, which thus prospered.

## Reunification and Maturity

In 589 the Sui finally reunited China and its two Buddhisms. The South contributed the scholastic schools of thought, whereas the North brought a legacy of state regulation, Sangha bureaucracy, state monasteries, mass piety, meditation, and Vinaya. The cross-fertilization helped form so-called sects or schools, each with its own founder, defined membership, core doctrines, and in some cases rules. Although disputes had arisen over doctrine, it was apparently the connection with state intervention and property that initiated the process. Zhiyi (538–597), the founder of Tiantai, was granted half the taxes of Shifeng County by Emperor Xuan of Chen in 577 for the expenses of his assembly. Thus, his influence dominated Mount Tiantai, and later the Sui emperor became his patron. Zhiyi's pupil, Guanding (561–632), created a lineage of masters back to the Buddha, initiating the issue of "family lineages," or genealogies, in East Asian Buddhism. Guanding also wrote a special code of discipline or procedures for the Tiantai monasteries to supplement the Vinaya. Up until this time, and in a sense to the present, a monastery could house teachers of several theoretical systems. The monastery "belonged" to the "school" or lineage (zong) of its abbot, and when he resigned the master of another school could become abbot. However, as emperors and officials began to donate land and tax revenues to specific monasteries, the property was jealously guarded and passed on to the heir or senior disciple. Emperor Yang of Sui (605–618) established monasteries under specified masters to teach a particular doctrine or sūtra as heads of assemblies (zhongzhu), and this might have forged a nexus between doctrines, lineages and monastic property to induce "sectarian" divisions within the Sangha.

During the Tang dynasty, when Buddhist monasticism matured, four aspects of monastic regulation were prevalent: the formal Vinaya of a theoretically autonomous order, the supplementary bodhisattva or Mahāyāna precepts, the informal rules governing individual monasteries formed in response to the Chinese environment; and the state laws governing the Sangha.

A problem for the Chinese was which Vinaya to use. At least four Vinaya codes had been translated by the first decades of the fifth century. By the sixth century the Dharmaguptaka Vinaya (sifenlü) dominated, as it was easier to understand. It was adopted by Daoxuan (596–667), the founder of the Nanshan school of Vinaya. Two other schools were based on the Dharmaguptaka Vinaya. Daoxuan's grand-pupil, Daoan (654–717), gained an informal edict from Emperor Zhongzong in 709 to have the Dharmaguptaka Vinaya made the code governing the entire Sangha. Later, in 778 or 781, Emperor Daizong ordered 14 leading Vinaya specialists from the three schools to synthesize their conflicting interpretations. This left the Nanshan school the only Vinaya school, and its supremacy in discipline and monastic codes lasted until the end of the dynasty. Eventually, in the Song dynasty, it was subsumed by the Chan monastic rules, the

View of niches, Feilaifeng Buddhist grottoes, near Hangzhou, Zhejiang, China, late 14th century.
Photo courtesy of Marylin M. Rhie

qinggui, which remained the supreme but supplementary code until modern times.

However, it was widely appreciated by the fifth century that these Vinaya codes were not Mahāyāna in spirit and thus were deficient. A movement grew in the sixth century, based partly on Indian texts in translations and partly on Chinese apocrypha, to formulate a supplementary set of precepts suitable for the bodhisattva, who could be a layperson or cleric. These vows were not meant for the regulation of monasteries but rather emphasized personal intention over physical and verbal activities. The vow was intended not to achieve personal liberation but to save all beings. The Dharmaguptaka Vinaya divided the precepts into performance, external form, the rule itself, and the mental acceptance of the rules. The last of these had been a matter of dispute, and Daoxuan, following the lead of Huiguang (468–537), to make his Vinaya conform to Mahāyāna, stated that the embodiment or mental essence of the precepts were seeds in the unconscious (ālayavijñāna) and that the divergence between Mahāyāna and non-Mahāyāna precepts were due to differences in ability and opportunity. These ideas contributed to the ideas on precepts and monastic regulation.

Furthermore, many regulations were not sanctioned by the Vinaya but had become customary in various monasteries because of the difficulties of maintaining Indian practices in a Chinese environment. Because clergy were not permitted in Chinese culture to beg for food, donors gave money or land, or else monks had to cultivate fields. They also participated in construction, mourned their parents, held personal wealth, supervised estates, and lent money or grain, all activities prohibited by the Vinaya. Thus, these practices were gradually codified in the custom of some monasteries.

The most significant factor was the state. Sangha autonomy was lost, as monks had to pay homage to the ruler, from 760 calling themselves "your subject" when addressing the sovereign. During the early Tang dynasty, the Sangha was severely subordinated to state authority, which issued special legal codes governing the clergy (daosengge) in 637, taxed the clergy, and limited their numbers by instituting qualifying examinations and ordination certificates, which changed from being a proof of status as a member of the order to being a permit for ordination. The clergy were punished by the state for breaches of secular and Buddhist law, and only minor infringements of the monastic discipline were handled by the order. The monastic officers were reduced to peripheral roles, and the Sangha lost its remaining autonomy. Yet enforcement of this state-imposed regulation was strict only when the government was efficient or threatened, and in later dynasties the laws were used only as warnings. Because ordination became more difficult when the state limited clerical numbers, many aspirants to the Sangha had to begin as apprentices (*dongzi*, aged 7 to 15) and then became acolytes (*xingzhe*), still untonsured. One could be tonsured only as a novice (*shami*) at 20, but as the state restricted numbers, some remained acolytes until middle age before gaining an ordination certificate. This created abuses, as even *shami* might be required to perform physical labor in the monasteries, and the state sold these certificates when the treasury needed funds. This abuse was widespread in the Song dynasty.

Although the clergy were not taxed as individuals, when the Tang allocated land to them the tax was paid by the monastery where the cleric was registered on the grounds that the Vinaya prohibited private property. Because of the wealth of the monasteries and the Chan custom of hereditary successions of abbots, the Southern Song strengthened the position of abbot by having them "publicly selected" or appointed by the state. Abbots were required to enforce stricter controls over monastic wealth and clerics' movements, and they became part of the tax collection system. Southern Song also established a system of major, imperially controlled Chan monasteries, the so-called five mountains and ten monasteries in southeastern China. Their abbots were appointed by imperial decree, and their role was to pray for the emperor and state. Thus, a form of state Buddhism was perpetuated, and later dynasties adopted similar policies.

Two forms of monastery and cleric resulted, forms that survived into the 20th century. The clerical "proletariat" lived in small, privately owned monasteries. The monastery was inherited by the ordination disciples of its "abbot." The clerical "elite" tended to live in the "large public monasteries" (*shifang conglin*), which were the common property of the entire Sangha, where Vinaya and Chan monastic procedures were strictly observed. Their large estates and populations required a complex bureaucracy in imitation of secular administration, and the abbots were selected by consultation, vote, or lot. All monks were tonsured in hereditary monasteries and joined a tonsure "family." This was not ordination as a novice (*shami*), for full ordination as a monk (*shamen*) was not legal until the age of 20. This came only after years of training, and ordinands were supposed to have state certification. Full ordination tended to occur at the public monasteries.

The monasteries only nominally belonged to "sects." Lineage counted for far more than doctrine, so a monastery might lecture on Tiantai doctrine, ordain according to the Vinaya school rit-

ual, live under a Chan monastic rule, and practice Pure Land devotions. Monasteries were largely autonomous when the state allowed and were not controlled by the order, which had no central administration. Monasteries went through cycles of construction, decay, and restoration or reconstruction. Strong abbots and strict discipline led to prosperity, the reverse to decline. The hereditary monasteries provided the rites for the dead, and some monasteries became pilgrimage and tourist destinations. Others put on plays and at festival times became fairgrounds. However, the large public monasteries often maintained an exclusion of all but earnest believers and genuine members of the Sangha.

JOHN JORGENSEN

*See also* Buddhism: Inculturation; Buddhist Schools/Traditions: China; Chan/Zen: China; Critiques of Buddhist Monasticism: Confucian; Critiques of Buddhist Monasticism: Indo-Tibetan; Daoism: Influence on Buddhism; Economics: Buddhist; Holy Men/Holy Women: Buddhist Perspectives; Initiation: Buddhist Perspectives; Libraries: Buddhist; Manuscript Production: Buddhist; Missionaries: Buddhist; Mountain Monasteries, Buddhist; Pilgrims to India, Chinese; Social Services: Buddhist; Taiwan

**Further Reading**

Ch'ên, Kenneth, *Buddhism in China: A Historical Survey*, Princeton, New Jersey: Princeton University Press, 1964

Cole, Alan, *Mothers and Sons in Chinese Buddhism*, Stanford, California: Stanford University Press, 1998

Kimura, Eiichi, editor, *Eon kenkyū*, Tokyo: Sōbunsha, 1962

Moroto, Tatsuo, *Chūgoku Bukkyō seidoshi no kenkyū*, Tokyo: Hirakawa Shuppansha, 1990

Ōchō, Enichi, editor, *Hokugi Bukkyō no kenkyū*, Kyoto: Heirakuji shoten, 1970

Ren, Jiyu, *Han Tang Fojiao sixiang lunji*, Peking: Renmin chubanshe, 1963

Tang, Yongtong, "Lun Zhongguo Fojiao wu shizong," *Xiandai Foxue* 4 (1964)

Tōdō, Kyōshun, and Shioiri Ryōdō, *Kan minzoku no Bukkyō: Bukkyō denrai kara Zui Tō made (Ajia Bukkyōshi: Chūgoku hen 1)*, Tokyo: Kōsei Shuppansha, 1975

Tsai, Kathryn, "The Chinese Buddhist Monastic Order for Women," *Historical Reflections/Réflexions Historiques* 8:3 (1981)

Tsai, Kathryn, translator, *Lives of the Nuns: Biographies of Chinese Buddhist Nuns from the Fourth to Sixth Centuries*, Honolulu: University of Hawaii Press, 1994

Tso, Sze-bong, "The Transformation of Buddhist Vinaya in China," Ph.D. Diss., Australian National University, 1982

Ui, Hakuju, *Ui Hakuju chosaku senshū*, Tokyo: Daitō Shuppansha, 1966

Weinstein, Stanley, *Buddhism under the T'ang*, Cambridge and New York: Cambridge University Press, 1987

Welch, Holmes, *The Practice of Chinese Buddhism 1900–1950*, Cambridge, Massachusetts: Harvard University Press, 1967

Welch, Holmes, *The Buddhist Revival in China*, Cambridge, Massachusetts: Harvard University Press, 1968

Wright, Arthur F., *Buddhism in Chinese History*, Stanford, California: Stanford University Press, 1959

Wright, Arthur F., *Studies in Chinese Buddhism*, edited by Robert M. Somers, New Haven, Connecticut: Yale University Press, 1990

Zürcher, Erik, *The Buddhist Conquest of China: The Spread and Adaptation of Buddhism in Early Medieval China*, Leiden: Brill, and New York: Humanities Press, 1959

# Chinul 1158–1210

## Korean founder of Chogye School of Sŏn Buddhism

As the founder of Korea's preeminent Chogye Order school of Sŏn (Chinese, Chan; Japanese, Zen) Buddhism, Chinul's impact on monasticism from Koryŏ times until today remains unparalleled. Posthumously conferred the title "National Preceptor Puril Pojo" ("the Universally Illuminating Buddha Sun") at his death at age 53 by King Huijong, an ardent follower, Chinul innovated a distinctive Korean tradition of conjoint Kyo (doctrinal study) and Sŏn (meditation practice), which radiated from his base at Susŏnsa in South Chŏlla province to virtually every corner of the Korean peninsula.

Born into an educated but low gentry family near the Koryŏ capital in Hwanghae province of present-day North Korea, we presume that Chinul left home to begin his religious profession in his teens during the turbulence of mid-dynasty times characterized by merciless power struggles, military coups, and disrupted social conditions. The Buddhist *sangha* was in serious moral decline after centuries of royal patronage and consequent misuse of power and wealth. Dividing the Buddhist clergy was a major contention between scholastic Kyo sects that favored Hwaŏm (Avataṃsaka) or Ch'ŏnt'ae (Tiantai) theory and Sŏn practice sects that were derived from disciples of Chinese master Ma-tsu Tao-i (Mazu Daoyi, 707–786). However, all temples catered to the ceremonial demands of noble patrons and their desire for ritualistic merit making.

Chinul rebelled against such disharmony and decadence early in his career. He devoted his life to reforming Korean Buddhist practice and faith first by attempting to foster a model "Concentration (*samādhi*) and Wisdom (*prajñā*) Society" (1188) with like-minded colleagues deep in the mountains, mentally and physically distant from the material concerns of the worldly *sangha* and its supporters. Growing numbers of followers led to the establishment of "The Society for the Cultivation of Sŏn" (Susŏnsa) and the reconstruction of an old temple renamed the same (1197–1205). The mountain on which it was built was renamed "Chogye" by the king, after the name of the mountain where the famous sixth patriarch of China once taught. This temple is now called Songgwangsa, the Sangha Jewel Monastery of today's Chogye Order. It is here that Chinul composed his mature work on the gradual cultivation of *samādhi* and *prajñā* in a way that also required strict adherence to the monastic precepts.

Although ordained in the Sagul-san lineage of the Nine Mountains School of Sŏn, Chinul did not study under a Sŏn master, nor did he receive formal transmission from a recognized adept. Rather he studied the sūtras, commentaries, and records of Chan masters independently and in an eclectic spirit, unconstrained by sectarian bias. Unlike the great Silla scholastic Wŏnhyo (617–686), who lived five centuries earlier, we have detailed accounts of the master's times and inner life in his own words. Chinul's contribution to Korean monastic cultivation was aptly carried on through the leadership of his brilliant disciple, Hyesim (1178–1234), posthumously called national Master Chin'gak, after his master's death in the Susŏnsa community in 1210. Chinul was the first of a succession of 16 national masters over 108 years that established Susŏnsa as a major center of Korean Buddhist monasticism during the Koryŏ period and inspired the Korean *sangha* from the Yi dynasty (1392–1910) until the present.

*Major Works by Chinul*

Chinul's major transformative religious experiences were inspired by what he read in scriptures (in Chinese) himself at different stages of his career.

His first major work, *Kwŏnsu chŏnghye kyŏlsa mun* (*Encouragement to Practice: The Compact of the Concentration and Wisdom Community*), rails against dependence on the "other power" of Amitābha Buddha and employs numerous quotations to persuade readers to trust that originally they too are an "enlightened buddhas" and that all that is necessary is to recover that state of perfection.

*Kye cho'sim hagin mun* (*Admonitions to Beginning Students*) is the first text given to Korean postulants today, and it provides the standard of conduct for all Sŏn monasteries and establishes ethical behavior as the basis for Sŏn cultivation. *Susim kyŏl* (*Secrets on Cultivating the Mind*), written between 1203 and 1205, is considered the most popular and influential Sŏn texts today and reveals two major elements of Chinul's approach to practice: sudden awakening followed by gradual and simultaneous cultivation of concentration and insight or wisdom.

*Chinsim Chiksŏl* (*Straight Talk on the True Mind*), composed about the same time as *Secrets*, explores the cultivation of "no-mind" as a means of controlling the deluded mind and provides techniques suited to practitioners of differing capacities.

Chinul's magnum opus, *Pŏpchip pyŏrhaeng nok chŏryo pyŏngip sagi* (*Excerpts from the Dharma Collection and Separate Circulation Record with Personal Notes*), was composed at the culmination of his intense vocation in 1209, a year before his death. It is a basic text studied in the lecture halls of Korean monasteries today and is said to be comparable in influence to Thomas Aquinas' *Summa theologica* (1260s) in Western medieval Christianity. It is a grand overview and analytical evaluation of the various discussions of approaches to enlightenment extant in China and Korea in Chinul's time.

FRANK M. TEDESCO

*See also* Buddhism: Inculturation; Buddhist Schools/Traditions: Korea; Chan/Zen: Korea; Kōan; Korea: History; Korea: Sites; Wŏnhyo

## Biography

Founder of the Chogye School of Korean Sŏn (Zen) Buddhism, Chinul was ordained at age 7 and by 1182 was advocating mountain retreats as an escape from decadent monasteries. On Chogye Mountain Chinul composed works of synthesis inspired by reading the works of Chinese masters and his own personal illuminations. His writings revitalized Buddhism in Korea and made Sŏn the preeminent school there.

## Major Works

(All translations in Robert E. Buswell, editor, *The Korean Approach to Zen: The Collected Works of Chinul*, 1983)

*Kwŏnsu chŏnghye kyŏlsa mun*, 1190; as *Encouragement to Practice: The Compact of the Concentration and Wisdom Community*, 1983
*Susim kyŏl*, 1203–1205; as *Secrets on Cultivating the Mind*, 1983
*Chinsim Chiksŏl*, 1205; as *Straight Talk on the True Mind*, 1983
*Kye cho'sim hagin mun*, 1205; as *Admonitions to Beginning Students*, 1983
*Pŏpchip pyŏrhaeng nok chŏryo pyŏngip sagi*, 1209; as *Excerpts from the Dharma Collection and Separate Circulation Record with Personal Notes*, 1983

## Further Reading

Buswell, Robert E., *The Zen Monastic Experience: Buddhist Practice in Contemporary Korea*, Princeton, New Jersey: Princeton University Press, 1992
Buswell, Robert E., editor, *The Korean Approach to Zen: The Collected Works of Chinul*, Honolulu: University of Hawaii Press, 1983; abridged as *Tracing Back the Radiance: Chinul's Korean Way of Zen* (Classics in East Asian Buddhism), Honolulu: University of Hawaii Press, 1991
Keel, Hee-Sung, *Chinul: The Founder of Korean Sŏn Tradition* (Berkeley Buddhist Studies Series, 6), Berkeley: Center for South and Southeast Asian Studies, University of California at Berkeley, Institute of Buddhist Studies, 1984
Ko, Ik-chin, "Chinul's Explanation of Emptiness in the Meditation School," in *Buddhism in Koryŏ: A Royal Religion* (Korea Research Monograph, 22), edited by Lewis Lancaster, Kikun Suh, and Chai-Shin Yu, Berkeley: Institute of East Asian Studies, University of California, 1996
Moon, Simon Young-suck, *Korean and American Monastic Practices: A Comparative Case Study*, Lewiston, New York: Mellen Press, 1998
Shim, Jae-Ryong, *The Philosophical Foundation of Korean Zen Buddhism: The Integration of Sŏn and Kyo by Chinul, 1158–1210*, Seoul: T'aehaksa, 1981
Shim, Jae-Ryong, "Sŏn Buddhist Tradition in Korea – as Represented by Chinul's Pojo Sŏn," *Korea Journal* 21:8 (1981)

# Christianity: Overview

In contemporary English, the word *monk* is frequently used to designate anyone living a dedicated religious life regardless of religious belief. Within the Roman Catholic Church its canon law identifies a variety of types of religious life, each having specific characteristics. Although the term *monk* may be found frequently in popular use, some religious societies bear other official designations; for example, the Franciscans are, properly speaking, "friars," although many will speak of them as "monks." This article limits its discussion to the religious life as followed by canons regular, monks, and friars. Groups identified as clerks regular (e.g., the Jesuits or Camillians) or as "institutes of apostolic life" (e.g., the Christian Brothers or the Daughters of Charity) are not discussed.

## Historical Background

In Christian history the word *monk*, coming from the Greek *monos* and meaning "one who lives alone," began to be used around the fourth century. It was applied mainly to anchorites or hermits within Christianity. Quickly the word began to denote anyone who lived an ascetic life, whether alone or in a community, whether Christian or not. In our contemporary world we find references to "monks" in non-Christian traditions, such as the Buddhist or Hindu.

Beginning without an identifying label, men and women in pre-Christian times would take on themselves an ascetic way of life that followed a spiritual path set forth by a religious leader or teacher (e.g., the prophet Elijah, Hosea, or John the Baptizer). Commentators on monastic movements often suggest that a specified way of living a religious life develops when people respond to the spiritual and moral aspirations found in the human heart.

## Christian Monastic Beginnings

Some historians suggest that Christian monasticism began as a movement in the early fourth century. With Emperor Constantine's (306–337) proclamation of the "Edict of Milan" in 313, the persecution and death of Christian men and women largely came to an end. Some desired a "white martyrdom" and sought ways in which they could give themselves totally to Christ and thus follow the spirit of the early martyrs who had witnessed to the saving work of Jesus Christ.

Others suggest that monasticism arose in the late third century during a time of religious enthusiasm in Egypt. There is general agreement that individuals who desired to live an intense Christian life found it necessary to withdraw from home and city because of the demands and distractions found there. Monastic men and women saw a need to live fully the "renunciation of the world" that they had promised in Baptism, having within themselves a strong desire to achieve a union with God on this earth.

Daily activities for these ascetics would be directed to prayer and simple work (such as the making of baskets), which allowed the Spirit of God to work in their lives. Each monastic wanted to possess the Holy Spirit and be led to purity of heart. By this way of life, the soul would be cleansed of sin, pride, and self-seeking.

The basic elements and beliefs of the Christian faith began to diverge in the details of worship and religious customs. As Christians found themselves in a variety of cultures, Eastern and Western, Christian monasticism came to be expressed in a variety of ways in its external practices, lifestyles, and liturgical expressions.

Christian monastic prayer, whether in the East or the West, was built on the recitation of the Psalms, found in the Hebrew Scriptures, for these inspired poetic compositions focused on the movements of the human heart. Early monastics were laypeople who were not tied to any ministry or function within the structured Christian Church as it existed in the communities near which they lived. Stories are told of monks who would hide themselves lest they be found by a local bishop and be pressured to be ordained and then be required to undertake ecclesial ministries.

Two early theologians of the ascetic life, Clement of Alexandria (c. 150–c. 251) and Origen (c. 185–254), set the stage for much that would follow in the development of Christian monasticism. Saint Pachomius (c. 290–346) was the first to draw monks together in a community, or "cenobitic," structure, writing what some consider the oldest monastic rule of life. This rule presumed the possession of goods in common as well as celibacy along with obedience to a spiritual leader. John Cassian (c. 360–after 430) and Evagrius Ponticus (346–399) are identified as early monastic writers, and their works and views have been studied and commented on by monastic scholars down to our own day.

Saint Antony of Egypt (c. 251–356) is credited with being an initial model for the Christian monastic movement as we know it today mainly because the *Life of Saint Antony*, written by St. Athanasius (c. 296–373), provided a model of austerity and renunciation.

In time monastic groups formed in the desert areas of Judaea because of associations with the ministry as well as the death and resurrection of Christ. In Asia Minor St. Basil the Great (c. 330–379) and his brother, St. Gregory of Nyssa (c. 350–c. 395), along with Basil's close friend St. Gregory of Nazianzus (329/30–389/90), established a way of monastic living.

The spread of monastic life was heavily influenced by political conditions of the age. For example, when St. Athanasius was exiled to various parts of the Roman Empire as a result of his work against the Arian heresy (e.g., 336 to Trier, 339–346 to Rome, and 356–362 to the desert), he influenced the establishment of monastic groups.

### The Rule of St. Augustine

Although strictly speaking not a member of the monastic movement, St. Augustine (354–430), as bishop of Hippo in Africa, composed a Rule for Men (RV) because he desired his clergy to live in common near the cathedral church, and this lifestyle included the sharing of goods. A number of documents exist that claim to be the "Rule of St. Augustine," although scholars seriously question whether any of these came from his pen, having their origin long after his death, although attributed to him. Most accept the RV as originating with Augustine, and mention of this document is made here because of its enormous influence

on the spiritual base for subsequent movements, especially groups of canons regular.

### Monastic Development in the West

With the establishment of a monastery at Monte Cassino, Italy, and the synthesizing of monastic traditions into a structured way of life, St. Benedict of Nursia (c. 480–c. 550) becomes a key figure in the history of Western monasticism. Benedict's journey from an eremitic life in a cave at Subiaco to his establishment of 12 small monastic groups there before his move to Monte Cassino provides a background for understanding the monastic way of life sketched out in his Rule for Monks (RB). Most scholars believe that Benedict based his work on the Rule of the Master (RM), a longer document lacking Benedict's sense of discretion and balance. The RB is recognized for its abiding influence in the history of Western civilization mainly as "wisdom literature" rather than as legislation. Benedict calls his way "the beginning of monastic life" and refers his monks to other sources: the Bible itself, the "Conferences, Institutes, and Lives of the Fathers," and the Rule of St. Basil.

From the RB itself it is apparent that Benedict foresaw the possible influence of his structure beyond the foundation at Monte Cassino. For example, a reference is made that the abbot may make adjustments in the clothing or the food provided for the monks, depending on the climate of the area or the burden of manual labor. Benedict's own monastery faced destruction shortly after the founder's death. The monks found their way to Rome, where the rule was adapted to conditions there. The future Pope St. Gregory the Great (590–604) gave his ancestral home on the Caelian Hill of Rome for the foundation of a monastery and joined that community. As pope he would send St. Augustine (d. 604) and a group of monks to England, and these men brought with them monastic traditions and practices. With the first monastery established at Canterbury, monasticism took root, and groups went forth to establish other centers. York developed as a most important center in northern England. Some claim that the English Christian Church was a heavily monastic church, as the monasteries became the focal points of ecclesiastical life.

From its foundation and into the eighth century, one could not speak of a "monastic order." First of all no common rule existed, and monastic men and women followed a variety of rules and practices. In many cases a monastic group would follow what might well be described as "mixed rules," or bits and pieces taken from a variety of sources. Mention may be made also of a variety of Celtic rules (e.g., those of St. Ailbe or St. Columban [d. 615]), which also influenced monastic living in Ireland.

### Monastic Growth in the West

In the late seventh and into the eighth century, Anglo-Saxon missionaries to the Continent appear to be followers of the RB, and at the same time the monasteries in the West began to change in both their general structure and their influence. From being a gathering of some 12 to 20 people, monasteries became complex units with 100 or more monks, having large property holdings, a school, a place for guests, and even a hospital. In some cases people who secured the monks' livelihood surrounded the monastery itself by involvement with monastic works – agricultural as well as artistic.

By the year 800 monasteries following Benedict's Rule within the broad empire of Charlemagne (France, Germany, and a large part of Italy) were at the center of intellectual and ecclesiastical activity. From the monastery at York came Alcuin (c. 740–804), a counselor to the emperor and a monk who would further in every way possible the development of studies within every monastery. These centers of activity gradually became more involved in worldly affairs, and this spirit also would influence the monastic life and observance.

A new figure arose in the person of Abbot Benedict of Aniane (c. 750–821), after St. Benedict himself probably the most crucial figure in Benedictine history. He gradually persuaded monasteries to follow one tradition, eliminating the various observances and interpretations. He placed great emphasis on the contemplative nature of the monastic life and emphasized the gradual elimination of the "external" students in the monastic school, namely, those who were not really interested in pursuing a vocation within the monastic life.

A meeting of abbots and monks of the empire was held at Aachen in 817, and here regulations were enacted and promulgated throughout the empire with the support of Emperor Louis the Pious (814–840). A change was gradually taking place in that whereas the original ideal of the RM had expected most monastic members to remain laymen, with only a few priests ordained to serve the community, now Benedictine monasticism began to display a higher proportion of clerics.

The gradual acquisition of lands and the success of agricultural and artistic endeavors helped make monastic properties desirable to feudal lords. In addition Norse invasions began to destroy monasteries in France, but after a short period of decline monasticism began to rebuild. Within France itself the abbey of Cluny in Burgundy (founded 910) was developing as the center of a major movement. Although nobility had donated the land for this abbey, it was free to elect it own abbot as prescribed by the Rule, and the property was placed under the protection of the Apostolic see in Rome. This granted Cluny a unique opportunity to develop its own future while drawing into its way of life a wide number of monasteries seeking to shed external influences and pressures. At the same time all affiliated abbeys stood under the direct control of the abbot of Cluny. However, this reform tended to create a problem for monastic living because the Cluniac life did not favor the balance visualized by the Rule: prayer, work, and sacred reading. Instead the Cluniac monk began to see his existence as focused on long periods of formal community prayer and little or no manual labor or *lectio divina*.

## The Monastic Day

The RB attempts to provide a structured day that follows the cycle of nature, making the winter horarium different from the summer one. Desiring that "all be done by daylight," time is provided for "the work of God" (the Divine Office or Liturgy of the Hours), for *lectio divina* (the meditative reading of Scripture and the Church fathers), and manual labor.

In winter an ordinary day would include the following:

| | |
|---|---|
| 2:00 a.m. | Rise for the nocturns |
| 2:10–3:30 | Nocturns |
| 3:30–5:00 | *Lectio divina* |
| 5:00–5:45 | Lauds |
| 5:45–8:15 | *Lectio divina*, study of the Psalms, including the office of prime when work assignments were given. Monks met in the chapter room, where a chapter of the Rule was read and the abbot could give an instruction. |
| 8:15–2:30 | Work, broken up by terce, sext, and none (about 10 minutes each) |
| 2:30–3:15 | Dinner |
| 3:15–4:15 | *Lectio divina* |
| 4:15–5:15 | Vespers, light supper, short reading from the fathers, compline (night prayer) |
| 5:15 | Retire |

## Reforms and New Ways of Life

It has been claimed that the RB has never been lived exactly as written except at Monte Cassino during the author's life. Over time modifications to the Rule were made, accommodating the needs of the times or the geographic area. Benedict himself allows the abbot of the community to make modifications in the timetable, in the quantity of food and drink (e.g., wine), and even in the arrangements of the Psalms prayed at the Divine Office.

The Cluniac system seemed to be growing by leaps and bounds, having five saintly abbots ruling for a period of over 200 years (Odo 927–943, Majolus 954–994, Odilo 999–1048, Hugh 1049–1109, and Peter the Venerable 1122–1156). Nonetheless individual Cluniac monks sought to restore aspects of Benedict's ideals by emphasizing specific aspects of the RB.

Saint Romuald (950–1027) left a Cluniac monastery to begin an eremitic observance in the mountainous region of Camaldoli near Arezzo in Italy. Saint John Gualbert (990–1073), originally a Cluniac and then a monk at Camaldoli, was founder of a monastery at Vallombrosa near Florence, where there was perpetual silence, strict monastic enclosure, and no manual labor.

During this period one also sees movements that did not originate with existing monasteries but that developed monastic observances. For example, St. Bruno (c. 1032–1101) abandoned life as a teacher and scholar and joined a group of hermits in a forest in France, some of whom would be key in the future founding of a new way of monastic life under the RB at Cîteaux. With two companions Bruno left the forest community for a remote mountainous area in what today is the Grande Chartreuse, the central house of the Carthusian Hermits.

A few of Bruno's former companions in the forest decided to start monastic life anew with a strong emphasis on solitude, poverty, and exact observance of the RB as they interpreted it at Molesmes. Harmful influences from feudalism, wealthy benefactors, and other social elements caused about 21 men to leave Molesmes for the "desert called Cîteaux." This took place in 1098, and the movement spread quickly as a result of the charismatic St. Bernard (1090–1153). An interesting development takes place during this period with the establishment of the *conversi*, or lay brothers, whose prayer life did not include the Divine Office in choir and who spent greater time in manual labor. While following the RB with their own interpretations, the "Charter of Charity" governed the relations between monasteries, setting up a system whereby visitations would be conducted to preserve the observances prescribed. In time the Order of Cistercians would find themselves with people moving into another reform after the Council of Trent (1545–1563), that of Armand de Rancé (1626–1700) at the abbey of La Trappe, forming what today is the Order of Cistercians of Strict Observance, or the Trappists.

## The Beginnings of Canons Secular and Regular

Outside of European cathedral and collegiate churches, canons secular are little known. "Chapters of Canons" who pray the Divine Office in a cathedral serve also as advisers to the local bishop. Until the 12th century bishops were chosen by popular acclaim of clergy and laity. Because many cathedral churches developed alongside monasteries of Benedictine monks, the idea of having a group of men responsible for the Divine Office and the Eucharist almost naturally led to nonmonastic cathedrals having a nonmonastic group, the canons, whose prayer and service resembled that of monks.

From about the middle of the 11th century, cathedral communities began to share a common life and adopted the Rule of St. Augustine as their spiritual base. As indicated earlier Augustine developed a simple rule for the clergy of his diocese of Hippo to live together, being "of one heart and mind with all things in common." In our own day we have as an example the Canons Regular of the Lateran, a group that has spread beyond their cathedral in Rome to minister in the United States. A number of canons regular groups belong to the Confederation of St. Augustine for mutual support.

Some saintly men founded groups of canons regular that today function, at least in externals, as do monks: living in community, praying the Divine Office, and engaging in apostolic ministry. Two of the more well known are the Canons Regular of Prémontré (Premonstratensians or Norbertines), founded in 1120, and the Canons Regular of the Holy Cross (Crosiers), founded in 1211.

## The Rise of the Friars

As is the case with many religious movements, the foundation of groups known as friars came as a result of social and economic change. Urbanization created a need that could not be met by monks with their vow of stability, which committed them to remain in an established community. The two best known, the Friars Minor (founded by St. Francis of Assisi in 1212) and the Friars Preachers (founded by St. Dominic in 1216), provided itinerant preachers and, with the rise of the universities, philosophical and theological professors. Saint Thomas Aquinas (c. 1225–1274), Duns Scotus (c. 1265–1308), and St. Bonaventure (c. 1217–1274) were friars. Other groups of friars developed during the 13th century, helping fill the needs of the Church. Carmelites, Trinitarians and Mercedarians (both founded for the redemption of Christians taken captive by Muslims), Servites, Augustinian Friars, and the Brothers of St. John of God (Hospitallers) comprise the more well known groups of friars.

## Secularization and the French Revolution

As David Knowles (1896–1974) explains, "At the end of the domination of Napoleon I the monastic order, and in particular the traditional Benedictine family, was in worse case than at any time since the days of Benedict himself. The Reformation had cut off all abbeys in the Northern countries and the French Revolution and Napoleon had accounted for the rest" (Knowles, 1969). With the dissolution of more than 1,000 Benedictine and Cistercian monasteries, monasticism almost did not exist as the calendar announced the beginning of the 19th century.

It is interesting that one of the key figures in the monastic revival was a diocesan priest, Prosper Guéranger (1805–1875), who started in 1833 with the restoration of the Abbey of Solesmes in France. From this community, known for its research in and restoration of Gregorian chant, came abbeys in France, England, Spain, Belgium, Italy, Canada, Mexico, and Argentina and on the island of Martinique.

Another growth pattern emerged as some very small and almost dying monasteries, such as those of Subiaco and Finalpia in Italy, were refounded. Under Pope Pius IX (1846–1878), these helped develop the Cassinese Congregation of Primitive Observance, to which was joined some of the more famous abbeys such as Montserrat in Spain. King Ludwig I (1825–1848) in Bavaria was responsible for helping restore the Bavarian Congregation and the Abbey of Metten, which in turn incited development of St. Vincent Archabbey by Boniface Wimmer (1809–1887) as well as the American Cassinese Congregation, formed by monasteries emanating from the Latrobe, Pennsylvania, community. Two communities in Switzerland made foundations in the United States, and these developed into the Swiss-American Congregation.

## Monastic Life in the Eastern Christian Churches

With the beginnings of monastic life in the East, especially the eremitic and cenobitic foundations along the Nile in Egypt, monasteries within this tradition continued in a quite different way than was the case in the West. "Monastic traditions" rather than a "monastic rule" became the base for life and operation. Using the writings of St. Pachomius (c. 290–346) as a foundation, they would read the instructions and Long Rules of St. Basil (c. 330–379) and the writings of other monastic fathers and mothers.

The monastery of St. Theodore of Stoudios in Constantinople had a great influence in the development of Eastern monasteries.

The greatest thrust came with the founding of the *lavra*, or association of monasteries, on Mount Athos in Greece in 963. Fostered initially by Emperor Nicephorus II Phocas (963–969), a community of *lavra*s continues today and operates within the structures of Orthodox Churches. Monasteries there differ in language and ethnicity, although the life structure is similar, and the monasteries are autonomous, although an association exists of monastic superiors who agree to the basic operational principles and interactions.

Within the Catholic Eastern Churches, one finds "Studite" monastic communities within the Byzantine Ukrainian tradition being revitalized in L'viv, Ukraine, part of the former Soviet Union. These men lived an "underground" monastic life under Communism and now seek to return to the spirit of their founder. The Order of St. Basil the Great (Basilian Fathers and Brothers), although considered monastic, are structured more according to the lines of the clerks regular, having a general superior and being divided into provinces. Basilians have been active in the United States and Canada, usually ministering to immigrants from Eastern Europe who belonged to the Catholic Ukrainian Church there at the turn of the 20th century.

Within the Maronite Catholic Church are two communities of monks following tradition that developed over time in Lebanon. They too are active in ministerial service to people from their homeland who have immigrated to the United States.

*Monastic Life in Protestant Christian Churches*

As explained by Owen Chadwick (1965), "The Protestant state varied in their attitudes to the monasteries. They were agreed that the monastic life was a mistaken form of Christian life, but whether or not it should therefore be suppressed is a matter of disagreement." In places where Reformation activity was strong, monastic men and women were encouraged to return to secular life and work. Martin Luther (1483–1546) himself was an Augustinian friar (not a cloistered monk), and his negative reaction was to monastic communities that were strictly contemplative in nature and did not engage in apostolic work, such as teaching or parochial ministry.

In the 20th century some leaders within mainline Protestant communions founded monastic communities following the early traditions in Christianity. Within the Protestant Episcopal Church, Benedictine life began in England with the foundations of the abbeys of Nashdom and Prinknash. Abbot Aelred Carlisle (1874–1955) entered the Catholic Church with a number of his monks, and the original Nashdom community remains viable and made a foundation in the United States that continues as St. Gregory's Abbey in Three Rivers, Michigan. A Lutheran community of Benedictines continues its attempt to form a stable community.

Known to most of the world because of its music and pilgrimages of young people, the monastery of Taizé in Burgundy, France, founded by Brother Roger Schutz within the Calvinist tradition and, with a rule developed by him and his brothers, continues to flourish.

DAVID TURNER, O.S.B.

*See also* Augustinian Rule; Basil the Great, St.; Benedict of Aniane, St.; Benedict of Nursia, St.; Benedictines: General or Male; Celtic Monasticism; Cluniacs; Cluny, Abbots of; Holy Men/Holy Women: Christian Perspectives; Lectio Divina; Liturgy: Western Christian; Monastery, Christian; Orders (Religious), Origin of; Origins: Comparative Perspectives; Orthodox Monasticism; Regulations: Christian Perspectives; Spirituality: Western Christian

**Further Reading**

Chadwick, Owen, *The Reformation* (Pelican History of the Church, volume 3), Baltimore, Maryland: Penguin Books, 1964; London: Hodder and Stoughton, 1965

Chapman, John, *Saint Benedict and the Sixth Century*, New York and London: Longmans, Green, 1929

Hilpisch, Stephanus, *Benedictinism through Changing Centuries*, Collegeville, Minnesota: St. John's Abbey Press, 1958

Kardong, Terrence, *The Benedictines* (Religious Order Series, volume 1), Wilmington, Delaware: Glazier, 1988

Knowles, David, *Christian Monasticism* (World University Library), New York: McGraw-Hill, and London: Weidenfeld and Nicolson, 1969

Rippinger, Joel, *The Benedictine Order in the United States: An Interpretive History*, Collegeville, Minnesota: Liturgical Press, 1990

Schuster, Ildefonso, *St. Benedict and His Times*, St. Louis, Missouri, and London: Herder, 1951

# Chrysostom, John, St. 349–407

Christian patriarch of Constantinople and renowned orator

Bishop at Antioch and, later, patriarch of Constantinople, John is one of the most celebrated preachers in Christian history (the sobriquet "Chrysostom," applied to him since the fifth century, means "golden mouth"). When he was a young man, his widowed mother, Anthusa, begged him not to leave her twice bereft when, forsaking a bureaucratic career, he sought to enter "the blessed life of monks and the true philosophy" (*De Sacerdotio* 1.2 [*Sources chrétiennes* 272.62]). Declining to enter one of the varied conclaves of Syrian monasticism then thriving in the immediate environs of Antioch, John acquiesced to her wishes through a compromise: he stayed in the city but joined the *asceterion* (ascetic academy) of Diodore of Tarsus (d. 390), where he practiced spiritual disciplines and studied the Scriptures, learning the principles of Antiochene exegesis. More historical and literary, the latter approach to the text largely eschewed the allegorizing associated with the Alexandrines. Inhabiting what was not properly a monastery, Diodore's students lived and worked in the midst of a bustling city but shared a brotherhood marked by prayer, study, and commitment to ascetic practices, such as celibacy. This whetted John's appetite for deeper monastic experiences, first in a cenobitic compound on Mount Silpios with an elderly hermit as his spiritual guide (372–376) and later in solitary seclusion in a remote cave. There he lived as an anchorite for two years (376–378), praying constantly, abstaining from sleep, and memorizing the New Testament. After this period, because of his fractured health (and, some suggest, his sense of a worldly duty incompatible with solitary retreat), John returned to the city and entered ecclesiastical service to his bishop, Meletios (d. 381). From that point (378) John began a career in pastoral ministry and church leadership marked by celebrated preaching and fervent commitment to inculcating ascetic values among the laity. Having been ordained in 386, John retained the abstemious habits and temperament forged in his youth. His uncompromising attitudes, fervent advocacy for the poor, and bombastic outbursts made formidable enemies from the time he was forcibly installed as patriarch of Constantinople in 398. Exiled twice on trumped-up charges, he died by forced march in Pontus in 407.

Chrysostom was revered among later monastics, especially in the East, both because of the allure of his personality and life story (he was vindicated almost immediately following his death) and because of the powerful exhortations to virtue found throughout his enormous literary corpus. Although John never wrote a systematic treatise on monasticism, among his earliest writings (all in Greek) are several praising the life of a monk in the face of potential deserters (*Adhortationes ad Theodorum lapsum 1 and 2*) and outright detractors (*Adversus oppugnatores vitae monasticae*; *Comparatio regis et monachi*). The latter work was long thought to be of questionable authorship but recently has been claimed as authentic (Hunter, 1988). He also composed treatises on particular virtues (*De eleemosuna* and *De compunctione ad Demetrium*; *De compunctione ad Stelechium*) and devoted several to various celibate lifestyles (*De virginitate*; *Ad viduam juniorem 1–2*; *Contra eos qui subintroductas habent*). Throughout his exegetical and other writings, Chrysostom often held up monasteries as the embodiment of the perfect community life of the Jerusalem Church (Acts 2), extolling monks as exemplars of "the angelic way of life," but he could also criticize the monastic lifestyle when it became so focused on detachment from the world and individual spiritual attainment that it did not contribute to the salvation and well-being of others.

This major tension in Christian monastic life – competition between desert and city as the proper arena of work for the gospel – defined John's life and his literary works. Chrysostom's most significant contribution is his idealistic vision of a Christian social order that sought to unite desert and city in a democratized, laicized monastic community rooted in the piety of each family unit (see Brown, 1988). All his writings – treatises, homilies expounding Scripture, and letters – are permeated with enthusiasm for an ascetic lifestyle to be practiced not in retreat from the world but in and among the tasks of everyday life. John constantly exhorts a lay audience to practice the monastic virtues of celibacy, almsgiving, voluntary poverty, fasting, penitence, habitual prayer, and biblical study. He insisted that, with the exception of virginity, these practices were not the sole province of monk or bishop but of the community of the baptized, who, although saved by Christ, must participate in that salvific activity through the proper exercise of their own free will by living the "philosophical" or "angelic" life of ascetics. For them monasteries served as a "lighthouse," a shining example of the potential for lived virtue.

Chrysostom's writings were abundantly copied, translated, and preserved in the monasteries of both East and West, where they served as hortatory kindling for future monastic communities. Nearly 4,000 manuscripts are extant. His writings on ascetic topics (listed previously) were transmitted in a separate *Corpus Asceticum* already by the ninth century (see Dumortier, 1955). Chrysostom's exegetical homilies, the most extensively preserved of those by any patristic interpreter, bequeathed to each new generation John's moralizing style of interpretation, in which biblical figures are viewed as exemplars of monastic virtues for all time. His letters too, such as those to his friend Olympias tenderly counseling her against "the tyranny of despondency" to which an ascetic might succumb, were preserved and treasured. The "Liturgy of St. John Chrysostom," although not actually composed by him, became the basis for Greek Orthodox liturgical piety from the Middle Ages and is still in use today. Even as Chrysostom claimed St. Paul as his spiritual mentor, others, such as John Cassian (c. 360–after 430), were to claim Chrysostom as theirs. Cassian (whom Chrysostom ordained a deacon at Constantinople around 404) was a pivotal figure in the dissemination of Chrysostom's spiritual teaching to the West, where he went as Chrysostom's special envoy to Pope Innocent I (402–417) and stayed, founding monasteries and transmitting what he had learned among Eastern monastics through his *De institutis coenobiorum* and *Collationes*.

John Chrysostom's ambiguous legacy – that of a polished urban preacher par excellence who propounded a vision of ascetic living extending beyond an elite corps of monks to all Christians – embodies many of the tensions (theological, sociological, and cultural) inherent in the rise of Christian monastic movements in the fourth century.

MARGARET M. MITCHELL

*See also* Asceticism: Christian Perspectives; Cassian, John; Istanbul, Turkey; Jerusalem, Israel; Liturgy: Eastern Christian; Origins: Eastern Christian; Syria; Transvestite Saints

## Biography

Trained as a Greek-speaking orator at Antioch, John could not at first fulfill his desire to become a monastic because of the wishes of his mother. To appease her he at first practiced ascetic disciplines at home, and subsequently in a rustic monastic community (372–376) and in a cave with a hermit (376–378). Following his return to the city, he was ordained deacon at Antioch in 381 and priest in 386. His renown as a preacher posthumously earned him the name "Golden Mouth." Reluctantly made bishop of Constantinople in 398, he was ousted five years later due to intrigues fomented by Theophilus, Patriarch of Alexandria. Banished to Armenia and then to Pontus, he died en route. He has been called the greatest of all Biblical expositors. The Liturgy (in Greek) ascribed to him in the Eastern Orthodox Church derives from Antioch but post-dates Chrysostom.

## Major Works

Exegetical Homilies on Biblical Books, in Migne, editor, *Patrologia Graeca*, vols. 53–64, 1859–1860; also in *Nicene and Post-Nicene Fathers*, vols. 10–14, various translators, 1888–1889

*De Sacerdotio*, in *Sources chrétiennes*, volume 272, edited by Anne-Marie Malingrey, 1980; also in *Nicene and Post-Nicene Fathers*, volume 9, translated by W.R.W. Stephens, 1889

*Adhortationes ad Theodorum lapsum 1 and 2*, in *Sources chrétiennes*, volume 117, edited by Jean Dumortier, 1966; also in *Nicene and Post-Nicene Fathers*, volume 9, translated by W.R.W. Stephens, 1889

*Adversus oppugnatores vitae monasticae*, in Migne, editor, *Patrologia Graeca*, volume 47, 1858

*Comparatio regis et monachi*, in Migne, editor, *Patrologia Graeca*, volume 47, 1858

*De virginitate*, in *Sources chrétiennes*, volume 125, edited by Herbert Musurillo, 1966

*Ad viduam juniorem 1–2*, in *Sources chrétiennes*, volume 138, edited by Bernard Grillet, 1968; also in *Nicene and Post-Nicene Fathers*, volume 9, translated by W.R.W. Stephens, 1889

*Contra eos qui subintroductas habent*, in Migne, editor, *Patrologia Graeca*, volume 47, 1858

*De eleemosyna*, in Migne, editor, *Patrologia Graeca*, volume 51, 1859

*De compunctione ad Demetrium*, in Migne, editor, *Patrologia Graeca*, volume 47, 1858

*De compunctione ad Stelechium*, in Migne, editor, *Patrologia Graeca*, volume 47, 1858

## Further Reading

Brandle, R., "Johannes Chrysostomus I," *Reallexicon für Antike und Christentum* 139–140 (1997) (contains most recent bibliography)

Brown, Peter, *The Body and Society: Men, Women and Sexual Renunciation in Early Christianity*, New York: Columbia University Press, 1988; London: Faber, 1989

Clark, Elizabeth A., *Jerome, Chrysostom, and Friends: Essays and Translations*, Lewiston, New York: Mellen Press, 1979

Dumortier, J., "L'auteur présumé du corpus asceticum des S. Jean Chrysostome," *Journal of Theological Studies* 6 (1955)

Festugière, A.J., *Antioche païenne et chrétienne: Libanius, Chrysostome et les moines de Syrie*, Paris: de Boccard, 1959

Hunter, David G., *A Comparison Between a King and a Monk/Against the Opponents of the Monastic Life: Two Treatises*, Lewiston, New York: Mellen Press, 1988

Kelly, J.N.D., *Golden Mouth: The Story of John Chrysostom – Ascetic, Preacher, Bishop*, Ithaca, New York: Cornell University Press, and London: Duckworth, 1995

Leroux, Jean-Marie, "Monachisme et communauté chrétienne d'après Saint Jean Chrysostom," in *Théologie de la Vie Monastique*, Paris: Aubier, 1961

Leroux, Jean-Marie, "Saint Jean Chrysostome et le monachisme," in *Jean Chrysostome et Augustin*, edited by Charles Kannengiesser, Paris: Beauchesne, 1975

Maur, Ivo auf der, *Mönchtum und Glaubensverkündigung in den Schriften des hl. Johannes Chrysostomus*, Freiburg im Breisgau: Universitäts Verlag, 1959

Shore, Sally Rieger, *John Chrysostom, "On Virginity" and "Against Remarriage,"* New York: Mellen Press, 1983

Wenger, Antoine, "Jean Chrysostome," in *Dictionnaire de spiritualité, ascétique et mystique: Doctrine et histoire*, volume 8, edited by M. Viller, et al., Paris: Beauchesne, 1974 (contains bibliography of older works)

## Related Web Sites

*www.ccel.wheaton.edu/Fathers2/* and *www.stmichael.org/Fathers/StJohnC/* (selected writings in English translation from *Nicene and Post-Nicene Fathers*, series 1)

*www.knight.org/advent/cathen/08452b.htm*

# Chu-hung. *See* Zhuhong

# Church Councils, Recent Catholic

Only two general councils of the Roman Catholic Church have been held since the Council of Trent in the 16th century: the First Vatican Council (1869–1870) and the Second Vatican Council (1962–1965). Although schemata had already been drawn up that dealt with the monastic and other religious orders in the Church, the First Vatican Council never took up the subject because the outbreak of the Franco-Prussian War made it necessary to suspend the council before this and many other issues could be considered. Nevertheless the mere fact that Pope Pius IX (1846–1878) had announced his plans for a general council had its impact on monasticism, for various meetings of abbots were convened in the late 1860s to discuss concerns to be brought to the council. Among the changes desired was greater cooperation among the monasteries while avoiding too much centralization. To some extent this desire was realized several decades later when Pope Leo XIII (1878–1903) founded the athenaeum Sant'Anselmo, an international Benedictine house of studies in Rome, and set at its head an abbot-primate with certain limited powers of supervision.

Much more was accomplished at the Second Vatican Council, convened under the leadership of Pope John XXIII (1958–1963) on 11 October 1962. Of the council's 16 documents, the centerpiece is the Dogmatic Constitution on the Church, *Lumen Gentium*, the sixth chapter of which discusses those members of the Church known as "religious," that is, those who profess the evangelical counsels of poverty, celibate chastity, and obedience. Monastic men and women are not named as such in this constitution, but their way of life is considered in a later document of the council, the Decree on the Appropriate Renewal of Religious Life (*Perfectae Caritatis*), which was promulgated on 28 October 1965.

Two main principles underlie the teaching of this decree: a return to the sources of Christian life and to the original inspiration of the institutes (this refers in particular to the following of Christ as set forth in the gospel and to the spirit and aims [charism] of the founder of each religious order or congregation) and an adaptation of the institute to the changed conditions of the times. Before discussing particular types of religious orders, the decree emphasizes that all members of these institutes should have both a "contemplative" and an "active" aspect to their lives: by the former "they cleave to God with mind and heart," whereas by the latter they seek to spread the kingdom of God (para. 5).

This usage of the language of "contemplation" as something that should characterize the lives of *all* religious then gives way to a more institutional usage, for paragraph 7 speaks specifically of those institutes that are "entirely ordered toward contemplation" through the strict practice of "solitude and silence, constant prayer and willing penance." No particular religious orders are named, either here or elsewhere in the decree, but the reference clearly includes ones that are monastic in origin (such as the Carthusians and Trappists) as well as some that arose from the mendicant movement (such as the Poor Clares and Discalced Carmelite nuns). The council speaks of these groups as having an honored place in the Church, which "they enlarge through their hidden apostolic fruitfulness."

This paragraph is followed by one dealing with institutes of a very different sort, those in which "apostolic and charitable activity is of the very nature of religious life." During the time when the decree was going through various drafts prior to its eventual submission to the entire council for approval, this rather stark division into "contemplative" and "active" institutes alarmed some persons, including members of monastic congregations who considered themselves contemplatives but who were also engaged in various apostolic activities, such as the conducting of schools. It was felt that the schema was too simplistic and would jeopardize the continued exercise of such activities by juridically pushing such communities in the direction of those named in paragraph 7 as having their lives "*entirely* ordered toward contemplation." The objections carried the day, so that the final draft included some additional paragraphs in which still other forms of religious life were named. The first of these addenda, paragraph 9, begins with a specific reference to monastic life, teaching that it is the principal duty of monks to offer God "a service at once humble and noble within the walls of the monastery" but adding that this may be done in several ways: either by the monks dedicating themselves "entirely to divine worship in the contemplative life" or by legitimately undertaking "some apostolic or charitable activity." Members of monastic communities, no less than those belonging to other religious orders or congregations, are likewise called on both to "renew their ancient beneficent traditions" and to "adapt them to the present-day needs of souls" (para. 9).

The directives found in this short decree were necessarily of the most general sort. More specific directives were published nine months later when Pope Paul VI (1963–1978) issued a *Motu proprio* giving norms for implementing this and several other decrees of the council. Perhaps the most significant directive was that the various religious institutes of the Church were to convene general chapter meetings of their leadership within two or at most three years to determine the particular ways in which they would both return to the sources and adapt to contemporary conditions. As monastic chapters met not only within that time frame but in subsequent years as well, a number of major changes came about. Among the most notable was a common (although not universal) move away from the traditional Latin Liturgy of the Hours (the Divine Office) to one using vernacular languages; in most cases this was accompanied by a reduction in the number of daily liturgical services from the seven or eight specified in the Benedictine Rule to about half that number. Equally significant was the general abandonment of the status of lay brothers and lay sisters, who had formerly been quite distinct from "choir monks" and "choir nuns" both in monastic garb and in the kind of prayer prayed in common. It cannot be denied that some monks and nuns regretted these and other changes and that some experiments in monastic living went far beyond anything that the council fathers had envisioned, but on the whole the changes have taken firm root within Roman Catholic monasticism and may rightly be considered among the most significant changes wrought by the Second Vatican Council.

JAMES A. WISEMAN, O.S.B.

*See also* Abbot Primate, Benedictine; Casel, Odo; Charism; Liturgical Movement 1830–1980; Marmion, Columba; Meditation: Christian Perspectives; Office, Daily: Western Christian; Papacy: Papal Pronouncements

## Further Reading

Alberigo, Giuseppe, and Joseph A. Komonchak, editors, *History of Vatican II*, 5 vols., Maryknoll, New York: Orbis, 1995–

Flannery, Austin, editor, *Vatican Council II: The Conciliar and Post Conciliar Documents*, Northport, New York: Costello, and Dublin: Dominican, 1975; 2nd edition, 1996

Galot, Jean, *Renouveau de la vie consacrée*, Paris: Lethielleux, 1966

Leclercq, Jean, "The Contemplative Life and Monasticism in the Light of Vatican II," *Cistercian Studies* 2:1 (1967)

Neenan, Benedict, "The Abbots Meeting at Salzburg: Benedictine Reform Efforts and Vatican I," *Annuarium Historiae Conciliorum* 24 (1992)

O'Connor, Edward, "Vatican II and the Renewal of Religious Life," *Review for Religious* 26:3 (1967)

Pennington, M. Basil, "Vatican II and the Contemplative Life," *Homiletic and Pastoral Review* 67:6–7 (1966–1967)

Wulf, Friedrich, "Decree on the Appropriate Renewal of the Religious Life," in *Commentary on the Documents of Vatican II*, volume 2, edited by Herbert Vorgrimler et al., New York: Herder and Herder, 1967; London: Burns and Oates, 1968

# Church Design. *See* Architecture: Armenian Monasteries; Architecture: Eastern Christian Monasteries; Architecture: Western Christian Monasteries

# Cistercians: Female

Although no evidence exists that women were among the founders at Cîteaux who had come from Molesme, women certainly had been at Molesme itself – and a number of them would be moved to the house of Jully around 1113. Jully seems to have been under the personal care of Bernard of Clairvaux (1190–1253) until the 1140s, when Eugenius III (1145–1153) tied it more strictly to Molesme. A house of women was also founded by Stephen Harding (d. 1134), abbot of Cîteaux, at le Tart, in the early 1120s. Indeed many houses that would adopt Cistercian practices and eventually became part of the Cistercian Order had women's houses associated with them. A number, such as Obazine and Coyroux (which were together incorporated before 1165), had been double houses at the outset. Many Cistercian men's houses had originally been part of double communities in which the associated houses of women became part of the Order of Fontevraud. Others were originally parts of congregations, such as that of Savigny, in which women's houses were the earliest founded; the entire congregation of Savigny would be incorporated by the Cistercians in the late 1150s.

It has been accepted for some time that many houses for Cistercian women were founded in the early 13th century; their numbers may have come to exceed those of men's houses in the Cistercian Order by the mid–13th century. The conditions under which houses for women were founded or affiliated become increasingly clear in statutes for the first half of the 13th century. This happened because Cistercian abbots in the general chapter (much like the men of other orders of the time) attempted to reduce their responsibilities for the "*cura monialium*" by limiting the conditions under which houses of women could be founded or incorporated. However, such communities of nuns continued to be founded, often by a group of notable ruling women at the time, including the countesses of Flanders, Jeanne and Marguerite; the queen of France, Blanche of Castile, whose parents had founded the royal house of Cistercians nuns of Las Huelgas at Burgos in the 1180s; the countess Isabelle of Chartres; and Matilda the Great, countess of Auxerre and Nevers. Indeed the years of the most favorable official treatment of Cistercian women by the Order's general chapter coincide almost precisely with the years in which Blanche of Castile (1188–1252), as daughter-in-law of Philip Augustus, queen of Louis VIII (1223–1226), and queen regent and later queen mother for Louis IX (1226–1270), held power of various sorts in France.

The relationship of women's houses to the rest of the Order became increasingly regularized after 1250. Many houses of women that previously had been treated as priories were elevated to abbey status, and their prioresses became abbesses. Limits were set on size according to resources. Many houses that had once been equal in status to neighboring houses of men as part of double communities were treated as daughters of such nearby abbeys for men, and visitation by the abbots of those neighboring houses of men was imposed. Such visitation often replaced that by the bishops who had often been active founders and patrons of these women's houses. Obviously not all these changes were to the liking of the women's houses; they often protested bitterly against being subjected to visitors who were at the same time their nearest rivals for property and patronage. Moreover as women's houses became tied to neighboring houses of monks, the possibilities of collective action by women's houses decreased because links between houses of nuns in what had once been seen as filiations, such as that of le Tart or that of St.-Antoine, were broken. Even the annual chapter at le Tart, which had in fact exercised very little independent power, was discontinued after the 13th century.

Whereas the situation for the 13th century and later is more clear, conflicting evidence about the 12th century has allowed traditional historians to assert that no Cistercian nuns existed during that golden age of the Cistercians. Such assertions are incorrect. In the mid–12th century, Herman of Tournai tells us that although Norbert of Xanten (c. 1080–1134) had monks and nuns living under the same roof at Prémontré, Bernard of Clairvaux did not approve of such double communities. Herman's statement, found in an account that also describes the women of a monastery at Montreuil who were following the practices of Cîteaux and working in the fields like the brothers of Cîteaux, does not state that Bernard did not approve of women's houses or women's monastic ambitions, only that he preferred separate houses. By the last decades of the 12th century, reinterpretation of more neutral material read it as attacks on religious women. Thus, remarks made by Bernard of Clairvaux that have more to do with his tendency to meddle were reread to attribute considerable misogyny to him; this is not necessarily found in his original remarks.

Similarly references to houses of nuns said to be "following the Rule of Saint Benedict according to the practices of Cîteaux" do not denote some sort of "imitation" Cistercians. These same phrases are found in papal privileges confirming the possessions of all houses of 12th-century Cistercians, women and men alike. A few women, such as the anchoress Yvette of Huy (1158–1228), adapted Cistercian customs to what were not cenobitic lives, but most so-called imitation Cistercian women were in fact as authentically Cistercian as were the monks who had received the same privileges in identical words. Indeed arguments that no houses of Cistercian women existed in the 12th century, if they were applied to men's houses, would lead to the conclusion that no Cistercian Order existed for much of the 12th century. In fact investigation of women's houses has led to considerable rethinking of just when that Order was created. If, as now seems likely, an Order was created around 1165, it had women in it from the start.

CONSTANCE HOFFMAN BERMAN

*See also* Bernard of Clairvaux, St.; Cistercians: General or Male; Double Houses, Western Christian; Fontevraud, France; France: History; Liturgy: Western Christian; Orders (Religious), Origin of; Premonstratensian Canons

## Further Reading

Berman, Constance H., "Abbeys for Cistercian Nuns in the Ecclesiastical Province of Sens: Foundation, Endowment and

Economic Activities of the Earlier Foundations," *Revue Mabillon* 73 (1997)

Berman, Constance H., "Cistercian Nuns and Tithes," *Cîteaux* 49 (1998)

Berman, Constance H., "Were There Twelfth-Century Cistercian Nuns?" *Church History* 68 (1999)

Berman, Constance H., *The Cistercian Evolution: The Invention of a Religious Order in the Twelfth-Century*, Philadelphia: University of Pennsylvania Press, 2000

Berman, Constance H., "The Labors of Hercules, the Cartulary, Church and Abbey of La Cour-Notre-Dame-de-Michery," *The Journal of Medieval History* (January 2000)

Carpenter, Jennifer, "Juette of Huy, Recluse and Other (1158–1228): Children and Mothering in the Saintly Life," in *Power of the Weak: Studies on Medieval Women*, edited by Carpenter and Sally-Beth MacLean, Urbana: University of Illinois Press, 1995

Degler-Spengler, Brigitte, "The Incorporation of Cistercian Nuns into The Order in the Twelfth and Thirteenth Century," in *Hidden Springs*, edited by John A. Nichols and Lillian Thomas Shank, Kalamazoo, Michigan: Cistercian Publications, 1995

Johnson, Penelope D., *Equal in Monastic Profession: Religious Women in Medieval France*, Chicago: University of Chicago Press, 1991

McNamara, Jo Ann Kay, *Sisters in Arms: Catholic Nuns Through Two Millennia*, Cambridge, Massachusetts: Harvard University Press, 1996

Venarde, Bruce, *Women's Monasticism and Medieval Society: Nunneries in France and England, 890–1215*, Ithaca, New York: Cornell University Press, 1997

# Cistercians: General or Male

## Foundation and Early Leaders

The Cistercians would eventually be the most successful of the many new religious communities of the 12th century, all of which sought a simpler and more authentic way of monastic life. They envisioned themselves returning to the Rule of St. Benedict of Nursia, stripped of the accretions of centuries. However, with their strongly eremitic impulses, being based on a combination of readings of the *Sayings of the Desert Fathers and Mothers* and notions of the life of the early Apostles, these reformers were also innovators. Probably the most important accomplishment of the Cistercians' religious fervor lay in transforming large numbers of independent reform communities into the most successful of all the new religious orders and in inventing the very notion of such a religious order.

The standard account of Cistercian origins tells that in 1098 a new foundation was made by the restless monastic reformer Robert of Molesme (c. 1027–1111), who had founded a reform house earlier, in 1075, at Molesme. Soon Robert was recalled by the monks of Molesme, but some of those who had followed him to Cîteaux stayed at the new place, which eventually became a separate and independent monastic community. The legitimacy of this new foundation at Cîteaux is stridently defended

in the later Cistercian foundation account called the *Exordium Parvum*, which cites a number of papal and episcopal letters in its praise; they were possibly concocted for that very purpose, for none of them exists outside the context of this account. Much debate exists about the dating of this and other "primitive documents" of the Cistercians, but the earliest surviving manuscripts come only from the 1160s.

In non-Cistercian sources the earliest references to the new community at Cîteaux come from the 1130s, when both Orderic Vitalis (1075–c. 1142) and William of Malmesbury (c. 1090–c. 1143) describe the austerities of this community headed by an Englishman, Stephen Harding (d. 1134), who was abbot at Cîteaux from around 1108 until just before his death. The reputation of the new community at Cîteaux for reformed monasticism was sufficient to attract a number of adult converts in the 1110s, among them the future abbot of Clairvaux, Bernard of Fontaine (1090–1153). Bernard is reputed to have entered with a number of his friends and relations. Those men urged their wives and sisters to enter the nearby abbey for women at Jully, another offshoot of the sometimes double house of Molesme.

Bernard soon was sent to be abbot at a daughter house at Clairvaux. There his writings and discussion of the practice of charity and equitable treatment of individuals within the monastic community would make him a leader in the movement of reform. He also became involved in Church politics, starting with his promotion of the candidacy of Innocent II (1130–1143) during the Anacletian schism; Innocent would reward Clairvaux and other abbeys subject to Bernard with exemption from certain ecclesiastical tithes. Although Bernard's writings on *The Song of Songs* have served as inspiration for much later mysticism, his preaching in favor of Innocent II (by attacks on rival Pope Anacletus II because he was descended from Jews) – as well as his preaching for the Second Crusade against Cathars in southern France and against intellectuals such as Peter Abelard (1079–1142/43) and Gilbert of la Porré (c. 1080–1154) – suggests a less inspiring side to his character. He was not above interference in ecclesiastical elections, such as that at York, and he was shameless in his promotion of monks from Clairvaux for episcopal promotion. Despite his protestations it is difficult to believe that Bernard did not actively campaign for the election as Pope Eugenius III (1145–1153) of the monk from Clairvaux, Bernardo Pignatelli, a native of Pisa who had entered Clairvaux after hearing Bernard's preaching.

## Spread of the Order

Despite traditional images of widespread Cistercian growth by emanation from Burgundy, in fact recent work has shown that most houses later attached to the Cistercians had existed earlier as independently founded reform communities. Such reform houses only gradually coalesced during the 12th century into a religious order. At first Bernard's preaching must have induced interest in certain Cistercian customs that limited liturgical practices and offered lay brother regulations. These customs made it possible to adapt traditional Benedictine practice to the 12th-century interest in escaping traditional manorial regimes. After

Cloister, Cistercian Abbey of Lilienfeld, Austria, 13th century.
Photo courtesy of Chris Schabel

having adopted such customs, independently founded reform houses began to be transformed into daughters, as happened earliest for Clairvaux and elsewhere in Burgundy. The transformation of preexisting houses into an order was not simple, and to date the process remains obscure because of the tendency to rewrite foundation documents to fit standard narratives. Clearly the process provided the emerging order with many accumulated resources of both property and personnel.

It is likely that by Bernard's death in 1153 the power of Clairvaux had become a menace to other houses of the Cistercian practice. Indeed it appears that much of the order-building of the third quarter of the 12th century can be seen as attempting to bring the powerful abbey of Clairvaux under control. This was accomplished not only by the establishment of an egalitarian assembly of all abbots of houses under the Cistercian practice, the general chapter, but also by the appointment of a committee of three (later four) abbots of the earliest daughters of Cîteaux (those of la Ferté, Pontigny, Clairvaux, and later Morimond) as overseers of Cîteaux itself. Clairvaux was gradually submerged within the larger group by such actions. Although the need to organize visitation internally would lead to the creation of filiation trees, it is likely that even before privileges of exemption

from episcopal visitation were granted to the Cistercians by the papacy in the 1180s, Clairvaux's filiation was beginning to be rivaled by those of the other three first daughter houses of Cîteaux. Each of these, with Cîteaux itself, would be organized as filiations for the purpose of internal visitations. These new filiations, like that filiation or congregation that began to be attached to Clairvaux by Bernard, would come to rival Clairvaux and its daughters. Indeed Morimond would prove especially adept in its attraction of existing congregations to its filiation in the last quarter of the 12th century.

However, such filiations and the filiation trees documenting them were established only at the end of the 12th century and finalized only in the early years of the 13th. They have often been misconstrued as evidence of how the "order" grew, but careful examination of their evidence, along with that of local administrative charters, shows that the miraculous growth of the Cistercians came largely by incorporation. In the first half of the 12th century, both Cîteaux and Clairvaux began to gather congregations of daughter houses and a few granddaughter houses, mostly in Burgundy or through patrons with Burgundian ties. Among them, for example, was the abbey of Bonnevaux, founded by the future Calixtus II (1119–1124), Guy de Bour-

Water course, Fountains Abbey (Cistercian), North Yorkshire, England, 12th century. The diverting of streams made the Cistercians the "Romans of the 12th century."
Photo courtesy of Chris Schabel

cian houses in all things except monastic vows; they were to be in charge of the satellite farms or granges so that monks could remain within the monastic enclosure. Although these lay brothers (*conversi*) were to be equal in status to the choir monks, they spent much more time at their agricultural duties and heavy manual labor – something that was recognized through providing them larger daily portions of food. They were often illiterate and had no ambitions to become either monks or priests. The management as a distinct group of these adult converts to the religious life – a custom never envisioned by St. Benedict of Nursia in his original rule – and provision for a shortened liturgical practice necessary for the universal practice of manual labor began to be codified into liturgical order books called *Ecclesiastica Officia* possibly by 1135 and into lay brother treatises by the 1150s. At about this time, around 1150, such Cistercian practices concerning lay brothers and liturgy began to be adopted by independent reformers who would in turn eventually become Cistercians.

Such monastic reform groups founded independently in many parts of Europe beyond Burgundy were similar in their reform origins to the monasteries at Cîteaux and Clairvaux. They often were eremitic and often had origins as double communities of both monks and nuns. These groups gradually coalesced into a new supramonastic group, a religious order, with an annual, universal general chapter of all abbots; written constitutional and legislative documents; the privilege of internal visitation in place

Interior of the infirmary, Cistercian Abbey at Ourscamp, Aisne, France, c. 1230.
Photo courtesy of Chris Schabel

gogne, who made that foundation in the Diocese of Vienne around 1118, when he was still archbishop there. However, such apostolic foundation, in which groups of 6 or 12 monks and an abbot (or the equivalent numbers of nuns and an abbess) were sent out to found a new colony, were the exception rather than the rule. Much more often incorporation fed the order's growth.

### Cistercian Reform Ideas

The most important change effected by the new religious communities of the 12th century was the combination of reduced liturgical practice with emphasis on manual labor in the lives of all members of a monastic community. Included was recruitment not by oblation of children but by adult conversion as well as rhetoric about the equitable treatment of a new type of monk who had converted to the religious life as an adult and often only after a career as a knight or a peasant. The earliest legislation explains that these lay brothers were equal to the monks of Cister-

Gothic cloister, Zwettl Abbey (Cistercian), Lower Austria, 1217.
Photo courtesy of the Austrian National Tourist Office

of episcopal visitation; and eventually organizational charts for the practice of such visitation on which all houses were placed (often arbitrarily) on filiation trees as mother or daughter houses. In this emerging order there would be, by the early 13th century, more than 500 houses of monks and by the mid–13th century an equal or possibly even greater number of houses of nuns.

## Cistercian Agriculture

The Cistercians of the 12th century formulated images of themselves as having founded their houses in the words of the Rule of St. Benedict, "far from cities, castles, and human habitations." They produced early art showing monks and lay brothers cutting down trees and working in the fields. They have often been identified as the monastic pioneers par excellence of the 12th century. In such hypotheses these pioneering monks brought civilization (and agricultural technology) to the previously uncleared and unsettled wildernesses of Western Europe as they established new communities of monks and nuns on the frontiers. This has been a long-held image of the Cistercians, but it is false. It wrongly ascribes to such organized groups of monks and nuns much agricultural labor that had in fact been done by their immediate, often anonymous predecessors, including peasant villagers attempting to eke out a little more land from the waste, and ephemeral eremitic groups.

Such self-images might have been promoted by the successors of the earliest Cistercian reformers because those later Cistercians did indeed find themselves and their abbeys and granges in isolated sites. However, they had forgotten that such isolation had been created by the careful managerial efforts of their predecessors, who had often systematically removed earlier inhabitants from their lands, transforming any number of peasants into lay brothers and lay sisters as they did so. The notion that such Cistercian communities had been founded in previously unoccupied lands seems also to have been appealing because it seemed to justify the extensive tithe privileges that had been granted to these new monks and nuns, assuring them that such tithes had not been owned earlier. In fact such exemptions from tithes were almost always achieved in the 12th century only by extensive repurchase of those rights through the same managerial efforts that had removed peasant cultivators and extinguished claims of owners to lands that became Cistercian granges. Once tithes were repurchased, only the exemption remained, and the repurchasing efforts were too easily forgotten.

Added confusion ensues because such images of Cistercians as pioneers might have had some basis in reality in certain areas of Europe, especially with regard to 13th-century foundations of houses for monks on the fringes of the new Christian Europe (e.g., in Scandinavia, the Baltic lands, Wales, Scotland, Ireland, and even the Iberian Peninsula). Ironically images of pioneering might be somewhat justified also with regard to houses of nuns founded in the 13th century, even in areas of northern France that had long been cleared and settled, but these were on very marginal lands that were all that 13th-century founders of houses of nuns had available to give. But these are exceptions.

Most foundations of those reform communities for religious men and women that would coalesce into a Cistercian Order by the last decades of the 12th century had in fact been founded in areas that had been already cleared, settled, and cultivated, often long before Cistercian or pre-Cistercian acquisition. Thus, much less credit for the great expansion of the Western European economy of the 11th and later centuries must be given to the Cistercians than was once thought. Indeed in terms of the clearance and reclamation movement following A.D. 1000, Cistercians, as it has been colorfully stated by Professor Fossier (1983), "were the last on the train, nearly missing it as it left the station."

If houses of 12th-century Cistercians usually became quickly wealthy, it was not because they were pioneers, although it might have been because they had granges. Such isolated farms – satellites of monasteries but within a limited distance from each community – were the fabled Cistercian granges on which huge agricultural profits were seen as being had, but laborers on those granges were the key. Any agricultural efficiency in such Cistercian grange agriculture was brought about through exploiting a new type of monk, the adult convert, in some cases a local knight tired of the military life who converted to the Cistercians and became an adept manager of Cistercian resources in a territory in which he had long had power of command. Only gradually would the Order succeed in insisting that such knights must become choir monks. Other effective adult converts were the earlier agricultural tenants on lands being compacted by Cistercians into granges; these peasants, who were now offered religious life as *conversi* of Cistercian houses, not only were efficient agricultural laborers on lands that they knew well but also offered to the Cistercians a labor force without the usual dependency costs of agricultural tenants. No pregnant wives or young children had to be supported, and at first few elderly members depended on them. The difficulty lay in maintaining adequate numbers of such laborers. They were recruited through Cistercian land acquisition, but when land acquisition ended, such lay brothers, an agricultural force of celibates ostentatiously not reproducing, could not provide a new generation of laborers as tenant families once had.

The pioneering image of the Cistercians has been influenced by images of the empty American frontier, but the Europe into which the Cistercians ventured was no more empty than were the Great Plains of the American Midwest. In general, early Cistercian growth did not occur, as was once thought, because monks and nuns were reaping the unexpected bumper crops of fertile lands never before cultivated. Rather Cistercians prospered because of managerial prowess in reconstituting large, compact properties, called granges, out of many fragmented holdings. Cistercians also met new demand from growing urban centers for meat, cheese, and animal products, which they marketed along with grain in tithe- and toll-exempt circumstances. Indeed this rural Order was closely linked to urban growth and its success to growing urban demand. Many Cistercians reaped as well the benefits of widespread incorporation. Not only had most houses of the 12th-century Order been established communities with extensive personnel and properties before they were affiliated, but many such established monastic communities also swallowed the properties and resources from smaller eremitic communities that were reduced to granges by the larger, more powerful communities.

CONSTANCE HOFFMAN BERMAN

See also Agriculture, Western Christian; Animals, Attitude toward: Christian Perspectives; Architecture: Western Christian Monasteries; Bernard of Clairvaux, St.; Christianity: Overview; Double Houses, Western Christian; England: Sites; Fishing and Fish Culture, Western Christian; France: History; Historiography, Recent: Western Christian; Lay Brothers and Lay Sisters, Christian; Liturgy: Western Christian; Monastery, Christian; Monastics and the World, Medieval; Orders (Religious), Origin of; Scandinavia; Spain; Spirituality: Western Christian; Trappists

## Further Reading

Auberger, Jean-Baptiste, L'unanimité cistercienne primitive: Mythe ou réalité?, Achel, Belgium: Editions Sine Parvulos, 1986

Berman, Constance H., "Cistercian Development and the Order's Acquisition of Churches and Tithes in Southern France," Revue bénédictine 91 (1981)

Berman, Constance H., Medieval Agriculture, the Southern French Countryside, and the Early Cistercians: A Study of Forty-Three Monasteries, Philadelphia: American Philosophical Society, 1986

Berman, Constance H., The Cistercian Evolution: The Invention of a Religious Order in the Twelfth-Century, Philadelphia: University of Pennsylvania Press, 2000

Bredero, Adriaan, Bernard of Clairvaux: Between Cult and History, Edinburgh: Clark, 1996; Grand Rapids, Michigan: Eerdmans, 1997

Constable, Giles, Three Studies in Medieval Religious and Social Thought, Cambridge and New York: Cambridge University Press, 1995 (see especially "Three Orders of Society")

Constable, Giles, The Reformation of the Twelfth Century, Cambridge and New York: Cambridge University Press, 1996

Cowdrey, H.E.J., "'Quidam Frater Stephanus Nomine, Anglicus Natione': The English Background of Stephen Harding," Revue bénédictine 101 (1991)

Fossier, Robert, "L'économie cistercienne dans les plaines du nord-ouest d'Europe," in Flaran: L'économie cistercienne, Auch, 1983

Lekai, Louis J., The Cistercians: Ideals and Reality, Kent, Ohio: Kent State University Press, 1977

Little, Lester K., Religious Poverty and the Profit Economy in Medieval Europe, Ithaca, New York: Cornell University Press, and London: Elek, 1978

Newman, Martha, The Boundaries of Charity: Cistercian Culture and Ecclesiastical Reform, 1098–1180, Stanford, California: Stanford University Press, 1996

Stock, Brian, The Implications of Literacy: Written Language and Models of Interpretation in the Eleventh and Twelfth Centuries, Princeton, New Jersey: Princeton University Press, 1983

# Cîteaux, France

The monastery of Cîteaux, France, the mother house of the Cistercian Order, was founded in 1098 by Robert of Molesme (c. 1027–1111). Robert, with about 20 other monks, had left the Benedictine abbey of Molesme (Côte d'Or) in search of a life based strictly on the rule of St. Benedict, and the monastery they founded was known simply as the New Monastery. The monastery's first site, at La Forgeotte, proved unsatisfactory, so the abbey was soon moved about a mile south to its present location and by 1119 was being referred to as Cîteaux, the old name for the new site.

After a hesitant start the new monastery met with unexpected success, and an ambitious building program was carried out throughout the 12th and subsequent centuries. A splendid new library was completed in 1509, a new definitorium (a building associated with the Cistercian general chapter, which was held annually, in theory, at Cîteaux) was constructed toward the end of the 17th century, and plans were made in the 18th century for an enormous rebuilding of the entire abbey that would have transformed it into a sort of monastic Versailles. Work on this grandiose project – the vision of the architect Samson-Nicolas Lenoir (1737–1810) – began in 1760, but by 1772 only half of one neoclassical wing had been completed, and even that is about 300 feet in length. The project was abandoned in 1776, and the French Revolution put an end to all such plans.

The Revolution was not the first time Cîteaux had been ravaged. The abbey had been hit hard by the Black Death (1348–1350), it had suffered during the Hundred Years' War (1337–1453; more than once the monks had been forced to seek refuge in Dijon), it had been burned and pillaged twice during the Wars of Religion (1559–1598), and it had been plundered by imperial troops in 1636. However, these problems were nothing compared to the wholesale destruction that occurred following the Revolution.

In 1791 the monks were expelled, the abbey was sold, and the medieval buildings were slowly demolished. The most important structures to survive were the 16th-century library, the 17th-century definitorium, and the 18th-century wing designed by Lenoir. During the 19th century, the buildings housed a theater, a sugar refinery, a phalanstery (a socialist agricultural community based on the ideas of Charles Fourier [1772–1837]), and a school for juvenile delinquents. Between 1860 and 1862, when the abbey was a school, a new church was built to the north of the Lenoir wing.

In 1898 the site was purchased by the Cistercians of the Strict Observance (Trappists), who established themselves in the Lenoir wing and reintroduced the regular round of monastic offices. For a century they used the 19th-century church, but that was remodeled from 1997 to 1998. There is a guest house at the abbey and the 16th-century library has been restored. However, because Cîteaux is once again an active monastic community, access to the buildings is understandably restricted, and the visitor must remember that the abbey is not a museum but a house of prayer.

DAVID N. BELL

From left to right: Abbey church, cloister gate, and reception hall (18th century), Abbey, Cîteaux (Côte d'Or), France.
Photo courtesy of Mary Schaefer

*See also* Bernard of Clairvaux, St.; Cistercians; France; Orders (Religious), Origin of

## Further Reading

Cîteaux: Commentarii cistercienses, and Association Bourguignonne des Sociétés Savantes, editors, *Pour une histoire monumentale de l'abbaye de Cîteaux 1098–1998*, Vitreux, France: Revue Cîteaux, commentarii cistercienses, Abbaye d'Acey, 1998

Conrad, Abbot of Eberbach, *Exordium magnum Cisterciense, sive, Narratio de initio Cisterciensis ordinis*, edited by Bruno Griesser, Turnhout: Brepols, 1994

Conrad, Abbot of Eberbach, *Le Grand Exorde de Cîteaux, ou Récit des débuts de l'Ordre Cistercien*, translated by Anthelmette Piébourg, Turnhout: Brepols, 1998

King, Archdale A., *Cîteaux and Her Elder Daughters*, London: Burns and Oates, 1954

Lackner, Bede K., *The Eleventh-Century Background of Cîteaux*, Washington, D.C.: Consortium Press, 1972

Lekai, Louis J., *The Cistercians: Ideals and Reality*, Kent, Ohio: Kent State University Press, 1977

Lekai, Louis J., *Nicolas Cotheret's Annals of Cîteaux*, Kalamazoo, Michigan: Cistercian Publications, 1982

Waddell, Chrysogonus, *Legislative and Narrative Texts from Early Cîteaux: An Edition, Translation, and Commentary*, Brecht: Cîteaux: Commentarii cistercienses, 1999

# Clare of Assisi, St. 1193/94–1253

Companion of St. Francis and foundress of the Poor Clares

Born of Ortolana di Fiumi and Faverone Offreduccio, Clare was the third of their five children, although the sources contain no certain facts about Clare's early years. Sometime before Palm Sunday 1212, Francis of Assisi (1181/82–1226) became so impressed by Clare's reputation for holiness that he "did desire to see and speak with Clare" to persuade her to follow his newly formed group of friars. "At the insistent entreaty of the holy father," Clare decided to commit "herself to the guidance of Francis," and thus she "laid the foundation of the Order of the Poor Ladies" (Pennacchi, 1910). She made her profession to Francis and his friars at their community house in Portiuncula on the night of 18 March 1212.

Francis found lodging for her first at the Benedictine convent near Basta, then in Panso, but because she had not joined Francis' group in order to become a Benedictine, she was dissatisfied and restless to move on. Her sister Agnes soon joined her, and together they moved to a house adjacent to the church of San Damiano. Others joined, and Clare became the superior of the Poor Ladies, as they were called. The only contemporary description of Clare's group is that of Jacques de Vitry, who observes that "the brothers minor and the sisters minor" all "live just like the first community" in urban hospices, were self-supporting, and accepted no wages (Huygens, 1960). Clare expected the women's lives to be identical to the men's, especially in the practice of poverty. Francis agreed, promising Clare "both through himself and through his religious to have for us always the same loving care and social solitude as he has for the brothers" (Quarracchi Franciscans, 1897, *Regula* 6.2). However, once opposition to Clare's Poor Ladies arose, Francis did not come to their aid despite being the one who had recruited Clare. Instead Clare had to seek protection from Innocent III (1198–1216). Clare petitioned the pope for a bull to protect the women's right to live Franciscan poverty. The resultant bull, *The Privilege of Seraphic Poverty*, identified the main characteristics of the Poor Ladies as poverty and imitation of Christ and warned under pain of excommunication, deposition, and damnation that no one was to force them to receive possessions. It was indeed a unique bull, for never before or since was a women's order so encircled by papal privilege and protection.

Soon after the bull was issued, the opposition began its efforts to modify Clare's form of life. In 1218 Hugolino Segni persuaded the new pope, Honorius III (1216–1227), to make Clare's monasteries the property of Rome and to impose a modified Benedictine

Cloister of the "Canticle of the Creatures," Church of San Damiano, Assisi, Italy, early 13th century. St. Clare lived here from about 1214 until her death in 1253.
Photo courtesy of Mary Schaefer

Simone Martini (1284–1344). Left: St. Clare. S. Chiara, Assisi, Italy.
Photo courtesy of Alinari/Art Resource, New York

rule on them that ignored the practice of poverty and mandated enclosure. We have no record of Clare's reaction to enclosure, but we do know that she entered battle to preserve poverty. A decade later Clare was still fighting Hugolino's (now Pope Gregory IX's [1227–1241]) attempt to make her "consent to some possessions," an attempt that "she wholeheartedly resisted and refused to agree." She justified her refusal by proclaiming, "Never do I wish to be released from following as closely as possible in the footsteps of Jesus Christ" (Pennacchi, 1910). Unable to deter Clare from a life of poverty and imitation of Christ, Gregory changed tactics and tried instead to discourage others from following her example. In 1228 he reissued Innocent's *Privilege* in a radically altered form that in effect nullified it. Poverty now was merely tolerated, and only in Clare's own monastery, and then only if the community agreed. Moreover Innocent's threat of excommunication, deposition, and eternal punishment for transgressors was replaced with a mild chastisement. In 1229 Gregory began enforcing his policy by obliging a Poor Ladies' monastery near Clare's to accept land and possessions, and he continued is-

View of the Umbrian countryside, Convent of San Damiano, Assisi, Italy, early 13th century. From this doorway St. Clare repelled the Saracen troops unleashed by Emperor Frederick II c. 1241.
Photo courtesy of Mary Schaefer

grasp of the theology of witness and its significance in religious life. To Clare the health of her order depended on its ability to bear witness to society, "for the Lord himself has set us an example and mirror for others, even for our own sisters whom the Lord has called to our life, in order that they themselves may then become mirrors and examples in the world" (Becker, 1985). Because Clare realized that witness could be rendered in any form of life, she adjusted easily to enclosure. What the Poor Clares must not do was to abandon their obligation to bear witness by the example of their lives, an obligation that Clare herself fulfilled both as a mendicant in her early years and as a cloistered nun in her later years.

In the early years of the 15th century, Colette of Corbie (1381–1447) initiated a reform within the Poor Clares to return them to Clare's original vision. Colette's reform spread throughout the male and female branches of the Franciscan family, but eventually these reform monasteries adopted a new rule; the women became known as Colettines, the men as Colettan. What remains of Clare's vision of monastic life after the mandated changes of the late medieval period is still lived today throughout the world in the enclosed monasteries of the Poor Clares.

PATRICIA RANFT

*See also* Assisi, Italy; Catherine of Bologna, St.; Francis of Assisi, St.; Franciscans: Female

## Biography

At about age 18, Clare of the Offreduccio family of Assisi renounced all possessions and joined Francis at the Portiuncula. Francis placed her for a short time in two Benedictine houses until a small house next to the restored church of San Damiano became available for her and her companions. From c. 1215 until her death 38 years later she served here as abbess of the Poor Clares. Her rule was the most austere yet adopted by women monastics. At her request in 1228 Gregory IX granted to three of her houses the "Privilegium paupertatis," which authorized those three houses and only those to live entirely on alms. She struggled for the rest of her life to win the same privilege of communal poverty for other houses of the rapidly spreading Order, finally succeeding just two days before her death. St. Clare was canonized two years after her death.

## Major Works

Rule of the Poor Clares
Four letters

## Further Reading

Becker, Marie-France, et al., *Ecrits* (Sources chrétiennes, number 325), Paris: Editions du Cerf, 1985
Franciscans, editors, *Seraphicae legislationis textus originales*, Ad Claras Aquas: Typographia Collegii S. Bonaventurae, 1897
Huygens, R.B.C., editor, *Lettres de Jacques de Vitry, 1160/1170–1240, évêque de Saint-Jean d'Acre*, Leiden: Brill, 1960
Pennacchi, Francesco, editor, *Legenda sanctae Clarae virginis: tratta dal Ms. 338 della Bibl. Communale di Assisi*, Assisi: Tipografia Metastasio, 1910

suing similar mandates until the end of his pontificate. Clare held fast, and in a letter to Agnes of Prague she counseled Agnes, in a veiled reference to her own struggle with the papacy, to persevere in the observation of poverty and imitation of Christ no matter who might try to dissuade her. Clare encapsulated the two guiding principles of poverty and imitation of Christ in a rule and for years petitioned the papacy to have the rule approved. She sought the rule's approval literally until she was on her deathbed, and hours before she died the papacy approved it. It was at best a token gesture, for ten years later a papal bull, *Beata Clara*, imposed a new rule authorizing the holding of property and funds on all 120 Poor Ladies' monasteries except that of Clare and Agnes. The approval of Clare's rule, however meaningless it was in the pursuit of a women's mendicant order, is significant in monastic history because it is the first approved rule written by a woman for women.

Although her rule disappeared, Clare's imprint on the Poor Clares (as they became known as after Clare's death) was permanent. Few if any medieval religious founders had a better

# Claustration (Cloister), Rules of

The Council of Tours in 567 decreed that monasteries should construct a place, or schola, where the monastic community could meet to read and discuss matters, all under the watchful eye of the abbot or prior. This schola, or cloister, was formed when it was realized that the most economical way of achieving exclusivity was to erect the essential monastic buildings – church, dormitory, refectory, and storehouse – to form a square or inner court. Thus, the cloister became the cornerstone of monastic life, enabling it to develop in exclusivity, protected from the outside world. Isolation was possible because even though the cloister was an inner enclosure, it was self-sufficient, for it had its own stores as well as a common area.

Because isolation was the key to making a religious community into a true corporative entity, it was the emergence of the cloister that made it possible for the soul, seeking Christ, to live in seclusion according to Benedict's dictates. For monastics, besides having access to all the buildings within the cloistral area, it was the cloister that safeguarded and guaranteed separation from the world. Indeed seclusion was considered absolutely necessary if the individual monk was to achieve oneness with the

Divine, by abstracting himself from the world in such a way as to behold it objectively.

Thus, to find seclusion the individual had first to withdraw from the world, and if the postulant was not going to be a hermit, it was essential to withdraw to an isolated place or to an isolation inherent in the buildings themselves. This isolation worked in two ways. First, the designs eventually formed the standard monastic plan and deliberately isolated the community from the world. Second, the rule of silence isolated the monks from one another, so that in the Christian monastic context each individual monk could seek a closer union with God.

A controlled and impersonal environment enabled the monks to live undisturbed in a truly corporative life to the end that they might worship together in choir as if in one mystical body. Such a setting thus formed the physical basis on which monks evolved an ever higher spirituality free from secular contagion yet designed so as not to go unnoticed by society at large.

Chapter 66 of the Rule of St. Benedict requires that everything necessary for the monks to live the communal life be on hand within the cloister, relieving monastics from ever needing to leave the enclosure. Chapter 67 of the Rule forbids monks to leave the enclosure, and any monk who goes beyond the bounds

Dormitory, Abbey of Eberbach (Cistercian), Oestrich, Rheingau, Germany, 1270–1345. In the film *The Name of the Rose* (1986) this dormitory was the Scriptorium.
Photo courtesy of Chris Schabel

Corridor with Benedictine monk, Melk Abbey, Lower Austria, rebuilt early 18th century.
Photo courtesy of the Austrian National Tourist Office

of the monastery, without the abbot's permission, would be punished. Moreover the cloister provided the choir monks with an ideal place in which to dwell in silence, in meditation, and in prayer – the essence of monastic life. Indeed chapter 4 of the Rule states that the workshop wherein the monks should fulfill the Rule – and all that it implies relative to the monastic life – is the enclosure, or cloister, of the monastery. It is what ensures stability to the community.

By living according to the Rule and the constitutions of the order, monks are fulfilling the first goal of the cloister, which is to maintain the communal life, the cloister symbolizing monastic life itself. The cloister also symbolizes the three vows – of poverty, chastity, and obedience – as well as the vow of stability. Moreover monks are expected to follow the customaries of the house. As the monk is obliged by his profession to avoid the outer world at all costs, another goal of the cloister was to protect the sacred (the church and monastery) from the profane (the outside world).

How could the outside world be kept from filtering into the cloister? It was with this in mind that the assembly at Aachen in 816–817 decreed that there should be no school in the cloister except for child oblates. Thus, all secular clerks and laypeople had to be excluded. Furthermore canon 598 positively forbids any woman, even a relative, to enter the enclosure of monks under any pretext unless she is the wife of a king, regent, or president. The intention of this prohibition was to preserve the peace and segregation of the monastic enclosure.

According to canon 600, the only people allowed in a cloister of contemplative nuns are the local bishop, the regional superior on his visitation, the confessor, rulers of states with wives and retinues, cardinals, physicians and surgeons (when necessary), and others whose services are needed. The bishop is to be accompanied by two clerics of a mature age.

Even today monastic life remains less rigid for men than for women, even though monks scarcely ever leave the monastic grounds except in emergencies or attending conferences. In addition rooms are provided where visitors may be received and talk freely to the monks during certain periods. In a convent of contemplative nuns, the situation is the complete opposite. The grill separating nuns from their visitors is still to be found in these convents, as it is in their churches. The grill is the symbol of their voluntary withdrawal from the world.

Because seclusion was the goal of the cloister (i.e., so that the monks might never be seen by the public), their processional route in the interior of the church from the chapter house to the choir was usually obscured from public view by means of wainscoting across the aisles and at the crossing so as to extend the rood screen. In effect this meant that the transepts, with the presbytery, also formed part of the cloister and thus were subject to its rules as well.

PHILIP E. MCWILLIAMS

*See also* Abbess, Christian; Architecture: Western Christian Monasteries; Benedictines: Female; Carmelites: Female; Cistercians: Female; Dominicans: Female; France: History; Franciscans: Female; Gender Studies: Christian Perspectives; Hermits: Western Christian; Monastery, Christian; Monastics and the World, Medieval; Oblates; Reformation; Women's Monasteries: Western Christian

**Further Reading**

Butler, Edward Cuthbert, *Benedictine Monachism: Studies in Benedictine Life and Rule*, London and New York: Longmans, Green, 1919; 2nd edition, Cambridge: Speculum Historiale, and New York: Barnes and Noble, 1924

Delatte, Paul, *The Rule of St. Benedict: A Commentary*, translated by Justin McCann, London: Burns, Oates and Washbourne, and New York: Benzinger, 1921

Knowles, David, *The Monastic Order in England: A History of Its Development from the Times of St. Dunstan to the Fourth Lateran Council, 943–1216*, Cambridge: Cambridge University Press, 1940; 2nd edition, 1963; New York: Cambridge University Press, 1976

Lawrence, C.H., *Medieval Monasticism: Forms of Religious Life in Western Europe in the Middle Ages*, London and New York: Longman, 1984; 2nd edition, 1989

Levi, Peter, *The Frontiers of Paradise: A Study of Monks and Monasteries*, London: Collins Harvill, 1987; New York: Weidenfeld and Nicolson, 1988

Moorhouse, Geoffrey, *Against All Reason*, New York: Stein and Day, and London: Weidenfeld and Nicolson, 1969

Stewart, Columba, *Prayer and Community: The Benedictine Tradition* (Traditions of Christian Spirituality), Maryknoll, New York: Orbis Books, and London: Darton, Longman and Todd, 1998

# Climacus, John, St. c. 570–649

Abbot at Mount Sinai and mystical author

The precise dates of the life of St. John Climacus are difficult to determine with certainty. The principal source, apart from the *Ladder of Divine Ascent* of John himself, is the *Life of John* written by a monk named Daniel of Raithou. However, Daniel does not provide any chronology, and he explicitly states that he does not even know John's place of origin. Until the current century, scholars generally accepted that John lived during the sixth century, but it now appears more reasonable to regard John as a seventh-century author and to consider the *Ladder* an ascetic synthesis comparable to the theological synthesis of Maximus the Confessor (c. 580–662).

Possibly born into a noble family, John enjoyed a good education, which his biographer describes as "wide learning." After moving to Mount Sinai at an early age, John experienced all three early traditional forms of monastic life, spending some time at first in obedience to an elder, later also as an abbot for 40 years of the renowned monastery on Mount Sinai, and finally for a long period as a hermit in the Sinaite desert, where he was greatly respected. A fresco in the church of the monastery to this day depicts him with a square halo, suggesting that it was painted while the saint was still alive or soon after his death.

When already quite advanced in age, John wrote the *Ladder* at the request of John, abbot of a nearby monastery in Raithou. The original title of the work was *Spiritual Tablets*, derived from a parallel with the prophet Moses. The *Ladder* consists of 30 steps, as a supplement to which John also composed a short treatise titled *To the Shepherd*, describing the task of the abbot or spiritual elder and likewise addressed to John of Raithou.

The audience is clearly a monastic one, but the *Ladder* is the work of a former hermit who had personal contact with monks living in community and who now, as spiritual elder and perhaps already abbot, understood well the tribulations faced by such monks. Writers of John's generation seem to have had an instinct that they were living at the end of an epoch, one that summed up the teaching of the preceding centuries but that was at the same time open minded, forward looking, and somewhat unprecedented. In this way, the *Ladder* has influenced many monks and married people alike over the centuries.

The style and structure of the *Ladder* give an impression of disjointedness, yet a certain subtlety exists in it. Doctrinal themes overflow into practical ones: the purely ascetic is continually being raised to the mystical and theological level. Nevertheless, the explicitly theological statements are not very frequent. Indeed, whatever deliberate patterns might be discerned in his work, no systematization exists in any formal discursive sense.

The basic image used in the *Ladder* is that found in Gen. 28:12. The use of the "ladder" in the spiritual life is found in earlier Christian authors and even in antiquity, but it is far more fully developed in John, and it is precisely this image that gives the book its distinct flavor and unity. It also influenced later iconography in monastery churches and refectories, especially from the 11th century onward.

The *Ladder* is a work that reflects a direct and personal experience on the author's part. However, it is also a book impregnated with tradition – a work of synthesis, integrating into a single whole many disparate strands of previous tradition. Obviously much indebted to the Palestinian school of Gaza (early sixth century), John could be seen as a continuator or successor of this school of spirituality. It could even be said that John lays down the foundations for a new spiritual school, the so-called Sinaite school, which is commonly restricted to Hesychius (7th to 8th century?) and Philotheus (9th to 10th century?). The Sinaite tradition deeply influenced the 14th-century Hesychasts.

JOHN CHRYSSAVGIS

Sucevița Monastery, Romania, 16th century, exterior wall painting of the eastern apse showing the Heavenly Ladder of St. John Climacus.
Photo courtesy of Mary Schaefer

*See also* Egypt; Hesychasm; Humanism, Christian; Maximus the Greek, St.; Mount Sinai, Egypt; Orthodox Monasticism: Byzantine; Spirituality: Eastern Christian; Vision, Mystical: Eastern Christian

### Biography
Renowned for his writings on spirituality, John spent his adult years from age 16 in the Monastery at Mount Sinai, where he became abbot at age 60. His name Climacus comes from the Greek word for ladder (*klimax*).

### Major Work
*Ladder of Divine Ascent*, edited by C. Luibheid and N. Russell, with an introduction by Kallistos Ware, 1982

### Further Reading
Bogdanovic, D., *Jean Climaque dans la littérature byzantin et la littérature serbe ancienne*, Belgrade: Institut d'Etudes Byzantines, 1968 (in Russian, but containing a summary in French)
Chryssavgis, John, *Ascent to Heaven: The Theology of the Human Person According to St. John of the Ladder*, Brookline, Massachusetts: Holy Cross Orthodox Press, 1989
Hausherr, Irénée, "La théologie du monachisme chez saint Jean Climaque," in *Théologie de la vie monastique: études sur la tradition Patristique*, Paris: Aubier, 1961; also in *Études de Spiritualité Orientale*, Rome: Pontificium Institutium Studiorum Orientalium Typis Pontificiae Universitatis Gregorianne, 1969
Heppell, M., "Introduction to the English translation by Archimandrite Lazarus [Moore]," in *The Ladder of Divine Ascent*, London: Faber, 1959
Völker, W., *Scala Paradisi: Eine Studie zu Johannes Climacus und zugleich eine Vorstudie zu Symeon dem Neuen Theologen*, Wiesbaden: Steiner, 1968

# Cloister. *See* Claustration (Cloister), Rules of

# Clothing: Buddhist Perspectives

Buddhist monastic clothing consists of three primary garments: an inner skirt, a vestlike shirt, and an outer robe. The outer robe might be insulated. Nuns wear an additional bodice and skirt. In ancient India these were dyed a deep yellow, or ochre, but later robe colors varied in different cultures from ochre to deep burgundy. Monks and nuns might wear a belt or cord around the waist and footwear appropriate to their environment and weather conditions. Hats, gloves, and overcoats are allowed in severe climates. Although the precise nature of the original monastic garments during Buddha's lifetime is unknown, the styles of the basic skirt, shirt, and robe of the early institutionalized community most likely were not dissimilar to clothing common in ancient Indian society.

Early monks and nuns were allowed four basic necessities: alms food, lodging, medicine, and clothing. The presentation of robes to monks and nuns was an important part of the ordination ceremony, as was the disposal of monastic robes after death. Newly ordained monks either brought fabric for the ordination ritual or were given robes by their preceptors. Worn-out robes were replaced when necessary from the monastery's supplies by the monk assigned to that task. Robes of deceased monks could be inherited, burned in cremation ceremonies, or buried.

Originally Buddhists made their robes from dusty pieces of cloth (pamsukūla) discarded in cemeteries or in heaps by villagers. These pieces were washed, dyed, and sewn together in acknowledgment of worldly conventions of hygiene, health, and propriety and at the same time in renunciation of luxury garments and membership in the lay community. In time there were so many donations of fabric and so many new monks that collecting discarded cloth proved no longer practical. The result was that Buddhists began to accept donations of cloth from the lay community. The problem then arose to develop rituals to sanctify robes that replaced the tradition of using only discards and at the same time to make sure that the Buddhists were recognizable to the larger community.

Recognition of the Buddhist community was an important issue because religious renunciation and uniform clothing were not restricted to Buddhists; early Jain and Hindu renunciates had similar traditions. As the Buddhist communities expanded in area and numbers, they developed behavioral and dress codes that distinguished them from adherents of other Indian religions. The codes set out parameters for materials deemed acceptable for monastic garments, their colors, the associated rituals, and doctrinal reasons for their dress code. All the specific rules were implemented from the perspectives of Buddhist worldview and its position in society.

Monastic clothing was designed to be a public sign of renunciation of social conventions and lifestyles, but at the same time garments were a sign of acceptance of conventions concerning human physical necessities and an acknowledgement of conventional social propriety. The very fact that Buddhists wore any garments at all set them apart from some of their more ascetic Indian cousins, such as Digambara Jains. Buddhists prohibited public nudity, as such a practice was extreme in its denial of needs for protection from the elements and in its rejection of social behavioral standards. Guidelines for acceptable fabrics and for receiving, washing, sewing, and dyeing garments were formulated to preserve the identifiable separateness of the Buddhist

community at the same time as preserving its commitment to engagement with lay culture.

All the variations in dress and rituals were pragmatic responses to situations that confronted the new community. For example, Buddhists accepted lay donations of cloth for robes but in a compromise allowed only robes made of cloth that was first cut to pieces and then sewn together so as to signal nonattachment to worldly values. This tradition survives to the present day; modern monks will wear garments of acceptable fabrics, but the fabric will be cut up and sewn together regardless of the quality of the fabric. In addition to robes made of discarded cloth, acceptable fabrics were linen, cotton, silk, wool, coarse hemp cloth, and canvas. All were washed, dyed, cut into pieces, and resewn.

As the monastic community grew, everything associated with robes had to be carefully specified and standardized, from the number of garments, the materials they were made of, where they came from, their colors, and how they were to be discarded. The Vinaya often includes detailed anecdotes that illustrate the situations that stimulated changes in monastic garments. The guidelines concerning monastic dress naturally grew in number. The many rules pertaining to robes are included in the "Donated Fabrics" (kathina) and "Robes" (cīvara) sections of the Vinaya, in the section "Leather Accessories" (carma), and in several other places throughout the Vinaya literature.

The Kathina section contains guidelines for accepting community donations of fabric for monks' robes. Evidently these took place on a very large scale and involved many different kinds of cloth, in different colors, given at different times of the year, and sometimes included tailored garments. Buddha and very likely his successors strove to maintain the uniformity of style and the doctrinal guidelines for propriety and Buddhist pragmatism and at the same time had to acknowledge increasing numbers of monks and nuns spread across a very large territory with diverse climates, economies, and cultures. Thus, the list of allowances and prohibitions in the literature is very long and detailed, and many variations exist. The text specifies the end of the rainy season retreat as the correct time for lay supporters to offer new material for monks' robes. Given the physical need of the monks and the doctrine that enables lay followers to accrue merit by donating to the Buddhist community, the monastic authorities felt compelled to specify guidelines for the acceptance of new robe material.

The guidelines in the sections on robes are case specific, and the literature sometimes includes stories that illustrate the reasons for the allowance or prohibition of specific items and on other occasions list only the results. In addition to the acceptance of lay donations after the monsoon retreat, specific guidelines are given for the storage and distribution of robe material, for dyeing, for use of animal skins and materials that affected the lives of living beings, and for a wide of variety of materials that contain a rich store of information about early Indian culture. The Vinaya texts also include descriptions of situations from places outside the Buddha's homeland. For example, monks and nuns in different cultures and climates were allowed different clothing items to meet the practical requirements of their environments. This shows a flexibility in Buddhist monasticism based on the doctrine that acknowledges worldly conventions. In this view inflexible adherence to formal structures, in this case monastic dress codes, is counterproductive and inconsistent with Buddha's teaching, so a tension existed between the constant need to maintain the integrity and identifiability of the monastic order and the need to adjust the rules on the basis of the changing needs of the community. Thus, the rules for monastic clothing exemplify the Buddhist doctrine of the "middle way," that is, between strict adherence to invariable absolute rules and pragmatic adjustments to the changing world.

PAUL NIETUPSKI

*See also* Gender Studies: Buddhist Perspectives; Hygiene: Buddhist Perspectives; Novices, Theravādin Rituals for; Regulations: Buddhist Perspectives; Rules, Buddhist (Vinaya); Saṅgha; Sexuality: Buddhist Perspectives

## Further Reading

Horner, Isaline B., translator, *Book of the Discipline*, 6 vols., London: Pali Text Society, 1951; reprint, 1992

Wijayaratna, Môhan, *Buddhist Monastic Life: According to the Texts of the Theravāda Tradition*, translated by C. Grangier and S. Collins, Cambridge and New York: Cambridge University Press, 1990

# Clothing: Christian Perspectives

With the emergence of monasticism, the custom gradually developed for monastics to wear a special type of dress called a habit (Latin, *habitus*, "dress" or "costume"). It distinguished monastics from laypeople and through its humbleness and poverty became the outward sign of the religious life. From the High Middle Ages, the form and color of the habit has continued to distinguish particular orders.

The habit was first worn in the fourth century by monks living in a community (cenobites) as a sign of the official beginning of an individual's monastic life. Its appearance was close to that of the contemporary dress of the poor. It was to be simple, menial, and sober, as Augustine and Jerome stipulated, as well as suitable for local conditions and climate, as Benedict of Nursia required.

The symbolism of the habit developed gradually. As early as the fifth century, it symbolized both the act of religious profession viewed as a second baptism and an individual's participation in the Passion of Christ (sometimes expressed through the very form of habit) as well as commitment to poverty, self-denial, and the ascetic ideal. The black or off-white habit of undyed wool was the symbol of humility. Hildegard of Bingen's view of the habit as the sign of contempt for the world (*contemptus mundi*) became widely accepted. The monk's cowl or hood was often described and depicted as a characteristic element of monastic vesture. It signified a monk's rejection of the world to which he was supposed to close his eyes and ears.

From the 13th century on, the right and obligation to wear a habit became subject to Church regulations, initially strict and later eased because of practical demands. The *Codex Iuris Canonici* (*CIC*) of 1917 required each monastic order to have its own distinctive habit to be worn only by its members. To alter the habit's form required the Vatican's permission. The Second Vatican Council (1962–1965) has relaxed regulations pertaining to the habit. As the outward sign of the consecrated life, it is to be characterized by simplicity, modesty, poverty, and aesthetic appearance and to be suitable to the conditions of time and place as well as the kind of service performed.

Pope Innocent III (1198–1216) is said to have remarked that "it is not the habit but religious profession that makes the monk." This reflected the contemporary practice of serving a novitiate in secular clothes and putting on the habit as a sign of joining a monastic order during the ceremony accompanying the taking of vows. The custom was formalized by Benedict of Nursia, who recommended in his Rule that after taking vows the monk should be "stripped of his clothes and dressed in monastic vestments" (58.26). However, in the late Middle Ages the dress of novices became similar to that of professed monks. This development was sanctioned by the Council of Trent in 1563 (*Conc. Trid. sess 25, De regul. . . . c. 15*), which required a novice to wear the order's habit for one year during the novitiate period. This requirement was abolished by the 1917 *CIC*, and the 1970 *Ordo professionis religiosae* restored the traditional principle of combining the ceremonial taking of vows with presenting the newly professed monk with the order's habit. The members and candidates of the monastic institute have the right to wear its habit, and in certain cases so do the members of the so-called third orders.

Since the 13th century Church law has obliged all monks and nuns to wear the habit. This obligation was further emphasized by the Council of Vienne (1311–1312), which introduced the sanction of excommunication *latae sententiae*. It was only the 1917 *CIC* that abolished penal sanctions while at the same time retaining the obligation to wear the habit and reducing the number of exceptions (which had increased especially since the Council of Trent, *sess 25, De regul.*, c. 19). The 1983 *CIC* states that monks should wear the habit of their institute according to its regulations.

Early habits resembled the dress of Egyptian peasants and comprised a sleeveless linen tunic (*lebiton*) worn with the linen cloth or leather belt or girdle; a goat hide covered the shoulders (*melote*), and head veil bore the monastery's symbol (*kukulion*). There was also a wooden staff. Such was the basic model for the habit in both Western and Eastern Christian monasticism.

In the Western Church the principal elements of a monk's habit were the tunic, the cincture or girdle, the scapular, and the cowl or hood; the nun's costume comprised the tunic, the scapular, and the head veil (*CIC* of 1917) and wimple. The basic element of the habit was an ankle-long tunic (*kolobion*, *lebiton*, *chiton*, or *podriasnik*) made of linen, wool, or burlap cloth and worn girdled. In antiquity it was worn also to bed. It was sleeveless or had short sleeves so as to remind the monk that he had no hands for evil deeds. The cincture or girdle, in the form of a leather belt, sash of cloth, or a cord, was worn around the usually loose tunic and symbolized the mortification of the monk's bodily desires. The scapular consisted of two narrow rectangular pieces of cloth joined at the shoulders, of knee or ankle length, with an opening for the head and sometimes including an attached hood or cowl. According to the Rule of St. Benedict (c. 55), the scapular was worn to work. Its cruciform shape symbolized the mortification of the body encouraged by Jesus. However, it was not worn by Cluniacs or Franciscans, among others. The hood or cowl covering the head and shoulders was worn by monks already in antiquity, both during the day and night, symbolizing childlike innocence, simplicity, and God's grace. The head veil symbolized a nun's "marriage" to Jesus, and the tradition of taking the veil reached back to the early Christian rite of the consecration of virgins.

In the Eastern Church the habit of the monks comprises the tunic, the girdle, and the *skadion* (*kamilavka* or *skuffia*), a cylindrical head covering. The nuns wear a head veil, leaving only the face exposed. In the Byzantine tradition the so-called *paramandia* (*analambano*, *analav*, or *paramant*), a rectangular piece of cloth with the representation of the Passion of Christ, was worn on the shoulders under the tunic. The monk of intermediate grade (one who has taken the ordinary vows, the so-called lower or small *schima*) wears the tunic: *skadion* and *klobuk* (black head covering with a veil). The fully professed monk (*megaloschimnik*) wears the *kukulion* (a type of hood with the embroidered Instruments of the Passion) and the *analvos* (a garment resembling the Western scapular but with no historical connections with it). During the liturgy the monk wears the loose mantle, called *mandyas* (*mantia*). The habit is supplemented by the *vervica* (*czotki*), a rosary, made of wood or wool, that is used to say the Lord's Prayer. During the liturgy Archimandrites wear the so-called *palica* (a square piece of cloth with the image of the cross, symbolizing the religious leader's spiritual sword).

In the Western Church the monastic habit developed from the traditions of antiquity and under the influence of the Rule of Benedict of Nursia. The latter enumerates things indispensable to a monk: "a *cucullus*, tunic, stockings, shoes, girdle, knife, stylus, needle, handkerchief, writing-tablets." The Rule goes on: "in moderate climate a *cucullus* and tunic should suffice, in wintertime the *cucullus* of woolen cloth, in summertime of a lighter fabric or worn out, a scapular to wear for work, as well as stockings and shoes. . . . All the monk needs are two tunics and two *cuculli* so he could wash them and change for the night. . . . The monk dispatched outside the monastery should receive a pair of trousers from the vestry which he will give back upon his return" (c. 55).

The monk's habit comprised a tunic and a hood or cowl. Over the tunic he wore a scapular (for work) or a *cucullus*, a loose outer mantle with wide, long sleeves (worn in choir by

some monastic orders, such as the Benedictines). The choir robes included also a surplice (white outer robe) and an *almuce* (shoulder cape). Instead of trousers a monk wore the short *femoralia* and stockings with shoes or sandals (*kalepodia*). Sometimes a type of vest called a *stofiola* was worn under the habit. The most common colors have been black, brown, white or gray, and occasionally blue. Orthodox monks dress only in black or white. Over time, with the emergence of new orders, the number and variety of habits greatly increased. Some assumed very intricate forms, a trend reversed by the reforms introduced by the Second Vatican Council.

Abbots carry the crook-shaped pastoral staff, called a crosier, its symbolism referring to the Tree of Life and, according to John Cassian (*Patrologia Latina* 49.76), providing the defense against evil spirits and sins as well as recalling the Passion of Christ. In certain circumstances abbots may wear pontificals (the insignia of the episcopal order).

At present a number of religious institutes do not use the habit. Their members, according to the institute's regulations, wear secular clothes that do not set them apart from the lay community.

MAREK DERWICH

*See also* Benedict of Nursia, St.; Benedictines: General or Male; Cassian, John; Hildegard of Bingen, St.; Jerome, St.; Origins; Regulations: Christian Perspectives; Visual Arts, Western Christian: Liturgical Furnishings

**Further Reading**

Augé, Matias, *L'abito religioso: Studio storico e psico-sociologico dell'abbigliamento religioso*, Rome: Istituto di teologia della vita religiosa "Claretianum," 1977; also published in *Claretinum* 16 (1976) and 17 (1977)

Barwig, Regis N., *Changing Habits*, New York: Pageant Press, 1970

da Gangi, B., "De habito ecclesiastico oggi," *Palestra del Clero* 45 (1966)

Dello Jacono, Joseph M., *De habitu ecclesiastico: Dissertatio historico-critica*, Rome, 1953

Moulin, Léo, *La vie quotidienne des religieux au Moyen Âge: Xe–XVe siècle*, Paris: Hachette, 1978

Oppenheim, Philippus, *Das Mönchskleid im christlichen Altertum*, Freiburg im Breisgau: Herder, 1931

Patthof, Gregor, "Habitus non facit monachum, sed professio. Die susceptio habitus und ihre Rechtsfolgen bis zum Konzil v. Trient," in *Studien und Mitteilungen zur Geschichte des Benediktinerordens und zeiner Zweige* 108 (1997)

Trichet, Louis, *Le costume du clergé: Ses origines et son évolution en France d'apres les règlements de l'Église*, Paris: Cerf, 1986

# Cluniacs

The Order of Cluny emanated from monastic reforms initiated at Cluny, an independent Benedictine abbey founded in 909 by Duke William I of Aquitaine (r. 886–918). Monasteries reformed by Cluny were expected to follow the common *ordo* once they joined the Order. The *ordo* regulated every detail of life and liturgy, and during the illustrious days of the Order all Cluniac houses followed the same daily office (*horarium*) and liturgical calendar as Cluny.

Under St. Hugh (abbot, 1049–1109), the Order was approved by the Cluniac Pope Urban II (1088–1099). Because of its rapid expansion, constitutions to supplement the Rule of St. Benedict were needed to manage the Order. The Farfa customary illustrates the extent to which dependencies were encouraged to emulate the spirit of the mother house, yet the constitutions necessary to organize and administer the Order properly were never introduced.

Apart from abbeys such as Vézelay, Hugh consolidated the Order by reducing most dependencies to the status of priories. The abbot of Cluny appointed all Cluniac superiors, often from within the community at Cluny. The abbot of Cluny, as father of all Cluniac communities, could take control of any house. Thus, the Cluniac Order was more like an extended community of priories dependent on Cluny, as verified by the language of charters.

From France the Order expanded into Lombardy, England, and Spain. Reasons for its expansion were the spiritual influence of Cluny and its liturgy, together with the belief that monasticism provided the road to salvation. In 1300 its remarkable growth ended abruptly under Abbot Pons de Melgueil. Although the number of Cluniac houses cannot be known exactly, it is reckoned that the Order of Cluny had 1,450 (or more) houses throughout Europe and 1,300 in France. Yet naming all of them has inherent problems, for many of them had earlier histories, so names and dedications did change. Another problem is that some monasteries followed the customs of Cluny yet remained autonomous (Fleury is an example), whereas Reading accepted Cluniacs as abbots. Others sent monks to Cluny to imbibe its spirit and then introduce it at home, as John of Farfa did by copying the Cluniac customary. As an additional difficulty, place names often change.

The phenomenal growth of the Order made it impossible for one abbot to rule. In 1132 Peter the Venerable (1092/94–1156) called the first general chapter; in 1200 Hugh V introduced statutes and in 1202 attempted to start general chapters. In 1231 Pope Gregory IX (1227–1241) tried to impose general chapters and regular visitations on the Order, the general chapter being designed to replace the personal leadership of the abbot of Cluny. Provinces were inaugurated at this time. Apart from the bond of allegiance between individual houses and the abbot of Cluny, what really kept the Cluniac Order together were the

Kenneth Conant's model of Cluny III (1086–1131), located in the Granary (Farinier), Cluny (Saône-et-Loire), France.
Photo courtesy of Mary Schaefer

common observances, the appointment of priors, and the making of profession at Cluny.

One of the Order's hallmarks was its freedom from outside interference. In 1016 Pope Benedict VIII (1012–1024) issued a bull giving Cluniac dependencies the same immunity from diocesan control as Cluny itself. Later, in 1024, Pope John XIX (1024–1032) extended this immunity to all Cluniac monks wherever they were. The reality was that the relationship of each house to Cluny had to be adjusted, as outside authorities and benefactors modified the degree of independence of foundations.

To counter threats to the Order during the Hundred Years' War, the abbots were elected from the great families of France, and during the 16th-century wars of religion the commendatory system was introduced. Later, Cardinals Richelieu (1585–1642) and Mazarin (1602–1661) were abbots *in commendam*. By 1622 the Order of Cluny was at a low ebb. Vain attempts at reform divided the Order into the Ancient and the Strict Observances, Cluny itself leading the Strict Observance. By 1768 the Order consisted of only 37 houses. The Order of the Ancient Observance was suppressed in 1788. During the French Revolution the Order of Cluny finally disappeared with the closing down of Cluny itself in 1790, when the community contained only 35 monks.

The Order's greatest achievement stems from its foundation as a reformed Benedictine house whose spirituality influenced countless other monasteries. That influence emanated from its expansive liturgy, especially the eucharistic celebration, which Hugh perceived as the Order's unifying element. By his profession a Cluniac became a monk of Cluny, the raison d'être of the Order. Thus, talented monks could be sent to and from Cluny to hold office anywhere.

The Cluniac concept of unity was apparent in other ways as well. When a monastery joined the Order, major building projects usually followed in order to create a presbytery befitting the Order's established ritual. Cluny's prestige was such even outside France that ground plans of her dependents and the quality of their architecture very often resembled those of Cluny; for example, Lewes was a miniature of Cluny II. It can also be said that Cluniac architecture made an enormous contribution to the Romanesque. Furthermore Cluniac iconographic and decorative schemes, known to us from books that they read and wrote, demonstrate the intellectual interests of the Order.

The custom of having all novices make profession at Cluny created problems, so that it was not always adhered to. Eventually it became a formality. In addition the term *Cluniac* became so common that problems of identity arose. Moreover the concept of the Order meant that every Cluniac house regarded itself as a little Cluny, which manifestly was not the case. Nor did the Cluniac customaries provide the basis for the creation of a full-fledged order, such as the Cistercians.

On the whole the overcentralization of the Order was its downfall, for despite the fact that all houses had to be self-sufficient, they were in fact only dependencies, relying on the mother house for guidance and leadership. The time-consuming liturgy prevented any real intellectual activity and impeded moving be-

yond its original reforming activities: simplicity, eucharistic liturgy, and artistic excellence. The latter shows in the sculpture of Cluny III, now exhibited in the Musée de Cluny, Paris, and in the renowned illuminated manuscripts.

PHILIP E. McWILLIAMS

*See also* Cluny, Abbots of; Cluny, France; England: Sites; Fishing and Fish Culture, Western Christian; France: History; German Benedictine Reform, Medieval; Governance: Christian Perspectives; Gregory VII; Historiography, Recent: Western Christian; Liturgy: Western Christian; Orders (Religious), Origin of; Regulations: Christian Perspectives; Spain: History

### Further Reading

Burton, Janet E., *Medieval Monasticism: Monasticism in the Medieval West: From Its Origins to the Coming of the Friars* (Headstart History Papers), Witney: Headstart History, 1996

Constable, Giles, *Cluniac Studies* (Collected Studies Series, 109), London: Variorum Reprints, 1980

Duckett, G.F., *Charters and Records among the Archives of the Ancient Abbey of Cluni from 1077 to 1534: Illustrative of the Acts of Some of Our Early Kings; and All the Abbey's English Foundations*, 2 vols., Wolff, 1880

Evans, Joan, *Monastic Life at Cluny, 910–1157*, London: Oxford University Press, 1931; Hamden, Connecticut: Archon Books, 1968

Evans, Joan, *The Romanesque Architecture of the Order of Cluny*, Cambridge: University Press, 1938; reprint, New York: AMS Press, 1971; Farnborough, Hampshire: Gregg, 1972

Horn, Walter, and Ernest Born, *The Plan of St. Gall: A Study of the Architecture and Economy of and Life in a Paradigmatic Carolingian Monastery* (California Studies in the History of Art, 19), 3 vols., Berkeley: University of California Press, 1979

Hunt, Noreen, *Cluny under Saint Hugh, 1049–1109*, London: Arnold, 1967; Notre Dame, Indiana: University of Notre Dame Press, 1968

Hunt, Noreen, editor, *Cluniac Monasticism in the Central Middle Ages* (Readings in European History), London: Macmillan, and Hamden, Connecticut: Archon Books, 1971

# Cluny, Abbots of

The abbey of Cluny led the recovery of European monasticism, which had suffered badly during the violence of the late ninth century. Its devotion to the Rule of St. Benedict was exemplary, and by 1100 its abbot was one of the leading figures in European society, heading a great family of houses spread across Europe. Enormous attention has focused on this network, the Cluniac Order, and it has been widely supposed that institutional innovation was a vital cause of Cluny's growth. However, for a century after its foundation Cluny was essentially a Benedictine house, although a very famous one. Its site was given in 909 by William the Pious, duke of Aquitaine, who conferred on his new

Model of Cluny III, 11th–12th century.
Photo courtesy of Lonchampt/CNMHS

foundation an immunity from incursions by secular officers, and this has been seen as a vital element in its success. However, Vézelay had received much the same privileges 40 years before, and it and other houses had also been given the kind of papal protection that Cluny first began to receive in 1031. The great difference was that Cluny enjoyed papal protection continuously, owing mainly to the personalities and prestige of the abbots. Moreover, from 909 to 1109 Cluny was ruled by only six abbots whose longevity enormously enhanced their influence.

The first abbot, Berno (c. 850), began his career during the political fragmentation and invasions that characterized the late ninth century. Like Gerard of Brogne (880–959), who began a monastic reform in Flanders around 914, Berno was a young nobleman who aspired to be a monk and knew that he could count on the support of others of his class. Berno trained as a monk at St. Martin of Autun, imbibing the spirit of St. Benedict

of Aniane (c. 750–821), who had reformed the Benedictine houses of France in the early ninth century. The prescriptions of the Aniane reform constituted the core of Cluny's later customs. After ruling Baume, Berno founded Gigny on his own lands around 890, and such was his reputation for sanctity that William, duke of Aquitaine, turned to him to establish the new house at his hunting lodge of Cluny.

Among those whom his reputation attracted was Odo from Tours, whom Berno designated as abbot (927–942) to succeed him, inaugurating a custom of designation that safeguarded the succession on the death of an abbot by establishing an accepted successor. Odo's personal sanctity attracted papal support, and he was called in to reform monasteries in France and Italy, earning the title Restorer of Monasteries in the work of Flodoard. His designated successor, Aymard (942–954), was a saintly man, but blindness forced him to pass the abbacy to Majolus

(954–994), who was a great reformer of monasteries in France and Italy and recruited extraordinarily able followers, such as St. William of Volpiano, who began a new circle of reformed houses centered on Dijon. Such was Majolus's reputation that he was an adviser of the Emperor Otto II (973–983) and is reputed to have refused both the bishopric of Besançon and the papal tiara.

His successor, Odilo (994–1049), was a friend and adviser of kings and popes, and Emperor Henry II sent his coronation regalia to Cluny in token of his regard. Great organizational change took place under Odilo. Monasteries that were founded or reformed by Cluny became priories that were permanently subjected to the abbot of Cluny. In this way what had been a loose network of abbeys, living by the customs of Cluny, was welded into an order that, at its zenith, comprised at least 400 houses. A primary reason for this was the desire that all should enjoy the extensive privileges that the papacy and others had showered on Cluny. This systematic reorganization of Cluny came at a time of continuing expansion, notably into Spain. At the same time Cluniac spiritual life was also developed. The Cluniacs had always cultivated the nobility, assuring them of the efficacy of their prayers in freeing both the living and the dead from the burden of sin, and Odilo's establishment of the Feast of All Souls was an extension of this practice. It was to become a feast across all Christendom.

Under Odilo's successor, St. Hugh (1049–1109), Cluny reached its apogee. Its influence extended all over Europe, most notably into Germany and England. The Cluniacs also diversified, establishing a house of nuns at Marcigny in 1056. The new church at Cluny, consecrated in 1095 by Urban II (1088–1099), was the greatest in all Christendom after Haghia Sophia at Constantinople. Its building was financed largely by tributes from Spanish monarchs who, notably after the fall of Toledo in 1085, desired to build connections with this spiritual powerhouse. Such ties wielded enormous influence as the *reconquista* proceeded. Hugh was the friend and adviser of kings and emperors, but relations with Gregory VII (1073–1085) were strained because Hugh remained rooted in a world respectful of lay influence in the Church.

Indeed the tide of change was turning against Cluny. By the mid–11th century gifts to the abbey were drying up, and a new spirit was abroad that demanded a simpler and more personal religiosity. Abbot Pons of Melgueil (1109–1122) behaved with an arrogance that divided the Cluniacs and alienated potential friends. His successor, Peter the Venerable (1122–1156), was the last notable abbot, having been a fine scholar and a man of great spiritual integrity who carried out considerable reforms in the Order. However, he is best known for his defense of traditional Benedictinism against St. Bernard (c. 1090–1153). Despite his vigor and learning, it was evident by the end of his life that new orders and new ways of looking at religion were triumphing and that Cluny had passed its moment of greatness.

Cluny owed its spectacular rise to many factors, but the wise leadership of long-lived abbots likely was decisive in focusing the attention of Europe on this great house and impelling it to the forefront in the wave of monastic reform that swept Europe in the 10th and 11th centuries.

JOHN FRANCE

*See also* Benedict of Aniane, St.; Benedictines; Bernard of Clairvaux, St.; Christianity: Overview; Cluniacs; France: History; German Benedictine Reform, Medieval; Historiography, Recent: Western Christian; Liturgy: Western Christian; Monastics and the World, Medieval; Spain: History; Travelers: Western Christian; William of Hirsau

**Further Reading**

Arni, C. Edson, *Masons and Sculptors in Romanesque Burgundy: The New Aesthetic of Cluny III*, University Park: Pennsylvania State University Press, 1983

*Colloque Pierre Abélard-Pierre le Vénérable,* Paris: Éditions du Centre national de la recherche scientifique, 1975

Constable, Giles, *Cluniac Studies*, London: Variorum, 1980

Cowdrey, H.E.J., *The Cluniacs and the Gregorian Reform*, Oxford: Clarendon Press, 1970

Hunt, Noreen, *Cluny Under St. Hugh, 1049–1109*, London: Arnold, 1967; Notre Dame, Indiana: University of Notre Dame Press, 1968

Hunt, Noreen, compiler, *Cluniac Monasticism in the Central Middle Ages*, London: Macmillan, and Hampden, Connecticut: Archon, 1971

Joannes of Cluny, *St. Odo of Cluny: Being the Life of St. Gerald of Cluny*, translated by G. Sitwell, New York: Sheed and Ward, 1958

Rosenwein, Barbara H., *To Be the Neighbor of St. Peter: The Social Meaning of Cluny's Property 909–1049*, Ithaca, New York: Cornell University Press, 1989

Valous, Guy de, *Le monachisme clunisien des origines au XVe siècle*, Paris: Picard, 1970

# Cluny, France

In 909 when Duke William I of Aquitaine (r. 886–918) decided to found an abbey, Benedictine monasticism was at a low ebb. He deliberately chose Berno (909–926), abbot of Baume, a well-known monastic reformer. William offered Berno any site he wanted, and Berno chose Cluny. Situated northwest of Mâcon, Cluny was remote and calm enough to miss the political upheavals of the day, an ideal place for an independent abbey to grow in peace. With no cathedral city or large monastery nearby, Cluny established itself without difficulty.

The choice of Berno as abbot was crucial, for the spiritual life begun at Cluny in the tenth century not only breathed new life into Benedictine monasticism but eventually gave support to the religious ideals of Pope Gregory VII (1073–1085).

William made Cluny the property of Sts. Peter and Paul, putting the abbey directly under the Holy See, thus freeing it from all outside interference. Indeed the Lateran Council of 1080 declared that no one had any power whatsoever over Cluny. Even though Cluny became a valuable ally of the papacy, St. Hugh (1024–1109; abbot, 1049–1109) maintained its inde-

Model of Cluny III, 11th–12th century.
Photo courtesy of Lonchampt/CNMHS

pendence even from the pope. Yet this remarkable degree of independence did not survive either the economic difficulties of the 12th century or the fiscal exactions of later kings and popes.

Cluny, as an autonomous Benedictine monastery, followed the Rule of St. Benedict but emphasized regular observance more than did most contemporaries. In addition, because of Berno's indebtedness to Benedict of Aniane (c. 750–821) and other Carolingian monastic reforms, Cluny found itself in the forefront of monastic tradition and as a center of Benedictine renewal was directly responsible for the reforming of many monasteries.

In its first 200 years, Cluny had only six abbots – the single most important factor in its history. All were men of longevity, outstanding holiness, and exceptional administrative ability. Berno had no plans to create a monastic order ruled from Cluny. Odo (926–944) followed Berno. He continued the traditions of Baume, establishing the strong liturgical tradition at Cluny. A

Bull of John XI (931–935) in 931 put Cluny and other abbeys in the forefront of monastic reform, but Odo made better use of these privileges than did other contemporaries. Aymard (944–965) came after Odo, then Mayeul (965–994). He was a contemplative man of great holiness, the first to be sainted. He reformed many more monasteries and built Cluny II (c. 955–981). Odilo (994–1049) followed. He is sometimes seen as the greatest abbot. Through his influence the number of reformed monasteries throughout France increased considerably, and many became subject to Cluny. Odilo rebuilt the monastic buildings, and at his death Cluny was perhaps the grandest monastery in Europe.

Hugh of Semur (1049–1109), the first abbot to be elected, was a man of deep piety who exercised immense influence on his contemporaries. By his time the prestige of both Cluny and its abbot were well established. Indeed so influential was Cluny that

South transept of the Abbey Church, Cluny (Saône-et-Loire), France,
11th–12th century.
Photo courtesy of Lonchampt/CNMHS

Hugh's advice was sought on crucial matters, even becoming the
mediator at Canossa between Pope Gregory VII and Emperor
Henry IV (1056–1106). Cluny III, the greatest basilica of its day,
was begun by Hugh in 1085 and dedicated in 1130. Following
destruction in the French Revolution, one transept is all that remains of this once incomparable church.

Hugh's abbacy also witnessed the greatest increase in the
number of Cluniac dependencies. When Cluniac Pope Urban II
(1088–1099) officially recognized the Cluniac family as a separate monastic Order of Cluny, Hugh became the first abbot of all
Cluniac monks. The belief that monasticism provided the surest
road to salvation possibly explains Cluny's expansion. However,
no evidence of any plans for a spiritual "empire" exists, and indeed Hugh refused to send monks to England and Spain when
first invited to do so. He preferred to invoke the spiritual influence of Cluny in order to reform individual houses rather than to
impose a system. The expansion of Cluny ended by 1300, by
which time it is said to have held 1,450 dependent houses across
Europe and 1,300 in France alone. Indeed from the beginning of
the 14th century, houses tended to break away, until the Order
was left with only 35 by 1790.

Those early abbots gave Cluny exceptional stability and continuity, providing the impetus to reform monasticism. Cluny had

a clear concept of monastic life that, together with its emphasis
on the *opus Dei*, the eucharistic celebration in particular, combined to make it an important liturgical center. The splendor of
Hugh's great basilica enhanced the liturgy at Cluny, where the
sanctuary symbolized the heavenly Jerusalem. The interaction of
the liturgy with the architecture helped make Cluny spiritually
and liturgically unique.

Life at Cluny centered around the Eucharist, but her overde-
velopment of the liturgy adversely affected the daily office (*horarium*), such that Cluny lost its initial simplicity and inevitably
its influence. The community had little time for reading and less
for literary work, thus preventing Cluny from becoming an important house of learning. Nevertheless the sculpture and decoration of Cluny III show that it was not indifferent to visual
culture.

Cluny became famous as a place of pilgrimage – second only
to St. Peter's in Rome and often seen as a substitute for it. To fulfill a vow to St. Peter, William de Warenne (d. 1088) went instead to Cluny, a visit that affected him so profoundly that in
1077 he founded the famous Cluniac priory at Lewes in Sussex.

Cluny's preeminence lasted from its foundation in 910 to the
end of the abbacy of Peter the Venerable in 1156. From then
until 1790, when the monks left during the French Revolution, it
played a relatively minor role. Because Cluny was a major European institution, it cannot be ignored in any study of European
history of the period. The fact that the site was excavated over a
40-year period is indicative of the importance of Cluny III in any
study of monastic architecture.

PHILIP E. MCWILLIAMS

*See also* Abbot: Christian; Architecture: Western Christian
Monasteries; Benedict of Aniane, St.; Benedictines: General or
Male; Cluniacs; Cluny, Abbots of; Fishing and Fish Culture,
Western Christian; France; German Benedictine Reform, Me-
dieval; Gregory VII; Historiography, Recent: Western Christian;
Hymnographers; Liturgy: Western Christian; Missionaries:
Christian; Relics, Christian Monastic; Spain: History; Visual
Arts, Western Christian: Sculpture

## Further Reading

Burton, Janet E., *Medieval Monasticism: Monasticism in the
    Medieval West: From Its Origins to the Coming of the Friars*
    (Headstart History Papers), Witney: Headstart History,
    1996
Conant, Kenneth John, "Medieval Academy Excavations at
    Cluny," *Speculum* 4 (1929)
Conant, Kenneth John, *Carolingian and Romanesque
    Architecture, 800 to 1200* (Pelican History of Art, Z13),
    Baltimore, Maryland, and Harmondsworth, Middlesex:
    Penguin Books, 1959; 4th edition, New Haven, Connecticut,
    and London: Yale University Press, 1978
Constable, Giles, *Cluniac Studies* (Collected Studies Series,
    109), London: Variorum Reprints, 1980
Duckett, G.F., *Charters and Records among the Archives of the
    Ancient Abbey of Cluni from 1077 to 1534: Illustrative of
    the Acts of Some of Our Early Kings; and All the Abbey's
    English Foundations*, 2 vols., Wolff, 1880

Evans, Joan, *Monastic Life at Cluny, 910–1157*, London: Oxford University Press, 1931; Hamden, Connecticut: Archon Books, 1968

Evans, Joan, *The Romanesque Architecture of the Order of Cluny*, Cambridge: University Press, 1938; reprint, New York: AMS Press, 1971; Farnborough, Hampshire: Gregg, 1972

Horn, Walter, and Ernest Born, *The Plan of St. Gall: A Study of the Architecture and Economy of and Life in a Paradigmatic Carolingian Monastery* (California Studies in the History of Art, 19), 3 vols., Berkeley: University of California Press, 1979

Hunt, Noreen, *Cluny under Saint Hugh, 1049–1109*, London: Arnold, 1967; Notre Dame, Indiana: University of Notre Dame Press, 1968

Hunt, Noreen, editor, *Cluniac Monasticism in the Central Middle Ages* (Readings in European History), London: Macmillan, and Hamden, Connecticut: Archon Books, 1971

*Speculum* 6 (1931)

*Speculum* 45 (1970)

Viroy, Jean, *L'Abbey de Cluny*, Paris: Laurens, 1957

# Collegeville, Minnesota

The township of Collegeville in Stearns County in central Minnesota was established in 1880 and named by Abbot Alexius Edelbrock, O.S.B. (1875–1889), of Saint John's Abbey. It is one of the most rugged sections of the Midwest, originally covered with woods and lakes. The impact of the glaciers is visible everywhere. Clay deposits are also much in evidence, and the manufacture of bricks would later become commonplace. Collegeville was about 12 miles from the growing city of St. Cloud and 80 miles from the current metropolitan area of Minneapolis and St. Paul.

Collegeville became the final site in 1867 for the development of Saint John's Abbey and University, which is located in section 1 of the township on the shores of the scenic lake now known as the Sagatagan. Possibly this is an Ojibwa word, meaning "spunk" or "punk," a shelflike, hard fungus used for tinder and obtained by Native Americans from trees near the lake before the appearance of European settlers. At present the population of the entire township is 3,274, of which 215 are members of Saint John's Abbey and about 1,700 are students of the university. The abbey owns about 2,400 acres in this township.

As a religious community, Saint John's can trace its roots to the Monastery of Monte Cassino in Italy (established by St. Benedict of Nursia), where in 529 he formulated his rule, which men and women could follow in all climates and ages. It emphasized Christ-centered living, including worship and work in community and rendering humanitarian service. In the following centuries Benedictine communities spread into northern Europe, and in 801 Charlemagne fostered the foundation of Metten on the Danube River in Bavaria. This was the monastery from which the first Benedictine monks came to the United States in

Alcuin Deutsch, O.S.B., Abbot of Saint John's Abbey, 1921–1950.
Photo courtesy of Saint John's Abbey Archives

1846 under the leadership of Boniface Wimmer, O.S.B. (1809–1887), who founded St. Vincent Abbey in Latrobe, Pennsylvania. In 1856 he dispatched the first group of monks, five in number, to Minnesota to found a monastery to care for an increasing number of German immigrants.

From the first days in Minnesota, the monks emphasized worship, meeting daily in the morning, noon, and evening for the recitation of the Divine Office and the offering of the Eucharist. By 1882 they had erected a spacious Romanesque church in the "Indian Bush," where the liturgy could be presented with care and splendor. The bricks used in the construction of the church were prepared in kilns located on the abbey grounds. Its entrance was flanked by twin towers, 150 feet in height, which became a symbol for the institution. In time three colorful and informative rose windows and an inspirational painting of Christ as the Way, the Truth, and the Life, by Brother Clement Frischauf, O.S.B. (1869–1944), a monk-painter and an exponent of the original Beuronese school of art, graced the interior. This painting encouraged the viewer to turn to prayer and meditation and has proved to be an exemplary piece of Christian art.

Aerial view of Saint John's Abbey and University, 1996.
Photo courtesy of Saint John's Abbey Archives

By the 1950s great growth in the community, numbering now 309 monks and a student population of 1,177, made the church, which admitted only 400 people, inadequate. An outstanding international architect, Marcel Breuer, was chosen as the designer with the enthusiastic support of Abbot Baldwin Dworschak, O.S.B. (1950–1971). Construction began in 1958. The plans called for replacing the twin towers, symbolic of Saint John's past, with a new, startling 100-foot landmark: a concrete banner serving as a bell carrier and reflector of light. Work on the new church advanced rapidly, and the dedication took place in August 1961. The majestic structure could accommodate a congregation of 2,000. The abbey now had a church large enough to allow the entire student body to attend a religious service with the monastic community. The baptistry, the altar, and the abbot's throne established a sacramental axis around which the plan of the church was organized. Despite the vast size, no one felt far removed from the altar. The church is most striking when large groups are worshiping.

Work, as part of the Benedictine way of life, has featured teaching, pastoral activities, publications, and promotion of the arts and crafts. In March 1857, a year after the arrival of the

monks, they obtained a charter from the territorial legislature. Classes were begun on 10 November with one professor and five students. The pursuit of the liberal arts and seminary studies and the development of a practical curriculum that would meet the needs of the immigrants in central Minnesota and the upper Midwest were emphasized. On 5 March 1869 the Minnesota State Legislature granted the Saint John's administration the power "to confer degrees and grant such diplomas in their discretion as are usual in colleges and universities." In 1883 the original charter was amended to give Saint John's the title of university. Since then, growth has been steady, and at present the College of Saint Benedict for women, sponsored by a monastery of Benedictine nuns, and Saint John's University of men, located four miles away, have a common curriculum, identical degree requirements, and a single academic calendar. All academic departments are joint, and classes are offered throughout the day on both campuses, which are linked by free bus service. The colleges now enroll 3,600 students, Saint Benedict's 1,900 women and Saint John's 1,700 men. The combined faculties include about 270 professors, among them a sizable number of Benedictines. Saint John's Abbey also sponsors a School of Theology and Seminary offering masters degrees in theology, pastoral ministry, liturgical and Benedictine studies, and liturgical music. Both the College of Saint Benedict and Saint John's University are accredited by the North Central Association of Colleges and Secondary Schools.

Other developments at Saint John's have been numerous. The Liturgical Press, created in 1926 during the administration of Abbot Alcuin Deutsch, O.S.B. (1921–1950), is a leading publisher of pastoral resources in the areas of scripture, liturgy, sacraments, and family life. The Hill Monastic Manuscript Library, founded in 1964, contains 20 million pages of microfilmed documentation from archives in Europe and Africa, a project ardently supported by the university's president, the Reverend Colman Barry, O.S.B. (1964–1971). The Institute for Ecumenical Research, founded in 1967, provides a residential center for research and writing by men and women from many religious faiths. Minnesota Public Radio (KSJR), founded at Saint John's in 1967, is currently the largest and most successful public radio system in the United States. A pottery studio was initiated in 1979 by the university's president, the Reverend Michael Blecker, O.S.B. (1971–1981), and is now directed by Richard Bresnahan. This alumnus and master potter, who studied under Nakazato Takaski in Japan, developed the largest wood-burning kiln in the United States on the campus. The Episcopal House of Prayer was built in 1989 during the administration of Abbot Jerome Theisen, O.S.B. (1979–1992), on five acres of land leased to the Episcopal Diocese of Minnesota by the monks of Saint John's Abbey where people can pray together in a unique way. The Interfaith Sexual Trauma Institute (ISTI) was created in 1994 by Saint John's Abbey and University and inspired by Abbot Timothy Kelly, O.S.B. (1992 to present), as a sponsored program in partnership with a national interdenominational leadership board "to facilitate the building of healthy, safe and trustworthy communities of faith." In 1998 an *Arca Artium*, containing more than 30,000 books by great scribes, printers, illustrators, and engravers, was opened to scholars and researchers, having been collected by a community member, Brother Oblate Frank Kacmarcik, a well-known teacher, liturgical designer, graphic artist, typographer, and calligrapher.

Pastoral activity has always been an important aspect of the work pursued by the Saint John's community. During the first 100 years, monks served in 113 parishes and 146 missions and chaplaincies in the upper Midwest, New York, Kentucky, the Bahamas, Puerto Rico, Mexico, and Japan. Emphasis on the developing liturgical movement from the 1920s during the administration of recent abbots, beginning with Alcuin Deutsch, O.S.B. (1921–1950), has been very significant in supporting popular participation, the rearrangement of the sanctuary, and meaningful changes in the Roman Catholic Church's worship endorsed by the Second Vatican Council (1962–1965). Few if any monasteries anywhere sponsor so many religious and cultural initiatives as does Saint John's.

VINCENT TEGEDER, O.S.B.

*See also* Liturgical Movement 1830–1980; Liturgy: Western Christian

**Further Reading**

Barry, Colman J., *Worship and Work: Saint John's Abbey and University 1856–1992*, Collegeville, Minnesota: Liturgical Press, 1992
Franklin, R.W., *Virgil Michel: American Catholic*, Collegeville, Minnesota: St. John's Abbey, 1956; reprint, Collegeville, Minnesota: Liturgical Press, 1988
Krey, August C., "Monte Cassino, Metten and Minnesota," *Minnesota History* 8 (1927)
Stewart, Columba, *Prayer and Community: The Benedictine Tradition*, Maryknoll, New York: Orbis Books, 1998; London: Darton, Longman and Todd, 1998
Tegeder, Vincent, "St. John's Abbey (Collegeville, Minnesota)," in *The Encyclopedia of American Catholic History*, edited by Michael Glazier and Thomas Shelley, Collegeville, Minnesota: Liturgical Press, 1997
Tegeder, Vincent, "St. John's University (Collegeville, Minnesota)," in *The Encyclopedia of American Catholic History*, edited by Michael Glazier and Thomas Shelley, Collegeville, Minnesota: Liturgical Press, 1997

# Columba, St. 521–597

Irish Christian founder of the monastery on Iona and Celtic missionary

Columba (Dove) is the Latinized form of the Irish name Columcille (Dove of the Church). This sixth-century Irish monk is well noted throughout history and has had considerable influence, but the exact facts of his life and mission are uncertain. The main source is the *Vita Columbae* (*Life of Columba*), written a century after his death by the ninth abbot of Iona, Adomnán (628–704). More hagiography than history, this work reflects the importance accorded to Columba in three books dedicated to his prophecies, miracles, and visions. The *Historia Ecclesiastica* (*The Ecclesiastical History of the English People*) by the Venerable Bede (673–735) pays great tribute to Columba but lacks accuracy in its knowledge of events in Ireland and Scotland. The various annals of later times, plus many Donegal traditions, attest further to the significance of this charismatic leader. A late 12th-century Irish life of Columcille by an anonymous Derry-based author corroborates some previous knowledge of the saint. Finally, a 16th-century encyclopedic life of Columba, *Betha Colum Cille*, by Manus O'Donnell contains many of the well-known but unauthenticated legends about Columba even while confirming some of the events surrounding his life.

Columba's monastic training is said to have come from being a disciple of Finnian, who might have been Finnian of Moville (Down) or Finnian of Clonnard (Westmeath), the latter known as the patriarch of Irish monasticism. He became a monk under St. Mobhi in the monastery of Glasnevin near Dublin, and was ordained a priest and continued to live in Ireland some years before his departure for the isles of Alba, then part of the Irish Dál Riata grouping.

Adomnán calls Columba "the father and founder of many monasteries," and his influence on the Celtic Church in both Ireland and England is to be found in this assertion. His greatest legacy is the foundation in 563 of the monastery on Iona, an island in the Inner Hebrides. This community flourished as a spiritual center for centuries. Other monasteries in England were founded from here, including the abbey of Lindisfarne (or Holy Island) on the Northumbrian coast, led by St. Aidan (d. 651), as well as Whitby and Melrose. The authority of Columba was invoked in the ensuing conflict over the Celtic dating of Easter versus the Roman custom at the Synod of Whitby (684). It is believed that Iona might not have been Columba's earliest foundation in what later became known as Scotland. That merit might belong to the abbey of Hinba on a still unidentified island. Other monasteries founded on Alba were Mag-Luinge, Artchain, and Bledach, all on the island of Tiree; Elena, on another island; and Cella Diuni, near Loch Arne on the mainland.

The Columban family of monasteries was a group of foundations that continued the spirit and direction of this saintly monk. O'Donnell claims that Columba personally began 300 monasteries, but this is surely an exaggeration. Many of these were established back in Ireland, and it is disputed which ones Columba really established. It is not likely that he found Derry, which appears to be a later foundation, but it is likely that he personally founded Durrow (Offaly) some time after Iona, around 580. Other Irish monasteries of the family include Kells, which was founded in 804 to provide safety from Iona monks fleeing from Viking raids and which received the *Book of Kells*, probably executed at Iona. The list of Irish monasteries in the Columban line include Raphne (Donegal) in 817; Rechru; Swords, near Dublin; Drumcliff (Sligo); Moone (Kildare); and Tory Island, off Donegal.

The monastic tradition of Columba, from which much of successive Celtic monasticism derived, involved an interlocking of both cenobitic and eremitic customs. Monks often lived alone in separate huts and came together for common prayer in an oratory. The entire monastery was a monastic village of many small buildings. These were simple wooden or wattle huts that were built to serve as guest house, oratory, refectory, library, and scriptorium as well as various sheds and barns for works in addition to the individual cells. Columba's own cell is marked at Iona on a small rocky knoll outside the present church.

A severe asceticism of fasting, keeping vigils, hard work, and silence belonged to this regimen. However, poetry and song were important ingredients as well. Many of the traditions portray Columba as a scribe who spent much time copying psalms and other manuscripts. One manuscript, the *Cathach*, a copy of the psalter (and the oldest surviving Irish manuscript), is attributed to him, as is the development of the particular calligraphic style of the Irish majuscule. Columba's respect for poetry is also remembered in his championing of the bards in Ireland at the Synod of Drum Ceat in Derry (590). Another aspect of his monasticism was pilgrimage. Much movement occurred between these monasteries, and Columba is known to have visited many communities. His departure for Iona is likely to have been a pilgrimage in search of a contemplative setting or even an adventure of "white martyrdom" rather than a departure for some penitential purpose, as a later legend declared.

Various writings are attributed to Columba, but none with surety. The Rule of Columba is a short collection of maxims and ascetic guidelines emphasizing the three monastic daily works of reading, labor, and prayer. The *Altus Prosator* (Father, Most High) has the best claim to be his own poetry, being a reflection on creation and sin. Other poems attributed to Columba include *Adjutor laborantium* (Helper of Workers), *Noli, Pater* (Do Not, Father), and *In te Christe credentium* (In You, Christ of Believers). At the least these testify to a tradition of Columba as a poet and writer.

Admiration and a cult for Columba soon passed into Celtic tradition. He is known as one of the three patrons of Ireland along with Patrick and Brigit (c. 453–c. 524). Thursday, the day of his birth in 521, has been celebrated as Columba's Day, and special prayers are said to him on that day. He is remembered in various roles as a friend of animals, as one who crowned kings, and as a wise and very discerning spiritual father. He was a strong charismatic character, a Christian warrior and hero, a poet and scribe, and a monk who led an intense ascetic and spiritual life.

TIMOTHY J. JOYCE, O.S.B.

*See also* Aidan, St.; Asceticism: Christian Perspectives; Botany; Brigit, St.; Celtic Monasticism; Iona, Scotland; Island Monasteries, Christian; Lindisfarne/Holy Isle, England; Missionaries: Christian; Pilgrimages, Christian: Western Europe; Scotland; Whitby, England

## Biography
Born of Irish royal lineage, Columba studied with among others St. Finnian. In 563 he sailed from Northern Ireland northward to Britain, settling on the island of Iona. From there he missionized in Scotland and founded a monastery at Durrow, Ireland. He made the monastery at Iona synonymous with the best in Celtic monasticism.

## Major Works
Hymns
Poetry

## Further Reading
Anderson, A.O., and M.O. Anderson, editors, *Adomnáns Life of Columba*, Oxford and New York: Clarendon Press, 1990 (with Latin text, translation, and notes)
Venerable Bede, *The Ecclesiastical History of the English People: The Greater Chronicle: Bede's Letter to Egbert*, edited by Judith McClure and Roger Collins, Oxford and New York: Oxford University Press, 1994
Bradley, Ian, *Columba, Pilgrim and Penitent, 597–1997*, Glasgow: Wild Goose, 1996
Clancy, Thomas Owen, and Gilbert Markus, *Iona: The Earliest Poetry of a Celtic Monastery*, Edinburgh: Edinburgh University Press, 1995 (the texts of poems are attributed to Columba)

De Paor, Marie, and Liam De Paor, *Early Christian Ireland*, London and New York: Thames and Hudson, 1978

Herbert, Máire, *Iona, Kells and Derry: The History and Hagiography of the Monastic Familia of Columba*, Oxford and New York: Clarendon Press, 1988; reprint, Dublin and Portland, Oregon: Four Courts Press, 1996 (contains translation of the 12th-century life of Columba)

Lacey, Brian, *Colum Cille and the Columban Tradition*, Dublin: Four Courts Press, 1997

Marsden, John, *The Illustrated Life of Columba*, translated by John Gregory, Edinburgh: Floris Books, 1995

O'Donnell, Manus, *Betha Colum Cille*, edited and translated by A. O'Kelleher and G. Schoepperle, Urbana: University of Illinois Press, 1918; reprint, Dublin: School of Celtic Studies, 1994

Whiteside, Leslie, *In Search of Columba*, Dublin and Blackrock, Colorado: Columba Press, 1997

# Columban, St. c. 543–615

Irish Christian monk and missionary to Europe

Columban (or Columbanus) was the greatest of the sixth-century Irish missionaries to the European mainland. Over a long life he combined brilliance, charm, courage, and fierce determination with unflinching austerity and a profound perception of the divine presence, leaving an indelible impression on the subsequent history of Western monasticism in what is now France, Belgium, Germany, Austria, Switzerland, and Italy. His literary legacy endures in a remarkable collection of letters, sermons, poems, and scriptural commentaries and in his monastic rule and penitential. His Life, composed around 641 by Jonas, an Italian monk of Columban's last foundation at Bobbio and dozens of sites across Western Europe that bear his name, form the basis of what is known about this outstanding monastic figure.

Columban was born around 543 in Leinster. His mother, Jonas relates, dreamed before his birth that the sun would arise from her breast to illuminate the world. Marked from an early age for a monastic education, Columban first studied grammar, rhetoric, geometry, and scripture. Around 560 he traveled to Lough Erne to continue his studies under St. Sinell, one of the Twelve Apostles of Ireland, at his monastery on Cleenish Island. However, his own call to the monastic life took him to St. Comgall's monastery at Bangor, which was famed for its austerity.

After many years at Bangor, Columban sought permission from Comgall to sail to the European mainland as a *peregrinus pro Christo*, a monastic evangelist. Around 589 he set off with 12 companions. Local place names (St. Columb Major and St. Columb Minor) suggest that the missionaries first landed in Cornwall, crossed the pennisula on foot, and set sail again for "Frankland," arriving near St.-Malo in Brittany. A host of sites, from the northern village of St.-Coulomb to several southern churches and places near Vannes, testify to the activity of the missionaries over a considerable period of time. Eventually, they attracted the attention of the Merovingian court. Reinforcing his band with a number of Breton disciples, Columban traveled to Rheims (or Orleans) at the request of King Guthram, a grandson of Clovis, who urged him to found a monastery in the Vosges region.

Columban chose a ruined Roman fort called Anagrates (modern Annegray), where under conditions of great hardship he and his monks tilled the soil and rebuilt the walls. There Columban's monastic rule also began to take shape. Eventual success and the growing number of monks led to additional foundations, notably at Luxeuil and Fontaine. Over the next century more than 100 new monasteries would follow Columban's rule.

The success of the Irish mission led to friction with Frankish bishops who, although negligent of their pastoral duties, were jealous of their prerogatives and suspicious of outlandish Irish customs regarding tonsure, fasting, and the dating of Easter, among others. Charges of teaching unorthodox doctrine were eventually laid against Columban and his monks. In 600 he defended the Irish customs in a striking letter to Pope St. Gregory I (590–604) in which he emphasized Ireland's constant fidelity to the Church of Rome. However, when summoned before a local synod at Châlon-sur-Saône in 603, he politely declined to attend.

In 610, in the midst of Merovingian dynastic struggles, Columban's refusal to recognize the illegitimate sons of Theuderich II, now king of Burgundy, led to forced exile for all the Irish monks, mainly because of the hatred of the old queen, the infamous Brunhilde. However, when the ship bearing Columban and his monks to Ireland was unable to leave port at Nantes, the captain put them ashore. They journeyed first to Neustria, where King Chlotar, Theuderich's cousin, invited them to remain, but by then Columban had decided to go south to labor among the Lombards of northern Italy, beyond the realm of the feuding and meddlesome Franks. Avoiding Burgundy, he and his companions traveled east to Austrasia, where they were welcomed by Theuderich's estranged brother, King Theudebert II, who offered land for a new foundation near Lake Constance.

At one point on their journey south, the Irish mission and even the monks' lives were endangered by the zeal of St. Gall, one of Columban's original companions, who set fire to a heathen shrine and destroyed all the offerings. Routed by the native people, the monks eventually located an abandoned site on the Austrian shore of Lake Constance near modern Bregenz. After two years Columban continued his migration south. Theuderich had captured and executed Theudebert, and although he and Queen Brunhilde would soon be killed themselves, for the time being they controlled the Frankish realms to the Italian frontier.

Just prior to the monks' departure, according to a ninth-century account by Walafrid Strabo (c. 808–849), Gall begged to remain behind because of illness. Exasperated, Columban released him but forbade him to offer Mass as long as Columban remained alive. That would not be long, for he died within three years after sending Gall his pastoral staff as a sign of forgiveness. In the meantime Columban had established his last monastery at Bobbio in the Appennines, where he had been given land by King Agiluf of Milan. In time it would house a famed library and grow in importance under the Benedictine rule, which replaced that of Columban.

Like his penitential, Columban's rule seems severe by modern standards and was considered so in his own time. However, the rule sought to mitigate the ascetic practices of zealous monks eager to emulate Christ and the martyrs of old, as the penitential attempted to create a more uniform and equitable system of ecclesiastical penalties. On both counts they succeeded, until they were supplanted by the more lenient Benedictine rule and new codes of canon law.

Columban's spirituality, learning, and poetic temperament emerge more clearly in his poems, letters, and commentaries, a considerable number of which have survived. Both his name and his influence also live on in the Columban Fathers, an Irish missionary congregation founded in 1917. It has been claimed that even the family name of Christopher Columbus derives from northern Italian devotion to this outstanding monastic leader. Honored by inclusion in the universal canon of saints, Columban's feast is celebrated on 23 November.

RICHARD WOODS, O.P.

*See also* Benedict of Nursia, St.; Bobbio, Italy; Celtic Monasticism; Exile, Western Christian; France: History; Gregory I (the Great), St.; Ireland: History; Libraries: Western Christian; Liturgy: Western Christian; Missionaries: Christian; Office, Daily: Western Christian; Origins: Western Christian; St. Gallen, Switzerland; Walafrid Strabo

### Biography

Columban left his monastery at Bangor, County Down, Ireland, c. 590, never to return. He established monasteries across Northern Gaul, stretching from Annegray and Luxeuil to Lake Constance. Together with St. Gall, he re-Christianized areas of Northern Gaul and began missionary work among pagans on Lake Constance. Around 612 he withdrew into the Apennines south of Piacenza and established a monastery at Bobbio, where he died in 615.

### Major Work

*Penitential of St. Columbanus* (volume 5 of *The Irish Penitentials*), edited by Ludwig Bieler, 1963

### Further Reading

Duckett, Eleanor, *The Wandering Saints of the Early Middle Ages*, New York: Norton, 1959; as *The Wandering Saints*, London: Catholic Book Club, 1960

Ní Mheara, Róisín, *In Search of Irish Saints: The Peregrinatio pro Christo*, Dublin and Portland, Oregon: Four Courts Press, 1994

Ó Fiaich, Tomás, *Columbanus in His Own Words*, Dublin: Veritas, 1974

Walker, G.S.M., editor and translator, *Sancti Columbani Opera*, Dublin: Dublin Institute for Advanced Studies, 1957

# Compostela, Spain. *See* Santiago de Compostela, Spain

# Congregations, Benedictine

In the late Middle Ages, decline and reform ran in tandem with Christian monasticism. Both the Fourth Lateran Council of 1215 and, more than a century later, the Cistercian pope, Benedict XII (1334–1342), with his bull *Summa Magistri* of 1336, had attempted to reinvigorate the old Benedictine houses by dividing them into provinces and insisting on regular general chapters and visitations. These efforts were largely a failure, mainly because the 14th century also saw the diffusion of a new scourge: the papal practice of handing over abbeys *in commendam* (literally, "into care") to a layman or a cleric (usually not a member of the order concerned) who thereby became the theoretical abbot and, in most cases, proceeded to appropriate the major part of the monastery's income to himself. Financially undermined and deprived of any genuine, let alone benevolent, leadership, the effects of this policy on the Benedictine monasteries was generally disastrous – materially, spiritually, and morally.

However, some commendatory abbots proved exceptions to the rule. One such was a 26-year-old Venetian nobleman, Ludovico Barbo (1382–1443), who in 1408 was given *in commendam* by Pope Gregory XII the moribund abbey of St. Giustina in Padua. Most untypically, in the following year Barbo made his monastic profession and was blessed as abbot. His program of monastic renewal soon attracted both novices and the interest of other Benedictine houses, but only after the election of his friend, Gabriele Condulmaro, as Pope Eugenius IV (1431–1447) did his radical ideas for the structure of a new reform congregation overcome lingering opposition.

In the novel constitutions for the Congregation of St. Giustina (known, after the adhesion of Monte Cassino in 1505, as the Cassinese Congregation), the lifelong Benedictine abbot was replaced by an annual superior, and the supreme, governing authority was given over to an annual general chapter. The latter elected a small group of definitors, who in turn appointed the abbots and visitators. In another major departure from traditional Benedictine practice, monastic profession was to be made to the congregation as a whole, not to the individual monastery. In fact, the monks were frequently transferred from house to house, as friars were in the mendicant orders. These sweeping changes were justified on the grounds that, first, the individual abbeys had long shown themselves incapable of reform (even if decreed by a provincial chapter) and, second, that this new arrangement left no loophole through which a commendatory abbot might be appointed. However, the new style of spirituality – the *devotio moderna* of the Rhineland and the Low Countries (although some scholars would now challenge this attribution) – that was promoted within the congregation by Barbo was perhaps an equally important change, as it gave a preponderant place to systematic, private meditation and prayer instead of to the choral office.

The Cassinese also placed great emphasis on study and scholarship, maintaining close links with leading Italian humanists. Moreover, until the suppressions of the late 18th and early 19th centuries, even though its great days seemed to be over, the congregation, which recruited almost exclusively from the nobility and the urban patriciate (2,238 professions were made between 1700 and 1799 alone), was to remain the wealthiest and most numerous and prestigious of all the Italian monastic bodies. However, by then its constitutional structure had long exercised a profound influence on Benedictines far outside the peninsula.

This first occurred in Spain toward the end of the 15th century, when its rulers, Ferdinand and Isabella, sought to transform a local reform movement centered on the priory of St. Benito at Valladolid (in northern Castile) into a formally structured congregation that might spearhead a renewal of Benedictine houses throughout their kingdom. Bowing to both royal and papal pressure, these Spanish monks eventually adopted the St. Giustina model, but they had no intention of following it slavishly. They much preferred to sing the daily office than to largely recite it as their Italian counterparts did. In addition, within the Congregation of Valladolid, the general chapter was to be held every three years, not annually; the abbot general himself, not special appointees, would carry out the visitation of the monasteries; and, most important, monastic profession was still to be made to the individual house, not to the congregation. In terms of spirituality, the key figure was Garcia di Cisneros (1455–1510), abbot of Montserrat and later a cardinal, who drew heavily on *devotio moderna* authors and whose classic work was to influence St. Ignatius Loyola (1491–1556). By the mid–16th century, more than 40 Spanish monasteries had joined the congregation. More than 300 years later, in 1789, 45 abbeys still belonged to it, with 1,575 choir monks, 190 *conversi* (lay brothers), and 13 hermits.

Growing up under the umbrella of the Congregation of Valladolid in the early 17th century were three monasteries (priories) of English Catholic exiles, in Flanders, Lorraine, and Paris. In 1619, after years of tortuous negotiations, these monks formed, and were approved of as, the English Benedictine Congregation, whose constitutional framework was again essentially that of the Cassinese, handed down with certain Valladolid modifications. However, the English Benedictines added some peculiarities of their own. Although ultimate authority was to rest with a general chapter that met four times per year, the president of the congregation also wielded considerable power, receiving all professions and especially dispatching monks (most of them, in fact) to "the mission" in Protestant England.

In 1604, the French-speaking Congregation of Sts. Vanne and Hydulphe, which followed the Cassinese constitutions more closely than any of their other imitators, had been formed in Lorraine. However, 14 years later, and partly for political reasons, the most famous of all the Benedictine groups in this line, the Congregation of St. Maur, was founded within France itself.

Despite papal pressure, all these new congregations in the Latin countries of Europe showed a general reluctance to forge strong links with convents of Benedictine women. Although statutes for nuns following the Cassinese observance were drawn up in the 16th century and had widespread influence in Italy – for example, in 1583 Pope Gregory XIII (1572–1585) prescribed triennial superiors for all convents in the peninsula – the number of communities that achieved actual incorporation was very limited. In any case, these enjoyed no voting rights, had no representation at general chapters (although they were obliged to submit fully to their decisions), and could not accept novices without the permission of the abbot president and the visitors. This situation was to be repeated within the Congregation of Valladolid, whereas the Vannists and the Maurists showed even less interest. However, in 17th-century France a number of female Benedictine communities managed to form two congregations of their own. One, on the centralized Cassinese model and with temporary superiors, was the Congregation of Our Lady of Calvary (1617), which still exists today in a reduced form. The second (also still extant), the Benedictine Nuns of the Perpetual Adoration of the Blessed Sacrament, founded in 1651 by Catherine de Bar in Paris (and approved in 1676), was perhaps less a congregation and more a union of monasteries following the same observance.

The development of Benedictine congregations in the German-speaking lands of central Europe followed a quite different course from the one thus far described. Although there, as in Italy, the spirit of reform emanating from the conciliar movement had been felt, the push toward a centralized structure was absent, perhaps partly because the *commendam* system had never gained the ascendancy that it enjoyed elsewhere.

In 1433, Johann Dederoth (d. 1439), a reforming abbot who was familiar with the new developments in Italy, took office at Bursfeld in Hanover and began an energetic campaign against the generally lax monastic observance in northern Germany. With the assistance of Johannes Rode (c. 1358–1439), an ex-Carthusian who was appointed to reform the ancient abbey of St. Matthias in Trier, he successfully persuaded other Benedictine houses to adopt the same austere discipline that he had imposed at Bursfeld. Papal approval was forthcoming in 1459 for the new congregation, which ten years later already comprised about 36 abbeys (94 were represented at the general chapter of 1530). The abbot of Bursfeld was always president of the congregation (thus its name, the Bursfeld Union), but the individual houses remained autonomous. The monks still made profession to these, not to the congregation, and continued to elect their own lifelong superiors. General chapters were held annually and visitations every second year. To encourage studies, the congregation established a college near the university in Cologne. Moreover, scholars estimate that by the year 1500, over 60 female Benedictine communities were under Bursfeld influence to varying degrees as well. Somewhat less than half this number not only followed its liturgical calendar and observances but also paid a tax to the congregation and had their elected superiors confirmed by its authorities. If the local bishop agreed, they might also receive Bursfeld confessors and visitors. However, the issue of episcopal jurisdiction was a thorny one, and no convents of nuns seem to have ever been officially incorporated.

With the Reformation, Bursfeld itself and almost half the constituent monasteries passed into Protestant hands. However, the remainder survived this shock as well as the calamities of the Thirty Years' War (1618–1648), not succumbing until the

Cloister, Monastery of San Giovanni Evangelista (Benedictine), Parma, Italy, 16th century. The monastery was a leader in the reform movement of the Cassinese Congregation.
Photo courtesy of the Editor

general suppression of German monasteries in the first years of the 19th century.

The constitutional structure of the Bursfeld Union was of great significance in both the short and the long term. In the short term, this decentralized, federalist structure that preserved local autonomy was adopted after the Tridentine decrees began to have an effect in southern Germany where only voluntary associations of monasteries had hitherto existed, following the reformed observances emanating from Kastl (Upper Palatinate) or Melk (Austria), and where the Bursfeld Union's attempts to expand southward had been unsuccessful.

The Bursfeld monasteries themselves had not been exempt from diocesan authority, and such exemption was also highly contentious for the Benedictines in the south. Only the Swiss Congregation (the most loosely structured of all) and the Bavarian Congregation (in 1684, after a century's struggle simply to come into existence) managed to secure it. Even in the latter case, the prince-bishop of Passau prevented the monasteries in the Bavarian part of his diocese from joining. Similar opposition also meant that the Austrian Benedictine congregation (ap-

proved in 1625) had only a nominal existence, as eight (of the eleven) member monasteries stood within the same diocese and were forbidden to send representatives to general chapters or to receive canonical visitations. Moreover, although the various Benedictine congregations in Austria, Bavaria, and Swabia cooperated in sending students and professors to the Benedictine University in Salzburg (founded in 1617), political and regional differences prevented any closer association. Each congregation had distinctive features. Abbots in Germany came mainly from the middle class, not the nobility, and the Bavarian Congregation included an especially high proportion of brewers' sons, not to mention a common novitiate. In the Congregation of Swabia (1603) – as distinct from the Congregation of Lower Swabia, formed in the face of fierce opposition from the prince-bishop of Augsburg (1685) – half the abbeys were also tiny independent states within the Holy Roman Empire.

In the longer term as well, this "German" style of Benedictine congregation was the one that presaged the future. Thus, by the end of the 19th century, the English Congregation and, by the early 20th, the Cassinese both abandoned their centralized structures for a more federalist system, whereas the major new congregations that arose in the years between 1837 and 1904 – the Congregation of France (Solesmes), the Cassinese of the Primitive Observance (Subiaco Congregation), the Beuronese, the St. Ottilien, and the two large Benedictine congregations in the United States – were variations on a model that can be traced back ultimately to Bursfeld and, in a sense, even to the Fourth Lateran Council (1215).

Almost all the monastic ancien régime – antiquated, intricate, and richly patterned as it was – came crashing down in the late 18th and early 19th centuries. Groups such as the Vannists, the Maurists, the Bursfeld Union, and the two congregations of Swabia (to name only a few) simply disappeared forever. Thus, the partial suppressions carried out by the Habsburg emperor, Joseph II (1780–1790), and similarly "enlightened" governments in some of the Italian states, plus the even more disastrous consequences of the French Revolution (and their diffusion in the wake of Napoleon's armies), had resulted in the almost total destruction of the old congregations.

However, a few survived. The Swiss hung on in their mountain fastnesses (although they were to lose half their monasteries later in the 19th century). The Austrian Congregation still existed, but under close state supervision and with most of its monks living out on parishes. Ironically, the English Benedictines found a refuge in their Protestant homeland, while a few former Cassinese abbeys held out in Sicily.

Some attempts at simple restoration were made as well. In Munich, King Ludwig I (1825–1848) regretted the attitudes of his predecessor and, from 1830 on, began to steadily restore the old Bavarian Congregation. In Italy, Pope Pius VII (1800–1823), himself a Cassinese monk, aided the reestablishment of various congregations both within his own territories and throughout the peninsula as a whole. The Cassinese regained some important monasteries but remained only a shadow of their former selves.

However, neither the survivors nor the restored congregations provided the driving force for Benedictine reconstruction during the 19th century. Instead, this came from entirely new foundations, the two most important of which were instituted by former secular priests: Prosper Guéranger (1805–1875) at Solesmes (in western France) in 1833 and the two Wolter brothers, Maurus and Placidus, at Beuron (in southwestern Germany) 30 years later.

Both Solesmes and Beuron were characterized in part by a romantic neomedievalism and a strong attachment to ultramontane Catholicism and the political right wing (the latter being an important source of their financing). However, although the Wolter brothers were greatly influenced by Guéranger's ideas, they also differed from them in some respects. The abbot of Beuron, unlike his counterpart at Solesmes, was not the permanent (i.e., ex officio) abbot president of his congregation. The Beuronese were also far more ready to admit lay brothers, more open to guests and pilgrims, and, at least until World War I, much more dynamic. Thus, the Beuronese congregation expanded rapidly in Germany, Belgium, England, and the Austrian Empire. In the nick of time, it also rescued and took temporary control of the dying Brazilian Congregation (founded in 1827). The congregation seemed to sweep all before it, its success and almost aggressive self-confidence inspiring both admiration and fear among other Benedictines. This was especially the case after Pope Leo XIII (1878–1903) founded an international Benedictine college (St. Anselmo) in Rome in 1880, and 13 years later a Benedictine confederation (encompassing the existing congregations), both headed by an "abbot primate," an entirely new monastic species. Although largely a figurehead without real power, this prelate came to enjoy growing prestige and a certain supervisory capacity. Almost inevitably, the first two holders of the post were Beuronese monks, as were many of the professors at St. Anselmo, and the outlook and customs of the Beuronese congregation undoubtedly exerted some influence on early generations of students at the college. Understandably perhaps, the French abbeys, whether of the Solesmes or the Subiaco affiliation, refused to send their students to Rome.

In Italy, Pietro Casaretto (1810–1878), a sickly, neurotic, but very determined Cassinese monk, attempted a reform movement within his own congregation, emphasizing a more disciplined, austere lifestyle (e.g., in terms of diet and timetable) and a new impetus toward foreign missions. In 1867 this movement detached itself from the Cassinese and became an independent congregation, the Cassinese of the Primitive Observance (more recently known as the Subiaco Congregation). It included many new houses that had been founded outside Italy (in France, Spain, England, Belgium, and later Germany) and even outside Europe. Casaretto himself had favored a very centralized structure, with temporary superiors appointed by a general chapter held only every 12 years. Much power was to reside in the abbot general of the congregation (initially himself). With the waning of Casaretto's influence, most of this fell away, and the constitutions of 1880 established a fairly traditional federal system with independent abbeys and supposedly lifelong abbots, although some traces of the earlier approach remained. Thus, the Subiaco congregation is still divided into provinces, each with its own abbot visitator.

The international missionary outlook that provided one aspect of this congregation's identity was soon surpassed in intensity by that of a relatively new Benedictine group that was founded specifically for the foreign missions and especially for the German colonies in East Africa. It had been brought into being in 1884 by Andreas Amrhein, a Beuronese monk. In 1887 he transferred his operations to St. Ottilien, and five years later this monastery became an abbey. (The abbot of St. Ottilien is always, ipso facto, the president of the same-named congregation.) The latter was accepted into the Benedictine Confederation in 1904, and today it has abbeys in the three German-speaking lands of central Europe and in Africa, Asia, and North and South America. Early in the 20th century, it and the other two German congregations, the Bavarian and the Beuronese, stood out from all others because of their veritable armies of bearded lay brothers (a clear majority in each case). However, even in 1995 the non-ordained remained an overwhelming majority within the Congregation of St. Ottilien.

Several of the new 19th-century congregations – those of France (Solesmes), Beuron, and the Cassinese of the Primitive Observance – plus more ancient bodies, such as the English Benedictines, were mixed congregations of men's and women's monasteries, the latter always being in the minority. However, in such congregations only the monks had active and passive voting rights, as is still largely the case.

In terms of congregational developments, the period between the two world wars was perhaps most notable for the secession from the Congregation of Beuron of its three abbeys in Belgium (1920), which then together formed a separate Belgian Congregation. This was later known as the Congregation of the Annunciation, and eventually it rivaled the Congregations of Subiaco and St. Ottilien in its international character if not in size.

More recently, since the Second Vatican Council (1962–1965), a number of additional congregations (most rather small) have also become part of the Benedictine Confederation. Several of these are centuries-old institutes that began as reform movements in medieval Italy and developed into separate monastic orders: the Vallombrosans, the Camaldolese, and the Sylvestrines. (These, like the Olivetans, who had already joined in 1960, still tend to be more centrally organized than most other Benedictines.) Others were new regional realignments of existing monasteries. Thus, three of the four abbeys of the Solesmes congregation in the Netherlands formed a separate Netherlands Congregation in 1969. In Argentina and Chile six monasteries, belonging to four different Benedictine congregations, united in a new Congregation of Cono-Sur in 1976.

The following are the three largest of the 23 congregations of monks (including novices) within the Benedictine Confederation, with statistics indicating their size, first in 1960 and then in 1995: the Subiaco (1,846 and 1,287), the American Cassinese (1,998 and 1,167), and the St. Ottilien (1,250 and 1,086). At the other end of the scale, in 1995, was the Slavic congregation, consisting of four monasteries and 29 monks in the Czech Republic and Croatia. It needs to be emphasized that a great diversity of style exists not only between the various congregations (e.g., between the pastoral and educational work of congregations in Anglo-Saxon and German-speaking lands on the one hand and the enclosed, contemplative life of the French monasteries on the other) but also within the same congregation (e.g., within the Subiaco Congregation). A small handful of male communities within the Benedictine Confederation still remain outside any congregation and depend directly on the abbot primate.

In contrast, in the 19th and 20th centuries, most of the nuns' convents were in this position (as they had been throughout Benedictine history) and were subject to local diocesan jurisdiction. Moreover, although often affiliated to the Benedictine Confederation, they still cannot be full voting members of it. In 1980 five-sixths of all such houses were in Europe and one-third in Italy. (In 1995 these Italian convents were still 114 in number, with 1,848 professed nuns and only 32 novices.) In recent decades the Roman authorities have attempted to lessen their isolation by encouraging the formation of regional federations.

Finally, a highly significant development from the mid–19th century onward has been the appearance of congregations of "active" Benedictine sisters (sorores). Eight of these congregations were founded between 1850 and 1900 and a further 23 in the following 80 years. Active in schools, hospitals, and missionary and pastoral endeavor, they varied greatly in size and were usually differentiated from the Benedictine nuns (moniales) in terms of their work, degrees of strictness of enclosure, and whether they took solemn or simple vows. In many cases this distinction was very tenuous, and it has become even more so with the promulgation of the new Code of Canon Law in 1983. Most of these bodies are independent, "modern" religious congregations in their own right, and most all have been affiliated to the confederation only since the 1960s. More numerous than either the monks (8,182) or the nuns (7,179), they numbered 10,208 professed members in 1995.

TERENCE KAVENAGH

See also Benedictines; Beuron, Germany: German Benedictine Reform, Medieval; Maurists; Monte Cassino, Italy; Patrons, Christian: Lay; Spain: History; United States: Western Christian

## Further Reading

Die Bayerische Benediktiner-Kongregation 1684–1984, special issue of Studien und Mitteilungen zur Geschichte des Benediktiner-Ordens und seiner Zweige 95:3–4 (1984)

Catalogus Monasteriorum O.S.B., 18th edition, Rome: Centro Studi S. Anselmo, 1995

Chaussy, Yves, Les Bénédictins de Saint-Maur, 2 vols., Paris: Études Augustiniennes, 1989

Collett, Barry, Italian Benedictine Scholars and the Reformation: The Congregation of Santa Giustina of Padua, Oxford and New York: Clarendon Press, 1985

Heutger, Nicolaus, Bursfelde und seine Reformklöster in Niedersachsen, Hildesheim: August Lax Verlagsbuchandlung, 1969

Knowles, David, From Pachomius to Ignatius: A Study in the Constitutional History of the Religious Orders, Oxford: Clarendon Press, 1966

Lunn, David, The English Benedictines, 1540–1688: From Reformation to Revolution, London: Burns and Oates, and New York: Barnes and Noble, 1980

Rees, Daniel, "The Bendictine Revival in the Nineteenth Century," in Benedict's Disciples, edited by David Hugh Farmer, Leominster, Herefordshire: Fowler Wright, 1980

Schmitz, Philibert, Histoire de l' Ordre de Saint-Benôit, volumes 3, 4, and 7, Maredsous, Belgium: Les Éditions de Maredsous, 1948

Sieber, Gottfried, The Benedictine Congregation of St. Ottilien: A Short History of the Monasteries, General Chapters, and Constitutions: Biographies of Its Superior Generals, St. Ottilien, Bavaria: EOS, 1992

Trolese, F.G., editor, Riforma della Chiesa, cultura e spiritualità nel Quattrocento Veneto: atti del convegno per il VI centenario della nascità di Ludovico Barbo, 1382–1443: Padova, Venezia, Treviso, 19–24 settembre 1982, Cesena, Italy: Badia di Santa Maria del Monte, 1984

Zaragoza Pascual, Ernesto, *Los Generales de la Congregación de San Benito de Valladolid*, 6 vols., Silos, Burgos: Abadia de Sato Domingo, 1973–1987

# Contemporary Issues: Buddhist

Because modernity has brought major social and economic changes to the Buddhist world, Buddhist monasticism faces significant and interesting challenges in the contemporary world. First is a shifting geographical base. On the one hand 20th-century history has proved devastating for Buddhism in some of its traditional strongholds. Suppression of Buddhism or mass defections from it have grave implications for monastics, who remain dependent on the surrounding lay community both for economic support and new recruits. Monastics cannot carry on in the face of lay Buddhism's demise or decline. On the other hand in the 20th century Buddhism has become established in a new geographical base – Europe, North America, and other parts of the world settled by immigrants of European descent.

During the 20th century, China, once the home of many important Buddhist monasteries and nunneries, has been secularized by its communist government, which dismisses traditional religion as "superstition." Japanese Buddhism was somewhat moribund at the beginning of the 20th century. Government support of Shintō through the end of World War II and the rise of many new religions since then have not helped. However, the greatest change in the status of Buddhism occurred in Tibet. Until the middle of the 20th century, Buddhism was the chief cultural force in the nation, and Tibet had a very large monastic population. The Chinese takeover, finalized in 1959, wrought great changes. Many of the most important Buddhist leaders fled into exile, and in Tibet the Chinese government has pursued a rigorous policy of secularization and suppression of Buddhism as well as of the Tibetan people in general. Chinese and Tibetan Buddhist monasteries and temples sustained major damage during the Cultural Revolution (1966–1976) as well, when many priceless treasures were destroyed and numerous monasteries razed.

In other parts of the Buddhist world, economic changes have proven more significant. In Southeast Asian Theravāda Buddhist countries, the political authorities have continued their traditional support of Buddhism and Buddhist monasteries, but a prosperous modern economy makes monkhood an unappealing career for most ambitious men. For example, Thai monasteries seldom have monks who are not either students taking advantage of a free education in the monastic setting or old men. The prosperous economy of Taiwan has produced a somewhat different effect. Pious lay businessmen continue their traditional economic support of monastic institutions to earn merit and in hopes of continued business success. Thus, monasteries are often prosperous, but they recruit far more nuns than monks. Women do not have the same opportunities in the secular economy, and many women resist a traditional patriarchal marriage. By contrast the open doors of a nunnery, where they can receive education and govern themselves, are quite attractive. Korea also has a modern, prosperous economy, exerting the same impact on monasticism. In addition Christian missionaries have been very successful in Korea, so that today the country is equally divided between Buddhists and Christians. A small fanatical group of Christians who believe that their newly adopted religion mandates them to destroy "graven images" burned many Buddhist temples and some Catholic churches in the 1990s.

Another major development in the 20th century was the development of Western Buddhism. Buddhist immigrants from all parts of the Buddhist world have been building monasteries and temples in the Western countries in which they have resettled. In addition many Europeans and European-Americans have converted to various schools of Buddhism. At this point most Western Buddhists are laypeople rather than monastics, but monastic-like meditation centers where people live temporarily and practice meditation are common, and some monasteries have been started.

Internationally one of the crucial issues facing Buddhist monasticism is the low status and poor conditions of the nuns' order in most of the Buddhist world. Because of patriarchal tradition in Asian Buddhist countries, monks received much more economic support than nuns and were far better educated. Consequently men were the major teachers and famous leaders. This fed a downward spiral for nuns. It was widely believed that lay donors earned more merit by supporting more worthy rather than less worthy monastics – and in this regard uneducated nuns could hardly compete with famous male scholars and meditation masters. In addition a career as a monk was thought to be more prestigious than one as a nun. Families welcomed their sons' decision to become monks and often placed them in monasteries at a young age, whereas they did not feel the same way about their daughters. Nuns were often despised as unfortunate rejects from society.

Because of these prejudices the nuns' order not only declined but vanished in many parts of the Buddhist world. To become a fully ordained nun requires an ordination ceremony that can be conferred only in the presence of ten fully ordained nuns. If the number of fully ordained nuns falls below ten, it can be very difficult to revive the nuns' order, especially if male authorities are opposed to that reintroduction. The nuns' ordination went from India to Sri Lanka early in the history of Buddhism and from there to China. From China it spread to Korea, but the full nuns' ordination never was transmitted to Tibet or to Thailand and the other Theravāda countries. Eventually it died out in Sri Lanka. Thus, in the modern world China and Korea remain the main sanctuaries in which nuns are still fully ordained, although the much less respected novice ordination, or the even less respected ordination as a lay nun, is available in all parts of the Buddhist world.

In the 1980s and 1990s, partly in response to feminist movements, these conditions began to change. As already noted, nuns' orders are flourishing in Taiwan and Korea. However, the

Theravāda male hierarchy in Southeast Asia and Sri Lanka is adamantly opposed to reintroducing the nuns' full ordination by receiving it from Chinese or Korean lineages, arguing that these Mahāyāna lineages are untrustworthy and might not be authentic. Some Chinese male authorities have made a point of providing an opportunity for nuns to be ordained outside Taiwan, making it easier for some women to receive ordination. Tibetan male authorities are much less opposed to reviving the nuns' order and usually recognize the validity of ordinations conferred on nuns who receive their precepts from non-Tibetan sources. In Tibetan Buddhism the levels of education and economic support received by nuns has begun to improve slowly. Some nuns now receive the same philosophical training as monks and will begin to assume greater teaching responsibilities. Among Western converts to Buddhism, there are relatively few nuns, but one of the best-known Western teachers of Buddhism, Pema Chodron, is an American nun who practices in a Tibetan lineage.

Another major issue facing monastic Buddhism in contemporary times is the changing role of Buddhist laity, bringing with it a shift in the relationship between monastic and lay Buddhists. Traditionally monastics were highly revered and socially privileged. They had a symbiotic relationship with laypeople, who earned merit by supporting monastics, while monastics provided much of the education and spiritual comfort that laypeople received. In this exchange it was the laypeople who were thought to receive the most. That is because monastics gave lay donors the opportunity to earn merit so that good fortune could continue or improve and bad fortune be reversed.

However, the role of Buddhist laity is changing in many ways, and it is unclear to what extent this traditional relationship will survive. Western Buddhism, in which dedicated lay practitioners take on disciplines of meditation and study that were traditionally the province of monastics, provides one model of how change might occur. In the Western context this has meant that many people who otherwise might become monastics (if that were the only route to advanced studies and meditation practices) remain lay Buddhists, in part because Western monasteries lack the traditional financial base. People who do become monastics often face great difficulties economically. Simply not enough laypeople have the financial resources both to support their own study and practice and to endow monasteries, and few wealthy Buddhist lay donors prefer to support monastics as a means of gaining merit for themselves. This situation could be temporary, a first-generation phenomenon. Many commentators suggest that because traditionally it is thought that Buddhism is not truly established in a country until a large and firm monastic community is in place, Western Buddhism will be on shaky ground until a larger and more economically secure monastic community emerges. However, Western Buddhism could also be pioneering a new model of serious lay Buddhist practice. Because historically in a number of settings the decline of lay Buddhism and Buddhism's heavy emphasis and reliance on monastics has proved to be a weakness that can lead to Buddhism's demise, this Western development might assist Buddhism's long-term development.

Lay meditation movements flourish in Asia as well. However, because of the traditional reverence for monastics in Asian countries, decline of the monastic community, if it occurs, would probably arise from different causes. Because the traditional merit-making system is well in place, it is unlikely that wealthy Buddhist businessmen would stop supporting monastics. Growth of Asian lay meditation movements could help the monastic community in certain ways. Lay practitioners will undoubtedly look to monks and nuns who possess advanced Buddhist training in scholarship and meditation as their teachers. A more likely scenario for the decline of monasticism is lack of recruits. As already noted, economic changes have made the monastery a less appealing place for many men who are pursuing new economic opportunities. Even in Buddhist countries in which monasteries still give primary education to impoverished boys, the latter often leave as soon as they become adults. In other Buddhist countries secular education is simply more attractive because it provides direct entry into the modern economic world. However, this change can also yield beneficial effects for Buddhist monasticism. First, those monks who remain in monasteries will have a genuine spiritual vocation and will no longer be using the monastery to escape rural poverty, forced labor, or army service. It is well known that traditionally monasteries harbored many men whose spiritual inclinations were less than exemplary. Second, as already noted, in some Buddhist countries nunhood is becoming increasingly attractive to women as nuns gain ground in educational opportunities and prestige and as women's traditional role as subservient wife in a patriarchal marriage becomes less attractive and more avoidable. This change redresses a problematic imbalance within traditional monasticism.

Monks and nuns are also looking to make changes in the services that they perform for society. Rather than simply being passive recipients of lay generosity in return for transmitting some traditional teachings, it has been suggested that monks and nuns should supply more social services to the poor and underprivileged and should provide firmer moral leadership concerning uniquely modern issues. The Dalai Lama's leadership in promoting peace and his commentary on modern social issues could serve as a model for such a new monasticism. The practice of some Thai monks who have ordained trees as monks to try to stop harmful logging practices is another example. In countries where monks are highly respected, this practice does stop loggers not because a monk performed this deed but because loggers will not desecrate monastic robes even if they are worn by trees rather than men.

The emergence of the Engaged Buddhist movement in most parts of the Buddhist world will encourage this development. This movement places a high priority on Buddhist social activism and social protest against consumerism, global capitalism, environmental degradation, and patriarchy. In addition to the Dalai Lama (1935– ), the late Bhikku Buddhadasa (1906–1993) of Thailand and Thích Nhát Hanh (1926– ) of Vietnam, among others, have been outstanding monastic leaders of this movement. Lay leaders, such as Sulak Sivaraksha of Thailand and

A.T. Ariyratna of Sri Lanka, are equally important. Besides introducing a new model of Buddhist social activism, this movement also embodies a new model of monastic-lay relations, as monastics and laypeople work together as equal colleagues rather than in a traditional relationship of hierarchical deference. As democracy and Western ideas of equality become more and more normative throughout the world, such egalitarian relationships between monastics and laypeople will spread. One can see a foreshadowing of this development in the Western controversies surrounding the role of the guru or spiritual master, often a monastic. Western Buddhists, who often are committed to democracy and egalitarianism, challenge the traditional authority.

RITA M. GROSS

*See also* Buddhadāsa; Buddhism: Western; Critiques of Buddhist Monasticism: Japanese; Dalai Lama (Tenzin Gyatso); Dialogue, Intermonastic: Buddhist Perspectives; Economics: Buddhist; Nhát Hanh, Thích; Patrons, Buddhist; Peace Movements, Buddhist; Persecution: Buddhist Perspectives; Sri Lanka: Recent Changes; Virtues, Buddhist; Zen and the West

### Further Reading

Dumoulin, Heinrich, and John C. Maraldo, editors, *The Cultural, Political and Religious Significance of Buddhism in the Modern World*, New York: Collier, and London: Collier Macmillan, 1976
Gross, Rita M., *Buddhism After Patriarchy: A Feminist History, Analysis, and Reconstruction of Buddhism*, Albany: State University of New York Press, 1993
Queen, Christopher S., and Sallie B. King, editors, *Engaged Buddhism: Buddhist Liberation Movements in Asia*, Albany: State University of New York Press, 1996
Swearer, Donald K., *The Buddhist World of Southeast Asia*, Albany: State University of New York Press, 1995
Tsomo, Karma Lekshe, editor, *Sakyadhita: Daughters of the Buddha*, Ithaca, New York: Snow Lion, 1988

## Contemporary Issues: Western Christian

Monasticism, as defined in this volume, has been the main outlet for organized lay religious virtuosity in both Eastern Christianity and Buddhism (Weber, 1958). Initially, this was also true for religious virtuosity in Western Christianity. However, a new form of active religious life emerged in the West after 1200 (for male orders) or 1500 (for female groups). Instead of an organized communal life of prayer, study, and work within the monastery compound, the active groups involved themselves in evangelization, education, and various social or health care apostolates. These external activities might have been a response to critics, especially the Protestant reformers, who considered traditional monasticism a useless and parasitic way of life. From the mid–16th century on, the membership of active communities within Roman Catholicism grew to exceed, by several orders of magnitude, those that continued to maintain a traditional monastic lifestyle. In the United States even the Benedictine

monastic foundations were often involved in external apostolates that were generally indistinguishable from those of the active communities. Male monastics worked as parish priests and ran academies or seminaries, whereas the women taught in parish schools, administered and staffed hospitals, or engaged in various social services. Prior to the mid-1950s most of the Benedictine women's foundations in the United States did not even recite the monastic Divine Office, having substituted a plethora of 19th-century devotional prayers. By 1967, of the over 1,400,000 men and women in Catholic religious communities worldwide, fewer than 5 percent were members of contemplative orders – the only orders that continued to live a traditional monastic lifestyle. Furthermore, the communities engaged in active apostolates were rapidly jettisoning many of the monastic components that had crept into their own lifestyles.

The major trend since 1965 that has affected all religious communities in Roman Catholicism, both active apostolic and monastic, has been declining membership. In some parts of the world, this decline has been precipitous: a 37 percent drop in North and Central America between 1967 and 1996, a 32 percent drop in Europe, a 35 percent drop in Australia, and a 10 percent drop in South America. In other areas membership has risen, most notably in eastern and southern Asia (up 21 percent) and in Africa (up 22 percent). Many explanations have been advanced to account for these demographic fluctuations, ranging from the expansion of educational and occupational opportunities in Western secular society (Ebaugh, 1993; Ebaugh et al., 1996) to the loss of identity and purpose within the orders themselves (Finke, 1997; Nygren and Ukeritis, 1993). Initially at least, monastic religious orders shared in the decline. The number of monastics worldwide fell 5 percent between 1965 and 1970, while the number of Benedictines in the United States fell 24 percent between 1964 and 1974.

A second trend, the reclamation of the monastic lifestyle, has also occurred during this period, not only within traditionally "monastic" orders such as the Benedictines but also among newly founded Catholic groups and even within Protestantism, in which apart from Anglicanism any form of monastic practice had been absent for over 400 years. Of 170 new religious communities and lay movements begun in the U.S. Catholic Church since 1965, 53 (31 percent) practice eremitical or cenobitical forms of monasticism and do not engage in active external apostolates (Center for Applied Research in the Apostolate, 1999). A directory of 39 new religious groups in France (Pingault, 1989) contains a similar proportion (30 percent) of new monastic communities, whereas at least 26 percent of the 65 new communities in Quebec appear to lead monastic lifestyles (Van Lier, 1998). These percentages are at least twice as large as the proportion of contemplative monastic communities among the religious orders founded between 1600 and 1950. Monastic groups are also being founded or expanded within the Anglican/Episcopalian Churches in England and North America and within the Lutheran Church in Germany, including a foundation in Martin Luther's former priory (Halkenhauser, 1996). The 1997 directory of Anglican religious communities in North America contains entries for 25 communities, 11 of which are mainly monastic, whereas four others combine monastic and apostolic elements. Three of the currently monastic Anglican orders were originally engaged in external apostolates but have shifted to a more monastic lifestyle in recent years.

Some evidence exists that the reclamation of the monastic lifestyle is ameliorating the drop in membership. Contemplative communities such as the Carmelites and the Trappists appear to be declining at a less rapid rate than the active communities, and some are even growing. Religious orders whose members continue to live communal or monastic lives have rates of new members that are over four times higher than those who do not (Finke, 1997). A growing hunger is apparent in many postindustrial Western countries for precisely the kind of contemplative space and spiritual mentoring that monasteries provide. In contrast, the increasing bureaucratic standardization and government regulation of religious schools, hospitals, and social agencies render them less attractive locales for the distinctive ministry of the apostolic orders. As increasingly more lay workers and administrators replace the ever-diminishing number of sisters, brothers, and religious-order priests in these institutions and as the remaining religious members begin to work elsewhere, the purpose (charism) of an apostolic order's corporate existence can become alienated from the institutions that it had originally been founded to run. One nationwide U.S. study found that the members of active religious communities expressed less role clarity than did the members of monastic and contemplative orders (Nygren and Ukeritis, 1993). New members are less likely to join religious communities whose identity and goals are ambiguous.

Thus, available evidence appears to indicate that the outlook for monastic religious life in Europe and North America is more promising than the projected future of the apostolic orders there. On the other hand, among Catholics of Africa and Asia the apostolic orders continue to grow.

However, this relatively optimistic assessment does not mean that the monastic orders do not face serious issues and problems that must be resolved in the near future. A key dilemma, occurring worldwide, is how to reconcile the renewed appreciation for monastic observance with the demands of the active apostolates that many of these orders have inherited from earlier periods. Many male monasteries have traditionally supplied priests to a number of far-flung parishes. This not only withdraws members from participation in the daily life and prayer of the community but also often leads to role confusion among the priests so assigned, who have been found by several studies to have "diocesan priest values" rather than those of monastic life (Wittberg, 1994). Some male monasteries have even found it difficult to persuade their newer members to accept ordination, precisely because these young men desire monastic rather than parish life. In turn this refusal of priestly office leads to leadership difficulties for the male groups, as canon law requires that the abbot or prior of a community be ordained. In addition, the seminaries, schools, or other institutions traditionally run by both male and female monastic communities now have mainly lay staffs with standards and policies dictated by governments or professional associations. As with the active orders, the connection between the school and the monastery can become less clear. Some schools might also serve a mainly wealthy clientele, and this can be a further source of ideological strain for the sponsoring monastery. Finally, as the attractiveness of monastic prayer and contemplation becomes more keenly felt, fewer of a monastery's members might be willing to accept full-time positions in these ministries. Because administrative roles are especially time consuming and require ever more specialized credentials, it might be especially difficult to attract monastic members to fill them.

The dilemma of articulating a sponsored apostolate within monastic life interfaces with a second dilemma: that of financial solvency. As an increasing proportion of their membership ages, both monastic and active orders must provide for their elderly. A 1997 study by the National Religious Retirement Office in the United States found that only 15 of the 165 men's communities and 60 of the 533 women's communities in that country were adequately funded for retirement expenses, whereas nearly 70 of the men's and more than 175 of the women's orders were between 81 percent and 100 percent underfunded. Providing for a monastery's elderly is even more difficult if younger members desire to work part time at nonadministrative positions to participate more fully in monastic life.

A third dilemma stems from the ways in which monastic life goes against the accepted values and assumptions of an increasingly individualistic Western culture. For example, many Americans no longer possess the skills for living in community, even if they desire what they romantically imagine such a lifestyle to be. Some monastics have complained of an influx of naive and idealistic applicants whose unrealistic expectations and subsequent departures are felt to be disruptive. A conflict also exists between monastic authority and the accepted Western values of team management and consensus decision making. This can result both in frustration for the prior or prioress and in discontent and alienation among the members. Finally, few monasteries are able to meet the traditional monastic ideal of self-sufficiency by providing all the labor necessary to run their facilities. This leads to a burgeoning staff of lay cooks, groundskeepers, secretaries, nurses, development officers, and investment portfolio managers, all of whom, taken together, might outnumber the actual monastics. Many monasteries have a faction of their membership who express discomfort at this state of affairs.

As more established orders reclaim their monastic traditions and as growing numbers of new monasteries, both Catholic and Protestant, are founded, it becomes possible to make some tentative predictions about the future of Christian Monasticism in the West. The difficulties of common life for individualistic westerners has led, in many places, to a rise in eremitical monasticism in addition to the more common cenobitic variant. For example, both the male and the female branches of the Carmelites have spun off laurae of hermits in recent years, and this trend is likely to continue. Another pronounced and innovative tendency is the reclamation of the ancient tradition of mixed monasteries containing both male and female members or both vowed celibate and married members in a single common life. This development has been especially common in the new communities recently founded in North America and Europe (see Pingault, 1989; Wittberg, 1996; Van Lier, 1998). Among many of the established, single-sex monasteries, programs of lay oblates have experienced a resurgence. The hunger among the laity for spirituality and contemplation often leads monastics to a more active involvement in spiritual mentoring or to providing training centers for various prayer movements. However, as with the more traditional active apostolates that they had formerly operated, involvement with the laity in these spirituality movements can ultimately impinge on monastic responsibilities, leading to strain and tension.

Finally, the intellectual tenor of monastic life appears to be undergoing a subtle but profound transformation. With fewer members involved in educational, health care, or social service apostolates and with more members shifting to spiritual mentoring, to contemplation, or to religious art, writing, or music, it has become less common for monastics to obtain advanced degrees in secular topics. When members, especially of the newly founded groups, speak of engaging in study or research, they almost always are referring to areas such as ascetic and mystical theology, iconography, or the reclamation of Gregorian chant. These endeavors are valuable in preserving the Church's long spiritual tradition, and because some authors have found that advanced education in secular subjects has led to decreased role clarity among religious order members in the past (Nygren and Ukeritis, 1993), concentrating on spiritual studies might be more beneficial for monastic identity. However, many older monastics express a sense of loss for the richness that a highly educated community, with members having backgrounds in biology, astronomy, anthropology, English literature, and economics, could experience. As the older monastics die, few young members express an interest in advanced study in these "secular" areas.

Religious virtuosity in Western Christianity appears to be undergoing a fundamental shift away from the activist/apostolic variant that has been normative in both Roman Catholicism and Protestantism since the Reformation and back to the monastic model that has been the traditional form in other traditions. Thus, contemporary Western Christian monastics are faced with the challenges posed by this shift: how to rework their traditions so as to be faithful to the old while adapting to the new, whether to detach themselves from their former institutions, and what balance to strike between involvement in spiritual mentoring of the laity and communal presence. Although none of these are easily resolved issues and although many monasteries, both new and old, might not resolve them successfully, these are dilemmas of growth and change, not of stagnation and decay.

PATRICIA WITTBERG

*See also* Benedictines: Female; Dialogue, Intermonastic: Christian Perspectives; Governance: Christian Perspectives

## Further Reading

Center for Applied Research in the Apostolate, *Emerging Religious Communities in the United States*, Washington, D.C.: Georgetown University, 1999

Ebaugh, Helen Rose, "The Growth and Decline of Catholic Religious Orders of Women Worldwide: The Impact of Women's Opportunity Structures," *Journal for the Scientific Study of Religion* 32:1 (1993)

Ebaugh, Helen Rose, Jon Lorence, and Janet S. Chafetz, "The Growth and Decline of the Population of Catholic Nuns Cross-Nationally, 1960–1990," *Journal for the Scientific Study of Religion* 35:2 (1996)

Finke, Roger, "An Orderly Return to Tradition: Explaining the Recruitment of Members into Catholic Religious Orders," *Journal for the Scientific Study of Religion* 36:2 (1997)

Halkenhauser, Johannes, "Protestant Religious Communities Today," *Religious Life Review* 35:6 (1996)

Nygren, David, and Miriam D. Ukeritis, *The Future of Catholic Religious Orders in the United States: Transformation and Commitment*, Westport, Connecticut: Praeger, 1993

Pingault, Pascal, *Renouveau de l'église: Les communautés nouvelles*, Paris: Fayard, 1989

Van Lier, Rick, *Les nouvelles communautés religieuses dans l'eglise Catholique du Quebec*, 3rd edition, Quebec: Université Laval, 1998

Weber, Max, *From Max Weber: Essays in Sociology*, translated and edited by H.H. Garth and C.W. Mills, New York: Oxford University Press, 1958

Wittberg, Patricia, *The Rise and Fall of Catholic Religious Orders: A Social Movement Perspective*, Albany: State University of New York Press, 1994

Wittberg, Patricia, "'Real' Religious Communities: A Study of Authentication in New Roman Catholic Religious Orders," in *The Issue of Authenticity in the Study of Religion*, edited by Lewis F. Carter and David G. Bromley, Greenwich, Connecticut, and London: JAI Press, 1996

## Related Web Sites

*http://www.geocities.com/Wellesley/1114/* (Sistersite)
*http://www.osb.org/osb/* (Order of St. Benedict)
*http://www.wthree.com/corl/index.html* (Conference on Religious Life in the Americas [Anglican])

# Cosmogony, Gnostic. *See* Gnostic Cosmogony in Buddhism

# Councils, Buddhist

The beginning of Buddhist history, as reported by Theravāda Buddhists, was marked by three important councils. The first was held at Rājagrha around 486 B.C., that is, shortly after the death of the Buddha. According to the Theravāda scriptures, Kāśyapa, who had been concerned about maintaining discipline within the community (*saṅgha*), asked the monk Upāli to recite the rules that were to be followed by the monks. The answer he gave is believed to be what constitutes today the book of discipline (*Vinayapiṭaka*). Ānanda was also asked to report all the teachings he heard from the Buddha. He would have then recited all the texts that make up the book of discourses (*Sūtrapiṭaka*). According to certain sources, even the books of advanced doctrines (*Abhidharmapiṭaka*) were recited during this council, so that the whole of the Three Baskets (Tripiṭaka) would have been collected at that time.

The existence of this council is recognized by all Buddhist traditions, but details about it are very contradictory and uncertain. For example, it is highly unlikely, considering the content of *Abhidharmapiṭaka*, that this part of the Theravāda scriptures was compiled at that time. The first council was obviously an attempt to establish the authenticity of the Buddhist Canon. It is quite possible to imagine that the immediate followers of the Buddha felt a need to assemble to ensure the continuity of their community by fixing the various teachings and instructions given by its founder. Thus, the historical importance of this event lies more in its disclosure of the attitudes and concerns of the first Buddhists than in the description of the event itself.

The second council took place at Vaiśali one century later, around 386 B.C. A large number of monks from the Eastern regions, where Vaiśali is situated, began to advocate, in the reign of King Kālāśoka, some ten points that were, according to the orthodox monks, considered to be a departure from the rules of the book of discipline. The tenth point, which advocated that gold and silver could be accepted from the hands of laypeople, seems to have been a central issue of debate. The monks from the Western regions disapproved of these innovations and brought the matter before a meeting of 700 monks under the presidency of Revata. The ten points for discussion were interpreted differently by the attending monks. As the matter could not be decided in open meeting, they ultimately left it to be decided by a select committee on which each side was represented by four members. These members finally decided the matter against the Vaiśali monks. According to the Theravāda account of this event, the "lax" monks were defeated but remained stubborn and some time later convened their own council, breaking away from the orthodox monks, the Sthavira (the Elders). The group of monks that seceded was later called the Mahāsaṅghika (the members of the great community). For the Theravāda Buddhists this is when the first schism within the community of monks occurred. However, according to the Mahāsaṅghika, the stimulus for the first great division involved an entirely different issue.

Apart from giving an account of how the first schism of the Buddhist community happened according to the Theravāda tradition, this second council informs us of a certain tension between monks who favored asceticism and those who wanted to settle down and live in stable communities. For example, the point about receiving gold and that concerning gardening (third point) pertained only to monks who were established in monasteries and certainly not to those who were still wandering. This council can also give us some information about the dating of the compilation of Theravāda code of discipline. The Vinaya is now very explicit about the question of receiving gold and silver; consequently the rule about handling gold might not have been formulated clearly at the time of the meeting at Vaiśali.

The third council, recognized only by the Theravāda Buddhists, was held at Patāliputra around 250 B.C. The main function of this council appears to have been the purification of the community from pseudo-monks who had swollen its ranks, likely because of the relatively comfortable life it offered. According to the tradition Emperor Aśoka himself is believed to have conducted that purification. The undesirable monks were expelled on the basis of their heretical views, which incidentally are the 64 views mentioned in the *Brahmajālasutta* of the *Dīgha Nikāya* (the collection of Long Discourses). Another reason behind this meeting was a serious doctrinal difference. Two groups were in opposition to each other on an issue relative to the nature of the dharmas, namely, whether primary elements support sense experience. One group, called Vibhajyavāda, held that the elements were impermanent, and the other group, called Sarvāstivāda, believed that they were incorruptible. The Vibhajyavāda are the direct predecessors of the Theravāda Buddhists.

The history of this council is not well known, and many of its details are contested by modern scholars. For example, it is difficult to imagine that Aśoka was personally involved in it. Nevertheless, as Gombrich (1988) argues, "Buddhist kings ever after Aśoka saw it as their duty to act as Defender of the Faith – to use the Christian phrase – by expelling malefactors to purify the Sangha. For a Buddhist, to defend the faith is to defend the Sangha."

In summary, the Buddhist accounts of the councils are so inconsistent and contradictory that they cannot be considered objective accounts of any historical value. However, despite their historical unreliability they do reveal some of the circumstances that furthered consolidation of the Buddhist Theravāda tradition.

FRANCIS BRASSARD

*See also* Arhat; Aśoka; Buddhist Schools/Traditions: South Asia; Disciples, Early Buddhist; Discourses (Suttas): Theravāda; Master and Pupil: Buddhist Perspectives; Patrons, Buddhist: India; Rules, Buddhist (Vinaya): Historical

## Further Reading

Bareau, André, *Les premiers conciles bouddhiques*, Paris: Presses universitaires de France, 1955

Bechert, Heinz, and Richard Gombrich, editors, *The World of Buddhism*, New York: Facts on File, and London: Thames and Hudson, 1984

Gombrich, Richard, *Theravāda Buddhism*, London and New York: Routledge and Kegan Paul, 1988

La Vallée Poussin, Louis de, *The Buddhist Councils*, Calcutta: Bagchi, 1976

Lamotte, Etienne, *Histoire du Bouddhisme indien*, Louvain: Publications universitaires, Institut orientale, 1958

Prebish, Charles S., "A Review of Scholarship on the Buddhist Councils," *Journal of Asian Studies* 33 (February 1974)

Warder, Anthony K., *Indian Buddhism*, 2nd edition, Delhi: Motilal Banarsidass, 1980

# Councils, Christian. *See* Church Councils, Recent Catholic

CRITIQUES 333

# Critiques of Buddhist Monasticism: Confucian

Confucian scholars were the most vehement and unrelenting critics of Buddhism in eastern Asia. Most typically they focused their attacks on Buddhism's socio-religious practices, especially those pertaining to or deriving from monasticism. Early on Confucian critiques of Buddhist monasticism centered around five themes: (1) the absence of sanction for Buddhist monasticism in the ancient Confucian canon, the *Five Classics*; (2) the unfilial nature of ascetic self-immolation, occasionally practiced but typically sanctioned by monastic orders; (3) the anti-familial nature of celibacy, often expected of monastic renunciants; (4) the unnaturalness of human renunciation of worldly pleasures; and (5) the politically problematic withdrawal of monks and nuns from the realm of government authority. Despite their critiques of monasticism, Confucians throughout the history of East Asia did engage in practices meant to facilitate achievement of spiritual enlightenment and moral perfection. Such practices arguably were similar to some of those promoted by Buddhist monasticism.

One of the earliest and most significant Confucian critics of Buddhist monasticism was the Tang dynasty (618–907) scholar Han Yu (768–824). His "Memorial on the Bone of the Buddha" argued that Buddhism was nothing more than a cult of barbarians that had infiltrated China during an age of imperial decline. Addressing his "Memorial" to the reigning Tang emperor, Han Yu encouraged him to destroy a supposed relic of the Buddha, an alleged finger bone that had been allowed into the imperial palace. Han Yu argued that if the emperor did not "distance himself" from such icons, his people would begin practicing self-immolation, abandon their families, and discard their occupations to become Buddhists, all in an effort to follow the emperor in worshiping the Buddha. Consequently, Han Yu claimed, Chinese traditions would be seriously corrupted if not destroyed.

In an essay "Yuan dao" (translated as "What Is the True Way" and "The Original Way"), Han Yu asserted that Buddhists violated natural human law and seriously undermined the foundations of the familial and political order in seeking spiritual perfection by "escaping from the world, the state, and the family." Although Han Yu did not directly influence the Tang persecution of Buddhist monastic establishments in 845, the latter was rationalized in distinctly Confucian terms that echoed many of his critiques. In particular Emperor Wuzong's (r. 841–846) "Edict on the Suppression of Buddhism" condemned the proliferation of Buddhist monasteries and the destructive drain that such expansion caused for family life and the political realm.

Most Song dynasty (960–1279) neo-Confucians followed Han Yu's criticisms of Buddhist monasticism. Zhu Xi (1130–1200) was by far the most influential and innovative of these later critics. Zhu charged that Buddhist monastic distaste for the world and human affairs resulted from a fundamental selfishness. Furthermore Zhu claimed that Buddhists were guilty of the most extreme crimes imaginable insofar as they discarded, through their devotion to monasticism, the bonds between ruler and minister, father and son, and husband and wife. The same

was true, Zhu added, because of the Buddhists' abandonment of the ethical virtues associated with family morality. Zhu observed that even when Buddhists concerned themselves with practical affairs, they did so without any affection, the latter having been banished because of their devotion to total emptiness. Such devotion led Buddhists to conclude that the moral principles inherent in reality were of no consequence. Insightfully Zhu added that the Buddhist tendency to organize monastic groups reflected the inescapability of society despite the ostensible and ultimately superficial efforts of Buddhists to divorce themselves from it through monasticism.

In Korea with the reign of King Kongmin (r. 1351–1374) in the late Koryŏ dynasty (918–1392), neo-Confucian attacks on Buddhism became more salient features of the religio-philosophical arena. The scholar Chong Mong-ju (1337–1392) praised Confucians for their natural lifestyles, which included eating, drinking, and sex, while condemning Buddhists for abandoning their families, leaving their spouses, and devoting themselves to meditating in isolated caves. Such a way of life, Chong argued, was not normal. To check the spread of Buddhist ritual, Chong advocated laws promoting the establishment of ancestral shrines for family-centered worship. With the Chosŏn dynasty (1392–1910), attacks on Buddhism became even more systematic. In addition to denouncing Buddhists for having undermined the family and state and branding Buddhist teachings as extreme heresies, many Chosŏn neo-Confucians proposed that Buddhist monks be defrocked and inducted into military service, their property allocated to the military, their slaves assigned to government agencies, their metal icons converted into coinage, their presses appropriated for publication of Confucian literature, and their monastic compounds used as government storehouses, post offices, and schools. Such attacks notwithstanding, neither Buddhism nor its monasteries were eliminated from the increasingly neo-Confucian intellectual world of Chosŏn Korea.

Confucianism was introduced to the Japanese archipelago along with Buddhism in the mid–sixth century and existed alongside it throughout the medieval period. Despite this rather symbiotic relationship, some early Confucian scholars were outspoken critics of Buddhism and especially of its monasticism. Miyoshi Kiyotsura (848–919), an imperial councillor, submitted a memorial to Emperor Daigo (r. 897–930) in 914 advocating disestablishment of Buddhism because of the severe socio-economic drain that its tax-exempt monasteries caused for the imperial state. Nevertheless Buddhism flourished until the late 16th century.

During the Tokugawa period (1600–1867), Japan's early modern era, Confucian opposition to Buddhism became a pervasive characteristic of the non-Buddhist religio-philosophical realm. Itō Jinsai (1627–1705), a Kyoto scholar who advocated a return to the original teachings of Confucius, criticized Buddhism, noting that its emergence in China had signaled the end of an age of peace and prosperity and the beginning of chronic socio-political chaos. In the late Tokugawa period, Shōji Noriyoshi (1793–1857), a merchant-scholar of political economy based in Hizen (now Nagasaki), argued that Buddhism was a useless, parasitic, and profoundly dangerous teaching. Like Jinsai, Shōji claimed that Buddhist institutions, especially its monastic establishments, led to socio-political disorder if not utter anarchy. In particular Shōji was convinced that Buddhist concern with leaving the secular world and devoting oneself to spiritual discipline made them irresponsible. However, whereas Jinsai cited Chinese history as proof, Shōji focused on the negative impact of Buddhist monastic values in Japanese history, noting the crimes – including assassination, patricide, riots, and revolts – that flowed from it. In advancing this analysis Shōji extolled Confucianism as a teaching that promoted knowledge, harmony, and a healthy, family-based socio-political order. Shōji's critique of Buddhism, along with others that typified much of late Tokugawa discourse, set the stage for the persecution by the Meiji imperial regime (1868–1912) of Buddhism as an institutional and ideological force and its elevation of Shintō as a national religion.

Despite Confucian attacks on Buddhist monasticism, significant evidence exists that Confucians incorporated elements of Buddhist spiritual practices integral to monasticism into their praxis. Most noteworthy in this regard was "quiet sitting" (Chinese, *jingzuo*; Japanese, *seiza*), a form of neo-Confucian meditation by which practitioners can supposedly perceive the pristine ethical basis of human nature. This practice apparently developed as the neo-Confucian response to the Chan (Japanese, Zen) Buddhist practice of sitting in meditation (Chinese, *zuochan*; Japanese, *zazen*) and the accompanying belief that during such meditation the practitioner could grasp the essential emptiness of everything. The neo-Confucian reinterpretation of the spiritual significance of meditative practice shows that despite their pointed polemics against Buddhist monasticism they were also concerned with providing forms of practical retreat for the spiritual growth, development, and full realization of individuals.

JOHN ALLEN TUCKER

*See also* Anticlericalism: Buddhist Perspectives; Buddhism: Inculturation; Buddhist Schools/Traditions: China; Celibacy: Buddhist; Chan/Zen: Japan; China; Economics: Buddhist; Holy Men in Power (Hierocrats), Buddhist; Japan: History; Korea: History; Monasticism, Definitions of: Buddhist Perspectives; Persecution: Buddhist Perspectives; Prophethood, Japanese Buddhist; Scholastics, Buddhist; Self-Immolation, Buddhist; Social Services: Buddhist

**Further Reading**

Bouchez, Daniel, "Buddhism and Neo-Confucianism in Kim Manjung's Random Essays," in *The Rise of Neo-Confucianism in Korea*, edited by Wm. Theodore de Bary and JaHyun Kim Haboush, New York: Columbia University Press, 1985

Chan, Wing-tsit, "Chu Hsi and Buddhism," in *Chu Hsi: New Studies*, edited by Wing-tsit Chan, Honolulu: University of Hawaii Press, 1989

Ching, Julia, *Chinese Religions*, Maryknoll, New York: Orbis, and London: Macmillan, 1993

de Bary, William Theodore, *The Buddhist Tradition in India, China, and Japan*, New York: Modern Library, 1969; reprint, New York: Vintage, 1972

Deuchler, Martina, "Reject the False and Uphold the Straight: Attitudes Toward Heterodox Thought in Early Yi Korea," in *The Rise of Neo-Confucianism in Korea*, edited by William Theodore de Bary and JaHyun Kim Haboush, New York: Columbia University Press, 1985

Deuchler, Martina, *The Confucian Transformation of Korea: A Study of Society and Ideology*, Cambridge, Massachusetts: Council on East Asian Studies, Harvard University, 1992

Fu, Charles Wei-hsun, "Chu Hsi On Buddhism," in *Chu Hsi and Neo-Confucianism*, edited by Wing-tsit Chan, Honolulu: University of Hawaii Press, 1986

Ketelaar, James Edward, *Of Heretics and Martyrs in Meiji Japan: Buddhism and Its Persecution*, Princeton, New Jersey: Princeton University Press, 1990

Kiyotsura, Miyoshi, "Statement of Opinion on Twelve Matters, 914," in *Japan: A Documentary History*, volume 1: *The Dawn of History to the Late Tokugawa Period*, by David J. Lu, Armonk, New York, and London: M.E. Sharpe, 1997

Sargeant, Galen Eugene, *Tchou Hi contre le Bouddhisme*, Paris: Imprimerie Nationale, 1955

# Critiques of Buddhist Monasticism: Indo-Tibetan

To a certain extent the Buddhist tradition developed as a reactionary movement in critique of Vedic ritualism, the caste system, and the philosophical doctrine of an eternal soul (*ātman*) prevalent in early India. Opposed to the extremes of the brahmin householder life on the one hand and the asceticism of Jains on the other, the way of life taught by the historical Buddha was nonetheless grounded in the Indian cultural matrix at that time, and the monastic tradition that arose from these teachings shared much in common with Hinduism and Jainism. Although lively doctrinal debate took place between these Indian religious traditions, Buddhist monastics managed to live in relatively harmonious, pluralistic relations with their neighbors for almost a thousand years after the life of the Buddha. However, the world-renouncing ways of Buddhist monks and nuns drew periodic attacks from brahmins, who felt that homelessness should be reserved for the later years of life. For example, during the eighth century their putative other-worldly attitudes were the target of the philosophers Śaṅkara and Kumārila Bhaṭṭa, who produced influential critiques of Mahāyāna Buddhism, especially the Yogācāra school's "mind-only" philosophy, which targeted this doctrine as a wrongful rejection of the objective world. Evidence also exists of brahmanic persecution of Buddhists, for example, by King Puṣyamitra, who overthrew the Mauryan Empire during the first century B.C.; King Sudhanvan, who ruled southern India during the eighth century A.D.; and King Mihirakula of Kashmir, who was famous for murdering Buddhist monks. From among Jain communities Buddhist monastics were criticized for being too moderate in their austerities. Unlike Buddhists Jains observed extremely strict lifestyle requirements, such as nudity, self-mortification, and frequent periods of fasting, and they were strongly opposed to the establishment of permanent residences and monasteries. Furthermore because Jains refused to take life for any reason, most Jains were critical of Buddhist formulations of compassion and nonviolence for being less than absolute. For example, the medieval Jain philosophers Haribhadra and Alanka argued that Buddhist ideals of compassion and self-sacrifice, illustrated by past-life stories of Buddha offering his body to hungry animals, were inherently violent and even murderous.

When Buddhist monasteries flourished in India, Buddhist monks and nuns were commonly criticized for indulging in earthly pleasures, such as wealth, sex, and rich foods. This line of critique was deployed by a variety of people, including Buddhists themselves, as witnessed in the writings of the seventh-century Chinese pilgrim Yixing. Furthermore Mahāyāna Buddhists argued against the older schools of Buddhism for imputing to monastics greater capacity for salvation than to the lay population, and advocates of the older schools would protest that the Mahāyānists were merely bodhisattva worshipers. All types of Buddhist monasteries became a target of the Muslim troops that swept through India from the 8th to the 13th century. Like the central Asian Hephthalites, the "White Hun" conquerors of the fifth century, these Muslim invaders plundered and destroyed countless monasteries, killing monks and nuns and burning Buddhist texts. The Muslim missionaries were instructed to seek out and dispel false gods and idolaters, including those of Hindus and Jains as well. For example, Buddhist monastic life in Bihar received a violent blow from General Muhammed Bakhtyar during the 11th century, and the armies of Bakhtyar Khalji and Muhammed Al Ghauri destroyed hundreds of Buddhist sites during the 12th and 13th centuries, ranging from the smallest shrines to the greatest monastic universities. By the 13th century the Buddhist order had disappeared almost entirely from its Indian homeland. Although no consensus exists among modern Buddhists and scholars about the primary cause for its demise, it appears to have been the result of a number of contributing factors, including the Muslim siege, the assimilative influence of Hindu Śaivism and Vaiṣṇavism, and the loss of royal patronage.

However, in Sri Lanka, where the waning of Buddhist institutions from the 6th to the 11th century paralleled their demise in India, Buddhist monasticism was revitalized from the 12th to the 14th century until it was suppressed by Christian missionaries. Beginning in the late 15th century, the arrival of Portuguese colonists, who, like the Muslims, were instructed to obliterate idols on the island, resulted in mass destruction of Buddhist temples and texts and the slaughter of monastics. Rival Dutch forces displayed a similar lack of mercy for Buddhism in the 17th century, and had it not been for Buddhist revival movements during recent centuries in Sri Lanka and India, Buddhist monasticism might not exist in these countries today.

During the eighth century, when it was beginning to decline in India, Buddhist monasticism was first taking form in Tibet, where it would establish itself as a central axis of Tibetan culture for more than a millennium. However, before gaining a stronghold in this region Buddhism faced a weighty nativist critique by indigenous Bön tradition advocates in the ninth-century royal courts that led to a suppression of the "foreign" religion for about 100 years. Eventually the Bön religion developed a monastic system of its own, and Buddhist monasteries were allowed to develop until becoming the mainstay of the Tibetan economy and government from the 15th to the 17th century. Before Chinese Communists overthrew the Dalai Lama's sovereignty in 1959, more than 2,500 monasteries and 800 nunneries belonged to the Buddhist order in Tibet, providing homes for around 10 to 15 percent of the population who were monks and 2 to 5 percent who were nuns.

The current Communist rulers of Tibet expound a characteristically Marxist critique of Buddhist monasticism and its influence on the Tibetan and Chinese peoples, having declared the Buddhist religion an "opiate of the people," a great hoax constructed to delude them about the greed, thievery, and exploits of their aristocratic Buddhist leaders. Resembling the polemic of Confucians in earlier centuries, Communist criticisms assail the utilitarian efficacy of monastic life, portraying the monasteries as antisocial, parasitic drains on the productivity and progress of society. The Communist conquerors of Tibet claim that the Buddhist religion, like others in their domain, promises future salvation from suffering to keep the lower classes satisfied with their present condition, in servitude of feudal lama rulers. Accordingly the "false refuge" offered by Buddhism, geared originally toward primitive humanity's fear of natural forces, is wielded by its bourgeois leaders as a political tool of oppression, cloaked in the guise of religion, that serves to preserve their power and authority. Communist critics, such as Ren Jiyu, are especially virulent against the Yogācāra and Chinese Huayan schools, as their idealism and focus on harmony is so contrary to the materialism and emphasis on class struggle propagated by Marxists. Communist leaders in China argue to this day that their actions in Tibet have been mainly liberative in nature, as they have ensured for the Tibetan people freedom *from* religion.

On the basis of their critique, the Communist government of China has implemented a radical suppression of religion in their domain in an attempt to purge the country of primitive superstitions and unpatriotic religious leaders. Since the Tibetan revolt of 1959, when the Dalai Lama fled to India, Tibetan Buddhist and Bön monastics have faced incessant persecution by their Communist rulers, who use military force to disempower and integrate them into a "homogeneous" Chinese society. Caught in the throes of cultural genocide, Buddhist monks and nuns are regularly subjected to labor camps, torture, public humiliation, and inquisitions concerning their allegiance to the Dalai Lama. The Dalai Lama's exiled government in Dharamsala, India, estimates that one-and-a-half-million Tibetans have died as a result of Chinese occupation and that at least 6,000 Tibetan monasteries have been destroyed or converted to military barracks, hospitals, and prisons, and religious artifacts have been reduced to ashes. Today Tibetan Buddhist monasticism subsists in diaspora in India, Nepal, Bhutan, Sikkim, Europe, and the United States more securely than it does in its Tibetan homeland.

TALINE GOORJIAN

*See also* Ashram, Influence of; Bön Monasticism; Buddhist Schools/Traditions: South Asia; Dharamsala, India (Tibetan); Discourses (Sūtras): Mahāyāna; Jain Monasticism and Buddhist Monasticism; Pilgrims to India, Chinese; Sri Lanka: History; Tibet: History

**Further Reading**

Bush, Richard C., Jr., *Religion in Communist China*, Nashville, Tennessee: Abingdon Press, 1970

Donnet, Pierre-Antoine, *Tibet mort ou vif*, Paris: Gallimard, 1990; revised edition, 1992; as *Tibet: Survival in Question*, translated by Tica Broch, London: Oxford University Press, 1994

Dutt, Sukumar, *Buddhist Monks and Monasteries of India: Their History and Their Contribution to Indian Culture*, London: Allen and Unwin, 1962

Goldstein, Melvyn C., and Matthew T. Kapstein, editors, *Buddhism in Contemporary Tibet: Religious Revival and Cultural Identity*, Berkeley: University of California Press, 1998

Granoff, Phyllis, "The Violence of Non-Violence: A Study of Some Jain Responses to Non-Jain Religious Practice," *Journal of the International Association of Buddhist Studies* 15:1 (1992)

Hazra, Kanai Lal, *The Rise and Decline of Buddhism in India*, New Delhi: Munshiram Manoharlal, 1995

Joshi, Lal Mani, *Studies in the Buddhistic Culture of India during the 7th and 8th Centuries A.D.*, Delhi: Motilal Banarsidass, 1967; 2nd edition, 1977

Smith, Bardwell L., editor, *Religion and Legitimation of Power in Sri Lanka*, Chambersburg, Pennsylvania: ANIMA Books, 1978

Tambiah, Stanley Jeyaraja, *Buddhism Betrayed? Religion, Politics, and Violence in Sri Lanka*, Chicago: University of Chicago Press, 1992

Welch, Holmes, *Buddhism Under Mao*, Cambridge, Massachusetts: Harvard University Press, 1972

Winius, George D., *The Fatal History of Portuguese Ceylon: Transition to Dutch Rule*, Cambridge, Massachusetts: Harvard University Press, 1971

**Related Web Site**

*http://www.tibet.com*

# Critiques of Buddhist Monasticism: Japanese

Since the embrace of Buddhism as a national religion by Prince Shōtoku (c. 573–621), the Buddhist monastic tradition has played a pivotal role in the development of Japanese culture, spirituality, education, and government policy. The centrality that it has enjoyed in Japan for over a thousand years is due largely to the syncretic approach of early monastics who sought to incorporate native rituals,h terminologies, and Shintō deities (*kami*) into the Buddhist framework rather than displace them. By the 17th century these uniquely Japanese forms of Buddhism assumed a powerful mediating position between government and society when the Tokugawa Shōgunate issued a command proscribing Catholicism and requiring households to affiliate themselves with Buddhist temples. On the basis of this parochial system (*danka seido*), Buddhist institutions in Japan acquired a dominant hold on the people and a share in temporal authority, which subsisted until a new government system emerged during the Meiji Restoration of 1868.

The Meiji transformation of Japan was spurred on by the arrival of Commodore Matthew Perry's ships in Edo Bay of Uraga during 1852, forcing the closed state of the Tokugawa to open its borders to the outside world, with all its scientific discourse, colonial endeavors, and technological developments. In response to these external pressures, the Japanese people initiated a process of radical modernization, including a sweeping revision of the relationship between Buddhism and the state. To gain leverage against foreign powers and to assert their position as a strong nation-state in the globalized 19th-century world, the newly born Meiji government took action against certain elements of Japanese culture deemed "nonnative," including the Buddhist priesthood, monastic institution, and religion in general. Scapegoated as a foreign, corrupting presence in Japan, useful only for funerary and festival services, the Buddhist order was systematically disempowered as thousands of priests and monastics were forced to disrobe and urged to marry. Over 40,000 temples, monasteries, and shrines were dismantled, and the metal from their bells, statues, and artifacts was melted for military use. The national polity (*kokutai*) of the Meiji state rested in part on the intention of "abolishing Buddhism and destroying its teachings" (*haibutsu kishaku*).

These Buddhist suppressions were part of a larger agenda of the Meiji government that sought the "separation of Buddhism and Shintō" (*shimbutsu bunri*) to purify the native Shintō tradition with which the Meiji state had identified. Having been historically blended together with Buddhism, a condition known during early Meiji as "two-sided Shintō" (*ryōbu shintō*), modern, state Shintō was reconstructed by the architects of the new government specifically for the purposes of restoring the imperial rule (*ōseifukko*) of the Meiji emperor, the embodiment of Shintō divinity. The critique of Buddhism and Buddhist monasticism put forth by the newly severed state Shintō and its corresponding imperial government was leveled on a number of fronts. With a nativist appeal the foreign status of Buddhism was asserted, on political and economic bases the power and wealth of Buddhist institutions were attacked, and for spiritual reasons the religiosity of Buddhist priests and monastics was reproached as degenerate and retrogressive. Buddhist priests and monastics were also criticized for being antisocial, parasitic, and superstitious, and the monastic system in general was denounced by Meiji advocates as a hindrance to the scientific and technological advancement of modern Japan.

In response to these criticisms, late 19th- and early 20th-century Buddhists in Japan reevaluated and redirected the thrust of their tradition to equip it for survival in a rapidly changing Japanese society. The resulting "new Buddhism" (*shin bukkyō*) propagated by these Buddhist reformists was fashioned in accordance with the lexicon of state Shintō and current trends toward modernization; it was geared toward the rationalist, universalizing discourse of science and away from the insulation and sectarianism of monastic life. Heralded as a modern, socially engaged, cosmopolitan tradition, these new Buddhist movements were promoted as thoroughly empiricist and scientific in their approach to life, having been purified of superstitious residues from their pre-Meiji past. Thus, to affirm the relevance and utility of Buddhism in a contemporary Japanese context, Buddhist apologists emphasized the aspects of their tradition that resonated with Meiji objectives, such as the historical association between Zen and the samurai warrior ethic (*bushido*) while participating themselves in the criticism of institutionalized monasticism.

This strain of internalized critique was especially pronounced in the case of Zen Buddhism, as ecumenical priests and scholars such as Shaku Sōen, D.T. Suzuki (1870–1966), and leaders of the Kyoto school strove to dissociate the notion of Zen as a kind of "experience" (*keiken*) from its monastic legacy. Resonant with contemporary notions of religious experience popularized by figures such as William James and Friedrich Schleiermacher in the West, who themselves were influenced by Enlightenment critiques of institutionalized religion, this abstracted and essentialized notion of Zen was constructed in opposition to the specificity of monastic ritual. Although it was pitted against the very tradition that it was claimed to represent, the revised, laicized version of Zen was marketed in the West and Meiji Japan itself as an expression of both Buddhism's universalism and of Japanese uniqueness (*nihonjinron*).

Recently the polemic over Buddhism and Buddhist monasticism in modern Japan has flowered into a full-scale dialectic as contemporary scholars have turned a critical eye to the decontextualized depiction of Japanese Buddhism, and especially Zen, propagated by Meiji Buddhist apologists. On the basis of erroneous interpretations of Buddhist principles, these critics say, Buddhism was employed to justify Japan's involvement in World War II, as exemplified by the actual participation of Zen priests in wartime efforts. Furthermore, led by Hakamaya Noriaki and Matsumoto Shirō, a new wave of scholarship known as "critical Buddhism" has emerged from Japan that questions the legitimacy and ethics of the monistic Japanese Buddhist doctrines of Buddha nature and original enlightenment (*hongaku shisō*). Although they are themselves influenced by the anti-institutionalism of Meiji apologists on the one hand and Meiji critics on the other, contemporary Japanese Buddhists have emerged from an era of tremendous adversity with a strong but self-critical acceptance of their long-standing monastic heritage.

TALINE GOORJIAN

*See also* Anticlericalism: Buddhist Perspectives; Buddhist Schools/Traditions: Japan; Critiques of Buddhist Monasticism: Confucian; Economics: Buddhist; Japan: History; Laicization of Spirituality: Buddhist Perspectives; Monasticism, Definitions of: Buddhist Perspectives; Nation-Building and Japanese Buddhism; Rennyo; Scholastics, Buddhist; Shikoku, the Pilgrimage Island of Japan; Shinran; Suzuki, Daisetz Teitaro; Syncretism in Japan, Buddhist

**Further Reading**
Duus, Peter, editor, *The Cambridge History of Japan*, Cambridge and New York: Cambridge University Press, 1988
Fader, Larry A., "Zen in the West: Historical and Philosophical Implications of the 1893 Chicago World's Parliament of Religions," *Eastern Buddhist* 15:1 (1982)
Heisig, James W., and John C. Maraldo, editors, *Rude Awakenings: Zen, the Kyoto School, & the Question of Nationalism*, Honolulu: University of Hawaii Press, 1995
Hubbard, Jamie, and Paul L. Swanson, *Pruning the Bodhi Tree: The Storm Over Critical Buddhism*, Honolulu: University of Hawaii Press, 1997
Ketelaar, James Edward, *Heretics and Martyrs in Meiji Japan: Buddhism and Its Persecution*, Princeton, New Jersey: Princeton University Press, 1990
Sharf, Robert H., "The Zen of Japanese Nationalism," in *Curators of the Buddha: The Study of Buddhism under Colonialism*, edited by Donald S. Lopez, Chicago: University of Chicago Press, 1995

# Critiques of Western Christian Monasticism

By the latter 15th century, monasticism had held sway in Western Europe for nearly a thousand years. At the heart of the original monastic ideal was the lifetime commitment of monks and nuns to withdraw from the world to seek spiritual perfection through prayer and rigorous self-denial. They hoped thereby better to serve God, to intercede on behalf of their fellow Christians, and ultimately to ensure their own salvation. However, from the 11th century on there had been mounting criticisms of the human shortcomings of the cloistered, especially their perceived failure to adhere to monastic discipline.

By far the most damaging censures of monasticism began in the early 16th century. The sharp satiric thrusts of the Dutch humanist Erasmus overlapped with the formidable theological challenge posed by the German reformer Martin Luther. These chief representatives of the Renaissance and Reformation movements, respectively, indicted medieval monasticism on a whole range of charges that would be taken to a further rhetorical level in the 18th century by the French rationalist Voltaire.

Erasmus, Luther, and Voltaire, each in his way, conveyed to several generations of Europeans a special contempt for medieval asceticism. They contributed much to the discrediting of the monastic enterprise, and, with the help of like-minded colleagues, they threatened for a time to bring it down. Examination of the views of these three major critics will indicate the main grounds for their hostility to the monastic institution.

Erasmus (c. 1466–1536) was educated in a series of semi-monastic Dutch schools before the early death of his parents led his guardians to enter him in an Augustinian Canons' monastery near his native Rotterdam. He seems to have been content enough at first with the monastic routine. At the monastery he found the leisure and the discipline to acquire an excellent knowledge of the pagan classics and to polish a fine Latin style that would soon provide his passport back to the world. In 1492 he took his formal monastic vows and was ordained a priest of the Order of Augustinian Canons.

However, Erasmus had already experienced disillusionment with the monastic life. Years later, in 1516, he recalled this experience in a letter to a friend:

I was thrust into a life for which
I was averse both in mind and body;
in mind, because I shrank from ceremonies and was fond
   of liberty;
in body, because my constitution was not adapted to such
   trials.

He came to detest the fasting, the extensive rituals, and the narrow outlook of his fellow monks. In short he came to feel like a person "buried alive while breathing."

In 1495 Erasmus used a temporary assignment writing letters for a local bishop as a permanent way out of his monastic commitment. Within a year he was at the University of Paris and would never return to the monastery. At Paris he studied medieval theology with growing impatience while making contacts with budding humanists who, like himself, were enchanted with the pre-Christian world of Greece and Rome.

Then in 1500 an encounter in England with the eminent Christian humanist John Colet (1466?–1519) inspired Erasmus to consider how he could apply his linguistic and scholarly talents toward a spiritual revival of the Catholic Church. In 1504 he proposed in his *Handbook of the Christian Faith* a humanist reform program that combined Christian and pagan elements of reform in a synthesis that he called the "Philosophy of Christ." This involved a simple nondoctrinal spirituality based largely on Christ's Sermon on the Mount integrated with the best ethical teachings of the pre-Christian Greeks and Romans. Erasmus believed that such a condensed, secularized Christianity, greatly downplaying traditional Church dogma, ritual, and asceticism, would prove more effective in people's lives.

In trying to make Christianity more compatible with the pagan classical tradition, Erasmus emphasized the primary character of the faith as an ethical way of life rooted more in freedom and love than in rigid doctrine and trivial practices. The Church, and especially monasticism, became prime targets of his dissatisfaction. Erasmus pointed out, often with satiric scorn, how many monks and nuns fell short of observing their monastic vows and rules.

The friars came in for particular derision as "beggar tyrants" because of their aggressive tactics in the streets. In his popular satire *The Praise of Folly* (1509), Erasmus refers to "fat, lazy, hypocritical friars" and describes "universally loathed" but "gloriously self-satisfied tribes of monks" who paid more attention to rivalries with other orders than to their proper monastic duties.

However, Erasmus' objection to monasticism ran beyond moral abuses. It was the monastic concept itself that most disturbed him. The ascetic ideal ran directly counter to the principles of his "Philosophy of Christ." Erasmus had pressed the contrast succinctly in his *Handbook*:

[Monks] of the most distinguished
orders hold that the essence of
perfection lies in ceremonies, in a fixed amount of psalm
   singing
and in manual labor. [But] the
monastic life should not be equated with the virtuous life.
It is just one type of life.

Further, special vows of poverty, celibacy, and obedience, which are human creations, "add very little to one who [has] observed the first and only vow we take in baptism, not to man but to Christ." Erasmus recommended the relaxation of the vow of celibacy for clergy.

Finally, if monks want to live solely on fish, vegetables, and eggs, that was their business, but "they ought not regard themselves as virtuous because of [this]." Clearly the ascetic life for Erasmus in the early 16th century was no longer the preferred way to salvation. He offered instead an impassioned invitation to a revitalized spirituality in the world based on the Gospels and on a secular ethic drawn from the ancient Roman philosopher Cicero (106–43 B.C.), among others.

Erasmus had found the monk's life unbearable. For him it involved, at best, only a succession of mechanical rituals and, at worst, an occasion for laxity and corruption. Although he never advocated the destruction of the monastic system, he regarded it as a medieval relic that should be allowed to expire.

In sum complex rituals, monastic vows, and ascetic practices had little place in the Erasmian version of Christianity. In addition the transcendent theological dimension of Christianity was repudiated in this minimalist program for Christian renewal. Erasmus' "Philosophy of Christ" effectively drained away the ascetic essence of monasticism. His treatises and his vivid stories and satires about the monks generated much of the highly charged atmosphere that would influence, among others, the young Luther.

Martin Luther (1483–1546) was a generation younger than Erasmus. The son of a miner, Luther at 22 joined a reformed order of Augustinian Friars at Erfurt in his native Saxony. In 1507 he was ordained a priest. However, the extreme privations he imposed on himself to win God's favor brought him no closer to satisfying the God whose anger he experienced. As Luther later wrote, "I tortured myself with prayer, fasting, vigils, and freezing. The cold alone might have killed me." He also practiced self-flagellation, hoping by such heroic acts to compel God to relieve him from his burden of guilt. Nothing availed. Luther felt that, in justice, God had to condemn him for his sins, and he could never assure himself of God's mercy.

As a last resort Luther's religious superior, Johannes von Staupitz (c. 1468–1524), assigned him to teach a course on the Bible at the newly opened Saxon University of Wittenberg. There in 1515, or a little later, Luther found in St. Paul's Letter to the Romans (1:17) the solution to his dilemma between the justice and the mercy of God. The passage read, "The just (or righteous) shall live by faith." Luther construed this to mean that Christians must believe by faith alone that God in his infinite mercy could save sinners despite their utter unworthiness and quite independently of any merit on their part or any pious works they might perform.

On the basis of the passage in Romans and of other biblical sources, Luther deemed a whole range of Catholic teachings and practices to be untenable. By 1520 he had completely rejected the Catholic system of salvation based on the efficacy of good works in cooperation with the grace of God. In Luther's view human nature was so depraved by original sin that individuals could do nothing on their own to attain justification in God's eyes. The traditional seven sacraments of the medieval Church and its extensive array of religious ceremonies, pilgrimages, and charitable enterprises could no longer be regarded as wellsprings of grace conducive to salvation.

Luther then applied his principle of justification by faith alone to the medieval institution of monasticism. In 1521 he published his fully developed views on the subject in a treatise titled *On Monastic Vows*.

Like so much else in Catholic tradition, Luther found the three standard monastic vows of poverty, celibacy, and obedience to be merely human "works" purported to earn merit toward salvation. Thus, he saw the monastic vow as yet another blasphemous appropriation of a divine prerogative that denied God the freedom to be God in deciding who would be saved. In addition he saw those who lived by rigid monastic rules and liturgies as so many Pharisees bound by an external master, the letter of the Law. Christians, Luther insisted, must serve God voluntarily from inward conviction, not because of formal vows. Once liberated from the Law, including vows, Christians would then do good works entirely for the glory of God and not for any hope of reward.

Taking the three vows individually, Luther discerned grave practical as well as theological deficiencies. Regarding the vow of obedience to one's monastic superior, Luther argued that it stood in clear violation of the gospel message that a Christian should be a servant to all and not bound to any one person. As for the vow of poverty, it had never been properly understood. True evangelical poverty prescribed that a monastery's resources be managed for the benefit of others. However, in reality greedy monks sought too often to preserve at all costs their property and status, ignoring the needs of orphans and others in the community.

It is above all in his theological discussion of celibacy that Luther laid the ax to the root of the monastic establishment. Apart from its discredited status as a "work," Luther found no clear scriptural authority for a vow of celibacy or indeed for celibacy in general as a precondition for the religious life. He insisted that neither Jesus nor Paul had recommended celibacy over the marriage state. For example, in Matthew 19:11–12 Jesus emphasized that the celibate life should be entirely voluntary. Finally Luther declared that the vow of celibacy defied common sense because, given human weakness, the vow was impossible to observe.

Thus, to break such illegitimate vows is no sin, notwithstanding the judgment of Catholic authority and public opinion. In place of the medieval ideal of contemplation and ascetic withdrawal from the world, Luther substituted an active role in the world for all Christians in service to others. His contention that all Christians became priests through baptism directly challenged the medieval hierarchy of clergy and laity. For Luther the new standard of holiness became the vocation of the Christian laity to marriage and family rather than to a life of withdrawal based on monastic celibacy.

The impact of Luther's treatise and similar writings was immediate and lasting. A contemporary credited *On Monastic Vows* with "emptying the cloisters." A large-scale exodus followed during the 1520s as thousands of monks and nuns deserted their monasteries and convents. Secular priests defected as well. Former monks provided the nascent Protestant movement with valuable leadership. The Benedictines alone lost 800 of their 3,000 houses. The number of monks sank overall to less than half of pre-Reformation levels even as monasticism virtually disappeared in Henry VIII's England. Most of the former monks and nuns, especially in Germany, chose marriage and family as their new context of Christian service.

Martin Luther had fused a centuries-old critique of monastic abuses with the revolutionary element of a theological principle, justification by faith alone, to call into question the very essence of the monastic enterprise. The Catholic Council of Trent (1545–1563) addressed many of the most flagrant abuses in monastic life while affirming, contrary to Luther, that monastic vows and activities were valid sources of spiritual merit. However, in the wake of the Reformation a series of brutal religious wars ravaged the European Continent and further eroded the prestige of Western Christianity, both Protestant and Catholic. Meanwhile dramatic breakthroughs were achieved in the realm of science, culminating in the work of the English mathematician Isaac Newton (1642–1727). The Scientific Revolution placed the study of natural phenomena on an empirical, mathematically verifiable basis that tended to diminish significantly the relevance of religious authority in understanding the physical world.

Disgust and dismay at the warring religious factions, coupled with the rise of a new scientific method grounded in controlled observation, experiment, and reason, created among the educated an atmosphere that favored tolerance, common sense, and a secular focus in matters of religion.

This is the world in which Voltaire came of age in the early 18th century. For close to 50 years as philosopher, playwright, novelist, and critic, Voltaire (1694–1778) would be a dominant intellectual force in European society. Born in Paris, the son of a lawyer, François Marie Arouet took the pen name Voltaire as a young man. After a rebellious youth he received a classical education at the Jesuit College in Paris, where he began to polish the style and the proficiency in satire that would make his fortune.

During a self-imposed exile to England from 1726 to 1729, Voltaire encountered the ideas and methods of the new science as found especially in Isaac Newton, supplemented by the potent political and religious ideas of the philosopher John Locke (1632–1704). He returned to France in 1729 as a deist in the tradition of Locke and Newton. He had also become a fervent convert to the promise of the new science and a believer in civil and religious liberty on the English model.

Voltaire popularized these ideas in books and pamphlets that won him international fame. As a deist he believed that the world was a great machine that operated on scientifically verifiable mathematical laws that required a divine "mechanic" to keep it running. However, Voltaire's God, although conscious, did not intervene miraculously in human affairs, nor did he answer prayers.

Voltaire found much to admire in Locke's rational approach to religion. Reason, common sense, and concrete experience were the best guides in religion as in other areas of life. In addition, like Locke (and Erasmus), Voltaire would virtually eliminate the role of doctrine and ritual in religion. In a society where political and religious differences had proven destructive to social harmony, Voltaire urged a humane tolerance as the most rational approach. In this enterprise he had many collaborators in his fellow philosophes. These were French writers and popularizers of "enlightened" ideas based on the secular values of the new science and on Locke's philosophy.

Yet up to 1750 Voltaire had rarely expressed in print his private disdain for the Christian faith. However, several events of the 1750s and 1760s roused him to open warfare with Christianity and especially with the Catholic Church. In 1759 the *Encyclopedia*, the leading publication of the *philosophes* in France, was suppressed by the Church with state support. That same year the king of France, Louis XV (1715–1774), responded to the alarm of the Catholic hierarchy at the rising tide of unbelief in the land by making it a capital offense to criticize the French Church. Voltaire was enraged. Finally two notorious cases of French Protestants persecuted by Catholic authorities fortified Voltaire's conviction that the Catholic Church, above all, had to be eliminated from the enlightened society he envisioned.

In treatises such as *On Toleration* (1763), in novels such as *Candide* (1759), and in dozens of pamphlets and letters, Voltaire attacked Catholicism not only for its perceived abuses but also for its doctrines and its mystical, otherworldly outlook as reflected most distinctly in monasticism. The sophisticated satire of Voltaire's earlier writings now acquired a much harsher edge of anger and invective. He began and ended many of his letters and pamphlets on various topics with the words "Crush the Infamous!," by which he meant the fanaticism and superstition he identified most closely with the Catholic Church.

In Voltaire's view Catholicism was the product of phony miracles, superstition-laden relics, and preposterous doctrines that had been concocted by a cynical priesthood to deceive the credu-

lous. Here Voltaire's penchant for the outrageous bon mot was irrepressible: "The first clergyman was the first rascal who met the first fool." It was the "infamous" Catholic Church that Voltaire and his fellow *philosophes* sought to expose through the cool light of reason. Further to Voltaire only a "reasonable" religion was acceptable, one that eliminated any revealed religion. Nonetheless he insisted that some form of rational religion based on deism was essential for social and political control.

As for monasticism it fell under Voltaire's general condemnation of Christianity. The spirit of the Enlightenment was not congenial to the traditional Christian contemplative life. Above all Voltaire regarded monasticism from a purely secular vantage. Not only was it irrational, but it constituted an intolerable material drain on society with "vast numbers" of monks and nuns living like parasites off the industry of the lay populace. According to Voltaire this dreary state of affairs had begun during the "Dark Ages," when lazy people averse to life's challenges had "crept into monasteries," where they infected one another with neurotic fantasies of women, devils, and gods.

However, monks were guilty of much worse. A character in Voltaire's novel *Candide* observes, "What, have you no monks to dispute . . . [and] to burn people not of the same opinion as themselves?" As for the relationship of virtue to the monastic life, Voltaire has no illusions: a hermit monk might be a saint in his life of extreme self-denial, but he is not virtuous. He is so "only when he performs some act from which others benefit." For Voltaire there must be a perceptible, material benefit for society at large. To be sure engrained hostility to monasticism was not restricted to Voltaire and his *philosophes* in France. "Enlightened" principles and Voltaire's own example inspired similar literary broadsides across Europe.

Erasmus, Luther, and Voltaire, the three archcritics of monasticism in the early modern period, reached their conclusions from very different perspectives.

Erasmus the Christian humanist reformer sought to revitalize the Western Church from within. Repelled by the maze of Church rituals that he believed obscured the meaning of Christianity, Erasmus hoped to supersede these components of the old order with a much simpler, more biblical Christianity that engaged the world directly at the practical moral level. Erasmus' antagonism to the monastic tradition arose from a personal loathing for the ascetic ideal. He found this value diametrically opposed to his secularizing objective. Nonetheless he would at least tolerate many medieval traditions. He believed that monasticism should simply be left to wither away.

More radically Luther aimed at transforming Western Christianity on the basis of a revolutionary theology that rejected monasticism and its ascetic culture as both unscriptural and unnatural. "Justification by faith alone" was the fulcrum that Luther hoped would overturn the monastic system, break down the traditional distinction between clergy and laity, and bring biblical precepts more directly into the mainstream of daily Christian life.

For his part Voltaire sought neither to reform nor to restructure the Western Church. He longed to destroy it, including the monastic institution that had been so integral a part of its history. Voltaire's core axioms of reason and the scientific method allowed no place for a mystical, ascetic life of the cloister, especially one that was not materially productive.

None of the three early modern critics found anything positive to say about the history of monasticism. Its major contributions to education and agriculture were simply ignored. Further the exaggeration natural to the genre of satire sometimes led Erasmus and especially Voltaire to caricatures of life in the monastery. Accounts of the many monks and nuns faithful to their vocations are not to be found among the lurid tales of gross negligence and misconduct. However, in fairness the hostility of the three writers derived more from matters of principle than from reports of corruption in the cloister. It was the ascetic ideal itself that they found insupportable. Each shared in varying degrees the conviction that the secular realm was inherently superior to the monastic.

The monastic enterprise would, of course, endure into the modern world after weathering the onslaughts not only of the eminent critics noted but also of writers and politicians from the era of the French Revolution on. The monastery remains an attractive alternative for both Catholic and Orthodox Christians seeking a transcendental experience of God in a contemplative environment away from the pressing material concerns of secular society. Nonetheless the debate from Erasmus to Voltaire regarding the role of asceticism in Western Christianity would contribute a significant thread to the much broader transition of European society from the medieval to the modern phases of its history. Yet when all was said and done, a prominent place would remain for the venerable Christian institution of monasticism.

DONALD D. SULLIVAN

*See also* Anticlericalism: Christian Perspectives; Asceticism: Christian Perspectives; Augustinian Canons; Augustinian Friars/Hermits; Celibacy: Christian; Dissolution of Monasteries; Fasting: Western Christian; Germany: History; Laicization of Spirituality: Christian Perspectives; Luther, Martin; Reformation; Self-Mutilation, Christian

**Further Reading**

Barnett, S.J., *Idol Temples and Crafty Priests: The Origins of Enlightenment Anticlericalism*, London: Macmillan, and New York: St. Martin's Press, 1999

Dipple, Geoffrey, *Antifraternalism and Anticlericalism in the German Reformation*, Aldershot, England: Scolar Press, and Brookfield, Vermont: Ashgate, 1996

Erasmus, *The Praise of Folly*, Ann Arbor: University of Michigan Press, 1958

Knowles, David, *The Religious Orders in England*, Cambridge: Cambridge University Press, 1959; New York: Cambridge University Press, 1979

Lohse, Bernhard, *Mönchtum und Reformation: Luthers Auseinandersetzung mit dem Mönchsideal des Mittelalters*, Göttingen: Vandenhoeck and Ruprecht, 1963

Luther, Martin, "Judgment . . . on Monastic Vows," edited and translated by James Atkinson in *The Christian in Society* I, Philadelphia: The Fortress Press, 1966

Morley, John, *Voltaire*, 2nd edition, New York: Appleton, and London: Chapman and Hall, 1872; revised edition, London: Macmillan, 1921

Pomeau, René, *La religion de Voltaire*. Paris: Nizet, 1956; revised edition, 1986

Rice, Eugene F., "Erasmus and the Religious Tradition, 1495–1499," *Journal of the History of Ideas* 11 (1950)

Stamm, Heinz-Meinolf, *Luthers Stellung zum Ordensleben*, Wiesbaden: Steiner, 1980

Voltaire, *Candide*, Boston: Bedford/St. Martin's, 1999

# Croatia (Hrvatska)

Croatia is a mainly Catholic country whose religious as well as economic, political, and cultural history has been marked by the establishment of monastic orders, the most important being the Benedictine, the Franciscan, and the Dominican. However, it is reported that as early as 356 Christian monastic communities, influenced by Egyptian monasticism, settled on the Dalmatian coast, which is a part of present-day Croatia. This article focuses on the Dalmatian region. The Benedictine Order, the oldest monastic community in Croatia, established its first monastery in 852 in Rižinice, near Split. From the 10th to the 13th century (the golden age of Croatian monasticism), the Benedictines founded more than 40 monasteries, mainly in and around the major cities of the Dalmatian coast (Zadar, Trogir, Sibenik, Split, and Dubrovnik). The Franciscans first came to Croatia in 1214 (Trogir), whereas the Dominicans founded their first important monastery in 1225 (Dubrovnik). Among the other monastic orders that settled in Croatia were the Paulist, the Augustinian, the Cistercian, and the Capuchin. Among the monastic communities for women, we can count the Benedictines, the Carmelites, and the Poor Clares.

The most ancient monasteries to be visited in Croatia are situated on the Dalmatian coast and on the islands. For example, in Zadar is the Benedictine monastery of St. Chrysogonus, which was built according to the Romanesque style and whose church was consecrated in 1175. This monastery played an important role, as did the Benedictines in general, in disseminating literary culture in Croatia through its scriptoria. It was also an important center of glagolitic (i.e. Dalmatian alphabet) liturgy. Also in Zadar is the monastery of St. Mary with cartularies and manuscript archives. This Benedictine monastery for nuns, whose foundation can be traced back as early as 1065, is also interesting for its Romanesque bell tower built in 1105 and for the reliquaries of its church. Very close to it one finds the Franciscan monastery of St. Francis with its Renaissance cloister (16th century) and a single-naved church (13th century), which is considered to be one of the oldest Gothic monuments in Croatia. This monastery has also a collection of about ten manuscripts with miniatures from the 13th century.

Going south from Zadar on the Dalmatian coast, one reaches Trogir, formally a Greek colony and then a fortified Roman harbor. In Trogir the Benedictine nuns were well represented with three monasteries: two for the nobility (St. Nicholas and St.

Peter) and one for the commoners (St. Michael). Today only the St. Nicholas monastery is still active. This monastery, previously known as St. Dujam, was founded in 1064. In addition to its collection of Christian religious art, St. Nicholas boasts the marble relief *Kairos*, the Greek divinity of the fleeting moment. Like the Benedictine monks the nuns were very active spreading culture and writing in Croatia. In their abbeys one could find schools in which young women learned grammar (*artes liberales*) and handicrafts. The Dominican monastery in Trogir is also worth visiting. It was founded in 1265 and is still occupied. Its church contains one of the most precious funerary monuments of the Renaissance style preserved in Dalmatia.

Another region important for the development of monasticism in Croatia is the city of Split and its surrounding islands. This city, which is now the most important in Dalmatia, is the seat of Diocletian's palace, probably one of the best-preserved structures of the late Antique period. Especially noteworthy in Split are the Franciscan monasteries with their cloisters, dating from the 13th and 15th centuries. However, it is on the islands that one finds the most interesting monasteries to visit. For example, Hvar has a Franciscan monastery with a Renaissance-style cloister and bell tower. It also has a rich collection of church objects and a precious painting of the Last Supper that contributed to the fame of the island. Close to Hvar is the island of Brač, where one finds a Dominican monastery with its Gothic church. Today all these monasteries, which are still occupied, have been partly converted into museums. The region of Split is also interesting for its ruins of convents and churches, giving evidence of a Christian presence preceding the arrival of the Slavs.

A final region of importance is the medieval city of Dubrovnik with its ramparts and narrow streets accessible only to pedestrians. Long a rival of Venice, this city was always an important center of religious and cultural activities sustained by the various monastic communities that settled there. Some of the monasteries, such as the Benedictine monastery on the island of Lokrum, lie in ruins, but others, especially the Franciscan and the Dominican convents, are still active. The first is especially interesting for its cloister, which is built in transitional Romanesque-Gothic style, and its adjacent pharmacy, which is one of the oldest in Europe (1317) and is still serving the local population. The Dominican monastery is renowned for its library, which contains manuscripts dating back to the moment it was established (1225). Fortunately both monasteries, despite the fact that they were specifically targeted by the Yugoslav army during its aggression against Croatia in 1992–1993, kept most of their treasured collections undamaged. However, some parts of the architectural structure were badly hit.

This description of some of the important monasteries of Croatia has dealt mainly with those established in Dalmatia. However, it should be noted that other regions of Croatia – such as Zagorje, where the capital Zagreb is situated, and the area between the Drava and Sava Rivers – bear witness to monastic activities as early as the 13th century.

As is the case elsewhere in the Catholic world, the number of monks and nuns is decreasing in Croatia. For this reason many monasteries are almost deserted, and some have even been converted into hotels, such as the Benedictine monastery on the island of Mljet.

FRANCIS BRASSARD

*See also* Benedictines; Dominicans; Franciscans

**Further Reading**

Dusa, Joan, *The Medieval Dalmatian Episcopal Cities: Development and Transformation*, New York: Peter Lang, 1991

Ivančević, Radovan, *Art Treasures of Croatia*, Belgrade: Jugoslovenska revija, 1986; 2nd edition, Zagreb: I.T.P. Motovun, 1993

Šanjek, Franjo, *Crkva i kršćanstvo u Hrvata, srednji vijek*, Zagreb: Kršćanska sadasnjost, 1993

# Crusades

In 1095 Pope Urban II (1088–1099) launched the First Crusade, which captured Jerusalem from Islam and founded a group of Latin principalities in the East whose defense, support, or restoration became a common concern of all Latin Christians down to the 16th century. Urban II was a Benedictine monk who had risen to be prior of Cluny, and it seems a paradox that one vowed to the religious life should have launched such a bloody series of wars. However, Christianity had no simple doctrine of war, and churchmen in the 11th century were increasingly trying to harness the violence of their world to Christian ends. The papacy took a highly pragmatic view of violence and frequently waged war for political ends in, for example, southern Italy. Successive popes endorsed the growing notion that war against nonbelievers, notably in Spain and on the eastern frontier of Germany, was meritorious. The Great Reform of the Church, which got under way in the last quarter of the 11th century, witnessed an effort by the popes to influence political developments by military force to shape society to the end of salvation. This was justified by the "theologians of violence," notably Anselm of Lucca (c. 1035–1086). Emerging from this process was the idea of a papal monarchy with a universal dominion. Its main architects, Gregory VII (1073–1085) and Urban II, were Benedictine monks. The Orthodox Church, which was the dominant religious force in the Byzantine Empire centered on Constantinople, was reluctant to recognize this supremacy. However, by 1071 this empire had lost Asia Minor to an Islam resurgent under the Turks. Urban II followed the example of Gregory VII in seeking to assert supremacy over the Orthodox by offering military aid against Islam when, in 1095, Alexius I Comnenus (1081–1118) asked for his assistance.

Urban II was successful because he was able to appeal to the piety of the upper classes. This expressed itself especially in pilgrimage, which was the form in which the great expedition of 1095 was cast. This journey to liberate Jerusalem was undertaken by a vow, just like a pilgrimage, and its accomplishment

Inner walls (from the southwest), Crac des Chevaliers (Hospitallers), Syria, first half of the 13th century.
Photo courtesy of Chris Schabel

offered to all who participated an indulgence, the hope of eternal life: the First Crusade was literally a penitential war in which every step forward and every blow was an act of penance that would free a participant's soul from hell. Urban came from the lesser nobility of France, and his appeal was shrewdly pitched to their piety and to the powerful sense of property so typical of a landed group, for this was to be war waged for the recovery of God's territory: Jerusalem and the Holy Land. Moreover, those who joined in this righteous war could enjoy rightful plunder and the riches of the East.

Urban's message of salvation by war did not have a universal appeal, but it was powerfully reinforced by monasteries whose intimate contact with some of the nobility and knights was influential in bringing numbers of them to take the cross. Moreover, monasteries made loans to and purchased property from intending crusaders, enabling them to depart. This intimate relationship between crusading families and monasteries would long continue to shape the attitudes of the European upper class toward the crusade. For example, in the mid–13th century the crusader chronicler Joinville would seek blessing from his local abbot.

However, the contribution of monasticism to the Crusades extended further than this. Monks went on crusade and sometimes,

like the Cistercian abbot of Vaux on the Fourth, had a powerful influence. The success of the First Crusade was so stunning that it had to be explained as part of the Divine Dispensation, and a systematic ideology was worked out to argue this. The "Idea of the Crusade" was developed largely by monastic writers, such as Robert of Rheims and Guibert of Nogent (c. 1053/65–c. 1125), in the generation after 1099. This forged the crusading ideology that became fused into chivalry, the moral code of the European upper class that emerged in the 12th century.

These monastic writers who forged the image of the crusade inevitably shaped it in their own form: Robert of Rheims portrayed Godfrey of Bouillon (d. 1100) as a devout man, "a monk, you would have thought, rather than a knight." Devout laymen who were dedicated to the service of the Holy Land formed themselves into a military order, the Temple, taking vows as monks yet living to fight the Islamic enemy. What to us appears a paradox, the fighting monk, arose quite naturally from the needs of 12th-century Jerusalem and the mental world in which men lived. So powerful was its example that the hospital, originally formed to look after the poor, also became militarized, and other orders arose in imitation all over Western Europe.

In terms of the crusade, medieval monasticism played a very active role in influencing the lay world. Saint Bernard was

Interior of gallery or cloister, with door to the Great Hall, Crac des Chevaliers (Hospitallers), Syria, c. 1250.
Photo courtesy of Chris Schabel

perhaps the greatest monk of the 12th century. His spiritual eminence gave both him and his order, the Cistercians, enormous authority. He helped shape the Rule of the Temple. His eloquence was enlisted by the papacy to preach the Second Crusade when crusader-held Edessa fell in 1144. Bernard's preaching elicited this enormous military expedition, and he was widely blamed for its failure.

It has often been remarked that the papacy and the crusading movement were bound together in an intimate relationship. However, an equally intimate connection had already existed between crusading and monasticism. Monks and monasteries were a powerful force in the launching of the First Crusade, the preaching of later crusades, and the development of the crusading ideal. Their wealth was a resource that often was put at the disposal of participants, and their Benedictine rule formed a basis for those most individual of all crusader institutions: the military orders. By the 13th century the papacy was deploying the dynamic new mendicant orders to preach the crusade, and new forms of piety and religious observation began to displace the Benedictines in the affections of the laity. By the 13th century

European society and its attitudes were being transformed, not least by the rise of monarchical states, and this created enormous challenges for both Benedictine monasticism and the crusading movement.

JOHN FRANCE

*See also* Bernard of Clairvaux, St.; Cathars; Cluny, Abbots of; France: History; Hospitallers (Knights of Malta since 1530); Israel/Palestine; Jerusalem, Israel; Mount Athos, Greece; Papacy: Monastic Popes; Pilgrimages, Christian: Near East; Warrior Monks: Christian

**Further Reading**

Barber, Malcolm, *The New Knighthood: A History of the Order of the Temple*, Cambridge and New York: Cambridge University Press, 1994

Blake, E.O., "The Formation of the 'Crusade Idea'," *Journal of Ecclesiastical History* 21 (1970)

Bull, Marcus, *Knightly Piety and the Lay Response to the First Crusade*, Oxford: Clarendon Press, and New York: Oxford University Press, 1993

Constable, G., "The Second Crusade as Seen by Contemporaries," *Traditio* 9 (1953)

Cowdrey, H.E.J., "Pope Urban's Preaching of the First Crusade," *History* 55 (1970)

Cowdrey, H.E.J., "Cluny and the First Crusade," *Revue Bénédictine* 83 (1973)

Cowdrey, H.E.J., "Pope Gregory VII's 'Crusading' Plans of 1074," in *Outremer: Studies in the History of the Crusading Kingdom of Jerusalem Presented to Joshua Prawer*, edited by B.Z. Kedar, H.E. Mayer, and R.C. Smail, Jerusalem: Yad Izhak Ben-Zvi Institute, 1982

Flori, Jean, *L'essor de la chevalerie, XIe–XIIe siècles*, Geneva: Droz, 1986

Maier, Christoph T., *Preaching the Crusades: Mendicant Friars and the Cross in the Thirteenth Century*, Cambridge and New York: Cambridge University Press, 1994

Riley-Smith, J., *The First Crusaders, 1095–1131*, Cambridge and New York: Cambridge University Press, 1997

# Cuthbert, St. c. 636–687

### English Christian monk, missionary, and bishop of Lindisfarne

Saint Cuthbert is known from an anonymous life, written around 700, which was brushed up by Bede (c. 673–735), who left us a prose and a verse text. Cuthbert was the product of the Irish missions to the Northumbrians. He received an ascetic upbringing at Melrose and followed Eata (who was a pupil of Aidan [d. 651], the early Irish evangelist of Northumbria) to the monastery of Lindisfarne, where both an abbot and a bishop resided. Theodore made Cuthbert the bishop of Lindisfarne in 685, and Cuthbert used the office to inspire missionary and eremitical activity in Northumbria.

His episcopate lasted only two years, during the last period of which he shut himself away on the Outer Farne, a barren islet off the Northumbrian coast, where he was cut off for days on end by the rough seas. When he was finally found on one such occasion, he had not been able to rise for five days, and his only food had been a few onions, his feet were ulcerated, and his body was badly wasted by malnutrition. His death shortly afterward can hardly have been unexpected. Bede, the greatest writer of Anglo-Saxon England, commemorated Cuthbert as a saint. His qualities were such as to place him as a worthy disciple of Jesus through his self-sacrifice and lack of concern for his own material needs.

However, Cuthbert's bodily remains, in contrast, were to be the focus of intense attention. They were reinterred several times, first in 698, when new vestments were placed on the body, which had rapidly become the focus of a major cult. The remains stayed where they were for a hundred years, but in 793 the monastery was subjected to a Viking raid. The body was untouched, and the monks returned, but so did the Vikings during their takeover of the Northumbrian kingdom in 875. Cuthbert's body was carried away when the monks evacuated. For seven years the body was carted about the kingdom until the monks settled at Chester Le Street in 883. Here the body attracted pilgrims and gifts, including an embroidered stole from King Athelstan (927–939). In 995 the body was transferred again to Ripon and then to Durham. The relics became the focus of the great cathedral built after the Norman Conquest, when the body was transferred to new shrine behind the high altar in 1104. In 1372 a new, grander shrine was built of rare stones.

Under Henry VIII (1509–1547), this shrine, which had been one of the most prominent in England, was despoiled of its adornments. The body was found incorrupt. However, the tomb was allowed to remain, and to dispel rumors that the remains had been lost at this time, the tomb was reopened in 1827. An ivory comb, portable altar, and pectoral cross from the seventh century were found in the tomb together with remains of the original wooden coffin. These items are now on show in the Chapter Library of Durham Cathedral. A final opening of the tomb took place in 1899, when the bones were examined scientifically and their age was verified. Apart from the remarkable artifacts preserved to the current day, the ongoing importance of Cuthbert's cult has been as a focus for regional pride in northern England and for Durham Cathedral in particular.

DOMINIC JANES

*See also* Animals, Attitude toward: Christian Perspectives; Bede, St.; England: Sites; Exile, Western Christian; Lindisfarne/Holy Isle, England

**Biography**
Cuthbert became a monk at Melrose, Scotland. In 661 he went with Eata to Ripon, but returned when Alchfrith of Northumbria turned that house over to Wilfrid. He became prior of Melrose and then of Lindisfarne, where he became bishop in 685. He spent part of his time in missionary activities and part in private prayer and contemplation. He died engaged in the latter activity on the Outer Farne Islands near Lindisfarne on 20 March 687. The Lindisfarne Gospels were dedicated to God and to Cuthbert.

**Further Reading**
Aird, William, *St. Cuthbert and the Normans*, Woodbridge, Suffolk: Boydell Brewer, 1999
Battiscombe, C.F., editor, *The Relics of St. Cuthbert: Studies by Various Authors*, Oxford: Oxford University Press, 1956
Bonner, Gerald, et al., editors, *St. Cuthbert, His Cult and His Community: To* A.D. *1200*, Woodbridge, Suffolk, and Wolfeboro, New Hampshire: Boydell Press, 1989
Colgrave, Bertram, editor and translator, *Two Lives of Saint Cuthbert: Texts*, Cambridge: Cambridge University Press, 1940; reprint, 1985

# Cyprus

Monastic history in Cyprus can be divided into five major periods. Each of these is discussed in the following.

### 300–1191
Monasticism has had a long history in Cyprus. Traditionally, Sts. Nicholas and Eutychios, participants in the Council of Nicaea, founded the first Cypriot monastery, Ayia Moni (Holy Monastery), in the hills behind Paphos, around 300. During Constantine's reign two more were established where the Roman governor Calocaerus introduced a special breed of cat to combat the poisonous snakes: St. Nicholas of the Cats (c. 325), on the Akrotiri Peninsula, and Stavrovouni (Holy Cross Mountain, c. 327), which stands atop an isolated mountain peak and is named after the Cross of the Penitent Thief brought there by Constantine's mother, the Empress Helena.

Because of the island's proximity to Egypt and Syria, Monophysite or former Monophysite monks resided on seventh-century Cyprus. The Chalcedonian monk Isidore of Cappadocia was a repentant Monophysite, but others, such as John the Egyptian, Bishop Paul of Edessa, and Cyrrhus of Edessa, appear to have remained Monophysite. The latter probably came to Cyprus as refugees from the Persian invasions or to learn Greek, as patristic texts indicate that Cyprus was both a refuge and a

Premonstratensian Abbey of Bellapais, northern Cyprus, 14th century, sacked 1570. The dormitory is on the upper floor above the chapter house.
Photo courtesy of Chris Schabel

center for the dissemination of Greek for monks from the eastern Roman provinces. It seems that most monks and monasteries on the island were Chalcedonian, and the overall numbers were so great that Cyprus was dubbed the "Island of the Saints" (i.e., monks in that period). Among the Chalcedonians were hagiographers of note, such as Bishop Paul of Paphos, Anthony of the monastery of Khoviza, and above all Leontios of Neapolis, the author of the extant lives of Sts. John and Symeon.

We know from contemporary narratives or archaeological excavations that the monasteries of Symboulos near Kourion, St. Barnabas near Famagusta, Styllos near Cape Gata, and Agros in the Troodos Mountains were among the active houses. The monk Anastasios of Sinai's detailed knowledge of the island's geography and people and his interest in Cypriot prisoners near the Dead Sea of Palestine who were transported there as a result of Arab raids on Cyprus from 649 to 650 indicate his possible Cypriot origins.

In the later seventh century, the unsettled conditions resulting from Arab raids and the Iconoclast persecution of eighth-century Byzantium encouraged monasticism on Cyprus, which from 647 to 965 enjoyed internal autonomy, simply paying taxes to both the Byzantines and the Muslim Arabs. Refugees from the Iconoclast persecution founded the now defunct houses of Panayia (Our Lady) ton Katharon and Panayia Absinthiotissa, both

named after Constantinopolitan sites. This is probably also true for the Antiphonetes Monastery near Kyrenia. Perhaps refugee monks from Muslim Palestine set up the monastery of Yialia near Arsinoe, which later benefited from the patronage of the Georgian Queen Thamar (1184–1213).

Byzantium reannexed Cyprus in 965, and by the 11th and 12th centuries, when the most important of the present houses were established, 33 monasteries were functioning. The greatest of all is Kykko, founded just before 1100 on a beautiful site in the Troodos Mountains by Esaias, with the urging and support of Manual Butumites, whom Esaias cured of sciatica. Esaias also cured the daughter of the emperor Alexios Comnenos (1081–1118) of the same disorder, and the monastery was given the Icon of the Virgin, the holiest in Cyprus, one of only three attributed to St. Luke. Farther east in the Troodos massif lies Makhairas, another powerful monastery, which the Palestinian monk Neilos established around 1148 on an attractive spot. Grants of money and land from the Emperor Manuel Comnenos made the house important early on, and through St. Neilos, its first abbot, who became bishop of Tamassos and archbishop of Cyprus, Makhairas acquired fame.

A third important establishment from this period is New Zion, founded by the most famous monk in Cypriot history, St. Neophytos, whose name the house bears today. Born in 1134

**Church of the Monastery of the Archangel Gabriel, near Nicosia, Cyprus, 12th–17th century.**
**Photo courtesy of Chris Schabel**

near Kato Lefkara, Neophytos received a basic education and around 1170 chose a pleasant site in a valley near Paphos to dig his own rock-cut cell, where he attracted followers, and the monastery came into being. In his cell Neophytos was a fairly prolific writer, and his works are often interesting for their commentary on current events: he criticized Isaac Comnenos, a tyrannous usurper who took over the island in 1184 and lamented the conquest by Richard the Lionheart in 1191 and the subsequent trials of the Orthodox Church and Greek Cypriot populace. Neophytos' cell remains today with contemporary wall paintings.

Two major monasteries of this period no longer function. Saint John Chrysostom (Koutsovendi) in the Kyrenia Mountains was probably a late tenth-century foundation where Neophytos was a novice, and St. George of Mangana, a daughter house of its famous namesake in Constantinople, was established near Nicosia after 1054. It became the wealthiest Greek monastery under Latin rule until the Venetians demolished it in 1567 in preparation for the defense of Nicosia against the Turks.

### Latin Rule, 1191–1571

With King Richard's conquest and his sale of Cyprus to Guy de Lusignan in 1192, Cyprus entered the Frankish phase of its history. Orthodox monasteries, such as St. Neophytos, usually were not despoiled of their property, and Makhairas and Mangana actually prospered under the Latins. Nevertheless, at least two houses (Stavrovouni and Episkopia) were taken over by Latins, and Kykko lost some dependencies. Moreover, the departure or relative impoverishment of the Byzantine nobility on the island and the conquest of Constantinople in 1204 in the Fourth Crusade removed their primary sources of patronage. Following the establishment of the Latin Church in 1196 and agreements between it and the Lusignan crown and nobles in 1220 and 1223, the number of Greek monks was limited, and restrictions were placed on Greek serfs' ability to become monks.

Latin and Greek monasteries in Palestine and Sinai had daughter houses and estates on Cyprus from which they received revenues. For the Greeks, St. Catherine of Sinai possessed the church of St. Symeon in Famagusta, and the Palestinian abbey of St. Theodosios had dependencies in the Limassol and Paphos districts. Latin examples include the Benedictine houses of St. Lazarus and St. Mary of Dragonaria, both of which were nunneries in Nicosia, and the powerful Stavrovouni, which remained an important pilgrimage goal because of the cross. Cistercian foundations from Syria, all in or near Nicosia, include the nunneries St. Theodore and St. Mary Magdalene and the men's houses St. Blaise and Beaulieu. Like Stavrovouni, Beaulieu wielded considerable political power.

Monastery of Panayia tou Arakos at Laghoudhera, Mount Adelphi, Cyprus, 12th century.
Photo courtesy of Chris Schabel

Around 1200 a house of Augustinian Canons Regular was established on the Orthodox site of Episkopia in a magnificent location between the Kyrenia Mountains and the north coast. The house, known today as Bellapais, joined the Premonstratensian order shortly afterward. Bellapais occupies a special place in the monastic and architectural history of Cyprus. One canon, Hugh of Fagiano, became Latin archbishop of Nicosia in 1251 and successfully upheld the primacy of the Cypriot Latin Church over its Greek counterpart, a primacy confirmed by both Churches in the papal bull of 1260, *Bulla Cypria*. Several members of the Armenian royal house were at times among Bellapais' canons from 1270 to around 1308: Kings Hayton I and II and Hayton I's nephew, Hayton the historian, an ambassador for the usurper Amaury, the brother of Henry I, from 1307 to 1308. The patronage of the kings of Cyprus Hugh III (1267–1284), buried at Bellapais, and Hugh IV (1324–1359) ensured that the house played an important political role and that the monastery's buildings, purely Gothic, were among the most splendid on the island. The intact church of the 13th century and the partially ruined conventual buildings, largely from the 14th, rival Fountains and Rievaulx for their romantic beauty in their exotic setting.

The four major mendicant orders each established houses in most or all of the four episcopal sees of Cyprus: Nicosia, Famagusta, Limassol, and Paphos. The power of the abbots of Bellapais, Stavrovouni, and Beaulieu was matched by that of the leaders of the Franciscan and Dominican orders on Cyprus, and mendicants often filled the ranks of the higher secular clergy and enjoyed royal favor. The two main mendicant orders arrived on Cyprus in the 1220s (Francis himself probably visited the island during the Fifth Crusade), the Carmelites and Augustinians coming later in the century.

Much of the Latin architectural heritage has been lost. The Benedictines had already abandoned Stavrovouni following the Mameluke invasion of 1426, and it eventually reverted to Greek monks. Like Mangana, Beaulieu was destroyed by the Venetians during the construction of the present walls in 1567. Excavations in the early 20th century revealed the classic Cistercian plan, with the refectory perpendicular to the ecclesiastical south cloister walk. The main houses of the Franciscans and Dominicans were also demolished, although medieval visitors attest to their magnificence, especially of the Dominicans' house, the beneficiary of much royal patronage, which rivaled Bellapais. However, Franciscan ruins can be found at Paphos and Famagusta. The Augustinian Hermits' 14th-century church in Nicosia, now the Omeriyeh Mosque, is the most important Gothic structure in the government-controlled area of Cyprus, but it was damaged by the Turkish bombardment during the siege of 1570. The ruined Carmelite church in Famagusta and the church of the Benedictine house of Our Lady of Tyre in Nicosia also remain, although in Turkish military zones.

Relations between the Latin and Orthodox Churches of Cyprus were never harmonious, but only one mortal clash took place between them, and that early on. In 1228 a Dominican named Andrew visited the Orthodox monastery of Panayia Kan-

tariotissa on the Karpas Peninsula in the northeast. There Andrew engaged in a discussion with the monks, two of whom, John and Konon, came from a monastery on Mount Athos. The discussion became heated over the issue of the validity of unleavened bread, which the Orthodox denied. Challenged to trial by ordeal, Andrew chose instead to take the matter to Archbishop Eustorge of Nicosia, who informed Pope Gregory IX (1227–1241). It was decided that the monks, 13 of them, should be treated as heretics, and partly because of the chaos of civil war on the island between Emperor Frederick II (1209–1250) and family Ibelin, in 1231 Andrew himself was able to obtain the execution, or martyrdom, of the monks. They were dragged by horses through the riverbed of the Pedhiaios, which runs through Nicosia, before being burned. Generally, relations were not so bad, and in fact Pope John XXII (1316–1334) protected Mangana and St. Catherine of Sinai from Latin high-handedness.

At its height, Latin monasticism on Cyprus must have been represented by close to 30 houses. Most of the Latin orders remained on the island during the Venetian period (1489–1571), although in a reduced and lax state. Linguistic, religious, and social differences between the Frankish rulers and the largely Greek population were decreasing already in the middle of the 14th century, and Orthodox monasteries were again the beneficiaries of patronage. In the 15th century Helen Paleologina, the Greek queen of John II of Cyprus, encouraged refugee monks from Constantinople to settle there and enriched Mangana with estates. Close to 60 Orthodox houses were active at the Turkish conquest. The Maronites and other religious communities were also represented on the island, as the Armenian monastery at Halevga near Mount Pentadaktylos attests.

### Turkish Rule 1571–1878

Latin houses on Cyprus were suppressed along with the secular Latin Church. The Franciscans slowly returned to the island from 1596, serving the local Maronites, establishing schools, and engaging in missionary activity. Today the order is active in the main government-controlled towns, where Spanish Franciscans provide Roman Catholic services in their mainly Baroque churches of the 19th century, mostly to foreign workers from the Philippines and Sri Lanka. At some point during Turkish rule, an Islamic community of the Whirling Dervishes sect, with a lifestyle that can be termed monastic in some respects, was established in Nicosia. The house was active until the 20th century, and its 17th-century building is now a museum in the Turkish-occupied zone of Nicosia.

The Turkish conquerors initially sequestered the Greek monasteries, but the Greeks were soon allowed to repurchase them, and by the late 18th century they had become prosperous when some 78 functioning houses are recorded. Saint Neophytos, virtually abandoned by 1610, recovered under Abbot Leontios and flourishes to this day. The Turks torched Stavrovouni in 1570, but it rebounded quickly. It was rebuilt in present form in the 19th century, adopted the Athonite rule from 1889 onward, and is now regarded as the strictest of the active Greek monasteries, reintroducing the prohibition against female visitors in 1988.

Kykko expanded after 1700 but was destroyed by fire in 1751 and 1813. Makhairas, also impoverished during the early Turkish period, had restored its finances by the early 19th century, although it had to be rebuilt following a devastating fire in 1892.

Generally, the monasteries played an important role in reinforcing the religious and, later, ethnic identity of the subject population, not least by providing a basic education to neighboring youths. Accordingly, in retribution for the Greek Cypriot monks' support of the Greek war of independence, the major monasteries were sacked in 1821, and Governor Küchük Mehmed martyred the monks of Stavrovouni and the abbots of Kykko, St. Neophytos, and other houses. The main houses again recovered, but the later Turkish rule took its toll, and by 1878 only about ten houses thrived; many of the smaller monasteries had been abandoned and had their lands absorbed by the big houses or sold to individuals or bishoprics for economic exploitation.

*English Rule, 1878–1960*
This was a period of revival and increasing prosperity for monasteries, which retained their political role. Monks were involved in the EOKA struggle against the British (1955–1959). In 1957 Gregorios Afxentiou, second in command of the EOKA guerillas and today considered a hero by the Greek Cypriots, was burned alive by the British in a hideout near Makheras, having refused to surrender. The British occupied Kykko in 1956. Archbishop Makarios III, the spiritual leader of the Greek Cypriots in the EOKA struggle and the first president of the Republic of Cyprus (1960–1977), had been, under the name Michael Mouskos, a novice at Kykko.

*Since Independence*
Cypriot Orthodox monasticism, especially female houses, continued to revive after the island gained independence in 1960, but in 1974 Turkey invaded Cyprus and since then has occupied the northern 38 percent of the island. The effect on monasticism has been dramatic. The five active monasteries in occupied Cyprus, some with centuries of inhabitance, had to be evacuated, with the exception of the monastery of the Apostle Andrew (served by one priest) at the tip of the Karpass Peninsula. Thus, important houses founded before the Frankish conquest, such as St. John Chrysostom and, on the north coast, Akheiropiitos ("built without hands") stand empty. Monasteries in the government-controlled areas have absorbed some refugee monks, such as those of St. Barnabas, who now reside at Stavrovouni. Sites under Turkish control that have great touristic value, such as Bellapais and St. Barnabas, have been maintained, but others have suffered neglect and even severe depredations, including the theft of icons and wall paintings, especially in the first few years after the invasion. Recently, plans were unveiled to turn the Armenian monastery at Halevga into a hotel. However, in the past couple of years, the Turkish authorities have allowed pilgrimages of otherwise banned Greek Cypriots to the Apostle Andrew monastery.

Orthodox monasticism in the government-controlled areas attempts to redefine its role in a rapidly modernizing society coping with the consequences of invasion. It has its problems, such as the recruitment of suitable male novices, and it is occasionally involved in the scandals that plague the church of Cyprus. However, unlike monasticism in many Western countries, monasticism in Cyprus remains alive and prosperous, being intimately intertwined in the island's affairs. As of 1995, 14 nunneries were functioning, with about 65 nuns, but that number grows yearly. Seven male houses were active, including about 80 monks and novices, a number that appears to have stabilized. However, their numbers belie their financial resources and political power, which are impressive, as is their energy. Pilgrims and tourists frequent the functioning houses, where the monks and nuns engage in farming, wine making, iconography and icon preservation, manuscript binding and conservation, and the writing of ecclesiastical history or theological homilies. Kykko, the richest and most powerful, leads the way; it and its dependencies run a school of Byzantine music, a new museum, a library with a manuscript collection, a conference center, and a research institute with important publications.

Vitality has had its negative side from the point of view of historical preservation. Modern alterations to the big houses occur regularly; for example, at Stavrovouni new cells have been built in apparent violation of codes for historical buildings. In most cases the older structure itself is not of great intrinsic interest, but St. Nicholas of the Cats and the Carmelite church of Karmi at Pano Polemidhia, both medieval, are suffering from tasteless and destructive modernization. Nevertheless, these are signs of religious vitality, and the award-winning restoration of Panayia Eleousa (Our Lady of Mercy) at Sindi in the Paphos district shows that where houses are derelict, proper historical conservation can be exercised.

*Monasteries to Visit*
Most of the important Orthodox houses were destroyed not once but several times. What remains is generally of interest for icons or the site itself, as for Stavrovouni, Makhairas, Kykko, and St. Neophytos, all functioning men's houses. For a working nunnery, visit St. Herakleidios, south of Nicosia. Ayia Napa in the southeast and Panayia Eleousa at Sindi are now defunct but are architecturally interesting, as is Archangel Gabriel, a Kykko dependency. On the northern slopes of the Troodos Mountains, St. John Lambadistis in Kalopanayiotis and Panayia tou Arakos (Our Lady of the Wild Vetches), a defunct house in Laghoudhera, contain fine wall paintings. Accommodation at functioning houses is often available, but check in advance for restricted access to women or men. Of the Latin orders, see the Augustinian Hermits' church in Nicosia (now the Omeriyeh Mosque). Because only day visits to the Turkish-occupied area are legal, a visit to Bellapais alone is recommended at present.

CHRIS SCHABEL AND NICHOLAS COUREAS

*See also* Iconoclasm (Controversy); Israel/Palestine; Istanbul, Turkey; Libraries: Eastern Christian; Orthodox Monasticism: Byzantine

## Further Reading

Coureas, Nicholas, *The Latin Church in Cyprus, 1195–1312*, Aldershot, Hampshire, and Brookfield, Vermont: Ashgate, 1997

Dikigoropoulos, A.I., "Cyprus 'Betwixt Greeks and Saracens' A.D. 647–695," Ph.D. Diss., University of Oxford, 1961

Enlart, Camille, *Gothic Art and the Renaissance in Cyprus*, translated by David Hunt, London: Trigraph, 1987

Galatariotou, Catia, *The Making of a Saint: The Life, Times, and Sanctification of Neophytos the Recluse*, Cambridge and New York: Cambridge University Press, 1991

Gunnis, Rupert, *Historic Cyprus: A Guide to Its Towns and Villages, Monasteries and Castles*, London: Methuen, 1936

Hackett, John, *A History of the Orthodox Church of Cyprus from the Coming of the Apostles Paul and Barnabas to the Commencement of the British Occupation* (A.D. 45– A.D. 1878): Together with Some Account of the Latin and Other Churches Existing in the Island, London: Methuen, 1901; reprint, New York: Franklin, 1972

Jeffery, George, *A Description of the Historic Monuments of Cyprus: Studies in the Archaeology and Architecture of the Island*, Nicosia, Cyprus: Government Printing Office, 1918; reprint, London: Zeno, 1983

Papageorgiou, Athanasios, *The Autocephalous Church of Cyprus: A Catalogue of the Exhibition*, Nicosia, Cyprus: Archbishop Makarios III Foundation, 1995

Stylianou, Andreas, and Judith Stylianou, *The Painted Churches of Cyprus*, Stourbridge: Mark and Moody, 1964; Chicago: Argonaut, 1967

# Czech Republic

From the ninth century Bohemia was Christianized by missionaries, among them monks who came from the area of the Archdiocese of Salzburg (Dioceses of Regensburg and Passau) and for some time in the second half of the ninth century also by St. Cyril (826–869) and Methodius (c. 815–885). Monks were appointed the first bishops of the first Czech Diocese of Prague, established in 973–976. At the same time, around 973, the first Czech monastery came into being; it was a nunnery at St. George's church in the Hradčany in Prague, founded by a Přemyslid princess, Mlada-Maria.

In 993 St. Adalbert (d. 997), a monk and the second bishop of Prague, established the Benedictine abbey in Břevnov near Prague; this abbey still exists. The next Benedictine abbey was founded by Prince Boleslav III (999–1003) in Ostrov u Davle. The establishment of the bishopric and large abbeys confirmed the status of Bohemia as a Christian state.

By the mid–12th century about ten Benedictine abbeys were founded. They played a crucial role in medieval Bohemia, especially in the area of culture. Quite interesting was an abbey of "Slavonic" Benedictines using a Slavic liturgy. Their liturgy was in Old Church Slavonic, and they used the Glagolitic in writing. Their abbey was founded in Sázava by St. Prokop (d. 1053), a hermit who enjoyed the support of Prince Vratislav II (1061–1092), on whose death the Benedictines using the Slavic liturgy were expelled and their place was taken by the Latin monks from Břevnov. An abbey in Kladruby, founded in the early 12th century, maintained ties with the abbey in Zwiefalten, which participated in the Hirsau reform movement.

Around 1140 Jindřich Zdík (d. 1050), the bishop of Olomouc, invited the Augustinian Canons of Jerusalem to settle in a monastery in Strahov near Prague. Around 1143 a congregation of Premonstratensians from Steinfeld was established there as well. The abbey in Strahov was the first and most important Premonstratensian monastery in central Europe. By the end of the 12th century, more than a dozen Premonstratensian monasteries, male and female, were founded. In 1142 the first Cistercian abbey was established in Siedlec; soon the Cistercians settled in many other places in Bohemia. Their abbeys were founded even in the 14th century. In the second half of the 12th century, military orders came to Bohemia: the Hospitallers from 1169, Augustinian Canons of the Holy Sepulchre of Jerusalem before 1188, and the Teutonic Order before 1204. By the end of the 12th century, about 40 monasteries existed in Bohemia.

From around 1225 mendicant orders appeared in Bohemia, first the Dominicans, then the Franciscans, then the Augustinian Hermits from the second half of the 13th century, and finally the Carmelites from the mid–14th century. Overall the mendicant orders had about 50 monasteries in the 13th century, and in the 14th century they established 20 more. In the 13th century arrived the Templars and the hospital orders. In 1237 blessed Agnes, the daughter of King Přemysl I (1197–1230), founded the Order of the Red Star Knights of the Cross at a hospital in Prague. This order later became quite widespread in central Europe. As for the female orders, there were numerous foundations of monasteries of the Premonstratensians and the Cistercians, then the Poor Clares, Dominican Sisters, and the Magdalenes. About 150 monasteries were in existence in 1300.

The first half of the 14th century was marked by a bitter conflict between the mendicant orders and secular clergy. It resulted in a bloody riot in Prague in 1334, directed against the mendicant orders. Trying to counterbalance the mendicant orders, John IV of Dražic, the bishop of Prague, founded a monastery of Augustinian Canons in Roudnice in 1333. The abbey of Roudnice supplied the base of further monastic foundations and formed a large congregation that became an important center of the Church and monastic reform, exerting its influence over all of central Europe. Its resonance emerged in the reform of the Benedictine abbey in Kastl.

In 1342 King John of Luxembourg (1310–1346) founded near Prague the first charterhouse in Bohemia. Emperor Charles IV (1346–1378) was a great patron of monasticism. In the New Town of Prague, which was his foundation, he founded abbeys of the Benedictines, Premonstratensian Nuns, Poor Clares, Carmelites, Augustinian Hermits (Female), Servites (Ordo Servorum Mariae), and Canons Regular as well as the famous monastery Emaus (Na Slovenach), established for Benedictine monks from Dalmatia who were using the Slavic liturgy. He also founded the abbeys of the Celestine Order in Ojvíně (Lusatia) and of the Carmelites in Tachově.

On the death of Charles IV, some tension affected monasteries in connection with the growing Church reform movement at the time of the Hussite movement. The very existence of monasteries was put in doubt by Matthias of Janova (d. 1394). The Hussite Revolution (1419–1434) seriously damaged and greatly depopulated most of the monasteries in Bohemia. Less damage was inflicted on monasteries in Moravia and Silesia (at that time a part of the kingdom of Bohemia), which remained outside the area governed by the Hussites.

In the aftermath of the Compacts of Lipany (1434), monasteries were slowly restored in Bohemia, yet the atmosphere remained inauspicious. There were very few new foundations of monasteries of the Augustinian Canons, Carmelites, Franciscan Observants (after 1454), or the Paulite Fathers (from 1491 Předni Vyton). If in 1400 the number of all monasteries in Bohemia (apart from Silesia) can be estimated at 220, in 1500 there were only about 165.

The Reformation drastically affected monastic life in Silesia and Bohemia, where a few dozen monasteries, especially of the mendicant orders, were suppressed. This situation changed when Bohemia became a part of the Habsburg Empire (1526–1918). After the battle of the White Mountain in 1620 and the defeat of the Czech uprising by the Habsburgs, Bohemia underwent a process of imposed re-Catholicization.

Already from the mid–16th century, and especially after 1620, new orders appeared in Bohemia that focused on active involvement in society. The Jesuits, who came to Prague with Peter Canisius (1521–1597) in 1556, were busy in education, preaching, and ministering to the upper echelons of society. In 1562 they established in Prague the Collegium Clementinum, which had the right to confer academic degrees. In the 18th century they had over 20 monasteries and more than a dozen colleges. From 1640 the Piarists were involved in education. An important role was played by the Capuchins, summoned by Laurence of Brindisi (d. 1619). They were involved in country missions and in ministry in parishes. Other orders active during that period included the Discalced Augustinian Canons, Barnabites, Brothers Hospitallers of St. John de Deo, Franciscans, Minims, Paulite Fathers, Servites, and Theatines; among the female orders were the Elizabethan Nuns, Carmelite Sisters, Ursulines, and Visitandines. In 1725 an eremitic order, the Ivanités (Congregatio fratrum eremitarum divi Ivani), was established in Bohemia, only to be suppressed in 1782.

Older orders were still of great importance, especially in the field of culture and scholarship. The Premonstratensians of Strahov founded the famous Collegium Norbertanum in Prague. Benedictine abbeys in Broumov, Břevnov, and Rajhrad were centers of art and scholarship. The Benedictines, Premonstratensians, and Augustinian Hermits were the mainstay of Czech Enlightenment Catholicism and Josephinism. An abbey of the Celestine Nuns in Choustnikove Hradiště (the so-called Czech Port Royal) was the center of Jansenism.

The abolition of monasteries conducted in 1782 and 1785 by Emperor Joseph II (1780–1790) caused great losses. Half the male monasteries and more than two-thirds of all nunneries were dissolved. Monastic life started to revive from the 1830s, and a breakthrough occurred in 1850, when Josephinism was officially rejected. The Redemptorists from Vienna headed by St. Clement Hofbauer (Dworzak, 1751–1820) played an important role in restoring monasticism. In Bohemia, as elsewhere in Europe, new forms of monastic life appeared, in particular congregations of clerks regular and female congregations. Around 1912, there were 122 male monasteries in Bohemia in which 1,079 priests and 411 other monks lived, and 410 nunneries with 5,632 nuns. The total population of Bohemia consisted of 7.26 million Catholics and 400,000 persons outside the Catholic Church.

Monasticism was suppressed on the Communist takeover in 1948. At that time about 3,000 monks and 12,200 nuns resided in Czechoslovakia. In 1950, during so-called Operation K, all monasteries were abolished, and monks and nuns were transferred to a few select abbeys to die out. These abbeys were abolished in 1955. Nevertheless a few female congregations continued through the Communist era, tolerated by the state authorities. In 1968 about 8,000 nuns and monks remained. Monastic life revived after 1989. Monasteries could recover their property because they had been illegally abolished in 1950. In 1994, 22 male and 29 female religious orders and congregations were in existence.

*Monasteries to Visit*

Brno (churches of the Franciscans and the Augustinian Hermits); Kutná Hora (churches of the Jesuits and the Ursulines); Prague (Břevnov, Emaus, Strahov, St. Agnes monastery [the Poor Clares], St. George monastery [the Benedictine Nuns], Clementinum [the Jesuits], the church of Virgin Mary Triumphant [the Capuchins], the church of Virgin Mary under the Chain [the Hospitallers]); former Benedictine abbeys in Broumov, Kladruby, Ostrov u Davle, Sázava; Cistercians in Osek, Plasy, Sedlec, Vyšší Brod, and Zlatá Koruna; and Premonstratensians in Milevsko and Teplá.

MAREK DERWICH

*See also* Augustinian Canons; Augustinian Friars/Hermits; Austria; Benedictines; Capuchins; Carmelites, Cistercians; Dominicans; Franciscans; Orthodox Monasticism: Slavic; Pilgrimages, Christian: Eastern Europe; Poland; Premonstratensian Canons; Reformation; Templars; Teutonic Order

## Further Reading

*Archiv für Kirchengeschichte von Böhmen-Mähren-Schlesien*, 1967–

David, Pierre, "Bohême," in *Dictionnaire d'histoire et de géographie ecclésiastique*, volume 9, Paris: Letouzey et Ané, 1937

Derwich, Marek, and Lesław Spychała et al., "State of Research on a Daily Life of Monks and Canons Regular in East-Central Europe during the Middle and Modern Ages," in *La vie quotidienne des moines et chanoines réguliers au Moyen Âge et Temps modernes: Actes du Premier Colloque International du L.A.R.H.C.O.R.: Wrocław-Ksiaz, 30 novembre–4 décembre 1994*, by L.A.R.H.C.O.R. Colloque international, Wrocław: Institut d'Histoire de l'Université de Wrocław, 1995

Hofmann, Johannes, editor, *Tausend Jahre Benediktiner in den Klöstern Břevnov, Braunau und Rohr*, St. Ottilien: EOS Verlag, 1993

Jirásko, Ludek, *Geistliche Orden und Kongregationen in den böhmischen Kronländern*, Prague: Fénix, 1991

Joos, Rainer, "Zwiefalten und Kloster Kladrau (Kladruby) in Böhmen," in *900 Jahre Benediktinerabtei Zwiefalten*, edited by Hermann Josef Pretsch, Ulm: Süddeutsche Verlagsgesellschaft, 1990

Kuthan, Jiří, *Die mittelalterliche Baukunst der Zisterzienser in Böhmen und in Mähren*, Munich: Deutscher Kunstverlag, 1982

*Řeholní život v českých zemích: Řeholni řady a kongregace, sekulárni instituty a společnosti apoštolského života v Česke republice* (History of Religious Orders in Czech Territories: Religious Orders and Congregations, Institutes of Apostolic Life in the Czech Republic), Kostelní Vydří: Karmelitánské Nakladelství, 1997

Seibt, Ferdinand, editor, *Bohemia Sacra*, Düsseldorf: Pädagogischer Verlag Schwann, 1974

Seibt, Ferdinand, editor, *Kaiser Karl IV, Staatsmann und Mären*, Munich: Prestel, 1978

*Tausend Jahre Bistum Prag, 973–1973*, Munich: Ackermann-Gemeinde, 1974

Vais, J., "Die Kartäuser in den Böhmischen Ländern," *Analecta Cartusiana*, 1:2 (1989)

Vlček, Pavel, and Petr Sommer et al., *Encyklopedie českých klàsterů* (Encyclopedia of Czech Monasteries), Praha: Libri, 1997

# Częstochowa (Jasna Góra), Poland

Częstochowa is a city in southern Poland with a Paulite monastery on Jasna Góra and a sanctuary devoted to the cult of the Virgin Mary in Poland. In 1382 Prince Władysław of Opole handed over to a group of 16 Paulite fathers of the Hungarian monastery Márianosztatra a parish church of the Nativity of the Virgin located on a hill called Jasna Góra (Clarus Mons) near the existing town of Częstochowa. Owing to the subsequent endowments of King Władysław Jagiełło (1386–1434) and his wife, Jadwiga, the monastery was founded on 24 February 1393. From the first half of the 15th century it remained a pilgrimage center, with the monks active in preaching and ministry. The monastery presided over the Polish province of the Paulite fathers and in 1493 acquired the right to self-government. In the first half of the 17th century, the Tridentine reform was introduced. New fortifications were erected that later would play an important role in the war with Sweden from 1655 to 1660.

The close of the 17th century saw the peak of the monastery's splendor, whereas the reforms of the Age of Enlightenment diminished its popularity. The monastery suffered severe repression inflicted by the czarist authorities following the fall of the January uprising (1864). During the revival of the 1920s, Polish bishops and the Apostolic see became involved. New statutes for the monastery were drawn at that time. Under Communist rule that was introduced in Poland in the aftermath of World War II, the monks from Jasna Góra followed the instructions of Cardinal Stefan Wyszyński (1901–1981), primate of Poland, and focused on propagating the nation's spiritual renewal through the cult of the Virgin Mary.

In 1384 the monastery's founder, Prince Władysław of Opole, donated a painting of the hodegetria type, showing the Virgin holding the Child on her left arm, executed in tempera on wood. It was probably brought from Bełz (Ruthenia), which had been conquered in 1377 by Władysław of Opole, at that time the governor of Ruthenia (1372–1379). The painting's earlier history remains unknown. The oldest records, dated to around 1474, contain only unreliable legends (see Kowalewicz, 1983). In 1430 the painting was severely damaged during an attempted robbery. In 1434 King Władysław Jagiełło had it restored and decorated in Krakow and then brought back to Częstochowa in a solemn procession. These events influenced the later development of the cult of the painting.

Another important stage in this development began with the successful defense of the monastery and the Jasna Góra sanctuary led by Prior Augustyn Kordecki. He fought off the besieging Swedish army (18 November to 26 December 1655) during the so-called Swedish deluge, when almost all Poland was occupied. Our Lady of Częstochowa was perceived as the advocate of defense and credited for the subsequent victory, itself of great significance for the country. Since that time devotion to Our Lady of Częstochowa has continued to play an extraordinary role in Polish spirituality. She was honored as the Queen of Poland (e.g., S. Kobierzycki, *Obsidio Clari Montis*, 1659). This aspect of the cult of Our Lady of Częstochowa was further emphasized by crowning the painting with papal crowns on 8 September 1717. It became a custom to dedicate oneself and the whole nation to her protection. This practice acquired great importance in the period following the Third Partition of Poland, when no independent Polish state existed (1795–1918), as well as during the Communist era (1945–1989). The climax came in 1956 with the so-called Jasna Góra Vows of the Nation, that is, a solemn act of allegiance to the Virgin Mary the Queen of Poland, delivered at Jasna Góra on 26 August by Polish bishops and the nation. More than a million people gathered on the 300th anniversary of the so-called vows of King Jan Kazimierz II (1656), proclaiming the Virgin Mary as Queen of Poland (see Wyszyński, 1962). At present the sanctuary continues to attract numerous pilgrims and functions as a gathering place for the faithful, especially youth. On 15 August 1991 the sixth World Youth Day was celebrated there and was attended by Pope John Paul II, who paid visits to the sanctuary in 1979, 1983, 1987, 1991, and 1997. Every year about two million pilgrims from Poland and abroad visit the sanctuary.

Today the Jasna Góra sanctuary consists of the monastery of the Paulite fathers, a late-Baroque basilica church, the Miraculous Painting Chapel, Armory, Treasury, Refectory, and Stations of the Cross.

MAREK DERWICH

See also Kiev (Kyiv), Ukraine; Pilgrimages, Christian: Eastern Europe; Poland

## Further Reading

Bausenhart, K., *Maria, die Königin Polens: Ursprungsgeschichte der Erwählung Mariens zur Königin Polen und ihre Wirkungsgeschichte auf das religiöse Leben des Volkes*, Münster West., 1977

"Jasna Góra," in *Encyklopedia Katolicka*, volume 7, Lublin: TNKUL, 1997

"Jasna Góra im Leben der Nation und der Kirche in Polen," *Das katholische Leben in Polen* 12:8–9 (1977)

Kowalewicz, Henryk, editor, *Najstarsze historie o Częstochowskim obrazie Panny Maryi, XV i XVI wiek* (The Oldest Relations about the Virgin Mary Painting of Częstochowa, 15th and 16th Centuries), Warsaw: PAX, 1983

*Studia Claromontana* 1–18 (1981–1998)

Świdziński, S., "Die älteste Quellen zur legendären Geschichte des wundertätigen Bildes der Mutter Gottes von Jasna Góra in Tschenstochau und ihre kritische Beleuchtung," *Ephemerides Mariologicae* 26:4 (1976)

Szafraniec, Kazimierz, *Z dziejów Jasnej Góry* (From the History of Jasna Góra), Warsaw: ATK, 1980

Weidhaas Hermann, *Czenstochau: Stadt, Kloster und Marienbild*, Leipzig: Seeman, 1966

Wojciechowski, Leszek, "Najstarsze klasztory paulinów w Polsce. Fundacja – uposażenie – rozwój do około 1430 roku" (The Oldest Monasteries of the Paulites in Poland: Their Foundation, Endowment and Development to c. 1430), *Studia Claromonatana* 11 (1991)

Wyrwas, S., "Dzieje kultu NMP Królowej Polski. Studium historyczne" (History of the Devotion to Virgin Mary the Queen of Poland: A Historical Study), in *Studia z dziejów liturgii w Polsce*, volume 2, Lublin: TNKUL, 1976

Wyszyński, S., *Wielka Nowenna Tysiąclecia* (The Great Novena of the Millennium), Poznań, 1962

Zbudniewek, Janusz, "Jasna Góra in der Zeit der zwei polnischen Nationalaufstände," in *De cultu Mariano saeculis XIX–XX: Acta Congressus Mariologici-Mariani Internationalis in sanctuario Kevelaer (Germania) anno 1987 celebrati*, volume 6, Rome: Pontificia Academia Mariana Internationalis, 1991

# D

## Daily Office. *See* Office, Daily

## Dalai Lama (Tenzin Gyatso) 1935–

Tibetan Buddhist leader

Tenzin Gyatso, the Fourteenth Dalai Lama, was born on 6 July 1935 in Taktser in the Amdo region of Tibet. His full name is Jampel Ngawang Lobsang Yeshe Tenzin, and the title Dalai Lama means "precious ocean of wisdom" or "unsurpassed in wisdom." The term *Dalai* itself is Mongolian, and the title was first given to Sonam Gyatso, the Third Dalai Lama, by the Mongol prince Altan Qan in the 16th century. The Tibetan word *Gyatso* is itself the equivalent of the term *Dalai*. The Fourteenth Dalai Lama is also the head of the Gelukpa, one of the four primary traditions or schools of Tibetan Buddhism. The Dalai Lama is the spiritual and temporal leader of Tibet living in exile with his government in Dharamsala, Himachal Pradesh, India. China invaded Tibet in 1950, and the Dalai Lama attempted to coexist with the colonial power, but conditions went from bad to worse. After a serious uprising in March 1959 in Tibet, he fled with 100,000 of his countrymen to India. In 1989 the Dalai Lama was awarded the Nobel Peace Prize for his untiring efforts to resolve the conflict with China through nonviolent dialogue.

At the age of two, Tenzin Gyatso was recognized as the 14th reincarnation of the Dalai Lama and thus as the successor to the "Great Thirteenth," as his predecessor had been known. Brought to Lhasa in 1939, he was enthroned at the Potala Palace in 1940. Under the guidance of his three tutors – Ling Rinpoche (the former abbot of Gyuto monastery), Trijang Rinpoche of Sera Je, and the celebrated scholar Kuna Lama Tenzin Gyaltsen – he pursued his education and monastic formation at the Norbulingka and Potala palaces. He studied logic and Buddhist philosophy, with emphasis on Prajñāpāramitā, Mādhyamaka, Abhidharma, and Vinaya. History, astrology, tantra, and poetry were also added, and his study of tantra was especially thorough. At the age of 24 he was awarded the Lharampa Geshe degree, a doctorate in Buddhist philosophy and practice, the highest degree in the Gelukpa monastic educational system. He started learning English while still a teenager. Because of the emerging problems with China, the Dalai Lama was made to accept his full temporal powers, with their numerous responsibilities and functions, at the age of 16.

Over the years since his exile, the Dalai Lama has traveled extensively, especially in the West, where he has taught the dharma. He has presented teachings, given retreats and empowerments, and taken part in major conferences, becoming a well-known figure around the world. He has lectured on the nature of compassion and wisdom at great length and in many contexts. He has tried to convey this central teaching of Mahāyāna Buddhism and has embodied it in his own life and example. Once at a news conference he was put on the spot by an aggressive journalist who asked him what his religion was all about, as he was trying to understand what motivated the Dalai Lama. The Dalai Lama looked at him with love and responded, "It's really very simple; my religion is kindness!" So indicative of his deeper convictions, this kindness has been a constant theme that he expresses in his principle of universal responsibility. On numerous occasions in various parts of the world and in diverse settings, the Dalai Lama has offered this teaching with clarity, eloquence, and depth of perception. This notion of responsibility affects every person and community on earth. He maintains that universal responsibility is both collective and individual. Each person has a responsibility to the whole planet because all of us are sustained by it. We must do something in our lives that enhances it in some way; it might be by embracing a more simple lifestyle, thus affecting the ecology of the earth in a positive way. Similarly the human family has a universal responsibility for the planet on all levels of need. Governments, every institution and organization, and all the religions of the world bear this same sacred responsibility. No one can escape from it, and no one can be a passive observer. Everyone must participate, especially in relation to the environment, or the natural world. Again this teaching on universal responsibility is a profound witness of commitment to compassion, and this is compassion on a global scale involving all human beings.

The Dalai Lama has also worked untiringly on the issue of peace. His great contribution here is his unceasing example and teaching on the necessity of nonviolence. One of the most significant documents of this is the "Universal Declaration on

Tenzin Gyatso, the 14th Dalai Lama.
Photo courtesy of John Powers

ligions and the Temple of Understanding in New York City. It was at the Parliament of the World's Religions in Chicago on 4 September 1993 that the Dalai Lama and other Buddhist monastics took part in an important dialogue with Christian monks and nuns around the theme "Śūnyatā and Kenosis: The Arising of Universal Compassion in the Spiritual Journey." Then, in the summer of 1996 in Kentucky at Thomas Merton's monastery, a follow-up meeting, called "The Gethsemani Encounter," was held. The proceedings appeared in 1997 under the same title, edited by Donald Mitchell. Like Pope John XXIII (1958–1963), the Dalai Lama has touched many hearts.

WAYNE TEASDALE

*See also* Buddhist Schools/Traditions: Tibet; Critiques of Buddhist Monasticism: Indo-Tibetan; Dharamsala, India (Tibetan); Dialogue, Intermonastic: Christian Perspectives; Keating, Thomas; Lhasa, Tibet; Liturgy: Buddhist; Nhát Hanh, Thích; Peace Movements, Buddhist; Persecution: Buddhist Perspectives; Self-Immolation, Buddhist; Tibet: History; Tibetan Lineages: Gelukpa

## Biography

Tenzin Gyatso, head of the Gelukpa lineage of Tibet, was recognized as such at age two and installed in the Potala Palace, Lhasa, where he lived until obliged to flee with thousands of followers in 1959. He settled in Dharamsala, India, which has become a center for Tibetans in exile. The Dalai Lama's worldwide travels advocating peace won him the Nobel Peace Prize in 1989. He is one of the world's best known religious leaders.

## Major Works

*Freedom in Exile: The Autobiography of the Dalai Lama*, 1990
*A Flash of Lightning in the Dark of Night: A Guide to the Bodhisattva's Way of Life*, 1994
*The Path to Enlightenment*, edited and translated by Glenn Mullin, 1995
*The World of Tibetan Buddhism: An Overview of Its Philosophy and Practice*, translated by Geshe Thupten Jinpa, 1995
*The Spirit of Tibet, Vision for Human Liberation: Selected Speeches and Writings of H.H. The Dalai Lama*, edited by A.A. Shiromany, 1996
*The Buddha Nature: Death and Eternal Soul in Buddhism*, 1997
*The Joy of Living and Dying in Peace*, 1997

## Further Reading

Craig, Mary, *Kundun: A Biography of the Family of the Dalai Lama*, Washington, D.C.: Counterpoint, and London: HarperCollins, 1997

Nonviolence," entered into with the Monastic Interreligious Dialogue (MID) under the leadership of Abbot Thomas Keating (1923– ). The Dalai Lama and MID coauthored this insightful and persuasive document, which is a sort of declaration of independence of religion from war making. It was signed formally in Santa Fe, New Mexico, on 2 April 1991. The declaration attempts to provide perspective and a context for the future that emphasizes our interconnectedness.

The Dalai Lama has also been a continuous participant in interfaith organizations, such as the Parliament of the World's Re-

# Damian, Peter, St. 1007–1072

Italian Benedictine scholar, poet, and monastic reformer

Saint Peter Damian, monk, prior, and then cardinal and finally Doctor of the Church, occupies a central place in medieval Western monasticism. A learned writer and poet, an ascetic, and a rigorous reformer of monasticism and the Church, his work bore fruit in the reform program of the Fourth Lateran Council (1215). Like St. Romuald (c. 950–1027), whose biography he wrote, Peter was born in Ravenna (in 1007), and the Eastern Christian spirituality of that place exerted a strong impact on him. He was the youngest of six children or more of a poor family and suffered a difficult childhood. His older brother facilitated his studies at Faenza and Parma. Peter became a brilliant Latinist and went on to teach rhetoric at Ravenna. He was then ordained and entered the rigorous hermitage of Fonte Avellana sometime after 1034. In 1043 he was elected prior and began improving the library and physical structure, drawing up a body of constitutions that defined their austere observance. He erected or reformed a series of hermitages and monasteries and organized them into a congregation that lasted until 1569, when it was united with that of Camaldoli. He was very influenced by Camaldoli's founder, St. Romuald, and Peter's biography of Romuald expressed and deepened his veneration. His work as church reformer on behalf of popes and the Roman Curia occupied much of his attention and energies and caused him to travel widely and have contact with emperors and kings as well as abbots and bishops. He died in 1072 at the age of 65 and is buried in the cathedral of Faenza.

Peter was one of the chief proponents of austere asceticism, which attempted to counteract the self-indulgence of the times. He advocated fasting and discipline for monks and clergy, noting St. Paul's analogy of the athlete who disciplines his body to win a merely earthly crown. He wrote a scathing tract against homosexual practices that Pope Alexander II (1061–1073) discreetly locked up. At least one scholar (Lester Little in 1976) has argued that Peter was possibly a repressed homosexual, a hypothesis that would explain the intensity of his writing on the subject. His spiritual writings depend heavily on Scripture, which he interprets typologically, and on Augustine's sacramental theology. Other fonts are Origen (c. 185–c. 254), from whom he quotes entire sections, Gregory the Great, and, in the specifically monastic tradition, the *Sayings of the Desert Fathers*, Cassian, the Rule of St. Benedict, and Romuald. In this regard he is remembered today mainly for his theology of the Christian community as bound together in the one Body of Christ and, in balance with this, his promotion of Christian solitude, which he likened to a return to paradise but also to a descent into the lion's den. He expressed the theology of community as well as solitude in his lyrical treatise "The Lord Be with You":

> The Church of Christ is united in all her parts by such a bond of love that her several members form a single body, and in each one the whole Church is mystically present; so that the whole Church universal may rightly be called the one bride of Christ, and on the other hand every single soul can, because of the mystical effect of the sacrament, be regarded as the whole Church.

ROBERT HALE, O.S.B. CAM.

*See also* Camaldolese; Cassian, John; Devotions, Western Christian; Gregory I (the Great), St.; Hermits: Western Christian; Hymnographers; Self-Mutilation, Christian

## Biography

Born at Ravenna, Peter studied in Faenza and Parma before entering a hermitage at Fonte Avellana in 1035. As prior there from 1043, he founded new monasteries and preached against clerics' simony (purchase of office). An advocate of the "apostolic life" without property, he promoted ecclesiastical reform and performed diplomatic missions. Although he was never officially canonized, in 1828 Leo XII proclaimed him "Doctor of the Church."

## Major Works

"The Lord Be with You," Opus. XI
"On Monastic Perfection," Opus. XIII
"On the Institutes of His Congregation," Opus. XV

## Further Reading

Blum, Owen, *St. Peter Damian: His Teaching on the Spiritual Life*, Washington, D.C.: Catholic University of America Press, 1947
Calati, Benedetto, "Pierre Damien," in *Dictionnaire de spiritualité, ascétique et mystique: Doctrine et histoire*, volume 12, Paris: Beauchesne, 1937–1995
Ignesti, Bernardo, *S. Pier Damiano e i suoi discepoli*, Siena: Edizioni Cantagalli, 1972
Leclercq, Jean, *Saint Pierre Damien: Ermite et homme d'église*, Rome: Edizioni di storia e Letteratura, 1960
Little, Lester K., "The Personal Development of Peter Damian," in *Order and Innovation in the Middle Ages: Essays in Honor of Joseph R. Strayer*, edited by William C. Jordan, Bruce McNab, and Teofilo F. Ruiz, Princeton, New Jersey: Princeton University Press, 1976
Mansueto della Santa, *Ricerche sull'idea monastica di San Pier Damiano*, Arezzo: Edizioni Camaldoli, 1961
*S. Pier Damiani: Atti del Convegno di Studi nel IX centenario della morte: Faenza, 30 settembre–1 ottobre, 1972*, Faenza: Società Torricelliana di Scienze e Lettere, 1973

# Daoism: Influence on Buddhism

When Buddhism was first introduced into China around the beginning of our era, the Chinese saw it as yet another sect of Daoism. This was due mainly to the meditational techniques, especially the breathing exercises found in scriptures such as the *Anbanshouyi jing* (Sūtra on the Mindfulness of Breathing). Under the Eastern Han (25–220) both Huang-Lao (the Yellow Emperor and the deified Laozi) and the Buddha were worshiped in conjunction.

Terminology taken mainly from the Lao-Zhuang tradition of Daoism played an important role in the early translations of Buddhist scriptures into Chinese and to a certain extent influenced the ways in which the Chinese came to understand some of the key concepts of the foreign religion. This process found its most direct expression in the method of translation known as "matching the meaning" (geyi). During the Eastern Jin dynasty (317–420), which ruled in the southern part of China, Lao-Zhuang Daoism and the Yi jing (Book of Changes) continued to make its impact on Buddhism through the tradition of xuanxue, or "obscure learning," a development that has wrongly been labeled "Neo-Daoism." The xuanxue was sufficiently influential to effect a special Daoistic imprint on the Chinese interpretation of the prajñāpāramitā sūtras. This also found its way into the writings of Sengzhao (c. 383–414), the most illustrious of Kumārajīva's (344–413) disciples, and is most apparent in the way he understood the mādhyamaka doctrine of emptiness as well as his speculations on the relationship between essence and function (ti-yong).

In the second half of the Nanbeizhao period (386–581), certain aspects of Daoist notions of millennialism were absorbed into growing Buddhist interest in messianism. A seminal scripture in this development was the Shouluo biqiu jian Yueguang tongzi (Scripture on the Monk Shouluo Meeting with Prince Moonlight), an apocryphal work of the sixth century. It contains both messianism and a vision of the apocalypse.

One of the most significant Daoist elements that the Chinese Buddhists took over was the concept of a spirit/soul (shen) that was immortal and subject to rebirth. In this manner they inadvertently came close to the Hindu doctrine of brahman/atman and thus introduced a line of thought that was essentially alien to the Indian Buddhist tradition.

The traditional Buddhist concept of the natural relationship between a cause and its effect was also altered in China partly because of influence from Daoism. The way that the law of karma was thought to operate did not always follow the Indian principles of cause and effect but rather can best be described as containing a strong element of externally operating agents, such as belief in a heavenly bureaucracy that rewards and punishes people for their deeds. According to this line of thinking, causality becomes a predefined moral guarantee for a sort of absolute "Heavenly Justice" that overrules karma as such. In this manner

A Daoist "Lonely Saint" (toksong) often found in Korean monasteries, distinguishable by his bald head and long eyebrows. Dongch'un-sa Monastery in Chunchon, South Korea.
Photo courtesy of John Powers

karma becomes rather inconsistent and random and, ceasing to be a natural law, becomes a matter of individual fate.

Among later Buddhist schools, Chan absorbed certain elements from both the *Daode jing* and to a lesser extent the *Zhuangzi*, which in various ways influenced the development of Chan doctrines and philosophy. Strongest was the concept of *wuwei*, or nonactivity, which in the early Southern Chan context was understood as the ideal attitude to practice. As such it became mixed up with certain notions of emptiness in accordance with the Sinitic interpretation of *prajñāpāramitā* and played an important role in the formation of the key concept of "no mind" (*wuxin*). Thus, the *Daode jing* continued to be read and studied by Buddhist monks.

Perhaps the strongest influence from Daoism emerged in the esoteric Buddhist tradition. The use of talismans (*fu*) and talismanic seals (*fuyin*) is one of the most important Daoist practices that the Buddhists in China took over. It is not known exactly when the use of paper charms became common in Chinese Buddhism, but by the early Tang dynasty this Daoist practice had become an integrated part of the general makeup of Buddhism. Attempts at locating talismans in the traditional Indian Buddhist material have hitherto proved futile, and undoubtedly the talismanic tradition in East Asian Buddhism embodies an original Chinese development that later spread to Korea and Japan. In any case, all surviving examples, without exception, contain a mixture of standard Chinese characters and corrupted characters in the form of a chart or diagram. It is no wonder that Buddhists, foreign as well as native, should seek to incorporate such a highly popular Chinese practice into their own, and thus it is not surprising that we find an extensive use of talismans in connection with the growing apocryphal Buddhist literature. Furthermore, because the lore surrounding the use of talismans is closely related to beliefs in magic and supernatural events, it is within a mainly ritual Buddhist context that the popularity of the written and printed charms should be seen. This is no coincidence, as it is precisely in the ritual sphere that charms were used by the Daoists. Thus, one of the most obvious points of interchange between Buddhist and Daoist beliefs was in the context of ritual practices, and to this esoteric Buddhism was eminently suited. Therefore, it is mainly within the esoteric Buddhist tradition that we find the use of talismans, and nearly always within a ritual – or ritualized – context.

HENRIK H. SØRENSEN

*See also* Buddhism: Inculturation; Chan/Zen: China; China; Critiques of Buddhist Monasticism: Confucian; Daoxuan (Tsaohsüan); Hermits: Buddhist; Kōan; Mountain Monasteries, Buddhist; Taiwan

## Further Reading

Abe, Stanley K., "Heterological Visions: Northern Wei Daoist Sculpture from Shaanxi Province," *Cahiers d'Extrême-Asie* 9 (1996–1997)
Benn, Charles, "Religious Aspects of Emperor Hsüan-tsung's Taoist Ideology," in *Buddhist and Taoist Practice in Medieval Chinese Society*, edited by David W. Chappell, Honolulu: University of Hawaii Press, 1987
Bokenkamp, Stephen R., "The Yao Boduo Stele as Evidence for 'Dao-Buddhism' of the Early Lingbao Scriptures," *Cahiers d'Extrême-Asie* 9 (1996–1997)
Bokenkamp, Stephen R., with a contribution by Peter Nickerson, *Early Daoist Scriptures*, Berkeley: University of California Press, 1997
Ch'ên, Kenneth, *Buddhism in China: A Historical Survey*, Princeton, New Jersey: Princeton University Press, 1964
Guofan, Gao, *Dunhuang minsu xue* (A Study of Folk Customs in Dunhuang), Shanghai: Shanghai wenyi chuban she, 1989
Kobayashi, Masayoshi, *Riku-chō dōkyōshi kenkyū* (A Study on the History of the Daoist Religion During the Six Dynasties), Tokyo: Sōbunsha, 1990
Kobayashi, Masayoshi, "The Establishment of the Taoist Religion (Tao-chiao) and Its Structure," *Acta Asiatica* 68 (1995)
Liu, Yang, "Cliff Sculpture: Iconographic Innovations of Tang Daoist Art in Sichuan Province," *Orientations* (September 1997)
Lü, Jianfu, *Zhongguo mijiao shi* (The History of Esoteric Buddhism in China), Beijing: Zhongguo shehui kexue chubanshe, 1995
Maeda, Shigeki, "The Evolution of the Way of the Celestial Master: Its Early View of Divinities," *Acta Asiatica* 68 (1995)
Ozaki, Masaharu, "The History of the Evolution of Taoist Scriptures," *Acta Asiatica* 68 (1995)
Schipper, Kristofer M., "Taoist Ordination Ranks in the Tunhuang Manuscripts," in *Religion und Philosophie in Ostasien: Festschrift für Hans Steininger zum 65. Geburtstag*, edited by G. Naundorf, K. Pohl, and H. Schmidt, Würzburg: Könighausen und Neumann, 1985
Sørensen, Henrik Hjort, "Divine Scrutiny of Human Morals in an Early Chinese Buddhist Sūtra: A Study of the Si tianwang jing (T. 590)," *SCEAR* 8 (1995)
Strickmann, Michel, *Mantras et mandarins: Le bouddhisme tantrique en Chine*, Paris: Gallimard, 1996
Sunayama, Minoru, *Zui Tō Dōkyō shisōshi kenkyū* (Studies in the History of Daoist Thought in the Sui-Tang Period), Tokyo: Hirakawa Shuppansha, 1990
Verellen, Franciscus, "Evidential Miracles in Support of Taoism," *T'oung Pao* 78 (1992)
Xiao, Dengfu, *Daojiao xingdou fuyin yu fojiao mijiao* (Astral Talismanic Seals in Daoism and Buddhist Esotericism), Taipei: Xinwenfeng, 1992
Xiao, Dengfu, *Daojiao shuyi yu mijiao dianji* (Daoist Ritual Practices and Textual Sources of Esoteric Buddhism), Taipei: Xinwenfeng, 1993
Xiao, Dengfu, *Daojiao yu mizong* (Daoism and Esoteric Buddhism), Taipei: Xinwenfeng, 1993
Zürcher, Erik, "Prince Moonlight: Messianism and Eschatology in Early Medieval Chinese Buddhism," *T'oung Pao* 63:1–3 (1982)

# Daoxuan (Tao-hsüan) 596–667

Chinese Buddhist historian and commentator on vinayas

Daoxuan compiled a very influential commentary on Buddhist monastic codes (vinayas), *Sifenlü shanfan buque xingshi chao* (T.

1804; Summarized Account of Monastic Conducts, Based on the Dharmagupta *Vinaya*, Redundancies Removed and Gaps Filled from Other Sources), and founded an important school of vinaya studies. Whereas the two other vinaya schools that had been founded under the Tang dynasty (618–907) declined, Daoxuan's school, called *Nanshanzong* (Mount Zhongnan school), prospered into the Song period (960–1279); important subcommentaries to Daoxuan's work were composed then. Daoxuan's commentary takes as its basis the vinaya of the Dharmagupta school, which had become more popular than the vinaya of the Sarvāstivāda school by Daoxuan's time in medieval China. However, Daoxuan adopted the methodology of supplementing the contents of this vinaya with extensive quotations not only from the vinayas of other Indian Buddhist schools but also from other scriptural sources, including Mahāyāna sūtras. Thus, Daoxuan's commentary illustrates how the Chinese Buddhist community, which followed the Mahāyāna (Greater Vehicle) teaching, read the literature on monastic codes that were compiled and preserved among the so-called Hīnayāna (Smaller Vehicle) schools.

Daoxuan is also known as a historian of Buddhism. His biographical collection, *Xugaoseng zhuan* (T. 2060; Further Biographies of Eminent Monks), contains 485 entries, to many of which a variety of 219 secondary biographies are appended. This collection continues the earlier, smaller work by Huijiao (497–554) that collected 257 biographies and 243 secondary biographies for the period 67–519. In turn Daoxuan's work was succeeded by the collection that Zanning (919–1001) prepared under imperial request and presented to the court in 988. These three collections define the history of medieval Chinese Buddhism, each dividing the biographies into ten categories based on the nature of the subjects' specialization and achievements. Daoxuan also compiled an extensive collection of historical documents (*Guanhongming ji*, T. 2103) and a catalog of Buddhist literature (*Tatang neidian lu*, T. 2149), here continuing and expanding the scope of similar works by an earlier eminent historian, Sengyou (445–518). In fact Daoxuan was believed to have been a reincarnation of Sengyou: according to Daoxuan's biography, found in Zanning's collection, when Daoxuan's mother became pregnant, she had a dream in which an Indian monk told her that she was carrying Sengyou in her womb.

Daoxuan's family is said to have come from Dantu (in present-day Jiangsu province) or Changcheng (in Zhejiang province) in southern China. Daoxuan first studied in the capital city of Chang'an (present-day Xian) under Huijun (564–637) of the Rijansi temple. In his biography of Hujun, Daoxuan mentions that he had stayed in close contact with Huijun until Huijun's death in 642. Daoxuan also studied under a prominent vinaya teacher, Zhishou (567–635), who was widely known for his study of Dharmagupta vinaya. Daoxuan later withdrew into the Fangchang valley on Mount Zhongnan, outside the capital city, where he is said to have befriended a famous Daoist and doctor, Sun Simao (d. 682). Daoxuan first drafted his previously mentioned vinaya commentary around 628, about the time that the founding emperor of Tang briefly persecuted the Buddhist community (Weinstein, 1987). Daoxuan then embarked on a pro-

longed journey that took him all over China and that lasted more than ten years (630–642). In the course of his travels, Daoxuan consulted a number of vinaya authorities and produced a revised version of the commentary in 636 (Fujiyoshi, 1979a). On his return Daoxuan settled at the Fengdesi temple on Mount Zhongnan, where important works on the vinaya and other subjects were composed.

According to its preface Daoxuan's biographical collection was first completed in 645; sources for this collection, such as stūpa inscriptions of prominent monks, must have been collected in the course of Daoxuan's extended travel. However, Daoxuan continued to collect additional biographies, and the version known today contains a large amount of later material, including an important biography of the famous monk Xuanzang (602–664) that describes the subject's death and funeral (Fujiyoshi, 1979a, 1992b; Ibuki, 1989). In the same year (645), Xuanzang returned from his extensive travel in India and central Asia and began his translation project at the Hongfusi temple in the capital city; many scholars were called to assist in this project. Daoxuan too was called to the capital to work on the project, although he returned to Mount Zhongnan the following year.

The Ximingsi temple, which Emperor Taizong (r. 626–649) built for the benefit of his crown prince in the capital city of Chang'an, was completed in 658, and both Xuanzang and Daoxuan moved there. Xuanzang had played an important role in the establishment of this temple, although his stay in this temple was brief; Daoxuan was appointed as the head monk (*shangzuo*) and stayed there for several years. In 662 Emperor Kaozong cautiously ordered his ministers to discuss the controversial issue of requiring monks to pay respect to the throne and to their parents. The monastic community, led by Daoxuan at the Ximingsi temple, refused forcefully, and in the end the emperor abandoned his attempt to bring the monastic community more closely under state control. Daoxuan argued first by reviewing how previous rulers had supported Buddhism and acknowledged the transcendence of the monastic community over worldly power. He then pointed out that the vinaya and other scriptures, used for ordination of monks and nuns, explicitly forbade them to pay respect to laypeople (Weinstein, 1987).

In 664, at age 69, Daoxuan withdrew into the Jingyesi temple on Mount Zhongnan, where he produced a number of works, including the *Hongming ji*, the *Tatang neidian lu*, and a collection of Chinese Buddhist miracle stories. In 667 Daoxuan established an ordination platform on Mount Zhongnan, a project that brought his many years of vinaya study to an appropriate conclusion. Daoxuan died the same year.

Some time before the end of his life, Daoxuan is said to have been visited by some gods who commended his writings on vinaya while correcting some of the mistakes. These gods are also said to have instructed Daoxuan on several topics, showing him such works as the detailed account, said to have existed in heaven, of the famous Jetavana temple, where the Buddha Śākymuni stayed frequently. They are also said to have answered Daoxuan's questions on the origins of many sacred sites in China and of miraculous Buddha images in China, such as those attributed to Indian King Aśoka. Accounts of these encounters survive in works attributed to Daoxuan and his collaborator Daoshi (dates unknown).

KOICHI SHINOHARA

*See also* Animals, Attitude toward: Buddhist Perspectives; Aśoka; Buddhist Schools/Traditions: China; China; Daoism: Influence on Buddhism; Pilgrims to India, Chinese; Regulations: Buddhist Perspectives; Rules, Buddhist (Vinaya): Historical; Scholastics, Buddhist; Stūpa

## Biography

A renowned scholar and historian of Buddhism, Daoxuan came from southern China and studied with several authorities on the vinaya as well as with a Daoist. At the beginning of the Tang dynasty he traveled for ten years all over China, and then revised his commentary on the vinaya. Later he traveled to India and Central Asia before settling in the capital city of Chang'an. He combatted the emperor's attempt to exact veneration from monastics.

## Major Works

*Sifenlü shanfan buque xingshi chao* (Summarized Account of Monastic Conducts, Based on the Dharmagupta *Vinaya*, Redundancies Removed and Gaps Filled from Other Sources)

*Xugaoseng zhuan* (Further Biographies of Eminent Monks)

## Further Reading

Fujiyoshi, Masumi, "Dōsen no yugyō to nisan no chosaku ni tsuite (2)," *Sanzö* 190 (1979)

Fujiyoshi, Masumi, "Zoku kōsōden, genjoden no seirtsu: shinhakken no kōshōji bon wo megutte," *Ōyōshigaku* 5 (1979)

Fujiyoshi, Masumi, "Bannen no Dōsen," *Kansaidaigaku bungaku ronshu* 41 (1992)

Fujiyoshi, Masumi, "Dōsen no nyūshoku to kōshū zoku kōsōden," *Kansaidagaku bungaku ronshū* 42 (1992)

Ibuki, Atsushi, "Zoku kōsōden no sōkō ni kansuru kenkyū," *Tōyōno shisō to shūkyō* 7 (1989)

Shinohara, Koichi, "The *Ruijing lu*: An Analysis of Its Sources," *The Journal of the International Association for Buddhist Studies* 14 (1991)

Shinohara, Koichi, "Changing Roles for Miraculous Images: A Study of the Miracle Image Section in Daoxuan's 'Collected Records'," *Images, Miracles, and Authority in Asian Religious Traditions*, edited by Richard Davis, Boulder, Colorado: Westview Press, 1998

Weinstein, Stanley, *Buddhism under the T'ang*, Cambridge and New York: Cambridge University Press, 1987

# David, St. d. 601

## Reputed founder of monasteries and patron saint of Wales

David (Latin name for the Welsh "Dewi") is the patron of Wales, but of his life we know almost nothing. His name indicates that he was a Briton – one of the Celtic-speaking inhabitants of England later called the Welsh. Traditionally he is said to have lived in the sixth century and died in 601. However, this date is based on the mid-tenth-century *Annales Cambriae* (*Annals of Wales*),

which records 458 for his birth and thus makes him 160 years old at his death! In fact David might have lived at any time during the fifth or sixth century. Our earliest literary references to him are Irish calendars from around 800 that record his feast day as 1 March (still his feast in the Latin Church), but no more. Evidence from Church dedications indicates a cult focused in southwestern Wales, with devotion to him spreading from there along the southern Welsh coast and into Cornwall and Ireland. Although he is traditionally identified as a monk-bishop, the *Annales Cambriae* identify him simply as a bishop; descriptions of him as a monk appear only later.

The legendary David, a saint identified by wonders from before his birth who functions as an ascetic monk, a champion of orthodoxy, and a thaumaturge, is first found in the Latin *Vita Davidis* (*Life of David*) by Rhigyfarch ap Sullian of the late 11th century. Written to support the independence of the Welsh see of St. David's against encroachment by Norman-controlled Canterbury, the *Vita* portrays a glorious saintly past for Wales under a great heavenly intercessor whose life offers many of the events typical of powerful saints. It is on this *Vita* that all other statements about David (in both Latin – e.g., Geoffrey of Monmouth [d. 1154] – and Welsh) rest.

Rhigyfarch portrays David as a founder of monasteries who becomes a great preacher and bishop acknowledged by other saints (e.g., Patrick) and validated by miracles. David's work begins with the foundation of 12 monasteries (*Vita*, 13), the one in which David dwells being noted for austerity and regularity. Later, when his monks are tempted by women dancing naked nearby, David is presented as immune from temptations "of the flesh" and as able to inspire his monks to resist the temptresses (*Vita*, 17). On another occasion, when someone tries to poison David, he is warned miraculously and so is preserved (*Vita*, 37–38). All these stories pattern David on St. Benedict as depicted in Gregory the Great's *Dialogi*. Likewise the image of David as a youth with a dove on his shoulder teaching him (*Vita*, 8) and later inspiring him as a preacher (*Vita*, 52) is modeled on Paul the Deacon's (c. 720–c. 800) story of the dove explaining the Scriptures to Gregory the Great (*Vita S. Gregorii*, 28). The legend of David shows that in the late 11th century, even for secular clerics such as Rhigyfarch, monasticism embodied the ideal of holiness. The portrayal of David epitomizes the triumph of hagiographic conventions.

THOMAS O'LOUGHLIN

*See also* Hagiography: Christian Perspectives; Wales

## Biography

The patron saint of Wales is known almost entirely from legend. Stories about him emulate accounts of other monastic saints. He is reported to have founded many monasteries, although he may have been not a monk-bishop but only a bishop. Few beloved figures are so scantily documented.

## Further Reading

Davies, Wendy, "Property Rights and Property Claims in Welsh 'Vitae' of the Eleventh Century," in *Hagiographie Cultures et Sociétés IVe - XIIe siècles: Actes du Colloque organise à Nanterre et à Paris, 2–5 mai 1979*, Paris: Études Augustiniennes, 1981

Davies, Wendy, *Wales in the Early Middle Ages*, Leicester and Atlantic Highlands, New Jersey: Leicester University Press, 1982

Lapidge, Michael, and R. Sharpe, *A Bibliography of Celtic-Latin Literature, 400–1200*, Dublin: Royal Irish Academy, 1985

O'Loughlin, Thomas, "Rhigyfarch's *Vita Dauidis*: An *Apparatus biblicus*," *Studia Celtica* 32 (1998)

Rhygyfarch, *Life of St. David: The Basic Mid Twelfth-Century Latin Text with Introduction, Critical Apparatus and Translation*, edited by John W. James, Cardiff: Wales University Press, 1967

# Dead, Intercession for. *See* Intercession for the Dead, Buddhist

# Death: Buddhist Perspectives

The idea of death is fundamental to the spiritual practices of all Buddhists. The Buddha is said to have started his teaching career by discussing death and impermanence (his first discourse at Benares) and to have finished it by saying, "All conditioned things are of a nature to decay – strive on untiringly" (*Dīgha Nikāya* II 156). The emphasis on death within Buddhism led early Western scholars to view Buddhist philosophy as inherently pessimistic. Against this interpretation other scholars have argued that Buddhism might disparage life but that in compensation it offers something more rewarding: immortality. Thus, if Buddhists cultivate a pessimistic outlook of life, it is not because they ultimately despise it but rather because they want to experience the best it has to offer.

The idea of death has been used in various ways by Buddhists, each serving a specific purpose in the context of spiritual practices. For example, in the Theravāda tradition the cultivation of the awareness that death is an inherent consequence of life has been used to apprehend fully the First Noble Truth taught by the Buddha: "Everything is suffering (*sabbam dukkham*)"; that is, everything is impermanent, without self and ultimately unsatisfactory. This cultivation of awareness is also called "the practice of discriminative insight" (Vetter, 1988) and as such is a direct means to acquisition of the liberating wisdom that frees one from ignorance (*avidyā*), the same ignorance that keeps one caught in the cycle of death and rebirth. In other words one becomes free from impermanence by meditating on the fact that everything is impermanent.

In practice this meditation on death took two distinct but interrelated forms. The first aims at actualizing the inevitability of death and is known within the Theravāda tradition as *marana-sati*. The second tries to bring about an awareness of impermanence by focusing one's attention on the different stages of decomposition of the human body. This form of meditation is called "meditation on the impure" (*aśubha-bhāvanā*) and is also used to eradicate any emotional attachment or physical attraction one has toward the human body. In ancient times Buddhist monks would go to battlefields or charnel grounds to practice these meditations, but today, as reported by Boisvert (1996), they go to morgues and hospitals, where postmortem examinations are performed.

A second important use of the idea of death within Buddhism is to instill a sense of urgency. In numerous passages from both the Theravāda and the Mahāyāna literature, one is reminded that death can occur at any moment, so that one should not forgo any moment to walk along the Buddhist path. In the *Bodhicaryāvatāra*, a Mahāyāna text of the eighth century, one is told that we are constantly under the surveillance of the Lord of Death. We might come to the mouth of death even today, so that one should abandon lethargy and the life of enjoyments, sleep, and pleasures and get on with practice as though today were the last day of life (chap. 7). In this context meditation on the idea of death is used to develop an attitude that helps a Buddhist aspirant to progress spiritually. In this regard Atiśa (982–1054), one of the most important transmitters of Buddhism to Tibet, is said to have told his students that "for a person who is unaware of death, meditation has little power, but a person who is mindful of death and impermanence progresses steadily and makes the most of every precious moment" (Powers, 1995). These meditations on the inevitability and the suddenness of death are often practiced in conjunction with reflections on the opportune time (*kṣaṇa*) that aim at making one aware of the great opportunity one enjoys in having been reborn as a human being and not as a ghost or even as a god.

A third application of the idea of death is worth mentioning within the context of Buddhist spirituality. This third use has more to do with death per se than with the idea of it, and it is to be found exclusively within the tantric tradition of Tibetan Buddhism. It appears that skilled tantric practitioners can indeed take control over the process of death. This can be done by recognizing the true nature of the mind and understanding the complex network of channels and energy that flows within the body. Tantric meditations are also practiced to simulate the process of death so that when actual death occurs one is prepared to go through, without being terrified, the different stages, known as *Bardo*, leading to spiritual emancipation or, when one is unfit for it, to rebirth. Thus, for tantric Buddhists the death of the body is only the end of one's grosser levels of consciousness; the more subtle ones become manifest, and one retains a certain level of lucidity for some time. For this reason Tibetans have elaborated a complex ritual of dying in which, among other things, the deceased is cared for (*rje 'dzin* practice) during a period of 49 days, the amount of time after which consciousness has to find a place of rebirth.

Despite the fact that Buddhists of every tradition allow the idea of death to play a central role within their spiritual practices, they do not value it so highly as to encourage suicide as the final step toward liberation, as might be the case in certain other religious traditions (e.g., Jainism and Catharism). However, to some extent one can see in the self-sacrifice of the bodhisattva an attempt to esteem martyrdom, but this interpretation may be a misunderstanding of the spiritual context in which such an act finds its significance. In other words, as it is the case with the idea of death, the idea of self-sacrifice is mainly a theme for one's meditation. As such, it is used to cultivate compassion toward other sentient beings.

FRANCIS BRASSARD

*See also* Aum Shinrikyō; Buddhist Schools/Traditions: Japan; Death Rituals, Buddhist; Intercession for the Dead, Buddhist; Liturgy: Buddhist; Mahāyāna; Meditation, Buddhist Perspectives; Origins: Comparative Perspectives; Pure Land Buddhism; Self-Immolation, Buddhist; Social Services: Buddhist; Spirituality: Buddhist

## Further Reading

Boisvert, Mathieu, "Death as Meditation Subject in the Theravāda Tradition," *Buddhist Studies Review* 13:1 (1996)
Powers, John, *Introduction to Tibetan Buddhism*, Ithaca, New York: Snow Lion, 1995
Santideva, *A Guide to the Bodhisattva Way of Life: Bodhicaryāvatāra*, translated by A. Vesna Wallace and B. Alan Wallace, Ithaca, New York: Snow Lion, 1997
Vetter, Tilmann, *The Ideas and Meditative Practices of Early Buddhism*, Leiden and New York: Brill, 1988
Walshe, Maurice, translator, *Thus Have I Heard: The Long Discourses of the Buddha Dīgha Nikāya*, London: Wisdom, 1987

# Death: Christian Perspectives

The Christian Bible rejects materialism and teaches that although God has created us as bodily beings, we are distinguished from other bodily creatures by also being *persons*, that is, creatures having spiritual intelligences and free wills directly created by God (Gen. 2:7). The Bible leaves open the question whether God not only has used human parents to produce the human body but also has unleashed some vast evolutionary process to produce the human species. The Christian Bible also rejects theories common in other philosophies and religions that consider the body to be evil or simply the temporary garment of the soul. The Bible rejects all theories of anthropological dualism and reincarnation.

Consequently the Bible denies that the Creator intended human death (Gen. 2:16–17; Wisd. of Sol. 1:13) and attributes this tragic inevitability to human sin incurred through temptation undergone by those created, purely spiritual beings – the Fallen Angels (Gen. 3:1–20; Rom. 5:12–14). Liability to death need not be understood as due exclusively to the sin of the first human couple but also to the whole accumulation of human evil – the wars, the lusts, the pride, and the tyranny of all human history. These evils have separated the human race from its original intimate relation with God that would have preserved us from the death to which our bodily condition unaided is liable.

Thus, for the Christian Bible death as the prime consequence of sin requires a Redeemer to free humankind. Early and medieval theologians understood literally the notion that without sin no one would have died. However, some modern theologians hold that, although humans would have died naturally even if there had been no fall, in that case "death would have no sting" (1 Cor. 15:55–56) because it would involve a painless and peaceful transition to immortality. Others have speculated that even if medical technology were to postpone death indefinitely, the threat of death would always remain.

In monastic theology meditation on death was often recommended but exclusively in the perspective of the Resurrection and of immortal life with God in Christ. This reached its height in the spirituality of a reformer of the Cistercians, Abbot Armand-Jean de Rancé (1626–1700), who is often pictured meditating on a skull. Although such preoccupation with death has been denounced as morbid, it is noteworthy that the philosopher Martin Heidegger (1889–1976), from an entirely secular perspective, reasoned that without this confrontation with mortality human existence remains inauthentic. Thus, monastic theology centered on the Augustinian dictum that knowledge of self and of God should be directed not toward death and despair but toward an ever more profound hope. However, this hope rested not on confidence in the good works required by the monastic rule, as Luther denounced it, but on a thoroughly Christian hope rooted in utter dependence on the grace of Christ. Saint Benedict (c. 480–c. 550) and St. Bernard of Clairvaux (1090–1153) dwelled constantly on humility as the special virtue of the monastic because it freed him not only from ambition and envy but also from all trust in his own righteousness. Similar reflections are to be found in the writings of Benedictine nuns, such as St. Hildegard of Bingen (1098–1179), St. Gertrude the Great (1256–c. 1302), and St. Mechtild of Hackeborn (1241/42–1298/99).

Indeed hope of eternal life leads in those advanced in holiness to a longing for death as the open door to the fullness of life. Thus, St. John of the Cross (1542–1591) says,

> When . . . the [purified]soul feels itself very near to going forth in the perfect possession of its kingdom, since it sees itself to be pure and rich and prepared for this, God permits it in this state to see His beauty and entrusts it with the gifts and virtues that He has given it, and all this turns into love and praise, since there is no leaven to corrupt the mass.

However, such a happy death, according to St. John, is possible only if the Christian has passed successfully through the purifications that he calls the twofold "Dark Nights." These are, first, the "Dark Night of the Soul" (the lower psychic faculties with its moral virtues) and, second, the "Dark Night of the Spirit" (the higher psyche with its theological virtues). The experience of these "nights" is a kind of living death in which the negative aspects of dying are overcome so that what unfolds in actual physical death is positive and joyful.

Thus, it is not surprising that in the sacraments the Church has provided a means of celebrating the mystery of death. This sacrament in its primitive form is described in the Epistle of St. James (5:14–15; cf. Mark 16:15):

> Is anyone among you sick? He should summon the presbyters of the church, and they should pray over him and anoint him with oil in the name of the Lord, and the prayer of faith will save the sick person, and the Lord will raise him up. If he has committed any sins they will be forgiven.

In time this sacrament was called "Extreme Unction" and was often feared and delayed as an omen of death. It was frequently practiced as a purely private rite. However, the Second Vatican Council (1962–1965) restored a better understanding by calling it simply "The Sacrament of the Anointing of the Sick" and provided that it might be administered whenever death from an internal cause looms. The sacrament might or might not exercise a physical effect of healing, but, if worthily received, it strengthens against fear of death and buttresses hope for eternal life. It should, if possible, be a public rite so as to express the concern of the whole Church. At the time of actual death, after the anointing, if the Christian is still conscious, the reception of the Eucharist as *Viaticum* ("for the journey") is the appropriate rite of actual passage.

In monastic liturgy, prayers for the dying and the dead have always had an important place, typified by the recitation of Psalm 130, the *De Profundis* ("Out of the Depths"). A special Office of the Dead is regularly recited as well, Masses for the Dead (*Requiem* Masses) are offered, and processions to the monastery cemetery take place not only at funerals but also at other times as reminders to pray for the dead. Such prayers are offered for members of the community and for relatives of the monks, benefactors of the monastery, and all the dying and deceased. This is an expression of the "Communion of Saints" of the Apostles' Creed.

BENEDICT M. ASHLEY, O.P.

*See also* Hildegard of Bingen, St.; John of the Cross, St.; Liturgy: Western Christian; Luther, Martin; Origins: Comparative Perspectives; Rancé, Armand-Jean de; Relics, Christian Monastic

### Further Reading
Bardos, Panos, *History of Thanatology*, Washington, D.C.: University Press of America, 1981
Becker, Ernst, *The Denial of Death*, New York: Free Press, 1973
Binski, Paul, *Medieval Death: Ritual and Representation*, Ithaca, New York: Cornell University Press, 1998
Coward, Harold, *Life after Death in World Religions*, Maryknoll, New York: Orbis Books, 1997
Greinmacher, Rovert, and Alois Miller, editors, *The Experience of Dying, Concilium*, New York: Herder and Herder, 1974
Grelot, Pierre, "Mort," in *Dictionnaire de spiritualité ascetique et mystique: Doctrine et histoire*, volume 10, Paris: Beauchesne, 1980

# Death Rituals, Buddhist

Sinhalese Buddhists characterize the uncertainty of human life by comparing it to a drop of water at the tip of a blade of grass; as demonstrated by the theory of impermanence (Pāli, *anicca*), they believe that sooner or later that drop of water will fall. Just as a flame goes out in the absence of oil, so human life fades away when the conditions are exhausted. With a strong belief in an infinite cycle of births and deaths (Pāli, *saṃsāra*), death is often viewed as only a temporary absence from this world, as the conclusion of one more episode in the process of changing one's place in the cycle of births and deaths. Thus, from the Theravāda Buddhist perspective each person needs always to be psychologically ready for the moment of death.

Buddhists have devised predeath rituals as well as postdeath rituals. The predeath ritual common among Sri Lankan Buddhists is the *jīvadāna pinkama* or *godāne* (offering made while one is alive); it is an offering made to the Buddhist monastic community in the hope of making one's own life better after death. During the course of the ritual, relatives visit the temple and conduct a Buddhist monk to their house for a short sermon. Whereas the *dāna* (giving) is the primary act, the monk's preaching (Sinhalese, *baṇa*) articulates the religious path and makes the devotees ready to enjoy the positive results of their meritorious actions. The next day they offer to the *saṅgha* (monastic community) various kinds of gifts, including household goods. At the end of the ceremony, the relatives express in words their soteriological wish: "We make this offering on behalf of our father 'Puñchirāla' in order that he may be reborn in the world of gods, and finally attain the eternal rest of *nirvāṇa*."

The funeral ritual held a few days after one's death is called *paṃsukūle*, a rite based on the ancient Buddhist practice of offering a "dust cloth" (Pāli, *paṃsukūle*) to the *saṅgha* in the name of the dead person. It is an important ritual meant for securing a safe journey for the dead person as well as for consoling the relatives. The crucial feature in a Buddhist funeral is the short sermon (Sinhalese, *paṃsukūle baṇa*) given to remind everyone of the uncertainty of human life. Because a relative's death is a time of grieving, Buddhist preaching at death rituals is meant above all to console the surviving relatives. It gives an opportunity for the survivors to reflect on the nature of death, to contemplate the impermanence of human life and of all conditioned things in the world, and to receive guidance for reorienting one's own life from the lessons learned at the funeral ceremony.

Burial urns (*budo*s) for deceased Korean monks and nuns, Bugui-sa in North Kyŏngsang province, South Korea.
Photo courtesy of John Powers

In funeral rituals Theravāda Buddhist monastics remind their devotees of the inevitability of death and the transience of human life by reciting a very popular Pāli canonical *gāthā* (verse) as a meditative reflection on death:

> *aniccā vata saṅkhārā uppāda vaya dhammino*
> *uppajjitvā nirujjhantī tesaṃ vūpasamo sukho.*
> Conditioned things are indeed impermanent;
> their nature is rising and falling down;
> having arisen, they pass away;
> their cessation is pleasant.

These brief words of the Buddha explain the fundamental tenet of Buddhism: the doctrine of impermanence. In the Theravāda context death becomes an occasion at which one's life and contributions are judged and evaluated by one's community. Thus, for every Buddhist, even for those who do not seriously practice their religion, a religious ceremony at death is considered essential.

In Sri Lanka, after the formal funeral rites, the dead are commemorated on several occasions: on the seventh day, the 45th day, the third month, the first year, and annually thereafter. The rituals performed on these occasions vary enormously, depend-

ing on the financial resources of the sponsors; however, most of these rituals have one basic structure.

The seventh-day memorial for the benefit of the dead relative often consists of (1) a "sermon for remembrance" (Sinhalese, *mataka baṇa*) delivered on the night of the sixth day, (2) a communal meal (Sinhalese, *saṅgikadāna*) offered to the monastic community on the seventh day, and (3) a short benedictory sermon called *bhuktānumodanā baṇa* (preaching for giving thanks) highlighting the benefits accumulated by the living relatives both for themselves and for the dead person. Buddhist monks' sermons at life-cycle rituals evoke the benefits accrued by both giver and receiver and make the donor happier by causing him or her to reflect on his or her own meritorious actions. The "dedication of merit" (Pāli, *puññānumodanā*) concludes such rituals. The account given by Robert Knox (1681), a British prisoner in 17th-century Sri Lanka, stands as one of the earliest vivid descriptions of postdeath rituals in Sri Lanka.

In Japanese Buddhism, after the funeral rites, memorial services are held on the seventh, 49th, and 100th days. After the first-year anniversary until the 50-year memorial, services are held in years ending with odd numbers 3 and 7. Funeral and memorial rites being the most important religious functions of

Totems for deceased general (left) and a deceased nun (right), Bugui-sa Monastery, North Kyŏngsang province, South Korea. The nun's epitaph records in her own writing reflections on her long life and states that death holds no terror for her.
Photo courtesy of John Powers

Japanese Buddhist monastics, the purpose of such rituals is to ensure a safe journey for the dead spirit from the defiled state of death to a wholesome state in paradise. This paradise-oriented belief obliges the Japanese to identify both the Buddha and the dead person as *hotoke*, which means literally "Buddha." For ensuring a safe journey, correct funeral rituals are crucial; for this purpose the Japanese Buddhist monastic grants a posthumous Buddhist name (Japanese, *kaimyō*) to the deceased and recites Buddhist sūtras. After inscribing the *kaimyō* on a memorial tablet (Japanese, *ihai*), the *ihai* is enshrined in the family Buddhist alter (Japanese, *butsudan*) for veneration. During the *Obon* (Sanskrit, *ullambana*) festival, the souls of the ancestors are invited to the *butsudan* in the evening of 13 August and are escorted back to the other world on 16 August. During this period Buddhist monks are invited to recite sūtras in front of the family *butsudan*. Whereas both Theravāda and Mahāyāna traditions respect the ancestors, current Japanese Buddhism focuses exclusively on the cult of the dead. By reciting Buddhist sūtras for the dead and maintaining temple cemeteries, Japanese Buddhist monastics have produced one of the most sophisticated institutionalized systems of treating the dead.

MAHINDA DEEGALLE

*See also* Death: Buddhist Perspectives; Intercession for the Dead, Buddhist; Japan: History; Liturgy: Buddhist; Prayer: Buddhist Perspectives; Social Services: Buddhist; Sri Lanka: History; Stūpa

## Further Reading

Ashikaga, Ensho, "The Festival for the Spirits of the Dead in Japan," *Western Folklore* 9 (1950)

Deegalle, Mahinda, *Baṇa: Buddhist Preaching in Sri Lanka (Special Focus on the Two-Pulpit Tradition)*, Ph.D. Diss., University of Chicago, 1995

Dickson, J.F., "Notes Illustrative of Buddhism as the Daily Religion of the Buddhists of Ceylon, and Some Account of Their Ceremonies After Death," *Journal of the Royal Asiatic Society (Ceylon)* 8 (1884)

Dun, Kyaw, "Burmese Funeral Rites," *Journal of the Burmese Research Society* 7 (1917)

Knox, Robert, *An Historical Relation of the Island Ceylon, in the East Indies: Together with an Account of the Detaining in Captivity of the Author and Divers Other Englishmen Now Living There, and of the Author's Miraculous Escape*, London: Richard Chiswell, 1681; as *An Historical Relation of Ceylon*, 2nd edition, Dehiwala: Tisara Prakāśakayō, 1966

Lloyd, A., "Death and Disposal of the Dead: Japanese," in *Encyclopaedia of Religion and Ethics*, 13 vols., edited by James Hastings, New York: Scribner's Sons, 1908–1926

Spiro, Melford E., *Buddhism and Society: A Great Tradition and Its Burmese Vicissitudes*, New York: Harper and Row, 1970; London: Allen and Unwin, 1971; 2nd edition, Berkeley: University of California Press, 1982

Tambiah, Stanley J., *Buddhism and the Spirit Cults in North-East Thailand*, Cambridge: Cambridge University Press, 1970

Visser, Marinus Willhem De, *Ancient Buddhism in Japan: Sutras and Ceremonies in Use in the Seventh and Eighth Centuries* A.D. and Their History in Later Times, 2 vols., Paris: Geuthner, 1928–1935

Welch, Holmes H., *The Practice of Chinese Buddhism, 1900–1950*, Cambridge, Massachusetts: Harvard University Press, 1967

Wells, Kenneth Elmer, *Thai Buddhism, Its Rites and Activities*, Bangkok: Bangkok Times Press, 1939; New York: AMS Press, 1982

Wylie, Turrell, "Mortuary Customs at Sa-skya, Tibet," *Harvard Journal of Asiatic Studies* 25 (1964–1965)

Yetts, W. Perceval, "Notes on the Disposal of Buddhist Dead in China," *Journal of the Royal Asiatic Society* (1911)

# Deities, Buddhist

From a certain point of view, the phrase "Buddhist deities" is an oxymoron. Buddhism proclaims itself "nontheistic," and its founder, Siddartha Gautama, the Buddha (traditional dates subject to scholarly dispute, 563–483 B.C.), proclaimed that he was neither a deity nor an incarnation of a deity but simply an "awakened one." This Buddhist claim means two things that set Buddhism apart from other religions. First, there is no creator of the universe and no beginning of time. Instead Buddhism posits that from "beginningless time," or saṃsāra (cyclic existence), all beings have endlessly wandered on the "wheel of birth and death." However, Buddhism also posits a way to end this cycle of death and rebirth. Perfect understanding of *anātman* (the absence of any permanent abiding self, soul, or ego) will end the craving and grasping that keep the saṃsāric cycle turning. Especially in early Buddhism the monastic lifestyle was said to be, if not essential, at least very helpful to attaining such understanding and equanimity. Second, there is no vicarious atonement or external agent of freedom from saṃsāra. Instead each individual must experience for him- or herself the understanding and detachment that bring liberation. No matter what practices developed in later forms of Buddhism to make it easier to attain enlightening understanding, no version of Buddhism, including Japanese Pure Land Buddhism, ever revoked this principle of needing to experience enlightenment for oneself.

However, if these two common understandings of deity as "creator" and "savior" are excepted, Buddhism does speak of "deities" and has so from its beginnings. Three distinct ways of speaking of deities are found in this nontheistic religion. "Worldly spirits" are the first type of deity. These beings also exist within the saṃsāric wheel of birth and death but are far more powerful and long-lived than human beings. Some worldly spirits are local deities associated with specific places; such local spirits are recognized in all forms of Buddhism. Second, personifications of Buddhist ideal qualities, such as wisdom and compassion, who function like deities and might be mistaken for deities by unknowledgeable outsiders, are common, especially in Mahāyāna Buddhist countries. Although Buddhist philosophy would not attribute independent, metaphysical existence to such beings, they are very important in the religious lives of both laypeople and monastics. Third, the term *deity* is used in a very specialized sense in Vajrayāna Buddhism. In that form of Buddhism, deities, as personifications of enlightened mind, are frequently used in meditation practices in which a meditator visualizes both him- or her self and the phenomenal world as that deity. Like the personifications of wisdom and compassion, such *yidam*s (meditation deities) do not exist independently but arise out of emptiness (*śūnyatā*). Meditation deities are essential to Vajrayāna Buddhist practice for all serious meditators, whether monastic or lay. Thus, Buddhist "deities" offer a very interesting alternative to what most religions posit about deities.

Interior of Vairocana Buddha Hall with main altar and Vairocana Buddha gilt bronze statue (1.77 meters in height), Pulguksa Temple, Kyŏngju, Kyŏngsang-bukdo, Unified Silla period, late eighth century. Photo courtesy of Marylin M. Rhie

Putuo (sometimes equated with Maitreya), Feilaifeng Buddhist grottoes, near Hangzhou, Zhejiang, China, late 14th century.
Photo courtesy of Marylin M. Rhie

Worldly spirits have been recognized from Buddhism's earliest days, at least according to the stories it tells about its origins. After Siddartha's enlightenment experience he despaired of teaching what he had learned because he thought that it went so much against the grain of usual human wants and needs that no one would pay attention to his message. At that point several gods came down from their heavenly abode to convince the Buddha that several people were almost ready to reach enlightenment and would, indeed, respond to his teaching. Thus, in a sense the very existence of the Buddhist religion is mythically attributed to the prompting of these gods.

It is important to understand that such "gods" and the "heavens" they inhabit are part of Indian cosmology. They were taken for granted in Indian Buddhism, as they are in the contemporary forms of Buddhism closest to its Indian origins, especially Tibetan Buddhism. But no matter how powerful and long-lived such gods might be and no matter how pleasant their lives, because they are still in saṃsāra they are impermanent, subject to death as gods and rebirth into another of the six realms of existence. Their status as gods is attributed to positive karma accrued through good deeds in past lives. However, because they are not enlightened and remain subject to rebirth, such a rebirth

is not sought by knowledgeable Buddhists, including most monastics. Monastics did accept the existence of such gods as readily as anyone else; in fact the follies of seeking rebirth as a god could provide sermon material for monastics.

Buddhism also accommodated the beliefs of preexisting religions by accepting as worldly spirits and protectors of the dharma those deities who were already venerated by local inhabitants. Such beings could be quite powerful and, unlike the Buddha, were willing to grant various favors to those who venerated them, although they could not grant the ultimate boon: enlightenment. In keeping with the nontheistic character of Buddhism, enlightenment came only through an individual's direct experience of egolessness (anātman) and emptiness (śūnyatā). Because of their worldly power, local deities are often quite popular, especially with laypeople, and monastics do not discourage these popular practices.

In most countries to which Buddhism migrated, a comfortable symbiosis between these local deities and Buddhism developed quite easily. For example, in Thailand one sees "spirit houses" everywhere. These are miniature dwellings, often quite elaborate and beautiful, at which offerings are left for the local deities by devotees who have prayed to them for specific worldly

local spirits and protectors is very much part of contemporary Tibetan Buddhism, practiced by monastics and laypeople alike.

The second kind of Buddhist deity is venerated only in Mahāyāna Buddhism. Often called "celestial bodhisattvas and buddhas" in older literature, they are extremely prevalent. Part of the Mahāyāna reformulation of Buddhism, which began about 500 years after the origins of Buddhism and which owed much to the work of Indian monastics, included developing a pantheon of mythical buddhas and bodhisattvas. In keeping with Buddhist nontheism, sacred narratives about all these beings tell of human beings who were inspired to take the bodhisattva vow to help all sentient beings attain enlightenment. Their current exalted position is due only to their own progress on the path, and their main function is to facilitate meditators' progress along the path to enlightenment.

Many celestial buddhas and bodhisattvas are personifications of the primary Mahāyāna virtues: wisdom and compassion. The most often invoked personification of wisdom is Bodhisattva Mañjuśrī, often depicted with a sword that cuts delusion in one hand and a book in the other. He is regularly invoked by students in Tibetan monasteries, and Japanese students facing "examination hell" go to Mañjuśrī's temple to pray for wit and help. Personifications of compassion abound. One of the most prevalent is Avalokiteśvara with his thousand eyes that see the needs of beings everywhere and his thousand arms that help in multiple situations at once. Two female personifications of compassion, who may be alternate forms of Avalokiteśvara, are, if anything, even more popular. Tārā is the universally beloved protector of Tibet and helper in all situations of need, whether

Jizō statues, Ise Peninsula, Japan. In Japan the Mahāyāna deity Jizō (Sanskrit, Kṣitigarbha) is associated with helping aborted fetuses, and his statue appears in their cemeteries.
Photo courtesy of David Moore

benefits. Local deities are also honored in other Theravādin Buddhist countries. Japan offers the best example of such thoroughgoing symbiosis. Most Japanese people, including most monastics (who are usually called "priests" in Japanese Buddhism), practice both Shintō and Buddhism to some extent. Virtually every Japanese Buddhist temple or monastery has a shrine to the local deities, called *kami*, near its entrance. This small shrine to the *kami* is essential; as deities of the place, they own and control the land on which the temple or monastery stands and must be asked for permission to build and maintain the Buddhist structure. Tibetan Buddhism also recognizes many local deities. Stories of the transmission of Buddhism to Tibet are filled with tales of how local deities, initially opposed to Buddhism, were tamed in a combat with a great Buddhist meditation master, who was sometimes a monastic, after which they swore to become protectors of the Buddhist dharma. Honoring these

Virupaksa, guardian of the west, who has a red skin and holds a *nāga* (serpent) and wish-fulfilling jewel (*cintā-mani*). At the entrance to Tongdo-sa, South Korea's largest monastery.
Photo courtesy of John Powers

A Korean pantheon of deities common in Korean monasteries, showing divinized ancestors and personifications of the stars of the zodiac. Bun-sa Monastery, North Kyŏngsang province, South Korea.
Photo courtesy of John Powers

worldly or more spiritual. In China and Japan, where she is known as Kwan-yin or Kannon, she is especially concerned with the woes of women. Often women pray to her for male children, and she is one of the few Buddhist deities sometimes depicted with a baby. (Japanese portrayals of Bodhisattva Jizō also show him with children. Because he rescues beings from hell, he is especially connected with protecting stillborn or aborted fetuses and young children who die.) Buddha Amitābha, another popular personification of compassion, features above all in Japanese Pure Land Buddhism. This uniquely Japanese form of Buddhism was developed by the monk Hōnen (1133–1212) and his disciple Shinran (1173–1262), who abandoned his monastic vows. However, the story of Amitābha originated in Indian Mahāyāna sūtra (one class of Buddhist scriptures) literature. As a human bodhisattva he vowed to use the infinite storehouse of merit that he would eventually accumulate to conjure a "Pure Land." Rebirth in his Pure Land would be easy and enlightenment there even easier. Because he has completed the journey to Buddhahood, his Pure Land now exists, and rebirth there is commonly sought by both monastics and laypeople of the Pure Land denomination.

The most specialized Buddhist deities are the so-called meditation deities (yidams) of Tibetan Vajrayāna Buddhism, an esoteric form of Buddhism. Teachings about and permission to practice the visualizations of these esoteric yidams are relatively restricted, but because Vajrayāna is the dominant form of Buddhism in Tibet, most monastics know about yidams and do yidam practice. To understand yidams it is essential to realize that they are personifications of enlightened mind. Thus, they are not external to the meditator but are a portrayal of that meditator as an enlightened being. Yidams are frequently portrayed in Tibetan art and are rather bizarre looking from a conventional point of view. They are usually a vivid primary color – red, blue, and green are common. They often have multiple faces, arms, and legs. They are portrayed seminude but bedecked with many ornaments. They can be portrayed in a peaceful demeanor, but more often they are fierce, even terrifying. One would not want to meet such a yidam uninitiated to his or her practice. Female and male yidams are equally common; they are portrayed either individually or joined in sexual union, the famous yab-yum (father-mother) icon. (Yes, monastics do these sexual visualizations.) However, the point is not the literal appearance of the *yidam*. Each detail of their iconography carries symbolic meanings; these symbolic meanings are the true point of these practices. When a meditator visualizes him- or herself as *yidam* or visualizes the phenomenal world as *yidam*, the meditator is not trying to become, for example, a red woman, the portrayal of the *yidam* Vajrayoginī. Rather the meditator, in seeing herself as Vajrayoginī, is attempting to uncover her own true nature, which has been obscured by the habitual patterns developed over many lifetimes in saṃsāra, and to manifest the qualities symbolized by Vajrayoginī's iconography.

In Vajrayāna Buddhism the guru is considered to be even more important than the *yidam* because without the guru no practitioner would be introduced to *yidam* practice. Tibetan literature includes numerous stories of students who mistakenly venerated the *yidam* rather than the guru when presented with the guru's command to pick one over the other. If the *yidam* is a "deity" (although not a deity with independent metaphysical existence), what does that make the guru? The question is awkward, especially in light of frequent Vajrayāna Buddhist claims that gurus have qualities that many would associate with deities, such as the ability to perform miracles and the ability to hear and respond to the requests of devotees. One could make a cogent case that the guru is the functional equivalent of a deity in Vajrayāna Buddhism, but that does not mean that the guru is the philosophical equivalent of a deity. Like the Buddha the guru is a human being who has gone through a long, arduous training process to reach his or her highly developed state. As such gurus demonstrate the fullness of human potential; they are not agents of salvation external to the world or to life shared by all sentient beings. Devotion to gurus, which is said to be necessary to the successful practice of Vajrayāna Buddhism, involves aspiration to become like the guru, not worship of a metaphysically existing entity that exists independently of the phenomenal world.

RITA M. GROSS

*See also* Asceticism: Buddhist Perspectives; Buddhism: Inculturation; Buddhist Schools/Traditions: China; Buddhist Schools/Traditions: Japan; Holy Men/Holy Women: Buddhist Perspectives; Hōnen; Images: Buddhist Perspectives; Initiation: Buddhist Perspectives; Japan: History; Mantras; Prayer: Buddhist Perspectives; Pure Land Buddhism; Shinran; Thailand; Tibet: History; Vajrayāna Buddhism in Nepal; Visual Arts, Buddhist

## Further Reading

Chandra, Lokesh, *Transcendental Art of Tibet*, New Delhi: International Academy of Indian Culture, 1996

Dobbins, James C., *Jodo Shinshu: Shin Buddhism in Medieval Japan*, Bloomington: Indiana University Press, 1989

Getty, Alice, *The Gods of Northern Buddhism*, Rutland, Vermont, and Tokyo: Tuttle, 1962

Gómez, Luis O., translator, *The Land of Bliss: The Paradise of the Buddha of Measureless Light*, Honolulu: University of Hawaii Press, 1996

Landaw, Jonathan, and Andy Weber, *Images of Enlightenment: Tibetan Art in Practice*, Ithaca, New York: Snow Lion, 1993

Picken, Stuart D.B., *Buddhism: Japan's Cultural Identity*, Tokyo and New York: Kodansha International, 1982

Tambiah, Stanley J., *Buddhism and the Spirit Cults of North-East Thailand*, Cambridge: Cambridge University Press, 1970

# Denmark. *See* Scandinavia

# Desert Fathers

The term "Desert Fathers" is traditionally used to designate the fourth- to fifth-century hermit monks of Egypt. Sometimes the word is used more broadly to include cenobites (those who lived in community) and other geographical regions, such as Sinai and Palestine. The literature associated with them includes some material about women, although this was not a "double monasticism," in which men and women pursued the monastic life alongside each other.

More narrowly the term denotes monks who lived an anchoritic (hermit) or semi-anchoritic life in Egypt. Their model was St. Antony (c. 251–356), whose life by Athanasius (c. 296–373) presents many of the elements characteristic of desert monasticism. Links to Antony, even if tenuous, were prized as marks of an authentic monastic pedigree. The tradition exemplified by Antony and his original followers was handed on to newcomers by a succession of teachers. These revered elders (each described as a *geron*, "old man," and titled *Abba*, "father") provided inspiration, discernment, and instruction to those who had come as apprentices in the monastic life.

What we know about the daily life of the Desert Fathers comes largely from the *Apophthegmata patrum* (*Sayings of the Fathers*). Thousands of these dicta and stories have been preserved in various collections and languages. Although the monks were typically speakers of Coptic, the native Egyptian language, the sayings were recorded in Greek and later edited into alphabetical and topical collections, perhaps in sixth-century Palestine. Two historical and biographical compendia, also written in Greek, contain important background and contextual information: the anonymous *Historia monachorum in Aegypto* (late fourth century; *History of the Monks of Egypt* [*HM*]) and the *Historia lausiaca* (c. 419; *Lausiac History* [*HL*]) of Palladius (c. 364–420/30).

The Desert Fathers are associated especially with two sites in the desert west of the Nile: Nitria and Scetis. Both areas were mostly flat and topographically uninteresting, featuring brackish pools that contained deposits of natron, which was prized by ancients for its usefulness as a detergent (cf. Jer. 2:22). Also known as Pernouj (preserved as al-Barnouj, the name of the modern town on the site), Nitria took its more common name from the local product. Nitria was the largest monastic settlement, likely because it was accessible by boat from Alexandria (about 40 miles away) by a canal that is now silted up. Like other monastic settlements Nitria was sometimes called "the mountain," more a symbolic than a topographical attribution. It was founded by Amoun, an Egyptian who went there perhaps as early as the 320s and soon gathered disciples around him. The most famous of these was Pambo (d. 373), a classic monastic frontiersman who once declared, "The monk's garment should be such that he could throw it out of his cell for three days and no one would take it." The large monastic population at Nitria (in the thousands, according to *HL* and Jerome, but great in any case) prompted the establishment of a quieter outpost called Kellia ("The Cells"). Tradition has St. Antony visiting Amoun at Nitria and assisting him in choosing a location a day's walk (about 11 miles) to the south for those wanting greater solitude. Among the prominent figures linked to Kellia were Macarius of Alexandria, who was its priest in the late fourth century, and the learned monks Ammonius and Evagrius Ponticus, members of the most famous (and controversial) of the many subgroups at the settlement. The monks of Kellia typically spent the weekdays in solitude, gathering together at the main church on the weekend for liturgy and a common meal.

Kellia is the monastic site most thoroughly explored by modern archaeologists, and its physical evidence can help in understanding life in any of the Egyptian monastic colonies. According to *HM*, the hermitages at Kellia were distributed so that the monks could not hear one another when chanting the Psalms. Modern excavations have located some 600 cells scattered across the site, normally separated from each other by at least 300 feet. Dating the remains is difficult, as is their correlation to the literary sources; the textual data are mostly from the fourth to early fifth centuries, although the site was occupied for another 500 years. Excavations suggest that the earliest cells were dug into the soil and had simple graduated vault roofs made of mud brick without mortar. Some cells were clearly intended for single occupancy, whereas others accommodated several hermits. Later dwellings were more elaborate, and complexes of cells associated with their own churches developed as soon as the original fourth-century pattern of individual cells around a single church began to give way to a more varied array.

Scetis, the modern wadi al-Natrun, was the figurative center of desert monasticism. Much harder to visit in ancient times than Nitria or Kellia, Scetis represented the ideal of separation from the world and keen asceticism depicted so vividly in the *Apophthegmata patrum*. The name is Coptic, and the meaning is uncertain; it likely signifies "oasis of natron," although another tradition interprets it as "scale of the heart." The founder was Macarius the Egyptian ("the Great," d. 390; often confused in the literature with Macarius of Alexandria), who came to Scetis about the same time Amoun went to Nitria. Among his followers were the famous monks known from the *Apophthegmata*: Sisoes, who later moved to Antony's Inner Mountain; the priest Isidore; Paphnutius, whose nickname was "the Buffalo"; and later the beloved John the Short, the converted Nubian brigand Moses, the aptly named Poemen ("Shepherd"), and the austere Arsenius. The monastic pattern at Scetis was similar to that of Nitria or, perhaps more precisely, of Kellia, with groups of hermits guided by recognized masters of the life. Traditionally, four "congregations" existed, each led by an elder. The head of Macarius' circle served as overseer of the whole. It was in Scetis that the young John Cassian (c. 360–after 430) spent several years, having arrived in the late 380s. Because travel to Scetis required passage overland, it was visited much less frequently by pilgrims than was Nitria, and the two sites were often confused in the literature.

Although Nitria-Kellia and Scetis were the two major centers of monastic settlement, the monks moved freely between them and to other sites, such as Antony's monastery at Pispir near the Nile or farther south to Antinoe, or beyond to Sinai or even Gaza and Palestine. Geographical stability was not essential to the life, and relocation for the sake of greater solitude or to consult a famous elder was common. Yet not all monks learned the life at one of the major centers. The famous sites owe their prominence to numbers and to the abundant literary evidence related to them.

These monks did not follow written rules or share communal norms as cenobites did. This fact makes describing their way of life in generic terms a risky endeavor. Nonetheless, common traits can be seen among monks living throughout Egypt, the Sinai, Gaza, and Palestine. The fundamental practices of nighttime vigil, regular times of prayer, manual labor, a single daily meal in mid-afternoon, and abstaining from meat were typical. These disciplines were taken seriously but applied flexibly according to circumstances and abilities. Fasts were broken for the sake of hospitality, and differences of background would determine standards of rigor (Arsenius was allowed a pillow because of his pampered upbringing). The great teachers modeled an asceticism tempered by spiritual freedom. Little trace of esoteric mysticism exists in desert literature. The spirituality was shaped by biblical texts that the monks memorized, prayed throughout the day, and sought to imitate in behavior. Psalmody was chanted at certain hours of day and night, and other biblical texts were recited during work, while traveling, or when doing routine chores. These customs created an atmosphere in which the Bible became the principal frame of reference for everything they did.

Such freedom was possible because of the relationship of spiritual guidance that made monks accountable to a discerning elder. Through regular consultations the monks shared their preoccupations and struggles, identifying blocks to inner freedom ("self-will") that could be surrendered through faithful dedication to the monastic way of life ("obedience"). The sayings suggest that the psychological insight of the abbas was astonishing, the fruit of a high degree of self-knowledge and an ability to listen attentively to others. Celibacy, physical disciplines, and separation from family and normal society were undertaken as a way to create inner room for spiritual transformation. The repentance that had originally motivated a move to the desert continued in daily recommitment to the monastic life, following Antony's dictum that a monk must make a new beginning each day while being aware that death could come at any moment.

The result, the elders insisted, was love for God and for other people. This love was manifested in tenderness between elder and disciple and in hospitality. Hospitality was an expected and frequent part of their life. Notwithstanding the emphasis on solitude, the desert monks were highly social people who visited one another for the sake of spiritual consultation and encouragement. All the stories and sayings we possess derive from these encounters. The degree of interaction and communal activity varied from circle to circle, although the nonclerical nature of monasticism in the early period required gathering with other groups of monks for the Eucharist, which, according to Egyptian custom, was celebrated on Saturdays and Sundays. The social atmosphere of desert spirituality was filled with the admonition "do not judge another." A danger in a highly disciplined life lay in mistaking means for ends and in condemning those who fell short. The most moving of the stories concern astonishing acts of compassion in which a sympathetic elder turned back the priggish rush to judgment by those unable to forgive.

The golden age of Nitria and Scetis lasted less than a century. Those first decades produced the monks and sayings that still occupy a central place in monastic spirituality. Theological, ideological, and ecclesiastical rifts eventually divided the monks like everyone else. Nitria-Kellia and to a lesser extent Scetis were split at the end of the fourth century by a controversy over teachings associated with Origen (c. 185–254) that led to the departure of some of the most famous monks for Palestine and Constantinople. Like the Egyptian Church as a whole, the monks were divided after the Council of Chalcedon (451) into opposing factions. Meanwhile marauding raiders devastated Scetis three times in the first half of the fifth century. During the Islamic period (after 640), the process of attrition that affected the entire Christian East eroded the monasteries as well. Perhaps already in the ninth century, Nitria-Kellia had been abandoned, and the population of Scetis, gathered into a few monasteries, dwindled slowly in the following centuries to a handful. In the second half of the 20th century, an unexpected explosion of recruits to the four surviving monasteries made them centers of theological and cultural activity for the Coptic minority of Egypt.

The legacy of the desert tradition was not only local. Through its own literature, the accounts of outsiders who visited, and the monastic forms that it inspired, the life of the Desert Fathers provided the grounding for all later Christian monasticism. Even cenobitic monks have looked to Antony and his heirs for examples of total dedication to God and humble service of others. In the West, through Latin translation of Greek texts and the transmission of Eastern monastic tradition through bicultural writers such as John Cassian, the Desert Fathers have played a major role in shaping the very understanding of what it means to follow the monastic path. Saint Benedict knew of the tradition and drew from it for his own Rule; Irish monasticism was deeply influenced by stories from Egypt, and successive monastic reforms have revived basic elements of the life described in those early sources. Even today the sayings and stories from fourth- to fifth-century Egypt are the most popular of all Christian monastic literature.

COLUMBA STEWART, O.S.B.

*See also* Antony, St.; Asceticism: Christian Perspectives; Benedict of Nursia, St.; Cassian, John; Desert Mothers; Egypt; Evagrius Ponticus; Hagiography: Eastern Christian; Hermits: Eastern Christian; Hospitality, Christian; Mount Sinai, Egypt; Origins; Pilgrimages, Christian: Near East; Recluses, Western Christian; Self-Mutilation, Christian; Transvestite Saints

## Further Reading

Burton-Christie, Douglas, *The Word in the Desert*, New York: Oxford University Press, 1993

Chitty, Derwas, *The Desert a City*, Oxford: Blackwell, and Crestwood, New York: St. Vladimir's Seminary Press, 1966

Evelyn-White, H.G., *The Monasteries of the Wadi'n Natrun*, New York: Arno Press, 1973

Gould, Graham, *The Desert Fathers on Monastic Community*, Oxford and New York: Oxford University Press, 1993

Guillaumont, Antoine, et al., "Kellia," in *Coptic Encyclopedia*, volume 5, New York: Macmillan, and Toronto: Collier Macmillan Canada, 1991

*Historia monachorum in Aegypto* (HM), translated by Norman Russell, in *The Lives of the Desert Fathers*, Oxford: Mowbray, and Kalamazoo, Michigan: Cistercian Publications, 1980

Palladius, *Historia lausiaca* (HL), translated by R.T. Meyer, in *Palladius: The Lausiac History*, Westminster, Maryland: Newman Press, 1965

Regnault, Lucien, et al., *Les sentences des Pères du désert*, 5 vols., Solesmes: Abbaye Saint-Pierre, 1966–1985

Ward, Benedicta, *Sayings of the Desert Fathers: The Alphabetical Collection*, London: Mowbray, and Kalamazoo, Michigan: Cistercian Publications, 1975

# Desert Mothers

The Desert Mothers were Christian women ascetics who lived in monastic communities or, more rarely, as solitaries during the fourth and fifth centuries A.D., principally in the deserts of Egypt, Palestine, and Syria. Some few women who practiced asceticism in places other than the desert and exerted a formative influence on women's involvement in the ascetic-monastic movement during this period may also be considered under this designation.

The extant sources for the lives and teachings of the Desert Mothers are slight in comparison to those available for their male counterparts. No sources are directly attributable to the women themselves or their female contemporaries. In the case of both male and female ascetics in these centuries, little reliable demographic information exists. What can be known about the Desert Mothers derives mainly from four sources: the "sayings of the Desert Mothers" found among the various collections of the *Apophthegmata patrum/Verba seniorum* (Sayings of the Fathers or Elders), chapters about women ascetics in the *Lausiac History* of Palladius (c. 364–420/30), vitae of ascetic women from this period, and stories and vitae of courtesans or harlots who became exemplars of repentance and desert asceticism.

## Sayings of the Desert Mothers

The Alphabetical Collection of the *Apophthegmata patrum* contains 47 sayings attributed to three ammas (mothers): Theodora, Syncletica, and Sarah. The disparity with the 986 sayings of 120 abbas (fathers) is only partially explained by the supposition that men greatly outnumbered women in the practice of desert asceticism. The sayings have been filtered through the editorial eye and ear of the (presumably) male redactor. The collection likely attained its current form toward the end of the sixth century, with some sayings dating back to the mid–fourth century.

Ten sayings are attributed to Theodora, the amma of a community of women near Alexandria. A number of them report theological conversations with abbas (the "old men") and monks as well as with the archbishop of Alexandria. Several of Syncletica's 27 sayings suggest that she was addressing a community of women ascetics. Many show a surprising richness of images and analogies and perhaps experience: they range from seafaring examples of wind and sea and boats to homely tasks such as washing clothes. In contrast Sarah's nine sayings reveal a solitary who lived by a river for 60 years – without looking at it. Although the monks and abbas acknowledged her as an anchorite, she was sharply challenged by some of the old men; her replies were equally pointed.

## The Lausiac History

Written in 419 or 420, the *Lausiac History* presents biographical sketches of ascetic men and women (mostly from the Egyptian desert) known to Palladius or whose stories were recounted to him by contemporaries; it comments on several monastic communities as well. Among the 12 women to whom he devotes chapters or parts of chapters, Melania the Elder and Melania the Younger are perhaps the best known; Olympias is also significant. Paula and her daughter Eustochium are among the aristocratic virgins and widows enumerated in one chapter. Palladius also records stories of several nameless women, exemplars of ascetic virtue or of the fall from grace, and a tale of conflict in one women's monastery.

## Vitae of Ascetic Women

The vitae of holy women provide further detail and some embroidery about desert asceticism in this period. Jerome's *Letter* 108 to Eustochium (370–c. 419) is a memorial of her mother, Paula (347–404), who was his disciple, patron, and cofounder in 386 of the double monastery in Bethlehem, where they pursued the study of the Scriptures along with a life of ascetic renunciation; she was also an avid pilgrim to the holy places of Palestine and Egypt and to the holy men of the desert. Although no vita of Melania the Elder (c. 345–410) exists, she is the subject of three chapters in the *Lausiac History* and is mentioned in numerous contemporary texts. Introduced to asceticism by Jerome (c. 345–420), she became the patron and colleague of the scholar Rufinus (c. 345–411), journeyed through Egypt and Palestine, and in the 370s founded a monastery on the Mount of Olives in Jerusalem. There is a vita of her granddaughter, Melania the Younger (c. 383–438/39), written by the monk Gerontius. The younger Melania embraced the ascetic life and persuaded her husband to do likewise; they dispensed their considerable fortune in works of charity and patronage throughout the empire and especially in and around Jerusalem.

Saint Macrina (c. 327–380), sister of Gregory of Nyssa (c. 330–c. 395) and Basil the Great (c. 330–379), was not, strictly speaking a Desert Mother, as the women's monastery that she founded with her mother and female servants was on the family's estate in rural Cappadocia. However, Gregory's *Life of Macrina* was a foundational text of female monasticism in the East and requires mention here. Olympias (c. 360/70– after 404), deaconess of Constantinople, founder of a women's monastery there, and friend and ally of John Chrysostom (c. 347–407), also belongs to urban asceticism. Her influence as a patron of bishops, clergy, and monks and nuns was extensive; her reputation for charity and chastity was well known. The anonymously authored *Life of Olympias* extended her fame; she is noted in other contemporary texts, and a seventh-century narration exists of the transfer of her relics, written by the nun Sergia.

The *Life of St. Syncletica* by pseudo-Athanasius is less a life than a collection of teachings attributed to her. Whether this Syncletica is an actual historical woman is uncertain; it is even less likely that she is to be identified with the Syncletica of the sayings collections. Brief vitae of four Syrian women ascetics found in the *Lives of the Eastern Saints* by John of Ephesus (c. 507–586) also should be noted: Mary and Euphemia lived primarily in cities and frequented the holy places of Jerusalem regularly, as did Susan, who later entered a monastery near Gaza; only Anastasia belongs to the desert (of mid-sixth-century Scete), but her story is of questionable historical value.

## Stories of Desert Harlots

More exemplary than biographical, stories of repentant courtesans or harlots reveal the ways in which their male authors/redactors perceived women ascetics. The women in these stories – Pelagia the Harlot, Maria the Niece of Abraham, Mary of Egypt, and Thaïs – represent both the fallen state of sexual sin and the grace of repentance. With the exception of Maria, they lived in isolation after their conversions: Thaïs was immured in a cell for three years, Mary was a solitary in the Jordanian desert for 47 years, and Pelagia disguised herself as a monk and remained undiscovered until her death.

FRANCINE CARDMAN

*See also* Desert Fathers; Egypt; Hermits: Eastern Christian; Origins: Eastern Christian; Israel/Palestine; Syria; Transvestite Saints; Women's Monasteries: Eastern Christian

## Further Reading

Brock, Sebastian, and Susan Ashbrook Harvey, editors, *Holy Women of the Syrian Orient* (The Transformation of the Classical Heritage, 13), Berkeley: University of California Press, 1987; updated edition, 1998

Cameron, Averil, "Desert Mothers: Women Ascetics in Early Christian Egypt," in *Women as Teachers and Disciples in Traditional and New Religions* (Studies in Women and

Admont Abbey (Benedictine), Styria, rebuilt 18th century.
Photo courtesy of the Austrian National Tourist Office

**St. Florian Abbey (Augustinian Canons), Upper Austria, rebuilt 18th century.**
Photo courtesy of the Austrian National Tourist Office

**Klosterneuburg Abbey (Augustinian Canons), 11th century, rebuilt early 18th century.**
Photo courtesy of the Austrian National Tourist Office

Melk Abbey (Benedictine), Lower Austria, rebuilt 18th century.
Photo courtesy of the Austrian National Tourist Office

Library, Admont Abbey (Benedictine), Styria, 18th century.
Photo courtesy of the Austrian National Tourist Office

Library, Melk Abbey (Benedictine), Lower Austria, early 18th century.
Photo courtesy of the Austrian National Tourist Office

Library, Altenburg Abbey (Benedictine), Lower Austria, 18th century.
Photo courtesy of the Austrian National Tourist Office

Library, Zwettl Abbey (Cistercian), Lower Austria, 18th century.
Photo courtesy of the Austrian National Tourist Office

Library, Schlägl Abbey (Premonstratensian), Upper Austria, 18th century.
Photo courtesy of the Austrian National Tourist Office

Abbey, Lilienfeld, Austria, 13th century.
Photo courtesy of Chris Schabel

Fountains Abbey, North Yorkshire, England, c. 1170. Seats in the form of stairs line the left wall.
Photo courtesy of Chris Schabel

Abbey, Fossanova, near Priverno, Lazio, Italy, late 12th century.
Photo courtesy of Chris Schabel

Cistercian abbey, Fossanova, near Priverno, Lazio, Italy, late
12th century.
Photo courtesy of Chris Schabel

Cistercian abbey, Maulbronn, Baden-Württemberg, Germany,
13th century.
Photo courtesy of Chris Schabel

Benedictine abbey, since 1541 a cathedral, Gloucester, England,
c. 1370.
Photo courtesy of Chris Schabel

SS. Giovanni e Paolo, Venice, Italy, 1260–1385.
Photo courtesy of Chris Schabel

Santa Maria Novella, Florence, Italy, 1278–1350, with the top register added by Alberti, 1456–1470.
Photo courtesy of Chris Schabel

Interior, Santa Maria Novella, Florence, Italy, 1278–1350.
Photo courtesy of Chris Schabel

Interior, Santa Maria sopra Minerva, Rome, c. 1280, renovated in the 15th century.
Photo courtesy of Chris Schabel

Gateway and tower, Evesham Abbey (Benedictine), Evesham, Worcestershire, early 16th century.
Photo courtesy of Chris Schabel

Abbey church, Buildwas Abbey (Cistercian), Shropshire, 12th century.
Photo courtesy of Chris Schabel

Abbey church, Furness Abbey (Cistercian), Lancashire, 12th century.
Photo courtesy of Chris Schabel

Facade, San Xavier del Bac, southern Arizona, 1797. The earlier Jesuit foundation became Franciscan during the 18th century.
Photo courtesy of Chris Schabel

San Jose de Tumacacori, southern Arizona, 1697. Built by Jesuits, transferred to Franciscans in the 18th century.
Photo courtesy of Chris Schabel

Facade, San Jose y San Miguel de Aguayo Convent, San Antonio, Texas, 1720.
Photo courtesy of Chris Schabel

Two-storied cloister, Franciscan convent, Valladolid, Yucatan, Mexico, mid–16th century.
Photo courtesy of Chris Schabel

Franciscan convent, Izamal, Yucatan, Mexico, mid–16th century.
Photo courtesy of Chris Schabel

Two-storied cloister, Franciscan convent, Cusco, Peru, mid–16th century. Said to be the oldest colonial structure in the city.
Photo courtesy of Chris Schabel

View of the south garden from the west side of the meditation hall, Daisen-in, Daitokuji, Kyoto, c. early 16th century, Muromachi period.
Photo courtesy of Marylin M. Rhie

Small side garden, Ryūkō-in, Daitokuji, Kyoto.
Photo courtesy of Marylin M. Rhie

Detail of the garden designed by Sesshū Tōyō (1420–1506), Jōeji temple, Yamaguchi City, early 16th century, Muromachi period.
Photo courtesy of Marylin M. Rhie

Katbui is an image of Maitreya carved out of the mountainside in South Kyŏngsang province.
Photo courtesy of John Powers

Part of a rook at Unhae-sa Monastery in North Kyŏngsang province.
Photo courtesy of John Powers

A dragon figure at Hansan-sa Monastery, South Kyŏngsang province.
Photo courtesy of John Powers

Doorway at Sojae-sa Monastery in South Kyŏngsang province.
Photo courtesy of John Powers

The main cliff (east side), Maiji Shan (Corn-rick Mountain), Tianshui, Gansu province. Buddhist caves date from the early 5th–15th centuries.
Photo courtesy of Marylin M. Rhie

Entrance to the Buddhist caves of the front Mountain area, Wenshu-shan (Mountain of Mañjuśrī Bodhisattva), Jiuquan, Gansu province. Buddhist caves date from the early fifth century and later.
Photo courtesy of Marylin M. Rhie

Caves and temple buildings at the Mogaoku Grottoes, Dunhuang, Gansu province. Founded in A.D. 366 and active in the opening of caves until the Yuan dynasty. Present wooden temple facade dates from the Ming dynasty (1368–1644).
Photo courtesy of Marylin M. Rhie

Religion, volume 32), edited by Elizabeth Puttick and Peter B. Clarke, Lewiston, New York: Mellen Press, 1993

Clark, Elizabeth A., translator, "The Life of Olympias," in her *Jerome, Chrysostom, and Friends: Essays and Translations* (Studies in Women and Religion, volume 2), New York: Mellen Press, 1979; 2nd edition, 1982

Clark, Elizabeth A., translator, "Sergia's Narration Concerning St. Olympias," in her *Jerome, Chrysostom, and Friends: Essays and Translations* (Studies in Women and Religion, volume 2), New York: Mellen Press, 1979; 2nd edition, 1982

Clark, Elizabeth A., *The Life of Melania, the Younger: Introduction, Translation, and Commentary* (Studies in Women and Religion, volume 14), New York: Mellen Press, 1984

Elm, Susanna, *Virgins of God: The Making of Asceticism in Late Antiquity* (Oxford Classical Monographs), Oxford and New York: Oxford University Press, 1994

*Palladius: The Lausiac History* (Ancient Christian Writers, number 34), translated and annotated by Robert T. Meyer, New York: Newman Press, 1964

Petersen, Joan M., translator, "Letters of Saint Jerome to Ascetic Women in the Roman Empire," in *Handmaids of the Lord: Contemporary Descriptions of Feminine Asceticism in the First Six Christian Centuries* (Cistercian Studies Series, number 143), Kalamazoo, Michigan: Cistercian Publications, 1996

Pseudo-Athanasius, "The Life and Activity of the Holy and Blessed Teacher Syncletica," translated by Elizabeth A. Castelli, in *Ascetic Behavior in Greco-Roman Antiquity: A Sourcebook* (Studies in Antiquity and Christianity), edited by Vincent L. Wimbush, Minneapolis, Minnesota: Fortress Press, 1990

Ward, Benedicta, *The Sayings of the Desert Fathers: The Alphabetical Collection* (Cistercian Studies Series, number 59), London: Mowbray, and Kalamazoo, Michigan: Cistercian Publications, 1975; revised edition, London: Mowbray, 1981; Kalamazoo, Michigan: Cistercian Publications, 1984

Ward, Benedicta, *Harlots of the Desert: A Study of Repentance in Early Monastic Sources* (Cistercian Studies Series, number 106), Kalamazoo, Michigan: Cistercian Publications, and Oxford: Mowbray, 1987

# Devotions, Western Christian

This article describes forms of pious meditations and devotional exercises that developed in Roman Catholic monasticism. The central devotion exercised in the old Benedictine monasteries was the *ruminatio*, that is, the half-loud reading and repeating of and reflecting on biblical texts, especially the Psalms (*meditatio* in medieval Latin included the study of the Bible, private praying, and contemplation). *Ruminatio* was understood, according to Cassian (*Institutes* 2, 15, 1), as a task for both the mouth and the heart of the religious. Also during the early Middle Ages, the praying of the canonical hours, which structures the life in any

convent, became a standard devotion of monks and nuns until today.

With the beginning of the Central Middle Ages, there emerged a completely new concentration of monastic meditation on the person and life of Jesus the man. Several meditations of Anselm of Canterbury (c. 1033–1109), written around 1100, are among the first testimonies of a new experience of Jesus "our brother." Intensive devotion to His Passion seems to be still some years earlier, as some writings of Peter Damian (1007–1072) show. A remarkable "fragmentation" of Christ's body took place, when the reverence paid to the Five Wounds was developed, at first it seems, by Bernard of Clairvaux (1090–1153), but in a much more haptic way during the late Middle Ages and especially the Counter-Reformation. Also the devotion to the Heart of the Savior and that of Mary had its roots in a convent, Helfta in Saxony, where at the end of the 13th century two mystics evolved this veneration, namely, Gertrud the Great (1256–c. 1302) and Mechthild (c. 1207–1282) of Hackeborn. Nuptial mysticism was at the core of Bernard's spirituality. On the basis of the *Song of Songs*, it became a devotion practiced with affective prayers and meditation for many later monks and, even more, for nuns, culminating not seldom in visionary experiences and the *unio mystica*. Although not without forerunners, especially among the Cistercians, the devotion to the sorrows and the joys of the Virgin, expressed by means of praying the rosary, was a comparatively late invention. It was propagated most successfully by the Dominican inquisitor Jakob Sprenger, better known as the coauthor of the *Hammer of Witches*, who in 1475 founded a brotherhood of the rosary in Cologne, from whence this devotion spread to the entire Catholic world.

Another group of monastic devotions pertains to asceticism. In the early Middle Ages, the Irish monks were famous for the immersions in cold water that they used to discipline their bodies. Self-flagellation, called *disciplina* because of its origin in monastic penitence, did not become popular in the monasteries before the 11th century, when Peter Damian recommended this devotion warmly in his treatise *De laude flagellorum* (In Praise of the Lashes). During the late Middle Ages and the early modern period through the beginning of the 20th century, self-flagellation was common in the more severe orders, as were fasting and silence.

It is important to note that at first many of these devotions were practiced exclusively in monasteries but later were taken over by pious laypeople. From the 13th to the 16th century, they prayed the hours, for which splendidly illuminated books of hours were created. Devotion to the Passion became common for the laypeople of the late Middle Ages. Many vernacular prayers were written, and many panels with the man of sorrows were painted for them. The Oratorian Jean Eudes (1601–1680) inaugurated the official cult of the Sacred Heart in 1670, which was propagated far and wide by Margaret Mary Alacoque (1647–1690) of the Order of the Visitation. It was also during the late Middle Ages that semireligious and laypeople followed the monks and nuns in their more severe ascetic practices, as we

Wooden stalls, Chapel of St. Bonaventure, Greggio (Lazio), Italy, 1220s. St. Francis visited this site in 1224 and inaugurated the Christmas creche.
Photo courtesy of Mary Schaefer

know from many a saint's lay life (e.g., Dorothy of Montau). Often lay brotherhoods and third orders affiliated to the religious orders functioned as intermediaries between the monastic world and the secular one.

PETER DINZELBACHER

*See also* Anselm, St.; Bernard of Clairaux, St.; Damian, Peter, St.; Gender Studies: Christian Perspectives; Holy Men/Holy Women: Christian Perspectives; Lectio Divina; Martyrs: Western Christian; Meditation: Christian Perspectives; Monastics and the World, Medieval; Mystics, German Monastic: Female; Recluses, Western Christian; Relics, Christian Monastic; Transvestite Saints; Visitandines

**Further Reading**

Berlière, Ursmer, *La dévotion au Sacré-Coeur dans l'Ordre de S. Benoit* (Collection "Pax," volume 10), Paris: Desclée de Brouwer, 1923

Dinzelbacher, Peter, *Christliche Mystik im Abendland: Ihre Geschichte von den Anfängen bis zum Ende des Mittelalters*, Paderborn: Schöningh, 1994

Dinzelbacher, Peter, editor, *Handbuch der Religionsgeschichte Deutschlands*, 6 vols., Paderborn: Schöningh, 2000–

Gougaud, Louis, *Devotional and Ascetic Practices in the Middle Ages*, London: Burns Oates and Washbourne, 1927

Leclercq, Jean, *The Love of Learning and the Desire for God: A Study of Monastic Culture*, New York: Fordham University Press, 1961; 2nd edition, London: SPCK, 1978; 3rd edition, New York: Fordham University Press, 1982

Leidenmüller, S., "Die Herz-Jesu-Verehrung bei Albert dem Grossen und im Dominikanerorden," *Jahrbuch für salesianische Studien* 17 (1981)

Richstätter, Carl, *Christusfrömmigkeit in ihrer historischen Entfaltung: ein quellenmässiger Beitrag zur Geschichte des Gebetes und des mystischen Innenlebens der Kirche*, Cologne: Bächem, 1949

Richstätter, Karl, *Die Herz-Jesu-Verehrung des deutschen Mittelalters: nach gedruckten und ungedruckten Quellen*, Paderborn: Bonifacius-Druckerei, 1919; 2nd edition, Regensburg: Kösel and Pustet, 1924

Winston-Allen, Anne, *Stories of the Rose: The Making of the Rosary in the Middle Ages*, University Park: Pennsylvania State University Press, 1997

# Dhamma. *See* Dharma

# Dharamsala, India (Tibetan)

Dharamsala, India, is home to the administration of the Tibetan government in exile and to several thousand of the over 100,000 Tibetan refugees in India. The headquarters of the Kagra district in Himachel Pradesh, it was originally an English hill station in the foothills of the Dhauladhar Range of the Himalayan Mountains. Dharamsala proper is a small commercial hub in the valley, at 4,100 feet, whereas Macleod Ganj, at 5,900 feet, has become the Tibetan area. It is the center of Tibetan culture in India and one of 54 agricultural and agro-industrial-based refugee communities for Tibetan immigrants. Macleod Ganj was founded by the English in 1856 and named after Sir Donald Macleod, who became lieutenant governor.

Tenzin Gyatso (1935– ), the 14th Dalai Lama of Tibet, and his cabinet administer the affairs of Tibet's government in exile from his home and headquarters in Dharamsala. The Dalai Lama fled Chinese-occupied Tibet in 1959 seeking asylum in India under increasing Chinese crackdowns on protest and threats to his own life. The government took up residence in Dharamsala in 1960 after the government of India offered the small hill station to the Tibetan refugees. Shortly thereafter a democratic constitution was drawn up providing for free elections, a bill of rights, a representative government, an independent judiciary, and, at the Dalai Lama's own request, diminished political power for himself. The constitution remains in draft form in the hope that someday it will be implemented in Tibet. The government of Tibet in exile, although not officially recognized by India, operates as a functioning government and is recognized by most Tibetans. It consists of a cabinet (the *Kashag*) of senior officials, a body of elected representatives from each region of Tibet, a national working committee, administrative offices, a council on religious and cultural affairs, a home and rehabilitation office, a council for Tibetan education, and a number of other offices and committees.

Being the political hub of Tibet in exile, Dharamsala is a center of protest against Chinese occupation of Tibet and of campaigns for Tibetan autonomy and human rights. A number of Tibetan groups make Dharamsala the center of their work on human rights and Tibetan freedom. For example, the Tibetan Women's Association campaigns for women's rights in Tibet. The government in exile itself publishes regular reports on events and activities among Tibetans in Tibet, often alleging Chinese abuses of power directed toward Tibetans. Many Tibetans still travel to Dharamsala from Tibet, crossing the Himalayas to escape Chinese rule.

Because of its efforts to preserve Tibetan culture and religion, as well as being the Dalai Lama's home, Dharamsala has been called "Little Lhasa," after the ancient Tibetan capital. Because of these preservation efforts, it is a major destination and point of interest not only for Tibetans themselves but also for scholars of Tibetan culture and religion. The Library of Tibetan Works and Archives contains the largest collection of Tibetan literature in the world as well as a substantial selection of literature in English on Buddhism and Tibetan culture. Thus, it is an important international resource for scholars. The library publishes books in Tibetan and English and houses a collection of artifacts and works of art brought from Tibet to India. Six monasteries operate in Dharamsala, all attempting to re-create the traditions, architecture, and aesthetics of the monasteries of Tibet, most of which were destroyed during the cultural revolution. The Namgyal monastery, next to the Dalai Lama's residence, is a prominent Gelukpa center for Buddhist monastic training, drawing many Tibetan monks. The Buddhist School of Dialectics trains monks in the lively art of Tibetan Buddhist debate. A medical center and institute for the study and practice of Tibetan medicine was created in Dharamsala as well and was then joined with an astrological center. The Tibetan Children's Village, established at Dharamsala immediately after the Dalai Lama's arrival, enrolls and cares for Tibetan orphans. Dharamsala also has a number of schools for children that teach both modern, secular education and traditional Tibetan culture and religion. The Tibetan Dance and Drama Society preserves traditional dances and folk opera.

Dharamsala remains a popular destination for more casual tourists interested in Tibet and Buddhism. At the Library of Tibetan Works and Archives, they can attend the many lectures given to the public by Tibetan monks and take beginning courses in meditation. Westerners also study meditation at a number of retreat centers, such as the Tushita Retreat Center and a Vipassana center that hosts residential retreats. The Dalai Lama gives public talks in March, drawing crowds to Dharamsala from around the world. When he is not traveling, he regularly uses his residence to meet with refugees who have recently arrived from Tibet as well as scholars, seekers, and tourists. Indeed the Dalai Lama himself is one of the main attractions for Tibetans, Indians, and westerners in Dharamsala.

DAVID L. MCMAHAN

*See also* Buddhist Schools/Traditions: Tibet; Critiques of Buddhist Monasticism: Indo-Tibetan; Dalai Lama (Tenzin Gyatso); Lhasa, Tibet; Peace Movements, Buddhist; Tibet; Tibetan Lineages

## Further Reading

*The Constitution of Tibet*, New Delhi: Bureau of H.H. the Dalai Lama, 1963
Dalai Lama XIV, *Freedom in Exile: The Autobiography of the Dalai Lama*, New York: HarperCollins, 1990; as *Freedom in Exile: The Autobiography of His Holiness the Dalai Lama of Tibet*, London: Hodder and Stoughton, 1990
Goodman, Michael Harris, *The Last Dalai Lama: A Biography*, London: Sidgwick and Jackson, 1986; Boston: Shambhala, 1987
Nowak, Margaret, *Tibetan Refugees: Youth and the New Generation of Meaning*, New Brunswick, New Jersey: Rutgers University Press, 1984
Powers, John, *Introduction to Tibetan Buddhism*, Ithaca, New York: Snow Lion, 1995
*Tibetans in Exile, 1959–1969*, Bureau of H.H. the Dalai Lama, Dharamsala, India, 1969

# Dharma

No term is more important in Buddhism than the word *dharma*. As with most fundamental religious terms, it is difficult to give a concise, accurate paraphrase of this term. The eminent Buddhalogist Edward Conze lists seven major meanings for it. This brief discussion will focus on two meanings.

First, *dharma* is used most often in its singular form in the ordinary Buddhist discourse of both monastics and laypeople. Used in that way the term has many connotations and can be translated in a number of different ways, all of them accurate. All these meanings circle around the dharma as "truth." Fundamentally *dharma* designates all the religious, metaphysical, spiritual, and moral teachings of Buddhism, which are held to be universal truths and not just Buddhist ideas. Because it means "everything that is true," dharma is vast. It is also no great surprise that Buddhists disagree about what exactly that truth is.

Conceived as truth, *dharma* frequently refers to the second of the "Three Refuges" or "Three Jewels" in the formula the Buddha, the dharma, and the *saṅgha*. The ancient formula "I go for refuge to the Buddha; I go for refuge to the dharma; I go for refuge to the *saṅgha*," repeated three times in the proper ritual context, changes one into a Buddhist, a follower of the dharma. In ceremonies for taking refuge vows, it is often explained that the Buddha is one's model, the dharma is the teachings and practices of the Buddhist path, and the *saṅgha* is the community of those who walk this path. Thus, the dharma, in a certain sense, includes the other two refuges because Buddhist teachings incorporate many teachings about the Buddha and the *saṅgha*. In this sense dharma is a refuge because it provides a sure method for finding freedom from the suffering of saṃsāra (cyclic existence).

Westerners might tend to regard *dharma* as a term equivalent to *religion*, but for that Buddhists usually prefer the term *Buddhadharma*. If a single-word English translation is required, many Buddhists prefer the translation *law* over the term *religion*. The term *law*, in the sense of Cosmic Law (i.e., the way things work independent of human constructions), is chosen because of its impersonality and its freedom from human artifice or divine revelation. Dharma is always there, like the laws of nature. From time to time it is discovered by extraordinary humans – the Buddhas of the three eras – and then taught to humans from generation to generation, for as long as the pure dharma is remembered and practiced. Everything taught in the dharma, no matter how nonempirical it might seem to non-Buddhists, is regarded as something that advanced practitioners would experience as "natural," not "supernatural."

A second basic meaning of the term *dharma* is the entire corpus of the Buddha's teachings. Considerable disagreement exists among the various branches of Buddhism as to exactly what the Buddha's teachings include. Although all schools of Buddhism ascribe their dharma to the Buddha, throughout the historical development of Buddhadharma many new elements entered Buddhist teachings, and the meaning of the term *Buddha* itself changed. Nevertheless all schools accept certain teachings attributed to the historical Buddha – the four Noble Truths, the Eight-

fold Path, and Co-dependent Co-arising – as genuine dharma. Theravāda Buddhists regard all other Buddhist teachings as later fabrications introduced by backsliding students. However, schools of Buddhism that developed later espouse a sacred history which claims that the historical Buddha, recognizing the limitations of his current students, taught Mahāyāna teachings of emptiness (*śūnyatā*) secretly to a few especially astute students and made arrangements for these teachings to be hidden until Buddhists in general were more ready to understand them. Schools that developed still later attribute their dharma to visions in which the Buddha gives an especially highly developed practitioner even more advanced teachings. This kind of sacred history is common to all later schools of Buddhism. Although these "histories" might seem to outsiders or to adherents of older forms of Buddhism to be fabrications, advocates of the newer schools of Buddhism argue that their dharma embodies the full unfolding of the implications of the basic dharma originally taught by the Buddha. The Buddha's skillful means in teaching enabled him to gear particular teachings to his audience, but the entire dharma is nevertheless contained in them. The metaphor of a lotus opening is frequently used to explain this process. The early teachings of the Buddha resemble a closed lotus; all its petals are already there, albeit hidden. Later developments simply represent the opening of the lotus and do not introduce some new, fabricated dharma.

The term *dharma* is also used in the plural in a much more technical sense that would not be part of the everyday discourse of most ordinary Buddhists. Its usage as a technical philosophical term – *dharmas* – would be limited in most cases to scholar-monks. However, the central meaning of *dharma* as "what is true" still adheres to this more technical use of the term. The dharmas (the term is always used in the plural in this context) are the real existents as opposed to the illusory appearances. According to Buddhist teachings ordinary people grow up conditioned to believe that the self and other phenomena exist as real entities, but analysis shows that they do not. Phenomena are made up of parts, are ever changing, and exist only as a result of causes and conditions. Thus, self and phenomena have no reality of their own and enjoy no independent existence apart from their causes and constituents. Although self and phenomena are mere illusory appearances, we cling to them as real existents, thus causing our own misery. By analyzing, that is, by looking beneath appearance, we discover the dharmas, the real existents or elements (somewhat as in atomic theory) that constitute the self and phenomena. Such analysis is the first step to understanding reality and gaining freedom.

According to the dominant school of Buddhist philosophy that uses this type of analysis, 75 dharmas account for everything one experiences. They can be classified in various ways to show how we mistake a bundle of dharmas for a solid entity, a real self or a real phenomenon. According to earlier schools of Buddhist philosophy, these dharmas themselves truly exist. Even that assertion was disputed by Mahāyāna philosophers, who claimed that even the dharmas lack true existence but rather exist only conventionally at the level of relative truth. Fundamentally, however, according to Mahāyāna philosophy, an all-pervading emptiness (*śūnyatā*) characterizes everything, including even those minute atoms of experience – the dharmas. This statement belongs to the dharma, in the first sense of the term *dharma*, according to Mahāyāna Buddhism.

RITA M. GROSS

*See also* Buddhist Schools/Traditions: South Asia; Buddhist Schools/Traditions: Tibet; Discourses (Sūtras): Mahāyāna; Discourses (Suttas): Theravāda; Mahāyāna; Master and Pupil: Buddhist Perspectives; Regulations: Buddhist Perspectives

**Further Reading**

Conze, Edward, *Buddhist Thought in India: Three Phases of Buddhist Philosophy*, London: Allen and Unwin, 1962; Ann Arbor: University of Michigan Press, 1967

Kalu, Rinpoche, *The Dharma That Illuminates All Beings Impartially Like the Light of the Sun and the Moon*, Albany: State University of New York Press, 1986

Rahula, Walpola, *What the Buddha Taught*, Bedford: Gordon Fraser Gallery, 1967; New York: Grove Press, 1974

Schcherbatskoi, F.I., *The Central Conception of Buddhism and the Meaning of the Word "Dharma,"* Delhi: Motilal Barnarsidass, 1970

Skorupski, Taduesz, "Buddhist Dharma and Dharmas," in *The Encyclopedia of Religion*, volume 4, edited by Mircea Eliade, et al., New York: Macmillian, 1987

# Dharmapāla, Anagārika 1864–1933

Sri Lankan Buddhist monk, reformer, and missionary

An influential advocate and exemplar of the 19th-century Buddhist revival in Sri Lanka, prodigious traveler, missionary and campaigner, and model of what has come to be known as "Protestant Buddhism," Dharmapāla exercised considerable influence on Buddhist monasticism, especially in Sri Lanka. Five dimensions of his career are noteworthy: (1) his self-styled designation – *anagārika*, (2) the campaign to restore and redeem the ancient Buddhist sites of India, (3) his reformist call to the laity, (4) support of women renunciants, and (5) his emphasis on Sinhala Buddhist nationhood.

Don David Hewavitarana, as he then was known, grew up in the English-speaking middle class of Colombo, Sri Lanka. At 20 years, influenced both by Sinhala revivalists such as the Venerable Mohoṭṭivatte Guṇānanda and theosophists from the West (most notably Henry Steel Olcott and Madame Blavatsky), he opted for a celibate but socially involved lifestyle by taking the name *Anagārika* (one who is not a householder). Originally a designation for monks, Dharmapāla made it a liminal state between laity and monasticism, combining renunciation of family ties with activism. Although the term has never been widely used, the ideal it represents remains widespread.

In 1891 Dharmapāla visited Bodh Gayā and Sārnāth in northern India. Shocked at their neglected and desecrated state, he vowed to restore those holy sites to Buddhism. Consequently he founded the Mahabodhi Society in Sri Lanka in May 1891 and started the *Mahabodhi Journal* in 1892. So began a lengthy struggle to wrest Bodh Gayā from its Hindu owners and to establish resident monastic groups at both sites. Support was enlisted during extensive travels in Asia and the West. Today the Mahabodhi Society is a worldwide network responsible for the work of overseas Sinhala Buddhist monasteries.

The Buddhism that Dharmapāla advocated for laypeople was characterized by a "this-worldly asceticism" marked by a strict code of ethics and etiquette. This required meditation and the belief that *nibbāna* was attainable in this life and also required eschewing "non-Buddhist" practices (many of them traditional). The first two encroached into areas of practice traditionally monopolized by monasticism, leading to a new lay/monastic dynamic in which the laity took greater control over their spiritual life and expected more sophisticated teaching from monastic teachers. Indirectly this shift has had a marked effect on Theravāda monasticism in Sri Lanka and worldwide.

In the United States in 1887 Dharmapāla met Countess Mirando de Souza Canavarro, a convert from Roman Catholicism. With his help she established in Sri Lanka a community for woman renunciants. Although it did not last long, the initiative contributed to the eventual reestablishment of an order of contemporary nuns in the country.

In 1906 Dharmapāla started *Sinhala Bauddhaya* (the Sinhala Buddhist), a journal that invoked language, race, and religion as factors capable of inspiring Sri Lankan Buddhists to resist Christianity, imperialism, and other non-Sinhala influences. In 1915, the year of anti-Muslim riots, the journal was banned, only to be restarted in 1922, and Dharmapāla was exiled from Sri Lanka until that year. Sri Lanka's merciless ethnic conflict in the post-1950 period has placed Dharmapāla's form of Sinhala Buddhist nationalism under judgment because it discounted religious diversity in Sri Lanka and has inspired some later nationalist movements, supported by sections of the monastic community, that have opposed agreements to devolve power to Tamil-majority areas. However, Dharmapāla's movement is best understood as a reaction to British imperial domination motivated by a passionate concern for the welfare of Buddhists and the promotion of Buddhism. Today Dharmapāla is revered as defender of Buddhism and national hero by many within the Sri Lankan monastic community.

ELIZABETH J. HARRIS

*See also* Bodh Gayā, India; Buddhism: Western; Buddhist Schools/Traditions: South Asia; Sri Lanka; Ten-Precept Mothers as Theravādin Nuns; Theravādin Monks, Modern Western

**Biography**

Don David Hewavitarana was born in Colombo, Sri Lanka, into the middle class. Collaborating with the early Theosophists, particularly Henry Steel Olcott, in 1881 he took the name Dharmapāla ("Guardian of the Truth") and headed the Buddhist section of the Theosophical Society. Ten years later he established the Mahabodhi Society in Sri Lanka and started its journal (*Mahabodhi Journal*) the next year. In 1893 he addressed the World Parliament of Religions in Chicago. He worked to restore Buddhist sites in India and Sri Lanka. In 1906 he founded the *Sinhala Bauddhaya*, which advocated resistance to foreign religions and culture. From 1915 to 1920 colonial authorities interned him in Calcutta. Following his return to Sri Lanka in 1922, he suffered ill health, but in 1925–1926 he made a final lecture tour to England and the United States.

## Major Works

*The Arya Dharma of Sakya Muni, Gautama, Buddha*, 1917
*The Life and Teachings of the Buddha*, 2nd edition, 1918
*Buddhism in Its Relationship with Hinduism*, 1928

## Further Reading

Bartholomeusz, Tessa, *Women under the Bo Tree: Buddhist Nuns in Sri Lanka*, Cambridge, New York, and Melbourne: Cambridge University Press, 1994

Bartholomeusz, Tessa, and Chandra R. De Silva, editors, *Buddhist Fundamentalism and Minority Identities in Sri Lanka*, Albany: State University of New York Press, 1998

Bond, George D., *The Buddhist Revival in Sri Lanka: Religious Tradition, Reinterpretation and Response*, Columbia: University of South Carolina Press, 1988

Gokhale, B.G., "Anagārika Dharmapāla: Toward Modernity Through Tradition in Ceylon," in *Tradition and Change in Theravāda Buddhism*, edited by Bardwell L. Smith, Leiden: Brill, 1973

Gombrich, Richard, and Gananath Obeyesekere, *Buddhism Transformed: Religious Change in Sri Lanka*, Princeton, New Jersey: Princeton University Press, 1988

Guruge, Ananda, editor, *Return to Righteousness: A Collection of Speeches, Essays, and Letters of the Anagārika Dharmapāla*, Colombo: Ministry of Education and Cultural Affairs, 1965

Obeyesekere, Gananath, "Personal Identity and Cultural Crisis: The Case of Anagārika Dharmapāla of Sri Lanka," in *The Biographical Process: Studies in the History and Psychology of Religion*, edited by Frank Reynolds and Donald Capps, The Hague: Mouton, 1976

Tambiah, Stanley Jeyaraja, *Buddhism Betrayed? Religion, Politics and Violence in Sri Lanka*, Chicago: University of Chicago Press, 1992

# Dialogue, Intermonastic: Buddhist Perspectives

A notable feature of the rich exchange between Christians and Buddhists has been the importance of the role played by contemplatives. As Gilbert Hardy (1990) points out, the dynamic force behind Buddhist-Christian dialogue has been provided largely by men and women in monastic orders or by those in active orders with an interest in contemplative practice (the Jesuit Enomiya-Lassalle immediately comes to mind). This development is per-

haps not unexpected, for Christianity and Buddhism are, among the world's major religions, the two that have always maintained the strongest monastic traditions. Especially since the initiation of programs such as the East-West Spiritual Exchange (Tōzai Reisei Koryū), in which Christian and Zen Buddhist monastics spend time in each other's monasteries, we can increasingly say, with Hardy, that "the spirit of reconciliation is supplanting long ingrained prejudices, and jealously guarded spiritual insights are now being shared with ease and simplicity."

For all of this, however, a noticeable asymmetry has remained in the Buddhist-Christian monastic dialogue so far. Although library shelves strain under the load of books by Christians writing on the benefits of Buddhist praxis and thought for the Christian spiritual life, and although countless Christians have taken up Buddhist forms of meditation as part of their life of prayer, there seems to be very little evidence of influence in the opposite direction – Buddhists appear virtually unaffected by the Christian input, at least as far as contemplative practices are concerned (the question of Christian influence on recent Buddhist social activism is an entirely different issue). To the best of my knowledge, no books exist by Buddhists promoting the techniques of Christian prayer as a possible contribution to Buddhist spirituality, nor do any reexaminations of Buddhism from a Christian perspective. Quite the contrary, Buddhist books on Christianity tend to be simply reinterpretations of the Christ figure and Christian spiritual practices from a Buddhist perspective, along the lines of "Christ as bodhisattva" and "grace as mindfulness."

It is possible to see in this asymmetry a certain cultural nationalism, and it would be hard to deny that such factors do exist. In ten years of living as a monk at a Japanese Rinzai Zen monastery, I saw no overt interest in Christianity among any of the monks I knew; several of the masters had read and admired the Gospels or such mystics as Meister Eckhart (c. 1260–1327), but that was about the extent of it. Despite overtures from the Christian side since the Second Vatican Council (1962–1965), and despite the warming personal relations between monastics on both sides, many Zen Buddhists continue to perceive Christianity as an aggressively missionary faith, with dialogue being yet another, albeit gentler, method of proselytization.

Also working against the adoption of Christian elements is the strong conservative grain in present-day Zen. The various Rinzai teaching lines have rigidified, with masters feeling duty-bound to pass on the koans, their answers, and the various accoutrements such as "capping phrases" in exactly the same way as they received them. Even advanced Zen monks from other teaching lines are required to redo their koan work from the very beginning if they start with a new master (this reexamination is generally quite rapid, as the basic thrust of the koans remains the same in the various lines). Thus, as an institution Zen monasticism has little natural inclination toward adopting new approaches from outside the tradition.

However, the most basic factor in the apparent asymmetry of the Buddhist-Christian exchange relates, I believe, to a basic difference between what Christian contemplatives have been adopting from Buddhism and what Buddhists might be expected to adopt from Christianity in return. In many ways the two traditions have much in common; although on the surface the spirituality of Christian monasticism may appear quite devotional in contrast to the radical detachment of Zen, essentially all monastic asceticism involves, as Hardy (1990) notes, "an 'emptying' of the self – *kenosis* – in order to reach the fullness of life." This is a point emphasized repeatedly in virtually every book on what has come to be called "Christian Zen." Works by Meister Eckhart and Johannes Tauler (c. 1300–1361) as well as the *Cloud of Unknowing* (14th century) are extensively quoted to show that apophatic spirituality – "the way of negation," of pure empty consciousness – has always been an essential part of the Christian mystical path.

The difference is that, whereas in Christianity the apophatic tradition – once a central part of the spiritual path – has largely died out after centuries of neglect (see Jäger, 1995, pp. 3, 126–130), in Zen Buddhism the negative path has remained the primary focus of praxis. Zen has thus retained its "methodology of emptying" – the sophisticated methods for facilitating contemplation using posture, breathing, and mental devices such as the koan – and it is primarily these that the Christian practitioners of Zen have adopted. As authors such as Hugo Enomiya-Lassalle, Thomas Hand, Elaine MacInnes, and Willigis Jäger have emphasized – and as I have often heard Zen masters themselves say – this methodology of emptying can be utilized independently of doctrinal content, making it as suitable for a Christian apophatic approach as for a Buddhist one. Thus, the use of Zen meditation techniques (as well as those of other Buddhist traditions, such as *vipassana*) has been part not so much of an infusion of Buddhist thought into Christianity as of a return to the apophatic origins of Christian contemplative prayer. The influence from Buddhism to Christianity, in other words, has been largely on the level not of doctrine but of technique; the elements of Buddhist thought that have accompanied this infusion of technique have, if anything, simply supported the wisdom of original Christian apophatic spirituality.

The question then arises: what elements of Christian spirituality might a Zen Buddhist want to adopt (again the question here involves contemplation, not social action)? If writers such as Enomiya-Lassalle and Jäger are correct that the spiritual consciousness emerging in the present age is one in which the contemplative outlook will play a greater part, then, in a situation in which even Christian contemplatives are turning to Buddhism for guidance in practices long lost in their own tradition, it is questionable whether Christianity has much to offer the average Zen practitioner. Similar questions arise with regard even to devotional practices, for Buddhists already possess devotional paths in the Pure Land traditions every bit as sophisticated as those in Christianity. Thus, on the level of spiritual praxis – that is, on the level that Christians have been borrowing from Buddhism – there is little that Buddhists could reasonably be expected to adopt.

One possible area in which Japanese Zen monasticism might eventually adopt elements from the Christian monastic tradition is that of lifestyle. Zen monastics I know who have spent time in Christian monasteries often express admiration for the lifetime vocations, for the strong sense of community, and for the balanced approach of work and study found in the contemplative orders. Some of the less formal training monasteries have initiated changes in the daily schedule based on Christian monastic practice, but this is an exception. It remains to be seen whether the Zen Buddhist institution as a whole will ever demonstrate such flexibility.

All in all there is no need to see the Buddhist-Christian dialogue as a one-way street. Japanese Zen Buddhists now have a much more open attitude toward Christianity than they did prior to the Second Vatican Council and have proved themselves willing to guide Christian practitioners of Zen for as long as the latter are willing to persevere. This is a heartening start, given the antipathy that prevailed between the two traditions until quite recently.

THOMAS L. KIRCHNER

*See also* Buddhist Schools/Traditions: Japan; Contemporary Issues: Buddhist; Dalai Lama (Tenzin Gyatso); Japan: History; Kōan; Master and Pupil: Buddhist Perspectives; Meditation; Peace Movements, Buddhist; Retreat, Christian; Spirituality: Buddhist; Spirituality: Western Christian; Vision, Mystical: Western Christian

## Further Reading

Dalai Lama, *The Good Heart*, Boston: Wisdom, 1996; London: Rider, 1997

Enomiya-Lassalle, Hugo M., *Zen Meditation for Christians* (Religious Encounters: East and West), La Salle, Illinois: Open Court, 1974

Griffiths, Paul J., editor, *Christianity through Non-Christian Eyes* (Faith Meets Faith Series), Maryknoll, New York: Orbis Books, 1990

Hand, Thomas G., and Chwen Jiuan A. Lee, *A Taste of Water: Christianity through Taoist-Buddhist Eyes*, New York: Paulist Press, 1990

Hardy, Gilbert G., *Monastic Quest and Interreligious Dialogue*, New York: Lang, 1990

Jäger, Willigis, *Search for the Meaning of Life: Essays and Reflections on the Mystical Experience*, Liguori, Missouri: Triumph Books, 1995

Lefebure, Leo D., *The Buddha and the Christ: Explorations in Buddhist and Christian Dialogue* (Faith Meets Faith Series), Maryknoll, New York: Orbis Books, 1993

MacInnes, Elaine, *Light Sitting in Light: A Christian's Experience in Zen*, London: Fount, 1996

Mitchell, Donald W., and James Wiseman, editors, *The Gethsemani Encounter: A Dialogue on the Spiritual Life by Buddhist and Christian Monastics*, New York: Continuum, 1997

Nhát Hanh, Thích, *Living Buddha, Living Christ*, New York: Riverhead Books, and London: Rider, 1995

# Dialogue, Intermonastic: Christian Perspectives

Dialogue is always a communication between two.
Dialogue at depth is communion – unity, oneness.

## Dialogue

Dialogue at any level demands respect and reverence, openness and a listening heart, trust and sincerity, sensitivity and interest, concern and compassion, a sharing and caring, and a willingness to be changed. Religious dialogue involves a sharing with another's spirituality, that is, the personal experience of being grasped by the Spirit – the very locus or meeting point for in-depth interreligious dialogue. The chosen or inherited "outer form" of our spirituality is the articulation of this forum of the spirit known as religion with its creed, cult, code, and community.

Thus, interreligious dialogue requires a true grounding in one's own religious beliefs and a witnessing to our living out the deepest implications of those beliefs. Without such we cannot recognize that grasp of the Spirit in our own depths or in anyone else. For too long religion itself has been a barrier to unity, peace, and harmony in the human family. An "intrareligious" dialogue is demanded of those entering into an exchange between the religions designed to bring about inner transformation – a purging of our prejudices, pettiness, competitiveness, and all the forms of that ignorance that blur "the truth that clouds the purity of our consciousness" (Tagore, 1913). Yet interreligious dialogue between people of various religions will become even more important as we move into the future striving together to move beyond boundaries of religion, race, sex, and politics toward human and cosmic healing, wholeness, and holiness.

For Christians in centuries past, interfaith dialogue had been the task of a few pioneers (Brahmabandhab Upadyaya [1861–1907], A.J. Appasamy [late 19th century], and H.A. Krishna Pillai [1827–1900]), both in Asia and in the West, until the coming of Swami Vivekananda (1863–1902) in 1893 to the first World's Parliament of Religions in Chicago. This event was not only a milestone in communication, understanding, and unity but also an internationally recognized moment in the integrative process of East-West dialogue – communion, but not without in-house struggles and misunderstandings within the various religions. Its fruits are still forthcoming!

## Intermonastic Dialogue

Understanding is frequently defined as the goal of interreligious dialogue in contrast to the polemic of denouncing another's position or the apologetic defending of one's own position. Christian monastics see the goal of the dialogue as understanding that fructifies through love in unity, oneness, and being of one mind and one heart (Abhishiktananda, 1976). At a summit conference in Calcutta, Thomas Merton (1915–1968), a Trappist who pioneered the way in East-West intermonastic dialogue in our day, affirmed this goal of unity – oneness in the dialogue. For him

communication was essential to the dialogical process, even communication beyond words. At the deepest level of communication there is no longer communication, he discovered, but communion. Deeply convinced that we are all already one but that we imagine that we are not, he said, "What we have to recover is our original unity. What we have to be is what we are" (Merton, 1973). Interreligious dialogue is itself a mutual call to awaken to our oneness.

This original unity, this oneness, from a Christian perspective has to do with the very ground of being. Created by the One in both image and likeness, we are called to be one people, sourced from the One and called to return to the One whom we call God, the Absolute, the Divine, Allah, the hidden Power, the Source, the Beyond, the Transcendent, and Ultimate Reality, with a thousand other attempts to name the unnameable One:

> This "Oneness of being," in which all opposites are reconciled is the supreme insight of the perennial philosophy. It cannot be known by reason, but where the heart is opened in faith to the supreme Reality, it is known with intellectual clarity. (Griffiths, 1994)

Christians, Jews, Muslims, peoples of the Book, and even Hindus ultimately believe in One God in dialogue with us, calling us to our Center. "I am the Lord your God. . . . Listen, oh Israel, the Lord our God is one God" (Deut. 6:4); "I have loved you with an everlasting love so I am constant in my affection for you" (Jer. 31:3); "As the Father has loved me, so I love you. Remain in my love" (John 15:9); and "Only God is God and Muhammad is his Prophet" (Muslim saying).

Christians believe that there are three Persons in the one God; for Hindus there are many manifestations, both male and female, of the One who is Beyond all. Whether we look to Jesus and the prophets of the Bible for our inspiration, to the prophet Muhammad, or to the Buddha, we discover this same message: people of every race, sex, or creed – we are all one human family, all sacred images of the One true Source deserving to enjoy the same human rights.

For Christians a second and perhaps even greater milestone in and clarion call to dialogue was *Nostra Aetate*, a document of the Second Vatican Council (1962–1965), wherein the Roman Catholic Church for the first time publicly affirmed truth in the scriptures and teachings of other religions. "Rejecting nothing that is true and holy in these religions," the Church exhorted its followers to act with prudence through dialogue and collaboration with followers of other religions and in witness of Christian faith and life so as to recognize, preserve, and promote, even to reverence, and revere the good things, both spiritual and moral, and even the social and cultural values found among these people. In the Church's task of promoting unity and love among all peoples and nations, the Council considered in this document mainly what all of us have in common and what promotes fellowship among us. For the Church teaches that all peoples constitute a single community and have a single origin, as God has made the whole human race dwell over the face of the earth. The final goal also is One: God. Divine providence and manifestations of goodness, God's saving designs extend to all peoples, toward the day when the elect will be united in that Holy City, ablaze with the Divine splendor where nations will walk in God's light (Rev. 21:10–23). Thus, this Council not only wholeheartedly endorsed and published this document on the Roman Church's relations with other religions but also inaugurated a special secretariat to engage in authentic interreligious dialogue. Eventually the Church called on monastics to be the "bridge" at the contemplative level of the dialogue, for it is at that deep level of prayer/contemplation where religions truly meet.

Monasticism itself is a phenomenon surfacing in many religious traditions. It corresponds to what is most interior in every person. Deep within everyone dwells the "monastic archetype" with its potential for inner prayer and unity. Monastics are those who dedicate their lives to this search for unity, for oneness through contemplation. However, intermonastic dialogue is not the prerogative only of monks. Many who live deeply the contemplative life in other walks of life have entered into the sacred exchanges with those of religions other than Christianity. The contemplative life is recognized to be a life mainly of unity because a contemplative is one who has transcended divisions to reach a unity beyond all divisions (Merton, 1984).

Perhaps this is why intermonastic dialogue flourishes between monastics and those whose lives are committed to contemplation. Bede Griffiths (1907–1993), an English Benedictine who lived as an Indian sannyasi for 35 years in southern India, called "unity beyond duality" our very birthright. We are being called to recover it: "As long as you think rationally you will have a dualistic attitude but when you stop the mind (through meditation) you discover the unifying principle behind everything" (Griffiths, 1992).

*Threefold Unity*
Christians believe that the eternal call to unity is threefold: we are called, created, and invited to be united with God, the Ultimate, the Absolute; we are called to wholeness and unity within ourselves; and we are called to a unity with one another and with the whole cosmos. All three facets of this eternal call are interrelated and hold vital ramifications for face-to-face dialogue.

1. Unity with God: The call to union with God, to divinization or deification (*theosis*), rang clearly in the early Christian Church and even before the coming of the Christian era. Unity in God is the relationship of the Divine Persons, and we are invited by grace to share in this Mystery of Love: "I have called you by your name, you are mine. You are precious in my sight and I love you" (Isa. 43), the prophet proclaimed in God's name. However, until the coming of Christ in human flesh the enablement of response to this call was not readily available. Belief in this awesome gift of deification and divinization for each of us has waned and has been all but submerged since the 18th century by rationalism, relativism, and the reign of science with its demythologizing critique of revelation today. Gregory Palamas (c. 1296–1359) and other Eastern Christian writers found this ex-

quisite, original divine offer central to their Christianity (Palamas, 1983). We of the West have yet to retrieve it. Jesus, when accused of being only a man and making himself "God," replied, "Is it not written in your law 'I have said: You are gods'" (Ps. 82:6, John 10:34). Indeed we are capacities for God. We have been created for union with God, an enablement, a gift of grace.

This union of God with the human person results in a divine humanity, first and foremost and uniquely in Jesus Christ. By his death and resurrection and the imparting of his Spirit to us through baptism, Jesus transmitted this divine nature to human persons. What Jesus is by nature (i.e., divine) we share in through grace. Baptism is actually a participation in the divine unity, an awakening and enkindling of the luminous core of our personhood (Barnhart, 1999). For Christians Christ is the central symbol embodying all reality. He is the light that illumines everyone coming into this world, fully divine, fully human, the very manifestation of the Godhead. He is further the symbol of the divinization of the entire universe. However, Christians do not have a monopoly on the knowledge of Christ. Other intuitions or glimpses of the Christ exist in other religions and cultures waiting to be discovered by us. It is for Christians to discern in those insights of others "lights of the same Mystery." Thus, the study of, and the dialogue with, other religions becomes "imperative for an adequate self-understanding of the Christian faith today" (Panikkar, 1992).

Both Christian and non-Christian mystics speak of this union of the human and the divine. At the height of contemplative love, one can hear this "eternal call of unity" and to Unity beckoning the beloved on to claim its original unity with an understanding pervaded with eternal resplendence (Ruusbroec, 1952, 1985). "Give me your mind, give me your heart, you shall indeed come to me" (Bhagavad Gita 18:65). These words from the Hindu tradition find an echo in the Hebrew Scriptures, "My son, give me your heart" (Prov. 23:26), and again, "I have loved you with an everlasting love" (Deut. 31:3). Rumi (1207–1273), the Sufi mystic, insisted that "lovers don't finally meet somewhere. They're in each other all along"(*Open Secret*, Versions of Rumi, 1984, no. 1246). Even more directly apropos, Jesus, in the Gospel of John, promises, "If you or anyone loves me, keep my word and my father will love you and we shall come to you and make our home in you" (John 14:23). And again, "Abide in me as I abide in you" (John 15:4). Christians do believe in the persistent inner drawing toward divine intimacy, seeing Christ himself as the Unifier in whom all unification takes place in the power of the Spirit. He is not only the inviter but the very invitation, the empowerer, the accompanier, and the reward of human/divine union. He comes, and his reward is with him (Isa. 62:11); "God is his worship, God is his offering offered by God in the fire of God" (Bhagavad Gita 4:24).

2. Unity within Ourselves: We are also called to wholeness and unity within ourselves – a necessary condition for divinization and divine union. The Buddha taught the practice of the eightfold path to his followers to correct our delusive wanderings from wholeness and to promote our practice of right

relationship with all that is. From a Christian perspective Ireneaus (c. 130–c. 200) has often been quoted as saying that "the glory of God is man/woman fully alive" – a succinct description of wholeness and inner unity. "God's interior speech comes from within in the unity of our spirit" (Ruusbroec, 1952). However, from early on we have been out of touch with our original unity and have actually fallen from it – a fall from the unity of the contemplative vision into the multiplicity, complications, and distractions of worldly existence. Thus, our minds are enslaved in concern for the transient, illusory, and trivial in life so that we can no longer see our own true "face" or know ourselves in the spirit and in God. We are no longer aware of the "image" that we are. Thus, we are exiled from our God and our innermost Self, left pitifully dependent on self-observation and self-assertion (Merton, 1983), and thus we are encrusted with an ego born out of fear and of defense mechanisms that pain and frighten us.

Yet down under, at our center, we have a true Self that corresponds to the presence of Ultimate Reality and through which we fully participate with body, soul, and spirit in the divine and Ultimate Source. The great gift of the Hindu tradition to humanity is the discovery of this Self, the *atman*, the ground of universal being. "It is not reached by thought; on the contrary, it is only reached by transcending thought" (Griffiths, 1977).

Hindus believe that *atman*, my true Self, is one with Brahman, not separate from myself. "Thou art That!" is one of the "great sayings" in their scriptures. The exchange of such teachings and the in-depth sharing of practices, successes, and failures in dismantling the false self offer light and understanding, peace and harmony, to one another. This is one area in which dialogue with other religions is a mutual boon to those involved in it.

In Zen practice, although there is no belief in a true Self as such, we are offered a method for emptying the mind of self-centeredness and delusive thoughts, realizing oneness with the very practice, plunging ourselves in the path toward wisdom, knowing existentially "who I am" and where I am. Be here now! The Way is already accomplished: we have only to taste the presence. What we are seeking is already here! Christians, while noting differences, find much correspondence with the practice of the sacrament of the present moment, recognizing and surrendering to the Divine in the "now" (DeCaussade, 1981; Brother Lawrence, 1887). Saint Paul, in acknowledging his true Self, cried out, "I live now not I, but Christ lives in me" (Gal. 2:20). For Christians Jesus Christ, the divine Word, becomes human; he is the Unifier, through his Spirit, in whom all unification takes place.

3. Unity with Others/Cosmos: Called to be one mind and one heart with one another and with the whole earth, we glance back from where we have come. Tribal oneness had its blessings and curses until "the individual" began to stand tall on the horizon. Individual growth was a great blessing until we encountered individualism as an excess of this emergence. We urgently need the best of both of these stances, the tribal and the individual, so as to go forward together (Cousins, 1992). Reverence and respect

for life and reverence for one another as sisters and brothers of the one and only human family are fruits of inner conversion and contemplative meditation, prayer that fetters out the selfish and negative and engenders and enhances the positive within us. "Out of the abundance of the heart the mouth speaks"(Matt: 12:34), Jesus told his disciples. Until the "fettering out" has begun, we are not ready for interreligious dialogue – i.e., to reverence life in ourselves, in one another, and in the earth.

In true dialogue, challenged by face-to-face sharing, communication becomes communion, oneness. Clingings; insisting on opinions of "I, me, mine"; and prejudices, racial or political, all fade as two people sincerely share from the ground of their being what is most sacred to them while reverencing the other. From a Christian perspective Christ left his followers a new and single commandment: To love one another as he loves us – which is unto death (John 13:34). About this same death process he proclaimed that no greater love can anyone have than to lay down one's life for another (John 15:13). And this he did for each and all of us while praying that we might be one as he is one with the Father, that we may be one in him and with each other, that all may be one (John 17:21). True dialogue is a kind of laying down of one's life for the other – a death to the ego-self that opens one up to an experience of resurrection in the true Self.

In this effort at oneness, the "encounter of otherness," Christians are called to the service of reconciliation wherein Christ becomes the very "mystery of union" (Panikkar, 1992). Forgiveness and reconciliation will bring us with new eyes to revere and respect one another. Only then can we reverence and respect the earth and tend and till it together with gentleness and nonviolent love.

*Conclusion*

Interreligious dialogue consists of four levels of participation. Everyone can and should be engaged in the first, which is the dialogue of life – working and living side by side with one another, anticipating needs, sharing the good things of the earth, and caring about one another in respectful and compassionate love. The second, the dialogue of solidarity, is a working together for the betterment of the community and society in peace and justice and for the advancement of human rights and happiness for all. The third, the dialogue of scholarship, includes conferences, research, and writings among scholars involved in interfaith dialogue. Finally, the dialogue of communion is dialogue at the deepest level of sharing, the dialogue of spirituality or spiritual exchange. Wherever we find or choose our involvement in the dialogue with others, we need to be gratefully and attentively aware of the "eternal call to unity."

"God's work in the emptiness of the soul is eternal!" (Ruusbroec, 1985).

M. PASCALINE COFF, O.S.B.

*See also* Contemporary Issues: Western Christian; Dalai Lama (Tenzin Gyatso); Griffiths, Bede; Keating, Thomas; Kōan; Le Saux, Henri; Meditation: Buddhist Perspectives; Merton, Thomas; Mystics, German Monastic; Palamas, Gregory, St.;

Schutz, Roger; Spirituality: Western Christian; Vision, Mystical: Eastern Christian

**Further Reading**

Abhishiktananda, Swami, *Hindu-Christian Meeting Point, within the Cave of the Heart*, Paris: Éditions du Seuil, 1966; revised edition, New Delhi: ISPCK, 1976

Barnhart, Bruno, *Second Simplicity*, New York: Paulist Press, 1999

Cousins, Ewert, *Christ of the 21st Century*, Rockport, Massachusetts: Element, 1992

Dalai Lama XIV, *The Good Heart: A Buddhist Perspective on the Teachings of Jesus*, Boston: Wisdom, 1996

DeCaussade, Jean Pierre, *The Sacrament of the Present Moment*, translated by Kitty Muggeridge, London: Fount, 1981; San Francisco: Harper, 1982; revised edition, 1989

Gioia, Francesco, editor, *Il Dialogo Interreligioso nel magistero pontificio*, Vatican: Vatican Library, 1994; as *Interreligious Dialogue: The Official Teaching of the Catholic Church (1963–1995)*, Boston: Pauline Books and Media, 1997

Griffiths, Bede, *Return to the Center*, Springfield, Illinois: Templegate, 1977

Griffiths, Bede, *The New Creation in Christ*, London: Darton, Longman and Todd, and Springfield, Illinois: Templegate, 1992

Griffiths, Bede, *Universal Wisdom: A Journey Through the Sacred Wisdom of the World*, San Francisco: HarperSanFrancisco, and London: Fount, 1994

Jalal al-Din Rumi, Maulana, *Open Secret: Versions of Rumi*, translated by John Moyne and Coleman Barks, Putney, Vermont: Threshold Books, 1984; London: Shambhala, 1999

Lawrence, Brother, *The Practice of the Presence of God*, London: Masters, 1887; New York: Revell, 1895; reprint, Mount Vernon, New York: Peter Pauper Press, 1963

Merton, Thomas, *The Asian Journal of Thomas Merton*, New York: New Directions, 1973; London: Sheldon Press, 1974

Merton, Thomas, "Inner Experience," *Cistercian Studies* 1 (1983) and 7 (1984)

Mitchell, Donald, and James Wiseman, editors, *The Gethsemani Encounter: A Dialogue on the Spiritual Life by Buddhist and Christian Monastics*, New York: Continuum, 1997

Palamas, Gregory, *The Triads*, edited by John Meyendorff, translated by Nicholas Gendle, New York: Paulist Press, and London: SPCK, 1983

Panikkar, Raimundo, *The Intrareligious Dialogue*, New York: Paulist Press, 1978; revised edition, 1999

Panikkar, Raimundo, "A Theophany for Our Times," *Theology Digest* 39:1 (Spring 1992)

Ruusbroec, Jan van, *The Spiritual Espousals*, translated by Helen Rolfson, New York: Harper, and London: Faber, 1952; reprint, Collegeville, Minnesota: The Liturgical Press, 1995

Ruusbroec, Jan van, *John Ruusbroec: The Spiritual Espousals and Other Works*, introduction and translation by James A. Wiseman, New York: Paulist Press, 1985

Tagore, Rabindranath, *Sadhana: The Realisation of Life*, London: Macmillan, 1913; New York: Macmillan, 1914; reprint, Tucson, Arizona: Omen Communications, 1972

Walker, Susan, editor, *Speaking of Silence: Christians and Buddhists on the Contemplative Way*, New York: Paulist Press, 1987

**Related Web Sites**

*http://www.gtu.edu/library/LibEcumenism.html#northam* (an excellent interfaith dialogue web site resource from the Graduate Theological Union Library at Berkeley, California)

*http://fas.harvard.edu/~pluralsm/* (the Pluralism Project provides numerous links to a wide variety of leading sites)

*http://ww.aar-site,org/scripts/AAR/members/elists.html* (the American Academy of Religion offers this web link for participants who are scholars interested in various web discussion groups)

*http://www.acusd.edu/theo/hcs-1/* (Society for Hindu-Christian Studies site)

*http://bedegriffiths.com* (Bede Griffiths Associates are offering this web site resource for Interreligious Contemplative Dialogue, highlighting the writings of Bede Griffiths)

# Dionysius the Pseudo-Areopagite c. 500

Author of mystical treatises

The *Corpus Dionysiacum* (*CD*) is usually discussed in the context of philosophical theology, or else it is wrongly but still persistently held up (or denounced) as the fountainhead of Christian mysticism. For over a century Western scholarship has been preoccupied with the nature of the debt that this late fifth- or early sixth-century body of writings owes to two pagan Neoplatonists, Iamblichus of Chalcis (d. c. 330) and Proclus Diadochus (d. 486). It is true that the pseudonymous author known previously as Pseudo-Dionysius knew and used these philosophers and that he was so vitally interested in the experience of God that he favored the language of apophaticism, as in the extraordinary series of "nots" that conclude his vastly influential little treatise *The Mystical Theology* (*MT*). It is also true that later thinkers in the Christian West, most notably the Scholastics of the 13th century (e.g., Thomas Aquinas and Bonaventure), read him mainly as an authority for systematic theology, whereas the later medieval mystics (e.g., Meister Eckhart [c. 1260–c. 1328] and the author of *The Cloud of Unknowing*) appeal to Dionysius' apophatic mysticism in support of their accounts of the ways to divine encounter. In addition to these two options, medieval churchmen often cite the Areopagite's treatises on the hierarchies (a word he seems to have invented) to support the authority of the clergy. These three identities – philosopher-theologian, mystic, and advocate of church order – turn up in the Western reception as largely independent of one another. Modern scholarship has often struggled in consequence with the coherence or, more precisely, the perceived incoherence of the Dionysian vision. For example, how is the direct encounter with God in the darkness of unknowing (*MT*) to be reconciled with the rigid maintenance of angelic and clerical mediation in the treatises on the *Celestial Hierarchy* (*CH*) and the *Ecclesiastical Hierarchy* (*EH*)? In addition, how, if at all, is the profession (or pretense) of Christian faith to be squared with the dependence on non-Christian philosophers so evident, for example, in the treatise on the *Divine Names* (*DN*).

Perhaps the key to a resolution of these difficulties lies in the Eastern, especially Syrian Christian and specifically monastic background of the Dionysian corpus. The appearance of "monks" (*monachoi*) in *EH* VI and *Ep* VIII of the *CD* strikes the modern reader as a glaring anachronism in texts that claim to be the work of a disciple of St. Paul (see Acts 17). However, on closer inspection and seen against the Syrian Christian background, this apparent anachronism turns out to be highly revealing. Dionysius' monks do not resemble the organized communities of Pachomius, the semi-anchorites of Scete, or the hermits of Antony's type. Neither do they reflect the similar structuring of ascetic life that had sprung up in Syria in imitation of the Egyptian models during the late fourth and fifth centuries. We find neither withdrawal (*anachoresis*) from the larger society nor the enclosure – or *Sonderwelt*, in Karl Heussi's phrase – so typical of monasticism's fourth-century emergence. Rather, the Dionysian monk is presented as a part of the local Christian community, worshiping at the parish church, even assigned a specific place in the liturgical assembly, and both emphatically subordinated to the presiding bishop. Also, and for the first time in Greek Christian literature, the monk receives his tonsure from the clergy as a specifically priestly action (i.e., as a "sacrament") that Dionysus goes on to associate with baptism. These features, notably the last, accord remarkably well with the Syrian institution of the *bnai qeiama*, which appears in the writings of Aphrahat of Persia (fl. 330s) and Ephrem Syrus (d. 373) as an already ancient feature of Syriac-speaking Christianity. The Syrian "single-ones" (*ihidaye*) were bound together in a covenant (*qeiama*) to live lives of prayer and charity but continued to share in the liturgical and day-to-day life of their fellow believers and made their vows of chastity on the occasion of their baptism. Moreover, the term *ihidaye* very likely stands behind the Greek *monachos* as early as the second-century Gospel of Thomas. Indeed, the Greek word might be a calque, at least in its Christian usage, on the Syriac term.

Thus, if *monk* is a genuinely ancient term in Syrian Christianity, the Dionysian emphasis on the ascetic's place within the liturgy and on subordination to the bishop reflects later developments, most notably the question of charismatic authority and the problems that the latter posed for episcopal rule and sacramental life. To be sure these concerns are already present in such earlier classics as Athanasius' *Life of Antony* and Basil the Great's *Rules* as well as in the Messalian crisis of the fourth and fifth centuries with its attendant episcopal condemnations. Put in Dionysian terms the problem is precisely that of the apparent antinomy between the *EH*'s insistence on clerical mediation through the liturgy and the direct experience of God in the *MT*. However, the resolution of that antinomy likewise lies in earlier Syrian or Syrian-inspired ascetic literature. Ephrem Syrus' *Hymns on Paradise* adumbrates, and the late fourth-century Syriac work the *Book of Steps* (*Liber Graduum*) fleshes out, an account of Christian worship as the image or icon at once of the angelic liturgy and of the individual believer's soul. The Macarian Homilies, written in Greek at the close of the fourth century, take up exactly the same idea of the liturgy as the divinely established icon of heaven and of the heart. We can then trace this theme at work throughout fifth and early sixth centuries in Syriac writings, for example, in the *Lives* of Bishop Rabbula of Edessa (d. 436) and Symeon Stylites (d. 452); in the homily of Pseudo-Ephrem "On the Hermits and Desert Dwellers" and of Jacob of Sarug "On the Chariot That Ezekiel the Prophet Saw"; in the Chorepiscopus Balai's poem "On the Consecration of the Church at Qennishrin"; and in Bishop Babai's homily "On the Domed Church at Edessa" (the latter two from the early sixth century).

Dionysius fits exactly into this Syrian Christian, mainly monastic continuum. Even his borrowings from the late Neoplatonists discover their context (*Sitz im Leben*) here, especially in Iamblichus' and Proclus' common defense of "ineffable rites" (i.e., theurgy) as the indispensible aide for the soul's encounter with the divine. The ascent of Moses into the darkness of unknowing that begins the *MT* discovers its correlate in the *EH*'s contemplation of the Church's sanctuary, of "Jesus, our most divine altar," in whom, Dionysius tells us, the believers are "consecrated and mystically consumed [*holokautomenoi*]" and thus have "access [*prosagoge*]" to the divine mystery (*EH* IV.12). The entire Dionysian project might be summed up by the Psalm verse that began the old Roman Mass – *et introibo ad altare dei* – in which the altar answers, first, to the visible table of the Eucharist; second, to the heavenly sanctuary and throne of Christ's divinity; and, third, to Christ's presence hidden within the inmost being of the baptized Christian. Thus, the contemplative ascent to heaven, into the cloud of Sinai, is simultaneously the believer's progressive entry into the mystery that is present both on the Church's altar and within his or her own soul. This triple aspect of the liturgy as itself holy and as mediating the presence of heaven to the soul, at least on this side of the eschaton (see *DN* I.4), governs the *CD* throughout. We find it announced in the corpus' opening chapter (*CH* I.3) and reprised in its concluding words, addressed to the Apostle John at Patmos (*Ep* X). Thus, the Dionysian hierarchies feature a certain multivalence. They shimmer somewhere between objective reality and subjective truth. However, their overall purpose is to affirm the divine establishment of the bishop and the bishop's liturgy not only as visible images of heaven and guarantors of church order but as guides toward and reflections of that inward ordering of the soul that alone can allow for divine encounter. In short, the ascetic solitary needs the Church and its sacraments, and Dionysius' whole effort is to demonstrate why this is so. The fact that his demonstration came out of a tradition that itself had monastic origins and that was over a century old at the time of the *CD*'s composition goes far toward explaining why, aside from the aura of the apostolic pseudonym, Dionysius came so quickly to be accorded immense authority in the Christian East and especially by the monks.

HIEROMONK ALEXANDER GOLITZIN

*See also* Albertus Magnus, St.; Asceticism: Christian Perspectives; Hesychasm; Macarian Homilies; Scholastics, Buddhist; Spirituality: Eastern Christian; Syria; Vision, Mystical: Eastern Christian

## Biography

The name derives from a false attribution of a body of mystical texts written in Greek around 500 A.D. Nothing is known of the author's life. From the time of a council in 533 at Constantinople until at least the 16th century these works were ascribed to Dionysius the Areopagite mentioned as being Paul's companion in Athens in Acts 17:34. The Dionysian Corpus formulated Neoplatonic mysticism in a manner that has exercised enduring influence.

## Major Works

Note: all works are written in Greek.
*Celestial Hierarchy*
*Ecclesiastical Hierarchy*
*Divine Names*
*Mystical Theology*

These writings and others are collected in *Pseudo-Dionysius: The Complete Works*, translated into English by C. Liubheid, with notes by P.E. Rorem, 1987.

## Further Reading

de Andia, Ysabel, *Henosis: L'Union à Dieu chez Denys l'Aréopagite*, Leiden and New York: Brill, 1996

Gersh, Stephen, *From Iamblichus to Eriugena: An Investigation of the Prehistory and Evolution of the Pseudo-Dionysian Tradition*, Leiden: Brill, 1978

Golitzin, Alexander G., *Et introibo ad altare dei: The Mystagogy of Dionysius Areopagita, with Special Reference to Its Predecessors in the Eastern Christian Tradition*, Thessalonica: Patriarchal Institute of Patristic Studies, 1994

Golitzin, Alexander G., "Hierarchy Versus Anarchy? Dionysius Areopagita, Symeon the New Theologian, Nicetas Stethatos, and Their Common Roots in Ascetical Tradition," *St. Vladimir's Theological Quarterly* 38:2 (1994)

Louth, A., *Denys the Areopagite*, Wilton, Connecticut: Morehouse-Barlow, and London: Chapman, 1989

Rist, J.M., "Pseudo-Dionysius, Neoplatonism, and the Weakness of the Soul," in *From Athens to Chartres: Neoplatonism and Medieval Thought: Studies in Honour of Edouard Jeanneau*, edited by H.J. Westra, Leiden and New York: Brill, 1992

Roques, René, *L'Univers Dionysien: Structure hiérarchique du monde selon le Pseudo-Denys*, Paris: Aubier, 1954

Rorem, Paul E., *Biblical and Liturgical Symbols within the Pseudo-Dionysian Synthesis*, Toronto: Pontifical Institute of Mediaeval Studies, 1984

Rorem, Paul E., *Pseudo-Dionysius: A Commentary on the Texts and an Introduction to Their Influence*, Oxford and New York: Oxford University Press, 1993

# Disciples, Early Buddhist

The Buddha renounced the worldly life in search of a path to *nibbāna* (i.e., final deliverance from suffering) and after his enlightenment took on the burden of teaching in order to guide others to the same goal that he himself had reached. Testifying to his success, he says that he has more than 500 monk and nun disciples who have attained supreme release and many more disciples, both monastic and laity, who have entered the irreversible path to liberation (*MN* 73, I 490–491). This article surveys the achievements of four distinguished monks and several prominent nuns who ranked at the forefront of the earliest *sangha*. If the sketch of the nuns is comparatively brief, this reflects the proportion of information in the sources. No comparison is made with non-Theravādin sources (which differ in details), nor is any attempt made to assess the material from a modern, critical point of view.

### Sāriputta and Mahāmoggallāna

The two main disciples can be treated together, for they were constant companions from infancy to death. The two were born on the same day in adjoining villages near Rājagaha (present-day Rajgir in Bihar) to families connected by a close bond of friendship. In their boyhood they were intimate friends, and on reaching maturity they jointly decided to go forth seeking a path to deliverance. After a fruitless search across India, they arrived back at Rājagaha shortly after the Buddha began his ministry. One day Sāriputta met by chance the arahant Assaji, who taught him a pithy stanza of Dhamma that brought him to the first stage of enlightenment: stream-entry. Sāriputta told his friend about this meeting, and Moggallāna also attained stream-entry.

Together they went to meet the Buddha and were admitted into the order. Each new monk then went off into solitude. Moggallāna reached arahantship (i.e., the final goal) after a week of diligent meditation. Sāriputta contemplated a wider range of principles and thus took two weeks to reach the goal. On the evening of Sāriputta's attainment, the Buddha assembled the *sangha* and named the two friends his chief disciples: Sāriputta, the foremost with respect to wisdom, and Moggallāna, the foremost with respect to spiritual powers.

The two monks accompanied the Buddha throughout his ministry, assisting him in the administration of the *sangha* and the promulgation of the Dhamma. The Buddha called them "the standard and model for my monk disciples" and urged the other monks to associate with them. Sāriputta generally trained the younger monks to reach stream-entry, after which he would direct them to Moggallāna, who would guide them to arahantship. Thus, the Buddha said that Sāriputta is like a mother who gives birth and Moggallāna like a wet nurse who nurtures the child (*MN* 141, III 248).

Because of their different aptitudes, the two disciples played different roles in the *sangha*. Sāriputta, as foremost in wisdom, was charged with the systematic analysis and classification of the teaching. We can see his mind at work in several *sutta*s, such as *MN* 9, *MN* 28, and *MN* 141. In two late *sutta*s, *DN* 33 and 34, he compresses the manifold doctrines of Buddhism into two comprehensive schemes to ensure their easy transmission to posterity. The commentaries also credit Sariputta with the codification of the Abhidhamma Piṭaka.

On the other hand, Moggallāna excelled in spiritual powers, such as clairvoyance, clairaudience, mind reading, telekinesis,

A Chinese statue of the Buddha's companion Ānanda, probably from the Tang dynasty.
**Photo courtesy of John Powers**

and psychokinesis. Guided by compassion he often used these powers to remove obstacles to the spread of the Dhamma and to transform beings who were inaccessible to verbal instruction. His feats are described at *MN* 37, *MN* 50, *SN* 6:5, *SN* 40:10, and *SN* 51:14, and elsewhere he gives inspiring discourses on points of monastic training (*MN* 15, *SN* 35:202).

Both Sāriputta and Moggallāna predeceased the Buddha. Sāriputta passed away peacefully on an October full moon after converting his aged mother to the Dhamma. Two weeks later

Moggallāna was brutally murdered, the karmic fruit of a terrible crime he had committed in a distant past life. After another six months the Master himself expired.

### Mahākassapa

Although the Buddha refused to appoint a personal successor, following his demise the monastic community came to look on one solitary elder as their tower of strength. This was Mahākassapa, "the Master's counterpart," who assumed the presidency of the First Buddhist Council.

Mahākassapa came from a wealthy brahmin family. From his youth he longed for a life of renunciation, but against his wishes his parents compelled him to marry. His bride, Bhaddā Kapilānī, shared his aspiration for an ascetic life, and thus the couple never consummated their marriage. After the death of their parents, they donned saffron robes and slipped away from their estate, intent on finding a guide to enlightenment.

Kassapa met the Buddha first, sitting beneath a tree, and recognized at once that this was his master. The Buddha ordained him, gave him a concise teaching, and exchanged robes with him, a unique honor not bestowed on any other disciple. Seven days later Kassapa attained arahantship. Meanwhile Bhaddā too had met the Buddha and became his follower, although she would be ordained a nun only five years later, when the order of nuns was created. After her ordination she too quickly realized arahantship.

Within the *sangha* Mahākassapa was the disciple foremost in the ascetic practices. Although the Buddha condemned self-mortification, he permitted the monks to observe a number of austerities that promoted simple living and renunciation. These include using only robes made from rags, eating only food collected on almsround, and living only in forests. Kassapa observed these practices scrupulously throughout his life and thus became a model of contentment and detachment.

A whole chapter about Mahākassapa is found at *SN*, chapter 16. In several *sutta*s the Buddha invites him to admonish the monks and praises him for his mastery over the meditative absorptions and the higher knowledges. At times Kassapa appears stern, especially in his treatment of Ānanda, the Buddha's amiable younger cousin, but his intention was always to keep alive the true spirit of the Dhamma. Mahākassapa also has to his credit 40 verses in the *Theragāthā* (Verses of the Elders) that reveal a different side to his character: an eloquent poet acutely sensitive to natural beauty.

Kassapa played a special role after the Buddha's *parinibbāna*. Aware that, with the Master gone, unscrupulous monks might try to corrupt the teachings, he convened a council of 500 arahants to rehearse the Dhamma and the Vinaya (the doctrine and the discipline). The product of this council was the first recension of the Buddhist Canon. The Pali tradition is silent about his death, but in the Northern Buddhist tradition it is believed that he sits in meditative trance inside Mount Kukkutapāda, awaiting the future Buddha Maitreya.

### Ānanda

When the Buddha was 55 years of age, he felt the need for a reliable attendant. The post fell to his younger cousin Ānanda, who had gone forth as a monk after the Buddha visited their home city and quickly attained stream-entry. For 25 years after the appointment, Ānanda lovingly served the Master in deed, word, and thought. He cleaned his dwelling, brought him food and water, mended his robes, and attended on him in illness. He also served as secretary, facilitating the Buddha's relations with the other monks and the laity.

Besides his devoted service to the Buddha, Ānanda had another gift as well: a prodigious memory that could retain anything that crossed his mind. This gift, crucial in an age when sacred literature was always transmitted orally, equipped Ānanda for his special role as "the treasurer of the Dhamma." Ānanda memorized all the discourses ever spoken by the Buddha and trained others to memorize them as well.

Ānanda was an eloquent speaker, and several of his discourses are recorded in the canon (*DN* 10; *MN* 53, 88, 108; *SN* 35:117; *AN* 4:161). More often he appears as the Buddha's interlocutor, questioning him and replying to his questions. His most memorable role, which would have surely won him an Oscar as best supporting actor, occurs in the Mahāparinibbāna Sutta (*DN* 16), "The Last Days of the Buddha," where in his grief and despondency on the Lord's passing he conveys most poignantly the sentiments of the whole Buddhist world.

Ānanda did not attain arahantship during the Buddha's lifetime, but after his death, spurred on by Mahākassapa, he reached the supreme goal on the very eve of the First Buddhist Council, which he attended as a stainless one. At the council he was responsible for the recension of the *sutta*s. If it were not for Ānanda's unique memory, his devotion to the Buddha, and his love of learning, it is questionable whether the Buddha's teachings would have long survived his death.

### Eminent Nuns

The first woman to receive ordination as a nun (*bhikkhunī*) was Mahāpajāpatī Gotamī, the Buddha's aunt and foster mother (his natural mother died seven days after his birth). Earlier, at Kapilavatthu, the Buddha had rejected her request to establish an order of nuns, but she followed him to Vesālī along with many noble women, and through the kind intercession of Ānanda her wish was granted. In a short time Gotamī attained arahantship and was appointed "the foremost among the nuns of long standing." For the rest of her life she served as a "mother superior" to the order of nuns and guided many younger women to enlightenment.

Within the nuns' order the Buddha appointed two nuns as "models and standards" for the others to emulate, female counterparts of Sāriputta and Moggallāna. These were Khemā and Uppalavaṇṇā, the former foremost in wisdom and the latter in spiritual powers. Other distinguished nuns were Dhammadinnā, the foremost preacher, whose masterly discourse (*MN* 44) was approved by the Buddha himself; Bhaddā Kapilānī, Kassapa's former wife, who excelled in the recollection of past lives; Bhaddā Kuṇḍalakesā, a former wandering debater, who became the chief of those with quick understanding; and Paṭācārā, who came to the Buddha in despair after losing her husband, two sons, and parents in quick succession and after her

ordination became the foremost nun specializing in monastic discipline.

BHIKKHU BODHI

Abbreviations: *DN* = *Dīgha Nikāya* (by number of *sutta*); *MN* = *Majjhima Nikāya* (by number of *sutta*); *SN* = *Saṃyutta Nikāya* (by chapter and *sutta* number); *AN* = *Aṅguttara Nikāya* (by chapter and *sutta* number). *Sutta* references to the *Nikāya*s are followed where relevant by the volume and page number in the roman-script edition published by the Pali Text Society.

*See also* Arhat; Asceticism: Buddhist Perspectives; Buddha (Śākyamuni); Buddhism: Overview; Buddhist Schools/Traditions: South Asia; Councils, Buddhist; Food: Buddhist Perspectives; Hermits: Buddhist; Holy Men in Power (Hierocrats), Buddhist; Liturgy: Buddhist; Mahāpajāpatī Gotamī; Master and Pupil: Buddhist Perspectives; Origins: Comparative Perspectives; Patrons, Buddhist: India; Pilgrims to India, Chinese; Rules, Buddhist (Vinaya): Historical; Saṅgha; Travelers: Buddhist

### Further Reading

Dhammapala, Acariya, *The Commentary on the Verses of the Therīs*, translated by William Pruitt, Oxford: Pali Text Society, 1998

Lamotte, Etienne, *History of Indian Buddhism: From the Origins to the Śaka Era*, translated by Sara Webb-Boin, Louvain-la-Neuve: Universite Catholique de Louvain, Institut Orientaliste, 1988

Malalasekera, G.P., *Dictionary of Pāli Proper Names*, 2 vols., London: Murray, 1937–1938; reprint, London: Pali Text Society, 1960; Boston: Pali Text Society, 1974

Nyanaponika, Thera, *Great Disciples of the Buddha*, Boston: Wisdom Publications, and Kandy, Sri Lanka: Buddhist Publication Society, 1997

Ray, Reginald A., *Buddhist Saints of India: A Study in Buddhist Values and Orientations*, New York: Oxford University Press, 1994

# Discipleship, Christian. *See* Master and Pupil: Christian Perspectives

# Discourses (Sūtras): Mahāyāna

### Overview

The term *Mahāyāna sūtra* refers to a body of Buddhist scriptural literature produced in India over a period of approximately 500 years (c. A.D. 100–600). Formally and contextually these scriptures claim to be the words of the Buddha Śākyamuni and to contain the authoritative statements of buddhas, bodhisattvas, and deities. Historically they are overall younger than the sūtras contained in the canonical collections of non-Mahāyāna schools, such as the Pāli Tipiṭaka collection of the Theravāda. The identity of the community that produced these texts, or their functional *Sitz im Leben*, are matters of contention among scholars. However, some agreement exists that most were produced by monastic communities or lay groups closely associated with them. In support of this hypothesis one may note that Mahāyāna sūtras are filled with references to the monastic ideal and with comments on the proper behavior of monks (nuns are mentioned less frequently if at all). Even when Mahāyāna sūtras contain criticisms of monastic behavior, they tend to imply that their critiques aim to uphold the true monastic virtue, not to reject the monastic life. An important exception, discussed here, is the *Vimalakīrti-nirdeśa* (often called "the Vimalakirti Sūtra").

Mahāyāna sūtras generally glorify the ascetic ideals of Buddhism. When they challenge the monastic establishment or monastic practice, they seem to refer specifically to the practices of certain Buddhist groups that have generally (although inaccurately and pejoratively) been identified as the followers of the "inferior vehicle," or Hīnayāna. The objects of this criticism, called in these texts *śrāvaka*s, or "disciples," are in most cases

Octagonal 12-storied Pagoda of Kumārajīva (d. A.D. 409 or 411), Luoshisi (Kumārajīva temple), Wuwei, Gansu province, China, brick, repaired in 1934, 32 meters. Kumārajīva translated Mahāyāna discourses into Chinese.
Photo courtesy of Marylin M. Rhie

straw men or literary conceits who represent the antithesis of the Mahāyāna ethical and monastic ideal. They are not members of actual communities.

### The Construction of a Polemic Distinction

As suggested here, discussing Mahāyāna sūtras presents several problems of historiography and often leads to a confusion between polemical discourse and possible references to actual practices. These problems form three sets. First, there are formal difficulties relating to the nature and setting of the sūtra genre. Second, the history of Mahāyāna presents special problems, most notably because "Mahāyāna" is not a distinct social entity (e.g., a sect) but rather a polemical stance in terms of an amorphous, perhaps imaginary group of rivals. To complicate matters this undefined rival group that is the target of so much derision has come to be identified, mistakenly, unfairly, and only in modern times with the various forms of Theravāda Buddhism found in Southeast Asia. Our third problem is that Mahāyāna sūtras are not attempts at doing history or recording monastic life – they are normative and mythic texts. Indeed the very term *Mahāyāna* might be a retrospective idealization of earlier beliefs and practices. Thus, we cannot easily derive from these texts historical information about anything, let alone about monastic life in classical India.

In the face of these difficulties, contemporary scholars of Indian Buddhism generally shun the sharp contrast delineated in the sūtras between Mahāyāna and Hīnayāna (not to mention the contrast with Theravāda, which has no foundation in the sūtras). For the first century of the modern study of Buddhism (roughly 1860 to 1960), the distinction between Mahāyāna and Hīnayāna ran as a leading motif in conceptions of Buddhist history. However, the distinction is based on a polemical, not a historical, set of categories. Only one side of the debate – and an ill-defined side at that – created such categories.

The Mahāyāna/Hīnayāna distinction corresponds to little out there in the world of religious institutions. First, it excludes everything non-Mahāyāna that happened in India (other than possible Indian antecedents of Theravāda). Second, it wrongly implies that there is more in common between the liturgy of, say, a fifth-century Indian Mahāsāṅghika, a 14th-century Tibetan "Vajrayānist," and a 20th-century Japanese layman than there is between the Mahāsāṅghika and the Theravāda Buddhist. Finally, it has contributed to a simplistic view of Mahāyāna as a lay and altruistic ideal (if not a practice) in contrast to a putative monastic and self-centered Hīnayāna.

### Content and Interpretation

Despite all these qualifications, we can learn much, albeit in a necessarily tentative mode, about Mahāyāna from the statements and narratives found in the Mahāyāna sūtras. Naturally anything deduced from these fundamentally prescriptive and mythical texts must confront the evidence of archaeology and independent historical witnesses, scant as this evidence might be.

For example, a close reading of Mahāyāna sūtras should disprove two common scholarly myths. One is that they are distil-

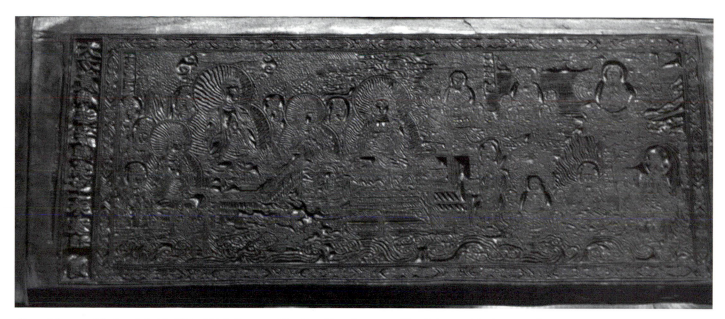

One of the woodblocks of the Buddhist Tripiṭaka, carved in the mid–13th century, Koryŏ dynasty, Haeinsa temple, Mount Kaya, Kyŏngsang-namdo. Photo courtesy of Marylin M. Rhie

lations of Mahāyāna philosophy. Although they contain much of Buddhist philosophy and often parallel the rhetoric, terminology, and dialectics of the scholastic tradition, they are religious texts that provide inspiration and materials for ritual and devotion as much as they do doctrinal guidance. Although it is true that these religious texts often (although not overwhelmingly, and still less always) contain statements reminiscent of the dialectics of the philosopher, these usually occur embedded in a rhetoric of religious authority, commitment, and devotion. The social contexts of this rhetoric can be inferred from the silent witness of Indian archaeology and the testimony of the Chinese pilgrims.

Mahāyāna sūtras also explode the myth of lay Mahāyāna. It has long been argued that Mahāyāna Buddhism was a lay movement if not a lay revolution. However, the Mahāyāna sūtras for the most part offer prescriptions for the monastic life and present clearly ascetic ideals. Even when the sūtras do speak of the life of the virtuous layperson (male or female), the ideal is monastic if not ascetic: the layperson is asked to lead a life that imitates life in the monastery. This sort of prescription has been called a "monachized" ideal of lay life, whereas the tendency to modify or soften the ascetic stance of these texts has been called the "laicization" of the monastic ideal (Robinson, 1966). Laicization and monachization are two dimensions of the same phenomenon: the religious and ethical ideal of the Buddhist is defined as somehow intermediate between the ascetic life of the ideal monk and the presumed life affirmation and freedom of the layman. Thus, laicization is not simply a tendency to criticize certain extremes of the monastic ideal, suggesting that the layperson might be better able to follow the true Buddhist path. It also conceives of the ideal saint in terms that are lay or perhaps even iconoclastic. For example, the monk might be presented in terms that suggest that the truly virtuous monk does

not conform to the externals of monastic rule but is somehow able to practice them internally. In India both aspects of laicization play a major role in the development of Buddhist tantra. In eastern Asia these ideal rhetorical moves found a practical counterpart in the eventual laicization, in practice, of Mahāyāna in Japan. That is, in the Japanese case the monk often was displaced by the lay minister.

The delicate balance between these two tendencies is embodied in a text that became very popular in eastern Asia: the *Vimalakīrti-nirdeśa*. This Mahāyāna sūtra presents a harsh criticism of Buddhist monasticism and proposes that its main character, the layman Vimalakirti, is the true embodiment of the Mahāyāna ideal. This text was central to the development of lay devotion and practice in eastern Asia but seems to have been less influential in India and certainly in Tibet. Western and Japanese scholars who have assumed that this text is an accurate account of the social situation in India and not merely a polemical stance might have projected onto the Indian scene a fragment of eastern Asian history.

Another common misconception that is suggested by the polemical rhetoric of Mahāyāna sūtras but that is not supported by a critical reading of this literature is the stereotype of Mahāyāna as a movement of practical compassion. The historical evidence does not support the presumed sharp contrast between the selfish Hīnayāna monk and the compassionate Mahāyāna bodhisattva, especially if the latter is conceived as a lay bodhisattva. The monks of the so-called Hīnayāna schools were also engaged in a constant interaction with the lay population, who contributed worldly support in exchange for instruction, religious merit, and services that included medical assistance and public education. Moreover some of the early Hīnayāna schools also speak of the ideal of the compassionate bodhisattva. The Mahāyāna texts, in turn, offer a mixed picture of Mahāyāna as a doctrine of compassion. Although many texts speak of the bodhisattva's limitless compassion, little is said of the bodhisattva's compassion in practical terms.

For explicit statements on the ethics of the bodhisattva, we must turn to the scholastic treatises known as *śāstra*s. Two such texts that feature prominently in the ethics of the bodhisattva are the *Bodhisattvabhūmi* of Asaṅga and the *Catuḥśataka* of Āryadeva. The latter, for example, speaks of the bodhisattva's dedication to public works and works of public charity. The *Bodhisattvabhūmi* distinguishes three levels in the Mahāyāna Buddhist ethical ideal. The first level, the morality of restraint, is represented by the rules of natural morality, applicable to monks and laymen alike, and by the monastic code established by the Buddha as the foundation of monastic practice. The second level, the morality of cultivation, refers to the cultivation of good qualities through a life of monastic perfection and meditation. The third and highest level is that of altruism: the morality of serving the interests of other sentient beings. This schema is, naturally, an exegetical one, but it captures various aspects of the interface between monasticism and ethics in the sūtras. One should note, furthermore, that no level corresponds exclusively to a monastic or a lay life.

The *Bodhisattvabhūmi* also suggests a close link between the ethical and the monastic ideals of Mahāyāna. In the sūtra literature furthermore, monasticism meets, or combines with, both ritual and ethical ideals, and this characteristic meeting of ideals occurs likewise in the *śāstra*s. For example, the seventh-century (?) Indian Mahāyāna scholastic Śāntideva writes both on the philosophy of Mahāyāna and on its practice as a spiritual path. He also argues for the conception of this path as the central message of the Mahāyāna sūtras. Śāntideva compiled an anthology of extracts from the Mahāyāna sūtras titled the "Compendium of Instructions," or *Śikṣāsamuccaya*. This work gives us an approximate idea of the ways in which Mahāyāna sūtras were incorporated into a doctrinal and ritual system of Buddhist practice. A similar function is served by another anthology, this one of doubtful or unclear authorship, the *Sūtrasamuccaya*, attributed to Śāntideva or to Nāgārjuna. Both of these anthologies also highlight the tensions generated by an ethical ideal that is still dominated by a monastic model.

### Fragments of Monastic Rule

Some Mahāyāna sūtras and portions of sūtras are also considered to be Mahāyāna equivalents to the earlier monastic code or vinayas. Thus, one hears occasionally the expression "Bodhisattva Vinaya." There is, strictly speaking, no such thing as a monastic code (vinaya) specific to the Mahāyāna: all Mahāyāna schools rely on one of the vinayas produced by the Hīnayāna. However, the Mahāyāna tradition proposes that the bodhisattva vows require a special formulation of the vinaya. This formulation is sometimes purely ideal or exegetical, but is sometimes identified with specific texts. A number of texts are sometimes mentioned as constituting the code, or *prātimokṣa* of the Bodhisattva, and as representing both ritual and ethical texts.

Sūtras that may be classified under this category include the *Daśadharmaka*, the *Bodhisattva Piṭaka*, and the *Upāli-paripṛc-*

*chā*. Nevertheless such texts do not represent strict substitutes for the ancient monastic codes, much less descriptions of monastic life. Rather they are in practice conceived as supplements to the monastic code and monastic practice, and they frame or place the restraints of monastic life within a Mahāyāna ritual and ethical context. As already noted the foundation for monastic rule is still found in the older (pre-Mahāyāna) vinayas and in the *śāstra*s. Among the latter, Śāntideva's *Bodhicaryāvatāra* stands out as the embodiment of the Mahāyāna fusion of ethical, ritual, and monastic ideals.

In China we find a so-called apocryphal sūtra, the *Brahmajāla Sūtra* (the presumed Sanskrit title, *Brahmajāla*, is of course like the Sūtra itself, a Chinese creation; the Chinese title is *Fanwanjing*). It is, like the three Indian sūtras mentioned previously, an attempt to reword traditional rules of monastic and lay demeanor in terms that better respond to the ideals of Mahāyāna.

### Life in the Monastery

Although the sūtras refer to monks and laypeople, they contain no descriptions of life in the monastery. Mahāyāna sūtras may contain ideal prescriptions of what the monk should be, but they do not deal with the concrete situation of the monk and the monastic establishment. Similarly the sūtras prescribe a variety of meditational practices but say close to nothing regarding actual practices or the integration of meditation into the daily life of the monastery. Some sūtras present tidbits of monastic ritual, and we know that some of these texts became the foundation or the textual basis for monastic and lay rituals.

Unfortunately Mahāyāna sūtras do not provide enough information for us to construct a reliable history of monasticism or even of lay-monk relations. This is not to say that Mahāyāna sūtras can be read or conceived as completely divorced from the monastic institutions that probably served as the ground or the background for their composition. The sūtras abound in references to the demands of the monastic code and to interactions between lay supporters and monks, they often mention the habits of the fallen as well as those of the ideal monk, and they abound in references to the material life of the monastery. Unfortunately they only imply or allude to this monastic background in terms that are so abstract that we cannot reliably reconstruct the social life of these institutions on the basis of Mahāyāna sūtras alone.

LUIS O. GÓMEZ

*See also* Asaṅga; Bodhisattva; Buddha (Śākyamuni); Buddhism: Overview; Critiques of Buddhist Monasticism: Indo-Tibetan; Daoxuan (Tao-hsüan); Discourses (Suttas): Theravāda; Laicization of Spirituality: Buddhist Perspectives; Liturgy: Buddhist; Mahāyāna; Mantras; Manuscript Production: Buddhist; Tiantai/Tendai: Japan

### Further Reading

Bendall, Cecil, and W.H.D. Rouse, translators, *Śikshā-Samuccaya: A Compendium of Buddhist Doctrine* (Indian Texts Series), London: Murray, 1922; reprint, Delhi: Motilal Banarsidass, 1971

Beresford, Brian C., editor and translator, *Mahāyāna Purification: The "Confession Sūtra," with Commentary by*

*Ārya Nāgārjuna, and the "Practice of Vajrasattva," with Sādhana, Supplemented by Verbally Transmitted Commentaries from Geshe Ngawang Dhargyey . . . [et al.]* (Meditational Series), Dharamsala: Translation Bureau of the Library of Tibetan Works and Archives, 1980

Beresford, Brian C., et al., editors and translators, *Āryaśūra's Aspiration, with Commentary by His Holiness the II Dalai Lama, and a Meditation on Compassion by His Holiness the XIV Dalai Lama*, Dharamsala: Library of Tibetan Works and Archives, 1979; reprint, 1981

Crosby, Kate, and Andrew Skilton, translators, *The Bodhicaryāvatāra* (World's Classics), general introduction by Paul Williams, Oxford and New York: Oxford University Press, 1995

Hirakawa, Akira, "The Rise of Mahāyāna Buddhism and Its Relationship to the Worship of Stupas," *Memoirs of the Research Department of the Tōyō Bunko* 22 (1963)

Hirakawa, Akira, *A History of Indian Buddhism: From Śākyamuni to Early Mahāyāna* (Asian Studies at Hawaii, number 36), translated and edited by Paul Groner, Honolulu: University of Hawaii Press, 1990

Lamotte, Étienne, editor and translator, *The Teaching of Vimalakīrti (Vimalakīrtinirdeśa): From the French Translation with Introd. and Notes (L'enseignement de Vimalakirti)* (Sacred Books of the Buddhists, volume 32), rendered into English by Sara Boin, London: Pali Text Society, and Boston: Routledge and Kegan Paul, 1976

Lang, Karen, editor and translator, *Āryadeva's Catuḥśataka: On the Bodhisattva's Cultivation of Merit and Knowledge* (Indiske Studier, 7), Copenhagen: Akademisk, 1986

Robinson, Richard H., "The Religion of the Householder Bodhisattva," *Bharati* (1966)

Tatz, Mark, editor and translator, *Difficult Beginnings: Three Works on the Bodhisattva Path*, Boston: Shambhala, 1985

Tatz, Mark, editor and translator, *Asanga's Chapter on Ethics with the Commentary of Tsong-Kha-Pa: The Basic Path to Awakening, the Complete Bodhisattva* (Studies in Asian Thought and Religion, volume 4), Lewiston, New York: Mellen Press, 1986

# Discourses (Suttas): Theravāda

The Sutta Piṭaka, the Basket of Discourses, contains records of the Buddha's sermons as well as discourses by his foremost disciples, such as Sāriputta, Moggallāna, and Ānanda. The *suttas* (Pāli for Sanskrit *sūtras*) are distributed into four major collections: the *Dīgha Nikāya*, or Long Discourses, with 34 *suttas*; the *Majjhima Nikāya*, or Middle Length Discourses, with 152 *suttas*; the *Saṃyutta Nikāya*, or Connected Discourses, 56 chapters of short, thematically related *suttas*; and the *Aṅguttara Nikāya*, or Numerical Discourses, 11 chapters of short *suttas* arranged according to a progressive numeric scheme. A fifth collection, the *Khuddaka Nikāya*, consists of miscellaneous short texts, mainly in verse, among them the popular *Dhammapada*.

The goal of the Buddhist training, as articulated in the *suttas*, is the attainment of *nibbāna*, the extinction of suffering here and now and ultimate release from samsara, the round of rebirths. Because the Buddha emphasized that renunciation is an essential condition for the fulfillment of the training, the *suttas* often focus on the proper practice of the monastic life as the most effective vehicle for realizing the final goal. In his reports of his own quest for enlightenment, the Buddha presents himself as the supreme exemplar of the monastic career, the model for all his monks and nuns to emulate. In *MN* 26 he tells how, while leading the household life, he perceived the dangers in sensuality and "went forth from home into homelessness seeking the undefiled supreme security from bondage, Nibbāna." Both *MN* 12 and *MN* 36 give us graphic accounts of the useless austerities he practiced before discovering the true path to awakening. In his first sermon (*SN* 56:11), he announces that those who have entered the homeless life should avoid two futile extremes – sensual indulgence and self-mortification – and instead follow "the middle way," the Noble Eightfold Path, which leads to enlightenment and release.

The Eightfold Path, which gives us a broad outline of Buddhist spiritual training, consists of eight factors woven into a harmonious whole: right view, right intention, right speech, right action, right livelihood, right effort, right mindfulness, and right concentration. The factors are consistently defined in the *suttas* by stock formulas (at *DN* 22, II 312–313; *MN* 141, III 251–252; and *SN* 45:8, V 8–10). Although the Buddha says that the practice of the Noble Eightfold Path is in principle open to people from any mode of life, whether monks or laypeople, he also emphasizes that the household life invariably impedes the quest for *nibbāna* by fostering a host of mundane attachments. Thus, he himself took up the life of a monk, and after his enlightenment he established an order of monks and nuns for those wanting to devote themselves single-mindedly to the task of self-purification.

In the *suttas* the Buddha often formulates the practice of the Noble Eightfold Path in various ways designed specifically for the renunciant monk. This article surveys the most common version of this training. However, this idealized picture of the Buddhist monk's life might convey the impression that the training is an exclusively individual affair pursued in a social vacuum. To correct this impression this article examines several *suttas* that show that, far from merely teaching a path to personal liberation for solitary renunciants, the Buddha took it as integral to his mission to found a *saṅgha*, a monastic community, to carry on his message. Finally, in case these two pictures seem incompatible, this article briefly discusses still another *sutta* that shows how the two images merge into one in a way that benefits the individual monk, the monastic community, and the wider world.

The first scheme gives us a picture of the monk's "gradual training," so called because it leads by stages all the way from the starting point to the goal. This scheme is found in an extended version at *DN* 2, in a more compact version at *MN* 27 and 51, and with variants at *MN* 39, 53, 107, and 125. The summary given here is based on the version of *MN* 27 (I 179–184) and *MN* 51 (I 344–348).

The sequence opens with the arising of a Buddha in the world and his teaching of the Dhamma (Sanskrit, Dharma). When a young man hears the teaching and gains faith, he goes forth into the homeless life and undertakes training as a monk.

The training unfolds in three stages: virtue, concentration, and wisdom. Virtue is implemented by observing the monastic rules, the most basic of which inculcate noninjury, nonstealing, celibacy, and truthfulness. The next three steps internalize the process of purification by providing a bridge from virtue to concentration. These are contentment with simple robes and alms food, restraint of the senses, and mindfulness and clear comprehension. Other versions insert here moderation in eating and vigilance as well.

Based on this purified virtue and restraint, the monk goes off into seclusion and practices meditation. His first task is to overcome the five mental hindrances: sensual desire, anger, sloth, restlessness, and doubt. When the hindrances are suppressed, he enters and dwells in the exalted states of mental unification, called the *jhāna*s. The *sutta*s enumerate four *jhāna*s, each loftier and more sublime than its predecessor. These are always described by the same stock formulas, which are sometimes illuminated by similes of striking beauty (*DN* 2, I 74–76; *MN* 39, I 276–278). Sometimes four higher meditative absorptions are mentioned, called the "formless attainments" (e.g., at *MN* 8, I 41), and these carry the process of mental unification still further. This completes the training in concentration.

However, concentration is not the end of the Buddhist path, and thus the monk must proceed to develop wisdom. With his mind purified by the practice of the *jhāna*s, he recollects his previous lives even over thousands of world cycles. Next he perceives how beings pass away and are reborn in accordance with their *kamma* (Sanskrit, *karma*), or deeds. The longer version of the scheme describes several other "super-knowledges," including supernormal powers, the divine ear, and thought reading (*DN* 2, I 76–81; *MN* 6, I 34–35). Finally he penetrates with insight the Four Noble Truths, the highest teaching of the Buddha, and thereby his mind is liberated from the "taints" (*āsava*), the primordial defilements that sustain the round of rebirths. This is the "taintless liberation of mind, liberation by wisdom," the highest goal of the holy life.

The *sutta* passage on the gradual training is extremely concise, compressing into its brief compass what in lived experience is really a protracted struggle for wisdom and self-mastery. To fill in this outline, numerous other *sutta*s could be cited that give us detailed close-ups of the stages treated so elliptically in the preceding discussion. The *Aṅguttara Nikāya* is an especially rich source of short *sutta*s that highlight the demands of mental training; for example, *AN* 3:100 minutely compares the purification of the mind to the process of refining gold. Although the gradual training sequence condenses the entire development of insight into two sentences, a fuller picture of the practice is given by the *Satipaṭṭhāna Sutta* (*DN* 22, *MN* 10), in which the Buddha expounds the "four establishments of mindfulness": contemplation of body, feelings, mind, and mental phenomena. The terrain to be penetrated by insight is explored most extensively in the *Saṃyutta Nikāya* in the chapters on dependent origination (12), the elements (14), the aggregates (22), the sense bases (35), and the Four Noble Truths (56).

The portrait of the monk's life given here might suggest that the Buddhist monastic journey is a solitary undertaking. However, this account is abstracted from its living context. In the background, hidden behind the words, lies the momentous fact that the Buddha created a *saṅgha* as the support and field for the monastic journey. Hidden from view as well is the Vinaya regulation making it obligatory for a newly ordained monk to spend five years of guidance under a teacher who will train him and direct his spiritual development. When Ānanda came to the Buddha and said that, in his view, good friendship is half the holy life, the Master corrected him and said that good friendship is the entire holy life (*SN* 45:2, V 2).

The Buddha laid down not only procedures for ordination and methods of meditation but also an entire body of communal rules and regulations designed to foster the spiritual growth of his monks and nuns. Although these rules themselves are the province of the Vinaya rather than the Sutta Piṭaka, several *sutta*s describe the spirit that should animate them. Three such texts lay down lucid guidelines to communal harmony, promulgated toward the close of the Master's life when the survival of a leaderless *saṅgha* was to become an urgent concern. One is *MN* 103, in which the Buddha instructs the monks to meet to rehearse the teachings and provides guidelines for ironing out disagreements that might arise over their letter and meaning. The general principle is that the two opposing positions should be carefully compared by all the monks, errors should be politely corrected, and, if disagreement persists, senior monks known for their impartiality should adjudicate.

Another *sutta* is *MN* 104, which opens after the death of the Jain leader Nigaṇṭha Nātaputta. A report has reached the Buddhist monks that Nātaputta's followers have split into two contentious factions, and the monks come to the Buddha anxious that such a fate might befall their own community. To prevent this from happening, the Buddha teaches the monks about the "six roots of disputes," which are actually 12 states arranged in pairs: anger and vindictiveness, contempt and presumption, envy and avarice, deceit and hypocrisy, evil wishes and wrong views, and opinionatedness and obstinacy. The Buddha enjoins the monks to self-scrutiny to ensure that such defilements do not arise in themselves; if they do arise, the monks should abandon them and strive to prevent their arising in the future. As a positive counterpart he then teaches the "six qualities of harmony and respect": loving deeds, loving speech, loving thoughts, the sharing of rightful gains, the observance of common precepts, and maintaining "the view that is noble and emancipating and leads to the extinction of suffering."

Still another text relevant to communal harmony is the opening scene of the *Mahāparinibbāna Sutta* (*DN* 16, II 76–77), "The Last Days of the Buddha." Here, to prepare the *saṅgha* for his departure from this world, the Buddha teaches the monks "seven principles of non-decline": the monks should (1) frequently meet in assembly, (2) conduct the affairs of the order in concord, (3) train in accordance with the precepts, (4) respect and heed wise elders, (5) avoid falling victim to craving, (6) seek out forest dwellings, and (7) welcome virtuous visiting monks and treat them with hospitality.

Although the two pictures just sketched might appear discrepant in emphasis, another *sutta* (*MN* 31), short and beautiful, shows how their images converge. The scene is a forest reserve called the Gosiṅga Wood, where three monks – Anuruddha, Nandiya, and Kimbila – have been living. The Buddha comes to visit them and asks how they are faring. The monks reply, "We are living in concord, with mutual appreciation, without disputes, blending like milk and water, viewing each other with kindly eyes." The Buddha asks how they manage to live like this, and the monks answer that they set up loving deeds, words, and thoughts toward one another, subordinate their own desires to those of their companions, and dwell "different in body but one in mind." They share their alms food, silently perform their duties, and meet every five days for an all-night discussion of the teachings. By living in this way, the *sutta* continues, all three monks have mastered the successive stages of meditation and reached final liberation of the mind. Speaking in their praise the Buddha declares, "If the world should remember these three young monks with confident heart, that would lead to the welfare and happiness of the world for a long time. These three young monks are practicing for the welfare and happiness of the many, out of compassion for the world, for the good, welfare, and happiness of gods and humans."

BHIKKHU BODHI

Abbreviations: *DN = Dīgha Nikāya* (by number of *sutta*); *MN = Majjhima Nikāya* (by number of *sutta*); *SN = Saṃyutta Nikāya* (by chapter and *sutta* number); *AN = Aṅguttara Nikāya*. *Sutta* references to the *Nikāyas* are followed where relevant by the volume and page number in the roman-script edition published by the Pali Text Society.

*See also* Arhat; Asceticism: Buddhist Perspectives; Buddha (Śākyamuni); Buddhism: Overview; Buddhist Schools/Traditions: South Asia; Councils, Buddhist; Dharma; Disciples, Early Buddhist; Liturgy: Buddhist; Master and Pupil: Buddhist Perspectives; Patrons, Buddhist: India; Prophethood, Japanese Buddhist; Repentance Rituals, Buddhist; Rules, Buddhist (Vinaya): Historical; Saṅgha

**Further Reading**

Bodhi, Bhikkhu, editor, *The Middle Length Discourses of the Buddha: A New Translation of the Majjhima Nikāya*, translated by Bhikkhu Ñāṇamoli, Boston: Wisdom Publications, 1995

Hinuber, Oskar von, *A Handbook of Pāli Literature, Indian Philology, and South Asian Studies*, volume 2, Berlin and New York: de Gruyter, 1996

Ireland, John D., translator, *The Udana and the Itivuttaka*, Kandy, Sri Lanka: Buddhist Publication Society, 1997

Norman, K.R., *Pāli Literature*, Wiesbaden: Otto Harrassowitz, 1983

Rhys Davids, Caroline A.F., and F.L. Woodward, translators, *The Book of the Kindred Sayings (Saṃyutta-nikāya)*, 5 vols., London: Oxford University Press, 1917–1930

Walshe, Maurice, translator, *The Long Discourses of the Buddha: A Translation of the Dīgha Nikāya*, Boston: Wisdom Publications, 1995

Webb, Russell, editor, *An Analysis of the Pāli Canon*, Kandy, Sri Lanka: Buddhist Publication Society, 1975; 2nd edition, 1991

Woodward, F.L., and E.M. Hare, translators, *The Book of the Gradual Sayings (Aṅguttara Nikāya)*, 5 vols., London: Oxford University Press, 1932–1936; New York: Luzac, 1955

# Dissolution of Monasteries: Continental Europe

In almost every part of Europe and the British Isles where the Protestant Reformation carried the day, monasteries and convents were closed, suppressed, dissolved, sold or disbanded, and abandoned. The story has been told in detail for Britain (by Knowles, Youings, and Bettey, among others) because of the relatively uniform nature of events there: Henry VIII's directives were the law of the entire land, and they were carried out, in

Facade of the Abbey Church of Saint-Jean-des-Vignes (Benedictine), Soissons, France, 13th and 14th centuries. Around 1810 local inhabitants preserved the facade against the desire of the bishop, who wished to use the stones for repair of the cathedral.
Photo courtesy of Chris Schabel

Donato Bramante, Cloister, Monastery of Sant'Ambrogio (Benedictine 784–c. 1470 and then Cistercian until dissolved by Napoleon in 1797), Milan, Italy, early 16th century. Since 1931 the University of the Sacred Heart has abided here.
Photo courtesy of the Editor

stages to be sure, with firmness and consequence. Undergraduates delight in the obviously mercenary goals that helped drive the confiscation of monastic property – raising money and rewarding loyal retainers in particular.

The situation on the Continent was quite different. Not only did certain kinds of monastic houses survive the Reformation as Protestant institutions (beguinages, "ladies foundations" [*Damenstifte*], houses of deaconesses, and the two military orders of the Teutonic Knights and Knights of St. John), but the story of suppression follows the long, drawn-out contours of the Reformation itself. Many territories adopted Protestant Church structures only later in the 16th century (e.g., Albertine Saxony and the newly "united" Netherlands). Augsburg, an imperial city with "parity of confessions" (*paritätische Reichsstadt*), was a testing ground for coexistence. Some houses were only "protestantized," not dissolved, and were "secularized" only much later; attempts to secularize particular houses failed (e.g., the house of the Teutonic Knights at Marburg in 1543). In those territories where the Reformation succeeded, only to be rolled back by the triumphant south German wave of the Catholic Reformation in the later 16th and early 17th centuries (e.g., Tyrol, parts of Austria and Bavaria, and Bohemia), monasteries were refounded and

restaffed. The Roman Catholic Church suppressed certain houses and orders in the course of the early modern period as a response to internal reform movements. The "enlightened" imperial government in Vienna contributed to this trend in the later 18th century, as did the French Revolution. In 1803 all the remaining quasi-autonomous ecclesiastical territories in the Holy Roman Empire were dissolved and their property given to the new territorial lords (along with all but six of the imperial cities and a handful of soon-to-be-dissolved *Damenstifte*).

Martin Luther's (1483–1546) many writings in favor of marriage and against monastic vows in the early 1520s laid the foundation for the dissolution of monastic houses. His insistence, so eagerly accepted by both reforming lay and ecclesiastical factions, that vows of celibacy were invalid because impractical and against human nature and thus that marriage was not merely the correct but the ideal state for human beings added an immediate incentive, at least according to much of the scholarly literature. The "good works" performed by regular monks and nuns were, for Luther, as null and void as any others not done out of faith. Luther laid aside his monastic garb in October 1524. In June 1525 he took as his wife a former nun, Katharina von Bora (1499–1552). Luther's own former monastic house at Wittenberg was so caught up in Luther's movement that it dissolved it-self, leaving Luther and Katharina to found a family in its large rooms. The remaining monasteries and nunneries in Electoral Saxony were among the first to be dissolved, leading quickly to a wildfire of suppressions in the new "evangelical" cities and terri-tories. The mendicant friars were especially disliked in towns, as they provided much of the resistance to evangelical preaching and restructuring there. Philip of Hesse followed suit in 1527–1528, although he had introduced the Reformation in 1524. A certain delay, as in England, between the formal act es-tablishing the reformed religion and the practical consequences concerning monastic houses seems not to have been uncommon. The close connections between monastic houses and elite fami-lies on the one hand and the important economic and political roles played by monasteries on the other help explain the reti-cence and delays associated with carrying out one of the most obvious and fundamental reforms flowing from evangelical the-ology. However, in most cities the monastic houses were sup-pressed along with the Mass, and the former residents were allowed to choose between conforming to the new order (be-coming tax-paying ministers, burghers, or housefathers or housemothers) or leaving. Rural monasteries that were immedi-ate to the empire (*reichsunmittelbar*) tended to survive, although many were attacked (and some suppressed) by neighboring towns for reasons of theological, political, or even commercial opposition: St. Gallen by its town or Weingarten by the Swabian city of Ravensburg.

As in Britain the confiscations served two masters: the theolo-gians and the secular princes or authorities. The example of Zurich, examined in detail by Lee Wandel, provides a number of lessons: the reforms of Ulrich Zwingli (1484–1531) necessitated dissolution for moral and theological reasons. However, confis-cated monastic and ecclesiastical property not only filled city coffers but also opened new avenues to social control for the pa-trician and burgher elite. The old charitable institutions, espe-cially those run by monastic houses, had been open to all. Charity dispensed by a city commission was limited not only to those deemed to be "deserving" poor but also to native or local residents – outsiders and the able-bodied were abruptly ex-cluded. The refunctionalization of the old ecclesiastical infra-structure had massive consequences in extra-religious fields.

Dissolution, then, took many forms on the Continent. In fact a better term might be the "evangelization" or "decatholiciza-tion" of monasteries. Not only did certain kinds of monastic and

Garden of the former Discalced Carmelite Convent of Saint-Joseph-des-Carmes, Paris. The convent was used as a prison 1790–1797, and the garden witnessed the massacre of 115 priests in September 1792.
Photo courtesy of the Editor

Nave of the Benedictine Abbey Church of Jumièges, Normandy, France, 1020–1067. The church was consecrated in the presence of William the Conqueror in 1067 and dissolved in the 1790s.
Photo courtesy of the Editor

Cloister, former Carmelite monastery, occupied since 1888 by the Arrigo Boito Conservatory of Music, Parma, Italy, 17th century.
Photo courtesy of the Editor

quasi-monastic institutions become "evangelical" and thus survive the Reformation, but many houses, both Protestant and Catholic, retained their political power as territorial authorities (corporate ecclesiastical lords). The unique political autonomy of many ecclesiastical units in the empire saved them from Reformation imposed "from above" by a territorial prince or city council or at least from dissolution. Not surprisingly, in the six or seven large ethnolinguistic areas (*nationes*) in Continental Europe that were affected by the Protestant Reformation, widely differing timetables and many local variations made the "dissolution" of the monasteries anything but a simple process.

ANDREW GOW

*See also* Austria; Critiques of Western Christian Monasticism; Germany: History; Protestant Monasticism: Lutheran; Reformation; St. Gallen, Switzerland; Scandinavia; Spain: History; Switzerland; Vadstena, Sweden

**Further Reading**

Félix, Maurice, *Congrégations religieuses; Étude historique et juridique*, Paris: Rousseau, 1908

Fritz, Gerhard, *Stadt und Kloster Murrhardt im Spätmittelalter und in der Reformationszeit* (Forschungen aus Württembergisch Franken, 34), Sigmaringen: Thorbecke, 1990

Hankel, Hans Peter, *Die reichsunmittelbaren evangelischen Damenstifte im Alten Reich und ihr Ende: eine vergleichende Untersuchung* (European University Studies, series 3,

History and Allied Studies, volume 712), New York: Lang, 1996

Schaal, Katharina, *Das Deutschordenshaus Marburg in der Reformationszeit: der Säkularisationsversuch und die Inventare von 1543* (Untersuchungen und Materialien zur Verfassungs- und Landesgeschichte, 15), Marburg: Elwert, 1996

Schepper, G. de, *La réorganisation des paroisses et la suppression des couvents dans les Pays-Bas autrichiens sous le règne de Joseph II* (Université de Louvain. Recueil de travaux d'histoire et de philologie, 3rd series, fascicle 8), Louvain: Bibliothèque de l'Université, 1942

# Dissolution of Monasteries: England, Ireland, and Wales

Between 1535 and 1540 all the monastic foundations in England, Wales, and Ireland were closed. This process, known as the "dissolution," began as a bid to enrich the crown and turned, in the hands of Thomas Cromwell (c. 1485–1540), into an attack on the monastic life, "superstitious" idolatry, and pilgrimages. In the first stage of the dissolution, small foundations that were accused of dissolute lifestyles and valued at less than £200 were suppressed. In the second stage all the greater houses were convinced to surrender themselves to the king, and the ancient practice of monasticism ended by 1540. Monasticism returned to England in reign of Mary Tudor (1553–1558), only to be abolished once more by Elizabeth I (1558–1603) in 1559, ending monasticism in those realms until the 19th century.

Before the dissolution, Cistericans, Gilbertines, Carthusians, Cluniacs, Premonstratensian Canons, Austin Canons, Bridgettines, Poor Clares, Benedictines, Augustinian Canonesses, Premonstratensian Canonesses, Cluniac nuns, Friars Observant (Franciscan), Knights of St. John, and Dominicans existed in England, Ireland, and Wales. Individual houses had been dissolved before, as happened when Cardinal Wolsey (1472/74–1530) founded what became Christ Church, Oxford. However, no order had suffered complete dissolution until the Friars Observant's denunciation of Henry VIII's divorce in 1533 from Katherine of Aragon and resistance to the royal supremacy over the Church brought many to a violent end. Their seven English houses, with about 200 religious, were dissolved by the end of August 1534. Many were executed or imprisoned, and many others fled the country.

Henry VIII (1509–1547) seems to have taken the lesson taught by the seizure of these friaries to heart through the prompting of Cromwell, his chief minister. Cromwell realized that his king's need for money and his own desire for reformation of the Church could walk hand in hand. The result was a government campaign to discover the value of ecclesiastical property and to "prove" the corruption of monastic life.

As supreme head of the Church in England, Henry VIII ordered the preparation of the *Valor Eccleisiasticus*, an inventory of the wealth of the church in England, Ireland, and Wales. Carried out in the spring and summer of 1535, it was designed to maximize the king's revenue from the annual tax on ecclesiastical income given to the king by the Act of First Fruits and Tenths approved by Parliament. The ecclesiastical tax was collected by the newly established Court of First Fruits and Tenths. When the value of the churches and monastic foundations had been determined, another inquisition was launched from 1535 to 1536 that aimed specifically at the religious. Acting as Cromwell's men, the commissioners were instructed to look for moral laxity and superstition in the monasteries.

One result was the *Compendium Compertorum* (Book of Findings), which was created by Thomas Lee (or Leigh) and Richard Layton for the province of York. This report, whose accuracy has been strongly questioned, reported on five items for each monastery: (1) the names of religious who were guilty of offenses against the vow of chastity; (2) the names of those who wanted to be released from their vows; (3) the "superstition" of the house, that is, the relics housed there; (4) the name of the "founder," actually the heir of the founder, who was assumed to be the patron of the house because it provided spiritual benefits to his family; and (5) the income and debts of the house. Lee and Layton found moral laxity everywhere they went. The reality of this laxity is debatable, although Claire Cross' and Noreen Vicker's recent prosopographical study of Yorkshire monastics led them to conclude that the *Compendium* cannot be dismissed out of hand as a work of propaganda. Whatever its validity, it provided a pretext for the first round of dissolutions.

In 1536 Parliament passed 27 Hen. VIII, c. 28, an act whereby all religious houses of monks, canons, and nuns that could not dispend manors, lands, tenements, and hereditaments above the clear annual value of £200 were given to the king's highness. The act announced that because "manifest sin, vicious, carnal and abominable living" were practiced by the inmates of houses having less than £200 income per year and fewer than 12 inhabitants, those small foundations would be dissolved.

To carry out the dissolution, Parliament established the Court of Augmentations of the Revenue of the King's Crown (27 Henry VIII, c. 27). Charged with overseeing the dismantling of the small monasteries, it took control of their lands and became responsible for their debts.

In April 1536 commissioners were appointed for every shire and charged with carrying out the dissolutions. The members of each house were given the choice of either continuing as religious by transferring to one of the large houses that was not being dissolved or taking a pension and being absolved of their vows of poverty and obedience. Although they were allowed to leave the religious life, they were not absolved of their vow of chastity, creating legal confusions in later years when some married. All those who took pensions were enrolled in the Court of Augmentations, which paid their annuities.

A few small houses received exemptions either because the community purchased it or because some houses had to be left open to receive those who chose to continue the religious life. In Wales three Cistercian houses were left open for the refugees, but each was made to pay for the privilege. For example, Whitland paid £400 and went heavily into debt. Other small monasteries survived because they were daughter houses of larger

Nave of church, Fountains Abbey (Cistercian), North Yorkshire, England, 12th century.
Photo courtesy of Chris Schabel

institutions. Little immediate resistance was raised to the clo-sures. Many of the patrons of these small houses were no longer connected with the founders' families, so the closures did not deprive them personally of spiritual benefits. Moreover, care was taken not to disturb the local management of the monastic lands, and in many cases they quickly passed to local families. The number of petitions for grants of particular monastic prop-erties suggests that the local gentry saw the dissolution as an opportunity.

In all, 172 men's houses and 244 women's houses were sup-pressed by the act of 1536. Plotted on a map, the dissolved houses form a distinct pattern. In many parts of England, very few small monastic foundations existed. Most of those dissolved were in East Anglia, Lincolnshire, and the East Riding of York-shire, where two-thirds of the monasteries disappeared. Of the 130 houses that existed before the act, only 43 remained by late 1536.

The relationship between the dissolutions and the rebellions that flared up in Lincolnshire and the north is debatable. The people of those regions were discontented for many reasons. Nonetheless, the rebels in Lincolnshire demanded that no more abbeys be suppressed. The Pilgrimage of Grace in Yorkshire made three demands about the monasteries in their Pontrefact articles: that the suppressed ones be restored, that the Francis-cans Observant be revived, and that Lee and Layton be punished for their lies about the state of the monasteries. The rebels re-opened some of the closed houses, and some abbots and monks responded enthusiastically. At Sawley the abbot and brothers immediately resumed the religious life, allowing their house to be used as a communication center by the rebels. Four other con-vents were noted by the king as being involved in the revolt, and the abbots of some of the larger houses were implicated as well. In the aftermath a number of abbots were executed and their houses forfeited. Jervaulx, Kirkstead, Whalley, and Bridlington were seized and closed.

At Furness in Lancashire the abbot voluntarily turned his house over to the crown, setting a precedent for the dissolutions that followed. Charged with supporting the rebels, he quickly

**West range, Fountains Abbey (Cistercian), North Yorkshire, England, 12th century.**
**Photo courtesy of Chris Schabel**

deeded the abbey to the king, establishing the principle that a monastic house was the personal property of those who lived there. Accordingly, they could deed it away if they so chose.

Many chose to do so, but under heavy government pressure. Although at first no concerted plan seemed to be in place to close all the monasteries, the seizures and surrenders in the aftermath of the revolts in early 1537 encouraged the reform party to think about doing so. In November 1537 Lewes in Sussex was surrendered by its prior, after which the pace of closures increased, with voluntary surrenders coming faster and faster until Waltham surrendered on 23 March 1540, ending monasticism in England.

In this second round of closures, a Protestant explanation was invoked. Whereas in the first round the pretense that the monasteries were not living a holy enough life was the excuse for closure, the second round was aimed at extirpating "dumb ceremonies" and "superstition." After the dissolution of Lewes, no monk or nun was again offered the chance to continue in religion.

Each surrender was the result of a negotiation between the king's commissioners and the monks and nuns about the fate of the religious' "private" property. However, the commissioners were under orders to dissolve all monastic foundations, so only the terms of the surrenders were debatable.

In this round the friaries went as well, and they went quietly. Although they must have remembered Henry VIII's harsh treat-

ment of the Friars Observant, fearing like treatment, they had another reason. Many of the friars were already inclined toward Protestantism. The preaching orders had many members who were more sympathetic to some tenets of reformed theology. Already living and preaching in the world, they found the transition easier. Perhaps the same sympathies contributed to the poverty of many of the friaries that, being dependent on local alms, were in severely poor condition. Their surrenders were hastened by unsubtle pressure used in the West and South by Bishop Richard Ingworth of Dover, a former friar himself. He offered the friars there a choice of much stricter discipline or dissolution. Dissolution was the universal choice. His method was so effective that in Wales it took him only three weeks to secure the surrender of all the friars in the principality. The friaries had little property to support their members, so the released friars received very small pensions.

The last Welsh order to be dissolved was the Knights of St. John. Their commandery at Slebech was surrendered in 1540.

In Ireland the timing and pattern of the dissolution was different. In the Pale, Wexford, Ormond, and the southwestern ports, the dissolution was totally effective. Beginning in 1536 the small houses and the daughter houses of suppressed English monasteries were dissolved. The process was interrupted by the Geraldine League shortly thereafter but began again in 1539, as ordered in Henry VIII's commission for dissolution issued in

**Church with floor tiles, Byland Abbey (Cistercian), North Yorkshire, England, 13th century.**
Photo courtesy of Chris Schabel

April of that year. In this round the Knights Hospitallers and the mendicant houses were dissolved. A final phase (1541–1543) closed a few more houses but did not complete the dissolution. It is estimated that, although the dissolution was complete in some counties, only 55 percent of the 140 monasteries and 40 percent of the some 400 mendicant houses in Ireland were closed.

No resistance was raised to the closures in Ireland, where monasticism was very weak. No more than six Irish house had more than six monks at the time, and many monks were no longer living their vows, having married, abandoned their habits, or converted their offices into hereditary possessions. However, the mendicants were doing well in the towns. In many places both English and Gaelic lords were quick to obtain monastic properties. Perhaps the person most rewarded by the dissolution was the grand master of the Hospitallers, Sir John Rawson, who was made Viscount Clontarf, given all the Hopsitaller lands there, and granted a pension of 500 Irish marks in exchange for his cooperation.

The fate of the expelled religious everywhere was portrayed with much pious pathos by 19th-century historians, such as Cardinal Gasquet, but recent research has complicated the story and made it less pathetic. All ex-monastics were given pensions, being paid by the Court of Augmentations on the basis of their rank in their house and the wealth of the house. A legal fiction that allowed voluntary surrender viewed monastic property as the possession of the monks of a particular house, giving them the right to be paid for their property. Because they "voluntarily" swapped their property with the crown, they received a pension in exchange.

Ecclesiastical employment was available for many of the male ex-religious. Some stayed where they were, serving as cathedral canons and secular priests. Others embraced the Protestant faith and began careers as preachers and administrators in the new establishment.

In Yorkshire, where the concentration of religious was greatest with about 610 monks and canons, a considerable number manifested a sense of community after the dissolution. Carthusians seemed especially wedded to their vows. Some were executed for resisting the royal supremacy, and many fled, dispersing to houses in Scotland and on the Continent. Many of them ended their lives at Sheen Anglorum in Bruges. When monasticism was restored under Mary, a number of Carthusians resumed their habits. Four of the brothers of Monk Bretton continued to live together and observe the rule in a rented house, keeping their library intact – by buying it back from the crown – until the last of them died 36 years later. A similar pattern is visible among some of Yorkshire's nearly 230 nuns. At least two small communities of nuns stuck together after their houses were taken.

However, significant numbers of the religious embraced the changes brought by the dissolution. Although the 1539 Act of Six Articles ordered them to keep their vows of chastity, in 1549 Parliament granted them the right to marry. Mary took it away in 1554, surveying the former religious in 1556 with the intention of returning them to the newly reestablished monasteries. The survey found that perhaps 20 percent of monks and nuns had married by then. Many of those, under pressure from the regime, repudiated their spouses.

For some the transition from monk to cleric was almost seamless, often being arranged before their houses were dissolved. Heads of houses did what they could to provide for themselves, their fellows, and their families out of the properties of their houses. Frequently granting leases and advowsons to ensure their own financial futures, they sometimes enriched their families, although they often gave property, such as copes, stoles, and communion plates, to persons who could expected to safeguard and return it. Monks serving in monastic cathedrals, such as Norwich, Durham, Worcester, and Canterbury, often turned into secular canons in the same cathedrals. In Oxford, Gloucester, Chester, and Peterborough, abbots and priors surrendered their houses to become bishops in those dioceses. The flood of ex-monastics into secular livings depressed the demand for

Chapter house entrance, Furness Abbey (Cistercian), Lancashire, England, 12th century.
Photo courtesy of Chris Schabel

clergy, contributing perhaps to the sharp decline of ordinations in the 1540s and 1550s.

Nuns, whose pensions were generally smaller than the men's, had a more difficult time returning to the world. Forbidden to marry until Edward VI (1547–1553) changed the law, they had few ways to supplement their incomes. Many were forced to return home to their relatives. Some did marry, but Mary's commissioners forced them to separate from their husbands. After Elizabeth came to the throne, some resumed their married states. Nonetheless, the nuns' houses were, as a group, poorer than those of the monks, so their pensions were smaller, their prospects were grimmer, and the track they leave in history was much fainter.

When Mary became queen, she was intent on restoring England to Catholicism. Parliament agreed, but only after she had accepted the proviso that property taken from the Church in the dissolution would remain in lay hands. Cardinal Pole (1500–1588) had insisted that restoration be made as an act of contrition, but the lawmakers disagreed. In return for the land, Mary got the repeal of all the ecclesiastical legislation of Henry VIII and Edward VI all the way back to the time before the Reformation. After the repeal became law in January 1555, she began to act on her plan to restore monasticism in England. This was not easy to do, as 15 years had passed since the last monks and nuns left their houses and very little property was available to support the refounded houses. Nonetheless, the Benedictines were returned to Westminster Abbey, the Carthusians to Sheen, the Franciscan Observants to Greenwich, the Dominicans to Smithfield, the Dominican nuns to Dartford, and the male and female Bridgettines to Sion. At the same time Mary abolished the Court of Augmentations, uniting it with the Exchequer.

These new foundations were swept away by Elizabeth's first Parliament. By 1 Eliz. I, c. 24, all monastic property was once more annexed to the crown. This act denounced the monastics as persons attempting to reduce the realm to "darkness and superstition," ending legal tolerance of their presence in the Tudor kingdoms. Once more the religious were granted pensions by the crown, which assumed the debts of the dissolved houses. By the 1570s even the memory of monasticism in England and Wales was fading fast.

NORMAN L. JONES

*See also* Archaeology: Western Europe; Augustinian Friars/Hermits; Cathedral Priories; Critiques of Western Christian Monasticism; England; Exile, Western Christian; Ireland: History; Reformation; Wales

## Further Reading

Baskerville, Geoffrey, *English Monks and the Suppression of the Monasteries*, New Haven, Connecticut: Yale University Press, and London: Cape, 1937

Ruins of Glastonbury Abbey, Glastonbury, England, 13th century. Dissolved in 1539, the abbey was despoiled as a stone quarry until 1830. Since 1908 the site has been owned by the Church of England.
Photo courtesy of the Editor

Bradshaw, Brendan, *The Dissolution of the Religious Orders in Ireland Under Henry VIII*, London and New York: Cambridge University Press, 1974

Cross, Claire, and Noreen Vickers, *Monks, Friars and Nuns in Sixteenth-Century Yorkshire*, Leeds: Yorkshire Archaeological Society, 1995

Gasquet, F.A., Cardinal, *Henry VIII and the English Monasteries: An Attempt to Illustrate the History of Their Suppression*, London: Hodges, 1888; Freeport, New York: Books for Libraries Press, 1972

Jack, Sybil, "The Last Days of the Smaller Monasteries," *Journal of Ecclesiastical History* 21 (1970)

Knowles, David, *The Religious Orders in England*, volume 3: *The Tudor Age*, Cambridge: Cambridge University Press, 1959; New York: Cambridge University Press, 1979

Thompson, Benjamin, "Monasteries and Their Patrons at Foundation and Dissolution," *Transactions of the Royal Historical Society* 4 (1994)

Woodward, G.W.O., *The Dissolution of the Monasteries*, London: Blanford Press, 1966; New York: Walker, 1967

Youings, Joyce, *The Dissolution of the Monasteries*, London: Allen and Unwin, and New York: Barnes and Noble, 1971

# Dissolution of Monasteries: Scotland

The nearly 100 Roman Catholic religious houses of Scotland first became objects of physical destruction in the 1530s. These religious houses represented the old religion, with its emphasis on the physical in the form of masses, sacraments, devotions, and festivals. The reformers, most notably George Wishart (c. 1513–1546) and John Knox (c. 1513–1572), saw the destruction of the contents and fabric of monastic buildings and even parish churches in Scotland as symbolic of the overthrow of superstition and idolatry. Such destruction would usher in a return to the pure message of the Gospel. This reforming zeal was abetted by local lords eager to add to their property and political power and by English rulers anxious to neutralize a traditional rival.

The destruction involved two phases. The first phase – before 1559 – saw the "casting down," or destruction, of altars and furnishings. The second phase – after 1559 – saw the unroofing and rapid deterioration of the buildings themselves. As early as 1533 a Walter Stuart was summoned before the archbishop of

Glasgow to explain damage to a statue of the Virgin in the Observant Friars' church in Ayr. In 1537 two men were sought for "hangeing of the image of St. Francis" in Dundee and Perth. In 1540–1541 the Scottish Parliament declared that no one should cut down the images of saints. However, in 1542, owing to the death of James V and the flirtation of the regent (the earl of Arran) with Protestantism, reform preachers grew bolder, and the violence against monastic property increased.

The friars, especially the Franciscan Observants, quickly became the favorite target of such violence. They lived in towns, where Lutheran influence was stronger; they were landlords who could be unpopular in any economic depression; and they were in the forefront of the anti-Lutheran campaign. Although lack of religious observance might be one of the rallying cries of those anxious to eliminate the monasteries, it was the more observant houses who posed the most serious threat to Lutheran ideas and who thus (as in England) were the first to be attacked. One convent destroyed was that of the Dominican nuns in Edinburgh, who were widely known for their strict observance. Riots in Dundee in 1543 saw at least one abbey sacked, and in Edinburgh the townspeople saved the Dominican priory from destruction.

In 1543 Cardinal David Beaton's star was on the rise, and Catholicism regrouped. The earl of Arran abjured his Protestantism, and the proposed marriage of Mary Stuart (1542–1587) to Edward VI (1547–1553) of England was repudiated. The English countered by invading the southern part of Scotland several times during the next few years, beginning with the "Rough Wooing" of 1544. These invasions did extensive damage to the monasteries from Edinburgh to the southern borders, including serious damage to Holyrood and the Dominican priory in Edinburgh and to monasteries in Kelso, Melrose, Dryburgh, and Jedburgh in the Borders. In 1547 the abbey of Balmerino was attacked on Christmas night.

However, most of the damage done to the friaries and monasteries in the war zone was not irreparable, and most of them eventually recovered from these assaults. Blackfriars, the Dominican priory in Edinburgh, housed a provincial council in 1549. Jedburgh held an ordination in 1550. Melrose, which the English claimed to have destroyed, kept up a normal monastic life until 1560. Materially the English invasions did nothing that would have remained permanent, but they had the effect of destabilizing the country and allowing the revolutionary forces to gain strength.

Thus, outbursts of iconoclasm grew more frequent. People were arrested for breaking statues in Edinburgh in 1556. In 1558 Elizabeth came to the throne of England, further emboldening the

Abbey of St. Mary (Premonstratensian), Dryburgh, Berwickshire, Scotland, 12th-century church with 15th-century gatehouse in the foreground.
Photo courtesy of Chris Schabel

reformers, so much so that civil war seemed imminent in Scotland. Early in 1559 a "Beggars' Summons" appeared on the doors of many friars' churches – a manifesto of sorts threatening the religious orders with confiscation of property in the name of the poor. In May 1559 John Knox returned to Scotland. Almost immediately he organized an assault on several houses in Perth, destroying altars, statues, pictures, and furnishings. From Perth he moved through Fife toward St. Andrew's, where the Franciscan and Dominican churches were destroyed and the cathedral's artistically rich interior was savaged. The monasteries of Scone and Lindores were then wrecked, and the Lords of the Congregation, as the reforming party was known, continued the destruction in Stirling and Edinburgh.

The traditional explanation for the dissolution of the Scottish monasteries – namely, that they had fallen into disrepair from neglect and that the "rascal multitude" and the English finished the job – is no longer satisfactory. Modern research has shown that the monasteries and friaries in Scotland were, like their counterparts in England, in relatively good shape both internally and externally. Buildings were being maintained and repaired right up to 1560, and recruits were still entering in respectable numbers – both of which are signs of a healthy religious life.

A system of commendators – abbots imposed on monasteries by the Scottish crown or nobility – did not help the public image or the religious life of the monasteries. Six of James V's illegitimate sons were imposed on monasteries. By 1560 nearly two-thirds of the monasteries had commendators as their leaders. Although some of these commendators took their jobs seriously and provided excellent leadership, many (such as James Stuart, the commendator of both Kelso and Melrose) neglected their monasteries and disposed of monastic property to their own or their family's advantage. This system, and that of granting "feus" (heritable leases), hastened and made permanent the transition from monastic to private property.

After the destruction of their monasteries, the monks themselves went in several directions. Some became Presbyterian ministers or readers, others fled to the Continent to rejoin their orders or take over houses in decline (three Scottish monasteries existed in southern Germany), and others held out for a time in Scotland itself. By 1580 few if any large monastic buildings remained intact. Monasticism would not return to Scotland until 1862.

JOHN C. VIDMAR

See also Critiques of Western Christian Monasticism; Dominicans: Female; England: History; Franciscans: General or Male; Luther, Martin; Persecution: Christian Perspectives; Reformation; Scotland

**Further Reading**

Cowan, Ian B., and David E. Easson, *Medieval Religious Houses: Scotland*, London: Longmans, Green, 1957; 2nd edition, London and New York: Longman, 1976
Dilworth, Mark, *Scottish Monasteries in the Late Middle Ages*, Edinburgh: Edinburgh University Press, 1995
Donaldson, Gordon, *Scotland: James V to James VII*, Edinburgh: Oliver and Boyd, 1965; New York: Praeger, 1966
McRoberts, David, "Material Destruction Caused by the Scottish Reformation," in *Essays on the Scottish Reformation 1513–1625*, edited by McRoberts, Glasgow: Burns, 1962
Ross, Antony, "Some Notes on the Religious Orders in Pre-Reformation Scotland," in *Essays on the Scottish Reformation 1513–1625*, edited by David McRoberts, Glasgow: Burns, 1962

# Dōgen 1200–1253

Japanese Buddhist philosopher, monk, and founder of Japan's Sōtō Zen school

Dōgen, the founder within Japan of the Sōtō school of Zen, was a Japanese Buddhist philosopher-monk whose trajectory of experience and teaching emphatically prioritized the monastic mode of life. He was also the author of a major, multifascicled treatise, the *Shōbōgenzō* (Treasury of the Eye of the Authentic Dharma), a work that, probably more than any text in the Japanese Buddhist tradition, has attracted the attention of philosophers in both Europe and North America during the 20th century.

Born within the court nobility of Kyoto, Japan's longtime capital, Dōgen was orphaned by the age of eight and, as was then customary, was sent into monastic life. Trained at the Tendai center on Mount Hiei, he became increasingly interested in the Zen forms of Buddhism that then were still fairly new to Japan and traveled in 1223 to China, where he met Rujing, the teacher regarded by him as the most authentic Zen master there. Returning to Japan in 1227, he lived in temples on the outskirts of the capital but in 1243 left the capital to reside in far-off Echizen, a place of harsh winters. In its mountains he founded Eihei-ji, the monastic complex that today remains as the base of Japanese Zen in this line. In 1240 he began work on the *Shōbōgenzō*, a text with a complicated and somewhat debated composition history. He died in 1253.

By the time he left the capital to establish a monastery in a remote area, Dōgen had come to hold what here will be called the perspective of "autotelic monasticism," meaning that the rewards of the monastic life are taken as intrinsic to it rather than as means to other goals, either material or spiritual. A distinctive mark of Dōgen was his emphatic rejection of all kinds of instrumentalism. This meant that when he insisted on the value of "sitting meditation" exactly in the manner of Śākyamuni (the Buddha), Dōgen viewed such an activity, undertaken with the body as well as with the mind, as a totally effective recapitulation of Śākyamuni's body and mind in the enlightened state. Thus, Dōgen outlined rules for the monastic life as ones that give an organized structure to meditation so conceived.

In his "Bendōwa" (Lecture Concerning Pursuit of the Way), Dōgen claimed to have learned this principle of noninstrumentality from his Chinese teacher:

In China I myself saw the great monasteries there, places with meditation halls in which 500 to 600 or even one or two thousand monks could gather. They sat meditating day and night. I asked my teacher, the abbot who had received the seal of authentic Dharma transmission, what was the essential teaching of the Buddha. He answered that it consisted in recognizing that practice and enlightenment are not two separate stages.

Another formulation in the same text is, "To practice is to exercise enlightenment." The focus in these, one consistently maintained within the Dōgen oeuvre, is on the disciplines, rituals, and "austerities" incumbent on the monk not as things to be endured so as to reach the telos of spiritual attainment but as identical with such practices.

This implies that neither the monastic nor the person viewing such activities from outside should consider these as "hardships" or as processes of pain. In fact pain does not become a term of value, likely because to make it so would refurbish the illusion of the "self" of the person in asceticism. Probably because *zazen* (sitting in the lotus posture with concentrated breath, mind, and body) was for him the paradigmatic Buddhist activity, Dōgen's unrelenting emphasis was on the joy intrinsic to all forms of Buddhist regimen and ritual.

Consequently, much of the *Shōbōgenzō* and his statements in the posthumously edited *Eihei-kōroku* consist in taking up aspects of monastic life – the putting on of robes and chanting of sūtras but also more "lowly" activities, such as preparing and eating meals or going to the privy – and in describing them as playful and ecstatic modes in which enlightenment is articulated in the mind and body of the practitioners. Supposed "deprivations" are revalorized as well – as, for example, in the "Dōtoku" (Expression of the Way) fascicle's discussion of a monk's protracted silence:

Do not take a dislike to your maintenance of silence. Your non-speaking gives articulation to the whole of the truth. You sit in silent meditation for a lifetime or two – not just for a couple hours now and a couple more later. . . . Thus a whole lifetime lived without leaving the monastery is a lifetime without lacunae in the expression of truth. . . . To remain speechless is not to be inarticulate; the very speechlessness of persons in perpetual silence is itself expressive.

This is the fashion in which Dōgen validated the monastic mode as unparalleled.

Modern critics suggest that Dōgen's decision to move his monastery away from the capital and into the mountains in 1243 was the result of having lost against Rinzai monks in competition for patronage. However, taken as the real reason, this would assume that he would have preferred to remain in the city.

It also overlooks what had been in earlier statements by him a steadily growing preference for monastic life in mountains rather than urban settings. His stance combined two things: a stated emphasis on how his Chinese master had disdained the compromises entailed by patronage from kings and his own strong sense that natural phenomena in their own modality are practitioners of the Buddhist way. The latter is perhaps most powerfully articulated in his "Sansui-kyō" (Sūtra of Mountains and Waters), composed in 1240:

Mountains are the dwelling place of great saints in a way that transcends the categories of past and present. Great saints and sages fused their bodies and their minds with the mountains. Thus the mountains themselves express sagehood and saintliness. Therefore when going into the mountains one should not expect to find sagehood only in the humans gathered there [as distinct from the mountains themselves]. Sagacity is not to be met in that way. It is comprised, rather, of the mountains themselves and in the way in which they too are practitioners of the enlightened way.

Such emphasis on natural phenomena as what might be called "co-monastics" was in conformity to Dōgen's acceptance of the infinity of space and time, which was part of the Indian Buddhist heritage. However, it was also another articulation of his rejection of instrumentality. Nature was not to be merely a *context* for human religious praxis, since instrumentalism of that type would encourage the species egotism of humans. These points were summarized in a justly respected formulation within Dōgen's "Genjō kōan" (Actualizing the Dharma): "To study the truth of Buddhism is to study the self. To rightly study the self consists of forgetting the self. And to forget the self is to be actively together with the myraid phenomena of the universe."

WILLIAM R. LaFLEUR

*See also* Buddhist Schools/Traditions: Japan; Chan/Zen: Japan; Eisai (Yosai); Japan: History; Kōan; Kyoto, Japan; Mount Hiei, Japan; Tiantai/Tendai: Japan

## Biography

Scion of an aristocratic family, Dōgen entered the Tendai monastery on Mount Hiei at age 13. Assailed by doubt he left to study under Eisai (1141–1215) and then to study in China 1223–1227 under Rujing. Back in Japan he lived first near Kyoto and in 1243 departed for distant Eihei-ji in on the northern seacoast. There he established a Sōtō Zen monastery and wrote the *Shōbōgenzō* (Treasury of the Eye of the Authentic Dharma). He insisted that *zazen* – meditating in the lotus position – is the core of Buddhism and not merely a "means" to enlightenment.

## Major Works

*Eihei-kōroku*, as *The Eihei-kōroku*, translated by Yūhō Yokoi, 1987

*Shōbōgenzō*, as *Master Dogen's Shobogenzo*, translated by Gudo Nishijima and Chodo Cross, 1994

## Further Reading

Abe, Masao, *A Study of Dōgen: His Philosophy and Religion*, edited by Steven Heine, Albany: State University of New York Press, 1992

Bielefeldt, Carl, *Dōgen's Manuals of Zen Meditation*, Berkeley: University of California Press, 1988

Heine, Steven, *Dōgen and the Kōan Tradition: A Tale of Two Shōbōgenzō Texts*, Albany: State University of New York Press, 1994

Kodera, Takashi James, *Dōgen's Formative Years in China: An Historical Study and Annotated Translation of the Hōkyō-ki*, Boulder, Colorado: Prajña Press, and London: Routledge and Kegan Paul, 1980

LaFleur, William R., editor, *Dōgen Studies*, Honolulu: University of Hawaii Press, 1985

Tanahashi, Kazuaki, editor, *Moon in a Dewdrop*, San Francisco: North Point Press, 1985; Longmead: Element Books, 1988

# Dominic, St. c. 1172–1221

## Spanish founder of the Dominican Order

Dominic was born in Caleruega, Old Castile. He studied theology at Palencia and then became a canon of the cathedral chapter at Osma, which followed a strict observance under the rule of St. Augustine. Even then Dominic was known for his detachment, intense prayer, and deep concern for others. In 1203 and again from 1205 to 1206, Dominic accompanied his bishop, Diego d'Azevedo, on a diplomatic mission to the north of Germany or to Denmark, concerning the marriage of Alfonso VIII's son. Experiences gathered on the way made a profound impression on the two men. While passing through the south of France, they witnessed the deplorable condition of the Church and the success of Catharism. Then, when they had arrived at their destination, they became acquainted with a plan to evangelize the Baltic regions.

Diego and Dominic spent the winter of 1205 in Rome, where they shared their experiences with Pope Innocent III (1198–1216). Diego was now so eager to preach the gospel to pagans that he asked to be relieved of his diocese to become a missionary, but he was refused. They probably also discussed the situation in Languedoc, which was very much on the pope's mind. Continuing their journey homeward, they again passed through Languedoc, arriving at Castelnau in June 1206 in time to participate in a meeting of Cistercians that included three papal legates: Peter of Castelnau (d. 1208) and Master Ralph, monks of Fontfroide, and Arnold Amaury, abbot of Cîteaux. In obedience to the pope, the Cistercians had been conducting a preaching campaign against the Cathars and the Waldensians since 1204. They rated the effort a failure and were about to give up when Diego boldly explained why they had failed. The legates conducted themselves in a manner befitting their high office. They rode on horseback and were accompanied by armed guards. (They were also involved with civil authorities in the prosecution of heresy.) The heretics, by contrast, relied solely on preaching, traveled on foot, and lived from hand to mouth. The austerity of their appearance caused many to believe that they were the true successors of the apostles. In the future, Diego advised, they must adopt the more evangelical style of the heretics. Diego and Dominic took the lead, and the Cistercians followed with some misgivings, which they communicated to the pope.

Innocent's response, dated 17 November 1206, was addressed to Master Ralph, ordering him to proceed in the very way recommended by Diego: "imitating the poverty of the poor Christ, in wretched dress and ardent spirit, reaching out to the wretched, drawing them away from error by word and example." During much of 1207, about 30 Cistercians, along with Diego and Dominic, engaged in mendicant preaching, touring towns on foot and debating with heretical leaders. Diego was so persuasive in a debate at Pamiers that he convinced Durand of Huesca, some fellow Waldensians, and the presiding judge to return to the Church. However, by summer's end most of the Cistercians had returned to their monasteries. Diego left for Spain in September to bring back financial support but died there on 30 December. Then, provoked by the intransigence of Raymond VI, count of Toulouse (rl. 1194–1222), and by the murder of a papal legate, in which the count was implicated, Innocent ordered the Albigensian Crusade in 1209. In the wake of the war, a council held at Avignon urged bishops to devote themselves all the more to preaching and to seek help from qualified others.

Thus, in the summer of 1215, Fulk, the bishop of Toulouse, offered official recognition and financial support to Dominic and his few companions, instituting them as a mendicant preaching band in his diocese "to uproot heresy, expel vices, teach the creed, and instill sound morals." In short, he gave official recognition to what Dominic was already doing and had embraced as his vocation. When Fulk departed in September for the Fourth Lateran Council, he took Dominic with him, confident that Innocent would approve of his initiative. In fact, Fulk's action reflected the council's mandate to appoint priests in every diocese dedicated exclusively to preaching and hearing confessions (c. 10). As expected, Innocent did approve and was prepared to offer Dominic and his followers papal confirmation, but he advised them first to choose a rule from those already approved. Evidently, he wanted to spare them possible suppression under c. 13 of the council, which forbade new forms of religious orders. Innocent died before they could report their choice. However, confirmation came from Innocent's successor, Honorius III (1216–1227). A bull of 22 December 1216 established Dominic's band of preachers as a papally exempt order of canons under the rule of St. Augustine. Evangelization was to be the primary mission of the "preachers," as a bull of 21 January 1217 called them. The steps taken from Innocent's authorization in 1206 of mendicant preaching to combat heresy to the establishment of the Order of Preachers and the universalization of its mission corresponded exactly to Dominic's own growing awareness of the Church's needs and the expansion of his apostolic vision. He personally collaborated in the formulation of those two bulls and in many others that would bring the new order to full realization.

Fra Angelico, Detail of St. Dominic from Jesus in Pretoria. Museum of San Marco, Florence, Italy, 1441.
Photo courtesy of Alinari/Art Resource, New York

It is a measure of Dominic's faith in divine guidance that, once he had received papal confirmation, he scattered his few followers to found priories in Paris, Bologna, Madrid, and Rome. Paris and Bologna were chosen with a view to recruitment. The two great university cities teemed with students and the best of Europe's scholars. Recruits drawn from their ranks would be ready for assignment without much additional preparation. The first Dominicans arrived in Paris on 12 September 1217 and in Bologna in April of 1218. While Dominic was preaching in Rome, Cardinal Ugolino, the great promoter of the mendicants and future Pope Gregory IX (1227–1241), introduced Reginald of Orleans to him. Reginald was a canon and a professor of ecclesiastical law at the University of Paris. After meeting Dominic, he joined the order and was soon sent to Bologna to take charge of the priory and to conduct a preaching mission. When Dominic visited Bologna in the summer of 1219, he found the community well established and already engaged in study. A much larger church had been given to the community to accommodate the crowds that came to hear Reginald, and a new priory had to be built to house the many vocations he attracted. Because the community in Paris was not faring as well, Dominic sent Reginald to them and personally took over formation of the new recruits.

From the very beginning, Dominic emphasized the lifelong study of Scripture and theology as an indispensable prerequisite for the order's primary task of preaching. He wanted every house to have a resident lecturer in theology to instruct the brothers. The general chapter held in Bologna in 1220 legislated on education and established the first Dominican school of theology at the Bologna priory. The powerful attraction of the universities on men of learning had left many cities entirely without teachers. In years to come these priory schools, with their resident masters and lectures open to outsiders, would do much to fill the void.

In addition to foundations for men, Dominic established houses for women. Indeed, the first foundation he was associated with was opened for women at Prouille in 1207. Diego had observed that women were sometimes driven by poverty into the arms of the Cathars, so he created a Catholic institution to receive them. As a vowed community with a regular liturgical life, Prouille served Dominic and his friars for years as a place of refreshment and refuge. In 1219 he took responsibility for a monastery of nuns at San Sisto in Rome, and he established another in Madrid. (A letter addressed to the prioress and nuns of Madrid is the only written work of Dominic to survive.) Dominic received the profession of Diana d'Andalò, a Bologna aristocrat, but the foundation she proposed did not materialize until after Dominic's death. Under his successor, Jordan of Saxony, a great number of women, especially in Germany, would seek affiliation with the order. The women's branch of the Dominicans would become known as the Second Order.

Dominic guided the friars through two general chapters that completed the work of foundation. The Chapter of 1220 set down the organizational structure and the process of decision making. The general chapter was given supreme legislative authority over mission and members. The Chapter of 1221 determined a geographical structure for the order that provided a pattern for growth. Five provinces were erected in Europe: Spain, Provence, France, Lombardy, and the Roman province, each with its prior provincial and chapter; missions were created in Hungary, Germany, England, Scandinavia, Poland, and Greece. An eyewitness reports that even as his brothers were being sent forth to preach among pagans, Dominic was letting his beard grow as a sign that he was ready to join them. He had never lost his desire to spread the gospel in foreign lands.

Between 1220 and 1221, when not engaged in the business of the order, Dominic joined his brothers in combatting heresy in northern Italy. Since 1217 Cardinal Ugolino had been assigned as papal legate to Lombardy, which had become a stronghold of the Cathars and the Waldensians, many of them refugees from the Albigensian Crusade. This was the work that had initiated his preaching career. In late July 1221 Dominic returned to Bologna completely exhausted. He was only about 50 years old when he died in the priory on 6 August 1221. True to his commitment to poverty, he ended his days on someone else's bed. Even in Bologna he had reserved nothing for his own use. Cardinal Ugolino conducted his funeral, and later, as Gregory IX, he sent a papal commission to Bologna to investigate the life and merits of Dominic as part of the canonization process. The testimonies given by his confreres bear loving witness to his intensely Christlike life, spent in poverty and in bodily austerities, constant in prayerful vigils and tireless in zeal for the salvation of others. The beautifully inspiring *Nine Ways of Prayer of St. Dominic*, an anonymous work written after 1260, is based on such eyewitness accounts. Dominic was canonized by Pope Gregory on 3 July 1234, the same pope who had canonized Francis of Assisi (1181/82–1226) on 16 July 1228.

The Order of Preachers and the Order of Friars Minor, the two great mendicant orders of the Middle Ages, developed side by side and belong to the history of the *vita apostolica*, which was an intense current of Christian spirituality that identified apostolic life with voluntary poverty and itinerant preaching: radical separation from the world and a deep sense of mission to the world. A simplicity and literalness were apparent in Francis' personal response to the Gospel that did not translate easily into a rule for a community. Harsh controversies broke out, even during his lifetime, over the interpretation of his aims. The genius of Dominic was to provide his followers with an institutional structure for effectively transmitting his charism that combined contemplation, community, study, and pastoral work, especially preaching. As a centralized, international organization, the structure of the Order of Preachers bore many similarities to medieval military orders and provided a model for future apostolic orders.

At the time of the Fourth Lateran Council, Innocent was painfully aware that the main obstacles to the reform desired by the council were unworthy and negligent ministers and a neglected and ignorant laity. The mendicant orders proved to be a providential remedy for those maladies. The Dominicans and the Franciscans helped to revolutionize pastoral care as preachers, confessors, spiritual directors, and founders of lay confraternities. They were also active in the life of the universities as theologians and teachers. The Dominicans continued to combat heresy by mendicant preaching, the only method Dominic considered warranted by the gospel. Dominican involvement in the papal inquisition, which was imposed on them by popes, beginning with Gregory IX, was clearly not in keeping with Dominic's example.

PHILIP TIMKO, O.S.B.

*See also* Augustinian Rule; Cistericans; Dominicans; Education of Christian Monastics; France: History; Heretics, Christian; Self-Mutilation, Christian; Spain: History

## Biography

Born in Castile, Spain, Dominic joined the Augustinian Canons of Osma and traveled thence in 1203–1205 to Northern Europe. On his return trip, he preached against the Albigensians in Languedoc, pioneering a new mode of itinerant mendicant preaching. In 1215 he was put in charge of these mendicant preachers at Toulouse, France. Between 1216 and 1218 Honorius III recognized them as the Order of Preachers (O.P.). In 1217 they established a priory at the University of Paris. The first general chapter was held at Bologna in 1220, where Dominic died in 1221. The church of San Domenico in that city houses his tomb.

## Further Reading

Koudelka, Vladimir J., *Dominic*, translated and edited by C. Fissler and Simon Tugwell, London: Darton, Longman and Todd, 1997 (includes an introduction to historical and hagiographical sources as well as a selection of primary documents)

"St. Dominic," in *Butler's Lives of the Saints*, new full edition, revised by John Cumming, Collegeville, Minnesota: Liturgical Press, 1998

Tugwell, Simon, editor, *Early Dominicans: Selected Writings*, with an introduction by Tugwell, New York: Paulist Press, and London: SPCK, 1982

Vicaire, Marie-Humbert, *Saint Dominic and His Times*, translated by Kathleen Pond, London: Darton, Longman and Todd, and New York: McGraw-Hill, 1964

Vicaire, Marie-Humbert, *The Genius of St. Dominic: A Collection of Study-Essays*, edited by Peter B. Lobo, Dublin: Dominican Publications, 1990

# Dominicans: Female

Communities of Dominican women have existed alongside those of men since the inception of the Order of Friars Preachers. While preaching against the Albigensians in southern France, Dominic (c. 1172–1221) obtained episcopal permission in 1206 to establish a community at Prouille for religious women, many of whom were converts from the heretical sect. In 1218 and 1219 he assisted in the founding of houses for women in Madrid and Rome (St. Sixto). Like their male counterparts the women followed a version of the Augustinian rule adapted by Dominic, but none of these women's communities was officially accepted into the Dominican Order during the early years. In 1220 Dominic attempted to obtain permission for the incorporation into the Order of the foundation of St. Agnes in Bologna, where his spiritual friend and charge Diana d'Andalo resided, but his efforts met with limited success.

During the first half-century of their existence, the Dominican women's communities continued to be accorded an ambiguous reception from the First Order of Dominicans. In 1224 the chapter general at Paris suspended the foundation of female houses, an act that was repeated in 1228, 1235, and 1256. Nonetheless, leaders among the Order of Preachers, including Jordan of Saxony (b. late 12th century, d. 1237), Dominic's successor, and Hugh of St. Cher (c. 1190–1263) encouraged and supported the establishment of houses for religious women. In 1259 the Constitutions of the Sisters, formulated by Humbert of Romans (c. 1200–1277), were approved. Finally, in 1267 the pope reaffirmed the Dominican friars' role in the care of religious women (*cura monialium*) but exempted them from material responsibility for the women's communities. With this act nuns became fully incorporated as the Second Order of Dominicans.

The regular life of Dominican men emphasized the importance of poverty and the significance of study in achieving the goals of preaching and otherwise ministering to those outside the monastery. By contrast the nuns led a contemplative life in enclosure. Although not permitted to preach, Dominican women were encouraged to pursue intellectual activities. Many wrote works about their own lives and their houses, and their communities became centers for the copying and illuminating of manuscripts.

The dramatic increase in the number of religious women in the 13th century can be explained in part as a response to the *Frauenfrage*, that is, the question of what to do with the surplus female population that had resulted in part from the Crusades and other military activities. The growth also reflected the fact that the religious life provided women with educational opportunities and security not accessible in the secular world. However valid, these demographic and social reasons do not fully account for the remarkable piety and devotion of religious women of the age.

By the beginning of the 14th century, almost 150 Dominican convents existed in Western Europe; of these approximately half were located in the two German Dominican provinces of Teutonia and Saxony. In these regions the mystical tradition profoundly affected Dominican nuns. The women experienced a personal relationship with God that manifested itself in visions, revelations, and other ecstatic experiences. Guided and supported by Dominican preachers, such as Meister Eckhart (c. 1260–c. 1328), John Tauler (c. 1300–1361), and Henry Suso (c. 1295–1366), the women recorded personal experiences and those of others in their community using the vernacular. Sisters, such as Christina Ebner (1277–1356), her kinswoman Margaret Ebner (c. 1291–1351), Adelheid Langmann (1306–1375), and Elsbeth Stagel (d. c. 1360), composed autobiographies, biographies of sisters in the community (*Schwesternbücher*), and letters that documented the intense spirituality of Dominican women of the age. The Dominican vow of monastic observances involving ascetic practices, such as fasting, also exerted a profound impact on the religious life of the women of the Order at this time.

The Black Death of the mid–14th century decimated the general population as well as that of the traditional and mendicant orders. Despite social, political, and ecclesiastical upheaval, the century witnessed the flourishing of the Third Order of Dominicans, especially around Cologne and in various urban areas in Italy. The tertiaries devoted themselves to the religious life but were not necessarily bound by the monastic tradition. Catherine of Siena (1347–1380), patron saint of Italy, was a member of the Third Order; in 1970 Pope Paul VI (1963–1978) declared her a Doctor of the Church. A mystic as well as an ecclesiastical emissary, Catherine inspired within the Order reforms that her confessor Raymond of Capua (c. 1330–1399) later championed.

Reform led to a schism within the Order between Conventuals and Observants. Although the dissent contributed to a period of crisis in the First Order, the Second Order continued to thrive throughout the 14th and 15th centuries. In Germany the reform led to renewed attention to the lives and writings of the spiritually blessed Dominican women of previous generations, and in Italy the canonization in 1461 of Catherine of Siena revived interest in the Third Order. As a consequence of the Reformation, the Order declined in the 16th century. However, the 17th century witnessed the resurgence among Dominican women renowned for their sanctity. The tradition flourished especially in Spain and in the recently colonized and converted regions of Latin America with women such as St. Rose of Lima (1586–1614).

In Europe the Order suffered renewed decline in the 18th century as a result of political upheaval, and many women's communities were closed. During the 19th century the Third Order experienced a period of growth, especially in the United States, England, and France. Whereas the nuns of the Second Order remained in enclosure, women of the Third Order became involved in missionary activities and the care of the sick and the poor. After the death of her husband, Mother Alphonsa Lathrop (1851–1926), daughter of Nathaniel Hawthorne, took vows in 1900 and established the Dominican congregation of St. Rose of Lima, or Servants of Relief for Incurable Cancer. In 1912 Mary Josephine Rogers (d. 1955) founded the first house of the Teresians, who in 1920 became the Foreign Mission Sisters of St. Dominic (Dominicans of the Third Order). Commonly known by the name of the mother house in New York, the Maryknoll Sisters engage in missionary work throughout the world.

Within the last century the ranks of Dominican women have become eight times as large as those of Dominican men – indisputable evidence that the Second and Third Orders of Dominicans continue to thrive.

DEBRA L. STOUDT

## Further Reading

Ashley, Benedict M., *The Dominicans*, Collegeville, Minnesota: Liturgical Press, 1990

Coakley, John, "Friars as Confidants in Medieval Dominican Hagiography," in *Images of Sainthood in Medieval Europe*, edited by Renate Blumenfeld-Kosinski and Timea Szell, Ithaca, New York: Cornell University Press, 1991

*Early Dominicans: Selected Writings*, translated with an introduction by Simon Tugwell, New York: Paulist Press, and London: SPCK, 1982

Eckenstein, Lina, *Woman Under Monasticism: Chapters on Saint-Lore and Convent Life Between* A.D. 500 *and* A.D. 1500, Cambridge: Cambridge University Press, 1896; New York: Russell and Russell, 1963

Grundmann, Herbert, *Religious Movements in the Middle Ages: The Historical Links Between Heresy, the Mendicant Orders, and the Women's Religious Movement in the Twelfth and Thirteenth Century, with the Historical Foundations of German Mysticism*, translated by Steven Rowan, Notre Dame, Indiana: University of Notre Dame Press, 1995

Hinnebusch, William A., *The History of the Dominican Order*, 2 vols., Staten Island, New York: Alba House, 1966

Lewis, Gertrud Jaron, *By Women, for Women, about Women: The Sister-Books of Fourteenth-Century Germany*, Toronto: Pontifical Institute of Mediaeval Studies, 1996

McNamara, Jo Ann Kay, *Sisters in Arms: Catholic Nuns Through Two Millennia*, Cambridge, Massachusetts: Harvard University Press, 1996

Wilms, Hieronymus, *Geschichte der deutschen Dominikanerinnen 1206–1916*, Dülmen: Laumann, 1920

# Dominicans: General or Male

The Dominicans, or Order of Preachers, were a product of the religious and intellectual ferment of the 12th and 13th centuries. The currents of that period included an emphasis on the humanity of Jesus, whose earthly life (including his poverty) might be imitated, and the development of the Scholastic method of reconciling potentially discordant texts by the careful use of formal logic. The Dominicans were part of a larger movement toward poverty, mendicancy, preaching, and intensive study that produced a new form of monasticism, one favoring mobility over stability and apostolate over withdrawal from the world. This movement produced many of the great intellectuals of the Middle Ages (including Thomas Aquinas), important spiritual writings, and popular preaching but also aroused intense opposition from entrenched interests. Later these friars, with the Franciscans and others, would be active in the New World. Only with the coming of the Jesuits would the Dominicans lose their place at the forefront of Roman Catholic intellectual life.

### The Founder and His Spiritual Family

Dominic, a son of Castile, was born around 1170. As a student he earned a reputation for charity, and he was recruited for the cathedral chapter in Osma. In 1203 Dominic accompanied his bishop, Diego, on a diplomatic mission to Denmark. On their return journey, they passed through Languedoc, where they encountered entrenched groups of heretics. Diego opted for poverty, mendicancy, preaching, and disputation as means of winning back souls, and, when he returned to Osma, he left Dominic to continue the work. A small family of religious, male and female, grew up around Dominic.

Although the religious wars (the Albigensian Crusade) erupted soon thereafter, Dominic continued his work of preaching. To buttress this work he went to the Fourth Lateran Council (1215), winning papal approval for his Order of Preachers. They adopted the rule of St. Augustine, supplementing it with their own legislation and customs, and evolved their own liturgical calendar, practices, and offices.

A decision by Dominic to scatter his followers throughout Western Europe (1221) instead of keeping them in the troubled Midi led to the establishment of convents of Friars Preachers in many cities and towns. These convents were linked into provinces and the provinces into a order. The master general and the general chapters were to oversee not only religious life but also a chain of houses of study that would provide a theological training for the brothers. The most talented of these were given advanced theological training and assigned not only to preach but to teach as well. Among the places in which the order was planted was Paris, where Dominican masters taught theology at the university. Reginald of Orleans, one of the earliest university-trained men to join the order, recruited such future luminaries as Jordan of Saxony (d. 1237), the founder's successor as master general of the order, and Moneta of Cremona, an early apologist against the heresies of the day.

Dominic did not live to see all of this accomplished by the time of his death in 1221. The founder came to be venerated for his sanctity, and he was canonized in 1234. An elaborate shrine was erected in the friars' church in Bologna to house the founder's relics. He was depicted in Dominican art in the order's black-and-white habit, often with a star on his forehead (based on a vision that his mother was reported to have had before the saint's birth) or clinging to the foot of the cross. Depictions of him as an inquisitor were few and late in origin. The order itself developed a pun, *domini canes* ("the Lord's dogs"), to express their self-identification as the dogs guarding the flock from the wolves of heresy.

### The Work of the Friars

Although not all Dominicans engaged in the effort, preaching remained at the heart of the order's apostolate. Preaching tools were created to help in preparation for this vital effort, and because the hearing of confessions could follow preaching, the friars also prepared manuals for confessors. These means made the Dominicans and the other mendicants attractive to large numbers; and some friars failed in tact, preaching at the time of the parochial mass. Moreover, mendicant confessors, being well trained, drew the faithful away from confessing to their parish priests. Both of these issues, involving monastics in parish work, caused considerable criticism of the friars and led to fierce resistance. Another source of tension was the desire of parish priests to prohibit friars from accepting the dead for burial, or at least

Pulpit (17th century) in Dominican Basilica of Sainte Madeleine (13th century), of St.-Maximin-La-Ste.-Baume, France.
Photo courtesy of the Editor

to get a share of bequests and offerings. The papacy made frequent efforts to negotiate or to impose compromises, but it complicated matters as well by giving the friars privileges exempting them from local ecclesiastical jurisdictions.

The teaching work of the friars also led to both success and controversy. Dominican teachers offered courses at their convents, but some also taught at universities. Among the most notable of these masters were Thomas Aquinas (c. 1225–1274) and Albertus Magnus (d. 1280). The involvement of Dominicans in the reception of Aristotle into the curriculum was controversial, as was their placing obedience to their order ahead of adherence to the regulations of the corporation of masters at the University of Paris. Pamphlet warfare erupted, focusing on issues of Christian perfection and leading the friars to look to Rome for protection, but the issue of the extent of papal power, especially in the granting of privileges, made the Preachers the foremost apologists for the Roman primacy, understood in a monarchic sense. The use of Aristotle in the schools also led to conflicts between

Green cloister (14th century) of the Dominican Church of Santa Maria Novella, Florence, Italy.
Photo courtesy of the Editor

Dominicans and Franciscans, especially over the authority of the works of Thomas Aquinas. (The order soon took steps to promote fidelity to Thomas' teachings.)

This apparatus of convents and schools, teachers, preachers, and confessors depended on the alms and offerings of the faithful. This required that some friars focus on gathering offerings. These questors could fall into shoddy practices, and even the honest ones were involved in the distribution of indulgences. Eventually, this would lead the Preachers into direct conflict with Martin Luther (1483–1546), but they were criticized on occasion long before that. The financial burden of the questors was increased by the tendency of the order to build large churches to accommodate audiences gathering to hear popular preachers.

Another effort of the friars was the defense of the faith through service as inquisitors. The work of the Inquisition was judicial in nature, and it usually was assigned to men of mature years. Manuals were written for this work as well, most notably by Bernard Gui and Nicholas Eymeric. Inquisitors were not pop-

ular, and one, Peter Martyr (c. 1200–1252), is depicted as a martyr with his head split open by an edged weapon.

Nor were Dominicans always found among the prosecutors of heretics. The bold speculative mystic Meister Eckhart was accused of heresy for his teachings on the union of the soul with the divine. One of the particulars in John XXII's bull of condemnation (1329) was that Eckhart preached his doctrines in the German vernacular. However, other German Dominican mystics, men and women alike, managed to escape such a winnowing.

The Dominicans continued in their role as papal apologists through the Great Schism and the conciliar crisis down to the age of the Reformation. Among the most notable Dominican papal apologists were Leonardo Dati, who argued the papal case at the Council of Constance (1414–1418), and Cardinal Juan de Torquemada (1388–1468). The latter, besides being the author of the influential *Summa de Ecclesia*, was a promoter of religious observance, a patron of the arts, and an early supporter of the art of printing in the Italian context.

### The Observant Movement, the Renaissance, and the Reformation

Even aside from conflicts with the secular clergy (Critics) or Franciscans, the Dominicans eventually came to be regarded as having fallen away from their primitive purity. Pope Benedict XII (1334–1342) attempted to impose a reform early in the 14th century, but eventually the order found its own remedy. Raymond of Capua (c. 1330–1399), once a spiritual adviser to Catherine of Siena (c. 1347–1380), became leader of an effort to promote stricter observance of the rule and customs. Certain abuses involving exemptions from poverty and common life were targeted for curtailment. By the early 15th century, individual Observant convents were becoming linked in congregations apart from the long-established provincial life of the Conventuals.

In Italy the most influential Observant congregation was that based in Lombardy, but Tuscany became one of the most notable seats of Observant life. Fiesole became a spiritual seat of the Observants, forming St. Antoninus, who served as bishop of Florence, and the painter Fra Angelico (1395/1400–1455). With the help of the Medici, the Observants took over St. Marco in Florence, in the monastic cells of which Angelico executed many outstanding frescoes. At a later date St. Marco was also the seat of the contentious friar Girolamo Savonarola (1452–1498), who, like Vincent Ferrer, is also an example of the continued success of Dominicans as preachers to large audiences. Moreover, the friars were active in spreading recitation of the rosary.

The Renaissance also saw a revival of interest in the fortunes of Thomas Aquinas. His liturgical cult was given greater prominence in papal Rome despite sniping by the humanism Lorenzo Valla (c. 1406–1457), and leading expositors of his thought included Thomas of Gaeta (Cajetan, 1480–1547), who composed an influential commentary on the *Summa Theologiae*. Cajetan, a Conventual, was attacked by some Observants for being too independent in his interpretation of the Angelic Doctor's teachings. Cajetan also was involved in the earliest controversies surrounding Martin Luther. Other Friars Preachers would be involved in the polemics inspired by the Reformation. (Among these was Silvester Prierias, an Observant opponent of Cajetan in the quarrel over Thomism, who was the first to equate Luther's questioning of indulgences with attacking the papacy.) Dominican involvement in the defense of the established religious order would culminate in the election of one of their own to reign as Pope Pius V (1566–1572). Pius was zealous in implementing the reforms of the Council of Trent (1545–1563) by, for example, establishing seminaries and enacting the purification of liturgical practices. He also lived to see the defeat of the Turks at the battle of Lepanto (1571).

Thomism also flourished in Spain, where Francisco de Vitoria (1483–1546) made the *Summa* the centerpiece of theological teaching in his classroom at Salamanca. Dominican respect for natural law made their theologians in Spain sympathetic to arguments that the indigenous inhabitants of the New World were full human beings with rights. This was no matter of idle chatter. Friars in St. Domingo were the first critics of the Spanish Conquest and its impact on local populations. This record of protest drew Bartolomé de Las Casas (1484–1566) into the Order of Preachers, where he found wide (but not unanimous) support that included the stand taken for the rights of the Indians at the Junta of Valladolid by Domingo de Soto and other followers of Vitoria. These "jurist theologians" also were among the figures cited by Hugo Grotius in his classic works on international law.

However, Spain also bred the order that would displace the Dominicans as the intellectual leaders of Roman Catholicism: the Society of Jesus. The Jesuits soon became entangled in disputes with the Preachers, including the controversy over grace and free will and predestination and divine foreknowledge that pitted the Dominican Domingo Báñez (1528–1604) against the Jesuit Luis de Molina (1535–1600).

The Dominicans also were intimately involved in the activities of the Spanish Inquisition, beginning with the involvement of Tomas, nephew of Cardinal Juan de Torquemada, in the effort to hunt out supposed crypto-Jews among the *conversos* of the Iberian Peninsula. The Inquisition was zealous in hunting out suspected heretics, but the tribunal that was active in the Basque country in the 17th century was surprisingly lenient with accused witches. (In contrast, Italian and German Dominicans often were zealous for the apprehension of witches.)

### The Later Fortunes of the Order

After the 16th century the Dominicans became enmeshed in certain developments usually associated with absolutism. General chapters met less and less frequently, eventually being slated for every sixth year, and the powers of the master general grew, until chapters met only to elect to that office. The masters came to reside in Rome, sending streams of letters and orders out to the provinces. They also obtained the right to review the acts of provincial chapters. Moreover, pomp increased as new masters general were chosen who were the sons of aristocratic families. However, the masters found their own powers circumscribed by those of papally appointed cardinal protectors and by direct papal intervention.

In the wake of the Reformation, the order was strongest in Spain, France, and Italy. Other portions of the order were harmed by the wars of central Europe, including the Thirty Years' War, and by the incursions of the Turks. Some new ground was gained in Russia and the New World, but provincial boundaries were moved to accommodate various secular regimes. The masters general did continue promoting both reform and studies. Moreover, the friars continued their efforts to promote orthodoxy, and friars composed elaborate commentaries on the *Summa Theologiae*. Some friars also became active in the writing of ecclesiastical history, including the history of the Order of Preachers. Nonetheless, Dominicans of the 17th century rarely were in the forefront of European thought. These trends, including active work in the missions, continued during the 18th century, but secular regimes gradually became hostile to the religious orders. Many monastic houses were closed, and some liturgical practices were suppressed, even by Catholic rulers, such as the Habsburg Emperor Joseph II (1780–1790). (Ironically, the apostolate of the friars in England and Ireland was becoming more tolerated just as these moves against the orders were being made on the Continent.)

Worse was to come, especially with the beginning of the French Revolution. The move to close monastic houses gained

Nave, Convent of La Tourette, L'Arbresle (Rhone), France, designed by Le Corbusier, 1957–1960.
Photo courtesy of J. Feuillie/CNMHS

momentum. In France, all orders were suppressed in 1790. Territories occupied by the armies of the Revolution often saw similar measures, and German princes began seizing the order's properties. Napoleon (1799–1814/15) spread similar measures throughout northern Italy and the Papal States. The order itself splintered when dissident Spanish friars rejected the order's leadership. Spain pressured Pius VI (1775–1799) into dividing the order into two jurisdictions (1804). However, the Spanish wing of the order suffered badly from the Napoleonic Wars and the independence movements in Latin America. (The revolutionary governments often attacked the orders as reactionary elements.) Even the governments of Spain and Portugal turned against the Dominicans in the 1830s.

However, after the fall of Napoleon, Dominican fortunes revived in northern and Eastern Europe, although both numbers and houses remained comparatively few. Moreover, the Dominican apostolate was in sore need of being revived. A new province was established in France under the leadership of Henri Lacordaire (1802–1861), and the friars established a new ministry in the United States. Finally, the order received strong leadership when Pius IX (1846–1878) named Vincent Jandel, one of Lacordaire's followers, first vicar general and then master general. A long process of promoting unity, restoring common life, reforming studies, and renewing apostolic labors was begun. Jandel carried on despite loss of some convents to liberal measures taken in newly united Italy by the Savoy regime and continued reverses in Latin America. Promotion of the rosary also was resumed, and new missionaries were sent to lands as far away as Australia. By 1872 the near century of crisis at last was over.

The Dominican order gained in numbers following Jandel's tenure. A mere 3,474 Dominicans in 1876 rose to 10,150 by 1963. New provinces were founded in North America, Australia, and other far places. Other provinces, even in largely Protestant countries, flourished. The anti-Catholic policies of rulers such as Bismarck hurt the friars, and the totalitarian regimes of either political extreme prevalent during the mid–20th century were hostile to monastics. Missionary efforts often suffered from nationalist uprisings and independence movements throughout the world. Ironically, the misfortunes suffered in the world's trouble spots seem to have hurt the Dominican family less than did uncertainties and upheavals arising after the Second Vatican Council (1962–1965) undertook its work of renewal. The order's numbers declined sharply for a time after the council and more gradually thereafter, but some growth has been experienced in recent years, especially in areas of strong missionary efforts, such as Africa, and in countries once behind the Iron Curtain. In addition, the order's leadership has taken measures to increase the flexibility of the Dominican family in dealing with changed situations, including the fostering of cooperation across provincial borders. Moreover, a new emphasis on poverty is being discussed.

The Dominican order, beginning with Jandel's reforms, also gave renewed attention to its program of study. Educational institutions were founded or updated. Biblical studies received particular attention, as did the systematic study of Thomism.

Publications by friars, including those by luminaries such as Yves Congar (1904–1995), increased in quantity and quality. Preaching received continued attention, but new media, such as film, radio, and television, became tools of an updated apostolate. Moreover, new houses of study have been founded in Africa and Latin America. The family of Dominic has endured through the 20th century, whereas once, around the middle of the 19th, it seemed doomed to fail.

THOMAS M. IZBICKI

See also Albertus Magnus, St.; Dominic, St.; Eckhart, Meister; Florence, Italy; France: History; Franciscans; Liturgy: Western Christian; Savonarola, Girolamo; Spain: History; Theology, Western Christian: Dominican; Thomas Aquinas, St.; Visual Arts, Western Christian: Painting

**Further Reading**

*Bullarium Ordinis FF. Praedicatorum: Sub auspiciis SS. D.N.D. Benedicti XIII, pontificis maximi, e jusdem ordinis,* 8 vols., Rome: Ex Typographia Hieronymi Mainardi, 1729

Canetti, Luigi, *L'invenzione della memoria: Il culto e l'immagine di Domenico nella storia dei primi frati Predicatori,* Spoleto: Centro Italiano di Studi sull'Alto Medioevo, 1996

Douie, Decima, *The Conflict Between the Seculars and the Mendicants at the University of Paris in the Thirteenth Century,* London: Aquin Press, 1954

*Early Dominicans: Selected Writings,* translated with an introduction by Simon Tugwell, New York: Paulist Press, and London: SPCK, 1982

Galbraith, Georgina R., *The Constitution of the Dominican Order 1216 to 1360,* Manchester, London, and New York: University Press, 1925

Hinnebusch, William A., *The History of the Dominican Order,* 2 vols., Staten Island, New York: Alba House, 1966

Hinnebusch, William A., *The Dominicans: A Short History,* Staten Island, New York: Alba House, 1975; Dublin: Dominican, 1985

Koudelka, Vladimir J., *Dominic,* translated and edited by C. Fissler and Simon Tugwell, London: Darton, Longman and Todd, 1997

Mortier, D.A., *Histoire des maîtres généraux de l'ordre des Frères Prêcheurs,* 8 vols., Paris: Picara, 1902–1920

Vicaire, M-H., *Histoire de Saint Dominique: Un homme évangélique,* 2 vols., Paris: Éditions du Cerf, 1957

# Double Houses, Western Christian

The designation "double house" has been applied to Western Christian monasteries by modern scholars to categorize medieval institutions that incorporated monastic women and men together under a single monastic official, theoretically an abbess. The term was not employed in the Middle Ages, and it has been distorted to cover a range of often dissimilar arrangements, so that its modern utility is highly questionable.

Experiments with chaste, communal, regular (governed by a monastic *regula*, or rule) religious life from their beginnings in the fourth-century Egyptian desert tended to involve men and women together. When St. Pachomius (c. 290–346) wrote his Rule, he institutionalized women and men living side by side, sharing the monastic life at Tabennisi under his direction. Even when the early monastic framers wrote rules exclusively for their male followers, as did St. Benedict of Nursia (c. 480–c. 550), his Rule was stretched unofficially to cover his sister, St. Scholastica (c. 480–c. 543), who lived the monastic life near Benedict's monastery of Monte Cassino.

Several powerful forces drove these early Christian ascetics either to institutionalize religious men and women into community or to allow them informally to live contiguous, parallel monastic lives. First, family mattered in premodern Europe; kinship bonds were the cement of early medieval society, and it was within families that deep religious fervor seems often to have flourished. Thus, sisters and brothers tended to want to share the religious life together. In addition, the hardships of renouncing property, autonomy, and sexuality could be borne more easily with the companionship and understanding of like-minded monastics of the opposite sex for support. Third, the sacramental needs of women required the presence of a male priest, so that placing religious men close by nuns made practical sense. Such kinship imperatives and personal and sacramental needs were authenticated by the Scriptural model of Christ living among his male and female followers. Thus, the authority of the apostolic tradition supported the gender sharing of monastic life.

The history of the so-called double house can be seen as one wave in the cycle of ebb and flow that marks the history of Christian monasticism. After the initial experiments in the desert, the monastic ideal spread to the Byzantine East and the Latin West and, in its first great flush in the West during the seventh century, often produced foundations that incorporated men and women into dual communities. Royal and aristocratic ladies in Gaul founded and ruled dual abbeys, such as Faremoutiers and Jouarre, often with support from their brothers. They set a pattern that caught on in England; sisters and brothers often acted together to found and lead dual houses, and many such institutions were ruled by powerful, noble abbesses, such as St. Hilda (614–680), who founded and ran Whitby Abbey in its most brilliant early years. In the eighth century the pattern spread to eastern Europe, where, for example, the dual German monastery of Heidenheim was originally ruled by a brother-sister team of St. Wynnebald (d. 761) and St. Walburga (c. 710–774), who, after her brother's death, ruled alone.

The Viking and Magyar invasions of the ninth and tenth centuries damaged or destroyed many of the early monastic foundations, and when they were reinstituted the tendency was to replace joint houses with single-sex houses, usually of men. At least 18 dual-sex houses suffered this fate in England, among them Whitby Abbey. The Church on the Continent followed suit; many joint abbeys were revived by rebuilding and refurbishing the buildings, replacing the monks with canons while choosing pointedly not to restore nuns to the institutions. The tendency to see male spirituality as superior to that of women was encouraged in general by the reform movement of the 10th

and 11th centuries and especially by vigorous conciliar legislation against the association of women and men within monastic institutions.

Yet despite the rejection of institutionalized dual abbeys, the forces that impelled monastic men and women to live and work together led willy-nilly to informal associations, even in the teeth of ecclesiastical resistance. Mothers and wives of men professing as monks were sometimes accepted into abbeys as were, for example, three women at St. Anselm's (c. 1033–1109) great male Abbey of Bec in the second half of the 11th century. Many other French, German, and Dutch Benedictine male communities also had women associated with them; sometimes these were professed nuns, and at other times the affiliated women were of a less clearly defined status. It could and did work the other way as well: canons and monks could reside in a convent, as did a group of canons at the convent of Stixwould in Lincolnshire in the 12th century and a half dozen monks at the nunnery of St.-Säens near Rouen in the 13th. Indeed the nuns of prosperous convents in the central Middle Ages liked to have their own resident priests. The nuns of Notre-Dame in Saintes had a dependent chapter, known as the Canons of St.-Pallais, right outside the abbey's walls to serve their sacramental needs.

By the beginning of the 12th century, when a strong wind of apostolic fervor was blowing across Europe, the dual monastery had its third and final institutional vogue. Three major experiments to create ways of pairing male and female monastics in one institution under a single head were tried – two in France and one in England – only one of which survived in the pattern originally intended right up to the French Revolution.

Robert Arbrissel (c. 1045–1116) was a wandering charismatic preacher in central France who collected around him bands of penitential men and women. When the gossip about his coed contingent became overwhelming in 1100–1101, he somewhat unwillingly established his followers in a dual monastery in western France at Fontevraud. He placed a mature, aristocratic widow as abbess in charge over the mixed group of religious women and men from diverse backgrounds; Fontevraud incorporated a house of noble choir-nuns, lay sisters, monks who served the nuns, and penitent prostitutes. Somewhat surprisingly to contemporaries, Fontevraud flourished, spawned daughter houses, and triumphantly continued into the late 18th century as a prosperous, successful "double house."

The 12th century was rich in dynamic reformers, another of whom, St. Norbert of Xanten (c.1080–1134), drew followers of both sexes with his preaching of the *vita apostolica*. Although Norbert never intended to be a monastic innovator, his solution in 1120 for dealing with his band of followers was to enclose the women within a convent next to the house of canons that he had already established at Prémontré in northern France. He instituted an abbot over the dual houses, which were separate and unequal. To the canons fell singing the liturgical offices and to the nuns listening to the canons, washing and mending their habits, and living a tightly enclosed existence to prevent any scandal. Prémontré developed into an order with special strength in the Low Countries, but the Premonstratensian canons found

Abbey of Geras-Pernegg (Premonstratensian), Lower Austria, rebuilt later 17th century. The abbey was founded c. 1153 as a double house. Photo courtesy of the Austrian National Tourist Office

their sisters an irksome burden. The women were required in 1137 to relocate at a distance from the canons' monasteries, and then in 1197–1198 the chapter went the final step and voted to admit no more women, effectively ending the Norbertine experiment in parallel religious life.

The third foray into monastic gender-sharing in the 12th century was, as in Norbert's case, a rather haphazard arrangement that grew unpredictably. Saint Gilbert of Sempringham (c. 1080–1189), an English country priest, might have originally intended to found an order for men, but the recruits who eagerly offered themselves were seven young women whom he set up in a small cloister in 1131. Then, finding that his nuns would need to be out and about to tend to business if no other provisions were made, Gilbert established a group of lay sisters, so the choir nuns could be rigorously cloistered. However, that did not suffice for the fledgling convent, which needed manpower to work fields as well as priests for the sacramental life; to meet these needs Gilbert created two more entities: a group of lay brothers to serve the nuns with manual labor and canons for the commu-

nity's spiritual care. However, by the late 12th century the ideal was already crumbling as increasingly new Gilbertine houses were founded for canons alone.

By the early 13th century, the era of enthusiastic experimentation in institutionalizing the shared monastic life for men and women was all but at an end. However, monastic women and men continued to live in a variety of parallel patterns that met diverse pragmatic needs. These can be grouped loosely into three categories. First, monasteries of both men and women continued irregular noninstitutional arrangements by which a monastery allowed one or a few members of the opposite gender to live under its protection. Second, women's houses, when rich enough, continued to support subordinate groups of monks or chapters of canons, although the men often resented the abbess's authority and struggled to claim more power and institutional autonomy by the later Middle Ages. Fontevraud, although often misnamed a "double house," falls into this second category as an abbey whose nuns triumphantly maintained control over brothers and canons, likely through the suasion of the choir nuns' extremely high birth, wealth, and influence. The third type of dual-monastic or quasi-monastic institution, one that continued through the later Middle Ages, was the hospital, or leper house, which used nursing sisters to do the actual caring for the sick alongside priests who attended to the souls of the patients.

Western medieval monasticism experienced three periods of formally institutionalized dual-sex monasteries, first in the opening days of the fourth century, then in the renewal of the seventh century, and finally during the reforming era of the 12th century; thus, the most idealistic association of monastic women and men occurred during times of experimentation and/or renewal. In addition, an almost continuous medieval tradition existed of associating monastics together to meet diverse needs. This rich variety and wide range of expectations for the association of professed men and women argue for the abandonment of the term *double monastery* – with its associated expectation that a unified institution is being described – in favor of using descriptive specificity to delineate the arrangements for particular houses and rules.

PENELOPE D. JOHNSON

*See also* Benedictines: Female; Cistercians: General or Male; Desert Fathers; Fontevraud, France; France: History; Gilbertines; Hilda, St.; Holy Men/Holy Women: Christian Perspectives; Lay Brothers and Lay Sisters, Christian; Liturgy: Western Christian; Monte Cassino, Italy; Origins: Eastern Christian; Pachomius, St.; Premonstratensian Canons; Whitby, England; Women's Monasteries: Western Christian

## Further Reading

Bateson, Mary, "Origin and Early History of Double Monasteries," *Transactions of the Royal Historical Society* 13 (1899)
Berlière, Ursmer, "Les monastères doubles aux XIIe et XIIIe siècles," *Académie royale de Belgique, Classe des lettres et des sciences morales et politiques* 18 (1923)

Elkins, Sharon K., *Holy Women of Twelfth-Century England*, Chapel Hill: University of North Carolina Press, 1988

Elm, Kaspar, and Michel Parisse, editors, *Doppelklöster und andere Formen des Symbiose männlicher und weiblicher Religiösen im Mittelalter*, Berlin: Duncker and Humblot, 1992

Gold, Penny S., "Male/Female Cooperation: The Example of Fontevrault," in *Medieval Religious Women*, volume 1: *Distant Echoes*, edited by John A. Nichols and Lillian Thomas Shank, Kalamazoo, Michigan: Cistercian Publications, 1984

Hilpisch, Stephanus, *Die Doppelklöster: Entstehung und Organisation*, Munster: Aschendorff, 1928

Johnson, Penelope D., *Equal in Monastic Profession: Religious Women in Medieval France*, Chicago: University of Chicago Press, 1991

Mitchell, Barbara, "Anglo-Saxon Double Monasteries," *History Today* 45 (1995)

Thompson, Sally, *Women Religious: The Founding of English Nunneries After the Norman Conquest*, Oxford: Clarendon Press, and New York: Oxford University Press, 1991

# E

## Echternach, Luxembourg

Echternach is an abbey (and a small town that developed around the abbey) in the lower Sûre valley in the grand duchy of Luxembourg. The early history of the abbey is closely related to the Anglo-Saxon missionary Willibrord (d. 736), its founder and first abbot. In 697–698, Willibrord received from Abbess Irmina of Oeren, mother-in-law of the *major domus* Pepin II (687–714), her half of the family villa at Echternach, which already included a church, a small monastery (*monasteriolum*), and a *xenodochium* for wandering monks. This donation was complemented a few years later by Pepin II and his wife, Plectrudis, who gave their half of the estate to Willibrord. Thanks to numerous donations made to the monastery by the local aristocracy of Toxandria and Hesse, Echternach accumulated vast resources and thus became the most important ecclesiastical foundation in the Mosel region of Austrasia. A new monastery was constructed at Echternach between 704 and 706 to replace the inadequate buildings of the small one given to Willibrord and his companions by Irmina. In 739 Willibrord died in Utrecht, and, according to his will, his body was transferred to the basilica of Echternach, and all the gifts he had received personally were left to the monastery. Under Willibrord's successors Echternach continued to grow. Gifts were continuously bestowed on the monastery by various aristocrats and especially by members of the Carolingian family. With Pepin III's accession to the Frankish throne in 751, Echternach became a royal monastery and from then was under the protection of the Carolingian kings.

Throughout the eighth century Echternach was a home for Anglo-Saxon and Irish pilgrims and monks and a center for the mission to the Frisians. Although it is clear that from a fairly early stage the monks at Echternach strictly followed a certain rule, it is unclear whether this rule was the rule of St. Benedict or the so-called mixed rule. However, little doubt exists that after the monastic reforms led by Benedict of Aniane (c. 750–821) and supported by Emperor Louis the Pious (814–840), Echternach followed the Benedictine rule. Around 848 to 850 the abbey was converted into a collegiate community ruled by a lay abbot. This situation changed in 973, when, at the request of Count Siegfried of Luxembourg, Emperor Otto I (936–973) sent 40 monks from St.-Maximin (Trier) to reform Echternach according to the Cluniac model. After a long period of decline during the late 13th, 14th, and 15th centuries, another group of monks from St.-Maximin (Trier) arrived at Echternach in 1493 to reform the abbey. The dissolution of Echternach took place in 1797 during the French Revolution.

At a fairly early stage of the monastery's history, a scriptorium was established at Echternach. This scriptorium was a meeting point for various Insular and Continental styles and methods, and consequently it became one of the most prolific scriptoria in northern Francia. In the course of the eighth and the ninth centuries, the scriptorium at Echternach grew immensely, reaching its peak under Abbot Humbert (1028–1051). During the abbacy of Regimbert (1051–1081) and Thiofrid (1081–1110), Echternach was also a prolific center of intellectual activity.

Today one can still see in Echternach the impressive quadrilateral buildings of the abbey (built from 1727 to 1731) as well as the 11th-century basilica, which was built on the site of the Carolingian church and enlarged in the 13th century. Massive works of restoration ensued in this church after its destruction in World War II. The only Carolingian remains are in the crypt, where the tomb of St. Willibrord is located.

YITZHAK HEN

*See also* Germany: History; Manuscript Production: Christian; Netherlands; Patrons, Christian: Royal; Willibrord, St.

## Further Reading

Ferrari, Michele Camillo, *Sancti Willibrordi venerantes memoriam: Echternacher Schreiber und Schriftsteller von den Angelsachsen bis Johann Bertels*, Luxembourg: Publications du CLUDEM, 1994

Ferrari, Michele Camillo, Jean Schroeder, and Henri Trauffler, editors, *Die Abtei Echternach 698–1998*, Luxembourg: Publications du CLUDEM, 1999

Krier, J., and R. Wagner, "Zur Frühgeschichte des Willibrordus-Klosters in Echternach," *Hémecht* 37 (1985)

Schroeder, Jean, "Echternach im Spiegel der europäischen Geschichtsforschung," *Echternacher Studien* 1 (1979)

Schroeder, Jean, "Echternach in Forschung und Literatur," *Echternacher Studien* 2 (1982) and *Echternacher Studien* 3 (1985)

Schroeder, Jean, and Henri Trauffler, *Die Anfänge der Abtei Echternach*, Luxembourg: Publications du CLUDEM, 1996

Spang, P., "Saint Willibrord et l'abbaye d'Echternach dans l'historiographie luxembourgeoise," *Hémecht* 42 (1990)

Wampach, Camillus, *Geschichte der Grundherrschaft Echternach im Frühmittelalter*, 2 vols., Luxembourg: Luxemburger Kunstdruckerei, 1929

# Eckhart, Meister c. 1260–1328

## German Dominican theologian

Eckhart of Hochheim was born in northeastern Germany near Erfurt. Nothing is known of his birth or childhood, although it has long been held that he came from a knightly family. About the age of 15, he entered the Order of Preachers (Dominicans) at Erfurt. After initial studies, he was sent in 1280 to the *studium generale* in Cologne, where he met the aged Albertus Magnus (d. 1280), the master of Thomas Aquinas (c. 1225–1274). Albert died a few months later, but Eckhart was surely taught some by his disciples. An ardent if selective Thomist, Eckhart, like many of Albert's students, more strongly favored the ancient tradition of Christian Neoplatonism.

After finishing his studies at Cologne, Eckhart was ordained to the priesthood, probably in 1293. He was then sent to Paris to lecture on the *Sentences* of Peter Lombard (c. 1100–1160) and to begin studies for the coveted title of master. Even so, he was elected to important positions in the Dominican Order. A year after arriving in Paris, he was elected prior at Erfurt. About the same time he was appointed vicar of Thuringia. Finally, in 1302 Eckhart was granted the title of *Magister in Theologia*, the highest academic honor of the age. As *Meister* (Master) Eckhart, he remains the only medieval figure still known by that title today.

After a year in Paris as regent master, Eckhart was elected head of the new province of Saxony, which included Erfurt. He was also entrusted with the spiritual guidance of the Dominican nuns of the region. In 1307 the Chapter of Strasbourg appointed Eckhart vicar of Bohemia and commissioned him to reform its Dominican houses. Between 1309 and 1310 he founded three new communities. His subsequent election as provincial of the Teutonian province was overturned by the general chapter in Naples. Sent back to Paris in 1311, he again occupied the Chair for Externs, a rare privilege. About that time Eckhart began his great but unfinished *Opus tripartitum* (The Three-Part Work), which he intended to be his crowning academic achievement. However, in 1313 he was recalled to Germany to be professor of theology, spiritual director, and preacher in Strasbourg. In 1314 he was elected prior of the Dominican community. Soon afterward the master of the Order named him vicar and once more placed Eckhart over the Dominican nuns of the region.

In 1322 Eckhart was recalled to Cologne as regent master of the *studium generale*. Three years later, during an inquisition by the archbishop of Cologne, he was summoned to defend himself against charges of preaching heresy. For over a year Eckhart protested his innocence, arguing that the charges were lodged out of envy. When the verdict went against him, he appealed to Pope John XXII (1316–1334). Then, at the age of 67 or 68, Eckhart and several companions walked 500 miles to plead his case at the papal court in Avignon.

Eckhart died before a verdict was reached, according to some accounts on the feast of St. Thomas Aquinas, 28 January 1328. He had first retracted anything that could be proved heretical in his teachings, but he also continued to deny that his intention or doctrine was in fact contrary to Christian faith. However, at the archbishop's insistence a papal bull of condemnation was issued in March 1329. Many of Eckhart's writings were subsequently lost or destroyed, and not even his gravesite has been discovered. However, his memory and doctrine were preserved by his Dominican disciples, Henry Suso (c. 1295–1366) and John Tauler (d. 1361), and other members of the informal group of mystics known as the Friends of God. Eventually, Eckhart came once more to be held in esteem, especially among German Dominicans.

At the general chapter of the Dominican Order held in Mexico City in 1992, the delegates received the report of a panel of expert scholars commissioned ten years before to review the condemnation of 1329. The panel concluded that Eckhart needed no "rehabilitation" in the juridical sense, for neither he nor his doctrine had in strict fact been condemned. Moreover, the bull itself had been officially restricted to the Archdiocese of Cologne. In March of the following year, the master of the Order, Fr. Damian Byrne, formally requested Cardinal Joseph Ratzinger to abrogate the bull of condemnation.

## Eckhart's Influence

Eckhart's philosophical teaching is only slowly being recovered and appreciated. However, his spiritual teaching soon became a major resource for Christian mystics for centuries to come. Relying on thorough knowledge of Scripture, of the spiritual theology of Alexandria, of the teachings of the Cappadocian fathers, and of the Dionysian writings, Eckhart fused Thomistic, Arabic, and Jewish elements into a great mystical synthesis. Radically apophatic in his approach, Eckhart asserted that nothing could describe either God or the soul. Thus, becoming one with God by ridding the mind of all images and the heart of all attachments was the true and only work to which the human spirit is called. Such a spiritual "way" calls for no special practices, such as penances, pilgrimages, or other works. Eckhart's spirituality remained a "wayless way."

Despite the condemnation of 1329, Eckhart's doctrine remained a powerful spiritual force. Even when combating what they perceived as erroneous or heretical elements in Rhineland mysticism, Jan van Ruusbroec (1293–1381) and Gerard Groote (1340–1384) end by repeating many of Eckhart's characteristic doctrines. Cardinal Nicholas of Cusa (1401–1464) found Eckhart's teaching attractive but hazardous to the uninstructed. Through the works of Suso and Tauler, Eckhart's teaching indirectly influenced later Catholic mystics, such as the Carmelites, St. Teresa of Avila (1515–1582) and St. John of the Cross (1542–1591), the Jesuit St. Peter Canisius (1521–1597), and the Passionist founder, St. Paul of the Cross (1694–1775), as well as

Martin Luther (1483–1546) and other Protestant reformers. The Anabaptist tradition also retained many of Eckhart's teachings. His influence is found in the Pietist movement of the 17th and 18th centuries and in the writings of Jacob Boehme (1575–1624) and especially Angelus Silesius (Johannes Scheffler, 1624–1677). In the 19th century Romantic poets and idealist philosophers from Clemens Brentano to Hegel appealed to Eckhart. In the mid–20th century an attempt to claim Eckhart as a proto-Aryan by the Nazi movement in Germany came to nothing. In more recent times Eckhart has attracted attention in Hindu and Buddhist circles as well as among Christian thinkers and spiritual seekers in Europe and the Americas.

RICHARD WOODS, O.P.

*See also* Albertus Magnus, St.; Carmelites; Dominicans; John of the Cross, St.; Spirituality: Western Christian; Teresa of Avila, St.; Vision, Mystical: Western Christian

## Biography

Having entered the Dominican house at Erfurt, Thuringia, Eckhart was sent to study at Paris and probably also with Albertus Magnus in Cologne. For three periods (1293–1294, 1302–1303, 1311–1313) he taught in Paris. In the intervals he served as Dominican prior in Erfurt. After 1313 he lived in Strasbourg until 1323 and thereafter in Cologne. He wrote treatises in both Latin and German. In 1326 Eckhart was tried before the archbishop of Cologne but died before his appeal to the pope could be heard. A year after his death Pope John XXII condemned 17 propositions taken from his writings as heretical. He influenced the Rhineland mystics, and ranks as one of the most influential medieval theologians never to have been canonized.

## Major Works

*Opus tripartitum* (exists only in fragments)
*Buch der göttlichen Tröstung*
*Predigt vom edlen Menschen*
*Meister Eckhart: Die deutschen und lateinischen Werke*, 11 vols., 1936–
*Meister Eckhart: German Sermons and Treatises*, 3 vols., translated by M. O'C. Walshe, 1979–1981
*Meister Eckhart: The Essential Sermons, Commentaries, Treatises and Defense*, edited and translated by Bernard McGinn and Edmund Colledge, 1981

## Further Reading

Davies, Oliver, *Meister Eckhart: Mystical Theologian*, London: SPCK, 1991
McGinn, Bernard, "Meister Eckhart's Condemnation Reconsidered," *The Thomist* 44 (1980)
McGinn, Bernard, with Frank Tobin and Elvira Borgstädt, editors and translators, *Meister Eckhart: Teacher and Preacher*, preface by Kenneth Northcott, New York: Paulist Press, 1987
Tobin, Frank, *Meister Eckhart: Thought and Language*, Philadelphia: University of Pennsylvania Press, 1986
Woods, Richard, *Eckhart's Way*, Wilmington, Delaware: Glazier, 1986

## Related Web Site

*http://www.op.org/eckhart* (Eckhart Society, Chicago and London)

# Economic Justice, Buddhist

Almost all Theravāda countries in postcolonial times have identified themselves with a socialist platform. Some went fully Marxist, and some German and Russian scholars claim that Buddhism, with its "no-soul" doctrine, is basically a materialist philosophy. However, the deeper reason is the Buddhist principle of equality and of "distributory justice" in economic matters. Tomomatsu Entai, the "radio boshi" trained in France, wrote the definitive work, *Bukkyō ni okeru "bunkei" genri to jissai* (1965; The Principle and the Reality of "Equal Division and Distribution" in Buddhism).

Just as the early Christian Church was for a while "communist," that is, it held property in common, so Buddhist monks have from the start answered the call to "sell all that you have and give it away" that St. Antony heeded. Buddhist monks renounced all worldly possessions and on principle "shared and shared alike." However, monks do not produce; they live off donations, so the principles of Buddhist economics address not the ethos of production – Max Weber's area of interest – but that of distribution. The basic rule is simple: every member is to have an equal share of whatever is donated to the *sangha*. The Buddha held to this principle so strictly that during his lifetime it meant sharing everything with everyone, including the laity and even other ascetics in the vicinity. That was before any sense of Buddhist versus non-Buddhist had set in. That also meant an equal share for everyone regardless of age and standing, so that even a seven-year-old novice would receive an adult amount of food, and the Buddha himself would take not an iota more. However impractical, this egalitarian ideal lived on as an ideal.

Adjustments of course must be made. Some donated goods are not divisible (e.g., a cart), some are held in perpetuity (housing), and sometimes one must consider not the entire *sangha* but only the local one or only those monks present (at a meager feast). Even now monks take turns being invited to lay offerings of good food. Soon enough, however, the legal ownership of permanent properties had to be settled. Does ownership last for one generation? Or are properties withdrawable by the donor? Do they belong to the universal *sangha*, or only the local community? And who, in the early days, counts as a regular "returnee" year after year to the same monsoon retreat? Who later are the permanent residents? And how long should the courtesy of "free room and board" last for a wayfaring monk who drops in? With some exercise of judiciousness these issues could be resolved without jeopardizing the spirit of "share and share alike."

More troublesome were two other developments: royal patronage and the postmortem idealization of the Buddha. Royal patronage is, as the phrase goes, "honey laced with poison." It is both boon and bane. Left to itself the *sangha* could adjudicate how the gifts should be divided, but from the start it could only educate a donor; it could not dictate the donor's will. A donor can freely specify an end use for his gift, and the housekeeping monk is legally bound by it. What often happens is that people make personal gifts to a relative who has chosen to retire into a village monastery. Such giving is considered "bad form," and the pious know well enough to balance that with a general gift made to the entire order. Still this meant that in most monasteries monks vowed to poverty usually end up being not equally poor. The difference might be minimal (e.g., a better mattress), and ideally brethren should rejoice in and not envy a fellow monastic's good fortune. However, monks not being perfect, seeds of envy and greed could sprout, and anyone reading an account of how Chinese monks get into a bidding war over goods left by a deceased member might be overly judgmental. But such incidents are only a harmless break in the ascetic routine, and they show how monastic rules governing the disposition of such property are still being observed to a laudable degree.

The greater danger came from royal donors. Kings accustomed to making their own laws often rode roughshod over the vinaya, and monastic prelates, especially political appointees, proved too willing to comply or to compromise, or else they were forced to do so. The Aśoka legend is filled with such conflicts, but the long and short of it is that monks in royal favor get lavish gifts, an offer that is hard to refuse. Thus, Kumārajīva (c. 344–413) at Kucha received a special allotment of grain and meat given him by the king, and once the end use of the royal gifts is specified, even a saint would need royal permission to rededicate its use. When Aśoka supposedly purified the *saṅgha* by instituting qualifying examinations, the seeds were sown of a system of state temples with abbots appointed at and sent down from the capital. Meritocracy then clashes with equality. The notion that scholarly abhidharmists who passed the more difficult examination in philosophy received larger state stipends is a legend spread by learned monks later, but that story only exposes a subsequent development. Soon a privileged ecclesiastical hierarchy rose that dropped the early ideal of "share and share alike." A widening gap between high clerics and monks working with the people would at times unleash reforms and even reformations.

The other economic imbalance was caused, unexpectedly, by the Buddha himself. According to his principle of equal distribution, when gifts are made out to the Three Jewels, a formula demands that one-third go to the Buddha. This allocation was fine when the Buddha was alive, for he would share it with his community, but not so after his passing, when there was no way to divine his will. With the nonphysical Buddha now having no material needs but having title to one-third of such gifts, equality bred inequality. By law the Buddha's degradable gifts have to rot at or around his reliquary, and neither the monks nor the poor in need could ever touch it. The *saṅgha* could borrow goods from the Buddha, but it is stipulated that that must be repaid in kind, with interest, it is hoped. Worse, the *saṅgha* had, in order to justify donation, argued that it is better to give to monks than to beggars. Why? Because a purer monk can do more spiritual good than can a vulgar beggar. This makes sense when both types of mendicants had to compete for the same resources, but soon enough well-fed monks were living in fairly comfortable monasteries while starving beggars gathered outside the gates. In addition the same rule means that giving to the Buddha, who is purer by far, would win the lay donor even more merit than would giving to monks. The situation then rose wherein the Buddha Jewel was draining donations away from the *saṅgha*. Something like that must have happened in early Buddhist history because the sectarian Buddhists tried to modify the rule regarding the separation of the Three Jewels. To retrieve resources lost to the Buddha, some sectarians recalled how when he was alive the Buddha was also a member of the *saṅgha*, and thus he is still so. Another group, hoping to gain access to the donation, wanted to designate the Buddha as the "head of the *saṅgha*," but the doctrine of separation remained strict. Monks of the *saṅgha* could not hang their clothes to sun near the stūpa of the Buddha, a stream could not flow through their separate grounds, and so on. Today few Theravādins know that such rules existed. The problem of separation has largely been resolved by having monks sponsor stūpa projects and control the fund-raising. Most surviving early stūpas record that arrangement, although, as in China, the money came from the laity.

In an early Mahāyāna text the *Upāsakaśīla Sūtra* (Scripture of Precepts for the Layman), a case was made for setting up a separate "poverty field" to aid the needy. This call was taken to heart in early sixth-century China when China was reliving the same trauma as Indian Buddhism once had. That is, the Buddha temples at the northern capital were siphoning off resources from the rural *saṅgha*-households. Meanwhile stūpas themselves were often left unattended and crumbling because no one wanted to refurbish what was another family's "merit field." In addition, in private temples (i.e., family chapels) monks found themselves becoming mere "hire-ins" who were slighted, even mistreated, by the powerful patrons of the Buddha. To right such wrongs a Chinese apocryphon, the *Xiangfa Jueyijing* (*Hsiang-fa chüeh-i ching*; Sūtra to Resolve Doubts in the Age of the Semblance Dharma), appeared between 517 and 520. It criticized the misplaced piety, lamented the waste, and called actively for "helping the widowed and the orphaned." It renamed the "field of poverty" the "field of compassion" and had the Buddha saying that "it is better to aid the widowed and orphaned in that field of compassion" than to shower more gifts on the already well-endowed Three Jewels in the "field of reverence." This rewrote the early principle of "equal distribution," for now finally gifts go "to each according to his need."

The Three Periods Sect picked this message up and urged people to donate "nonstop" to an Inexhaustible Treasure run by the sect leaders for the welfare of all. The donors were advised to commit themselves to a "universal donation" in the "universal teaching" of the Last Age. "Universal donation" translates into a donation without a specified end user or end use. This allowed the sect to channel resources wherever need was the greatest. This experiment in unconditional gift making was so successful that the storehouses holding the Inexhaustible Treasure lived up to the name. It and the religious fervor behind it so threatened the state that the state did move in, closed it down, and had the sect banned. By the ninth century A.D., that legacy had disappeared, and the memory of a second historical struggle between Buddha and *sangha* over the principle of "equal distribution" was lost. By then the temple manorial system operated fairly much like the secular one. Scholars working to recover Chinese Buddhist economic history have relied mainly on the Dunhuang (Tun-huang) documents from the ninth century on. They can tell us much about the actual mechanics of the estates, their administration, the land and serf ownership, the primary industries, and the incomes and expenditures, but even Jacques Gernet (1956) has overlooked what Tomomatsu has uncovered in principle and tersely in fact.

Tenantization changed the fundamental relationship between monk and laity. Gone was the design of previous *sangha*-households that had experimented with a religious manorial system in which rural monastics looked out for the interest of lay peasant householders. Monks and laymen supported one another in an interdependence necessitated in part by that age of chaos during which Buddhism provided a refuge from both spiritual and material ill. It sheltered the peasants from both the state and the powerful magnate families. Peace restored the authority due to those two contending forces, and the monasteries themselves had to adjust to the ways of the worldly institutions. After the Tang period (618–907), the forest monks saw their ascetic "mountain retreats" turning into proprietary institutions. The Chan lineages relied on those abbots who headed these "mountain gates" (schools, sects) with support from local patrons. A new lineage could spring only from an independent monastery and the necessary landholdings. Abbots were regularly enshrined to mark their special standing. The official clerical bureaucracy staffed by monks had long disappeared by the middle of the Tang period, when civil authorities had taken over that supervisory role, and the end of official state support in the Ming period ended any and all pretense of a national *sangha*. Very much decentralized and with monastic ownership and local autonomy being jealously guarded, innovations and reforms became extremely difficult to launch, as attested to in modern attempts at reform. In China dreams of "share and share alike" survived in millenarian movements and that of equal distribution flourished in lay-run "mutual aid" societies.

WHALEN LAI

*See also* Aśoka; Buddha (Śākyamuni); China; Patrons, Buddhist; Saṅgha

## Further Reading

Gernet, Jacques, *Les aspects économiques du Bouddhisme dans la société chinoise du Ve au Xe siècle*, Paris: École francaise d'Extrême-Orient, 1956; as *Buddhism in Chinese Society: An Economic History from the Fifth to the Tenth Century*, New York: Columbia University Press, 1995
Lai, Whalen, "Dating the *Hsiang-fa Chüeh-i Ching*," *Annual Memoir of Otani University Shin Buddhist Comprehensive Research Institute* 4 (1986)
Schopen, Gregory, "Deaths, Funerals, and the Disposition of Monastic Property in a Monastic Code," in *Buddhism in Practice*, edited by Donald Lopez, Jr., Princeton, New Jersey: Princeton University Press, 1995
Tokuno, Kyoko, "The Book of Resolving Doubts Concerning the Semblance Dharma," in *Buddhism in Practice*, edited by Donald Lopez, Jr., Princeton, New Jersey: Princeton University Press, 1995
Twitchett, Dennis C., "The Monasteries and China's Economy in Medieval Times," *Bulletin of the School of Oriental and African Studies* 19:3 (1957)
Yang, Lien-sheng, "Buddhist Monasteries and Four Money-Lending Institutions in China," *Harvard Journal of Asian Studies* 13 (1950)

# Economics: Buddhist

Generally it can be said that historians of Buddhism have tended to focus on the history of ideas and philosophical organization. Less attention has been given to social practices and the role of Buddhism in broader social structures. One manner in which to address this imbalance is to look at Buddhist economic practices, a topic little understood and rarely studied. Buddhism, in any of its geographic variations, was never merely a set of doctrines and religious practices but has always been a complex social phenomenon, actively engaged in a multitude of activities, from the philosophical to the political and economic. The Buddhist world was immense, encompassing regions in southern and Southeast Asia from Laos, Cambodia, India, Burma (Myanmar), Sri Lanka (Ceylon), Vietnam, and Thailand up through eastern Asia and Tibet, China, Korea, Japan, and Taiwan. Buddhism has exerted a powerful economic influence on all these societies.

For the purposes of this article, the term *economics* refers to social practices undertaken by Buddhists that generated income and were connected to mechanisms of exchange. Exchange occurred when someone donated something to a monastery (e.g., land, harvest, or money) and in return received either religious services or, more commonly, "merit." Merit could be used to improve one's lot in life or that of deceased family members in the afterlife. From the monastery's perspective the transfer of merit was tied to processes of accumulation, specifically, the accumulation of land. The relationship between Buddhism and economics centers on the relationship between Buddhist monasteries and land. Historically Buddhists have engaged in many commercial activities, but land has always been the foundation of their economic power.

In early Indian Buddhism many monks supported themselves in part by begging, a social practice that allowed them to move around. Food given to a monk earned merit for the donor. Nonetheless, since its early days in India, Buddhism faced an ideological dilemma: whereas the ideal monk was penniless, ascetic, and uninterested in material goods, monasteries required funding in order to promote the Dharma. For this reason donations were essential to the success of the monastic community ( *sangha*). Perhaps the most important concept motivating the laity to contribute to Buddhist monasteries was the notion of religious merit. A gift to the *sangha* was a way for the patron to earn merit for one's past, present, and future. The *sangha* was the great "field of merit," and any donation to the *sangha* earned merit. Thus, an economy of exchange was instituted. In principle monasteries were not allowed to dispose of any gift given to them. Disposing of a gift donated to the *saṅgha* canceled the merit earned by the patron. Historically throughout Asia the practice of gift giving and the concept of merit led to an accumulation process that came to be the defining economic characteristic of Buddhism.

From its beginnings in the sixth century B.C., Buddhism was transportable and was never attached to a specific locale, and monks and laypeople were encouraged to proselytize. When Buddhism spread throughout Asia, it moved along the major trade routes, and Buddhist monks traveled the same roads as merchants. Buddhism and commerce became closely linked, and Buddhist monasteries and monks were frequently associated with merchants or guilds. The ideal of the monk as a peripatetic notwithstanding, monks in India and Sri Lanka were sometimes men of considerable wealth and property, including land. Although Buddhist monks morally renounced their claims to all personal and private possessions, this was not a legal act with legal ramifications. Buddhist monks possessed and used private wealth. Inscriptional records of all periods show monks and

nuns as active and substantial donors almost everywhere in India. Whereas many of the vinayas forbade private wealth and worldly possessions, some did not. Whether monks could own land was open to interpretation. Not only did different sets of monastic regulations give different opinions on the issue, but the mental state of the owner was considered key for determining the propriety of ownership. Thus, interpretation was a key factor in how rules for monks were read. For example, traditionally monks were forbidden from cultivating their land because of the risk of inadvertently killing living creatures in the soil. In early Indian Buddhism monks could consume food only if received from someone as a donation. The vinaya strictly forbade cultivating land, and yet this was later reinterpreted by Chan monks in China who called for monks to work in their own fields. Nor did Buddhist doctrine interfere with types of economic exchange now considered exploitative. For example, in China during the Tang period (618–907) it was quite common for individuals with excessive debt to mortgage themselves out to Buddhist monasteries as temple workers. Many monasteries owned temple slaves who worked their land. Monasteries also employed tenant farmers and used novices who had not yet been fully or-

A monk planting crops at a monastery on Dobong-san mountain near Seoul, South Korea.
Photo courtesy of John Powers

dained as monks. One scholar suggests that "good intention" was a relational social determinant that had profound implications for the social order and was often invoked to explain or justify the actions of monks.

For Chinese Buddhists the issue of wealth was never separated from the issue of land: both formed part of an accumulation process that began at least as early as the fourth century. Donations to Buddhist monks – which usually meant to the *saṅgha* as a whole – contributed to the accumulation of monastic wealth, as did usury, which quickly became a widespread practice among Buddhists throughout Asia. In China, where patronage was a major source of income, Buddhist monasteries, partly because of their production of wealth, became associated with the nobility and have always been associated with wealthy and powerful families. By at least the sixth century, Chinese Buddhists developed what came to be referred to as the "Inexhaustible Treasuries" (*wujincang*) – storehouses of gifts, goods, and items of value. Loans from these treasuries were regularly lent out to merchants at high interest rates and generated immense profits for many Chinese Buddhist monasteries. The Inexhaustible Treasuries became one of the principle commercial activities of the larger Chinese Buddhist monasteries in which a surplus value was used to sustain the monastic community. Religious festivals and market fairs were frequently held in the same place in China, and Buddhist monks were very active in trading. Some of the commercial activities Chinese Buddhist monks engaged in include tea production, salt trade, silver smelting, pawnshops and lotteries in which, for example, the robes of a deceased famous abbot associated with a specific monastery might be sold for profit. Buddhist monasteries held auctions; produced paper, ink sticks, and inkstones; and were actively engaged in the printing and production of books. Certain monasteries became well known as medical dispensaries, and certain monks gained fame as medical doctors. Other monasteries produced silk, selling it at a profit. Still others engaged in embroidery practices (convents were the primary producers in this area), and some produced lead powder, operated hostels, and made and sold food. It was quite common for larger Chinese Buddhist monasteries to establish oil presses to add to their overall income. Very few social institutions had the financial capability and technological knowledge to run such facilities. The impact on the local people, who for the most part had neither sufficient human resources nor sufficient capital to establish and operate oil presses or mills, was considerable. In medieval China oil was an extremely important product used for cooking, lighting, and cosmetics; in ship construction; in the manufacture of weapons and lacquered goods; in rust prevention; in construction; and in the manufacture of ink. Milling was an industry that was quite common among the many economic operations in which monasteries were engaged. Certain Buddhist monasteries had the expertise to grind grain products to a fine powder and sell them to the local people. This was clearly a technology to which very few social groups in China had access. Some wealthy landowners would have had the required technology, as did the larger Buddhist monasteries. During the Song period (960–

1279), milling practices were common in the larger Buddhist monasteries.

Having left India on the trade routes, Buddhism spread throughout eastern Asia. From China Buddhism first entered Korea in the fourth century, and, like Buddhists elsewhere in Asia, the Korean *saṅgha* quickly became involved in a variety of economic activities; again a principal focus was land accumulation. Very little research has been done on Korean Buddhism and economics. In 538 Buddhism entered Japan, and its status became defined by the Taiho code of 701. Japanese Buddhism became economically powerful. The imperium granted tax revenues to temples, and monasteries owned considerable land. By the 14th century monasteries were involved in commercial activities such as brewing sake and lending money and worked closely with merchant guilds. Some temples arbitrated disputes between merchants and even controlled trading rights in certain areas. At various times in history, Buddhism's economic power in China, Japan, and Korea and in other parts of the Buddhist world prompted severe crackdowns on their institutions by governments, resulting in massive land confiscations; for example, Japan in the 16th century, China in the ninth century, and Korea in the 15th century experienced widespread Buddhist persecutions. In most cases the argument was made that Buddhist monasteries controlled too much land. Buddhist monks in China were deeply involved in all the exchange processes pertaining to land, so much so that one scholar of Chinese history has argued that the profound changes in the Chinese economy between the fifth and the tenth century were due in part to the influence of Buddhism. In China monasteries were often subjected to crackdowns that sought to take back the precious metals used in their Buddha statues. However, in almost all cases, after suffering severe economic and religiously disruptive setbacks following these crackdowns, Buddhism for the most part would recover and renew its economic strength – a testament to the degree to which monasteries had become integrated into society.

In the 20th century in mainland China, first the Nationalist government and then the Communist Party systematically dismantled the economic foundations of monastic Buddhism, confiscating huge amounts of land. It remains to be seen what the final outcome of this will be. In other parts of Asia, Buddhism is still as much involved with socioeconomic activities as ever. For example, powerful Taiwanese Buddhist organizations own land in Japan and the United States and actively seek to increase their economic base. The exchange of merit is still at the core of Buddhist economics, and Buddhist capital continues to exchange hands: hospitals are established, universities founded, and charities organized. Engaging in economic activities was and continues to be as much a part of everyday Buddhist life as any other Buddhist activity. More research is needed on the complex relations between Buddhism and economics, the interaction between Buddhist doctrine and economic practices, the role of ritual in socioeconomic practices, and the processes of commodification of objects for exchange, such as land. Buddhist economic practices highlight the gap that exists between doctrinal representation and social practice. Focusing on Buddhist social practices, the everyday actions of Buddhists, the institutional organization of Buddhist monasteries, Buddhist commercial activities, exchanges of capital, and interactions with the mundane world can provide us with a more balanced understanding of Buddhism and the various roles that it performed in different societies.

MICHAEL J. WALSH

*See also* Buddhist Schools/Traditions: Japan; China; Clothing: Buddhist Perspectives; Economic Justice, Buddhist; Food: Buddhist Perspectives; Governance: Buddhist Perspecives; Japan: History; Rules, Buddhist (Vinaya): Historical; Saṅgha; Social Services: Buddhist; Virtues, Buddhist

**Further Reading**

Brook, Timothy, *Praying for Power: Buddhism and the Formation of Gentry Society in Late-Ming China*, Cambridge, Massachusetts: Council on East Asian Studies, Harvard University, 1993

Ch'en, Kenneth K.S., *The Chinese Transformation of Buddhism*, Princeton, New Jersey: Princeton University Press, 1973

Gernet, Jacques, *Buddhism in Chinese Society: An Economic History from the Fifth to the Tenth Centuries*, translated by Franciscus Verellen, New York: Columbia University Press, 1995

Gombrich, Richard F., *Theravāda Buddhism: A Social History from Ancient Benares to Modern Colombo*, London and New York: Routledge, 1988

Huang, Minzhi, *Songdai fojiao shehui jingjishi lunji* (Essays on the Socioeconomic History of Buddhism during the Song Dynasty), Taipei: Taiwan xueshengshu, 1989

Quan Hanshu. "Songdai siyuan suo jingying zhi gongchangye" (Commercial Activities of Song Dynasty Buddhist Monasteries), in *Beijing daxue sishi zhou nianji nianlun wenji yibian*, Beijing: Beijing University, 1939

Schopen, Gregory, "Monastic Law Meets the Real World: A Monk's Continuing Right to Inherit Family Property in India," *History of Religions* 35:2 (November 1995)

Schopen, Gregory, *Bones, Stones, and Buddhist Monks: Collected Papers on the Archaeology, Epigraphy, and Texts of Monastic Buddhism in India*, Honolulu: University of Hawaii Press, 1997

Twitchett, Denis, "Monastic Estates in T'ang China," *Asia Major* 5 (1956)

Yang, Lien-Sheng, *Studies in Chinese Institutional History*, Cambridge, Massachusetts: Harvard University Press, 1961

# Economics: Christian

Economics is the study of the production, distribution (or provision), and consumption of goods and services. In modern times it usually has been categorized among the social sciences. Historically, however, more often it has functioned as a philosophy. When theologians treat economics, the study ordinarily is accounted a dimension of morals. Christian economics assays the treatment and administration of goods and services according to gospel standards and magisterial pronouncements, especially specific ecclesial instructions on religion's conception of temporalities, labor, and finances. In terms of this last category, through special instructions, popes since Leo XIII (1878–1903) have created an especially fruitful body of thought. Notably through social encyclicals they have articulated a perspective constituent to a specifically Christian response to economics in the modern world.

Monasticism has elaborated on Christian economics by proposing and advocating an understanding peculiar to its own situation, namely, how economic issues are understood and treated by men and women who have *chosen* to live in poverty. Thereby the monastics redefine the issues and purposes of economics, and they conclude that because poverty – both voluntary and involuntary – is imitative of Christ, it is thus an issue pertinent to (although not necessarily binding on) all Christians.

The cloistered perspective has taken two principal courses: the mendicant and the monastic. These are not antithetical; rather they offer different approaches to meeting the same gospel ideal. For mendicants especially economics is a prominent concern. The word *mendicants* indicates beggars. This begging constitutes for them an immediate and absolute mode of entrusting the supply of provisions to the movement of God. Thus, their mendicancy colors the way in which they are enfolded in providence.

The traditionally monastic perspective propounds a different understanding of economics' pertinence. Mendicants tend to emphasize the biblical injunction not to amass treasure against the prospect of the morrow, whereas monastics account the goods and holdings of the monastery as constituting what God *has* provided. The monks hold that the rubrics of their poverty disencumber them from temporal concerns. For both mendicants and monastics, these temporalities are understood as God's provision.

The language used by these congregations can be employed to illustrate the distinction between them. Mendicant literature often refers to "detachment" from temporalities. Detachment entails a divorce between the friars and any intrinsic value found in the goods and services they use. The mendicants are not acquisitive or possessive. However, in the monastic view, epitomized by *Regula Benedicti* (the monastic Rule of St. Benedict), providence's provisions are understood differently. Rather than detachment St. Benedict (c. 480–550) proposes that the monk regard temporalities disinterestedly. Such items are tools (*ferramenta*), or means intended to promote the good of all and not only of individuals. Thus, Benedict wants them to be treated reverently, as if indeed they were "vessels of the altar." The difference between these two outlooks is not great theoretically, but it affects the practice exercised toward the cloister's economics.

A provocative irony exists in poverty's role in Christian monastic economics. For both mendicants and monastics, poverty is a crucial virtue, chosen and embraced for the sake of the heavenly kingdom. Yet at the same time, the monk regards the poor with compassion, often seeking to alleviate their burden. He longs to ease the poverty of others while choosing its weight for himself.

Especially among more active orders, the poor are often addressed through some form of external social action. For the more cloistered bodies, care for the poor is usually approached through domestic endeavor. That is important, as Benedict prescribes that a monk's good works should be undertaken in "the environment of the cloister and stability of the community." Assistance of the poor assumes various forms. For example, it is common to supply the monastery's porter (*portarius*, "the monk who answers the door") with wherewithal for giving small-scale financial aid. The poor who call at the monastery might be given a meal. Some abbeys also have a tradition of setting aside a number of rooms for wayfarers.

The poor who call at the monastery are considered guests (*hospites*). For Benedictines in particular that invokes an elaborate and important protocol. Receiving guests is especially vital to the monastic vision. In his *Regula* Benedict urges that all such visitors be received as Christ. His recommendations include such features as a greeting by the superior or guest-master, the recitation of Scripture or passages from the *Regula*, the washing of hands, and conventions for dining and speaking. Benedict intends that the guest should be welcomed, of course, but also edified. That, too, is part of the monastic economic vision because it is an act of charity, enriching the poor spiritually.

When guests are present, the common order of the cloister continues (with some allowance for exceptions). However, it is not unusual for elaborate special provisions to be readied for those who visit. Saint Walburga (c. 710–779), a Benedictine nun who participated in the monastic evangelization of the German peoples, is often cited as the Order's exemplar in welcoming the poor. She established a room in her monastery to store clothing that might be given to the poor and another chamber where such guests might dine. In addition she ordained that while the poor ate, the *Regula* or gospel should be read to them so that "the soul as well as the body may be fed."

Another prominent factor in monastic economics is the ambition to identify with the poor (as well as with Christ who chose to be poor). In this the mendicant orders are especially strong. In particular Franciscan economics (indebted to the Order's founder, St. Francis of Assisi [1181/82–1226]) derives substance from the friars' uncompromising fraternity with the poor.

Monastic poverty has both a corporate and an individual dimension. Of these, corporate poverty has proven the more vexing aspect, being contentiously debated through the centuries. The term *corporate poverty* refers to the economic status and practices of the monastery. Models, principles, and aspirations vary. For example, St. Francis urged strict, absolute poverty, remembering Christ's lack of even a place to rest His head. However, practical concerns and Church influence brought about considerable compromise of that approach, even before Francis' death. Saint Dominic (c. 1170–1221) sponsored a poverty that allowed greater attention to the imperative of certain necessities. He permitted the acquisition of goods pertinent to the work whereunto his followers were called and also what was needed for the healthful (albeit modest) maintenance of the workers.

Followers of *Regula Benedicti* (e.g., Benedictines, Cistercians, and Camaldolese) developed their concept of corporate poverty along different lines. Benedict provided a variety of injunctions that influenced the issue. For example, he prescribed that the monks' produce should be underpriced so that "in all things God may be glorified." Yet such principles have been subjected to centuries of accommodation and adaptation. The core of the Benedictine philosophy, as it has developed, is that the monk ought not be preoccupied with temporalities. Thus, the monastery is equipped with adequate provisions, and these are committed readily to reasonable use. Although superfluity is not sought, the presence of a secure domestic environment is considered to benefit monastic spirituality and ambitions. The reasoning is this: were a person to live in such need that food, clothing, shelter, or other necessities are wanting, these factors would command the monk's attention, distracting him from his mindfulness of divinity. In such cases, it is suggested, the monk's poverty would detract from rather than serve his religious life and purpose.

For monastics a tradition has developed that allows individual cloisters to hold substantial acreage (a practice probably indebted to the monks' reliance on monastic farms for sustenance and income). This has occasioned the most volatile of modern monastic economic issues. It is now common practice for monks to use their property for external, even commercial, enterprises. Thus, they profit from mercantile activity rather than from their labor. The difference is significant, as Benedict explicitly calls for the monks to live by "the work of their hands." This revision of Benedict's economic insight has led some monastic communities to seek income from investments or other interest-bearing transactions. Although common today, such practices cannot be justified in terms of the Benedictine *Regula*. Indeed it has been argued that in the Christian personalist movement (e.g., Catholic Worker houses [1933 and later]) of the 20th century, a greater fidelity exists to the economics of the *Regula*, purely considered, than is practiced at some modern monasteries. Various personalist leaders (e.g., Peter Maurin, 1877–1949) have explicitly conceded the inspiration that they drew from Benedict's thought.

However, individual poverty is the more crucial economic element in monastic life. Benedict's admonition – perhaps the most strongly worded prescription in *Regula Benedicti* – is that the "vice of private ownership" ought to be extirpated, "ripped out by the roots and removed from the cloister." He then outlines the wherewithal with which the monk should be satisfied, listing the measure and type of food, clothing, bedding, and personal implements (e.g., knife, stylus, tablet, and handkerchief). All are issued from the common store, seeking to address need rather than equivalence (Acts 4:35). Great care is taken to cast this as justice and wise provisioning rather than as deprivation or sparsity. Thus, the *Regula* also holds that adaptations in diet, clothing, and other arrangements ought to be made as circumstances recommend. Further adjustments are allowed for reason of climate, season, or the rigor of work. However, Benedict does say that the brothers should be content with whatever is issued to them, even if it be the "meanest and least" allotment. Thus, Benedict strives to avoid harshness that might distract the monk and induce him to dwell on temporal concerns. Satisfaction of *needs*, he proposes, should avert murmuring.

To further this objective Benedict urges the officers of the monastery to have compassion for the weak. In particular he demands that the cellarer (the monk who has charge of the monastery's goods) should exhibit benevolence and kindness. Through dicta such as these, Benedict makes his economic insight more practicable and congenial. The humane and compassionate character of Benedict's provisions is especially evident in his admonition that the abbot (who administers the community and represents Christ to the monks) should prefer to be loved rather than feared.

The economic theory deployed in monastic life is specifically Christian on every level from conception to execution, and the cloister itself affords a clearly defined environment wherein these principles and ambitions will be realized. The monastic insight is that all matters of production, distribution, and consumption of created things, as well as all services of or by created beings, figure in some way into the course of providence. They are means of advancing a divinely centered vocation. God provides for the monks, who in turn are to use this materiel according to the monastic insight, conscientiously and with integrity. The emphasis in monastic Christian economics falls not on amassing or commanding temporal wherewithal. Instead its principles seek to address human need in a context and manner that is consistent with the monastic vocation. In keeping with this, monasticism intends to color economics rather than allow economics to determine the character of the cloister.

PASCHAL BAUMSTEIN, O.S.B.

*See also* Agriculture, Western Christian; Benedictines: General or Male; Dominic, St.; Dominicans: General or Male; Francis of Assisi, St.; Franciscans: General or Male; Hospitality, Christian; Papacy: Papal Pronouncements; Social Services: Western Christian

## Further Reading

Fry, Timothy, editor, *RB 1980: The Rule of St. Benedict in Latin and English with Notes*, Collegeville, Minnesota: Liturgical Press, 1981

Maurin, Peter, *Easy Essays* (Catholic Worker Penny Pamphlets [series]), New York: Catholic Worker Press, 1934; London: Sheed and Ward, 1938

Mounier, Emmanuel, *A Personalist Manifesto*, translated by the monks of Saint John's Abbey, London and New York: Longmans, Green, 1938

Pesch, Heinrich, *Liberalismus, Socialismus und Christliche Gesellschaftsordnung* (Die Sociale Frage: beleuchtet durch die "Stimmen aus Maria-Laach," 12–13), Freiburg im Breisgau: Herdersche Verlagshandlung, 1899

Schumpeter, Joseph Alois, *History of Economic Analysis*, edited by Elizabeth Boody Schumpeter, London: Allen and Unwin, 1952; New York: Oxford University Press, 1954

# Education of Christian Monastics

The male monastic orders organized huge educational pyramids for the purpose of educating their members in the High Middle Ages and early Renaissance (1200 to 1500). Female monastics depended on their own individual convents for most of their schooling.

## Schools for Male Monastics

As the most important monastic orders expanded from their origins, they faced the daunting task of educating their members. The friar who was destined to preach the word of God (the Dominican goal) needed to know the word of God, and this meant study. Even the Franciscans, after some hesitation, accepted the necessity of educating their members. Thus, the major religious orders, especially the Dominicans, the Franciscans, and the Augustinian Hermits, erected elaborate and similar educational edifices. The Carmelites, Cistercians, Servites (Servants of Mary), and other orders followed with similar but smaller structures. The mendicant orders began to erect this educational structure by the second quarter of the 13th century, and it was fully in place by the fourth quarter of the century.

The minimum age for novices was 18 (with some exceptions), so as a condition of admission the orders demanded that novices have some learning. Nevertheless, novices' education was often minimal, and so the monastic orders directed each convent to establish a school, consisting of a single teacher who taught the younger members. After a year's novitiate and making a profession of vows, the young members of the convent began classes. For the Dominicans the classes consisted of daily lectures on the Bible and the *Sentences* of Peter Lombard, along with daily repetition exercises of what was learned and a weekly disputation (formal debate) covering the week's material, always in Latin. The convent provided training in Latin for those who lacked knowledge of it. For the Dominicans, attending classes remained a lifetime obligation.

After two years of studying the Bible and Lombard's *Sentences*, those with greater aptitude for learning were sent to a provincial school (*studium*). These schools were in designated convents within the province and were administered by the provincial leadership of the order. (A province was a large administrative unit of the order, sometimes encompassing dozens or perhaps a hundred or more convents, as in the Dominican province of central Italy or that for all of England.) Provincial schools were open to members from all the convents in the province, and local convents sent designated members to these schools. Provincial schools often moved from one convent to another to take advantage of the presence of a teacher or better library resources. Provincial schools (*studia*) were of three levels. The lowest were sometimes called "arts" schools but taught logic on the basis of Aristotle's logical works and standard medieval manuals. Logic was the basic methodological tool for Scholastic learning. After two or three years in the logic school, gifted students studied for another two years at a provincial school for philosophy, where they studied Aristotle's philosophical texts, especially the *Physics* and *On the Soul*. The curriculum was a combination of natural philosophy, focusing on the material world, and metaphysics, the study of being, which was seen as preparation for theology. After two years of study at a provincial philosophy school, a few favored students advanced to provincial theological schools, if the order had them, where they studied the Bible and Lombard's *Sentences* for another two years or so.

Whereas the number of schools was large, the size of the local or provincial school was very small: six, eight, or perhaps ten students taught by one lecturer. Nor did a student necessarily study continuously year after year. His local convent might call him back to teach or for some other task. Indeed, the major goal of all the schools was to train friars for service to the order, especially teaching.

At the apex of the educational structure were an order's "general schools" (*studia generalia*). These were theological schools that were under the direction of the highest leadership of the order; this leadership was expressed through general chapter meetings every few years in which the general of the order, provincial priors, and delegates decided policy. General schools were found in some of the most important convents of the order and seldom moved. Attendance was limited to members of the order who had passed through the lower schools and by quotas. For example, in 1316 the Dominicans decreed that each province (which might comprise thousands of members) might send two students to each general school of the order. Either the home convent or the province paid the expenses of members sent to the general schools. Practically all the future leaders of the order (i.e., generals, provincial priors, and the leading scholars) studied in general schools.

General schools taught theology through the familiar combination of lectures on the Bible and lectures on Lombard's *Sentences* and the usual repetition exercises and disputations. Unlike the lower schools, general schools likely had two or more lecturers, and a few secular priests and the occasional layman probably attended as well. Dante Alighieri (1265–1321), who was never a friar, might have studied theology at the Dominican general school of St. Maria Novella in Florence.

By the middle of the 14th century, the Franciscans had about 30 general schools across Europe, the Dominicans about 20, the Augustinian Hermits about 20, the Carmelites about 16, and the smaller mendicant orders fewer. Each of the major orders added one or a few more in the 15th century, often establishing a new general house alongside a newly founded university.

*Monastic Education and the Universities*
The emphasis on Latin, the logical and philosophical works of Aristotle, the Bible, and Lombard's *Sentences* by the schools of the male religious orders imitated the university curriculum. This is because Aristotle penetrated all areas of higher learning in the West in the 13th century, when both the religious orders and the universities were organizing education. Male monastic orders and their schools existed both adjacent to and inside universities.

Most religious order general schools were located in convents in university towns – clear evidence of the attraction of universities. For example, all the major religious orders and many minor ones had general schools in Paris and Oxford. However, locating a religious order general school in a convent in a university town

did not necessarily mean that the school was part of the university. Relations between order and university varied greatly, and professorships were individual appointments. For example, in 1230 John of St. Giles, a professor at the University of Paris, announced in the middle of a lecture that he was joining the Dominican order. Thus, he finished his lecture as a Dominican, and the order had a university professor. In time many members of mendicant orders became university teachers in universities that specialized in the teaching of theology, mainly at Paris, Oxford, Cambridge, and Cologne, and in universities in central Europe. As the mendicant orders became more involved in study and teaching, some professorships of theology were reserved for them. The most famous mendicant order scholars moved back and forth between their own order schools and university professorships. For example, the Dominican Thomas Aquinas (c. 1225–1274) taught at the University of Paris, his fellow Dominican Albertus Magnus (d. 1280) taught at the University of Cologne, and the Franciscan John Duns Scotus (c. 1265–1308) taught at the universities of Paris and Cologne, and they all taught in the schools of their orders.

In northern European universities, such as Paris and Oxford, where most of the undergraduate instruction took place in colleges (residences with instruction for young arts students under the direction of secular authorities or monastics), the religious orders established such colleges in addition to convents for their own members. They did so partly because mendicant order friars were excluded from studying in the Faculty of Arts at Paris. The result was that many male monastics studied in northern European university towns, sometimes as university students and sometimes as students at the order's general school located there. By the early 16th century, between 1,500 and 2,000 members of 13 religious orders were to be found in Paris studying either arts or theology at some level.

However, universities emphasizing law and medicine, which included all those in Italy, southern France, and many in Spain, had few members of mendicant orders as either students or professors. Because the universities of southern Europe taught very little theology, friars taught theology to their own students in convent *studia* located in university towns. Yet neither the teachers nor the students of the convents were members of the university community, and very few individual monastics enrolled to study arts, medicine, or law in southern European universities. Eventually, in the late 15th and the 16th centuries, most Italian universities added two monastics to their faculties, typically a Dominican to teach Thomist theology and a Franciscan or an Augustinian Hermit to teach Scotist theology.

*Education of Female Monastics*
Female monastics could not erect pyramids of schools because they lived in single, local convents with minimal organizational ties with other convents, even those of the same order. They did not attend universities, nor could they attend schools outside the convent, because the papal constitution *Periculoso* (1298) imposed cloistering on all nuns who professed solemn vows. Although medieval cloistering was not always rigid, it restricted

the movements of most nuns. Only the so-called beguines lived uncloistered lives. On the border between professed nuns and laywomen, beguines lived a voluntary life of poverty, chastity, prayer, and good works without solemn vows. They lived either alone or together in apartments or houses, praying together, doing good works, and earning their living by tasks such as weaving and spinning. For example, St. Catherine of Siena (1347–1380) was a third-order Dominican who initially lived as a cenobite in a room in her father's house before embarking on extensive travel and writing prolifically.

For nuns professing solemn vows, female monastic education depended greatly on the tradition, commitment, and educational resources of the local convent and the determination of an individual nun. Despite the difficulties, medieval and Renaissance Europe had numerous educated nuns, including many mystics and spiritual writers, some of whom read and wrote Latin.

They learned in various ways. Many girls and women entering the convent brought their education with them. Because elementary literacy and a minimum age (typically 16, although not always observed) were often prerequisites for entering a convent, parents with daughters intended for the convent saw that they received prior schooling. In addition, many adult women, sometimes with considerable education and experience, entered convents as widows. Convents that attracted upper-class women were likely to have better-educated nuns.

Many female convents educated lay girls as long-term residents without vows. By the 14th century, Italian urban parents, especially widowers, often sent girls to a female monastery to be raised and educated. Once in the convent, the girl was subject to its rules, including cloistering. They lived and learned in the monastery for several years until removed, perhaps to be married. Some professed vows and remained. Obviously, the convent had to have a teacher to instruct them and the novices.

Typical female monastic education, whether for lay girls, novices, or professed nuns, was not extensive. It consisted of learning to read and write in the vernacular as well as sewing and singing. Most of the books known to have been available in convents were vernacular religious texts, such as saints' lives. The *Officium Beatae Mariae Virginis* (Little Office of Our Lady, also called the Book of Hours or Rosary) was probably the most commonly read Latin work. A combination of small breviary and prayer book, the *Officium* contained psalms, prayers, hymns, and litanies, many in praise of Mary. Nuns read or memorized the prayers.

Although professed nuns were not allowed to leave the monastery to study, male spiritual advisers, some of them university-trained mendicant order friars, were allowed to come to them. Although no evidence exists that they taught nuns on a regular basis, they could offer intellectual and spiritual guidance and reading matter to the exceptional nun. Many famous mystics and spiritual writers wrote under the urging and guidance of spiritual advisers or dictated to them. Finally, the music that was sung, performed, and sometimes composed by nuns offers evidence of intellectual accomplishment. Some nuns might have sung without being able to read words or music, but more complex musical performance, such as singing polyphonic music to the accompaniment of an organ or instruments, required the ability to read music and Latin.

Despite the numerous barriers, it is likely that most nuns possessed at least vernacular literacy. A few fragmentary studies from late 16th-century Italy show that the literacy rate (usually 50 percent to 75 percent) for nuns was much higher than that of the male or female populations outside the monastery.

PAUL F. GRENDLER

*See also* Alcuin; Augustinian Friars/Hermits; Dominicans; France: History; Franciscans; Libraries: Western Christian; Scholars, Benedictine; Women's Monasteries: Western Christian

**Further Reading**
Note: information on the education of female monastics must be gleaned from a variety of fragmentary and elusive sources.

Farge, James K., *Orthodoxy and Reform in Early Reformation France: The Faculty of Theology of Paris, 1500–1543*, Leiden: Brill, 1985

Gutierrez, David, *The Augustinians in the Middle Ages 1256–1356*, translated by Arthur J. Ennis, Villanova, Pennsylvania: Augustinian Historical Institute, 1984

Gutierrez, David, *The Augustinians in the Middle Ages 1357–1517*, translated by Thomas Martin, Villanova, Pennsylvania: Augustinian Historical Institute, 1983

Hinnebush, William, *The History of the Dominican Order*, volume 2: *Intellectual and Cultural Life to 1500*, New York: Alba House, 1973

Lickteig, Franz-Bernard, *The German Carmelites at the Medieval Universities*, Rome: Institutum Carmleitanum, 1981

Moorman, John, *A History of the Franciscan Order from Its Origins to the Year 1517*, Oxford: Clarendon Press, 1968; Chicago: Franciscan Herald Press, 1988

Mulcahey, M. Michèle, *"First the Bow Is Bent in Study" – Dominican Education Before 1350*, Toronto: Pontifical Institute of Mediaeval Studies, 1998

*Le scuole degli ordini mendicanti (secoli XIII–XIV)*, Todi: Presso l'Accademia Tudertina, 1978

# Egypt

*Early Development*

Egypt was long believed to be the place of origin for organized Christian monasticism. Athanasius' *Life of Antony* (written c. 356–357) implied as much, and it was widely read by Christians at the time of its composition and in succeeding centuries. Ascetic practice in Syria is now better understood and appreciated, but Egypt remains crucial to the study of Christian monasticism. Basic questions are raised. Why did organized monasticism develop in Christianity during the fourth century, and why did this happen in Egypt? A preference for asceticism (in the sense of withdrawal from society, combined with fasting, vigils, and extended prayer) is found among various groups in Egypt prior to the fourth century. Philo of Alexandria (c. 20 B.C–c. A.D. 50), in *On the Contemplative Life,* praises the prayerful life of the Jewish *Therapeutae* in the first century, and the life of Plotinus (c. 205–270), whose early years were spent in Egypt, indicates a preference for asceticism in some pagan philosophical circles. A strong current of asceticism existed in the first centuries of Christianity in Egypt: Eusebius of Caesarea (c. 260–c. 340), in his *Ecclesiastical History,* assumes that Philo's *Therapeutae* are Christians; Gnostic Christians, such as Valentinus (second century A.D.), recommend ascetic practices in the second century; and Origen (c. 185–253), Christian scholar and theologian in Egypt and Palestine, was renowned for his severe asceticism. Ascetic practice was common among various groups in Egypt from the first through the third century.

Changes appear in the late third century in Egypt. Larger numbers of Christians take up an ascetic life, somewhat separated from society, and experiment with different forms of organization so as to create Christian monasticism. The reasons for this change are still debated. Some saw the monk as successor to the martyr, as Christianity became first tolerated and then state sanctioned; others saw the monks as refugees from the economic pressures of the empire. Native Egyptian resistance to Greco-Roman cultural hegemony has also been proposed as an explanation of the development. Recently it has been understood as a response to the religious and social needs of late antiquity in Egypt.

According to the *Life of Antony,* the saint (252–356), having heard the gospel injunction to "go, sell what you have" and "follow me" (Matt. 19:21), disposed of his property and took up a life of prayer and asceticism on the outskirts of his village. This might be an idealized version of Antony's actions, but it is clear that others who were already living in this way were available as role models. This village-based, small-scale monasticism is becoming better known through study of documentary papyri: men and women left their families and lived in small groups in towns and villages, supporting themselves with handicrafts, to lead a celibate life of prayer and ascetic practice. Antony began this way but gradually sought greater separation from settled Egypt and founded two sites with his disciples that continued as monastic foundations for centuries: the Outer Mountain at Pispir and the Inner Mountain near the Red Sea at Mount Qulzum. Antony and his followers lived in separate cells with no rule but curtailed food and sleep to devote themselves to prayer. Antony offered guidance, as did other experienced monks, and all worked to support themselves. The letters of Antony show him advising groups of monks in other places, especially Arsinoe in the Fayyum.

By the early fourth century, groups of monks gathered in the Nitrian desert and adopted the same practices as at Antony's settlements. Nitria, located about 30 miles southeast of Alexandria, was founded in the 330s by Amoun. Kellia, somewhat farther into the desert, was also founded by Amoun on the advice of Antony; it has been scientifically excavated, revealing many details of the living conditions of monks in the semi-eremitic colonies. Kellia was informally led in the fourth century by Macarius of Alexandria (346–394) and became home to Evagrius Ponticus (346–399), an influential speculative theologian and monastic theorist. Scetis, the site farthest from cultivated land, was founded by Macarius the Egyptian (c. 300–c. 390) around 330. The Nitrian sites provide the setting for most of the *Sayings of the Fathers* (*Apophthegmata Patrum*), which were compiled in the late fifth century, and the question remains whether they convey the attitudes of the early period. The same environment and material is the main source for Palladius (c. 346–420/30) (*Lausiac History*), the anonymous *History of the Monks of Egypt,* and the monastic works of John Cassian (c. 360–after 430) (*Conferences* and *Institutes*). The textual history of the *Sayings* is complicated and still being explicated; meanwhile scholars have focused on determining the reliability of individual sayings, and some of these are generally rated higher than previously. The monastic ideology of the Nitrian communities, as recorded in the *Sayings,* exalted the relationship between abba (father) and disciple. The new monk lived close to an abba who taught him how to fast, how to pass the time in his cell, and how to make the handicrafts that would support him. In turn the disciple told the abba about harmful thoughts or actions that interfered with his efforts. The abba taught by example, and his authority derived from his years of monastic experience, as no common rule existed. Monks lived in separate cells and gathered only for worship and a shared meal on Saturdays and Sundays.

Farther up the Nile, about 370 miles south of Alexandria, Pachomius (c. 290–346) began a monastic career similar to that of Antony and the Nitrians but ended as the leader of a cenobitic community living under a common rule. A *Life of Pachomius* survives in several versions, as does a set of rules, collected and translated by Jerome (c. 345–420), but these sources were produced after the death of Pachomius, so it is difficult to recover the facts of his early life and work. Pachomius was drafted into the army in 312–313 and, while encamped at Thebes, was impressed by Christian acts of charity toward the conscripts. After release from the army, he sought instruction in Christianity and baptism at Chenoboskion and then spent three years in the village, sharing a life of service, labor, and Scripture with a few others. This is the village-based asceticism recorded in the papyri. Pachomius left this setting and spent some time as the disciple of Palamon, an older hermit – the Nitrian model. He left Palamon after receiving a divine sign to found a community at Tabennisi, a semi-deserted village. Other would-be monks joined Pachomius there, and after a series of stages that are quite unclear in the sources, he created a system in which new members applied to join the community, received the monastic habit, and followed rules governing life in the community. All this evolved over a period of 10 to 15 years. Pachomius eventually ruled 11 monastic houses (some for men and some for women) from the headquarters at Pbow, and by the end of the fourth century the Pachomian movement included about 7,000 people. After his death the monasteries were led by close associates, Theodore and Horsiesius, who also left writings that address issues of community life.

Another center of communal monasticism developed down the Nile in the region of Akhmim (Greek, Panopolis). The White Monastery, located across the Nile from Akhmim and about 93 miles northwest of Thebes, developed from a settlement of ascetics led by Pgol on the mountain of Atribah (the escarpment at the edge of the cultivated land of the Nile Valley). Pgol's nephew Shenoudi assumed leadership when Pgol died (c. 385) and transformed the settlement into a highly organized monastic compound. During his very long lifetime, Shenoudi (d. 465) created a new type of cenobitic monasticism. First, the monastic rule at the White Monastery was stricter than that of the Pachomians, and it was enforced with strong measures, including corporal punishment. Second, Shenoudi became involved in the affairs of neighboring communities: offering refuge in the monastery in times of attacks by the Blemmyes, supporting the rights of the poor against the exploitation of wealthy landowners, and raiding pagan sites. He preached regularly to both monks and laypeople, offering advice on Christian conduct and guidance in the current doctrinal disputes. Origen, Mani, Melitius, and Nestorius are all condemned by Shenoudi, who demonstrates that he was familiar with the controversies of the period. He left a large body of work in Coptic, written in a powerful, highly individual style, but because none of it was translated until the late 19th to early 20th century, Shenoudi, unlike Pachomius, remained unknown outside Egypt.

The strong foundation of monasticism in Egypt was threatened by several forces in the fifth century. Theophilus, the bishop of Alexandria in 385–412, attacked the Origenist views of certain leading monks in the Nitrian communities and forced them into exile in 400. He may have acted in the context of a broader ecclesiastical power struggle, but the effect was to remove certain intellectual leaders from the monasteries. Raids by desert barbarians against Scetis are recorded in 407, 434, and 444. However, most significant at this time was the split between Chalcedonian and Monophysite doctrine that divided the entire Church in Egypt. When the Council of Chalcedon (451) deposed Dioscorus (d. 454), the patriarch of Alexandria, who rejected the Chalcedonian formula and held to a strict one-nature Christology based on the teaching of Cyril of Alexandria (d. 444), a crisis struck monasteries in Egypt. Athanasius and the patriarchs who succeeded him had maintained close ties to the monasteries through visits and written communication; thus, most monks supported Dioscorus against the council. However, some supported the new Chalcedonian patriarch, and the ensuing schism divided the monastic movement for centuries. At first some monasteries were entirely Chalcedonian (Canopus, a Pachomian-style monastery near Alexandria), some entirely Monophysite (Enaton), and some divided (in Kellia and Scetis). Despite many attempts to reconcile the two doctrinal camps aided by imperial support for Chalcedonian leaders in Egypt, the Monophysite (or anti-Chalcedonian) party strengthened in the monasteries. Kellia and Scetis became entirely Monophysite, and ties grew between Monophysite monks in Egypt and Syria, as illustrated by the founding of the Monastery of the Syrians in Scetis in the early sixth century. The *Panegyric on Apollo* (by

Stephen, bishop of Heracleopolis Magna, sixth century) describes the outcome when Emperor Justinian (527–565) installs a Chalcedonian abbot at Pbow: Apollo, the anti-Chalcedonian abbot, leaves and founds a new monastery. The Pachomian movement centered on Pbow gradually fades from the historical record. By the late sixth century, ties between the Monophysite patriarch and Monophysite monasteries were strong, and most bishops were chosen from the monasteries. Bedouin raids devastated Scetis again in 577, but other evidence points to the strength of the monasteries: bequests to cenobitic communities were common, and new semi-eremitic communities appeared (Monastery of Epiphanius, west of Thebes, c. 580–640).

### After the Arab Conquest

The Arab conquest of Egypt in 642 interrupted and altered the development of monasticism in Egypt. In contrast the Persian conquest in 616 had proved to be a brief, destructive interregnum. Reasons for the success of a small Arab force in expelling the Byzantine army from Egypt have been long debated; disaffection and disloyalty of the anti-Chalcedonian, native Egyptian, Coptic-speaking population is often cited, but this explanation is inadequate, and internal weakness of the Byzantine Empire must be considered. The new Muslim rulers of Egypt exercised little immediate impact on the monasteries and on the Egyptian Church as a whole, which was now solidly Monophysite with a small Chalcedonian minority (also termed Melkites). At first the rulers were concerned mainly with collecting the taxes payable by all non-Muslim subjects, but gradually the burden of inferior status and occasional sharp bursts of persecution by anti-Christian rulers produced large-scale conversion to Islam. Present-day Egypt is more than 90 percent Muslim.

Certain periods stand out in the history of monasticism after the Arab conquest. This history can be reconstructed in part through contemporary sources, such as *The Churches and Monasteries of Egypt and Some Neighbouring Countries* by Abu al-Makarim, written between 1177 and 1204 (a work previously attributed to Abu Salih the Armenian), and *A Short History of the Copts and of Their Church* by Taqiy al-Din al-Maqrizi (1364–1442). Evidence exists of increased pressure on the monasteries over taxation in the eighth century, and extensive destruction of churches and cells occurred in the Wadi'n Natrun in 817. However, as a result of new construction the monasteries of Scetis acquired walled compounds in place of scattered cells and have largely retained this form to the present day. Non-Copts who were also Monophysites increased their presence in the monasteries at this time: Syrians (at the Monastery of the Syrians, as noted previously), Armenians at a site near the Monastery of John Colobos, and Ethiopians. Armenian inscriptions witness to a presence at the White Monastery in Upper Egypt in the 12th and 13th centuries.

The rule of the Bahri Mamluks (1260–1382) was especially notable for discrimination against Christians, including the destruction of churches and monasteries; conversion to Islam accompanied these measures, and thus Maqrizi's work (c. 1440) is a record of monasticism in decline. The monasteries of the

Wadi'n Natrun showed the effects of plague, famine (in 1348–1349 and 1374), and loss of endowments in the 14th century. Maqrizi enumerated monastic houses in existence, although with few monks; some disappeared soon after he wrote.

Europeans began to visit Egypt in the 17th century and record their impressions: Wansleben in 1672–1673, Denon with Napoleon in 1798, and others. The Christian population had become a small minority, and few monks and active monasteries remained. Egyptian Christians formed an independent Church that was firmly anti-Chalcedonian and led by the patriarch, although a small Melkite (Chalcedonian) group remained, and other Christian denominations (Catholics and Protestants) were represented beginning in the 18th and 19th centuries. Ties between the patriarch of Alexandria and the monasteries that had been created in the time of Athanasius (328–373) became even more important after the Arab conquest. From the 5th through the 13th century, the patriarch was chosen mainly from the monks of the Monastery of St. Macarius (Wadi'n Natrun), in the 14th and 15th from the Monastery of the Holy Virgin (al-Muharraq), in the 17th through the 19th from the Monastery of St. Antony (on the Red Sea), and in the 20th from monasteries in the Wadi'n Natrun.

## Modern Period

The 20th century, especially the last 50 years, has been a period of revitalization for the monasteries, and this development is closely linked to the person and the plans of the patriarch. As nationalist sentiment and desire for modernization grew in Egypt, the Coptic Orthodox Church was threatened, and new leaders, who often had been trained in the monasteries, introduced reforms. Cyril (patriarch 1959–1971), who spent years in the Monastery of Baramus (Wadi'n Natrun) and as a hermit before his election, believed that improved monastic discipline would strengthen the entire Egyptian Church and ordered all monks to return to their monasteries to fulfill their vows. Shenouda III (patriarch 1971 to present) was first a monk in the Monastery of the Syrians and then spent six years as a hermit near the Monastery of St. Bishoi; during his patriarchate the numbers of monks and nuns has continued to grow. Other individuals who consciously modeled themselves on the Desert Fathers by living as hermits in isolated cells were selected for leadership positions in monasteries, for example, Matta al-Meskin, a leader at the Monastery of St. Macarius, Wadi'n Natrun. Thus, a revival that began in the monasteries in the 1940s and that was manifest in the convents in the 1950s has increased the monastic population in all the sites that are still active. For example, between 1960 and 1990 the population of the Monastery of St. Macarius grew from 12 to 105 monks (for numbers in other monasteries c. 1990, see Cannuyer, 1990). An effort has been made to repopulate old sites (e.g., the White Monastery) that had ceased to function. The modern monastic revival has been influenced more by the semi-eremitic example of the Desert Fathers, in which groups of monks live in close proximity to offer mutual support, than by the more hierarchical, rule-based system of the Pachomians. The convent of the Daughters of Mary in Beni Soueif houses nuns who work outside the convent as teachers and nurses; this seems to show the influence of Catholic women's religious orders, although an Egyptian precedent exists in the support that Shenoudi gave to the surrounding community by means of the White Monastery.

## Sites: Ancient and Modern

Given the wide distribution of monasticism in Egypt from the fourth century (if not earlier), it is impossible to inventory all sites briefly. At the peak of monastic development in the fifth and sixth centuries, certain regions were most important (modern names or main site in parentheses): Mareotis (west of Alexandria), Nitrian desert (including Wadi'n Natrun), Pispir (Outer Mount of Antony), Arsinoe (Fayyum area), Arabian Desert (near the Red Sea, Monasteries of St. Antony and St. Paul), Oxyrhynchus (Beni Soueif), Antinoe (Ansina), Lycopolis (Asyut), Panopolis (Sohag and Akhmim, the Red and White Monasteries), and Thebaid (Pachomian communities). Archaeological investigation has been concentrated in the Nitrian sites, whereas other areas have received much briefer surveys.

The modern monastic revival has taken place mainly in those regions that maintained a continuous monastic presence: Wadi'n Natrun, Arabian Desert, Fayyum, and Asyut. The Monastery of St. Menas, in the Mareotis region, was refounded in 1959 on the ancient site and has become a fairly large community (55 monks in 1989). In contrast convents are located in towns and cities without these ancient associations: four in Cairo and three in other towns (Bilqas, Tantah, and Beni Soueif). Other ancient monastic sites have been resettled by a handful of monks. Thus, monastic sites in Egypt are either functioning monasteries, which in some cases receive visitors, or ruins awaiting scientific study.

JANET TIMBIE

*See also* Antony, St.; Archaeology: Near East; Armenia; Asceticism: Christian Perspectives; Desert Fathers; Desert Mothers; Evagrius Ponticus; Hagiography: Eastern Christian; Hermits: Eastern Christian; Island Monasteries, Christian; Office, Daily: Eastern Christian; Origins: Comparative Perspectives; Origins: Eastern Christian; Pachomius, St.; Pilgrimages, Christian: Near East; Shenoute of Atripe; Spirituality: Eastern Christian; Syria; Transvestite Saints; Women's Monasteries: Eastern Christian

## Further Reading

Bagnall, Roger S., *Egypt in Late Antiquity*, Princeton, New Jersey: Princeton University Press, 1993
Cannuyer, Christian, *Les Coptes*, Brussels: Éditions Brepols, 1990; revised edition, 1996
Chitty, Derwas J., *The Desert a City*, Oxford: Blackwell, 1966; Crestwood, New York: St. Vladimir's Seminary Press, 1966
*The Churches and Monasteries of Egypt and Some Neighbouring Countries*, translated by B.T.A. Evetts, Oxford: Clarendon Press, 1895
Doorn-Harder, Pieternella van, *Contemporary Coptic Nuns*, Columbia: University of South Carolina Press, 1995
Evelyn-White, Hugh G., *The Monasteries of the Wadi'n Natrun*, volumes 2 and 3, New York: Metropolitan Museum of Art, 1932–1933

Gould, Graham, *The Desert Fathers on Monastic Community*, Oxford: Clarendon Press, and New York: Oxford University Press, 1993

Kamil, Murad, *Aspects de l'Égypte copte*, Berlin: Akademie-Verlag, 1965

Leipoldt, Johannes, *Schenute von Atripe und die Entstehung des National-Aegyptischen Christentums*, Leipzig: Hinrichs, 1903

Maqrizi, Ahmad ibn Ali, *A Short History of the Copts and of Their Church*, translated by S.C. Malan, London: Nutt, 1873

Meinardus, Otto F.A., *Monks and Monasteries of the Egyptian Deserts*, Cairo: American University Press at Cairo, 1961; revised edition, 1989

Mottier, Yvette, and Nathalie Bosson, *Les Kellia: Ermitages coptes en Basse-Égypte*, Geneva: Éditions du Tricorne, 1989

Rousseau, Philip, *Pachomius*, Berkeley: University of California Press, 1985; updated, 1999

Timm, Stefan, *Das christlich-koptische Ägypten in arabischen Zeit*, 6 vols., Wiesbaden: Reichert, 1984–1992

Veilleux, Armand, editor and translator, *Pachomian Koinonia*, 3 vols., Kalamazoo, Michigan: Cistercian Publications, 1980–1982

# Einsiedeln, Switzerland

This Swiss abbey-*nullius*, located about 19 miles south of Zurich in the canton of Schwyz, began with two hermits, Blessed Benno (d. 940), a canon of Strassburg and later bishop of Metz, and Blessed Eberhard, also a canon of Strassburg, who formed the growing number of hermits into a community of monks following the Rule of St. Benedict around 934. The monastery was built on the site of the hermitage of St. Meinrad (d. 861), a monk of Reichenau in Lake Constance, who had been put to death by brigands. Dedicated to Our Lady of the Hermits, Einsiedeln received lands and privileges from the local nobility and Emperor Otto I (936–973) and other Saxon emperors. In the 10th and 11th centuries, monks of Einsiedeln were chosen as abbots and bishops to serve in other places. Einsiedeln also founded other houses, such as Petershausen in Constance (983), Muri (1027), and Hirsau (1065). The abbot became a prince of the Holy Roman Empire. By the end of the Middle Ages, entrance into the community was restricted to sons of the nobility.

In the Middle Ages the cell of St. Meinrad became the shrine of the Black Virgin, an object of pilgrimage for much of the German-speaking area in southern Germany, Switzerland, and Alsace. The "chapel of graces," a neoclassical structure constructed in 1807 with elements from the former structure and located in the nave of the grand abbey church, is today one of the most important Marian shrines in Europe.

Between 1516 and 1518 Ulrich Zwingli (1484–1531) was one of the pilgrim preachers at Einsiedeln. From that post he went to Zurich, where he openly launched the Swiss reform. The monastic community at the time consisted of two monks: Abbot Conrad III von Hohenrechberg, who lived on his horse farm away from the abbey, and the administrator, Diebold von Geroldseck, who eventually joined Zwingli in the reform movement. With the resignation in 1526 of Abbot Conrad III at the instigation of the townspeople, Louis Blarer, a monk of St. Gall, became abbot under irregular circumstances. Entry into the community ceased to be restricted to nobles. Joachim Eichhorn (d. 1569), also a monk of St. Gall, succeeded as abbot and restored the prosperity of the community.

During the 18th century the church and the monastic buildings were rebuilt in the baroque style. At the end of the century, in 1798, French revolutionary soldiers suppressed the monastery. The statue of the Black Virgin was hidden, and the monks dispersed, to be reestablished some six years later. During the past 150 years, Einsiedeln has established St. Meinrad Archabbey, New Subiaco Abbey, and Assumption Abbey in the United States and Los Toldos Abbey in Argentina. Today Einsiedeln is the spiritual center of Catholic Switzerland, internationally renowned for its pilgrimage and its baroque splendor. The abbey of Einsiedeln has introduced the cause for beatification of Brother Meinrad Eugster, who died in 1925, acclaimed by all for his sanctity.

CYPRIAN DAVIS, O.S.B.

*See also* Abbeys, Territorial; Reichenau; St. Gallen, Switzerland; Switzerland

## Further Reading

*Annales Einsiedlenses: Monumenta Germaniae Historica: Scriptorum*, volume 3 (137–149), Hanover: Hiersemann, 1839; reprint, New York: Kraus Reprint, 1963

Böck, Hanna, *Einsiedeln: Das Kloster und seine Geschichte*, Zurich: Artemis, 1989

*Chronique d'Einsidlen, ou, Histoire de l'Abbaye Princière, de la sainte chapelle, et du pèlerinage de Notre Dame des Hermites*, Einsiedeln: Benziger, 1787

Holzherr, Georg, *Einsiedeln: The Monastery and Church of Our Lady of the Hermits from the Carolingian Period to the Present*, Zurich: Schnell and Steiner, 1988

Schmid, Alfred, editor, *Corolla Heremitana: Neue Beiträge zur Kunst und Geschichte Einsiedelns und der Innerschweiz*, Olten: Walter-Verlag, 1964

Zürcher, Johannus Chrysostomus, *Man of God – Brother Meinrad Eugster*, translated by Gerard Ellspermann, Einsiedeln: Benziger, 1976

# Eisai (Yosai) 1141–1215

Japanese Zen monk and reformer

Recognized as the introducer of the Rinzai Zen tradition to Japan, Eisai is the founder of the Senkō lineage within the 24 branches of the current Rinzai school. The personage of Myōan Eisai has three dimensions: he was (1) an important monastic innovator in thought and practice at a time of major tension and change in Japanese Buddhism, (2) a major Kamakura-period Buddhist activist in the world of shifting court/warrior political power and culture, and (3) a pivotal link between the flourishing Chan traditions of Song China and the subsequent Rinzai lineages in Japan.

Myōan Eisai was born on 22 April 1141 in the Kaya family in Kibutsu in the province of Bitchū (present-day Okayama prefecture) as the son of a shrine priest of the Kibutsu shrine and given the name Senjumaru. From age 11 he began a lifelong interest in Buddhist scriptural study by reading major pre-Mahāyāna Buddhist commentary literature under the monk Seishin at the Kaya district temple Annyōji.

The dominant Buddhism of this age was based in the classical court-centered Heian culture of Kyoto. Its centers included the transplanted Tang Chinese encyclopedic/esoteric Tendai (Chinese, Tiantai) university-like school on the Mount Hiei range due northeast of the capital and the esoteric Shingon school to the distant southeast on the Mount Kōya range. Eisai ascended Mount Hiei when he was 13 or 14 years old to take tonsure with Tendai ordination (the "All-encompassing Mahāyāna Precepts," or *endon-kai*), receiving the Buddhist name Eisai (Brilliance from the West). At Seishin's death in 1157, he moved to his disciple Semmei to receive the esoteric Akasagarbha memory-deepening initiation (*gumonjiho*), studied Tendai doctrine under Ūben and esoterism under Kikō of Hōki, and underwent the Tendai esoteric initiation (*abhiseka*) from Geni on Mount Hiei. From 1161 to 1168 he trained in various Tendai esoteric practices, leaving by merchant ship for Song-dynasty China in early April 1168. He spent about three to four months touring the Tiantai school headquarters on Mount Tiantai (including the Chan monastery Wan-nien-ssu) and returned to Japan in September, beginning a period of intense writing (his *Shukke-taikō* [Outlines for Monastics], *Taikō-ketsu* [Esoteric Orally-Transmitted Essentials of the Womb-Repository Realm], *Tetsuganji-sōken-engi* [Origins of the Building of Tetsuganji], *Nyutō-shukyō-gammon* [Petition to Collect Tang Scriptures], and so on), scripture copying, receiving additional esoteric ordinations, and performing various esoteric rituals for rainfall and exorcism.

By April 1187 he was back in Song China, intending to visit the great sites of the historical Buddha in India, but was unsuccessful and instead laid plans for fund-raising campaigns to supervise the rebuilding of several Chinese pagodas and monastic structures. He began the second major Buddhist practice of his life – Zen sitting meditation and koan work under the 18th-generation master Xu-an Huai-chang of the Lin-qi Chan school's Huang-long lineage at Mount Tian-long (in present-day Chekiang) – receiving a surplice, staff, kneeling cloth, whisk, authentication of realization and authorization as "Dharma-heir" (*yin-zheng*), and possibly the name Myōan (Brilliant Seclusion) at this time.

He returned to Japan by July 1187, beginning a period of monastery construction and remodeling that would occupy the rest of his life. He first built a small chapel at Hirado, the Fuju-an, where he practiced Zen on the basis of the Chan monastic standards (*jing-gui*; Japanese, *shingi*); subsequently he erected Shofukuji (recognized as the first Zen temple in Japan), Chiekoji in Hizen, and Tōrinji and Tokumonji in Chikuzen; rebuilt Senkō-in in Chikugo; and sent funds to rebuild the Chien-fo-ko on Mount Tien-lung.

In 1194 the court issued an edict prohibiting both Eisai and Dainichi Nōnin from propagating the "Daruma school" (the Bodhi-"dharma" Zen tradition). Eisai was attacked by the (Tendai?) monk Rōben of Kyozaki, who called for a justification of this advocacy of Zen before a monastic assembly on Mount Hiei. Eisai responded by writing his most famous work, the *Kōzen-gokoku-ron* (Declaration to Promote Zen Practice to Safeguard the Country), and *Mirai-ki* (Predictions for the Future), appealing to the court to rescind the edict.

In 1199 Eisai moved to the new northern warrior capital of Kamakura, engaging in such ritual activity as the one-year death commemoration of shōgun Minamoto Yoritomo, Buddhist image-eye-opening, and so on. Minamoto's widow, Masako, and current shōgun Yoriie invited Eisai to propagate Zen, funding in 1200 his construction of Jūfukuji, the first Kamakura Zen monastery (built in Kamegadani on the site of the villa of the murdered Minamoto Yoshitomo). By 1202 Yoriie invited Eisai to Kyoto to construct the first Kyoto Zen temple, Kenninji, to which Eisai added two distinct structures to practice three traditions side by side: his original Tendai school in the Shikan-in, esoteric Buddhism at the Shingon-in, and Zen at Kenninji proper. By 1203 Sanetomo, the third shōgun, began his long-term patronage; Kenninji became a court-sponsored monastery (*kanji*). Eisai wrote his *Kissa-yōjō-ki* (Drinking Tea for a Long Life) for this ailing shōgun in 1211. In the final 12 years of his life, he initiated monks of various schools in esoteric initiations (*abhishekha*) and taught them Zen meditation, produced copies of the Buddhist Canon, restored temples, and preached major sermons by invitation. He died on 5 July 1215. He had been honored with the name Yōjōbo (either while in China or subsequently by the Japanese court) and thus was the founder of the Tendai school's Yōjō lineage and was awarded the posthumous title of Nationwide Master of a Thousand Lights (*Senkō-kokushi*).

As a monastic innovator Eisai was born into the classical court-centered Heian-period Buddhist world of the doctrinal and practice eclecticism and esoterism of the Tendai and Shingon schools. He combined (1) a strong Nara-period Buddhist sense of preceding Indian and Chinese Buddhist scriptures, doctrines, deities, and rituals with (2) a characteristically Heian-period Japanese sense of a universe powered by indigenous deities (*kami*), spirits, ghosts, and demons who needed to be controlled by esoteric Buddhist practice and (3) the new mainland Zen sitting meditation, koan practice, and monastic regulations. Eisai synthesized these trends into an interesting Buddhism that was transitional between previous classical Heian esoterism and subsequent medieval Zen, Pure Land, and Nichiren practice relating to a broader warrior and peasant base. Eisai's eclecticism is usually described as a combination of "Tendai all-encompassing bodhisattva ordination (*endon-kai*)/esoterism/Zen meditation and monastic regulations." This syncretism is important because it is the source of subsequent positive and negative Japanese Buddhist assessments or images of Eisai.

One major positive evaluation sees Eisai to have been fully aware of the independence and vigor of the Chinese Chan tradition as well as of the accommodating practice syncretism characteristic of post-Tang Chinese Buddhism. (His own Chan master, Xu-an Huai-chang, practiced just such an esoteric/Chan combination himself at Mount Tian-long.) Yet this assessment also recognizes the entrenched ecclesiastical power that the Tendai school exercised in the Heian court (based on its northeasterly location to the capital and its vast esoteric resources to contain ill fortunes, bad karma, and vengeful spirits from civil political and social machinations). Above all this "Eisai" had to accommodate the entrenched classical Nara and Heian schools, so he introduced Zen to reform Tendai, accommodating opposition by means of his Tendai/esoteric/Zen synthesis. His major work, the *Kōzen-gokoku-ron* (Declaration to Promote Zen Practice to Safeguard the Country), consists of a justification of the new Zen practice as a restoration of Tendai completeness. It aims to renew the Tendai bodhisattva morality (*śīla-Vinaya*), the vigor of monastic practice (Zen monastic standards), and meditative depth (*zazen* and koan practice), centered on the major Zen theme of the Buddha-heart/mind. Another highly positive assessment sees Eisai as not only the formal introducer of Rinzai Zen as a lineage in Japan but also the earliest advocate of Zen culture (very much characteristic of Rinzai practice). "Zen culture" includes not only monastic life but also the subsequent major developments known as the Zen arts, crafts, and martial arts. Eisai's concern with Zen monastic standards (*shingi*) in his practice after 1187 clearly promotes the former aspect of Zen culture; his return to Japan with tea and cultivating tea plants as part of Zen monasticism is seen as a pioneer effort in what has been generalized as the medieval Japanese secularization of Zen monastic forms and rituals in literature, tea ceremony, ink wash, and calligraphy.

Yet these same efforts can be read with two highly negative evaluations as well (especially in comparison to the Sōtō Zen tradition's image of its founder Dōgen's course some decades later). Dōgen was largely unsuccessful in attracting court and warrior patronage and so founded the central Sōtō monastery, Eiheiji, near the far western Japanese seacoast. The Sōtō school obscured this failure by crediting Dōgen with establishing a Zen tradition quite separate from Tendai and Shingon practice remote from both court and warrior power. In comparison Eisai has often been criticized for contaminating the Song Zen he introduced with Heian esoteric practices and ideology and for being unable to construct any actual physically separate Zen monasteries. This ignores the preceding model of the esoteric Zen of Eisai's own Chan master, Hsü-an. However, such criticism is compromised as well by the strains of esoteric ritual and theory to be found within the Sōtō Zen experience itself. Such esoteric elements would be in place by the time of Dōgen's disciple Tettsū Gikai (1219–1309) and the revivalist Keizan Jōkin (1268–1325). It should also be noted that the image of the purity and distinctness of an "uncontaminated" Zen is part of the modern nativist idealization of Japanese Zen to the West propounded by the philosopher Daisetz Suzuki (1870–1966). These views reflect the severe cultural changes forced on Japan in undergoing modernization from 1868 through the 1920s and subsequent apologetics during the nativist isolationism of the war years.

Eisai the Buddhist activist displayed a balance during the 13th-century shift from court to warrior power but clearly cultivated early warrior support after his second trip to China. He sought to thwart Tendai/court obstruction in establishing Zen practice under any terms and used the personal patronage of the second and third shōguns to secure a foundation for the new tradition (both in Kamakura and in the court- and Tendai-dominated capital of Kyoto). In a sense Eisai combines monastic innovation with successfully playing shogunal patronage off against court and Tendai Buddhist power. He deserves credit as the earliest introducer of any formal lineage-authenticated Zen practice in Japan.

DENNIS LISHKA

*See also* Buddhist Schools/Traditions: Japan; Chan/Zen: China; Chan/Zen: Japan; China; Critiques of Buddhist Monasticism: Japanese; Dōgen; Esoteric Buddhism in China and Japan; Japan: History; Kyoto, Japan; Mount Hiei, Japan; Mount Kōya, Japan; Nation-Building and Japanese Buddhism; Suzuki, Daisetz Teitaro; Tiantai/Tendai: Japan; Zen, Arts of

## Biography

A brilliant synthesizer of traditions and initiator of Rinzai Zen in Japan, Eisai started as a Tendai monk at Mount Hiei before spending a period of less than a year in China (1168). He stayed there beginning in 1187 for four years to study Chan and then returned to found Shofukuji Monastery (Japan's first Zen temple) in Kyoto as well as Jūfukuji (1200) in Kamakura. He pioneered what became known as "Zen culture" and introduced tea into Japan.

## Major Work

*Kōzen-gokoku-ron* (Declaration to Promote Zen Practice to Safeguard the Country)

## Further Reading

Dumoulin, Heinrich, *Zen Buddhism: A History*, volume 2: *Japan*, New York: Macmillan, and London: Collier Macmillan, 1990

*Eisai zenji to Rinzai-shū* (Zen master Eisai and the Rinzai School), edited by Hirano Sōjō and Kato Shōshun, Tokyo: Furukawa Kobunkan, 1985

*Nihon no zen goroku – 1: Eisai* (Japanese Zen Records – 1: Eisai), Furuta Shōkin, Tokyo: Kōdansha, 1977

Welter, Albert, "Eisai's Promotion of Zen for the Protection of the Country," in *Religions of Japan in Practice*, edited by George J. Tanabe, Jr., Princeton, New Jersey: Princeton University Press, 1999

# Elders, Russian Monastic (Startsi)

The spiritual elder, or *starets* (plural, *startsi*, related to the Russia word *starik*, or "old man"), is a tradition that can be traced back to the desert hermits of the early Church. The use of the Greek equivalent, *geron*, dates from the fourth century. A starets is usually a monk or nun (and occasionally a layperson) who holds no official ecclesiastical office but who is sought out by the people as a spiritual counselor because of his holiness. Occasionally, a starets is appointed as successor by an existing starets, but usually the starets becomes a spiritual elder because, like the prophetic and charismatic calling that it is, he is recognized as one by the people. It should be emphasized that he rarely seeks to become a starets; indeed, he usually strenuously resists the call. The spiritual gifts of a starets include the ability to discern spiritual truth (discernment = *diakrisis*) and to see into the souls of their spiritual children, the ability to love others and to take on their suffering, and the ability to transform or transfigure the world through miracles and visions. However, these miracles and visions are always tempered by discernment and sobriety and are secondary to the spiritual life lived in humility and purity. The spiritual elder is rooted in the tradition of spiritual paternity and is one who begins as a disciple to a spiritual teacher. The spiritual elder is profoundly aware of being a selfless instrument of God's will, and to that end he embodies the Eucharistic life of the Church, the Scriptures, and the teachings of the Holy Fathers. He always seeks to humble and empty himself (*kenosis*) to be a conduit for the workings of the Holy Spirit. He prays continually, usually in the *Hesychast* (*hesychia* = stillness) contemplative tradition using the Jesus Prayer, or prayer of the heart ("Lord Jesus Christ, Son of God, have mercy on me a sinner"), and his prayer, although contemplative and interior, is an intercession for the salvation of all sinners. He is separated from the world through asceticism and constant prayer yet ultimately united with God's creation through love. He continually wars against pride and arrogance to achieve perfect humility, which leads to simplicity and the love for all. God calls him to a ministry of reconciliation and healing. The spiritual elder always respects the will of the individual when that will is exercised responsibly, and he always strives toward the divination (*theosis*) of human nature.

The earliest Russian startsi probably date back to the Christianization of Russia in the tenth century, but their names are unrecorded. The first prominent starets to be documented is Nilus (Maikov) of Sora (1433–1508), a proponent of hesychasm and the founder of the Athonite form of *skete* life in Russia. He was a disciple of the starets Paisy Jaroslavov. Nil's monastic rule emphasizes poverty, simplicity, and contemplative prayer as practiced on Mount Athos, where he had lived. In effect his *skete* was an embodiment of Athonite ascetic ideals transplanted on Russian soil. What we know about him is derived largely from his writings: the *Predanie*, a short list of concrete rules of conduct for his monks, and the *Ustav* (Rule), his most important work, which is not technically a rule but an ascetic treatise compiled, as the title of the introduction states, "From the Writings of the Holy Fathers on Mental Activity" (i.e., unceasing prayer). Several letters concerning spiritual advice have also survived. Nil's *skete* was a community of huts surrounding a church located in a swampy area on the Sora River about ten miles from the Kirillo-Belozerski Monastery in northern Russia. The monks lived in groups of two or three, usually a starets with disciples.

They focused primarily on unceasing prayer and the study, translation, and editing of Scripture and the writings of the Holy Fathers, the combination of which Byzantine tradition termed the "Divine Writings." The monks came together as a community only for church services. The starets was an essential component in Nil's community. He taught that a spiritual father was one who lived the Gospel teachings and other holy writings and was thereby able to discern the true from the false for the novice. Nil left no living tradition of his *skete* community, yet through the influence of his writings he stands as the first great model of the Russian elder.

Paisy Velichkovsky (1722–1794) was a Poltavan who became a monk in 1746 on Mount Athos, where he absorbed the Sinaite and Athonite traditions of hesychasm that he was to champion so successfully among the Slavs. In complementary fashion he was also strongly influenced by the works of Nil Sorsky. On Mount Athos he attracted a following of Slavs and Romanians that grew so large that he had to move to Moldavia – first to Dragomirna, then to Sekul, and finally to Neamt, where he established large monasteries modeled after life on Mount Athos. Among the duties of his monks was to revise and translate works of the Latin fathers, mostly Greek and some Latin. Paisy translated from Greek to Slavonic the *Philokalia*: the treasure trove of Sinaite and Athonite hesychasm. In his own writings Paisy owes much to Sora, both in style and content. The overall effect of Paisy's writings and his training of spiritual elders was to create a revival of the Hesychast tradition in Russia, taking up where Sorsky had left off in the late 15th and early 16th centuries. He is called the founder of *starchestvo*, the movement of spiritual direction that involves total revelation of thoughts and obedience to the elder. Later it became established in Russia, especially at Optino Monastery in Kozelsk. He was proclaimed a saint in 1988, and his feast day is 15 November.

Tikhon (Sokolov) of Zadonsk (1724–1783) offers a striking contrast to both Sorsky and Paisy. He was a professor at the Novgorod seminary, where he had studied. He took his monastic vows in 1758 and in 1761 was appointed an assistant bishop in the Novgorod diocese, then bishop of Voronezh in 1763. In 1769 he retired into seclusion at the Zadonsk monastery, where he lived the rest of his life. He was known for his considerable pastoral gifts and devoted much of his life to aiding the poor and afflicted. He was strongly influenced by Western ideas, especially the writings of the Lutheran mystic Johann Arndt (1555–1621) and Joseph Hall (1574–1656), the Anglican bishop of Norwich, yet he still held fast to the precepts of the Orthodox Church. He was not a hesychast, although his prayer life showed affinities to it. What distinguishes Tikhon as a great starets is compassion for sufferers and a wonderful ability to discern the divine image in all those he encountered. Staretz Zosima in Dostoevsky's *Brat'ia Karamazovy* (1880; *Brothers Karamazov*) is generally considered to be a combination of Tikhon and elder Amvrosy of Optina monastery. Tikhon was canonized in 1861, and his feast day is 13 August.

Dosithea (1749–1810), a nun of Ivanovsky Convent in Moscow, was known as "The Royal Recluse." Although not known technically as a starets (or staritsa, as women are called), she was an important spiritual influence on many people. She counseled, among others, Timothy Putilov and his brother Thomas to consult disciples of Paisy at Novospassky monastery in Moscow. Timothy became Abbot Moses of Optino monastery, and Thomas became Abbot Isaiah of Sarov monastery. She was the only daughter of Empress Elisabeth (1741–1762) and Field Marshall Count Alexis Rasumovsky. Dosithea was Princess Augusta Tarakanov before her profession as a nun. At the death of her mother in 1762, her father sent her to Europe to protect her from court intrigues. In 1773 an impostor posed as the princess and fell out with Empress Catherine II (1762–1796), who had her kidnapped and put in prison in St. Petersburg, where she died on 4 December 1775. Troubles in the country prompted the empress to bring the real Princess Augusta back to Russia in 1785. She was kidnapped from her home in Europe and brought to St. Petersburg. The empress forced her to become a nun in Ivanovsky Monastery, where she was confined as a recluse under the professed name of Dosithea. No one was allowed to see her but the abbess, her confessor, and the metropolitan of Moscow. After the death of Catherine II, she was allowed visitors and became much sought as a spiritual adviser because of her great virtue and spiritual gifts.

Seraphim of Sarov (1759–1833), the monk-priest and starets, is one of the most revered of all Russian saints. Born at Kursk, he entered the monastery of Sarov in Tambov province at age 19. He was under the spiritual guidance of Fr. Joseph, the monastery's treasurer. For 15 years he lived the ordinary life of the community, then he became a deacon and eventually priest. Following the fourth-century monastic rule of St. Pachomius of Egypt, he lived in seclusion from 1794 to 1825, first as a hermit in the surrounding forest and then as a recluse in a small cell in the monastery. While living in his hut in the forest, he practiced severe ascetic feats, including spending 1,000 days standing, kneeling, and praying on rocks in the ancient Stylite tradition. He fasted and prayed continually, especially the Publican's prayer and the Jesus Prayer. He sought to discipline his body and mind to empty himself and to be filled with the Holy Spirit. It was his means to salvation. In 1825 he opened his cell to visitors and became a starets to all the people. Through great ascetic deprivation and suffering, he became a man filled with heavenly joy who infused others with joy. He became literally transfigured by the uncreated light of God. He had uncanny gifts: prophetic insight into the spiritual needs of his visitors, of healing them physically and spiritually, and of foreseeing the future. In turn he was counseled and healed by many visions of the Mother of God (*Theotokos*). He was canonized in 1903, and his feast day is 2 January.

Staritsa Anastasia Logacheva (1809–1875) led a dramatic ascetic life after the model of St. Seraphim of Sarov. She was born to peasant parents in the village of Kudlei in central Russia. At age eight she was left to the care of relatives and soon after sought the life of a religious recluse. From the age of 12, she regularly fasted, prayed, and pursued solitude. She spent much her time in a cave that she had dug in the hillside of a ravine. In 1826, at the age of 17, she made a pilgrimage to Sarov monas-

tery to seek Seraphim's blessing to be a hermit. In visionary fashion he chose her out of a crowd of pilgrims and told her that her time had not yet come. She returned to him several years later and was told to seek guidance from the monks of the Monastery of the Caves in Kiev, which she did. Shortly before Seraphim's death in 1833, she returned a third time, and he blessed her mission, telling her to settle in a place where she could smell burning palms and to quell her bodily desire by wearing chains. However, he also told her not to abandon her aging parents, who had abandoned her. She cared for them for 17 years. When they died she gave away everything and became a cave-dwelling hermit in a remote area among the fragrance of burning palms. To open herself to God, she fasted, slept little, and prayed the Jesus Prayer unceasingly. She read one complete Gospel every day, as St. Seraphim did, and, also like him, undertook strenuous ascetic feats. At one point she fasted for 40 days on a rock while praying with her arms outstretched like a cross. Another time she was seen standing on an anthill covered in insects and blood. Later she was forced to move her hut into Kudlei, where she learned to live in the desert of interiority. Some years later she joined the Ardotov monastery and came to terms with cenobitic life. From 1863 she spent the remainder of her life as a professed nun in the Nikolaevsky women's community in Siberia. Anastasia was a spiritual elder true to the example of St. Seraphim. From the deprivations of her asceticism and peasant life, she became a woman who was sought out for her wisdom, holiness, and joy.

Paraskeva Ivanova (19th century) is an example of a fool for Christ who was revered as a staritsa. She was a nun of the Diveyevo Convent, "without whose advice nothing was ever undertaken in that monastic community" (Kontzevich, 1989).

Optina Monastery in Kozelsk in central Russia was the most spiritually influential of all Russian monastic institutions. Its fame is based almost entirely on its legendary startsi, who lived at Optina Pusteyn, the ascetic community attached to the monastery. Of special note are the startsi Leonid Nagolkin (1768–1841), Macary Ivanov (1788–1860), and Amvrosy Grenkov (1812–1891). It was they, along with Moses Putilov (1782–1862) and Isaac Antimonov (1809–1894), the two great Optino abbots, who developed the school of *starchestvo* (spiritual direction). Starets Leonid, who had been influenced by Fr. Theodore, a disciple of Paisy, first introduced *starchestvo* at Optino. It involves the daily revelation to the starets of a person's every thought, intention, and temptation and in turn the acceptance the starets' counsel without question. In short one was required to reveal everything to him and to seek his advice in everything. At Optina the practice of *starchestvo* began with Starets Leonid's spiritual direction of the abbot, monks, and postulants. Eventually, large crowds of visitors and pilgrims were drawn to Optina to be included in the process, causing much scandal among the other monks. At one point Leonid was ordered to stop giving *starchestvo* to all comers but eventually was allowed to resume. The spiritual life at Optina proved very influential among writers and intellectuals. A.S. Khomiakov (1804–1860) and Nikolai Gogol (1809–1852) were in close contact with Starets Macary and came to Optina. Dostoevsky, Tolstoy, and Vladimir Soloviev (1853–1900) visited Starets Macary. Starets Amvrosy is often said to be a model for Starets Zosima in Dostoevsky's *Brothers Karamazov*, and Optina Monastery is often said to be the novel's monastery. Other Optina startsi continued the tradition, including Anatoly, Joseph (1837–1911), Barsanuthius, and finally Nectarius, who died expelled from Optina when the Soviets closed it in 1928. However, none of the subsequent startsi approaches the greatness of the first three.

Another Russian monastic center of importance to the development of spiritual eldership is Valamo (Russian, *Valaam*) on Valamo Island in Lake Ladoga. In addition to the main monastery, many *sketes* and hermitages were spread out over various islands of the Valamo archipelago of the lake. Founded in the 14th century by the hermits Sergios and Germanos (possibly from Mount Athos), the monastery was dedicated to the Transfiguration of Christ. It became a prominent center of Russian monasticism in the 15th century. It was dissolved in 1618 but reopened by Peter the Great (1689–1725) in 1718, after which it became enormously popular as a place of pilgrimage. The monastery had three degrees of monastic life: the majority lived the strict cenobitic life of the central monastery; others, who had some experience in monastic life, lived the semi-eremitic life in *sketes*; and the most experienced were allowed to live the solitary life in hermitages. After 1918 the monastery came under the jurisdiction of the autonomous Greek Orthodox Church of Finland. In 1940 the monks were evacuated to Heinavesi in Finnish Karelia, which is now known as New Valamo. Some of its important spiritual elders include Abbot Nazarius Anosov (1735–1809), who began reorganizing Valamo in 1781; Abbot Barlaam, who professed at Valamo in 1789, became its abbot in 1839, and retired to Optina in 1839; Abbot Damaskin (1795–1881); John of Valaam (1873–1958); Igumen (superior) Chariton of Valamo, compiler of *The Art of Prayer*; Fr. John of Petchenga; Hieroschimonk Luke; and Fr. Michael, recluse of Uusi Valamo (d. 1962).

Ignatius Brianchininoff (1807–1867), whose birth name was Dimitri, was a member of the nobility. In 1822 he was sent to the Imperial School of Engineers in St. Petersburg to prepare for a position in the army corps of engineers. While at school he came to the attention of Czar Nicholas I, who took great interest in his career and provided for his education. At his time he came under the spiritual tutelage of Fr. Athanasius of the St. Alexander Nevsky Laura in St. Petersburg. When Dimitri asked permission to leave school for the monastic life, the czar denied his request. He was commissioned as an officer in the engineer corps in 1827, and this eventually caused a physical and spiritual breakdown in him. He was allowed to leave the service and immediately began to pursue the life of a monk. Ignatius was deeply drawn to Optina Monastery and its precepts of spiritual direction. He knew and was influenced by Leonid Nagolkin, the first great Optina starets. At Semigorodsky Monastery he was professed as a monk in 1831 and was ordained priest the following year. From there he was sent to Pelshem-Lopotov Monastery near Vologda, but when the czar learned about his situation, he ordered him to return to St. Petersburg. Nicholas' esteem for the 27-year-old priest-monk was so high that he immediately appointed him archimandrite (superior) of the prestigious St.

Sergius Monastery in Petersburg. Ignatius remained there for 24 years, until he was made bishop of the Caucasus and the Black Sea in 1857. In the same year he published his Russian translation of the *Philokalia*. However, his health failed, and he was allowed to retire in 1861 to live out his last six years in the Nicolo-Babaevski Monastery. Ignatius, like his younger contemporary Theophan the Recluse, was a prolific writer steeped in patristics who saw himself as the conservator of a great spiritual tradition rather than an originator. His collected works take up several volumes, including a very influential tract on the Jesus Prayer. Both Ignatius and Theophan lived intense spiritual lives shaped by hesychasm, and this quality is reflected in their writings, their relations with others, and their profound influence on Russian monasticism.

Theophan the Recluse (1815–1894) was born George Vasilievich Govorov at Chernavsk in central Russia. The son of a parish priest, he himself was ordained priest-monk in 1841. While attending the attending the Theological Academy of Kiev from 1837 to 1841, he came under the influence of Fr. Partheny, a starets of Petcherskaya Lavra in Kiev. He taught in various theological seminaries until 1847. From 1847 to 1854 he served the Russian Spiritual Mission in Jerusalem and from 1856 to 1867 in Constantinople. He was consecrated bishop of Tambov in 1859 and translated to Vladimir in 1863. In 1866 he retired to the monastery of Vyshi, first as a monk and then a hermit. Theophan was instrumental in promulgating hesychasm, especially the Jesus Prayer. He translated Greek and Latin spiritual writings into Russian. Of special importance are the *Philokalia* (1876–1890) and Lorenzo Scupoli's *Unseen Warfare*, which he translated and revised from the edition by Nicodemus of the Holy Mountain. Theophan's importance as a starets derives from his massive correspondence and his spiritual writings. From 1872 to the end of his life, he was a complete recluse who had physical contact with almost no one. However, he spent many hours every day in his seclusion, responding to the large number of letters received from all over Russia. These correspondents, mostly women, were his spiritual children. He was canonized in 1988, his feast day is 10 January.

*The Way of a Pilgrim* was first published in 1884 in Kazan under its Russian title *Sincere Tales of a Pilgrim to His Spiritual Father*. The book was very popular in Russia before the Revolution and for many years has been very popular and influential in the West. The book is especially helpful as an introduction to hesychasm, the Jesus Prayer, *Dobrotolubiye* (the much-expanded Russian translation of the *Philokalia* by Theophan the Recluse), and *starchestvo* (spiritual direction involving total revelation of thoughts and obedience to the elder).

The following are examples of 20th century Russian spiritual elders. Starets Silouan Antonov (1866–1938) joined St. Panteleimon Monastery on Mount Athos in 1892. His enormous gifts as a spiritual elder evolved from intense spiritual searching and suffering. His spiritual maxim was "keep thy mind in hell, and despair not." His disciple was Archimandrite Sophrony Sakharov (1896–1993), who moved to Europe from Russia in 1921. He studied at St. Sergius Orthodox Theological Institute in Paris but became disillusioned with academic life and settled at St.

Panteleimon Monastery on Mount Athos, where for eight years he was under the spiritual guidance of Starets Silouan. After Silouan's death in 1938, he became a cave-dwelling anchorite-priest. Later he was called as confessor and spiritual father to the monks of St. Paul Monastery. He founded the Stavropegic Monastery of St. John the Baptist in Tolleshunt, Essex, England, where he was abbot and abbot emeritus until his death. He published several volumes related to Starets Silouan and also wrote numerous works on the spiritual life. John (Maximovich), archbishop of San Francisco and Shanghai (1896–1966), was a wonder-worker and fool for Christ. His body is enshrined in the Joy of All Who Sorrow Cathedral on Geary Street in San Francisco. In many ways he exhibited the spiritual gifts of the earlier Russian startsi. He was especially renown for the intensity of his intercessory prayer and for his mystical ability to intuit and answer the thoughts of his spiritual children. The life of Fr. Arseny (1893–1973) became known through a *samizdat* collection, now published as *Father Arseny, 1893–1973: Priest, Prisoner, Spiritual Father. Being the Narratives Compiled by His Spiritual Father*. It is a soul-shaking account of life in Stalin's prison camps and the spiritual heroism that grew out of them. One can only hope that much more will be heard from Fr. Arseny's spiritual children.

MICHAEL D. PETERSON

*See also* Hermits: Eastern Christian; Hesychasm; Isaac the Syrian (Isaac of Nineveh), St.; Master and Pupil: Christian Perspectives; Mount Athos, Greece; Mount Sinai, Egypt; Nilus of Sora, St.; Paisy Velichkovsky; Philokalia; Pilgrimages, Christian: Eastern Europe; Russia: History; Russia: Recent Changes; Seraphim of Sarov, St.; Spirituality: Eastern Christian; Vision, Mystical: Eastern Christian

**Further Reading**

Behr-Sigel, Elisabeth, "Hesychasm and the Western Impact in Russia: St. Tikhon of Zadonsk (1724–1783)," in *Christian Spirituality: Post-Reformation and Modern*, edited by Louis Dupre, Don E. Saliers, and John Meyendorff, New York: Crossroad, 1989

Bolshakoff, Serge, *Russian Mystics*, Kalamazoo, Michigan: Cistercian Publications, 1977

Bolshakoff, Serge, and M. Basil Pennington, *In Search of True Wisdom: Visits to Eastern Spiritual Fathers*, Garden City, New York: Doubleday, 1979

Brianchaninov, Ignatius, *On the Prayer of Jesus: From the Ascetic Essays of Bishop Ignatius Brianchaninov*, translated by Father Lazarus Moore, London: Watkins, 1952; Rockport, Massachusetts: Elements, 1993

Dunlop, John B., *Staretz Amvrosy: Model for Dostoevsky's Staretz Zossima*, Belmont, Massachusetts: Nordland, 1972

Ellis, Jane, *An Early Soviet Saint: The Life of Father Zachariah*, Springfield, Illinois: Templegate, 1977

*Father Arseny, 1893–1973: Priest, Prisoner, Spiritual Father: Being the Narratives Compiled by the Servant of God Alexander Concerning His Spiritual Father*, translated by Vera Bouteneff, Crestwood, New York: St. Vladimir's Seminary Press, 1998

Hackel, Sergei, "Trial and Victory: The Spiritual Tradition of Modern Russia," in *Christian Spirituality: Post-Reformation and Modern*, edited by Louis Dupre, Don E. Saliers, and John Meyendorff, New York: Crossroad, 1989

Ivanov, Makary, *Russian Letters of Direction, 1834–1860*, selection, translations, and foreword by Iulia de Beausobre, Westminster: Dacre Press, 1944; reprint, Crestwood, New York: St. Vladimir's Seminary Press, 1994

John of Valaam, *Christ Is in Our Midst: Letters from a Russian Monk*, translated by Esther Williams, foreword by Metropolitan Anthony of Sourozh, Crestwood, NewYork: St. Vladimir's Seminary Press, and London: Darton, Longman and Todd, 1980

Khariton, Hegumen of Valaamskii Spaso-Preobrazhenskii monastyr', compiler, *The Art of Prayer: An Orthodox Anthology*, translated by E. Kadloubovsky and E.M. Palmer, edited with an introduction by Timothy Ware, London: Faber, 1966

Kontzevich, I.M., "Eldership," *Epiphany* 9 (Summer 1989)

Maloney, George A., *Russian Hesychasm: The Spirituality of Nil Sorskij*, The Hague: Mouton, 1973

Meehan, Brenda, *Holy Women of Russia: The Lives of Five Orthodox Women Offer Spiritual Guidance for Today*, San Francisco: HarperSanFrancisco, 1993

Rees, Catherine, "A Pilgrimage to Optina Today," *Sourozh* 44 (June 1991)

Rose, Seraphim, and Abbot Herman, *Blessed John, the Wonderworker: A Preliminary Account of the Life and Miracles of Archbishop John Maximovitch*, compiled and edited by the St. Herman of Alaska Brotherhood, Platina, California: St. Herman of Alaska Brotherhood, 1979; 3rd edition, 1987

Siluan, Monk, *Wisdom from Mount Athos: The Writings of Starets Silouan, 1866–1938*, compiled by Archimandrite Sophrony, translated by Rosemary Edmonds, London: Mowbrays, 1974

Sofrony, Archimandrite, *His Life Is Mine*, translated by Rosemary Edmonds, London: Mowbrays, 1977

Spidlik, Tomas, "The Theological Renewal of the Russian Startsi," *Communio* 15 (Spring 1988)

Stanton, Leonard J., *The Optina Pustyn Monastery in the Russian Literary Imagination: Iconic Vision in Works by Dostoevsky, Gogol, Tolstoy, and Others*, New York: Peter Lang, 1995

Ware, Kallistos, "The Spiritual Father in Orthodox Christianity," *Cross Currents* 24:2–3 (Summer/Fall 1974)

*The Way of a Pilgrim and The Pilgrim Continues His Way: A New Translation*, translated by Helen Bacovcin, New York: Image Books, 1992

*Writings from the Philokalia on Prayer of the Heart*, translated by E. Kadloubovsky and G.E.H. Palmer, London: Faber and Faber, 1951; Boston: Faber and Faber, 1992

# Elizabeth of Schönau 1129–1164

German Benedictine nun and visionary

Elizabeth of Schönau belonged to a well-established Rhenish family with connections to the Count of Laurenburg, founder in 1114 of the Benedictine priory (later abbey) at Schönau in Hesse. Eventually a double monastery, Schönau was part of the Hirsau reform movement (1080–1150), which emphasized the interaction between monasteries and local bishops and lay nobles. Entering there at age 12, Elizabeth was nourished in an atmosphere that valued spiritual renewal, women's monastic life, and service to the broader church and world.

In 1152, five years after her profession, Elizabeth began experiencing ecstatic visions that continued to the end of her life. Hesitant at first to reveal them for fear of ridicule, she eventually made them known to the nuns and to her abbot at Schönau but, most important, to her brother Ekbert, who became a monk at Schönau in 1155, dedicating his life to editing and disseminating her work. His role has been controversial but has recently been carefully analyzed by Anne L. Clark. Although Ekbert exerted a tremendous influence on Elizabeth, helping her grow in self-confidence regarding her visionary vocation and, to an extent, even helping shape the theological content of her visions, we can trust that the works he edited are fundamentally those of Elizabeth.

Like that of her contemporary Hildegard of Bingen (1098–1179), Elizabeth's visionary experience resembles the prophetic tradition of Ezekiel, Daniel, and the Apocalypse, prompting her to condemn abuses in church and society, notably the Cathar heresy and clergy negligence. Elizabeth was influenced to an extent by Hildegard, visiting the older seer in 1156 and corresponding with her on several occasions. Elizabeth's *Liber Viarum Dei* especially shows affinities with Hildegard's *Scivias*. However, Elizabeth's visionary corpus is neither as idiosyncratic nor as grandiose as Hildegard's. Instead, it simply reveals her grounding in traditional Benedictine liturgical piety. Her visions occurred usually during the celebration of the eucharist or the recitation of the divine office, during which Elizabeth would converse with the saint whose feast was celebrated that day. At the end of the vision, Elizabeth often proclaimed a scriptural verse or other utterance connected with the content of the vision.

Elizabeth and her visions were celebrated during and after her lifetime. Elected superior of the Schönau nuns in 1157, she was consulted widely for spiritual advice by ecclesial and secular leaders. Manuscripts of her writings circulated in England, France, and Germany and were translated into Anglo-Norman, Provençal, German, and Icelandic. In all, 145 known manuscripts survive, 45 of which contain her complete corpus. Her visions might have added substantially to the development of the doctrine of purgatory; more certain is their contribution to the doctrine of Mary's assumption. Elizabeth's creative reworking of the legend of St. Ursula and the 11,000 virgin martyrs of Cologne was extremely popular. Extant in 69 medieval manuscripts, it became the basis for the version in Voragine's *Golden Legend* (1265); influenced later versions, such as that in Bokenham's *Legendys of Hooly Wummen*; and inspired numerous art cycles depicting the life of St. Ursula. Although efforts for Elizabeth's canonization were unsuccessful, local popular devotion to her continued long after her death. Her name was added to the Roman martyrology in 1584 with a feast day of 18 June.

JOAN M. NUTH

*See also* Germany: History; Hildegard of Bingen, St.; Mystics, German Monastic: Female; Vision, Mystical: Western Christian

## Biography

A Benedictine nun in the double house at Schönau (Taunus), in the 1140s and 1150s Elizabeth underwent visions, which her brother Ekbert, a Benedictine, recorded. She lived a stringent asceticism, and her "visions" exercised wide influence.

## Major Works

*Liber Viarum Dei*
*Visiones*
*Letters*

## Further Reading

Clark, Anne L., *Elisabeth of Schönau: A Twelfth Century Visionary*, Philadelphia: University of Pennsylvania Press, 1992

Clark, Anne, "Repression or Collaboration? The Case of Elisabeth and Ekbert of Schönau," in *Christendom and Its Discontents: Exclusion, Persecution, and Rebellion, 1000–1500*, edited by Scott L. Waugh and Peter D. Diehl, Cambridge and New York: Cambridge University Press, 1996

Dean, Ruth J., "Elizabeth, Abbess of Schönau, and Roger of Ford," *Modern Philology* 41:4 (1944)

Kerby-Fulton, Kathryn, and Dyan Elliott, "Self-Image and the Visionary Role in Two Letters from the Correspondence of Elizabeth of Schönau and Hildegard of Bingen," *Vox Benedictina* 2 (1985)

O'Dell, M. Colman, "Elizabeth of Schönau and Hildegard of Bingen: Prophets of the Lord," in *Medieval Religious Women (Peace Weavers)*, volume 2, edited by John A. Nicols and Lillian Thomas Shank, Kalamazoo, Michigan: Cistercian Publications, 1987

Petroff, Elizabeth Alvilda, "Visionaries of the Early Twelfth Century: Christina of Markyate, Hildegard of Bingen, and St. Elisabeth of Schönau," in *Medieval Women's Visionary Literature*, edited by Elizabeth Alvilda Petroff, Oxford and New York: Oxford University Press, 1986

Roth, F.W.E., editor, *Die Visionen der hl. Elisabeth und die Schriften der Aebte Ekbert und Emecho von Schönau*, Brünn: Studien aus dem Benediktiner- und Cistercienser-Orden, 1884

Thiébaux, Marcelle, "Handmaid of God: Elisabeth of Schönau," in *The Writings of Medieval Women: An Anthology*, 2nd edition, edited and translated by Marcelle Thiébaux, New York: Garland, 1994

Wiethaus, Ulrike, "In Search of Medieval Women's Friendships: Hildegard of Bingen's Letters to Her Female Contemporaries," in *Maps of Flesh and Light: The Religious Experience of Medieval Women Mystics*, edited by Ulrike Wiethaus, Syracuse, New York: Syracuse University Press, 1993

# England: History

Monasticism was established from two directions in Anglo-Saxon England: from east and west. From the east came Roman cenobitism, for Augustine, leading the mission of Pope Gregory the Great, was himself a monk and his center of activity was the monastery that he established in Canterbury. However, from a different direction was derived Celtic monasticism. King Oswald (634–642) of Northumbria invited a mission from Iona, the community founded by St. Columba that proselytized in the 630s, its center being at the community established by Aidan (d. 651) at Lindisfarne. The two forms of monasticism differed substantially: the Roman with the emphasis on communal life but the Celtic eremitical and the Celtic more ascetic. The outward manifestation was a different tonsure and the liturgical one the different computation of Easter. The confusion was resolved in 664 at Whitby at the expense of the Celtic. Much of what is known of these early phases of monasticism in England is derived from the *Historia Ecclesiastica*, compiled by St. Bede (c. 673–735) in his monastery of Jarrow in Northumbria.

By the eighth century, the vitality of monasticism had declined, having been further attenuated by the Viking incursions from the 790s. After an initial attempt by Alfred (871–899) to restore monastic fortunes, the resuscitation of English monasticism was achieved by Edgar (959–973). Its revitalization was the object of the king and three monks, Dunstan, abbot of Glastonbury (d. 988); Æthelwold, abbot of Abingdon (d. 984); and Oswald (d. 992), who were later translated to the sees of Canterbury, Winchester, and Worcester, respectively. This tenth-century monastic reform was predicated on the *Regularis Concordia*, the adopted rule of St. Benedict, which had been introduced around 970 at Winchester. From its base in the south and west of England, the Wessex heartland, this rule was transferred to Benedictine houses in the east, for example, to Ramsey, Crowland, Thorney, Ely, and Peterborough. By the end of the millennium, some 40 houses had been established or reestablished with the new rule but all south of the River Trent. All these houses were associated with the royal family and thus fell within royal patronage. Thereafter, other Benedictine houses were founded but with nonroyal patronage, again roughly south of the Trent. In this general process the cathedral chapters of several sees were established as regular, that is, with Benedictine monks.

Monasticism in the north experienced a revival in the late 11th century through the relationship between the dioceses of Worcester and York, both held by St. Oswald and St. Wulfstan (c. 1009–1095). The ultimate result of the association, after the resolution of a conflict, was the colonization of northern monasteries from Worcester diocese. One of the knights of William de Percy, Reinfred, was so impressed by the remains of the old monastery at Whitby that he determined to take the religious life and entered the Benedictine house at Evesham in Worcester diocese. At Evesham he came into contact with Aldwine, prior of Winchcombe, and Ælfwig, a monk of Evesham, the three resolving to restore the "golden days" of monasticism of Bede in the north. They revived monasticism first at Jarrow, then at Whitby, and finally at Wearmouth. When William of St.-Calais acceded to the see of Durham, he intended to replace the secular canons of the cathedral with regulars (monks). Accordingly, in 1083 the monks of the newly established or reestablished houses of

Monkwearmouth-Jarrow were invited to Durham to replace the secular canons.

This revival of northern monasticism was probably inspired by a mixture of motives, not least the political aim of replacing the English clerics in a remote region that had not been easily placated. However, it has been suggested that nostalgic reflection on the Bedan past of northern monasticism was also an inspiration.

The Norman attitude toward pre-Conquest Benedictine religious houses was probably ambiguous. Lanfranc (c. 1010–1089), archbishop of Canterbury, the first of the Norman prelates of the whole *ecclesia Anglicana*, strove to establish regular cathedral chapters in some of the diocesan centers, for which he instituted his *Monastic Constitutions*. Matthew argued that the first generations of Norman superior lords were not interested in English houses and were intent instead on patronizing the religious houses of their French patrimonies by founding cells of those houses in England. Nevertheless, Cownie (1998) has recently contended that some of these lords patronized the pre-Conquest Benedictine religious houses, attempting to establish with them the sort of associations that they had maintained with western French religious houses. Equally, Ridyard has revealed that these pre-Conquest Benedictine religious houses had no aversion to the Old English saints. A small number of religious houses was founded by Normans in the late 11th century with no connection with Norman houses but with Cluny. The responses of the Normans now seem to have then been diverse.

In the 12th century ensued a great wave of monastic foundations, commencing with the introduction of the Austin Canons (Black Canons) into England toward the end of the 12th century. The earliest houses – such as St. Botolph in Colchester, St. Mary in Huntingdon, St. Giles in Cambridge, and St. Gregory in Canterbury – followed a strict common life and discipline but cannot be said to have yet adopted the rule of St. Augustine. This rule was acquired more formally after around 1100 in these four houses and in the prolific number of houses of the Order to be established in the early 12th century. Many foundations were associated with the court of Henry I (1100–1135) and his first consort, Matilda (d. 1118), both of whom were responsible for foundations. The *curiales* and *novi homines* of Henry I followed this example. The episcopacy also sponsored the new order, and several houses had episcopal founders. Several of the new houses were refoundations in which Austin Canons displaced secular canons; in some cases the new house appropriated a college of secular canons. Thus, patronage of the Austin Canons ensued from a number of different reasons: the attractiveness of a new order to lay founders, the association with the royal court, the prospective ministry by the regular canons (important, perhaps, for the episcopal founders, especially in those cases in which colleges of secular canons were replaced), and the low cost of endowment, as not only were many of the houses very small and their estates marginal but part of the endowment consisted of returning to the Church what was the Church's, that is, appropriated parish churches. Perhaps the last point contained a dual consideration: limited cost but also the expectation of a more effective pastoral ministry (which failed to materialize). Such was the popularity of the Austin Canons that the number of their houses came to rival those of the Black Monks.

To some extent, the continued expansion of the Black Canons was truncated by the arrival of the Cistercians, the White Monks, who entered England with the foundation of Waverley in 1128. Although the chapter general of 1152 prohibited the foundation of new houses of the Order, some other foundations occurred in England so that ultimately more than 80 houses of the Order existed in Britain. However, the first association of the White Monks was with the baronial families of the early 12th century, especially during the "Anarchy" of King Stephen's reign (1135–1154), so it is possible that one motive (among many) in the foundation of Cistercian houses was political, that is, to promote the representation of baronial territorial integrity through the foundation and patronage of a new religious house. Indeed, some of the houses, such as Garendon and Sawtry, were founded on disputed land. To some extent such rivalry might have informed the foundations by the Beaumont twins, especially Waleran, count of Meulan, and the brothers, the earls of Chester and (Roumare) Lincoln, who contested the Midlands.

The Black Canons having become established earlier in the 12th century, the White Canons (Premonstratensians) appeared first in 1143 at Newhouse. By 1267 in England 37 abbeys, three nunneries, and six cells existed, or more than two-thirds of the abbeys in that country. Important for the expansion of the White Canons was the kinship connection of knightly families and of members of the administrative cadre of Henry II (1154–1189), such as Ranulf de Glanvill, the chief justiciar.

The military orders were also established in England in the early to mid–12th century: the Templars, initially in London, around 1128, and the Hospitallers in Clerkenwell in the capital in 1144. Thus, much of the 12th century was a time of a succession of waves of eclectic orders acceding to England. For women as well, the 12th century presented new opportunities for personal devotion through the common religious life.

By the late 13th century, 142 nunneries existed in England, only ten of which were unambiguously pre-Conquest foundations. However, their development abounds in obscurities, surrounding the precise nature of their foundation and the order to which they belonged. Some of this ambiguity emanated from the instability of the association between nunneries and male religious houses, as female religious relied on male religious for liturgical arrangements. Many of the pre-Conquest nunneries existed in double houses, and this solution was somewhat returned to by the Gilbertine Order in the 12th century. The Gilbertines were peculiar to England, having been initiated by Gilbert of Sempringham (c. 1083–1189), a priest who arranged for a number of women in the parish of Sempringham (Lincolnshire) to live the communal, religious existence. In 1131 he provided a cell near the parish church for their use. By around 1139 this anchorage was transformed into a priory, and in the same year, Bishop Alexander of Lincoln founded an associated house at Haverholme. These houses were set on a new footing after 1147 when males were admitted, the nuns following the

Benedictine rule (after the Cistercians had refused to supervise female houses) and the males the rule of St. Augustine. The Order expanded but remained largely concentrated in Lincolnshire and Yorkshire with a few outliers, such as Shouldham in Norfolk.

Nunneries affiliated to Fontevraud were few in England, but their foundation reflects the political as well as spiritual motives that coalesced in founders' minds. Kintbury was possibly established in 1154 but moved to Nuneaton by 1157. It had been founded by the earl of Leicester and his wife, Amice, who entered the house. In seeking to provide for other religious women, her motivation might well have been spiritual and personal. It has also been suggested that the foundation marked the political reconciliation of the earl with Henry II and and the integration of an English baron back into the Angevin Empire. Another house affiliated to Fontevraud, Amesbury, was a refoundation by Henry II in 1177 as an act of contrition after the death of Beckett. The expansive foundation of religious houses in England was substantially complete by around 1200, with but a trickle of new foundations thereafter. The complex history of English religious houses in the late Middle Ages is still under explored. Barrie Dobson suggested that one of the contributory problems in the later Middle Ages was the disassociation of religious house from local gentry, a loss of an important local, sustaining relationship. Monks and canons were generally of an inferior position to the local gentry. Consequently, the defenders of religious houses were not there in support at the dissolution. A similar line of argument has been expounded by Benjamin Thompson, who suggests that the demographic changes that affected patronal families through the late Middle Ages further weakened the association between religious houses and their natural defenders. The force of that circumstance was illustrated by the aristocratic plan of 1529 to appropriate the landed estates of religious houses, so that the dissolution of small houses was delayed until 1536, although Cardinal Wolsey (1472/74–1530) had suppressed and confiscated a few houses for the endowment of his educational college. The turn of the larger houses arrived in 1539.

The later fortunes of English religious houses can perhaps be best illustrated by the Benedictine experience. Despite a short revival at Westminster under Mary, English monasticism continued in exile from 1558 until the late 18th century. The English Benedictine congregation maintained a continuous link with English medieval monasticism throughout that exile. From 1605 to 1607, a community of monks in exile was founded as the monastery of St. Gregory the Great at Douai in northern France, housing English and Welsh monks trained abroad. In 1793, when Douai was suppressed, the English monks crossed the English Channel and finally settled at Stratton-on-the Fosse near Bath in 1814. Because the penal laws against Catholics were not enforced, they could establish the house now known as Downside Abbey, which is the senior monastery in the English congregation. Similarly, the nuns in exile at Cambrai since 1625, imprisoned in 1795 by the French revolutionaries, returned to establish Stanbrook. Nuns who had moved from Cambrai to

Paris in 1651 were also imprisoned and then released in 1795. They settled first in Dorset, then at Cannington (Somerset), and finally in 1836 at Colwich. During the 19th century and later, other houses of the Order were founded, such as Ampleforth (1802), Alton (1895), Belmont (1858), Curzon House (1921), and Worth (1933). Certain others were reestablishments of monks at medieval sites, such as Buckfast (1882) and Prinknash (1928). Thus, the English Benedictine congregation now comprises three nunneries and 11 male houses.

DAVE POSTLES

*See also* Anselm, St.; Archaeology: Western Europe; Architecture: Western Christian Monasteries; Augustinian Canons; Augustinian Rule; Bede, St.; Dissolution of Monasteries: England, Ireland, and Wales; Double Houses, Western Christian; Exile, Western Christian; Gilbertines; Gregory I (the Great), St.; Lanfranc; Libraries: Western Christian; Lindisfarne/Holy Isle, England; Reform, Tenth-Century Anglo-Saxon Monastic; Whitby, England

## Further Reading

Burton, Janet, *Monastic and Religious Orders in Britain 1000–1300*, Cambridge and New York: Cambridge University Press, 1994

Colvin, Howard M., *The White Canons in England*, Oxford: Clarendon Press, 1951

Cownie, Emma, *Religious Patronage in Anglo-Norman England 1066–1135*, Rochester, New York: Boydell Press, 1998

Dickinson, J.C., *The Origins of the Austin Canons and Their Introduction into England*, London: SPCK, 1950

Thompson, Sally, *Women Religious: The Founding of English Nunneries After the Norman Conquest*, Oxford and New York: Oxford University Press, 1991

# England: Sites

Benedictine monasticism first arrived in England in A.D. 597, when Gregory the Great (590–604) sent the Augustine of Canterbury to Kent to Christianize the Britons. The remains of the Sts. Peter and Paul church can still be seen within the ruins of St. Augustine's monastery behind Canterbury Cathedral.

Monasticism entered its golden age in England when Benedict Biscop (c. 628–689/90) founded Jarrow in 678 and Monkwearmoth (Tyne and Wear) in 674. The Venerable Bede (c. 673–735) entered the community at the age of seven and spent his life there. The church at Monkwearmoth still stands, as do parts of the Saxon monastery church at Jarrow, which is still in use today, and the outlines of the domestic buildings.

Whitby Abbey (North Yorks), located on the cliffs by the sea, played an important role in this era. Whitby was a double monastery founded in 657 by Hilda (614–680), one of the most remarkable women of the age. Her monastery hosted the Synod of Whitby in 664. Although the Danes destroyed Hilda's Whitby, the ninth-century quarters of the nuns have recently been excavated, and there are substantial ruins of the postconquest

church, including the spectacular east facade from the 13th century, the 14th-century nave, the low walls of the cloister, part of the abbot's house, and the earthworks of the precinct.

The invasion of the Danes brought the decline and near extinction of monastic life. In the tenth century, monastic life was revived, largely through the efforts of St. Dunstan (c. 909–988). Dunstan was born near Glastonbury Abbey (Somerset), which was reputed to house the relics of St. Brigit and St. Patrick. Gastonbury had been both a Celtic and a Saxon monastery; Dunstan revived monasticism there under the *Regularis Concordia*. Nothing remains of Dunstan's monastery, but the church, cloister ranges, abbot's kitchen, and gatehouse from the postconquest community built during the reign of Henry II (1154–1189) still stand. During this phase of building, a tomb containing two skeletons thought to be those of King Arthur and Guinevere was discovered; the remains were later stolen during the dissolution of the monasteries. A thorn tree there is believed to be descended from a thorn from the staff of Joseph of Arimathea, who, according to legend, brought the Holy Grail to England and founded Glastonbury as the first Christian church there. At the time of the Domesday survey, Glastonbury was the wealthiest house in England.

The Norman period brought a revival of monastic life. Lindisfarne priory (Northumberland), built on the site of St. Cuthbert's church, was founded in 1083 as a Benedictine house. The ruins of Bury St. Edmunds (Suffolk), one of the wealthiest houses in medieval England, date from the 12th century and include the abbey church, two gatehouses, and a precinct wall. They are preserved in a public garden. The most well known remnant of medieval Benedictine monasticism in England is Westminster Abbey (London), founded as a royal *Eigenkloster* and built on the site of an Anglo-Saxon Benedictine monastery. It was completed in 1065 for Edward the Confessor (1042–1066); since that time every monarch but Edward V and Edward VIII has been crowned here, including William the Conqueror (1066–1089), who defeated Edward's successor Harold at the battle of Hastings in 1066. Westminster Abbey houses the coronation throne and, until recently, the Stone of Scone. All that remains of the Confessor's church is the Pryx Chamber. The abbey was home to such notable figures as Gilbert Crispin, who was abbot there for 30 years. Henry III (1216–1272) rebuilt the Norman end of the abbey to house the shrine of Edward the Confessor, and it became a popular destination for pilgrimages. The cloisters also date from this period. The abbey church also houses the tombs of several monarchs, including Edward III, Henry VII, Mary I, Elizabeth the Great, Mary Queen of Scots, and the two princes of the tower as well as many famous figures in English history, such as Newton, Chaucer, Blake, Lord Byron, Handel, and the unknown warrior. It is also renowned for its beautiful French Gothic nave and the circular vaulting of the Henry VII chapel. During the English Reformation, Westminster Abbey was one of six monasteries that were not dissolved; today the abbey is a royal church.

William the Conqueror founded Battle Abbey (Sussex) as an act of penance for the death of King Harold, whose body was

South transept, Kirkstall Abbey (Cistercian), Leeds, South Yorkshire, England, 12th century. This is the most fully preserved Cistercian site in England.
Photo courtesy of Chris Schabel

mutilated by the Normans. The high altar was built on the very site where Harold died. At the time of the dissolution, it was one of the more prosperous houses in England. Most of the ruins date from the 13th century. Some walls of the church and chapter house survive, along with latrines and reredorters, and the east and west ranges of the cloister buildings are still present. The west range is now a private school.

The Cluniacs established several foundations during this period. Their first foundation was Lewes Priory (Sussex), the partial remains of whose east and south cloisters survive. Other substantial ruins remain at Monk Bretton Priory (South Yorks), whose church, cloister, and gatehouse still stand; Castle Acre Priory (Swaffham), whose west facade, nave, transepts, choir, east range (including the chapter house), dorter, and reredorter are well preserved (the west range has been restored and includes the cellarium); and Lenten Priory (Nottinghamshire), very little of whose remains survive.

The Augustinian Canons also made several foundations in England during the Norman period, including Thornton Abbey (Humberside), founded in 1139 and whose most notable remains are the 14th-century gatehouse; Thornholme Priory (Humberside), much of whose precinct remains largely com-

plete; Kirkham Priory (North Yorks), much of whose cloister buildings and 14th-century gatehouse remain; and Waltham Abbey (Essex), whose ruins are less substantial.

The growth of new orders in the 12th century led to the foundation of the first Cistercian house in England, Waverly Abbey (Surrey), in 1128. In 1132, 12 monks from Clairvaux and their abbot, William, settled on land donated by Walter Espec on the Rye River north of York and founded Rievaulx Abbey (North Yorks). Its most famous resident was Aelred (1109–1167), who became abbot in 1147. At its height the abbey probably had some 400 monks and lay brothers living within its walls. The abbey began to decline in the 13th century, was sacked by the Scots in the 14th century, and was dissolved by Henry VIII (1509–1547) in 1538. It is one of the better-preserved ruins in England. Reconstruction of the abbey began in 1919; even so, fewer than half of the 72 buildings listed in the suppression of 1538 survive, and only 15 acres of the original 92 acres once enclosed within the abbey precinct survive. Other remains include the nave of the abbey church, which, oddly enough, is aligned on a southeast-to-northwest axis. It dates from the 12th and 13th centuries and is one of the oldest extant Cistercian churches in Europe. Other remaining structures include the largely intact

Benedictine abbey, since 1541 a cathedral, Gloucester, England. The fan-vaulted cloister walk dates from c. 1370.
Photo courtesy of Chris Schabel

13th-century presbytery and its flying buttresses; the transepts; the cloister, built before Aelred's abbacy; the outlines of the chapter house, refectory, dormitory, and lay brothers' range; and the ruins of the founding abbot William's shrine.

After a visit from monks from Rievaulx in 1132, Richard, prior of St. Mary's of York, presented a petition proposing Cistercian-style reforms that was met with refusal by the abbot. Richard and 13 monks left St. Mary's and founded Fountains Abbey (North Yorks) on a plot of land given to them by Archbishop Thurston three miles from Ripon on the Skell River. Although life was very harsh in the beginning, the abbey eventually became one of the wealthiest houses in England. The ruins of the abbey are the most extensive monastic site still standing in England and are marked by such structures as the Great Perpendicular Tower of Marmaduke Huby, the magnificent nave of the abbey church, the enormous lay brothers' range on the west end (in which the wool was stored), the guest houses, the warming room, the cloister, and numerous smaller rooms. The abbey was purchased in 1540 by Sir Richard Gresham and later was resold

to Stephen Proctor, who built Fountains Hall out of stone from the abbey's ruins. In 1768 Fountains Hall and the ruins of Fountains Abbey were sold to William Aislabie, who, true to the fashion of the times, incorporated the remains of the abbey into the landscape of his estate.

Kirkstall Abbey (West Yorks) was another important Cistercian foundation and is one of the best-preserved sites in England. Its remains include the nave, cloister, abbot's house, and less well preserved remains of other structures, such as the guest house. Cleeve Abbey (Somerset), founded in 1190, has been restored. Its east and south cloister ranges include a chapter house, warming room, and refectory. Roche Abbey (South Yorks) and Jervaulx Abbey (North Yorks), other important Cistercian sites founded in 1147 and 1156, are not as well preserved. The Cistercians also absorbed many foundations of the Savignac Order, including Buildwas Abbey (Shropshire); Furness Abbey (Cumbria), most of whose substantial ruins date from the 12th century; and Byland Abbey (North Yorks), a foundation of Furness Abbey.

Dormitory, Battle Abbey (Benedictine), Sussex, England, 13th century. Founded by William the Conqueror on the site of the battle of Hastings (1066).
Photo courtesy of Chris Schabel

**Water course at Fountains Abbey (Cistercian), North Yorkshire, England, 12th century.**
**Photo courtesy of Chris Schabel**

The new orders included the Knights Templars, whose London Temple church is very well preserved, and the Carthusians, who founded houses in England known as charterhouses. Henry II (1154–1189) founded the first Carthusian house in England, Witham Priory (Somerset), as an act of penance for the murder of Thomas á Becket (c. 1120–1170). The most extensive remains of a Carthusian charterhouse are found at Mount Grace Priory (North Yorks), which dates from 1398 and boasts such famous residents as Sir Thomas More. The church, cloisters, and inner and outer courtyards survive. The London charterhouse was another important Carthusian foundation; its cloister, church, and chapter house still stand. The Premonstratensian canons also founded several houses, the most substantial ruins of which are Easby Abbey (North Yorkshire) and Egglestone Abbey (County Durham).

Bath Abbey (Somerset), founded as a Benedictine priory in 970, has a spectacular church dating from the 16th century. It is one of the last great churches built before the dissolution of the monasteries under Henry VIII, which almost completely obliterated all traces of monasticism in England. Several Benedictine cathedral priories built during the Norman period were converted to cathedrals with a dean and a chapter of canons in the wake of the English Reformation. These include Gloucester Cathedral, built in the late 14th century; Ely Cathedral, begun in 1090; and Chester Cathedral, from the late 13th century. Durham Cathedral, begun in 1093 to house the relics of St. Cuthbert (c. 636–687), is an important example of the Transitional style and has a restored Norman chapter house, refectory, and monks' dorter. Norwich Cathedral, begun in 1096, is a spectacular example of Romanesque architecture with later Perpendicular elements. Among the more well known and well preserved sites are St. Albans Cathedral, begun in 1077; Peterborough Cathedral, begun in 1117, housing the tomb of Henry VIII's first wife, Catherine of Aragon; and Winchester Cathedral, housing the relics of Cnut. Tewkesbury Abbey church survived the dissolution, and its Despenser Chantry is the earliest example of Perpendicular fan vaulting.

Whereas these monastic sites were converted to cathedrals, other monasteries were simply destroyed or converted to estates, such as the Augustinian priory of St. Osyth (Essex). Many English monastics fled to the Continent and founded such houses as Douai; when the French Revolution erupted in 1789, many displaced Continental monastics in turn went to England, where they brought about a revival of monastic life. Many great foundations of today, such as the Benedictine houses Ampleforth, Downside, and Woolhampton Abbeys, date from this period.

The revival of monastic life in England links the past with the present and serves as a reminder of the achievements of the many once-great foundations whose ruins dot the countryside.

*Monasteries to Visit*
Battle Abbey
Byland Abbey
Cleeve Abbey
Fountains Abbey
Furness Abbey
Kirkstall Abbey
Lindisfarne Priory
Mount Grace Priory
Rievaulx Abbey

DEBORAH VESS

*See also* Aelred of Rievaulx, St.; Bede, St.; Cluniacs; Cuthbert, St.; Dissolution of Monasteries: England, Ireland, and Wales; Gregory I (the Great), St.; Hilda, St.; Island Monasteries, Christian; Lindisfarne/Holy Isle, England; Reform, Tenth-Century Anglo-Saxon Monastic; Whitby, England

## Further Reading

Burton, Janet E., *Monastic and Religious Orders in Britain, 1000–1300* (Cambridge Medieval Textbooks), Cambridge and New York: Cambridge University Press, 1994

Burton, Janet E., *The Monastic Order in Yorkshire, 1069–1215* (Cambridge Studies in Medieval Life and Thought, 4th series), Cambridge and New York: Cambridge University Press, 1999

Cook, Olive, *English Abbeys and Priories*, New York: Viking Press, and London: Thames and Hudson, 1960

Coppack, Glyn, *English Heritage Book of Abbeys and Priories*, London: Batsford/English Heritage, 1990

Fergusson, Peter, *Architecture of Solitude: Cistercian Abbeys in Twelfth-Century England*, Princeton, New Jersey: Princeton University Press, 1984

Knowles, David, *The Monastic Order in England: A History of Its Development from the Times of St. Dunstan to the Fourth Lateran Council, 943–1216*, Cambridge: Cambridge University Press, 1940; 2nd edition, Cambridge: Cambridge University Press, 1963; New York: Cambridge University Press, 1976

Lillich, Meredith P., editor, *Studies in Cistercian Art and Architecture* (Cistercian Studies Series), 4 vols., Kalamazoo, Michigan: Cistercian Publications, 1982–1993

Platt, Colin, *The Abbeys and Priories of Medieval England*, New York: Fordham University Press, and London: Secker and Warburg, 1984

Robinson, David, and Janet Burton, *The Cistercian Abbeys of Britain: Far from the Concourse of Men* (Cistercian Studies Series, number 179), Kalamazoo, Michigan: Cistercian Publications, and London: Batsford, 1998

Robinson, Joseph Armitage, *Gilbert Crispin, Abbot of Westminster: A Study of the Abbey under Norman Rule*, Cambridge: University Press, 1911

Taunton, Ethelred, *The English Black Monks of St. Benedict: A Sketch of Their History from the Coming of St. Augustine to the Present Day*, 2 vols., London: Nimmo, and New York: Longmans, Green, 1897

Wardrop, Joan, *Fountains Abbey and Its Benefactors, 1132–1300* (Cistercian Studies Series, number 91), Kalamazoo, Michigan: Cistercian Publications, 1987

# Ennin 794–864

Japanese Tendai Buddhist abbot

The Japanese Tendai (Chinese, Tiantai) priest Ennin (known posthumously as Jikaku Daishi) was a disciple of Saichō and the third abbot of the Enryakuji temple complex on Mount Hiei, the center of Japanese Tendai Buddhism. Ennin is noted for promoting esoteric (Shingon) rituals within Tendai practice. He also contributed to the development of Pure Land rituals through the introduction of meditation practices focusing on the physical attributes of Amida Buddha.

Ennin was born into the regionally powerful Mibu family of Shimotsuke province (present-day Tochigi province). In 808, at age 15, he became a student of Saichō on Mount Hiei. Under Saichō's tutelage he studied the *Maka shikan* (Chinese, *Mohezhiguan*) – a central Tendai treatise written by the sect's Chinese founder Zhiyi (Chih-i, 538–597) – and other important Tendai works as well as Tendai meditation techniques. In 816 he received the full precepts at the Tōdaiji ordination platform in Nara. Around 833, as a result of assiduous ascetic practice, Ennin became sick and resigned himself to an apparently inevitable death. For three years he secluded himself in a simple hermitage in the Yokawa area of Mount Hiei, eventually recovering his former health. His place of retreat later became the Shuryōgon'in temple, a site of ascetic activity for subsequent Tendai monastics, most notably the famous mid-Heian-period monk Genshin (942–1017).

After recovering, Ennin was selected as a scholar-monk to travel to Tang China to study Buddhism. He departed for China in 838 and returned to Japan in 847. He wrote about his experiences in a detailed diary, the *Nittō guhō junrei gyōki* (*Ennin's Diary: The Record of a Pilgrimage to China in Search of the Law*). This text chronicles his stays at Mount Wutai and at the capital of Changan, where he studied esoteric Buddhist doctrine. Ennin's intended destination had been Mount Tiantai, the center of Chinese Tendai, where he had hoped to obtain answers to doctrinal questions related to Tendai. Because of internal Chinese politics, he was never granted permission to visit Mount Tiantai. One especially interesting section of his diary describes the Buddhist persecutions that occurred under the reign of Emperor Wuzong in 845. Despite his difficulties in China, he returned to Japan, carrying with him esoteric sūtras and ritual manuals that became important to the further development of Tendai esotericism (Taimitsu).

After his return to Japan, Ennin enjoyed the patronage of aristocrats and the imperial court. In 848 he was appointed one of ten official court priests to serve at the imperial palace's Buddhist hall. Monks appointed to this honored position were chosen from among those known for their strict adherence to monastic precepts and for their erudition. Then, in 854, Ennin was appointed head abbot of Enryakuji.

Through his supervision of the construction of numerous temples, including the development of the Yokawa area of Mount Hiei that became a center for ascetic practice, Ennin's legacy includes the great expansion of the Tendai monastic complex on Mount Hiei. Doctrinally and ritually Ennin moved Tendai further toward esoteric Buddhism by performing esoteric initiation and other rituals at the Enryakuji complex. He also made important contributions to the subsequent development of Pure Land practices in Japan through his inauguration of the constantly walking meditation (jōgyō zanmai). A variation on a similar practice set forth by Zhiyi, this contemplative ritual consists of a 90-day circumambulatory meditation on the physical form of Amida Buddha as a means of leading the practitioner to enlightenment.

WILLIAM E. DEAL

See also Buddhist Schools/Traditions: Japan; Mount Hiei, Japan; Mount Wutai, China; Mountain Monasteries, Buddhist; Pure Land Buddhism; Saichō

### Biography

Having become a disciple of Saichō at age 15, Ennin endured ill health before he entered seclusion on Mount Hiei. In 838 he traveled to China, including Mount Wutai, to return to Japan only in 847. Seven years later he became head abbot at Enryakuji on Mount Hiei, where he expanded the role of Tendai.

### Major Work

Nittō guhō junrei gyōki; as Ennin's Diary: The Record of a Pilgrimage to China in Search of the Law, translated by Edwin O. Reischauer, 1955

### Further Reading

Reischauer, Edwin O., Ennin's Travels in T'ang China, New York: Ronald Press, 1955
Saitō, Enshin, translator, Jikaku Daishi Den: The Biography of Jikaku Daishi Ennin, Tokyo: Sankibō Busshorin, 1992
Waley, Arthur, "Ennin and Ensai," in his The Real Tripitaka and Other Pieces, New York: Macmillan, and London: Allen and Unwin, 1952

# Esoteric Buddhism in China and Japan

### China

The earliest traces of esoteric Buddhism in China – mostly in the form of incantations and dhāraṇīs – come from several important canonical and nonesoteric sūtras of the Mahāyāna persuasion that were translated between the late second century and early fourth century. From the fifth to the sixth century, a growing number of dhāraṇī scriptures were being introduced to the Chinese Buddhists. In this new material the use of dhāraṇīs encapsulated the purport of the scriptures. In the course of this development, the esoteric tradition both took over and influenced Daoism.

The Tang dynasty (618–907) represents the high point in esoteric Buddhist practice in China, and its doctrines and rituals influenced virtually all Buddhist traditions in the realm. At that time it was represented by the Zhenyan school, which propounded a fairly systematic and structured form of esoteric Buddhism complete with elaborate rituals that included methods such as the use of mudras, maṇḍalas, complex visualizations, and dhāraṇīs. At that time its leaders were the three ācāryas Śubhākarasimha (637–735), Vajrabodhi (669–741), and Amoghavajra (705–774), all of whom were influential at the Tang court. Although their brand of esoteric Buddhism was multifaceted, their teachings centered on the Mahāvairocana Sūtra and the Vajraśekhara. Several of the largest temples in the twin capitals of Chang'an and Luoyang, including the Anguo Temple, the Da Xingshan Temple, and the Qinglong Temple, belonged to Zhenyan Buddhism.

By the middle of the eighth century, Zhenyan Buddhism held an almost complete sway over the Tang court and at the same time exerted a considerable influence on the other Buddhist schools in the empire. This influence reached far beyond Chang'an and Luoyang. Tiantai monks in the twin capitals came under increasing influence from the rituals and esoteric practices taught in Zhenyan Buddhism, and gradually these gained in popularity, although they do not appear to have entirely supplanted traditional Tiantai teachings. When Saichō (767–822), the illustrious founder of the Japanese Tendai school, stayed in China, he received esoteric initiations at a number of Tiantai temples.

When the Huichang Suppression of Buddhism took place between 844 and 845, most of the large Zhenyan temples in Chang'an and Luoyang were destroyed. This heralded the end of the Zhenyan school, although more syncretic and unstructured forms of esoteric Buddhist practice continued in the provinces. Especially in Sichuan a strong esoteric tradition developed at the end of the Tang and continued in force until the end of the Song dynasty (960–1279). During the Yuan and early Ming dynasties, Tibetan Lamaism was introduced into China, and under the Qing (1644–1911) it became the official religion of the Manchu rulers.

### Japan

Esoteric Buddhism (mikkyō) was introduced into Japan during the Nara period (710–794), but it was not until after Saichō and Kūkai (774–835) had journeyed to China to study that a systematic transmission of Zhenyan Buddhism to Japan took place. Although its practices began to influence the hitherto exoteric Tendai Buddhism, Kūkai's Shingon school was based entirely on esoteric Buddhism. The esoteric aspect within the Tendai school is commonly known as Taimitsu.

Kūkai studied under Huiguo (746–805), a disciple of Amoghavajra. On his return to Japan, he received strong support from the imperial court and was granted large landholdings both within Kyoto and on Mount Kōya to the south of the capital. The largest Shingon temples that Kūkai built were Toji in the Heian capital and Kongobuji on Mount Kōya.

Kūkai wrote a number of important works, including the Sokushin jōbutsu gi (Attaining Enlightenment in This Very Life), the Hizō hōyaku (The Precious Key to the Esoteric Treasure), and the Shōji jissō gi (The Meanings of Sound, Word, and Reality). Although he is considered as having inherited the direct

Main shrine hall, Tafosi, Zhangye, Gansu province, China, Xixia dynasty, 12th century.
Photo courtesy of Marylin M. Rhie

transmission of the Zhenyan school, Kūkai was in fact an original thinker who contributed actively to the development of Shingon doctrine and ritual practices. Among the concepts he developed was the *samādhī*, in which the adepts identifies himself with Mahāvairocana through a complex and highly detailed process. On a more folk-religious level, Kūkai is celebrated as a thaumaturge, and his life story is intimately connected with numerous local legends. The famous Shikōku pilgrimage to the holy sites (including temples, caves, and waterfalls), which is associated with his life, is one of the enduring elements in popular Shingon practice.

However varied, Shingon practices center around the dual maṇḍalas, the Vajradhātu and the Garbhadhātu, which symbolize universal and individual enlightenment, respectively. As in Zen Buddhism a cardinal doctrine in Shingon was belief in the attainment of Buddhahood in one lifetime. *Homa (goma)*, or fire sacrifices, play a central part in both Shingon and Tendai rituals.

During the Kamakura period (1192–1333), a heterodox branch of Shingon Buddhism arose. It was called the Tachikawa sect, and its followers practiced a combination of Shingon rituals and Daoistic longevity techniques that involved ritualized sex. Because of its unorthodox practices and widespread popularity, the Tachikawa sect was eventually suppressed.

Following the Muromachi period (1338–1573) the Shingon tradition gradually declined, and although it has remained up to this day, it no longer commands a large following, nor is it especially influential. At present most of its temples function as museums.

HENRIK H. SØRENSEN

*See also* Buddhist Schools/Traditions: China; Buddhist Schools/Traditions: Japan; China; Daoism: Influence on Buddhism; Deities, Buddhist; Eisai (Yosai); Ennin; Hermits: Buddhist; Holy Men/Holy Women: Buddhist Perspectives; Kūkai; Kyoto, Japan; Liturgy: Buddhist; Mantras; Mount Kōya, Japan; Mount Meru; Pure Land Buddhism; Saichō; Sexuality: Buddhist Perspectives; Shikoku, the Pilgrimage Island of Japan; Vajrayāna Buddhism in Nepal

**Further Reading**

Astley, Ian, "An Example of Vajrasattva in the Sino-Japanese Tantric Buddhist Tradition," *Studies in Central and East Asian Religions* 1 (1988)
Astley, Ian, *The Rishukyō: The Sino-Japanese Tantric Prajñāpāramitā in 150 Verses: Amoghavajra's Version*, Buddhica Britannica Series Continua III, Tring: Institute of Buddhist Studies, 1991

Lanterns, inscribed with the names of benefactors, Daimyō-ō-in Temple, Mount Kōya, Japan. This is the headquarters of the Shingon sect founded by Kūkai.
Photo courtesy of David Moore

Astley, Ian, "Some Random Remarks on the History of Esoteric Buddhism in East Asia," in *Perspectives on Japan and Korea*, edited by Arne Kalland and Henrik H. Sørensen, Nordic Proceedings in Asian Studies 1, Copenhagen: Nordic Institute of Asian Studies, 1991

Chandra, Lokesh, *The Thousand-Armed Avalokiteśvara*, New Delhi: Abhinav, Indira Gandhi National Centre for the Arts, 1988

Chou, I-liang, "Tantrism in China," *Harvard Journal of Asian Studies* 8 (1945)

Goepper, Roger, *Aizen-Myōō: The Esoteric King of Lust: An Iconological Study*, Zürich: Artibus Asiae, Museum Rietberg, 1993

Groner, Paul, *Saichō: The Establishment of the Japanese Tendai School*, Berkeley: Institute of Buddhist Studies, Center for South and Southeast Asian Studies, University of California at Berkeley, 1984

Gulik, R.H. van, *Hayagriva: The Mantrayanic Aspect of Horse-Cult in China and Japan*, Leiden: Brill, 1935

Ishida, Hisatoyo, *Esoteric Buddhist Painting*, Tokyo and New York: Kodansha, 1987

Karmay, Heather, *Early Sino-Tibetan Art*, Warminster: Aris and Phillips, 1975

Kūkai, *Kūkai: Major Works*, translated by Yoshito S. Hakeda, New York: Columbia University Press, 1972

Lü Jianfu, *Zhongguo mijiao shi* (The History of Esoteric Buddhism in China), Beijing: Zhongguo shehui kexue chubanshe, 1995

Matsunaga, Daigan, and Alicia Matsunaga, *Foundation of Japanese Buddhism*, 2 vols., Los Angeles: Buddhist Books International, 1974

Matsunaga, Yūkei, *Mikkyō no rekishi* (The History of Esoteric Buddhism), Kyoto-shi: Heirakuji Shoten, 1969

Mevissen, Gerd J.R., "The Indian Connection: Images of Deified Spells in the Arts of Northern Buddhism, Part I," *Silk Road Art and Archaeology* 1 (1990); "Part II," *Silk Road Art and Archaeology* 2 (1991/92)

Orzech, Charles D., "Puns on the Humane King: Analogy and Application in an East Asian Apocryphon," *JOAS* 109:1 (1989)

Orzech, Charles D., "Seeing Chen-yen Buddhism: Traditional Scholarship and the Vajrayāna in China," *History of Religions* 29:2 (1989)

Orzech, Charles D., "Esoteric Buddhism and the Shishi in China," in *The Esoteric Buddhist Tradition*, edited by H.H. Sørensen, Copenhagen and Aarhus: Seminar for Buddhist Studies, 1994

Osabe, Kazuo, *Ichigyō zenji no kenkyū* (A Study of the Chan Master Yixing), Kobe: Kobe Shoka Daigaku Gakujutsu Kenkyukai, 1963

Osabe, Kazuo, *Tōdai mikkyōshi zakkō* (History of Esoteric Buddhism during the Tang Dynasty), Kobe: Kobe Shoka Daigaku Gakujutsu Kenkyukai, 1971

Osabe, Kazuo, *Tō Sō mikkyō shi ronkō* (Essays on the History of Esoteric Buddhism during the Tang and Song), Kobe: Kobe Joshi Daigaku Tozai Bunka Keneyujo, and Kyoto: Hatsu Baijo Nagato Bunshōdō, 1982

Payne, Richard Karl, *The Tantric Ritual of Japan: Feeding the Gods: The Shongon Fire Ritual*, Delhi: Pradeep Kumar Goel, 1991

Reis-Habito, Maria, "The Repentance Ritual of the Thousand-Armed Guanyin," *SCEAR* (1991)

Reis-Habito, Maria, *Die Dhāraṇi des Grossen Erbarmens des Bodhisattva Avalokiteśvara mit tausend Händen und Augen: Übersetzung und Untersuchung ihrer textlichen Grundlage sowie Erforschung ihres Kultes in China*, Nettetal: Steyler Verlag, 1993

Reis-Habito, Maria, "The Great Compassion Dhāraṇi," in *The Esoteric Buddhist Tradition*, edited by H.H. Sørensen, Copenhagen and Aarhus: Seminar for Buddhist Studies, 1994

Shi Jinbo, *Xixia fojiao shilu* (An Abbreviated History of Buddhism under the Xixia), Yinchuan: Ningxia renmin chubanshe, 1988

*Shingon: Die Kunst des geheimen Buddhismus in Japan*, compiled by Roger Goepper et al., Cologne: Museum für Ostasiatische Kunst der Stadt Köln, 1988

Sørensen, Henrik H., "Typology and Iconography in the Esoteric Buddhist Art of Dunhuang," *Silk Road Art and Archaeology* 2 (1991/92)

Sørensen, Henrik H., editor, *The Esoteric Buddhist Tradition*, Copenhagen and Aarhus: Seminar for Buddhist Studies, 1994

Strickmann, Michel, "Homa in East Asia," in *Agni, the Vedic Ritual of the Fire Altar*, edited by Frits Staal, 2 vols., Berkeley, California: Asian Humanities Press, 1982

Strickmann, Michel, *Mantras et mandarins: Le bouddhisme tantrique en Chine*, Paris: Gallimard, 1996

Weinstein, Stanley, *Buddhism under the T'ang*, Cambridge and New York: Cambridge University Press, 1987

Xiao Dengfu, *Daojiao xingdou fuyin yu fojiao mijiao* (Astral Talismanic Seals in Daoism and Buddhist Esotericism), Taipei: Xinwenfeng, 1992

Xiao Dengfu, *Daojiao shuyi yu mijiao dianji* (Daoist Ritual Practices and Textual Sources of Esoteric Buddhism), Taipei: Xinwenfeng, 1993

Xiao Dengfu, *Daojiao yu mizong* (Daoism and Esoteric Buddhism), Taipei: Xinwenfeng, 1993

Yamamoto, Chikyō, *Introduction to the Maṇḍala*, Kyoto: Dōhōsha, 1980

Yoritomi, Motohiro, *Chūgoku mikkyō no kenkyū* (Studies in Chinese Esoteric Buddhism), Tokyo: Daitōshuppansha, 1979

# Ethiopia

### Christianity in Ethiopia

The history of Christianity in historical Ethiopia (i.e., the Federal Republic of Ethiopia and Eritrea) and the perception of the faith by its followers make Ethiopian monasticism a fascinating subject of investigation. Although historians might believe otherwise, it is monks, Christian holy men, more than anyone else who have been responsible for the spread of Christianity in Ethiopia. This article examines the history, practice, and influence of monastics in Ethiopia.

Because Ethiopia is located so close to the Middle East, the cradle of Christianity, some of the region's inhabitants must have known about or even embraced the new religion as soon as it started to spread outside its country of birth. Tyranus Rufinus, the fourth-century historian, takes note of this fact when he narrates his widely accepted history of the beginning of Christianity in Ethiopia.

According to Rufinus (c. 345–410), Meropius, a certain philosophy teacher of Tyre (in present-day Lebanon), set out on a voyage in the direction of India, taking with him two of his students, Frumentius and Aedesius. Because of an accident that befell their vessel at an Ethiopian (Indian, according to Rufinus) seaport (possibly Adulis), all passengers, save for the two students, perished. The coastal guards took the two children to the palace in the capital city of Aksum (Axum), where the king made Frumentius his secretary and Aedesius his butler.

When the king died, the dowager queen entrusted Frumentius with the upbringing of the royal princes. This authority must have given Frumentius the opportunity to convert the palace to his faith, Christianity. Furthermore, he used his good offices to encourage the Christians in town (possibly merchants from the Middle East who had arrived in Ethiopia before him) to organize themselves into a worshiping community, building an oratory to which a school for children was also attached.

When Frumentius and Aedesius were permitted to leave Ethiopia, Aedesius returned to his homeland and became the pastor of one of its churches. However, Frumentius went to Alexandria to ask the archbishop, Athanasius (296–373), to look after the incipient church in Ethiopia. Having studied the application, Athanasius (and his bishops) decided to ordain Frumentius himself bishop of Aksum, seeing that he knew the country and people better than anyone else. Thus, Frumentius became the first bishop of Ethiopia and its apostle. The Synaxarium of the Ethiopian Church states that he returned to Ethiopia and preached the peace (*sälam*) of Christ in all its regions; for this reason he was called Abba Sälama (Father Peace).

In fact, the local sources contain no information of any significance about Frumentius. His story, as told by Rufinus and subsequently repeated by Greek historians (e.g., Socrates, Sozomen, and Theodore the Lector), was brought to the Ethiopians as a homily by an anonymous writer, evidently one of its Metropolitans (a Copt) who knew the Greek source(s). He begins his homily with these words: "It is my pleasure to tell you how your land, the land of the Ag'azi, became Christian, as we have found [it] written down, how all your lands became Christian."

It is also doubtful whether "Sälama" is really Frumentius and whether he was so called because he preached peace (*sälam*). If this were true, he would have been called Sälam, the Ethiopic word for "peace," not Sälama, which is Arabic and a common Arabic name. Undoubtedly Frumentius was a bishop consecrated for Ethiopia by St. Athanasius, but the local tradition has no memory of him and his efforts to Christianize Ethiopia.

## Monks from the Byzantine World

The Christianization of Ethiopia that has continued to this day must have resulted from the efforts of monks who came to Ethiopia from the Mediterranean or Byzantine world, individually and in groups, and their Ethiopian followers and successors. Of these Yoḥanni, the founder of the monastery of Däbrä Sina (Mount Sinai), and Mätta', the founder of Däbrä Libanos (Mount Lebanon in Tegray), are reported as having come as individuals. The records are not specific on the date of their arrival in Ethiopia. The fact that their names are Arabic (Yoḥanni for John or Yohannes and Mätta' for Mathew or Matthaios/Maththaios) would suggest that they came to Ethiopia after the Arabic conquest of Egypt in A.D. 642. However, this could be a reflection of the time when their hagiographies were compiled rather than of the time when they flourished. In fact, Mätta''s hagiography states that he came to Ethiopia on the recommendation of Abbot Pachomius of Egypt, who lived around A.D. 290–346. This is about the time when Frumentius was ordained bishop of Aksum.

Several groups of monks have been identified as having come from the Byzantine realm between the fifth and seventh centuries and having settled in Ethiopia. Church historians suspect that at least one group, locally called the Nine Saints, came to Ethiopia to keep the Ethiopian Church on the side of the Monophysites when controversy concerning the relationship of humanity and divinity in Christ erupted in the Universal Church and was not settled to the satisfaction of all at the Council of Chalcedon in 451. Nothing is certain. Locally the Nine Saints are remembered more for having strengthened the faith and spread monasticism than for having engaged in Christological disputes. However, it is very interesting to note that the local sources maintain that this particular group of monks came to Ethiopia leading a large group of hierarchically organized Christians and bringing their books with them.

"Their books," according to Abba Giyorgis of Sägla, one of the most authoritative native scholars who lived between the 14th and the 15th centuries, are the New Testament Scriptures: "They [the Ethiopians] received the New Testament Scripture when the righteous of [the New] Rome came [to Ethiopia bringing their books with them]." It is possible that "their books" also included service books and educational materials for their doctrine of "one nature" in Christ, the Christological dogma of the non-Chalcedonians. Furthermore, it is significant to note that among the first works translated into the Ge'ez (Gə'əz) language was the monastic rule of Pachomius, the founder of cenobitic monasticism.

Of the monks who came to Ethiopia from the Byzantine regions and introduced monasticism, each founding a monastery, the Church remembers the following ten with great reverence. All but the first constitute the Nine Saints.

1. Libanos/Mätta': He heard the call to lead a monastic life on the night of his wedding. He left his parent's house by night and went to Mount Olivet, where Pachomius, the Egyptian archi-mandrite, was living. The order to go to Ethiopia came from Abba Pachomius. There is a suggestion that once settled in Ethiopia, he helped in the translation of one of the Gospels to Ge'ez. He and another (Ethiopian) monk founded a monastery in Hawzen (in Tegray) and built a church that they dedicated to the Holy Cross. Lebanon/Mätta' is commemorated on 3 Ṭerr (Tubah), or 28/29 December (Julian) or 11/12 January (Gregorian; the second dates, 29 December and 12 January, refer to leap years).

2. Arägawi/Zämika'el: His names – the only one of the Nine Saints who has a Ge'ez name – mean "The Elder" and "[The Devotee] of Michael," respectively. He was the leader of the Nine Saints during their journey from Egypt to Ethiopia. Tradition maintains that he received the monastic garb from Theodore, disciple of Pachomius. He founded the celebrated monastery of Däbrä Damo in Tegray. The saint used a long serpent as a rope to ascend the impregnable summit of Mount Damo, where he built his monastery. Today people use real rope to climb it as well as to transport whatever the monastery needs. King Gäbrä Mäsqäl (558–588) was present when later the church was consecrated, and St. Yared's hymn for it is still chanted on the day of its founder's commemoration, 14 Ṭəqəmt (Babah), or 11 October (Julian) or 24/25 October (Gregorian). His mother, Edna, came with the group and founded a nunnery for girls, Betä Dänagəl (House of the Virgin), nearby.

3. Ṗänṭälewon (Pantaleon): Ṗänṭälewon is remembered for having helped King Kaleb (in 525) by his prayers when the monarch crossed the Red Sea to rescue the Christian community in Najran from the persecution of Zu Nuas (or Phinnehas), the Jewish ruler of Arabia. He is called "Ṗänṭälewon of the Cell" for having never left his narrow cell after he entered it, 45 years before his death. Ṗänṭälewon is commemorated on 6 Ṭəqəmt (Babah), or 16/17 October.

4. Yəsḥaq (Isaac)/Gärima: He was probably a prince. He left his parents' palace to come to Ethiopia at the invitation of Abba Ṗänṭälewon. His monastery is at Mädära, near Adwa, in Tegray. Yəsḥaq/Gärima is remembered on 17 Säne (Ba'unah), or 24 June.

5. Afṣe: His hagiographer does not provide us with much historical information; he has him ascending to heaven like Elijah. His feast is celebrated on 29 Gənbot (Bashans), or 6 June.

6. Gubba: He founded his hermitage west of Mädära (where Yəsḥaq's monastery stood), but we have no trace of it today. Gubba is remembered, with Abba Afṣe, on 29 Gənbot (Bashans), or 6 June.

7. Alef: Tradition ascribes to Alef the founding of Däbrä Halle Luya in Tegray. His hagiographer has no more information about him than what he writes about the other monks in general: how they came to Ethiopia and where they settled. Alef is commemorated on 11 Mäggabit (Barahmat), or 20 March.

8. Yəm'ata: Not much is known about Yəm'ata, either, other than that he was one of the Nine Saints. His feast is on 28 Ṭəqəmt (Babah), or 7/8 November.

9. Liqanos: Liqanos built his hermitage, the Däbrä Qonaṣəl, north of Aksum. Today it is called Däbrä Liqanos, "Monastery (or Mountain) of Liqanos." Liqanos is remembered twice a year, on 25 Ḥedar (Hatur) and 4 Ṭərr (Tubah), or 4/5 December and 12/13 January.

10. Səhma: He settled southeast of Adwa, but his monastery did not survive. He is remembered on 16 Ṭərr (Ṭuhab), or 24/25 January.

Every Ethiopian monk prides himself on tracing his monastic genealogy to one of these monastic saints, but most of them trace their lines to Arägawi/Zämika'el through Yoḥanni, the seventh abbot of Däbrä Damo. Yoḥanni's spiritual sons – Iyyäsus Mo'a (of Amhara), Täklä Haymanot (of Shoa), and Danə'el (of Tegray) – are the three luminaries whose disciples dominated the history of Ethiopian monasticism.

Cosmos Indicopleustes, an Egyptian monk, reports that when he visited the Red Sea coastal regions of Ethiopia around A.D. 525, churches and monasteries flourished everywhere in the country. However, by the tenth century Aksum lay in ruins. No credible cause has been reported; a revolt of the non-Christian subjects against the power of the Church has been suggested. A woman called Isato or Gudit, both probably derogatory names given to her by her opponents, is credited with the leadership of the revolt and devastation. Whatever the cause and magnitude of the calamity, by this time Christianity was well rooted in the country.

A new dynasty, the Zagʷe, rose from the ruins and held charge of Church and state until A.D. 1270. History credits this dynasty with the building of the rock-hewn churches in Lasta, but no record exists of the dynasty's contribution to the spread of Christianity. Instead this was the work of monks of the next dynasty, the so-called Solomonic dynasty.

### Monks of the Solomonic Dynasty

Those who established the Solomonic dynasty in 1270 did not acknowledge that the dynasty was a new one; rather they claimed that they had restored the old dynasty, which had ruled from Aksum until Aksum was destroyed. They called it Solomonic, claiming the monarchs' descent from the King Solomon of Israel and the Queen of Sheba (or the South), who, tradition claims, was an Ethiopian queen. When she visited King Solomon (cf. 1 Kings 10:1–13; 2 Chron. 9:1–12), she conceived by him a child whom she called Menelik. This Menelik inherited his mother's throne and supposedly established the earlier Solomonic dynasty, which, it was believed, had ruled Ethiopia until Aksum was destroyed and the dynasty overthrown.

When Aksum was destroyed, the legitimate heir to the throne fled to the south and wandered for a long time from place to place. One of his descendants, Yəkunno Amlak, was able to win the support of all the leading monasteries and raise an army to overthrow the Zagʷe and establish/restore the Solomonic/Aksumite dynasty in 1270, this time in Amhara, not in Tegray, where Aksum is located.

### In Amhara and Shoa

The two important monastic leaders who collaborated with Yəkunno Amlak when he revolted against the Zagʷe were Iyyäsus Mo'a, founder of the Monastery of Däbrä Ḥayq Ǝstifanos in Amhara, and Täklä Haymanot, founder of the Monastery of Däbrä Asbo/ Däbrä Libanos in Shoa. The Church, on whose behalf the two monks conspired, must have been well rewarded in return. According to tradition it was allowed to collect a third of the national revenue, asrat, or "tithe." The prevailing saying has been "a third for the King, a third for the Church, and a third for the tiller," but asrat means "tithe" (i.e., tenth), not "third."

Iyyäsus Mo'a hailed from a religious family in Amhara. When he felt the call to dedicate his life to Christ, he traveled to Tegray around 1241 and joined the monastic community of Däbrä Damo, a monastery founded by the leader of the Nine Saints. Iyyäsus Mo'a served in the community for seven years as a novice and later as a monk under Abba Yoḥanni, the seventh abbot after its founder. He carried out difficult assignments with the admiration and approval of the abbot. He then moved south and settled on the island of Lake Ḥayq in Amhara, where he served in the church dedicated to St. Stephen (Ǝstifanos) the Protomartyr.

Iyyäsus Mo'a's presence on the island invigorated the education of the Christian community there. Many students from Amhara and Shoa, including Yəkunno Amlak, attended his school. Däbrä Ḥayq became one of the important centers of Ethiopian traditional education for years. Its monks contributed immensely to the growth of Ethiopic literature by translating into Ge'ez religious books, especially lives of the saints, martyrs, and Desert Fathers of the Universal Church that are recognized as such by the Coptic Church of Alexandria. Thanks to the generous grant of land that the monastery received from the rulers, the monks were free from the labor of tilling the land, which they leased instead to farming communities.

Täklä Haymanot came from a rich family in Shoa. He was about to establish a family when he was called by the Holy Spirit while on a hunting trip. He returned immediately from the field, distributed his property to the needy, and went out to preach the gospel to the heathens. He converted many to Christianity, including King Motäläme, who previously had invaded Christian enclaves and plundered them. Then Täklä Haymanot made a pilgrimage to the monastic centers in the north, notably to Däbrä Ḥayq in Amhara and Däbrä Damo in Tegray, the monastery established by the leader of the Nine Saints.

At Däbrä Ḥayq he served seven years under Abba Iyyäsus Mo'a, who gave him the first level of monastic garb. Then he traveled to Däbrä Damo in Tegray, apparently to settle there for the rest of his life. However, Abba Yoḥanni bestowed on him the higher level of monasticism and advised him to return to his homeland, Shoa, where the Church needed him to strengthen the

Christians in their faith and bring the light of the gospel to the surrounding pagan regions.

In Shoa, in the south, Täklä Haymanot recruited young men, mostly from among his nephews and other relatives, and made them zealous monks who went out and evangelized the heathens. After years of hard work in the service of the gospel, Täklä Haymanot and his followers chose an impressive place on the steep bank of the Jema River, where they founded the Monastery of Asbo. They settled there, with a cell designated for their leader, where he spent his life standing in prayer day and night, as a result of which one of his legs became atrophied and broke off. Accordingly Täklä Haymanot is depicted with a leg broken off and three wings on each side. (In hagiography people are transformed physically when they attain perfection in righteousness. Some grow wings to be able to fly and join the community of angels; some shine "seven times brighter than the sun.") Täklä Haymanot died in 1313 of a certain epidemic that devastated his nascent monastic community.

The remaining followers of Täklä Haymanot, monks and nuns, known as *bak*ʷ*r* (first-born), lived together in one place until the abbot noticed the need for a separate place for the nuns. They built a nunnery adjacent to the monastery, following the example of Edna, the mother of Arägawi/Zämika'el, who had founded a nunnery when her son established the monastery of Däbrä Damo.

Following the example of their predecessors, the next generation of Däbrä Asbo monks, called Betä Wäs, continued to preach the gospel to the adjacent communities until around 1340. At this time Metropolitan Ya'əqob (c. 1336–1344) summoned them to his palace and inquired about the situation of the Church in the south. He then chose 12 from among them, corresponding to the number of the disciples of Christ, and divided the south among them. He made Filəppos, the abbot of the monastery, their head (representing St. Peter). They received the title of *nəburä əd*. They executed their assignment with much success, some even founding monasteries. They made retreats once a year, coming back to Däbrä Asbo/Däbrä Libanos on the memorial day of their spiritual father.

It is to be remembered that until 1951, the metropolitan (i.e., the spiritual head of the Ethiopian Orthodox Church) was a Copt (Egyptian), whereas the administrative head, titled *itchege* (*əčäge*), was the abbot of Däbrä Libanos.

### In Tegray

Tegray, which included the major part of today's Eritrea, was the center of the Church and the state until Aksum, the capital city, was destroyed in the ninth/tenth century. Most of the ancient monasteries are to be found in this region. During the Solomonic dynasty two monasteries in Tegray, the Monasteries of Abba Danə'el (in Gärä'alta) and Ewosṭatewos in Särä'e, rose to prominence when Abba Ewosṭatewos (1273–1332), the spiritual son of the former, challenged the Church authorities for having violated the commandment for the observance of Saturday as the Sabbath of the Lord. He went all the way to Cairo (Egypt) and beyond to Cyprus and Armenia in search of support for his cause. He could not accept the abolition of the Sabbath in violation of the Ten Commandments and the Apostolic Constitutions. His followers even refused ordination as deacons and priests until they forced the Church to accept officially their position in a council held in 1450.

A century after Metropolitan Ya'əqob, the north was organized by Emperor Zär'a Ya'əqob (1434–1468), who divided the region according to the number of monasteries there and assigned a region for each to evangelize. However, the emperor was not always on friendly terms with some of the monasteries. A case in point was his confrontation with the movement of the Ǝsṭifanosites (Stephanites).

Around 1429 Abba Ǝsṭifanos was expelled from his monastery of Däbrä 'Abbay in Shire, Tegray, when he protested against the fact that the community had abandoned austerity, the core principle of monastic life. His movement was of a fundamentalist nature. He and his followers established their own monastery where they led the strictest form of monastic life. Another practice that they likewise shunned (and that brought them great trouble) was prostration before the monarch, which he demanded even at the mention of his name, and before holy icons (especially the Madonna and Child) and the cross. The emperor's reverence for the icon of the Blessed Virgin bordered on idolatry. Their challenge to the authority of the land was heard everywhere. Thus, the emperor was concerned that these monks might set a bad example for his other Christian subjects, which indeed they had. He persecuted them with the utmost severity. Today Istifanos has no followers to champion his tenets, but his monastery of Gunda Gunde is reputed to possess important manuscripts.

### The Concept and Impact of Monasticism

Ethiopian Christianity can be characterized as a monastic religion, with strict observance of austerity, especially in fasting, which includes abstaining from animal products for about two-thirds of the year. The impact of these "immigrant" monks so early in the history of the faith in the country and the spread of monasticism alongside Christianity could be responsible for this. Monasticism is understood and accepted as a higher form of Christianity to which all the faithful aspire. Tradition in later times has made it easy for the faithful to take this path: today any Christian can take the monastic garb at any age and, if he or she so wishes, stay at home, keeping his or her worldly property. The requirement for taking the garb is a vow to lead a celibate life after (not necessarily also before) becoming a monk or nun. One prays to live so that one feels no need for a person of the other gender as an intimate partner.

There is no minimum age required for being accepted to monastic life. Because monasteries are centers of education for all levels, students attending school there are encouraged by the community to join it as monks. The monastic ritual has prayers for three-year-old children. Couples who are unable to have children vow to give their child to a monastery if the wife should be enabled to bear one. Such children are bound to become monks or nuns. They believe that they were born to serve God in whatever way the community charts for them.

The sources suggest that a layman is first tested during three years working for the monastery and participating in the spiritual life of the community. If he is found to be suitable for monasticism, he is clothed with a *qamis* (tunic or monastic habit) and girdled with a *qənat* (cinture), which is a leather cord. The *askema* (from the Greek for "scapular"), made of leather, and the *qob* (monastic cap) are received at the highest grade of monasticism.

There are two words meaning monastery: *däbr* and *gädam*. *Däbr* means "mountain" or "mount," as in "Mount Sinai," and *gädam* means "wilderness," as in John the Baptist as "the voice of the one crying in the wilderness." The history of the two names is not clear; but it is obvious that each referred, at least initially, to the topography where monasteries were built. However, we have *däbr* monasteries not only on top of mountains, such as Däbrä Damo in Tegray, but also in lower places, such as Däbrä Libanos in Shoa (the "ä" suffixed to *däbr* is a genitive marker meaning "of"). Today any monastery can be called a *gädam*; *gädam* simply means "monastery." *Däbr*, on the other hand, refers to a "monastery on top of a mountain" or to a major monastery (not in size but in significance) that is recognized as such by the authorities of the Church and state. The rulers of the land appointed their heads. Thus, the name *däbr* indicates that a monastery with this name is a *däbr* in the second or even the first meaning.

The concept of monasticism involves rejection of this world, that is, rejection of the physical comforts that this world offers. Thus, the first step in founding a monastery is to remove oneself as far as possible from regions settled by people and to establish the monastic settlement at a place not easily accessible to worldly people.

### Types of Monasticism

Both types of monasticism – anchoritism, according to the tradition established by St. Antony (d. 356) and St. Paul of Thebes (d. 340), and cenobitism, according to the Rule of St. Pachomius (d. 346) – are known and practiced in Ethiopia. The monastic rule of St. Pachomius may have regulated communal life at the beginning, but today copies of it exist in hardly any monasteries. Each monastery has its own rule, but some practices are common to all.

The cenobitic communities emphasize praying, working, and dining together. All (save the old) divide the labor needed to maintain the community, including tilling the land, fetching water and firewood, baking, cooking, and shopping. When a person joins the community, he or she yields to the monastery every piece of property that he or she brings with him or her. Monastics eat together and pray together. They are not allowed to have any food in their cells. If visitors bring anything edible, the host has to bring the offerings to the communal table. In some *däbr* monasteries the horologion is recited 24 hours of the day, so the monks take turns keeping the prayer uninterrupted.

Members of a cenobitic community are at no time allowed to leave the monastery without the knowledge and permission of the *mäggabi*, or prior. When on a mission (e.g., to the market and government offices), they go in groups of two or three in order to guard each other from the temptations of the evil spirit. If the monastery is a *gädam* (i.e., not an official *däbr*), it elects its own officers who serve for an indefinite time. Only circumstances oblige the community to elect replacements. Monasteries are completely independent of higher authorities in the state or the Church. At times they even have challenged the definition of the Orthodox faith when theological disputes erupted.

Anchorites are of two types: followers of St. Antony and followers of St. Paul of Thebes. The followers of St. Antony lead a semiprivate life within the monastery, reminiscent of the idiorrythmic monasticism of Mount Athos in Greece. If cooked food is not provided from the communal kitchen, each has his or her private house where he or she prepares his or her meal from the foodstuff supplied by the monastery. They can own private property, such as offerings of any kind (food and money) brought by their visitors. They receive from the communal treasury a limited amount of money for other needs, such as clothes.

The followers of St. Paul of Thebes are a subclass of the anchorites; they are called *baḥtawiyan* (singular, *baḥtawi*, "a loner"). These lead a most precarious life in a monastery composed of cells. Members of such a monastery hold nothing in common other than the fact that they live in one compound. They do not know one another, as there is no occasion for them to meet. They own nothing other than what they put on, a jar for water, and a plate for receiving food. They dedicate their time totally to prayers and private worship, such as prostrating oneself to the ground (*səgdät*) hundreds of times a day. Their meal comes, when it comes, from the nearby monasteries and villages. They go without food for days if no one provides it. The messengers put the meal at the door of the cell. They know that the *baḥtawi* is still alive if the food of the previous day has been consumed.

One type of *baḥtawiyan* are the *gəḥuśan* (singular, *gəḥuś*, "the withdrawn"). No one knows where they are. They withdraw from their monasteries and live in the forests. They are met occasionally by hunters and herdsmen even though they try to hide. They live on what the wild plants offer. It is not uncommon that human bones, with hand crosses and other Christian artifacts near them, are found in the forests of the Christian highland. It is impossible to tell whether predators found them dead or alive.

### Power of the Monks

More often than not, anchorites come out of their caves and forests and go to the world to admonish the Christians and warn the "generation of vipers . . . to flee from the wrath to come." The nation's political and spiritual leaders do not like the *baḥtawiyan* who come to the world because they consider the leaders to be the archvipers. When the anchorites fearlessly castigate the rulers, the latter arrest them and keep them in prison.

The faithful firmly believe that individual monks as well as the monastic communities are endowed with spiritual power that works wonders. The *baḥtawiyan* bring messages of warning and glad tidings from the Lord to pious people. Whenever people see a monk, they wish to be visited by him. The stories of famous historical figures begin with *baḥtawiyan* appearing to their pious parents and telling them that a child will be born to them who will rise to greatness.

In order to win the favor and secure the prayers of the monasteries, rulers (kings and governors) lavish land on the monasteries. The land grants that the monasteries received in the course of their history freed monks from manual labor, especially from working in the fields. They leased their properties to farming families in exchange for food and drink (homemade beer) that the monastic community received once a year on the memorial day of one of the saints. Some monasteries became so rich that farmers who possessed monastic land took turns in providing the community's annual food supply in this manner. This freedom gave the time to read and meditate on what they call collectively the *Gännät* (Garden) or the *Mäṣəḥafä Mänäkosat* (Book of the Monks) or *Apophthegmata Patrum* (*Sayings of the Fathers*).

The large monasteries owned daughter monasteries, and because of the size of the land grants they received, the country was divided into monastic realms or dioceses rather than bishoprics. (There is no record that Ethiopia before this century had more than at most two bishops at any one time.) As owners of such estates, monasteries had their own courts – until 1974, when the military government nationalized all properties – to hear cases of the farmers who live on their estates.

During the reign of Emperor Zär'a Ya'əqob (1434–1468), the abbots of the major monasteries became members of the Royal Council, advising the monarch on the administration of the state, of which the Church was a part. For the abbots this meant neglecting the spiritual needs of their communities.

It is difficult to know the number of monasteries in today's Ethiopia. The Church's central administration in Addis Ababa keeps a register of churches but not of monasteries. Monasteries are listed in the register, but only when they have churches. Furthermore, not all centers with the name *däbr* or *gädam* have monastic communities. Some are defunct monasteries, with only their churches remaining to serve the surrounding communities. For the purpose of this article, it will suffice to mention the following:

Eritrea: Däbrä Bizän, Däbrä Sina, Ṣä'ada Amba, Gunda Gunde

Tegray: Däbrä Damo, Däbrä 'Abbay, Däbrä Bänkol, Däbrä Ṣärabi, Samu'el of Qoyyäṣa, Samu'el of Allelo, Abba Gärima, Abba Pänṭälewon, Abba Liqanos, Abba Alef, Abba Libanos, Abraha Aṣbḥa

Bägemdər: Waldəbba, Maḥbärä Ṣəllase, Säqʷar, Mändäbba, Gälila, Ṭana Qirqos, Betä Ləhem, Däbrä Bərhan Ṣəllase, Qoma

Gojjam: Märṭulä Maryam, Däbrä Dəmaḥ, Däbrä Wärq, Däbrä Mäwi', Moṭa Giyorgis, Daga Əstifanos, Kəbran Gäbrə'el,

Ǝnnarga Ṣəllase, Däbrä Ṣəmmuna, Gʷänj Ṣəlalo, Washära, Qoga, Mängəstä Sämayat

Wollo: Lalibäla, Gəshän, Tädbabä Maryam, Atronəsä Maryam, Däbrä Ḥayq Əstifanos, Ashätän Maryam, Gännätä Maryam, Abba Giyorgis Zägasətcha, Abunä Aron Däbrä Betel

Shoa: Däbrä Libanos, Zəqʷala, Ǝttisa Täklä Haymanot, Däbrä Bəśrat, Järr Ṣəllase, Däbrä Bäggə', Männagäsha Maryam, Addis 'Aläm, Miṭaq 'Amanu'el

Harerge: Asäbot (Däbrä Wägäg)

Middle East: Ethiopian monks have lived in the Middle East, especially in Egypt and the Holy Land (Palestine), since the early Middle Ages, building their own monasteries. However, the dangers of travel from Ethiopia through countries inhabited by peoples hostile to their religion has made it difficult to maintain a continued presence there. Today Ethiopian monks in Egypt live in Coptic monasteries with the Coptic monks. However, in Israel and Palestine they have several monasteries adequately populated. As a result Jerusalem (with its surroundings) is an archbishopric, connected to the past through Dayr Sulṭan, near the Church of the Holy Sepulchre, and with Däbrä Gännät as its administrative center.

GETATCHEW HAILE

*See also* Armenia; Desert Fathers; Egypt; Fasting: Eastern Christian; Hagiography: Eastern Christian; Hermits: Eastern Christian; Israel/Palestine; Orthodox Monasticism: Byzantine; Women's Monasteries: Eastern Christian

## Further Reading

Arras, Victor, editor and translator, *Collectio Monastica* (Corpus Scriptorum Christianorum Orientalium, Scriptores Aethiopici, volumes 238–239), 2 vols., Louvain: Secrétariat du Corpus SCO, 1963

Arras, Victor, editor and translator, *Patericon Aethiopice* (Corpus Scriptorum Christianorum, volumes 277–278), 2 vols., Louvain: Secrétariat du Corpus SCO, 1967

Athanasius, Saint, Patriarch of Alexandria, *Apologie à l'Empereur Constance. Apologie pour sa fuite* (Sources Chrétiennes, number 56), translated by Jan M. Szymusiak, Paris: Editions du Cerf, 1958

Budge, E.A. Wallis, *The Book of the Saints of the Ethiopian Church*, volume 4, Cambridge: University Press, 1928; New York: Olms, 1976

Cerulli, Enrico, "Gli abbati di Dabra Libānos, capi del monachismo etiopico, secondo la 'lista rimata' (sec. XIV–XVIII)," *Orientalia* 12–14 (1943–1945)

Cerulli, Enrico, *Etiopi in Palestina; Storia della comunità etiopica di Gerusalemme* (Collezione scientifica e documentaria, volumes 12, 14), 2 vols., Rome: Liberia dello Stato, 1943–1947

Cerulli, Enrico, "Il monachismo in Etiopia," *Orientalia Christiana Analecta* 153 (1958)

Conti Rossini, Carlo, "L'omilia di Yohannes, vescovo d'Aksum, in onore di Garimâ," in *Actes du onzième Congrès international des orientalistes: Paris, 1897*, Paris: Imprimerie National: Leroux, 1898

Conti Rossini, Carlo, "Il Gadla Libānos," *Ricordo di un soggiorno in Eritrea* 3 (1903)

Conti Rossini, Carlo, editor, *Vitae sanctorum antiquiorum I: Acta Yārēd [Gadla Yared, seu Acta Sancti Yārēd] et Panṭalēwon [Gadla Panṭalēwon, seu Acta Sancti Pantaleonis]* (Corpus Scriptorum Christianorum Orientalium, volumes 26–27, Scriptores Aethiopici, 9–10), 2 vols., Louvain: Durbecq, 1955

Dillmann, August, "Zur Geschichte der axumitischen Reiches im vierten bis sechsten Jahrhundert," *Abhandlungen der Königlichen Akademie der Wissenschaften zu Berlin, Philosophisch-historische Klasse* 1 (1880)

Getatchew Haile, "The Homily in Honour of St. Frumentius, Bishop of Aksum," *Analecta Ballandiana* 97 (1979)

Getatchew Haile, "The Monastic Genealogy of the Line of Täklä Haymanot of Shoa," *Rassegna di Studi Etiopici* 29 (1982–1983)

Getatchew Haile, "The Homily of Abba Eləyas, Bishop of Aksum on Mäṭṭaʿ," *Analecta Bollandiana* 108 (1990)

Getatchew Haile, "A Fragment on the Monastic Fathers of the Ethiopian Church," *Orbis Aethiopicum* (1992)

Guidi, Ignazio, editor, *Il "Gadla Aragâwi," Memoria del socio Ignazio Guidi* (Memorie della Classe di scienze morali, storiche e filologiche, volume 2, part 1a), Rome: Tip. della R. Accademia dei Lincei, 1895

Kaplan, Steven, *The Monastic Holy Man and the Christianization of Early Solomonic Ethiopia* (Studien zur Kulturkunde, 73), Wiesbaden: Steiner, 1984

Kinefe-Rigb Zelleke, "Bibliography of the Ethiopic Hagiographical Traditions," *Journal of Ethiopian Studies* 8:2 (1975)

Pedersen, Kirsten, *The History of the Ethiopian Community in the Holy Land from the Time of Emperor Tewodros II till 1974* (Studia oecumenica Hierosolymitana, volume 2), Jerusalem: Ecumenical Institute for Theological Research – Tantur, 1983

Rainieri, Osvaldo, "'Gadla Ṣādqān' or 'Vita dei Giusti,' Missionari dell' Etiopia nel sesto secolo," *Nicolaus* 6 (1978)

Rufini Aquileiensis Presbyteri, *Historia Ecclesiasticae*, edited by J.P. Migne, *Patrologia Latina*, volume 21, cols. 478–480

Sergew Hable Selassie, *Ancient and Medieval Ethiopian History to 1270*, Addis Ababa: Haile Sellassie I University, 1972

Socrates Scholasticus, *Ecclesiastical History: A History of the Church in Seven Books, from the Accession of Constantine to A.D. 305, the 38th Year of Theodosius II: Including a Period of 140 Years* (Greek Ecclesiastical Historians of the First Six Centuries of the Christian Era, volume 3), London: Bagster, 1844

Taddesse Tamrat, "Some Notes on the Fifteenth Century Stephanite 'Heresy' in the Ethiopian Church," *Rassegna di Studi Etiopici* 22 (1966)

Taddesse Tamrat, *Church and State in Ethiopia, 1270–1527* (Oxford Studies in African Affairs), Oxford: Clarendon Press, 1972

Ullendorff, Edward, *Ethiopia and the Bible* (Schweich Lectures, 1967), London: Oxford University Press for the British Academy, 1968

Yaqob, Beyene, *Giyorgis di Saglā Il Libro del Mistero (Maṣḥafa mesṭir)* (Corpus Scriptorum Christianorum Orientalium, volume 515, Scriptores Aethiopici, tomus 89), Louvain: Louvanii in Aedibus E. Peeters, 1990

# Evagrius Ponticus c. 345–399

Middle Eastern Christian monk and participant in Origenist controversy

Evagrius was born in a Christian family in the province of Pontus, most likely around 345. Sometime after 370 St. Basil of Caesarea (c. 330–379) ordained his father rural bishop in Cappadocia and himself lector of the church in Caesarea. After the death of Basil in 379, Evagrius joined St. Gregory of Nazianzus (329/30–389/90) as deacon in Constantinople. After two years Evagrius fled from Constantinople to Jerusalem, where he stayed with Melania and Rufinus on the Mount of Olives. On their advice he continued to Egypt and settled in Nitria in the desert to the southeast of Alexandria. Here he became the disciple of St. Macarius the Great (c. 300–c. 390) and Abba Pambo. Later he became, together with the four tall brothers, the most prominent member of the intellectual circle later denounced as Origenists. Among his disciples were John Cassian (c. 360–after 430) and Palladius (c. 364–420/30). He died after 17 years in the desert in January 399, just before the first Origenist controversy reached the desert and led to the expulsion of his associates and disciples. The most important sources on his life are the *Historia Lausiaca*, his vita, and his own writings, especially his many personal letters.

Through his many writings Evagrius occupies a central position in the history of Christian spirituality. He was the first to present systematically the spiritual tradition of the Egyptian desert and integrate it into an Alexandrian theological framework. His preference for the genre of collections of sayings, *kephalaia*, arranged in series, became an important model for later spiritual writings, especially the *centuria*, which is a series of 100 chapters, known from the *Philokalia*. His works on ascetic practice, especially the treatises *Praktikos*, *On Prayer*, and *On the Eight Thoughts*, were rapidly translated into other languages and have been read throughout the history of monasticism, some of them under the name Nilus of Ancyra. Most important are his psychological insights and systematic treatment of spiritual progress from *ascesis* (exercise) through *apatheia* (indifference) and *agape* (love) to *theoria* (vision). He had a seminal impact on the growth of Palestinian and Syriac monastic tradition, and his influence on the writings of Cassian and Diadochus of Photike, as well as on authors such as Dionysius the Pseudo-Areopagite and Maximus the Confessor, is clearly visible. He also wrote numerous letters to, among others, Melania, Rufinus, John of Jerusalem, and Gregory of Nazianzus and produced scholia on the Psalms, the Proverbs, and other biblical books. In his speculative works he developed the cosmology of Origen in ways that led to his denunciation at the ecumenical council of Constantinople in 553. Readers of later monastic authors are often warned against reading his works. For this reason many of his texts are preserved only among the non-Chalcedonian Churches, mainly in Syriac and later Arabic translations. Hitherto completely neglected in the West, Evagrius is rapidly gaining an audience in academic and spiritual circles.

SAMUEL RUBENSON

*See also* Basil the Great, St.; Cappadocia, Turkey; Cassian, John; Desert Fathers; Dionysius the Pseudo-Areopagite; Egypt; Gregory of Nazianzus, St.; Hermits: Eastern Christian; Humanism, Christian; Israel/Palestine; Istanbul, Turkey; Jerusalem, Israel; John of Damascus, St.; Manuscript Production: Christian; Origins: Comparative Perspectives; Origins: Eastern Christian; Philokalia; Spirituality: Eastern Christian; Theology, Eastern Christian; Vision, Mystical: Eastern Christian

## Biography

Born in Pontus, Asia Minor, Evagrius was ordained deacon by St. Gregory of Nazianzus and became a preacher in Constantinople. In 382 he left for the Desert of Nitria in Egypt, where he lived out his life as a disciple of St. Macarius of Egypt. After 553 his writings were condemned for espousing the views of Origen. As a result his writings are preserved only in Latin and Syriac translations. The first Christian monastic to write voluminously, Evagrius became a major source for our knowledge of the Desert Fathers and Mothers.

## Major Works

*Ad monachos*
*Antirrhetikos*
*Apophthegms*
*Gnostic Chapters*
*Gnostikos*
*Letters*
*On Evil Thoughts*
*On Prayer*
*On the Eight Thoughts*
*Praktikos*

## Further Reading

Bunge, Gabriel, "Évagre le Pontique et les deux Macaire," *Irénikon* 56 (1983)
Bunge, Gabriel, "Origenismus – Gnostizismus: Zur geistesgeschichtlichen Einordnung des Evagrios Pontikos," *VC* 40 (1988)
Clark, Elizabeth, *The Origenist Controversy: The Cultural Construction of an Early Christian Debate*, Princeton, New Jersey: Princeton University Press, 1992
Driscoll, Jeremy, *The "Ad Monachos" of Evagrius Ponticus: Its Structure and a Select Commentary*, Rome: Benedictina Edizioni Abbazia S. Paolo, 1991
Guillaumont, Antoine, *Les "Kephalaia gnostica" d'Évagre le Pontique et l'histoire de l'origénisme chez les Grecs et chez les Syriens*, Paris: Éditions du Seuil, 1962
Ponticus, Evagrius, *Briefe aus der Wüste*, Trier: Paulinus-Verlag, 1986

# Examinations, Theravādin

Monasticism is often divided into two main orientations, not necessarily exclusive: study and contemplation. Buddhist monasticism makes no exception to the rule. This becomes evident to anyone who studies Burmese monastic institutions: certain lineages give precedence to study (*pariyatti*), whereas others give precedence to meditation (*paṭipatti*). In fact Burmese monasticism has been so important in Myanmar that it has become an institution in itself, with regular examinations that, in the past, were led by the various schools (Burmese, *gaṇ*; Pāli, *gaṇa*, *nikāya*) and, in modern days, taken care of mainly by the national government.

If a novice or a monk has been ordained within a school emphasizing *pariyatti*, he might dedicate most of his daily activities to study. One of the most esteemed academic titles that one can earn is that of *dhammācariya* (teacher of the *dhamma*). However, it is compulsory to undergo many preliminary steps before one can sit for this prestigious exam. The first qualification that one must obtain on the way to the *dhammācariya* is the *pahtama-nge* (the first little), followed logically by the *pahtama-lat* (the first middle) and the *pahtama-gyi* (the first great). The very best students will need at least five years to complete these preliminary exams. There is no age restriction for any of these; an 11-year-old novice may sit for the *pahtama-gyi*, and a 36-year-old monk wishing to be admitted for the *dhammācariya* must first start with the *pahtama-nge*.

Most of these exams are conducted just before the *Thengyan*, the water festival that occurs around mid-April. These three days of festivities and religious celebrations (feasts offered to the monks, *shinpiyu*) mark the beginning of the Burmese new year and start only after the *dhammācariya* is completed. Each of these exams is offered annually and demands intense preparation in the days preceding the event. From their village monastery, where many candidates have spent most of their lives, novices and monks need to prepare for the journey that will take them to the institution where the exam is conducted. Thus, stress is inherent in the process, but the excitement associated with this academic pilgrimage renders it more bearable.

The present-day Union of Myanmar is divided into seven states (Kachin, Chin, Shan, Rakhine, Kayah, Kayin, and Mon) and seven divisions (Sagaing, Mandalay, Magwe, Bago, Ayeyarwady, Taninthayi, and Yangon). Only the divisions of Mandalay and Ayeyarwady have more than two cities/villages where the exams are hosted. This implies that candidates from certain regions need to embark on extended travel to reach the town where the exam is held. No exam whatsoever is conducted in the Taninthayi division or the Chin and Kayin states. Chin's nonrepresentation is no surprise, for the state represents a feeble percentage of the Union of Myanmar's population, and 99 percent of the Chins are Christians, animists, or Pau Chin Hau, the latter being based on the worship of a divinity called Pasian. The Kayin state is mainly Christian with a strong Buddhist representation; on the other hand, the Taninthayi division is essentially Buddhist. However, these two southeastern regions bordering

Thailand are somewhat isolated from the rest of the country, and the presence of Kayin rebels might render difficult, if not impossible, the organization of government-led exams.

All the monastic exams follow basically the same pattern: they are usually composed of two questions on *abhidhamma* (philosophical texts), two on *vinaya* (disciplinary texts), and two on *sutta* (discourses), each of these categories being further divided into ten subquestions. The candidate might be asked to write out some passages from memory, to correct grammar, to explain a passage in detail, or to give a critical account of a specific text. The exam is usually held over six days, each day being assigned a three-hour period during which one question with its ten subdivisions must be correctly answered. Government exams are written. As with the preliminary examinations, the *dhammācariya* is divided into two categories, each one higher than the previous one: *sāsanadhajadhammācariya* and *sāsanadhajasiripavaradhammācariya*. It is also important to mention that two nongovernmental organizations also hold the annual *dhammācariya* exam, differing from the government's in that an oral is also required: the Sakyasiha of Mandalay and the Cetiyan Gaṇ of Yangon are monastic organizations whose examinations hold a much higher status than that of the government exams.

The *dhammācariya* exam is very difficult to pass, so very few monks proceed to the highest Burmese exam, known as the *tipiṭakadhāra* (bearer of the three baskets), in which, to succeed, the monk must demonstrate that he knows by heart the entire Pāli Canon with its three genres: *vinaya*, *sutta*, and *abhidhamma*. Even the *Guinness Book of Records* mentions this brilliant achievement of memory! This exam is much more complex than the previous one, for the candidate is examined for 33 days and is entitled to only three errors a day in his recitation. It is by far the most exacting exam throughout the Union of Myanmar, and only a few diligent monks participate in this annual event, held in December at Kabaye Paya in Yangon.

MATHIEU BOISVERT AND MATTHEW KOSUTA

*See also* Burma (Myanmar); Discourses (Suttas): Theravāda; Festivals, Buddhist; Governance: Buddhist Perspectives; Korea: History; Meditation: Buddhist Perspectives; Novices, Theravādin Rituals for; Scholastics, Buddhist

Note: no secondary sources on this topic are available in English or French.

# Exile, Western Christian

Withdrawal from the world is an inherent part of the monastic call, and all Christians are called on to be pilgrims, that is, aliens resident in this world whose true citizenship is in heaven. Exile as a self-imposed ascetic practice was characteristic of Celtic monks, especially those from Ireland, whose *peregrinatio* took them and their faith and sometimes their learning to all corners of the known world. An Irish medieval *peregrinus* undertook not only to visit a shrine but also to leave his homeland either permanently or for a prolonged period. Although motivated mainly by a personal quest for perfection, such exile also involved a missionary endeavor to promote the kingdom of Christ on earth. Columban (d. 615) was not the first Irish *peregrinus*, but he likely was the most influential. Through exile he and his fellow monks exerted a profound influence on the establishment of the monastic life in France, Germany, and Italy and contributed greatly to the Carolingian Renaissance. The growing dominance in the ninth and tenth centuries of the Benedictine charism of stability, encouraged by the same renaissance, together with the decline of native Irish tradition, brought the heroic age of the movement to an end. The Schottenklöster network remained as an abiding memorial. The name by which the pilgrim monks were known (and that they used to describe themselves) was *Scoti*, and a continuing flow of Irish monks into Germany led to the establishment at Ratisbon, Würzburg, and elsewhere of Irish monasteries in exile: Schottenklöster. A post-Reformation reflection of the *peregrinus* tradition was the foundation of Irish colleges and religious communities throughout mainland Europe.

Ireland's identity as a monastic church helps to make its influence understandable, but the English too were intrepid "pilgrims." Saint Boniface's (c. 673–754) contribution to the evangelization of Germany and to the propagation of the Benedictine Rule was second to none. Of course, not all exiles from their homelands or monastic houses were voluntary. Sometimes exile was precipitated by persecution. The community of St. Cuthbert (c. 636–687) abandoned their exposed island monastery at Lindisfarne on account of the Viking raids that began in the 790s. Carrying the body of Cuthbert, they roamed about Northumbria in the ninth century before settling first at Chester-le-Street in 883 and finally at Durham in 995.

Within 50 years of Henry VIII's dissolution of the monasteries (1539), the English Reformation gave impetus for the foundation of a great network of religious communities with exclusively English and Welsh membership in exile in Continental Europe. The earliest of these communities was the English College for the training of secular clergy, which opened at Douai in the Spanish Netherlands in 1568. This was followed by the opening of the English Jesuit College at St. Omer in 1593 and the beginning of the Jesuit mission to England. Both the secular colleges and their Jesuit counterparts viewed the period of exile as temporary, and both were dedicated to the reconversion of England.

A third force emerged among the English Benedictines, whose revival began in exile. Their Continental houses at Douai (1607), Dieulouard, Lorraine (1608), Paris (1615), and Lambspring (1644) in Germany, the latter formerly a *Schottenkloster*, began as separate foundations. It took a generation of controversy to reconstruct a revived English Benedictine Congregation. This was due in part to conflicts with seculars and Jesuits and also to the differing claims of the French, Italian, and Spanish Benedictine monasteries at which the first post-Reformation English monks had been professed. In 1619 an English Benedictine Congregation was reconstituted on lines very different from its medieval counterpart. The latter had been a federation of autonomous houses, but the new congregation took its model from the reformed monastic congregations of the 15th century. It remained more centralized, even if by the papal bull *Plantata* (1633) it received all the privileges of the medieval congregation.

The English Benedictines were exceptional in combining two distinct systems of monastic government: the missioners served in England (for whose formation and training the Congregation mainly existed) under provincials, whereas the conventuals lived in monasteries under priors (only Lambspring was an abbey). All came under the authority of the president-general and ultimately under the general chapter, which met every four years. The monasteries themselves were strictly observant. Life on the mission continued amid constant fear of death and harassment throughout most of the 17th century. Three of the 40 English martyrs canonized by Pope Paul VI in 1970 were Benedictines: Alban Roe, John Roberts, and Ambrose Barlow. In a sense the English Benedictines, like other religious drawn from the English Catholic community, endured a double exile, first from their native country by entering a monastery abroad and second from those very monasteries once posted on the mission. The first exile could be a prolonged one. Most monks began their connection with their communities as pupils in monastic schools where "church students" destined for the priesthood mingled with lay students. This intermingling of laity with future priests strengthened the cohesive mentality of the English Catholics, who saw themselves proudly as "recusants," that is, those who refuse (*recusare*) to accept the state religion. Few or no visits home were permitted for English Catholic students in the Continental schools.

The English Friars, like the Benedictines, were revived during the recusant period. They lived a life similar in model to that of the exiled monks with schools, missions in England, and a house of formation on the Continent that could also serve as a "safehouse" in a time of persecution. The Dominicans were fortunate in having Cardinal Philip Howard, a Dominican himself, as their chief benefactor. In 1697 he founded an English house at Louvain, supplementing the priory at Bornten in the Low Countries established in 1658. The Franciscan Observants opened a friary at Douai in 1629, but like the Dominicans they never mustered the manpower of the Benedictines, who statistically fell far behind the Seculars and Jesuits. English Carmelites were even fewer in number. Among the Irish, who boasted a far more vital and populous native church, the Friars were far stronger. For example, in 1739 the Irish Augustinian Friars acquired as a training college the church of San Matteo in Rome close to the Irish Dominicans, who had already settled at San Clemente. From there, before the end of the 18th century, they had already sent Augustinians to the United States, beginning the *peregrinatio* of so many Irish clergy to the New World.

The Irish Augustinians of San Matteo regarded James Stuart (1688–1766), "the old Pretender," as their chief benefactor. By adhering to the Stuarts long after it had become a lost cause, Anglophone communities abroad showed how profound their exile was and how isolated they were from the political mainstream of their own countries. This was especially true of the women. Eng-

English convent, Bruges, Belgium, 18th century.
Photo courtesy of the Editor

lishwomen who wanted to pursue a religious life in the period from the Reformation to the French Revolution had to accept lifelong exile as well as enclosure as part of their vocation. The only exception was a few sisters of Mary Ward's (1585–1645) Institute of the Blessed Virgin Mary who worked undercover in England. Even Mary Ward's Institute, first established at St. Omer in 1609, had the great majority of its sisters resident outside England. A group of over 20 English communities were established, many of them in Flanders, where they came under Spanish and in some cases French protection following the expansion of French territory during the reign of Louis XIV (1643–1715). Only one of these exiled religious communities had migrated as a community from England: the Bridgettine Syon Abbey. This royal foundation, established in 1419 on the Thames River at Twickenham, not far from London, had been dissolved by Henry VIII in 1539 and briefly revived under Mary Tudor (1553–1558) in 1557. It pursued a peripatetic life until 1594, when the sisters settled in Lisbon, Portugal, where they were to remain until the Napoleonic Wars.

All the other communities were new, although they represented the older orders rather than the new Counter-Reformation ones. The first to be "revived" was the Benedictines, in 1598 at Brussels, from which a number of foundations were made. Much depended on local support and Church approval, and all the exiled communities were to remain small and poor. Among the communities founded from Brussels was that for Irish nuns at Ypres. It remained in exile until the bombardment of World War II forced its removal to Ireland, where it is now settled as Kylemore Abbey. The female English foundation at Cambrai in 1623, closely associated with the revival of the English male Benedictine Congregation, had as its spiritual director Dom Augustine Baker (1575–1641). His emphasis on contemplative prayer corresponded closely to the needs of a convent always to some extent cut off by language and culture from its local church. The Cambrai community – which eventually settled at Stanbrook, near Worcester, England, in 1835 – made a foundation in 1651 in Paris. The latter is now settled at Colwich in the English Midlands. In its turn Stanbrook was instrumental in the foundation of monasteries in 1849 in Australia at Rydalmere, New South Wales, now at Jamberoo, and in Brazil at São Paulo. The latter has several daughter houses. Mission and exile seem closely related.

The Franciscan tradition was well represented. In 1609 a Poor Clare convent was established at Gravelines, in the Low Countries, from which in 1625 an Irish daughter house was founded. Originally in exile, this community established itself near Dublin by the end of the 1620s and became the mother house of many foundations. Gravelines also had three English daughter houses, at Aire (1629), Rouen (1644), and Dunkirk (1652). A Franciscan Third Order house was established in 1628 at Brussels and later translated to nearby Nieuport. From 1661 the Paris English Franciscan house was a Conceptionist convent, called the Blue Nuns on account of their habit. Like the men, even the most retired of English women's orders on the Continent operated schools for recruitment and incomes, and the Paris one likely was the most successful and well attended such establishment. At least until 1789 Paris provided an agreeable place for exile.

Dominican nuns had their centers as well, notably a house in Brussels founded by Cardinal Howard in 1669. Carmelite English women were more numerous than their male counterparts, with foundations at Antwerp (1619), Lierne (1648), and Hoogstraele (1678). The Augustinian canonesses had foundations at Louvain (1609), Bruges (1629), and Paris (1633). The Bruges foundation, in its historic buildings, is the only one of these exiled communities to remain still (1999) in exile, although many were to survive their transplantation to England. Located on the Fossé St.-Victor, the Paris convent remained there throughout the French Revolution and continued as a community and school until the early years of the 20th century. Among its alumni was George Sand (1804–1876), the novelist, whose autobiography includes a vivid recollection of her school days. The Canonesses of the Holy Sepulchre, established at Liège in

1642, left the Continent in 1793 and returned to England, settling at New Hall in Essex.

The French Revolution and the wars that followed brought an end to this English church in exile, and, following years of difficulty and unsettlement, many of the communities were reestablished at home. They retained something of their Continental character, especially in the early days. For example, among the English Benedictines the search for new spheres of operation continued. In Australia the first two archbishops of Sydney were Downside monks, Bede Polding and Bede Vaughan; the Douai monastery had relocated to Downside in Somerset. The island of Mauritius boosted a succession of English Benedictine bishops. Such activity, which continued alongside "missions" and education in England, probably owed more to the expanding missionary impetus of the British Empire and the need to secure an income for a string of struggling communities bereft of their Continental fundings than to any lingering longing for exile.

It was one of the ironies of the French revolutionary period that many French Catholics sought refuge in the very country, England, that had exiled by law so many of its citizens since the Reformation. About 7,000 French priests arrived in the early 1790s, many to remain until their deaths. A considerable number of individual religious arrived in England, albeit few communities. Before 1789 the Bourbons, in line with the dictates of Enlightenment thought, had reformed most of their monasteries out of existence. The exceptions were a small group of Carthusians who settled near Shaftesbury in Dorset, a whole convent of French Benedictine nuns who came from Montargis to Norfolk by way of Brighton, and the Cistercian community that settled at Lulworth in Dorset.

This last group were part of the extraordinary band of monks (and nuns) who gathered around Augustin de Lestrange (1754–1827), who as former novice master of La Grande Trappe refounded his monastery at Valsainte, Switzerland, in 1791, becoming abbot in 1794. Fired by "the holy will of God," he attracted numerous disciples – of whom those in Lulworth were but a few – and conducted the two-year (1798–1800) "monastic odyssey," which kept his followers together as true *peregrinates*, or a "monastery on wheels." In the rationalistic climate of the 19th century, Lestrange's witness to the monastic way led to a great revival of his Cistercian Order in its Trappist guise. His example was to revitalize that tradition around the world.

Attempts by anticlerical governments in Europe to suppress religious orders by driving them into exile have, in the modern period, been less than successful. Bismarck's *Kulturkampf*, which saw religious orders being exiled from Germany in the 1870s, misfired and led to a strengthening of the Catholic Church and the repeal of most of the laws by 1887. In France the Laws of Association, passed between 1901 and 1903, sought the expulsion of all religious orders. Ultimately this too was to be a dead letter, but in the long term it allowed a growth in foundations outside these countries, especially in the Anglophone world.

In the 20th century atheistic communism has led to enforced exile. In 1949 in China the religious orders were well developed, with the Franciscans, for example, totaling 757 members. Some of these have gone into exile, but more have sunk without a trace. Among Russian exiled communities is the Orthodox Monastery of Valamo. Captured by the Russians in 1940, the monks moved from the Valamo Islands to Heinävesi in Finland, where they built a new monastery that has become a symbol of the revival of the Orthodox tradition in Finland.

Voluntary wandering religious, such as the Celtic *peregrinatus*, found a counterpart in the 18th- and 19th-century Russian *stranichestvo*, but as we have seen, most exiles in the monastic tradition have been coerced by political or religious persecution.

AIDAN BELLENGER

*See also* Baker, Augustine; Boniface, St.; Celtic Monasticism; Columban, St.; Congregations, Benedictine; Cuthbert, St.; Dissolution of Monasteries: England, Ireland, and Wales; England: History; Lindisfarne/Holy Island; More, Gertrude; Reformation; Rome and the Papacy

**Further Reading**

Anson, Peter F., *The Religious Orders and Congregations of Great Britain and Ireland*, Worcester: Stanbrook Abbey Press, 1949

Bellenger, Dominic Aidan, *The French Exiled Clergy in the British Isles after 1789*, Bath: Downside Abbey, 1986

Dilworth, Mark, *The Scots in Franconia: A Century of Monastic Life*, Edinburgh: Scottish Academic Press, and Totowa, New Jersey: Rowman and Littlefield, 1974

Guilday, Peter, *The English Catholic Refugees on the Continent 1558–1795*, London and New York: Longmans, Green 1914

Kervingant, Marie T., *Des Moniales face à la Révolution française*, Paris: Beauchesne, 1989

Lainio, Eino, and Niilo Kohoner, *Valamo and Its Message*, Helsinki: Valamo-Seura, and London: Nicholas, 1983

Mackey, James P., editor, *An Introduction to Celtic Christianity*, Edinburgh: Clark, 1989

Martin, F.X., and Clare O'Reilly, *The Irish Augustinians in Rome, 1656–1994 and Irish Augustinian Missions Throughout the World*, Rome: St. Patricks, and Dublin: Augustinian House of Studies, 1994

Rees, Daniel, editor, *Monks of England: The Benedictines in England from Augustine to the Present Day*, London: SPCK, 1997

Whelan, Basil, *Historic English Convents of To-Day*, London: Burns, Oates and Washbourne, 1936

# F

## Farming, Christian. *See* Agriculture, Western Christian

## Fasting: Buddhist

This Buddhist ritual, largely limited to certain hours of holy days and to fixed days of specific months, was regarded as doctrinally significant by the time of the Second Council in North India. Fasting became a religious ritual in a two-meal-a-day culture only after affluent conditions prevailed and fasting could be ritualized as intentional deprivation. Buddhists apparently borrowed fasting from Hindu abstention practices, and the practice had become well established and canonical by the fourth century B.C. since the issue of a sect of monks failing to observe the hours of fasting came up at the Second Council at Vesālī (Vaiśālī).

Fasting as a religious experience has been explained in several ways: symbolically remembering and sharing with those who are less fortunate, further sanctification of holy and other designated days by a physically depriving activity, marking observance of holy vows, intensifying the religious experience through exercising the will and subjecting the body to abnormal stress, identification with the struggle of Gautama before enlightenment, and simply a practice inherited from ancient abstention and purification practices.

In the so-called ten moral precepts of Buddhism, number 6 is the injunction not to eat at unseasonable times. All devout Buddhists follow the first five (the original precepts: prohibitions against killing, stealing, excessive sexual practices, lying, and drinking to intoxication), and many of the five later additions. However, these last precepts (abstention from personal adornments, sleep on sumptuous beds, and owning gold or silver) are regarded as being on a different moral plane, as more applicable to cloistered individuals than to the lay population. Attitudes toward eating have therefore fallen into the secondary – and less demanding – group and are practiced largely by the clergy.

Buddhists adopted pre-Buddhist fasting days relative to the lunar calendar, on the 1st, 8th, 15th, and 23rd days of the month, that is to say, the full moon, the new moon, and the days evenly spaced between (Sanskrit, *Upavasatha*). Observed like sabbaths these days are reserved in most Buddhist countries for special group ceremonies, readings of particular texts, confessions, head shaving, changing of clothes, and fasting from midday until dawn. In Japan (Japanese, *Fusatsu*) it has been more customary to hold the meetings of the monks on the 15th and 30th days of the month. The most holy day is *Vaiśākha* (Sanskrit), or Wesak, the day of the full moon that occurs in April or May and that is regarded by many traditional Buddhists as the day of Buddha's birth, renunciation, enlightenment, and *parinirvāṇa*. Japanese celebrate the birth of Buddha on 8 April.

The *Dhūtanga* (Japanese, *Jūni-zuda*) are the 12 rules (sometimes 13) of Buddhist mendicant living. Number 4 requires eating food at only one place, number 5 requires eating from only one container (i.e., these two imply no seconds), and number 6 requires not eating after noontime. Drinking water, however, is permitted. The Japanese term *tosō* (throwing away everything), referring to this frugal life, has been used for wanderers begging for alms and preaching on street corners.

Fasting in the Chinese and Japanese context can be synonymous with abstention from the eating of meat, for vegetarian feasts and fasting go by the same written character (*jai* [*chai*]; Japanese, *monoimi*). These meager meals for monks, with invited laypeople, often entailed huge ceremonies – the attendants numbering in the thousands – in the Sui (590–618) and Tang (T'ang) (618–906) dynasties in China and from the seventh century through the eighth century in Japan, usually on invitation of the court. They were held for a variety of reasons, some annually, and others for special events, such as thanksgiving occasions and because of natural or other threats to national stability or the state. The conventional scheduled fasting pattern was called the "three long months" and the "six fasting days," fasting taking place the first 15 days of the 1st, 5th, and 9th months (thus they seemed longer) and the 8th, 14th, 15th, 23rd, 29th, and 30th days of every month. Animals were not to be killed and criminals not executed during these times. Fasting could occupy 81 days a year, to which could be added other days when circumstances demanded it.

Total fasting (*danjiki*) for a given length of time, such as a week, is an ordeal included in the qualifications of becoming an *ajari* (Sanskrit, *ācārya*), usually translated as a teacher, but a rare teacher who reached a very distinguished rank in the Shingon and Tendai sects. Fasting may be accompanied by other ascetic practices, such as fire walking. At this stage in their spiritual development, *ajari* are credited with the powers of exorcism.

Several temples in northern Japan house mummified remains of individuals (*sokushim-butsu*, "self-mummified Buddhas") who fasted or reduced their food intake to certain floral stuff as a result of vows. This method of gaining spiritual power guaranteed entry into nirvana with the Buddha. The corpses are in Yamagata prefecture, a strong Shugendō (mountain asceticism) area known for the white-garbed *yamabushi*, whose ascents of sacred mountains have traditionally been carried out under excruciating, life-threatening conditions. In their case Mount Yudono (altitude c. 5,000 feet), in the southwest of the prefecture, was the scene of their endeavors. The Buddhist connection is usually with the Shingon sect and its esoteric practices. Like the *yamabushi* these fasting ascetics were not necessarily cloistered men, but their efforts gained them sainthood and preservation in the temple.

From introduced religious practices, various prohibitions evolved against the eating of meat, salt, or grains (rice, wheat, millet, barley, and beans), the so-called Five Cereals. It is unlikely that Shintō contributed anything to these restrictions, as its appreciation of life and those things that made it most enjoyable were in constant conflict with Buddhist views of moderation, and the rejection of the grains is on record before all of them were cultivated in Japan.

By avoiding grains and meat, little was left on the menu except grass, nuts, berries, tree bark, leaves, and pine needles. Vows were made for a lean diet of 1,000, 2,000, or 3,000 days, with a progressive reduction in quantity of "food" until it was given up altogether. Death often came before the vow was consummated.

In principle, after wasting away, preferably dying in a yoga position, such an individual was buried in a wooden coffin and then exhumed three years later. The totally desiccated corpse was dressed in abbot's robes, displayed in a temple, and treated like a seated Buddhist image, the object of offerings of incense, flowers, and prayers. Recognition of their sacrifices imparted power to others. Tombstone dates and temple notes place the practice from the 18th through the 19th century. The remains are preserved in otherwise little known temples in the cities of Sakata and Tsuruoka: Chūren-ji, Dainichi-bō, Kaikō-ji, and Nangaku-ji.

However, for those not planning a terminal ritual, the records suggest that by maintaining a certain consumption level, longevity was in many cases actually enhanced. Best known are the tree eaters (*mokujiki*), one of whom, an 18th-century itinerant named Mokujiki, left his mark because he reimbursed his hosts for his lodgings with hastily carved wooden images. Mokujiki died in 1810 in his early 90s. Hundreds of these Buddhist deity figures are prized collectors' items today.

J. EDWARD KIDDER, JR.

*See also* Asceticism: Buddhist Perspectives; Councils, Buddhist; Festivals, Buddhist; Food: Buddhist Perspectives; Japan: History; Mount Hiei, Japan; Rules, Buddhist (Vinaya)

**Further Reading**

Blacker, Carmen, *The Catalpa Bow: A Study of Shamanistic Practices in Japan*, London: Unwin Hyman, 1975; 2nd edition, 1986
Ch'en, Kenneth, *Buddhism in China: A Historical Survey*, Princeton, New Jersey: Princeton University Press, 1964
Hori, Ichiro, "Self-mummified Buddhas in Japan," *History of Religions* 1:2 (1961)
Ling, T.O., "Councils," "Fasting, Fasts," and "Holy Days," in *A Dictionary of Buddhism*, New York: Charles Scribner's Sons, 1972

# Fasting: Eastern Christian

Fasting plays a vital role in the spiritual life of all members of the Eastern Christian Churches – monks and nuns, clergy, and laity alike. Fasting is almost the same throughout the year for monastics and laity, except that laity fast on all ordinary Wednesdays and Fridays, whereas monks and nuns include Mondays as well. Technically, fasting on these days means abstinence from all meat, meat and dairy products (lard, eggs, butter, milk, and cheese), fish (other than shellfish), olive oil, and alcoholic beverages. It also means that the amount of food should be moderated and that no food should be eaten between meals. Many individuals eat only one meal on a fast day. Other fast days in the Byzantine tradition to which these limitations apply are the following: the Eve of the Feast of the Lord's Nativity (new calendar, 24 December; old calendar, 6 January), the Eve of Theophany (5 and 18 January), the Feast of the Beheading of St. John the Baptist (29 August and 11 September), and the Feast of the Exaltation of the Cross (14 and 27 September).

The guidelines vary for special fasting seasons. For the Advent, or Nativity, Fast (15 and 28 November, 24 December, and 6 January) and the Apostles' Fast (Monday after All Saints Day to 29 June and 6 January), Wednesdays and Fridays are strict fasts, as usual. For the other days of the week, no meat or meat and dairy products are permitted, although fish, wine, and olive oil are. Abstinence becomes stricter in the last weeks of the Nativity Fast. Fish is not permitted, and olive oil and wine are permitted only on Saturdays and Sundays. During the Dormition Fast (August 1–14 and 14–27) no meat, meat or dairy products, fish (except shellfish), olive oil, or wine are permitted. On the Feast of the Transfiguration, which occurs during this fast, fish, wine, and oil are permitted; if the Dormition Feast falls on a Wednesday or Friday, fish, wine, and oil may be used for those days, but meat and meat and dairy products are not permitted.

A fourfold pattern emerges during the Great Lenten Fast before Pascha or Easter (a moveable feast): Meat-Fare Week, in which only wine and oil are prohibited on Wednesday and Friday; Cheese-Fare Week, in which all meat and meat products are prohibited; Great Lent (four weeks from the Sunday of Orthodoxy to Lazarus Saturday); and Holy Week (from Palm Sunday on). Both Great Lent and Holy Week are strict fast periods. Eating is done in great moderation, and all meat, meat and dairy products, fish, olive oil, and wine are omitted from the diet. The first week of Lent and Holy Week are especially restrictive periods. Wine and oil are permitted on all Saturdays and Sundays except Holy Saturday, which is considered a very strict fast day. Other exceptions include the Feasts of the Annunciation, which fall during Great Lent, and Palm Sunday. Wine and oil are permitted on the Forefeast and the Leavetaking of the Annunciation to the Most-Holy Theotokos, whereas fish, wine, and oil are permitted on the day of the Annunciation and on Palm Sunday.

In addition, food is completely abstained from before receiving Holy Communion, at least from the previous midnight onward. On days when the Pre-Sanctified Liturgy is offered in the evening, the allowance is often made for individuals to abstain beginning at noon. Allowances for fasting in general are made for health and other justifiable reasons. Several of the early monastic rules indicate that exceptions were always made for the less able, and in general fasting tended to be simpler than in later times. According to rule 5 of St. Pachomius (c. 290–346), sick monks were allowed to have as much food as they needed. On the other hand, the healthy monks abstained on Wednesdays and Fridays and during the Passover and the 50 days of Eastertide. On all other days a common table was set at noon and again at dinnertime for the tired, the old, the very young, and those suffering from the extreme desert heat. Some chose to eat at both meals, some only at one, and others took only a little bread for their sustenance. Also, those who did not wish to partake at the common table could receive bread, water, and salt in their cells on a daily basis or every other day, as they chose. The shorter rules of Basil the Great (c. 330–379) also counsel moderation, saying that excessive fasting endangers the ability to work. Therefore, fasting and eating must be done according to the dictates of piety and according to God's commandments to serve his glory. Fasting and eating are for sustenance, never to surfeit, so that one can be God's servant.

The foregoing is an overview of the guidelines of fasting in the Byzantine tradition. The Armenian, Coptic, Ethiopian, and East and West Syrian traditions are similar but also include a pre-Lenten Fast of Nineveh and exclude other days. In all the Eastern Christian traditions, it is essential to understand that fasting from food and drink is not a self-contained, rule-bound entity unto itself. As Bishop Kallistos (Ware) points out, "The tendency to over-emphasize external rules about food in a legalistic way, and the opposite tendency to scorn these rules as outdated and unnecessary, are both alike to be deplored as a betrayal of true Orthodoxy. In both cases the proper balance between the outward and the inward has been impaired" (Ware, 1984). Rather, fasting is an ascetic tool – a way to train and discipline the body – with the aim to bring one closer to God. One fasts not only with the stomach but also with the whole body. Above all, one must fast from sin.

Some of the temptations that the Fathers warn against include vanity, for which fasting is done to please men and self rather than God (Basil the Great, Diadokos, and others). Maximos the Confessor (c. 580–662) counsels that fasting must be integrally connected with prayer and almsgiving because fasting weakens sensual desire, whereas almsgiving soothes the soul's inflamed disposition, and prayer purifies the intellect and enables contemplation. John Climacus (c. 570–649) says that fasting must be coupled with obedience because fasting begins the process of sensuality's destruction, whereas obedience completes it through humility. Ephrem the Syrian (c. 306–373) commends fasting with the mouth and heart so that, while abstaining, one does not indulge in what is destructive to the self. He also recommends Scripture as a guide to judge which fast reconciles one to God and which one angers Him. True prayer can also be judged this way. Isaac of Nineveh (d. c. 700) also couples prayer with fasting, saying that fasting is the father of prayer when fasting is accomplished through discernment. Diadokos of Photiki (c. 400–c. 486) reminds us that fasting is about self-control and humility and exhorts against despising food, as self-control rather than food is the real issue. He recommends moderation in fasting as well as eating because excessive fasting causes dejection and distraction. Mark the Hermit (d. c. 430), in his little treatise *On Fasting* (unavailable in English), warns against taking pride in accomplishments of self-restraint because if a man truly knows himself, he will know how little he knows. Until a man knows himself, he cannot attain the knowledge of God. Finally, John Chrysostom (c. 347–407), in his sermon on fasting, warns us that the importance of fasting is not only giving up food but also stopping sinful practices. Fasting is devalued by abstaining only from food. If a person is in need, help him; if you are tempted to jealousy, abstain from it. More than only the mouth, the true fast involves the eyes, ears, feet, hands, and whole body. Abstain from greed (hands); avoid unnecessary pleasures (feet); do not behold what is forbidden (eyes); avoid the lewd, evil, and false talk of others (ears); and, beyond abstaining from food, avoid foul language and telling lies about others (mouth). He concludes with this question: what is the purpose of abstaining from flesh meats when "you bite and devour your fellow man?"

MICHAEL D. PETERSON

*See also* Asceticism: Christian Perspectives; Basil the Great, St.; Cathars; Climacus, John, St.; Food: Christian Perspectives; Hermits: Eastern Christian; Isaac the Syrian (Isaac of Nineveh), St.; Maximus the Greek, St.; Office, Daily: Eastern Christian; Orthodox Monasticism: Byzantine; Pachomius, St.

## Further Reading

Berzonsky, Vladimir, "What Fasting Is and Is Not," *Sourozh* 44 (June 1991)

Dura, Ioan, "The Canons of the Sixth Ecumenical Synod Concerning Fasting and Their Application to the Present Needs of the Orthodox Faithful," *Greek Orthodox Theological Review* 40 (Spring-Summer 1995)

Grimm, Veronika, *From Feasting to Fasting: The Evolution of a Sin: Attitudes to Food in Late Antiquity*, London and New York: Routledge, 1996

Musurillo, Herbert, "The Problem of Ascetical Fasting in the Greek Patristic Writers," *Traditio: Studies in Ancient and Medieval History, Thought and Religion* 12 (1956)

Sophrony, Archimandrite, "Principles of Orthodox Asceticism,"
in *The Orthodox Ethos: Essays in Honor of the Centenary
of the Greek Orthodox Archdiocese of North America*,
edited by Angelos J. Philippou, Oxford: Holywell Press,
1964
Theodore the Studite, "On Fasting and Dispassion," translated
by Archimandrite Ephrem, *Sourozh* 47 (1992)
Vellian, Jacob, "Lenten Fast of the East Syrians," in *A Tribute
to Arthur Vööbus: Studies in Early Christian Literature and
Its Environment, Primarily in the Syrian East*, edited by
Robert H. Fischer, Chicago: Lutheran School of Theology at
Chicago, 1977
Ware, Kallistos, "The Meaning of the Great Fast," in *The
Lenten Triodion*, translated from the original Greek by
Mother Mary and Kallistos Ware, London and Boston:
Faber and Faber, 1984
"When We Fast: An Orthodox Perspective," *One World* 121
(December 1986)

# Fasting: Western Christian

Monastic fasting must be seen as a variant and development of
fasting within Christianity as a whole. Thus, one must begin
with the Scriptures, for fasting continually understood itself by
reference to them – and a few notable texts – as both its justification and its explanation. In texts such as 1 Samuel 31:13, fasting is a basic expression of mourning after a death, and this
mutated into the ascetic notion of mourning after one's own or
others' sins. Fasting also expresses repentance after sin as an attempt "to repay the cost" and repair the damage of sin, and although many passages were cited, Joel 1:14 was that most often
recalled liturgically. In such cases fasting was seen as a way of
averting divine punishment. By extension this was seen to link
fasting and prayer (e.g., Ps. 35:13), by which fasting added force
to petitions by showing one's seriousness. Thus, public fasts
were a means by which the community sought God's help and
deliverance (e.g., Judg. 20:26). However, the most striking fast
was as a preparation for entering into the presence of God in
order to receive revelation: thus, Moses' fast of 40 days and 40
nights (Exod. 34:28) was seen to prefigure both Christ's fast
(Matt. 4:2) and the fasts of those who would enter into a closer
relationship with God. Thus, there was a similar fast before bap-
tism/Easter (which was recalled each year by Lent), and the ability to fast was a prerequisite of a monastic vocation (*Historia
Lausiaca* 18.13).

Jesus himself seems to have taken a casual attitude to fasting
(see Mark 2:18), but from the start the Church saw regular fasting as part of its prayer and discipline. In the *Didache* (mid first
century), it is accepted that Christians fast twice weekly, and the
practice is justified by the notion that Jesus condemned hypocritical fasting (8.1). This theme is found in a more developed form
in Matthew 6:16–18, where true piety consists in almsgiving,
prayer, and fasting, which is done not "as with the hypocrites"
to gain admiration but rather is witnessed only by God. Chris-

Interior of refectory, St. Bavo's Abbey (Benedictine), Ghent, Belgium,
12th century. Tombstones are visible on the floor.
Photo courtesy of Chris Schabel

tian writers developed this notion of three interlocked ascetic
practices (prayer, fasting, and alms) as the key to holiness, and
early monasticism simply expanded on this by seeing them as the
foundations for a whole lifestyle.

Athanasius (c. 296–373) said that studying Antony's life was
a guide to monastic asceticism (*Vita*, preface), and accordingly
fasting is shown as a special part of his life and that of his disciples, for one of the abbot's duties was to watch over the monks'
fasts (chap. 4). However, whereas in the *Vita* we see the earlier
Christian theme of fasting linked with prayer (chaps. 5, 40), we
also find a new note of suspicion of matter as inducing spiritual
weakness and a loss of self-control. Thus, the enjoyment of food
becomes a demonic snare against which Antony (c. 251–356)
fortifies his body by fasting (chap. 5) and thus gains greater self-
control by making himself less susceptible to bodily pleasure
(chap. 7); and, as the monk is the latter-day martyr, so fasting is
part of his continual daily martyrdom (chap. 47). The notion of
the clash of the monk and the demons runs throughout this influential text – presented as patterned on Christ's fast in the

**Refectory, Cistercian abbey at Maulbronn, Baden-Württemberg, Germany, 13th century.**
**Photo courtesy of Chris Schabel**

wilderness when he was tempted when hungry (Matt. 4:1–11) – and fasting lures both the demons and Satan himself to come and torment the saint. However, having brought about the engagement, Antony conquers them through prayer (chap. 40). Fasting is not only a shield (chap. 5) but also a weapon against the demons who fear it as bringing them destruction (chap. 30). These themes resurface in the *Historia Lausiaca* (c. 419) and Jerome's vitae and through them became an integral part of monastic teaching and self-understanding. Thus, the additional monastic fasts came to be seen as a distinctive mark of holiness.

Although the twin themes of fasting as assisting self-control and matter as a distraction to the spirit were found in Athanasius, it was from John Cassian (c. 360–after 430) that they received their theoretical expression. His writings present the fullest treatment of fasting and were looked to as basic teaching until modern times. Although he was anxious to distinguish monastic fasting from the rejection of matter as evil and from the practices among non-Christian philosophical cults (*Conlationes* 21.13–14), he de facto adopted many of their ideas. Moreover he took over from Greek medical theory the notion of "contraries healed by contraries" and within this framework presented fasting as the contrary remedy not only to gluttony but to other bodily indulgences as well, for Christ's desert fast showed that those faults could be overcome (*Conlationes* 5.4–5).

Thus, fasting became a medicine for a range of sins, distractions, and temptations; and, developing on the notion of fasting as a weapon and a form of petition, this medicine not only repaired past damage but also inoculated for the future. Thus, gluttony was one of the "eight principal vices," and the appropriate balance came from fasting, which cured the vice, let its damage become visible to the sinner, and strengthened him for the future (*Instituta* 5; *Conlationes* 5.4). However, Cassian was concerned that fasting might become an end in itself (*Conlatio* 21.13) or a vice through wrong intention (*Conlatio* 16.19) or so excessive that it produced harm (*Conlationes* 2.17, 21.18); thus, it needed to be seen simply as a tool (*Conlationes* 21.14, 21.17), one to be used wisely as part of an overall asceticism. Cassian also provides important information about the regulation of fasting, its links with the liturgy, and differences in practice emerging between East and West (*Instituta* 3.9; *Conlationes* 21.11, 19–36). However, one effect of Cassian's work was to emphasize the link between fasting and reparation after sin through the use of penitential books, and this eventually led to a general understanding of fasting mainly as a penitential discipline.

THOMAS O'LOUGHLIN

*See also* Antony, St.; Asceticism: Christian Perspectives; Cassian, John; Food: Christian Perspectives; Holy Men/Holy Women:

Refectory, Abbey of Saint-Jean-des-Vignes (Benedictine), Soissons, 13th century.
Photo courtesy of Chris Schabel

Christian Perspectives; Penitential Books; Prayer: Christian Perspectives

### Further Reading

McNeill, John T., "Medicine for Sin as Prescribed in the Penitentials," *Church History* 1 (1932)
Stewart, Columba, *Cassian the Monk* (Oxford Studies in Historical Theology), New York: Oxford University Press, 1998

# Festivals, Buddhist

Often centered around a monastery or shrine, festivals (*pūjās*) are occasions for Buddhist communities to affirm their group identity and faith while enjoying the merriment of parades, talent competitions, dancing, and feasting. Buddhists might set out on great pilgrimages to participate in these collective rituals that remember the anniversary of a specific event and reenact the legends and myths of Buddhist culture. During the festivities special merit can be accrued by lay attendees through acts of devotion, such as giving offerings to monks and nuns, prostrating, reciting prayers, or living as a monastic for that day. Some of the most delicious meals of the year are served at these events; dishes include the thick Chinese New Year's porridge called Laba and the Tibetan Zho curds served to monks after their summer retreat. Other common elements in Buddhist festivals are lights and water, processions of a sacred object (such as a Buddha image or relic), and the oration of a sermon particular to that occasion. Being transitional moments that seal off the past and give birth to new beginnings, festivals regularize the opportunity for both monastic and lay Buddhists to review their values and spiritual commitments and to learn more about the history and teachings of their religion.

Festivals order time and integrate human life with the passing seasons. Although many Asian countries have recently adopted the Western Gregorian calendar, most Buddhist festivals are based on lunar calendars, with the new moon marking the beginning of every month. In addition to lunar and Gregorian calendar systems, timetables vary further among nations. For example, Tibetan and Chinese Buddhists adhere to a hexagenary (60-year) cycle, wherein each year represents the combination of an animal and an element. Most Southeast Asian countries, including Sri Lanka and Nepal, rely on a solar calendar originating in India. Theravāda Buddhists also recognize a Buddhist Era–dating system that traces back to the Buddha's death around the fifth century B.C. On the basis of this chronology, the New Year festival for the 2,500th year B.E. took place in 1956. The complexity of these calendaring systems can be witnessed in places such as Nepal, where calendars are commonly constructed with all three manners of dating. As a result of these different styles of measuring time, diverse communities of Buddhists might observe the same festival on different occasions. For example, in Southeast Asia the New Year festival takes place in either April or December, whereas in China and Tibet it is dated according to a lunar calendar, occurring in China on the new moon in late January or early February and in Tibet on the new moon in late February. Although New Year festivals, such as those of harvest time, are not strictly Buddhist in nature, Buddhists often incorporate religious elements into this celebration, and the rituals of any New Year's gathering, although culturally specific, will commonly be led by a monk or a nun. This is especially noticeable when the government is nominally Buddhist, as in Thailand and in the former nation of Tibet, where New Year ceremonies would traditionally involve a rededication of the country to Buddhism.

Monastic calendars are traditionally structured by two regular elements: the four sacred *uposatha* (Sinhalese, *poya*) days per month, which fall on the new, full, and quarter moons, and the annual monsoon rains retreat (*varṣāvāsana*; Pāli, *vassa*). Originally the *uposatha* days, held on the new and full moons, were occasions for monastics to gather together and confess any digressions from the monastic code of discipline (vinaya). This tradition is not strictly observed in modern times, but the *uposatha*s, comparable to the Christian Sunday, are still considered to be the most sacred days of the week, and it is common for lay Buddhists to observe the lifestyle of a monastic during such days. Most Buddhist festivals, with the exception of New Year's events, are held on *uposatha* days, especially on the most auspicious full-moon day (*purnima*), and among Indian and Southeast Asian Buddhists festivals are often named after the lunar month in which that full moon is couched.

Although parallels to the rains retreat exist in regions that have no monsoons, such as the Tibetan summer retreat (dbyar gnes), this tradition and the rites that accompany it are most emphasized among Theravāda communities in southern and Southeast Asia, where the rains generally extend from July to October. Some Buddhists hold celebrations at the beginning of the retreat, such as the Thai festival known as Khao Pansa, during which the monastics are presented with practical requisites for the retreat. Especially popular in the northeastern Thai cities of Ubon and Ratchathani are the elaborate candle competitions held during Pansa, when large floats bearing these wax sculptures of Buddhist imagery are led through town and offered to the monasteries. On the last full moon of the retreat in October, a festival takes place honoring the anniversary of Buddha's descent from heaven, where he once spent a rainy season teaching his mother. This occasion is known as Lhabap Tüchen (hla babs dus chen) in Tibet and as Thadinjut in Burma, where great light displays are held in remembrance of the heavenly torches that lit his way home. The Kaṭhina festival that celebrates the formal ending (*pavāraṇā*) of this retreat is held within the next month and marks the greatest merit-making day of the year for lay Buddhists. During this occasion monks and nuns who have successfully completed this contemplation time are presented by the laity with new robes (*kaṭhina*). In Thailand the robes are patched together from old cloth and disinfected with plant and tree-bark extracts, resulting in a dye ranging from yellow to brown, and in Burma it is traditional for young girls to weave the robes together. Most often the *kaṭhina* are carried to the monastery in elaborate processions, accompanied by paper-money trees, drummers, dancers, and offerings of new bowls and food.

Perhaps the most celebrated festival throughout the Buddhist world is Vaishākha Purnima (Sinhalese, Wesak), also known as Buddha Jayanti, which celebrates the life and enlightenment of the historical Buddha, Śākyamuni. However, differences exist regarding the emphases and dates of this festival among denominations. For example, for Theravāda Buddhists it commemorates his birth, enlightenment, and death into final nirvāṇa, whereas Chinese Buddhists emphasize his birth, and in Japan separate celebrations are held for his birth, Buddha Day, or Flower Festival (Hanamatsuri), and his death, Nirvāṇa Day (Nehan E). Known in Burma as Kahsoung and in Tibet as Saga Dawa (Sa ga zla ba), this event occurs in most places on the full moon of the second lunar month of Vaishākha, usually falling in late May or early June. The Nepalese Newar Buddhists embrace

A monk performing a 'cham dance at Phyang Monastery, Ladakh, India, during a summer festival.
Photo courtesy of John Powers

both the Vaishākha festival as inherited from a modernist Theravāda movement and a month-long Guṃlā celebration during late August or early September that commemorates the same events. A great deal of local variation colors these events, as, for example, the vehicles used to process a Buddha image, such as the elephant used in Bodhnath, Nepal. In addition to these differences, it is typical on this day for Buddhists to bathe a Buddha image and to water a Bodhi tree, the type of banyan tree under which the Buddha awakened. Temples, monasteries, and shrines are decorated with garlands, balloons, and paper lanterns or oil lamps, a reminder of the Buddha's enlightenment. Popular sites for this festival are the Indian cities of Lumbini, where the Buddha was born; Bodh Gayā, where he was enlightened; and

Kushinagara, where he died, although many other locations are sought out on this day, such as the stūpas in Anurādhapura, Sri Lanka, and Kathmandu, Nepal. Some Buddhists also commemorate his cremation, such as those from Thailand who hold a festival eight days after Vaishākha that is known as Wan Atthami, during which robed monastics lead candle-lit processions like strings of prayer beads around their shrines.

Although no festival commemorating events in the Buddha's life is canonically prescribed, Buddhists honor many such anniversaries with celebration. For example, festivals are held to commemorate the Buddha's first sermon on the Four Noble Truths, at which a group of five ascetics became his first followers. This event is thus recognized as the birth of the Buddhist order (sangha) and the first turning of the wheel of the doctrine (dharmacakra). In India, where it also signifies the Buddha's first renunciation of household life, this festival falls on the full moon of the fourth lunar month of Ashadi (Pāli, Asala), corresponding to late July, and is thus known as Ashadi Purnima. The city of Sārnāth near Benares, India, having been the area of this first sermon, is the most bustling location in India for the Ashadi festival. For Tibetan Buddhists, who call it Chökhor (chos 'khor) or Trugpa Tsezhi (drug pa tshes bzhi), this occasion is held about the same time of the year but takes place on the fourth day of the sixth lunar month according to Tibetan calendars. The format for this event is similar to that of Vaishākha, with many processions and offerings given to monastics, such as scarves, food, lit wicks, and oil or butter for lamps. A similar celebration takes place on the full moon of late February, known in Thailand as Maka Bucha, which remembers the Buddha's last sermon to a spontaneous gathering of 1,250 disciples, an event also known as the Four Miracles Assembly. Maka Bucha is the largest festival of lights in northern Thailand and Laos.

Great diversity exists among the many local festivals that adorn the Buddhist calendar. In southern and Southeast Asia, these occasions are mainly Theravāda in nature. In Sri Lanka the holiday named Poson honors the advent of Buddhism on the island when Mahinda, the son of Emperor Aśoka, arrived and converted Sri Lanka's king. Falling on the full moon of the third lunar month, usually in June or July, Buddhist monastics all over Sri Lanka lead processions of Mahinda's image on this day. A festival honoring the arrival of Sanghamitta, Mahinda's sister, who began the order of nuns in Sri Lanka, is held in the full moon of late December. One is also held in September at Mahinyangana, commemorating the anniversary of the Buddha's three visits to Sri Lanka. In late July or early August is a large celebration known as Asala Perahara, during which the Buddha's tooth relic is paraded through the city of Kandy. Although this event is led mainly by lay Buddhists, monks might be present as observers. Veneration of relics is also the theme of an annual fair held during the November full moon by the temple Wat Sraket at the Golden Mount in Bangkok. During October Thai Buddhists celebrate Chak Phra, the pulling of the Buddha image, which is an especially elaborate occasion in the city of Surat Thani, where the image is mounted on a decorative barge

designed as a water serpent (nāga) and floated down the Tapi River. At the dawn of April rains, water splashing and boat racing are found at the Songkran festival throughout Thailand, when everyone wants to sprinkle a monastic with perfumed water.

In the mainly Mahāyāna countries of eastern Asia, the popular Ghost Festival, known in Chinese as Yulanpen or Zhong Yuan, in Korean as Manghon Il, and in Japanese as Obon, is held at the end of the summer retreat in August. Characterized by offerings of food and scripture-recitation made to deceased relatives and hungry ghosts (pretas; Chinese, egui), this occasion is nominally Buddhist but largely coextensive with local spiritualism and indigenous traditions such as Daoism. For seven days honoring one's ancestors is the theme, as both monastic and lay Buddhists enjoy reenactments of the adventures of Mulian, who journeyed through the afterworlds in search of saving his deceased mother from hell. Elements of this festival can be witnessed in nearly all countries with Chinese influence, such as the Sembahjang Hantu ritual in Java and the Pudu ceremony in Hawaii.

Vajrayāna Buddhists from places such as Tibet, Nepal, Bhutan, and Mongolia also observe their own unique anniversaries, such as the death of the Gelukpa leader Tsongkhapa in November. During the first month of the New Year, a festival instituted by Tsongkhapa in 1409, known as the Great Prayer or Mönlam Chenmo (smon lam chen mo), is held. Unique to Tibetan celebrations are the elaborate butter sculpture offerings, which are very tall, intricate appliqué designs held by scaffolding frames. Also unique are the Tibetan ritual dances known as Cham ('chams) and the dancers' masks ('bag). Before Communist occupation, the capital city of Lhasa was a popular site of pilgrimage for celebrations, but today most Tibetan Buddhist festivals are observed only by exiled Tibetans in other parts the world.

TALINE GOORJIAN

See also Bodh Gayā, India; China; Examinations, Theravādin; Japan; Korea: Sites; Liturgy: Buddhist; Nepal; Novices, Theravādin Rituals for; Pilgrimages, Buddhist; Sri Lanka; Thailand; Tibet; Timekeeping: Buddhist Perspectives

## Further Reading

Anderson, Mary M., *The Festivals of Nepal*, London: Allen and Unwin, 1971

Gerson, Ruth, *Traditional Festivals in Thailand*, Kuala Lumpur and New York: Oxford University Press, 1996

Gombrich, Richard, "Buddhist Festivals," in *Festivals in World Religions*, edited by Alan Brown, London and New York: Longman, 1986

Jinaratana, Neluwe, "Buddhist Festivals," in *A Panorama of Indian Buddhism: Selections from the Maha Bodhi Journal, 1892–1992*, edited by D.C. Ahir, Delhi: Sri Satguru, 1995

Kapstein, Matthew T., "A Pilgrimage of Rebirth Reborn: The 1992 Celebration of Drigung Powa Chenmo," in *Buddhism in Contemporary Tibet: Religious Revival and Cultural Identity*, edited by Melvyn C. Goldstein and Matthew T. Kapstein, Berkeley: University of California Press, 1998

Lewis, Todd T., "Contributions to the Study of Popular Buddhism: The Newar Buddhist Festival of Guṃlā Dharma," *Journal of the International Association of Buddhist Studies* 16:2 (1993)

Nash, Manning, "Ritual and Ceremonial Cycle in Upper Burma," in *Anthropological Studies in Theravāda Buddhism*, New Haven, Connecticut: Yale University, 1966

Richardson, Hugh, *Ceremonies of the Lhasa Year*, London: Serindia, 1993

Teiser, Stephen F., *The Ghost Festival in Medieval China*, Princeton, New Jersey: Princeton University Press, 1988

## Related Web Sites

*http://library.advanced.org/10131/ladakh_fairsandfestivals.html*
*http://www.buddhanet.net/festival.htm*

# Fishing and Fish Culture, Western Christian

The Western tradition of Christian asceticism accepted consumption of fish in place of animal flesh; the Eastern monastic tradition did not. Thus, the modern imagination peculiarly associates medieval Western monks with the eating, catching, and rearing of fish. Historical evidence replaces simple hyperbole with more complex realities: fish often had greater importance in religious diets than in those of the laity; yet, despite greater historical continuity of monastic estates, monks and nuns exploited their local wild and artificial fisheries in much the same way as lay contemporaries.

Early Christians associated fish with the purifying element water and with the Greek anagram ΙΧΘΎΩΣ for Christ. Late Roman churchmen set historically formative models for eating fish. Benedict of Nursia (c. 480–550), whose Rule (c. 540) adjusted fierce Eastern asceticism to a harsher Western environment, forbade (chaps. 36 and 39) healthy monks from eating the flesh of quadrupeds ("meat"). Benedict's silence regarding fish let monastics substitute it for the prohibited "flesh." When the learned senatorial politician Cassiodorus (485–580) entered monastic retirement at his family estate of Vivarium on Italy's southern coast, his community enjoyed the fish from natural rocky coves that had been modified to keep local catches alive. Isidore of Seville (c. 560–636) justified such practices on grounds of the purity of fish, creatures that contemporaries believed reproduced without sexual congress. Later authorities reiterated Isidore's reasoning to explain both the prominence of fish in monastic diets and the general Western practice of consuming fish during meatless Friday and Lenten "fasts." Still ideology and custom permitted rather than required monks and pious laity to eat fish.

Fragmentary and incidental reports indicate the real, if bounded, interest of early medieval ascetics in catching, storing,

and eating fish. Gregory of Tours (538/39–594) tells that a sixth-century recluse in Auvergne, St. Caluppa, occasionally fished for his own food, whereupon God saw to it that the fish came straight to him. In the 740s Frankish strongman Pepin the Short (747–768) gave the abbey of Flavigny a fishery on the Saône River in return for daily recitation of a psalm. Contemporaries also connected the mid-eighth-century foundation of an abbey on the Bavarian alpine lake Tegernsee to the familiarity of its noble Franco-Bavarian founders with the rich fishery there. Such acts confirm not only a link between monasteries and fish supplies but also lay use of these resources. Early medieval and Carolingian monks stood out more for avoiding meat than for consuming fish. Indeed Carolingian and Anglo-Saxon monastic legislation is noteworthy more for nutritionally unbalanced emphasis on vegetable foods, mainly bread and beans, than for frequent rations of fish. Nevertheless ninth-century Bobbio and Prüm had rich fisheries worked by their subjects on Lake Garda and the Moselle and Meuse Rivers, respectively.

During the central Middle Ages, monastic reforms ascribed greater value to fish in the diet, especially if reluctant monks were to be won away from the meat-rich tastes of the lay elite. Tenth-century reformers Olpert of Gembloux and Odo of Cluny (c. 879–942) each reportedly arranged a small artificial pond beside the house so that their monks' grudging acquiescence in dietary abstinence could be reinforced with a constant supply of fresh fish. Most fishes that arrived in measured portions several times a week on Cluniac tables were caught from natural local waters by lay fishers subject to the abbey; a few types (squid and herring) came salted and barreled from the far-distant sea. Store ponds at Cluny, which reared no fish during its 11th-century apogee of prestige, were located along the Grosne River with easy access to the fish kitchen. Artificial tanks measuring hundreds of square yards for live storage of fish are typical of medieval monastic sites from Spain and Italy to England and Poland. The architecture at the fishpond of Kremsmünster is renowned. Abbots and their communities struggled with lay neighbors to control the rich fisheries associated with weirs and mill dams, where migratory varieties, such as salmon, eel, shad, and sturgeon, concentrated for easy capture.

A second wave of reformers, notably Cistercians and Carthusians, turned in disgust against the pseudo-ascetic luxury of monks whose rich meals of fish followed the letter but not the spirit of the Rule. A 12th-century tale jibed that on Judgment Day St. Benedict would recognize his true sons, the Cistercians, from their bellies full of beans and vegetables while repudiating the salmon- and pike-stuffed Benedictines. Indeed despite later myth early Cistercians ate little if any expensive fish, and it was generations, even centuries, before some of their characteristic valley sites became artificial fish farms. Twelfth- and 13th-century rations document the slow entry of fish into the diet as treats ("pittances") that benefactors endowed for special occasions. Fishing most often gets mentioned in early Cistercian charters when a lay seigneur granted sharply limited rights of use on waters that he owned – such as Clairvaux received from the

Bartolomeo Carlone and Jakob Prandtauer, Baroque Fish Pond (Fischbehalter), Stift Kremsmünster (Benedictine), Upper Austria, 1692–1717.
Photo courtesy of the Austrian National Tourist Office

lord of Joinville on the Marne River in 1216 – or as one of the legal appurtenances included in a grant of land and lordship – as Zarnowiec convent, founded in 1248, received over its own Pomeranian lake and river flowing into the nearby Baltic. Czech and Polish princes also gave monasteries entire existing communities of fishers whose dues in kind would now supply the monks or nuns, and the lord of Joinville made very plain that the privileges of Clairvaux did not extend to his own artificial fishponds. Neither fishing nor fish culture was peculiar to monastic institutions in medieval Europe.

By the High and later Middle Ages, some monasteries controlled large natural fisheries. Five of Tintern Abbey's manors operated weirs to catch salmon and eel as well as bank and stream nets on the Severn. Tegernsee owned many nets and traps on its lake in 1023 and in the 13th century received dues in fish from some tenants. From at the latest the 1440s until it was secularized in 1803, Tegernsee employed seven to nine full-time fishers. By around 1200 Cistercian houses in northwestern Spain owned boats to fish sardines in local estuaries as well as facilities to process the catch. Although many houses finally gave up direct operation and leased their fisheries to professionals, monastic communities retained such interest in fishing that they are a principal source for early written information and eventually for

Europe's first full-fledged instructional manuals on how to catch fish.

European transition from store ponds to fully artificial fish farms probably first occurred in early 12th-century France. There spread across later medieval Europe a sophisticated technology for manipulation of water in numerous and sometimes very large artificial ponds and of specially chosen fish – since the 13th century mainly exotic carp (*Cyprinus carpio*) originating from the lower Danube. Although in most regions monastic landowners took an active part, their practices did not differ much from those of their lay neighbors. Yet over time the greater stability and durability of monastic estates enabled them to build capital infrastructure and keep it going, so that in places without easy access to marine fishes some houses developed major fish-farming enterprises. By around 1200 Chaalis in Valois had more than ten ponds covering more than 38 hectares at the abbey site and further areas underwater at granges on the Thîeve River. Still in operation in the 14th century, the enterprise fell into disuse before 1700. Heilsbronn near Nürnberg in Franconia began acquiring existing ponds during the late 13th century – more than 100 years after its foundation – and was artificially stocking small fish by 1340. When secularized early in the Reformation, Heilsbronn ran a total of 72 large and small ponds. In

Bartolomeo Carlone and Jakob Prandtauer, Baroque Fish Pond (Fischbehalter), Stift Kremsmünster (Benedictine), Upper Austria, 1692–1717.
Photo courtesy of the Austrian National Tourist Office

Yorkshire the Cistercians at Byland built ponds covering more than 25 hectares during two major campaigns of the 1150s to 1170s and the 1220s to 1230s. Few English monasteries operated ponds large enough to serve domestic needs, much less to permit important sales of fish. As English marine fisheries grew to supply even inland consumers, monastic ponds there fell into disuse. However, Continental houses, like their lay neighbors, could and did run very large enterprises that yielded major incomes. Zwettl, a Cistercian community in northern Lower Austria, continues to rear and market carp, trout, and other fishes today.

As the Middle Ages drew to a close, Church officials more willingly sanctioned the bending, although not the complete abandoning, of monastic dietary rules. For example, for two generations preceding the dissolution of Westminster Abbey only half the resident brethren had to dine in the refectory according to the letter of the Rule, consuming a tasty variety of sea fishes bought on the London market. Others ate meat with impunity in the infirmary or under some constraint in a "misericord" located both physically and ideologically halfway between infirmary and refectory. Monks at 16th-century Tegernsee, who enjoyed the fine fishes of their alpine location, refused ducal and even papal offers of similar relaxation of the Rule. Having recovered from religious and political revolt, monks in the old Benedictine house at Ename in 17th-century Flanders ate freshwater fishes reared artificially or caught from the Scheldt by their own employees and, as they had since the 1300s, marine varieties that officials bought at neighboring Oudenaarde.

RICHARD C. HOFFMANN

*See also* Austria; Benedict of Nursia, St.; Bobbio, Italy; Carthusians; Cistercians; Cluniacs; Cluny, France; Fasting: Western Christian; Food: Christian Perspectives; Regulations: Christian Perspectives; Seasons, Liturgical: Western Christian

## Further Reading

Benoit, Paul, and Monique Wabont, "Mittelalterliche Wasserversorgung in Frankreich: Eine Fallstudie: Die Zisterzienser," in *Die Wasserversorgung im Mittelalter*, edited by Klaus Grewe, Mainz: Phillipp von Zabern, 1991

Blary, François, *Le domaine de Chaalis, XIIe–XIVe siècles: Approches archéologiques des établissements agricoles et industriels d'une abbaye cistercienne*, Paris: Éditions du CTHS, 1989

Bond, C.J., "Monastic Fisheries," in *Medieval Fish, Fisheries and Fishponds in England*, 2 vols., edited by Michael Aston, Oxford: BAR, 1988

Currie, Christopher K., "The Role of Fishponds in the Monastic Economy," in *The Archaeology of Rural Monasteries*, edited by Roberta Gilchrist and Harold Mytum, Oxford: BAR, 1989

Hoffmann, Richard C., "Medieval Cistercian Fisheries, Natural and Artificial," in *L'espace cistercien*, edited by Léon Pressouyre, Paris: Ministère de l'Enseignement supérieur et de la Recherche, Comité des travaux historiques et scientifiques, 1994

Hoffmann, Richard C., *Fishers' Craft and Lettered Art: Tracts on Fishing from the End of the Middle Ages*, Toronto and Buffalo, New York: University of Toronto Press, 1997

McDonnell, J., *Inland Fisheries in Medieval Yorkshire, 1066–1300*, York: Borthwick Institute of Historical Research, University of York, 1981

Rosenlund, Knud, "The Fish-Bone Material from a Medieval Danish Monastery and an 18th century Mission Station in Greenland – An Investigation of Materials with a Known Key," in *2èmes Rencontres d'archéo-ichtyologie*, edited by Nathalie Desse-Berset, Paris: Editions du CNRS, 1984

Seidenspinner, Wolfgang, "Das maulbronner Wassersystem - Relikt zisterziensischer Agrarwirtschaft und Wasserbautechnik im heutigen Landschaftsbild," *Denkmalpflege in Baden-Württemberg* 18 (1989)

Van Neer, Wim, and Anton Ervynck, "Food Rules and Status: Patterns of Fish Consumption in a Monastic Community (Ename, Belgium)," *Archaeofauna* 5 (1996)

Verdon, Jean, "Recherches sur la pêche et la pisciculture en occident durant le haut moyen age," in *Actes du 102e Congrès national des sociétés savantes (Limoges, 1977): Section d'archéologie et d'histoire de l'art: Le Limousin: Études Archéologiques*, Paris: SEVPEN, 1979

Zug Tucci, Hannelore, "Il mondo medievale dei pesci tra realta' e immaginazione," in *L'uomo di fronte al mondo animale nell'alto Medioevo*, 2 vols., Spoleto: Presso la sede del Centro Italiano, 1985

# Flagellation. *See* Self-Mutilation, Christian

# Florence, Italy

As a city more often identified with economic enterprise during the Middle Ages and with secular – even pagan – culture during the Renaissance, Florence might not evoke the history of monasticism in an obvious way. However, such an impression would be mistaken. The city's topography, and that of its hinterland, discloses a large number of monastic sites, many of which are now difficult to recognize because they were secularized in the late 18th and 19th centuries and turned over to other uses. For example, the Dominican church of S. Maria Novella is well known, as is its inner cloister (1350), the "Chiostro Verde," with its frescoes by Paolo Uccello (1396–1475) and others; few are aware that beyond there is a larger cloister, the "Chiostro Grande," now used as a police academy. Moreover the growth of traffic and the priorities of modern tourism have led visitors to neglect monastic establishments, especially in the suburbs.

Florence well reflects the history of the monastic orders. Benedictine foundations can be documented outside the city, at Ripoli, from the eighth century and, closer to the city center, at the Badia Fiorentina, the "abbey of Florence," from the tenth century. The Umiliati were established at Ognissanti in 1251, the Carmelites at S. Maria del Carmine in 1268, and the Carthusians outside the city at Galluzzo in 1341. The mendicant orders were quickly in place from the 13th century, with the Augustinians at S. Spirito, the Franciscans at S. Croce, and the Dominicans at S. Maria Novella. The Dominicans were later associated with a powerful Observationist movement, leading to the foundation of S. Domenico at Fiesole (1406) and S. Marco, taken over from the Silvestrine Order in 1437.

However, Florence's association with monastic reform dates from much earlier. Saint John Gualbert (S. Giovanni Gualberto, c. 990–1073), a Florentine monk at the Benedictine house of S. Miniato al Monte, became involved in wider movements for renewal in the Church and initiated a reformed Benedictinism at his retreat east of Florence at Vallombrosa around 1000. Further foundations were quickly established nearer the city, at S. Salvi (1048) and Passignano (1049). Another form of Benedictine reform influential in Florence was begun by a monk from Ravenna, St. Romuald (San Romualdo, c. 952–1027), who established a house at Camaldoli in the early 11th century; the monastery was then in the territory of Florence's neighbor, Arezzo, but from 1384 the area came under Florentine rule. The Order of Servites was founded by seven prominent Florentine citizens around 1240, with houses in both the country (Montesenario) and the city (Ss. Annunziata). The Florentine St. Philip Benizi (San Filippo Benizi, 1233–1285) helped establish the Servites in Tuscany and beyond. The Olivetani, whose order originated in the territory of Siena in the early 14th century, were established at S. Bartolomeo a Monte Oliveto in 1377. Indeed the frequency of local attempts at reform might explain why the Cluniac and Cistercian Orders remained marginal in the history of Florentine monasticism.

There are further indications of the strength of the monastic ideal in Florence. Orders of nuns were established, in the case of the Servites by S. Juliana (1270–1341), the niece of one of the Order's founders. The moral and spiritual preaching of the friars had a great appeal. From the 13th century lay confraternities were often associated with monastic houses, as with that dedicated to Mary and Agnes at the Carmine. Guilds extended patronage, as in the case of the woolen cloth manufacturers, the Arte della Lana, to the Franciscan hermitage of La Verna. The Orders also enjoyed the patronage of powerful local and regional families. In the 15th century the Medici were generous benefactors, especially of the Observant Dominicans at S. Marco and the Servites at Ss. Annunziata, and the tomb monuments and family chapels in such churches as S. Maria Novella, S. Croce, and the Badia Fiorentina reveal them to have become and remained pantheons to Florentine society.

Finally Florentine monasticism did not become atrophied, a point that can be better appreciated when religious art and architecture are seen in context, as expressions of piety and indicators of the vitality of the communities concerned. If major building work – cloisters, conventual buildings, bell towers, and churches – tended to be medieval or Renaissance in date, architectural and decorative schemes can often be traced, stretching from the Middle Ages to the 18th century, as at S. Maria del Carmine. During the Renaissance patrons engaged leading architects to work on monastic buildings, as Cosimo de' Medici did with Michelozzo (1396–1472) at S. Marco and Giovanni Rucellai with Alberti (1404–1472) at S. Maria Novella.

The cultural contributions of the monastic orders themselves remained considerable and would loom even larger if the study of sacred music in Florence were more advanced. The Camaldolese monk and prolific painter Lorenzo Monaco (c. 1370–1425) drew on a tradition of manuscript illuminating at S. Maria degli Angeli. The Dominican painters Fra Angelico (c. 1400–1455) and Fra Bartolomeo (c. 1475–1517) also worked beyond the confines of the cloister. Important libraries were accumulated, as at Vallombrosa and S. Marco, and if some figures such as the Dominicans Giovanni Dominici (1355–1419) and the Ferrarese friar Girolamo Savonarola (1452–1498) opposed the culture of the Renaissance, others could reconcile the new learning with the old, such as the Camaldolese Ambrogio Traversari (1386–1439) or the Dominican Antonio Pierozzi (St. Antonius, 1389–1459). The lay humanist scholar Cristoforo Landino (1424–1492) could set his Neoplatonic dialogue, the *Disputationes Camaldulenses* (1474), at the headquarters of the Dominican Order.

JOHN EASTON LAW

*See also* Architecture: Western Christian Monasteries; Camaldolese; Dominicans: General or Male; Gualbert, John, St.; Savonarola, Girolamo; Servites; Vallombrosans; Visual Arts, Western Christian: Book Arts before the Renaissance; Visual Arts, Western Christian: Painting

**Further Reading**

Bosi, Roberto, *Monasteri Italiani*, Bologna: Calderini, 1990
Busignani, Alberto, and Raffaello Bencini, *Le Chiese di Firenze*, 4 vols., Florence: Sansoni, 1974–1988
Clarke, G., "Ambrogio Traversari: Artistic Advisor in Early Fifteenth Century Florence?" *Renaissance Studies* 11:3 (1997)
Eisenberg, Marvin, *Lorenzo Monaco*, Princeton, New Jersey: Princeton University Press, 1989
*Firenze e Provincia* (Guida d'Italia del T.C.I.), Milan: Touring Club Italiano, 1993
Hood, William, *Fra Angelico at San Marco*, New Haven, Connecticut: Yale University Press, and London: BCA, 1993
Lesnick, Daniel Richard, *Preaching in Medieval Florence: The Social World of Franciscan and Dominican Spirituality*, Athens: University of Georgia Press, 1989
Paatz, Walter, and Elizabeth Valentiner Paatz, *Die Kirchen von Florenz, Ein kunstgeschichtliches Handbuch*, 6 vols., Frankfurt am Main: Klostermann, 1952–1955
Penco, Gregorio, *Storia del Monachesimo in Italia dalle origini alla fine del Medio Evo* (Tempi e figure, 31), Rome: Edizioni Paoline, 1961; 3rd edition, Milan: Jaca, 1995
Polizzotto, Lorenzo, *The Elect Nation: The Savonarolan Movement in Florence, 1494–1545* (Oxford-Warburg Studies), New York: Oxford University Press, and Oxford: Clarendon Press, 1994
Pope-Hennessy, John Wyndham, *Fra Angelico*, New York and London: Phaidon Press, 1952; 2nd edition, Ithaca, New York: Cornell University Press, and London: Phaidon Press, 1974
Rolfi, Gianfranco, et al., *La Chiesa e La Città a Firenze nel XV secolo*, Florence: Silvana, 1992
Verdon, Timothy, and John Henderson, *Christianity and the Renaissance: Image and Religious Imagination in the Quattrocento*, Syracuse, New York: Syracuse University Press, 1990
Weinstein, Donald, *Savonarola and Florence: Prophecy and Patriotism in the Renaissance*, Princeton, New Jersey: Princeton University Press, 1970
Zeppegno, Luciano, *Le Chiese di Firenze: dalle splendide chiese-museo del centro cittadino alle sconosciute pievi del contado: una guida che ricompone tutte le tessere di quel meraviglioso mosaico che è Firenze* (Italia nostra, 4), Rome: Newton Compton, 1976; 2nd edition, 1991

# Fontevraud, France

The foundation of Fontevraud may be traced to the charismatic and idiosyncratic wandering preacher Robert of Arbrissel (c. 1045–1116). Robert, a native of Brittany educated in Paris, had been an archdeacon, a hermit, and founder of a house of canons before beginning his last career as an errant evangelist with the blessing of Pope Urban II (1088–1099) in 1096. Robert attracted many disciples male and female, who lived in informal religious communities or followed Robert on his journeys. Sharply criticized for his unorthodox behavior and the close association of women and men in his entourage – some historians have noted the compatibility of Robert's special mission to women and the new ideals of troubadour poetry – Robert bowed to pressure and, with the help of Bishop Peter II of Poitiers, established a monastery in the little valley of Fontevraud (*Fons Evraldi*), on the border of the dioceses of Poitiers, Tours, and Angers in western France. A more traditional but still unusual arrangement resulted from the compromise of Robert's ideals and the impulse toward order and regularization typical of ecclesiastical mentality of the era. Fontevraud was to be a community under a rule, but one that welcomed all sorts and conditions of women, "poor and noble, widows and virgins, elderly and youthful, whores and those who rejected men" in the words of Robert's biographer Baudri of Dol. That some of these women fled husbands to follow the charismatic preacher did not help the reputation of Robert's movement, especially since Robert sometimes refused to send them back.

From its foundation in 1100 or 1101, Fontevraud functioned as a "double monastery," a mixed community of men and women, perhaps modeled on those of early medieval times. Women led the community; Robert had no interest in serving as a monk or abbot and, when the new house appeared to be on firm ground organizationally and financially, he returned to the apostolate, leaving in charge Hersende of Montsoreau and Petronilla of Chemillé, both of local aristocratic families and among Robert's early followers. Approved by pontifical bull in 1106, Fontevraud already had begun to gather a federation of daughter houses, some founded by Robert himself, each similarly mixed communities headed by a female superior. When Robert reorganized the community again in 1115 to reflect the existence of about 15 priories, he made Petronilla of Chemillé (possibly one of those women who had fled married life) the first abbess of Fontevraud and head of the burgeoning order.

Nave of the Abbey Church of Fontevraud (Maine-et-Loire), 12th century, with the tombs of Henry II of England (1154–1189) and Eleanor of Aquitaine (c. 1122–1204).
Photo courtesy of J. Feuillie/CNMHS

Exterior of the kitchen, Abbey Church of Fontevraud (Maine-et-Loire), 12th century.
Photo courtesy of J. Feuillie/CNMHS

Abbess Petronilla presided over Fontevraud until her death in 1149, making the Order of Fontevraud what it remained until the French Revolution: the largest and wealthiest federation of monasteries for women in Roman Christendom. Combining spirituality and practicality, the roles of Mary and Martha much beloved of 12th-century exegetes, Petronilla guided the growth of Fontevraud and its order, furthering the transformation of Robert's original vision. Pope Calixtus II consecrated the choir and transept of the Romanesque abbey church in 1119, and the remainder of the structure was probably finished in Petronilla's time. By the time the first abbess died, Fontevraud had some 50 French priories. The number grew to more than 70 in the following decades and included houses in southern England and Aragon.

The aristocratic character of the order became ever more prominent after the death of Robert of Arbrissel. Fontevraud attracted the patronage of Count Fulk V of Anjou, later the king of Jerusalem (d. 1142), whose daughter Mathilda was the second abbess from 1149 to 1155. Fulk's grandson Henry Plantagenet, king of England (1154–1189) and, through inheritance and marriage to Eleanor of Aquitaine (c. 1122–1204), lord of a vast

Continental realm, was a special protector and generous patron of the house, leaving to Fontevraud on his death the princely sum of 2,000 marks. Henry, Eleanor, their son King Richard the Lionheart, and their daughter-in-law Isabelle of Angoulême were buried at Fontevraud. Two abbesses of the 13th century were of English royal blood, and there were numerous abbesses of the French royal family of the Capetians and its successor dynasty, the Bourbons. The unorthodox aspects of Fontevraud's origins were eclipsed by its status as a prestigious mother house and home to many members of royal and princely families.

Fontevraud experienced community tensions from the middle of the 13th century, as some monks did not want to live under the control of a woman and the aristocratic nuns frequently complained about the rigor of their religious lives. The disruptions of the Hundred Years War (1337–1453) did nothing to stem internal disorder or simplify management of vast and scattered properties. Of several attempts to reform and reestablish the abbesses' control, the most significant was perhaps that of Renée of Bourbon, who succeeded in imposing papal-sanctioned statutes on the mother house and a number of recalcitrant priories. Abbess Renée also undertook an ambitious building plan continued by her successors. In the century and a half before the French Revolution, Fontevraud experienced a new period of renown and royal favor; King Louis XV (1715–1774) entrusted the abbess with the education of four daughters.

Fontevraud, like other French monasteries, suffered attack in the wake of the French Revolution. In 1792 the monastery compound was sacked and the community dispersed. Napoleon turned the abbey into a prison in 1804, which it remained until 1963. The site is now preserved as a historical monument. There remain numerous buildings from both 12th-century and early modern construction programs, making Fontevraud today one of the most notable monastic complexes in France. Of particular importance are the handsome Romanesque abbey church, with nave and chevet measuring nearly 90 meters, housing the Plantagenet tombs, and the unique 12th-century octagonal kitchen.

BRUCE L. VENARDE

*See also* Benedictines: Female; Cistercians: Female; Double Houses, Western Christian; France; Heloise; Women's Monasteries: Western Christian

**Further Reading**

Bienvenu, Jean-Marc, "Aux origines d'un ordre religieux: Robert d'Arbrissel et la fondation de Fontevraud," *Cahiers d'histoire* 20 (1975)
Gold, Penny S., "Male/Female Cooperation: The Example of Fontevrault," in *Medieval Religious Women*, volume 1: *Distant Echoes*, edited by John A. Nichols and Lillian Thomas Shank, Kalamazoo, Michigan: Cistercian Publications, 1984
*Histoire de l'Ordre de Fontevrault (1100–1908)*, 3 vols., Auch: Cocharaux, 1911–1915
Smith, Jacqueline, "*Procurator Mulierum*: Robert of Arbrissel's Relations with Women," in *Medieval Women*, edited by Derek Baker, Oxford: Blackwell, 1978
Tunc, Suzanne, *Les femmes au pouvoir: deux abbesses de Fontevraud aux XIIe et XVII siècles*, Paris: Editions du Cerf, 1993
Venarde, Bruce L., *Women's Monasticism and Medieval Society: Nunneries in France and England, 890–1215*, Ithaca, New York: Cornell University Press, 1997

# Food: Buddhist Perspectives

Food and the proper means of obtaining it has been a central concern to Buddhists from the time of the Buddha. Legend has it that the young prince who would go on to become the awakened one ("Buddha") renounced the pleasures of life in the palace and eventually took up a life of extreme austerity, subsisting on only one grain of rice per day. He became so emaciated that one could see the outline of his spinal cord in the concave of his abdomen. One day he fainted and on recovering realized that his self-denial had gotten him nowhere. Like trying to tie knots in the air, such mortifications brought him no closer to awakening than had the hedonistic life of the palace. Clearly the starving man is as preoccupied with food as is the gourmand who spends hours considering the merits of each possible dish. And so the young prince Siddhartha is said to have discovered the Middle Way between the extremes of self-denial and self-indulgence. He began eating normally so as to be free of the psychic bondage that comes with excessive preoccupation with food. Although the legend of the discovery of the Middle Way might be a later interpretation added to biographies of the Buddha as a way of differentiating Buddhists from their more ascetically inclined Jain rivals, this characterization of Buddhism as the Middle Way and the attitude toward food that it implies have become key elements of the self-understanding of Buddhists throughout Asia.

As the Buddha gained followers after his awakening, he established a monastic community of mendicants entirely dependent on food and clothing offered by others. The earliest Buddhist monastic codes mandate that Buddhist monks (and nuns, with the establishment of the order of nuns somewhat late in the life of the Buddha) eat only food received at the hands of another. For these monks and nuns obtaining food not produced by their own labor was so central to their identity that they were known as "beggars" (a literal translation of the Pāli and Sanskrit terms for "monk" and "nun"). The earliest monks and nuns in India led a peripatetic existence, traveling from place to place to avoid depleting the resources of any one community. Following the dictum common to many renunciant groups existing at the time of the Buddha, the Buddhist renouncer was to acquire food in the manner of the honey bee, which flies from flower to flower and takes only a sip of nectar at each. Begging for alms during daily almsrounds provided basic sustenance. Monks and nuns went in search of alms with a begging bowl early in the morning, going from house to house without exception, visiting the homes of rich and poor. They were to stand in silence at the donor's door. If they were given something, they were to accept it regardless of quantity and quality. Buddhist monastics were also invited to the homes of lay followers for meals.

By their method of obtaining food, Buddhist renouncers in India distinguished themselves from their brahmanic (proto-Hindu) counterparts, who ate roots and berries. Should Buddhist monks and nuns find some food, they were not to eat it, according to monastic regulations. Veena Das suggests that such regulations meant that Buddhist monastics were encouraged to remain creatures of culture rather than behaving, like their non-Buddhist counterparts, as creatures of nature (Das, 1985). In addition the necessity of remaining close to the settled world of towns and villages in their travels provided monks and nuns with ample opportunities for interaction with the laity. For the lay giver the opportunity to feed monks and nuns was (and remains) a crucial means of developing the virtue of generosity (*dāna*) and earning the merit by which to gain a better birth after death. For the monastic recipient the daily almsround was not only a means of assisting laity in their quest to earn merit but also an occasion for meditation.

Food occupies a central place in Buddhist philosophy, and thus meditation on food is essential to the mental discipline of monastic life. Food is said to be the foundation of all life – both present life and future lives. Buddhist philosophers recognize four types of food: (1) material food; (2) the food of sense contact; (3) the food of the mind, or volition; and (4) consciousness, which sustains both body and mind. All four types of food are to be approached with great caution, for the consumption of these foods can generate endless craving. The *Saṃyutta Nikāya*, a collection of discourses attributed to the Buddha, says that one should regard taking food and drink with the same horror that parents, having run out of provisions while crossing a vast jungle, would experience at the prospect of having to eat their only child. Likewise one should view the other sustainers of psychophysical existence with aversion. Such aversion is not an end in itself. However, as an antidote to passion, aversion is a necessary preliminary, a prerequisite for awakening. Buddhaghosa – the fifth-century Theravāda commentator who is often considered the premier spokesman of monastic Buddhism – describes how the daily almsround can be regarded meditatively as an occasion to overcome attachment to the pleasures of food and to develop a salutary sense of aversion toward food and the other sustainers of life. In his *Visuddhimagga* (*The Path of Purification*), Buddhaghosa suggests that a monk setting off on an almsround should attend to a variety of unpleasant sights and smells on the way. Noting lizard droppings on the floor of the monastery and bird droppings on the monastery door, he should also observe that the threshold is stained by mucus and saliva and the bodily wastes of sick novices who have relieved themselves just outside the door. The monk must cross over vile-smelling cesspools full of decomposing matter. Flies light on his skin and his begging bowl. People might fill his bowl with stale and putrid foods. Should he receive choice, tasty foods (as is likely to be the case, since lay supporters earn merit by giving monks and nuns high-quality food in generous portions), the sensual appeal of

such foods can be decreased by mixing everything together into a uniform paste. Clearly food is to be ingested as a necessity, not as an end in itself. Food is best understood as medicine for the body. Thus, monastic reflections on food such as Buddhaghosa's recognize its value as a means of subsistence but discourage the ingestion of food as a source of sensual pleasure.

Turning to the question of diet, one can see in Buddhism overall a tendency to promote vegetarianism. Buddhism arose in part as a critique of the brahmanic sacrificial religion of ancient India in which animals were ritually slaughtered and offered to the deities. Rather than attempting to gain merit by the violent destruction of the lives of animals, the ideal sacrifice that the Buddha promoted takes the form of self-discipline in thought and action. Buddhism teaches respect for all living creatures. Monastic codes not only forbid the killing of animals but also dictate a high level of awareness of the harm done to lower life forms in daily human activity. For example, monks and nuns were to remain in one location and suspend their travels during the monsoon season to avoid stepping on the plethora of worms and other lower life forms that thrive in the muddy roads, and they were also to avoid the use of water in which small creatures are living. The Buddha is said to have spoken against butchers and fishers and recommended that lay Buddhists avoid such occupations in accordance with the precept to avoid taking life (the first of five precepts taken by all lay Buddhists). Nevertheless this emphasis on compassion toward animals did not necessarily require vegetarianism among early Buddhists in India, nor is vegetarianism universal among all Buddhists today. Although some of the Buddha's followers proposed a rule of strict vegetarianism, this rule would have caused difficulties for monks and nuns begging in some regions of India and southern Asia. The ecology of the mountainous areas of southern Asia (such as Nepal and Tibet) does not permit a wholly vegetarian diet. Thus, in southern Asia and Tibet meat dishes given to a monk or nun are to be accepted unless the meat was specially prepared for the donation. However, in those areas of Asia where the environment permits a totally vegetarian diet, Buddhists have tended to practice vegetarianism. Vegetarianism is strongly advocated by the Mahāyāna tradition, with its emphasis on compassion as the primary virtue. Mahāyāna texts often point out the interconnectedness of all life, suggesting that at one time or another in the cycle of rebirth we were once related as family members to those fish and mammals that we thoughtlessly kill for our dinner tables. Mahāyāna texts give pride of place to legends of the past lives of the Buddha in which, out of compassion for starving animals, he offered his own body as food for these animals. In China, where the Mahāyāna tradition gained dominance early on, vegetarianism quickly became the norm for both lay and monastic Buddhists despite the resistance of Confucians, who viewed the eating of animals as an appropriate recognition of the human's place in the divine scheme of things. The great Buddhist monastic kitchens of China developed such vegetarian staples as tofu in the attempt to provide a completely plant-based diet.

Another aspect of compassionate eating that developed in eastern Asia is the practice of feeding hungry ghosts. Hungry ghosts are beings who, because of greediness in past lives, have huge, ravenous stomachs and tiny, needlelike throats. They suffer constant hunger and thirst as a result. In the heyday of monasticism in China, monks and nuns offered a portion of their meals to hungry ghosts before feeding themselves.

LIZ WILSON

*See also* Animals, Attitude toward: Buddhist Perspectives; Asceticism: Buddhist Perspectives; Aśoka; Body: Buddhist Perspectives; Buddhist Schools/Traditions; Disciples, Early Buddhist; Fasting: Buddhist; Gestures, Buddhist; Hygiene: Buddhist Perspectives; Mahāyāna; Novices, Theravādin Rituals for; Regulations: Buddhist Perspectives; Rules, Buddhist (Vinaya): Historical; Self-Immolation, Buddhist

## Further Reading

Chapple, Christopher Key, *Nonviolence to Animals, Earth, and Self in Asian Traditions*, Albany: State University of New York Press, 1993

Das, Veena, "Paradigms of Body Symbolism: An Analysis of Selected Themes in Hindu Culture," in *Indian Religion*, edited by Richard Burghart and Audrey Canthe, London: Curzon Press, and New York: St. Martin's Press, 1985

Feer, L., editor, *Saṃyutta Nikāya, or The Book of the Kindred Sayings*, volume 2, London: Pali Text Society, 1884–1898

Khare, R.S., editor, *The Eternal Food: Gastronomic Ideas and Experiences of Hindus and Buddhists*, Albany: State University of New York Press, 1993

Rhys Davids, C.A.F., editor, *The Visuddhi-magga of Buddhaghosa*, 2 vols., London: Pali Text Society, 1920–1921; reprint, London and Boston: Routledge and Kegan Paul, 1975

Smith, Brian K., "Eaters, Food, and Social Hierarchy in Ancient India: A Dietary Guide to a Revolution of Values," *Journal of the American Academy of Religion* 58:2 (1990)

Wijayaratna, Môhan, *Buddhist Monastic Life: According to the Texts of the Theravāda Tradition*, translated by Claude Grangier and Steven Collins, Cambridge and New York: Cambridge University Press, 1990

# Food: Christian Perspectives

The reduction of a person's intake of food by making a little suffice accords with early Christian conceptions of poverty. The New Testament mentions the dietary components of the common people – bread, fish, and wine – which subsequently became part of the myth and symbolic vocabulary of the Christian faith. The asceticism characterizing early Christianity finds expression in the description of John the Baptist, who lived as a hermit in the desert and survived with the little food found in his natural habitat (Matt. 3:4). In a description by the Essene sect, we find a dominant trend of abstaining from material possessions and choosing poverty as a desirable lifestyle. Josephus Flavius claimed that the Essenes conducted a Pythagorean lifestyle (*Antiquities* 15.371), whereby vegetarianism was one of its important principles. The main component of the Essene diet was the loaves of bread that they were served at their communal

Kitchen, Benedictine abbey, Glastonbury, Somerset, England, 14th century.
Photo courtesy of Chris Schabel

meals (*War* 2.130). These and other features indicate a connection between the Essenes and the first Christians in Judaea at the end of the Second Temple period.

The hagiographical literature developed in the monasteries of Egypt, Syria, and Palestine is the main source for learning about the dietary customs of the early Christians. In the regulations of the early monasteries of Syria (fifth to sixth century A.D.), it is stipulated that abstention from meat was required to fulfill the principles of Christianity with utmost devotion. The communal meal was conceived as a continuation of the liturgies and communal prayer wherein speaking was forbidden and a homily was delivered: "While the brothers dine, a homily shall be read in order that with the body also the soul might be nourished" (Vööbus, *Rules for the Monks in Persia*, 1960). Unlike the common people, who ate meat, stringent observance of this custom by monastics is corroborated by the archaeological evidence from various monasteries that contains no animal bones. Grinding stones, oil presses, and wine presses that were found attest to foods customarily eaten in the monastic communities.

Granary, Cistercian abbey at Maulbronn, Baden-Württemberg, Germany, 13th century.
Photo courtesy of Chris Schabel

The three main food components in the monks' diet were bread, wine, and oil. Bread was also the staple food of the recluse monks living in the depths of the desert. Wheat grain ground with basalt grinding stones operated by the monks was stored in silos. The bakery was one of the most important installations in the monastery; its ovens were dome shaped with a semicircular opening at the top. In the Monastery of the Holy Bush (St. Catherine's) in Sinai, a sixth-century baking oven has been preserved intact. Its floor and ceiling were made of baked clay bricks. As illustrated in various mosaics from the Byzantine period (as in the Church of the Bread and Fishes at 'Ein Tabgha [Heptapegon] north of the Sea of Galilee), the loaves of bread were small and round.

Monks also ate seasonal vegetables, raw or cooked. The hagiographical sources mention soaked legumes, lupine seeds, a lentil dish, and a special one made of beans (*pisarion*) as well as carobs, dates, and figs, which could be preserved and stored for a long time. Oil and wine were also components of the monks' diet, as evidenced by the remains of wine and oil presses found in many monasteries. *Eukration*, a warm wine spiced with pepper, cinnamon, and fennel seeds, is mentioned in the sources and was especially important to monks living in the desert during the cold winter months.

The diet of monks and of the common people living in the countryside contained edible wild plants. The *Manouthion* plant gathered by monks should be identified with the tumble thistle (*Gundelia tournefortii*), which grows in the spring and to this day is considered by the fellahin in the villages to be a tasty and nutritious food component. Other wild plants, such as saltbush, capers, and reed and palm hearts, were also consumed by monks for their nutritious value. It appears that edible wild plants contributed to the quality of the customary diet among the monks and among other inhabitants in the Byzantine period.

YIZHAR HIRSCHFELD

*See also* Asceticism: Christian Perspectives; Biblical Figures and Practices; Botany; Devotions, Western Christian; Egypt; Fasting: Eastern Christian; Fasting: Western Christian; Liturgy: Eastern Christian; Mount Sinai, Egypt; Offices, Daily: Western Christian; Origins: Eastern Christian; Syria

**Further Reading**

Dar, Shimon, "Food and Archaeology in Romano-Byzantine Palestine," in *Food in Antiquity*, edited by John Wilkins, F.D. Harvey, and Mike Dobson, Exeter: University of Exeter Press, 1995

Dembinska, Maria, "A Comparison of Food Consumption between Some Eastern and Western Monasteries in the Fourth–Twelfth Centuries," *Byzantion* 55 (1985)

Hirschfeld, Yizhar, "The Importance of Bread in the Diet of Monks in the Judean Desert," *Byzantion* 66 (1996)

Vööbus, Arthur, compiler, *Syriac and Arabic Documents*, Stockholm: Etse, 1960

# Forest Masters

Before Thailand became a modern nation-state in the late 19th century, the region was made up of many small, culturally diverse kingdoms. Villages were often framed by immense tracts of jungle, forest, or savanna. If a village was situated near a great forest, a forest monastery was likely to be an integral part of the religious life of that rural community. Phatthalung, now a province in southern Thailand, was once a principality encompassing 298 forest monasteries (*wat*s). Spread over a wide geographic area, these *wat*s displayed considerable ethnic and cultural diversity. Theravāda Buddhism, the region's dominant religion, consisted of a wide range of local traditions and monastic lineages. Monks lived in *wat*s located in towns, villages, and forests. While some were scholars and others more concerned with meditation practice, virtually all the revered *ajan*s (teachers) were socially engaged: responsibility to the lay community was intrinsic to settled monastics as well as forest monks. There were also reclusive forest monks who focused mainly on meditative and yogic practices.

Once Siam became a centralized nation-state, the Dhammayut Order, founded in the 1820s by Mongkut (later King Rama IV), became the model for state Buddhism. This order emphasized the study of the Pāli Canon and strict observance of the Vinaya (the monastic rules of discipline). All other Buddhist traditions within Siam were lumped together under one disparaging label: Mahanikai.

With the passage of the Sangha Act of 1902, monks of all local traditions were placed under the control of the government in Bangkok. Wandering forest monks were instructed to cease wandering, settle in monasteries, and accept the new curriculum formulated by Mongkut's son, Wachirayan, head of the Dhammayut Order. To *sangha* authorities in Bangkok, the ideal *bhikkhu* (monk) was a scholar and administrator, true to the new Vinaya. To monks of the forest tradition, the ideal *bhikkhu* was a homeless renunciant seeking liberation from the endless cycle of rebirths. This ideal, harkening back to the Buddha's time, inspired several of the most revered forest masters of the 20th century: Mun Phurithatto (1870–1949), Buddhadasa (1906–1993), and Cha Suphattho (1918–1992).

Mun and Cha shared similar ethnic and social backgrounds. They grew up among rice farmers in Lao-speaking villages in Ubon province in northeastern Thailand. When Mun came of age, state Buddhism, standard textbooks, and secular education did not yet exist. As a novice in the village *wat*, Mun studied palm-leaf texts that contained local history, literature, and Buddhist teachings. In 1892 he moved to the town of Ubon and was reordained as a monk in the Dhammayut Order, attracted by its strict discipline, although the rewards of academic study and ecclesiastical appointments did not interest him. Mun devoted his time to meditation, wandering alone or in the company of other monks through the wilds of the Thai, Lao, and Shan states and beyond. Eventually his skill and reputation as *kammatthāna* (meditation) teacher and the widespread belief in his shamanistic healing powers encouraged large numbers of monks to seek him out. For most of his life, he was peripatetic. Not until he was in his 70s did Mun settle into a forest hermitage.

Mun observed many of the 13 ascetic practices (Pāli, *dhūtanga*) that were integral to local traditions. These included wearing robes made of cast-off rags and dwelling in forest cemeteries or the wilderness. To most people the forest was a fearsome, dangerous place full of wild animals, malevolent spirits, and diseases. It was Mun's conviction that nature – trees, rivers, caves, snakes, tigers, *nāga*s (serpent deities of the underworld), and *phi*s (spirits or ghosts) – is the best teacher to put *dhamma* texts to the test.

Buddhadasa (Ngu'am Indapanno) was born to a modest Chinese-Thai merchant family in the town of Chaiya in southern Thailand. He was educated at the local *wat* as a temple boy before attending a government school. He left school after six years, when his father died, to run the family store. Because he had access to books and opportunities to discuss *dhamma*, by the time he was ordained as a monk (1926) he had read and discussed all the basic texts and had acquired considerable knowledge of the larger world.

Like other young monks of his day, Ngu'am was drawn to the state monastic curriculum and went to study Pāli at a prestigious *wat* in Bangkok. When he read the (nonrequired) Tipiṭaka (Pāli Canon), he became aware of the contradiction between the way of life of the monks who followed state Buddhism and that of the Buddha's original disciples. Yearning for peace and simplicity, Ngu'am returned to his hometown and in 1932 moved into an abandoned *wat* in a nearby forest. There he established Suan Mokkhabalarama (The Garden of the Power of Liberation) and took the name Buddhadasa. In working to integrate textual study and meditation practice, Buddhadasa regarded the wilderness in which he lived and observed ascetic practices as his teacher. As a writer and preacher, Buddhadasa appealed to villagers as well as educated urbanites who were spiritually unfulfilled by modern life.

Cha, two generations younger than Mun, was also educated in the village *wat*. Cha was a temple boy and a novice, but he spent only one year in a secular school. At the age of 20, he was ordained as a monk and went to a monastery in a district town of Ubon to study Bangkok's curriculum. The deaths of his father and brother led Cha to question the academic vocation and to begin the search for a meditation master. In 1949 he met Ajan Mun.

The forest tradition of Mun was known for emphasizing meditation and strict observance of the Vinaya. Although he espoused Mun's teachings and practices, Cha never joined the Dhammayut Order. He lived as a peripatetic for some time, then settled in a forest *wat* near his village where he undertook the training of monks and novices. Eventually he set up an international forest monastery, also in Ubon, to train Western monks.

All three forest masters were critical of institutional Buddhism, which elevated textual learning above meditation practice and social responsibility. Their disciples were among the first to protest the destruction of forests and to advocate conservation. Respect for the instructional value of the natural world was at the forefront of the *ajans*' teachings; they drew on nature to reveal the interconnectedness of all life forms. They were down-to-earth, teaching with warmth and humor by using analogies and similes drawn from everyday life to elucidate principles such as nonattachment or selflessness or to reveal the less obvious aspects of greed: aversion and delusion.

The lives of these forest teachers reveal their concern for the welfare of people. Mun and his disciples were often called on to provide herbal and spiritual remedies to remote villagers suffering from illness or fear. Cha and Buddhadasa opened doors to monks and laypeople of the world community. Buddhadasa boldly articulated the need for dhammic socialism, envisioned as a network of communities committed to ecological and moral principles and conceived as an alternative to the dehumanizing power of corporate capitalism, global uniformity, and the media-induced obsession with sex and violence. His teachings have inspired social and environmental movements in many countries.

Cha's gifts as a teacher have resulted in the extension of the Thai-Lao forest tradition abroad. Monasteries in his lineage have been established by his Western disciples in England, Switzerland, Italy, Australia, New Zealand, and the United States. "Liberation Park" is being established in the Midwest under an American disciple of Buddhadasa. A venerable tradition that came close to being lost in Thailand is now being given a chance to flourish in areas that have remained, until recently, largely untouched by Theravāda Buddhism.

KAMALA TIYAVANICH

*See also* Bangkok, Thailand; Buddhadāsa; Disciples, Early Buddhist; Hermits: Buddhist; Holy Men in Power (Hierocrats), Buddhist; Mongkut; Mun, Ajahn; Novices, Theravādin Rituals for; Origins: Comparative Perspectives; Saṅgha; Thailand; Theravādin Monks, Modern Western

## Further Reading

Buddhadasa, Phra Thepwisutthimethi (Ngu'am), *The First Ten Years of Suan Mokkh*, translated by Mongkol Dejnakarintra, Bangkok: Niti Issaranititham, 1990

Jayasaro Bhikkhu, *Ubon Mani* (Jewel of Ubon), Bangkok: Khurusapha, 1992

Kohler, Nicholas P., editor, *Radical Conservatism: Buddhism in the Contemporary World: Articles in Honour of Bhikkhu Buddhadasa's 84th Birthday Anniversary*, Bangkok: Sathirakoses-Nagapradipa Foundation, 1990

Kornfield, Jack, *Living Dharma: Teachings of Twelve Buddhist Masters*, Boston: Shambhala, 1996

Kornfield, Jack, and Paul Breiter, editors, *A Still Forest Pool: The Insight Meditation of Achaan* Chah (A Quest Book), Wheaton, Illinois: Theosophical Publishing House, 1985

Nyanasampanno, Boowa, "An Account on the Dhutanga Kammathana Bhikkhus," in *Buddhism in Thailand*, Bangkok: Thai Watana Panich Press, 1980

Santikaro Bhikkhu, "Buddhadasa Bhikkhu: Life and Society through the Natural Eyes of Voidness," in *Engaged Buddhism: Buddhist Liberation Movements in Asia*, edited by Christopher S. Queen and Sallie B. King, Albany: State University of New York Press, 1996

Santikaro Bhikkhu, "The Four Noble Truths of Dhammic Socialism," in *Entering the Realm of Reality: Towards Dhammic Societies*, edited by Jonathan Watts, Alan Senauke, and Santikaro Bhikkhu, Bangkok: Suksit Siam, 1997

Santikaro Bhikkhu, editor, *Heartwood of the Bodhi Tree: The Buddha's Teaching on Voidness*, translated by Dhammavicayo, Boston: Wisdom, 1994

Swearer, Donald, editor, *Me and Mine: Selected Essays of Bhikkhu Buddhadasa* (SUNY Series in Buddhist Studies), Albany: State University of New York Press, 1989

Tambiah, Stanley J., *The Buddhist Saints of the Forest and the Cult of Amulets: A Study in Charisma, Hagiography, Sectarianism, and Millennial Buddhism* (Cambridge Studies in Social Anthropology, 49), Cambridge and New York: Cambridge University Press, 1984

Taylor, Jim L., *Forest Monks and the Nation-State: An Anthropological and Historical Study in Northeastern Thailand* (Social Issues in Southeast Asia), Singapore: Institute of Southeast Asian Studies, 1993

Tiyavanich, Kamala, *Forest Recollections: Wandering Monks in Twentieth-Century Thailand*, Honolulu: University of Hawaii Press, 1997

Yansampanno, Bua, *The Venerable Phra Acharn Mun Bhuridatta Thera, Meditation Master*, translated by Siri Buddhasukh, Bangkok: Mahamakut Rajavidyalaya Press, 1976

# France: History

*Foundations*

Monasticism has a long history in France. There were monks in the lands that became France as early as the fourth century, when the soldier-recluse Martin of Tours (d. 397) came to Gaul and founded religious communities at Ligugé and Tours. At the turn of the fifth century, John Cassian (c. 360–after 430) reflected on the merits of the eremitic and cenobitic forms of ascetic life, bearing in mind the experience of monks in Gaul as well as of God's athletes in the Eastern deserts. In addition the ascetic ideal already informed the department of St. Germain of Auxerre (d. 437/38) and Caesarius of Arles (c. 470–542), who were leaders in conversion and pastoral ministry in fifth-century Gaul. The later insistence on self-abnegation as a test of true conversion owes something to the example of priests and monks in the age before the dynastic foundations of France. Caesarius founded monasteries for women and men at Arles. In the sixth century Merovingian patronage was responsible for the foundations of St. Vincent (which became Saint-Germain-des Prés) at

Paris; Saint-Médard of Soissons; and Sainte-Croix of Poitiers. The example of Eastern desert asceticism long persisted at Lérins and Marseille, where the fathers lived in loose association without communal discipline.

A new age of monastic foundation followed the conversion of King Clovis (481–511) to Christianity in the later fifth century. The tendency was favored by the model of ascetic conversion and by elite patronage. Frankish magnates endowed congregations of monks in the northeast, and the wish to be buried in ascetic company persisted during Merovingian times. However, this was the age of royal foundations, of houses favored by kings and queens whose lavish patronage left permanent marks in religious tradition. Among notable religious women were Geneviève, who promoted the cult of St. Denis at Paris; Queen Chrotechildis, who became an exemplary nun after converting her husband, Clovis; and Queen Radegunde (c. 518–587), who drew on the observance of Lérins in founding her nunnery at Poitiers in 547. Kings established monks in the houses that became Saint-Germain-des Prés in Paris and Saint-Bénigne in Dijon.

Little is known about the rules of these houses, whose ancestral tie to the desert traditions weakened with time. It is possible that the Rule of St. Benedict of Nursia (c. 480–c. 550), composed in Italy in the earlier sixth century, had some diffusion in Gaul. However, it is unlikely that either Benedict or his source, the "Rule of the Master," drew on Gallic tradition. Monks were subject to the supervision of bishops, one of whom, Ferialus of Uzès, compiled a rule for local use that emphasizes obedience and associative virtues. With the multiplication of ascetic communities, the monks became guardians of relics not only at Tours but also at Poitiers, Lyons, Trier, Arles, and Toulouse By the early seventh century, the cloak of St. Martin was treasured by Merovingian kings, who, however, now favored St. Denis of Paris over the cult of St. Martin. The growing popularity of such cults was connected with the continuing task of conversion, wherein relics became patrimonial wealth in which lay families could invest. Already lay benefactors found it difficult to think of donated property as wholly alienated.

This was not yet Benedictine monasticism, although the principles of a house-focused cenobitism continued to spread. New vitality was imparted by the mission of Columban (d. 615), who came from Ireland with disciples in 590 and founded Luxueil as a holy fueling station for the conversion of tepid Christians as well as of pagans. Putting himself under the Frankish king's protection, Columban imposed his own rules of ascetic conduct, which were more demanding of personal repentance than was the Benedictine Rule; and he was among the first Christian leaders to preach a faith in God above all saints. This was not to reject the sanctity of relics, which he saw to be an inspirational element of Frankish life. From Luxueil spread a new religious fervor, as Columban's disciples Audoen, Otmar, Bertin, and Eligius became founder saints themselves in Rouen, St. Omer, Paris, and Noyon, respectively. This impulse persisted in the seventh century, when Queen Bathildis endowed monks at Corbie and nuns at Chelles. Especially symptomatic was the career of St. Amand, a tireless traveler who found backsliding Christians everywhere, including at the king's court, where Dagobert (629–639) began to wonder whether this loose cannon could be entrusted with religious discipline among Christians as well as with preaching to the unconverted. With Amand "the monkish conception of mission combined with the ascetic life takes on new force" (Wallace-Hadrill, 1983). Northern Frankland became a mission field.

In the eighth century this field, spreading northward and eastward, became a fertile but dangerous zone of initial conversion. The Columbanic ideal of penitential reform weakened to the point that zealous missionaries were appalled by the laxity of faith and observance in western Frankland. In 744 the Carolingian mayor of the palace, Pepin III the Short (747–768), held a reforming council at Soissons in which monks and nuns were enjoined to live in observance of their Rules. They were enabled to recover lost patrimonies, a regulation that points to a new problem in monastic history: the temptation felt by kings and lay magnates to seize property from those they were appointed to protect.

### The Carolingian Ages

When Pepin III's son Charlemagne (768–814) came to power, it was already clear that monastic discipline was hard to sustain beyond the lifetimes of founder saints. Yet monasticism seemed now more important than ever for public welfare. The monastic life in western Frankland best known to us in the eighth and ninth centuries is that of the greater monasteries whose interests and wealth were essential to the workings of the monarchy. This was a novelty, for after Columban's time, as the Merovingian hold on power weakened, the bishops had in many places secured the disciplinary and patrimonial supervision of monasteries. Kings and magnates alike resisted this, and the rise of the Carolingian family entailed a struggle with bishops for patrimonial control of monasteries. The reforming councils of the 740s marked a stage in the early success of the Frankish mayors. Under King Pepin III and Charlemagne, the royal protectorate of major houses became systematic if not yet exclusive.

That is why monastic reform was central to Carolingian royal enterprise. Charlemagne viewed his monks as intermediaries between God and the people, involved in a synergy of royal command and devout prayer aimed at promoting the welfare and salvation of Christians There were monks, such as Alcuin of York (c. 740–804), among the courtiers whom he exploited to develop a vast program of moral, legal, and doctrinal reformation. Under Louis the Pious (814–840), this program was brought to bear more emphatically on the monastic life. Louis had for his mentor a monk named Benedict (c. 750–821), who had professed religion at Aniane, southern France, before coming to the king's notice. Already under Charlemagne he had sought to bind monks and nuns to the Benedictine Rule. In councils directed by Benedict of Aniane in 802 and 813, the Rule of St. Benedict was made mandatory; that it was thought necessary to read the Rule to the abbots assembled at Reims suggests that it was still imperfectly familiar to them. The era of mixed rules was not quite over. In fact the first efforts to place the cathedral clergy under a monastic regimen went back to the time of Bishop Chrodegang of Metz (d. 766), who had founded the abbey of Gorze (748) under a strictly Benedictine observance. Later he established his episcopal clergy as "canonical clerks" (*clerici canonici*) according to a common life influenced by Benedict's Rule.

Important new regulations for monks, nuns, and canons came out of the great councils of Aachen in 816 and 817. In these a distinction between their observances was drawn with insistent clarity. With the emperor's support the reformers imposed compliance with St. Benedict's Office, that is, the specified devotions and readings. The continuous singing of the Psalms was reduced, whereas the extent of prayers was permitted to increase beyond that stipulated in the Rule. Following heated debate it was agreed to limit monastic schooling to children destined for the monastic life, and abbots were enjoined to renounce the perquisites of power in favor of a conventual life in the community. The reforms of Aachen were a little too doctrinaire fully to succeed, nor were political circumstances in the turbulent ninth century conducive to a vision of peace and order. Monastic schools continued to educate non-monastic-bound children in small numbers while the constraints of provincial diversity worked against the ideal of a single monastic custom to supplement the Rule. Nevertheless the Rule of St. Benedict "became the foundation of monastic identity" (De Jong, 1995). The monastic reform promoted by Louis the Pious was a bold effort to create a politically united Christian Church to match the imperial unity decreed in 817. Legates were sent out from the imperial court to verify compliance with the regulations.

In promoting the Benedictine Rule, the Carolingian monastic reforms sought to compensate for, and even to insulate from, the pressures of the world. The Rule itself, together with Pope Gregory's *Pastoral Care*, defined the abbot's role as functionally official. It preserved a Roman bureaucratic order. However, the tendency of society was for power to be exercised as proprietary and personal. This was not a new issue, but the demands of lordship and familial interest in the ninth century were sufficient to subvert the notion of the abbot humbly serving his fellow monks Not all lay abbots were unworthy. Einhard (c. 770–840), the biographer of Charlemagne, instituted a division of lands between abbot and monks at St. Peter of Ghent such as would prove influential elsewhere; yet this institution did more to excite rivalry than to foster ascetic withdrawal. It is not accidental that the notion of "cloister" (*claustrum*) as referring to sacrosanct space reserved for monks became normal in the ninth century, from which time it denoted sheltered space on the south side of the church, often adjoining the dormitory and refectory. The so-called Plan of St. Gall survives from the early ninth century to show how the building and spaces of a large Frankish monastery were arranged.

Thus, the Benedictine house was ordered in contrast to the turbulent aristocratic world outside. Obedience to the abbot and humility were central, a self-discipline evidently more difficult for adult novices than for children. Young boys were molded into the habits of silence and prayer, their memories filled with

psalms and petitions. By the ninth century, when the liturgy was expanding and new altars were multiplying in dependence on religious houses, monks sometimes – and in some places in large numbers – took holy orders. Moreover, by a practice known mainly from monasteries of Lothair's Middle Kingdom, cults of the dead encouraged monks to create networks of liturgical commemoration – a ceaseless enterprise in prayer, in which founders' kinfolk, the king and his counts, and increasingly the families of donors turned the monasteries into "powerhouses of prayer."

### Cluny

By the later ninth century, not only were monks living in more places in western Frankland than ever before, they were often living in fear of external attack, their patrimonies vulnerable to shiploads of Vikings rowing up the rivers or descending on Flemish fenlands. The congregation of Saint-Philibert, founded in the seventh century on the isle of Noirmoutier, sought refuge on the mainland toward 815–819; by 836 the harassment was bad enough to force the monks further inland, and indeed they undertook a long series of further moves northward and eastward until at last, having put all of Auvergne between themselves and their assailants, they found asylum with their relics at Tournus. Richer and less mobile communities suffered the loss of patrimonies scattered throughout the empire; the monks of Saint-Wandrille, driven from their house in the lower Seine valley, were restored only in the 11th century under Duke Richard II, when a new Norman community of more local and less vulnerable patrimony took shape. Nor were Normans the only invaders. Monasteries in Provence felt the sting of Muslim pirates, some of whom captured for ransom Abbot Maieul of Cluny as late as 972; the Magyars violated monastic property in Lorraine.

Carolingian reforming zeal was flagging in the houses of monks and regular canons that survived the invasions. The pressures of lay benefactors were relentless, and bishops, such as those at Nantes and Le Puy, acquired lordships over convenient monasteries. Perhaps most symptomatic was the recognition of proprietors of monastic patrimony as lay abbots. Not even the Carolingian rules prevented lay magnates from serving God after their fashion. Toward 890 Count Gerald of Auvergne founded a monastery at Aurillac. Other nobles did likewise in their domains, so that by 930 something like a monastic renovation was under way. One Gerard of Namur founded a house at Brogne in 914, becoming its abbot and subjecting his flock to the Benedictine Rule. In Upper Lorraine a noble-born clerk named John established a more austere observance in a new house at Gorze. These reforming impulses rapidly spread, reaching Normandy when a disciple of Gerard was charged by Duke Richard I (942–996) to reestablish Benedictine observance at Saint-Wandrille and Saint-Ouen of Rouen and to institute it at Mont-St.-Michel.

The most influential center of reform was Cluny, founded in 910 by Duke William the Pious of Aquitaine (ruled 886–918) and the monk Berno. The latter was a Burgundian noble who had endowed monks at Gigny, then taken vows himself at Autun and assumed direction of growing congregations at Gigny and

Baume. What Duke William contributed was the estate of Cluny; and in the presence of bishops and lay notables he endowed a monastery destined to a prodigious future. The monks were to be subject to the apostles Peter and Paul to the exclusion of all other secular powers. Bringing monks from his other houses, Berno (abbot, 910–926) set about reviving the Benedictine usages: chant of psalms, observance of silence, and the old rules concerning diet, clothing, and chastity. His success at Cluny, seen at once to be a model house, speedily won him gifts of other monasteries, whose princely proprietors wanted to horn in on his reforming zeal and repute.

Berno was the first of a long series of great abbots who dominated Cluny – and, in some respects, Western Christendom – for the next two centuries. Odo (927–942) set the example for an itinerant abbacy, bringing reforming ideals to Aquitaine and Italy and writing about God and the saints. Maieul (954–994) and Odilo (994–1049) made the Cluniac observance famous throughout France and beyond (except in Germany, where the emperors retained full control of the monasteries). Monks of Cluny accompanied the abbots; one or two of them would remain in the houses or cells they visited to ensure compliance. Because canon law forbade abbots to accumulate offices, it became usual to vest the abbacy of reformed houses in the abbot of Cluny. In this practice, as also in the common customs added to the Rule, might be traced the beginnings of an order of affiliated monasteries. Many dozens of Benedictine houses came under Cluniac direction, such as Fleury and Saint-Maur-des-Fossés.

Cluny's was a theocratic monasticism, oriented to a sanctified world of religious kingship yet insistent on a jurisdictional autonomy that marked a departure from Carolingian practice. The abbots advised and admonished rulers, the monks prayed incessantly for the living and the dead, while the lay faithful invested in the assurance of salvation through their gifts or their conversions to the monastic estate. The Cluniacs worked at charity. Saint Odo established a cult of Martin of Tours (remembered for sharing his cloak with the poor Christ), and St. Odilo sold the monks' vases and jewels to help the poor. Admission to the congregation was not gratuitous, which is one reason that both monks and nuns were the offspring of elite families. What Cluny added to the Benedictine Rule was a custom of life and worship (the *ordo cluniacensis*) that was distinctive and famous. Silence, prayer, and work were of foremost value, with notable emphasis on collective prayer. The liturgical offices grew longer yet also more various and ceremonious. It was a liturgy suited to a devotionalism more ritually public than self-searching. Cluny was not in the forefront of intellectual achievement, although monks read, copied, and decorated manuscripts while some of her abbots followed St. Odo's example in writing on the religious life. During the time of Hugh (1049–1109), Cluny achieved a pinnacle of prestige and success, becoming a "refuge for penitents" (Morris, 1989) and associating noble families in the brotherhood of the monks. The congregation collected tribute from King Alfonso VI of León and built a vast new church to accommodate laypersons and pilgrims together with choir monks. However, it was a problematic prosperity bound up with the openness of religious appeal and observance to the world. The

balance of ends and means collapsed under Abbot Pons (1109–1122), to be restored incompletely under Peter the Venerable (1122–1156).

Some of the houses to which the Cluniac customs spread became centers of reform in their own right. At Fleury, where by virtue of a pious fraud the relics of St Benedict of Nursia had been deposited, the great abbot Abbo (c. 954–1004) cultivated the new scholastic learning of Reims and Paris. He was himself a noted writer on law and morals. Whereas at Cluny, subject only to the Roman See, the exemption of the monks from worldly jurisdictions became a characteristic tenet, it was at Fleury under Abbo that exemption from episcopal authority became (again) a foremost issue. At Dijon the monks of Saint-Bénigne came under the direction of William of Volpiano, a Cluniac monk born in Italy who introduced the customs of Cluny and served as abbot for 40 years. More austerely ascetic than his contemporary Odilo, he succeeded nonetheless in supervising some 1,200 monks scattered in far-flung lands. In Normandy he restored the lapsed congregations at Fécamp, Saint-Ouen (Rouen), Jumièges, and Mont-St.-Michel, and he founded Bernay. In southern France Cluniac hegemony sometimes met resistance, as at Saint-Pierre of Moissac, or competition, as from both Saint-Victor of Marseille and Moissac. Saint-Victor became the leader of a monastic confederation in its own right.

Cluny's role in the larger movement of ecclesiastical reform has been much debated. What is clear is that the moral influence of her great abbots, incessantly traveling, preaching, and denouncing worldly sins, moved many people who chose not to renounce the world. Moreover the cause of monastic exemption resonated with resentment at lay domination of churches. Few worried that churches passed from lay lords to monastic patrimonies, much as this might detract from Benedictine austerity. Abbot Hugh was in close touch with Pope Gregory VII (1073–1085), who claimed that Cluny was St Peter's "own particular property."

### The 12th Century

By this time two wider tendencies were challenging Cluny's ascendancy in France. The growth of population together with increasing wealth meant that monastic communities other than those subject to Cluny began to prosper, winning recognition in multiplying spheres of provincial lordship. Moreover generations of preaching, much of it by monks, was creating a more reflective, questioning faith in many Christians, especially in those devout enough to enter the monastic life. The Gregorian reform movement of the 1070s encouraged people to worry about the deportment of priests and to revere apostolic poverty, two positions that would later be branded heretical. Inner compunction came to seem important, a means to impose on Christians a more subjectively engaged devotionalism as well as militant service for the faith.

From such impulses sprang a host of new religious foundations. Not since the postapostolic age had so many people sought to renounce the world as solitaries as in the 11th century. In France the eremitic life soon attracted converts so as to assume cenobitic forms. Monasteries originated in this way at

Fontevraud, Savigny, and Tiron, with affiliated houses and cells creating new religious orders in time. Fontevraud was the foundation (1101) of Robert of Arbrissel (c. 1045–1116), sometime student, preacher, and hermit, and it provided a house for women as well as for men. Within two decades it had become the flourishing center of a congregation of 15 monasteries in western France, all of them mainly but not exclusively female. Women's monastic foundations, far from declining in the age of the reforming Church, as was once thought, multiplied fourfold from 1070 to 1170 (Venarde, 1997).

Likewise arising from eremitic inspiration were the Orders of Grandmont and the Grande Chartreuse. Stephen of Muret (c. 1054–1125/25) founded a hermitage at Muret (Limousin) that was moved to Grandmont in 1125, received customs under Prior Stephen of Liciac (1139–1163), and eventually spun off some 150 dependent houses in France and England. The Carthusian Order arose from the foundation of La Grande Chartreuse by Bruno of Cologne (c. 1032–1101) in 1084. The Carthusians were severely rigorous hermits disposed in cells and assembling only in worship. Prior Guigo (1109–1136) wrote the first customs, and in his time affiliated cells began to multiply, notably in Burgundy. Of altogether different character were the military orders associated with the First Crusade (1095) and its consequences. The Knights of the Temple (Templars) arose from the impulse of a French knight named Hugh of Payns around 1119; he organized a small brotherhood of men under religious vows aimed at defending the pilgrim roads to Jerusalem. The Knights of St. John of Jerusalem (Hospitallers), having begun as a charitable mission for the care of the sick, likewise assumed military responsibilities. Although both orders remained centered in Jerusalem, both acquired important patrimonies and convents in Western lands, including France.

By far the most successful of the new orders was that of Cîteaux (Cistercium), a place in Burgundy. Not only did it grow with unparalleled speed, but it influenced or even absorbed other movements while its religious tenets remolded the prevailing spirituality. For as with most forms of monasticism, success entailed the contradiction of withdrawal that shakes the world. Bernard of Clairvaux (1090–1153), who took vows at Cîteaux in 1113, was soon joined by his Burgundian knightly kinsmen. In 1115 he became abbot of Clairvaux, was soon thereafter a celebrated preacher and controversialist, and by the 1130s functioned as little less than the moral arbiter of Europe.

The first Cistercians were monks who seceded from the new (1075) Benedictine house of Molesme in 1098. Some of them, including their leader Robert, returned to Molesme, leaving a precarious remnant of eight who persevered at Cîteaux under two abbots, including the Englishman Stephen Harding (1109–1122). In Stephen's time came the first expansion, with new foundations at La Ferté (1113), Pontigny (1114), and Morimond and Clairvaux (1115). From these daughter houses sprang yet more congregations in a spiraling multiplication extending far beyond Burgundy and France, amounting to some 344 houses by 1152. In that year the general chapter prohibited further foundations, a decree better observed in France than elsewhere.

The Cistercian movement marked a reaction against the customs that had overgrown the Benedictine Rule. Insistence on a literal observance of the Rule can be traced back to the secession from Molesme, but quite possibly it became a central tenet only in St. Bernard's day. On the assumption that the Rule forbade what it did not explicitly authorize, a more severely ascetic regime was required, a life more nearly resembling that of the poor Christ. Wearing undyed wool, the "White Monks" looked different from old Benedictines, the "Black Monks." More problematic was the restoration of work to the daily regimen and the rejection of incomes from sources, such as churches and mills, not mentioned by the Rule. Yet the Cistercians in their turn had to compromise with the Rule. They wanted only men old enough to decide for themselves. They established lay brothers (conversi), as the Cluniacs had done, to help manage necessities, but they excluded lay brothers from company with choir monks. The most considerable departure from the Benedictine Rule lay in the decision, prescribed in the "Charter of Charity" (1119), to associate all Cistercian abbots in systematic supervision and visitation. Each year the abbots were to assemble at Cîteaux while each house was to be visited by the abbot of its founder house. The multiple abbots made of each house the isle of repose ordained by St. Benedict, but it was not easy for abbots of distant houses to assemble annually.

The personal magnetism and brilliance of St. Bernard largely explains the early success of the Cistercians. Preaching, admonishing, and persuading, he drew hundreds of men to the Order. The statutory visitation of daughter houses would alone have kept him on the road, for Clairvaux was by far the most prolific parent of such offspring. Otherwise Bernard's influence multiplied outside the cloister, his letters, sermons, and theological tracts reaching enlarged circles of the faithful responsive to a newly emotional and subjective spirituality. Yet there was timely new logic in his way of rethinking St. Benedict's steps of humility, and the "reason" emergent in his age is visible also in the economic structuring of Cistercian resources. Many houses were set up in frontier lands that could be managed as consolidated farms by the lay brothers and hired laborers.

The revival of apostolic values among reformers and hermits helps explain the concurrent renewal of a common life appropriate to priests. The Rule of Aachen (816) having generally lapsed, the 11th century witnessed a variety of experimental practices. In 1039 the bishop of Avignon permitted four canons to live together in the church of Saint-Ruf, and this model of religious life spread widely. The Roman reformers advocated "the apostolic, that is the common life" (Council of 1059), and during the next generation many communities came to base their observance on texts attributed to St. Augustine. Toward 1100 the popes could distinguish clearly between secular clergy and canons having property and regular clergy imitating the apostolic life and comprising monks and canons. The "canons regular" were those living under the Augustinian Rule. The cathedral clergies of France were generally reluctant to submit to this more austere observance. Apart from two or three southern bishoprics, only Sées in Normandy instituted a regular chapter. This was instigated by Saint-Victor of Paris, itself a model for Augustinian regularity in

Refectory, Abbey Church of Saint-Jean-des-Vignes (Benedictine), Soissons, France, 13th and 14th centuries.
Photo courtesy of Chris Schabel

collegiate churches, and, like Saint-Ruf, its practice was open to imitation elsewhere. The most remarkable new impulse of this sort, rooted in the works of hermits and itinerant preachers and influenced by the Cistercians, was that of Prémontré, founded by Norbert of Xanten (1080/85–1134). The Premonstratensians, as Augustinian canons living the apostolic life of personal renunciation, rapidly won followers in northeastern France and beyond.

By 1200 the "Benedictine centuries" were over. Many of the Christian reformers had been monks, and many of these down to 1150 had been elected popes. However, there were no real successors to Peter the Venerable or Bernard of Clairvaux. Outwardly the old Benedictines, now often called "Black Monks" by reason of the habits they wore, prospered. Abbot Suger of Saint-Denis (1122–1251), yet another great figure of his passing generation, achieved stunning success as manager and architect, realizing the worldly monastic life with conspicuous brilliance. However, he too had no such admirable successor; moreover he epitomized the excesses and failings of the old monastic way that reformers had long inveighed against. Saint Bernard excoriated the Cluniacs for excesses of table and dress contrary to the Rule; Abbot Peter responded with dignity that his monks at least displayed charity. The quarrel droned on, not without eloquence but quite without resolution; by the 1180s critics such as Walter Map (1130/35–1209/10) could disparage monks, Black and

White, with equal vehemence. The "crisis of monasticism," as some have termed it, had occurred earlier and cut deeper. Many people in growing populations who had felt excluded from the Benedictine life sought the new outlets offered by ascetic preachers and the apostolic model. Increasing wealth called into question a traditional model of elite humility, pushing charity and the pastoral office to the fore. Survival, revival, and innovation were the marks of a varied monastic life at its apogee in 12th-century France.

### The Later Middle Ages

At the turn of the 13th century, Pope Innocent III (1198–1216) viewed the monastic orders as an asset to be used for the good of the Church. He appointed two Cistercian monks to a legatine commission to preach against heretics in southern France, but he knew that problems existed in the monastic life. An investigation disclosed that the abbot of Vézelay, one of the most illustrious Cluniac houses, was an incontinent simoniac dissipating the monks' patrimony. Similar abuses turned up in the most venerable Cistercian abbeys as well as in the Orders of Grandmont and Prémontré.

However, Innocent III faced larger problems than those of the religious orders. The measures taken to improve monastic discipline at the Fourth Lateran Council (1215) witnessed to the strength as well as the weakness of a luxuriant growth. Two measures above all should be noted. First, the council ordained that orders hitherto lacking a periodic assembly of conventual heads should institute such forthwith. This was a commendation of a Cistercian innovation over against the Black Monks, and explicitly so, for the canon further enjoined that neighboring Cistercian abbots were to serve as advisers in the new assemblies. The federative ideal was to prevail against the self-sufficient Benedictine house. Second, the council prohibited any further replication of religious houses, meaning that novices were henceforth to choose one of the established modes of religious life and could not join new ones. This prohibition, which like the first affected France as part of Christendom, must be understood in relation to the most salient innovation of the 13th century: the institution of the Orders of St. Dominic and St. Francis.

Dominic of Calaruega (c. 1172–1221) accompanied his Spanish bishop in preaching against the heretics in southern France (1206–1207). By 1212 it was clear that he and, in Italy, Francis of Assisi (1181/82–1226) commanded substantial followings of men willing to renounce personal possessions and to preach and teach "by word and example." Pope Innocent III was prepared to distinguish these groups of Poor Men from some previous ones who had been denounced as heretics, but he was also responsive to the fears of bishops that mendicant preachers would usurp priestly functions. Thus, although in 1215 an injunction against new orders was politic, it was accompanied by a provision for the appointment of suitable preachers in cathedral cities, a provision that was to be the opening for a vast new enterprise. By the 1220s Franciscan and Dominican houses were being established in France; the Dominicans, followed by the Franciscans, organized federatively, setting up supervisory provinces and assembling in periodic chapters. The Dominican life and observance were modeled on those of the Augustinian Canons. Dominic's followers continued to serve in the campaigns against heresy, especially against the Cathars in southern France. By the 1240s mendicant friars from both new orders were being appointed to commissions of inquiry; and when he returned from the crusade of 1248–1254, King Louis IX (1226–1270) was influenced by Franciscan spirituality in his public works. Educated men of both orders multiplied (against the counsel of the Spiritual Franciscans), and in France the Franciscan Bonaventura (c. 1217–1274) and the Dominican Thomas Aquinas (c. 1225–1274) rose to occupy professorships of theology at Paris. The mendicant orders rode the crest of urbanism and human fertility. Houses for pious women, who were often called beguines, had already been established in northern towns. Other mendicant groups included the Carmelites and Augustinian friars; more important than these in France were the Friars of the Sack, founded in 1251. Auxiliary associations for men and women, such as the Poor Clares, were organized.

Meanwhile the old orders carried on. They found it difficult to maintain discipline. When the (Franciscan) Archbishop Eudes Rigaud of Rouen traversed Normandy toward 1260, he found backsliding and sexual misconduct in many of the abbeys, priories, and nunneries. This cannot have been abnormal; what was new was that a written record was kept. Benedictines of all kinds survived as privileged elements in growing societies. The mendicants enjoyed the advantages of novelty, of closer touch with powerful ideals; yet even this advantage had weakened by 1300, when the Franciscans were riven by internal dispute. In the old orders the numbers of vocations fell in the later Middle Ages, and the old practice of pious donation was reduced and diverted to the mendicant friars. Men and women, especially of the nobility, took up livings in old religious houses. By the later 14th century, writers everywhere held monks and friars in suspicion or contempt. The abbots of Cluny had their town houses (that of Paris still exists); even the Cistercians had lost their prestigious esprit. By this time their piety had been diffused in a lay society acculturated to monastic spirituality. French monks were forced from their houses by the Hundred Years' War, afflicted and reduced by the Plague. The popes of Avignon began to appoint candidates to abbacies as a matter of financial privilege, and the institution of commendatory abbots would persist until the French Revolution. France was not immune to humanist currents from Italy, and in some few places a new penchant for bookish piety can be traced in the 15th century.

*Modern Times*

Only in the past century has monastic life recovered from the blows of modernity. Although many religious houses in France survived the disorders of the 16th century and some others were established thereafter, few survived the French Revolution. Cîteaux, for example, was pulled to pieces in 1791, and the remains were sold. In 1563 the Council of Trent had required existing monasteries to join or re-form in congregations, and such federations served to maintain traditions even as they now partook of politics. Through periodic chapters and visitations, good observance was generally restored. The congregation of Saint-Maur (1621–1792) upheld the Benedictine Rule while engaging in teaching, preaching, and exemplary historical scholarship. The Jesuits, organized in the years 1539–1540 as a bulwark of Roman Catholic reformation (and suppressed in 1763), might be regarded as a new order or clerks regular; however, they pointedly departed from medieval principles of voluntary associative life, and their activist role in France came into conflict with congregations supportive of Gallicanism (i.e., advocacy of French privileges). Among these were the reformed Cistercians of the Strict Observance, dating from 1664 at La Trappe, whose practice forced a split from Cistercians of the Common Observance. Virtually ended by the Revolution, Cistercian life in both reformed traditions was restored in the 19th century – monks of the Strict Observance, or Trappists, restored Cîteaux in 1898 – and carries on today. Monks content with the Rule of St. Benedict likewise made a new start in the 19th century, often assuming roles in educational and pastoral work. Solesmes, a Benedictine community refounded in 1833 by Prosper Guéranger in an ancient convent, became known for its work in liturgy and music.

Monasticism in modern France is an adaptation and a survival. The new impulses – for example, in history and liturgy – however admirable, even indispensable, represent human pur-

suits that would seem to subvert the quest for eternity. The profoundly vital ages unfolded between the careers of Benedict of
Aniane and Bernard of Clairvaux together with the prayers of
the monks they led. The religious life in France was then a matter of life and death. Yet even then the needs as well as the temptations of the world enticed monks and nuns. Missionaries
almost from the start, they became teachers, singers, and scholars during their most creatively religious phase. Little is heard
before modern times of a specifically French monasticism. Dynastic historiography dated back to Suger's day at Saint-Denis;
for patriotism we wait for the 14th century or, among monks,
even later. The religious orders in medieval France had little use
for political boundaries, and the modern ones hardly differ in
this respect.

THOMAS N. BISSON

*See also* Abelard, Peter; Alcuin; Architecture: Western Christian
Monasteries; Augustinian Canons; Benedict of Aniane, St.; Bene-
dict of Nursia, St.; Beguines; Bruno, St.; Caesarius of Arles, St.;
Carmelites; Carthusians; Cathars; Cistercians; Claustration
(Cloister), Rules of; Cluny, Abbots of; Cluny, France; Columban,
St.; Dominic, St.; Dominicans; Fontevraud, France; Francis of
Assisi, St.; Franciscans; Grandmontines; Guéranger, Prosper;
Heloise; Hospitallers (Knights of Malta since 1530); Lérins,
France; Liturgy: Western Christian; Martin of Tours, St.; Mau-
rists; Mont-St.-Michel, France; Orders (Religious), Origin of;
Origins: Western Christian; Patrons, Christian; Premonstraten-
sian Canons; Radegunde, St.; Solesmes, France; Suger; Templars;
Trappists; Victorines; Warrior Monks: Christian

**Further Reading**

Constable, Giles, *The Reformation of the Twelfth Century*,
  Cambridge: Cambridge University Press, 1996
De Jong, Mayke, "Carolingian Monasticism: The Power of
  Prayer," *The New Cambridge Medieval History: Volume II,
  c. 700–c. 900*, edited by Rosamond McKitterick, Cambridge
  and New York: Cambridge University Press, 1995
Hunt, Noreen, editor, *Cluniac Monasticism in the Central
  Middle Ages*, London: Macmillan, and Hamden,
  Connecticut: Archon, 1971
Lemarignier, Jean-François, "Political and Monastic Structures
  in France at the End of the Tenth and the Beginning of the
  Eleventh Century," translated by Fredric L. Cheyette in
  *Lordship and Community in Medieval Europe: Selected
  Readings*, New York: Holt, Rinehart, and Winston, 1968
Morris, Colin, *The Papal Monarchy: The Western Church from
  1050 to 1250*, Oxford: Clarendon Press, and New York:
  Oxford University Press, 1989
Prinz, Friedrich, *Frühes Mönchtum im Frankenreich: Kultur
  und Gesellschaft in Gallien, den Rheinlanden und Bayern
  am Beispiel der monastischen Entwicklung (4. bis 8.
  Jahrhundert)*, Vienna: Oldenbourg, 1965; 2nd edition,
  Munich: Oldenbourg, 1988
Southern, Richard W., *Western Society and the Church in the
  Middle Ages*, Harmondsworth: Penguin, and Grand Rapids,
  Michigan: Eerdmans, 1970
Venarde, Bruce L., *Women's Monasticism and Medieval
  Society: Nunneries in France and England, 890–1215*,
  Ithaca, New York: Cornell University Press, 1997
Wallace-Hadrill, John M., *The Frankish Church*, Oxford:
  Clarendon Press, and New York: Oxford University Press,
  1983

# France: Sites

Alongside Italy and Ireland contemporary France is undoubtedly
the land in which there has been the greatest efflorescence of the
major monastic movements of western Christianity: St. Martin
at Ligugé (c. 360), St. Honaratus at Lérins (c. 410), St. Columban at Luxeuil (c. 590), Duke William of Aquitaine and Berno at
Cluny (909–910), St. Bruno at La Grande-Chartreuse (1084),
Robert d'Arbrissel at Fontevraud (1101), St. Robert of Molesme
at Cîteaux (1098), St. Bernard at Clairvaux (1115), St. Norbert
at Prémontré (1120), Armand-Jean Le Bouthillier de Rancé at La
Trappe (reformed in 1664), and so on. However, of all the
houses founded by these prestigious pioneers, only Fontevraud
remains in its original buildings. Some of the other houses still
have homogeneous ensembles of buildings, but most of these
are of a relatively late date (the 17th century at La Grande-
Chartreuse, the 18th at Prémontré, and the 19th at Lérins and
La Trappe). Elsewhere the monasteries are composite – as at
Ligugé, where one can, however, see beneath the floor of the former abbey church, now the parish church, the remains of early
Christian and early medieval buildings – or else very fragmentary, as at Luxeuil, Cluny, Cîteaux, and Clairvaux.

Nevertheless France remains among the countries that are
richest in monastic monuments. Many sites have been damaged
by the passage of time or the contempt of human beings, notably
as a result of being nationalized during the French Revolution,
when monasteries transformed into prisons, hospitals, or
schools or sold and neglected by new owners. Yet some of the
most prestigious monasteries have been admirably restored, including Mont-St.-Michel, the abbey church of Saint-Denis, and
the monumental complex of Fontevraud. Visiting conditions
vary enormously. In some cases visits are completely forbidden
either for religious reasons, as at La Grande-Chartreuse, which
remains the headquarters of the Carthusian Order, or for secular
reasons, as at Clairvaux, which has become a national prison. In
other cases visits are restricted to certain times of the year, in
particular where monastic communities are still functioning.
However, many old monasteries, whether they have become
public or private property, are open to visitors on the usual conditions and at the usual times. Indeed, so many exist that only a
very limited selection of them can be presented here. This will be
done region by region on the assumption that visitors who are
pressed for time should make their own choice in their turn. In
any case it is Burgundy and Normandy that offer the greatest
concentration and the finest selection of centers of French
monasticism.

*Paris and the Île de France*
From among the earliest medieval monastic sites of the Parisian
region, only the memorial crypt of the convent of Jouarre (seventh century) has been preserved, with its superb tombs (seventh

to eighth century) of its first abbess, Theodechilde, and her brother, Bishop Agilbert. However, some of these very old monasteries became prestigious royal abbeys, and several generations of kings were buried in their churches, such as Saint-Germain-des-Prés in Paris and, most notably, in Saint-Denis, where the two abbey churches, now absorbed into the urban sprawl, are masterpieces: the first (11th to 12th century) of Parisian Romanesque art and the second (12th to 13th century) of French Gothic.

As for the countryside of the Île de France, one may admire above all the remains of such Cistercian abbeys as Les Vaux de Cernay, Chaalis, Longpont, or Ourscamps, which were founded in the 12th century and of which only the ruins of their medieval churches and certain convent or abbey buildings remain. In addition Royaumont, a royal foundation of the 13th century, retains its ruined church, its cloister in its original state, and some of the buildings that surrounded them, in particular kitchens and a refectory as well as a pleasing abbot's residence from the 18th century that is situated at a slight distance from the older remains.

### The Loire Valley

The Loire basin witnessed the development of some of the most important and prestigious monasteries in Western Europe. The oldest of them, Marmoutier, was founded by St. Martin in 372, but only a few, not very interesting vestiges of it remain. By contrast at Fleury, which became known as Saint-Benoît-sur-Loire in 672, when the remains of St. Benedict were transferred there from Monte Cassino, monastic buildings remain, now occupied by a Benedictine community, and there is an imposing abbey church (11th to 12th century) that has a bell-tower porch decorated with superb Romanesque capitals. Finally, at Fontevraud, founded by Robert d'Arbrissel in 1099, there remains a remarkably homogeneous ensemble of buildings, notably including a church roofed with domes on pendentives, where one may admire the recumbent effigies of Henry II Plantagenet, Eleanor of Aquitaine, and Richard the Lionheart.

However, one may well wish to leave the river valley in order to go and admire two other sites. To the south, in Berry, stands the very beautiful Cistercian abbey of Noirlac, which retains its church (12th century) and its monastic buildings (12th to 13th century) grouped around its cloister. To the north the abbey of Solesmes stands on the banks of the Sarthe: formerly a modest medieval priory, in 1837 it was given over to the monastic life and became the birthplace of the revival of Benedictinism and the Gregorian liturgy in France.

### Brittany

In the historic heart of Brittany, close to the Loire estuary and south of Nantes, can be found Saint-Philbert de Grand-Lieu, formerly a daughter house of the abbey of Noirmoutier. Its abbey church, with very distinctive Carolingian forms inspired by Roman architecture, dates back to the ninth century; it once housed the body of St. Philibert, which was brought there by the monks of Noirmoutier when they fled from invading Vikings. However, it is at the other end of Brittany that one will find the most venerated site of Breton monasticism, at Landevennec, an establishment of the Celtic tradition founded in the sixth century by St. Guénolé but totally rebuilt in the Romanesque period. In 1958 a Benedictine community was established close to the medieval monastery, which has been subjected to systematic excavation: the results have been collected in a small museum. Elsewhere in Brittany one can visit the remains of the Benedictine monastery of Redon, founded in 832, and in particular its church (11th to 12th century), which is dominated by a monumental square tower; the austere medieval abbey churches, set amid greenery, that are the only remains of the Cistercian monasteries of Boquen and Relecq; the abbey of Daoulas, founded by the Order of Canons of St. Augustine in the 12th century; and the Premonstratensian abbey of Beauport, founded in the 13th century.

### Normandy

Normandy is among the regions of France that are richest in monastic history. The ancient foundations of the Seine Valley, Fontenelle/Saint-Wandrille and Jumièges, date back to the middle of the seventh century, and the former is still very much alive. The Benedictine community at Fontenelle/Saint-Wandrille, in the shadow of an old and now ruined abbey church, still uses the 14th-century cloister and the chambers that surround it, which are both Romanesque (such as the 12th-century refectory) and "classical" (i.e., rebuilt in the 17th century following the norms of the Maurist reform). Jumièges was founded by St. Philibert in a bend of the Seine: the ruins of its two churches, Saint-Pierre (St. Peter, late tenth century) and Notre-Dame (Our Lady, 11th century), still attract large numbers of visitors interested in the distinctive qualities of their pre-Romanesque and Romanesque Norman art or drawn by the romantic charm of their superb surroundings.

Another generation of Norman abbeys began with the Benedictine foundations promoted by the aristocracy, in particular by the family of the Dukes of Normandy, in the 10th, 11th, and 12th centuries (although in fact these were often transformations of older churches). At Fécamp, which Duke Richard II made into a Benedictine abbey in 1001, the monumental church (12th to 13th century) still exists. Cerisy-la-Fôret, founded in 1032 by Duke Robert, still has its fine Romanesque abbey church. At Le Bec-Helluoin, founded by Herluin in 1035, the tower of the medieval abbey church and the Maurist buildings of the 17th century are now occupied by a community of Olivetan Benedictines. At Saint-Georges-de-Boscherville, built on the initiative of the lords of Tancarville (1050–1114), one may still admire the church and the chapter house (11th to 12th century) that dominate the Seine. Lessay, founded by the lords of La Haye du Puits in 1056, has a beautiful Romanesque abbey church and monastic buildings from the 18th century. The Abbaye-aux-Hommes (Abbey for Men) and the Abbaye-aux-Femmes (Abbey for Women) in Caen, dedicated to Saint-Étienne (St. Stephen) and La Trinité (the Trinity), respectively, were founded in the 1060s by Duke William (the Conqueror) and Duchess Matilda in expiation for their marriage, which the ecclesiastical authorities had judged to be consanguinous. Both of these abbeys retain monumental churches, each with a facade dominated by twin towers and an interior lit through a lantern tower as well as 17th-century monastic buildings with sumptuous woodcarving and decoration. At Hambye, founded around 1145 by Guillaume Paynel, one may still admire the ruins of the 13th-century abbey church and several old monastic buildings.

Finally, and most important, there is the abbey of Mont-St.-Michel. In the eighth century an oratory was founded on this site by Bishop Aubert of Avranches; it was served by a small community of clerics. Duke Richard I created a Benedictine monastery in its place in 966. Its first church, known as Notre-Dame-sous-terre (Our Lady under the Ground), dates from the end of the tenth century and can still be seen, although it has been buried under later buildings, notably the new abbey church that still crowns the summit of the hill. Additions have been made to this church in every period, including its Romanesque nave (11th century), its flamboyant choir (15th to 16th century), and its spire (19th century). The church is surrounded by buildings that harmonize with the rocks, notably the late medieval abbot's residence, which dominates the southern aspect, and the monastic buildings to the north, which include the outstanding 13th-century "Merveille" ("Marvel"), with its cloister, refectory, and rooms for work and ceremonial.

### The North and Picardy

Only a little remains of the most famous abbeys founded north of Gaul in the Merovingian and Carolingian periods, including fragments of the Gothic facade at Saint-Bertin, an elaborate tower at Saint-Amand, and some of the arches of the abbey church at Corbie. Saint-Riquier alone has conserved a superb monumental ensemble from the Middle Ages. In particular the remains of its famous Carolingian church, known through a miniature in Hariulf's chronicle, and the tomb of Charlemagne's son-in-law Angilbert, who, as secular abbot, conceived its construction, have been discovered beneath the flamboyant church of the 15th and early 16th centuries, with its facade animated by numerous sculptures. Few medieval vestiges remain of the great foundations of the 12th century other than an imposing building for monks on the Cistercian site of Vaucelles. By contrast the abbeys of Valloires and Prémontré display some magnificent baroque ensembles from the 18th century.

### Champagne, Lorraine, Alsace, and the Franche-Comté

Traveling east, one arrives at Reims, where one may admire the abbey church of Saint-Rémi, which was built over the tomb of the bishop who baptized King Clovis and is a masterpiece of the Romanesque and early Gothic styles of the Champagne region (12th to 13th century). The Premonstratensian abbey at Pont-à-Mousson was reconstructed in a somewhat baroque version of the classical style during the 18th century.

In Alsace, just over the border from Lorraine, stands Marmoutier, a seventh-century foundation: its abbey church, fronted with a facade of the 11th to 12th century, is one of the three great masterpieces of Alsatian Romanesque, along with Murbach and Ottmarsheim. Murbach was a Benedictine foundation of the eighth century that grew wealthy on its considerable endowments of land; its abbot became a prince of the Holy Roman Empire. The transept, choir, and two towers of the 12th-century abbey church have survived amid the forest of Vosges. Ottmarsheim, a Benedictine convent founded on the banks of the Upper Rhine around 1030, is distinctive because of the shape of its 11th-century church, an octagon inspired by the imperial chapel at Aachen.

In the Franche-Comté the only site that really must be visited is that of Baume-les-Messieurs, a Colombanian foundation of the seventh century that became a Benedictine abbey and then a college of regular canons. Its medieval church and abbatial buildings stand in a row at the edge of the monastic estate at the foot of a mountain.

### Burgundy

The history of monasticism in Burgundy dates back to the very early Middle Ages. It is said that Queen Clotilde ordered the building of its first monastery, in the sixth century, over the tomb of the bishop Saint-Germain-d'Auxerre. Placed under the Benedictine Rule, this abbey reached its intellectual and artistic apogee in the ninth century with the development of a very brilliant school and the construction of a new crypt, which may still be admired beneath the present Gothic church. At Flavigny, an eighth-century foundation, there remain the lower parts of a church built in the ninth century. At Tournus, a small seventh-century monastery, the monks of Noirmoutier, fleeing the Vikings and their earlier refuge at Grand-Lieu, installed the relics of St. Philibert in 875; the privileges and donations that followed gave the monastery a new impetus that culminated in the construction of the superb abbey church, from the 10th to the 12th century, and of the new monastic buildings of the 12th and 13th centuries. The history of Vézelay is almost as long, as it was founded in the middle of the ninth century; two centuries later, however, it passed under the control of Cluny and reached its apogee with the rebuilding of its abbey church, which has a Romanesque nave, narthex, and tympanum (12th century) and a Gothic choir (early 13th century).

Indeed the foundation of Cluny in 909–910 had far-reaching effects on the history of monasticism in Burgundy, as it drew earlier foundations under its control and also promoted the establishment of numerous priories. Of the mother abbey itself, once the most important monastery in Western Europe, there remains no more than one transept and a tower of the abbey church built at the end of the 11th century (and known as Cluny III) and a granary from the end of the 13th century that is now a lapidary museum. However, thanks to some of its priories, one can still glimpse today the distinctiveness of Cluny art, although not so much at the priory of La Charité-sur-Loire, which is almost as dilapidated as the mother house, as at the priories of Charlieu, with its Romanesque tympanum, Berzé-La-Ville, with its murals, and, above all, Paray-Le-Monial, with its perfectly preserved abbey church, a smaller version of Cluny III.

Burgundy was the birthplace of the Cistercian movement, which arose precisely as a reaction against the artistic and intellectual luxury of Cluny. Only a few buildings remain at Cîteaux, still given over to the monastic life, but at Pontigny, the second daughter abbey of Cîteaux, one will find a very beautiful abbey church of the early Gothic period (end of the 12th century), which in fact is not at all Cistercian, as its choir is surrounded by an ambulatory and chapels radiating from it. Fontenay, founded in 1118 by St. Bernard of Clairvaux (1090–1153), is an outstanding and completely homogeneous example of the "Bernardine" architecture of the 12th century, preserved almost in its entirety with its church, its cloister, its chapter house, its monastic buildings, and even its forge.

### The Lyonnais, the Alps, and Provence

In the Lyonnais region one should see, to the north of Lyon, Ambronay, a Benedictine foundation of the ninth century that retains its large Gothic church, its cloister, and its chapter house, and south of Lyon, Saint-André-le-Bas at Vienne, a sixth-century foundation, with its 12th-century church and cloister.

The Alpine valleys were available for those who sought to flee from the world, and many new foundations emerged there at the time of the great monastic development of the 11th and 12th centuries. The most famous is St. Bruno's foundation at La Grande-Chartreuse. One cannot visit its 17th-century buildings, but a small museum displays the Carthusians' rigorous way of life. One may also admire, to the north of the massif, remains of the 13th-century church and, in particular, the 14th-century cloister, decorated with superb Italian frescoes at the beginning of the 15th century, at the Augustinian abbey of Abondance. On the banks of Lake Le Bourget stands the abbey of Hautecombe, a Cistercian foundation of the 12th century, and the mausoleum of the Counts of Savoy, which was completely rebuilt in the 19th century in a neo-Gothic style. To the south of the massif, in the upper valley of the Durance, is the priory of Ganagobie, an offshoot of Cluny, which has a church and a cloister with fine Romanesque sculptures and mosaics.

From Ganagobie one can leave the Alps and enter Provence, where one can see the remains of two very old foundations from the fifth century: the crypt of Saint-Victor in Marseille and the medieval fragments of Saint-Honorat at Lérins, which are surrounded by 19th-century reconstructions. However, one may prefer to visit the abbey of Montmajour, a Benedictine foundation of the tenth century that retains a church and monastic buildings from the 12th century, and above all the three Cistercian sister abbeys of Provence, Le Thoronet, Sénanque, and Silvacane. All three have preserved typically Bernardine monumental ensembles of the 12th or early 13th century in all their original harmony and surroundings.

### Languedoc and the Toulouse Region

On the western side of the lower valley of the Rhone can be found the 14th-century Carthusian monastery of Villeneuve-lès-Avignon, which benefited from its close proximity to the residence of the popes at Avignon, and the Benedictine monastery of Saint-Gilles-du-Gard, founded in the eighth century, of which a crypt and a superb monumental facade, sculpted in the 12th century, have been preserved. One may then be interested in taking a detour in order to visit, in the hinterland of Montpellier, two centers of Carolingian monasticism: Aniane, of which nothing remains but which, thanks to its abbot, Benedict (c. 750–821), was the birthplace of the Benedictine reform imposed by Louis the Pious (814–840) throughout the whole of his empire, and, very close by, Gellone, known today as Saint-Guilhem-du-Désert, founded by Charlemagne's cousin William of Aquitaine: its 11th-century abbey church still adorns the small square in the town, but its cloister is to be found today in the Cloisters Museum in New York. Fontfroide, a Cistercian foundation near Narbonne, has retained its ensemble of buildings from the 12th to the 13th century almost intact, but their elegance and discreet decor are not entirely in keeping with the austerity demanded by Bernard of Clairvaux.

In the Roussillon region, at the foot of the eastern Pyrenees, several monastic foundations from the 9th to the 11th century have left us some gems of medieval architecture. At Serrabone a magnificently isolated priory, the church (11th to 12th century) has a richly decorated pink marble gallery. At Saint-Michel-de-Cuxa, the church (10th to 12th century) is flanked by a typically Catalan square tower that inspired the one constructed at the Cloisters Museum in New York: it is there that one can also find half the cloister, with its fine sculpted capitals, no longer to be seen in its original location. Isolated on a rocky peak, Saint-Martin-du-Canigou has a church and a cloister from the 10th to the 11th century. Finally, at Arles-sur-Tech there are a Romanesque church and a beautiful Gothic cloister.

The Toulouse region is also very rich in remains. The immense monastic basilica of Saint-Sernin de Toulouse, a masterpiece of southern French Romanesque art of the 11th and 12th centuries, is outstanding because of its alternating use of brick and stone. The austere house of preaching friars in Toulouse, known as Jacobins, is in a pure Gothic style of the 13th century. To the northwest stands the abbey of Moissac, a seventh-century Benedictine foundation that reached its apogee in the late 11th and early 12th centuries with the construction of the church, the cloister, and the church doors: decorating the central pier of the south door is a figure of the prophet Jeremiah, perhaps the supreme masterpiece of French Romanesque sculpture. The abbey of Flaran is a well-preserved example of the small Cistercian monasteries of the 12th and 13th centuries.

### The Atlantic Seaboard

Atlantic France retains beautiful ruins, surrounded by greenery, from the numerous Benedictine foundations of the 10th and 11th centuries – such as La Sauve Majeure in the Bordelais region, Fontdouce in Saintonge, and Maillezais in lower Poitou – and from the houses of the Cistercians and regular canons founded in the 12th century, such as the Chateliers in Ré, La Couronne in Angoumois, and Sablonceaux in Saintonge. Fortunately, however, some of these monasteries have been preserved in their urban or semi-urban surroundings and have bequeathed to us some of the greatest masterpieces of French Romanesque art: the Abbaye-aux-Dames at Saintes, with its church and tower from the 11th to the 12th century; Saint-Hilaire at Poitiers, with its 11th-century nave and 12th-century choir; and, most notably, Saint-Savin-sur-Gartempe, which has the finest set of Romanesque frescoes in France on the vault of its magnificent nave (11th to 12th century).

*Central France, the Auvergne, and Their Borderlands*
We will end our journey into the heart of French monasticism by way of the Massif Central, starting with a group of abbey, priory, and collegial churches in the Auvergne: Notre-Dame du Port at Clermont-Ferrand, Saint-Austremoine at Issoire, Saint-Julien at Brioude, and Saint-Nectaire or Orcival. They were all built in the 12th century. The use of volcanic stones gives their Romanesque style an authentic austerity as well as a family resemblance. Saint-Julien and Saint-Nectaire were daughter houses of a great abbey situated in southeastern Auvergne, La Chaise-Dieu, founded in 1043 by Robert de Turlande, who made it the headquarters of an important congregation. By and large its remaining buildings – church, cloister, and monastic structures – date from the 14th century. They contain several treasures of late medieval art, notably a celebrated 15th-century fresco of the Dance of Death. However, it is in southwestern Auvergne that one will find a final and admirable example of monastic art and influence at Sainte-Foy in Conques. The austere abbey church of this eighth-century foundation possesses a superb sculpted tympanum depicting the Last Judgment and a treasure house of religious gold- and silverware containing numerous reliquaries, such as a famous statue of St. Foy.

STÉPHANE LEBECQ

*See also* Architecture: Western Christian Monasteries; Cluny, France; Fontevraud, France; Island Monasteries, Christian; Lérins, France; Mont-St.-Michel, France; Solesmes, France

**Further Reading**

Bottineau, Yves, *L'art baroque*, Paris: Citadelles/Mazenod, 1986

Durliat, Jean, *Des Barbares à l'an mil*, Paris: Citadelles/Mazenod, 1985

Durliat, Jean, *L'art roman*, Paris: Citadelles/Mazenod, 1993

Erlande-Brandenburg, Alain, *L'art gothique*, Paris: Citadelles/Mazenod, 1983

Erlande-Brandenburg, Alain, and Anne-Bénédicte Merel-Brandenburg, *Histoire de l'architecture française du Moyen Age à la Renaissance (IVe siècle–début XVIe siècle)*, Paris: Caisse Nationale des Monuments Historiques et des Sites, 1995

Taralon, Jean, *La France des abbayes*, Paris: Hachette Réalités, 1978

# Francis of Assisi, St. 1181–1226

Italian founder of the Franciscan Order, beloved saint

Saint Francis of Assisi was the son of Pietro di Bernardone and his wife, Pica, or Giovanna, who was probably of French origin. Baptized John, the child received the name Francis from his father, perhaps as a pet name meaning "the little Frenchman." As a cloth merchant, Pietro traveled frequently in France. At this time, French fashions, popular literature, and religious ideas were quite influential in Italy. It is highly likely that Pietro gained much more than commercial benefits from his travel in France and not unlikely that Francis was exposed to these influences at home from both his parents. According to his earliest biographer, Thomas of Celano (c. 1190–1260), Francis led a somewhat dissolute life as a youth, enjoyed singing and dancing, and was popular among the young people of Assisi. He aspired to be numbered among the nobility, not an unusual characteristic among the upwardly mobile merchant class of late 12th- and 13th-century Italy. However, we should probably exercise caution in accepting too literally this picture of Francis, as the topos of a misspent youth was standard fare among hagiographers and hearkened back to the *Confessions* of St. Augustine of Hippo (354–430). What seems most evident is that Francis was a natural leader.

The great crisis of his life came in 1202–1203, when he was captured and held prisoner in neighboring Perugia. However, his conversion seems to have been gradual. Only in 1205, when he set out on a knightly quest to join Walter of Brienne's expedition against Markward of Anweiler, the German ministerial who had been condemned by Pope Innocent III (1198–1216) as a rebel against King Frederick of Sicily, did he begin seriously to question the direction of his life and decided to return home. He dramatically altered his lifestyle, symbolized by his embrace and kissing of a leper whom he met.

Throughout his life, Francis combined a remarkable gift to penetrate directly to the heart of fundamental issues with directness of action, often of a very concrete form. Thus, when he perceived that Christ spoke to him from the cross in the church of San Damiano, he took his words literally and began to gather materials to repair local churches. He gave the poor money from the sale of goods in his father's shop, incurring the wrath of his father for taking it without permission. Chiara Frugoni has suggested that Francis' father might have been a usurer, and this could account for Francis' taking money to make restitution by giving it to the poor. This might also explain the deepening crisis in his relations with his father, culminating in the scene in which, in the presence of the local bishop, he removed his clothes and declared himself emancipated from his father's guardianship.

Not surprisingly, Francis gathered about himself a group of like-minded men. Possibly, some women were also among those attracted by his religious message. In 1212, Francis aided Clare of Assisi (1193/94–1253), who formed a community of these female followers, that developed later as the second order of Franciscans. Francis reflected the new religious spirit that was capturing the popular imagination not only in Italy but in the north as well. In 1199, Pope Innocent III had canonized the Cremonese merchant Homobonus (c. 1120–1197), whom he singled out for his deeply religious life and his service to his community and the poor. Homobonus had belonged to a lay religious confraternity. Such confraternities were seed-beds of new religious devotions and concern for the poor. In addition, numerous houses of the *Humiliati* (priests and laity dedicated to an active religious life) existed, and historians have begun to multiply other examples. Where such groups were once regarded as exceptional and thought to be tainted with heresy, we now know that they were part of this swelling religiosity among the clergy and laity that was inspired by the notion of making the monastic ideal of the imitation of Christ more generally present in the Christian community. This process inevitably provoked some opposition and even led some into conflict with their bishops and into heresy, but that was not true of the majority. Still, the fear of heresy was strong. Many in the church were quick to label new forms of piety, especially those that involved the laity in preaching and Bible reading, as heretical. Francis seems to have been aware of these risks from a very early date.

At some unknown date in 1209 or 1210, with the support of his bishop and the help of a friendly cardinal, John of St. Paul, he was able to secure some kind of preliminary approval from Pope Innocent III. Although the sources have seen this as recognition of a new religious order, the tone taken by the pope suggests that what was involved was a grant of protection to Francis and his companions, not unlike that accorded to others involved in the establishment of new communities around this time. The rule that Francis submitted was not promulgated in the manner in which other rules were in this period, suggesting that formal recognition of the Franciscan order was delayed. Innocent might well have ordered that Francis and his companions receive the tonsure, and it is virtually certain that he granted them permission to preach, probably under the same terms as those accorded other lay groups. These steps would have been entirely consistent with the policies that he was developing with regard to other religious groups in these years, and they were necessary to delineate those who enjoyed some form of official ecclesiastical sanction from those who did not. Opposition to new religious rules surfaced at the Fourth Lateran Council in 1215 and combined with Francis's determination that his order should have its own rule to add to the delay.

Although the message of Francis of Assisi was not entirely unique and the religious community that he founded had other counterparts, none flourished in the same way as did the Order of Minor Brothers, as he called his group. Behind that phenomenon lay his own extraordinary personality. He was not merely one of the most charismatic figures of his age but also one of the few who was able to transmit this characteristic to future generations, even centuries after his death. Permission to preach unleashed the pent-up spiritual energy of Francis on much of central and northern Italy. The brief notices of his preaching that we have reveal the impossibility that contemporaries felt trying to describe the impact of his words. What is evident is that they were so overwhelmed by the man that they could scarcely take in what he was saying. During these years, the order underwent a dramatic growth that necessitated organization into provinces, even before it had received final approval of its rule.

Francis envisaged his order as a community of equals committed to the imitation of Christ and his apostles. Drawing on the apostolic poverty movement, which flourished among both clergy and laity in the second half of the 12th century, Francis in-

corporated both the flexibility of organization that characterized many of these groups and a particular emphasis on voluntary poverty as he believed it had been practiced by Christ and his apostles. Francis embraced poverty to demonstrate his separation from the world, but, in contrast to the Catharist or Albigensian heretics, he placed a singular value on the natural world created by God. On the practical level, the poverty of his followers contrasted with the apparent wealth of the monastic order. However, we should not view Francis as rejecting the monastic view of poverty as much as adapting it to the new circumstances of urban society. Francis' order was urban in character, and most of its members were drawn from the same background as Francis, at least for the first generation of its existence. Francis had the gift of personifying his objectives. He spoke always in concrete terms of "Madonna Povertà" (My Lady Poverty), just as he spoke of brother sun and sister moon in his "Canticle of the Sun." This figurative language, so alien to modern ears, was highly effective in reaching medieval audiences because it heightened the contrast between Francis' position and that of his opponents among the heretics without forcing a confrontation. Francis was deeply committed to the church and seemed to have had a profound understanding of the central doctrines of Christian theology, but he encapsulated them in an imagery that had an appeal to the masses. For example, the symbol of Francis preaching to the birds reaches to the very core of his approach in the way in which he united all of nature under the Divine Creator.

Francis had a missionary vision of his role and that of his order. In 1219, after at least one or two earlier efforts to reach out to the Muslim world, he journeyed to Damietta, Egypt, where a crusader army was encamped before the city. The accounts in the first and second lives by Thomas of Celano and in James of Vitry's sixth letter provide almost no historical insight into this mission except to describe how Francis preached to the assembled crusaders and, with the permission of Cardinal Pelagius of Albano, the papal legate, crossed the lines to the Muslim camp. In all probability, this occurred during a time of truce. Some have suggested that Francis was received by the sultan because he was thought to bring terms of peace. More likely, he delivered a message similar to that he had preached to the crusaders and consistent with a letter that Pope Innocent III had written earlier to Al-Adil, the brother of Saladin and father of the reigning sultan, al-Malik al-Kāmil. This was a message of peace to be achieved through conversion to the Christian faith. Undoubtedly, because of his character as a Christian mystic, Francis was accorded an honorable reception. Moreover, al-Kāmil's policy was directed to securing terms with the crusaders at this time to free himself to pursue his ambition to unite the inheritance of Saladin in Syria to the sultanate of Egypt. Although Francis' mission brought no tangible results, certainly not along the lines he might have hoped for, it might have served a useful purpose in keeping negotiations alive for a time. Certainly, the crusaders were at a rather low state during this period. From that perspective, this mission should not be regarded as having been without value.

When Francis left Egypt, he journeyed first to the Holy Land and then, learning that his young community was in difficulty, returned to Italy. Clearly, the growth of an order required an effective organization. Francis sought the appointment of a cardinal protector in the person of Cardinal Ugolino (c. 1148–1241) of Ostia, a personal friend and supporter. He also appointed Peter Cattani as his vicar and devoted himself to the preparation of a rule. The rule that was presented to the Chapter of the Mats in Assisi in 1221 failed to pass muster with the Roman Curia. The main objections concerned the lack of a clear constitutional framework and especially the lack of sufficient preparation for the religious life for new members. With the aid of Cardinal Ugolino, in a procedure that was by this time quite normal for new religious orders, the rule was revised and submitted once more to the Curia and Pope Honorius III (1216–1227), who promulgated it in 1223. Honorius made special mention of the approval by Pope Innocent III; the approval had probably been introduced in the curial discussion as a way of bypassing the prohibition against new religious rules in canon 13 of the Fourth Lateran Council. Clearly, both Ugolino and the Pope were strong supporters of the work of Francis. In light of later controversies within the order and the debates among modern scholars since Paul Sabatier in the late 19th century about the relationship between Francis and the hierarchy of the church, the question of the rule has assumed a very considerable importance, certainly greater than was warranted by the actual circumstances surrounding its promulgation. For some of the early followers of Francis, who regarded themselves as keepers of his ideals and for the Spiritual Franciscans in the second half of the 13th century, the changes in the rules, although approved by Francis himself and never departing from his own goals in essentials, proved to be a strong stick in internal debates, especially when united to the argument that the order had departed from Francis' conception of poverty. However, these debates emerged only after his death.

The last years of Francis' life were devoted to preaching, prayer, and efforts to inspire and direct his followers. On Christmas in 1223, in Greccio, he presented a tableau of the Nativity, which became the first crib. Francis never moved far from the poetic and dramatic roots of his early life. These formed an essential part of his secret in touching the lives of the masses. His transformation of the abstract into the concrete achieved its most profound realization in his reception of the stigmata (the five wounds of Christ), on his own body on Monte La Verna on 24 September 1224. Finally, worn out, blind, and physically ill, Francis died on 4 October 1226. Less than two years later, on 16 July 1228, his old friend Ugolino, now Pope Gregory IX, canonized him as a saint.

In death, Francis remained as influential a figure as he was in life, thanks in large measure to the spread of his order. The image of Francis, which rapidly appeared in the houses and churches of the order, carried a message that preserved essential features of his life and the legends that rapidly grew up around it. Although Francis left no extensive body of writings, the frescoes of Giotto (c. 1267–1337) and his school at Assisi, Florence, and Padua, as well as the works of other masters, provided concrete witness of the message of the saint. Although that message was somewhat distorted by disputes and legends, the figure of Francis himself seemed always to emerge clearly with its charism intact. It was this charismatic character that also helped feed the divisions that developed within the order. Following the death of Francis, works such as the *Legend of the Three Companions* appeared with the aim of establishing a particular view of Francis. *The Second Life of St. Francis* (1246–1247), by Thomas of Celano, also belonged to this genre. By midcentury, the Franciscans were also influenced by the prophetic writings of Joachim of Fiore (c. 1135–1202), which were interpreted in apocalyptic terms in the *Eternal Gospel* (1254) by the Gerard of Borgo San Donnino (d. 1276) and the *Lectura super Apocalipsim* of Peter John Olivi (c. 1248–1298). The Spiritual Franciscans, drawing on these elements, were increasingly critical of those members of the order, whom they regarded as departing from Francis' view of poverty. This debate has remained a central issue in writings about Francis and the order. Unfortunately, early on the statements of Francis were taken out of the context of contemporary discussions on the nature of monastic poverty, to which they clearly belonged, and put into a broader context of criticism of the relationship between the church and property, a subject that Francis seems never to have addressed. The issue was, at least in part, influential in the 15th century reform movement (led by such friars as Bernardino of Siena [1380–1444]) that produced the Observantine movement (Brown Franciscans) and the 16th century reform that led to the establishment of the Capuchins. The enormous popularity of Francis is also evident in the establishment of Franciscan communities within the Anglican and Episcopalian Church as well as the proliferation of communities of men and women devoted to Francis within the Roman Catholic Church.

JAMES M. POWELL

*See also* Assisi, Italy; Bonaventure, St.; Capuchins; Clare of Assisi, St.; Crusades; Franciscans: General or Male; Hagiography: Western Christian; Theology, Western Christian: Franciscan

## Biography

Son of a cloth merchant in Assisi, Francis worked in his father's business until age 20. In 1202 he was held captive in neighboring Perugia for a year during a border dispute. Between 1204 and 1208 he broke with his former life, as he repaired churches. Around 1208 at the church of Portiuncula below Assisi he heard a call from Matthew 10:7–19 to abandon all property. In 1209 in Rome he received papal approval for the rule he had drawn up for his 12 followers. These "friars minor" expanded rapidly. In 1212 St. Clare founded a similar community in Assisi. In 1217 the Order was divided into provinces, but during Francis' absence in Egypt in 1219 dissension broke out, obliging him to restate his rule. In 1224 on Mount La Verna he received the Stigmata, and two years later he died at the Portiuncula. Few figures in the history of Christianity have equaled Francis in power of attracting followers.

## Major Works

*St. Francis of Assisi: Writings and Early Biographies: English Omnibus of the Sources for the Life of St. Francis*, edited by Marion A. Habig, 3rd revised edition, 1973 (contains Francis' "Canticle of the Sun" and "Salutation of the Blessed Virgin Mary" as well as a valuable bibliography)

## Further Reading

Armstrong, Edward A., *St. Francis: Nature Mystic*, Berkeley: University of California Press, 1973

Cuthbert, Father, *Life of St. Francis of Assisi*, London and New York: Longmans, Green, 1912; reprint, 1960

Englebert, Omer, *St. Francis of Assisi: A Biography*, London: Burns Oates, and New York: Longmans, Green, 1950; reprint, Chicago: Franciscan Herald Press, 1965

Fortini, A., *Nuova vita di San Francesco*, 5 vols., Assisi: Edizioni Assisi, 1959

Frugoni, Chiara, *Francis of Assisi: A Life*, London: SCM, and New York: Continuum, 1998

Jacobus de Vitriaco, *Lettres de Jacques de Vitry, 1160/1240, évêque de Saint-Jean d'Acre*, edited by R.B.C. Huygens, Leiden: Brill, 1960

Lambert, Malcolm, *Franciscan Poverty: The Doctrine of the Absolute Poverty of Christ and the Apostles in the Franciscan Order, 1210–1323*, London: SPCK, 1961

Pasquazi, Silvio, editor, *San Francesco e il Francescanesimo nelle letteratura italiana dal Rinascimento al Romanticismo*, Rome: Bulzoni Editore, 1990

Powell, James M., "The Papacy and the Early Franciscans," *Franciscan Studies* 36 (1976)

Powell, James, M., "San Francesco d'Assisi e la quinta crociata: Una missione di pace," *Schede Medievali* 4 (1983)

Sabatier, Paul, *The Life of St. Francis of Assisi*, New York: Scribner, and London: Hodder and Stoughton, 1894; revised edition, 1930

# Francis of Paola, St. 1416–1507

Italian-French Christian ascetic and founder of the Order of Minims

This much admired ascetic was born 27 March 1416 at Paola on the Tyrrhenian coast of Calabria, Italy, and died 2 April 1507 at Plessis-lès-Tours on the Loire River in Touraine, France. Son of a landowner, Giacomo Alessio, and his wife, Vienna di Fuscaldo, Francis was named after St. Francis of Assisi (1181/82–1226), to whom his parents had prayed to have a son after 15 years of marriage. An abscess in the infant's left eye was cured after his parents vowed to offer him as an oblate for one year to a Franciscan monastery. He was raised in a pious, austere family and educated in a local monastery and by an archpriest. At 13 years of age, he spent one year as an oblate in the Franciscan monastery of St. Marco Argentano (about 12 miles from Paola), whose guardian was a disciple of St. Giacomo della Marca. The evidence he gave of preternatural gifts (bilocation, not being burned by hot embers, and so on) drew the attention of the friars and local bishop, but despite the friars' pleadings he returned to

Paola after the vow was fulfilled. In 1429 he went on a pilgrimage with his parents to various holy sites in Assisi, Loreto, and Rome, where he personally criticized Cardinal Giuliano Cesarini for his pomp. On his return to Paola, Francis adopted the lifestyle of an independent hermit, living in a hut on his parents' land and devoting himself to prayer, work, and fasting (eating only vegetables and roots but beans on feast days). Because people came in increasing numbers to see this joyous and serene teenage hermit who was barefooted and dressed in rags, he repeatedly withdrew farther into the forest. By 1436, with the permission of the archbishop of Cosenza, he gathered around him a group of neighboring hermits and fresh recruits, among whom, later in 1450, was his widowed father, who chose him as their spiritual guide. Having adopted a cenobitic lifestyle, he founded monasteries in Poterno, Spezzano, and Corigliano. His fame spread as he cured numerous persons of their ailments and spoke out courageously in defense of the poor and oppressed. King Ferrante (1458–1494) of Naples sent troops to arrest him, but reportedly he became invisible to them as he prayed before the Eucharist. His crossing the straits of Messina in 1464 by using his mantle as a boat – a feat witnessed by many – led Pius XII (1939–1958) in 1943 to declare him the patron saint of Italian sailors.

Francis' reputation as a miracle-worker led to a papal inquest and the eventual approbation of his congregation. Although Francis declined in 1473 to mitigate his austerities, Paul II (1464–1471) was prepared to approve his rule but died first; in 1474 his successor, Sixtus IV (1471–1484), after another inquest, gave papal approbation to a rule that the archbishop of Cosenza, Pirro Caracciolo, had already approved in 1471. This early rule, which seems to have been derived from that of the Hermits of Fra Pietro di Pisa, prescribed fasting, complete abstinence from meat and its by-products (e.g., milk and eggs), and the vows of chastity, obedience (with the election of a hermit as superior), and poverty (begging and not touching money). The canonist, priest, and fellow hermit Baldassare Spina apparently helped him write the rule. In these early documents the congregation was called the Poor Hermit Friars of Francis of Paola.

The latter part of Francis' career was spent in France. He was sent there by Sixtus IV, who was responding to a request of the gravely ill Louis XI (1461–1483) that the miracle-working hermit come to his bedside. At the French court Francis maintained his austere lifestyle, became spiritual adviser to members of the royal family, founded new monasteries, and worked on his rule. The version approved in 1493, in which his followers are called the Hermits of the Order of Minims ("the least"; Franciscans had called themselves "lesser friars"), continued to be based on the rule of the Hermits of Fra Pietro di Pisa with elements borrowed from the rules of the Amadeite Congregation of the Franciscans, the Augustinians, and the Benedictines. The version of 1501 urged religious perfection and prescribed a simple lifestyle, fraternal correction, and a harsh asceticism involving a fourth vow of total and perpetual abstinence. Revised by Francis to allow for a second order of cloistered nuns and a third order of laypersons, this rule was approved by Julius II (1503–1513) in

1506 and adopted by the first general chapter meeting in Rome (1507/8). By the death of its founder in 1507, the order had simplified its name to Minims. It possessed 33 monasteries and convents: 14 in France, 12 in Italy, four in Spain, two in Germany, and one in Bohemia.

At the urgings of Queen Anne of France, whose daughter Claude was cured in 1507 of a deadly fever through the intercession of the recently deceased Francis, the canonical process for his canonization was initiated in 1512 in Tours and Cosenza. Leo X (1513–1521) declared Francis a blessed in 1513 and a saint in 1519.

Francis became a very popular saint in Italy, France, and Spain. Numerous churches were dedicated to him, and he was adopted as the patron of Spain, Naples, Calabria, and Sicily. Noted artists, such as Reni, Ribera, Murillo, Velasquez, Goya, and Rubens, painted his portrait, and musicians such as Scarlatti and Liszt dedicated compositions to honor him. His reputation for sanctity rested on his love of God and neighbor; on his practice of prayer, humility, poverty, and extreme asceticism; and on his miracles and outspoken defense of the poor and oppressed. The order of Minims that he founded, which exists to this day, has never mitigated the austerity of his rule.

NELSON H. MINNICH

*See also* Asceticism: Christian Perspectives; France: History; Francis of Assisi, St.; Franciscans: General or Male

## Biography

After living for a year as a boy with the Franciscans, the young Calabrian withdrew to a cave near Paola. He attracted others to live as hermits, and c. 1435 they began to live in community. The Order of Minims (Ordo Fratrum Minimorum) can be dated from 1471 and had its rule confirmed by Pope Sixtus IV in 1474. In the 1480s King Louis XI (1461–1483) invited the holy man to France, where he dwelt near the court for many years. Having served as spiritual director of King Charles VIII (1483–1498), he died in France in 1507.

## Selected Works

*Centuria di lettere del glorioso patriarca S. Francesco di Paola fondatore dell'ordine dei minimi*, edited by Francesco (Preste) da Longobardi, Rome, 1655 (for a scholarly critique of the authenticity of these letters, see Ernesto Pontieri, "Il problema critico della Lettere di San Francesco di Paola," in his *Per la storia di Ferrante I d'Aragona*, Naples, 1947; 2nd edition, 1969)

*Opuscula quaedam, Epistolae, Oracula, Sententiae*, edited by Francesco da Scelì, Naples, 1624; 2nd edition, 1692

*Regulae*, in *S. Minimorum Ordinis S. Francisci de Paula Regulae*, edited by Giuseppe Roberti, Rome, 1906

## Further Reading

Capponi, Francesco, *S. Francesco di Paola: Sulla vita: Amor che tutto muove*, Rome: Tip. Agostiniana, 1954 (originally published in Genoa, 1926)

Fiot, Robert, *Jean Bourdichon et Saint François de Paule*, Tours: Typolitho Gibert-Clarey, 1961

Fiot, Robert, *Saint François de Paule à Amboise*, Tours: Association de amis de Saint François de Paule, Club Gutenberg, 1975

Galuzzi, Alessandro M., *Origini dell' Ordine dei Minimi*, Rome: Libreria editrice della Pontificia Università Lateranense, 1967

Galuzzi, Alessandro M., "La 'Societas pauperum heremitarum' di Paola dalla 'Decet nos' (30.11.1470) alla conferma pontificia (17.5.1474)," *Bollettino ufficiale dell' Ordine dei Minimi* 22 (1976)

Roberti, Giuseppe M., *S. Francesco di Paola, Fondatore dell' Ordine dei Minimi (1416–1507): Storia della sua vita*, Rome: Off. Pol. Laziale, 1915; 2nd edition, Rome: Curia Generalizia dell' Ordine dei Minimi in S. Francesco di Paolo ai Monti, 1963

Russo, Francesco, *Bibliografia di S. Francesco di Paola*, Rome: Curia Generalizia dell' Ordine dei Minimi in S. Francesco di Paolo ai Monti, 1957–1967

Simi, Gino J., and Mario M. Segreti, *Saint Francis of Paola: God's Miracle Worker Supreme, 1416–1507*, Rockford, Illinois: TAN Books, 1977

Vezin, Gilberto, *Saint François de Paule, fondateur des Minimes, et la France*, Paris: La pensée universelle, 1971

# Franciscans: Female

The Franciscan tradition intersects with the feminine monastic heritage in three different expressions that have existed since the early 13th century. The first of these is the cloistered life of the nuns who follow the Rule of St. Clare of Assisi or its derivatives. The second is the small number of enclosed monasteries of women who follow the Rule of the Third Order Regular of St. Francis. Finally, throughout the centuries individual women or small communities have lived an eremitic form of life. Often on the fringes of better-known institutes of Franciscan nuns, this last group embodies the inclination toward solitary contemplation that was central to both Francis and Clare of Assisi.

*The Poor Clares*

Three years after Francis (1181/82–1226) received papal confirmation of his proposal for a new religious brotherhood in 1209, Clare di Favarone di Offreducio (1193/94–1253) sought the spiritual guidance of Francis and his companions. A member of one of Assisi's most aristocratic families, she embraced as her own goal the new "Franciscan" insertion into the lives of the urban poor. From the first, however, key aspects of her form of life stood in sharp contrast to that of Francis and his itinerant brothers, who initially rejected stable houses in favor of a mobile life of preaching.

Following a ceremony of investiture on Palm Sunday, 1212, Clare lived in two different settings of women religious. The first was the Benedictine monastery of St. Paul in Bastia. In this monastery she benefited from canonical sanctuary when threatened with removal by the patriarchs of her family. When the initial threat to her incorporation into the Franciscan movement abated, she joined a small household of dedicated women living in St. Angelo in Panzo adjoining Assisi. This was the home of a group of "bizzoche" women. (The name is indicative of the wooden clogs that characterized their simple dress.) They were the Italian equivalent of the beguines who were gaining prominence in the Low Countries at this same period. There Clare, now accompanied by her sister Agnes, continued to resist her family and to discern a paradigm for living that would embody her inspiration. Whatever the reason for her sojourn in Panzo, it did not provide a permanent solution to her needs.

Clare finally took residence in the small monastery of St. Damian, situated a short distance below the city of Assisi. Francis had restored the ruined edifice prior to 1209 and had prophesied that it would house a famous community of holy women (see St. Francis' *Legend of the Three Companions*, 1964). Clare's small sisterhood began to flourish soon after her arrival sometime in 1212. It is evident that she did not begin her community with a fully documented rule. A letter from Jacques de Vitry (1160/70–1240) in 1216 describes what might be the early outlines of the life of the Poor Sisters that he observed while traveling in Umbria. "The women live near the cities in various hospices. They accept nothing, but live from the work of their hands. In fact, they are very much offended and disturbed because they are honored by the clergy and laity more than they deserve." Various interpretations of this text have given rise to a debate about the degree to which these sisters engaged in active service to the needy or led a life of strict separation from society in the initial years of the community.

The "rule" of these first years was equivalent to the *propositum* of Francis. Certain exhortations that he addressed to the sisters have been recorded. They were *The Form of Life Given by Francis to Clare and Her Sisters* (1212/1213) and *The Last Will Written for Clare and the Poor Ladies* (1226). Meanwhile Francis' Rule was redacted to include the expanding needs of his fraternity in 1221, and a new edition was approved by Honorius III (1216–1227) in 1223. We surmise that the "Poor Sisters" lived by their own extrapolations of this text, which figures as a primary source in the Rule that St. Clare wrote 30 years later.

Other ecclesiastical norms influenced the regimen that gradually emerged in St. Damian. After the close of the Fourth Lateran Council in 1215, the papal legate to central Italy, Cardinal Hugolino dei Conti di Segni, insisted that Clare accept his legislation, which offered Church protection in exchange for episcopal regulation. Although sympathetic to the pastoral potential of the Franciscan movement, the cardinal had little room in his program for small urban convents that did not correspond to strict reforms that he favored in female monastic houses. This "rule," based on the Rule of St. Benedict, was ultimately adopted by numerous communities in the Umbrian valley. Clare resisted but found a solution that allowed her to accept it while retaining her primary affiliation with the Franciscan brothers.

When this cardinal ascended the papal throne in 1227 and took the name Gregory IX (1227–1241), he continued his efforts to bring Clare and her affiliates into the orbit of his reforms. He demoted the standard of poverty espoused by Clare and gave Cistercian monks rights of visitation. A small number of monasteries insisted on the strict adherence to Clare's formula of poverty and mutual relationships with the Friars Minor. Most notable among these was the monastery founded in Prague in 1233 by Agnes, daughter of the royal Premysl dynasty of Bohemia. Other monasteries accommodated to the "Hugolinian" rule and accepted property. Hugolino/Gregory – taking advantage of the early arrangement that gave him jurisdiction over St. Damian – referred to these convents as belonging to the "Order of St. Damian." The attribution implied fidelity to Clare's project and person while driving a wedge between her convents and others who chose the papal program in place of hers. The papal rule contained strict interpretations of enclosure and multiplied protective regulations. The text contains many references to dangers of abuse and laxity, extensive times of silence, regulation of visitors, physical protection of doors and windows, and entrance into the cloister.

In 1247 Pope Innocent IV (1243–1254) issued another rule for the Poor Sisters, hoping to clarify ambiguous provisions of

Dormitory, Convent of San Damiano, Assisi, Italy, early 13th century. Here the Poor Clares lived from about 1214 until they moved to the newly completed Santa Chiara in the 1260s.
Photo courtesy of Mary Schaefer

his predecessor's legislation. This rule also conferred ownership of property, a permission opposed to Clare's most intense convictions. This rule was rejected by St. Damian's and its affiliates. Clare then composed a "Form of Life," or rule, which clearly advanced her specific understanding of evangelical life for women living in small, stable communities without property. Her text addresses the structures of an enclosed monastic life. However, a tone of dire warning and command gives way to a generous allowance for the exercise of discretion on the part of the abbess. She is able, for example, to permit egress for "a useful, reasonable, evident and approved purpose" (Rule of St. Clare 2:11). Careful comparison of Clare's language and vocabulary indicates the pastoral and prudent adjustments that she made to the requirements of enclosed life for the women of her era. This text was approved by Innocent IV in 1253 just prior to the death of Clare. This was the first legislative text by a woman to be pontifically approved.

Subsequent rules, such as those written by Isabel of Longchamps in 1259 and Pope Urban IV (1261–1264) in 1263, codified obligations of the friars and/or the requirements of poverty and enclosure. The "Urbanist" rule was widely disseminated and introduced the name "Poor Clares." Despite such efforts to dictate the perfection of observance, the Clares fell into decline in various places and to varying degrees but emerged from such troubles under the leadership of bold and saintly abbesses who were usually supported by leading friars in various epochs of reform. Two notable periods are the 15th century, in which St. Colette of Corbie (1381–1447), St. Eustochia of Messina (1432–1468), St. Catherine of Bologna (1413–1463), and Bl. Camilla Baptista Varani (d. 1524) led renewals. The Conceptionists, founded by St. Beatrice da Silva (d. c. 1492), and the Annunciationists, founded by Bl. Joan of Valois (d. 1505), enjoy strong historical ties to the Poor Clare tradition. In 1538 a new branch of Capuchin Poor Clare sisters was founded by Maria Lorenzo Longo in Naples. Following the losses suffered during the height of the Reformation, new growth occurred as monasteries became missionary outposts in the New World. The liberal suppressions that marked Western Europe in successive waves from the 17th to the 19th century damaged the Poor Clare presence. Its renaissance was due to the labors of such women as Marie-Dominique Berlamont (d. 1871) in Belgium and England, Marie-Claire Bouillevaux (d. 1871) in France, and Mother Magdalen Bentivoglio, who came with her sister, Constance, to the United States in 1875.

Through the centuries the Sisters of St. Clare have continued to live an enclosed monastic vocation in which the combination of experiential poverty, mutual charity, and contemplation forms the ideal path of discipleship. Although autonomous, each monastery can participate in a federation whose roots lie in a particular reform or affiliation with a branch of friars. These federations offer educational and other forms of assistance to member monasteries. Each jurisdiction of friars (Coventual, Capuchin, or Observant) provides friars at international and regional levels dedicated to work with the members of the "Second Order," as the Poor Clares are also known.

### Third Order Regular

In the Third Order Regular branch of the Franciscans – a branch of congregations of vowed women or men dedicated to works of mercy and prayer – there exist a small number of enclosed monasteries. Most of these are found in Western Europe and Mexico. Since the 14th century women of the Third Order of St. Francis gathered in small congregations and typically combined a life of contemplation with work to alleviate social and personal misfortune. The Council of Trent (1545–1563) decreed enclosure for all such female institutes. Although many adopted only a partial observance of enclosure so as not to inhibit apostolic work, a small number did embrace a completely cloistered form of living. In the late 20th century fewer than 100 such convents existed. Efforts to force acceptance of the Poor Clare Rule in place of the more elastic Third Order Regular Rule resulted in the transfer of many such small cloisters to the ranks of the Second Order.

A new Third Order Regular Rule, approved by John Paul II in 1982, specifically acknowledges the option of an enclosed monastic life for Franciscan women distinct from that of the Second Order. This group of cloistered Franciscan sisters has remained relatively unknown even within the Franciscan family. Friars of the Third Order Regular maintain official bonds with several of these monasteries. New educational programs concerning the Third Order tradition of monastic and contemplative dedication might foster new expressions in the 21st century.

### Solitary Religious

In addition to Franciscan women who have lived a monastic life in the Second or Third Order, there have been women who have lived a public dedication to a life of intercessory prayer and spiritual direction. Although they were not foundresses or members of monasteries, their actual life program drew heavily on the monastic traditions and wisdom. These they promoted in hermitages, anchor holds, or some other alternative space that declared radical separation from family and society. Designations such as "Beguine," "inclusae," "reclusae," and "bizzoche" are associated with these women. Whereas some might have been part of local and unregulated communities, others lived in solitary settings, often in defiance of normative expectations of Church authorities. Saint Margaret of Cortona (1247–1297), St. Angela of Foligno (1248–1309), and St. Umiliana de Cerchi (1219–1246) figure among early examples.

Although these women did not embrace monastic life, they created important alternatives between the landed monasteries of the Benedictine tradition, the small penitential fraternities whose members were encumbered with normal domestic and commercial pursuits, and the completely regulated enclosure of the Poor Clares. Recent research has uncovered the rich variety of these urban religious women who created unusual vehicles of contemplative living that borrowed from monastic discipline while creating a new synthesis of its elements. A resurgence of interest in the eremitic component of the Franciscan vocation has stimulated modern research and innovative renewal in Franciscan convents and friaries. Thus, the future of the Franciscan experience of monastic life holds the promise of continued fidelity to the rich traditions of the Second and Third Order combined with fertile possibilities for a radical reappropriation of the contemplative life in new or renewed forms.

MARGARET CARNEY, O.S.F., S.T.D.

*See also* Beguines; Catherine of Bologna, St.; Clare of Assisi, St.; Claustration (Cloister), Rules of; Francis of Assisi, St.; Hermits: Western Christian; Liturgy: Western Christian

**Further Reading**

Alberzoni, Maria Pia, "Nequaquam a Christi sequela in perpetuum absolvi desidero: Clare between Charism and Institution," translated by Nancy Celaschi, *Greyfriars Review* 12 (1998)

Armstrong, Regis J., editor, *Clare of Assisi: Early Documents*, New York: Paulist Press, 1988

Carney, Margaret, *The First Franciscan Woman: Clare of Assisi and Her Form of Life*, Quincy, Illinois: Franciscan Press, 1993

Cirino, André, and Josef Raischl, *Franciscan Solitude*, St. Bonaventure, New York: Franciscan Institute, 1995

Gennaro, Clara, "Clare, Agnes and the First Sisters: From the 'Pauperes dominae' of San Damiano to the Poor Clares," translated by Lori Pieper, *Greyfriars Review* 9:3 (1995)

McKelvie, Roberta Agnes, *Retrieving a Living Tradition: Angelina of Montegiove, Franciscan, Tertiary, Beguine*, St. Bonaventure, New York: Franciscan Institute, 1997

Moorman, John, *A History of the Franciscan Order: From Its Origins to the Year 1517*, Oxford: Clarendon Press, 1968; Chicago: Franciscan Herald Press, 1988

Pazzelli, Raffaele, *The Franciscan Sisters: Outlines of History and Spirituality*, translated by Aidan Mullaney, Steubenville, Ohio: Franciscan University Press, 1993

Pazzelli, Raffaele, "La vita claustrale nel Terzo Ordine Regolare di San Francesco," *Analecta*, T.O.R. 27:156 (1996)

Sensi, Mario, "The Women's Recluse Movement in Umbria during the 13th and 14th Centuries," translated by Edward Hagman, *Greyfriars Review* 8:3 (1994)

# Franciscans: General or Male

The Franciscans include all the religious communities inspired by the life and work of St. Francis of Assisi (1181/82–1226). More specifically, *Franciscan* refers to the order founded by Francis between about 1205 and 1210 that followed the rule of life composed by the saint. Francis called his followers the Order of Friars Minor (*Ordo Fratrum Minorum*), which means the "order of lesser brothers." In the Italian urban communities of the late 12th and early 13th centuries, the word *minor* referred to those who played little role in the social or political life of the communes. Francis attracted both male and female followers as early as 1205. By 1209 or 1210, there were 12 men, including himself. Less is know about his female followers at this time. Francis journeyed to Rome to seek papal protection and approval for the rule he had composed for his new community.

This rule, which is no longer extant, was composed of significant gospel verses and some practical arrangements. At a period when the composition of such rules was quite common for both lay communities and new religious orders, the action of Francis was not at all unusual. Aided by his own bishop, Guido, who was in Rome at this time, and supported by Cardinal John of St. Paul, Francis was received by Pope Innocent III (1198–1216).

This event has been enshrined in legend. By the middle of the 13th century, there was already a legend of a vision of the pope in which he dreamed that Francis was holding up a collapsing church of St. John Lateran, an image pregnant with meaning because the Lateran basilica was the cathedral of Rome and the mother church of the West, having been built by Emperor Constantine (306–337) following his conversion to Christianity. The historical meaning of Francis' journey to Rome has been much more problematic, but such a journey was not unusual. Other groups had sought papal protection and approval for their rules in the late 12th and early 13th centuries, most notably the Order of the Most Holy Trinity, founded by John of Matha (d. 1213); the Hospitaller order of the Holy Spirit of Montpellier; and the *Humiliati*. One of the principal reasons for seeking papal protection was to ensure that gifts of property made to the communities were protected from local authorities. In Francis' case, his community possessed no property, making the usual letter of protection unnecessary. However, the pope did not promulgate the rule proposed by Francis at this time.

Innocent III seems to have solved the problem that confronted him by ordering that members of the fledgling community be given the clerical tonsure, thus denoting their status and making it visible to everyone that they were under the protection and jurisdiction of the church. The fact that he did not issue a bull (i.e., a letter under seal) approving the rule has been from the very early period a cause of concern and controversy. However, if we examine other rules from this period, we find that it was quite usual for the early draft of the rule to be submitted to a committee of bishops and abbots appointed by the pope (but probably composed of men acquainted with the aims of the founders) to be put into an acceptable form. Innocent III's instructions to Francis that he should return later and that he would take further steps might well be read in this light. The oral approval of the rule would then be more tentative than some would argue.

Already in the lifetime of Francis, the rapid growth of the order soon outstripped the early provisions that Francis had made. In fact, growth was probably an impediment to producing a finished form of the rule. Moreover, Francis himself was engaged mainly in visiting and directing the increasingly far-flung communities of the order. In 1217, this growth made necessary the division of the order into provinces. Francis himself had traveled in France and Spain. He contemplated a personal missionary voyage to Morocco but decided to send some of the brothers. These were the first Franciscan martyrs. In 1219, he traveled to Egypt, where he preached to the crusaders at Damietta and in the camp of the Sultan al-Kāmil. He also visited Acre and the Franciscans established there. On his return to Italy, he faced the need to address the organizational questions that were now most pressing. The appointment of Peter Cattani, one his original followers, as vicar general seems to have been aimed at placating the early members of the community, who were now overwhelmed by the more recent members.

The rule of 1221, often referred to as the *regula non bullata* because it was not promulgated by the pope, was the product of Francis' efforts to set forth his ideal in a way that would be accepted by the main factions in the order, which now had about 3,000 members. Historians have tried to explain the history of the rule in various ways. In the late 19th century, the brilliant French Protestant scholar Paul Sabatier, whose *The Life of St. Francis of Assisi* (1894) remains very popular, presented an interpretation that placed Francis at the beginning of the Protestant tradition and viewed the making of the rule as a struggle between Francis the rebel and an unreformed papacy bent on undermining his work. Although the Sabatier thesis is no longer tenable, its influence lingers. Above all has been a tendency to make the issue of poverty central to the discussions over the rule rather than recognizing that this issue was the result of internal conflicts mainly after the death of Francis. The rule of 1221 was approved by the Chapter of the Mats, held in 1221 at Assisi.

What has been especially distorted by Sabatier and remains a matter of contention is the fact that this rule was not promulgated. Instead, Francis, working with the cardinal protector of the order, Ugolino of Ostia (c. 1148–1241), and members of the community, in a manner not very different from that of other founders, redacted the final version of the rule that was promulgated by Pope Honorius III (1216–1227) on 29 November 1223, in the bull *Solet annuere*. Although Sabatier attempted to depict this redaction as a departure from the spirit of St. Francis, contemporary sources strongly suggest that the main reason for its preparation lay in the need to give the rule a clearer juridical form. It preserved the important statements of Francis' own ideals. Undoubtedly, it was a compromise, but that compromise emerged from within the order itself rather than from the side of the papacy or Cardinal Ugolino, both of whom strongly supported Francis' views on poverty despite their radical departure from traditional monastic forms. In *Solet annuere*, Honorius invoked Innocent III's oral approval to ensure that the Franciscan rule would not be prohibited by canon 13 of the Fourth Lateran Council, which forbade the proliferation of new religious rules. Moreover, Honorius was quick to avail the papacy of the new order.

When Francis died on 4 October 1226, the Franciscan order already enjoyed enormous popularity not only in Italy but throughout Europe and even in the Near East. Although unresolved tensions remained within the order that resulted in increasing conflicts, these seem to have had only a minimal impact on its external image. During the 1220s, Franciscan preaching, exemplified in St. Anthony of Padua (1188/95–1231), reached out especially to the people of the cities. The close ties between the Franciscan message and the civic culture of northern Italy are exemplified by the role that the Franciscans played in the "Alleluia" of 1233 – that preaching mission aimed at bringing peace and harmony to the public life of the communes. Although no direct proof is possible, the mission's impact might well have been felt on the writings of the Brescian *causidicus*, Albertanus of Brescia, whose efforts to probe the causes of conflict and promote its resolution produced some of the most original thinking of the period. His lay sermons were delivered in the church of San Giorgio in Brescia, the first church in that city run by the Franciscans. Just as Francis himself had become a model for the urban classes of central and northern Italy, his order reflected the transformation of medieval society as it became more urban, forging the intellectual tools that would be needed to produce stronger institutions and to underpin Western Catholicism in an age of great rationality and giving tongue to those whose voices were often unheard, namely, the growing population of urban lower classes. Already in the 13th century, the order established missions along the Silk Road and in China itself. The first archbishop of Beijing was a Franciscan. However, these missions came to an end with the collapse of the Mongol Empire.

Facade, showing St. Francis receiving the stigmata, former monastic church of San Francesco, Reggio Emilia, Italy, c. 1725.
Photo courtesy of the Editor

Despite its achievements, the order was not able to resolve its internal conflicts, which, to a considerable degree, arose from a tension between those who sought a simpler contemplative life based on a complete commitment to poverty and those who embraced the mission of the order as it had evolved even during the life of Francis himself. In 1230, a group of friars, representing mainly the ministers, approached Pope Gregory IX, seeking a solution to the continued internal strife. The pope avoided the extremes and, in the papal bull *Quo elongati*, rejected the contention of those who insisted that the Testament of St. Francis should have equal force with the rule. In fact, no foundation existed for that assertion. The pope then dealt with the issue of property, which would remain in the ownership of the donors, and ordered that *nuntii* (syndics) should have charge of the money of the order. Regardless of the fact that this arrangement continued the effort of the papacy to ensure that the intention of the founder was met, even though the provisions were a major departure from monastic practice, it served only to solidify the positions of the factions.

Brother Elias, who had been appointed vicar general by Francis in 1221 and had been replaced by an elected minister general in 1227, was elected minister general in 1232, only to fall victim to the turbulence within the order and his own lapses in judgment in 1239. During the second half of the 13th century, minister generals, such as Haymo of Faversham and Bonaventure of Bagnorea (c. 1217–1274), the great Paris theologian, tried to rule with the support of a moderate majority. Papal efforts to resolve the problems associated with poverty met with continuing frustration. The Spiritual Franciscans increasingly resorted to external political powers to gain support for their cause. Not even the election of a Franciscan pope, Nicholas IV (1288–1292), brought a cessation to conflict; in fact, it seemed to add tinder to the fire. The Spirituals increasingly turned to apocalyptic writings, such as those of Joachim of Fiore (1135–1202), a Calabrian Cistercian, and his 13th-century popularizer, Gerard of Borgo San Donnino, for inspiration. In the early 14th century, internal tensions reached the point that they boiled over onto the political factionalism of the period. Conflict arose between Pope John XXII (1316–1334) and the Franciscans over the ownership of property by Christ and his apostles. The pope labeled the proposition that Christ and the apostles had no property heretical in the papal bull *Cum inter nonnullos*. Because the pope had already declared in *Ad conditorem* that the Franciscans should hold their property in the same way as other orders, the Spirituals vehemently attacked the position of the pope. The court of Ludwig IV (1294–1347) of Bavaria became a center for dissidents.

Like other religious orders, the Franciscans were influenced by the Observant reforms of the late 14th and early 15th centuries. The period following the Black Death – as well as during the recurrent waves of plague that devastated Europe throughout this period and, to a lesser degree, well into the 17th century – witnessed a widespread religious revival. Dissatisfaction was everywhere with the current religious practice and a desire to restore the religious zeal and practice found in the early church or, in the case of the orders, in the primitive practices of their own communities. The mendicant orders were singled out, in part because of the competition they offered to the secular clergy and in part because of their influence in the political sphere. Already in the 13th century, powerful critics were objecting to the role of the mendicants in the universities. What complicated the reform movement within the Franciscans was the long history of disputes over the meaning of the rule. The Franciscan were by no means the only order to split over the issue of observance, but most of the orders managed to accommodate those who wanted stricter interpretations of the rule within the community. In the case of the Trinitarians, the observance ultimately became the norm for the order. In the case of the Franciscans, the efforts to settle previous disputes inhibited any such solution because factional lines were already hardened. Pope Martin V (1417–1431), in yet another compromise, abrogated *Ad conditorem* and restored papal control over the property of the order through syndics. In response to dissatisfaction over this decision, in 1430 he convoked a general chapter of the order in Assisi to try to resolve disputes. The Martinian constitutions were largely the work of St. John of Capistrano (1386–1456), one of the leading Observants. Again disputes broke out, and in 1443, in response to the request of the Observants, they were again provided with their own superiors. The move toward separation of the Observants from the Conventuals (as those who accepted the papal privileges of the order were called) was well under way in the mid–15th century. Finally, Pope Leo X (1513–1521) brought about separation by the papal bull *Ite et vos* of 31 May 1517. Although for a short time an effort was made to retain a fiction of a single order by making the Conventual superior (called the master general) subject to the approval of the Observant superior (now called minister general), that soon lapsed. The 16th century also saw the foundation of the Capuchins and their separation from the order to form a third independent branch of the first order of Franciscans. During this same period, various reform groups, some with roots as far back as the 15th century, came into existence in France, Germany, and Spain. Thus, in the modern period, the history of the Franciscans not only includes these three orders and the reform groups that remained subject to one or another of them, the second order (the Poor Clares, for women), and the third order for the laity; it also came to encompass many communities of men and women who embraced the spirit of St. Francis and proclaimed themselves his followers.

The Capuchins owe their foundation to Matteo da Bascio, who in 1525 obtained verbal authorization to wear a habit with a distinctive hood and to lead the life of an itinerant preacher while remaining in the order. With the patronage of the Duchess of Camerina, a niece of Pope Clement VII (1523–1534), the Capuchins gradually gained greater independence until in 1536 the order was approved by Pope Paul III (1534–1539), who left it under the jurisdiction of the Observants. The defection in 1542 of Bernardino Ochino (1487–1564), the vicar general of the order, to Protestantism almost wrecked it, but it weathered the storm. The Capuchins fit in well with the spirit of the Counter Reformation. They were staunch defenders of the faith. In the

17th century, they were very active as missionaries in the Middle and Far East as well as in the New World. In 1616, the order gained full independence. The popularity of the Capuchins was enormous, but in the late 18th and early 19th centuries, following attacks by Freemasons and the impact of the French Revolution, their numbers declined sharply. In addition to their missionary work, modern Capuchins are engaged mainly in preaching and parochial work.

The modern history of the Conventuals (the Black Franciscans) has been closely tied to political events in those countries in which they worked. In Assisi, they continued to hold the great basilica of St. Francis, built to house his tomb between 1227 and 1230. Like other religious orders, they were expelled from missionary work in Spain, Portugal, and the lands controlled by these powers. As a result of the French Revolution, they also suffered in France. They remained active in the 18th and 19th centuries in eastern Europe, with missions in Lithuania and Russia. They have worked in the United States since 1852.

The modern history of the Observants (Brown Franciscans) is tied to a number of reforms that led to a continuing division within the community, although not to the foundation of separate orders, except in the case of the Capuchins. In France, the 16th century saw the foundation of the Recollects, who spread to the Low Countries and Germany. Likewise, communities of Discalced and Reformed friars were formed, mainly in Spain and Italy. As with the Capuchins and the Conventuals, the Observants suffered substantial losses in the 18th century and during the Revolutionary and Napoleonic periods. In Latin America, where they had been especially active as missionaries, newly independent governments moved to suppress religous communities. In the 19th century, the Franciscans in Germany and Italy were subjected to intense political pressures. Under these circumstances, given the drastic decline in numbers and in houses, the pressure to unify all the reform groups under one set of constitutions won approval in 1897. No longer were the various groups under the Observants identified, except as members of the Order of Friars Minor.

The Franciscans have exercised a major influence on the religious, intellectual, and cultural life of the West. From the very beginning, they contributed to a new imagery that found its highest expression in the work of Giotto (c. 1267–1337) and his school but that evolved into a popular mass art that has survived into modern times. This art captured the intimate relationship between the divine and ordinary life and gave it a concrete expression. It took themes, such as the humanity of Christ, that had become popular in the 12th century and universalized their message. The roots of the early Franciscans in the urban culture of central and northern Italy helped give their work a distinctive character. Drawing on the ideas of the Parisian schools, they addressed those moral issues that were of concern to the people of the towns, such as usury, poverty, and urban violence. Theologians such as St. Bonaventure and Duns Scotus (c. 1265–1308) made the strains of mystical theology that had flourished in monasticism in the 12th century more accessible to the Christian community as a whole, aided by the learned preaching of the friars. They became the archetypical figures of missionaries to the native peoples of the New World. In the 18th century, Junipero Serra (1713–1784) created the chain of missions that became the foundation for California. In the late 18th and 19th centuries, controversy swirled over their efforts. Often they were presented in popular writing as superstitious, ignorant, and backward looking. More recently, some critics, influenced by modern anthropological research, have indicted missionaries, the friars among them, for their policies toward the Indians. At the same time, the Franciscans have expanded their work in education, social welfare, and health care while maintaining their roles in the missions, parish work, and preaching. Like other religious orders, their numbers declined in the second half of the 20th century, but the spirit of St. Francis remains a vital element both within the Franciscans and in society at large.

JAMES M. POWELL

See also Assisi, Italy; Capuchins; Dominicans; France: History; Francis of Assisi, St.; Joachim of Fiore; Liturgy: Western Christian; Poland; Reformation

## Further Reading

Brooke, Rosalind B., *Early Franciscan Government: Elias to Bonaventure*, Cambridge: Cambridge University Press, 1959

Di Fonzo, L., "Francescani," in *Dizionario degli Istituti di Perfezione*, volume 4, edited by Giancarlo Rocca, Rome: Paoline, 1997

Esser, Kajetan, *Origins of the Franciscan Order*, translated by Aedan Daly and Irina Lynch, Chicago: Franciscan Herald Press, 1970

Gratien de Paris, *Histoire de la fondation et de l'évolution de l'ordre des frères mineurs au XIIIe siècle*, Rome: Istituto storico dei Capuccini, 1982

Grundmann, Herbert, *Religious Movements in the Middle Ages: The Historical Links Between Heresy, the Mendicant Orders, and the Women's Religious Movement in the Twelfth and Thirteenth Century, with the Historical Foundations of German Mysticism*, translated by Steven Rowan, Notre Dame, Indiana: University of Notre Dame Press, 1995

Holzapfel, Heribert, *The History of the Franciscan Order*, translated by Antoine Tibesar and Gervase Brinkmann, Teutopolis, Illinois: St. Joseph Seminary, 1948

Huber, Raphael, *A Documented History of the Franciscan Order*, Milwaukee, Wisconsin, and Washington, D.C.: Nowing Publishing Apostolate, 1944

Lynch, C.J., "Franciscans," in *New Catholic Encyclopedia*, volume 6, Washington D.C.: Catholic University of America Press, 1967

Mac Vicar, T., "Franciscans, Capuchin," in *New Catholic Encyclopedia*, volume 6, Washington D.C.: Catholic University of America Press, 1967

Moorman, John, *A History of the Franciscan Order from Its Origins to the Year 1517*, Oxford: Clarendon Press, 1968; Chicago, Franciscan Herald Press, 1988

Scudder, V.D., *The Franciscan Adventure: A Study of the First Hundred Years of the Order of St. Francis of Assisi*, New York: Dutton, and London: Dent, 1931

Smith, J., "Franciscans, Conventual," in *New Catholic Encyclopedia*, volume 6, Washington D.C.: Catholic University of America Press, 1967

Wadding, Luke, *Annales Minorum*, 29 vols., Florence: Ad Claras Aquas (Quaracchi), 1931–

# Fugitive Religious

In the Middle Ages, professed religious who, without dispensation, returned to the world were variously called *fugitivi*, *vagabundi*, and *vagantes*, but to popes, bishops, religious superiors, canon lawyers, and others more widely they were more properly called *apostatae* (apostates). In modern usage the word *apostate* is applied almost exclusively to a baptized Christian who has abandoned the Christian faith. This modern usage was only one of its meanings in the medieval period, when a distinction was made between *apostasia a fide* (apostasy from the faith) and *apostasia a religione* (apostasy from the religious life). As early as about 1160, Stephen of Tournai, the canonist, observed that in his time the word *apostasy* was used usually to refer to a person who, after taking religious vows, returns to the world. And it was in this sense that the word has continued to be used into the 21st century, although in recent centuries this usage was confined almost exclusively to canon lawyers. During the Middle Ages the terms *fugitive* and *apostate* were synonymous. Early modern commentators began to distinguish the two. For them an apostate was a professed religious who left with the intention of not returning, whereas a fugitive was a professed religious who left but with the intention of returning. This distinction parallels the military distinction between a soldier who deserts and a soldier who goes AWOL (absent without official leave). This distinction received legal sanction in the *Codex iuris canonici* (Code of Canon Law) of 1918. The medieval meaning of apostasy is presumed in the present article.

The abandonment of the religious life is as old as monasticism itself. John Cassian (c. 360–after 430), writing in 417–418 from his experience in both Eastern and Western monasticism, reported that a monk might try to flee his monastery undetected at night under cover of darkness. At St. Benedict's community at Subiaco, the devil was said to have led a monk away. The great Rule of St. Benedict, itself so formative of monastic practices and attitudes for more than a thousand years, recognized the fugitive monk as a problem even in the sixth century:

> If a brother through his own fault leaves the monastery and then wishes to return, he should first promise to make full amends for his leaving. When received, he is to take the lowest place to test his humility. If he should leave a second time, he should be received back, and even a third time, but after that he should know that there is no possibility of return. (chap. 29)

This chapter was read for centuries and continues to be read in Benedictine monasteries throughout the Christian world, a constant reminder of the possibility of flight into apostasy. When in the 12th century canon law became organized as an academic discipline, religious apostasy was seen as a crime. Gratian, in his *Decretum* (1140), held that apostate religious ought to be compelled to return to their religious houses. The most important canon law book of the Middle Ages, the *Liber extra* (1234) of Pope Gregory IX (1227–1241), urged superiors to excommunicate apostates. In 1298 Pope Boniface VIII (1294–1303) made excommunication an automatic penalty, incurred by the very act of apostasy without need of a superior imposing it. And so it remained an ipso facto penalty.

Two elements were necessary for canonical apostasy. First, the person must be a professed religious, and, second, the person must leave with the intention of not returning. The first element is not as simple as might appear at first sight. For profession as a religious, a person had to be of legal age, unmarried, and *compos mentis*. Thus, if underage, not single, or not mentally competent, even though solemn vows had been taken, a person did not become a religious. The profession was defective and invalid, and thus that person could not become an apostate. Stated simply: no profession, no apostasy.

The canonical age for entry into a religious community was 12 for girls and 14 for boys, the same ages required for valid marriage. Because it was required from the mid–12th century that a year of probation (*annus probacionis*) precede profession, the minimum age for profession was 13 and 15. Many cases could be cited of "religious" who claimed that they were not apostates because they had been underage at the time of profession. For example, in 1445 John Hawtyen claimed that when he was only eight years old he was admitted to the Carmelite priory in London and that when he ran away he was considered an apostate. In any case, his mother brought him back, weeping, to the priory, and he was later adjudged not a religious (and thus not an apostate). Religious might also claim that their vows were invalid because they had been married at the time of profession. For example, in 1268 a probationary monk at St. Mary's Abbey in York was asked to leave when the abbot discovered that he had a wife who was still living. Occasionally a religious might even lie, claiming falsely to be married, so that he could leave without incurring canonical penalties. An Augustinian canon of Hexham Priory in far northern England did this but later repented (in 1350), confessing his guilt and seeking readmission. In fact he had been an apostate since he had left after having been validly professed.

The second element required that the professed religious actually abandon the religious life. It was not enough merely to wander without permission to the local village for an evening's entertainment and, being distracted, not return for several days. Actual abandonment of the life was required for apostasy. Such was presumed when a religious abandoned the religious habit and wore instead secular clothes. The common formula used was *habitu spreto* (having spurned the habit). In the Holy Year of 1350, the prior of Westminster Abbey went as a pilgrim to Rome. As he traveled through hostile France, for safety's sake he wore secular clothes, but, once at Rome, fearing that he would be considered an apostate, he secured a papal letter of reconciliation. It was not unknown for an apostate religious to continue wearing the religious habit, although he had no intention of returning, which serves to underline the fact that it was rejection of the religious life itself (if not of the habit) that constituted apostasy.

Popes repeatedly urged religious superiors to seek out runaway religious and to effect their return to their monasteries. The two classic text are the decretals *Ne religiosi vagandi* (1234) of Gregory IX and *Pastor bonus* (1335) of Benedict XII (1334–1342). In some cases the superiors made no effort to reclaim their lost sheep, for troublesome monks might easily upset the peace of a community. The nuns of a convent at Florence said that they would all leave if they were forced to accept back a particular nun. Many times there were forcible returns, as when the secular arm was invoked to capture apostates and bring them back to their houses for punishment (*ad castigandum*). Standard punishment included fasting for a period of 40 days, public flagellation, and additional prayers (not uncommonly an extra recitation of the Psalter each week). To these, other penalties (including exile) could be added, depending on the circumstances.

One study covering England for the 250 years before the dissolution of the religious houses in the 1530s discovered over 1,100 allegedly apostate religious, reckoned to be about 1 percent of the religious population for those years. Yet given the incompleteness of the surviving records, the actual percentage might have been 4 or 5 percent. No pattern can be seen: apostate religious came from every order in proportion to the size of the order (excepting the Carthusians), from houses of every size, and from every part of the country. Apostates constituted a perennial but not dominant feature of the ecclesiastical landscape of those centuries. Why apostates left we can never know with certainty, for records seldom mention their motives, and the historian cannot look into the souls of others. Here we are on the thin ice of supposition and even conjecture. Like so many human decisions, the decision to abandon the religious life likely owed much to mixed motives. One should look to the restrictions imposed by the vows of poverty, chastity, and obedience but also, beyond them, to the possibility for many of a boredom resulting from living a life in confined circumstances among the same people day after day for years and even decades, all the while repeating formulas and rituals, the repetition of which must have challenged even the most devout to invest them with spiritual meaning. Yet, for all that, the stereotype of a monk fleeing over the abbey walls late at night with a bag filled with monastic silver and with the neighbor's daughter waiting on the other side distorts the historical reality, for, although such a monk can be found, he is hardly representative. The stories that survive frequently concern tragic circumstances of men and women who felt trapped in unhappy circumstances and who chose illegal egress as a solution to their all- too-human predicament.

F. DONALD LOGAN

*See also* Benedict of Nursia, St.; Cassian, John; Monastics and the World, Medieval; Subiaco, Italy

## Further Reading

Bouché, J., "Apostasie de religion," in *Dictionnarie de droit canonique*, volume 1, Paris: Letouzey et Ané, 1935

Harper-Bill, Christopher, "Monastic Apostasy in Late Medieval England," *Journal of Ecclesiastical History* 32 (1981)

Hoffmeister, Philip, "Die Strafen für den Apostata a Religione," *Studia Gratiana* 8 (1962)

Logan, F. Donald, *Runaway Religious in Medieval England, c. 1240–1540*, Cambridge and New York: Cambridge University Press, 1996

Mayali, Laurent, "Du vagabondage à l'apostasie: Le moine fugitive dans la société médiévale," in *Religiöse Devianz*, edited by Dieter Simon, Frankfurt: Klostermann, 1990

Power, Eileen, *Medieval English Nunneries*, Cambridge: Cambridge University Press, 1922; New York: Biblo and Tannen, 1964

Riesner, Albert J., *Apostates and Fugitives from Religious Institutes*, Washington, D.C.: Catholic University of America Press, 1942

# Fujii, Nichidatsu (Nittatsu) 1885–1985

## Japanese Buddhist monk and peace activist

The Japanese Buddhist monk Nichidatsu Fujii, although guided by the teachings of Nichiren (founder of the Nichiren school of Buddhism in the Kamakura period), did not lead his life by following the doctrines of the established Nichirenshu. Fujii was a founder of Nipponzan Myōhōji (literally, "the Japanese Mountain Dhamma Temple"), which is known for its efforts following World War II to build *Bussharitō* (the Stūpa [tower] of the Relics of Buddha) throughout Asia. These Peace Pagodas are now found throughout the world. The monks of the Nipponzan Myōhōji practice *shodai*, that is, hitting a drum and chanting *namu myōhō renge kyō* (faith in the *Lotus Sūtra*). A meeting with Mahatma Gandhi (1869–1948) profoundly influenced Fujii to become involved in peace movements.

His autobiographical information is found in his book *Waga Hibōryoku: Fujii Nittatsu-Jijoden* (1972; *My Non-Violence: An Autobiography of a Japanese Buddhist*). While still young he became interested in Nichiren and became a monk at the age of 19. Afterward he studied not only the teachings and doctrines of the Nichirenshu but also those of the Pure Land and the Zen schools. Yet Fujii's power derived not from his studies but mainly from his understanding of Nichiren's teaching through his ascetic practices, such as fastings, sleep deprivation, and subjecting his body to cold showers under waterfalls in the mountains, all without following the instructions and orders of others. In this sense he belonged to a tradition of private ascetics called *hijiri*, who can be traced back to the early sixth century. Once, while he was practicing a ten-day-long fasting-and-waking period in the mountain, he had a vision in which he saw Jōgyō Bosatsu (Viśiṣṭacāritra-bodhisattva) carrying the Buddha in the figure of a little child. After this experience Fujii vowed before the Kasuga shrine in Nara that he would spend the rest of his life as an ascetic propagating the teachings of Buddha, especially through the teachings of Nichiren. During World War II he started to go abroad (e.g., to Manchuria, China, and India) to spread the *Odaimoku* (the title of the *Lotus Sūtra*) not by

Monks of Nipponzan Myōhōji chanting in honor of the *Lotus Sūtra* at the Peace Pagoda, North Leverett, Massachusetts. The stūpa was built c. 1985.
Photo courtesy of the Editor

making public sermons but by walking on streets while hitting a drum and chanting *namu myōhō renge kyō*.

After World War II Fujii attended the Second International Peace Conference for Religion in 1954. He was awarded a Prize for the Mission Effort of the Buddhism in 1969 and the Sri Lanka President's Peace Prize in 1983. As a part of the peace movement, Fujii led protests against the construction of Narita International Airport and also against the expansion the U.S. Air Force base in Tachikawa, Tokyo. His work to construct some 50 temples of the relics of Buddha continued and spread into European countries and the United States. Such a Peace Pagoda exists in North Leverett, Massachusetts. Even after his death his followers continue the efforts to construct these temples and the peace movement in Japan and abroad. His sermons made before his death are printed along with recent reports by the members in the monthly publications of the Nipponzan Myōhōji.

TAKESHI KIMURA

*See also* Buddhist Schools/Traditions: Japan; Nara; Japan; Nation-Building and Japanese Buddhism; Peace Movements, Buddhist; Prophethood, Japanese Buddhist; Pure Land Buddhism

## Biography

The founder of the Nichiren Buddhist Peace Pagoda movement became a monk at age 19. After extensive self-imposed austerities in the manner of the mountain ascetics, he vowed to

spread the teachings of the Buddha, emphasizing peace. After World War II, he joined many protests and won peace prizes. He initiated the Peace Pagodas, more than 50 of which were built around the world.

## Major Works

*Dokku*, 1961
*Waga Hibōryoku: Fujii Nittatsu-Jijoden*, 1972; as *My Non-Violence: An Autobiography of a Japanese Buddhist*, translated by T. Yamaori, 1975
*Bukkyo to Sekai Heiwa*, 1980; as *Buddhism for World Peace*, translated by Yumiko Miyazaki, 1980

## Further Reading

Fujii, Nichidatsu, *Buddhism for World Peace*, translated by Yumiko Miyazaki, Tokyo: Japan-Bharat Sarvodaya Mitrata Sangha, 1980

# Fulda, Germany

Founded in 744 by Boniface (c. 675–754) as the flagship monastery of the Anglo-Saxon mission to central Germany, Fulda received a royal endowment of land "four miles in every

Saint Michael's Church, Benedictine abbey, Fulda, Hesse, Germany, c. A.D. 800.
Photo courtesy of Chris Schabel

Cathedral on the site of Benedictine abbey, Fulda, Hesse, Germany, 18th century.
Photo courtesy of Chris Schabel

direction" from the site of the monastery itself so as to comprise an estate of some 50 square miles. Under direct royal and papal protection, Fulda became one of the richest and most powerful Benedictine houses of medieval Germany until its decline in the 13th century, with landholdings scattered over a vast area from northern Italy to Frisia and from Alsace-Lorraine to the eastern parts of Germany. A massive new church and conventual buildings were constructed in the early ninth century and modeled on Old St. Peter's, the church being reoriented with its apse and the relocated tomb of St. Boniface at the west end, the claustral buildings behind them, and an atrium at the east end. This church was dedicated in 819 and survived with alterations until the present Baroque Dom was built by Johann Dientzenhofer between 1704 and 1712. In 1752 the church was raised to cathedral rank, and the prince abbots, who already enjoyed episcopal status, became prince bishops of Fulda.

To the north of the main church, another small church, consecrated in 822 and dedicated to St. Michael, was built to serve as the cemetery chapel for the monks. It consisted of a crypt surmounted by a turriform circular "nave" with a concentric ambulatory at the main arcade level. Verse *tituli* for the altars were provided by Rabanus Maurus (c. 780–856), one of which implies a conscious attempt to imitate the Holy Sepulchre church in Jerusalem. A copy of Adamnán's *De locis sanctis* (c. 700), which

includes a detailed description of the Sepulchre church, appears in a late medieval Fulda library list and might have been there early enough to have influenced the design of St. Michael's. By the end of the 11th century at the latest, a model sepulchre and relics of the Holy Land formed part of the accoutrements of St. Michael's, but the former was unfortunately demolished in the 18th century, leaving no unambiguous archaeological evidence.

From an early date an influential scriptorium existed at Fulda whose style of handwriting embraced both Insular and Continental traditions. The monastery was also well known as a literary center. Its reputation was established when Rabanus was head of the school there, one of whose pupils was the theologian, hagiographer, and poet Walafrid Strabo (c. 808–849); another, Otfried (d. c. 875), wrote a celebrated gospel harmony in verse, the *Evangelienbuch* (c. 863–871).

The monastery was secularized in 1803, and its buildings were converted to use as a seminary, and these are not generally accessible to the public. Saint Michael's church, including the original Carolingian crypt, is used for normal church services and is otherwise open to the public on application. The cathedral is generally open to the public. The long north-to-south flanking chambers at the west end incorporate substantial walling from the Carolingian church, which is best seen by visiting the subterranean museum, which houses early architectural fragments, liturgical vessels and reliquaries, vestments, and statuary.

DAVID PARSONS

*See also* Alcuin; Boniface, St.; German Benedictine Reform, Medieval; Germany: History; Manuscript Production: Christian; Missionaries: Christian; Rabanus Maurus

## Further Reading

Ellger, Otfried, *Die Michaelskirche zu Fulda als Zeugnis der Totensorge: zur Konzeption einer Friedhofs- und Grabkirche im karolingischen Kloster Fulda*, Fulda: Parzeller, 1989

Parsons, David, "Sites and Monuments of the Anglo-Saxon Mission in Central Germany," *Archaeological Journal* 140 (1983)

Parsons, David, "Fulda, Hessen," in *The Dictionary of Art*, edited by Jane Turner, volume 11, New York: Grove, 1996

Parsons, David, "The Churches of the Anglo-Saxon Missionaries in Southern Germany: A Review of the Evidence," *Early Medieval Europe* 8:1 (1999)

Pralle, Ludwig, *Fulda: Dom und Abteibezirk*, Königstein im Taunus: K.R. Langewiesche Nachfolger, 1974

# G

## Gampopa 1079–1153

Tibetan Buddhist monk and founder of Karma
Kagyü school

The lineage chant of the Karma Kagyü school of Tibetan Buddhism, chanted every morning by its practitioners, honors the forebears of the lineage. The chant begins, "Great Vajradhara, Tilo, Naro, Marpa, Milarepa, Lord of Dharma Gampopa, Knower of the Three Times Omniscient Karmapa." This chant well illustrates the significance of Gampopa (1079–1153) in the formation of the entire Kagyü school, one of the four main schools of Tibetan Buddhism. Prior to him semi-legendary wandering yogis without an institutional base dominated; after him a strong monastic institutional base was in place, headed by successive lineage holders considered to be rebirths of one another, each of whom was called "the Karmapa."

Gampopa was a successful physician in his early life, happily married, and the father of two children. When plague struck his region, he worked tirelessly to cure people, only to lose his own son and daughter to the epidemic. Then his wife became sick with the same disease but clung desperately to her life. When Gampopa asked her to what she was attached and why she would not let herself die a peaceful death, she replied that she did not want him to remarry and forget her. He replied that he had already learned the lesson of impermanence and the unsatisfactoriness of saṃsāra (cyclic existence) from all the suffering he had witnessed, and he promised to devote the rest of his life to dharma practice, whether she lived or died. To further reassure her he took a vow that he would become a monk after her death.

Gampopa immediately fulfilled his vow and took ordination in a monastery that specialized in the teachings of Atiśa (982–1054), an Indian teacher who had visited Tibet and taught there beginning in 1042. Atiśa's teachings, systematized as the Kadampa school (which influenced both the Kagyü and the Geluk lineages of Tibetan Buddhism), included important Mahāyāna teachings called *lojong* (mind training.) Consisting of numerous slogans helpful to training in Mahāyāna ethical disciplines, these Seven Points of Mind Training remain influential to the present day. Gampopa mastered these teachings and later included them in the systematic training program that he developed for Kagyü practitioners.

However, Gampopa was destined for a more inclusive path and a larger role in the development of Tibetan Buddhism. After gaining proficiency in the Kadampa teachings, he began to dream of a greenish yogi, and at the same time his meditation deepened considerably. His monastic colleagues, when told of the dreams, warned him that yogis are dangerous people and that such dreams are caused by demons. They urged him to receive a blessing and to adopt a practice to counter these dreams. Gampopa followed their advice, but the dreams increased in frequency. Meanwhile the great yogi Milarepa (1040–1123) had been asked by his students to name a successor because he was getting old and the students feared for the survival of his teachings and high level of realization. That night Milarepa dreamed of the student who would be able to receive all his teachings and continue his lineage; he would be a fully ordained monk who was also called "Physician." Sometime later Gampopa heard the name "Milarepa" for the first time and fainted because of the intensity of his karmic connection with Milarepa. Soon thereafter he left the monastery to find Milarepa, after promising his monastic colleagues that he would forever uphold their monastic traditions notwithstanding his future associations with the yogi Milarepa.

The story of how Milarepa and Gampopa met is often told. After a harrowing journey Gampopa finally neared the abode of Milarepa and asked local people to direct him to his teacher. On hearing that the clairvoyant Milarepa already knew he was coming and had made preparations for his arrival, Gampopa became proud of himself. He expected to meet Milarepa the next day; instead he was met by one of Milarepa's senior disciples and told that because of his pride he would have to wait to meet his guru until he was no longer full of himself. After two weeks of solitary practice, he was finally fit to meet his teacher. Milarepa was drinking liquor out of a human skull cup. He gave the vessel to Gampopa and told him to drink the rest. Gampopa, realizing that many people were watching, hesitated; his monastic vows forbade him to drink alcohol. Milarepa's challenge "Don't think so much. Just drink it" is one of the most famous lines in the Kagyü order's stories of its heroes and founders.

Despite the fact that Gampopa was clearly destined to become Milarepa's successor and despite all the training he had already received, Gampopa still needed to receive further teachings and empowerments from Milarepa and to practice intensively. Gampopa's Kadampa training had not given him the profound Tantric practices transmitted from the cosmic Buddha Vajradhara to the first Indian lineage holder Tilopa. In turn the latter had transmitted them to the Indian scholar Naropa, who had given them to the Tibetan translator Marpa, from whom Milarepa had received them. Gampopa was personally trained by Milarepa for some time, but eventually he was commanded to leave Milarepa's presence and to continue meditation practice in central Tibet until he achieved full realization. Milarepa died relatively soon after they parted company, and Gampopa continued to practice for 13 years before he eventually achieved full realization. He then practiced in retreat for seven more years.

Finally it became clear to Gampopa that he had a responsibility to teach what he had learned, and disciples quickly gathered around him. It is said that never before in the history of Tibet had there been so large a gathering of dharma students as at his thriving monastic community. The cotton-clad yogis whom he instructed continued to dwell in caves emulating the lifestyle of Milarepa, and large numbers of ordinary laypeople also came to him for instruction. By the time Gampopa died, the way in which he had organized the Kagyü order, systematized monastic training, and combined the Kadampa teachings with the Tantric Mahamudra teachings of Milarepa meant that Tibetan Buddhism was more secure and stable than it had ever been before. The success of the second transmission of Buddhism to Tibet was assured.

Gampopa's immediate successor was responsible for one of the most famous and enduring features of Tibetan Buddhism. This disciple, Dusum Khyenpa (1110–1193), was perhaps even more accomplished than Gampopa. During his lifetime he became known as Karmapa "Person of Action," and before he died he gave a sealed envelope to a trusted student. It contained instructions on how to find him again after his rebirth. That incarnation was the second Karmapa, and this succession of rebirths has continued to the present day. Thus, the first lineage of "reincarnating lamas" came into existence; this institution, unique to Tibetan Buddhism, was soon adopted by many other great teachers. Today the most famous such lama is the Dalai Lama, head of the Gelukpa order.

In addition to his organizational genius and his teaching ability, Gampopa left his mark on Tibetan Buddhism through writings. His primary work, translated into English with the title *Gems of Dharma, Jewels of Freedom*, is one of the most widely used manuals about Mahāyāna Buddhism ever written. In addition to its primary place in the curriculum studied by Tibetan students of Buddhism, in recent years it has become a principal text for Western Buddhists. Gampopa's importance as a systematizer and transmitter of the Tibetan Buddhist teachings and practices available in his day is unparalleled.

RITA M. GROSS

*See also* Buddhist Schools/Traditions: Tibet; Hagiography: Buddhist Perspectives; Ladakh, India; Mahāyāna; Master and Pupil: Buddhist Perspectives; Milarepa; Monasticism, Definitions of: Buddhist Perspectives; Sakya Pandita (Sapen); Tibet: History; Tibetan Lineages: Kagyü

**Biography**

An institutionalizer of the Kagyü lineage, Gampopa was a physician and husband in early life. After the death of his wife, he studied with Atiśa before becoming a disciple and successor of the great yogi Milarepa. Legend tells of Gampopa's subsequent years of ascetic practice before he established a monastery and systematized the training of monks.

**Major Work**

*The Jewel Ornament of Liberation*, edited and translated by Herbert V. Guenther, 1971; also translated as *Gems of Dharma, Jewels of Freedom*, translated by Ken and Katia Holmes, 1995

**Further Reading**

Nalanda Translation Committee under the Direction of Chogyam Trungpa, *The Rain of Wisdom . . . The Vajra Songs of the Kagyu Gurus*, Boulder, Colorado: Shambhala, 1980; London: Shambhala, 1981

Stewart, Jampa Mackenzie, *The Life of Gampopa: The Incomparable Dharma Lord of Tibet*, Ithaca, New York: Snow Lion, 1995

# Gardening, Christian. *See* Agriculture, Western Christian

# Gardens: Buddhist Perspectives

Buddhist garden design in Asian cultures can be classified either according to historical periods or different schools of Buddhism or by the chief cultural influence of the geographic location. The most spectacular and best known examples of Buddhist gardens are Chinese ones – often with symbolism borrowed from Daoist and other local cults referring to the parallel between the garden and the landscape. Japanese garden and space planning, which has been a focus of interest in garden design studies worldwide, developed from traditional Chinese garden design, which presented the landscape in miniature. In Japanese tradition sand was substituted for water, representing the movement of the water waves around the rocks in the designed space.

The history of Chinese gardens is related to visual arts such as ink painting and calligraphy, in which ink and paper evoke natural forces. The presentation takes a dynamic form instead of the more stable one of a painting. Interaction between internal and external changes in the garden is part of the plan. Imitation of natural landscape in Chinese visual arts has a long history of which the garden design is only one. Paintings exemplify how the sequence of scenes and the relation between these sequences has a deep religious or philosophical meaning related to different stages of a spiritual path – as, for example, in the famous ox-herding series of paintings – which can be related to the garden design in both the Chinese and the Japanese tradition of gardens. The external or natural landscape evoked parallel movements in

The "boat" rock, east garden of the Daisen-in, Daitokuji temple, Kyoto, Japan. The garden is said to have been designed by Abbot Kogaku Kokushi in the early 16th century, Muromachi period.
Photo courtesy of Marylin M. Rhie

the mind stream. Interaction between landscape and mind can be seen as a path of cognitive moments, and therefore the design of garden paths assumed a very sophisticated expression in the Buddhist and Chinese culture. Landscape elements were classified into different types according to the characteristics of solidity, color, and movement as well as in relation to one another, and these different classifications were used to facilitate the design process. Gardening and landscape design expressed different dynamics in the landscape, which developed also into specific *feng shui* practices, in both a logical-mathematical and a more intuitive form.

Chinese garden art influenced Southeast Asian cultures, whereas during the colonial period Western interest focused on adapting the garden design language to Western garden design, especially the British style. In Asian cultures the influence has differed because of the strong presence of local symbolism that became assimilated to the new art forms. Natural elements and orientation practices of exterior space vary according to the locations and functions of the space.

Japanese garden design is best known from Zen gardens of high aesthetic value that emphasize the time perspective in the garden arts. The symbolism of impermanence is expressed in Chinese garden art by structuring the stages, whose transition is differentiated by colors, by more stable elements (e.g., rocks), by more dynamic elements (e.g., water and wind), and by sounds as well as by living beings, such as small animals and insects. In Japan the concept of impermanence is expressed through the task of keeping the space unchanged as long as possible by analogy with meditative experience where perceptions remain unchanged for a certain time. This approach can be seen as one of the comparative keys for reading the garden design language of Japanese tradition. In each Asian country indigenous culture affected Buddhist gardens in interaction usually with holy sites or inside the monasteries as well as in the art of locating monasteries in the right kind of landscape.

For example, in Indonesia during the Central Javanese period, known as one of the great Buddhist kingdoms of the past, the time-space hierarchy in landscape and garden art is organized with specific attention to the perceptions of the equator and sharp shadows. Horizontal and vertical visual effects in this landscape are united to the practical needs of the garden as a resting place.

Mandala landscape is an interesting form of conceptual Buddhist garden design that extends into landscapes, above all in Nepal, Tibet, and Bhutan. Likewise in ancient kingdoms of Southeast Asia, temples such as Angkor Wat have the mandala

Byōdō-in, Hōōdō, Kyoto, Japan.
Photo courtesy of John C. Huntington, the Huntington Archive

built inside the complex, and Borobudur in central Java was seen as the focus of a larger maṇḍala encompassing the landscape without external limits.

In conclusion Buddhist gardens can be defined as places for transformation where the perceiver of the garden becomes the gardener himself, the gardener of an inner landscape. Buddhist gardens can be seen as integral parts of the architecture as well as places where architectural elements are considered animate and inanimate constituents of the palace or buildings while the external surrounding area can be considered a garden. As in maṇḍala design there are different levels of space – external, intermediate, and inner – that can be divided into smaller units of the general design. For example, in Theravāda tradition space is sometimes divided into two main parts, a narrow path that leads to a widening of the perspectives on the next level. Examples of this include Sinhalese Charles Correa's architectural concept as differentiation between starting and arrival view as well as the example of the urban design for Kapilavastu (which is to be completed in the near future). The Buddha Śākyamuni's birthplace in today's Nepal, designed by Kenzō Tange, exemplifies Japanese Buddhist influence on architectural landscape design. In Mahāyāna Buddhism the landscape is considered the Bud-

dha's noble eightfold path and can be divided into horizontal levels and vertical landscapes. Highly elaborate landscape design can be found in the Vajrayāna tradition, in which different levels are perceived as cosmological presentations and provide symbols of the spiritual path of the perceiver. Physical gardens and mental gardens are considered complementary and function at different levels. The physical garden can evoke the mental garden, and the mental garden becomes a matrix for the future development of other gardens or views. The physical garden can comprise a small portion of a landscape, or it can duplicate the landscape in miniature, as in bonsai gardening. The experiential moment between observer and the subject is the essence of Buddhist garden design.

The complementarity of spaces functions between gardens and cemeteries. Because cemeteries can be considered as spaces dedicated to passing away and gardens as resting places, the complementarity gets expressed in space design. Similarly, according to different stages of the process of passing away, the garden can consist of other gardens, such as visual, taste, touch, and thought gardens. One of the important approaches to the external spaces is the direction of arrival and the related tradition of circumambulation of sacred places done clockwise or counterclockwise, depending on the ceremony. Different traditions contain practices in which cemeteries have a deep meaning and are contained as one part of the exercise, whereas in others the garden can evoke the Pure Land by dividing gardens into transient and timeless gardens.

In Tibetan Tangkas the gardens are accompanied by cemeteries, direction guardians, clouds, mythic animals, guardians, and other creations that characterize each direction of the space.

We can find the earliest example of a Buddhist monastic attitude toward landscaping in the Vinaya Pacittiya, part II, number 11: "Damaging of a living plant is to be confessed."

LAURA PORCEDDU

*See also* Aśoka; Chan/Zen: Japan; Zen, Arts of

## Further Reading

Japanese gardens:

Asano, K., G. Takakuwa, and R.F. Dickinson, *Invitation to Japanese Gardens*, Rutland, Vermont: Tuttle, 1970

Slawson, David A., *Japanese Gardens*, Tokyo and New York: Kodansha, 1987

Treib, M. Hermann, *A Guide to the Gardens of Kyoto*, Tokyo: Shufunomotomo, 1980

Chinese gardens:

Chen Lifang, *The Garden Art of China*, Portland, Oregon: Timber Press, 1986

Clunas, Craig, *Fruitful Sites*, Durham, North Carolina: Duke University Press, 1996

Johnston, R. Stewart, *Scholar Gardens of China*, Cambridge and New York: Cambridge University Press, 1991

Kwok, D.W.Y., *The Urbane Imagination*, Dubuque, Iowa: Kendall/Hunt, 1997

Tsu, Frances Ya-sing, *Landscape Design in Chinese Gardens*, New York: McGraw-Hill, 1988

Zen gardens:

Davidson, A.K., *The Art of Zen Gardens*, New York: J.P. Tarcher/Perigee, 1992

Harte, Sunnive, *Zen Gardening*, New York: Stewart Tabori and Chang, 1999

Wright, Thomas, *Zen Gardens: Kyoto's Nature Revealed*, Kyoto: Mitsumura Suiko Shoin, 1990

Buddhist landscape:

Eck, L. Diana, *The Imagined Landscape*, Delhi: Motilal Banarsidass, 1998

MacDonald, A.W., *Mandala and Landscape*, Delhi: Motilal Banarsidass, 1997

Shepherd Slusser, Mary, *Nepal Mandala: A Cultural Study of the Kathmandu Valley*, Delhi: Motilal Banarsidass, 1998

# Gardens: Christian Perspectives

Gardens have a long history in the Christian Church. What is surprising is how little has been written about monastic gardening in contemporary literature. The first monks in the deserts of Egypt and Palestine practiced the biblical mandate that one must eat from the labor of one's own hands, a sentiment to be echoed a few centuries later by St. Benedict in his Rule: "They are true monks who live by the labor of their hands, as did the Fathers and Apostles." One of the very first monks, St. Antony (c. 270–356), who has been called the Father of Monasticism, wrote of gardening in his journal: "These vines and the little trees did he plant; the pool did he contrive, with much labor for the watering of his garden; with his rake did he break up the earth for many years." Thus, gardening came to be seen as a way to elevate the human spirit of the monk to the ultimate Creator of beauty. Almost from the beginning of the movement, many monastic communities have had a garden set aside for meditation. Sometimes these areas consisted of covered, or "cloistered," arbors separated from the gardens proper by arches, which created frames for viewing the beauty of the garden. By the Middle Ages many cloisters were laid out with formal gardens, ornamental fountains, and pools, perhaps remnants of more primitive watering courses. The pools also provided fish for fast days. Although gardens were primarily utilitarian, most were also tranquil places designed to inspire meditation on the grandeur of the Creator and, if we are to believe the writings of some, such as St. Hildegard of Bingen (1098–1179), they could be places where mystical experiences took place. For example, Gregor Mendel (1822–1884), an Augustinian canon, began to formulate the laws of genetics while strolling through the cloister gardens and meditating on the different flowers of the sweet-pea patch and how the Lord allowed for so much variety.

However, in time the Roman Church began to think of the appreciation of the beauty of flowers as "heathenish" and the cultivation of herbs as "Satanic," a predilection happily not followed by the Eastern or the Celtic Church and, from historical evidence, apparently not by all Roman Church monasteries. In the early sixth century, St. Benedict (c. 480–c. 550) is known to have had a monastic rose garden, or "Rosary." Not until late in the sixth century did this practice begin to wane. Perhaps this rejection was prompted by the fact that as the Roman Church moved north, it came across the Celts and others who practiced what the Church considered witchcraft, namely, the use of herbs in aid of healing. When the Roman Church finally accepted the cultivation of flowers and herbs, thus coming full circle back to St. Antony, clerics realized that plants offer powerful symbols of various Christian virtues. In this way monastics were able, or so they thought, to combat those uses that were considered Satanic. The saints and especially the Virgin Mary benefited by these virtuous associations. By the late Middle Ages, many Roman Catholic monasteries featured what came to be known as "Saint's Gardens" or "Mary Gardens." These evolved eventually into today's small shrines surrounded by flowerbeds and foliage. The first reference to an actual garden dedicated to Mary is found in the life of the Irish patron of gardening, St. Fiacre (d. c. 670). We are told that the saint tended a small garden that he built in honor of "Our Lady" at his monastery in France, which became famous as a hospice for the poor and infirm. The first reference to a monastic "Mary Garden" by name is found in the accounting records of a 15th-century monastic community at Norwich Priory in England. The first record of a flower actually named for Mary is found in a 1373 English recipe for a spell to ward off the plague. In this recipe the herb calendula, or pot marigold, is called *seint mary gouldes* (St. Mary's Gold). It is important, the recipe claims, that *seint mary gouldes* be brewed while one is saying a certain prayer, or charm. Ironically here was the very sort of incantation that the Roman Church had hoped to stop. Unfortunately the Roman Church's practice of associating flowers with Christian virtues unleashed disarray among those who studied horticulture, causing a lack of uniformity among the common names of herbs. For example, what Celts and Anglo-Saxons knew as meadowsweet became known as Bride's wort or Mary's wort in honor of the Virgin Mary.

Until the 13th century monastic communities were mainly vegetarian, with the monks raising most of the produce. Other than worship, "gardening" was the primary task of most monastics. Sites chosen for the monastic retreat were usually wild and inaccessible. Gradually forests were cleared, and the land was worked into farms and gardens. However, by the Middle Ages monasteries associated with the Benedictine Black Monks ceased agricultural production and, to some extent, the study of plants, and gardens became more ornamental than productive. Into this void came the 12th-century reform movement of the Cistercians, who sought to reestablish the "old order" of agriculture and gardening.

We are fortunate to possess detailed drawings of the layout of the gardens of the monastery of St. Gall in Switzerland. The plan provides much information about what seems to be a typical ninth- or tenth-century monastic garden. Saint Gall's 16 garden beds contained medicinal and pot herbs along with ornamentals, trees (fruit and nut), and various fruit and grapevines. The beds produced an astonishing variety: onions, leek, coriander, dill, poppies (papaver and magones), radish, chard, garlic, shallot, parsley, chervil, lettuce, peppermint, parsnips, cabbage, fennel, lily, rose, climbing bean, pepperwort, costmary, Greek hay, rosemary, mint (menthe), sage, rue, iris (gladiola), pennyroyal, cumin, lovage, and watercress. Records from other monastic communities suggest that to these may be added dandelion, wild carrot, primrose, sweet violet, viola, calendula, thyme, marigold, nuts, and legumes. Almost all gardens incorporated ornamental and fruit-bearing trees and vines. With the possible exception of the physic (i.e., medicinal) garden, it was the practice, at least up to the High Middle Ages, not to segregate flowers, herbs, and vegetables into separate plots. At St. Gall's, as in many monasteries, it was the task of the monks, in addition to gardening, to copy ancient herbals and to re-create the old healing formulas. One of the first of these works, *De cultura hortorum* (On the Cultivation of Gardens), by Walafrid Strabo (c. 808–849), abbot of Reichenau, sings in poetic form the spiritual virtues of gardening, a "holy occupation." In the 12th century Hildegard of Bingen wrote two volumes on the nutritional and medicinal value of plants, echoing praises of gardening from the time of St. Antony down to Walafrid. She stated a truth that all sought to practice: things of Creation dwell in harmony. There is a rhythm of the seasons, an inner goodness of Creation and its laws, working together to maintain balance.

*Site to Visit*
The Cloisters, New York, New York: A re-created medieval cloistered garden.

FRANK A. MILLS

*See also* Agriculture, Western Christian; Botany; Hildegard of Bingen, St.; Island Monasteries, Christian; Meditation: Christian Perspectives; Pharmacology; Reichenau; St. Gallen, Switzerland; Walafrid Strabo

**Further Reading**

Hildegard of Bingen, *The Ordo Virtutum of Hildegard of Bingen: Critical Studies*, Kalamazoo, Michigan: Medieval Institute Publications, Western Michigan University, 1992

Hildegard of Bingen, *The Letters of Hildegard of Bingen*, 2 vols., edited by Joseph L. Baird, New York: Oxford University Press, 1998

Horn, Walter W., and Ernest Born, *The Plan of St. Gall: A Study of the Architecture and Economy of and Life in a Paradigmatic Carolingian Monastery*, Berkeley: University of California Press, 1979 (this volume contains the garden plans found in the monastery of St. Gall library [Stiftsbibliothek, Ms. 1092])

Payne, R., and W. Blunt, *The Hortus of Walafrid Strabo*, Pittsburgh, Pennsylvania: University of Pittsburgh Press, 1966

Rubenson, Samuel, *The Letters of St. Antony: Monasticism and the Making of a Saint* (Studies in Antiquity and Christianity), Minneapolis, Minnesota: Fortress Press, 1995

Schipperges, Heinrich, *Hildegard of Bingen: Healing and the Nature of the Cosmos*, translated by John A. Broadwin, Princeton, New Jersey: Wiener, 1997

Whiteman, Robin, and Rob Talbot, *Brother Cadfael's Herb Garden: An Illustrated Companion to Medieval Plants and Their Uses*, Boston: Little, Brown, 1996

Wilds, Nancy, *Church Grounds and Gardens*, New York: Seabury Press, 1964

# Gelukpa. *See* Tibetan Lineages: Gelukpa

# Gender Studies: Buddhist Perspectives

Women are faced with contradictory images of the feminine within the textual traditions of all Buddhist schools. Passages that present women as intellectually weak, sexually uncontrolled, or suitable only for the role of submissive wife are not difficult to find. The following words from the Pāli Canon are an obvious example:

Monks, women end their life unsated and unreplete with two things. What two? Sexual intercourse and child-birth. These are the two things. (*Aṅguttara Nikāya*, I 76)

Counteracting this androcentric strand is material connected with the early nuns or *bhikkhuni*s (Sanskrit, *bhikṣuṇī*s). The texts credit some of them with communicating the very word of the Buddha (*Buddhavacana*). Some nuns openly claim spiritual equality with their male counterparts. The *Therīgāthā*, a collection of their poems found in the Pāli Canon, presents strong, liberated women who give voice to the central Buddhist message that enlightenment is not gendered.

Within the historical tradition a similar pattern is found. Many women in Asia are encouraged to believe that their gender is the fruit of bad *kamma* (Sanskrit, *karma*, "action") in a previous birth, and in some countries there are religious duties that women are normally debarred from, such as carrying relics. The loss or absence of a recognized *Bhikkhunī* order in most Theravāda Buddhist countries has fostered a dualism that links the feminine with production and the masculine with the spiritual, the latter heightened through the symbol of the monastic robe. Yet before European imperialism women in certain Buddhist countries, such as Burma and Sri Lanka, had legal and social rights far in advance of their Western counterparts. In Mahāyāna Taiwan, nuns today outnumber monks, and in some forms of Buddhism powerful images of the feminine feature both in popular devotion and advanced meditation practice.

When Buddhist women have looked at this situation through the lens of gender studies, a number of concerns familiar in feminist approaches to religion have arisen: a need to rediscover women's histories and to reinterpret holy texts, a campaign for equal rights within authority structures or a search for new forms of authority, exploration into the nature of consciousness and the construction of identity, and affirming the body. Present within these categories is a variety of approaches, ranging from those that seek to defend Buddhism's historical record as pro-woman to those that recognize patriarchy and seek the transformation of Buddhism through feminism or through a return to the Buddha's original vision.

Defense of Buddhism's historical record became imperative in response to the criticism that Buddhism received, particularly during the 19th century, from Western missionaries. In 1890 Samuel Langdon, a Methodist missionary in Sri Lanka, wrote,

> We find the women generally the most bigotedly attached to the heathen faiths, of which they know next to nothing, and which are responsible in great measure for their degraded position. (*My Happy Valley*)

In response to this legacy, some Buddhist women in the 20th century rose to defend their faith as liberative to women and far less patriarchal than Christianity with its male God and male ordination lineage. Isaline Horner's 1930 study is still a classic. Lorna Devaraja, a Sri Lankan professor of history, has given papers in Asia and the West, arguing through a comparative method that affirmation of women has been written into Buddhist text and history through, for example, desegregation of the sexes in public space, legal codes favorable to women, possession by women of socio-economic and political influence, and the existence of a vibrant woman's monasticism.

Spirited defense of women within Buddhism animates a number of studies that have sought to uncover the lost history of Buddhist women. For example, Dr. Hema Goonatileke, a Sri Lankan academic based in the 1990s at the Buddhist Institute in Phnom Penh, has used the biographies of unsung royal Buddhist women in Cambodian history to emphasize that it is women who have often been responsible for keeping Buddhism alive during war and conflict (see "Rediscovering Cambodian Buddhist Women of the Past," given at the 5th International Conference of Sakyadhītā, December 1997–January 1998, Phnom Penh).

Publications of the Gender Project at the Social Scientists Association in Colombo (1990s) have uncovered the role of Buddhist women in initiating education for women in Asia. Susan Murcott's *The First Buddhist Women* (1991) movingly attempts to re-create the stories of the nuns represented in the *Therīgāthā*. Their lives as wives, mothers, old women, or prostitutes/courtesans and their transformation into wise women and religious teachers are convincingly put on record, together with a new translation of their verses.

Especially in Asia an early challenge for Buddhist women was the lack of higher ordination for women monastics in Theravāda countries, such as Burma, Cambodia, Sri Lanka, and Thailand. This absence stimulated studies that both uncovered women's history and campaigned for the restoration of lost rights. The writings of Dr. Chatsumarn Kabilsingh, a Thai academic and feminist, have been central to this. Her doctoral dissertation, "A Comparative Study of the Bhikkhunī Pātimokkha" (1984), compared the Theravāda rule of discipline for nuns with several rules of discipline within Mahāyāna Buddhism. She demonstrated that differences between them were negligible and that contemporary Mahāyāna nuns were following a rule of life very similar to the one that Theravāda nuns would follow if higher ordination were allowed them. Her aim was to demonstrate that there can be no objection on grounds of lineage to Mahāyāna nuns ordaining Theravāda nuns and therefore that the argument of those who claimed Mahāyāna Buddhism was too degenerate or different to serve in renewing a Theravāda monasticism was untenable.

Academic theory was confirmed by experience when, in 1986, Hema Goonatileke visited China from Sri Lanka and declared in the Sri Lankan press on her return that Chinese nuns followed a rule almost identical to that of Theravāda ("Vinaya Tradition in China is Theravāda," *Sunday Observer*, Colombo, 14 June 1986). Such writings did much to foster action undertaken mainly by members of the international women's organization Sakyadhītā, which in the last two decades of the 20th century led to some Theravāda nuns gaining higher ordination in ceremonies in America, India, and Sri Lanka for the first time since around the 11th century.

Pressure for the recovery of higher ordination for nuns in the Theravāda and Vajrayāna traditions was and is a call for the feminine to be included in the powerful Buddhist image of the monastic robe and for the dualism linking male with spiritual and female with reproduction to cease. It has also involved an appeal for the reevaluation of Buddhist texts in the light of gender awareness and of the Buddha's known willingness to confer ordination on women. Several approaches have unfolded. Kabilsingh, in *Thai Women in Buddhism* (1991), concentrates both on transmission – that the texts were recorded and preserved by men for men, "according to their own subjective standards of what was important" – and on the influence of Indian cultural and social norms on the Buddha. She implies that it was not impossible that the Buddha could, at times, have got it wrong! Rita Gross, in *Buddhism after Patriarchy* (1993), seeks to create from the texts a "usable" Buddhist past, free from what she sees as a quadruple androcentrism, which includes ignoring stories of Buddhist women in a male-dominated form of transmission. She is therefore willing to jettison stories concerning women that are incompatible with "fundamental Buddhist values," for example, Mahāyāna myths that show women magically transforming themselves into males before attaining Buddhahood. A rigorous sifting process is encouraged to create a heritage that enhances women.

The recovery of women's history, reinterpretation of the texts, and campaigning for a more visible woman's component in sacred space all envision a transformed Buddhism in the present, capable of giving women self-confidence. These are activist concerns, which normally do not emphasize the issues of identity, consciousness, and body, which have preoccupied some schools of gender studies in the West. Yet the latter have not been absent from Buddhist studies, although they have been addressed more frequently by Western Buddhists than those in Asia. For example, a problem connected with appreciation of the body is Theravāda Buddhism's tendency to project its appraisal of the material as impermanent and prone to decay onto the image of a woman's body. The *Mahādukkhakhanda Sutta* (*Majjhima Nikāya*, I 88–89) takes the listener through the cycle of human existence, from youthful beauty to death, using a woman's life to the point where she is "swollen, discoloured, decomposing," and beyond. That this affected the self-image of the early Buddhist nuns is suggested by Kathryn Blackstone in *Women in the Footsteps of the Buddha* (1998), a comparative study of the *Therīgāthā* and the *Theragāthā*, verses by the early monks. The monks, she found, rarely applied the doctrine of impermanence to their own bodies but projected it onto women. On the other hand the nuns did not, in like manner, project impermanence onto men but looked inward, personalizing the aging process into what became a negative self-image. Yet she also found that the women were more concerned with community and personal relationships than were the men. It is an area that deserves more study.

Two important Western voices that have proposed interaction between Buddhism and feminism are Rita Gross and Anne Klein. In *Buddhism after Patriarchy*, Gross emphasizes the need for a feminist revaluation of Buddhism in the conviction that, although the tradition is sexist, it is not irreparably so. She identifies four similarities between Buddhism and feminism. Both begin with experience and move to theory, which becomes the expression of experience. Both are willing to go against the grain

to pursue truth. Both use the first two to explore how mental processes can block or enhance liberation. Both speak of liberation as the aim of human existence. This means, she argues, that Buddhism and feminism can mutually transform each other. In the reconstruction that follows, she looks toward a postpatriarchal future for Buddhism in which gender equality is built into the very fabric, leading to a transformation of both lay and monastic Buddhism. With reference to the latter, women should train with men, she suggests, and the large gulf between lay and ordained should be broken down.

In *Meeting the Great Bliss Queen* (1995), Anne Klein concentrates on feminist discourse concerning self and identity. Feminist theory, she explains, is divided between the postmodernist claim that the self is a constructed entity and the assertion that there is an essential feminine spirit to be discovered by each woman. Likewise, she continues, Buddhist philosophy is divided between the view that liberation is something that arises developmentally through cause and effect and the apparently contradictory claim that it is something that is already existent inside oneself, waiting to be uncovered. Weaving between Western and Eastern constructions of self, she then suggests a way of reconciling these approaches through the image of the Great Bliss Queen, a powerful *dakini* (a female muse of enlightenment) in the Tibetan Nyingma tradition. What many feminists lack, she emphasizes, is Buddhism's understanding both of how the mind is and of the power of "innate awareness" uncovered through mindfulness. The meditation practices connected with the Great Bliss Queen are then held up as one way of helping Western feminists achieve a connectedness that does not undermine creativity and a mindfulness that creates inner coherence and destroys dualistic categories.

Literature by and about Buddhist women is rapidly expanding. Whether or not monasticism is the theme, this literature feeds into the lives of Buddhist women monastics. The potential for cross-fertilization between gender studies and Buddhism and indeed their mutual transformation through this interaction is great. Yet the enormity of the practical task facing women if patriarchal structures are to be transformed within society and within each woman's psyche should not be forgotten.

ELIZABETH J. HARRIS

*See also* Buddhist Schools/Tradtions; Burma (Myanmar); Celibacy: Buddhist; Deities, Buddhist; Disciples, Early Buddhist; Hygiene: Buddhist Perspectives; Rules, Buddhist (Vinaya): Historical; Sexuality: Buddhist Perspectives; Sri Lanka; Ten-Precept Mothers as Theravādin Nuns; Thailand; Tibet

## Further Reading

Bartholomeusz, Tessa, *Women under the Bo Tree: Buddhist Nuns in Sri Lanka*, Cambridge and New York: Cambridge University Press, 1994

Batchelor, Martine, *Walking on Lotus Flowers: Buddhist Women Working, Loving and Meditating*, London: Thorsons, 1996

Blackstone, Kathryn R., *Women in the Footsteps of the Buddha: Struggle for Liberation in the Therigatha*, Richmond, Surrey: Curzon, 1998

Devaraja, Lorna, "The Position of Women in Buddhism: With Special Reference to Pre-Colonial Sri Lanka," in *Faith Renewed II: A Report on The Second Asian Women's Consultation on Interfaith Dialogue, November 1–7, 1991, Colombo, Sri Lanka*, Seoul: Asian Women's Resource Centre for Culture and Theology, 1992

Friedman, Lenore, and Susan Moon, editors, *Being Bodies: Buddhist Women and the Paradox of Enlightenment*, Boston and London: Shambala, 1997

Gross, Rita, *Buddhism after Patriarchy: A Feminist History, Analysis and Reconstruction of Buddhism*, Albany: State University of New York Press, 1993

Horner, Isaline B., *Women under Primitive Buddhism*, London: Routledge, 1930; reprint, Delhi: Motilal Barnasidass, 1975

Kabilsingh, Chatsumarn, "A Comparative Study of the Bhikkhunī Pātimokkha," in *Oriental Research Studies*, volume 28, Varanasi: Chaukhamba Orientalia, 1984

Kabilsingh, Chatsumarn, *Thai Women in Buddhism*, Berkeley, California: Parallax Press, 1991

Klein, Anne Carolyn, *Meeting the Great Bliss Queen: Buddhists, Feminists and the Art of the Self*, Boston: Beacon Press, 1995

Macy, Joanna, *World as Lover, World as Self*, Berkeley, California: Parallax Press, 1991

Murcott, Susan, *The First Buddhist Women: Translations and Commentary on the Therīgāthā*, Berkeley, California: Parallax Press, 1991

Paul, Diana Y., *Women in Buddhism: Images of the Feminine in Mahāyāna Buddhism*, Berkeley, California: Asian Humanities Press, 1979

Tampoe, Manel, *The Story of Selestina Dias: Buddhist Female Philanthropy and Education*, Colombo, Sri Lanka: Social Scientists' Association, 1997

Tsomo, Karma Lekshe, editor, *Buddhism Through American Women's Eyes*, Ithaca, New York: Snow Lion, 1995

# Gender Studies: Christian Perspectives

Recently much attention has been given to issues of gender within all segments of literary, historical, and spiritual studies. The impact of gender studies on issues of Christian monasticism has been extensive. Merely gazing over a list of recent scholarly works will impart understanding of current concerns with gender and sexuality as they pertain to Christian monasticism and spirituality in general.

Although current debates are indeed important and have a great bearing on how we understand any literary or historical tradition, it is naive to assume that gender issues are only of recent concern with respect to Christian spirituality itself or to the history of Christian monasticism.

A few names and ideas are crucial to any understanding of this topic. First, perhaps, is the cult of the Virgin Mary, in a sense the first Christian "mystic" and a powerful focus for most of the devotional texts written in the Christian world. Mary is endlessly fascinating to Christians and scholars alike. She is the source and subject of innumerable poems, hymns, prayers, and sermons. Her presence has brought to the patriarchal world of the Church and of Christianity itself a gender balance and a voice for the feminine that no other figure within Christianity has achieved. Not associated with temptation and sin, like Eve; not associated (however inaccurately) with prostitution, like Mary Magdalene; and not fallen and redeemed at all but formed as a unique and sinless woman, Mary should stand as the primary inspiration of any work associated with gender and Christianity.

Mary's influence in monasticism is wide, although of course not as wide as that of Christ. The life of the religious woman and man would have involved constant self-analysis and reflection on the *imitatio Christi*. Thus, although monastic women would surely have striven to emulate Mary's purity and faith in their lives and devotional practices, it seems as if the cynosure of much monastic contemplation was the body of Christ and not the soul of Mary. Examples abound in monastic literature of men *and women* addressing their devotion and desire to Christ – portraying themselves as his lover, his spouse, or his child. Rarely does the active devotion of, for example, anchoritic spirituality center solely on Mary. Thus, acts of devotion, and the content of so many devotional texts, present a paradox with respect to gender issues; that is, both men and women are drawn in desire and love to the body and presence of Christ. Christ himself is often feminized in depictions of his passion, and the speakers of many devotional texts (most notably, of course, the sermons of Bernard of Clairvaux [1090–1153]) feminize themselves as spouses, lovers, and brides of Christ.

The issue of the personal expression of gender is also closely tied to monasticism and to medieval Christian devotions. Monastic life curtailed contact between the sexes. Although marriage was possible early on in the religious life, by the 13th century all religious orders expressly forbade any unnecessary contact among men and women. Such orders and rules also prohibited close, intimate contact within the same gender, with the term "particular friendship" being applied to such relationships. Particular friendships were very closely watched and often disrupted by monastic authority. Looking back now, one might assume that this was because of a desire to prevent sexual activity among the religious, especially homosexual acts within gender-restricted cloisters. The idea that such prohibition succeeded – that rules were enough to prohibit the expression of sexuality and desire – is unrealistic. Undoubtedly friendships and sexual relationships did unfold within monastic houses throughout the Middle Ages as well as into the modern age. However, more interesting is not the fact of such relationships but the means by which so many members of religious orders sublimated their physical longings into the realm of spirituality.

Again and again, throughout monastic writings, authors describe their feelings of love for Christ as erotic, matrimonial desire. An example appears in the anchoritic text *On Wel Swude God Urieson of God Almihti* (c. 1250), in which the speaker expresses her spiritual desire through earthly metaphors of love and sexuality: "Illuminate my darkened heart, / give my dwelling brightness, and brighten my soul / that is sooty, and make her worthy of thy sweet / winning. Kindle me with the blaze of your radiant / love. Let me be your lover; teach me to love thee, living lord" (author's translation). The spiritual desire for union that is part of all mystical experiences is translated here into the language of heterosexual desire and love. What made such a transition abundant in medieval literature was not a less sophisticated understanding of love and marriage, as has been argued, but rather a need to formulate inexpressible feelings of transcendence and desire through the always flawed medium of human language. Language seems to fail us when we attempt to speak to the deepest emotions of human experience. It is just so with the gendered, spiritual desire of medieval (and often contemporary) religious writing. The expression of love so deeply felt, desired, and ultimately won by the medieval mystic is beyond words – it is extralinguistic. Nevertheless its expression must employ the language of men and thus invoke metaphors that will go only so far, hence the use of sexual and erotic language: such language is the closest the writers can get to what they experienced in their transcendent pursuit of the presence of the Divine.

Other names and issues that seem crucial to an understanding of gender with respect to Christian spirituality include the letters of Abelard (1079–1142/43) and Heloise (c. 1100–1163/64), in which the 12th-century lovers-turned-monastic Christians express their love and sexual desire and the conflict these pose for their continued well-being. Abelard, a priest and teacher forced by circumstance to jettison his amorous past, writes with authority to Heloise about his wish for her to love only God and not him. Heloise, on the other hand, remains subject to passion and is unwilling to relinquish the feelings of desire that she and Abelard have shared. She writes of her love for Abelard surpassing her love for God. In a sense their lives reflect a basic tension within monastic life throughout the medieval and modern world: the tension between living in the world and denying its presence. This is a tension that has often troubled and frustrated Christians of both genders throughout Western history.

Modern concerns about Christianity and gender have remained within these basic areas: the devotion of both genders to the gendered body and passion of Christ, the problem of sexuality within religious life, and the proliferation of sexual language within expressions of spiritual desire. Although such concerns might take different forms in the modern world, they have been with us throughout the history of Christianity.

SUSANNAH MARY CHEWNING

*See also* Abelard, Peter; Devotions, Western Christian; Desert Mothers; Heloise; Historiography, Recent: Western Christian; Holy Men/Holy Women: Christian Perspectives; Transvestite Saints; Vision, Mystical: Western Christian

**Further Reading**

Boswell, John, *Same-Sex Unions in Pre-Modern Europe*, New York: Villard Books, 1994; as *The Marriage of Likeness: Same-Sex Unions in Pre-Modern Europe*, London: HarperCollins, 1995

Bynum, Caroline Walker, *Jesus as Mother: Studies in the Spirituality of the High Middle Ages* (Publications of the Center for Medieval and Renaissance Studies, 16), Berkeley: University of California Press, 1982

Cahill, Lisa Sowle, *Women and Sexuality* (Madeleva Lecture in Spirituality), New York: Paulist Press, 1992

Murphy, Sheila M., *A Delicate Dance: Sexuality, Celibacy, and Relationships among Catholic Clergy and Religious*, New York: Crossroad, 1992

Newman, Barbara, *From Virile Woman to WomanChrist: Studies in Medieval Religion and Literature* (Middle Ages Series), Philadelphia: University of Pennsylvania Press, 1995

Watt, Diane, editor, *Medieval Women in Their Communities*, Buffalo, New York: University of Toronto Press, and Cardiff: University of Wales Press, 1997

# German Benedictine Reform, Medieval

The issue of Benedictine monastic reform has been overshadowed by the two great Burgundian reform movements of Cluny and Cîteaux. The reality of monastic life in the European Middle Ages was much richer and more diversified, owing especially to several German reform groups, including the Gorzian movement, the Young Gorzians, and the reform associated with Hirsau. Because Germany's political environment was much more stable than that of 10th- and 11th-century France, these Germanic movements never attempted to free themselves of imperial or local noble controls and thus developed along a very different path from that of Cluny. The most striking difference is that monasteries of all three German reforms maintained their autonomy rather than forming a Cluniac-style confederation under the rule of a single abbot. Also noteworthy is that the German reforms were consistently more open and friendlier toward lay society than were Cluny and its daughter houses.

German Benedictine reform can be said to begin with the refoundation of Gorze near Metz in 933. Bishop Adalbero of Metz turned over the crumbling, largely abandoned monastery to Ainold and six companions, all men seeking a more vigorous ascetic life than could be found in Germany at the time. With Adalbero's support Gorze rapidly attracted like-minded monks, apparently using the reform program of Benedict of Aniane (c. 750–821) as its model for the monastic life. Gorzian monasticism, also called the Lotharingian reform, spread rapidly. Already around 934, when the duke of Lorraine decided to reform St. Maximin in Trier, he took two Gorzian monks to act as teachers to his new community. Saint Maximin in turn became an especially important source of the reform, as did Lorsch and St. Evre, Toul. This became the model for the Gorzian reform. Older reformed houses would supply all or some personnel to houses that nobles or bishops were founding or reforming in their own territories. In part students educated in Gorzian monastic schools who later became bishops spread the reform in their own dioceses; the school of Gorze itself was especially influential in this regard. These reformed houses were not "given" to Gorze or other reform centers, nor were they given to an outside authority as Cluny was turned over to St. Peter. Instead

Gorzian-reformed monasteries remained the property of whichever noble had brought in the reformers. Thus, although the number of houses following Gorzian practices in the 10th and 11th centuries eventually reached at least 160 in Germany, Hungary, and the Slavic lands bordering on the empire, they had no official connection to one another. The only thing that marked them out was a common way of life.

The Gorzian reformed practices, like those of France and Italy, were a development of Benedict of Aniane's ninth-century legislation. The reformers advocated long hours of corporate prayer, separation from the world, and careful observance of the Benedictine Rule. Differences from Cluny's observance appear mostly in details, such as the type of habit worn, how frequently monks should shave, and the shape of the monastic tonsure. However, extant writings for the Gorzian reform circle do express different attitudes toward the world outside the cloister than do Cluniac works. One cannot avoid the impression that Gorzian monks were more optimistic in their views about secular society. Especially because many Gorzian houses were imperial monasteries, the monks were drawn into missionary work on the eastern frontier. For example, the St. Maximin monk Adalbert of Magdeburg was sent on a mission to Kiev by Emperor Otto I (936–973); other St. Maximin monks formed the original and probably evangelizing community of St. Mauritius, Magdeburg; and the monk John of Gorze was even sent on an embassy to the caliph of Cordoba.

The fruitful alliance between monasteries and lay rulers and nobility continued with the offshoot of the Gorzian reform known as the Young Gorzian movement. This movement is associated especially with the abbots Richard of St. Vanne (Verdun), Poppo of Lorsch (or Stablo), and William of St. Bénigne, Dijon, all active in the early 11th century. These reformers are linked by the mixture of Gorzian and Cluniac usages at their houses, by the patronage of Emperor Henry II (1002–1024), and by a shared interest in lay affairs. The emperor gave both Richard and his disciple Poppo sweeping authority to reform imperial monasteries, some of which already followed Gorzian customs. This led at times to conflict, as when Fulda was taken over only with the help of imperial troops in 1013 and the community dispersed and when the monks of Corvey rebelled in 1014 to defend their customs, leading to the imprisonment of 17 monks. This of course points to the great weakness of the Gorzian dependence on proprietors: a monastery could be forced to change its observance on a whim, besides the more obvious dangers of lay exactions and encroachments. In this case no evidence really exists that the monks so violently reformed were living a lax or nonmonastic life. Although there is a hint that greater asceticism was introduced, the crux of the Young Gorzian reform appears to have been that the reformers were introducing *different* customs. There is a hint that some of these customs were Cluniac. At least the monks being reformed complained that the new practices violated the Benedictine Rule, a criticism also made especially of Cluniac clothing and tonsuring. The Young Gorzian reform also disrupted the autonomy of individual abbots and monasteries, which until that time had been the norm

in Germany. Richard of St. Vanne eventually governed 21 monasteries. Poppo went even further: Emperor Conrad II (1024–1039) gave the reformer control of all imperial monasteries (about 100 houses) in 1039. In both cases, however, the reformers distributed most of the monasteries entrusted to them to disciples who became abbots and largely free of juridical ties to the founder. One should also note that neither of these cases constitutes a true monastic confederation; they were personal unions of groups of monasteries under an individual, and the monasteries involved regained their autonomy with the reformer's death. However, even such a temporary alliance suggests that German rulers were strongly attracted by the scope and systematic nature of Cluniac monasticism, and it was difficult for German Benedictine houses to compete.

The Young Gorzian reform was not, however, Cluniac. The reformed houses practiced a mixture of Cluniac and Lotharingian customs. This can be traced most clearly at William of Dijon's main house of St. Bénigne, Dijon. William himself spent time as a monk in Cluny before receiving this monastery. He appears to have picked his favorite practices from both the Cluniac and the Gorzian way of life and went on to found other mixed-practice monasteries. However, what most distinguishes William's reform work is that, like other Young Gorzian reformers, he was less suspicious of the laity than Cluny was. The Young Gorzians were open to the practice of lay advocates taking care of monastic work outside the cloister, a tradition firmly opposed by the abbots of Cluny. This can almost certainly be attributed to the different conditions of Germany and France. Whereas France was sinking into feudal anarchy, Germany enjoyed one of the strongest governments of the Middle Ages, and German emperors supported monasteries and protected them from lay depredations besides appointing competent and reasonably pious bishops. Thus, German monasteries simply did not need to fight for independence from the laity and band together for protection as did Cluny. The Young Gorzians, in their world friendliness, also opened their monasteries to the laity in an unprecedented fashion. Laypeople, even women, are known to have participated in monastic processions and to have dined in monastic refectories. Richard of St. Vanne expanded his monastery significantly, apparently to make it more suitable for large numbers of pilgrims. Richard even led a large pilgrimage, including hundreds of laymen, to Jerusalem. All three reformers also became involved in the cause of ecclesiastical reform, William especially arguing strongly that it was a true monk's duty to interfere for the benefit of those outside the monastic life.

Even when a new monastic reform movement in Germany imposed what the sources insist was pure Cluniac observance, the resulting religious life was distinguishable from that at houses of the Cluniac confederation. The new reform leader was Hirsau in the diocese of Speyer, refounded around 1065 by the count of Calw. Like other reform leaders Abbot William of Hirsau (c. 1026–1091) soon received other monasteries to reform, and he usually accomplished this by giving one of his disciples the abbacy rather than maintaining personal control. Unlike the other reformed monasteries discussed in this article, Hirsau was liberated from its proprietary status and placed under papal authority, apparently in emulation of Cluny. However, it was not made subject to the abbot of Cluny and clearly followed an independent policy, especially during the disruptions of the investiture controversy. Under Abbot William, Hirsau became a center of the papal reform movement. Besides William himself, who was a zealous papal supporter, many of the rank-and-file Hirsau monks became involved in preaching. There are even accounts that they passed through enemy lines to further the papal cause against the emperor. After William's death Hirsau's daughter house St. George's in the Black Forest became the leader of the ecclesiastical reform movement in southern Germany under its abbot, Theoger.

With the Hirsau reform family, German monastic concern for the laity reached an apex. Besides playing an extremely active role in the investiture controversy, preaching for the pope and his reform program, the Hirsauer monks as well as abbots were active in more general reform of secular society. William is said to have convinced whole villages to take up a semi-monastic life; Pope Urban II (1088–1099) took these new communities under his protection in 1091. Theoger of St. George's is even supposed to have organized women into communal life. However, by the 1090s the Hirsau monasteries began to dissociate themselves from these activities in the world, responding to a barrage of criticism that took Cluniac monasticism as its ideal. The fading of Hirsau's world friendliness marks the end of a long chapter of German Benedictine history, as new religious orders came to take over such duties toward secular society, gradually leaving German Benedictine monasticism as a quiet backwater barely distinguishable from that in other lands.

PHYLLIS G. JESTICE

*See also* Abbot: Christian; Benedictines: General or Male; Cluniacs; Cluny, Abbots of; Congregations, Benedictine; Fulda, Germany; Germany; Gregory VII; Monastics and the World, Medieval; Orders (Religious), Origins of; William of Hirsau

**Further Reading**

Benz, Karl J., "Heinrich II und Cluny," *Revue bénédictine* 84 (1974)

Bulst, Neithard, *Untersuchungen zu den Klosterreformen Wilhelms von Dijon (962–1031)* (Pariser Historische Studien, 11), Bonn: Röhrscheid, 1973

Dauphin, Hubert, *Le Bienheureux Richard, Abbé de Saint-Vanne de Verdun, 1046* (Bibliothèque de la Revue d'histoire ecclésiastique, fascicle 24), Louvain: Bureaux de la Revue, Bibliothèque de l'université, 1946

Hallinger, Kassius, *Gorze-Kluny: Studien zu den monastischen Lebensformen und Gegensätzen im Hochmittelalter* (Studia Anselmiana, philosophica, theologica, fascicles 22–25), 2 vols., Rome: Herder, 1950–1951

Jakobs, Hermann, *Die Hirsauer, Ihre Ausbreitung und Rechtsstellung im Zeitalter des Investiturstreites* (Kölner historische Abhandlungen, 4), Cologne: Böhlau, 1961

Jestice, Phyllis G., "The Gorzian Reform and the Light under the Bushel," *Viator* 24 (1993)

Kottje, Raymund, and Helmut Maurer, editors, *Monastische Reformen im 9. und 10. Jahrhundert* (Vorträge und Forschungen, 38), Sigmaringen: Thorbecke, 1989

Leclercq, Jean, "Jean de Gorze et la vie religieuse au Xe siècle," in *Saint Chrodegang, communications présentées au Colloque tenu à Metz à l'occasion du douzième centenaire de sa mort*, Metz: Éditions Le Lorrain, 1967

Schieffer, Theodor, "Cluniazensische oder gorzische Reformbewegung?," *Archiv für mittelrheinische Kirchengeschichte* 4 (1952)

Wisplinghoff, Erich, *Untersuchungen zur frühen Geschichte der Abtei S. Maximin bei Trier von den Anfängen bis etwa 1150* (Quellen und Abhandlungen zur mittelrheinischen Kirchengeschichte, 12), Mainz: Gesellschaft für mittelrheinische Kirchengeschichte, 1970

# Germany: History

Monasticism and Christianity came simultaneously to Germany in the early Middle Ages. The first Christian missionaries to evangelize the territories beyond the Rhine were mostly Anglo-Saxon monks who began their proselytizing endeavors around 650. Because Germany had not been part of the Roman Empire, dioceses were organized around monasteries rather than cities. These monasteries served as the bases for future missionary activity and episcopal control. The most eminent of the Anglo-Saxon missionaries who worked in Germany was Wynfrith (c. 675–754), who evangelized Germany in cooperation with the papacy and with the Carolingian family. In 719 he was named bishop and took a new name, Boniface. For the next 35 years, Boniface preached the gospel and founded monasteries in Germany, the most important being the house of Fulda, which came to be a center of scholarship. However, traditional paganism still had its adherents in Germany, especially among the Saxons and Frisians, who murdered Boniface in 754. The Christian church in Germany, along with the monasteries, were taken under the protection of the Carolingian monarchy during the reign of Charlemagne (768–814), who after several savage campaigns subdued the Saxons and forced them to accept the faith.

During the reign of Charlemagne, German monks, some of whom the emperor summoned to his palace school at Aachen, became part of the intellectual and cultural elite of the Carolingian Empire. Walafrid Strabo (c. 808–849) became abbot of the important monastery of Reichenau and was a famed composer of Latin poetry. Einhard (c. 770–840), a monk of Fulda, wrote the most popular biography of Charlemagne. Later in the ninth century, Regino, abbot of Prüm (892–899), wrote a chronicle of the Viking invasions. The monks in German scriptoria busily copied books containing the learning of pagan antiquity and of the Latin fathers of the church. Fulda's library contained 110 books; the monastic library of Reichenau came to possess more than 400. However, the scholars and scribes of this era produced little original literature. They were more skillful at preserving the learning of the past.

Exterior of church, Abbey of Eberbach (Cistercian), Oestrich, Rheingau, Germany, 1270–1345.
Photo courtesy of Chris Schabel

The German monks were also involved in the controversies of the era. For example, Rabanus Maurus (c. 780–856) was involved in the *filioque* argument with the Greek church that took place at the Synod of Aachen in 808. The Franks described the procession of the Holy Spirit in the Nicene Creed as being from the "Father and the Son" (*ex patre filioque*), whereas the Greeks believed the procession to be from the Father only. A Saxon monk named Gottschalk (c. 804–c. 869), one of the more creative minds of the ninth century, initiated a controversy with his teaching on the idea of predestination. Gottschalk taught that God had predestined some to everlasting life, others to eternal perdition. The sacraments do nothing to avail the wicked, and no one who is good could be damned. In 838 the synod of Quierzy decided that Gottschalk's teaching contradicted the decrees of the Council of Orange (529), which for three centuries had been accepted as the orthodox view on predestination. Gottschalk was flogged and imprisoned for his error. He never recanted. Gottschalk's opinions instigated the composition of a great literature on the subject of predestination that mostly supported the traditional teaching, that is, that men and women have the free will to choose the good or the evil. God knows from all eternity what will be chosen, but his knowledge of it does not cause the decision.

This great era of cultural achievement was nonetheless short-lived. The era of the Viking and Magyar invasions (c. 850–950) were ruinous to many monasteries. Because monasteries were virtually undefended, raiders targeted them first. Monasteries searched about for protectors (called advocates, usually the local lord and his private army of warriors), but that protection came at a price. The advocate assumed the privileges and immunities of the monastery as well as the right to name the abbot. Between the depredations of raiders and the demands of the advocates, many monasteries became vacant, and in those that remained, monastic observance was often lax.

By the turn of the tenth century, monastic reformers of the monasteries had begun to agitate for restoration. The first cries for reform came from the duchy of Lotharingia, where the high aristocracy demanded renewal of the monasteries. The reformers believed that the rule of St. Benedict was the only licit monastic rule and that monasteries must be freed from their oppressors. The center of the early German monastic reform movement was the monastery of Gorze, which had been all but destroyed by the raiders. The monastery had come into the possession of Bishop Adalbero of Metz, who in 933 handed control of the monastery over to a group of reforming monks. These monks lived in Gorze according to the Benedictine rule and within two years were

Chapter house, Cistercian abbey at Maulbronn, Baden-Württemberg, Germany, 13th century.
Photo courtesy of Chris Schabel

sending their brethren to introduce reform into other German monasteries. One hundred and fifty monasteries were reformed according to the impulses unleashed by Gorze. Unlike Cluny in France, which was under the direct protection of the pope, reformed monasteries in Lotharingia were subject to the jurisdiction of the local bishop. Because they continued to recognize episcopal jurisdiction and owned churches and chapels themselves, the German reformed monasteries greatly influenced the diocesan clergy. Other important reform movements emerged in the 11th century, such as that originating out of the foundation of Hirsau (1049).

With the installation of Leo IX (1048–1054) as pope by his cousin, the emperor Henry III (1039–1056), monastic reform ideas became part of papal ideology. Leo had been part of the reform movement in Germany, and he brought a number of important reformers with him to Rome, such as Hildebrand, the Lotharingian monk who later became Pope Gregory VII (1073–1085). Along with men such as Hildebrand, Leo, in close cooperation with the emperor, worked to remove the abuses of simony and clerical marriage from the priesthood. In effect, these papal reformers wanted to make the diocesan clergy more like reformed monks, separated as far as possible from ties to secular society, and celibate. When Hildebrand, who was a more

radical reformer than Leo IX had been, became pope Gregory VII in 1073, lay investiture was added to the abuses troubling the Catholic Church. Gregory insisted that laymen should have no role in the appointment of bishops, and this contributed to the outbreak of the investiture controversy with Henry IV (1056–1106). During the investiture controversy, which lasted until 1122, German monasteries were divided in their allegiances. The unreformed monasteries were largely on the side of the emperor, whereas reformed monasteries were split into pro-papal and pro-imperial parties. Because many of the reformed monasteries still had strong ties to the imperial church, they could not oppose the emperor. However, other reformed monasteries blamed the emperor for the abuses in the church and for persecuting Gregory VII, who had tried to purify the church of abuse.

By the end of the investiture controversy, the mantle of reform in Catholic Europe had passed to the Cistercians, who never became a great force in German church affairs. Traditional Benedictine houses continued to prosper and command many resources. The next great religious movement in Germany arrived with the mendicant orders in the early 13th century. Both the Franciscans and the Augustinians founded numerous convents across Germany, but the Dominicans quickly assumed leadership of the religious life in Germany. The Dominicans proved to be especially attractive to sons of the urban patriciate. They became the intellectual and spiritual leaders of Germany for the rest of the Middle Ages not only through their substantial erudition but also through their pastoral caretaking of religious women, who constituted another powerful movement in German religious life.

By the 15th century another set of reforming impulses, which had been released in part by the scandal of the Great Schism (1378–1417), led to the division in Germany and elsewhere of the religious orders into branches known as Conventual and Observant. Many reformers had despaired of renewing the whole church but hoped that parts of the church could be reformed, such as individual dioceses or religious orders. Devotional movements, such as the Brethren of the Common Life in the Low Countries, greatly influenced the thinking of these reformers. Conventuals argued for a liberal interpretation of their rule, whereas Observants insisted on a literal interpretation. Observant monks and friars constituted important reform groups within the later medieval church. Along with the Observants, the Carthusians, whose strict ascetic life was famous, attracted many candidates.

The Protestant Reformation destroyed monasticism, along with Catholicism, in much of Germany. Luther himself wrote a treatise, *De votis monasticis* (1521; On Monastic Vows), wherein he taught that celibacy and asceticism were contrary to Scripture. A life of good works made no sense to evangelical Protestants, so in regions where Lutheranism or, later, Calvinism replaced Catholicism, the monasteries were in time dissolved. Monasteries were suppressed in one of two ways. First, monastic lands were seized, giving the monks no way of making a living. They were then turned out of the monastery and usually given a pension from the appropriated monastic lands. Many either migrated to Catholic territories or took teaching positions in their native regions. Second, monasteries were allowed to die a natural death. No monastery could survive more than a few generations in a mainly Protestant region because new candidates for the religious life were no longer available. Monasteries were suppressed after territorial princes, urban governing councils, or the monks themselves had adopted the Protestant faith, such as Albert of Brandenburg, grand master of the Teutonic Knights, who secularized the lands of the order and became a Prussian duke. By the end of the 16th century, only 800 out of 3,000 Benedictine monasteries remained in Germany. The Augustinians lost nearly every single German convent.

Recovery for religious life came a bit more slowly in Germany than it did in southern Europe. However, by the 1620s the Catholic Reform, or Counter-Reformation, began to bear fruit. The Counter-Reformation followed on the victories of the Catholic Habsburg rulers in the Thirty Years' War. Emperor Ferdinand II (1619–1637) was a devout Catholic who was determined to restore Catholicism to Germany after war broke out between himself and the great Protestant principalities of Germany. Ferdinand's armies occupied northern Germany in 1626, and a number of monasteries there were reestablished. His Edict of Restitution (1629) enacted the return of lands seized from the monasteries during the Reformation. By the end of 1631, 150 Catholic churches and monasteries had been refounded. However, Ferdinand's restoration was brief, as his high-handedness in dealing with the defeated German Protestant princes prompted the invasion of the Swedish King Gustavus Adolphus (1611–1632), whose small but highly trained armies swept the imperial forces from northern Germany, and Ferdinand was compelled to nullify the Edict of Restitution in 1635.

Nonetheless, what remained of German religious life was being reformed and renewed, so that in the 18th century, German monasticism might have been the healthiest in Catholic Europe as the momentum initiated by the Counter-Reformation continued. Many small orders of teaching monks and nuns, inspired by the example of the Society of Jesus, came into existence, such that activist religious orders tended to attract more candidates than the contemplative orders. Benedictine houses were famed for their scholarly activities, having produced great folio volumes on German regional and monastic history between 1750 and 1800. Their libraries were the envy of Europe.

The Enlightenment of the 18th-century threatened the institutions of the Catholic Church even more dangerously than had the Reformation. For Enlightenment deists and atheists, the religious life was folly, the most odious superstition. Through Enlightenment influence the Habsburg Emperor Joseph II (1780–1790) came to believe that the religious orders, especially the large international ones, were a threat to the stability of the state, and he subjected the church in his realm to tighter control. He dissolved 700 out of 2,163 monasteries in the Habsburg territories, and in so doing provided an example to future governments formed by the principles of the Enlightenment.

The French Revolution posed a great threat to German monasticism. Unlike Emperor Joseph, the French National Convention (1792–1795) was in its most radical phase anti-Christian and imperialist, which in turn drove many clergymen all over Europe into the antirevolutionary camp. Furthermore, republican ideology maintained that monastic vows limited personal liberty. The French Republic went to war against the crowns of Europe beginning in 1792 and by 1794 had occupied the Rhineland, a mostly Catholic region of Germany. French military leaders in this sector, among them many Catholics, decided that because the people were devoted to the monks, no monasteries should be dissolved. Even on the right bank of the Rhine, where resistance to French occupation was greater, no monasteries were suppressed before 1797.

However, with the advent of Napoleon Bonaparte (1799–1815), the ancient role of the Catholic Church in Germany was destroyed. Napoleon secularized the ancient prince-bishoprics and gave their lands over to secular rulers. He suppressed all independent monasteries (mostly small ones) whose lands were likewise given over to secular rulers or public welfare institutions, such as schools and hospitals. In monasteries scheduled for suppression, a commission would read a patent to the monks. Their goods were then inventoried and the monks informed of their future. The great German monastic libraries were given to scholarly state-owned libraries. Napoleon's victories prompted German kings to suppress monasteries in their domains in order either to use the resources thus obtained for defense against Napoleon or to provide his armies with allied troops. Bishops and abbots raised formal protests against the secularizations but were powerless to stop them. Because much of peasant participation in Catholic worship involved the making of pilgrimages to monasteries with especially revered relics, they too resented the suppressions. The fate of the monasteries of Cologne typified those throughout Germany: two became government offices, 14 became factories or warehouses, and two became military barracks. Bishops who were reorganizing their dioceses sometimes acquired the buildings of suppressed monasteries; their splendid buildings could be purchased cheaply for parochial churches and worship. Thus had monastic churches served before suppression, but because of ancient immunities their resources had often been beyond effective control of the bishop. Because secularization of the monasteries and prince-bishoprics destroyed the ancestral political, social, and religious organization of Germany, the Habsburg Emperor Franz I (1792–1835) proclaimed the Holy Roman Empire dissolved in 1806.

Nonetheless, the devotion of German Catholics to monasticism survived the liberal onslaught, and a monastic recovery in Germany followed soon after the defeat of Napoleon in 1815. The monks continued to draw patrons from all ranks of German Catholic society. The dissolution of the Holy Roman Empire in 1806 also meant that now monks could draw support from Protestant rulers. Part of the purpose of the empire had been to maintain religious spheres of influence within which one denomination dominated. After the dissolution of the empire, more Catholics came under Protestant rule, and some Protestants came under Catholic rule. Protestant rulers often showed their goodwill toward new Catholic subjects by benevolence to monks. The religious configuration especially of Prussia became even more complex as the 19th century wore on, as Catholic Poles seeking employment in new industrial jobs migrated westward. Indeed, most Prussian monks were Poles. Kaiser Wilhelm II (1888–1918) gave an altar to the Benedictine monastery church of Beuron because he needed the support of Catholics against the socialists. Beuron, which had been reestablished as a Catholic monastery in 1863 after having been suppressed by Napoleon, became important in the modern liturgical movement.

On the other hand, German monasteries still had enemies, the most powerful of whom was Otto von Bismarck, who served as imperial chancellor from 1871 to 1890. Bismarck distrusted the Catholics, against whom he directed his Kulturkampf. He too expelled all monks and nuns (except those who cared for the ill) from Prussia in 1875; 605 monks were expelled from the diocese of Cologne. The policy of Kulturkampf proved disastrous for the German government. German Catholics formed one-third of German society and a solid voting block in the Reichstag. Polish Catholics denounced what they believed an attack not only on their religion but on their nationality as well. By 1890 Bismarck and Pope Leo XIII (1878–1903) agreed that re-strictions on monasteries would be lifted, but by then the Kulturkampf had tied the German monasteries more closely to their principal protector: the pope.

Monasticism in Germany continued to flourish into the 20th century; many monasteries became tourist attractions in addition to being pilgrimage sites. During the Weimar Republic, the last legal restrictions on monasteries proclaimed during the Kulturkampf were repealed and a number of new monasteries opened. After Adolf Hitler seized power in 1933, he did not disturb the monasteries, although he was convinced that a confrontation with the Catholic Church in Germany was inevitable. When World War II broke out in 1939, Nazi authorities imposed a closer surveillance on both bishops and monks, as church authorities denounced the crimes of the regime. From September 1940 until July 1941, more than 100 monasteries were closed, but Hitler stopped the suppressions when the bishops protested. In the closing months of war, as the Allied armies invaded Germany, monasteries bore their brunt of destruction and death.

In the years after the war, monasteries in what became East Germany languished under an oppressive communist regime, whereas those in West Germany prospered and played an important role in developments in the Catholic Church as a whole. As leaders of the liturgical movement, the Benedictines of Maria Laach greatly influenced the proceedings of the Second Vatican Council. German monks continued their important charitable work of teaching and caring for the poor. However, after Vatican II the number of German monks declined precipitously and remained low until the end of the 1990s.

ROBERT W. SHAFFERN

See also Augustinian Friars/Hermits; Beuron, Germany; Boniface, St.; Dissoluton of Monasteries: Continental Europe; Dominicans; Franciscans; Fulda, Germany; German Benedictine Reform, Medieval; Gregory VII; Luther, Martin; Maria Laach, Germany; Monastics and the World, Medieval; Walafrid Strabo; William of Hirsau; Wolter, Maurus; Wolter, Placidus

## Further Reading

Blumenthal, Uta-Renate, The Investiture Controversy: Church and Monarchy from the Ninth to the Twelfth Century, Philadelphia: University of Pennsylvania Press, 1988

Chadwick, Owen, The Popes and European Revolution, Oxford and New York: Clarendon Press, 1981

Chadwick, Owen, A History of the Popes, 1830–1914, Oxford and New York: Clarendon Press, 1998

Freed, John, The Friars and German Society in the Thirteenth Century, Cambridge, Massachusetts: Mediaeval Academy of America, 1977

Hirsch, Hans, "The Constitutional History of the Reformed Monasteries During the Investiture Contest," in Mediaeval Germany: 911–1250: Essays by German Historians, 2 vols., edited by Geoffrey Barraclough, Oxford: Blackwell, 1948

Laistner, M.L.W., Thought and Letters in Western Europe, A.D. 500 to 900, Ithaca, New York: Cornell University Press, and London: Methuen, 1957

Läpple, Alfred, Klöster und Orden in Deutschland, Munich: Delphin, 1985

Oakley, Francis, *The Western Church in the Later Middle Ages*, Ithaca, New York: Cornell University Press, 1979

Tellenbach, Gerd, *The Church in Western Europe from the Tenth to the Early Twelfth Century*, translated by Timothy Reuter, Cambridge and New York: Cambridge University Press, 1993

Van Engen, John, *Rupert of Deutz*, Berkeley: University of California Press, 1983

# Germany: Sites

*Introduction*

The peculiar history of Germany has made for a very uneven survival of the many monasteries that were a feature of the medieval landscape. Until the late 19th century, Germany consisted of a large number of electorates, principalities, dukedoms, and petty states that despite conquests and alliances remained largely independent of one another. The famous Reformation-period doctrine of *cuius regio, eius religio* led to a patchwork of Roman Catholic and Protestant states, depending on the whim of individual rulers or their perception of what would be politically advantageous. In the unreformed states monasteries continued to flourish. In states where Lutheranism or Calvinism was dominant, monasteries were dissolved, as they were in England. The variable pattern of monastic survival that this produced was further confused during the Napoleonic period (1799–1815), when many more monasteries were secularized. Some of the monastic buildings and their churches were put to new, in some cases inappropriate, uses. For example, the Cistercian monastery at Haina became a lunatic asylum, and St. Peter's at Erfurt became a military barracks, with the church used as a munitions store; the charterhouse at Nürnberg was converted into a museum in 1866, and more recently semi-ruined sites, such as that at Bad Hersfeld, have become open-air theatres. Although a great deal survives and can be visited, the geographical spread is uneven. Towns such as Cologne and Erfurt offer rich pickings, whereas the visitor to Berlin is hard put even to locate the small Franciscan house left in ruins since World War II.

*Origins: Monasteries of the Pre- and Early Romanesque Periods*

The early medieval geography of Germany has also played a part in the way monasteries developed. Much of the country as defined today emerged from the Roman period quite untouched by Roman civilization and military rule. The empire extended no farther east than the Rhine and no farther north than the Danube, although parts of southwestern Germany were also Roman territory, as the exact line of the frontier (*limes*) between the two rivers varied from time to time. The considerable western and southern "fringe" areas followed the rest of the Roman Empire in accepting Christianity in the fourth century, and in towns such as Trier, Cologne, and Regensburg evidence exists for churches and monasteries from an early date. At Bonn and Xanten in the Rhineland, religious communities sprang up in the former Roman cemeteries on the discovery of martyrs' graves.

The cult centers developed into churches with accommodation for the religious and for the pilgrims who came to venerate the saints' shrines. Traders followed the pilgrims, and market settlements grew up; the fort at Bonn and the *colonia* at Xanten were eventually abandoned, and the medieval towns developed at some distance from the original Roman sites. Especially at Xanten it is possible for the visitor to appreciate the extent of "settlement drift"; the Roman town has been largely undisturbed by later developments and has been restored in recent years as an archaeological theme park. Standing on the ramparts one can now see the minster and town of Xanten several hundred meters to the south.

However, beyond the *limes* Germany remained unromanized and pagan, and it was left to missionaries from other parts of Europe to convert the people and to set up churches and monasteries. Frankish missionaries operated in the context of Merovingian and Carolingian military campaigns to the east of the Rhine; the Irish followers and successors of Columban (d. 615) worked mainly in the former Roman areas of the south; the Anglo-Saxons under Winfrith (St. Boniface, c. 675–754) broke new ground in Hessen and Thuringia, founding important monasteries, such as Fulda in 744.

The earliest places of worship tended to reuse Roman building materials or even to convert entire Roman buildings to Christian purposes, for example, in Trier, an imperial capital, where a major palace (said to be that of St. Helena, mother of Constantine the Great) was reduced in size to become the cathedral. Despite many later rebuildings, much of the Roman masonry is still easily identifiable in the standing fabric. A short boat ride away is Pfalzel, where a minor rural palace (*palatiolum*, thus the name Pfalzel) was turned into a nunnery by a member of the Carolingian dynasty. Some rooms of the villa became the church and others the conventual buildings. The latter are now private houses and offices but can be viewed from the outside and show significant remains of Roman masonry.

The Reichenau, an island in Lake Constance accessible by causeway, supported a major monastery with at least three separate churches. Saint George at Oberzell preserves the earliest evidence, with much of the church building dating from the late ninth century and extensive mural painting from the late tenth. At Mittelzell the major monastic church of Sts. Mary and Mark was first built in the early eighth century and rebuilt in the early ninth, with extensions continuing until the late tenth. However, the church that remains is a basilica of the first half of the 11th century. Saint Peter at Niederzell is a fully Romanesque building with baroque embellishments, but a fragment of a carved stone screen panel survives from the ninth century. The Reichenau monastery was famous and influential and had a flourishing scriptorium that produced the famous parchment plan of St. Gallen (c. 830).

Another important Carolingian monastery has been revealed by excavation at Lorsch, where parts of a later monastic church still stand. However, best known is the so-called Torhalle (gatehouse) or Königshalle (royal hall), a small two-storied triple-arched building with rich Roman-derived decoration externally

Gatehouse, Abbey of Lorsch (founded by Benedictines, 764), near Worms (Rhineland), Germany, c. 800.
Photo courtesy of Mary Schaefer

and *trompe l'oeil* paintings in the upper chamber. In Westphalia the church at Corvey still incorporates the late ninth-century westwork, with its vaulted ground-floor chamber and upper galleries, on the walls of which early musical notation has been discovered.

The tenth-century convent at Gernrode on the east side of the Harz Mountains was originally built for canonesses who attended worship in galleries over the side aisles that opened to the nave through arcades, an early example of the three-tier elevation in a medieval church. Part of the later cloister still exists to the south of the church. Canonesses were also catered for in the 11th-century church of St. Maria im Kapitol in Cologne.

### The Monastic Orders in the Full Middle Ages

#### 1. Benedictines and Cluniacs

The early medieval house at Hirsau, to the north of the Black Forest (surviving ninth-century carved stonework) was refounded in 1065, and the church was rebuilt shortly afterward to adapt it to the Cluniac liturgy. Saint Aurelius, the main church, survives, but the church of Sts. Peter and Paul and the accompanying claustral buildings are in ruins. At Maria Laach, in the Eifel, a house for Cluniac monks was founded in the late 11th century, with further building campaigns in the mid and late 12th; it is a good example of mature German Romanesque.

It is still a working monastery, and guided tours are offered. Saint Peter's at Erfurt (Thuringia) was converted from a collegiate church to a Benedictine monastery in 1060 and came under the influence of Hirsau later in the century. Roughly contemporary with this is the refounded early medieval nunnery on the Fraueninsel in the Chiemsee, between Munich and Salzburg (Austria). Boat trips can be taken to this still functioning convent.

The 12th and early 13th centuries saw the building or rebuilding of many Benedictine monasteries, for example, in Cologne at Great St. Martin's and at nearby Brauweiler. In Lower Saxony are St. Godehard at Hildesheim and the former abbey at Königslutter, where part of the Romanesque cloister survives with elaborate carved columns and capitals. The 12th-century monastery at Weingarten, some 20 miles north of the Austrian end of Lake Constance, was remodeled in the baroque style in the 18th century. It had been a major pilgrimage goal on account of its relic of the Holy Blood and has become a center for Roman Catholic education. Its famous medieval library was dispersed at secularization; two late 11th-century gospel books are now in the Pierpont Morgan Collection in New York.

#### 2. Cistercians

The Cistercians were well represented in Germany, and several of their houses have survived to a greater or lesser extent. Well-preserved complexes from the 12th century can be found in the Rheingau at Eberbach near Eltville; at Haina in north Hessen, where at the Reformation the monastery was converted by the local ruler into a hospice for the poor and sick ("a copybook example of the idiosyncratic architecture of the Cistercians"); and at Bad Maulbronn (Baden-Württemberg), where the monastery became a Protestant school after the dissolution of the monasteries and is a major contender for the title of best-preserved medieval monastery north of the Alps. At Chorin, to the northeast of Berlin, an impressive church and extensive conventual buildings of mid-13th-century date, all in brick, survive in typical Cistercian rural isolation.

### 3. Carthusians
In the German-speaking area Carthusian foundations tended to concentrate in and around southern Styria, now part of Slovenia. The few charterhouses to have survived in present-day Germany are good examples of the semi-eremitic philosophy of the Order. The best examples are in Nürnberg, which was founded in 1330 and became a museum in the 19th century; it can be visited during normal museum opening hours. In Erfurt the first charterhouse was built in timber in the 1370s; the church was replaced in stone by 1380 and the claustral buildings in the 15th century, followed by the chapter house in 1503 and some rebuilding in the early 18th century.

### Canons Regular

### 1. Augustinians
The best-preserved house is at Bad Reichenhall in Bavaria, close to Salzburg and the Austrian border. The late Romanesque church has cloister and conventual buildings to the south; the elaborate architectural decor is Italianate in style. The double monastery (i.e., for both sexes) at Barsinghausen near Hanover also has claustral buildings, and the 13th-century church preserves a gallery for the canonesses in the south transept.

### 2. Premonstratensians
The cathedral at Brandenburg took in the canons from St. Gotthardt's, now the parish church, which retains the typically austere Romanesque façade of its original occupants. The cathedral has late Romanesque claustral buildings to the north, which house the Dommuseum, where medieval textiles and illuminated manuscripts are on display. About 20 miles northeast of Brandenburg lies Jerichow, whose brick church is mainly in a plain Romanesque style but with Gothic additions and a crypt with elaborately carved capitals. The monastic museum occupies the claustral ranges and displays archaeological and documentary material relevant to the site and its surroundings.

### 3. The Military Orders
No significant remains of the Templars exist. The Hospitallers, with their medical preoccupations, developed multipurpose buildings combining church and hospital, often of two or three stories, as at Niederwiesel and Neckarelz. The Teutonic Knights were especially active in the northeast, and some of their houses are in present-day Poland or Lithuania. However, the key site is Marburg, where they embraced the cult of St. Elisabeth; buildings of the close around her church include the House of the Order and other of the Knights' properties, most of which are now in the possession of the university.

### The Friars

### 1. The Dominicans
The Order is represented at a large number of places in Germany. The Thüringer Museum occupies their buildings in Eisenach, just east of the border between Hessen and the former East Germany. Thirty miles farther east, at Erfurt, the Predigerkirche (preaching church) has become the city's main Protestant place of worship. Inside a plain exterior the church exhibits Gothic harmony and many late medieval features. At Neuruppin, some 40 miles northeast of Berlin, the brick church shows various periods of building from the mid–13th to the 14th century. At Constance the early Gothic cloister now houses the Inselhotel. The church at Lambrecht, dating from the 14th century, has a western gallery for the nuns.

### 2. The Franciscans
A smaller number of impressive Franciscan friaries survive. The small house at Berlin in the Nicholaiviertel was bombed during World War II and has been deliberately left as a ruin. However, more substantial remains can be found at Erfurt, where the Barfüsserkirche was another victim of the bombing; again the nave has been left as a controlled ruin, but the chancel has been restored as a small museum and houses some of the original medieval glass. Saint Katharine's church in Lübeck, just inland from the Baltic coast, has survived intact. It has a rich west façade and several unusual features, including a two-storied chancel, a Tintoretto altarpiece, and a series of 20th-century sculptures of great interest. The conventual buildings have been a school since the 16th century, and the church is a museum, as is the former Franciscan house at Zittau, close to the borders with both Poland and the Czech Republic.

### 3. The Augustinian Friars and the Carmelites
Confusingly Erfurt had an Augustinian friary as well as a collegiate church for Augustinian canons. The most famous member of the friars' community was Martin Luther (1483–1546), whose reconstructed cell can be visited as part of a guided tour. The nave of the friary church in Trier was demolished in 1811, but the 14th-century choir remains; this bears a close resemblance to the Carmelite church in the same city, which was progressively demolished in the 19th and 20th centuries, leaving the claustral buildings of the mid-16th, remodeled in the baroque style. Another baroque gem is the Carmelite church in Regensburg.

### Sites to Visit
Key: E = early medieval (up to the end of the 11th century), A = Augustinian Canons, AF = Austin Friars, B = Benedictines, C = Cistercians, Ca = Carthusians, Cl = Cluniacs, D = Dominicans, F = Franciscans, N = nuns or canonesses, P = Premonstratensians, T = Knights of the Teutonic Order

Chorin (C)

Cologne: Gross St. Martin (B); St. Maria im Kapitol (EN); St. Barbara (Ca); Brauweiler, St. Nicholas (B)

Constance (D)

Corvey (E)

Erfurt: St. Peter (B); Reglerkirche (A); Barfüsserkirche (F); Predigerkirche (D); Augustinerkloster (AF); St. Salvator (Ca)

Fulda (E, B)

Gernrode (E, N)

Hildesheim: St. Godehard (B); St. Michael (E)

Hirsau (E, Cl)

Jerichow (P)

Lambrecht (DN)

Lorsch (E)

Marburg (T)

Maria Laach (Cl)

(Bad) Maulbronn (C)

Neuruppin (D)

Nuremberg (Ca)

Pfalzel (E)

(The) Reichenau (E, B)

(Bad) Reichenhall (A)

Zittau (F)

DAVID PARSONS

*See also* Architecture: Western Christian Monasteries; Benedictines; Boniface, St.; Carthusians; Cistercians; Cluniacs; Columban, St.; Dissolution of Monasteries: Continental Europe; Dominicans; Franciscans; Fulda, Germany; German Benedictine Reform, Medieval; Hospitallers (Knights of Malta since 1530); Luther, Martin; Maria Laach, Germany; Premonstratensian Canons; Reformation; Reichenau; St. Gallen, Switzerland; Teutonic Order; William of Hirsau

## Further Reading

Binding, G., and M. Untermann, *Kleine Kunstgeschichte der mittelalterlichen Ordensbaukunst in Deutschland*, Darmstadt: Wissenschaftliche Buchgesellschaft, 1985

Braunfels, W., *Monasteries of Western Europe*, London and New York: Thames and Hudson, 1993

Conant, Kenneth J., *Carolingian and Romanesque Architecture, 800 to 1200*, 2nd edition, Harmondsworth and New York: Penguin, 1987

Romanò, Cesare, *Abteien und Klöster in Europa*, Augsburg: Pattloch, 1997 (see pages 174–211)

# Gestures, Buddhist

Gestures may be categorized in a variety of overlapping ways, for example, iconographic gestures (as seen in images); ritual gestures (as performed by oneself or others, in some cases identical to the gestures of images); gestures of greeting (when meeting other people or in devotional acts, i.e., greeting the Buddha); gestures of communication (such as when taking food or to avoid speaking); and taboo gestures (such as pointing one's foot at a Buddha image). Gestural systems are every bit as complex and fluid as spoken language. This article considers the significance of two categories: mudra and greeting gestures.

The most symbolically weighted category of gesture in Buddhism is mudra (Sanskrit, "seal" or "sign"; Chinese, *yin-xiang*; Japanese, *inzo, ingei*), usually referring to a gesture of the hands. These set positions have been codified with set meanings: protection, fearlessness, salutation, preaching, sprinkling ambrosia, menacing, homage, charity, and calling others to witness. For example, the *namaskāra*, with hands in front and palms together, a widely recognized gesture of greeting; *vitarka*, a gesture of argument; *bhutadamana*, "awe inspiring"; and *dhyāna* or *samādhi*, indicating meditation. Some of the mudra are associated with specific deities, although many are widely diffused in iconography and ritual. Specific mudra also invoke specific deities and their powers; for example, the healing Buddha Bhaisajyaguru is depicted performing a *dhyāna-mudra* (meditation gesture, the left hand in his lap, palm up, with a bowl of medicine resting on it), showing meditation to be the source of healing (the bowl of medicine serves as a metaphor for the healing power of the dharma). Other elements of the Buddha's gestural system include nods of the head, calm smiles, beams of light from his body, and patting good monks on their heads.

The Japanese Shingon monk Kūkai (774–835) classified mudra (as well as body movements, incense smell, and the taste of certain herbs) as the "body" part of the "Three Mysteries" (body, speech, and mind). Speech refers to mantras, and mind refers to visualizations. Although the teachings of the Buddha may be preached in any number of expedient ways, including by translating Sanskrit into local dialects and employing whatever gestures are conducive to enlightenment, the mudra claims a special status because they replicate the actual physical form of the Buddha, just as the mantra replicates the actual sounds uttered by Buddha. When performed correctly the practitioner reproduces the physical movements of the Buddha, thereby enacting enlightenment. This performed Buddhahood is known as *sokushin jobutsu*, or "becoming a Buddha in this very body." Recent scholarship has highlighted the performative aspect of the attainment of Buddhahood in contrast to intellectualized or mystical versions of Buddhism common in much scholarly and popular literature.

The most common gesture in a Buddhist (indeed Asian) context is the *namaskāra* or *namaste* (which is actually what one might say as one performs this greeting) (Japanese *gasshō*, or in Thailand the *wai*). This gesture is made by pressing together the palms of the hands in front of the body. Although it is similar to the Christian gesture of prayer (especially common since the late Middle Ages), no evidence exists of any direct influence in either direction. This *namaskāra* gesture is an excellent example of the performance of social distinctions. In most cases the exact height of the hands generally indicates the actor's perceived or intended social position with respect to the other person: the hands are raised higher toward people "higher up" than oneself. For example, a *wai* to the king of Thailand would involve placing one's hands almost above one's head. A *wai* to a fully ordained monk

Gyuto monks (Gelukpa lineage) doing hand mudras.
Photo courtesy of John Powers

is usually at the forehead. An adult's *wai* made in response to a child's greeting is at heart level. Special devotion might be shown by placing one's hands on the feet of the monk. As with the spatial distinction of height, the timing of this gesture is also important: the subordinate initiates the gesture. Thus, in theory one never responds to a *wai* with hands any higher.

Conversely, the fact that monks do not *wai* to laity (not even to the king) signifies that monkhood is an ideal social order "outside of the world." However, members of the ordained community continue to perform obeisance to each other, and Buddhist scriptures encode the orthodox hierarchy: all nuns, no matter how senior, bow to all monks, no matter how junior. Novices bow to the fully ordained. In cases in which the relative seniority of two monks is unclear or ambiguous or in which each perceives the other to be more worthy, an elaborate game of inverted one-upmanship – one might even say "one-downmanship" – takes place, as each tries to *wai* first, and higher.

Buddhist monastic guides reveal an elaborate regimen of body control, especially a mindful control of the hands; rules prohibit flapping the arms around, standing with arms akimbo, carelessly scratching or blowing one's nose when in the presence of superiors, tickling people, and so on. Gestures should also be controlled at mealtimes; there are rules in the *Prātimokṣa*, for example, against licking the fingers, scraping the bowl with fin-

gers, or sticking the tongue out. The activities of seeing, pointing, and touching are strongly rule-governed. The control of gestures is part of a more encompassing effort to mindfully discipline the entire body as well as speech and mind. As with control of the hands, there is a range of prescribed postures for the body, called *āsana*. These refer to the postures of yoga, the best known being the *padmāsana*, or "lotus position." When circumambulating an image or sacred site, one should move clockwise with palms together and with one's right shoulder to the object of reverence, possibly with that shoulder bared.

Finally, to the extent that some Buddhist monastic traditions produced (or are associated with) martial arts traditions, the category of gesture overlaps with the *kata*, or set martial arts positions. The category of gesture also overlaps with holding objects in the hands, where the objects carry rich symbolic meanings (e.g., the willow twig and vase of Guanshiyin in eastern Asia). Iconographic guidebooks establish set meanings for the objects.

ERIC REINDERS

*See also* Images: Buddhist Perspectives; Kūkai; Liturgy: Buddhist; Mantras; Mount Meru; Stūpa; Visual Arts, Buddhist

### Further Reading

Frédéric, Louis, *Buddhism*, Paris and New York: Flammarion, 1995

Gordon, Antoinette K., *The Iconography of Tibetan Lamaism*, Rutland, Vermont: Charles E. Tuttle, 1959; reprint, New York: Paragon, 1972

Saunders, E. Dale, *Mudra: A Study of Symbolic Gestures in Japanese Buddhist Sculpture*, New York: Pantheon, and London: Routledge and Kegan Paul, 1960

Sharf, Robert H., "Buddhist Modernism and the Rhetoric of Meditative Experience," *Numen* 42 (1995)

*Taisho shinshu daizokyo* (Buddhist Canon of the Taisho Era), edited under the direction of Takakusu Junjiro, Watanabe Kaigyoku, and Ono Gemyo, Tokyo: Taisho issaikyo kankokai, 1924–1935 (see pictorial section in volume 8)

# Gethsemani, Kentucky

Located in Nelson County at Trappist, Kentucky (50 miles south of Louisville), the Abbey of Gethsemani is the oldest monastery of the Cistercians of the Strict Observance (popularly known as Trappists) in the United States. It was founded on 21 December 1848 by French Cistercian monks from the Abbey of Melleray in Brittany. Through friendship with Bishop Benedict Flaget of Bardstown/Louisville, the 45 French monks were invited to come to the Diocese of Louisville and settle on property purchased from the Sisters of Loretto in the heart of the "Holy Land of Kentucky."

Dom Eutropius Proust, the founder and first abbot of Gethsemani, led the pioneer monks until his resignation in 1860, when he returned to Melleray in France. He later became abbot of Tre Fontane in Rome, where he died in 1874. The first years saw very few vocations and even fewer from those who persevered. The first American-born choir monk to persevere was Frederic Dunne, who was elected fifth abbot in 1935. He received Thomas Merton (Fr. Louis, 1915–1968) into the novitiate in December of 1941. Merton's writings, especially *The Seven Storey Mountain* (1948), would exert a profound effect on the monastic life as well as on the church at large. Vocations greatly increased in the years following its publication, which coincided with the end of World War II.

Gethsemani's expansion began during the abbacy of Dom Frederic Dunne with the foundation of the Monastery of the Holy Spirit in Conyers, Georgia, in 1945 and Holy Trinity Abbey in Huntsville, Utah, in 1947. Following the death of Dom Frederic Dunne in August 1948, Dom James Fox, founding superior of the first foundation in Conyers, Georgia, was elected sixth abbot of Gethsemani. The expansion continued with a third foundation in 1949 at Mepkin, Moncks Corner, South Carolina, and a fourth one in 1951 at Genesee, Piffard, New York. Gethsemani launched a fifth foundation, New Clairvaux, in 1955 in the Sacramento Valley, at Vina, California. In 1966, Gethsemani assumed the paternity of a foundation near Santiago, Chile, originally begun by St. Joseph's Abbey, Spencer, Massachusetts. Since then, the monks have moved to a more isolated location in Chile at Rancagua and have renamed the monastery Miraflores.

From its earliest days the monks of Gethsemani welcomed visitors and retreatants and for about 50 years conducted a school for boys on the property. The latter burned down in 1912, never to be rebuilt. By then enough schools existed in that part of Kentucky so that the monks could concentrate on their specific vocation: the contemplative life of prayer in silence and solitude. Men and (since 1989) women retreatants are welcomed at Gethsemani for some days of retreat during which they are encouraged to follow the prayer life of the community.

PATRICK HART, O.C.S.O.

*See also* Dalai Lama (Tenzin Gyatso); Merton, Thomas; Trappists; United States: Western Christian

**Further Reading**

Aprile, Dianne, *The Abbey of Gethsemani: Place of Peace and Paradox*, Louisville, Kentucky: Trout Lily Press, 1998

Flanagan, Raymond, *Burnt Out Incense*, New York: Kennedy, 1949

Kelty, Matthew, *Aspects of the Monastic Calling*, Trappist, Kentucky: Abbey of Gethsemani, 1975

Merton, Thomas, *The Waters of Siloe*, New York: Harcourt Brace, 1949

# Gilbertines

In 1131 in Lincolnshire, England, Gilbert of Sempringham (c. 1089–1189), a priest, built dwellings and a cloister on his inherited land so that seven women could lead a religious life. Wanting these women to be enclosed, Gilbert added serving women, with a distinctive religious habit and a modified religious life. They were called lay sisters (*conversae*) in imitation of the Cistercian lay brothers (*conversi*). To perform heavy manual labor and tend the fields, Gilbert next added lay brothers to Sempringham.

By 1139 Gilbert had established a second community at Haverholme on land given by Alexander, the bishop of Lincoln, who had ordained him. In 1147, concerned with overseeing these two communities, Gilbert traveled to France to ask the Cistercians to accept the responsibility. When the Cistercians refused, Gilbert returned and added a fourth group, priests following the Augustinian Rule. By 1154 Gilbert had established seven additional communities – Alvingham, Bullington, Catley, Nun Ormsby, and Sixhills in Lincolnshire; Watton in Yorkshire; and Chicksands in Bedfordshire – each containing all four groups: Benedictine nuns, Augustinian canons, lay sisters, and lay brothers. By then the men also had a house of their own, Malton in Yorkshire; and in Lincoln, canons, lay brothers, and lay sisters tended a Gilbertine hospital. This rapid increase indicates the Order's popularity but also corresponds to the period of the most rapid growth of female monasticism in England.

Many economic charters survive, but information about the Order comes mainly from two lengthy documents of the early 13th century. Completed in 1205, three years after Pope Innocent III (1198–1216) declared Gilbert to be a saint, the *Vita of*

*Gilbert* emphasizes his role in the Order and relates the miracles attributed to him. *The Institutes of the Gilbertine Order*, surviving in a version finished by 1223, contains almost 200 sections detailing how the Order was supposed to function.

According to the *Institutes* the head of the Order was the master (*magister*), who had final say in all legal and economic matters. He was the only man allowed to speak privately with the sisters. Three male and three female inspectors (*circatores* and *circatrices*, respectively) aided him by visiting the houses every year; the Order was exempt from episcopal supervision. The *magister* appointed the prior of each house, and the nuns elected three prioresses who held the office in rotation. The prior and three other men oversaw all buying and selling, but the nuns were consulted, kept receipts, and held the treasury. A general chapter convened annually at Sempringham Priory to make major decisions. On the death of the *magister*, both male and female leaders met to elect his successor, with the final selection being made by canons alone. Although the *Institutes* attempted to balance the roles of the women and men, ultimate authority resided in the *magister*, and thus nuns had less power than was typical in Benedictine houses.

The *Vita* and the *Institutes* reveal how the early 13th-century Gilbertines viewed themselves. However, these documents are so late that scholars debate issues concerning the Order's early history. How influential in it were the Cistercians? When were the extensive rules segregating the sexes enacted? Was the Order as unique as the documents claimed? Because the early 13th century was a time of greater supervision of female religious life, many regulations in the *Institutes* might have been recent promulgations.

Certainly by the early 13th century, the Gilbertines needed to defend their organization. Around 1165 an affair between a nun and a brother of Watton raised questions about the effectiveness of Gilbert's segregation of the sexes. The Gilbertine arrangement was further threatened about the same time by a revolt of some lay brothers against the authority of the canons. The emphasis in Gilbert's *Vita* and the *Institutes* on the careful government of the communities, the rigorous segregation of the sexes, and the cooperation of the four groups might have been partly a response to these crises. Praising their order in biblical terms, these documents present the Gilbertines as a new creation in which old and young, women and men, monastics and clerics, and literate and illiterate live together in harmony.

The greatest lacunae in the sources concern the Gilbertine women. Many names have been preserved, but no women's writings survive. Gilbert's *Vita* says that the women's desire for religious life led to the founding of Sempringham, but later women's initiatives are not recounted. We do not know the nuns' attitude toward their strict enclosure, whether the lay sisters resented remaining servants, or whether the women were content to have canons assume the major leadership roles. Given the Order's early popularity, we can assume that women found it appealing, but they remain enigmas to us.

After the early rapid expansion, the pace of new foundations slowed. By 1200 one more house for both sexes had been founded (Shouldham in Norfolk), and the maximum number of inhabitants had been fixed: Watton was permitted the most, 140 women and 70 men, and Catley the fewest, 60 women and 35 men. Fifteen hundred men and women might have been Gilbertines at that time. All-male houses continued to be established; by 1230 ten existed, as many as those for both sexes. Eventually 14 all-male houses were in existence for canons alone or serving as charitable institutions. Although invited to Rome and briefly attempted in Scotland, the Gilbertines remained an exclusively English order, mainly in Lincolnshire.

The Gilbertine expansion and decline paralleled that of other Benedictine and Augustinian houses, losing popularity in the 13th century to new religious orders and suffering a large population loss in the Black Death of 1348–1349. However, most Gilbertine communities survived until 1535, including all ten of the 12th-century houses for both sexes. Three were among the wealthiest female houses. By late 1539 all had been dissolved. Although the women never wielded as much power as the men, and although the houses for men alone grew to outnumber those for both sexes, the arrangement that Gilbert devised in the mid–12th century survived until it met the fate of all English monasteries under King Henry VIII (1509–1547).

SHARON K. ELKINS

*See also* Augustinian Rule; Cistercians; Dissolution of Monasteries: England, Ireland, and Wales; Double Houses, Western Christian; Lay Brothers and Lay Sisters, Christian

**Further Reading**

Constable, Giles, "Aelred of Rievaulx and the Nun of Watton: An Episode in the Early History of the Gilbertines," in *Medieval Women*, edited by Derek Baker, Oxford: Blackwell, 1978

Elkins, Sharon, *Holy Women of Twelfth-Century England*, Chapel Hill: University of North Carolina Press, 1988

Foreville, Raymonde, *Un procès de canonisation à l'aube du XIII siècle (1201–1202), le Livre de saint Gilbert de Sempringham*, Paris: Bloud et Gay, 1943

Foreville, Raymonde, and Gillian Keir, editors, *The Book of St. Gilbert*, Oxford: Clarendon Press, and New York: Oxford University Press, 1987

Golding, Brian, *Gilbert of Sempringham and the Gilbertine Order c. 1130–c. 1300*, Oxford: Clarendon Press, and New York: Oxford University Press, 1995

Knowles, David, "The Revolt of the Lay Brothers of Sempringham," *English Historical Review* 50 (1935)

Thompson, Sally, *Women Religious: The Founding of English Nunneries after the Norman Conquest*, Oxford: Clarendon Press, and New York: Oxford University Press, 1991

# Gnostic Cosmogony in Buddhism

That the *Wisdom Sūtra*, which founded the Mahāyāna tradition, had affinities with the Gnostics on the Silk Road has long been suspected. Both idolized a feminine Wisdom: *sophia*, as the creative principle accompanying God, and *prajñā*, as the "mother of buddhas and bodhisattvas." Motifs of light and darkness and the cave appear in both. Although the early Church characterized some Gnostics as hedonists or antinomians, those positions were more the exception than the rule. Instead, to the extent that they subscribed to a body-soul dualism, Gnostics tended to favor asceticism.

Whether ascetics will become eremites or cenobites, itinerants, or settled communities depends on a crucial distinction. In societies well disposed toward communion with the dead ("sarcophiliac") and in which "feeding the dead" expands also into "feeding the poor," law and social justice tend to prevail. In societies in which death pollution is highly feared ("sarcophobic") and in which the dead are scattered and afforded no communion, a quest for spiritual deliverance from the body and body politics, from law and authorities, tends to dominate. That line divides the Jews from the Gnostics and separates Rome to the West from the Silk Road to the East with the Syrian Church being divided in the middle. In Latin Europe practices such as prayers on behalf of the dead and conversing with the intimate departed built up a greater "sociability." There church dramas and guild performances would usher in the modern theater – except for a "sarcophobic" Germany that had failed to sanctify a common dead. Without a profound sense of a human community in the hereafter, celebration of universal brotherhood on this side is unlikely.

Is there a way to gauge how Buddhism stands in these matters? How self-sufficient or how sociable are her Gnostics? What justice is afforded by her Law? Of these two religions on the Silk Road – Gnosticism and Buddhism – it is hard to know who influenced whom, when, and how. Not many travelers are as well known and as well attested to as the Iranian Mani (216–276). This article considers one apparent overlap: a Buddhist cosmogony that reads strangely similar to the Gnostics.

Buddhism accepted as given the cycles of rebirth. Because saṃsāra is rooted in ignorance, it can be severed by wisdom. A formula runs that ignorance has no beginning but may have an end, whereas enlightenment has a beginning and no end; however, saṃsāra by itself is without beginning or end. It just rolls on and on and on, from time immemorial to time everlasting. On these grounds Buddhism ought to entertain no cosmogony. However, the *Agama Sūtra* (Scripture of Origin) does postulate such a beginning, and it reads like a Gnostic version of the Fall. The Gnostics usually tell of a remote (alien, hidden, and absent) God far above the dark Demiurge who created this world. The distant God is separated from that lower deity by a host of spiritual beings, sometimes called the Aeons. Man himself is an alien sojourning on this earth, an "inn for the night." He might carry inside his fleshly garment a precious pearl, a divine spark that came from that Lightworld on high. That light, dispersed in some primordial time, has fallen and is now trapped in this world of matter that the evil Demiurge created. Light is held hostage by the cosmic powers, sometimes known as the Archons. All is lost until this ignorant (dazed, drunk, asleep, lost, wandering, and homesick) soul is awakened by a Messenger sent to call him home. The soul is given the secret of the soul's origin, its fall, and its destined end. With that the soul-lights escape from this lower realm and return, united, to the Lightworld.

The Buddhist myth of origin tells likewise of how, in the beginning, there were these Radiant Gods in the realm of form. That is a realm above the realm of desires that we now inhabit. These beings of pure light – one rank away from the realm of desires – have sublime form but no gross desire. Somehow they fell from that Lightworld as a consequence of a desire to smell the fragrances of the earth and of a wish to dine on its substance. This scene is a Buddhist rewriting of the ancient Vedic "fire sacrifice": the fragrant smoke of a burnt animal rises skyward; it delights and lures the gods to come down to partake in the sacrificial offering. That eating caused the Radiant Gods to take on the nature of what they ate; they lost their radiance and gained a quasi-materiality. In a logic reminiscent even of Isaac Luria's 16th-century Kabbalah, there was a "shrinkage" and an "expulsion." The exit of these Gods from their radiant rank meant a shrinkage in that domain that in turn made it possible for the rank just below them, that of Brahmas, or creator gods, to expand. The Radiant God that first fell into this space soon saw more likenesses of himself, that is, of other Radiant Gods falling into that space. He mistook them to be his own mental creation. This explanation is similar to that offered by the Gnostic Valentinians (second century A.D.), who held that the first Creation came about when the Mind begins to have Thoughts of its own. Those Thoughts then split themselves off into separate entities so as to start the chain of Aeons going. Thus, cognitive subject-object dualism broke up the primal unity of the One.

For the *Agama Sūtra* this story explains the advent of the Hindu creator-god Brahma. However, being anti-monist and anti-monotheist the Buddhist scripture had these fallen Radiant Gods thinking they were multiple Creator Gods. There is actually no Creation as such; there are just these "fallen angels of the Lightworld," who, on seeing copies of themselves, thought that they were the Creators. They then became the Demiurges responsible for creating the lower world, that is, the realm of desires where all sentient beings are trapped.

This Buddhist cosmogony justifies an ascetic project for Buddhist monastics. To reverse the fall monks should avoid desire, minimize material contact, and eat only one meal a day – that is, just enough to keep "body and soul" (or rather "no soul," to be exact) together. A taboo exists against strong spices and meat of any kind because saṃsāra is basically a "food chain," a fact familiar to early hunting cultures, in which life is a matter of eating or being eaten. In Buddhist iconography saṃsāra is such a uroboric cycle of "life and death," a snake biting (swallowing) its own tail, and Mara the Evil Demiurge is the devourer, holding the six paths of rebirth in his open jaws. Early farming cultures avoided kill-and-be-killed by growing grains, and ascetics in the East Gangetic plain lived up to that pacifist, vegetarian ideal. Although Gnostic influence cannot be ruled out in this Buddhist myth of origins, it can be viewed instead as a rational retelling of the second of the four Noble Truths, that craving causes suffering, thus responding to and rewriting Hindu cosmogony. Hindus accepted cosmic cycles, at the end of which everything dissolves into the ocean except for Brahma, the Creator God, who survives the deluge (or a holocaust) intact. He sleeps through a long, long night and wakes up to create the world anew.

WHALEN LAI

*See also* Asceticism: Buddhist Perspectives; Buddhist Schools/Traditions: Tibet; Deities, Buddhist; Economic Justice, Buddhist; Mount Meru; Stūpa; Tibetan Lineages

**Further Reading**

Conze, Edward, *Thirty Years of Buddhist Studies: Selected Essays*, Oxford: Cassirer, 1967; Columbia: University of South Carolina Press, 1968
Jonas, Hans, *The Gnostic Religion: The Message of the Alien God and the Beginnings of Christianity*, 2nd edition, Boston: Beacon Press, 1958
Layton, Bentley, *The Gnostic Scriptures: A New Translation with Annotations and Introductions*, Garden City, New York: Doubleday, 1987
Logan, Alastair H.B., *Gnostic Truth and Christian Heresy: A Study in the History of Gnosticism*, Edinburgh: Clark, 1996
Rudolph, Kurt, *Gnosis: The Nature and History of an Ancient Religion*, Edinburgh: Clark, 1983

# Governance: Buddhist Perspectives

Buddhist monasteries are to be self-governed by the objective rules of the monastic code (vinaya). That aspect of internal government is covered elsewhere in this encyclopedia under "Rules, Buddhist." This article focuses on the external relationship of *saṅgha* to the state. The full historical spectrum being too extensive, only a telescoped analysis of the fundamental dynamics is offered here.

The Buddha renounced the world; this ex-prince became a wandering ascetic. First he joined other ascetics, then he decided to go at it alone, only to return, enlightened, to teach others the way to *nirvāṇa*; later he founded a community of monks. The monastic is above the laws of the land, and the layman is soundly under their rule. A two-tiered structure, referred to as *nibbānic (nirvāṇic)* and *kammatic (karmatic)* Buddhism by Melford Spiro, resulted. This is the first paradigm:

| Monastic | Nirvāṇa as goal | Self-governed | Path of wisdom |
|---|---|---|---|
| Layman | Karma restricted | Caste duty and law | Path of works |

The monastic free from the world works at attaining wisdom and liberation. The layman, castebound still, seeks better rebirth by performing good works, above all by supporting the *saṅgha*. Monastic Buddhism is "otherworldly mystical," and monks being nonviolent and nonpolitical should avoid the battlefield. They are not even to approach rulers and kings.

However, that classic model of a monk/lay divide was transgressed. The Buddha being not only a world renouncer but also the world conqueror, his dharma could possibly rule both worlds. If so, equality within the monastic brotherhood could inspire similar social experiments in the lay world. After all, during the Buddha's lifetime both monk and layperson looked up to him for guidance. After his death both groups supported the relic cult and his idealization. The Buddha's eventual apotheosis made possible a third path: liberation by faith. In this scheme a devotee seeks the grace of merit transference from the merit-rich Buddha, resulting in a second paradigm with a tripartite structure and the Buddha mediating and rising above the lay/monastic divide:

| Monastic | World renunciate | Path of wisdom |
|---|---|---|
| Buddha | World conquering | Path of devotion |
| Layman | World subject | Path of works |

The world-conquering aspect of the Buddha helped to revise the monk's previous nonpolitical stand. For although monastics should not go courting worldly rulers, worldly rulers are not discouraged from seeking edification through monks; and, because a regal Buddha attracted regal patrons, the two wheels of the dharma – that of Buddha and king – could cross paths. If Emperor Constantine (A.D. 306–337) made it possible for the churches to develop "social teachings," so King Aśoka's (third century B.C.) patronage also changed the character of otherworldly Buddhism. Kings generally hated religious dissension. They desired some (but not an overly complicated) doctrinal unity and worked best with an ecclesiastical hierarchy similar to the secular officialdom. Thus, Aśoka supposedly called a Third Council, settled sectarian disputes, purged the impure elements, and set up qualifying examinations to reward successful candidates. He also adopted Buddhist principles for his reign, issued edicts propagating the dharma, and dispatched ambassadors of goodwill around and sent out missionaries abroad. The following is a paradigm of Aśokan rule:

**Buddha (Relic) as Foundation of Polity**

| *Saṅgha* | State |
|---|---|
| *Saṅgharāja* in the capital | Next to king as rāja |
| Top ecclesiastical hierarchy | Government hierarchy |
| Monk qualifying board | State temple bureau |
| State-supported temple | Regional administration |
| Officially appointed abbot | Local state official |
| Popular nonstate temple | (No state office at this low level) |
| Familiar village monastery | |

The Aśokan legend underwrites the Theravādin ecclesiastical structure. The system has the Buddha on top and the king and a *saṅgharāja* (papist head) below him. The king enjoys the Buddha's blessing, but the coronation ritual tends to remain brahmanical. The *saṅgharāja* resides at the capital, housed in the national temple next to the royal palace. He is supposed to be elected from below but in effect is appointed by the king. The king as royal patron must approve the candidate. Under this spiritual head of the *sangha* stands a network of state temples that run parallel to and often are located next to the regional administrative offices. The temples reach down only as far as the secular posts do. Monks who passed a state board examination at the capital on the basis of their (largely objective book) learning would be appointed to these prestigious and rather comfortable temples. However, these official temples are less well attended (except by officials on business or during festive celebrations) than the nonstate temples in the same city that house abbots of recognized piety who enjoy popular support. These temples are supported by the local patrons, and more common people visit them. Down at the villages are small, spartan monasteries. Set just on the outskirts of the village, they are familiar to all, as one's own uncle and other kinsmen might have chosen to retire therein. The more gifted young monks there might be sent off to better learning facilities; some could end up serving in the state temples. Although Theravādin in tone this pattern is found also in Mahāyānist Far East, being basically a combination of the primitive *sangha* that was built up "from below" with the majestic *sangha* imposed "from above." The network of state temples might be tight or loose. It can vary from being monolithic (i.e., a single pyramid) to being decentralized (with centrifugal satellites).

The ideal Aśokan balance of secular power and religious authority (two columns and two tiers) might not last, for inherent tensions exist in the arrangement as well as different ways in which those tensions might play out. The cultural variations are so many that we can present only a summary of the key options. One problem is the king. Notwithstanding the mutual attraction of Buddha and king – these world conquerors share the same set of supernatural marks – kings are not Buddhas. They are not even monks, only laymen. Granted that the two wheels of the dharma – of king and Buddha – should resemble "the two wings of a bird," an ambitious king might try to usurp the prerogatives of the Buddha. According to the early monastic code, the king being a layman has neither the right nor the authority to supervise the *sangha*. He cannot adjudicate its internal disputes, and even less can he purge unwholesome elements as Aśoka supposedly did. The *sangha* may consult a royal patron, but a monk is always the king's superior.

That tension emerges in the wider Aśokan legends. Aśoka is derided as ugly or dark skinned, impure or foul smelling, and bloodied and murderous, before and sometimes even after his famous change of heart. He is remembered for failing to enforce consensus within the *sangha*, at which point he had to call in the Great Tissa. Thus, unlike the caesaropapist Constantine at the Council of Nicaea (325), it is Tissa and not Aśoka who chaired the Third Council. Aśoka was also put in his place by a miracle-working seven-year-old novice. The king bowed to the boy and conceded that he must do so in public. Like the drama of Henry II and Thomas à Becket, Aśoka even had to apologize openly for inadvertently causing the death of two monks when his agents acted overzealously against them. These condemnations of the king no doubt came from the pen of a monk-critic.

Not that kings would take such derision lying down. In an eternal tug-of-war between *sangha* and state, the king might maneuver himself into having the upper hand. A king might acquire a monk's credentials by entering the order. That can involve a pious, temporary routine, or it might turn, as it did later in Japan, into "cloistered rule" – by which a king pulls the political strings while officially in seclusion. Alternatively, the king might line up with one monastic faction against another. This could be to enhance his political clout, to promote a program of monastic reform, or both. Bolder still the king might turn from being a defender of the faith to being an active vicar of the *sangha*, say, by supervising the ordination of monks himself; or a king might claim to have received the dharma directly from the Buddha, thus challenging the *sangha*'s right to be the sole custodian of the dharma. Quite often a king is rumored to possess some supernatural marks, making him into a potential cosmic king who will usher in the Future Buddha. More simply he might be honored as a bodhisattva, meaning that he would become a Buddha in the future. In the most radical move, the king might unite the two wheels of the dharma, claiming to be both king and Tathāgata (i.e., the Buddha). Not that the monks upholding the monastic prerogative would take such royal hubris lying down. Both can play the same game. In Tibetan theocracy the Dalai Lama as Avalokiteśvara incarnate rules Tibet as both priest and king, and almost always, lurking in the wings, is the perennial notion of someone claiming to be the Future Buddha. A long history of millennium hopes has existed, peaceful or otherwise, in both Theravāda and Mahāyāna cultures.

Regal claims to the Buddha's titles must be probed on a case-by-case basis to see what they actually entail in practice. Some regal claims are only symbolic and hardly affect the autonomy of the *sangha*. Some royal humility might mask more questionable designs, for medieval politics is often a strange mix of piety and ambition. A few evil monks deserve a Rasputin-like reputation; others are maligned because they happen to counsel female rulers, and the defenders of patriarchal bloodlines hated both. A healthy jostling between this-worldly power and otherworldly authority might keep both *sangha* and state in check. An exemplary *sangharāja* elected with popular support is always better than a political appointee, and a single pope might hold his ground against the king better than a council of ten elders. In addition, having a distinct and separate clerical bureau protects the *sangha* better than does placing the *sangha* under local civil bureaucratic control. What has so far not been covered in this discussion are two less "governable" figures in the Buddhist tradition: the forest dweller and the wayfaring monk. The former inspires awe by his devotion to ascetic practice. While he stays put, the people flock to him in droves. As with the series of monastic reforms in the Latin Church, these "pure souls" in the social margins could revitalize the monastic establishments and, like the Cistercians, might end up supplying candidates for popes and *sangharāja*s. The wayfaring monk also operates outside the regular channel of control. Unlike the forest monk the wayfarer refuses to stay put; he goes to the people instead. His mobility sets a good example for the lay pilgrim; his popular preaching might foster a different kind of reformation. For that and the "one-man" institution of the Holy Man, see "Holy Men in Power (Hierocrats), Buddhist."

WHALEN LAI

*See also* Abbot: Buddhist; Anticlericalism: Buddhist Perspectives; Asceticism: Buddhist Perspectives; Aśoka; Buddha (Śākyamuni); Dalai Lama (Tenzin Gyatso); Desert Fathers; Examinations, Theravādin; Holy Men in Power (Hierocrats), Buddhist; Monasticism, Definitions of: Buddhist Perspectives; Patrons, Buddhist; Prophethood, Japanese Buddhist; Saichō; Saṅgha; Sri Lanka: History; Tibet: History

### Further Reading

Brück, Michael von, and Whalen Lai, *Buddhismus und Christentum: Geschichte, Konfrontation, Dialog*, Munich: Beck, 1997

Carrithers, Michael, *The Forest Monks of Sri Lanka*, Delhi: Oxford, 1983

Kloppenborg, Ria, *The Paccekabuddha: A Buddhist Ascetic*, Leiden: Brill, 1974

Spiro, Melford E., *Buddhism and Society: A Great Tradition and Its Burmese Vicissitudes*, New York: Harper and Row, 1970; London: Allen and Unwin, 1971; 2nd expanded edition, Berkeley: University of California Press, 1982

Tambiah, Stanley Jeyaraja, *World Conqueror and World Renouncer: A Study of Buddhism and Polity in Thailand against a Historical Background*, Cambridge and New York: Cambridge University Press, 1976

Weber, Max, *Religion of India*, Glencoe, Illinois: Free Press, 1958

# Governance: Christian Perspectives

The common pattern of government for a religious community is an abbot or prior as superior and various officials with delegated responsibility for different aspects of the community's life. However, the exact way in which this model has been implemented has varied. The style of government reflects the charism of the founder, the customs and habits that the order acquires over the passage of time, and the way in which authority is exercised in the surrounding secular culture. In recent years religious communities have adopted more democratic practices influenced by the prevailing secular culture.

## Historical Development

### 1. Early Hermits

When groups of disciples began to gather around St. Antony (c. 251–356) and the other hermits in Upper Egypt at the end of the third century, little systematic organization existed. A person seeking the eremitic life would attach himself to an experienced hermit for guidance and spiritual direction; most of the time, however, he would live alone, in his own cell, responsible for his own daily routine. With the increasing numbers of adherents, more organization became required, and St. Antony is said to have composed a rule for his followers containing the principles and pattern for monastic life.

In the communities founded by Pachomius (c. 290–346), the monks lived in groups or houses under a local superior. These local superiors related to the overall superior of the monastery, initially Pachomius himself. Although the monks would assemble to pray and listen to the scriptures, and although their manual work was directed the local superior, each monk retained a great deal of freedom for organizing his day and for planning time spent in prayer or spiritual reading. Pachomius saw himself not as a director but as the servant of his monks, and he sought to merge into the background. He viewed his role as providing the framework within which individual monks could live a life of prayer and closeness to God. In advice given to Theodore of Alexandria, he emphasized that a superior should have concern for the sick, be a model in observing the rules, seek to outstrip his subjects in the spiritual life, and admonish wrongdoers "privately and with patience."

### 2. Monasteries

In the West, where the Rule of Benedict of Nursia quickly became the norm for monastic life, the abbot was to be a father figure for his monks, leading them by word and example (Rule 2.11–12) and caring for them like a shepherd (Rule 2.7–10). Initially Benedict followed Pachomius and decreed that there should be deans, each with responsibility for a group of ten monks (Rule 21.1–2). However, the pattern of government soon shifted to a more hierarchical or feudal pattern by which authority is divided according to function. Under the abbot there is a prior who acts as his deputy and takes care of the practical day-to-day running of the monastery assisted by a range of officials, each with his own function, such as the sacristan, cellarer, novice master, and infirmarian.

In the Pachomian and Benedictine models, each monastery is independent and functions as an autonomous unit although linked by fraternal bonds with other monasteries of the same order. Only in later centuries have more formal links developed among different groupings of monasteries, usually foundations made from a central house such as Cluny or Cîteaux, having an overall president and some form of centralized activity.

### 3. Mendicant Orders

Unlike monks for whom the monastery is a refuge from the world, the friars seek to serve the secular world; the Franciscans give priority to the preaching of the gospel and the Dominicans to teaching and counteracting heresy. Thus, the mendicant orders adopt a more integrated approach in which the communities or friaries in a country or geographic region are organized as a province and the provinces form a unified religious order. Individual friaries use many of the same monastic terms, with overall authority vested in a prior (or guardian for the Franciscans) assisted by a subprior and others, such as novice master, sacristan, and bursar. Over all the friaries in a "province," there is a prior provincial and uniting all the provinces a prior general (or master general for the Dominicans).

### 4. Later Orders

Many of the religious orders founded after the Reformation tended to be more integrated and centralized. As a former soldier, St. Ignatius of Loyola (c. 1491–1556) used aspects of his military experience in his vision for the Society of Jesus. In addition to the three vows of poverty, obedience, and chastity, Ignatius added a fourth vow of obedience to the pope, seeing his new society as a band of warriors ready to be deployed by the papacy wherever the need was greatest.

Other post-Reformation religious orders were more oriented toward specific apostolates, frequently running large institutions, such as schools, orphanages, or hospitals. These religious orders took their pattern of governance from more bureaucratic models although adopting different terminologies. Instead of abbot or abbess, the newer orders used the term *superior* while preserving the original paternal/maternal image by adding the prefix *father* superior or *mother* superior. In orders running large institutions, there emerged a dual hierarchy divided between a superior and officials responsible for the conventual life and a head mistress or matron over the institution that the community directed. In such situations, an individual could be the principal of a large school during the working day and then return to be a simple religious in an abbey or a convent.

### 5. Recent Foundations

Religious communities founded in the 20th century have looked to more radical forms of religious life with emphasis on being present in the world – as opposed to the cloistered separation of earlier ages – and on adopting a simple lifestyle without large buildings or institutions. The new congregations live in small communities with little formal structure, and although there might be a superior, the emphasis is on sharing and reaching a consensus. Obedience is seen less as obeying an individual authority figure and more as a response to the decisions of the whole community.

### Sociological Perspectives

### 1. Models of Authority

From a sociological perspective the style of government that religious orders adopt usually reflects the prevailing pattern within the contemporary secular society. Pachomian monasteries are idealized, celibate towns directed by a "head man" and his officials. Benedict, in turn, systematized the government of a monastery, dividing the roles and the responsibilities, but his structure has many of the features of the emerging feudal pattern of his age.

In the early 13th century, the mendicant orders adopted an international approach, taking their inspiration from the developing commercial world of their time. It is noteworthy that Francis of Assisi's father was a merchant, for it is the interlocking, international structure of the merchant businesses that influenced the organization of Francis' order. For Ignatius of Loyola it was the structure of the army that inspired his vision for the Jesuits, whereas for the later orders, especially the large orders of women, it was the running of large institutions that gave them a pattern. Some orders, such as the Sisters of Mercy, began as individual, independent convents, serving the needs of their local area, and only in recent years have they linked together in a larger, more structured organization. More recently the model of a political cell or task group has influenced smaller religious communities who work together as a team of equals, seeking to improve society by their presence as they stand alongside the poor and disadvantaged.

Following the changing models of religious life, authority has been exercised in different ways. Pachomius aimed to be a retiring, unobtrusive father figure who inspired and encouraged his monks. Benedict built on this foundation and emphasized the role of the abbot as the father to his community. However, with the growth of the Benedictine and related orders (e.g., Cistercians and Carthusians), the political and economic importance of abbeys grew. Inevitably the abbot became a local magnate or "spiritual lord," distancing himself from the community by living in separate, more sumptuous quarters, "appropriate" to his dignity and role.

Being unendowed and relying on charity, the mendicant orders initially were able to avoid this problem, and friaries sought to be simple, poor communities where the superior led by example. Before long, however, as friars began to serve on diplomatic missions by both Church and state, superiors of provinces or local priories were tempted to emphasize the dignity of their offices. Conversely individual friars began to discover ways to avoid the obligations of religious life, and doctors of theology were notable for securing privileges and exemptions.

In later centuries the social work carried out by the religious orders led to a prioritizing of service and a concern for efficiency. In this climate an emphasis fell on obedience and an unquestioning following of rules. An individual's faithfulness to his vocation as a religious and thus to God was seen in willingness to conform, to set aside individuality and to give oneself totally to the order's apostolate.

More recently the changing pattern of society in the 20th century and, in the Roman Catholic Church, the unleashing of new ideas following the Second Vatican Council (1962–1965) has led to a reevaluation of the nature of authority and the exercise of government in a religious order. With authority being challenged in secular society, religious orders are looking afresh at their system of government. More democratic styles of leadership have introduced open discussion and a searching for consensus. The superior is not so much an authority figure as he or she is a facilitator who serves the community and assists its members to exercise their talents. Some smaller communities have experimented with "leaderless" communities where there is no superior and decisions are reached democratically.

## 2. Democracy

From the earliest times there has always been an element of democracy within monastic life. Benedict legislated for the election of abbots by "the whole community . . . or by some part of the community, no matter how small which possesses sounder judgement," whereas the Carmelite Rule (c. 1210) directs that the prior shall be "chosen for the office by common consent or that of the greater and maturer part." In the mendicant orders priors provincial and priors general were elected by delegates meeting in a chapter, whereas local priors were appointed. Other orders have mostly followed this pattern, although some have adopted a greater degree of centralization with provincials appointed by a general council.

During the Middle Ages there was no fixed term for abbots or superiors, and individuals commonly remained in office for life. The same applied in general to the mendicant orders, although there was a certain amount of movement of priors from house to house. In more recent years most religious orders have elected superiors for a fixed term, commonly three years for a local superior and six years for a major superior. Most orders allow a superior to be reelected for a further term, but a third consecutive term is either forbidden or allowed only with special permission.

Elections within Roman Catholic orders have normally followed what is known as canonical procedure, that is, three votations where a candidate is elected at the first or second votation if he or she secures an absolute majority. Otherwise at the third votation the candidate with a relative majority, that is, the greatest number of votes, is declared elected.

Most monasteries or orders in their initial years gave voting rights to all full members, that is, to those who had made a monastic profession; new entrants or novices were excluded. However, with the increasing clericalization of the Roman Catholic Church in the 12th and 13th centuries, voting rights were restricted to the clerical members of religious orders (i.e., priests and those proceeding to orders) or to choir sisters in convents, whereas the lay brothers and sisters were disenfranchised and declared ineligible for any positions of authority. Following the Second Vatican Council, most religious orders have restored voting rights to all professed members, although despite requests from some orders, the bar on lay brothers becoming superiors in clerical orders has been upheld by the Vatican authorities.

## Psychological Perspectives

Commonly the authority figure in a religious community has been viewed as a paternal/maternal figure. For Benedict the abbot holds "the place of Christ in the monastery" (Rule 2.2): he is God's delegate, and in obeying his commands the individual monks or religious are obeying God himself. Thus, in order to reach perfection each individual must obey wholeheartedly and unreservedly. Where the superior is conscious of his fallibility and seeks to exercise the loving care of God, such a model has

great value, but where the superior becomes overconcerned with conformity or with the apostolate, there are dangers. Where the superior is overvalued as a father figure, the idealized view of the individual monk or nun as an "obedient child" – the converse of a father figure – can lead to an undervaluing of the stature of the individual and of adult professional qualities.

In the modern centuries, superiors have frequently been chosen for their administrative talents, that is, for their ability to direct large institutions or apostolates. It is the ability of the individual to direct the apostolic activities of others that has been preeminent and not the role as paternal or maternal figure. More recently emphasis has shifted to the image of the superior-as-facilitator, one who enables the activities of others and seeks to release their talents in the service of God.

RICHARD COPSEY, O.CARM.

*See also* Abbess, Christian; Abbot: Christian; Desert Fathers; France: History; Gregory I (the Great), St.; Gregory VII; Monastics and the World, Medieval; Officials: Western Christian; Orders (Religious), Origin of; Papacy: Papal Pronouncements; Patrons, Christian: Royal

## Further Reading

Albert, Saint, Patriarch of Jerusalem, *The Rule of Saint Albert*, edited and translated by Bebe Edwards, Boars Hill: Carmelite Fathers, 1966 (*http://www.carmelnet.org*)

Basil, Saint, Bishop of Caesarea, *The Ascetic Works of Saint Basil* (Translation of Christian Literature. Series 1: Greek Texts), translated by W.K.L. Clarke, New York: Macmillan, and London: Society for Promoting Christian Knowledge, 1925

*Code of Canon Law*, Book 2, Part 3, Section 1, Title 2, Chapter 2, Washington, D.C.: Canon Law Society of America, 1983 (*http://www.prairienet.org/nrpcatholic/cicmenu.html*)

Francis, of Assisi, Saint, *Francis and Clare: The Complete Works* (Classics of Western Spirituality), translated by Regis J. Armstrong and Ignatius C. Brady, New York: Paulist Press, and London: SPCK, 1982 (*http://www.listserv.american.edu/catholic/franciscan/rules/*)

Giabbani, A., "Autoritá," in *Dizionario degli Istituti di Perfezione*, Rome: Edizioni Paoline, 1974

Vogüé, Adalbert de, editor, *The Rule of Saint Benedict, a Doctrinal and Spiritual Commentary* (Cistercian Studies Series, number 54), Kalamazoo, Michigan: Cistercian Publications, 1983 (*http://www.osb.org*)

The particular regulations for each order are usually contained in a constitution or other documents that are circulated only internally. The Jesuits, however, have published the documents of their last General Congregation on the web: *http://maple.lemoyne.edu/~bucko/sj_docs*

# Grandmontines

The Grandmontines drew their inspiration from Stephen of Muret, who, around 1078, established a hermitage in the forest of Muret near Limoges in the French province of Limousin.

Stephen was a solitary with no intention of founding a religious order, but when he died in 1124 he left a considerable number of followers and was eventually venerated as the Father of the Order of Grandmont. In 1125 the little community was evicted from Muret, but a benefactor gave them an alternative site in the vicinity. This cold and barren hillside, known as Grandmont, gave its name to both the Order and its mother house.

The simplicity and holiness of the lives led by the first generation of Grandmontines, combined with their reputation for generosity toward the poor, caused them to become familiarly known as the *Bonshommes*. Their fame soon spread beyond the Limousin and attracted numerous benefactors, notably Henry II, Plantagenet (1154–1189). So great was the king's admiration for

**Grandmontine Church of Comberoumal (Aveyron), France.**
**Photo courtesy of Carole Hutchison**

the Order that he expressed the desire to be buried at Grandmont. At the time of his death in 1189, the simple priory church was deemed unworthy of a king, so he was buried in the prestigious abbey church of Fontevraud. The same year Stephen of Muret was canonized, and his remains were translated to a shrine incorporated in the high altar at Grandmont.

Through the efforts of Stephen's closest companion, Hugues Lacerta, and a second Stephen, Stephen Liciac the dynamic fourth prior (1140–1150), the hermits constituted a religious order. Together they compiled the Rule of Grandmont, based on the daily homilies preached by Stephen to his companions and faithfully remembered by them. The most cited maxim of Stephen is that "the only rule is the Gospel of Christ," and throughout its length the Rule quotes extensively from this divine source. The brethren were expected to live like the apostles and desert fathers in conditions of extreme poverty. Communities were never to exceed 13, including three or four choir monks and the remainder lay brethren. The only real superior within the Order was the prior of Grandmont. The daughter houses were known as cells, and each was jointly headed by a spiritual director (corrector) and a lay brother (curiosis) who were responsible for temporalities. Total equality existed whereby choir and lay brethren used a single choir, deliberated together in chapter meetings, and shared the same refectory and dormitory. The inspiration of Stephen of Muret had devised a completely new form of religious life in which the communal life of monks was combined with the solitude and poverty of hermits. Emphasis was diverted from ritual and ceremony to silent contemplation and communion with God. The Rule received papal approval in 1156.

By the close of Stephen Liciac's priorate, 40 cells existed, a number that increased to 165 in the mid–13th century. Only five were founded outside France: three in England and two in Navarre, now Spain. Such rapid growth was not without problems. A crisis occurred in 1185 and was prolonged through several generations, by which time the reputation of the Order was in shreds.

This unhappy sequence of events was attributable to the unusual status of the lay brethren. As time went by they had made themselves masters within the cells and were asserting authority over the choir brothers, many of whom were priests and, naturally enough, resented this state of affairs. In 1187 the tension became so acute that 200 Grandmontines defected and sought refuge in other religious houses. Calm was restored during the priorate of Gerard Ithier (1188–1198), an attractive and competent figure who authored *The Mirror of Grandmont*. However, following his death quarrelling resumed and continued intermittently throughout the 13th century despite a whole series of papal interventions. Finally, in 1317, Pope John XXII (1316–1334) acted ruthlessly to terminate the crisis. A traditional monastic hierarchy was imposed. Henceforth the prior of Grandmont would hold abbatial status, and 39 of the daughter houses were designated priories, whose priors additionally were responsible for a number of dependent cells. Not only were the lay brethren deprived of authority, but they became totally subservient to the choir monks. The Order was effectively transformed into a traditional coenobitic institute, and its unique eremitical and democratic character disappeared forever.

The 17th century witnessed a reform led by Dom Charles Frémon that became known as the strict observance. Six houses joined him in returning to the primitive observance of the Rule of Grandmont and the severe austerities that it prescribed. The reform was peacefully achieved, and the strict observants maintained their allegiance to the abbot of Grandmont, who became the abbot general.

In the late 18th century, both branches of the Order fell victim to the Commission des Réguliers, a body appointed by the king to investigate the affairs of all religious institutions in France. The commission had papal approval, and any religious establishment found wanting for either laxity or insufficient numbers was referred to Rome for suppression. The reform movement hastened the demise of the Order of Grandmont, as neither branch possessed houses with communities large enough to satisfy the commissioners. In 1772 the fate of the Grandmontines was sealed, and the last abbot put up a valiant legal fight, but to no avail. When he died in 1787, the Order of Grandmont died with him.

The Grandmontines have left an outstanding architectural legacy. More than 50 sites retain interesting vestiges, and 16 extant churches reveal their unique church plan. The nave is always a single-aisled, tunnel-vaulted structure terminating in an apse that encloses the sanctuary. The building is lit by only four windows: three in the sanctuary and a fourth in the west wall. Light streams into the sanctuary, where the concentration of brightness is intensified by the fact that it is marginally broader and higher than the nave.

CAROLE A. HUTCHISON

*See also* Fontevraud, France; France: History; Hermits: Western Christian; Orders (Religious), Origin of

**Further Reading**

Becquet, Dom Jean, *Études Grandmontaines*, Paris: Musée du pays d'Ussel, 1998
Doll, Deborah, translator, *The Maxims of Stephen of Muret*, Kalamazoo, Michigan: Cistercian Publications, 1999
Hutchison, Carole A., *The Hermit Monks of Grandmont*, Kalamazoo, Michigan: Cistercian Publications, 1989

# Greece

The oldest Christian monastic communities of modern Greece date from the Middle Ages, most of them from the 11th and 12th centuries. Possibly monasteries developed in the later Roman Empire, but none have left any traces. In comparison to the number of foundations in Constantinople, Anatolia, Syria, Palestine, or Egypt, Greeks of the ancient homeland show a marked lack of enthusiasm for adopting the ascetic life.

The invasions of Greece might explain why this happened. In 396 the Visigoths struck Athens and Corinth and devastated the countryside. The most serious and long-lasting damage occurred after 582 when Avar and Slavic tribes descended into the peninsula, marking an end to what remained of the great classical cities of Greece. The Slavs settled in the interior, and only the larger cities on the eastern seaboard remained under the rule of the Christian emperors in Constantinople.

From the late eighth century, a series of Byzantine campaigns commenced that extended over the next two centuries, and with it came a gradual re-Christianization of the country. The land was now sufficiently secure to allow individual ascetics, who welcomed the opportunity to distance themselves from the policies of iconoclast emperors in the capital, to settle on the Greek peninsula or one of the Aegean islands. When men such as Loukas of Aegina and Nikon the Penitent attracted disciples, cenobitic monasticism was born in the land that is now modern Greece.

By this time Byzantine monasticism was already a finished product. It drew on several traditions: Egyptian, Anatolian, Palestinian, and Constantinopolitan. The Egyptian St. Antony the Abbot (c. 251–356), the first to take up the ascetic life, was always a model for Byzantine monks and nuns. *The Life of Antony the Abbot*, attributed to St. Athanasios (c. 296–373), was spiritual reading in every major monastery of the Byzantine world. Saint Pachomios (c. 290–346), also an Egyptian, sponsored the establishment of cenobitic monasticism, in which monks should lead a common life under the direction of an abbot. A combination of these two forms of the ascetic life appeared in the *lavra*, where individuals would live solitary lives during the week but gather together for the liturgy and common prayer on Sundays and great feast days.

Greek monks of the Middle Ages were also the custodians of the wisdom of St. Basil the Great (c. 330–379), bishop of Caesarea in Cappadocia in the late fourth century. Basil, although an admirer of the Egyptians, put even more emphasis on the need for monastic community life (*koinobion*). He believed strongly that his brotherhoods and sisterhoods (he avoided calling them monks) should form communities following a daily schedule of prayer and work. Basil saw too many opportunities for eccentric behavior in both the hermetic ideal of Antony and the *lavra*. The ordered existence of the *koinobion* would prevent such aberrations as sometimes happened among Syrian monks. Basil's advice was well taken in the Greek world, where cenobitic monasticism prevailed but always in tension with the *lavra*. Despite official disapproval certain individuals always regarded the cenobitic life merely as an introduction to a more perfect hermetic life.

The Palestinian monastery of Mar Sabas also contributed to Byzantine monasticism. Founded near Jerusalem in 483, Mar Sabas attracted hundreds of followers to imitate its structure, which gave more latitude to the individual monk than envisaged in the admonitions of St. Basil.

The influence of Constantinople's great monasteries on monasticism everywhere in the Byzantine world can hardly be exaggerated. This influence resulted both from admiration for the capital's many monasteries and their sainted founders and from

Monastery of the Presentation of Mary, Amorgos, Greece, founded by Emperor Alexios I Komnenos (1081–1111).
Photo courtesy of Charles Frazee

legislation promulgated under the emperor's name. The *Novels of Emperor Justinian* (527–565) legislated at length on monasticism. His edicts required that monks live in cenobitic monasteries and limited the number of solitaries permitted to exist within the enclosure. Monks were required to pray, work, eat, and sleep according to a daily schedule under the direction of an abbot. The emperor also forbade double monasteries in which monks and nuns shared the same church and sometimes the same refectory and kitchen. Novices who sought admission to the monastery had to prove themselves over a three-year period before they were invested in the monastic *schema*, the tunic that identified a monk.

Monasteries had to receive the approval of the local bishop before they could function, an order that first appeared in the legislation of the Council of Chalcedon of 451. Justinian continued the tradition that everyone except runaway slaves and government officials still on duty had to be accepted into the monastery or convent. Only if they proved troublesome could they be expelled. Both civil and canon law emphasized that monks and nuns were to stay put in their houses, and only for a very serious reason (e.g., an abbot adopting a heretical opinion) was one allowed to leave. In fact this law proved to be too difficult to enforce. The individualism of the Byzantine monk and nun caused frequent transfers to occur.

One characteristic of monastic life in Byzantium was the radical egalitarianism of the monastery and convent. In theory no class distinctions were admitted, but it was often the case that applicants from the aristocracy received better accommodations and special privileges on entrance. In time the more mature monks sought to distinguish among themselves, wearing the *great schema* with a cowl and scapular, whereas more recent candidates wore a *small schema* to show that they had not yet proven themselves. Abbots assigned the more difficult manual tasks to illiterate monks.

At the head of every monastery was an abbot, called the *hegoumen* or archimandrite. He was elected for a life term by the monks in the community, although it was not unknown that Byzantine emperors or governors often promoted their favorites to this position. The *hegoumen*'s principal role was to act as spiritual director of the monastery and its confessor. In consultation with the monks, the *hegoumen* appointed other officials: the *oikonomos*, the financial officer; the *chartophylax*, the supervisor of the archives and the monastery's clerical officer; and the *bibliophylax*, the librarian. The abbot was generally but not necessarily a priest. Each monastery contained several priests to offer the liturgy and confer the sacraments, but most monks were never ordained. The abbot enforced the discipline of the community, assigning to rule breakers penances of days of fasting, solitary confinement, or even expulsion.

Convents had a similar organization with an abbess acting as superior. Young girls joined the convent at a minimum of 16 years of age, but each convent had its share of widows. After completing their novitiate, they donned a black tunic, the *himation*, over which an outer cloak, the *mandylas*, was worn. The head covering was a veil that allowed only the face to show. The bishop appointed chaplains for a convent's liturgical ceremonies.

For their protection women's convents were located in urban settings where they became part of the larger community. Custom dictated that in Byzantine convents little interest be shown in the arts or in intellectual matters.

Church councils also voiced concern for legislation on monasteries and convents. In 692 the Council in Trullo at Constantinople required that a boy reach ten years of age before admission and extended by a year the time of novitiate. To provide greater security for monks and nuns, it forbade the alienation of monastic lands into secular estates.

Other emperors followed Justinian in continuing to legislate on monastic life. All Byzantine rulers knew how popular and important monasteries had become and felt a responsibility to make sure that their members lived up to the ideals they embraced. In addition the emperors were very concerned over the management of farm lands donated to monasteries in bequests and acted to discourage too great a diversion of revenue from the state treasury. One reason behind the eighth-century imperial promotion of iconoclasm was an attempt to limit the estates under monastic control.

The patriarchs of Constantinople were also concerned about the monasteries and convents of the empire. Monasteries

A monastic church, Mistra, Greece, later Byzantine period.
Photo courtesy of Charles Frazee

founded by a patriarch, known as *stauropegia*, were exempt from the jurisdiction of the local bishop. In return the *stauropegia* sent a fee to the patriarchate that in late Byzantine times provided a significant amount of revenue.

Even for those who chose the ascetic life, society was never too distant, providing both moral and physical support. Because monks and nuns had renounced the desires and ambitions of this world, they became more attractive to those whose cares centered on it. Monasteries and convents in the cities welcomed large numbers of daily visitors, and those in the countryside, especially if they were pilgrimage sites, were never isolated from the outside world. Rather than rely on their parish or diocesan clergy, Byzantine people trusted above all the prayers of monks and nuns to pave their way into eternity.

The primary goal of monastics was to strive to become more like God. Eastern Christian spirituality showed little interest in original sin, which so preoccupied Western Christian thought. Rather the Christian life involved a pursuit of perfection, for God was already present in the human person at birth; the monk and nun were simply striving to make the divine presence more evident through a life of asceticism. Material things were not evil; it was precisely because they were good that a person might follow a vocation that gave up family, private possessions, and even one's own will for the sake of finding the higher good of union with God in this world. *Apatheia*, or lack of concern for power, riches, or marriage, was always considered one of the highest virtues because it led to *theosis*, becoming one with the divine nature. In this transformation a person found true freedom.

The daily life of the monk and nun followed a pattern of life that made each day similar to the one that preceded it. Every morning before dawn the day began with *orthros*. Subsequently at three-hour intervals the monks and nuns gathered in the monastery church, the *katholikon*, to continue their public prayer until at sundown the final vespers, the *lychnikon*, closed the activities of the day. The lighting of the evening candles and lamps signified Christ, the light of the world. The abbot or one of the priests of the monastery offered the liturgy on Sundays and feast days, but it was not, as in the Latin Church, a daily event. The content of the public prayers of the monks or nuns was made up of the Psalms, litanies, antiphons, and scriptural lessons. At least one-third of the year was a time of fasting when only one full meal was taken at 3:00 p.m., and all-night vigils preceded great holy days. *Proskynesis*, or full body prostration, was a form of private devotion that monks and nuns repeated many times as a form of prayer.

Every Byzantine monastery and convent had certain physical features to make it possible for its inhabitants to pursue their lives' purpose. The church, or *katholikon*, was always at the center of the enclosure, as prayer was of the essence of monastic life. Close by were the living quarters of the monks or nuns (individual sleeping rooms, or cells) but also in some foundations a common dormitory where people slept on straw mats. A refectory large enough to hold all members of the community provided a place for taking meals. Attached to the refectory were the kitchen and sometimes a bakery. Usually a bathhouse, a latrine, an infirmary, and a laundry room were present. Animals occupied stables, and warehouses held the tools of the community. In Byzantine times monasteries and convents led the rest of society in understanding the mechanics of plumbing and heating, in building ducts for hot air, and in constructing extensive basins and drains.

Larger monasteries, which without good reason often carried the name *lavra*, were meant to be self-sufficient. Therefore, monks and nuns skilled in crafts such as leather working, pottery, carpentry, textiles, and metalworking for liturgical vessels continued to practice their specialties. Icon painters were in great demand, as were scribes who copied manuscripts for the library. Most of the monks were farmers whose lives differed little from that of the peasants living near the enclosure.

Because monastic estates often lay at a distance from the monastery, certain monks comprised a *metochion*, a monastery in miniature, that housed the workers needed to till the fields there. *Metochia* were also found in cities where two or three monks oversaw a hostel for their community's visitors. Sometimes a monastery in decline opted to become a *metochion* of a large monastery. Several monks with the permission of the abbot might voluntarily abandon the central monastery for greater solitude in a *skete*, which gave them freedom to develop their own regimen.

A monastic founder, known after the eighth century as the *ktetor*, usually drew up a constitution for his monks that was known as the monastery's *typikon*. Women founders did the same for their convents. Eighteen *typika* are still extant for monasteries in Greece dating from the 11th through the 15th century. The *typika* sought to lay down the rules for the monastery, addressing such issues as the choice of officials, the daily schedule, the diet and dress required, and the calendar of liturgical celebrations. They vary in length and content, as each *ktetor* had his or her own ideas on how the establishment should function. The *typikon* often included a list of the monastery's property in a document known as the *brebion*.

Two *typika* became exemplars for the first founders of the Greek monasteries of the Middle Ages. The earliest, which had a wide circulation (although it was constantly amended), originated in Mar Sabas' Palestinian monastery. The other model was the work of Theodore of Stoudios (759–826), who devised his *typikon* for the monastic community that he headed in Constantinople. Written down in 826 after Theodore's death, it was considered so well done that it competed with Mar Sabas' constitution. As might be expected various combinations of these two rules appeared, for the *ktetor* was permitted to arrange matters as he or she saw fit. Unlike in the West, a variety of monastic religious orders never appeared in the Greek world, as the *typika* already allowed great flexibility.

Throughout the Middle Ages Thessalonike was the major city of Greece, far outdistancing Athens and Corinth in importance. Therefore, it is not surprising that David (d. 535), the first known hermit in Greece, should seek solitude nearby. In his Life it is said that he had come to Greece from Mesopotamia, living many years in the pursuit of the ascetic life until his death. Some time before 700, disciples sought out his grave, dedicating their

Kaiseriani Monastery, outside Athens. The former cloister is now a museum.
Photo courtesy of Charles Frazee

establishment to St. Theodore and St. Merkourios, later called Hosios David. It is also known as St. Theodora's because the monastery, at one time a convent, was once her home. Another institution in Thessalonike was the Latomou monastery. It receives mention in the biography of Joseph the Hymnographer (c. 810–886), who came there for spiritual guidance around 830. The monks used a much earlier church, dating from the end of the fifth century, for their *katholikon*. The Latomou church, with a fifth-century mosaic of Christ, is still extant in the modern city. It is the oldest surviving domed-cross structure in Greece.

Around 866 John Kolobos established a monastery near Ierissos on the isthmus of Mount Athos. He dedicated his monastery to St. John the Baptist, and Emperor Basil I (867–886) issued a grant of privileges to its monks, but the monastery did not have a long life, lasting for only a century.

During the tenth century, with the countryside reclaimed from Slavic invaders and cities once more centers of economic activity, it was possible for monks and nuns to find security for their institutions and patrons to help in their establishment. Hosios Loukas is preeminent among the monasteries of central Greece built at this time. The monastery holds the tomb of Blessed Loukas, a hermit of the tenth century who became fa-

mous for his healing powers. Loukas' tomb is in the larger of the two monastic churches located there and is still protected by guardian monks. The *katholikon*'s mosaics are the oldest program surviving in modern Greece with 140 images decorating its walls and ceiling. The architecture of the church is octagonal with squinches (triangular supports) holding up the dome. Because of earthquakes architects have had to rebuild the dome several times, with the latest reconstruction completed in 1964. Some scholars argue that Emperor Constantine IX (1042–1055) provided the funds needed for the project. Others credit Emperor Romanos II (956–963) for its patronage, claiming that he hoped to be buried next to the tomb of Blessed Loukas.

The smaller church, of cross-and-square construction, is the older of the two, with a lantern on its roof rather than the usual dome. Apparently this was an addition put on it when Cistercian monks shared the monastery with the Greeks in the 13th century. Now dedicated to the Dormition of Mary, the Mother of God (Greek, *Theotokos*), it once was the church of St. Barbara.

The cluster of monasteries on the Holy Mountain, Mount Athos, makes it the premier monastic center of modern Greece. Saint Athanasios of Trebizon (c. 920–1003) founded the first monastery there in the tenth century. Like many other bright young men of the times, Athanasios traveled to Constantinople, where he completed his education, and decided to enter the monastic life. In the capital he befriended the soon-to-be emperor Nikephoros II Phokas (963–969). With Nikephoros' encouragement in 962, Athanasios left Constantinople to begin a monastery near the tip of the peninsula of Mount Athos. The peninsula, about 25 miles long and about a mile and a half-mile wide, already was home for a group of hermits who had settled in caves within the forest that covered the mountain's sides. Athanasios encouraged them to join him in a cenobitic community. Because he had imperial support and financial aid (as Nikephoros intended to retire there after his tenure as emperor finished), his foundation prospered. Athanasios drew up a *typikon* to govern the life of the monks. It became so admired that since his day the Athonite constitution has become the standard for all subsequent monastic foundations in Greece. Within a few years other monasteries sprouted on Mount Athos, notably Iveron and Vatopedi, until eventually the Holy Mountain of Mount Athos became the most important center of the ascetic life in all the Eastern Christian world, a title that it holds to this day.

The tenth century also witnessed a flourishing of monastic institutions in other parts of Greece. Nikephoros II Phokas furnished funds for a monastery, the Panchrantou, on the island of Andros. In Athens the *katholikon* of the Petrake monastic church dates from about 975, making it one of the capital's oldest Byzantine monuments. Three other monasteries in the vicinity of Athens came into existence a bit later. One, built on Mount Hymmetos probably in the late 11th century, is Kaisariani. Now a museum, it became noted for its spring, the source of the Ilisos, that furnished ancient Athens with its water supply. The second, located about six miles south of Athens, is at Daphni on the main road between Athens and Corinth. The date of the monastery's construction is unknown, but its world-famous mosaics, the work of artists brought in from Constantinople, date from the late 11th century. The earliest mention of the monastery is in a document of 1048. The third establishment, Hosios Meletios, with well-fortified walls still surrounding the enclosure, was built close to the border between Attica and Boeotia.

The foundation of new monasteries and convents accelerated during the 11th century. In Thessalonike the Akapniou monastery appeared, possibly on the city acropolis. Founded by St. Photios of Thessaly, its name shows that its patrons were from the wealthy Byzantine Akapnes family.

Two important monasteries appeared on the Dodecanese islands of the Aegean Sea during the 12th century: Nea Moni on Chios and the Monastery of John the Theologian on Patmos. Around 1049 two hermits, Niketas and John, settled on Chios. Learning of the opportunities to establish a monastery there, Emperor Constantine IX (1042–1055) donated funds for the property and the construction of the *katholikon*. The original mosaics at New Moni are still in place. Later the monks raised a tower for defense against pirates.

In 1088 Emperor Alexios I Komnenos (1081–1111) became the principal benefactor so that his friend Christodoulos could establish a community on the barren island of Patmos. Its importance lay in the fact that it was here that John, author of the Book of Revelation in the New Testament, had written his visions. The Patmos monastery acquired large revenues owing to its estates and exemption from certain forms of taxation. The Patmos community collected a significant number of manuscripts and icons and a variety of ecclesiastical vessels. A strong wall, built about the monastery, made it so well defended that it was never taken by any invader. On the rugged coast of the island of Amorgos, Alexios endowed the construction of the Monastery of the Presentation. Today it houses just three aged monks.

Early in the 13th century, Latin Catholics arrived in Greece as a result of the Crusader and Venetian capture of Constantinople in 1204 during the Fourth Crusade. Pope Innocent III (1198–1216) believed that this event offered an opportunity to effect a reconciliation between the Greek and Latin Churches and requested that Cistercian monks set up houses in Greece. The pope presumed that the simplicity of the White Monks in the Greek countryside would further this goal. By 1225 the Cistercians occupied 12 houses from Constantinople to the Peloponnesus. Usually the monks preferred to build their own monasteries, but in some places, such as at Hosios Loukas, they formed a double community. In some circumstances the Western monks ousted the Greeks, taking over their buildings. This was the case in Thessalonike at the Choriatou monastery, and around 1207 French monks arrived at Daphni. During their residence they added an exonarthex to the *katholikon* and built a small cloister to the south of the church. The ruins of two Cistercian Gothic churches remain in the Peloponnesus: at Zaraka, near Lake Stymphalia, and in the eastern part of the peninsula where Our Lady of Issova was located.

During the Latin occupation most of the monasteries in Greece stayed in native hands: Nea Moni of Areia near Nauplion, Kaisariani, and Akapaniou in Thessalonike, which in fact was placed under papal protection by Pope Innocent III. The monasteries of Mount Athos were also secure.

The Latin occupation of Greece lasted in some parts of the country until the Ottoman Turkish conquest of 1458, but by that time Daphni was the sole surviving Cistercian foundation. Today it is a museum that attracts art enthusiasts from all over the world. On Venetian-held Crete the Dominican and Franciscan friars built churches wherever a Catholic community was large enough to support their presence. The Knight Hospitallers of St. John made the island of Rhodes their headquarters for several centuries until the Ottomans expelled them in the 16th century. When the Italians took Rhodes from the Turks in the early 20th century, Mussolini ordered a major restoration of the old city, including the inns of the Knights and the grand master's palace.

During the late Middle Ages, new Byzantine monastic communities flourished at Mistra, overlooking the site of ancient Sparta in Lakedaemonia. Although French Prince William II Villehardouin built it to be his capital, after 1262 it came under Byzantine control, unleashing a rash of construction. Seven churches with frescoes remain, the best in all of Greece to have survived from this last flowering of Byzantine art. The nuns of the Pantanassa monastery still provide hospitality to guests visiting the site.

One more cluster of monasteries appeared in the 14th century at Meteora ("floating in the air"). This site offers the modern traveler one of the most dramatic landscapes in all of Greece. Meteora's bare-stone, almost inaccessible spires rise 400 to 500 feet. Many monks who first settled here were refugees from Mount Athos who had increasingly come under attack from Turkish raids.

Another Athanasios was now to make his mark in the monastic history of Greece. He settled on one of the peaks, first as a hermit and then with his disciples at the Great Meteoron, where he composed a short *typikon* for his disciples. When the son of the Serbian king, John-Ioasaph Uroš (c. 1373–1423), took up residence at the Grand Meteoron, it attracted considerable support from his countrymen.

Two developments affected the monastic life on Mount Athos in the 14th century and, because of its influence, the other monasteries of Greece. The first was the introduction around 1390 of idiorrythmic monastic life, in which a person was allowed to hold private property, buy his own food and clothes, eat meat, and live in his own quarters. When a sufficient number of monks adopted the idiorrythmic life, a monastery dispensed with its abbot and chose a council, the *synaxis*, to govern its affairs. The second event was the overwhelming popularity of Hesychasm as an ideal form of monastic prayer. Hesychasts found God in the private recitation of the Jesus Prayer until they professed to share in the Divine Light that the apostles saw at the Transfiguration of Christ on Mount Tabor. This turn to mysticism necessarily minimized the importance of the traditional public offices of the monastic community.

In 1458 Sultan Mehmed II (1451–1481) led his Ottoman forces into Greece, commencing a long occupation of the country. For the most part the initial Turkish period brought many difficulties to the Greek monks, nuns, and their monasteries. Some suffered destruction, whereas others lost their revenues or counted so few occupants that they had no choice but to be absorbed into larger congregations. Thessalonike's Hosios David's church became a mosque, as did many other urban monastic churches.

However, the situation was not completely bleak. The citizens of Athens were wise enough to depute the abbot of Kaisariani to offer Mehmed II the keys to the city, saving it from destruction and earning tax-exempt status for the monastery as long as it existed. Patmos fared even better. Mehmed II commissioned its abbot to collect the island's taxes, and in 1461 Pope Pius II (1458–1464) placed it under his protection.

At Meteora a golden age unfolded in the 16th century when as many as 24 establishments clung to its peaks. In 1578 the Pendeli Monastery was founded just outside Athens, today one of the country's most prestigious institutions, as it often serves as a conference center for the activities of the Orthodox Church of Greece. Dozens of small monasteries continued to be started during the Turkish period, although their prospects were limited, and, because of their poverty, few outlived the life of the founder.

Patrons were still to be found among wealthy Greeks. They provided funds for the restoration of the frescoes to be seen in the monastic churches of the island in Ioannina's lake and those in Kaisariani. The bishop of Larisa was able to endow a monastery near Trikkala, the Monastery of the Great Gates. Amid the small gains made under the Turks, a large majority of Greek monks and nuns longed for the day when they would be rid of their Muslim rulers.

When the Greek Revolution of 1821 broke out, many monks abandoned their monasteries to take up arms against the Turks. Tradition has it that Bishop Germanos of Old Patras first raised the flag of independent Greece at the Ayia Lavra near Kalavrita. Monks associated with the struggle for freedom often suffered cruel tortures and death, so that at the end of the war in 1830 many monasteries stood empty, their inhabitants scattered. Mount Athos sat out the revolution, as did the monasteries of Meteora, and after the peace settlement remained within Ottoman territory. Therefore, the monasteries of independent Greece, limited to a small area north of the Gulf of Corinth, the Peloponnesus, and the Aegean islands were the only ones affected when the young Bavarian King Otto I (1832–1862) arrived in Nauplion to become sovereign of the kingdom of Greece. With him came advisers from Munich who had little use for monasteries. One of their first legislative acts was to dissolve the small monasteries and confiscate their lands. Of the nearly 600 establishments prior to the revolution, only 151 were allowed to continue. The government compressed the remaining convents into a handful of institutions.

In the 19th century Western European travelers visiting Greek monasteries both inside and outside the country shared the opinion that they were in a terrible state of ignorance and poverty. What monasteries did cultivate was enthusiasm for extending of the Greek state to include areas still under Ottoman rule. On Crete monasteries were central to the independence movement, best demonstrated during the outbreak of hostilities in 1866. The abbot and monks of Arkadi blew themselves up along with the refugees who had fled to them for safety rather than surrender to the Turkish forces besieging the monastery.

In the early 20th century, Greek monastic life attracted few candidates from any but the peasant class, resulting in continued stagnation. Even on Mount Athos and Meteora, a melancholy atmosphere descended on the communities, where buildings constructed to hold hundreds of monks or nuns held only a dozen. After the terrible years of World War II, civil war engulfed Greece, causing even more damage to monasteries and convents. However, once stability returned most monasteries revived, and the government initiated restoration work in the more historic institutions. Better-educated candidates appeared at monastery doors seeking admission, some from the Greek diaspora in the Americas and Australia. In fact dozens of new foundations have appeared in the past two decades.

Statistics for the year 2000 show that about 950 monks and 2,500 nuns now live in about 400 active Greek monastic institutions. Well over half the men live in the 20 monasteries of Mount Athos, whereas the rest are scattered throughout the country. Tourists so overwhelmed Meteora that all but a handful of monks have abandoned their peaks and made off for the quiet of the Holy Mountain. Recent legislation will limit access to Mount Athos lest it suffer the same fate. In Attica the Monastery of the Paraclete flourishes, as does the Kouvara Monastery of the Transfiguration, a center of Old Calendarists, a schismatic group that refuses to accept the stance of the official Church in adopting the Gregorian calendar, except for the dating of Easter. The Old Calendarists now hold the allegiance of over 100 monasteries and convents.

The Church of Greece is making every attempt to encourage vocations to the monastic life. Church leaders recognize that it was in the monasteries and convents that the Christian faith survived many difficult times and affirm that in the future a place for those who choose the ascetic life must always exist.

CHARLES A. FRAZEE

See also Antony, St.; Archaeology: Near East; Basil the Great, St.; Cappadocia, Turkey; Fasting: Eastern Christian; Hagiography: Eastern Christian; Hesychasm; Hymnographers; Iconoclasm (Controversy); Island Monasteries, Christian; Israel/Palestine; Istanbul, Turkey; Lavra; Libraries: Eastern Christian; Liturgy: Eastern Christian; Meteora, Thessaly, Greece; Mount Athos, Greece; Orthodox Monasticism: Byzantine; Palamas, Gregory, St.; Theodore of Stoudios, St.

## Further Reading

Curzon, Robert, *Visits to Monasteries in the Levant*, New York: Putnam, 1850; London: Milford, 1916

Hellier, Chris A., *Monasteries of Greece*, London: Tauris Parke Books, and New York: St. Martin's Press, 1996

Janin, Raymond, *La géographie ecclésiastique de l'empire byzantin*, volume 2: *Les églises et les monastères des grands centres byzantins*, 3 vols., Paris: Institut Français d'Etudes Byzantines, 1953–1981

Kokkines, Spyros, *Ta Monasteria tes Hellados*, 2nd edition, Athens: Vivliopoleion tes Hestias, 1993

Kokores, Demetrios, *Orthodoxa Hellenika Monasteria*, 2nd edition, Athens: Eptalophos AVEE, 1997

Morris, Rosemary, *Monks and Laymen in Byzantium, 843–1118*, Cambridge and New York: Cambridge University Press, 1995

Nichol, Donald, *Meteora: The Rock Monasteries of Thessaly*, revised edition, London: Variorum, 1975

Panagopoulos, Beata, *Cistercian and Mendicant Monasteries in Medieval Greece*, Chicago: University of Chicago Press, 1979

Runciman, Steven, *Mistra: Byzantine Capital of the Peloponnese*, London: Thames and Hudson, 1980

## Related Web Site

*http://platon.uoa.gr/-oudt/htm/english/orthos/.htm*

## Gregorian Chant. *See* Plainchant

# Gregory I (the Great), St. c. 540–604

*Roman monk and highly influential pope*

Gregory was born into a devout aristocratic family. He became prefect of Rome (head of the civil administration) at an unusually early age around 573 but soon resigned his office and founded seven monasteries on family properties, retiring to one of them on the Caelian Hill as a monk. Around 578 he was ordained deacon and in 579 sent as apocrisiarius (papal representative) to the imperial court at Constantinople. He tried to secure help for Italy against the Lombards (who had invaded Italy a decade before) while also establishing a liaison with the Church in Constantinople. He lived in community with a household of monks in the ambassador's residence. Around 585 he returned to Rome and his monastery, where he became a leading adviser of the pope. He was elected pope himself in 590, the first monk to hold the office. Reluctant to leave his monastery, he established a monastic and clerical household and dismissed lay servants from his staff, urging this on other bishops. Italy faced a grave crisis. The Lombards had brought war and, with it, disease and famine. A power vacuum existed in Rome with the breakdown of the civil administration. Thus, Gregory found himself at the forefront of temporal as well as spiritual affairs until his death in 604.

His remarkable energy, versatility, and skill as a political as well as ecclesiastical leader and administrator can be seen in his correspondence, which was exceptionally extensive; 854 letters survive. He reorganized the estates belonging to the papacy in Italy, Sicily, Gaul, North Africa, and Dalmatia to supply the needs of famine- and disease-ridden Italy. He negotiated treaties and raised troops. He tried to improve the organization and discipline of the clergy, laying down a code for the election and conduct of bishops while striving to enforce clerical celibacy. Although he accepted the sovereignty of the emperor in Constantinople, he steadfastly refused to acknowledge the title of ecumenical patriarch used by the bishop of Constantinople, which he saw as an infringement on the prerogatives of the bishops of Rome. Tireless in asserting Rome's claims to jurisdiction, he adopted the title used by popes ever since: Servant of the Servants of God.

One of his lasting achievements was the establishment of the Church at Canterbury, England, by sending a mission of monks from Rome in 596, led by Augustine (d. 604/09), the prior or Gregory's own monastery of St. Andrew. This was the first successful papal initiative to regain for Christianity territory lost to the pagan barbarians when the Western Roman Empire fell. In Canterbury Augustine established a monastery dedicated to St. Peter and St. Paul that was also a royal mausoleum and a cathedral dedicated as Christ Church that became the center of pastoral and missionary work. The concept and the dedications chosen for these foundations show their Roman origins, although Augustine was encouraged by Gregory to incorporate influences and personnel from Gaul. Gregory was as closely involved in the project as he could be at such a distance and re-inforced Augustine with more clergy in 601. The strategy of the mission was to establish centers from which Christianity could be established, and in this it was highly successful. The English always regarded Augustine as the apostle of England.

Gregory was a great, if not strikingly original, spiritual and theological writer. He wrote in a variety of genres. For popular edification his *Dialogi* (*Dialogues*) recite the lives and miracles of the Italian saints, mostly hermits and monks. It included the earliest biography of Benedict of Nursia (c. 480–c. 550), a fact that guaranteed the book's lasting renown. To guide the clergy in their work, he wrote *Regula Pastoralis* (*Pastoral Care*), which sets up the ideal of the bishop as the shepherd of souls. It was translated into Greek in his own lifetime and remained a classic handbook throughout the Middle Ages. His homilies also became immensely influential and were repeatedly quoted by later writers and used as exemplars by later sermon writers. His *Moralia in Job* (*Morals on the Book of Job*) is his greatest work of mystical theology and the foundation for his reputation as one of the major Western mystical writers.

In Gregory's time monasteries composed their own rules eclectically from a variety of sources. He probably knew the Rule of Benedict, which he praises briefly in the *Dialogues*, but his monasteries would have been equally influenced by the Rules of Basil and the Master and customs drawn from other houses. Gregory's monasteries were urban rather than rural and probably harsher than Benedict's, with more fasting and perhaps a more rigorous attitude to faults. Gregory was always a great advocate and protector of monastic life. As pope he sought to protect monasteries from seizure of property or interference by bishops, clergy, laymen, or even Roman Church officials. He wanted monasteries to choose their own abbots and tried to safeguard their authority – for example, by preventing monks from being removed from monasteries without their permission – while confining bishops' rights over them to spiritual matters. He fixed a minimum age for abbesses and prescribed a two-year novitiate (Benedict had one year, Justinian three). He was concerned with disciplinary issues such as vagrancy, private property, and women visiting or residing on monastic property, requiring bishops, abbots, rectors, or even special commissions to deal with abuses. He wanted secular officials appointed to handle the business of monasteries, and although he allowed monks to be ordained for the internal sacramental needs of the community, he made a very sharp distinction between monastic and pastoral vocations.

Later centuries saw the inflation or anachronistic definition of his achievements. When the monasteries of Western Europe adopted the Rule of Benedict, Gregory came to be said to have been a Benedictine, especially as he was the author of the first *Life* of Benedict. Although no monk was elected pope again until 672, he was later seen as the prototype of the Benedictine reformer-pope, an ideal emulated especially in the 11th century. His modest liturgical reforms led to his being described as the author of the medieval liturgy. Plainchant was commonly called Gregorian chant after him. He did enhance the development of the papacy by defending its prerogatives and enlarging its role both civil and ecclesiastical, but his letters and reputation later earned him the anachronistic reputation as the architect of the monarchical medieval papacy. His mystical theology was profoundly and permanently influential in the West. His distinction between the contemplative and active lives and his emphasis on the need for penance and compunction to unite the Christian with the sacrifice of Christ became hallmarks of the Western tradition.

BERNARD GREEN, O.S.B.

*See also* Benedict of Nursia, St.; Benedictines: General or Male; England: History; Governance: Christian Perspectives; Hagiography: Christian Perspectives; Hagiography: Western Christian; Island Monasteries, Christian; Istanbul, Turkey; Monastics and the World, Medieval; Origins: Western Christian; Plainchant; Regulations: Christian Perspectives; Vision, Mystical: Western Christian

## Biography

Son of a Roman Senator, Gregory became Prefect of Rome before c. 574. He sold his property and joined a monastery there that he himself had founded. From c. 579 to 585 he served as papal representative at Constantinople. Having returned to his monastery in Rome, in 590 he was elected pope. Few if any popes have exercised greater lasting influence. Styling himself the "servant of the servants of God," he made peace with the invading Lombards, administered the estates of the church with great skill, dispatched St. Augustine to evangelize in England, and promoted Benedictine monasticism. His promotion of plainchant at the Schola cantorum led to his name being attached to it, although "Gregorian chant" as we know it evolved for centuries after him.

## Major Works

*Regula Pastoralis*, c. 591; as *Pastoral Care*, translated by Henry Davis, 1950

*Dialogi*, c. 593; as *Dialogues*, translated by Odo John Zimmerman, 1959 (Book II contains the *Life and Miracles of St. Benedict*)

*Moralia in Job*; as *Morals on the Book of Job*, 1844–1850

Letters

## Further Reading

Dagens, Claude, *Saint Gregoire le Grand: Culture et expérience chrétiennes*, Paris: Études Augustiniennes, 1977

Markus, Robert, *Gregory the Great and His World*, Cambridge and New York: Cambridge University Press, 1997

Richards, Jeffrey, *Consul of God*, London and Boston: Routledge and Kegan Paul, 1980

Straw, Carole, *Gregory the Great: Perfection in Imperfection*, Berkeley: University of California Press, 1988

# Gregory VII c. 1015–1085

Italian Benedictine reformer and pope

The monk Hildebrand, who reigned as Pope Gregory VII (1073–1085), is known mostly as the pope who launched the investiture controversy, the great struggle between German emperor and papacy that decisively influenced the future of both the empire and the Western Church. Less often considered is the fact that Gregory was the most notorious European monk of the 11th century. He was part of an unprecedented run of monks who became pope, from Nicholas II's election in 1059 until the death of Gelasius II in 1119. However, more than with any other pope in this period, the fact that Gregory VII was a monk played a crucial role in creating a new attitude toward monastic involvement in the world.

The German emperor Henry IV (1056–1106), in his letter of 1076 that calls for Gregory's deposition, addresses him as "Hildebrand, not pope by God's ordination, but false monk" (Morrison, 1971). Hildebrand had certainly lived an irregular monastic life by earlier standards. Having made his monastic profession at a Roman monastery, he entered papal service at an early age. As archdeacon of the Roman Church, he was sent on missions by several popes and was even accused by critics of commanding the papal army. Although many other monks of the time were in papal service, Hildebrand's high visibility and volatile character made him a natural target for traditionalists who argued that monks had no business becoming actively involved in secular matters. They should stay in their monasteries and serve the rest of humanity through prayers, not polemics. Worst of all, unlike his predecessor Gregory I (590–604), Hildebrand had voluntarily left monastic life, motivated by self-will instead of compulsion. That Pope Gregory continued to wear the Benedictine habit as pope only made his behavior appear more outrageous.

Gregory and his supporters insisted that the needs of the Church superseded adherence to the Benedictine Rule. Already in the 1060s Hildebrand defended the Vallombrosans in their stand against the simonist bishop of Florence, arguing that witness to the truth took precedence over monastic quiet and stability. As pope Gregory continued to advocate monastic activity in favor of Church reform, strongly supporting the active congregations of Vallombrosa and Hirsau, licensing monks as wandering preachers, and apparently quarreling with Abbot Hugh of Cluny (r. 1049–1109) over the latter's failure to throw Cluniac support behind the papally sponsored reform movement. As Gregory's supporter Manegold of Lautenbach wrote, Gregory answered a call from God, to give up the quietude of monastic life for the greater good. Gregory contended that other monks should do the same.

For monks the most important long-term effect of Gregory's pontificate was the establishment of a principle: popes, in their overarching concern for the Catholic Church, have a right to use even monks as their tools. A papal license is stronger than the Benedictine Rule, and the monk's vow of obedience outweighs Benedict's injunction to stability. In future generations the appeal to obedience was used to justify many nonmonastic activities.

PHYLLIS G. JESTICE

See also Benedictines: General or Male; Canons Regular, Origins of; Cluniacs; Cluny, Abbots of; German Benedictine Reform, Medieval; Liturgy: Western Christian; Monastics and the World, Medieval; Netherlands; Vallombrosans; William of Hirsau

## Biography

Hildebrand, the future reforming pope, was born in Tuscany and took vows as a Benedictine. From 1046 to 1049 he lived in Germany in exile with Pope Gregory VI. From 1049 until his own election as pontiff in 1073 he administered papal property and guided a series of reforming popes. He campaigned against simony and sexual immorality among clerics. A bitter conflict with Emperor Henry IV (1056–1106) lasted from 1076 until Gregory's death in exile at Salerno in 1085. Throughout his pontificate Gregory wore the robes of a Benedictine.

## Major Works

Letters (in *Registrum*)

## Further Reading

Cowdrey, H.E.J., *Pope Gregory VII, 1073–1085*, New York: Oxford University Press, and Oxford: Clarendon Press, 1998

Fichtenau, Heinrich, "Cluny und der Mönch Hildebrand (Gregor VII)," in his *Beiträge zur Mediävistik: ausgew. Aufsätze*, volume 3, Stuttgart: Hiersemann, 1986

Jestice, Phyllis G., *Wayward Monks and the Religious Revolution of the Eleventh Century* (Brill's Studies in Intellectual History, volume 76), Leiden and New York: Brill, 1997

Morghen, Raffaello, *Gregorio VII e la riforma della Chiesa nel secolo XI* (Storia, 2), Palermo: Palumbo, 1974

Morrison, Karl, editor, *The Investiture Controversy: Issues, Ideals, and Results* (European Problem Studies), New York: Holt, Rinehart and Winston, 1971

Robinson, Ian S., *Authority and Resistance in the Investiture Contest: The Polemical Literature of the Late Eleventh Century*, Manchester, Greater Manchester: Manchester University Press, and New York: Holmes and Meier, 1978

# Gregory of Nazianzus, St. c. 329–390

Cappadocian Christian theologian and advocate of Nicene orthodoxy

Gregory of Nazianzus, or "The Theologian," as he is more commonly known in the Eastern Church, is one of the most important of the circle of the Cappadocian theologians writing in the generation after Athanasius of Alexandria (c. 296–373). He was the close friend of Basil of Caesarea (c. 330–379) and Gregory Nyssa (c. 330–c. 395) and was deeply involved in the ascetic reflections that came from the various members of this closely knit Christian clan. His mother, Nonna, was a visionary and austere

Christian matron who had converted her wealthy spouse, Gregory the Elder, and encouraged his patronage of the local Christians to the extent that he was elected bishop of Nazianzus. The education devoted to their sons, Gregory and Caesarius, was lavish. Apart from studies in local schools, where he first made the acquaintance of Basil, Gregory studied in Palestine and especially Athens, where he seems to have been baptized, and drew Basil into some form of ascetic Christian lifestyle with him while they studied together with the Christian professor of rhetoric, Prohaeresius. Basil was dissatisfied with Athenian life and returned home, and soon afterward, in 358, Gregory and Caesarius were recalled to Cappadocia. Basil had intended to devote himself to a political career, but the death of his father and the influence of his sister Macrina (c. 327–379) induced Basil to join the ascetic experiment on his family estates at Annesi in the Pontic region. Already one of the most learned Christians of his age, Gregory determined to continue at home the ascetic life he had begun and also to devote himself to advanced studies of literature. The extent of his reading in both pagan and Christian sources is seen in all his work. He was especially devoted to the metaphysical and ascetic ideas of Origen (c. 185–c. 254), whose tradition he was responsible for softening so that it might enter into the mainstream of the dogmatic and monastic traditions of later Christian orthodoxy.

Basil invited him to share the monastic life at Annesi, but Gregory's visits there, amusingly described in his letters, convinced him that the lifestyle was not suited to his own ideas. Nevertheless, the time spent with Basil saw their compilation of the *Philokalia*, a florilegium of inspiring passages from Origen that prioritized the great Alexandrian's mystical and ascetic thought. Gregory soon after returned to his father's estates, where in 361 he was pressured into accepting ordination as a priest, an event that he interpreted (at least in the immediate aftermath) as ruining his aspirations to live a life of seclusion. His father seems to have regarded his ascetic withdrawal, on the family-owned hill settlement at nearby Karbala, with some impatience. Gregory's own writings, even years after the event, show that he regarded the imposition of orders as tantamount to "tyranny" over him. His initial reaction to the ordination was to flee to Basil for advice. The latter counseled him to make his peace at home, and in the following year Gregory returned, on his own terms, only to find the local church in a serious dispute. It is difficult to interpret the exact cause, but some kind of theological confession had been accepted by Bishop Gregory on behalf of the local Church, and an influential group of local ascetics had withdrawn their communion. It also seems that they had been offended by the young Gregory's flight from their area, hoping that he would have represented monastic interests on the presbyteral council. Gregory's early orations are dedicated to the cause of reconciliation between his family and these local ascetics; in these orations he seems to have been successful, aided by Basil. In turn he supported Basil's cause when the latter aspired to the metropolitan see of Caesarea, and at first he thought he might assist Basil in advancing the latter's ideas for a philanthropically oriented and monastically directed Church life. He delivered important orations in support of the hospice that Basil was building at Caesarea, but soon afterward Basil's machinations to establish Gregory in an auxiliary see at Sasima turned their relationship sour. Gregory retired to Nazianzus to assist his ailing father as auxiliary bishop. In his final years he played a major part in the prelude to the Council of Constantinople and its theology of the Holy Spirit when he delivered his famous *Theological Orations* in Constantinople between 379 and 381. After a long retirement on his estates in failing health, he died around 390, leaving a large body of theological and poetic work of the highest quality.

Gregory is most famous in Christian history for seminal contributions to Christology and to Trinitarian doctrine, but his role in the foundations of ascetic theory should not be overlooked. He was the most extensively read Christian author throughout the long centuries of Byzantium, and his ideas were massively influential. Gregory argues that the true ascetic life should be one of quiet withdrawal from the affairs of the world. This can be done anywhere, in city or the village, but it needs to be done in such a way that ascetics can devote their time to constant study and reflection. Gregory sees mental dedication to the study of godly things as the quintessential purification of the soul, comparable to purification of the body through moderate ascesis, prayer, and celibate fidelity. The soul and body that have thus been purified prepare the Christian for the vision of God. Only those who have been admitted to the light of the Presence are qualified to teach others. It is an interesting claim for a pattern of authority that was to become increasingly standard after him – that Church leaders in episcopal sees ought to be chosen from the ranks of educated monastics. Gregory's understanding of the ascetic life as a dynamic progress toward the luminous vision of God and as a path that ought to be followed with a wide degree of personal freedom, allowing large amounts of time to be dedicated to the service of scholarship and quietness (*hesychia*), laid a pattern for most of what was to follow in Byzantine monastic theory. He himself needs to be considered in the increasingly rare class of Christian elite aristocrats pursuing the perfect life of withdrawal.

JOHN McGUCKIN

*See also* Basil the Great, St.; Cappadocia, Turkey; Gregory of Nyssa, St.; Hymnographers; Israel/Palestine; Macrina, St.; Origins: Eastern Christian; Spirituality: Eastern Christian; Theology, Eastern Christian; Transvestite Saints; Vision, Mystical: Eastern Christian

## Biography

Son of the Bishop of Nazianzus, Gregory studied at Athens together with his lifelong friend St. Basil. Having become a monastic, in the early 360s he was unwillingly ordained priest and ten years later bishop of a village in Cappadocia. In 379 he preached at Constantinople in favor of Nicene orthodoxy and during the Council of Constantinople in 381 was elected bishop of that city. He resigned almost at once in order to retire to his estate at Nazianzus. Known simply as the "Theologian," Gregory ranks as one of the three Cappadocian Fathers.

## Major Works

*St. Gregory Nazianzen: Orations and Letters*, edited by Charles
G. Browne and Edwin H. Gifford, translated by James E.
Swallow, 1955

*St. Gregory Nazianzen: Select Poems*, edited by J.A. McGuckin,
1986, 1989, and 1995

*Faith Gives Fullness to Reasoning: The Five Theological
Orations of Gregory Nazianzen*, edited by Frederick W.
Norris, 1991

Gregory also compiled the *Philokalia* (an anthology of works
by Origen) with Basil.

## Further Reading

Ellverson, Anna-Stina, *The Dual Nature of Man: A Study in the
Theological Anthropology of Gregory of Nazianzus*,
Uppsala, Sweden: Almquist and Wiksell, 1981

McGuckin, J.A., "Perceiving Light from Light in Light: The
Trinitarian Theology of St. Gregory the Theologian," *Greek
Orthodox Theological Review* 39:1 (1994)

McGuckin, J.A., "The Vision of God in St. Gregory
Nazianzen," in *Studia Patristica*, Leuven: Peeters, 1996

Ruether, Rosemary R., *Gregory of Nazianzus: Rhetor and
Philosopher*, Oxford: Clarendon Press, 1969

Winslow, Donald F., *The Dynamics of Salvation: A Study in
Gregory of Nazianzus*, Cambridge, Massachusetts:
Philadelphia Patristic Foundation, 1979

# Gregory of Nyssa, St. c. 330–c. 395

Cappadocian Christian theologian and writer
on mysticism

Born into a prominent Christian family in Cappadocia, Gregory
of Nyssa was the younger brother of Basil the Great (c. 330–
379). With Gregory of Nazianzus (329/30–389/90), they championed Nicene orthodoxy in the fourth century. The most brilliant and subtle thinker (and the most prolific author) of these
Cappadocian Fathers, Gregory of Nyssa wrote works on asceticism and mysticism that supplied theoretical undergirding for
the monastic movement organized by his brother.

Scholars disagree about who Gregory's principal educational
mentor might have been, whether his brother Basil or the pagan
Libanius. However, Gregory undoubtedly was prodigiously
learned in the classical authors, in the Christian Scriptures, and
in contemporary culture. His works give unmistakable evidence
of wide scholarship as well as practical experience of the world.
Almost certainly married, he probably never lived the monastic
life, although he wrote in praise of it.

Under Basil's urging, Gregory turned from a career as teacher
of rhetoric to devote himself to the service of the Church. In 372
Basil appointed Gregory bishop of Nyssa. In 379 Basil died, before his younger brother had manifested the distinctiveness in
thought and speculation for which he became known. Gregory
took up Basil's mantle of theological and ecclesiastical leadership. He played a prominent role at the Council of Constantino-

ple (381) and in the following years authored several doctrinal
treatises while engaging in administrative duties. From the late
380s on, his writings focused on mystical spirituality.

These writings demonstrated extraordinary originality and
thorough mastery of the subject. As always in his works, emphasis fell on the infinitude and incomprehensibility of God: in these
later works Gregory emphasized the mystical implications of this
fundamental orientation. He urged that the Christian life is one
of unceasing ascent of the soul to union with God. In Gregory's
two books on the titles of the Psalms, he expounded the analogy
of a ladder leading upward toward perfection; he also used this
analogy in his treatment of the Beatitudes. The ladder analogy
subsequently became a favorite among monastic writers, particularly John Climacus (c. 570–c. 649).

Gregory's homilies on the Canticles presented the book as a
rhapsody on the union of love between God and the human soul.
Whereas others (notably Origen) had approached the book in
this fashion, Gregory's mystical exegesis set the pattern that was
followed by numerous monastic authors in subsequent centuries.

However, the crowning achievement of Gregory's mystical
writings was *De Vita Moysis* (*The Life of Moses*). In this work
Gregory gave little attention to prayer, meditation, or other specific disciplines of spirituality. Instead, he focused on the elements in Moses' life that encouraged withdrawal from human
affairs to seek God, the asceticism and contemplation that allow
one to ascend toward God, and the necessity of returning to
offer service in human society. In this work Gregory presented
the Christian life as an eternal progress and in so doing offered a
direct counter to the ideal of static unity urged by Plato and Origen. Especially within Eastern Orthodoxy this emphasis has
shaped the understanding of the Christian life.

JAMES R. PAYTON, JR.

*See also* Basil the Great, St.; Cappadocia, Turkey; Gregory of
Nazianzus, St.; Isaac the Syrian (Isaac of Nineveh), St.; Macrina,
St.; Origins: Eastern Christian; Spirituality: Eastern Christian;
Theology, Eastern Christian; Transvestite Saints; Vision, Mysti-
cal: Eastern Christian

## Biography

Brother of St. Basil and St. Macrina, and one of the three
"Cappadocian Fathers," Gregory trained as an orator. He
became bishop of Nyssa, Cappadocia, in 372, from which
position Arians deposed him c. 376. He served briefly as bishop
of Sebaste c. 380 before working to combat Arianism in the
diocese of Pontus. A prolific writer, Gregory upheld Nicene
orthodoxy while perpetuating themes of Origen. He died soon
after attending a Council in Constantinople in 394.

## Selected Works

*Contra Eunomium*
*De Oratione Dominica*
*Epistulae*
*In Canticum Canticorum*
*In Inscriptiones Psalmorum*
*Opera Ascetica*
*Opera Dogmatica Minora*
*Sermones*

*The Lord's Prayer; The Beatitudes*, translated and annotated by Hilda C. Graef, 1954

*Two Rediscovered Works of Ancient Christian Literature: Gregory of Nyssa and Macarius*, edited by Werner Jaeger, 1954

*Gregorii Nysseni Opera*, edited by Werner Jaeger and Hermannus Langerbeck, 10 vols., 1960–1992

*From Glory to Glory: Texts from Gregory of Nyssa's Mystical Writings*, edited by Jean Daniélou and Herbert Musurillo, 1961

*De Vita Moysis*, edited by Herbert Musurillo, 1964; as *The Life of Moses*, translated and with an introduction and notes by Abraham J. Malherbe and Everett Ferguson, 1978

## Further Reading

Balthasar, Hans Urs von, *Presence and Thought: An Essay on the Religious Philosophy of Gregory of Nyssa*, San Francisco: Ignatius Press, 1997

Daniélou, Jean, *Platonisme et théologie mystique: Essai sur la doctrine spirituelle de saint Grégoire de Nysse*, Paris: Aubier, Éditions Montaigne, 1944

Migne, J.P., editor, *Patrologia Graeca*, volumes 44–46, Paris: Migne, 1857

Mühlenberg, Ekkehard, *Die Unendlichkeit Gottes bei Gregor von Nyssa: Gregors Kritik am Gottesbegriff der klassischen Metaphysik*, Göttingen: Vandenhoeck and Ruprecht, 1966

Völker, Walther, *Gregor von Nyssa als Mystiker*, Wiesbaden: Steiner, 1955

# Griffiths, Bede 1907–1993

English Benedictine author and leader of the Christian ashram movement in India

Bede Griffiths was born Alan Richard Griffiths of a middle-class Anglican family in England. He was educated at Oxford, where he and C.S. Lewis, his tutor, became great friends. In 1931 he entered the Catholic Church and, a month later, Prinknash Abbey in Gloucestershire. His early life, education, conversion, and monastic experience in England are recorded in his autobiography, *The Golden String* (1954), whose title was inspired by Blake's poem "Heaven's Gate." *The Golden String* is really a phenomenology of an inner spiritual and intellectual journey from agnosticism to faith and then to Catholicism.

After 25 years of monastic life in England, Griffiths accepted the challenge to cofound a Benedictine monastery in India. An Indian monk, Father Benedict Alapatt, invited him into this venture. As he was leaving for the subcontinent in 1955, he wrote to a friend, "I am going out to India to seek the other half of my soul." He was referring to the intuitive, feminine, mystical dimension of his being. His first joint attempt to establish a Benedictine community failed, but then, in 1958 with Father Francis Mahieu, a Belgian Cistercian, he founded Kurisumala Ashram in Kerala on the southwest coast. Griffiths stayed there for ten years, serving as novice master, professor, and guest master. Then in 1968, Henri Le Saux, O.S.B. (Abhishiktananda, 1910–

1973), the cofounder of Shantivanam Ashram, asked Kurisumala Ashram to assume responsibility also for Shantivanam. Griffiths was sent, serving there as superior until his death in May 1993.

Under his visionary leadership the community grew into a stable and viable monastic presence in Tamil Nadu in southern India. In 1980 Griffiths became a Camaldolese Benedictine and in 1982 brought the community of Shantivanam into the congregation. Shantivanam, also known as Saccidananda Ashram, was dedicated to the Holy Trinity, which was conceived as a hybrid of Catholic monastic life and Hindu *sannyasa*, that is, the life of renunciation. Such a process of inculturation had been encouraged by the Second Vatican Council, culminating in sporadic experimentation spanning two centuries.

Griffiths was a mystic, a prophet, and an icon of love. He experienced deeply intense intimacy with the Divine, which he expressed in the personalist terms of the Catholic tradition, notably in the language of the Spanish mystics with their emphasis on love. In a letter to me in 1990, he wrote, "I find myself in the Void (the Emptiness, or *Shunyata* of the Buddhists), but the Void is totally saturated with love." His mystical experience and the inner process he went through bridged the gap between Christian contemplation and Buddhist Emptiness.

In his prophetic mode, Griffiths endlessly addressed the task of the Church in terms of the other traditions. He identified this task as one of careful assimilation of their spiritual treasures, much as the early fathers of the Church had absorbed Greek philosophy when developing Christian theology as a vehicle for the gospel. He remained an unceasing critic of ecclesial abuse of power, especially by Rome. Furthermore, Griffiths often spoke of the coming new synthesis of science, mysticism, and faith; this is the subject of his book *A New Vision of Reality: Western Science, Eastern Mysticism and Christian Faith* (1989). Finally, Griffiths was truly an icon of love working across cultures. In himself he reversed the attitude of the English toward Indians, helping Christians esteem the Hindu ideal of renunciation.

WAYNE TEASDALE

*See also* Ashram, Influence of; Dialogue, Intermonastic: Christian Perspectives; India: Christian; Le Saux, Henri; Vision, Mystical: Western Christian

## Biography

Upon graduation from Oxford University, Griffiths moved to the Cotswolds in search of a simpler life. In 1931 he converted from the Anglican to the Roman Catholic Church and joined the Benedictines at Prinknash Abbey. After serving as prior at Farnborough from 1947 to 1952, he traveled in 1955 to India to emulate Henri Le Saux (1910–1973) and Jules Monchanin (1895–1957). From 1958 to 1968 he lived at Kurisumala ashram in Kerala. In 1968 Griffiths took over leadership of the Saccidananda Ashram that the two Frenchmen had cofounded in Tamil Nadu 20 years before. He remained a Benedictine living as a sannyasi, publishing numerous treatises on the interaction of Christian and Hindu thought. He is revered as leader of the Christian ashram movement.

## Major Works

*The Golden String: An Autobiography*, 1954; revised edition, 1980

*Christ in India: Essays Towards a Hindu-Christian Dialogue*, 1966

*Return to the Center*, 1976

*The Marriage of East and West: A Sequel to the Golden String*, 1982

*A New Vision of Reality: Western Science, Eastern Mysticism and Christian Faith*, edited by Felicity Edwards, 1989

*Universal Wisdom*, edited by Roland Ropers, 1993

## Further Reading

du Boulay, Shirley, *Beyond the Darkness: A Biography of Bede Griffiths*, New York: Doubleday, and London: Rider, 1998

Teasdale, Wayne, *Toward a Christian Vedanta: The Encounter of Hinduism and Christianity According to Bede Griffiths*, Bangalore: Asian Trading Corp., 1987

# Gualbert, John, St. before 1000–1073

Italian Christian monk, reformer, and founder of the Vallombrosan Order

According to the hagiographic tradition, the founder of the Vallombrosan Order was born in Petrojo near Florence. His father was one Gualbert (Visdomini?) of a rich noble family. A turning point in John Gualbert's spiritual life occurred one Good Friday when he forgave the killer of a relative, eschewing the vendetta custom that required him to take revenge. Against his father's will he became a Benedictine monk at San Miniato abbey near Florence at the age of 19. Protesting the simoniac election of abbot Obert (c. 1035), he left this monastery on the advice of hermit Teuzo and, in search of a secluded place suitable for strict observance of St. Benedict's Rule, visited a number of abbeys, including that of Camaldoli.

Finally Gualbert settled at Asquabella (later Vallombrosa) near Florence (c. 1036). His following grew as the community was joined by other monks from San Miniato and by lay Florentines. In time their arrival necessitated the founding of a new monastery. On 27 January 1037 a Florentine notary and clerk named Albert gave the monks traveling to Vallombrosa an estate, and on 3 July 1039 Ita, the abbess of San Ellero, donated ground where the monastery could be erected. Among those involved in the founding of the abbey were also the Emperor Conrad II (1024–1039), who visited Florence in 1038, and Bishop Ruodo of Paderborn, who possibly consecrated the abbey church (1038?). Gualbert was appointed provost (first mentioned in 1043) and then abbot, probably on the occasion of meeting Pope Leo IX (1048–1054) at Passignano in 1050 (the title confirmed in 1068). The new congregation was confirmed by Pope Victor II (1057–1059) in 1055. From 1040 a number of monasteries subordinated to Vallombrosa abbey were founded (e.g., San Salvi, Moscheta, and Passignano). As a sign of humility, Gualbert never became a priest.

Thanks to Gualbert, Vallombrosa became a local center not only of monastic reform but also of movements to reform the Church, the suppression of simony being a primary goal. On this issue Gualbert collaborated with several popes and also with St. Peter Damian (1007–1072) and Hubert of Silva Candida, among others. His activities, including preaching, evoked considerable hostility among those opposing reform. He is known to have participated in the deposition from office of one Guarino, a simoniac abbot of Settimo (1068). Gualbert was also involved in a dramatic conflict with Pietro Mezzabarba, archbishop of Florence (1061–1068), and having incited the Florentines to rise up against the archbishop brought about his deposition.

Gualbert strove to implement the idea of communal life, an idea inspired by the fathers of the Church, especially St. Basil, and based on strict observance of St. Benedict's Rule. He made a provision for *conversi*, whose efforts freed monks from manual labor. Another novelty was the centralized administration of abbeys subordinated to Vallombrosa, inspired by Cluny. Nevertheless, it was Rodolph, Gualbert's successor, who created the congregation of Vallombrosa.

Gualbert died on 12 July 1073 at San Arcangelo abbey in Passignano (Chianti) and was buried there. He was canonized on 1 October 1193 by Pope Celestine III (1191–1198). He is patron saint of Italian foresters (since 1951) and of foresters from the city of Sao Paolo, Brazil (since 1957).

MAREK DERWICH

*See also* Basil the Great, St.; Benedictines; Cluniacs; Cluny, France; Florence, Italy; Vallombrosans

## Biography

John joined the Benedictine house of San Miniato, Florence, but withdrew c. 1036 and settled in the Valley of Vallombrosa in the Apennines east of Florence c. 1040. Monks gathered around him to live a semi-eremitical life under strict observance of the Rule of St. Benedict. The Vallombrosan Order emerged there. He employed *conversi* to perform manual labor. Throughout his career he battled against the practice of simony (i.e., purchase of clerical office).

## Major Works

Gualbert left two letters. The first was addressed to Bishop Herman of Volterra (edited in *Patrologia Latina* 146.792d–794). The second was his spiritual testament (edited in *Patrologia Latina* 146.700–701). Gualbert was only a user and not the author of an 11th-century *Book of Prayers* (edited in *Patrologia Latina* 146.971–979; also edited by A. Salvini, 1933).

## Further Reading

Three earliest *Lives* of John Gualbert are among the important works of medieval hagiography. The first was written by Andrew of Parma, abbot of Strumi (d. 1101 or 1102; *Bibliotheca Hagiographica Latina* 4397; edited in *Patrologia Latina* 147.765–812; also edited by F. Baethgen, in *Monumenta Germaniae Historica, Scriptores Rerum Germanicarum* 30:2 [1934] pp. 1080–1104), the second composed by an anonymous disciple of Gualbert

Andrea Orcagna, *St. John Gualberto and Episodes from His Life*, Cappella di S. Silvestro, S. Croce, Florence, Italy, 14th century.
Photo courtesy of Alinari/Art Resource, New York

(*Bibliotheca Hagiographica Latina* 4399; edited by R. Davidsohn, in *Forschungen zur älteren Geschichte von Florenz*, 1896, pp. 55–60; also edited by F. Baethgen, in *Monumenta Germaniae Historica, Scriptores Rerum Germanicarum* 30:2 [1934] pp. 1104–1110), and the third authored by St. Atto, abbot of Vallombrosa, later bishop of Pistoia (d. 1153; *Bibliotheca Hagiographica Latina* 4398a; edited in *Patrologia Latina* 146.671–706).

Boesch, Gajano, S., "Giovanni Gualberto e la vita comune del clero nelle biografie di Andrea de Strumi e di Atto di Valombrosa," in *La vita comune del clero nei secoli XI e XII, Atti della Settimana di studio: Mendola, settembre 1959*, volume 2, Milan: Società editrice Vita e pensiero, 1962

Casini, S., *Storia di S. Giovanni Gualberto Florentino*, Florence, 1934

Degl'Innocenti, Antonella, "Le vite antiche di Giovanni Gualberto, cronologia e modelli agiografici," *Studi Medievali* 25 (1984)

Di Re, P., *Giovanni Gualberto nelle fonti dei secoli XI–XII*, Rome, 1974

Lucchesi, E., *S. Giovanni Gualberto: Dai boschi d'Italia alle foreste del Brasile*, Florence, 1959

Miccoli, Giovanni, *Pietro Igneo: Studi sull'età gregoriana*, Rome: Nella sede dell'Istituto, 1960

Quilici, B., "Giovanni Gualberto e la sua riforma monastica," *Archivo Storico Italiano* 99:1–2 (1941); 99:3–4 (1941–1942); 100:1–2 (1942–1943)

Salvini, A., *S. Giovanni Gualberto*, Bari, 1961 [1943]

Spinelli, Giovanni, and Giustino Rossi, editors, *Alle origini di Vallombrosa: Giovanni Gualberto nella società dell'XI secolo*, Novara: Europía, and Milan: Jaca Book, 1984

Vasaturo, R. Nicola, *Vallombrosa: L'abbazia e la congregazione: Note storiche*, Vallombrosa: Edizioni Vallombrosa, 1994

Wilmart, André, "Le manuel de prières de saint Jean Gualbert," *Revue Bénédictine* 48 (1936)

# Guéranger, Prosper 1805–1875

French Benedictine liturgical reformer and expert
on plainchant

The monastic founder and liturgist was born at Sablé-sur-Sarthe near Le Mans, France, on 4 April 1805 and died at the Abbey of Solesmes in Sablé on 30 January 1875. Guéranger was the son of the local schoolmaster at Sablé, and his general education was under the direction of his father until the age of 13. In 1818 he was sent to study at the Collège Royal at Angers, and in 1822 he entered the seminary of Le Mans. Guéranger was ordained priest for the Diocese of Le Mans on 7 October 1827.

The life and work of Guéranger can be understood as a response to the political and religious environment in which he lived. Significant characteristics of this environment include the total suppression of monastic life in the wake of the French Revolution, the precarious situation of the Catholic Church in France after the Revolution, the French Church's split between Gallican and Ultramontane (i.e. papal) loyalties, and widespread usage of neo-Gallican liturgical rites. Guéranger's refoundation of Benedictine life at Solesmes with its liturgical emphasis and concomitant restoration of Gregorian chant is best understood in these contexts.

Guéranger had developed a passion for reading by the age of seven, and by the time he was ordained he had digested a great number of the works of the Fathers and of the Roman Catholic tradition. A major influence on the intellectual formation of Guéranger was exercised by the Abbé Félicité de Lamennais (1782–1854), whom he considered a brave, eloquent, and passionate defender of the rights of the Roman Catholic Church. Already in 1821, before he had entered the seminary, Guéranger had read Lamennais' *Essai sur l'indifférence en matière de religion* (1817–1823; Essay on Indifference in Matters of Religion). By 1830 Guéranger was contributing articles to Lamennais' journal *Mémorial Catholique*, and in 1831 Guéranger had published *De l'élection et de la nomination des évêques* (On the Selection and Nomination of Bishops), in which he discussed the role of the state in the appointment of bishops. The young priest sent a copy to Lamennais for approval. Thus, Guéranger's ultramontanism (i.e., advocacy of papal centralization against national autonomy) was in many respects influenced by that of Lamennais. However, Guéranger progressed beyond Lamennais through reading Philippe-Olympe Gerbert's *Considérations sur le dogme générateur de la piété catholique* (1829; Considerations on Dogma as the Source of Catholic Piety), which translated Lamennais into the concrete language of sacramental theology.

Guéranger's liturgical work must be viewed in light of the numerous neo-Gallican diocesan liturgies that survived in France until the 1850s. These neo-Gallican rites had developed between 1670 and 1840, and because of the reorganization of dioceses after the Revolution, more than one might be employed in a single diocese. Unlike the various medieval Roman-Gallican liturgies that Guéranger defended, the neo-Gallican rites, in his mind, were tainted by modernity, individualism, elitism, and nationalism. These characteristics stood in stark contrast to the sense of tradition, community, objectivity, and international solidarity that Guéranger discerned in the medieval Roman-Gallican liturgies and the Tridentine liturgical books.

Guéranger's liturgical piety had already been evident in his youth, for he knew a large part of the liturgy of Le Mans by heart before he left for Angers in 1818. It was at Angers that his liturgical horizons began to broaden, and subsequently he began to be impressed by both the Roman liturgy as a bearer of tradition and the Roman chants. Further study led him to appreciate the medieval Roman-Gallican rites. Guéranger deeply valued the dogmatic character of the liturgy, and his insistence on this dogmatic stability led him to esteem the liturgy as both a witness to tradition and the living voice of tradition.

Guéranger's interest in monastic life developed slowly. It was first awakened in 1824 while he was still in the seminary. Having become familiar with the learned editions edited by the Benedictines of the Congregation of St. Maur, he felt called to that type of scholarly religious life. He discussed this prospect with M. Heurtebize, one of his professors in the seminary at Le Mans, who admitted to also being interested in Benedictine life. Because it was not possible to become a Benedictine in France at that time, the two men discussed the possibility of entering at Monte Cassino in Italy, but nothing came of these youthful aspirations. Three years later, on the day of his ordination to the priesthood at Tours, Guéranger visited the ruined abbey of Marmoutier and prayed that God might raise up men to restore such ruined places and defend the liberty of the Church. Four years later, in the spring of 1831 the priory buildings of Solesmes, which he had known from his youth, were put up for sale. This was the turning point for Guéranger's vocation. The priory buildings were in danger of being destroyed, and Guéranger marshaled all his forces to preserve the former Benedictine monastery in his native town.

Guéranger's monastic calling can be considered a true charism. With no monastic training and no experience of religious community, he approached his bishop on 29 November 1831 with a proposal to restore Solesmes as a Benedictine monastery and center of ecclesiastical learning. Two principles guided Guéranger and Solesmes from the very beginning: (1) the celebration of the liturgy was to take precedence over every other activity of the monastery, and (2) Benedictine life involved a commitment to serious study of the things of God for the sanctification of the monk and service of the Church. The liturgical mission of Solesmes was confirmed by Pope Gregory XVI (1831–1846) in 1837 in the apostolic brief *Innumeras inter*, in which he stated that Solesmes was "to revive pure traditions of worship." This liturgical mission was carried out with emphases on tradition, community, objectivity, and international solidarity.

On 11 July 1833 Guéranger, with one companion, Abbé Fonteinne, who was also a diocesan priest, restored monastic life at Solesmes. The monastic foundation at Solesmes was traditional in that it looked to the past for its models, but it was up-to-date as well, as it sought to establish a revived community life appropriate to the conditions of the time. Sixth-century monks had lived in social conditions rather similar to those that surrounded Solesmes at the time of its restoration; that is, social chaos ensued in the conflict between a dying culture and the forces of radical social change. The success of Solesmes showed how Benedictine monasteries could contribute to solidifying Catholic culture and evangelizing secular society.

Guéranger's efforts at refounding Benedictine life in France were confirmed on 14 July 1837, when the Holy See officially approved the foundation of Solesmes and established the Congregation of France, as the Solesmes Congregation was initially known. On 26 July 1837 Dom Guéranger professed his vows as a Benedictine at St. Paul's-outside-the-Walls in Rome.

Although Guéranger's foundation at Solesmes was traditional and although he valued highly the study of ecclesiastical and monastic tradition, he was critical of those who, disillusioned with the present and skeptical about the future, studied history and archaeology as a form of escapism. In Guéranger's view, the past should be studied in order to understand the present and to discern how things should be.

Guéranger's influence on Benedictine monasticism and liturgical practice in the Catholic Church cannot be overestimated. The monastery of Solesmes grew into a congregation that was canonically erected in 1837. In 1995 the Solesmes Congregation numbered 18 monasteries of monks with 746 members and eight monasteries of nuns with 281 members. The Congregation of Solesmes spread beyond the borders of France into Spain, Luxembourg, England, Holland, Canada, Senegal, the French Antilles, and the United States.

Guéranger's influence in the monastic world was extended significantly when Maurus and Placidus Wolter, the founders of the Benedictine monastery at Beuron, Germany (1863), took monastic life at Solesmes as the model for their own foundation and transposed it into a German setting. Through his connections with Beuron, Guéranger influenced directly and in significant ways all the monasteries of the Beuronese Congregation as well as those founded from or shaped in some way by Beuronese practice. These include the Congregation of the Annunciation (formerly the Belgian Congregation), the Congregation of St. Ottilien, and the Brazilian Congregation. In 1995 fully one-third of all Benedictine monks belonged to monasteries either founded by Guéranger or significantly influenced by him.

*Sacrosanctum concilium*, the Constitution on the Sacred Liturgy of the Second Vatican Council (4 December 1963), which decreed the renewal of the Latin liturgy of the Catholic Church, was shaped significantly by the liturgical mission fostered so assiduously by Guéranger, Solesmes, and the monasteries formed in their liturgical tradition.

KURT BELSOLE, O.S.B.

*See also* Beuron, Germany; Congregations, Benedictine; France: History; Liturgical Movement 1830–1980; Liturgy: Western Christian; Maurists; Music: Christian Perspectives; Office, Daily: Western Christian; Scholars, Benedictine; Wolter, Maurus; Wolter, Placidus

## Biography

Born at Sablé-sur-Sarthe near Le Mans, France, Guéranger became a priest in that diocese in 1827. Inspired by the Church Fathers and contemporary writers, he aspired to make the liturgy a vehicle of authenticity. When the priory buildings of Solesmes in his hometown came up for sale in 1831, he undertook to establish Solesmes as a center of Benedictine renewal. The monastery re-opened in 1833 and ignited liturgical reform, not least in alliance with the Wolter brothers at Beuron. Solesmes is renowned above all for research on plainchant.

## Major Works

*Institutions liturgiques*, 3 vols., 1840–1851
*L'Année liturgique*, 9 vols., 1841–1866; as *The Liturgical Year*, volumes 1–12 translated by Laurence Shepherd, volumes 13–15 translated by Stanbrook Abbey, 1883–1903
*Religious and Monastic Life Explained*, translated by Jerome Veth, 1908
*The Spirit of Solesmes*, 1997

## Further Reading

Franklin, R.W., "Guéranger: A View on the Centenary of His Death," *Worship* 49:6 (1975)
Franklin, R.W., "Guéranger and Pastoral Liturgy," *Worship* 50:2 (1976)
Franklin, R.W., "Guéranger and Variety in Unity," *Worship* 51:5 (1977)
Franklin, R.W. "The Nineteenth Century Liturgical Movement," *Worship* 53:1 (1979)
Johnson, Cuthbert, "Prosper Guéranger, Abbot of Solesmes," *Questions Liturgiques* 64 (1983)
Johnson, Cuthbert, *Prosper Guéranger (1805–1875): A Liturgical Theologian*, Rome: Pontificio Ateneo S. Anslemo, 1984
Pfaff, Maurus, "Dom Prosper Guéranger Abt von Solesmes," *Erbe und Auftrag* 51 (1975)
Pfaff, Maurus, "Dom Prosper Guéranger und Maurus Wolter," in *Commentaria in s. Regulam*, edited by Jean Gribomont, Rome: Edizioni Abbazia S. Paolo, 1982
Rees, Daniel, "The Benedictine Revival in the Nineteenth Century," in *Benedict's Disciples*, edited by D.H. Farmer, Leominster, Herefordshire: Fowler Wright, 1980; Harrisburg, Pennsylvania: Gracewing, 1995
Soltner, Louis, "Beuron und Dom Guéranger," *Erbe und Auftrag* 51 (1975)
Soltner, Louis, *Solesmes and Dom Guéranger, 1805–1875*, translated by Joseph O'Connor, Orleans, Massachusetts: Paraclete, 1995
Ward, Anthony, "Jean-Claude Colin on Prosper Guéranger: 'Dom Guéranger rend un service immense à l'Église'," *Ephemerides Liturgicae* 103 (1989)

# Guigo I 1083–1136

French prior of La Grande-Chartreuse, legislator,
and author

Also known as Guigues de Châtel, the fifth prior of La Grande-Chartreuse worked also as legislator and spiritual writer. According to tradition he was born at the Sancti Romani castle in the Diocese of Valence. Modern scholars identify this place with St.-Romain-de-Mordanne in the commune of St.-Barthélémy-le-Plain (Ardèche) or with St.-Romain-de-Leprs, about 6 miles to the south.

Guigo became a monk at La Grande-Chartreuse in 1106, becoming prior three years later. He performed this duty until his death on 27 July 1136. After an avalanche destroyed the monastery in 1132, Guigo rebuilt it on the present site. Very active, he was a friend of Peter the Venerable (1092/94–1156) and Bernard of Clairvaux (1090–1153).

While he was prior the Carthusians, who until then owned only two monasteries far removed from each other (La Grande-Chartreuse in the French Alps and Santa Maria della Torre in Calabria), grew into a real order. At least seven new charterhouses were founded. Apart from Guigo's energy and talents, this quick development owed much to the unwavering support given to the Order by St. Hugh I, bishop of Grenoble (d. 1 April 1132). The *Life of Hugh* was written by Guigo at the request of Pope Innocent II (1130–1143) for the purpose of his canonization, which was pronounced in 1135.

The most important work by Guigo is *Consuetudines Cartusiae* (The Customs of the Carthusians), written in 1121–1128 at the joint request of St. Hugh, bishop of Grenoble; three priors of new charterhouses (Bernhard of Portes, Humbert of St.-Sulpice, and Milo of Meyriat); and Peter the Venerable. In 1133 it received the approval of Pope Innocent II. It consists of 80 short chapters concerned with liturgy (1–8), monks (9–41), *conversi* (42–76), fugitives and *numerus clausus* (77–79), and the glory of the sequestered life. It builds on the ancient monastic tradition, on the Rule of St. Benedict, and on the liturgical habits of the regular canons of St. Ruf. The work was printed for the first time in 1510 together with monastic statutes by John Amorbach at the request of the general chapter of the Carthusians. *Consuetudines Cartusiae* was approved by the first general chapter of the Carthusians (1140 or 1141) as binding on the Order and have since functioned as a rule.

Between 1109 and 1115 Guigo wrote 476 meditations. Nine of his letters are also extant. Among those of particular interest is "Lettre à un amie sur la vie solitaire" (Letter to a Friend on the Secluded Life), which summarizes Guigo's views on the Carthusian vocation.

MAREK DERWICH

*See also* Bernard of Clairvaux, St.; Carthusains; Cluny, Abbots of; France: History; Liturgy: Western Christian; Regulations: Christian Perspectives

## Biography

Born near Valence in the Valley of the Rhone, Guigo entered La Grande-Chartreuse at age 23 in 1106 and served as its fifth prior from 1109 until his death in 1136. He compiled the Carthusian Customary for use by daughter houses.

## Major Works

*Consuetudines Cartusiae*, in *Patrologia Latina*, volume 153; as *Coutumes de Chartreuse* (Sources Chrétiennes, 313), edited by M. Laporte, 1984

*Meditationes*, edited by A. Wilmart, in *Études de Philosophie Médievale* 22 (1936); as *Guiges Ier, prieur de Chartreuse, Les Meditations Chartreuse* (Sources Chrétiennes, 308), edited by M. Laporte, 1983; as *The Meditations of Guigo, Prior of the Charterhouse*, translated and with an introduction by A.G. Mursell, 1995

*Vita sancti Hugonis gratianopolitani episcopi*, in *Patrologia Latina*, volume 153; also edited by Ch. Bellet, 1889; as "Vie de Saint Hugues, Évêque de Grenoble, l'Ami des Moines," translated by M.A. Chomel, annotated and with an introduction by B. Bligny, *Analecta Cartusiana* 112/113 (1986)

Guigo edited the *Letters* of Jerome.

## Further Reading

Un chartreux, "La jeunesse de Guigues le Chartreux," *Revue drômoise* 83 (1983)

Dubois, Jacques, "Les institutions monastiques du XIIe siècle: À propos des coutumes de Chartreuse rédigées par Guignes et éditées par un Chartreux," *Revue d'histoire de l'Église de France* 72 (1986); also in Dubois' *Aspects de la vie monastique en France au Moyen Âge*, Aldershot, Hampshire, and Brookfield, Vermont: Variorum, 1993

Gilson, Étienne, "Présentation de Guiges I," *La Vie spirituelle, ascétique et mystique* 40 (1934)

Gruys, Albert, *Cartusiana: Un instrument heuristique*, volume 1: *Bibliographie générale, auteurs cartusiens*, Paris: CNRS, 1976

Hacquard, G., "La vie cartusienne d'après le prieur Guiges I," *Revue des sciences religieuse de l'Université de Strasbourg* 31 (1957)

Hacquard, G., "Lettre du prieur Guigues Ier à un amie sur la vie solitaire," *Analecta Cartusiana* 82 (1980)

Mursell, Gordon, *The Theology of the Carthusian Life in the Writings of St. Bruno and Guido I*, Salzburg: Institut für Anglistik und Amerikanistik, Universität Salzburg, 1988

Poisson, A., *La doctrine monastique des Coutumes de Guiges*, Paris, 1961

Raby, F.J.E., "Guigo I, prior of the Grande Chartreuse 'To Himself'," *Laudate* 15 (1937)

Rieder, Bruno, *Eus locum dabit: Studien zur Theologie des Kartäuserpriors Guigo I: (1083–1136)*, Paderborn: Schöningh, 1997

Tugwell, Simon, *The Ways of Imperfection*, London: Darton, Longman and Todd, and Springfield, Illinois: Templegate, 1984

Voilin, H., "Un penseur inconnu: Guigues le chartreux," *Bulletin mensuel de l'Académie Delphinale de Grenoble* 8:4 (1972)

Wilmart, André, "Les écrits spirituels des deux Guigues," *Revue d'ascétique et de mystique* 5 (1924); reprinted in Wilmart's *Auteurs Spirituels et Textes Dévots du Moyen Âge latin*, Paris: Bloud et Gay, 1932

## Gyatso, Tenzin. *See* Dalai Lama

# H

**Habit.** *See* Clothing: Christian Perspectives

## Hagiography: Buddhist Perspectives

Buddhist hagiography resembled its Christian counterpart in many ways. Both were didactic, provided exemplars of conduct, commemorated the deaths of the saints, celebrated the potency of their relics, and were written by the faithful, engaged "historians." Yet the subjects differed considerably. Christian saints tended to be martyrs, whereas Indian Buddhist saints tended to be renouncers. This was because Buddhists were motivated by the promise of escape from sufferings caused by desire, Christians by the promise of salvation by passing the trials set by God. Moreover, Buddhist hagiography was founded on four totally different premises.

First, the doctrine of rebirth meant that each life, or cluster of lives, was but one in a succession of lives. The lineage of rebirths of what might be called a "complex of consciousness" justified the writing of a series of hagiographies. Souls were held not to exist, so no individual egos were possible. Rebirths were narrated in company with those with whom a person had shared karmic affinities, such as family members, companions, or even enemies. The rebirths were thought to express the transmission of teachings. Thus, the earliest forms of Indian Buddhist hagiography were the *jātaka*s, or the previous lives of the Buddha remembered and related by him to illustrate the consequences of moral actions and the doctrine of rebirth itself. A connected genre were the *avadāna*, the lives of arhats (saints, "stream winners") and disciples through their rebirths, which told how they ineluctably attained sainthood after making a vow that was confirmed by Buddha in one of his incarnations.

Second, the course of these lives was governed by causation, that is, by the action of karma or deeds and their results. The Buddha or paragon, as a human being, had to overcome the consequences of his past deeds and so exemplified causation. Originally, no biography of the Buddha existed; in an attempt to avoid deification, he was not even depicted graphically. However, as popular devotion intensified, a biography was gradually pieced out of the incidents in the sūtras and vinaya (rules of discipline) that supplied the context for a doctrine or monastic rule. Later, motifs from the myths of Indian heroes were incorporated into the hagiography, giving it a more supernatural dimension.

Third, no divine intervention in the karmic "moral patterning" existed because the Buddha was held not to have experienced divine revelation but rather to have realized the laws of the universe. Although gods exist in Buddhist cosmology, they too are subject to the workings of karma. Thus, the supernatural is always subsidiary and its assistance merely the outcome of the saint's accumulated merit.

Fourth, time was conceived to be cyclical, unfolding in a spiral, and lacked the unilinear, teleological trajectory familiar in Christian thought. Thus, each buddha and saint, along with his associates, repeated approximately the same life course. By the fifth century the life of the Buddha became relatively fixed, and in East Asia the hagiography was summarized in eight set scenes (*baxiang*), both in literature and art. The lives of the saints were patterned similarly, for they imitated Buddha, and accounts are given of their previous lives, their vow, its acceptance by the Buddha in a prediction, and the working through in this human life of the remaining influences of past evil actions and the elimination of their consequences by means of the saint's achievements. The lives of local saints were more historically immediate substitutes for that of the Buddha and were not so hidden as to disguise the model. This hagiography grew out of the feeling that the Śākyamuni Buddha was in the distant past, that the Maitreya Buddha (the coming buddha) in the far future, and that the timeless Corpus of the Dharma (*Dharmakāya*, a notion that in Mahāyāna meant the body of the Buddha as principle, one that could be manifested in various forms in all the parallel worlds of sentient existence) had to be revealed in more recent or accessible saints, preferably living in the country of the hagiographer. The earlier, imperfect rebirths and their culmination in sainthood also promised everyone that they too had the potential to become a saint and gain deliverance. The final Indic development, the genealogies (*vaṃśa*), organized these lives and rebirths into a cogent order, furnished the Buddha with a royal lineage, and displayed some sense of the transmission of the teachings and monastic rules. Thus, the mature Indic hagiography of the Buddha had four components: *jātaka*s, genealogies, career from birth to enlightenment through to ministry, and the prelude to and death events, plus the history of his relics.

Indic hagiography tended to ignore secular time and circumstances, such as dates, family names, and years as a monk. The saints lived in an almost seamless, uniform cosmos, perhaps reflective of the timeless states of meditation and the moral patterning of karma. Thus, even as late as the hagiographies of the tantric *siddha*s (awakened ones) written in the later 11th and early 12th centuries, the narrative follows a ritualized, repetitive pattern. The Indian hagiographies became the models for those of Southeast Asia and Tibet. The Tibetans developed this to its conclusion in their *'khruṅs-rab* (histories of incarnation), in which they claimed to be able to discern the previous rebirths of a saint. They even permitted simultaneous lives for the same "personality," as the cosmos is timeless and saints are unfettered by it. Their whole concept of biography, as *rnam-thar* (the course to liberation), displays the rationale of Buddhist hagiography.

In Sinitic or East Asian Buddhism, hagiographies were influenced by both the Indic tradition and Confucian historiography, which required of its *liezhuan* (connected biographies) a grounding in secular time and mundane reality. This had an effect on Buddhist hagiography similar to the results of demands made of Christian authors of vitae from the 13th century onward to provide evidence for canonization: attention to time, place, sources, verification, and "historical fact." Sinitic hagiography tended to humanize its subjects, for Confucians were wary of the supernatural, and many wrote the sources that hagiographies were based on, but this did not preclude Buddhist inclusion of the supernatural into the mundane life course. The lives were conventions, grouped into types that exemplified the living out of a role – a notion that muffled the personality. Here too the initiators of most early hagiographies were the Vinaya teachers, who wanted to illustrate proper behavior and monastic conduct. Later, competition between Buddhist "schools" in East Asia produced a plethora of hagiographies. Chan especially wrote histories of the "transmission of the lamp" (*chuandeng*) or enlightened mind, reducing hagiographies to the essentials of the occasions of enlightenment in a bare historical skeleton. The Chinese veneration of transmission rather than of creativity reinforced Indic "moral patterning" to create the impression of the unchanging identity of the teachings. East Asian hagiography also introduced fear of the degeneration of Buddhism in the so-called end period of the dharma (*mofa*). This presentiment of negative change resulted in time taking on greater significance and coming to resemble more, in Japan especially, the Christian notions of the millennium and the Second Coming.

JOHN JORGENSEN

*See also* Body: Buddhist Perspectives; Buddha (Śākyamuni); Buddhist Schools/Traditions; Tibetan Lineages

## Further Reading

Bekker-Nielsen, Hans, Peter Foote, Jørgen Højgaard Jørgensen, and Tore Nyberg, editors, *Hagiography and Medieval Literature: A Symposium*, Odense: Odense University Press, 1981

Frauwallner, Erik, *The Earliest Buddhist Vinaya and the Beginnings of Buddhist Literature*, Rome: Is. M.E.O., 1956
Goodrich, Michael, *Vita Perfecta: The Ideal of Sainthood in the Thirteenth Century*, Stuttgart: Anton Hiersemann, 1982
Granoff, Phyllis, and Koichi Shinohara, editors, *Monks and Magicians: Religious Biographies in Asia*, Oakville, Ontario: Mosaic Press, 1988
Jorgensen, John, "Korean Buddhist Historiography," *Pulgyo Yŏn'gu* 14 (1997)
Kakhun, Sok, compiler, *Lives of Eminent Korean Monks: The Haedong kosŭng chŏn*, translated by Peter Lee, Cambridge, Massachusetts: Harvard University Press, 1969
Nattier, Jan, *Once Upon a Future Time: Studies in a Buddhist Prophecy of Decline*, Berkeley, California: Asian Humanities Press, 1991
Reynolds, Frank, "The Many Lives of the Buddha," in *The Biographical Process: Studies in the History and Psychology of Religion*, edited by Frank E. Reynolds and Donald Capps, The Hague: Mouton, 1976
Robinson, James B., translator, *Buddha's Lions: The Lives of the Eighty-Four Siddhas*, Berkeley, California: Dharma, 1979
Schober, Juliane, editor, *Sacred Biography in the Buddhist Traditions of South and Southeast Asia*, Honolulu: University of Hawaii Press, 1997
Tambiah, Stanley Jeyeraja, *The Buddhist Saints of the Forest and the Cult of Amulets: A Study in Charisma, Hagiography, Sectarianism, and Millennial Buddhism*, Cambridge: Cambridge University Press, 1984
Ts'ao Shih-pang, "Zhongguo Fojiao shizhuan yu mulu yuanchu Lüxue shamen zhi tandao," *Xinya xuebao* (*Hsin-Ya Hsüeh-Pao*) 6:1 (1964), 7:1 (1965), 7:2 (1966)
Vostrikov, Andrei I., *Tibetan Historical Literature*, translated by Harish Chandra Gupta, Calcutta: Indian Studies Past and Present, 1970; Richmond, Surrey: Curzon Press, 1994
Warder, Anthony K., *An Introduction to Indian Historiography*, Bombay: Popular Prakashan, 1972
Wright, Arthur F., "Biography and Hagiography: Hui-chiao's 'Lives of Eminent Monks'," in *Silver Jubilee Volume of the Zinbun Kagaku kenkyusyo*, Kyoto: Kyoto University, 1954; reprinted in *Studies in Chinese Buddhism*, edited by Robert M. Somers, New Haven, Connecticut: Yale University Press, 1990
Wright, Dale S., "Historical Understanding: The Chan Buddhist Transmission Narratives and Modern Historiography," *History and Theory* 31:1 (1992)

# Hagiography: Christian Perspectives

The early spread of monasticism owes more to hagiography as a means of communicating its ideals and practices than to anything else. It was the rapid spread of the lives (vitae as a literary form) of the early desert monks that led to familiarity with them as Christian heroes and models for imitation. The first, and paradigmatic, vita of Antony of Egypt (c. 251–356) was written shortly after Antony's death by Athanasius (c. 296–373). It recounts Antony's vocation and asceticism but especially his conflicts with demons. It is victory over them that makes him a man of Christian *arete/virtus* (prowess). Athanasius' aim is clear from his preface: once you know Antony's struggles and how he won them, "you will be able to train with zeal to imitate him." Athanasius assumes that a way of life is learned better through imitation of lifestyle and habit than through a theoretical presentation, "for Antony's life is an appropriate guide to monks in asceticism." Thus, the rationale of the vita is moral rather than historical, and any information that proves useful for understanding Antony's biography is incidental. However, the mode of presentation is historical rather than systematic: thus, when Athanasius laid out an ascetic scheme (16–34) that was in effect the first monastic rule, he put it into Antony's mouth, giving it a *Sitz-im-Leben* as a long sermon. Translated into Latin around 360 by Evagrius of Antioch (c. 320–394), this text exerted influence throughout the empire within decades, as Augustine witnesses. It was later translated into Syriac, Armenian, and Arabic.

Jerome (c. 345–420) next added to monastic hagiography, inspired directly by Athanasius. His life of Paul of Thebes (written c. 376) was to determine who had been the first desert hermit. Around 391 Jerome wrote vitae of Malchus and Hilarion. Although his purpose is moral in all three, the later ones more obviously supply a guide to being a hermit as well as describe the routine of a group of ascetics, all this interspersed with the miracles of these Palestinian monks. These vitae were popular in Latin and were translated into Greek, Coptic, Syriac, Armenian, Old Slavonic, Ethiopian, and Arabic.

The third highly influential piece of hagiography was Palladius' *Historia Lausiaca* (c. 419–420). Inspired by Athanasius (cf. 8, 6), Palladius (c. 364–420/30) stated that his aim was to provide learners with models of imitation from those strong in faith and ascetic endurance (see Palladius' Letter to Lausus). He supplied 71 such models by name and uniquely included women, even depicting them teaching men (55, 1). His influence shows in the range of translation: Latin, Coptic, Syriac, Armenian, Ethiopian, Arabic, and even Old Sogdian.

Hagiography remained a favorite means of inculcating the monastic life. The success of Cassian's writings is due in large part to their hagiographic setting. Later the spread of Benedict's fame was due to hagiography in Gregory the Great's *Dialogi*. Everywhere that monasticism spread, so did the practice of treasuring and writing vitae, as the works by Adomnán (on Columba), Bede (on Cuthbert), and Rhigyfarch (on David) in the British Isles testify. This influence owed partly to the vitae's attractiveness as stories but also to structural features within monasticism. Insofar as a monk is a disciple of an elder who already knows through experience the monastic life, so

Rock of the Stigmata, mounted in the Chapel of St. Bonaventure, La Verna (Tuscany), Italy. Said to be the rock on which St. Francis received the stigmata in September 1224.
Photo courtesy of Mary Schaefer

hagiography provided proven masters for imitation. This notion became built into monastic routine through the value placed on reading vitae as an activity. For example, Benedict's rule stipulates that on nonfasting days the monks are to sit together after supper and listen "to Cassian's *Collations* and the Lives of the Fathers" for edification (42).

As a genre hagiography shares some features with ancient biography and aretology and some surface similarities with modern biographies but should not be confused with either. Although vitae often feature a temporal sequence (childhood, adulthood, and death) and have often been viewed by historians as biographies, historical details should be construed as accidental. The intention was not to narrate the events of a life but to show that God is "glorified in his saints" (1 Thess. 1:10). Events are recorded so as to make this plain. If a saint is a heroic Christian, he is also a man of power, for through him Christ has worked miracles. Thus, a saint is one who can be looked on as an exemplar and imitated (cf. 1 Cor. 11:1). To this end the material is arranged, sermons and lessons are put in his mouth, and the spiritual contest is narrated. The saint as teacher relies not on learning, for many vitae have the topos of "the holy fool" (cf. 2 Cor. 11), but on his own lived experience. Often it is his triumph over demons that gives him authority. Vitae portray the saint as one who has "fought the good fight . . . finished the race . . . kept the faith" (2 Tim. 4:7), "not . . . against flesh and blood, but against the principalities, against the powers, against the world rulers of this present darkness, against the spiritual hosts of wickedness in the heavenly places" (Eph. 6:12). Thus, vitae should be read on a mythic level as regards the miraculous element, often on a liturgical level as regards times and significant events, and on a moral level as showing the superiority of the ascetic life over ordinary Christian life. Writers assumed that the way to wisdom could be revealed more perfectly by description than by prescription, and this hortatory purpose should be seen as primary.

Vitae present us with a hermeneutical task of great complexity. They did succeed in persuading many to choose the monastic life. Followers mimicked even small details (e.g., Irish monks copied the stone cells built, according to Palladius, by Dorotheus), and vitae could lead to religious conversion (see Augustine, *Confessiones* 8, 6–8 on Athanasius). Yet many readers today find vitae repellent: their miracles might seem incredible and detrimental to faith, their accounts of demons might seem silly or evidence for psychological disorders (e.g., *Vita Antonii* 8), and tales involving chastity evidence a profound antibody fascination. Vitae vividly show the shift in worldviews between the patristic period and ours. This "gap" raises an existential question: if many aspects of the monastic life grew to prominence largely because they were presented as ideals in these vitae, and if we no longer find these documents religiously credible, then perhaps those ideals themselves must be reexamined. "The example of the holy fathers" becomes for us problematic.

THOMAS O'LOUGHLIN

*See also* Antony, St.; Asceticism: Christian Perspectives; Benedict of Nursia, St.; Cassian, John; Gregory I (the Great), St.; Hagiography: Eastern Christian; Hagiography: Western Christian; Origins: Eastern Christian; Spirituality: Eastern Christian; Transvestite Saints

**Further Reading**
Butler, Cuthbert, editor, *The Lausiac History of Palladius: A Critical Discussion Together with Notes on Early Egyptian Monasticism*, Cambridge: Cambridge University Press, 1898
Butler, Cuthbert, editor, *The Lausiac History of Palladius: The Greek Text Edited with Introduction and Notes*, Cambridge: Cambridge University Press, 1904
Cusack, Pierce, *An Interpretation of the Second Dialogue of Gregory the Great: Hagiography and St. Benedict*, Lewiston, New York: Mellen Press, 1993
Deferrari, Roy J., editor, *Early Christian Biographies* (Athanasius, *Life of Antony*, translated by Mary Emily Keenan; Jerome, *Lives of Paul, Hilarion*, and *Malchus*, translated by Marie Liguori Ewald), Washington, D.C.: Catholic University of America Press, 1952
Delehaye, Hippolyte, *The Legends of the Saints*, translated by Donald Attwater and introduced by Thomas O'Loughlin, reprint, Dublin and Portland, Oregon: Four Courts Press, 1998
Driver, Steve, "From Palestinian Ignorance to Egyptian Wisdom: Jerome and Cassian on the Monastic Life," *American Benedictine Review* 48 (1997)
Meyer, Robert T., editor, *Palladius: The Lausiac History*, Westminster, Maryland: Newman Press, 1965
Oldfather, William Abbott, editor, *Studies in the Text Tradition of St. Jerome's Vitae Patrum*, Urbana: University of Illinois Press, 1943
Petersen, Joan M., *The Dialogues of Gregory the Great in Their Late Antique Cultural Background*, Toronto: Pontifical Institute of Mediaeval Studies, 1984

# Hagiography: Eastern Christian

Hagiography is one of the genres of Eastern ecclesiastical literature. In plain terms hagiography is the biography of a holy person enriched sometimes with a list of posthumous miracles performed by the saint's relic. Its roots go back to the period of the persecutions of Christians. Modern Orthodox Christianity continues the tradition, and a number of hagiographies written about modern saints have been produced even in the 20th century in Orthodox Christian countries (e.g., Greece and Russia). Since its appearance hagiography has served numerous purposes, the major ones being as follows: (1) establishing the holiness of a virtuous person (although the case here is not clear; i.e., was a person canonized as a result, among other things, of the existence of his hagiographic account, or did the canonization of a person demand the creation of a life?); (2) commemorating the deeds and the virtuous life of an established saint; (3) honoring a saint; (4) edifying and entertaining the faithful; and (5) serving liturgical purposes, that is, the vita of the saint (or more often an abridged version of it called *synaxary note*) was read on the commemoration day in the course of the liturgy.

The earliest form of hagiography is the *martyrion*, the account of the trial and execution of the early Christian martyrs. After the cessation of the persecutions, another major type of hagiography appears among the early monastic circles of Egypt in the fourth century. This is the life (vita) proper of a particular saint. The earliest exponent of this type is the famous fourth-century *Life of St. Antony* (*Vita Antonii*) attributed to Athanasius (c. 296–373), patriarch of Alexandria. Since the appearance of this type of hagiography, the vast majority of the saints' lives up to modern times have dealt with holy persons who lived part if not all of their adult lives in the monastic habit. For example, 53 lives and *synaxary notes* for saints of the ninth century are preserved. Only four of these narrate the life of laypersons who achieved sanctity. Two more lives describe the career of ecclesiastical officials (*Life of John of Polyboton* and *Theokletos of Lacedaimon*), whereas the remaining 47 are lives of monks.

The third form of hagiography that also appeared in Egypt is the *Sayings of the Fathers* (*Apophthegmata Patrum*), that is, collections of short stories that display the wisdom of early hermits. Probably after the seventh century, collections of posthumous miracles performed by relics of saints appear as a separate type. In later centuries encomia and panegyrics, usually based on already existing lives, form the latest development in hagiography. Most of the Eastern hagiographies are written in Greek, but numerous ones exist as well written in Syriac, Coptic, Armenian, Georgian, and Arabic. After the major separations that occurred in the Eastern Church with the secession of the Nestorian and Monophysite Churches from the mid–fifth to mid–sixth century, Greek becomes by far the dominant language in hagiography (later Arabic covered a small portion).

The first lives, namely, these of Saint Antony (c. 251–356) and St. Pachomius (c. 290–346), not only establish hagiography as a literary genre but also contain the bulk of information about the formation of Christian monasticism. Although preceded by a number of earlier solitary monks, Antony stands as the founder of Egyptian solitary monasticism. The *Vita Antonii* traces the major steps in his monastic career. Antony flees from his village to the desert and devotes himself to rigorous mortification of the flesh. He spends long periods sleepless and under a strict fasting regimen; he fights the demons and tames the wild beasts. In the sequel disciples gather around Antony, and his role becomes more public. He persuades many to take monastic vows and performs a number of healing miracles. He even defends Christianity against pagans and gets involved in the ecclesiastical developments of his times. In terms of content this is roughly the model followed by most later hagiographers.

The various lives of St. Pachomius record the development of the communal (cenobitic) monastic life in Tabennesi of Upper Egypt. Pachomius organized large monastic communities of thousands of people living under common rules. Monks lived in a walled camp divided into "houses," spent much time in manual labor, worshiped, prayed and ate together, and practiced obedience to the monastic superior along with poverty and abstinence.

The spread of monasticism to neighboring Palestine and Syria is recorded in the hagiographic work of Cyril of Scythopolis (sixth-century author) and Theodorete of Cyrus (c. 393–c. 460), respectively. In fifth-century Palestine we witness the institution of the *lavra*, a form of monasticism combining solitary with communal ascetic life. The monks of the *lavra* lived in individual cells or caves and gathered every Sunday at the communal church and refectory to celebrate the Eucharist and eat together. The founders of the *lavra* system were Euthymius (377–473) and Sabas the Great (439–532). Their lives are among the works of Cyril of Scythopolis.

In Syria monasticism developed on a solitary basis, and Theodorete, bishop of Cyrus, in his *Philotheos Historia*, includes the account of the deeds of 30 saints. Symeon the Elder Stylite (c. 390–459) figures prominently among them for his rigorous practices. He spent the major part of his ascetic life standing on a pillar (*stylos*, thus "stylite") exposed to the elements of nature and constantly praying and fasting. Although very few in numbers, imitators of Symeon the Elder appeared through the later centuries, and as late a saint as the 11th-century Lazaros Galesiotes spent part of his monastic life on a pillar. Even Constantinople acquired its own stylite saint, Daniel, in the fifth century. Saint Daniel's life, written around 500, is a rich source of information pertaining to the Church and political history of the fifth century.

In Syria originates another rare case of a holy man: the holy fool. Symeon of Emesa, or Symeon the Fool, whose life was written by the seventh-century Cypriot bishop Leontios of Neapolis, spent half his life as a strict ascetic. Then he returned to the civilized world, only to behave in a manner that defied all social conventions. The author of this vita assures us that Symeon behaved so first to conceal his holiness and second to entice to repentance those who needed his help the most, namely, the marginal elements of the society (e.g., prostitutes and innkeepers).

The period up to the first half of the seventh century concludes with the excellent hagiographies written by some highly educated monks and ecclesiastics, such as Sophronios of Jerusalem, John Moschos, Leontios of Neapolis, and John the Almsgiver. John Moschos (c. 550–619/34) has become famous as the author of the *Pratum Spirituale* (*Leimonarion*). This work is a collection of short stories that resemble much the *Sayings of the Fathers* in form and contain all the memorable narratives and sayings that Moschos jotted down in his peregrinations among the major monastic centers of Egypt, Palestine, and Syria.

Hagiography entered a period of decline after the expansion of Islam in the Eastern parts of the Old Roman world during the second half of the seventh century. However, a remarkable regeneration took place just around the end of the eighth century, and hagiography flourished from the 9th to the 11th century. The hagiography of this period is characterized by a heavy focus on monasticism, something that reflects the general flourishing of Byzantine monasticism at that time. The lives of monk-saints written usually if not exclusively by fellow monks or disciples appear with much greater frequency than in the previous period. The vitae of Blasios of Amorion, Plato of Sakkoudion, Theodore of Studios, and Nicholas of Studios and possibly that of Niketas of Medicion are all products of the Monastery of Studios in

Constantinople. The lives of Constantine the Jew, Eustratios of Agauros, Ioannikios (two), Peter of Atroa, and a few others originate from the monastic milieu of Mount Olympus in Bithynia.

Monastic heroes that prevailed in this period were people who built new monasteries or restored abandoned ones, such as Theodore of Stoudios, Theophanes the Confessor, Athanasios of Athos, and Lazaros of Mount Galesion. The character of the pious married woman who finds salvation by taking monastic vows provided the subject matter for a number of lives as well (e.g., Athanasia of Aegina, Theodora of Thessalonike, Anna-Euphemianos, and Mary the Younger). A third cluster of lives records the career of major patriarchs of this period, many of whom had taken monastic vows before their ascent to the patriarchal throne. These include the lives of Tarasios (exceptionally a layman before his consecration), Nikephoros I, Methodios I, Ignatios I, and Euthymios I and the funeral oration to Anthony Kauleas by Nikephoros the Philosopher. These lives do not result from as systematic a plan as do the continuous entries in the Roman *Liber Pontificalis*, but they are much more extensive and are written in high literary style.

Apart from the creation of numerous new saints' lives, the tenth century witnessed also a major movement of collecting and editing earlier lives. Niketas David Paphlagon and Symeon Metaphrastes excelled in this field. However, modern scholars regret these attempts at homogenizing and elevating the style of the earlier lives, especially those carried out by Symeon, because they resulted in the loss of the stylistic particularities of earlier hagiographers.

Hagiography in Slavic languages appears for the first time in the context of the Christianization of the Slavs in Moravia (second half of ninth century). Methodios (c. 815–885) and Cyril/ Constantine (826–869), the evangelists of the Slavs, probably translated, among other liturgical texts, the *Sayings of the Fathers* into Old Slavonic. The tradition of translations of Greek saints' lives into Slavonic continued with the life of Constantine/Cyril and Methodios. Later in the same century, this tradition was transplanted in Bulgaria, and the anonymous life of Naoum of Ochrid was written in Bulgarian by that time. Hagiographic production begins in Russia at the time of Prince Jaroslav the Wise of Kiev (1019–1054). Translations of Greek saints' lives, whose authors are mostly unknown to us, were created then. The Russian monk Nestor composed two Russian vitae: the life of the first abbot of the Kiev Crypt Monastery, St. Feodosij (d. 1073), and the life of Princes Boris and Gleb, who were murdered in 1015 and later canonized.

For Greek-speaking Christianity the period from the 11th to the mid–13th century marks another era of relative decline in hagiography. Few lives were written during these years, but it seems that some interesting traits of monasticism still survived. Stylites and holy fools are still attested in these lives (e.g., those of Lazaros of Galesion and Leontios of Jerusalem). Significant saints also appear on the periphery of the Christian world, such as Neophytos the Recluse in Cyprus. On the other hand a rather critical stance seems to develop toward monasticism on the part of educated Byzantines of that period. In turn this tendency might be connected to the fact that official Church and political

authority tried to make monks and solitary holy persons conform to established norms. This is evident among other hagiographies in the 12th-century life of Cyril Phileotes. The decline continues well into the 13th century. The fall of Constantinople to the Latins of the Fourth Crusade in 1204 might largely account for this fact. In any case the scant hagiography that exists for the 13th century narrates the lives of much earlier saints. However, a notable exception is the peculiar case of the autobiography of Nikephoros Blemmydes (1197/98–1272). A learned monk who spent his life in Nicaea, he eventually decided to write his own life, as no monk of the monastery that he had founded volunteered to fulfill that task. Needless to say Nikephoros was never canonized, but his autobiography is one of the most informative pieces of "hagiographic" literature for the period of the empire of Nicaea (1204–1261).

Despite the temporary decline hagiographic production picks up pace after the reconquest of Constantinople by Michael Palaeologos in 1261. The last two centuries of the Orthodox Christian Byzantine Empire witnessed a revival of hagiography. Not only were contemporary holy men commemorated in vitae and encomia, but a considerable number of earlier saints' lives were recast in newer versions. According to A.-M. Talbot's account, 36 lives were devoted to 32 contemporary holy men, whereas 45 different authors rewrote about 125 earlier saints' lives. These figures are by no means exhaustive. Most of the saints of the Palaeologan period were of monastic background; some of them attained high ecclesiastical status, such as Patriarch Athanasius I of Constantinople. Three or four were neomartyrs (e.g., St. Niketas the Younger) who were executed by the Muslims. Others established their holiness through opposition to the Union of the Orthodox and Catholic Churches proclaimed at Lyons in 1274 and later by supporting Hesychasm in the mid–14th century (e.g., Gregory Palamas). The credibility of the holy person that had been temporarily disputed in the Comnenian era (11th to 12th century) was reestablished, and the solitary wandering monk figures prominently among those celebrated in these hagiographies (e.g., St. Maximos Kausokalybites). Most of the authors of these lives were monks or churchmen, usually disciples of the saint they eulogized. Theoktistos of Studios and Joseph Kalothetos were two monks who wrote lives of Patriarch Athanasios I of Constantinople (r. 1289–1293 and 1303–1310).

On the other hand new vitae of old saints were written in a creative wave that borrowed much from the methodology of the tenth-century hagiographer Symeon Metaphrastes (e.g., Constantine Acropolites [fl. 1294–1321], who was hailed as the New Metaphrastes). With few exceptions these authors were not monks but, rather, well-educated people of the period. Their convictions were anti-Unionist, and among them figures one of the few female authors of Byzantium: Theodora Raoulaina wrote the vita of the brothers Theophanes and Theodore Graptoi, two Palestinian monks who had been tortured during the second Iconoclasm (830s) with iambic verses being tattooed on their foreheads.

After the fall of Constantinople to the Ottoman Turks in 1453, new crops of saints appear to multiply the ranks of the already established neomartyrs. Most of them died as a result of Muslim persecutions that were directed not only against the former Byzantine Church but also against the other Oriental Churches (Armenian, Syrian, Chaldean, Coptic, and Ethiopian). The Russian Church also has its own neomartyrs from the times of the Tatar invasions. Among these newly created saints in the period between the 15th and the 19th century, monks figure, as always, prominently. Most famous are the lives of the Thessalian monk Damianos, who was martyred in 1566, and the pious Athenian matron, Philothee Venizelou. She founded two monasteries in Athens, and she finally met with death after horrible tortures in 1589 because she had hosted four Christians whom the Turks wanted to convert to Islam. The Russian Church has canonized a number of monks and churchmen of that period, such as Philip, metropolitan of Moscow, who was martyred for the freedom of the Church under Ivan IV (1533–1584), and John of Kazan, who was killed by the Tatars in 1529.

In the Greek Church canonization of holy persons has never ceased, and even the 20th century has witnessed the presence of saintly people, such as the monk and later metropolitan (briefly of Pentapolis in Egypt) Nektarios of Aegina (d. 1920; proclaimed a saint on 20 April 1961). However, the hagiography of neomartyrs comprises a rather documentary piece of literature with no high stylistic aspirations like those of its Byzantine predecessors. Although the language is within the style frame of Orthodox Greek liturgical diction, what prevails is the recital of the bare facts, punctuated usually with detailed accounts of the tortures.

ALEXANDER ALEXAKIS

*See also* Antony, St.; Desert Fathers; Egypt; Ethiopia; Greece; Hermits: Eastern Christian; Holy Men/Holy Women: Christian Perspectives; Istanbul, Turkey; Libraries: Eastern Christian; Liturgy: Eastern Christian; Martyrs: Eastern Christian; Origins: Eastern Christian; Orthodox Monasticism; Regulations: Christian Perspectives; Relics, Christian Monastic; Russia; Sabas, St.; Seasons, Liturgical: Eastern Christian; Stylites; Theodore of Studios, St.; Transvestite Saints

### Further Reading

Repertories of Hagiographical Texts:
Halkin, François, *Bibliotheca hagiographica graeca Subsidia Hagiographica*, Brussels: Société des Bollandistes, 1957; reprint, 1985
Halkin, François, *Novum Auctarium*, Brussels: Société des Bollandistes, 1984 (a complete repertory of hagiographic texts in Greek before A.D. 1453)
Peeters, P., *Bibliotheca hagiographica orientalis*, Brussels: Apud editores, 1910; reprint, Brussels: Société des Bollandistes, 1970 (a repertory of hagiographic texts in Arabic, Armenian, Coptic, Ethiopic, and Syriac)

Repertories of Saints:
*Bibliotheca Sanctorum*, 13 vols., Rome: Istituto Giovanni XXIII nella Pontificia Università lateranense, Città Nuova Editrice, 1961–1970

Editions of Hagiographies:
Bollandus, Ioannes, *Acta Sanctorum Quotquot toto orbe coluntur, vel a Catholicis scriptoribus celebrantur quae ex latinis & graecis aliarumque gentium antiquis monumentis*, 67 vols., Paris: Palmé, 1863–1940

Secondary Bibliography:
Aigrain, René, *L'hagiographie: Ses sources, ses méthodes, son histoire*, Paris: Bloud et Gay, 1953
Brown, Peter, "The Rise and Function of the Holy Man in Late Antiquity," *Journal of Roman Studies* 61 (1971)
Delehaye, Hippolyte, *Cinq leçons sur la méthode hagiographique*, Brussels: Société des Bollandistes, 1934
Delehaye, Hippolyte, *Les passions des martyrs et les genres littéraires*, Brussels: Société des Bollandistes, 1966
Hackel, Sergei, *The Byzantine Saint: University of Birmingham, Fourteenth Spring Symposium of Byzantine Studies*, London: Fellowship of St. Alban and St. Sergius, 1981
Krueger, Derek, *Symeon the Holy Fool: Leontius's "Life" and the Late Antique City*, Berkeley: University of California Press, 1996
Salaville, S., "Pour un répertoire des Néo-Saints de l'Église Orientale," *Byzantion* 20 (1950)
Talbot, Alice-Mary, "Old Wine in New Bottles: The Rewriting of Saints' Lives in the Palaeologan Period," in *The Twilight of Byzantium: Aspects of Cultural and Religious History in the Late Byzantine Empire: Papers from the Colloquium Held at Princeton University, 8–9 May 1989*, edited by Slobodan Curcic and Doula Mouriki, Princeton, New Jersey: Department of Art and Archaeology, Program in Hellenic Studies, 1991

### Related Web Sites

*http://www.kbr.be/~socboll/index.html* (The www page of the Society of the Bollandists, exclusively dedicated to the study of Saints. Contains many links to related sites.)
*http://www.bway.net/~halsall/texts/vittrans.html* (Survey of Translations of Byzantine Saints' Lives [ordered by century in which saint lived]. This survey includes translations into modern Western European languages of Greek vitae; both published works and works in progress are listed.)
*http://cygnus.uwa.edu.au/~jgrapsas/pages/main.htm* (Orthodox Church of Australia; calendar of yearly feasts with abbreviated Saints' Lives translated into English.)

## Hagiography: Western Christian

The genus of hagiographic writing is older than monasticism, dating back to the Greek vitae of pagan holy men, the apocrypha of the Old and New Testaments, and the *passiones* of the martyrs of the old Church. During the early and High Middle Ages, the writing of "biographies" of charismatic men and women was done primarily in monasteries, and this for two reasons. On the one hand, during and after the great migrations, Latin traditions survived here only, and on the other hand, the most typical holy figures of this epoch were the abbot, the nun, and the eremite.

Although the *Vita of St. Martin* by Sulpicius Severus (c. 360–c. 430) became the most important general model for Latin hagiography, the best-known legend of a monk was the *Vita of*

*St. Benedict of Nursia*, published as book 2 of the late sixth-century *Dialogi*, a work ascribed most often, but not without contradiction, to Pope Gregory I (590–604). The number of Latin vitae of abbots or abbesses written by a monk or a nun during the Middle Ages is legion; they all usually follow the same pattern, treating at first the life of the hero (very briefly his youth and more profusely his life and miracles after the conversion) and ending with the *miracula post mortem*. Two interesting examples are the anonymous life of the Irishman Fursey (d. c. 650), who died as abbot of the Frankish monastery Lagny (this text integrated the saint's autobiographical visions), and the life of abbess Lioba of Tauberbischofsheim (d. c. 782), written by Rudolf of Fulda, O.S.B., around 838, according to the information of four pupils.

Each monastic order favored the writing of the lives of its own saints. These were used for reading aloud during meals and for preaching to pilgrims. In the late 11th and 12th centuries, a semi-hagiographic tradition existed of autobiographical accounts written by Benedictines (e.g., Othloh of St. Emmeram, Guibert of Nogent, Suger of St. Denis, and Peter Abelard), later renewed by the Dominican Henry Suso (c. 1295–1366).

With the coming of the friars, who intensified preaching, collections of the Dominican saints' lives became more sought after; it was a Dominican, Jacopo of Voragine (Varazze; c. 1230–1298), who wrote the most popular work of this type, the *Golden Legend* (c. 1260). It was soon translated into all vernacular languages and shaped the iconography of the saints in painting and sculpture as well. It goes without saying that countless individual vitae kept being written. Some authors specialized in providing hagiographic texts on request, as did Johann Gielemans (d. 1487), who compiled literally thousands of saints' lives.

The oldest vernacular songs about saints, such as the Old French Sainte Eulalie (late ninth century), the contemporary Old High German Georgslied, and those in the Old English Vercelli Book (c. 975), probably were composed and copied by monks. However, most later vernacular hagiography is due to lay authors, such as Hendric of Veldeke in Maasland, Hartmann of Aue, Germany, or, less often, secular priests, such as Gonzalo de Berceo in Spain. However, still one or another monk created a saint's legend in his native tongue, as did Beneit of St. Alban, O.S.B., author of a poem on St. Thomas Becket (c. 1185), or Lamprecht of Regensburg, who, on the point of converting to the Friars Minor, wrote a German version of Thomas of Celano's life of St. Francis around 1238.

Considering the general skepticism of older historians toward monastic (and other) hagiography of the Middle Ages, it is vital to note that the genre indeed contains fictitious texts (e.g., the lives of the Apostles) and texts of very little historical value (e.g., the stories of many martyrs), written centuries after the supposed lifetime of the texts' heroes. In addition, however, numerous vitae, especially from the 12th century on, were written by religious who had been in personal contact with the saint and who give authentic information. Thus, St. Bernard of Clairvaux wrote the life of his friend Malachy of Armagh. Bernard's own vita was written, Bernard being still alive, by blessed William of St. Thierry, O.S.B. (later O.Cist.), a man who was very close to the famous Cistercian. For similar reasons lives, such as those of St. Francis by blessed Thomas of Celano, O.F.M.; of St. Catherine of Siena, O.P.Tert., by her confessor blessed Raymond of Capua, O.P.; and of the recluse St. Dorothy of Montau by her confessor Johannes Marienwerder, T.O., are serious historical sources, notwithstanding the conventions of the hagiographic genre.

In the early modern period, it was the Jesuits who launched the most important hagiographic enterprise, namely, the collection of all the vitae of Catholic saints in the many-volumed *Acta Sanctorum* (1643– ), organized according to the calendar. As this work has remained unfinished, the group, originally founded by Jean Bolland (1596–1665), is still active today, their work proceeding very slowly. In addition, the *Acta Sanctorum Ordinis Sancti Benedicti* by Jean Mabillon (1632–1707), published in 1668–1701, should be mentioned. These tasks had been begun in an apologetic spirit, namely, to counteract Protestant criticism of what Luther had called *Lügende* (a fantasy word combined from *Legende* and *Lüge*, "lie"), but they marked the first efforts to create critical editions of this literary genre. From the 19th century on, historical work with hagiographic texts became more the task of secular historians, especially medievalists, yet some important monastic scholars remained in this field (e.g., Hippolyte Delehaye, S.J.; Boudouin Gaiffier, S.J.; and Jean Leclercq, O.S.B.). However, in the last quarter of the 20th century, the main efforts concerning monastic hagiography were undertaken by secular historians who value the wealth of information that hagiographic texts offer for the study of mentalities, everyday life, and cultural history. The leading groups now work at Italian universities, where they publish learned journals and organize specialized congresses. Today no one can deal seriously with hagiography without knowing the recent Italian secondary literature.

PETER DINZELBACHER

*See also* Bede, St.; Benedictines; Gregory I (the Great), St.; Historiography, Recent: Western Christian; Holy Men/Holy Women: Christian Perspectives; Leclercq, Jean; Maurists; Pilgrimages, Christian: Western Europe; Relics, Christian Monastic

## Further Reading

*Bibliotheca hagiographica latina antiquae et mediae aetatis* (Subsidia hagiographica, number 6), 2 vols., Brussels: Société des Bollandistes, 1898–1901; supplements, 1911, 1986

*Bibliotheca Sanctorum*, 13 vols., Rome: Istituto Giovanni XXIII nella Pontificia Università lateranense, 1961–1970

Blumenfeld-Kosinski, Renate, and Timea Szell, editors, *Images of Sainthood in Medieval Europe*, Ithaca, New York: Cornell University Press, 1991

Boesch Gajano, Sofia, editor, *Raccolte di vite di santi dal XIII als XVIII secolo: strutture, messaggi, fruizioni* (Collana del Dipartimento di studi storici dal Medioevo all'età Contemporanea, 5), Fasano di Brindisi: Schena, 1990

Boesch Gajano, Sofia, editor, *Santità, culti, agiografia: temi e prospettive: atti del I Convegno di studio dell'Associazione italiana per lo studio della santità, dei culti e dell'agiografia, Roma, 24–26 ottobre 1996*, Rome: Viella, 1997

Caffiero, Marina, et al., editors, *Modelli di santità e modelli di comportamento: contrasti, intersezioni, complementarità* (Sacro/santo, 10), Turin: Rosenberg and Sellier, 1994

Chiovaro, Francesco, editor, *Histoire des saints et de la sainteté Chrétienne*, Paris: Hachette, 1986

Dinzelbacher, Peter, and Dieter Bauer, editors, *Heiligenverehrung in Geschichte und Gegenwart*, Ostfildern: Schwabenverlag, 1990

Dubois, Jacques, and Jean Loup Lemaître, *Sources et méthodes de l'hagiographie médiévale*, Paris: Cerf, 1993

Farmer, David H., *The Oxford Dictionary of Saints*, Oxford: Clarendon Press, 1978; New York: Oxford University Press, 1982; 4th edition, Oxford and New York: Oxford University Press, 1997

*Les fonctions des saints dans le monde occidental (IIIe–XIIIe siècle): actes du colloque* (Collection de l'École française de Rome, 149), Rome: École française, 1991

Goodich, Michael, *Vita perfecta: The Ideal of Sainthood in the Thirteenth Century* (Monographien zur Geschichte des Mittelalters, 25), Stuttgart: Hiersemann, 1982

Grégoire, Réginald, *Manuale di agiologia: introduzione alla letteratura agiografica* (Bibliotheca Montisfani, volume 12), Fabriano: Monastero San Silvestro Abate, 1987; 2nd edition, 1996

Knowles, David, "The Bollandists," in his *Great Historical Enterprises*, London: Nelson, 1959; New York: Nelson, 1962

Leonardi, Claudio, "Agiografia," in *Lo spazio letterario del medioevo* 1:2, edited by Guglielmo Cavallo et al., Rome: Salerno, 1992

*Models of Holiness in Medieval Sermons: Proceedings of the International Symposium (Kalamazoo 4–7 May 1995)* (Textes et études du Moyen Âge, 5), Louvain-la-Neuve: Fédération internationale des Instituts d'études médiévales, 1996

Peeters, P., *L'oeuvre des Bollandistes* (Mémoires de la Classe des lettres), Brussels: Bureaux de la Société des Bollandistes, 1920

Philippart, Guy, editor, *Hagiographies: Histoire internationale de la littérature hagiographique latine et vernaculaire en Occident des origines à 1550 = International History of the Latin and Vernacular Hagiographical Literature in the West from Its Origins to 1550* (Corpus Christianorum. Hagiographies, 1), Turnhout: Brepols, 1994–

Sicari, Antonio, *Il grande libro dei ritratti di santi* (Già e non ancora, 324), Milan: Jaca Books, 1997

Spijker, Ienje Van 't, *Als door een speciaal stempel: Traditie en vernieuwing in heiligenlevens uit Noordwest-Frankrijk, 1050–1150* (Middeleeuwse studies en bronnen, 23), Hilversum: Verloren, 1990

Vauchez, André, *La sainteté en Occident aux derniers siècles du Moyen Age: d'après les procès de canonisation et les documents hagiographiques* (Bibliothèque des écoles françaises d'Athènes et de Rome), Rome: École française, 1981; revised edition, 1988

Wilson, Stephen, editor, *Saints and Their Cults: Studies in Religious Sociology, Folklore, and History*, Cambridge and New York: Cambridge University Press, 1983

Indispensable are the specialized reviews: *Analecta Bollandiana*, Brussels: Société des Bollandistes, 1882– ; *Hagiographica: Rivista di agiografia e biografia della Società internationale per lo studio del Medio Evo latino = Journal of Hagiography and Biography of Società internazionale per lo studio del Medio Evo latino*, Turnhout: Brepols, 1994– ; *Sanctorum. Bolletino dell'associazione italiana per lo studio della santità, dei culti e dell'agiografia*, Rome, 1996–

# Haid, Leo Michael 1849–1924

U.S. Benedictine, Catholic bishop, educator, and author

Baptized Michael Hite (the surname's spelling was later changed), Haid had association with the Order of St. Benedict from his earliest days: Michael was born in the Benedictine parish attached to St. Vincent Abbey (Latrobe, Pennsylvania), baptized in the monastery's church, and educated at the abbey from age 12 (1861) onward. In 1868 Michael was received into the Benedictine novitiate at St. Vincent, taking the name Leo in religion. He professed monastic vows in 1869, and solemn vows and priestly ordination followed in 1872. Father Leo then taught in his monastery's schools and served as their chaplain until his election as abbot of the newly independent Maryhelp (Belmont) Abbey in North Carolina (1885).

Unacquainted with Maryhelp and believing himself too young and inexperienced for abbatial office, Haid accepted his promotion reluctantly. Further cause for concern arose when, on arriving in North Carolina, he found that his monastery was a grimly ramshackle hovel with a small clapboard chapel and an unproductive farm. The Carolina college's enrollment totaled only 27 boys that year, and the monks on-site included only one other priest, five clerics, and (soon afterward) four brothers. Nonetheless, refusing to succumb to the dispiriting prospects of his abbey, Haid, reigning for 39 years, led his monks effectively in cultivating a prosperous monastic estate. Sponsoring a zealously Benedictine character, Maryhelp grew to more than 70 monks, with a stately complex of buildings, hundreds of pupils, and a unique self-contained diocesan territory. Under Haid's leadership, which he characterized as abbatial paternity, his Carolina abbey became one of the most prodigious successes in early American monasticism.

Haid's achievement in establishing a Catholic foothold in the most heavily Protestant state in the country won national and international attention and resulted in his promotion to the episcopacy. In 1887 Abbot Leo was named titular bishop of Messene and vicar-apostolic of North Carolina. However, he countered his nomination by refusing to be separated from his monastery or to relinquish his duties as abbot. In time – after intervention by James Cardinal Gibbons (the vicariate's provincial) – Rome acquiesced to Haid's conditions, agreeing that on his receipt of episcopal consecration (1888) he might serve simultaneously as both abbot and bishop.

Despite his episcopal rank Haid maintained his focus on the cloister and before long had won international prominence in the Order of St. Benedict. This recognition first arose at Rome's 1893 abbots' congress, called by Pope Leo XIII (1878–1903) to

Abbot-Bishop Leo Michael Haid, O.S.B., D.D. (1849–1924), was a Benedictine monk, abbot, bishop, abbot-*nullius*, Pontifical Count, Assistant at the Pontifical Throne, Praeses of the American Cassinese Congregation of the Order of Saint Benedict, an educator, and playwright.
Photo courtesy of Belmont Abbey Archives

invigorate the Benedictine Confederation and to create the office of abbot-primate. Throughout the congress' deliberations, Haid vociferously fought against proposals to endow the primacy with real powers. The abbot-bishop's contention, successfully argued, was that a grant to the primate of any actual jurisdiction would prove antithetical to the autonomy enjoyed by individual Benedictine monasteries.

Haid's other principal contribution to Benedictine theory and practice surfaced in the administration of the Church in North Carolina. The abbot-bishop was troubled by the incessant need of securing additional priests to staff his vicariate (an expansive territory that extended over more than 49,000 square miles). Worried that future bishops might seek to employ Belmont's monks in parishes, Abbot Leo succeeded in convincing Rome in 1910 to define his monastery as *abbatia nullius dioecesis* (an abbey of no diocese). Haid argued that juridical separation was necessary in missionary territory such as the Carolinas, for without it parochial demands would surely compromise monastic integrity.

Even in death Haid's preference for the monastic life was in evidence. When he died in 1924, he was found to have specified interment among the graves of his monks rather than in the precincts of one of his cathedrals.

PASCHAL BAUMSTEIN, O.S.B.

*See also* Abbot: Christian; United States: Western Christian

## Biography

Leo Michael Haid, a Benedictine monk (1868–1924), abbot (1885–1924), abbot-*nullius* (1910–1924), and Catholic bishop (1887/88–1924), was a distinguished American monastic prelate who is noted for reigning concurrently and coterminiously over his monastery and two diocesan jurisdictions. In addition, he served two terms as *praeses* of the American Cassinese congregation of Benedictine monks (1890–1896) and acted as president of his monastery's college, seminary, four preparatory academies, and two industrial schools. He was also a noted orator, published playwright, and a proponent of a respected philosophy of Benedictine education.

## Further Reading

Note: the Haid papers have been collected in the Archives of Belmont Abbey (North Carolina).

Baumstein, Paschal, *My Lord of Belmont: A Biography of Leo Haid*, King's Mountain, North Carolina: Herald House, 1985; reprint, Charlotte, North Carolina: Laney-Smith, 1995

Baumstein, Paschal, "A Conflict of Miters: The Diverse Polities and Cathedral Abbey of Bishop Haid, Leo," *Word and Spirit* 14 (1992)

Baumstein, Paschal, "An Abbatial Diocese in the United States," *Catholic Historical Review* LXXICX (1993)

Oetgen, Jerome, *An American Abbot: Boniface Wimmer, O.S.B., 1809–1887*, Latrobe, Pennsylvania: Archabbey Press, 1976; revised edition, Washington, D.C.: Catholic University of America Press, 1997

# Hakuin c. 1685–1768

## Japanese Rinzai Zen master

In the last three centuries in Japan, Hakuin Ekaku has been the most influential master of the Rinzai school. Although preceded by many notable Chinese and Japanese masters, back to the founder of the Rinzai school in China (Linji), Hakuin was to become the most significant Rinzai master of his day and down to the present. Nearly all Rinzai masters today trace their dharma lineage to Hakuin, his kōan system, his methods of Zen practice, and his understanding of enlightenment (satori, kenshō). Rinzai Zen is Hakuin Zen.

One of the reasons for Hakuin's considerable influence was the dynamic of his personal experience and spiritual development. As a small child he had begun to suffer from anxiety, depression, and self-doubt. At the age of seven he was profoundly troubled on hearing a sermon from a Tendai Buddhist text on the "eight hot hells." Convinced that he was doomed, he began seeking answers and peace of mind, spending extraordinary amounts of time visiting Buddhist temples, chanting sūtras, studying texts, and meditating. By his early teens he had become convinced that his only hope lay in monkhood, but his parents denied him permission. Despite their efforts at redirecting his interests and activities, Hakuin became even more convinced that the monastic life was the only way out, and at age 15 his parents acquiesced in his wishes.

Although this step is hardly unusual in Buddhism, inasmuch as monastic practice has been central to Buddhism from its inception, Hakuin approached Zen teachers and the monastic life with the desperation of a drowning man. For most of the next nine years he took his soul searchings from master to master in monastery, temple, and hermitage. He manifested all the symptoms that William James identified as characteristics of "soul-sickness" and the "divided self": melancholy, dread, depression, anxiety, guilt, inner conflict, doubt, and despair.

Hakuin's first major breakthrough did not occur until he was 24, an event that he describes in his *Orategama* as like the smashing of a sheet of ice or jade tower that had imprisoned him. To his enlightenment experience he gave the description "Great Joy" (*daikangi*), which he subsequently argued is a spiritual state that can be attained only by first going through Great Doubt (*daigi*) and Great Death (*daishi*), with the aid of kōan meditation (*kanna* Zen).

As a result of his personal odyssey, Hakuin advocated a thoroughgoing use of the kōan as a device for developing and intensifying doubt (the "great ball of doubt"). The degree of enlightenment, he argued, was in proportion to the degree of prevenient doubt: "Great doubt, great enlightenment; small doubt, small enlightenment." To this end he gave strong emphasis to rigorous monastic discipline, military-like techniques of verbal and physical abuse, and especially an unrelenting concentration on the kōan.

Thus, Hakuin gave unprecedented attention to the kōan system, which had long been a feature of the Rinzai school. Meditation for Hakuin was kōan meditation. One's assigned kōan was to become the focus of one's being day and night, within the meditation hall and without. By fixing one's whole being on the kōan, an inner transformation eventually should occur, and one can then experience the joy and peace of new insight (*kenshō*) into one's "Buddha nature."

Although the *Mu* kōan ("Does a dog have Buddha-nature? No!") had been commonly used as a starter kōan, Hakuin preferred one of this own devising: "What is the sound of one hand clapping?" After having one's first satori, one would then meditate on further kōans that were designed to precipitate further insights and resolutions. No single satori could be expected to root out all psychological and spiritual problems. For Hakuin, then, the whole of one's practice was to be centered in kōan study and for the whole of one's life. This was supported by his own experience of subsequent satoris, emerging out of other kōans he had been working on.

Although Hakuin systematized kōans and kōan study to accommodate the needs of different levels and types of realization, he strongly emphasized the unpredictability of the satori. One could not predetermine or control or guarantee the time, place, or outcome. This too was corroborated by his personal experience of great and small satoris and in a variety of contexts: during an illness, in a rainstorm, after being beaten with a broom by an elderly woman, "listening" to falling snow, hearing the buzzing of an insect, during a dream, while reading a Chinese text, doing walking meditation (*kinhin*) in a monastery hall, and so on. With all this he stood squarely in the Zen tradition of "sudden enlightenment," which is traceable not only back to Rinzai (Linji) but also to the Sixth Patriarch Huineng (A.D. 637–715).

Like the founders and reformers of many Christian orders, Hakuin advocated a strict, uncompromising discipline accompanied by a thoroughgoing commitment and resolve. His Zen was heroic, tough-minded, and courageous – not, as he would say, for cowards and weaklings. "Dead sitting," half-hearted practice, hollow rituals, and timid spirit were the enemies with which he contended so passionately. Yet he had great compassion for the common people, spending the last 50 years of his life as abbot of the small Zen temple in the rural village of his youth – Hara in the Shizouka district. As his fame spread and would-be disciples came from far and wide, he could have become abbot of the Rinzai headquarters in Kyoto, Myoshin-ji. However, he elected to remain in close touch with peasantry and villagers as counselor, educator, preacher, author of popular tracts, and even songwriter, artist, and poet for the education and uplifting of the common people.

Because of the vividness and dramatic character of Hakuin's own religious experiences, the impress of his strong personality and example, his profound convictions so ably expressed, his exuberant style and manifold gifts, and his wedding of the twin Buddhist virtues of wisdom and compassion, Rinzai Zen in Japan became, and has been ever since, Hakuin Zen.

CONRAD HYERS

*See also* Asceticism: Buddhist Perspectives; Buddhist Schools/Traditions: Japan; Chan/Zen: Japan; Japan: History; Kōan; Zen, Arts of

## Biography

A preeminent master of the Rinzai ("sudden enlightenment") school of Zen, Hakuin entered the first of many monasteries at age 15. Years of rigorous questing led to his emphasis as a teacher on strict discipline, incessant focus on the kōan, and constant meditation.

## Major Works

*Orategama*

*The Zen Master Hakuin: Selected Writings*, edited by Philip Yampolsky, 1971

*The Essential Teachings of Zen Master Hakuin*, translated by Norman Waddell, 1994

## Further Reading

Dumoulin, Heinrich, *Zen Enlightenment: Origins and Meaning*, translated by John Maraldo, New York: Weatherhill, 1979

Dumoulin, Heinrich, *Zen Buddhism: A History*, volume 2 revised, translated by James W. Heisig and Paul Knitter, New York: McMillan, and London: Collier Macmillan, 1990

Hau Hoo, *The Sound of One Hand: Two Hundred Eighty One Zen Kōans and Answers*, translated by Yoel Hoffman, New York: Basic Books, 1975

Hyers, Conrad, *Once-Born, Twice-Born Zen: The Soto and Rinzai Schools of Japan*, Wolfeboro, New Hampshire: Longwood Academic, 1989; revised, Durango, Colorado: Longwood Academic, 1991

James, William, *The Varieties of Religious Experience*, New York and London: Longmans, Green, 1902

Kapleau, Philip, *Three Pillars of Zen*, Boston: Beacon Press, 1965; 25th anniversary edition, New York: Anchor Books, 1989

Miura, Isshu, and Ruth Fuller Sasaki, *Zen Dust: The History of the Kōan and Kōan Study in Rinzai (Lin-chi) Zen*, New York: Harcourt, Brace and World, 1966

Suzuki, D.T., "Dōgen, Hakuin, Bankei: Three Types of Thought in Japanese Zen," *Eastern Buddhist* 9:1 and 9:2 (1976)

# Heloise c. 1100–1163/64

French Christian abbess and letter writer

Heloise's fame today comes mainly from her association with Peter Abelard (1079–1142/43), who was first her teacher, then her husband, and later her spiritual director. In her age, however, Heloise was renowned as one of the most learned women in Europe and was one of most respected abbesses of the time.

Heloise was born in 1100 or 1101. Nothing is known of her parents, except her mother's name, Hersinde, which is listed in the necrology of the Paraclete. Heloise grew up in the Benedictine monastery of St. Marie of Argenteuil, six miles northwest of Paris. At the age of 17, she went to Paris to live with her uncle Fulbert, a canon of Notre Dame. She was very well educated, as Abelard twice mentions in his letters that Heloise knew Greek and Hebrew as well as Latin. Heloise's abilities were truly remarkable in an era in which women had few opportunities for education and advancement; even Abelard knew little or no Greek and no Hebrew.

Heloise's intellectual abilities attracted the attention of Abelard, who was then master of the schools of Paris and in his mid-30s. According to Abelard's autobiography, *Historia Calamitatum* (1132–1133), his conquest of Heloise was callous; he asked her uncle for lodging, and Fulbert quickly agreed to the arrangement to further his niece's education. Abelard and Heloise began a passionate affair; Abelard became bored with his teaching and wrote love songs that were sung throughout the streets of Paris. Because Abelard had a reputation for continence, Fulbert initially dismissed rumors of their affair. When he discovered the truth, he tried to separate the lovers, but Heloise became pregnant. Abelard took her to his home in Brittany, where she gave birth to their son Astrolabe.

Abelard offered to marry Heloise, provided that the marriage be kept a secret. Although his status as a canon of Paris did not prohibit him from marrying, advancement in the Church would have been impossible to a married man. Although Fulbert agreed to Abelard's terms, Heloise adamantly opposed the idea. She argued that a secret marriage would not satisfy her uncle because the scandal had already been made public. Further, she argued that the distractions of married life would detract from Abelard's contemplative life as a philosopher. Drawing on the ideas of Cicero and Seneca, Heloise argued that the philosophical life was best lived by solitaries. She insisted that formal marriage was superfluous, for, as in the spiritual friendships described in Cicero's *De Amicitia*, love is given freely and disinterestedly. She stated that she would rather be Abelard's whore than his wife.

Ultimately, however, Heloise gave in to Abelard, entrusted Astrolabe to Abelard's sister, and returned with him to Paris, where they were secretly married. Just as Heloise had predicted, Fulbert leaked the news of the marriage, and Abelard removed Heloise to Argenteuil. For unknown reasons Abelard forced her to wear the postulant's habit, which was not required for her to stay. Assuming that Abelard had forced Heloise to take vows, Fulbert had his men break into Abelard's room one night and castrate him. Abelard saw this event as punishment from God, and he took vows at St. Denis; although she had no monastic vocation, Heloise obeyed Abelard's wishes and took vows at Argenteuil.

The first mention of her after these events comes in 1128, when Abelard discovered that Abbot Suger of St. Denis (1081–1151) had claimed Argenteuil. Heloise was then prioress and perhaps had been since 1123. Abelard installed the nuns in the Paraclete near Nogent-sur-Seine in 1129, and Heloise later became the first abbess of that community. Shortly thereafter Heloise came across a copy of Abelard's *Historia Calamitatum* and began to correspond with him. Although some scholars, such as John F. Benton, have charged that the letters were fabrications, the consensus of scholars now is that the letters are authentic. In her letters she chastised Abelard for failing to respond to her on intimate terms appropriate for spouses and wrote at great length of her inability to forget her love for him and convert to the monastic life. She distinguished between outer appearances and the inner life so eloquently that Etienne Gilson has attributed the origin of Abelard's intentional ethics in the *Scito te Ipsum* to Heloise. Peter Dronke has also pointed out that Heloise's mastery of rhetoric exceeded that of her master.

In the fifth letter of the correspondence, according to Betty Radice's numbering, Heloise seemingly resigned herself to her vocation and requested that Abelard write a history of nuns and provide her community with a rule suitable for women. Although some scholars, such as D.W. Robertson and Peter von Moos, interpret her request as a sign of her final conversion to the religious life, other scholars point to many missing dimensions of traditional conversion letters. The inscription of the letter, *Domino specialiter, sua singulariter* (God's own in species, his own as), is ambiguous; one is unsure whether *dominus* refers to Abelard or God and whether Heloise refers to her unique identity as Abelard's wife or to her identity as the Bride of Christ.

At any rate, Heloise argued that the Rule of St. Benedict could not be followed comfortably by women. She argued that the clothing, diet, and manual labor prescribed by the Rule were inappropriate for women's physical needs, questioned the appropriateness of having priests come for the night readings, wondered whether the abbess can function as an abbot at the guest table and during prayers, and requested that concessions be made in the ordering of the Psalms to accommodate "the weaker sex." These statements are puzzling, as the Rule allowed for freedom of interpretation in different circumstances, and customaries of individual institutions regularly adapted the Rule to suit specific needs of women. Heloise herself was clearly aware of this, for her discussion of meat and wine conceded that Benedict allowed consumption of these items out of reverence for the customs of the times, even when Scripture and the writings of the Fathers seemed to forbid them. Linda Georgiana has suggested that Heloise was criticizing the ability of monastic practices to regulate the inner life.

Abelard responded with a letter glorifying women's roles as equal to those of clerics and gave the nuns a rule that they appear never to have followed. Although Abelard also responded to several questions posed by Heloise and sent sermons and verses to her, the two do not appear to have had any further personal contact. Heloise died on 16 May 1163 or 1164, having outlived Abelard by 21 years. Under her leadership the Paraclete established six daughter houses and became one of the most respected houses in Europe. She corresponded with Peter the Venerable (1092/94–1156), who esteemed her as a woman of exceptional wisdom and virtue. In death Heloise was finally reunited with her husband. According to legend, when the tomb was opened, Abelard extended his arms to greet her.

DEBORAH VESS

See also Abelard, Peter; Animals, Attitude toward: Christian Perspectives; France: History; Gender Studies: Christian Perspectives; Women's Monasteries: Western Christian

## Biography

Educated at the Benedictine monastery of Argenteuil near Paris, Heloise learned Latin, Greek, and Hebrew. After moving at age 17 to the home of her uncle Fulbert in Paris, she fell in love with the prestigious scholar Abelard, then in his mid-30s. When she became pregnant, Abelard took her to his home in Brittany, where she bore their son Astrolabe. Initially Heloise rejected Abelard's proposal of a secret marriage, preferring spiritual friendship, but eventually she acceded. When news of the marriage leaked out, Abelard forced her to become a monastic postulant, and Fulbert ordered his men to castrate Abelard. Thereupon Abelard took vows at St. Denis and Heloise at Argenteuil. After becoming prioress there, she moved her community to the Paraclete almost 50 miles southeast of Paris. In her first letters to Abelard, she expressed her difficulty in accepting monastic life and later asked Abelard to write a Rule suited to women. Heloise outlived Abelard by more than 20 years.

## Major Works

"The Personal Letters of Abelard and Heloise" (in Latin), edited by J.T. Muckle, in *Medieval Studies* 15 (1953)

"The Letter of Heloise on Religious Life and Abelard's First Reply" (in Latin), edited by J.T. Muckle, in *Medieval Studies* 17 (1955)

## Further Reading

Benton, John F., "Fraud, Fiction and Borrowing in the Correspondence of Abelard and Heloise," in *Pierre Abelard, Pierre le Vénérable*, Paris: Éditions du centre national de la recherche scientifique, 1975

Dronke, Peter, "Heloise," in *Women Writers of the Middle Ages*, edited by Dronke, Cambridge and New York: Cambridge University Press, 1984

Georgiana, Linda, "Any Corner of Heaven: Heloise's Critique of Monasticism," *Medieval Studies* 49 (1987)

Gilson, Etienne, *Heloise and Abelard*, reprint, Ann Arbor: University of Michigan Press, 1972

McLaughlin, Mary Martin, "Abelard as Autobiographer: The Motives and Meaning of His *Story of Calamities*," *Speculum* 42 (1967)

McLaughlin, Mary Martin, "Abelard and the Dignity of Women: Twelfth Century 'Feminism' in Theory and Practice," in *Pierre Abelard, Pierre le Vénérable*, Paris: Éditions du centre national de la recherche scientifique, 1975

McNamer, Elizabeth, *The Education of Heloise*, Lewiston, New York: Edwin Mellen Press, 1992

Newman, Barbara, "Authority, Authenticity, and the Repression of Heloise," *Journal of Medieval and Renaissance Studies* 22 (1992)

Radice, Betty, "The French Scholar-Lover Heloise," *Medieval Women Writers*, edited by Katharina Wilson, Athens: University of Georgia Press, 1984

Southern, R.W., "The Letters of Abelard and Heloise," in *Medieval Humanism and Other Studies*, Oxford: Blackwell, 1970

Waddell, Chrysogonus, editor, *The Paraclete Statutes: Institutiones Nostrae*, Trappist, Kentucky: Gethsemani Abbey, 1987

# Heretics, Christian

In the course of its long history, Christian monasticism inevitably produced a number of heretics, that is, those who were judged by ecclesiastical authorities to deviate from the publicly pronounced teaching of the Church. This article does not enumerate all monastics accused of heresy but rather deals with heresies directly related to monasticism or those in which monastics, by the nature of their vocation, played a great role.

Monasticism rose to prominence in the fourth century, and it did so in two forms: cenobitic or communal monasticism (from the Greek *koinos*, common, and *bios*, life), and eremitic monasticism, that of hermits. The latter was much admired by Christians, largely because of the career of St. Antony of Egypt (251?–356), whose life was written by the patriarch of

Alexandria, Athanasius (c. 296–373). However, another important bishop, Basil of Caesarea (c. 330–379), doubted the Christian character of eremiticism. He rested his opposition on the communal nature of Christianity. For him the Church is at base a community, called together to do God's work in the world. Like all early Christian writers, Basil loathed heresy not only because of its false doctrines but also because it broke up the unity of the Church. He feared that the much lionized eremiticism likewise damaged Christian unity because hermits cut themselves off from the community, the sacraments, the liturgy, and the world, which Christ had come to save. Because most of the hermits were illiterate peasants, they also cut themselves off from the Scriptures, which were read to them from the pulpits they scorned. The ever-pastoral Basil also harbored spiritual concerns for hermits. They deprived themselves of fraternal correction when they fell into faults and from fraternal assistance in time of temptation. For him, monks should be cenobites. Indeed, so seriously did Basil take cenobitism that he wrote a rule for monks that became the standard rule for monks of the Orthodox Churches.

However, Basil did not win many others to his view. Eremitic monasticism survived and held its high place, even in the eyes of cenobites. The Anglo-Saxon Benedictine, the Venerable Bede (673–735), recounted how Melrose monastery provided space within its grounds for those who wanted to be hermits.

Athanasius saw hermits in a very different light from Basil, and his *Life of St. Antony* immortalized the Egyptian hermit. This bishop is best known for his lifelong struggle against the Arian heretics (who denied the divinity of Christ). When the Arians drove him from his see, he found refuge in the desert among the monks, both cenobites and hermits, who proved to be his strongest supporters. The patriarch praised their unwavering orthodoxy, aligning it to their saintliness, although it might have arisen also from ignorance. Most monks were poorly educated brothers who went to the desert at an early age and simply could not follow theological debates. Orthodox writers always accused the heretics of innovations and novelties, and the monks might have seen Athanasius as the upholder of the traditional faith.

Athanasius and his allies, supporters of the Ecumenical Council of Nicaea (325), eventually defeated the Arians, and by the end of the fourth century Nicene teaching had become the touchstone of orthodoxy and was anachronistically applied to writers who had died before the Arian controversy had even begun. One of these was Origen of Alexandria (c. 185–c. 253), a great spiritual writer and a pioneering theologian. In 393 an ignorant, self-appointed heresy hunter, Epiphanius of Salamis (c. 315–403), demanded that the monks of Palestine, admirers of Origen, join him in condemning the deceased Alexandrian. Not too many did, but among them was the Latin monk Jerome (c. 342–c. 420), an avid polemicist. He helped Epiphanius in his attack on bishop John of Jerusalem (c. 352–417), who continued to support Origen's teachings.

In 400 the growing controversy attracted an unscrupulous ecclesiastical politician, Theophilus, patriarch of Alexandria (385–412). A former adherent of Origen, he denounced him and lined up support for this about-face among conservative Egyptian monks. In 402 he accused four prominent Egyptian monks, the Tall Brothers, of Origenist sympathies. The brothers fled to Constantinople, where a former monk, John Chrysostom (c. 347–407), held the episcopal chair. Now masterminding the whole affair, Theophilus engineered the deposition and exile of John Chrysostom and the condemnation of Origen's theology, thus asserting the triumph of Alexandria over the upstart see of Constantinople. He had used some monks to aid his designs while simultaneously condemning and persecuting others. However, this drama had another act to play.

Resentful of Theophilus, some Palestinian monks secretly continued to read Origen's works. In 542 word of this reached the Byzantine Emperor Justinian (527–565), who condemned Origen's teaching in 543 with an imperial proclamation and again in 553 at an ecumenical council, Constantinople II. The pious emperor also instituted heresy hunting in Palestinian monasteries.

While the Eastern monks were involved in the Origenist controversy, Western monks faced the problem of Pelagianism. Pelagius (c. 354–c. 420) was an British monk who had left his homeland and become a spiritual adviser to a noble Roman family. Most of what we know about his teaching survives in the writings of his opponent, Augustine of Hippo (354–430). Pelagius taught that humans could so discipline themselves that they could be saved by their own free wills and without divine grace, adding, however, that few had actually done this. On the other hand, Augustine believed that original sin had corrupted human nature, including the will, and that no one could be saved by free will alone. Only divine grace could save people, who literally could do nothing to deserve that grace. God gave it freely to those whom he wanted to save, and he knew before he even created the world to whom he would give it. This amounts to predestination.

The powerful and influential African bishop easily routed the British monk, who went into exile. Although most Westerners found Pelagius' teaching extreme, many, especially Western monks, held strong reservations about Augustinian predestinationism. The Gallic monks in Marseilles and Lérins became the focal point of opposition.

Augustine had envisioned a lost world, the Garden of Eden before the Fall. Although Christ had saved humanity from the consequences of the primal disobedience, return to an Edenlike state was impossible, yet Eden loomed large in monastic imagery. Adam and Eve's murderous son, Cain, had built the first city, and monks abandoned urban civilization for the desert, forest, and offshore islands. Egyptian accounts told of monks who went about literally naked and others almost so, a symbolic return to the pristine state of humanity before the Fall. Many monks feared that predestinationism would devalue their lives and calling. Why abandon civilization, why fast and pray unceasingly, why bind oneself to a monastic rule when Augustine's God had settled everything in advance?

John Cassian (c. 360–435) of Marseilles disagreed with Pelagianism but indirectly criticized Augustine, insisting that God wants all people to be saved and not only the Augustinian elect. Furthermore, Cassian allowed for the possibility that free will could cooperate with grace. Following him, monks at Lérins, such as the author Vincent (d. c. 450) and a monastery alumnus, Faustus, bishop of Riez (c. 408–495), went further, arguing that because God had created human nature, nothing, not even sin, could destroy it completely. Thus, although grace is necessary for salvation, the human will, on its own, can cooperate with grace and even prepare the individual to accept it. Since the 17th century this position has borne the unfair and inaccurate label of Semi-Pelagianism.

The Augustinians rejected the Gallic monks' views out of hand. If the will could accept the grace that God offered, it was doing something good without grace, an impossibility for them. Although the African's views triumphed in the larger Western Church, the Semi-Pelagian view held its own in Gaul until the 520s, when an African bishop, Fulgentius of Ruspe (467–533), attacked the views of the Lérins' alumnus, Faustus, as heretical. Another monastery alumnus, Caesarius, bishop of Arles (c. 470–542), presided at the Second Council of Orange (529), which rejected Faustus' teaching, insisting that only grace could move the will toward the good. In a small bow to Gallic monastic tradition, the council refrained from commenting on predestination.

The transformation of Western monastic views on this question occurred steadily throughout the early Middle Ages, and by the ninth century another monk, the Saxon Gottschalk of Fulda (c. 804–c. 869), found himself condemned as a heretic by a council of Carolingian bishops in 849 for teaching double predestinationism, claiming that God had predestined not only some to salvation but also the nonelect to damnation. As John Calvin would later point out, this was the logical conclusion of predestination to salvation, even if Augustine had avoided saying it.

Although individual Christian monks continued to be involved in heresy, after the general codification of monasticism through the Basilian rule in the East and the Benedictine rule in the West, monastic involvement in heretical disputes rarely reached a grand scale. Yet sometimes an entire monastic house, even a prominent one, could fall under suspicion.

In the 14th century the monks of Mount Athos in Greece practiced Hesychasm, the constant repetition of the Jesus Prayer ("Lord Jesus Christ, Son of God, have mercy on me"). They insisted on specific bodily positions and regulated breathing to aid the intensity of the prayer. The Hesychasts aspired to a vision of the Divine Light that might even be seen by the bodily eyes of a blessed few. Around 1340 a Greek monk in Calabria named Barlaam denounced Hesychasm as outright superstition. The Athonite Hesychast Gregory of Palamas (c. 1296–1359) mounted a spirited defense of the practice that eventually became part of the Orthodox tradition.

Often opponents would try to associate monasticism itself with heretical ascetical movements. Monasticism and asceticism were linked from the beginning, but ascetic extremism appeared much earlier. In the second century the Ebionites and several Gnostic sects devalued the importance of the material world and of the body, contradicting the biblical teaching that God had created the material world and saw that it was good, that he had fashioned the bodies of Adam and Eve, and that Jesus took on a body to save this world. Some monks never felt comfortable with their bodies, but Christian monks as a group followed Scripture and accepted the material, although they rejected materialism. Yet when the dualist Manichees became prominent in the West in the fourth century, Jerome complained that monasticism's enemies saw a Manichee in everyone who practiced physical self-denial.

At the same time in the East, the Messalian movement began. Also called the "Euchites" (those who pray), the Messalians prayed incessantly for the elimination of carnal passions. In 431 the Ecumenical Council of Ephesus condemned their prayer book, the *Asketikon*. The movement faded in popularity after that but survived until the seventh century.

In the Middle Ages extremist asceticism dwelt only on the fringes of the Church, and ecclesiastical authorities rarely associated it with the by then well established Benedictine or Basilian monasticism. For example, the dualist Cathars, objects of vicious persecution and even a so-called "crusade" in Languedoc during the early 13th century, exercised little influence beyond the Mediterranean littoral in France, northeastern Spain, and northwestern Italy.

Although not an actual heresy, "elitism" on the part of many early monks called monasticism's Christian character into question. Jerome claimed that monks would occupy a higher place in heaven than married people, and he never hid his disdain for the secular clergy of Rome. When one of his spiritual advisees, a noble young woman named Blesilla, died from the austerities that he imposed on her, the Roman populace ranted against the *detestabile genus monachorum* (loathsome race of monks). However, with the modern monastic acknowledgment of differing vocations, such elitism is rare.

Modern research into heresy has proven that "heretics" were often believers trying out new ideas that appeared threatening to those who believed that Christianity could and should never change. It is not surprising that the supposed heresies in which monks were involved appeared early in monastic history when the monks were still finding their place in the larger community.

JOSEPH F. KELLY

*See also* Antony, St.; Asceticism: Christian Perspectives; Basil the Great, St.; Bede, St.; Caesarius of Arles, St.; Cassian, John; Cathars; Desert Fathers; Hermits: Eastern Christian: Hermits: Western Christian; Hesychasm; Israel/Palestine; Lérins, France; Mount Athos, Greece; Spirituality: Eastern Christian

## Further Reading

Athanasius, *The Life of Saint Antony*, edited and translated by Robert Meyer, Westminster, Maryland: Newman Press, 1950

Basil of Caesarea, *Ascetical Works*, translated by Monica Wagner, Washington, D.C.: Catholic University of America Press, 1950

Clark, Elizabeth, *The Origenist Controversy: The Cultural Construction of an Early Christian Debate*, Princeton, New Jersey: Princeton University Press, 1992

Fedwick, Paul, editor, *Basil of Caesarea: Christian, Humanist, Ascetic*, 2 vols., Toronto: Pontifical Institute of Mediaeval Studies, 1981

Kelly, J.N.D., *Jerome: His Life, Times, and Controversies*, San Francisco: Harper and Row, 1975

Lambert, Macolm, *The Cathars*, Oxford and Malden, Massachusetts: Blackwell, 1998

Lieu, Samuel, *Manichaeism in Mesopotamia and the Roman East*, Leiden and New York: Brill, 1994

Logan, Alastair H.B., *Gnostic Truth and Christian Heresy: A Study in the History of Gnosticism*, Edinburgh: T & T Clark, 1996

Meyendorff, John, *Gregory Palamas*, New York: Paulist Press, 1998

Rees, Brinley R., *Pelagius: A Reluctant Heretic*, Woodbridge, England, and Wolfeboro, New Hampshire: Boydell Press, 1988

Rousseau, Philip, *Ascetics, Authority and the Church in the Age of Jerome and Cassian*, Oxford and New York: Oxford University Press, 1978

Smith, Thomas, *De Gratia: Faustus of Riez's Treatise on Grace and Its Place in the History of Theology*, Notre Dame, Indiana: University of Notre Dame Press, 1990

Stewart, Columba, *"Working the Heart of the Earth": The Messalian Controversy in History, Texts, and Language to A.D. 431*, Oxford: Clarendon Press, and New York: Oxford University Press, 1991

Stewart, Columba, *Cassian the Monk*, New York: Oxford University Press, 1998

Weaver, Rebecca H., *Divine Grace and Human Agency: A Study of the Semi-Pelagian Controversy*, Macon, Georgia: Mercer University Press, 1996

# Hermits: Buddhist

The Buddhist order (*saṅgha*) started as a loose confraternity of itinerant almsmen (*bhikṣu*). In its initial period Buddhism did not constitute an organized community and was distinguished from other sects only by its orientation toward a particular leader, namely, the Buddha, and his teaching (dharma). The concept of the *bhikṣu* was already fully developed in the early Upanishads and originally required abandonment of both personal belongings and fixed abode. The establishment of monastic institutions was not envisioned by the Buddha, and the early Buddhist *bhikṣu*s assembled only once a year to spend the rainy season in a single place. However, some monks preferred to retire to the forests instead of spending the rainy season in the community. These forest dwellers (*āraṇyaka*) may be regarded as the prototypes of all Buddhist anchorites. The Buddha himself is the model of the Buddhist forest dweller inasmuch as he attained enlightenment while sitting at the foot of a tree (*vṛkṣa-mūlika*) an expression that became a technical term for anchoritism. Thus, forest dwelling or anchoritism remained an option even after the steadily growing movement of Buddhist wandering almsmen had changed into an order of cenobites.

A forest dweller might live alone or be accompanied by a few like-minded practitioners or disciples. Also, he cannot isolate himself completely from society because, not being allowed to provide for his own sustenance, he depends on alms offered by laypeople. The *Visuddhimagga* (59) distinguishes three classes of forest dwellers, corresponding to the strictness of their seclusion: (1) those who always meet the dawn in the forest, (2) those who live in a village during the rainy season, and (3) those who also spend the winter months in villages. According to the Pāli Canon of the Theravāda school, the Buddha warned against false motives for anchoritism, such as folly and blindness, evil desires and longings, foolishness and mental disturbance, and the desire to be praised by the Buddhas and their disciples. Praiseworthy, however, are hermits whose wants are few and who desire only seclusion. The practice of forest dwelling is included in the standard lists of 12 or 13 ascetic options (*dhūtāṅga*). Three of the ascetic options directly refer to a secluded life: (1) living in a forest, (2) sitting under a tree, and (3) residing in an unsheltered place.

Although itinerancy was the original lifestyle of a *bhikṣu*, it was eventually superseded by anchoritism and especially cenobitism. Choice of one of these options should be made on the basis of personal preference. The *Vanapattha Sutta* (*Majjhima Nikāya* 17) says that a *bhikṣu* may dwell in a forest or quit it or dwell anywhere in a village, a township, or a country, as long as such dwelling is conducive to his spiritual cultivation. The dual structure of the Buddhist clergy, formed by anchorites and cenobites, refers to the two main duties of a *bhikṣu* – to meditate and to instruct – and is maintained especially in Theravāda countries up to the present. A monk living in towns and villages is expected to teach the laity and preserve the dharma, whereas hermits should occupy themselves with meditation. Many anchorites turned their backs on the monasteries because they felt that the luxurious life in a monastic community was not conducive to the attainment of enlightenment and that the daily duties of an ordinary monk obstructed religious practice. From the earliest times hermits have been admired as saints (arhat) by the laity. This can lead to the paradoxical situation that an ascetic, who has chosen a life of solitude and poverty, is visited by numerous pilgrims and receives all kinds of offerings. Thus, a considerable danger of misuse exists.

In China hermits and mountain ascetics were likewise held in high esteem. People believed that the anchorites' awe-inspiring asceticism and their strange religious practices endowed them with supernatural faculties, such as banning demons, curing illnesses, and stopping famines. Chinese Buddhist mountain ascetics were strongly influenced by indigenous mountain cults as well as by Daoist recluses. The Buddhist ideal of an undisturbed meditative life gradually amalgamated with the Daoist goals of longevity, complete freedom, and harmony with nature. Buddhist hermits frequently adopted Daoist dietetic practices, such as abstention from grain, and occasionally committed self-mutilation or self-immolation. Evidently many hermits in China deviated considerably from the old Buddhist ideal of moderation, that is, to avoid the dangerous path of suffering and enjoyment.

Like most elements in Japanese culture, Buddhist anchoritism in Japan was deeply influenced by the Chinese paradigm. Buddhist hermits in Japan practiced a highly syncretic cult of mountain asceticism and religious itinerancy. Many of those practitioners who preferred not to live in a monastery traveled from one holy site to another, whereas others settled in caves or simple huts on sacred mountains; used moss, bark, paper, and deer skins as clothing; and carried priests staffs with antlers. They often practiced extreme asceticism and were esteemed as powerful thaumaturgists, healers, and exorcists. They were respectfully called sages (*hijiri*) or superior/holy men (*shōnin*). The 13th paragraph of the laws for monks and nuns (*sōniryō*), issued in the eighth century, endorses the option of temporal anchoritism if it is for the purpose of meditation and spiritual purification, if a proper application has been filed, and if superiors have given permission. The local authorities had to be kept informed. With the decline of state control over the Buddhist order, the deterioration of the official ordination system, the decadence of monastic life, and increasing social unrest, the number of illegally practicing hermits and itinerant monks grew rapidly from around the 11th century and contributed much to the Buddhist reform movements of the 13th century. Mountain asceticism was eventually institutionalized by the major branches of esoteric Buddhism (Tendai and Shingon).

The dual structure of the Buddhist *saṅgha* was also preserved in Tibet. Although huge monasteries that housed up to tens of thousands of monks characterized Lamaism before the Chinese occupation of Tibet, in addition there had always been practitioners who forsook communal life and chose caves as their abodes. They strove to cultivate spiritual and supernatural faculties and to commit themselves to severe asceticism. Especially the Kagyü sect (bKa' brgyud pa) and the Nyingma sect (rNying ma pa) have promoted extreme forms of seclusion, namely, the practice of immurement. Many practitioners of these traditions have had themselves immured in caves or special hermitages, some of which are completely dark, for a fixed period of customarily seven or sometimes five years. Their contact with the outer world is confined to the reception of food offerings through a narrow slot in the wall.

CHRISTOPH KLEINE

*See also* Buddhadāsa; Buddhist Schools/Traditions: China; Buddhist Schools/Traditions: Japan; Daoism: Influence on Buddhism; Forest Masters; Holy Men/Holy Women: Buddhist Perspectives; Holy Men in Power (Hierocrats), Buddhist; Monasticism, Definitions of: Buddhist Perspectives; Mountain Monasteries, Buddhist; Origins: Comparative Perspectives; Sexuality: Buddhist Perspectives

**Further Reading**

Dutt, Sukumar, *Buddhist Monks and Monasteries of India: Their History and Their Contribution to Indian Culture*, London: Allen and Unwin, 1962

Gombrich, Richard, *Theravada Buddhism: A Social History from Ancient Benares to Modern Colombo*, London and New York: Routledge, 1988; reprint, 1995

Hori, Ichiro, "On the Concept of Hijiri (Holy-Man)," Part I: *Numen* 5:2 (1958); Part II: *Numen* 5:3 (1958)

Hori, Ichiro, "Self-Mummified Buddhas in Japan: An Aspect of the Shugen-dō ('Mountain Asceticism') Sect," *History of Religions* 1:2 (1961)

Karunaratna, Upali, "Araññaka," in *Encyclopedia of Buddhism: Volume II*, edited by G.P. Malalasekera, Colombo: The Government Press, 1966

Kieschnick, John, *The Eminent Monk: Buddhist Ideals in Medieval Chinese Hagiography*, Honolulu: University of Hawaii Press, 1997

Kleine, Christoph, "Hermits and Ascetics in Ancient Japan: The Concept of Hijiri Reconsidered," *Japanese Religions* 22:2 (1997)

Taylor, James L., "The Textualization of a Monastic Tradition: Forest Monks, Lineage, and the Biographical Process in Thailand," in *Sacred Biography in the Buddhist Traditions of South and Southeast Asia*, edited by Juliane Schober, Honolulu: University of Hawaii Press, 1997

Tucci, Giuseppe, *The Religions of Tibet*, Berkeley: University of California Press, and London: Routledge, 1980

Tyler, Royall, and Paul L. Swanson, editors, "Shugendo and Mountain Religion in Japan," *Japanese Journal of Religious Studies* 16:2–3 (1989)

# Hermits: Eastern Christian

The monastic life in its Christian form has existed almost as long as has Christianity itself. It has shown different stages in its evolution from the first hermits of the Egyptian desert to the later, more organized and communal monastic units. In its origins in the late third and early fourth centuries, Christian monasticism was concentrated in Egypt, closely followed by settlements in Palestine. Monasticism has taken three main forms, all of which are still to be found in the Orthodox Church today. The first of these forms is that of the hermits – ascetics leading the solitary life in huts or caves and even in tombs, among the branches of trees, or on the tops of pillars. It was to this eremitic mode of life that the word *monasticism* was first applied to denote properly the life of lonely isolation. Similarly, the word *monk* (from Greek *monos*, meaning "alone" or "solitary") was initially restricted – before it applied to all who "left the world," whether they lived alone or in community – to a hermit or anchorite. A hermit's withdrawal from the everyday world and search for seclusion and isolation was motivated by a desire to pursue a disciplined life of extreme asceticism amounting almost to a form of voluntary martyrdom. It was believed that the purging of unworthy thoughts and actions through unceasing prayer would lead to a knowledge of God.

However, historical evidence has shown that asceticism had entered Egyptian life long before the rise of hermits and monasticism there, but no evidence exists to show how extensive it was among the people in general. In Egypt ascetic practices were known and pursued even before the fourth century by non-Christian ascetics who despised the world and its pleasures, forsook the haunts of humanity, and retired to solitude, where they fasted, meditated, and pursued a celibate life. This was the case also in Syria and Palestine, places where, in the course of time, the Christian eremitic mode of monasticism emerged as well. In these regions certain cults inculcated discipline, demanded strict asceticism, practiced self-mutilation, or demanded purification of the soul from the contamination by the senses.

Nevertheless, the origin of Christian hermits does not lie in mere imitation of a non-Christian system. Although asceticism thrived in Alexandria and other towns of Egypt, where a number of pagan cults already influenced ascetic tendencies, it was Christianity that epitomized a tendency toward the desert. It was Christianity that made hermits multiply and the eremitic mode of life spread. Moreover, when Christianity reached the various races living in Egypt, it came to minds, of the most earnest, who had been already taught to look on the world and life through ascetic eyes. Because they regarded asceticism as the highest ideal, Christianity would tend to come to these people through ascetic channels.

Even from the days of Christ, Christians had been conscious of a certain feeling of isolation from the world. The examples of Elijah, John the Baptist, St. Paul, and similar figures from the Scriptures who had sought the desert, at least for a time, exemplified a tendency toward a life of isolation in the desert. In the course of time this tendency was strengthened by the opposition and persecution of the state and by its growing corruption and laxity. Hermits multiplied at times of stress and persecution. However, as the third century proceeded attitudes toward the desert developed along two lines: First, in the words of Dionysius, bishop of Alexandria, "in the Decian persecution great distress came upon the church and the multitude wandered in the deserts and mountains and perished by hunger and thirst and cold and sickness and robbers and wild beasts." Thus, it is clear that a large number of Christians sought refuge in the deserts of Egypt (c. A.D. 250), and we can suppose that some of the more ascetic remained there after the persecutions had ended and helped turn men's minds to the desert as a refuge from the ills of life. Second, and more important, was the custom that had grown up by around 270 of hermits living in solitude near their villages, at a time when not many cells yet existed in Egypt and no monk at all knew of the distant desert. This ascetic mode of living was pursued by all who wanted to give heed to themselves and to practice discipline in solitude near their own villages. Occupying a small dwelling built by themselves, they could live a life of prayer and contemplation free from the dangers of society and provide for their few wants by cultivating a small piece of ground or by weaving mats for sale. Yet this mode of life did not satisfy the more aspiring spirits, who gradually preferred to live as hermits further away from the village and the distraction of visitors.

Of special importance for the rise and growth of Eastern Christian asceticism was the worldliness of the Church, which became evident after recognition under Constantine (306–337).

This was felt with keen sorrow and disappointment by the more earnest, for whom the eremitic life represented a desire to return to the lofty ideals of the New Testament. As a protest against the secularization of the Church, men turned away to live the Christian life in the desert.

Another reason to account for the increase of hermits at the beginning of the fourth century was the nominal Christianization of the Roman Empire and subsequently the cessation of persecutions. The ascetics now sought to win the martyr's crown of heavenly glory – which their predecessors in the time of persecutions had gained more quickly and easily by a bloody death – in the burning deserts and caverns of Egypt and Syria, amid the pains of self-torture and the mortification of natural desires and relentless battles with demons.

Some early Christians hermits, feeling disgusted by the lawlessness prevailing in the country, came to realize the City of God in the desert and the cell and, in contrast to the luxury, sensuality, and disorder of the world, led peaceful lives of poverty, chastity, and prayer. However, others became hermits for dire reasons because of the loss or confiscation of their possessions, the perils of death, the loss of dear ones, the burden of taxation, or the law's pressure.

The great model of the eremitic life is the founder of monasticism himself, St. Antony of Egypt (251–356). His life as a hermit has been described by Athanasius (c. 296–373), bishop of Alexandria, and this document has always remained the standard of the monastic ideal. The *Vita Antonii* defined the whole later development of monasticism in the Church. Saint Athanasius saw Antony as the first hermit. Outwardly Antony's life followed a very simple pattern. He was born in Egypt (c. 251) into a Coptic Christian family. When still very young he was shaken by the words of the Gospel. He gave away all his property and devoted himself entirely to ascetic feats, starting in his own village but very soon withdrawing into the desert, where he spent 20 years in complete solitude. He learned from visiting the hermits of whom he had heard and set himself to imitate their respective virtues. Athanasius has described this period of his life, often very realistically, as a ceaseless struggle with the devil. Unlettered, he was assiduous in manual work, working to provide for himself and for those in need. No doubt certain individuals had acted in a similar way before, but Antony differed from predecessors both in the determination and sanctity of a long life and in his gift for inspiring and guiding others. A stream of imitators soon became a flood of people begging him to tell them the secret of his life. He found, like other hermits before him, that a life of solitude was by no means free from temptations, but he overcame these by constant prayer and greater severity of life. His food was the simplest: bread, salt, and water. Sleep was reduced to minimum; often he spent whole nights awake, and when he did sleep he usually used the bare ground instead of his rush mat. The notion of Antony's perfection – seen as a return to humanity's natural condition – became a constant teaching of Eastern Christian ascetics. Of great importance were the powers that Antony exhibited at that point: healing the sick, casting out demons, and using the grace of speech to comfort the sorrowful,

Church of St. Symeon Stylites, near Aleppo, Syria, late fifth century. Remains of the saint's pillar stand in the octagonal crossing.
Photo courtesy of Chris Schabel

to reconcile those at variance, and to urge all to put nothing in the world before the love of Christ. He persuaded many to choose the solitary life, and he emerged from his seclusion to become their teacher and leader. Henceforth "monasteries" arose in the mountains, and the desert was inhabited by solitaries. However, these monasteries were solitary cells, not abodes of groups of monks. Antony initiated a type of hermit involved in public life, one determined to hearten the persecuted Christians, to give support to the confessors in court even by exposing himself to arrest.

As Antony attracted more and more disciples and visitors, there began what may be called the golden age of Egyptian hermit life from around 330 to 440. The first fathers of the desert lived alone or by twos and threes in caves, huts, or brick-built cells, supporting themselves on the produce of vegetable patches and small fields while making baskets of palm fronds that they sold to visitors or agents. The money bought other necessaries of life. Their time was spent in prayer, in work and in reading, and in memorizing the Scriptures. Such a life, if it were to be satisfying and fruitful, demanded an uncommon degree of psychological stability and self-control.

It is said that Antony's monasteries – which appeared as a kind of a small gathering of hermits – were a step forward from the completely solitary life. However, their degree of communal organization must not be exaggerated. Gradually, a loose voluntary system emerged by which each hermit lived his own life in a large collection of cells. The progenitor of this system was Antony's "Outer Monastery," a kind of community of gatekeepers guarding the approach to the saint (superior hermit). Similarly, later in the century a community of monks kept the key to the approach to the three-chambered cell on the cliffs, where John of Lycopolis (one of the most famous and illustrious strict solitaries) remained enclosed for 48 years. The approach was thrown open to visitors only on Saturdays and Sundays.

The fourth century showed a strong tendency to develop from the strictly eremitic life to a common life. It was found that the intense individualism of the solitary life involved serious spiritual dangers, especially for young monks. A loss of character often accompanies a life of isolation when no mingling takes place among diverse temperaments and experiences, faults go uncorrected, and no restraints are imposed on the will. In addition lawlessness made isolation dangerous for the lonely hermit.

The first stage of this transition was Antony's establishment of so-called associations of eremites. Drawn together by longing for human companionship and by difficulties and dangers of a solitary life, these hermits lived in clusters of cells and were to some extent under the influence and guidance of an elder to whom they voluntarily attached themselves. This form of monastic life stood halfway between the hermits and the community life founded by St. Pachomius of Egypt (286–346). It was a semi-eremitic life, a kind of middle way that, instead of a single highly organized community, provided a loosely knit group of small settlements, each containing perhaps two to six members. The great centers of the semi-eremitic life in Egypt were Nitria and Scetis, which by the end of the fourth century had produced many outstanding monks: Ammon (d. c. 350) the founder of Nitria, Macarius of Egypt (c. 300–c. 390), Macarius of Alexandria (d. 394), Evagrius Ponticus (c. 345–399), and Arsenius the Great. Other smaller centers of the semi-eremitic type were Pispir, Chenoboskion, Cellia or Cells, and Scete.

Once in existence monastic life spread rapidly to Palestine and Syria. In the fifth and sixth centuries, leadership in the monastic movement shifted to Palestine, with St. Euthymius the Great (d. 473) and his disciple St. Sabas (439–532). Palestine had its great pioneer in Hilarion (291–371), who derived his enthusiasm from Egypt. He pursued a hermit's life on the Egyptian model at Gaza. After almost 50 years in solitude, he journeyed around the western Mediterranean in a vain attempt to escape from his clients. A great number of disciples joined him, and around 330 monasteries started to spring up throughout the land. Gaza and Eleutheropolis became important monastic centers there, retaining their Egyptian links.

Monasteries were soon founded in the holy places in Palestine, and the arrival of Jerome (c. 345–420) and his group of noble Roman ladies attracted recruits. The mountainous desert east of Jerusalem proved as attractive to anchorites and hermits, as did that of Egypt; the *lavra* (hermit group) rather than the Pachomian cenobium (community) became the norm. In the *lavra* a number of caverns or huts at a distance from one another housed hermits under the direction of a saintly elder. A row or cluster of solitary cells stood around a common center, including a bakery and a church where the ascetics would assemble on Sundays and for the vigil of Saturday night, followed by the Eucharist, a common meal, and the apportioning of provisions and work for the week. In Syria, St. Ephrem (306–373) theologian and poet, founded the school of Edessa with a monastic framework of vowed students who would perform spiritual service for the surrounding hermits. In general Syria and Mesopotamia witnessed extreme ascetic models characterized by strange self-inflicted austerities. In Syria two types of asceticism prevailed: one that followed in its basic lines the Egyptian model and a native one characterized by individualism and spiritual extremes.

The second kind included strange classes of solitaries chained to rocks either in a cave or in the open air and the still stranger stationary monks (stylites), who remained motionless either on the ground or on a pillar. Of these last the most celebrated was Symeon the Elder (389–459), who remained for more than 30 years on his 30-foot-high column near Antioch. He was a true saint who gave to those who gathered around his pedestal wise and temperate advice on spiritual and human problems.

In Asia Minor the monastic model that spread was that of the Basilian kind, that is, one with a moderate but fully regulated degree of community life. This model was founded by Basil of Caesarea (c. 330–379), himself a bishop. In this the way of the solitary or hermit, although not excluded, was reserved for the more experienced monks. The Basilian kind of monasticism became dominant in the Byzantine Empire, although hermits and extreme ascetics of the pillar-saint type were not unknown there. It is said that Byzantine monasticism accommodated different ascetic models, ranging from the eremitic to the large cenobitic house. The most popular kind of monasticism in the middle Byzantine period was termed "hybrid" monasticism, a combination of elements drawn from both the lavriote and the cenobitic traditions.

Byzantine monastic life in this period proved much more flexible than this model allows. As in the early days of the movement, throughout the Middle Ages monasticism expressed itself in various ways. Cenobitic houses of all sizes existed, varying from the large imperial foundations, such as the 12th-century Pantocrator of John II Comnenus (1118–1143), to the very small ones set up by villagers. Groups of monks lived for most of the week independently as hermits in their own separate cells, meeting together on Saturdays and Sundays and accepting the guidance of a more experienced monk. Such groups resembled the original *lavra*s and became known as *kellia*, a number of which might accept a common spiritual leader and form a *skete* directly linked to a cenobitic house. In addition completely solitary hermits lived entirely on their own, a life considered suitable only for the more experienced. All forms might flourish in the vicinity of a cenobitic house, or even within its surrounding walls. In this sense hermits did not live independently but belonged to a cenobitic system. Many solitaries adopted such isolation only for the later part of their monastic life. As they became more experienced, they would withdraw from the common life of their house, perhaps to a cell in its grounds, to some distant island, or to a mountain cave such as abounded on Mount Athos, where hermits were well established by the mid–ninth century. In the late Middle Ages, a further monastic association developed in which several monks were grouped into families living together and owning private property. Under a common superior, normally the different groups met only for services in the chapel. This system was called "idiorrythmic," that is, based on a private individual routine.

The contrasting forms of Byzantine monasticism can be classified in relation to geography. The fertile, flat lands bordering the Sea of Marmara and the Aegean Sea supported large communal houses (such as those founded by St. Theodore of Stoudios [759–826]). By the end of the ninth century, these existed in western Asia Minor as well as in the region around Mount Olympos (the Monastery of Sakkoudion and the monastery of St. John the Baptist in Constantinople). By contrast the inhospitable ranges to the east provided a natural setting for hermits and solitaries seeking *eremia* (solitude), a prerequisite for followers of the kind of life first led by St.

Antony, whose progression ever higher into the mountainous wilderness of Egypt, as he entered advanced planes of spiritual experience, remained the exemplar both for later Byzantine hermits and for many monastic founders.

However, many, such as the Stoudites, doubted that solitary wrestling with temptations provided the best method of achieving a spiritual life. The model of the solitary hermit suffered a worse setback through Justinian legislation, which banned the foundation of noncenobitic houses while allowing a few monks to lead a hermit's life, but only within their religious community.

Many of the most influential monastic founders of Asia Minor, including those of houses on Athos and Patmos, founded houses that followed the age-old lavriote tradition. They wanted the possibility of individual spiritual experience not to replace that offered by the cenobium but to exist in addition to it. As in many other areas of Byzantine life, the concept of hierarchy came to pervade monasticism. Men could progress from communal life to the status of a solitary within the community and finally to that of a hermit.

Lavriote monasticism spread in the 10th and 11th centuries, and evidence shows that many monastic founders wanted to include these opportunities for individual asceticism in the regulations that they drew up for their houses. This lavriote way of life can also be seen in the monastic centers of western Asia Minor founded on the holy mountains of Olympos, Latras, Mykale, Kyminas, and Galesion.

In the tenth century the most famous center of Byzantine monasticism was established by St. Athanasios (c. 920–1003) at Mount Athos (the "Holy Mountain"), a rocky peninsula in northern Greece jutting out into the Aegean Sea. In the ninth century Athos was a place of hermits and small religious groups rather than large houses. In the course of time, more permanent houses were established to the north of the peninsula, and solitary hermits lived side by side with monastic groups. Later John Tzimiskes' *Typikon* – a document regulating life on Athos issued between 970 and 972 – put an end to the period of individual, solitary asceticism there. Henceforth the priors (*hegoumenoi*) alone were to decide on suitable candidates for the solitary life in each monastery. Without recruits the number of hermits dwindled, and it is probable that some of them formed themselves into communities. Athanasios the Athonite favored the system of *lavra* that combined the elements of communal monasticism with opportunities for individual seclusion. During the 13th century Athos witnessed a decline of cenobitic houses as an idiorrythmic way of life came to prevail.

By the 12th century many customs of hermits or stylites continued, but in a new context. The strict lavriote tradition was compromised to accommodate growing numbers of postulants. On the other hand, the cenobitic tradition was modified to allow for the existence of a few "advanced" monks as solitaries outside the walls. In the following years the communal aspect of the "mixed" houses prevailed, a tradition that survives today. The outstanding contribution of the lavriote-influenced houses to Byzantine and post-Byzantine monasticism was this element of

flexibility. It allowed the individual full opportunity to begin his spiritual development within a community without denying him the eventual opportunity of progression to the solitary life of a hermit.

MARIA ROUMBALOU

*See also* Antony, St.; Desert Fathers; Desert Mothers; Egypt; Ethiopia; Evagrius Ponticus; Hagiography: Eastern Christian; Israel/Palestine; Island Monasteries, Christian; Istanbul, Turkey; Lavra; Macarian Homilies; Meteora, Thessaly, Greece; Mount Athos, Greece; Origins: Comparative Perspectives; Origins: Eastern Christian; Orthodox Monasticism: Byzantine; Pachomius, St.; Pilgrimages, Christian: Near East; Recluses, Western Christian; Russia: History; Spirituality: Eastern Christian; Stylites; Syria; Theodore of Stoudios, St.

**Further Reading**
Brown, Peter, *Society and the Holy in Late Antiquity*, Berkeley: University of California Press, and London: Faber and Faber, 1982
Burton-Christie, Douglas, *The Word in the Desert: Scripture and the Quest for Holiness in Early Christian Monasticism*, New York: Oxford University Press, 1993
Chitty, Derwas, *The Desert a City*, Oxford: Blackwell, and Crestwood, New York: St. Vladimir's Seminary Press, 1966
Dawkins, M.E., *The Monks of Athos*, London: Allen and Unwin, 1936
Dodds, E.R., *Pagan and Christian in an Age of Anxiety: Some Aspects of Religious Experience from Marcus Aurelius to Constantine*, Cambridge: Cambridge University Press, and New York: Norton, 1965
Gould, Graham, *The Desert Fathers on Monastic Community*, Oxford: Clarendon Press, and New York: Oxford University Press, 1993
Lietzmann, Hans, *A History of the Early Church*, volume 4, translated by B.L. Woolf, London: Nicholson and Watson, and New York: Scribner, 1937
Morris, Rosemary, *Monks and Laymen in Byzantium, 843–1118*, Cambridge and New York: Cambridge University Press, 1995
Rostovtzeff, Michael, *Social and Economic History of the Roman Empire*, Oxford: Clarendon Press, 1926

# Hermits: Western Christian

A straightforward dichotomy between eremitism and the Western monastic tradition is false. Etymologically, the solitary (*monos*, "monk") withdraws (*anachorein*, thus "anchorite") to the desert (*eremus*, which gives rise to "hermit"). Although in response to specific historical developments, the words *monk*, *anchorite*, and *hermit* have come to have different meanings, the vocations they describe all look to a common origin in the deserts of the East, and all, in ways subtly distinct both from one another and from other historical manifestations of themselves, share a commitment to a hidden life of asceticism and contemplation. Two dichotomies recur throughout the vocations' history: (1) between the life of the hermit as unstructured, even anarchic, and that of the monk as characterized, above all, by order, and (2) between the communal life (cenobitism) of monks and the solitude of the hermit. The latter dichotomy, at least, is an oversimplification: throughout their history, the lives of monastic institutions, in the same way as individual monastic vocations, have always involved a negotiation between the competing claims of solitude and communion, the eremitic and the cenobitic.

The eremitic ideal seems to have been introduced to the West by Athanasius (c. 296–373), an exile from his bishopric of Alexandria first in Trier and then, from 339, in Rome. He offered both the personal testimony of a friend of Pachomius (c. 290–346) and Serapion and later his *Life of St. Antony*, the hagiographic classic that inspired not only the conversion of Augustine but also a host of literary descendants of which Jerome's *Life of St. Paul the First Hermit* (377?) was only the first and most influential. Early in the next century, these two lives were joined by the reminiscences of John Cassian (c. 360–433), newly settled in the West at Marseilles, that are contained in his *Institutes* and *Conferences* and in 424 by the *Life of St. Martin* by Sulpicius Severus (c. 316–397), the Hungarian-born bishop of Tours and founder of Gaul's first communities of hermits at Ligugé and Marmoutier.

In its transmission to the temperate West, the ideal found its realization not in the desert but in the wilderness and isolation of the ocean, the fens, or the forest. The search for "a desert in the ocean" was an important feature of early Celtic eremitism, and the islands of Lérins off Cannes were home to one of the first and longest-lived Western eremitic settlements; in England the fenland county of Norfolk boasted more medieval solitaries than any other, and the 12th-century *Life of St. Bernard of Tiron* described the forests of northwestern France as "virtually a second Egypt." Although the hermit was thus situated at the margins of society, he was not outside it; like the Holy Man of antiquity, he was endowed by his liminality with an important mediatory and cohesive function that occasionally expressed itself in more tangible form than prayerful intercession alone. Wulfric of Haselbury (England), a 12th-century enclosed solitary, served his village community as arbitrator, healer, and agent for poor relief (perhaps even as banker) and as a link between the worlds of the villagers and of their Norman overlord.

The Rule of St. Benedict (c. 540) classifies monks into cenobites and hermits or anchorites (both of which are to be commended) and sabaraites and gyrovagues (which are not). It makes provision, by way of exception, for hermits:

who not in the first fervour of their conversion, but after long probation in a monastery, having learnt in association with many brethren how to fight against the devil, go out well-armed from the ranks of the community to the solitary combat of the desert. They are able now to live without the help of others, and by their own strength and God's assistance to fight against the temptations of mind and body. (c. 1)

Because the Rule is so heavily weighted toward the cenobitic life, it is easy to forget that Benedict saw it only as preparatory to the superior life of the hermit. His own monastery of Monte Cassino probably had hermitages associated with it, and throughout the Middle Ages it was common for Benedictine monasteries to make provision for monks who wanted to live a solitary life. Cluny, in opposition to which many of the new eremitic communities were to define themselves, had a number of hermits living under its protection during the 11th and 12th centuries in hermit chapels, some of which are still extant. However, it became common for monastic authors to emphasize that the hermit life was for the few. In his Rule for Solitaries (late ninth century), Grimlaicus warned that "to enter the solitary life is the highest perfection; to live imperfectly in solitude is to incur the greatest damnation."

In the 11th and 12th centuries, the eremitic ideal was proclaimed anew by reformers disillusioned with the worldliness and perceived liturgical self-indulgence of Cluniac Benedictinism. Casting their initiatives as a return to monasticism's desert origins, men such as Romuald (c. 950–1027) embraced a form of eremitism that emphasized austerity, asceticism, and withdrawal to isolated locations above total solitude. Often accompanied and invariably joined by further companions, they founded monasteries and in some cases new religious orders. This movement began in Italy and overran France but made itself felt across all Western Europe, from Hungary to Portugal to northern England. Out of this movement were born the great orders of Cîteaux, Prémontré, and Chartres as well as the Camaldolese, Grandmontines, Savigniacs, Vallombrosans, and the order of Fontevraud. Of the new orders, the Carthusians and the Camaldolese have retained their eremitic character to this day; most of the other eremitic foundations of this period became, more or less quickly, victims of their own success in that increased size necessitated rules, customs, and reintegration into the institution of cenobitic monasticism. However, the temptation to see in this a teleology (i.e., to view cenobitism as the natural state of monastic man) is likely to be resisted because it is to treat cenobitism as an absolute instead of attending to the reality of the 12th century's many new monasticisms, each achieving in its own way the necessary balance between the individual and the monastic community.

At about the same time as the new monastic orders were becoming established, a terminological distinction emerged between hermits and anchorites. The word *anchorite*, which the Rule of St. Benedict had used interchangeably with *hermit*, now comes, with its synonym *recluse*, to describe one perpetually enclosed within a cell. Although the vocation is amply recorded in early sources, such as Gregory of Tours' *History of the Franks* (c. 591), and was legislated for in several of the early councils, its great popularity belongs to the 12th and 13th centuries. Monks occasionally became recluses, but this way of life was more often entered into by secular priests, laymen, and especially women (most of them laywomen), who seem to have outnumbered men in the vocation throughout its history. The female bias in anchoritism, although sometimes overstated, stands in sharp contrast to the almost total exclusion of women from the vocation of hermit. Some anchorites' cells (reclusories or anchorholds) were attached to monastic churches, sometimes with arrangements for the provision of the necessities of life from the monasteries' resources; however, most were secular foundations that were situated adjoining parish churches or in purely civic locations, such as at town gates.

Although ceremonies for the enclosure of anchorites were accompanied by the Office of the Dead and included a ritual walling up of the door to the reclusory, surviving remains suggest that dwellings were not overly cramped, and legislative and other documentary material allows for a garden, servants, and domestic animals. Indeed, the author of the 15th-century English *Speculum Inclusorum* (Mirror for Recluses) feels that it is necessary to include a warning directed at those of his readers who might choose the life of an anchorite because they think that it is an existence more comfortable than that they presently enjoy.

The period of greatest popularity of the anchoritic vocation was also that in which the life of the hermit suffered a severe decline in esteem. Late-medieval eremitism (like, to a lesser degree, eremitism of all periods) is characterized above all by diversity: although monks still left behind communal life to enter the spiritual combat of the hermitage and solitaries still fled the world to island and woodland retreats, most hermits from the 14th century onward seem to have entertained less lofty spiritual ambitions and were employed in what would later be defined as public works: mending roads, keeping bridges, tending lighthouses, or acting as caretakers of outlying chapels or sites of pilgrimage. Moreover, in seeking alms for their maintenance in this work they became implicated in the period's obsessions with the evils first of religious mendicancy and later of vagrancy. A good index of their social decline is afforded by their depiction in literature: whereas in the High Middle Ages the hermit was an important figure in the chansons de geste and the courtly romances, by the end of the period he inhabits the world of satire, folktale, and balladry. Already in this period calls were being made for greater regulation of the eremitic vocation, and in England evidence exists for closer episcopal supervision of hermits during the last century before the Reformation.

The religious upheaval of the 16th century saw the end of hermit life in those countries that embraced Protestantism. It also provoked a return to the desert ideal among a number of the existing religious orders. The Order of Camaldoli was reformed under the influence of Paolo Giustiniani (1476–1528), and the eremitic element in early Franciscanism was rekindled by the foundation of the Capuchins, whose rule was approved in 1529. Inspired by Teresa of Avila (1515–1582) and John of the Cross (1542–1591), the newly seceded Discalced Carmelites, recalling the order's origins on Mount Carmel, established their first "desert" convent at Bolarque (Spain) in 1592. In France the end of the wars of religion was accompanied by a remarkable efflorescence of hermit vocations and hermitage building. As in the late Middle Ages, concerns were voiced about the unstructured nature of the life, and in the mid–17th century men such as Michel de St.-Sabine and Frère Jean-Jacques reformed her-

mitages and drew up constitutions that were adopted by diocesans for the governance of all solitaries under their jurisdiction. The prudence of such measures could be argued on the evidence of the eremitic community of Port-Royal (southwest of Paris; colonized from 1633), which was not only unconventional and highly fashionable but also a hotbed of Jansenist heresy. Such moves to regularize the solitary vocation culminated in the inclusion by Pope Benedict XIV (1740–1758) of a section on hermits and recluses in his authoritative compendium of canon law, *De synodo dioecesana*, in 1748.

The year 1748 also saw the birth of the pilgrim-hermit St. Benedict Joseph Labre. However, by the time of his death in Rome in 1783, the solitary life was already in decline, being regarded with incomprehension by a new Age of Reason, and the destruction of the Napoleonic Wars was about to engulf the remaining hermitages along with much else in Europe's religious life. Since that time vocations to the hermit life have existed – some have been celebrated, such as that of Charles de Foucauld (1858–1916), the "Hermit of the Sahara" and posthumous founder of the Little Brothers and Little Sisters of Jesus, and that of John C. Hawes (1876–1956), the "Hermit of Cat Island" (Bahamas) – but none has approached an eremitic movement. A possible exception is the burgeoning of the solitary life in the United States marked by the Carthusian foundation at Whitingham, Vermont, in 1951; the Camaldolese at Big Sur, California, in 1958; and the Trappist Thomas Merton's withdrawal to his woodland hermitage, which he began in the 1950s and made full time in 1965. In addition, the Anglican Church has seen a number of 20th-century experiments in the solitary life, including in the 1920s and 1930s a number of anchoresses in contact with Fr. William Sirr, hermit at Glasshampton Park, Worcestershire, and the establishment in 1967 by the Oxford-based Community of the Sisters of the Love of God (founded in 1906) of a *lavra*-style settlement in Kent.

E.A. JONES

*See also* Benedict of Nursia, St.; Camaldolese; Carmelites; Cassian, John; Celtic Monasticism; Claustration (Cloister), Rules of; Desert Fathers; Desert Mothers; Egypt; Island Monasteries, Christian; Jansenist Controversy; Jerome, St.; Lérins, France; Martin of Tours, St.; Monte Cassino, Italy; Origins: Western Christian; Pachomius, St.; Recluses, Western Christian; Social Services: Western Christian

## Further Reading

Anson, Peter F., *The Call of the Desert: The Solitary Life in the Christian Church*, London: SPCK, and New York: Morehouse-Barow, 1964

Clay, Rotha M., *The Hermits and Anchorites of England*, London: Methuen, 1914; Detroit, Michigan: Singing Tree Press, 1968

Constable, Giles, "Eremitical Forms of Monastic Life," in *Istituzioni monastiche e istituzioni canonicali in Occidente (1123–1215): Atti della Settimana internazionale di studio, Mendola, 28 agosto–3 settembre 1977*, Milan: Vita e Pensiero, 1980

Doyère, Pierre, "Erémitisme en Occident," in *Dictionnaire de spiritualité, ascétique et mystique: Doctrine et histoire*, volume 4, Paris: Beauchesne, 1937–1995

LeGoff, Jacques, "The Wilderness in the Medieval West," in *The Medieval Imagination*, translated by Arthur Goldhammer, Chicago: University of Chicago Press, 1988

*L'Eremitismo in Occidente nei Secoli XI e XII: Atti della seconda Settimana internazionale di studio, Mendola, 30 agosto–6 settembre 1962*, Milan: Società editrice Vita e Pensiero, 1965

Leyser, Henrietta, *Hermits and the New Monasticism: A Study of Religious Communities in Western Europe, 1000–1150*, London: Macmillan, and New York: St. Martin's Press, 1984

Mayr-Harting, Henry, "Functions of a Twelfth-Century Recluse," *History* 60 (1975)

McCann, Justin, editor and translator, *The Rule of Saint Benedict: In Latin and English*, London: Burns, Oates, 1952

Sainsaulieu, Jean, *Les Ermites français*, Paris: Éditions du Cerf, 1974

Sheils, W.J., editor, *Monks, Hermits and the Ascetic Tradition: Papers Read at the 1984 Summer Meeting and the 1985 Winter Meeting of the Ecclesiastical History Society*, Oxford: Blackwell, 1985

Warren, Ann K., *Anchorites and Their Patrons in Medieval England*, Berkeley: University of California Press, 1985

# Hesychasm

The term *Hesychasm* (from the Greek word *hesychazein*, "to be quiet, or at rest") has at least four distinct meanings in the history of monastic life and spirituality. These four meanings are by no means contradictory, but neither are they identical. However, all four can be connected in some way to the person and the writings of Gregory Palamas (1296–1359), who stands as a link between the earlier and later spiritual tradition of the Christian East. These four meanings are outlined here.

First, *Hesychasm* signifies, in general, the phenomenon of monasticism based on the eremitic or hermit life. In this sense, the word denotes the experience that begins in fourth-century Egypt and is based on the lifestyle of Antony the Great. It is the way of silence, which seeks, through radical withdrawal from society, to overcome the divisions and tensions within and thus become "simple" (cf. Matt. 6:22) and "single," which might have been one of the original meanings of the word *monk* (*monos, monastikos, monachos*). The way of contemplation and prayer are articulated in the writings of Evagrius Ponticus (346–399). This is perhaps the classical definition of *Hesychasm*.

Second, it is associated in more recent times with the theology of Gregory Palamas and often is used interchangeably with *palamism*. In this sense, the word signifies the articulation by Palamas of the way of mystical experience and divine knowledge through a vision of the uncreated light. Appealing to recognized patristic authorities and specifically to the Cappadocian Fathers and Dionysius the Pseudo-Areopagite, Palamas argued that God

transcends our understanding, being "above all essence" and "above all name." Palamas emphasizes the traditional distinction between essence (i.e., the inner being) and energies (i.e., outward revelation) in God and claims that from this life we are able to have a direct knowledge of God's energies, a mystical union in this age with God face to face. This experience is manifested in the form of a vision of divine light, as this is observed in the lives of the saints and most notably revealed at the Transfiguration of Christ, which is an anticipation of the last times. As in the teaching of Symeon the New Theologian (949–1022), for Gregory this light is nonimaginary and yet nonmaterial, both invisible and visible, uncreated and infinite.

Third, it is related by contemporary authors to the psychosomatic methods of prayer. Although it is incorrect to reduce the phenomenon of Hesychasm to these methods, such practices were the point of much controversy in the 14th century; Barlaam the Calabrian (c. 1290–1348) denounced the way of prayer among the monks of Mount Athos, whom he disdainfully called "people with their souls in their navels." It was Palamas who accepted being the spokesman of the monks, underlining the participation of the entire person – body and soul – in the mystical experience. He appeals to the Incarnation and refers to the Eucharist in developing a doctrine of salvation that includes and involves the human body and all material creation. Although not dwelling on the method of prayer as such – which he believes to be merely a useful technique for beginners in the spiritual life – Palamas claims that the human body does not simply see the divine light but itself becomes transfigured into light. Once again, the understanding is that what occurs completely on the Last Day can be anticipated "even now," "so far as this possible." If the second meaning of *Hesychasm* implies an eschatological consequence to silence, this third meaning has clear anthropological and cosmological implications in relation to salvation in Christ.

Finally, *Hesychasm*, beyond its more narrowly religious connotations, also designates a social, cultural, and political ideology that originated in Byzantium in the 14th century but that left an impact on the intellectual, social, and artistic development of the churches and peoples where the Byzantines "exported" their civilization. The fierce conflict between Barlaam and Palamas, especially from 1337 to 1341, revived a long-standing intellectual and spiritual clash between the more "extreme," contemplative monks and the more "moderate," educated humanists. The former suspected, whereas the latter admired, classical Greek philosophy and secular learning.

The theology and spirituality of Hesychasm contains a dynamic tradition centered on silence. One of the key texts for the appreciation of *hesychia*, or silence, is the *Ladder of Divine Ascent*, written by the seventh-century abbot of the Sinaite monastery of St. Catherine, John Climacus (c. 570–c. 649). The *Ladder* has an entire step (no. 27) devoted to *hesychia* that proved influential over the centuries, especially among the Hesychast writers of the 14th century who defended this tradition on Mount Athos.

In the *Ladder*, it immediately becomes clear that *hesychia* has two levels: an outward (John speaks of "the door of the cell") and an inward ("the door of the tongue") (*Step* 27,17 PG88:1100). On the outward level, silence signifies external, physical withdrawal from noise, an outward way of solitude as compared with a communal way of life. In this sense, *hesychia* is practiced in the eremitic or semi-eremitic forms of monastic life. On the inward level, silence denotes an inner disposition, the spiritual withdrawal from earthly visions and forms. The Hesychast is the one who is concentrated on God. Clearly, the two senses overlap, but they are not the same. In the first half of the sixth century, Barsanuphius the Elder writes that "silence does not consist of keeping your mouth shut" (*Letter* 554).

The understanding is that the Hesychast confines within the body the power of the soul. The Hesychast is not dispersed but concentrated on a single point or person: God. Therefore, the true definition of silence is not outward but inward. Drawing on Basil's famous *Second Letter* on spirituality, we might say that the Hesychast is the one who tries to move from multiplicity to simplicity, from diversity to unity. "The kingdom of God is within you" (Luke 17:21): the Hesychast realizes this inwardly and intensely, and here silence connects with apophatic (i.e., negative) theology. The apophatic way applies both to theology and to prayer. God is a mystery above and beyond our understanding and even our experience. Silence is a fitting way of addressing God in prayer, as it constitutes an imageless, wordless attitude whereby the Hesychast no longer simply says prayer but is prayer all the time.

The Jesus Prayer – otherwise known as "pure prayer," "prayer of the intellect," or "prayer of the heart" – is the way with which such silence has been practiced for centuries in the Christian East. The essential words of this prayer are "Lord Jesus Christ have mercy on me." The origins of this prayer can be sought in Nitria and Scetis of fourth-century Egypt. The fundamental elements of the Jesus Prayer are precisely the discipline of repetition, the emphasis on penitence, the teaching of imageless prayer, the devotion to the Holy Name of Jesus, the use of a specific formula (probably dating from the sixth or seventh century), and the linking of this formula with the rhythm of breathing (a technique found as early as the 13th century).

JOHN CHRYSSAVGIS

*See also* Basil the Great, St.; Climacus, John, St.; Greece; Humanism, Christian; Meditation: Christian Perspectives; Mount Athos, Greece; Origins: Comparative Perspectives; Orthodox Monasticism; Paisy Velichkovsky; Palamas, Gregory, St.; Philokalia; Russia: History; Spirituality: Eastern Christian; Vision, Mystical: Eastern Christian; Visual Arts, Eastern Christian: Painting

## Further Reading

Behr-Sigel, Elisabeth, *The Place of the Heart: An Introduction to Orthodox Spirituality*, Torrance, California: Oakwood, 1992
Hausherr, Irénée, *Hésychasme et prière*, Rome: Pont Institutum Studiorum, 1966
Mantzarides, Georgios, *The Deification of Man: St. Gregory Palamas and the Orthodox Tradition*, Crestwood, New York: St. Vladimir's Seminary Press, 1984
Meyendorff, John, *A Study of Gregory Palamas*, London: Faith Press, 1964; Crestwood, New York: St. Vladimir's Seminary Press, 1974
Meyendorff, John, *Byzantine Hesychasm: Historical, Theological, and Social Problems*, London: Variorum Reprints, 1974
Meyendorff, John, *St. Gregory Palamas and Orthodox Spirituality*, New York: St. Vladimir's Seminary Press, 1974
Ware, K., "The Spirituality of the *Philokalia*," *Sobornost. Incorporating Eastern Churches Review* 13:1 (1991)

# Hierocrats. *See* Holy Men in Power (Hierocrats), Buddhist

# Hilda, St. 614–680

English Christian nun and abbess at Whitby

Saint Hilda is renowned as a pioneer of female monasticism in England who established one of the first double monasteries (containing both female and male religious) at Whitby in the kingdom of Northumbria. Most of what we know about her comes from the *Historia Ecclesiastica* of St. Bede (c. 673–735). Hilda was a member of the Deiran royal house (one of the two rival dynasties fighting for control of Northumbria) and was born while her father, Hereric, was in exile. At the age of 33, around 647, she decided to enter the religious life and was intending to join her sister in the Frankish monastery of Chelles when she was persuaded by Bishop Aidan (d. 651) of Lindisfarne to become one of the first female religious in the kingdom of Northumbria. At first she lived with a few companions on the banks of the River Wear but subsequently took over a community at Hartlepool that had been established by Heiu, the first Northumbrian woman to enter the religious life. In 655 Hilda was entrusted with the upbringing of Ælfflaed, the daughter of King Oswy of Northumbria and her own first cousin once removed, whom the king had vowed to the religious life if he was victorious in battle. Two years later she acquired the estate of Streanæshalch, later known as Whitby, and subsequently a daughter community was founded nearby at Hackness.

Under Hilda, Whitby became one of the foremost monasteries in Northumbria and a major center of learning in both Latin and Old English. The *Vita S. Gregorii*, the first Latin saint's life to be produced in England, was written there shortly after her death, and it was at Whitby that Caedmon (d. c. 680) composed the earliest religious verse in Old English. Five of the men she trained became bishops, and in 664 the important synod, where it was decided that the Northumbrian Church would recognize the authority of Canterbury rather than Iona, was held in the monastery. In 671 King Oswy was buried at Whitby. He was

Ruins of Whitby Abbey Church (12th–13th century), Whitby, Northumbria, England.
Photo courtesy of the Editor

from the Bernician royal family but had married Hilda's cousin Eanflaed, who subsequently retired to Whitby and became joint abbess with her daughter Ælfflaed on Hilda's death. Oswy's patronage of Whitby (in Deira) can be seen as part of his attempts to reconcile the rival Bernician and Deiran royal houses. Hilda died on 17 November 680, and her feast is widely commemorated in Anglo-Saxon calendars; in the tenth century her relics were translated to the monastery of Glastonbury. Although her preeminence undoubtedly owed much to her royal birth, she was also an inspirational leader. Bede praises her for her wisdom and says that all who knew her "used to call her mother because of her outstanding devotion and grace" (IV, 23). She has been an inspiration for other women who have entered the church, some of whom have taken her name, and for pioneers of women's education, including the founders of St. Hilda's College, Oxford, in 1893.

BARBARA YORKE

*See also* Abbess, Christian; Bede, St.; Double Houses, Western Christian; England; Liturgy: Western Christian; Whitby, England; Women's Monasteries: Western Christian

## Biography

Descended from one of the royal families of Northumbria, Hilda wished to join her sister at a monastery near Paris, but was recalled by St. Aidan to become abbess at Hartlepool in 649. In 657 she founded a double monastery at Streanaeshalch, which the Danes later renamed Whitby. At the synod there in 664, she sided with the losing party that defended Celtic modes of dating, but she readily accepted the decision in favor of Roman customs.

## Further Reading

Blair, Peter Hunter, "Whitby as a Centre of Learning in the Seventh Century," in *Learning and Literature in Anglo-Saxon England: Studies Presented to Peter Clemoes on the Occasion of His Sixty-Fifth Birthday*, edited by Michael Lapidge and Helmut Gneuss, Cambridge and New York: Cambridge University Press, 1985

Colgrave, Bertram, editor, *The Earliest Life of Gregory the Great by an Anonymous Monk of Whitby*, Cambridge: Cambridge University Press, and Lawrence: University of Kansas Press, 1968

Colgrave, Bertram, and Roger Mynors, editors, *Bede's Ecclesiastical History of the English People*, Oxford: Clarendon Press, 1969

Fell, Christine, "Hilda, Abbess of Streonæshalch," in *Hagiography and Medieval Literature: A Symposium*, edited by Hans Bekker-Nielsen, Odense: Odense University Press, 1981

Hollis, Stephanie, *Anglo-Saxon Women and the Church: Sharing a Common Fate*, Woodbridge, Suffolk, and Rochester, New York: Boydell Press, 1992

Wormald, Patrick, "St. Hilda, Saint and Scholar (614–80)," in *A Celebration of the Education of Women*, edited by Jane Mellanby, Oxford: St. Hilda's College, 1993

# Hildegard of Bingen, St. 1098–1179

German Benedictine poet, composer, educator, and visionary

Hildegard of Bingen, born into a family of Rhineland free nobility in 1098, is a key figure for understanding the changing aspects of 12th-century monasticism. At an early age (probably when she was ten years old, in 1108) she was enclosed with the anchoress Jutta of Spanheim in a cell attached to the monastery of Disibodenberg in the Diocese of Mainz. This monastery had undergone various changes of allegiance since its putative founding by a wandering Irish bishop, St. Disibod, in the seventh century. Most recently it had been returned to the Benedictine fold by Archbishop Ruthard, who expelled a company of canons from the site and colonized it with monks from his own foundation of St. James at Mainz, a monastery influenced by the Hirsau reform.

Here Hildegard was raised in an atmosphere of rigorous asceticism by her older mentor, taught the Psalms, and introduced to the Benedictine way of life. The fame of Jutta and her pupil attracted further recruits to the anchorage, which was transformed by degrees into a small convent for women alongside the male monastery. When Jutta died in 1136, Hildegard was elected *magistra* by the sisters and took over the running of the establishment, subject to the authority of the abbot of Disibodenberg. Between 1136 and about 1149, various tensions developed between the two groups because of overcrowding at the hilltop site and because of Hildegard's acknowledgment of her prophetic powers and the commencement of her writing career and subsequent recognition by Pope Eugenius II (1145–1153) at the Synod of Trier in 1148–1149. Empowered by these circumstances she announced that she had been commanded by God to move her nuns to a deserted site at Rupertsberg, a hill overlooking the confluence of the Nahe and Rhine Rivers at Bingen, about 18 miles from Disibodenberg. This news was not welcomed by the monks of the parent house. It was not until they had been convinced that the divine will was involved by a spectacular illness in which Hildegard took to her bed, speechless and immobile, that they agreed to the plan. Thus, Hildegard, with the moral and financial support of Archbishop Henry of Mainz and Richardis, marchioness of Stade, transferred with 18 of her nuns to Rupertsberg in 1150.

Despite initial difficulties caused by the undeveloped nature of the site, complaints from the nuns, and further resistance from the monks, Hildegard succeeded in establishing her new convent. This was admiringly described by Guibert of Gembloux in the 1170s as having places for 50 sisters, running water in the workshops, and a constant stream of visitors.

Equable relations with Disibodenberg took some time to reestablish. It seems that Hildegard was always regarded and indeed regarded herself as in some way subject to the abbot of the parent house. Yet by 1158 she had established virtual independence from them in matters of nuns' dowries, lay advocacy, and election of the superior, and the abbot was to afford spiritual services to the nuns by providing a provost of their choice. The only extant reference to her as abbess of Rupertsberg comes in the privilege of 1163 given by Emperor Frederick Barbarossa (1152–1190). The term most frequently used is *magistra* (mistress) of the nuns at Rupertsberg. A few years later she founded a second convent across the Rhine at Eibingen. This convent might have been for women of less exalted social station than those at Rupertsberg, although comparatively little is known about this foundation (except that it was established on the site of a former convent of canonesses).

Despite establishing two convents Hildegard should not be considered as having founded her own order. She always declared herself a staunch follower of St. Benedict, although some of her practices might have surprised him. These are the subject of an interesting interchange of letters between Hildegard and a canoness from Andernach, Tenxwind, who, as the sister of Richard of Springiersbach, represented the new austerity of the stricter wing of the Augustinians. Tenxwind takes Hildegard to task for the elaborate clothing that she allows her nuns to wear on festal days (long white silk veils and crowns over their unbound hair) and for the social exclusivity of her nuns. In this way it would seem that Tenxwind was representing the new spirit of reform with its emphasis on the simplicity and egalitarian nature of the *vita apostolica*, whereas Hildegard represents the more traditional connection of the Benedictines with the high nobility and social privilege.

During her lifetime Hildegard served as adviser and confidant to a wide range of people, from popes and emperors to heads of religious houses and their rank-and-file members. She corresponded with monastics of most orders, including the reforming Cistercians, such as Bernard of Clairvaux (1090–1153); with the new orders of canons (including a cordial exchange with Richard of Springiersbach); and with numerous heads of Benedictine houses, both male and female. She also visited monasteries on several extended trips and tried to settle their problems. She wrote a short commentary on the Benedictine Rule for a group of monks who cannot now be positively identified. The commentary displays a humane and commonsense interpretation of Benedict's work, which, she was wont to claim, had been inspired by the Holy Spirit, while Benedict was "a second Moses." Indeed, the keynote of her advice to monastics of all kinds is moderation, in contrast, it seems, to the practices of her mentor, Jutta.

Although Hildegard's reputation among the Benedictines has always been high, it suffered somewhat during the later Middle Ages among the mendicant orders because of the varying interpretations given her prophecies. After her death these were collected by the Cistercian Gebeno of Eberbach and issued under the title *Pentachronon*. Their use in antifraternal polemics led, for example, to her denigration by the Franciscan archbishop of Canterbury, John Pecham (c. 1225–1292), in the late 13th century.

Although the abbey at Rupertsberg was destroyed in the Swedish wars and now remains only as a series of fragmentary arches incorporated into a much later building (presently used as a business that sells office equipment), the physical remains of her establishment at Eibingen (after serving, among other things, as an arsenal) were reclaimed in the 19th century for the religious purposes of the parish of Eibingen. However, her main spiritual legacy continues somewhat further from the river at the Abtei St. Hildegard, refounded at Eibingen from the Beuron Benedictine community in the early years of the 20th century. The abbey has been active in furthering the study of Hildegard's works ever since.

SABINA FLANAGAN

*See also* Benedictines: Female; Bernard of Clairvaux, St.; Beuron, Germany; Botany; Death: Christian Perspectives; Gardens: Christian Perspectives; Germany; Hymnographers; Liturgy: Western Christian; Music: Christian Perspectives; Pharmacology; Scholars, Benedictine; Spirituality: Western Christian; Women's Monasteries: Western Christian

## Biography

At around age eight Hildegard was placed in the care of Blessed Jutta, a recluse at a Benedictine monastery at Disibodenberg, Germany. In 1136 Hildegard succeeded Jutta as *magistra*. Around 1150 her community moved to a newly built convent at Rupertsberg, near Bingen. From the early 1140s she recorded her visions and Latin poems, which have won wide attention in the 20th century.

## Major Works

*Scivias*, 1141–1151
*Liber vitae meritorum*, 1158–1163; as *The Book of the Rewards of Life*, translated by Bruce W. Hozeski, 1994
*Liber divinorum operum*, 1163–1173/74
77 songs (*carmina*)

## Further Reading

Burnett, Charles, and Peter Dronke, editors, *Hildegard of Bingen: The Context of Her Thought and Art*, London: Warburg Institute, 1998
Dronke, Peter, "Hildegard of Bingen," in *Women Writers of the Middle Ages: A Critical Study of Texts from Perpetua (d. 203) to Marguerite Porete (d. 1310)*, edited by Dronke, Cambridge and New York: Cambridge University Press, 1984

Flanagan, Sabina, *Hildegard of Bingen, 1098–1179: A Visionary Life*, London and New York: Routledge, 1989; 2nd edition, 1998
Flanagan, Sabina, "'For God Distinguishes the People on Earth as in Heaven': Hildegard of Bingen's Social Ideas," *Journal of Religious History* 22 (1998)
Haverkamp, Alfred, "Tenxwind von Andernach und Hildegard von Bingen: Zwei 'Weltanschauungen' in der Mitte des 12. Jahrhunderts," in *Institutionen, Kultur und Gesellschaft im Mittelalter*, edited by Lutz Fenske et al., Sigmaringen: Thorbecke, 1984
Hotchin, Julie, "Enclosure and Containment: Jutta and Hildegard at St. Disibod," *Magistra* 2 (1996)
Kerby-Fulton, Kathryn, "Hildegard of Bingen and Antimendicant Propaganda," *Traditio* 43 (1987)
Mews, Constant, "Seeing Is Believing: Hildegard of Bingen and the *Life of Jutta, Scivias*, and the *Commentary on the Rule of Benedict*," *Tjurunga* 51 (1996)
Newman, Barbara, *Sister of Wisdom: St. Hildegard's Theology of the Feminine*, Berkeley: University of California Press, 1987
Newman, Barbara, editor, *Voice of the Living Light: Hildegard of Bingen and Her World*, Berkeley: University of California Press, 1998
Schrader, Marianna, and Adelgundis Führkötter, *Die Echtheit des Schrifttums der Heiligen Hildegard von Bingen*, Cologne: Böhlau, 1956

# Historiography, Recent: Eastern Christian

Eastern Orthodox historiography of the last 150 years might be described in a number of different ways, and the topic is of large proportions. This article divides history writers into five groups: Slavophiles, ecclesiastical historians of the 19th century, professors at St. Sergius (Paris), "Oxbridge" professors, and professors at northeastern American seminaries. Because members of each group show certain temporal, geographical, and social traits in common, if not theological and hermeneutical agendas, the divisions appear useful. However, many excellent histories were written during this same period by people who do not fit easily into any of these categories. To address this situation a sixth section is devoted here to significant authors and their works not previously categorized.

*The Slavophiles and Soloviev*
While Greece and the Balkans were fighting for freedom against the Ottoman Empire, the Slavophiles in Russia developed as an articulate theological group. Although known not as historiographers but mainly as theologians and philosophers, they followed Russian Orthodox tradition in such a way as to forge an epistemology and hermeneutic distinct from that of nationalistic Westernizers and neo-Scholastics who otherwise dominated the Orthodox East. The Slavophiles tended to draw a strict dichotomy between idealized Russisms (things Russian) and dominant German trends, such as pantheism and romanticism.

Prominent among the Slavophiles were A. Khomiakov, I. and P. Kireevsky, K. and I. Aksakov, and Iu. Samarin, as well as others. In addition to the premier essay "The Church is One," focusing on the unity and *Sobornost* (Catholicity) of the Church, Alexis Khomiakov (1804–1860) wrote *L'Église latine et le protestantisme au point de vue de l'Église d'Orient* and his unfinished world *History* ("Semiramis") in three volumes (Riasanovsky, *Russia and the West*, 1952), both of which were published posthumously. Konstantine Aksakov (1817–1860), in a collection of published and unpublished articles on various topics, was responsible for the Slavophile Russian history. Peter Kireevsky (1808–1856) brought out ten volumes of epics, folklore, and spiritual literature, *Songs Collected by P.V. Kireevsky*. The project appears to have first been conceived as a collection of historical and literary monuments by a large circle of Moscovite Slavophiles, but it came under intense political and religious censorship and a change of scope. Iurii Samarin's (1819–1876) masters thesis, a critique of the spiritual regulation of Peter I (1689–1725) and Westernizing influences in the Orthodox Church, remained influential for a century.

Vladimir Soloviev (1853–1900) stood in direct continuity with the Slavophiles but developed his thought ecumenically – in defiance of his roots – as he expanded philosophically toward the West. Again he is not identified mainly as a historian, as was his father, Sergei Soloviev (1820–1879), one of the premier 19th-century Westernizers and author of the 29-volume *History of Russia*. Vladimir wrote *La Russie et l'Église Universelle* (*Russia and the Universal Church*) and an additional corpus of a dozen major philosophical and theosophical works. He helped inspire the return of the Russian intelligentsia to the Orthodox Church in the 20th century, including Sergius Bulgakov and Pavel Florensky.

*Ecclesiastical Historians of the 19th (and Early 20th) Century*
Had we not begun our overview with the Slavophiles, we would have discovered the first modern Eastern Orthodox ecclesiastical historian only a few decades earlier in the person of Metropolitan Platon Levshin (1737–1812). The ecclesiastical historians are characterized by multivolume collections of primary sources or complete histories on a given topic. Each monastery was expected to chronicle its own history, but it would always be connected with a larger geographical and chronological scheme. E.E. Golubinskii appears to be the Church historian most often consulted by specialists today. One could make the case that Platonov and Kliuchevsky, along with Kondakov, were more influential among their many students at the turn of the century (Vernadsky, *Russian Historiography*) and in Europe after the Russian Revolution. Most of the works are available only in Russian, but the topics covered regularly include the Balkans, Greece, and Turkey.

*Complete Collection of the Laws of the Russian Empire*; *Complete Collection of Russian Chronicles*; *Documents of the Imperial Society of Russian History and Antiquities at Moscow University*; *Documents Collected by the Archeographic Expedi-* tion of the Academy of Sciences; *Historical Acts and Supplements to Historical Acts*; *Russian Historical Library*; Makarii Bulgakov, *The History of the Kiev Theological Academy* (1843), *History of the Russian Schism of Old Belief* (1854), *The History of the Russian Church* (1857–1882); Evgenii Golubinskii, *A History of the Russian Church* (in Russian, 2 vols., 1900), *A Short Outline of the History of the Orthodox Church of Bulgaria, Serbia, and Romania* (in Russian, 1871); Filaret Gumilevskii, *History of the Russian Church* (6th edition, 1895), *Survey of Russian Spiritual Literature* (1884); Nikolai Kapterev, *The Nature of Russian Relations with the Orthodox East in the XVI and XVII Centuries* (1884/1968), *Patriarch Nikon and His Opponents in the Matter of Reforming Church Rituals* (1887); Vasilii Kliuchevsky, *Ancient Russian Hagiographies as Historical Sources* (1872), *Course of Russian History* (1921); Nikodim Kondakov, *Iconography of Our Lord God and Savior, Jesus Christ: A Historical and Iconographical Essay* (in Russian, 1905); Mikhail Priselkov, *Essays on the Ecclesiastical-Political History of Kievan Rus' X–XII cc.* (1913); Sergei Platonov, *Lectures* (8th edition, 1913), *Essays on the History of the Time of Troubles in the State of Muscovy in the XVI–XVII Centuries*; Petr Znamenskii, *Educational Guide to the History of the Russian Church* (1904), *Ecclesiastical Schools in Russia Prior to the Reform of 1808* (1881).

*Professors at St. Sergius Orthodox Theological Institute*
The "Spiritual Academy" of Berlin and the activities of the Russian Students Christian Movement coalesced in 1925 under the leadership of Metropolitan Evlogii Georgievskii. Staffed by the most distinguished faculty of Eastern scholars in the 20th century, the St. Sergius Orthodox Theological Institute in Paris exercised a powerful influence inside and outside the Orthodox *oikoumene* and produced a huge theological and historical corpus (Zernov, *Russian Émigré Authors*, 1973).

One can discern several dynamic historiographical trajectories in their works. First, all members voiced an adverse reaction to Marxism and Leninism, and Berdiaev and Bulgakov – both former Marxists – had written strong condemnatory evaluations before arriving in Paris. Second, the group was self-conscious about its own unique intellectual and spiritual repository and took this responsibility seriously, writing in ways that had been curtailed previously by czarist censors and forbidden under Lenin and Stalin. Third, as immigrants in Paris the members were forced to engage issues alive in the West. This rapprochement included a strong presence in ecumenical circles and a lively dialogue with Roman Catholic theologians who would later attend the Second Vatican Council (1962–1965). Fourth, Church history – and all history – for the writers stood under the sway of transcendent events, such as the Parousia of the Holy Spirit, the Incarnation, the Eucharist, and the Resurrection. Afanasiev and Berdiaev, although not historians, made these points explicit in different ways. Fifth, history and its sources were preferred over theological systems, and even programmatic history was made accountable to original sources. A. Kartashev, V. Lossky, and G. Florovsky reevaluated Christian history by a reliance on "patristics" in the Eastern sense of the field's purview: all fathers and mothers of the Church in all centuries. This reevaluation, sometimes referred to as Florovsky's "Neo-Patristic Synthesis," did not eschew any substantive controversial category and resonated with a similar movement among (French) Roman Catholics.

Nikolai Afanasiev, Thesis: "The Power of the State in the Ecumenical Councils" (in Serbian, 1927), *Trapeza Gospodnia* (*The Lord's Supper*, 1952); Nicholai Berdiaev, *The Meaning of History* (1923); Sergei Bulgakov, *The Orthodox Church* (1935); Olivier Clément, *Byzance et le christianisme* (1964); Anton V. Kartashev, *Essays on the History of the Russian Church* (in Russian, 1959), *The Ecumenical Councils* (in Russian, 2 vols., 1963); Basil (Vsevolod) Krivocheine, *In the Light of Christ: Saint Symeon, the New Theologian* (translated 1986); Nicholas O. Lossky, *History of Russian Philosophy* (1951); Vladimir Lossky, *The Mystical Theology of the Eastern Church* (1957); Myrrha Lot-Borodine, *La Déification de l'homme, selon la doctrine des Pères grecs* (1970), *Un Maître de la spiritualité byzantine au XIVe siècle, Nicolas Cabasilas* (1958); Léonide Ouspensky, *The Meaning of Icons* (with Vladimir Lossky, translated 1952), *The Theology of the Icon* (2 vols., translated 1978).

### "Oxbridge" Professors

The English-speaking world owes a great debt of gratitude to Oxford and Cambridge scholars who consistently engaged topics left untreated in many major Western universities and seminaries (e.g., the "Dark Ages" through the "Reformation" in the East). In most Western curricula today, even graduate and seminary historical studies continue to jump from Augustine to Luther in the West (with a brief pause for the Crusades and Thomas Aquinas) and ignore the East completely. The Oxbridge professors are to be commended for their high quality of scholarship and balance in treating later Byzantine, Arabic, and Slavic studies. Of these histories the highly recommended *Orthodox Church* by Bishop Kallistos (Timothy) Ware has been the most influential.

Derek Baker, editor, *The Orthodox Churches and the West* (1976); Richard Clogg, editor, *Greece in the 1980s* (1983); Methodios Fouyas, *Orthodoxy, Roman Catholicism and Anglicanism* (1972); Charles Frazee, *The Orthodox Church and Independent Greece* (1969); Joan Mervyn Hussey, *Church & Learning in the Byzantine Empire, 867–1185* (1963), *The Byzantine Empire* (1966), *The Orthodox Church in the Byzantine Empire* (1986); Sir John Lawrence, *A History of Russia* (7th revised edition, 1993); John Mason Neale, *A History of the Holy Eastern Church* (1847–1873); Dimitry Obolensky, *Bogomils* (1948), *Byzantium and the Slavs* (1971), *The Byzantine Commonwealth* (1971), *Six Byzantine Portraits* (1988); William Palmer, *The Patriarch and the Tsar* (6 vols., 1876); Michael Rostovtzeff, *Ancient Decorative Art in South Russia* (1914), *An Outline of the History of the Ancient World* (1963); Steven Runciman, *A History of the Crusades* (3 vols., 1951–1954), *Eastern Schism* (1955), *The Sicilian Vespers* (1958), *Fall of Con-*

*stantinople, 1453* (1965), *The Great Church in Captivity* (1968), *Last Byzantine Renaissance* (1970), *The Byzantine Theocracy* (1977); Philip Sherrard, *Church, Papacy and Schism* (1978); A. P. Vlasto, *The Entry of the Slavs into Christendom* (1970); Kallistos Ware, *Eustratios Argenti: A Study of the Greek Church Under Turkish Rule* (1964), *The Orthodox Way* (1979); Nicolas Zernov, *Eastern Christendom* (1961), *The Russian Religious Renaissance of the Twentieth Century* (1963), *The Russians and Their Church* (1945, 3rd edition 1978).

### Professors at Northeastern American Seminaries

Georges Florovsky (1893–1979) left St. Sergius to teach at St. Vladimir's Orthodox Theological Seminary, Holy Cross Greek Orthodox School of Theology, and Harvard Divinity School and wrote a theological history that covers all periods from the Apostolic fathers to the present as well as other books and articles constituting a 54-page bibliography. Other scholars, such as John Meyendorff, Jaroslav Pelikan, and Georges Barrois, also completed far-reaching studies, the latter two before they entered the Orthodox Church. Most histories by professors of northeastern American seminaries have been written within the last 30 years and tend toward the genre of introduction or apologias while invariably presenting information new to Western readers.

Georges Barrois, *Manuel d'Archéologie Biblique* (2 vols., 1939, 1953); George Bebis, *Nicodemos of the Holy Mountain* (1989); John Lawrence Boojamra, *Church Reform in the Late Byzantine Empire* (1980); *Dumbarton Oaks Bibliographies* (1973– ), *Papers* (1941– ), *Studies* (1950– ), *Texts* (1967– ); John Erickson, *The Challenge of Our Past: Essays in Orthodox Canon Law and Church History* (1991); George Fedotov, *The Russian Church Since the Revolution* (1928), *Saints of Ancient Russia, X–XVII* (1931), *A Treasury of Russian Spirituality* (1948), *The Russian Religious Mind* (2 vols., 1946, 1966); Georges Florovsky, *Ways of Russian Theology* (2 vols., 1979), *Collected Works* (14 vols., 1972– ); Stanley Harakas, *Let Mercy Abound: A Chronicle of Greek Orthodox Social Concerns* (1983); Vasiliki Limberis, *Divine Heiress: The Virgin Mary and the Creation of Christian Constantinople* (1994); John Meyendorff, *Living Tradition* (1978), *Byzantium and the Rise of Russia* (1981), *Imperial Unity and Christian Divisions* (1989), *The Orthodox Church* (4th edition 1996), *Rome, Constantinople, Moscow* (1996); Jaroslav Pelikan, *The Christian Tradition: A History of the Development of Doctrine* (5 vols., 1971–1989); John Romanides, *Franks, Romans, Feudalism, and Doctrine* (1981); Alexander Schmemann, *The Historical Road of Eastern Orthodoxy* (1963), *Russian Theology, 1920–1965: A Bibliographical Survey* (1969); Constance Tarasar, editor, *Orthodox America, 1794–1976* (1975); Michael Vaporis, *Some Aspects of the History of the Ecumenical Patriarchate of Constantinople in the Seventeenth and Eighteenth Centuries* (1969).

### Previously Unclassified Studies

Wassilij Alexeev, *Materials for the History of the Russian Orthodox Church in the U.S.S.R.* (1954–1955); Aziz Atiya, editor,

*Coptic Encyclopedia* (1991); James Billington, *The Icon and the Axe: An Interpretive History of Russian Culture* (1970); James Cunningham, *A Vanquished Hope: The Movement for Church Renewal in Russia, 1905–1906* (1981); Mircea Eliade, editor, *The Encyclopedia of Religion* (1987); Deno Geanakoplos, *A Short History of the Ecumenical Patriarchate of Constantinople 330–1990* (2nd revised edition, 1990); Vlad Georgescu, *The Romanians: A History* (translated 1990); Chrestos Giannaras, *The Modern Greek Identity* (in Greek, 1978), *Orthodoxy and the West* (in Greek, 1996); André Grabar, *Christian Iconography: A Study of Its Origins* (translated 1961); Raphael Hawaweeny, *An Historical Glance at the Brotherhood of the Holy Sepulchre* (translated 1996); A. Martinos, *Thriskevtiki kai Ithiki Enyklopaideia* (12 vols., 1962–1968); Metropolitan Maximos of Sardes, *The Oecumenical Patriarchate in the Orthodox Church: A Study in the History and Canons of the Church* (translated 1976); George Ostrogorsky, *History of the Byzantine State* (translated 1986); Athanasios Paliouras, editor, *Oecumenical Patriarchate* (1989); Aristeides Papadakis, *Crisis in Byzantium* (1997); Justin Popovich, *The Truth about the Serbian Orthodox Church and Communist Yugoslavia* (in Serbian, 1990); Andrzej Poppe, *The Rise of Christian Russia* (1982); Dimitry Pospielovsky, *The Orthodox Church in the History of Russia* (1998), *The Russian Church Under the Soviet Regime 1917–1982* (2 vols., 1984), *Soviet Studies on the Church and the Believer's Response to Atheism* (1988); Omeljan Pritsak, *The Origin of Rus'* (1981); Michael Prokurat, Alexander Golitzin, Michael D. Peterson, *Historical Dictionary of the Orthodox Church* (1996); Nicholas Riasanovsky, *A History of Russia* (6th edition, 1999); Sophia Senyk, *A History of the Church in Ukraine* (1993); Igor Smolitsch, *Geschichte der russischen Kirche, 1700–1917* (1964–1991); Dumitru Staniloae, *Philokalia* (translation and commentary in Romanian); Alexander Vasiliev, *History of the Byzantine Empire, 324–1453* (2 vols., 1952); Paul Verghese, *Koptisches Christentum* (1973), *Die Syrischen Kirchen in Indien* (1974), *A Light Too Bright: The Enlightenment Today* (1992); George Vernadsky, *A History of Russia* (1969), *Kievan Russia* (1948); Andrzej Walicki, *A History of Russian Thought from the Enlightenment to Marxism* (translated 1979); Vasilii Zenkovsky, *A History of Russian Philosophy* (translated 1953).

MICHAEL PROKURAT

*See also* Archaeology: Near East; Bulgaria; Greece; Hagiography: Eastern Christian; Libraries: Eastern Christian; Martyrs: Eastern Christian; Orthodox Monasticism; Russia; Serbia; Theology, Eastern Christian; Ukraine; Women's Monasteries: Eastern Christian

## Further Reading

Afanasiev, Nikolai N., "The Power of the State in the Ecumenical Councils," Masters Thesis, Belgrade University, 1927

Alexeev, Wassilij, *Materials for the History of the Russian Orthodox Church in the U.S.S.R.*, New York: Research Program on the U.S.S.R., 1954–1955

Atiya, Aziz S., *A History of Eastern Christianity*, Notre Dame, Indiana: University of Notre Dame Press, 1967; London: Methuen, 1968

Atiya, Aziz S., editor, *Coptic Encyclopedia*, New York: Macmillan, 1991

Barrois, Georges A., *Manuel d'Archéologie Biblique*, 2 vols., Paris: Picard, 1939, 1953

Bebis, George S., *Nicodemos of the Holy Mountain*, Mahwah, New Jersey: Paulist Press, 1989

Berdiaev, Nikolai, *The Meaning of History*, London: Centenary Press, and Cleveland, Ohio: World, 1936

Blane, Andrew, editor, *Georges Florovsky: Russian Intellectual and Orthodox Churchman*, Crestwood, New York: St. Vladimir's Seminary Press, 1993

Boojamra, John Lawrence, *Church Reform in the Late Byzantine Empire: A Study of the Patriarchate of Athanasois of Constantinople*, Brookline, Massachusetts: Hellenic College Press, 1980

Bulgakov, Makarii, *The History of the Kiev Theological Academy*, Kiev: Kiev Theological Academy, 1843

Bulgakov, Makarii, *History of the Russian Schism of Old Belief*, Petersburg: Petersburg Theological Academy, 1854

Bulgakov, Makarii, *The History of the Russian Church*, 13 vols., Moscow: Ecclesiastical Publications, 1857–1882

Bulgakov, Sergei, *The Orthodox Church*, Florida: Three Hierarchs Seminary Press, 1977

Clément, Olivier, *Byzance et le christianisme*, Paris: Presses Universitaires de France, 1964

Christoff, Peter K., *Introduction to Nineteenth Century Russian Slavophilism*, 4 vols., The Hague/Paris: Mouton et al., 1961–1991; Princeton, New Jersey: Princeton University Press, 1961

Constantelos, Demetrios J., *Understanding the Greek Orthodox Church*, New York: The Seabury Press, 1982; 3rd edition, Brookline, Massachusetts: Hellenic College Press, 1998

Cunningham, James W., *A Vanquished Hope: The Movement for Church Renewal in Russia, 1905–1906*, Crestwood, New York: St. Vladimir's Seminary Press, 1981

*Dumbarton Oaks Bibliographies* (1973– )

*Dumbarton Oaks Papers* (1941– )

*Dumbarton Oaks Studies* (1950– )

*Dumbarton Oaks Texts* (1967– )

Erickson, John H., *The Orthodox Church in History*, 5 vols., Crestwood, New York: SVS Press, 1989–

Erickson, John H., *The Challenge of Our Past: Essays in Orthodox Canon Law and Church History*, Crestwood, New York: St. Vladimir's Seminary Press, 1991

Fedotov, George P., *The Russian Church Since the Revolution*, London and New York: SPCK, 1928

Fedotov, George P., *Saints of Ancient Russia, X–XVII*, Paris: YMCA Press, 1931

Fedotov, George P., *The Russian Religious Mind*, 2 vols., Cambridge, Massachusetts: Harvard University Press, 1946, 1966

Fedotov, George P., editor, *A Treasury of Russian Spirituality*, New York: Sheed and Ward, 1948; London: Sheed and Ward, 1950

FitzGerald, Thomas E., *The Orthodox Church*, Westport, Connecticut: Greenwood Press, 1995

Florovsky, Georges, *The Collected Works of Georges Florovsky*, 14 vols., Belmont, Massachusetts: Nordland, 1972–

Florovsky, Georges, "The Predicament of the Christian Historian," in *Christianity and Culture*, volume 2, *The Collected Works of Georges Florovsky*, Belmont, Massachusetts: Nordland, 1974

Florovsky, Georges, *Ways of Russian Theology*, 2 vols., Belmont, Massachusetts: Nordland, 1979

Geanakoplos, Deno, *A Short History of the Ecumenical Patriarchate of Constantinople (330–1990): "First Among Equals" in the Eastern Orthodox Church*, New York: Greek Orthodox Archdiocese of North and South America, 1983; 2nd edition, Brookline, Massachusetts: Holy Cross Orthodox Press, 1990

Georgescu, Vlad, *The Romanians: A History*, Columbus, Ohio: Ohio State University Press, 1990

Georgievskii, Evlogii, *Put' Moei Zhizni. Vospominaniia Mitropolita Evlogiia, Izlozhennye po Ego Rasskazam T. Manukhinoi* (My Life's Path: The Memoirs of Metropolitan Evlogii, Based on His Own Accounts by T. Manukhina), Paris: YMCA Press, 1947

Giannaras, Chrestos, *He neoellenike tautoteta* (The Modern Greek Identity), Athens: Ekdoseis Gregore, 1978

Giannaras, Chrestos, *Orthodoxia kai dyse ste neotere Hellada* (Orthodoxy and the West), Athens: Ekdoseis Domos, 1996

Golubinskii, Evgenii E., *Istoriya Russkoi Tserkvi* (A History of the Russian Church), 2 vols., Moscow, 1900; reprint, The Hague: Mouton, 1969

Golubinskii, Evgenii E., *Kratkii Ocherk Istorii Pravoslavnoi Tserkvi Bolgarskoi, Serbskoi, i Rumynskoi* (A Short Outline of the History of the Orthodox Church of Bulgaria, Serbia, and Romania), Moscow: Ecclesiastical Publications, 1871

Grabar, André, *Christian Iconography: A Study of Its Origins*, Princeton, New Jersey: Princeton University Press, 1961; London: Routledge, 1969

Hammond, Peter, *The Waters of Marah: The Present State of the Greek Church*, London and New York: Macmillan, 1956

Harakas, Stanley S., *Let Mercy Abound: Social Concern in the Greek Orthodox Church*, Brookline, Massachusetts: Holy Cross Orthodox Press, 1983

Hawaweeny, Rt. Rev. Raphael, *An Historical Glance at the Brotherhood of the Holy Sepulchre*, translated by Michel Najim, Torrance, California: Oakwood Publications, 1996 (originally published in Arabic under the pseudonym Sheikh 'Abl El Ahad Eshshaf, 1893)

Hussey, Joan Mervyn, *Church and Learning in the Byzantine Empire, 867–1185*, New York: Russell and Russell, 1963

Hussey, Joan Mervyn, *The Byzantine Empire*, Cambridge: Cambridge University Press, 1966

Hussey, Joan Mervyn, *The Orthodox Church in the Byzantine Empire*, Oxford: Clarendon Press, 1986

Karmiris, John N., editor, *Ta Dogmatika Kai Symbolika Mnemeia tes Orthodoxou Katholikes Ekklesias*, 2nd edition, 2 vols., Graz: Druck, 1968

Kartashev, Anton V., *Ocherki po Istorii Russkoi Tserkvi* (Essays on the History of the Russian Church), 2 vols., Paris: YMCA Press, 1959; Moscow: Nauka, 1991

Kartashev, Anton V., *Vselenskie Sobory* (The Ecumenical Councils), 2 vols., Paris: Izd. Osobago Komiteta pod Predsiedatelstvom Episkopa Silvestra, 1963

Khomiakov, Alexis S., *L'Église latine et le protestantisme au point de vue de l'Église d'Orient*, Lausanne, Switzerland: Berda, 1872; Farnborough, United Kingdom: Gregg, 1969

Kondakov, Nikodim, *Ikonografiia Gospoda Boga i Spasa Nashego Iisusa Khrista. Istoricheskii i Ikonograficheskii Ocherk* (Iconography of Our Lord God and Savior, Jesus Christ: A Historical and Iconographical Essay), C.-Peterburg: Tovarishchestvo R. Golike i A. Vil'borg, 1905

Krivocheine, Basil (Vsevolod), *Dans la Lumière du Christ*, Chevetogne, Belgique: Éditions de Chevetogne, 1980; as *In the Light of Christ: Saint Symeon, the New Theologian*, Crestwood, New York: SVS Press, 1986

Lawrence, John, *A History of Russia*, New York: Farrar, Strauss, Cudahy, 1960; 7th edition, New York: Meridian, 1993

Limberis, Vasiliki, *Divine Heiress: The Virgin Mary and the Creation of Christian Constantinople*, London and New York: Routledge, 1994

Lossky, Nicholas O., *History of Russian Philosophy*, New York: International Universities Press, Inc., 1951

Lossky, Vladimir, "Tradition and Traditions," in *In the Image and Likeness of God*, Crestwood, New York: St. Vladimir's Seminary Press, 1985

Lot, Myrrha Borodine, *La Déification de l'homme, selon la doctrine des Pères grecs*, Paris: Cerf, 1970

Lot, Myrrha Borodine, *Un Maître de la spiritualité byzantine au XIVe siècle, Nicolas Cabasilas*, Paris: Orante, 1958

Makarii, Metropolitan of Moscow, *Istorija Russkoj Cerkvi v 12 Tomach*, Dusseldorf: Brucken, 1968

Maloney, George A., *A History of Orthodox Theology since 1453*, Belmont, Massachusetts: Nordland, 1976

Maximos, Metropolitan of Sardes, *The Oecumenical Patriarchate in the Orthodox Church: A Study in the History and Canons of the Church*, Thessaloniki: Patriarchal Institute for Patristic Studies, 1976

Meyendorff, John, *The Orthodox Church: Its Past and Its Role in the World Today*, New York: Pantheon, and London: Darton, 1962; 4th edition, Crestwood, New York: St. Vladimir's Seminary Press, 1996

Meyendorff, John, *Living Tradition*, Crestwood, New York: St. Vladimir's Seminary Press, 1978

Meyendorff, John, *Byzantium and the Rise of Russia: A Study of Byzantino-Russian Relations in the Fourteenth Century*, Cambridge and New York: Cambridge University Press, 1981

Meyendorff, John, *Imperial Unity and Christian Divisions*, Crestwood, New York: St. Vladimir's Seminary Press, 1989

Meyendorff, John, *Rome, Constantinople, Moscow: Historical and Theological Studies*, Crestwood, New York: St. Vladimir's Seminary Press, 1996

Neale, John Mason, *A History of the Holy Eastern Church*, 5 vols., London: Masters, 1847–1873

Obolensky, Dimitry, *Bogomils: A Study in Balkan Neo-Manichaeism*, Cambridge: Cambridge University Press, 1948; New York: AMS, 1978

Obolensky, Dimitry, *Byzantium and the Slavs*, London: Variorum, 1971; Crestwood, New York: St. Vladimir's Seminary Press, 1994

Obolensky, Dimitry, *The Byzantine Commonwealth: Eastern Europe 500–1453*, Crestwood, New York: St. Vladimir's

Seminary Press, and London: Weidenfeld, 1971; new edition, London: Phoenix Giant, 1999

Obolensky, Dimitry, *Six Byzantine Portraits*, Oxford: Clarendon Press, and New York: Oxford University Press, 1988

Ostrogorsky, George, *History of the Byzantine State*, London: Blackwell, 1986

Ouspensky, Léonide, *The Meaning of Icons*, Boston: Boston Book and Art Shop, 1952; 2nd edition, Crestwood, New York: St. Vladimir's Seminary Press, 1982

Ouspensky, Léonide, *The Theology of the Icon*, 2 vols., Crestwood, New York: St. Vladimir's Seminary Press, 1978

Paliouras, Athanasois, editor, *Oecumenical Patriarchate: The Great Church of Christ*, Geneva: Orthodox Center, 1989

Palmer, William, *The Patriarch and the Tsar*, 6 vols., London: Trubner, 1871–1876

Papadakis, Aristeides, *Crisis in Byzantium*, New York: Fordham University Press, 1983; revised edition, Crestwood, New York: St. Vladimir's University Press, 1997

Papademetriou, George, editor, *Introduction to St. Gregory Palamas*, New York: Philosophical Library, 1973

Pelikan, Jaroslav, *The Christian Tradition: A History of the Development of Doctrine*, volume 1: *The Emergence of Christian Tradition (100–600)*, Chicago: University of Chicago Press, 1971

Pelikan, Jaroslav, *The Vindication of Tradition*, New Haven, Connecticut: Yale University Press, 1984

Popovich, Justin, *Istina o Srpskoj Pravoslavnoj Crkvi u Komunistickoj Jugoslaviji* (The Truth about the Serbian Orthodox Church and Communist Yugoslavia), Grayslake, Illinois: The Free Serbian Orthodox Diocese of the U.S.A. and Canada, 1990

Poppe, Andrzej, *The Rise of Christian Russia*, London: Variorum, 1982

Pospielovsky, Dimitry, *The Orthodox Church in the History of Russia*, Crestwood, New York: St Vladimir's Seminary Press, 1998

Pospielovsky, Dimitry, *The Russian Church Under the Soviet Regime 1917–1982*, 2 vols., Crestwood, New York: St. Vladimir's Seminary Press, 1984

Pospielovsky, Dimitry, *Soviet Studies on the Church and the Believer's Response to Atheism*, New York: St. Martin's Press, and London: Macmillan, 1988

Pritsak, Omeljan, *The Origin of Rus'*, Cambridge, Massachusetts: Harvard University Press, 1981

Ramet, Pedro, editor, *Eastern Christianity and Politics in the Twentieth Century*, volume 1, *Christianity Under Stress*, Durham, North Carolina: Duke University Press, 1988

Riasanovsky, Nicholas V., *Russia and the West in the Teaching of the Slavophiles*, Cambridge, Massachusetts: Harvard University Press, 1952

Riasanovsky, Nicholas V., *A History of Russia*, New York: Oxford University Press, 1963; 6th edition, 1999

Romanides, Ioannes, *Franks, Romans, Feudalism, and Doctrine: An Interplay Between Theology and Society*, Brookline, Massachusetts: Holy Cross Orthodox Press, 1981

Rostovtzeff, Michael I., *Ancient Decorative Art in South Russia*, Petersburg: Archeological Commission, 1914

Rostovtzeff, Michael I., *An Outline of the History of the Ancient World (Ocherk Istorii Drevniago Mira)*,

volume 1: selections, translated by J.D. Duff, edited by Elias J. Bickerman, New York: Oxford University Press, 1963

Runciman, Steven, *A History of the Crusades*, 3 vols., Cambridge: Cambridge University Press, 1951–1954

Runciman, Steven, *Eastern Schism*, Oxford: Clarendon Press, 1955; New York: AMS, 1983

Runciman, Steven, *The Sicilian Vespers: A History of the Mediterranean World in the Later Thirteenth Century*, Cambridge: Cambridge University Press, 1958; Baltimore, Maryland: Penguin, 1960

Runciman, Steven, *Fall of Constantinople, 1453*, Cambridge: Cambridge University Press, 1965; New York: Cambridge University Press, 1990

Runciman, Steven, *The Great Church in Captivity: A Study of the Patriarchate of Constantinople from the Eve of the Turkish Conquest to the Greek War of Independence*, London: Cambridge University Press, 1968; New York: Cambridge University Press, 1985

Runciman, Steven, *Last Byzantine Renaissance*, Cambridge: Cambridge University Press, 1970

Runciman, Steven, *The Byzantine Theocracy*, Cambridge and New York: Cambridge University Press, 1977

Schmemann, Alexander, *The Historical Road of Eastern Orthodoxy*, New York: Chekhov, 1954; London: Harvill Press, 1963

Senyk, Sophia, *A History of the Church in Ukraine*, Rome: Pontificio Istituto Orientale, 1993

Sherrard, Philip, *Church, Papacy and Schism*, London: SPCK, 1978

Smolitsch, Igor, *Geschichte der russischen Kirche, 1700–1917*, Leiden: E.J. Brill, 1964–1991

Soloviev, Vladimir, *Russia and the Universal Church*, translated by Herbert Rees, London: Bles, 1948

Staniloae, Dumitru, *Philokalia*, Bucharest: Editura Institutului Biblic, 1900–

Tarasar, Constance J., editor, *Orthodox America 1794–1976*, Syosset, New York: The Orthodox Church in America Department of History and Archives, 1975

Vaporis, Michael, *Some Aspects of the History of the Ecumenical Patriarchate of Constantinople in the Seventeenth and Eighteenth Centuries: A Study of the Ziskind MS. No. 22 of the Yale University Library*, New York: Greek Orthodox Archdiocese, 1969

Vasiliev, Alexander, *History of the Byzantine Empire, 324–1453*, 2 vols., Madison: University of Wisconsin Press, and Oxford: Blackwell, 1952

Verghese, Paul, *Koptisches Christentum*, Stuttgart: Evangelisches Verlagswerk, 1973

Verghese, Paul, *Die Syrischen Kirchen in Indien*, Stuttgart: Evangelisches Verlagswerk, 1974

Verghese, Paul, *A Light Too Bright: The Enlightenment Today: An Assessment of the Values of the European Enlightenment and a Search for New Foundations*, Albany: State University of New York Press, 1992

Vernadsky, George, *A History of Russia*, 5 vols., New Haven, Connecticut: Yale University Press, 1943–1969

Vernadsky, George, *Russian Historiography: A History*, edited by Sergei Pushkarev, translated by Nicklas Lupinin, Belmont, Massachusetts: Nordland, 1978

Walicki, Andrzej, *A History of Russian Thought from the Enlightenment to Marxism*, translated from the Polish by Hilda Andrews-Rusiecka, Stanford, California: Stanford University Press, 1979; Oxford: Clarendon Press, 1980

Ware, Kallistos, *The Orthodox Church*, Baltimore, Maryland: Penguin, 1963; Harmondsworth: Penguin, 1969; 2nd edition, London and New York: Penguin, 1993

Ware, Kallistos, *Eustratios Argenti: A Study of the Greek Church Under Turkish Rule*, Oxford: Clarendon Press, 1964; Willits, California: Eastern Orthodox Books, 1974

Ware, Kallsitos, *The Orthodox Way*, London: Mowbrays, and Crestwood, New York: St. Vladimir's Seminary Press, 1979; revised edition, 1998

Ware, Kallistos, "Tradition and Traditions," in *Dictionary of the Ecumenical Movement*, edited by Nicholas Lossky et al., Geneva: World Council of Churches, and Grand Rapids, Michigan: Eerdmans, 1991

Zenkovsky, V.V., *A History of Russian Philosophy*, 2 vols., London: Routledge., 1953

Zernov, Nicholas, *The Russians and Their Church*, London: SPCK, and New York: Macmillan, 1945; 3rd edition, London: SPCK, 1978

Zernov, Nicholas, *Eastern Christendom*, New York: Putnam, and London: Weidenfeld, 1961

Zernov, Nicholas, *The Russian Religious Renaissance of the Twentieth Century*, London: Darton, and New York: Harper and Row, 1963

Zernov, Nicolas, *Russian Émigré Authors: A Biographical Index and Bibliography of Their Works on Theology, Religious Philosophy, Church History and Orthodox Culture, 1921–1972*, Boston: G.K. Hall, 1973

# Historiography, Recent: Western Christian

Scholarly study of Western Christian monasticism, which began in Europe more than three centuries ago, remains vital at the start of the third millennium. A proliferation of projects and publications of both traditional and innovative nature has characterized monastic history during the last 30 years. In many ways the history of monasticism is like any other historical subject: a great deal more is being written about it than a generation ago, new work has moved along many paths, and it is harder than ever to keep track of directions in research. To generalize – the necessary evil of a brief summary, which can canvass only a few important trends and mention a handful of studies – it is perhaps useful to think of recent work in monastic history as breaking down barriers. The cloister wall has proven to be extremely permeable, literally and figuratively, as historians consider the practices, influences, and significance of monastics and monasticism in Western culture from various disciplinary and interdisciplinary perspectives. Coinherence of methodologies and approaches has produced creative interactions between a centuries-old tradition of monastic history, with its focus on institutional developments and notable individuals, and a new range of sacred and profane topics, from ascetic spirituality to modern labor politics. Thus, recent scholarship has given impetus to investigation of the larger social meanings, broadly defined, of monastic people and monastic life across the centuries.

In 1974 Giles Constable's essay "The Study of Monastic History Today" noted a "real need for a sociological and comparative approach" to break down old dichotomous clichés: eremitism and cenobitism, action and contemplation, errancy and permanence. Constable found that "some beginnings have been made towards the study of what may be called monastic ecology: the mutual relations between monasteries and their environment." The literature he cited in this connection was mostly by German-language scholars. One of the most influential of these, although not specifically a study of monasticism, was Herbert Grundmann's innovative 1935 work, the expanded 1961 edition of which has recently been translated into English as *Religious Movements in the Middle Ages: The Historical Links between Heresy, the Mendicant Orders, and the Women's Religious Movement in the Twelfth and Thirteenth Century, with the Historical Foundations of German Mysticism*. At the title suggests, Grundmann was a juxtaposer: he posited common religious and material contexts for orthodox and heretical movements in 12th- and 13th-century Europe, connected these movements and traced their links to contemporary women's spiritual and religious activities (on which very little had previously been written at all), and finally found in female affective religion a necessary precursor of the flowering of later medieval German mysticism. Grundmann broke new ground by looking at both doctrinal issues and socioeconomic developments to evaluate and account for the religious environment of the European past. His project stepped beyond conventional intellectual boundaries and defied ready categorization: Robert E. Lerner's introduction to the English translation calls it a founding text in the "religious-historical branch of cultural history" while noting its influence on subsequent accounts of the medieval mendicants and women religious, to note only the two topics most interesting to students of monasticism.

A second, expanded edition of Grundmann's book was printed in 1961, just a few years after David Knowles (1896–1974) completed his four massive volumes on the monastic history of England from the 10th century to the 16th. The encyclopedic work of the Benedictine Knowles marked perhaps the apogee of the great tradition of institutional monastic history written by monks reaching back to 17th-century France. It was the secular Grundmann and his "ecological" approach that set new directions. In the wake of Grundmann's investigative model, historians of monasticism after World War II and especially after 1960 increasingly took a broader view of their subject, but it was not until 1978 that a similarly foundational project appeared in English. Lester K. Little's *Religious Poverty and the Profit Economy in Medieval Europe* drew heavily on European studies of Grundmann and others, especially the French Dominican scholar Marie-Dominique Chenu (1895–1990). Little examined the relations between a money economy, the urban milieu, and the spirituality of poverty in Europe, from about 1000 to about 1300. The central sections of the book reinterpreted the history of Western Christian monasticism in this era.

In place of the standard narrative of waves of religious and spiritual innovation, decadence, and reform, Little offered an interpretation of monastic history that responded to evolving economic situations and structures, with the problem of religious poverty in an increasing wealthy society his central theme. All three sets of dichotomies that Constable had regarded as limiting the scope of monastic history evaporated in Little's sweeping approach. In addition Little's narrative elided the distinction between monks and friars, one still preserved in Constable's 1976 *Medieval Monasticism: A Select Bibliography*.

In the years since, many scholars have followed Little in situating monasticism firmly within the society around it, looking at the connections between monastics and the world for which they prayed as they sought their own salvation. For example, rather than concentrating on the classic themes of Cluniac organization and of spirituality, Barbara H. Rosenwein (1982) found outside the cloister, in the chaotic world of tenth-century Europe, an essential framework for explaining the initial success of Cluny. In a separate study (1989) Rosenwein closely traced the history of Cluny's landed estates to uncover spiritual and material values common to the monks and their secular neighbors. Most recently, Dominique Iogna-Prat (1998) has returned to Cluniac thought, specifically Abbot Peter the Venerable's (1092/94–1156) commentaries on heretics and non-Christians. Here the old subjects of Cluniac self-conception and spirituality are recast in terms of larger patterns of thought about the position of monasticism and the Church in the whole society and the relationship of those ecclesiastical conceptions to European ideas about inclusion and exclusion. Such a study represents both tradition, in its close reading of theological texts, and the newer sociological and comparative approach that Constable championed.

Thus, expansion of old conceptual confines does not mean that traditional approaches to monastic history have been correspondingly eclipsed or perennial themes dismissed. Indeed the pursuit of monastic history from institutional and national perspectives continues to thrive. In the United States, Cistercian Publications has brought into print more than 300 titles in monastic history during the last three decades. These include both translations of monastic authors and modern scholarly studies. The latter address the entire chronological range of monastic history, from its origins in the late antique Mediterranean to the 20th century, from Desert Fathers and Desert Mothers to Thomas Merton (1915–1968). The emphasis falls on Cistercian life and thought in the Middle Ages, but in keeping with the new inclusive vision of monastic studies, Cistercian Publications' list includes more than just Cistercian history and features books by both religious and secular scholars.

A great deal of important work also continues to appear in the pages of scholarly journals focused on a single monastic order or congregation. Several periodicals on mendicant history are published in Europe, and Cistercian history is the focus of serials published in Italy, Austria, Belgium, and the United States. *Analecta Praemonstratensia* concentrates on the long history of the so-called white canons from their origins in the 12th century,

and the Carthusian monks and nuns are the subject of their own journal as well. The larger Benedictine contribution is even more widely represented, divided between sharply focused periodicals such as *Regulae Benedicti studia* (on monastic rules) or *Vox benedictina* (on monastic women) and those such as *American Benedictine Review* that do not restrict themselves to strictly Benedictine or even monastic subject matter. These few references could easily be multiplied.

Recent monographic work has further shown how long-lived themes and theses in institutional monastic history can be reviewed and revised. The place of Cistercians in 12th-century society provides one example. In the last 15 years, the work of Constance H. Berman and Constance B. Bouchard has demolished the once-standard account of Cistercian monks as fleers of the world for the "desert" of European hinterlands, supposedly acting on separatist and self-impoverishing impulses articulated by many 12th-century monks. Instead, less self-conscious historical records show that Cistercians did not settle in the wildernesses and were in fact eager and even innovative participants in the economic boom of the 12th century. From another perspective Martha G. Newman (1996) has argued that Cistercian spirituality had a dual character: it involved not only individual contemplation and salvation but also a conception of the right ordering of the world that often led its adherents into extensive activity outside the cloister.

Nationally themed scholarly enterprises and publication series frequently include a great deal of material on monastic history. More than a century after it was conceived, the *Monasticon Belge* is now complete in eight large volumes that specifically address the history of Belgian monastic institutions in dozens of entries, many of them the product of archival and bibliographic investigation so extensive that they are miniature monographs. Various volumes of *Helvetia Sacra*, a series on the religious history of Switzerland, cover monastic life from the early Middle Ages to the 20th century. The same is true for the series *Italia Sacra* and *Germania Sacra*, which include numerous monographs on monastic houses across the medieval and modern centuries. The *Dictionnaire d'histoire et de géographie ecclésiastiques* (which first began to appear in 1912 and is only now moving into the middle of the alphabet) is universal in scope but contains extremely helpful short entries on themes, individuals, movements, and ideals in Christian monastic history, with emphasis on the French contribution.

Two characteristics of writing about recent monastic history deserve special notice. First, burgeoning scholarship on monastic women might represent the single most striking development of the last generation. In the 30 years or so after the first edition (1935) of Grundmann's *Religious Movements in the Middle Ages*, very little new scholarship on women in religion appeared, a failing vigorously addressed in the decades since, as women have become a major focus of all arenas of historical investigation. A substantial bibliography of work now examines monastic women from the early days in Egypt to our own times in the vastly expanded "West"; for example, more than one scholar has specifically identified her work as a contribution to that very history of English women's monasticism that David Knowles mostly neglected. Perhaps because women in the Western tradition have always been closely associated with the world, especially the human body and sexuality, studies on women and monasticism have, even more than other aspects of monastic history, tended toward the "relational," that is, toward considering women's religious experience in relation to social structure, gender ideology, or (following Grundmann) spirituality. Here a few titles can give an idea of a rich literature that defies brief description: Cordula Nolte, *Conversio und Christianitas: Frauen in der Christianisierung vom 5. bis 8. Jahrhundert* (1995; on women and the conversion of Europe in the early Middle Ages); Barbara Newman, *Sister of Wisdom: St. Hildegard's Theology of the Feminine* (1987); Caroline Walker Bynum, *Holy Feast and Holy Fast: The Religious Significance of Food to Medieval Women* (1987); Kathryn Burns, *Colonial Habits: Convents and the Spiritual Economy of Cuzco, Peru* (1999); Marie de la Trinité Kervingant, *Des moniales face à la Révolution française: Aux origines des Cisterciennes-Trappistines* (1989; on the re-creation of women's monasticism after the violent dismantling of regular religious life in Revolutionary France); and Carol K. Coburn and Martha Smith, *Spirited Lives: How Nuns Shaped Catholic Culture and American Life, 1836–1920* (1999). In 1996 Jo Ann Kay McNamara published *Sisters in Arms: Catholic Nuns through Two Millennia*, a narrative survey of female religious life from antiquity to the pontificate of John Paul II.

The second important feature of recent monastic historiography is that some of the most interesting new work on monasticism regularly appears in books whose central focus is another subject. To take only a few examples, John Bernhardt's recent study (1993) of the German monarchy in the central Middle Ages concluded that the kings relied heavily on monastic institutions and their inhabitants, male and female, in preserving and augmenting royal authority over a large territory. In such a book politics, monasticism, and gender all meet together. Two recent studies on preaching by Christoph T. Maier (1994) and Daniel R. Lesnick (1989) consider the relationship of Franciscans and Dominicans to, respectively, the ideal and reality of 13th-century crusading and the social and economic climate of late medieval Florence. The titles of those books signal their importance for monastic history, but that is not always the case. John Boswell's *Christianity, Social Tolerance, and Homosexuality: Gay People in Western Europe from the Beginning of the Christian Era to the Fourteenth Century* (1980), a pioneering work in what is currently termed queer studies, rests heavily on evidence from the monastic literary and cultural milieus.

The paradigm of "oblique monastic history" is especially notable for the postmedieval era. A typical strategy has been to frame books as discussions of monastic contributions to various historical subjects – for example, humanist and posthumanist Catholic education, organized labor in the industrial era, nursing, or the European settlement and cultural domination of the Americas – rather than as books on monastic life and thought per se. That is not to say that no books focus on monasteries and monastics since the 15th century, as quite a number do, some of

which are mentioned above. However, here even more than in late antique and medieval monastic history, the focus is less on the nature of cloistered religious life and thought than on its share and stake in a variety of social and cultural movements.

The trends just summarized have sometimes brought frustration in the wake of productivity, and so a few cautions are perhaps in order. It has become a habit among monastic historians to deplore the failure of any given book to consider its subject equally fully from all angles. To caricature a bit: there is a schism between those who have no patience for what they view as sexually repressed people worrying about how many angels can dance on the head of a pin and those who see the determined focus on monastic life in the context of the world, the flesh, and the devil as condescending to and dismissive of the most significant accomplishments of Catholic religious across the centuries. More concretely, monastic historians often criticize one another for insufficient attention either to theological and spiritual concerns or to social conditions. Although it is clear that the linking of secular and religious history has been enormously fertile, it might also be the case that it will be the rare scholar who can manage to write with genuine sensitivity to religious and worldly contexts. One such scholar is Giles Constable, whose 1996 *The Reformation of the Twelfth Century* considers the relation of monastic individuals and institutions to each other and to religious thought and change and the connections of all these actors and changes to extramonastic historical change as well. The breathless quality of that precis is intentional: the book is a marvelously observant discussion of an era when, as Constable put it, "links between people and between the individual and God were loosened and where the boundaries between the sacred and the profane . . . were redefined within the course of less than a long lifetime." However, only that far could one renowned scholar, summing up decades of perceptive reading and exposition, advance toward a comprehensive statement about the nature and importance of monastic life in one time and place. To make conclusions about causes, for example, Constable found impossible; for him it was not viable to ask, as Lester Little explicitly did, "Why?" McNamara's story of Catholic nuns from Mediterranean antiquity to late 20th-century America coheres primarily by dint of its author's passionate political agenda, her *longue dureé* view of monastic women who, engaged in constant struggle with male authority, over many centuries laid the groundwork for modern feminism. Has monastic history reached a stage where closely argued syntheses and interpretations are untenable? Is writing in light of strong ideological conviction – a venerable technique of Christian history, after all – the only way to counter the centripetal tendencies that characterize monastic historiography no less than academic historiography in general? If so, that is perhaps the price of doing what R.W. Southern 30 years ago urged ecclesiastical historians to do: study the history of religion "as an aspect of secular history" to understand better the limitations and opportunities of religious people and institutions. By the same token, following that formula, as so many have done, has given monastic history a whole new set of subjects and approaches, broadened its scope, renewed its ability to consider old subjects, and created new ones. Integration and completeness are more difficult than ever, but in the face of such fruitfulness it is hard to lament the end of coherence.

BRUCE L. VENARDE

See also Archaeology: Western Europe; Benedictines; Cluniacs; Cluny, France; Dominicans; Franciscans; Hagiography: Western Christian; Knowles, M. David; Leclercq, Jean; Orders (Religious), Origin of; Women's Monasteries: Western Christian

**Further Reading**

Note: this list includes only works mentioned or quoted in the foregoing essay.

Berman, Constance H., *Medieval Agriculture, the Southern French Society, and the Early Cistercians: A Study of Forty-three Monasteries*, Philadelphia: American Philosophical Society, 1986

Bernhardt, John W., *Itinerant Kingship and Royal Monasteries in Early Medieval Germany: c. 936–1075*, Cambridge and New York: Cambridge University Press, 1993

Boswell, John, *Christianity, Social Tolerance, and Homosexuality: Gay People in Western Europe from the Beginning of the Christian Era to the Fourteenth Century*, Chicago: University of Chicago Press, 1980

Bouchard, Constance B., *Holy Entrepreneurs: Cistercians, Knights, and Economic Exchange in Twelfth-Century Burgundy*, Ithaca, New York: Cornell University Press, 1991

Burns, Kathryn, *Colonial Habits: Convents and the Spiritual Economy of Cuzco, Peru*, Durham, North Carolina: Duke University Press, 1999

Bynum, Caroline Walker, *Holy Feast and Holy Fast: The Religious Significance of Food to Medieval Women*, Berkeley: University of California Press, 1987

Chenu, Marie-Dominique, *Nature, Man, and Society in the Twelfth Century: Essays on New Theological Perspectives in the Latin West*, translated by Jerome Taylor and Lester K. Little, Chicago: University of Chicago Press, 1957

Coburn, Carol K., and Martha Smith, *Spirited Lives: How Nuns Shaped Catholic Culture and American Life, 1836–1920*, Chapel Hill: University of North Carolina Press, 1999

Constable, Giles, "The Study of Monastic History Today," in *Essays on the Reconstruction of Medieval History*, edited by Vaclav Mudroch and G.S. Couse, Montreal: McGill-Queen's University Press, 1974

Constable, Giles, *Medieval Monasticism: A Select Bibliography*, Toronto and Buffalo, New York: University of Toronto Press, 1976

Constable, Giles, *The Reformation of the Twelfth Century*, Cambridge and New York: Cambridge University Press, 1996

Grundmann, Herbert, *Religious Movements in the Middle Ages: The Historical Links between Heresy, the Mendicant Orders, and the Women's Religious Movement in the Twelfth and Thirteenth Century, with the Historical Foundations of German Mysticism*, translated by Steven Rowan with an introduction by Robert E. Lerner, Notre Dame, Indiana: University of Notre Dame Press, 1995

Iogna-Prat, Dominique, *Ordonner et exclure: Cluny et la société chrétienne face à l'hérésie, au judaïsme et à l'islam, 1000–1150*, Paris: Aubier, 1998

Kervingant, Marie de la Trinité, *Des moniales face à la Révolution française: Aux origines des Cisterciennes-Trappistines*, Paris: Beauchesne, 1989

Knowles, David, *The Monastic Order in England: A History of Its Development from the Times of St. Dunstan to the Fourth Lateran Council, 943–1216*, Cambridge: Cambridge University Press, 1940; 2nd edition, Cambridge and New York: Cambridge University Press, 1976

Knowles, David, *The Religious Orders in England*, 3 vols., Cambridge: Cambridge University Press, 1948–1959

Lesnick, Daniel R., *Preaching in Medieval Florence: The Social World of Franciscan and Dominican Spirituality*, Athens: University of Georgia Press, 1989

Little, Lester K., *Religious Poverty and the Profit Economy in Medieval Europe*, Ithaca, New York: Cornell University Press, and London: Elek, 1978

Maier, Christoph T., *Preaching the Crusades: Mendicant Friars and the Cross in the Thirteenth Century*, Cambridge and New York: Cambridge University Press, 1994

McNamara, Jo Ann Kay, *Sisters in Arms: Catholic Nuns through Two Millennia*, Cambridge, Massachusetts: Harvard University Press, 1996

Newman, Barbara, *Sister of Wisdom: St. Hildegard's Theology of the Feminine*, Berkeley: University of California Press, and Aldershot: Scolar, 1987

Newman, Martha G., *The Boundaries of Charity: Cistercian Culture and Ecclesiastical Reform, 1099–1180*, Stanford, California: Stanford University Press, 1996

Nolte, Cordula, *Conversio und Christianitas: Frauen in der Christianisierung vom 5. bis 8. Jahrhundert*, Stuttgart: Hiersemann, 1995

Rosenwein, Barbara H., *Rhinoceros Bound: Cluny in the Tenth Century*, Philadelphia: University of Pennsylvania Press, 1982

Rosenwein, Barbara H., *To Be the Neighbor of Saint Peter: The Social Meaning of Cluny's Property, 909–1049*, Ithaca, New York: Cornell University Press, 1989

Southern, R.W., *Western Society and the Church in the Middle Ages*, Harmondsworth: Penguin, and Grand Rapids, Michigan: Eerdmans, 1970

# Holy Island, England. *See* Lindisfarne/Holy Island, England

# Holy Men/Holy Women: Buddhist Perspectives

Buddhist terminology has no proper equivalent of the Christian term *saint*, *holy man*, or *holy woman*. However, Buddhists of all times have venerated outstanding persons for their religious achievements, worshiped their relics, and honored their memories by writing hagiographic accounts of their lives or by creating images of them. Thus, it is safe to assume that there exists a concept of holy person in Buddhism that can be compared to the Christian notion. At the core of the Christian saint's identity lies the tension between imitability and inimitability, between likeness to us and otherness than us (Cohn, 1986). This holds true for the various types of holy person in Buddhism as well. In some cases imitability and likeness to us dominate, whereas in other cases inimitability and otherness than us are prevalent.

The prototype of all holy persons in Buddhism is Siddhartha Gautama, the Buddha Śākyamuni himself. All Buddhists who strive for religious perfection (i.e., holiness) follow his example in one way or another. Thus, the specific religious ideals of holiness are molded on the model of the Buddha's achievements. These are mainly perfect insight, compassion and sympathy for all suffering beings, and freedom from every kind of attachments.

Immediately after the Buddha's death, and increasingly since the reign of the Mauryan ruler Aśoka (r. 272–232 B.C.), a pronounced relic cult around the remains of Śākyamuni's cremated body prospered in India and subsequently spread to neighboring countries. However, following his complete extinction (parinirvāṇa) the Buddha became inapproachable, and a need for more recognizably human holy persons was strongly felt by the believers.

The prototypical personification of holiness in early Buddhism and in the Theravāda tradition is the arhat (worthy of worship). Like the Buddha an arhat has gained insight in the true nature of things. He knows for certain that he has overcome all defilements and passions that hitherto bound him to the cycle of birth and death and that he will attain nirvāṇa instantly after the present life. Some of the immediate disciples of the Buddha, such as Kāśyapa, Maudgalyāyana, and others, are venerated as the first arhats. In principle arhatship was attainable for men and women, for monastics and laypeople. The best-known female arhat is the Buddha's aunt and foster-mother Mahāprajāpatī Gautamī, who purportedly persuaded her nephew to consent to the establishment of an order of nuns. In addition to Mahāprajāpatī Gautamī the Buddha's natural mother Māyā as well as his wife are revered as prototypical female saints. However, when Buddhism gradually developed into an elite monastic religion, a tendency became apparent to deny women's and laypeople's potentials of attaining arhatship.

People's craving for accessible holy beings led eventually to a belief that some arhats had not vanished into nirvāṇa but, on the Buddha's command, functioned as defenders of the religion and could be called on in times of crisis. According to tradition it was a dispute over the degree of the arhats' infallibility that, among other things, lead to the first schism of the Buddhist order about 100 years after the Buddha's death.

The tendency to restrict arhatship to monks might, among other factors, have contributed to the establishment of Great Vehicle (mahāyāna) Buddhism and its specific ideal of holy men and holy women. The classic holy person of the Mahāyāna is the "enlightenment being" (bodhisattva). The bodhisattva did not entirely replace the arhat as a holy person in Mahāyāna but consigned him to a second-class position. The term bodhisattva denotes a variety of beings who, in contrast to arhats, have vowed to lead all sentient beings to enlightenment. Consequently followers of the Mahāyāna accuse the arhat of being selfish. Furthermore the arhat's nirvāṇa is considered inferior or preliminary to the "supreme and perfect enlightenment" (anuttara-samyak-sambodhi) of the bodhisattva. Bodhisattvas are typically depicted as noble laymen. The concept of the bodhisattva was by no means unknown to early Buddhism, but the designation referred exclusively to the Buddha in his former incarnations, when he was proceeding on his way to Buddhahood and was working for the liberation of sentient beings.

The authoritative texts of Mahāyāna Buddhism depict a large variety of bodhisattvas as well as various stages of bodhisattvahood. However, in the context of Buddhist concepts of holy persons it is reasonable to leave aside bodhisattvas who are regarded as transcendent godlike beings, such as Avalokiteśvara, Mañjuśrī, and so on, and confine the survey to historical or semi-historical figures venerated as bodhisattvas. However, even when transcendent bodhisattvas are excluded, the term bodhisattva comprises quite divergent types of spiritually advanced figures. Rulers such as Shōmu (r. 724–749) of Japan and Khri-srong-lde-btsan (740–c. 798) of Tibet were believed to be incarnations of Mañjuśrī. The Tibetan tradition regards King Srong-btsan sgampo (r. c. 620–649) as well as the Dalai Lamas up to the present as manifestations of Avalokiteśvara, and the Sri Lankan kings between the 4th and the 11th century were likewise believed to be bodhisattvas. Chinese Empress Wu (r. 684–704) and Burmese King Alaungpaya (r. 1752–1760) claimed to be incarnations of the future Buddha Maitreya. Besides such sacred rulers great philosophers (e.g., Nāgārjuna and Vasubandhu), founders of monastic orders or doctrinal traditions, and pious laypeople and faithful benefactors are venerated as bodhisattvas. At times the designation bodhisattva is even used to denote a follower of the Mahāyāna in general, in contrast to the "hearer" (śrāvaka) of the so-called Lesser Vehicle (hīnayāna).

In addition to the classical types of holy persons of the Hīnayāna and Mahāyāna (arhat and bodhisattva, respectively), Tantric, or so-called Diamond Vehicle (vajrayāna), Buddhism invented a new class of holy persons, namely, the fully perfected ones (mahāsiddha). A mahāsiddha is a male or female practitioner who is revered for his or her accomplishments of spiritual and thaumaturgic faculties. From the standpoint of Tantric Buddhism, the arhat represents a monk who has perfected the self-discipline of the Hīnayāna, the bodhisattva represents altruism and perfect insight into the sublime doctrines of the Mahāyāna, and the mahāsiddha is an often noncelibate and antinomian practitioner who has fully mastered the esoteric teachings and Tantric rituals. Thereby he or she embodies the particular ideals of Vajrayāna Buddhism. The well-known legend of the Indian scholar-monk Śāntirakṣita, who failed in subjugating the hostile demons of Tibet, establishes a precedent for the superiority of the mahāsiddha over the learned monk. In the end it was the mahāsiddha Padmasambhava (eighth century) who succeeded in performing the national exorcism. In analogy to the development of the bodhisattva ideal in early Mahāyāna Buddhism, the invention of the *mahāsiddha* type in the Vajrayāna tradition can be seen partly as a response to a growing tendency in developed Mahāyāna to emphasize the ideal of the educated monastic to the disadvantage of lay practitioners. The more that established Buddhism tended to emphasize the inimitability and otherness of holy persons, the more laypeople longed for an accessible ideal of holiness.

The specific notion of a sacred ruler of the world, known as a "wheel-turning" (*cakravartin*) monarch, appears quite early in Buddhism. In many ways the *cakravartin* is the secular or political counterpart of a Buddha and shares many of the latter's characteristics. The perfect ruler who acts in accordance with Buddhist ideals and passionately supports Buddhism is best personified by King Aśoka, who is regarded as an iron-wheel-turning (i.e., armed, *balacakravartin*) monarch in Pāli literature and is thus identified with the left hand of the Buddha. Some monarchs, such as Burmese King Bodawpaya (r. 1781–1819), declared themselves *cakravartin* to legitimize their reigns. Like Buddhahood the rank of a *cakravartin* is restricted to the male.

Besides these classic types of holy men and holy women, there exist numerous persons who are venerated for superior thaumaturgic or spiritual faculties, rigorous asceticism, contributions to the spread or institutionalization of Buddhism (e.g., through the establishment of temples and monasteries), or simply exemplary piety. Chinese Buddhists have produced countless hagiographies of eminent monks and, to a much lesser extent, nuns. Although apparently not all these monks and nuns were cultically revered, it is justifiable to define them as holy persons because of their being protagonists of hagiographic accounts and because they functioned as models of perfect behavior and as objects of veneration.

The compilers of the three paradigmatic collections of Chinese Life Accounts of Eminent Monks (*Gaoseng zhuan*) distinguish, with slight variations, ten categories of venerable practitioners: (1) translators, (2) exegetes, (3) thaumaturgists, (4) meditators, (5) experts in monastic discipline, (6) self-immolators, (7) recitators, (8) benefactors, (9) hymnodists, and (10) preachers. These ten categories do not represent a set of clear-cut and mutually exclusive types of holy men but refer rather to the preeminent faculties and virtues of the protagonists and at the same time to the most highly esteemed ideals of medieval Chinese Buddhism. In simplified terms we can distinguish three dominant virtues of a Buddhist monk in medieval China: (1) asceticism, (2) thaumaturgy, and (3) scholarship. Whereas the three collections (*Gaoseng zhuan*) contain far more than 1,000 hagiographies of monks, only one collection of nuns' lives is extant, containing a mere 65 stories. This discrepancy clearly indicates the inferior role of female monastics in Buddhism and the misogynistic attitude of both the religion and the societies in which it was established.

The emergence of competing schools and sects in China gradually caused changes in the ideals of holiness. Emphasis was laid on persons who contributed to the founding and growth of a particular tradition (e.g., founders of temples and monasteries and influential commentators) or who represented the respective religious virtues of that tradition. For example, in Chan Buddhism the eccentric enlightened master gained priority over the virtuous scholar monk. Even the arhat cult was revived by Chan Buddhists, although the bizarre-looking arhats in China resemble Daoist immortals (*xian*) rather than Hīnayāna saints.

The second major strand of Chinese Buddhism, the Pure Land school (*jingtu zong*), emphasized yet another ideal of holiness. Hagiographic accounts of this tradition, more than ever before, celebrated pious believers who put all their faith in the salvific grace of the Buddha Amitāyus or Amitābha, who finally invites them to his Pure Land of Utmost Bliss (*jile jingtu*). The popular Pure Land cult in eastern Asia brought about a considerable democratization of the ideal of holiness. Although still subordinate to the monastics, pious laypeople increasingly became objects of veneration, and their lives were seen as models to be followed. The most extreme manifestation of the pious lay-believer type is the wonderfully good person (*myōkōnin*) of 19th-century Japan. *Myōkōnin* were typically simple and illiterate laypeople whose everyday lives were rooted in a firm faith in and gratitude for Amida Buddha's grace.

Especially in Japan the founders of religious orders and denominations have been elevated to the status of holy beings. Their images are placed on the altars of temples or private houses side by side with those of the central Buddha. For example, the Pure Land school (Jōdo-shū) regards its alleged founder, Hōnen (1133–1212), as Mahāsthāmaprāpta, one of the two attending bodhisattvas of Amida Buddha, whereas the followers of the Nichiren schools claim that Nichiren (1222–1282) was none other than the bodhisattva Viśiṣṭacārita.

Buddhists of all times have revered the holy hermit who practices severe austerities in remote mountains and forests and cultivates thaumaturgic faculties. Such ascetics are believed to be powerful miracle workers and have functioned as healers and exorcists. In times when the reputation of ordinary monastics had significantly declined, the laity tended to regard the extramonastic mountain ascetics and itinerant monks as holy men par excellence. In Japan these practitioners were accordingly called *hijiri* (sage or saint) or, more frequently, *shōnin* (holy or venerable person). In Southeast Asia the designations arhat and hermit (literally, forest dweller, *āraṇyaka*) are often used interchangeably.

Closely related to holy recluses, a special cult centering on self-immolators arose. So-called body renouncers jumped to death from the cliffs of sacred mountains or trees, cremated or drowned themselves, or offered their flesh to wild beasts. Their bodily remains were highly esteemed as powerful relics. As in medieval Christianity relics became valuable objects of trade and theft. A peculiar kind of relic cult centered around the mummies of great saints to whom the power of stopping famines was assigned. In China the mummy of the sixth Chan patriarch, Huineng (638–713), became the object of a distinctive relic cult. Some practitioners (*gyōnin*) of a particular sect of mountain asceticism in the northeastern regions of Japan had their disciples bury them alive and later mummify their bodies by smoke. These self-immolators are venerated as great saints who have become Buddhas in their own bodies (*sokushin jōbutsu*) to the present day.

CHRISTOPH KLEINE

*See also* Arhat; Aśoka; Buddha (Śākyamuni); Buddhādasa; Buddhist Schools/Traditions: Japan; Buddhist Schools/Traditions: Tibet; Death Rituals, Buddhist; Deities, Buddhist; Disciples, Early Buddhist; Esoteric Buddhism in China and Japan; Gender Studies: Buddhist Perspectives; Hagiography: Buddhist Perspectives; Hermits: Buddhist; Hōnen; Huineng; Prayer: Buddhist Perspectives; Self-Immolation, Buddhist

**Further Reading**

Chou, Chu-chia, G.P. Malalasekera, and W.G. Weeraratne, "Arahant," in *Encyclopedia of Buddhism: Volume II*, edited by G.P. Malalasekera, Colombo: The Government Press, 1966

Cohn, Robert L., "Sainthood," in *The Encyclopedia of Religion*, 16 vols., edited by M. Eliade, New York: Macmillan, 1986; London: Collier, 1993

Faure, Bernard, "Relics and Flesh Bodies: The Creation of Ch'ang Pilgrimage Sites," in *Pilgrims and Sacred Sites in China*, edited by Susan Naquin and Chün-Fang Yü, Berkeley: University of California Press, 1992

Katz, Nathan, *Buddhist Images of Human Perfection: The Arahant of the Sutta Piṭaka Compared with the Bodhisattva and the Mahāsiddha*, Delhi: Motilal Banarsidass, 1982; 2nd edition, 1989

Kawamura, Leslie S., editor, *The Bodhisattva Doctrine in Buddhism*, Waterloo, Ontario: Wilfred Laurier University Press, 1981

Kieschnick, John, *The Eminent Monk: Buddhist Ideals in Medieval Chinese Hagiography*, Honolulu: University of Hawaii Press, 1997

Nanayakkara, S.K., "Cakravartin," in *Encyclopedia of Buddhism: Volume III*, edited by G.P. Malalasekera, Colombo: The Government Press, 1971

Strong, John S., *The Legend and Cult of Upagupta: Sanskrit Buddhism in North India and Southeast Asia*, Princeton, New Jersey: Princeton University Press, 1992

Suzuki, Daisetz Teitaro, *Shin Buddhism*, New York: Harper and Row, and London: Allen and Unwin, 1970

Tambiah, Stanley J., "The Buddhist Arahant: Classical Paradigm and Modern Thai Manifestations," in *Saints and Virtues*, edited by John Stratton Hawley, Berkeley: University of California Press, 1987

# Holy Men/Holy Women: Christian Perspectives

The Hebrew Bible provides enduring models for Jewish and Christian lives, for example, Abraham and Sarah, who longed for a child, and the prophets Miriam, Aaron, and Moses. Hannah, Isaiah, Jeremiah, Ruth, and Esther each sought God's will in their lives and prayed for the deliverance of their people. Assimilated into the Christian faith, figures of the ancient Testament became models of Christian sanctity celebrated in story, sculpture, and stained glass.

The New Testament presents Jesus as a prophet of the Kingdom of God, a friend of the poor and sinners, and a teacher who advocates reform. With his execution his movement seemed to fail until his followers, Mary Magdalene and the women, Peter and the apostles, Stephen and the gentiles, and Paul and some pharisees, galvanized by their belief that Jesus was still alive, began to spread his teachings and a communal way of life as described in the Acts of the Apostles. Ultimately their teaching that Jesus was the Son of God led to a break with rabbinic Judaism that in the synagogues of the Diaspora survived the destruction of the Second Temple (A.D. 70). Meanwhile in Ethiopia, South India, Rome, Spain, and France, some of Jesus' followers were believed to have settled as missionaries, becoming after a time local saints and martyrs revered by converts who lived there.

Among the next generations of Christian holy men and women were martyrs, such as Ignatius of Antioch (c. 35–c. 107), who begged his friends not to interfere, and Perpetua, who defied her pagan father when she was arrested with her entire household of Christian converts. Her slave Felicitas gave birth to a child in prison, and both women gave their nursing infants to relatives to raise before they were killed in the arena at Carthage around 202. Perpetua's diary depicts prison conditions, the solace of friendship and shared sacraments, and the dreams by which she understood her fate.

Missionary preachers in Celtic, Latin, and Greek along the trade routes included a slave named Blandina, who perished valiantly with the martyrs of Lyons in 177. Many of these martyrs were Montanists who risked all to keep alive the egalitarian spirit of the early Church, still advocating women and men as prophets and teachers in tension with the developing clerical hierarchy. Although the Roman Empire became officially Christian with Constantine (306–337), the faith spread slowly and imperfectly in northern Europe, where generations of missionaries and martyrs bequeathed their names, relics, and reputations to local churches at their burial. Their sanctity was confirmed in hagiography that recounted the miracles that ensued after their deaths.

Ascetics, living in community, alone in the desert, or wandering as evangelists, replaced the martyrs as ideal saints after the threat of Christian persecutions diminished. Jerome (c. 345–420) retired to the Holy Land with a group of rich, scholarly Roman women to produce the Vulgate edition of the Bible. Egeria, from Bordeaux, wrote in awestruck tones of the many virgins and ascetics she encountered on her pilgrimage (c. 381–384) to holy places mentioned the Bible. She commented on how little these persons ate and how often they prayed as they tried to imitate Jesus and the apostles.

Bishop Athanasius of Alexandria (c. 296–373) drafted the *Life of St. Antony*, depicting his fierce battles against demons in the desert and Christ's appearance that saved him. Antony (c. 251–356), as early as 270, had left his sister with a group of ascetic women in Alexandria of whom she later became superior. Such urban ascetic communities were popping up in the cities of the empire, supplementing the earlier underground house churches.

John Cassian (c. 360–after 430) returned to Marseilles from an extensive tour of Eastern communities with advice for those desiring eremitic and communal forms of ascetic life. The sayings and lives of the Desert Fathers and Desert Mothers promoted very fierce forms of asceticism for those who aspired to sanctity.

Macrina (c. 327–380) urged her brother, Bishop Basil of Caesaria (c. 330–379), to provide rules to guide her, her mother, and a brother who wished to turn their estates and household into an ascetic community dedicated to serving the poor. Basil; their brother Gregory of Nyssa (c. 330–c. 395), who wrote of Macrina's *Life*; a friend named Gregory of Nazianzus (329/30–389/90); Augustine of Hippo; John Chrysostom; Martin of Tours; and many male fourth-century ascetics were drafted as bishops of an increasingly organized Church under the aegis of the emperors. Wealthy Italian magnates, such as Paulinus of Nola (355–431) and Cassiodorus (485/90–c. 580), turned their estates into scholarly Christian communities of married couples, single ascetics, and virgins. With his conversion Augustine (354–430) adopted a celibate life and tried to organize communities first for his philosophical friends and later for his clergy as bishop of Hippo. Bishop Caesarius of Arles (c. 470–542) developed a rule for male and female communities that emphasized enclosure and separation from society. Martin of Tours (d. 397) favored a semi-eremitic lifestyle that spread to the Celtic lands of Brittany, Wales, Scotland, and Ireland. These ascetic founders and bishops became the models for generations of Christian saints who were nurtured in these protomonastic communities.

Meanwhile in Constantinople the golden-tongued preacher John Chrysostom (c. 347–407) tried by his lively sermons to reform the morality of sophisticated Christian Romans. He cultivated a deep friendship with a woman deacon and patron, Olympias, who stood by him during imperial persecutions for his Trinitarian beliefs that eventually led to his death. John tried to discourage unmarried male and female ascetics from living celibate lives as couples for fear that it would bring scandal on the Church. However, this lifestyle persisted for some time in various parts of the empire, for it was seen as the most difficult and thus most meritorious form of the ascetic and saintly life, to which celibacy was the key.

During the Gothic invasions an extremely wealthy couple, Melania and Pinianus, were driven from Italy and advised by Augustine of Hippo to dedicate the riches they had saved to the founding of monasteries. Bishops such as Ambrose, Leo I, and Gregory I increasingly took responsibility for governing their people. Pope Gregory I (590–604) demonstrated holiness as he ministered in famine and plague, provided a manual of pastoral care for his bishops, and sent monk-missionaries to revive Christianity in Anglo-Saxon England. His *Dialogues* on the life of St. Benedict and his propagation of the Benedictine Rule offered new guides for would-be saints, as did the immensely influential *Life of St. Martin* by Sulpicius Severus (c. 360–c. 430).

Grotto of St. Francis, Eremo delle Carceri, near Asissi, Italy. St. Francis prayed in this grotto while on retreat.
**Photo courtesy of Mary Schaefer**

No process of canonization yet existed, and the people acclaimed their saints by flocking to shrines and attesting to miracles. The saint often became more powerful after death than in life as others acted in his or her name. The late antique saint might be a noble, powerful bishop, or ruler (some holy queens qualified), one who cultivated humility in imitation of Christ, and was often an evangelist and healer. Bishops encouraged cults of local saints and consolidated their authority over the people by building churches, displaying relics, and creating rituals and festivals of the saints.

With Benedict's Rule, which was accepted only gradually, we can speak of cenobitic monasticism in the West. The Rule wanted monks and nuns to live in community and discouraged but did not eliminate wandering bands of evangelist-ascetics. It also decreed that monks and nuns spend many years in community before adopting the hermit life, an option that nonetheless remained popular and influential throughout the Middle Ages. Benedictine monastics vowed stability to one community, conversion of life, and obedience to their abbots and abbesses. Prayer, work, and study were part of their daily lives, and guests were to be received as if they were Christ. By far the majority of saints in the early Middle Ages came out of the monasteries.

Benedictine monasteries retained strong ties with the surrounding Christian communities on whom they depended for support. Many lay patrons emulated monastic virtues and participated in the liturgies and prayers provided by the religious. Often they entered monasteries later in life or pledged their children as oblates or novices.

Semi-eremitic communities persisted, and the Celtic practice of penitential pilgrimage brought missionary monks and nuns from Ireland and England back to evangelize the Continent in the seventh century. Hilda of Whitby (614–680) and other influential abbesses ruled over monasteries of men and women, renowned for their studies, that became nurseries of bishops and missionaries. Bishop Boniface (c. 675–754) and his relative the nun Leoba (d. c. 782) are the best remembered of the Anglo-Saxon missionary saints. She weathered many crises as abbess of a community of nuns that planted the faith among the Germans. Lay aristocrats built chapels and monasteries to venerate the miracles of their local saints and martyrs and with clergy commemorated their deeds in charters, hagiography, and art.

Scholars have called the period 650–750 a golden age of women saints, especially queens, who patronized the Church and the poor and lived holy lives. The most famous of all was Queen Radegunde (c. 518–587), who was captured in Spain and forcibly married to King Clothar. She did her duty as a wife but siphoned their resources into care of the poor. She eventually escaped when the king killed her brother and founded the monastery of the Holy Cross in Poitiers, where with his eventual acquiescence she was able to finish her life in holy seclusion, as described by her poet and chaplain friend Fortunatus and the nun Bodonivia. Magnificent 11th-century illuminated manuscripts of her vita helped keep her memory alive throughout the Middle Ages.

The biographies of Carolingian kings aspired to present them as saints, although that proved difficult, as they pursued conquest and sometimes violently forced conversions to Christianity. Manuals, such as that of the Carolingian mother Dhuoda and Jonas of Orlean's *Advice to the Laity*, advocated a lay regimen of prayer that was nearly monastic. Dhuoda's son, William, was to honor God, the king, and his father to govern with justice and to care for the poor. Count Gerald of Aurillac, as described by Abbot Odo of Cluny (c. 879–942), received the poor into his home for meals, freed captives and serfs, ruled justly with a minimum of violence, and founded a monastery, although he refused to become a monk because of his responsibilities as count. When Benedict of Aniane (c. 750–821) experienced conversion, he considered becoming a poor pilgrim, shepherd, or shoemaker while using his revenues to support the poor.

Although most early medieval saints were from the nobility, voluntary poverty had a powerful attraction for them. Conversions, especially of young women, occurred during childhood and might be announced to their parents in portents and dreams. Girls were married at a very young age, and resisting marriage was a constant theme for the aspiring saint. The 12th-century

holy woman Christina of Markyate was beaten by her mother and locked in at night with her fiancé before she managed to escape and live secretly with hermits until an annulment could be procured.

Men were more likely to be converted in adolescence, sometimes after a wild life, when they too opted for celibacy. A noble youth who was an elder or only son could not easily give up warfare or marriage and often had to put his aspirations to a holy life on hold while he fulfilled family ambitions. Adult conversions of men and women were rare and difficult, and those of even the lesser nobility often went unnoticed until new patterns emerged in the 12th-century.

Twelfth-century holy people participated in an evangelical revival as followers of popular preachers, such as Robert of Arbrissel (c. 1045–1116); rich and poor, men and women, took to the roads together, ultimately forming a religious community. Some, such as the Paraclete and Fontevraud, came to be ruled by an abbess but included subcommunities of men and women from all walks of life. Many holy men and women were never recognized by the Church, which had begun to develop an official process of canonization, because they became leaders of so-called heretical groups, such as the Cathars and the Waldensians. The most fervent saints of the 12th century sought to emulate the life of the apostles and to go "naked with the naked Christ."

Women were counted as nearly a quarter of the 12th- and 13th-century saints and were among the most prominent. Especially remarkable were mystics, some of whom were nuns (e.g., Hildegard of Bingen [1098–1179], abbess, physician, preacher, and consummate musician) whereas others were recluses or beguines (e.g., Marie of Oignies). Marie and her husband had nursed lepers together but ultimately separated when she joined a group of *Mulieris sanctae*, who lived an informal religious life without permanent vows and served the sick and the poor.

These holy women exercised spiritual authority because of their respected visions and prophecies and stood up to priests, abbots, and bishops when they deemed it necessary, but they also attracted the interest of male spiritual guides and biographers who protected and nurtured them. Holy women were preoccupied with their inner lives, being devoted to the Eucharist, which often they could only view, since receiving might trigger ecstasies. They cared for the poor in person when possible, or else they prayed, fasted, and assumed the sufferings of those in Purgatory when enclosed. Their own bodies became battlegrounds of holiness and freedom, as some rebelled against the wealth and power of their parents by adopting fierce ascetic regimens.

By the 13th century a great variety of options existed for men among canons, hermits, monks, and friars. The most severe were the Cistercians and the Carthusians, who sought to live apart from the world. The new mendicant orders following Francis (1181/82–1226) and Dominic (c. 1172–1221) worked among the poor of the growing cities. However, in urban areas a new lay saint might emerge from the wealthy middle classes who did not necessarily join a religious community. A holy merchant or landholder might accept the spiritual guidance of a chaplain and use his wealth and energy to better his city and rescue increasing numbers of marginalized persons there, such as beggars and prostitutes.

Lay confraternities provided men and women the support of religious community. For example, those of the rosary encouraged lengthy meditations on the lives of Mary and Christ as well as mantric recitations of set prayers on their beads. More frequent use of the sacraments, such as penance and the Eucharist, and an increasing number of vernacular devotional guides, culminating in Thomas à Kempis' (c. 1380–1471) *Imitation of Christ*, provided married laymen and laywomen with the tools to live lives esteemed as holy by their peers.

The Protestant Reformation denounced the veneration of saints and declared the married couple and home to be the center of Christian life and education. The Catholic Church again chose for canonization those who led religious orders, such as Ignatius of Loyola (1491–1556) and Teresa of Avila (1515–1582). Supernatural phenomena were often denounced as diabolical rather than holy; women and some men were executed as witches by both Protestants and Catholics, and even those of exemplary lives feared the scrutiny of inquisitions. Nonetheless some early Christian parameters of sanctity have persisted into modern times, even into the 20th century. Many would point to Edith Stein or Dietrich Bonhoeffer (who resisted Nazi tyranny), Dorothy Day or Mother Teresa (who cared for the poorest of the poor), and Thomas Merton or the Dalai Lama (who have promoted meditation, compassion, and the meeting of East and West) as saints for our day.

MARY S. SKINNER

*See also* Basil the Great, St.; Benedict of Nursia, St.; Boniface, St.; Caesarius of Arles, St.; Cassian, John; Cassiodorus; Cathars; Chrysostom, John, St.; Devotions, Western Christian; Gregory I (the Great), St.; Hagiography: Western Christian; Hilda, St.; Hildegard of Bingen, St.; Macrina, St.; Martyrs: Western Christian; Missionaries: Christian; Oblates; Origins: Comparative Perspectives; Radegunde, St.; Recluses, Western Christian; Reformation; Spirituality: Eastern Christian; Teresa of Avila, St.; Transvestite Saints; Vision, Mystical: Eastern Christian; Visual Arts, Eastern Christian: Painting

**Further Reading**

Blumanfeld-Kozinski, Renate, and Timea Szell, editors, *Images of Sainthood in Medieval Europe*, Ithaca, New York: Cornell University Press, 1991 (see especially essays by Vauchez, Carrasco, McNamara, Cokeley, Uitti, Robertson, and Kieckhefer)

Brown, Peter, *The Cult of the Saints*, Chicago: University of Chicago Press, and London: SCM Press, 1981

Brown, Peter, *Body and Society: Men, Women, and Sexual Renunciation in Early Christianity*, New York: Columbia University Press, 1988; London: Faber, 1989

Bynum, Caroline, *Holy Feast and Holy Fast*, Berkeley: University of California Press, 1987

Goodich, Michael, *Vita Perfecta, The Ideal of Sainthood in the Thirteenth Century*, Stuttgart: Hiersemann, 1982

Jestice, Phyllis, *Wayward Monks and the Religious Revolution of the Eleventh Century*, Leiden and New York: Brill, 1997

Kieckhefer, Richard, *Unquiet Souls: Fourteenth-Century Saints and Their Religious Milieu*, Chicago: University of Chicago Press, 1984

Kitchen, John, *Saints' Lives and the Rhetoric of Gender*, New York: Oxford University Press, 1998

Little, Lester, *Religious Poverty and the Profit Economy in Medieval Europe*, Ithaca, New York: Cornell University Press, and London: Elek, 1978

Poulin, Joseph-Claude, *L'ideal de Sainteté dans l'Aquitaine Carolingienne, d'après les Sources Hagiographiques, 750–795*, Quebec: Presses de l'Université Laval, 1975

Sticca, Sandro, editor, *Saints: Studies in Hagiography*, Binghamton, New York: Medieval and Renaissance Texts and Studies, 1996

Vauchez, Andre, *La Sainteté en Occident aux Derniers Siècles du Moyen Age*, Rome: École française de Rome, 1981; revised edition, 1988; as *Sainthood in the Later Middle Ages*, Cambridge and New York: Cambridge University Press, 1997

Vauchez, Andre, *Les Laïcs au Moyen Age: Pratiques et Expériences Religieuses*, Paris: Cerf, 1987; as *The Laity in the Middle Ages: Religious Beliefs and Devotional Practices*, Notre Dame, Indiana: University of Notre Dame Press, 1993

Weinstein, Donald and Rudolph Bell, *Saints and Society: The Two Worlds of Western Christendom, 1000–1700*, Chicago: University of Chicago Press, 1982

# Holy Men in Power (Hierocrats), Buddhist

Royal patronage of Buddhism by King Aśoka changed the character of Buddhism for good. A world-renouncing tradition was transformed materially into a world-conquering force. A balance between *saṅgha* and state might be struck, but that balance worked better in the southern path. There Theravāda was the only lineage school, and it survived relatively unopposed by an undeveloped indigenous culture. Northwestern India, a major base of future Mahāyāna, was different. It was culturally complex and politically advanced but fluid. Out of that situation came a more conflictual form of hierocracy in which holy men wielded power.

Spirituality can be either sedentary or mobile. Syrian Christianity had pillar saints and anchorites or hermits; it also had itinerant holy men; the Desert Fathers in Egypt tended to live in settled communities as cenobites. In India the Jains considered karma to be a kind of physical stuff. To remove karma (action, matter, and movement), the ascetic might refuse to eat and make a virtue of standing absolutely still. Buddhism endorsed immobility as well; Ākṣobhya Buddha is the Immovable Worthy in an ascetic Pure Land in the East, but even more strongly Mahāyāna endorsed mobility. The formula "*nirvāṇa* is *saṃsāra*" underwrites a nonabiding *nirvāṇa*: it is wherever the bodhisattva happens to be. All these notions went back to the historical Buddha, who had sworn not to move from under the Bodhi Tree until he was enlightened, but he soon became enlightened – he removed more than just karma – and he moved on. The *sangha* later also combined wayfaring (nine months of the year) with settling down (during the monsoon retreat). Under Aśokan patronage the settled community prospered, becoming urbane and worldly. When Constantine (306–337) supported the Church, which also became more worldly, the Desert Fathers protested by trekking into the desert. Under Aśoka it seems that forest monks grew; they too left the cities to cultivate meditation in the hills. Legends about these so-called *pratyekabuddha*s described them as men of few words who talked in enigmas. They kept up humble mendicancy, being truly poor in both body and spirit. At the same time Subhūti, a disciple of the Buddha known for "loving the forest life," began belatedly to call attention to himself. This arhat of the Hīnayāna camp would be recruited retrospectively by Mahāyāna to be the Buddha's mouthpiece; he revealed the Emptiness of Wisdom achieved by the bodhisattva. For the Theravādin *sangha*, this call of the forest is a temporary option, an occasional ascetic retreat, and something the whole community could do during the monsoon season. (A full-time institution of forest monks was revived in Sri Lanka as late as the 20th century by German-born Buddhist monks.)

Sedentary Theravāda in the South could better support these marginal forest monks. War-torn northern India instead favored hierocrats, or "holy men in office." There a darker picture of kingship prevailed. Kings were both bane and boon. They could destroy the *sangha* as easily as they could support it. In the Sarvāstivāda *Aśoka Avadāna*, it is prophesied that no one less than a future descendent of Aśoka would destroy the dharma. Instead of depicting a gentler king working with a leader of an orderly *sangha*, the North dramatized a violent king opposed by a lone ascetic such as Upagupta. Not only did ephemeral kingdoms rise and fall there, but foreign rulers neglected a basic Indian courtesy – namely, that a king should never openly involve a renunciate in war. Instead the northern rulers employed holy men the way in which Persian kings did their court magi. King Kanishka was a second Aśoka but an unrepentant killer. He had Aśvaghosa (second century) serving in his court. From there, traveling with traders and soldiers, the monk itinerant and the holy man brought the dharma by way of the Silk Road into China. Mobility then became prized over immobility, portability (of relics and images) over the fixed sanctity (of shrines patronized by segmented, sedentary groups).

Nomadic invaders brought hierocracy into China in 316. Between then and 439 was a "century of the holy man." Bloodied killers and men of peace operated side by side, like the lion and the lamb. Sinners and saints made strange but workable political bedfellows. The records call all major monks of renown in North China "king-makers." They were all "war prophets," even against their own protestation. These renunciates did not endorse war or violence but only appeared to do so. That is because the Mahāyāna *Sūtra of the Golden Light* had promised rulers (in northwestern India) that anyone who supported the dharma would be protected in turn by the Four Heavenly Kings.

Thus, in pious retrospect every victory was credited to divine protection, whereas any loss was ascribed to human failings.

Thus, like the Syrian holy men in late antiquity who served as "rural patrons," these holy men in a barbarianized North China acted as "national preceptors." They worked miracles by brokering peace between hostile parties, securing concessions from both the barbarian invaders (central Asian Buddhists) and the much harassed Chinese population. The latter gratefully converted overnight en masse to the faith. Ruler and subjects who could not trust one another now could do so; they would separately pledge loyalty to the holy man – in exchange for his protection, both divine and human. The sad side of the story is that these pillars of the various states inevitably became booty in war. Capturing a holy man with due reverence – while putting him under virtual house arrest and forcing him into concubinage in the case of Kumārajīva (c. 344–413) – meant capturing whole populations who had pledged themselves to the holy man. Thus, for an entire century all contenders for control of North China waged wars in a mad scramble to enlist these saints to be national preceptors.

The phenomenon of the holy man in European late antiquity was misunderstood until Peter Brown unraveled its dynamics. Likewise the century of holy man in China has been misread to date. This hierocratic institution, being inherently unstable, could not last. It ended when North China was reunited under a single rule in 439. They outlived their utility now that the traditional avenue for meditating between ruler and the ruled was restored. However, later periods of renewed conflict with foreign rulers, such as under the Mongols, could bring back this institution for a while. Otherwise for most Buddhist cultures in time of peace, the Aśokan model of rule offered the more reasonable standard.

WHALEN LAI

*See also* Buddhist Schools/Traditions: Japan; China; Disciples, Early Buddhist; Forest Masters; Governance: Buddhist Perspectives; Holy Men/Holy Women: Buddhist Perspectives; Saichō; Theravādin Monks, Modern Western

## Further Reading

Brown, Peter, *The Cult of Saints: Its Rise and Function in Latin Christianity*, Chicago: University of Chicago Press, and London: SCM Press, 1981

Brown, Peter, *Society and the Holy in Late Antiquity*, Berkeley: University of California Press, and London: Faber, 1982

Lai, Whalen, "Subhūti, Forest Monks and the Aṣṭasāhasrikā Prajñāpāramitā: A Third Hypothesis to Mahāyāna Genesis," *The Journal of Religious Studies* (India), 28:2 (1997)

Nattier, Jan, *Once Upon a Future Time*, Berkeley, California: Asian Humanities Press, 1991

Strong, John, *The Legend of King Asoka: A Study and Translation of the Asokavadana*, Princeton, New Jersey: Princeton University Press, 1983

Strong, John, *The Legend and Cult of Upagupta: Sanskrit Buddhism in North India and Southeast Asia*, Princeton, New Jersey: Princeton University Press, 1992

Tambiah, Stanley Jeyaraja, *The Buddhist Saints of the Forest and the Cult of Amulets: A Study in Charisma, Hagiography, Sectarianism, and Millennial Buddhism*, Cambridge and New York: Cambridge University Press, 1984

# Hōnen 1133–1212

Japanese Tendai monk and founder of Japanese Pure Land school of Buddhism

The Japanese Pure Land school (Jōdo-shū) claims Hōnen (Genkū) as its founder. He is the first of five monks (Shinran, Eisai, Dōgen, and Nichiren) from whom later the so-called Kamakura new Buddhist schools were derived (Jōdo-shinshū, Rinzai-shū, Sōtō-shū, and Nichiren-shū). Hōnen lived during the transition from the Heian to the Kamakura period, a time of social, economic, and religio-philosophical changes during which the warrior class developed an alternative center of power in Kamakura and assumed many functions of the imperial court government in Kyoto.

Born in what is today Okayama prefecture, Hōnen was sent to Mount Hiei, the center of Japanese Tendai Buddhism, at the age of 12 and was ordained a few years later. He later withdrew (*tonsei*) from the increasingly secularized monastic center to the remote Kurodani temple on Mount Hiei to study and practice under Eikū, an adherent of the Pure Land tradition within Tendai. After completing the required 12-year period of uninterrupted residence on the mountain, as part of his "search for the dharma and the cultivation of practice" he undertook trips to temples in and around Kyoto and Nara. In 1175 he left Mount Hiei (but not the order), first practicing with a *nembutsu* practitioner in the western mountains of Kyoto and later settling on its eastern slopes. Here he became active in teaching monks, nuns, and laypeople, and a group of followers gathered around him. His teaching of the exclusive practice of the vocal *nembutsu* (*senju nenbutsu, shōmyō nenbutsu*) as well as his growing movement (called *ikkō senju*) caused sharp criticism first from within his order and then from Nara's Kōfuku-ji. It seems that the libertinistic behavior of a few of his followers eventually provoked the court to defrock Hōnen and some of his disciples and send them into exile in 1207. Hōnen later was rehabilitated; he returned to Kyoto in 1211 and died the following year.

Hōnen's spiritual path began with his search for a sure practice for attaining liberation from the cycle of birth and death. This was accompanied by a sense of living in a time of crisis because he, like many other contemporary Buddhists, believed that the decadent, so-called end period of the dharma (*mappō*) had arrived, during which attaining awakening was thought to be impossible. Among his earlier works are four interpretations of Genshin's *Ōjō yōshū* (Teachings Essential for Birth), or the Tendai systematization of Pure Land thought, in which Hōnen repeatedly attempted to squeeze out the "essential" or "necessary" practice for certain birth into Amida's Pure Land. He found his answer in a quotation from Shandao that says that all practitioners who keep Amida continuously concentrated in mind (*nembutsu*) will certainly attain birth in the Pure Land, whereas those employing miscellaneous practices cannot be assured of it. Hōnen understood Shandao's "concentrated" (meditative) practice as "exclusive" (*moppara*), leading him to teach the exclusive vocal *nembutsu*. In his main work, the *Senchaku hongan nembutsu shū* (Passages on the Selection of the Nembutsu in the Original Vow), he systematically developed his teaching by first elaborating Daochuo's distinction between Pure Land and the Holy Path, the latter comprising (for Hōnen) all Buddhist practices other than the *nembutsu*. He explained his teaching of the vocal *nembutsu* mainly on the basis of an eclectic selection of quotations from Shandao's works (whose overall emphasis, however, was on the meditative *nembutsu*). Hōnen found a doctrinal basis for the exclusive *nembutsu* in Zhiqian's Chinese translation of the *Sūtra of Immeasurable Life*, according to which Amida "selected" (*senchaku*) the *nembutsu* for gaining birth in his land. The term *selection* allowed Hōnen to advocate the exclusive practice of the *nembutsu* and the abandonment of all other practices. Because it is "easy," it can be performed by all "ordinary human beings" and thus "equally" leads to liberation, whereas the other practices are "difficult" and thus do not yield this result.

Although Hōnen shared with many Buddhists of his time a concern for ordinary laypeople, his approach was fundamentally different. Whereas traditional schools hold that a variety of practices meet the different spiritual capacities (*ki*) of people, Hōnen argued for the lowest common denominator (the *nembutsu*) and its exclusiveness. He thereby developed a new paradigm for classifying the various Buddhist teachings and practices (*kyōsō hanjaku*). Whereas Tendai upheld an inclusive-hierarchical model that comprised a broad variety of teachings and practices with the *Lotus Sūtra* on the top, Hōnen polarized Pure Land and Holy Path teachings, or *nembutsu* and other practices, thus forcing practitioners to choose between the two. The other acclaimed founders of the new Kamakura Buddhism basically followed the same paradigm by selecting just one practice and teaching while excluding others. Whereas the established schools tended to react conservatively to the critical period of *mappō* by emphasizing worship of the (historical) Śākyamuni and strict adherence to monastic rules, Hōnen advocated a new model for liberation from suffering that resulted in a renewal movement in Japanese Buddhism.

Hōnen's teachings threatened the very basis of the established schools, which naturally reacted vigorously to those teachings. Although libertinistic tendencies seem to be evident in his movement, Hōnen himself adhered strictly to monastic rules and also administered the precepts for laypeople (*jukai*). Hōnen did not deny the value of keeping precepts and performing other practices as such as many of his followers and critics claimed. Rather, he criticized their being done in the (for him, false) expectation that they would certainly lead to liberation from the cycle of birth and death. One of his disciples, Shinran (1173–1262), went further, marrying a nun and referring to himself as "neither monk nor lay." He provided the teaching basis for the first doc-trinally founded form of lay Buddhism in Japan (which later be-came Jōdo-shinshū, the True Pure Land school) in contrast to the pragmatically motivated development of Japanese Buddhism after the Meiji persecution of Buddhism.

Hōnen himself intended to establish a "doctrinal school" of Pure Land (*rikkyō kaishū*), but he never attempted to organize an independent religious organization as the present-day Jōdo-shū claims (Kleine, 1996). A first attempt to gain independence can be seen in the case of Hōnen's disciple Ryūkan (1148–1227), who held ordinations without approval, although the government soon confiscated the ordination certificates. It was Shōgei (1341–1420) of Jōdo-shū's Chinzei branch who first received of-ficial permission to conduct ordinations. This marks the begin-ning of an independent school called Jōdo-shū (Kleine, 1996).

MARTIN REPP

*See also* Buddhist Schools/Traditions: Japan; Dōgen; Eisai (Yosai); Holy Men/Holy Women: Buddhist Perspectives; Kyoto, Japan; Mount Hiei, Japan; Nara, Japan; Nation-Building and Japanese Buddhism; Nembutsu; Pure Land Buddhism; Rennyo; Shinran; Tiantai/Tendai: Japan

### Biography

Hōnen, a monk of the Japanese Tendai school, taught that by exclusively calling on Amida's name (*nembutsu*) one assuredly would attain birth in the Pure Land of this Buddha. His teaching provided the doctrinal foundation for what later became the Pure Land school (Jōdo-shū) in Japan. One of his disciples, Shinran, was claimed as founder of the True Pure Land school (Jōdo-shinshū).

### Major Works

*Senchaku hongan nembutsu shū*; as *Hōnen's "Senchakushu": Passages on the Selection of the Nembutsu in the Original Vow*, edited and translated by the *Senchakushu* English Translation Project, 1998

*Ichimai kishōmon* (a one-page outline of his teaching)

### Further Reading

Coates, Harper H., and Ryugaku Ishizuka, *Honen the Buddhist Saint: His Life and Teaching*, 5 vols., Kyoto: Society for the Publication of Sacred Books of the World, 1925

Ikawa, Jōkei, editor, *Hōnen Shōnin den zenshū*, Kyoto: Hōnen Shōnin den Zenshū Kankōkai, 1978 (complete collection of Hōnen Shōnin's biographies)

Ishii, Kyōdō, editor, *Shōwa shinshu Hōnen Shōnin zenshū*, Kyoto: Heirakuji Shoten, 1955 (Shōwa period new edition of the complete collection of Hōnen Shōnin's works)

Kleine, Christoph, *Hōnens Buddhismus des Reinen Landes: Reform, Reformation oder Häresie?*, Frankfurt and New York: Peter Lang, 1996

Repp, Martin, "The Supreme Dharma for the Meanest People: A Study of Hōnen's Interpretation of the 'Three Pure Land Sūtras'," *Japanese Religions* 21:1 (1996)

Repp, Martin, "Wie wird man seiner Hingeburt gewiss? Eine Untersuchung zum Reinen Land Buddhismus der Heian und Kamakura Zeit," *Kirisuto-kyō kenkyū* 16 (1996)

Senchakushū English Translation Project, translators and editors, *Hōnen's "Senchakushū": Passages on the Selection of the Nembutsu in the Original Vow (Senchaku hongan nembutsu shū)*, Honolulu: University of Hawaii Press, and Tokyo: Sōgō Bukkyō Kenkyūjo, Taishō University, 1998

# Hospitality, Christian

Hospitality is one of the basic virtues of the monastic life. Ac-cording to the Rule of St. Benedict, "All guests who arrive should be received as Christ, for he himself will say, *I was a stranger and you took me in* (Matt 25:35)" (RB 53.1). Although Benedict's chapter on hospitality is based on the teaching of Jesus, his treatise reflects the ancient desert theme of hospital-ity, beautifully expressed in the story of Abraham offering hospital-ity to the three strangers at Mamre in Genesis 18. The story was popular with the Desert Fathers.

The New Testament word for hospitality, *philoxenia* (Rom. 12:13; Heb. 13:2), literally means "love for strangers." It is derived from the Greek *xenos*, which means "guest," or "stranger," as well as "host." In Greek culture (cf. *Odyssey* 6:121) as well as Hebrew, hospitality was a sacred duty, for the stranger was vulnerable, away from the support of tribe or peo-ple. The Israelites never forgot that they had once been strangers in the land of Egypt (Deut. 10:19); their law taught them God's special concern for the orphan, the widow, the stranger in the land (Exod. 22:20–21; Deut. 10:18; Jer. 7:6). In addition to the story of Abraham's guests at Mamre are stories of rewards re-ceived by those who practice hospitality. In welcoming the strangers at Mamre, Abraham is welcoming God, who blesses him with the promise that his barren wife Sara would give birth to a son. For feeding and sheltering Elijah, the widow of Zarephath was sustained through the famine and received her son back from the dead (1 Kings 17:19–24). The New Testament represents the guest-host relationship that is constitutive of hos-pitality in multiple ways that link Jesus, others, and God. The Gospels reflect the important role that table fellowship played in the ministry of Jesus; that tradition, in which Jesus is both guest and host, shows that no one is excluded from God's reign. In Matthew 25:31–46, Jesus identifies himself with the last and the least; whatever done to welcome, feed, or shelter them is done to him. Thus, charity becomes theophany. The early Church, in continuing the table-fellowship tradition, came to recognize the risen Jesus present "in the breaking of the bread" (Luke 24:35). The author of the Letter to the Hebrews writes, "Do not neglect hospitality, for through it some have unknowingly entertained angels" (Heb. 13:2). In the third and fourth centuries, hospital-ity was regarded as a fundamental Christian virtue expressed both through personal charity and institutionally through the es-tablishment of hospitals and hospices.

Offering hospitality was a basic part of the monastic life from the beginning; the Desert Fathers understood it as an obligation of charity, but some authors are more reserved about guests. Basil (330–379) was cautious; his rules provided for welcoming guests but in a way that did not interfere with the ascetic life of the monastery (Longer Rule XX). John Cassian (360–435), an important link between Eastern and Western monasticism, saw that hospitality could be a burden for the hermit, but he also spoke of it as duty; a monk should break his fast to entertain a visitor (*Institutes* 5.23); to receive another is to receive Christ (*Institutes* 5.24). The Rule of the Master, source for much of Benedict's Rule, is highly suspicious of guests; after two days they were to be put to work or sent on their way (RM 78). Two brothers were to be assigned to keep watch on them, even at night, to protect the goods of the monastery (RM 79).

The spirit of Benedict's chapter on hospitality is quite different. He begins with the biblical idea of receiving God in the guest, especially in the poor; this idea is repeated three times in the first 15 verses. Guests should be received, prayed with, given the sign of peace, and have their hands and feet washed. The actual ritual of welcome was probably mediated by the monastic travelogue that Rufinus translated in 404 as *Historia Monachorum in Aegypto*. Although the first verse in RB 53 says that "all" (*omnes*) guests should be received, qualifications begin in the second. Commentators agree that this should be understood as referring to fellow monks and orthodox Christians, not heretics (Arians) or non-Christians. The remaining verses (16–23) are concerned with more practical details. Benedict observes that guests are never in short supply in the monastery and tend to arrive at odd hours (RB 53.16). The kitchen for the abbot and guests should be separate from that of the monks so as not to disturb the brothers. The guest quarters should be well managed with beds ready, and monks not assigned to caring for guests should not speak with them beyond a humble greeting and to ask for a blessing. The monasteries that followed Benedict's Rule were well served by it, functioning as hostels for travelers and pilgrims throughout the medieval period. The guest master at Cluny had to deal with a steady stream of visitors, among them prelates and members of the nobility. The guest house built by Odilo (994–1048) had beds for 45 male guests in one wing and 30 for women in another. However, monastic hospitality is always more than civic virtue, as it is rooted in a biblical vision of the divine presence in the stranger, especially in the last and the least.

THOMAS P. RAUSCH, S.J.

*See also* Benedict of Nursia, St.; Cluny, Abbots of; Fasting: Western Christian; France; Origins: Comparative Perspectives; Pilgrimages, Christian

## Further Reading

Gould, Graham, *The Desert Fathers on Monastic Community*, Oxford and New York: Clarendon Press, 1993

Greer, Rowan A., "Hospitality in the First Five Centuries of the Church," *Monastic Studies* 10 (1974)

Kardong, Terrence G., "To Receive All as Christ," *Cistercian Studies* 19 (1984)

Kardong, Terrence G., *Benedict's Rule: A Translation and Commentary*, Collegeville, Minnesota: Liturgical Press, 1996

Koenig, John, *New Testament Hospitality: Partnership with Strangers as Promise and Mission*, Philadelphia: Fortress Press, 1985

# Hospitallers (Knights of Malta since 1530)

The Sovereign Order of St. John of Jerusalem, Rhodes and Malta originated as a hospice, or "hospital," for pilgrims in Jerusalem before the arrival of the First Crusade in 1099. Although later generations of Hospitallers claimed that the foundation went back to pre-Christian times, contemporary sources indicate that it was founded in the second half of the 11th century by Amalfi merchants. Later sources suggested that the original dedication was to St. John the Almoner, but in fact the hospice was probably dedicated from the first to St. John the Baptist. It was originally dependent on the monastery of St. Mary of the Latins in Jerusalem, but by 1099 it seems to have been self-governing. As yet it was little different from the many other religious hospitals founded in Europe during the central Middle Ages.

The first known administrator of this hospital of St. John was one Gerard, whose origins are unknown. A cult of a blessed Gerard, apparently the founder, existed at the hospital's house at Manosque by 1283, but later attempts to obtain his canonization failed. Gerard was said to have been imprisoned by the Muslim authorities in Jerusalem for his aid to the crusaders while they besieged the city in July 1099. After Jerusalem fell, Gerard and his hospice received donations from the victorious crusaders in the East and also in southern France and Italy at important points on the pilgrim routes to the East and on the pilgrim route to the shrine of St. James of Compostela at Santiago. By 1113, when Gerard's hospital was given papal recognition by Paschal II (1099–1118), it had become an international organization, based in Jerusalem and supported by a network of houses in Europe. During the first half of the 12th century, successive popes took the order under papal protection, granting it exemption from episcopal jurisdiction.

The first rule of the order, recorded by Raymond du Puy, second master of the hospital (1120–1260), was based on the rule of St. Augustine, giving a simple outline of a religious life. The rule emphasized that the purpose of the order was to serve the sick and the poor and that the Hospitallers were serfs, or slaves, of the poor. However, the military needs of the Crusader States were such that by the 1130s the Hospitallers were also hiring mercenaries to protect pilgrims on the road to the holy places and were undertaking the defense of castles. The papacy was slow to acknowledge that this development in the order's activities was valid, and Pope Alexander III (1159–1181) wrote urging the brothers not to take up arms but to continue in their original vocation. This militarization not only met a need for military personnel in the East but also encouraged donations in the West. After their active military role in campaigns against

Gallery or cloister, Crac des Chevaliers, Syria, first half of the 13th century. The Hospitallers held and rebuilt this ancient fortress 1142–1271.
Photo courtesy of Chris Schabel

Saladin and during the Third Crusade, the Hospitallers were generally recognized in the West as a military order alongside the Templars. With the Teutonic order after 1198, these two international military orders shared the burden of the defense of Latin Christian territory in the East, were often cited together (and confused with each other) by chroniclers, and were regarded as rivals, although in fact they made great efforts to cooperate with each other.

Like the Templars, the Hospitallers played an important role in every crusading expedition to the Holy Land from the time of their militarization and also became actively involved in the Iberian *Reconquista*. The order continued its care for the sick and poor in the East alongside its military activities; its infirmary formed part of its headquarters, initially in Jerusalem and then, after the loss of Jerusalem to Saladin in 1187, in Acre. The order also maintained some hospices in the West. In Europe the Hospitallers were endowed with property and privileges by those who wanted to assist their military and hospitable work, and, like the Templars, brothers of the order were taken into the service of popes and kings.

The order originally attracted recruits mainly from the lesser knightly and from nonknightly classes, men as well as women, although by the early modern period it had changed to being an aristocratic order. Women's houses and double houses of men and women existed in the hospital by the 1180s; the great convent of Sigena in Aragon was founded in 1187 and received its own rule, becoming the standard rule for houses of Hospitaller women. These were enclosed houses; the sisters of the hospital did not care for the sick.

With the loss of the kingdom of Jerusalem in 1291, the Hospitallers moved their headquarters and infirmary to Cyprus, where, with the Templars, they attempted to organize a new crusade. Whereas the Templars were unable to arouse support for a large expedition and their bridgehead at Ruad was lost to the Muslims in 1302, the Hospitallers eventually set out with a small expedition that succeeded in capturing the island of Rhodes from its Greek Orthodox rulers. In 1310 they moved their headquarters to Rhodes. Although how much this conquest would benefit Western Christendom was debatable, the Hospitallers were active in the crusading cause at the very time that the Templars and the Teutonic order were undergoing papal investigation for heresy.

Convinced of the Hospitallers' crusading credentials, Pope Clement V (1305–1314) decided that the property of the Templars should be given to the Hospitallers to ensure its continued use in the crusading cause. The pope was unprepared for the

Keep of Kolossi Castle, west of Limassol, Cyprus, built 1454 to replace a fortress of c. 1300.
Photo courtesy of Chris Schabel

howl of indignation from bishops and secular rulers who protested that the Order of the Hospital was corrupt and inefficient and in need of root-and-branch reform. They argued that giving it the Templars' lands would make it still more arrogant while doing nothing for the crusade. Eventually, the Hospitallers secured the Templars' lands in return for a promise of reform that was never carried out and for a large payment to King Philip IV (1285–1314) of France for his expenses in bringing the charges against the Templars that probably was never paid in full. The next few decades saw the Hospitallers facing serious financial difficulties in the wake of their conquest of Rhodes. Added to this, the order did not receive all the Templars' lands, either because patrons or kings refused to give them up or, in Portugal and Valencia, because they were used as the basis of new military orders.

The 14th century was a time of reorientation for the Hospitallers, who were adapting to the new circumstances of a naval war against the Muslims while nationalistic and localizing tendencies among their European houses often meant that dues were not sent to Rhodes. The order's financial problems, added to an internal crisis that led to the deposition of Grand Master Fulk de Villaret in 1317, prompted greater papal intervention in

the internal affairs of the order. In 1343 Pope Clement VI (1342–1352) wrote to the grand master, calling for internal reform of the order and a greater commitment to military action; in 1355 Pope Innocent VI (1352–1362) wrote in similar terms. Both popes threatened that if the Hospitallers did not become more effective, they would take back the Templars' lands and use them to form a new military order. In 1373 Pope Gregory XI (1370–1378) set up an investigation into the Hospitallers' resources in Europe that revealed that the order had severe problems that were hindering its effectiveness against the Muslims. However, the order's internal problems were not the only hindrance; popes interfered with the running of the order, as in 1377 when Pope Gregory XI imposed Juan Fernández de Heredia as grand master. The Great Schism (1378–1417) divided the order into two obediences. In addition, wars between Genoa and Venice and the Hundred Years' War between England and France prevented the launch of major expeditions against the Muslims.

Despite these problems, the Hospitallers were active at sea against the Muslims and from the 1330s played a major role in the crusading naval leagues. They excelled in the capture of Smyrna in 1344 and in financing its defense; from 1374 they were made solely responsible for the defense of the city until it was lost to Tamerlane in 1402. The Hospitallers were involved in the crusades of Peter I of Cyprus and also in Latin Greece, especially in Achaea, which they leased from Queen Joanna of Naples in 1376 but were forced to withdraw in 1381. The order continued to seek a base in Achaea and to be involved in crusading efforts in the Balkans into the early 15th century. After the loss of Smyrna, a new castle was built on the Turkish mainland at Bodrum that enabled the Hospitallers to publicize in the West their military activity against the Turks.

In the 15th century Rhodes itself came under attack from the Muslims: from the Mamluks of Egypt in 1440 and 1444, while a series of raids on the Rhodian islands by Ottoman Turks reached a climax in the siege of 1480, which the Hospitallers, under Grand Master Pierre d'Aubusson, resisted successfully. In 1482 a treaty with the Ottoman pretender Jem paved the way for a peace treaty with the sultan that remained secure until Jem's death in 1395. Although the Hospitallers were increasingly isolated in the eastern Mediterranean following the conquest of Constantinople by the Ottomans in 1453, they maintained naval pressure on the Muslim powers through the *corso*, a kind of licensed holy-war piracy, and in 1510 defeated the Mamluks in a sea battle. However, in 1522 the Ottoman Sultan Suleiman the Magnificent (1520–1566) led an attack on Rhodes. Because of a lack of support from the West, the Hospitallers were forced to surrender the island.

The emperor Charles V (1519–1558) offered the Hospitallers the island of Malta as their new headquarters against the Turks. This was taken up in 1530. The island soon came into the front line in the war between the emperor and the sultan for control of the Mediterranean, and in 1565 Sultan Suleiman sent an expeditionary force against Malta. Following a heroic defense under Grand Master Jean de la Valette, the order was finally relieved by a Spanish force led by Don García de Toledo, Philip II of Spain's viceroy in Sicily. Secure in Malta, the Hospitallers capitalized on the goodwill engendered by their success to solicit donations from European donors to finance the fortification of the island. Their new capital city was named Valetta after its founder.

The Hospitallers no longer represented the whole of Christendom against the Muslims. With the Reformation the English *langue* of the order was dissolved, and the order in the Netherlands, Brandenburg, and Sweden became Protestant. The Hospitallers continued to take a major part in Catholic naval leagues against the Turks and maintained the *corso* against the Turks and those who traded with them, leading to serious diplomatic confrontations with the Venetians. In mainland Europe, Hospitallers acted as ambassadors and had close contacts with rulers and popes.

Although by the 18th century some (especially Venetian ambassadors) might declare it an anachronism, the Order of Malta still enjoyed great prestige in Europe. Some brothers were actively engaged in charitable and missionary work and, appropriately, medical research. However, as the order remained mainly French, the French Revolution dealt it a serious blow. In 1792

the National Assembly confiscated the order's property in France. When Napoleon attacked Malta in 1798, the brothers were divided on whether to resist or fight; the grand master, Ferdinand von Hompesch, decided to surrender.

The Hospitallers were again without a base. In 1834 they established their headquarters in Rome and reorganized the order to meet the needs of the modern world. Today the Order of Malta remains formally a military order, but its function is once again the care of the sick poor: it runs hospitals, clinics, and dispensaries and raises money for these purposes worldwide. Four Protestant orders are associated with the Catholic Sovereign order, in Germany, Sweden, the Netherlands, and Britain. In recent years the government of Malta has allowed the Sovereign order to reestablish a presence on Malta, and an embassy has been established in Valetta.

HELEN J. NICHOLSON

*See also* Augustinian Rule; Crusades; Cyprus; Dissolution of Monasteries: Continental Europe; Germany: Sites; Israel/Palestine; Jerusalem, Israel; Orders (Religious), Origin of; Pilgrimages, Christian: Near East; Santiago de Compostela, Spain; Scandinavia; Spain: History; Templars; Teutonic Order; Warrior Monks: Christian

## Further Reading

Barber, Malcolm, editor, *The Military Orders: Fighting for the Faith and Caring for the Sick*, Aldershot, England, and Brookfield, Vermont: Variorum, 1994

Forey, Alan, *The Military Orders: From the Twelfth to the Early Fourteenth Centuries*, London: Macmillan, 1992

Forey, Alan, *Military Orders and Crusades*, Aldershot, England, and Brookfield, Vermont: Variorum, 1994

Luttrell, Anthony, *The Hospitallers in Cyprus, Rhodes, Greece and the West (1291–1440)*, London: Variorum, 1978

Luttrell, Anthony, *Latin Greece, the Hospitallers and the Crusades, 1291–1400*, London: Variorum, 1982

Luttrell, Anthony, *The Hospitallers of Rhodes and Their Mediterranean World*, Aldershot, England, and Brookfield, Vermont: Variorum, 1992

Luttrell, Anthony, *The Hospitaller State on Rhodes and Its Western Provinces, 1306–1462*, Aldershot, England, and Brookfield, Vermont: Variorum, 1999

Mallia-Milanes, Victor, *Venice and Hospitaller Malta, 1530–1798: Aspects of a Relationship*, Marsa, Malta: Publishers Enterprises Group, 1992

Mallia-Milanes, Victor, editor, *Hospitaller Malta, 1530–1798: Studies on Early Modern Malta and the Order of St. John of Jerusalem*, Msida, Malta: Mireva, 1993

Nicholson, Helen, *Templars, Hospitallers and Teutonic Knights: Images of the Military Orders, 1128–1291*, Leicester: Leicester University Press, and New York: St. Martin's Press, 1993

Nicholson, Helen, editor, *The Military Orders*, volume 2, *Welfare and Warfare*, Aldershot, England, and Brookfield, Vermont: Ashgate, 1998

Riley-Smith, Jonathan, *The Knights of St. John in Jerusalem and Cyprus, c. 1050–1310*, London: Macmillan, and New York: St. Martin's Press, 1967

# Hrosthwitha c. 932–1000

Saxon Benedictine nun, playwright, and poet

All that is known of Hrosthwitha is what can be inferred from her works and from her situation as a Benedictine nun at the imperial Saxon foundation at Gandersheim. This evidence reveals her to have been at once remarkable and conventional. Her originality lay in the choice of genres in which she wrote, whereas her conventionality lay in the lessons that her works intended to convey.

The splendid education that Hrosthwitha received at Gandersheim reflects the medieval Benedictines' commitment to preserving and spreading classical learning. Hrosthwitha became a skilled Latin poet who made a unique contribution to the didactic mission of her order. Her main interest was hagiography, conceived both as homiletic and, perhaps, as elaboration of the Benedictine office. Her earliest works were a series of poems narrating both saints' legends and apocryphal accounts of the life of Mary and the ascension of Christ. Later in life her literary reputation led her friends to urge her to try her hand at history in the form of epic poetry. She produced a long piece, lauding the reign of Otto I (936–973), as well as a history of the early years of her cloister. Today, however, her reputation rests on her most original compositions: six plays that she says she composed in the style of the Roman playwright Terence (c. 195–159 B.C.).

Hrosthwitha wrote not out of admiration for Terence but rather to counter his influence. Finding his descriptions of women distasteful, she wanted to provide her readers with superior models of female heroism. Women are the main protagonists of her plays, and their plots demonstrate the options for heroism that were available to women in the three roles to which medieval society confined them: virgin, wife, and whore. Hrosthwitha believed that martyrdom (especially in the defense of virginity or as a reparation for its loss) was a woman's highest calling. Her plays celebrate virgins who fight off both suitors and rapists and whores who reclaim their virtue by acts of monumental self-denial. In her plays, no less than in her legends, marriage was the calling that she found most difficult to appreciate. Many of her female characters equate marriage with pollution. Like St. Jerome (354–420), Hrosthwitha claims that motherhood redeems itself only by producing virgins to be dedicated to the religious life. Only virgins could attain the highest realms of heaven and thereby become brides of Christ. Lesser rewards awaited other good women. For Hrosthwitha the ascetic's repudiation of sexuality was the foundation of spiritual life for both genders. Monastics who read her works were no doubt confirmed in their faith that theirs was the superior human calling.

Hrosthwitha's compositions do not seem to have circulated widely or exercised much influence. Most survive today in a single manuscript from the early 11th century, whereas some fragments of a few of her plays come from the 12th. Her works were not widely known until the 16th century, when the humanist Conrad Celtes (1459–1508) published her work. Subsequently, scholars expressed doubt that a woman of the tenth century could have acquired Hrosthwitha's impressive education and suggested that Celtes must have forged her work as a joke. However, modern textual analysis has confirmed its (and her) authenticity.

A. DANIEL FRANKFORTER

*See also* Germany: History; Humanism, Christian; Jerome, St.; Women's Monasteries: Western Christian

## Biography

This German Christian poet came from a noble Saxon family and lived as a canoness in the Abbey of Gandersheim. Her poems in Latin are modeled on those of Horace, Virgil, and Ovid, and her plays on those of Plautus and Terence. Her writings were rediscovered by the humanist Conrad Celtes at Ratisbon and published in 1501.

## Major Works

*Hrotsvithae Opera*, edited by Helena Homeyer, 1970

*The Plays of Hrotsvit of Gandersheim*, edited by Katharina Wilson, 1989

*Hrotsvit of Gandersheim: A Florilegium of Her Works*, edited by Katharina Wilson, 1998

## Further Reading

Dronke, Peter, *Women Writers of the Middle Ages: A Critical Study of Texts From Perpetua (213) to Marguerite Porete (1310)*, Cambridge and New York: Cambridge University Press, 1984

Frankforter, A. Daniel, "Hroswitha of Gandersheim and the Destiny of Women," *The Historian* 41:2 (1979)

Jackson, W.T.H., *Medieval Literature: A History and Guide*, New York: Collier-Macmillan, 1967

Kronenberg, Kurt, *Roswitha von Gandersheim, Leben und Werk*, Bad Gandersheim: Hertel, 1962

Nagel, Bert, *Hrotsvit von Gandersheim*, Stuttgart: Metzler, 1965

Wemple, Suzanne F., *Women in Frankish Society*, Philadelphia: University of Pennsylvania, 1981

Wilson, Katharina, *Hrotsvit of Gandersheim: The Ethics of Authorial Stance*, Leiden and New York: Brill, 1988

Zeydel, Edwin, "The Authenticity of Hrotsvitha's Works," *Modern Language Notes* 69 (1946)

# Huaihai (Huai-hai) 720–814

Chinese Chan monk

Huaihai, whose family name was Chang, was born in Changle in present-day Fuzhou province, China. Having received his ordination, he stayed for many years in the Fucha Monastery in Lujiang (present-day Anhui province). He is reported to have moved to Jiangxi province when he learned that Ma Zudao was preaching in Nankang. Wandering from monastery to monastery in Jiangxi province, he finally went to reside at Baizhang Mountain (Longxing district in present-day Jiangxi province). Here he died after having instructed for more than 20 years.

Tradition credits Huaihai, known as "the great wise one of the Baizhang Mountain," with the compilation of the rules of monastic discipline for Chan monks. These rules, called the Pure Rules of Baizhang (Baizhang Qinggui), combine what is useful of the existing rules of Hīnayāna and Mahāyāna. The claim that Huaihai was the creator of Chan rules is contradicted by the historical fact that, in his time, Chan monks, when already living in monasteries, lived together with other, non-Chan monks, who were organized according to the rules of the Vinaya school. Only gradually were distinctive Chinese (Chan-)rules added. Analysis of historical records reveals that some rules might need to be linked to Huaihai but that no real codex with his name ever existed. A real set of Chan monastic rules dates only from the Song dynasty (960–1279).

A positive factor for the growth of Chan monasteries, especially in the Song dynasty, has been that Chan monks were engaged in physical labor. This explains the most famous of Huaihai's rules: "One day without working is one day without food." As the number of Chan monks increased, with figures of over 1,000 monks in one monastery, disagreements between the two groups of monks (Chan and non-Chan) living in one monastery undoubtedly increased, necessitating the establishment of new rules. As the number of Chan devotees began to outnumber the original monks in the monastery, Chan monks pushed through their own Chinese rules that differed from the rules of the Vinaya school. These (Song-)rules are attributed to Huaihai and are called the Pure Rules for Chan Monasteries (Chanyuan Qinggui). Another name for the rules is the Pure Rules for Chan Monasteries of Baizhang (Baizhang Conglin Qinggui). These rules are the oldest extant set of Chan rules and are a major source for our knowledge of the organization of Chan monasteries at the end of the Northern Song dynasty (960–1127). They became standard for all monasteries in China (including non-Chan monasteries) as well as for Chan (Zen) monasteries in Japan, where the rules were imported in 1356.

After having been modified in the Southern Song dynasty (1127–1279), a new version of the rules was written under the Mongol Yuan dynasty (1279–1368). It has been observed that the rule "One day without working is one day without food" was then no longer followed. The Yuan version of the Pure Rules was also used in the Ming dynasty.

BART DESSEIN

*See also* Buddhist Schools/Traditions: China; Chan/Zen: China; China; Mahāyāna; Rules, Buddhist (Vinaya)

**Biography**

To this eighth-century Chan monk have been ascribed (mistakenly) the rules known as the Pure Rules of Baizhang. He lived in various monasteries in Lujiang and later in Jiangxi province.

**Further Reading**

Colcutt, Martin, *Five Mountains: The Rinzai Zen Monastic Institution in Medieval Japan*, Boston: Harvard University Press, 1981

Demiéville, Paul, *Choix d'études bouddhiques*, Leiden: Brill, 1973

Dumoulin, Heinrich, "Die Entwicklung des chinesischen Chan nach Hui-neng im Lichte des Wu-men-kuan," *Monumenta Serica* 6 (1941)

Dumoulin, Heinrich, *Geschichte des Zen-Buddhismus*, volume 1, *Indien und China*, Bern: Francke, 1985

Edkins, Joseph, *Chinese Buddhism: A Volume of Sketches, Historical, Descriptive and Critical*, Boston: Hodder and Stoughton, 1880; London: Kegan Paul, Trench, Trübner, 1893

Fritz, Claudia, *Die Verwaltungsstruktur der Chan-Klöster in der späten Yuan-Zeit: Das 4. Buch der Chixiu Baizhang qinggui, übersetz, annotiert und mit einer Einleitung Versehen*, Bern: Peter Lang, 1994

Groot, J.J.M. de, *Le code du Mahāyāna en Chine: son influence sur la vie monacale et sur le monde laïque*, Amsterdam: Müller, 1893

Hackman, Heinrich, "Pai chang ch'ing kuei: The Rules of Buddhist Monastic Life in China," *T'oung Pao* 9 (1908)

Lopez, Donald, editor, *Buddhism in Practice*, Princeton, New Jersey: Princeton University Press, 1995

# Huineng trad. 638–713

Reputed Chinese founder of Southern Chan

In Chan tradition Huineng was the founder of Southern Chan and, as sixth patriarch (*liuzu*), the true heir of Hongren (d. 674). Since the tenth century, with few exceptions, all Chan monks claimed a lineage traced through Huineng and Bodhidharma back to Śākyamuni. As the figurehead of Southern Chan, Huineng, or rather his image, was crucial.

Yet until his self-proclaimed heir, Shenhui (684–758), launched a vitriolic propaganda campaign in 730 around the metropolitan region, Huineng was known only as a parochial teacher from the remote South, just one of the ten disciples of Hongren. Shenhui, who had studied under Shenxiu (d. 706), an influential student of Hongren, dismissed Shenxiu's "Northern Chan" as compromised, inadequate gradualism and exalted Huineng's "Southern Chan" orthodox subitism. Shenhui and his epigones forged an image for Huineng out of a factual vacuum by contrasting him to the tall, aristocratic, scholarly, and metropolitan Shenxiu and by modeling his career roughly on those of Hongren and the unlikely and uncrowned sage Confucius. Having proposed a Confucian "imperial" lineage for Chan, Shenhui became wedded to the Confucian paradigm. Thus, Huineng was depicted in the hagiography that evolved between the 730s and 780s as a short, ugly hillbilly who was the son of peasants or a disgraced, exiled official. He was either orphaned when three years old or supported his widowed mother by selling firewood, and he mixed with uncivilized hunter tribes. Hearing a customer chant the *Jin'gangjing* (Diamond Sūtra), he was moved to study with Hongren, but as an illiterate lay youth he had to hull grain. In an initial interview with Hongren, he asserted that even a hunting Liao tribesman from beyond the pale like himself possessed the Buddha nature and so was no different in spiritual potential to Hongren. This so impressed Hongren that when, according to the *Liuzu Tanjing* (Platform Sūtra of the Sixth Patriarch), Huineng composed a verse superior to Shenxiu's verse, Hongren gave him the symbols of the patriarchal succession. Hongren's pupils, incredulous, pursued him, but he escaped south and into seclusion in the hills and in one version was tonsured in 676 by Yinzong in Canton. Huineng taught at Baolin Monastery (later named Nanhua, "South China," Monastery) until his death, refusing to attend court and surviving assassination attempts. He prepared for his own death, which was accompanied by miracles.

This portrayal of the attainment of buddhahood by an illiterate, rustic layman was appealing because it affirmed the universality of the potential to become buddha. It divided the community, but in 816 the emperor granted Huineng a posthumous title, confirming the sixth patriarch claim, which probably had been imperially sanctioned as early as 770. Thereafter Chan proponents promoted new visions of Huineng. They attributed to him the *Platform Sūtra*, the only sūtra not preached by Buddha, thus elevating Huineng to the status of a living buddha. The sūtra's content was moderated, its sermons were emphasized, and its style was polished. Thus, it was included in the Continued Buddhist Canon and reprinted many times from 1012 on. By the Ming dynasty several leading literati wrote commentaries on it. A commentary on the *Diamond Sūtra* was also attributed to Huineng, and that sūtra is recited to this day in Chan monasteries on the grounds that Huineng was enlightened by this sūtra and had recommended it. Thus, Huineng's writings became part of literary Chan and yet still appealed to meritocratic sentiment. The Huineng hagiography also appeared in Chan biographical collections that bore the Song imperial imprimatur, and Huineng was given honorific titles by three Song emperors.

Another promotional tactic was employed by the monastic community of Nanhua Monastery, which from the 780s, at the latest, claimed to possess a lacquer body-cast of Huineng, and this "mummy" was reputedly the object of several attempted thefts, once by a monk from Silla in 722. As a result Ssanggye Monastery in South Korea claims to possess the "crown" (*uṣṇīṣa*) of Huineng's head. The mummy is of a real person, and it is still enshrined in Nanhua, although in 1477 it was shifted from its stūpa (at the relic's request in a dream) into the Hall of the Sixth Patriarch. This relic was credited with powers against drought and was paraded around Shaozhou and Canton as late as the 16th century as a rain god. Huineng was said to have created springs throughout the region. His mummy was even used as a palladium by the Southern Han (918–971) rulers, and it was brought to the Song court in 1032. His precedent led to a tradition of eminent monks being lacquered as "flesh body" (*roushen*) mummies. Huineng's secondary relics – his bowl, the robe of transmission, and a rock weight – were venerated at Nanhua, although other monasteries tried to forge a connection and their own Huineng relics. This promotion succeeded, for Silla monks visited Nanhua in the eighth and ninth centuries,

and Matteo Ricci (1522–1610) wrote that pilgrims flocked there from all over China. Nanhua Monastery was the major pilgrimage destination of South China, and Huineng became one of the most popular figures in Chinese culture. His hagiography was extended in Song and Yuan times to elevate him from human patriarch to a Buddhist deity. Thus, in the latter hagiographies he was made a member of an illustrious clan, was miraculously born after a six-year pregnancy on the same day as the Buddha's birthday, did not drink his mother's milk but divine ambrosia, and was unharmed by sword blows; his relics had supernatural powers.

The legacy of Huineng is twofold. First, the hagiographical image and teachings of the *Platform Sūtra* asserted that anyone, even an illiterate layperson, could see the Buddha nature and be enlightened at once without lengthy, arduous study by using formless precepts and unfettered meditation. This egalitarian streak proved subversive to the extent that the state required monks to be proficient in at least several scriptures, yet this was undermined by the literary quality and doctrinal subtleties of the text. Huineng's followers sinicized Buddhism, in that the religious (anti-)hero Huineng became a living Chinese buddha with his own sūtra and seemed all the more familiar, because he was partly modeled on the sage Confucius. Second, the Huineng relic as deity made Nanhua Monastery one of the major pilgrimage sites of China. The relic and monastery gained the protection even of emperors such as Genghis Khan (1206–1227). This monastery was a pillar of Chan and was restored by the famous Hanshan Deqing (1546–1623) and Xuyun (c. 1840–1959).

JOHN JORGENSEN

*See also* Hakuin; Holy Men/Holy Women: Buddhist Perspectives; Vietnam

## Biography

The legend of the sixth patriarch of Southern Chan was fashioned by his self-proclaimed successor Shenhui (684–758), who used the legends to overshadow the Northern School. Very little is known about Huineng apart from posthumous legends, which hail him as an exemplar of sudden awakening in contrast to the Northern School's advocacy of gradual awakening.

## Major Work

The *Platform Sūtra* was posthumously attributed to Huineng.

## Further Reading

Chŏng, Sŏngbon, "Yukjo Tan'gyŏng ŭi sŏngnip kwa chemunje," in *Yukjo Tan'gyŏng ŭi se'gye*, edited by Kim Chi'gyŏn, Seoul: Minjoksa, 1989

Ding, Fubao, *Liuzu Fabao Tanjing jianzhu*, n.p., 1919

Faure, Bernard, "Relics and Flesh Bodies: The Creation of Ch'an Pilgrimage Sites," in *Pilgrims and Sacred Sites in China*, edited by Susan Naquin and Chün-fang Yü, Berkeley: University of California Press, 1992

Guangdongsheng Bowuguan, compilers, *Nanhua Si*, Beijing: Wenwu chubanshe, 1990

Komazawa Daigaku Zenshūshi kenkyūkai, *Enō kenkyū*, Tokyo: Daishūkan shoten, 1978

McRae, John, "The Legend of Hui-neng and the Mandate of Heaven: An Illiterate Sage and the Unlikely Emperor," in *Fo Kuang Shan Report of International Conference in Ch'an Buddhism*, Kaohsiung: FoKuang, 1990

McRae, John R., "The Story of Early Ch'an," in *Zen: Tradition and Transition*, edited by Kenneth Kraft, New York: Grove Press, 1988; London: Rider, 1989

Nagashima, Takayuki, *Truths and Fabrications in Religion: An Investigation from Documents of the Zen (Ch'an) Sect*, London: Probsthain, 1978

Nihon Miira Kenkyū Gurūpu, editors, *Nihon Chūgoku miira shinkō no kenkyū*, Tokyo: Heibonsha, 1993

Yampolsky, Philip B., *The Platform Sūtra of the Sixth Patriarch*, New York: Columbia University Press, 1967

Zhang, Mantao, editor, *Liuzu Tanjing yanjiu lunji*, Taipei: Dasheng wenhua chubanshe, 1976

# Huiyuan (Hui-yüan) 334–416

## Founder of Chinese Pure Land Buddhism

Huiyuan was born in the house of Jia in Loufan Yanmen (present-day Daizhou in Shanxi province). In his youth he studied Confucian classics as well as Daoist literature. Because of political troubles he was unable to move to southern China to pursue these studies. This forced him to take up Buddhist studies, in which he soon excelled. At age 20, at the instigation of Dao'an (312–385), he left home to become a religious mendicant. Around 380 he settled at Mount Lu (Jiujiang district in present-day Jiangxi province), which under his guidance developed into the most famous center of Buddhism in southern China. Although Huiyuan is reported never to have left Mount Lu until his death in 416, it is known that the mountain became the meeting place for monks and laymen, including Buddhist-minded Confucianist literati and members of the highest gentry. Thus, the life of Huiyuan is representative for the period of early Chinese "gentry Buddhism."

Gentry Buddhism is characteristic of the series of minor Chinese dynasties that ruled southern China after the fall of the Han dynasty in 220. The traditional Chinese cultural elite in these regions turned away from Confucianism and had their minds opened to Daoism and the new Buddhist faith. Huiyuan played an important role as a middleman between the Buddhist world and the Chinese intellectual elite, and undoubtedly his greatest contribution to Chinese Buddhism is in making Buddhism acceptable to the Chinese literati. Because members of both the Chinese and the non-Chinese courts that governed northern China frequented Mount Lu, an increasing number of laypeople were attracted to the doctrine as well.

The presence of lay followers had some important consequences. One of these concerns the "obeisance to the throne" of lay followers and monks. Huiyuan claimed that because lay followers were still functioning in society, naturally they must be loyal to the throne. On the other hand, Buddhist monks, he said, have retreated from society and thus are no longer subject to common jurisprudence. In 404 Huiyuan even wrote the treatise *Shamen Bujing Wangzhe Lun* (Buddhist Monks Do Not Have to Pay Respect to the Emperor). Huiyuan's prestige helped to give Buddhist monasteries an independent position in Chinese society. Another important consequence was that to make Buddhist scriptures comprehensible for the Chinese people, Daoist (as well as Confucianist) concepts especially were used. This style of writing is called *geyi* (matching meanings). Finally, the accentuation of devotion and the use of statues helped laypeople in their concentration. Thus, it is reported that on 11 September 402, Huiyuan, together with an assembly of 123 monks and lay followers (including some important literati), made a vow in front of a statue of Amitābha to be reborn in his Western Paradise. It is claimed that this event is the beginning of Chinese Pure Land Buddhism, and Huiyuan is seen as the founder and first patriarch of that school.

Huiyuan's biography informs us that he felt distressed because of the poor condition of Vinaya texts. Thus, he is reported to have sent some of his disciples to the West to collect more Vinaya texts. It was also at his request that, at the beginning of the fifth century, the translation of the Vinaya of the Sarvāstivādins was completed by Dharmaruci, this work having been left uncompleted because of the death of Puṇyatara. The emergence of a Buddhist clergy that set in from the fifth century was undoubtedly facilitated by the existence of complete Chinese Vinayas. In addition, Huiyuan is credited with the *Fashe Jiedu* (Rules for the Buddhist Community).

BART DESSEIN

*See also* Buddhist Schools/Traditions: China; China; Missionaries: Buddhist; Rules, Buddhist (Vinaya)

## Biography

One of the earliest Buddhist monks in China, Huiyuan became a disciple of Dao'an from 355 to 378. Thereafter he settled for good on Mount Lu in Southern China. In 402 he founded the White Lotus school, in which monastics and lay people vowed to be reborn in Amida Buddha's Pure Land. He is considered the founder of Chinese Pure Land Buddhism.

## Major Works

*Fashe Jiedu* (Rules for the Buddhist Community)
*Shamen Bujing Wangzhe Lun* (Buddhist Monks Do Not Have to Pay Respect to the Emperor)

## Further Reading

Bagchi, Prabodh Chandra, *India and China: A Thousand Years of Cultural Relations*, New York: Philosophical Library, 1951; Westport, Connecticut: Greenwood Press, 1971

Chen, Kenneth, *Buddhism in China: A Historical Survey*, Princeton, New Jersey: Princeton University Press, 1964

Demiéville, Paul, "La pénétration du Bouddhisme dans la tradition philosophique Chinoise," *Cahiers d'Histoire Mondiale* 3:1 (1956)

Hurvitz, Leon, "'Render unto Caesar' in Early Chinese Buddhism: Hui-yüan's Treatise on the Exemption of the Buddhist Clergy from the Requirements of Civil Etiquette," *Sino-Indian Studies* 5 (1957)

Inouye, Ichii, "Rozan-bunka to Eon," *Shien* 9 (1934)

Liebenthal, Walther, "Shih Hui-yüan's Buddhism," *Journal of the American Oriental Society* 70 (1950)

Liebenthal, Walther, "The Immortality of the Soul in Chinese Thought," *Monumenta Nipponica* 8 (1952)

Ryōon, Kubota, *Shina Ju Dō Butsu Kōshōshi*, Tokyo: Daito Shuppansha, 1943

Sčuckij, J., "Ein Dauist im chinesischen Buddhismus," *Sinica* 15 (1940)

Tokiwa, Daijō, *Shina ni Okeru Bukkyō to Jukyō Dōkyō*, Tokyo: Toyo Bunko, 1930

Tsukamoto, Zenryū, *A History of Early Buddhism: From Its Introduction to the Death of Hui-yüan*, 2 vols., translated by Leon Hurvitz, Tokyo and New York: Kodansha International, 1985

Zürcher, Erich, *The Buddhist Conquest of China: The Spread and Adaptation of Buddhism in Early Medieval China*, 2 vols., Leiden: Brill, and New York: Humanist Press, 1959

# Humanism, Christian

If positive engagement with ancient pagan literature is taken as the main criterion of humanism, then monastic humanism has been very common, for, notwithstanding Jerome's experience of being torn between Christ and Cicero (*Epistola* 22.30), classical studies have been an important part of monastic culture at least since the time of the Cappadocian Fathers. Throughout the centuries Eastern and Western ascetics have appreciated, preserved, and transmitted classical Greek and Latin literature. However, so numerous and diverse were the reasons that the religious found for studying the classics that an attempt to catalog them as a taxonomy of monastic humanism becomes tedious. Furthermore, the term's derivation from the Renaissance notion of *studia humanitatis* (grammar, poetry, rhetoric, history, and moral philosophy) makes this understanding of humanism too narrow for the purpose at hand. Because that curriculum developed in a particular set of historical circumstances, and because modern assessments of the 15th-century *umanisti* in some ways also reflect the particular concerns of the 19th-century German scholars who singled them out, humanism understood in this way offers a constricted view into the culture of monasticism.

Equally time-bound is the theme of human dignity so often mentioned as an element of humanism. The Renaissance curriculum of classical studies corresponded to a diminished view of the lasting consequences of original sin and a high estimation of man's place in nature and the cosmos. Although this theme achieved a new intensity in the 15th century, its elements were much older. Even before Socrates "brought philosophy down from heaven to earth" by focusing on the soul and human excellence, Hellenic myth celebrated the human invention or discovery of the arts. Later in the ancient world, man was viewed as microcosm, as the likeness of god (*Corpus Hermeticum*), as a fragment of god (Epictetus), or even as god (*Somnium Scipionis*). However instructive it might be to follow the transmission and career of these ideas in Christian monasticism, such an effort could be described rather as a preface to the study of Renaissance or modern culture than as a contribution to our knowledge of monastic humanism. Certainly some classical ideas about the dignity of man resonated in monastic culture from the start, but in the absence of a parallel consideration of doctrines of man's chronic post-lapsarian ignorance and impotence, a study of human dignity will yield misleading results. More important, although ancient ideas of human dignity sometimes resemble Christian themes of ascent and deification (*theosis*), in no way do they connect with the theme of descent and suffering (*kenosis*). The awareness of the Son's self-emptying and descent into abandonment, which deeply informs monastic renunciation, humility, and obedience, is unintelligible within the framework of antique conceptions of civic virtue or philosophical excellence.

More satisfying than the theme of human dignity is the broader question of the spirit in which the religious resorted to the classics. Jean Leclercq (1911–1993) described an integral humanism that cultivated in human beings an increase of the influence of Jesus, the one perfect Man, in a process that will be consummated outside history. Leclercq insisted that the monastic culture of the Western Middle Ages reconciled this eschatological humanism with what he sometimes called the love of learning. This "historical humanism . . . seeks in the writings of the past lessons capable of contributing to man's harmonious development" (Leclercq, 1961). The religious gained from the classics a sensibility attuned to worldly and metaphysical beauty and also acquired a refinement of speech and sentiment needed for self-examination. According to this view the works of Anselm of Canterbury (c. 1033–1109) exhibit a synthesis of classical culture and monastic practice in a style and mode of expression that amply reflect their author's orientation toward that highest form of humanism in which man and God are united, namely, the Incarnation. Behind this reconciliation of the two humanisms is the *reductio artium ad theologiam* (leading of secular disciplines back to theology), according to which Christianity fulfills and completes earlier, fragmentary understandings of the universe. This incorporation of the partial truths (*logoi*) of pagan knowledge into the wholeness of Christ the Logos was a facet of Eastern monasticism from the time of the Cappadocian Fathers. Western ascetics from Cassiodorus (c. 485/90–c. 581) to Erasmus (1466/69–1536) found a clear statement of the idea in Augustine's *De vera religione* and *De doctrina christiana*.

Robert Bultot (1963–1964) has challenged Leclercq's thesis by withholding the term *humanism* from any Christian culture that fails to uphold the autonomy of the secular disciplines and at least a provisional finality of human values. The ontological foundation of Anselm's contempt for the world (*contemptus mundi*) was an awareness of the disproportion between God and finite being. Anselm disqualified the latter in the order of values without inquiring after its essence or its particular significance. When nature as a whole lacks the density of a stable, immanent principle, human nature too tends to be viewed exclusively in the light of man's supernatural end. Anselm seems to accept the hyperspiritualist myth of primitive human beings as contemplative

souls, a view that Bultot describes as "angelic anthropology."
The ecclesiology that Anselm developed around this "angelic anthropology" often identifies Christian life with monastic life and
has certain other predictable consequences, including degradation of the status of marriage, family, and secular pursuits. An
outlook such as Anselm's precludes the development of a Christian humanism based on passages such as Psalm 8:5–8 ("Yet you
have made them a little lower than God. . . . You have given
them dominion over the works of your hands . . .") and its
echoes in 1 Corinthians 15:27 and Ephesians 1:22. Although
Leclercq and Bultot advance the discussion by highlighting the
new intellectual and spiritual contexts in which the classics were
assimilated, any scholarly framework in which the same evidence leads to opposite conclusions has a limited value.

The point here is not to deny classical studies and the theme
of human dignity a place in the discussion of monastic humanism but to suggest that these issues are most helpful when subordinated to the question of what it is to be a human being. By
drawing theological anthropology in its historical dimension to
the center of the discussion of monastic humanism, as Glenn
Olsen (1990) has done for medieval humanism, it becomes possible to gain a more nuanced sense of the ways in which monastic culture selected and employed the resources at its disposal,
including the classics and ideas about human dignity, to accomplish specifically Christian and ascetic objectives. Focusing more
carefully on a given period's understanding of what it means to
be human helps disclose hope and possibility alongside the misery and sin proper to man. Although any concept of Christian
humanism must encompass both misery and hope, it is in hermitage and cloister, where the eschatological horizon is always
present, that the sense of man as being caught between two
worlds is especially keen. Whatever paradox or even oxymoron
"monastic humanism" exhibits in an ethos that is at once world-
fleeing and world-affirming derives from the cosmic paradox of
Christ's glorification through abasement, for assimilation to the
self-abasing Christ is the aim of the religious.

A fundamental aspect of this anthropology must be the
changing estimation of the human body between late antiquity
and the early modern period. Apprehensiveness about the body,
as well as doubts about the character and density of psychosomatic unity that were an important feature of ancient thought,
affected Christian monasticism almost from the start. Because
the main issues involved in this topic are considered elsewhere in
this volume, here it suffices to point out the body's relevance to
the history of monastic humanism.

The status of the heart (kardia, cor) is another basic question
that arises in relation to the changing concept of what it is to be
human. Ancient high culture tended to view the rational mind
(nous, mens, ratio) as the essential faculty of man and to emphasize the intellect's role as pilot of the irrational faculties and
steward of the senses, whether in leading the philosophical life of
contemplation or the civic life of practical reason. Once again
this nexus of ideas helped shape early Christian doctrines of the
human person. It continued to influence even those patristic and
medieval authors who were aware of a psychology that was

more in keeping with Scripture, which featured the heart (lev or
levav, kardia) as the spiritual summit of man and the locus of his
contact with divine grace. In ancient Hebrew and New Testament usage, the heart is not only the center of moral, religious,
and spiritual activity but also the seat of thought, planning, volition, memory, and imagination. By contrast Scripture associates
the emotions, including love and hate, and the desires, such as
hunger and thirst, with the soul rather than the heart. The gradual process of amalgamation and interpenetration that began
when Greco-Roman and Judeo-Christian psychological teachings converged in late antiquity proved decisive for the subsequent history of spirituality and religion in both the East and the
West.

Several branches of the tradition continued to be mainly intellectual. A case in point is Evagrius Ponticus (345–399), who
propounded an Origenist cosmology of procession from and return to the unity of the primitive monad. The latter's nature is
that of pure intelligence. His mystical theology included a series
of profound psychological reflections based on years of ascetic
experience. His version of the Aristotelian understanding of man
as rational animal is the claim that human beings achieve their
complete self-realization as the image of God when the purified
human mind perceives God in contemplation (theoria, gnosis).
The life of ascetic praxis aims at purifying the soul's passions to
allow the unencumbered mind to rise in contemplation. Like a
mirror, the soul that has arrived at perfect knowledge of the
Trinity in higher contemplation reflects the light of the divine
presence and thereby comes to resemble the divine archetype.

A new synthesis that focused on the heart eventually emerged
from the tension between the platonizing image of the human
person as hierarchy of members and faculties and the Stoic doctrine of man as centered on a single ruling principle located in
the depths of the heart. Many Stoics and some ancient medical
authorities thought of the ruling principle in human beings as
the pneuma, or spark, of the divine Logos. Just as the Logos
could be equated with the sun as center of the cosmos, so the
center of man the microcosm is said to be the heart, "the Logos
in us." Having no form of its own, the divine spark manifests itself in different modes according to the activities and operations
of the various parts of the human mind and body. Origen (c.
185–c. 254) and other Christian authors adopted this more unified image of the human person by assimilating the Stoic Logos
to the Logos of the Gospel of John. In turn the possibility of integrating the nonrational faculties, such as the affections, will,
and senses, in an account of the human person that centers on
the heart gradually became apparent.

Maximus the Confessor (580–662) reoriented Evagrian ascetic mysticism in a sacramental and Christocentric approach to
prayer that proved decisive in Byzantine monasticism. He shared
Evagrius' view that contemplation is man's proper end but elaborated this idea in light of an account of the human person more
consonant with Scripture and with ancient views of man outside
the platonic tradition. Maximus found the latter epitomized in
the treatise of the late fourth-century Nemesius of Emesa.
Rather than picture highest prayer as equivalent to the

Hans Holbein the Younger, *Erasmus*, Louvre, Paris, France, c. 1523–1524.
Photo courtesy of Alinari/Art Resource, New York

restoration of pure *nous* (mind), Maximus wrote that "he who truly loves God prays entirely without distraction, and he who prays entirely without distraction loves God truly." He considered dispassionate knowledge of God insufficient in the absence of a love (*agape*) so powerful that it draws the human person away from all subordinate goods and toward divine goodness. This emphasis on the "blessed passion" of love has implications for monastic practice as well as for contemplation. Just as both goodness and truth are attributes of God, so spiritual intelligence is part of man's life. As a consequence, ascetic struggle and the acquisition of virtues acquire a more central and abiding role in Maximus' account of the ascent to God than Evagrius had allowed.

The Greek monastic tradition in which *theosis* brings not illumination of the disembodied intellect but transfiguration of the whole person culminated in Gregory Palamas (1296–1350). He wrote in defense of the monks of Mount Athos who practiced a form of prayer known as Hesychasm, which comprised the constant repetition of a simple "prayer of the heart" combined with a breathing technique meant to unify body and soul in a single, encompassing act of prayer. Although the notion of total absorption in a short prayer called "the memory of Jesus" can be traced back to the fourth century, John Climacus (580–650) is the earliest known author to link the utterance of the prayer with the natural rhythm of breathing. The Athonite Hesychasts came under attack from the Greek Calabrian philosopher Barlaam (c. 1290–1348) for claiming to gain spiritual knowledge of God through the body. They insisted that such communion is not the province of a mystical elite but is open to anyone who practices the technique (always assuming divine grace) regardless of education or calling. Because Barlaam held that a formation in classical studies is prerequisite to that higher theology that alone can yield knowledge of God, this polemic has often been represented as a conflict between Barlaam's humanism and the ascetic, world-fleeing spirituality of the monks. However, Gregory Palamas can be depicted as hostile to humanism only if one begins with strictly noetic and anticorporeal assumptions about what it means to be human.

Early in the history of cenobitic monasticism, intersubjective spiritual development was related to the heart. Unlike Antony (c. 251–356), who viewed community as the nursery of *askesis*, to be left behind when a more rigorous solitary discipline became possible, Pachomius (c. 290–346) understood community as the setting for ongoing improvement. Taking Acts 4:32 ("Now the whole group of those who believed were of one heart and soul, and no one claimed private ownership of any possessions, but everything they owned was held in common.") as a guiding principle, he promoted communion (*koinonia*), in which monks give mutual assistance and even assume responsibility for one another's spiritual growth. It is characteristic of the Pachomian literature to look for ways to mediate the disjunction between caution, self-knowledge, and self-control on the one hand and generosity, selflessness, and surrender to God's influence on the other. This literature examines that mediation for fresh insights about how the individual should interact with oth-

ers. Thus, the spiritual life becomes a dynamic process in which divinity gradually fills the heart and in which the vision of God becomes a vision of God in neighbor. As Pachomius said, there is no greater vision than "to see the invisible God in a visible man, his temple."

Like Pachomius, Basil (c. 330–379) invoked the communion of Acts 2:44 and the unity of heart and soul of Acts 4:32 as the ground for prohibiting all noncenobitic forms of monasticism. However, Basil went beyond the Egyptian abbot by presenting passages such as John 13:34 ("I give you a new commandment: to love one another.") against the background of Aristotelian and wider Hellenic assumptions about the essentially social character of human nature. In the *paideia*-centered culture of ancient Athens, as this had been adapted in the Hellenistic and Roman periods, Basil and the other Cappadocian Fathers found a model of systematic human formation according to a standard of excellence (*arete*), along with terminology, imagery, and concepts that could be applied within the cloister. Although its New Testament roots distinguish the Christian idea of reform from *paideia* as well as from various other ideologies of renewal known in antiquity, certain features of Pauline reform could be expressed or amplified in terms borrowed from the ancient practice of education (*paideia*). This optimism about the unification of all knowledge in a cosmic whole also underlies the rule that the ninth-century *hegumenos* Theodore (759–826) wrote for the monks of the Studion, a community in Constantinople whose social and liturgical inflection later became central in Byzantine civilization.

The monasticism introduced in the West by John Cassian (c. 360–after 430) reflected Basilian and Pachomian traditions in its focus on the monk's heart and on the charity that unifies individuals in a body of brotherly love (*corpus fraternitatis*). Although he considered *anchoresis* the more advanced form, Cassian held that cenobitic monks lead the apostolic life recorded in Acts 2:44 and 4:32, a linkage that he affirmed both as a matter of spiritual affiliation and as a continuous historical development. His normative emphasis on the hierarchical relation between master and disciple did not prevent him from acknowledging the horizontal dimension of communal life, in which experience of renunciation of the world and reintegration into community of friends eventually render the monk fit to enter the presence of the Divine Persons. Pre-12th-century Benedictine sources seldom focus on horizontal relations within the monastery. Even so the enhanced standing of the art of Latin grammar among Benedictines often betrayed an awareness that all distinctively human pursuits depend on man's use of language. Schoolmasters followed Augustine, albeit with fewer reservations than he, in affirming the validity and worth of the secular disciplines as parts of a surpassing Christian whole. As Alcuin (c. 740–804) put it, like the seven columns on the porch of the temple of holy wisdom, the arts afford access to the sacred precinct within.

The interest in heart, will, and affections in 12th-century spirituality coincided with more extensive and more intimate familiarity with classical and patristic literature. The numerous commentaries and homilies based on the Song of Songs produced in Cistercian monasteries attest to this fact, as do the several treatises on the nature and dignity of love written by central figures such as Aelred of Rievaulx (1109–1167), William of St. Thierry (1075/80–1148), and Bernard of Clairvaux (1090–1153). Nor were heart and love exclusively involved in the ascent toward contemplation; interest in the affections also manifested the Cistercian and general 12th-century awareness of the Trinitarian economy and the humanity of Christ. Following an insight of Origen, Bernard wrote that although the Father cannot suffer, in giving his Son to suffer He experiences compassion. Both Aelred and William of St. Thierry wrote meditations on the Lord's humanity and on the Passion, and in turn this concern for suffering undertaken out of love had implications for the understanding of cenobitic life. Discovering the image of God in other selves as well as through introspection, Cistercian authors expressed their discovery in an idiom shaped by familiarity with the classics. Although his dialogue *On Spiritual Friendship* incorporated large portions of Cicero's *On Friendship*, Aelred read Cicero in light of the Song of Songs, the wisdom literature of the Old Testament, and the writings of Ambrose and Jerome.

In the Renaissance Erasmus (1466/69–1536) drew together several of these strands into a humanist primitivism that stemmed from his Christian psychology. Impressed with what he took to be the purity and simplicity of the apostolic Church, Erasmus criticized the formality and materialism of late medieval piety and called for a restoration of the spiritual and transcendent worship of the primitive Church. Reform would involve persuading people to subordinate external observances to an inward imitation of Christ (*imitatio Christi*). To ensure that modern readers encounter the Lord's authentic teachings, Erasmus applied to the Gospels and Fathers the critical philological methods that devotees of the *studia humanitatis* had developed for understanding ancient pagan texts. His edition of the Greek New Testament enjoyed widespread success and became the foundation for vernacular translations, such as that of Martin Luther (1483–1546). In addition to their technical contribution to the study of the Bible and Fathers, *studia humanitatis* provided an excellent means for developing human spiritual potential on a broad front. Spiritualizing metaphysical convictions sometimes led Erasmus to speak of containing, voiding, or neutralizing the affections. However, usually he took a more generous approach in which the passions and emotions could be redirected and channeled in support of the struggle against vice and of gradual habituation to virtue. Because of its power to arouse admiration and stir the inclinations, eloquence, whether that of the ancient orators and poets or that of the classically versed Greek and Latin Fathers, is pivotal in the Erasmian understanding of moral reform. In short the anxiety of Jerome, one of Erasmus' favorite authors, that love of pagan literature might stifle growth in discipleship of Christ points less directly to the essential issues of monastic humanism than does Jerome's observation that whereas Plato considered the intellect to be the center of man, Christ taught that it is the heart (*Epistola* 64.1).

DAVID APPLEBY

*See also* Alcuin; Anselm, St.; Climacus, John, St.; Education of Christian Monastics; Evagrius Ponticus; Hesychasm; Leclercq, Jean; Libraries: Western Christian; Liturgy: Eastern Christian; Maximus the Greek, St.; Pachomius, St.; Scholars, Benedictine; Spirituality: Western Christian

## Further Reading

Bouyer, Louis, *Erasmus and the Humanist Experiment*, translated by Francis X. Murphy, London: Chapman, 1959

Bultot, Robert, *Christianisme et valeurs humaines: La doctrine du mépris du monde, en occident, de S. Ambroise à Innocent III*, volume 4: *Le XIe siècle*, Louvain: Éditions Nauwelaerts, 1963–1964

Jaeger, Werner, *Early Christianity and Greek Paideia*, Cambridge, Massachusetts: Belknap Press, 1961; London: Oxford University Press, 1969

Leclercq, Jean, *The Love of Learning and the Desire for God*, translated by Catharine Misrahi, New York: Fordham University Press, 1961; reprint, London: SPCK, 1978

Leonardi, Claudio, editor, *Gli umanesimi medievali, Atti del II Congresso dell'Internationales Mittellateinerkomitee*, Florence: SISMEL edizioni del Galluzzo, 1998

Olsen, Glenn W., "Twelfth-Century Humanism Reconsidered: The Case of St. Bernard," *Studi Medievali* 31:1 (1990)

Tsirpanlis, Constantine N., "Byzantine Humanism and Hesychasm in the Thirteenth and Fourteenth Centuries: Synthesis or Antithesis, Reformation or Revolution?" *The Patristic and Byzantine Review* 12 (1993)

# Hume, Basil 1923–1999

English Benedictine priest, abbot, and archbishop of Westminster

The son of a distinguished Scottish Presbyterian physician and his French wife, George Hume was brought up in Newcastle and educated at Ampleforth. He entered the monastery at Ampleforth in 1941, receiving the name Basil, and subsequently studied modern history at Oxford and theology at Fribourg in Switzerland. Ordained a priest in 1950, he taught theology in the monastery and modern languages in the school at Ampleforth, becoming a housemaster in 1955. In 1963, at the age of 40, he was elected abbot of Ampleforth, the largest Benedictine community in the British Isles, then numbering 153 monks.

About half the community was resident at Ampleforth, where their main work was teaching in two boarding schools with about 750 boys. The other half of the monks were resident on over 20 parishes with nearly 40,000 parishioners and at a dependent priory in the United States that became independent in 1973. Thus, the scale of Abbot Hume's responsibilities was considerable, extending beyond the cloister into the daily lives of ordinary people. A sympathetic listener and intuitive, gifted leader, Abbot Hume proved successful at leading his community through a time of rapid, unprecedented change. He modernized life in the monastery without startling innovations while coping with the needs and problems of different individuals with considerable sensitivity. His teaching on monastic life was humane, tolerant, and pragmatic. A selection of his monastic conferences was published, *Searching for God* (1977).

His appointment as archbishop of Westminster in 1976 came as a surprise. The 18th- and 19th-century contribution by Benedictines to the English and Welsh hierarchy had been considerable but was largely forgotten. Some feared that a monk might be aloof, but Cardinal Hume demonstrated a compassion and openness bred of years of community living. As a monk he was seen less as a representative of Church authority than as a man of God who could talk unaffectedly of prayer and the spiritual life. As a Benedictine he was recognized as having roots deep in the spiritual history of the nation, a fact that allowed him to play an ecumenical role more naturally than his predecessors. Notwithstanding his parentage he was widely perceived as being very English – a quality not always associated with Catholicism – but his knowledge of German and fluency in French had also gained him, most unusually for an English bishop, a major European role. Within his own diocese devolution of power owed much to his monastic experience.

In 1998 his mandatory resignation at the age of 75 was refused by Rome. His 22 years at Westminster had established him as the senior religious figure in England, immensely popular and instantly recognizable. His influence behind the scenes in political circles is widely believed to have been extensive. Despite a decline in numbers Catholicism has assumed a more central position in English life during the last quarter of the 20th century, the Hume years. He died of cancer after a brief illness, still in office, in June 1999. Eulogies came from all sectors of the British public and from around the world.

BERNARD GREEN, O.S.B.

*See also* Abbot: Christian; England: History; Monk-Bishops

## Biography

Son of a Scottish physician and French mother, George Hume was educated at the Benedictine monastery of Ampleforth in Yorkshire. He entered the monastery in 1941, taking the name Basil. Having studied at Oxford and Fribourg in Switzerland, he was ordained in 1950 and taught at the school of Ampleforth, becoming abbot there in 1963, only to be named Archbishop of Westminster in 1976. As chief prelate of England until his death in June 1999, Cardinal Hume brought Benedictine kindliness and ecumenism to that office.

## Major Works

*Searching for God*, 1977
*In Praise of St. Benedict*, 1981
*To Be a Pilgrim*, 1984

## Further Reading

Butler, Carolyn, editor, *Basil Hume by His Friends*, London: Fount, 1998
Castle, Tony, editor, *Basil Hume, a Portrait*, London: Collins, 1986
Stanford, Peter, *Cardinal Hume and the Changing Face of English Catholicism*, London and New York: Geoffrey Chapman, 1993

# Humor: Buddhist

The question of the association of humor with Buddhist life and practice arose fairly early in the history of Buddhism. Buddhist scholastics debated the question whether the Buddha ever laughed, as some sūtras seemed to suggest, and if so in what sense and for what reasons. The prevailing opinion was that the Buddha did laugh on certain occasions, but only in the most restrained and refined sense. Using the dramatic classifications of Bharata (fourth century) in which six classes of laughter were arranged in hierarchical fashion from the nearly imperceptible smile to the raucous guffaw, Buddhist scholars allowed that the Buddha would have used only the most refined and restrained expression. On the common assumption that the source of laughter is the pleasurable, the issue was joined as to whether this pleasure arose from observing the exalted truths of enlightenment and Buddhahood or from escaping the bonds of ignorance and desire. It was Buddhadatta's thesis in the *Abhidhammavatara* that the Buddha's laughter arose from the degraded and not the sublime and thus involved seeing the folly of one's unenlightened existence in the light of newfound truth and liberation. However, this still seems to imply an enjoyment of sublime wisdom, not just liberation from suffering.

One finds a variety of forms of laughter and humor in Buddhist literature, art, and practice that run up and down Bharata's scale. Coming out of the yogic practice that Buddhism shares with other sannyāsin movements is the comic association of meditating monks with sitting frogs. The frog motif accompanied the spread of Buddhism into China, Korea, and Japan. The animal scroll by the Japanese abbot Toba-sojo (1053–1140) depicts monkeys, foxes, and rabbits in the posturings of monks, priests, and laypeople chanting before a large bullfrog Buddha on an altar, seated on cabbage leaves instead of the traditional lotus flower. The "meditating frog" ink sketch by Zen master Sengai (1750–1837) carries the accompanying calligraphy: "If by sitting in meditation (*zazen*) one becomes a Buddha." The frog grasps the point and smiles (i.e., "all frogs are Buddhas"). The human observer also gets the point: "sitting in meditation alone will not bring about Buddhahood."

Comical human figures are also found in Buddhist literature and art. Chinese legend grows around the monk Bu-tai (d. 916), a fat, jolly person who, because of his size and playful temperament, had difficulty sitting in meditation or conforming to monastic discipline. Leaving the monastic life he wandered from village to village, playing games with children and bringing them sweets and trinkets in his linen (sack), not unlike an Oriental Santa Claus. Eventually he is seen as a Buddha of happiness and good luck. Some claimed he was an incognito appearance of the next historical Buddha, Maitreya. With large belly and broad grin, he is commonly found in Buddhist temples and in the pictorial arts as a bringer of good fortune and good cheer. In the monastery he still symbolizes the freedom and enjoyment of enlightenment.

Other individuals have also served as "holy fools" in ways similar to the Holy Fool tradition in the Greek and Russian Or-

and as a "skillful means" (*upāya*) of leading toward Buddhist goals. Masters were often noted for their strange behavior and odd teaching methods: shouting, kicking, striking, roaring, and laughing. Questions would often be answered in such eccentric ways or by holding up a finger, responding unintelligibly, or walking out of the room. Kakua, one of the early Japanese monks to travel to China to study Chan, was invited on his return to explain the teaching before the emperor. He produced a flute from his robe, blew one note, bowed, and excused himself.

The first Chinese patriarch of the Chan tradition is Bodhidharma, who is credited with bringing Chan (*dhyāna*) teaching from India to China in the early fifth century. Although he is usually depicted as an intense, stern, no-nonsense figure, he is also credited with using humor to challenge common assumptions and to point out the follies of the desiring self – as in the tale of his audience before the emperor, who asks how much merit he might expect to gain from all his support for Buddhism, only to be told, "No merit whatsoever!" On the one hand, Bodhidharma is the epitome of seriousness, having zealously meditated against the wall of a cave until, according to legend, his legs fell off. On the other hand, he thereby becomes the legless *daruma* doll in popular culture that, however struck, bobs straight up again in comic flexibility.

Much of Buddhist humor is iconoclastic in character. Because the sources of evil and suffering are identified as the ego – its desires and attachments – the foolishness of these forms of bondage and ignorance are natural targets of humor. In the Zen tradition this iconoclasm is extended to Buddhist scripture, acts of piety, revered patriarchs, and even the Buddha himself. All are potential contexts for self-congratulation, and all are objects of desire and attachment. Thus, the Chinese sixth patriarch is depicted tearing up a sūtra scroll, or Lin-ji, founder of the Lin-ji (Rinzai) sect, advises, "If you meet a Buddha, kill the Buddha; if you meet a patriarch, kill the patriarch." Even the central focus of the Zen (meditation) school in meditation can become a potential occasion for pride and pretension, grasping and clinging. Thus, it too is fair game for humor, and humor is an expression of true understanding – as in the many comic sketches of Bodhidharma meditating intensely or the advice of an early Chan master: "Speech is blasphemy, silence is a lie. Beyond speech and silence is the way out."

Many Zen anecdotes present the master laughing uproariously in response to a question or the monk laughing loudly in the moment of sudden enlightenment. It is said of one Chinese monk that, in answer to his question about Buddhist teaching, the master kicked him in the chest. As a result the monk was enlightened and afterward commented, "Ever since my master kicked me in the chest I have been unable to stop laughing." Writes the later master Sengai, "Unexpectedly discovering the way of life in the midst of death, he bursts out in hearty laughter."

CONRAD HYERS

*See also* Bodhidharma; Buddha (Śākyamuni); Buddhist Schools/Traditions; Chan/Zen: China; Chan/Zen: Japan; China; Japan: History; Kōan; Visual Arts, Buddhist

A shamanic guardian figure typical of those found at the entrance to Korean monasteries.
Photo courtesy of John Powers

thodox Churches and Western figures such as the Franciscan Friar Juniper. Their foolishness suggested a higher wisdom and spirituality, whereas the conventional wisdom of the sane and sensible majority was seen as foolishness. A figure of the Sōtō school of Zen in Japan was nicknamed Ryōkan (Great Fool) and was noted for playing with children and composing poems about lice. It was he who, on being confronted by a burglar in his mountain retreat, apologized for having nothing worth stealing, gave him his extra robe, and afterward wrote, "The robber, failing to carry away the moon, it shines in through my window."

The largest number of examples of Buddhist humor is to be found in the Chan/Zen tradition. Its largely anecdotal literature, and its art, especially the ink sketches, contain many instances of the uses of humor as an appropriate expression of Buddhist life

## Further Reading

Addiss, Stephen, *The Art of Zen*, New York: Abrams, 1989

Hyers, Conrad, *Zen and the Comic Spirit*, Philadelphia: Westminster, 1973; London: Rider, 1974; as *The Laughing Buddha: Zen and the Comic Spirit*, Wolfeboro, New Hampshire: Longwood Academic, 1989

Hyers, Conrad, "Humor in Taoist and Zen Art," *Asian Art and Culture* 7:3 (1994)

Suzuki, D.T., *Sengai: The Zen Master*, Greenwich, Connecticut: New York Graphic Society, and London: Faber, 1971

Tanahashi, Kazuski, *Penetrating Laughter, Hakuin's Zen and Art*, Woodstock, New York: Overlook Press, 1984

Tao-yuan, Shih, *The Transmission of the Lamp: Early Masters*, translated by Sohaku Ogata, Wolfeboro, New Hampshire: Longwood Academic, 1989

# Humor: Christian

The history of humor in the Church and its monastic traditions is one of ambivalence. On the one hand humor has been viewed as inappropriate and dangerous relative to sacred places and concerns and to the rigors of spiritual discipline. Holiness seems to require the utmost in seriousness, whereas laughter and the comic suggest a lack of sincerity and reverence, even outright sacrilege. On this scale humor may be located in the outer courts of the temple or in the informality of the vestibule but hardly in the Holy of Holies.

Thus did John Chrysostom (c. 347–407) preach in 390, "This world is not a theater in which we can laugh, and we are not assembled in order to burst into peals of laughter, but to weep for our sins." The sixth-century Rule of St. Benedict warns, "As for coarse jests and idle works or words that lead to laughter, these we condemn with a perpetual ban." Or, in the context of Quaker pietism, Robert Barclay insisted in his *Apology for the True Christian Divinity* (1676),

> It is not lawful to use games, sports, nor among other things comedies among Christians, under the notion of recreations, which do not agree with Christian silence, gravity, and sobriety; for laughing, sporting, gaming, mocking, jesting, vain talking, etc. is not Christian liberty nor harmless mirth.

Plato, in his *Republic*, rejected a comic art that so easily arouses rebelliousness in the populace, and he counsels the guardians of his ideal republic not to indulge in boisterous laughter or play the fool. Aristotle, however, took a more balanced view, distinguishing between liberal and illiberal forms of humor. Humor can move toward the ugly and grotesque or toward the friendly gesture and beauty of a smile. Through humor, tensions can be released and aggressions diverted, but humor can also increase tensions and serve as a tool of aggression. Humor can encourage a larger perspective and humbler posture, or it can reinforce prejudice and inflate a sense of superiority – as racist, sexist, and ethnic jokes so often do.

Anything good can be turned to evil purposes, and so with humor. We thus find not only misgivings over the negative possibilities of humor but also many examples of positive uses of humor in the Christian tradition. Jesus used a scathing ironic humor against the pride and hypocrisy of fellow Pharisees as the blind leading the blind, cleaning the outside of the cup but not the dregs within, and praising past prophets while plotting to kill present ones (Matt. 23). Jesus could also use a gentler humor in his teaching about the follies of judging others: "First take the log out of your own eye, and then you will see clearly to take the speck of dust out of your brother's eye" (Matt. 7:5). One could find no clearer example of the magnanimity and inclusiveness of a liberal humor than in Jesus' dealings with women and children, his working and healing on the sabbath, and his reaching out to the marginal and outcast: tax collectors, Samaritans, prodigals, adulterers, and prostitutes.

Saint Paul not only refers to the gospel and to the preaching of the cross as foolishness to those of worldly wisdom but in doing so uses the term *moira*, which in the Greco-Roman world is associated with fools, clowns, mimes, and comedians (morons). Paul thus initiates an introduction of the fool tradition into Christianity. Similarly when Dante (1265–1321) comes to write his great drama of salvation and human destiny, he titles it the *Commedia*. In it the descent into hell is the result of the worldly foolishness of self-centeredness and self-aggrandizement. Instead of gaining more in riches, power, and esteem, the damned actually become smaller and poorer of soul – themes dear to the heart of all monastic traditions.

In the *Commedia* each level of the *Inferno* is smaller and more stifling than the previous one, whereas those who are moving toward *Paradiso* are those whose spirits are turned outward to God and to others, partaking in the foolishness of divine mercy and grace. If Hell is the most tragic place, Heaven is the most comic place, as those who are there are the more selfless, open, and free. Good humor corresponds with faith, hope, and love and with the joyful celebration and liberation they bring. As Dante exclaimed on approaching the eighth level of heaven, "I seemed to see the Universe alight with a single smile."

Both the criticisms and the encomia of humor can be seen as appropriate to Christian faith and life. Negative forms of humor are those that might be associated with the descent into Hell: profanity, sacrilege, frivolity, sarcasm, cynicism, pride, and self-justification. "Eat, drink and be merry, for tomorrow we die." Positive forms of humor are those that lead heavenward, being more self-deprecating, inclusive of others, compassionate, and celebratory.

This outward and upward movement of the comic spirit is manifest in the ancient custom in Eastern Orthodox circles of setting aside the day after Easter as a day of laughter and playfulness, with feasting, games, and dancing in the churchyard and a sharing of jokes and anecdotes in the church. Such behavior is seen as appropriate because of the big joke that God pulled on

Satan in the resurrection. To God belongs the last laugh, and all are free to laugh and be playful, for their faith and trust is in God and God's victory.

Gregory, third-century bishop of Palestine, introduced secular amusements in conjunction with commemorations of the martyrs, arguing that the martyrs were honored by playfulness and laughter, which their martyrdoms had made possible. The same Chrysostom who warned about laughter and playfulness thought otherwise in a sermon on the Pauline verse "Rejoice in the Lord always," advocating a spirit of joyfulness that laughed to scorn the sorrows that could drag the spirit down.

The fourth-century abbot Apollo taught that the result of penance should not be melancholy or sadness but cheerfulness and celebration, as constituting much better testimony to God's love and forgiveness. Similarly St. John Climacus (c. 570–c. 649) wrote that God does not desire mournfulness but that "we should rejoice with laughter in our soul." Saint Bruno (c. 1032–1101), founder of the Carthusian Order, was noted for his cheerful disposition. This was seen by him and his followers as especially important for those engaged in the rigors of monastic training. Saint Teresa of Avila (1515–1582) prayed for deliverance from "somber, serious, sullen saints." A host of similar examples could be given of those appreciating and expressing humor and laughter throughout the history of the Church and monasticism down to more recent stellar examples, such as Pope John the XXIII and Thomas Merton (1915–1968).

Despite the common image of monks and church authorities as spoilsports and killjoys, the fact is that many have taken the name Hilary (Hilarius), including three early figures who were canonized, one of whom also became a Doctor of the Church and another who became pope. In Greek the word *hilarion* suggested cheerfulness and a merry disposition. The Latin *hilarius* has a more elated and expressive connotation, leading to the boisterous implications of the English "hilarity." After all, the earliest Christians were accused of drunkenness and are described in the Book of Acts as having "glad and generous hearts, praising God and having favor with all the people" (Acts 2:46–47).

These associations with *hilarius* and *moira* led also to a "holy fool" tradition in both the Eastern and the Western Church. As early as the sixth century – and probably much earlier – a type of spirituality developed in which the expression of piety involved eccentric, foolish, childlike behavior and in some cases feigned or real madness. The monk or priest or wanderer manifested sincerity not by a display of wisdom or sanctity but by becoming an object of mockery.

As simpletons, the holy fools challenged elaborate pomp and ceremony and derided endless theological disputation over mysteries that by definition were mysteries. Like Thomas à Kempis (c. 1380–1471) in his *Imitation of Christ* (1418), they exemplified a simple, childlike faith and simplicity of daily life. They humbled themselves in comic identification with the humility and humiliation of Jesus. As with St. Francis (1181/82–1226) and the early Franciscans, who called themselves the world's

fools (*mundi moriones*), the holy fools withdrew from the riches and power and splendor of the world and Church – and in some cases monasteries as well – to follow in the footsteps of a penniless wanderer who had been hailed as king by being given mock robes and a crown of thorns and a cross for a throne.

Although the theme of the laughing savior is probably Gnostic in origin, a number of depictions of the smiling Christ are to be found in the art of the Church, such as the wooden crucifix dating from the 12th century in the Cistercian monastery of Lérins, France. Although the immediate context of the crucifixion suggested a decisive conquest by the forces of evil and injustice, calling for the profoundest anguish and grief, the larger context was one of celebration, as the resurrection victory and the ultimate triumph belongs to God. Although there is "a time to weep, and a time to laugh, a time to mourn, and a time to dance" (Eccles. 3:4), the last word is given to laughter and dancing.

CONRAD HYERS

*See also* Bruno, St.; Chrysostom, John, St.; Climacus, John, St.; Martyrs: Western Christian; Merton, Thomas; Teresa of Avila, St.

## Further Reading

Cormier, Henri, *The Humor of Jesus*, translated by the Society of St. Paul, New York: Alba House, 1977

Cox, Harvey, *The Feast of Fools: A Theological Essay on Festivity and Fantasy*, Cambridge, Massachusetts: Harvard University Press, 1969

Hyers, M. Conrad, *And God Created Laughter: The Bible as Divine Comedy*, Atlanta, Georgia: Knox Press, 1987

Hyers, M. Conrad, *The Spirituality of Comedy: Comic Heroism in a Tragic World*, New Brunswick, New Jersey: Transaction, 1996

Jónsson, Jakob, *Humour and Irony in the New Testament*, Reykjavík: Bókaútgáfa Menningarsjóls, 1965; New York: Humanities Press, 1966

Samra, Cal, *The Joyful Christ: The Healing Power of Humor*, San Francisco: Harper and Row, 1986

Saward, John, *Perfect Fools: Folly for Christ's Sake in Catholic and Orthodox Spirituality*, Oxford and New York: Oxford University Press, 1980

Trueblood, Elton, *The Humor of Christ*, New York: Harper and Row, 1964

# Hungary

Tradition has it that King Stephen I (St. Stephen; 997–1038) introduced Christianity into what is now Hungary. The truth of the matter is that King Stephen was a proponent of the Roman version, and even in this it was not Stephen but his father, Géza (972–997), baptized by St. Adalbert of Prague, who introduced Roman Christianity by inviting German missionary monks. Nevertheless, Stephen, who as a child was baptized and educated by Adalbert, and his consort, Giesela, the sister of Emperor Henry II (1002–1024), contributed heavily to the evangelization of Hungary by inviting German and Italian

Crypt, Benedictine monastery, Pannonhalma, Hungary, 13th century.
Photo courtesy of Chris Schabel

missionaries, along with the monk scholar St. Gerard of Csanád, into the country. In all instances the missionaries, like Adalbert, followed the Cluniac reform movement. In 1000, with the approval of Emperor Otto III (983–1002), Pope Sylvester II (999–1003) crowned Stephen as Christian King Stephen I, and the Hungarian state was born.

Early in the Christian era, the region belonged to the Roman provinces of Pannonia and Dacia, and from accounts of martyrdoms and remains of artifacts it is evident that Christianity flourished at an early date. Archaeological and Byzantine records indicate that sizable Christian communities existed, lasting at least through the rule of the Avars (sixth to eighth century). These Christian traditions were inherited by the Slavs and apparently passed on to the Magyars (Hungarians). Géza's wife, a Byzantine Christian, was undoubtedly influential in bringing her husband to Christianity, albeit in the Roman version. Because both Pannonia and Dacia harbored a mixture of Celto-Slavic peoples and their major towns lay on ancient trade routes, it is also probable, although no evidence exists, that wandering Irish missionary monks of the ninth century might have established small monastic hermitages in the region. Be that as it may, it was Stephen who first organized the Church into two archdioceses, eight dioceses, and five Benedictine abbeys, most notably

Pannonhalma. In 1050 Stephen's son, Andrew I, established Hungary's oldest still extant monastic community at Tihany. From the capital Esztergom, rooted in this strong ecclesiastical structure, Stephen resisted the still strong influences of the native religion and Byzantine Christianity. Under the Árpád dynasty the archbishops, bishops, and abbots became a potent political force, the dynasty and the Church buttressing each other until being defeated by the Turks at the Battle of Mohács (1526). In all, a little over 40 Árpáds became saints or blessed, indicating the depths of the Árpád spirituality.

Little is known about Turkish Hungary other than that the country was in disarray not only from being conquered by the Turks but also from political infighting among the Hungarians themselves. That the Catholic Church and its monastic institutions survived at all during this period is due mainly to the ministry of the Franciscans, who had their work doubly cut out for them. The Order not only sought to restore Catholic devotion but also had to deal with the inroads of the Protestant Reformation. The Reformation was of little concern to the Turks, but they granted less toleration to Catholicism than to Protestantism. On the other hand, the people responded heartily to the Reformation. By the middle of the 16th century, only about 300 Catholic priests and religious remained in Hungary. During the second half of the century, the Counterreformation was in full swing, the key role being played by the Jesuits, who were welcomed into the royal territories of Hungary, and in those areas the people began to return to the Catholic Church. However, for the most part the Serbian, Romanian, and Ruthenian (Ukrainian) populations remained faithful to the Orthodox Church.

During the 18th century Hungary was incorporated into the Habsburg Empire, resulting in a resurgence of Catholic influence. Emperor Charles VI (1711–1740) granted to Protestants full religious liberty (which had been taken away Leopold I) but required them to restore Catholic churches and monasteries. Under Charles VI education was promoted. Most prominent of the teachers were the Jesuits, but the Hermits of St. Paul, Benedictines, Cistercians, Premonstratensians, and Piarists were present as well. The Piarists inaugurated the teaching of Hungarian history and literature. Maria Theresa (1740–1780) and her son Joseph II (1780–1790), seeking to promote enlightened humanism, reversed the course by suppressing religious orders and seeking to make the Church an instrument of the state – a policy known as Josephinism. Ironically, during this time most of Hungary's intellectuals, poets, and writers increasingly came from the monastic orders.

With the coming of communism in 1945, many of the clergy and religious were openly hostile to the new government. The communists retaliated in 1945 by confiscating Church lands and in 1948 by dissolving 59 of 63 Catholic orders, taking over the running of all schools. In 1950 about 2,500 monks and nuns, about one-quarter of the total, were deported, even though the Catholic Church in the same year made, under coercion, an oath of loyalty to the communist constitution. The Catholic Church and the government finally reached an accommodation in 1964, the first of its kind in a communist state. The agreement certified certain episcopal appointments, and in turn the Vatican agreed that Church officials would be allowed to take an oath of allegiance to the constitution and conceded the state's right to approve the selection of certain Church officials. However, the oath was binding only where the laws of the state did not conflict with the tenets of the Church.

Following the accord church posts were filled, parish churches reopened, and the monastic orders reestablished. By the late 1980s Benedictines, Franciscans, Piarists, and Our Lady's School Sisters were once again functioning in limited numbers. In 1986, for the first time since the coming of the communist state, a new order of nuns, the sisters of Our Lady of Hungary, received permission to organize. Following the collapse of communism, these orders are showing remarkable gains.

### Religious Orders

Today most of the Benedictine monasteries of the Hungarian Congregation resemble the Cluniac model, even though the Congregation of Cluny no longer exists. After the entry of the Benedictines into Hungary around 1000 came the Premonstratensians (1130), Cistercians (1142), the Canons Regular of St. Augustine (1198), and the Franciscans (1232), who by 1300 had over 50 houses. An order native to Hungary, the Hermits of St. Paul (1250), spread to Italy, Germany, Austria, Poland, Lithuania, and Sweden. Later the Knights Hospitallers (Malta) and the Teutonic Knights, Carthusians, Carmelites, Capuchins, Dominicans, Sisters of Salvator, and Our Lady's School Sisters established orders in Hungary as well. Many of the monastic settlements became the nuclei of new towns, hospitals, and centers of learning.

### Sites

A few stone carvings and the crypt are all that remain of the original Benedictine Abbey at Tihany (1050). The crypt remains almost in its original form and is the burial place of Andrew I, the abbey's benefactor. The church at Máriabesnyö (1761) contains a 12th- to 13th-century ivory carving of the Virgin Mary with the Holy Child in her arms. Legend has it that the discovery of this carving was brought about by a dream of the wife of the landowner. Today thousands of faithful Hungarians make pilgrimages to the shrine, the care of which is given to Capuchin monks and Salvator Sisters, both of whom maintain houses nearby.

FRANK A. MILLS

*See also* Austria; Benedictines; Cluny, France; Franciscans; Pilgrimages, Christian: Eastern Europe; Reformation

*Further Reading*
Balics, L., *The History of the Catholic Church in Hungary*, 3 vols., Budapest, 1885–1890
Galter, Alberto, *The Red Book of the Persecuted Church*, Westminster, Maryland: Newman Press, 1953
Harmatta, J., "A magyarság õstörténete" (The Prehistory of the Hungarians), *Magyar Tudomány* 35 (1990)
Jászay, Magda, *A kereszténység védõbástyája-olasz szemmel: Olasz kortárs írók a XV–XVIII: századi Magyarországról* (The Bulwark of Christianity: Italian Contemporary Writers on 15th–18th century Hungary), Budapest: Nemzeti Tankönyvkiadó, 1996
Moravcsik, Gyula, *Byzantium and The Magyars*, Amsterdam: Hakkett, 1970
Moravcsik, Gyula, editor, *Constantine Porphyrogenitus, De Administrando Imperio* (The Imperial Administration), translated by R.J.H. Jenkins, London: Athlone Press, 1962
Nagy, T., *The History of Christianity in Hungary*, Budapest, 1939

# Hygiene: Buddhist Perspectives

Hygiene in Buddhist monasticism was a matter of either ritual or personal physical cleanliness. Practices designed for ritual purity and simple functions for personal cleanliness were validated by Buddhist doctrine, although few rules were designated specifically for personal cleanliness. The most important point is that the idea of hygiene, whether a complex ritual and symbolic process or simply a matter of physical cleanliness, indicates that Buddhists acknowledged the importance of worldly conventions. Theirs was not a system that denied all conventions of the world as illusory. Other Indian religious groups had ideas of purity and profanity and of personal hygiene, but Buddhists were careful to affirm the philosophical validity of conventional processes for individuals, always orienting the rules toward spiritual progress.

Buddhism evolved in a society with established ideas about what was pure and what was profane. Archaeological evidence from the pre-Buddhist Indus valley civilizations suggests that ritual bathing was practiced in large public facilities, likely for religious reasons, and remains of water systems in private homes indicate that personal hygiene was also a concern. In later Hindu traditions ritual bathing was and continues to be an important practice, mainly for religious reasons, that is, for spiritual cleanliness and incidentally for personal hygiene. Buddhism inherited, but only with modifications, many of the Indian ideas about ritual purity and personal hygiene. For example, the Hindu caste system preserved systems of social and religious purity by which only upper castes would have access to religious teachings. Lower castes and persons outside the system handled things considered ritually impure, including corpses and soiled garments.

Buddhism inherited brahmanical ideas of social hierarchy but modified them to accord with the Buddhist priority of individual inner religious development. Unlike brahmanical cultures Buddhist monastic communities included persons from all castes and both men and women, albeit separated by gender. Although these communities modified the Indian caste structure, they preserved a different kind of hierarchical structure. Buddhist monastic communities replaced the caste system with one based on year of ordination. Previously ordained monks enjoyed rights and privileges higher in status than monks ordained later, and monks were categorically of higher status and privilege than nuns. In effect seniority and gender provided criteria for social status and increased access to "pure" teachings and exemption from "impure" duties. This was not a purely egalitarian system.

Ritual purity aside specific rules for personal hygiene for all Buddhist monks were not a normal part of Indian religious cultures. For example, practitioners of Jainism believed that all worldly action, including ritual purifications and personal hygiene, only perpetuated suffering and continued rebirth. Consequently Jains refrained from, for example, washing or cleaning their teeth. In contrast to the Jain and other Indian ascetic groups, the Buddhists believed that worldly action was significant and related to progress on the path to enlightenment. This is evident in such everyday practices as bathing, oral hygiene, washing robe material before tailoring, and replacing robes when worn out. Moreover, in contrast to the early brahmanical concept of external ritual activity and the Jain and ascetic rejection of all worldly activity, the Buddhists sought to purify themselves by external ethical actions based on internal ethical thoughts. Buddhists believed that by eliminating neurotic attachment to objects as well as anger and ignorance, they would rid themselves of suffering and make progress on the path to enlightenment. This process of eliminating undesirable or impure activities of body, speech, and mind, including all forms of sexual expression, was accomplished by the exercise of ethical behavior, the accumulation of wisdom, and concentration, all inherently good and pure actions.

Another factor important for attention to purity and hygiene in Buddhist monasteries was very likely Buddhist awareness and inclusion of medical practices in their large and rapidly growing communities. As medical innovators Buddhist monks were aware that contamination of water and food, for example, caused diseases. Thus, the Buddha, often referred to as the "Great Physician," ordered that his communities pay attention to cleanliness in their living environments and in personal hygiene.

In general rules for physical and material cleanliness were not emphasized in Buddhism. All rules for ritual purity and personal hygiene for monks and nuns were designed to promote mental and spiritual development. Hygiene was recommended or required only when it was considered conducive to progress on the path to Buddhist enlightenment. Bathing, oral hygiene, housecleaning, clothes washing, personal cleanliness, and medical treatments were all sanctioned in Buddhist monasteries, but only as secondary practices to promote mental development and growth on the path to enlightenment.

PAUL NIETUPSKI

*See also* Ashram, Influence of; Body: Buddhist Perspectives; Jain Monasticism and Buddhist Monasticism; Medicine, Buddhist; Regulations (Vinaya): Historical; Sexuality: Buddhist Perspectives; Social Services: Buddhist

### Further Reading

Gombrich, Richard F., *Theravāda Buddhism: A Social History from Ancient Benares to Modern Columbo*, London and New York: Routledge, 1988
Wijayaratna, Mohan, *Buddhist Monastic Life: According to the Texts of the Theravada Tradition*, Cambridge and New York: Cambridge University Press, 1990

# Hygiene: Christian Perspectives

The sources on hygiene in Eastern (i.e., Byzantine) monasticism are principally rules and acts of foundation of monasteries (the so-called *typika*) that specify all the details of life, including care for hygiene. There are also lives of saints, which are not necessarily reliable because of the nature of the genre, ascetic treatises (especially by founders of monasteries), and historical accounts and literary works (especially by the fathers of the Church). Archaeology confirms the textual data at least in part through evidence of fountains, aqueducts, and cisterns for water supply. A recent analysis of the state of health of the current monastic population at Mount Athos provides comparative material because of continuity from the late Byzantine epoch to the present.

In the classical world care for hygiene was part of daily life and took different forms: baths, diet, and exercises of the body and of the soul. Whereas diet and gymnastic have been theorized since Herodikos of Selymbria (c. 500–430/20 B.C.), hygiene, considered as dealing with preservation of health, became an independent part of medicine only with the empiricist school (third century B.C.). Its principles of full accomplishment of bodily well-being were systematically applied in Roman life from the first century B.C. Treatises were written on the topic up to Galen (A.D. 129–c. 216), and their contents were summarized in the late-antique encyclopedias of medicine, such as that of Aetios (fl. c. 530–560 A.D.) and further reproduced in Byzantium.

Thanks to his miracles of healing, Christ was compared with Asclepius, and the early Christians seemed to value body, health, and hygiene – above all because of belief in the resurrection of body – even though pagans dismissed Christianity as a religion for sick people. From the fourth century A.D. on, classical medicine, having been at first rejected, was progressively assimilated; however, its inspiration was transformed, as it was considered a gift of God. The fathers of the Church often used the medical comparisons and the concept of hygiene in presenting the message of salvation.

At the same time the luxury of bathing was denounced in the ascetic literature, in which the theme of *alousia* (i.e., nonbathing) appeared, and even to the point of forbidding baths in the monastic rules of Pachomius (d. A.D. 346) and of Athanasius (d. A.D. 373). Although these were exceptions – in the monastic rules by Basil of Caesarea (A.D. 329/30–379) there is no prohibition – frequent use of baths was discouraged, especially for healthy people, by means of a pseudo-medical theory of weakness of the body caused by excessive bathing. The rule was that of moderate use, as was the case for food as well; in case of illness bathing was permitted because it contributed to recovery. Contradictorily some ascetics of the sixth and seventh centuries practiced common bathing with women, not for hygiene but as an exercise aimed to reinforce their resistance to earthly temptations.

The further history of bath regulation shows the evolution of the concept of hygiene in a monastic context: in 1054–1070, the Evergetis, a male monastery of Constantinople, introduced warm baths that were permitted at any time for the sick and three times a year for healthy monks. In the capital this trend was reinforced, for the nuns (Kecharitomene, 1110–1016) as well as for the monks (Pantokrator, 1136), with even a higher frequency (12 and 24 times a year, respectively). At first the provinces echoed this movement (as at Kosmosoteira, near Bera, 1152, and at Heliou Bomon, near Bursa, 1162, where bathing was allowed 12 times a year) and even amplified it (as at Areia, near Nauplia, 1162, with weekly frequency). However, around the mid–12th century a return of rigorism appeared in a patriarchal institution of Constantinople (Phoberos, 1144), where bathing was allowed only for the sick. Confirmed in the province during the Latin occupation of Constantinople (Neophytos in Cyprus, 1214), the prohibition was then justified by a danger, especially for young monks, and an explicit reference to Pachomius. Bathing reappeared after the restoration of 1261 but

with a lower frequency (four times a year), in Constantinople (Lips, 1294–1301, and Bebaia Elpis, 1327–1335), and in the province (Memoikeion, near Serres, 1332), even though it was specified that for the nuns (Lips) it should be done especially by the young ones. Bathing was permitted for the sick and the elderly according to a doctor's prescription and, in Menmoikeion, whenever it seemed proper to the superior.

Eastern monasticism thus approached hygiene in an evolutive way: in contrast to a classical heritage of full bodily accomplishment, at first it rejected hygiene, even though at the same time more equilibrated positions were taken in theology. An attempt was made from the mid–11th century on to introduce the practice of hygiene for monastic life, an attempt that did not last long, however, as ancient rigorism reappeared. Thus, there were two opposite attitudes toward hygiene, both aimed at canceling the notion of body, either by forbidding its care (even in the approach to God, in contrast to the use of ablutions in Islam) or by trying to satisfy it, especially for medical reasons. Even though the former won out, the victory was ambivalent, as mortification itself was considered a way of caring for the body.

ALAIN TOUWAIDE

*See also* Asceticism: Christian Perspectives; Fasting: Eastern Christian; Mount Athos, Greece

## Further Reading

Berger, Albrecht, *Das Bad in der byzantinischen Zeit*, Munich: Universität, Institut für Byzantinistik und neugriechische Philologie, 1982

Frings, Hermann, "Medizin und Arzt bei den griechischen Kirchenvätern bis Chrysostomos," Ph.D. diss., Bonn, 1959

Grotzfeld, Heinz, *Das Bad im arabisch-islamischen Mittelalter. Eine kulturgeschichtliche Studie*, Wiesbaden: Harrassowitz, 1970

Kottek, Samuel, "Hygiene and Healing among the Jews in the Post-Biblical Period: A Partial Reconstruction," in *Rise and Decline of the Roman World*, part 2, volume 37.3, edited by Wolfgang Haase and Hildegard Temporini, Berlin and New York: de Gruyter, 1996

Leven, Karl-Heinz, *Medizinisches bei Eusebios von Kaisareia*, Düsseldorf: Triltsch, 1987

Orlandos, Anastasios, *Monasteriake architektonike*, Athens: s.l., 1926; 2nd edition, 1958

Schultz, Titus, *Medizin auf dem Berg Athos*, Düsseldorf: Triltsch, 1989

Söllner, Albert, *Die hygienischen Anschauungen des römischen Architekten Vitruvius; ein Beitrag zur antiken Hygiene*, Jena: Gustaf Fischer, 1913

Temkin, Owsei, *Hippocrates in a World of Pagans and Christians*, Baltimore, Maryland: Johns Hopkins University Press, 1991

Volk, Robert, *Gesundheitswesen und Wohltätigkeit im Spiegel der byzantinischen Klostertypika*, Munich: Universität, Institut für Byzantinistik und neugriechische Philologie, 1983

Wöhrle, Georg, *Studien zur Theorie der antiken Gesundheitslehre*, Stuttgart: Franz Steiner, 1990

# Hymnographers

The term *hymnody* is taken from the Greek *hymnodia*, which literally means "hymn-song." The term *hymnographer* is taken from the Greek *hymnodos*, which literally means "hymn-singer" or "hymn-poet." This article surveys major exemplars in the East and the West down to 1300.

Still recent in its origin, hymnology is the science of hymnody and of hymnographers. It was not until the 19th century that energy was committed to investigate and classify the vast amount of Latin hymnody buried in the numerous surviving medieval manuscripts. The publication of the *Analecta Hymnica Media Aevi*, begun in 1886 in Leipzig and completed in 58 volumes in 1992, only lays the groundwork for future researchers in this area. The hymnody and hymnographers of the Orient (i.e., Armenian, Greek, and Syrian material) remains for the most part uninvestigated and unpublished.

The widest meaning of the noun *hymn* is praise of God in public worship through song. The earliest Christians borrowed this custom from the Jewish faith, so that the liturgical hymns of both Christians and Jews were similar during the first centuries after Christ. Using mainly the psalms and canticles from the Old and New Testaments, the congregation would participate in the worship service by intoning responses, refrains, alleluias, hosannas, doxologies, acclamations, the Trisagion, and especially the *Kyrie eleison*.

The *Constitutiones apostolicae*, although referred to as hymns, are actually prayers or prose songs, yet they deserve a closer examination. The morning hymn, or *hymnus angelicus*, is the *Gloria in excelsis Deo*, composed prior to A.D. 150, which St. Athanasius (c. 296–373) translated into Latin and inserted into the Western liturgy. The evening hymn is a shorter form of the *Gloria in excelsis Deo*, using the first verse of Psalm 112 as an introduction. The Greek hymn for grace at meals begins *Eulogetos ei, Kyrie, ho trephon me ek neotetos mou, ho didous trophen pase sarki*, clearly originating from Scriptures. The Candlelight hymn, as it is known, was described as old already by St. Basil (c. 330–379) and is much more rhythmic and metrical in construction.

## Early History

The earliest historical evidence of Christian hymnographers emerges in the fourth century, beginning in the East and appearing soon afterward in the West. Because of the activity of heretics who incorporated beautiful music with erroneous doctrine into their services, hymns soon became a popular form of Christian folk song that the Church decided to counteract by composing hymns of their own. Saint Ephraem the Syrian (c. 306–373) was the first to produce hymns as an antidote to heretical hymns. He was intensely prolific, composing at least 85 hymns on the subject of death alone and many others on topics such as faith, paradise, and Christmas. At least 65 of his hymns are directed against various heretics. Syriac hymnody, although nonexistent after the conquest of Syria by the Arabs in the seventh century, has survived to the present day in the Syriac liturgy.

Although many points of contact exist between the Eastern and Western Churches, and although hymnographers of both liturgies emerged at approximately the same time, separate paths were taken from the very beginning despite common characteristics. Saint Hilary of Poitiers (c. 315–367/68) tried to compose Latin hymns in imitation of St. Ephraem but was unsuccessful because the music did not appeal to popular taste. Only three or four fragments of his hymns survive. Saint Gregory of Nazianzus (329/30–389/90) was more successful writing Greek hymnody.

Saint Ambrose, bishop of Milan (c. 339–397), has been regarded as the father of Latin hymnody. Fourteen genuine hymns have survived that are attributed to him, including four that are used daily at terce, sext, and none in the Roman breviary. They provided a form and model for all later breviary hymns: *Aeterna Christi munera*, *Splendor paternae gloriae*, and *Aeterne rerum conditor*. Early hymnody had to effect a compromise between the quantitative principles of classical verse and the accentual or rhythmic principles of popular music. Saint Ambrose combined these two principles by choosing the iambic dimeter as his most common metrical pulse on the grounds that it was the most natural and popular meter. He usually avoids conflicts between word and verse accent, and this contributes to the lasting popularity of his hymns. In fact his strophe of four iambic dimeters became so popular among other hymnographers that the type became known as the *hymnus Ambrosianus*, although the original inspiration for this verse type probably emanated from the *versus saturnius*, the favorite meter of the profane popular poetry of the Romans. Saint Augustine (354–430) was deeply impressed by the hymns of St. Ambrose.

The hymns of Aurelius Prudentius (348–c. 410) stand in contrast to those of St. Ambrose, as they were devised for private devotion and are highly poetic. He composed two books of hymns: the *Kathemerion* and the *Peristephanon*. The Mozarabic liturgy incorporated some of Prudentius' martyr hymns in its services. In the Roman service the hymns for lauds on Tuesday, Wednesday, and Thursday are by Prudentius: *Ales diei nuntius*, *Nox et tenebrae et nubili*, and *Lux ecce surgit aurea*. The hymn for the Feast of the Holy Innocents, *Salvete flores martyrum*, is also by Prudentius.

The increased number of festivals introduced into the liturgy in the fifth century necessitated more hymns. Bishop Paulinus of Nola (353/55–431), Pope Gelasius I (492–496), and the poet Caedilius Sedulius (c. 450) all composed in the *hymnus Ambrosianus* style. The development of eight-strophe hymns also became standardized at this time. Venantius Fortunatus, bishop of Poitiers (c. 530–c. 610), was a prominent hymnographer in the Frankish dynasty of the Merovingians. Two of his hymns on the Crucifixion, *Pange lingua gloriosi* and *Vexilla regis prodeunt*, and one on the Blessed Virgin Mary, *Quem terra, pontus, aethera*, are still in the Roman liturgy.

After Prudentius the Mozarabic liturgy generated an active tradition of well over 200 hymns independent of the Roman rite. Almost all the hymnographers responsible for this production were Spanish bishops: Isidore of Seville (c. 560–636), Branlio of Saragossa (d. 651), Eugenius II of Toledo (d. 657),

Quiricus of Barcelona (d. 666), and Cyxilla of Toledo (d. c. 783).

A different hymn tradition developed in the ancient Irish Church. Most were for private or monastic use, and rhyme and alliteration rather than classical meter dominated in hymn composition. The oldest hymn written in Ireland, and the oldest purely rhythmical Latin hymn, was by St. Secundus or Sechnall (d. c. 448) and was dedicated to St. Patrick. Saint Gildas (d. 569); St. Columba (c. 521–597); St. Columban (d. 615); St. Ultan of Ardgreccan (d. 656); Colman Mac Murchon, abbot of Maghbile (d. c. 731); Oengus Mac Tipraite (c. 741); Cuchuimne (c. 746); and St. Maobruain, abbot of Tallaght (d. 792), were all prolific in the Irish hymn tradition. No Irish Latin hymn was adopted into the Roman liturgy.

Greek hymnody after St. Gregory of Nazianzus was constructed on the ancient classical forms and exploited the delicacies and lyricism of the Greek language. Synesius (c. 370–c. 413) wrote at least 12 hymns that betray somewhat their author's Neoplatonist tendencies. However, it is the ingenious Romanos (d. c. 560) who is considered the real founder of Greek hymnody. About 80 hymns of this greatest of Byzantine poets survive to the present day. The artistic form of the *contakia* consists of 20 or 30 strophes of uniform structure to which is attached at least one or more strophes of varying structure. Every strophe is followed by a refrain of one or two short lines. His Christmas hymn, *He parthenos semeron*, was performed every year at the imperial court until the 12th century by a double choir from Haghia Sophia and the Church of the Apostles. It is more like a dramatic oratorio and helped Romanos earn the surname *ho melodos*. After Romanos a number of Greek ecclesiastics continued the *contakia* tradition, the main ones being Patriarch Sophronius of Jerusalem (629); St. Andrew, archbishop of Crete (d. c. 726); St. Joseph the Hymnographer (c. 810–886); and St. Theodore (d. 866), abbot of the great monastery of Stoudios at Constantinople, which in the late ninth century became a nursery of hymnography and hymnographers. The Greek hymnographers also invented the canon, a hymn composed of eight to nine different songs, each with a peculiar construction of three or more strophes. One canon hymn in particular had over 250 strophes and was called *ho megas kanon*. Even women hymnographers rank highly in the Greek tradition. The talented poetess Kassia (early ninth century) founded a convent where she wrote both sacred and profane poetry, as did the celebrated German nun Hroswitha von Gandersheim (tenth century) after her. A revision of the Greek hymnal in the ninth century was a disastrous event, as many wonderful *contakia* were dropped from the liturgy in favor of the canons, and the hymns that remained were "improved." By the 11th century the Greek liturgy had ceased to develop.

## Western Hymnody

Even as hymnody declined in the Eastern liturgy, a vigorous revival of hymnody was occurring in the Western liturgy from the 9th to the 13th century. The Carolingian Empire was the impetus behind this renaissance through its acceptance and adoption of the Roman liturgy and chant as the only official Christian rite. Many of Charlemagne's court poets were the impetus for the renewed hymnody: Paul the Deacon (c. 720–c. 800); Paulinus of Aquileia (c. 730–802); Alcuin, abbot of St. Martin of Tours (c. 740–804); Theodulf, bishop of Orleans (c. 750–821); and Rabanus, abbot of Fulda (c. 780–856). Students of Rabanus who became hymnographers include Walafrid Strabo (c. 808–849), Gottschalk of Orbais (d. 869), and Hermanric of Ellwangen (d. 874).

By the tenth century monastic hymnographers were leaders in a new type of hymnody, namely, that of the metrical and rhythmical offices. This development occurred in the Frankish area containing the abbeys of St.-Amand, Landevenec, St.-Omer, and Prum. Hucbald (d. 930), the main hymnodist at St.-Amand, was the inventor of the *ars organizandi*. Landevenec housed the monk Clemens (c. 870) and the abbot Gurdestin (d. 884), whereas Prüm was represented by Wandalbert (d. c. 870). However, it was the school of St. Gall that produced the most famous and talented singers and hymnologists and cultivated the new metrical forms of sequence and trope. Those monks whose influence and talent created the St. Gall legacy were Ratpert (d. after 884), Waldrammus (d. c. 900), Tutilo (d. 898), Notker Balbulus (d. 912), Abbot Hartman (d. 925), Ekkehard I (d. 973), Notker Physicus (d. 975), and Hermann Contractus (d. 1054).

In the 10th and 11th centuries, the new hymnody flourished. At the abbey of Cluny, monastics such as Odo (c. 879–942) and Odilo (961/62–1049) led the way for other talented French hymnographers of this time period, such as Fulbert of Chartres (d. 1029), Ademar of Chabannes (d. 1034), Ordorannus of Sens (d. 1045), Rainald of St. Maurice of Angers (d. c. 1074), Eusebius Bruno of Angers (d. 1081), and Berengar of Tours (c. 1010–1088). The German monasteries produced Arnold of Vohburg (d. c. 1035), Heribert of Eischastadt (d. 1042), Berno of Reichenau (d. 1048), Othlo of St. Emmeram in Ratisbon (d. 1072), Gottschalk of Limburg (d. 1098), and Bruno (d. 1054), count of Egisheim, later Pope Leo IX. In England, Wulfstan of Winchester (d. 990) and St. Anselm, archbishop of Canterbury (c. 1033–1109), were the most prominent hymn writers. In Italy, Wido of Ivrea (11th century), Alberich of Monte Cassino (d. 1088), Alphanus of Salerno (d. 1085), and St. Peter Damian (1007–1072) stand out among the many hymnodists.

## Zenith and Decline

The 12th and 13th centuries unleashed such a wealth of hymn production that only a few of the hymnographers can be mentioned. The language of the hymns became more elegant, the poetic forms richer, the rhyme purer, and the rhythm more regular. In addition the newly founded monastic orders contributed new talent to the ranks of hymn writers. In France can be mentioned Peter Abelard, abbot of St. Gildas (1079–1142/43), who composed a complete hymnbook for his convent to the Paraclete; Peter the Venerable, abbot of Cluny (1092/94–1156); and St. Bernard of Clairvaux (1090–1153). The zenith of rhythmical hymns was reached by the community of St. Victor in Paris, led by its prolific hymnographer Adam of St. Victor (d. 1142). His sequences and proses survive in many forms to the present day.

In Germany should be mentioned St. Hildegard von Bingen (1098–1179), the most prominent and prolific female monastic composer of the Middle Ages. In England there was Alexander Neckam, abbot of Cirencester (d. 1217), and John Peckham, archbishop of Canterbury (d. 1274). Italy was represented by the works of Thomas of Capua (d. 1243), St. Thomas Aquinas (c. 1225–1274), and the supposed Franciscan monastic composer of the *Stabat mater*.

The revision of the Roman breviary under Pope Boniface (1294–1303) effectively banned almost all the rhythmical hymns from the Roman liturgy. This action undermined the further production of hymns until the Protestant Reformation of the 16th century, when this popular form of religious song was once again revived and disseminated to the masses.

BRADFORD LEE EDEN

*See also* Alcuin; Ambrose, St.; Basil the Great, St.; Ireland; Isidore of Seville, St.; Liturgy: Celtic; Liturgy: Eastern Christian; Liturgy: Western Christian; Music: Christian Perspectives; Plainchant; Rabanus Maurus; St. Gallen, Switzerland; Spain: History; Spirituality: Eastern Christian; Victorines; Walafrid Strabo

**Further Reading**

*Analecta Hymnica*, 55 vols., 1886–1922

"Hymnody and Hymnology," in *The Catholic Encyclopedia*, Internet version

Music, David W., *Hymnology: A Collection of Source Readings*, Lanham, Maryland: Scarecrow Press, 1996

Reynolds, William Jensen, *A Survey of Christian Hymnody*, New York: Holt, Rinehart, and Winston, 1963; 3rd edition, Carol Stream, Illinois: Hope Publishing, 1987

Szoverffy, Joseph, *Across the Centuries: Latin Poetry, Irish Legends, and Hymnody between Late Antiquity and the Sixteenth Century: Harvard Lectures and Other Studies*, Boston: Classica Folia Editions, 1988

# I

## Iconoclasm (Controversy)

In the eighth and ninth centuries, a movement arose in the Byzantine Empire that was opposed to icons – the pictorial representations of Jesus Christ or the saints. The controversy over this opposition – called "iconoclasm" – racked both the empire and the Church within it for more than a century. The controversy came in two stages: "first iconoclasm" lasted from 726 to 787 and "second iconoclasm" from 813 to 843. The main protagonists of iconoclasm were the Byzantine emperors, and the main defenders of icons – "iconophiles" (or "iconodules") – were monks.

In the pre-Nicene period Christian religious art developed from modest beginnings in symbols (the cross, loaves and bread, and a fish [the Greek word *ichthus* being an acrostic for "Jesus Christ, God's Son, Savior"]) to the more representational art found in the catacombs. With the legalization of Christianity in the Roman Empire, Christian art was free to develop. Although three-dimensional statuary did not become common over the next few centuries, religious art flourished in tapestries and in two-dimensional paintings. The latter, which came to be known as "icons," became increasingly prevalent in the centuries after Justinian the Great (527–565). Most of those who painted icons were monks, many of whom used icons extensively in their spirituality, and monasteries often became repositories of icon collections. This religious art elicited divergent assessments. Various figures – for example, Eusebius of Caesarea (c. 260–c. 340) – expressed opposition to such religious imagery either as an unwarranted materialization of a purely spiritual Christian worship or as a violation of the second commandment of the Decalogue; however, others defended religious imagery. In the iconoclastic controversy of the eighth and ninth centuries, the issue was joined and resolved.

In the early eighth century, several bishops in eastern Asia Minor spoke out against icons. Their objections attracted notice but not support in the capital, until Leo III (717–741, known as the Isaurian) – whose family roots were in eastern Asia Minor – became emperor. His military leadership brought an end to a lengthy period of defeat and weakness in the Byzantine Empire. He ascribed that period of decline to divine judgment on the toleration of religious imagery. A major component of his determined approach to resuscitating the empire was iconoclasm.

The controversy began in 726, with the emperor publicly denouncing icons; in 730 he enacted an imperial decree forbidding them and demanding their destruction. Hoping that imperial influence would persuade his subjects to eliminate icons and thus invite divine blessing on the empire again, Leo made extensive use of the privilege accorded Byzantine emperors of delivering sermons, and in them he denounced icons. However, he found that both the populace of Constantinople and the vast majority of the monks, who by that time exercised immense influence in Byzantine society, opposed his stance. Reaction was intense and immediate in much of the empire: crowds in the capital city violently interrupted attempts to remove conspicuous icons, and iconophiles offered spirited defenses of religious imagery. Leo's son, Constantine V (741–775), carried on the imperial opposition to icons: indeed, he became iconoclasm's main spokesman, arguing against icons in no fewer than 13 publications. In 754 he summoned a council to Hiereia that officially condemned icons.

However, imperial support for iconoclasm went considerably beyond decree and argument. From 730 on icons were destroyed and iconophiles persecuted. The imperial will was so widely carried out that, with the exception of the Monastery of St. Catherine at Mount Sinai, virtually no icons have survived from the period before iconoclasm. The persecution against iconophiles was no less vigorous: many monks were imprisoned, mutilated, or exiled; prominent iconophiles were executed; and at one point monks were herded into the Hippodrome in Constantinople, surrounded by prostitutes from the city, and faced with the choice of either marriage to one or death. The longer iconoclasm continued, the more it became a crusade against monasticism.

The three main spokesmen for iconophilism were monks. The first of them, St. John of Damascus (c. 675–c. 749), presented his case during first iconoclasm. Appealing to passages in the Old Testament, he argued that God was not absolutely opposed to religious imagery, as witnessed by the cherubim carved and overlaid with gold on the cover of the Ark of the Covenant. More significantly for the course of the controversy, John of Damascus refocused the argument onto Christology (and thus the question of salvation): if God's Son had genuinely become human, as the six previous ecumenical councils had declared, then that incarnate person could be portrayed pictorially. According to the Damascene, the divine prohibition of image making had in view the coming incarnation: God forbade any merely human attempts at imaging God, as God himself would send his own image. Thus, obedience to the divine commandment now entailed making representations of the incarnate one. He went on to explain how icons could properly be used in Christian devotion.

In 787 the iconophile Irene – regent for her young son, Constantine VI (780–797) – called a council that repudiated iconoclasm (with its 754 council) and endorsed icons. However, this council – Nicea II, subsequently endorsed as the seventh ecumenical council – did not answer all the questions raised by iconoclasts during the course of the controversy. This left the door open for the renewal of iconoclasm in 813: Emperor Leo V (813–820), following the example of his namesake, adjudged recent problems in the empire to be divine judgment on toleration of icons. However, no iconoclast spokesman emerged to rebut John of Damascus or the two iconophile leaders of second iconoclasm, Theodore of Stoudios (759–826, abbot of the Stoudios monastery in Constantinople) and Patriarch Nicephorus I (758–828, who was deposed as patriarch for iconophilism and became a monk). Building on the Damascene's arguments, these two completed the task of refuting iconoclasm. In 843 the iconophile Theodora – regent for her young son, Michael III (842–867) – summoned a council that endorsed the decisions of Nicea II and solemnly rehabilitated icons. This event is commemorated in Orthodox churches on the first Sunday of Lent as the Triumph of Orthodoxy.

JAMES R. PAYTON, JR.

See also Alcuin; Images; Istanbul, Turkey; Liturgy: Eastern Christian; Meditation: Christian Perspectives; Mount Athos, Greece; Orthodox Monasticism: Byzantine; Spirituality: Eastern Christian; Theodore of Stoudios, St.; Theology, Eastern Christian; Vision, Mystical: Eastern Christian; Visual Arts, Eastern Christian: Painting

**Further Reading**

Alexander, P.J., *The Patriarch Nicephorus of Constantinople: Ecclesiastical Policy and Image Worship in the Byzantine Empire*, Oxford: Clarendon Press, 1958; New York: AMS Press, 1980

Geischer, Hans-Jürgen, editor, *Der byzantinische Bilderstreit: Texte zur Kirchen- und Theologiegeschichte*, volume 9, Gütersloh: Gütersloher Verlagshaus, 1968

Giakalis, Ambrosios, *Images of the Divine: The Theology of Icons at the Seventh Ecumenical Council*, Leiden and New York: Brill, 1994

Hennephof, Herman, compiler, *Textus byzantini ad iconomachiam pertinentes*, Leiden: Brill, 1969

John of Damascus, Saint, *On the Divine Images: Three Apologies Against Those Who Attack the Divine Images*, translated by David Anderson, Crestwood, New York: St. Vladimir's Seminary Press, 1980

Ostrogorski, Georgiji, *Studien zur Geschichte der byzantinischen Bilderstreites*, Breslau: Marcus, 1929

Ostrogorski, Georgiji, *The History of the Byzantine State*, 3rd edition, translated by Joan Hussey, New Brunswick, New Jersey: Rutgers University Press, 1969

Parry, Kenneth, *Depicting the Word: Byzantine Iconophile Thought of the Eighth and Ninth Centuries*, Leiden and New York: Brill, 1996

Pelikan, Jaroslav, *The Spirit of Eastern Christendom (600–1700)*, Chicago: University of Chicago Press, 1974

Pelikan, Jaroslav, *Imago Dei: The Byzantine Apologia for Icons*, Princeton, New Jersey: Princeton University Press, 1990

Sahas, Daniel, editor, *Icon and Logos: Sources in Eighth-Century Iconoclasm*, Toronto and London: University of Toronto Press, 1986

Theodore the Studite, Saint, *On the Holy Icons*, translated by Catherine P. Roth, Crestwood, New York: St. Vladimir's Seminary Press, 1981

# Icons, Christian. *See* Images: Christian Perspectives

# Images: Buddhist Perspectives

The Iconoclastic Controversy that shook the Eastern Church arose out of a distinct cultural context. The way in which it was settled would divide Byzantine piety and practice from those in the Latin Church areas. Proponents seeking a ban of the icon were justifiably concerned with reactions from the Jewish and the Muslim communities, which staunchly opposed the use of images as idolatry. The Monophysites, who held that there is only one – the divine – nature in the person of Christ, also objected to any overly humanlike depiction. The Syrian Church and the Gnostics further east on the Silk Road shared that sentiment. They were wary of images of God or Christ. Because Silk Road Christianity crossed paths with Mahāyāna, which although supposedly docetic welcomes images, an understanding of their similarities and differences should be enlightening.

Buddhism was originally aniconic. No image of the Buddha was permitted. If his presence was required in early Buddhist art, he would be represented by a symbol such as a lotus, a footprint, or a dharma wheel. This rejection of a formal representation derives from the doctrine of *anātman* (no-self) and of *nirvāṇa* (personal extinction). Being ontologically negative, neither could be depicted. The Enlightened One also has only a "single nature" of *bodhi*, or wisdom. Because wisdom is transpersonal, it transcends the visible prince Siddhārtha who discovered it. Thus, even the pre-enlightened prince, to the extent that he is a project of that enlightened destiny, is not objectified. A depiction of the prince leaving home on a horse shows only the white horse with an invisible rider topped off by a regal canopy. Thus, one follows the Buddha in reverence; one does not idolize him.

This aniconism accords well with early Buddhist monastic spirituality. The monks who walked in the Buddha's footsteps had their minds focused on the eternal, universal, and thus impersonal dharma. As aids to single-pointed mindfulness (medita-

Śākyamuni Buddha in a monumental statue (4.8 meters) known as Ango-in, late sixth century. This is the oldest Buddhist image in Japan.
Photo courtesy of David Moore

tion), they made use of color, geometric shape, light, and mental recollection, but no sculptured image for visualization yet existed. That would come later. For the moment the dictum "Follow the Dharma, not the person" held, and just as the Logos is there before and after the person Jesus, so the dharma pre- and postdates Gautama, being "good in the beginning, in the middle, and in the end." There is no "Dharma Buddha" as there is "Christ Logos." Whereas Christianity had a triune formula in the doctrine of the Trinity, sectarian Buddhism held instead a doctrine of the separation of the Three Jewels. Buddha, dharma, and *saṅgha* are three, not one. Despite the Buddha once having said, "Those who have seen me have seen the Dharma," that provided no pretext to collapse the exemplar of the path with the end point of that path. The early Church produced theology (*theos* + *logos*), which reflects on God. Early Buddhism produced only abhidharma (*abhi* + *dharma*), which reflects on reality. The monk elders stayed faithful to the universal Truth; their rituals involved no liturgical worship of the Buddha. This would change with Mahāyāna. There was a cult of relics, but a relic is not image, and in the oral transmission of the dharma, Truth is a disembodied Voice that was "heard" (sūtra); it was not even written down as "scripture." Both Buddha and dharma remained invisible.

The advent of images changed all that. The three-dimensional statue came with the Apollo figure brought in by the Alexandrine troops. The first Buddha image copied from it then appeared at Gandhāra. At roughly the same time an indigenous Buddha image was sculptured at nearby Mathura. What has been said of the image's impact on Hinduism is instructive here. Once the form of God became available, the Hindu *śruti* and *smṛti* (the canon of the "heard" and the "remembered," respectively) faced stiff competition from the *murti* (the visible form) of the living God. Thereafter popular *pūja* image worship outpaced classic Vedic sacrifice. Likewise, once the form of the Buddha became available, the Buddhist audible sūtra also faced stiff competition from the living image of the Buddha. For it is only human that talking person to person to the dharma wheel is awkward. It is much easier to supplicate one on one a divine form.

For better or worse the Buddha image would elicit a more emotional faith that would have wider lay appeal. The image would also change the impassivity at the heart of monastic piety. This shift from relic to image was concurrent with a shift from the oral to the written. By the time the Pāli Canon closed in Sri Lanka, the Mahāyāna pantheon of Buddhas and bodhisattvas was exploding in the north. However, why, when the Christian

Buddha in meditation, Daitokuji Zen temple, Kyoto, Japan,
16th century.
Photo courtesy of John C. Huntington, the Huntington Archive

Gnostics on the Silk Road rejected the use of images, did the Buddhist Gnostics (docetic Mahāyāna) find no problem with it? The reason has to do with the peculiar nature of the Greek icon and the specific design of the Buddha statue.

The Greek icon, however stereotyped it might appear to outsiders, is crafted with sufficient human likeness as to ensure individuality. Even when the icon is of the Risen Christ – a wistful, skyward spirit bathed in aura and halo – it is still identifiable with the flesh-and-blood Jesus who had walked the earth. What in the eyes of the Monophysites looms as the danger of conflating the divine essence with the material facade of the human was overcome by Byzantine monk-artists who obeyed a basic requirement of the icon, namely, that an icon must be two-dimensional. This erases any suggestion of *material* thickness, for there was a very real fear that demons (the gods of the pagan cults) might once more freely inhabit any material image and graven idol. This docetic fear of matter contaminating spirit is present in Buddhism. All Buddha images must be brought to life – animated by spirit – through a consecration rite. (This is standard practice in nearly all religions; the Greeks were the one exception, for they never animated their sculptures.) However, the fear that any excessive human likeness would misrepresent the divine is alleviated in Mahāyāna. That is because no one looking up at a much idealized Buddha image would think that he is looking at a mortal. Beyond the historical fact that the Buddha is of the "two legged" (human) species, confusing that "embodiment of nirvanic peace" with any known sentient being was unlikely. The mature Buddha image, with all its iconographic marks intact, moved away decisively from the model that was the classic Apollo figure. It has reversed the Greek premise. The Greeks worked to capture divinity within the limits of the human physique; they accomplished that by elevating the classic nude to its most ideal. Matter and form fused into one mathematically perfect and divinely proportioned entity. No such ideal nude, the result of an artistic apotheosis, ever existed in reality. All earthly nudes are its imperfect copies. Christianity had just cause to be wary of that pagan ideal. Buddhist artists faced with the Apollo figure did their best to reconstitute the image in another way.

Thus, they intentionally "rounded off" the muscular body, "dissolved away" the naturalistic fold of the tunic, and added those "elephantine ears" and other "animalian" icons or marks (the Buddha is supposed to embody the best marks of various living species) to come up with a supermundane Buddhakāya. Only very rarely do images of the Buddha depict him as an emasculated "skin and bone" extreme ascetic taken from his pre-enlightened days – before he trod the Middle Path. Of biographical interest only, this form, like those of the 16 arhats, is not usually featured as an object of worship. The ideal Buddha image must possess all those extraordinary (84 major and 32 minor) marks that it shares with the Cosmic King. It is an impiety and an abomination to render an incomplete set or to keep, as collectors now do, only a bust or a half torso of the Buddha, virtually beheading or truncating the Holy One. As a result all Buddhas basically look alike. Their individual careers are distinguished by any additional vows they made; one tells them apart by specific iconographic marks or by the attendant figures.

Identical in wisdom, Buddhas can be classified according to the Three Bodies theory. These can be compared with some Christian counterparts:

| Dharmakāya: | Law-body | Wisdom | Formless, impersonal |
|---|---|---|---|
| Sambhogakāya: | Bliss-body or recompense-body | For self and others | Transcendental form and with compassion |
| Nirmaṇakāya: | Transformation-body | For others | Doceto-didactic form |

The law-body is similar to the eternal, impersonal Logos; the transformation-body is similar to the person Jesus functioning as a docetic shadow on earth; the bliss-body mediates the two, combining the personal and the transcendental, more like the transfigured Jesus or the risen Christ. In theory Dharmakāya, being formless, can have no formal image – with one exception, namely, Vairocana, the Sun Buddha as the one and only Dharmakāya Buddha.

The history of the various Buddha images and their vicissitudes is too complex to unravel here. However, one handle to making sense of a "circuit of Buddhas" in the Far Eastern Buddhist history is to imagine a certain parallel to "high and low Christology" in Europe. The Christ figure started off as "low" (closer to humanity as in Jewish Adoptionism) and rose higher and higher in time (closer to God, first through Incarnationism). When Christ was perceived in a preeminently judgmental role (on the Judgmental Seat), so fear-inducing and remote, a host of secondary mediators (i.e., Mary and the saints) rose to play the new intercessors between Man and God. That was before the Reformation. Luther then reestablished the Christ on the Cross as the one and only mediator and in the process brought him once more closer to mankind. The rehumanization of the Christ figure had already commenced earlier in the Gothic depiction of the suffering Jesus with blood dripping from his nailed palms – something unthinkable to the Orthodox Church, which uses a cross but not a crucifix. This progression in perception (not affecting the Nicene creed itself) can be mapped by a curve of "transcendentalization and rehumanization" as follows:

high Christology
(on the Judgment Seat)

| cosmic Christ | Mary and the saints |
| (on the apse) | (around the choir) |
| low Christology | Christ rehumanized |
| (image of the good shepherd) | (image of the suffering Jesus) |

In Mahāyāna we can map this curve by employing two known sets of attributes of the Buddha – mundane/transmundane and wisdom/compassion – as follows:

|  | Wisdom | Compassion |
|---|---|---|
| transmundane | Vairocana (law-body) Wreath school | Amitābha (bliss-body) Pure Land school |
| mundane | Śākyamuni (transform-body) Lotus school | Zen patriarch (human buddha) Zen school |

Imagine a similar curve rising from the lower left box and peaking in the center between the upper two boxes before dipping down in time into the lower left one marked by Zen. If so, then Buddhology, like Christology, also began on a "low" note, with the Theravāda tradition echoing the early historical thesis that the one-time prince Śākyamuni Buddha was basically a teacher of the dharma. This marks the early aniconic phase. The Buddha figure then climbed increasingly "high" on the upward curve. It reached eternal status already in the *Lotus Sūtra*, well celebrated in carvings and images. However, Śākyamuni Buddha would be overtaken in time by other, still more transmundane Buddhas. This is seen in the two upper boxes with Vairocana representing the Dharmakāya Wisdom and Amitābha representing the Body of Blissful Recompense (the offering of a Pure Land paradise to the faithful). At the end of the downward curve on the lower

right is the Zen tradition. There too a secularizing trend opted for a "rehumanization of the Buddha." In Zen paintings of the Buddha, this first patriarch – sans halo, sans aura, sans elephantine ears, and the rest of the supernatural marks – looks very much like you and me. It returns the Buddha to a human dimension of a lord and master with whom, like the suffering Jesus, the follower could more easily identify – to die on the cross with the Lord and to rise like him one day, or, to repeat the same enlightenment experience as the Buddha, now as in the beginning.

WHALEN LAI

*See also* Buddha (Śākyamuni); China; Gestures, Buddhist; Iconoclasm (Controversy); Kyoto, Japan; Liturgy: Buddhist; Mount Meru; Patrons, Buddhist; Pilgrims to India, Chinese; Scholastics, Buddhist; Sexuality: Buddhist Perspectives; Stūpa; Visual Arts, Buddhist; Worship Space: Buddhist Perspectives

## Further Reading

Belting, Hans, *Likeness and Presence: A History of the Image before the Era of Art*, Chicago: University of Chicago Press, 1994

Coomaraswamy, Ananda Kentish, *Elements of Buddhist Iconography*, Cambridge, Massachusetts: Harvard University Press, 1935; 2nd edition, New Delhi: Munshiram Manoharlal, 1972

Coomaraswamy, Ananda Kentish, *Why Exhibit Works of Art?* London: Luzac, 1943; as *Christian and Oriental Philosophy of Art*, New York: Dover, 1956

Getty, Alice, *The Gods of Northern Buddhism: Their History, Iconography, and Progressive Evolution through the Northern Buddhist Countries*, Oxford: Clarendon Press, 1914; 2nd edition, 1928; reprint of 2nd edition, Rutland, Vermont: Charles E. Tuttle, 1962

# Images: Christian Perspectives

Jewish Scriptures prohibited the making of images of God on the grounds that divine power could not be confined by either earthly materials or the inadequacies of human artistry. These writings were deeply implicated in the emergence of Christianity, and the earliest Christians observed exhortations from the books of Exodus and Leviticus to avoid the use of images and idols. However, from around A.D. 200 a Greco-Roman tradition that was well disposed to imagery slowly prevailed against Old Testament ideas, first in private contexts and then in public buildings. The new attitude was reinforced by the fact that Christianity introduced a new dimension in its ideas of the divine: the notion of the Incarnation. Belief in the divinity of Jesus as the sacred Word-made-flesh provided many with the theological means to contemplate the picturing of God. Manufacture of Christian art increased from around the fourth century. Monasteries became key centers for the production, display, and dissemination of art and art styles throughout the Holy Land, the far reaches of the Byzantine Empire, and the countries of Western Europe.

The function and meaning of such art cannot be understood in merely secular terms. Monastic imagery in the form of painting, stained-glass windows, illuminated manuscripts, and so on has complemented both sacred texts and liturgy in depicting and promoting spiritual experience. Often the sacred art of a monastery takes on special significance from its geographical and architectural setting. The sixth-century monastery of St. Catherine at Mount Sinai attracted (and still attracts) many pilgrims who stepped out of the desert into a church whose architecture and mosaics delineate a pathway into the heart of the building. Just as the church contained images of Moses as well as a relic of the burning bush, so the monastery's location enabled it to highlight the imagined site of the original biblical event.

One of the most important and influential forms of Christian art, and one that has been closely associated with monastic communities, is the icon (Greek, *eikon*, "image"). An icon is a stylized painting on a wooden panel, usually of Christ or a saint, and is produced according to strict devotional as well as artistic rules. The result is an image that in certain respects is an embodiment of what it depicts. Icons emerged in the second half of the fourth century and became especially important in the Eastern Orthodox Churches. The earliest examples to have survived come from the early Byzantine period and have been preserved in St. Catherine's Monastery on Mount Sinai and in places in Egypt.

Such images of holy figures served a number of functions. The veneration of saints was given its original impetus by monasticism, and this attitude contributed to the desire to represent spiritual exemplars as realistically as possible to provide a form of immediate access to the saint. A number of early Church fathers spoke of Christian pictorial art as a didactic and hortatory aid, and in the eighth and ninth centuries St. Basil's (c. 329–379) dictum that "the honor shown to the image is conveyed to its model" became a slogan for supporters of the deployment of such images. According to some of the defenders of icons, to depict the features of a holy personage was not to produce a mere work of art; rather, it was a form of piety, enabling the artist to make contact with the energies emanating from the person being portrayed.

These emphases continued in monastic communities in subsequent centuries. In medieval Russia during the Middle Ages, icon painting was considered the highest form of art: to devote oneself to painting icons was to serve God. The monastic communities of Mount Athos might have been important disseminators of the idea that icon painting was a form of sacred vocation, almost a liturgy in paint, and certainly some of the best icon painters in the Orthodox world were monks. Others lived in close contact with monks and bishops. One of the most famous of all icon painters, Andrei Rublev (1369/70–before 1427), spent his early life as a lay brother in a Russian monastery where he worked as apprentice to an icon painter.

Icons were and still are located within liturgical practices, thus transcending ordinary portraits in their use: they might be carried in liturgical processions, kissed during ritual, and re-garded as a visual embodiment of the divine beings they represent. Traditionally Byzantine icons present a face-on, frontal view of their subjects, thus facilitating a straightforward encounter of the central figure with the believer. The power of such images is recounted in miracle discourses. For example, a number of stories have been told at Mount Athos of Turks who shot at or defaced icons but subsequently repented and became monks.

The power of images, defended in one interpretation of biblical texts, was nevertheless challenged by influential figures in the Church. In 726 or 730 iconoclasm became the official doctrine of the empire and remained in force until 780. It was revived again in 814 and lasted until 842. During the period of iconoclasm, it was forbidden to include figural works of art in the decoration of churches, so that mosaics and paintings were restricted to formal compositions or symbols, such as the cross. According to some believers an idolatry implicit in icon use had incurred divine displeasure and thus contributed to the success of Muslim attacks on the Byzantine Empire. The iconoclast movement might also have been promoted by those seeking to restrict the growing power of the monasteries, as attacks on images could provide veiled justification for their dissolution. The iconoclast emperors were all of Eastern (i.e. non-Greek) origin and were perhaps influenced by the nonrepresentational character of Islamic art.

Despite the power of the iconoclast movement in the Byzantine Empire, monasteries provided an important forum for the continuation of the production of religious images. Indeed they tended to oppose the movement, and various examples exist of images produced for monasteries at a time when such art was officially banned. Monastic paintings from the period survive in rock-cut chapels and sometimes also in larger built churches in Cappadocia. The region as a whole seems to have been little affected by the iconoclast ban and likely was located far enough away from the great cities to ignore the iconoclasts' decrees with impunity. Some icons preserved at the monastery of St. Catherine on Mount Sinai may have been produced during the period of iconoclasm, distance from urban centers again affording a degree of protection.

With regard to Western Christianity, during the Middle Ages the monasteries in Europe flourished as centers of art, culture, and science. In Italy and southern France, classical Roman, early Christian, and Byzantine traditions contributed to the development of Romanesque art. Illumination of manuscripts played a leading role in the genesis of the Romanesque style (as well as providing a source of income for monasteries) and rapidly became a source of models for wall painting, stained glass, goldsmith's work, and sculpture; yet, as in the East during an earlier period, to some believers sacred images were objects of distrust as much as veneration. In the 12th century St. Bernard of Clairvaux (1090–1153) criticized any monastic art that diverted the attention of monks away from unity with God. For Bernard an essential question was whether decoration achieved its proper goal of enhancing the meaning of a building in the glorification of the Lord. Waves of iconoclasm emerged in Europe during the 16th century as part of a Protestant theological and physical attack on what were perceived as the idolatrous images, rituals, and sacraments of the Catholic Church. Reforming theologians such as Zwingli (1484–1531) argued that the Eucharist itself was an idol, much like other carnal objects, such as relics and icons. In many parts of Europe, theological arguments for reform reinforced a politically charged desire to expropriate the influence and wealth of monasteries and shrines, and many of these were destroyed throughout northern Europe. Orthodoxy, on the other hand, having carried out its disputes many centuries earlier, never rejected the sensual world of icons, incense, or liturgical drama.

Monastic use of images echoes that in other areas of Christianity in many but not all ways. Unlike in parish churches monastic representations of biblical scenes, divinity, saints, and so on are often produced for private rather than general consumption. In other words they reflect the tightly knit and sometimes highly learned character of monastic life and devotion. Monasteries have had the resources and motivation to create or commission some of the most powerful visual representations of divinity that exist in the Christian world; yet, ironically perhaps, their inhabitants have sometimes felt the need to restrict access to such representations in order to preserve the integrity and contemplative quality of life in a cloistered community. Obscure iconography and subject matter as well as esoteric symbolism are characteristic of much monastic imagery. Thus, the taste of early hermits in Cappadocia during the period of iconoclasm is reflected in unfamiliar apocryphal scenes and complicated biblical cycles. The monks did not try to make the Bible story clear for laity, nor were they especially concerned with making beautiful pictures out of the more important scenes, as would artists who operated under the patronage of emperors or nobles. Religious dogma appeared more important than beauty, simple exegesis, or fine art. Again much of the art on Mount Athos in past centuries has been concerned with depicting doctrine rather than evoking beauty and elegance. Meanwhile in the medieval West symbolism was itself an intellectual craft, and the complex nature of messages produced through decoration emphasized monastic seclusion and its search for the divine.

The sometimes inward-looking, obscure character of monastic imagery has not precluded the intrusion of highly secular, politically charged, and rather obvious messages into some artistic work. A monastery church near Vladimir in Russia has a 17th-century Last Judgment that depicts the Swedes, the Poles, and the Tatars among the condemned: these were the enemies against whom the Russians were fighting at the time. Depictions of Psalm 149 were also used to convey the notion of Orthodox Christian victory in battle over unbelievers. The nations and peoples on whom vengeance was exercised in the psalm could be represented as Muslims, the archetypal unbelievers of the period.

Images remain important in monastic life today, and the production of icons and other forms of sacred art continues. Thus, monks on Mount Athos might earn their living by icon painting and handicrafts. Debates are still current among the monks of St. Catherine as to whether the awkward location of certain images in the monastic church has hindered the spiritual life of the community. The liturgical life in Christianity, like that of Buddhism but unlike that of Islam or Judaism, widely encourages the incorporation of images of the divine into worship. However, the history of Christian monasticism is distinctive not only because the contemplation of images has prevailed within both Eastern and Western traditions but also because monks have regarded the production of such images as furthering the glory of God.

SIMON COLEMAN

*See also* Basil the Great, St.; Bernard of Clairvaux, St.; Cappadocia, Turkey; Iconoclasm (Controversy); Mount Athos, Greece; Mount Sinai, Egypt; Orthodox Monasticism; Spirituality: Eastern Christian; Visual Arts, Eastern Christian: Painting; Visual Arts, Western Christian: Painting; Vocation, Christian

## Further Reading

Cormack, Robin, *Writing in Gold: Byzantine Society and Its Icons*, London: George Philip, and New York: Oxford, 1985

Elsner, John, "The Viewer and the Vision: The Case of the Sinai Apse," *Art History* 17 (1994)

Freedberg, David, *The Power of Images: Studies in the History and Theory of Response*, Chicago: University of Chicago Press, 1989

Koch, Guntram, *Early Christian Art and Architecture: An Introduction*, London: SCM Press, 1996

Lawrence, C.H., *Medieval Monasticism: Forms of Religious Life in Western Europe in the Middle Ages*, London and New York: Longman, 1984; 2nd edition, 1989

Mango, Cyril, *The Art of the Byzantine Empire 312–1453*, Englewood Cliffs, New Jersey: Prentice-Hall, 1972; Toronto: University of Toronto Press, 1986

Milis, Ludo, *Angelic Monks and Earthly Men: Monasticism and Its Meaning to Medieval Society*, Woodbridge and Rochester, New York: Boydell Press, 1992

Pelikan, J., *Imago Dei: The Byzantine Apologia for Icons*, Princeton, New Jersey: Princeton University Press, 1990

Schiemenz, Günter, "The Painted Psalms of Athos," in *Mount Athos and Byzantine Monasticism*, edited by Anthony Bryer and Mary Cunningham, Aldershot and Brookfield, Vermont: Variorum, 1996

Talbot Rice, D., *Byzantine Art*, Oxford: Clarendon Press, 1935; Baltimore, Maryland: Penguin, 1948; revised and expanded edition, Harmondsworth: Penguin, 1968

# India. *See* Ajaṇṭā, India; Bodh Gayā, India; Buddhist Schools/Traditions: India; Dharamsala, India (Tibetan); Ladakh, India; Nālandā, India; Patrons, Buddhist: India; Visual Arts, Buddhist: India

# India: Christian

India, at one billion people the second most populous country in the world, is a religiously pluralist society. Besides the dominant Hinduism, local tribal, Muslim, Buddhist, Jain, Jewish, and Christian religions are found (the last, 2.6 percent of the total, is concentrated in the south, especially Kerala). Jains and Buddhists as well as Christians practice lifelong monasticism; Hindus may renounce their former way of life and become monks (and outcastes) in the fourth stage of their spiritual journey.

The Kerala (southwest) coast of India was visited before the Christian era by westerners. A colony of mercantile Jews settled at Cochin. The Thomas (Syriac) Christians trace their origins to the apostle Thomas ("doubting Thomas"), popularly believed to have landed on the Malabar coast in A.D. 52 and to have been martyred on the east coast at Madras (Chennai) in 72. They maintained contacts with churches in Edessa, Chaldea, Persia, and Mesopotamia.

In 1321 a French Dominican and four Franciscans reached India; the latter were martyred. The Portuguese arrived with Vasco da Gama in 1498, bringing Franciscan friars and Latin Christianity to Goa; they were surprised by the presence of ancient Eastern churches. The Jesuit mission began in earnest with the arrival in 1542 of St. Francis Xavier. His three-year preaching campaign yielded abundant baptisms; other Latin efforts were ineffectual. Subsequent Roman missionary effort concentrated on ending the independent existence of the Indo-"Syrian" churches. Latinization of the Thomas Christians was hastened by the Synod of Diamper (1599). The Syro-Malabar Church and its religious orders became the most Latin of all the Eastern churches in communion with Rome.

### Forerunners of Christian Sannyāsic Monasticism

Sannyāsa (Sanskrit, "to give up") originated in the Hindu monastic and mystical tradition with the forest dwellers (rishis, or Vedic seers) who practiced asceticism and meditation to attain enlightenment and discover the Transcendent One in the "cave of the heart." Mystical wisdom is acquired from a spiritual master (guru). Robert de Nobili, S.J. (1577–1656), has been called the "father of Christian sannyāsa." Having arrived in Goa in 1605, De Nobili vowed to live as a sannyāsi. He fasted, dressed as a Brahmin, prayed in Hindu style, and studied Tamil and Sanskrit in order to read the Vedas, developing theological terms suitable for the Indian context. His mission was directed toward upper-caste Hindus and offered no alternative to the strict caste system.

In 1831 three Syro-Malabar priests established the Carmelites of Mary Immaculate (C.M.I.) to combine contemplation and service, especially spiritual guidance, with sannyāsic elements. In 1897 the Hindu Ramakrishna movement was founded as an activist ashram to offer selfless public service. Brahmabandhab Upadhyay (1861–1907), a Brahmin convert to Catholicism (1891), became a sannyāsi (1894) and synthesized Christian monasticism with the Vedas, suggesting that the Trinity be equated with Saccidānanda (Sat-Cit-Ananda), the divine name. His Kasthalic Matha (Catholic Monastery, 1900) was forced to disband. The first Christian ashram was founded in 1918. Bethany ashram is Orthodox Syrian, now with Anglican monastic influence. Ashrams founded by Mahatma Gandhi (1869–1948) were reformist and inspired in 1921 Christukula (Tamil Nadu) and Christa Seva Sangha (Pune) Protestant ashrams. The ashram may be either a monastic "house" or a retreat center held together by personal relationships of guru and disciples. Visitors are welcomed. Protestant ashrams tend to greater social activism; the Catholic ones are more contemplative. Interreligious as well as ecumenical worship is a common feature.

### Recent Foundations

In the spirit of Upadhyay, Jules Monchanin (1895–1957) made advaita (nonduality) and praise of the Trinity the goal of Shantivanam Ashram (Grove of Peace), founded at Kulitalai on the Kavery River. Many visited but few stayed. In 1950 Henri Le Saux, O.S.B. (1910–1973), called Abhishiktananda, "Bliss of Christ," arrived. The two sought to grasp "the authentic Hindu search for God in order to Christianize it," starting with themselves. After Monchanin died in France, Le Saux moved to a hermitage in the Himalayas to study at the feet of Hindu masters. Bede Griffiths, O.S.B. (1906–1992), had founded Kurisumala Ashram (1958) in Kottayam, Kerala, with the Belgian Cistercian Francis Mahieu. Griffiths became the spiritual teacher (acharya) of Shantivanam in 1968.

The example of a Hindu monk, Brahmachari, influenced the vocation of Thomas Merton (1915–1968), who would become an ardent participant in monastic interreligious dialogue.

### Typical Women's Communities

The Franciscan Missionaries of Mary were founded in 1877 at Ootacamund (British hill station, Tamil Nadu) by Hélène de Chappotin de Neuville (1839–1904) to combine contemplation and action. An entirely Indian branch of St. Bridget of Sweden's order (1370) is the Order of the Most Holy Savior (Bridgettines), founded in Rome (1911) by Elisabeth Hesselblad (1870–1957). Their contemplative semi-enclosed monastic life is dedicated to liturgical prayer, especially for the reunion of Christians. Each monastery includes a guest house and women's hostel open to all faiths, with occupational training centers. Bridgettine houses in South India are in Bangalore, Mysore, Pallavaram (Chennai), Goa, Kalamassery (Cochin), and Trivandrum.

MARY M. SCHAEFER

See also Ashram, Influence of; Bridgettines; Griffiths, Bede; Le Saux, Henri; Merton, Thomas

## Further Reading

Abhishiktananda, Swami, *Prayer*, London: SPCK, 1967; new and enlarged edition, Delhi: SPCK, 1993

Abhishiktananda, Swami, *Saccidananda: A Christian Approach to Advaitic Experience*, Delhi: SPCK-LPH, 1974

Abhishiktananda, Swami, "The Significance of India for Camaldolese Monasticism," *The American Benedictine Review* 40 (1989)

Griffiths, Bede, *The Marriage of East and West*, London: Collins, and Springfield, Illinois: Templegate, 1982

Lefébure, Marcus, "India of the Heart," *New Blackfriars* 68 (1987)

Lipski, Alexander, *Thomas Merton and Asia: His Quest for Utopia*, Kalamazoo, Michigan: Cistercian Publications, 1983

Neill, Stephen, *The Story of the Christian Church in India and Pakistan*, Grand Rapids, Michigan: Eerdmans, 1970

Neill, Stephen, *A History of Christianity in India: The Beginnings to* A.D. *1707*, Cambridge and New York: Cambridge University Press, 1984

Neill, Stephen, *A History of Christianity in India, 1707–1858*, Cambridge and New York: Cambridge University Press, 1985

Pennington, M. Basil, *Monastic Journey to India*, New York: Seabury Press, 1982

Ralston, Helen, *Christian Ashrams: A New Religious Movement in Contemporary India*, Lewiston, New York: Mellen Press, 1987

Raverty, Aaron, "Monastic Interreligious Dialogue: Tibet, Nepal, and Northern India," *Cisterican Studies Quarterly* 32:2 (1997)

*The Space in the Heart of the Lotus: Bede Griffiths: A Benedictine in India*, videocassette, Encinitas, California: Inner Directions, 1987

Teasdale, Wayne Robert, *Toward a Christian Vedanta: The Encounter of Hinduism and Christianity According to Bede Griffiths*, Bangalore: Asian Trading Corporation, 1987

Vandana, *Gurus, Ashrams, and Christians*, London: Darton, Longman and Todd, 1978

Vandana Mataji, editor, *Christian Ashrams: A Movement with a Future?* Delhi: SPCK, 1993

Weber, J.G., editor and translator, *In Quest of the Absolute: The Life and Work of Jules Monchanin*, Kalamazoo, Michigan: Cistercian Publications, 1977

*The Wisdom of a Prophet*, videocassette, Perth, Western Australia: MTI Films, 1992

# India: Sites

The importance of *place* in the Indian Buddhist imagination becomes apparent every time one reads the opening of a sūtra. "Thus have I heard," Ānanda narrates, "at one time the Blessed One was staying in . . ." This stock frame might be finished with the name of Śrāvastī, where Śākyamuni frequented a grove donated to the *saṅgha* by Anāthapiṇḍada; or the location might be the glade belonging to Āmrapālī, a courtesan in Vaiśālī; or, again, perhaps Śākyamuni was at the Nyagrodha garden, a gift from his father on the outskirts of Kapilavastu, his childhood home. These are only three of the locales identified in the Buddhist sūtras' introductory cliché. For example, the collection of Pāli *sutta*s names 81 separate places, ranging from capital cities through settled towns to rural hamlets. This variety of place-names reminds us that Śākyamuni wandered the roads of north-central India throughout his 45-year career as a teacher. Although few of the 81 places are repeated, five are named with great frequency. The restricted universe of commonly named places reminds us that Śākyamuni was also a settler. The Buddha's life and teachings were fixed in the very buildings that his *saṅgha* inhabited. Through the 17 centuries that Buddhism flourished on the Indian subcontinent, Śākyamuni's fame, stories of his lives (past and present), and teachings spread from Nāgapaṭṭinam, near the southern tip, to Taxila, at the headwaters of the Indus. Thus, India can be mapped as a Buddhist land whose places unfold a history extending to the present day, when pilgrims and tourists from six continents forge new identities and communities in their encounter with some very old sites.

It should come as no surprise that Śākyamuni Buddha's sacred biography was closely connected to a theoretical and ritual valorization of certain places in particular. The *Mahāparinirvāṇa sūtra*, accepted by Buddhists as a record of Śākyamuni's final months, stipulates four locations that a devout Buddhist must visit during his or her life: the site of the Buddha's birth, of his awakening, of his first teaching, and of his death. This sūtra does not name or map these four sites. However, other literary and archaeological sources identify the locales. Siddhārtha Gautama was born in Lumbinī, he awakened in Bodh Gayā, he first taught in Sārnāth, and he died in Kuśinagara. Indeed, scholastic writings on the Buddha's biography represent these places as cosmically significant in their own right. Geographical happenstance played little role in a Buddha's earthly life. For Buddhist scholastics the Deer Park in Sārnāth, for example, was the only place that Śākyamuni could have given his first teaching. Similarly, the tree beneath which Śākyamuni realized supreme knowledge was necessarily located in Uruvilvā, near the bank of the Nairañjanā River.

The village known to Buddhist literature as Uruvilvā is now called Bodh Gayā. As is the case with the other major monastic pilgrimage sites associated with Śākyamuni's life in India, Bodh Gayā is located in the Gangetic basin, in the modern state of Bihar. From the third century B.C., when Emperor Aśoka is said to have visited, until the present day, Bodh Gayā has been the most significant site in Buddhist India. A specimen of *Ficus religiosus* standing within an enclosure behind the Mahābodhi temple holds special import: it is said to be an ancestor of the original tree beneath which Śākyamuni gained awakening after he overcame the forces of desire, anger, and ignorance. Directly to the east of this tree (where Śākyamuni himself would have sat) lies a stone platform, reputed to have been set there by Aśoka around 260 B.C. Although the seventh-century Chinese pilgrim Xuanzang ascribes the Mahābodhi temple to Aśoka as well, the structure that stands today is a modern reconstruction of an edifice that probably dates to the sixth century A.D., itself installed over earlier stone and wood structures. Numerous smaller shrines, marking significant events during the first seven weeks of Śākyamuni's buddhahood, fill the bougainvillea-lined park that surrounds the main temple.

**Dhamekh Stūpa in the Deer Park, Sārnāth, India, fourth–sixth century A.D., enveloping a smaller stūpa built during the reign of Aśoka.**
**Photo courtesy of John Powers**

Although Bodh Gayā is a primary pilgrimage destination for all Buddhists, historically the site has had a special relationship with devotees from the island of Sri Lanka. For example, the current Bodhi tree descends from a grafting of the original tree that was preserved in Anurādhapura, a hospice was built for Sri Lankan monks and pilgrims in the fourth century, and a 13th-century Tibetan pilgrim named Dharmasvāmin describes the site as controlled by Sri Lankan Theravādins during the twilight of Buddhist India. After a hiatus of several centuries (during which the Mahābodhi compound was controlled by Śaivites), this historical relationship was renewed in 1891, when a Sri Lankan layman named Dharmapāla (1864–1933) founded the Mahā-bodhi Society; Dharmapāla's goal was realized in 1953, when Buddhists once again took control of the Mahābodhi temple. Beyond the restoration of the central temple itself, the most impressive and exciting effect of Dharmapāla's activities has been the transformation of Bodh Gayā into a truly international town. Currently, almost every majority-Buddhist country has at least one monastery in the vicinity, and many run programs that cater both to pilgrims from their native lands and to "foreign" tourists.

Like Bodh Gayā other sites associated with Śākyamuni Buddha's biography also lead a double life: the edifice they provide for contemporary Buddhism is supported by the remains of ancient shrines and monasteries. Lumbinī (modern Rummindei), the site of the Buddha's birth, is located in southern Nepal and holds a pillar erected by Aśoka himself. Among the ruined monasteries to be found at Kuśīnagara (modern Kasia in Uttar Pradesh), the most important mark the site where Śākyamuni at-

tained complete nirvāṇa and the site of his cremation. Sārnāth, long a center for Buddhist art, culture, and learning, is rich in the remains of monastic establishments dedicated to serving pilgrims and tourists attracted by memorials to Śākyamuni's initial teaching of the Four Noble Truths.

In addition to the four pilgrimage spots named in the *Mahā-parinirvāṇa sūtra*, the Indian states of Bihar and Uttar Pradesh are covered by important reminders that these territories were once the heartland of a Buddhist India. Especially noteworthy among these many sites is Nālandā, a great monastic university on the outskirts of Rajgir in Bihar. This town had early importance as the birthplace and repository for the relics of Śāriputra, Śākyamuni's foremost disciple. However, Nālandā became increasingly prominent in the fifth century A.D., when the Gupta kings began an extensive project of building temples and monasteries. By the time of Xuanzang in the seventh century, Nālandā was India's preeminent educational institution and had an international reputation. However, whereas the nearby monasteries at Bodh Gayā were associated with the Theravāda sect, Nālandā became the great seat of Mahāyāna and, later, Tantric thought. Other sites in these two states, significant within the history of Buddhist monasticism, include Śrāvastī, Vaiśālī, and Kauśāmbī.

The earliest material evidence we have for Buddhism's presence in India dates to Aśoka, and the distribution pattern of this king's pillar and stone edicts reveals that by the third century B.C. Buddhist monasteries were not limited to the Gangetic basin. In the state of Madhya Pradesh, two of the most significant sites have cores that date to roughly this period: Sāñcī and Bhārhut. Sāñcī was founded by Aśoka himself, who had once been a viceroy in the nearby city of Ujjain. He had the top of a hill flattened, built a stone brick stūpa, and erected a polished-sandstone pillar. Several centuries later Aśoka's stūpa was dressed in stone and surrounded by carved rails and gates. Sāñcī flourished until the 12th century; evidence for every important development in Buddhist art and architecture can be found at the site. In addition to numerous stūpas and temples, the hill is dotted with numerous monastic dwellings. Bhārhut, the second major site in Madhya Pradesh, is not worth visiting. Like Sāñcī, Bhārhut was used as a monastic habitation for more than a millennium. Unlike Sāñcī, Bhārhut's monuments and habitations were razed by local villagers foraging for building materials. In the 19th century Sir Alexander Cunningham gathered what he could and deposited the remains at the Indian Museum in Calcutta. Although both Sāñcī and Bhārhut were long-lived monastic institutions, they are known mainly for their Śuṅga-period artifacts (second to first century B.C.), whose inscriptions reveal Buddhism to have been a popular religion patronized by craftsmen and farmers as well as kings.

The southernmost site having historical importance for Buddhism is the port city of Nāgapattinam in Tamil Nadu. Historically, Nāgapattinam was noteworthy for its ties to China, whose kings and notables built monasteries for pilgrims far from home. Today little tangible remains of Nāgapattinam's Buddhist heritage. The last vestige, a multistoried Chinese-style pagoda, stood until 1857, when it was razed by Jesuits.

In the state of Andhra Pradesh, the Krishna River valley holds two important monastic complexes: Amarāvatī and Nāgārjunakoṇḍa. Although neither site can be associated with Aśoka directly, the introduction of Buddhism to this region dates no later than the Mauryan period. Of these two sites Amarāvatī started earlier and declined later; we know that a monk from Sri Lanka restored a shrine in Amarāvatī in the 14th century. Amarāvatī is best known for its great stūpa, whose modest core was enlarged and embellished in the second century A.D. during the Śātavāhana dynasty. As with Bhārhut, most of Amarāvatī's treasures do not remain in situ but rather in the Madras Government Museum. Nevertheless, one cannot overestimate the importance of Amarāvatī in the history of Indian Buddhism. Associated with the Mahāsāṅghika sect, this site might well have been an early center for the development of Mahāyāna doctrine. Additionally, the *Kālacakra Tantra* identifies Amarāvatī (under the ancient name Dhānyakaṭaka) as the place of its composition. The 14th Dalai Lama (1935– ) has traversed the world, offering initiations into this system of Tantric practice, keeping the name of Dhānyakaṭaka alive. Not far from Amarāvatī, the monastic complex at Nāgārjunakoṇḍa dates from the third and fourth centuries A.D. and owes its primary patronage to the grand dames of the local Ikṣvāku rulers, who knew this site by the name Vijayapurī. The monasteries of Nāgārjunakoṇḍa filled a valley of about 23 square miles, making it one of the largest Buddhist sites in India. Tragically, this valley was submerged in the 1960s to serve as a reservoir. Large-scale excavations were undertaken from 1954 to 1960. Several monasteries and monuments were reconstructed on the peak of Nāgārjunakoṇḍa hill, which is now an island in the middle of the reservoir accessible by a regular ferry.

As we have seen in other regions of the subcontinent, the state of Maharashtra first enters history through the monuments of King Aśoka. However, whereas freestanding structures dominate at Indian Buddhist sites elsewhere, Maharashtra's ancient traders, kings, monks, and nuns used their wealth to commission rock-cut cave monasteries and shrines. Physical restrictions imposed by the living rock were more than overcome by the technical proficiency and artistic mastery of Maharashtra's stone workers. The Buddhist sites of Maharashtra represent a broad diversity of architectures, scales, and functions, ranging in complexity from simple rough-hewn cells to the grand, painted monastery and palaces found at Ajanṭā. Each one of the region's monastic sites has its special attractions and charms. Highlights include the sculpted goddesses at the Aurangabad caves; the caitya at Karla, described in an inscription as "the most excellent rock-mansion in India"; the monastic graveyard at Kanheri, located in a northen suburb of Mumbai; the caves at Ellora, whose three-story complexes stand harmoniously beside Hindu and Jain excavations; and Ajaṇṭā, which is unique for its simultaneous preservation of architectural forms, sculpture, inscriptions, and painting.

The rock-cut monasteries of Maharashtra can be dated from the second century B.C. through the eighth century A.D. However, that is not the end of Maharashtra's Buddhist history. In 1956 Dr. Bimrao Ramji Ambedkar (1891–1956), an author of the Indian constitution and a leader of India's untouchables, converted to Buddhism, starting a wave of mass conversions among the untouchables, especially in Maharashtra. Since that time Ambedkar's home in Bombay and the place at which he first declared himself a Buddhist in Nagpur have become important sites for the Ambedkar Buddhists. A modern resurgence of Buddhism in India has also been fostered by the increasing presence of Tibetans in the wake of China's invasion.

*Monasteries to Visit*
Nearly every state in India preserves relics of the subcontinent's Buddhist past. The most concentrated set of sites will be found in the Gangetic basin, where Śākyamuni lived and taught. Sārnāth, near the city of Varanasi, is most accessible, with Bodh Gayā and Nālandā a half a day away. Cave-monasteries dot Maharashtra's landscape: Kanheri can be reached by public transportation in Mumbai, and both Ajaṇṭā and Ellora, doubtless the most commonly visited Buddhist sites in India, are day trips from Aurangabad. By comparison most of the sites in the Krishna valley are difficult of access and, accordingly, receive significantly less attention from visitors and scholars. Ratnagiri, in the state of Orissa, bears ample witness to Buddhism's second millennium in India. Finally, northern Pakistan, known to ancient Buddhism as Gandhāra, was a center for Buddhist monasticism. Important sites include Taxila, Manikyala, Shah-ji-ki-dheri, and Takht-i-Bahi.

RICHARD S. COHEN

## Further Reading

Aitken, Molly Emma, editor, *Meeting the Buddha: On Pilgrimage in Buddhist India*, New York: Riverhead Books, 1995

Dutt, Sukumar, *Buddhist Monks and Monasteries of India: Their History and Their Contribution to Indian Culture*, London: Allen and Unwin, 1962

Huntington, John C., "Sowing the Seeds of the Lotus: A Journey to the Great Pilgrimage Sites of Buddhism," *Orientations* 16:11, 17:2, 17:3, 17:7, and 17:9 (1985–1986)

Huntington, Susan L., *The Art of Ancient India: Buddhist, Hindu, Jain*, New York: Weatherhill, 1985

Mitchell, George, editor, *The Penguin Guide to the Monuments of India*, volume 1: *Buddhist, Jain, Hindu*, London and New York: Viking, 1989

Mitra, Debala, *Buddhist Monuments*, Calcutta: Sahitya Samsad, 1971

Nagao, Gadjin, "The Architectural Tradition in Buddhist Monasticism," in *Studies in Buddhist Art of South Asia*, edited by A.K. Narain, New Delhi: Kanak Publications, 1985

Sarkar, H., *Studies in Early Buddhist Architecture of India*, Delhi: Munshiram Manoharlal, 1966

Schopen, Gregory, *Bones, Stones, and Buddhist Monks: Collected Papers on the Archaeology, Epigraphy, and Texts of Monastic Buddhism in India*, Honolulu: University of Hawaii Press, 1997

Xuanzang, *Si-yu-ki: Buddhist Records of the Western World: Translated from the Chinese of Hiuen Tsiang* (A.D. 629), translated by Samuel Beal, Delhi: Munshiram Manoharlal, 1969

# Initiation: Buddhist Perspectives

Patterns of conversion/initiation in Buddhism can tell us much about changes in the monastic institution and its lifestyle ideal. However, because it is not possible to cover the whole span of this topic from India to Japan, the longer and better-kept records from Buddhist China will be used to cast light on the history of conversion as a whole. One of the points made by Arthur D. Nock in his classic study *Conversion* (1933) is that unlike the mystery cults, the Christian faith elicits a clear *metanoia* (change of mind) by virtue of its call for a break with the past and for a total commitment in all aspects of life. Buddhism made a similarly total demand. It also laid out a full new life for the convert. In China it carved out a separate and distinct identity, much more than did the concurrent Daoist movements, and in the early fifth century the layman Zong Bing (Tsung Ping) expressed that *metanoia* well in his *Mingfolun* (Ming-fo-lun, Essay on Enlightenment) when he confessed that it was "not he who found the Light (of the Buddha); it is the Light that found him."

The Buddha being a renunciate and Buddhism being a monastic tradition, conversion was understood initially as the act of leaving home. Modeled after the great "going forth" of the Buddha, this is the first of the four stations in his legendary life – the other three being enlightenment, commencing teaching, and the final extinction. Renunciation means "turning away" from an old way of life and embarking on a new one. It is seen as "entering the stream" that would lead to fording over to the "other shore" (*nirvāṇa*). This rite of passage is reenacted in all Buddhist traditions and informs its classic understanding of conversion. The experience might and should be personally transformative, but understood institutionally it is the act of simply entering the order. Thus, as with medieval Christianity only monks and nuns had this special "calling." Laymen, as Max Weber noted, had yet to assume a *Beruf* (calling). So too the layman Zong Bing, his experience of a transformation notwithstanding, had not been "called away."

Only a monk embarking on a new life was given a new name to mark his joining a new family. He received his "precept name" from his precept master. Counted only as a novice who had taken on ten basic precepts (five more than the laity), he awaits a full ordination, allowed only after age 20, when he would take on the 250 or so rules of the full vinaya. The date of his full ordination was duly recorded, for that would determine his seniority in the new brotherhood. That full set of monastic precepts is held in such sacred trust that it is a secret not to be divulged to the laity. (China would later replace the 250 rules with its own set of Zen monastic precepts.) The formal rite of his full ordination is usually conducted in company with many others like him and at a larger (regional or higher) temple under a more reputable precept master, although that relationship is not as warm as the one with his original precept master. Other intimate master-disciple relationships might rise out of one's later search for a spiritual master. In such contexts initiate-initiator roles might be reversed. Thus, Kumārajīva (d. c. 412) was tutored under a Sarvāstivāda master before he was converted to Mahāyāna Emptiness by a Mahāyāna master. His previous Sarvāstivāda master confronted him, but, after having converted to Mahāyāna too, he conceded that he should now learn from Kumārajīva instead. India as a whole constitutes such a "free market" of ideas. A master defeated by another could bring his own disciples into the new camp.

With conversion in China understood as initiation into the order, we must interpret the dynamics as they are told in the various Lives of Eminent Monks. These collective lives cannot help but follow the paradigmatic life of the Buddha. Typical of the Chinese account of a monk's life are the following. First comes his secular name and family background, although some low-born who rose to eminent status might have no erstwhile family background to report. Then come some early signs of monastic inclination or future expertise; the story of the Siddhārtha has its fill of such. Even this aspect, always colorful, is not indispensable. What is a "must" – unless for some reason the data were not available – is the time (age), the place (monastery), and the tutelage of the person's initiation into the order, perhaps a note on his later formal reception of the full precepts. Then follow the highlights of his career; these vary with his proven expertise. Finally comes a narrative of his death, and this should emit some aura of sanctity to remind us of the *parinirvāna* of the Buddha. What is not necessary – and rarely told in the average hagiographies – is some dramatic episode of personal "awakening." The earlier assumption about a holy life might be in force here, namely, that with multiple rebirths what matters is that a person has "left the world" during this life. His final "crossing of the stream" in some future life can wait.

A report of the historical shifts in Chinese conversion patterns based on these Lives of Eminent Monks was made by Miyakawa Hisayuki in *Rokuchō shūkyōshi* (1974; Religious History of the Six Dynasties). Although the data are limited and not always balanced, the shifts accord well enough with other known changes in the monastic institution so as to deserve mention. Simply stated, until the 400s the early Chinese converts seem to have come from among the better-educated class; conversions tended to occur at a more mature age and were often triggered by the lure of new ideas. The star converts of the early *saṅgha* look like the early Church fathers: they set the course for the new faith. This top-heavy picture reminds us that, with the *saṅgha* not yet being materially well endowed, it is quite natural for the dharma (intellectual ideas) to seduce the erudite minds of independently wealthy patrons. Their prestige and standing in the society was needed to help make the faith respectable and legitimate. Once the *saṅgha* took root in China and could raise the resources to recruit one and all, a new class of converts rose. These were men from the general population, many suffering the pain of dislocation brought about by invasions. These converts had to make hard, personal decisions about joining a fellowship of renunciates that their parents and neighbors still held in low esteem. However, the existential struggle also made for creative minds that spearheaded innovations in the sixth century, although some of that spiritual vigor was lost by the 600s precisely because the *saṅgha* had become so entrenched by then as to appear a bit too worldly and comfortable. More younger sons of notables again entered the order, which had become an alternative avenue of upward mobility and self-aggrandizement. With China reunited and prosperous, that secular bent even received the stamp of approval from Sinitic Mahāyāna schools.

Interestingly what triggered many conversions by then was not the abstract philosophy of Emptiness or the personal suffering of the dispossessed but rather the beauty of images and the grandeur of temples. An example is that of a small child who was brought to a temple. The beauty of a Buddha image so moved him that he supposedly stayed for good. Because an image is a living Buddha, the perfect marks thereon are divine form and grace. These could effect an "aesthetic" conversion that overwhelms the senses; it is due more to passion and awe than to intellectual fascination or painful renunciation. However, most likely it was a pious mother who brought her child to the temple, so that the child was presocialized into her devotion. Her allowing the child to stay behind could easily be her wish. Much to her spiritual merit, she might even have pledged the child to the Buddha before it was born. With such socialized conversions came a notable drop in the average age of entry for

converts during the Tang dynasty, and by the 14th century (during the Ming dynasty) the very young age was due mainly to inbreeding; that is, having fallen out of favor with the ruling elite, the monastery was recruiting its future monks from the pool of orphans brought under its charge. With fewer bright young minds then volunteering to become monks (most preferred advancement through the civil examination system), the overall quality of monks in late dynastic China declined. Such are the leads provided by Miyakawa's finding.

However, the final judgment needs to be qualified. At the end of the medieval Buddhist period, roughly from 800 to 1200, a new type of conversion arose, and these were registered in a new genre. It is a "crisis conversion" involving a clash of wills and a sudden leap in the dark. The old idea of conversion, understood as a ritualized passage into the orders, was being overshadowed by the new conversion, seen now as a dramatic and self-validating "transformative experience." The mood is not unlike what happened in late medieval Europe with some mystics (St. John of the Cross and St. Theresa) or among those sectarians within the Reformation who considered a person not truly Christian unless he or she was personally "reborn." Institutional membership (of the church type) was no longer deemed sufficient; a person must be so moved by the spirit as to be "baptized anew." Around the 700s in China, the Zen tradition began to redefine what "true discipleship" of the Buddha meant. Membership in the open "physical *saṅgha*" was not enough. Now one had also to be in a secret "spiritual lineage," an unbroken "mind-to-mind" transmission, passing from the Buddha down, from patriarch to patriarch, to one's own spiritual master. True conversion is not dated by the time of entry into the order but now involves a moment of sudden illumination and total enlightenment. Not unlike a "leap of faith," this "leap of wisdom" is a wager in the dark. It involves a renunciation of reason during a battle of wills – not man's foolish pride against God's free grace but a Zen student running up against a wall of an impossible assignment (later the koan) from his master, a living Buddha whose word, however nonsensical, is Law. It is all or nothing. Breaking that impasse liberates totally. Around that inner "turmoil and turnover" that marks the Zen enlightenment rose a new poetic, a new rhetoric, and a new form of conversional biography. The "encounter dialogues" during the mind-to-mind transmission between master and disciple later evolved into the so-called koan system. Memories of the "dead words" of the grand masters provide the dilemmas used to rekindle the living wisdom, even if that would involve abusing texts and deconstructing conversations.

Now the persons whom Ernst Troeltsch called the "church type" will always have misgivings about such "sectarian" claims to a special dispensation validated by a "holier than thou" peak experience, but we cannot hope to resolve that difference in opinion. The irony perhaps is that such "sudden enlightenment" or conversion experience must have existed in some measure before in both the East and the West. We do not get to hear of it because it unfolded in a very private conversation between a monk-in-training and his spiritual master. Zen made public what had once been private; it created an "open secret" of the kōan (public court case). One reason that Zen dialogues (truncated later into bare-bone "heading phrases") are so senseless is because as snippets of an exchange they presume certain tacit rules of the game, but these codes or cues are strategically left out.

In the West we can actually see a similar shift from the Lutheran sermon as the preaching of the Word of God (soliciting a decision for or against) to the Puritan's use of testimony. The latter, the retelling in public of personal conversions, then fuels more such emotional outpourings of the uncontrollable Spirit. Zen also counts on its testimonials of sudden enlightenment to trigger more of the same. Both perpetuate and precipitate a sense of crisis so as to generate the radical change of heart, and that Zen non/sense (semantics) still works (pragmatics) magic to this day. Now the religion of grace, notes Paul Tillich, is a religion of paradox. Thus, perhaps it is not unreasonable that along with Zen mysticism there rose also Pure Land faith. The latter catapulted its own (often lay) charismatics who also publicize their "reborn" experiences. Their collective lives contain these new signposts, first an encounter with a "good friend" who relates the "good news" of Amitābha's "free grace." That leads to the chanting of the Buddha's name so as to attain, at the deathbed, the "salvation from hell" and the "deliverance to paradise." These "testimonials" are also retold to solicit more faith of the same. The cases of "evil men gaining birth in Pure Land" might best move the hearts of proud men. With this as with Zen, institutional conversion is not required. In theory any layperson could just as well be surprised by the thunder of Zen silence or the amazing grace of Pure Land.

WHALEN LAI

See also Buddhism: Overview; Chan/Zen; Kōan; Master and Pupil: Buddhist Perspectives; Monasticism, Definitions of: Buddhist Perspectives; Novices, Theravādin Rituals for; Origins: Comparative Perspectives; Rules, Buddhist (Vinaya): Historical; Saichō; Saṅgha; Visual Arts, Buddhist: Tibet

**Further Reading**

Hui-chiao, Shih, *Biographies des moines éminents de Houei-kiao: Kao seng tchouan*, edited by Robert Shih, Louvain: Institut Orientaliste, bibliothèque l'Université, 1968

Lai, Whalen, "The Three Jewels in China," in *Buddhist Spirituality: Indian, Southeast Asian, Tibetan, and Early Chinese*, edited by Takeuchi Yoshinori, New York: Crossroad, 1993

Lai, Whalen, "Legends of Births and the Later Pure Land Tradition," in *The Pure Land Tradition: History and Development*, edited by James Foard, Michael Solomon, and Richard K. Payne, Berkeley: Regents of the University of California, 1996

McRae, John, *The Northern School and the Formation of Early Ch'an Buddhism*, Honolulu: University of Hawaii Press, 1986

Troeltsch, Ernst, *The Social Teaching of the Christian Churches*, New York: Macmillan, and London: Allen and Unwin, 1931

# Initiation: Christian Perspectives

## Components

The process of initiation or entry into a monastic community or religious congregation typically consists of four stages:

1. an initial process of probation or discernment before the candidate is admitted into the community
2. a simple ceremony of admission into community life
3. a period of training and further discernment within the community, commonly called a novitiate
4. a rite of profession when the candidate formally declares his or her intention to adopt the monastic life, is accepted by the community, and makes a public declaration of the monastic vows

Over the years this transition from secular life has become more differentiated, partly through caution as monastic communities seek to avoid unsuitable candidates and partly through the realization that individuals need more time to avoid hasty or immature decisions.

## Initial Period of Probation

Soon after beginning to dwell as hermits in the Egyptian desert, Paul, Antony (c. 251–356), and their companions began to attract disciples. Many, inspired by their example, sought to live close to them, following the eremitic life but with no formal organization and thus no explicit process of initiation. In fact such disciples were frequently not welcomed as they disturbed the solitude of the early hermits, some of whom sought to escape their presence by retreating into even greater solitude. However, as awareness arose that a new religious movement had begun, the selection and training of new disciples came to be seen as part of ensuring a continuing movement. In addition as soon as hermits began to live in monastic communities, the process by which persons joined the community needed to be clarified and regulated.

*Eligibility*: An early problem arose concerning those who sought to enter a monastic community from frivolous, transient, or unworthy motives. These were often impelled by momentary enthusiasm and quickly lost their desire to remain. Such entrants served only to disturb the more committed monks and needed to be dissuaded. Similarly, for obvious reasons, heretics and serious criminals were not welcome. Others were seen as not being free to make the choice of a religious life. Slaves and serfs were judged to be under the control of others, whereas those in public service or the army had commitments from which they could not be released. This same reason prevented the admission of married persons without the agreement of their spouses. Finally, young boys were excluded because of their lack of maturity and because, as minors, they were still subject to their parents. Thus, very quickly, as the early religious communities elaborated their organization and rules, a process of careful selection of new members emerged.

*Preliminary testing*: In order to exclude those who sought entrance from frivolous or transient motives, the early monastic communities tended to make the process of admission difficult and humbling so that entrants had to exhibit some perseverance before being accepted. As Benedict wrote in his Rule, "To him that newly cometh to change his life, let not an easy entrance be granted."

John Cassian (c. 360–after 430) records that, in the Egyptian monasteries, applicants were forced to lie on the ground outside the gates for ten days or more while monks from the community strove to dissuade them by shouting insults. During this period the applicant was given the psalms and the liturgy to be learnt. By enduring this treatment an applicant demonstrated patience and humility. Only after this probation was satisfactorily completed was an applicant accepted into the monastery.

Benedict, in his Rule, modified this somewhat harsh approach. He wrote, "If he that cometh persevere in knocking, and after four or five days is seen patiently to endure the wrongs done him and the difficulties made about his coming in, and to persist in his petition, let entrance him be granted him." The newly accepted applicant was then lodged in the guest house for a few days until he could begin his year of probation. In later centuries religious orders adopted a more humane approach, and St. Francis (1181/82–1226), in his first Rule, states that "postulants are to be received kindly."

In the 20th century religious orders have tended to apply more sophisticated selection procedures. Most candidates are expected to have a period of contact with the order or congregation of one to two years while they get to know the order and after which the candidate makes a formal application to be accepted. At this point most applicants are routinely expected to undergo some professional assessments, usually a medical and a psychological examination, followed by a formal interview by the order itself. Modern religious orders are especially concerned with psychological suitability of applicants in order to be sure that candidates possess the necessary personality and other qualities to endure the demands of the religious vocation. Particular care is taken to identify candidates who have a history of mental illness or instability. Considerable research has been done in recent years on the psychological characteristics of those seeking to enter religious life and on the effectiveness of selection procedures.

Throughout the centuries there have always been reasons for religious communities to ease their admission procedures. In the early years of a new monastic movement, there appears to be a need to make entry easier in order to accommodate the large numbers seeking entrance; at other times it is anxiety aroused by a diminishing number of vocations that leads a community or congregation to accept applicants who would otherwise have been rejected. Cluny suffered a decline in the 11th century when they began to accept large numbers without adequate probation or training. In some cases a probation of only a few hours was demanded. For the converse reason, following the Black Death, many religious orders lowered their standards in order to replenish the numbers in their communities. In England, for example, there are numerous instances in the 14th and 15th centuries of monasteries accepting boys below the minimum age of 14 years. In the late 20th century, the diminishing number of vocations has frequently tempted religious communities to take candidates who, in more flourishing times, would have been rejected.

### Admission to Community Life

The moment of formal entrance to a religious community is normally marked by a religious ceremony in which the candidate presents himself before the community and publicly asks to be accepted. Commonly the candidate lies prostrate on the ground while making this request to indicate humility. The religious superior responds on behalf of the community, explaining the demands of the monastic life to ensure that the candidate understands what he is undertaking and asking the candidate whether he is willing to accept these.

Traditionally, once the candidate had formally declared his intention before the whole community, his adoption of the monastic life was sealed by removal of his secular clothes and his exchanging them for a religious habit. This change of clothing symbolized leaving off of the ways of the world and adopting a new lifestyle. In recent years many orders have delayed the adoption of the religious habit until the candidate makes his or her profession of the vows after the novitiate.

As the theology of religious life developed, other symbolic aspects were stressed. For women the image of religious life as a mystical marriage with Christ began to be emphasized. Women candidates were dressed as brides during the entrance ceremony to signify that they were being "married" to Christ until, at the conclusion, the white dresses were replaced by religious habits. Following the Second Vatican Council (1962–1965), this aspect has been discontinued in Roman Catholic orders. Using the same imagery, in some male and female orders candidates are given a wedding ring to symbolize the dedication of themselves to God.

### Postulancy and Novitiate

In the early centuries it was quickly appreciated that new entrants needed a period of instruction in how to live the monastic life and that, during this period, a further process of discernment would take place. In Pachomius' monasteries this period of probation within the community lasted for three years before a candidate was finally accepted as a full-fledged monk. In Benedict's Rule the period of probation was reduced to one year, which became a norm for many centuries. At three moments during the year, Benedict instructed that the Rule should be read to the novice and he should be asked whether he wished to leave. Finally, at the end of the year, at the third reading of the Rule, the novice was told that from that day forward he would be bound by the Rule for life.

In many orders the religious habit of the new novice differed in some way from that of the professed religious to signify that he or she was still under probation. For religious sisters it was common for postulants to wear a simple black dress. On entry to the formal novitiate, this dress was exchanged for a religious habit but with a white veil instead of the black worn by professed religious. The black veil was adopted only after profession. In recent years many religious orders have decided that novices shall continue to wear secular dress until profession.

During the novitiate an experienced member of the community is normally designated as novice master or mistress with the responsibility for training the novices. Traditionally there has been a certain amount of separation of the novices from the other members of the community. This served to create an atmosphere of quiet and reflection and to preserve novices from the influence of any relaxation of the monastic ideals on the part of the older members of the community. During the novitiate there is normally no academic study, but rather the focus is on learning the daily routine of religious life, the rule and constitutions of the congregation, the performance of the liturgy, and an introduction to the practice of prayer and meditation.

*Profession*

Traditionally, following the pattern set by Benedict, after satisfactory completion of one year in the novitiate, the individual formally presents himself before the community to ask to be accepted as a full member. After a preliminary interrogation and possibly a declaration that the novitiate has been satisfactorily completed, the novice places himself before the superior and requests permission to make profession of the monastic vows. In the Benedictine tradition these vows are of stability, conversion of life, and obedience, whereas most other orders take the better-known and more common vows of poverty, chastity, and obedience. Once these have been professed and a written copy of them has been signed by the novice, he or she is clothed in the full habit of the professed religious. For religious communities that do not wear a distinctive habit, this clothing is usually replaced by the wearing of some symbol – a badge, medal, or wedding ring – that indicates the person's acceptance as a fully professed member of the religious community.

The shape and pattern of this public profession of vows varies from one religious institute to another. In the Iona Community, which follows the Protestant tradition, the ceremony whereby an associate member becomes a full member of community is called a "hallowing." The individual, moreover, makes an annual statement of his intention to remain with the community.

Originally the vows professed after the novitiate were considered final and binding for the rest of the individual's life. As expressed in the Benedictine Rule, the novice knows "that he is now bound by the law of the Rule, so that from this day forward, he cannot depart from the Monastery, nor shake off from his neck the yoke of the Rule." During the medieval period the wearing of the habit was considered a public sign of the intention to be a religious, and if it was worn for a whole year, the individual was considered a full religious even though no public profession had taken place.

Following the Council of Trent (1545–1563), the period of probation has been extended by delaying the taking of solemn or final vows. After the novitiate candidates normally make vows that are renewed after three years (or every year). Only after a period of three to six years is the candidate allowed to make final profession for life. In many of the newer religious orders, lifetime vows are not taken, and the members renew their vows each year.

RICHARD COPSEY, O.CARM.

*See also* Benedict of Nursia, St.; Cassian, John; Church Councils, Recent Catholic; Orders (Religious), Origin of; Regulations: Christian Perspectives; Seasons, Liturgical: Western Christian; Women's Monasteries: Western Christian

**Further Reading**

Albert, Saint, Patriarch of Jerusalem, *The Rule of Saint Albert*, edited and translated by Bebe Edwards, Boars Hill: Carmelite Fathers, 1966 (*http://www.carmelnet.org*)

Basil, Saint, Bishop of Caesarea, *The Ascetic Works of Saint Basil* (Translation of Christian Literature. Series 1: Greek Texts), translated by W.K.L. Clarke, New York: Macmillan, and London: Society for Promoting Christian Knowledge, 1925

*Code of Canon Law*, Book 2, Part 3, Section 1, Title 2, Chapter 3, Washington, D.C.: Canon Law Society of America, 1983 (*http://www.prairienet.org/nrpcatholic/cicmenu.html*)

Francis, of Assisi, Saint, *Francis and Clare: The Complete Works* (Classics of Western Spirituality), translated by Regis J. Armstrong and Ignatius C. Brady, New York: Paulist Press, and London: SPCK, 1982 (*http://www.listserv.american.edu/catholic/franciscan/rules/*)

Vogüé, Adalbert de, editor, *The Rule of Saint Benedict, a Doctrinal and Spiritual Commentary* (Cistercian Studies Series, number 54), Kalamazoo, Michigan: Cistercian Publications, 1983 (*http://www.osb.org*)

# Intercession for the Dead, Buddhist

In all Buddhist countries Buddhist monks are invited to help "make merits" during lay funerals. This remains a major source of income everywhere. However, originally in India, where samsara was a common belief after the country's axial age, it is believed that a person dies, only to be reborn in a new life. Because he or she will be held responsible for his or her actions anew, there is no reason for the dead to require intercession. Any intercession would have to be limited to the interim between death and rebirth; and, because Hindus cremate the dead or discard the corpse in water, there are no remains, no enshrinement, no lasting ancestral worship, and no continual feeding of the dead. However, there is a holdover rite from early Vedic times, the *śraddhā*, which involves rolling rice balls to create a spiritual body for the departed, even though, logically speaking, this practice is at odds with Upaniṣadic belief in saṃsāra. However, that is not an issue for Buddhism, as the Buddha discontinued that brahmanic rite. He put nothing in its place.

Yet clearly his final words – "Shed no tear" and "Be a light unto yourself" – were not enough to satisfy the laymen who, at the death of a family member, wanted tearfully to "do something" for the beloved dead. What happened eventually is that a Buddhist family would call in monks instead of the brahmins and feed them instead of the Hindu priests, and the monks in return would help the family "make merit." Theravāda would not speak of "merit transference," for that is a Mahāyāna rewriting of the rule that karma, good or bad, is individual and merits cannot be transferred. Theravāda calls intercession for the dead part of the donation piety of "giving," namely, sharing merit and rejoicing in sharing. Usually the ritual lasts seven days. The full interim of 49 days between rebirths is observed in Tibet. During Bardo the dead person receives the gnosis from the *Book of the Dead*, so as to accomplish a safe passage to a better rebirth or even liberation itself.

Strictly speaking, intercession as a legal move presumes some kind of judgment. Nomads of Buddhist central Asia had no permanent burials and no regular ancestral worship, nor had they experience with law courts. However, Confucian China had emphasized ancestral worship and maintained a pre-Buddhist belief in "earth prisons" (hells) overseen by magistrates in an underground bureaucracy similar to the one on earth (and in heaven). Burdened by rites to feed the dead, China also had a more heightened fear that underfed ancestors and unmourned dead might become "hungry ghosts." Thus, by the sixth century A.D. at the Ghost Festival (the Chinese Halloween), Buddhists emulated the legend of Mu-lien (Mogallāna). This disciple of the Buddha had saved his mother from hell. During her life she had refused mendicants food and had become a hungry ghost – a *preta* with a large stomach and a tiny neck whose insatiable appetite cannot be quenched because any food put into her mouth turned instantly into burning coal. The Ghost Festival sponsors generous feeding of monks, beggars, wandering goblins, and all those dead who are released from hell on that 15th night of the seventh moon. Filial sons sponsored such feasts for their ancestors' sake. By the Ming dynasty (1368–1644), most monks had become specialists in the Yogācāra rite for "opening up the burning mouth," and the staging of the "Water and Land

A ceremony of prayers for the dead held one year after the death of a relative.
Photo courtesy of David Moore

Assembly" – a Buddhist ritual for those who had died un-mourned at sea and on land – became a major undertaking and the grandest of ceremonies.

Like the cult of purgatory in the Catholic West, the Chinese cult helps to underwrite a cosmic community between saints (who are uncommon and undead) and the common dead. The common, or shared, dead now support the living as much as the living support the dead. That project went contrary to the neo-Confucianism of the Song period (960–1279). The latter cam-paigned to return China to the classical norm of mourning only for one's own dead. That resulted in Ming cities permitting many urban poor to die unclaimed, unmourned, and unburied, and the city could not cremate them because the neo-Confucian state viewed cremation as a "barbaric" custom. These rotting bodies of the polluted dead ended up in beggars' graves next to the tem-ple of the city god. Uncared for and unfed, they returned as hun-gry ghosts, vengeful spirits, and lost souls, on both land and sea, to haunt the conscience of the living. They required all those Bud-dhist rituals that the neo-Confucians thought to supplant.

However, matters grew worse. By late dynastic China the "earth prisons" were no longer anything like Buddhist purgato-ries, that is, places for working off one's bad karma. They had become places of permanent incarceration and full-scale infer-nos. Intercession by monks ceased in the courts of the much more secular Ten Kings of Hell; prayer lost out to the Chinese version of "indulgences," that is, paper money, paper gold, and paper silver, offered to bribe the runners and oil the machinery of (in)justice down under. As an alternative, just as Christ once harrowed hell, a popular and dramatic remedy is to have figures such as Mu-lien, the Buddha, Avalokiteśvara, Kṣitagarbha, or Daoist counterparts storm the citadels of hell to get poor souls released. Korea inherited that cult of the Ten Kings after her neo-Confucians had followed China and returned Korea to a society segmented by clear, blood lineages.

Japan never had that classical Confucian norm to return to, as it had always accepted nonkin heirs and cared for nonkin dead. Moreover Japan did not give up the cremation fire that pu-rifies the polluted dead. After the Kamakura period (1185–1333), devotees of the Pure Land got to go straight thither with-out all that embattled detour through hell. Japan grants her dead a rather smooth passage into becoming *kami* (gods) *hotoke* (buddha) after only a year. Registered since the Tokugawa at local *bodaiji* (temples), all Japanese are guaranteed family plots for their cremated remains. At the price of a proper donation, the dead are given a postmortem precept name previously re-served for monks. All graves are marked with a *sutoba* (stūpa reliquary) as if the common dead had also left behind "uncom-mon" relics. In short Japan knew sanctified common dead, but not polluted, familial dead. Secular, family names do not even appear on gravestones. Enjoying a monopoly of funeral services, Japanese Buddhists also evolved a lengthy series of memorial ceremonies, making Japan in some ways the most Buddhist of Far Eastern cultures.

WHALEN LAI

*See also* Asia, Central; China; Death: Buddhist Perspectives; Death Rituals, Buddhist; Deities, Buddhist; Japan; Liturgy: Bud-dhist; Tibetan Lineages

**Further Reading**

Ariès, Phillippe, *The Hours of Our Death*, New York: Knopf, and London: Allen and Unwin, 1981

Lai, Whalen, "Rethinking the Chinese Family: Wandering Ghosts and Eternal Parents," in *The Ideal in the World's Religions*, edited by Robert Carter and Sheldon Isenberg, St. Paul, Minnesota: Paragon House, 1997

McDermott, James, "Is There Group Karma in Theravāda Buddhism?" *Numen* 23 (1976)

Schmitt, Jean-Claude, *Ghosts in the Middle Ages: The Living and the Dead in Medieval Society*, translated by Teresa Lavender Fagan, Chicago: University of Chicago Press, 1998

Teiser, Steven, *The Ghost Festival in Medieval China*, Princeton, New Jersey: Princeton University Press, 1988

Teiser, Steven, *The Scripture of the Ten Kings and the Making of Purgatory in Medieval Chinese Buddhism*, Honolulu: University of Hawaii Press, 1994

Williams, Paul, *Mahāyāna Buddhism: The Doctrinal Foundations*, London and New York: Routledge, 1989

# Intermonastic Dialogue. *See* Dialogue, Intermonastic

# Internet, Buddhist and Christian

*The Internet Matrix*

The Internet came of age during the final decade of the 20th cen-tury. Conceived initially as a military command system and then as an academic computing network, it eventually became a pop-ular general-purpose tool for a number of everyday operations. These include electronic transactions (e-commerce, on-line data input, telecommuting, and entertainment), interpersonal com-munication, information storage, information finding, and long-distance information access. Within less than 30 years, its phenomenal growth (up to 90 percent per year) transformed the original set of four networked computers (in December 1969) into the massive network of networks linking 43.2 million machines (in December 1998) and over 160 million people worldwide.

As a device for finding and accessing remotely stored data and as a medium for worldwide publication of documents, the Internet is a novel and revolutionary tool. It drastically redefines the relationships, some of them centuries old, formed between people (both as individuals and as groups) and information. The speed, energy, ease, and miniscule cost with which text, graphic, and acoustic information can be now created, copied, collated, formatted, and presented for the use by the global audience are unparalleled. Thus, it is likely that the Internet's long-term effect on the organization of human knowledge and on patterns of social interaction will be as powerful as the earlier and cumulative effects of writing (c. 3500 B.C.), printing (China and Korea in the 11th century and Germany in the mid–15th century), wired and wireless communications, photography, sound recording, and cinematography (mid– to late 19th century).

On-line catalogs in the Library of Congress (www.loc.gov) reveal, among 117 million records, the bibliographical details of some 3,050 individual publications on the specialist topic of Christian and Buddhist monasticism. Assuming an average of 200 pages per publication, the library's catalogs talk about a collection comprising some 610,000 pages, or 2.6 gigabytes of text. In contrast, in November 1998 the Internet provided constant and direct access to full contents of some 6.4 gigabytes of monasticism-related information. This consisted of 640,000 unique pages concerned with monastic people and institutions (among the then total 420 million pages on the Web). According to the AltaVista search engine (www.altavista.com), about 115,000 (18 percent) of these pages dealt with Buddhist monasticism, whereas the remaining 525,000 or (82 percent of the sample) dealt with Christian monasticism.

Present-day libraries store, catalog, and lend to approved readers data in the form of physical objects (i.e., books and periodicals). Such information is usually of high quality but is slow moving, largely uncopyable, and very difficult to search. Electronic documents handled over the Internet are easy to search, cross-reference, and duplicate. Moreover, digital documents and images are largely freely available to anyone, anytime and anyplace, and often within seconds. However, their major drawback is their disappointingly low quality. Most of the current on-line data are notoriously unreliable and the organization and documentation poor. Ominously, the criteria of truthfulness, objectivity, factual evidence, and freedom from errors of omission and commission are still not key issues on the Internet. Instead, the ease with which information can be tracked down and copied, connection speeds, and the monetary cost of data and their novelty and entertainment value seem to be the prime concerns.

Throughout this article, data and trends, unless marked otherwise, refer to the situation on the Internet in late 1998. Most of the observations refer to Web-based resources constructed in European languages. The term *monastery* is applied to both male and female houses. This article deals only with developments involving official monastic organizations. Thus, no attempt is made to discuss the parallel networked universe of lay groups that are inspired by the contemplative traditions of either of the two religions. Finally, cited here are mainly those on-line projects that seem most likely to continue to operate in the next five to ten years.

## Degrees of On-Line Monastic Presence

Digital networked documents that pertain to Buddhist and Christian monasticism form two large and distinct groups: mate-

rials created within and materials created without the context of monastic life. The first group consists of about 40 percent Buddhist and 47 percent Christian Web pages. These documents have been created by the monks and nuns themselves to introduce and describe their communities, to communicate and interlink with one another, and to contact and instruct unspecified but potentially numerous and interested members of the general public.

Monasteries, in the course of their discovery and colonization of the Internet, seem to go through the following sequence of phases:

1. *Isolation.* Contacts with the world are accomplished through travel, visits, and exchange of written or printed materials.

2. *Traditional technology.* Phones, faxes, and radio transmitters are used. (For example, in 1998 the Meteora group of monasteries in Thessaly, Greece, appeared to have phones but no presence on the Internet.) Electronic files are produced on stand-alone computers, and initial experiments with e-mail are conducted.

3. *Incipient networking.* E-mail is used regularly, but the addresses are cryptic (e.g., jxm306@ . . .). The first personal and corporate home pages are established on servers run by nearby friendly academic, nongovernmental, and commercial organizations. The sites are monolingual. Monasteries initially place their files within impromptu, haphazardly labeled subdirectories (e.g., the Russian Orthodox Monastery in Colorado uses ra.nilenet.com/~russmonk). Subsequently, the more meaningfully labeled directories are used (e.g., the Hosshin-ji Zen Monastery in Fushihara, Japan, uses www.semui.co.jp/hosshinji, and the Abhayagiri Forest Monastery in California uses www.dharmanet.org/Abhayagiri). Resources are developed by in-house boffins and maintained on an ad hoc basis.

4. *Regular networking.* E-mail addresses assume legible formats (e.g., john.martin@ . . .). The number and variety of Web documents grow steadily. Complicated file structures, ornamental graphics, video files, animations, sound effects, and Java scripts are used and abused. Interactive input pages, on-line databases, localized search engines, and "cyberstores" become common. Sites continue to be monolingual. Monasteries register dedicated, often eponymous domain names. For example, the Dharma Drum Monastery in Ching Shan, Taiwan, uses www.ddm.org.tw; the Chi Lin Nunnery in Hong Kong uses www.chilinnunnery.org.hk; the Namgyal Monastery (i.e., H.H. Dalai Lama's personal one) in Dharamsala, India, uses www.namgyal.org; the Kopan Monastery in Kathmandu, Nepal, uses www.kopan-monastery.com; the St. Anthony Coptic Orthodox Monastery in California uses www.samn.com; the Hermitage of the Exaltation of the Holy Cross (Russian Orthodox) in St. Louis, Missouri, uses holycross-hermitage.com; and Tyniec (Benedictine) Abbey in Kraków, Poland, uses www.tyniec.mm.com.pl. Regularly maintained resources are developed by friendly volunteers and commercial firms.

5. *Expert networking.* Digital maturity is reached. E-mail addresses are used to distinguish persons (e.g., john.martin@ . . .)

and functions (e.g., porter@ . . . , abbot@ . . . , scriptorium@ . . . , or it-support@ . . .). On-line documents become shorter and greatly simplified. Their universal legibility and minimal transmission times start being appreciated. Documents are provided in more than one language. The more ornamental pages are also available in the plain-text formats. Information services are used for systematic and thoughtful interaction with on-line visitors. Monasteries are able manage their own Internet connectivity. In-house information technology (IT) teams are established. Electronic scriptoria explore the best methods for the creation of e-texts and strategies for effective hypertext publishing. Monasteries organize Internet workshops and training courses. They provide design and maintenance of information systems and high-accuracy data conversion services both to other monasteries and to the outside world. Key expert centers emerge (e.g., the Monastery of Christ in the Desert in New Mexico at www.christdesert.org and the College of St. Benedict and St. John's University in Minnesota at www.csbsju.edu).

The exact timing and speed with which an organization will move from one technological phase to another are dictated by the interplay of many concurrent factors. Internal factors involve the presence of the in-house IT savvy, financial resources, and an openness to and interest in the world. The internal dynamics of the monastic group itself also play a role. The essential external factors include the availability of a reliable supply of electricity (from a grid, generator, or solar panels), an inexpensive yet sturdy telephone network, the presence of Internet connectivity providers in the country, and the absence of an adverse political climate or administrative regulations.

Clearly, the reasons for which three, say, Buddhist monasteries, each located in a different country (e.g., Scotland, India, and Tibet), might or might not have an on-line presence are bound to be different in each case.

### The Structure of a Monastic Web Site

Corporate monastic Web pages belonging to a given faith are always situated within the context of concentrically nested and interdependent information fields. These are (1) the world of paper and other nondigital, nonnetworked information; (2) the Internet as a whole; (3) the Web-based cyberspace; (4) the whole of the Buddhist (Christian) cyberspace; (5) the monastic Buddhist (Christian) cyberspace; (6) the cyberspace of a given monastic lineage/order; and (7) a Web site belonging to a given community. The Buddhist and Christian parts of the monastic Internet exist in almost complete isolation from each other. Only very recently did the Monastic Interreligious Dialogue (MID; www.osb.org/osb/intl/mid), a task group established in 1978, begin the on-line charting and documentation of emerging conversations, encounters, and mutual exchanges between monastics of different religions.

On the whole, monastic information systems, regardless of their denomination or religion, have very similar architectures. About 12 component elements are organized in roughly the same manner.

The advertised entry point to the monastic corporate site is through a (1) carefully designed home page. The page has a simple and easy to remember address. For example, the Shasta Abbey (Order of Buddhist Contemplatives) Monastery in California uses www.oncon.org. The home page is almost always adorned with an impressive logo. The self-activating sound files (with suitable chants or music) and animated images also tend to be provided. Such electronic gadgetry commonly is excessive and badly integrated so that it overloads and crashes visitors' browsers.

The home page leads to a fivefold group of factual documents: (2) the community's objectives and brief history; (3) a page with postal and e-mail addresses, phone and fax numbers, and instructions on how to reach the place by train, bus, or car; (4) schedules of regular internal activities; (5) details of events, training courses, and spiritual retreats that are open to public; and (6) information on schools or colleges that the monastery or convent might operate and for which separate sets of factual pages are developed (e.g., www.drba.org for the Dharma Realm Buddhist Association in California and www.shc.ac.th for the Sacred Heart Convent School in Bangkok, Thailand).

Next come links from the home page to documents that are aimed at the education and involvement of electronic visitors. These links offer a weary cyber traveler a modicum of electronic hospitality. Buddhist sites tend to include short but illustrated (7) biographies of the founders or main teachers and (8) pages containing collections of his or her Dharma talks. However, Christian sites that tend to include the biographical details of the monastery's current members are not common. Instead, information is provided about the order's founders, and a link is given to an external site, usually an academic one (see the following section on lay resources), with a collection of e-texts of the founder's key religious writings.

In both traditions an important part is played by (9) electronic outreach. Christian sites publish Web pages with general spiritual advice and counsel and supplement them with analyses of Christian monastic ideals. These are frequently followed by details of vocational opportunities and formative programs. Additionally, a page specializing in computer-mediated prayers might be provided. For example, the Monks of Adoration (St. Augustine) in Massachusetts (www.monksofadoration.org) offer, through the RealAudio narrowcasting software, an on-line edition of Chanted Rosary and a live Webcam filming their chapel. Other monasteries seem to favor less flamboyant contacts. For example, since 1995 Zen Mountain Monastery in New York State (www.zen-mtn.org) runs a "Cybermonk" service "where a senior monastic is available through e-mail (cybermonk@zen-mtn.org) to answer your Dharma questions." Similarly, the Order of St. Benedict in Collegeville, Minnesota (www.osb.org/osb, established in April 1995), invites electronic visitors to "send or leave a message in the 'Pilgrims' Parlor' or join the discussion about *lectio divina* at the 'Tabula' (i.e. local electronic message board)."

Well-established Buddhist and Christian monastic Websites might run (10) electronic shops that are a part of the monastery's fund-raising programs. Cyberstores sell mainly inspirational books and CDs with religious music. Frequently, the book and CD sales are accomplished with the aid of such on-line behemoths as Amazon.com and Barnes & Noble, which pay their monastic affiliates a 5 to 15 percent commission on each purchase. In addition, Buddhist on-line shops sell altar supplies, meditation cushions, statues of the Buddhas, and refrigerator magnets. On the other hand, their Christian counterparts tend to specialize in gourmet foodstuffs and "monastery blend" coffee and teas. Orders and credit card payments can be submitted by fax or e-mail from anywhere in the world. Undoubtedly because of the Internet, even the most isolated monastic community can have the same access and the same exposure to the world as its counterparts from densely populated metropolises.

Once the monastery's use of the Internet has matured, it is likely that it will place on-line some of its (11) newsletters and magazines. A directory of Benedictine electronic resources, maintained by the Sacred Heart Monastery in Richardton, North Dakota (www.rc.net/bismarck/shm), lists 31 on-line journals and newsletters produced by the houses in the United States. In contrast, on-line Buddhist monastic journals are less common. A catalog of electronic serials maintained by the Buddhist Studies WWW Virtual Library (www.ciolek.com/WWWVL-Buddhism.html) points to the existence of about 50 Buddhist on-line periodicals, but only ten of them are produced within the monastic context.

The final element of a monastic Web site is a (12) directory of links to related Internet resources. Christian sites, quite wisely, tend to abstain from individual cataloging efforts. Instead, they make a link to directories provided by their parent organizations. For example, the Catholic Information Center on Internet (www.catholic.net) and the Anglicans Online (www.anglican.org) manage comprehensive lists of their religious orders that have a presence on the Internet. The headquarters of the Cistercian Order of the Strict (Trappist) Observance (www.ocistso.org) maintains an authoritative directory of its orders' Internet addresses. Similar services are centrally supplied by the regional headquarters of the Orders of St. Benedict (www.osb.org/osb), Dominicans (www-oslo.op.org), Carmelites (www.carmelnet.org), Franciscans (www.ofm.org), and the (Hospitallers) Order of Malta (198.62.75.1). Up-to-date and consolidated lists of the on-line Orthodox monasteries (www.nettinker.com/monasteries/monline.htm) also exist. Finally, incipient and thus somewhat chaotic registers are kept by the Coptic Society of St. Shenouda the Archimandrite (www.stshenouda.com).

For the Buddhist Internet such monastic-run central facilities have not yet evolved. With the exception of the services of the Chogye Order in Korea (www.buddhism.or.kr) or the single-handed efforts of a Theravādin monk Ven. Pannyavaro, who maintains BuddhaNet in Sydney, Australia (www.buddhanet.net), each Buddhist site keeps its own catalog of monastic resources. By doing so, each site by and large replicates the work already done by other Buddhist sites. Thus, the need for author-

itative and up-to-date central catalogs are filled by the non-monastic initiatives, such as DharmaNet's (www.dharmanet.org) directories of U.S. and overseas lay and monastic Dharma centers and the register maintained at the International Research Institute for Zen Buddhism in Kyoto, Japan (www.iijnet.or.jp/iriz/irizhtml/centers/country.htm).

*Monastic Attitudes toward the Internet*

Although e-mail has been used by religious organizations since the early 1980s, it is only from late 1993 onward (since the advent of the Web) that the Internet became a factor significantly affecting the life and operations of all communities in all parts of the world. Interestingly, despite the emergence of many thousands of Buddhist monastic information systems, these do not seem to have a clearly stated policy regarding the use of the Internet as such. In addition, no public discussion has taken place regarding the nature and range of on-line interactions between various monastic groups. Like the Internet itself, Buddhist cyberspace continues to be polycentric, individualistic, unconscious, and uncoordinated. However, a very different strategy has begun to evolve among the Roman Catholic orders.

In February 1997 the Benedictine Internet Commission (BIC) (www.osb.org/osb/bic) was formed to consider how rapidly developing technology can best be used to extend the Benedictine way of life and make it accessible to people throughout the world. The 21-person expert team of monks and nuns from the United States, England, and Germany commenced the task by reviewing, through meetings and e-mail exchanges, the pros and cons of the monastic Internet. The arguments in favor of the Internet are extension of hospitality, connectivity, information exchange, vocation outreach, oblate information, resource sharing, prayers, visibility, and formation. The negative aspects were also identified: addiction to browsing and e-mail, intrusiveness, cost, lack of expertise and equipment, untrustworthy or low-quality information, and the loss of the subtleties of face-to-face communication. Members of the BIC have also organized a "Monasticism and Technology" forum, a series of training seminars, and a "Monastic WebWeaver's Retreat."

The BIC's final report, accepted in October 1998 by the Presidents of the OSB Federation, emphasized the need for "being prudent stewards of this new tool of the monastery." The report identified five areas of special importance to the monastic houses today: (1) the need to expand their monastic digital and network literacy; (2) the opportunity to interconnect monasteries; (3) the application of technology to enhance and expand the scope of monasteries' ministries and hospitality, including electronic hospitality; (4) the promotion of global awareness among monasteries, especially those in developing countries and isolated areas; and (5) the emergence of new technologies and new issues in monastic formation. The report made 16 specific recommendations that advocated the widespread, systematic, informed, thoughtful, ethical, productive, creative, and community-orientated (i.e., cooperative) application of the Internet to monastic purposes. The recommendations were made so that, to quote the report's words, "we are not directed by the tools themselves, become addicted to their use, or use them inappropriately. We must be on guard not to allow their use to become a divisive force in our communities or make us elitist, dividing us from those without the same access" (Benedictine Internet Commission, 1998).

The BIC was subsequently transformed into a permanent section of the American Benedictine Academy (www.osb.org/osb/acad/aba) and was charged with providing technical advice and help to interested abbots and prioresses. The Benedictines' pioneering work undoubtedly will greatly inform any policy discussions yet to be undertaken by other orders.

*Lay Resources with Information about Monasticism*
In addition to the on-line resources developed by the monastics themselves, 60 percent of related Buddhist and 53 percent of Christian documents have been built by lay users of the Internet. Nonmonastic materials form three subgroups: (1) details of publications that can be purchased on- and off-line from academic and commercial booksellers (5 percent of Buddhist and 4 percent of Christian resources fall into this category); (2) popular information resources, such as news and promotions of tourist attractions (Buddhism 45 percent, Christianity 27 percent); and (3) materials associated with the scholarly endeavors of research institutes and universities (Buddhism 10 percent, Christianity 22 percent).

The contributions of university presses, publishers, and booksellers are mainly in the form of public access on-line catalogs and databases of relevant books. Such digital resources amply supplement catalogs issued by monastic publishers (e.g., St. Austin Press at www.saintaustin.org and Franciscan Printing Press at fpp@p-ol.com).

On-line news is distributed daily by numerous national and local electronic newspapers. The topics range from sensational headlines, such as "The Case of the Nefarious Nuns," "Romanian Police Beat Nuns at 1997 Christmas Mass," and "Vietnam's Monks Return to Forefront of Protests," to more inspirational stories, such as "Buddhist Nuns Dedicate New Nunnery," "Jewish-Christian Relations: Jewish 'Convent Children' Thank Their Saviours," and "Sister Scholastica Celebrates Her 100th Birthday."

Ample tourist information is mounted on-line by tour operators, government culture-promotion agencies, and large numbers of nostalgic travelers. About 25 percent of all on-line photographs and texts belonging to this category advertise the monastic complexes of Greece. The monasteries of Tibet, Russia, and Ireland claim another 25 percent of the promotions. The next 25 percent of those amateurish and semiprofessional travel e-leaflets are dedicated to monasteries in the United States, England, Italy, Nepal, and Mexico. The remaining percentage of the on-line "tourism, heritage and culture" materials covers monastic architecture and art from other parts of the world.

The most dependable lay resources are those created and maintained within academic contexts. Such materials provide critical and scholarly accounts and analyses of the history, organization, and significance of the monastic institutions of both faiths. A prominent role in these is played by specialist electronic agoras and discussion groups that are managed through numerous mailing list servers belonging to universities and occasionally commercial organizations. In late 1998, among some 137,000 electronic agoras worldwide, nine lists dealt with Christian monasticism and four with Buddhism.

Among the Christian lists, only one, OSB-L@vm.marist.edu (Benedictine Order), is dedicated to monastic subscribers. Other lists, such as OP-L@op.org (Dominican laity, established in August 1994, 50 subscribers) and ASSISI-L@american.edu (Franciscan Order, date of establishment unknown, 237 subscribers), although designed for the monastics, are open to lay participants as well. This trend is repeated by SISTER-L@listserv.syr.edu (history and concerns of Catholic women religious, date of establishment unknown, 1,126 subscribers) and ORTHODOX@listserv.indiana.edu (Orthodox Christianity, established in the autumn of 1989, 1,180 subscribers). A highly specialized service is provided by the electronic discussion group FORMER-NUNS@onelist.com (needs and interests of former members of women's religious communities, established in March 1998, 45 subscribers). This is a forum only for women from Catholic and other backgrounds. Finally, nuggets of useful information can be found on SPIRITUS@maelstrom.stjohns.edu (Christian contemplative tradition, established in March 1997, 130 subscribers) and MARONITE@onelist.com (Maronite Christianity, established in June 1998, eight subscribers).

Only one of the existing Buddhist lists seems to specialize in monastic topics: UPASIKA@lists.best.com (lay practitioners associated with the Theravādin "Forest Sangha" monasteries, established in February 1997, 70 subscribers). Other lists are more general and focus either on Buddhism as a whole (e.g., BUDDHA-L@ulkyvm.louisville.edu, Buddhist academic list, established in October 1991, 710 subscribers) or on the activities of one of its major schools (DHAMMA-LIST@quantrum.com.my, Theravāda Buddhism, and ZENBUDDHISM@vivanewmexico.com, Ch'an/Zen academic list, established in August 1993, 295 subscribers).

In addition to mailing lists are on-line research articles, book reviews, and rare specialist journals, for example, *Magistra: A Journal of Women's Spirituality in History*, established in July 1995 (www.faculty.de.gcsu.edu/~dvess/magistra.htm), and the *Journal of Buddhist Ethics*, established in 1994 (jbe.la.psu.edu), which also acts as the primary distributor for the first public domain electronic version of the Pāli Canon, compiled in Sri Lanka. Another cluster of lay materials, modified on annual basis, is formed by the on-line lecture notes and syllabi of courses. Christian monasticism is usually covered by courses on Western civilization, medieval art and architecture, medieval history, early church history, theology, or even the business and cultural environment in Egypt. On the other hand, Buddhist monasticism tends to be handled by units on religious studies, world religions, or the history of Buddhism or as a part of the more specialized courses, such as the sociology of rulership and religion or the anthropology of China.

Important data are additionally provided by on-line bibliographies, ranging from catalogs of the Greek manuscripts of the Philotheou (Mount Athos) Monastery (abacus.bates. edu/~rallison), medieval and early modern deeds (www.law. harvard.edu/library), and the Hill Monastic Manuscript Library Collection (www.csbsju.edu) to bibliographies of the rule of St. Benedict (www.osb.org), English and Irish monasticism (both at h-net2.msu.edu/~albion), patristics and early Church history (www.slu.edu/libraries), hermits, and Latin Church institutions (both at orb.rhodes.edu) to bibliographies of Buddhist religion (here-and-now.org/buddrel), Sinhala (Sri Lankan) Buddhism (jbe.la.psu.edu/4/deeg1.html), koan studies(www.ciolek.com/ WWWVL-Zen.html), and Chinese cultural studies (academic. brooklyn.cuny.edu/core9/phalsall/chinbib.html).

Related to bibliographies are directories of expert Internet resources: Matrix (women and Christian religious communities, 500–1500, matrix.divinity.yale.edu), NetSerf (medieval research, netserf.cua.edu/research), Argos: Ancient and Medieval Internet (argos.evansville.edu), and Project Muse (humanities' searchable on-line journals, muse.jhu.edu/muse.html). Some sites have hagiographies, such as Biographical Sketches of Memorable Christians of the Past (justus.anglican.org/resources/bio), and archives of pertinent electronic texts and images, such as Encyclopedia Coptica (cs-www.bu.edu/faculty/best/pub/cn), the 38 volumes of the Christian Classics Ethereal Library (ccel. wheaton.edu), patristic files (www.sewanee.edu/Theology/patristicsw/alphalist.html), the Illuminated Medieval Manuscripts site (medieval.arthistory.sbc.edu), and a catalog of illuminated manuscripts on the Web (forum.inet.fi/adlit/manus.htm), the files of the Electronic Buddhist Text Initiative (EBTI; www. human.toyogakuen-u.ac.jp/~acmuller/ebti.htm), the on-line repositories of the Center for Buddhist Studies at the National Taiwan University (ccbs.ntu.edu.tw), the Huntington Archive of Buddhist and Related Art (kaladarshan.arts.ohio-state.edu), and the galleries of the Asian Arts Online Journal (asianart.com).

Finally, valuable and pertinent reference materials can be found on-line at public access sites, such as the Catholic Encyclopedia (www.knight.org/advent), ORB Online Encyclopedia (orb.rhodes.edu), and the Early Church On-Line Encyclopedia (Ecole) Initiative (cedar.evansville.edu/~ecoleweb). No equivalent on-line encyclopedias deal explicitly with Buddhism. However, some of the introductory information for that religious tradition and its monastic life can be gleaned from commercial information servers, often residing on restricted-access subnetworks, such as Grolier or the Encyclopaedia Britannica.

T. MATTHEW CIOLEK

*See also* Archives, Western Christian; Dialogue, Intermonastic: Christian Perspectives; Libraries: Western Christian

**Further Reading**

Benedictine Internet Commission, *Final Report*, 15 January 1998: *www.osb.org/osb/bic/report.html*
Ciolek, T. Matthew, and Irena M. Goltz, editors, "The Internet Studies Page," in *Information Quality WWW Virtual Library*, 1999: *www.ciolek.com/WWWVL-InfoQuality.html*
Gilster, Paul, *Digital Literacy*, New York: Wiley Computer Publishing, 1997
Ojeda-Zapata, Julio, "Monks on the Net," *St. Paul Pioneer Press*, 1 October 1995: *www.osb.org/osb/ppress.html*
Zakon, Robert H., *Hobbes' Internet Timeline*, 1998: *info.isoc.org/guest/zakon/Internet/History/HIT.html*

# Iona, Scotland

Iona (in Gaelic *Ì* or *Ì Choluim Chille*, "of Columba") is an island, measuring about one by three miles, off the southwestern coast of Mull in the Inner Hebrides. Reaching it today requires two ferry crossings, but it was central and easily accessible when transport was usually by sea. Saint Columba (Colum Cille), born of royal stock in Donegal (c. 521), came to Iona in 563 and founded a monastery. Iona was in Dalriada, itself an expansion of Gaelic-speaking *Scoti* from Ireland into present-day Scotland, making hardly tenable St. Bede's statement that in 565 Iona was given to Columba by the Pictish king. Quickly, Iona became the focal point of a network of monasteries, and Columba's prestige was confirmed when the king of Dalriada came to him in 574 for Christian inauguration of his rule.

Iona's *paruchia* (sphere of authority) comprised all Scottish Dalriada as well as parts of Ireland and gradually extended into other parts of Scotland. Columba, although simply a priest, was the undisputed leader and as abbot had monk-bishops subject to him. Although his main apostolate was monastic and centered in Dalriada, he approached the Pictish king in Inverness and with his consent preached and baptized in Pictland, as did some of his monks, and the mission to Pictland expanded greatly after his death in 597. Iona extended its supremacy over all of northern and eastern Scotland; then, in 634, Aidan (d. 651), a monk of Iona, became bishop in Northumbria, with Lindisfarne as his seat. Almost all of Scotland and part of northeastern England were in Iona's *paruchia*.

However, in 664, after the decision at Whitby in favor of Roman over Celtic custom, the conservative monks in Northumbria returned to Iona. Despite the efforts of Adomnán (abbot 679–704), the Iona monks refused to accept the Whitby decision until 717. However, Iona's headship remained, although Lindisfarne's influence spread in eastern Scotland, and episcopal rather than abbatial control increased. Iona itself remained a sanctuary for exiles, penitents, and pilgrims and a center of culture and learning. Cumméne (abbot c. 657–669) was author of a penitential book and a work on Columba; Adomnán used the latter for his *Life of Columba* and also wrote about the Holy Land, *De Locis Sanctis*. Early chronicles were compiled in Iona. More remarkably, the celebrated *Book of Kells* (c. 800), an illustrated gospel book, was penned in Iona, and the superb stone standing crosses were sculpted there.

In 795, Iona was plundered by Vikings, and in 806 the community was massacred. Part of Columba's relics was taken in 849 to Dunkeld, which became the religious capital of Scotland, although Iona remained the spiritual center and the burial place of the Scottish kings. Abbot and monks were again massacred in 986. A century later, Queen St. Margaret (c. 1046–1093) is said to have given aid to Iona, and in 1164 Culdees were living alongside the monks. Pilgrims are recorded on the island up to 1200.

In the 12th century, the Scottish Church was transformed by the establishment of territorial bishoprics and Continental-style monasteries. In 1203, Iona became Benedictine, although not without violent opposition from Columban monasteries in Ireland. It was now in the diocese of Sodor, in the metropolitan province of Nidaros (Norway). Iona's status was anomalous, for it was given exemption from episcopal authority as well as from Benedictine chapters in Scotland, and the abbot was granted the miter. Only traces have remained of the Celtic monastery, which comprised individual cells and some simple communal buildings, the whole enclosed within a boundary wall. The usual medieval buildings were now erected; these were quite small but strikingly beautiful: church, cloisters, chapter house, and so on in durable stone. Evidence exists that women had a place in early Iona but not an establishment. Now a nunnery of Augustinian canonesses was founded.

In the 15th century, Iona was still imperfectly integrated into Scotland. The lordship of the Isles was dominant rather than the Scottish crown. Evidence exists of Irish architectural influence and masons' work, and Iona itself was the home of a distinctive school of sculpture. The children of Iona abbots and their noble concubines were entering the abbey and nunnery, seemingly a reversion to some ancient form of tribal monasticism, against which the monks successfully petitioned Rome. As a result of the Great Schism, Sodor had both a Scottish and an English bishop, but the only cathedral was on the Isle of Man. Therefore, in 1499, Iona abbey became the cathedral of the Scottish diocese of the Isles, with the bishop holding Iona *in commendam*, that is, with full abbatial powers despite not being a monk. Scions of two powerful local families, Campbells and Macleans, competed for the dual prelacy.

In 1560, the Reformation put an end to monastic life, and the community died out, but the church remained the Protestant cathedral. In 1609 the bishop issued the "Statutes of Iona," which contained far-reaching measures of religious, social, and cultural reform. Although the abbey buildings later became ruinous, Iona's aura as a sacred place persisted, leading the poet Wordsworth to compose four sonnets on Iona and Dr. Samuel Johnson in 1773 to declare, "That man is little to be envied whose patriotism would not gain force upon the plain of Marathon, or whose piety would not grow warmer among the ruins of Iona."

In modern times, the medieval buildings have been restored. In 1874–1875 the foundations of the abbey and nunnery were cleared and some repairs begun, and in 1899 a trusteeship was formed to restore the church for use by all Christian denominations. Since 1979 the island has been in the care of the National Trust for Scotland. However, the main event was the formation of the Iona Community by the Reverend George MacLeod (1895–1991) in 1938. The abbey is now restored and lived in

and has become a center for ecumenical activities. A Catholic house of prayer has also been recently built. In 1997, the centenary of Columba's death, Iona attracted countless groups and pilgrims.

MARK DILWORTH O.S.B.

*See also* Columba, St.; Dissolution of Monasteries: Scotland; Ireland: History; Island Monasteries, Christian; Liturgy: Celtic; Scotland

## Further Reading

*Argyll: An Inventory of the Ancient Monuments*, volume 4: *Iona*, Edinburgh: Royal Commission on the Ancient and Historical Monuments of Scotland, 1982

Cameron, Nigel M. de S., editor, *Dictionary of Scottish Church History and Theology*, Edinburgh: T. and T. Clark, and Downers Grove, Illinois: InterVarsity Press, 1993

Clancy, Thomas Owen, and Gilbert Márkus, *Iona: The Earliest Poetry of a Celtic Monastery*, Edinburgh: Edinburgh University Press, 1995

Cowan, Ian B., and David E. Easson, *Medieval Religious Houses: Scotland*, London and New York: Longman, 1957; 2nd edition, 1976

Dilworth, Mark, "Iona Abbey and the Reformation," *Scottish Gaelic Studies* 12:1 (1971)

Ferguson, Ron, *Chasing the Wild Goose*, London: Collins, 1988; revised edition as *Chasing the Wild Goose: The Story of the Iona Community*, Wild Goose Publications, 1998

Herbert, Máire, *Iona, Kells, and Derry: The History and Hagiography of the Monastic Familia of Columba*, Oxford: Clarendon Press, and New York: Oxford University Press, 1988

Ritchie, Anna, *Iona*, London: Batsford, and Edinburgh: Historical Scotland, 1997

# Ippen 1239–1289

## Japanese founder of Ji sect of Pure Land Buddhism

Ippen (also Chishin) was an itinerant practitioner of Pure Land Buddhism who was devoted to the *nembutsu* (the invocation of Amida Buddha's name) and the founder of an itinerant order of followers, the Jishū (Time Order, referring to the constant practice of *nembutsu*). Born on the island of Shikoku to a warrior clan that had suffered a severe reversal of fortunes, Ippen embarked on the life of "a holy man that has abandoned the world," the main characteristic of which was incessant wayfaring (*yugyō*). From the outset he seems to have distributed paper amulets on which was printed Amida's name, and in a religious vision on Mount Kōya he learned that through these amulets rather than through any faith or morality everyone might achieve rebirth into Amida's Pure Land. From this experience he took the name Ippen, which means the "instant (invocation)," and distributed his amulets in all areas of significant Japanese population and at every great religious center of his day. In time he attracted a band of fellow wayfarers, which grew into the

Jishū. (Originally, the Jishū included men and women together, but within a generation they had become segregated.) In 1279 Ippen and the Jishū first performed the *nembutsu* dance to indicate that in a single *nembutsu*, human and Buddha, this world and the next, all became one. Ippen's biography is contained in the *Ippen Hijiri-e* (1299; Illustrated Record of the Holy Man Ippen), a set of 12 scrolls that is a masterpiece of Japanese painting and one of the leading sources for the study of medieval life.

Ippen and the memory of his life transformed the world of Buddhist wayfarers in medieval Japan. Before him these professional religious itinerants had been organized by the great temples as fund-raisers who distributed amulets and solicited contributions on their travels. Distinguished from regular monks, these itinerants were based in separate institutions on temple grounds while remaining under the jurisdiction of temple authorities. Ippen's career transformed their practice in two ways. First, he provided them with a spiritual justification for their wayfaring lives. Life on the road no longer served only the pragmatic ends of fund-raising; it now constituted the supreme response to Amida Buddha's vow to save all who invoke his name. Second, because of this new religious ideology and Ippen's own extensive travels, Ippen's biography served to unite these itinerants institutionally into the Jishū regardless of their temple base.

As the largest itinerant order of medieval Japan, Ippen's Jishū extended its influence far beyond the life of the road. Already in the 14th century, Jishū members had allied themselves with warrior bands to administer Buddhist services for the battlefield dead. From this association the Jishū enjoyed the patronage of the *shōgun*, and its members were frequently part of the cultural entourage of elite warriors in the 15th and 16th centuries. With the fall of the Ashikaga Shōgunate in 1573, the Jishū's fortunes declined and by the 17th century it had reconstituted itself as one of the smaller Buddhist sects. However, it continued to be led by the Wayfaring Saint (*yugyō shōnin*) who traveled the country, only now in great luxury. Today the head of the sect's main branch is still designated the Wayfaring Saint, but the term does not reflect his actual religious discipline.

JAMES H. FOARD

*See also* Japan: History; Mount Kōya, Japan; Pure Land Buddhism; Shikoku, the Pilgrimage Island of Japan; Temple, Buddhist; Warrior Monks: Buddhist

**Biography**

Having studied Pure Land Buddhism as a youth, Ippen embarked on a lifetime of wandering ministry throughout Japan. He founded the Ji sect of Pure Land Buddhism, emphasizing the six-hour invocation of the *nembutsu* every day. Although the Jishū diminished in importance, Ippen's practice of dancing while reciting the *nembutsu* influenced Japanese theater. Approaching death, he burned all of his writings in the belief that they all amount to the Namu Amida Butsu.

**Major Works**

*Ippen Shonin Goroku* (Record of Ippen)

**Further Reading**

Foard, James H., "Prefiguration and Narrative in Medieval Hagiography: The *Ippen Hijiri-e*," in *Flowing Traces: Buddhism and the Literary and Visual Arts of Japan*, edited by James H. Sanford, William R. LaFleur, and Masatoshi Nagatomi, Princeton, New Jersey: Princeton University Press, 1992

Foard, James H., "Ippen and Pure Land Wayfarers in Medieval Japan," in *The Pure Land Tradition: History and Development*, edited by James H. Foard, Michael Solomon, and Richard K. Payne, Berkeley: Regents of the University of California, 1996

Hirota, Dennis, *No Abode: The Record of Ippen*, Kyoto and San Francisco: Ryukoko University, 1986; reprint, Honolulu: University of Hawaii Press, 1997

Imai, Masaharu, *Jishū Seiritsushi no Kenkyū* (Studies in the History of the Formation of the Jishū), Tokyo: Yoshikawa Kōbunkan, 1981

Kanai, Kiyomitsu, *Ippen to Jishū Kyōdan* (Ippen and the Jishū Order), Tokyo: Kadokawa Shoten, 1975

Ōhashi, Shunnō, *Jishū no Seiritsu to Tenkai* (The Formation and Development of the Jishū), Tokyo: Yoshikawa Kōbunkan, 1973

Tachibana, Shundō, *Jishūshi Ronkō* (A Study of Jishū History), Kyoto: Hōzōkan, 1975

# Ireland: History

Christian communities existed in Ireland before Patrick's return in the mid– or late fifth century, and the *Life of St. Declan* mentions four bishops: Declan, Ciarán, Ailbe, and Ibar, of whom the latter two are certainly later. However, a well-organized church had not taken hold. Even Patrick's mission, following the brief and largely failed attempt by Palladius in 431, was not immediately successful. Assisted by several companions (who most likely were monks ordained and functioning as secular clergy), he eventually won sufficient converts to inaugurate a stable organization based on Roman diocesan structures, including a hierarchy of bishops, priests, and deacons. He did not found monasteries. Nevertheless, within a century the dominant form of Irish Christianity was not diocesan but monastic in form.

The flowering of Irish monasticism in the sixth and seventh centuries was a consequence of the British and Irish exchange during the fifth century. Monks frequently traveled between Ninian's (c. 360–432) first great center, Candida Casa in northwestern Britain, and several Irish monasteries. Later, Irish monks studied under St. David (c. 520–588) at Menevia, and Gildas (c. 500–570) seems to have traveled to Ireland to help organize monastic discipline.

Although monasticism came to England and then to Ireland from Gaul, its character was Egyptian – decentralized, pluralistic, and loosely organized. Resembling settlements or small villages, some monasteries admitted both men and women, married laypersons as well as celibates, and a variety of support personnel. Abbots were sometimes married, and leadership was

Mellifont Abbey (Cistercian), County Louth, Ireland, 13th century. This was the earliest Cistercian house in Ireland.
Photo courtesy of Mary Schaefer

often handed down through families. The lifestyle tended to be coenobitical; that is, the monks lived in separate cells or huts but participated in common prayer, meals, and other functions. However, a tendency existed among the more austere ascetics to become hermits in the strict sense, separating from others to undergo what came to be called the "green martyrdom," living in remote, isolated places (*díaearts*) alone with God.

This quest for an intense, self-sacrificing form of testimony was further expressed by the "white martyrdom," or voluntary exile and death in an alien land undergone out of love for the homeless Christ. In its extreme form the white martyrdom meant a life of perpetual pilgrimage. Sometimes these holy wanderers would set themselves adrift at sea in rudderless boats to go where winds and Providence would carry them.

The earliest Irish monastery was most likely St. Enda's (c. 450–535) foundation on the Aran Islands. Among his disciples were Finnian of Moville (c. 495–579), Eugene of Ardstraw (d. 618), and Tighearnach of Clones. Saint Finnian of Clonard (d. 549), the "teacher of the saints of Ireland," inspired a number of other founders, known as the Twelve Apostles of Ireland, including Columba (Columcille, c. 521–597), Ciarán of Clonmacnois (d. 549), Brendan of Clonfert (c. 484–577), Molaise (Laserian, d. c. 638), Cainneach (517–600), Sinell of Cleenish, and Brendan of Birr (490–573).

A third wave of monastic foundations launched Bangor, founded by St. Comgall (c. 516–603); Glendalough, founded by Kevin (d. 618); Tuam, founded by Jarlath (d. c. 650); and Cork, founded by Bairre (d. 704). Monasteries for women were founded by Brigit (fifth or sixth century) at Kildare, the most famous and, within a century, one of the most influential (and in fact a double monastery); by Moninna at Killeevy before the end of the fifth century; by Ita (c. 480–570) at Killeady in County Limerick; and by Samthann (d. 739) at Clonbroney in County Longford.

Although a "typical" Irish monastery might number up to 1,000 inmates, its layout was comparatively simple. A wall, more symbolic than defensive, encompassed a group of diverse buildings. Both monks and their lay associates slept and prayed privately in small cells that were constructed originally of wood or wattles and mud and eventually of stone. Two or three monks might share a cell, but many dwelt alone. Communal buildings included a church, kitchen, refectory, and guest house. Within the perimeter of the enclosure were barns, stables, smithies, and craft shops. In most respects an Irish monastery resembled a small village.

Abbots and abbesses governed the monasteries, being assisted by a group of senior monks or nuns responsible for important tasks, such as material upkeep of the buildings, instruction of

Round tower at St. Kevin's Monastery, Glendalough (County Wicklow), Ireland, 11th–12th century.
Photo courtesy of Mary Schaefer

novices, copying of manuscripts, and care of guests. The abbot or abbess was also assisted by a minister who acted as a secretary and adviser.

The monastic diet was spare. Although excavations have produced quantities of beef and pork bones near monastic settlements, the monks themselves subsisted on a fare of bread, cereals, vegetables, and water. Beer, fish, honey, milk, and butter were sometimes permitted, although in the more rigorous monasteries, such as that of Comgall at Bangor and Mel Ruain at Tallaght, these were permitted only on suitable and infrequent occasions. The monks' garb was a long white tunic that was covered in cold weather by a woolen cloak and hood. Sandals were worn when necessary. Manual labor, an essential part of Irish monastic discipline, included farming, fishing, building, brewing, and weaving.

Because of its origins in Gaul and Britain – especially at Tours, Lérins, Auxerre, and Candida Casa – Irish monasticism was Latin in its language and liturgy. The formal liturgy consisted of the celebration of the Mass and the singing of the Hours, the midnight office being the longest. The role of Scripture was especially conspicuous. The Bible was used for liturgical, devotional purposes and, above all, study, exegesis, and

commentary. The magnificently illuminated Gospels of Kells, Durrow, Lindisfarne, and other monasteries not only represent the artistic genius of the Celtic monks in calligraphy, portraiture, and abstract design but also testify to the importance that they accorded to the Word of God. Although these undisputed masterpieces might have been used for liturgical celebrations, missals were also created for this purpose at a very early period.

In addition to official books, a vast literature illustrates the intensely personal devotion and informal liturgies of the monks and people at large, such as the small *Pocket Gospels*, which could be taken on journeys or pilgrimage. Artistic accomplishment soon extended to graphic and plastic expression, such as the great carved stone crosses that most likely marked the inner boundary of the monastic "cloister" and the superb examples of metalwork, such as the Ardagh chalice, jeweled book covers, and shrines for the bells, staves, and belts of sainted founders.

Scribes and scholars not only copied, read, and commented on scripture but also studied grammar, rhetoric, and the works of the classical pagan poets, especially Virgil and Horace. They also preserved the writings of the Latin fathers: Ambrose, Augustine, Jerome, Cassian, and Gregory, among others. Some knew at least a little Greek. The monks recorded even the pre-Christian myths and sagas of the Celts from the oral versions of the bardic schools, thus preserving for subsequent generations the Book of Invasions, the Ulster Cycle, and the Fenian Cycle, the earliest of all nonclassical European mythologies.

From the beginning, vigorous ascetic discipline typified Celtic monasticism. Today such asceticism might appear extreme, but in those demanding times it would have seemed less so. Although attracted to the wilderness and *dísearts* of solitary communion with God, the monks were not antisocial, and their ascetic example accomplished a truly missionary function in a heroic age. Whether as ordinary forms of penitence or imposed as punishment for infractions of the rule, such practices included fasting, silence, sleep deprivation, repeated genuflections, praying for extended periods with outstretched arms, and whippings, usually on the palm with a leather strap.

Another aspect of Irish monastic practice was strong emphasis on pastoral care and spiritual development. Preaching and solitary witness were among the principal monastic activities. Monks also provided spiritual counsel, especially in the person of the *Anamchara* (soul-friend), at once confessor, adviser, and spiritual companion. Education and fostering, hospitality to travelers, and the protection of refugees were important works of justice. Sacramental ministry was advanced by the development of penitentials, which sought to regulate and harmonize as well as mitigate the assignment of penances to both monks and laypersons.

Concern for others led to the first great missionary impulse of the postapostolic Church. The Irish missions to pagan areas of Scotland, England, and the Continent began more as a form of solitary witness rather than as direct evangelization. However, as Christianity spread northward and eastward from Ireland, Scotland, and England, a true missionary effort developed. Hundreds of monks and nuns abandoned Ireland forever to spread the Gospel among Franks, Goths, Lombards, Huns, Slavs, and

Temple Dowling (Teampull Dooling), Clonmacnois (County Offaly), Ireland, 10th century, rebuilt 14th century.
Photo courtesy of Mary Schaefer

other pagan peoples. By the ninth century wandering monastic scholars succeeded the missionaries, returning the light of learning as well as faith to much of Western Europe, especially at the court school of Charlemagne and his successors.

### Decline and Fall

For over 200 years, beginning in 795, Viking raiders plundered the coasts and navigable river areas of Ireland, sacking and burning monasteries and often massacring the inhabitants. Irish warlords and pirates had looted monasteries before. A significant motive lay in the fact that monasteries were often used by nearby dwellers to store valuables as well as grain. Monasteries also housed highly ornamented church vessels, book covers, and liturgical instruments of surpassing value as well as beauty. However, the Viking terror was calculated and systematic as well as ruthless, aiming at eventual subjugation and colonization and thus bringing the golden age of Irish monasticism to an end.

Monasteries rebuilt and recovered, only to be repeatedly destroyed, and by the time the Viking terror had abated, the weakened Irish Church faced a new and formidable opponent. Although the language and tone of the Celtic churches was Latin and loyalty to Rome was undeniable, as St. Columban (d. 615) pointed out in his famous letter to Gregory I (590–604), the Irish Church and its monasteries differed in many respects from

Roman practice if not belief. After the Synod of Whitby in England in 664, which asserted the primacy of the new Roman methods of computing the date of Easter, the shape of the tonsure, and the role of bishops, the Irish Church had little difficulty bringing itself into uniformity with the rest of the Western churches. By the end of the first millenium, all resistance to the Gregorian reform had disappeared. However, the decline of the Celtic Church was past remedy for other reasons. The tribal character of Irish monasticism had introduced elements of factionalism, favoritism, and ultimately political control. By the 12th century, after the Plantagenet conquest of Ireland, the need for ecclesiastical reform was apparent. The greatest and most saintly figure of the Irish Church at that time, St. Malachy of Armagh (1094–1148), introduced Cistercian monks into Ireland and supported reform efforts that effectively ended the hegemony of the Irish monasteries. Saint Laurence O'Toole (d. 1180), a monk of Glendalough and then archbishop of Dublin during the Anglo-Norman Conquest, similarly promoted the cause of reform, bringing the Irish Church further under English influence.

By the end of the 12th century, dioceses ruled by bishops supplanted the old order. Some monasteries, such as Glendalough, became episcopal sees. Others were converted to use as parish churches or simply evolved into towns, including Armagh, Kildare, Kells, and Derry. Some of the greatest monasteries were simply abandoned, eventually falling into ruin, as with Clonmacnois, Durrow, and Monasterboice. In the following century the arrival of Continental mendicant orders, such as the Augustinians, Franciscans, and Dominicans, further eroded old Irish monasticism.

Although the remaining monasteries and most religious houses were devastated during the Tudor period, beginning in 1536 with their suppression by Henry VIII (1509–1547), mendicant orders continued to serve the pastoral needs of the people until the mid-17th-century persecution of Oliver Cromwell and the Puritans, during which great numbers of Franciscans, Dominicans, Jesuits, and other religious and diocesan priests, along with scores of lay Catholics, either fled or died as martyrs. However, Irish religious houses survived on the Continent and clandestine pastoral activity continued in Ireland throughout the 18th century, until Catholic relief acts permitted the restoration of religious institutions between 1791 and 1793.

Today Cistercian monasteries such as Mount Melleray in County Waterford (1832), Mount St. Joseph in County Tipperary (1878), Mellifont Abbey in County Louth (1938), and the only Benedictine monastery in Ireland, Glenstal Abbey in County Limerick (1927), are well established. Ancient sites can still be seen in every area of the island, including (among many others) Armagh in County Armagh, Clonmacnois in County Offaly, Clonfert and Inishmore in County Galway, Glendalough in County Wicklow, Jerpoint Abbey in County Kilkenny, Old Melifont Abbey and Monasterboice in County Louth, Kells in County Meath, Boyle Abbey in County Roscommon, and the beehive huts and Gallarus Oratory on the Dingle Peninsula in County Kerry. Off the Kerry coast, Skellig Michael, with its dramatically tiered stone huts, is accessible by boat in clement weather.

RICHARD WOODS, O.P.

*See also* Abbess, Christian; Asceticism: Christian Perspectives; Brigit, St.; Celtic Monasticism; Cistercians; Egypt; Exile, Western Christian; Hermits: Western Christian; Hymnographers; Lérins, France; Libraries: Western Christian; Liturgy: Celtic; Liturgy: Western Christian; Manuscript Production: Western Christian; Marmion, Columba; Missionaries: Christian; Origins: Western Christian; Penitential Books; Visual Arts, Western Christian: Sculpture; Whitby, England

### Further Reading

Bitel, Lisa, *Isle of the Saints: Monastic Settlement and Christian Community in Early Ireland*, Ithaca, New York: Cornell University Press, 1990

de Paor, Máire, and Liam de Paor, *Early Christian Ireland*, London: Thames and Hudson, 1964; New York: Thames and Hudson, 1978

Hughes, Kathleen, *Early Christian Ireland: Introduction to the Sources*, Ithaca, New York: Cornell University Press, and London: Hodder and Stoughton, 1972

Hughes, Kathleen, and Ann Hamlin, *Celtic Monasticism: The Modern Traveler to the Early Irish Church*, New York: Seabury, 1981

Manning, Conleth, *Early Irish Monasteries*, Dublin: Country House, 1995

McNeill, John T., *The Celtic Churches: A History*, A.D. 200–1200, Chicago: University of Chicago Press, 1974

O'Sullivan, Jeremiah, "Old Ireland and Her Monasticism," in *Old Ireland*, edited by Robert McNally, New York: Fordham University Press, and Dublin: Gill, 1965

Ryan, John, *Irish Monasticism: Origins and Early Development*, Dublin: Four Courts Press, and Ithaca, New York: Cornell University Press, 1972

Sheehy, M.P., "Concerning the Origin of Early Medieval Irish Monasticism," *Irish Theological Quarterly* 29 (1962)

For lives of the Irish saints, see Heist, W.W., *Vitae Sanctorum Hiberniae*, Subsidia Hagiographica 28, Brussels, 1965, and the now classic translations by Charles Plummer of the Latin and Irish versions: *Vitae Sanctorum Hiberniae*, 2 vols., Oxford: Clarendon Press, 1910; and *Bethada Náem nÉrenn*, 2 vols., Oxford: Clarendon Press, 1922

### Related Web Site

*http://www.ucc.ie/celt/* (University College, Cork)

**Cross of the Scriptures and Cathedral, Clonmacnois (County Offaly), Ireland, 11th century.**
**Photo courtesy of Mary Schaefer**

# Ireland: Sites

Fifteen hundred years of monasticism in Ireland have left extensive remains throughout this island. This article surveys these remains in three historical periods: (1) ancient Irish monasteries (5th to 12th century), (2) Anglo-Norman Irish monasteries (12th to 16th century), and (3) modern monastic foundations (19th to 20th century).

*Ancient Irish Monasteries (5th to 12th Century)*
Following the evangelizing work of St. Patrick, the Church in Ireland quickly became a monastic Church. The centers of church were not diocese or parish but monastic villages under the leadership of abbot or abbess. Consequently, these centuries are marked by monastic foundations all over Ireland. Because the earliest monastic buildings in Ireland were constructed in wood or wattle and mud, nothing remains of the original edifices. However, stone structures still survive that were built in later times on the original sites. Hundreds of simple stone "bee-

**Gallarus Oratory, Kilmakedar, Dingle Peninsula (County Kerry), Ireland, eighth or ninth century. The dry rubble masonry models a shape resembling an upturned boat.**
**Photo courtesy of Mary Schaefer**

hive" (*clochan*) structures are to be found scattered over the southwest, especially in Kerry. The oldest extent chapel is the Gallarus Oratory (seventh or eighth century) on the Dingle Peninsula, a drystone building with a corbeled roof rising directly without break from the walls. The most spectacular monastic remains are to be found on the rocky precipice of the island of Skellig Michael, eight miles off the coast of Kerry, where six beehive cells, two oratories, sculptures, and a cemetery are to be found. This site was inhabited by monks for about 700 years, having been interrupted at times by Viking raids. Other ancient monastic sites continue to be unearthed, such as at Riesk near Ballyferriter in Kerry, where cross-decorated slabs were uncovered in the 1970s, leading to the further remains of a monastic enclosure.

The earliest identified Irish monastic founder was St. Enda (d. 520). A chapel is the only remainder of his monastery on Inismor, the largest of the Aran Islands. Many other monastic ruins can be found on this island, including the impressive sculptures and gravestones at the so-called Seven Churches. Another island, farther north off the coast of Sligo and much more difficult to access, is Inismurray, where a stone-walled enclosure and a cluster of oratories and *clochans* are easily definable, reminding us of its ninth-century founder, St. Molaise. The remains of a holy well and oratory are still to be seen on the top of Mount Brandon, north of Dingle in Kerry, and the site of St. Brendan's hermitage.

The four great ecclesiastical centers and points of pilgrimage in Ireland were Armagh, Kildare, Clonmacnois, and Glendalough. Nothing of monastic interest is left at Armagh, which is noted more for being the primatial see of St. Patrick. In Kildare (which means "Church of the Oak" and points to a pre-Christian Druidic center), St. Brigit (fifth or sixth century) founded a double monastery of men and women that rose to be a large monastic city. Today a high tower remains next to the Anglican Cathedral, and St. Brigit's well outside the town remains a point of pilgrimage. Saint Ciarán (d. 549), disciple of Enda, founded the great center of Clonmacnois, which is strategically situated at the nodal point of the Ireland's east-west roadway with the north-south traffic of the Shannon River. Extensive remains here include oratories, high crosses, and sculptures, some of which are now kept in a museum and interpretive center. Saint Ciarán died only six months after this foundation. A modern sculpture at the site "The Pilgrim" commemorates this circumstance. Interpretive facilities are also to be found at the much more extensive grounds and remains of Glendalough in County Wicklow, where St. Kevin (d. 618) began his monastery, one that became a great university as well as a spiritual center. A round tower, the ruins of a cathedral, several churches, St. Kevin's cross, St. Kevin's kitchen, and his sacred cave are impressive remains at this site.

Monasteries that came from the line of Columba (c. 521–597), founder of Iona, include Kells (County Meath), where crosses, a round tower, and St. Columba's house remain, and Durrow (County Offaly), where only a high cross and a holy well are left. A high cross also marks the Columban foundation of Moone in Kildare. The great Columban foundation of Derry

St. Kevin's Kitchen, Glendalough (County Wicklow), Ireland, sacked by the Danes in the early 11th century. This two-story oratory (11th–12th century) had a sacristy added in the foreground and a bell tower in the rear.
Photo courtesy of Mary Schaefer

today lies beneath the Protestant Cathedral. His monastery of Drumcliff in Sligo is marked by a high cross and a cemetery, where the poet W.B. Yeats (1865–1939) lies at rest. The greatest high crosses in Ireland are to be found at Monasterboice (County Louth), founded by St. Buite around 520. This site includes the outstanding Muirdach's cross, the so-called great high cross (21 feet high), and two churches and a round tower.

A monastic reform movement, called *Céili Dé*, or "Culdees," occurred in Ireland in the eighth century. Its leading advocate was St. Maelruain, from northern Tipperary, who in 774 founded the monastery of Tallaght, south of Dublin. This movement had great promise but was cut short by the Viking invasions that began at the end of the eighth century. Some monastic remains can be traced at Tallaght.

*Anglo-Norman Irish Monasteries (12th to 16th Century)*
Internal loss of fervor, secularist control, lack of charismatic leaders, and Viking attacks led to the weakening of the old Irish monasteries. The 12th century brought internal Church reform and then the significant occurrence of the Norman invasion, beginning in 1169. Outside influence from England and the Continent now began to dominate Ireland.

The earliest reference to Benedictines in Ireland is from 1085 to 1096 at Christ Church, Dublin. It seems probable that the first Irish Benedictine monks had become Benedictines in German monasteries and then returned to Ireland to bring the Rule of St. Benedict to their homeland. The so-called *Schottenklöster*, a group of Irish Benedictine monasteries in southern Germany, were to be found in such places as Ratisbon and Würzburg. Monasteries founded by Benedictine monks from the German monasteries and from communities in France included Erenagh (County Down) in 1127, Cashel and Ross Carberry (County Cork) in 1134, St. Mary's in Dublin in 1139, and Downpatrick (County Down). Most of these and some others succumbed to the Vikings or the Black Death (around 1350) or became Cistercian. The only Benedictine remains to be identified in Ireland are at Fore (County Westmeath), founded around 1200 and closed in the Reformation in 1539.

During the 12th century extensive ecclesiastical reforms brought Ireland more in conformity with the Church on the Continent. Saint Malachy (1094–1114), the archbishop of Armagh, was a confidant of St. Bernard of Clairvaux (1090–1153) and brought to Ireland both the Cistercian monks and the French canons regular of St. Augustine of Arrouaise. Many of

**High crosses with Christian graveslabs, churchyard, Kells (County Meath), Ireland, 10th–11th century.**
**Photo courtesy of Mary Schaefer**

these new European communities took over or absorbed previous Irish monastic settlements. The Cistercian white monks began 39 new houses between 1142 and 1273, 13 of which were already Irish monasteries. The canons of St. Augustine, also very monastic and similar in lifestyle to the Cistercians (though more pastorally oriented) founded 96 new houses, 57 of which had been Irish monasteries. Among the latter were the great monastic centers of Clonmacnois and Glendalough.

The first Cistercian monastery was at Mellifont (County Louth), which was built on a new rectangular and impressive plan that had been previously unknown in Ireland. A well-preserved lavabo is among the ruins to be seen there today. Various degrees of monastic ruins can also be found at the Cistercian abbey sites of Boyle (Roscommon), Corcormoe (Clare), Dunbrody (Wexford), and Knockmoy (Tipperary). Very striking sculptures are to be found on the arcade of the cloister remains at Jerpoint (Kilkenny). The abbeys of Holy Cross (Tipperary) and Duiske (Kilenney) are unique in that they were better preserved, experienced some rebuilding, and have been restored recently to serve as both parish churches and monastic museums.

The canons of St. Augustine were to be found especially in western Ireland. Cong Abbey (Mayo) has some interesting remains. The abbey of Ballintubber (Mayo) has been called "the

abbey that refused to die," as Catholics gathered secretly even after dissolution to celebrate Mass there. The church and chapter rooms have been restored as part of an ongoing restoration, and Ballintubber now serves as both parish church and retreat center.

All these communities began with great fervor and superior organization but were weakened by tension and conflict between the native Gaelic Irish and the new immigrant Anglo-Norman monks. Other religious communities from the Continent soon followed these two groups, including the more apostolic Dominicans, Franciscans, and Carmelites. Some confusion exists in identifying their religious houses (and remains), as the title of abbey is sometimes used where a friary is really meant. For example, Quin Abbey in Clare is a Franciscan friary from the 15th century that has impressive remains.

*Modern Monastic Foundations (19th to 20th Century)*
The 16th-century dissolution of the monasteries under King Henry VIII (1509–1547) effectively ended monasticism in Ireland. The 18th-century penal laws continued to make monastic foundations impossible. None of this stopped Irish men and women from embracing the monastic vocation, but now they went to the Continent to do so. A number of these became Cis-

tercian monks of the Abbey of Melleray in Brittany, the old Celtic region of France. Following the Catholic relief acts of 1782, 1792, and 1793, Catholic emancipation took place in Ireland in 1829. Within three years 60 Irish monks from Melleray established the monastery of Mount Melleray on the slopes of the Knockmealdown Mountains north of Cappoquin in County Waterford (1832). This community eventually established six daughter houses: four in Ireland and one each in the United States and New Zealand. A monastery of about 45 monks with farm and guest house continues to thrive today. Their first foundation was Mount St. Joseph Abbey at Roscrea in Tipperary (1878), which opened a school for boys in 1905. In 1965 this community founded a monastery at Bolton in Kildare. Other foundations were made by Roscrea in Scotland and Australia. The two Irish communities of Roscrea and Bolton number about 38 and 14 monks, respectively.

Another significant foundation from Mount Melleray was made in 1938 at Mellifont Abbey (County Louth). The monastery was built close to the ruins of Old Mellifont Abbey, the protomonastery of the Cistercians in Ireland. It is dedicated to Our Lady and St. Malachy and numbers about 27 monks. The only monastic settlement in Northern Ireland was founded by Mount Melleray at Portglenone in the Diocese of Down. Known as Our Lady of Bethlehem Abbey, this monastery has no external apostolate but an open guest house and confessional chapel available to the many pilgrims who visit this community of 28 monks.

Cistercian nuns are also to be found in Ireland today. Their one community was founded in 1932 at Glencairn on the banks of the Blackwater River near Lismore (County Waterford). Saint Mary's Abbey, as it is known, was founded from Holy Cross Abbey, Stapelhill, in Dorset (England). The community has made foundations in the United States and Nigeria and still numbers about 40 nuns in Ireland.

Following dissolution Irish vocations were also to be found in European Benedictine communities. In 1665 the Belgium Benedictine nuns of Ghent founded a community that became known as the Irish Dames of Ypres, where they lived until the building was shelled out in 1914 during World War I. The nuns took refuge in England and then came in 1916 to MacMine (County Wexford). In 1922 the community moved to Kylmore Abbey, Connemara (County Galway), where they established a secondary school of girls. Today they have a community of 29 nuns. In 1993 a newer community of nuns came to St. Benedicts Mount at Cobh (County Cork), a small community of seven nuns, established from Tyburn Convent in London.

In the late 19th century, a diocesan priest of Dublin, Joseph Marmion (1858–1923), left his native Ireland to become a Benedictine monk at the Abbey of Maredsous in Belgium. Dom Columba Marmion eventually became the abbot of Maredsous. Within four years of his death, his desire to bring Benedictines back to Ireland was brought to fruition in the foundation of Glenstal Abbey near Limerick City. The community was dedicated to Marmion's own patrons: St. Joseph and St. Columba. It was established on grounds near the medieval Cistercian monastery of Owney, and the monks took over a 19th century mock Norman castle. The community now has about 60 monks and has established a priory in Nigeria. A secondary school for boys, ecumenical gatherings, an active guest house, and an exquisite icon chapel have marked this community's life in Ireland.

*Monasteries to Visit*
The modern Cistercian and Benedictine communities are generally open to visitors. Among the ancient Celtic sites that are especially worthwhile to see are Skellig Michael, Clonmacnois, Glendalough, and Monasterboice. Medieval ruins of great interest include Mellifont, Jerpoint, Holy Cross, and Ballintubber.

TIMOTHY J. JOYCE, O.S.B.

*See also* Augustinian Canons; Brigit, St.; Cistercians; Columba, St.; Ireland: History; Island Monasteries, Christian; Marmion, Columba

### Further Reading

Beattie, Gordon, *The Benedictine and Cistercian Monastic Yearbook*, York: Ampleforth Abbey, 1998
Carville, Geraldine, *The Occupation of Celtic Sites in Medieval Ireland by the Canons Regular of St. Augustine and the Cistercians*, Kalamazoo, Michigan: Cistercian Publications, 1982
Gwynn, Aubrey, and R. Neville Hadcock, *Medieval Religious Houses: Ireland*, Harlow: Longmans, 1976; Dublin: Irish Academic Press, 1988
Hughes, Kathleen, and Ann Hamlin, *Celtic Monasticism: The Modern Traveler to the Early Irish Church*, New York: Seabury Press, 1981
Manning, Conleth, *Early Irish Monasteries*, Dublin: Country House, 1995
O'Brien, Jacqueline, and Peter Harbison, *Ancient Ireland: From Prehistory to the Middle Ages*, New York: Oxford University Press, and London: Weidenfeld and Nicolson, 1996
O'Reilly, Séan, *Irish Churches and Monasteries: An Historical and Architectural Guide*, Cork: Collins Press, 1997
Ryan, John, *Irish Monasticism: Origins and Early Development*, Dublin: Four Courts Press, and New York: Longmans and Green, 1931; reprint, Dublin: Four Courts Press, 1992
Stalley, Roger, *The Cistercian Monasteries of Ireland: An Account of the History, Art, and Architecture of the White Monks in Ireland from 1142–1540*, New Haven, Connecticut: Yale University Press, 1987

# Isaac the Syrian (Isaac of Nineveh), St.

## d. c. 700

Middle Eastern Christian monk, author, and influence on Eastern Orthodox monasticism

According to *The Book of Chastity* by Isho'denah (a ninth-century East Syrian source), Isaac was born in Qatar on the western shore of the Persian Gulf. He was a member of the

Church of the East, commonly known as "Nestorian" because of the sharply Dyophysite Christological positions that it held (although historically it had little or nothing to do with Nestorius). Isaac was ordained a bishop of Nineveh by Catholicos George (660–680). After he had held this office for five months, he resigned and ascended the mountain of Matout (in Huzistan province in present-day Iran). Then he moved to the monastery of Rabban Shabur. An anonymous West Syrian source of uncertain date specifies that in his old age Isaac became blind and because of that was called "second Didymos" after Didymos the Great, an Alexandrian theologian of the fourth century. The exact dates of Isaac's birth and death are not known.

Isaac's literary legacy consists of ascetic and mystical homilies written in Syriac. A large number of them were translated into Greek at the end of the eighth or the beginning of the ninth century in the Lavra of St. Sabas in Palestine. From the Greek this collection of Isaac's writings was translated into Georgian (tenth century), Slavonic (14th), and Latin (15th) and, in turn, from Latin into Portuguese, Spanish, Catalan, French, and Italian (15th and 16th century). Isaac's name became widely known and appreciated throughout the Christian East and West, especially in monastic circles. His ascetic and mystical homilies influenced many monastic writers, including Nilus of Sora (1433–1508), Nicodemos the Hagiorite (c. 1749–1809), and Theophane the Recluse (1815–1894). Dostoyevsky was deeply influenced by Isaac's homilies and used some of them as source material for "the writings of Elder Zosima" in *The Brothers Karamazov* (1879–1880).

In 1983 a new collection of Isaac's writings ("Second Part") was discovered by the Oxford Syrian scholar Sebastian Brock. It consists of 41 chapters, of which one (chap. III) is divided into 400 "Chapters on Knowledge." The original text of chapters I to III still awaits publication, whereas chapters IV to XLI were published in 1995 with an English translation.

The main theme of Isaac's theology is that of divine love. God Himself, in Isaac's understanding, is first of all immeasurable and boundless love. Divine love is beyond human understanding and stands above description in words. It is the main reason for the creation of the universe and is the driving force behind the whole of creation. Divine love dwells at the foundation of the universe, it governs the world, and it will lead the world to a glorious outcome when the latter will be entirely "consumed" by the Godhead. God loves equally the righteous and sinners, angels and demons. God's love toward fallen angels does not diminish as a result of their fall, and it is not less than the fullness of love that He has toward other angels.

If God is love by His nature, everyone who has acquired perfect love and mercy towards all of creation thereby becomes godlike. Characteristic in this connection is Isaac's famous text on the "merciful heart," that attainment through which one can become like God:

And what is a merciful heart? It is the heart's burning for the sake of the entire creation, for men, for birds, for animals, for demons, and for every created thing; and by the

recollection of them the eyes of a merciful man pour forth abundant tears. From the strong and vehement mercy which grips his heart and from his great compassion, his heart is humbled and he cannot bear to hear or to see any injury or slight sorrow in creation. For this reason he offers up tearful prayer continually even for irrational beasts, for the enemies of the truth, and for those who harm him, that they be protected and receive mercy. And in like manner he even prays for the family of reptiles because of the great compassion that burns without measure in his heart in the likeness of God.

Thus, the "merciful heart" in a person is the image and likeness of God's mercy, which embraces the whole of creation – people, animals, reptiles, and demons. With God there in no hatred toward anyone but rather all-embracing love, which does not distinguish between righteous and sinner, between a friend of truth and an enemy of truth, or between angel and demon.

Another characteristic theme of Isaac is that of solitude and renunciation of the world. Solitude in Isaac is not a synonym for celibacy and the eremitic life. Rather it is first and foremost an experience of union with God. Solitude is one's internal experience of living within oneself through withdrawal into one's inner person, something that is necessary for uniting oneself with God. At the same time it is the experience of renouncing the "other," even if it is a friend or a relative. Finally it is an experience of withdrawal from the world and renunciation of it to achieve union with God. Solitude can be painful, full of inner suffering, but without this experience one can never come close to the fullness of life in God.

Other ascetic and mystical themes discussed by Isaac of Nineveh touch on bitter tears of repentance and sweet tears of compunction, humility and flight from the world, struggling with passions and enduring temptations, feeling despair and experiencing abandonment by God, "stillness of mind" and "spiritual prayer," contemplation and illumination by the divine light, and mystical wonder and "inebriation" by the love of God. Isaac's writings contain many recommendations concerning prayer as well as many details regarding the practice of prayer in his own time and milieu. Thus, polemicizing against the Messalians, he speaks of the importance of the outward aspects of prayer, of prayer before the Cross, of prostrations and veneration of the Cross, of reading aloud, of night prayer, of prayer with one's own words, and of prayer for the world.

Isaac's teaching on the torments of Gehenna and on universal salvation is of special interest. In his eschatological insights Isaac comes close to Gregory of Nyssa (c. 330–c. 395). According to Isaac the torment of Gehenna is not eternal. Gehenna is regarded by Isaac as a kind of purgatory rather than a hell: it is conceived and established for the salvation of both human beings and angels. After being punished for a certain period in Gehenna, sinners and even demons will be saved by God: "It is clear . . . that demons will not remain in their demonic state, and sinners will not remain in their sins; rather, He is going to bring them to a single equal state of perfection in relationship to His own Being

– in a state in which the holy angels are now, in perfection of love and passionless mind." All those who have fallen away from God will eventually return to Him because of the temporary and short torment in Gehenna that is prepared for them so that they can purify themselves through the fire of suffering and repentance. Having passed through this purification by fire, they will attain to the angelic state: "Maybe they will be raised to a perfection even greater than that in which the angels now exist; for all are going to exist in a single love, a single purpose, a single will, and a single perfect state of knowledge."

In modern times the popularity and influence of Isaac of Nineveh continues to grow. He is one of the most widely read spiritual writers among monks on Mount Athos. His name is known to every monk in Russia, and he is venerated as a saint in the Russian Church (which is quite a unique case, seeing that he was a "Nestorian" bishop). His writings have played a key role in the recent revival of Coptic monasticism. Even outside the monastic milieu, the writings of Isaac are very well known. Isaac's writings have crossed not only the boundaries of time but also confessional barriers. As early as the ninth century, they were read by the Byzantine and Syrian Orthodox as well as the Church of the East. In the 15th century Isaac broke into the Catholic world while remaining one of the most popular ascetic writers of the Eastern Orthodox Church. At present Isaac's writings draw the attention of Christians who belong to different denominations.

One of the secrets of this ecumenical reception lies in the fact that Isaac is always speaking of God's love, which has no boundaries, which is beyond any concept of justice or requital, which underwent crucifixion for the salvation of the whole world, and which leads all created beings to salvation. In every epoch the Christian world needs to be reminded of this universal love of God for His creation because in every epoch a strong tendency exists within Christianity to replace the religion of love and freedom that was brought by Jesus with a religion of slavery and fear. Isaac reminds modern Christians that it is not out of fear of punishment or out of hope for future reward that we are to keep God's commandments but out of our love for God.

HILARION ALFEYEV

See also Elders, Russian Monastic (Startsi); Gregory of Nyssa, St.; Hesychasm; Lavra; Mount Athos, Greece; Nestorian Monasticism; Nilus of Sora, St.; Russia: Recent Changes; Spirituality: Eastern Christian; Syria; Vision, Mystical: Eastern Christian

## Biography

Isaac of Nineveh was born in Qatar. Having served for just five months as bishop of Nineveh, he retired to the mountain of Matout in Iran. Later he dwelt at the monastery of Rabban Shabur. His homilies written in Syriac and translated into Greek became a major source for Eastern Orthodox spirituality, particularly in Russia.

## Major Works

*Le Livre de la Chasteté*, edited by J.B. Chabot, 1896
*Mar Isaacus Ninevita: De perfectione religiosa*, 1909
*Mystic Treaties by Isaac of Nineveh*, translated from Bedjan's Syriac text with an introduction and registers by A.J. Wensinck, 1923

*The Ascetical Homilies of Saint Isaac the Syrian*, translated by D. Miller, 1984
*The Heart of Compassion*, edited by A.M. Allchin, 1989
*On Ascetical Life*, translated by M. Hansbury, 1989
*Isaac of Nineveh (Isaac the Syrian), "The Second Part,"* chapters IV–XLI, translated by Sebastian P. Brock, 1995

## Further Reading

Alfeyev, H., "Prayer in St. Isaac of Nineveh," in *Prayer and Spirituality in the Early Church*, volume 1, edited by Pauline Allen, et al., Queensland, Australia: Centre for Early Christian Education, 1998
Alfeyev, H., *The World of Isaac the Syrian*, Kalamazoo, Michigan: Cistercian Publications, 2000
Assemani, J.B., *Bibliotheca Orientalis*, vols. 1–3, Rome, 1719
Bettiolo, P., "Avec la charité comme but: Dieu et création dans la méditation d'Isaac de Ninive," *Irénikon* 63 (1990)
Brock, Sebastian P., "St. Isaac of Nineveh and Syriac Spirituality," *Sobornost* 7:2 (1975)
Brock, Sebastian P., "Isaac of Nineveh: Some Newly Discovered Works," *Sobornost/Eastern Churches Review* 8:1 (1986)
Brock, Sebastian P., *Spirituality in Syriac Tradition*, Kottayam, India: St. Ephrem Ecumenical Research Institute, 1989
Brock, Sebastian P., "Lost – and Found: Part II of the Works of St. Isaac of Nineveh," *Studia Patristica* 19:4 (1990)
Bunge, G., "Mar Isaak von Ninive und sein 'Buch der Gnade,'" *Ostkirchliche Studien* 34 (1985)
Chabot, J.B., *De sancti Isaaci Ninevitae*, Paris, 1892
Khalifé-Hachem, E., "La prière pure et la prière spirituelle selon Isaac de Ninive," in *Mémorial Mgr Gabriel Khouri-Sarkis*, Louvain: Impr. orientaliste, 1969
Khalifé-Hachem, E., "Isaac de Ninive," in *Dictionnaire de Spiritualité ascétique et mystique: Doctrine et histoire*, volume 7, Paris: Beauchesne, 1971
Khalifé-Hachem, E., "L'âme et les passions des hommes d'après un texte d'Isaac de Ninive," *Parole d'Orient* 12 (1984–1985)
Licher, D.A., "Tears and Contemplation in Isaac of Nineveh," *Diakonia* 11 (1976)
Tsirpanlis, C.N., "Praxis and Theoria: The Heart, Love and Light Mysticism in Saint Isaac the Syrian," *Patristic and Byzantine Review* 6 (1987)

# Isidore of Seville, St. c. 560–636

Christian bishop of Seville and author

Among all the churchmen of Visigothic Spain, Isidore of Seville was undoubtedly the most distinguished bishop and the most prolific author.

The course and chronology of Isidore's early life is confused and uncertain. He was born around 560 to a family of probable Byzantine origins from Cartagena who migrated to Seville sometime in the mid–sixth century. He had two brothers, Leander (bishop of Seville, c. 584–599/600) and Fulgentius (bishop of Ecija), and a sister, Florentina, who became a nun. After the death of his parents, Isidore was educated under the supervision of his elder brother, Leander, possibly in a monastery. However, this must not be taken to imply that Isidore was a monk. No evidence exists to confirm this assertion, and it might well be that Isidore and his brothers led a self-imposed ascetic life in their own household, as was common among many aristocrats in the fourth and fifth centuries.

In 599 or 600 Leander died, and Isidore succeeded his brother to the see of Seville. From then on our knowledge of his career and activities is much more certain and accurate. As the metropolitan of the ecclesiastical province of Baetica, Isidore presided in 619 over the Second Council of Seville, and in 633 he presided over the Fourth ("national") Council of Toledo, which made a remarkable attempt to reorganize the Visigothic Church and to regularize religious life throughout Spain and Septimania. The canons of these two councils clearly reflect Isidore's own vision and his organizing abilities. Isidore had close and confident relations with most of the Visigothic kings under whom he served, and from the time of Sisebut (611/612–620) until his death in 636, Isidore appears in our sources as the king's most intimate advisor on ecclesiastical matters and as the foremost intellectual figure in the whole of Visigothic Spain. He was canonized in 1598 and was declared a Doctor of the Church in 1722. In 1999 after much study the Pontifical Council for Social Communications declared Isidore of Seville to be the patron saint of the Internet.

Isidore of Seville was an extremely prolific author. His vast literary inheritance includes historical compositions, that is, *Chronicon* (Chronicle) and *Historia Gothorum, Wandalorum et Suevorum* (History of the Goths, the Vandals and the Sueves); a continuation to Jerome's and Gennadius' *De viris illustribus* (On Famous Men); introductory exegetical aids to the study of the Scriptures; theological treatises, such as *De fide catholica contra Judaeos* (On the Christian Faith against the Jews); scientific works, such as *De natura rerum* (On the Nature of Things); encyclopedic compositions, the most famous of which are *Etymologiae sive origines* (Etymologies or Origins) and *Differentiae sive proprietate sermonum* (Differences, or on the Meaning of Words); and manuals of Christian faith and practice, the most celebrated of which are the *Sententiae* and *De ecclesiasticiis officiis* (On the Offices of the Church). Although the chronology of Isidore's writings is not at all clear, it seems that most were composed only after he was elected to the see of Seville. Furthermore, the authenticity of many other compositions that in the past were attributed to Isidore is still questionable.

Isidore of Seville was also a central figure in the history of Visigothic monasticism. Between the years 615 and 618, he composed a rule (*Regula monachorum*) for the monks of a certain (still unidentified) monastery in the vicinity of Seville. This small treatise, written in 24 chapters and in a simple language and style, was designed to guide the monks in various matters regarding their way of life, their duties, the election of an abbot, and so on. Isidore's main sources for the rule, as for many of his theological and exegetical works, were Augustine (354–430) and Pope Gregory the Great (590–602), although it is obvious that he also used some earlier monastic sources, including the rule of St. Benedict. Nevertheless, Isidore's idea of a monastic community was in some respects rather different from that of Benedict. For example, although according to the rule of St. Benedict manual labor in the monastery's fields and vineyard was part and parcel of monastic life, Isidore states in his rule that the monks should provide for their own food (e.g., work in the monastery's garden) and help the poor but should not do any construction work or works in the fields. These labors were to be done by slaves. Undoubtedly, such a regulation is a consequence of the prosperous economic situation of the monasteries in Visigothic Spain but still it points to a significant difference in the monastic ideal.

From his rule and from various other passages scattered in his writings, it appears that Isidore envisaged the monastic community as an intellectual center. Like Augustine and Benedict, Isidore made prayer and reading obligatory for all monks. In his rule he provided for three hours of reading every day and directed the monks to borrow their books from the librarian (*sacrarius*) each day at the first hour and return them after vespers. However, he also provided for a daily period (after vespers) in which the monks should meditate together and discuss various questions concerning their sacred readings. These assemblies, according to Isidore, are to be presided over by the abbot, who should also explain to everyone the meaning of difficult passages or theological issues.

The influence of Isidore's writings and thought on the medieval Church was enormous. His fame reached far beyond the Iberian Peninsula, and his works were read throughout the medieval West (including Ireland and Anglo-Saxon England). By the eighth century Isidore's compositions were found in almost every library on the Continent, and his influence on Carolingian theologians and later thinkers is amply documented but still has to be fully explored. Isidore's *Etymologiae*, to give just one example, became the standard reference book throughout Europe shortly after its publication, and it held this status unsurpassed throughout the Middle Ages. However, Isidore's monastic rule was less influential than the rest of his writings. Although it enjoyed a vast circulation in Spain, especially in the northeastern regions of the Iberian Peninsula it was almost unknown elsewhere on the Continent.

YITZHAK HEN

*See also* Animals, Attitude toward: Christian Perspectives; Benedict of Nursia, St.; Bobbio, Italy; Lectio Divina; Scholars, Benedictine; Spain: History

## Biography

Born into the nobility of Cartagena, Spain, Isidore fled to Seville and grew up under the supervision of his brother, the monk Leander, who became Bishop of Seville c. 580, Isidore succeeded him in that office c. 600, during which time he enjoyed the support of the Visigoth kings. A prodigious administrator and scholar, he strengthened the church in Spain and left a vast corpus of writings, which circulated throughout the Middle Ages. He was canonized in 1598.

## Major Works

*Etymologiae*
*De natura rerum*
*Sententiae*
*De ecclesiasticiis officiis*
*Synonyma*
*De viris illustribus*

## Further Reading

Cazier, Pierre, *Isidore de Séville et la naissance de l'Espagne catholique*, Paris: Beauchesne, 1994
Collins, Roger, *Early Medieval Spain: Unity in Diversity, 400–1000*, London: Macmillan, and New York: St. Martin's Press, 1983; revised edition, 1995
Díaz y Díaz, Manuel, "Aspectos de la tradición de la regula Isidori," *Studia Monastica* 7 (1965)
Fontaiene, Jacques, *Isidore de Séville et la culture classique dans l'Espagne wisigothique*, 3 vols., Paris: Études Augustiniennes, 1959–1983
Fontaiene, Jacques, "La vocation monastique selon saint Isidore de Séville," in *Théologie de la vie monastique*, Paris, 1961
Frank, K.S., "Isidor von Sevilla Regula Monachorum und ihre Quellen," *Römische Quartalschrift für christliche Altertumskunde und für Kirchengeschichte* 67 (1972)
Hillgarth, J.N., "The Position of Isidorian Studies: A Critical Review of Literature, 1936–1975," *Studi Medievali* 24 (1983)
Hillgarth, J.N., "Isidorian Studies," *Studi Medievali* 31 (1990)

# Island Monasteries, Christian

Early monasticism meant withdrawal from the city (the paradigm of life in antiquity: *civitas*, "civilization") to the desert, and monasticism's essential quality was being "apart from the city." Wildernesses surrounding cities were abundant in Palestine and Egypt, but when monasticism spread into Europe a substitute was needed, and small islands in the sea offered an obvious choice. These islands were usually small – so that the monks could be the only inhabitants – yet close enough to land to make access convenient, and in these features a structural correspondence exists between them and the desert monasteries of Egypt.

*The Mediterranean*

The earliest example of an island monastery appears to be Lérins in southern Gaul (now the Île St. Honorat, about 2 miles off Cannes). Its founder, Honoratus, had spent time with monks in the East and, on returning to Gaul around 410, chose this island as a place where he could live like a desert ascetic. Honoratus' model seems to have been that of a Palestinian *lavra*, and he and his companions intended to live as hermits. However, it was not long before an important cenobium had grown there, with families (e.g., Eucherius of Lyons) retiring there. Meanwhile those wanting to live as anchorites did so in isolated cells apart from the main community. Eucherius (d. c. 450) arrived there sometime after 410 and described the monastery memorably: "My

Lérins . . . sprinkled with waters, green with grasses, sparkling with flowers, a paradise of pleasant things for the eyes and nose . . ." (*De laude heremi* 42). By evoking a mixture of the paradise of Genesis 2 and the ideal garden of the classical poets, Eucherius envisioned the island as a small world where humanity, previously ejected from a garden into a hostile world through sin (Gen. 3:17–18, 24), can now through Christ leave that world for paradise. To be a monk there is to have a foretaste of heaven. Lérins rose to be an influential school: Eucherius, Vincent of Lérins (d. before 450), and Salvian of Marseille (c. 400–c. 480) taught there, and for several centuries the island kept alive its image as a place of learning and holiness. John Cassian (c. 360–after 430) was a friend of Eucherius, and when we now read his accounts of desert monasteries, already adapted to the situation of southern Gaul, we should infer that he probably had an island like Lérins in mind when he described communities in the Egyptian desert. Certainly it was in places such as Lérins that Cassian's works became major monastic resources. Lérins' success spawned other island monasteries around the northern rim of the Mediterranean in the following centuries, all imitating it.

Franciscan sanctuary, Island of Santa Maria di Barbana, lagoon of Grado, Friuli, Italy, 20th century. Having welcomed a hermitage in the sixth century, the island housed Benedictines from c. 1000 to 1450 and since then Franciscans.
Photo courtesy of the Editor

St. Michael's Mount, Cornwall, England. In 1047 Edward the Confessor placed a chapel here under the protection of Mont-St.-Michel in Normandy.
Photo courtesy of Chris Schabel

These include Capraria (present-day Capraia off Sicily), Gorgona, Palmaria, Galinaria (present-day Galinara, where, according to Sulpitius Severus [*Vita* 6], Martin of Tours fled), the Hyères in the Ligurian Sea, and Nisita near Naples. Gregory the Great (*Dialogi* 4.31) knew of hermits on the Lipari Islands.

In the Greek world, although many monasteries existed on islands (e.g., Patmos), there were fewer where an entire island became identical with its monastery. However, the most significant example is not an island but "almost an island": the peninsula of Mount Athos. Although younger than Lérins, its *sketes* share the same inspiration, for it is reached by boat, and in governing the entire area by its own constitution it exhibits the urge to build a small world where the larger's values do not apply. The other example is the Princes' Isles in the Sea of Marmara near Istanbul. In Byzantine times these islands were known as "Papadonisia" (the monks' archipelago) because of their monasteries. Like Lérins they are close to the city yet in another world. The first monastery was built by Emperor Justin II (565–578) in 569, and soon many monasteries of monks and nuns existed that provided both a retreat and an ecclesiastical prison for deposed rulers and patriarchs. The monasteries survived until the mid–19th century.

*Northwestern Europe*
When and where the first island monastery in northern seas was established remains in dispute. Fifth- and sixth-century remains

have been found on Caldey Island off Pembrokeshire, Wales, but it is unclear whether they are monastic. We are on safer ground historically with Iona off Mull, Scotland. Established by Columba (c. 521–597) in the later sixth century, Iona grew to head a federation of houses in Ireland, Scotland, and England. In the context of island monasteries, we should note that Iona itself harbored the main cenobitic monastery – although according to Adomnán's *Vita Columbae* the monks lived in individual cells in conscious imitation of the desert communities – and on other nearby islands were located hermitages and islands of penitence. Indeed Adomnán (c. 624–704) recounts the story of a monk called Cormac, who repeatedly sailed northward "to search for a desert-hermitage (*herimum*) in the ocean" (*Vita* 2.42). Thus, Adomnán explicitly parallels an island monastery with one in the desert. It was from Iona that the Aidan (d. 651) went to set up another famous island monastery on Lindisfarne (now Holy Island) off Northumberland, and around the same time we know that a monastery of Irish and Anglo-Saxon monks existed on Inisbofin off Mayo (Bede, *Historia ecclesiastica* 4.4).

Hagiography from this period shows that island monasteries were perceived to have a specifically religious character rather than just to be convenient lonely places. Many hermitages existed on land. Island monasteries provided special schools of holiness presided over by fathers modeled on those described in Cassian and Palladius (Muirchú, *Vita Patricii* 1.26). They offered ideal penitential retreats for converting one's way of life and preparing for a missionary's life. This evidence, alongside Adomnán's statements about Cormac, show that islands and living in the ocean took on a particular value in their spirituality. Trusting one's life to a frail craft on the mighty sea was seen as an act of trust in God and abandonment to providence. On the sea one had to rely on God's blessing for one's security, and one's direction was set not so much by the personal will as by the disposal of grace. It is from this perspective that we view the travels of Irish monks to Iceland and other islands (e.g., the Faroes) in the eighth century (Dicuil, *De mensura orbis terrae* 7.11–15, writing in 825) and the spectacular monastic cells from the same period on Skellig Michael off Kerry. It is this place that might have inspired the "Michael" dedications to Mont-St.-Michel in Normandy (ninth century) and St. Michael's Mount in Cornwall (tenth century). The numerous other islands off the European coast (e.g., Inis Murray off Sligo and the Scilly Isles off Cornwall) or on islands in rivers (Inishcaltra in the Shannon, Rheinau in the Rhine, and Reichenau in Lake Constance) all testify to a widely recognized suitability within many strands of Western monasticism of small islands as monastery locations.

### The Island as a Symbol

Apart from its obvious isolation, that is, the sea replacing the desert's sand, an island is a complex monastic symbol. An island is cut off from the rest of the world; as such it comprises a microcosm of the earth, and it becomes a world in itself and can symbolize either the Kingdom, a utopia, or a dystopia. Just as the earthly inhabited land mass (the *orbis terrarum*) is a hemisphere surrounded by the ocean, so the island is a small roundel of land set in the sea. This symbolic role can be seen in Eucherius' *De laude heremi*, in which the island is a type of paradise, a place where Christ's plan for life can be realized in miniature, supplying a foretaste of heaven. Here is a land where peace reigns, where praise ascends like incense (cf. Ps. 141:2), where the Law is meditated on (cf. Ps. 1:2), and where the inhabitants are given to contemplation. As the tiny land mass of the island now is, so the gigantic land mass of the three continents should become. A similar image of the island can be seen in Adomnán's *Vita Columbae*: from Iona proceed the Word of God, missions of peace, and examples of holiness to the surrounding territories. The island monastery is a liminal place marking the boundary between tended land and the limitless ocean. An entry point and an outpost, it is a place of safe retreat and a place of penitential exile. It belongs partly to the inhabited world of the mainland and yet remains wholly apart. All these resonances of place make an island an ideal religious site, as these qualities correspond directly to the role of the monastery within larger Christian society. Reversing the symbolism

Inchmahome Priory (Augustinian Canons), on an island in the Lake of Menteith, near Callander, Scotland, 13th century.
Photo courtesy of Chris Schabel

Cloister of the Benedictine Abbey of Mont-St.-Michel (Manche), France, 11th–12th century.
Photo courtesy of J. Feuillie/CNMHS

a monastery is an island of calm in the turmoil of the world's sea.

Because most monastic islands lie close to land, they can be seen as on its edge or frontier, and so they exercise an apotropaic function. Set at the limits of Christ's mission from beyond, when demons come to assault the Church, islands function as forts holding the demons at a distance. Monasteries such as Skellig Michael and Mont-St.-Michel dedicated to the Archangel Michael (the conqueror of the demons) seem to indicate that this was part of these island hermits' task. Those sites where a monastery was perched high up on a rocky outcrop (e.g., Bardsey or Lindisfarne in addition to the Michael dedications) can be understood as places where monks carried spiritual warfare up into the domain of the evil "aerial animals" (St. Augustine's name for demons) so that the latter cannot "wander throughout the world for the ruin of souls" (traditional Catholic prayer to St. Michael).

The island can also stand for dystopia – a place of evil within a landscape of fear. Here the classic example is the island of Volcano in the Lipari Islands. This was the place of terror and the "gates of hell" (cf. Matt. 16:18) discussed by Gregory the Great (*Dialogi* 4.28–31). Here an island marks the transition between this world and Death, just as an island monastery marks the boundary between this world and Life. In a less extreme form, the island is the place that is "cut-off from the land of the living" (cf. Isa. 53:8, Jer. 11:19, and Ezek. 26:20) and so can become a place of extreme penitence.

The challenge of reaching an island is also significant, for it demands braving the sea and weather in a small craft. This setting forth requires trust in divine care (cf. Matt. 8:23–27) and is analogous to putting oneself in God's hands and relying on providence (e.g., Jonah). Reaching the destination can be seen to depend mainly on grace, and it is within that framework that the task of rowing or sailing took place. On the water the monk saw God's mighty forces of which he sang (Ps. 107:23–25) and could challenge the evil beasts (Leviathan) that dwelt in the deeps.

All these symbols occur in the ninth-century allegory of the monastic life, the *Navigatio sancti Brendani*, in which a group of monks who want to know both what to choose and what to avoid in life visit a series of islands in the ocean. Each island visited represents a spiritual condition (ranging from the New Jerusalem to the entrance to hell) or a degree of monastic fervor. In those that are anticipations of heaven, the monks are obedient and sing the liturgy in harmony, whereas on other islands monastic disorder and the chaos of sin dominate: each state of the soul is as distinct as an island.

*Modern Examples*

Islands hold a special lure for people who seek space in which to reflect and pray, and on several that held medieval monasteries attempts have been made at a revival. In 1859 Cistercians settled on Lérins, and their monastery continues today. In 1906 a group led by Aelred Carlyle (1874–1955) established a monastery on Caldey Island. They left the island in 1928 for Prinknash, England, but were replaced by Cistercians. Although in general less interest is shown in living a monk's life on islands, many are now pilgrimage sites and places of retreat, notably Iona.

THOMAS O'LOUGHLIN

*See also* Aidan, St.; Columba, St.; Cyprus; Hermits: Eastern Christian; Iona, Scotland; Lérins, France; Lindisfarne/Holy Island, England; Mont-St.-Michel, France; Mount Athos, Greece; Origins: Western Christian; Scandinavia; Scotland

## Further Reading

Horn, Walter, Jenny White Marshall, and Grellan D. Rourke, *The Forgotten Hermitage of Skellig Michael*, Berkeley: University of California Press, 1990

O'Loughlin, Thomas, "The Symbol Gives Life: Eucherius of Lyons' Formula for Exegesis," in *Scriptural Interpretation in the Fathers: Letter and Spirit*, edited by Thomas Finan and Vincent Twomey, Dublin and Portland, Oregon: Four Courts Press, 1995

O'Loughlin, Thomas, "'The Gates of Hell': From Metaphor to Fact," *Milltown Studies* 38 (1996)

O'Loughlin, Thomas, "The View from Iona: Adomnán's Mental Maps," *Peritia* 10 (1996)

O'Loughlin, Thomas, "Living in the Ocean," in *Studies in the Cult of Saint Columba*, edited by Cormac Bourke, Dublin: Four Courts Press, 1997

O'Loughlin, Thomas, "Distant Islands: The Topography of Holiness in the *Navigatio sancti Brendani*," in *The Medieval Mystical Tradition: England, Ireland, Wales*, edited by Marion Glasscoe, Exeter: Exeter University, 1999

Riché, Pierre, *Education and Culture in the Barbarian West*, translated by John J. Contreni, Columbia: University of South Carolina Press, 1976

Thomas, Charles, "Hermits on Islands or Priests in a Landscape?" *Cornish Studies* 6 (1978)

Wooding, Jonathan, "St. Brendan's Boat: Dead Hides and the Living Sea in Columban and Related Hagiography," in *Studies in Irish Hagiography*, edited by John Carey, Máire Herbert, and Pádraig Ó Riann, Dublin: Four Courts Press, 1999

# Israel/Palestine

## History

Palestine can justifiably be called the crucible of Christian monasticism. Although it was the desert of Egypt that provided a landscape for both the anchoritic asceticism of Antony (251?–356) and the cenobitic monasticism of Pachomius (c. 290–346), it was in Palestine, and especially in the Judaean desert, that the two distinct ideals fused to form a model for monastic life that could be transplanted throughout the Christian world.

Historically, monasticism in Palestine began with the development of pilgrimage to the holy sites and has remained closely linked to pilgrimage to this day. The building in the fourth century of the Church of the Holy Sepulchre and other shrine churches in Jerusalem and the Church of the Nativity in Bethlehem provided a focus for pilgrim devotion. However, until imperial patronage of the holy sites had permeated Palestine, the Christians remained a minority group in the population without the resources to support a monastic network as extensive as that in Syria and Egypt. Palestinian monasticism centered on the Judaean desert, which stretched east of Jerusalem to Jericho and to the south as far as the Herodion. The region enjoyed its own biblical associations, such as the place of Christ's baptism at the Jordan River and the Mount of Temptation near Jericho. Moreover, the Judaean desert was less extensive and less harsh than the Egyptian one. Withdrawal from urban civilization was possible without a total loss of contact, for most monks in Palestine never dwelt more than a day's walk from Jerusalem. The pilgrimage tradition brought human contact as well, so that the monasteries that favored a cenobitic model, such as that of Theodosius (423–529), developed the functions of caring for pilgrims alongside the more central ones of meditation and prayer. The special character of Palestinian monasticism is further demonstrated by the development of a distinctive form of ascetic life, the *lavra*, in which the needs of anchoritism and cenobitism are combined.

It is impossible to assign a precise date to the first monastic foundations in Palestine, but the pilgrimage account of Egeria (380s) gives monks an important role in facilitating the devotions of pilgrims at the holy sites. Among claimants to be the founders of Palestinian monasticism are Hilarion, a follower of Antony's anchoritic model who built up a community of hermits in Gaza (307–330), and Chariton, who initiated the *lavra* type in the Judaean desert in the early fourth century and is associated with sites north of Jerusalem (Pharan), near Jericho (Douka), and deep in the desert, near Herodion. During the early fifth century, an urban monastic form, based in Jerusalem and combining devotion to the holy sites with social work, also emerged. Most of the important figures associated with early foundations appear not to have been natives of Palestine. For example, Chariton and Euthymius were from Asia Minor, whereas Latin monastic colonies were founded by Jerome (c. 345–420) and Rufinus with their disciples Paula (347–404) and Melania (d. c. 410) in the late fourth century. This diversity is a further reflection of the link between monasticism in the Holy Land and pilgrimage to the holy sites.

The fifth and sixth centuries saw considerable expansion in the numbers of monastic foundations in Palestine. Most of this activity took place in the Judaean desert, although Gaza, the Sea of Galilee, and the Sinai Peninsula were also settled by monks. The most important monastic figures of the fifth century were Euthymius (377–473), founder of a *lavra* at Khan al-Ahmar/Mishor Adumim; his friend Theoctistus; Theodosius the Coenobiarch (423–529), founder of a cenobitic monastery east of Bethlehem; and the Cappadocian monk Sabas (439–532), whose Great Lavra in the Kidron Valley southeast of Jerusalem proved to be the most enduring of all Palestinian monastic foundations.

The Palestinian monasteries, partly because of their proximity to Jerusalem itself, became involved during the fifth and sixth centuries in theological controversy. Following the lead taken by Euthymius and Sabas, the monasteries presented a foundation for Chalcedonian orthodoxy to take root in Palestine after the Council of Chalcedon (451) and the subsequent fragmentation of the Church in the eastern Mediterranean. Further controversy occurred in the sixth century. Dissenters from Sabas' views established a community at the New Lavra in 507 whose geographical remove from the network of existing monasteries in the desert reflects a more speculative approach to theology, as seen in their espousal of Origenism. The liturgical traditions and prayer life of the Palestinian monasteries were rendered complex by the ethnic diversity of the monks themselves; for example, Sabas' Great Lavra allowed Armenian monks to celebrate part of the liturgy in Armenian, whereas Theodosius established separate chapels for monks using different liturgical languages. Climatic and topographical conditions circumscribed the capacity of monks to engage in cultivation of the land. Recent archaeological research at Mar Sabas has shown that gardens were laid down, and it was possible to plant vineyards and olive groves in the Jordan valley around Jericho. However, much of the manual labor carried out by monks consisted of basket and rope making.

Historians now agree that the "golden age" of Palestinian monasticism was coming to an end even before the invasions of the Persians (614–628) and Arabs (634), partly because of theological tensions. However, the invasions, especially the Persian, which was accompanied by violence against monks, hastened a decline. Yet the Islamic domination of Palestine was not incompatible with the continuity of monastic life, especially at Mar Sabas. A group of monks, notably John of Damascus (c. 655–c. 750) from the 730s to the 750s, Theodore Abu Qurra from around 750 to 825, and Stephen the Sabaite, attest to the vitality of the intellectual life in the Judaean desert. A rupture seems to have occurred between the ninth and the end of the 11th centuries, and by 1099, when the First Crusade brought in its wake a Frankish settlement of the Holy Land, only Mar Sabas was still functioning.

The Frankish settlement proved to be sympathetic to the indigenous monastic tradition. Under a Latin ecclesiastical hierarchy and with the financial patronage of Emperor Manuel Comnenus (1142–80), a number of ancient monasteries were revived, including St. Euthymius, St. John the Baptist, St. George Choziba, and Kalamon. The revival took the form not only of rebuilding monasteries but also of cultivating ruins and adopting old anchoritic practices, as, for example, witnessed by the Greek pilgrim John Phokas (1185). Frankish tolerance might have arisen in part because, with the exception of a community at Chariton's site at Douka, the Franks were not greatly interested in the desert. Their own monastic presence in the Holy Land was restricted largely to a few eremitical communities, such as Pal-

maria in Galilee; a scattering of Cistercian houses, such as Belmont and Salvatio; and the maintenance of the few Benedictine houses that had pre-dated the First Crusade, notably St. Mary Latin in Jerusalem. Some new houses were founded, such as the nunneries at Bethany and St. Anne in Jerusalem. However, the Franks concentrated on maintaining and embellishing the shrine churches, most of which were given cathedral status and, in line with cathedrals in the West, staffed by regular canons. The most innovative features of the Frankish monastic presence were the military orders, which combined contemplative and martial functions as a development of the emerging ethics of holy war and chivalry in the West. One eremitical community, on Mount Carmel, that probably included indigenous Christians as well as Franks in an early stage (c. 1180s–1214) developed into the Carmelite order of friars. The expulsion of the Franks by the Muslims in 1291 eventually resulted in Frankish representation at the holy sites being restricted to the Franciscans.

Throughout the Frankish period, the confessional diversity that had been so early a characteristic of Palestinian monasticism continued in the Armenian monastery of St. James, the Syrian Orthodox foundation of Mary Magdalene, and Coptic, Ethiopian, and Georgian monasteries in Jerusalem. The different confessions maintain a precarious relationship in the holy sites to the present day, although tensions between Orthodox, Franciscans, and Armenians have often been grave. The Mamluk conquests of the 13th century restricted but did not prevent access to the holy sites. After centuries for which our knowledge of monasticism in Palestine is obscure, a new Western colonization began in the 19th century, marked, for example, by the settlement of Russian and French monks in Jerusalem. However, the political climate since 1948 has exposed the indigenous Christianity in Israel to tensions from which recovery may prove difficult. The liturgical life at monasteries such as Mar Sabas, Choziba, and Dair Hajla (Kalamon) remains strong, partly because of the recruitment of Orthodox monks from the United States and Slavic countries. Nevertheless, the effects of two generations of emigration have left the indigenous Christian community in Israel weaker than ever. It is to be hoped that this depopulation will not lead the distinguished history of monasticism in the Holy Land to extinction.

*Sites*

Only one Palestinian monastery, the Great Lavra of St. Sabas (498), has survived from its foundation without rupture as a functioning religious community. Sabas spent 12 years in the *lavra* of Theoctistus before periods of solitude and wandering in the desert. In 483 his cave dwelling in the wadi Kidron, southeast of Jerusalem, began to attract disciples. In 490 Sabas dedicated a large cave as a church, and between 491 and 501 a hospice, bakery, and reservoir were added. During the sixth century the Great Lavra had as many as 300 monks. The bones of the monks that were killed in the Persian invasion of 614 can still be seen in the martyrium, but despite this setback the monastery survived to enjoy a period of liturgical and intellectual brilliance in the eighth and ninth centuries. Many of the present buildings date from post-earthquake reconstruction in the 19th century. The monastery of Theodosius the Coenobiarch, about halfway between Bethlehem and Mar Sabas, was founded in 479. At its peak in the early sixth century, a community of 400 monks lived here, serving four churches and maintaining a pilgrims' hostel and hospitals. The reconstruction of 1893, known as Deir Dosi, stands on the same spot but is much smaller.

To the east of Jerusalem stand the ruins of two other foundations of the same period. Euthymius (377–473) came to Palestine from Armenia and was a disciple of Chariton at Pharan before founding a *lavra* with Theoctistus. The monastery at Khan al-Ahmar/Mishor Adumim, off the Jerusalem-Jericho road, was founded in 428. Relations between the two foundations were close, and Euthymius specified that monks who wanted to join his *lavra* must first serve an apprenticeship with Theoctistus. After his death the *lavra* became a cenobitic monastery. Cyril of Scythopolis, the most important literary source for early desert monasticism, lived here in the mid–sixth century. Another example of the desert *coenobium* is the recently excavated monastery of Martyrius, which, like that of Euthymius, is now surrounded by modern development. The ground plan, preserved almost in its entirety, allows the visitor to understand perfectly the organization of a monastery of this period, with its pilgrims' hostel, bathhouse, refectory, burial cave, and church. Martyrius, a Cappadocian, arrived in Palestine in 457 and entered the *lavra* of Euthymius before founding his own monastery. In 478 he became patriarch of Jerusalem but continued to direct the development of the monastery.

Another surviving example of a desert monastery is St. George of Choziba, a *lavra* founded by John of Thebes around 480 in the wadi Qilt, between Jerusalem and Jericho. This was one of the monasteries that was revived during the 12th century. Another site that was revived under the crusaders was the monastery at the Mount of Temptation (Jebel Quruntul), outside Jericho. Originally, the site was settled by Douka in 340 but was abandoned after the Persian invasion, only to be resettled by Frankish hermits before 1116. The present occupied buildings are 19th-century reconstructions. Virtually nothing survives of the Frankish monastic presence in the 12th to 13th centuries, but the oratory and some cells from the 13th-century hermitage on Mount Carmel give an indication of how Western monks developed their own version of the Byzantine *lavra*. Here hermits lived in individual cells and joined together daily for communal worship in the oratory.

ANDREW JOTISCHKY

*See also* Armenia; Desert Mothers; Egypt; Ethiopia; Hermits: Eastern Christian; Jerome, St.; Jerusalem, Israel; Lavra; Libraries: Western Christian; Office, Daily: Eastern Christian; Origins: Eastern Christian; Pilgrimages, Christian: Near East; Syria; Warrior Monks: Christian

**Further Reading**

Binns, John, *Ascetics and Ambassadors of Christ: The Monasteries of Palestine, 314–631*, Oxford and New York: Clarendon Press, 1994
Chitty, Derwas, *The Desert a City: An Introduction to the Study of Egyptian and Palestinian Monasticism under the Christian Empire*, Oxford: Basil Blackwell, and Crestwood, New York: St. Vladimir's Seminary Press, 1966
Cyril of Scythopolis, *Lives of the Monks of Palestine*, translated by R.M. Price, Kalamazoo, Michigan: Cistercian Publications, 1991
Flusin, Bernard, *Saint Anastase le Perse et l'histoire de la Palestine au début du VIIe siècle*, Paris: CNRS, 1992
Hirschfeld, Yizhar, *The Judean Desert Monasteries in the Byzantine Period*, New Haven, Connecticut: Yale University Press, 1992
Hunt, E.D., *Holy Land Pilgrimage in the Later Roman Empire, A.D. 312–460*, Oxford: Clarendon Press, 1982
Jotischky, Andrew, *The Perfection of Solitude: Hermits and Monks in the Crusader States*, University Park: Penn State University Press, 1995
Patrich, Joseph, *Sabas, Leader of Palestinian Monasticism: A Comparative Study in Eastern Monasticism, Fourth to Seventh Centuries*, Washington D.C.: Dumbarton Oaks Research Library and Collection, 1995
Perrone, Lorenzo, *La chiesa di Palestina e le controversie christologiche: Dal Concilio di Efeso (431) al secondo Concilio di Costantinopoli (553)*, Brescia: Paideia, 1980
Perrone, Lorenzo, "Monasticism in the Holy Land: From the Beginnings to the Crusaders," *Proche-Orient Chrétien* 45 (1995)

# Istanbul, Turkey

Istanbul was once a major center of monasticism, when, known as Constantinople, it served as the capital of the late Roman or Byzantine Empire. From 323 until its capture by the Ottoman Turks in 1453, Constantinople was the most important patriarchate of the eastern Mediterranean. Because it held the residence of both emperor and patriarch, the city attracted patrons who were the great benefactors of monastic institutions.

In the Byzantine world the monks and nuns became the ideal Christians – those who were intent on living a life of perfection. Many wealthy people, including members of the imperial family, often took vows and were clothed in the monastic habit as death approached. It would be hard to overestimate the importance of the monk and nun in Constantinople, where schools, hospitals, hospices, and the copying of manuscripts occupied the time not spent in prayer.

Around 382, on the invitation of Emperor Theodosius I (379–395), Isaac, a Syrian anchorite, formed the first orthodox monastic community in Constantinople. He located it outside Constantine's walls, in the eastern Psamathia quarter, near the Golden Gate. One of his disciples was Dalmatios, an officer in the imperial guard. It was he who endowed the community and, on Isaac's death in 406, succeeded him as abbot of the monastery, which subsequently took his name. Its abbot, with the title of archimandrite, acted as titular head of all the city's monks.

Exterior of the church of the Holy Savior in Chora, Istanbul. The church contains the best preserved mosaics of any extant church in the city.
**Photo courtesy of Charles Frazee**

Around 420 the Byzantine capital welcomed Alexander, also a Syrian, who arrived with his disciples. Alexander took literally Jesus' admonition to pray always, so he required that the liturgical offices in his community never stop. The Eucharistic liturgy and the chanting of psalms, hymns, and prayers gave the impression that the monks never slept, so they received the name *akoimetoi* ("the sleepless ones"). In fact, the monks rotated the offices among themselves in different shifts, for the community grew to about 300 individuals. In 463, on the invitation of Studius, consul of the East, they were given a residence and church dedicated to St. John the Baptist. The Stoudios monastery was one of several monasteries built in the fifth century as a wave of enthusiasm for the monastic life swept Constantinople. Recruits came from all over the empire – Egyptians, Syrians, and Armenians – imparting an ethnic flavor to some of these institutions.

In Justinian's day (527–565) the number of monasteries in Constantinople reached 68, with an additional 40 located in Chalcedon, across the Bosporus. Cenobitic institutions were added to a number of hermits, stylites, and holy fools that made

the Byzantine capital also the monastic capital of the urban Christian world.

After 726 Constantinople's monastic life was violently shaken when Emperor Leo III (717–741) began his attack on the icons. Many historians regard iconoclasm as a not-so-subtle attack on monks, for too many potential soldiers and taxpayers and their estates were lost because of the large number of recruits to the religious life. Although some monks supported the imperial policy, most suffered harassment and exile because of their resistance to iconoclasm. Leo III's son Constantine V (741–775) vigorously persecuted the capital's monks, most of whom left the capital for Mount Olympos (now Ulu Dâg) in Bithynia.

Two remarkable persons, Plato and Theodore (759–826), lived in monasteries on Mount Olympos, and after the Seventh Ecumenical Council had restored the icons in 787, they were prepared to return to the city on the invitation of Empress Irene (797–802). She gave Theodore and Plato the monastery of Stoudios for themselves and their followers, as too few *akoimetoi* remained. New enthusiasm for the monastic life brought hundreds of novices into the community until it numbered 700 monks. Theodore laid down strong lines of administration, set rigid prescriptions for the daily offices, and added to the monastic enclosure a hospital, school, scriptorium, and workshop for icon painters.

The daily life of the Studite monk followed a pattern based on the counsels of St. Basil the Great (c. 330–379) as interpreted by Theodore. Several hours before dawn the monks arose from the reed mats on which they slept in the monastic dormitory. They hurried to the darkened church, where they prayed in silence until the officiating priest incensed the building. Then followed the night prayer, the *mesonyktikon*, and the dawn office, the *orthros*. While the service was in progress, the abbot proceeded to a secluded place in the church, and each monk who felt the need to do so confessed his faults. The office finished, then, on three days of the week, Theodore gave an instruction. This completed, the monks spent the remainder of the day at work and prayer. Just before midday the Eucharist was offered and afterward the main meal eaten. Abstinence was kept throughout the year, and fasting (when only one meal was permitted) came on Wednesdays and Fridays and every day during Lenten and other seasons of fasting. All the monks wore the same habits, exchanging them once a week for a clean ones.

The other monasteries of Constantinople could not have varied their programs too much from that of Stoudios. Each monastery followed its own *typikon*, a constitution that the founder prescribed, but abbots were allowed a certain latitude to amplify or limit what the *typikon* of their monasteries required. Many monasteries held miraculous icons, such as that of the Hodegon Monastery east of Hagia Sophia near the seawalls. Its treasure was thought to be St. Luke's picture of Mary, the Virgin Hodegetria, the most important icon of the city. In the twelfth century a Jewish traveler to Constantinople claimed that the city boasted as many monasteries as days in the year.

In 1204 soldiers of the Fourth Crusade captured Constantinople, and many of the major monasteries of the city passed into the hands of Latin monks and friars. On the return of Constantinople to a Byzantine emperor in 1261, the great monasteries were left impoverished, and many of the smaller ones disappeared. Emperor Michael VIII Palaiologos (1234?–1282) combined those that were left into more viable institutions. His widowed daughter Maria, who had been sent off to marry the son of the Mongol Khan Hulagu, returned to Constantinople and endowed a convent whose church, St. Mary of the Mongols, is the one monastic building still in Christian ownership, located in the Fener district of modern Istanbul.

The most outstanding example of monastic churches endowed in the 14th century is known as Holy Savior in Chora, built between 1316 and 1321, just inside the Theodosian walls. In one of the brilliant mosaics of the building, Theodore Metochites, an officer at the court, is pictured donating the church after its restoration. For a visitor to modern Istanbul, the Chora monastery (now Kariye Camii museum) is the best choice for observing the past glories of Byzantium. The monasteries in this final period of Christian Constantinople were less numerous and definitely poorer, as they shared in the general decline of the Byzantine world.

In 1453 the Ottoman Turks captured Constantinople, eventually making it their capital. Few monasteries survived the conquest, and those that did eventually disappeared. None remain today. Several monastic churches that became mosques are still extant in Istanbul, but most are in ruins.

CHARLES A. FRAZEE

*See also* Archaeology: Near East; Architecture: Eastern Christian Monasteries; Basil the Great, St.; Hagiography: Eastern Christian; Hymnographers; Iconoclasm (Controversy); Island Monasteries, Christian; Liturgy: Eastern Christian; Mount Athos, Greece; Origins: Eastern Christian; Pilgrimages, Christian: Eastern Europe; Pilgrimages, Christian: Near East; Syria; Theodore of Stoudios, St.; Visual Arts, Eastern Christian: Painting

**Further Reading**
Charanis, Peter, "The Monk as an Element of Byzantine Society," *Dumbarton Oaks Papers* 4 (1948)
Dagron, G., "Les moines et la ville: Le monachisme à Constantinople jusqu'au concile de Chalcédonie (451)," *Travaux et Mémoires* 4 (1970)
Frazee, Charles, "St. Theodore of Stoudios and Ninth-Century Monasticism in Constantinople," *Studia Monastica* 23:1 (1981)
Janin, Raymond, *La géographie ecclésiastique de l'empire byzantin*, volume 3: *Les églises et monastères*, Paris: Institut français d'études byzantines, 1953; 2nd edition, 1969
Lemerle, Paul, *Cinq études sur le XIe siècle byzantin*, Paris: Centre national de la recherche scientifique, 1977
Maclagan, Michael, *The City of Constantinople*, London: Thames and Hudson, and New York: Praeger, 1968
Mango, Cyril, *Le développement urbain de Constantinople: IVe–VIIe siècles*, Paris: de Boucard, 1990
Miller, Timothy, *The Birth of the Hospital in the Byzantine Empire*, Baltimore: Johns Hopkins University Press, 1985
Talbot, A-M., "An Introduction to Byzantine Monasticism," *Illinois Classical Studies* 12:2 (1987)

# Italian Benedictine Saints. *See* Saints, Italian Benedictine

# Italo-Greek Monasticism

During the period in which southern Italy and Sicily were culturally, politically, and religiously the Western extreme of the Byzantine Empire, indigenous Italo-Greek monasticism flourished, above all in Calabria. The spiritual life, structure, and ideals of this monasticism are known through a series of lives of Italo-Greek monks written between the 10th and 12th centuries. These lives (Greek, *Bioi*) portray some of the most influential of these monks, especially those who fled to Calabria during the time of the increasing Muslim occupation of Sicily.

In the 10th and 11th centuries, two regions harbored Italo-Greek monastic life: the Merkourion and the Latinianon, both in Calabria. The Merkourion was particularly suitable for the establishment of monastic settlements. Located along the valley of the Lao River, it has dense forests, mountains, ravines with abundant fresh water, and many natural grottoes and caves. Here some of the best-known Italo-Greek monks, such as Phantinos and his spiritual son, Neilos of Rossano, and the monastic family of Christopher and his sons, Sabas and Makarios, lived their monastic calling. The basic structure of their life was eremitic, but many of these hermits attracted disciples, and some of them even organized monasteries where their disciples live a communal life.

The earliest of these monastic saints whose life we possess is Elias the Younger (832–903). He was born in Enna in Sicily and after a long pilgrimage moved to Taormina and then to Salinas in Calabria, where he and his disciple Daniel lived in solitude, gradually gathering other monks. Eventually Elias was summoned to come to the emperor in Constantinople but died on his journey there. The *Life of Elias the Speleot* (the cave dweller; c. 860–c. 960) recalls a man born in Reggio in Calabria who around the age of 18 decided that he must renounce all his possessions and become a monk. He entered the monastic life in Sicily but returned to Reggio, where he met Elias the Younger and Daniel. He established a monastery in a cave for his disciples. To this day this cave remains a pilgrimage site. The lives of the monastic family of Christopher and his wife, Kale, and their sons, Sabas and Makarios (tenth century), from Collesano in Sicily recount the story of an entire family who entered the monastic life in Sicily and then moved to Calabria to escape the Saracens. Sabas and Makarios settled in the Merkourion, and, beginning as hermits, Sabas gradually gathered many monks around him while spending five days of the week in solitude. He finally became head of many monks in the surrounding regions in a type of monastic federation. Eventually Sabas moved farther north to Salerno and then traveled to Rome, where he died. Makarios then became head of the monastic federation.

The longest and most complete life is that of Neilos the Younger (910–1004) of Rossano in Calabria. This is the

The Catholicon (monastic church), Monastery of St. Mary Nea Odigetria, known as the Patirion, Rossano, Calabria, Italy, 12th century.
Photo courtesy of David Hester

The Catholicon (monastic church) of the monastery at Stilo, Calabria, Italy.
Photo courtesy of David Hester

Mosaic over the entrance to the nave of the Catholicon, Monastery of Grottaferrata, Latium, Italy, 12th century. The small figure is thought to represent the Italo-Greek monk Bartholomew the Younger, builder of the church.
Photo courtesy of David Hester

masterpiece of Italo-Greek hagiographic literature. Written by one of Neilos' disciples, it furnishes details about the culture, history, personalities, and daily monastic life of tenth-century southern Italy. In it one finds some of the great historical personalities of the era. Neilos began as a disciple of St. Phantinos but received permission to live as a hermit. He collected some disciples, the most important of whom was Blessed Stephen, who remained with him all his life. The life contains a detailed account of the stay of Neilos near the Benedictine monastery of Monte Cassino. Initially Neilos distrusted the monks there as foreigners, but gradually he changed his opinion. He then composed a service in honor of St. Benedict and held a long discussion with the monks about differences between the Greeks and the Latins. Neilos then departed for Rome, where be became involved in a dispute between a pope and an antipope and the German Emperor Otto III (983–1002). At the end of his life, Neilos established a monastery at Grottaferrata in the Alban Hills south of Rome. This monastery is the only Italo-Greek monastery still functioning.

The final major life of an Italo-Greek monk is that of Bartholomew of Simeri (1050/60–1130). Here again the author, a monastic contemporary, showed a grasp of history and drama, mentioning many important Byzantine and Norman historical figures. The life describes the situation of the Italo-Greek monks at the beginning of the Norman period in the late 11th century, when the Norman royalty were actively involved in Italo-Greek culture. Bartholomew began the monastic life by joining a hermit who taught him how to live the monastic life. He became a hermit, living in a cave and practicing strict asceticism. He attracted followers and was planning to abandon them when he had a vision that told him to build a monastery at Rossano, the Patirion. Queen Adelaide, widow of Roger I (1072–1101) and regent for Roger II, helped Bartholomew in this project. After the Normans placed southern Italy again under the authority of the Patriarchate of Rome, Bartholomew traveled to Rome, where the pope exempted his monastery from the control of the local bishop. He then journeyed to Constantinople, where Emperor Alexius I Comnenus (1081–1118) gave him many gifts and books for the monastery. He also visited Mount Athos to fulfill a request to reform a monastery. When he returned to Italy, he was summoned by the Norman king, Roger II (1103–1154), before whom a miracle took place at the end of the promontory in Messina's harbor. The king built a monastery, Most Holy Savior, at the site of the miracle. This monastery became the head of many of the Italo-Greek monasteries in Sicily and Calabria, initiating the cenobitic transformation of Italo-Greek monasticism.

These are not the only Italo-Greek monks whose deeds are recorded. Some other monks whose lives remain are Leo-Luke of Corleone, Luke of Demena, Bitalios of Castronovo, Gregory of Cassano, Phantinos the Younger, Nikodemos of Kellarana, Bartholomew the Younger (the builder of the monastery church at Grottaferrata), Philaret the Younger of Seminara, and John Theristes.

After the Norman occupation of southern Italy and Sicily (1072–1091), both Italo-Greek monasticism and Italo-Greek society were gradually transformed. Monasticism developed in a strongly cenobitic direction with an emphasis on monks living together in monasteries linked in large monastic confederations. An even greater transformation occurred in Italo-Greek society as the Italo-Greeks were gradually Latinized, becoming part of the Latin Church, and their culture was gradually absorbed into Latin culture. Eventually the monastic life of the Italo-Greeks declined so much that during visitations made to the Italo-Greek monasteries in 1457–1458, most of the monks were found to be Latins, who could no longer celebrate the church services or read the few remaining Greek books found in the libraries. At this time a new migration of Albanian Orthodox exiles came to Calabria and Sicily to continue the legacy of Byzantine Christianity in Italy.

DAVID PAUL HESTER

*See also* Hagiography: Eastern Christian; Istanbul, Turkey; Monte Cassino, Italy; Mount Athos, Greece; Orthodox Monasticism: Byzantine

### Further Reading

*Bollettino della Badia Greca di Grottaferrata*, Grottaferrata, Italy: Scuola Tipografica Italo-Orientale "S. Nilo," 1947–

Ferrante, Nicola, *Santi Italogreci in Calabria*, Reggio Calabria: Edizioni Parallelo 38, 1981

Gay, Giulio, *L'Italia meridionale e l'Empero Bizantino dall'avvento di Basilio I alla resa di Bari ai Normanni (867–1071)*, Firenze, 1917

Giovanelli, Germano, editor, *Vita di S. Nilo, fondatore e patrono di Grottaferrata*, Grottaferrata: Badia di Grottaferrata, 1966

Guillou, André, *Aspetti della civiltà bizantina in Italia: Società e cultura*, Bari: Ecumenica Editrice, 1976

Hester, David, *Monasticism and Spirituality of the Italo-Greeks*, Thessaloniki: Patriarchal Institute of Patristic Studies, 1992

# Italy. *See* Assisi, Italy; Bobbio, Italy; Florence, Italy; Monte Cassino, Italy; Subiaco, Italy

# J

## Jain Monasticism and Buddhist Monasticism

Strong similarities exist between the code of monastic behavior applicable to Jain monks and that applying in Buddhist monastic life. In all likelihood this similarity in monastic codes is not due to mutual borrowing or imitation but rather shows that each of these rival religious groups modeled its monastic rules on preexisting codes of ascetic behavior. Gautama Buddha, founder of Buddhism, and Vardhamana Mahavira (Vārdhamāna Mahāvīra), the great teacher of the Jains, were contemporaries. They lived in the same area of eastern India (ancient Magadha, present-day Bihar), and the religious movements each separately set in motion coexisted from the time of these religious teachers until the disappearance of Buddhism from India sometime before A.D. 1400. Jainism's unbroken history continues in India up to today. Judging from the literary remains, the Jain and Buddhist monastic movements appear to owe more to preexisting modes of ascetic/monastic behavior than to mutual interaction. The three major anti-ritualistic traditions – Brahmanical asceticism, Buddhist monachism, and Jain monachism – that emerged in the valley of the Ganges by about the fifth century B.C. are likely to have sprung from shared roots: all three teach the importance of karma in determining rebirth and the need to seek personal liberation (*moksha*) from that round of rebirth (*samsara*), and, although their soteriologies differ, all three have at their core mendicancy, lifelong celibacy, and homeless wandering.

In studying the monastic practice of either the Buddhists or the Jains, setting the early Buddhist model beside the Jain reveals the parallel and occasionally independent developments within each. In both movements the role of the monastic community (monks and nuns) was from the beginning absolutely central, although the precise nature of that role has been the subject of considerable debate. Much has been written about the nature of early Buddhism, but less attention has been paid to the relationships that exist between it and Jainism or the similarities and differences in the parallel monastic traditions. No comprehensive study of the monastic practices of early Jainism has yet been undertaken (and still less of its medieval or modern monastic traditions). In some external matters we can see that the Buddhists did take care to distinguish themselves from other groups. For example, in the *Mahavagga* of the Buddhist Vinaya-pitaka (I.70), rules forbid Buddhist monks to go without robe or bowl lest they give the impression of belonging to other sects. In color too the ruddy robes of the Buddhist monk contrast against the undyed cloth of the Shvetambara Jain monk. Jain monks were allowed alms bowls made of gourds or wood, whereas Buddhists were not permitted bowls of wood. Notwithstanding these matters of external appearance, the core monastic rules of both sects (as detailed in literary remains) have much in common and are more likely to have come from a common source than to have been copied from each other.

In India the three ascetic/monastic traditions – the Vedic-Brahmanical, the Buddhist, and the Jain – have transmitted separate streams of literary material stating normative rules for individual behavior. Being the oldest detailed evidence, these sources must be the starting point of any comparison of Buddhist and Jain monastic practice. However, literary evidence is not the only source for information on the two monastic traditions. Gregory Schopen (1997) has made a number of studies of Buddhist monastic practice, setting inscriptional sources against literary ones. No such comprehensive studies have yet been attempted using the considerable quantity of Jain inscriptional materials.

The rules of the Vedic-Brahmanical tradition are contained in the extensive *dharmashastra* (*dharmaśāstra*) literature in Sanskrit that has been exhaustively studied by P.V. Kane (1930–1962). Although this tradition did not evolve monastic groupings on the scale of the other two, the rules for ascetic behavior given in these sources are strikingly similar to those found in the Jain and Buddhist sources. The oldest of the *dharmashastra*s has been dated to 600 to 400 B.C. (Derrett, 1973), but most scholars are unwilling to say more than that the oldest of these were likely to have been composed by the beginning of the fourth century B.C. (Olivelle, 1993).

For the Buddhist tradition the monastic code (Vinaya) of the Theravāda school preserved in Pāli is the oldest of the complete extant versions. It was first written down around 100 B.C. in Sri Lanka, although it was not given its current form until the time of the scholiast Buddhaghosa (fifth century A.D.). It too has been studied in some detail. The code of behavior transmitted by this sole surviving descendent of the "Hīnayāna" Buddhist sects was equally fundamental for the equivalent codes of the Mahāyāna sects.

The discipline texts of the Jains are more problematic and have received less attention, partly because the rules are more scattered (Tatia, 1981) and partly because printed versions have been difficult to obtain (especially the commentaries). Some Jain monks oppose the publication of these texts because they are viewed as relevant only to monks and nuns and not suitable for lay individuals. For the Shvetambara Jains, the Angas, the Cheyasuttas, and the Mulasuttas (all in Prakrit), together with their exegetical literature (in Sanskrit), play the same role as the Vinaya texts do for the Buddhists. In particular three works preserved in the Shvetambara "canon" – the *Ayara-*, *Kappa-*, and *Vavahara-sutta*s – are generally regarded as giving the rules valid for Jain monks and nuns, although section 3 of the *Dasaveyaliya* also contains rules for monastic behavior. The Digambara Jains maintain that the earliest scriptures were lost but that the rules for Digambara monks are given in such works as Kundakunda's *Niyamasara* and the *Mulacara* (further sources are listed in Prasad, 1972). The dating of the Jain texts is problematic, as most contain several layers of material, but there is no reason to doubt that much of the material goes back to the time of Mahavira.

Comparing the literary sources for Jain and Buddhist monastic rules raises a larger question concerning the ultimate origins of the ascetic tradition itself in ancient India. Given the relative chronologies and the extensive overlapping of teachings and practices, Jainism and Buddhism have to be seen as emerging within the context of that ascetic tradition. A number of theories have been proposed about origins, but no academic consensus has yet developed. For early generations of scholars, the most likely explanation for the parallels in monastic rules found in Jain and Buddhist texts was that both had borrowed them from the codes developed for ascetics within the (Aryan) Vedic-Brahmanical tradition. The clearest statement of this is by Hermann Jacobi (1884): five undertakings are valid for all Buddhists (lay and monastic, although with a few strengthenings for monastic use):

(1) not to harm living beings
(2) not to take what is not given
(3) not to have wrong conduct in sexual matters (this means celibacy for monastic individuals)
(4) not to indulge in false speech
(5) not to take intoxicants

The parallels when compared with the five primary rules for Jain monks are obvious:

(1) not to destroy life
(2) not to lie
(3) not to take what is not given
(4) celibacy
(5) not to have any worldly possessions

Jacobi went on to point out that the Jain series matched more closely that of the Vedic-Brahmanical ascetics:

(1) not injuring living beings
(2) truthfulness
(3) not taking the property of others
(4) continence
(5) liberality

Jacobi added that it would have been unlikely for the Jains to imitate the Buddhists, who were, after all, their rivals when they had the older more respected model of the Brahmanic ascetics to copy. Max Müller, H. Kern, Albrecht Weber, E.W.O. Windisch, and H. Oldenberg all supported this initial model.

Early in the 20th century, T.W. Rhys Davids, P. Deussen, and R. Garbe (Bronkhorst, 1993) traced the origin of asceticism in India to a reaction against the religion of the Vedas, viewing Buddhism, Jainism, and the Vedic-Brahmanical Upanishad literature as new movements defining themselves in opposition to the main religious current with its focus on sacrifice and household life. The discovery of the pre-Vedic Indus centers of urbanization led some scholars – Sukumar Dutt, Étienne Lamotte, G.C. Pande, and A.K. Warder – to develop this thesis and propose a non-Vedic (non-Aryan) origin for Indian asceticism. Johannes Bronkhorst (1993) has attempted to synthesize these two viewpoints and suggested that Indian asceticism emerged from two sources, one Vedic and the other non-Vedic. However, the proposal of dual sources has not been universally accepted, Olivelle preferring to say that "the most we can say is that the ascetic traditions contain beliefs and practices not contained in the early [V]edic literature, and that they are in many ways opposed to the central [V]edic ideas" (*Rules and Regulations of Brahmanical Asceticism: Yatidharmasamuccaya of Yadava Prakasa*, edited and translated by Patrick Olivelle, 1995). Olivelle had earlier opposed the notion of Buddhist and Jain monastic codes having borrowed from Vedic-Brahmanical sources on the grounds of chronology but had accepted that the strong parallels between the movements demonstrated a remarkable uniformity in life pattern for the three different types of ascetics (1974).

Whatever the origins of Indian asceticism, the close parallels found in the three traditions indicate some kind of common source. Although accounts of individuals transferring allegiance from one sect to the other exist, it is unlikely that such converts could have influenced the fundamental monastic codes of Jainism or Buddhism, which are ascribed to the founders themselves. The Buddha and Mahavira both underwent training with groups of ascetics before they founded their own monastic groupings, and they would have been exposed to preexisting codes of ascetic practice during that time. However, whether the Jains and Buddhists drew directly from the Vedic-Brahmanical model cannot be proven.

Detailed comparative studies based on Vedic-Brahmanical, Jain, and Buddhist sources have been made by Colette Caillat (1965), Nand Kishore Prasad (1972), and more recently by Thomas Oberlies (1997). Caillat focused on the rules for confession of breaches of Jain monastic discipline and subsequent atonement. Although Prasad's study is detailed, his conclusions are rather general and tend to repeat earlier judgments. Oberlies has made a preliminary but indicative study focusing on the rules regulating the life of a pupil (whether of the Veda, or a Jain or Buddhist novice), a monk's/ascetic's permitted paraphernalia, and the rules for dwelling places and alms gathering. In addition to the already identified parallelism of rules, Oberlies has shown that where the monastic codes of the Jains and the Buddhists diverge, the conservative Jains tend to retain the older forms of rules, at times increasing their severity, whereas the rules formulated for Buddhists show a tendency to innovation and increased flexibility. This accords with the widespread Jain view of Buddhist monastic law that the Buddhists were less stringent about matters that the Jains considered to be important (i.e., matters of food and the practice of austerities) and thus that the Buddhist monastics were corrupt (Dundas, 1992). In the light of the very different subsequent histories of these two movements (Buddhism became a pan-Asian religion, whereas Jainism never spread beyond India), it is hard to resist suggesting that the flexibility of Buddhist monastic behavior might have been one of the factors aiding the spread of Buddhism, whereas the rigidity of Jain practice, especially in regard to accepting food, can be seen as curtailing its ability to proselytize.

ROYCE WILES

*See also* Ashram, Influence of; Buddhism: Overview; Critiques of Buddhist Monasticism: Indo-Tibetan; Hygiene: Buddhist Perspectives; Master and Pupil: Buddhist Perspectives; Rules, Buddhist (Vinaya): Historical

**Further Reading**

Bronkhorst, Johannes, *The Two Sources of Indian Asceticism* (Schweizer Asiatische Studien, volume 13), New York: Lang, 1993

Caillat, Colette, *Les Éxpiations dans le Ritual Ancien des Religieux Jaina* (Publications de l'Institut de Civilisation indienne, série in-8, fascicle 25), Paris: Éditions de Boccard, 1965; as *Atonements in the Ancient Ritual of the Jaina Monks* (Lalbhai Dalpatbhai series, 49), Ahmedabad: L.D. Institute of Indology, 1975

Deo, Shantaram Bhalchandra, *History of Jaina Monachism from Inscriptions and Literature* (Deccan College Dissertation Series, 17), Poona: Deccan College Post-graduate and Research Institute, 1956

Derrett, J. Duncan M., *Dharmaśāstra and Juridical Literature*, Wiesbaden: Otto Harrassowitz, 1973

Dundas, Paul, *The Jains*, London: Routledge, 1992

Jacobi, Hermann, *Gaina Sūtras* (Sacred Books of the East, volume 22), part 1, Oxford: Oxford University Press, 1884; New York: Scribner, 1901

Kane, P.V., *History of Dharmaśāstra*, Poona: Bhandarkar Oriental Research Institute, 1930–1962, revised edition 1968–

Oberlies, Thomas, "Neuer Wein in alten Schläuchen?: Zur Geschichte der buddhistischen Ordensregeln," *Bulletin d'Études Indiennes* 15 (1997)

Olivelle, Patrick, *The Origin and the Early Development of Buddhist Monachism*, Colombo: Gunasena, 1974

Olivelle, Patrick, *The Āśrama System: The History and Hermeneutics of a Religious Institution*, Oxford and New York: Oxford University Press, 1993

Prasad, Nand Kishore, *Studies in Buddhist and Jaina Monachism* (Prakrit Jaina Institute Research Publication Series, volume 9), Vaishali: Research Institute of Prakrit, Jainology and Ahimsa, 1972

Schopen, Gregory, *Bones, Stones, and Buddhist Monks: Collected Papers on the Archaeology, Epigraphy, and Texts of Monastic Buddhism in India* (Studies in the Buddhist Traditions), Honolulu: University of Hawaii Press, 1997

Tatia, Nathmal, and Muni Mahendrakumar, *Aspects of Jaina Monasticism*, New Delhi: Today and Tomorrow's Printers, 1981

# Jansenist Controversy

Jansenism was a 17th-century movement within Roman Catholicism that proved especially popular among monastics in France and was condemned as heretical. It arose out of the writing of the Dutch theologian Cornelius Jansen (1585–1638), who died as bishop of Ypres. In his *Augustinus* (1638) Jansen deplored what he believed to be a stale moral theology that had been impoverished by ceremonialism and semi-Pelagianism (i.e., the doctrine that God grants grace in response to human behavior). Jansen emphasized humankind's utter dependence on God and insisted that salvation comes solely through the love of God, which in turn creates faith. That love is effected by conversion, which is the gratuitous gift of God. Jansen taught that without special grace, human beings are too sinful to follow God's commandments. Because he also taught that the operation of God's grace was irresistible, Jansen came to be accused of a kind of predestinarianism akin to that of Calvinism, although he insisted on his loyalty to the Catholic Church. The title of his treatise *Augustinus* betrays the influence of the African father of the Church on his thought.

Jansenism became popular in France because of the efforts of capable disciples, most of whom were vowed religious. Jean Duvergier, abbé de St.-Cyran (1581–1643), first spread the views of his friend Jansen throughout France. He enlisted the aid of the influential Arnauld family, especially Angélique Arnauld (1591–1661), who was prioress of the Benedictine convent of Port-Royal near Versailles, which remained a center of the Jansenist movement until the dissolution of the convent by the French government in 1705. However, during the 17th century Angélique's rigorous reform of Port-Royal attracted so many postulants that the nuns opened a second convent in Paris. Her brother Antoine Arnauld (1612–1694), a Sorbonne-educated priest, was possibly Jansenism's most influential intellectual. His work *Concerning Frequent Communion* (1643) was read more widely than Jansen's own *Augustinus*.

Just as Gallicanism sought the independence of the French Church from papal control, so Jansenism sought the Church's purification; indeed Jansenism enjoyed more popularity among Gallican than ultramontane (i.e., pro-papal) clergy. In this respect Jansenism marked a reaction against the Jesuits' handling of pastoral care. The Jesuits, who were confessors to Europe's royal families (Louis XIV's confessor was a Jesuit), favored a more lenient approach to the examination of conscience. As formulated by Luis de Molina (1535–1600), Jesuit doctrine held that severity in pastoral counseling would alienate those who most needed the Church, so they contended that confessors should grant absolution for the slightest of good grounds – an idea that became known as the doctrine of probabilism. Jansenist critics countered that confessors had to be severe, lest sins go unrepented and unpunished. Whereas Jesuits emphasized God's mercy and love toward penitents, Jansenists emphasized the gravity of human sinfulness and the majesty of God's justice. Their pastoral motto was *tutior pars sequenda est* (the safer course must be followed), by which they meant that penitents must examine their conduct very strictly, lest sins go unconfessed. As confessors Jansenists imposed harsher penances and counseled greater austerity than did Jesuits. Gallican Jansenist clergy summoned papal aid in their attack on probabilism, which the papacy condemned in 1665, 1666, and 1679. The Jesuits were ordered to permit in their seminaries both criticism of their pastoral counseling and alternative training for confessors. Jansenists also quarreled with their Jesuit antagonists over reception of communion. The Jesuits counseled frequent reception of the Eucharist, but the Jansenists believed that communion should be received no more than once a month. The great mathematician Blaise Pascal (1623–1662) ridiculed the Jesuits in his "Provincial Letters" (1656–1657).

Moreover, in mid-17th-century France, the Jansenist controversy raged in many ways less as a theological controversy than as an occasion for the settling of scores between various factions of the Roman Catholic Church. Gallican clergy used Jansenist ideas to buttress their French-centered vision of Church government against the ultramontane orders, and Dominicans accused the Jesuits of furthering moral degradation through casuistry based on probabilism. By 1660 a potent alliance of the French monarchy under Louis XIV (1643–1715), the papacy, and the Society of Jesus combined to attack Jansenism. Earlier the religious founders St. Francis de Sales (1567–1622) and St. Vincent de Paul (1581–1660) had already expressed doubts about Jansenism's orthodoxy. In 1660 Louis XIV ordered the General Assembly of the Clergy to mount a strategy for the eradication of Jansenism. The following year the assembly suggested that holders of French benefices be compelled to sign a formula condemning Jansenist ideas. Many Jansenist leaders went underground. The nuns of Port-Royal became a favorite target of royal displeasure. In 1665 Pope Alexander VII (1655–1667) commanded Jansenists to submit to papal discipline and to renounce their ideas. By 1668 a lull in the conflict ensued from negotiations that devised formulas that allowed those who resisted either the king or the pope to submit with dignity. The period that followed was known as the "Peace of the Church" (1669–1679).

However, the peace was insecure, and by the beginning of the 18th century Louis' insistence on orthodoxy unleashed another attack on Jansenism. When a Jansenist posed to the Sorbonne the question of whether the condemnation of the book *Augustinus* might be received with respectful silence, new suspicions of Jansenist subversion of right teaching reawakened with violence. The king suggested to the pope that they work together to root out Jansenism for good. Thus, in 1705 Pope Clement XI (1700–1721) condemned respectful silence. The king was more severe, having had Port-Royal desecrated. Although the king successfully destroyed Jansenism as a movement, its influence on the French Church lasted well into the 18th century and beyond.

ROBERT W. SHAFFERN

*See also* Asceticism: Christian Perspectives; France

**Further Reading**

Abercrombie, Nigel, *The Origins of Jansenism* (Oxford Studies in Modern Languages and Literature), Oxford: Clarendon Press, 1936
Doyle, William, *Jansenism: Catholic Resistance to Authority: From the Reformation to the French Revolution* (Studies in European History), New York: St. Martin's Press, 1999
Gastellier, Fabian, *Angélique Arnauld*, Paris: Fayard, 1998
Maire, Catherine-Laurence, *De la cause de Dieu à la cause de la nation: le jansénisme au XVIIIe siècle* (Bibliothèque des histoires), Paris: Gallimard, 1998
Van Hove, Brian, "Jansenism and Liturgical Reform," *American Benedictine Review* 44 (1993)
Van Kley, Dale K., *The Jansenists and the Expulsion of the Jesuits from France, 1757–1765* (Yale Historical Publications, Miscellany, 107), New Haven, Connecticut: Yale University Press, 1975

# Japan: History

The history of monasticism (*sōin seido*) in Japan begins with the arrival of Buddhism from Korea and China, as neither Daoism nor Japanese Shintō found institutional expression in any form of regulated cloistered communities. According to the *Nihon Shōki*, an eighth-century chronicle, the official date of Buddhism's introduction into Japan was 552 (or 538, as argued by some scholars), when a Korean mission presented several Buddhist images and scriptures to the Japanese emperor. After initial struggles Buddhism was accepted and promoted by the powerful Soga clan, led by Soga no Umako (d. 626), who is said to have had in 584 the nun Zenshinni and two others enroll in a sanctuary within the Ishikawa residence under the direction of a Korean monk. In 593 the monastery Gangōji (also called Asuka-dera or Hōkōji) was built, and after its completion in 596 two Korean monks were appointed to head it. Soga no Umako's niece, Empress Suiko (554–628), and her regent prince, Shōtoku (574–622), who is credited with the foundation of Shitennōji (593) and Hōryūji (Ikarugadera, 607), and some clan chieftains favored the surge of several hundred monastic foundations.

*Nara Period*

Sanron, Jōjitsu, Hossō, Kusha, Ritsu, and Kegon – the so-called Six Nara Sects – established themselves during the seventh and eighth centuries. They were not mutually exclusive but rather emphasized the exegesis of different texts. Most of these conformed to official expectations and devoted their activities to textual studies and prayer ceremonies. Three of these sects – Hossō, Ritsu, and Kegon – have survived until today.

## 1. Sanron

In 625 the Korean monk Hye-kwan (Ekan) and in 701 Gembō and Dōji introduced the teachings of the Chinese San-lun school to Japan, where it became known as the Sanron school, literally "Three Treatises," named after the following: (1) the *Mādhyamika-śāstra* (*Chūron*, "Treatise of the Middle Way"), attributed to Indian philosopher Nāgārjuna; (2) the *Dvādaśa-mukha-śāstra* (*Jūnimonron*, "Treatise of the 12 Gates"), also attributed to Nāgārjuna; and (3) the *Śata-śāstra* (*Hyakuron*, "100 Treatises"), by Nāgārjuna's disciple Āryadeva.

Sanron's central theme was emptiness (*kū*): the various phenomena, eternal (*mui*) or produced through causation (*ui*), are all subordinate to the principle of origination and destruction and thus lack real substance. This idea is elaborated in the so-called middle path of eightfold negation (*happū-chūdō*): nonbirth, nonextinction, noncessation, nonpermanence, nonuniformity, nondiversity, noncoming, and nongoing. By negating these negations themselves, the illusory character of secular truth – that everything is regarded as different from every other thing and existent – is revealed, and the ultimate aspect of truth – that everything is equal and void – will be understood (*shinzoku-nitai*).

Sanron doctrines were often studied together with Jōjitsu teachings. Hye-kwan and his disciple Chizō taught at Gangōji, and a rival branch was established at Daianji (also called Kudara Daiji, Takechi Daiji, and Daikan Daiji), where Dōji was appointed preceptor in 729. Sanron and Jōjitsu were both rather text-centered schools. They declined rapidly after the ninth century despite their great influence on Japanese Buddhist thought and disappeared entirely in the 14th century.

## 2. Jōjitsu

The Chinese Cheng-shi sect, regarded as a Hīnāyana school, was also imported by Hye-kwan in 625. The *Satyasiddhi-śāstra* (*Jōjitsuron*, "Treatise on Establishing Reality") by Harivarman (third to fourth century) is the basis of its doctrines and gave the school its name.

Negating the distinction between the all-things-nonexistent and all-things-existent theories, Jōjitsu maintains that neither mind nor matter exists. Worldly reality is but an instantaneous flash of a present moment, according to Jōjitsu; past and future do not exist. All phenomena can be reduced by gradual reduction to infinitesimal elements and thus to emptiness, so that

The Hōōdō (Phoenix Hall), Byōdō-in, Uji (near Kyoto), Japan, mid–11th century, Heian period.
**Photo courtesy of Marylin M. Rhie**

emptiness exists antithetically to existence. The absolute truth, which is thought to be identical with absolute emptiness, is to be established by suppressing the three attachments: (1) to the elements, (2) to all things insubstantial and nominal, and (3) to emptiness itself. Jōjitsu doctrines were studied in conjunction with the Sanron sect, but an independent religious body was never established.

### 3. Kusha

Chitsū and Chitatsu are credited with first introducing the Chinese Ju-she sect to Japan in 658; a second transmission took place in 735 by Gembō. Focusing mainly on the *Abhidharmakośa* (*Abhidatsuma kusharon*, "Quintessence of the Law"), Kusha, often labeled "realistic school," maintains that the existence of past, present, and future are separate and real but non-continuous entities connected in a causal relationship. The transmigration of the elements through time shapes, albeit momentarily, all phenomena, including human beings. Kusha regards the study of the basic Buddhist concept of the Four Noble Truths (*shitai*) as the key to deliverance. Owing to its small number of followers, Kusha never was independent, but it became an appendage of the Hossō school in 793.

### 4. Hossō

An offspring of the Chinese Faxiang is the Hossō school (also called Yuishiki-shu, Ōreinjitsu-shu, Jion-shu, Usō-shu, or Sō-shu). Hossō ("Characteristics of the Dharma") was brought over to Japan four times: in 653 or 660 by Dōshō; in 658 by Zhitong (Chitsū) and Zhida (Chitatsu); in 703 by Zhifeng (Chihō), Zhiluan (Chiran), and Zhixiong (Chiyū); and in 735 by Xuanfang (Gembō).

Dōshō and his pupil Gyōgi at Hōryūji belonged to the so-called transmission of the Southern Monastery. However, the later transmission of the Northern Monastery, taught at Kōfukuji, was considered the orthodox one. Yakushiji, founded in 681 by Emperor Temmu, figured as another center of the sect.

Hossō, which teaches that nothing exists outside the mind, draws on the principles of the *Vijñāptimātratā-śāstra* (*Yuishiki-iron*, "Treatises on the Idea of Ideation") by Vasubandhu (fourth century) and the *Yogāchāryābhūmiśāstra* (*Yugaron*, "Treatises on Yoga") by Asaṅga (fourth century). According to Hossō, the phenomenal world, including the "self," is merely a product of ideation, which is also the origin of the Chain of Cause and Effect. The middle path lies in (1) recognizing the illusory and temporary character of "reality," (2) accepting that all phenomena are but an ideation and subsequently void, and (3) aiming to discover the ultimate truth beyond the emptiness of nonexistence and ideated reality.

Hossō flourished mainly during the Nara period, when especially Gyōgi attracted many followers by spreading the message of Buddhist salvation among the masses. His irregular practices led to a temporary condemnation by the government. Another Hossō monk, Gembō, was exiled in 745 for supporting an attempted coup d'état, and the Hossō monk Dōkyō (d. 772) nearly

became emperor when Empress Kōken tried to install him on the throne in 761. The beginning of the Heian period, marked by the transfer of the capital to Heiankyō in 794, led to the decline of the sect, although Yakushiji, Kōfukuji, and Hōryūji remained centers of Buddhist studies.

In 1998 Hossō had 577,000 followers and maintained 37 temples headed by Yakushiji and Kōfukuji. Hōryūji seceded in 1950, becoming the head temple of the Shōtoku sect.

### 5. Ritsu

When the Japanese government resumed dispatching embassies to China in 732, it also sought from China an authority on rules and monastic discipline in an effort to regulate and control its own rapidly growing Buddhist community. Jian-zhen (Ganjin, 688–763), a monk of the Chinese Lü sect (Ritsu-shu, meaning "school of rules"), responded to the invitation, reaching Japan in 754. Once there, he established the Ritsu sect, which teaches that observance of the Mahāyāna precepts is the way to attain Buddhahood.

An earlier attempt to gain control of the Buddhist community had been made when Empress Suiko appointed registrars (*sōjō* and *sōzu*) to supervise monks and nuns. Additional steps in establishing secular control through an administrative framework were taken by promulgating the "Regulations for Monks and Nuns" (*sōniryō*) within the Taihō Codex (701) and the Yōrō Codex (718). There were 250 rules for monks and 348 for nuns. The regulations stipulated, for example, that every monk and nun (1) be trained and ordained only in ways approved by the state, (2) reside only in temples and refrain from religious activity outside the temple, and (3) obey the civil and canon law. It was prohibited (1) to become a "private monk or nun" (*shidō*) or help or encourage others to do so; (2) to build unauthorized hermitages, temples, or monasteries; (3) to conduct unauthorized religious activity, fortune-telling, or proselytizing; (4) to interfere with state affairs; (5) to arouse the common people; (6) to study books on military tactics and strategy; (7) to drink liquor or eat proscribed food; (8) to consort with members of the opposite sex; (9) to plead civil suits in clerical dress; (10) to lend their names to laypeople to avoid taxes; and (11) to accumulate private property and wealth. Government control over tonsuring (*tokudo*) and ordination (*jukai*) was executed by the Ministry of Civil Affairs (*jibushō*), which appointed the registrar-general of monks (*sōgō*).

Reviving these rules, Ganjin established an ordination platform (*kaidan-in*) at Tōdaiji, where he conferred bodhisattva precepts on more than 400 people, including Empress Kōken (718–770) and retired Emperor Shōmu (701–756). In 758 Ganjin was granted the title Great Preceptor (*daiwajō*). In 759 Tōshōdaiji was established, becoming the new headquarters of the Ritsu sect.

Later two more *kaidan-in* were established at Yakushiji and Kanzeonji; as a result, Ritsu flourished during the Heian period. A schism occurred later, in the Kamakura period, when Shunjō (1166–1227) became head of the so-called Hokkyō Ritsu (Ritsu of the northern capital, Kyoto), and Kakujō (1194–1249), Eizon

The Daibutsuden (Great Buddha Hall), Tōdaiji, Nara, Japan, originally built in mid–eighth century, rebuilt in the early Kamakura period, late 12th to early 13th century. Contains the mid-eighth-century colossal bronze Roshana Buddha.
Photo courtesy of Marylin M. Rhie

(1201–1290), and Ninshō (1217–1303) led the Shingon-influenced Nankyō Ritsu (Ritsu of the southern capital, Nara).

Today the sect has 91 temples and 106,000 followers, headed by Tōshōdaiji.

### 6. Kegon

The Hua-yan (Kegon) sect was transmitted in 736 by Daoxuan (Dōsen, 596–667) and in 740 by the Korean priest Sim-Pyong (Shinjō, d. 742). It is founded on the principles of the *Avatamsaka-sūtra* (*Kegon-kyō*, "Flower Ornament Sūtra"), which, according to Kegon, contains the Buddha's supreme teachings. Kegon follows the doctrines of the "Ten Profound Gates" (*jūgemmon*), which explain the ten characteristics of the phenomenal world as being correlative, interdependent, and mutually originating. It also teaches the "Six Characteristics of Everything" (*rokusō*): universality/specialization, similarity/diversity, and integration/differentiation.

Kegon's dogma aims at tracing the sameness of everything: all things at all times compose one entity, and all things possess emptiness (i.e., absolute truth) and thus are able to realize Buddha nature. Kegon-shu attempts to fit all previous Buddhist teachings into its own system, labeling them as partial aspects of the truth, which Kegon claims to expound in its entirety.

Tōdaiji, presiding today over 47 other temples, is the center of the sect.

### Heian Period (794–1185)

For reasons not yet entirely understood, the capital was transferred from Nara to Nagaoka in 784 and from there to Heian Kyō (present-day Kyoto) in 794, marking the beginning of the Heian period. However, it has been argued that the growing influence of the Buddhist sects on politics was a major reason for the move. Emperor Kammu tried, to no great avail, to limit the number of clerics and temples and to restrict land sales to religious organizations, targeting mainly the Nara sects.

However, the new Buddhist sects, Tendai and Shingon, soon gained in strength, government support, and funding, and although their respective centers were situated beyond the capital precincts, they began to have an impact on secular as well as religious matters.

### 1. Tendai

Tendai was founded by Saichō (767–822; posthumously Dengyō Daishi), who, dissatisfied with ecclesiastical life in Nara, in 804 received imperial permission to search in China for the best form of Buddhism. Saichō focused on the Tiantai (Tendai) school but studied also Zhenyan (Shingon) and Chan (Zen) doctrines. After his return to Japan in 805, he established Tendai on Mount Hiei outside Kyoto, where his former humble mountain retreat grew into a religious community of some 3,000 temples located around Enryakuji.

Based on the *Hokkekyō* ("The Lotus Sūtra"), Tendai systematizes all scriptures and previous doctrines, interpreting them as different stages of a revelation progressively disclosed by the Buddha according to the growing understanding of his followers and culminating in Tendai's teachings. Its doctrines (*kyōmon*) state that there are three levels of existence:

(1) the temporary (*ke*), forming the material world, and
(2) the void (*kū*), being the eternal negative aspect of the temporary.

Both the void and the temporary – being preconditions for each other – are transcended by

(3) the middle (*chū*), which alone exists absolutely.

The dogma was framed by a set of rules governing religious praxis. Saichō required from his disciples a 12-year monastic training on Mount Hiei, including prayers, confession of sins, and penance.

Claiming the perfect teaching, Saichō was uncompromising toward the established sects, especially Shingon, although he and Kūkai had a friendly relationship in the beginning. His petition for a separate ordination system stirred further opposition and failed to win the court's approval until after Saichō's death in 822.

Among Saichō's successors, Ennin (794–864) and Enchin (814–891) were the most prominent. They managed to revive Tendai, which had been increasingly influenced by Shingon doctrines. However, in the tenth century a bitter, even warlike dispute developed between monks of Ennin's line and those of Enchin's line, leading to the establishment of Onjōji (Miidera) at the foot of Mount Hiei. By 1100 all the Tendai monasteries had standing armies and not only fought among themselves and against other sects but also took sides in the civil wars. Finally, in 1571, warlord Oda Nobunaga ended their influence by destroying Enryakuji.

Although Tendai recovered from this blow, it never regained its former prominence. Today Tendai maintains 5,093 temples and counts 216,277 clergy and 6,388,000 lay members.

## 2. Shingon

Maintaining 12,369 temples with 13,231,000 followers in various branches, Shingon (also called Shingon-darani, Maṇḍala, Himitsu, or Yoga sect) remains in 1998 one of the major sects in Japan.

It was imported in 806 and systematized by Kūkai (774–835; posthumously Kōbō Daishi), one of the most charismatic figures in Japanese history, to whom are attributed several cultural accomplishments, including the invention of one of the Japanese syllabic writing systems. In establishing Shingon, literally "true word," he succeeded in introducing esoteric Buddhism (*mikkyō*), a school with a very complex set of rules, dogmas, and mysterious practices that nevertheless became popular in wide sections of the population.

Shingon's teachings are based mainly on the *Mahavairocana-sūtra* (*Dainichikyō*, "Sūtra of the Great Sun Buddha") and the *Vajraśekhara-sūtra* (*Kongōchōkyō*, "Diamond Sūtra"). It claims, in contrast to other schools, that Buddhist teachings are derived from the Mahavairocana Buddha (Dainichi Nyorai, "Great Sun Buddha"), who is seen as the absolute in his truth, infinity, and omnipresence, the historical Buddha being merely one of his many manifestations.

Dainichi Nyorai unites two aspects of the truth: (1) the "Womb Realm" (*Taizōkai*), signifying the phenomenal world in its diversity and inconstancy, the source of five of the six Great Elements (earth, water, fire, wind, and space), and (2) the "Diamond Realm" (*Kongōkai*) of perfect wisdom, the indestructible essence of the world and the source of the sixth element, the mind. Dainichi Nyorai is surrounded by multitudes of buddhas, bodhisattvas, and spiritual powers. He is at once the source of all existence and of enlightenment, which can be attained by adepts who follow the Three Mystic Treasures (*sammitsu*) concerning (1) rules (*giki*), governing invocation, offering, manual signs, and mantras; (2) speech (*go*), reciting mantras, which symbolize the essence of the speech of Dainichi Nyorai; and (3) mind (*i*), thinking, feeling, imagining, visualizing, listening, and ceasing the activities of mind. Some of these religious exercises are rather simple to follow, so that despite its general complexity and mysteriousness, Shingon appealed to the masses as well as to a growing cenobitic community.

Aiding the sect's success were Kūkai's charisma and his ability to compromise with the Nara sects, as well as the fact that Dainichi Nyorai came to be identified by Shintō followers with the Sun Goddess, forming the syncretist Ryōbu Shintō. In 816 Emperor Saga granted the sect permission to build its center at Kongōbunji on Mount Kōya. Another important temple was Tōji, close to the capital, which was presented to Kūkai in 823.

About 300 years after Kūkai's death, differences in rituals led to a first schism, when Kakuban (1095–1143) established the Dai Dembōin on Mount Kōya. Another 140 years later Raiyu (1226–1304) advocated a new theory concerning the source of the esoteric Buddhist sūtras. The ensuing controversy led to the establishment of Negoroji, which became the headquarters of the New Shingon sect.

Warlord Toyotomi Hideyoshi razed Negoroji during the civil wars in 1585. After that the Buzan branch of New Shingon maintained its center at Chōkokuji (or Hasedera), while the Chizan branch was concentrated at Chishakuin. Both sites are still extant.

Today Old Shingon includes the Tōji, Daigo, Daikakuji, Omuro, Sennyūji, Yamashina, and Zentsūji subsects.

## 3. Zen

The last Buddhist sects to emerge favoring a cenobitic life were the Zen sects: Rinzai (founded by Eisai [1141–1215]), Sōtō (Dōgen Kigen [1200–1253]), and Ōbaku (Ingen [1592–1673]).

Long before these became independent schools, Zen (i.e., seated meditation) was a part of the teaching and practice of other schools; Eisai's temple, for example, Kenninji in Kyoto, developed into a place where Tendai, Shingon, and other doctrines were taught.

It was not until Nampo Jōmyō (posthumously Daiō Kokushi, 1235–1308), Shūhō Myōchō (posthumously Daitō Kokushi, 1282–1337), and Kanzan Egen (posthumously Kanzan Kokushi, 1277–1360) that Rinzai became truly independent. Their temples, Kenchōji, Daitokuji, and Myōshinji in Kyoto, remain the centers of Rinzai today. Hakuin Ekaku (1685–1768) laid the foundation for today's Rinzai by systematizing the practice of Kōan.

In 1998 Rinzai had 5,876 temples, 6,086 clergy, and 1,388,000 followers.

Generally speaking, Zen desists from Mahāyāna intellectualism, discourages rationalization, and promotes religious practice, aiming to achieve the direct perception of self and reality (Buddhahood). Thus, Dōgen taught that seated meditation is the only suitable way to attain enlightenment (satori), interpreting satori to be more a process than a permanent state. Sōtō-Zen also maintains a complex set of rules governing daily life, thus following the example of the historical Buddha.

The sect is taught in 14,702 temples and employs 16,661 clergy to look after 1,579,000 followers.

In the 16th century the last addition from the Chinese Zen schools arrived in Japan. The Ōbaku sect has much in common with the Rinzai school, but it also esteems invocation of the *nembutsu* formula that had been promoted by several Pure Land sects. Ingen maintained the unity of scriptures and Zen (*kyōzen ichi*) and held on to Chinese monastic rules. Today the sect has 464 temples, 458 clergy, and 353,000 followers, led by Mampukuji.

Despite their success, especially among the warrior class, Zen and the other sects could not stop the countermovement of various Pure Land sects that rejected monasticism and religious speculation and promoted faith as the only way to salvation. The most prominent of these leaders were Hōnen (1133–1212), the founder of the Pure Land or Jōdo sect; Shinran (1173–1263), the founder of the True Pure Land or Jōdo-Shin sect; and Nichiren (1222–1282), the founder of the Hokke or Lotus sect. Together these sects have more than 43,823,000 followers in Japan.

Other reasons for the decline of monasticism in Japan were the previously mentioned warlike disputes among some of the sects and the long civil war that ended at the beginning of the 17th century, when the Tokugawa shogunate came to power. Tokugawa's decision to ban Christianity and to isolate the country, a ban that was enforced until 1868, deprived Buddhism of spiritual challenges and so led to stagnation.

The Meiji Restoration saw a temporary anti-Buddhist movement in favor of Shintoism. In many parts of Japan, Buddhist institutions were vandalized and clergy laicized. These circumstances and the reappearance of Christianity inspired monks such as Fukuda Gyōkai (1806–1888) and Shaku Unshō (1827–1909) to lead a reform movement in favor of monastic rules. Although there are now fewer cenobitic communities in Japan than in earlier times, a remarkable number remain.

CLAUDIA MARRA

*See also* Asaṅga; Asceticism: Buddhist Perspectives; Buddhism: Inculturation; Buddhist Schools/Traditions: Japan; Chan/Zen: Japan; Critiques of Buddhist Monasticism: Confucian; Critiques of Buddhist Monasticism: Japanese; Death Rituals, Buddhist; Dōgen; Eisai (Yosai); Ennin; Hakuin; Hōnen; Kōan; Kūkai; Kyoto, Japan; Libraries: Buddhist; Manuscript Production: Buddhist; Marathon Monks; Mountain Monasteries, Buddhist; Nation-Building and Japanese Buddhism; Patrons, Buddhist: Japan; Peace Movements, Buddhist; Rennyo; Saichō; Shinran; Suzuki, Daisetz Teitaro; Syncretism in Japan, Buddhist; Visual Arts, Buddhist: Japan; Warrior Monks: Buddhist; Zen, Arts of; Zen and the West

## Further Reading

Asahi Shuppansha, editor, *Asahi Nenkan 1998*, Tokyo, 1998

Brown, Delmer M., editor, *The Cambridge History of Japan*, Cambridge and New York: Cambridge University Press, 1993

Brüll, Lydia, *Die japanische Philosophie*, Darmstadt: Wissenschaftliche Buchgesellschaft, 1989

Collcutt, Martin, *Five Mountains: The Rinzai Zen Monastic Institution in Medieval Japan*, Cambridge, Massachusetts: Harvard University Press, 1981

Dumoulin, Heinrich, *Zen Buddhism: A History*, 2 vols., New York: Macmillan, and London: Collier, 1988–1990

Hammitzsch, Horst, editor, *Japan-Handbuch*, Wiesbaden: Steiner, 1981; 3rd edition, Stuttgart: Steiner, 1990

*Japanese-English Buddhist Dictionary*, Tokyo: Daitō Shuppansha, 1965

Mizuno, Kogen, *Essentials of Buddhism: Basic Terminology and Concepts of Buddhist Philosophy and Practice*, Tokyo: Kosei, 1996

Sato, Giei, and Eshin Nishimura, *Unsui: A Diary of Zen Monastic Life*, Honolulu: University of Hawaii Press, 1973

Saunders, E. Dale, *Buddhism in Japan*, Philadelphia: University of Pennsylvania Press, 1964

Suzuki, D.T., *The Training of the Zen Buddhist Monk*, Kyoto: Eastern Buddhist Society, 1934; New York: University Books, 1959

Watanabe, Shoko, *Japanese Buddhism*, Tokyo: Kokusai Bunka Shinkokai, 1964; 3rd edition, 1970

## Related Web Sites

*http://darkwing.uoregon.edu/~felsing/jstuff/bud.html*
*http://online.anu.edu.au/asianstudies/buddhism/buddhism.html*
*http://www.ciolek.com/WWWVL-Buddhism.html*
*http://www.daiwa-foundation.org.uk/*
*http://www.human.toyogakuen-u.ac.jp/~acmuller/index.html*
*http://www.iijnet.or.jp/iriz/irizhtml/irizhome.htm*
*http://www.jsnet.org/*
*http://www.nichibun.ac.jp/*
*http://www.uwyo.edu/A&S/RELSTDS/budglent.htm*

# Japan: Sites

Because many Buddhist temples exist in Japan, a presentation of some of the headquarters of the various Buddhist schools, where the monks dwell, work, study, and conduct major ceremonies, is most valuable. Japan has 13 major schools of Buddhism (Ritsu, Kegon, Hossō, Tendai, Shingon, Jōdo, Rinzai, Sōtō, Ōbaku, Jōdoshin, Nichiren, Yūzū Nenbutsu, and Ji). Each school has various subschools and each subschool its own headquarters. The Japanese periods referred to here are as follows: the Nara (710–784), the Heian (794–1185), the Kamakura (1192–1333), the Muromachi (1392–1573), the Edo (1600–1868), and the Meiji (1868–1912). After the name of the headquarters temple, the name of the mountain, if relevant, is stated and the prefecture in which it is located, followed by the name of the respective Buddhist school.

### Tōshōdaiji, Nara (Ritsu [Vinaya] School)

Emperor Shōmu founded this temple for a Chinese monk called Ganjin (Chinese, Jian-zhen), who had attempted to come to Japan to transmit the Ritsu five times in vain because of shipwrecks and other calamities and had lost his eyesight. He succeeded the sixth time, in 754. Ganjin held an initiation ceremony for Shōmu and others in front of the Daibutsu-den of Tōdaiji in 754. The construction of Tōshōdaiji was completed in 759, and the imperial court and the aristocrats' families protected and gave support to Tōshōdaiji. After the middle of the Heian period, it lost some prominence, but in the middle of the Kamakura period, a monk called Kakusei revived the temple. After a period of some decline in the Muromachi period, the Edo government revived Tōshōdaiji. In the Meiji period, following a vinaya revitalization movement by Unshou, the temple was again revived.

Today Tōshōdaiji represents the Ritsu (vinaya) tradition, closely associated with Theravāda Buddhism, a rarity among the Mahāyāna Buddhism traditions of Japan.

### Tōdaiji, Nara (Kegon [Chinese, Hua-yan] School)

Tōdaiji is known for its great Vairocana Buddha, whose height is 53 feet and whose construction was brought about by the Emperor Shōmu's imperial ordinance. The Kegon school of Buddhism was a flourishing school in the Nara period, whose basic sūtra is the *Kegongyō* (Flower Wreath Sūtra; Sanskrit, *Buddhāvatamsaka-nāma-mahāvaipulya-sūtra*). The building and the statue of the great Buddha were burned down and restored several times. The Kegon school lost its influence in the Heian period, as Tendai and Shingon gained support from the court and the aristocratic classes. Through the Kamakura period Koben and Gyonen revived it, and in the Edo period Houtan (1659–1738) attempted to revive it. Today monks still practice the religious life, even though the site is the center of tourism in Nara.

### Enryakuji, Hieizan, Shiga (Tendai [Chinese, Tiantai] School)

Enryakuji has been a center for Buddhist religious practice since the Heian period. The founders of new schools of Buddhism during the Kamakura period were originally trained at Hieizan. In 788 Saichō erected a temple that in 823 was named Enryakuji by Emperor Saga. Saichō (767–822) established Enryakuji as the center of the Tendai school but could not obtain imperial permission for Enryakuji to perform ordination ceremonies, which were allowed only at some official temples, such as Tōdaiji. After his death imperial permission was granted.

On Mount Hiei, Enryakuji encompasses three districts: the eastern area, the western area, and Yokokawa (the northern area). According to Saichō's original ninth-century plan, Enryakuji contained only the eastern and the western. Saichō's disciple Ennin (794–864) developed the Yokokawa area. Ennin also went to China to learn more about Buddhism and brought back many Tantric scriptures. Eventually he became the third head of Enryakuji. At about the same time, the other monk, named Enchin (814–891), also went to China to study Tantric Buddhism and brought various Tantric scriptures back to Enryakuji. Later he became the fifth head of Enryakuji and revived a nearby temple, Onjōji. Under the third head, Ennin, and the fifth, Enchin, Enryakuji flourished as the center of the Tantric (Vajrayāna) teaching of the Tendai school (*taimitsu*), appealing to the aristocratic classes. After Enchin died, the followers of Ennin's branch and those of Enchin's branch battled over control of the mountain, and followers of Enchin's branch left Hieizan and moved to Onjōji. The two branches finally split; those who remained in Hieizan were called the *sammon* (the mountain faction), and those who left Hieizan and moved to Onjōji were called *jimon* (the temple faction). Following this split Enryakuji went into a slow decline that spanned several decades.

In the tenth century the monk Ryōgen, the future 18th abbot, revived Enryakuji through his acquaintance with Fujiwarano Morosuke, the grandfather of Fujiwarano Michinaga. The Fujiwara clan gave financial support to Enryakuji. Morosuke's son Jinzen became Ryōgen's disciple and succeeded him as 19th abbot. After Jinzen became the head, those who came from aristocratic families, especially the Fujiwara clan, monopolized Enryakuji and aristocratized it. New factions separated aristocratic and plebian groups of monks.

Ryōgen had a disciple named Genshin who wrote *Ōjō Yōshū*, a book that focused on the belief in Amitābha-Buddha. Hōnen and Shinran would emerge from this tradition.

As the Tendai school flourished, Hieizan attracted various groups of monks. Among them, *sōhei* (warrior-monks) or *yamahōshi* (mountain monks) were notorious for their violent behavior, destroying buildings and temples and challenging *samurai* (warriors). They carried the portable shrine (*mikoshi*) around the town and demanded that their pleas be accepted by the court. They threatened violence if their pleas were not heard. They also participated in attacking and burning Onjōji.

The Enryakuji finally became so powerful that in the 16th century Oda Nobunaga, a feudal lord attempting to unify Japan, began to view it as a threat and attacked and destroyed it. Later the buildings were restored. Today rigorous religious practices continue at Enryakuji. Enryakuji on Mount Hiei is also known for its monks' *sennichi kaihōgyō* (thousand-day wandering in the mountain). Participants are called "marathon monks" in popular English usage.

Even on Miyajima (Shrine Island) a Buddhist pagoda towers over the Shintō complex. Completed by the Taira clan patriarch Kiyomori at the end of the Heian Period (1168), Miyajima is in the Seto Inland Sea close to Hiroshima Prefecture. Its huge gate (*torii*) is a watergate that can be walked under at low tide. One of the traditional three most beautiful sights in Japan.
Photo courtesy of Steve McCarty

*Kongōbuji, Kōya-san, Wakayama (Shingon [Tantric or Esoteric Buddhism] School)*

Kōya-san is a general name for the Buddhism monastic complex of more than 110 temples and monasteries of the Shingon school on Mount Kōya. Kōya-san was known for prohibiting women to enter the mountain precinct.

Before Kūkai built Kongōbuji in the 9th century, he practiced religious life at Tōji and Jingoji in Kyoto. Emperor Saga gave Mount Kōya to Kūkai in 816. He founded Kongōbuji in the same year, but its construction did not proceed promptly. The main temple complex was built under the second abbot, Shinzen (804–891), and Kongōbuji did not prosper financially for some time.

Two issues arose at the initial stage of development of Kōya-san. One was the matter of *Shingonshū Nenbundosha*, that is, the regulation that all students had to study and train for ordination at Kōya-san (and not at the other Shingon temples, Tōji and Jingoji). This regulation was instituted to prevent the decline of Kōya-san, which was located far from Kyoto. However, gradually this regulation was disregarded, and in 897 Tōji succeeded in obtaining four students for training. Another issue was the ownership of *Sanjūchō Sakusu* (30 notebooks), which were writ-

ten by Kūkai while he was studying in China. Initially these 30 notebooks were stored at Tōji and borrowed by Shinzen and brought to Kōya-san. When he borrowed them a second time, he did not return them to Tōji because a Tendai monk was in charge of Tōji. Because these 30 notebooks were a source of authority, Tōji and Kongōbuji disputed their possession for about 40 years. In the end the 30 notebooks were returned to Tōji.

Kōya-san's fame spread in the 10th century along with belief in Kūkai's *Nyūjō*, that is, the belief that Kūkai did not die but that, having attained *nibbāna*, he was still alive and was wandering through the country teaching Buddhism. The number of pilgrimages to Kōya-san increased as this belief spread. From the Heian period to the Momoyama period, many aristocrats, shogunates, and feudal lords visited the mountain.

Around the 11th century belief in Kūkai's *Nyūjō* became associated with belief in the descent of Maitreya (the Future Buddha). The combination of these beliefs led to the custom of leaving one's own hair and the ashes of cremated bones at the temple, a practice that continues today. At the same time the practice of burying the sūtra in the ground on the Kōya-san became popular. By the 13th century the temple complex on the Kōya-san was constructed and organized as it is today. About

Courtyard of the Hōryūji temple with the Kondō (left), the five-storied pagoda (right), and the entrance gate (center), Nara, Japan. Founded A.D. 607, the buildings were rebuilt in the second half of the seventh century.
Photo courtesy of Marylin M. Rhie

3,000 monks were studying and working on Kōya-san at that time.

In the 12th century, as belief in the Jōdo Pure Land and in the Mappō (the end of the era, 2,000 years after the Buddha's death) spread and extended its influence to Kōya-san, the abbot Kakuban led a reform movement to integrate belief in the Jōdo (the Pure Land) into Shingon teachings, that is, *Himitsu-Nen-butsu* (Esoteric Nembutsu). Kōya-san attracted a number of Pure Land Buddhists who formed communities of ascetic worshipers. Gradually three major groups emerged on Kōya-san: the *Gakuryogata* (monks), who studied and practiced; the *Gy-ōningata* (service personnel), who took care of the food preparation, cleaning, and maintenance of the buildings; and the *Hijirigata* (wanderers), who lived ascetically and kept aloof from temple society.

Kōya-san continued to flourish under the patronage of successive shogunates, although setbacks occurred, such as Oda Nobunaga's 16th-century attack and massacre of 100 monks. During the Edo period each of the three groups attempted to establish superiority over the others by seeking close connection with the Tokugawa shogunates. After the Meiji Restoration, the prohibition of women's entry into Kōya-san was officially over-

turned. Kōya-san remains one of the most important religious sites in Japan.

*Chion'in, Kyoto (Jōdo [Pure Land] School)*
The head temple of Jōdo school of Buddhism included the site where Hōnen (1133–1212), the founder of the Jōdo school, settled to proclaim his new teachings after leaving Mount Hiei in 1175. It is also the site where he died after returning from exile. The original temple in memory of Hōnen was built in 1234 by his disciple Genchi (1183–1238). The temple was destroyed several times, especially during the Ōnin War (1183–1238), which ravaged Kyoto. After it was destroyed by fire in 1633, it was rebuilt by the third Tokugawa shōgun.

*Honganji, Kyoto (Jōdoshin [True Pure Land] School)*
The Honganji (Temple of the Original Vow) originated in a small memorial chapel enshrining an image of Shinran (1173–1263), built in 1272 by his daughter Kakushin Ni (1224–1283). This location is now part of Chion'in. In 1282 Kakushin Ni donated this property to a community of faithful. Her grandson Kakunyo Sōhō (1270–1351) obtained for the mausoleum the status of a temple, and it was redesignated Honganji in 1321.

Kakunyo asserted the Honganji's preeminence among True Pure Land schools by claiming direct descent from Shinran, Kakushin Ni, and his grandson Nyoshin (1235–1300). The Honganji's fourth to seventh heads continued to assert special status.

The eighth head, Rennyo Kenju (1415–1499), established the Honganji as the preeminent place of the True Pure Land school. His pastoral letters, written in simple language, preached a return to Shinran's original doctrine of salvation through faith in the grace of Buddha Amida, the Buddha of Infinite Light (Sanskrit, Amitābha-Buddha). The rapid expansion of the Honganji school caused conflict with Mount Hiei, and Rennyo moved to Hokuriku (northern Honshū) to set up a new center. During the Ōnin War, Honganji's armed leagues (the *Ikkōikki*) emerged as a powerful force in Japanese politics when adherents of the temple intervened militarily in the Hokuriku's regional conflicts. Because his fellows ignored his appeal not to act militarily, Rennyo returned to the Kansai region and built another temple headquarters at Yamashina.

Through the Sengoku-Momoyama period, the Honganji changed the location of its headquarters. In 1549 the imperial court appointed the tenth head, Shōnyo Kōkyō, to be the provisional high priest of Buddhism. In 1560 the 11th head, Kennyo Kōsa, obtained the status of an imperial abbacy for the Honganji.

In the late 16th century, Toyotomi Hideyoshi, who unified Japan, ordered Kyōnyo, the 12th head, to resign (just one year after he had succeeded to power) and assigned his younger brother Suinyo to be the head. Yet after Tokugawa Ieyasu defeated the Toyoyomi family and reunified Japan in 1600, in 1602 he gave the nearby lands to Kyōnyo to build a new temple. Kyōnyo established his own branch of the Honganji, which was known as the Higashi (East) Honganji. The Honganji subsequently split into two separate branches. Later both the Higashi Honganji and the Nishi (West) Honganji suffered internal doctrinal disputes.

### Eiheiji, Fukui (Sōtō Zen School)

The temple was founded in 1243 by the Zen master Dōgen (1200–1253) to train monks in the tradition of the Sōtō school of Zen Buddhism, which Dōgen had learned from his Chinese master T'ien-t'ung Ju-ching. Initially Dōgen was teaching Zen in Kyoto. Yet, when he wrote a doctrinal piece and presented it to the court, the monks of Enryakuji who were asked to read and judge it got angry at Dōgen and destroyed his temple. Then he left Kyoto and went to the Echizen area and built a temple. First called Daibutsuji, two years later it was renamed Eiheiji.

At Eiheiji, Dōgen wrote not only theoretical and religious pieces but also instructive and regulatory manuals for the social and institutional aspects of Eiheiji. Dōgen's two foci of concern (theoretical and institutional) became a source of future quarrels between the third head, named Gikai, who wanted to expand and establish the institutional side of the temple, and the group led by a monk named Gien, who wanted to focus on religious practice. Finally a schism emerged from this conflict, and the Gikai faction moved out of Eiheiji to another temple. Because of this quarrel Eiheiji lost its local patrons and many followers. During the late 14th century, it went into decline and was badly damaged by fire in 1473. In 1573 it was attacked by the True Pure Land followers (*Ikkōikki*) and burned down.

Only in the early 17th century did it reemerge as the preeminent center of Sōtō Zen, and through the 17th century it was reconstructed and expanded. Today about 70 buildings exist at Eiheiji, which continues to be the major Sōtō Zen institution and is known for its rigorous monastic discipline.

### Daitokuji, Kyoto (Rinzai Zen School)

This is the head temple of the Daitokuji branch of the Rinzai Zen school. The temple was originally a small monastery built by Sōhō Myōchō in 1315. In 1325, at the request of retired Emperor Hanazono (1297–1348), the monastery became a supplication hall for the imperial court. After it was included in the first rank of the Gozan (the Five Mountains) in 1333, the Ashikaga shōgun Takauji, acting in league with opponents of the temple, placed it in the lowest rank of the system in 1386. Daitokuji decided to step out of the official system of the Gozan in 1431 and became independent.

The original temples were destroyed by fire in 1453 and also by the Ōnin War (1183–1238). Daitokuji produced two popular Zen monks, Ikkyu Sōjun (1394–1481) and Takuan Sōhō (1573–1645). After the Meiji Restoration of 1868, the Daitokuji went into decline and in 1876 became an independent temple of the Daitokuji branch of the Rinzai school. Later it reemerged as an important temple for the Zen Buddhism.

### Kuonji, Minobusan, Yamanashi (Nichiren School)

When Nichiren (1222–1282), the Kamakura-period prophet devoted to the *Lotus Sūtra*, found that the Kamakura shogunate government did not accept his teaching after he had returned from his second exile on the island of Sado, he withdrew to Mount Minobu in 1274. He stayed in a small building there, writing several books and giving instructions to his followers. After eight years he went to a warmer area to restore his health but died on the way. His bones were buried in the Kuonji.

In the 16th century the feudal lord of Takeda accepted the faith of Nichiren school. In the 17th century, strife between two factions (Fuju-fuse [Neither Give nor Receive] and Ju-fuse [Receive but Not Give]) arose in the Nichiren school. Because the military government of Edo suppressed the former, Kuonji was established as the central temple for the Nichiren school through the Edo period.

In 1693 the 31st head, Nichidatsu, established ties with the imperial family, which allowed the head of the Kuonji to wear the purple cloth. During the Edo period the Kuonji received less financial support from the shogunate. During the 19th century fires destroyed the temple complex, yet the latter half of the Meiji period witnessed the restoration of the Kuonji and the establishment of its educational facility.

*Kenchōji, Kamakura (Rinzai Zen School)*

Kenchōji was founded around 1248 and was the headquarters of the Kenchōji branch of the Rinzai Zen school during the Kamakura period. It was supported by the Hojo clan and was designated among the first rank of the Kamukura Five Mountains system by Ashikaga Shogunate Yoshimitsu in 1386. The building complex was burned down several times. The monks who dwelled at Kenchōji exercised some influence on the Five Mountain literature, a literary movement that composed poems in Chinese characters. Kenchōji also published several books concerning Zen teachings and the Buddhist sūtras. With the support of the political rulers, Kenchōji flourished throughout the Muromachi and Edo periods.

Readers who would like to visit any of these temples are advised to make contact with any of them prior to their visitation, as each has a different policy concerning accepting visitors. Readers should check other reference books and tourist guides for non-headquarters temples open to foreign visitors.

TAKESHI KIMURA

*See also* Buddhist Schools/Traditions: Japan; Chan/Zen: Japan; Dōgen; Ennin; Hōnen; Kūkai; Kyoto, Japan; Marathon Monks; Mount Hiei, Japan; Mount Kōya, Japan; Nara, Japan; Patrons, Buddhist: Japan; Pure Land Buddhism; Rennyo; Saichō; Shikoku, the Pilgrimage Island of Japan; Shinran; Syncretism in Japan, Buddhist; Tiantai/Tendai: Japan; Warrior Monks: Buddhist; Zen, Arts of

**Further Reading**

Hanayama, Shinsho, *A History of Japanese Buddhism*, translated and edited by Kosho Yamamoto, 3rd edition, Tokyo: Bukkyo Dendo Kyokai, 1973

Kitagawa, Joseph M., *On Understanding Japanese Religion*, Princeton, New Jersey: Princeton University Press, 1987

Kiyota, Minoru, editor, *Japanese Buddhism: Its Tradition, New Religions and Interaction with Christianity*, Tokyo and Los Angeles, California: Buddhist Books International, 1987

Roth, Martin, and John Stevens, *Zen Guide: Where to Meditate in Japan*, New York: Weatherhill, 1985

Steinilber-Oberlin, Emile, *The Buddhist Sects of Japan: Their History, Philosophical Doctrines and Sanctuaries*, translated by Marc Lugé, London: Allen and Unwin, 1938; Westport, Connecticut: Greenwood Press, 1976

Usui, Shiro, *A Pilgrim's Guide to Forty-Six Temples*, New York: Weatherhill, 1990

# Jerome, St. c. 345–420

Christian abbot, scholar, and translator of the Bible

Jerome, whose work as a Bible translator created the core of the Vulgate and thus shaped Western culture well into the modern period, also influenced the development of monasticism in the West. In part this came about through his work as a translator: the Vulgate became the basis for chanting and meditation, thereby forming monastic spirituality, and his translation of Pachomian writings brought the earliest forms of cenobitic monasticism to the attention of Latin readers. In so doing he influenced the Rule of St. Benedict and all subsequent monasticism in the West. However, Jerome was also a monk, and his original works on asceticism, as well as his exegetical works, are informed by his monastic experience in the East and the West at the end of the fourth century.

Born in Strido in Dalmatia around 345 (the earlier date of 331 is recorded by Prosper of Aquitaine and affirmed by Kelly [1975] but is rejected by most scholars), Jerome received the classical education appropriate for the son of a propertied family. In 360–367 he continued his studies in Rome, expecting to become a civil servant, and was baptized. This career path then took him to Trier, the capital of Gaul, and at this point his ascetic and religious interests began to dominate. Some early monastic influence might have been felt at Trier, as it had previously been the site of Athanasius' exile (335), for at this point (370) Jerome abandoned career prospects and moved to Aquileia (near Venice) in the company of ascetically minded friends (Rufinus, Bonosus, Chromatius, and Heliodorus). In Aquileia Jerome followed the established program of the urban ascetic – celibacy, fasting, and prayer – while copying Christian classics available there.

Jerome left Aquileia in 373 in the company of Evagrius of Antioch (c. 320–c. 394) and headed to Syria, where he had direct contact with Eastern forms of monasticism while living as a hermit in the desert of Chalcis (375–377). However, before going to Chalcis Jerome wrote letters praising certain aspects of asceticism and expressing views that must have been formed in the West (see Rousseau, 1978). Jerome wrote that the monk inhabits "a city delightful above all others" (Letter 2 to the hermit Theodosius) and that Bonosus, who has taken up the ascetic life on an island, has "enrolled himself in a new city" (Letter 3 to Rufinus). These views (and perhaps the famous nightmare in which divine judgment ruled him a Ciceronian and not a Christian) led him to withdraw from Antioch and join the monastic "society" of Chalcis. Monks were scattered over the region in individual cells to fast and pray, with only occasional contact. Letters written at this time (375–377) indicate that Jerome saw these conditions as necessary for the Christian ascetic: the ascetic must leave family and possessions and live in solitude (Letter 14); he should remain apart from doctrinal controversy, as his proper role is to weep in "chains, dirt, disordered hair" (Letter 17).

Yet while in Chalcis Jerome continued his scholarly work and thus modeled a different role for future Christian monks. He improved his knowledge of Greek, began Hebrew studies, and learned the spoken language of the Syrian monks with whom he lived (Letter 7). He asked for books (Letter 5) and employed copyists to augment his personal library, and other writings show that Jerome and the monks of Chalcis were deeply involved in the doctrinal controversy that split the Church in Antioch; Jerome wrote to Pope Damasus I (366–384) asking for guidance on whom to support as bishop (Letters 15 and 16). His decision to support Paulinus as bishop, combined with his refusal to accept the new Eastern formula of three hypostases, made Jerome a target of hostility in Chalcis, and he left the desert in 376–377. Earlier he had praised the desert as the best possible place for the Christian ascetic (Letters 2 and 17); from now on he would be drawn closer to cities where the wealthy could practice asceticism, becoming an adviser to upper-class men and women on ascetic doctrine and practice while progressing as a biblical translator and exegete.

The theoretical basis of Jerome's asceticism was shaped by contacts he made after leaving Chalcis. Returning to Antioch he was ordained by Paulinus. By 380 Jerome was in Constantinople, where he came under the influence of Gregory of Nazianzus (329/30–389/90) (praised by Jerome, *On Famous Men* 117) and translated Greek texts, including the works of Origen (c. 185–c. 254). His early theoretical writings on asceticism were shaped largely by Origenism: because bodies were ephemeral, Christians could live even now as "spirits" as long as they rejected sexual relations and the demands of family and property (see Brown, 1988). Returning to Rome, from 382 to 385 Jerome had ample opportunity to exert influence. As adviser to Damasus, he translated Greek patristic texts and began to work on a new Latin Bible. As adviser to a group of aristocratic women, the widows

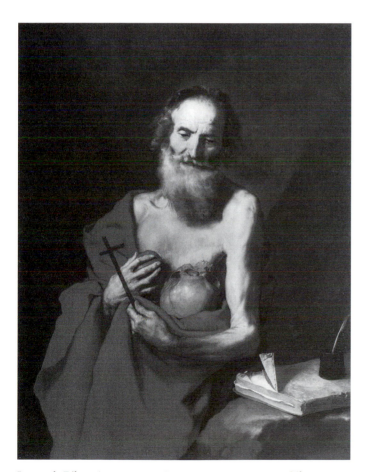

Jusepe de Ribera (1591–1652), St. Jerome, c. 1628–1640. Oil on canvas, 129 x 100.3 cm. The Cleveland Museum of Art, 1999, Mr. and Mrs. William H. Marlatt Fund, 1961.219.
Photo courtesy of The Cleveland Museum of Art

Marcella and Paula and their daughters, he guided their home-based ascetic practice and Bible study.

The letter to Eustochium, Paula's daughter (Letter 22, written 384), set out principles to guide the choice of an ascetic life and gave practical advice on conduct. The letter is actually a treatise meant for wide circulation, and in it Jerome argues that virginity is the condition willed by God, whereas sex and marriage came about only after the Fall. The belief that the serious Christian was celibate had been circulating for centuries; Jerome gave it impact by promoting the idea in aristocratic circles and portraying the ideal of spiritual marriage to Christ in a vivid way (Letter 22.25–26), using imagery from the Song of Songs.

Work on an improved Latin Bible began at the request of Damasus in 383–384, first with a revised version of the Gospels based on Old Latin and Greek (these became the Vulgate Gospels) and then a revision of the Psalms (version lost). Jerome left Rome in 385 after the death of Damasus and traveled to the East, touring the Holy Land and the monastic sites in the Nitrian Desert of Egypt before settling in Bethlehem in an ascetic community with Paula and Eustochium in a nearby women's community (described in Letter 108). Jerome continued his Hebrew studies, going deeper in an effort to improve the Latin Bible. He could now consult Origen's *Hexapla* (a six-column biblical text allowing comparison of Hebrew and various Greek versions); using this he revised the Psalter (a version that became known as the Gallican Psalter and became part of the Vulgate) and then other biblical books. Around 390 Jerome realized that it was preferable to produce a fresh translation based directly on the Hebrew Scriptures rather than to revise the Old Latin. At the same time he argued that only the 22 books of the Jewish canon were Scripture; others (e.g., Wisdom, Ecclesiasticus, and Judith) should be read for edification only. Working from the Hebrew with the aid of the *Hexapla*, he began by translating the Book of Samuel and the Book of Kings and then progressed to the Psalter (completed in 393), the Book of Prophets, and the Book of Job; the Octateuch was completed in 404. Jerome did not produce a fresh translation of every biblical book: in the New Testament he translated only the Gospels; in the Old Testament some books were simply revised. Rufinus the Syrian (c. 345–411), an associate of Jerome, may have produced the translation of the remaining New Testament books that formed the Vulgate. Cassiodorus (485/90–c. 580) played a role in ordering the work of Jerome and others into a single Bible, but the process continued past the eighth century.

The quality of his biblical translations varies. Jerome claimed that his translation aimed to produce "sense for sense" (Letter 106.29), yet the end product is sometimes very literal and sometimes approaches paraphrase (Sparks [1970] summarizes these characteristics). The importance of Jerome's translation for monasticism lay in the fact that by means of this text he crafted a Christian Latin – simple, with strong Hebrew flavor – that permeated monasteries in the West and shaped their spirituality. In Benedictine monasteries the office ensured that nine times a day the monks would hear lengthy biblical passages as well as chant the Psalms. Thus, they spoke or chanted Jerome's language into the 20th century, when modern-language translations replaced Latin in most monastic practice. In 1965 Thomas Merton (1915–1968), writer and Trappist monk, praised "the incomparable sound of the Vulgate" and affirmed, "The Latin psalter is for me! It is a deep communion with the Lord and His saints, of my Latin Church" (Merton, 1997). This communion rests in part on the work of Jerome.

Commentaries on biblical books followed the translations, often at the specific request of friends. Jerome also produced surveys of Christian history and literature at several different points in his career, mainly on the basis of the works of Eusebius (*Chronicle* extended to 378; the *Book of Places* and *Book of Names*; *On Famous Men* in 393). Poorly preserved monastic works, such as the letters of Antony (c. 251–356), are given a *terminus* by a citation in *On Famous Men* (88). He also wrote polemical treatises: against the Nicene rigorist Lucifer of Cagliari (c. 382); against John of Jerusalem and Rufinus for Origenism; against Helvidius (c. 383), Jovinian (394), and Vigilantius (c. 406); and against the Pelagians (c. 410) for in various ways devaluing virginity and the monastic life. The latter group of polemics is useful for marking the development in Jerome's thinking about the significance of virginity and other ascetic practices in Christian life. Anti-Origenist since 393, he came to doubt that Christians could attain perfection or a "passionless" state in this life even through the strictest asceticism (*Dialogue against the Pelagians* 2.24).

Jerome also wrote or translated a group of works that fostered the development of monastic life. A group of three works records the lives of Christian hermits: *Life of Paul* (374–375), *Life of Hilarion* (390), and *Life of Malchus* (391). Once considered "romances" by critics, they are now thought to have a historical core, yet the subject's biography is subordinated to other interests. As a founder of monasticism, Paul is portrayed as a rival to Antony. Hilarion follows Antony's example (22 years in the desert, then a public career of wonder-working in the service of the Church), but the events of his life are grouped thematically to illustrate ascetic practices. Malchus demonstrates the importance of guarding virginity, even when threatened.

When Jerome settled in Bethlehem (386) in a monastery that he organized, paired with a women's community supervised by Paula (described in Letter 108), he acted as its abbot. It was organized on cenobitic lines: the monks lived in cells; met for meals, prayers, and instruction; obeyed superiors; and worked to support themselves. This is the Pachomian model that Jerome praised in the letter to Eustochium (Letter 22); later, at the time of Paula's death in 404, he translated a collection of Pachomian writings into Latin (from Greek on the basis of a Coptic original) for the benefit of Western monks interested in communal monasticism. Jerome's translation of the Rule of Pachomius contributed substantially to Vigilius' Eastern Rule (c. 420), and the translation also circulated in Italy in a shortened version. By this means the Rule of Pachomius was able to influence the Rule of St. Benedict (c. sixth century). Jerome died in 420, a polemicist to the end – a very late work is a fierce attack on the Pelagians (Letter 154) – but his biblical scholarship and role in the preservation of early monastic texts stand as his greatest contributions to the development of Christian monasticism.

JANET TIMBIE

*See also* Benedict of Nursia, St.; Desert Mothers; Gregory of Nazianzus, St.; Humanism, Christian; Israel/Palestine; Jerusalem, Israel; Libraries: Western Christian; Origins: Eastern Christian; Origins: Western Christian; Pachomius, St.; Transvestite Saints

## Biography

Born near Aquileia in Friuli (northeast of Venice), Jerome was baptized in Rome and then devoted himself to an ascetic life in Aquileia. Around 374 he set out for Palestine, only to linger in Antioch and the Syrian desert, where he learned Hebrew. After being ordained in Antioch, he returned to Rome, where from 382 to 385 he worked as secretary to Pope Damasus I (366–384). In 386 Jerome settled in Bethlehem, Palestine, as head of a new men's monastery. There he translated the Bible into Latin (a task first undertaken on the Psalms for Pope Damasus), wrote commentaries on the Bible, and engaged in extensive correspondence. Jerome's name soon became synonymous with philological Biblical scholarship.

## Major Works

*Chronicon* (Chronicle), edited by R. Helm, in *Griechischen Christlichen Schriftsteller*, volume 47, 1956

*De viris illustribus* (On Famous Men), edited by E.C. Richardson, in *Texte und Untersuchungen*, volume 14, 1896; translated by E.C. Richardson, in *Select Library of Nicene and Post-Nicene Fathers*, series 2, volume 3, 1892

*Dogmatic and Polemical Works*, translated by John N. Hritzu, in *Fathers of the Church*, volume 53, 1965

*Epistolae* (Letters), edited by I. Hilberg, *Corpus Scriptorum Ecclesiasticorum Latinorum*, volume 54, 1910–1918; translated by C.C. Mierow, in *Fathers of the Church*, volume 33, 1963

*Hebraicae Quaestiones in Libro Geneseos* (Hebrew Questions in the Book of Genesis), edited by P. de Lagarde, in *Corpus Christianorum, Series Latina*, volume 72, 1959

*Homilies*, edited by G. Morin, *Corpus Christianorum, Series Latina*, volume 78, 1958; translated by M.L. Ewald, in *Fathers of the Church*, volumes 48 and 57, 1964–1966

*Onomastica: Liber locorum, Liber nominum* (Book of Places, Book of Names), edited by P. de Lagarde, 1870

*Prologus Galeatus: The Middle English Bible; Prefatory Epistles of St. Jerome*, edited by C. Lindberg, 1978

*Vita S. Hilarionis, Vita Malchi, Vita Pauli* (Lives of St. Hilarion, Malchus, and Paul), edited by J.P. Migne, in *Patrologia Latina*, volume 23; translated by M.L. Ewald, in *Fathers of the Church*, volume 15, 1952

*Vulgate* (Latin translation of the Old and New Testaments), 1452–1455, edited by R. Weber, 1983

## Further Reading

Boon, Amand, editor, *Pachomiana Latina*, Louvain: Bureaux de la Revue, 1932

Brown, Peter, *The Body and Society: Men, Women, and Sexual Renunciation in Early Christianity*, New York: Columbia University Press, 1988

Cavallera, Ferdinand, *Saint Jérôme, sa vie et son oeuvre*, 2 vols., Louvain: Champion, 1922

Clark, Elizabeth A., *The Origenist Controversy: The Cultural Construction of an Early Christian Debate*, Princeton, New Jersey: Princeton University Press, 1992

Coleiro, E., "St. Jerome's Lives of the Hermits," *Vigiliae Christianae* 11 (1957)

Kelly, J.N.D., *Jerome: His Life, Writings, and Controversies*, New York: Harper and Row, and London: Duckworth, 1975

Merton, Thomas, *Dancing in the Water of Life*, volume 5: *The Journals of Thomas Merton*, edited by Robert E. Daggy, San Francisco: HarperSanFrancisco, 1997

Rousseau, Philip, *Ascetics, Authority and the Church in the Age of Jerome and Cassian*, Oxford and New York: Oxford University Press, 1978

Sparks, H.F.D., "Jerome as Biblical Scholar," in *Cambridge History of the Bible*, volume 1, edited by P.R. Ackroyd and C.F. Evans, Cambridge: Cambridge University Press, 1970

# Jerusalem, Israel

Jerusalem, a city central to three faiths – Judaism, Christianity, and Islam – can lay claim to being the most sacred place on the planet. In the past 3,000 years, since it was made the location of the Ark of the Covenant by King David, the city has come to be seen as the center of the earth, or its navel, and has acted as a powerful religious magnet. The word *Jerusalem*, which probably means the foundation of the Semitic god Shalem, would in the Middle Ages be translated as the city or vision of peace (shalom) and be revered by members of all three faiths as a final resting place. To Christian monks especially, it became the Alpha and the Omega, or the place of origin of their religion and the site of the Last Judgment, the location onto which would descend the heavenly Jerusalem.

From the origins of Christian monasticism in the third and fourth centuries, monks were drawn to Jerusalem and often lived in communities awaiting Christ's return in places associated with the final days of his earthly ministry. Constantine (306–337), the first Christian emperor, built several large churches at these sites in the 320s and 330s, notably the church of the Holy Sepulcher, a great basilica built over the places of Christ's passion and burial. The emperor's mother, St. Helena (c. 255–c. 330), supposedly had found the very cross on which Christ had been crucified. This precious item, which would become the most important relic of the Christian centuries and the principal symbol of Christendom, was preserved in this church. Constantine and Helena also built a large basilica, the Eleona, on the Mount of Olives at the place where Christ had instructed his disciples about the end of the world and near the point where he had ascended to heaven. It was late in the fourth century that a church of the Ascension, octagonal in shape and surmounted by a great cross, was built on that spot. In the same period the wealthy matron Melania the Elder (d. c. 410) and her spiritual adviser, Rufinus (c. 345–411), built a number of monasteries and oratories on the Mount of Olives and many hospices to house the growing number of pilgrims.

In the first half of the fifth century, the empress Eudocia, wife of Valentinian III (425–455), proved a generous patron of the religious of Jerusalem and built a large number of churches, monasteries, and hospices there. Her contemporary Melania the Younger (383–439) also had constructed on the Mount of Olives and elsewhere in the city a number of monasteries and oratories dedicated to the apostles, martyrs, and other saints. This significant increase in the number of monks and of religious communities in Jerusalem must be seen in the context of the rapid growth of the monastic population in Palestine and Syria in the period.

In the sixth century Justinian (527–565) included the Holy City in his large-scale building program in the Roman Empire. He erected the church of St. Mary the New, the Nea, which boasted a large monastic community that ran hospitals and hospices for both men and women pilgrims. Justinian was the last great Christian imperial builder before the Crusades and constructed in the city hospices and branches of the many monastic establishments found near it in Palestine. The imperial building program of Justinian and his predecessors is readily evident in the sixth-century *Madaba Map* mosaic, found in the trans-Jordan region, which portrays numerous places in Jerusalem, including many of the churches that had monks associated with them.

A number of the churches of Jerusalem and their religious communities were destroyed or severely damaged in the Persian conquest of the city in 614. Constantine's great church of the Holy Sepulcher is included in this list, and the True Cross was taken to Persia, where it would remain until Heraclius (610–641) restored it in 628 after his conquest of the Persians. The Roman restoration of control over Jerusalem would be brief, for in 638 the forces of Islam took the city. During the first centuries of their occupation, they built on the Temple Mount the celebrated Dome of the Rock and the Aqsa mosque and permitted the return of the Jews. Also during this period the Christians were allowed to restore a number of their churches and religious communities.

That Jerusalem continued to be important in the West in the eighth and ninth centuries is evident in the actions of Charlemagne (768–814) with respect to the Holy City. Around 800 he exchanged envoys and gifts with both the patriarch of Jerusalem, who sent him the keys of the church of the Holy Sepulcher, and the Muslim ruler Harun al-Rashid (786–809). That he received a protectorate over the Holy Land is highly unlikely, but he did send enough wealth to Jerusalem to support Western religious communities there and to sponsor the building of a hospice for pilgrims from the West. This funding supported a Latin community of religious at the church of the Holy Sepulcher. A memorandum written for the emperor in 808 on the houses and monasteries of Jerusalem records churches and religious communities, with the number of members, and bears clear witness to the Western emperor's keen interest in and support of Jerusalem, a connection that would grow even greater in subsequent centuries through the development of the legend of Charlemagne.

In the ensuing period, before Jerusalem fell to the Latin crusaders, the Holy City came under the control of the Fatimid dynasty in Egypt. Muslims, Jews, and Christians continued to worship at the sites holy to each, although increasingly during this period the Mount of Olives became the most important center of Jewish public prayer. It also drew growing numbers of Western Christian pilgrims with millennial expectations. A violent disturbance in 1009 corroborated for many the proximity of the end when the Fatimid caliph, al-Hakim (996–1021), ordered the destruction of the church of the Holy Sepulcher and persecuted both Christians and Jews. The apprehension was further exacerbated in 1033 when a great earthquake damaged many of the churches, monasteries, and convents in and around Jerusalem.

In the early 1070s the Seljuk Turks became masters of the city. Their conquest contributed significantly to the summoning of the First Crusade, which swept over Jerusalem in July 1099. During nearly a century of crusader control of the Holy City, much rebuilding of Christian structures, both churches and monasteries, took place. The crusaders converted the Dome of the Rock and the Aqsa mosque, called by them "the Temple," into Christian churches. The latter became the center of a new militant monastic society, the Knights of the Temple. The other militant religious order that was born in Jerusalem during the crusader occupation was the Knights of St. John of the Hospital (the Hospitallers), who cared for pilgrims and the Christian sick and like the Templars sought to defend Jerusalem from the Muslim threat that grew rapidly during the 12th century.

On the retaking of Jerusalem by the Islamic forces under Saladin in 1187, with relatively little damage to the city, the Muslims restored the Dome of the Rock and the Aqsa mosque. The diminishing of Christian communities in the Holy City was marked by Muslim takeover of a number of Christian structures, such as the Benedictine house of nuns dedicated to St. Anne. By the time of the peaceful assuming of control of the city by the Ottoman Turks in 1516, the Christian presence had been severely reduced, that of Western rites even more than of the Eastern. Because in 1453 the patriarch of Constantinople had been made the head of all Christians in the Ottoman Empire, it is hardly surprising that the number of Greek religious houses remained relatively numerous, with at least 14 in the 18th and 19th centuries, many of which served as hospices for the Christian pilgrims who came mainly from the East. Armenian, Coptic, and Abyssinian houses were also important. As for Western Christians the Franciscans remained the most visible force, especially at the Holy Sepulcher, and conducted many visitors on the Via Dolorosa.

The entrance of British General Edmund Allenby into Jerusalem in December 1917 ended Turkish rule and resulted in the appearance of modern Western-oriented Jerusalem, which has become a bone of contention in the post–World War II state of Israel. Although not as prominent as the Jewish and Islamic presences in the Holy City during the past 50 years, the Chris-

tian communities continue their traditional association with the sites linked to the life of Christ and to the early Christian Church. These places have drawn an ever increasing number of Christian pilgrims, including in 1964 that of Pope Paul VI (1963–1978), the first bishop of Rome to visit Jerusalem since St. Peter.

Over the centuries the attraction of Jerusalem as the Alpha and the Omega for Christianity has drawn countless pilgrims to the Holy City, including many monks hoping to establish themselves there or simply wanting a foretaste of the Last Days. The Psalms, recited daily in the Divine Office, and the liturgy in general heightened that longing to return to the source. Hagiography and the accounts of earlier pilgrims also strengthened this desire. Relics from the Holy Land, especially pieces of the True Cross, increased the longing to have some tangible contact with the sacred site. From the fourth century on, large numbers of pilgrims, including many monks, traveled to the Holy City after reading biblical commentaries and letters by St. Jerome (c. 345–420). These pilgrims enhanced the economic well-being of the monasteries and hospices where they stayed. The pilgrims also acquired relics, such as the most highly prized pieces of the True Cross or other commemorative items made and offered by the religious communities.

After the Muslim conquest of 638, the city became a magnet for pilgrims of the three faiths, whose members harbored deep suspicions and fears of the actions of members of the other faiths and even of Christians of different sects. Riots and disturbances were frequent. One cause of contention lay in the miracle of the Descent of the Holy Fire, which occurred annually on Holy Saturday before Easter, when the flame mysteriously appeared and reignited the vigil lights at the church of the Holy Sepulcher. In the course of the centuries, this occurrence became a central moment in the Holy Week observance in Jerusalem, especially among Greek Orthodox Christians. It was this "miracle," which the Muslim observers viewed with deep suspicion, that purportedly caused Caliph al-Hakim to have the church destroyed in 1009.

To many Christians, especially in the West, Hakim's actions only confirmed the apocalyptic expectations that were widespread during the 10th and 11th centuries and that caused so many pilgrims, as reported by the chronicler Ralph Glaber, to go to Jerusalem and await the Second Coming. Similar fears have caused some Christians in the late 20th century to follow the same path. Their activities in Jerusalem have been viewed with much anxiety by both Jews and Muslims.

The United Nations partition of the city in 1947 created an international city, a *corpus separatum*. In many ways this action acknowledged the special nature of this very sacred place. Although its future is clouded by continuing animosity, now especially between Jews and Arabs, Jerusalem will remain a deeply holy site offering to many a vision of peace that is to come.

DANIEL F. CALLAHAN

*See also* Crusades; Desert Mothers; Hagiography: Eastern Christian; Hospitallers (Knights of Malta since 1530); Israel/Palestine;

Jerome, St.; Liturgy: Western Christian; Office, Daily: Western Christian; Origins: Eastern Christian; Pilgrimages, Christian: Near East; Relics, Christian Monastic; Syria; Templars; Warrior Monks: Christian

## Further Reading

Asali, Kamil J., editor, *Jerusalem in History: 3000 B.C. to the Present Day*, London and New York: Kegan Paul, 1997

Callahan, Daniel F., "Jerusalem in the Monastic Imaginations of the Early Eleventh Century," *The Haskins Society Journal* 6 (1994)

Canard, Marius, "La destruction de l'Église de la Résurrection par le calife Hâkim et l'histoire de la descente du feu sacré," *Byzantion* 35 (1965)

Coüasnon, Charles, *The Church of the Holy Sepulchre in Jerusalem*, translated by J.-P.B. and Claude Ross, London: Oxford University Press, 1974

Murphy-O'Connor, Jerome, *The Holy Land: An Archaeological Guide from Earliest Times to 1700*, 2nd edition, Oxford and New York: Oxford University Press, 1986

Peters, Francis E., *Jerusalem: The Holy City in the Eyes of Chroniclers, Visitors, Pilgrims, and Prophets from the Days of Abraham to the Beginnings of Modern Times*, Princeton, New Jersey: Princeton University Press, 1985

Peters, Francis E., *The Distant Shrine: The Islamic Centuries in Jerusalem*, New York: AMS Press, 1993

Prawer, Joshua, and Haggai Ben-Shammai, editors, *The History of Jerusalem: The Early Muslim Period, 638–1099*, New York: New York University Press, 1996

Vincent, Hugues, and Felix Marie Abel, *Jérusalem nouvelle*, Paris: Lecoffre, 1914

Walker, Peter W.L., *Holy City, Holy Places?: Christian Attitudes to Jerusalem and the Holy Land in the Fourth Century*, Oxford: Clarendon Press, 1989; New York: Oxford University Press, 1990

Wilken, Robert L., *The Land Called Holy: Palestine in Christian History and Thought*, New Haven, Connecticut: Yale University Press, 1992

Wilkinson, John, *Jerusalem Pilgrims Before the Crusades*, Jerusalem: Ariel, and Warminster: Aris and Phillips, 1977

# Joachim of Fiore c. 1135–1202

Italian Benedictine and Cistercian monk, founder of the "Florensians," theologian, and historian

Although best known and influential for his novel three-*status* theology of history, Joachim of Fiore was himself a devout practitioner, a restless and determined innovator, and a subtle theologian of the monastic life. Born to a notary of the Sicilian court and made a junior chancery official himself, Joachim was transformed by a pilgrimage he made to the Holy Land in 1167. After dedicating his life to God, Joachim spent some time as a hermit, first near a Greek monastery on Mount Etna, Sicily, then in Calabria. Around 1171, he became a monk at the Benedictine house at Corazzo, of which he became prior, then abbot in the years 1176–1177. Having become abbot of the house, Joachim soon began a difficult campaign to have Corazzo incorporated into the Cistercian Order, convinced at this point in his life that the Cistercian Order represented the highest form of the monastic life. (The house was incorporated in 1188 only after Joachim's departure.) While at the Cistercian house of Casamari in 1183, Joachim had two visions that launched him on his career as an apocalyptic prophet and scriptural exegete. As the decade wore on, Joachim slowly became more deeply involved with his writing and increasingly disenchanted with his administrative work as abbot of Corazzo.

In this context, the Abbot of Fiore wrote his monastic treatise *De vita sancti Benedicti et de Officio divino secundum eius Doctrinam*, a work of interest in several respects. First, it is cast in the form of an exegesis of Gregory the Great's *Life of Benedict* (*Dialogues*, Book II). Second, Joachim expresses his oft-repeated thoughts about the historical significance of monasticism. Third, he makes a number of critical comments about the Cistercian Order, which he was then preparing (in imitation of Benedict, he believed) to leave in order to create a new monastic institution.

In fact, in 1188, Joachim launched his efforts to create a new monastic community in the mountains of Calabria. He began by founding the house of San Giovanni in Fiore, the first house of what was to become the Congregation of Fiore, or "Florensians." Ultimately, about 40 houses would be established, although many of these eventually returned to the Cistercian Order. Despite the fact that the Florensian houses observed many Cistercian practices and that Joachim heralded Bernard as a sign of the imminent transformation of the monastic order, his departure from Corazzo alienated him from Cîteaux, which condemned him at its General Chapter in 1192. Interestingly, Joachim seems to have regarded the Florensian order to be as much a transitional order as was the Cistercian.

The journey from hermit to Benedictine to Cistercian to founder of the "Florensians" exemplifies a crucial biographical and theological theme for Joachim, whose life was shaped by a ceaseless quest for the perfect form of the monastic life. This quest was itself inspired partly by Joachim's conviction that, in the coming third age or *status* of salvation history, the monastic order itself would be transformed and perfected. Although questions about Joachim's vision of the monastic utopia of the third age remain debated (partly because it is depicted in visual form in his *figurae*), it seems clear that he did not envisage a radical departure from the structure and institutions of the medieval church, as some of his interpreters have suggested. What is even clearer is that Joachim saw the structure of world history in terms of the appearance and evolution of the institution and practice of monasticism. Indeed, for Joachim, monasticism – or monasticism in its highest form – was the end and meaning of salvation history.

KEVIN MADIGAN

*See also* Cistercians; Crusades; Franciscans: General or Male; Heretics, Christian; Savonarola, Girolamo

## Biography

Born near Cosenza, Calabria. Joachim traveled to Palestine before entering the Benedictine (soon to become Cistercian) monastery at Corazzo (near Crotone, Calabria). Elected abbot there in 1177, he left office and received papal permission to establish his own congregation in the Sila mountains of Calabria. His periodizing of history into Trinitarian segments (Age of the Father = Old Testament, Age of the Son = New Testament, Age of the Holy Spirit soon to begin) fascinated successive generations, including the Spiritual Franciscans and Dante. Joachim's doctrines were condemned in 1255 and 1263.

## Major Works

Liber de Concordia Novi ac vetris Testamenti
Expositio in Apocalypsim
Psalterium decem Chordarum

## Further Reading

McGinn, Bernard, *The Calabrian Abbot: Joachim of Fiore in the History of Western Thought*, New York: Macmillan, 1985
McGinn, Bernard, editor and translator, *Apocalyptic Spirituality*, New York: Paulist Press, and London: SPCK, 1979
Reeves, Marjorie, *The Influence of Prophecy in the Later Middle Ages: A Study in Joachimism*, Oxford: Clarendon Press, 1969; revised edition, Notre Dame, Indiana: University of Notre Dame Press, 1993
Reeves, Marjorie, "The Originality and Influence of Joachim of Fiore," *Traditio* 36 (1980)
Wessley, Stephen E., *Joachim of Fiore and Monastic Reform*, New York: Peter Lang, 1990
West, Delno, editor, *Joachim of Fiore in Christian Thought: Essays on the Influence of the Calabrian Prophet*, New York: Burt Franklin, 1975

# John of Damascus, St. c. 655–c. 750

## Christian monk and theologian

John of Damascus (Yanan ibn Mansur) was a member of a high-ranking Christian family and followed his father in office at the court of the Islamic caliph at Damascus, probably representing Christian affairs there. He lived sometime between 655 and 750. The proposed death date is fairly secure, but his birth might have been later than the traditional supposition, perhaps sometime nearer 670. It is difficult to tell, as the traditional life dates from the 11th century and has many questionable elements. John resigned his post around 725, probably because of political pressures, and became a monk at Mar Saba monastery near Bethlehem, where he eventually was ordained priest. Between 726 and 730, in the time that the veneration of images had been proscribed by Emperor Leo (717–741) at Constantinople, John wrote three discourses in defense of icons, which became important resources for later generations of Orthodox theologians. He was anathematized by the Iconoclastic Synod of 753, but Mar Saba was then out of the political reach of the Byzantine court,

and John continued preaching to great effect in the churches of Jerusalem. The icon venerators, eventually to be victorious, hailed him at the Second Council of Nicaea in 787 as a heroic confessor. His connecting of the theology of icon to incarnational Christology was a notable aspect of his apologia.

One of his fellow monks, Cosmas the Melodist (c. 675–c. 751), later the bishop of Maiuma, encouraged John to write a systematic compilation of Christian theology. This became his most important work: *The Fount of Knowledge*. It has the hallmark of a scholastic compendium made up of three parts: on philosophy, on heresies, and on the Orthodox faith. The last section soon assumed the status of a one-volume authority on Orthodox theology and also exerted a massive influence on the medieval Western Church, not least because it was a primary source for Thomas Aquinas in his *Summa Theologiae*. John's other large work was the *Sacra Parallela*, now preserved only in fragments. It is a great compilation of scriptural and patristic texts relating to the ascetic and moral life – a veritable monastic florilegium.

Mar Saba was an important center at this period for the coming together of foundational elements of Byzantine liturgical offices. The liturgy of the Great Church at Constantinople was influential, but so too was the monastic *Typikon* of Mar Saba. John himself made an important contribution to this process not only in his rhetorical sermons (especially those devoted to the honor of the Virgin Mary) but especially in his hymn writing. Many of the hymns now attributed to him may not be authentic, for his success attracted imitators, but his modeling of hymnography was important for the liturgical shaping of monastic forms of prayer.

All his writing was designed as an aid to monastics living the life of perfection. Theological knowledge (i.e., orthodoxy) was essential to the ascetic task as he and previous Byzantine theologians saw it. He also wrote on the connection between ascetic endeavor and theological vision. His homily on the Transfiguration is an example of his thought here. John teaches, following Gregory of Nazianzus (c. 330–379) and Evagrius Ponticus (349–399), that the monk's life is a progress toward the divine vision. Such a life is based on purity of heart that arises out from asceticism and bears fruit in love. When the monk has arrived through disciplined ascetic training to the stability of pure love, then the potential is given for the disciple to contemplate God and see Him, to whom all life turns for its being. John's concept of ascesis is that the monk needs a twofold preparation: *praxis* (ascetic deeds and training) and *theoria* (how to envision God correctly, i.e., in an orthodox theological manner). He sees discipleship as a progressive conforming to the image of God in Christ. This progress is advanced by association with other disciples (monastic elders) who have already begun to embody the image of the Lord in their lives and characters. For John the true saints have imaged Christ so faithfully that they have become archetypal. In this assimilation little that is idiosyncratic remains in their lives. So too the monastic who achieves the goal of individual perfection in Christ will be conformed also to the prior tradition of the saints, both concretely and intellectually. This explains why, for John, individuality in thought or behavior was hardly a virtue to be striven for. He was a great synthesizer and compiler by design and intent. It is in this, and not for any originality he might have had, that he assumes importance in the history of theology and monastic spirituality. His feast day is celebrated in the Christian calendar on 4 December.

JOHN MCGUCKIN

*See also* Evagrius Ponticus; Iconoclasm (Controversy); Hymnographers; Israel/Palestine; Jerusalem, Israel; Liturgy: Eastern Christian; Spirituality: Eastern Christian; Theology, Eastern Christian; Thomas Aquinas, St.; Visual Arts, Eastern Christian: Painting

## Biography

Born into a wealthy Greek-speaking Christian family in Damascus, John held a position at the court of Umayyad caliph. Around 725 he resigned to become a monk at the monastery of St. Sabas near Jerusalem. He defended the use of images during the Iconoclastic Controversy. His seminal work *The Fount of Knowledge* was written at the urging of a fellow monk, the hymnist Cosmas the Melodist. Among other achievements, he is the first Christian theologian to be well acquainted with Islam.

## Major Works

*Sacra Parallela*
*Exposition of the Orthodox Faith*, translated by S.D.F. Salmond (in Saint Hilary's *Select Works*), 1899
*Writings (The Fount of Knowledge)*, translated by Frederick H. Chase, 1958
*On the Divine Images: Three Apologies Against Those Who Attack the Divine Images*, translated by David Anderson, 1980
Hymns

## Further Reading

McGuckin, John A., *The Transfiguration of Christ in Scripture and Tradition*, Lewiston, New York: Mellen Press, 1987
Nasrallah, Joseph, St. *Jean de Damas: Son Époque, sa vie, son oeuvre*, Harissa, Lebanon: Imp. Saint Paul, 1950
O'Rourke-Boyle, M., "Christ the Eikon in the Apologies for Holy Images of John of Damascus," *Greek Orthodox Theological Review* 15 (1970)
Sahas, Daniel J., *John of Damascus on Islam: The "Heresy of the Ishmaelites,"* Leiden: Brill, 1972

# John of the Cross, St. 1542–1591

## Spanish Carmelite, poet, and mystic

Born John of (Juan de) Yepes in 1542 in the village of Fontiveros in Castile, Spain, the future St. John of the Cross was the second son of poor weavers. His father, who had married beneath his social station, died when John was seven years of age, necessitating a move by his mother and her two young children to Arevalo and then to Medina del Campo. As a child, John began his education at the local College for the Children of Doctrine, then continued it under the Jesuits at their school in Medina. During this time he enjoyed the patronage of a wealthy nobleman who apparently intended to groom him for a benefice as chaplain of the local hospital.

However, in 1563, John took the habit of the Carmelite order in Medina del Campo and professed his vows a year later as Friar John of St. Matthias. At the time of his entrance, the Constitutions of 1462 governed the lives of the friars. Tracing their history to the hermits of Mount Carmel in the Holy Land, the Carmelites had mitigated the rule of the order when they moved to Europe in the 13th century. These changes included abandonment of the eremitical for the mendicant tradition, the foundation of houses in cities rather than deserts, meals taken in common, reduction of abstinence from meat, and a shortening of the periods of silence to the time between Compline and Prime.

After profession, John was sent to study the liberal arts at the University of Salamanca and resided at the order's College of St. Andrew in the city. His successful completion of the three-year course of study was capped by his ordination in 1567. It was at about this time that he met St. Teresa of Avila (1515–1582), who had already begun the reform of the Carmelite women. Having disclosed to her his desire to enter the Carthusians so that he could follow a more contemplative life, he was persuaded to wait and to consider initiating a reform of the Carmelite men along the lines of the Teresian model. In November 1568, John, in the company of the former prior of Medina del Campo and a lay brother, established the first house of what would eventually become the Discalced Carmelites in the tiny hamlet of Duruelo. Henceforth, he would be known as John of the Cross.

The rule that he adopted followed closely that embraced by St. Teresa. It exceeded the strict observance of the rule as mitigated by Eugenius IV (1431–1447) and attempted to imitate as much as possible that observed by the earliest hermits of Mount Carmel. At Duruelo, John and his companions combined the demands of contemplation with an active apostolate among the local community, where they preached and provided the sacraments. Within the monastery they practiced an austere form of the ascetic life, including strict abstinence from meat, continuous fasting, wearing of a rough serge habit, and going barefoot (thus the name "Discalced"). Long periods of silence, coupled with individual prayer and work, occupied the greater part of the day, but periods for recreation were also mandated for by the rule. The ancient liturgy of the Holy Sepulchre, the cult of the Virgin of Carmel, and obedience to "the Father of the Order" were included as well. Despite the rigors of the primitive rule, many new postulants as well as professed members of the Observance joined the reform. John of the Cross served as the first master of novices, one of many posts that he eventually filled in the order.

Although one of the cofounders of the Discalced Carmelites, John did not take an active part in the administrative struggles that soon engulfed the order. The tensions between the Observants (Calced or Mitigated) and the Discalced eventually led to his seizure by the Calced and his imprisonment in 1578 under extremely harsh conditions in Toledo. While there, he composed his great mystical poems, to which he later added prose commentaries. The proclamation of him in 1926 as a Doctor of the Church is based on these works and their elucidation of mystical prayer.

Both the poetry and the commentaries were written in vernacular Spanish, utilizing the language and the poetic forms characteristic of Renaissance literature in Spain. Because the commentaries were composed in response to questions put to him regarding the deeper meaning of the mystical poems, the use of Spanish rather than Latin ensured ready access to their teachings by their target audience: the nuns and monks of the Reform. As the Discalced Carmelites spread throughout Europe and the Americas, translation of his complete works followed, so that by the early 17th century they could be found in Latin, French, Italian, and the original Spanish.

John of the Cross' principal contribution to monasticism lay in the realm of spiritual direction. During his lifetime, he earned a reputation as an astute confessor and director of souls. His activity in this regard extended to both monastics and the laity. His ability to guide both individuals and other spiritual directors in ways that encouraged contemplative prayer and outlined the many approaches to mysticism was remarked on by many of those who knew him.

After his death in 1591 in Ubeda, the influence of his teaching emanated from his writings. Thus, his most enduring influence on monasticism is the collection of works on the mystical way. Two treatises, titled *Subida del Monte Carmelo* (1579–1585; *The Ascent of Mount Carmel*) and the *Noche oscura* (1582–1585; *Dark Night*), provide commentary on the poem known also as the "Dark Night" (1579–1581). In these works, John explains the purification of the senses and the spirit, which he deems to be necessary first steps to mystical advancement. The *Cantico espiritual* (1578–1584; *Spiritual Canticle*) describes all the stages of the mystic way, from asceticism to mystical marriage. The *Llama de amor viva* (1585–1587; *Living Flame of Love*) focuses on the transforming union experienced at the final stage of mystical prayer. These works provide spiritual directors and individuals a comprehensive explanation of the many approaches to mysticism. The extent of John's influence on later monastics as well as lay people is far-reaching. Among monastics it is evident in the writings of such Carmelite writers as St. Thérèse of Lisieux (1873–1897) and St. Theresa Benedicta of the Cross (Edith Stein, 1891–1942). Others influenced by his works include Thomas Merton (1915–1968), Charles de Foucauld (1858–1916), and Karol Wotijla (John Paul II, 1920– ). John of the Cross' works have drawn equal interest from a wide range of readers from diverse religious backgrounds, including representatives of the Anglican and Lutheran traditions as well as adherents of Judaism, Islam, Hinduism, and Buddhism.

ELIZABETH TERESA HOWE

*See also* Carmelites; Spirituality: Western Christian; Teresa of Avila, St.; Thérèse of Lisieux, St.; Vision, Mystical: Western Christian

## Biography

One of the most influential poets of Christian mysticism, John of the Cross lived as a Carmelite from 1563. He joined St. Teresa in founding the Discalced Carmelites, and from 1572–1577 was confessor at her convent in Avila. After many trials, including nine months' imprisonment in 1577–1578, he served as prior of Carmelite houses in Granada (1582) and Segovia (1588). His Spanish-language poems and treatises differentiate three stages of mystical ascent and disseminated notions such as "the dark night of the soul."

## Major Works

*Cantico espiritual*, 1578–1584; translated as *Spiritual Canticle*

*Subida del Monte Carmelo*, 1579–1585; translated as *The Ascent of Mount Carmel*

*Noche oscura*, 1582–1585; translated as *Dark Night*

*Llama de amor viva*, 1585–1587; translated as *Living Flame of Love*

*The Complete Works of Saint John of the Cross*, translated and edited by E. Allison Peers from the critical edition of Silverio de Santa Teresa, 3 vols., 1934

*The Collected Works of St. John of the Cross*, translated and edited by Kieran Kavanaugh and Otilio Rodriguez, 1973

## Further Reading

Baruzi, Jean, *Saint Jean de la Croix et le problème de l'expérience mystique*, Paris: Alcan, 1931

*The Book of the Foundations*, volume 3, *The Complete Works of St. Teresa of Jesus*, translated and edited by E. Allison Peers, London: Sheed and Ward, 1972

Bruno de Jésus-Marie, *St. John of the Cross*, edited and translated by Benedict Zimmerman, New York: Sheed and Ward, 1932

Crisogóno de Jesús, *The Life of St. John of the Cross*, translated by Kathleen Pond, New York: Harper, and London: Longmans, 1958

Efren de la Madre de Dios, and Otger Steggink, *Tiempo y vida de San Juan de la Cruz*, Madrid: Biblioteca de Autores Christianos, 1992

Ruano, Lucinio, editor, *Vida y obras de San Juan de la Cruz . . . Biografía*, 7th edition, Madrid: La Editorial Católica, 1973

# Joseph of Volokolamsk, St. 1439/40–1515

Russian leader of the "Possessor" monastic movement

Joseph of Volokolamsk (elsewhere, Joseph of Volotsk, Joseph of Volok; Russian, Iosif Volotskii), founder and *hegumen* (abbot) of the Volokolamsk Monastery (Church of the Dormition) and Rule, is best known in Russian history as the leader of the "Possessor" monastic movement. Possessors believed in extensive church holdings and close cooperation with secular authority in order to do God's work. Their main opponent was Nilus of Sora (Russian, Nil Sorskii, c. 1433–1508), who, as leader of the "Non-Possessors," minimized church holdings, preferred a separation between church and state, and espoused the contemplative ideal of Hesychasm that he had learned on Mount Athos.

The question of land ownership in 15th- to 16th-century Muscovy involved not only collaboration with the state but also the possession of villages and of the peasants who inhabited them.

Joseph, né Ivan Sanin, was born into a family that owned the village Iazvishche about 70 miles northwest of Moscow. Contemporary family members included several male and female monastics, ascetics, iconographers, and high-ranking clergy. The boy had a good memory, and at age seven began to study and pray at the Volokolamsk Monastery dedicated to the feast of the Elevation of the Cross. At 20, after becoming first reader and then cantor and living at three different monasteries, he was tonsured monk and instructed by Paphnutius of Borovsk, a spiritual grandchild (a disciple of a disciple) of St. Sergius of Radonezh (c. 1314–1392). Paphnutius, later canonized, distinguished himself as abbot, spiritual father, and estate manager with connections to nobility. At his death in 1477, this role passed to Hegumen Joseph.

Inexplicably, Joseph then traveled to several other monasteries and later returned to his boyhood countryside with seven brethren to build a monastery devoted to the Dormition of the Theotokos (Mother of God). The task took almost 30 years to complete and was funded by nobility and Archbishop Gennadius of Novgorod. Their cenobitic rule, written by Joseph, addressed the needs of a Possessor monastery in a way that the few, extant Slavic rules of other monasteries could not. (For the entire Extended Rule with comparisons to the Brief Rule, see Goldfrank, 1983.)

Synods in 1490 and 1504 condemned the so-called Judaizing heresy, a movement in Novgorod and Moscow that included translations of biblical books directly and exclusively from the Hebrew. The "Judaizers" were led by Zechariah (Slavic, Skharia), possibly a Crimean Karaite Jew, who taught, for example, that Christ was a prophet, the messianic prophecies were unfulfilled, and the Church is unnecessary. Joseph, the Possessors' champion (along with Archbishop Gennadius of Novgorod), wrote against four heretical practices: anti-Trinitarian and anti-Incarnational theology, iconoclasm and opposition to worship, opposition to monasticism as devoid of divine blessing, and criticism of the failure of septimillennialist Christian apocalyptic eschatology (A.D. 1492, or year 7000 after Creation in the then current Jewish and Byzantine calendrical reckoning). Eventually, all these polemics were edited into Joseph's magnum opus, *Prosvetitel' ili oblichenie eresi zhidovstvuiushchikh* (The Enlightener, or Accusation of Heresy against the Judaizers).

During the 16th century the kingdom of Muscovite Russ, or Great Russia, began to coalesce. In 1502–1503 Grand Prince Ivan III (1462–1505) was on the verge of confiscating monastic lands. This bold move was supported in part by the Non-Possessors (i.e., the Trans-Volgan Elders) and especially by Nilus of Sora. Quite naturally Joseph wrote against the proposal. In defense of his position, he cited the following arguments: confiscation was without precedent; it was prohibited by Canon Law, and legal strictures existed against it; a Byzantine and Slavic tradition of philanthropy to monasteries existed that went back to Emperor Constantine I (306–337); intercessory services performed by monastic communities were expected by benefactors to endure in perpetuity and therefore had a God-protected status; and monastic villages were necessary to attract to monasticism aristocrats who would then serve as future prelates. The Non-Possessors disputed these arguments, especially those pertaining to monastic villages in which monks controlled others' lives and properties.

In an ironic turn of events, in March 1507 Hegumen Joseph composed an official will and gave his monastery to Grand Prince Vasilii III (sole ruler, 1505–1533). In return the prince was to guard the Rule of the monastery and to expel malcontents. This established Possessor monasticism by lodging it under the patronage of the ruling family. Vasilii accepted this role and also welcomed Josephite piety. The next *hegumen* after Joseph, the loyal Josephite Daniel of Riazan, later became the Metropolitan of Moscow (1522–1539). Joseph, canonized locally in 1579 and more universally in 1591, became a favorite saint of the Romanov dynasty and was favored well into the next century.

Joseph educated monks for service in the Church and state in high office, and Muscovy expanded in the 16th century under this leadership. In fact the Russian Church as a whole can be described as Josephite throughout the 16th century in its Possessor attitudes, new monastic foundations, and rules. In the 17th century both Old Believers and centrist czars invoked Joseph's name to support traditionalism and imperial monarchy. The Josephite movement waned in the 18th and 19th centuries under the influence of the Enlightenment and discussion of egalitarian human freedoms. Although both Joseph and Nilus were canonized (Nilus only in the 19th century), Joseph's "establishment" position better accommodated the rising centralization of the Muscovite state, whereas many of Nilus' disciples were condemned as heretics.

MICHAEL PROKURAT

*See also* Hesychasm; Moscow, Russia; Mount Athos, Greece; Nilus of Sora, St.; Orthodox Monasticism: Slavic; Russia: History; Russia: Sites; Sergius of Radonezh, St.; Visual Arts, Eastern Christian: Painting

## Biography
Born northwest of Moscow, Joseph studied with Paphnutius of Borovsk at a monastery in Volokolamsk. Thereafter Joseph visited several other monasteries before returning to Volokolamsk to found a new monastery dedicated to the Dormition of the Virgin. As a leader of the Possessor movement, Joseph collaborated with lay rulers in administering extensive land holdings. He was opposed by the "Non-Possessors" led by Nilus of Sora, who pursued Hesychasm and sought separation of church and state.

## Major Works
*Prosvetitel' ili oblichenie eresi zhidovstvuiushchikh* (The Enlightener, or Accusation of Heresy against the Judaizers), 4th edition, 1903
*Poslanii'a Iosifa Volotskogo* (The Letters of Joseph Volotsky), edited by A.A. Zimin and Ia. S. Lur'e, 1959

*The Monastic Rule of Iosif Volotsky* (Cistercian Studies Series 36), edited and translated by David M. Goldfrank, 1983

*Poslanie ikonopisetsu*, edited by Hierodeacon Roman (A.G.) Tamburg, 1994

## Further Reading

Billington, James H., *The Icon and the Axe: An Interpretive History of Russian Culture*, New York: Knopf, 1966

Fedotov, Georgii P., *The Russian Religious Mind*, volume 2: *The Middle Ages, the Thirteenth to the Fifteenth Centuries*, edited by John Meyendorff, Cambridge, Massachusetts: Harvard University Press, 1966

Nevostruev, K., *Chteniya v Obshchestve Lyubitelei Dukhovnago Prosveshcheniya* (Readings in the Society of Spiritual Enlightenment), Moscow, 1865 (contains three lives of St. Joseph)

Riasanovsky, Nicholas V., *A History of Russia*, 5th edition, New York: Oxford University Press, 1993

Ware, Timothy, *The Orthodox Church, New Edition*, London and New York: Penguin, 1993

# Julian of Norwich c. 1342–after 1416

## English anchoress, mystic, and author

Julian of Norwich, an anchoress, lived in a cell attached to the Church of St. Julian in Norwich, England, sometime before 1413 until her death around 1416. She was a mystic, visionary, and teacher of prayer and is the first woman known to have written in English prose. She likely was named for the church to which her cell was attached. Some wills attest to her identity, and a short passage in the *Book of Margery Kempe* (1430s) confirms that she was highly regarded as a spiritual guide. No other biographical details remain, except for what she narrates in her writing. She was 30 years of age in 1373, putting her birth date at 1342. She recounts that in 1373 she fell victim to an illness that brought her near death. After a sudden recovery she received a series of experiences that she called "showings" (and at times "revelations") that centered on the Passion of Christ and encompassed the work of the Creation, the inner life of the Trinity, the mystery of Redemption, and the "oneing" of humanity with God. Fifteen years after the initial showings, she arrived at a synthesis of what the visions meant and was assured that "Love was our Lord's Meaning." In 1393, after 20 years of prayer and reflection, she received further insights.

Julian's account of her visions and of her reflections and insights flowing from them is preserved in two forms: a short text (S) and a long text (L). None of the original manuscripts is extant. A copy of S, Amherst (A), was made in the 15th century (London, MS British Museum Additional 37790); L exists in Paris (P) (MS Bibliothèque Nationale Fonds anglais 40), in Sloane1 (London, BM Sloane 2499), and in Sloane2 (London, BM Sloane 3705), and P was copied in the late 16th or early 17th century and S1 and S2 in the 17th and 18th centuries respectively. Some fragments are also extant, as is an abridged version (Westminster Cathedral Treasury MS 4). The long-text

manuscripts appear to have been in the Benedictine nuns' libraries in Paris and Cambrai and perhaps were copied there. The first printed text, by R.F.S. Cressy, O.S.B. (London, 1670), is thought to be based on P. In his "Dedicatory Epistle," Cressy recommends his book to a widow, Lady Mary Blount, thus signaling interest in Julian beyond the monasteries.

The formal rite of enclosure for an anchorite symbolized death to the world and committed the candidate to a life of prayer and penance. Regarding penance, Julian's teaching departs from the harsh tradition of narrow asceticism. She tells others that "all our living is a profitable penance." Indeed, "we ought meekly and patiently put up with and endure the penance that God himself gives us – keeping in mind his blessed passion." As to prayer, she did not follow her contemporaries in dividing prayer into fixed types and stages. Her focus was on the prayer of "beholding," a contemplative stance fostered by sustained attention to the goodness of God in all things. Such prayer includes loving attention to God dwelling within the human soul. She believes that God wants his lovers to take more joy in God's presence than to expend sorrow for frequent failings.

However, sin was a major concern for her because it seemed to be contrary to the goodness of God. A mysterious showing, that of the Lord and the Servant, was granted her to ease her anguish over this matter. She was then able to depart from the prevailing theology of salvation in her time, that of Anselm of Canterbury (c. 1033–1109).

Although minor echoes exist in Julian's long text of the teachings of Anselm, she differs radically from him on the mystery of salvation. Anselm held that the justice of God demanded the death of the God-man, Jesus, so as to restore humanity to the state forfeited through sin. Julian teaches that Jesus endured Crucifixion and death out of love in order to bring humanity into the new creation, a state surpassing that which had been lost. We are redeemed because the Son of God shares his own life with us by assuming humanity in his personal existence as a human being. It is then possible for us to come into mystical union with Christ. Through unity with the one body, humanity is always in God's unchanging love. Thus, God promises that despite the evil in the world, all things ultimately will be well.

Although in a canonical state herself, Julian did not concern herself with the accepted distinctions between the active life and the contemplative life. Instead, she addressed herself to her "even Christians," that is, to all who seek God in love, and she offered comfort to all. She did not deal with what was proper to hermits and anchoresses. In this she differed sharply from her contemporaries, such as Walter Hilton (c. 1343–1396), who believed in special rewards and singular honors for those who had embraced such a state of life in the church.

Julian is especially renowned for her teaching on the motherhood of God, which she applies to the Trinity and to Jesus Christ as man. Although missing from the short text, the theme appears in chapters 59 to 64 in the long text. The metaphor is based in Scripture and has a long history in Christian teaching, but Julian surpasses all her predecessors in her comprehensive and theological use of it. For her the metaphor reveals the intimacy that God in the Trinity establishes with creatures and portrays the solidarity of Christ with all humanity. The threefold motherhood gives humanity its birth in creation, its "new beginning" in the Incarnation, and its "new beginning without end" in bliss.

Thomas Merton (1915–1968) ranks Julian as the greatest of the English mystics. Her work is now admired for literary excellence, for inclusion of feminine metaphors for God, and for theological depth, and her text serves as a guide to contemplative prayer. Julian prayer groups are widespread, and a reconstructed form of her cell is a place of pilgrimage.

RITAMARY BRADLEY, S.F.C.C.

*See also* Anselm, St.; Asceticism: Christian Perspectives; England: History; Hermits: Western Christian; Merton, Thomas

## Biography

This most renowned of anchoresses left scant record of her life. She lived probably at St. Julian's church, Norwich, East Anglia. The first version of her *Showings or Revelations of Divine Love* was written soon after 1373, and the Long Text was completed no earlier than 1393. She was familiar with the writings of Dionysius the Pseudo-Areopagite.

## Major Works

*Showings or Revelations of Divine Love*, c. 1373; Long Text c. 1393 (see Further Reading section below for recent editions)

## Further Reading

Baker, Denise Nowakoski, *Julian of Norwich's Showings: From Vision to Book*, Princeton, New Jersey: Princeton University Press, 1994

Beer, Frances, editor, *Julian of Norwich: Revelations of Divine Love, translated from British Library Additional MS 37790; The Motherhood of God: An Excerpt, translated from British Library MS Sloane 2477*, Cambridge: D.S. Brewer, 1998

Bradley, Ritamary, *Julian's Way: A Practical Commentary on Julian of Norwich*, London: HarperCollins Religious, 1992

Clark, John P.H., "Fiducia in Julian of Norwich, II," *Downside Review* 95 (1979)

Colledge, Edmund, and James Walsh, editors, *A Book of Showings to the Anchoress Julian of Norwich*, Toronto: Pontifical Institute of Mediaeval Studies, 1978

Colledge, Edmund, and James Walsh, translators, *Julian of Norwich Showings*, New York: Paulist Press, 1978

Crampton, Georgia Ronan, editor, *The Shewings of Julian of Norwich*, Kalamazoo, Michigan: Medieval Institute Publications, 1993

Julian of Norwich, *A Revelation of Love*, edited by Marion Glasscoe, Exeter: University of Exeter Press, 1976

McEntire, Sandra, editor, *Julian of Norwich: A Book of Essays*, New York: Garland, 1998

Nuth, Joan M., *Wisdom's Daughter: The Theology of Julian of Norwich*, New York: Crossroad, 1991

Pepler, Conrad, *The English Religious Heritage*, London: Blackfriars, and St. Louis, Missouri: Herder, 1958

Savage, Anne, and Nicholas Watson, editors, *Anchoritic Spirituality: Ancrene Wisse and Associated Works*, New York: Paulist Press, 1991

# K

## Kagyü. *See* Tibetan Lineages: Kagyü

## Kandy, Sri Lanka

The city of Kandy (Sinhala, *Mahānuwara*, or "Great City"), with a population of about 110,000 in 1999, became an important center of Theravāda Buddhist monasticism in the middle of the 18th century and remains so today. As the last of the traditional Sinhala royal capitals, Kandy is also home to the *Daladā Maligāva*, or "Temple of the Tooth-Relic." Since at least the 12th century in the capital of Polonnaruva, the *Daladā* has been regarded as the palladium of the Sinhala Buddhist people. Possession of and tribute to the *Daladā*, in addition to patronage of the *sangha*, conferred legitimacy on Buddhist kingship in the eyes of the Sinhalese. To this day pilgrimage to the *Daladā Maligāva* remains one of the most popular religious practices among the laity. Following the English disestablishment of Lankan kingship in 1815, custodianship of the *Daladā* became the responsibility of the *Mahānayaka*s (supreme monastic incumbents) of the Asgiriya and Malvatta *nikāya*s, the two chapters of the Buddhist *sangha* in Kandy that claim to represent the continuation of orthodox Theravāda monasticism in Sri Lanka.

Traditionally the chief centers and administrative powers of Buddhist monasticism in Sri Lanka were located in royal capitals, first for about 13 centuries in Anurādhapura (third through the tenth century) and then in Polonnaruva for two (11th through the 13th century). The proximity of monastic centers to royal capitals expressed the function of Buddhist kings who regarded themselves as the chief laymen or patrons of the *sangha*. Following the demise of Polonnaruva kingship, during which time the *sangha* had been reconstituted as thoroughly Theravādin, the political strengths as well as the fortunes of the *sangha* declined rather precipitously, except for a brief period of revival during the 15th century at Köttē (just east of present-day Colombo). The kingdom of Kandy was legitimately established during the last decade of the 16th century by Vimaladharmasurya I following a series of intrigues against Portuguese designs on power. Although he and his namesake successor (Vimaladharmasurya II about 100 years later) made sustained attempts to revive the moribund community of monks by importing *bhikkhu*s from Burma to reestablish the *upasampada* (ordination) monastic lineage of Theravāda, it was not until the middle of the 18th century that the Asgiriya and Malvatta chapters were finally reconstituted in an orthodox manner. This was achieved, ironically, under the sponsorship of Kīrti Śrī Rājasinha (1751–1782), a king of Tamil Śaivite origins who, at the urging of a largely self-motivated and reform-minded monk, Valivita Saranamkara, successfully imported Siamese monks from Thailand to reestablish legitimate monastic ordination lines and *sima*s (purified monastic boundaries).

Kīrti Śrī proceeded to invest almost all his limited wealth into refurbishing Kandyan temples and promoting Buddhist rites, including the *Äsala Perahera*, the annual ritual in which the *Daladā* processes ceremonially through the streets of Kandy. Under Saranamkara, who became a *Sangharāja* (literally, "king of the *sangha*"), vinaya disciplinary rules again began to be celebrated every other week in *pāṭimōkkah* recitations. In addition meditation practices were reemphasized, Pāli language and grammar were again taught and Sinhala translations of Pāli texts accomplished, and a centralized monastic authority was established in Kandy.

Following Saranamkara's death in 1778, authority devolved to the respective *Mahānayaka*s of the Asgiriya and Malvatta *nikāya*s. These two *viharaya*s remain the orthodox centers of the Siyam (indicating the Siamese origins) *nikāya* to this day where ordination ceremonies are carried out between the full moons of May and June each year within their premises. Most Buddhist temples and incumbent monks in the central highlands are linked to one of these two monastic chapters. Others are affiliated with the low-country-dominated Amarapura or Ramañña *nikāya*s, which in the 19th century were established to accommodate monastics from caste ranks other than those of the majority rice-growing caste, the *goyigāma*, who alone are admitted to the Siyam *nikāya*.

JOHN HOLT

*See also* Anurādhapura, Sri Lanka; Liturgy: Buddhist; Pilgrimages, Buddhist; Pilgrims to India, Chinese; Sri Lanka: Sites; Thailand; Theravādin Monks, Modern Western

### Further Reading

Dewaraja, Lorna, *A Study of the Political, Administrative and Social Structure of the Kandyan Kingdom of Ceylon,*

*1707–1760*, Colombo: Lake House, 1972; as *The Kandyan Kingdom of Sri Lanka, 1707–1761*, Colombo: Lake House, 1988

Gombrich, Richard, *Precept and Practice: Traditional Buddhism in the Rural Highlands of Ceylon*, Oxford: Clarendon Press, 1971; 2nd edition, Delhi: Motilal Banarsidass, 1991; London and New York: Kegan Paul, 1995

Holt, John, *The Religious World of Kīrti Śrī: Buddhism, Art and Politics in Late Medieval Sri Lanka*, New York: Oxford University Press, 1996

Malalgoda, Kitsiri, *Buddhism in Sinhalese Society, 1750–1900*, Berkeley: University of California Press, 1976

Seneviratne, H.L., *Rituals of the Kandyan State*, Cambridge and New York: Cambridge University Press, 1978

# Kathmandu Valley, Nepal

With Sanskrit inscriptions and Indic material culture datable back to the fifth century A.D., this large valley, roughly 20 miles in diameter at an altitude of 4,500 feet, became a center where both Hindu and Buddhist monasticism have flourished up until the present. Until 1769 "Nepal" referred to the Kathmandu Valley alone, but when the modern state was formed that year and the valley became its capital, a new definition began so that there needs to be historical precision about the term. This article focuses on the contemporary monastic complexes in the valley; the article "Nepal: History" recounts the premodern history of the state and valley region, and the article "Nepal: Sites" surveys the current monastic sites in the modern nation.

As was the case from the earliest records, monastic traditions in the Kathmandu Valley today include those of Hinduism and a multitude of Buddhist schools. Most monasteries were built by the Newars, the earliest attested ethnic group of the region who speak a Tibeto-Burman language and whose culture was shaped mainly by Indian influences from the south. Buddhist monasticism in the Kathmandu Valley was later diversified by the immigration of Buddhists from outside: by Tibetan monks who established branches of their monastic schools, mostly after 1400, and in the 20th century by reformist missionary Theravādins from Sri Lanka and Southeast Asia.

As was the case elsewhere in Asia and throughout the world, valley monasteries grew around important political and trade centers that were sustained by extremely fertile soils and abundant monsoon rains. The dominant walled city-states – Kathmandu, Bhaktapur, Patan, and Kirtipur – became the main sites for these institutions, as did several regional pilgrimage sites: the hilltop Svayambhū stūpa, Cabahil and Bauddha for Buddhists, and the riverside Paśupati complex for Hindus.

## Newar Buddhist Monasticism

By the later Malla era (1475–1769), there was a "domestication" of the Newar *saṅgha* as "monks" became householders whose patrilineages became castes that, with only a few exceptions, did not admit outsiders. These Newar "householder monks," who called themselves *Bare* (from the Sanskrit term *Vande* or *vandanā*, an ancient Indic term of respect for monks), adopted the caste names *śakyabhikṣu* and *vajrācārya*. Their major role became the performance of rituals drawing on deities and powers of the Vajrayāna Buddhist tradition. To be an adult member of the Newar *saṅgha*, the men must undergo first (in local parlance) *śrāvaka*-styled celibate ordination (usually taking three days) and then Mahāyāna-styled initiation into the *bodhisattva saṅgha*. Like married Tibetan lamas of the Nyingmapa Order, the *vajrācārya* priests serve the community's ritual needs, with some specializing in textual study, medicine, astrology, and meditation. At its peak Newar Buddhist monasticism included more than 300 monastery sites.

Once the Newar kings were ousted by the Shah dynasty from Gorkha, who unified the modern state in 1769, discrimination against Buddhists and the changes in land tenure laws undermined the tenancy system that had supported this Newar monastic system. Today, of the 300 monasteries still documented, roughly 10 percent have all but disappeared, and more than 50 percent are in perilous structural condition.

The cities of Kathmandu and Patan have a system of main monasteries (*mu bāhā*), 18 and 15, respectively. Every householder monk is ordained in one of these. However, many must perform their ritual duties (and may live in) one the several hundred branch monasteries affiliated with the main monasteries. (Bhaktapur and other smaller towns have *bāhā*s, but all are independent entities.) Newar monasteries are now ruled simply by the seniormost male members of their individual *saṅgha*s.

## Theravāda Buddhism

Newars who became disenchanted with their indigenous Mahāyāna culture and monasticism since 1930 have supported the establishment of Theravāda Buddhist reform institutions. Beginning with the Anandakuti monastery at Svayambhū for monks and the Dharmakirti dormitory for "nuns" in central Kathmandu, Newars have been ordained and then renounced the householder life to live in these institutions, joined by teaching monks from Sri Lanka and nuns from Burma. (Technically the ancient order of nuns, the *bhikkhuni saṅgha*, has died in the Theravāda countries; the term *anāgārika* is used locally, although the women conform to the Vinaya rules, including celibacy.) These institutions have been instrumental in promoting the modernist "Protestant Buddhism" originating in colonial Sri Lanka: they have subtly critiqued the Newar and Tibetan Mahāyāna beliefs and practices while seeking to revive the faith by promoting textual study and vernacular translations, scheduling popular preaching, and spreading the practice of lay meditation. Other independent meditation centers started by Goenka, a lay teacher from India, have since the early 1980s gained considerable popularity. Theravāda monasteries and meditation centers are now found in most major valley towns.

## Tibetan Buddhism

The Kathmandu Valley has been especially affected by the diaspora of Tibetan teachers since 1959, when tens of thousands of disciples followed the Dalai Lama into exile to escape Chinese rule. Several reasons have led to this region becoming one of the most important centers of Tibetan Buddhism in the world. First, one of the largest concentrations of Tibetan refugees settled in the Kathmandu Valley, and they have focused on building institutions for their communities. Given the wealth generated by the carpet-weaving industry, some of the profits have built and expanded the initial structures. Second, many of the most affluent Tibeto-Burman Buddhists from across Nepal have in the last decades chosen to establish homes in the valley for both business and political purposes. Prominent donors from this community have bought lands and built monasteries that have tended to draw monks or nuns from their home regions. Finally, as Tibetan Buddhism has become increasingly attractive to westerners, prominent Tibetan lamas oriented to them – and funded by their donations – have established "Dharma centers" that in most ways resemble traditional monasteries. Here one can find textual study and meditation being pursued by both ethnic Tibetans and westerners clad in red robes.

TODD T. LEWIS

*See also* Initiation: Buddhist Perspectives; Ladakh, India; Manuscript Production: Buddhist; Mount Meru; Nepal; Sri Lanka: History; Stūpa; Tibet: History; Tibetan Lineages: Nyingma; Vajrayāna Buddhism in Nepal; Visual Arts, Buddhist: Nepal

**Further Reading**

Gellner, David N., *Monk, Householder, and Tantric Priest: Newar Buddhism and Its Hierarchy of Ritual* (Cambridge Studies in Social and Cultural Anthropology, 84), Cambridge and New York: Cambridge University Press, 1992

Lienhard, Siegfried, "Nepal: The Survival of Indian Buddhism in a Himalayan Kingdom," in *The World of Buddhism: Buddhist Monks and Nuns in Society and Culture*, edited by Heinz Bechert and Richard F. Gombrich, New York: Facts on File, and London: Thames and Hudson, 1984

Locke, John K., *Buddhist Monasteries of Nepal: A Survey of the Bahas and Bahis of the Kathmandu Valley*, Kathmandu: Sahayogi Press, 1985

Snellgrove, David, "Buddhism in Nepal," in his *Indo-Tibetan Buddhism: Indian Buddhists and Their Tibetan Successors*, volume 2, Boston: Shambhala, and London: Serindia, 1987

Toffin, Gérard, *Société et Religion chez les Newar du Népal* (Cahiers Népalais), Paris: Editions du Centre national de la recherche scientifique, 1984

# Keating, Thomas 1923–

## U.S. Trappist and leader in ecumenical and interreligious dialogue

Thomas Keating, an American Trappist monk, grew up in New York city in an upper-class Catholic family. He attended Yale and Fordham Universities, taking his degree in English. In 1944 he entered the Cistercians at Our Lady of the Valley Abbey in Valley Falls, Rhode Island. He professed his solemn vows in the spring of 1949 and was ordained a priest in June of the same year. In 1950 the community moved to Spencer, Massachusetts, and took the name St. Joseph's Abbey. It attracted so many vocations that it became necessary to establish a number of foundations, one of which, St. Benedict's Monastery in Snowmass, Colorado, Keating served as prior from 1958 to 1961. In 1961 he was elected abbot of Spencer. So visionary was his leadership that his abbacy, which spanned 20 years, has been referred to as the golden age of Spencer.

Keating's tenure as abbot saw many innovations and experiments. He shepherded the community through the difficult years of the Second Vatican Council (1962–1965) and its aftermath. Just as the Church was opening itself up to other religions, this brilliant, saintly abbot opened his monastery to spiritual impulses from the East. He invited Tibetan, Japanese, and Hindu masters as well as mystical theologians from the Eastern Orthodox Church to give substantial input to the Spencer community. In this way Keating encouraged a deep ecumenism that allowed exploration of other spiritualities, emphasizing always an experiential approach. He resigned as abbot in 1981 and moved back to Snowmass to direct souls in contemplation, to pursue interreligious dialogue, and to write.

In 1984 Keating launched two initiatives: Contemplative Outreach and the Snowmass Conference. The former is dedicated to spreading knowledge of Christian contemplative experience through promotion of centering prayer and a solid conceptual background and the latter to interfaith encounter built around spiritual practice. Contemplative Outreach now has a global network of contemplatives, mainly laypeople, living their lives in the world.

From 1985 to 1992 Keating chaired Monastic Interreligious Dialogue (MID), formerly the North American Board for East-West Dialogue, and during this time the board expanded and deepened relations with Tibetans and their Buddhist tradition. Out of this relationship came an important document coauthored with the Dalai Lama, the *Universal Declaration on Nonviolence* (1991). Keating's work in the Snowmass Conference, MID, and the Naropa Institute distinguishes him as a leader whose contributions to interfaith encounter will endure.

WAYNE TEASDALE

*See also* Cistercians; Dalai Lama (Tenzin Gyatso); Dialogue, Intermonastic: Christian Perspectives; Meditation: Christian Perspectives; United States: Western Christian

**Biography**

This American Trappist grew up in New York City and graduated from Fordham University. He entered a Cistercian house in Rhode Island in 1944. When it moved to Spencer, Massachusetts in 1950, it became St. Joseph's Abbey. From 1961 to 1981 Keating served as its Abbot. Active in ecumenical and later interreligious gatherings, Thomas Keating has been a leader in intermonastic dialogue.

**Major Works**
*Open Mind, Open Heart: The Contemplative Dimension of the*
   *Gospel,* 1986
*The Mystery of Christ: The Liturgy as Spiritual Experience,*
   1987
*Invitation to Love: The Way of Christian Contemplation,* 1992
*Intimacy with God,* 1994

**Further Reading**
Teasdale, Wayne, "Thomas Keating: An American
   Contemplative Sage," *The Canadian Catholic Review* 15:9
   (October 1997)

# Kiev (Kyiv), Ukraine

Kyiv was the seat of the grand princedom of Kyivan Rus', the
first state of the Eastern Slavs, which flourished from the 9th to
the 13th century. With the conversion of the population to
Christianity around 988, the city became the center of a distinctive ecclesial tradition that adapted the model of Byzantine
Christianity to the Slavic context. The Christian cultures of Russia, Ukraine, and Belarus trace their origins back to a common
source in tenth-century Kyiv.

Some of the oldest monasteries of Rus' were established in
the capital city and in the surrounding region, foremost among
them being the Vydubyts'ky, the Mezhyhiria, and the Kyivan
Caves monasteries.

The Kyiv-Vydubyts'ky Monastery of St. Michael the
Archangel (988–992) stands in the southern part of Kyiv. According to legend the first metropolitan of Kyiv, Michael,
founded the Church of St. Michael, and subsequently Prince
Vsevolod Yaroslavovych founded the monastery. Among the
monastery's *hegumen*s in the pre-Mongol period was Nestor,
the chronicler of Kyivan Rus'. The world-renowned icon of the
Blessed Virgin of Częstochowa traces its origins to the Kyiv Vydubyts'ky Monastery in the early 17th century. Noteworthy
*hegumen*s included St. Theodosius Uhlytsky (1668–1688), later
the archbishop of Chernihiv.

Two features distinguished the Vydubyts'ky Monastery: internal discipline and social activism. The assembly of monks not
only elected a *hegumen* but could also depose him, as occurred
on three occasions. The monastery's social philanthropy consisted of running schools, a hospital, an orphanage, and a home
for elderly priests. Points of interest in the territory include
traces of a protective wall (12th century), the Church of the Annunciation and its surrounding cemetery, and the Church of the
Transfiguration.

The Mezhyhiria (Mezhyhors'k) Monastery of the Transfiguration (c. 988), in Berestovo-Vyshhorod north of Kyiv, is one of
the oldest monasteries in Ukraine. In 1672 the monastery accepted the Zaporozhian Cossacks under its pastoral care, and its
monks served as military chaplains and ran a military hospital.
Supported by 17th-century benefactors Petro Mohyla and Het-

man Bohdan Khmelnyts'ky, the monastery acquired a prominence second only to that of the Kyivan Caves. Restored again in
the 18th century, it was destroyed by the Soviets in 1930.

The Caves Monastery of Kyiv (1051), founded by St. Anthony (c. 983–1072), is perhaps the most important monastery
of the Kyivan Rus' period. Situated in the southern part of Kyiv
and overlooking the Dnipro River, the monastery's buildings and
caves occupy two hills and the valley between them. Saint Anthony of the Caves, born in Liubech north of Kyiv, entered the
monastic life at Mount Athos. Returning to Kyiv he settled in a
cave used previously by Metropolitan Hilarion. When his spiritual life attracted a community, he appointed St. Varlaam as the
first *hegumen* and resumed an idiorhythmic life in another cave.
Varlaam was succeeded as *hegumen* by Anthony's disciple, St.
Theodosius (c. 1036–74), under whose leadership the monastery
flourished. In the late 11th and early 12th centuries, notable residents of the monastery included Alipy, the first iconographer of
Kyivan Rus', and Nestor, author of the *Life of Theodosius* and

**Gateway, Monastery of the Caves (Petcherskaia Lavra), Kiev, Ukraine,
17th century.**
**Photo courtesy of Robert E. Jones**

Monastery of the Caves (Petcherskaia Lavra), Kiev, Ukraine, 17th century.
Photo courtesy of Robert E. Jones

the *Primary Chronicle*. The 13th-century Caves monk Polikarp was a compiler of the *Kyivan Caves Paterikon*, an instructional collection of stories about the monastery's early brethren.

The first half of the 17th century was an auspicious time for the Caves Monastery. Enlightened archimandrites, especially Petro Mohyla (1596–1646), promoted great advances in education. In the peace concluded between Poland and Muscovy (1667), the Caves Monastery came under the latter's influence, and by 1688 the patriarchate in Moscow took over ecclesiastical control.

On the eve of the Russian Revolution (1917), the Caves Monastery housed over 1,200 monks and novices and was one of the most famous spiritual centers of Kyivan Christianity; here pilgrims venerated relics of the holy brethren. Under Soviet rule the monastery was nationalized and transformed into a cultural-historical reserve. By 1929 its monastic life was terminated. Reopened during World War II and shut down by the Soviets in 1964, the Caves Monastery was permitted to restore its monastic life in 1988, as Ukraine commemorated the millennium of Kyivan Christianity.

Of special interest at the Caves Monastery are the churches of the Nativity of the Virgin and of the Conception of the Virgin (17th century), an 18th-century belfry, the wells of St. Anthony and St. Theodosius, underground passages and caves containing

the churches of the Nativity of Christ and of St. Theodosius (11th century), and relics of the monastery's saints.

The Kytaivs'ky Holy Trinity Hermitage Monastery (12th century) is about five miles south of Kyiv. In its vicinity are the site of the 10th-century fortified town of Kytaievo ("Kytai," from Tatar for "fortress"), a cemetery, and caves. In the 17th century a *skyt*, or *skete* (hermitage), was established here and used by monks from the nearby Caves Monastery. Since the 18th century distinguished monks such as Dosifei and Theophil, a "holy fool," as well as the starets Paisii of the Lavra, lived here, and a number of monks were buried in the cemetery. The monastery remained active until 1930, when it was transformed into a hostel for invalids. In 1990 the main church of the Holy Trinity (1767) was reconsecrated and began to function as an Orthodox parish.

The Hlynets'k Monastery (11th century), about nine miles south of Kyiv, was destroyed by the Mongols. Its remains constitute the cave of St. Theodosius, who apparently prayed there, and traces of a church building. In the 19th century the *skete* of the Blessed Virgin was founded on the site, old caves were excavated, and two churches were built.

Saint Cyril's Monastery (12th century), founded by Prince Vsevolod Olhovych, was destroyed by Mongols and rebuilt in 1605. Secularized in 1785 it was turned into a hospital and home for the handicapped. In 1929 it was designated a museum. Saint Cyril's Church contains fine 12th-century frescoes.

Saint Florian's Convent (15th century), in the Podil district of Kyiv, was home to nuns from aristocratic families. After the Russian Revolution it was closed for religious use. It reopened again as a convent after World War II.

The Epiphany Brotherhood Monastery (1616), also in the Podil district of Kyiv, was established by nobles, clerics, and Cossacks and was conceived as an Orthodox stronghold against Roman Catholicism. Its *hegumen*s, among them the colorful preacher and later archbishop of Novgorod, Theophan Prokopovych (1681–1736), were also rectors of the affiliated brotherhood school of the same name that developed into the Kyivan Mohyla Academy. In the post-Soviet period the site became home to the restored Academy.

Other Kyivan monasteries include St. Andrew's (11th century, destroyed 1240) and St. Michael the Golden-Domed (1108, destroyed in 1934 and recently reconstructed). The St. Nicholas Pustynnyi Monastery (12th century), located on a hill in Kyiv near Askold's Tomb, numbered about 50 monks and novices before the Russian Revolution. In the 1930s it was dismantled and replaced with park kiosks.

ANDRII S. KRAWCHUK

*See also* Archaeology: Russia; Architecture: Eastern Christian Monasteries; Bulgaria; Częstochowa (Jasna Góra), Poland; Hermits: Eastern Christian; Libraries: Eastern Christian; Martyrs: Eastern Christian; Mount Athos, Greece; Orthodox Monasticism; Pilgrimages, Christian: Eastern Europe; Russia: History; Theodosius of Kiev, St.; Ukraine

**Further Reading**

Denisov, L.I., *Pravoslavnye Monastyri rossiiskoi imperii*, Moscow: Izdanie A.D. Stupina, 1908

Hewryk, Titus D., *The Lost Architecture of Kiev*, New York: Ukrainian Museum, 1982

Karsim, Inna, "The Kytaivska Pustyn' (Kyivan-Kytaiivskyi Holy Trinity Monastery)," *Logos: A Journal of Eastern Christian Studies* 40:1–2 (1999)

Libackyj, Anfir, *The Ancient Monasteries of Kiev Rus'*, New York: Vantage Press, 1978

Prestel, David K., "Anthony of the Caves," in *The Modern Encyclopedia of Religions in Russia and the Soviet Union*, edited by Paul D. Steeves, volume 2, Gulf Breeze, Florida: Academic International Press, 1990

Prestel, David K., "Caves Monastery of Kiev," in *The Modern Encyclopedia of Religions in Russia and the Soviet Union*, edited by Paul D. Steeves, volume 5, Gulf Breeze, Florida: Academic International Press, 1993

Senyk, Sophia, *Women's Monasteries in Ukraine and Belorussia to the Period of Suppressions*, Rome: Pont. Institutum Studiorum Orientalum, 1983

Senyk, Sophia, "Monasticism," in her *A History of the Church in Ukraine*, volume 1: *To the End of the Thirteenth Century*, Rome: Pontificio Istituto Orientale, 1993

Titov, F., "O zagranichnykh monastyriakh Kievskoi eparkhii XVII–XVIII vv.," *Trudy Kievskoi Dukhovnoi Akademii* (1905)

Zinkewych, Osyp, and Andrew Sorokowski, editors and compilers, *A Thousand Years of Christianity in Ukraine: An Encyclopedic Chronology*, New York: Smoloskyp Publishers, 1988

# Knights of Malta. *See* Hospitallers (Knights of Malta since 1530)

# Knowles, M. David 1896–1974

English Benedictine historian of medieval monasticism

David Knowles, a Benedictine monk and Catholic priest, was one of the 20th century's foremost British medievalists of religion. At university he trained in classics and focused on literature, but an interest in the U.S. Civil War soon induced him to turn to historical studies. However, after the appearance of his first book (*The American Civil War: A Brief Sketch*, 1926), Knowles' refocused his research on the medieval period.

Christened Michael Clive in his native Studley (Warwickshire), Knowles attended West House School (Edgbaston, 1906–1910) in youth and then enrolled (1910–1914) as a scholar under the Benedictine monks of Downside. Discerning a monastic vocation he entered the Downside novitiate on taking his diploma (1914). Under his religious name (David), he professed the monastic vows (1915 and 1918) and was ordained priest (1922). Studies at Cambridge (Christ's College, 1919–1922) and St. Anselmo (Rome, 1922–1923) followed, after which he assumed various duties in the abbey and school at Downside (1923–1933), including a distinguished tenure as editor of *Downside Review* (1929–1933).

When Knowles assumed direction of the *Review*, it was a Benedictine *quodlibet* (this-and-that) that was respected but not really distinguished. Rather than seeking to advance scholarship, it acted as a forum of monastic commentary. However, with Knowles as editor a different tone emerged. He transformed the *Review* from a newsletter into a substantial, albeit small, journal of serious retrospection and learned analysis. His format featured a series of scholarly, monastic essays that were rendered in accessible prose. Content focused on the diverse historical elements that had germinated the Benedictine resurgence of the 19th and 20th centuries. Knowles' *Downside Review* was an immediate success, and its impact was widespread. Especially noteworthy was the interest that the *Review* awakened in the Norman abbey of Bec, a distinguished cloister that for centuries had been overlooked in favor of its more populous and prosperous contemporary, Cluny.

In these years the English Congregation of Benedictines was especially occupied with parochial work. Knowles objected to that orientation loudly and repeatedly, urging a more traditionally contemplative life. However, his recommendations came to naught and resulted in Dom David's assignment to residence at Ealing Priory (London, 1933–1939), where, it was hoped, his disruptive influence might be muted.

At Ealing, Knowles immersed himself in research that resulted in his masterwork, *The Monastic Order in England* (1939/40, revised 1963). Ordinarily, a book on England's abbeys of 943 to 1216, written by a monk, would have proven too limited and too parochial to achieve broad scholarly prominence. However, Knowles turned his monastic preserve into an asset. For example, he designed the second section of *Monastic Order* as an inquiry into the "interior polity of the black monks." In this book he brought a practical, experiential perspective to his analysis of contemporary records. The result, critics conceded, was a narrative that could have been executed only by a scholar who had personally experienced the rubrics of cloistered life.

Knowles also lent an appealing freshness to the deployment of primary sources. He commonly integrated unusually lengthy sections of original texts into *Monastic Order*'s narrative. Rendered in his own eloquent translations, these passages were transformed from obscure references into vital components of a chronicle both vivid and pertinent. They exemplified the undercurrent that would flow through all of Knowles' best work, namely, its literary merit. Knowles' writing won reviews as glowing as those that greeted his scholarship.

Regrettably, the eminence that Knowles won with *The Monastic Order in England* contrasted with the seeming dissolution of his Benedictine vocation. In 1939 Knowles left his monastery illicitly, taking a flat near his psychotherapist, Dr. Elizabeth Kornerup. Ipso facto excommunication resulted from which he would not be released until 1952. In 1944 Knowles was granted a fellowship at Peterhouse (Cambridge), where he found academic life congenial and accepted regular promotions in the following years. This ascendency culminated eventually in his appointment to the university's Regius Chair of Modern History (1954–1963).

Throughout his career Knowles was active in learned societies; he was admitted to the British Academy and served as president of the Royal Historical Society (1956–1960). However, he always gave primacy to his writings. Renowned for the felicity of their prose as well as their scholarship, these were prolific and varied. Among his most noted works are *The Religious Orders in England* (1948, 1955, and 1959) and two volumes on English mystics (1927 and 1961). In addition, Knowles' research on Archbishop Thomas Becket (c. 1120–1170) and his episcopal contemporaries proved especially fruitful.

In this last regard, in the study of Thomas Becket, the Knowles method produced some of its most auspicious assessments. Dom David restated the struggles of 1162–1170 to reveal how the maneuverings of king and primate were often defined and even brokered by machinations in the English episcopate. Especially the figure of Gilbert Foliot (c. 1110–1187), bishop of Hereford (1148–1163), rival for Canterbury, and then bishop of London (1163–1187), emerged as influential. Knowles interpreted the principals in these conflicts as figures of astounding

rigidity. Nonetheless, he argued, the situation was exacerbated by misunderstanding more than by stubbornness. He contended that a crucial disparity existed in the weight that each party assigned when estimating the issues. In particular, Knowles says, Foliot never grasped how Becket's shift of allegiance (from king to God, from state to Church) had recast the conflict and deepened its consequence. A critical lack of spiritual depth existed in Foliot, debilitating him from perceiving the serious, divine content that had transformed the substance of the struggle. In particular, says Knowles, it created a discrepancy in perception that concealed from Foliot the critical redefinition of the problem that (unexpectedly) had won the embrace of Becket (with the full weight of his famed faculty for rigid adherence). Dom David's evaluation of this conflict, it can be suggested, is peculiarly appropriate to the genius of a monastic scholar and is the sort of radically revisionist perspective that typifies his analyses.

Late in his career, in the 1960s, Knowles published a series of books that revived the format he had used so effectively in the *Downside Review* of the early 1930s. These volumes were collections of diverse, brief, but serious selections from Knowles' essays and addresses and were issued for a general audience. *Saints and Scholars* (1962), a collection of 25 literary portraits of medieval figures, features mainly learned Benedictines. *Great Historical Enterprises* (1963) draws attention to various scholarly and cultural activities that demonstrate the compatibility of intellectual endeavor with Church purpose. Of particular note in that volume is his 27-page depiction of the Maurists, arguably the greatest movement in the history of Benedictine scholarship. *From Pachomius to Ignatius* (1966) surveys various religious orders according to their respective charters or constitutions.

Knowles employed his eloquence as more than a medium of presentation: it was also a scholarly tool. In particular, his voice was used effectively in redirecting the focus of historical analyses. For example, when dealing with figures of significant intellectual attainment (e.g., Bernard of Clairvaux), Knowles eschewed conventional restatements of his subject's learned elocutions. Instead, he wanted to know how the person's intellect had participated in effecting his character. Although Knowles sometimes dealt with abstract thought directly (e.g., *The Evolution of Mediaeval Thought* [1962], based on a series of lectures), he believed that the historian's art turned on consideration of a person's merit and substance more than on human activities and achievements.

Knowles' contribution to scholarly theory and enterprise has helped to shape a distinct field of historical inquiry. Known as "intellectual history," this school of scholarship enriches historical narrative by incorporating standards of assessment and appraisal that had previously been reserved to biographers. Its approach was articulated most eloquently in Dom David's inaugural lecture as Regius Professor, titled "The Historian and Character" (17 November 1954).

Knowles contributed a provocative concept of spiritual stability to monastic theory. His argument was that a person who truly and properly inculcates the content of his monastic rule is able to remain a monk regardless of location, even when outside the cloister ("*ubique terrarum*," in Knowles' phrase). He believed that this was not a license for extracloistral activity but rather an inherently Benedictine faculty that is implicit in chapter 50 of *Regula Benedicti*. Significantly, Knowles first articulated this theory in *The Benedictines* (1929), published before, rather than in justification of, his own prolonged absence from the cloister.

Knowles died while still living under Dr. Kornerup's attentive oversight. He had made only one visit to Downside since his departure 35 years before but had lent to his abbey's reputation the renown earned by his scholarly achievements.

Paschal Baumstein, O.S.B.

*See also* Benedictines: General or Male; Butler, Cuthbert; Chapman, John; England: History; Historiography, Recent: Western Christian; Leclercq, Jean

## Biography

The distinguished historian of Western Christian monasticism was educated at Downside Abbey, where he became a monk in 1914. Desiring to found a new community free from duties of teaching school, Knowles failed to win papal approval of this project in 1934. From 1939 he lived apart from the community (to which he was, however, formally reconciled in 1952). From 1947 to 1963 he served professor at the University of Cambridge.

## Selected Works

Note: the following entries comprise the principal constituents of the Knowles bibliography (n.b., many of Knowles' major essays and addresses were collected in volumes included *infra*, e.g., in *Historian and Character, Saints and Scholars, Great Historical Enterprises, From Pachomius to Ignatius*):

*The American Civil War: A Brief Sketch*, 1926
*The English Mystics*, 1927
*The Benedictines*, 1929
"Essays in Monastic History," *Downside Review* (1931–1934)
"The Monastic Horarium, 970–1120," *Downside Review* (1933)
"Abbot Cuthbert Butler, 1858–1934," *Downside Review* (1934)
"Bec and Her Great Men," *Downside Review* (1934)
*The Monastic Order in England: A History of Its Development from the Times of Saint Dunstan to the Fourth Lateran Council, 940–1216*, 1939/40; revised edition, 1963
*The Religious Houses of Medieval England*, 1940
*The Religious Orders in England*, 1948, 1955, 1959 (volume 3 was abridged as *Bare Ruined Choirs: The Dissolution of the English Monasteries*, 1959 and 1976)
*The Episcopal Colleagues of Archbishop Thomas Becket*, 1951
*The Monastic Constitutions of Lanfranc* (Latin text with parallel translation), 1951
*Monastic Sites From the Air* (coauthored with J.K. St. Joseph), Cambridge Air Surveys, volume 1, 1952
*Medieval Religious Houses: England and Wales* (coauthored with R. Neville Hadcock), 1953; revised edition, 1971
*Charterhouse: The Medieval Foundation in the Light of Recent Discoveries* (coauthored with W.F. Grimes), 1954

*The Historical Context of the Philosophical Works of Saint Thomas Aquinas*, Aquinas Society of London, paper no. 30 (a paper read to the Aquinas Society of London in 1956), 1958
"The Need for Catholic Historical Scholarship," *The Dublin Review* (1958)
"Saint Benedict," *The Month* (1960)
*The English Mystical Tradition*, 1961
*The Evolution of Medieval Thought*, 1962
*Saints and Scholars*, 1962
*Great Historical Enterprises and Problems in Early Monastic History*, 1963
*The Historian and Character*, 1963
*From Pachomius to Ignatius: A Study in the Constitutional History of the Religious Orders*, 1966
*What Is Mysticism?* (U.S. edition entitled *The Nature of Mysticism*), 1967
*The Middle Ages* (written with D. Obolensky), The Christian Centuries, volume 2, 1969
*Thomas Becket*, 1970
*The Heads of Religious Houses: England and Wales, 940–1216* (coauthored with C.N.L. Brooke and Vera London), 1972

## Further Reading

Biggs, Anselm, "Great Benedictines: David Knowles, a Sad Life, a Brilliant Mind," *Crescat* (1987)
Brooke, Christopher, et al., *David Knowles Remembered*, Cambridge: Cambridge University Press, 1991
Morey, Adrian, *David Knowles: A Memoir*, London: Darton, Longman and Todd, 1979
Patin, W.A., "Curriculum Vitae," in *"The Historian and Character" and Other Essays by David Knowles*, edited by C.N.L. Brooke and Giles Constable, Cambridge: Cambridge University Press, 1963

# Kōan

*Overview*

A kōan is a statement invoked in Zen Buddhism for the direct and immediate realization of the ultimate truth of selflessness. Sometimes the statement is an action, such as bowing or sticking out one's tongue to indicate fear or surprise. Thus, although a kōan can be defined as a statement, it need not be verbal. Masters took to shouting and even to striking monks – as well as nuns and laypeople – often in a compassionate attempt to help the inquirer break through his or her delusional self-attachment by an immediate and dramatic *embodiment* of the living truth itself rather than verbal discourse *about* it. These active demonstrations and verbal expressions – often prosaic, sometimes iconoclastic and humorous, occasionally even scatological – originally resulted from spontaneous exchanges known as *mondō* in Japanese (literally "question and answer"). Such impromptu exchanges were eventually written down – others were embellished or even created – to provide teaching materials for the nascent Zen sect.

Four related but discernible aspects of kōan usage can be described: problem, challenge, probe, and expression. Initially the kōan is a seemingly unsolvable *problem* that the ego-self is nevertheless *challenged* to resolve. The ego-self as it is can in no way fully comprehend, let alone resolve, a kōan, for it is never a mere paradoxical device or witty maxim that can be considered objectively. Rather, when seriously grappled with, a kōan actually confronts us with the fundamental fact of our own untenability – that we cannot come to rest as we are – that the ego-self itself is, finally, unbearable. This is the true and only "content" of a kōan as problem-challenge. This is well illustrated in a legendary *mondō* between Bodhidharma (d. 532) – an Indian Buddhist monk who traveled to China and is considered the 28th Indian patriarch and first Chinese patriarch of Zen Buddhism – and a Chinese monk who becomes the second patriarch of Chinese Zen. The learned and mature Chinese Buddhist monk states that he himself has not yet found peace and begs Bodhidharma to pacify him. Bodhidharma replies, "Bring forth this self which is not at peace, and I will pacify it!" Fully gripped by the kōan, it is resolved through a religious realization or breakthrough known as awakening, or satori. Kōan are then used positively to *probe*, to broaden, and to deepen the realization until it can be freely and fully *expressed*.

Although emphasis is put on "sitting Zen" (*zazen*) as a means of struggling with the kōan, the practicer eventually is unable to extricate himself/herself from the kōan even while engaged in the activities of daily life. Of the numerous examples of Zen awakening recorded, none occurred during the simple practice of *zazen*; rather it is occasioned by a discrete act or event. Thus, although the initial losing of one's ego-self is a necessary prerequisite, the ensuing awakening to selflessness (as the formless, original self of all) constitutes the actual breakthrough and resolving – or dissolving – of the kōan.

### Etymology

Etymologically the Japanese word *kōan* (Chinese, *gong'an*) referred to a public document or public case used as a legal precedent in court: by according with Law or Truth (Sanskrit, *Dharma*), kōan put a stop to private understanding and subjective interpretations. This juridical sense can be discerned in some of the earliest extant usages of the term, for example, when an approaching monk is admonished by the master: "It's a clearly manifest kōan [Japanese, *genjō kōan*], but I release you from 30 blows." In effect the problem lies in the monk's very way of being in coming to the master, an "obvious crime," but the master releases him from the punishment he deserves. In the 13th century the Japanese master Dōgen (1200–1253) used the term *genjō kōan* in a creative and rhetorical manner for the title and subject of the first fascicle of his *Shōbōgenzō*, a work central to Sōtō Zen. Although Rinzai Zen is better known for its use of kōan as problem-challenge, Sōtō has also made such use of kōan in its own unique manner, especially as probe-expression.

### Historical Survey

Toward the end of the Tang dynasty (618–907) in China, outstanding Buddhist masters loosely associated with the emerging Zen (Chinese, *Chan*) sect came to favor familiar colloquial Chinese expressions when lecturing and especially in responding to questions. Some of these terms were borrowed from Daoism. In this way the Chinese genius developed kōan as a religious tool to realize the ultimate truth of selflessness concretely in the world at hand. This preference for "directly pointing" rather than more roundabout and abstract, traditional Buddhist formulas can be traced back to teachings attributed to Bodhidharma. A quatrain attributed to him describes Zen's unique spirit and teaching method:

Without relying on words or letters,
Independently transmitted apart from any teachings;
Directly pointing to the human self,
[Formless, selfless original] nature is seen and awakening
    attained.

In this spirit almost anything could be – and often was – taken up as the subject for a potentially awakening encounter. The two most famous examples are as follows: (1) In Tang China a monk, knowing that the sūtras state that all living beings have the awakened or Buddha nature, asks his master whether the dog in front of them has it. The master responds, "No." This is widely known as the Mu kōan, after the Japanese pronunciation of the master's answer. With this kōan the untenability of self is presented in terms of the duality of affirmation-negation: neither will do. (2) Almost 1,000 years later the Japanese Rinzai Zen master Hakuin (1686–1769) formulated the kōan "You know the sound of two hands clapping – What is the sound of one hand?" Here the untenability of self is presented in terms of the duality of sound-silence: again neither will do. Unlike the Mu kōan, Hakuin's kōan has no explicit Buddhist reference and thus is not so susceptible to metaphysical misinterpretation. Hakuin's interrogatory phrasing was also more effective in arousing the "great doubt" necessary to penetrate kōan, rather than the mere repetition of the word *Mu!* which the earlier kōan succumbed to over the centuries. Today these are the two most basic kōan given to Rinzai Zen monks upon entering the monastery.

Set questions soon became a kind of lingua franca among wandering Buddhist monks. Common examples are as follows: "Why did the founding patriarch [Bodhidharma] come from the West?" or simply, "What is an awakened one [Pāli/Sanskrit, *Buddha*]?" Masters responded in ways designed to help inquirers realize directly who and what they are rather than discuss preconceived notions of why Bodhidharma came from India to China or who "Buddha" was. When the Tang master Linji (d. 867), known in Japanese as Rinzai, the father of Rinzai Zen, was asked about Bodhidharma's intention in coming from the West, he exclaimed, "If there is any intent, you can never save yourself." When an earlier master was asked the same question, he responded, "Why don't you just ask the intention of yourself?"

The increased use of "old case" kōan during the Northern and Southern Song dynasties (960–1279) is attributed to the increase in the number and the decrease in the quality of seekers, most of whom were monks. The Zen sect now flourished, and increasing numbers of people visited masters and studied under them. Earlier seekers, mature in their practice and already burning with their own religious problem, occasionally awakened through a single impromptu *mondō* with a master. Now inquirers were usually given previously formulated kōan to help them plumb the depths. Meanwhile masters compiled, arranged, and rearranged kōan collections. A rich poetic and literary tradition replaced the earlier freshness and vigor, resulting in the classic collections of kōan cases with appended poems and comments, including those known and used today as "The Blue Cliff Record" and "The Gateless Barrier" (Japanese, *Hekigan-roku* and *Mumonkan*, respectively).

Chinese master Dahui (1089–1163), in rejecting this burgeoning literary preoccupation, championed the use of kōan in what came to be termed "introspecting-the-kōan" in contrast to the "silent-illumination" associated with Sōtō Zen. It was introduced to Korea by Chinul (1158–1210), founder of the Korean tradition of Sŏn, or Zen, and at about the same time to Japan by immigrant Chinese monks and Japanese monks who had practiced in China. In this practice the turning word or point of the kōan was to be introspected ever more deeply until one awakened to its true intent. With the Mu kōan mentioned previously, the master's answer "No!" is the turning word or point. The practicer is not to cogitate over or meditate on its objective meaning but constantly to introspect in the sense of completely giving oneself up and subjectively stripping away everything by boring into and *being* it. Thus, the kōan is not an intellectual puzzle or verbal riddle to be figured out. Kōan were specifically designed to be impervious not only to the intellect but also to emotion and will. Although on the surface kōan might seem alien to more traditional religious – even Buddhist – approaches, the ultimate intent remains the same, for only by being utterly divested or "empty" (Sanskrit, *śūnya*) can awakening occur.

*Modern Trends*
In the Edo era (1603–1867) of Japan, Hakuin further systematized and organized the various kōan, giving special attention to an initial kōan as a means of arousing the "great doubt" and final "great death [of ego-self]," which culminates in awakening, or satori; other more difficult and complex kōan would then be used for post-satori practice under a master to further probe and more clearly express it. Hakuin's spiritual descendants developed the present kōan curricula now in use in Rinzai monasteries. These curricula, depending on the lineage, include hundreds or even thousands of kōan that must be seen into as one essential requirement for becoming a Zen master.

The word *kōan*, like other Japanese Zen terms, including *mondō*, *satori*, *zazen*, and *Zen* itself, has become an English word found in college dictionaries. In the process of Zen's introduction to the West over the 20th century and more recent popularization worldwide, Japanese interpreters such as D.T. Suzuki (1870–1966) have rendered Western phrases (e.g., from the Bible) as kōan. Saint Augustine's "Our heart is restless until it rests in Thee" from the opening of his *Confessions* can function like a kōan simply by appending the challenge "Show this 'Thee'!" Today many westerners, including Catholic monks and nuns, have turned to a popular form of Zen practice that includes kōan combined with a renewed interest in Christian mysticism.

Shin'ichi Hisamatsu (1889–1980), an outstanding Japanese Zen layman and philosopher, has given the sharpest and most penetrating critique of the pervasive abuse of kōan to invoke mere transcendent states or spiritual insights rather than the religious great death-great awakening. Hisamatsu emphasized the crucial importance of what he termed the fundamental kōan: "Right now as you are – however you are – will not do; what do you do?" Rather than advocating a reform movement in contemporary Japanese Zen, this can be viewed more accurately as an explicit contemporary restatement of the original spirit out of which kōan developed.

JEFF SHORE

*See also* Bodhidharma; Buddhist Schools/Traditions: China; Buddhist Schools/Traditions: Japan; Chan/Zen: China; Chan/Zen: Japan; Chinul; Dialogue, Intermonastic: Buddhist Perspectives; Dōgen; Hakuin; Humor: Buddhist; Initiation: Buddhist Perspectives; Laicization of Spirituality: Buddhist Perspectives; Suzuki, Daisetz Teitaro; Zen, Arts of

**Further Reading**

Akizuki, Ryomin, "Patriarch Zen and the Koan: An Introduction to Zen Training," translated by Jeff Shore, *Chanoyu Quarterly* 72 (1993)

Buswell, Robert E., *The Zen Monastic Experience: Buddhist Practice in Contemporary Korea*, Princeton, New Jersey: Princeton University Press, 1992

DeMartino, Richard, "The Human Situation and Zen Buddhism," in *Zen Buddhism and Psychoanalysis*, New York: Harper, 1960

Dogen, "Shobogenzo Genjokoan," translated by Norman Waddell and Masao Abe, *The Eastern Buddhist*, new series, 5:2 (October 1972)

Dumoulin, Heinrich, *Zen Buddhism: A History*, 2 vols., London: Collier Macmillan, and New York: Macmillan, 1988–1990

Hakuin, *The Zen Master Hakuin: Selected Writings*, translated by Philip B. Yampolsky, New York: Columbia University Press, 1971

Hakuin, *The Essential Teachings of Zen Master Hakuin*, translated by Norman Waddell, Boston: Shambhala, 1994

Heine, Steven, *Dogen and the Koan Tradition: A Tale of Two Shobogenzo Texts*, Albany: State University of New York Press, 1994

Hisamatsu, Shin'ichi, "Zen: Its Meaning for Modern Civilization" translated by Richard DeMartino and Gishin Tokiwa, *The Eastern Buddhist*, new series, 1:1 (September 1965)

Hisamatsu, Shin'ichi, "True Sitting: A Discussion with Hisamatsu Shin'ichi," translated by Jeff Shore, *The Eastern Buddhist*, new series, 31:1 (1998)

Kadowaki, J.K., *Zen and the Bible: A Priest's Experience*, translated by Joan Rieck, London and Boston: Routledge and Kegan Paul, 1980

Lin-chi, *The Zen Teaching of Rinzai: The Record of Rinzai*, translated by Burton Watson, Berkeley, California: Shambhala, 1976

Miura, Isshu, and Ruth Fuller Sasaki, *Zen Dust: The History of the Koan and Koan Study in Rinzai (Lin-chi) Zen*, New York: Harcourt, Brace and World, 1966

Shibayama, Zenkei, *Zen Comments on the Mumonkan*, translated by Sumiko Kudo, New York: Harper and Row, 1974

Shore, Jeff, "Koan Zen from the Inside," *Hanazono Daigaku Bungakubu Kenkyukiyo* 28 (1996)

Suzuki, D.T., *Essays in Zen Buddhism* (second series), London: Luzac, 1933; New York: Samuel Weiser, 1971

Suzuki, D.T., *An Introduction to Zen Buddhism*, London and New York: Rider, 1949; revised edition, 1992

# Korea: History

## Buddhism of the Three Kingdoms Period

Buddhism was introduced into the Korean peninsula from China during the fourth century A.D. At that time Korea was divided into three contending kingdoms: the northern state of Koguryŏ (c. 250–668), western Paekche (c. 300–660), and the southeastern state of Silla (c. 300–936). Over the centuries Buddhism replaced shamanism as the national faith and spread from the higher classes of society to the commoners.

Buddhism in the Three Kingdoms Period was mainly a religion for the nobility and the upper classes. In terms of doctrines and practices, it was based largely on Chinese Buddhist developments. It included strong elements of shamanism, including spirit worship, totemism, and animism. Monks and nuns were recruited from important noble families as well as from the royal houses. Buddhism was valued for providing divine protection of the realm, and large temples and monasteries were established in or near the capitals of the Three Kingdoms.

## Buddhism under Unified Silla

In 668 the kingdom of Silla brought the peninsula under its sway after many years of bloody struggle. By then Buddhism had penetrated into all aspects of the medieval Korean society, including its art, literature, and architecture. The court and gentry invested large sums of money in the construction of temples and pagodas that are said to have dominated the skyline of Kyŏngju, the Silla capital. Among the most famous temples in Korea is Pulguk Temple, which was constructed in the middle of the eighth century, and the celebrated artificial cave-sanctuary, the Sŏkkuram Grotto, containing a large statue of Śākyamuni Buddha. The increased contact with Tang China resulted in large numbers of Korean monks going abroad to study the doctrines of Chinese Buddhism, and in time even Korean temples were established in China proper.

Unified Silla (668–936) is generally considered the golden age of Korean Buddhism. The important sects were the Kyeyul (Vinaya), Pŏpsŏng (Dharma Nature), the Hwaŏm (Flower Garland), the Pŏpsang (Dharmalakṣana), and several lineages of Sŏn Buddhism. In addition, Ch'ŏnt'ae (Tiantai), Ch'ŏngt'o (Jingtu), and esoteric Buddhism (*milgyo*) were also active in Korean at that time.

## Koryŏ Buddhism

The Koryŏ dynasty (918–1392) continued to venerate Buddhism, as had the previous dynasty, and the kings maintained close ties with the masters and eminent monks of the most influential sects. Ch'ŏnt'ae Buddhism was formally introduced in Korea by the Hwaŏm monk Uich'ŏn (1055–1101), who had traveled to China in the 1080s collecting Buddhist scriptures. Back in Korea he sought to unify the various Buddhist schools under Ch'ŏnt'ae Buddhism, but his attempt was foiled by adherents of traditional Sŏn Buddhism.

The first edition of the Korean Buddhist Tripiṭaka was published during the 11th century as a means to secure divine protection against invasions by the Khitans. During the Mongol invasion in the 13th century, all the wooden blocks were burned. In 1231 a new set of blocks was carved under royal auspices. This set is kept in Haein Temple and is the oldest complete set of the Mahāyāna Buddhist canon extant today.

The monastic community under the Koryŏ was organized to accord with both social norms and the Buddhist moral code: the vinaya. Because of the importance and influence of Buddhism on almost every aspect of Koryŏ society, it was both common and popular for every sort of person to embark on a religious career, and many examples can be found of sons and daughters from the royal family and the nobility who chose to join the *sangha*. In many cases these upper-class monks and nuns rose to high positions within the monastic community, and several became leading figures within the tradition. A fairly substantial amount of sacred literature from their hands remains as a testimony of their achievements.

Throughout most of the dynasty, it was obligatory for Buddhist novices to pass an official examination to become monks and nuns. The curriculum in these exams consisted of demonstrating one's knowledge of certain Buddhist scriptures and possibly a certain liturgical proficiency. These monastic entrance exams consisted of different grades, and the highest type of religious office required a considerable mastery of Buddhist doctrines and practices. This examination system can be traced back to early part of the dynasty prior to the unification of the peninsula in 936. Not until the middle of the 10th century did a systematization of the Buddhist examination take place. The Buddhist examination system was modeled on that of the civil examination and was divided into several stages. Monks who passed the highest examinations held a status within the Buddhist bureaucracy comparable to that of government officials. These monks most often had high social backgrounds and belonged to the absolute elite of the Koryŏ *sangha*.

During the 12th century Korean Sŏn Buddhism underwent a revival that was due partly to the efforts of Chinul (1158–1210), who organized an influential Sŏn Buddhist association. His extensive writings combined Sŏn, Pure Land, and Hwaŏm doctrines and were highly influential in his own time. Later Sŏn masters based themselves on a Korean version of Linji Chan (Imje).

Buddhism flourished at the royal court in Kaegyŏng (present-day Kaesŏng), where gigantic rituals and lectures on Buddhist scriptures were held annually. At these events it was common for

Pusŏksa temple, Yungp'ung-gun, Kyŏngsang-bukdo, founded in the Unified Silla period by the Hwaŏm monk Uisang in c. A.D. 670s during the reign of King Munmu (660–681). Main shrine hall rebuilt in Koryŏ dynasty, 12th–13th century.
Photo courtesy of Marylin M. Rhie

several thousand monks to partake of large banquets inside the palace. Esoteric practices were dominant in connection with court Buddhism.

Under the Koryŏ Buddhist monasteries became very powerful and wealthy. In addition to temple lands, they owned and operated water mills, oil mills, printing houses, and so on, and the Buddhist communities were deeply involved in commerce and politics.

*Buddhism under the Chosŏn*
With the establishment of the Chosŏn dynasty (1392–1910), Confucian reformers began confiscating temple lands and reducing the number of temples and monks. However, Buddhism continued to function until the middle of the 15th century, when it was subjected to heavy restrictions and general suppression. A brief Buddhist revival occurred during the middle of the 16th century.

In the 16th and 17th centuries, a large number of eminent monks arose, among whom the most important are Houng Pou (d. 1566) and Hyŭjŏng (1522–1604). It appears that Hyŭjŏng followed in the footsteps of Chinul with regard to Sŏn doctrine, although in practice he was closer to the late Koryŏ tradition. However, his importance rests mainly on the fact that most of

the later Sŏn lineages trace themselves back to him. Hyŭjŏng is also famous for having organized armies of monks to fight against the Japanese Hideyoshi invasion of 1592–1598.

During the second half of the Chosŏn dynasty, Buddhism declined sharply. Few masters of significance appeared amid general poverty of the monasteries and low social status of the Buddhist clergy. At the beginning of the 1880s, Japanese Buddhist missionaries arrived in Korea as part of Japanese imperialist tactics and quickly succeeded in winning converts among the Korean population. Although the actual motives of the Japanese Buddhist missionaries are not in doubt, these missionaries succeeded in lifting the Confucian ban on Buddhism in 1895, a development that gave a great impetus toward its restoration. At that time the master Kyŏnghŏ (1849–1912) actively promoted traditional Sŏn practices and revived several training centers. In addition he founded Buddhist societies for the education of the laity. Many of Kyŏnghŏ's disciples contributed to the Buddhist renaissance that took place during the Japanese colonial period.

*Buddhism during the Japanese Colonial Period*
In 1910 Korea was formally annexed by Japan, and consequently Korean Buddhism came under the influence of its Japanese counterpart. The Japanese colonial government controlled

all the major temples in the country and also appointed the abbots. As a result Korean Buddhism became divided into a pro-Japanese and an anti-Japanese faction. Nevertheless Buddhism was able to continue its revival, during which several Buddhist journals of a high scholarly standard were published. These journals were the products of a new class of Buddhist intellectuals, including Yi Nŭnghwa (1869–1943) and Han Yongun (1879–1944).

In 1935 the modern Chogye Order was formally founded. Several leading members of the Order belonged to the anti-Japanese faction, but it also included monks with close connections to the colonial government. Later the pro-Japanese monks founded the T'aego Order. These monks gradually became married priests in accordance with a Japanese custom dating back to the Meiji Restoration of the 1880s.

### Korean Buddhism Today

Following the Japanese defeat in 1945 and the division of the country in 1950 at the outbreak of the Korean War, Korean Buddhism has seen a steady increase in adherents. In addition to the dominant Chogye and Neo-Ch'ŏnt'ae Orders, more than 25 "new" or reformed schools of Buddhism have appeared since 1945. According to recent statistics active Buddhists constitute around 15 million, which marks a sharp rise since the 1980s.

Despite an apparent increase of Buddhists in recent years, the general standard of the monks' training and spiritual motivation is declining. This is a result mainly of the increasing difficulties facing Korean Buddhism in providing a meaningful spiritual alternative to the problems and anxieties facing people in a modern industrialized society. In addition fierce competition from Protestant Christianity for new converts has forced Buddhism to use new and often unsavory strategies that run counter to its basic doctrines.

HENRIK H. SØRENSEN

*See also* Buddhism: Inculturation; Buddhist Schools/Traditions: Korea; Chan/Zen: Korea; China; Chinul; Critiques of Buddhist Monasticism: Confucian; Economics: Buddhist; Japan: History; Korea: Sites; Wŏnhyo

### Further Reading

Buswell, Robert E., *The Zen Monastic Experience: Buddhist Practice in Contemporary Korea*, Princeton, New Jersey: Princeton University Press, 1992

Chinul, *The Korean Approach to Zen: The Collected Works of Chinul*, edited by Robert E. Buswell, Honolulu: University of Hawaii Press, 1983

Choi Byŏng-hŏn (Ch'oe Pyŏnghŏn), "Significance of the Foundation of Susŏnsa in the History of Korean Buddhism," *Seoul Journal of Korean Studies* 1 (1988)

Han Kidu, *Han'guk sŏn sasang yŏngu* (A Study of the Thought of Korean Sŏn Buddhism), Iri: Wongwang taehakkyo, 1974

*Han'guk pulgyo sasangsa: Sungsan Pak Kil-chin paksa hwagap kinyŏm* (Festschrift on the Occasion of Prof. Sungsan Pak Kilchin's Sixtieth Birthday: The History of Korean Buddhist Thought), Chonbuk Iri-si: Won Pulgyo Sasang Yon'guwon, 1975

*Han'guk pulgyo sasang sa yŏngu* (Studies in the History of Korean Buddhist Thought), Seoul: Tongguk Taehakkyŏ ch'ulp'an bu, 1983

Hŏ Hŭngsik, *Koryŏ pulgyo sa yŏngu* (A Study of the History of Koryŏ Buddhism), Seoul: Ilcho kak, 1986

Hŏ Hŭngsik, *Han'guk chungse pulgyo sa yŏngu* (Studies in the Buddhist History of Medieval Korea), Seoul: Ilcho kak, 1994

Iryon, Samguk, *Yusa: Legends and History of the Three Kingdoms of Ancient Korea*, translated by Ha Tae-Hung and Grafton K. Mintz, Seoul: Yonsei University Press, 1972

Kil Hŭisŏng, "State and Sangha in Korean History," *Korea Journal* 21:8 (1981)

Korean Buddhist Research Institute, editors, *Buddhist Thought in Korea*, Seoul: Dongguk University Press, 1994

Lancaster, Lewis R., and C.S. Yu, editors, *Introduction of Buddhism to Korea: New Cultural Patterns*, Berkeley, California: Asian Humanities Press, 1989

Lancaster, Lewis R., and C.S. Yu, editors, *Assimilation of Buddhism in Korea: Religious Maturity and Innovation in the Silla Dynasty*, Berkeley, California: Asian Humanities Press, 1991

Yi, Nŭnghwa, *Chosŏn pulgyo t'ongsa* (Comprehensive History of Korean Buddhism), 2 vols., Kyongsong: Sinmun'gwan, 1918; reprint, Seoul: Poyŏnkak, 1979

# Korea: Recent Changes

Despised, oppressed, excluded, and unable to enter the capital, Buddhist monks saw their social and geographic isolation end in 1895 through pressure from Japanese Buddhist clergy, agents of Japanese colonialism. After Japan annexed Korea in 1910, the Korean Sangha struggled to resist Japanese attempts to control Buddhism, especially after the patriarch of the newly united Sangha, Yi Hoe-gwang, agreed to subordinate the order to Japanese Sōtō Zen. Dissidents invoked orthodoxy and inheritance of the Imje (Japanese, Rinzai) lineage. The colonial authorities then ordered all monasteries organized under 30 main monasteries and headed by government-approved abbots with new dictatorial powers. No longer elected by the residents, the abbots converted common monastic into private property and adopted Japanese practices permitting married clergy and meat-eating, thus violating orthodox monastic regulations. This divisive tactic succeeded because the Sangha had long been separated into *sap'ansung* – administrators and laboring monks who had paid the onerous taxes of the old regime – and the *ip'ansung*, who studied doctrine and meditated. The law on monasteries further marginalized the dissident Sŏn (Chinese, Chan, "meditation") monks. They were excluded from all but 19 of the 1,363 monasteries and by 1922 numbered only ten percent of the 7,100 clergy. The meditation clergy established the Sŏn Hag'wŏn (Meditation Academy) to find practice sites and launch an anti-Japanese purification campaign, which lasted into the 1970s. In 1941, T'aego Monastery was built in Seoul as the headquarters of Korean Buddhism, now unified as the Chogye order.

**A statue of Maitreya at Pogun-sa in Seoul, South Korea.
Photo courtesy of John Powers**

After liberation and the division of Korea in 1945, the 500 celibates claimed orthodoxy and influenced the South Korean president in 1954 to order the expulsion of the 7,000 married clergy from the monasteries. In 1969, following a series of bitter legal and physical battles, the celibates, who enjoyed public support and increased numbers, forced the married clergy to relinquish T'aego Monastery, now renamed Chogye Monastery. In 1970 the married clergy seceded to form the T'aego order. The cost to the celibates was continued internal disputes and government abuse of monastic property, most of which had been lost in the 1950 land reforms. Government intervention in 1980 led to the arrest of Sangha leaders and the violation of monastic sanctity. A so-called "masses Buddhism" of young monks who sought revitalization through a socialist Buddhism of welfare and resistance emerged in response. In 1988 the laws governing monastic properties were repealed, and in 1994 radical monks physically ousted the conservative leaders from Chogye Monastery for funding the presidential campaign of the Protestant Kim Young-sam. Meanwhile, in 1988 an independent university for the Sangha was established and in 1989 a broadcasting service initiated. In 1990 the number of denominations increased to 26,

with 17,656 monks and 7,549 nuns in 9,231 monasteries and hermitages in South Korea.

Around 1945 in communist North Korea, there were 1,600 clergy and 403 monasteries, but after the devastation of the Korean War, confiscation of all land, the mobilization of everyone into production, and antireligion campaigns, only a few elderly clergy and Buddhist front organizations have remained. After a thaw in 1989, virtually all the 300 clergy were married and untonsured. They wore suits and lived in villages near the 60 surviving monasteries, preserving elements of colonial Buddhism in a time warp.

JOHN JORGENSEN

*See also* Chan/Zen: Korea; Japan: History; Korea: History; Korea: Sites; Self-Immolation, Buddhist; United States: Buddhist

**Further Reading**

Buswell, Robert E., *The Zen Monastic Experience: Buddhist Practice in Contemporary Korea*, Princeton, New Jersey: Princeton University Press, 1992

Jorgensen, John, "A Social Analysis of Korean Buddhism and Its Future Prospects," in *Han'guk Pulgyo ŭi chwap'yo/The Direction of Korean Buddhism*, edited and published by Nogwŏn Sŭnim Kohŭi kinyŏm haksul nonch'ong kanhaeng wiwŏnhoe, Kimch'ŏn, 1997

Kang Sŏkju and Pak Kyŏnghun, *Pulgyo kŭnse paegnyŏn*, Seoul: Chung'ang Ilbo Tonghyang, 1980

Mok Chŏngbae, "Kŭn. Hyŏndae," in *Han'guk Pulgyo Ch'ongnam*, compiled by Han'guk Pulgyo Ch'ongnam p'yŏnch'an wiwŏnhoe, Seoul: Puljisa, 1993

Mok Jeong-bae, "Buddhism in Modern Korea," *Korea Journal* 33:3 (Autumn 1993)

Shim Jae-ryong, "Buddhist Responses to Modern Transformation of Society in Korea," *Korea Journal* 33:3 (Autumn 1993)

Sin Pŏpt'a, "Nam Puk Pulgyo kyoryu wa chŏnmang," in *Han'guk Pulgyo Ch'ongnam*, compiled by Han'guk Pulgyo Ch'ongnam p'yŏnch'an wiwŏnhoe, Seoul: Puljisa, 1993

Tedesco, Frank M., "Sleeping Wisdom Awakens: Korean Buddhism in the 1990s," *Korea Journal* 33:3 (Autumn 1993)

Yi Kiyŏng, "Han'guk Pulgyo ŭi hoego wa chŏnmang," in *Han'guk Pulgyo Ch'ongnam*, compiled by Han'guk Pulgyo Ch'ongnam p'yŏnch'an wiwŏnhoe, Seoul: Puljisa, 1993

# Korea: Sites

Anyone visiting Korea to explore Buddhist sites at the start of the 21st century will be pleased to discover that Korea's monastic tradition is still very much alive despite many challenges that have confronted it since the first temples were built in Koguryŏ 16 centuries ago. Many features of traditional Korean monastic life are still maintained in the innumerable ancient but often rebuilt temple complexes and hermitages that are ensconced in mountains throughout the southern half of the peninsula. Aspects of traditional monasticism can also be found in modern, urban temples and propagation centers that cater to laypeople who have migrated to Seoul and other cities as part of the massive population shift that all but emptied the countryside in Korea's forced march toward economic development during the last few decades.

Many layers of Korean history can be read in a tour of the country's major monasteries and lesser-known Buddhist sites, but they are not readily apparent to visitors who are unfamiliar with the complexity of the peninsula's past. Many sites have been leveled by war, and much outstanding Buddhist art has been stolen as well. A brief historical overview might help bring a clearer understanding of the richness of Korea's Buddhist heritage as revealed in its extant institutions.

The fortunes of Buddhist monasteries on the Korean peninsula has ebbed and flowed dramatically since Buddhism was officially introduced to Korea from China in A.D. 372. Generally, for about a millennium since its arrival in Koguryŏ, when the first temples for foreign missionaries were built by King Sosurim near the northern edge of the peninsula, Buddhism was favored by successive royal courts and the aristocracy during the periods of the Three Kingdoms, the Unified Silla (668–936) and the Koryŏ (936–1392). Leaders welcomed the prestige that Bud-

dhism enjoyed in powerful neighboring regimes like China as well as the support that it gave the state as an agency for worldly and spiritual protection (*hoguk pulgyo*) and a unifying national ideology (*t'ongil pulgyo*). Although not infrequently savaged by incursions of the Chinese, Khitans, Mongols, and Manchus from the north and Japanese marauders by sea, for centuries monastic complexes were constructed, maintained, renovated, and rebuilt in the cities and in mountains. However, with the advent of the Yi, or Chosŏn, dynasty (1392–1910) in the late 14th century, Buddhist clergy and their temples fell out of favor with the royal court and the exclusivist neo-Confucian literati class that guided it. Buddhism's power and prestige, which was at a pinnacle in the Koryŏ, was legislated to the lowest level of society in the Chosŏn. Monks and nuns were forced to take refuge in mountain monasteries whether or not they were disposed to scriptural scholarship or proponents of direct meditation experience. Kyo (Doctrine) and Sŏn (Meditation) schools were progressively reduced and consolidated from 11, to 7, to 2, and finally to no sectarian identity by government decree. Monasteries in the mountains that had been mainly Sŏn practice centers became residences for monks and nuns of all schools. Differences among temple traditions and lineage virtually disappeared in practice.

Vairocana Buddha Hall and courtyard, Pulguksa Temple, Kyŏngju, Kyŏngsang-bukdo, Unified Silla period, late eighth century.
Photo courtesy of Marylin M. Rhie

Although Japanese pressure on the last Yi dynasty royalty at the end of the 19th century helped raise the status of Buddhist clergy from the lowest rung of the Chosŏn class hierarchy, it also planted seeds of conflict within the *sangha* during 35 years of Japanese colonial rule (1910–1945) and afterward. The imperial government, following Meiji reforms, favored married clergy over traditionally celibate monks and nuns for important positions in the monastic hierarchy. The issue of the propriety of celibate versus married clergy and complex disputes regarding legal disposition or control of temples and monastic properties have led to periodic purification reform movements (*ch'ŏnghwa kyehyŏk undong*, 1954–1962) within the *sangha* and some highly publicized brawls and schisms in recent history, perhaps the most significant of which was the withdrawal of married clergy from the Chogye Order (Taehan Pulgyo Chogye-jong) to form the independent T'aego Order (Han'guk Pulgyo T'aego-jong) in 1970. Much to the dismay of laypeople, echoes of discord over control of temples and their financial influence within Chogye Order administration have continued into the present.

With the demise of imperial Japan and the end of World War II in 1945, liberation brought national division, which split the relatively homogeneous Korean people into two ideologically opposed camps that collided shortly afterward in the bloody three-year Korean War (1950–1953), which devastated most population centers and monastic sites throughout the country. The long, uneasy truce after the catastrophic clash has sharpened the political (and psychological) division severely, causing an almost impenetrable cleavage that persists into the 21st century as a last vestige of Cold War military brinkmanship.

The reclusive, atheistic, and Stalinist North is officially known as the Democratic Peoples' Republic of Korea. With about 80 percent of the land uninhabited mountains, the country is divided from China by the Yalu and Tumen Rivers to the north and from South Korea by the narrow, heavily armed so-called demilitarized zone (DMZ) to the south. The North has four seasons, with winters colder and drier than in the southern half of the peninsula. As in South Korea the spring and autumn seasons are the best in which to visit monasteries because of the temperate weather. The changing colors of the autumn leaves of the heavily forested mountains in both the North and the South make ventures to mountain retreats an aesthetic delight. Certain Buddhist sites in the North, such as the monastery P'yohyunsa in the Diamond Mountains, which was destroyed during the Korean War, have been repaired or rebuilt by the state. The activities of officially designated Buddhist clergy and a few ancient monastic sites are strictly regulated by the central government for propaganda purposes. We presume that they are no more than a facade of traditional Korean religion to accommodate the tourist trade and to mollify certain international "watchdog" organizations through contrived examples of religious freedom.

The overt practice of Buddhism in the North seems to be minimal. For decades citizens there have not been allowed to express themselves freely, communicate with one another, or travel within or outside their country. Foreign visitors are restricted to government-prescribed itineraries in the company of authorized guides and interpreters. Veneration of the late Kim Il Sung and his ruling son, Kim Jong Il, and their materialistic ideology of *juche* (self-sufficiency) dominate all thinking and action in the North. The early economic success of the communist state after the civil war has given way to serious contraction, especially since the termination of external aid with the disappearance of Soviet support. There have been repeated agricultural failures due to mismanagement and natural disasters.

Two sites worth visiting are in the famous Diamond Mountains. They are the once royally favored P'yohunsa Monastery (erected in 670), which is renowned for a central image of Pŏpki Posal (Bodhisattva Born of Truth from the Avatamsaka Sūtra) that is enshrined in its main Dharma Hall, called Panyabojŏn (Wisdom Jewel Hall), and Chŏngyangsa Monastery, with its Hŏlsŏngnu pavilion, from which it is said that 12,000 peaks of inner Kŭmgangsan (Diamond Mountains) can be seen. In the Myohyangsan Mountains can be found Pohyŏnsa Monastery, which was erected in 968 and restored at least six times since then. At its height in the Koryŏ, it had 24 buildings. It is now called a "History Museum" and is on the government-designated domestic and foreign VIP tourist circuit. Its holds a rare 13-story pagoda. This site is especially famous for its association with the great monk Sŏsan Taesa and 5,000 monk-soldiers (*ŭibyŏng*, "righteous armies") who successfully defended Korea against Japanese marauders at the time of the Hideyoshi invasions in the last decade of the 16th century. A special hall (Such'ungsa) is dedicated to their achievements as well as memorial stones and other artifacts. Special modern-day Buddhist "national unification" ceremonies have been performed here by so-called North Korean monks with conventional haircuts (not shaven headed), wearing traditional red *kasa* over stylized, monastic robes.

Sŏngbulsa Monastery in Hwanghaedo province was established in 898 by the influential geomancer National Master Tosŏn Kuksa. At its height it had 20 monks' residential buildings, many hermitages, and 15 stone pagodas. The surviving dharma halls were erected in the 14th century. Koryŏ-period decorated beams (*t'anch'ŏng* painting) are among the oldest styles surviving in North Korea. Sŏkwangsa in South Hamgyŏng province was allegedly founded in 1386 by Yi Sŏnggye, founder of the Chosŏn dynasty, on the advice of Muhak Taesa, who predicted Yi's ascendancy to power in a dream.

Much more accessible to visitors is the better-known nation to the south of the DMZ. In contrast to the North, the successfully capitalist and newly democratized South, officially called the Republic of Korea, has been considered an "Asian tiger" and "a miracle on the Han River" because of its rapid industrial development and real per capita growth in the last decades of the 20th century. Despite the financial crisis of 1997 that required massive loans from international agencies such as the International Monetary Fund (IMF), the general wealth of the South Korean population (about 46 million) has been able to support religious growth of all kinds, with the number of avowed Catholic and Protestant believers swelling so much as to equal and even edge slightly ahead of Buddhists in recent polls. Church

Kneeling Bodhisattva sculpture (180 cm in height) and octagonal nine-storied pagoda (15.15 meters in height), Wŏljŏngsa, Mount Odae, Py'ŏnggch'ang-gun, Kangwŏndo, mid–tenth century, Koryŏ dynasty, both granite.
Photo courtesy of Marylin M. Rhie

building has become a growth industry in tandem with the booming housing construction industry. Massive Catholic churches compete with a profusion of Protestant ones, replete with towers and crosses, more often than not puncturing the evening skyline in red neon.

The Buddhist community in South Korea has been very much a part of the rapid economic development of the country since the 1970s. Urban Buddhist propagation centers with resident clergy affiliated with large monasteries have also expanded and multiplied in the major cities, and the mountain monasteries have undergone renovations and expansion, with paved access roads, electricity, telephones, modern plumbing and flush toilets, oil and gas heating rather than traditional wood or charcoal, satellite dishes, new buildings for conferences and overnight guests, youth programs, and so on.

Be that as it may, the traditional, seasonal monastic retreat cycle follows the lunar calendar (summer, mid-fourth to mid-

seventh lunar month [ha' angŏ]; winter, mid-tenth to mid-first [dong angŏ]) and is still carefully observed at Sŏn (Zen) practice centers (sŏnwŏn) around the country. There are over 90 registered sŏnwŏn in the Chogye Order alone with about 1,600 monks and nuns in seasonal attendance, averaging a few dozen practitioners per meditation hall (sŏnbang), ranging from as few as five to over 80 per monastery. Serious visitors must make arrangements well in advance to visit certain monasteries or meditation precincts within the complexes during these periods. Participants, who must have at least taken novice (Korean, sami; Sanskrit, śramaṇera) vows, commit to remain the entire three-month period and abide by the strenuous schedule of discipline aptly called "tight rules" (kyŏlche): rising from the often shared sleeping floor at 3 a.m., chanting, sitting still for numerous sessions, taking formal meals and performing menial work around the monastery grounds and maintaining silence throughout the day and evening, and finally retiring at 9 p.m. or later. Unnecessary talk, reading, and visitors, even for short-term practice, are not permitted.

Spring and autumn are considered free seasons, a time of "loose rules" (haeje). Monks and nuns are unconfined and can "do many things" (manhaeng), such as traveling on pilgrimage to other temples around Korea and touring holy sites abroad, depending on the wishes and means of their sponsors or their own resources.

The four-year educational programs at scriptural lecture halls (kangwŏn or sŭngha taehak) for novices as well as further, advanced study for pigu and piguni (fully ordained monks and nuns) at the larger monasteries have been modeled on that of secular institutions. Those clergy wishing careers in Buddhist-related academics can apply to study at the Central Sangha College (Chungang Sungga Taehakkyo) in Seoul and the new Kimp'o campus or at Korea's premier Buddhist school of higher education, Dongguk University, with campuses in Seoul and Kyŏngju. These institutions are important for training Buddhist leaders and are definitely worth visiting in addition to the monasteries.

Those who wish to acquire a better grasp of Korean Buddhist monastic life are advised to observe the tradition over a change of practice seasons, such as in the spring from the beginning of the fourth lunar month through preparations for the major holiday of Buddha's Birthday (puch'ŏnim o-shinnal), including a great lantern parade festival for clergy and laypeople everywhere on the eighth day of the fourth month, and into the beginning of the summer retreat that begins around the 15th of the month. Late summer can also be of interest with the end of the summer retreat on the Buddhist holiday of Ullambana, the Festival for the Dead (Korean, ulanpun-jeil or paekchung) on the 15th of the seventh lunar month. Be advised, however, that one month later is Ch'usŏk, the Korean native and Confucian Harvest Moon holiday, when families reunite in their hometowns and most business in Korea comes to a halt for a week. Half the population seems to shift from the cities to the countryside in their automobiles, and all domestic transportation is booked months in advance. Traveling to rural monasteries can be challenging at this time as well as at Lunar New Year all over Asia. Visitors might want to remain at a monastic site of their choice during this period.

After visitors have arrived at Kimpo Airport near Seoul, the precincts of the very active Chogyesa Temple and Chogye Order Headquarters in downtown Seoul are a "must" visit because of their importance as representatives of Korea's largest Buddhist order and the place from which so much national and international news about Korean Buddhism emanates. There are about 1,700 large and small temples in the Chogye Order and over 13,000 registered Chogye clergy in 1993. Almost all the well-known, historically important sites are Chogye affiliated. Of the many other active Chogye sites in Seoul, one might consider visits to Chosŏn-period Hwagyesa Temple in the temple-rich Samgaksan area in the northern part of Seoul. It is the monastic base of Korean Buddhism's most successful international propagation association, the Kwanum School of Zen, with its founder, the Venerable Seung Sahn, who resides there. Nearby, too, is Tosŏnsa, the "temple of patriotic penance," named after the renowned and influential Silla master and expert in geomancy (Korean, *p'ungsu*; Chinese, *feng-shui*) Tosŏn. This temple was much favored by the pious wife of late President Pak Chung Hee. Other signs of Chogye Order vitality are modern-style urban temples, such as Kuryŏngsa, the Seoul branch temple of the Buddha Jewel monastery T'ongdosa, the socially progressive Nŭngin Sŏnwŏn across the road, and the renovated Pongŭnsa Temple complex near the towering Korea Trade Center in newly developed southern Seoul. The various socially engaged activities of the Join Together Society (JTS) in Sŏch'o-dong in Seoul and the Han Maum Sŏnwŏn, founded by the charismatic nun the Venerable Tae Haeng in suburban Anyang, are also worth looking into to get a broader perspective of the tradition in renewal.

Other Buddhist sites of note in Seoul are Pongwŏnsa, a monastic complex of the T'aego Order, which rightfully boasts of preserving and transmitting ancient Koryŏ Buddhist arts, music, and dance. This order claims nearly 2,500 temples, mostly very small, family-style chapels, and about 4,700 clergy. The growth of the recently revived Ch'ŏnt'ae (Tiantai) Order can also be discerned in its modern Seoul branch center Kwanmunsa, which reflects the devotional fervor of the Order's huge Kuinsa Monastery, which can accommodate about 10,000 people.

Visitors to Seoul must also take advantage of the insights that can be gained into the Korean monastic tradition by watching the Buddhist cable television station BTN-TV in Korean and occasional special programs about Buddhism on Arirang-TV, an English-language station. Videotapes of monastic life, such as at the austere *bhiksuni* temple Unmunsa, and of significant events, such as the cremation ceremonies of high monks, have also been produced by the Buddhist radio station BBS (Pulgyo pangsong). Tours organized by the Royal Asiatic Society Korea Branch can provide opportunities to visit Buddhist sites off the beaten track. These trips are usually led by long-term resident expatriates and scholarly specialists of uncommon experience.

The most internationally renowned Buddhist sites in Korea are on the UNESCO World Heritage List. They are Haeinsa Monastery and its unique woodblock library of the Tripitaka Koreana, the Great 80,000 Sūtra Depository (P'almandaejanggyŏng), and the beautifully carved Buddhist sculpture in the stone grotto Sŏkkuram near the Pulguksa Monastery in the city of Kyŏngju, the ancient capital of the Unified Silla. Kyŏngju is a kind of "Buddha Land" itself with innumerable sites and remains. Visitors will be well advised to explore its surprising wealth of ancient Buddhist artifacts and should allow ample time to do so.

South Korea is a small country with modern highways and good, yet relatively inexpensive, public transportation. Most monastic sites and sacred places can be easily reached.

*Major Monasteries and Sites to Visit*
Chogyesa and Chogye Order Headquarters: Kyŏnji-dong, downtown Seoul

Chogye Order Ch'ongnims: large monasteries that encompass *sŏnwŏn*, *kangwŏn*, *yulwŏn* (vinaya center), and *yŏmbulwŏn* (Pure Land devotional center)

T'ongdosa: "Buddha Jewel Monastery," established by Chajang in 646 to enshrine Buddha's relics. The Main Hall does not have a Buddha image but rather a window looking out to a stūpa that enshrines relics of the Buddha brought to Korea from China by the Vinaya Master Chajang

Haeinsa: "Dharma Jewel Monastery," a UNESCO World Heritage site of the Tripitaka Koreana woodblock library and home of the late Chogye Order patriarch Sŏngch'ŏl Songgwangsa: "Sangha Jewel Monastery," associated with Koryŏ National Master Chinul (Pŏmnyŏnsa, near Chogyesa, is its Seoul branch temple)

Sudŏksa: renowned for the 20th century's influential Sŏn Master Kyŏnghŏ and his renowned student Mangong, who died there in 1946 (the major lineages responsible for the revival of modern Sŏn Buddhism derive from them)

Paegyangsa: newly restored and active monastery with socially progressive leadership; site of a recent Assembly of Sŏn Masters and an Internet-televised, international conference on Korean Sŏn in 1998

Kyŏngju: capital of the Buddhist Unified Silla dynasty
    Sŏkkuram Grotto
    Pulguksa: its famous pagodas Tabo T'ap and Sŏkka T'ap
    Punhwangsa: associated with Wŏnhyo
    Hwangryongsa: associated with Chajang and the nine-story wooden pagoda destroyed by 13th-century Mongol invasions
    Kyŏngju National Museum

Piguni monasteries

    Unmunsa: ordained women's training center; 250 students in a four-year course

    Chongamsa: 200 students in a four-year course

Sŏnamsa: T'aego Order Ch'ŏngnim on Chogyesan, near the Chogye Order Songgwangsa

Kuinsa: large Ch'ŏnt'ae devotional center

FRANK M. TEDESCO

*See also* Buddhist Schools/Traditions: Korea; Chan/Zen: Korea; Chinul; Korea: History; Korea: Recent Changes

## Further Reading

Buswell, Robert E., *The Zen Monastic Experience: Buddhist Practice in Contemporary Korea*, Princeton, New Jersey: Princeton University Press, 1992

Chŏng, T'ae-hyŏk, and Sin Pŏpt'a, *Pukhan pulgyo tapsagi*, Seoul: Minjoksa, 1994

Korean Buddhism Chogye Order, *Korean Buddhism*, Seoul: Korean Buddhist Chogye Order, 1996

Taehan Pulgyo Chogyejong Kyoyugwŏn Pulhak yŏnguso, *Kangwŏn ch'ongnam*, Seoul: Taehan Pulgyo Chogyejong Kyoyugwon, 1997

Yun, Kyong-nyol, *Namsan: Discovering the Ancient Wonder of Kyongju's Mt. Namsan*, translated by Charles Mark Mueller, Seoul: Buddha Land, 1994

## Related Web Sites

The Internet now allows users access to basic and frequently updated information about the major monasteries and sacred places in Korea. However, most sites are in Korean language and require Korean software to appreciate fully. Informative English-language web sites are:

*http://www.buddhapia.com/eng/*
*http://www.buddhism.or.kr* and *http://www.dharmanet.net* (the main Chogye Order sites)

Large and small temples are coming on-line all the time.

# Kūkai 774–835

Founder of Japanese Esoteric Buddhism (Shingon)

As a pilgrim walks through the ancient cemetery of Okunoin on Mount Kōya (Kōya-san), amidst the towering cryptomeria (Japanese cedar) trees while passing several hundred thousand tombstones and monuments, he eventually crosses the Mimyonohashi Bridge, which spans the Tamagawa River. Now, in the most sacred area of Mount Kōya, he approaches the Torodo Hall, lit by hundreds of oil lamps that are offered to Kūkai and where Buddhist rituals routinely take place dedicated to his memory. Directly behind this hall, between incense urns, the

path ends, and the pilgrim stands with others already praying in front of the Gobyō Grave, the mausoleum of Kūkai. He remains, some believers say, within the tomb in perpetual *samādhi* (meditation).

Whether Kūkai (posthumously Kōbō Daishi) still meditates or not, his contributions to Japanese Buddhism and culture remain unrivaled in Japanese history. It is certainly true, as the tourist brochure *A Guide to Kōyasan* states, "Kūkai's memory lives throughout Japan to this day. Even in remote places, the name Daishi is a household word."

Perhaps the reason that Kūkai's fame persists is that his life's work extends beyond the seminal contributions he made to Japanese Buddhism, and includes significant works in linguistics (he is often credited with developing the *kana* syllabary, although he is actually more responsible for its wider acceptance), education, poetry, calligraphy (he is considered one of the great calligraphy masters [*shosei*] in Japanese history), lexicography, pilgrimages (credited with originating the famed Shikoku pilgrimage), and sculpture. Indeed one can argue that Kūkai made contributions to his native culture unrivaled by any other monk in the history of world monasticism.

Kūkai (birth name Tōtomono or Mao) was born to an aristocratic family at Byōbugaura in Sanuki province in Shikoku. The Saeki-Ōtomo clan was an ancient clan and a noble house. However, Kūkai, like Gautama Buddha before him, took no solace in a privileged birth but rather pursued college at the capital, where he avidly studied Chinese classics and history.

At college he was exposed to Buddhist scriptures and perhaps grew discontented at merely reading the words and not confronting the reality behind them. We do know that he soon became a Buddhist layperson and began to write. His first work, the *Sangō Shīki* (798; Indications of the Goals of the Three Teachings), was a text that drew distinctions between Confucianism, Daoism, and Buddhism. His biography suggests that, although a layperson, Kūkai began at this time a pattern that he would maintain for the remainder of his life: arduous practice as a devoted Buddhist (akin to the mountain ascetics of the time) while interspersing this asceticism with forays into worldly life. From early in his life as a Buddhist, Kūkai emphasized monastic practice both for himself and for members of his sect.

The search for personal truth led Kūkai to China, a common path for many Japanese Buddhist founders during the formative periods of Japanese Buddhism. He studied under Hui-kuo (Keika, 746–805), learning the intricacies of esoteric Buddhism. Within three months of his meeting of Hui-kuo, Kūkai was permitted the final initiation (Sanskrit, *abhiṣeka*; Japanese, *kanjo*) and thus was recognized as accomplished in esoteric Buddhism. From this experience he was emboldened and understood that his life's work was to bring this dharma (teaching) back to Japan.

He returned to Japan in 806, bearing such items as sūtras, maṇḍalas, and ritual instruments necessary to spreading esoteric Buddhism, and eventually came to be installed (in 809) as the abbot at Takaosanji (now Jingoji). Kūkai established himself as a

**Representative statue of Kūkai (Kōbō Daishi), holding the ritual *vajra*, as Kūkai's Shingon is a form of Esoteric Buddhism like that of Tibet.**
**Photo courtesy of Steve McCarty**

significant personage in the early Heian artistic society in Kyoto, and Emperor Saga (r. 809–823) favored Kūkai by requesting examples of his artistic work (calligraphy and poetry).

As abbot of Takaosanji, Kūkai began the perpetuation of his teachings in Japan by performing the initiatory rite of *abhiṣeka*. From the performance of initiatory rituals, he was able to establish the *saṅgha* (community) of monks and begin to organize the monastic rule. In 813 he wrote *Konin no goryakukai* (The Admonishments of Konin), which was designed as a guide for his monastic order. During this period at Takaosanji, Kūkai produced a rich outpouring of writings (eventually a corpus consisting of more than 50 texts) that further extended his growing reputation among contemporaries and, even more important, provided the scriptural support of what came to be called Shingon (True Word) Buddhism in Japan.

Yet Kūkai longed to create a sacred space that would allow the full flowering of *Mikkyō* Buddhism (esoteric Buddhism) that he envisioned for the Japanese people. In 816 he asked for Emperor Saga's permission to construct a monastic community on Mount Kōya. He wrote of the choice of Kōya to be the axis for his teaching:

When young, I, Kūkai, often walked through mountainous areas and crossed many rivers. There is a quiet, open place called Kōya located two days' walk to the west from a point that is one day's walk south from Yoshino. . . . High peaks surround Kōya in all four directions; no human tracks, still less trails, are to be seen there. I should like to clear the wilderness in order to build a monastery there for the practice of meditation, for the benefit of the nation and of those who desire to discipline themselves. (*Kūkai: Major Works*, 1972)

In 819 Kūkai began construction of a monastic center on Mount Kōya. The construction and influence of this monastic center dominated the remainder of his life. In 823, with the bequeathing of Tōji as the Kyoto headquarters of Shingon Buddhism, Kūkai had the structure in place for Shingon Buddhism to prosper.

As befits an esoteric tradition, Shingon cosmology is indispensable to its monasticism. From his earliest writings Kūkai was interested in making distinctions between the philosophies of the day. In his writing *Hizō hōyaku* (The Precious Key to the Secret Treasury), Kūkai draws a systematic distinction between

Buddhist perspectives by connecting different schools with different stages, culminating in the highest philosophy, which he equated with the esoteric resolution. In this work, human consciousness is said to develop through ten stages – from the lowest level of the "goatish" mind to the highest stage of human consciousness that transcends the lower levels, culminating in the Buddhist resolution of Awakening (nirvāṇa). Although Kūkai clearly distinguishes between Buddhist (and other religious) views, he also readily utilizes a confluence of Buddhist thought in formulating his esoteric position.

Kūkai's tantric, religio-philosophy is based on his own existential realization. His ideas are informed by two sūtras and two śāstras: the *Mahāvairocana Sūtra* (Japanese, *Dainichikyo*) and *Vajraśekhara Sūtra* (Japanese, *Kongocho-kyo*) and the *Bodhicitta Śāstra* and *Commentary on the Awakening of Mahāyāna Faith*. In addition, Kūkai's thought is strongly influenced by the Mahāyāna philosophies of Mādhyamika and Yogācāra Buddhism.

Within Kūkai's writings we find an elaboration of the *trikaya* (three-body) theory that has ancestry within Mahāyāna Buddhism. In explicating the *nirmānakāya* (physical form of Buddha), *sambhogakāya* (celestial forms of buddhas and bodhisattvas), and *dharmakāya* (Universal Buddha form/structure) conceptions, Kūkai argues that Gautama Buddha as *nirmānakāya* is a manifestation of *dharmakāya* (personified as *Mahāvairocana*; Japanese, *Dainichi*). That is, the historical Gautama Buddha was a form of *dharmakāya*, yet *dharmakāya* extends beyond the physical so as to function as the substratum of the Universe. Thus, it includes all buddhas, bodhisattvas, and our own original nature. Kūkai further renders all material existence as constructed of six elements (Japanese, *Roku-dai*): earth, water, fire, wind, space, and mind (a similar articulation is found in other tantric writings). These elements serve two purposes in Kūkai's thought: first to connect mind (*citta*) and matter (*rūpa*) as ontologically inseparable to illuminate the essence of all reality, namely, harmony of the six elements (Japanese,

Cave temple barely visible behind autumn leaves at Iwayaji (Cliff Hut Temple), number 45 of the 88 sacred places of Shikoku, high in the mountains where Kūkai is believed to have practiced asceticism.
Photo courtesy of Steve McCarty

Devotees praying to Kōbō Daishi (Kūkai) outside the Okunoin, Mount Kōya, Japan.
Photo courtesy of David Moore

*Rokudai-enyū*), and second to serve as an epistemological truth that is utilized in monastic practice.

With the matrix that gives form to Gautama Buddha as part of *Dharmakāya-Mahāvairocana*, Kūkai consequently argues that one's own Buddha nature (the idea that one is inherently Awakened) is also identical with *Dharmakāya-Mahāvairocana* and is "in our mind," as Kūkai puts it. In truth *Dharmakāya-Mahāvairocana* does not exist apart from one's mind and yet is not circumscribed by the individual mind either. One could say that, for Kūkai, reality is such that although a distinction appears to exist between subject and object, this is a conventional, erroneous perception. In truth, one mind encompasses all reality. For the Shingon aspirant, the goal is to actualize the dormant human consciousness, represented as Buddha nature, that in response realizes this consciousness as a natural, primordial truth. This paradoxical reality represents authentic reality and is able to be grasped, in Kūkai's understanding, only through meditational practice.

Thus, his prescribed monastic practice focuses on realizing the Buddha nature that is inherent in all things, thereby at the same time actualizing the compassion and wisdom that comprise the original Awakening (*hongaku*) that is in principle (*rigu*) possessed by all persons. Human personal consciousness is, in principle, awakened to the ultimate reality of *Dharmakāya-Mahāvairocana*. In a word, one's consciousness is simultaneously identical with and paradoxically, at the same time, different from ultimate reality. Unfortunately one's personal consciousness is delusional (*kleśa*) and misconceives the nature of reality. It wrongly sees only an objectification of a unique subjective self, failing to understand that our true nature is this original Awakening. This articulation of Buddhist soteriology can be exegetically drawn from the Four Noble Truths of Buddhism and is familiar to disciples of exoteric Buddhist orientation. The nonoppositional reality of all things is revealed. The uncovering of one's Buddha nature can be rendered as the actualization of *anātman* (selfless-self, or, in personalistic terms, the I and not-I consciousness that is nirvāṇa).

What is critically important for Kūkai is that one come both to realize the problem of human existence and then move to actualize the resolution to that problem. As Kūkai's dictum insists, we should be about "attaining enlightenment in this very existence (*sokushin jobutsu*)," and he believes that the esoteric path is more efficient than the exoteric path of Buddhism in accomplishing this goal.

Shingon Buddhism provides a rich monastic practice that deploys an elaborate symbolism, ritualism, and iconography. Kūkai's practice focuses on observation of precepts and on meditation. In regard to precepts he refers to both esoteric and exoteric precepts. The exoteric ones are those, ten in number, that are usually binding on Mahāyāna monastics. However, the esoteric precepts are those that are encompassed in vows that are taken prior to the initiatory *abhiṣeka* ritual. In summary, these esoteric precepts enjoin the preceptor to hold to the dharma, strive unceasingly for Awakening, display compassion to all sentient creatures, and proselytize the teachings of the True Buddhism to others.

The primary tools used for Shingon practice are activities of the body, speech, and mind – referred to as the three secrets (Japanese, *san-mitsu*). Provided with privileged information, the monastic engages in strictly prescribed articulation of how to move his fingers (mudra), what sounds to utter (mantra), and what to think or visualize (maṇḍala). Through the practice of daily meditation, the acolyte strives to meditate as *Mahāvairocana* meditates. This is done to actualize knowledge that the three secrets are likewise embodied in the personification of Ultimate Reality that is *Mahāvairocana*. Eventually this knowledge comes to efface the differences between the acolyte and *Dharmakāya-Mahāvairocana*.

Shingon Buddhism additionally utilizes what is termed "A-ji meditation." In this meditation, the symbolic meaning is twofold: "A" is the first letter of Devanāgāri (Sanskrit script) and yet also is a sign of negation, or emptiness. In sum "A" is a symbol for *Dharmakāya-Mahāvairocana*, and this meditation strives for insight into the nature of the meditator's relationship with reality. This insight negates the notion of independent selfhood.

The maṇḍala is a particular symbol of Kūkai's Buddhism and the metaphysical heart of the Shingon Buddhist altar. As one faces the altar, the *Vajradhātu* (Japanese, *Kongōkai*) maṇḍala hangs on the left and the *Garbhakośa* (Japanese, *Taizōkai*) maṇḍala on the right. With detailed and expansive iconography, these maṇḍalas symbolize the Buddhist Universe by illustrating Buddhist deities and related mudras. Although these maṇḍalas have a pedagogical function, their fuller meaning can be discerned only by the believer as he strives to engage the maṇḍala as an embodiment of his True Nature.

Operating about 3,800 temples, Shingon Buddhism is not restricted to Japan. Shingon has also established a foreign missionary presence that includes *sangha* in such countries as Thailand, Brazil, Canada, and the United States. However, the center of Kūkai's Buddhism remains the temple complex on Kōya-san. Many Shingon temples – at one point, more than a thousand existed – still extend over the sacred mountain, and the Buddhist practices that Shingon monastics and devoted believers engage in as part of each morning service continue to vibrate before their respective *butsudan* (Buddhist altar), just as they have done for a thousand years. Similarly Kūkai's unparalleled contributions to Japanese Buddhism, monasticism, and culture continue to vibrate throughout Japan and will likely do so for millennia yet to come.

LESLIE D. ALLDRITT

*See also* Buddhist Schools/Traditions: Japan; Deities, Buddhist; Esoteric Buddhism in China and Japan; Japan; Kyoto, Japan; Liturgy: Buddhist; Maṇḍala; Meditation: Buddhist Perspectives; Mount Kōya, Japan; Mountain Monasteries, Buddhist; Saichō; Shikoku, the Pilgrimage Island of Japan

## Biography

The founder of Japanese Esoteric Buddhism (Shingon) studied in China in 804–805. Upon his return he interacted with Saicho, the founder of Tendai in Japan. In 816 Emperor Saga granted to Kūkai Mount Kōya and in 823 Tōji, an imperial temple in Kyoto. The temples on Mount Kōya celebrate his memory.

## Major Works

*Sango Shiki* (Indications of the Goals of the Three Teachings), 798

*Konin no goryakukai* (The Admonishments of Konin), 813

*Hizō hōyaku* (The Precious Key to the Secret Treasury)

*Kūkai: Major Works*, translated by Yoshito S. Hakeda, 1972

*Kōbō Daishi Kūkai Zenshū* (The Complete Works of Kōbō Daishi), 8 vols., 1983–1986

## Further Reading

Abe, Ryuichi, *The Weaving of Mantra: Kūkai and the Construction of Esoteric Buddhist Discourse*, New York: Columbia University Press, 1999

Hayasaka, Akira, *Kūkai*, Tokyo: Daiwa Shobo, 1984

Kiyota, Minoru, *Tantric Concept of Bodhicitta: A Buddhist Experiential Philosophy (an Exposition Based upon the Mahavariocana-sutra, Boddhicitta-sastra and Sokushin-jobutsu-gi)*, Madison, Wisconsin: South Asian Area Center, 1982

Odin, Steve, "Aesthetic Symbolism in Japanese Shingon Buddhism," in *Sacred Interconnections*, edited by David Griffen, Albany: State University of New York Press, 1990

Shaner, David, "Bodymind Experience in Japanese Buddhism: A Phenomenological Study of Kūkai and Dōgen," Ph.D. Diss., University of Hawaii, 1980

Snodgrass, Adrian, *The Matrix and Diamond World Mandalas in Shingon Buddhism*, New Dehli: Aditya Prakashan, 1988

Yamasaki, Taiko, *Shingon: Japanese Esoteric Buddhism*, Boulder, Colorado: Shambhala, 1988

# Kyiv, Ukraine. *See* Kiev (Kyiv), Ukraine

# Kyoto, Japan

Kyoto became officially designated by this name in 1868, when the capital was moved to Edo and named Tōkyō, East Capital. Kyōto then became the capital (*kyō*) (of) capital(s) (*to*). Although it was called Heian-kyō in Chinese fashion, the capital of peace and tranquility, when founded in 794, popular language after about the 12th century used Kyōto.

The new city was the outcome of an intensifying feud between Emperor Kammu (r. 781–806) and the Nara clergy, mainly the successive heads of the huge Tōdai-ji, whose host of monks was a formidable and frightening political force. They claimed a divinely endowed monopoly on ordinations, had a large network of temple connections and real estate in 23 provinces, and held household fiefs and other wealth exceeding that of the royal family. When Kammu censured the seven great Nara temples in 796, they were listed in this order: Tōdai-ji, Kō-fuku-ji, Gankō-ji, Daian-ji, Yakushi-ji, Saidai-ji, and Hōryū-ji. However, only two years later, when he designated "official" temples (*kan-ji*) (i.e., those qualified for full government support), he added Shitennō-ji (in Osaka), Gūfuku-ji (former Kawara-dera in Asuka, Nara prefecture), and Sūfuku-ji (in Otsu, Shiga prefecture) to the list but dropped Tōdai-ji to second from last. His intentions had by then become clear.

The restraining orders to temples had failed to accomplish his goals, and Kammu decided to isolate them from political affairs by moving the capital. He did this to Nagaoka in 784, but in too much haste. The choice of site was poor – much of it too low and subject to flooding – the transfer was badly managed, and the engineer of the move was assassinated by a disaffected prince, leaving the specter of a vindictive spirit haunting the area. Heian was the next stop for the capital, where it remained for more than 1,000 years.

Selection was well made, conforming admirably to the Chinese geomantic ideal of a symmetrical plan protected by three mountains and supplied by two rivers. The south is easily accessible across relatively level ground. As laid out, the checkerboard measured about 3.1 miles north to south and about 2.8 miles east to west. This brought the Kamo River right through the city, so its course was redirected the equivalent of two and a half blocks to join the Takano River on the north edge of the city and to flow along its eastern edge. Communication within the city then improved, but the additional water frequently caused serious flooding. As at Nara the eastern side was much preferred, and slowly the population gravitated across the river toward Higashiyama. The palace, in the north, was later moved toward the east at one of the several times it needed rebuilding in order to keep it in the middle of the city.

Emperor Kammu's prejudices were demonstrated in the virtual elimination of temples from the city, with the exception of two in the south on either side of the main street. A few temples had notable records as welfare agencies, and this left the city without such services. These two were guardian temples for Heian: the Tō-ji, East Temple, officially titled Kyō-ō-gokoku-ji, (State-Protecting Temple), finished by Kōbō Daishi around 823, founder of the esoteric Shingon sect, and the Sai-ji, West Temple, about which rather little is known except that it was wiped out in a fire in 1223. The former served as a major inn for official visitors waiting to be received at the court and as a center of political negotiations. Fortunately, despite destruction in the civil war in 1486, many important wooden statues of the ninth century were saved, and the temple was rebuilt after 1605, the five-story pagoda, at 185 feet, being the tallest in Japan.

Kammu supported the embryonic temple of the Tendai sect on Mount Hiei (later known as Enryaku-ji) in the northeastern part of the city as protector against the attack route of evil spirits and fostered the construction of other esoteric temples in rural locations. Emperor Saga (r. 810–823) followed the same calculated course, but when the Fujiwara family found a way to control the court by marrying their daughters to emperors, the entire picture changed. Fujiwara Yoshifusa held the office of regent (sesshō) from 858, and the powerful family then proceeded to build numerous Amida halls and, later, temples for retirement to await entry into the Pure Land Western Paradise of Amida. Temples sprang up in city blocks and on the outskirts.

This development was accompanied by the growth of the shōen system, the untaxed private estates resulting from the breakdown of central controls and the rise of the practice of hiring peasants to protect their landholdings. Some temples employed and trained their own monk-soldiers (sōhei), often with socially disastrous results. Even emperors acquired shōen. The Fujiwara court enjoyed a new level of luxury – a cultural high point in Japanese history – with literature and the arts thriving under their patronage. They followed the specifications in the Ōjōyōshū (Rebirth in the Pure Land [of Amida]), a description of the way to salvation by Priest Genshin of the Tendai sect, in which the devotee recited the name of the Buddha (nembutsu) while meditating intently on the image of Amida Buddha. The rote system came to be known as the Easy Path.

The simplicity of the beliefs and the promise of rich spiritual rewards inspired hordes of pilgrims to take to the roads to Nara and to the Nantō Shichidaiji (The Seven Great Temples of the Southern Capital), where Buddhist traditions were felt to be most profound. The practice was abandoned only after the roads became unsafe in the civil wars of the 14th century.

The start of the retreat-retirement-memorial temple complex was a villa built by Fujiwara Michinaga that he gave to his son Yorimichi and converted to a temple in 1052. This is the Phoenix Hall (Hōō-dō) of the Byōdō-in in Uji, south of Kyoto, named after the legendary bird of resurrection, a bronze pair sitting on the ends of its roof ridge and the shape of the building and its extended galleries, fronting the Western Paradise pond, said to resemble an alighting bird. The Phoenix Hall itself was erected in 1053. Yorimichi resigned his kampaku (civil dictator) position in 1068, took the tonsure, and lived in the Byōdō-in. There he worshiped the statue of Amida Buddha by the sculptor Jōchō, dying six years later.

Especially notable were the vast temples in the Shirakawa district of Kyoto, north of Sanjō, to which the rulers retired after abdication, took the vows, and lived a politically active life. They had their own cabinets and advisers in a system known as insei (cloistered government). Almost 20 temples were clustered at Shirakawa by the middle of the 12th century, and these embodied all the developments in Pure Land architecture and associated icons. At the least, most had Amida halls with nine images for the nine states of Amida's paradise, Yakushi halls with seven images, Godaimyō halls with five images of esoteric deities, a Middle Island, and a pagoda. All were sooner or later destroyed by fires of natural or human causes.

Several uprisings marked the decline of Fujiwara power. These uprisings were climaxed by the Gempei War (Gen = Minamoto, Pei = Taira) of 1180–1185, ushering in the so-called Kamakura period (1185–1333) and the start of 700 years of military rule. The wife of Minamoto Yoritomo (shōgun, 1192–1199) was a Hōjō with home base in the Kantō in eastern Japan. He selected the seaside town of Kamakura to establish his military government (bakufu), and the rulers titled themselves shikken (regent). All found that the country was ungovernable without control of Kyoto, so they stationed their garrison in the Rokuhara district there, an especially pleasant area on the east side. For security police stations were ranged throughout the city.

The rulers discovered their particular religious interests in the newly introduced Zen practices while the rank and file were accepting the nembutsu and dancing in the streets. Eisai (1141–1215), priest of Tendai, came back from China in 1191 and built the first Zen temple in Kyoto, Kennin-ji, south of Gion, between the Kamo River and the street now known as Higashiyama-dōri. At the request of the Hōjō regent, he erected the Jūfuku-ji in Kamakura, a step that led to the adoption of Zen by the warrior class as a self-disciplining method. This was Rinzai Zen, which emphasizes kōan (questions and answers) and expects sudden

Interior, Daitoku-ji Zen temple, Kyoto, Japan, 16th century.
Photo courtesy of John C. Huntington, the Huntington Archive

enlightenment. The Sōtō Zen that was brought in by Dōgen (1200–1253) a quarter of a century later emphasized meditation while sitting cross-legged (*zazen*) in order to find one's inner self. Admittedly it was expected to be a slow and arduous process. Confrontations with Kyoto's traditional clergy led Dōgen to leave, and he founded the Eihei-ji in Fukui prefecture, a very substantial Zen training center today.

The Hōjō constructed large Zen temples in the hills of Kamakura, notably the Kenchō-ji (1253) and Engaku-ji (1282), each embodying new Chinese features in arrangement of buildings and architectural details, inviting distinguished Chinese priests to head them. They were preoccupied with organizing the defenses against the attempted invasions by the Mongols (1274 and 1281), the latter temple a thanks offering for sending the kamikaze, the divine winds that saved the day. A group of Rinzai temples in Kamakura became the Gozan (Five Mountain temples), with a companion set of nunneries that wielded considerable power.

Kyoto is home to the main medieval sects. Hōnen (1133–1212), a priest of the Enryaku-ji, preached the gospel that became the Jōdo-shū (Pure Land sect), detaching the worship of Amida from the inventory of Tendai thought, although the sect was not formally authorized until around the end of the 16th century. Its essence is the saving grace of Amida, rebirth in paradise requiring only the invocation of his name. The Chion-in, one of Kyoto's largest temples, is its center. Shinran (1173–1262), Hōnen's follower, is revered as the founder of Jōdo Shinshū (True Pure Land sect). His anticlerical attitude – he married and wore commoner's clothes – was inimical to Kyoto's conservative establishments, and he moved to Hōjō home territory, where he had phenomenal success among the farming class. After a variety of political difficulties, the Hongan-ji temple settled in Kyoto, then was forced to split, the Nishi-hongan-ji and the Higashi-hongan-ji heading two branches of the sect.

The Ashikaga occupation of Kyoto (1333) inaugurated two centuries of civil wars that were started by a dispute over selecting the emperor. Two held the throne, known as the Nambokuchō (Southern and Northern Courts) period (1336–1392). The second Ashikaga shōgun took up residence in the Muromachi district of Kyoto, giving the name to the Muromachi period (1334–1568). The Ashikaga built great Zen temples in the surrounding hills and found cultural and economic advisers among the priests. The connections with Ming China were close, and large Zen temples became major art centers, the training grounds for black-ink (*sumi-e*) and related styles of painting. Zen monasteries sprang up throughout the country, their public service in the form of schools (*terakoya*) in which young boys were taught the basics of reading and writing.

The listing varies, but the main great Gozan temples were the Nanzen-ji, erected on the spot of a former detached palace; Shōkoku-ji, the Ashikaga family temple; Kennin-ji, supported by the Hōjō; Tōfuku-ji, the Kujō family temple, Fujiwara descendants; and Tenryū-ji, begun in 1339 by Ashikaga Takauji (1305–1358) to placate the spirit of Emperor Go-daigo, who had died the year before. Two shōguns in particular, Ashikaga Yoshimitsu (1358–1408) and Yoshimasa (1436–1490), have left their villas, almost all that remain of their retirement temple complexes.

Kyoto had become more cosmopolitan, the power of the aristocracy slipping, to be replaced by that of the merchants, who slowly but surely organized themselves for protection from looting, concentrating their occupations in blocks (*machi*). Uprisings among the peasants were brutally suppressed. Earthquakes, fires, floods, famines, and plagues created havoc, breeding constant lawlessness, and conditions reached their lowest point in the inconclusive Ōnin War (1467–1477), ten years of willful destruction with the Shōkoku-ji a special target, the opposing armies barracked in temples on either side of the city. The Enryaku-ji's monk-army on Mount Hiei mauled Kyoto at night. Two-thirds of the population had died or fled. Inevitably few city temples remained intact.

This miserable state of affairs was terminated when Oda Nobunaga (1534–1582) captured Kyoto, unified the country, put down the farmers' revolts (*ikkō ikki*) instigated by adherents of the Jōdo Shin-shū, and burned the Tendai temples on Mount Hiei and killed countless monks. After Nobunaga's assassination Toyotomi Hideyoshi (1536–1598) took on the task of reconstructing Kyoto. The Tokugawa (1603–1868) generally sustained his policies. Writers referred to much of the area as uncultivated open country, a few temples standing but in ruins. Many changes were made, including narrowing streets to make them more difficult to fight through, but Toyotomi was, in fact, intent on disassembling the social structure to eliminate further opposition. The independence of the *machi* groups, which maintained a Buddhist temple and even locked themselves within walled areas at dark, was too much. Large numbers of people were displaced, temples were clustered (thus names such as Teramachi now), and an *odoi* was built, a somewhat oblong moated wall surrounding a large part of the inner city. People were assigned space, and the gates were bolted at night. However, renaissance must have been fairly rapid, as a document of 1624 gives a population figure of 410,000. A disastrous fire burned most of the enclosed city in 1708.

The Meiji government (1868–1912) moved the capital to Tokyo and "redesigned" the old city of Kyoto, restoring some of its earlier features. With the advent of Western-style buildings, the appearance of the city changed dramatically, but ordinances on the height of buildings have kept the skyline low and modest in a situation quite unique in Japan. Several east-west streets were widened as firebreaks during World War II, but the city was untouched and has blossomed. Most of the old temples are prospering religious institutions today and are regarded as the strongest single component in local politics. The city was so rich in its arts that, for all the destruction, the quantity that has survived is staggering, making Kyoto one of the most visited cities in the world.

J. EDWARD KIDDER, JR.

*See also* Architecture: Structural Monasteries in East Asia; Chan/Zen: Japan; Dōgen; Eisai (Yosai); Esoteric Buddhism in China and Japan; Hōnen; Mount Hiei, Japan; Nara, Japan; Nembutsu; Pure Land Buddhism; Rennyo; Saichō; Shinran; Temple, Buddhist; Tiantai/Tendai: Japan; Topography, Sacred (Buddhist); Visual Arts, Buddhist: Japan; Warrior Monks: Buddhist; Zen, Arts of

## Further Reading

Hall, John, *Japan: From Prehistory to Modern Times*, Tokyo: Tuttle, 1971

Hall, John, "Kyoto as Historical Background," in *Medieval Japan: Essays in Institutional History*, edited by John Hall and Jeffrey Mass, New Haven, Connecticut: Yale University Press, 1974

Hayashi, Tatsusaburo, with George Elison, "Kyoto in the Muromachi Age," in *Japan in the Muromachi Age*, edited by John Hall and Takeshi Toyoda, Berkeley: University of California Press, 1977

Kidder, J. Edward, *Japanese Temples: Sculpture, Paintings, Gardens, and Architecture*, Tokyo: Bijutsu Shuppan-sha, and London: Thames and Hudson, 1964

Ponsonby-Fane, R.A.B., *Kyoto: Its History and Vicissitudes since Its Foundation in 792 to 1868*, Hong Kong: Rumford Printing Press, 1931; revised edition as *Kyoto, the Old Capital of Japan (792–1869)*, Kyoto: The Ponsonby Memorial Society, 1956

Sansom, George, *A History of Japan to 1334*, Stanford, California: Stanford University Press, 1958

Sansom, George, *A History of Japan, 1334–1615*, Stanford, California: Stanford University Press, 1961

Yamamura, Kozo, editor, *Medieval Japan*, volume 3, *The Cambridge History of Japan*, Cambridge and New York: Cambridge University Press, 1990

*Zenkoku jiin meikan* (Nationwide Directory of Temples), revised edition, 4 vols., Tokyo: Zen Nihon Bukkyokai Jiin Meikan Kankokai, 1970

# L

## La Trappe, France

The foundation of La Trappe dates from 1122, when Rotrou III, count of the Perche, vowed to build a monastery in memory of his wife and brother-in-law, both of whom had perished two years earlier in the wreck of the *White Ship*. The first building was simply a small chapel, and it was some years before the monastery itself was constructed and the count invited the Savigniac religious of Breuil-Benoît (Eure) to the new foundation. The date at which the brethren first came to the site is uncertain, but by 1140 La Trappe was a Savigniac abbey, and when the Savigniac houses united with the Order of Cîteaux in 1147, La Trappe became a Cistercian house in the line of Clairvaux.

Few details of the medieval buildings are known, and from the 14th century to the 17th, the history of the abbey is depressing. It was deserted in 1361; pillaged, burned, or both by the English in 1376, 1382, 1434, and 1469; disastrously neglected under a series of commendatory abbots; and, at the time when Armand-Jean de Rancé (1626–1700) became its regular abbot, in a state of decay, both materially and morally. The buildings were ruinous, and no more than six monks were living there in undisciplined squalor.

Rancé therefore arranged for all but one of these monks to be sent elsewhere and then embarked on an extensive program of repair and rebuilding. Under his administration the abbey flourished and achieved prosperity and renown, although both came to an end with the French Revolution.

The decree ordering the suppression of the religious orders in France had been issued in 1790, but the inhabitants of the area around La Trappe, together with the religious of the abbey led by Dom Augustin de Lestrange (1754–1827), petitioned that the abbey be excepted. After considering the matter for almost a year, the authorities decided against the request, and Lestrange and 22 other religious left the abbey on 10 May 1791 and made their way to Switzerland, where they founded La Val-Sainte and ensured the continuance of the Trappist way. However, La Trappe itself survived for another year and was finally closed on 3 June 1792.

During and after the Revolution, the abbey was almost completely destroyed, but in 1815, after the fall of Napoleon, Lestrange and a number of monks returned to France, purchased the remains, began an ambitious program of rebuilding, and refounded a new abbey on the ruins of the old. The new church was dedicated in 1832. However, in 1880 the monks were again expelled but soon returned, at which time the monastery was entirely rebuilt. The present neogothic church was consecrated on 30 August 1895.

Of the medieval buildings, only one survives: a 13th-century structure that might have been a mill or an industrial building.

The abbey has a guest house, and vistors may attend some of the monastic offices in the church, although entrance to the cloister and other monastic buildings is not permitted.

DAVID N. BELL

*See also* Asceticism: Christian Perspectives; Cistercians: General or Male; Rancé, Armand-Jean de; Trappists

### Further Reading

Charencey, Charles-Félix-Hyacinthe Gouhier, comte de, *Cartulaire de l'abbaye de Notre-Dame de la Trappe*, Alençon: Renaut de Broise, 1889

Charencey, Charles-Félix-Hyacinthe Gouhier, comte de, *Histoire de l'abbaye de la Grand-Trappe*, 2 vols., Mortagne: G. Meaux, 1896–1911

Dimier, Joseph, *La sombre Trappe: Les légendes et la vérité*, Abbaye S. Wandrille: Éditions de Fontenelle, 1946

Du Bois, Louis, *Histoire civile, religieuse et littéraire de l'abbaye de La Trappe*, Paris: Raynal, 1824

[Félibien, André], *Description de l'abbaye de La Trape: Nouvelle édition, avec figures*, Paris: Le Febvre, 1689

Guérout, Gérard, "La communauté de La Trappe face à la Révolution: 13 février 1790–3 juin 1792," *Cîteaux: Commentarii cistercienses* 40 (1989)

Krailsheimer, Alban J., *Armand-Jean de Rancé, Abbot of La Trappe: His Influence in the Cloister and the World*, Oxford: Clarendon Press, 1974

Krailsheimer, Alban J., *Rancé and the Trappist Legacy*, Kalamazoo, Michigan: Cistercian Publications, 1985

Tournoüer, Henri, *Bibliographie et iconographie de la Maison-Dieu Notre-Dame de La Trappe au diocèse de Séez, de A.-J. Le Bouthillier de Rancé . . . et en général de tous les religieux du même monastère*, 2 vols., Mortagne: Marchand et Gilles, 1894–1896

Aerial view of the Monastery of La Trappe.
Photo courtesy of Abbaye de La Trappe

# Labdron, Machig c. 1055–1153

Tibetan Buddhist teacher and originator of
*Chöd* meditation

Machig Labdron, one of the most important women teachers in the history of Tibetan Buddhism, is said to be the only Tibetan teacher whose teachings were taken from Tibet to India and practiced there; in every other case Buddhist teachings traveled from India to Tibet instead. She is famous as the originator of *Chöd* (cutting), a relatively esoteric practice in which one visualizes one's own body being cut up as an offering to needy, hungry sentient beings. Performed alone in frightening places, such as charnel grounds, this practice destroys ego-clinging and fear, thus liberating the practitioner. Today it is practiced in many schools of Tibetan Buddhism by both monastics and serious lay practitioners.

As is usually the case for revered practitioners of meditation, Tibetan literature includes a rich biographical tradition surrounding Machig Labdron. Discrepancies exist among the various biographies, but the outlines of Machig's life are clearly discernable. She was born around 1055, meaning that she lived during the second propagation of Buddhism to Tibet and was an active participant in those events. As is common in Tibetan stories of great practitioners, her birth and life were highly unusual by conventional standards. Her birth is attributed to the aspiration of an Indian male yogi to help convert the Tibetans. In his visions, a *ḍākiṇī* (female sky-goer) came to him and told him to transfer his consciousness into her heart-center so that, after killing his body, she could transport him to the womb of his future mother in Tibet. The mother experienced magnificent dreams and an easy birth; the girl baby was born with a third eye and other marks of extraordinary status clearly visible. In fact she is said to be an emanation of "the Great Mother of Wisdom," Prajñāpāramitā, and also of Ārya Tārā, one of the most beloved female buddhas of Tibetan tradition from whom she is said to have personally received some of her teachings.

In her youth she excelled first as a professional reader and then as a student of the Prajñāpāramitā (transcendent wisdom) sūtras. Living as a nun she studied with many teachers and was renowned for her understanding. Finally she sought Tantric initiation at the age of 20. During her initiation she went into a deep meditative state and simply vanished, floating through the walls of the temple and landing at the Tree of Serlag, a place inhabited by fierce magical beings. She tamed them and then was visited by many Tantric deities, culminating in the appearance of the Great Mother of Wisdom, followed by Ārya Tārā. She predicted that Machig's teachings would "become like the sun rising in the sky." Ārya Tārā also told Machig that an Indian yogi who was an emanation of the Buddha would soon arrive in Tibet and that she should take him as her consort.

Soon thereafter the Indian yogi arrived in Tibet. Machig went to meet him and eventually did become his consort. Her gurus had not only advised her to initiate the relationship but also predicted that great benefit for sentient beings would result from the union, and that in any case her consort, Thopa Bhadra, was not an ordinary being. At the age of 23, she began living with him and eventually gave birth to at least three children. Many people gossiped about Machig's liaison, complaining that she had broken her vows as a nun, although it is unclear whether she had ever actually taken ordination as a nun.

When she was 35, Machig left her children with her husband because she realized that it was time for her to return to her gurus and her dharma practice. She received more initiations and again showed signs of great realization. She began teaching Chöd. When she was 41, Ārya Tārā again appeared to Machig, bestowed an extremely profound initiation on her, and again predicted that her teachings would benefit many beings, both human and nonhuman. A year later she was reunited with her husband and children. The three children, two sons and a daughter, eventually became lineage-holders of her teachings and great teachers in their own right. At this reunion she and Thopa Bhadra compared their meditative experiences and sang songs of blessing to each other. Thopa Bhadra left for India the next day, his mission in her life complete, and her children went about their various retreats and meditation practices.

Machig's final test came from Indian pundits. By this time her fame and her teachings had reached India, and Indian Buddhist masters were skeptical that Machig was an emanation of Great Mother Wisdom, suspecting that she was an evil spirit incarnate instead. Three powerful yogis were chosen to go to Tibet to confront Machig and debate with her. Always an accomplished debater, Machig was able to answer all their questions and delivered many teachings. When challenged to prove the authenticity of her doctrines, she recounted her previous lives, ending with the story of the Indian yogi whose consciousness had been transferred to the womb of her mother. His body still lay intact in the cave in which the body had died, Machig said. She also told the Indian yogis exactly what would happen when his body was cremated. When they found the body and the cremation went as predicted, the Indian yogis finally conceded that, in this one case, a genuine teaching had originated in Tibet rather than in India.

For the rest of her long life, Machig taught her numerous students and helped innumerable patients suffering from various physical and mental diseases. She died in 1153 at the age of 99.

RITA M. GROSS

*See also* Meditation: Buddhist Perspectives; Tibet: History

## Biography

A great and long-lived woman teacher in Tibet, Machig is known through legends. She lived as a nun, then for 12 years as consort of an Indian yogi, and then as a teacher of a new technique of meditation known as *Chöd*.

## Further Reading

Allione, Tsultrim, *Women of Wisdom*, London and Boston: Routledge and Kegan Paul, 1984

Edou, Jerome, *Machig Labdrön and the Foundations of Chöd*, Ithaca, New York: Snow Lion, 1996

# Ladakh, India

The Himalayan kingdom of Ladakh and its sister region Zangskar (L. La-dwags; bZangs.dkar) represent one of the few regions where Tibetan Buddhist monasticism remains in its original institutional form. Located to the north of the western Himalayan range on the frontier of modern India, the region is isolated from all overland contact throughout most of the eight-month winter, when temperatures regularly drop to at least −20 degrees C.

The area's political geography – sandwiched between Pakistan, Kashmir, and Chinese-occupied Tibet – has placed religion at the center of its political identity for much of the last millennium. Ladakh's present status as part of the Indian state of Jammu and Kashmir has allowed it to maintain much of the Buddhist monastic culture of pre-invasion Tibet. However, even before 1959 Ladakh represented one of the most "clericalized" regions in the Tibetan Buddhist sphere; indeed, since the 15th century its religio-economic life has been dominated by a form of mass monasticism that even today accounts for 10 to 15 percent of the male population in many areas.

Monasteries (especially those built from the 14th century on) are usually located on pinnacles and mountainsides, their central temples surrounded by descending lines of monastic quarters. In general the monastic populations are recruited from local villages and households that act also as sponsors for monastic rites, often paying usufruct on monastic lands. In return monasteries perform rites on the laity's behalf, carrying out funerary, purificatory, and exorcistic rites (of the latter the most spectacular being the annual 'cham masked dances). Certain monasteries also have attendant oracles – laity or monks who become possessed by worldly but Buddhist protector deities to cure and to pronounce on urgent economic and political questions.

## History

Buddhism's history in the northwestern Himalaya is a long, checkered one. A satellite kingdom to the vast Buddhist Kushan Empire in Kashmir from the first century B.C. to the fifth century A.D., the region boasts many monolithic carvings and inscriptions from this era, especially the impressive Maitreya carving at

Rizong Monastery, Ladakh, India.
Photo courtesy of John Powers

Mulbek, the "gateway" to Ladakh. However, such influences have been almost entirely overlaid by two periods in the rise of Buddhism within Tibet itself: the so-called second diffusion of Buddhism to Tibet in the tenth century and Tibet's progressive and turbulent centralization as a Buddhist state under the rule of the Gelukpa (dGe-lugs-pa) Order and the Dalai Lamas from the 15th to the 17th century.

### The Second Diffusion

Responding to the edicts of the western Tibetan monk-king Ye-shes 'Od, who sought to reestablish monastic discipline in Tibet, Buddhist scholars journeyed across the western Himalaya to the monasteries of India, seeking to transmit Buddhist doctrine to the high plateau. Most noted amongst these was the translator, teacher, and shrine builder *lotsava* Rinchen Zangpo (Rin-chen bZang-po, 958–1055): many of the 108 shrines he is credited with building acted as the basis for subsequent monastic communities. Later the Tantric yogins Naropa and Marpa (Mar-pa, 1012–1096) – who, along with their spiritual descendents Milarepa (Mi-la-ras-pa, 1040–1123) and Gampopa (sGam-po-pa, 1079–1153), formed the basis of semi-monastic Kagyudpa (bKa'-rgyud-pa) tradition – journeyed through Ladakh: Naropa's supposed meditation cave is near Dzongkhul

(Dzong-khul) monastery, and Marpa's can still be visited at Stongde (Stong-sde).

### The Centralization of Tibet

The influence of such figures led to the rise of the Kadampa (bKa'-dams-pa) and Kagyudpa schools in the area from the 11th to the 13th century, with emphasis on the Drugpa ('Brug-pa, one of the six Kagyudpa schools). As with much of Tibet, political tension over this emphasis emerged, as the highly monastic Gelukpa Order (founded 1409), the spiritual descendents of the Kadampa, grew in confidence and wealth from its Lhasa center. Key Gelukpa luminaries, such as Changsems Sherab Zangpo (Byang-sems Shes-rabs bZang-po, hereafter Changsems), a disciple of Tsongkhapa himself, restored many decaying Kadampa establishments in Ladakh during the mid-1400s and "brought over" several Kagyudpa establishments to Gelukpa control. As Gelukpa power burgeoned during the following two centuries, Ladakhi royalty increasingly sided with the Kagyudpa, sponsoring large, politically powerful Drigung ('Bri-gung) and Drukpa monasteries.

In 1680, amid accusations that Gelukpa monks were being persecuted in Ladakh, the Fifth Dalai Lama (1617–1681) sent in Mongol forces to rout the king and centralize Ladakh's monastic

Tikse Monastery, Ladakh, India.
Photo courtesy of John Powers

structure under Tibetan administration. With the help of the Kashmir Moghuls, Ladakhi King Tsewang Namgyal (Tshedbang rNam-rgyal) repulsed the invaders, but the war's long-term impact on monasticism was huge. Tibetan reforms placed all Buddhist monasteries under Gelukpa ascendancy, and existing Gelukpa monasteries in the area entered the control of Drepung ('Bras-spungs) monastic university and Gyutö (br-Gyud-Stod) Tantric College outside Lhasa.

The following two centuries saw both the further systematization of the Gelukpa under Ngari Rinpoche's (mNga'-ris Rinpo-che) ownership (see the following discussion) and the undermining of kingly authority in the region as it passed first into the control of the Maharajas of Jammu and then into the sphere of British (later independent) India.

With many monks traveling to central Tibet to train for fully ordained status, monasticism in Ladakh became increasingly dependent on its larger neighbor. This came to a halt following the Chinese invasion of Tibet in 1950: the disappearance of institutional Buddhism in the Chinese Cultural Revolution of the 1960s isolated Ladakh's monasteries from their wider ecclesiastical infrastructures. This was compounded by the political sensitivity of Ladakh itself, which since 1962 has hosted a huge

Indian military presence and has been the subject of substantial incursions by Chinese and Pakistan forces.

The opening of Ladakh to tourism, begun in 1975, has brought mixed blessings to its monasteries. Although many monastic festivals have become tourist circuses, the increased revenue from tourism and foreign patrons has allowed for the renovation of older shrines and the founding of new monastic establishments (most recently the Gelukpa nunnery at Lingshed). More important, the 1980s and 1990s have witnessed a reintegration of Ladakhi monasteries into the newly founded Tibetan refugee monasteries and monastic universities in South India.

*Monastic "Families" and Traditions in Ladakh*
The complex folds of Ladakh's political history have left permanent marks on the form of Buddhism practiced there. Today Buddhist monastic establishments of all sizes are scattered across the region, from village shrines with one or two caretaker-monks to large educational and ritual complexes of 150 or more. Although the four major orders of Tibetan Buddhism are represented in Ladakh, the region's political history has meant that monastic life is dominated by the Gelukpa and Kagyudpa orders.

Although theoretically independent in financial terms, most of the monasteries exist as part of complex "families" of principal and branch monasteries owned by lineages of reincarnating high lamas. One of the largest such families of monasteries belongs to the lineage of Ngari Rinpoche and includes the following monastic complexes:

Karsha Chamspaling (dKar-cha Byams-pa-gLing: 140 monks; f. by P'agspa Sherabs [Phags-pa Shes-Rabs], brought over to Gelukpa c. 1440 by Changsems). Branches: Karsha Dorje-Dzong (dKar-cha rDo-rje-rDzong: nunnery, 20 nuns) and Khagsar, Purang, and Phags-pa.

P'uktal (Phug-dar: 60 monks; f. by P'agspa Sherabs, brought over by Changsems). Branches: Mune Diskitling (Mu-ni bDe-Skyid-gLing: 15 monks; f. c.1440 by Changsems).

Stongde Marpaling (Stong-sde Mar-pa-gling: 60 monks; f. c. 1040 by Marpa, brought over to Gelukpa by Lama Gyaltsen Lundrup Palazangpo [bLa-ma rGyal-mtshan-pa kLu-'grub dPal-bZang-po]; branch of Karsha Chamspaling until the 1940s).

Lingshed Kumbum (gLing-shed sKu-'bum: 65 monks; f. c.1440 by Changsems). Branches: Lingshed nunnery (12 nuns; f. 1998 by geshe Ngawang Changchub [dGe-bShes Nga-dbang Byang-chub]); permanently manned shrine rooms (one or two caretaker monks) in villages of Nyeraks, Skyumpada, Yulchung, and Dibling.

Likir Galdan Thargyaling (kLu-dkyil dGe-ldan Thar-rGyas-gLing: 100 monks; f. 1065 by Lama Duwang Chosje [Dus-dbang Chos-rJe], brought over by Kedrupje's [mKhas-grub-rje] disciple, Lhawang Lodros Sangpud [Lha-dbang bLo-gros Sangs-phud]).

With the exception of Likir, all these monasteries appear to have passed into the ownership of the Ngari Rinpoche lineage as a gift from the Ladakhi King Tsewang Namgyal (Tshe-dbang rNam-rGyal) to the Eighth Ngari Rinpoche in 1779. Following this, Rangdum Shadrup Dzamlingyan (Rang-lDum Sha-grup Dzam-gling-rgyan monastery: 40 monks) was built in 1783 to act as regional seat of the Ngari Rinpoche lineage and as "mother monastery" (ma-dgon) to the others, a symbolic position that it maintains today.

Largely because of the region's political history, such families of monastic institutions are found mainly among the Gelukpa and bKa'rgyud-pa orders in Ladakh. By owning incarnate lineage, these include the following:

Gelukpa

*Under Bakula Rinpoche*
Principal monastery: Spituk (dPe-thub:100 to 140 monks; f. by Kadampa, transformed into Gelukpa by Lama Lhawang Lo-

dros). Branches: Sankar, Stok Gurphug, and Sabu Tashi Gepel (Sa-phud bkra-shis dGe-phel).

*Under Khanpo Rinpoche*
Principal monastery: Tikse (Khrig-se: 80 monks; f. 1447 by Paldan Sherab [dPal-ldan Shes-rabs, Changsems' nephew]). Branches: Diskit (bDe-skyid: 100 monks, f. 1420 by Changsems).

*Under Lama Tsultrim Nyima (Tshul-Khrims Nyi-ma) and Sras Rinpoche*
Principal monastery: Rizong (Ri-dzong: 40 monks; f. 1843 by incumbent lineages); attached nunnery: Chulichan (20 nuns); branch at Samstanling (50 monks; f. 1850 by Lama Tsultrim Nyima).

Kagyudpa Order

*Under Skyabje Toldan Rinpoche ('Bri-gung)*
Principal monastery: Phyang Tashi Choszang (Phyi-dbang bKra-bshis Chos-bZang: 70 monks; f. c. 1531 by Chos-rje Danma Kunga); donor: King Jamyang Namgyal ('Jam-yang rNam-rgyal). Branches: Lamayuru Yungdrung T'arpaling (f. by Rinchen Zangpo, brought over by Chosje Danma Kunga; donor: King Jamyang Namgyal), Shyang, Sara, and Sechukul.

*Under Stakna Tulku Rinpoche ('Brug-pa)*
Principal monastery: Stakna (Stag-sna: 30 monks; f. 1580 by Chosje Jamyang Palkar [Chos-rje 'Jam-yang dPal-dkar]; donor: King Jamyang Namgyal). Branches: Takrimo (sTag-ri-mo), Bardan (Bar-gDan), and Sani (Sa-ni).

*Under Staksan Raschen (Stag-san Ras-chen) Rinpoche (Drugpa)*
Principal monastery: Hemis (f. c.1630 by Stagsan Raschen; donor: King Sengge Namgyal [Seng-ge rNam-rgyal]). Branches: Chemre T'egchoggon (Chem-'dre Theg-mChog-dGon: 300 monks), Wanla, Mulbhek, and others.

The less influential Sakya (Sa-skya) are represented by Matho monastery (dMang-tro: 60 monks; f. 15th century by Lama Drukpa Dorje ['Brug-pa rDo-rje]; no sitting incarnate is present, but Loding Khan Rinpoche fills the post) and the Nyingmapa (rNying-ma-pa) by Taktok Padmalinggon monastery (Brag-Thog Padma-gling-dgon, f. by Tsewang Norbu [Tshe-dbang Nor-bu]), which has various associated hermitages.

Each family shares central religious traditions that, although not excluding any one element, emphasize certain aspects of monastic training more than others. For example, within the Gelukpa those monasteries belonging to the Ngari Rinpoche lineage emphasize Tantric training and ritual (including large-scale exorcistic rites and masked dances), whereas those belonging to the Lama Tsultrim Nyima and Sras Rin-po-che lineages concentrate on the perfection of monastic discipline.

MARTIN A. MILLS

*See also* Gampopa; Liturgy: Buddhist; Milarepa; Tibet; Tibetan Lineages; Vajrayāna Buddhism in Nepal

**Further Reading**

Crook, J., and H. Osmaston, *Himalayan Buddhist Villages*, Bristol: University of Bristol Press, 1994
Snellgrove, D., and T. Skorupski, *The Cultural Heritage of Ladakh*, 2 vols., Warminster and Forest Grove, Oregon: Aris and Phillips, 1977–1980
Thub-bstan-dpal-ldan, Dge-slong, *A Brief Guide to the Buddhist Monasteries and Royal Castles of Ladakh*, Nanjangud: Kapila Power Press, 1976

# Laicization of Spirituality: Buddhist Perspectives

According to Theravāda Buddhism, monks are indispensable; they are necessary as a proof that the Buddha's teachings (Dharma) are valid and realizable. Lax behavior on the monks' parts will invariably mean that the religion itself is in decline. In fact the Buddha predicted that Buddhism would last for 5,000 years, and toward the end of that period monks would become so lax in their spiritual quest that they would have to put a small piece of yellow cloth around their necks to signify that they are still "monks"; in all other aspects, however, they would be no different from a layperson. And when no monks remain, neither will Buddhism.

The highest level of spiritual attainment in Buddhism, that of *arahant*, is not possible for a layperson. The religion lays out a detailed plan of spiritual development, starting from the ordinary person, who is still mired in the web of births and rebirths. Then the first step of spiritual attainment is the *Sotāpanna*, followed by the *Sakadāgāmī*, the *Anāgāmī*, and finally the *Arahant*. The *Sotāpanna* (one who has entered the stream) is one who understands the basic tenets of the Dharma but still has a number of defilements (*kilēsa*) and as a result will return in no more than seven future lives, including human ones. Then he or she will eventually attain *nibbāna*. The *Sakadāgāmī* (one who returns only once), like the *Sotāpanna*, will return in human form but will endure fewer lifetimes before attaining *nibbāna*. The *Anāgāmī* (one who will not return) will be reborn only once in heaven and will attain *nibbāna* there. The *Arahant* is one who has extinguished all desires and will not be reborn anywhere. As one who has completely extinguished all desires and defilements, the *Arahant* will loathe and despise the lay life (assuming that he or she is still a layperson at the time of attainment) so much that he or she has to become a monk immediately. However, it is possible for one who has attained the first three levels to remain a layperson, even though it becomes progressively more difficult as one advances up the spiritual ladder.

Nevertheless, this does not mean that the laypeople have no role to play. On the contrary they are very important and indeed necessary to the religion, for it is they who care for the monks' material needs so that they can continue their spiritual effort and demonstrate that the Dharma is relevant and valid. Monks are there to show the world that it is possible to go against the prevalent tendency to reify, to grab hold and to keep things intact. All these recourses maintain the cycle of births and rebirths, together with endless sufferings. Monks are supposed to de-reify, to let go and to take apart; in other words they provide living examples to laypeople that the way toward *nibbāna* is indeed possible. Laypeople are supposed to emulate the behavior of the monks so that they too can be released from saṃsāra (the cycle of rebirths) in their future lives. Services that they provide for the monks are meritorious and will help them attain the highest ideal more easily. Thus, monks and laypeople exist in symbiosis. Without the laypeople monks will not survive because they are forbidden by the Vinaya (rules prescribing the monks' behavior) to till the land or to engage in business of any kind. Laypeople in turn benefit from the monks' teachings and exemplary behaviors.

Laicization of spirituality is more problematic for Theravāda Buddhism than for Mahāyāna Buddhism. The former emphasizes individual discipline and spiritual attainment through following the Buddha's guidelines. According to Theravāda Buddhism the individual is solely responsible for his or her own spiritual attainment. The Buddha is only a teacher, a guide who shows the Way to beings, and it is up to the beings themselves to take up the arduous journey toward liberation. On the other hand, Mahāyāna Buddhism believes in a pantheon of bodhisattvas who aim to carry all the sentient beings across saṃsāra toward liberation. Thus, it is quite understandable that attempts to laicize spirituality should come more from the Mahāyāna side. If salvation is possible through help of the bodhisattvas, then it is not absolutely necessary to become a monk or a nun to achieve at least some level of attainment. Because the *arahant* ideal is given much less weight in Mahāyāna, the notion that one must become a monk simply to liberate oneself from saṃsāra is discounted. The ideal in becoming a monk is rather to become a bodhisattva and to help other beings. These are quite different ideals, and because one bodhisattva can help countless beings, it follows that the laity can achieve spiritual attainment more easily through the help of a bodhisattva than by becoming one.

However, many attempts have been made in Theravāda cultures to laicize spirituality to some extent, especially in recent years. The demands of modern life have made it almost impossible for the majority of Buddhists in Thailand to renounce their livelihood and take up the saffron robe, even for a short period. Thus, many temples now serve a growing number of Buddhists who have only a little time to spend but want to practice the Dharma closely. Many offer short retreats for a few days or weeks, and the practitioners are taught meditation by monks. Such retreats have become popular among those who would like to get away from the hectic life of the city for a while and to understand the Dharma fully. To signify their seriousness the practitioners usually must wear white robes and follow precepts close to those of the monks. For example, no eating is allowed after 12 noon each day. However, one can see that this is more a case of spiritualization of the laity than of laicization of the monastics.

SORAJ HONGLADAROM

*See also* Discourses (Sūtras): Mahāyāna; Prayer: Buddhist Perspectives; Pure Land Buddhism; Shinran; Spirituality: Buddhist

## Further Reading

*Buddhism in Thai Life*, Bangkok: National Identity Board, Prime Minister's Office, 1981

Lester, Robert C., *Theravada Buddhism in Southeast Asia*, Ann Arbor: University of Michigan Press, 1973

Na Rangsri, Sunthorn, *Putthapratyaa Chaak Phra Traipidok* (Buddhist Philosophy from the Tripiṭaka), Bangkok: Chulalongkorn University Press, 1998

Piker, Steven, *Buddhism and Modernization in Contemporary Thailand*, Leiden: Brill, 1973

Smith, Bardwell I., editor, *Religion and Legitimation of Power in Thailand, Laos, and Burma*, Chambersburg, Pennsylvania: ANIMA Books, 1978

Spiro, Melford E., *Buddhism and Society: A Great Tradition and Its Burmese Vicissitudes*, New York: Harper and Row, 1970; London: Allen and Unwin, 1971

Swearer, Donald, *Buddhism and Society in Southeast Asia*, Chambersburg, Pennsylvania: ANIMA Books, 1981

Tambiah, Stanley Jeyaraja, *World Conqueror and World Renouncer: A Study of Buddhism and Polity in Thailand Against a Historical Background*, Cambridge and New York: Cambridge University Press, 1976

Tambiah, Stanley Jeyaraja, *The Buddhist Saints of the Forest and the Cult of Amulets*, Cambridge and New York: Cambridge University Press, 1984

Wijayaratna, Mohan, *Buddhist Monastic Life: According to the Texts of the Theravada Tradition*, translated by Claude Grangier and Steven Collins, Cambridge and New York: Cambridge University Press, 1990

# Laicization of Spirituality: Christian Perspectives

In Buddhism, at least in the Theravāda tradition, those alone who have in this life taken a vow to "enter the Path" leading directly to nirvāṇa can hope to enter nirvāṇa at death. Others committed to Buddhism can expect to arrive at this final stage of freedom from the Wheel of Karma only in some future reincarnation. By way of contrast the Christian Gospel promises that all those who have taken the vows of baptism can hope to achieve the goal of their spiritual journey in a single lifetime. It is true that in Roman Catholicism this entry into the vision of God might take place not immediately at death but only after a period of purification (Purgatory), but those who die in the Lord are certain to pass through this purification to God prior to the Resurrection and Last Judgment. It follows also that those who die having rejected God's mercy have no further hope but, like the fallen angels, of their own free will have forever excluded themselves from God.

In the third century A.D., the great scholar Origen (c. 185–c. 254) speculated whether the notion of reincarnation might be assimilated into Christian doctrine, but this possibility was immediately and definitively rejected by the Church as incompatible with the doctrine of Resurrection. In certain Gnostic, Manichaean, and Albigensian heresies, it was maintained that only a group of "the perfect" can achieve holiness, whereas others of the sect must rely on the prayers of the perfect for salvation. This view was also rejected by the Catholic Church, although it did not disappear from popular belief.

However, in Roman Catholic Christianity there cannot be two essentially different types of spirituality. All the baptized are called to holiness, and all who remain true to their baptism at death or in Purgatory will achieve total holiness, although of different degrees, according to a person's degree of love of God at death. This Catholic doctrine is based on the command of Jesus in the Sermon on the Mount: "Be perfect as your heavenly Father is perfect." It is believed that he would not have given such a command without also offering the grace for all his disciples to fulfill it. Yet in the 17th century, to correct an exaggerated interest in mysticism then current, Alfonso Rodriguez, S.J. (1538–1616), proposed a distinction between an "ordinary way" of spirituality based on "active contemplation" and an "extraordinary way," to which only a few are called on the basis of "infused contemplation." Although for long widely accepted, this distinction is now largely abandoned, after being effectively refuted by Juan Arintero, O.P., and Réginald Garrigou-Lagrange, O.P. (1877–1964), who argued that "infused contemplation" is simply Christian faith operating at its fullness under the influence of the gifts of the Holy Spirit. Because these gifts are given to all Christians, all the baptized receive a general call to infused contemplation, although not all may actually progress in this life to the point of receiving a call to open themselves to this gift. However, further discussion of this subject has led to certain qualifications. For example, Garrigou-Lagrange noted that, as is evident in the biographies of some saints, those living the active life might sometimes achieve a higher degree of charity than those in the contemplative life and thus be at a higher degree of holiness. Yet their actual enjoyment of infused contemplation might be delayed by the circumstances of their charitable activities. Thus, they might not arrive at the fullness of infused contemplation until late in life, when they are freer for prayer. Moreover in some souls this form of contemplation might take more hidden forms than in others. Consequently spiritual directors should not conclude that those whose prayer remains merely active are spiritually retarded through some habit of sin.

Furthermore one should not without qualification accept the common view that distinguishes the Christian life of observance of the Ten Commandments from the more perfect life of the counsels. This was a questionable interpretation of the Gospel narrative (Mark 10:17–31; Matt. 19:16–30; Luke 18:18–30) in which Jesus tells the young man who has observed the Commandments that he ought also to "go and sell what you possess, give to the poor, and come follow me." In this view the "counsels" are taken to be celibacy, poverty, and obedience, which are vowed in the consecrated life of religious. However, these are merely means to better observance of the Commandments and are not appropriate for Christians in every vocation or circumstance. Rather all Christians alike are called to keep the Commandments and to grow in the faith, hope, and charity that comprise Christian holiness. Yet people might adopt different means to this growth, the counsels being preeminent, but their use remains a matter of free choice according to a person's individual vocation.

Thus, it would be entirely wrong to suppose that the consecrated life of the monastic or other forms of religious life are invested with a higher form of spirituality than the life of marriage or single life in the world. For all Roman Catholic Christians, spirituality means principally growth in the theological virtues of faith, hope, and love of God and neighbor and in the moral virtues that support them. Even the highest mystical prayer, we are told by St. John of the Cross (1542–1591), the great spiritual Doctor of the Church, are nothing but intense acts of faith, hope, and love. Other extraordinary phenomena, such as visions, revelations, the stigmata, and the working of miracles, do not of themselves constitute holiness but are given by God either to encourage the Christian to greater trust in God or to manifest the beauty and meaning of the Christian life to others. This deifying union (*theosis*) effected by these theological virtues is identical in earthly as in heavenly life, except that the union of faith is veiled, whereas the union of vision is face to face in the light of God. Whether on earth or in heaven, it is an immediate person-to-person union between the creature and its Creator.

Thus, the fundamental elements of spirituality must be the same for all Roman Catholic Christians, whether clerical, vowed, or lay. Yet life in the world that is proper to the laity as such presents specific problems that require appropriate modes of this fundamental spirituality. The Second Vatican Council (1962–1965), both in its *Dogmatic Constitution on the Church* (*Lumen Gentium*, 1964, chap. V) and more specifically in its *Decree on the Apostolate of Lay People* (*Apostolicam actuositatem*, 1965), explained the basis for such an authentic lay spirituality for Roman Catholics. After consultation with the entire episcopate, this was further formulated in the *Catechism of the Catholic Church*, issued by Pope John Paul II in 1994. These documents emphasize that the basis of a sound spirituality for those whose vocation is to a life in the world is first of all a deep respect for and understanding of the graces of their baptism. This also includes a profound appreciation of the graces of the sacrament of Confirmation and of Christian community in the Eucharist and for most laypersons the sacrament of Matrimony as well as of the sacraments of Reconciliation and Anointing of the Sick for their purification from sin. To be received fruitfully, these sacraments must be acts of Christian faith in response to the proclamation of the Gospel. Thus, they constitute both the celebration of the gifts of grace and their source for further growth in holiness. The laity, whose lives are not shaped by monastic rules but by the shifting requirements of domesticity and work that often leave little room even for prayer, are often tempted to use the sacraments only irregularly and prepare for them carelessly. Thus, they must develop a praxis of regular reception of the sacraments and communal worship. They must be vividly aware of the doctrine of the Communion of the Saints and the reality of the Church as the Body of Christ, in which all members are concerned for one another. A merely private, individualistic piety cannot be authentically Roman Catholic.

A second feature of lay spirituality must be learning to pray not only vocally but meditatively at times and in a manner compatible with one's occupations in the world. Although many techniques of prayer exist (and here something can be learned from non-Christian spiritualities), it is essential to understand that the goal of prayer is not some "experience" or "altered state of consciousness." It is the deifying union with God in the only way possible in this life, that is, in acts of faith, hope, and love. First, prayer must be a petition to God for an increase of his better gifts already given, through which we are able to come before him. Then prayer is thanksgiving for these gifts and praise of God not only for the divine generosity but also for the community of the Triune God itself in infinite power, truth, and love. Laypersons who take time in their busy lives for meditation thus come to know God as the source of all the good that they do each day in any activity, however humble or mundane that activity might be.

However, the spirituality of the laity does not render the tradition of monastic spirituality useless. In the Roman Catholic Church, the clergy and religious are at the service of the whole People of God in the building up of the Body of Christ (Eph. 2:19–22). Thomas Aquinas (c. 1225–1274) says that for contemplatives the rule should be *contemplare, et contemplata aliis tradere*, that is, "to contemplate in order to share with others what one has contemplated." Thus, through the ages a monastery has been and should continue to be a center of spiritual inspiration and renewal. Yet the laity ought to support monastic life and share with monks and nuns not only the problems but also the insights of the Holy Spirit in their own lives. For all Christians Christ remains the model to be imitated and the source of grace by which to be transformed into his image. Yet perhaps the recent development, mainly under the influence of liberation theology, of "basic communities" might in the future perform some of the animating functions exercised in the past by monasteries but will themselves still require centers of contemplative life. That monasteries can also serve ecumenism has been demonstrated in recent years, notably by the Taizé community. In so enormous a community as the Roman Catholic Church, centers of more intense communal and contemplative life serve to raise the level of participation by the laity as a whole.

BENEDICT M. ASHLEY, O.P.

*See also* Critiques of Western Christian Monasticism; Gnostic Cosmogony in Buddhism; Heretics, Christian; John of the Cross, St.; Thomas Aquinas, St.

## Further Reading
*Called and Gifted for the Third Millenium: Reflection of the U. S. Catholic Bishops on the Thirtieth Anniversary of the*

*Decree on the Apostolate of the Laity*, Washington, D.C.: United States Catholic Conference, 1999

Congar, Yves, *Lay People in the Church: A Study for a Theology of Laity*, 2nd edition, Westminster, Maryland: Newman Press, and London: Chapman, 1965 (a basic theological treatment)

Dean, Eric, *St. Benedict for the Laity*, Collegeville, Minnesota: Liturgical Press, 1989

Francis de Sales, Saint, *Introduction to the Devout Life*, edited by John Ryan, Garden City, New York: Doubleday Image Books, 1972 (a classic work on lay spirituality)

Morin, Douglas J., *No Less Zeal: A Spiritual Guide for Catholic Lay People*, Staten Island, New York: Alba House, 1993

Muto, Susan, and Adrian Van Kamm, *Commitment: Key to Christian Maturity*, New York: Paulist Press, 1989

Osborne, Kenan, *Ministry: Lay Ministry in the Roman Catholic Church, Its History and Theology*, New York: Paulist Press, 1993

Shaw, Russell, *Understanding Your Rights: Your Rights and Responsibilities in the Church*, Ann Arbor, Michigan: Servant, 1994

Vauchez, André, and Daniel E. Bornstein, editors, *The Laity in the Middle Ages: Religious Beliefs and Devotional Practices*, Notre Dame, Indiana: Notre Dame University Press, 1997

Wuthnow, Robert, *After Heaven: Spirituality in America since the 1950s*, Berkeley: University of California Press, 1998

# Lanfranc c. 1005–1089

First Norman archbishop of Canterbury, biblical scholar, and teacher

Lanfranc was born in Pavia, Lombardy, sometime around 1005. After a career in law at Pavia, he left Italy around 1030; from 1030 until 1039, when he became a teacher in Avranches, little is known of his life. Shortly thereafter he entered the monastery of Bec, Normandy. According to the *Vita Lanfranci*, his conversion came after an attack by bandits in which he vowed that if he escaped he would become a monastic. He apparently felt that life at Bec was not strict enough and resolved to leave and become a hermit. Abbot Herluin learned of his plan and persuaded him to stay.

Lanfranc served as prior of Bec from 1045 to 1063, developing a school there that became famous and won the patronage of many wealthy laymen. He was the teacher of Anselm (1033–1109), Ivo of Chartres (c. 1040–1115), the future Pope Alexander II (1061–1073), and several bishops and archbishops. He was highly skilled in the arts of the trivium and known for his efforts to correct biblical texts; as archbishop of Canterbury, he ensured that monastic churches possessed corrected texts of the Bible, which were still in use 100 years later. His biblical commentaries on the Pauline Epistles were influential in the schools of Laon and Paris and were still being copied a century after. His skills were amply demonstrated in the debate with Berengar of Tours (1010–1080), who denied the doctrine of the transubstan-

tiation. Lanfranc's *Liber de corpore et sanguine Domini* was noteworthy for its summary of patristic thought on the Eucharist, and it laid the groundwork for the modern understanding of the doctrine of transubstantiation.

Lanfranc became an adviser to Duke William of Normandy, who in 1063 appointed him abbot of St. Étienne in Caen. Here he educated, among others, the relatives of Pope Alexander II. The Norman Conquest in 1066 eventually brought Lanfranc to England. After a church council removed Stigand as archbishop of Canterbury in 1070, William invested his trusted adviser Lanfranc as the new archbishop. He received the pallium in 1071 from his former pupil Alexander II in Rome. He reorganized the English Church and established the primacy of Canterbury. Through his relationship as spiritual adviser to Queen Margaret of Scotland, he also helped reform the Church of Scotland and extended the influence of William and of Canterbury to Scotland.

Lanfranc was the single greatest influence on English monasticism from 1070 until his death in 1089. He drew many abbots from Bec and Caen; at the time of his death, the abbots of every important monastery were Normans. Under Lanfranc the number of monasteries grew by fifty percent, and monasticism was reformed according to the Norman model. Through his nephew Paul, abbot of St. Albans, he influenced the rebuilding of St. Albans, and his constitutions were imposed on the community. His constitutions were later also used at Croyland and Durham, influenced those of Westminster, and even had an influence in Norway. Although Lanfranc was not a strong supporter of monastic exemptions from diocesan control, he supported Bury St. Edmunds in the dispute with Herfast of Thetford and Ely in its dispute over land and rights with the bishop of Lincoln. As king's justice he played an important role in the monastic affairs of East Anglia and assisted in the recovery of monastic rights and property for the abbey of Ramsey. Lanfranc fought to preserve monastic chapters in the Cathedral churches. He obtained papal approval for the perpetual monastic status of the monks of Christ Church, Canterbury. He also encouraged Gundulf, former prior of St. Etienne, to establish monks as opposed to canons at Rochester.

Under Lanfranc new vocations to the monastic life almost doubled, and consequently many new building projects were begun. After a disastrous fire in 1067, he also rebuilt the church at Canterbury, constructed the monastic buildings, and surrounded the entire complex with a wall. Several other monasteries greatly expanded their buildings. Lanfranc continued to influence monastic learning in England. He brought Ernulf of St. Symphorien as schoolmaster at Canterbury, who built a monastic library and instilled French learning as opposed to the Anglo-Saxon traditions.

Lanfranc was renowned for his kindness and loving nature. No other archbishop but Dunstan (c. 909–988) exerted as important an effect on English monasticism, and when Lanfranc died in 1089, like Dunstan he was buried before the crucifix in Canterbury.

DEBORAH VESS

*See also* Anselm, St.; Cathedral Priories (England); England: History; France: History; Reform, Tenth-Century Anglo-Saxon Monastic

## Biography

Born in Pavia, the Lombard traveled to northern France, where in 1042 he entered the abbey of Bec. He became prior in 1045 and in 1063 abbot of William I's new monastery of St. Stephen in Caen. From 1070 to his death in 1089 he served as the first Norman Archbishop of Canterbury. His pupil and successor St. Anselm (c. 1033–1109) followed a remarkably similar career path from Lombardy via Bec to Canterbury. The two of them must be considered the Italians who most deeply influenced religious life in England.

## Major Works

*De corpore et sanguine Domini* (On the Body and Blood of Christ), 1060s

*The Monastic Constitutions of Lanfranc*, edited and translated by David Knowles, 1951

Biblical commentary

## Further Reading

Eadmer, *Eadmeri Historia Novorum in Anglia, et opuscula duo de vita Sancti Anselmi et quibusdam miraculis ejus* (Chronicles and Memorials of Great Britain and Ireland during the Middle Ages, number 81), London: Longmans, 1884

Gibson, Margaret, *Lanfranc of Bec*, Oxford: Clarendon Press, 1978

Knowles, David, *The Monastic Order in England: A History of Its Development from the Times of St. Dunstan to the Fourth Lateran Council, 943–1216*, Cambridge: Cambridge University Press, 1940; 2nd edition, Cambridge: Cambridge University Press, 1963; New York: Cambridge University Press, 1976

Knowles, David, *Saints and Scholars: Twenty-Five Medieval Portraits*, Cambridge: Cambridge University Press, 1962; Westport, Connecticut: Greenwood Press, 1988

Knowles, David, Christopher Nugent Brooke, and Vera C.M. London, *The Heads of Religious Houses, England and Wales: 940–1216*, Cambridge: Cambridge University Press, 1972

*Vita Lanfranci*, in *Patrologiae cursus completus. Series Latina*, volume 150, by J.P. Migne, Paris, 1844

William of Malmesbury, *Willelmi Malmesbiriensis monachi Gesta Regum Anglorum, atque Historia novella* (English Historical Society Publications), London: Sumptibus Societatis, 1840

William of Malmesbury, *Gesta Pontificum* (Rolls Series), London, 1870

# Latin America

## Overview

This topic is often neglected in the history of monasticism in part because monastic establishments in Latin America went from being centers of evangelization during the colonial period to marginal institutions in the independent secular states of Latin America. Furthermore the forms of spirituality most characteristic of Latin America thrived outside the monastic setting. There is also a persistent assumption that Latin American monasticism – outside the European metropol and the cultural influence of the elites – could not foster the quality of religious life worthy of histories of spirituality. Finally there is a persistent assumption that Latin America is a single cultural block and furthermore only an extension of Spanish (perhaps Portuguese!) traditions of spirituality.

Latin American monasticism is thus trapped by presuppositions that consider its colonial role as suspect and that at the same time discount the possibility of spirituality in the "hybrid" cultures of an empire's periphery. The assumption is that the goal of the monastic orders is a life of the mind and the spirit and that, therefore, intense sociopolitical involvement is tainted. Thus, the efforts of those working on the periphery were dismissed as unlikely to reach the heights of the metropol's learned monasteries.

### The Meeting of "Three" Cultures

The study of monasticism in Latin America in fact offers unique insights into unspoken values of class and culture, as well as of spiritual life, that often accompany the ideals of monasticism. During the 16th and 17th centuries, Latin American monasticism served – as it had earlier in Europe – as an agent of inculturation. Although it never attained the scholarly productivity of European monasticism during the late Middle Ages, Latin American monasticism often stimulated individual creativity and divergent or dissident voices. Thus, it served as a vehicle for the expression of a nonconformist and creative spirit in a sociopolitical environment that repeatedly stifled movements toward greater cultural openness. Moreover monasticism could play a dual role: as a vehicle for the imposition of European values and as a site for the development of creole awareness.

Even in its sociopolitical role as instrument of inculturation, Latin American monasticism served to modulate and at times soften the brutality of imperial conquest, especially by advocating more humane laws for the treatment of Native American populations and subsequently of African slaves. Monasticism thus engaged both sides in a turbulent encounter of two disparate forces: on the one hand the literate systems of powerful military and economic forces controlled by an elite of European descent and on the other the oral remnants of the traditions and values of populations that had been displaced, decimated, or marginalized.

### Colonial Monastic Establishments and Traditions

In most of Latin America, the process of evangelization was in the hands of the Dominican and Franciscan orders, with some contributions from the Augustinians and later the Jesuits (although the latter was not a monastic movement). The major intellectual impetus behind the Spanish Inquisition in Latin America came from Dominicans, who ironically took the lead in shielding Native Americans – their spirituality and their

Cloister of Augustinian convent at Yuriria, Guanajuato, Mexico,
16th century.
Photo courtesy of Chris Schabel

"magical" practices – from the rules of the Inquisition. Indeed the first discussions of God-given human rights in Spanish came from the pens of Dominicans in Salamanca and the Americas. The Dominican Fray Bartolomé de las Casas (1474–1566) traveled between the New and the Old Worlds in a desperate attempt to preserve the dignity of Spain's Native American subjects. At the University of Salamanca, Spain's great center of learning, Fray Francisco de Vitoria (c. 1486–1546) formulated a doctrine of human rights. Although of Christian inspiration it was motivated in part by the double shock of having to confront the cruelty of the Christians and the radical otherness of the diverse American populations.

However, these efforts did not weaken the essentially European character of monasticism in Latin America. As schools of European Christian values and language, the monasteries tended to avoid (and to fear) the cultural "miscegenation" that gradually produced a native Latin American culture and spirituality. The Janus-faced role of defender of European interests and edu-

cator of Native Americans and Africans led to relationships that are troubling from our perspective on social justice. For example, silver mined by Indians in Peru went to Spain to support the foundation of Teresa of Avila's nunneries (for which she was most grateful in her correspondence).

### The Traditions of Spirituality

Arguably spirituality, broadly understood as an inner quest for religious meaning, thrived best at the interface between the Christian and the Native American (and subsequently the African) views of the world – of divinity, of humanity, and of ritual links between the human and the divine. Nevertheless the monastery retained in the Americas a role similar to the one it held in Europe: a safe haven for the pursuit of individual and communal spirituality. This aspect of monasticism is embodied in a number of distinguished figures in the history of Latin American Christian spirituality.

This tradition found its earliest representative in Rosa de Lima (1586–1617), the first person of American birth to be canonized by the Roman Catholic Church (1617). Born Isabel de Flores, Rosa was canonized on the year of her death as the patron saint of Peru and of all South America. She epitomizes the pivotal role of women in the development of spirituality in the new continent but also embodies some of the motifs common in post-Reformation monastic mysticism: the visionary tradition, the cultivation of miracles, and the ideals of monastic purity.

To the same period belongs Martín de Porres (1579–1639), the Catholic Church's first saint "of color." He became a Dominican oblate (lay monastic) at Lima in 1610. His life is held up as an example of kindness and obedience. He tended the sick and established one of the first schools for Peruvians of non-European descent. Significantly, although he was beatified in 1837, he was not canonized until 1962 (under Pope John XXIII). Martín de Porres stands paradoxically at the tense interface between the ideals of the empire and the idealization of creole cultures. He epitomizes, as the word "creole" (little servant) suggests, the identification of spiritual humility with the subaltern citizen of the colonies. Poor, and the child of racial "mixture" (he was a mulatto, the illegitimate child of a Spanish grandee and a free black woman), Martín de Porres remained essentially a servant to the friars who enjoyed full ordination. And yet his position of poverty was soon idealized, in part by a popular devotion that understood his subservient role as the embodiment of monastic poverty, simplicity, and obedience. Needless to say his standing as a representative of these moral ideals in no way precluded major roles as performer of miracles and mystic visionary – his humility and racial background may even have enhanced these attributes.

Of course a monastic spirituality in the European mode was also open to native Latin Americans. Emblematic of this possibility is Teresa de los Andes (born Juanita Fernández Solar, 1860–1930), who was also canonized as a saint. She represents the tradition of Carmelite spirituality that developed in many parts of Spanish Latin America (including the poorer Caribbean

Dominican convent, Cusco, Peru, incorporating walls from the Inca Temple of the Sun, 17th century.
Photo courtesy of Chris Schabel

colonies of Cuba and Puerto Rico). Teresa de los Andes arguably embodies a truly native South American Catholic spirituality, especially the kind that developed at the turn of the 20th century in her native Chile, yet her style and doctrine reflect influences from contemporary Spanish and French spirituality.

A different dimension of the American adaptation of Christian spiritualities emerges in the figure of Mexico's Juana Inés de la Cruz (born Juana Inés de Asbaje, 1651–1695). She represents the monastery's role as a place of both learning and rebellion. One of Mexico's great lyric poets of the colonial period, she was a child prodigy and a distinguished scholar of theology, Latin, and Nahuatl (the Native American language of Mexico's central valley). She was one of the first female and feminist intellectual voices of Latin America. Although she distinguished herself at the viceroy's court and in various theological disputations, she eventually retired to become a recluse, pursuing her own spiritual quest and tending the sick and the poor.

## The Present and the Future

Latin American religion seems headed toward a cacophony of religious plurality, greater secularism, and increasing creolization. The future of monasticism in this context is uncertain. During the second half of the 20th century, religion in Latin America continued to play a major role as a force for cultural adaptation in two directions: the spread of European (and of North American) values and the revival, conservation, or adaptation of local values. These dual functions have played out on the stage of geopolitical conflict during the leftist revolutions that emerged and eventually collapsed throughout Latin America. Yet notable during this period was the absence of a major role for the monastery. The period of its central role in Latin American culture is past.

Nevertheless the ideals of the recluse as inspired religious voice and as the voice of justice for the oppressed resurfaced in the figure of Ernesto Cardenal (1925– ). Ordained as a Benedictine monk, he became Nicaragua's poet and hermit priest-prophet who spoke against the evils of commercialism and capitalism. His attempts at mystical and poetical solitude ended with his conversion to liberation theology and socialist ideals, which led to his becoming first spiritual inspirator of revolution and then minister of culture for the Sandinista government (1979–1990). In the end he quietly accepted the Pope's 1985 ruling suspending him from his priestly functions *a divinis*.

## Summary

The study of monasticism in Latin America offers an ideal opportunity to explore a number of crucial issues regarding the interface between spiritual ideals and historical realities. First, the history of this phase of Catholic monasticism exemplifies the connection between literate religion and the relationships that exist between metropolitan centers and imperial metropols to colonies, the periphery, and subaltern societies. Second, the study of these phenomena problematizes our perception of Latin America as a simple extension of a vaguely defined "Iberian" culture. Third, Latin American monasticism raises questions regarding our tendency to confuse political marginality (so-called backwaters of history) with spiritual slumber. Spiritual aspiration is not thwarted by isolation from centers of cultural power or by oppression, exploitation, neglect, poverty, or civil war. In places far from the great centers of learning, human beings have pursued the spiritual quest in ways that spiritually are of the same stuff as in the great historical centers that produced the most influential scholarship and monastic codes.

Luis O. Gómez

*See also* Carmelites: Female; Dominicans: General or Male; Franciscans: General or Male; Mercedarians; Peter of Alcántara, St.; Portugal; Spain: History; Spirituality: Western Christian; Teresa of Avila, St.

## Further Reading

The vast majority of the sources available on this topic are not in English. There is no general history focusing on traditions of spirituality in Latin American monasticism, much less a study of the interaction between the monastery and nonorthodox forms of popular spirituality.

Barrios Valdés, Marciano, *La espiritualidad chilena en tiempos de Santa Teresa de los Andes: 1860–1930* (Colección Encarnación, 10), Santiago de Chile: San Pablo, 1994

Borges Morán, Pedro, *Religiosos en Hispanoamérica* (Colecciones MAPFRE 1492. Colección Iglesia católica en el Nuevo Mundo), Madrid: Editorial MAPFRE, 1992

Bruno, Cayetano, *Las órdenes religiosas en la evangelización de las Indias* (Colección 500 años, 10), Rosario, Santa Fe, Argentina: Ediciones "Didascalia," 1992

Cardenal, Ernesto, *The Doubtful Strait = El estrecho dudoso*, Bloomington: Indiana University Press, 1995

Cavallini, Giuliana, *St. Martin de Porres: Apostle of Charity* (Cross and Crown Series of Spirituality, number 26), St. Louis, Missouri: Herder Books, 1963; reissued, Rockford, Illinois: Tan Books, 1979

Dussel, Enrique, *A History of the Church in Latin America: Colonialism to Liberation (1492–1979)*, translated and revised by Alan Neely, Grand Rapids, Michigan: Eerdmans, 1981

Dussel, Enrique, *Historia general de la Iglesia en América Latina, Tomo I.1: Introducción general a la historia de la Iglesia en América Latina* (El peso de los días, 10), Salamanca: Ediciones Sígeme, 1983

Flores Araoz, José, et al., *Santa Rosa de Lima y su tiempo* (Colección Arte y tesoros del Perú), Lima: Banco de Crédito del Perú, 1995

García-Rivera, Alex, *St. Martín de Porres: The "Little Stories" and the Semiotics of Culture* (Faith and Cultures Series), foreword by Virgil Elizondo, introduction by Robert J. Schreiter, Maryknoll, New York: Orbis Books, 1995

Gil de Muro, Eduardo Teófilo, *Cada vez que mire el mar: Una biografía de Teresa de Los Andes: Juanita Fernández Solar*, Santiago, Chile: Carmelo Teresiano, 1992

León Portilla, Miguel, *Los franciscanos vistos por el hombre náhuatl: Testimonios indígenas del siglo XVI* (Serie de cultura náhuatl. Monografias; number 21), Mexico: Universidad Nacional Autónoma de México, 1985

Merrim, Stephanie, editor, *Feminist Perspectives on Sor Juana Inés de la Cruz* (Latin American Literature and Culture Series), Detroit, Michigan: Wayne State University Press, 1991

Rowland, Christopher, editor, *The Cambridge Companion to Liberation Theology* (Cambridge Companions to Religion), Cambridge and New York: Cambridge University Press, 1999

Sievernich, Michael, *Conquista und Evangelisation: 500 Jahre Orden in Lateinamerika*, Mainz: Matthias-Grünewald-Verlag, 1992

# Lavra

The term *lavra* is used to designate that specific type of organization of a monastic community that can be viewed as a mean between the cell of the hermit and the monastery of the cenobite.

Before the word took on this technical designation, it indicated a city lane or an alley. Its usage in the monastic system might indicate the lane or path that each monk traversed from his individual cell to a central area where the monks met weekly, although the word has also been associated with the Arabic word *suq*, meaning "marketplace." In the 590s Evagrios Scholastikos (*Ecclesiastical History* I.21) defines a *lavra* as the place "where the dwelling place is distinct, but where the common life accomplishes a single goal – the love of God."

The *lavra* was a community of monks, under a single leader, who spent most of the week living in solitude in separate cells or in caves but who assembled once a week, normally on Saturday or Sunday, in a common central building complex that included a minimum of a church and a bakery and sometimes storage or service rooms. Infirmaries or hospices have been identified in the larger *lavra*s. Often the church was set apart from the other buildings to remove it from the commotion often attendant in the other buildings. The lack of evidence for any refectories suggests that meals were kept simple enough to be prepared in one of the service buildings. A subsequent modification of this system involved a full cenobium (monastery) in the central complex where younger monks resided and novices learned the monastic life until they were ready to go out and dwell in their own cells; the more advanced monks lived in the outerlying cells and came into the monastery complex each weekend. The entire area of such a complex ranged from about 10,000 to 1,200,000 square meters and accommodated up to 150 monks.

During the week the monks' daily regimen was taken up entirely with prayer and meditation, including various hours of prayer to which the entire community was called. The monks were located close enough to the center complex to hear the daily calls to prayer and close enough to one another to hear the community's collective voices raised in prayer. The monks spent most of the remaining parts of the day reciting Psalms, reading of the Bible, or engaged in private prayer, often while practicing some sort of simple manual craft, very often weaving straw mats or baskets or twining rope. The weekly gathering allowed the monks to celebrate the Liturgy of the Resurrection together and to collect new food supplies for the coming week.

The origin of the *lavra* is associated with Palestine, and the *lavra* served to distinguish Palestine from the more famous centers of Egypt and Syria. Although a number of sources witness to the history of this lifestyle, two stand out: the *Lives of the Monks of Palestine* by Cyril of Scythopolis (b. c. 525) and the *Pratum Spirituale* by John Moschus (c. 550–619 or 634). Although monastic life in both its cenobitic and its eremitic form flourished in Palestine from the early fourth century, four chronological periods in the history of the *lavra*s of Palestine can be distinguished: the beginnings in the fourth century; the period of expansion in the fifth century; the zenith, from the end of the fifth century into the seventh century; and the period of decline. In this early period it was Chariton who came to the Holy Land on pilgrimage and stayed and who is the traditional founder of three monasteries in Judaea, all of the *lavra* type: at Pharan in a cave where he had been held captive in a valley about five and a half miles northeast of Jerusalem, at Douka on the cliffs of Mount Quruntul overlooking Jericho from the west, and at Souka (this was also known as the Old Lavra) in a deep ravine northeast of the village of Tekoa.

Its subsequent growth owed much to the two great monks of Palestine: Euthymius (377–473) and Sabas (439–532). Euthymius fled his duties as head of the monks in the Diocese of Milytene and came to Jerusalem in 405, also as a pilgrim. He first established himself in the *lavra* of Pharan. He left this and, together with a fellow monk, Theoctistus, founded a number of other monasteries and *lavra*s, including the *lavra* on the cliff in Wadi Mukallik and another in the area of Mishor Adummim. The *lavra* system became centered around a monastery rather than a central church largely because of the efforts of Euthymius. He was followed in this by subsequent founders of *lavra*s, such as Gerasimus, John of Choziba, and Sabas. The period under the leadership of Euthymius was also notable for the great involvement of the Judaean monks in the Church establishment of Jerusalem. This very close relation between the two was of great mutual benefit, as steady financial assistance and support was in place for the monasteries while the monks rendered their aid and support to the orthodox patriarchs of Jerusalem against the anti-Chalcedonian party.

The height of Judaean monasticism was in the fifth and sixth centuries under the leadership of Theodosius (423–529) and Sabas, the father of Judaean monasticism. The two shared the duties of archimandrite over all the monks of Judaea, the first monks to hold this position: Theodosius for the cenobia and Sabas for the *lavra*s and the hermits. Sabas founded a *lavra* in the cliffs of the Kidron Valley near the cave in which he had been dwelling for several years. This was the beginnings of the so-called Great Lavra, which, because of Sabas, came to be the "chief of every *lavra* in Palestine." This *lavra* was located on the same cliffs on which the present-day monastery of Mar Saba is situated. Sabas is remembered for his expansion of the *lavra*s and his prolific building activity, setting up at least ten *lavra*s throughout the Judaean desert.

One remarkable characteristic of these Judaean *lavra*s was their international makeup. Nearly all of them seem to have been made up mainly of foreigners; very few inhabitants were native to Palestine. Of Euthymius' original 12 disciples, only one was from Palestine. Most of the monks in these *lavra*s came from districts of Asia Minor and from Armenia, Georgia, Cyprus, Greece, Italy, Mesopotamia, Syria, Arabia, and Egypt.

The decline of the *lavra*s was certainly hastened by the destruction wrought by the Persians during their invasions of the early seventh century. Only a few *lavra*s survived and then remained in existence until the early Middle Ages. Recent archaeological investigations have located the remains of 19 *lavra*s in the Judaean desert. Of these, ten were constructed on or near cliffs, whereas the other nine were constructed in level plain or plateau areas, including one atop Masada, and six in the broad plain around Jericho. Under the Greek Orthodox patriarchate of Jerusalem, a minor revival of Judaean monasticism occurred in the 19th century, but it was of short duration. Although no true *lavra* exists today, the term is given to certain cenobitic monasteries (e.g., the Lavra on Mount Athos) that enjoy a certain prestige because of either their historical importance or their size. This practice was also carried from Athos to Russia, where one can find several monasteries called *lavra*s.

EDWARD G. MATHEWS, JR.

*See also* Archaeology: Near East; Architecture: Eastern Christian Monasteries; Hagiography: Eastern Christian; Monastery, Christian; Mount Athos, Greece; Origins: Eastern Christian

## Further Reading

Binns, John, "The Distinctiveness of Palestinian Monasticism," in *Monastic Studies: The Continuity of Tradition*, edited by Judith Loades, Bangor: Headstart History, 1990

Binns, John, *Ascetics and Ambassadors of Christ: The Monasteries of Palestine, 314–631*, Oxford: Clarendon Press, 1994

Chitty, Derwas J., *The Desert a City*, Oxford: Blackwell, and Crestwood, New York: St. Vladimir's Seminary Press, 1966

Flusin, Bernard, *Miracle et Histoire dans l'Oeuvre de Cyrille de Scythopolis*, Paris: Études augustiniennes, 1983

Hirschfeld, Yizhar, "Les Laures du désert judéen," *Le Monde de la Bible* 68 (1989)

Hirschfeld, Yizhar, *The Judean Desert Monasteries in the Byzantine Period*, New Haven: Yale University Press, 1992

Hirschfeld, Yizhar, *The Palestinian Dwelling in the Roman-Byzantine Period*, Jerusalem: Franciscan Printing Press, 1995

Patrich, Joseph, *Sabas, Leader of Palestinian Monasticism: A Comparative Study in Eastern Monasticism, Fourth to Seventh Centuries*, Washington, D.C.: Dumbarton Oaks Research Library and Collection, 1995

# Lay Brothers and Lay Sisters, Christian

Lay brothers (*conversi*) and lay sisters (*conversae*) were a common feature in most monastic orders from the 12th century on. Although lay brothers and sisters were fully professed members of their orders, they did not participate in the *opus Dei*, the daily round of prayer that occupied the lives of monks and nuns. Medieval writers often saw the distinction between monks and nuns and these lay monastics in terms of the biblical story of the sisters Mary and Martha (Luke 10:38–42). Like Martha lay brothers and lay sisters attended to the daily agricultural and household chores of monastic communities, leaving the monks and nuns free to devote themselves entirely to prayer and contemplation, on the model of Mary. In the Middle Ages these men and women were usually from humble backgrounds and lacked the education and connections necessary to become fully professed monks or nuns.

Originally the term *conversus* was identified with a person who had been "converted" to the monastic life as an adult, as opposed to an *oblatus*, who had been "offered" to a monastery as a young child. Exactly when and where the term *conversus* began to be used in reference to lay brothers is unclear; by the mid–11th century men known as *fratres laici* existed at several monasteries in northern Italy and at the German abbey of Hirsau. These early lay brothers were bound by vows of poverty, obedience, and stability, but their status within their communities had not yet been formalized. Lay sisters probably trace their origins back to an earlier period than lay brothers and are first mentioned in ninth-century French sources.

Although lay brothers were incorporated into many orders, including the Carthusians, Gilbertines, Premonstratensians, and Grandmontines (and later the mendicant orders), it was the Cistercians who most fully developed the *conversi* as an institution. From the turn of the 12th century, lay brothers quickly became a fundamental component of Cistercian communities throughout Europe. Because the Cistercians supported themselves largely through agriculture and animal husbandry but did not believe in using landed serfs as Benedictines had traditionally done, lay brothers supplied the labor necessary to work Cistercian granges. In addition Cistercians especially welcomed craftsmen, such as blacksmiths, carpenters, and masons, as *conversi*.

Within the Cistercian Order lay brothers followed their own rule, the *Usus conversorum* (Use of the lay brothers), which, like the Benedictine Rule followed by Cistercian monks, dictated how they were to work, pray, eat, and dress. The *Usus* prescribed a regime of hard manual labor for the *conversi* and denied them many of the amenities that monks of the Order enjoyed. Lay brothers were to wear simple habits made from coarse materials, cover their beds only with the skins of sheep or goats, and wear beards without the "crown" of the monks' tonsure. In addition the consumption of alcoholic beverages on the granges where the *conversi* worked was strictly forbidden. *Conversi* were also barred from participating in the election of monastic officials. One of the most significant differences between the monks and the lay brothers was that the latter were required to remain illiterate and thus had little hope of ever attaining clerical status. They made their profession in the vernacular, and their education consisted only of memorizing a few short prayers.

Although lay sisters might have existed in an informal sense in the earlier Middle Ages, it was Gilbert of Sempringham (1083–1189), founder of the Gilbertine Order, who first organized such women under a monastic rule. In 1131 Gilbert founded a community of nuns at Sempringham, where, with the aim of shielding his charges from any contact with the secular world, he enclosed a group of female servants in the same cloister. These women soon became lay sisters; like lay brothers *conversae* were set apart from the nuns whom they served by distinct habits and by lack of education. At several so-called double houses of Gilbertine nuns and canons in England, lay sisters and lay brothers coexisted within the same communities, although care was taken to ensure that their contact was as minimal as was that between the nuns and the canons. Among the Gilbertines *conversae* were present not only in the monasteries of the Order but also in charity hospitals operated and supervised by affiliated priories for the care of the poor. If Gilbert's

addition of lay sisters to his Order was influenced by the example of the Cistercian lay brothers, some houses of Cistercian nuns incorporated lay sisters into their communities on the Gilbertine model.

Ideally the work performed by lay brothers and lay sisters was meant to facilitate prayer and contemplation of the monks and nuns whom they served. In actual practice, however, relations between *conversi* and choir monks and nuns were often fraught with tensions that occasionally erupted into violence. Of the 123 revolts that have been documented within the Cistercian Order between 1168 and 1308, at least 70 involved *conversi*, and the Gilbertine Order was thrown into chaos between 1165 and 1171 by a well-organized uprising of its brothers at the mother house of Sempringham. The complaints of rebellious lay brothers varied, ranging from the worldliness and corruption of monks and nuns to the prohibition against the consumption of beer on granges. Episcopal visitation records reveal that discord between lay sisters and nuns was not uncommon and was most often caused by the sisters' dissatisfaction with their perceived inferior status. Nuns frequently complained that the *conversae* had discarded their sheepskin cloaks and hoods and appropriated the nuns' habits for themselves; the sisters sometimes countered by impugning the nuns' morality in front of episcopal visitors.

Both revolts and the changing nature of Cistercian land tenure contributed to the widespread decline of the institution of lay brothers in the 14th and 15th centuries. As the Cistercians became increasingly involved in manorial and feudal systems of landholding, the labor of *conversi* ceased to be an essential component of the Order's economic well-being. However, both lay brothers and sisters have persisted in many orders down to the present day.

KATHERINE ALLEN SMITH

*See also* Agriculture, Western Christian; Beghards; Beguines; Cistercians: General or Male; Double Houses, Western Christian; Gilbertines; Liturgy: Western Christian; Monastics and the World, Medieval; Oblates; William of Hirsau

## Further Reading

Donnelly, James S., *The Decline of the Medieval Cistercian Laybrotherhood* (Fordham University History Series, number 3), New York: Fordham University Press, 1949

Elkins, Sharon K., "The Emergence of a Gilbertine Identity," in *Medieval Religious Women*, volume 1: *Distant Echoes* (Cistercian Studies Series, 71), edited by John A. Nichols and Lillian Thomas Shank, Kalamazoo, Michigan: Cistercian Publications, 1984

Golding, Brian, *Gilbert of Sempringham and the Gilbertine Order, c. 1130–c.1300*, New York: Oxford University Press, and Oxford: Clarendon Press, 1995

Knowles, David, "The Revolt of the Lay Brothers of Sempringham," *English Historical Review* 50 (1935)

Nichols, John A., "The Internal Organization of English Cistercian Nunneries," *Citeaux* 30 (1979)

Williams, David H., *The Cistercians in the Early Middle Ages*, Leominster: Gracewing, 1998

# Lay Patrons, Christian. *See* Patrons, Christian: Lay

# Laypeople. *See* Laicization of Spirituality; Lay Brothers and Lay Sisters, Christian

# Le Saux, Henri 1910–1973

French Benedictine founder of the ashram of Saccidananda and theologian

Henri Le Saux, who came to be called Abhishiktananda (the Bliss of the Anointed One, or the Bliss of Christ), was born of a good, sturdy middle-class family in Brittany. He became a Benedictine monk, entering the Abbey of Ste. Anne de Kergonan in Brittany in 1929. He made his solemn profession in 1935 and was ordained a priest in 1939. In 1947 he began writing to Jules Monchanin (1895–1957) and in 1948 went to India to join him. Monchanin was a saintly French priest who wanted to establish a Christian contemplative monastic community in southern India. In 1950 the two founded Saccidananda Ashram, or Shantivanam, on the banks of the sacred Kavery, the "Ganges of the south," and located in the village of Tannirpalli near the city of Trichy in Tamil Nadu. It was very primitive, poor, and simple, approximating the life of the Hindu renunciate in traditional Indian society (i.e., the average ashramic community). The community has always kept a basic commitment to a life of utter simplicity and renunciation, and this commitment was reaffirmed during the tenure of Bede Griffiths (1907–1993) as the prior of Shantivanam (1968–1993). The embracing of radical poverty expressed both solidarity with India's poor and renunciation of the world's goods, which is one of the hallmarks of Hindu monasticism as expressed in *sannyasa*. Le Saux's and Monchanin's ideal was to shed light on how the mystical life of India can be reconciled with the Christian experience of the inner life, and their aspiration was conveyed in this simple phrase: *advaita* and the Trinity. That focus never wavered.

Abhishiktananda and Monchanin went to Arunachala at Tirruvanamali, also in Tamil Nadu, to sit in the presence of Ramana Maharshi (1879–1950), one of modern India's greatest saints. Ramana was a *muni*, a silent seer who rarely spoke. As they sat in Ramana's presence, something awakened in Abhishiktananda as he experienced "eternal" India in this seer. Ramana was also a pure nondualist (an *advaitin*). Abhishiktananda clearly discerned the authenticity of India's mysticism in this sage, who for him incarnated the eternal reality of India's mystic sages of antiquity, the forest seers (*rishis*), the founders of the Hindu tradition. After Ramana's death Abhishiktananda would spend long periods in the caves of Arunachala absorbed in meditation. During one of these times, he was drawn into a vortex of

mystical depth out of which he never emerged. His whole inner experience from that point on took him deeper and deeper into *advaita*, pure nondual (unitive) awareness. In a number of his books, especially in *Sagesse hindoue, mystique chrétienne: Du Vedanta à la trinité* (1965; *Saccidananda: A Christian Approach to Advaitic Experience*), he was trying to reconcile his Christian faith and mysticism with his experience of Hindu *advaita*.

After Monchanin died in 1957, Abhishiktananda gravitated more and more into solitude. His attitude toward Shantivanam became strangely ambiguous, and his heart was no longer really there. In 1968 he turned Shantivanam over to Kurisumala Ashram under Griffiths' leadership, departing for his hermitage in Uttakashi in the Himalayas. He died in December 1973 after he had discovered, or so he believed, how the Trinity and *advaita* come together. Few Benedictines have ventured so far afield.

WAYNE TEASDALE

*See also* Griffiths, Bede; India: Christian

## Biography

Having lived as a Benedictine in Brittany, Le Saux moved to India in 1948, where with Jules Monchanin he founded the ashram of Saccidananda. After the death of Monchanin, Le Saux, now known as Swami Abhishiktananda, moved to a hermitage near the source of the Ganges. The Hindu master Ramana Maharshi (1879–1950) shaped Le Saux's interreligious experience. Le Saux's numerous writings incorporate categories of Advaita Vedanta into Christian theology.

## Major Works

*Sagesse hindoue, mystique chrétienne: Du Vedanta à la trinité*, 1965; translated as *Saccidananda: A Christian Approach to Advaitic Experience*, 1974
*La rencontre de l'hindouisme et du christianisme*, 1966
*Une messe aux sources du gange*, 1967
*Souvenirs d'Arunachala: Récit d'un ermite chrétien en terre hindoue*, 1978
*La montée au fond du coeur: Le journal intime du moine chrétien-sannyasi hindou, 1948–1973*, edited by R. Panikkar, 1986

## Further Reading

Davy, Marie-Madeleine, *Henri Le Saux, Swami Abhishiktânanda: Le passeur entre deux rives*, Paris: Éditions du Cerf, 1981
Lacombe, Olivier, *Indianité: Études historiques et comparatives sur la pensée indienne*, Paris: Belles Lettres, 1979 (see pages 129–148)
Teasdale, Wayne, "Abhishiktananda's Mystical Intuition of the Trinity," *Cistercian Studies* 17:1 (1983)

# Leclercq, Jean 1911–1993

French Benedictine scholar of medieval Christian monasticism

The great historian of Western medieval monasticism, Jean Leclercq, was born 31 January 1911 in Avesnes, France. He was the third of four children. He joined the Benedictine monastery of Clervaux in Luxembourg in 1928, was professed 29 June

1930, studied two years at Clervaux, did his military service at Metz from 1932 to 1933, and then studied theology at St. Anselmo in Rome from 1933 to 1937. Having begun work on his doctoral dissertation on Jean of Paris, he took courses in Paris from 1937 to 1938. He spent most of the war years at the Abbaye de la Source in Paris, where he made many useful contacts. At Etienne Gilson's suggestion Leclercq concentrated his studies on 11th- and 12th-century monasticism. In 1946 he published books on Peter of Celle, Peter the Venerable, and John of Fécamp as well as 20 articles.

Leclercq's *S. Bernard Mystique* (1948) and an article on an early manuscript of Bernard's works preserved at Engelberg helped earn him an invitation to edit the works of St. Bernard. He undertook this enormous task with the help of C.H. Talbot and Henri Rochais. This 30-year project, which involved traveling across Europe to examine manuscripts, ended with the publication of the eighth and last volume in 1977. In conjunction with his manuscript research for this edition, Leclercq published about 200 articles, the most important of which were collected in *Recueil d'études sur S. Bernard et ses écrits* (5 vols., 1962–1992). He identified some hitherto unknown works of Bernard, definitively excluded some unauthentic ones, and clarified the stages of writing and revision that Bernard's works had undergone.

In 1957 Leclercq published a version of a course of lectures he gave at St. Anselmo from 1955 to 1956, *Amour des lettres et le désir de Dieu* (*The Love of Learning and the Desire for God*). This erudite and entrancing book about the intellectual and spiritual life of medieval monks became something of a best-seller in Europe and North America. There and elsewhere he differentiated several types of medieval theology. The logical, deductive, speculative, and argumentative theology of scholasticism was preceded by a monastic theology that was literary, imaginative, rhetorical, and oriented toward contemplation and lifelong conversion.

Nothing monastic was alien to Leclercq. He published books and articles both on various eras and figures of monastic history and on monastic practice and prayer. He took great interest in innovative forms of monasticism, including the revival of eremitical life, urban monasticism, and liturgical adaptation. His total scholarly output includes over 40 books and 1,000 articles.

After World War II many Benedictine and Cistercian monasteries were founded in Africa, Asia, and South America. Leclercq worked in close association with the secretariat of AIM (Aide-Inter-Monastères) and traveled all over the world, giving lectures and advice to new monastic foundations.

Leclercq was also very active in interreligious monastic dialogues. He participated in the intermonastic dialogues at Bouake (1964), Bangkok (1968), Bangalore (1973), Kandy (1980), and Berkeley (1987). He was a founder of *Dialogue Interreligieux Monastique*.

Leclercq was unassuming, polite, and optimistic. He counted among his friends many great medievalists. He was encouraging to young students, especially monks. It was a cause of some sorrow to him that more young monks did not follow the paths he

had pioneered in the study of medieval monastic studies. He died in 1993, facing death with the same gentle humor that he had shown toward life. No one contributed more to the post-1960 flowering of scholarship about Western medieval monasticism.

HUGH FEISS, O.S.B.

*See also* Benedictines; Bernard of Clairvaux, St.; Cistercians; Hagiography: Western Christian; Historiography, Recent: Western Christian; Humanism, Christian; Knowles, M. David; Regulations: Christian Perspectives; Schools and Universities, Benedictine

## Biography

Born in northernmost France, this most prolific and beloved historian of medieval Cistercians and Benedictines was professed at the Benedictine monastery of Clervaux, Luxembourg, in 1930. Known above all for editing and commenting on the works of Bernard of Clairvaux, Leclercq wrote more than 40 books and 1,000 articles. He rivals in productivity his Benedictine namesake Henri Leclercq (1869–1945).

## Major Works

*S. Bernard Mystique*, 1948

*Amour des lettres et le désir de Dieu*, 1957; as *The Love of Learning and the Desire for God*, translated by Catharine Misrahi, 1961

*Sancti Bernardi Opera* (editor, in collaboration with C.H. Talbot and H. Rochais), 8 vols., 1957–1977

*Recueil d'études sur S. Bernard et ses écrits*, 5 vols., 1962–1992

*Aspects du monachisme, hier et aujourd'hui*, 1968; as *Aspects of Monasticism*, translated by Mary Dodd, 1978

*Vie religieuse et vie contemplative*, 1969; as *Contemplative Life*, translated by Elizabeth Funder, 1978

## Further Reading

Elder, E. Rozanne, editor, *The Joy of Learning and the Love of God: Essays in Honor of Jean Leclercq*, Kalamazoo, Michigan: Cistercian Publications, 1993 (bibliography by Michael Martin, pages 415–498)

Leclercq, Jean, "Discovering St. Bernard," *Monastic Studies* 16 (1985)

McGinn, Bernard, "Jean Leclercq's Contribution to Monastic Spirituality and Theology," *Monastic Studies* 16 (1985) (the entire issue is in honor of Dom Leclercq)

Severus, Emmanuel von, "In Memoriam Jean Leclercq O.S.B.," *Archiv für Liturgiewissenschaft* 37 (1995)

Truijen, Vincent, "In Memoriam Dom Jean Leclercq, O.S.B.," *Studien und Mitteilungen zur Geschichte des Benediktinerordens und seine Zweige* 105 (1994)

# Lectio Divina

Found most commonly but not exclusively in writings on monastic spirituality and originally equated with *sacra pagina*, the phrase *lectio divina* almost always refers to a "holy reading" of the Scriptures or (rather rarely) of the fathers of the Church or other spiritual writing requiring prayerful reflection on the text. It is a privileged means in monasticism, along with the liturgy and the work of the monastery, to lead to communion with God in prayer. *Lectio* aims to draw out the spiritual meaning of the Scriptures in order for the monk to grow in God's wisdom revealed through the Word. Thus, the kind of scriptural interpretation on which *lectio* is based is neither scientific nor historical-critical, nor is its reflection on the Word aimed at theological insight (in the modern sense of academic theology). Rather, it aims at disclosing the God who speaks through the Word and at shaping an appropriate response in thought, prayer, and the conduct of one's life. It is theological in the sense that it praises and acknowledges the God who reveals, and it responds to God by deepening conversion of mind and heart in life. It is dialogical in the sense that it restores the sacred Scriptures to their original status as proclamations to be heard and responded to. It reveres the Scriptures as divine address requiring a humble and forthright response. The monk does not engage in *lectio divina* for the sake of being intellectually informed or enlightened; rather, he or she engages in *lectio* truly to "listen" and respond to God's invitation to lead a fuller and richer life illumined by God's revealed Word and through God's gracious invitation and action.

The tradition of the Jewish *Shema* is pertinent here. The text of "Hear O Israel" (Deut. 6:4) and its repetition in daily Jewish prayer reveals the emphasis in the Jewish and Christian traditions of appreciating the Scriptures as God's announcement, which believers are to "hear" and assimilate again and again. Thus, the term *lectio* should be understood less as a cerebral comprehension of words on the "sacred page" and more as a means of "listening" and truly "hearing" God announcing revealed truth, the true good news of salvation. The way in which monastics practiced this holy reading during the patristic and early medieval eras was to speak the words aloud and to meditate on their meaning (*meditatio*) by repeating them and truly savoring their meaning. The term *rumination* describes this holy exercise. One literally "chewed over" the sacred text to savor and digest it. With the convenient duplication of the printed word (especially through printing), *lectio* came to be understood as a silent reflection on the scriptures done by monks in solitude.

The practice of *lectio divina* is attested as early as Origen (e.g., in his *Letter to Gregory the Thaumaturge*), Ambrose (*De Officiis Ministrorum*), Augustine (*Sermon 219*), and Jerome (*Letter to Eustochius*), among others. It receives significant exposition and emphasis in the Rule of St. Benedict, chapter 48 of which begins with "Idleness is the enemy of the soul. Therefore

A French Trappist engaged in *lectio divina*.
Photo courtesy of Frère Thomas, Abbaye de La Trappe

the brothers should have specified periods for manual labor as well as for prayerful reading" (*lectio divina*). The balance of the chapter presents an *horarium* for the daily manual labor and for *lectio*. In chapter 49 Benedict offers prescriptions for spiritual exercises during Lent in which he includes holy reading (*lectioni*).

Traditionally, in monasticism the practice of *lectio* leads the monk to deeper conversion of heart and obedience. Thus, it is not coincidental that the Virgin Mary becomes a model for monks of their life, especially in terms of "listening" to the word and obeying it. The notion that Mary received God's Word through the announcement that she would bear the Word made flesh (Luke 1:26–38) and that "she pondered" many things in her heart (Luke 2:19) exemplifies how she stands as a model listener and believer. Depictions of Mary praying over the Scriptures as Gabriel visited her to make his announcement envision how believers (not necessarily monks) should ponder God's Word, welcome it, and obey it ("let it be done to me according to your word"; Luke 1:37). That Mary invites others to obey God's Word is exemplified in her role at the wedding feast at Cana when she instructs the stewards to "do whatever he tells you" (John 2:5).

In contemporary monasticism the practice of *lectio* is associated with keeping silence and with practicing solitude. These traditional monastic observances are regarded as more pertinent today given the relative absence of silence in much contemporary culture. The outward disposition of being silent paves the way for a deepening penetration into the mystery of God through the holy reading of the Word. That monks are to be silent in order to "listen" to God's word is found throughout the Rule of St. Benedict, including its opening sentence: "Listen carefully, my son, to the master's instructions, and attend to them with the ear of your heart" (Prologue 1). As a consequence of this kind of "listening," the monk grows in obedience to God through the revealed and assimilated Word. It is no coincidence that in Latin grammar the word *audire* (to listen) means "to obey" when it is followed by the dative case. For the monk to listen leads to obedience, which is the fruit of listening to God's Word.

The precise texts or books of the Scriptures to be used for *lectio* are commonly not specified. However, some would argue that when Benedict uses the plural (*lectionibus*) in 48:13, he is referring to the readings to be used in the office of readings of the Liturgy. Nonetheless, one can legitimately make a connection between *lectio divina* and the monastic practice of listening to extensive Scripture readings at vigils (or matins or the office of readings in the present revision of the Liturgy of the Hours). However, it is also clear that the monk's *lectio* should not be restricted to the Liturgy, thus the repeated exhortations in monastic literature that monks apply themselves regularly to "holy reading" on their own.

The wider Church has been exposed to a kind of *lectio divina* after the Second Vatican Council through the practice of "scripture-sharing" prayer groups and the practice of what has been termed "centering prayer" (made popular by Basil Penning-

ton and Thomas Keating [1923– ], among others). Whereas some would see a continuation of *lectio* through the practices of "meditation" and mental prayer from the post-Reformation era through modern times, it is more commonly understood that *lectio* has been more characteristically a monastic practice. That it has become widely appreciated today as a way of praying over the Scriptures for a variety of people in the Church at large demonstrates the relative success of the biblical and liturgical movements that unfolded in the Church in the 20th century.

KEVIN W. IRWIN

*See also* Ambrose, St.; Benedict of Nursia, St.; Bible Interpretation; Devotions, Western Christian; Jerome, St.; Keating, Thomas; Meditation: Christian Perspectives; Orthodox Monasticism: Byzantine; Seasons, Liturgical: Western Christian; Spirituality: Western Christian; Visual Arts, Western Christian: Book Arts before the Renaissance

## Further Reading

Bacht, H., "Meditatio in den altesten Monchsquellen," *Geist und Leben* 28 (1955)

Boland, Andre, "Lectio divina et Lecture Spirituelle," in *Dictionnaire de Spiritualité, ascétique et mystique: Doctrine et histoire*, volume 9, Paris: Beauchesne, 1979

Casey, Michael, *Sacred Reading: The Ancient Art of Lectio Divina*, Ligouri, Missouri: Triumph Books, 1995

Cummings, Charles, *Monastic Practices*, Kalamazoo, Michigan: Cistercian Publications, 1986

Grant, Robert M., "Jewish Christianity in the Second Century," *Recherches de science religieuse* 60 (1972)

Heschel, Abraham, *God in Search of Man: A Philosophy of Judaism*, London: Calder, 1956; New York: Meridian Books, 1959

Leclercq, Jean, *The Love of Learning and the Desire for God: A Study of Monastic Culture*, New York: Fordham University Press, 1961; London: SPCK, 1976

Louf, Andre, *Teach Us To Pray: Learning a Little About God*, London: Darton, Longman and Todd, 1974; New York: Paulist Press, 1975

Mulholland, Robert, *Shaped by the Word: The Power of Scripture in Spiritual Formation*, Nashville, Tennessee: Upper Room, 1985

Pennington, Basil, *Lectio Divina: Renewing the Ancient Practice of Praying the Scriptures*, New York: Crossroad, 1998

Rouillard, Philippe, "Lectio divina," *Catholicisme* 7 (1969)

Todde, M., "Lettura e meditazione della Scrittura seconde la tradizione patristica," *Servitium* 7 (1973)

Vandenbroucke, Francois, "La lectio divina du 11 au 14 siecle," *Studia Monastica* 8 (1966)

# Lérins, France

Although a monastery still exists there today, during the fifth century the island of Lérins enjoyed a period of greatness that affected the course of monasticism in the Latin West. At that time many Western ecclesiastics were ambivalent about monasticism, fearful of the highly publicized and often undisciplined histrionics of some Eastern monks – fears that seemed justified by the disputes between the ascetic Jerome (c. 345–420) and the Roman clergy in the 380s and the stormy career of the monk-bishop Martin of Tours (d. 397). Lérins would change all that.

Now called St. Honorat, Lérins was a deserted island in the Mediterranean Sea off the modern Riviera due south of Cannes. Around 400 the priest Honoratus (c. 350–c. 430) settled there as an ascetic and by 410 had founded a community that also provided *cellulae* for hermits. Honoratus' cousin and successor as abbot, Hilary of Arles (401–449), provides what little we know of life in the community's earliest years, but because he does this in a funeral sermon for his cousin, the emphasis falls on Honoratus' virtues and his later, very brief career as a bishop. Eucherius of Lyons (c. 390–c. 450) wrote a panegyric, *De laude eremi*, that compares Lérins to a desert, making much of the desert theme in the Bible (Moses and John the Baptist) but telling little about daily life.

Lérins assumed importance because it became a virtual school for the Gallic episcopate. The monks had a reputation for sanctity, and the Gallic people often chose them to be their bishops. The roster of Lérins' episcopal alumni is remarkable. Having embraced ascetic continence, Eucherius of Lyons and his wife, Galla, moved to an adjacent island in 418. They sent their two sons, Salonius and Veranus, to be educated at Lérins, and Eucherius often visited the community for study and spiritual growth. Eucherius became bishop of Lyons in 434, and both his sons also became bishops. Another married nobleman who had embraced ascetic continence, Salvian, arrived on the island around 424; he eventually left to become a priest in Marseilles and then the city's bishop.

In 428 the founder Honoratus became bishop of Arles but died within two years; he was succeeded by his successor as abbot, Hilary, who held the See of Arles until 449. He traded in monastic humility for episcopal ambition, trying to raise Arles to metropolitan status, only to be thwarted by Pope Leo I the Great (440–461), who wanted no rival in the West. Maximus and Faustus became bishops of Riez, in 434 and 458, respectively, and Lupus held the See of Troyes from 427 to 478. By demonstrating to ecclesiastical leaders that monks could play a central role in the life of the Church, these Lérins alumni paved the way for the Western acceptance of monasticism.

Vincent of Lérins (d. c. 450) became famous for the Vincentian canon for orthodoxy: Christians should believe what has been believed everywhere, always, and by everyone (*quod ubique, quod semper, quod ab omnibus*). Vincent and other Lérins monks fought extremist interpretations of Augustine's predestinationism, earning the unfair and inaccurate label of Semi-Pelagians.

Lérins' greatness and importance faded quickly. Caesarius of Arles (c. 470–542) was its last great figure. The monastery adopted the Rule of St. Benedict in the seventh century, was pillaged several times by the Saracens in the Middle Ages, was confiscated by the revolutionary government in 1791 and

repurchased by a local bishop in 1859, and is now a Cistercian house.

JOSEPH F. KELLY

*See also* Desert Fathers; France; Heretics, Christian; Island Monasteries, Christian; Jerome, St.; Master and Pupil: Christian Perspectives; Origins: Western Christian; Spain: History

**Further Reading**

Chadwick, Nora, *Poetry and Letters in Early Christian Gaul*, London: Bowes and Bowes, 1955
Cooper-Marsden, A.C., *The History of the Islands of the Lérins*, Cambridge: Cambridge University Press, 1913
De Vogüé, Adalbert, "Les Débuts de la vie monastique à Lérins," *Revue d'histoire ecclésiastique* 88 (1993)
Hoare, F.R., *The Western Fathers*, London: Sheed and Ward, 1954 (includes *A Discourse on the Life of Saint Honoratus* by Hilary of Arles)
Leclercq, Henri, "Lérins," in *Dictionnaire d'Archéologie Chrétienne et de Liturgie*, volume 8:2, edited by Fernand Cahrol, Paris: Letouzy et Ané, 1907–1953
Pricoco, Salvatore, *L'isola dei santi*, Rome: Edizioni dell'Aleneo e Bizzarri, 1978
Prinz, Friedrich, *Frühes Mönchtum im Frankenreich*, Vienna: Oldenbourg, 1965
Van Dam, Raymond, *Saints and Their Miracles in Late Antique Gaul*, Princeton, New Jersey: Princeton University Press, 1993

# Lhasa, Tibet

Lhasa has been the capital of Tibet since the seventh century (before that time Yarlung served as the capital) and can still be considered the most important center for Tibetan cultural heritage today, notwithstanding the huge transformations in the social and physical structure of the town during the last three decades. Despite all, Lhasa retains its symbolic value as a religious capital, ranking with Rome, Jerusalem, and Mecca.

The small village named Ra-sa ("Ra" meaning "goat" in Tibetan) was changed in name and status when it was chosen as the political and religious capital by the Fifth Dalai Lama, Songsten Gampo. From a goat valley it became a hometown of the deities, Lha-sa. An unforgettable impact on the outside world was made by its reputation as a mysterious, inaccessible, and forbidden city. Access was extremely difficult because of both the geographical location and the political strategy of restricted communications, especially since the 19th century.

Descriptions of Lhasa from the first half of the 20th century may be found in *My Journey to Lhasa* (1927), by Alexandra David-Neel, who was the first European woman to visit Lhasa; *Seven Years in Tibet* (1947), by Heinrich Harrer, and the movie of the same title; *Lhasa* (1905), by Perceval Landon; and *Lhasa, the Holy City* (1938), by F. Spencer Chapman. The latter two writers assume the point of view of a foreign and outside observer, whereas the first two write from the perspective of personal experience.

**The Potala, until 1959 the winter palace of the Dalai Lamas, Lhasa, Tibet, 17th century.**
**Photo courtesy of John Powers**

Today's Lhasa has grown to ten times its original area, and the structure of the town has been shaped and directed by socialist space-planning principles, changing the physical and ideological priorities of the original town space. Sometimes these principles conflicted with conservation of the town's original structure. The initial town structure presented a clear center and four cardinal points that were marked by important religious buildings and surrounded by three concentric circumambulation paths (around the center of the town and the main temple). This scheme of town planning arranged space in a maṇḍala, with streets and palaces as the components, and recalls other Buddhist cities and temple buildings.

The symbolism of the universe with its center and surrounding fence is represented in the physiognomy of the land structure, into which built components, such as streets and palaces, are articulated. In this original space structure, the Jokhang temple (founded in 625) functions as the center of the town and remains to this day a very important place of pilgrimage.

The town's east-west axis is marked by Ganden monastery and Ngari Labrang. Norbu Linga palace (also called Summer palace) lies on the same axis. The north-south axis runs from Sera monastery (renowned because warrior-monks, or "dobdobs," used to live there) toward Samye monastery (which is situated between the town of Lhasa and the Samye River). The outer ring around the city is called Lingkor, whereas the inner ring runs around the main temple and constitutes the circumambulation path inside the main temple's courtyard.

The original town structure has undergone continuous upheaval since 1951, when the Chinese People's Liberation Army entered Lhasa for the first time. The transformation unfolded in five main phases, resulting today in a general configuration divided into two separate units, old town and suburbs, the latter occupying most of the town area and consisting of new structures. The guidelines for the transformations come from Plan Lhasa 2000. The six phases in the alteration of the town structure have been as follows: (1) 1950 to 1954: preliminary phase. (2) 1955 to 1959: introduction of external values as priorities above traditional values. (3) 1960 to 1966: transformation and division into counties for the purpose of centralizing administrative power; this centralization of power altered the original structure of the town, imposed transformations on the whole structure of the society, and divided the town into eight districts.

(4) 1966 to 1968: cultural revolution with systematic destruction of all representations of traditional values, such as temples and religious objects, including statues and holy scriptures. (5) 1969 to 1980: main phase of physical changes in roads, electricity, and residential buildings. (6) 1980 to the present: a massive development program, changing the town and landscape and introducing the concept of museum function for the monastic units.

To some extent renewal is being accomplished not with aggressive intervention but in harmony with original values. As a result of international agreements, three of the town's main buildings have been protected by a conservation plan: Potala palace and Jokhang and Ramoche temples. Other remarkable sites inside Lhasa are Norbu Linga palace; Ahetsangu, Drepung, and Sera monasteries; and characteristic outdoor spaces, such as Barkhor, the marketplace, and the celestial burial place on the east side of town.

Potala (meaning "peak") palace was built in three historical phases on the top of Mapori (red hill) close to the lake. The first phase resulted in the palace "Mapori" (pre–seventh century), which was destroyed during the war with the Mongols. The second phase began in 1645, when work commenced on a new structure, inspired by a renowned location in India, Cape Comorin. The third phase resulted in the famous palace we know today, with 1,000 rooms, red and white sections, and staircases of extraordinary framework. The structure of the walls slopes vertically inward with both static and aesthetic implications. The windows are arranged in a symbolic rhythm in sets of two and three and in the red section in a rhythm of five. The sections are also distinguished by gold-plated roofs on the red palace and terraced roofs on the white palace. These features have amazed foreign visitors since 1979, when visiting was again permitted.

LAURA PORCEDDU

See also Architecture: Buddhist Monasteries in Southern Asia; Buddhist Schools/Traditions: Tibet; Critiques of Buddhist Monasticism: Indo-Tibetan; Ladakh, India; Maṇḍala; Peace Movements, Buddhist; Tibet; Tibetan Lineages; Visual Arts, Buddhist: Tibet

**Further Reading**

Alexander, Andre, *The Old City of Lhasa*, Berlin: Tibet Heritage Fund, 1998

Azevedo, Pimpim de, *Tibetan Old Buildings and Urban Development in Lhasa 1948–1985–1998*, Berlin: Tibetan Heritage Fund, 1998 (included as an insert in Andre Alexander's *The Old City of Lhasa*)

Batchelor, Stephen, *The Tibet Guide*, London: Wisdom, 1987; revised edition, Boston: Wisdom, 1998

Brignoli, Frank J., and Christine Johnston Brignoli, *Lhasa, Tibet's Forbidden City*, Hong Kong: Peter Chancellor Designer Associates, 1987

Chapman, F. Spencer, *Lhasa, the Holy City*, London: Chatto and Windus, 1938; New York and London: Harper and Brothers, 1939; revised edition, as *Memoirs of a Mountaineer*, London: Chatto and Windus, 1951

David-Neel, Alexandra, *Voyage d'une Parisienne a Lhassa*, Paris: Plon, and, as *My Journey to Lhasa*, New York and London: Harper and Brothers, 1927; revised edition, London: Virago, 1983; reprint, Boston: Beacon Press, 1993

Landon, Perceval, *Lhasa*, 2 vols., Delhi: Kailash Publishers and London: Hurst and Blackett, and, as *The Opening of Tibet*, New York: Doubleday, Page, and Company, 1905; revised edition, London: Hurst and Blackett, 1906

*The Potala Palace of Tibet*, Hong Kong: Joint Publishing, 1982; revised edition, as *The Potala of Tibet*, London and Atlantic Highlands, New Jersey: Stacey, 1988

Richardson, Hugh Edward, *Ch'ing Dynasty Inscriptions at Lhasa*, Rome: Istituto italiano per il Medio ed Estremo oriente, 1974

Snellgrove, David, and Hugh Richardson, *A Cultural History of Tibet*, New York: Praeger, and London: Weidenfeld and Nicolson, 1968; revised edition, Boulder, Colorado: Prajna Press, 1980; reprint, Boston and London: Shambhala, 1986

Tsering Tsomo, *Urban Morphology of Lhasa, Tibet*, New Delhi: IPH, 1994

# Libraries: Buddhist

According to the seventh-century Chinese pilgrim Xuanzang, the great North Indian monastery complex at Nālandā possessed three multistory libraries in the early seventh century A.D. Although this may have been exceptional, substantial libraries certainly existed in many early Buddhist centers, but none of these are now extant, and their holdings and organization are a matter of conjecture.

We are on more solid ground when we turn our attention to eastern Asia. The *Annals of the Sui Dynasty* recount that in 518 Emperor Wu "made a large collection of 5,400 Buddhist canonical books and placed them in the Hualin Garden." A catalog was compiled at the time, although this was certainly not the first Chinese collection of Buddhist literature.

Copies of sacred texts donated to temples by wealthy Chinese laity were stored in so-called sūtra repositories. One standard design, apparently invented by the lay master Fu Tashi (497–569), consisted of a tall, octagonal, revolving cabinet (*chuan lun cang*) containing banks of keep drawers, hinged around a central pillar. It was easy to use and had the added advantage that it could be revolved by illiterate persons as a merit-making act. The magnificent revolving cabinet of the Nan chansi in Suzhou is said to have cost 10,000 strings of cash, with another 3,600 strings spent on its more than 5,000 manuscript scrolls. Completed in 863 it had 64 seats arranged around a central repository whose turning could be stopped only with the aid of a sturdy brake. Another celebrated repository at the Jin gesi on Mount Wutai contained the Tripiṭaka in over 6,000 fascicles written in gold and silver ink on dark-blue paper. Catalogs of the seventh to eighth century suggest that each drawer of a typical repository contained about ten scrolls.

In China, from 972, printed sacred texts began to assume a new stitched book shape, and different forms of library housing, usually large wooden closets, evolved. Libraries were usually located on the upper floor of one of the major halls of the monastery complex, often somewhere near the entrance to the precincts. Typically it consisted of cases containing the Tripiṭaka, a central altar containing a variety of images often including the bodhisattva Guanyin, and tables and chairs, including some arranged in an adjoining room for the use of visitors. The library usually also provided storage for wooden printing blocks as well as living quarters for the librarian and his assistant. It was not uncommon for such libraries to double up as One Thousand Buddha Halls (*Qian fodian*). A Platform for Drying Sūtras in the Sun (*shai jingtai*) was positioned just in front of the library. Here, on the sixth day of the sixth month, books were spread in the sunshine and cleaned. Although this task was performed by monks, laypeople also attended the event as a merit-making exercise.

The oldest Japanese Buddhist sūtra repository (*kyōzō*) appears to have been Prince Shōtoku's private study, the Yumedono (Dream Hall) at the Hōryūji on the outskirts of Nara, dating from the early seventh century. The Yumedono is supposed to have housed Shōtoku's manuscript copy of a treatise on three sūtras (*Sangyō gisho*), the first scholarly work by a native Japanese. However, the *kyōzō* of most early Japanese Buddhist temples, such as the Tōdaiji, Genkōji, and Kōfukuji, housed Chinese classics as well as Buddhist literature. Another early temple, the Enryakuji, established by Saichō in 788 as the headquarters

of the Tendai school, housed a collection of 230 writings in 460 volumes imported from China. Today this library is maintained in the city of Otsu near Mount Hiei.

In line with the ordinances of the Taihō Code of 701, the Zushoryō, the first archival library in Japanese history, was founded to store Buddhist images, scriptures, and other writings. Five copies of every book written or copied in temples were supposed to be lodged there. At its inception the Zushoryō provided some degree of general access, but after 728 entrance to those below high court rank was prohibited.

Written texts have been the object of extreme devotion in Japan, and this led to a highly protective attitude toward their custodianship. Indeed in all parts of the Buddhist world sacred writings must be carefully handled. They are placed on specially constructed stands for reading purposes, and women are forbidden from resting them on their laps. Some Buddhist libraries, such as the Shūgei Shuchiin, established by Kūkai in 828, did allow limited access to commoners, but the traditional position was that "the people must be made to obey and not to learn." Nevertheless a prominent convert to Buddhism, Isonokami no Yakatsugu (729–781), a Japanese ambassador to China, is renowned as the founder of Japan's first public library, the Untei, which consisted of a pavilion on the grounds of his family temple.

The ruling clan of eighth-century Japan encouraged the copying of Buddhist sūtras as a means of ensuring the prosperity of

One of a pair of halls built to contain the 13th-century Tripiṭaka woodblocks, Haeinsa temple, Mount Kaya, Kyŏngsang-namdo.
Photo courtesy of Marylin M. Rhie

Part of the Tibetan canon in Leh Gompa, Leh, Ladakh, India.
Photo courtesy of John Powers

the state and the welfare of the people. Because the presence of sacred writings was essential to the establishment of a temple, many new temples were established around this time. By the Kamakura period (1192–1333) sūtra copying was conducted mainly within the monastic libraries themselves, and by the 15th century many temples had a book room (*shoin*) that, apart from its function as a repository, was also used for reading and writing as well as for literary gatherings.

The history of Buddhist libraries in Southeast Asia is a little opaque. In Burma a Buddhist library is said to have been established in Pagan as early as the 11th century by King Anawrahta. This eventually evolved into the Pitaka Taik. In 1795 a British envoy to Burma described the royal library of Amarapura as the largest royal library between the Danube and China. In neighboring Thailand King Narai (1656–1688) appears to have ordered his royal scribes to gather together all known religious and legislative writings, thus establishing the Royal Library at Ayutthaya, which was subsequently destroyed by the Burmese invasion of 1767. However, the tradition of Southeast Asian royal libraries continued into the Chakri dynasty, when Rama I (1782–1809) had the Mondira Dhamma library of Buddhist scriptures built on the grounds of his new palace in Bangkok in 1783.

IAN HARRIS

*See also* Bangkok, Thailand; Burma (Myanmar); China; Discourses (Sūtras): Mahāyāna; Japan: Sites; Kūkai; Manuscript Production: Buddhist; Mount Wutai, China; Nālandā, India; Nara, Japan; Pilgrims to India, Chinese; Saichō; Tibetan Lineages: Sakya

### Further Reading
Welch, Theodore F., *Toshokan: Libraries in Japanese Society*, London: Bingley, and Chicago: American Library Association, 1976

# Libraries: Eastern Christian

The libraries of the Eastern Christian world are treated here in two large divisions: the Byzantine world (Greek) and the meta-Byzantine worlds of the Balkans and Russia (which used Church Slavonic). These libraries may be classified systematically into five categories, not all of which were found everywhere: (1) royal or palace libraries, (2) public libraries, (3) academic libraries, (4) personal libraries accumulated by private individuals (wealthy educated persons of high culture and scholars), and (5) monastic libraries. We will consider under Byzantine libraries first the capital, Constantinople, where the evidence is more abundant, and then the provinces, for which lack of evidence requires us to treat public, academic, and royal libraries together, as reflected in the resources used by provincial writers. For Russia and the Balkans, libraries and literacy are directly linked to the Christianization of those nations, meaning that monastic and church libraries constitute the main category. Finally, what remnants of these libraries are still to be found in their original locales are now being or have already been gathered into central national libraries for preservation.

### Constantinople: Palace Library

The Palace Library probably dates from soon after the establishment of the capital at Constantinople in 330, but no reliable evidence for this early period survives. As late as the ninth and tenth centuries, the Byzantine emperors Leo the Armenian (813–820) and Constantine Porphyrogenitos (913–957) had recourse to monastic libraries for ecclesiastical and patristic literature needed to deal with contemporary ecclesiastical issues. The Palace Library must have been seriously deficient in Christian resources. This omission may have been remedied under Emperor Porphyrogenitos. He apparently determined that the imperial library should match the comprehensiveness of the famed Alexandrian Library of the Hellenistic age, for he mentions in his *De legationibus* (I.25–27) that he had collected books from throughout the inhabited world.

The Palace Library was decimated in the sack of Constantinople by the crusaders in 1204, but some of it was probably salvaged and reassembled in the interim Nicaean kingdom, where Emperor John III (1222–1254) refounded the Palace Library as part of the cultivation of Byzantine culture there. After the reestablishment of the Byzantine capital in Constantinople in 1261, the royal library was reconstituted in one wing of the palace by Michael Palaeologus (1259–1282) until it was finally destroyed by the Ottoman Turks in 1453.

### University and School Libraries in Byzantium

The Justinianic code, in its attempt to regulate state-sponsored education (as opposed to private tutelage in the home), provided for professorships responsible for lectures delivered in the auditorium, but not for any centrally organized university system. It is understandable, then, that no evidence has survived for any central university library. Private acquisition of books by students seeking higher education was the rule, whether the students were home-schooled or educated in the state-subsidized system of higher education, and the Palace Library probably served the research needs of the university professors in the capital.

Few manuscripts survive from the long interim of instability and local military revolts (seventh to mid–ninth century). There is little record about education and none at all about libraries serving either higher education or the patriarchate until about 860, the beginning of the "Macedonian" renaissance, when Bardas, who served as Caesar (i.e. regent) under his nephew, Michael III (842–867), revived the imperial university in the

Magnaura Palace. In 863 he placed it under the direction of Leo the Philosopher (Emperor, 886–912), whose searches for books in the monasteries throughout Asia Minor demonstrate the increasing Christianization of Byzantine culture. Nevertheless, the generally "humanistic" character of the tradition of education continued to shape the core content of school and university libraries. As late as the 12th century the archbishop of Thessaloniki, Eustathius, a major proponent of education in that city, wrote a commentary on Homer emphasizing his importance as the foundation of Byzantine education.

Outside of Constantinople libraries are known to have been associated with numerous centers of learning throughout the empire. Not all of these would have included Christian literature. The famed library of Alexandria continued to serve the Museum until the Arab conquest of Egypt (639/40). Alexandria was also home to the prestigious medical school where Caesarius (c. 335–369) studied, while his older brother, Gregory of Nazianzus (329/30–389/90) was reading in the Alexandrian library. Although these libraries were not notably Christian ones, Berytus (Beirut) was famed for its law school, founded by Constantine IX (1042–1055) in 1045, where canon law was a central subject. The Beirut law school formed a legal triumvirate with Rome and Constantinople. Caesarea (modern Kayseri) was renowned for its theological library, reputed to have contained 30,000 volumes. Other centers of learning with libraries of Christian content included Antioch in Syria, Ephesus, and the theological school of Edessa, which was influential in the fifth-century Christological and later Monophysite controversies.

### The Patriarchal Libraries

Although the Patriarchal Academy in Constantinople was founded in the time of Theodosios II (408–450), no library is attested for that institution until the seventh century, when the patriarch Sergius (610–638) is said to have established one there. Early evidence for the library is very sparse. Theophanes Continuatus (3.14 = PG 109, 120A) mentions an episode in which the Patriarchal Library was consulted during the iconoclastic controversy, and Zonaras (15.12.1) reports that it burned in 726. Reestablished at an unknown date, it is next mentioned by Theodore Prodromos (Ms. Vat. Gr. 305, fol. 74v). A few references to books in this library and a few surviving manuscripts bearing ownership notes confirm its ongoing existence. Saint Cyril (d. 869), a student of Leo the Philosopher and himself a professor of philosophy, is said to have served for a time as director of the "Patriarchal Library at St. Sophia." (*Acta Sanctorum* October XI, 169, Bruxelles, 1864). The fate of the library after the Fourth Crusade (1204) is unknown, but the library is again attested by an ownership note in a copy of Sophocles and Pindar written in the 15th century (Ms. Vat. Gr. 1333, fol. 78v).

The Patriarchal Library probably retained the books of some of its patriarchs, many of whom were bibliophiles in possession of their own personal libraries. In addition, small libraries were probably associated with the various smaller schools in the capital under the direction of the patriarchate. The Patriarchal Library today occupies a site assigned to it in the 17th century by the Ottoman conquerors of Constantinople. Having survived intact the disastrous fire of 1951 that destroyed the rest of the Patriarchate's buildings, it is today a central repository for manuscripts from a number of monasteries, among them the Chalki Monasteries of the Panaghia Kamariotissa and the Holy Trinity, and the Theological School of Chalki.

Libraries from the Patriarchates of Jerusalem, Antioch, and Alexandria also house today a variety of collections consolidated from various churches and monasteries in more modern times. At Jerusalem, for example, are the collections from the Metochion of the Holy Sepulchre, Precious Cross, the Church of the Resurrection, the Monastery of Mar Ibrahim, and collections of some of its patriarchs, including the Patriarch Nikodemos.

### Public Libraries

While public libraries were well known in the classical era, and some references from the Byzantine era also survive, no evidence survives to indicate any significant Christian content in public libraries in the early Byzantine period. The library of Constantinople is reported to have burned twice, in 457 and again in the eighth century. From the ninth-century revival on, no trace of this library exists.

During the Latin occupation (1204–1261), with its wholesale destruction of the capital's libraries, the concept of the public library was revived in Nicaea, with special emphasis on the collection and preservation of Hellenic and Greek Christian literature. According to chronicler Theodore Skoutariotes (b. c. 1230, metropolitan of Kyzikos 1277–1282), Nicaean Emperor Theodore Doucas Lascaris (1254–1258) collected enough books for several libraries. Many were probably salvaged from the disaster in Constantinople. Skoutariotes treats this project as part of the restoration of the entire educational system.

### Personal Libraries

With books costing as much as a third of the annual salary of those civil servants who had the requisite education to want them, and with no developed book trade, only the wealthy could afford personal libraries, and the largest of these were small by modern standards. Photios (c. 810–c. 893), twice patriarch of Constantinople (858–867 and 877–886), describes some 280 books in his three-volume collection of reviews of the books that he had read. A significant proportion of these will have been from libraries to which he had access or via loans from friends rather than his own books. The personal library of Arethas (860–c. 935), archbishop of Caesarea in Cappadocia, who could afford to commission new copies of desired books, was large for its time, as indicated by the 24 books from his collection still identifiable today. Readers and scholars often copied books themselves or borrowed them to avoid the cost of commissioning new copies. Although many students probably sold their books to younger students to recoup their costs, volumes ac-

quired during their university years were often retained to become the core of small personal libraries.

Personal libraries suffered fates similar to public and imperial libraries. Michael Choniates (metropolitan of Athens, 1182–1204) lost his library in the sack of Athens in 1205 and despite considerable effort managed afterward to recover only a few items.

### Monastic Libraries

Monastic libraries played the largest role in preserving and making accessible classical, Byzantine, and ecclesiastical literature. Monasteries were to be found everywhere in Greek-speaking Christendom, and numerous monasteries in every significant city possessed libraries. Outside of the cities libraries were found in individual monasteries or clusters of monasteries at many "Holy Mountains" throughout the empire: Mount Olympus in Bithynia, the Holy Mountain near Rossano in southern Italy, the rock pinnacles of Meteora in central Greece, the monasteries on the Mountain of Moses in the Sinai, and – above all – the Holy Mountain, Athos. A few of these monasteries that continue to exist possess significant libraries that have remained intact since the Byzantine era (e.g., St. Catherine's monastery in the Sinai, the monasteries of Mount Athos and Meteora; and St. John's Monastery on Patmos). Urban or suburban monastic libraries often served as regional public and research libraries. These libraries were intended primarily to serve the liturgical needs of their monasteries, but they also sustained the work of monastic theologians and of teachers devoted to the preservation of Orthodox literature and literacy, most notably during the *Turkocratia* (the era of Ottoman rule, 1453–1822).

From the fourth-century beginnings of Christian monasticism among the hermits and *lavra*s of Egypt and Palestine, books comprised an important part of monastic life. They were read for edification and copied both as a source of support and as an ascetic exercise, as indicated by references in the *Apophthegmata Patrum* and John Moschus' (c. 550–619/34) *Pratum Spirituale*. Copying presumes the possession of exemplars. Although a hermit might find a market and income from copying one or two exemplars, the needs of monasteries were greater. Palestinian monasteries, such as the Great Lavra of Sabas founded in Palestine in the fifth century, were centers of anti-Origenist activity, an involvement that entailed not only writing of anti-Origenist tracts but also study and copying of patristic literature needed for resources. The Nag Hammadi codices survived from the library of a Pachomian monastery in Chenoboskion when they were hidden during an outbreak of violence related to controversies over Gnosticism. Justinianic legislation called for keeping collections of books in all monasteries for the use of the monks (Nov. 133.2), indicating that reading and study in these monastic centers was by Justinian's time (527–565) viewed as something to be expected. Monastic foundation charters and *typika* often mention books among the goods provided by the founder to meet the needs of the monastic life, in particular the Bibles, psalters, and liturgical books needed for the services as well as books of canon law and patristic literature to guide the abbots and elders of the monastery.

Monasteries naturally tended to become repositories for books – precious books dedicated to the monasteries by their owners for the salvation of their souls, books rescued from destruction elsewhere, and books left to monasteries by the monks who had owned them. The 14th-century foreign minister and scholar Theodore Metochites, preparing for his retirement to a life of scholarly writing at the Chora Monastery in Constantinople, built up its library to support his ongoing scholarly work there. The monks themselves produced personal copies of service books and edifying anthologies such as the *gerontika* (the ever evolving collections of *apophthegmata patrum*, edifying stories of the hermits and ascetics of the past as well as of more recent spiritual heroes of the monastery). Those monasteries that possessed the requisite relics, location, and fame to become pilgrimage sites tended to accumulate not only endowments and precious treasures but also larger libraries. Similarly, monasteries located in or around Constantinople or the regional capitals might double as public and academic libraries. Such monasteries were typically also major centers of book production, so that their libraries served as a stock of exemplars for their copyists and traveling scholars in search of books.

Monastic libraries were as likely to experience vicissitudes as were the city libraries. Libraries accumulated by wise and provident abbots of good education could suffer in later times the depredations of invaders, raiders, or pirates, or they could just as easily be despoiled by their own illiterate monks and abbots of later times who saw the books as financial assets when their monasteries fell into financial need. The archbishop of Thessaloniki, Eustathius (12th century), speaks to this problem of illiterate monks in his work on the reform of the monastic life:

> You treat this as a matter of trade, selling off this advantage you possess, indeed listening to the suggestions of the evil spirit who tells you "Sell these books of yours, spend the money as you please and follow me" . . . You illiterate fellow, why ever do you wish to reduce the library to the level of your own character? Just because you have no trace of culture, must you empty the library of the books that transmit it? (translated by Nigel G. Wilson [1967])

Shortly after this passage he mentions having requested at a local monastery permission to see a copy of the works of Gregory of Nazianzus famous for its calligraphy, only to be told that it had been sold, with the explanation, "What use was it to us?"

Rarely are monastic libraries represented today by surviving catalogs from the Byzantine and early post-Byzantine eras. At St. John Prodromos on Patmos, catalogs of 1201 (330 books), 1382 (300 books), and a partial catalog of 1580 (58 books, 22 of them new since 1382) give a sense of the size of this major monastic library. Ownership of books was typically documented only when a book was loaned or transferred to new ownership, and then in the book itself.

## Constantinopolitan Monastic Libraries

Among the most important of the Constantinopolitan monastic libraries was that of the Monastery of St. Theodore of Studios. Theodore (759–826) established a monastic system or rule that, in keeping with the tradition of the earliest Egyptian monasteries, required monks to read and provided for the production of books. Thus, over time the monastery accumulated a substantial library. Theodore's rule was adopted by a cluster of related monasteries, as a result of which it became standard for monasteries to possess libraries for monastic reading and edification and not merely the books required for services. From the Evergetis Monastery in Constantinople, the Kievan monasteries sent for copies when they began to be established in the ninth and tenth centuries. The Studite model also played a major role on Mount Athos, as evidenced by the Athonite adoption of Studite cenobitism – and by the Athonite libraries. The Monastery of Stoudios became a major center of book production in the tenth century, adopting and standardizing the then new minuscule script as a cost-saving measure for the production of books to replace the deteriorating earlier manuscripts written in majuscules. The monastery must have accumulated a significant library to support this mission and the program of reading by its monks. The monastic libraries at the capital played an important role in the various controversies and related councils that were held in the city.

## Libraries by Region

Thessaloniki must have had significant resources in its libraries to produce a student so erudite as St. Constantine (Cyril, 829–869), missionary to the Slavs and a student of Leo the Philosopher in Constantinople. The quality of the libraries in Thessaloniki continued through the 12th century, when the archbishop of Thessaloniki, Eustathius, could find and quote more than 400 different sources in his works. These libraries probably fell victim to the Norman sack of Thessaloniki in 1185, as described by Eustathius himself. Our knowledge of these libraries is limited to what can be derived from quotations from books found in those places by writers and scholars who were educated and flourished there.

In Asia Minor the monastic libraries of Trebizond, Mount Olympus in Bithynia, and Cappadocia were important regional resources.

The Library of St. Catherine's monastery, Sinai, a Justinianic foundation (constructed c. 548–565) remains today an important resource for scholars. From the time of the Arab conquest of the Sinai peninsula in the mid–seventh century until the 11th century, Sinai remained out of the orbit of Byzantine intellectual life.

In eastern Macedonia the Monastery of St. John Prodromos near Serres had a library of more than 400 volumes and the monastery of Kosinitsa on Mount Pangaion more than 260, until they were seized by the occupying Bulgarians in 1917. In

1923, in accordance with the 1919 Neuilly Accord, 259 manuscripts from these monasteries were returned to Greece, most of which were deposited in the National Library. Most of the remaining manuscripts are located today in the Ivan Dujcev Center in Sophia.

On Cyprus a number of mid-Byzantine monastic foundations had good libraries, including Kykkos, Machairas, St. John Chrysostom, Theotokos of Forbion (Asinou), Lagoudera, and the Enkleistra. Saint Neophytus, who founded the Enkleistra near Paphos, took pains in his *typikon* to protect his library by strict policies regarding use and forbidding alienation of books, which in his lifetime numbered about 150. These libraries grew during Turkish conquests of the mainland in the 14th to 15th century, when scribes from major centers such as Mount Olympus in Bithynia took refuge on Cyprus. Large libraries in the Kykkos and Machairas monasteries were destroyed by fires, the latter as recently as 1892. Only a small portion of the books from these middle and late Byzantine monastic libraries on Cyprus survive there. Most of these are preserved today not in monasteries but in the bishoprics, which began systematically to collect and preserve them during the 18th century. The library of the Monastery of St. John Chrysostom was transferred to the Patriarchal Library in Jerusalem.

The library of the Prodromos Monastery on Patmos contains some 330 manuscripts, the product of an active policy of collecting books by its abbots that began with its founding abbot, Christodoulos. Forced to flee from the Monastery of St. Paul in Latros when the Ottoman Turks overran that area in 1079, he brought as many of the manuscripts as he could with him to the capital, a quarter of which the emperor then allowed him to take to the new monastery on Patmos.

The Monasteries of Mount Athos are today famous for their libraries, which contain in excess of 10,000 manuscripts. The history of these libraries began in the year 963, when the Great Lavra of St. Athanasius was founded. This monastery was a Constantinopolitan-style cenobium in a world of hermits and *lavra*s. Athanasius' foundation introduced the Studite *Typikon* with its emphasis on reading. The Great Lavra is known to have developed two libraries: a main library and a "library of the catechumens." Other especially rich Athonite libraries include those of Iviron and Vatopedi. Some of the smaller monasteries also include significant libraries intact from an early date. The monastery of Philotheou (founded c. 991 as a hermitage; refounded as a cenobium in 1141) still preserves in its library some of the service books acquired at the time of its 12th-century refoundation. The Athonite libraries were busy and growing during the 14th-century Hesychast revival, when Athonite monks were searching Patristic literature to undergird the antiquity and legitimacy of the teachings of St. Gregory Palamas (c. 1296–1359). In the 16th century, when the Ottoman Turkish regime became oppressive (the era of the neomartyrs), the Athonite monastic libraries grew rapidly by preserving and recopying older manuscripts and producing a new generation of liturgical books. These 16th-century copies constitute a large proportion

of the Athonite libraries today. Great numbers of manuscripts from the Athonite libraries have migrated to European libraries or (by means of loans to the Russian Synodal Library) to the State Historical Museum in Moscow.

The Athonite monastic community was instrumental in the creation of an Orthodox literature for the recently converted Bulgarians, Serbs, Iberians (Georgians), and Russians, who in turn founded or patronized various monasteries on the Holy Mountain (Zographou, Chilandar, Iviron, and Panteleimonos, respectively). Other Athonite monasteries that ultimately remained Greek also had extended associations in the northern Balkans – Koutloumousi with the Voivodes of Wallachia and Philotheou with the Georgian kings of Kakhetia.

*Orthodox Libraries beyond Byzantium*

The foundation and growth of libraries in the Balkans and in Russia is directly related to the Christianization of those areas and to the translation of Orthodox Christian literature from Greek into Old Church Slavonic. Thus, these libraries were from the beginning associated mainly with monasteries and with the metropolitan churches where this activity was situated; they had no obligation to an educational system based on the continuity of classical Greek culture. Here the literature of Byzantine Orthodoxy was copied and translated into Old Church Slavonic. In the process the literature of Orthodox monasticism became the basis of a transnational literary culture. Bibles, liturgical books, homilies, saints' lives, and encomia served the cycle of the Church year; translations of the Greek patristic literature (especially of the fourth and fifth centuries), collections of sermons, *gerontika* (thematic anthologies of the gnomic wisdom of the anchorites of Egypt and Palestine and more recent monastic sages), and catechetical questions and answers supported theological education; apocryphal literature supplemented the Gospel history; Byzantine chronicles, tales of Alexander the Great, and Josephus' histories covering the entirety of world history as governed by divine providence set the stage for the emergence of the Balkans in the triumphal progress of Orthodoxy; the *Physiologus* exemplified allegorical revelation through the natural world; and the *Christian Topography* of Kosmas Indicopleustes constructed an Orthodox geography in travelogue form. Other factors that played a major role in the development of monastic libraries among the Slavs included the spread of Hesychasm in the 14th century, the systematic retranslation of all the literature previously translated from Greek, the standardization of orthography, and the liturgical revisions necessitated by the change from the Constantinopolitan to the Jerusalemite *Typikon*. The introduction of paper, which came into regular use in the mid-14th century, made the rapid growth of monastic libraries in both the Greek and the Slavic worlds feasible at the very moment when these factors created an increased need.

The monastic libraries among the Slavs are distinguished from their Greek counterparts by the conscious exclusion of Greek classical literature. The Greek classics had no comparable cultural role among Slavic-speaking peoples to justify their preservation and were rejected as the product of paganism. They are also distinguished by delayed exploitation of the technological revolution of printing. Although book printing in Cyrillic began at the end of the 15th century, the Muscovite tsardom did not enjoy the benefits of the new technology until the mid–16th century, as attested by the appearance at that time of important monastic print collections. In these regions the manuscript tradition continued unabated through the 19th century. Although the writing of manuscripts in monasteries continued also in Greece, it was clearly reduced to a minor role after the advent of printing.

## 1. Bulgaria

Although the Orthodox mission to the Slavs began with the short-lived mission to Moravia in the ninth century by Sts. Cyril and Methodios (the "Apostles and Enlighteners of the Slavs"), it gained real momentum first in Bulgaria with the foundation of monasteries possessing schools, programs of book production, and libraries.

The earliest monasteries in Bulgaria (ninth and early tenth centuries) were built following the conversion in 863 of King Boris (852–863). These early monasteries were located mostly in and near Ohrid and Preslav but also in the vicinity of the old capital, Pliska, where the Boyars continued to resist Christianization. Boris built seven metropolitan cathedrals; he founded and throughout his reign continued to build up the endowments of a number of monasteries that he founded, including the royal monastery of Tiča, where he eventually retired. At least eight monasteries flourished in and around the new Christian capital, Ohrid, during the reign of his son, Symeon (893–927). His Slavic bishop, St. Clement, a disciple of Sts. Cyril (826–869) and Methodios (c. 815–885), established a center at Lake Ohrid in Macedonia for training priests in Church Slavonic and for translation of Orthodox literature. Here, too, some of the earliest Church Slavonic literature was produced. Tiča became the seat of the second Slavic bishopric, in northeastern Bulgaria, completing the Slavicization of the Bulgarian Church (Fine, 1987).

Boris and Symeon provided for monastic libraries following the model of monastic administration prevalent in Constantinople and Thessaloniki. During the second half of the century, a second wave of monastic foundations in southern Bulgaria between the upper valleys of the Strymon and the Vardar Rivers in remote mountainous areas was influenced more by the contemporary development of monasticism on Mount Athos, whose monasteries were extensively invested in real estate in this region. In the tenth century the monasteries of Thessaloniki, Mount Athos, and Mount Olympus in Bithynia were international monastic foundations dedicated to the transmission of Byzantine Orthodoxy and its literature to the Slavs and other non-Greek peoples. To this Byzantine substrate the cults of the Bulgarian monastic founders and saints quickly added a unique Bulgarian and Slavic monastic and hagiologic literature.

This history of Slavic intellectual activity was temporarily interrupted by Byzantine Emperor Basil II's (976–1025) conquest and annexation of Bulgaria in 1018. The following Hellenization of the Slavic Church, under Greek Archbishop Theophylact of Ohrid (c. 1090–1109), meant the closing of the Slavic schools, replacement of Old Church Slavonic liturgy by Greek, and the systematic destruction of the Slavic manuscripts that had filled the libraries of Bulgaria. Not one of these Slavic manuscripts from before the Second Bulgarian Empire has survived.

In the 14th century the spread of Hesychast practices and theology played a very significant role in the formation of Slavic monasteries and the expansion of the content of their monastic libraries. In Bulgaria Gregory of Sinai (d. 1346), fleeing the barbarian raids on Athonite monasteries, settled in the monastery of Paroria, where he obtained the patronage of Czar John Alexander. There he attracted the Bulgarian abbot Theodosius of Trnovo, who dedicated himself to translating Gregory's Hesychast writings into Bulgarian. After Gregory's death Theodosius traveled to Mount Athos, Thessaloniki, and Berrhoia and established the monastery of Kefalarevo. There his disciples, including the monks Dionysius and John, translated the works of John Chrysostom (c. 347–407) and John Climacus (c. 570–c. 649), respectively. The patriarch, Euthymios, was a well-educated and prolific writer who supported the orthographic reforms of the late 14th century.

The Ottoman conquest of 1393 had a devastating effect on monastic libraries, but even so the resulting losses were not as exhaustive as those caused by the Byzantine policies of Hellenization following the conquests of Basil II.

## 2. Serbia

In the context of internal dispute between Nicene and Epirote powers during the Latin occupation of Constantinople, when the Serbian leader Stefan the "First Crowned" was developing closer ties with the Latin pope, an autocephalous national Orthodox church was created in Serbia by the Nicene patriarch. Sava (c. 1175–1235), King Stefan's brother, was appointed archbishop of Serbia in 1219. The great early Serbian monasteries were founded in rural wooded valleys, unlike the Athonite monasteries, but their organization was clearly Byzantine. Saint Sava organized the monastic life of the Studenica Monastery, which he founded, on the basis of the *typikon* of Evergetis Monastery, which he had found in use at Chilandar on Mount Athos. This model was followed in the other great early Serb monasteries: Žiča and Sopoćani and then in the later royal monasteries of Mileševa (13th-century foundation, home of the relics of St. Sava), Gračanica near Kosovo, and Polje and Dečani (both 14th-century foundations). As in Bulgaria the monasteries housed schools where a literate class of officials for chancellery duty could be trained. Likewise the monasteries produced the charters and other documents needed by the new church. They also extended the Christianization of the Serbs and established libraries to house the translation of traditional Byzantine Christian literature (especially sermons and saints' lives), which, together with liturgical books, constituted much of the content of these libraries. From the 13th century on, these libraries were enriched with increasing numbers of original Serbian works. The books in the Serbian libraries, both translations and original, were produced partly at the great Serbian Monastery on Mount Athos, Chilandar, and partly in the larger monasteries within Serbia. Among these major monastic institutions with libraries was that of Žiča, the monastery built by Stefan and first seat of the Serbian archbishop. Among the important early projects of translation was Sava's own edition of the *Byzantine Nomocanon of Fourteen Titles*, a compendium of Byzantine canon law. This Nomocanon had been in use in Byzantium since the seventh century, with modifications based on Aristinos' and John Zonaras' commentaries. Adapted to Serbian needs, the new nomocanon rejected the Byzantine subordination of Church to state in favor of an equal partnership. It also formed the basis of civil law in the young Serbian state.

By the 14th century, under Stephan Dušan, many Serbian monasteries, benefiting from the equal partnership of Church and state in Serbia, had acquired vast landholdings and large endowments. In these prosperous circumstances, as in Bulgaria, the Hesychast movement contributed to the growth of Serbian libraries, as Serb disciples of Gregory of Sinai carried on his work. Jakov, later metropolitan of Serres after its capture by Stephan Dušan, maintained ties with the Monastery of St. Catherine at Mount Sinai, reflected in the presence there today of several Old Church Slavonic manuscripts. Stefan Lazarević (1389–1427, despot 1402–1427) established a number of monasteries in Serbia that possessed significant libraries and contributed to the literary revival of that time. The Monastery of Resava (Manasija), founded in 1407, was intended specifically as a center for Hesychasts, whom Stefan revered. According to Constantine the Philosopher, the leading literary figure, scholar, and patron in the reign of Stefan, the despot endowed the monastery generously with books and icons. Although not a major literary center, it was typical in its dedication to translation and copying.

## 3. Romania

Romanian monasteries and the Romanian Orthodox Church played a unique role among Slavic-speaking Christians. Romania (Wallachia and Moldavia) was not overtaken by the Ottoman Turks. The monasteries, the schools that they supported, and the Romanian scribes who worked in them produced a prodigious number of books during the Ottoman era and served as a conduit for books from the Balkans to the Russians and Ukrainians. Their role during this time is reflected in the influence of the Romanians on Mount Athos at the Athonite Monastery of Koutloumousi and the continuing presence of Romanian *sketes* there today.

## 4. Kievan Rus' and Russia

Credit for the first library in Rus' is given to Iaroslav the Wise (1015–1054), son of Grand Prince Vladimir, who converted Kievan Rus' to Christianity. The *Primary Chronicle* (*Povest' vremennykh let*), the earliest surviving chronicle of Kievan Rus', reports that Iaroslav "loved books, and caused many books to be written out, and he placed them in the church of St. Sophia." This church, built between 1037 and 1047/48 to be the metropolitan cathedral, was placed under the jurisdiction of Metropolitan Ilarion (1051–c.1054). Metropolitan Ilarion was erudite in Greek and Slavonic and is now known especially for his "Homily on Law and Grace." As a repository for the rapidly growing body of Slavonic translations of Byzantine ecclesiastical literature, the cathedral served the needs of the clergy and of the first generation of Rus' who enjoyed a specifically Christian literacy. Much of this literature, whether in Slavonic translation or original, was already available to Rus' through the South Slavs. Extraordinary examples still extant of Rus'ian manuscripts, such as the 1056/57 Ostromir Gospels, copied in Novgorod, or the 1073 Miscellany of Grand Prince Sviatoslav, from Kiev, bear testimony to the rapid process of both Byzantine and Slavo-Byzantine acculturation.

The Kievan Monastery of the Caves is also noted for the original literary productivity of its monks, contributing an extended Slavonic monastic literature that became a new feature of monastic libraries in Rus'ian lands from the late 11th century on. Among the works that were common to these monasteries were Nestor's *Life of Feodosii of the Caves*, his *lection* on Boris and Gleb, the *paterik* of the Monastery of the Caves with its stories of its monastic heroes, and the *Primary Chronicle*. As Christianity spread outward from Kiev in the 12th century, so did the institutions of monasticism and monastic libraries.

After the Mongols reduced Kievan Rus', Moscow emerged in the late 14th century as the dominant political and cultural center. Moscow's alliance with the Mongols, paralleling Paleologan diplomatic ties with the Mongols against the Turks, laid the groundwork for expansion of new Orthodox territories, monasteries, and their libraries in Russia. After the fall of Constantinople in 1453, Moscow, being the only independent and powerful Orthodox state, saw itself as the defender of Orthodoxy. Thus, when Ottoman policy moved to eradicate Orthodoxy in the early 16th century, Grand Prince Basil III (1505–1533) committed himself to the translation and preservation of the Orthodox heritage. Moscow increasingly viewed its earlier literary and cultural heritage with a critical eye. In fact this was expressed by attempts to standardize liturgical and other texts. For example, Basil III invited Maximus the Greek (c. 1470–1556), of Vatopedi Monastery on Mount Athos, to come to Russia to "correct the books." Maximus spent the rest of his life in this activity.

### The Patriarchal Library

The Russian Patriarchal Library came into existence following the institution of the Russian patriarchate in Moscow in 1588 by Ecumenical Patriarch Jeremiah II. In the following century Patriarch Nikon of Moscow (1652–1658) undertook a reform of the Russian liturgy to bring it into conformity with Greek ritual. His envoy, Arseny Suchanov, traveled to the monasteries of Mount Athos and the Balkans collecting manuscripts for this project – manuscripts that made the new Patriarchal Library (today the Synodal Library) one of the richest collections of Greek manuscripts in the world, not to mention its wealth of Slavonic and other resources.

*Academic Libraries*

Academic libraries in Russia are a relatively late phenomenon. Among Orthodox educational institutions, the Moscow Theological Academy stands out as the most important Orthodox scholarly institution in Russia. In 1917 its library had some 300,000 volumes and 1,600 manuscript books. After the Revolution the academy was closed, and its library was nationalized under control of the Publichnaia Library – commonly called in Soviet days the Lenin Library and now the Russian State Library (in Moscow). Reestablished in 1947 the Theological Academy was moved to the Trinity Monastery of St. Sergius, but it was renamed the Sergeevskii filial of the Publichnaia Library. Its counterpart in Ukraine, the Kiev Theological Academy (Kievskaia dukhovnaia akademiia), with some 1,600 manuscripts prior to the Revolution, holds about 2,000 today. Many of these manuscripts, cataloged before the Revolution, came from Orthodox monasteries and churches in Ukraine, including the Pochaiv Assumption Monastery and the Melets' monastery in Volhynia. Yet another Orthodox academic library was the Vifansk Theological Library.

In the 1920s the collections of the Vifansk Theological Library and the library of the Trinity Monastery were combined with the library of the Moscow Theological Academy. However, in the 1930s all the rare religious manuscripts and most of the archives were moved to the Lenin Library, with the exception of some especially valuable codices that were allegedly sold by the Communist government. In 1947, with the reestablishment of the Theological Academy, the library was also reestablished, but it lacked the manuscripts and rare books of the Academy's original library.

In St. Petersburg the Library of the Theological Academy similarly centralized numerous other libraries, including those of the Monastery of Aleksandr Nevskii, the Sofia Cathedral of Novgorod, and the Kirillo-Belozerskii Monastery.

*Nationalization of the Old Monastic and Church Libraries*

The centralization of libraries from monasteries and churches, already evident in the Orthodox theological libraries mentioned previously, was advanced with the formation of the National Libraries. In Ukraine the central repository of the old Orthodox libraries was the Ukrainian National Library founded in 1918, known today, after many reorganizations, as the Vernadsky National and University Library of Ukraine. By 1919 a manuscript section had been formed as a centralized repository for manuscript collections in eastern Ukraine. Among the collections thus nationalized were those of the Kiev Monastery of the Caves (Kievo-Pechers'ka Lavra) and the Saint Sophia Cathedral in Kiev. Other noteworthy examples include the Monastery of St. Michael of the Golden Domes, the Kiev Vydubychi St. Michael, the Kiev Church of the Tithe, and the Nizhyn Annunciation Monastery. Integration of these collections into a central manuscript division obscured the distinctions of content and the lines of demarcation between the collections of the old libraries that had not been adequately cataloged. Other manuscripts known to have been in the monastic and church collections have disappeared, such as those of the St. Nicholas Hermitage Monastery and the St. Florus Women's Monastery in Kiev.

In Moscow the centralization of manuscript libraries is evidenced in the libraries of the Troitsko-Sergievskii Monastery and the Moscow Ecclesiastical Academy, now preserved in the Manuscript Division of the Russian State Library (formerly the Lenin State Library). Likewise manuscripts from the monastery of St. Nicolas (Nikol'skii Edinoverčhevskii Monastyr) are preserved along with the old Patriarchal (Synodal) library in the Historical State Museum.

Generally, under Communism virtually all original monastic and theological libraries, especially in the former Soviet Union, were nationalized and incorporated in state national and public libraries. This was less true for such libraries in the former Eastern Bloc nations. Today, after the fall of Communism, the future status of many of these nationalized and confiscated collections remains unresolved as the various churches and private individuals affected have begun attempts to recover what was taken.

ROBERT W. ALLISON

*See also* Istanbul, Turkey; Jerusalem, Israel; Meteora, Thessaly, Greece; Mount Athos, Greece; Mount Sinai, Egypt; Orthodox Monasticism

## Further Reading

Fine, John V.A., *The Late Medieval Balkans: A Critical Survey from the Late Twelfth Century to the Ottoman Conquest*, Ann Arbor: University of Michigan Press, 1987; Manchester, Greater Manchester: Manchester University Press, 1991

Franklin, Simon, and Jonathan Shepard, *The Emergence of Rus, 750–1200* (Longman History of Russia), London and New York: Longman, 1996

Grimsted, Patricia Kennedy, *Archives and Manuscript Repositories in the U.S.S.R., Moscow and Leningrad* (Columbia University, Studies of the Russian Institute), Princeton, New Jersey: Princeton University Press, 1972 (Moscow and Leningrad); Ukraine and Moldova, 1988

Jovanovic, Slobodan A., *A Guide to Yugoslav Libraries and Archives*, Columbus, Ohio: American Association for the Advancement of Slavic Studies, 1976

Mango, Cyril, "The Availability of Books in the Byzantine Empire, A.D. 750–850," in *Byzantine Books and Bookmen* (Dumbarton Oaks Colloquium, 1971), edited by Mango and Ihor Sevcenko, Washington, D.C.: Dumbarton Oaks Center for Byzantine Studies, 1975

Reynolds, L.D., and Nigel Guy Wilson, *Scribes and Scholars: A Guide to the Transmission of Greek and Latin Literature*, London: Oxford University Press, 1968; 2nd edition, New York: Clarendon Press, 1989; 3rd edition, New York: Oxford University Press, and Oxford: Clarendon Press, 1991

Thomson, Francis J., "The Nature of the Reception of Christian Byzantine Culture in Russia in the Tenth to Thirteenth Centuries and Its Implications for Russian Culture," *Slavica gandensia* 5 (1978)

Wilson, Nigel G., "The Libraries of the Byzantine World," *Greek, Roman and Byzantine Studies* 8 (1967)

Wilson, Nigel G., "Books and Readers in Byzantium," in *Byzantine Books and Bookmen* (Dumbarton Oaks Colloquium, 1971), edited by Cyril A. Mango and Ihor Sevcenko, Washington, D.C.: Dumbarton Oaks Center for Byzantine Studies, 1975

# Libraries: Western Christian

"A monastery without a library is a fort without an armory."

> – monastic adage, Western Europe

The first monastic libraries emerged in Egypt, a result of the individual efforts of scholars such as Origen (c. 185–c. 254), the size of the Christian community there, and the strong pre-Christian presence of libraries in that region. Monasteries under the direction of Pachomius (c. 290–346) and Shenoute (fifth century) required that members learn to read, and it was expected that they would borrow and study books from the community's collection. Coptic and Greek works were included. A library catalog from the Phobaimmon monastery, dating from around 600, was found in the 1970s. It includes about 80 titles and mentions the material on which the writing was done (usually papyrus and less often parchment.) Books of the Old and New Testaments, lectionaries, church canons, biography/hagiography, and the occasional medical book made up the collection (Krause, 1991).

The pattern in Eastern Christendom seems to have been quite similar. "Catalogs" were simply inventories of items held by the community. On occasion the personal library of a patriarch (Kazhdan and Browning, 1991) would include heretical books: evidently, before the printing press, controlling the circulation of works deemed unsavory was much simpler than now. The Rule of Pachomius (fourth century) stipulated that the *econome* (roughly equivalent to the Western abbot) had responsibility for the care of manuscripts and books. Surviving collections at Mount Athos and Mount Sinai provide some indication of the scope that collections attained (Witty, 1967).

Christianity grew as a way of life with a heavy dependence on tradition, and inevitably that tradition became a written one. As in so many other ways (e.g., law and transportation), the Christian way incorporated the accomplishments of Roman civilization with respect to books and libraries. According to Seneca, collecting for reading and display had become fashionable (Witty, 1967): "Nowadays a library takes rank with a bathroom as a necessary ornament of a house" (*De Tranquil. Animi*, ix: cited in Witty, 1967).

It appears that readings – from the Scriptures, from works of Christian instruction, and from the letters of Church leaders – were an integral part of Christian worship from the very beginning, and from that it fell out that the place where people gathered for services became the place where books were collected for use. This pattern seems already to have been established by the time of Jerome (c. 345–420) so that he assumes that wherever there was a congregation, there would be books. Logically enough, churches that became administratively central tended to accumulate the larger and better collections. Early examples include that at Jerusalem around 250 and slightly later in Caesarea (Palestine), Cirta (North Africa), Alexandria, and Rome.

Jerome's influence on the founding of the first "papal" library by his friend Pope Damasus I (366–384) at the Church of St. Lawrence was significant. The personal wealth of Popes Agapetus (535–536) and Gregory I (590–604) enlarged the scope of the collection further. Cassiodorus (485/90–c. 580), a contemporary of Agapetus, exercised perhaps a greater influence on libraries and scholarship than any other figure of the Middle Ages: his *Institutiones divinarum et saecularium literatum* was not only a guide to systematic reading but also a practical manual for the scriptorium (copying room). His work set a pattern for medieval libraries that endured until the Renaissance (Witty, 1967).

The Middle Ages saw far more disruption of libraries in the West than in the East, where the rising Islamic culture had its own highly learned tradition. In the West the center of gravity shifted around the seventh century from urban centers to monastic libraries. The great age of monastic libraries and scriptoria was between the 8th and 12th centuries. The inclusion of a library in the structure and life of a monastic order was articulated clearly in the Rule of St. Benedict (c. 540):

> Above all, let one or two seniors be appointed to go round the monastery at the hours when the brethren are engaged in reading and see that there be no slothful brother giving himself to idleness or to foolish talk and not applying himself to his reading, so that he is thus not only useless to himself but a distraction to others. If such a one be found, let him be corrected once and a second time. (Rule of St. Benedict, cited in Thurston, 1911)

Normally a mother house would provide such books as it could spare for any new monastery, and this would set in motion a period of great copying activity in the scriptorium of the new house. This pattern has left behind a traceable web of connections in styles of script and illustration from one center to another. Benefactors of a new monastic house would also commonly provide it with new books. Monasteries invested considerable time, energy, and skill in cultivating such treasures, indicated by the painstaking craftsmanship of the scribes, the periodic rebinding of volumes, and the careful attention devoted to compiling catalogs (Bruckner, 1965). Extant records indicate the energetic pace that was maintained in monastic scriptoria of this period.

Local collections varied somewhat in content according to local needs, but of course the greatest attention was paid to Holy Scripture, the works of the Fathers, and liturgical works needed for regular services. The latter would encompass sacramentaries, lectionaries, gospel books, *evangelistaria*, missals, and so on (Bruckner, 1965). A somewhat more public function was fulfilled by the maintenance of the *Liber vitae*, or records of deceased

Abbey of St. Mary (Premonstratensian), Dryburgh, Berwickshire, Scotland, 12th century. The doorway into the church from the cloister shows a book cupboard on the right.
Photo courtesy of Chris Schabel

members, together with those of relatives and community bene-factors. This type of literature gradually took on a life and structure of its own, as entries were arranged chronologically according to the Church calendar, with more material pertinent to individuals accumulating. To this were added feasts, masses, texts, and liturgical and homiletic material – all very specialized, time consuming, and expressive of considerable devotion.

The bibliographic needs of those monasteries that maintained schools were somewhat more sophisticated. Here would be included more extensive collections of Roman authors, Christian poets, and books on rhetoric, grammar, history, and so on. It is in this endeavor that the monastic libraries fulfilled a crucial role in ensuring that classical works were not lost to memory.

The need for more esoteric and far-reaching works – on astrology, law, medicine, and mathematics-was often met by an informal barter system whereby libraries were able to fill gaps in their own collections by trading duplicate or unneeded works for others of greater interest. "Thus until well into the 12th century . . . the monastic libraries were a significant mirror of intellectual movements and currents" (Bruckner, 1965).

By the standards and capacities of the period, a collection numbering more than a thousand would be considered very large. No monastic library approached its collection task with any idea of being comprehensive (as university libraries could and did prior to Gutenberg). Culling out of unnecessary or defective copies was common practice: quality and utility, not mass, were the priorities. The office of "librarian" was often formally defined as early as the eighth century. Catalogs varied as much in complexity as they did in size, ranging from a single sheet to much more complex registers. In some cases books were kept chained to the desks in which they were housed. The concern for security is further indicated by a librarian's responsibility for impressing the official stamp or label of the monastery on each volume. Organization was not elaborate and could usually be maintained by nothing more sophisticated than a parchment list glued to boards and hung on a wall.

The architecture of monastic libraries of this period provides further indication of the importance assigned to their use. Typically a large, pillared hall would serve as a reading room with built-in cupboards to store the books. Carrels for study were often set around the perimeter to take the greatest advantage of light. The plan for library construction at St. Gallen (present-day northeastern Switzerland) showed such detail and insight that copies were circulated in Europe and might well have influenced construction elsewhere. In brief this plan called for a two-story annex between the transept and the east choir. The lower floor

**Anteroom of the library, Monastery of San Giovanni Evangelista (Benedictine), Parma, Italy, 16th century.**
**Photo courtesy of the Editor**

was to serve as the scriptorium, the upper as the *bibliotheca*. Other monastic centers, such as Monte Cassino, had separate libraries, with the liturgical collection kept in proximity as close as possible to the sanctuary (Thurston, 1911).

During the 12th century the central importance of monastic libraries began to be supplanted by cathedral collections. This was a result of social change rather than of religious or ecclesiastical forces. Populations in Europe began to shift markedly toward the cities. This was accompanied by the emergence of the new bourgeoisie, who showed a strong interest in learning. The provision of learning opportunities for this group required an urban base and a lay orientation, neither of which the monasteries were in any position to provide. The convergence of these new realities with the rise of mendicant orders (e.g., the Franciscans) – monastics who preferred the public life of the town to the retirement of the cloister – meant a surprisingly rapid shift of focus away from monastic libraries and, for that matter, a new approach to "publishing." To borrow from today's usage, the approach of the cathedral libraries more closely resembled those of a "public library" than of an academic library.

Somewhat related to these trends – the rise of the bourgeoisie, population shifts toward the city, and the emergence of mendi-

cant orders – came the development of universities whose libraries tended to be much more encyclopedic in ambition than monastic libraries and drew further attention away from them. Among the religious orders the Dominicans and Franciscans were especially active in this new intellectual arena. Thus, as early as the end of the 13th century newer university libraries, such as that of the Sorbonne in Paris, dwarfed in size and scope the more selective, "niche" collections of the rural, monastic houses.

Mention has already been made of Monte Cassino, but it is important to draw attention to England, the setting where the monastic library seems to have come to its fullest flowering. More than one recent work has suggested that its position on the extremity of "civilization" engendered – especially among the Irish – both a stronger sense of determination and a greater insulation from cultural decline than elsewhere (Roy, *Islands of Storm*, 1991; Cahill, *How the Irish Saved Civilization*, 1995). In "saving civilization" – through the process of copying deteriorating manuscripts and preserving them so that when the time came they could be reintroduced to the Continent – monastic efforts kept alive the potential for a rebirth of civilization in a more favorable time. For example, Alcuin (c. 740–804), librarian of the great library of York, became a trusted confidante of Charlemagne (768–814) and thus had a direct effect on the revival of learning during his reign. Somewhat earlier the Celtic apostle Columban (d. 615) brought his library to Bobbio in Italy (Reynolds, 1968, 1991; O'Connor, 1921).

In addition to the missionary centers of Iona and Lindisfarne, monastic communities at Jarrow (home of the Venerable Bede), Wearmouth, and York in many ways exemplified the highest achievements of the great centuries of monastic libraries. These included the rapid and energetic expansions of library collections, the effort expended at bringing in new collections in whole from great distances, and most memorably the exquisite works from their scriptoria.

The experience of Benedict Biscop (c. 628–689/90), a distant protégé of the great Cassiodorus and eventually librarian at Jarrow, is instructive. At the age of 25, Biscop was outside the church, a rough soldier of fortune. When he turned to the monastic life, he took an active, almost obsessive interest in learning and books, and for the rest of his life he, not so much with formal education as with a kind of instinctive sense of what books were necessary, went everywhere and spared no effort or expense to build a great library; and, if the caliber of scholars that a library trains is any indicator of the library's quality, it can be said that he surpassed Cassiodorus himself. The monks of Jarrow made no less than three copies of the great Bible of Cassiodorus, of which only one survives: "it contains 2060 large folio pages and weighs 75 and 1/2 pounds; and it has been calculated that the three of them together required the skins of 1550 calves, not to speak of the silver and precious stones for their bindings, or the skilled labor of at least seven scribes over several years" (Southern, 1976). Southern goes on to say that "the library at Jarrow produced a scholar of the kind that Cassiodorus could only dream of in vain: Bede." In their time the libraries within the monastic tradition have served the mission and ideals of their communities. Yet what has often outlasted even the physical collections and buildings is their own ideal: "the power of the library is to bring order out of chaos" (Southern, 1976).

DAVID STEWART

See also Alcuin; Archives, Western Christian; Bede, St.; Cassiodorus; Celtic Monasticism; Egypt; Gregory I (the Great), St.; Hagiography; Manuscript Production: Christian; Maurists; Monte Cassino, Italy; Mount Athos, Greece; Mount Sinai, Egypt; Officials: Western Christian; St. Gallen, Switzerland; Schools and Universities, Benedictine; Visual Arts, Western Christian: Book Arts before the Renaissance

## Further Reading

Bruckner, A., "Libraries, Medieval," in *The New Catholic Encyclopedia*, volume 5, Washington, D.C.: Catholic University of America Press, 1965

Cahill, Thomas, *How the Irish Saved Civilization*, New York: Doubleday, and London: Hodder and Stoughton, 1995

Cahn, Walter, "The *Rule* and the Book: Cistercian Book Illumination in Burgundy and Champagne," in *Monasticism*

*and the Arts*, edited by Timothy G. Verdon, Syracuse, New York: Syracuse University Press, 1984

Cross, Claire, "Monastic Learning and Libraries in Sixteenth-century Yorkshire," in *Humanism and Reform: the Church in Europe, England, and Scotland, 1400–1643*, edited by James Kirk and James K. Cameron, Oxford and Cambridge, Massachusetts: Blackwell, 1991

Dawkins, R.M., "Notes on Life in the Monasteries of Mount Athos," *Harvard Theological Review* 46:3 (July 1953)

Jebb, Dom Philip, "The Archives of the English Benedictine Congregation Kept at St. Gregory's, Downside," *Downside Review* 312 (July 1975)

Kazhdan, Alexander, and Robert Browning, "Library," in *The Oxford Dictionary of Byzantium*, volume 5, edited by Alexander Kazhdan et al., Oxford and New York: Oxford University Press, 1991

Krause, Martin, "Libraries," in *The Coptic Encyclopedia*, volume 5, edited by Aziz S. Atiya, New York: Macmillan, 1991

O'Connor, John B., *Monasticism and Civilization*, New York: P.J. Kenedy, 1921

Ramsay, Nigel, "The Cathedral Archives and Library," in *A History of Canterbury Cathedral*, edited by Patrick Collinson et al., Oxford and New York: Oxford University Press, 1995

Reynolds, L.D., and N.G. Wilson, *Scribes and Scholars: A Guide to the Transmission of Greek and Latin Literature*, London: Oxford University Press, 1968; 3rd edition, Oxford: Clarendon Press, and New York: Oxford University Press, 1991

Roy, James Charles, *Islands of Storm*, Chester Springs, Pennsylvania: Dufour, and Dublin: Wolfhound Press, 1991

Southern, R.W., "A Benedictine Library in a Disordered World," *Downside Review* 94 (July 1976)

Thurston, Herbert, "Libraries," in *The Catholic Encyclopedia*, volume 8, edited by Charles G. Herberman et al., New York: Robert Appleton, 1911

Turner, D.H., editor, *The Benedictines in Britain*, New York: George Braziller, and London: The British Library, 1980

Witty, F.J., "Libraries, Ancient," in *New Catholic Encyclopedia*, volume 8, New York: McGraw-Hill, 1967

# Life Cycle, Christian

Jesus, who was born before Herod's death in 4 B.C. and probably was crucified in A.D. 30, was traditionally considered by Christians to have died at age 33, which thus was considered the age of perfect male maturity. Aristotle set this male maturity at 35. For women maturity was supposed to be reached earlier, as the possibility of bearing children seldom lasted beyond 45. The Old Testament reports advanced ages for the antediluvial patriarchs, apparently on the grounds that Adam would have been immortal if he had not sinned. Thus, Methusaleh, a descendant of Adam's virtuous son Seth, died before the Flood at the age of 969. After the Flood humankind was reduced to our present life span, yet sometimes the righteous lived to an advanced age, as did Moses, who died at 120, and in general long life was promised to those faithful to the Covenant (Deut. 30:20). After that, as Psalm 90:10 says, "Seventy is the sum of our years; eighty if we are strong." Yet in the late Book of Wisdom, this is modified by the declaration, "The just man, though he die early, shall be at rest, for age that is honorable comes not with the passing of time" (Wisd. of Sol. 4:7–8). Interestingly the older Jewish conception of the blessing of a long life is still evident in the stories of the monks of the desert. Saint Antony the Great was said to have died at 95.

At the other end of the life span, Jesus insisted that respect be given to children, and this had led to infant baptism. Moreover from the time of the *Didache* at the beginning of the second century A.D., abortion was forbidden to Christians in the baptismal catechesis. Under the influence of Aristotle's theory of "delayed hominization" of the embryo, the Roman Catholic Church, although it has always condemned abortion as a grave sin, long hesitated to declare when human life begins. However, in light of modern embryology it recently has adopted the view that the spiritual soul of each human person is created directly by God to impart human life at the moment of the fertilization of the human zygote. The celebration of the Feast of the Holy Innocents and the canonization of young martyrs has also contributed to this reverence for children.

Ancient monasteries, following the precedent of Samuel's reception in the Temple (1 Sam. 2:24–28) as a child offered to the Lord, often received "oblates" at a very early age. However, in 656 the Council of Toledo forbade the reception of boys under ten and required them to be free to leave at puberty. This was in part to permit care for the orphaned but also to educate the younger sons of noble families. Thomas Aquinas (c. 1225–1274) was an oblate of Monte Cassino, although he was never professed as a monk. In the Rule of St. Benedict, allowance is made for boy oblates (chaps. 30 and 59); for the sick, old men, and children as regards health and food (chaps. 36 and 37); and for those who find a command of the abbot impossible to carry out (chap. 68).

Most significant of all for a Christian understanding of the life cycle has been the sacramental system. Thomas Aquinas developed this view in the *Summa theologiae* (III, q.65, a.1, c). Here he suggests that in the order of spiritual growth baptism corresponds to human birth, confirmation to youth, and the Eucharist to maturity. Marriage and holy orders correspond to the service of the community by mature persons, penance to recovery from sickness, and the anointing of the sick to aging and death.

Another approach to understanding the life cycle in Christian terms is provided by the theory of the three ages or ways of spiritual growth that goes back to Origen (c. 185–c. 254) and is found in Gregory of Nyssa (c. 330–c. 395), Dionysius the Pseudo-Areopagite, and many other monastic writers. However, its full development unfolded with the Carmelites Teresa of Avila (1515–1582) and John of the Cross (1542–1591). According to this scheme the work of grace in the faithful Christian soul, especially in those who are able to persevere in contemplative prayer, takes the three forms of purgation, illumination, and union. Although the three processes go on simultaneously at all stages of Christian life, among beginners the first dominates, among those of solid virtue the second, and among the perfect the third. Thus, in a life in which spiritual progress is steady, the Christian passes through a purgative, then an illuminative, and finally a unitive stage that is the beginning of eternal life with God. These stages are demarcated by the experience that the purgative process, which like the other two is always present, takes the form of the "Dark Night of the Soul," marking the transition from the purgative to the illuminative way, and then of the "Dark Night of the Spirit," marking the transition from the illuminative to the unitive way. These stages of spiritual growth take different forms and proceed at different rates for different persons according to circumstances, vocations, and fidelity to prayer and virtuous living.

BENEDICT M. ASHLEY, O.P.

*See also* Antony, St.; Death: Christian Perspectives; Gregory of Nyssa, St.; John of the Cross, St.; Teresa of Avila, St.; Thomas Aquinas, St.

### Further Reading

Ariès, Philippe, *Centuries of Childhood: A Social History of Family Life*, New York: Random House, and London: Cape, 1962

Ariès, Philippe, *The Hour of Death*, New York: Knopf, and London: Allen Lane, 1981

Ariès, Philippe, et al., editors, *History of Private Life*, 5 vols., Cambridge, Massachusetts: Belknap Press at Harvard University Press, 1987–1991

Booth, Wayne C., *The Art of Growing Older: Writers on Living and Aging*, Chicago: University of Chicago Press, 1995

Lenz, Theodore, *The Person: His and Her Development Through Life*, revised edition, New York: Basic Books, 1997

Levi, Giovanni, and Jean-Claude Schmitt, editors, *A History of Young People in the West*, Cambridge, Massachusetts: Belknap Press at Harvard University Press, 1997

Rice, E. Philip, *Human Development: A Life-Span Approach*, 2nd edition, New York: Prentice Hall, 1995

# Lindisfarne/Holy Island, England

Lindisfarne is a spit of land cut off by the tide twice a day from the coast of Northumberland. In the late seventh and eighth centuries, the monastery at Lindisfarne was known throughout Western Europe for devotion and learning. Its monks traveled widely between the Firth of Forth and the Humber, preaching, teaching, and founding new religious centers. Among those educated at Lindisfarne were Chad (d. 672), Cedd (d. 664), and Wilfrid (634–709), all of whom were later recognized as saints. Aidan (d. 651), Finan (d. 661), Colman (d. 676), and Cuthbert (c. 636–687) were well-known bishops of Lindisfarne. The finest product of its culture, the Lindisfarne Gospels (c. 696–698), is a prime treasure of Anglo-Saxon illumination in the Celtic style. When in 698 the incorrupt body of Cuthbert was enshrined in

Ruins of Benedictine abbey (late 11th century), Lindisfarne Island. The parish church (12th–13th century) is on the right.
Photo courtesy of the Editor

the church, Lindisfarne became a major destination for pilgrimage. In 793 the church was destroyed by Vikings, sending a shock wave as far as the court of Charlemagne. Terrorized by further Viking raids, the monks abandoned the island in 875, taking with them their relics, including the body of Cuthbert, which was eventually buried at Durham.

The customs and worship of the monastery were at first those of Iona. At the Synod of Whitby (664), the Celtic date for Easter was vigorously defended by Colman, bishop of Lindisfarne. When it was agreed that Roman customs, including the date for Easter, would be followed in Northumbria, the Scots withdrew from Lindisfarne. Eata, an Englishman who had been a pupil of Aidan, was then appointed abbot, later becoming bishop. Although Bede (c. 673–735) sharply disapproved of the monks' adherence to the Celtic date for Easter, he painted an idealized picture of monastic life on Lindisfarne. He admired the austerity and poverty of the primitive monastery, which possessed only cattle and had few buildings except a chapel. Nothing remains of the Celtic foundation today.

In the 11th century Lindisfarne became known as Holy Island. In 1082 a monastic presence was reestablished on the island. Lindisfarne Priory developed as one of a number of "cells" maintained by monks from the great Benedictine cathedral-priory of Durham. The pillars of the church clearly show the dis-

tinctive style of the masons who worked on Durham Cathedral. The community remained small (likely not more than a dozen), but after Edward I's (1272–1307) invasion of Scotland in 1296 it was effectively in a war zone. Income declined to the point where only two or three monks could be supported. In 1537 the priory was closed by the commissioners of Henry VIII (1509–1547), and the buildings gradually fell into ruin.

The extensive and well-preserved remains seen by visitors today are mainly from the 12th and 13th centuries, when the priory flourished. Holy Island is a popular destination for contemporary pilgrims, who often choose to approach in the traditional manner, that is, barefoot across the sands.

NICHOLAS SAGOVSKY

*See also* Aidan, St.; Bede, St.; Celtic Monasticism; Cuthbert, St.; England: History; Island Monasteries, Christian; Reform, Tenth-Century Anglo-Saxon Monastic; Whitby, England

## Further Reading

Backhouse, Janet, *The Lindisfarne Gospels*, London: Phaidon Press, 1981
Bede, *Historia Ecclesiastica* (especially Books 3–5)
Bonner, Gerald, David Rollason, and Clare Stancliffe, *St. Cuthbert, His Cult and His Community: To A.D. 1200,*

Woodbridge, Suffolk, and Wolfeboro, New Hampshire: Boydell Press, 1989

Colgrave, Bertram, editor, *Two Lives of St. Cuthbert: Texts*, Cambridge and New York: Cambridge University Press, 1985

Magnusson, Magnus, *Lindisfarne, The Cradle Island*, Stocksfield, Great Britain, and Boston: Oriel Press, 1984

O'Sullivan, Deidre, and Robert Young, *English Heritage Book of Lindisfarne Holy Island*, London: Batsford/English Heritage, 1995

Raine, James, *The History and Antiquities of North Durham*, London: John Bowyer Nichols and Sons, 1852

# Liturgical Furnishings, Christian. *See* Visual Arts, Western Christian: Liturgical Furnishings

# Liturgical Movement 1830–1980

The liturgical reform legislated at the Second Vatican Council (1962–1965) had deep roots in several movements, some of them a century old by the time that the council began: a monastic reform, a popular liturgical movement, scholarly rediscoveries and reflections, and legislative approval and implementation. The monastic community actually made major contributions to all four areas. This article examines the significant contributions that the monastic community has made to that aspect of the renewal that began in the monasteries but that soon engaged the whole Church: the "liturgical movement."

### The Monastic Reform at Solesmes (1830–1904)

The suppression of the monasteries during the French Revolution (1792), plus the neo-Gallican liturgical experiments of French bishops who refused to implement the reforms mandated by the Council of Trent (1545–1563), provided a fertile field for a 19th-century monastic revival in France centered in the restored foundation at Solesmes. In a conservative reaction to neo-Gallican developments in religion, music, and art, Prosper Guéranger (1805–1875), a diocesan priest, reestablished in 1833 the ancient monastery of St.-Pierre at Solesmes, France, and dedicated himself to reinstating the Benedictine tradition. Central to Guéranger's project were his views that (1) monastic liturgy should center on the Mass and the Divine Office, following the Roman liturgy as he understood it especially from his earlier ministry as a chaplain to religious from Rome who were working in France and as expressed in his three-volume *Institutions liturgiques* (1840, 1841, 1851); (2) monastic life should center on the major feasts of the Church year, as reflected in his multivolume work *L'Année liturgique* (1841 and later); and (3) monastic liturgy should use chant rather than contemporary Church music, a decision that led the monks of Solesmes to become a central resource for chant research in 1870. Although his focus seemed to be primarily on monastic reform, Guéranger

also hoped that a reform of the monasteries would revive the French Church and would attract laypeople to participate in the Divine Office and Mass.

Toward the end of Guéranger's life, the Franco-German competitive spirit also contributed significantly to the direction of the monastic life at Solesmes. In 1872 the secular publisher Frederick Pustet of Ratisbon, Germany, obtained from Pius IX (1846–1878) permission to publish a comprehensive book of chants, together with a 30-year exclusive contract forbidding other publishers from producing "official" chant books. In France, beginning in 1862, the monks of Solesmes, led by Dom Joseph Pothier (1835–1923) and Dom Jausiens, began comparative studies of chant manuscripts that yielded, in 1880, the scholarly study *Les Mélodies grégoriennes d'après la tradition* and, in 1882, a *Graduale*. A copy of this *Graduale* was presented to Leo XIII (1878–1903) by Cardinal Pitra, an illustrious monk of Solesmes, but Pustet's 30-year privilege remained in force. In defense of the approach taken at Solesmes, Dom André Mocquereau (1849–1930) published a collection of photographic reproductions of the principal manuscripts of the gradual *Justus ut palma*, the first volume of *Paléographie musicale* (1889), to demonstrate the inadequacies of the chant manuscript used as the basis for the Pustet book and to promote the "Solesmes chant," which was based on more ancient manuscripts and better comparative techniques.

In 1904, by mandate of Pope Pius X (1903–1914), an official Vatican edition of all liturgical books containing chant was initiated. The copyrights for the chant books from Solesmes were ceded to the pope by three monks representing Solesmes (now in exile on the Isle of Wight) – Doms Mocquereau, Gagin, and Noetinger – but to their surprise Dom Pothier, now abbot of St.-Wandrille, served as chair of the Vatican chant committee and chose to base its work on an 1895 manuscript instead of more recent work. Eventually the committee was dissolved, and the monks of Solesmes were given formal responsibility for preparing revised versions of Gregorian chant. Monastic life at Solesmes centered more and more on chant research and prayerful execution of sung prayer.

### The Contribution of Other European Monasteries (1833–1909)

Although Guéranger's ideas about monastic reform lie at the root of many elements in the liturgical movement, our present vantage point shows that many of his liturgical positions were frequently undocumented, highly conservative, and often incorrect. Numerous members of the modern liturgical movement have wrestled to correct his positions, which had become firmly entrenched in popular understanding because of their widespread adoption in Solesmes' daughter monasteries and other Benedictine communities. From 1833 to 1900, Benedictine foundations, many founded or influenced by Solesmes, spread a version of Guéranger's vision of monastic reform based on the liturgy and with it the seeds of a liturgical renewal for the whole Church.

In Germany, the monastery at Beuron, founded in 1863 by Maurus and Placidus Wolter and famous for its art in a pseudo-Romanesque style, was inspired by the vision of Solesmes. Dom

Anselm Scott, following a French idea, published the first German-Latin Missal in 1884, the *Messbuch der hl. Kirche*, and the *Vesperbuch* quickly followed (1893). Each contained numerous explanations taken from Guéranger's *L'Année liturgique*.

Maredsous was a Belgian foundation (1872) of Beuron financed by the Desclée family. Dom Gerard von Caloen, rector of the abbey school, published the first French-Latin Missal, *Missel des fidèles* (1882). At the Eucharistic Congress in 1883, he suggested lay participation in the Mass and communion during Mass (radical ideas for which he was removed as rector). He founded the *Messager des fidèles* (later to become the *Revue Bénédictine*), the first publication founded specifically to promote the liturgical movement. Its main contributor, Dom Germain Morin, took on the conservative Guéranger. A later abbot of Maredsous (from 1909), the Irish monk Dom Columba Marmion (1858–1923), proclaimed through various writings a spirituality firmly based on the liturgical texts.

Maria Laach, a German foundation in the Rhineland, was taken over from the Jesuits in 1893 by monks from Beuron who developed the art style they carried from their home abbey. Dom Odo Casel (1886–1948), a monk of Maria Laach, wrote *Das christliche Kultmysterium* (1932; *The Mystery of Christian Worship*), which was to influence the thinking of the liturgical movement in the first decades of the 20th century, and he expanded his approach in the 15 volumes of *Jahrbuch für Liturgiewissenschaft* (1921–1941), which he edited. In theological circles of the day, the sacraments were seen as ceremonial, chiefly rubrical, and mainly the responsibility of canon lawyers, masters of ceremonies, and ritualists. Casel presented the sacraments (Greek, *mysterion*) as mysteries, internal actions of Christ. Although based incorrectly on the hypothesis that sacraments were rooted in Greek mystery cults, this thinking led to theories about the action of Christ in the sacraments offering praise to the Father and also to the new language that described the Church as the mystical body of Christ that acts in the sacraments. Like Guéranger's publications Casel's work was hotly contested for years, discredited by those opposed to the popular reforms offered by the advocates of the liturgy, and explained, corrected, and sometimes adamantly defended with a blind faith by supporters of the liturgical movement.

Mont-César, a foundation in Belgium (1899) by monks of Maredsous, was the monastery of Lambert Beauduin (1870–1963). Members of this monastery included Abbot Bernard Capelle, the cantor Dom Ildephonse Dirkx, and Dom Bernard Botte, who was to found the Institut Supérieur de Liturgie in Paris in 1945.

The Abbey of St Michael, Farnborough, England (1895), produced the scholarly work of its prior/first abbot Dom Fernand Cabrol (1855–1937), a monk of Solesmes. His study of the liturgy of Jerusalem in the fourth century based on the *Itinerarium Aetheriae* (*Travels of Egeria*), discovered by Gamurrini some ten years before (1884); his *Introduction aux études liturgiques*; and a little popular work, *Le Livre de la prière antique*, influenced a wide range of scholars. On a more compre-

hensive level are his *Monumenta ecclesiae liturgica* and the *Dictionnaire d'archéologie chrétienne et de liturgie*, begun in 1903 with Dom Henri Leclercq (1869–1945) and completed in 1953. In 1905 Dom Cabrol's series of lectures at the Institut Catholique in Paris outlined his method of historical research, establishing academic credibility for liturgical studies.

Monastic contributions to liturgical scholarship in the 19th and early 20th centuries were not limited to professed monastics or even to members of Roman Catholic communities. Edmund Bishop (1846–1917), briefly a monk of Downside Abbey and strongly influenced by his monastic experience, was the author of significant essays on the history of liturgy, especially on the introduction of the Roman Rite into Gaul. Many of these are collected in *Liturgica Historia: Papers on the Liturgy and Religious Life in the Western Church* (1918); his most famous essay, "The Genius of the Roman Rite," exerted a strong influence on the call for "noble simplicity" in the reform of the Second Vatican Council. Walter Howard Frere (1863–1938), a member of the Anglican monastic Community of the Resurrection who later became bishop of Truro, contributed significant studies of Reformation liturgical thought, the Russian Orthodox Church, and early Roman liturgy to the corpus of liturgical scholarship. The best-known Anglican liturgical scholar in the early 20th century may be Dom Gregory Dix (1901–1952), a monk of Nashdom Abbey, whose most significant work, *The Shape of the Liturgy* (1945), has influenced nearly every revision of the Eucharistic liturgy since World War II.

*The Popular Liturgical Movement (1909–1963)*
At the National Congress of Catholic Action held in 1909 at Malines, Belgium, Dom Lambert Beauduin, O.S.B., presented an address, "The Full Prayer of the Church," in which he issued a call for the active participation of the people in the work of the Church, especially in the liturgy, using a quote from Pius X's 1903 *motu proprio, Tra le sollecitudini*, which encouraged a lay involvement rooted in the "Church's most important and indispensable source, active participation in the sacred mysteries and in the public and solemn prayer of the Church." Some saw Beauduin's talk as a call for the "democratization" of the Church's worship. The unique characteristics of Beauduin's approach were that (1) it called for the active participation of the people; (2) it was popular, based on parochial ministry outside the monastery; (3) it translated theoretical ideas into popular language; and (4) it used mass media elements, publications, and conferences to motivate people and disseminate ideas.

Like Guéranger before him, Beauduin had been ordained as a diocesan priest (in 1897). Two years later he joined the Aumoniers du Travail, a priests' society for the care of workers. He joined the Benedictines at Mont-César in 1906, where he came under the influence of Columba Marmion. In addition to his own interest in liturgy, he had the resources of this abbey at his disposal. He founded *Questions liturgiques* (1909; later *Questions liturgiques et paroissales*), assisted by Brothers Antoine Pierard and Landaold de Waeghe. Beauduin published what came to be considered the "manifesto" of the popular liturgical movement, *La piété de l'Église* in 1914 (1926; *Liturgy, the Life of the Church*).

The beginning date of the popular movement in Germany is often given as 1918, the publication date for the first number of *Ecclesia Orans*, the well-known collection directed by Dom Ildefons Herwegen (1874–1946), abbot of Maria Laach (who was influenced by the scholarly Flemish journal *Liturgisch Tijdschrift*, begun by the Benedictines of Affligem, Brabant, in November 1910).

Although Benedictines certainly dominate this history, they were not the only monastics to make significant contributions. The Augustinian Canons of Klosterneuburg in Austria contributed to the popular liturgical movement, especially Pius Parsch (1884–1954) through his popular work on the Church year, *Das Jahr des Heiles* (1929; *The Church's Year of Grace*, 1953–1959). Parsch realized as a chaplain during World War I how little popular information on the liturgy was available to people, so he returned to Klosterneuburg to begin what came to be called the *Volksliturgisches Apostolat* (Popular Liturgical Apostolate). The monthly review *Bible and Liturgy* (intended for priests) and a weekly paper, *Live with the Church* (intended for laypeople), made Klosterneuburg a liturgical center for German-speaking countries. As early as 1934 Parsch began discussing a radical notion – the actual reform of liturgical rites, specifically a reform of the Easter Vigil. His first successful reform was a revised Austrian *Rituale* (1935), which was partially in the vernacular.

The influence of monastic communities on the popular liturgical movement extended well beyond the monks themselves. Countless leaders were formed by experiences of the liturgical life in monastic communities, such as Romano Guardini (1885–1968), whose best-known work, *The Spirit of the Liturgy*, was written while he was still a university student under the influence of the liturgy celebrated at Beuron.

The event that began the popular liturgical movement in the United States stands out: Dom Virgil Michel (1888–1938), a 33-year-old monk of St. John's Abbey in Collegeville, Minnesota, spent 19 months (February 1924 to August 1925) at the Benedictine College in Rome. From Solesmes he learned about the chant revival, from Maredsous publishing, and from Mont-César the popular movement. Most especially from Beauduin, his fellow Benedictine, who had mastered a style of writing, teaching, and publishing that emphasized clarity and mass communication, he learned method and content.

This nine-month visit changed Michel and, quite literally, the face of American Catholicism. On Michel's return to St. John's, Abbot Alcuin Deutsch supported the beginnings of an American liturgical movement by authorizing the foundation of the magazine *Orate Fratres* (later *Worship*) and The Liturgical Press, which began publishing The Popular Liturgical Library, a series of pamphlets and short treatments of elements connected with the liturgy. The press's first major text was the English version of Beauduin's only book, *La piété de l'Église* (1914), translated by Michel as *Liturgy, the Life of the Church* (1926). From 1926 to 1930 the press was directly under Virgil Michel's editorial control.

Between 1930 and his death in 1936, a number of events occurred that gave a particular shape to the early stages of the liturgical movement in the United States. First, Michel experienced a breakdown and was sent to recuperate in northern Minnesota, serving the Native Americans there (1930–1933). The Stock Market crash of 1929 and the subsequent Great Depression left more than ten million workers unemployed in the United States. When Michel returned to Collegeville to reassume the leadership of the liturgical apostate in 1933, he was deeply committed to wrestling with the results of the Depression. Just as Beauduin's liturgical program in Europe took root as part of the Catholic reaction to Marxism through the Catholic Worker Movement, so Michel recognized that the liturgical movement in the United States could not be separated from the social issues created by industrialized society, especially the concerns of workers; celebration of the liturgy could not be isolated from its setting in the modern world.

Editorials in *Orate Fratres* and the texts of publications coming from The Liturgical Press in the years between 1933 and 1938 were dominated by Michael's twin focus on liturgy and social reform and by the drive to popularize the linkage of these ideas. Michel died rather suddenly in 1938 and was replaced by Dom Godfrey Diekmann (1909– ) as editor of the magazine, soon retitled *Worship*, and as director of The Liturgical Press.

Diekmann was one of the planners who germinated the idea of a Liturgical Week at the Catechetical Congress (1939) in Cincinnati, when the section on liturgy quite spontaneously and unexpectedly outgrew the space allotted to it. The first Benedictine Liturgical Conference met in Chicago under the patronage of Archbishop (later Cardinal) Samuel Stritch in the Holy Name Cathedral School (21–25 October 1940) with 1,260 persons in attendance. Although under Benedictine auspices, speakers addressed such topics as the parish, parish worship, the Mass, the Divine Office, devotions, and artistic expression. After the success of that first week, Benedictine Liturgical Weeks were held in St. Paul, Minnesota (1941); in St. Meinrad, Indiana (1942); and at St. Procopius Abbey, Lisle, Illinois (1943).

In 1943 the Liturgical Conference replaced the Benedictine Liturgical Conference, and the popular liturgical movement in the United States disengaged itself from dependence on the monastic community for its lifeblood, although the popular movement and monasticism continued a close relationship through scholarship and in subsequent legislative reforms evident from the earliest days of the popular movement. Untold communities of religious woman, experienced in the liturgical movement, passed on their love and commitment to a life saturated with liturgical experiences through the Catholic school system, thus preparing the soil for the liturgical reform to come.

Although the primary visible effort at liturgical renewal in Europe after World War II began to shift to diocesan settings such as the Centre de Pastorale Liturgique (CPL) founded in

1943 in Paris, with its journal *La Maison-Dieu*, and the Liturgical Institute of Trier in postwar Germany (1947), with its publication *Liturgisches Jahrbuch*, the advocacy for liturgical renewal continued in partnership with the monastic communities.

Following the success of the first German National Liturgical Congress in 1950, the First International Liturgical Study Week was held at Maria Laach, sponsored jointly by the French CPL and the Liturgical Institute at Trier. About 30 persons from Western Europe addressed the topic of "The Problems of the Roman Missal." Mont-St.-Odile hosted the Second International Study Meeting (1952) with the theme "Modern Man and the Liturgy" – many ideas discussed here reappeared in the Vatican Council's Constitution *Gaudium et Spes* (*Church in the Modern World*). The Fourth International Study Week met at Mont-César/Louvain (1954) with the theme "Pericope System and Concelebration."

### From Liturgical Movement to Liturgical Reform and Renewal (1948–1980)

In 1948 Pope Pius XII (1939–1958) established a commission for liturgical reform that was in operation into 1960 working in absolute secrecy. Members included Dom Anselmo Albareda, O.S.B., prefect of the Vatican Library, and (after 1960) Abbot Cesario D'Amato of St. Paul's, Rome. This commission produced the Holy Week reforms, taking even the Congregation of Rites by surprise, and they worked on other reforms, including a new *Rituale*, which was set in print but never published because Pope John XXIII (1958–1963) had announced his intention to summon a council. The ready acceptance of the Holy Week reform, despite initial skepticism, made possible consideration of a total reform of the Roman Rite.

The Second Vatican Council, under the direction of Pope John XXIII, mandated a sweeping reform in the *Constitution on the Sacred Liturgy* (1963) and linked it with a concern for social justice – Virgil Michel's major concern along with liturgical renewal – as expressed in the *Pastoral Constitution on the Church in the Modern World* (1965). The preparatory commission for the liturgy schema at the council, the Conciliar Liturgical Committee, and the Consilium charged with implementing the liturgy constitution included as members, consultors, and advisers such well-known Benedictines as Bernard Botte (Belgium and the Institut Liturgique), Eugène Cardine (France and the Pontifical Institute of Sacred Music, Rome), Godfrey Diekmann (United States), Jean Leclercq (Luxembourg), Thierry Maertens (Belgium), Burkhard Neunheuser (Germany and Sant' Anselmo Liturgical Institute, Rome), Adrien Nocent (Belgium and Sant' Anselmo), Abbot Jean Prou (Solesmes), Polycarp Radó (Hungary), Abbot Pierre Salmon (Luxembourg and St. Jerome Monastery, Rome), Cipriano Vagaggini (Italy), Abbot Rembert Van Doren (Mont-César), and Abbot Primate Rembert Weakland. Abbot Karl Egger of the Canons Regular of the Lateran (CRL) also served on the reforming commissions.

The reform legislated at the Second Vatican Council spread into areas of the Church far beyond the initial dreams of Guéranger, Beauduin, Michel, or the numerous men and woman of the monastic communities who had shaped and refined those dreams. However, almost every person engaged – bishops and abbots, *periti* and ecumenical observers – had been directly influenced by liturgical celebrations experienced in monastic communities. Monastic life, worship, and the often hidden and dedicated work of monastic scholars directly influenced the ideas of the Second Vatican Council.

The implementation of the council directives influenced every monastery, especially as the general liturgical reforms mandated by the council brought into question the preservation of elements unique to monastic life, such as the daily office – a particular concern of Pope Paul VI (1963–1978). Through the work of Abbot Primate Weakland, the *Thesaurus Liturgiae Horarum Monasticae* was finally approved in 1977 for the Confederation of the Order of St. Benedict as a model for the renewal of the liturgy of the hours in monastic communities. The formation of the Benedictine Musicians of America in 1966, first of the men only and then of both men and women in 1974, developed the Benedictine Book of Song and provided an opportunity for religious in the United States to share their experiences of formulating music in the vernacular in the United States and Canada. The Monastic Liturgical Forum in 1989 grew from the Benedictine Musicians of America.

### Liturgy and Monasticism in the 21st Century

At the dawn of the 21st century, it is clear that the influence of monastic communities is the seed from which the current renewal of the Church has grown, begun with the hope expressed – as much as with the legislation mandated – by the Second Vatican Council. It was the council's hope that monastic life would prove to be the seedbed of the future Church: "The Council's wish is that the venerable institution of monastic life in both East and West should be faithfully maintained and radiate its authentic spirit ever more resplendently. For in the long course of the centuries it has earned the well-deserved respect of both the Church and human society. . . . Respecting the spirit of their own community, monks should renew their ancient traditions, the source of so much good, and so adapt them to the contemporary needs of souls that their monasteries will become like seedbeds for the growth of the Christian people" (*Perfectae caritatis*, number 9).

Joseph Gelineau, a contemporary liturgist, says, "The monastic charism is essential for the future of the Church: celibacy to signify waiting for the coming of the Bridegroom; continual prayer which makes vigilance incarnate until the return of the Master; detachment from the goods of this world with a view to the world that is to come and for the purposes of sharing between human brothers and sisters."

In the fourth and fifth centuries, monks from diverse backgrounds began to sing and pray while people were gathering, with those arriving gradually joining in until the arrival of the various ministers for the liturgy of the word and Eucharist. These monks or "ascetics" did not take on particular liturgical functions; their role was to safeguard the "gift" of living prayer in the midst of the people.

How many times on a Sunday morning, arriving for Sunday Eucharist, have I wished, "If only men and women of prayer were with us." In a Church that is becoming more and more scattered, how badly the Church's assemblies are in need of such a presence at their Sunday Eucharist! The liturgy proper to monks is the daily sanctification of the hours, but in our times the Sunday Eucharist is the liturgy urgently in need of a praying community.

VIRGIL C. FUNK

See also Beauduin, Lambert; Beuron, Germany; Church Councils, Recent Catholic; Collegeville, Minnesota; Guéranger, Prosper; Liturgy: Western Christian; Maria Laach, Germany; Music: Christian Perspectives; Office, Daily: Western Christian; Solesmes, France; Wolter, Maurus; Wolter, Placidus

**Further Reading**

Botte, Bernard, *From Silence to Participation: An Insider's View of Liturgical Renewal*, The Pastoral Press, 1978

Brinkhoff, L., "Chronicle of the Liturgical Movement," in *Liturgy in Development*, edited by Alting Von Geusau, London: Sheed and Ward, 1965; Westminster, Maryland: Newman Press, 1966

Bugnini, Annibale, *The Reform of the Liturgy 1948–1975*, translated by Matthew J. O'Connell, Collegeville, Minnesota: The Liturgical Press, 1990

Chandlee, H. Ellsworth, "The Liturgical Movement," in *The New Westminster Dictionary of Liturgy and Worship*, edited by J.G. Davies, Philadelphia: Westminster Press, 1986

Franklin, R.W., and Robert L. Spaeth, *Virgil Michel, American Catholic*, Collegeville, Minnesota: The Liturgical Press, 1988

Gelineau, Joseph, *Libres propos sur les Assemblées Liturgiques*, Paris: Les Éditions de L'atelier, 1999

Hall, Jeremy, "The American Liturgical Movement: The Early Years," *Worship* (1987)

Jounel, Pierre, "The History of the Liturgy," in *The Church at Prayer*, part 1: *Principles of the Liturgy*, Collegeville, Minnesota: The Liturgical Press, 1987

Jungmann, Joseph A., *The Mass of the Roman Rite: Its Origins and Development*, translated by Francis A. Brunner, revised Charles K. Riepe, New York: Benziger, 1959

Regan, Patrick, "How Did Liturgical Change Get Started . . . and Why?" *Pastoral Music* 8:2 (1984)

Rousseau, Olivier, *The Progress of the Liturgy, An Historical Sketch*, Westminster, Maryland: Newman Press, 1951

Tuzik, Robert L., editor, *How Firm a Foundation: Leaders of the Liturgical Movement*, Liturgy Training Publications, 1990

# Liturgical Seasons, Christian. *See* Seasons, Liturgical

# Liturgists, German Monastic

The tradition of German monastic liturgists began in the Carolingian era with Amalarius of Metz (c. 775–c. 850), who virtually initiated the allegorical interpretation of the Mass. Amalarius had been a student of Alcuin (c. 740–804) as a young man and was named bishop of Trier in 811. His episcopate ended in 813, when he was sent on a diplomatic mission to the Byzantine emperor. When he returned the post had been given to someone else. During the next 20 years, Amalarius composed the *Liber officialis*, in four books, an interpretation of the inward meaning of the Mass and the festivals of the liturgical year. In this book Amalarius used allegory, which had already been used by Scripture scholars since Origen (c. 185–c. 254) and by the Byzantine liturgist Germanus (c. 640–c. 733) of Constantinople, to interpret Christian worship. For example, during the Mass (the Roman rite, as Amalarius seems to have used an *ordo Romanus*) the consecrated Host was broken into three pieces. The priest placed one of the pieces in the chalice of consecrated water and wine, the second he reserved for communion, and the third remained on the altar. Amalarius taught that this division into three pieces signified Christ risen from the dead (that placed in the chalice), Christ who still walks on earth (that reserved for communion), and Christ lying in the tomb (that remaining on the altar). Although in 838 the Synod of Quierzy condemned Amalarius' method and opinions on the liturgy, his authority on liturgical subjects lasted until the end of the Middle Ages. The numerous extant manuscripts of the *Liber officialis* testify to his popularity. Because Amalarius borrowed much from the Latin and Greek fathers, their authority buttressed his own. Furthermore, the usefulness of the *Liber officialis* was unrivaled, as it was the first systematic attempt to explain the liturgy as a whole. Finally, that Amalarius interpreted the Roman rite contributed to the replacement of the Gallican and Germanic rites by the Roman.

The 11th century was the next era of creative German monastic liturgical studies. Berno, abbot of Reichenau, published a number of short liturgical commentaries between 1024 and 1032. His commentary on the Mass combined allegorical exposition with a chronological presentation of papal *auctoritates* obtained from the *Liber pontificalis*. Thus, Berno anticipated the important work of Bernhold of Constance (1054–1100), who initiated a new phase of liturgical scholarship with the publication of his *Micrologus de ecclesiasticis observantibus*. In the *Micrologus*, which was a pro-papal polemic during the investiture controversy, Bernhold abandoned the allegorical interpretation of the liturgy so as to better serve his purpose of championing the Roman over other rites of the Mass. Instead, Bernhold employed a new, historical approach to the study of liturgy. An array of patristic, papal, and conciliar texts supported his interpretation of the prayer texts and rubrics, much as a later monk, Gratian (d. by c. 1160), would organize these texts according to legal subjects. After Bernhold a canonistic tradition of liturgical interpretation coexisted with the allegorical tradition.

Moreover, during the same era German monastic authors writing exclusively for other monks revived the allegorical tradition. Honorius Augustodunensis (c.1075/1080–1156), whom scholars debate was either English or south German, depended on Amalarius but added new allegorical expositions that linked liturgical actions and rites with events in the life of Christ. In his *De divinis officiis*, Rupert of Deutz (c. 1075–1129) systematically interpreted the Benedictine liturgy. Unlike other liturgical commentators who began with the Mass and the liturgical calendar, Rupert began with the daily prayer of the monks. He wrote so that those who participated in the *opus Dei* could understand it. He was especially mindful of those of whom he was especially critical, namely, priest-monks who celebrated private masses for the favor of powerful nobles rather than for spiritual edification. According to Rupert, all prayers and readings should be understood in the light of the gospel for the day. He believed that the Holy Spirit had inspired the Benedictine liturgy, which was an allegory of salvation history. Rupert, whose life revolved around regular, daily prayer, reaffirmed the tradition of the Church fathers that declared that theological reasoning could take place only with reference to Christian worship (*Lex orandi est lex credendi*: the rule of prayer establishes the rule of faith). The number of extant manuscripts of the *De divinis officiis* ranks Rupert with the giants of medieval liturgical exposition. He exerted an important influence on the popular *De missarum mysteriis* of Lothario of Segni (1160/1161–1216), who later became Pope Innocent III. Only the work of the Frenchman William Durand (c. 1230–1296), who crafted a synthesis of the allegorical and canonistic methods, supplanted him. The success and influence of Durand's work discouraged innovative liturgical studies for the rest of the Middle Ages.

The historical maelstrom of the Reformation, the Thirty Years' War, and the French Revolution destroyed most of the monasteries in Germany, and of those that survived and flourished, most were involved in charitable endeavors, such as relief for the poor and education. The German Benedictines especially continued to produce important scholarly publications, but their labors were dedicated more often to monastic history than to liturgy. An important center of German monastic liturgical study reemerged only in the 20th century under the inspiration of the liturgical movement, which called for greater lay participation in worship and for reform of the liturgy itself. The Benedictine house of Maria Laach in the Rhineland became a center of liturgical scholarship. The formidable figures of Abbot Idlefonsus Herwegen (abbot, 1913–1946), Odo Casel (1886–1948), and Kunibert Möhlberg (1878–1963) made many contributions to liturgical scholarship. They edited a new and distinguished journal of liturgiology, *Ecclesia Orans* (from 1918); emphasized the mysterious reenactment in the Mass of Christ's salvific offering; and established a historical, archeological, and sociological context for liturgical development. They offered an alternative to the romantic notion of medieval liturgy popularized by the French liturgiologist Prosper Guéranger (1805–1875) and believed that, instead of representing the highest form of Christian worship, inappropriate innovations had corrupted the medieval liturgy. Liturgy should be pruned of such prayers and rites and restored to its apostolic simplicity. Thus, the monastic liturgiologists of Maria Laach influenced the liturgical reforms promulgated by the Second Vatican Council.

ROBERT W. SHAFFERN

*See also* Beuron, Germany; Casel, Odo; Guéranger, Prosper; Liturgical Movement 1830–1980; Liturgy: Western Christian; Maria Laach, Germany; Office, Daily: Western Christian

**Further Reading**

Laistner, M.L.W., *Thought and Letters in Western Europe*, A.D. 500–900, Ithaca, New York: Cornell University Press, and London: Methuen, 1957

Priests of St. Séverin (Paris) and St. Joseph (Nice), *What Is the Liturgical Movement?*, translated by Lancelot C. Sheppard, London: Burns and Oates, 1964

Thibodeau, Timothy, "The Influence of Canon Law on Liturgical Exposition, c. 1100–1300," *Sacris Erudiri* 37 (1997)

Van Engen, John, *Rupert of Deutz*, Berkeley: University of California Press, 1983

# Liturgy: Buddhist

*Doctrinal Approaches to Liturgy*

Although the liturgical worship of the Buddha has a history almost as long as that of Buddhism itself – and constitutes one of the dominant features of Buddhist religiosity – controversy over the doctrinal validity of such practices, especially within the monastic community, has vexed both Asian Buddhists and Western academic commentators in equal measure. For many the propitiation of a divine Buddha is at odds with the notion of an enlightened Śākyamuni who, through severing all contact with saṃsāric existence, ended the round of rebirth, suffering, and death. Because the Buddha is gone from the world, all worship and offering aimed at him should be empty ritualism, at odds with the Buddha's own teachings. Such views enjoy some scriptural authority; in the *Dīgha Nikāya* the dying Buddha explains to his disciple Ānanda,

> I am reaching my end. After my decease, may each of you be your own island, your own refuge; have no other refuge. . . . Do not waste your time, O Ānanda, in paying homage to my body; but concern yourself, with all diligence and application, with your own spiritual welfare.

Later interpreters have differed as to what this should mean in practice. In *The Questions of King Milinda*, the first-century philosopher Nāgasena argued that although the Buddha was indeed entirely free of earthly encumbrance and thus accepted no gift, pious acts toward his image and memory bore good fruit. Thus, worship could be effective because it was focused on a symbolic "reminder" (Pāli, *cetiya*) of the Buddha's attainment and teachings. Mahāyāna scholars later maintained the possibil-

**Bells in the main hall of Daimyō-ō-in on Mount Kōya, Japan, headquarters of the Shingon sect founded by Kūkai.**
**Photo courtesy of David Moore**

ity of a continuing ritual "presence" and efficacy of the Buddha to the faithful in certain, limited forms: while asserting that enlightenment entails a "snuffing out" of involvement with the saṃsāric world, philosophers such as Nāgārjuna (c. 150–250 A.D.) argued that the difference between saṃsāra and *nirvāṇa* was fundamentally illusory and was transcended by the nature of Buddhahood: thus, although the Buddha might ultimately transcend saṃsāra, he might also conventionally exist within it without contradiction. This philosophical perspective has been reified into the notion of the *tri-kāya*, or "three bodies," of the Buddha, wherein only the Buddha's mind existed beyond the phenomenal world while his karmic presence continued to manifest itself as divine and earthly forms that can be worshiped and propitiated.

However, the eventual upshot of much of this debate remained much the same across the Buddhist world: worship of the Buddha constituted a central "field of merit" for both lay and monastic populations. Moreover the Buddha's assertion that "He who sees the *dharma*, sees me" also retained its force in the sense that liturgical acts concentrated on the Buddha exist as one of a limited number of dependable *means of liberation* from saṃsāric existence. This emphasis on soteriology rather than mere reverence had three principal repercussions: First, the

iconic "presence" of the Buddha within ritual and artistic forms is often being represented in terms of symbols of his attainment, teaching, and wisdom – the wheel, the Bodhi Tree, or merely footprints. Second, the means of liberation was not limited to the person of the Buddha but also extended to his teachings and to the community of adepts, or *saṅgha*, who have gained some degree of spiritual realization through those teachings. Thus, most liturgical forms in both Theravādin and Mahāyāna Buddhism begin with the so-called Three Refuges:

I go for refuge to the Buddha,
I go for refuge to the Dharma,
I go for refuge to the Saṅgha.

Finally, this flexibility of symbolic presence meant that, just as a statue or relic represents the body of the Buddha, canonical texts represent his speech. The recitation of the scriptures, accompanied by the widespread use of Pāli and Sanskrit mantras, became a key index of the Buddha's presence as a fulcrum of liberation and is seen as a source of good karma and blessing in and of itself, a fact that leads most monks to spend most of their ritual lives in prodigious rounds of textual recitation.

Incense burner at Siong Lim Temple, Singapore.
Photo courtesy of John Powers

### Liturgy, Authority, and Pastoral Care

Actual liturgical practices within Buddhism – especially within the Mahāyāna traditions of China, where devotional practices to deities such as the Buddha Amitābha and the bodhisattva Kuan-yin proliferated – are far too varied to deal with comprehensively here. Thus, for the purposes of understanding, this article concentrates on Theravādin and Mahāyāna monasticism in Southeast Asia and Tibet. Here the annual calendars of most Buddhist monasteries usually include four key events: New Year; the celebration of the Buddha's birth, enlightenment, and death; the summer (or "monsoon") retreat; and the spring recitation of texts. These events highlight three identifiable but interweaving modes of monastic activity: first as an elite form of religious discipline, second as a center of ecclesiastical and (above all) scriptural authority, and third as a provider of ritual specialists to the social, agricultural, and economic needs of surrounding lay communities.

As regards the first activity, monastic life is held together by the disciplinary vows of the vinaya and is focused on the Buddha's life as the exemplar of monasticism, a combined emphasis

that informs both the communal nature of much Buddhist liturgy and its focus on relations with the Buddha: quotidian prayers and offerings are made to the Buddha, or in the Mahāyāna case Buddhas, within the main temple by the monastic community as a bounded whole, and, on the new and full moons, the community enters closed ceremony in the temple to recite their vows and confess infractions.

The second – scriptural authority – carries both scholastic and ritual dimensions. The scholastic study of scripture and commentary remains the purview of a tiny minority of monks, with scholastically adept (and financially well endowed) monks studying at elite monastic centers as a prelude to careers as teachers or administrators. However, this scholastic dimension is outweighed by the importance of recitation as a mode of scriptural authority, an authority that reinforced the third aspect of monastic ritual: the pastoral care of surrounding lay populations. For example, the spring recitation of scriptures, while often carried out in the monastery, is almost universally complemented by having monks recite in lay households and by performing ritual circumambulation of the village fields with the

Straw Chanting Center, Anurādhapura, Sri Lanka, rebuilt 20th century.
Photo courtesy of John C. Huntington, the Huntington Archive

scriptures. These acts are seen as doing more than merely expressing doctrinal truths; they are aimed explicitly at blessing and purifying households and fields for the upcoming harvest. Similar recitations are also carried out over the sick and at the inauguration of new buildings, business ventures, and organizations.

Throughout Asia rites carried out on behalf of lay sponsors very much dominate the life of the average Buddhist monk, whose role as renouncer is overshadowed by, and subsumed within, his role as ritual specialist. Rituals performed on behalf of lay communities are aimed mainly at consecration, purification, and protection from magical harm. Thus, Thai Buddhist monks conducting funerary rites (often seen as the sine qua non of pastoral responsibilities in Buddhist monasticism) will chant Buddhist sūtras that are designed to transfer karmic merit to the dead and *piritta* texts (themselves often Buddhist sūtras) that are designed to purify the households of laity who might have been affected by the ritual pollution associated with death and to protect the living from the return of the dead. Tibetan monks will recite also the Tibetan Book of the Dead to guide the deceased through to either liberation or a good rebirth and will perform "empowerment" ceremonies to consecrate the deceased with the powers of his tutelary Buddha, or *yidam* (see the following discussion).

The role of Buddhist liturgical practice in the protection of surrounding lay communities is most obvious in the performance of exorcistic rites. A common such rite in Mahāyāna communities is recitation of the *Bhāgavatiprajñapāramitāhridaya*, or Heart Sūtra – a contemplation of the nature of emptiness (*śūnyatā*) – attended by preliminary prayers to the Buddha, by mantras of purification, and by closing prayers that obstacles, hindrances, and demons be pacified. It is perhaps in this area of liturgical practice where the Central Asian forms of Buddhist monasticism, such as those practiced in Tibet and Mongolia, enter their own: whereas the most difficult and dangerous forms of exorcism are often left to noncelibate yogins in Tibetan regions, Buddhist monasteries in Tibet maintain a highly elaborate cycle of exorcisms, many of which are attended by highly colorful masked dances called '*cham*, often the center of large festivities.

### Guru Devotion and Vajrayāna Buddhism

The rise of Vajrayāna, or Tantric, Buddhism in India during the first millennium A.D. ushered in a new, highly ritualized form of Mahāyāna Buddhism. Incorporating Śaivite forms of worship such as guru devotion, deity yoga, Tantric empowerment, and most controversially sexual yoga into the Buddhist ritual corpus,

Vajrayāna remains one of the most disputed developments in Buddhism's history, marking a substantial divergence between Theravādin and Mahāyāna Buddhism. For early Western scholars of Buddhism, such as L.A. Waddell in the 1890s, this highly stylized form of Buddhism represented so great a corruption of Buddhism's earlier philosophical purity that they dubbed it "Lamaism" rather than a form of Buddhism. More recent scholars have seen such a reading as demonstrating an overconcern with the form, rather than the function, of Buddhist ritual, arguing instead that most of the later Vajrayāna Buddhist ceremonial involved a root-and-branch reconstruction of Śaivite ritual that maintained key symbolic structures while rebuilding their meaning and exegetical context to present a profoundly new vehicle for a wholly Buddhist soteriology.

Central to this transformation are two interlinked cosmological symbols that remain the centerpiece of Tibetan Buddhism to this day: the *lama* (Tibetan, *bla.ma*; Sanskrit, *guru*), or spiritual guide, and the *yidam* (Tibetan, *yi.dam*; Sanskrit, *istadevata*), or tutelary deity. Within the ritual context each of these is seen as being of Buddha status: indeed as spiritual guide the lama is identified with the *yidam* and becomes the principal object of worship and respect, being seen as the living source of the Buddhist dharma and thus superior even to celestial Buddhas. This dynamic is made concrete in the act of Tantric empowerment, or *wang* (Tibetan, *dbang*), whereby the lama as the archetypal spiritual teacher confers on the student the "seeds" (usually conveyed within key mantras) of the bodily, verbal, and mental qualities of the tutelary Buddha as well as his celestial palace, or maṇḍala, in a rite that combines consecration and symbolic rebirth.

The transmission of such empowerments is essential to much of the ritual authority of Tibetan Buddhist monastic communities, where the propitiation of central tutelary Buddhas – such as Yamantaka among the Gelukpa and the many forms of the "second Buddha" Guru Rinpoche Padmasambhava in Nyingmapa monasteries – occurs daily. Tantric worship of Buddhas – based around the structure of the so-called seven-limbed prayer (prostration, offerings, confession, rejoicing in merit, beseeching the Buddhas and bodhisattvas not to leave the world, requesting them to turn the wheel of dharma, and dedicating the resulting merit) – centers both on externally visualized Buddhas and on the adept as a *dag-skyed*, or "self-generated," Buddha. The performance of such rites and meditations is believed gradually to bestow the powers and wisdom of the *yidam* on the monk-meditator, enabling him to control lower Buddhist deities (especially the powerful and fierce *choskyong*, or dharma protector deities) and to coerce recalcitrant earth spirits and exorcise demons.

### Buddhist Liturgy and the Needs of Laity

The integration of lay interests into the ritual lives of monasteries has been the subject of much critical academic comment, taking as their lead Monier Monier-Williams' still resonant query as to whether such rituals constituted "true Buddhism." The prevalence of religious forms that either actively integrate or tacitly accept the propitiation of local and non-Buddhist deities and

spirits into the life of Buddhist monasticism has led some to argue that Buddhism is either inherently syncretic or at best accretive. In other words intellectual preoccupation with *mokṣa*, or liberation from worldly concerns, means that some room must be made for more mundane emotional and ritual needs, especially of the laity. Melford E. Spiro divided religious life in Buddhist countries into a variety of levels: *nibbānic* Buddhism (those religious forms aimed at attaining enlightenment), *kammatic* Buddhism (aimed at attaining a better rebirth in the next life), and *apotropaic* Buddhism (focused on attaining success and avoiding misfortune in this life). Ultimately this question remains an open one, but it is certainly the case that too dogmatic a distinction between soteriological and worldly concerns elides the degree to which many Buddhist forms incorporate all three motivations, often working in tandem.

MARTIN A. MILLS

*See also* Buddhist Schools/Traditions: Japan; Death Rituals, Buddhist; Deities, Buddhist; Esoteric Buddhism in China and Japan; Festivals, Buddhist; Images: Buddhist Perspectives; Mantras; Novices, Theravādin Rituals for; Prayer: Buddhist Perspectives; Regulations: Buddhist Perspectives; Repentance Rituals, Buddhist; Rules, Buddhist (Vinaya): Historical; Visual Arts, Buddhist: Tibet; Worship Space: Buddhist Perspectives

### Further Reading

Beyer, Stephen, *The Cult of Tara: Magic and Ritual in Tibet*, Berkeley: Regents of the University of California Press, 1973

Samuel, Geoffrey, *Civilized Shamans: Buddhism in Tibetan Societies*, Washington, D.C.: Smithsonian Institution Press, 1993

Spiro, Melford E., *Buddhism and Society: A Great Tradition and Its Burmese Vicissitudes*, New York: Harper and Row, 1970; London: Allen and Unwin, 1971; 2nd edition, Berkeley: University of California Press, 1982

Tambiah, Stanley J., *Buddhism and the Spirit Cults in North-East Thailand*, Cambridge: Cambridge University Press, 1970

# Liturgy: Celtic

Here liturgy is understood to be the public or sacramental-priestly worship of God, which involves the participation of the laity in the work of their redemption by Christ. Saint Patrick (*Confessio*, secs. 38–41) refers to the people of the Lord whom by divine mercy he has won from worship of idols to that of the true God.

Yet no distinct Celtic rite ever existed. From the extant liturgical sources (the seventh- and eighth-century mixed Gallican and Irish Bobbio Missal; the Antiphonary of Bangor, c. 700, and its "sister" manuscript, the Turin fragment; the Stowe Missal, written c. 800 and revised very soon after; the Book of Dimma, 750/850; the martyrologies of Óengus and of Tallaght, both c. 800; and some other few manuscripts), we cannot conclude that one Irish, much less one Celtic, liturgy existed or, on the other hand, that a multiplicity of liturgies did. Rather, as a result of the

Altar, monastery of Clonmacnois (County Offaly), Ireland, 20th century.
Photo courtesy of Mary Schaefer

development of monasticism beginning with the 6th century, the Irish Church between the 8th and the 12th century exhibited marked peculiarities in organization and government. However, whereas Kenney (1929) could assert that "monasticism was the basis of the Irish system," we should rather say today with Sharpe (1984) that one system existed in which monastic and nonmonastic churches overlapped. In this system the bishop, even if a monk himself, oversaw pastoral care. He ordained and appointed priests to cures, consecrated oil and chrism, received nuns, and went on visitation. Secular priests were obliged to baptize, offer mass and distribute communion, preach, give extreme unction, and perform requiem services. However, a shortage of secular clergy often caused monks to perform these services.

The Roman elements in the Stowe Missal have suggested to Gamber (1967), followed by Curran (1984), that the original core of the Irish liturgy was Roman, not Gallican, as many have thought. The Stowe and Bobbio Missals and the *Missale Francorum* share an early, and probably Irish, recension of the Roman canon. Patrick tells how he administered to thousands of neophytes the rites of initiation, baptism, and confirmation (followed presumably by mass, at which they communicated under both species, this being the climax of the ceremony of initiation in the fifth century). From the beginning a succession of bishops and clergy was maintained. The Irish divine office was originally the cathedral office, with the various grades of clergy joining laity to sing matins and vespers in church.

When communications with Rome, interrupted in the mid–fifth century, were reopened in the sixth, it became apparent that in certain liturgical and disciplinary matters (e.g., Easter tables, ordination of a bishop, and baptism) the English and Irish (or Insular) churches had not kept pace with developments on the Continent. The monastic churches of central or southern Ireland came to share the concern of the Roman mission (597) to Canterbury about this. The date of Easter was the important issue, and by around 636 southern Ireland had come into line with the Roman practice. The churches in Northumbria (also monastic) yielded at the Synod of Whitby in 664, after a time to be followed by northern Ireland. Iona held out until 716 and Wales until 768.

The monastic stamp now expressed itself strongly on the Insular liturgy. The sixth-century penitential of Uinniau (a Briton?) and that of Cummean (c. 650), both the work of monks, lay down that baptism is to be administered to children and is not to be repeated. The penitentials are very careful in legislating for the proper celebration of mass and for proper care of the reserved species. The Eucharist, "the sacrifice of salvation" (St. Gall), remains the central act of worship. Irish monks make their own contributions to the mass, with litanies and intercessory prayers, and to the office with, for example, a twofold vigil at midnight and early morning. The Irish self-confidence demonstrated here and also in the virtuoso composition of collects (in verse and prose) for the monastic office and of hymnody for the Eucharist and the office showed genuine creativity during the seventh and eighth centuries. Irish monastics excelled at Eucharistic devotion, liturgical inventiveness, and scholarship (biblical exegesis, theology, hagiography, computistics, legal tracts, and so on). This vitality sent missionaries out: Columba to Iona (563), Máelrubha from Bangor to Applecross, and Columban and Gall to the Continent. The liturgy inspired art forms open to outside influences: metalwork and crosses issuing from the monastic workshops, gospel books from the scriptoria, and the hymns and prayers already mentioned. At the same time Columban's foundations at Luxeuil and Bobbio helped open Irish liturgy to influences from Ambrosian Milan, Mozarabic Spain, southern Gaul, and even the East. The Rule of Columban, Adomnán's account of Iona, the Antiphonary of Bangor, and the "Voyage of Brendan" (ninth century?) between them make clear that the ascetic, "desert" monastic tradition had by the seventh century integrated into it the cathedral (or ecclesiastical) tradition. This fusion resulted in a monastic office that showed the Irish genius for austerity, eclecticism, and a devotion to Christ and his saving work that could rise to lyrical heights.

The system of private confession and penance that took root on the Continent in the eighth century is generally accepted as having had its origin in the Celtic Insular churches. Probably in the beginning a monastic practice, it was brought to the Continent and popularized there by Columban and other monks, Irish and Anglo-Saxon. A feature of the eighth-century Culdee (Céli Dé) reform was the emphasis placed on giving extreme unction and holy communion to the dying. The martyrologies of Óengus and of Tallaght, both from around 800, are the works of a church proud of its great past.

JOHN J. SILKE

*See also* Celtic Monasticism; Columban, St.; Ireland; Missionaries: Christian; Penitential Books; Wales; Whitby, England

## Further Reading

Bieler, Ludwig, editor, *The Irish Penitentials*, Dublin: Dublin Institute for Advanced Studies 5, 1975

Cabrol, Fernand, "Bangor (Antiphonaire de)," *Dictionnnaire d'archéologie chrétienne et de liturgie*, volume 2, Paris: Letouzey et Ané, 1903

Corish, Patrick, "The Pastoral Mission of the Early Irish Church," in *Léachtaí Cholm Cille* 2, Maynooth: An Sagart, 1971

Cosgrave, William, "How Celtic Penance Gave Us Personal Confession," *Doctrine and Life* 41 (1991)

Curran, Michael, *The Antiphonary of Bangor and the Early Irish Monastic Liturgy*, Blackrock, Co., Dublin: Irish Academic Press, 1984

Gamber, K., "Die irischen Messlibelli alz Zeugnis für die frühe römische Liturgie," *Römische Quartalschrift* 62 (1967)

Kenney, James F., *The Sources for the Early History of Ireland: An Introduction and Guide*, volume 1: *Ecclesiastical* (Records of Civilization, Sources and Studies), New York: Columbia University Press, 1929; revised edition, Dublin: Pádraic Ó Táilliúir, 1979

Sharpe, Richard, "Some Problems Concerning the Organization of the Church in Early Medieval Ireland," *Peritia* 3 (1984)

Warren, Frederick E., *The Liturgy and Ritual of the Celtic Church*, 2nd edition, edited by Jane Stevenson, Woodbridge, Suffolk, and Wolfeboro, New Hampshire: Boydell Press, 1987

# Liturgy: Eastern Christian

The term *liturgy* itself requires a few preliminary remarks concerning its original meaning, how it evolved, and what it came to mean during the Byzantine era (330–1453). Neither ideas nor institutions emerge from nothing. History is evolutionary and carries much within it that can be traced back to remote antiquity. Byzantine institutions and civilization in general owed much not only to Christianity but also to the cultural milieu and intellectual inheritance from ancient Hellenism.

The term *liturgy*, from the Greek *leitourgia*, means "service," an act or work (*ergon*) performed by or for people (*laios*, *leiton*). In classical Athens and other city-states, the term was used in a range of technical, political, social, and religious senses. In a city-state wealthy people were expected to sponsor public functions, such as theatrical performances, athletic contests, and musical, festival, and religious ceremonies for the benefit of the public.

From the classical centuries through the Hellenistic and Roman periods, the term was used extensively. The translators of the Hebrew Bible into Greek (the Septuagint version of the Bible (third–second century B.C.), which was the official Bible of the Greek-speaking Church of the medieval centuries) use the infinitive *leitourgein* more than 100 times and the noun *leitourgia* 50 times in the sense it was used in classical times. For example, in the book of Numbers (2:21–24) we read,

> The Lord said to Moses, take a census of the sons of Gerson . . . all who can enter the service [*leitourgein*] to do the

work in the tent of meeting. This is the service [*leitourgia*] of the families of the Gersonites in serving [*leitourgein*] and bearing burdens . . .

New Testament writers use both infinitive and noun in a similar context. Saint Luke writes that when Zachariah's "time of service [*tes leitourgias autou*] was ended, he went to his house" (Luke 1:23). Saint Paul, writing about raising money for the poor in Jerusalem, adds that the rendering of this service (*diakonia tes leitourgias*) does more than supply the wants of the saints (2 Cor. 9:12). References to liturgy as service both to people and to God, as worship, as system of worship, and as public performance of sacrificial rites appear frequently in the early Christian literature. It is in the sense of sacrificial service (i.e., as Eucharist) that it is mostly used in the Byzantine Church and religious life.

The Liturgy epitomizes the dogma, doctrine, code of ethics, cult, community structure, and metaphysical or transcendent vision of Greek or Eastern Orthodox Christianity as it developed in the course of a millennium. Briefly, these six categories are used here in specific contexts. *Dogma* describes the accepted and codified faith of the community; *doctrine* refers to theological teachings that undergo development; *code* is used to describe ethical imperatives and the rules of and obligations toward action; *cult* involves ritual and symbolic movement and activity in the execution of the liturgy, such as processions, candles, signs, and censer; and *community structure* explains the nature of relationships among the followers of the common faith, that is, the principles that bind individual believers into a living organism and structured organization: the Church.

The Liturgy comprises more than a narrative and reenactment of the mystery of Christ's life; it is an unfolding Christian interpretation and understanding of history whose vision is the ultimate union of the human person with the Transcendent God through Jesus Christ. The Transcendent invites, and humans respond, thus fulfilling a quest to go beyond the surface of daily experience. The offering of the chalice, Communion, points to the Transcendent and reveals that the ultimate destiny of human existence is to achieve *theosis*, an eternal life in the Transcendent.

Liturgy in the Byzantine era meant more than the service of the Eucharist. The term was employed to emphasize the corporate character of liturgical rituals, including baptism, marriage, funerals, other sacraments, and sacramentals. The prayer life of the Byzantine Church incorporated a set of corporate rituals that formed a coherent structure and addressed diverse spiritual and physical needs of the people, religious as well as social, noetic as well as intellectual desires and quests.

The cycle of liturgical services included Bible readings, the Word of God, but also the Word-of-God illustrated iconography; readings but also homilies; and symbols but also icons – a coordination of visible and invisible realities, the macrocosm reduced to a microcosm. A liturgy brings together the physical and the metaphysical, the created and the uncreated, and especially Divinity and humanity. The variety of the liturgical forms that we find in the Byzantine religious life provided a synthesis of and a compromise between the rites practiced in the imperial Cathedral of Hagia Sophia, which exerted an overwhelming influence throughout the empire and elsewhere, and the practices in monasteries, such as the Studion in Constantinople, which had synthesized Palestinian and Constantinopolitan liturgical practices.

By the fourth century *liturgy* had acquired a specific meaning and was referred to as the Sacrament (or *Mysterion*) of the Eucharist; it was identified with the Last Supper of Christ. Nevertheless, some 20 volumes of hymns, services, sacraments, liturgies, and prayers, such as the *Menaia* (services for the saints of the month), *Triodion, Pentikostarion, Euchologion,* and *Oktoechos,* show that Liturgy assumed various forms. The Greek Church had embraced the totality of life through a variety of liturgical services. Services at the birth of a child, at the opening of schools for classes, at the installation of public officials, or at the seeding of fields and the reaping of crops; services for forgiveness of sins and for health of body and soul; and texts of sacraments and sacramental services for baptism, chrismation, marriage, and so on provide ample evidence that liturgical life was a daily experience for the Orthodox subjects of the Byzantine Empire. The Church never made a clear distinction between sacraments (*mysteria*) and sacramentals (*hierai akolouthiae*); all were intended to consecrate some aspect of life and the cosmos as a whole.

The daily life of the people, whether dwellers in large cities such as Constantinople, Thessalonike, Nicaea, Ephesos, or Trapezous or inhabitants of provincial towns or the countryside involved daily religious services and the Eucharistic liturgy proper. The ecclesiastical calendar includes daily commemorations of celestial and earthly beings – members of the Church triumphant and of the Church militant. Angelic hosts, prophets of the old dispensation, apostles, church fathers, martyrs, saints of the desert (both male and female), "unmercenary" physicians, the ancestors of Christ on the side of his mother, and other members of the congregation "who have fallen asleep in the hope of resurrection to eternal life" are commemorated as participants in the prayer life of the faithful.

The liturgy recapitulated the whole economy of God – God's providence and acts in history from the moment of humanity's disobedience to God's direct intervention in the person of Jesus the Christ. Eucharistic liturgy was perceived as the mystery of God's love. Throughout the Liturgy God is described as *philanthropos* (lover of humankind), *eleemon* (merciful), *oiktirmon* or *panoiktirmon* (compassionate or most compassionate), *euergetes* (benefactor), *Soter* (saviour), and the *monos philanthropos*

Sucevița Monastery, Romania, 16th century. A sister is calling to prayer by beating the wooden semantron.
Photo courtesy of Mary Schaefer

(the only true lover of humankind). It is out of love for humanity that God assumed humanity to save the human. (John 3:16) God's justice is mitigated by God's love and compassion for his creation.

Six major Eucharistic liturgies were present during the Byzantine era: the Liturgy of Iakovos (James), the Liturgy of Mark, the Liturgy of Clement, the Liturgy of St. Basil, the Liturgy of John Chrysostom, and the Liturgy of the Presanctified Gifts. Of these the liturgy falsely attributed to Clement was written in Syria and was incorporated in the *Diatagai ton Hagion Apostolon* (Instructions of the Twelve Apostles). It was never adopted by the Greek Church. The most widely used liturgy was that attributed to St. John Chrysostom (354–407), followed by St. Basil's, which is celebrated ten times during the year, and that of the Presanctified Gifts, a special liturgy celebrated every Wednesday and Friday of the Great Lent – the 40-day Lent before Easter.

The central point of every one of these liturgies is the sacrifice of Christ, who becomes the link between Divinity and humanity and secures his *koinonia* (communion) with his people and establishes a *koinonia* among the faithful themselves. For this reason the liturgy was perceived as a corporate worship of God in Christ. In the early Church the liturgy was called a *synaxis*, a gathering of the faithful for Bible reading, Communion, and a meal. The spirit that dominates every act of the Liturgy is the notion of God's *philanthropia*, that is, God's attributes becoming manifested in God's love for the creation, including humankind. The atmosphere created is intended to elevate the human spirit to spiritual concerns. The faithful situate themselves among the spiritualized personalities of the Old and the New Testaments, apostles and martyrs, Church intellectual fathers, and illiterate anchorites of the desert. All these personages are depicted in abstract icons, lighted with flickering candles, bathed in sweet-smelling incense, and enveloped by music and hymns that strengthen the faith, augment hope, and bind people in love. The visible and invisible choruses of believers join under a common mantle of eternity. In other words the liturgy is a highly spiritual experience bringing together the created and the uncreated, those living in time and those who have entered eternity.

In theory at least, the liturgy was for all, and it was in the liturgy and the sharing of the same cup that the unity of the community was proclaimed. Emperors and poor peasants, patriarchs and humble monks, queens and servant girls, and generals and ordinary soldiers shared from the same cup. The sharing exemplified one invisible but real kingdom in heaven, one visible but real kingdom on earth. Sunday liturgy especially was the supreme spiritual experience for Byzantine society, whether in cities and towns or villages and farm communities. The text of the liturgy constitutes a mirror of Orthodox Christianity's spirit and incorporates all the characteristics of Orthodox worship.

For nearly six centuries the liturgy attributed to St. Basil dominated the liturgical cycle, but after the 11th century it was St. John Chrysostom's Liturgy that was conducted more frequently than any other. It includes a sequence of readings, prayers, and petitions that were enriched in the course of time, and it evolved to epitomize the whole realm of spirituality and unfold the philosophy of history held by the medieval Greek world. Petition after petition, prayer after prayer, and symbols and reenactments embrace concerns for the totality of the cosmos and reveal a deep interest for cosmic salvation.

Saint John's Liturgy is a step-by-step ascent from the material to the immaterial, from the created to the uncreated. As a mirror of Orthodoxy's philosophy of history, the liturgy is an account and reenactment of God's invasion of human history – from the moment of creation, to re-creation through the God-made-human event, to the *eschaton* (end of time) and the return of the cosmos to its pristine immateriality and humankind's state of *theosis* when God will be in all and all in God.

Saint John's Liturgy is divided into three interrelated sections: the service of the *Prothesis* (preparation) and *Orthros* (matins), the service of catechumens or liturgy of the Word, and the Liturgy of the Eucharist or "the Mystery." The *Orthros* includes a series of Psalm readings, petitions, gospel pericopes, the Magnificat, hymn singing, and doxology. More than any of these steps, the *prothesis* (preparation) of the gifts and the bread and wine of the Eucharist best express the sense of history that Orthodoxy proclaims.

Whereas the *Orthros*/matins service opens with an apophatic (inexpressible) invocation of an undefined God, proclaiming "Blessed is our God at all times, now and always and for ever and ever," the Eucharistic liturgy starts with a *cataphasis* (declaration) of the Triune God, God one in essence but three in persons. Thus, "Blessed be the Kingdom of the Father and the Son and the Holy Spirit, now and always and for ever and ever."

Although the Old Testament progressively reveals what God is, in that text God remains the unknown God, the obscure one, present in word but absent from humanity's religious knowledge and experience. It was the incarnation of the Logos and the descent of the Spirit that confirmed the triune nature of God as Creator, Redeemer, and Sanctifier. The *Orthros*/matins is preparatory and anticipatory and includes more Bible readings from the Old Testament, such as Psalms, hymns imbued with Old Testament imagery and prophetic sayings, but also the Magnificat and several Christian hymns of later centuries.

Old Testament thinking is not absent from the Eucharist proper, especially in the first part, which includes passages from Psalms and prophetic utterances; but the biblical structure of the liturgy and the Bible readings depend much more on the New Testament, on the fulfillment of prophecy and expectation.

Although the liturgy's prayers are saturated with biblical passages, allusions, names, and imagery, they also abound in philosophical apophatic terminology. Terms describing God or Christ as *aphatos* (unutterable), *atreptos* (unchangeable), *analloiotos* (with no essential change), *anaimaktos* (bloodless), *philanthropos* (lover of the human being), *anekphrastos* (ineffable), *aperinoetos* (beyond understanding), *aoratos* (invisible), *akataleptos* (incomprehensible), *aei on* (always existing), or *osautos on* (always the same) are found seldomly in the Bible but frequently in Greek classical literature and philosophy. The influence of Greek thought in the prayer life of Byzantine Christianity becomes clear when one remembers that in the Greek East cultural continuity existed between non-Christian and Christian Hellenism and that the Eastern Church never divorced itself from its Greek linguistic and cultural heritage.

The liturgy constitutes the center of the Church's life and offers the fullest manifestation of its ecclesiology, its doctrine, its major ethical teachings, and its eschatology. For some Greek Church fathers and theologians with a more mystical bent, such as Dionysios the Pseudo-Areopagite (c. 500), Maximos the Confessor (c. 580–662), Nicholas Kabasilas (b. c. 1322), Symeon of Thessalonike (d. 1429), and Gregory Palamas (c. 1296–1359), the Liturgy provided the opportunity for a personal, mystical, and total consummation in divinization (*theosis*) of the individual believer here on earth. Both symbol and reality, the Divine Liturgy working through Scripture and Eucharist, the word and the mystery, elevates the believer to a higher state of existence where one gains an intimate and profound communion with God, who provides the gifts, leads to the variety of services, and activates all to the common good (cf. 1 Cor. 12:4–11).

Although the core texts of the liturgies are attributed to major Church fathers, such as Basil the Great (c. 330–379) and John Chrysostom, several sacramental services (baptism, marriage, and so on) and *akolouthies* (church services such as the *paraklesis*, the *apodeipnon*, or compline and services for saints' days) were composed by known and many unknown monks and nuns. Joseph the hymnographer (c. 810–886), Kosmas (c. 675–c. 751), John of Damascus (c. 655–c. 750), Andrew of Crete (c. 660–740), Theodore of Stoudios (759–820), Theophanes (c. 775–845), and the nun Kassia (Kassiane, early ninth century) are a few of the major contributors to hymnology and the prayer life of the Church. Every church service has evolved and has been enriched by members of the monastic world.

Liturgy and liturgical services and feasts served not only spiritual needs but also social and economic ones. Such activities provided opportunities for people to socialize, to meet relatives and friends, and to see dignitaries of both the Church and the imperial court as well as to express disappointments and frustrations. They provided forms of relaxation if not entertainment. On the other hand, the liturgy and other liturgical services required the presence of furniture and the use of utensils. The extensive use of candles, oil, icons, incense, wax, and clerical vestments provided economic opportunities and the employment of people – technicians, tailors, painters, and beekeepers – who made a living for themselves and their families.

The interrelationship between religious, social, and economic needs is clearly revealed in the following account by a mid-fifth-century orator who wrote of the *panegyris* of St. Thekla. The *panegyris* began and ended with a liturgy. In the final liturgy,

> all rushed, citizen and foreigner, man, woman, and child, governor and governed, general and soldier, leader of the mob and individual, both young and old, sailor and farmer and everyone simply who was anxious, all rushed to come together, to pray to God, to beseech the Virgin, and having partaken of the holy mysteries [i.e., the Eucharist] to go away blessed and as someone renewed in

body and soul. Then they banqueted and set to discussing the wonders of the *panegyris*. One participant praised its brilliance, another the size of the crowd, yet another the harmony of the psalmody, another the duration of the vigil, and so they continued commenting on the liturgy and prayer, the shoving of the crowd, the shouting, and the quarreling. One man commented on the fact that he was inspired by a beautiful young woman that he saw during the celebration and was consumed by the thought of having his pleasure with her so that he could only offer prayers to this end. It seems also that at the dismissal of the service gifts were given by the attendants of the sanctuary to the pious (needy).

Thus, a liturgy was celebrated for the renewal of body and soul; it attracted crowds, dignitaries, and ordinary people; it included prayers and gossip, praise for the brilliance of the service and the knowledge of the teachers, praise for the harmony of the psalmody, but also complaints about the duration of the rite; and it included prayers for the attraction of a bride and distribution of charities to the pious needy. A liturgy-*panegyris* involved the total human being exercising all one's strengths and all one's weaknesses.

Similar descriptions of the *panegyris* as a religious-social-economic phenomenon are provided by authors of the 9th, 11th, 12th, and later centuries. However, it is to be noted that these unique celebrations were observed during the annual memories of local saints, such as St. John the Theologian, St. Thekla, or St. Demetrios, and not on a regular Sunday, the Lord's Day. These liturgical-social-commercial celebrations had their parallel in the ancient Greek world and indicate cultural continuity between pagan and Christian Hellenism. This relationship between the religious and so-called secular concerns is understood when we bear in mind that the Byzantine Church sought not to destroy but to transform and consecrate culture. Liturgy and liturgical life had no other purpose except to sanctify the totality of the human person and one's environment.

DEMETRIOS J. CONSTANTELOS

*See also* Hagiography: Eastern Christian; Hymnographers; Iconoclasm (Controversy); Istanbul, Turkey; Meditation: Christian Perspectives; New Skete, New York; Orthodox Monasticism: Byzantine; Seasons, Liturgical: Eastern Christian; Spirituality: Eastern Christian; Visual Arts, Eastern Christian: Painting; Worship Space: Christian Perspectives

## Further Reading

Brightman, Frank E., *Liturgies Eastern and Western*, volume 1: *Eastern Liturgies*, Oxford: Clarendon Press, 1896

Cabasilas, Nicholas, *A Commentary on the Divine Liturgy*, translated by J.M. Hussey and P.A. McNulty, London: SPCK, 1966

Calivas, Alkiviades, "An Introduction to the Divine Liturgy," in *The Divine Liturgy of Saint John Chrysostom*, translated by the Faculty of Hellenic College/Holy Cross Greek Orthodox School of Theology, Brookline, Massachusetts: Holy Cross Orthodox Press, 1985

Contos, Leonides, *The Liturgikon* (Greek text with an English translation), Northridge, California: Narthex Press, 1996

Constantelos, Demetrios J., *Understanding the Greek Orthodox Church*, Brookline, Massachusetts: Hellenic College Press, 1998

Meyendorff, John, "The Liturgy: A Clue to the Mind of Worldwide Orthodoxy," in *Orthodox Theology and Diakonia*, edited by Demetrios J. Constantelos, Brookline, Massachusetts: Hellenic College Press, 1981

Raya, Joseph, and José de Vinck, translators, *Byzantine Daily Worship*, Allendale, New Jersey: Alleluia Press, 1968

Schmemann, Alexander, *Introduction to Liturgical Theology*, London: Faith Press, and Portland, Maine: American Orthodox Press, 1966

# Liturgy: Western Christian

Early monasticism, a lay movement, sought to respond to the New Testament counsel to "pray always" (Luke 18:1, 1 Thess. 5:17, Acts 2:42), doing so in community. It was distinguished by the daily recitation of the Liturgy of the Hours rather than by celebration of the Eucharist. A rule for laymen attributed to St. Augustine (354–430) exhorts, "'Persevere faithfully in prayer' (Col. 4:2) at the hours and times appointed" (2.1). This rule is given body in the *Ordo monasterii* 2 (Regulations for a Monastery). Of Augustinian provenance it details prayer for early morning, terce, sext, none, vespers, and the night. It is perhaps the earliest text to prescribe the content of the hours.

Praying the hours is the distinctive characteristic of monasticism. However, this article focuses on celebrations of the Eucharist (the Mass) and the related communion service outside of Mass in major monastic families of the West as differentiated from the Roman cathedral or parochial Eucharistic rite. With the ordination of increasing numbers of monks in the Carolingian period, the Eucharist gained an important place in the *opus Dei*. Some reference is also made to rites within the Eucharistic liturgy in which women figured as subjects: the consecration of virgins, ordination to the diaconate, and ordination as abbess. Other liturgies celebrated in monasteries include those of confession and reconciliation, anointing of the sick, rites for the dying, and the Office of the Dead.

## I. Mass and Communion Services: Early Rules

In the early period a monastic community might not include a single priest. In fact some banned the admission of priests or required that they not exercise their orders. Within a monastery the Eucharist might be celebrated infrequently.

### Rule of the Master

The early sixth-century Rule of the Master provides for the Liturgy of the Hours; Mass takes place in the monastery oratory only on the patronal feast and at the blessing of an abbot. For Sunday Mass the monks go to the parish church. Within the monastery communion (of both bread and wine) is distributed daily by the lay abbot. The short communion service including the kiss of peace breaks the fast; usually it follows none and precedes the common meal.

### Rule of Benedict

The bishops of Rome founded monasteries to ensure a regimen of continuing prayer in the city basilicas. The resulting hybrid formed of cathedral and monastic offices inspired Benedict's sequence of vigils (nocturns and matins), lauds, prime, terce, sext, none, vespers, and compline. The Rule of Benedict prescribed a balanced diet of *lectio divina*, prayer, and work. Like the Rule of the Master, the Rule of Benedict (c. 530–560) seems not to presume a regular Mass. *Missa* (chaps. 17, 35, 38, and 60) might mean a liturgical dismissal, whereas chapter 38.2 and 63 probably refer to the kiss of peace and communion "outside of Mass." However, the abbot is now permitted to choose one of the monks to be ordained presbyter or deacon (chap. 62). Later

Apse, Church of SS. Quattro Coronati (the Four Crowned Ones), Rome, Italy. The fresco is by Giovanni di San Giovanni, 1630. Enclosed Augustinian nuns are shown in front of the altar.
**Photo courtesy of Mary Schaefer**

practice would have a conventional Mass celebrated on Sundays and feast days.

An early 12th-century psalter from Benedict's monastery at Monte Cassino contains a service for communion (of both bread and wine) comprised of introduction with invocations, three chanted psalms, litany, Our Father, Creed, general confession, and prayers with a trinitarian focus surrounding the communion rite. The same order was used in a convent of Benedictine nuns at Benevento. A 10th- or 11th-century *ordo* (ms. 25 from Auxerre in France) uses the feminine gender. These communion services, which include a penitential rite, complete the monastic diet of Scripture read in choir.

### Rules of Caesarius, Columban

In sixth-century Gaul some monks were ordained to serve the community, Mass was celebrated within the monastery, and communion was not received daily except during Easter week. Confession to abbot or abbess was a feature of the Columban rule. Around 629, Luxeuil, a Celtic monastic center founded by St. Columban (d. 615), adopted a rule combining those of Columban and Benedict. Continuous worship was maintained, with 75 psalms said each night in winter. This "mixed observance" was found at the nunnery of Jouarre-en-Brie, founded in the seventh century; its crypt with tombs is the only preserved Merovingian monastic interior.

### Women's Liturgical Activity

Women's contribution to the development of liturgical rites has for the most part gone unnoticed and unrecorded. Founder and ruler of a double monastery of hermits and anchoresses grouped about a church, St. Hilda of Whitby (614–680) hosted the synod of 663/664. She supported the Northumbrian and Irish customs but accepted the synod's decision for the Roman date of Easter and thus Roman liturgical practice.

What more recent times came to consider as extraordinary or even aberrant customs were acceptable when liturgical books included ordination rites for women deacons (8th to 11th century in Benedictine convents in the region of Rome) and ordination rites for abbesses that paralleled those for abbots. Extant insignia of crown, ring, crosier, and liturgical chair testify to the liturgical presidency exercised by the quasi-episcopal abbess of the first convent to adopt the Rule of Benedict in Germanic lands: Nonnberg Abbey in Salzburg (founded c. 700). Such abbesses exercised the juridical functions of a bishop over lands, parishes, and priest-chaplains. The crosier was a symbol of their pastoral office.

### II. Carolingian Renaissance

At the end of the eighth century, the monastery of St. Riquier, Centula (northern France), constituted a "holy city" of 7,000, of which 300 were monks, 100 children, 110 soldiers, and many families, all ruled by Abbot Angilbert. The monks were fully occupied in prayer. To the Rule of Benedict were added rituals, litanies, and processions around the monastery's three great

Presbytery, Abbey Church (Benedictine), Vézelay (Yonne), France, 12th century.
**Photo courtesy of Mary Schaefer**

churches and five minor chapels. Two conventual masses (part of the required office) were said daily.

The contribution of Benedict of Aniane (c. 750–821), the Carolingian Benedictine reformer supported by Louis the Pious (814–840), is disputed. He seems to have given impetus to the addition of lengthy liturgical practices so that monastic life was almost reduced to liturgical and ceremonial functions. The Synod of Aachen (817) made the Rule of Benedict normative; from this time almost all monks were members of the Benedictine family.

The vow of stability (residence in one monastery for life) encouraged significant architectural design of liturgical and living space. An ideal plan of a monastery and its double-apsed church, copied between 816 and 832, was sent from Abbot Haito of Reichenau to Abbot Gozbert of St. Gall. The part of the church accessible to serfs and lay visitors housed numerous altars; it was screened off from the "monk's church," which occupied the two eastern bays of the nave, the transept crossing, and the presbytery. Partitions created small chapel areas, each with its altar, within the nave. Altars in the west and east apses honored St. Peter and St. Paul. The high altar in the presbytery was dedicated to the Virgin and St. Gall; against the transept's east wall, two altars were dedicated to the saintly patrons of the two monastic traditions that shaped the Swiss monastery: Benedict and Columban. Ten altars in the nave housed relics; here was a place for the private Masses that multiplied with relics' acquisition. Monks were ordained as priests to provide the Masses that petitioned God's good favor and honored the relics of saints. Losing its balance of prayer, work, and *lectio divina* designed for vowed laypersons, monastic life was becoming clericalized.

## III. Cluniac Reform

Liturgical observances had already accumulated prior to the Cluniac reform. It seems to have been usual for a monastery to have two daily Masses (a conventual and a *missa matutinalis*, one in early morning), two litanies, and 75 psalms on ordinary days and 138 on feast days (as opposed to St. Benedict's 150 over the week). The monk spent more time in choir than in his cell. On solemn days elements of the cathedral office (lights, ceremony, and vestments) were used. Other monasteries besides Cluny celebrated *laus perennis*, the "perennial praise" of uninterrupted liturgy, made possible by three shifts of monks and choirboys.

Cluny (founded 910) was a centralized order under the direct authority of the abbot of Cluny; all vows were made to him and superiors appointed by him. As abbot, Hugh the Great (1049–1109) introduced minor changes into the liturgy. Numerous ministries allowed both the lettered and the unlettered to participate. "The Lord abbot . . . ordered them . . . to serve in the church, namely, that those who understand this read and chant; and the others who are not able, carry candlesticks and thuribles." Cluny, although not liturgically innovative, developed a maximalist liturgical observance. Its calendar and *horarium* (daily schedule) were typical of the 11th-century monastic world. Altogether 210 psalms were said daily in winter.

In the lifetime of St. Hugh, Cluny's Mass rite resembled the relatively unadorned *ordo romanus primus*, the Roman rite of the seventh to eighth century, with perhaps some Gallican elaborations. The chant was simple, without repetitions or ceremonial ornament. The 11th-century solemn Cluniac Mass on Sundays and feasts (following terce) was distinguished by the variety of ministries for the liturgy of the word. At the offertory the abbot brought five hosts and some wine, which were incensed along with the altar. The sole offertory prayer was *Suscipe Sancte Trinitas*; the priest said *Orate pro me* without response. The Roman Canon was said, without elevation or genuflection at the consecration, through to the doxology. While the deacon broke the large hosts, peace was exchanged, the monks coming forward in procession. The priest received the host and then gave general communion by intinction. The communicant prostrated

**Organ and choir stalls, Abbey Church of Notre-Dame de la Maigrauge (Cistercian nuns), Fribourg, Switzerland, mid–13th century.
Photo courtesy of Mary Schaefer**

or bowed profoundly before receiving communion standing and then kissed the priest's hands. On returning to the altar, the priest consumed the remaining consecrated wine. The ablutions of chalice and fingers by priest, deacon, and subdeacon were elaborate. After the *Ite, missa est* (dismissal) the ministers returned to the sacristy.

The *missa matutinalis* and conventual Mass on ordinary days were less elaborate but had more collects and a longer offertory procession. On these less solemn occasions, all the monks came forward, bringing bread and wine that they received from the sacristan, thus respecting old Roman custom. The Creed, presumably as a substitute for communion, was said only when the laity were present. On fast days Mass was said after none, in the late afternoon or early evening. The *De divinis officiis* (*Patrologia Latina* 170.11–332), an influential Mass commentary throughout the 12th century, was written around 1116 by a black monk, Rupert of Deutz (c. 1075–1129/30). *De sacrificio missae* (*Patrologia Latina* 180.853–856) is the only liturgical Mass commentary attributable to a monk of the great abbey of Cluny.

Romanesque architectural and sculptural invention had reached its height in Cluny III (1088–1130) and Vézelay (nave 1120–1132, Cluniac). Cluny attracted much criticism on account of its attention to liturgy. Following a visit in 1063, St. Peter Damian (1007–1072), himself a monk, criticized what would become the second-largest church in Christendom (after St. Peter's) for its liturgical splendor and lengthy offices and its monks for lack of penance and mortification. A wise abbot, Peter the Venerable (1092/94–1156), responded temperately to a similar criticism by St. Bernard of Clairvaux (1090–1153). Such liturgical observance was its own kind of asceticism.

The Benedictine abbey at Rupertsberg (Rhineland, 12th century) benefited from St. Hildegard of Bingen's (1098–1179) compositions for the liturgy: 77 liturgical songs (the *Symphonia*), unique chant with antiphons and responsories (see *Scivias* III.13), and a liturgical drama. On solemn occasions, perhaps for communion, the nuns wore crowns, rings, and veils at the liturgy.

### Augustinian Rule

The Rule of St. Augustine circulated in the 11th century. It was adopted by communities of canons regular inspired by Gregory VII's (1073–1085) reform of clergy. Communities of canonesses also followed this rule, perhaps living in separate dwellings around the parish church. Their abbess was consecrated by the bishop in a rite that resembled that for a deacon. She participated in diocesan and regional synods and appointed her own chapter of canons. The Rule of St. Augustine proved apt for the double monasteries of men and women that came into existence during this period. Some elements were also usable for those following the anchoritic life (see the 13th-century *Ancrene Wisse*, Parts I and VIII). Although they heard Mass every day, according to this rule anchoresses were to receive communion with the frequency of Augustinian lay brothers, that is, 15 times a year.

Square chevet (apsidal east end), Abbey of Fontenay (Cistercian), Fontenay (Côte d'Or), France, 1139–1147. This is the oldest extant Cistercian abbey and shows St. Bernard's preferred plan for a church. Photo courtesy of Mary Schaefer

### IV. The Monastic 12th Century

Toward the end of the 11th century, a number of at first isolated reforms were inspired by the eremitic ideal: Camaldoli (founded by Romuald, c. 950–1027), Vallombrosa around 1030 (John Gualbert), Fonte Avellana (Peter Damian, d. 1072), Grandmont (Étienne de Muret, 1074), Molesme (Robert, 1075), Grande Chartreuse (Bruno, 1084), Fontevraud (Robert d'Abrissel, 1096), and Cîteaux (Robert of Molesme, 1098). By the early 12th century, these had developed into forms of cenobitic monasticism based on the Rule of St. Benedict. The new reforming orders shared a number of characteristics. In liturgy they pruned accretions and repetitions, turned to earlier (especially patristic) sources, and reduced or eliminated ecclesiastical compositions in favor of Scripture. The material success of ascetic monasticism in the 12th century is displayed in brilliantly designed and ornamented churches either monastic (Moissac and Vézelay) or inspired by monastic architecture (churches of the pilgrimage roads that imitate Cluny, e.g., the cathedral of St. Lazare, Autun).

### Cistercians

Cistercians were the puritanical offshoot of the Benedictine stock, advocating adherence to "the integrity of the Rule," its very letter. They pruned everything from the office that had been added by their predecessors. Their thoroughgoing liturgical reform is shown in Stephen Harding's (abbot 1108–1133) correction of the Vulgate against the Hebrew text with the help of Jewish rabbis, by the restoration of Ambrosian hymns and chants to the office (thus reducing the repertoire of hymns), and by recourse to Metz for the supposed chant of Gregory the Great for their antiphonary. The early *Carta Caritatis* (Charter of Charity) prescribed that all monasteries follow the usages of the New Monastery (Cîteaux), sharing common texts for both office and Mass, so that they might "live with one love, under one Rule and in the same observances." Chant was highly prized. Saint Bernard of Clairvaux himself organized the editing of Stephen Harding's earlier Cistercian antiphonary, which had been based on the Metz tradition, "correcting" it (c. 1147) according to rules of music theory and especially the living chant tradition to achieve "authenticity," uniformity, and sobriety. The number of feasts was reduced. The work of God in choir comprised seven canonical hours plus the Office of the Dead (on weekdays from 1134). For choir monks there was only one conventual Mass daily, except for Sundays and feast days without manual labor; however, a Mass for the dead was soon added.

Before St. Bernard's death a procession preceding the conventual Mass was introduced for Ascension Day and in 1223 for the Assumption; then processions for Palm Sunday and Purification were added. These took place in the cloister at three stations: outside the chapter house, in front of the refectory, and at the door of the church, as at the Cistercian abbey of Notre-Dame de la Maigrauge, Fribourg (Switzerland), where on Assumption Day (15 August) both nuns and congregation process through the cloister using the 13th-century chants of the house.

Fontenay (founded 1119, church erected 1139–1147), the oldest extant Cistercian abbey, shows the plan preferred by St. Bernard. The facade was unassuming, like a stone barn. In contrast to the radiating ambulatory of the Cluniac pilgrimage churches, the eastern end was square, giving place for only one altar near the center of the sanctuary and a small rectangular choir. Additional altars were erected in four or six lateral chapels created on the east side of the transept. Cistercian architectural style was a Burgundian half-Gothic, which, with the rapid diffusion of the order, became "international half-Gothic." Sculpture (1124) and stone towers were forbidden (1157); colored glass was to be removed (1182) and replaced with grisaille.

A tunnel vault with no clerestory and vaulted aisles provided the wonderful acoustics appreciated by Bernard, while light flowed in from windows in the austere west facade and east end. A stair in the south transept led directly to the large dormitory over chapter house and hall. The lay brothers assembled in the west end of the nave, separated by a screen from the crossing and choir reserved for the choir-monks.

Simplicity was legislated in altar linens and vestments. Only stole and maniple might be of silk; chasubles were of one color; dalmatics and tunics were not used. The chalice and reed for communion might be silver or gold plated. Crucifixes were to be wooden and painted, without a sculpted figure. These provisions were continued in the *Institutes* (before 1152). Two candelabra of iron flanked an unadorned altar; thuribles were of iron or copper. The *Ecclesiastica officia* (Book of Usages, 1220–1230) included liturgical instructions. Outsiders were not admitted to the office, confession, communion, or conventual Mass; indeed they were not to be allowed within the church, which was subdivided by a rood screen separating the east end of the nave, transept crossing, and choir – all reserved for the choir-monk – from the west end of the nave for the lay brothers. (The rule categorically excluding laymen was not always observed.) Two al-

tars against the west side of the rood screen provided for the services attended by the lay brothers.

Careful study of extant early Cistercian Eucharistic texts indicates that a Cluniac *ordo missae* was their source as it was also for the Carthusian Mass; in turn the Gallo-Roman rite of the use of Lyons lay behind Cluniac usage. The early liturgy of the New Monastery around 1100 was that of Molesme by virtue of Robert's founding of both; he had brought with him from Molesme a *capella* (vestments, vessels, and liturgical books). These appurtenances were to remain at the New Monastery, except for an office book (*breviarium*, perhaps an office lectionary) to be copied before it was returned. Molesme's Liturgy of the Hours came from the abbey of Marmoutier (a leader of 11th-century reform) by way of Robert's earlier monastery, Moutier-la-Celle.

Mass was celebrated after prime (winter) or terce (summer). There were three types of celebrations: the solemn conventual Mass with deacon, subdeacon, and a subminister; a ferial Mass in which the priest was assisted by a deacon or a subdeacon; and a private Mass, for which the priest needed a cleric and a lay assistant. In early usages priest and ministers never genuflected; they made a profound bow. The conventual Mass began like a canonical hour with the Lord's Prayer and the sign of the cross. Until the offertory, when the gifts and altar were incensed, the presider intoned only Gloria and Credo and said the orations. All else was done by ministers and choir. The priest did not say what was read or chanted by others. Until 1232 there was neither elevation nor genuflection during the Canon, except that during the doxology host and chalice were elevated by priest and deacon. The kiss of peace was given only to communicants. Communion in both kinds was obligatory on Christmas, Holy Thursday, Easter, and Pentecost until 1261, when the chalice was reserved to the ministers.

On Sundays and other major feasts the priest-monk communicated if he had not celebrated during the week; priests could celebrate as they wished, except when required to do so as hebdomadary. (However, only one Mass per altar each day was allowed.) Brothers received communion seven times annually, attended Mass and assisted at the office only on Sundays and feasts. Communion was from hosts consecrated at the Mass. Hosts for communion of the sick were suspended above the altar (see the Eucharistic dove at Hauterive, monastery of the Common Observance reopened in 1938) or on a column in the presbytery. Priest-monks might offer Mass privately or abstain from daily private Mass in the interests of work. Saint Bernard was exceptional in saying Mass every day. The learned abbot Isaac of Stella wrote a commentary on the Canon of the Mass (*Patrologia Latina* 194.1889–1896) that reveals the individualistic clerical piety cultivated in the Cistercian communitarian solitude.

Confession was weekly, the abbot hearing the annual confession. Anointing of the sick was administered before viaticum (communion for the dying). Immediately after death the body was washed, clothed in the monastic habit, and placed in the choir of the church. The continuous psalter was begun; if possible Mass was said, then the corpse was borne out the north transept door (Fontenay, north transept) and interred in the earth without a coffin, having been incensed and sprinkled along with the grave. The brothers then returned to the church to pray the penitential psalms.

Abbots had faculties to confer minor orders. At first they were forbidden to bless nuns; later this rule was interpreted to forbid only the consecration of virgins, reserved to the bishop. The abbot of Cîteaux could bless abbots and abbesses. In the 15th century abbots received the *pontificalia* and jurisdiction to confer the diaconate.

The 12th century marked the high point of Cistercian austerity and success. Pontigny (rebuilt with polygonal apse and ambulatory with radiating chapels 1185–1210) is the best surviving example of the rebuilt church at Clairvaux (1153–1174). In the 13th century the number of feasts was greatly augmented. In 1608 the Cistercian breviary was revised to follow the Roman liturgical reforms of Pius V (1566–1572). The general chapter decree in 1618 that priests conform to the Roman missal caused dissent.

Convents of nuns following the Cistercian rule multiplied after 1125. For some time the monks remained aloof. However, the obligation of enclosure for nuns from the 13th century required that abbots assume charge of Cistercian nunneries. Until the Council of Trent (1545–1563), clerics willing to work as chaplains were trained in Cistercian liturgy and spirituality in a monastery, then took their vows at a convent to whose abbess they promised obedience. Lay brothers were also attached in this way. A bull of Innocent III (1198–1216) in 1210 ended the ancient custom at the royal Spanish abbey of Las Huelgas of nuns manifesting conscience to the abbess. The writings of St. Gertrude the Great (1256–1302), one of the 13th-century Cistercian mystics of Helfta, reveal a profound and original mysticism shaped by the liturgy. Her visions (sometimes with herself as priest) often took place during the singing of the hours. She understood herself as graced to declare forgiveness of sins.

### Premonstratensians

The Premonstratensian Order, founded in northern France in 1120 by St. Norbert (c. 1080–1134), later bishop of Magdeburg, originated as a mixed community of men and women under the patronage and rule of St. Augustine, but very early women were excluded. Houses spread rapidly. Under Cistercian influence the White Canons lost some of their active apostolic character, becoming more monastic. Their connection to Cistercians is indicated by a sermon on the Mass (*Patrologia Latina* 177.455–470), preached in chapter at Cîteaux by one Richard the Premonstratensian.

A complete liturgical code was worked out from 1126 to 1131 by Blessed Hugh, first abbot of Premontré. The oldest extant text of the *ordinarius* dates from the last quarter of the 12th century. Liturgical legislation shaped the Order's spirit, with insistence upon uniformity of liturgical books and observances. Premonstratensian chant offered an important alternative to Gregorian; public choral office was the distinguishing feature.

Eucharistic dove, Abbey of Hauterive (Cistercian), near Fribourg, Switzerland. Founded 1138, disbanded 1848, refounded 1938. Photo courtesy of Mary Schaefer

Not purely Roman and not beholden to either Lyons or Paris, the Roman-Germanic pontifical of the tenth century seems to be the root of the Premonstratensian Mass rite. The priest recited privately whatever was sung. In 1290 three daily Masses were prescribed. Saint Norbert had celebrated Mass daily, but this could not have been the practice of the majority of the priests, as the church at Premontré had only nine altars. Laity could communicate. The liturgy was especially rich in Lent and Eastertide. Lent displayed a number of early Roman features; communion was customary on Holy Thursday, Good Friday, and Holy Saturday. During Eastertide the Sunday conventual Mass was that of Easter, the *missa matutina* that of the Sunday. Corpus Christi was a solemnity (1322) with procession and multiple Benedictions of the Blessed Sacrament during Mass and vespers (17th century). Increasing adherence to Roman customs was found in the early 17th century and again in 1749.

### Carthusians

Founded by St. Bruno (c. 1032–1101) at Chartreuse in the Alps in 1084, this small eremitic order has never needed reform. The *Consuetudines Cartusiae* (c. 1127) by Guigo (1083–1136), fifth prior of Chartreuse, is the oldest liturgical and disciplinary document of the Order. It reduced and revised the monastic traditions. Reading from Scripture and not ecclesiastical compositions was given high priority. Liturgical books and rite were drawn from the use of Lyons when not from monastic tradition.

Only vespers and matins were sung communally in the church. As at Lyons the office on the Sunday after Pentecost was the same as for the feast, thus putting the Sunday offices a week behind the Roman office. The antiphonary was monastic, that is, reduced Roman with some Gallicanisms. The lessons were taken almost exclusively from the Bible, which was read annually in its entirety. There were no processions, and no feasts were transferred, sometimes occasioning a mélange of feast and Sunday.

Because solitaries, according to Guigo, should not spend too much time in the study of chant, the *recordatio*, an exercise to prepare the chant, was used as at Lyons. The night office was chanted by heart. Two cantors (*cantores chori*) directed the choir, and an *emendator* corrected any error by repeating it correctly. The office was to be sung elegantly and with lively voice (*rotunda et viva voce cantemus* according to the *Statuta antiqua*); no musical instruments were allowed. Correct pronunciation, accent, and spelling were of concern. In the 17th and 18th centuries, the chant came to be executed in a heavy and monotonous tone.

In the 12th century the sung conventual Mass was not celebrated every day; there were about 200 annually. A shortage of priests in the early years corresponded to the vocation to solitude.

A single candle served for Mass; rarely, two candles were used. From 1127 the *asperges* rite – the blessing and sprinkling of water around the altar, then on the monks, and then on the laity at the door of the choir – was decreed for Sundays. There was no blessing after the dismissal, which was given by the deacon, the priest's only assistant. As in the Gallican liturgy, the Masses for the Vigil and Day of Christmas included a lesson from Isaiah before the epistle, which was read by a monk who came from his stall; the deacon chanted the gospel. Having prepared the gifts the deacon incensed the altar. On Sundays the deacon consumed the host that had been reserved the previous week for the sick. Guigo designed a straw for taking the precious blood.

In the 13th century a number of feasts were added, along with a daily conventual Mass (or even two). A new compilation of liturgical rules (1259) fused those of 1127 and 1222/23 and ended the period of evolution; later it came to be called *Statuta antiqua*. The priest never knelt at the altar; he held his hands elevated and extended in the form of the crucified (*in modum crucifixi*) throughout the Canon. The elevation of the host was now mentioned, and the corporal that covered the chalice pulled back a little at the consecration of the wine. A special candle might be held behind the priest at the elevation so that the host could be seen. In 1271 a window in the choir screen was allowed, to be opened at the moment of the elevation to allow laity to glimpse the host. In the late 16th century the liturgy was seriously modified, and in 1603 the Carthusian missal was "corrected" to the Roman missal of Pius V (1566–1572).

Carthusian nuns make solemn profession in the rite of the consecration of virgins presided over by the bishop. This ancient rite includes for them the bestowal of maniple, stole, and cross. Their chanting of the epistle at Mass and gospel at matins even with priests present were functions of subdeacon and deacon and were occasionally challenged.

### Carmelites

The Carmelite Order has claimed as its "founder" the prophet Elijah. Certainly its origins were in the Holy Land and specifically Mount Carmel, where solitaries lived in its many caves. By the mid–12th century the hermits' cells were clustered to comprise a *lavra* around a chapel. Their Augustinian-derived rule was given them by St. Albert of Vercelli, patriarch of Jerusalem, around 1210. They recited the Divine Office according to the rite of the Holy Sepulchre and gathered in the oratory for daily Mass. This rite was not Eastern but rather the one then in use at the Holy Sepulchre in Jerusalem, mainly that of Paris. Processions on feasts linked to the Jerusalem holy sites were colored by their locale. At the solemn Sunday Mass, the Easter proper replaced the regular Sundays after Pentecost. However, the basilica ceremonies were necessarily adjusted toward simplicity, and poverty remained characteristic of Carmelite churches and liturgical appointments; a *flabellum* (fan or flyswatter), a functional necessity in the Holy Land, remained a distinguishing ornament in later liturgies.

Unsettled conditions in the Holy Land led to migrations of small groups of Carmelites to Europe as early as 1238, where they became mendicant friars with a rule influenced by the Dominican. Their devotion to Mary resulted in numerous feasts dedicated to her. Around 1312 Sibert de Beka removed Dominican elements from the Carmelite rite. During the 14th century the *Salve regina* came to be recited at the end of Mass. Priests were to celebrate at least three times weekly (1462).

### V. The Friars

The 12th-century monastic liturgical reforms had returned to biblical and liturgical sources, pruning and simplifying conventual worship. The 13th century saw the addition of feasts and a growth that paralleled the general religious culture, frequently obscuring the earlier liturgical simplicity. This is true for Cistercians, Premonstratensians, and Carthusians. Two mendicant orders founded early in the century were to reorient the Church's apostolic activity and displace monastic leadership. For both preaching stood at the forefront of their ministry.

### Franciscans

Saint Francis of Assisi (1181/82–1226) reversed the tendency to liturgical growth that had overtaken even the 12th-century reforming orders. He preferred that the friars pray as they had before their "conversion": those in holy orders and thus bound to public prayer "according to the use of the Roman court," the lettered lay brothers from the psalter, unlettered clerics and lay brothers the Creed, the Our Father (24 at matins), and Glory be by heart. In the Earlier Rule of 1221, Francis enjoins that "all the brothers, whether clerical or lay, should celebrate the Divine Office, the praises and prayers, as is required of them. The clerical brothers should celebrate the office and say it for the living and the dead according to the custom of the clergy. . . . And they may have only the books necessary to fulfill their office. And the lay brothers who know how to read the psalter may have it. But those who do not know how to read should not have any book" (chap. 3).

The Later Rule of 1223 specifies the obligation of those who were clerics to "celebrate the Divine Office according to the rite of the holy Roman Church, except for the Psalter, for which reason they may have breviaries" (chap. 3). Francis wanted the friars to possess no unnecessary books. The large and varied office books of other orders were replaced by one-volume breviaries containing the texts and by missals with the simple and brief Mass of the Roman Curia. The mendicant vocation required that breviaries be portable; in the hands of these itinerants, the office of the Roman Curia spread rapidly. Francis composed a devotional Office of the Passion to correspond with the canonical Liturgy of the Hours.

Francis, who had been ordained a deacon, wanted only one Mass to be celebrated per day in each house. If there were more priests in the house (in the early days there were very few), let one, Francis counseled, be content with the celebration of another. In other words, priests were not to say private Masses. The penitential discipline of confessing sins to a priest or, in the absence of a priest, to a brother was enjoined before receiving communion (chap. 20).

The liturgical observances of the enclosed Poor Ladies (Poor Clares) founded by St. Clare of Assisi (1193/94–1253) followed closely Francis' Rule. "The Sisters who can read shall celebrate the Divine Office according to the custom of the Friars Minor; for this they may have breviaries, but they are to read it without singing. And those who . . . are not able to read and pray the Hours, may . . . say the Our Father's." The nuns were to confess at least twelve times a year and receive communion seven times annually (chap. 3).

### Dominicans

The Order of Preachers (Dominicans) founded by St. Dominic (c. 1171–1221) in the region of Toulouse, France, were canons regular following the Rule of St. Augustine. The Dominican friar was described by Stephen of Salanhac (d. 1290) as "a canon by profession, a monk in the austerity of his life, and an apostle by his office of preacher." From their founding Dominicans placed great store in intellectual training, preaching to the intelligentsia and to heretics. (Their barnlike hall-churches were designed for preaching.) They counted in their number theologians of the first rank: St. Thomas Aquinas (c. 1225–1274) and St. Albert the Great (d. c. 1280). A relative simplicity was the keynote of their

primitive liturgy, and its unity, stability, and precision led orders, dioceses, and even countries to adopt or adapt it. In the interests of study, lessons and Mass were to be brief but recollected; but secondary elements of 13th-century liturgy – graduals, litanies, processions, and daily Offices of the Dead and of the Virgin – were not suppressed.

The Dominican rite was "unified" by a commission of four friars, drawn from France, England, Lombardy, and Germany in 1245; it was codified (1254–1256), not without opposition, under Humbert de Romans (c. 1200–1277), master-general. The prototype, containing 14 books and still extant in Rome, was mostly the Roman rite of the late 12th century. In 1267 a papal bull reserved changes to the Holy See.

As in most medieval rites, the chalice was prepared with wine and water before the short *Confiteor*. The host and chalice were offered together, with a single prayer, at the offertory. Only the consecrated host was elevated, and there was no elevation at the doxology. After the consecration the priest extended his arms in the form of a cross. The priest communicated himself with the host using the left hand. Solemn Mass was distinguished from the Roman by special locations (and sometimes stances) of the ministers; prescribed hand gestures showed concern for rubrical exactness. Some prayer texts were Roman variants, others were dropped, and there were many differences in ceremonial details. The 16th century found Dominicans still with rubrical consciousness.

The Dominican martyrology was at base Usuard's (c. 875). Dominicans were involved with the feast of Corpus Christi from the start, when Cardinal Hugh of St. Cher (c. 1190–1263) endorsed it in 1251; Thomas Aquinas composed the office.

### VI. Modern Monastic Liturgical Renewal

If Benedictine monastic liturgy is essentially the Liturgy of the Hours, with larger monasteries and priories developing their own forms, it is also the Eucharistic liturgy of the diocesan cathedral; only the calendar is specifically monastic. Thus, Benedictine monasticism has been influential in establishing and continuing the modern liturgical movement: Solesmes (under Abbot Guéranger), Beuron (Abbots Maurus and Placidus Wolter), and the Belgian abbeys (Lambert Beauduin). Maria Laach pioneered the celebration of Good Friday and Easter liturgies (Abbot Ildefons Herwegen, Odo Casel).

### VII. Late 20th Century

Since the Second Vatican Council (1962–1965), the larger Benedictine abbeys and priories have renewed office and Mass customs. Saint John's Abbey in Collegeville, Minnesota, has been a center for Roman Catholic and ecumenical liturgical renewal in North America through scholarship, teaching, and publishing. Its abbey church by Marcel Breuer and Pier Luigi Nervi was liturgically daring in 1960. The sung office on Sundays and feasts is of recent composition. At St. Benedict's Monastery in St.

Joseph, Minnesota, a 19th-century German baroque-style church was remodeled by the sisters and the liturgical consultant Frank Kacmarcik to provide a centrally placed altar and ambo, with presider's chair facing across to the organ in the opposite transept. Liturgy of the Hours, the daily liturgical expression of Benedictine women, is celebrated in a separate room with facing benches.

Experiments in liturgical enculturation are often found in monastic settings. Women's communities may incorporate liturgical dance into office or Eucharist (e.g., Poor Clares in Africa or Canada and Camaldoli nuns in Rome).

MARY M. SCHAEFER

*See also* Abbess, Christian; Augustinian Rule; Benedictines; Bernard of Clairvaux, St.; Carmelites; Carthusians; Cistercians; Cluniacs; Collegeville, Minnesota; Dominic, St.; Dominicans; France: History; Francis of Assisi, St.; Franciscans; Hilda, St.; Hildegard of Bingen, St.; Lectio Divina; Office, Daily: Western Christian; Plainchant; Prayer: Christian Perspectives; Premonstratensian Canons; Relics, Christian Monastic; St. Riquier, France; Seasons, Liturgical: Western Christian; Visual Arts, Western Christian: Liturgical Furnishings; Women's Monasteries: Western Christian; Worship Space: Christian Perspectives

## Further Reading

Cabrol, Fernand, editor, *Dictionnaire d'archéologie chrétienne et de liturgie*, 15 vols., Paris: Letouzey et Ané, 1903–1953

Dubois, J., "Office des heures et messe dans la tradition monastique," *La Maison-Dieu* 135 (1978)

Eberle, Luke, translator, *The Rule of the Master = Regula Magistri* (Cistercian Studies Series, 6), Kalamazoo, Michigan: Cistercian Publications, 1977

Fink, Peter, editor, *The New Dictionary of Sacramental Worship*, Collegeville, Minnesota: Liturgical Press, 1990

Fry, Timothy, editor, *RB 1980: The Rule of St. Benedict in Latin and English with Notes*, Collegeville, Minnesota: Liturgical Press, 1981

Hughes, Andrew, *Medieval Manuscripts for Mass and Office: A Guide to Their Organization and Terminology*, Buffalo, New York: University of Toronto Press, 1982

Hunt, Noreen, *Cluny under Saint Hugh, 1049–1109*, London: Arnold, 1967; Notre Dame, Indiana: University of Notre Dame Press, 1968

King, Archdale A., *Liturgies of the Religious Orders* (Rites of Western Christendom), London and New York: Longmans, Green, 1955

Lackner, Bede K., "The Liturgy of Early Cîteaux," in *Studies in Medieval Cistercian History* (Cistercian Studies Series, number 13), Spencer, Massachusetts: Cistercian Publications, 1971

Lawless, George, *Augustine of Hippo and His Monastic Rule*, New York: Oxford University Press, and Oxford: Clarendon Press, 1987

Leclercq, Jean, "Eucharistic Celebrations without Priests in the Middle Ages," *Worship* 55:2 (March 1981)

Lekai, Louis J., *The Cistercians: Ideals and Reality*, Kent, Ohio: Kent State University Press, 1977

Pfaff, Richard William, *Medieval Latin Liturgy: A Select Bibliography* (Toronto Medieval Bibliographies, 9), Buffalo, New York: University of Toronto Press, 1982

Savage, Anne, and Nicholas Watson, *Anchoritic Spirituality: Ancrene Wisse and Associated Works* (Classics of Western Spirituality), New York: Paulist Press, 1991

Taft, Robert, "The Frequency of the Eucharist throughout History," in *Can We Always Celebrate the Eucharist?* (Concilium, 152), edited by Mary Collins et al., Edinburgh: Clark, and New York: Seabury Press, 1982

Tirot, Paul, *Un "Ordo Missae" monastique: Cluny, Cîteaux, La Chartreuse* (Bibliotheca "Ephemerides Liturgicae," "Subsidia," 21), Rome: CLV-Edizioni Liturgiche, 1981

Van Dijk, Stephen Joseph Peter, and Joan Hazelden Walker, *The Origins of the Modern Roman Liturgy: The Liturgy of the Papal Court and the Franciscan Order in the Thirteenth Century*, Westminster, Maryland: Newman Press, 1960

Van Dijk, Stephen Joseph Peter, editor, *Sources of the Modern Roman Liturgy; The Ordinals by Haymo of Faversham and Related Documents (1243–1307)* (Studia et documenta Franciscana, 1–2), 2 vols., Leiden: Brill, 1963

Vogel, Cyrille, *Medieval Liturgy: An Introduction to the Sources* (NPM Studies in Church Music and Liturgy), translated and revised by William Storey and Niels Rasmussen, Washington, D.C.: Pastoral Press, 1986

Waddell, Chrysogonus, "The Quest for the Liturgy of Early Cîteaux: A Progress Report," *Liturgy OCSO* 31:2–3 (1998)

# Luther, Martin 1483–1546

German Augustinian friar, priest, theologian, and founder of the Protestant Reformation

Martin Luther became an Augustinian monk in Erfurt in 1505 after receiving the masters degree there at age 21. In 1508 he was appointed to teach at Wittenberg, where he received the doctorate in 1512 and taught until his death. The Reformation is said to have begun in 1517 when he posted the 95 theses concerning indulgences, but it was not until he married in 1525 that he relinquished his identity as a monk. His major statement on monasticism was *De votis monasticis Martini Lutheri iudicium* (1521; Judgment of Martin Luther on Monastic Vows).

Luther did not completely reject monasticism in this treatise, nor have the Church traditions that follow his teachings. Certainly monasticism has been rare in Protestant history, but that is due to other than purely theological reasons. Luther's was a conservative reformation that rejected only what he considered to be intolerable aspects of his contemporary Church. That left much practice and many institutions in the optional category of "adiaphora," that is, things that do not affect salvation and can vary widely. As long as no higher righteousness or winning of salvation or second baptism was ascribed to monastic status, the latter was accepted and even encouraged by Luther and the Lutheran confessional writings.

vows made under false pretenses. This provided consolation to former monastics as well as a public justification of their actions.

For Luther it was not monastic life itself that was problematic but rather the theology of vows. In the discussion of monastic vows, Luther was concerned with three questions: To whom is the vow made? Is it possible to fulfill vows? and How are the vows related to the responsibilities of all Christians?

The monastic theology of the late Middle Ages held the monastic vow to be one made to God and argued on that basis that it took priority over all other commitments and could not be reversed. Luther disagreed by rejecting the relevance for Christians of the Old Testament notion of vows to God, noting the absence of such vows in the New Testament. Instead, monastic vows must be understood as promises made to other people and as such not of the same degree of theological significance or legal status as a vow to God would be. Here Luther's thought

Lucas Cranach the Elder, *Martin Luther,* Uffizi, Florence, Italy, 1529.
Photo courtesy of Alinari/Art Resource, New York

Chapter house, Augustinian Friars' house, Erfurt, Germany, 14th century. Luther lived in this Augustinian house 1505–1508 and was ordained here 1507.
Photo courtesy of Chris Schabel

Luther's negative statements on monasticism came in reaction against a bias in favor of monastic life that he saw in the theology and piety of the late Middle Ages. He thought that ordinary married life was demeaned to second-class religious status and that monastic vows were held to all but guarantee salvation. Nothing distressed Luther more than the idea that one could work one's way into heaven, and he found that sentiment pervading much monastic piety.

The immediate cause of the treatise on monastic vows was the plight of many monks and nuns who had accepted the Reformation preaching. They now considered their vows to have been based on false doctrine and no longer binding. Thus, many left their communities, and many of these got married, including eventually Luther himself and his wife, Katherine of Bora. In this treatise Luther gave a theological warrant for the repudiation of

**Tomb of Martin Luther (19th century), Schlosskirche, Wittenberg, Germany.**
**Photo courtesy of the Editor**

seems to be confirmed by Benedict. In chapter 58 of the Rule of St. Benedict, the monastic profession is made to the community "in the presence of God." The subsequent ritual of prostration is made in turn before each of the monks.

To assert that vows are not made to God does not repudiate the possibility of a commitment to monastic life but does eliminate its absolute priority and subordinates it to the assessing of responsibilities that inevitably occurs in the complexity of human life. As a life choice monasticism might be a possibility among others, but it has no special status before God and might even prove less productive in services of love.

The second element of Luther's critique of vows centers on the great difficulty for most people of maintaining true chastity. He certainly does not deny that people should and can be celibate for certain periods of life, but he assumes that lifelong chastity is a gift from God alone that a person can accept but can never undertake to achieve by exercise of will without special grace. Thus, one does not vow chastity so much as one hopes and prays for the grace of discipline and wisdom in sexual mat-

ters. Because he felt that the ability to be chastely celibate was rare, Luther, in an appendix to this treatise, cites 1 Timothy 5:9 on the early Church's institution of "widows" and concludes that no one under age 60 should be asked to promise celibacy.

The third focus of concern with vows lies in the traditional notion of evangelical counsels, a compromise position on marriage and monastic life that is still offensive to the spirit of the Reformation. In this perspective marriage is not wrong, but celibacy and monastic life are better. Against this Luther refers to the example of St. Francis, who said that he wanted his followers simply to live according to the Gospel. This implies no extra or special expectations of monks. Nothing more than love is or can be commanded.

Luther's reading of the Bible deems only obedience to parents and love of the neighbor to be absolute. Thus, one's obligations to family and society must take precedence over a desire to live in a monastery. The ordinary structures of life, the ones seen in the Bible, are the usual callings of Christians in which they serve others. Monastic rules, insofar as they impose new institutions and demands, add obligations and vocations to Christian living that have no biblical warrant. If monks think that through their added programs they earn more of God's favor or transcend ordinary life, they sin against God's grace and love. Luther felt that monastic life was easier, more pleasant, and less ascetic than was being a parent, spouse, worker, and citizen in the less ordered and less secure arenas of lay activity. Earthly vocation for Luther is irrelevant to salvation, but the callings of life should offer opportunities for services of love to other humans in gratitude for God's love and forgiveness.

Even though the arguments in Luther's treatise on monastic vows seem quite negative, monastic communities with reformed theology continued to exist in Lutheran areas and were supported by Luther himself. The community at Moellenbeck, Lower Saxony, converted to Reformation teachings in 1558 and continued to exist until 1675. Earlier, when the city senate of Herford, Westphalia, proposed to abolish its monastic communities in 1532, Luther wrote a letter in defense of them. He commended their praiseworthy customs and was pleased that as long as members lived and believed in accord with the Gospel, the communities should continue.

GEORGE WECKMAN

See also Augustinian Friars/Hermits; Bible Interpretation; Critiques of Western Christian Monasticisim; Death: Christian Perspectives; Dissolution of Monasteries: Continental Europe; Francis of Assisi, St.; Germany: History; Protestant Monasticism: Lutheran; Reformation

## Biography

Son of a miner in Saxony, Martin Luther studied at Erfurt University 1501–1505 before becoming an Augustinian Hermit there. Ordained priest in 1507, a year later he became professor of moral philosophy at the new University of Wittenberg, Saxony. In 1510 he spent a month in Rome, and in 1511 became a professor of biblical exegesis at Wittenberg, a position he held for the next 35 years. Between 1514 and 1519 he became convinced that man can be saved ("justified" before God) only by God's mercy (grace) and not by human deeds. Luther's break with the medieval church proceeded gradually, culminating in 1525 when he introduced a reformed liturgy in Wittenberg and married, thereby ceasing to be an Augustinian Hermit. Heirs of the Protestant Reformation regard Luther as the initiator and founder of what became the Lutheran ("evangelisch") Church.

## Major Works

*An den christlichen Adel deutscher Nation* (Address to the Christian Nobles of the German Nation), 1520
*De Captivitate Babylonica Ecclesiae I* (On the Babylonian Captivity of the Church), 1520
*Von der Freiheit eines Christenmenschen* (On the Freedom of a Christian), 1520
*De votis monasticis Martini Lutheri iudicium* (Judgment of Martin Luther on Monastic Vows), 1521
Translation of the Bible into German

## Further Reading

Biot, Francois, *The Rise of Protestant Monasticism*, Baltimore: Helicon, 1963
Erikson, Erik H., *Young Man Luther: A Study in Psychoanalysis and History*, New York: Norton, and London: Faber, 1958
Luther, Martin, *Table Talk* (Luther's Works, American Edition, volume 54), Philadelphia: Fortress Press, 1967
Oberman, Heiko A., *Luther: Man between God and the Devil*, New Haven, Connecticut: Yale University Press, 1989
Wingren, Gustaf, *Luther on Vocation*, Philadelphia: Muhlenberg Press, 1957

# Lutheran Monasticism. *See* Protestant Monasticism: Lutheran